A t Table: Values of t_α

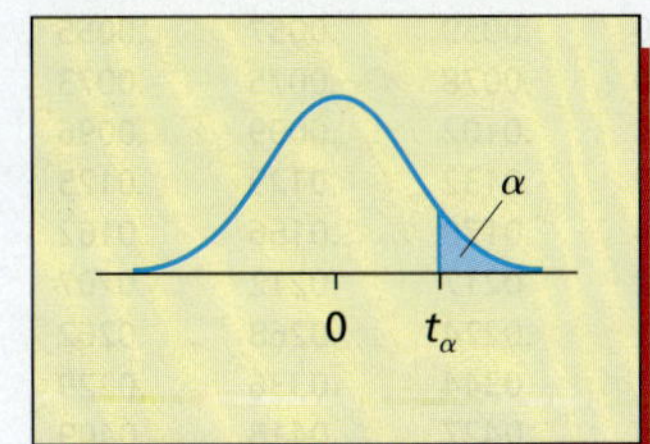

df	$t_{.100}$	$t_{.050}$	$t_{.025}$	$t_{.010}$	$t_{.005}$	$t_{.001}$	$t_{.0005}$
1	3.078	6.314	12.706	31.821	63.657	318.31	636.62
2	1.886	2.920	4.303	6.965	9.925	22.326	31.598
3	1.638	2.353	3.182	4.541	5.841	10.213	12.924
4	1.533	2.132	2.776	3.747	4.604	7.173	8.610
5	1.476	2.015	2.571	3.365	4.032	5.893	6.869
6	1.440	1.943	2.447	3.143	3.707	5.208	5.959
7	1.415	1.895	2.365	2.998	3.499	4.785	5.408
8	1.397	1.860	2.306	2.896	3.355	4.501	5.041
9	1.383	1.833	2.262	2.821	3.250	4.297	4.781
10	1.372	1.812	2.228	2.764	3.169	4.144	4.587
11	1.363	1.796	2.201	2.718	3.106	4.025	4.437
12	1.356	1.782	2.179	2.681	3.055	3.930	4.318
13	1.350	1.771	2.160	2.650	3.012	3.852	4.221
14	1.345	1.761	2.145	2.624	2.977	3.787	4.140
15	1.341	1.753	2.131	2.602	2.947	3.733	4.073
16	1.337	1.746	2.120	2.583	2.921	3.686	4.015
17	1.333	1.740	2.110	2.567	2.898	3.646	3.965
18	1.330	1.734	2.101	2.552	2.878	3.610	3.922
19	1.328	1.729	2.093	2.539	2.861	3.579	3.883
20	1.325	1.725	2.086	2.528	2.845	3.552	3.850
21	1.323	1.721	2.080	2.518	2.831	3.527	3.819
22	1.321	1.717	2.074	2.508	2.819	3.505	3.792
23	1.319	1.714	2.069	2.500	2.807	3.485	3.767
24	1.318	1.711	2.064	2.492	2.797	3.467	3.745
25	1.316	1.708	2.060	2.485	2.787	3.450	3.725
26	1.315	1.706	2.056	2.479	2.779	3.435	3.707
27	1.314	1.703	2.052	2.473	2.771	3.421	3.690
28	1.313	1.701	2.048	2.467	2.763	3.408	3.674
29	1.311	1.699	2.045	2.462	2.756	3.396	3.659
30	1.310	1.697	2.042	2.457	2.750	3.385	3.646
40	1.303	1.684	2.021	2.423	2.704	3.307	3.551
60	1.296	1.671	2.000	2.390	2.660	3.232	3.460
120	1.289	1.658	1.980	2.358	2.617	3.160	3.373
∞	1.282	1.645	1.960	2.326	2.576	3.090	3.291

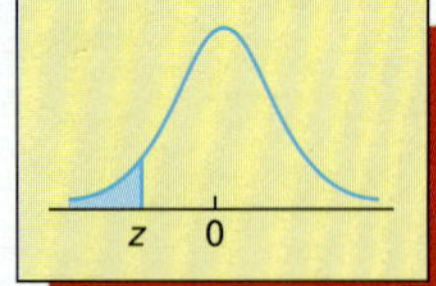

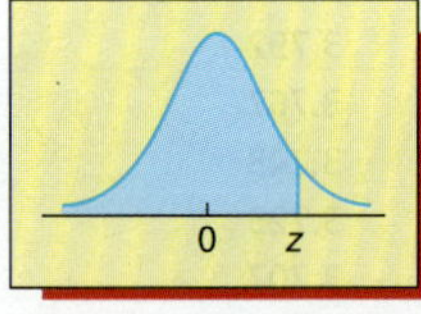

Cumulative Areas under the Standard Normal Curve

z	.00	.01	.02	.03	.04	.05	.06	.07	.08	.09
−3.4	.0003	.0003	.0003	.0003	.0003	.0003	.0003	.0003	.0003	.0002
−3.3	.0005	.0005	.0005	.0004	.0004	.0004	.0004	.0004	.0004	.0003
−3.2	.0007	.0007	.0006	.0006	.0006	.0006	.0006	.0005	.0005	.0005
−3.1	.0010	.0009	.0009	.0009	.0008	.0008	.0008	.0008	.0007	.0007
−3.0	.0013	.0013	.0013	.0012	.0012	.0011	.0011	.0011	.0010	.0010
−2.9	.0019	.0018	.0018	.0017	.0016	.0016	.0015	.0015	.0014	.0014
−2.8	.0026	.0025	.0024	.0023	.0023	.0022	.0021	.0021	.0020	.0019
−2.7	.0035	.0034	.0033	.0032	.0031	.0030	.0029	.0028	.0027	.0026
−2.6	.0047	.0045	.0044	.0043	.0041	.0040	.0039	.0038	.0037	.0036
−2.5	.0062	.0060	.0059	.0057	.0055	.0054	.0052	.0051	.0049	.0048
−2.4	.0082	.0080	.0078	.0075	.0073	.0071	.0069	.0068	.0066	.0064
−2.3	.0107	.0104	.0102	.0099	.0096	.0094	.0091	.0089	.0087	.0084
−2.2	.0139	.0136	.0132	.0129	.0125	.0122	.0119	.0116	.0113	.0110
−2.1	.0179	.0174	.0170	.0166	.0162	.0158	.0154	.0150	.0146	.0143
−2.0	.0228	.0222	.0217	.0212	.0207	.0202	.0197	.0192	.0188	.0183
−1.9	.0287	.0281	.0274	.0268	.0262	.0256	.0250	.0244	.0239	.0233
−1.8	.0359	.0351	.0344	.0336	.0329	.0322	.0314	.0307	.0301	.0294
−1.7	.0446	.0436	.0427	.0418	.0409	.0401	.0392	.0384	.0375	.0367
−1.6	.0548	.0537	.0526	.0516	.0505	.0495	.0485	.0475	.0465	.0455
−1.5	.0668	.0655	.0643	.0630	.0618	.0606	.0594	.0582	.0571	.0559
−1.4	.0808	.0793	.0778	.0764	.0749	.0735	.0721	.0708	.0694	.0681
−1.3	.0968	.0951	.0934	.0918	.0901	.0885	.0869	.0853	.0838	.0823
−1.2	.1151	.1131	.1112	.1093	.1075	.1056	.1038	.1020	.1003	.0985
−1.1	.1357	.1335	.1314	.1292	.1271	.1251	.1230	.1210	.1190	.1170
−1.0	.1587	.1562	.1539	.1515	.1492	.1469	.1446	.1423	.1401	.1379
−0.9	.1841	.1814	.1788	.1762	.1736	.1711	.1685	.1660	.1635	.1611
−0.8	.2119	.2090	.2061	.2033	.2005	.1977	.1949	.1922	.1894	.1867
−0.7	.2420	.2389	.2358	.2327	.2296	.2266	.2236	.2206	.2177	.2148
−0.6	.2743	.2709	.2676	.2643	.2611	.2578	.2546	.2514	.2483	.2451
−0.5	.3085	.3050	.3015	.2981	.2946	.2912	.2877	.2843	.2810	.2776
−0.4	.3446	.3409	.3372	.3336	.3300	.3264	.3228	.3192	.3156	.3121
−0.3	.3821	.3783	.3745	.3707	.3669	.3632	.3594	.3557	.3520	.3483
−0.2	.4207	.4168	.4129	.4090	.4052	.4013	.3974	.3936	.3897	.3859
−0.1	.4602	.4562	.4522	.4483	.4443	.4404	.4364	.4325	.4286	.4247
−0.0	.5000	.4960	.4920	.4880	.4840	.4801	.4761	.4721	.4681	.4641
0.0	.5000	.5040	.5080	.5120	.5160	.5199	.5239	.5279	.5319	.5359
0.1	.5398	.5438	.5478	.5517	.5557	.5596	.5636	.5675	.5714	.5753
0.2	.5793	.5832	.5871	.5910	.5948	.5987	.6026	.6064	.6103	.6141
0.3	.6179	.6217	.6255	.6293	.6331	.6368	.6406	.6443	.6480	.6517
0.4	.6554	.6591	.6628	.6664	.6700	.6736	.6772	.6808	.6844	.6879
0.5	.6915	.6950	.6985	.7019	.7054	.7088	.7123	.7157	.7190	.7224
0.6	.7257	.7291	.7324	.7357	.7389	.7422	.7454	.7486	.7517	.7549
0.7	.7580	.7611	.7642	.7673	.7704	.7734	.7764	.7794	.7823	.7852
0.8	.7881	.7910	.7939	.7967	.7995	.8023	.8051	.8078	.8106	.8133
0.9	.8159	.8186	.8212	.8238	.8264	.8289	.8315	.8340	.8365	.8389
1.0	.8413	.8438	.8461	.8485	.8508	.8531	.8554	.8577	.8599	.8621
1.1	.8643	.8665	.8686	.8708	.8729	.8749	.8770	.8790	.8810	.8830
1.2	.8849	.8869	.8888	.8907	.8925	.8944	.8962	.8980	.8997	.9015
1.3	.9032	.9049	.9066	.9082	.9099	.9115	.9131	.9147	.9162	.9177
1.4	.9192	.9207	.9222	.9236	.9251	.9265	.9279	.9292	.9306	.9319
1.5	.9332	.9345	.9357	.9370	.9382	.9394	.9406	.9418	.9429	.9441
1.6	.9452	.9463	.9474	.9484	.9495	.9505	.9515	.9525	.9535	.9545
1.7	.9554	.9564	.9573	.9582	.9591	.9599	.9608	.9616	.9625	.9633
1.8	.9641	.9649	.9656	.9664	.9671	.9678	.9686	.9693	.9699	.9706
1.9	.9713	.9719	.9726	.9732	.9738	.9744	.9750	.9756	.9761	.9767
2.0	.9772	.9778	.9783	.9788	.9793	.9798	.9803	.9808	.9812	.9817
2.1	.9821	.9826	.9830	.9834	.9838	.9842	.9846	.9850	.9854	.9857
2.2	.9861	.9864	.9868	.9871	.9875	.9878	.9881	.9884	.9887	.9890
2.3	.9893	.9896	.9898	.9901	.9904	.9906	.9909	.9911	.9913	.9916
2.4	.9918	.9920	.9922	.9925	.9927	.9929	.9931	.9932	.9934	.9936
2.5	.9938	.9940	.9941	.9943	.9945	.9946	.9948	.9949	.9951	.9952
2.6	.9953	.9955	.9956	.9957	.9959	.9960	.9961	.9962	.9963	.9964
2.7	.9965	.9966	.9967	.9968	.9969	.9970	.9971	.9972	.9973	.9974
2.8	.9974	.9975	.9976	.9977	.9977	.9978	.9979	.9979	.9980	.9981
2.9	.9981	.9982	.9982	.9983	.9984	.9984	.9985	.9985	.9986	.9986
3.0	.9987	.9987	.9987	.9988	.9988	.9989	.9989	.9989	.9990	.9990
3.1	.9990	.9991	.9991	.9991	.9992	.9992	.9992	.9992	.9993	.9993
3.2	.9993	.9993	.9994	.9994	.9994	.9994	.9994	.9995	.9995	.9995
3.3	.9995	.9995	.9995	.9996	.9996	.9996	.9996	.9996	.9996	.9997
3.4	.9997	.9997	.9997	.9997	.9997	.9997	.9997	.9997	.9997	.9998

Business Statistics in Practice

FOURTH EDITION

The McGraw-Hill/Irwin Series: Operations and Decision Sciences

BUSINESS STATISTICS

Aczel and Sounderpandian,
Complete Business Statistics,
Sixth Edition

ALEKS Corporation,
ALEKS for Business Statistics,
First Edition

Alwan,
Statistical Process Analysis,
First Edition

Bowerman and O'Connell,
Business Statistics in Practice,
Fourth Edition

Bowerman, O'Connell, and Orris,
Essentials of Business Statistics,
First Edition

***Bryant and Smith,**
Practical Data Analysis: Case Studies in Business Statistics, Volumes I, II, and III

Cooper and Schindler,
Business Research Methods,
Ninth Edition

Delurgio,
Forecasting Principles and Applications,
First Edition

Doane and Seward,
Applied Statistics in Business and Economics,
First Edition

Doane,
LearningStats CD Rom,
First Edition, 1.2

Doane, Mathieson, and Tracy,
Visual Statistics,
Second Edition, 2.0

Gitlow, Oppenheim, Oppenheim, and Levine,
Quality Management,
Third Edition

Lind, Marchal, and Wathen,
Basic Statistics for Business and Economics,
Fifth Edition

Lind, Marchal, and Wathen,
Statistical Techniques in Business and Economics,
Twelfth Edition

Merchant, Goffinet, and Koehler,
Basic Statistics Using Excel for Office XP,
Third Edition

Kutner, Nachtsheim, Neter and Li,
Applied Linear Statistical Models,
Fifth Edition

Kutner, Nachtsheim, and Neter,
Applied Linear Regression Models,
Fourth Edition

Sahai and Khurshid,
Pocket Dictionary of Statistics,
First Edition

Siegel,
Practical Business Statistics,
Fifth Edition

Wilson, Keating, and John Galt Solutions, Inc.,
Business Forecasting,
Fifth Edition

Zagorsky,
Business Information,
First Edition

QUANTITATIVE METHODS AND MANAGEMENT SCIENCE

Hillier and Hillier,
Introduction to Management Science,
Second Edition

*Available only through McGraw-Hill's PRIMIS Digital Assets Library.

Bruce L. Bowerman

Richard T. O'Connell

Miami University

Business Statistics in Practice

FOURTH EDITION

with additional examples and exercises and selected appendices by
Steven C. Huchendorf

University of Minnesota

with MegaStat software and other contributions by
J. Burdene Orris

Butler University

Boston Burr Ridge, IL Dubuque, IA Madison, WI New York San Francisco St. Louis
Bangkok Bogotá Caracas Kuala Lumpur Lisbon London Madrid Mexico City
Milan Montreal New Delhi Santiago Seoul Singapore Sydney Taipei Toronto

The McGraw·Hill Companies

BUSINESS STATISTICS IN PRACTICE
International Edition 2007

Exclusive rights by McGraw-Hill Education (Asia), for manufacture and export. This book cannot be re-exported from the country to which it is sold by McGraw-Hill. The International Edition is not available in North America.

Published by McGraw-Hill/Irwin, a business unit of The McGraw-Hill Companies, Inc., 1221 Avenue of the Americas, New York, NY 10020.

10 09 08 07 06 05 04 03 02 01
20 09 08 07
CTP SLP

When ordering this title, use ISBN: 978- 007-126118-0 or MHID: 007-126118-4

Printed in Singapore

www.mhhe.com

Bruce L. Bowerman
To my wife, children, sister, and other family members:
Drena
Michael, Jinda, Benjamin, and Lex
Asa and Nicole
Susan
Fiona and Radeesa
Daphne, Chloe, and Edgar
Gwyneth and Tony

Richard T. O'Connell
To my wife and children:
Jean
Christopher and Bradley

About the Authors

Bruce L. Bowerman Bruce L. Bowerman is professor of decision sciences at Miami University in Oxford, Ohio. He received his Ph.D. degree in statistics from Iowa State University in 1974, and he has over 37 years of experience teaching basic statistics, regression analysis, time series forecasting, survey sampling, and design of experiments to both undergraduate and graduate students. In 1987 Professor Bowerman received an Outstanding Teaching award from the Miami University senior class, and in 1992 he received an Effective Educator award from the Richard T. Farmer School of Business Administration. Together with Richard T. O'Connell, Professor Bowerman has written 11 textbooks. These include *Forecasting and Time Series: An Applied Approach; Forecasting, Time Series, and Regression: An Applied Approach* (also coauthored with Anne B. Koehler); and *Linear Statistical Models: An Applied Approach.* The first edition of *Forecasting and Time Series* earned an Outstanding Academic Book award from *Choice* magazine. Professor Bowerman has also published a number of articles in applied stochastic processes, time series forecasting, and statistical education. In his spare time, Professor Bowerman enjoys watching movies and sports, playing tennis, and designing houses.

Richard T. O'Connell Richard T. O'Connell is associate professor of decision sciences at Miami University in Oxford, Ohio. He has more than 32 years of experience teaching basic statistics, statistical quality control and process improvement, regression analysis, time series forecasting, and design of experiments to both undergraduate and graduate business students. He also has extensive consulting experience and has taught workshops dealing with statistical process control and process improvement for a variety of companies in the Midwest. In 2000 Professor O'Connell received an Effective Educator award from the Richard T. Farmer School of Business Administration. Together with Bruce L. Bowerman, he has written 11 textbooks. These include *Forecasting and Time Series: An Applied Approach; Forecasting, Time Series, and Regression: An Applied Approach* (also coauthored with Anne B. Koehler); and *Linear Statistical Models: An Applied Approach.* Professor O'Connell has published a number of articles in the area of innovative statistical education. He is one of the first college instructors in the United States to integrate statistical process control and process improvement methodology into his basic business statistics course. He (with Professor Bowerman) has written several articles advocating this approach. He has also given presentations on this subject at meetings such as the Joint Statistical Meetings of the American Statistical Association and the Workshop on Total Quality Management: Developing Curricula and Research Agendas (sponsored by the Production and Operations Management Society). Professor O'Connell received an M.S. degree in decision sciences from Northwestern University in 1973, and he is currently a member of both the Decision Sciences Institute and the American Statistical Association. In his spare time, Professor O'Connell enjoys fishing, collecting 1950s and 1960s rock music, and following the Green Bay Packers and Purdue University sports.

Preface

In *Business Statistics in Practice, Fourth Edition,* we provide a modern, practical, and unique framework for teaching the first course in business statistics. This framework features case study and example driven discussions of all basic business statistics topics. In addition, we have endeavored to make this book the most clearly written, motivating, and easy to use business statistics text available. We have taken great pains to explain concepts simply from first principles. Therefore, the only prerequisite for this book is high school algebra.

Business Statistics in Practice has five attributes that make it an effective learning tool:

- A consistent theme of business improvement through statistical analysis.
- A unique use of "continuing" case studies that integrates different statistical areas.
- A real emphasis on the study of variation that stresses that the analysis of individual population observations is as important as the analysis of population means.
- A flexible topic flow that facilitates different topic choices and encourages different teaching approaches. In particular, since many courses give different emphases to probability, hypothesis testing, regression and statistical modeling, nonparametric statistics, and quality control, this book provides great flexibility with respect to how, when, and whether to cover these topics.
- A modern use of the statistical capabilities of the software packages MINITAB, Excel, and MegaStat (an Excel add-in package included on the text's student CD-ROM) that stresses statistical interpretation and reflects the use of these packages in the real world.

New to the fourth edition are

- *The cell phone case,* which is the first continuing case in Chapter 1 and discusses how a bank uses a random sample to estimate its cell phone costs. Using this estimate, the bank decides whether to outsource management of its wireless resources. This case should be particularly motivating to students because it addresses a real problem faced by both students and businesses—unpleasantly high cell phone bills.
- *Continuing cases with no need to refer back to previously given computer outputs.* Each time a continuing case is revisited, any needed computer output is included with the current case discussion. In addition, whenever possible the background information needed to understand the current analysis is provided, so the student does not need to refer back to previous material.
- *Business improvement icons* BI—placed in the page margins—that identify when an important business conclusion has been reached using statistical analysis. Each conclusion is also highlighted for additional emphasis.
- *Confidence intervals for and hypothesis tests about a population mean presented by using the σ known/σ unknown approach.* This approach simplifies the choice of z or t-based procedures and is consistent with computerized procedures provided by MINITAB, Excel, and MegaStat. A t distribution table with up to 100 degrees of freedom is given in Table A.4 of Appendix A. Confidence intervals for and hypothesis tests about the difference between two population means are also presented using the σ known/σ unknown approach.
- *Completely updated end of chapter computer appendices* that clearly show how to perform statistical analysis using MINITAB (Version 14), Microsoft Excel 2003, and the latest version of MegaStat.
- *Expanded coverage of sampling in Chapter 1.* We now discuss using both a random number table and computer generated random numbers to select a random sample. We also have added an optional section that introduces stratified, cluster, and systematic sampling and discusses the problems of undercoverage, nonresponse, and response bias.
- *A substantial number of new, real world data sets in the exercises,* particularly in the exercises of Chapter 1 (An Introduction to Business Statistics) and Chapter 2 (Descriptive Statistics).

- *An optional appendix on covariance and correlation.* This end of book appendix (Appendix B) can be covered either after covering scatter plots in Chapter 2 or before covering simple linear regression analysis in Chapter 11. Or, it can be omitted entirely without loss of continuity.
- *An optional appendix on normal probability plots.* This end of book appendix (Appendix D, Part 1) supplements the normal distribution discussion in Chapter 5.
- *A simpler and easier to understand example introducing sampling distributions.* This stock return example motivates the discussion of the sampling distribution of the sample mean in Chapter 6.
- *Increased emphasis on the concept of the margin of error* to better motivate the discussion of confidence intervals in Chapter 7.
- *A step-by-step hypothesis testing approach* that is used in almost all hypothesis testing examples in Chapter 8 (Hypothesis Testing) and Chapter 9 (Statistical Inferences Based on Two Samples). This approach consists of a seven-step procedure that is designed to break hypothesis testing down into small, easy to understand steps and to also clearly show how to use the book's hypothesis testing summary boxes. Although the seven-step procedure is not formally used after Chapter 9, the students' familiarity with the steps and summary boxes should enable them to successfully carry out hypothesis tests in later chapters.
- *Increased emphasis in Chapter 9 on the "unequal variances" t-based procedure for comparing two population means.* This procedure is becoming increasingly popular because it is available in most statistical software packages and is a very accurate approximation that does not require assuming equal population variances.
- *A simplified and improved discussion of simple and multiple regression analysis.* In simple regression (Chapter 11), we give more concise explanations of the simple linear regression model, least squares, and confidence and prediction intervals. In addition to using improved graphics, the chapter also provides the flexibility to cover simple coefficients of determination and correlation (Section 11.6) early or later in the chapter. In multiple regression (Chapter 12), we have refined the innovative, modular organization of the third edition. This will make it easier to selectively cover whatever multiple regression (and model building) topics are desired. We have also simplified the presentation of dummy variables and added a short section on *logistic regression.* In both the simple and multiple regression chapters, we have improved our explanations and use of MINITAB, Excel, and MegaStat regression outputs. Key outputs are more clearly annotated to help the beginner find needed regression quantities.
- *An optional appendix on Holt–Winters' exponential smoothing models.* This appendix (Appendix E) is now included in the book (and on the book's CD-ROM).

In addition, as in the third edition, there is an optional section in Chapter 5 that covers use of the cumulative normal table. Although (because of reviewer input) we use the standard normal table to explain confidence intervals and hypothesis tests based on the normal distribution, we have explicitly designed the figures illustrating normal curve areas so that the intervals and tests can also be explained using the cumulative normal table.

We now discuss in more detail the attributes that make *Business Statistics in Practice* an effective learning tool.

Business improvement through statistical analysis The ultimate goal of statistical analysis in business is business improvement. This theme is the foundation for the case studies and examples in this text, many of which are based on actual, real world situations. For example, consider the following synopses of three case studies.

- **The Cheese Spread Case:** The marketer of a soft cheese spread wishes to replace the spout on its plastic dispenser with a less expensive spout. The company uses confidence intervals to conclude that demand for the spread will remain sufficiently high when the change is made to make replacing the spout profitable.
- **The Trash Bag Case:** A leading producer of trash bags uses hypothesis testing to convince the standards and practices division of a major television network that advertising claims about its newest trash bag are valid.
- **The Fuel Consumption Case:** A natural gas company uses regression analysis to predict its city's natural gas needs accurately enough to avoid paying fines to a pipeline transmission system.

In each of these cases, statistical analysis leads to an informed action (replace the spout, advertise the claim, use the regression prediction procedure) that results in business improvement. Furthermore, we continue this theme throughout the presentation of all statistical techniques in this book. For instance, we use descriptive and inferential statistics to compare the risk and return characteristics of different investment choices in order to improve the way we manage an investment portfolio; we use statistical process control to improve manufacturing and service processes; and we use design of experiments to study the effects of several different advertising campaigns in order to improve how a product is marketed.

A unique continuity of presentation and use of case studies *Business Statistics in Practice* features a unique continuity of presentation that integrates different statistical areas. This integration is achieved by an early emphasis (in Chapters 1 and 2) on the difference between the population and the sample and by a continuing use of practical, realistic case studies that span not only individual chapters but also groups of chapters. Specifically, Chapter 1 shows how to select random (or approximately random) samples from populations and processes by introducing four case studies as examples and by presenting additional case studies as exercises. Then in Chapter 2 we show how to use descriptive statistics to estimate the important aspects of these populations and processes. We continue to employ these case studies through the probability and sampling distribution chapters until we use confidence intervals and hypothesis testing to make statistical inferences. Furthermore, we introduce new case studies in each and every chapter. For example, we introduce several case studies in our presentation of simple linear regression and then extend these case studies when we discuss multiple regression and model building to show how regression is used in the description, prediction, and control of business variables.

A real emphasis on the importance of variation *Business Statistics in Practice* emphasizes that since businesses must satisfy individual customers, the analysis of individual population observations—which is achieved by analyzing population variation—is as important as analyzing the population mean. Our discussion of variation begins in Chapter 1, where we intuitively examine the variation of sample data and use simple runs plots to evaluate statistical control. This discussion continues in Chapter 2, where we use the empirical rule to estimate tolerance intervals containing different percentages of population observations. For example, we use the empirical rule in the

- **Payment Time Case** to describe the variation of individual bill payment times around the estimated mean bill payment time for a new electronic billing system.
- **Marketing Research Case** to describe the variation of individual customer ratings of a new soft drink bottle design around the estimated mean rating of the new design.
- **Car Mileage Case** to describe the variation of individual gas mileages around the estimated mean mileage obtained by a new midsize car.

In addition, in the **coffee temperature case** we introduce the idea of process capability—determining whether almost all process observations fall within customer requirements—and in other case studies we consider the problems involved with describing the variation of highly skewed populations.

Our emphasis on variation continues throughout the book. For example, in Chapter 7 we clearly distinguish between a confidence interval for a population mean and a tolerance interval for a given percentage of individual population measurements. In Chapter 8 we discuss the effect of variation on the interpretation of a hypothesis test about the population mean. In Chapters 11 through 13 we show how prediction intervals can be used to evaluate the predictive capabilities of different regression and time series forecasting models. In addition, we demonstrate how prediction intervals are used to assess whether any individual population observations are "unusual" enough to suggest the need for process improvement. Finally, in Chapter 14 we present a complete discussion of statistical process control and improvement (including the six sigma philosophy adopted by Motorola, Inc., and a number of other prominent U.S. companies). Furthermore, in all of these chapters we use practical case studies to illustrate the ideas being presented.

A flexible topic flow Although the table of contents of this book reveals a rather standard topic organization, the book utilizes a flexible topic flow that facilitates different topic choices and encourages different teaching approaches. In particular, since different courses place different amounts of emphasis on probability, hypothesis testing, regression and statistical modeling, nonparametric statistics, and quality control, this book provides great flexibility with respect to how, when, and whether to cover these topics. Furthermore, in optional sections, appendices, and self-learning exercises, the book gives the student the opportunity to study more advanced topics in a concise and practical way. Thus, as we now discuss, courses with a wide variety of topic coverages and emphases can be taught using this book.

Probability The most minimal approach to probability would cover Section 3.1 (the concept of probability), Section 4.1 (random variables), Section 5.1 (continuous probability distributions), and Section 5.3 (the normal distribution, including an intuitive example of the addition rule for mutually exclusive events). These sections are the only prerequisites for Chapters 6 through 14 (sampling distributions, confidence intervals, hypothesis testing, experimental design, regression, time series forecasting, and quality control).

Instructors who wish to also cover discrete probability distributions (Chapter 4) have the option of doing this either with a fairly minimal probability background or with a complete probability background. The fairly minimal probability background consists of Section 3.1 (the concept of probability) and Section 3.2 (using sample spaces to find probabilities). Note that this background is sufficient because, since Example 4.2 of Chapter 4 intuitively illustrates the multiplication rule for independent events and the addition rule for mutually exclusive events in the context of finding a discrete probability distribution, it is not necessary to cover the complete discussion of probability rules given in Sections 3.3 and 3.4. Of course, this complete discussion is necessary background for covering chi-square tests of independence (Chapter 16) and Bayes' Theorem and decision theory (Chapter 17). Also, the complete discussion features the **AccuRatings Case,** which is a very motivating data driven application of the probability rules.

Hypothesis testing In the fourth edition we have used a seven-step procedure to break hypothesis testing down into small, easy-to-understand steps and to clearly show how to use the book's hypothesis testing summary boxes. In addition, we have fully and concisely integrated the discussion of using rejection points and p-values. The seven-step procedure shows how to use both approaches, and the hypothesis testing boxes summarize both rejection points and p-values for each test. We have also motivated the link between the approaches by considering how major television networks sometimes use different α values when evaluating advertising claims. We are aware of several courses that introduce hypothesis testing in the context of using p-values to test the significance of regression coefficients. This can be done in our book by totally skipping Chapter 8 and by noting that every section throughout the rest of the book includes self-contained summary boxes (and examples) that fully cover any needed confidence intervals and hypothesis tests. Also, Chapter 6 (sampling distributions) intuitively illustrates the use of p-values in the context of evaluating a claim about a population mean and in the context of evaluating a claim about a population proportion. Therefore, Chapter 6 can be used as an extremely short, intuitive introduction to p-values.

Regression and statistical modeling The fourth edition features an innovative organization of regression analysis that simplifies the flow of the overall discussion and makes it very easy to cover whatever regression topics are desired. As in the third edition, we have included an optional section on residual analysis at the end of the simple linear regression chapter (Chapter 11). In Chapter 12: Multiple Regression and Model Building, we have refined the modular organization of the third edition and have made it easier to cover whatever portions of multiple regression and model building are desired. As shown in a diagram on its opening page, Chapter 12 consists of four parts. Part 1: Basic Multiple Regression discusses the basic descriptive and inferential techniques of multiple regression analysis and would be a sufficient introduction to this topic for many introductory business statistics courses. After completing Part 1, the reader can study optional Part 2: Using Squared and Interaction Terms, optional Part 3: Dummy Variables and Advanced Statistical Inferences, and any section of optional Part 4: Model Building and Model Diagnostics. These optional parts can be covered in any order and without loss of continuity (note that Part 4 consists of four self-contained sections: model building and the effects of multicollinearity; residual analysis in multiple regression; diagnostics for detecting outlying and influential observations; and logistic regression). Furthermore, optional material covering model diagnostics and topics in some of the supplementary exercises tie key portions of the four parts together. This approach allows instructors to easily cover what they consider most important in courses with limited time devoted to regression analysis. Similarly, since many business statistics courses do not have substantial time to devote to experimental design (Chapter 10) and time series forecasting (Chapter 13), we have put great effort into making our presentation of these topics both complete and easy to get through.

Nonparametric statistics We have placed all of the nonparametric techniques covered in the book in Chapter 15. Furthermore, at the end of the discussion of each parametric technique in Chapters 8 through 11 we refer readers to the section in Chapter 15 that discusses the nonparametric technique that would be used if the assumptions for the parametric technique fail to hold. Therefore, the instructor has the option of integrating the discussion of nonparametric statistics into the main flow of Chapters 8 through 11.

Quality control Process improvement through control charts is discussed in Chapter 14. Thus, this topic is placed outside of the main flow of what might be regarded as classical statistics. However, since Chapter 14 has as its only prerequisite Chapter 6 on sampling distributions, the instructor has the option to cover Chapter 14 at any point after Chapter 6.

Optional Advanced Topics In optional sections, appendices, and self-learning exercises, the book gives the student the opportunity to study more advanced topics in a concise and practical way. Examination of the table of contents reveals that many of the more advanced topics—for example, counting rules (Appendix C, Part 1), the hypergeometric distribution (Appendix C, Part 2), covariance and correlation (Appendix B), normal probability plots (Appendix D, Part 1), the Poisson and exponential distributions (Sections 4.4 and 5.5), calculating the probability of a Type II error (Section 8.6), and statistical inferences for a population variance (Section 8.8)—are included in many other business statistics books. However, some of the more advanced topics, while not unique to this book, are less frequently covered in other basic statistics texts. These topics (the most advanced of which are discussed in CD-ROM Appendices F through L) are as follows:

- Properties of the Mean and Variance of a Random Variable, and the Covariance Between Two Random Variables (Appendix D, Part 2).
- Derivations of the Mean and the Variance of the Sample Mean and of the Mean and the Variance of the Sample Proportion (Appendix D, Part 3).
- Confidence Intervals for Parameters of Finite Populations (Section 7.5), including sample size determination (Exercise 7.57).
- An Introduction to Survey Sampling (Section 1.5); estimation formulas, optimal allocation, and sample size determination in stratified random sampling (Appendix F, Part 1); and estimation formulas in one- and two-stage cluster sampling and ratio estimation (Appendix F, Part 2).
- A Comparison of Confidence Intervals and Tolerance Intervals (Section 7.6).
- Using Matrix Algebra to Perform Regression Calculations (Appendix G).
- The regression approach to one-way analysis of variance (Exercise 12.45), and the regression approach to two-way analysis of variance (Appendix H).
- Advanced Model Diagnostics (Exercises 12.76 and 12.77) and Model Building with Squared and Interaction Terms (Exercise 12.74).
- Logistic Regression (Section 12.15) and Discriminant Analysis (Exercise 12.78).
- Factor Analysis, Cluster Analysis, and Multidimensional Scaling (Appendix I).
- The Box–Jenkins methodology, a fairly complete discussion featuring nonseasonal and seasonal modeling, using autocorrelated error term models in regression analysis, intervention analysis, and transfer function models (Appendix J).
- Individuals charts and c charts (Appendix L).

Furthermore, we have put great effort into making the discussion of all of the more advanced topics clear, concise, and easy to get through. This gives the instructor considerable flexibility in designing different business statistics courses. For example, a professor teaching a second course in business statistics can opt to either cover a variety of intermediate topics or present a more in-depth treatment of regression analysis and forecasting.

MINITAB, Excel, and MegaStat *Business Statistics in Practice, Fourth Edition,* features a modern use of the statistical capabilities of the software packages MINITAB, Excel, and the Excel add-in MegaStat. Throughout the book we provide an abundant number of outputs from all three packages in both examples and exercises that allow students to concentrate on statistical interpretations. This use of outputs is particularly prominent in statistical areas where hand calculations are impossible or impractical and where having students run their own programs (while theoretically optimal) would, because of time constraints, not allow them to see a wide variety of applications. These areas include descriptive statistics, ANOVA, regression, and time series forecasting. In addition, appendices at the end of each chapter show in detail how to use MINITAB, Excel, and MegaStat to implement the statistical techniques discussed in the chapter. For the fourth edition, the developer of MegaStat, Professor J. B. Orris of Butler University, has worked closely with us. We believe that MegaStat is the most comprehensive, accurate, and easy to use Excel add-in package in existence. In addition to remedying most of the computational problems associated with Excel Data Analysis Tools, MegaStat is also specifically designed to enhance the use of *Business Statistics in Practice.* For example,

- In addition to giving the usual descriptive statistics, frequency distributions, and histograms, MegaStat provides stem-and-leaf displays, box plots, dot plots, runs plots, normal plots, and output for the Empirical Rule (as well as tolerance intervals estimated to contain any specified percentage of individual observations). MegaStat also gives the option to calculate tolerance intervals and confidence intervals using the same dialog box. Therefore, students can better understand the crucial difference between these two types of intervals (as illustrated on pages 293 and 294).
- The MegaStat dialog box for every one and two sample hypothesis testing procedure for means and proportions allows the user to calculate a confidence interval for the population parameter being tested. Therefore, the student is encouraged to evaluate both statistical significance and practical importance. Such evaluation is a consistent theme of *Business Statistics in Practice* (in particular, see Chapters 8 and 9).
- MegaStat's one-way ANOVA, randomized block, and two-factor ANOVA procedures provide graphical output helping students to better analyze experimental data. In addition, each procedure provides easy to understand pairwise comparisons of population means using both Tukey procedures and individual t-tests. Such graphical analysis and pairwise comparisons are emphasized in Chapter 10.
- In addition to providing confidence intervals and prediction intervals in simple and multiple regression, MegaStat gives a full range of residual plots, normal plots, and outlying and influential observation diagnostics, as well as the variance inflation factors for the independent variables in a regression model. In addition, MegaStat provides an all possible regressions output that summarizes all well known model selection criteria, as well as the p-values for the independent variables. MegaStat also gives a stepwise selection procedure that provides more information than given by classical stepwise regression or backward elimination. MegaStat's regression capabilities are designed to enhance the regression coverage in Chapters 11 and 12. Furthermore, all of MegaStat's regression capabilities can be accessed in one very easy to use dialog box, allowing the student to carry out a wide range of regression procedures in a correct, informative, and simple way.

In addition, MegaStat is fully capable of performing analysis related to discrete and continuous probability distributions, time series forecasting, nonparametric statistics, chi-square tests, and statistical quality control charts—virtually all topics covered by *Business Statistics in Practice.* MegaStat is provided on the student CD-ROM.

Further Features The book's CD-ROM, in addition to containing the previously discussed advanced topic appendices and MegaStat, also features Excel templates, data files, tutorials, web links, self graded quizzes, PowerPoint presentations, and Visual Statistics 2.0 by Doane, Mathieson, and Tracy. Visual Statistics is a Windows software program that helps students learn statistics through interactive experimentation and visualization. Visual statistics icons in the text identify concepts that are further explained by Visual Statistics. This edition also features Homework Manager. This is an online electronic tutor customized to the text and available as an option to students.

In addition, the book has the following supplements: an instructor's solutions manual developed by Patrick Schur, Miami University, and test bank developed by Denise Krallman, Miami University (included on the instructor's edition CD-ROM and available in print format); a student study guide developed by Sandra Strassar, Valparaiso University (available in print format); and PowerPoint transparency masters developed by Ronny Richardson, Southern Polytechnic State University, with contributions by Harvey Singer, George Mason University.

Acknowledgments We wish to thank the many people who have helped to make this book a reality. First, we wish to thank Drena Bowerman, who spent many hours cutting and taping and making trips to the copy shop, so that we could complete the manuscript on time. Second, we wish to thank Professor J. B. Orris of Butler University. Professor Orris's hard work and dedication have made MegaStat a truly excellent statistical software package. In addition, his feedback and many intellectual contributions have greatly improved this book. Third, we wish to thank Professor Steven Huchendorf of the University of Minnesota. Professor Huchendorf provided a substantial number of new exercises for the fourth edition and helped tremendously in the development and writing of Appendix B: Covariance and Correlation and Appendix D (Part 1): Normal Probability Plots. He did this in a very timely fashion, and we really appreciate his work. Fourth, we wish to thank Professor Michael L. Hand of Willamette University, who is a coauthor of the second edition of this book. Although Professor Hand did not work on the fourth edition, we thank him for his contributions to the second edition and regard him as a valued friend and colleague. Finally, we wish to thank Professor Anne Koehler of Miami University. Professor Koehler wrote the original versions of the MINITAB and Excel appendices included in the text. The final appendices are largely based on her original versions. We cannot thank Professor Koehler enough for her selfless work, which is a hallmark of her career. We also wish to thank the people at McGraw-Hill/Irwin for their dedication to this book. These people include Executive Editor Scott Isenberg, who has made many excellent suggestions for developing the second, third, and fourth editions of this book and who is, in general, a very positive and helpful resource to the authors; Executive Editor Dick Hercher, who persuaded us initially to publish this book with McGraw-Hill/Irwin and who continues to offer sound advice and support with each revision of the book; Senior Developmental Editor Wanda Zeman, who has shown great dedication through four editions of this book (Wanda's many excellent ideas and tireless attention to detail have been instrumental in the continual improvement of the book); and Project Manager Laura Griffin, who has capably and diligently guided this book through its production, and who consistently proves to be a tremendous help to the authors.

We thank the many contributors who reviewed text chapters and/or provided helpful feedback at one of our reviewer conferences. We are grateful to all of them.

Sung Ahn, Washington State University
Arsene Aka, Catholic University of America
Charles Apigian, Middle Tennessee State University
Philip Boudreaux, University of Louisiana–Lafayette
Robert Brookshire, James Madison University
Wen Chiang, University of Tulsa
Ali Choudry, Florida International University
Howard Clayton, Auburn University
Richard Cox, University of Arkansas–Little Rock
Bradford Crain, Portland State University
Nandita Das, Lehigh University
Cassandra DiRienzo, Elon University
Anne Marie Drougas, Dominican University
Joy Field, Boston College
Gary Franko, Siena College
David Friesen, Midwestern State University
Thomas Groleau, Carthage College
Cindy Hinz, Saint Bonaventure University
Johnny Ho, Columbus State University
Steven Huchendorf, University of Minnesota
Peter Ittig, University of Massachusetts
Chun Jin, Central Connecticut University
Mark Karseig, Central Missouri State University

Ron Klimberg, Saint Joseph's University
Jennifer Kohn, Montclair State University
Maria Lambert, Pitt Community College
Constantine Loucopoulos, Northeastern State University
Brad McDonald, Northern Illinois University
Constance McLaren, Indiana State University
Jackie Miller, Ohio State University
John M. Miller, Sam Houston State University
Patricia A. Mullins, University of Wisconsin–Madison
Tappan K. Nayak, George Washington University
Sufi M. Nazem, University of Nebraska–Omaha
Gary Nelson, Central Community College–Columbus
Ceyhun Ozgur, Valparaiso University
Jayprakash Patankar, University of Akron
Deborah Primm, Jacksonville State University
Harold Rahmlon, Saint Joseph's University
Said E Said, East Carolina University
Scott Seipel, Middle Tennessee State University
Sankara Sethuraman, Augusta State University
Daniel Shimsak, University of Massachusetts–Boston
Walter Simmons, John Carroll University
Harvey Singer, George Mason University
Robert Smidt, California Polytechnic University
Toni Somers, Wayne State University
Robert Stevens, University of Louisiana–Monroe
Faye Teer, James Madison University
Dharma Thiruvaiyaru, Augusta State University
James Thorson, Southern Connecticut State University
Bijesh Tolia, Chicago State University
Akinori Tomahara, Queens College
Fan T. Tseng, University of Alabama–Huntsville
Lee Van Scyoc, University of Wisconsin–Oshkosh
William Warde, Oklahoma State University
Allen Webster, Bradley University
Mark Witkowski, University of Arkansas–Little Rock
Louis Woods, University of North Florida
Jack Yurkiewicz, Pace University
Jay Zagorsky, Boston University
Zhen Zhu, University of Central Oklahoma
Zhiwei Zhu, University of Louisiana–Lafayette

We also wish to thank the error checker, Don R. Robinson, Illinois State University, who was very helpful. Most important, we wish to thank our families for their acceptance, unconditional love, and support.

Bruce L. Bowerman
Richard T. O'Connell

Brief Table of Contents

Table of Contents

Chapter 13

Time Series Forecasting

Chapter 14

Process Improvement Using Control Charts

Guided Tour

Business Statistics in Practice, Fourth Edition, has been written with students' needs in mind. Its clear and understandable explanations and use of real world case studies and examples present content that business students can relate to. Because today's students learn in a visual and interactive way, the text is supplemented by a free student CD-ROM, containing a host of updated resources and helpful study aids. In addition, both students and instructors are provided with additional resources on the text website. Thus, students are given a number of statistical tools in a variety of ways and shown how these tools can be used to positively impact business and other organizations.

Chapter Introductions

Each chapter opens with a preview showing how the statistical topics to be discussed apply to real business problems. The continuing case examples that run throughout the book are briefly introduced along with the techniques that will be used to analyze them.

Visual Statistics 2.0

Visual Statistics, described later in the tour, helps students learn statistics through interactive experimentation and visualization. Concepts in the text that are treated in the Visual Statistics software program are identified by icon, with chapter reference, in the margin of the text next to the concept.

In Chapter 1 we saw that although we can sometimes take a census of an entire population, we often must randomly select a sample from a population. When we have taken a census or a sample, we typically wish to describe the observed data set. In particular, we describe a sample in order to make inferences about the sampled population.

In this chapter we learn about **descriptive statistics,** which is the science of describing the important characteristics of a population or sample. Generally, we look at several important aspects of a set of measurements. One such aspect is the **central tendency,** or middle, of the data set. For instance, we might estimate a typical bottle design rating in the marketing research case or a typical city driving mileage in the car mileage case. Another important aspect of a data set is the **variability,** or spread, of the data. For example, we might estimate the largest and smallest gas mileage that would likely be obtained when a new midsize car is purchased. Or, in the marketing research case we might measure the spread of the bottle design ratings. If the ratings are clustered closely together, consumers' ratings are much the same (or are consistent). If the ratings are spread far apart, then consumers have widely varying opinions of the new bottle design. A third important aspect of a data set is the **shape** of the population or sample. Looking at a data set's shape tells us how the population or sample is *distributed* over various values (more about this later). Still another important aspect is whether **outliers** exist. For instance, if there are outlying bottle design ratings, then several consumers have opinions about the design that are very different from the opinions of most of the sampled consumers. Descriptive statistics also involves using **graphical methods** to depict data sets and to study relationships between different variables.

In this chapter we use a variety of methods to describe the cell phone usages, bottle design ratings, coffee temperatures, and car mileages introduced in the cases of Chapter 1. In addition, we introduce three new cases:

The Payment Time Case: A management consulting firm assesses how effectively a new electronic billing system reduces bill payment times.

The Electronic Article Surveillance Case: A survey is used to study the unintended effects on consumer attitudes of false electronic article surveillance alarms.

The Marketing Ethics Case: A survey is conducted to study marketing researchers' attitudes toward violating confidentiality in marketing research studies.

2.1 Describing the Shape of a Distribution

We begin looking at the characteristics of a population by describing the population's overall pattern of variation. That is, we describe the shape of the distribution of population measurements. We often employ a sample of measurements taken from a population in order to infer what the population looks like.

VS CHAPTER 1

Several graphical methods—the **stem-and-leaf display,** the **histogram,** and the **dot plot**—are often used to portray shapes of distributions.

Stem-and-leaf displays We illustrate how to construct stem-and-leaf displays in the following examples.

Example 2.1 The Car Mileage Case

Table 2.1 presents the sample of 49 gas mileages that have been obtained by the new midsize model in Example 1.4 (page 15). To graphically portray the pattern of variation in these mileages, we can construct a stem-and-leaf display. In order to do this, we first notice that the sample mileages range from 29.8 to 33.3. For this data we will (somewhat arbitrarily) construct a display having the first two digits of the mileages—the whole numbers 29, 30, 31, 32, and 33—as the **stems.** These are placed in a column on the left side of the display as follows:

29
30
31
32
33

CHAPTER 2

Descriptive Statistics

Chapter Outline

Case Studies

The text provides a unique use of case studies that span individual chapters and groups of chapters. Cases are used to introduce the concepts, to demonstrate the methods, and to provide students with motivating exercises. These case studies help students see how statistics is used in business and can be used to improve processes.

Student Friendly Presentation

The authors have made improvements throughout the text to make learning easier for students. The following examples highlight some of these improvements.

Step-by-Step Hypothesis Testing Approach

This approach consists of a seven-step procedure designed to break hypothesis testing down into small, easy to understand steps. This procedure is used in almost all the examples in Chapters 8 and 9 and can be applied by students throughout the remainder of the text where hypothesis testing is done.

Testing a "greater than" alternative hypothesis by using a rejection point rule In Section 8.1 we explained how to set up appropriate null and alternative hypotheses. We also discussed how to specify a value for α, the probability of a Type I error (also called the **level of significance**) of the hypothesis test, and we introduced the idea of a test statistic. We can use these concepts to begin developing a seven step hypothesis testing procedure. We will introduce these steps in the context of the trash bag case and testing a "greater than" alternative hypothesis.

Step 1: State the null hypothesis H_0 and the alternative hypothesis H_a. In the trash bag case, we will test $H_0: \mu \leq 50$ versus $H_a: \mu > 50$. Here, μ is the mean breaking strength of the new trash bag.
Step 2: Specify the level of significance α. The television network will run the commercial stating that the new trash bag is stronger than the former bag if we can reject $H_0: \mu \leq 50$ in favor of $H_a: \mu > 50$ by setting α equal to .05.
Step 3: Select the test statistic. In order to test $H_0: \mu \leq 50$ versus $H_a: \mu > 50$, we will test the modified null hypothesis $H_0: \mu = 50$ versus $H_a: \mu > 50$. The idea here is that if there is sufficient evidence to reject the hypothesis that μ equals 50 in favor of $\mu > 50$, then there is certainly also sufficient evidence to reject the hypothesis that μ is less than or equal to 50. In order to test $H_0: \mu = 50$ versus $H_a: \mu > 50$, we will randomly select a sample of $n = 40$ new trash bags and calculate the mean $\bar{x}$ of the breaking strengths of these bags. We will then utilize the **test statistic**

$$z = \frac{\bar{x} - 50}{\sigma_{\bar{x}}} = \frac{\bar{x} - 50}{\sigma/\sqrt{n}}$$

A positive value of this test statistic results from an $\bar{x}$ that is greater than 50 and thus provides evidence against $H_0: \mu = 50$ and in favor of $H_a: \mu > 50$.
Step 4: Determine the rejection point rule for deciding whether to reject H_0. To decide how large the test statistic must be to reject H_0 in favor of H_a by setting the probability of a Type I error equal to α, we do the following:

- Place the probability of a Type I error, α, in the right-hand tail of the standard normal curve and use the normal table (see Table A.3, page 824) to find the normal point z_α. Here z_α, which we call a **rejection point** (or **critical point**), is the point on the horizontal axis under the standard normal curve that gives a right-hand tail area equal to α.
- **Reject $H_0: \mu = 50$ in favor of $H_a: \mu > 50$ if and only if the test statistic z is greater than the rejection point z_α.** (This is the **rejection point rule.**)

Greater Accessibility of Continuing Cases

Each time a continuing case is revisited, any needed computer output and, whenever possible, relevant background information is included with the current case discussion. Consequently, students seldom need to refer back to previously covered material in order to grasp the content included in a given case segment.

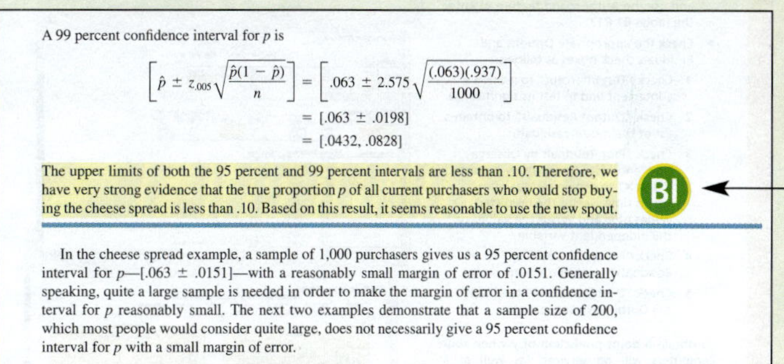
A 99 percent confidence interval for p is

$$\left[\hat{p} \pm z_{.005}\sqrt{\frac{\hat{p}(1-\hat{p})}{n}}\right] = \left[.063 \pm 2.575\sqrt{\frac{(.063)(.937)}{1000}}\right] = [.063 \pm .0198] = [.0432, .0828]$$

The upper limits of both the 95 percent and 99 percent intervals are less than .10. Therefore, we have very strong evidence that the true proportion p of all current purchasers who would stop buying the cheese spread is less than .10. Based on this result, it seems reasonable to use the new spout.

In the cheese spread example, a sample of 1,000 purchasers gives us a 95 percent confidence interval for p—[.063 ± .0151]—with a reasonably small margin of error of .0151. Generally speaking, quite a large sample is needed in order to make the margin of error in a confidence interval for p reasonably small. The next two examples demonstrate that a sample size of 200, which most people would consider quite large, does not necessarily give a 95 percent confidence interval for p with a small margin of error.

Business Improvement

Business improvement applications are identified by icons and are highlighted—to indicate when important business improvement conclusions have been reached using statistical analysis.

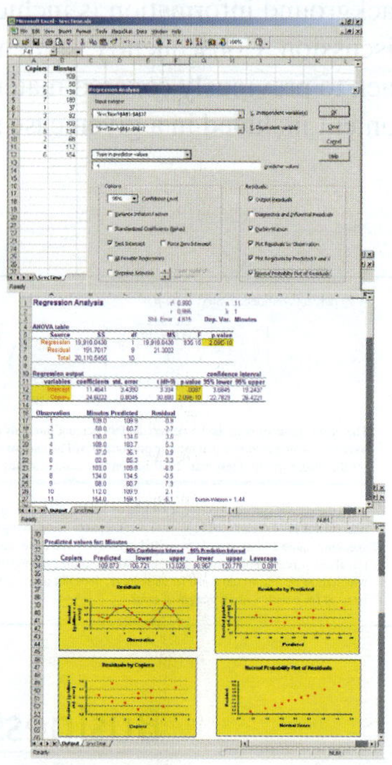
526 Chapter 11 Simple Linear Regression Analysis
Appendix 11.3 Simple Linear Regression Analysis Using MegaStat
The instructions in this section begin by describing the entry of data into an Excel worksheet. Alternatively, the data may be loaded directly from the data disk included with the text. The appropriate data file name is given at the top of each instruction block. Please refer to Appendix 1.2 for further information about entering data and saving and printing results in Excel. Please refer to Appendix 1.3 for more information about using MegaStat.
Simple linear regression for the service time data in Figure 11.14 on page 476 (data file: SrvcTime.xls):
Enter the service time data (page 456) with the numbers of copiers serviced in column A (with label Copiers) and the service times in column B (with label Minutes).
Select MegaStat : Correlation/Regression : Regression Analysis.
In the Regression Analysis dialog box, click in the "Independent variables" box and use the AutoExpand feature to enter the range A1.A12.
Click in the "Dependent variable" box and use the AutoExpand feature to enter the range B1.B12.
Check the appropriate Options and Residuals check boxes as follows:
1 Check "Test Intercept" to include a y-intercept and to test its significance.
2 Check "Output Residuals" to obtain a list of the model residuals.
3 Check "Plot Residuals by Observation" and "Plot Residuals by Predicted Y and X" to obtain residual plots versus time, versus the predicted values of y, and versus the values of the independent variable.
4 Check "Normal Probability Plot of Residuals" to obtain a normal plot.
5 Check "Durbin-Watson" to obtain the Durbin–Watson statistic.
To obtain a point prediction of y when four computers will be serviced (as well as a confidence interval and prediction interval):
Click on the drop-down menu above the Predictor Values box and select "Type in predictor values."
Type the value of the independent variable for which a prediction is desired (here equal to 4) into the "predictor values" box.
Select a desired level of confidence (here 95%) from the Confidence Level drop-down menu or type in a value.
Click OK in the Regression Analysis dialog box.

Excel/MINITAB/MegaStat Tutorials

The end of chapter appendices contain helpful tutorials that teach students how to carry out statistical analysis using Excel, MINITAB, and MegaStat. These tutorials include step-by-step instructions for performing almost every type of statistical method presented in the book. For additional help, video tutorials for Excel, MINITAB, and MegaStat are provided on the Student CD-ROM.

Excel, MINITAB, and MegaStat Output

Throughout the text, Excel, MINITAB, and MegaStat outputs illustrate how statistical analysis is done electronically.

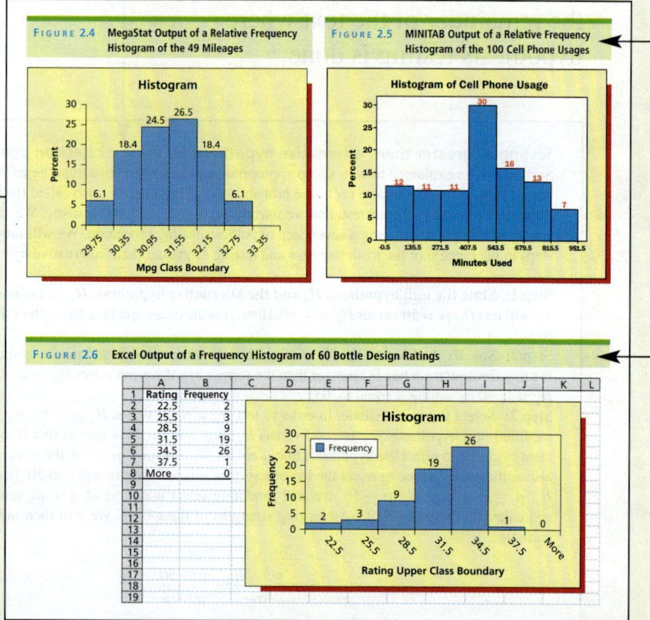
FIGURE 2.4 MegaStat Output of a Relative Frequency Histogram of the 49 Mileages
Histogram
Percent
Mpg Class Boundary
FIGURE 2.5 MINITAB Output of a Relative Frequency Histogram of the 100 Cell Phone Usages
Histogram of Cell Phone Usage
Percent
Minutes Used
FIGURE 2.6 Excel Output of a Frequency Histogram of 60 Bottle Design Ratings
Rating Frequency
Histogram
Frequency
Rating Upper Class Boundary

Exercises...

There are over 1000 exercises in the text. Many use real data from the current business literature. Data sets on the Student CD-ROM are identified by icon in the text. Within each chapter, exercises are broken into two parts—"Concepts" and "Methods and Applications." The methods and applications exercises vary in rigor from routine calculations to fairly sophisticated case study analysis. In addition, there are Internet exercises to help students make use of the Internet for gathering and using real data and supplementary exercises at the ends of chapters.

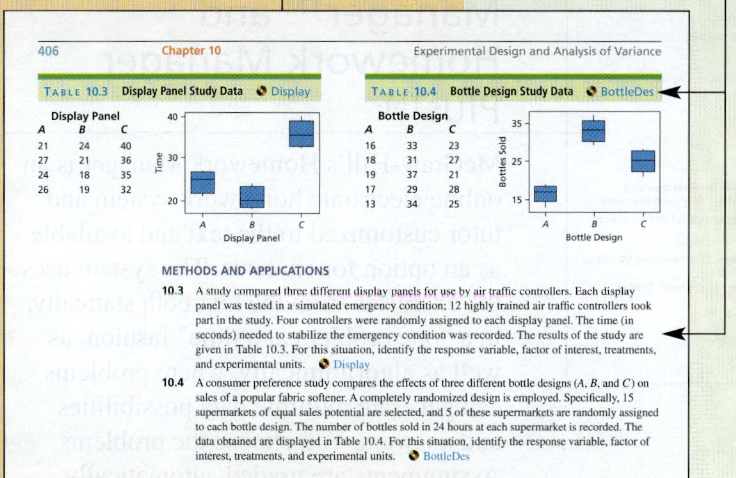

406 Chapter 10 Experimental Design and Analysis of Variance

Table 10.3 Display Panel Study Data Display

A	B	C
21	24	40
27	21	36
24	18	35
26	19	32

Table 10.4 Bottle Design Study Data BottleDes

A	B	C
16	33	23
18	31	27
19	37	21
17	29	28
13	34	25

METHODS AND APPLICATIONS

10.3 A study compared three different display panels for use by air traffic controllers. Each display panel was tested in a simulated emergency condition; 12 highly trained air traffic controllers took part in the study. Four controllers were randomly assigned to each display panel. The time (in seconds) needed to stabilize the emergency condition was recorded. The results of the study are given in Table 10.3. For this situation, identify the response variable, factor of interest, treatments, and experimental units. Display

10.4 A consumer preference study compares the effects of three different bottle designs (A, B, and C) on sales of a popular fabric softener. A completely randomized design is employed. Specifically, 15 supermarkets of equal sales potential are selected, and 5 of these supermarkets are randomly assigned to each bottle design. The number of bottles sold in 24 hours at each supermarket is recorded. The data obtained are displayed in Table 10.4. For this situation, identify the response variable, factor of interest, treatments, and experimental units. BottleDes

...And More Exercises

are found on the student text's website.

Boxed Equations, Formulas, and Definitions

Each chapter contains easy-to-find boxes that will help students identify and understand the key ideas in the chapter.

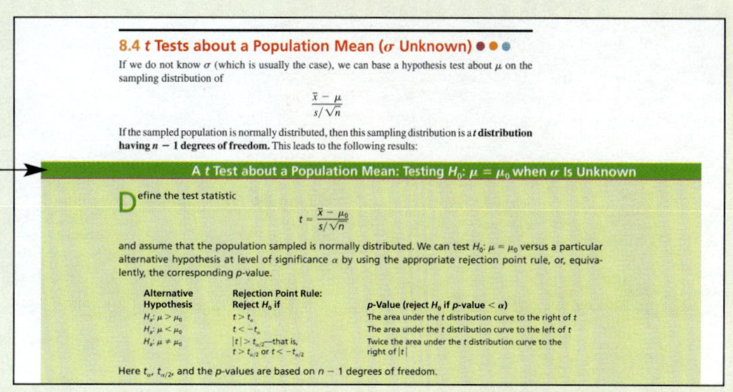

8.4 t Tests about a Population Mean (σ Unknown)

If we do not know σ (which is usually the case), we can base a hypothesis test about μ on the sampling distribution of

$$\frac{\bar{x} - \mu}{s/\sqrt{n}}$$

If the sampled population is normally distributed, then this sampling distribution is a **t distribution having $n - 1$ degrees of freedom.** This leads to the following results:

A t Test about a Population Mean: Testing $H_0: \mu = \mu_0$ when σ Is Unknown

Define the test statistic

$$t = \frac{\bar{x} - \mu_0}{s/\sqrt{n}}$$

and assume that the population sampled is normally distributed. We can test $H_0: \mu = \mu_0$ versus a particular alternative hypothesis at level of significance α by using the appropriate rejection point rule, or, equivalently, the corresponding p-value.

Alternative Hypothesis	Rejection Point Rule: Reject H_0 if	p-Value (reject H_0 if p-value $< \alpha$)
$H_a: \mu > \mu_0$	$t > t_\alpha$	The area under the t distribution curve to the right of t
$H_a: \mu < \mu_0$	$t < -t_\alpha$	The area under the t distribution curve to the left of t
$H_a: \mu \neq \mu_0$	$\lvert t \rvert > t_{\alpha/2}$—that is, $t > t_{\alpha/2}$ or $t < -t_{\alpha/2}$	Twice the area under the t distribution curve to the right of $\lvert t \rvert$

Here t_α, $t_{\alpha/2}$, and the p-values are based on $n - 1$ degrees of freedom.

Chapter Summary

In this chapter we studied **probability.** We began by defining an **event** to be an experimental outcome that may or may not occur and by defining the **probability of an event** to be a number that measures the likelihood that the event will occur. We learned that a probability is often interpreted as a **long-run relative frequency,** and we saw that probabilities can be found by examining **sample spaces** and by using **probability rules.** We learned several important probability rules—**addition rules, multiplication rules,** and the **rule of complements.** We also studied a special kind of probability called a **conditional probability,** which is the probability that one event will occur given that another event occurs, and we used probabilities to define **independent events.**

Glossary of Terms

complement (of an event): If A is an event, the complement of A is the event that A will not occur. (page 136)
conditional probability: The probability that one event will occur given that we know that another event occurs. (page 143)
dependent events: When the probability of one event is influenced by whether another event occurs, the events are said to be dependent. (page 146)
event: A set of sample space outcomes. (page 130)
experiment: A process of observation that has an uncertain outcome. (page 127)
independent events: When the probability of one event is not influenced by whether another event occurs, the events are said to be independent. (page 146)
mutually exclusive events: Events that have no sample space outcomes in common, and, therefore, cannot occur simultaneously. (page 139)
probability (of an event): A number that measures the chance, or likelihood, that an event will occur when an experiment is carried out. (page 131)
sample space: The set of all possible experimental outcomes (sample space outcomes). (page 129)
sample space outcome: A distinct outcome of an experiment (that is, an element in the sample space). (page 129)
subjective probability: A probability assessment that is based on experience, intuitive judgment, or expertise. (page 128)

Important Formulas

Probabilities when all sample space outcomes are equally likely: page 133
The rule of complements: page 136
The addition rule for two events: page 139
The addition rule for two mutually exclusive events: page 140
The addition rule for N mutually exclusive events: page 141
Conditional probability: page 144
The general multiplication rule: page 145
Independence: page 146
The multiplication rule for two independent events: page 147
The multiplication rule for N independent events: page 147

Supplementary Exercises

Exercises 3.34 through 3.37 are based on the following situation: An investor holds two stocks, each of which can rise (R), remain unchanged (U), or decline (D) on any particular day.

Chapter Ending Material

The end of each chapter includes a chapter summary, a comprehensive glossary of terms, and important formula references. The examples shown here are from Chapter 3, Probability.

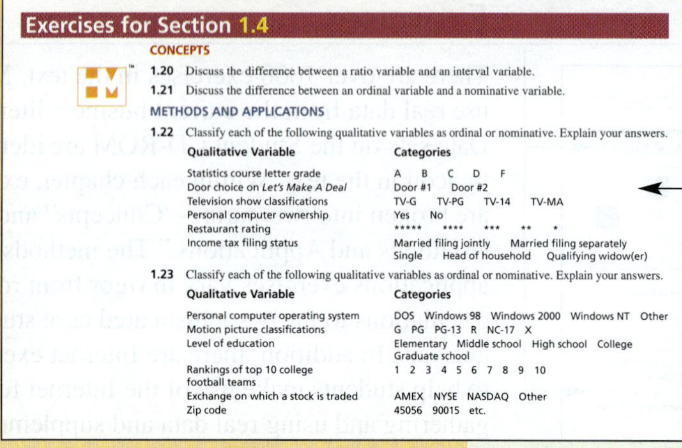

Exercises for Section 1.4

CONCEPTS

1.20 Discuss the difference between a ratio variable and an interval variable.

1.21 Discuss the difference between an ordinal variable and a nominative variable.

METHODS AND APPLICATIONS

1.22 Classify each of the following qualitative variables as ordinal or nominative. Explain your answers.

Qualitative Variable	Categories
Statistics course letter grade	A B C D F
Door choice on *Let's Make A Deal*	Door #1 Door #2
Television show classifications	TV-G TV-PG TV-14 TV-MA
Personal computer ownership	Yes No
Restaurant rating	***** **** *** ** *
Income tax filing status	Married filing jointly Married filing separately Single Head of household Qualifying widow(er)

1.23 Classify each of the following qualitative variables as ordinal or nominative. Explain your answers.

Qualitative Variable	Categories
Personal computer operating system	DOS Windows 98 Windows 2000 Windows NT Other
Motion picture classifications	G PG PG-13 R NC-17 X
Level of education	Elementary Middle school High school College Graduate school
Rankings of top 10 college football teams	1 2 3 4 5 6 7 8 9 10
Exchange on which a stock is traded	AMEX NYSE NASDAQ Other
Zip code	45056 90015 etc.

McGraw-Hill's Homework Manager™ and Homework Manager Plus™

McGraw-Hill's Homework Manager is an online electronic homework system and tutor customized to the text and available as an option for students. The system uses the exercises from the text both statically, in a "one problem at a time" fashion, as well as algorithmically, where problems can generate multiple data possibilities and answers. You choose the problems. Assignments are graded automatically and the results are stored in your private gradebook. Detailed results show you at a glance how each student does on an assignment or even on an individual problem. You can also monitor progress to see which students need extra help. A Homework Manager icon appears in the text next to those exercise sections available in Homework Manager.

Homework Manager Plus™ is available with the interactive online version of the textbook. It is integrated with the text so that students can review the relevant parts of the text while doing homework. The online text is identical to the printed version, including all figures and exhibits, and provides an interactive learning experience.

For Students

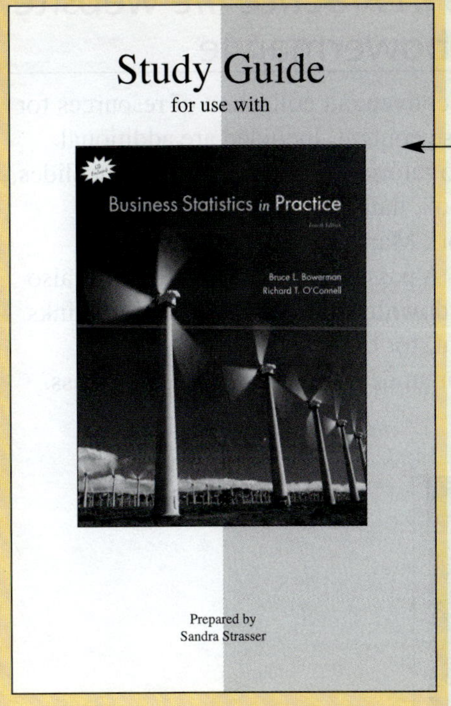

Study Guide
for use with
Business Statistics in Practice
Bruce L. Bowerman
Richard T. O'Connell
Prepared by
Sandra Strasser

Student Study Guide—0-07-319188-4 978-0-07-319188-1

This supplement for the student has been completely updated by Sandra Strassar, Valparaiso University, with the goal of helping students master the course content. It highlights the important ideas in the text and contains detailed tutorial solutions to some of the more challenging exercises. Each chapter includes key ideas, true/false questions, multiple choice questions, and problems, as well as solutions to these. A key feature is the inclusion of solutions using the new version of the Excel add-in MegaStat, which is included on the Student CD-ROM.

Student CD-ROM

Every new copy of the Fourth Edition is packaged with a free Student CD-ROM featuring self-quizzes, data sets identified by icons in the text, video tutorials in Excel, MINITAB, and MegaStat, PowerPoint presentation slides for easy note taking, MegaStat version 10 and the "Getting Started" Manual developed by J. B. Orris of Butler University, Visual Statistics 2.0, which is described later, Advanced Topics Appendices, Excel templates and Workbook, and web links to the text website and the McGraw-Hill Business Statistics website (BSC).

Business Statistics in Practice 4/e website
www.mhhe.com/bowerman4e

This text website contains a convenient collection of resources for students to help master course content. Included are additional exercises, self-quizzes, video tutorials, narrated PowerPoint slides, Excel templates and workbook, data sets, link to ALEKS, a self-paced tutorial, Homework Management, a coursework management tool, and more. A password protected section is also available to instructors with downloadable supplements and links to resources, such as PageOut, for creating a professional, interactive course website for students and instructors to access.

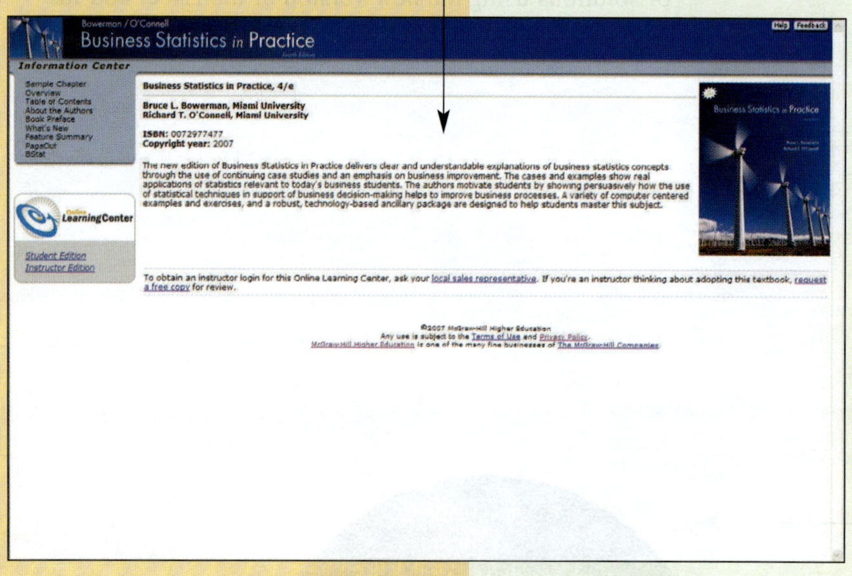

Visual Statistics, 2.0, by Doane, Mathieson, and Tracy This software program for Windows is designed for teaching and learning statistics concepts. It is included on the CD-ROM in both the student and instructor editions. The program is unique in that it is intended to help the instructor teach and students learn the concepts through interactive experimentation and visualization. Active learning is promoted through competency building exercises and individual and team projects. Visual Statistics contains 21 software modules and coordinating student worktext all on CD. A printed version of the worktext is also available. An icon appears in the text next to concepts that are further explained and illustrated through Visual Statistics. The samples below show a display of the content and a portion of the tutorial help included in the worktext.

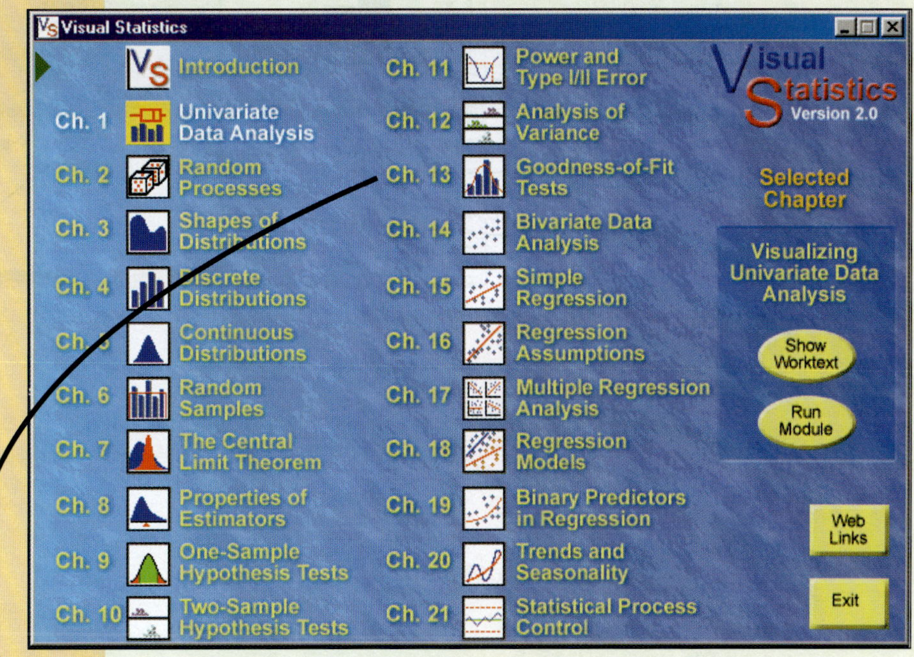

Orientation to Basic Features

This module does goodness-of-fit tests. You can analyze a variety of different data sets by selecting them from the Notebook or create your own using the data editor.

1. Opening screen Start the module by pressing its view button in the *Visual Statistics* menu. When the module is loaded, you will be in the introduction page of the Notebook. Read the questions this module enables you to answer and then click the **Concepts** tab to see the concepts that are covered. Click on the **Examples** tab, select **Class Projects,** select **Weight of D'Anjou Pears,** and press **OK.** Read the Hint that appears in the middle of the display and press **OK.** The upper left shows a frequency histogram with a normal distribution (the default). The Control Panel appears on the right. On the bottom left is a statistical summary that compares the sample with the specified theoretical distribution. On the lower right is a table of calculations for the chi-square test. Other displays may be chosen from the menu bar at the top of the screen or by right-clicking a display and using the menu. The flashing **Update Displays** button will indicate when you have changed one or more control settings.

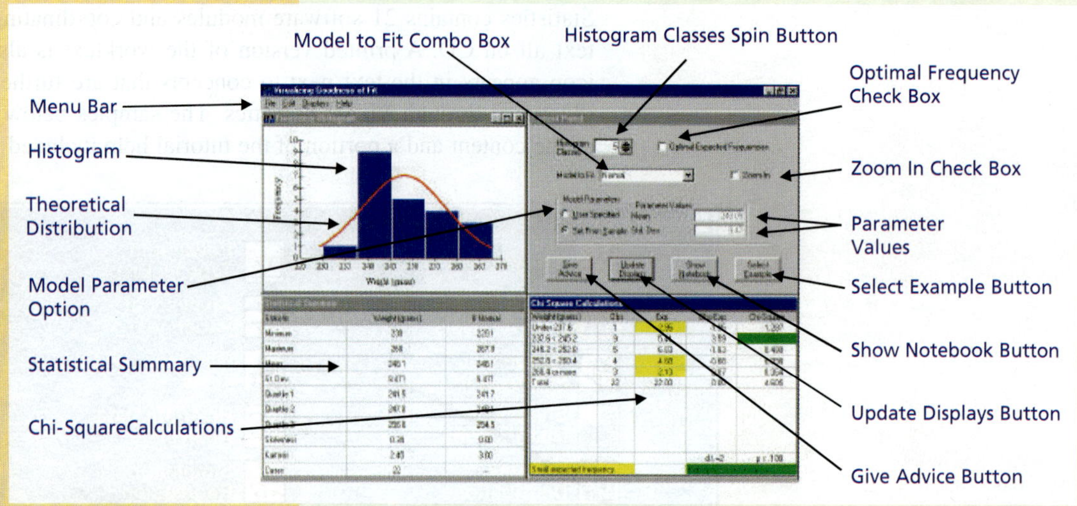

Business Statistics in Practice

FOURTH EDITION

CHAPTER 1

An Introduction to Business Statistics

Chapter Outline

The subject of **statistics** involves the study of how to collect, summarize, and interpret data. **Data** are numerical facts and figures from which conclusions can be drawn. Such conclusions are important to the decision-making processes of many professions and organizations. For example, government officials use conclusions drawn from the latest data on unemployment and inflation to make policy decisions. Financial planners use recent trends in stock market prices to make investment decisions. Businesses decide which products to develop and market by using data that reveal consumer preferences. Production supervisors use manufacturing data to evaluate, control, and improve product quality. Politicians rely on data from public opinion polls to formulate legislation and to devise campaign strategies. Physicians and hospitals use data on the effectiveness of drugs and surgical procedures to provide patients with the best possible treatment.

In this chapter we begin to see how we collect and analyze data. As we proceed through the chapter, we introduce several case studies. These case studies (and others to be introduced later) are revisited throughout later chapters as we learn the statistical methods needed to analyze the cases. Briefly, we will begin to study four cases:

C

The Cell Phone Case. A bank estimates its cellular phone costs and decides whether to outsource management of its wireless resources by studying the calling patterns of its employees.

The Marketing Research Case. A bottling company investigates consumer reaction to a new bottle design for one of its popular soft drinks.

The Coffee Temperature Case. A fast-food restaurant studies and monitors the temperature of the coffee it serves.

The Car Mileage Case. To determine if it qualifies for a federal tax credit based on fuel economy, an automaker studies the gas mileage of its new midsize model.

1.1 Populations and Samples

Statistical methods are very useful for learning about populations, which can be defined in various ways. We begin with the following definition:

A **population** is a set of existing units (usually people, objects, or events).

Examples of populations include (1) all of last year's graduates of Dartmouth College's Master of Business Administration program, (2) all consumers who bought a cellular phone last year, (3) all accounts receivable invoices accumulated last year by The Procter & Gamble Company, (4) all Lincoln Town Cars that were produced last year, and (5) all fires reported last month to the Tulsa, Oklahoma, fire department.

We usually focus on studying one or more characteristics of the population units.

Any characteristic of a population unit is called a **variable.**

For instance, if we study the starting salaries of last year's graduates of the Dartmouth College MBA program, the variable of interest is starting salary. If we study the gasoline mileages obtained in city driving by last year's Lincoln Town Car, the variable of interest is gasoline mileage in city driving.

We carry out a **measurement** to assign a **value** of a variable to each population unit. For example, we might measure the starting salary of an MBA graduate to the nearest dollar. Or we might measure the gasoline mileage obtained by a car in city driving to the nearest one-tenth of a mile per gallon by conducting a mileage test on a driving course prescribed by the Environmental Protection Agency (EPA). If the possible measurements are numbers that represent quantities (that is, "how much" or "how many"), then the variable is said to be **quantitative.** For example, starting salary and gasoline mileage are both quantitative. However, if we simply record into which of several categories a population unit falls, then the variable is said to be **qualitative** or **categorical.** Examples of categorical variables include (1) a person's gender, (2) the make of an automobile, and (3) whether a person who purchases a product is satisfied with the product.[1]

[1]Optional Section 1.4 discusses two types of quantitative variables (ratio and interval) and two types of qualitative variables (ordinal and nominative).

If we measure each and every population unit, we have a **population of measurements** (sometimes called **observations**). If the population is small, it is reasonable to do this. For instance, if 150 students graduated last year from the Dartmouth College MBA program, it might be feasible to survey the graduates and to record all of their starting salaries. In general:

If we examine all of the population measurements, we say that we are conducting a **census** of the population.

Often the population that we wish to study is very large, and it is too time-consuming or costly to conduct a census. In such a situation, we select and analyze a subset (or portion) of the population units.

A **sample** is a subset of the units in a population.

For example, suppose that 8,742 students graduated last year from a large state university. It would probably be too time-consuming to take a census of the population of all of their starting salaries. Therefore, we would select a sample of graduates, and we would obtain and record their starting salaries. When we measure the units in a sample, we say that we have a **sample of measurements.**

We often wish to describe a population or sample.

Descriptive statistics is the science of describing the important aspects of a set of measurements.

As an example, if we are studying a set of starting salaries, we might wish to describe (1) how large or small they tend to be, (2) what a typical salary might be, and (3) how much the salaries differ from each other.

When the population of interest is small and we can conduct a census of the population, we will be able to directly describe the important aspects of the population measurements. However, if the population is large and we need to select a sample from it, then we use what we call **statistical inference.**

Statistical inference is the science of using a sample of measurements to make generalizations about the important aspects of a population of measurements.

For instance, we might use a sample of starting salaries to **estimate** the important aspects of a population of starting salaries. In the next section, we begin to look at how statistical inference is carried out.

1.2 Sampling a Population of Existing Units

Random samples If the information contained in a sample is to accurately reflect the population under study, the sample should be **randomly selected** from the population. To intuitively illustrate random sampling, suppose that a small company employs 15 people and wishes to randomly select two of them to attend a convention. To make the random selections, we number the employees from 1 to 15, and we place in a hat 15 identical slips of paper numbered from 1 to 15. We thoroughly mix the slips of paper in the hat and, blindfolded, choose one. The number on the chosen slip of paper identifies the first randomly selected employee. Then, still blindfolded, we choose another slip of paper from the hat. The number on the second slip identifies the second randomly selected employee.

Of course, it is impractical to carry out such a procedure when the population is very large. It is easier to use a **random number table.** To show how to use such a table, we must more formally define a random sample.[2]

A **random sample** is selected so that, on each selection from the population, every unit remaining in the population on that selection has the same chance of being chosen.

To understand this definition, first note that we can randomly select a sample *with or without replacement.* If we **sample with replacement,** we place the unit chosen on any particular selection back into the population. Thus we give this unit a chance to be chosen on any succeeding

[2]Actually, there are several different kinds of random samples. The type we will define is sometimes called a *simple random sample.* For brevity's sake, however, we will use the term *random sample.*

selection. In such a case, all of the units in the population remain as candidates to be chosen for each and every selection. Randomly choosing two employees with replacement to attend a convention would make no sense because we wish to send two different employees to the convention. If we **sample without replacement,** we do not place the unit chosen on a particular selection back into the population. Thus we do not give this unit a chance to be selected on any succeeding selection. In this case, the units remaining as candidates for a particular selection are all of the units in the population except for those that have previously been selected. **It is best to sample without replacement.** Intuitively, because we will use the sample to learn about the population, sampling without replacement will give us the fullest possible look at the population. This is true because choosing the sample without replacement guarantees that all of the units in the sample will be different (and that we are looking at as many different units from the population as possible).

CHAPTER 1

In the following example, we illustrate how to use a random number table, or computer-generated random numbers, to select a random sample.

Example 1.1 The Cell Phone Case: Estimating Cell Phone Costs[3]

Businesses and college students have at least two things in common—both find cellular phones to be nearly indispensable because of their convenience and mobility, and both often rack up unpleasantly high cell phone bills. Students' high bills are usually the result of *overage*—a student uses more minutes than his or her plan allows. Businesses also lose money due to overage, and, in addition, lose money due to *underage* when some employees do not use all of the (already paid-for) minutes allowed by their plans. Because cellular carriers offer more than 10,000 rate plans, it is nearly impossible for a business to intelligently choose calling plans that will meet its needs at a reasonable cost.

Rising cell phone costs have forced companies having large numbers of cellular users to hire services to manage their cellular and other wireless resources. These cellular management services use sophisticated software and mathematical models to choose cost efficient cell phone plans for their clients. One such firm, MobileSense Inc. of Westlake Village, California, specializes in automated wireless cost management. According to Doug L. Stevens, Vice President of Sales and Marketing at MobileSense, cell phone carriers count on overage and underage to deliver almost half of their revenues. As a result, a company's typical cost of cell phone use can easily exceed 25 cents per minute. However, Mr. Stevens explains that by using MobileSense automated cost management to select calling plans, this cost can be reduced to 12 cents per minute or less.

In this case we will demonstrate how a bank can use a random sample of cell phone users to study its cellular phone costs. Based on this cost information, the bank will decide whether to hire a cellular management service to choose calling plans for the bank's employees. While the bank has over 10,000 employees on a variety of calling plans, the cellular management service suggests that by studying the calling patterns of cellular users on 500-minute plans, the bank can accurately assess whether its cell phone costs can be substantially reduced.

The bank has 2,136 employees on a 500-minute-per-month plan with a monthly cost of $50. The overage charge is 40 cents per minute, and there are additional charges for long distance and roaming. The bank will estimate its cellular cost per minute for this plan by examining the number of minutes used last month by each of 100 randomly selected employees on this 500-minute plan. According to the cellular management service, if the cellular cost per minute for the random sample of 100 employees is over 18 cents per minute, the bank should benefit from automated cellular management of its calling plans.

In order to randomly select the sample of 100 cell phone users, the bank will make a numbered list of the 2,136 users on the 500-minute plan. This list is called a **frame.** The bank can then use a **random number table,** such as Table 1.1(a), to select the needed sample. To see how this is done, notice that any single-digit number in the table is assumed to have been randomly selected from the digits 0 to 9. Any two-digit number in the table is assumed to have been randomly selected from the numbers 00 to 99. Any three-digit number is assumed to have been randomly

[3]The authors would like to thank Mr. Doug L. Stevens, Vice President of Sales and Marketing, at MobileSense Inc., Westlake Village, California, for his help in developing this case.

TABLE 1.1 Random Numbers

(a) A portion of a random number table

33276	85590	79936	56865	05859	90106	78188
03427	90511	69445	18663	72695	52180	90322
92737	27156	33488	36320	17617	30015	74952
85689	20285	52267	67689	93394	01511	89868
08178	74461	13916	47564	81056	97735	90707
51259	63990	16308	60756	92144	49442	40719
60268	44919	19885	55322	44819	01188	55157
94904	01915	04146	18594	29852	71585	64951
58586	17752	14513	83149	98736	23495	35749
09998	19509	06691	76988	13602	51851	58104
14346	61666	30168	90229	04734	59193	32812
74103	15227	25306	76468	26384	58151	44592
24200	64161	38005	94342	28728	35806	22851
87308	07684	00256	45834	15398	46557	18510
07351	86679	92420	60952	61280	50001	94953

(b) MINITAB output of 100 different, four-digit random numbers between 1 and 2136

705	1131	169	1703	1709	609
1990	766	1286	1977	222	43
1007	1902	1209	2091	1742	1152
111	69	2049	1448	659	338
1732	1650	7	388	613	1477
838	272	1227	154	18	320
1053	1466	2087	265	2107	1992
582	1787	2098	1581	397	1099
757	1699	567	1255	1959	407
354	1567	1533	1097	1299	277
663	40	585	1486	1021	532
1629	182	372	1144	1569	1981
1332	1500	743	1262	1759	955
1832	378	728	1102	667	1885
514	1128	1046	116	1160	1333
831	2036	918	1535	660	
928	1257	1468	503	468	

selected from the numbers 000 to 999, and so forth. Note that the table entries are segmented into groups of five to make the table easier to read. Because the total number of cell phone users on the 500-minute plan (2,136) is a four-digit number, we arbitrarily select any set of four digits in the table (we have circled these digits). This number, which is 0511, identifies the first randomly selected user. Then, moving in any direction from the 0511 (up, down, right, or left—it does not matter which), we select additional sets of four digits. These succeeding sets of digits identify additional randomly selected users. Here we arbitrarily move down from 0511 in the table. The first seven sets of four digits we obtain are

0511 7156 0285 4461 3990 4919 1915

(See Table 1.1(a)—these numbers are enclosed in a rectangle.) Since there are no users numbered 7156, 4461, 3990, or 4919 (remember only 2,136 users are on the 500-minute plan), we ignore these numbers. This implies that the first three randomly selected users are those numbered 0511, 0285, and 1915. Continuing this procedure, we can obtain the entire random sample of 100 users. Notice that, because we are sampling without replacement, we should ignore any set of four digits previously selected from the random number table.

While using a random number table is one way to select a random sample, this approach has a disadvantage that is illustrated by the current situation. Specifically, since most four-digit random numbers are not between 0001 and 2136, obtaining 100 different, four-digit random numbers between 0001 and 2136 will require ignoring a large number of random numbers in the random number table, and we will in fact need to use a random number table that is larger than Table 1.1(a). Although larger random number tables are readily available in books of mathematical and statistical tables, a good alternative is to use a computer software package, which can generate random numbers that are between whatever values we specify. For example, Table 1.1(b) gives the MINITAB output of 100 different, four-digit random numbers that are between 0001 and 2136 (note that the "leading 0's" are not included in these four digit numbers). If used, the random numbers in Table 1.1(b) identify the 100 employees that should form the random sample.

After the random sample of 100 employees is selected, the number of cellular minutes used by each employee during the month (the employee's *cellular usage*) is found and recorded. The 100 cellular-usage figures are given in Table 1.2. Looking at this table, we can see that there is substantial overage and underage—many employees used far more than 500 minutes, while many others failed to use all of the 500 minutes allowed by their plan. In Chapter 2 we will use these 100 usage figures to estimate the cellular cost per minute for the 500-minute plan.

TABLE 1.2 A Sample of Cellular Usages (in minutes) for 100 Randomly Selected Employees
CellUse

75	485	37	547	753	93	897	694	797	477
654	578	504	670	490	225	509	247	597	173
496	553	0	198	507	157	672	296	774	479
0	822	705	814	20	513	546	801	721	273
879	433	420	521	648	41	528	359	367	948
511	704	535	585	341	530	216	512	491	0
542	562	49	505	461	496	241	624	885	259
571	338	503	529	737	444	372	555	290	830
719	120	468	730	853	18	479	144	24	513
482	683	212	418	399	376	323	173	669	611

Approximately random samples In general, to take a random sample we must have a list, or **frame,** of all the population units. This is needed because we must be able to number the population units in order to make random selections from them (by, for example, using a random number table). In Example 1.1, where we wished to study a population of 2,136 cell phone users who were on the bank's 500-minute cellular plan, we were able to produce a frame (list) of the population units. Therefore, we were able to select a random sample. Sometimes, however, it is not possible to list and thus number all the units in a population. In such a situation we often select a **systematic sample,** which approximates a random sample.

Example 1.2 The Marketing Research Case: Rating a New Bottle Design[4]

The design of a package or bottle can have an important effect on a company's bottom line. For example, an article in the September 16, 2004, issue of *USA Today* reported that the introduction of a contoured 1.5-liter bottle for Coke drinks (including the reduced-calorie soft drink Coke C2) played a major role in Coca-Cola's failure to meet third-quarter earnings forecasts in 2004. According to the article, Coke's biggest bottler, Coca-Cola Enterprises, "said it would miss expectations because of the 1.5-liter bottle and the absence of common 2-liter and 12-pack sizes for C2 in supermarkets."[5]

In this case a brand group is studying whether changes should be made in the bottle design for a popular soft drink. To research consumer reaction to a new design, the brand group will use the "mall intercept method"[6] in which shoppers at a large metropolitan shopping mall are intercepted and asked to participate in a consumer survey. Each shopper will be exposed to the new bottle design and asked to rate the bottle image. Bottle image will be measured by combining consumers' responses to five items, with each response measured using a 7-point "Likert scale." The five items and the scale of possible responses are shown in Figure 1.1. Here, since we describe the least favorable response and the most favorable response (and we do not describe the responses between them), we say that the scale is "anchored" at its ends. Responses to the five items will be summed to obtain a composite score for each respondent. It follows that the minimum composite score possible is 5 and the maximum composite score possible is 35. Furthermore, experience has shown that the smallest acceptable composite score for a successful bottle design is 25.

In this situation, it is not possible to list and number each and every shopper at the mall while the study is being conducted. Consequently, we cannot use random numbers (as we did in the cell phone case) to obtain a random sample of shoppers. Instead, we can select a **systematic sample.** To do this, every 100th shopper passing a specified location in the mall will be invited to participate in the survey. Here, selecting every 100th shopper is arbitrary—we could select

[4] This case was motivated by an example in the book *Essentials of Marketing Research* by W. R. Dillon, T. J. Madden, and N. H. Firtle (Burr Ridge, IL: Richard D. Irwin, 1993). The authors also wish to thank Professor L. Unger of the Department of Marketing at Miami University for helpful discussions concerning how this type of marketing study would be carried out.

[5] Source: "Coke says earnings will come up short," by Theresa Howard, *USA Today*, September 16, 2004, p. 801.

[6] This is a commonly used research design. For example, see the Burke Marketing Research website at http://burke.com/about/inc_background.htm, Burke Marketing Research, March 26, 2005.

FIGURE 1.1 The Bottle Design Survey Instrument

Please circle the response that most accurately describes whether you agree or disagree with each statement about the bottle you have examined.

Statement	Strongly Disagree						Strongly Agree
The size of this bottle is convenient.	1	2	3	4	5	6	7
The contoured shape of this bottle easy to handle.	1	2	3	4	5	6	7
The label on this bottle is easy to read.	1	2	3	4	5	6	7
This bottle is easy to open.	1	2	3	4	5	6	7
Based on its overall appeal, I like this bottle design.	1	2	3	4	5	6	7

TABLE 1.3 A Sample of Bottle Design Ratings (Composite Scores for a Systematic Sample of 60 Shoppers)
Design

34	33	33	29	26	33	28	25	32	33
32	25	27	33	22	27	32	33	32	29
24	30	20	34	31	32	30	35	33	31
32	28	30	31	31	33	29	27	34	31
31	28	33	31	32	28	26	29	32	34
32	30	34	32	30	30	32	31	29	33

every 200th, every 300th, and so forth. By selecting every 100th shopper, it is probably reasonable to believe that the responses of the survey participants are not related. Therefore, it is reasonable to assume that the sampled shoppers obtained by the systematic sampling process make up an *approximate* random sample.

During a Tuesday afternoon and evening, a sample of 60 shoppers is selected by using the systematic sampling process. Each shopper is asked to rate the bottle design by responding to the five items in Figure 1.1, and a composite score is calculated for each shopper. The 60 composite scores obtained are given in Table 1.3. Since these scores range from 20 to 35, we might infer that *most* of the shoppers at the mall on the Tuesday afternoon and evening of the study would rate the new bottle design between 20 and 35. Furthermore, since 57 of the 60 composite scores are at least 25, we might estimate that the proportion of all shoppers at the mall on the Tuesday afternoon and evening who would give the bottle design a composite score of at least 25 is $57/60 = .95$. That is, we estimate that 95 percent of the shoppers would give the bottle design a composite score of at least 25.

In Chapter 2 we will see how to estimate a typical composite score and we will further analyze the composite scores in Table 1.3.

In some situations, we need to decide whether a sample taken from one population can be employed to make statistical inferences about another, related population. Often logical reasoning is used to do this. For instance, we might reason that the bottle design ratings given by shoppers at the mall on the Tuesday afternoon and evening of the research study would be representative of the ratings given by (1) shoppers at the same mall at other times, (2) shoppers at other malls, and (3) consumers in general. However, if we have no data or other information to back up this reasoning, making such generalizations is dangerous. In practice, marketing research firms choose locations and sampling times that data and experience indicate will produce a representative cross-section of consumers. To simplify our presentation, we will assume that this has been done in the bottle design case. Therefore, we will suppose that it is reasonable to use the 60 bottle design ratings in Table 1.3 to make statistical inferences about *all consumers*.

To conclude this section, we emphasize the importance of taking a random (or approximately random) sample. Statistical theory tells us that, when we select a random (or approximately random) sample, we can use the sample to make valid statistical inferences about the sampled population. However, if the sample is not random, we cannot do this. A classic example occurred prior to the presidential election of 1936, when the *Literary Digest* predicted that Alf Landon would defeat Franklin D. Roosevelt by a margin of 57 percent to 43 percent. Instead, Roosevelt won the election in a landslide. *Literary Digest*'s error was to sample names from telephone books and club membership rosters. In 1936 the country had not yet recovered from the Great Depression, and many unemployed and low-income people did not have phones or belong to clubs. The *Literary Digest*'s sampling procedure excluded these people, who overwhelmingly voted for Roosevelt. At this time, George Gallup, founder of the Gallup Poll, was beginning to establish his survey business. He used an approximately random sample to correctly predict Roosevelt's victory.

As another example, today's television and radio stations, as well as newspaper columnists, use **voluntary response samples.** In such samples, participants self-select—that is, whoever wishes to participate does so (usually expressing some opinion). These samples overrepresent people with strong (usually negative) opinions. For example, the advice columnist Ann Landers once asked her readers, "If you had it to do over again, would you have children?" Of the nearly 10,000 parents who *voluntarily* responded, 70 percent said that they would not. An approximately random sample taken a few months later found that 91 percent of parents would have children again. We further discuss random sampling in optional Section 1.5.

Exercises for Sections 1.1 and 1.2

CONCEPTS

1.1 Define a *population.* Give an example of a population that you might study when you start your career after graduating from college.

1.2 Define what we mean by a *variable,* and explain the difference between a quantitative variable and a qualitative (categorical) variable.

1.3 Below we list several variables. Which of these variables are quantitative and which are qualitative? Explain.

a The dollar amount on an accounts receivable invoice.
b The net profit for a company in 2005.
c The stock exchange on which a company's stock is traded.
d The national debt of the United States in 2005.
e The advertising medium (radio, television, or print) used to promote a product.

1.4 Explain the difference between a census and a sample.

1.5 Explain each of the following terms:

a Descriptive statistics.
b Statistical inference.
c Random sample.
d Systematic sample.

1.6 Explain why sampling without replacement is preferred to sampling with replacement.

METHODS AND APPLICATIONS

1.7 The **Forbes 2000** is a ranking of the world's biggest companies (measured on a composite of sales, profits, assets and market values) by the editors of *Forbes* magazine. Below we give the best performing U.S. companies in the food, drink and tobacco industry from the **Forbes 2000** as listed on the *Forbes* magazine website on February 2, 2005. BestPerf

Company	Sales (Billions $)	Profits (Billions $)	Company	Sales (Billions $)	Profits (Billions $)
Altria Group (1)	60.7	9.20	Pepsi Bottling Group (12)	10.3	0.42
Coca-Cola (2)	21.0	4.35	Tyson Foods (13)	25.2	0.36
PepsiCo (3)	27.0	3.49	Campbell Soup (14)	6.9	0.65
Anheuser-Busch (4)	14.1	2.08	Dean Foods (15)	9.2	0.36
Sara Lee (5)	18.7	1.11	Hershey Foods (16)	4.2	0.46
Coca-Cola Enterprises (6)	17.3	0.68	Wm Wrigley Jr (17)	3.1	0.45
General Mills (7)	10.8	1.00	Constellation Brands (18)	3.3	0.21
ConAgra Foods (8)	19.8	0.84	RJ Reynolds Tobacco (19)	5.3	−3.57
Archer Daniels (9)	31.7	0.49	UST (20)	1.7	0.49
Kellogg (10)	8.8	0.79	Hormel Foods (21)	4.2	0.19
HJ Heinz (11)	8.3	0.66	Brown-Forman (22)	2.5	0.25

Source: *Forbes,* 2/2/05.

Consider the random numbers given in the random number table of Table 1.1(a) on page 6. Starting in the upper left corner of Table 1.1(a) and moving down the two leftmost columns, we see that the first three two-digit numbers obtained are

33 03 92

TABLE 1.4 The Most Admired Company in Each of 30 Industries as Listed on the *Fortune* magazine website on March 14, 2005 MostAdm

	Company	Industry		Company	Industry
1	Alcoa	Metals	16	Intl. Business Machines	Computers
2	Anheuser-Busch	Beverages	17	International Paper	Forest & Paper Products
3	BASF	Chemicals	18	Johnson & Johnson	Pharmaceuticals
4	Berkshire Hathaway	Insurance: P & C	19	Lear	Motor Vehicle Parts
5	BHP Billiton	Mining, Crude-Oil Production	20	Northwestern Mutual	Insurance: Life, Health
6	BP	Petroleum Refining	21	PepsiCo	Consumer Food Products
7	Cardinal Health	Wholesalers: Health Care	22	Procter & Gamble	Household and Personal Products
8	Cisco Systems	Network Communications	23	RWE	Energy
9	Citigroup	Megabanks	24	Texas Instruments	Semiconductors
10	Continental Airlines	Airlines	25	Toyota Motor	Motor Vehicles
11	Walt Disney	Entertainment	26	United Technologies	Aerospace and Defense
12	FedEx	Delivery	27	Verizon Communications	Telecommunications
13	General Electric	Electronics	28	Vinci	Engineering, Construction
14	Home Depot	Specialty Retailers	29	Wal-Mart Stores	General Merchandisers
15	Illinois Tool Works	Industrial & Farm Equipment	30	Walgreen	Food & Drug Stores

Source: *Fortune*, March 14, 2005.

FIGURE 1.2 The Video Game Satisfaction Survey Instrument

Statement	Strongly Disagree						Strongly Agree
The game console of the XYZ-Box is well designed.	1	2	3	4	5	6	7
The game controller of the XYZ-Box is easy to handle.	1	2	3	4	5	6	7
The XYZ-Box has high quality graphics capabilities.	1	2	3	4	5	6	7
The XYZ-Box has high quality audio capabilities.	1	2	3	4	5	6	7
The XYZ-Box serves as a complete entertainment center.	1	2	3	4	5	6	7
There is a large selection of XYZ-Box games to choose from.	1	2	3	4	5	6	7
I am totally satisfied with my XYZ-Box game system.	1	2	3	4	5	6	7

Starting with these three random numbers, and moving down the two leftmost columns of Table 1.1(a) to find more two-digit random numbers, use Table 1.1 to randomly select five of these companies to be interviewed in detail about their business strategies. Hint: Note that we have numbered the companies in the *Forbes* list from 1 to 22.

1.8 Table 1.4 gives the most admired company in each of 30 industries as shown in the 2005 list of Global Most Admired Companies on the *Fortune* magazine website on March 14, 2005. Starting in the upper right corner of the random number table of Table 1.1(a) (page 6) and moving down the two rightmost columns, we see that the first three two-digit numbers obtained are

88 22 52

Starting with these three random numbers, and moving down the two rightmost columns of Table 1.1(a) to find more two-digit random numbers, use Table 1.1 to randomly select four of these industries for further study. MostAdm

1.9 THE VIDEO GAME SATISFACTION RATING CASE VideoGame

A company that produces and markets video game systems wishes to assess its customer's level of satisfaction with a relatively new model, the XYZ-Box. In the six months since the introduction of the model, the company has received 73,219 warranty registrations from purchasers. The company will randomly select 65 of these registrations and will conduct telephone interviews with the purchasers. Specifically, each purchaser will be asked to state his or her level of agreement with each of the seven statements listed on the survey instrument given in Figure 1.2. Here, the level of agreement for each statement is measured on a 7-point Likert scale. Purchaser satisfaction will be measured by adding the purchaser's responses to the seven statements. It follows that for each consumer the minimum composite score possible is 7 and the maximum is 49. Furthermore, experience has shown that a purchaser of a video game system is "very satisfied" if his or her composite score is at least 42.

TABLE 1.5 Composite Scores for the Video Game Satisfaction Rating Case VideoGame

39	44	46	44	44
45	42	45	44	42
38	46	45	45	47
42	40	46	44	43
42	47	43	46	45
41	44	47	48	
38	43	43	44	
42	45	41	41	
46	45	40	45	
44	40	43	44	
40	46	44	44	
39	41	41	44	
40	43	38	46	
42	39	43	39	
45	43	36	41	

TABLE 1.6 Waiting Times (in Minutes) for the Bank Customer Waiting Time Case WaitTime

1.6	6.2	3.2	5.6	7.9	6.1	7.2
6.6	5.4	6.5	4.4	1.1	3.8	7.3
5.6	4.9	2.3	4.5	7.2	10.7	4.1
5.1	5.4	8.7	6.7	2.9	7.5	6.7
3.9	.8	4.7	8.1	9.1	7.0	3.5
4.6	2.5	3.6	4.3	7.7	5.3	6.3
6.5	8.3	2.7	2.2	4.0	4.5	4.3
6.4	6.1	3.7	5.8	1.4	4.5	3.8
8.6	6.3	.4	8.6	7.8	1.8	5.1
4.2	6.8	10.2	2.0	5.2	3.7	5.5
5.8	9.8	2.8	8.0	8.4	4.0	
3.4	2.9	11.6	9.5	6.3	5.7	
9.3	10.9	4.3	1.3	4.4	2.4	
7.4	4.7	3.1	4.8	5.2	9.2	
1.8	3.9	5.8	9.9	7.4	5.0	

a Assume that the warranty registrations are numbered from 1 to 73,219 in a computer. Starting in the upper left corner of Table 1.1(a) and moving down the five leftmost columns, we see that the first three five-digit numbers obtained are

33276 03427 92737

Starting with these three random numbers and moving down the five leftmost columns of Table 1.1(a) to find more five-digit random numbers, use Table 1.1 to randomly select the numbers of the first 10 warranty registrations to be included in the sample of 65 registrations.

b Suppose that when the 65 customers are interviewed, their composite scores are obtained and are as given in Table 1.5. Using the data, estimate limits between which most of the 73,219 composite scores would fall. Also, estimate the proportion of the 73,219 composite scores that would be at least 42.

1.10 THE BANK CUSTOMER WAITING TIME CASE WaitTime

A bank manager has developed a new system to reduce the time customers spend waiting to be served by tellers during peak business hours. Typical waiting times during peak business hours under the current system are roughly 9 to 10 minutes. The bank manager hopes that the new system will lower typical waiting times to less than six minutes.

A 30-day trial of the new system is conducted. During the trial run, every 150th customer who arrives during peak business hours is selected until a systematic sample of 100 customers is obtained. Each of the sampled customers is observed, and the time spent waiting for teller service is recorded. The 100 waiting times obtained are given in Table 1.6. Moreover, the bank manager feels that this systematic sample is as representative as a random sample of waiting times would be. Using the data, estimate limits between which the waiting times of most of the customers arriving during peak business hours would be. Also, estimate the proportion of waiting times of customers arriving during peak business hours that are less than six minutes.

1.11 In an article titled "Turned Off" in the June 2–4, 1995, issue of *USA Weekend,* Dan Olmsted and Gigi Anders report on the results of a survey conducted by the magazine. Readers were invited to write in and answer several questions about sex and vulgarity on television. Olmsted and Anders summarized the survey results as follows:

> Nearly all of the 65,000 readers responding to our write-in survey say TV is too vulgar, too violent, and too racy. TV execs call it reality.

Some of the key survey results were as follows:

Survey Results

- 96% are very or somewhat concerned about SEX on TV.
- 97% are very or somewhat concerned about VULGAR LANGUAGE on TV.
- 97% are very or somewhat concerned about VIOLENCE on TV.

Note: Because participants were not chosen at random, the results of the write-in survey may not be scientific.

a Note the disclaimer at the bottom of the survey results. In a write-in survey, anyone who wishes to participate may respond to the survey questions. Therefore, the sample is not random and we say that the survey is "not scientific." What kind of people would be most likely to respond to a survey about TV sex and violence? Do the survey results agree with your answer?

b If a random sample of the general population were taken, do you think that its results would be the same? Why or why not? Similarly, for instance, do you think that 97 percent of the general population is "very or somewhat concerned about violence on TV"?

c Another result obtained in the write-in survey is as follows:

- Should "V-chips" be installed on TV sets so parents could easily block violent programming?

YES 90% NO 10%

If you planned to start a business manufacturing and marketing such V-chips (at a reasonable price), would you expect 90 percent of the general population to desire a V-chip? Why or why not?

1.3 Sampling a Process

A population is not always defined to be a set of *existing* units. Often we are interested in studying the population of all of the units that will be or could potentially be produced by a process.

A **process** is a sequence of operations that takes inputs (labor, materials, methods, machines, and so on) and turns them into outputs (products, services, and the like).

Processes produce output *over time*. For example, this year's Lincoln Town Car manufacturing process produces Lincoln Town Cars over time. Early in the model year, Ford Motor Company might wish to study the population of the city driving mileages of all Lincoln Town Cars that will be produced during the model year. Or, even more hypothetically, Ford might wish to study the population of the city driving mileages of all Lincoln Town Cars that could *potentially* be produced by this model year's manufacturing process. The first population is called a **finite population** because only a finite number of cars will be produced during the year. Any population of existing units is also finite. The second population is called an **infinite population** because the manufacturing process that produces this year's model could in theory always be used to build "one more car." That is, theoretically there is no limit to the number of cars that could be produced by this year's process. There are a multitude of other examples of finite or infinite hypothetical populations. For instance, we might study the population of all waiting times that will or could potentially be experienced by patients of a hospital emergency room. Or we might study the population of all the amounts of grape jelly that will be or could potentially be dispensed into 16-ounce jars by an automated filling machine. To study a population of potential process observations, we sample the process—usually at equally spaced time points—over time. This is illustrated in the following case.

Example 1.3 The Coffee Temperature Case: Monitoring Coffee Temperatures 

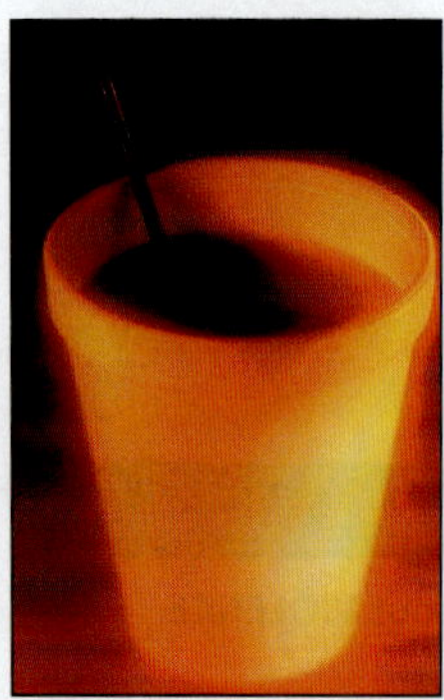

According to the website of the Association of Trial Lawyers of America,[7] Stella Liebeck of Albuquerque, New Mexico, was severely burned by McDonald's coffee in February 1992. Liebeck, who received third-degree burns over 6 percent of her body, was awarded $160,000 in compensatory damages and $480,000 in punitive damages. A postverdict investigation revealed that the coffee temperature at the local Albuquerque McDonald's had dropped from about 185°F before the trial to about 158° after the trial.

This case concerns coffee temperatures at a fast-food restaurant. Because of the possibility of future litigation and to possibly improve the coffee's taste, the restaurant wishes to study and monitor the temperature of the coffee it serves. To do this, the restaurant personnel measure the temperature of the coffee being dispensed (in degrees Fahrenheit) at half-hour intervals from 10 A.M. to 9:30 P.M. on a given day. Table 1.7 gives the 24 temperature measurements obtained in the time order that they were observed. Here, time equals 1 at 10 A.M. and 24 at 9:30 P.M.

[7] http://www.atla.org/consumermediaresources/tier3/press_room/facts/products/mcdonald's%20coffee.aspx, Association of Trial Lawyers of America, January 25, 2005.

TABLE 1.7 24 Coffee Temperatures Observed in Time Order (°F) Coffee

Time		Coffee Temperature	Time		Coffee Temperature	Time		Coffee Temperature
(10:00 A.M.)	1	163°F	(2:00 P.M.)	9	159°F	(6:00 P.M.)	17	158°F
	2	169		10	154		18	170
	3	156		11	167		19	155
	4	152		12	161		20	162
(12:00 noon)	5	165	(4:00 P.M.)	13	152	(8:00 P.M.)	21	156
	6	158		14	165		22	167
	7	157		15	161		23	155
	8	162		16	154		24	164

Examining Table 1.7, we see that the coffee temperatures range from 152° to 170°. Based on this, is it reasonable to conclude that the temperature of most of the coffee that will or could potentially be served by the restaurant will be between 152° and 170°? The answer is yes if the restaurant's coffee-making process operates consistently over time. That is, this process must be in a state of **statistical control.**

A process is in **statistical control** if it does not exhibit any unusual process variations. Often, this means that the process displays a **constant amount of variation** around a **constant,** or horizontal, **level.**

To assess whether a process is in statistical control, we sample the process often enough to detect unusual variations or instabilities. The fast-food restaurant has sampled the coffee-making process every half hour. In other situations, we sample processes with other frequencies—for example, every minute, every hour, or every day. In Chapter 14, where we discuss a systematic method for studying processes called **statistical process control (SPC),** we consider how to determine the sampling frequency for a process. Using the observed process measurements, we can then construct a **runs plot** (sometimes called a **time series plot**).

A **runs plot** is a graph of individual process measurements versus time.

Figure 1.3 shows the MINITAB and Excel outputs of a runs plot of the temperature data. (Some people call such a plot a **line chart** when the plot points are connected by line segments as in the Excel output.) Here we plot each coffee temperature on the vertical scale versus its corresponding time index on the horizontal scale. For instance, the first temperature (163°) is plotted versus time equals 1, the second temperature (169°) is plotted versus time equals 2, and so forth. The runs plot suggests that the temperatures exhibit a relatively constant amount of variation around a relatively constant level. That is, the center of the temperatures can be pretty much represented by a horizontal line (constant level)—see the line drawn through the plotted points—and the spread of the points around the line is staying about the same (constant variation). Note that the plot points tend to form a horizontal band. Therefore, the temperatures are in statistical control.

In general, assume that we have sampled a process at different (usually equally spaced) time points and made a runs plot of the resulting sample measurements. If the plot indicates that the process is in statistical control, and if it is reasonable to believe that the process will remain in control, then it is probably reasonable to regard the sample measurements as an approximately random sample from the population of all possible process measurements. Furthermore, since the process is remaining in statistical control, the process performance is **predictable.** This allows us to make statistical inferences about the population of all possible process measurements that will or potentially could result from using the process. For example, assuming that the coffee-making process will remain in statistical control, it is reasonable to conclude that the temperature of most of the coffee that will be or could potentially be served will be between 152° and 170°.

To emphasize the importance of statistical control, suppose that another fast-food restaurant observes the 24 coffee temperatures that are plotted versus time in Figure 1.4. These temperatures also range between 152° and 170°. However, we cannot infer from this that the temperature of most of the coffee that will be or could potentially be served by this other restaurant will be

FIGURE 1.3 MINITAB and Excel Runs Plots of Coffee Temperatures: The Process Is in Statistical Control

(a) The MINITAB output

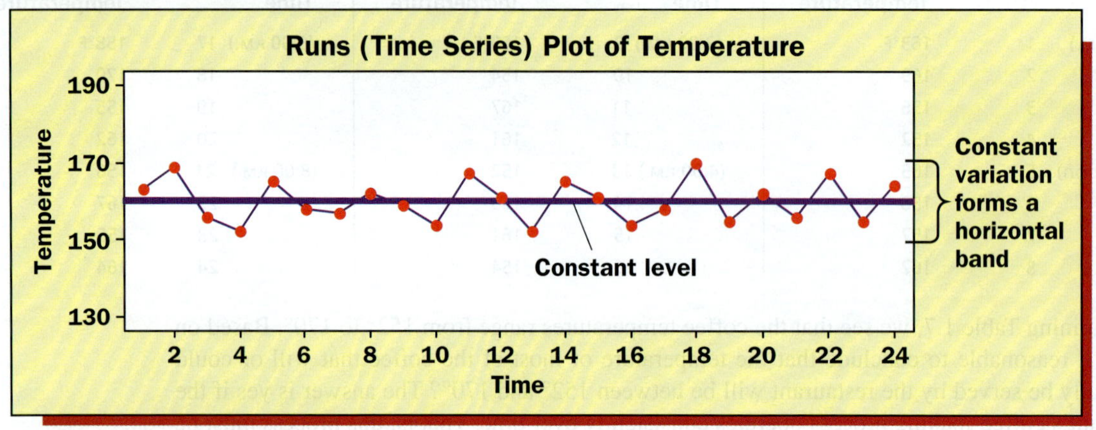

(b) The Excel output

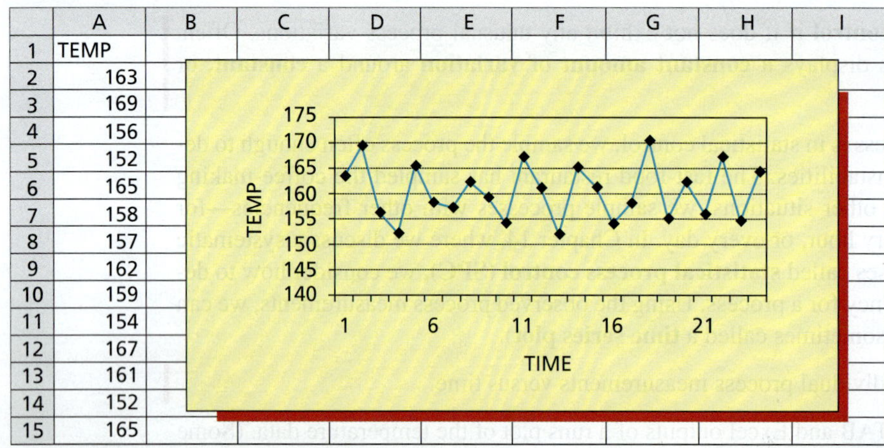

	A	B	C	D	E	F	G	H	I
1	TEMP								
2	163								
3	169								
4	156								
5	152								
6	165								
7	158								
8	157								
9	162								
10	159								
11	154								
12	167								
13	161								
14	152								
15	165								

FIGURE 1.4 A Runs Plot of Coffee Temperatures: The Process Level Is Decreasing

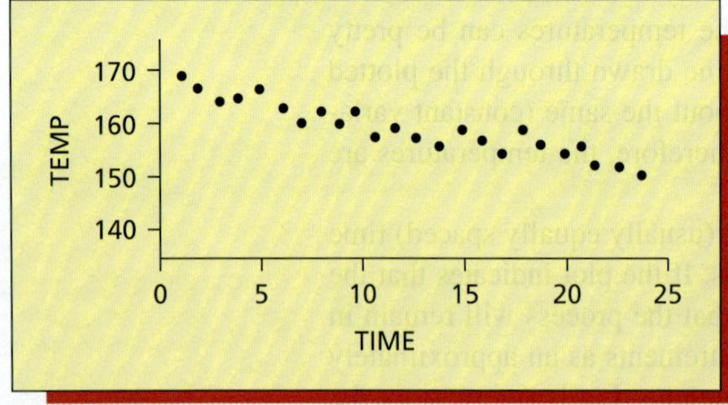

FIGURE 1.5 A Runs Plot of Coffee Temperatures: The Process Variation Is Increasing

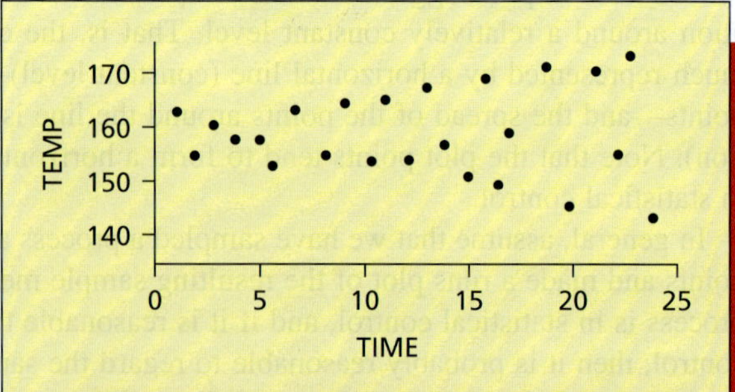

between 152° and 170°. This is because the downward trend in the runs plot of Figure 1.4 indicates that the coffee-making process is out of control and will soon produce temperatures below 152°. Another example of an out-of-control process is illustrated in Figure 1.5. Here, the coffee temperatures seem to fluctuate around a constant level but with increasing variation (notice that the plotted temperatures fan out as time advances). In general, the specific pattern of out-of-control behavior can suggest the reason for this behavior. For example, the downward trend in the runs plot of Figure 1.4 might suggest that the restaurant's coffeemaker has a defective heating element.

Visually inspecting a runs plot to check for statistical control can be tricky. One reason is that the scale of measurements on the vertical axis can influence whether the data appear to form a horizontal band. We will study better methods for detecting out-of-control behavior in Chapter 14. For now, we will simply emphasize that a process must be in statistical control in order to make valid statistical inferences about the population of all possible process observations. Also, note that being in statistical control does not necessarily imply that a process is **capable** of producing output that meets our requirements. For example, suppose that marketing research suggests that the fast-food restaurant's customers feel that coffee tastes best if its temperature is between 153° and 167°. Since Table 1.7 indicates that the temperature of some of the coffee it serves is not in this range (note that two of the temperatures are 152°, one is 169°, and another is 170°), the restaurant might take action to reduce the variation of the coffee temperatures.

The marketing research, and coffee temperature cases are both examples of using the **statistical process** to make a statistical inference. In the next case, we formally describe and illustrate this process.

Example 1.4 The Car Mileage Case: Estimating Mileage

C

In 2005 the U.S. Department of Energy (DOE) and the Environmental Protection Agency (EPA) emphasized the importance of auto fuel economy. *The Fuel Economy Guide,* available at the DOE website, discusses the effects of gasoline consumption on U.S. energy security and the economy as follows.[8]

> **Buying a more fuel efficient vehicle can help strengthen our national energy security by reducing our dependence on foreign oil.** Half of the oil used to produce the gasoline you put in your tank is imported. The United States uses about 20 million barrels of oil per day, two thirds of which is used for transportation. Petroleum imports cost us about $2 billion a week—that's money that could be used to fuel our own economy.

The *Guide* also discusses the effects of gasoline consumption on global warming:[9]

> Burning fossil fuels such as gasoline or diesel adds greenhouse gases, including carbon dioxide, to the earth's atmosphere. Greenhouse gases trap heat and thus warm the earth because they prevent a significant proportion of infrared radiation from escaping into space. Vehicles with lower fuel economy burn more fuel, creating more carbon dioxide. Every gallon of gasoline your vehicle burns puts 20 pounds of carbon dioxide into the atmosphere. You can reduce your contribution to global warming by choosing a vehicle with higher fuel economy.
>
> **By choosing a vehicle that achieves 25 miles per gallon rather than 20 miles per gallon, you can prevent the release of about 15 tons of greenhouse gas pollution over the lifetime of your vehicle.**

In this case study we consider a tax credit offered by the federal government to automakers for improving the fuel economy of midsize cars. According to *The Fuel Economy Guide—2005 Model Year,* virtually every midsize car equipped with an automatic transmission has an EPA combined city and highway mileage estimate of 26 miles per gallon (mpg) or less. Furthermore, the EPA has concluded that a 5 mpg increase in fuel economy is significant and feasible.[10] Therefore, the government has decided to offer the tax credit to any automaker selling a midsize model with an automatic transmission that achieves an EPA combined city and highway mileage estimate of at least 31 mpg. To find the combined city and highway mileage estimate for a particular car model, the EPA tests a sample of cars. The steps used to obtain this estimate are those used in the **statistical process** for making a statistical inference:

1 **Describe the practical problem of interest and the associated population or process to be studied.** Consider an automaker that has recently introduced a midsize model with an automatic transmission and wishes to demonstrate that this new model qualifies for the tax credit. The automaker will study the population of all cars of this type that will be or could potentially be produced.

[8]World Wide Web, http://www.fueleconomy.gov/feg/FEG2005intro.pdf, U.S. Department of Energy, January 25, 2005.
[9]World Wide Web, http://www.fueleconomy.gov/feg/FEG2005intro.pdf, U.S. Department of Energy, January 25, 2005.
[10]The authors wish to thank Jeff Alson of the EPA for this information.

TABLE 1.8 A Sample of 49 Mileages (Time Order Is Given by Reading Down the Columns from Left to Right) GasMiles

30.8	30.9	32.0	32.3	32.6
31.7	30.4	31.4	32.7	31.4
30.1	32.5	30.8	31.2	31.8
31.6	30.3	32.8	30.6	31.9
32.1	31.3	32.0	31.7	32.8
33.3	32.1	31.5	31.4	31.5
31.3	32.5	32.4	32.2	31.6
31.0	31.8	31.0	31.5	30.6
32.0	30.4	29.8	31.7	32.2
32.4	30.5	31.1	30.6	

FIGURE 1.6 MegaStat Output of a Runs Plot of the 49 Mileages

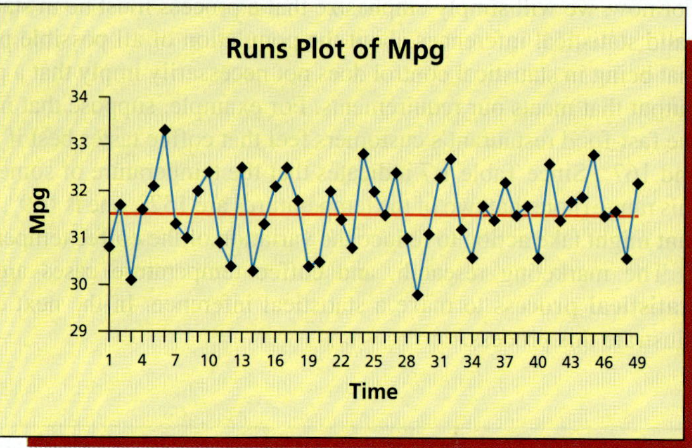

2 **Describe the variable of interest and how it will be measured.** The variable of interest is the EPA combined city and highway mileage of a car. This mileage is obtained by testing the car on a device similar to a giant treadmill. The device is used to simulate a 7.5-mile city driving trip and a 10-mile highway driving trip, and the resulting mileages are used to calculate the EPA combined mileage for the car.[11]

3 **Describe the sampling procedure.** The automaker selects a sample of 49 of the new midsize cars by randomly selecting one car from those produced during each of 49 consecutive production shifts. Here the sample size (49) is determined by statistical considerations to be discussed in Chapter 7. Each sampled car is subjected to the EPA test. The resulting sample of 49 combined city and highway mileages is given in Table 1.8 (in time order).

4 **Describe the statistical inference of interest.** The sample of 49 mileages will be used to estimate the "typical" EPA combined mileage for the population of all possible new midsize cars. The estimate obtained is the EPA combined city and highway mileage estimate for the new midsize model.

5 **Describe how the statistical inference will be made and evaluate the reliability of the inference.** Figure 1.6 gives the MegaStat output of a runs plot of the 49 mileages. The runs plot indicates that the mileages are in statistical control. If it is reasonable to believe that car mileages for this model will remain in control, we can make statistical inferences. For instance, because the mileages in Table 1.8 range from 29.8 to 33.3 mpg, we might infer that most of the new midsize cars will get combined city and highway mileages between 29.8 and 33.3 mpg. To estimate the "typical" EPA combined mileage for the population of all possible cars, we might visually draw a horizontal line through the "middle" of the plot points in Figure 1.6. When we do this, the horizontal line intersects the vertical axis at about 31.5 mpg. Therefore, we might conclude that the EPA combined city and highway mileage estimate for the new midsize model should be 31.5 mpg. Since this estimate exceeds the EPA standard of 31 mpg, we might also conclude that the automaker qualifies for the tax credit. However, the estimate is intuitive, so we do not have any information about its *reliability*. In Chapter 2 we will study more precise ways to both define and estimate a "typical" population value. Then in Chapters 3 through 7 we will study tools for assessing the reliability of estimation procedures and for estimating "with confidence."

[11]Since the EPA estimates that 55 percent of all driving is city driving, it calculates combined mileage by adding 55 percent of the city mileage test result to 45 percent of the highway mileage test result.

Exercises for Section 1.3

CONCEPTS

1.12 Define a *process*. Then give an example of a process you might study when you start your career after graduating from college.

1.13 Explain what it means to say that a process is in statistical control.

1.14 What is a runs plot? What does a runs plot look like when we sample and plot a process that is in statistical control?

METHODS AND APPLICATIONS

1.15 The data below give 18 measurements of a critical dimension for an automobile part (measurements in inches). Here one part has been randomly selected each hour from the previous hour's production, and the measurements are given in time order. AutoPart1

Hour	Measurement	Hour	Measurement
1	3.005	10	3.005
2	3.020	11	3.015
3	2.980	12	2.995
4	3.015	13	3.020
5	2.995	14	3.000
6	3.010	15	2.990
7	3.000	16	2.985
8	2.985	17	3.020
9	3.025	18	2.985

Construct a runs plot and determine if the process appears to be in statistical control.

1.16 Table 1.9 presents the time (in days) needed to settle the 67 homeowners' insurance claims handled by an Indiana insurance agent over a year. The claims are given in time order by loss date. ClaimSet

a Figure 1.7 shows a MINITAB runs plot of the claims data in Table 1.9. Does the claims-handling process seem to be in statistical control? Why or why not?

TABLE 1.9 Number of Days Required to Settle Homeowners' Insurance Claims (Claims Made from July 2, 2004 to June 25, 2005) ClaimSet

Claim	Loss Date	Days to Settle	Claim	Loss Date	Days to Settle	Claim	Loss Date	Days to Settle
1	7-2-04	111	24	11-5-04	34	47	3-5-05	70
2	7-6-04	35	25	11-13-04	25	48	3-5-05	67
3	7-11-04	23	26	11-21-04	22	49	3-6-05	81
4	7-12-04	42	27	11-23-04	14	50	3-6-05	92
5	7-16-04	54	28	11-25-04	20	51	3-6-05	96
6	7-27-04	50	29	12-1-04	32	52	3-6-05	85
7	8-1-04	41	30	12-8-04	27	53	3-7-05	83
8	8-13-04	12	31	12-10-04	23	54	3-7-05	102
9	8-20-04	8	32	12-20-04	35	55	3-19-05	23
10	8-20-04	11	33	12-23-04	29	56	3-27-05	11
11	8-28-04	11	34	12-31-04	25	57	4-1-05	8
12	9-3-04	31	35	12-31-04	18	58	4-11-05	11
13	9-10-04	35	36	12-31-04	16	59	4-15-05	35
14	9-17-04	14	37	1-5-05	23	60	4-19-05	29
15	9-18-04	14	38	1-8-05	26	61	5-2-05	80
16	9-29-04	27	39	1-16-05	30	62	5-15-05	18
17	10-4-04	14	40	1-18-05	36	63	5-25-05	58
18	10-6-04	23	41	1-22-05	42	64	6-6-05	4
19	10-15-04	47	42	1-25-05	45	65	6-12-05	5
20	10-23-04	17	43	1-27-05	43	66	6-24-05	15
21	10-25-04	21	44	2-5-05	39	67	6-25-05	19
22	10-30-04	18	45	2-9-05	53			
23	11-2-04	31	46	2-23-05	64			

FIGURE 1.7 MINITAB Runs Plot of the Insurance Claims Data for Exercise 1.16

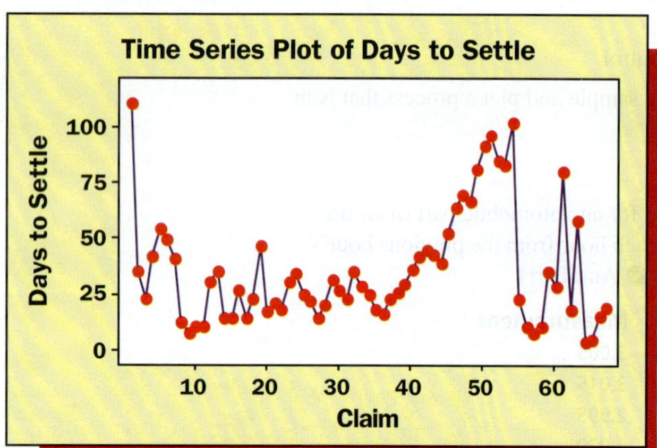

FIGURE 1.8 Runs Plot of Daily Percentages of Customers Waiting More Than One Minute to Be Seated (for Exercise 1.17)

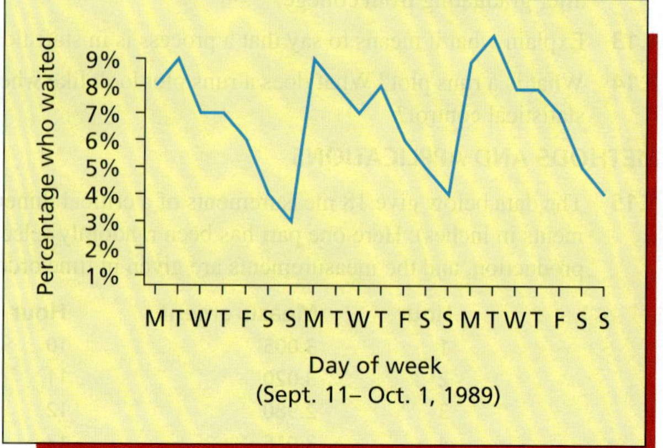

b In March of 2005, Indiana was hit by a widespread ice storm that caused heavy damage to homes in the area. Did this ice storm have a significant impact on the time needed to settle homeowners' claims? Should the agent consider improving procedures for handling claims in emergency situations? Why or why not?

1.17 In the article "Accelerating Improvement" published in *Quality Progress* (October 1991), Gaudard, Coates, and Freeman describe a restaurant that caters to business travelers and has a self-service breakfast buffet. Interested in customer satisfaction, the manager conducts a survey over a three-week period and finds that the main customer complaint is having to wait too long to be seated. On each day from September 11, 1989, to October 1, 1989, a problem-solving team records the percentage of patrons who must wait more than one minute to be seated. A runs plot of the daily percentages is shown in Figure 1.8.[12] What does the runs plot suggest?

1.18 THE TRASH BAG CASE[13] TrashBag

A company that produces and markets trash bags has developed an improved 30-gallon bag. The new bag is produced using a specially formulated plastic that is both stronger and more biodegradable than previously used plastics, and the company wishes to evaluate the strength of this bag. The *breaking strength* of a trash bag is considered to be the amount (in pounds) of a representative trash mix that when loaded into a bag suspended in the air will cause the bag to sustain significant damage (such as ripping or tearing). The company has decided to carry out a 40-hour pilot production run of the new bags. Each hour, at a randomly selected time during the hour, a bag is taken off the production line. The bag is then subjected to a *breaking strength test.* The 40 breaking strengths obtained during the pilot production run are given in Table 1.10, and an Excel runs plot of these breaking strengths is given in Figure 1.9.

a Do the 40 breaking strengths appear to be in statistical control? Explain.

b Estimate limits between which most of the breaking strengths of all trash bags would fall.

1.19 THE BANK CUSTOMER WAITING TIME CASE WaitTime

Recall that every 150th customer arriving during peak business hours was sampled until a systematic sample of 100 customers was obtained. This systematic sampling procedure is equivalent to sampling from a process. Figure 1.10 shows a MegaStat runs plot of the 100 waiting times in Table 1.6. Does the process appear to be in statistical control? Explain.

[12]The source of Figure 1.8 is M. Gaudard, R. Coates, and L. Freeman, "Accelerating Improvement," *Quality Progress,* October 1991, pp. 81–88. © 1991 American Society for Quality Control. Used with permission.

[13]This case is based on conversations by the authors with several employees working for a leading producer of trash bags. For purposes of confidentiality, we have withheld the company's name.

TABLE 1.10 Trash Bag Breaking Strengths TrashBag

48.5	52.5	50.7	49.4
52.3	47.5	48.2	51.9
53.5	50.9	51.5	52.0
50.5	49.8	49.0	48.8
50.3	50.0	51.7	46.8
49.6	50.8	53.2	51.3
51.0	53.0	51.1	49.3
48.3	50.9	52.6	54.0
50.6	49.9	51.2	49.2
50.2	50.1	49.5	51.4

FIGURE 1.9 Excel Runs Plot of Breaking Strengths for Exercise 1.18

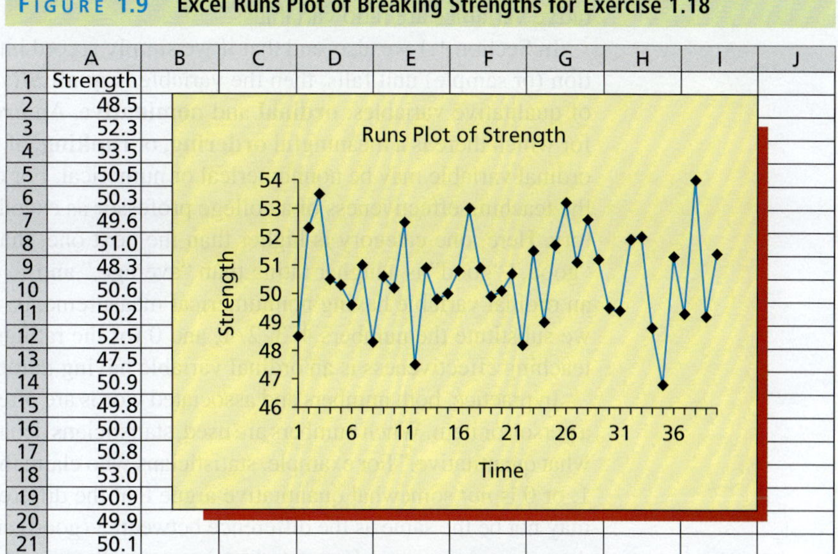

FIGURE 1.10 MegaStat Runs Plot of Waiting Times for Exercise 1.19

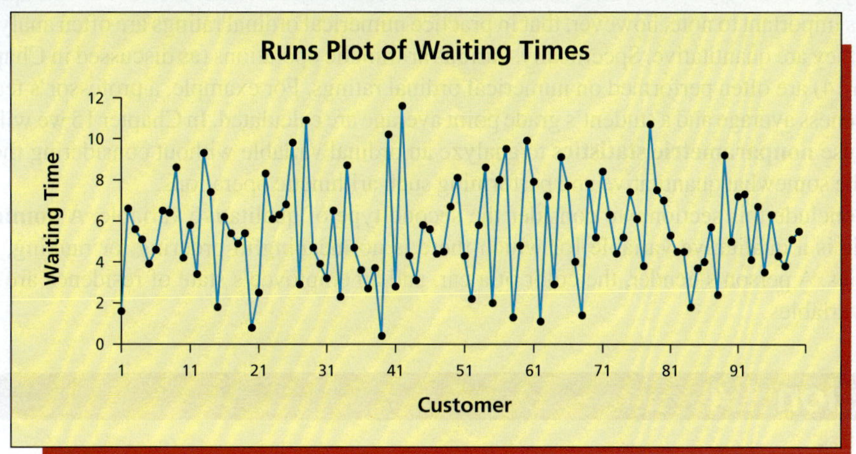

1.4 Ratio, Interval, Ordinal, and Nominative Scales of Measurement (Optional)

In Section 1.1 we said that a variable is **quantitative** if its possible values are **numbers that represent quantities** (that is, "how much" or "how many"). In general, a quantitative variable is measured on a scale having a **fixed unit of measurement** between its possible values. For example, if we measure employees' salaries to the nearest dollar, then one dollar is the fixed unit of measurement between different employees' salaries. There are two types of quantitative variables: **ratio** and **interval.** A **ratio variable** is a quantitative variable measured on a scale such that ratios of its values are meaningful and there is an inherently defined zero value. Variables such as salary, height, weight, time, and distance are ratio variables. For example, a distance of zero miles is "no distance at all," and a town that is 30 miles away is "twice as far" as a town that is 15 miles away.

An **interval variable** is a quantitative variable where ratios of its values are not meaningful and there is not an inherently defined zero value. Temperature (on the Fahrenheit scale) is an interval variable. For example, zero degrees Fahrenheit does not represent "no heat at all," just that it is very cold. Thus, there is no inherently defined zero value. Furthermore, ratios of temperatures are not meaningful. For example, it makes no sense to say that 60° is twice as warm as

30°. In practice, there are very few interval variables other than temperature. Almost all quantitative variables are ratio variables.

In Section 1.1 we also said that if we simply record into which of several categories a population (or sample) unit falls, then the variable is **qualitative** (or **categorical**). There are two types of qualitative variables: **ordinal** and **nominative.** An **ordinal variable** is a qualitative variable for which there is a meaningful **ordering,** or **ranking,** of the categories. The measurements of an ordinal variable may be nonnumerical or numerical. For example, a student may be asked to rate the teaching effectiveness of a college professor as excellent, good, average, poor, or unsatisfactory. Here, one category is higher than the next one; that is, "excellent" is a higher rating than "good," "good" is a higher rating than "average," and so on. Therefore, teaching effectiveness is an ordinal variable having nonnumerical measurements. On the other hand, if (as is often done) we substitute the numbers 4, 3, 2, 1, and 0 for the ratings excellent through unsatisfactory, then teaching effectiveness is an ordinal variable having numerical measurements.

In practice, both numbers and associated words are often presented to respondents asked to rate a person or item. When numbers are used, statisticians debate whether the ordinal variable is "somewhat quantitative." For example, statisticians who claim that teaching effectiveness rated as 4, 3, 2, 1, or 0 is *not* somewhat quantitative argue that the difference between 4 (excellent) and 3 (good) may not be the same as the difference between 3 (good) and 2 (average). Other statisticians argue that as soon as respondents (students) see equally spaced numbers (even though the numbers are described by words), their responses are affected enough to make the variable (teaching effectiveness) somewhat quantitative. Generally speaking, the specific words associated with the numbers probably substantially affect whether an ordinal variable may be considered somewhat quantitative. It is important to note, however, that in practice numerical ordinal ratings are often analyzed as though they are quantitative. Specifically, various arithmetic operations (as discussed in Chapters 2 through 14) are often performed on numerical ordinal ratings. For example, a professor's teaching effectiveness average and a student's grade point average are calculated. In Chapter 15 we will learn how to use **nonparametric statistics** to analyze an ordinal variable without considering the variable to be somewhat quantitative and performing such arithmetic operations.

To conclude this section, we consider the second type of qualitative variable. A **nominative variable** is a qualitative variable for which there is no meaningful ordering, or ranking, of the categories. A person's gender, the color of a car, and an employee's state of residence are nominative variables.

Exercises for Section 1.4

CONCEPTS

1.20 Discuss the difference between a ratio variable and an interval variable.

1.21 Discuss the difference between an ordinal variable and a nominative variable.

METHODS AND APPLICATIONS

1.22 Classify each of the following qualitative variables as ordinal or nominative. Explain your answers.

Qualitative Variable	Categories
Statistics course letter grade	A B C D F
Door choice on *Let's Make A Deal*	Door #1 Door #2
Television show classifications	TV-G TV-PG TV-14 TV-MA
Personal computer ownership	Yes No
Restaurant rating	***** **** *** ** *
Income tax filing status	Married filing jointly Married filing separately Single Head of household Qualifying widow(er)

1.23 Classify each of the following qualitative variables as ordinal or nominative. Explain your answers.

Qualitative Variable	Categories
Personal computer operating system	DOS Windows 98 Windows 2000 Windows NT Other
Motion picture classifications	G PG PG-13 R NC-17 X
Level of education	Elementary Middle school High school College Graduate school
Rankings of top 10 college football teams	1 2 3 4 5 6 7 8 9 10
Exchange on which a stock is traded	AMEX NYSE NASDAQ Other
Zip code	45056 90015 etc.

1.5 An Introduction to Survey Sampling (Optional)

Random sampling is not the only kind of sampling. Methods for obtaining a sample are called **sampling designs,** and the sample we take is sometimes called a **sample survey.** In this section we explain three sampling designs that are alternatives to random sampling—**stratified random sampling, cluster sampling,** and **systematic sampling.**

One common sampling design involves separately sampling important groups within a population. Then, the samples are combined to form the entire sample. This approach is the idea behind **stratified random sampling.**

In order to select a **stratified random sample,** we divide the population into nonoverlapping groups of similar units (people, objects, etc.). These groups are called **strata.** Then a random sample is selected from each stratum, and these samples are combined to form the full sample.

It is wise to stratify when the population consists of two or more groups that differ with respect to the variable of interest. For instance, consumers could be divided into strata based on gender, age, ethnic group, or income.

As an example, suppose that a department store chain proposes to open a new store in a location that would serve customers who live in a geographical region that consists of (1) an industrial city, (2) a suburban community, and (3) a rural area. In order to assess the potential profitability of the proposed store, the chain wishes to study the incomes of all households in the region. In addition, the chain wishes to estimate the proportion and the total number of households whose members would be likely to shop at the store. The department store chain feels that the industrial city, the suburban community, and the rural area differ with respect to income and the store's potential desirability. Therefore, it uses these subpopulations as strata and takes a stratified random sample.

Taking a stratified sample can be advantageous because such a sample takes advantage of the fact that units in the same stratum are similar to each other. It follows that a stratified sample can provide more accurate information than a random sample of the same size. As a simple example, if all of the units in each stratum were exactly the same, then examining only one unit in each stratum would allow us to describe the entire population. Furthermore, stratification can make a sample easier (or possible) to select. Recall that, in order to take a random sample, we must have a frame, or list, of all of the population units. Although a frame might not exist for the overall population, a frame might exist for each stratum. For example, suppose nearly all the households in the department store's geographical region have telephones. Although there might not be a telephone directory for the overall geographical region, there might be separate telephone directories for the industrial city, the suburb, and the rural area. Although we do not discuss how to analyze data from a stratified random sample in the main body of this text, we do so in Appendix F (Part I) on the CD-ROM that accompanies this book. For a more complete discussion of stratified random sampling, see Mendenhall, Schaeffer, and Ott (1986).

Sometimes it is advantageous to select a sample in stages. This is a common practice when selecting a sample from a very large geographical region. In such a case, a frame often does not exist. For instance, there is no single list of all registered voters in the United States. There is also no single list of all households in the United States. In this kind of situation, we can use **multistage cluster sampling.** To illustrate this procedure, suppose we wish to take a sample of registered voters from all registered voters in the United States. We might proceed as follows:

Stage 1: Randomly select a sample of counties from all of the counties in the United States.

Stage 2: Randomly select a sample of townships from each county selected in Stage 1.

Stage 3: Randomly select a sample of voting precincts from each township selected in Stage 2.

Stage 4: Randomly select a sample of registered voters from each voting precinct selected in Stage 3.

We use the term *cluster sampling* to describe this type of sampling because at each stage we "cluster" the voters into subpopulations. For instance, in Stage 1 we cluster the voters into counties, and in Stage 2 we cluster the voters in each selected county into townships. Also, notice that the random sampling at each stage can be carried out because there are lists of (1) all counties in the United States, (2) all townships in each county, (3) all voting precincts in each township, and (4) all registered voters in each voting precinct.

As another example, consider sampling the households in the United States. We might use Stages 1 and 2 above to select counties and townships within the selected counties. Then, if there is a telephone directory of the households in each township, we can randomly sample households from each selected township by using its telephone directory. Because *most* households today have telephones, and telephone directories are readily available, most national polls are now conducted by telephone.

It is sometimes a good idea to combine stratification with multistage cluster sampling. For example, suppose a national polling organization wants to estimate the proportion of all registered voters who favor a particular presidential candidate. Because the presidential preferences of voters might tend to vary by geographical region, the polling organization might divide the United States into regions (say, Eastern, Midwestern, Southern, and Western regions). The polling organization might then use these regions as strata, and might take a multistage cluster sample from each stratum (region).

The analysis of data produced by multistage cluster sampling can be quite complicated. We explain how to analyze data produced by one- and two-stage cluster sampling in Appendix F (Part 2) on the CD-ROM that accompanies this book. This appendix also includes a discussion of an additional survey sampling technique called *ratio estimation.* For a more detailed discussion of cluster sampling and ratio estimation, see Mendenhall, Schaeffer, and Ott (1986).

In order to select a random sample, we must number the units in a frame of all the population units. Then we use a random number table (or a random number generator on a computer) to make the selections. However, numbering all the population units can be quite time-consuming. Moreover, random sampling is used in the various stages of many complex sampling designs (requiring the numbering of numerous populations). Therefore, it is useful to have an alternative to random sampling. One such alternative is called **systematic sampling.** In order to systematically select a sample of n units without replacement from a frame of N units, we divide N by n and round the result down to the nearest whole number. Calling the rounded result ℓ, we then randomly select one unit from the first ℓ units in the frame—this is the first unit in the systematic sample. The remaining units in the sample are obtained by selecting every ℓth unit following the first (randomly selected) unit. For example, suppose we wish to sample a population of $N = 14{,}327$ allergists to investigate how often they have prescribed a particular drug during the last year. A medical society has a directory listing the 14,327 allergists, and we wish to draw a systematic sample of 500 allergists from this frame. Here we compute $14{,}327/500 = 28.654$, which is 28 when rounded down. Therefore, we number the first 28 allergists in the directory from 1 to 28, and we use a random number table to randomly select one of the first 28 allergists. Suppose we select allergist number 19. We interview allergist 19 and every 28th allergist in the frame thereafter, so we choose allergists 19, 47, 75, and so forth until we obtain our sample of 500 allergists. In this scheme, we must number the first 28 allergists, but we do not have to number the rest because we can "count off" every 28th allergist in the directory. Alternatively, we can measure the approximate amount of space in the directory that it takes to list 28 allergists. This measurement can then be used to select every 28th allergist.

In this book we concentrate on showing how to analyze data produced by *random sampling.* However, if the order of the population units in a frame is random with respect to the characteristic under study, then a systematic sample should be (approximately) a random sample and we can analyze the data produced by the systematic sample by using the same methods employed to analyze random samples. For instance, it would seem reasonable to assume that the alphabetically ordered allergists in a medical directory would be random (that is, have nothing to do with) the number of times the allergists prescribed a particular drug. Similarly, the alphabetically ordered people in a telephone directory would probably be random with respect to many of the people's characteristics that we might wish to study.

When we employ random sampling, we eliminate bias in the choice of the sample from a frame. However, a proper sampling design does not guarantee that the sample will produce accurate information. One potential problem is **undercoverage.**

Undercoverage occurs when some population units are excluded from the process of selecting the sample.

This problem occurs when we do not have a complete, accurate list of all the population units. For example, although telephone polls today are common, 7 to 8 percent of the people in the United States do not have telephones. In general, undercoverage usually causes low-income people to be underrepresented. If underrepresented groups differ from the rest of the population with respect to the characteristic under study, the survey results will be biased. Another potentially serious problem is **nonresponse.**

Nonresponse occurs when a population unit selected as part of the sample cannot be contacted or refuses to participate.

In some surveys, 35 percent or more of the selected individuals cannot be contacted—even when several callbacks are made. In such a case, other participants are often substituted for the people who cannot be contacted. If the substitute participants differ from the originally selected participants with respect to the characteristic under study, the survey will again be biased. Third, when people are asked potentially embarrassing questions, their responses might not be truthful. We then have what we call **response bias.** Fourth, the wording of the questions asked can influence the answers received. Slanted questions often evoke biased responses. For example, consider the following question:

Which of the following best describes your views on gun control?

1 The government should take away our guns, leaving us defenseless against heavily armed criminals.
2 We have the right to keep and bear arms.

This question is biased toward eliciting a response against gun control.

Exercises for Section 1.5

CONCEPTS

1.24 When is it appropriate to use stratified random sampling? What are strata, and how should strata be selected?

1.25 When is cluster sampling used? Why do we describe this type of sampling by using the term *cluster?*

1.26 Explain each of the following terms:
a Undercoverage **b** Nonresponse **c** Response bias

1.27 Explain how to take a systematic sample of 100 companies from the 1,853 companies that are members of an industry trade association.

1.28 Explain how a stratified random sample is selected. Discuss how you might define the strata to survey student opinion on a proposal to charge all students a $100 fee for a new university-run bus system that will provide transportation between off-campus apartments and campus locations.

1.29 Marketing researchers often use city blocks as clusters in cluster sampling. Using this fact, explain how a market researcher might use multistage cluster sampling to select a sample of consumers from all cities having a population of more than 10,000 in a large state having many such cities.

Chapter Summary

This chapter has introduced the idea of using **sample data** to make **statistical inferences**—that is, drawing conclusions about populations and processes by using sample data. We began by learning that a **population** is a set of existing units that we wish to study. We saw that, since many populations are too large to examine in their entirety, we often study a population by selecting a **sample,** which is a subset of the population units. Next we learned that, if the information contained in a sample is to accurately represent the population, then the sample should be **randomly selected** from the population, and we saw how **random numbers** (obtained from a **random number table**) can be used to select a **random sample.** We also learned that selecting a random sample requires a **frame** (that is, a list of all of the population units) and that, since a frame does not always exist, we sometimes select a **systematic sample.**

We continued this chapter by studying **processes.** We learned that to make statistical inferences about the population of all possible values of a variable that could be observed when using a process, the process must be in **statistical control.** We learned that a process is in statistical control if it does not exhibit any unusual process variations, and we demonstrated how we might sample a process and how to use a runs plot to try to judge whether a process is in control.

Next, in optional Section 1.4 we studied different types of quantitative and qualitative variables. We learned that there are two types of **quantitative variables—ratio variables,** which are measured on a scale such that ratios of its values are meaningful and there is an inherently defined zero value, and **interval variables,** for which ratios are not meaningful and there is no inherently defined zero value. We also saw that there are two types of **qualitative variables—ordinal variables,** for which there is a meaningful ordering of the categories, and **nominative variables,** for which there is no meaningful ordering of the categories.

We concluded this chapter with optional Section 1.5, which discusses **survey sampling.** We introduced **stratified random sampling,** in which we divide a population into groups **(strata)** and then select a random sample from each group. We also introduced **multistage cluster sampling,** which involves selecting a sample in stages, and we explained how to select a **systematic sample.** Finally, we discussed some potential problems encountered when conducting a sample survey—**undercoverage, nonresponse, response bias,** and **slanted questions.**

Glossary of Terms

categorical (qualitative) variable: A variable having values that indicate into which of several categories a population unit belongs. (page 3)
census: An examination of all the units in a population. (page 4)
cluster sampling (multistage cluster sampling): A sampling design in which we sequentially cluster population uints into subpopulations. (page 21)
descriptive statistics: The science of describing the important aspects of a set of measurements. (page 4)
finite population: A population that contains a finite number of units. (page 12)
frame: A list of all of the units in a population. This is needed in order to select a random sample. (page 5)
infinite population: A population that is defined so that there is no limit to the number of units that could potentially belong to the population. (page 12)
interval variable: A quantitative variable such that ratios of its values are not meaningful and for which there is not an inherently defined zero value. (page 19)
measurement: The process of assigning a value of a variable to each of the units in a population or sample. (page 3)
nominative variable: A qualitative variable for which there is no meaningful ordering, or ranking, of the categories. (page 20)
nonresponse: A situation in which population units selected to participate in a survey do not respond to the survey instrument. (page 23)
ordinal variable: A qualitative variable for which there is a meaningful ordering or ranking of the categories. (page 20)
population: A set of existing units (people, objects, events, or the like) that we wish to study. (page 3)
process: A sequence of operations that takes inputs and turns them into outputs. (page 12)
qualitative (categorical) variable: A variable having values that indicate into which of several categories a population unit belongs. (page 3)
quantitative variable: A variable having values that are numbers representing quantities. (page 3)
random number table: A table containing random digits that is often used to select a random sample. (page 4)
random sample: A sample selected so that, on each selection from the population, every unit remaining in the population on that selection has the same chance of being chosen. (page 4)
ratio variable: A quantitative variable such that ratios of its values are meaningful and for which there is an inherently defined zero value. (page 19)
response bias: A situation in which survey participants do not respond truthfully to the survey questions. (page 23)
runs plot: A graph of individual process measurements versus time. (page 13)
sample: A subset of the units in a population. (page 4)
sampling without replacement: A sampling procedure in which we do not place previously selected units back into the population and, therefore, do not give these units a chance to be chosen on succeeding selections. (page 5)
sampling with replacement: A sampling procedure in which we place any unit that has been chosen back into the population to give the unit a chance to be chosen on succeeding selections. (page 4)
statistical control: A state in which a process does not exhibit any unusual variations. Often this means that the process displays a uniform amount of variation around a constant, or horizontal, level. (page 13)
statistical inference: The science of using a sample of measurements to make generalizations about the important aspects of a population. (page 4)
statistical process control (SPC): A method for analyzing process data in which we monitor and study the process variation. The goal is to stabilize (and reduce) the amount of process variation. (page 13)
strata: The subpopulations in a stratified sampling design. (page 21)
stratified random sampling: A sampling design in which we divide a population into nonoverlapping subpopulations and then select a random sample from each subpopulation (stratum). (page 21)
systematic sample: A sample taken by moving systematically through the population. For instance, we might randomly select one of the first 200 population units and then systematically sample every 200th population unit thereafter. (page 7)
undercoverage: A situation in sampling in which some groups of population units are underrepresented. (page 22)
variable: A characteristic of a population unit. (page 3)

Supplementary Exercises

1.30 Some television stations attempt to gauge public opinion by posing a question on the air and asking viewers to call to give their opinions. Suppose that a particular television station asks viewers whether they support or oppose a proposed federal gun control law. Viewers are to call one of two 800 numbers to register support or opposition. When the results are tabulated, the station reports that 78 percent of those who called are opposed to the proposed law. What do you think of the sampling method used by the station? Do you think that the percentage of the entire population that opposes the proposed law is as high as the 78 percent of the sample that was opposed?

1.31 In early 1995, *The Milwaukee Sentinel,* a morning newspaper in Milwaukee, Wisconsin, and *The Milwaukee Journal,* an afternoon newspaper, merged to form *The Milwaukee Journal Sentinel.* Several weeks after the merger, a Milwaukee television station, WITI-TV, conducted a telephone call-in survey asking whether viewers liked the new *Journal Sentinel.* The survey was "not scientific" because any viewer wishing to call in could do so.

On April 26, 1995, Tim Cuprisin, in his "Inside TV & Radio" column in the *Journal Sentinel,* wrote the following comment:

> **WE DIDN'T CALL:** WITI-TV (Channel 6) did one of those polls—which they admit are unscientific—last week and found that 388 viewers like the new *Journal Sentinel* and 2,629 don't like it.
>
> We did our own unscientific poll on whether those Channel 6 surveys accurately reflect public opinion. The results: a full 100 percent of the respondents say absolutely, positively not.

Is Cuprisin's comment justified? Write a short paragraph explaining your answer.

1.32 Table 1.11 gives the "35 best companies to work for" as rated on the *Fortune* magazine website on March 14, 2005. Use random numbers to select a random sample of 10 of these companies. Justify that your sample is random by carefully explaining how you obtained it. List the random numbers you used and show how they gave your random sample.

1.33 A bank wishes to study the amount of time it takes to complete a withdrawal transaction from one of its ATMs (automated teller machines). On a particular day, 63 withdrawal transactions are observed between 10 A.M. and noon. The time required to complete each transaction is given in Table 1.12. Figure 1.11 shows an Excel runs plot of the 63 transaction times. Do the transaction times seem to be in statistical control? Why or why not? ATMTime

TABLE 1.11 *Fortune's* 35 Best Companies to Work for in March 2005 (for Exercise 1.32)

Rank	Company
1	Wegmans Food Markets
2	W.L. Gore
3	Republic Bancorp
4	Genentech
5	Xilinx
6	J.M. Smucker
7	S.C. Johnson & Son
8	Griffin Hospital
9	Alston & Bird
10	Vision Service Plan
11	Starbucks
12	Quicken Loans
13	Adobe Systems
14	CDW
15	Container Store
16	SAS Institute
17	Qualcomm
18	Robert W. Baird
19	QuikTrip
20	HomeBanc Mortgage
21	David Weekley Homes
22	TD Industries
23	Valero Energy
24	Network Appliance
25	JM Family Enterprises
26	American Century Investments
27	Cisco Systems
28	American Cast Iron Pipe
29	Stew Leonard's
30	Whole Foods Market
31	Baptist Health South Florida
32	Arnold & Porter
33	Amgen
34	American Fidelity Assurance
35	Goldman Sachs Group

Source: *Fortune,* 3/14/05.

TABLE 1.12 ATM Transaction Times (in Seconds) for 63 Withdrawals ATMTime

Transaction	Time	Transaction	Time	Transaction	Time
1	32	22	34	43	37
2	32	23	32	44	32
3	41	24	34	45	33
4	51	25	35	46	33
5	42	26	33	47	40
6	39	27	42	48	35
7	33	28	46	49	33
8	43	29	52	50	39
9	35	30	36	51	34
10	33	31	37	52	34
11	33	32	32	53	33
12	32	33	39	54	38
13	42	34	36	55	41
14	34	35	41	56	34
15	37	36	32	57	35
16	37	37	33	58	35
17	33	38	34	59	37
18	35	39	38	60	39
19	40	40	32	61	44
20	36	41	35	62	40
21	32	42	33	63	39

FIGURE 1.11 Excel Runs Plot of ATM Transaction Times for Exercise 1.33

	A
1	ATM TIME
2	32
3	32
4	41
5	51
6	42
7	39
8	33
9	43
10	35
11	33
12	33
13	32
14	42

FIGURE 1.12 **Runs Plot of the Cleveland Indians' Winning Percentages from 1915 through 2004 (for Exercise 1.34)**

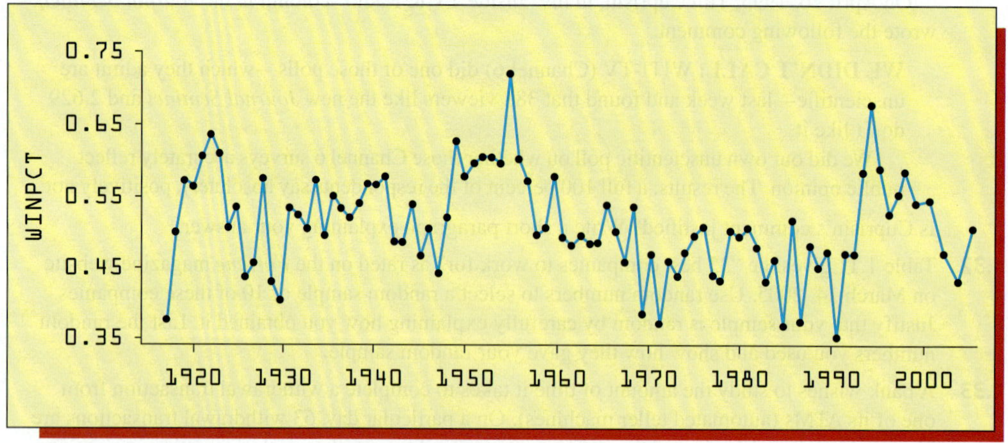

1.34 Figure 1.12 gives a runs plot of the Cleveland Indians' winning percentages from 1915 (when the team was renamed as the "Indians") to 2004. Many longtime Indians fans believe that the April 1959 trade of Rocky Colavito, a feared home-run hitter, for Detroit's Harvey Kuehn, a good average hitter without exceptional power, sent the team into a decline that lasted more than 30 years. Does the runs plot provide any evidence to support this opinion? Why or why not?

1.35 THE TRASH BAG CASE TrashBag

Recall that the company will carry out a 40-hour pilot production run of the new bags and will randomly select one bag each hour to be subjected to a breaking strength test.

a Explain how the company can use random numbers to randomly select the times during the 40 hours of the pilot production run at which bags will be tested. Hint: Suppose that a randomly selected time will be determined to the nearest minute.

b Use the following random numbers (obtained from Table 1.1) to select the times during the first five hours at which the first five bags to be tested will be taken from the production line: 61, 15, 64, 07, 86, 87, 57, 64, 66, 42, 59, 51.

MINITAB, Excel, and MegaStat for Statistics

In this book we use three types of software to carry out statistical analysis—MINITAB, Excel, and MegaStat. MINITAB is a computer package designed expressly for conducting statistical analysis. It is widely used at many colleges and universities, and in a large number of business organizations. Excel is, of course, a general purpose electronic spreadsheet program and analytical tool. The analysis ToolPak in Excel includes many procedures for performing various kinds of basic statistical analyses. MegaStat is an add-in package that is specifically designed for performing statistical analysis in the Excel spreadsheet environment. The principal advantage of Excel is that, because of its broad acceptance among students and professionals as a multipurpose analytical tool, it is both well known and widely available. The advantage of a special-purpose statistical software package like MINITAB is that it provides a far wider range of statistical procedures and it offers the experienced analyst a range of options to better control the analysis. The advantages of MegaStat include (1) its ability to perform a number of statistical calculations that are not automatically done by the procedures in the Excel ToolPak, and (2) features that make it easier to use than Excel for a wide variety of statistical analyses. In addition, the output obtained by using MegaStat is automatically placed in a standard Excel spreadsheet and can be edited by using any of the features in Excel. MegaStat can be copied from the CD-ROM included with this book. MINITAB, Excel, and MegaStat, through built-in functions, programming languages, and macros, offer almost limitless power. Here, we will limit our attention to procedures that are easily accessible via menus without resort to any special programming or advanced features.

Commonly used features of MINITAB, Excel, and MegaStat are presented in this chapter along with an initial application—to produce a time series or runs plot. You will find that the limited instructions included here, along with the built-in help features of all three software packages, will serve as a starting point from which you can discover a variety of other procedures and options. Much more detailed descriptions of MINITAB can be found in other sources, in particular in the manual *Meet MINITAB: Release 14 for Windows.* This manual is available in print and as a .pdf file, viewable using Adobe Acrobat Reader, on the MINITAB Inc. website (http://www.minitab.com/products/minitab/14/documentation/aspx). Similarly, there are a number of alternative reference materials for Microsoft Excel. Of course, an understanding of the related statistical concepts is essential to the effective use of any statistical software package.

The instructions in this book are based on MINITAB (Version 14) for Windows and Microsoft Excel 2003 as found in Microsoft Office 2003.

Appendix 1.1 ■ Getting Started With MINITAB

We begin with a look at some features of MINITAB that are common to most analyses. When the instructions call for a sequence of selections from a series of menus, the sequence will be presented in the following form:

Stat : Basic Statistics : Descriptive Statistics

This notation indicates that Stat is the first selection from the Minitab menu bar, next Basic Statistics is selected from the Stat pull-down menu, and finally Descriptive Statistics is selected from the Basic Statistics pull-down menu.

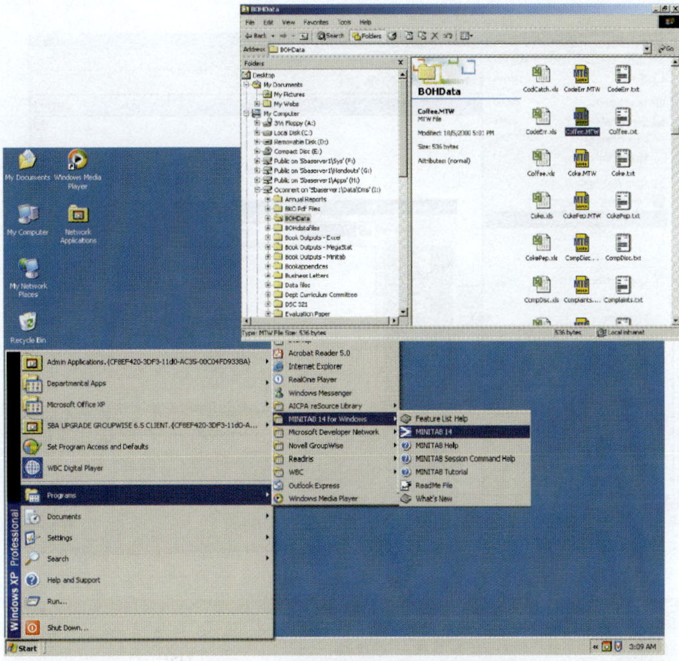

Starting MINITAB Procedures for starting MINITAB may vary from one installation to the next. If you are using a public computing laboratory, you may have to consult local documentation. For typical MINITAB installations, you will generally be able to start MINITAB with a sequence of selections from the Microsoft Windows Start menu something like the following:

- Select **Start : Programs : MINITAB 14 for Windows : Minitab 14**

You can also start MINITAB with a previously saved MINITAB worksheet (like Coffee.mtw or one of the many other data files from the CD-ROM included with this text) from the Windows Explorer by double-clicking on the worksheet's icon.

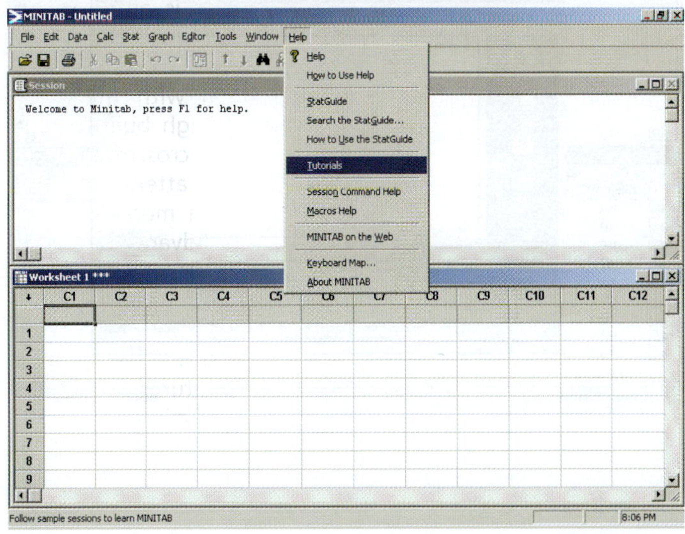

After you start MINITAB, the display is partitioned into two working windows. These windows serve the following functions:

- The "Session" window is the area where MINITAB commands and basic output are displayed.
- The "Data" window is a spreadsheet-style display where data can be entered and edited.

Help resources Like most Windows programs, MINITAB includes on-line help via a Help Menu. The Help feature includes standard Contents and Search entries as well as Tutorials that introduce MINITAB concepts and walk through some typical MINITAB sessions. Also included is a StatGuide that provides guidance for interpreting statistical tables and graphs in a practical, easy-to-understand way.

Entering data (entering the coffee temperature data in Table 1.7) from the keyboard:

- In the Data window, click on the cell directly below C1 and type a name for the variable, Temp, and press the Enter key.
- Starting in line 1 under column C1, type the values for the variable (coffee temperatures from Table 1.7 on page 13) down the column, pressing the Enter key after each number is typed.

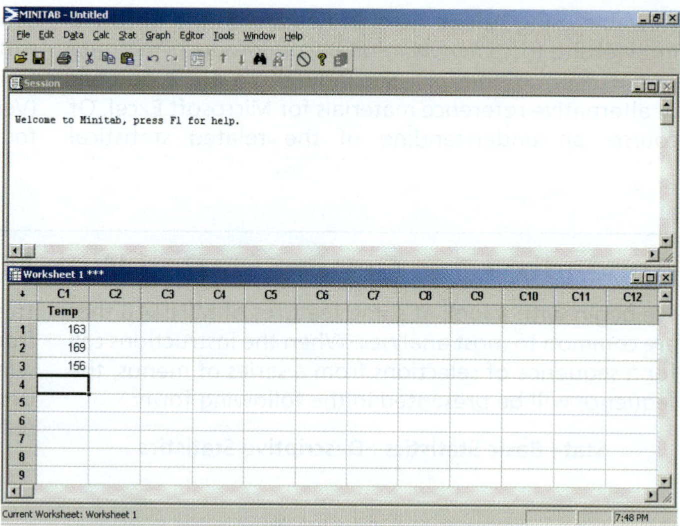

Saving data (saving the coffee temperature data):

- Select **File : Save Current Worksheet As**.
- In the "Save Worksheet As" dialog box, use the "Save in" pull-down menu to select the destination drive and folder. (Here we have selected the floppy drive, A:)
- Enter the desired file name in the File name box. (Here we have chosen the name Coffee. Minitab will automatically add the extension .mtw.)
- Click Save in the "Save Worksheet As" dialog box.

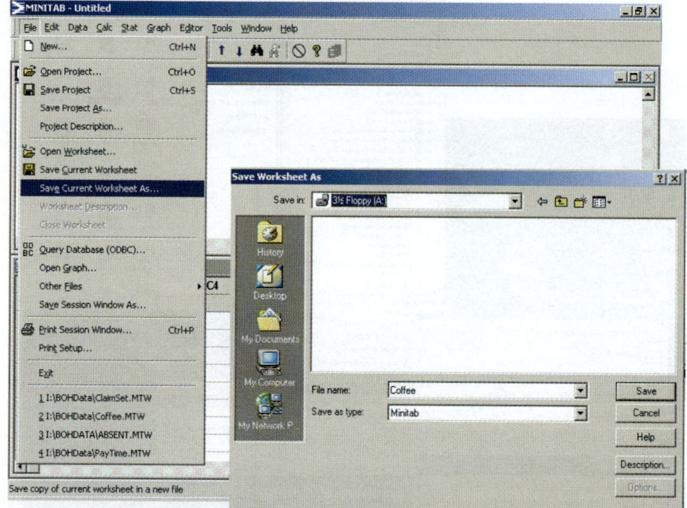

Retrieving a Minitab worksheet containing the coffee temperature data in Table 1.7 (data file: Coffee.mtw):

- Select **File : Open Worksheet**
- In the Open Worksheet dialog box, use the "Look in" pull-down menu to select the source drive and folder. (Here we have selected the floppy drive, A:)
- Select the desired file name in the File name box. (Here we have chosen the Minitab worksheet Coffee.Mtw)
- Click Open in the Open Worksheet dialog box.
- Minitab may display a dialog box with the message, "A copy of the content of this file will be added to the current project." If so, click OK.

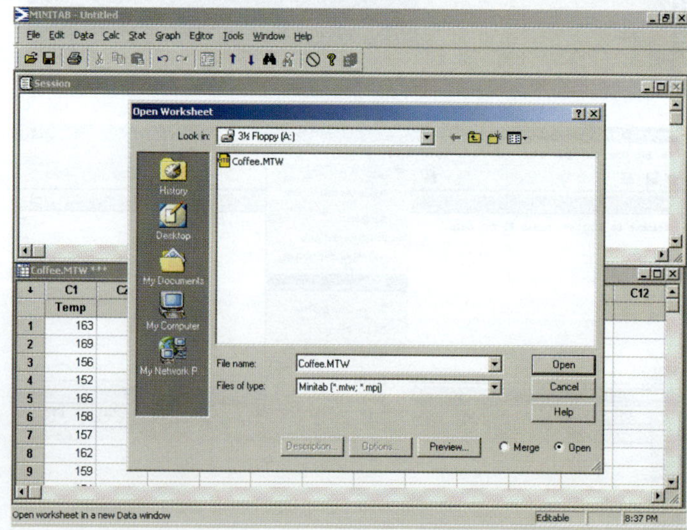

Creating a runs (or time series) plot similar to Figure 1.3(a) on page 14 (data file: Coffee.mtw):

- Select **Graph : Time Series Plot.**
- In the Time Series Plots dialog box, select Simple, which produces a time series plot of data in a single column. Click OK in the Time Series Plots dialog box.
- In the "Time Series Plot—Simple" dialog box, enter the name of the variable, Temp, into the Series box. Do this either by typing its name, by clicking on its name in the variables box on the left and then clicking on the Select button, or by double-clicking on its name in the variables box on the left.
- Click OK in the "Time Series Plot—Simple" dialog box.

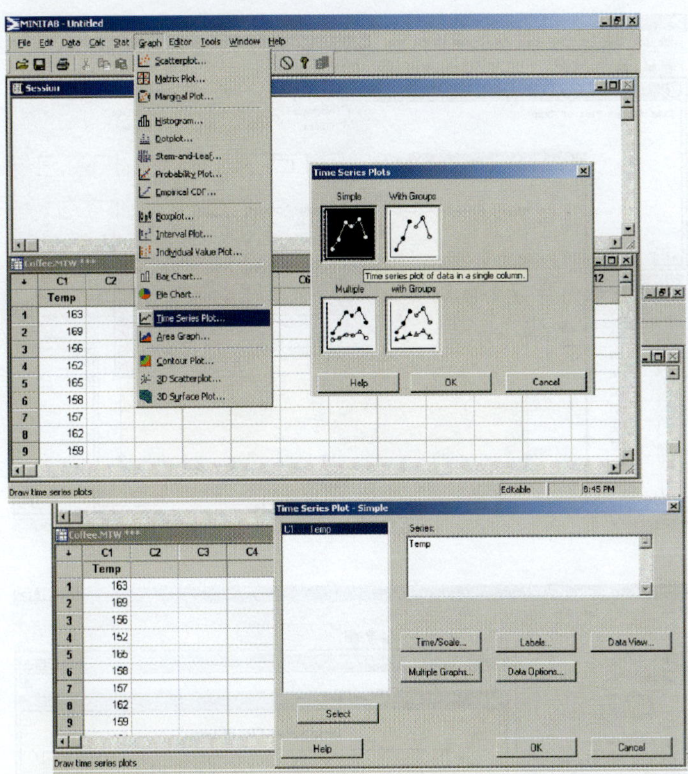

- **The runs (or time series) plot** will appear in a graphics window.

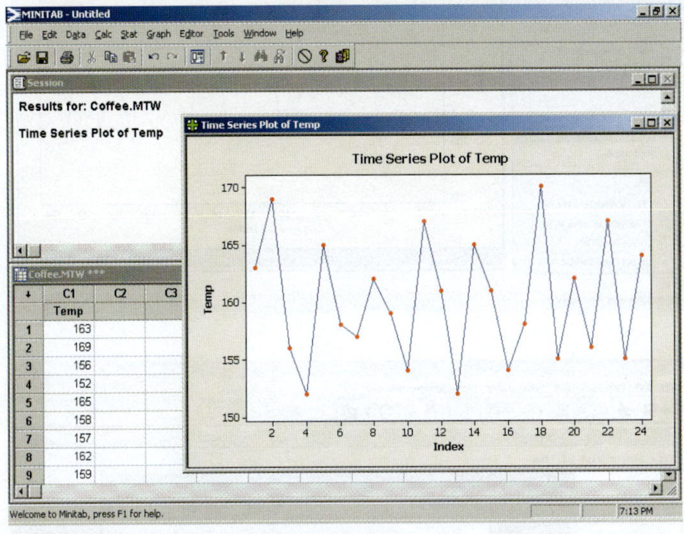

- **The graph can be edited** by right-clicking on the portion you wish to edit. For instance, here we have right-clicked on the data region. Selecting "Edit Data Region" from the pop up window yields a dialog box that allows you to edit this region. The x and y scales, x and y axis labels, title, plot symbols, connecting lines, data region, figure region, and so forth can all be edited by right-clicking on that particular portion of the graph.

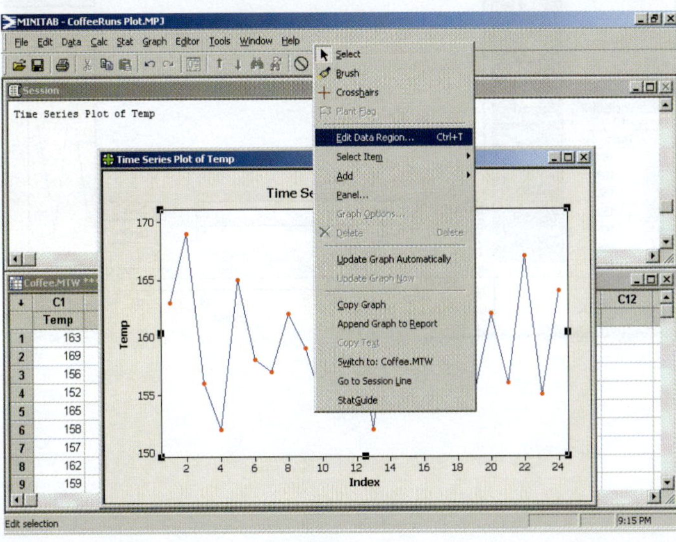

- For instance, here we have right-clicked on the data region and then selected "Edit Data Region" from the pop up menu. The Edit Data Region dialog box allows us to edit various attributes of this region. As shown, selecting Custom and clicking on the Background Color arrow allows us to change the background color of the data region.

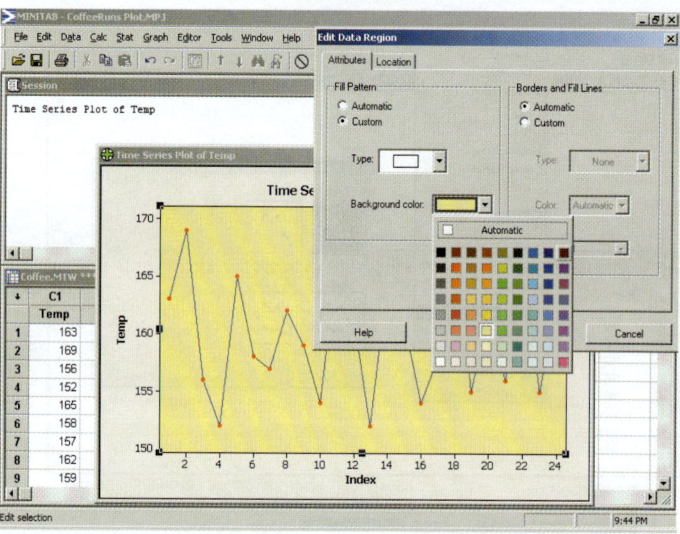

Printing a high-resolution graph similar to Figure 1.3(a) on page 14 (data file: Coffee.mtw):

- Click in the graphics window to select it as the active window.
- Select **File : Print Graph** to print the graph.
- Select the appropriate printer and click OK in the Print dialog box.
- When finished with the graph window, you can close it by clicking on the ☒ button in the upper right corner of the graphics window.

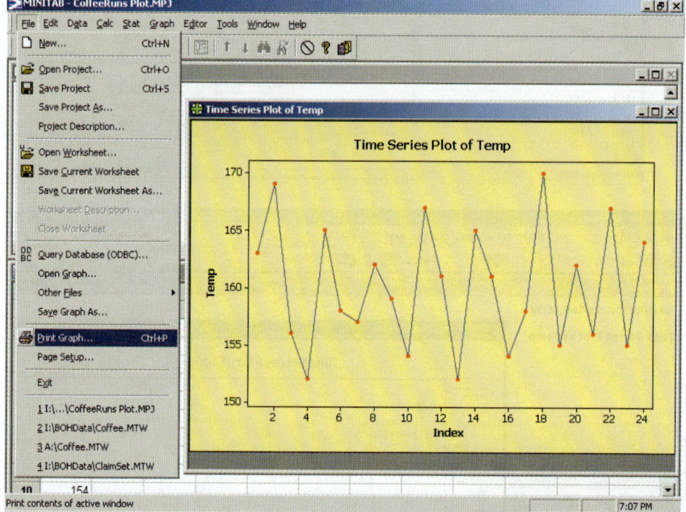

Saving the high-resolution graph:

- Select **File : Save Graph As.**
- In the "Save Graph As" dialog box, use the "Save in" pull-down menu to select the destination drive and folder (here we have selected the floppy drive, A:).
- Enter the desired file name in the File name box (here we have chosen the name Coffee). MINITAB will automatically add the extension .MGF.
- Click Save in the "Save Graph As" dialog box.

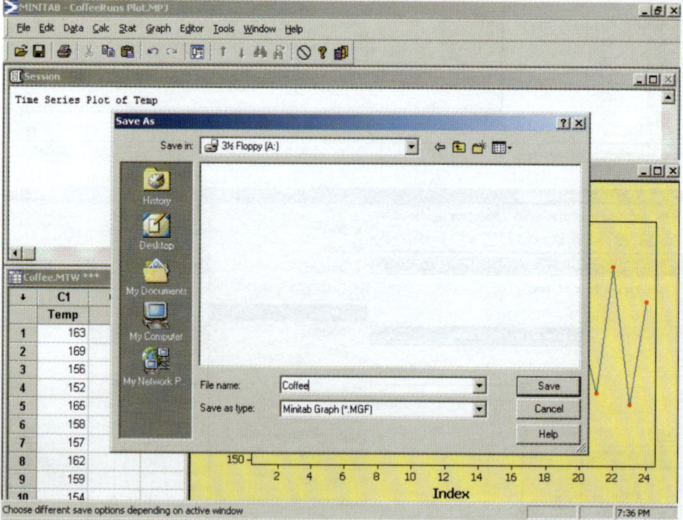

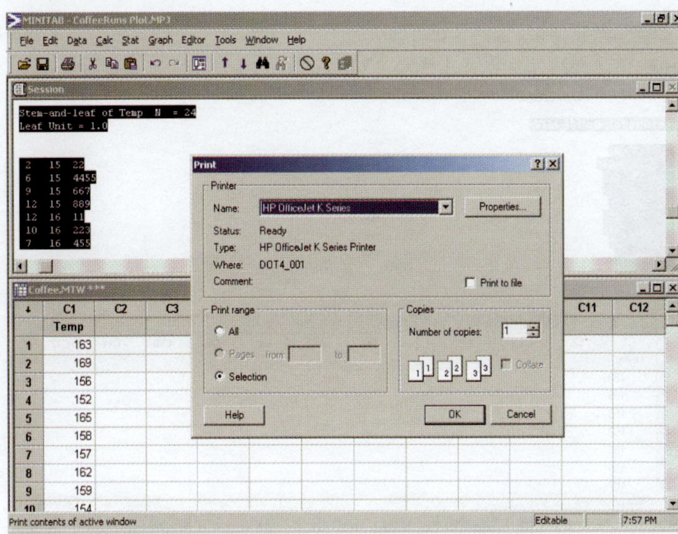

Printing data from the Session (shown) or Data window (data file: Coffee.mtw):

To print selected text from the Session window:

- Use the mouse to select the desired text.
- Select **File : Print Session Window.**
- In the Print dialog box, note that the Print range "Selection" option is selected. To print the entire Session window, select Print range "All".
- Click OK in Print dialog box.

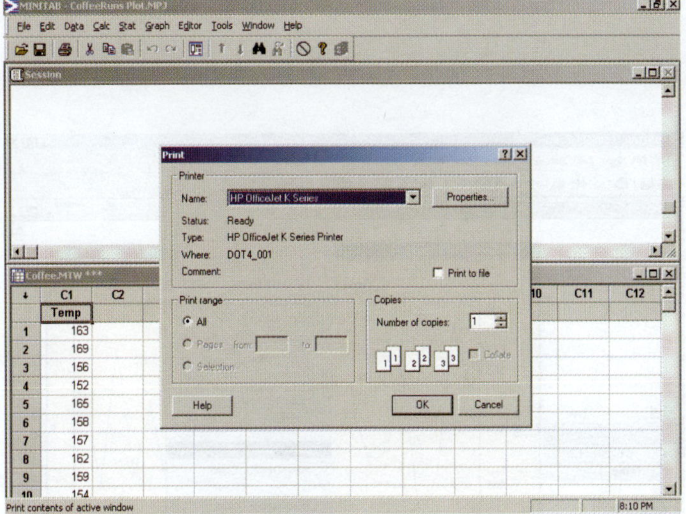

To print a Minitab worksheet from the data window:

- Click in the Data window to select it as active.
- Select **File : Print Worksheet.**
- Click OK in the Data Window Print Options dialog box.
- Click OK in the Print dialog box.

Including MINITAB output in reports The immediately preceding examples show how to print various types of output directly from MINITAB. Printing is a useful way to capture a quick hard-copy record of an analysis result. However, you may prefer at times to collect selected analysis results and arrange them with related narrative documentation in a report that can be saved and printed as a unit. This is easily accomplished by copying selected MINITAB results to the Windows clipboard and pasting them into your favorite word processor. Once copied to a word processor document, MINITAB results can be documented, edited, resized, and rearranged as desired into a cohesive record of your analysis. The following sequence of examples illustrates the process of collecting MINITAB output into a Microsoft Word document.

Copying session window output to a word processor document:

- Be sure to have a word processing document open to receive the results.
- Use the scroll bar on the right side of the Session window to locate the results to be copied and drag the mouse to select the desired output (selected output will be reverse-highlighted in black).
- Copy the selected output to the Windows clipboard by clicking the Copy icon on the MINITAB toolbar.
- Switch to your word processor document by clicking the button on the Windows task bar (here labeled MS Word Report.doc...).
- Click in your word processing document to position the cursor at the desired insertion point.
- Click the Paste button on the word processor power bar.
- Return to your MINITAB session by clicking the MINITAB button on the Windows task bar.

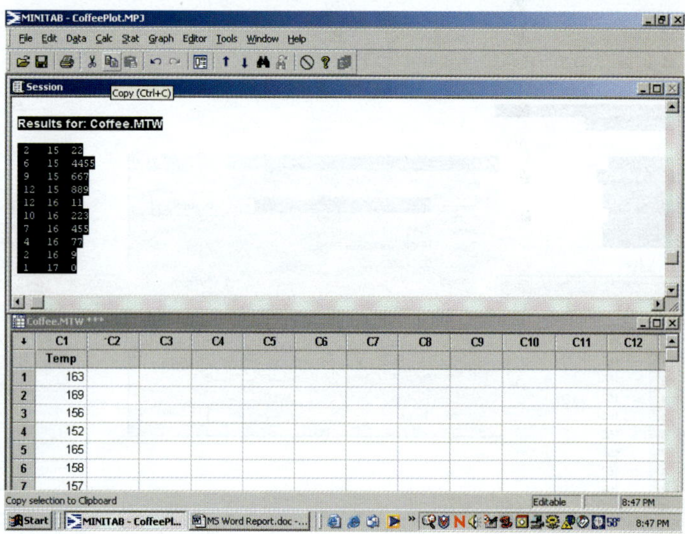

Copying high-resolution graphics output to a word processor document:

- Be sure to have a word processing document open to receive the results.
- Copy the selected contents of the high-resolution graphics window to the Windows clipboard by right-clicking in the graphics window and then clicking Copy Graph on the pop up menu.
- Switch to your word processor document by clicking the button on the Windows task bar (here labeled MS Word Report.doc...).
- Click in your word processing document to position the cursor at the desired insertion point.
- Click the Paste button on the word processor power bar.
- Return to your MINITAB session by clicking the MINITAB button on the Windows task bar.

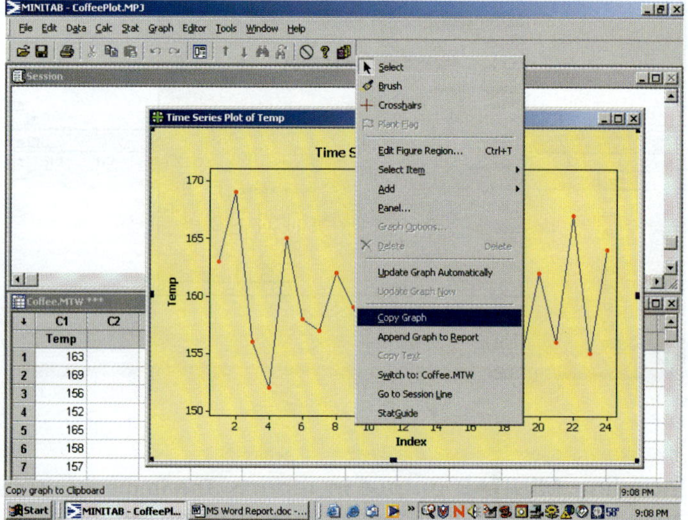

Results Here is how the copied results might appear in Microsoft Word. These results can be edited, resized, repositioned, and combined with your own additional documentation to create a cohesive record of your analysis.

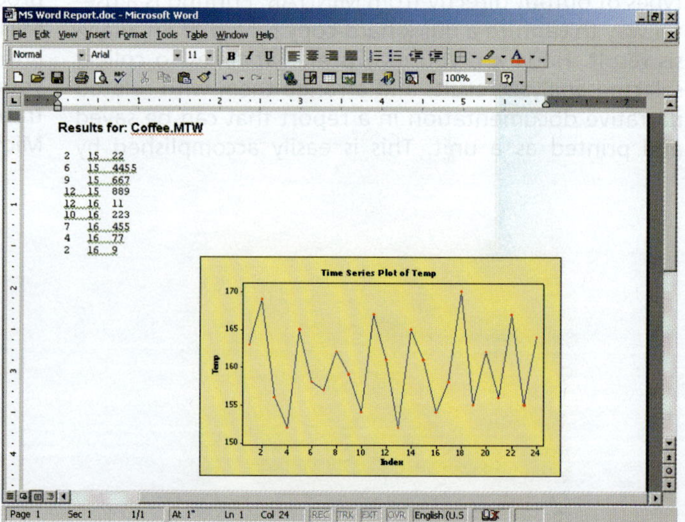

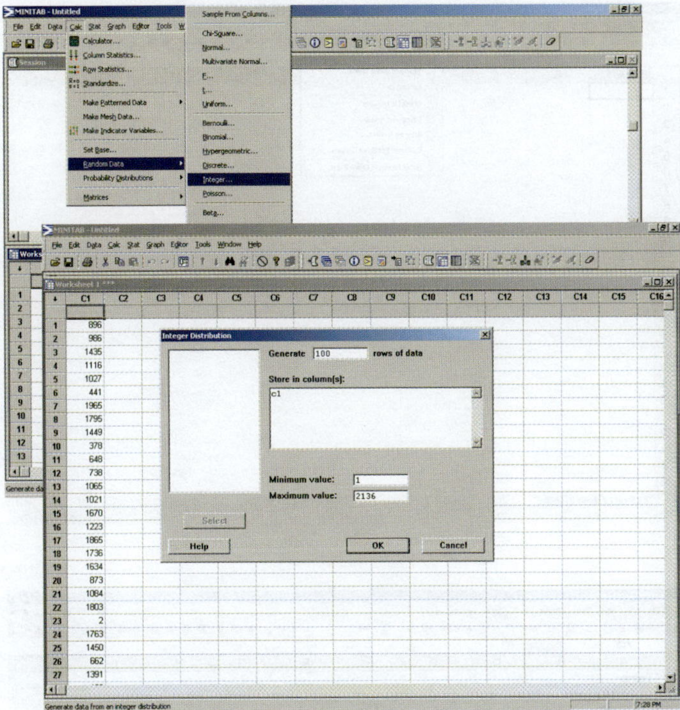

We complete this appendix by demonstrating how MINITAB can be used to generate a set of **random numbers** (as in Example 1.1 on page 5).

To create 100 random numbers between 1 and 2136 similar to those in Table 1.1(b) on page 6:

- Select **Calc : Random Data : Integer**
- In the Integer Distribution dialog box, enter 100 into the "Generate rows of data" window.
- Enter C1 into the "Store in column(s)" window.
- Enter 1 into the Minimum value box and enter 2136 into the Maximum value box.
- Click OK in the Integer Distribution dialog box.

The 100 random numbers will be placed in the Data Window in column C1. These numbers are generated with replacement. Repeated numbers would be skipped if the random numbers are being used to sample without replacement.

Appendix 1.2 ■ Getting Started with Excel

We begin with a look at some features of Excel that are common to many analyses. When the instructions call for a sequence of selections from a series of menus, the sequence will be presented in the following form:

Tools : Data Analysis : Descriptive Statistics

This notation indicates that Tools is the first selection from the Excel menu bar, next Data Analysis is selected from the Tools pull-down menu, and finally Descriptive Statistics is selected from the Data Analysis menu window.

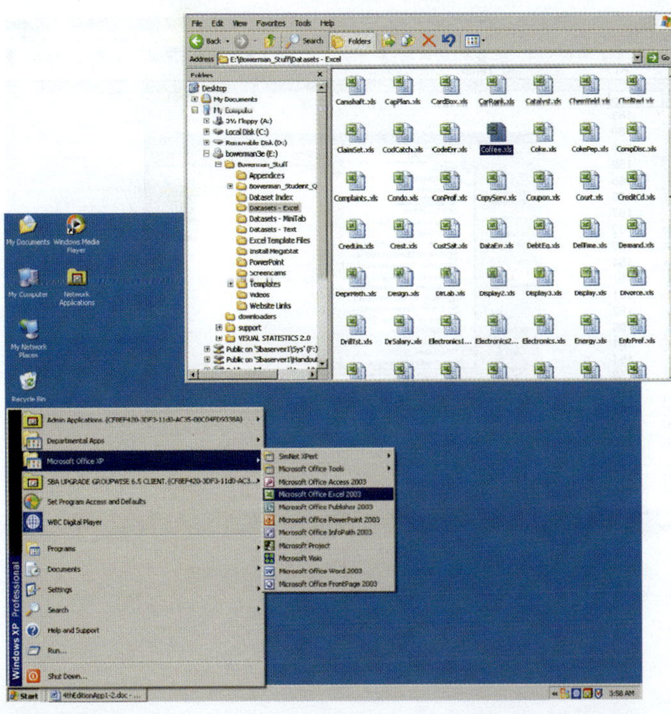

For many of the statistical and graphical procedures in Excel, it is necessary to provide a range of cells to specify the location of data in the spreadsheet. Generally, the range may be specified either by typing the cell locations directly into a dialog box or by dragging the selected range with the mouse. Though, for the experienced user, it is usually easier to use the mouse to select a range, the instructions that follow will, for precision and clarity, specify ranges by typing in cell locations. The selected range may include column or variable labels—labels at the tops of columns that serve to identify variables. When the selected range includes such labels, it is important to select the "Labels check box" in the analysis dialog box.

Starting Excel Procedures for starting Excel may vary from one installation to the next. If you are using a public computing laboratory, you may wish to consult local documentation. For typical Excel installations, you will generally be able to start Excel with a sequence of selections from the Microsoft Windows Start menu something like the following:

- Select **Start : Microsoft Office XP : Microsoft Office Excel 2003**

You can also start Excel with a previously saved Excel spreadsheet (like Coffee.xls or one of the other data files from the CD-ROM included with this text) from the Windows Explorer by double-clicking on the spreadsheet file's icon.

After starting Excel, the display will generally show a blank Excel workbook.

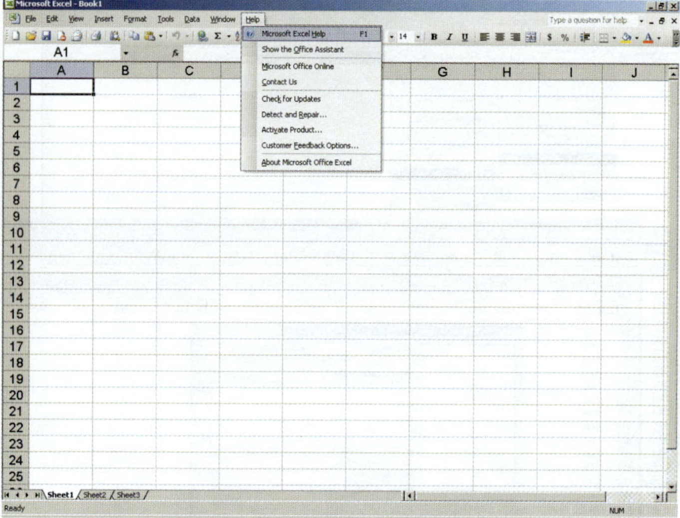

Help resources Like most Windows programs, Excel includes on-line help via a Help Menu that includes an Excel help wizard as well as a Contents and Index entry.

Entering data (entering the coffee temperature data in Table 1.7) from the keyboard (data file: Coffee.xls):

- In a new Excel workbook, click on cell A1 in Sheet1 and type a label—that is, a variable name—(here, Temp) for the coffee temperatures.
- Beginning in cell A2 (directly under the column label Temp) type the values for the variable (coffee temperatures from Table 1.7 on page 13) down the column, pressing the Enter key following each entry.

Saving data (saving the coffee temperature data):

- Select **File: Save As.**
- In the "Save As" dialog box, use the "Save in" drop-down menu to select the destination drive and folder (here we have selected the floppy drive, A:).
- Enter the desired file name in the "File name" box (here we have chosen the name Coffee). Excel will automatically add the extension .xls.
- Click Save in the "Save As" dialog box.

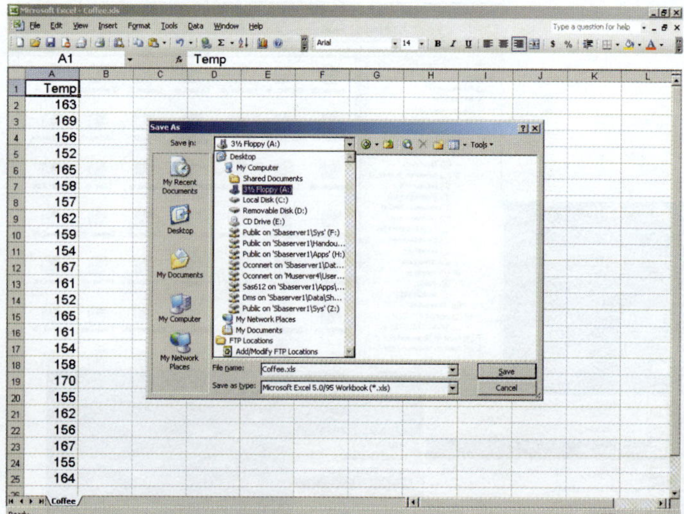

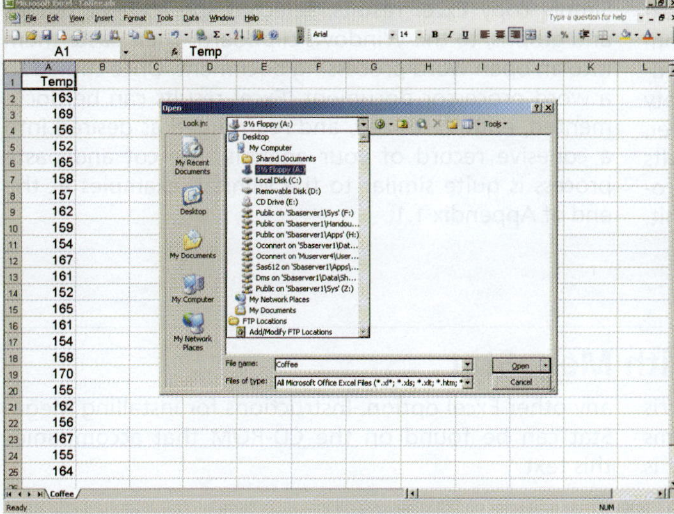

Retrieving an Excel spreadsheet containing the coffee temperature data in Table 1.7 on page 13 (data file: Coffee.xls):

- Select **File : Open**
- In the Open dialog box, use the "Look in" drop-down menu to select the source drive and folder (here we have selected the floppy drive, A:).
- Select the desired file name in the "File name" box (here we have chosen the Excel spreadsheet Coffee.xls).
- Click the Open button in the Open dialog box.

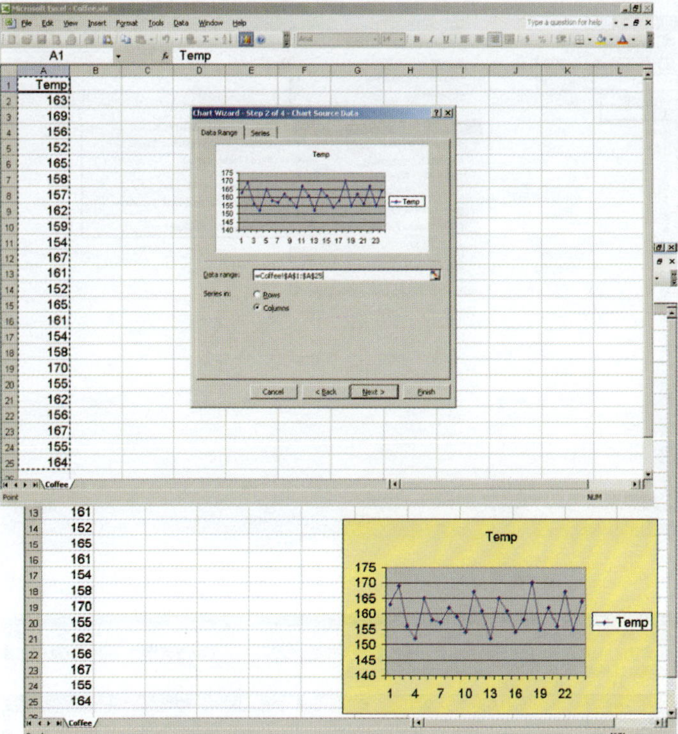

Creating a runs plot similar to Figure 1.3 (b) on page 14 (data file: Coffee.xls):

- Click the Chart Wizard button on the Excel toolbar.
- In the "Chart Wizard—Step 1 of 4" dialog box, click on Line in the Chart type menu and click Next>.
- In the Step 2 dialog box, be sure that the range in the Data Range box is the correct range for the data and label. If not, enter the correct range (here A1:A25) in the Data Range box.
- Under the "Series in" option, select Columns and click Next>.
- In the Step 3 dialog box, click Next>.
- In the Step 4 dialog box, click Finish.

The graph can be repositioned on the spreadsheet by dragging it with the mouse. The graph can be resized by dragging the sizing handles around the edge of the graph. Many formatting options are available by right-clicking various graph elements.

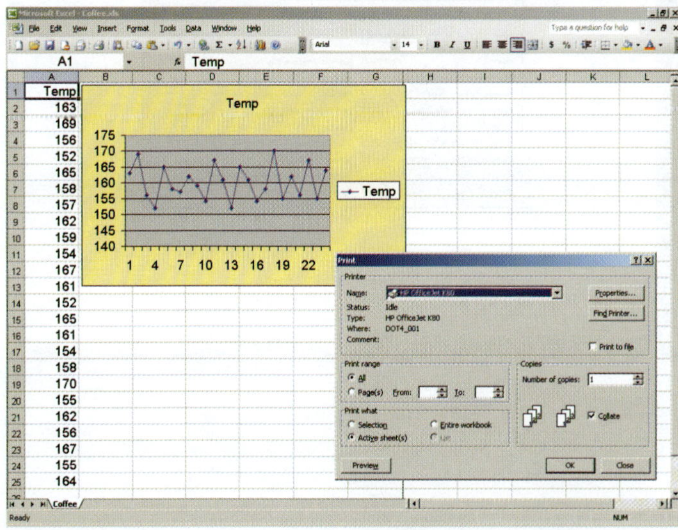

Printing a spreadsheet with embedded graph similar to Figure 1.3 (b) (data file: Coffee.xls):

- Click outside the graph to select the data and the graph for printing. (Click on the graph to select only the graph for printing.)
- Select **File : Print**.
- Click OK in the Print dialog box.

There are many print options available in Excel for printing—a selected range, selected sheets, or an entire workbook—making it possible to build and print fairly sophisticated reports directly from Excel.

Including Excel output in reports The preceding example showed how to print selected analysis results from Excel. Printing is a useful way to capture a quick hard-copy record of an analysis result and Excel offers a variety of options for building sophisticated reports. However, you may at times prefer to collect selected analysis results and arrange them with related narrative in a word processing document that can be saved and printed as a unit. Simply copy Excel results, selected spreadsheet ranges and graphs, to the Windows clipboard. Then paste them into an open word processing document. Once copied to a word processor document, Excel results can be documented, edited, resized, and rearranged as desired into a cohesive record of your analysis. The cut and paste process is quite similar to the Minitab examples at the end of Appendix 1.1.

Appendix 1.3 ■ Getting Started with MegaStat

MegaStat, which was developed by Professor J. B. Orris of Butler University, is an Excel add-in that performs statistical analyses within an Excel workbook. After it is installed, it appears on the Excel menu and works like any other Excel option. Instructions for installing MegaStat can be found on the CD-ROM that accompanies this text.

When you click on MegaStat on the Excel menu bar, the MegaStat menu appears as shown to the right. Most of the menu options display submenus. If a menu item is followed by an ellipsis (...), clicking it will display a dialog box for that option.

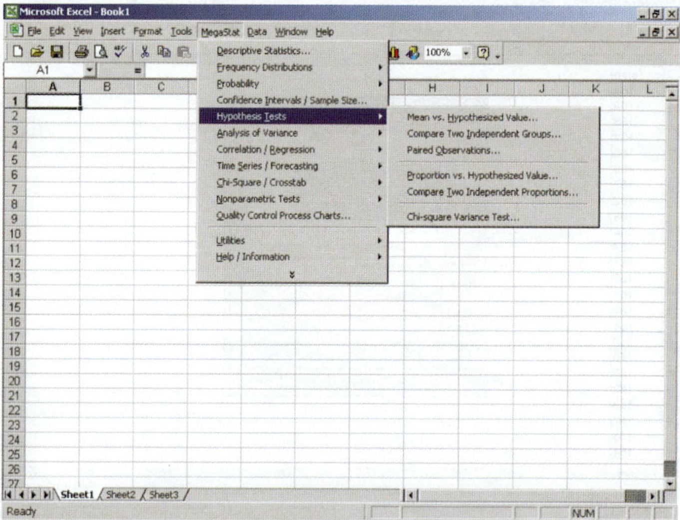

A dialog box allows you to specify the data to be used and other inputs and options. A typical dialog box is shown to the right.

After you have selected the needed data and options, click OK. The dialog box disappears, and MegaStat performs the analysis. Before we look at specific dialog boxes, we will describe some features that are common to all of the options. MegaStat use is intuitive and very much like other Excel operations; however, there are some features unique to MegaStat.

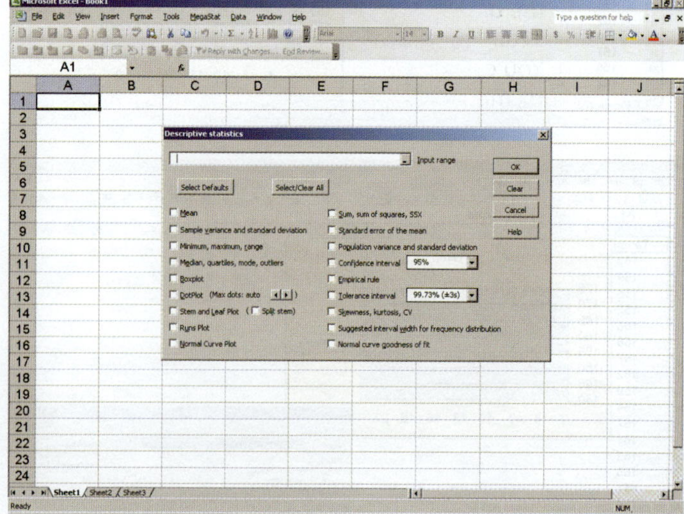

Data selection Most MegaStat dialog boxes have fields where you select input ranges that contain the data to be used. Such a field is shown in the dialog box just illustrated—it is the long horizontal window with the label **"Input range"** to its right. Input ranges can be selected using four methods:

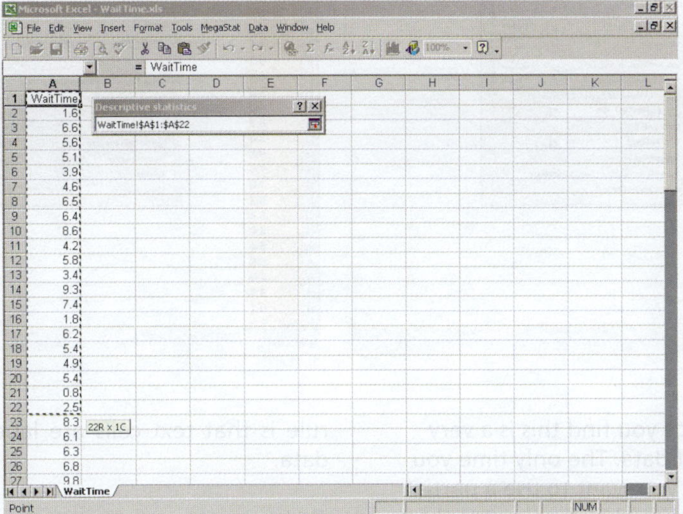

1 **Pointing and dragging with the mouse.** Simply select the desired data by pointing to it, left-clicking on the first data item, and dragging the cursor to select the rest of the data as illustrated above.

Since the dialog box pops up on the screen, it may block some of your data. You can move a dialog box around on the screen by placing the mouse pointer over the title bar (colored area at the top) and then clicking and holding the left mouse button while dragging the dialog box to a new location. You can even drag it partially off the screen.

You will also notice that when you start selecting data by dragging the mouse pointer, the dialog box will collapse to a smaller size to help you see the underlying data. It will automatically return to full size when you release the mouse button. You can also collapse and uncollapse the dialog box manually by clicking the collapse (-) button at the right end of the field. Clicking the button again will uncollapse the dialog box. (Never use the ☒ button to try to collapse or uncollapse a dialog box.)

2 **Using MegaStat's AutoExpand feature.** Pointing and dragging to select data can be tedious if you have a lot of data. When you drag the mouse down it is easy to overshoot the selection, and then you have to drag the mouse back until you get the area correctly selected. AutoExpand allows you to select data rapidly without having to drag through the entire column of data. Here is how it works:

a Make sure the input box has the focus (that is, click in it to make the input box active). An input box has the focus when the insertion pointer is blinking in it.

b Click in one cell of the column you want. If more than one column is being selected, drag the mouse across the columns.

c Right-click over the input field **or** left-click the label "Input range" to the right of the input box. The data range will expand to include all of the rows in the region where you selected one row.

This procedure is illustrated on the next page. In the left screenshot, we have left-clicked on one cell in the column of data labeled WaitTime. In the right screenshot, we see the result after we right-click over the input field or left-click on the label "Input range." Notice that the entire column of data has been selected in the right screenshot. This can be seen by examining the input field or by looking at the column of data.

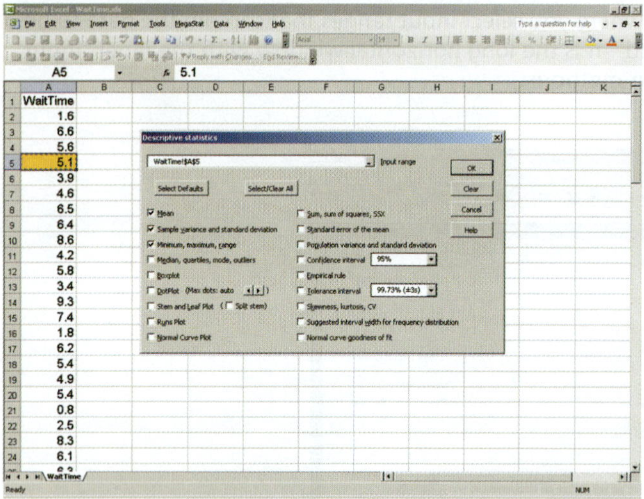

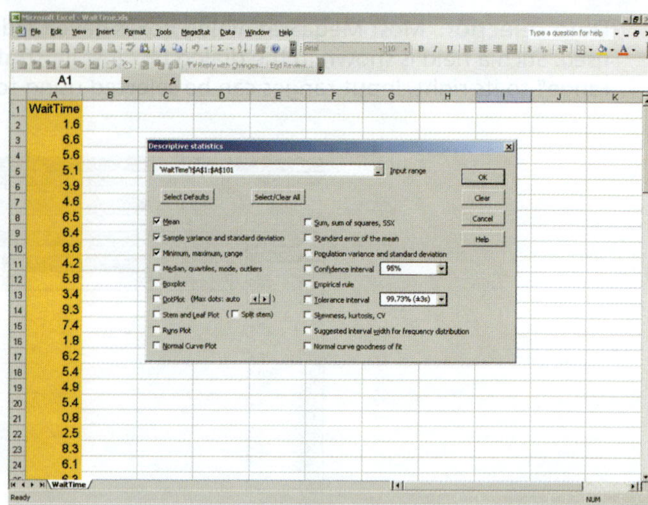

With a little practice you find this is a very efficient way to select data. The only time you cannot use it is when you want to use a partial column of data. You should also be aware that the AutoExpand stops when it finds a blank cell; thus any summations or other calculations at the bottom of a column would be selected.

Note: When using these methods of data selection, you may select variables in an alternate sequence by holding the CTRL key while making multiple selections.

3 **Typing the name of a named range.** If you have previously identified a range of cells using Excel's name box, you may use that name to specify a data range in a MegaStat dialog box. This method can be very useful if you are using the same data for several different statistical procedures.

4 **Typing a range address.** You may type any valid Excel range address—for example, A1:A101—into the input field. This is the most cumbersome way to specify data ranges, but it certainly works.

Data labels For most procedures, the first cell in each input range can be a label. If the first cell in a range is text, it is considered a label; if the first cell is a numeric value, it is considered data. If you want to use numbers as variable labels, you must enter the numbers as text by preceding them with a single quote mark—for instance, '2. Even though Excel stores times and dates as numbers, MegaStat will recognize them as labels if they are formatted as time/date values. If data labels are not part of the input range, the program automatically uses the cell immediately above the data range as a label if it contains a text value. If an option can consider the entire first row (or column) of an input range as labels, any numeric value in the row will cause the entire row to be treated as data. Finally, if the program detects sequential integers (1,2,3,...) in a location where you might want labels, it will display a warning message. Otherwise, the rule is that text cells are labels, and numeric cells are data.

Output When you click OK in a MegaStat dialog box, it performs some statistical analysis and needs a place to put its output. It looks for a worksheet named Output in the current Excel application. If it finds one, it goes to the end of it and appends its output; if it doesn't find an Output worksheet, it creates one. MegaStat never changes the user's worksheets; it only sends output to its Output sheet.

MegaStat attempts to format the output, but **remember that the Output sheet is just a standard Excel worksheet and can be modified in any way.** You can adjust column widths and change any formatting that you think needs improvement. You can insert, delete, and modify cells. You can copy all or part of the output to another worksheet or to another application such as a word processor.

When the program generates output, it adjusts column widths for the current output. If you have previous output from a different option already in the Output sheet, the column widths for the previous output may be altered. You can attempt to fix this by manually adjusting the column widths. Alternatively, you can make it a practice to always start a new Output sheet. The **Utilities menu** has options for deleting the Output sheet, for making a copy of it, and for starting a new one.

An example We now give an example of using MegaStat to carry out statistical analysis. When the instructions call for a sequence of selections from a series of menus, the sequence will be presented in the following form:

MegaStat: Probability: Counting Rules

This notation says that MegaStat is the first selection from the Excel menu bar; next Probability is selected from the MegaStat pull-down menu; and finally Counting Rules is selected from the Probability submenu.

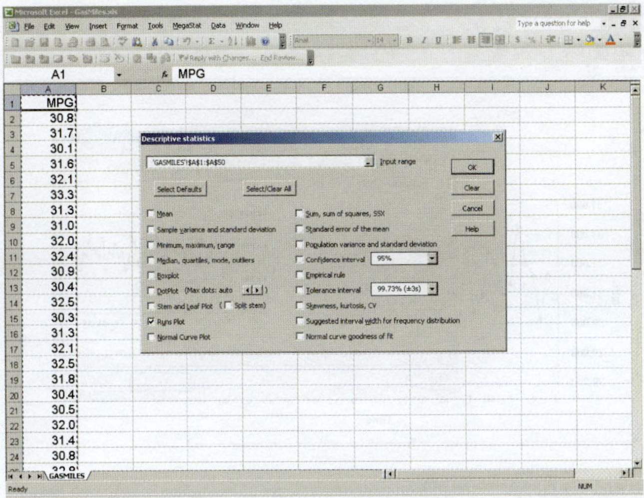

Creating a runs plot similar to Figure 1.6 on page 16 (data file: GasMiles.xls):

- In the Descriptive Statistics dialog box, enter the mileage data in Table 1.8 on page 16 into column A with the label MPG in cell A1 and with the 49 mileages in cells A2 through A50.
- Select **MegaStat : Descriptive Statistics.**
- Enter the range A1: A50 into the Input range box. The easiest way to do this is to use the MegaStat AutoExpand feature. Simply select one cell in column A (cell A4, for instance) by clicking on the cell. Then, either right-click in the Input range box or left-click on the label "Input range" to the right of the Input range box.
- Check the Runs Plot check box.
- Click OK in the Descriptive statistics dialog box.

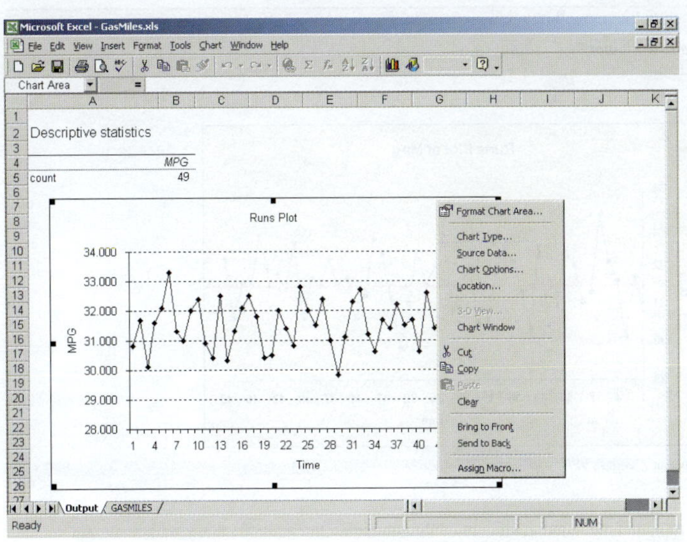

MegaStat places the resulting analysis (in this case the runs plot) in an output worksheet. This is a standard Excel worksheet, which can be edited using any of the usual Excel features.

For instance, by right-clicking on various portions of the runs plot graphic, you can edit the plot in many ways. Here we have right-clicked on the chart area. By now selecting **Format Chart Area,** we are able to edit the graphic in a variety of ways.

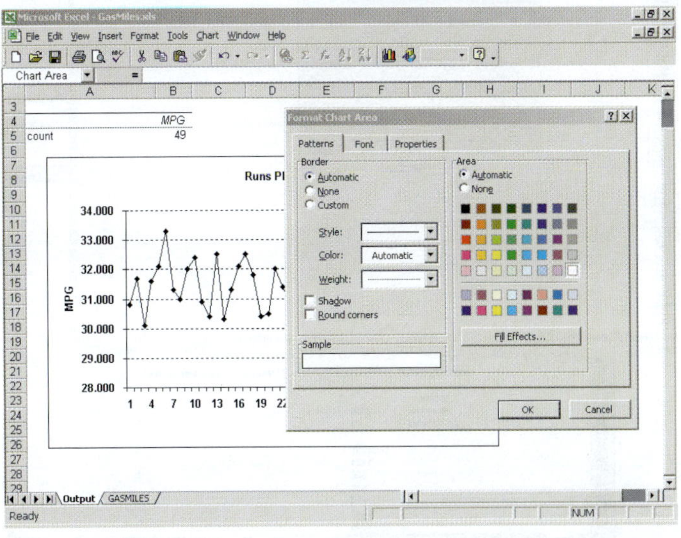

In the Format Chart Area dialog box, we can add color to the runs plot, change fonts, and edit the plot in many other ways.

When we right-click on the chart area and obtain the previously shown pull-down menu, we can alternatively select **Chart Options.** The Chart Options dialog box allows us to edit chart titles, axes and axis labels, data labels, and many other chart features.

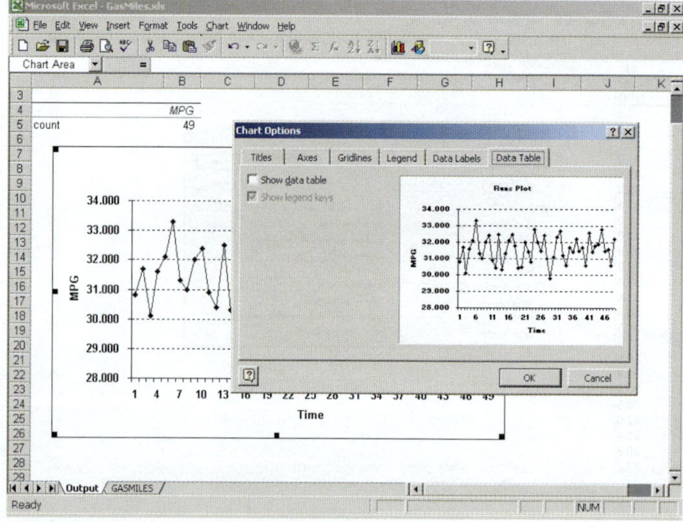

Our final edited runs plot as presented in the text is as follows.

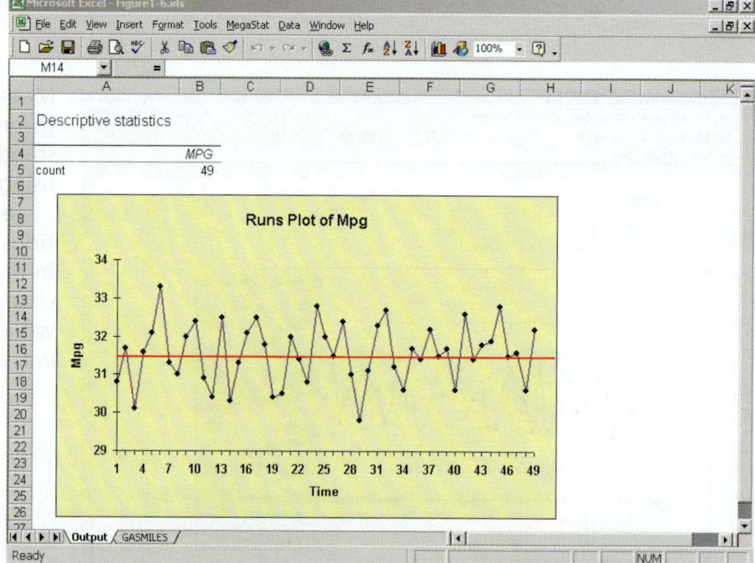

We complete this appendix by demonstrating how MegaStat can be used to generate a set of **random numbers** (as in Example 1.1 on page 5).

To create 100 random numbers between 1 and 2136 similar to those in Table 1.1(b) on page 6:

- Select **MegaStat : Generate Random Numbers ...**
- In the Random Number Generation dialog box, enter 100 into the "Number of values to be generated" window.
- Click the right arrow button to select 0 Decimal Places.
- Select the Uniform tab, and enter 1 into the Minimum box and enter 2136 into the Maximum box.
- Click OK in the Random Number Generation dialog box.

The 100 random numbers will be placed in the Output Sheet. These numbers are generated with replacement. Repeated numbers would be skipped if the random numbers are being used to sample without replacement.

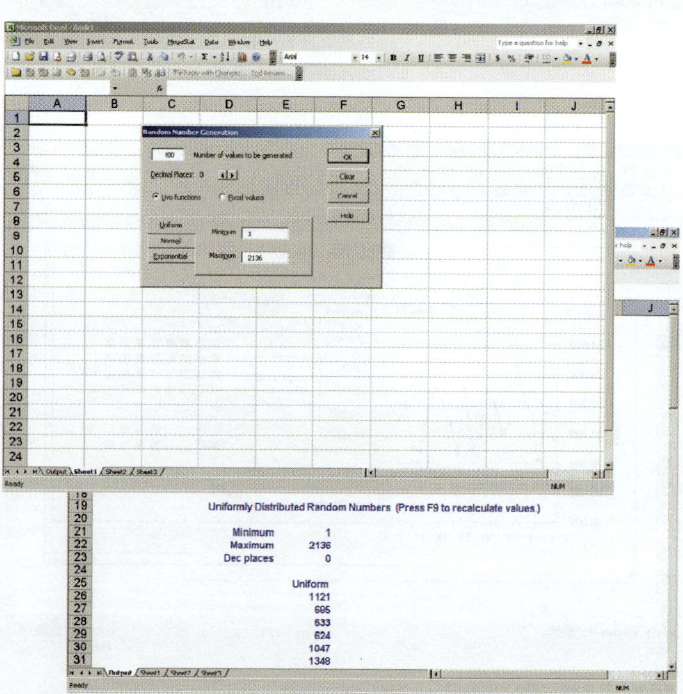

Appendix 1.4 ■ Introduction to Internet Exercises

The Internet and the World Wide Web provide a rich source of data and information on a limitless variety of subjects, among them government statistics, data about firms, and data about consumers. Though you probably have experience using the Internet, in this book we will use the Internet as a source of data for statistical analysis. We do this through Internet exercises in many chapters of this book. These exercises will ask you to go to a website, find appropriate data (and perhaps copy it) and then analyze the data.

The BSC: The McGraw-Hill/Irwin Business Statistics Center The BSC is a collection of Internet-based resources for teaching and learning about business statistics. It includes links to statistical publications, websites, software, and data sources. To go to the BSC, enter the Web address http://www.mhhe.com/business/opsci/bstat/ into your browser. There are also links to the BSC on the CD-ROM included with this text. To see a list of databases accessible through the BSC, click on the Data Bases button on the BSC home screen. Updated links to data and additional Internet exercises can also be found at this text's website—http://www.mhhe.com/business/opsci/bowerman/.

1.30 Internet Exercise

The website maintained by the U.S. Census Bureau provides a multitude of social, economic, and government data. In particular, this website houses selected data from the most recent *Statistical Abstract of the United States* (http://www.census.gov/statab/www/). Among these selected features are "Frequently Requested Tables" that can be accessed simply by clicking on the label.

- **a** Go to the U.S. Census Bureau website and open the "Frequently requested tables" from the *Statistical Abstract.* Find the table of "Consumer Price Indexes by Major Groups." (Note that in Chapter 17 we explain how price indexes are constructed.) Construct runs plots of (1) the price index for all items over time (years), (2) the price index for food over time, (3) the price index for fuel oil over time, and (4) the price index for electricity over time. For each runs plot, describe apparent trends in the price index.
- **b** By opening the "Frequently requested tables" from the *Statistical Abstract,* find the table of "Crimes and Crime Rates, by Type." Repeat the analysis of part (a) for each of (1) total violent crime rate (per 100,000 population) over time, (2) murder rate (per 100,000 population) over time, and (3) robbery rate (per 100,000 population) over time.

1.31 Internet Exercise

The website maintained by *Fortune* magazine (http://www.fortune.com) offers a wide selection of interesting business data. Included is the famous *Fortune* 500 List as well as many other company lists (America's Most Admired Companies, The *Fortune* Global 500, etc.).

- **a** Go to the *Fortune* website and find the *Fortune* 500 list. Consider the first 50 companies (ranked 1 through 50 by revenue) and select a random sample of 10 of the top 50 companies, using either a random number table (Table 1.1(a) on page 6) or random numbers obtained using MINITAB or MegaStat. Justify that your sample is a random sample by explaining exactly how the sample was selected.
- **b** Go to the *Fortune* website and find the *Fortune* Global 500 list. Select a systematic sample of 10 companies from this list. Explain exactly how the sample was selected.

CHAPTER 2

Descriptive Statistics

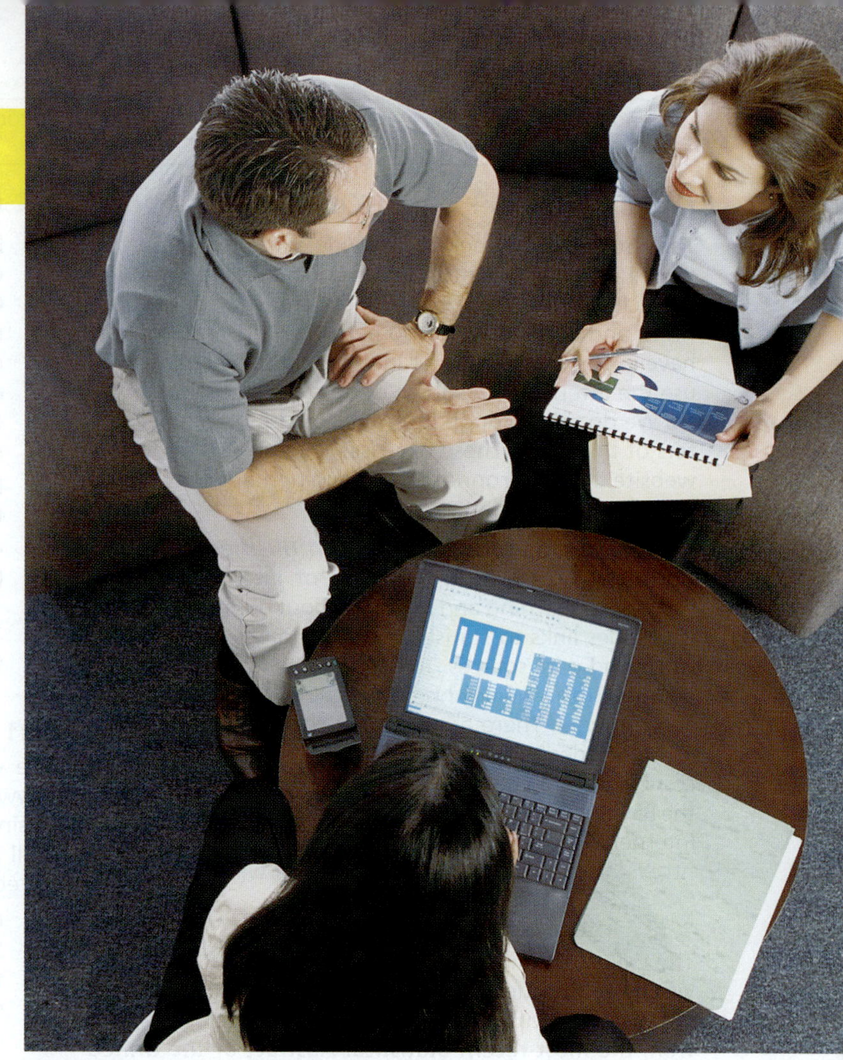

Chapter Outline

- **2.1** Describing the Shape of a Distribution
- **2.2** Describing Central Tendency
- **2.3** Measures of Variation
- **2.4** Percentiles, Quartiles, and Box-and-Whiskers Displays
- **2.5** Describing Qualitative Data
- **2.6** Using Scatter Plots to Study Relationships between Variables (Optional)
- **2.7** Misleading Graphs and Charts (Optional)
- **2.8** Weighted Means and Grouped Data (Optional)
- **2.9** The Geometric Mean (Optional)

In Chapter 1 we saw that although we can sometimes take a census of an entire population, we often must randomly select a sample from a population. When we have taken a census or a sample, we typically wish to describe the observed data set. In particular, we describe a sample in order to make inferences about the sampled population.

In this chapter we learn about **descriptive statistics,** which is the science of describing the important characteristics of a population or sample. Generally, we look at several important aspects of a set of measurements. One such aspect is the **central tendency,** or middle, of the data set. For instance, we might estimate a typical bottle design rating in the marketing research case or a typical city driving mileage in the car mileage case. Another important aspect of a data set is the **variability,** or spread, of the data. For example, we might estimate the largest and smallest gas mileage that would likely be obtained when a new midsize car is purchased. Or, in the marketing research case we might measure the spread of the bottle design ratings. If the ratings are clustered closely together, consumers' ratings are much the same (or are consistent). If the ratings are spread far apart, then consumers have widely varying opinions of the new bottle design. A third important aspect of a data set is the **shape** of the population or sample. Looking at a data set's shape tells us how the population or sample is *distributed* over various values (more about this later). Still another important aspect is whether **outliers** exist. For instance, if there are outlying bottle design ratings, then several consumers have opinions about the design that are very different from the opinions of most of the sampled consumers. Descriptive statistics also involves using **graphical methods** to depict data sets and to study relationships between different variables.

In this chapter we use a variety of methods to describe the cell phone usages, bottle design ratings, coffee temperatures, and car mileages introduced in the cases of Chapter 1. In addition, we introduce three new cases:

The Payment Time Case: A management consulting firm assesses how effectively a new electronic billing system reduces bill payment times.

The Electronic Article Surveillance Case: A survey is used to study the unintended effects on consumer attitudes of false electronic article surveillance alarms.

The Marketing Ethics Case: A survey is conducted to study marketing researchers' attitudes toward violating confidentiality in marketing research studies.

2.1 Describing the Shape of a Distribution

We begin looking at the characteristics of a population by describing the population's overall pattern of variation. That is, we describe the shape of the distribution of population measurements. We often employ a sample of measurements taken from a population in order to infer what the population looks like.

CHAPTER 1

Several graphical methods—the **stem-and-leaf display,** the **histogram,** and the **dot plot**—are often used to portray shapes of distributions.

Stem-and-leaf displays We illustrate how to construct stem-and-leaf displays in the following examples.

Example 2.1 The Car Mileage Case

Table 2.1 presents the sample of 49 gas mileages that have been obtained by the new midsize model in Example 1.4 (page 15). To graphically portray the pattern of variation in these mileages, we can construct a stem-and-leaf display. In order to do this, we first notice that the sample mileages range from 29.8 to 33.3. For this data we will (somewhat arbitrarily) construct a display having the first two digits of the mileages—the whole numbers 29, 30, 31, 32, and 33—as the **stems.** These are placed in a column on the left side of the display as follows:

29 |
30 |
31 |
32 |
33 |

TABLE 2.1 A Sample of 49 Mileages GasMiles

30.8	30.9	32.0	32.3	32.6
31.7	30.4	31.4	32.7	31.4
30.1	32.5	30.8	31.2	31.8
31.6	30.3	32.8	30.6	31.9
32.1	31.3	32.0	31.7	32.8
33.3	32.1	31.5	31.4	31.5
31.3	32.5	32.4	32.2	31.6
31.0	31.8	31.0	31.5	30.6
32.0	30.4	29.8	31.7	32.2
32.4	30.5	31.1	30.6	

The third (tenths place) digits of the mileages are the **leaves** of the display. These are placed in rows corresponding to the appropriate stems. Therefore, the first three mileages—30.8, 31.7, and 30.1—would be represented as

```
29 |
30 | 8 1
31 | 7
32 |
33 |
```

We continue this procedure, and we order the data within each row (although this is not required). We obtain the following stem-and-leaf display:

```
29 | 8
30 | 1 3 4 4 5 6 6 6 8 8 9
31 | 0 0 1 2 3 3 4 4 4 5 5 5 6 6 7 7 7 8 8 9
32 | 0 0 0 1 1 2 2 3 4 4 5 5 6 7 8 8
33 | 3
```

This display portrays the overall pattern of the variation of the sample mileages. It groups the mileages into classes, and it graphically illustrates how many mileages are in each class, as well as how the mileages are distributed within each class. The first class corresponds to the stem 29 and consists of the mileages from 29.0 to 29.9. There is one mileage—29.8—in this class. The second class corresponds to the stem 30 and consists of the mileages from 30.0 to 30.9. There are 11 mileages in this class. Similarly, the third, fourth, and fifth classes correspond to the stems 31, 32, and 33 and contain, respectively, 20 mileages, 16 mileages, and 1 mileage.

If we want a more detailed display, we can create more classes by using stems labeled as 29, 30*, 30, 31*, 31, 32*, 32, and 33*. Here, for instance, in the row labeled 30* we place the mileages from 30.0 to 30.4, and in the row labeled 30 we place the mileages from 30.5 to 30.9. Doing this, we obtain

```
29  | 8
30* | 1 3 4 4
30  | 5 6 6 6 8 8 9
31* | 0 0 1 2 3 3 4 4 4
31  | 5 5 5 6 6 7 7 7 8 8 9
32* | 0 0 0 1 1 2 2 3 4 4
32  | 5 5 6 7 8 8
33* | 3
```

Looking at the stem-and-leaf display, the distribution of sample mileages appears to be quite **symmetrical.** That is, the *upper portion* of the display (the portion corresponding to the stems 29, 30*, 30, and 31*) and the *lower portion* of the display (the portion corresponding to the stems 31, 32*, 32, and 33*) are nearly *mirror images* of each other. We will learn in later sections that symmetry or, more generally, the shape of the distribution of data influences how we measure both the central tendency and the variability of the data.

FIGURE 2.1 MINITAB and MegaStat Outputs of a Stem-and-Leaf Display of the 49 Mileages

```
Stem-and-Leaf Display: MPG

Stem-and-leaf of MPG   N = 49
Leaf Unit = 0.10

1     29  8
5     30  1344
12    30  5666889
21    31  001233444
(11)  31  55566777889
17    32  0001122344
7     32  556788
1     33  3
```

(a) The MINITAB Output

Stem and Leaf plot for MPG

stem unit = 1
leaf unit = 0.1

Frequency	Stem	Leaf
1	29	8
4	30	1344
7	30	5666889
9	31	001233444
11	31	55566777889
10	32	0001122344
6	32	556788
1	33	3
49		

(b) The MegaStat Output

Finally, Figure 2.1 gives MINITAB and MegaStat outputs of a stem-and-leaf display of the 49 sample mileages. These displays are identical to the latter of the two displays we set up by hand. In the MINITAB output, the leftmost column of numbers summarizes how many measurements (mileages) are in the various stems. For example, the 11 (in parentheses) tells us that the stem for 31.5 to 31.9 mpg includes 11 mileages; the 12 (no parentheses) tells us that a total of 12 mileages are at or below 30.9 mpg; the 7 tells us that a total of 7 mileages are at or above 32.5 mpg. In the MegaStat output, the leftmost column of numbers tells us how many measurements are in each of the stems. For instance, 7 mileages are in the stem for 30.5 to 30.9 mpg.

We summarize how to set up a stem-and-leaf display in the following box:

Constructing a Stem-and-Leaf Display

1 Decide what units will be used for the stems and the leaves. As a general rule, choose units for the stems so that there will be somewhere between 5 and 20 stems.

2 Place the stems in a column with the smallest stem at the top of the column and the largest stem at the bottom.

3 Enter the leaf for each measurement into the row corresponding to the proper stem. The leaves should be single-digit numbers (these can be rounded values that were originally more than one digit).

4 If desired, rearrange the leaves so that they are in increasing order from left to right.

Some stem-and-leaf displays do not appear symmetrical. This is illustrated in the next two examples.

Example 2.2 The Payment Time Case: Reducing Payment Times[1]

C

Major consulting firms such as Accenture, Ernst & Young Consulting, and Deloitte & Touche Consulting employ statistical analysis to assess the effectiveness of the systems they develop. This case concerns a consulting firm that developed a new computer-based, electronic billing system for a Hamilton, Ohio, trucking company that was experiencing problems with its billing and accounts receivable process. The trucking company's former billing system employed a computer to generate invoices, which were mailed to customers. However, customers were taking too long to make payments. The standard payment time for most industries is 30 days, where payment time is measured from the date on the invoice to the date payment is received.

[1]This case is based on a real problem encountered by a company that employs one of our former students. For purposes of confidentiality, we have withheld the company's name.

TABLE 2.2 A Sample of Payment Times (in Days) for 65 Randomly Selected Invoices PayTime

22	29	16	15	18	17	12	13	17	16	15
19	17	10	21	15	14	17	18	12	20	14
16	15	16	20	22	14	25	19	23	15	19
18	23	22	16	16	19	13	18	24	24	26
13	18	17	15	24	15	17	14	18	17	21
16	21	25	19	20	27	16	17	16	21	

Payment Times

```
10  0          } 
11             } Shorter "Tail"
12  00         }
13  000
14  0000
15  0000000
16  000000000
17  00000000
18  000000
19  00000
20  000
21  0000
22  000        }
23  00         }
24  000        }
25  00         }
26  0          } Longer "Tail"
27  0          }
28             }
29  0          }
```

Ratings

```
20  0
21
22  0
23
24  0
25  00
26  00
27  000
28  0000
29  00000
30  000000
31  00000000
32  00000000000
33  0000000000
34  00000
35  0
```

A number of the trucking company's customers were not meeting the 30-day standard. In fact, typical payment times were 39 days or more. To reduce payment times, the consulting firm installed a new billing system. This system sends invoices electronically from the trucking company's computer directly to the customer's computer and also allows customers to easily check and correct errors electronically.

The consulting firm intends to market the new billing system to other trucking companies if it can establish that the new system substantially reduces payment times. In order to assess the effectiveness of the system, the consulting firm will study the payment times for invoices processed during the first three months of the system's operation. During this period, 7,823 invoices are processed using the new system. To study the payment times of these invoices, the consulting firm numbers the invoices from 0001 to 7823 and uses random numbers to select a random sample of 65 invoices. The payment time for each of the sampled invoices is determined, and the resulting 65 payment times are given in Table 2.2.

In order to summarize the 65 payment times, the consulting firm decides to construct a stem-and-leaf display. Noting that the payment times range from 10 to 29 days and are expressed as whole numbers, we use these whole numbers as stems. Because a whole number, say 18, can be written as 18.0, we use the (implied) tenths-place digit, 0, as the leaf value. Therefore, the stem-and-leaf display is as shown in the left page margin under the heading "Payment Times." Looking at this display, we see that all of the sampled payment times are substantially less than the 39-day typical payment time of the former billing system. In addition, we see that the "tail" of the distribution consisting of the higher payment times is longer than the "tail" of the distribution consisting of the smaller payment times. This shows that a few of the payment times are somewhat larger than the rest. Here we say that the distribution seems to be *skewed* toward the larger payment times. Alternatively, we say that the distribution is *skewed with a tail to the right* because, if we turn the display sideways so that we are looking at it with the stems forming a number line, the longer tail would extend to the right.

Example 2.3 The Marketing Research Case

Consider the sample of 60 bottle design ratings in Table 1.3 (page 8). These bottle design ratings range from 20 to 35, so a stem-and-leaf display of the ratings is as shown in the left page margin under the heading "Ratings." Looking at this display, we see that the distribution of bottle design ratings seems to be skewed toward the smaller ratings. That is, we say the distribution is *skewed with a tail to the left.* This says that a few of the ratings are somewhat lower than the rest of the ratings.

Frequency distributions and histograms The **count of the number of measurements in a class** defined by a stem is called the **frequency** of the class. One advantage of a stem-and-leaf display is that it gives the frequencies of the different classes and also lists the specific measurements in each class. However, such listings for the different classes can be unwieldy if we are portraying a large number of measurements. For example, while it is convenient to display the 65 payment times using the stem-and-leaf display of Example 2.2, summarizing 500 payment times with the same type of format would be difficult.

When we have many measurements, it is best to group them into the classes of a **frequency distribution** and to display the data by using what is called a **histogram.** These are also useful for summarizing more moderately sized data sets (such as the 65 payment times). We illustrate this in the following example.

Example 2.4 The Payment Time Case

C

Here is a **frequency distribution** for the 65 payment times:

Class	Frequency
10–12	3
13–15	14
16–18	23
19–21	12
22–24	8
25–27	4
28–30	1

The frequency distribution divides the payment times into classes, and the **frequency** for each class tells us how many of the payment times are in each class. Note that the classes must be defined so that any particular payment time will fall into one and only one class. In order to group the payment times into the classes of a frequency distribution, we must first decide how many classes to use. A general rule says that the number of classes should be the smallest whole number K that makes the quantity 2^K greater than the total number of measurements n. Since $n = 65$, and since $2^6 = 64$ is less than 65 and $2^7 = 128$ is greater than 65, we should use $K = 7$ classes. We next find the length of each class by computing

$$\text{Class length} = \frac{\text{Largest measurement} - \text{Smallest measurement}}{K}$$

Since the largest and smallest payment times in Table 2.2 are 29 days and 10 days, the class length is $(29 - 10)/7 = 2.7143$. This says that, in order to include the smallest and largest payment times in the 7 classes, each class must have a length of at least 2.7143. To obtain a more convenient class length, we arbitrarily round this value up to 3. To form the first class, we start with the smallest payment time—10—and add 2 (one less than the class length 3) to obtain the class 10–12. To form the second class, we start with the payment time 13 and add 2 to obtain the class 13–15. Continuing this process, we find that the remaining 5 classes are 16–18, 19–21, 22–24, 25–27, and 28–30. Note that each class contains 3 payment times, where 3 is the class length. For example, the first class of 10–12 contains the 3 payment times 10, 11, and 12.

In general, the smallest and largest data values that can belong to a given class are called the **lower and upper class limits.** For example, the seventh class of 28–30 has a lower class limit of 28 and an upper class limit of 30. The largest **observed** payment time—29 days—is contained in this last class. In cases where the largest measurement is not contained in the last class, we simply add another class. Generally speaking, the guidelines we have given for forming classes are not inflexible rules. Rather, they are intended to help us find reasonable classes.

Once we have formed the classes, we record the number of measurements that fall into each class. To do this, we look at each measurement and place a check, or tally, to the right of the class into which the measurement falls. For example, since the first four payment times in Table 2.2 are 22, 19, 16, and 18, we obtain the first four checks shown in the following table:

Class	First 4 Checks	65 Checks	Frequency
10–12		///	3
13–15		~~////~~ ~~////~~ ////	14
16–18	//	~~////~~ ~~////~~ ~~////~~ ~~////~~ ///	23
19–21	/	~~////~~ ~~////~~ //	12
22–24	/	~~////~~ ///	8
25–27		////	4
28–30		/	1

If we examine all 65 payment times, we obtain the 65 checks shown above. To determine the **frequency** for a class, we count the number of checks for the class. Table 2.3 lists both the frequencies and the relative frequencies for the seven classes. The **relative frequency** of a class is the proportion (fraction) of the total number of measurements that are in the class. For example, there are 14 payment times in the second class, so its relative frequency is $14/65 = .2154$. This

TABLE 2.3 A Frequency Distribution and a Relative Frequency Distribution of the 65 Payment Times

Class	Frequency	Relative Frequency	Boundaries	Midpoint
10–12	3	3/65 = .0462	9.5, 12.5	11
13–15	14	14/65 = .2154	12.5, 15.5	14
16–18	23	23/65 = .3538	15.5, 18.5	17
19–21	12	12/65 = .1846	18.5, 21.5	20
22–24	8	8/65 = .1231	21.5, 24.5	23
25–27	4	4/65 = .0615	24.5, 27.5	26
28–30	1	1/65 = .0154	27.5, 30.5	29

FIGURE 2.2 MINITAB Output of a Frequency Histogram of the 65 Payment Times

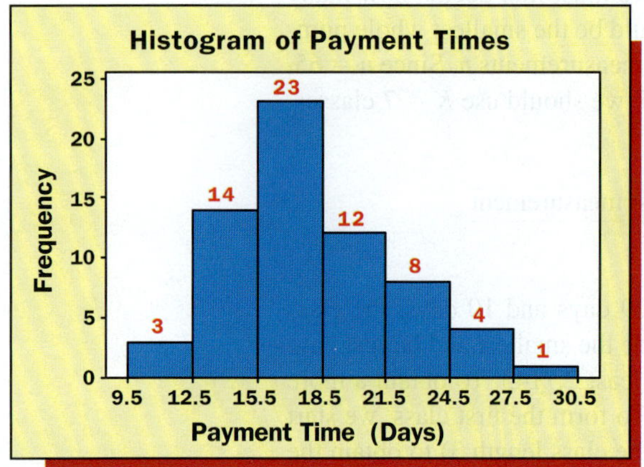

FIGURE 2.3 MINITAB Output of a Relative Frequency Histogram of the 65 Payment Times

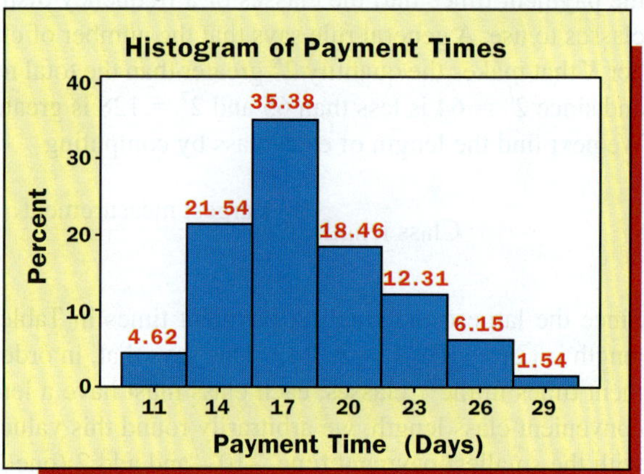

says that the proportion of the 65 payment times that are in the second class is .2154, or, equivalently, that 100(.2154)% = 21.54% of the payment times are in the second class. A list of all of the classes—along with each class frequency—is the previously given frequency distribution. A list of all of the classes—along with each class relative frequency—is called a **relative frequency distribution.**

To graphically portray the distribution of the payment times, we construct a **histogram.** To set up a **frequency histogram,** we draw rectangles representing the classes. Here the base of a rectangle describing a class represents the payment times in the class, and the height of the rectangle represents the class **frequency.** A **relative frequency histogram** is drawn in the same way, except that the height of the rectangle represents the **relative frequency** of the class. To construct these histograms, we employ what we call **class boundaries.** Consider, for example, the first and second classes. The upper class limit of the first class is 12, and the lower class limit of the second class is 13. The class boundary between these classes is halfway between these class limits—12.5. Likewise, the class boundary between the second and third classes is 15.5, which is halfway between the upper class limit of the second class, 15, and the lower class limit of the third class, 16. Table 2.3 gives all of the class boundaries for the 65 payment times. These boundaries are shown in Figure 2.2, which is a MINITAB output of a frequency histogram of the payment times. Note that the difference between the upper and lower class boundaries of a given class is the class length 3. Also, note that an alternative to using class boundaries to specify the classes is to use **class midpoints.** The midpoint of a class is the point halfway between the class limits (or boundaries). For example, the rightmost column in Table 2.3 gives the midpoints of the seven classes describing the payment times. These midpoints are shown in Figure 2.3, which is a MINITAB output of a relative frequency histogram of the payment times. Notice that MINITAB expresses the relative frequencies as **percentages.** For example, since the frequency and the relative frequency for the second class are 14 and 14/65 = .2154, the heights of the rectangles over the second class in Figures 2.2 and 2.3 are 14 and 21.54%.

TABLE 2.4 A Frequency Distribution and a Relative Frequency Distribution of the 49 Mileages

Class	Frequency	Relative Frequency	Boundaries	Midpoint
29.8–30.3	3	3/49 = .0612	29.75, 30.35	30.05
30.4–30.9	9	9/49 = .1837	30.35, 30.95	30.65
31.0–31.5	12	12/49 = .2449	30.95, 31.55	31.25
31.6–32.1	13	13/49 = .2653	31.55, 32.15	31.85
32.2–32.7	9	9/49 = .1837	32.15, 32.75	32.45
32.8–33.3	3	3/49 = .0612	32.75, 33.35	33.05

FIGURE 2.4 MegaStat Output of a Relative Frequency Histogram of the 49 Mileages

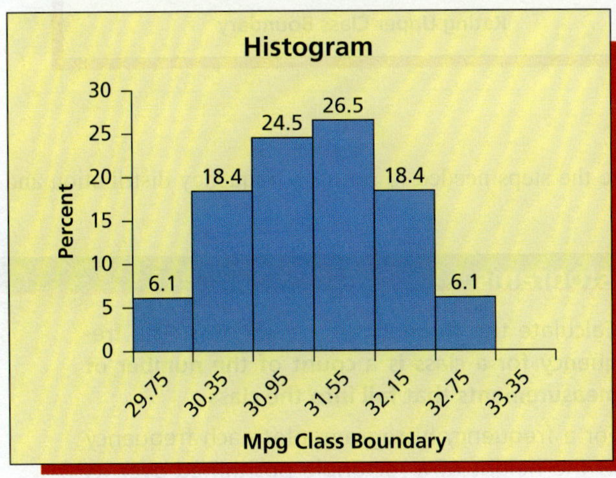

FIGURE 2.5 MINITAB Output of a Relative Frequency Histogram of the 100 Cell Phone Usages

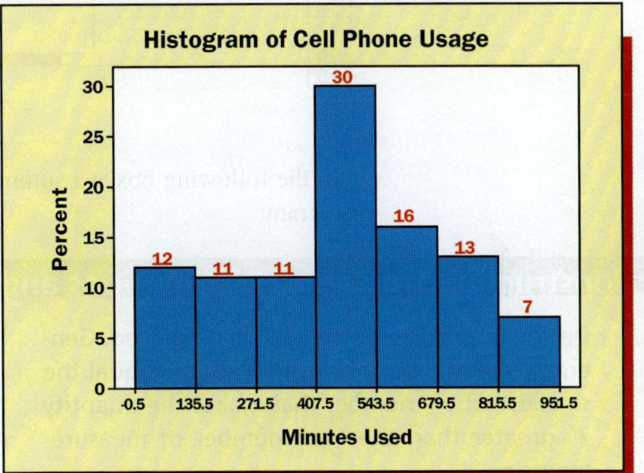

In general, we can have MINITAB, Excel, or MegaStat form a histogram by using classes that we specify or by having these computer packages automatically select classes for us. When specifying classes, we usually express the lower and upper class limits to the same decimal place accuracy as the observed data values. For example, since the payment times are measured to the nearest day and thus are integers, we use integer class limits of 10–12, 13–15, and so on. As another example, consider grouping the $n = 49$ gas mileages in Table 2.1 into the classes of a frequency distribution. Since $2^5 = 32$ is less than 49 and $2^6 = 64$ is greater than 49, we should use $K = 6$ classes. The largest and smallest mileages in Table 2.1 are 33.3 and 29.8, and so we find the class length by computing $(33.3 - 29.8)/6 = .5833$. To obtain a more convenient class length, we round this value up to .6, which is expressed to the same decimal place accuracy as the mileages. To form the first class, we start with the smallest mileage—29.8—and add .5 (one-tenth less than the class length .6) to obtain the class 29.8–30.3. To form the second class, we start with the mileage 30.4 and add .5 to obtain the class 30.4–30.9. Continuing this process, we obtain the 6 classes shown in Table 2.4. Here the largest mileage—33.3—is just barely included in the last class. If we group the 49 mileages into the classes, we obtain the frequencies and relative frequencies given in Table 2.4. A MegaStat output of a relative frequency histogram of the mileages is shown in Figure 2.4. This histogram uses the class boundaries as the labels on its horizontal axis.

Similar to a stem-and-leaf display, a histogram describes the overall pattern of variation displayed by the data. Examining the histogram in Figure 2.4, we see that the distribution of the 49 mileages appears quite symmetrical. On the other hand, the histograms in Figures 2.2 and 2.3 show that the payment times are somewhat skewed with a tail to the right. As another example, the MINITAB output in Figure 2.5 of a relative frequency histogram of the cell phone usages in Table 1.2 (page 7) shows that there is a cluster of usages near 500 minutes with a substantial number of usages both above and below this cluster. Finally, the Excel frequency histogram in Figure 2.6 indicates that the bottle design ratings in Table 1.3 (page 8) are skewed with a tail to the left. This Excel histogram uses the upper class boundaries as the labels on its horizontal axis.

FIGURE 2.6 Excel Output of a Frequency Histogram of 60 Bottle Design Ratings

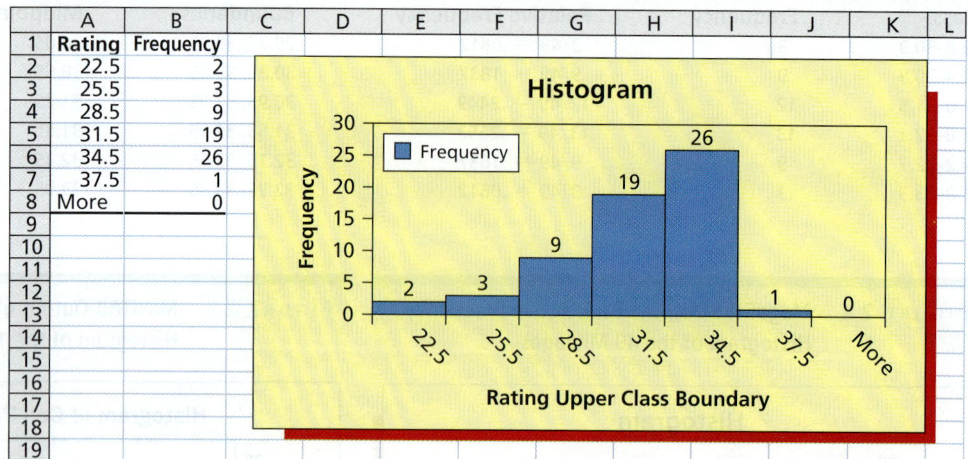

In the following box we summarize the steps needed to set up a frequency distribution and histogram:

Constructing Frequency Distributions and Histograms

1. Decide how many classes will be employed. Generally, the number of classes K should equal the smallest whole number that makes the quantity 2^K greater than the total number of measurements n.

2. Compute the **class length:**

$$\frac{\text{Largest measurement} - \text{Smallest measurement}}{K}$$

If desired, round this value to obtain a more convenient class length.

3. For each class, determine the **lower and upper class limits**—the smallest and largest measurements that can belong to the class.

4. Calculate **class boundaries.** These will be values halfway between the upper class limit of one class and the lower class limit of the next class.

5. Calculate the **frequency** for each class. **The frequency for a class is a count of the number of measurements that fall into the class.**

6. For a frequency histogram, plot each frequency as the height of a rectangle positioned over its corresponding class. Use the class boundaries to separate adjacent rectangles.

7. For a **relative frequency histogram,** plot each relative frequency as the height of a rectangle positioned over its corresponding class. **The relative frequency of a class is its frequency divided by the total number of measurements n.**

CHAPTER 1

Although we have given a procedure for determining the number of classes, it is often desirable to let the nature of the problem determine the classes. For example, to construct a histogram describing the ages of the residents of a certain city, it might be reasonable to use classes having 10-year lengths (that is, under 10 years, 10–19 years, 20–29 years, 30–39 years, and so on). In general, when constructing a histogram, the **area** of the rectangle positioned over a particular class should represent the **relative proportion of measurements in the class. When we use equal class lengths, this can be accomplished by making the height of the rectangle over a particular class represent the relative proportion of measurements in the class** (as described in the previous summary box for constructing histograms). This is because the area of a rectangle is its base multiplied by its height and because, if we are using equal class lengths, then the bases of all the rectangles over the various classes are the same.

As an example, in Figure 2.2 the height of the rectangle over the second class (the payment times from 13 to 15) is the class frequency 14, and the height of the rectangle over the first class (the payment times from 10 to 12) is the class frequency 3. These different heights tell us that the proportion of payment times in the second class, which is 14/65, is greater than the proportion of payment times in the first class, which is 3/65. It is desirable to use equal class lengths whenever the raw data (that is, all the actual measurements) are available. However, it is sometimes necessary to draw histograms with unequal class lengths, particularly when analyzing data published in the form of a frequency distribution having unequal class lengths. Often economic and social data are published in this form. In such a case, one must vary the rectangle heights to make the areas of the rectangles represent the relative proportions of measurements in the classes. How to do this is discussed in Exercise 2.11. Also discussed in this exercise is how to deal with **open-ended** classes. For example, if we are constructing a histogram describing the yearly incomes of U.S. households, an open-ended class could be households earning over $200,000 per year.

FIGURE 2.7 A Symmetrical, Bell-Shaped Curve

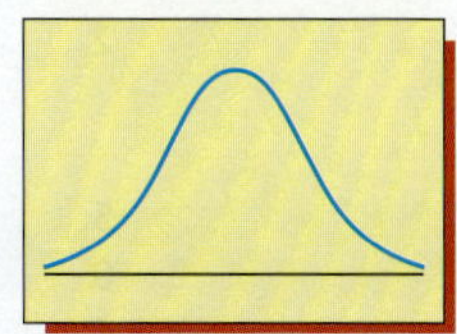

Some common population shapes Often we construct a stem-and-leaf display or histogram for a sample to make inferences about the shape of the sampled population. Sometimes it is useful to describe the shape of a population by using a smooth **curve.** For instance, the stem-and-leaf display and histogram for the sample mileages look quite symmetrical and **bell-shaped.** Therefore, it is reasonable to infer that the population of all mileages can be described by a symmetrical, bell-shaped curve. Such a curve is shown in Figure 2.7. Several different kinds of symmetrical, bell-shaped curves are used to describe populations. One such curve that is particularly useful is called the **normal curve.** We can graph a specific equation to obtain the normal curve. This equation will be given and discussed in Chapter 5.

FIGURE 2.8 A Normal Curve Describing the Mileages

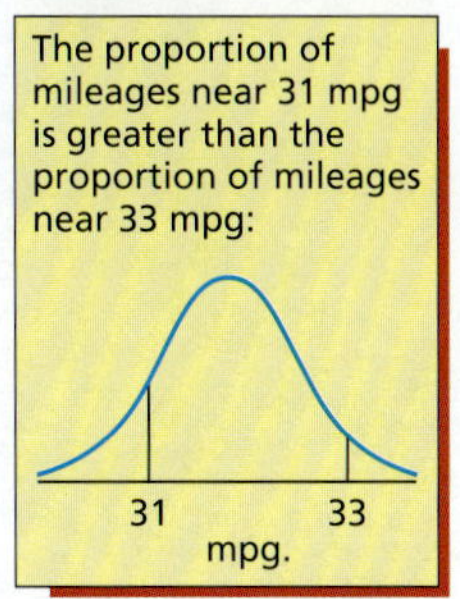
The proportion of mileages near 31 mpg is greater than the proportion of mileages near 33 mpg:
31
33
mpg.

To intuitively understand the normal curve, recall from our discussion of histograms that if we use classes of equal lengths, then the height of the rectangle over a given class represents the relative proportion of measurements in the class. Similarly, **the height of the normal curve over a given point represents the relative proportion of population measurements that are *near the given point.*** For example, Figure 2.8 illustrates a normal curve describing gas mileages. We see that the normal curve's height over the point 31 mpg is greater than its height over the point 33 mpg. This tells us that the proportion of mileages near 31 mpg is greater than the proportion of mileages near 33 mpg.

Many real populations are distributed according to the symmetrical, bell-shaped normal curve. We say that such populations are **normally distributed.** However, instead of being symmetrical and bell-shaped, the overall shape of a population may be skewed with a tail to the right, as is the curve in Figure 2.9, or with a tail to the left, as is the curve in Figure 2.10. Alternatively, many other population shapes are also possible. If the stem-and-leaf display and/or histogram of a random sample of measurements looks like one of these curves, this suggests that the curve describes the overall shape of the entire population of measurements. In this case, the curve is called the **relative frequency curve** that describes the population. Said another way, **the population is distributed according to the relative frequency curve.** For instance, the stem-and-leaf display and histogram we constructed for the 49 mileages suggest that the population of all mileages is distributed according to a normal relative frequency curve—that is, the mileages are normally distributed. As another example, the stem-and-leaf display and histogram we have constructed for the 65 payment times suggest that the population of all payment times is distributed according to a relative frequency curve that is skewed with a tail to the right. Finally, the stem-and-leaf display and histogram we constructed for the 60 bottle design ratings indicate that the population of all bottle design ratings is distributed according to a relative frequency curve that is skewed with a tail to the left. As shown in Figure 2.8, **the height of any relative frequency curve over a given point represents the relative proportion of population measurements that are *near the given point.***

FIGURE 2.9 A Curve That Is Skewed with a Tail to the Right

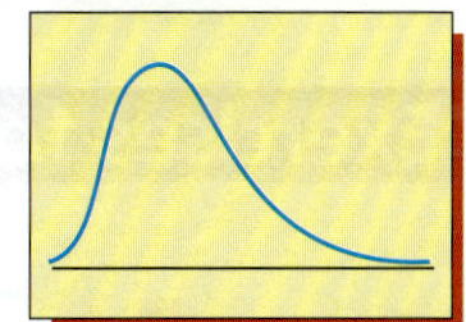

Further graphical techniques, and detecting outliers One of the authors of this book recently taught a course in business statistics to a class of 40 students. A comparison of the scores received by these students on the first two 100-point exams is given by the **back-to-back stem-and-leaf display** in Figure 2.11 and by the two **dot plots** in Figure 2.12. Note that to make each dot plot, we draw a number line on which we measure the exam scores. We then place dots above the number line to represent the exam scores. The number of dots located above a particular exam score indicates how many students received that exam score. After noticing the two-peaked appearance of the stem-and-leaf display and dot plot for Exam 1, the author investigated and

FIGURE 2.10 A Curve That Is Skewed with a Tail to the Left

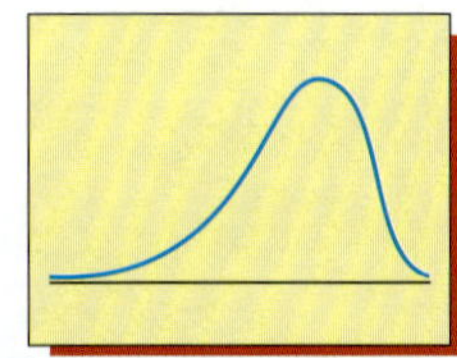

FIGURE 2.11 A Back-to-Back Stem-and-Leaf Display

Exam 1		Exam 2
2	3*	
	3	
	4*	
5	4	
0	5*	
8 6	5	5
4 4 3 1 1 0	6*	2 3
9 9 8 7 7 6 5	6	6 7 7
2	7*	1 3 4 4 4
8 6	7	5 6 7 7 8
3 3 1	8*	0 2 3 4
9 8 7 7 6 5	8	5 6 6 7 7 8 9
4 3 3 2 2 1 0 0	9*	0 1 1 2 3 3 4 4
8 6	9	5 7 9

FIGURE 2.12 Dot Plots of the Scores on Exams 1 and 2

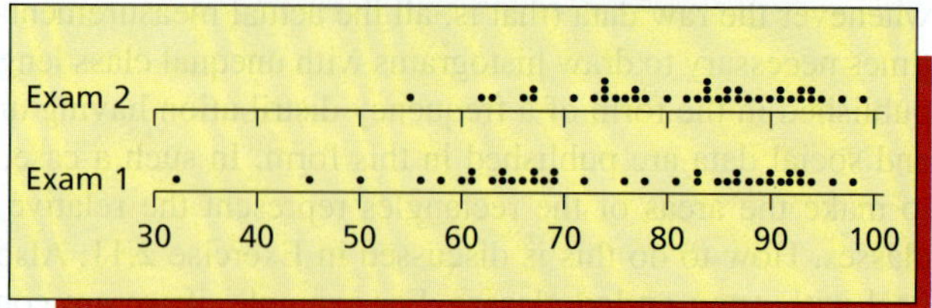

found that most of the students who scored less than 70 on the exam had not been attending class regularly. Because of this, the author implemented a mandatory attendance policy. The stem-and-leaf display and dot plot for Exam 2 are single-peaked and indicate a considerable improvement in student performance. Of course, this does not prove that the attendance policy was solely responsible for the improved performance. However, many students told the author that being *forced* to attend class improved their test scores.

Stem-and-leaf displays and dot plots are useful for detecting **outliers,** which are unusually large or small observations that are well separated from the remaining observations. For example, the stem-and-leaf display and dot plot for Exam 1 indicate that the score 32 seems unusually low. How we handle an outlier depends on its cause. If the outlier results from a measurement error or an error in recording or processing the data, it should be corrected. If the outlier cannot be corrected, it should be discarded. If an outlier is not the result of an error in measuring or recording the data, its cause may reveal important information. For example, the outlying exam score of 32 convinced the author that the student needed a tutor. After working with a tutor, the student showed considerable improvement on Exam 2. A more precise way to detect outliers is presented in Section 2.4.

Exercises for Section 2.1

CONCEPTS

2.1 What do each of the following population shapes look like? Explain each in words and then draw a picture to illustrate each shape.

a Symmetrical and bell-shaped. **b** Double-peaked.
c Skewed with a tail to the left. **d** Skewed with a tail to the right.

2.2 Explain

a How to construct a stem-and-leaf display; a histogram; a dot plot.
b How class limits, class boundaries, and class midpoints differ.
c What outliers are and how they are handled.

METHODS AND APPLICATIONS

2.3 *Forbes* magazine publishes the *Forbes* Platinum 400—a list of the "Best Big Companies in America" as selected by the magazine's writers and editors. Table 2.5 gives the best companies in the retailing industry as given in this list on the *Forbes* website on March 16, 2005.
ForbesPlat

a Construct a stem-and-leaf display of the profit margin percentages for the best performing retailers as given in Table 2.5. Use the whole numbers from 1 to 24 as the stems. Then describe the distribution of profit margins.

TABLE 2.5 The Best Performing Retailers from the *Forbes* Platinum 400 as Listed on the *Forbes* Magazine Website on March 16, 2005 ForbesPlat

Company	Total Return (%) Last 5 Years	Sales Growth (%) Last 12 Months	Profit Margin (%)	Return on Capital (%) Last 12 Months
Abercrombie & Fitch	9.5	12.6	10.9	25.7
Advance Auto Parts	25.5	11.3	5.0	17.0
Amer Eagle Outfitters	7.5	10.7	6.1	14.7
AnnTaylor Stores	3.7	21.7	5.9	11.6
Bed Bath & Beyond	20.1	21.5	9.2	22.8
Best Buy	8.1	17.4	3.3	21.7
CDW	14.0	27.7	4.0	20.6
Charming Shoppes	10.2	1.3	3.1	8.3
Claire's Stores	14.0	14.3	11.2	20.3
Costco Wholesale	2.0	13.1	1.8	0.0
CVS	3.4	14.3	3.2	11.2
Dollar General	2.1	11.7	4.4	18.3
Ebay	20.4	54.6	24.0	13.1
Electronics Boutique	13.2	26.5	2.9	19.2
Family Dollar Stores	11.9	11.2	5.0	19.7
Foot Locker	29.5	10.6	5.3	12.8
Fred's	30.8	12.8	2.2	9.2
Guitar Center	35.6	18.6	3.9	15.9
Home Depot	−4.3	13.5	6.9	19.8
Kohl's	5.8	12.9	5.9	11.5
Lowe's Cos	16.9	18.7	5.9	14.7
Michaels Stores	28.3	9.1	5.9	14.4
Neiman Marcus Group	20.7	14.4	5.8	12.7
O'Reilly Automotive	12.6	13.8	7.0	12.6
Pacific Sunwear	11.2	20.0	8.6	25.1
Pestmart	53.6	13.0	5.0	15.4
Regis	17.9	12.7	5.4	11.0
SCP Pool	45.8	14.8	5.2	20.8
Staples	6.4	11.5	4.7	15.2
Target	9.6	11.3	6.8	8.6
TJX Cos	14.5	15.4	4.9	33.4
Tractor Supply	48.9	18.3	3.6	16.5
United Auto Group	26.3	17.6	1.1	4.0
Walgreen	5.7	15.4	3.6	17.6
Williams-Sonoma	5.9	17.2	5.9	21.1

Source: *Forbes*, 3/16/05.

b Construct a stem-and-leaf display of the return on capital percentages for the retailers in Table 2.5. Use the whole numbers from 0 to 33 as the stems. Then describe the distribution of the returns.

c Compare the distributions of the profit margins and return on capital percentages.

2.4 The data in Table 2.6 concern the 30 fastest-growing companies as listed on March 16, 2005, on the *Fortune* magazine website. Fastgrow

a Figure 2.13 gives the MINITAB output of a stem-and-leaf display of the revenue growth rates for the 30 firms. Describe the shape of the distribution of growth rates.

b The price/earnings ratio of a firm is a multiplier applied to a firm's earnings per share (EPS) to determine the value of the firm's common stock. For instance, if a firm's earnings per share is \$5, and if its price/earnings ratio (or P/E ratio) is 10, then the market value of each share of common stock is (\$5)(10) = \$50. To quote Stanley B. Block and Geoffrey A. Hirt in their book *Foundations of Financial Management:*[2]

> The P/E ratio indicates expectations about the future of a company. Firms expected to provide returns greater than those for the market in general with equal or less risk often have P/E ratios higher than the market P/E ratio.

[2]Source: Excerpt from S. B. Block and G. A. Hirt, *Foundations of Financial Management*, p. 28.

TABLE 2.6 Data Concerning the 30 Fastest-Growing Companies as Listed on March 16, 2005 on the *Fortune* Magazine Website FastGrow

Rank	Company	EPS Growth*	Revenue Growth*	Total Return*
1	InVision Technologies	222%	93%	135%
2	eResearch Technology	256%	43%	218%
3	New Century Financial	85%	91%	89%
4	Central European Distribution	98%	49%	135%
5	eBay	92%	70%	39%
6	National Medical Health Card Sys	85%	44%	107%
7	Countrywide Financial	78%	71%	46%
8	Neoware Systems	76%	70%	47%
9	Friedman Billing Ramsey Group	93%	52%	44%
10	Bradley Pharmaceuticals	59%	59%	76%
11	Middleby	91%	33%	109%
12	Hovnanian Enterprises	71%	40%	69%
13	Websense	162%	60%	23%
14	Sanders Morris Harris Group	185%	35%	36%
15	Career Education	66%	51%	45%
16	American Healthways	167%	48%	28%
17	United PanAm Financial	65%	39%	62%
18	FTI Consulting	105%	61%	19%
19	Jarden	99%	25%	109%
20	Par Pharmaceutical	143%	87%	5%
21	Capital Title Group	84%	87%	21%
22	Advanced Neuromodulation	128%	46%	24%
23	Possis Medical	76%	38%	42%
24	Symantec	85%	30%	59%
25	ASV	128%	33%	32%
26	Chico's FAS	47%	43%	66%
27	Rewards Network	152%	29%	38%
28	Fidelity National Financial	64%	38%	38%
29	NetBank	107%	60%	−1%
30	Electronic Arts	254%	32%	24%

*3-year annual rate.

Source: *Fortune*, 3/16/05.

FIGURE 2.13 MINITAB Stem-and-Leaf Display of the 30 Revenue Growth Rates for Exercise 2.4(a)

```
Stem-and-leaf of Revenue Growth N = 30
Leaf Unit = 1.0

  2   2  59
  5   3  0233
  9   3  5889
 13   4  0334
(3)   4  689
 13   5  12
 11   5  9
 10   6  001
  7   6
  7   7  001
  4   7
  4   8
  4   8  77
  2   9  13
```

FIGURE 2.14 MegaStat Stem-and-Leaf Display of the 65 Satisfaction Ratings for Exercise 2.5

Stem and Leaf plot for Rating

stem unit = 1 leaf unit = 0.1

Frequency	Stem	Leaf
1	36	0
0	37	
3	38	000
4	39	0000
5	40	00000
6	41	000000
6	42	000000
8	43	00000000
12	44	000000000000
9	45	000000000
7	46	0000000
3	47	000
1	48	0
65		

In the figure below we give a dot plot of the P/E ratios for 29 of the 30 fastest-growing companies (the P/E ratio for one of the companies was not available to *Fortune*). Describe the distribution of P/E ratios.

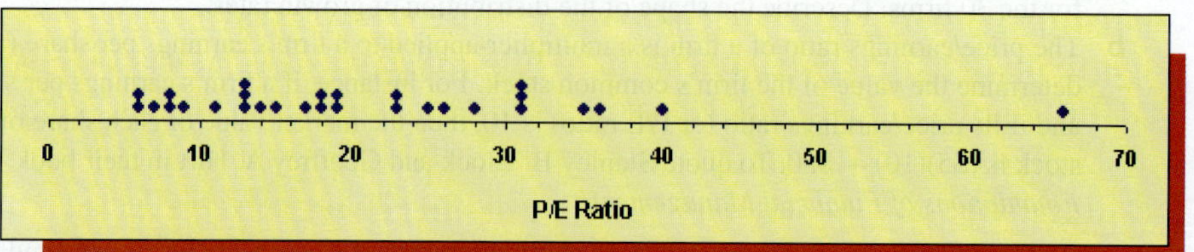

c Construct a dot plot of the total return percentages for the 30 fastest-growing companies and describe the distribution of return percentages.

2.5 THE VIDEO GAME SATISFACTION RATING CASE VideoGame

Recall that Table 1.5 (page 11) presents the satisfaction ratings for the XYZ-Box video game system that have been given by 65 randomly selected purchasers. Figure 2.14 gives the MegaStat output of

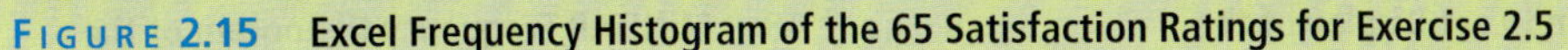

FIGURE 2.15 Excel Frequency Histogram of the 65 Satisfaction Ratings for Exercise 2.5

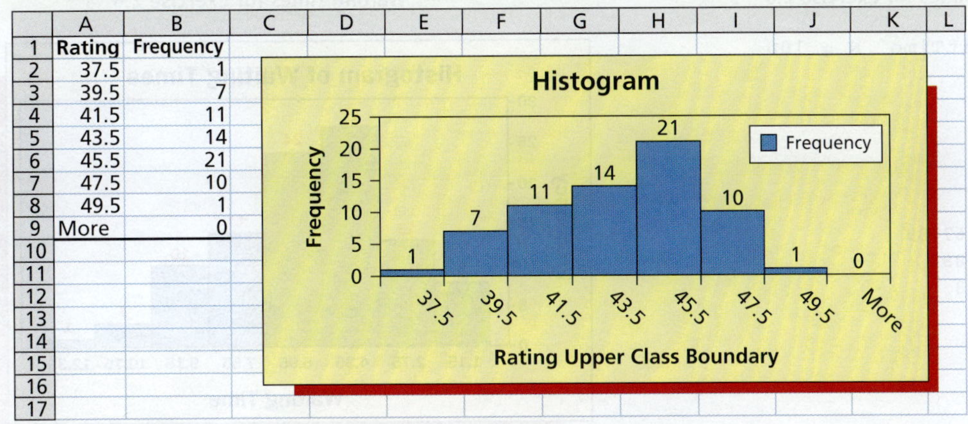

Rating	Frequency
37.5	1
39.5	7
41.5	11
43.5	14
45.5	21
47.5	10
49.5	1
More	0

FIGURE 2.16 Excel Frequency Histogram of the 100 Waiting Times for Exercise 2.6

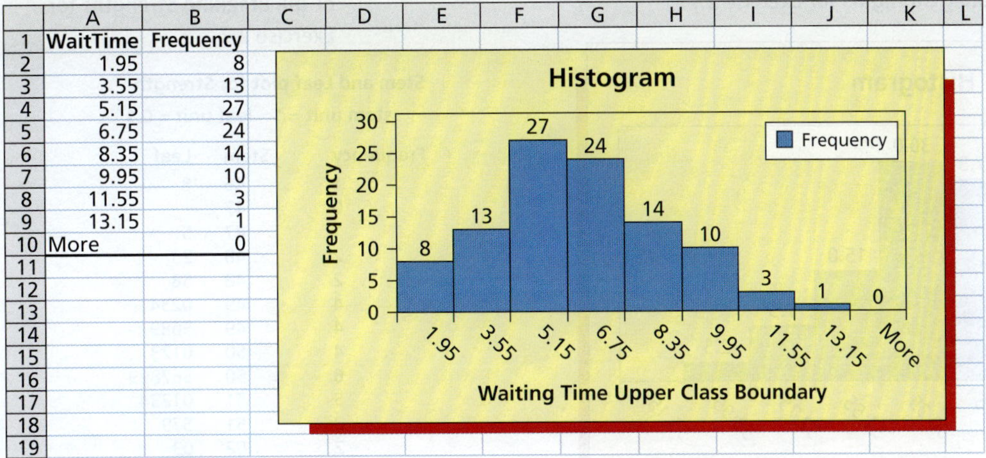

WaitTime	Frequency
1.95	8
3.55	13
5.15	27
6.75	24
8.35	14
9.95	10
11.55	3
13.15	1
More	0

a stem-and-leaf display, and Figure 2.15 gives the Excel output of a frequency histogram of the 65 satisfaction ratings.

a Verify that the classes and class frequencies given in Figure 2.15 are those obtained by using the histogram construction method discussed in this section.

b Using Figures 2.14 and 2.15, infer the shape of the relative frequency distribution describing the population of all possible customer satisfaction ratings for the XYZ-Box video game system.

c Construct a relative frequency histogram of the 65 satisfaction ratings.

2.6 THE BANK CUSTOMER WAITING TIME CASE WaitTime

Recall that Table 1.6 (page 11) presents the waiting times for teller service during peak business hours of 100 randomly selected bank customers. Figure 2.17 gives the MINITAB output of a stem-and-leaf display, and Figures 2.16 and 2.18 give the Excel and MINITAB outputs of a frequency histogram of the 100 waiting times.

a Verify that the class boundaries (in Figure 2.16), the class midpoints (in Figure 2.18), and the class frequencies are those obtained by using the histogram construction method discussed in this section.

b Using Figures 2.16, 2.17, and 2.18, infer the shape of the relative frequency distribution describing the population of all possible customer waiting times during peak business hours.

2.7 THE TRASH BAG CASE TrashBag

Recall that Table 1.10 (page 19) presents the breaking strengths of 40 trash bags selected during a 40-hour pilot production run. Figure 2.19 gives the MegaStat output of a relative frequency histogram and Figure 2.20 gives the MegaStat output of a stem-and-leaf display of the 40 breaking strengths.

FIGURE 2.17 MINITAB Stem-and-Leaf Display of the Waiting Times for Exercise 2.6

```
Stem-and-leaf of WaitTime   N = 100
Leaf Unit = 0.10

  2   0  48
  8   1  134688
 17   2  023457899
 28   3  12456778899
 45   4  00123334455567789
(15)  5  011223445667888
 40   6  1123334556778
 27   7  0223445789
 17   8  0134667
 10   9  123589
  4  10  279
  1  11  6
```

FIGURE 2.18 MINITAB Frequency Histogram of the Waiting Times for Exercise 2.6

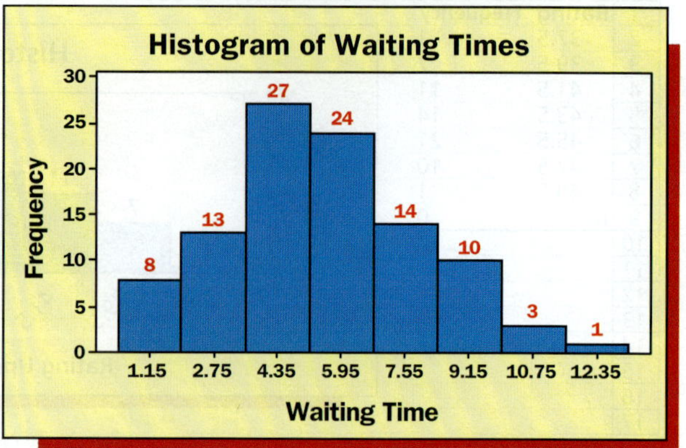

FIGURE 2.19 MegaStat Relative Frequency Histogram of the 40 Breaking Strengths for Exercise 2.7

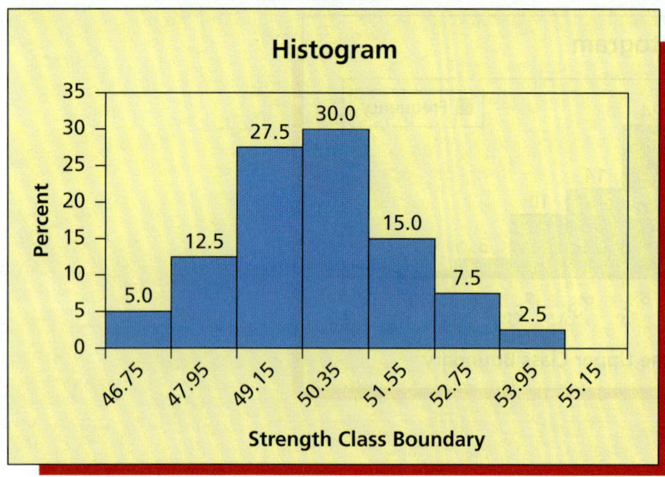

FIGURE 2.20 MegaStat Stem-and-Leaf Display of the Breaking Strengths for Exercise 2.7

Stem and Leaf plot for Strength

stem unit = 1 leaf unit = 0.1

Frequency	Stem	Leaf
1	46	8
0	47	
1	47	5
2	48	23
2	48	58
4	49	0234
4	49	5689
4	50	0123
6	50	567899
5	51	01234
3	51	579
2	52	03
2	52	56
2	53	02
1	53	5
1	54	0
40		

a Verify that the classes and class relative frequencies given in Figure 2.19 are those obtained by using the histogram construction method discussed in this section.

b Using Figures 2.19 and 2.20, infer the shape of the relative frequency distribution describing the population of all possible trash bag breaking strengths.

2.8 Consider Table 1.9 (page 17), which gives the numbers of days needed to settle 67 homeowners' insurance claims. ClaimSet

a Construct a stem-and-leaf display using the stems 00, 10, 20, . . . , 90, 100, 110.

b Figure 2.21 gives the MINITAB output of a frequency histogram of the 67 numbers of days to settle. Verify that the classes and class frequencies used in Figure 2.21 are those obtained by using the histogram construction method discussed in this section.

c Using the stem-and-leaf display and the histogram, describe the distribution of the numbers of days to settle. What caused the distribution to look like this (see Exercise 1.16 on pages 17 and 18)?

2.9 Babe Ruth's record of 60 home runs in a single year was broken by Roger Maris, who hit 61 home runs in 1961. The yearly home run totals for Ruth in his career as a New York Yankee are (arranged in increasing order) 22, 25, 34, 35, 41, 41, 46, 46, 46, 47, 49, 54, 54, 59, and 60. The yearly home run totals for Maris over his career in the American League are (arranged in increasing order) 8, 13, 14, 16, 23, 26, 28, 33, 39, and 61. Compare Ruth's and Maris's home run totals by constructing a back-to-back stem-and-leaf display. What would you conclude about Maris's record-breaking year? HomeRuns

FIGURE 2.21 MINITAB Frequency Histogram of the 67 Numbers of Days to Settle for Exercise 2.8

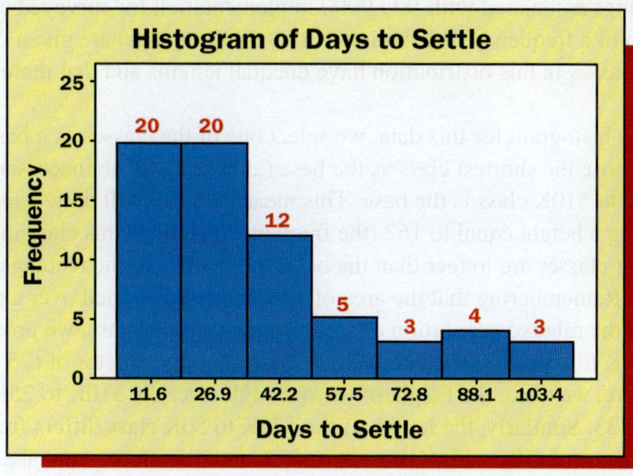

2.10 THE CIGARETTE ADVERTISEMENT CASE ModelAge

In an article in the *Journal of Marketing* (January 1992), Mazis, Ringold, Perry, and Denman discuss the perceived ages of models in cigarette advertisements.[3] To quote the authors:

> Most relevant to our study is the Cigarette Advertiser's Code, initiated by the tobacco industry in 1964. The code contains nine advertising principles related to young people, including the following provision (*Advertising Age* 1964): "Natural persons depicted as smokers in cigarette advertising shall be at least 25 years of age and shall not be dressed or otherwise made to appear to be less than 25 years of age."

Tobacco industry representatives have steadfastly maintained that code provisions are still being observed. A 1988 Tobacco Institute publication, "Three Decades of Initiatives by a Responsible Cigarette Industry," refers to the industry code as prohibiting advertising and promotion "directed at young people" and as "requiring that models in advertising must be, and must appear to be, at least 25 years old." John R. Nelson, Vice President of Corporate Affairs for Philip Morris, recently wrote, "We employ only adult models in our advertising who not only are but *look* over 25" (Nelson 1990). However, industry critics have charged that current cigarette advertising campaigns use unusually young-looking models, thereby violating the voluntary industry code.

Suppose that a sample of 50 people is randomly selected at a shopping mall. Each person in the sample is shown a typical cigarette advertisement and is asked to estimate the age of the model in the ad. The 50 perceived age estimates so obtained are as follows.

26	30	23	27	27	32	28	19	25	29
31	28	24	26	29	27	28	17	28	21
30	28	25	31	22	29	18	27	29	23
28	26	24	30	27	25	26	28	20	24
29	32	27	17	30	27	21	29	26	28

a Construct (1) a stem-and-leaf display, (2) a frequency histogram, and (3) a relative frequency histogram of the 50 perceived ages.

b Using your answer in part *a*, infer the shape of the relative frequency distribution describing the population of the ages that would be perceived by all possible shoppers.

c What percentage of the perceived ages are below the industry's code provision (of 25 years old)? Do you think that this percentage is too high?

2.11 In this exercise we consider how to deal with class lengths that are unequal (and with open-ended classes) when setting up histograms. Often data are published in this form and we wish to construct a histogram. An example is provided by data concerning the benefits of ISO 9000 registration published by CEEM Information Services. According to CEEM:[4]

> ISO 9000 is a series of international standards for quality assurance management systems. It establishes the organizational structure and processes for assuring that the production of goods or services meet a consistent and agreed-upon level of quality for a company's customers.

[3]Source: M. B. Mazis, D. J. Ringold, E. S. Perry, and D. W. Denman, "Perceived Age and Attractiveness of Models in Cigarette Advertisements," *Journal of Marketing* 56 (January 1992), pp. 22–37.

[4]Source: CEEM Information Services, Fairfax, Virginia. *Is ISO 9000 for You?*

ISO 9000

Annual Savings	Number of Companies
0 to \$10K	162
\$10K to 25K	62
\$25K to 50K	53
\$50K to 100K	60
\$100K to 150K	24
\$150K to 200K	19
\$200K to 250K	22
\$250K to 500K	21
(>\$500K)	37

Note: (K = 1000)

CEEM presents the results of a Quality Systems Update/Deloitte & Touche survey of ISO 9000–registered companies conducted in July 1993. Included in the results is a summary of the total annual savings associated with ISO 9000 implementation for surveyed companies. The findings (in the form of a frequency distribution of ISO 9000 savings) are given on the page margin. Notice that the classes in this distribution have unequal lengths and that there is an open-ended class (>\$500K).

To construct a histogram for this data, we select one of the classes as a base. It is often convenient to choose the shortest class as the base (although it is not necessary to do so). Using this choice, the 0 to \$10K class is the base. This means that we will draw a rectangle over the 0 to \$10K class having a height equal to 162 (the frequency given for this class in the published data). Because the other classes are longer than the base, the heights of the rectangles above these classes will be adjusted. Remembering that the area of a rectangle positioned over a particular class should represent the relative proportion of measurements in the class, we proceed as follows. The length of the \$10K to 25K class differs from the base class by a factor of $(25 - 10)/(10 - 0) = 3/2$, and, therefore, we make the height of the rectangle over the \$10K to 25K class equal to $(2/3)(62) = 41.333$. Similarly, the length of the \$25K to 50K class differs from the length of the base class by a factor of $(50 - 25)/(10 - 0) = 5/2$, and, therefore, we make the height of the rectangle over the \$25K to 50K class equal to $(2/5)(53) = 21.2$.

a Use the procedure just outlined to find the heights of the rectangles drawn over all the other classes (with the exception of the open-ended class, >\$500K).

b Draw the appropriate rectangles over the classes (except for >\$500K). Note that the \$250K to 500K class is a lot longer than the others. There is nothing wrong with this as long as we adjust its rectangle's height.

c We complete the histogram by placing a star (∗) to the right of \$500K on the scale of measurements and by noting "37" next to the ∗ to indicate 37 companies saved more than \$500K. Complete the histogram by doing this.

2.12 A basketball player practices free throws by taking 25 shots each day, and he records the number of shots missed each day in order to track his progress. The numbers of shots missed on days 1 through 30 are, respectively, 17, 15, 16, 18, 14, 15, 13, 12, 10, 11, 11, 10, 9, 10, 9, 9, 9, 10, 8, 10, 6, 8, 9, 8, 7, 9, 8, 7, 5, 8. Construct a stem-and-leaf display and runs plot of the numbers of missed shots. Do you think that the stem-and-leaf display is representative of the numbers of shots that the player will miss on future days? Why or why not? FreeThrw

2.2 Describing Central Tendency

The mean, median, and mode In addition to describing the shape of the distribution of a sample or population of measurements, we also describe the data set's **central tendency.** A measure of central tendency represents the *center* or *middle* of the data. Sometimes we think of a measure of central tendency as a *typical value.* However, as we will see, not all measures of central tendency are necessarily typical values.

One important measure of central tendency for a population of measurements is the **population mean.** We define it as follows:

The **population mean,** which is denoted μ and pronounced *mew,* is the average of the population measurements.

CHAPTER 3

More precisely, the population mean is calculated by adding all the population measurements and then dividing the resulting sum by the number of population measurements. For instance, we consider the population of profit margins for five of the best big companies in America as rated by *Forbes* magazine on its website on March 16, 2005. The companies and profit margins (to the nearest percent) are as follows:[5]

Company	Profit Margin (Percent)
Black & Decker	8%
Washington Post	10
Texas Instruments	15
Clorox	12
Foot Locker	5

[5]Source: *Forbes*, 3/16/05. © 2005 Forbes, Inc. Reprinted with permission.

The mean μ of this population of profit margins is

$$\mu = \frac{8 + 10 + 15 + 12 + 5}{5} = \frac{50}{5} = 10 \text{ percent}$$

Since this population of five profit margins is small, it is possible to compute the population mean. Often, however, a population is very large and we cannot obtain a measurement for each population unit. Therefore, we cannot compute the population mean. In such a case, we must estimate the population mean by using a sample of measurements.

In order to understand how to estimate a population mean, we must realize that the population mean is a **population parameter.**

A **population parameter** is a number calculated using the population measurements that describes some aspect of the population. That is, a population parameter is a descriptive measure of the population.

There are many population parameters, and we discuss several of them in this chapter. The simplest way to estimate a population parameter is to make what is called a **point estimate.**

A **point estimate** is a one-number estimate of the value of a population parameter.

Although a point estimate is a guess of a population parameter's value, it is not a *blind guess.* Rather, it is an educated guess based on sample data. One way to find a point estimate of a population parameter is to use a **sample statistic.**

A **sample statistic** is a number calculated using the sample measurements that describes some aspect of the sample. That is, a sample statistic is a descriptive measure of the sample.

The sample statistic that we use to estimate the population mean is the **sample mean,** which is denoted as $\bar{x}$ (pronounced *x bar*) and is the average of the sample measurements.

In order to write a formula for the sample mean, we employ the letter n to represent the number of sample measurements, and we refer to n as the **sample size.** Furthermore, we denote the sample measurements as $x_1, x_2, \ldots, x_n$. Here x_1 is the first sample measurement, x_2 is the second sample measurement, and so forth. We denote the last sample measurement as x_n. Moreover, when we write formulas we often use *summation notation* for convenience. For instance, we write the sum of the sample measurements

$$x_1 + x_2 + \cdots + x_n$$

as $\sum_{i=1}^{n} x_i$. Here the Greek letter sigma (Σ) says that we are writing out a sum of *like terms.* The general term x_i says that all the terms we are adding up look like x_i. The index $i = 1$ to n says that we let the subscript i in the general term x_i range from 1 to n, and we add up all these terms. Thus

$$\sum_{i=1}^{n} x_i = x_1 + x_2 + \cdots + x_n$$

We define the sample mean as follows:

The **sample mean** $\bar{x}$ is defined to be

$$\bar{x} = \frac{\sum_{i=1}^{n} x_i}{n} = \frac{x_1 + x_2 + \cdots + x_n}{n}$$

and is the **point estimate of the population mean** μ.

Example 2.5 The Car Mileage Case

C

In order to offer its tax credit, the federal government has decided to define the "typical" EPA combined city and highway mileage for a car model as the mean μ of the population of EPA combined mileages that would be obtained by all cars of this type. Here, using the mean to represent

a typical value is probably reasonable. We know that some individual cars will get mileages that are lower than the mean and some will get mileages that are above it. However, because there will be many thousands of these cars on the road, the mean mileage obtained by these cars is probably a reasonable way to represent the model's overall fuel economy. Therefore, the government will offer its tax credit to any automaker selling a midsize model equipped with an automatic transmission that achieves a mean EPA combined mileage of at least 31 mpg.

To demonstrate that its new midsize model qualifies for the tax credit, the automaker in this case study wishes to use the sample of 49 mileages to estimate μ, the model's mean mileage. Before calculating the mean of the entire sample of 49 mileages, we will illustrate the formulas involved by calculating the mean of the first five of these mileages. Table 2.1 (page 44) tells us that $x_1 = 30.8$, $x_2 = 31.7$, $x_3 = 30.1$, $x_4 = 31.6$, and $x_5 = 32.1$, so the sum of the first five mileages is

$$\sum_{i=1}^{5} x_i = x_1 + x_2 + x_3 + x_4 + x_5$$

$$= 30.8 + 31.7 + 30.1 + 31.6 + 32.1 = 156.3$$

Therefore, the mean of the first five mileages is

$$\bar{x} = \frac{\sum_{i=1}^{5} x_i}{5} = \frac{156.3}{5} = 31.26$$

Of course, intuitively, we are likely to obtain a more accurate point estimate of the population mean by using all of the available sample information. The sum of all 49 mileages can be verified to be

$$\sum_{i=1}^{49} x_i = x_1 + x_2 + \cdots + x_{49} = 30.8 + 31.7 + \cdots + 32.2 = 1{,}546.1$$

Therefore, the mean of the sample of 49 mileages is

$$\bar{x} = \frac{\sum_{i=1}^{49} x_i}{49} = \frac{1{,}546.1}{49} = 31.5531$$

BI

This point estimate says we estimate that the mean mileage that would be obtained by all of the new midsize cars that will or could potentially be produced this year is 31.5531 mpg. Unless we are extremely lucky, however, this sample mean will not exactly equal the average mileage that would be obtained by all cars. That is, the point estimate $\bar{x} = 31.5531$ mpg, which is based on the sample of 49 randomly selected mileages, probably does not exactly equal the population mean μ. Therefore, although $\bar{x} = 31.5531$ provides some evidence that μ is at least 31 and thus that the automaker should get the tax credit, it does not provide definitive evidence. In later chapters, we discuss how to assess the *reliability* of the sample mean and how to use a measure of reliability to decide whether sample information provides definitive evidence.

Another descriptive measure of the central tendency of a population or a sample of measurements is the **median.** Intuitively, the median divides a population or sample into two roughly equal parts. We calculate the median, which is denoted M_d, as follows:

Consider a population or a sample of measurements, and arrange the measurements in increasing order. The **median,** M_d, is found as follows:

1 If the number of measurements is odd, the median is the middlemost measurement in the ordering.

2 If the number of measurements is even, the median is the average of the two middlemost measurements in the ordering.

Example 2.6

A new medical clinic in a Midwestern city plans to pay internists a yearly salary of $180,000. The administrator of the clinic wishes to compare this salary with the salaries of internists in private practice in the Midwest. In order to do this, the administrator randomly selects a sample of $n = 13$ internists from thousands of such physicians in private practice in the Midwest. Each internist in the sample is asked to report his or her previous year's salary. The 13 salaries—arranged in increasing order and expressed in units of $1,000—are as follows:

127 132 138 141 144 146 (152) 154 162 171 177 192 241 DrSalary

Because the number of salaries is odd, the median of this sample is the middlemost salary in the ordering. Therefore, the median is 152 (it is circled). In this case there are six salaries below the median and six salaries above the median. Since the sample median equals 152, we estimate that the median salary of all internists in private practice in the Midwest is $152,000. The $180,000 salary to be offered by the clinic is substantially higher than this estimated median salary. Furthermore, because the $180,000 salary is higher than all but two salaries ($192,000 and $241,000) in the clinic's sample, we might conclude that this salary is quite competitive.

Example 2.7

The manufacturer of a DVD recorder randomly selects a sample of 20 purchasers who have owned the recorder for one year. Each purchaser in the sample is asked to rank his or her satisfaction with the recorder on the following 10-point scale:

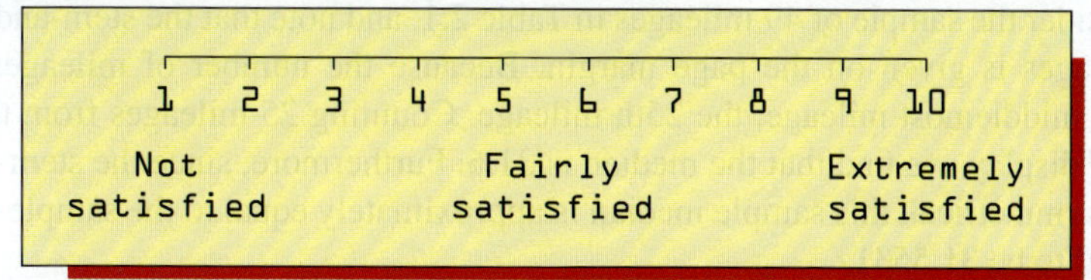

Suppose that the following rankings, arranged in increasing order, are obtained.

1 3 5 5 7 8 8 8 8 (8) (8) 9 9 9 9 9 10 10 10 10 DVDSat

Because the number of satisfaction ratings is even, the median of this sample is the average of the two middlemost ratings. Both of these ratings are 8—they are circled. Therefore, the median of this sample is 8, and we estimate that the median satisfaction rating of all the DVD recorder owners is 8. This estimated median satisfaction rating seems relatively high. Note, however, that there are four rather low individual satisfaction ratings: 1, 3, 5, and 5. This suggests that some DVD recorders may be of low quality. If the manufacturer wishes to satisfy all of its customers, the company must investigate the situation.

A third measure of the central tendency of a population or sample is the **mode,** which is denoted M_o.

The **mode,** M_o, of a population or sample of measurements is the measurement that occurs most frequently.

For example, the mode of the satisfaction ratings given in Example 2.7 is 8. This is because more purchasers (six) gave the DVD recorder a rating of 8 than any other rating. Sometimes the highest frequency occurs at two or more different measurements. When this happens, two or more modes exist. When exactly two modes exist, we say the data is *bimodal*. When more than two modes exist, we say the data is *multimodal*. Finally, when data are presented in classes (such as in a frequency histogram), the class having the highest frequency is called the *modal class*. For instance, the modal class for the histogram of mileages in Figure 2.4 (page 49) is the class from 31.55 mpg. to 32.15 mpg.

FIGURE 2.22 Relationships among the Mean μ, the Median M_d, and the Mode M_o

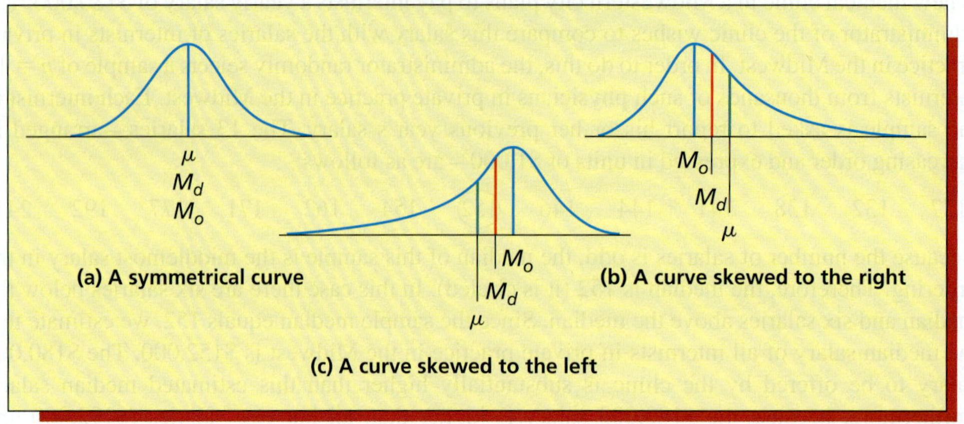

Comparing the mean, median, and mode In order to compare the mean, median, and mode, look at Figure 2.22. Part (a) of this figure depicts a population described by a symmetrical relative frequency curve. For such a population, the mean (μ), median (M_d), and mode (M_o) are all equal. Note that in this case all three of these quantities are located under the highest point of the curve. It follows that when the frequency distribution of a sample of measurements is approximately symmetrical, then the sample mean, median, and mode will be nearly the same. For instance, consider the sample of 49 mileages in Table 2.1, and note that the stem-and-leaf display of these mileages is given on the page margin. Because the number of mileages is odd, the median is the middlemost mileage, the 25th mileage. Counting 25 mileages from the top of the stem-and-leaf display, we find that the median is 31.6. Furthermore, since the stem-and-leaf display is fairly symmetrical, this sample median is approximately equal to the sample mean, which was calculated to be 31.5531.

Mileages

29	8
30	1344
30	5666889
31	001233444
(31)	555(6)6777889
32	0001122344
32	556788
33	3

Figure 2.22(b) depicts a population that is skewed to the right. Here the population mean is larger than the population median, and the population median is larger than the population mode (the mode is located under the highest point of the relative frequency curve). In this case the population mean *averages in* the large values in the upper tail of the distribution. Thus the population mean is more affected by these large values than is the population median. To understand this, note that the stem-and-leaf display of the sample of 13 internists' salaries in Example 2.6 is given on the page margin and is skewed to the right. Here the mean of the 13 salaries, which is 159.769 (or $159,769), is affected by *averaging in* the large salaries (192 and 241) in the right-hand tail of the distribution. Thus this mean is larger than the sample median, $152,000. The median is said to be **resistant** to the large salaries 192 and 241 because the value of the median is affected only by the fact that these salaries are the two largest salaries in the sample. The value of the median is not affected by the **exact sizes** of the salaries 192 and 241. For example, if the largest salary were smaller—say 200—the median would remain the same but the mean would decrease. If the largest salary were larger—say 300—the median would also remain the same but the mean would increase. Therefore, the median is resistant to large values but the mean is not. Similarly, the median is resistant to values that are much smaller than most of the measurements. In general, we say that **the median is resistant to extreme values.**

Salaries

12	7
13	2 8
14	1 4 6
(15)	(2) 4
16	2
17	1 7
18	
19	2
20	
21	
22	
23	
24	1

Figure 2.22(c) depicts a population that is skewed to the left. Here the population mean is smaller than the population median, and the population median is smaller than the population mode. In this case the population mean *averages in* the small values in the lower tail of the distribution, and the mean is more affected by these small values than is the median. For instance, the stem-and-leaf display of the sample of purchaser satisfaction ratings in Example 2.7 is given on the page margin and is skewed to the left. In this case, the mean of these ratings, which equals 7.7, is affected by *averaging in* the smaller ratings (1, 3, 5, and 5) in the left-hand tail of the distribution. Thus the mean is smaller than the sample median, 8.

Ratings

1	0
2	
3	0
4	
5	0 0
6	
7	0
(8)	0 0 0 0 (0)(0)
9	0 0 0 0 0
10	0 0 0 0

When a population is skewed to the right or left with a very long tail, the population mean can be substantially affected by the extreme population values in the tail of the distribution. In such a case, the population median might be better than the population mean as a measure of central tendency. For example, the yearly incomes of all people in the United States are skewed to the right with a very long tail. Furthermore, the very large incomes in this tail cause the mean yearly income to be inflated above the typical income earned by most Americans. Because of this, the median income is more representative of a typical U.S. income. The following case illustrates that the choice of the mean or the median as a measure of central tendency can depend on the purpose of the study being conducted.

Example 2.8 The Insurance Information Institute Case

In 1984 the Insurance Information Institute defended high liability insurance premiums by asserting that the mean reward in product liability cases exceeded one million dollars. Opponents of premium increases countered that the median award was only $271,000. The mean and median differed dramatically in this case because the mean was greatly inflated by a relatively few extremely large awards. From the point of view of reporting a *typical award* to the public, the median is probably superior. However, from the point of view of establishing premiums, the mean is probably superior. This is because the mean helps us determine the total amount that insurance companies paid out, which is the bottom line as far as the insurance industry is concerned. For example, if the mean award of one million dollars is based on 1,000 liability cases, then the insurance industry paid out a total of one billion dollars.

When a population is symmetrical or not highly skewed, then the population mean and the population median are either equal or roughly equal, and both provide a good measure of the population central tendency. In this situation, we usually make inferences about the population mean because much of statistical theory is based on the mean rather than the median. We illustrate these ideas in the following two cases, which also show that we can obtain the mean and the median by using MINITAB, Excel, and MegaStat outputs.

Example 2.9 The Payment Time Case

C

The MINITAB output in Figure 2.23 tells us that the mean and the median of the sample of 65 payment times are 18.108 days and 17 days, respectively. Because the stem-and-leaf display of the payment times in Example 2.2 is not highly skewed to the right, the sample mean is not much greater than the sample median. Therefore, using the mean as our measure of central tendency, we estimate that the mean payment time of all bills using the new billing system is 18.108 days. This is substantially less than the typical payment time of 39 days that had been experienced using the old billing system.

Example 2.10 The Marketing Research Case

The Excel output in Figure 2.24(a) tells us that the mean and the median of the sample of 60 bottle design ratings are 30.35 and 31, respectively. Because the stem-and-leaf display of the bottle design ratings in Example 2.3 is not highly skewed to the left, the sample mean is not much less than the sample median. Therefore, using the mean as our measure of central tendency, we estimate that the mean rating of the new bottle design that would be given by all consumers is 30.35. This is considerably higher than the minimum standard of 25 for a successful bottle design.

BI

To conclude this example, note that Figures 2.24(b), 2.24(c), and 2.25 give the Excel and MegaStat outputs of the previously discussed means and medians for the internists' salaries, customer satisfaction ratings, and mileages. Other quantities on the outputs will be discussed as we proceed through this chapter.

FIGURE 2.23 MINITAB Output of Statistics Describing the 65 Payment Times

```
Variable   Count      Mean    StDev   Variance
PayTime       65    18.108    3.961     15.691

Variable  Minimum       Q1   Median       Q3   Maximum   Range
PayTime    10.000   15.000   17.000   21.000    29.000  19.000
```

FIGURE 2.24 Excel Outputs of Statistics Describing Three Data Sets

(a) Statistics describing the 60 bottle design ratings

STATISTICS	
Mean	30.35
Standard Error	0.401146
Median	31
Mode	32
Standard Deviation	3.107263
Sample Variance	9.655085
Kurtosis	1.423397
Skewness	−1.17688
Range	15
Minimum	20
Maximum	35
Sum	1821
Count	60

(b) Statistics describing the 13 internists' salaries

STATISTICS	
Mean	159.7692
Standard Error	8.498985
Median	152
Mode	#N/A
Standard Deviation	30.64353
Sample Variance	939.0256
Kurtosis	3.409669
Skewness	1.695197
Range	114
Minimum	127
Maximum	241
Sum	2077
Count	13

(c) Statistics describing the 20 customer satisfaction ratings

STATISTICS	
Mean	7.7
Standard Error	0.543381
Median	8
Mode	8
Standard Deviation	2.430075
Sample Variance	5.905263
Kurtosis	2.128288
Skewness	−1.56682
Range	9
Minimum	1
Maximum	10
Sum	154
Count	20

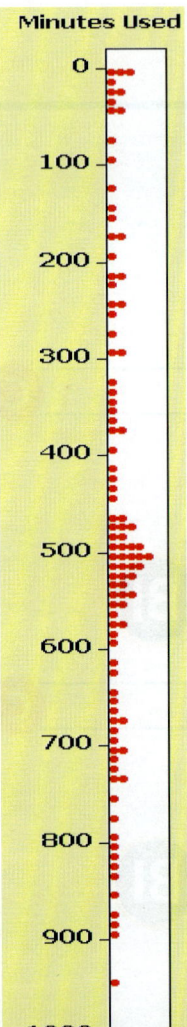

FIGURE 2.25 MegaStat Output of Statistics Describing the 49 Mileages

Descriptive statistics

	MPG	empirical rule	
count	49	mean − 1s	30.754
mean	31.553	mean + 1s	32.352
sample variance	0.639	percent in interval (68.26%)	63.3%
sample standard deviation	0.799	mean − 2s	29.955
minimum	29.8	mean + 2s	33.152
maximum	33.3	percent in interval (95.44%)	95.9%
range	3.5	mean − 3s	29.155
sum	1,546.100	mean + 3s	33.951
sum of squares	48,814.850	percent in interval (99.73%)	100.0%
deviation sum of squares (SS)	30.662		
1st quartile	31.000	low extremes	0
median	31.600	low outliers	0
3rd quartile	32.100	high outliers	0
interquartile range	1.100	high extremes	0
mode	31.700		

Example 2.11 The Cell Phone Case

Remember that if the cellular cost per minute for the random sample of 100 bank employees is over 18 cents per minute, the bank will benefit from automated cellular management of its calling plans. Last month's cellular usages for the 100 randomly selected employees are given in Table 1.2 (page 7), and a dot plot of these usages is given in the page margin. If we add together the usages, we find that the 100 employees used a total of 46,652 minutes. Since each employee was on a 500-minute plan that costs \$50, the base price of the cell phone plan for the 100 employees was 100(\$50) = \$5,000. Furthermore, 51 of the employees used more than the 500 minutes allowed. The sum of the cellular usages for these 51 employees can be calculated to be 33,150 minutes, which implies that the total number of overage minutes is 33,150 − 51(500) = 7,650. Since each overage minute is assessed a \$.40 charge, the total overage charge is 7,650(\$.40) = \$3,060. In addition, the 100 sampled employees were assessed \$1,257 of long distance and roaming charges. In summary, the 46,652 minutes used by the 100 sampled employees cost the bank a total of (\$5,000 + \$3,060 + \$1,257) = \$9,317. This works out to an average of \$9,317/46,652 = \$.1998, or 19.98 cents per minute. Because this average cellular cost per minute exceeds 18 cents per minute, the bank will hire the cellular management service to manage its calling plans.

BI

To conclude this section, note that the mean and the median convey useful information about a population having a relative frequency curve with a sufficiently regular shape. For instance, the mean and median would be useful in describing the mound-shaped, or single-peaked, distributions in Figure 2.22. However, these measures of central tendency do not adequately describe a double-peaked distribution. For example, the mean and the median of the exam scores in the double-peaked stem-and-leaf display of Figure 2.11 (page 52) are 75.225 and 77. Looking at the display, neither the mean nor the median represents a *typical* exam score. This is because the exam scores really have *no central value.* In this case the most important message conveyed by the double-peaked stem-and-leaf display is that the exam scores fall into two distinct groups.

Exercises for Section 2.2

CONCEPTS

2.13 Explain the difference between each of the following:

a A population parameter and its point estimate.

b A population mean and a corresponding sample mean.

2.14 Explain how the population mean, median, and mode compare when the population's relative frequency curve is

a Symmetrical.

b Skewed with a tail to the left.

c Skewed with a tail to the right.

d Normally distributed.

METHODS AND APPLICATIONS

2.15 Calculate the mean, median, and mode of each of the following populations of numbers:

a 9, 8, 10, 10, 12, 6, 11, 10, 12, 8

b 110, 120, 70, 90, 90, 100, 80, 130, 140

2.16 Calculate the mean, median, and mode for each of the following populations of numbers:

a 17, 23, 19, 20, 25, 18, 22, 15, 21, 20

b 505, 497, 501, 500, 507, 510, 501

2.17 THE VIDEO GAME SATISFACTION RATING CASE VideoGame

Recall that Table 1.5 (page 11) presents the satisfaction ratings for the XYZ-Box game system that have been given by 65 randomly selected purchasers. Figures 2.26 and 2.29(a) give the MINITAB and MegaStat outputs of statistics describing the 65 satisfaction ratings.

a Does the sample mean $\bar{x} = 42.954$ provide evidence that the mean of the population of all possible customer satisfaction ratings for the XYZ-Box is at least 42? (Recall that a "very satisfied" customer gives a rating that is at least 42.) Explain your answer.

b Use the stem-and-leaf display in Figure 2.14 (page 54) to verify that the median of the satisfaction ratings is 43. How do the mean and median compare? What does the stem-and-leaf display tell you about why they compare this way?

2.18 THE BANK CUSTOMER WAITING TIME CASE WaitTime

Recall that Table 1.6 (page 11) presents the waiting times for teller service during peak business hours of 100 randomly selected bank customers. Figures 2.27 and 2.29(b) give the MINITAB and MegaStat outputs of statistics describing the 100 waiting times.

a Does the sample mean $\bar{x} = 5.46$ provide evidence that the mean of the population of all possible customer waiting times during peak business hours is less than six minutes (as is desired by the bank manager)? Explain your answer.

b Use the stem-and-leaf display in Figure 2.17 (page 56) to verify that the median of the waiting times is 5.25. How do the mean and median compare? What does the stem-and-leaf display tell you about why they compare this way?

FIGURE 2.26 MINITAB Output of Statistics Describing the 65 Satisfaction Ratings

```
Variable   Count    Mean   StDev  Variance
Ratings       65  42.954   2.642     6.982

Variable  Minimum      Q1  Median      Q3  Maximum   Range
Ratings    36.000  41.000  43.000  45.000   48.000  12.000
```

FIGURE 2.27 MINITAB Output of Statistics Describing the 100 Waiting Times

Variable	Count	Mean	StDev	Variance
WaitTime	100	5.460	2.475	6.128

Variable	Minimum	Q1	Median	Q3	Maximum	Range
WaitTime	0.400	3.800	5.250	7.200	11.600	11.200

FIGURE 2.28 MINITAB Output of Statistics Describing the 40 Breaking Strengths

Variable	Count	Mean	StDev	Variance
Strength	40	50.575	1.644	2.702

Variable	Minimum	Q1	Median	Q3	Maximum	Range
Strength	46.800	49.425	50.650	51.650	54.000	7.200

FIGURE 2.29 MegaStat Outputs of Statistics Describing Three Data Sets

(a) Satisfaction rating statistics

Descriptive statistics

	Rating
count	65
mean	42.95
median	43.00
sample variance	6.98
sample standard deviation	2.64
minimum	36
maximum	48
range	12
empirical rule	
mean − 1s	40.31
mean + 1s	45.60
percent in interval (68.26%)	63.1%
mean − 2s	37.67
mean + 2s	48.24
percent in interval (95.44%)	98.5%
mean − 3s	35.03
mean + 3s	50.88
percent in interval (99.73%)	100.0%

(b) Waiting time statistics

Descriptive statistics

	WaitTime
count	100
mean	5.460
median	5.250
sample variance	6.128
sample standard deviation	2.475
minimum	0.4
maximum	11.6
range	11.2
empirical rule	
mean − 1s	2.985
mean + 1s	7.935
percent in interval (68.26%)	66.0%
mean − 2s	0.509
mean + 2s	10.411
percent in interval (95.44%)	96.0%
mean − 3s	−1.966
mean + 3s	12.886
percent in interval (99.73%)	100.0%

(c) Breaking strength statistics

Descriptive statistics

	Strength
count	40
mean	50.575
median	50.650
sample variance	2.702
sample standard deviation	1.644
minimum	46.8
maximum	54
range	7.2
empirical rule	
mean − 1s	48.931
mean + 1s	52.219
percent in interval (68.26%)	67.5%
mean − 2s	47.287
mean + 2s	53.863
percent in interval (95.44%)	95.0%
mean − 3s	45.644
mean + 3s	55.506
percent in interval (99.73%)	100.0%

2.19 THE TRASH BAG CASE TrashBag

Consider the trash bag problem. Suppose that an independent laboratory has tested 30-gallon trash bags and has found that none of the 30-gallon bags currently on the market have a mean breaking strength of 50 pounds or more. On the basis of these results, the producer of the new, improved trash bag feels sure that its 30-gallon bag will be the strongest such bag on the market if the new trash bag's mean breaking strength can be shown to be at least 50 pounds. Recall that Table 1.10 (page 19) presents the breaking strengths of 40 trash bags of the new type that were selected during a 40-hour pilot production run. Figures 2.28 and 2.29(c) give the MINITAB and MegaStat outputs of statistics describing the 40 breaking strengths.

a Does the sample mean $\bar{x} = 50.575$ provide evidence that the mean of the population of all possible trash bag breaking strengths is at least 50 pounds? Explain your answer.

b Use the stem-and-leaf display in Figure 2.20 (page 56) to verify that the median of the breaking strengths is 50.65. How do the mean and median compare? What does the stem-and-leaf display tell you about why they compare this way?

2.20 Consider Table 2.6 (page 54), which gives data concerning the 30 fastest-growing companies as listed on March 16, 2005 on the *Fortune* magazine website. FastGrow

a The mean and median of the EPS (earnings per share) growth percentages for the 30 fastest-growing companies can be found to be 114.1 and 92.5 respectively. By examining the actual EPS growth percentages in Table 2.6, explain why the mean is larger than the median.

TABLE 2.7 Data Comparing Lifestyles in the U.S. and Eight Other Countries LifeStyle

	Voters *Percentage Who Voted in Last National Election*	Income Tax *Highest Personal National Rate*	Video Rentals *Per Capita per Year*	PCs *Per 100 People*	Religion *Percentage of Households Who Attend Services Regularly*
U.S.	49.1%	40%	13.8	35.0	51.6%
Germany	82.2	56	2.1	17.0	20.0
France	68.9	54	0.9	16.0	N.A.
Britain	71.5	40	3.3	20.0	23.6
Netherlands	78.3	60	1.8	20.0	28.9
Sweden	78.6	55	2.1	18.0	10.0
Italy	85.0	46	0.7	11.5	55.8
Japan	58.8	50	7.5	14.0	N.A.
South Korea	63.9	44	N.A.	N.A.	N.A.

N.A.-Not available.

Source: "America vs. The New Europe: By The Numbers," *Fortune*, December 21, 1998, p. 156. Reprinted from the December 21, 1998, issue of *Fortune*, copyright 1998 Time, Inc. All rights reserved.

TABLE 2.8 Top 10 Websites in April 2004 as Rated by comScore Media Metrix WebVisit

	Unique Visitors April (04)
Yahoo! sites	113.2
Time Warner Network	111.8
MSN-Microsoft sites	110.1
Google sites	66
eBay	60.1
Amazon sites	39.1
Terra Lycos	38.4
About/Primedia	38.3
Excite Network	29
Viacom Online	28

Source: Courtesy of ComScore Networks. Copyright © 2004. All rights reserved.

b The mean and median of the revenue growth percentages for the 30 fastest-growing companies can be found to be 51.9 and 47, respectively. By examining the actual revenue growth percentages in Table 2.6, explain why the mean is somewhat larger than the median.

Exercises 2.21 through 2.25 refer to information in Table 2.7, which gives data concerning lifestyles in the United States and eight other countries. In each exercise (a) compute the appropriate mean and median; (b) compare the mean and median and explain what they say about skewness; (c) construct a dot plot and discuss what the dot plot says about skewness and whether this agrees with how the mean and median compare; (d) discuss how the United States compares to the mean and median. LifeStyle

2.21 Analyze the data concerning voters in Table 2.7 as described above. LifeStyle

2.22 Analyze the data concerning income tax rates in Table 2.7 as described above. LifeStyle

2.23 Analyze the data concerning video rentals in Table 2.7 as described above. LifeStyle

2.24 Analyze the data concerning PCs in Table 2.7 as described above. LifeStyle

2.25 Analyze the data concerning religion in Table 2.7 as described above. LifeStyle

2.26 Table 2.8 gives the number of unique visitors during April 2004 to the top 10 websites as rated by comScore Media Metrix, a division of comScore Networks, Inc. Compute the mean and median for the website data and compare them. What do they say about skewness? WebVisit

2.27 In 1998 the National Basketball Association (NBA) experienced a labor dispute that canceled almost half of the professional basketball season. The NBA owners, who were worried about escalating salaries because several star players had recently signed huge contracts, locked out the players and demanded that a salary cap be established. This led to discussion in the media about excessive player salaries. On October 30, 1998, an article titled "What does average salary really mean in the NBA?" by Jonathan Sills appeared in his Behind the Numbers column on the ESPN.com website. The article discussed the validity of some media claims about NBA player salaries. Figure 2.30 shows a frequency distribution of NBA salaries as presented in the Sills article. Use the frequency distribution to do the following:

a Compare the mean, median, and mode of the salaries and explain the relationship. Note that the minimum NBA salary at the time of the lockout was $272,500.

b Noting that 411 NBA players were under contract, estimate the percentage of players who earned more than the mean salary; more than the median salary.

c Below we give three quotes from news stories cited by Sills in his article. Comment on the validity of each statement.

"Last year, the NBA middle class made an average of $2.6 million. On that scale, I'd take the NBA lower class."—*Houston Chronicle*

"The players make an obscene amount of money—the median salary is well over $2 million!"—*St. Louis Post Dispatch*

"The players want us to believe they literally can't 'survive' on $2.6 million a year, the average salary in the NBA."—*Washington Post*

FIGURE 2.30 1997–98 NBA Salaries

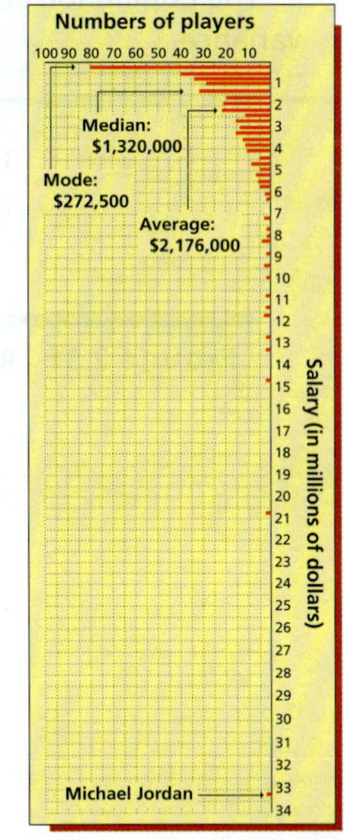

Source: Reprinted courtesy of ESPN.

2.3 Measures of Variation

Range, variance, and standard deviation In addition to estimating a population's central tendency, it is important to estimate the **variation** of the population's individual values. For example, Figure 2.31 shows two histograms. Each portrays the distribution of 20 repair times (in days) for personal computers at a major service center. Because the mean (and median and mode) of each distribution equals four days, the measures of central tendency do not indicate any difference between the American and National Service Centers. However, the repair times for the American Service Center are clustered quite closely together, whereas the repair times for the National Service Center are spread farther apart (the repair time might be as little as one day, but could also be as long as seven days). Therefore, we need measures of variation to express how the two distributions differ.

One way to measure the variation of a set of measurements is to calculate the *range*.

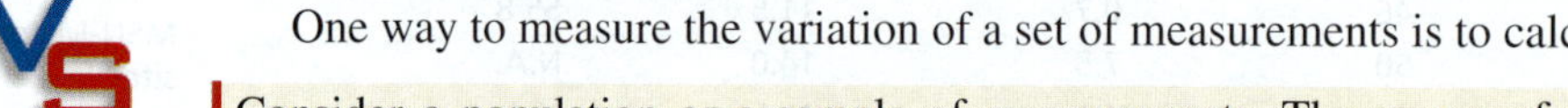

Consider a population or a sample of measurements. The **range** of the measurements is the largest measurement minus the smallest measurement.

In Figure 2.31, the smallest and largest repair times for the American Service Center are three days and five days; therefore, the range is $5 - 3 = 2$ days. On the other hand, the range for the National Service Center is $7 - 1 = 6$ days. The National Service Center's larger range indicates that this service center's repair times exhibit more variation.

In general, the range is not the best measure of a data set's variation. One reason is that it is based on only the smallest and largest measurements in the data set and therefore may reflect an extreme measurement that is not entirely representative of the data set's variation. For example, in the marketing research case, the smallest and largest ratings in the sample of 60 bottle design ratings are 20 and 35. However, to simply estimate that most bottle design ratings are between 20 and 35 misses the fact that 57, or 95 percent, of the 60 ratings are at least as large as the minimum rating of 25 for a successful bottle design. In general, to fully describe a population's variation, it is useful to estimate intervals that contain **different percentages** (for example, 70 percent, 95 percent, or almost 100 percent) of the individual population values. To estimate such intervals, we use the **population variance** and the **population standard deviation.**

The Population Variance and Standard Deviation

The **population variance** σ^2 (pronounced *sigma squared*) is the average of the squared deviations of the individual population measurements from the population mean μ.

The **population standard deviation** σ (pronounced *sigma*) is the positive square root of the population variance.

For example, consider again the population of profit margins for five of the best big companies in America as rated by *Forbes* magazine on its website on March 16, 2005. These profit margins

FIGURE 2.31 Repair Times for Personal Computers at Two Service Centers

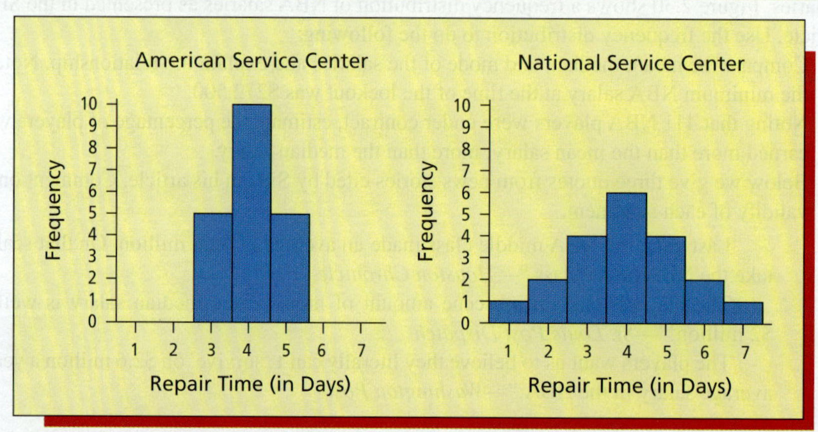

are 8%, 10%, 15%, 12%, and 5%. To calculate the variance and standard deviation of these profit margins, we first calculate the population mean to be

$$\mu = \frac{8 + 10 + 15 + 12 + 5}{5} = \frac{50}{5} = 10$$

Next, we calculate the deviations of the individual population measurements from the population mean $\mu = 10$ as follows:

$(8 - 10) = -2 \quad (10 - 10) = 0 \quad (15 - 10) = 5 \quad (12 - 10) = 2 \quad (5 - 10) = -5$

Then we compute the sum of the squares of these deviations:

$$(-2)^2 + (0)^2 + (5)^2 + (2)^2 + (-5)^2 = 4 + 0 + 25 + 4 + 25 = 58$$

Finally, we calculate the population variance σ^2, the average of the squared deviations, by dividing the sum of the squared deviations, 58, by the number of squared deviations, 5. That is, σ^2 equals $58/5 = 11.6$. Furthermore, this implies that the population standard deviation σ—the positive square root of σ^2—is $\sqrt{11.6} = 3.406$.

To see that the variance and standard deviation measure the variation, or spread, of the individual population measurements, suppose that the measurements are spread far apart. Then, many measurements will be far from the mean μ, many of the squared deviations from the mean will be large, and the sum of squared deviations will be large. It follows that the average of the squared deviations—the population variance—will be relatively large. On the other hand, if the population measurements are clustered close together, many measurements will be close to μ, many of the squared deviations from the mean will be small, and the average of the squared deviations—the population variance—will be small. Therefore, the more spread out the population measurements, the larger is the population variance, and the larger is the population standard deviation.

To further understand the population variance and standard deviation, note that one reason we square the deviations of the individual population measurements from the population mean is that the sum of the raw deviations themselves is zero. This is because the negative deviations cancel the positive deviations. For example, in the profit margin situation, the raw deviations are -2, 0, 5, 2, and -5, which sum to zero. Of course, we could make the deviations positive by finding their absolute values. We square the deviations instead because the resulting population variance and standard deviation have many important interpretations that we study throughout this book. Since the population variance is an average of squared deviations of the original population values, the variance is expressed in squared units of the original population values. On the other hand, the population standard deviation—the square root of the population variance—is expressed in the same units as the original population values. For example, the previously discussed profit margins are expressed in percentages. Therefore, the variance of these profit margins is $\sigma^2 = 11.6(\%)^2$, whereas the standard deviation is $\sigma = 3.406\%$. Since the population standard deviation is expressed in the same units as the population values, it is more often used to make practical interpretations about the variation of these values.

When a population is too large to measure all the population units, we estimate the population variance and the population standard deviation by the **sample variance** and the **sample standard deviation.** We calculate the sample variance by dividing the sum of the squared deviations of the sample measurements from the sample mean by $n - 1$, the sample size minus one. Although we might intuitively think that we should divide by n rather than $n - 1$, it can be shown that dividing by n tends to produce an estimate of the population variance that is too small. On the other hand, dividing by $n - 1$ tends to produce a larger estimate that we will show in Chapter 6 is more appropriate. Therefore, we obtain:

The Sample Variance and the Sample Standard Deviation

The **sample variance** s^2 (pronounced *s squared*) is defined to be

$$s^2 = \frac{\sum_{i=1}^{n}(x_i - \bar{x})^2}{n - 1} = \frac{(x_1 - \bar{x})^2 + (x_2 - \bar{x})^2 + \cdots + (x_n - \bar{x})^2}{n - 1}$$

and is the **point estimate of the population variance** σ^2.

The **sample standard deviation** $s = \sqrt{s^2}$ is the positive square root of the sample variance and is the **point estimate of the population standard deviation** σ.

Example 2.12 The Car Mileage Case

To illustrate the calculation of the sample variance and standard deviation, we begin by considering the first five mileages in Table 2.1 (page 44): $x_1 = 30.8$, $x_2 = 31.7$, $x_3 = 30.1$, $x_4 = 31.6$, and $x_5 = 32.1$. Since the mean of these five mileages is $\bar{x} = 31.26$, it follows that

$$\begin{aligned}\sum_{i=1}^{5}(x_i - \bar{x})^2 &= (x_1 - \bar{x})^2 + (x_2 - \bar{x})^2 + (x_3 - \bar{x})^2 + (x_4 - \bar{x})^2 + (x_5 - \bar{x})^2 \\ &= (30.8 - 31.26)^2 + (31.7 - 31.26)^2 + (30.1 - 31.26)^2 \\ &\quad + (31.6 - 31.26)^2 + (32.1 - 31.26)^2 \\ &= (-.46)^2 + (.44)^2 + (-1.16)^2 + (.34)^2 + (.84)^2 \\ &= 2.572\end{aligned}$$

Therefore, the variance and the standard deviation of the sample of the first five mileages are

$$s^2 = \frac{2.572}{5-1} = .643 \quad \text{and} \quad s = \sqrt{.643} = .8019$$

Of course, intuitively, we are likely to obtain more accurate point estimates of the population variance and standard deviation by using all the available sample information. Recall that the mean of all 49 mileages is $\bar{x} = 31.5531$. Using this sample mean, it can be verified that

$$\begin{aligned}\sum_{i=1}^{49}(x_i - \bar{x})^2 &= (x_1 - \bar{x})^2 + (x_2 - \bar{x})^2 + \cdots + (x_{49} - \bar{x})^2 \\ &= (30.8 - 31.5531)^2 + (31.7 - 31.5531)^2 + \cdots + (32.2 - 31.5531)^2 \\ &= (-.7531)^2 + (.1469)^2 + \cdots + (.6469)^2 \\ &= 30.66204\end{aligned}$$

Therefore, the variance and the standard deviation of the sample of 49 mileages are

$$s^2 = \frac{30.66204}{48} = .638793 \quad \text{and} \quad s = \sqrt{.638793} = .7992$$

Notice that the MegaStat output in Figure 2.25 (page 64) gives these quantities (rounded to three decimal places). Here $s^2 = .6388$ and $s = .7992$ are the point estimates of the variance, σ^2, and the standard deviation, σ, of the population of the mileages of all the cars that will be or could potentially be produced. Furthermore, the sample standard deviation is expressed in the same units as the sample values. Therefore $s = .7992$ mpg.

Before explaining how we can use s^2 and s in a practical way, we present a formula that makes it easier to compute s^2. This formula is useful when we are using a handheld calculator that is not equipped with a statistics mode to compute s^2.

The **sample variance** can be calculated using the *computational formula*

$$s^2 = \frac{1}{n-1}\left[\sum_{i=1}^{n} x_i^2 - \frac{\left(\sum_{i=1}^{n} x_i\right)^2}{n}\right]$$

Example 2.13 The Payment Time Case

Consider the sample of 65 payment times in Table 2.2 (page 46). Using this data, it can be verified that

$$\sum_{i=1}^{65} x_i = x_1 + x_2 + \cdots + x_{65} = 22 + 19 + \cdots + 21 = 1{,}177 \quad \text{and}$$

$$\sum_{i=1}^{65} x_i^2 = x_1^2 + x_2^2 + \cdots + x_{65}^2 = (22)^2 + (19)^2 + \cdots + (21)^2 = 22{,}317$$

Therefore,

$$s^2 = \frac{1}{(65-1)}\left[22317 - \frac{(1{,}177)^2}{65}\right]$$

$$= \frac{1{,}004.2464}{64} = 15.69135$$

and $s = \sqrt{s^2} = \sqrt{15.69135} = 3.9612$ days (see the MINITAB output in Figure 2.23 on page 63).

A practical interpretation: the Empirical Rule In the next box we give a practical interpretation of the population standard deviation. This interpretation is often referred to as the *Empirical Rule for a normally distributed population.*

The Empirical Rule for a Normally Distributed Population

If a population has **mean μ** and **standard deviation σ** and is **described by a normal curve,** then, as illustrated in Figure 2.32(a),

1 68.26 percent of the population measurements are within (plus or minus) one standard deviation of the mean and thus lie in the interval $[\mu - \sigma, \mu + \sigma] = [\mu \pm \sigma]$

2 95.44 percent of the population measurements are within (plus or minus) two standard deviations of the mean and thus lie in the interval $[\mu - 2\sigma, \mu + 2\sigma] = [\mu \pm 2\sigma]$

3 99.73 percent of the population measurements are within (plus or minus) three standard deviations of the mean and thus lie in the interval $[\mu - 3\sigma, \mu + 3\sigma] = [\mu \pm 3\sigma]$

FIGURE 2.32 The Empirical Rule and Tolerance Intervals

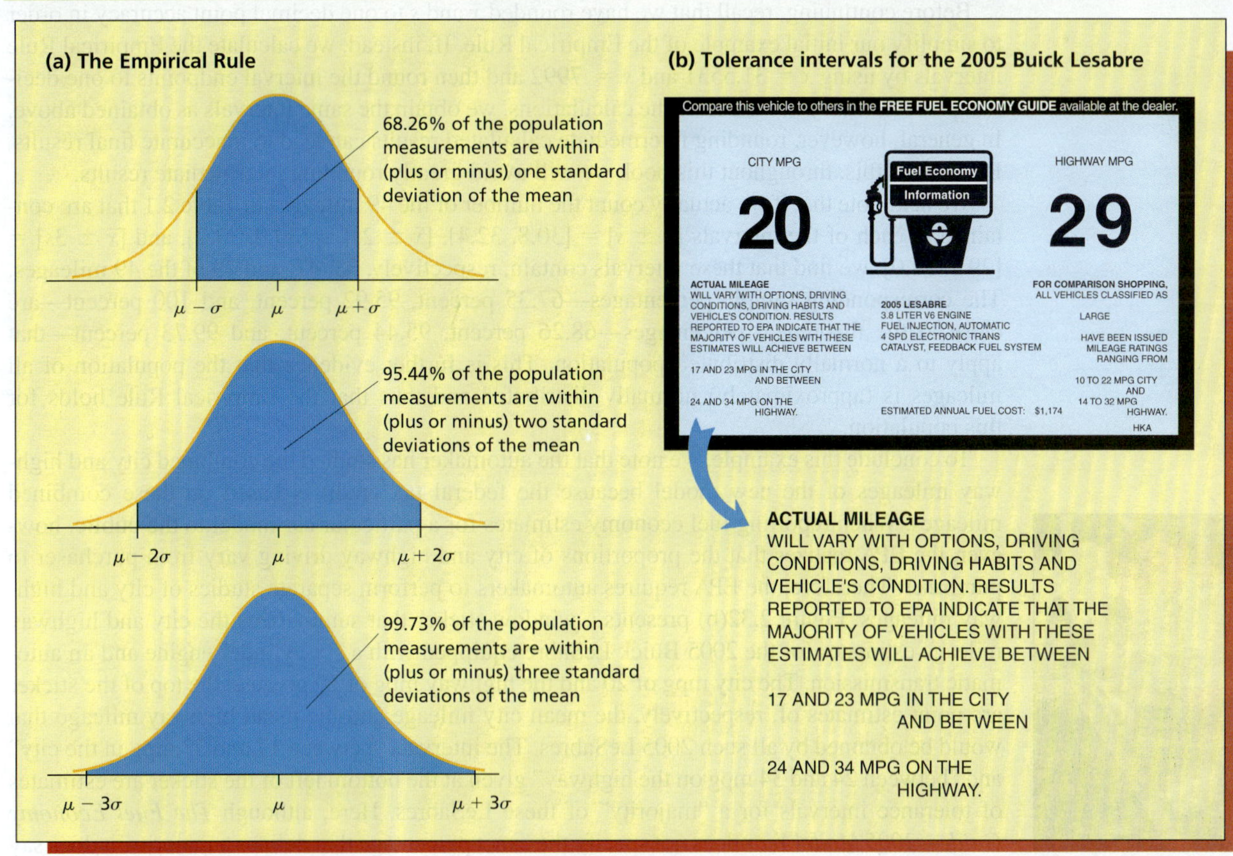

(a) The Empirical Rule
68.26% of the population measurements are within (plus or minus) one standard deviation of the mean
μ − σ
μ
μ + σ
95.44% of the population measurements are within (plus or minus) two standard deviations of the mean
μ − 2σ
μ
μ + 2σ
99.73% of the population measurements are within (plus or minus) three standard deviations of the mean
μ − 3σ
μ
μ + 3σ
(b) Tolerance intervals for the 2005 Buick Lesabre
Compare this vehicle to others in the FREE FUEL ECONOMY GUIDE available at the dealer.
CITY MPG
20
Fuel Economy
Information
HIGHWAY MPG
29
ACTUAL MILEAGE
WILL VARY WITH OPTIONS, DRIVING CONDITIONS, DRIVING HABITS AND VEHICLE'S CONDITION. RESULTS REPORTED TO EPA INDICATE THAT THE MAJORITY OF VEHICLES WITH THESE ESTIMATES WILL ACHIEVE BETWEEN
17 AND 23 MPG IN THE CITY AND BETWEEN
24 AND 34 MPG ON THE HIGHWAY.
2005 LESABRE
3.8 LITER V6 ENGINE
FUEL INJECTION, AUTOMATIC
4 SPD ELECTRONIC TRANS
CATALYST, FEEDBACK FUEL SYSTEM
ESTIMATED ANNUAL FUEL COST: $1,174
FOR COMPARISON SHOPPING, ALL VEHICLES CLASSIFIED AS
LARGE
HAVE BEEN ISSUED MILEAGE RATINGS RANGING FROM
10 TO 22 MPG CITY AND
14 TO 32 MPG HIGHWAY.
HKA
ACTUAL MILEAGE
WILL VARY WITH OPTIONS, DRIVING CONDITIONS, DRIVING HABITS AND VEHICLE'S CONDITION. RESULTS REPORTED TO EPA INDICATE THAT THE MAJORITY OF VEHICLES WITH THESE ESTIMATES WILL ACHIEVE BETWEEN
17 AND 23 MPG IN THE CITY AND BETWEEN
24 AND 34 MPG ON THE HIGHWAY.

In general, an interval that contains a specified percentage of the individual measurements in a population is called a **tolerance interval.** It follows that the one, two, and three standard deviation intervals around μ given in (1), (2), and (3) are tolerance intervals containing, respectively, 68.26 percent, 95.44 percent, and 99.73 percent of the measurements in a normally distributed population. Often we interpret the *three-sigma interval* $[\mu \pm 3\sigma]$ to be a tolerance interval that contains *almost all* of the measurements in a normally distributed population. Of course, we usually do not know the true values of μ and σ. Therefore, we must estimate the tolerance intervals by replacing μ and σ in these intervals by the mean $\bar{x}$ and standard deviation s of a sample that has been randomly selected from the normally distributed population.

Example 2.14 The Car Mileage Case

Again consider the sample of 49 mileages. We have seen that $\bar{x} = 31.5531$ and $s = .7992$ for this sample are the point estimates of the mean μ and the standard deviation σ of the population of all mileages. Furthermore, the stem-and-leaf display and histogram of the 49 mileages suggest that the population of all mileages is normally distributed. To more simply illustrate the Empirical Rule, we will round $\bar{x}$ to 31.6 and s to .8. It follows that, using the interval

1 $[\bar{x} \pm s] = [31.6 \pm .8] = [31.6 - .8, 31.6 + .8] = [30.8, 32.4]$, we estimate that 68.26 percent of all individual cars will obtain mileages between 30.8 mpg and 32.4 mpg.

2 $[\bar{x} \pm 2s] = [31.6 \pm 2(.8)] = [31.6 \pm 1.6] = [30.0, 33.2]$, we estimate that 95.44 percent of all individual cars will obtain mileages between 30.0 mpg and 33.2 mpg.

3 $[\bar{x} \pm 3s] = [31.6 \pm 3(.8)] = [31.6 \pm 2.4] = [29.2, 34.0]$, we estimate that 99.73 percent of all individual cars will obtain mileages between 29.2 mpg and 34.0 mpg.

Since the difference between the upper and lower limits of each tolerance interval is fairly small, we might conclude that the variability of the individual car mileages around the estimated mean mileage of 31.6 mpg is fairly small. Furthermore, the interval $[\bar{x} \pm 3s] = [29.2, 34.0]$ implies that almost any individual car that a customer might purchase this year will obtain a mileage between 29.2 mpg and 34.0 mpg.

Before continuing, recall that we have rounded $\bar{x}$ and s to one decimal point accuracy in order to simplify our initial example of the Empirical Rule. If, instead, we calculate the Empirical Rule intervals by using $\bar{x} = 31.5531$ and $s = .7992$ and then round the interval endpoints to one decimal place accuracy at the end of the calculations, we obtain the same intervals as obtained above. In general, however, rounding intermediate calculated results can lead to inaccurate final results. Because of this, throughout this book we will avoid greatly rounding intermediate results.

We next note that if we actually count the number of the 49 mileages in Table 2.1 that are contained in each of the intervals $[\bar{x} \pm s] = [30.8, 32.4]$, $[\bar{x} \pm 2s] = [30.0, 33.2]$, and $[\bar{x} \pm 3s] = [29.2, 34.0]$, we find that these intervals contain, respectively, 33, 47, and 49 of the 49 mileages. The corresponding sample percentages—67.35 percent, 95.92 percent, and 100 percent—are close to the theoretical percentages—68.26 percent, 95.44 percent, and 99.73 percent—that apply to a normally distributed population. This is further evidence that the population of all mileages is (approximately) normally distributed and thus that the Empirical Rule holds for this population.

To conclude this example, we note that the automaker has studied the combined city and highway mileages of the new model because the federal tax credit is based on these combined mileages. When reporting fuel economy estimates for a particular car model to the public, however, the EPA realizes that the proportions of city and highway driving vary from purchaser to purchaser. Therefore, the EPA requires automakers to perform separate studies of city and highway mileages. Figure 2.32(b) presents a window sticker that summarizes the city and highway mileage estimates for the 2005 Buick LeSabre equipped with a six-cylinder engine and an automatic transmission. The city mpg of 20 and the highway mpg of 29 given at the top of the sticker are point estimates of, respectively, the mean city mileage and the mean highway mileage that would be obtained by all such 2005 LeSabres. The intervals "between 17 and 23 mpg in the city" and "between 24 and 34 mpg on the highway" given at the bottom left of the sticker are estimates of tolerance intervals for a "majority" of these LeSabres. Here, although *The Fuel Economy Guide—2005 Model Year* does not specify the exact percentage that defines a majority, it does say that a majority should be interpreted to mean "most." Therefore, the first interval estimates that most LeSabres will obtain between 17 mpg and 23 mpg in city driving. Similarly, the second interval estimates that most LeSabres will obtain between 24 mpg and 34 mpg in highway driving.

A quality improvement application: meeting customer requirements Tolerance intervals are often used to determine whether customer requirements are being met. Customer requirements often specify that a quality characteristic must be inside an acceptable range of values called *specifications.* Specifications are written for *individual measurements.* For example, suppose that marketing research done by the fast-food restaurant of Example 1.3 (page 12) suggests that coffee tastes best if its temperature is between 153° and 167°. Therefore, the customer requirements (specifications) would say that the temperature of each individual cup of coffee must be between 153° and 167° (this specification would typically be written as $160° \pm 7°$).

If a process is able to consistently produce output that meets customer requirements (specifications), we say that the process is **capable** (of meeting the requirements). From a practical standpoint this means that *almost all* of the individual measurements must be within the specification limits. Furthermore, if the population of all process measurements is approximately normally distributed, it is common practice to conclude that a process that is in statistical control is capable of meeting customer requirements if the three-sigma tolerance interval estimate $[\bar{x} \pm 3s]$ is within the specification limits. We say this because, if this interval is within the specification limits, then we estimate that almost all (99.73 percent) of the process measurements are within the specification limits.

For example, recall that the runs plot of the 24 coffee temperatures in Figure 1.3 (page 14) indicates that the fast-food restaurant's coffee-making process is in statistical control. The mean and the standard deviation of these temperatures are $\bar{x} = 160.0833$ and $s = 5.3724$, and a stem-and-leaf display indicates that the temperatures are approximately normally distributed. It follows that we estimate that the interval

$$\begin{aligned}[\bar{x} \pm 3s] &= [160.0833 \pm 3(5.3724)]\\ &= [143.97, 176.20]\end{aligned}$$

contains 99.73 percent of all coffee temperatures. Since this interval tells us that some coffee temperatures are outside the customer specifications of 153° to 167°, the coffee-making process is not capable of meeting customer requirements. Here, although the process is exhibiting a constant amount of variation around a constant level (or mean), the constant amount of variation—as indicated by the standard deviation of $s = 5.3724$—is too large. Suppose that to reduce the standard deviation of the coffee temperatures, the restaurant tests a new coffeemaker. A sample of 24 coffee temperatures is in control and approximately normally distributed with a mean of $\bar{x} = 160.0174$ and a reduced standard deviation of $s = 2.1215$. It follows that we estimate that the interval

BI

$$\begin{aligned}[\bar{x} \pm 3s] &= [160.0174 \pm 3(2.1215)]\\ &= [153.65, 166.38]\end{aligned}$$

contains 99.73 percent of all coffee temperatures. We infer that almost all coffee temperatures produced by the new coffee-making process are within the customer specifications of 153° to 167°. Therefore, the improved process is capable of meeting customer requirements.

BI

Skewness and the Empirical Rule The Empirical Rule holds for normally distributed populations. In addition, this rule also approximately holds for populations having **mound-shaped** (single-peaked) distributions that are not very skewed to the right or left. For example, recall that the distribution of 65 payment times is somewhat but not highly skewed to the right. Moreover, the mean and the standard deviation of the payment times can be calculated to be $\bar{x} = 18.1077$ and $s = 3.9612$. If we actually count the number of payment times that are contained in each of the intervals $[\bar{x} \pm s] = [14.1, 22.1]$, $[\bar{x} \pm 2s] = [10.2, 26.0]$, and $[\bar{x} \pm 3s] = [6.2, 30.0]$, we find that these intervals contain, respectively, 45, 62, and 65 of the 65 payment times. The corresponding sample percentages—69.23 percent, 95.38 percent, and 100 percent—are close to the theoretical percentages—68.26 percent, 95.44 percent, and 99.73 percent—given by the Empirical Rule.

Therefore, we have evidence that the Empirical Rule approximately holds for the population of all bill payment times. It follows that we estimate that (1) 68.26 percent of all bill payment times will be between 14 days and 22 days, (2) 95.44 percent will be between 10 days and 26 days, and (3) 99.73 percent (that is, almost all) will be between 6 days and 30 days. These results indicate that the variability of the individual bill payment times around the estimated mean of 18.1077 days is reasonably small (note that, in making this conclusion, we take into account the fact that any population of bill payment times will exhibit some variability). Furthermore, because almost all bill payment times will be substantially less than the 39 days typical of the old billing system, we conclude that the new, computer-based electronic billing system is a substantial improvement.

In some situations, the skewness of a mound-shaped distribution of population measurements can make it tricky to know whether and how to use the Empirical Rule. For example, we previously concluded that the distribution of 60 bottle design ratings is somewhat but not highly skewed to the left. The mean and the standard deviation of the 60 bottle design ratings are $\bar{x} = 30.35$ and $s = 3.1073$. If we actually count the number of ratings contained in each of the intervals $[\bar{x} \pm s] = [27.2, 33.5]$, $[\bar{x} \pm 2s] = [24.1, 36.6]$, and $[\bar{x} \pm 3s] = [21, 39.7]$, we find that these intervals contain, respectively, 44, 57, and 59 of the 60 ratings. The corresponding sample percentages—73.33 percent, 95 percent, and 98.33 percent—are, respectively, greater than, approximately equal to, and less than the theoretical percentages—68.26 percent, 95.44 percent, and 99.73 percent—given by the Empirical Rule. Therefore, if we consider the population of all consumer ratings of the bottle design, we might estimate that (1) at least 68.26 percent of all ratings will be between 27 and 34, (2) approximately 95.44 percent of the ratings will be between 24 and 35 (a rating cannot exceed 35), and (3) fewer than 99.73 percent of the ratings will be between 21 and 35. Result (3), and the low ratings 20 and 22 in the left-hand tail of the stem-and-leaf display in Example 2.3 (page 46), suggest that the bottle design ratings distribution is too skewed to the left to use the Empirical Rule to make conclusions about almost all ratings. However, we are not necessarily concerned about almost all ratings, because the bottle design will be successful if it appeals to a large percentage of consumers. Results (1) and (2), which describe 68.26 percent and 95.44 percent of all consumer ratings, imply that large percentages of consumer ratings will exhibit reasonably small variability around the estimated mean rating of 30.35. This, and the fact that 57, or 95 percent, of the 60 ratings are at least as large as the minimum rating of 25 for a successful bottle design, suggest that the bottle design will be successful.

Chebyshev's Theorem If we fear that the Empirical Rule does not hold for a particular population, we can consider using **Chebyshev's Theorem** to find an interval that contains a specified percentage of the individual measurements in the population.

Chebyshev's Theorem

Consider any population that has mean μ and standard deviation σ. Then, for any value of k greater than 1, at least $100(1 - 1/k^2)\%$ of the population measurements lie in the interval $[\mu \pm k\sigma]$.

For example, if we choose k equal to 2, then at least $100(1 - 1/2^2)\% = 100(3/4)\% = 75\%$ of the population measurements lie in the interval $[\mu \pm 2\sigma]$. As another example, if we choose k equal to 3, then at least $100(1 - 1/3^2)\% = 100(8/9)\% = 88.89\%$ of the population measurements lie in the interval $[\mu \pm 3\sigma]$. As yet a third example, suppose that we wish to find an interval containing at least 99.73 percent of all population measurements. Here we would set $100(1 - 1/k^2)\%$ equal to 99.73%, which implies that $(1 - 1/k^2) = .9973$. If we solve for k, we find that $k = 19.25$. This says that at least 99.73 percent of all population measurements lie in the interval $[\mu \pm 19.25\sigma]$. Unless σ is extremely small, this interval will be so long that it will tell us very little about where the population measurements lie. We conclude that Chebyshev's Theorem can help us find an interval that contains a reasonably high percentage (such as 75 percent or 88.89 percent) of all population measurements. However, unless σ is extremely small, Chebyshev's Theorem will not provide a useful interval that contains almost all (say, 99.73 percent) of the population measurements.

Although Chebyshev's Theorem technically applies to any population, it is only of practical use when analyzing a **non-mound-shaped** (for example, a double-peaked) **population that is not extremely skewed to the right or left.** Why is this? First, **we would not use Chebyshev's**

Theorem to describe a mound-shaped population that is not very skewed because we can use the Empirical Rule to do this. In fact, the Empirical Rule is better for such a population because it gives us a shorter interval that will contain a given percentage of measurements. For example, if the Empirical Rule can be used to describe a population, the interval $[\mu \pm 3\sigma]$ will contain 99.73 percent of all measurements. On the other hand, if we use Chebyshev's Theorem, the interval $[\mu \pm 19.25\sigma]$ is needed. As another example, the Empirical Rule tells us that 95.44 percent of all measurements lie in the interval $[\mu \pm 2\sigma]$, whereas Chebyshev's Theorem tells us only that at least 75 percent of all measurements lie in this interval.

It is also not appropriate to use Chebyshev's Theorem—or any other result making use of the population standard deviation σ—to describe a population that is extremely skewed. This is because, if a population is extremely skewed, the measurements in the long tail to the left or right will greatly inflate σ. This implies that tolerance intervals calculated using σ will be so long that they are of little use. In this case, it is best to measure variation by using **percentiles,** which are discussed in the next section.

z-scores We can determine the relative location of any value in a population or sample by using the mean and standard deviation to compute the value's z-score. For any value x in a population or sample, the ***z*-score** corresponding to x is defined as follows:

***z*-score:**

$$z = \frac{x - \text{mean}}{\text{standard deviation}}$$

The z-score, which is also called the *standardized value,* is the number of standard deviations that x is from the mean. A positive z-score says that x is above (greater than) the mean, while a negative z-score says that x is below (less than) the mean. For instance, a z-score equal to 2.3 says that x is 2.3 standard deviations above the mean. Similarly, a z-score equal to -1.68 says that x is 1.68 standard deviations below the mean. A z-score equal to zero says that x equals the mean.

A z-score indicates the relative location of a value within a population or sample. For example, below we calculate the z-scores for each of the profit margins for five of the best big companies in America as rated by *Forbes* magazine on its website on March 25, 2005. Recall that for these five companies, the mean profit margin is 10% and the standard deviation is 3.406%.

Company	Profit margin, x	x − mean	z-score
Black & Decker	8%	$8 - 10 = -2$	$-2/3.406 = -.59$
Washington Post	10	$10 - 10 = 0$	$0/3.406 = 0$
Texas Instruments	15	$15 - 10 = 5$	$5/3.406 = 1.47$
Clorox	12	$12 - 10 = 2$	$2/3.406 = .59$
Foot Locker	5	$5 - 10 = -5$	$-5/3.406 = -1.47$

These z-scores tell us that the profit margin for Texas Instruments is the farthest above the mean. More specifically, this profit margin is 1.47 standard deviations above the mean. The profit margin for Foot Locker is the farthest below the mean—it is 1.47 standard deviations below the mean. Since the z-score for the Washington Post equals zero, its profit margin equals the mean.

Values in two different populations or samples having the same z-score are the same number of standard deviations from their respective means and, therefore, have the same relative locations. For example, suppose that the mean score on the midterm exam for students in Section A of a statistics course is 65 and the standard deviation of the scores is 10. Meanwhile, the mean score on the same exam for students in Section B is 80 and the standard deviation is 5. A student in Section A who scores an 85 and a student in Section B who scores a 90 have the same relative locations within their respective sections because their z-scores, $(85 - 65)/10 = 2$ and $(90 - 80)/5 = 2$, are equal.

The coefficient of variation Sometimes we need to measure the size of the standard deviation of a population or sample relative to the size of the population or sample mean. The **coefficient of variation,** which makes this comparison, is defined for a population or sample as follows:

$$\textbf{Coefficient of variation} = \frac{\text{standard deviation}}{\text{mean}} \times 100$$

The coefficient of variation compares populations or samples having different means and different standard deviations. For example, Morningstar.com[6] gives the mean and standard deviation[7] of the returns for each of the Morningstar Top 25 Large Growth Funds. As given on the Morningstar website, the mean return for the Strong Advisor Select A fund is 10.39 percent with a standard deviation of 16.18 percent, while the mean return for the Nations Marisco 21st Century fund is 17.7 percent with a standard deviation of 15.81 percent. It follows that the coefficient of variation for the Strong Advisor fund is $(16.18/10.39) \times 100 = 155.73$, and that the coefficient of variation for the Nations Marisco fund is $(15.81/17.7) \times 100 = 89.32$. This tells us that, for the Strong Advisor fund, the standard deviation is 155.73 percent of the value of its mean return. For the Nations Marisco fund, the standard deviation is 89.32 percent of the value of its mean return.

In the context of situations like the stock fund comparison, the coefficient of variation is often used as a measure of *risk* because it measures the variation of the returns (the standard deviation) relative to the size of the mean return. For instance, although the Strong Advisor fund and the Nations Marisco fund have comparable standard deviations (16.18 percent versus 15.81 percent), the Strong Advisor fund has a higher coefficient of variation than does the Nations Marisco fund (155.73 versus 89.32). This says that, *relative to the mean return,* the variation in returns for the Strong Advisor fund is higher. That is, we would conclude that investing in the Strong Advisor fund is riskier than investing in the Nations Marisco fund.

Exercises for Section 2.3

CONCEPTS

2.28 Define the range, variance, and standard deviation for a population.

2.29 Discuss how the variance and the standard deviation measure variation.

2.30 Why are the variance and standard deviation usually considered more effective measures of variation than the range?

2.31 The Empirical Rule for a normally distributed population and Chebyshev's Theorem have the same basic purpose. In your own words, explain what this purpose is.

2.32 When is a process capable, and what are process specification limits? Give an example of a situation in which process capability is important.

METHODS AND APPLICATIONS

2.33 Consider the following population of five numbers: 5, 8, 10, 12, 15. Calculate the range, variance, and standard deviation of this population.

2.34 Table 2.9 gives the percentage of homes sold during the fourth quarter of 2004 that a median income household could afford to purchase at the prevailing mortgage interest rate for six Texas metropolitan areas. The data were compiled by the National Association of Home Builders. Calculate the range, variance, and standard deviation of this population of affordability percentages. HouseAff

2.35 Table 2.10 gives data concerning the top 10 U.S. airlines (ranked by revenue) as listed on the *Fortune* magazine website on March 16, 2005. AirRev

a Calculate the population range, variance, and standard deviation of the 10 revenues and of the 10 profits (note that negative values are losses rather than profits).

b Using the population of profits, compute and interpret the z-score for each airline.

2.36 In order to control costs, a company wishes to study the amount of money its sales force spends entertaining clients. The following is a random sample of six entertainment expenses (dinner costs for four people) from expense reports submitted by members of the sales force. DinnerCost

$157 $132 $109 $145 $125 $139

a Calculate $\bar{x}$, s^2, and s for the expense data. In addition, show that the two different formulas for calculating s^2 give the same result.

b Assuming that the distribution of entertainment expenses is approximately normally distributed, calculate estimates of tolerance intervals containing 68.26 percent, 95.44 percent, and 99.73 percent of all entertainment expenses by the sales force.

[6]Source: http://poweredby.morningstar.com/Selectors/AolTop25/AolTop25List.html, March 17, 2005.

[7]Annualized return based on the last 36 monthly returns.

TABLE 2.9 Housing Affordability in Texas HouseAff

Metro Area	Percentage
Austin-San Marcos	66.8%
Dallas	66.4
El Paso	64.8
Houston	69.3
San Antonio	74.4
Fort Worth-Arlington	75.2

Data compiled by National Association of Home Builders.
Source: Housing Affordability in Texas from www.nahb.com/facts/hoi/2004_Q4/.

TABLE 2.10 The Top 10 Airlines (Ranked by Revenue) in 2004 AirRev

Airline	Revenue ($ Billions)	Profit ($ Millions)
American Airlines	17.4	−1228
United Airlines	13.7	−2808
Delta Airlines	13.3	−773
Northwest Airlines	9.5	248
Continental Airlines	8.9	38
US Airways Group	6.8	1461
Southwest Airlines	5.9	442
Alaska Air Group	2.4	14
America West Holdings	2.3	57
ExpressJet Holdings	1.3	108

Source: *Fortune 500*, 3/16/05.

c If a member of the sales force submits an entertainment expense (dinner cost for four) of $190, should this expense be considered unusually high (and possibly worthy of investigation by the company)? Explain your answer.

d Compute and interpret the z-score for each of the six entertainment expenses.

2.37 THE TRASH BAG CASE TrashBag

The mean and the standard deviation of the sample of 40 trash bag breaking strengths are $\bar{x} = 50.575$ and $s = 1.6438$.

a What do the stem-and-leaf display and histogram in Figures 2.19 and 2.20 (page 56) say about whether the Empirical Rule should be used to describe the trash bag breaking strengths?

b Use the Empirical Rule to calculate estimates of tolerance intervals containing 68.26 percent, 95.44 percent, and 99.73 percent of all possible trash bag breaking strengths.

c Does the estimate of a tolerance interval containing 99.73 percent of all breaking strengths provide evidence that almost any bag a customer might purchase will have a breaking strength that exceeds 45 pounds? Explain your answer.

d How do the percentages of the 40 breaking strengths in Table 1.10 (page 19) that actually fall into the intervals $[\bar{x} \pm s]$, $[\bar{x} \pm 2s]$, and $[\bar{x} \pm 3s]$ compare to those given by the Empirical Rule? Do these comparisons indicate that the statistical inferences you made in parts *b* and *c* are reasonably valid?

2.38 THE BANK CUSTOMER WAITING TIME CASE WaitTime

The mean and the standard deviation of the sample of 100 bank customer waiting times are $\bar{x} = 5.46$ and $s = 2.475$.

a What do the stem-and-leaf display and histogram in Figures 2.17 and 2.18 (page 56) say about whether the Empirical Rule should be used to describe the bank customer waiting times?

b Use the Empirical Rule to calculate estimates of tolerance intervals containing 68.26 percent, 95.44 percent, and 99.73 percent of all possible bank customer waiting times.

c Does the estimate of a tolerance interval containing 68.26 percent of all waiting times provide evidence that at least two-thirds of all customers will have to wait less than eight minutes for service? Explain your answer.

d How do the percentages of the 100 waiting times in Table 1.6 (page 11) that actually fall into the intervals $[\bar{x} \pm s]$, $[\bar{x} \pm 2s]$, and $[\bar{x} \pm 3s]$ compare to those given by the Empirical Rule? Do these comparisons indicate that the statistical inferences you made in parts *b* and *c* are reasonably valid?

2.39 THE VIDEO GAME SATISFACTION RATING CASE VideoGame

The mean and the standard deviation of the sample of 65 customer satisfaction ratings are $\bar{x} = 42.95$ and $s = 2.6424$.

a What do the stem-and-leaf display and histogram in Figures 2.14 and 2.15 (pages 54 and 55) say about whether the Empirical Rule should be used to describe the satisfaction ratings?

b Use the Empirical Rule to calculate estimates of tolerance intervals containing 68.26 percent, 95.44 percent, and 99.73 percent of all possible satisfaction ratings.

c Does the estimate of a tolerance interval containing 99.73 percent of all satisfaction ratings provide evidence that 99.73 percent of all customers will give a satisfaction rating for the XYZ-Box game system that is at least 35 (the minimal rating of a "satisfied" customer)? Explain your answer.

d How do the percentages of the 65 customer satisfaction ratings in Table 1.5 (page 11) that actually fall into the intervals $[\bar{x} \pm s]$, $[\bar{x} \pm 2s]$, and $[\bar{x} \pm 3s]$ compare to those given by the Empirical Rule? Do these comparisons indicate that the statistical inferences you made in parts *b* and *c* are reasonably valid?

2.40 Consider the 63 automatic teller machine (ATM) transaction times given in Table 1.12 (page 25).

a Construct a stem-and-leaf display for the 63 ATM transaction times. Describe the shape of the distribution of transaction times. ATMTime

b When we compute the sample mean and sample standard deviation for the transaction times, we find that $\bar{x} = 36.56$ and $s = 4.475$. Compute each of the intervals $[\bar{x} \pm s]$, $[\bar{x} \pm 2s]$, and $[\bar{x} \pm 3s]$. Then count the number of transaction times that actually fall into each interval and find the percentage of transaction times that actually fall into each interval.

c How do the percentages of transaction times that fall into the intervals $[\bar{x} \pm s]$, $[\bar{x} \pm 2s]$, and $[\bar{x} \pm 3s]$ compare to those given by the Empirical Rule? How do the percentages of transaction times that fall into the intervals $[\bar{x} \pm 2s]$ and $[\bar{x} \pm 3s]$ compare to those given by Chebyshev's Theorem?

d Explain why the Empirical Rule does not describe the transaction times extremely well.

2.41 The Morningstar Top Fund lists at the Morningstar.com website give the mean yearly return and the standard deviation of the returns for each of the listed funds. As given by Morningstar.com on March 17, 2005, the RS Internet Age Fund has a mean yearly return of 10.93 percent with a standard deviation of 41.96 percent; the Franklin Income A fund has a mean yearly return of 13 percent with a standard deviation of 9.36 percent; the Jacob Internet fund has a mean yearly return of 34.45 percent with a standard deviation of 41.16 percent.

a For each mutual fund, find an interval in which you would expect 95.44 percent of all yearly returns to fall. Assume returns are normally distributed.

b Using the intervals you computed in part *a*, compare the three mutual funds with respect to average yearly returns and with respect to variability of returns.

c Calculate the coefficient of variation for each mutual fund, and use your results to compare the funds with respect to risk. Which fund is riskier?

2.42 Consider the data concerning a critical dimension of an auto part given in Exercise 1.15 (page 17), and assume the process producing this part is in statistical control.

a When we compute the sample mean and sample standard deviation of the 18 dimensions, we obtain $\bar{x} = 3.0028$ and $s = .01437$. Assuming the dimensions are mound-shaped, use these values to compute an estimated tolerance interval that you would expect to contain almost all (99.73 percent) of the auto part's dimensions. Based on this interval, can we conclude that the process is capable of meeting specifications of 3.00 ± .03—that is, 2.97 to 3.03? Explain your answer.

b After a research and development program is carried out to improve the manufacturing process that produces the auto part, the following 18 measurements of the dimension are obtained (they are given in time order). Does the process appear to be in statistical control? Justify your answer. AutoPart2

Hour	Measurement (Inches)	Hour	Measurement (Inches)
1	3.010	10	3.005
2	3.005	11	2.995
3	2.990	12	2.995
4	3.010	13	3.010
5	2.995	14	3.000
6	2.990	15	2.990
7	3.000	16	2.995
8	2.990	17	3.010
9	3.010	18	3.000

c When we compute the sample mean and sample standard deviation of the 18 observed dimensions from the improved process, we obtain $\bar{x} = 3$ and $s = .00786$. Assuming the measurements are normally distributed, use these results to compute an estimated tolerance interval that you would expect to contain almost all (99.73 percent) of the dimensions produced by the improved process. Based on this interval, can we conclude that the improved process is capable of meeting specifications of 3.00 ± .03—that is, 2.97 to 3.03? Explain your answer.

2.4 Percentiles, Quartiles, and Box-and-Whiskers Displays

Percentiles, quartiles, and five-number displays In this section we consider **percentiles** and their applications. We begin by defining the ***p*th percentile.**

For a set of measurements arranged in increasing order, the ***p*th percentile** is a value such that p percent of the measurements fall at or below the value, and $(100 - p)$ percent of the measurements fall at or above the value.

There are various procedures for calculating percentiles. One procedure is as follows: To calculate the pth percentile for a set of n measurements, we first arrange the measurements in increasing order (by, for example, constructing a stem-and-leaf display). Then we calculate the index $i = (p/100)n$. If i is not an integer, the next integer greater than i denotes the position of the pth percentile in the ordered arrangement. If i is an integer, then the pth percentile is the average of the measurements in positions i and $i + 1$ in the ordered arrangement. For example, Figure 2.33(a) presents the stem-and-leaf display of the 65 payment times. In order to calculate the 75th percentile of these 65 payment times, we calculate the index $i = (75/100)65 = 48.75$. Because $i = 48.75$ is not an integer, the 75th percentile is the 49th payment time in the stem-and-leaf display. Counting up to the 49th payment time in this display, we find that the 75th percentile is 21 days (see Figure 2.33(a)). This implies that we estimate that approximately 75 percent of all payment times are less than or equal to 21 days. As another example, Figure 2.33(b) presents the stem-and-leaf display of the 60 bottle design ratings. In order to calculate the fifth percentile of these 60 ratings, we calculate the index $i = (5/100)60 = 3$. Because $i = 3$ is an integer, the fifth percentile is the average of the third and fourth ratings in the stem-and-leaf display. Counting up to these ratings in this display, we find that the fifth percentile is $(24 + 25)/2 = 24.5$ (see Figure 2.33(b)). Since any rating is a whole number, we estimate that approximately 5 percent of all ratings are 24 or less and that approximately 95 percent of all ratings are 25 or more.

In general, unless percentiles correspond to very high or very low percentages, they are resistant (like the median) to extreme values. For example, the 75th percentile of the payment times would remain 21 days even if the three largest payment times—26, 27, and 29—were, instead, 35, 56, and 84. On the other hand, the standard deviation in this situation would increase from 3.9612 to 10.2119. In general, if a population is highly skewed to the right or left, it can be best to describe the variation of the population by using various percentiles. For example, we might

FIGURE 2.33 Using Stem-and-Leaf Displays to Find Percentiles and Five-Number Summaries

(a) The 75th percentile of the 65 payment times, and a five-number summary

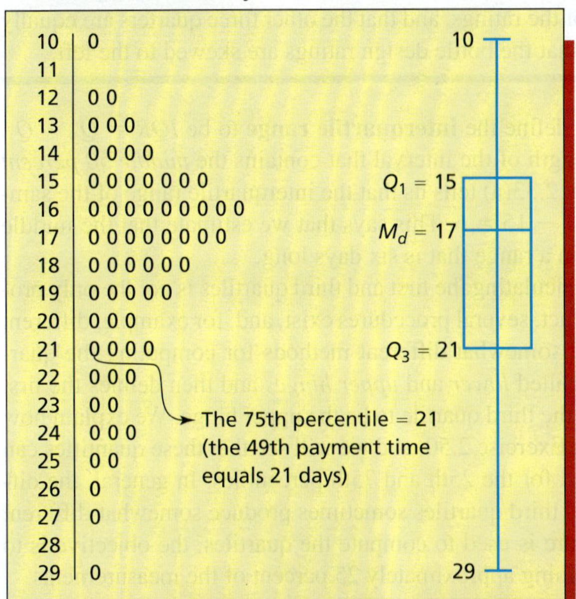

(b) The 5th percentile of the 60 bottle design ratings, and a five-number summary

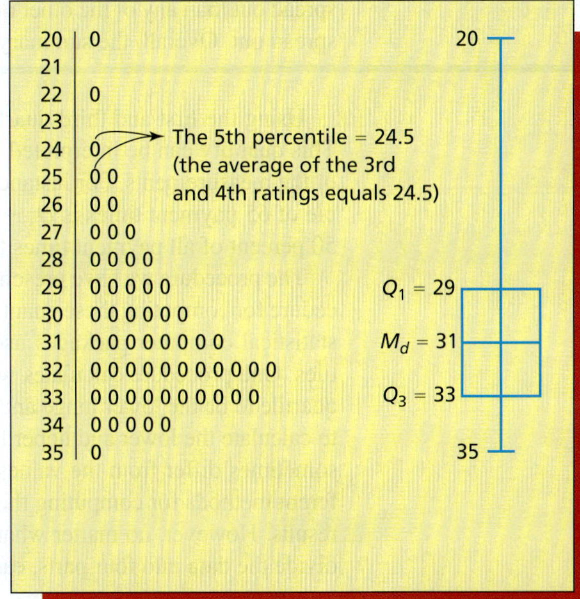

describe the variation of the yearly incomes of all people in the United States by using the 10th, 25th, 50th, 75th, and 90th percentiles of these incomes.

One appealing way to describe the variation of a set of measurements is to divide the data into four parts, each containing approximately 25 percent of the measurements. This can be done by defining the *first, second,* and *third quartiles* as follows:

The **first quartile,** denoted Q_1, is the **25th percentile.**
The **second quartile** (or **median**), denoted M_d, is the **50th percentile.**
The **third quartile,** denoted Q_3, is the **75th percentile.**

Note that the second quartile is simply another name for the median. Furthermore, the procedure we have described here that would be used to find the 50th percentile (second quartile) will always give the same result as the previously described (see Section 2.2) procedure for finding the median. For example, to find the second quartile of the 65 payment times, we find the 50th percentile by calculating $i = (50/100)65 = 32.5$, which says that the second quartile is the 33rd payment time in the stem-and-leaf display of Figure 2.33(a). Counting up to the 33rd payment time in the display, we find that the second quartile equals 17, which is the result we obtained for the median of the payment times in Example 2.9 (page 63).

Example 2.15 The Payment Time Case

Since $i = (25/100)65 = 16.25$, the first quartile (25th percentile) of the 65 payment times is the 17th payment time in the stem-and-leaf display of Figure 2.33(a). Therefore, $Q_1 = 15$. Remembering that the median of the payment times is 17, and that the 75th percentile of the payment times is 21, the quartiles are $Q_1 = 15$, $M_d = 17$, and $Q_3 = 21$.

We often describe a set of measurements by using a *five-number summary.* The summary consists of (1) the smallest measurement; (2) the first quartile, Q_1; (3) the median, M_d; (4) the third quartile, Q_3; and (5) the largest measurement. It is easy to graphically depict a five-number summary; we have done this for the 65 payment times alongside the stem-and-leaf display of Figure 2.33(a). Notice that we have drawn a vertical line extending from the smallest payment time to the largest payment time. In addition, a rectangle is drawn that extends from Q_1 to Q_3, and a horizontal line is drawn to indicate the location of the median. The summary divides the payment times into four parts, with the middle 50 percent of the payment times depicted by the rectangle. The summary indicates that the largest 25 percent of the payment times is more spread out than the smallest 25 percent of the payment times, and that the second-largest 25 percent of the payment times is more spread out than the second-smallest 25 percent of the payment times. Overall, the summary indicates that the payment times are somewhat skewed to the right.

As another example, for the 60 bottle design ratings, $Q_1 = 29$, $M_d = 31$, and $Q_3 = 33$. The graphical five-number summary of the ratings is shown alongside the stem-and-leaf display of the ratings in Figure 2.33(b). The summary shows that the smallest 25 percent of the ratings is more spread out than any of the other quarters of the ratings, and that the other three quarters are equally spread out. Overall, the summary shows that the bottle design ratings are skewed to the left.

Using the first and third quartiles, we define the **interquartile range** to be $IQR = Q_3 - Q_1$. This quantity can be interpreted as the length of the interval that contains the *middle 50 percent* of the measurements. For instance, Figure 2.33(a) tells us that the interquartile range of the sample of 65 payment times is $Q_3 - Q_1 = 21 - 15 = 6$. This says that we estimate that the middle 50 percent of all payment times fall within a range that is six days long.

The procedure we have presented for calculating the first and third quartiles is not the only procedure for computing these quantities. In fact, several procedures exist, and, for example, different statistical computer packages use several somewhat different methods for computing the quartiles. One procedure calculates what are called *lower* and *upper hinges* and then defines the first quartile to be the lower hinge and defines the third quartile to be the upper hinge. We explain how to calculate the lower and upper hinges in Exercise 2.50, and we will see that these quantities can sometimes differ from the values obtained for the 25th and 75th percentiles. In general, the different methods for computing the first and third quartiles sometimes produce somewhat different results. However, no matter what procedure is used to compute the quartiles, the objective is to divide the data into four parts, each containing approximately 25 percent of the measurements.

Box-and-whiskers displays (box plots) A more sophisticated modification of the graphical five-number summary is called a **box-and-whiskers display** (sometimes called a **box plot**). Such a display is constructed by using Q_1, M_d, Q_3, and the interquartile range. As an example, again consider the 20 customer satisfaction ratings

1 3 5 5 7 8 8 8 8 8 8 9 9 9 9 9 10 10 10 10

for which it can be shown that $Q_1 = 7.5$, $M_d = 8$, $Q_3 = 9$, and $IQR = Q_3 - Q_1 = 9 - 7.5 = 1.5$. To construct a box-and-whiskers display, we first draw a box that extends from Q_1 to Q_3. As shown in Figure 2.34(a), for the satisfaction ratings data this box extends from $Q_1 = 7.5$ to $Q_3 = 9$. The box contains the middle 50 percent of the data set. Next a vertical line is drawn through the box at the value of the median M_d (sometimes a plus sign (+) is plotted at the median instead of a vertical line). This line divides the data set into two roughly equal parts. We next define what we call **inner** and **outer fences.** The **inner fences** are located $1.5 \times IQR$ below Q_1 and $1.5 \times IQR$ above Q_3. For the satisfaction ratings data, the inner fences are

$$Q_1 - 1.5(IQR) = 7.5 - 1.5(1.5) = 5.25 \quad \text{and} \quad Q_3 + 1.5(IQR) = 9 + 1.5(1.5) = 11.25$$

(again see Figure 2.34(a)). The **outer fences** are located $3 \times IQR$ below Q_1 and $3 \times IQR$ above Q_3. For the satisfaction ratings data, the outer fences are

$$Q_1 - 3(IQR) = 7.5 - 3(1.5) = 3.0 \quad \text{and} \quad Q_3 + 3(IQR) = 9 + 3(1.5) = 13.5$$

FIGURE 2.34 A Box-and-Whiskers Display of the Satisfaction Ratings

(a) Constructing the display

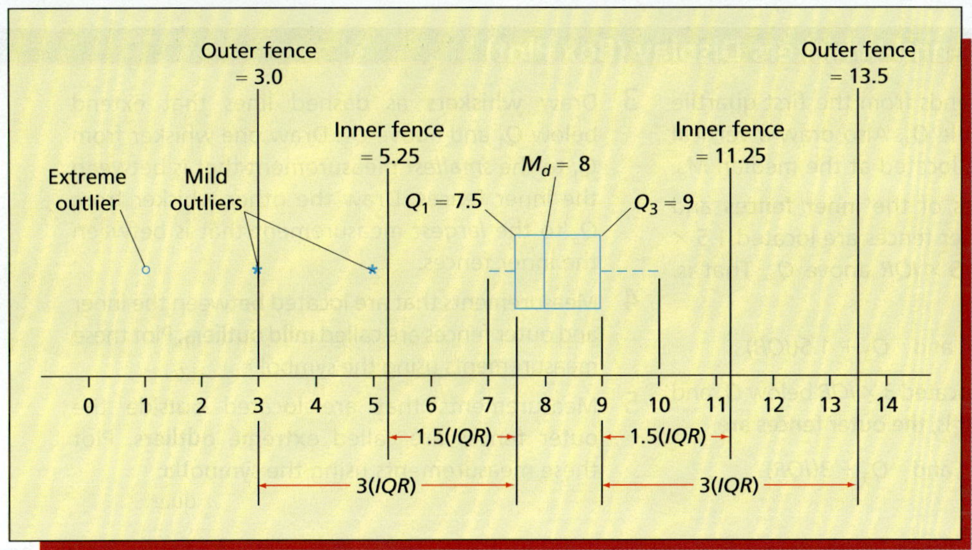

(b) MINITAB output

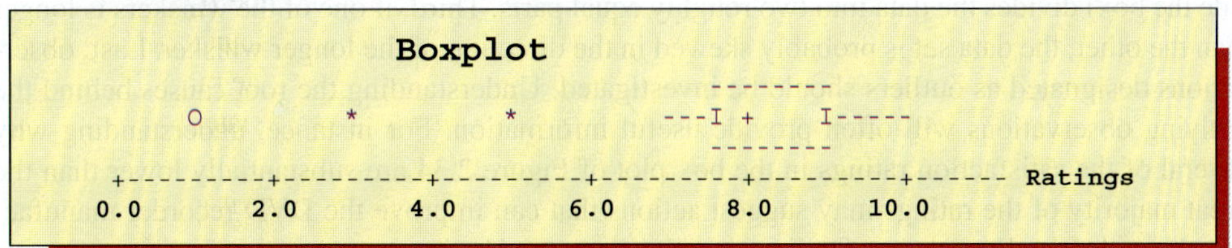

(c) MegaStat output

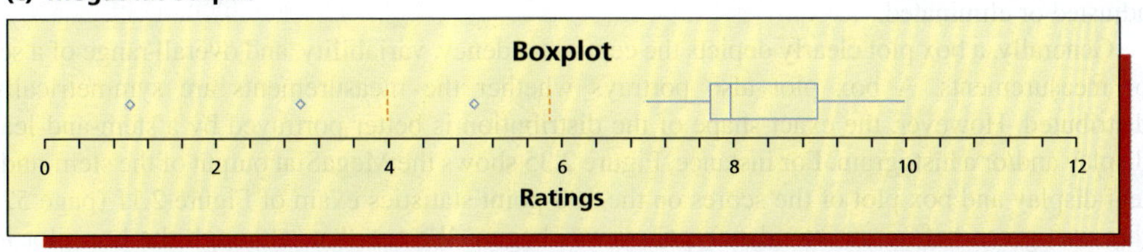

(these are also shown in Figure 2.34(a)). The inner and outer fences help us to draw the plot's **whiskers:** dashed lines extending below Q_1 and above Q_3 (as in Figure 2.34(a)). One whisker is drawn from Q_1 to the smallest measurement between the inner fences. For the satisfaction ratings data, this whisker extends from $Q_1 = 7.5$ down to 7, because 7 is the smallest rating between the inner fences 5.25 and 11.25. The other whisker is drawn from Q_3 to the largest measurement between the inner fences. For the satisfaction ratings data, this whisker extends from $Q_3 = 9$ up to 10, because 10 is the largest rating between the inner fences 5.25 and 11.25. The inner and outer fences are also used to identify **outliers.** An **outlier** is a measurement that is separated from (that is, different from) most of the other measurements in the data set. Measurements that are located between the inner and outer fences are considered to be **mild outliers,** whereas measurements that are located outside the outer fences are considered to be **extreme outliers.** We indicate the locations of mild outliers by plotting these measurements with the symbol $*$, and we indicate the locations of extreme outliers by plotting these measurements with the symbol o. For the satisfaction ratings data, the ratings 3 and 5 are mild outliers ($*$) because these ratings are between the inner fence of 5.25 and the outer fence of 3.0. The rating 1 is an extreme outlier (o) because this rating is outside the outer fence 3.0. These outliers are plotted in Figure 2.34(a). Parts (b) and (c) of Figure 2.34 give MINITAB and MegaStat outputs of the box-and-whiskers plot. Notice that MINITAB identifies the median by using a plus sign (+), while MegaStat uses a vertical line. In addition, MegaStat plots all outliers using the same symbol and marks the inner and outer fences using vertical dashed lines. Note here that MegaStat computes the quartiles Q_1 and Q_3 and the inner and outer fences using methods that differ slightly from the methods we have described. The MegaStat Help menus describe how the calculations are done. We now summarize how to construct a box-and-whiskers plot.

Constructing a Box-and-Whiskers Display (Box Plot)

1 Draw a **box** that extends from the first quartile Q_1 to the third quartile Q_3. Also draw a vertical line through the box located at the median M_d.

2 Determine the values of the **inner fences** and **outer fences.** The inner fences are located $1.5 \times IQR$ below Q_1 and $1.5 \times IQR$ above Q_3. That is, **the inner fences are**

$$Q_1 - 1.5(IQR) \quad \text{and} \quad Q_3 + 1.5(IQR)$$

The outer fences are located $3 \times IQR$ below Q_1 and $3 \times IQR$ above Q_3. That is, **the outer fences are**

$$Q_1 - 3(IQR) \quad \text{and} \quad Q_3 + 3(IQR)$$

3 Draw **whiskers** as dashed lines that extend below Q_1 and above Q_3. Draw one whisker from Q_1 to the *smallest* measurement that is between the inner fences. Draw the other whisker from Q_3 to the *largest* measurement that is between the inner fences.

4 Measurements that are located between the inner and outer fences are called **mild outliers.** Plot these measurements using the symbol $*$.

5 Measurements that are located outside the outer fences are called **extreme outliers.** Plot these measurements using the symbol o.

When interpreting a box-and-whiskers display, keep several points in mind. First, the box (between Q_1 and Q_3) contains the middle 50 percent of the data. Second, the median (which is inside the box) divides the data into two roughly equal parts. Third, if one of the whiskers is longer than the other, the data set is probably skewed in the direction of the longer whisker. Last, observations designated as outliers should be investigated. Understanding the root causes behind the outlying observations will often provide useful information. For instance, understanding why several of the satisfaction ratings in the box plot of Figure 2.34 are substantially lower than the great majority of the ratings may suggest actions that can improve the DVD recorder manufacturer's product and/or service. Outliers can also be caused by inaccurate measuring, reporting, or plotting of the data. Such possibilities should be investigated, and incorrect data should be adjusted or eliminated.

Generally, a box plot clearly depicts the central tendency, variability, and overall range of a set of measurements. A box plot also portrays whether the measurements are symmetrically distributed. However, the exact shape of the distribution is better portrayed by a stem-and-leaf display and/or a histogram. For instance, Figure 2.35 shows the MegaStat output of the stem-and-leaf display and box plot of the scores on the 100-point statistics exam of Figure 2.11 (page 52) that was given before an attendance policy was begun. We see that, although the box plot in Figure 2.35 tells us that the exam scores are somewhat skewed with a tail to the left, it does not

FIGURE 2.35 MegaStat Output of a Stem-and-Leaf Display and Box Plot of the Exam Scores

Stem and Leaf plot for ExamScore

stem unit = 10 leaf unit = 1

Frequency	Stem	Leaf
1	3	2
0	3	
0	4	
1	4	5
1	5	0
2	5	68
6	6	011344
7	6	5677899
1	7	2
2	7	68
3	8	133
6	8	567789
8	9	00122334
2	9	68
40		

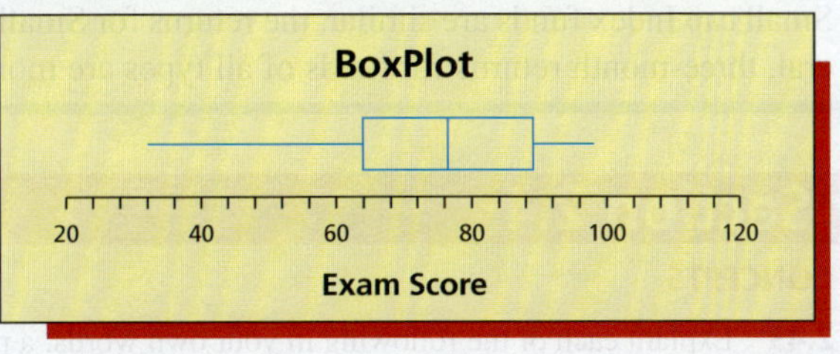

FIGURE 2.36 Graphical Comparison of the Performance of Mutual Funds by Using Five-Number Summaries

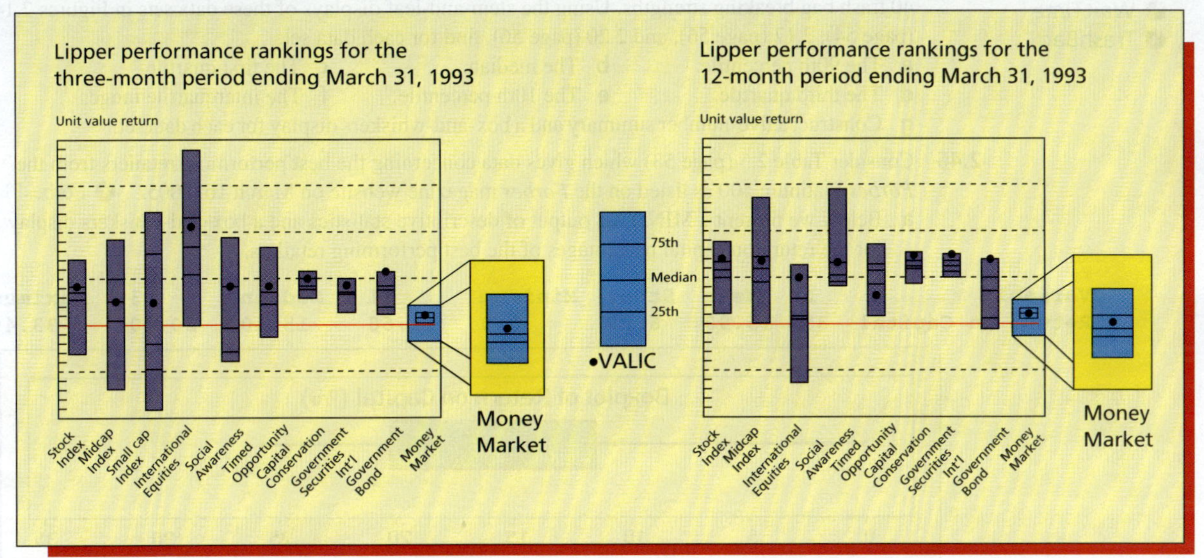

Source: Reprinted by permission of Lipper, Inc.

reveal the double-peaked nature of the exam score distribution. On the other hand, the stem-and-leaf display clearly shows that this distribution is double-peaked.

Graphical five-number summaries and box-and-whiskers displays are perhaps best used to compare different sets of measurements. We demonstrate this use of such displays in the following example.

Example 2.16 The VALIC Case

In July of 1993, the Variable Annuity Life Insurance Company (VALIC) sent its investors an analysis of the performance of its variable account mutual fund options relative to other variable annuity fund options in various categories (stock index, money market, and so forth). VALIC used the graphical five-number summaries in Figure 2.36 to summarize and compare performances. The dot within each five-number summary represents the return of the VALIC mutual fund option for that category. In explaining the plots, VALIC said

> The data show that all of VALIC's mutual fund options ranked at or above their respective category median return for the three-month period ending March 31, 1993. Also, eight of VALIC's mutual fund options ranked above their respective category median return for the 12-month period ending March 31, 1993.

Notice that the lengths of the five number summaries indicate performance variability for the various funds. For example, while the median three-month returns for Midcap Index funds and Small cap Index funds are similar, the returns for Small cap funds are more variable. Also, in general, three-month returns for funds of all types are more variable than 12-month returns.

Exercises for Section 2.4

CONCEPTS

2.43 Explain each of the following in your own words: a percentile; the first quartile, Q_1; the third quartile, Q_3; and the interquartile range, *IQR*.

2.44 Suppose that we are using a box-and-whiskers plot to depict a population or sample of measurements. How would you interpret each of the following?

a The whisker to the right is much longer than the whisker to the left.

b The interquartile range is much longer than either of the whiskers and there are no outliers.

c The distance between Q_1 and the median is far less than the distance between the median and Q_3.

d The interquartile range is very short.

METHODS AND APPLICATIONS

VideoGame
WaitTime
TrashBag

2.45 Consider the 65 game system satisfaction ratings, the 100 bank customer waiting times, and the 40 trash bag breaking strengths. Using the stem-and-leaf displays of these data sets in Figures 2.14 (page 54), 2.17 (page 56), and 2.20 (page 56), find for each data set:

a The 90th percentile. **b** The median. **c** The first quartile.
d The third quartile. **e** The 10th percentile. **f** The interquartile range.
g Construct a five-number summary and a box-and-whiskers display for each data set.

2.46 Consider Table 2.5 (page 53) which gives data concerning the best performing retailers from the *Forbes* Platinum 400 as listed on the *Forbes* magazine website on March 16, 2005. ForbesPlat

a Below we present a MINITAB output of descriptive statistics and a box-and-whiskers display for the return on capital percentages of the best performing retailers.

Variable	N	Mean	StDev	Minimum	Q1	Median	Q3	Maximum
Return on Capital	35	15.90	6.39	0.0	11.60	15.40	20.30	33.40

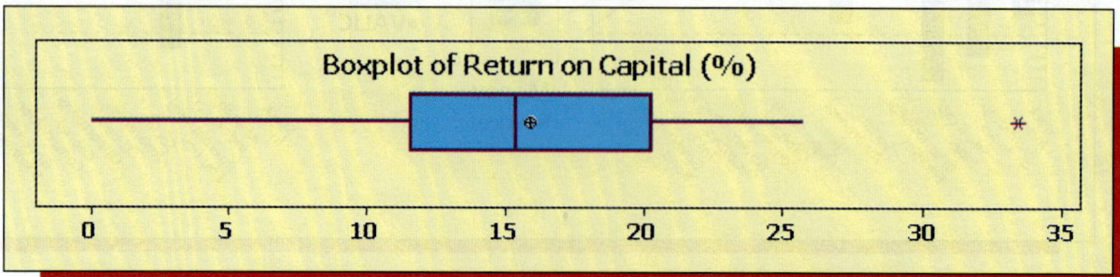

Using the MINITAB output, describe the distribution of the return on capital percentages with respect to central tendency, variability, skewness, and outliers.

b Below we present a MegaStat output of descriptive statistics and a box-and-whiskers display for the total return percentages of the 30 fastest growing companies as given on the *Fortune* magazine website on March 16, 2005. FastGrow

Total Return					
count	30	minimum	-1	1st quartile	29.00
mean	59.47	maximum	218	median	44.50
sample variance	2,183.02	range	219	3rd quartile	74.25
sample standard deviation	46.72			interquartile range	45.25

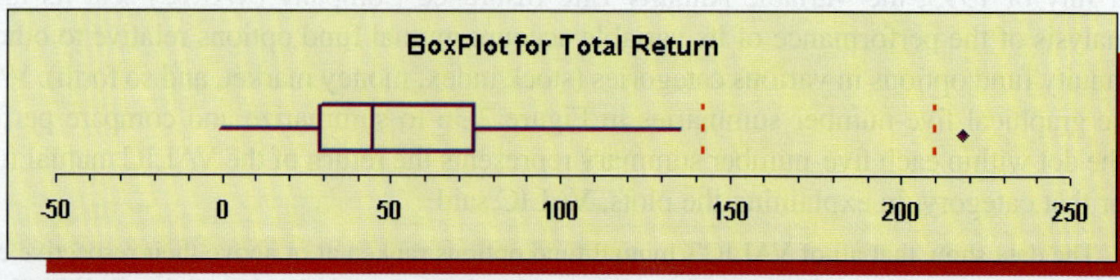

Using the MegaStat output, describe the distribution of the return on capital percentages with respect to central tendency, variability, skewness, and outliers.

2.47 On its website, the *Statesman Journal* newspaper (Salem, Oregon, 2005) reports mortgage loan interest rates for 30-year and 15-year fixed-rate mortgage loans for a number of Willamette Valley lending institutions. Of interest is whether there is any systematic difference between 30-year rates and 15-year rates (expressed as annual percentage rate or APR) and, if there is, what is the size of that difference. The following table displays the 30-year rate and the 15-year rate for each of nine lending institutions. Also given is the difference between the 30-year rate and the 15-year rate for each lending institution. To the right of the table are given side-by-side MINITAB box-and-whiskers plots of the 30-year rates and the 15-year rates and a MINITAB box-and-whiskers plot of the differences between the rates. Use the box-and-whiskers plots to compare the 30-year rates and the 15-year rates. Also, calculate the average of the differences between the rates. Mortgage

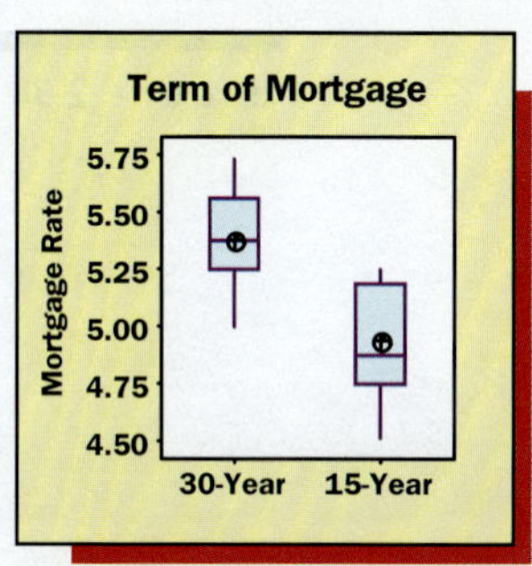

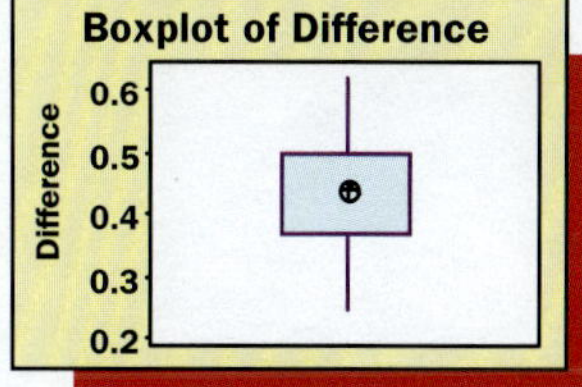

Lending Institution	30-Year	15-Year	Difference
Blue Ribbon Home Mortgage	5.375	4.750	0.625
Coast To Coast Mortgage Lending	5.250	4.750	0.500
Community Mortgage Services Inc.	5.000	4.500	0.500
Liberty Mortgage	5.375	4.875	0.500
Jim Morrison's MBI	5.250	4.875	0.375
Professional Valley Mortgage	5.250	5.000	0.250
Mortgage First	5.750	5.250	0.500
Professional Mortgage Corporation	5.500	5.125	0.375
Resident Lending Group Inc.	5.625	5.250	0.375

Source: http://online.statesmanjournal.com/mortrates.cfm

2.48 In the book *Business Research Methods,* Donald R. Cooper and C. William Emory present box-and-whiskers plots comparing the net profits of firms in five different industry sectors. Each plot (for a sector) was constructed using net profit figures for a sample of firms from the *Forbes* 500s. Figure 2.37 gives the five box-and-whiskers plots.

a Using the plots in Figure 2.37, write an analysis comparing net profits for the five sectors. Compare central tendency, variability, skewness, and outliers.

b For which sectors are net profits most variable? Least variable?

c Which sectors provide opportunities for the highest net profits?

2.49 Figure 2.38 gives seven pairs of five-number summaries presented in an article in the January 1995 issue of *Quality Progress.* In the article, authors Dale H. Myers and Jeffrey Heller discuss how AT&T has employed a quality award process (called the Chairman's Quality Award or CQA) to improve quality. To quote Myers and Heller:

> In 1989, AT&T began searching for a systematic process to achieve two major goals: aligning its business management systems more closely with customers' needs and integrating quality

FIGURE 2.37 Box-and-Whiskers Plots Comparing Net Profits for Five Industry Sectors (for Exercise 2.48)

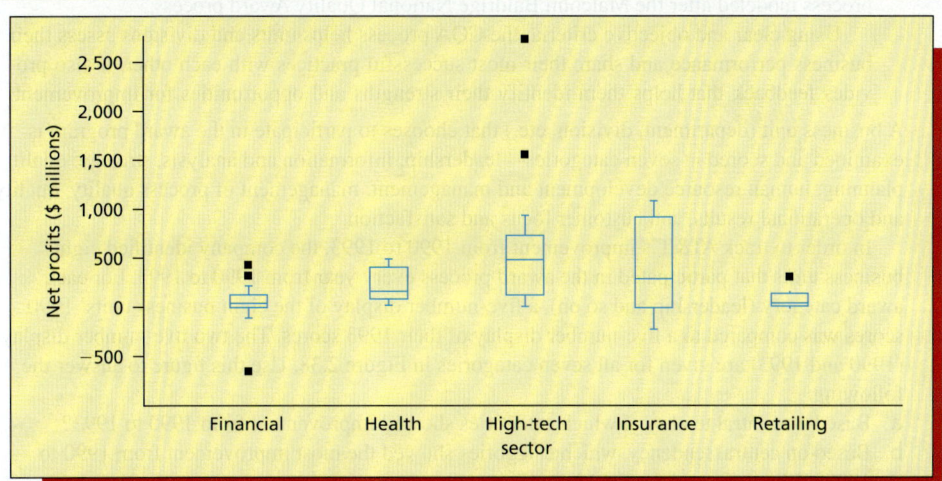

Data from: "The *Forbes* 500s Annual Directory," *Forbes,* April 30, 1990, pp. 221–434.

Source: D. R. Cooper and C. W. Emory, *Business Research Methods,* p. 409. Copyright © 1995. Reprinted by permission of McGraw-Hill Companies, Inc.

FIGURE 2.38 **Comparison of AT&T Chairman's Quality Award Scores from 1990 to 1993 for Eight Business Units (for Exercise 2.49)**

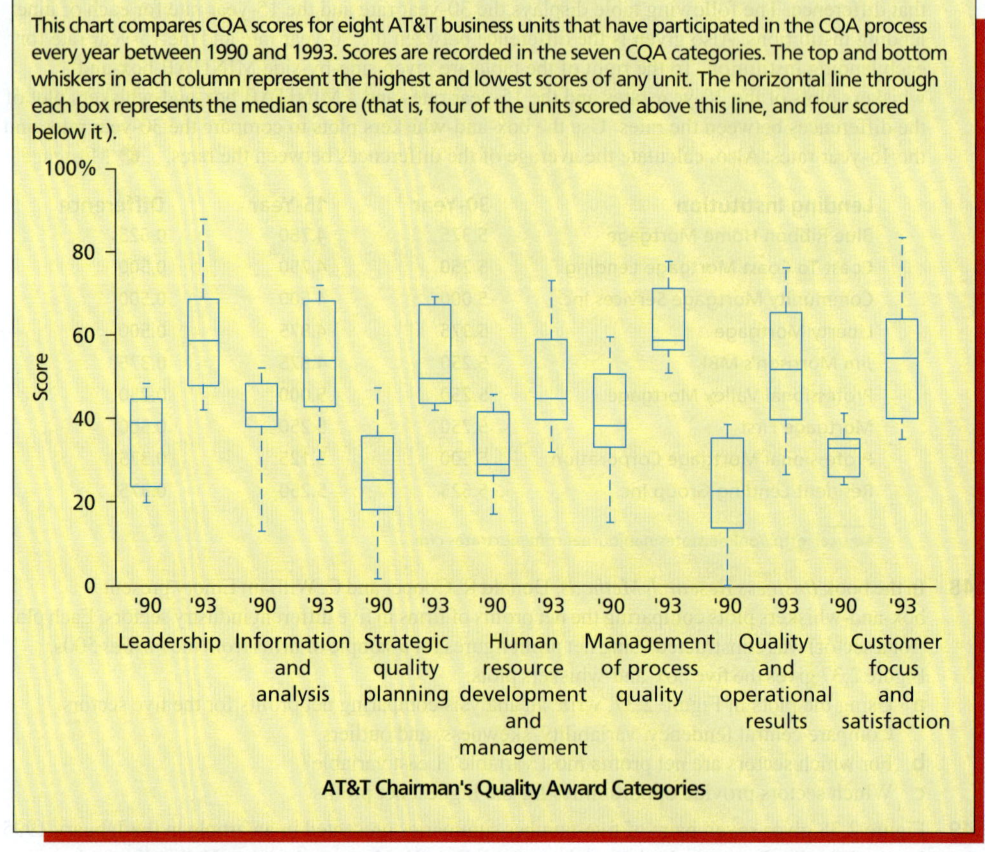
This chart compares CQA scores for eight AT&T business units that have participated in the CQA process every year between 1990 and 1993. Scores are recorded in the seven CQA categories. The top and bottom whiskers in each column represent the highest and lowest scores of any unit. The horizontal line through each box represents the median score (that is, four of the units scored above this line, and four scored below it).
100%
80
60
40
20
0
Score
'90 '93 '90 '93 '90 '93 '90 '93 '90 '93 '90 '93 '90 '93
Leadership
Information and analysis
Strategic quality planning
Human resource development and management
Management of process quality
Quality and operational results
Customer focus and satisfaction
AT&T Chairman's Quality Award Categories

Source: D. H. Myers and J. Heller, "The Dual Role of AT&T's Self-Assessment Process," *Quality Progress*, January 1995, pp. 79–83.

> principles into every business practice. AT&T wanted this new process to be based on clear and quantifiable standards so that its key building blocks—the business units and divisions—could objectively assess the strengths and shortcomings of their operations.
>
> Within a year, AT&T took its first major step into the world of objective self-assessment. The New Jersey–based telecommunications giant created a Chairman's Quality Award (CQA) process modeled after the Malcolm Baldrige National Quality Award process.[8]
>
> Using clear and objective criteria, the CQA process helps units and divisions assess their business performance and share their most successful practices with each other. It also provides feedback that helps them identify their strengths and opportunities for improvement.

A business unit (department, division, etc.) that chooses to participate in the award program is examined and scored in seven categories—leadership, information and analysis, strategic quality planning, human resource development and management, management of process quality, quality and operational results, and customer focus and satisfaction.

In order to track AT&T's improvement from 1990 to 1993, the company identified eight business units that participated in the award process every year from 1990 to 1993. For each award category (leadership and so on), a five-number display of the eight business units' 1990 scores was compared to a five-number display of their 1993 scores. The two five-number displays (1990 and 1993) are given for all seven categories in Figure 2.38. Use this figure to answer the following:

a Based on central tendency, which categories showed improvement from 1990 to 1993?

b Based on central tendency, which categories showed the most improvement from 1990 to 1993? Which showed the least improvement?

[8]We discuss the Malcolm Baldrige National Quality Award process in Chapter 14.

c In which categories did the variability of the CQA scores increase from 1990 to 1993? In which categories did the variability decrease? In which categories did the variability remain about the same from 1990 to 1993?

d In which categories did the nature of the skewness of the CQA scores change from 1990 to 1993? Interpret these changes.

2.50 In Section 2.4 we presented a commonly accepted way to compute the first, second, and third quartiles. Some statisticians, however, advocate an alternative method for computing Q_1 and Q_3. This method defines the first quartile, Q_1, as what is called the *lower hinge* and defines the third quartile, Q_3, as the *upper hinge*. In order to calculate these quantities for a set of n measurements, we first arrange the measurements in increasing order. Then, if n is even, the *lower hinge* is the median of the smallest $n/2$ measurements, and the *upper hinge* is the median of the largest $n/2$ measurements. If n is odd, we insert M_d into the data set to obtain a set of $n + 1$ measurements. Then the *lower hinge* is the median of the smallest $(n + 1)/2$ measurements, and the *upper hinge* is the median of the largest $(n + 1)/2$ measurements.

a Consider the sample of $n = 20$ customer satisfaction ratings:

1 3 5 5 7 8 8 8 8 8   8 9 9 9 9 9 10 10 10 10

The smallest 10 ratings   The largest 10 ratings

Using the method presented in Section 2.4 (pages 79 to 80), find Q_1 and Q_3. Then find the lower hinge and the upper hinge for the satisfaction ratings. How do your results compare? DVDSat

b Consider the following sample of $n = 11$ doctors' salaries (in thousands of dollars):

127 132 138 141 146 152 154 171 177 192 241

Using the method presented in Section 2.4, find Q_1 and Q_3. The median of the 11 salaries is M_d = 152. If we insert this median into the data set, we obtain the following set of $n + 1 = 12$ salaries:

127 132 138 141 146 152   152 154 171 177 192 241

The smallest 6 salaries   The largest 6 salaries

Find the lower hinge and the upper hinge for the salaries. Compare your values of Q_1 and Q_3 with the lower and upper hinges. DrSalary

c For the 11 doctors' salaries, which quantities (Q_1, M_d, and Q_3 as defined in Section 2.4) or (the lower hinge, M_d, and the upper hinge) in your opinion best divide the salaries into four parts?

2.5 Describing Qualitative Data

Bar charts and pie charts Recall that when we employ a **qualitative** or **categorical variable** we simply record into which of several categories a population element falls. For example, for each automobile produced in the United States we might record the manufacturer—Chrysler, Ford, General Motors, a Japanese manufacturer, or some other manufacturer. We often display such data graphically. For instance, Figure 2.39 gives the Excel output of a **bar chart** of the percentages of automobiles sold in the United States in 1997 by these manufacturers. Figure 2.40 gives the Excel output of a **pie chart** of these percentages, while Figure 2.41 gives a MINITAB bar chart comparing the percentages sold by the manufacturers in 1970 with the percentages sold in 1997. Figure 2.42 makes the same comparison by using two pie charts. Notice the declining percentages of automobiles sold by Chrysler, Ford, and General Motors, and the increased percentage of automobiles sold by Japanese manufacturers. We have emphasized the increase in the percentage sold by Japanese manufacturers by *exploding* their *pie slices* in Figure 2.42.

In general, bar charts and pie charts are convenient ways to summarize the percentages of population units that are contained in several different categories.

Estimating proportions Suppose that a population unit can fall into one of several categories. Often we are interested in a specific category, and, in such cases, we often wish to estimate

p = the proportion of all population elements that are contained in the category of interest

In order to estimate this proportion, we can randomly select a sample from the population. Then the **sample proportion**

$\hat{p}$ = the proportion of the sample elements that are contained in the category of interest

is a reasonable point estimate of the **population proportion** p.

FIGURE 2.39 An Excel Bar Chart of U.S. Automobile Sales in 1997 AutoShares97

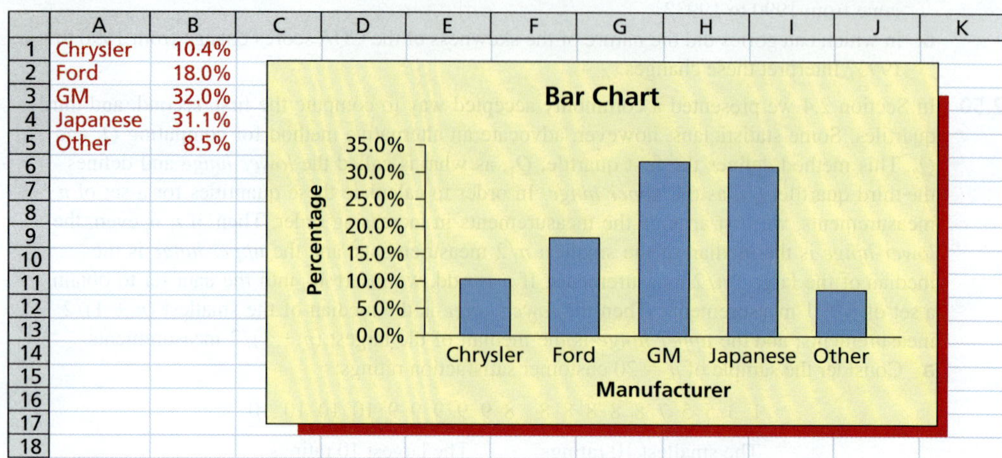

FIGURE 2.40 An Excel Pie Chart of U.S. Automobile Sales in 1997

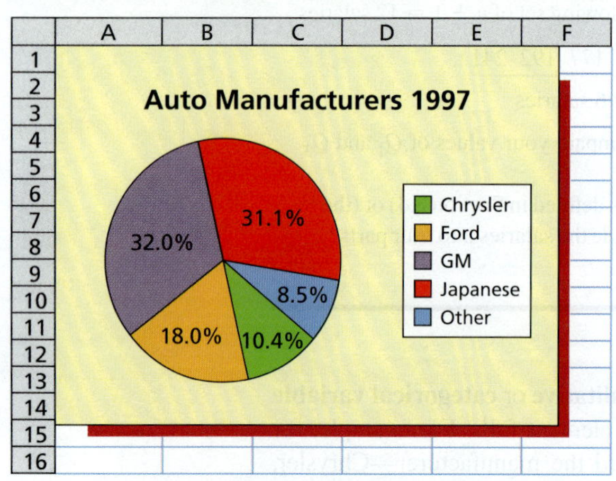

FIGURE 2.41 A MINITAB Bar Chart Comparing 1997 U.S. Automobile Sales with Those in 1970

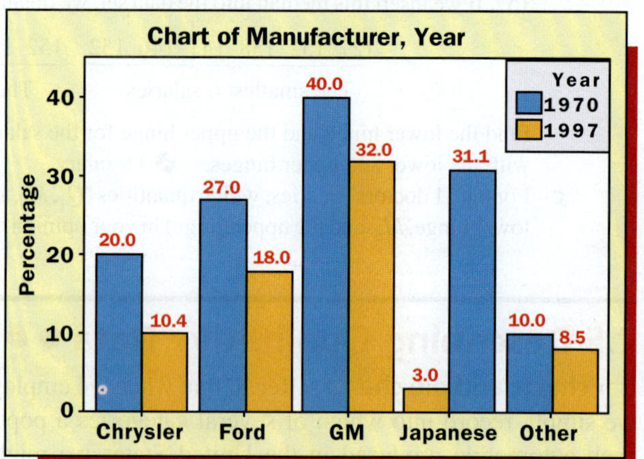

FIGURE 2.42 Two MINITAB Pie Charts Comparing the Percentages of Automobiles Sold by Different Manufacturers in 1970 with Those in 1997

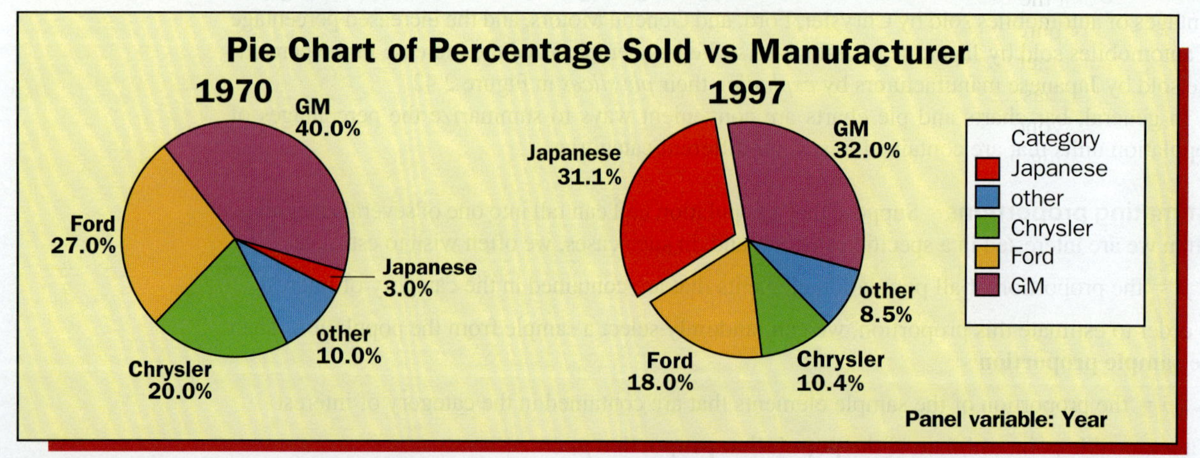

In the following examples, we introduce two new cases that illustrate estimating a population proportion p.

Example 2.17 The Marketing Ethics Case: Estimating Marketing Researchers' Disapproval Rates

In the book *Essentials of Marketing Research,* William R. Dillon, Thomas J. Madden, and Neil H. Firtle discuss a survey of marketing professionals, the results of which were originally published by Ishmael P. Akoah and Edward A. Riordan in the *Journal of Marketing Research.* In the study, marketing researchers were presented with various scenarios involving ethical issues such as confidentiality, conflict of interest, and social acceptability. The marketing researchers were asked to indicate whether they approved or disapproved of the actions described in each scenario. For instance, one scenario that involved the issue of confidentiality was described as follows:

> **Use of ultraviolet ink** A project director went to the marketing research director's office and requested permission to use an ultraviolet ink to precode a questionnaire for a mail survey. The project director pointed out that although the cover letter promised confidentiality, respondent identification was needed to permit adequate cross-tabulations of the data. The marketing research director gave approval.

Of the 205 marketing researchers who participated in the survey, 117 said they disapproved of the actions taken in the scenario.

In this situation we would like to make an inference about the population of all marketing researchers. Specifically, we wish to estimate the *population proportion*

p = the proportion of all marketing researchers who disapprove of the actions taken in the ultraviolet ink scenario

Since 117 of the 205 surveyed marketing researchers said they disapproved, the *sample proportion*

$$\hat{p} = \frac{117}{205} = .57$$

is the point estimate of p. This point estimate says we estimate that p, the proportion of all marketing researchers who disapprove, is .57. That is, we estimate that 57 percent of all marketing researchers disapprove of the actions taken in the ultraviolet ink scenario.

Example 2.18 The Electronic Article Surveillance Case: Estimating Consumer Reaction to False Alarms

In an article titled "Consumer Responses to Electronic Article Surveillance Alarms" in the *Journal of Retailing,* Scott Dawson studies the unintended effects of false electronic article surveillance alarms. As Dawson explains in the article, in 1990 estimated annual losses from shoplifting were $50 billion. Electronic article surveillance (EAS), an important weapon used by retailers to combat shoplifting, places a small sensor on an item of merchandise. If a shoplifter attempts to exit the store with the item, an electronic alarm is set off by the sensor. When an item is legitimately purchased, the sales clerk removes the sensor to prevent the alarm from sounding when the customer exits the store. Sometimes, however, the clerk forgets to remove the sensor during the purchase. This results in a false alarm when the customer exits—an embarrassing situation for everyone involved (especially the customer). Such false alarms occur quite frequently. In fact, according to Dawson's article "nearly half of all consumers have experienced an accidental EAS alarm."

Dawson conducted a survey to study consumer reaction to such false alarms. Based on a systematic random sample of 250 consumers, he found that 40 of these consumers said that, if they were to set off an EAS alarm because store personnel did not deactivate the merchandise, then "they would never shop at the store again."

Suppose we wish to estimate p, the population proportion of all consumers who would say they would never shop at the store again if subjected to an EAS false alarm. Since 40 of the 250 sampled consumers said they would never shop at the store again, the sample proportion $\hat{p} = 40/250 = .16$ is the point estimate of p. This point estimate says we estimate that 16 percent of all consumers would say they would never shop at the store again if subjected to an EAS false alarm.

Finally, suppose a retailer is considering the installation of an EAS system. In an attempt to convince the retailer to purchase the system, a company that markets EAS systems claims that no more than 5 percent of consumers would say that they would never shop at a store again if they were subjected to an EAS false alarm. Based on Dawson's survey results, the retailer would have a hard time believing this claim. That is, the sample proportion $\hat{p} = .16$ suggests that more than 5 percent of all consumers would say that they would never shop at the store again. But is the evidence here conclusive? We will address this question in later chapters.

The Pareto chart **Pareto charts** are used to help identify important quality problems and opportunities for process improvement. By using these charts we can prioritize problem-solving activities. The Pareto chart is named for Vilfredo Pareto (1848–1923), an Italian economist. Pareto suggested that, in many economies, most of the wealth is held by a small minority of the population. It has been found that the **"Pareto principle"** often applies to defects. That is, only a few defect types account for most of a product's quality problems.

Here, defects can be divided into two categories—the **"vital few"** and the **"trivial many."** The vital few are the small number of defects that account for a large percentage of the total, while the trivial many are the large number of defects that account for the small remaining percentage of the total. If the vital few defects are very costly to an organization, it may wish to work on eliminating their causes before working to solve other problems.

To illustrate the use of Pareto charts, suppose that a jelly producer wishes to evaluate the labels being placed on 16-ounce jars of grape jelly. Every day for two weeks, all defective labels found on inspection are classified by type of defect. If a label has more than one defect, we will record the type of defect that is most noticeable. The Excel output in Figure 2.43 presents the frequencies and percentages of the types of defects observed over the two-week period.

In general, the first step in setting up a **Pareto chart** summarizing data concerning types of defects (or categories) is to construct a frequency table like the one in Figure 2.43. Defects or categories should be listed at the left of the table in *decreasing order by frequencies*—the defect with the highest frequency will be at the top of the table, the defect with the second-highest frequency below the first, and so forth. If an "other" category is employed, it should be placed at the bottom of the table. The "other" category should not make up 50 percent or more of the total of the frequencies, and the frequency for the "other" category should not exceed the frequency for the defect at the top of the table. If the frequency for the "other" category is too high, data

FIGURE 2.43 Excel Frequency Table and Pareto Chart of Labeling Defects Labels

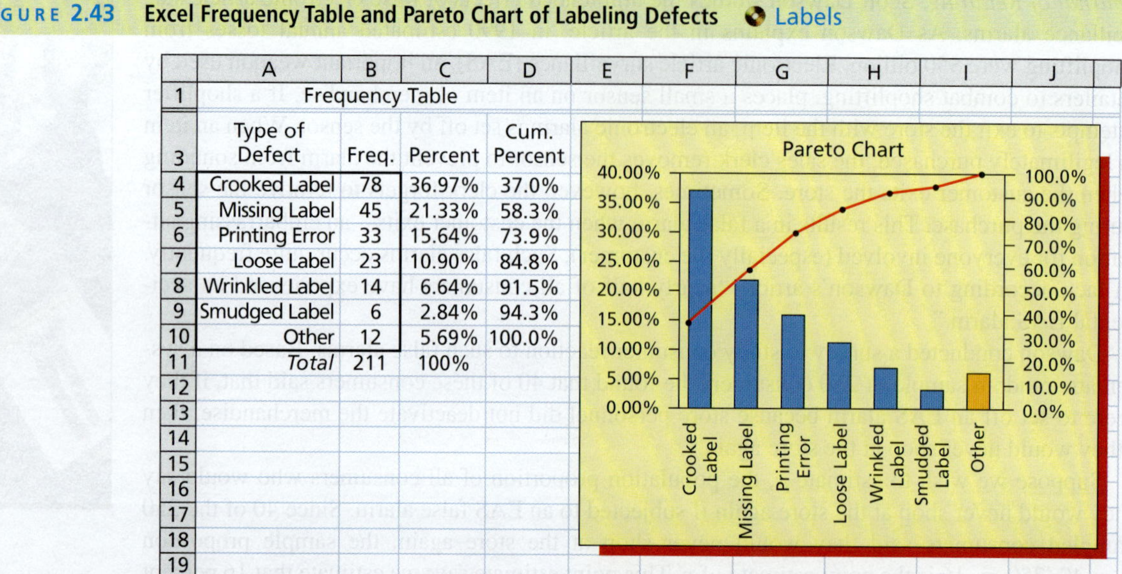

	A	B	C	D
1	Frequency Table			
3	Type of Defect	Freq.	Percent	Cum. Percent
4	Crooked Label	78	36.97%	37.0%
5	Missing Label	45	21.33%	58.3%
6	Printing Error	33	15.64%	73.9%
7	Loose Label	23	10.90%	84.8%
8	Wrinkled Label	14	6.64%	91.5%
9	Smudged Label	6	2.84%	94.3%
10	Other	12	5.69%	100.0%
11	*Total*	211	100%	

should be collected so that the "other" category can be broken down into new categories. Once the frequency and the percentage for each category are determined, a cumulative percentage for each category is computed. As illustrated in Figure 2.43, the cumulative percentage for a particular category is the sum of the percentages corresponding to the particular category and the categories that are above that category in the table.

The Pareto chart is a **bar chart.** Different kinds of defects or problems are listed on the horizontal scale. The heights of the bars on the vertical scale typically represent the frequency of occurrence (or the percentage of occurrence) for each defect or problem. The bars are arranged in decreasing height from left to right. Thus, the most frequent defect will be at the far left, the next most frequent defect to its right, and so forth. If an "other" category is employed, its bar is placed at the far right. The Pareto chart for the labeling defects data is given in Figure 2.43. Here the heights of the bars represent the percentages of occurrences for the different labeling defects, and the vertical scale on the far left corresponds to these percentages. The chart graphically illustrates that crooked labels, missing labels, and printing errors are the most frequent labeling defects.

As is also illustrated in Figure 2.43, a Pareto chart is sometimes augmented by plotting a **cumulative percentage point** for each bar in the Pareto chart. The vertical coordinate of this cumulative percentage point equals the cumulative percentage in the frequency table corresponding to the bar. The cumulative percentage points corresponding to the different bars are connected by line segments, and a vertical scale corresponding to the cumulative percentages is placed on the far right. Examining the cumulative percentage points in Figure 2.43, we see that crooked and missing labels make up 58.3 percent of the labeling defects and that crooked labels, missing labels, and printing errors make up 73.9 percent of the labeling defects.

Exercises for Section 2.5

CONCEPTS

2.51 Find an example of a pie chart or bar chart in a newspaper or magazine. Copy it, and hand it in with a written analysis of the information conveyed by the chart.

2.52 What is a population proportion? Give an example of a population proportion that might interest you in the profession you intend to enter.

METHODS AND APPLICATIONS

2.53 The National Automobile Dealers Association (NADA) publishes *AutoExec* magazine, which annually reports on new vehicle sales and market shares by manufacturer. As given on the *AutoExec* magazine website on March 17, 2005, new vehicle market shares for 2003 are as illustrated in the Excel bar chart of Figure 2.44(a) and the Excel pie chart of Figure 2.44(b). Using these Excel graphics, write an analysis explaining how new vehicle market shares have changed from 1997 (see Figure 2.42 on page 88) to 2003. AutoShares

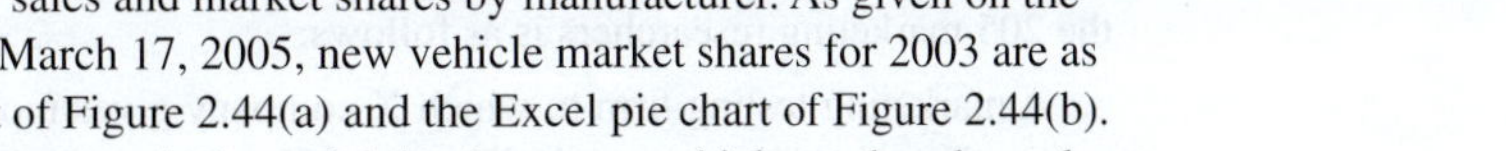

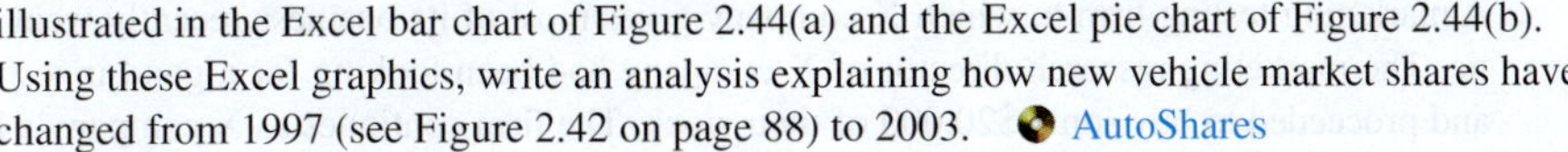

2.54 **a** On March 11, 2005, the Gallup Organization released the results of a CNN/USA Today/Gallup national poll regarding Internet usage in the United States. Each of 1,008 randomly selected adults was asked to respond to the following question:

> As you may know, there are Web sites known as "blogs" or "Web logs," where people sometimes post their thoughts. How familiar are you with "blogs"—very familiar, somewhat familiar, not too familiar, or not at all familiar?

The poll's results were as follows: Very familiar (7%); Somewhat familiar (19%); Not too familiar (18%); Not at all familiar (56%).[9] Use these data to construct a bar chart and a pie chart.

b On February 15, 2005, the Gallup Organization released the results of a Gallup UK poll regarding Internet usage in Great Britain. Each of 1,009 randomly selected UK adults was asked to respond to the following question:

> How much time, if at all, do you personally spend using the Internet—more than an hour a day, up to one hour a day, a few times a week, a few times a month or less, or never?

The poll's results were as follows: More than an hour a day (22%); Up to an hour a day (14%); A few times a week (15%); A few times a month or less (10%); Never (39%).[10] Use these data to construct a bar chart and a pie chart.

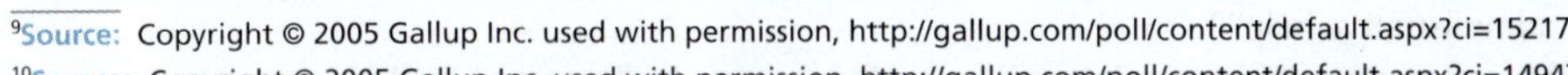

[9]Source: Copyright © 2005 Gallup Inc. used with permission, http://gallup.com/poll/content/default.aspx?ci=15217

[10]Source: Copyright © 2005 Gallup Inc. used with permission, http://gallup.com/poll/content/default.aspx?ci=14947

FIGURE 2.44 Excel Bar Chart and Pie Chart of 2003 U.S. New Vehicle Market Shares by Manufacturer (for Exercise 2.53) AutoShares

(a) The bar chart

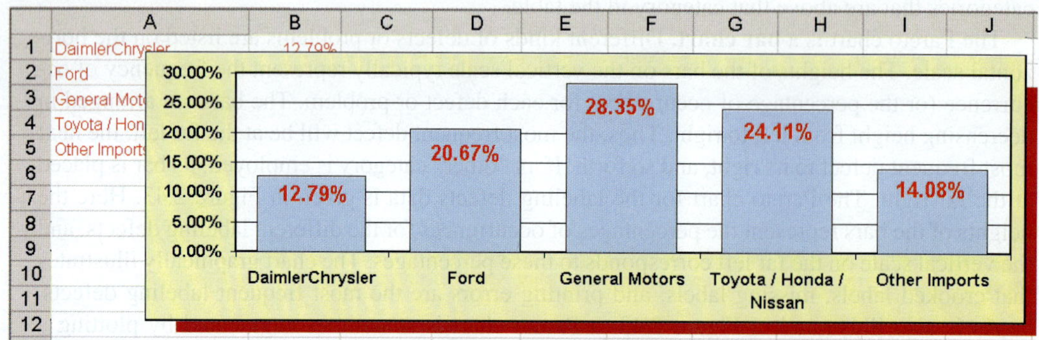

(b) The pie chart

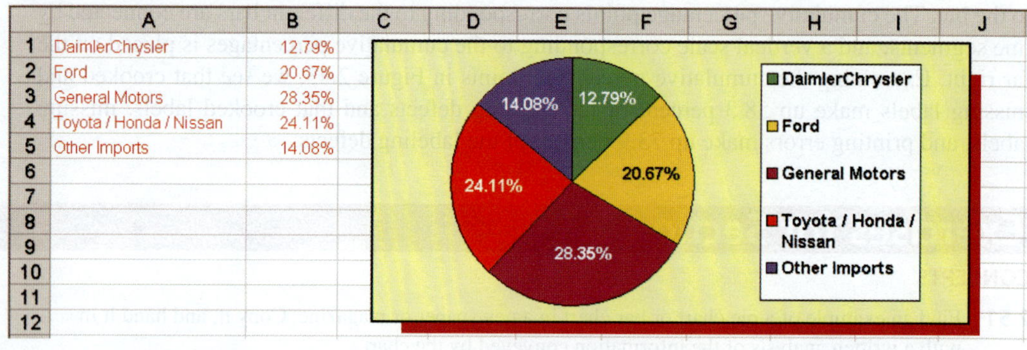

Source: http://www.nada.org, March 17, 2005.

2.55 THE MARKETING ETHICS CASE: CONFLICT OF INTEREST

Consider the marketing ethics case described in Example 2.17. One of the scenarios presented to the 205 marketing researchers is as follows:

> A marketing testing firm to which X company gives most of its business recently went public. The marketing research director of X company had been looking for a good investment and proceeded to buy some $20,000 of their stock. The firm continues as X company's leading supplier for testing.

Of the 205 marketing researchers who participated in the ethics survey, 111 said that they disapproved of the actions taken in the scenario. Use this sample result to compute a point estimate of the proportion of all marketing researchers who disapprove of the actions taken in this conflict of interest scenario.

2.56 In an article in *Quality Progress,* Barbara A. Cleary reports on improvements made in a software supplier's responses to customer calls. In this article, the author states:

> In an effort to improve its response time for these important customer-support calls, an inbound telephone inquiry team was formed at PQ Systems, Inc., a software and training organization in Dayton, Ohio. The team found that 88 percent of the customers' calls were already being answered immediately by the technical support group, but those who had to be called back had to wait an average of 56.6 minutes. No customer complaints had been registered, but the team believed that this response rate could be improved.

As part of its improvement process, the company studied the disposition of complete and incomplete calls to its technical support analysts. A call is considered complete if the customer's problem has been resolved; otherwise the call is incomplete. Figure 2.45 shows a Pareto chart analysis for the incomplete customer calls.

a What percentage of incomplete calls required "more investigation" by the analyst or "administrative help"?

b What percentage of incomplete calls actually presented a "new problem"?

c In light of your answers to *a* and *b*, can you make a suggestion?

FIGURE 2.45 **A Pareto Chart for Incomplete Customer Calls (for Exercise 2.56)**

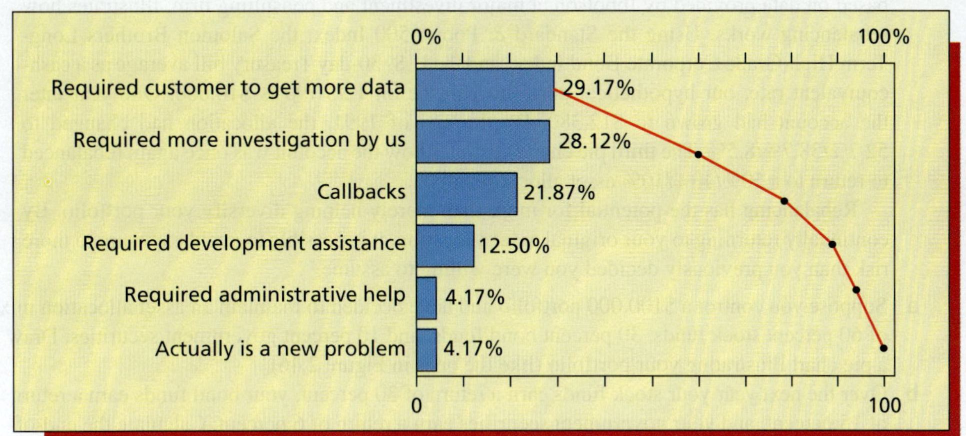

Source: B. A. Cleary, "Company Cares about Customers' Calls," *Quality Progress* (November 1993), pp. 60–73. Copyright © 1993 American Society for Quality Control. Used with permission.

FIGURE 2.46 **Using Pie Charts to Illustrate Portfolio Rebalancing (for Exercise 2.58)**

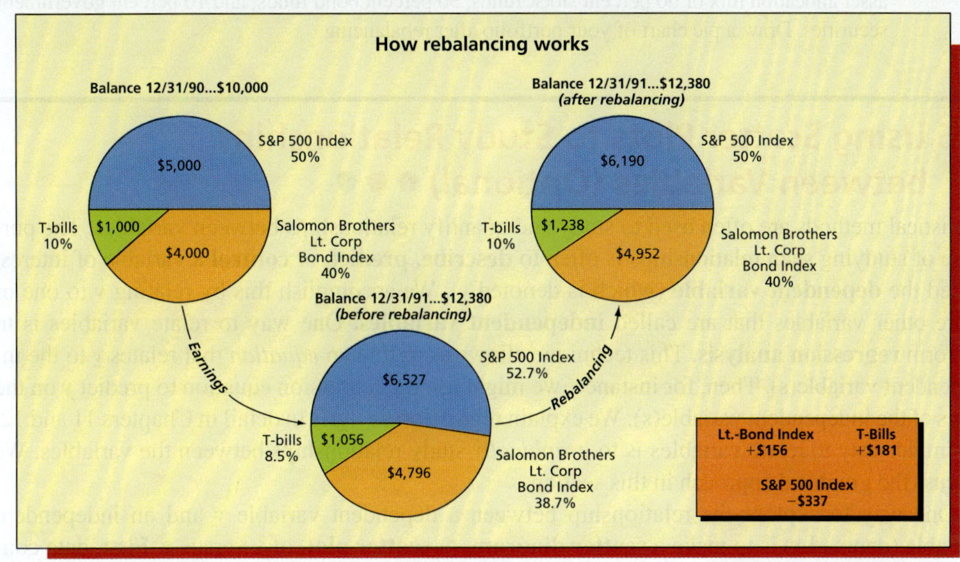

Source: The Variable Annuity Life Insurance Company, *VALIC* 6, no. 4 (Fall 1993).

2.57 On January 11, 2005 the Gallup Organization released the results of poll investigating how many Americans have private health insurance. The results showed that among Americans making less that $30,000 per year, 33% had private insurance, 50% were covered by Medicare/Medicaid, and 17% had no health insurance, while among Americans making $75,000 or more per year, 87% had private insurance, 9% were covered by Medicare/Medicaid, and 4% had no health insurance.[11] Use bar and pie charts to compare health coverage of the two income groups.

2.58 In the Fall 1993 issue of *VALIC Investment Digest,* the Variable Annuity Life Insurance Company used pie charts to illustrate an investment strategy called **rebalancing.** This strategy involves reviewing an investment portfolio annually to return the asset mix (stocks, bonds, Treasury bills, and so on) to a preselected allocation mix. VALIC describes rebalancing as follows (refer to the pie charts in Figure 2.46):

Rebalancing—A Strategy to Keep Your Allocation on Track

Once you've established your ideal asset allocation mix, many experts recommend that you review your portfolio at least once a year to make sure your portfolio remains consistent with your preselected asset allocation mix. This practice is referred to as *rebalancing*.

[11]Source: http://gallup.com/poll/content/default.aspx?ci=14581

For example, let's assume a moderate asset allocation mix of 50 percent equities funds, 40 percent bond funds, and 10 percent cash equivalent funds. The chart [see Figure 2.46] based on data provided by Ibbotson, a major investment and consulting firm, illustrates how rebalancing works. Using the Standard & Poor's 500 Index, the Salomon Brothers Long-Term High-Grade Corporate Bond Index, and the U.S. 30-day Treasury bill average as a cash-equivalent rate, our hypothetical portfolio balance on 12/31/90 is $10,000. One year later the account had grown to $12,380. By the end of 1991, the allocation had changed to 52.7%/38.7%/8.5%. The third pie chart illustrates how the account was once again rebalanced to return to a 50%/40%/10% asset allocation mix.

Rebalancing has the potential for more than merely helping diversify your portfolio. By continually returning to your original asset allocation, it is possible to avoid exposure to more risk than you previously decided you were willing to assume.

a Suppose you control a $100,000 portfolio and have decided to maintain an asset allocation mix of 60 percent stock funds, 30 percent bond funds, and 10 percent government securities. Draw a pie chart illustrating your portfolio (like the ones in Figure 2.46).

b Over the next year your stock funds earn a return of 30 percent, your bond funds earn a return of 15 percent, and your government securities earn a return of 6 percent. Calculate the end-of-year values of your stock funds, bond funds, and government securities. After calculating the end-of-year value of your entire portfolio, determine the asset allocation mix (percent stock funds, percent bond funds, and percent government securities) of your portfolio before rebalancing. Finally, draw an end-of-year pie chart of your portfolio before rebalancing.

c Rebalance your portfolio. That is, determine how much of the portfolio's end-of-year value must be invested in stock funds, bond funds, and government securities in order to restore your original asset allocation mix of 60 percent stock funds, 30 percent bond funds, and 10 percent government securities. Draw a pie chart of your portfolio after rebalancing.

CHAPTER 14

2.6 Using Scatter Plots to Study Relationships between Variables (Optional)

Statistical methods are often used to study and quantify relationships between variables. The purpose of studying such relationships is often to **describe, predict,** or **control** a variable of interest called the **dependent variable** (which is denoted y). We accomplish this by relating y to one or more other variables that are called **independent variables.** One way to relate variables is to perform **regression analysis.** This technique allows us to find an *equation* that relates y to the independent variable(s). Then, for instance, we might use the regression equation to predict y on the basis of the independent variable(s). We explain regression analysis in detail in Chapters 11 and 12. A simpler way to relate variables is to *graphically* study relationships between the variables. We discuss the graphical approach in this section.

One way to explore the relationship between a dependent variable y and an independent variable (denoted x) is to make a **scatter diagram,** or **scatter plot,** of y versus x. First, data concerning the two variables are observed in pairs. To construct the scatter plot, each value of y is plotted against its corresponding value of x. If y and x are related, the plot shows us the direction of the relationship. That is, y could be positively related to x (y increases as x increases) or y could be negatively related to x (y decreases as x increases).

Example 2.19

A manufacturer produces a bulk chemical product. Customer requirements state that this product must have a specified viscosity when melted at a temperature of 300°F (viscosity measures how thick and gooey the product is when melted). Chemical XB-135 is used in the production of this chemical product, and the company's chemists feel that the amount of chemical XB-135 may be related to viscosity. In order to verify and quantify this relationship, 24 batches of the product are produced. The amount (x) of chemical XB-135 (in pounds) is varied from batch to batch and the viscosity (y) obtained for each batch is measured. Table 2.11 gives (in time order) the values of x and the corresponding values of y obtained for the 24 batches. The MINITAB output of a scatter plot of y versus x is given in Figure 2.47. The scatter plot indicates a strong positive relationship between y and x—that is, as the amount of chemical XB-135 used is increased, the viscosity of the product increases. We must now be careful. It would be tempting to conclude that increases

TABLE 2.11 Viscosity Data for 24 Batches of a Chemical Product Produced on August 1, 2005
Viscosity

Batch	Pounds of Chemical XB-135 (x)	Viscosity (y)	Batch	Pounds of Chemical XB-135 (x)	Viscosity (y)
1	10.0	31.76	13	11.2	32.93
2	10.0	31.91	14	11.2	33.19
3	10.2	32.02	15	11.4	33.35
4	10.2	31.85	16	11.4	32.76
5	10.4	32.17	17	11.6	33.33
6	10.4	32.30	18	11.6	33.19
7	10.6	32.60	19	11.8	33.28
8	10.6	32.15	20	11.8	33.57
9	10.8	32.52	21	12.0	33.60
10	10.8	32.46	22	12.0	33.43
11	11.0	32.41	23	12.2	33.91
12	11.0	32.77	24	12.2	33.76

FIGURE 2.47 MINITAB Output of a Scatter Plot of Viscosity versus Amount of Chemical XB-135

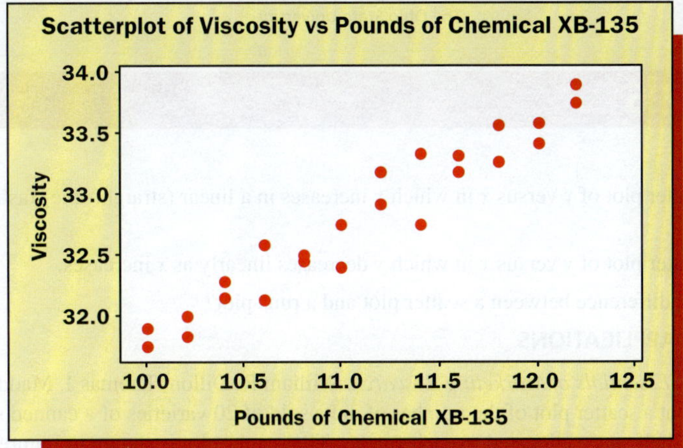

in the amount of chemical XB-135 *cause* increases in viscosity. However, this is not necessarily the case. Perhaps some other factor could be causing the apparent relationship. For instance, the 24 batches were produced in time order. If some other variable that affects viscosity (such as temperature or pressure in the reaction chamber, or the composition of a raw material) is changing over time, this change could be responsible for the observed increases in viscosity. Assuming that we have held other variables that may affect viscosity constant, the evidence supporting a cause-and-effect relationship may be quite strong. This is because the manufacturer has purposely varied the amount of chemical XB-135 used. However, it is really up to the scientific community to establish and understand any cause-and-effect relationship that may exist.

If we are convinced that we can control viscosity by changing the amount of chemical XB-135, we may wish to quantify the relationship between y and x. One way to do this is to calculate the **covariance** and the **correlation coefficient** between y and x. How this is done is discussed in Appendix B on page 841. We would also like to develop an equation relating y to x. This can be done by using regression analysis (see Chapter 11). With such an equation, we can predict y on the basis of x, and we can determine the amount of chemical XB-135 to use in order to achieve a specified viscosity.

Because the plot points in Figure 2.47 seem to fluctuate around a *straight line,* we say that there is a **straight line** (or **linear**) **relationship between y and x.** However, not all relationships are linear. For example, demand for a product, y, might increase at an increasing or decreasing rate as advertising expenditure to promote the product, x, increases. In this case, we say that there is a **curved relationship** between y and x. We discuss curved relationships in Chapter 12.

FIGURE 2.48 A Scatter Plot of Units Sold versus Shelf Space

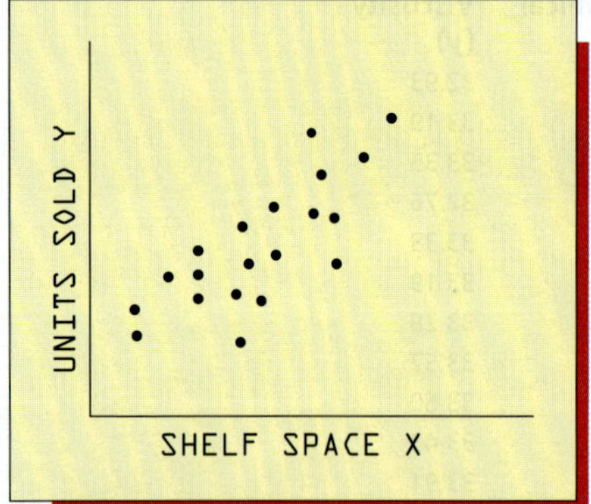

Source: W. R. Dillon, T. J. Madden, and N. H. Firtle. *Essentials of Marketing Research* (Burr Ridge, IL: Richard D. Irwin, Inc., 1993), p. 452. Copyright © 1993. Reprinted by permission of McGraw-Hill Companies, Inc.

FIGURE 2.49 Excel Output of the Mean Restaurant Ratings and a Scatter Plot of Mean Preference versus Mean Taste FastFood

	A	B	C	D	E	F
1	Restaurant	Meantaste	Meanconv	Meanfam	Meanprice	Meanpref
2	Borden Burger	3.5659	2.7005	2.5282	2.9372	4.2552
3	Hardee's	3.329	3.3483	2.7345	2.7513	4.0911
4	Burger King	2.4231	2.7377	2.3368	3.0761	3.0052
5	McDonald's	2.0895	1.938	1.4619	2.4884	2.2429
6	Wendy's	1.9661	2.892	2.3376	4.0814	2.5351
7	White Castle	3.8061	3.7242	2.6515	1.708	4.7812

Source: The Ohio State University.

Exercises for Section 2.6

CONCEPTS

2.59 Draw a scatter plot of y versus x in which y increases in a linear (straight-line) fashion as x increases.

2.60 Draw a scatter plot of y versus x in which y decreases linearly as x increases.

2.61 What is the difference between a scatter plot and a runs plot?

METHODS AND APPLICATIONS

2.62 In the book *Essentials of Marketing Research,* William R. Dillon, Thomas J. Madden, and Neil H. Firtle present a scatter plot of the number of units sold of 20 varieties of a canned soup versus the amount of shelf space allocated to each variety. The scatter plot is shown in Figure 2.48.

a Does there appear to be a relationship between y (units sold) and x (shelf space)? Does the relationship appear to be straight line (linear) or curved? How does y (units sold) change as x (shelf space) increases?

b If you were told that a variety of soup is allotted a small amount of shelf space, what would you guess about sales?

c Do you think that the amount of shelf space allocated to a variety causes sales to be higher or lower? Give an alternative explanation for the appearance of the scatter plot.

2.63 THE FAST-FOOD RESTAURANT RATING CASE FastFood

In the early 1990s researchers at The Ohio State University studied consumer ratings of fast-food restaurants. Each of 406 randomly selected individuals rated the six fast-food restaurants shown in the Excel output of Figure 2.49. Each individual gave each restaurant a rating of 1, 2, 3, 4, 5, or 6 on the basis of taste, convenience, familiarity, and price, and then ranked the restaurants from 1 through 6 on the basis of overall preference. In each case, 1 is the best rating and 6 the worst. The mean ratings given by the 406 individuals are given in Figure 2.49 along with a scatter plot of mean preference versus mean taste. Construct scatter plots of mean preference versus each of mean convenience, mean familiarity, and mean price. Then interpret all the scatter plots.

2.7 Misleading Graphs and Charts (Optional)

The statistical analyst's goal should be to present the most accurate and truthful portrayal of a data set that is possible. Such a presentation allows managers using the analysis to make informed decisions. However, it is possible to construct statistical summaries that are misleading. Although we do not advocate using misleading statistics, you should be aware of some of the

FIGURE 2.50 Two Bar Charts of the Mean Salaries at a Major University from 2002 to 2005

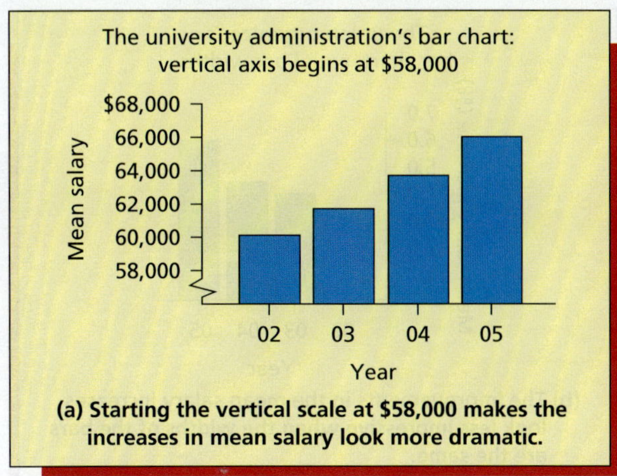

(a) Starting the vertical scale at $58,000 makes the increases in mean salary look more dramatic.

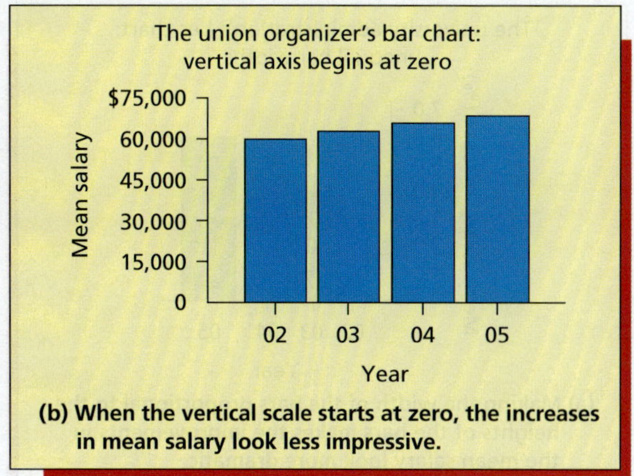

(b) When the vertical scale starts at zero, the increases in mean salary look less impressive.

ways statistical graphs and charts can be manipulated in order to distort the truth. By knowing what to look for, you can avoid being misled by a (we hope) small number of unscrupulous practitioners.

As an example, suppose that the faculty at a major university will soon vote on a proposal to join a union. Both the union organizers and the university administration plan to distribute recent salary statistics to the entire faculty. Suppose that the mean faculty salary at the university and the mean salary increase at the university (expressed as a percentage) for each of the years 2002 through 2005 are as follows:

Year	Mean Salary (All Ranks)	Mean Salary Increase (Percent)
2002	$60,000	3.0%
2003	61,600	4.0
2004	63,500	4.5
2005	66,100	6.0

The university administration does not want the faculty to unionize and, therefore, hopes to convince the faculty that substantial progress has been made to increase salaries without a union. On the other hand, the union organizers wish to portray the salary increases as minimal so that the faculty will feel the need to unionize.

Figure 2.50 gives two bar charts of the mean salaries at the university for each year from 2002 to 2005. Notice that in Figure 2.50(a) the administration has started the vertical scale of the bar chart at a salary of $58,000 by using a *scale break* (⌇). Alternatively, the chart could be set up without the scale break by simply starting the vertical scale at $58,000. Starting the vertical scale at a value far above zero makes the salary increases look more dramatic. Notice that when the union organizers present the bar chart in Figure 2.50(b), which has a vertical scale starting at zero, the salary increases look far less impressive.

Figure 2.51 presents two bar charts of the mean salary increases (in percentages) at the university for each year from 2002 to 2005. In Figure 2.51(a), the administration has made the widths of the bars representing the percentage increases proportional to their heights. This makes the upward movement in the mean salary increases look more dramatic because the observer's eye tends to compare the areas of the bars, while the improvements in the mean salary increases are really only proportional to the heights of the bars. When the union organizers present the bar chart of Figure 2.51(b), the improvements in the mean salary increases look less impressive because each bar has the same width.

Figure 2.52 gives two runs plots (also called **time series plots**) of the mean salary increases at the university from 2002 to 2005. In Figure 2.52(a) the administration has stretched the vertical axis of the graph. That is, the vertical axis is set up so that the distances between the percentages are large. This makes the upward trend of the mean salary increases appear to be steep.

FIGURE 2.51 Two Bar Charts of the Mean Salary Increases at a Major University from 2002 to 2005

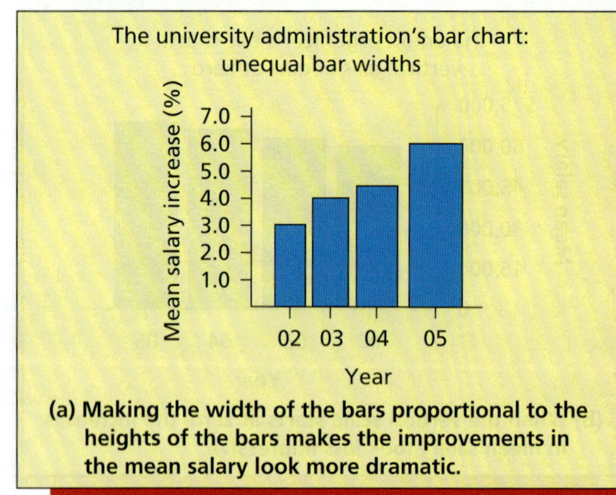

(a) Making the width of the bars proportional to the heights of the bars makes the improvements in the mean salary look more dramatic.

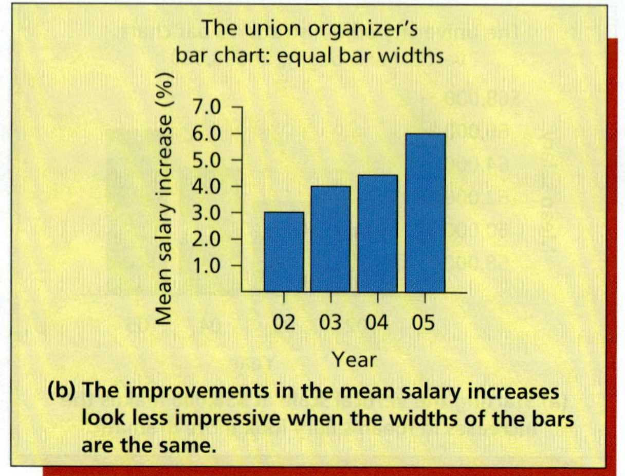

(b) The improvements in the mean salary increases look less impressive when the widths of the bars are the same.

FIGURE 2.52 Two Runs Plots of the Mean Salary Increases at a Major University from 2002 to 2005

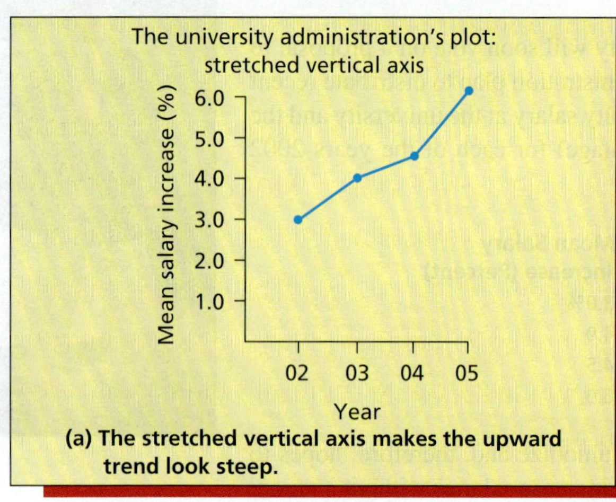

(a) The stretched vertical axis makes the upward trend look steep.

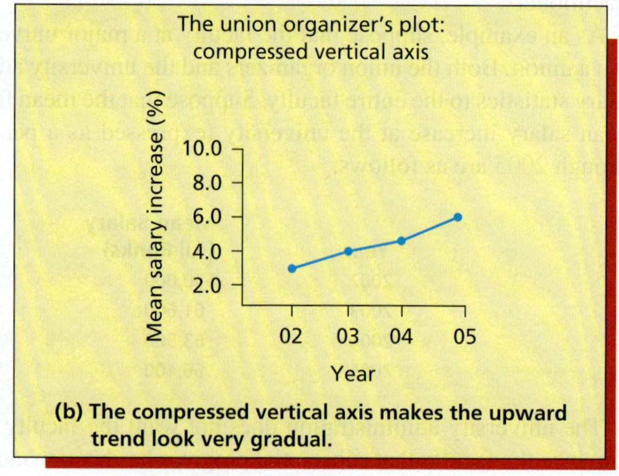

(b) The compressed vertical axis makes the upward trend look very gradual.

In Figure 2.52(b) the union organizers have compressed the vertical axis (that is, the distances between the percentages are small). This makes the upward trend of the mean salary increases appear to be gradual. As we will see in the exercises, stretching and compressing the horizontal axis in a runs plot can also greatly affect the impression given by the plot.

It is also possible to create totally different interpretations of the same statistical summary by simply using different labeling or captions. For example, consider the bar chart of mean salary increases in Figure 2.51(b). To create a favorable interpretation, the university administration might use the caption "Salary Increase Is Higher for the Fourth Year in a Row." On the other hand, the union organizers might create a negative impression by using the caption "Salary Increase Fails to Reach 10% for Fourth Straight Year."

In summary, we do not approve of using statistics to mislead and distort reality. Statistics should be used to present the most truthful and informative summary of the data that is possible. However, it is important to carefully study any statistical summary so that you will not be misled. Look for manipulations such as stretched or compressed axes on graphs, axes that do not begin at zero, and bar charts with bars of varying widths. Also, carefully think about assumptions, and make your own conclusions about the meaning of any statistical summary rather than relying on captions written by others. Doing these things will help you to see the truth and to make well-informed decisions.

Exercises for Section 2.7

CONCEPTS

2.64 When we construct a bar chart or graph, what is the effect of starting the vertical axis at a value that is far above zero? Explain.

2.65 Find an example of a misleading use of statistics in a newspaper, magazine, corporate annual report, or other source. Then explain why your example is misleading.

METHODS AND APPLICATIONS

2.66 Figure 2.53 gives two more time series plots of the previously discussed salary increases. In Figure 2.53(a) the administration has compressed the horizontal axis. In Figure 2.53(b) the union organizers have stretched the horizontal axis. Discuss the different impressions given by the two time series plots.

2.67 In the article "How to Display Data Badly" in the May 1984 issue of *The American Statistician,* Howard Wainer presents a *stacked bar chart* of the number of public and private elementary schools (1929–1970). This bar chart is given in Figure 2.54. Wainer also gives a line graph of the number of private elementary schools (1930–1970). This graph is shown in Figure 2.55.

FIGURE 2.53 Two Runs Plots of the Mean Salary Increases at a Major University from 2002 to 2005

(a) The administration's plot: compressed horizontal axis

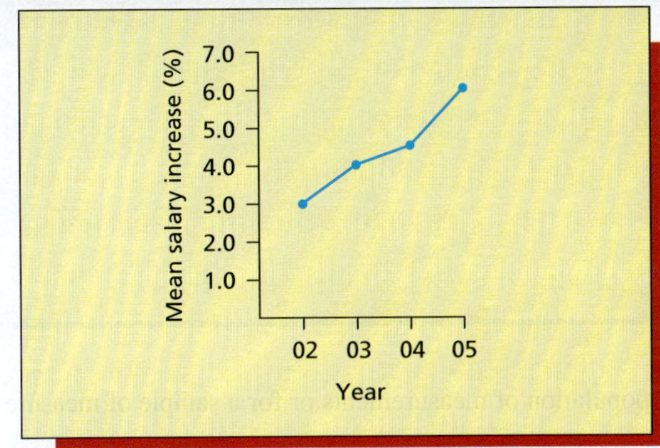

(b) The union organizers' plot: stretched horizontal axis

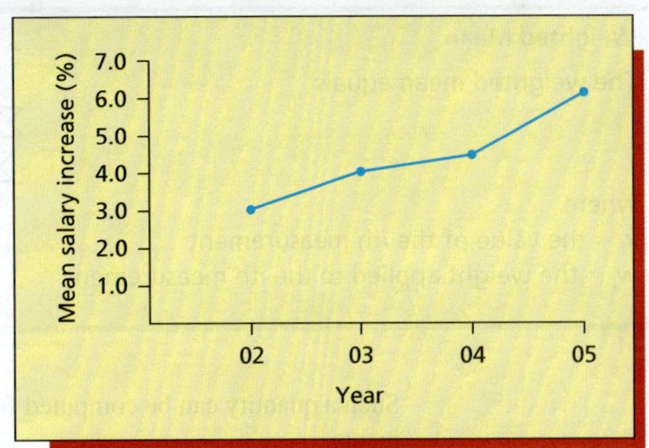

FIGURE 2.54 Wainer's Stacked Bar Chart

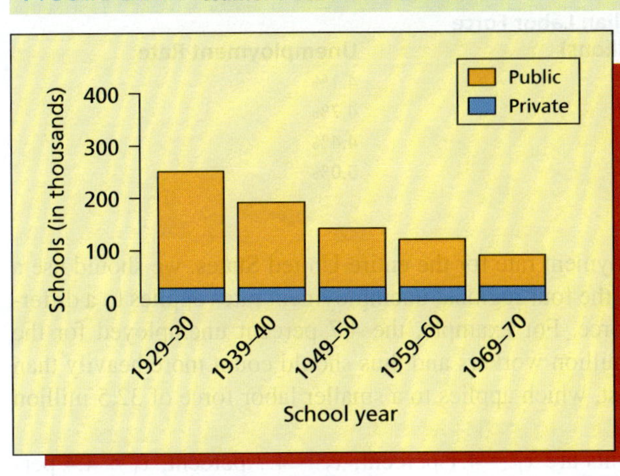

FIGURE 2.55 Wainer's Line Graph

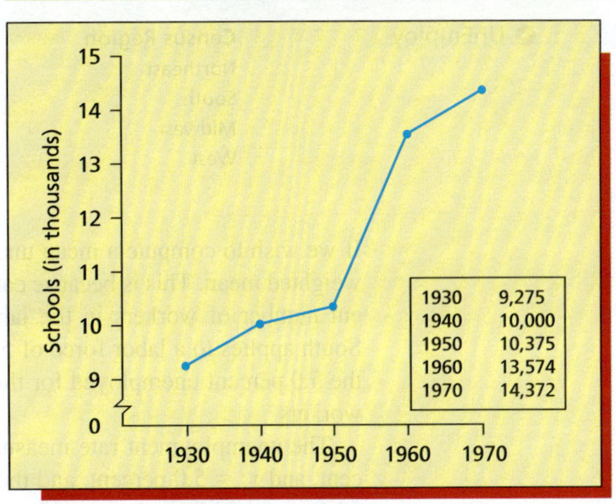

Source: H. Wainer, "How to Display Data Badly," *The American Statistician*, May 1984, pp. 137–147. Copyright © 1984 American Statistical Association. Used with permission.

a Looking at the bar chart of Figure 2.54, does there appear to be an increasing trend in the number of private elementary schools from 1930 to 1970?
b Looking at the line graph of Figure 2.55, does there appear to be an increasing trend in the number of private elementary schools from 1930 to 1970?
c Which portrayal of the data do you think is more appropriate? Explain why.
d Is either portrayal of the data entirely appropriate? Explain.

2.8 Weighted Means and Grouped Data (Optional)

Weighted means In Section 2.2 we studied the mean, which is an important measure of central tendency. In order to calculate a mean, we sum the population (or sample) measurements, and then divide this sum by the number of measurements in the population (or sample). When we do this, each measurement counts equally. That is, each measurement is given the same importance or weight.

Sometimes it makes sense to give different measurements unequal weights. In such a case, a measurement's weight reflects its importance, and the mean calculated using the unequal weights is called a **weighted mean.**

We calculate a weighted mean by multiplying each measurement by its weight, summing the resulting products, and dividing the resulting sum by the sum of the weights:

Weighted Mean

The weighted mean equals

$$\frac{\sum w_i x_i}{\sum w_i}$$

where
x_i = the value of the ith measurement
w_i = the weight applied to the ith measurement

Such a quantity can be computed for a population of measurements or for a sample of measurements.

In order to illustrate the need for a weighted mean and the required calculations, consider the June 2001 unemployment rates for various regions in the United States:[12]

UnEmploy

Census Region	Civilian Labor Force (Millions)	Unemployment Rate
Northeast	26.9	4.1%
South	50.6	4.7%
Midwest	34.7	4.4%
West	32.5	5.0%

If we wish to compute a mean unemployment rate for the entire United States, we should use a weighted mean. This is because each of the four regional unemployment rates applies to a different number of workers in the labor force. For example, the 4.7 percent unemployed for the South applies to a labor force of 50.6 million workers and thus should count more heavily than the 5.0 percent unemployed for the West, which applies to a smaller labor force of 32.5 million workers.

The unemployment rate measurements are $x_1 = 4.1$ percent, $x_2 = 4.7$ percent, $x_3 = 4.4$ percent, and $x_4 = 5.0$ percent, and the weights applied to these measurements are $w_1 = 26.9$, $w_2 = 50.6$, $w_3 = 34.7$, and $w_4 = 32.5$. That is, we are weighting the unemployment rates by the

[12]Source: U.S. Bureau of Labor Statistics, http://stats.bls.gov/news.release/laus.t01.htm, August 7, 2001.

regional labor force sizes. The weighted mean is computed as follows:

$$\mu = \frac{26.9(4.1) + 50.6(4.7) + 34.7(4.4) + 32.5(5.0)}{26.9 + 50.6 + 34.7 + 32.5}$$

$$= \frac{663.29}{144.7} = 4.58\%$$

In this case the unweighted mean of the four regional unemployment rates equals 4.55 percent. Therefore, the unweighted mean understates the U.S. unemployment rate by .03 percent (or understates U.S. unemployment by .0003(144.7 million) = 43,410 workers).

The weights chosen for calculating a weighted mean will vary depending on the situation. For example, in order to compute the mean percentage return for a portfolio of investments, the percentage returns for various investments might be weighted by the dollar amounts invested in each. Or in order to compute a mean profit margin for a company consisting of several divisions, the profit margins for the different divisions might be weighted by the sales volumes of the divisions. Again, the idea is to choose weights that represent the relative importance of the measurements in the population or sample.

Descriptive statistics for grouped data We usually calculate measures of central tendency and variability using the individual measurements in a population or sample. However, sometimes the only data available are in the form of a frequency distribution or a histogram. For example, newspapers and magazines often summarize data using frequency distributions and histograms without giving the individual measurements in a data set. Data summarized in frequency distribution or histogram form are often called **grouped data.** In this section we show how to compute descriptive statistics for such data.

Suppose we are given a frequency distribution summarizing a sample of 65 customer satisfaction ratings for a consumer product.

SatRatings

Satisfaction Rating	Frequency
36–38	4
39–41	15
42–44	25
45–47	19
48–50	2

Because we do not know each of the 65 individual satisfaction ratings, we cannot compute an exact value for the mean satisfaction rating. However, we can calculate an approximation of this mean. In order to do this, we use the midpoint of each class to represent the measurements in the class. When we do this, we are really assuming that the average of the measurements in each class equals the class midpoint. Letting M_i denote the midpoint of class i, and letting f_i denote the frequency of class i, we compute the mean by calculating a weighted mean of the class midpoints using the class frequencies as the weights. The logic here is that if f_i measurements are included in class i, then the midpoint of class i should count f_i times in the weighted mean. In this case, the sum of the weights equals the sum of the class frequencies, which equals the sample size. Therefore, we obtain the following equation for the sample mean of grouped data:

Sample Mean for Grouped Data

$$\bar{x} = \frac{\sum f_i M_i}{\sum f_i} = \frac{\sum f_i M_i}{n}$$

where

f_i = the frequency for class i

M_i = the midpoint for class i

$n = \sum f_i$ = the sample size

TABLE 2.12 Calculating the Sample Mean Satisfaction Rating

Satisfaction Rating	Frequency (f_i)	Class Midpoint (M_i)	f_iM_i
36–38	4	37	4(37) = 148
39–41	15	40	15(40) = 600
42–44	25	43	25(43) = 1,075
45–47	19	46	19(46) = 874
48–50	2	49	2(49) = 98
	$n = 65$		2,795

$$\bar{x} = \frac{\sum f_iM_i}{n} = \frac{2{,}795}{65} = 43$$

TABLE 2.13 Calculating the Sample Variance of the Satisfaction Ratings

Satisfaction Rating	Frequency f_i	Class Midpoint M_i	Deviation $(M_i - \bar{x})$	Squared Deviation $(M_i - \bar{x})^2$	$f_i(M_i - \bar{x})^2$
36–38	4	37	37 − 43 = −6	36	4(36) = 144
39–41	15	40	40 − 43 = −3	9	15(9) = 135
42–44	25	43	43 − 43 = 0	0	25(0) = 0
45–47	19	46	46 − 43 = 3	9	19(9) = 171
48–50	2	49	49 − 43 = 6	36	2(36) = 72
	65				$\sum f_i(M_i - \bar{x})^2 = 522$

$$s^2 = \text{sample variance} = \frac{\sum f_i(M_i - \bar{x})^2}{n - 1} = \frac{522}{65 - 1} = 8.15625$$

Table 2.12 summarizes the calculation of the mean satisfaction rating for the previously given frequency distribution of satisfaction ratings. Note that in this table each midpoint is halfway between its corresponding class limits. For example, for the first class $M_1 = (36 + 38)/2 = 37$. We find that the sample mean satisfaction rating is 43.

We can also compute an approximation of the sample variance for grouped data. Recall that when we compute the sample variance using individual measurements, we compute the squared deviation from the sample mean $(x_i - \bar{x})^2$ for each individual measurement x_i and then sum the squared deviations. For grouped data, we do not know each of the x_i values. Because of this, we again let the class midpoint M_i represent each measurement in class i. It follows that we compute the squared deviation $(M_i - \bar{x})^2$ for each class and then sum these squares, weighting each squared deviation by its corresponding class frequency f_i. That is, we approximate $\sum (x_i - \bar{x})^2$ by using $\sum f_i(M_i - \bar{x})^2$. Finally, we obtain the sample variance for the grouped data by dividing this quantity by the sample size minus 1. We summarize this calculation in the following box:

Sample Variance for Grouped Data

$$s^2 = \frac{\sum f_i(M_i - \bar{x})^2}{n - 1}$$

where $\bar{x}$ is the sample mean for the grouped data.

Table 2.13 illustrates calculating the sample variance of the previously given frequency distribution of satisfaction ratings. We find that the sample variance is $s^2 = 8.15625$ and, therefore, that the sample standard deviation is $s = \sqrt{8.15625} = 2.8559$.

Finally, although we have illustrated calculating the mean and variance for grouped data in the context of a sample, similar calculations can be done for a population of measurements. If we let

N be the size of the population, the grouped data formulas for the population mean and variance are given in the following box:

Population Mean for Grouped Data

$$\mu = \frac{\sum f_i M_i}{N}$$

Population Variance for Grouped Data

$$\sigma^2 = \frac{\sum f_i (M_i - \mu)^2}{N}$$

Exercises for Section 2.8

CONCEPTS

2.68 Consider calculating a student's grade point average using a scale where 4.0 represents an A and 0.0 represents an F. Explain why the grade point average is a weighted mean. What are the x_i values? What are the weights?

2.69 When we perform grouped data calculations, we represent the measurements in a class by using the midpoint of the class. Explain the assumption that is being made when we do this.

2.70 When we compute the mean, variance, and standard deviation using grouped data, the results obtained are approximations of the population (or sample) mean, variance, and standard deviation. Explain why this is true.

METHODS AND APPLICATIONS

2.71 According to the Morningstar.com website, the 2004 total return percentages for several popular funds were as follows: FundReturns

Fund	2004 Total Return %
Vanguard 500 Index	10.7
Wasatch Core Growth	21.7
Fidelity Stock Selector	9.9
Fidelity Dividend Growth	5.8
Janus Worldwide	5.5

Source: http://quicktake.morningstar.com/Fund/TotalReturns.asp, March 17,

Suppose that an investor had \$100,000 invested in the Vanguard 500 Index fund, \$500,000 invested in the Wasatch Core Growth fund, \$500,000 invested in the Fidelity Stock Selector fund, \$200,000 invested in the Fidelity Dividend Growth fund, and \$50,000 invested in the Janus Worldwide fund.

a Compute a weighted mean that measures the 2004 average total return for the investor's portfolio.

b Compare your weighted mean with the unweighted mean of the five total return percentages. Explain why they differ.

2.72 The following are the January 2005 unemployment rates and civilian labor force sizes for five states in the Midwest. UnEmpStates

State	Size of Civilian Labor Force (Millions)	Unemployment Rate (%)
Iowa	1.62	5.1
Michigan	5.09	7.1
Illinois	6.45	5.6
Indiana	3.18	5.4
Wisconsin	3.08	4.8

Source: United States Bureau of Labor Statistics, http://stats.bls.gov/, March 17, 2005.

a Using a weighted mean, compute an average unemployment rate for the five state region.

b Calculate the unweighted mean for the five unemployment rates. Explain why the weighted and unweighted means differ.

2.73 The following frequency distribution summarizes the weights of 195 fish caught by anglers participating in a professional bass fishing tournament. BassWeights

Weight (Pounds)	Frequency
1–3	53
4–6	118
7–9	21
10–12	3

a Calculate the (approximate) sample mean for this data.

b Calculate the (approximate) sample variance for this data.

2.74 The following is a frequency distribution summarizing earnings per share (EPS) growth data for the 30 fastest-growing firms as given on *Fortune* magazine's website on March 16, 2005. EPSGrowth

EPS Growth (Percent)	Frequency
0–49	1
50–99	17
100–149	5
150–199	4
200–249	1
250–299	2

Source: http://www.fortune.com, March 16, 2005.

Calculate the (approximate) population mean, variance, and standard deviation for these data.

2.75 The Data and Story Library website (a website devoted to applications of statistics) gives a histogram of the ages of a sample of 60 CEOs taken in 1993. We present the data in the form of a frequency distribution below. CEOAges

Age (Years)	Frequency
28–32	1
33–37	3
38–42	3
43–47	13
48–52	14
53–57	12
58–62	9
63–67	1
68–72	3
73–77	1

Source: http://lib.stat.cmu.edu/DASL/Stories/ceo.html, April 15, 2005.

Calculate the (approximate) sample mean, variance, and standard deviation of this data.

2.9 The Geometric Mean (Optional)

In Section 2.2 we defined the mean to be the average of a set of population or sample measurements. This mean is sometimes referred to as the arithmetic mean. While very useful, the arithmetic mean is not a good measure of the rate of change exhibited by a variable over time. To see this, consider the rate at which the value of an investment changes—its rate of return. Suppose that an initial investment of \$10,000 increases in value to \$20,000 at the end of one year and then decreases in value to its original \$10,000 value after two years. The rate of return for the first year, R_1, is

$$R_1 = \left(\frac{20{,}000 - 10{,}000}{10{,}000}\right) \times 100\% = 100\%$$

and the rate of return for the second year, R_2, is

$$R_2 = \left(\frac{10{,}000 - 20{,}000}{20{,}000}\right) \times 100\% = -50\%$$

Although the value of the investment at the beginning and end of the two-year period is the same, the arithmetic mean of the yearly rates of return is $(R_1 + R_2)/2 = (100\% + (-50\%))/2 = 25\%$. This arithmetic mean does not communicate the fact that the value of the investment is unchanged at the end of the two years.

To remedy this situation, we define the **geometric mean** of the returns to be **the constant return R_g, that yields the same wealth at the end of the investment period as do the actual returns.** In our example, this says that if we express R_g, R_1, and R_2 as decimal fractions (here $R_1 = 1$ and $R_2 = -.5$),

$$(1 + R_g)^2 \times 10{,}000 = (1 + R_1)(1 + R_2) \times 10{,}000$$

or

$$\begin{aligned} R_g &= \sqrt{(1 + R_1)(1 + R_2)} - 1 \\ &= \sqrt{(1 + 1)(1 + (-.5))} - 1 \\ &= \sqrt{1} - 1 = 0 \end{aligned}$$

Therefore, the geometric mean R_g expresses the fact that the value of the investment is unchanged after two years.

In general, if $R_1, R_2, \ldots, R_n$ are returns (expressed in decimal form) over n time periods:

The **geometric mean** of the returns $R_1, R_2, \ldots, R_n$ is

$$R_g = \sqrt[n]{(1 + R_1)(1 + R_2) \cdots (1 + R_n)} - 1$$

and the ending value of an initial investment I experiencing returns $R_1, R_2, \ldots, R_n$ is $I(1 + R_g)^n$.

As another example, suppose that in year 3 our investment's value increases to $25,000, which says that the rate of return for year 3 (expressed as a percentage) is

$$\begin{aligned} R_3 &= \left(\frac{25{,}000 - 10{,}000}{10{,}000}\right) \times 100\% \\ &= 150\% \end{aligned}$$

Since (expressed as decimals) $R_1 = 1$, $R_2 = -.5$, and $R_3 = 1.5$, the geometric mean return at the end of year 3 is

$$\begin{aligned} R_g &= \sqrt[3]{(1 + 1)(1 + (-.5))(1 + 1.5)} - 1 \\ &= 1.3572 - 1 \\ &= .3572 \end{aligned}$$

and the value of the investment after 3 years is

$$10{,}000\,(1 + .3572)^3 = \$25{,}000$$

Exercises for Section 2.9

CONCEPTS

2.76 In words, explain the interpretation of the geometric mean return for an investment.

2.77 If we know the initial value of an investment and its geometric mean return over a period of years, can we compute the ending value of the investment? If so, how?

METHODS AND APPLICATIONS

2.78 Suppose that a company's sales were $5,000,000 three years ago. Since that time sales have grown at annual rates of 10 percent, −10 percent, and 25 percent.

a Find the geometric mean growth rate of sales over this three-year period.

b Find the ending value of sales after this three-year period.

2.79 Suppose that a company's sales were $1,000,000 four years ago and are $4,000,000 at the end of the four years. Find the geometric mean growth rate of sales.

2.80 The Standard and Poor's 500 stock index is a commonly used measure of stock market performance in the United States. In the table below, we give the value of the S & P 500 index on the first day of market trading for each year from 2000 to 2005. S&P500

Year	S&P 500 Index
2000	1,455.22
2001	1,283.27
2002	1,154.67
2003	909.03
2004	1,108.48
2005	1,211.92

Source: http://table.finance.yahoo.com.

a Show that the percentage changes (rates of return) for the S&P 500 index for the years from 2000 to 2001 and from 2001 to 2002 are, respectively, −11.8 percent and −10.0 percent (that is, −.118 and −.100 expressed as decimal fractions).

b Find the rates of return for the S&P 500 index for each of the years: from 2002 to 2003; from 2003 to 2004; from 2004 to 2005.

c Calculate the geometric mean return for the S&P 500 index over the period from 2000 to 2005.

d Suppose that an investment of $1,000,000 is made in 2000 and that the portfolio performs with returns equal to those of the S&P 500 index. What is the investment portfolio worth in 2005?

2.81 According to the USA Statistics in Brief summary of U.S. census data, the amount of consumer credit outstanding (in billions of dollars) is as follows[13]:

1990 : $789 1995 : $1,096 2000 : $1,534

a Find the geometric mean five-year rate of increase in consumer credit outstanding.

b Use the geometric mean rate of increase to project the amount of consumer credit outstanding in 2005.

Chapter Summary

We began this chapter by studying how to depict the shape of the distribution of a data set. We learned that **stem-and-leaf displays** and **histograms** are useful graphics for portraying a data set's distribution. We also learned about some common population shapes. We saw that data sets often have shapes that are **symmetrical, skewed with a tail to the right,** or **skewed with a tail to the left.**

Next we presented and compared several measures of **central tendency.** We defined the **population mean** and we saw how to estimate the population mean by using a **sample mean.** We also defined the **median** and **mode,** and we compared the mean, median, and mode for symmetrical distributions and for distributions that are skewed to the right or left. We then studied measures of **variation** (or *spread*). We defined the **range, variance,** and **standard deviation,** and we saw how to estimate a population variance and standard deviation by using a sample. We learned that a good way to interpret the standard deviation when a population is (approximately) normally distributed is to use the **empirical rule,** and we applied this rule to assess **process capability.** We next studied **Chebyshev's Theorem,** which gives us intervals containing reasonably large fractions of the population units no matter what the population's shape might be. We also saw that, when a data set is highly skewed, it is best to use **percentiles** and **quartiles** to measure variation, and we learned how to construct a **box-and-whiskers plot** by using the quartiles.

[13]Source: http://www.census.gov/statlab/www/part5.html.

After learning how to measure and depict central tendency and variability, we presented several methods for portraying qualitative data. In particular, we used **bar charts** and **pie charts** for this purpose. We also discussed using a sample to estimate the proportion of population units that fall into a category of interest.

We concluded this chapter with several optional sections. First, we studied using **scatter plots** to examine relationships between variables. Next we discussed misleading graphs and statistics, and we explained some of the tactics that are commonly used to try to distort the truth. We also introduced the concept of a **weighted mean** and then explained how to compute descriptive statistics for **grouped data.** Finally, we showed how to calculate the **geometric mean** and demonstrated its interpretation.

Glossary of Terms

bar chart: A graphical display of categorical data (data in categories) made up of vertical or horizontal bars. (page 87)

box-and-whiskers display (box plot): A graphical portrayal of a data set that depicts both the central tendency and variability of the data. It is constructed using Q_1, M_d, and Q_3. (page 81)

capable process: A process that is able to consistently produce output that meets (or conforms to) specifications (requirements). (page 73)

central tendency: A term referring to the middle of a population or sample of measurements. (page 58)

Chebyshev's Theorem: A theorem that (for any population) allows us to find an interval that contains a specified percentage of the individual measurements in the population. (page 74)

coefficient of variation: A quantity that measures the variation of a population or sample relative to its mean. (page 75)

dependent variable (denoted y): A variable that we wish to describe, predict, or control. (page 94)

Empirical Rule: For a normally distributed population, this rule tells us that 68.26 percent, 95.44 percent, and 99.73 percent, respectively, of the population measurements are within one, two, and three standard deviations of the population mean. (page 71)

extreme outlier (in a box-and-whiskers display): Measurements located outside the outer fences. (page 82)

extreme value: A measurement in a population or sample that is different from most of the other measurements. (page 62)

first quartile (denoted Q_1): A value below which approximately 25 percent of the measurements lie; the 25th percentile. (page 80)

frequency: The count of the number of measurements in a class or of the number of measurements having a particular value. (page 46)

frequency distribution: A numerical summary that divides the values of a variable into classes and gives the number of values in each class. (page 46)

geometric mean: The constant return (or rate of change) that yields the same wealth at the end of several time periods as do actual returns. (page 105)

grouped data: Data presented in the form of a frequency distribution or a histogram. (page 101)

histogram: A graphical portrayal of a data set that shows the data set's distribution. It divides the data into classes and gives the frequency for each class. Histograms are particularly useful for summarizing large data sets. (page 46)

independent variable (denoted x): A predictor variable that can be used to describe, predict, or control a dependent variable. (page 94)

inner fences (in a box-and-whiskers display): Points located $1.5 \times IQR$ below Q_1 and $1.5 \times IQR$ above Q_3. (page 81)

interquartile range (denoted IQR): The difference between the third quartile and the first quartile (that is, $Q_3 - Q_1$). (page 80)

measure of variation: A descriptive measure of the spread of the values in a population or sample. (page 68)

median (denoted M_d): A measure of central tendency that divides a population or sample into two roughly equal parts. (page 60)

mild outlier (in a box-and-whiskers display): Measurements located between the inner and outer fences. (page 82)

mode (denoted M_o): The measurement in a sample or a population that occurs most frequently. (page 61)

mound-shaped: Description of a relative frequency curve that is "piled up in the middle." (page 73)

normal curve: A bell-shaped, symmetrical relative frequency curve. We will present the exact equation that gives this curve in Chapter 5. (page 51)

outlier: An unusually large or small observation that is well separated from the remaining observations. (page 52)

Pareto chart: A bar chart of the frequencies or percentages for various types of defects. These are used to identify opportunities for improvement. (page 90)

percentile: The value such that a specified percentage of the measurements in a population or sample fall at or below it. (page 79)

pie chart: A graphical display of categorical data (data in categories) made up of "pie slices." (page 87)

point estimate: A one-number estimate for the value of a population parameter. (page 59)

population mean (denoted μ): The average of a population of measurements. (page 58)

population parameter: A descriptive measure of a population. It is calculated using the population measurements. (page 59)

population proportion (denoted p): The proportion of population units that are contained in a category of interest. (page 87)

population standard deviation (denoted σ): The positive square root of the population variance. It is a measure of the variation of the population measurements. (page 68)

population variance (denoted σ^2): The average of the squared deviations of the individual population measurements from the population mean. It is a measure of the variation of the population measurements. (page 68)

range: The difference between the largest and smallest measurements in a population or sample. It is a simple measure of variation. (page 68)

relative frequency: The frequency of a class divided by the total number of measurements. (page 47)

relative frequency curve: A curve that describes the shape of a population of measurements. (page 51)

relative frequency histogram: A graphical portrayal of a data set that shows the data set's distribution. It divides the data into classes, gives the relative frequency for each class, and is particularly useful for summarizing large data sets. (page 48)

sample mean (denoted $\bar{x}$): The average of the measurements in a sample. It is the point estimate of the population mean. (page 59)

sample proportion (denoted $\hat{p}$): The proportion of sample elements that are contained in a category of interest. (page 87)
sample size (denoted n): The number of measurements in a sample. (page 59)
sample standard deviation (denoted s): The positive square root of the sample variance. It is the point estimate of the population standard deviation. (page 69)
sample statistic: A descriptive measure of a sample. It is calculated from the measurements in the sample. (page 59)
sample variance (denoted s^2): A measure of the variation of the sample measurements. It is the point estimate of the population variance. (page 69)
scatter plot: A plot of the values of a dependent variable y versus the values of an independent variable x. (page 94)
skewed to the left: Description of a relative frequency curve having a long tail to the left. (page 51)
skewed to the right: Description of a relative frequency curve having a long tail to the right. (page 51)
stem-and-leaf display: A graphical portrayal of a data set that shows the data set's distribution. It displays the data in the form of stems and leaves. (page 43)
third quartile (denoted Q_3): A value below which approximately 75 percent of the measurements lie; the 75th percentile. (page 80)
tolerance interval: An interval of numbers that contains a specified percentage of the individual measurements in a population. (page 72)
weighted mean: A mean where different measurements are given different weights based on their importance. (page 100)
z-score (of a measurement): The number of standard deviations that a measurement is from the mean. This quantity indicates the relative location of a measurement within its distribution. (page 75)

Important Formulas

The population mean, μ: page 58
The sample mean, $\bar{x}$: page 59
The median: page 60
The mode: page 61
The population range: page 68
The population variance, σ^2: page 68
The population standard deviation, σ: page 68
The sample variance, s^2: pages 69, 70
The sample standard deviation, s: page 69
Computational formula for s^2: page 70
The Empirical Rule: page 71
Chebyshev's Theorem: page 74
z-score: page 75
The coefficient of variation: page 75
The pth percentile: page 79
The quartiles: page 80
The weighted mean: page 100
Sample mean for grouped data: page 101
Sample variance for grouped data: page 102
Population mean for grouped data: page 103
Population variance for grouped data: page 103
The geometric mean: page 105

Supplementary Exercises

2.82 In the book *Modern Statistical Quality Control and Improvement,* Nicholas R. Farnum presents data concerning the elapsed times from the completion of medical lab tests until the results are recorded on patients' charts. Table 2.14 gives the times it took (in hours) to deliver and chart the results of 84 lab tests over one week. LabTest

a Construct a frequency histogram and a relative frequency histogram for the lab test waiting time data.

b Looking at the histogram, are most of the test results delivered and charted within several hours?

c Are there some deliveries with excessively long waiting times? Which deliveries might be investigated in order to discover reasons behind unusually long delays?

2.83 Figure 2.56 depicts data for a study of 80 software projects at NASA's Goddard Space Center. The figure shows the number of bugs per 1,000 lines of code from 1976 to 1990. Write a short paragraph describing how the reliability of the software has improved. Explain how the data indicate improvement.

2.84 **THE INVESTMENT CASE** InvestRet

The Fall 1995 issue of *Investment Digest,* a publication of The Variable Annuity Life Insurance Company of Houston, Texas, discusses the importance of portfolio diversification for long-term investors. The article states:

> While it is true that investment experts generally advise long-term investors to invest in variable investments, they also agree that the key to any sound investment portfolio is diversification. That is, investing in a variety of investments with differing levels of historical return and risk.

TABLE 2.14 Elapsed Time (in Hours) for Completing and Delivering Medical Lab Tests LabTest

6.1	8.7	1.1	4.0
2.1	3.9	2.2	5.0
2.1	7.1	4.3	8.8
3.5	1.2	3.2	1.3
1.3	9.3	4.2	7.3
5.7	6.5	4.4	16.2
1.3	1.3	3.0	2.7
15.7	4.9	2.0	5.2
3.9	13.9	1.8	2.2
8.4	5.2	11.9	3.0
24.0	24.5	24.8	24.0
1.7	4.4	2.5	16.2
17.8	2.9	4.0	6.7
5.3	8.3	2.8	5.2
17.5	1.1	3.0	8.3
1.2	1.1	4.5	4.4
5.0	2.6	12.7	5.7
4.7	5.1	2.6	1.6
3.4	8.1	2.4	16.7
4.8	1.7	1.9	12.1
9.1	5.6	13.0	6.4

Source: N. R. Farnum, *Modern Statistical Quality Control and Improvement*, p. 55. Reprinted by permission of Brooks/Cole, an imprint of the Wadsworth Group, a division of Thompson Learning. Fax 800-730-2215.

FIGURE 2.56 Software Performance at NASA's Goddard Space Center, 1976–1990

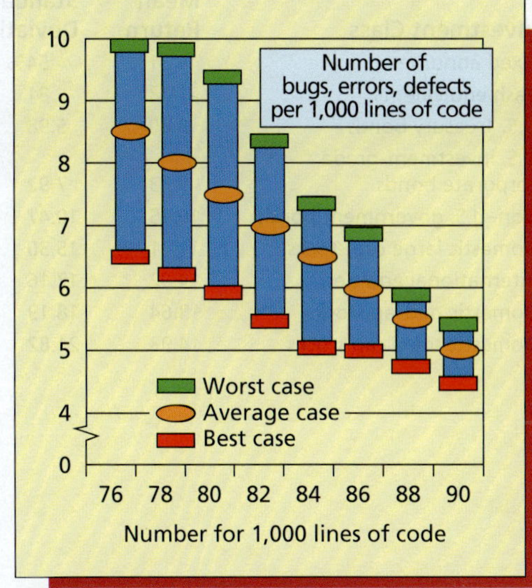

Source: Reprinted from the January 15, 1992, issue of *Business Week* by special permission. Copyright © 1992 by The McGraw-Hill Companies.

> Investment risk is often measured in terms of the volatility of an investment over time. When volatility, sometimes referred to as *standard deviation,* increases, so too does the level of return. Conversely, as risk (standard deviation) declines, so too do returns.

In order to explain the relationship between the return on an investment and its risk, *Investment Digest* presents a graph of mean return versus standard deviation (risk) for nine investment classes over the period from 1970 to 1994. This graph, which *Investment Digest* calls the "risk/return trade-off," is shown in Figure 2.57. The article says that this graph

> . . . illustrates the historical risk/return trade-off for a variety of investment classes over the 24-year period between 1970 and 1994.
>
> In the chart, cash equivalents and fixed annuities, for instance, had a standard deviation of 0.81% and 0.54% respectively, while posting returns of just over 7.73% and 8.31%. At the other end of the spectrum, domestic small-company stocks were quite volatile—with a standard deviation of 21.82%—but compensated for that increased volatility with a return of 14.93%.
>
> The answer seems to lie in asset allocation. Investment experts know the importance of asset allocation. In a nutshell, asset allocation is a method of creating a diversified portfolio of investments that minimize historical risk and maximize potential returns to help you meet your retirement goals and needs.

Suppose that, by reading off the graph of Figure 2.57, we obtain the mean return and standard deviation combinations for the various investment classes as shown in Table 2.15.

Further suppose that future returns in each investment class will behave as they have from 1970 to 1994. That is, for each investment class, regard the mean return and standard deviation in Table 2.15 as the population mean and the population standard deviation of all possible future returns. Then do the following:

a Assuming that future returns for the various investment classes are mound-shaped, for each investment class compute intervals that will contain approximately 68.26 percent and 99.73 percent of all future returns.

b Making no assumptions about the population shapes of future returns, for each investment class compute intervals that will contain at least 75 percent and 88.89 percent of all future returns.

c Assuming that future returns are mound-shaped, find

(1) An estimate of the maximum return that might be realized for each investment class.

(2) An estimate of the minimum return (or maximum loss) that might be realized for each investment class.

TABLE 2.15 Mean Return and Standard Deviation for Nine Investment Classes InvestRet

Investment Class	Mean Return	Standard Deviation
Fixed annuities	8.31%	.54%
Cash equivalents	7.73	.81
U.S. Treasury bonds	8.80	5.98
U.S. investment-grade corporate bonds	9.33	7.92
Non–U.S. government bonds	10.95	10.47
Domestic large cap stocks	11.71	15.30
International equities	14.02	17.16
Domestic midcap stocks	13.64	18.19
Domestic small cap stocks	14.93	21.82

FIGURE 2.57 The Risk/Return Trade-Off

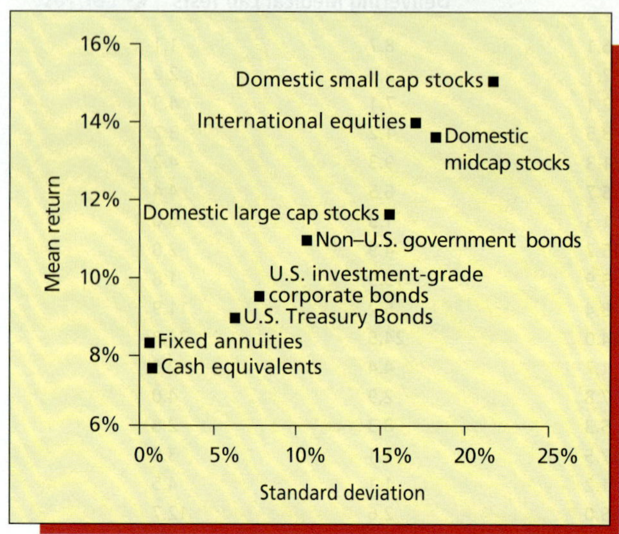

Source: The Variable Annuity Life Insurance Company, *VALIC* 9, (1995), no. 3.

d Assuming that future returns are mound-shaped, which two investment classes have the highest estimated maximum returns? What are the estimated minimum returns (maximum losses) for these investment classes?

e Assuming that future returns are mound-shaped, which two investment classes have the smallest estimated maximum returns? What are the estimated minimum returns for these investment classes?

f Calculate the coefficient of variation for each investment class and compare the investment classes with respect to risk. Which class is riskiest? Least risky?

2.85 Table 2.16 gives data concerning consumer complaints against U.S. airlines (1997–2003). Depict the data graphically. Then summarize what the data tell you about improvements in airline service from 1997 to 2003. AirComplaints

2.86 A filling process is supposed to fill jars with 16 ounces of grape jelly. Specifications state that each jar must contain between 15.95 and 16.05 ounces. A jar is selected from the process every half hour until a sample of 100 jars is obtained. When the fills of the jars are measured, we find $\bar{x} = 16.0024$ and $s = .02454$.

a Assume that the fill process is in statistical control, and also assume that the population of all jar fills is normally distributed. Determine whether the process is capable of meeting specifications by using an interval that you would expect to contain 99.73 percent of all fills.

b When the process is improved, it is found to be in statistical control. Moreover, a sample of 100 fills yields $\bar{x} = 16.0011$ and $s = .01328$. Is the improved process capable of meeting specifications? Justify your answer.

2.87 THE INTERNATIONAL BUSINESS TRAVEL EXPENSE CASE

Suppose that a large international corporation wishes to obtain its own "benchmark" for one-day travel expenses in Moscow. To do this, it records the one-day travel expenses for a random sample of 35 executives visiting Moscow. The mean and the standard deviation of these expenses are calculated to be $\bar{x} = \$538$ and $s = \$41$. Furthermore, a histogram shows that the expenses are approximately normally distributed.

a Find an interval that we estimate contains 99.73 percent of all one-day travel expenses in Moscow.

b If an executive submits an expense of $720 for a one-day stay in Moscow, should this expense be considered unusually high? Why or why not?

2.88 THE UNITED KINGDOM INSURANCE CASE

Figure 2.58 summarizes information concerning insurance expenditures of households in the United Kingdom in 1993.

a Approximately what percentage of households spent on life insurance?

b What is the approximate average expenditure (in UKL) per household on life insurance? Note: the averages given in Figure 2.58 are for households that spend in the class.

TABLE 2.16 Consumer Complaints against U.S. Airlines, 1997–2003 (for Exercise 2.85)
AirComplaints

Complaint Category	1997	1998	1999	2000	2001	2002	2003
Total	6,394	7,980	17,345	20,564	14,076	7,697	4,600
Flight problems[1]	1,699	2,270	6,449	8,698	5,048	1,808	1,049
Customer service[2]	1,418	1,716	3,657	4,074	2,531	1,478	584
Baggage	826	1,105	2,351	2,753	1,965	1,082	801
Ticketing/boarding[3]	904	805	1,329	1,405	1,310	898	643
Refunds	531	601	935	803	942	737	428
Fares[4]	195	276	584	708	568	436	243
Disability[5]	(NA)	331	520	612	457	420	323
Oversales[6]	414	387	673	759	539	364	223
Discrimination[7]	(NA)	(NA)	(NA)	(NA)	164	176	73
Advertising	57	39	57	42	42	43	13
Tours	13	23	28	25	11	([8])	([8])
Animals	(NA)	(NA)	(NA)	1	6	–	2
Smoking	5	([9])	([9])	([9])	([9])	([9])	([9])
Credit	1	([9])	([9])	([9])	([9])	([9])	([9])
Other	331	427	762	684	493	255	218

– Represents zero. NA Not available. [1]Cancellations, delays, etc. from schedule. [2]Unhelpful employees, inadequate meals or cabin service, treatment of delayed passengers. [3]Errors in reservations and ticketing; problems in making reservations and obtaining tickets. [4]Incorrect or incomplete information about fares, discount fare conditions, and availability, etc. [5]Prior to 1998, included in ticketing/boarding. [6]All bumping problems, whether or not airline complied with DOT regulations. [7]Allegations of discrimination by airlines due to factors other than disability, such as race, religion, national origin or sex. [8]Included in "Other" beginning 2002. [9]Included in "Other" beginning 1998.

Source: U.S. Department of Transportation, Aviation Consumer Protection Division, *Air Travel Consumer Report,* monthly. See Internet site <http://airconsumer.ost.dot.gov>.

FIGURE 2.58 Insurance Expenditures of Households in the United Kingdom (1993)

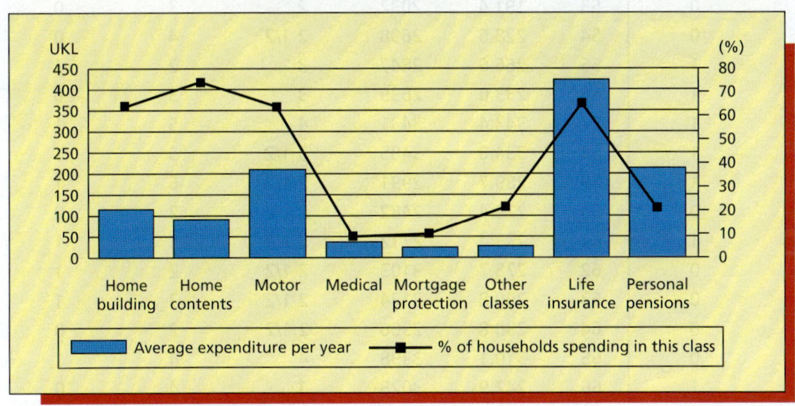

Source: CSO family expenditure survey.

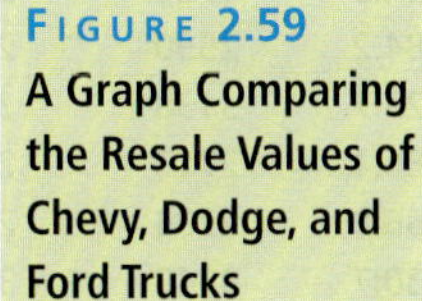

FIGURE 2.59 A Graph Comparing the Resale Values of Chevy, Dodge, and Ford Trucks

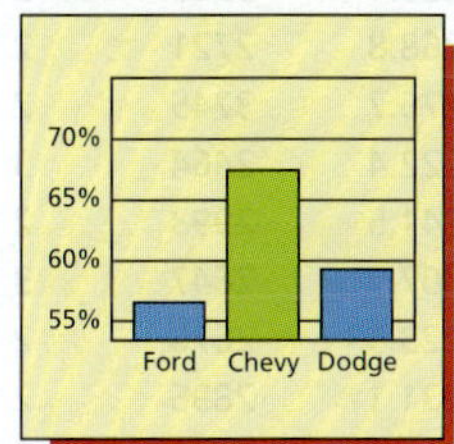

Source: Reprinted courtesy of General Motors Corporation.

2.89 Figure 2.59 was used in various Chevrolet magazine advertisements in 1997 to compare the overall resale values of Chevrolet, Dodge, and Ford trucks in the years from 1990 to 1997. What is somewhat misleading about this graph?

2.90 THE FLORIDA POOL HOME CASE

In Florida, real estate agents refer to homes having a swimming pool as *pool homes.* In this case, Sunshine Pools Inc. markets and installs pools throughout the state of Florida. The company wishes to estimate the percentage of a pool's cost that can be recouped by a buyer when he or she sells the home. For instance, if a homeowner purchases a pool for which the current selling price is $30,000 and then sells the home in the current real estate market for $20,000 more than the homeowner would get if the home did not have a pool, the homeowner has recouped $(20{,}000/30{,}000) \times 100\% = 66.67\%$ of the pool's cost. To make this estimate, the company randomly selects 80 homes from all of the homes sold in a Florida city (over the last six months) having a size between 2,000 and 3,500 square feet. For each sampled home, the following data are collected: selling price (in thousands of dollars); square footage; the number of bathrooms; a niceness rating (expressed as an integer from 1 to 7 and assigned by a real estate agent); and whether or not the home has a pool (1 = yes, 0 = no). The data are given in Table 2.17. Figure 2.60 gives descriptive statistics for the 43 homes having a pool and for the 37 homes that do not have a pool. PoolHome

a. Using Figure 2.60, compare the mean selling prices of the homes having a pool and the homes that do not have a pool. Using this data, and assuming that the average current selling price of the pools in the sample is \$32,500, estimate the percentage of a pool's cost that can be recouped when the home is sold.

b. The comparison you made in part (a) could be misleading. Noting that different homes have different square footages, numbers of bathrooms, and niceness ratings, explain why.

TABLE 2.17 The Florida Pool Home Data PoolHome

Home	Price ($1000s)	Size (Sq Feet)	Number of Bathrooms	Niceness Rating	Pool? yes=1; no=0	Home	Price ($1000s)	Size (Sq Feet)	Number of Bathrooms	Niceness Rating	Pool? yes=1; no=0
1	260.9	2666	2 1/2	7	0	41	285.6	2761	3	6	1
2	337.3	3418	3 1/2	6	1	42	216.1	2880	2 1/2	2	0
3	268.4	2945	2	5	1	43	261.3	3426	3	1	1
4	242.2	2942	2 1/2	3	1	44	236.4	2895	2 1/2	2	1
5	255.2	2798	3	3	1	45	267.5	2726	3	7	0
6	205.7	2210	2 1/2	2	0	46	220.2	2930	2 1/2	2	0
7	249.5	2209	2	7	0	47	300.1	3013	2 1/2	6	1
8	193.6	2465	2 1/2	1	0	48	260.0	2675	2	6	0
9	242.7	2955	2	4	1	49	277.5	2874	3 1/2	6	1
10	244.5	2722	2 1/2	5	0	50	274.9	2765	2 1/2	4	1
11	184.2	2590	2 1/2	1	0	51	259.8	3020	3 1/2	2	1
12	325.7	3138	3 1/2	7	1	52	235.0	2887	2 1/2	1	1
13	266.1	2713	2	7	0	53	191.4	2032	2	3	0
14	166.0	2284	2 1/2	2	0	54	228.5	2698	2 1/2	4	0
15	330.7	3140	3 1/2	6	1	55	266.6	2847	3	2	1
16	289.1	3205	2 1/2	3	1	56	233.0	2639	3	3	0
17	268.8	2721	2 1/2	6	1	57	343.4	3431	4	5	1
18	276.7	3245	2 1/2	2	1	58	334.0	3485	3 1/2	5	1
19	222.4	2464	3	3	1	59	289.7	2991	2 1/2	6	1
20	241.5	2993	2 1/2	1	0	60	228.4	2482	2 1/2	2	0
21	307.9	2647	3 1/2	6	1	61	233.4	2712	2 1/2	1	1
22	223.5	2670	2 1/2	4	0	62	275.7	3103	2 1/2	2	1
23	231.1	2895	2 1/2	3	0	63	290.8	3124	2 1/2	3	1
24	216.5	2643	2 1/2	3	0	64	230.8	2906	2 1/2	2	0
25	205.5	2915	2	1	0	65	310.1	3398	4	4	1
26	258.3	2800	3 1/2	2	1	66	247.9	3028	3	4	0
27	227.6	2557	2 1/2	3	1	67	249.9	2761	2	5	0
28	255.4	2805	2	3	1	68	220.5	2842	3	3	0
29	235.7	2878	2 1/2	4	0	69	226.2	2666	2 1/2	6	0
30	285.1	2795	3	7	1	70	313.7	2744	2 1/2	7	1
31	284.8	2748	2 1/2	7	1	71	210.1	2508	2 1/2	4	0
32	193.7	2256	2 1/2	2	0	72	244.9	2480	2 1/2	5	0
33	247.5	2659	2 1/2	2	1	73	235.8	2986	2 1/2	4	0
34	274.8	3241	3 1/2	4	1	74	263.2	2753	2 1/2	7	0
35	264.4	3166	3	3	1	75	280.2	2522	2 1/2	6	1
36	204.1	2466	2	2	0	76	290.8	2808	2 1/2	7	1
37	273.9	2945	2 1/2	5	1	77	235.4	2616	2 1/2	3	0
38	238.5	2727	3	1	1	78	190.3	2603	2 1/2	2	0
39	274.4	3141	4	4	1	79	234.4	2804	2 1/2	4	0
40	259.6	2552	2	7	1	80	238.7	2851	2 1/2	5	0

FIGURE 2.60 Descriptive Statistics for Homes With and Without Pools (for Exercise 2.90)

Descriptive statistics (Homes with Pools)	Price	Descriptive statistics (Homes without Pools)	Price
count	43	count	37
mean	276.056	mean	226.900
sample variance	937.821	sample variance	609.902
sample standard deviation	30.624	sample standard deviation	24.696
minimum	222.4	minimum	166
maximum	343.4	maximum	267.5
range	121	range	101.5

TABLE 2.18 Mortgage Loan Rates at Butler County, Ohio, Financial Institutions (February 1999)
OhioMort

Institution	15-Year	30-Year
Fifth/Third Bank	6.60 f	6.875 f
	5.50 v	6.375 v
First Southwestern	6.625 f	7.0 f
	6.0 v	6.75 v
LCNB	6.75 f	7.125 f
	5.75 v	6.5 v
Oxford Bank	6.75 f	7.25 f
	6.75 v	6.625 v
Union County National	6.75 f	6.875 f
	6.59 v	7.3775 v
Bank One	7.0 f	7.25 f
	6.0 v	6.75 v

2.91 Table 2.18 gives February 1999 mortgage loan rates at financial institutions in Butler County, Ohio, as obtained in a survey conducted by the authors. Rates for 15-year and 30-year mortgages are given, and rates for both fixed- and variable-rate loans are given. A fixed-rate (f) loan has an interest rate that stays the same for the term of the mortgage, whereas a variable-rate (v) loan's interest rate changes with the market during the term of the mortgage. By constructing appropriate box-and-whiskers plots and by placing them side by side for ready comparison, compare the following mortgage rate distributions on the basis of central tendency, variability, skewness, and outliers.

a Compare rates for 15-year mortgages versus rates for 30-year mortgages. OhioMort

b Compare rates for fixed-rate mortgages versus rates for variable-rate mortgages.

c Compare rates for four loan types: fixed 15-year mortgages, fixed 30-year mortgages, variable 15-year mortgages, and variable 30-year mortgages.

2.92 Internet Exercise

Overview: The Data and Story Library (DASL) houses a rich collection of data sets useful for teaching and learning statistics, from a variety of sources, contributed primarily by university faculty members. DASL can be reached through the BSC by clicking on the Data Bases button in the BSC home screen and by then clicking on the Data and Story Library link. The screen image to the right shows the BSC Data Base page. The DASL can also be reached directly using the url http://lib.stat.cmu.edu/DASL/. The objective of this exercise is to retrieve a data set of chief executive officer salaries and to construct selected graphical and numerical statistical summaries of the data.

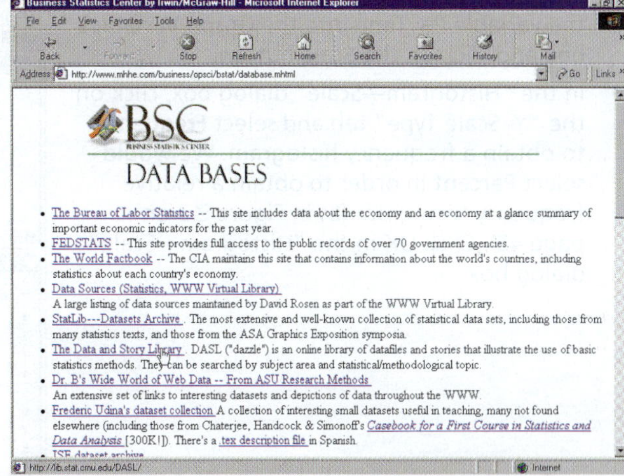

Appendix 2.1 ■ Descriptive Statistics Using MINITAB

The instructions in this section begin by describing the entry of data into the MINITAB data window. Alternatively, the data may be loaded directly from the data disk included with the text. The appropriate data file name is given at the top of each instruction block. Please refer to Appendix 1.1 for further information about entering data, saving data and printing results when using MINITAB.

- **Stem and leaf plot** in Figure 2.1 on page 45 (data file: GasMiles.mtw):
- Enter the mileage data from Table 2.1 (page 44) into column C1 with variable name MPG.
- Select **Graph : Stem-and-Leaf**
- In the Stem-and-Leaf dialog box, select the variable MPG into the Graph Variables box by clicking on MPG in the variables list and by then clicking the Select button (or by double clicking on MPG in the variables list or by typing MPG into the Variables box).
- Click OK in the Stem-and-Leaf dialog box.
- The stem-and-leaf plot appears in the Session window and can be selected for printing or copied and pasted to a word processing document. (See Appendix 1.1)

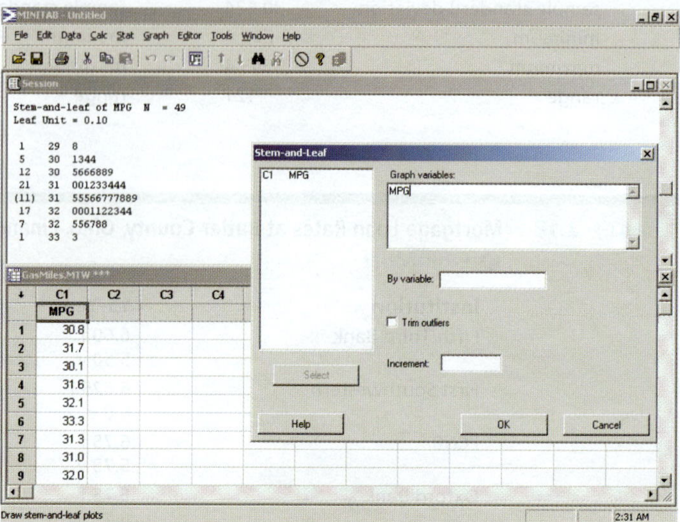

Frequency histogram of the payment times in Figure 2.2 on page 48 (data file: PayTime.mtw):

- Enter the payment time data from Table 2.2 (page 46) into column C1 with variable name PayTime.
- Select **Graph : Histogram**
- In the Histograms dialog box, select Simple (this selection is the default selection) and click OK in the Histograms dialog box.

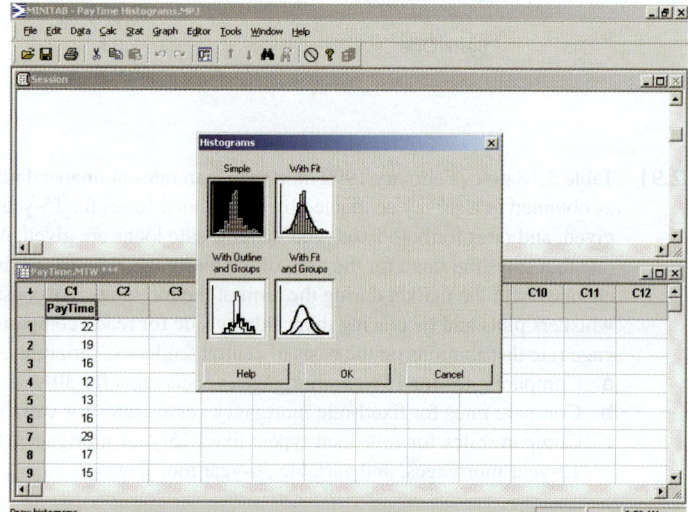

- In the "Histogram—Simple" dialog box, select the variable PayTime into the Graph Variables box and click on the Scale button.
- In the "Histogram—Scale" dialog box, click on the "Y- Scale Type" tab and select **Frequency** to obtain a frequency histogram. We would select **Percent** in order to obtain a relative frequency histogram (as in Figure 2.3 on page 48). Click OK in the "Histogram—Scale" dialog box.

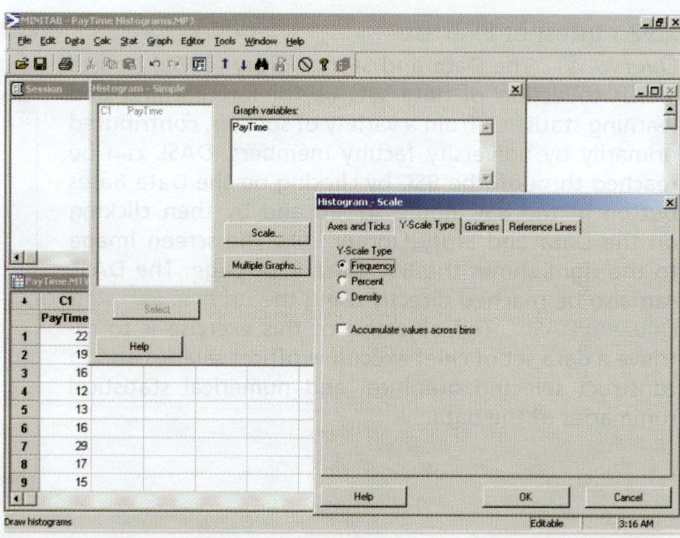

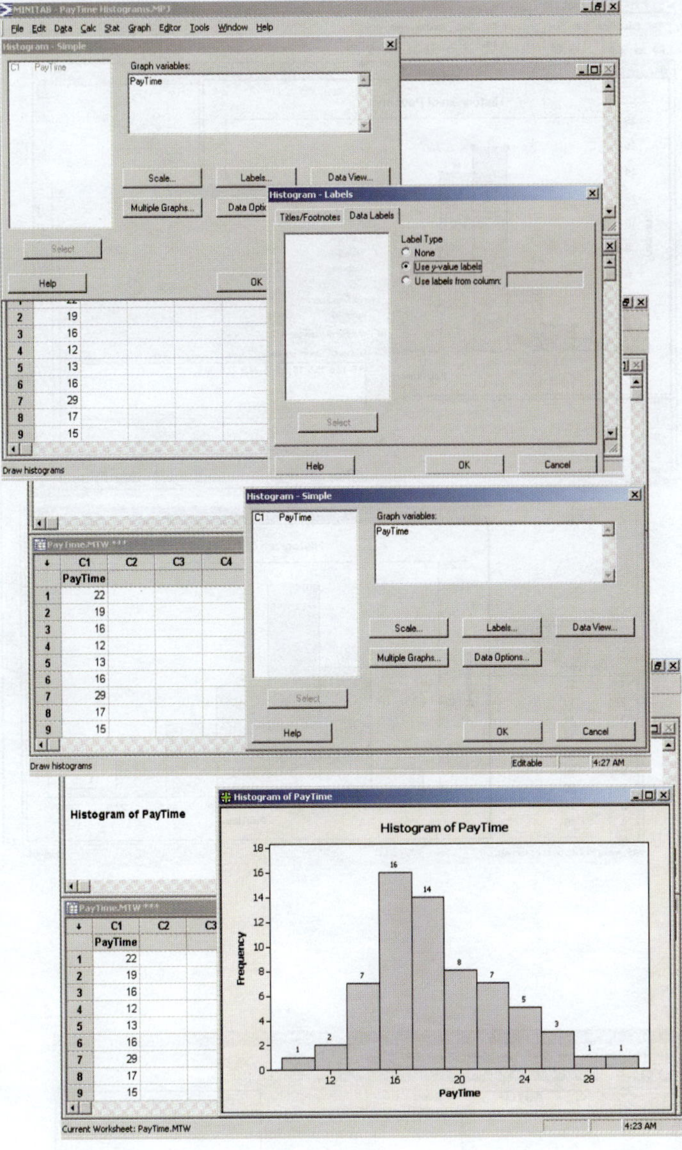

- To obtain **data labels** (the numbers at the tops of the histogram bars that indicate the heights of the bars—in this case the frequencies), click on the Labels button in the "Histogram—Simple" dialog box. In the "Histogram—Labels" dialog box, click on the Data Labels tab and select "Use y-value labels". Then click OK in the "Histogram—Labels" dialog box.

- To create the histogram, click OK in the "Histogram—Simple" dialog box. **The histogram will appear in a graphics window.**

- The histogram can be selected for printing or can be copied and pasted into a word processor document. (See Appendix 1.1.)
- Notice that MINITAB automatically defines classes for the histogram bars, and automatically provides labeled tick marks (here 12, 16, 20, 24 and 28) on the x-scale of the histogram. The automatically provided classes and x-scale ticks are not the same as those that would be obtained using the method of histogram construction presented in Section 2.1 of this book. However, we can edit the automatically constructed histogram to produce the histogram classes we have described in Section 2.1. This is sometimes called "binning."

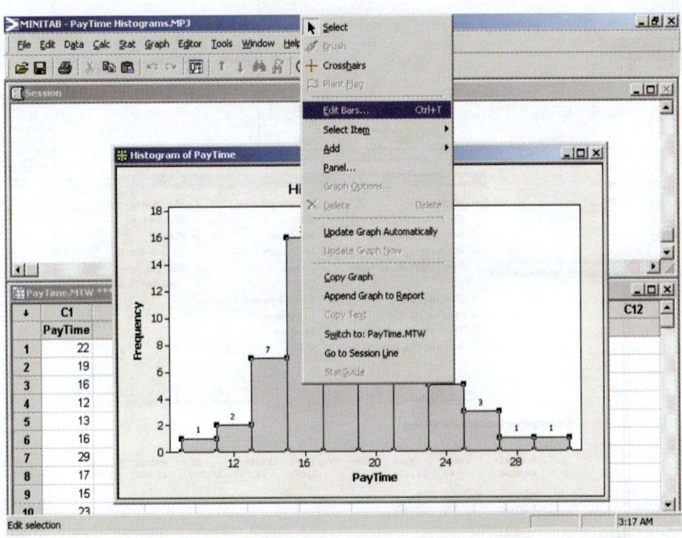

In order to obtain the histogram classes and the x-scale labeling shown in Figure 2.2 on page 48:

- Right click in the middle of any of the histogram bars.
- In the pop-up menu, select "Edit bars".

- In the "Edit Bars" dialog box, click on the Binning tab.
- Select the Interval Type to be Cutpoint to label the x-scale by using class boundaries as in Figure 2.2. If we wished to label the x-scale by using class midpoints as in Figure 2.3 on page 48, we would select the Interval Type to be Midpoint.
- Select the Interval Definition to be "Midpoint/Cutpoint positions."
- In the Midpoint/Cutpoint positions window, enter the class boundaries (or cutpoints)

  9.5 12.5 15.5 18.5 21.5 24.5 27.5 30.5

  as given in Table 2.3 (page 48) or shown in Figure 2.2.
- Click OK in the "Edit Bars" dialog box.
- The histogram in the graphics window will be edited to produce the class boundaries, histogram bars, and x-axis labels shown in Figure 2.2.
- The histogram can be further edited by right clicking on a desired portion of the histogram and by clicking on the Edit option in the resulting pop-up menu. A dialog box will appear that allows the analyst to edit many aspects of the selected portion of the graphic. For instance, the axis labels, histogram title, data and figure regions, and data labels may all be edited.

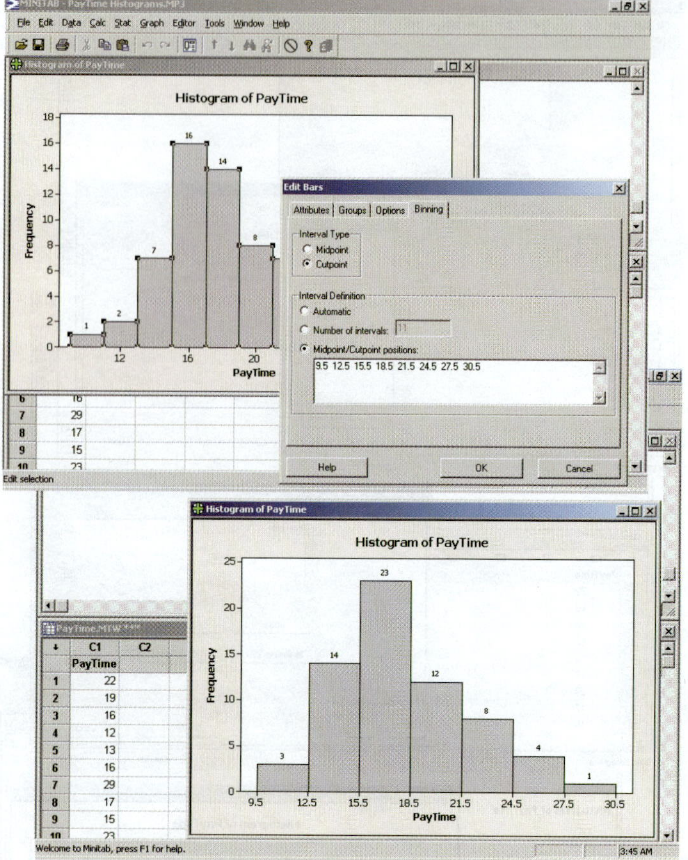

Numerical descriptive statistics in Figure 2.23 on page 63 (data file: PayTime.mtw):

- Enter the payment time data from Table 2.2 (page 46) into column C1 with variable name PayTime.
- Select **Stat : Basic Statistics : Display Descriptive Statistics.**
- In the Display Descriptive Statistics dialog box, select the variable Paytime into the Variables window.
- In the Display Descriptive Statistics dialog box, click on the Statistics button.
- In the "Descriptive Statistics—Statistics" dialog box, enter checkmarks in the checkboxes corresponding to the desired descriptive statistics. Here we have checked the mean, standard deviation, variance, first quartile, median, third quartile, minimum, maximum, range, and total checkboxes.
- Click OK in the "Descriptive Statistics—Statistics" dialog box.
- Click OK in the Display Descriptive Statistics dialog box.
- The requested descriptive statistics are displayed in the session window.

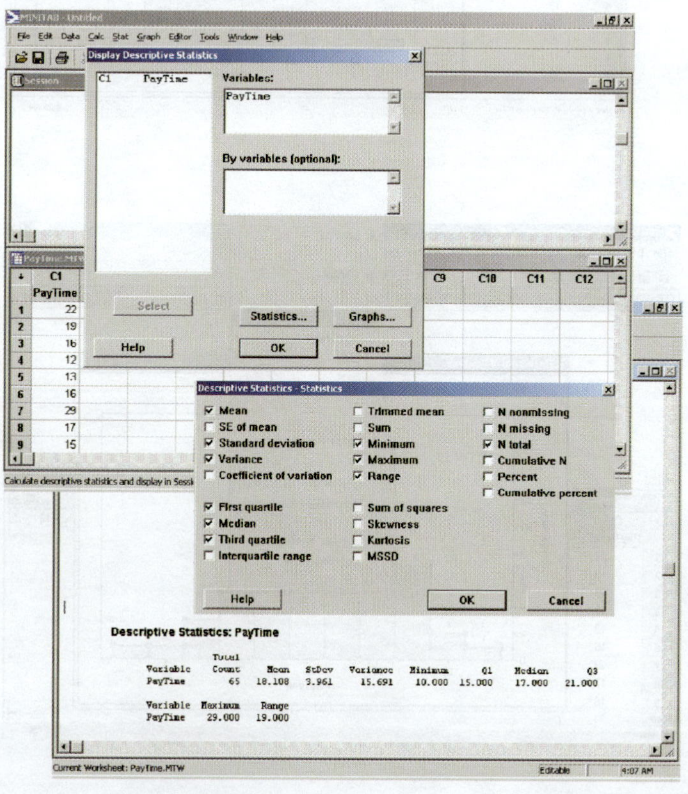

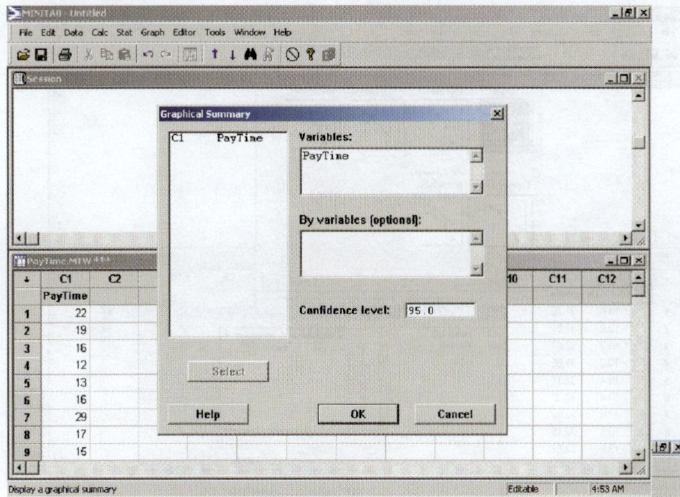

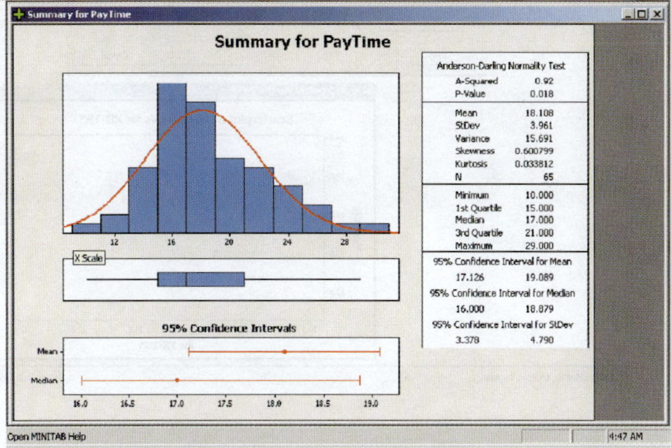

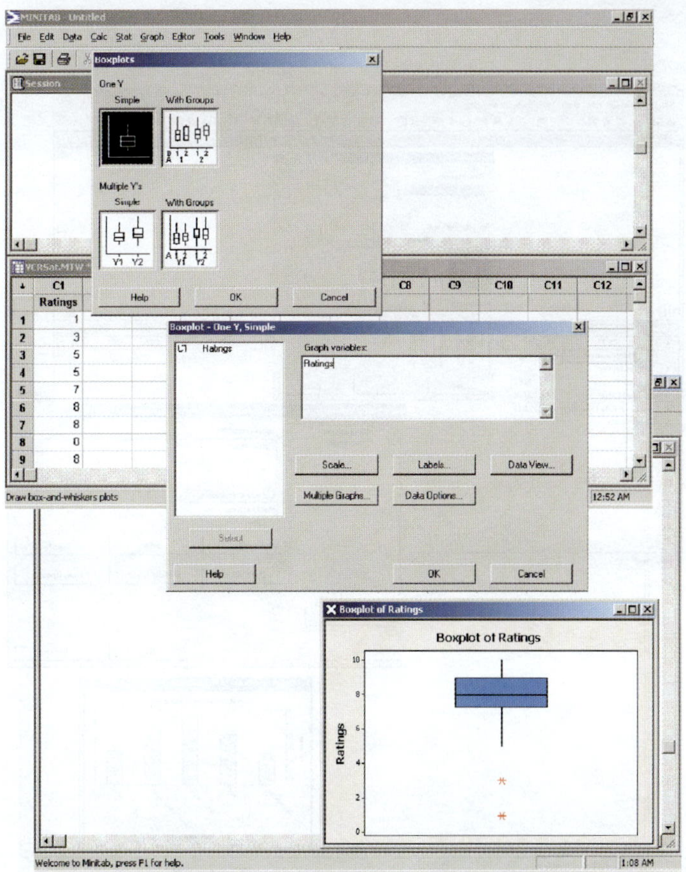

Minitab also offers a unique and informative graphical data summary that includes a histogram, a box plot, and numerical descriptive statistics as well as confidence intervals (discussed in Chapter 7) for the mean and the median.

To obtain the **graphical summary:**

- Select **Stat : Basic Statistics : Graphical Summary.**
- In the Graphical Summary dialog box, select the variable PayTime into the Variable window.
- Click OK in the Graphical Summary dialog box.
- The graphical data summary will appear in a high-resolution graphics window and can be selected for printing or can be copied and pasted to a word processor document. (See Appendix 1.1)

Box plot similar to Figure 2.34(b) on page 81 (data file: DVDSat.mtw):

- Enter the satisfaction rating data from page 61 into column C1 with variable name Ratings.
- Select **Graph : Boxplot**
- In the Boxplots dialog box, select "One Y Simple."
- In the "Boxplot—One Y, Simple" dialog box, select the variable Ratings into the Graph Variables window.
- Click OK in the "Boxplot—One Y, Simple" dialog box.
- The boxplot appears in a graphics window and can be selected for printing or can be copied and pasted into a word processor document.
- Note that the boxplot produced by MINITAB is constructed using methods somewhat different from those presented in Section 2.4 of this book. Consult the MINITAB help menu for a precise description of the boxplot construction method used. A boxplot that is constructed using the methods of Section 2.4 can be displayed in the Session window—rather than in a graphics window. Such a boxplot is called a **character boxplot.** Character graphs do not appear by default on the Graph pull-down menu in MINITAB 14. However, the **Character Graph** option can be added to the Graph pull-down menu. Instructions for doing this can be found in the MINITAB help menu—consult "Character graphs" in the help index.

Scatter plot in Figure 2.47 on page 95 (data file: Viscosity.mtw):

- Enter the viscosity data from Table 2.11 on page 95—pounds of chemical XB-135 with variable name "lbs XB-135" in column C1 and values of viscosity in column C2 with variable name Viscosity.
- Select **Graph : Scatterplot**
- In the Scatterplots dialog box, select Simple.
- Click OK in the Scatterplots dialog box.
- In the "Scatterplot—Simple" dialog box, select the variable Viscosity into the "Y variable" box in row 1 and select the variable "lbs XB-135" into the "X variable" box in row 1.
- Click OK in the "Scatterplot—Simple" dialog box.
- The scatterplot will appear in a graphics window and can be selected for printing or can be copied and pasted into a word processor document.
- Additional plots can be obtained by placing appropriate variable names in other rows in the "Y variable" and "X variable" boxes.

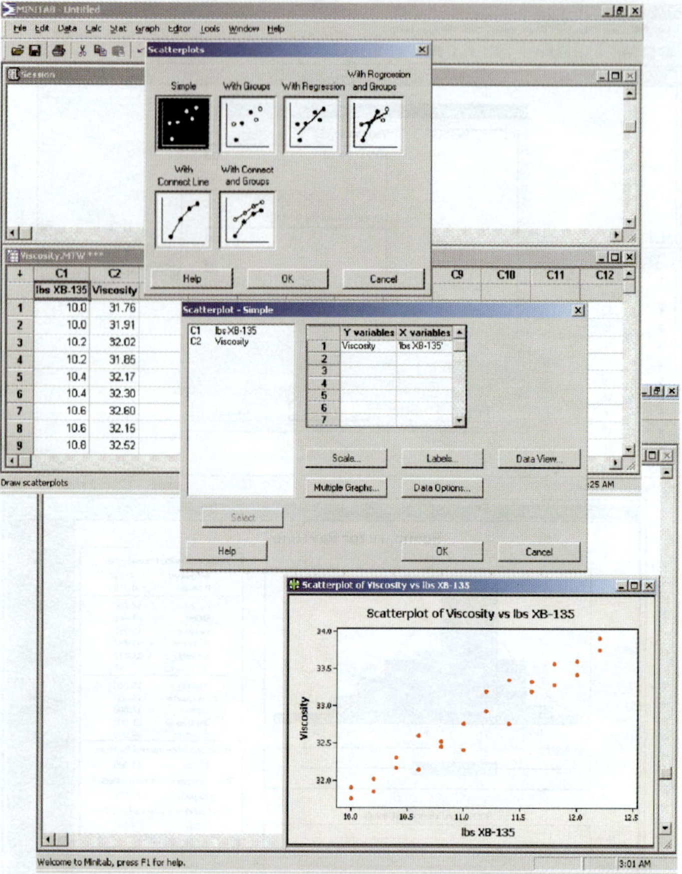

Bar chart of automobile sales percentages similar to that shown in Figure 2.44(a) on page 92:

- Enter the auto manufacturers into column C1 with variable name Manufacturer and the sales percentages into column C2 with variable name Percentage as shown in the screenshot.
- Select **Graph : Bar Chart.**
- In the Bar Charts dialog box, select "Values from a table" in the "Bars represent:" pull-down menu.
- In the Bar Charts dialog box, select "One column of values—Simple."
- Click OK in the Bar Charts dialog box.
- In the "Bar Chart—Values from a table, One column of values, Simple" dialog box, select the variable Percentage into the "Graph variables" window and select the variable Manufacturer into the "Categorical variable" window. Then click OK.
- The bar chart will appear in a graphics window and can be edited, selected for printing, or copied and pasted into a word processor document.

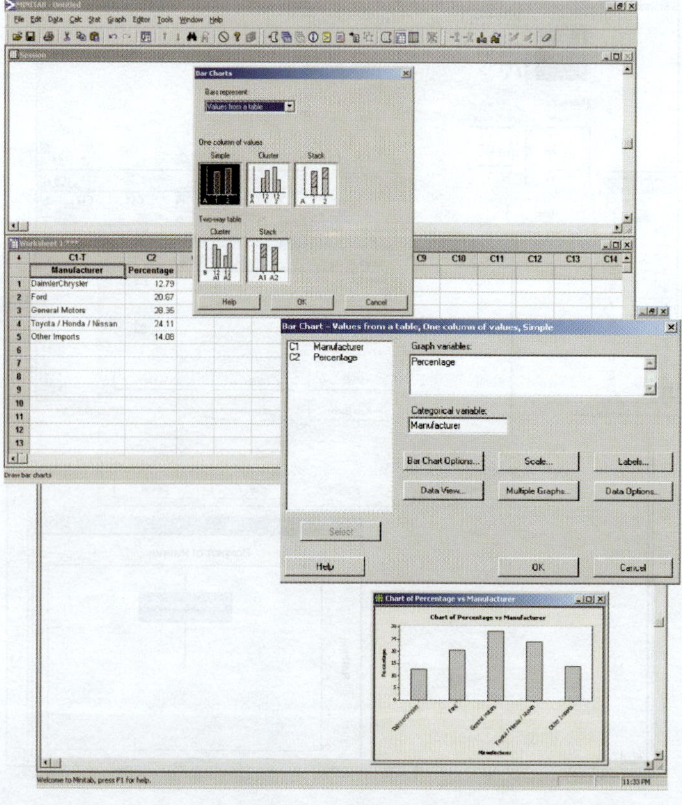

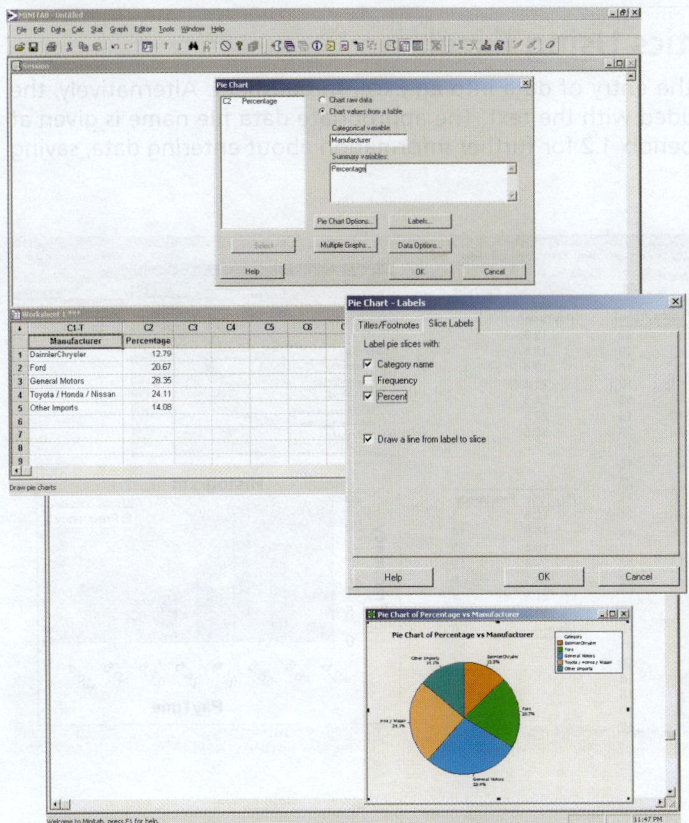

Pie chart of automobile sales percentages similar to that shown in Figure 2.44(b) on page 92:

- Enter the auto manufacturers into column C1 with variable name Manufacturer and the sales percentages into column C2 with variable name Percentage as shown in the screenshot.
- Select **Graph : Pie Chart.**
- In the Pie Chart dialog box, select "Chart values from a table" by clicking.
- Click in the "Categorical variable" window and enter the variable name Manufacturer.
- Enter the variable name Percentage into the "Summary variables" window.
- In the Pie Chart dialog box, click on the Labels button.
- In the "Pie Chart—Labels" dialog box, click on the Slice Labels tab.
- Place checkmarks in the Category name, Percent, and "Draw a line from label to slice" checkboxes.
- Click OK in the "Pie Chart—Labels" dialog box.
- Click OK in the Pie Chart dialog box.
- The pie chart will appear in a graphics window and can be edited, selected for printing, or copied and pasted into a word processor document.

Appendix 2.2 ■ Descriptive Statistics Using Excel

The instructions in this section begin by describing the entry of data into an Excel spreadsheet. Alternatively, the data may be loaded directly from the data disk included with the text. The appropriate data file name is given at the top of each instruction block. Please refer to Appendix 1.2 for further information about entering data, saving data, and printing results.

Frequency histogram for the payment times similar to Figure 2.2 on page 48 (data file: PayTime.xls):

- Enter the payment time data in Table 2.2 (page 46) into column A with the label PayTime in row 1 of column A (that is, in cell A1) and with the 65 payment times in cells A2 to A66.
- Enter the label (or variable name) PayTime in cell C1.
- Enter the upper class boundaries from Table 2.3 on page 48 (that is, 12.5, 15.5, 18.5, 21.5, 24.5, 27.5, and 30.5) into cells C2 to C8. (Skip this entry if you wish Excel to find **automatic** class limits).
- Select **Tools : Data Analysis : Histogram.** Note that if the Data Analysis option does not appear in the Tools pull-down menu, click on "Add ins" and install the Data Analysis Toolpak.
- Click OK in the Data Analysis dialog box.
- In the Histogram dialog box, enter the range A1.A66 into the "Input Range" box.
- In the "Bin Range" box enter the range, C1.C8. Leave this box blank if Excel is providing **automatic** class limits.
- Check the Labels checkbox.
- Click "Output Range" and enter a cell, say C12, in the "Output Range" box. The upper left portion of the output will be placed in the specified cell.
- Check the "Chart Output" checkbox.
- Click OK in the Histogram dialog box.
- Click on the histogram that now appears and use the mouse to resize the chart. In particular, enlarge the histogram until all of the upper class limits are displayed along the horizontal axis. If necessary, right-click on a horizontal axis label and reduce the font size in order to show all of the upper class limits.

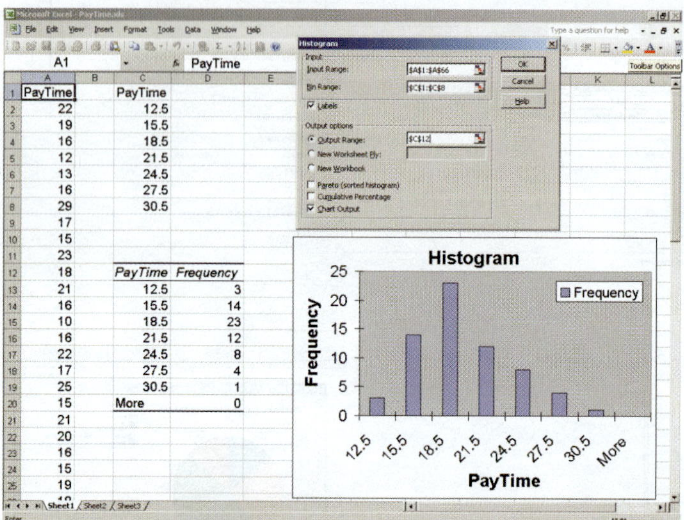

To remove the gaps between the bars (optional):

- Double click on any of the histogram bars.
- In the Format Data Series dialog box that appears, click on the Options tab.
- In the box for "Gap width", enter 0 (that is, zero).
- Click OK in the Format Data Series dialog box.
- The histogram can be selected for printing or can be copied-and-pasted to a word processing document. (See Appendix 1.2.)

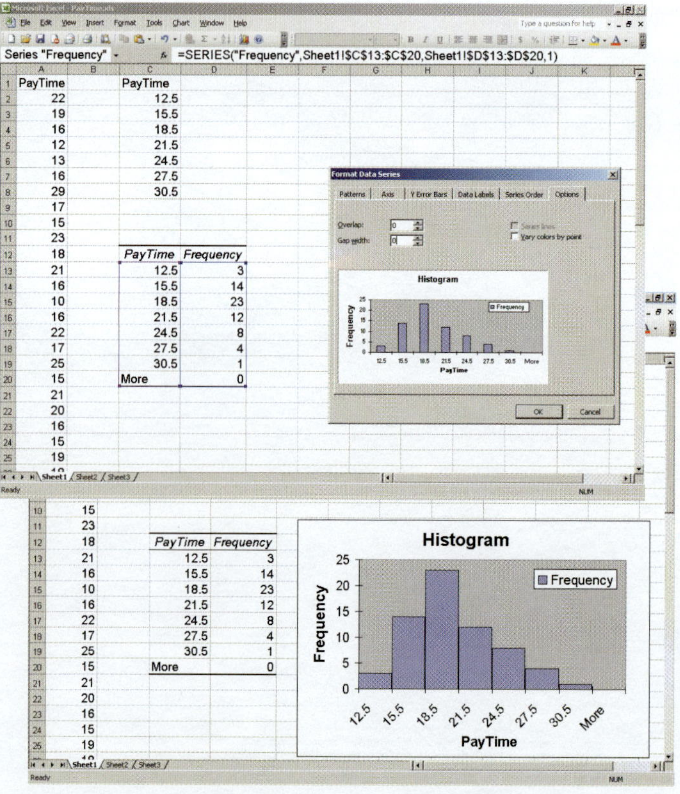

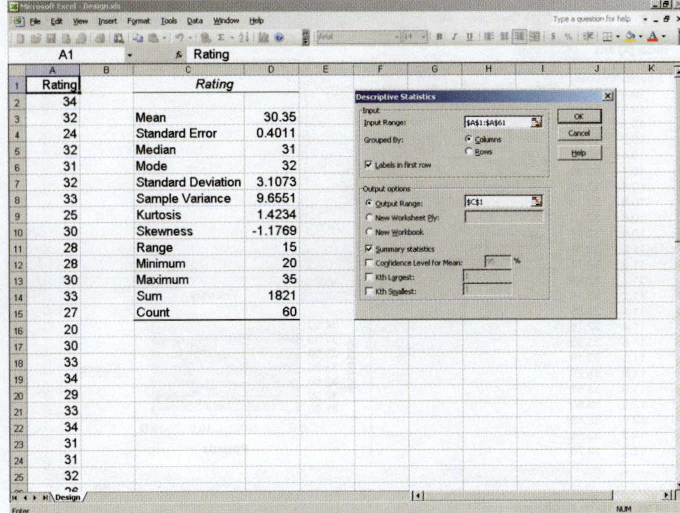

Numerical descriptive statistics for the bottle design ratings in Figure 2.24 (a) on page 64 (data file: Design.xls):

- Enter the bottle design ratings data into column A with the label Rating in cell A1 and with the 60 design ratings from Table 1.3 (page 8) in cells A2 to A61.
- Select **Tools : Data Analysis : Descriptive Statistics.**
- Click OK in the Data Analysis dialog box.
- Enter the range for the data, A1.A61, into the "Input Range" box.
- Check the "Labels in First Row" checkbox.
- Click "Output Range" and enter the cell for the upper left corner of the desired location of the output, say C1.
- Check the "Summary Statistics" checkbox.
- Click OK in the Descriptive Statistics dialog box.
- The descriptive statistics summary will appear in cells C1. D15. Drag the column C border to reveal complete labels for all statistics. The descriptive statistics can be printed directly from Excel or can be copied-and-pasted to a word processing document. (See Appendix 1.2)

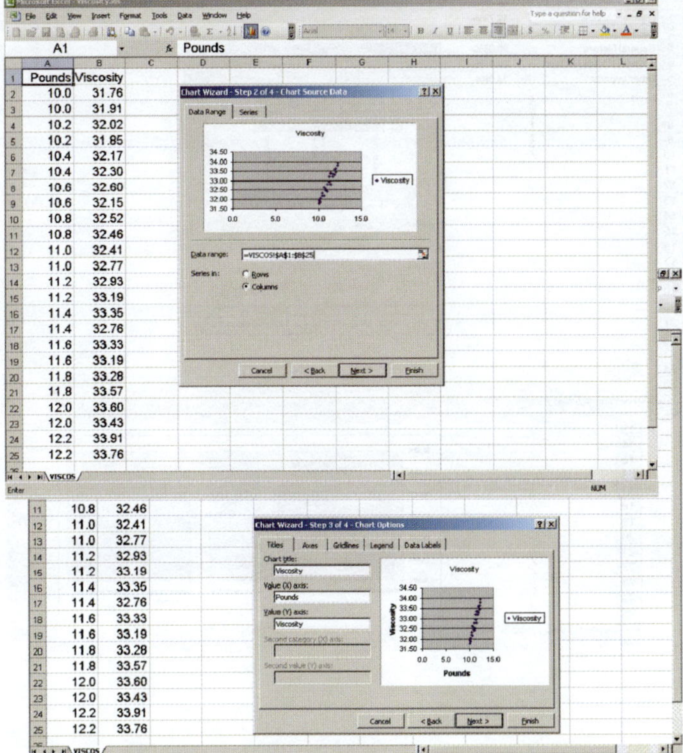

Scatter plot similar to Figure 2.47 on page 95 (data file: Viscosity.xls):

- Enter the viscosity data from Table 2.11 (page 95) into columns A and B. Place the label Pounds in cell A1 and enter the pounds of chemical figures into cells A2 to A25. Similarly, place the label Viscosity in cell B1 and enter the viscosity figures into cells B2 to B25. (Note: The order of the columns determines the axes in the plot. The variable for the vertical axis must be in the second column).
- Select the Chart Wizard from the toolbar.
- In the Step 1 dialog box, select "XY (Scatter)" from the Chart Type menu. Click Next.
- In the Step 2 dialog box, enter the data range of both columns combined, A1.B25, into the "Data range" box. Alternatively, click in the "Data range" box and select cells A1 through B25 with the mouse.
- Select the "Series in: Columns" option and click Next.
- In the Step 3 dialog box, enter Pounds in the "Value(X) Axis" box and enter Viscosity in the "Value(Y) Axis" box. Click Next.
- In the Step 4 dialog box, click Finish.
- Move the graph and resize it as desired by dragging edges with the mouse.

- Change the horizontal scale by double clicking on any of the numeric labels on the horizontal scale (for instance, double click on the 10). Then, in the Format Axis dialog box, click on the "Scale" tab and change the "minimum value" to 10. Click OK.
- The spreadsheet and scatter plot can be printed directly from Excel or can be copied-and-pasted to a word processing document. (See Appendix 1.2)

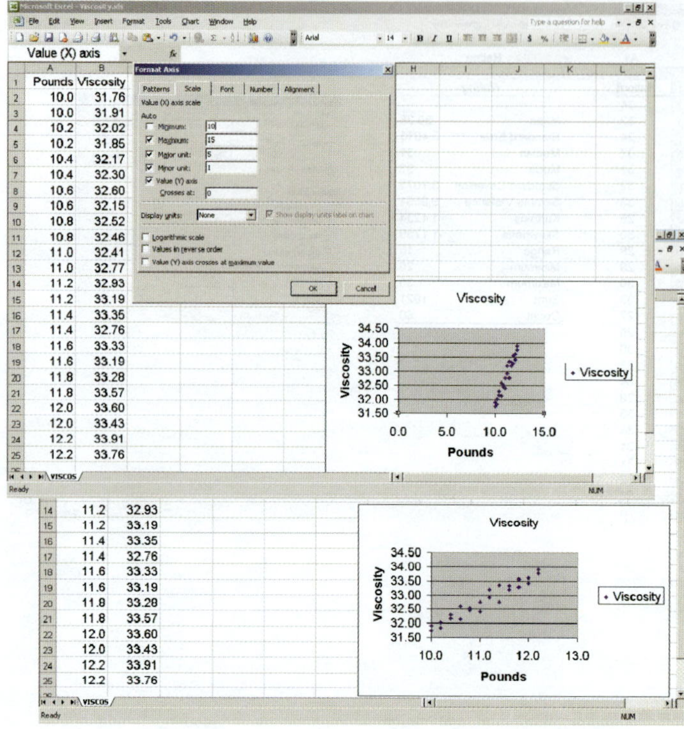

Bar chart for categorical data (auto manufacturer percentages) in Figure 2.44 (a) on page 92 (data file: AutoShares.xls):

- Enter the automobile sales data of Figure 2.44 into columns A and B as shown in the screenshot.
- Select the Chart Wizard from the toolbar.
- Select "Column" from the Chart Type menu and click Next.
- In the "Chart Wizard—Step 2 of 4" dialog box, enter A1.B4 into the "Data range" box.
- Select the "Series in: Columns" option.
- Click Finish in the "Source Data" dialog box.

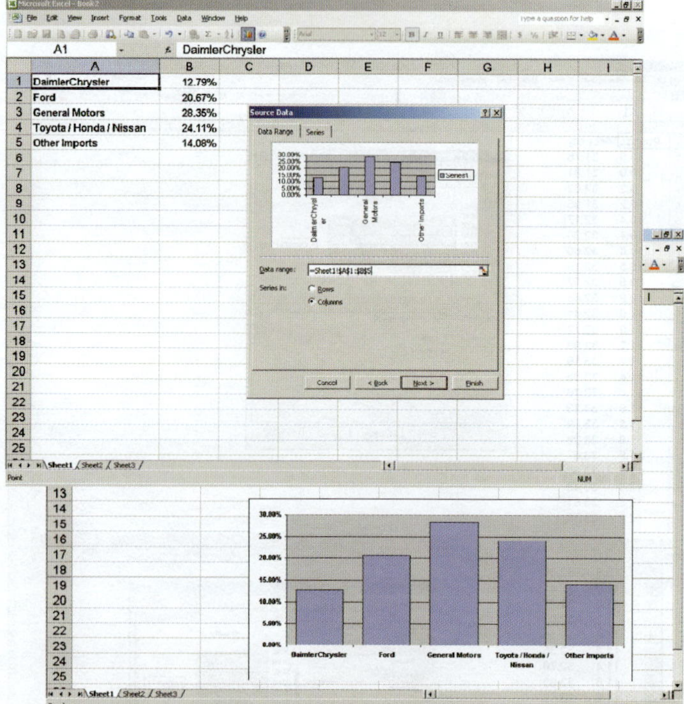

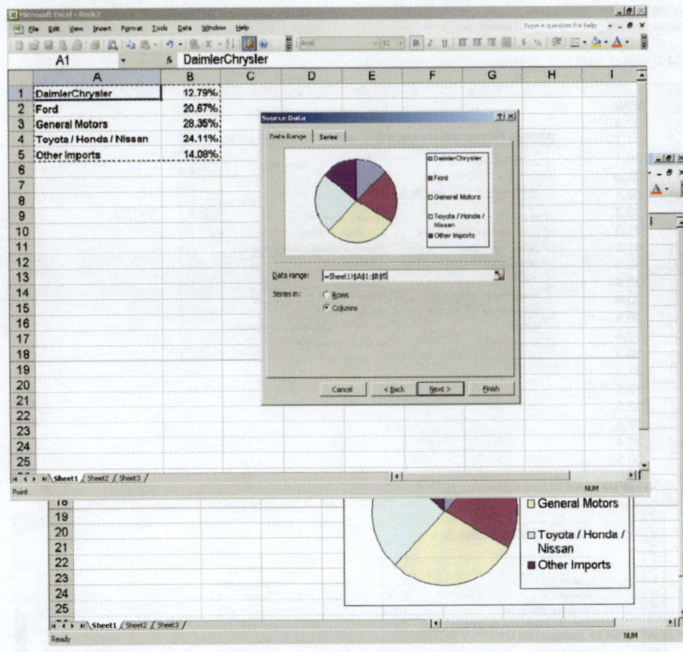

Pie Chart of auto manufacturer percentages in Figure 2.44(b) on page 92: (data file: AutoShares.xls):

- Enter the auto manufacturer data of Figure 2.44 into columns A and B as shown in the screenshot.
- Select the Chart Wizard from the toolbar.
- Select "Pie" from the Chart Type menu and click Next.
- In the "Chart Wizard—Step 2 of 4" dialog box, enter A1.B5 into the "Data range" box.
- Select the "Series in: Columns" option.
- Click Finish in the "Source Data" dialog box.

Appendix 2.3 ■ Descriptive Statistics Using MegaStat

The instructions in this section begin by describing the entry of data into an Excel worksheet. Alternatively, the data may be loaded directly from the data disk included with the text. The appropriate data file name is given at the top of each instruction block. Please refer to Appendix 1.2 for further information about entering data and saving and printing results in Excel. Please refer to Appendix 1.3 for more information about using MegaStat.

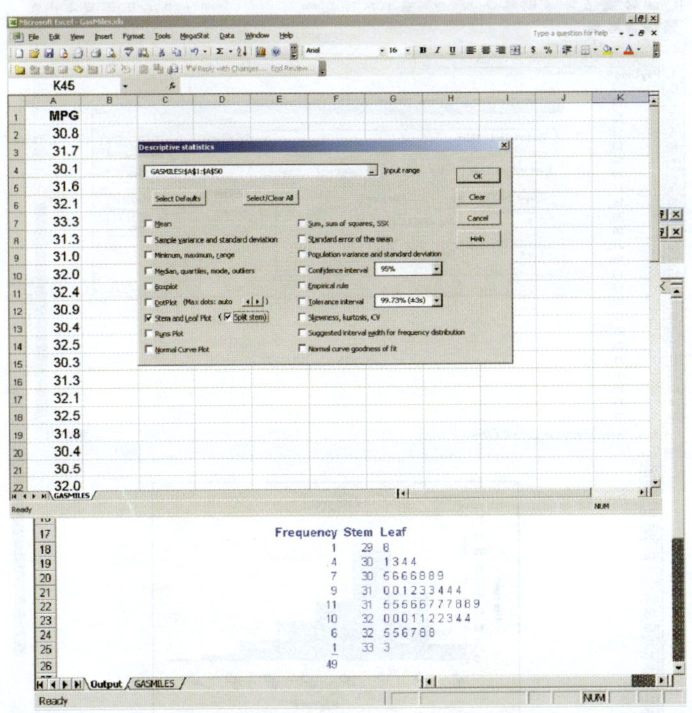

To analyze the gas mileage data in Table 2.1 on page 44 (data file: GasMiles.xls):

- Enter the mileage data from Table 2.1 into column A with the label MPG in cell A1 and with the 49 gas mileages in cells A2 to A50.

To produce the **Stem and Leaf display** in Figure 2.1(b) on page 45:

- Select **MegaStat : Descriptive Statistics.**
- In the "Descriptive Statistics" dialog box, use the autoexpand feature to enter the range A1.A50 into the Input Range box.
- Check the "Stem and Leaf Plot" checkbox.
- (Optional) Check the "Split Stem" checkbox—this depends on how you want the output to appear. You may wish to construct two plots—one with the Split Stem option and one without—and then choose the output you like best.
- Click OK in the "Descriptive Statistics" dialog box. The output will be placed in an Output worksheet.

In order to compute the **descriptive statistics** given in Figure 2.25 on page 64:

- Select **MegaStat : Descriptive Statistics.**
- In the "Descriptive Statistics" dialog box, check the checkboxes that correspond to the desired statistics. If tolerance intervals based on the empirical rule are desired, check the "Empirical Rule" checkbox.
- Click OK in the "Descriptive Statistics" dialog box.
- The output will be placed in an Output worksheet.

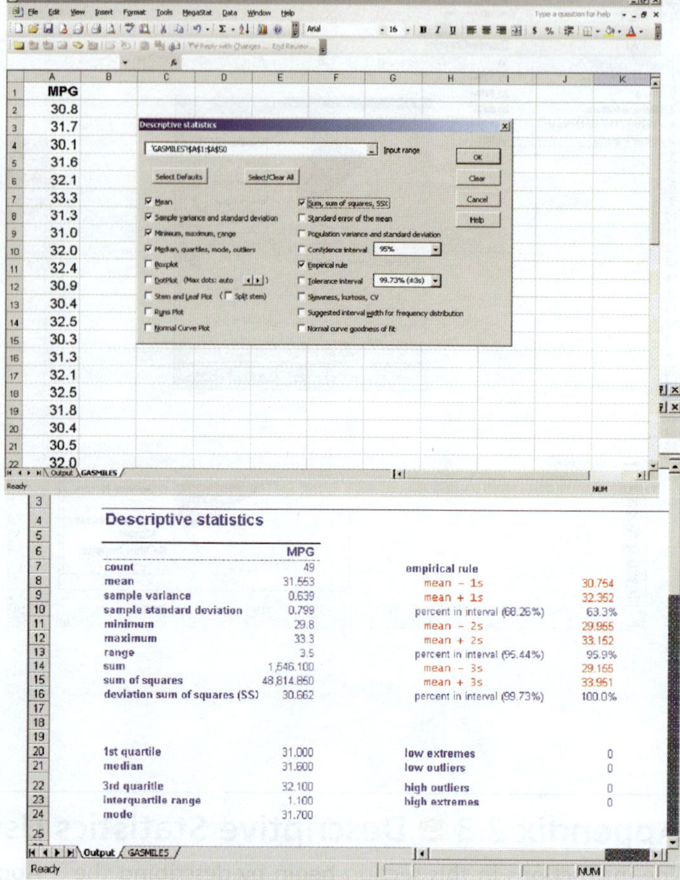

To produce a **histogram** of payment times similar to Figure 2.2 on page 48 (data file: PayTime.xls):

- Enter the payment time data in Table 2.2 on page 46 into column A with the label PayTime in cell A1 and with the 65 payment times in cells A2 to A66.
- Select **MegaStat : Frequency Distribution : Quantitative.**
- In the "Frequency Distribution—Quantitative" dialog box, use the autoexpand feature to enter the input range A1.A66 into the Input Range box.
- Enter the class width (in this case equal to 3) into the Interval Width box.
- Enter the lower boundary of the first—that is, leftmost—interval of the histogram (in this case equal to 9.5) into the appropriate box.
- Make sure that the Histogram checkbox is checked.
- Click OK in the "Frequency Distribution—Quantitative" dialog box.
- The histogram output will be placed in an output worksheet. The histogram can then be edited using any of the usual Excel editing features—for instance, see Appendix 1.3 for some of these features.

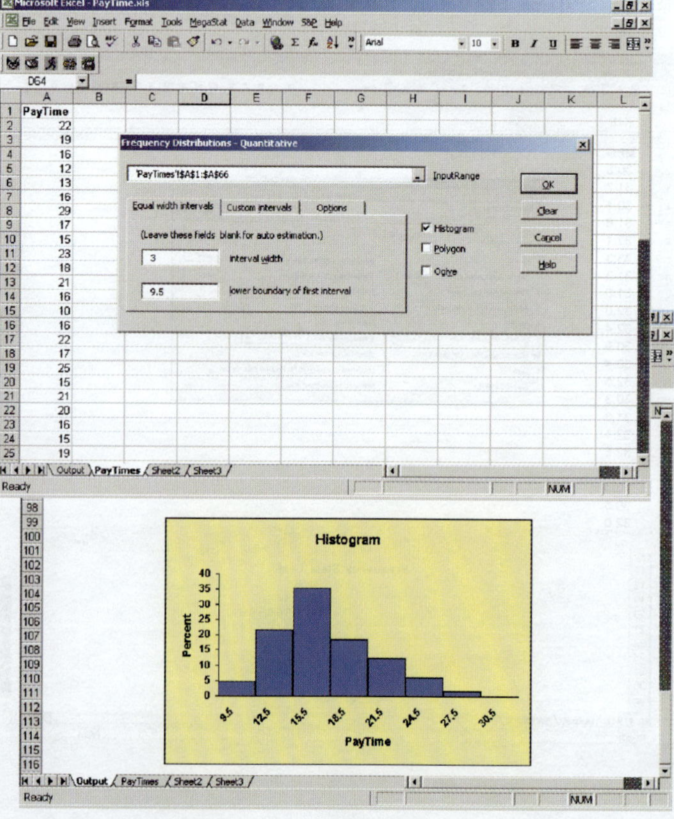

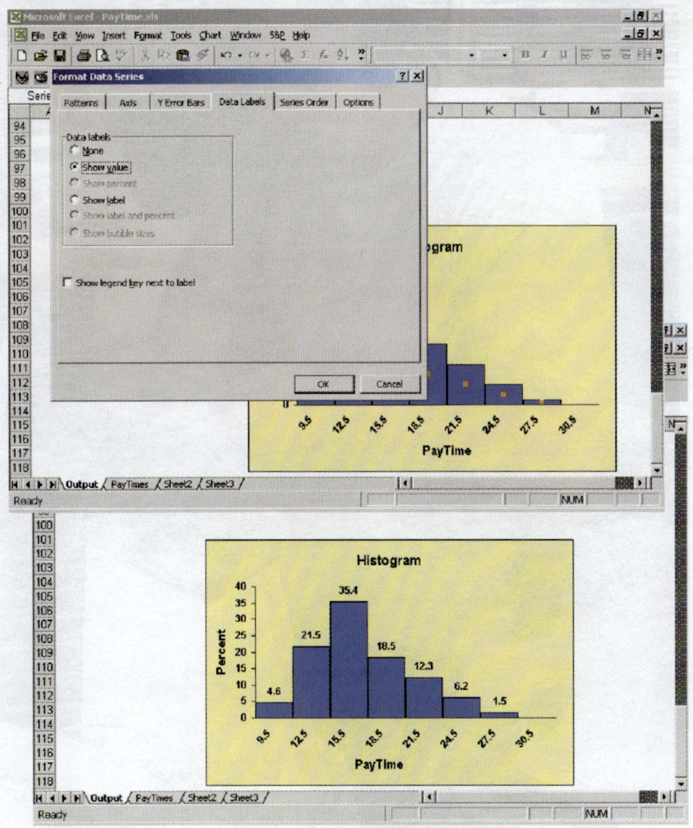

To place **data labels** above the histogram bars:

- Right click on any one of the histogram bars, and select "Format Data Series".
- In the "Format Data Series" dialog box, click on the Data Labels tab.
- Click on "Show value".
- Click OK in the "Format Data Series" dialog box.

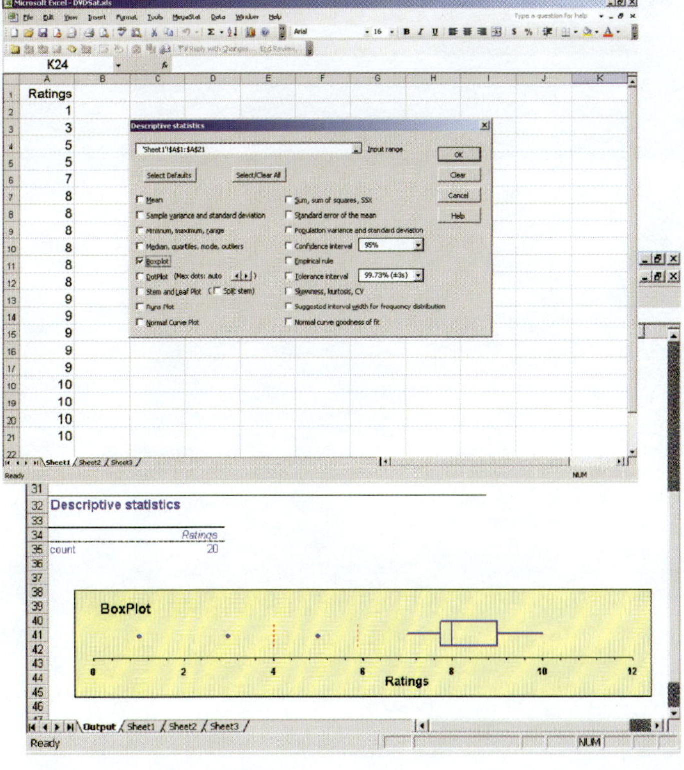

To construct the **box plot** of satisfaction ratings in Figure 2.34(c) on page 81 (data file: DVDSat.xls):

- Enter the satisfaction rating data on page 61 into column A with the label Ratings in cell A1 and with the 20 satisfaction ratings in cells A2 to A21.
- Select **MegaStat : Descriptive Statistics.**
- In the "Descriptive Statistics" dialog box, use the autoexpand feature to enter the input range A1.A21 into the Input Range box.
- Check the Boxplot checkbox.
- Click OK in the "Descriptive Statistics" dialog box.
- The boxplot output will be placed in an output worksheet, which can be edited using any of the usual Excel editing features.

CHAPTER 3

Probability

Chapter Outline

In Chapter 2 we explained how to use sample statistics as point estimates of population parameters. Starting in Chapter 6, we will focus on using sample statistics to make more sophisticated **statistical inferences** about population parameters. We will see that these statistical inferences are generalizations—based on calculating **probabilities**—about population parameters. In this chapter and in Chapters 4 and 5 we present the fundamental concepts about probability that are needed to understand how we make such statistical inferences. We begin our discussions in this chapter by considering rules for calculating probabilities.

In order to illustrate some of the concepts in this chapter, we will introduce a new case.

C

The AccuRatings Case: AccuRatings is a radio ratings service provided by Strategic Radio Research, a media research firm in Chicago, Illinois. AccuRatings clients include radio stations owned by CBS, Cap Cities/ABC, Group W, Tribune, and many other major broadcast groups across the United States and Canada. In addition, Strategic Radio Research is the primary research vendor for MTV/Music Television. Strategic has twice been named to the Inc. 500 list of fastest-growing privately held companies in America. Using portions of an AccuRatings report and the concepts of probability, we will analyze patterns of radio listenership in the Los Angeles market. We will also use Strategic Radio Research data and several *probability rules* to analyze the popularity of individual songs on a client's playlist.

3.1 The Concept of Probability

We use the concept of *probability* to deal with uncertainty. Intuitively, the probability of an event is a number that measures the chance, or likelihood, that the event will occur. For instance, the probability that your favorite football team will win its next game measures the likelihood of a victory. The probability of an event is always a number between 0 and 1. The closer an event's probability is to 1, the higher is the likelihood that the event will occur; the closer the event's probability is to 0, the smaller is the likelihood that the event will occur. For example, if you believe that the probability that your favorite football team will win its next game is .95, then you are almost sure that your team will win. However, if you believe that the probability of victory is only .10, then you have very little confidence that your team will win.

When performing statistical studies, we sometimes collect data by **performing a controlled experiment.** For instance, we might purposely vary the operating conditions of a manufacturing process in order to study the effects of these changes on the process output. Alternatively, we sometimes obtain data by **observing uncontrolled events.** For example, we might observe the closing price of a share of General Motors' stock every day for 30 trading days. In order to simplify our terminology, we will use the word *experiment* to refer to either method of data collection.

An **experiment** is any process of observation that has an uncertain outcome. The process must be defined so that on any single repetition of the experiment, *one and only one* of the possible outcomes will occur. The possible outcomes for an experiment are called **experimental outcomes.**

CHAPTER 2

For example, if the experiment consists of tossing a coin, the experimental outcomes are "head" and "tail." If the experiment consists of rolling a die, the experimental outcomes are 1, 2, 3, 4, 5, and 6. If the experiment consists of subjecting an automobile to a tailpipe emissions test, the experimental outcomes are pass and fail.

We often wish to assign probabilities to experimental outcomes. This can be done by several methods. Regardless of the method used, **probabilities must be assigned to the experimental outcomes so that two conditions are met:**

1. The probability assigned to each experimental outcome must be between 0 and 1. That is, if E represents an experimental outcome and if $P(E)$ represents the probability of this outcome, then $0 \le P(E) \le 1$.
2. The probabilities of all of the experimental outcomes must sum to 1.

Sometimes, when all of the experimental outcomes are equally likely, we can use logic to assign probabilities. This method, which is called the *classical method,* will be more fully discussed in the next section. As a simple example, consider the experiment of tossing a fair coin. Here, there are *two* equally likely experimental outcomes—head (H) and tail (T). Therefore, logic suggests that the probability of observing a head, denoted $P(H)$, is $1/2 = .5$, and that the probability of observing a tail, denoted $P(T)$, is also $1/2 = .5$. Notice that each probability is between 0 and 1. Furthermore, because H and T are all of the experimental outcomes, $P(H) + P(T) = 1$.

Probability is often interpreted to be a **long-run relative frequency.** As an example, consider repeatedly tossing a coin. If we get 6 heads in the first 10 tosses, then the relative frequency, or fraction, of heads is $6/10 = .6$. If we get 47 heads in the first 100 tosses, the relative frequency of heads is $47/100 = .47$. If we get 5,067 heads in the first 10,000 tosses, the relative frequency of heads is $5{,}067/10{,}000 = .5067$.[1] Since the relative frequency of heads is approaching (that is, getting closer to) .5, we might estimate that the probability of obtaining a head when tossing the coin is .5. When we say this, we mean that, if we tossed the coin an indefinitely large number of times (that is, a number of times *approaching infinity*), the relative frequency of heads obtained would approach .5. Of course, in actuality it is impossible to toss a coin (or perform any experiment) an indefinitely large number of times. Therefore, a relative frequency interpretation of probability is a mathematical idealization. To summarize, suppose that E is an experimental outcome that might occur when a particular experiment is performed. Then the probability that E will occur, $P(E)$, can be interpreted to be the number that would be approached by the relative frequency of E if we performed the experiment an indefinitely large number of times. It follows that we often think of a probability in terms of the percentage of the time the experimental outcome would occur in many repetitions of the experiment. For instance, when we say that the probability of obtaining a head when we toss a coin is .5, we are saying that, when we repeatedly toss the coin an indefinitely large number of times, we will obtain a head on 50 percent of the repetitions.

Sometimes it is either difficult or impossible to use the classical method to assign probabilities. Since we can often make a relative frequency interpretation of probability, we can estimate a probability by performing the experiment in which an outcome might occur many times. Then, we estimate the probability of the experimental outcome to be the proportion of the time that the outcome occurs during the many repetitions of the experiment. For example, to estimate the probability that a randomly selected consumer prefers Coca-Cola to all other soft drinks, we perform an experiment in which we ask a randomly selected consumer for his or her preference. There are two possible experimental outcomes: "prefers Coca-Cola" and "does not prefer Coca-Cola." However, we have no reason to believe that these experimental outcomes are equally likely, so we cannot use the classical method. We might perform the experiment, say, 1,000 times by surveying 1,000 randomly selected consumers. Then, if 140 of those surveyed said that they prefer Coca-Cola, we would estimate the probability that a randomly selected consumer prefers Coca-Cola to all other soft drinks to be $140/1{,}000 = .14$. This is called the *relative frequency method* for assigning probability.

If we cannot perform the experiment many times, we might estimate the probability by using our previous experience with similar situations, intuition, or special expertise that we may possess. For example, a company president might estimate the probability of success for a one-time business venture to be .7. Here, on the basis of knowledge of the success of previous similar ventures, the opinions of company personnel, and other pertinent information, the president believes that there is a 70 percent chance the venture will be successful.

When we use experience, intuitive judgement, or expertise to assess a probability, we call this a **subjective probability.** Such a probability may or may not have a relative frequency interpretation. For instance, when the company president estimates that the probability of a successful business venture is .7, this may mean that, if business conditions similar to those that are about to be encountered could be repeated many times, then the business venture would be successful in 70 percent of the repetitions. Or, the president may not be thinking in relative frequency terms but rather may consider the venture a "one-shot" proposition. We will discuss some other

[1]The English mathematician John Kerrich actually obtained this result when he tossed a coin 10,000 times while imprisoned by the Germans during World War II.

subjective probabilities later. However, the interpretations of statistical inferences we will explain in later chapters are based on the relative frequency interpretation of probability. For this reason, we will concentrate on this interpretation.

3.2 Sample Spaces and Events

In order to calculate probabilities by using the classical method, it is important to understand and use the idea of a *sample space*.

CHAPTER 2

The **sample space** of an experiment is the set of all possible experimental outcomes. The experimental outcomes in the sample space are often called **sample space outcomes.**

Example 3.1

A company is choosing a new chief executive officer (CEO). It has narrowed the list of candidates to four finalists (identified by last name only)—Adams, Chung, Hill, and Rankin. If we consider our experiment to be making a final choice of the company's CEO, then the experiment's sample space consists of the four possible experimental outcomes:

$A \equiv$ Adams is chosen as CEO.

$C \equiv$ Chung is chosen as CEO.

$H \equiv$ Hill is chosen as CEO.

$R \equiv$ Rankin is chosen as CEO.

Each of these outcomes is a sample space outcome, and the set of these sample space outcomes is the sample space.

Next, suppose that industry analysts feel (subjectively) that the probabilities that Adams, Chung, Hill, and Rankin will be chosen as CEO are .1, .2, .5, and .2, respectively. That is, in probability notation

$$P(A) = .1 \qquad P(C) = .2 \qquad P(H) = .5 \qquad \text{and} \qquad P(R) = .2$$

Notice that each probability assigned to a sample space outcome is between 0 and 1 and that the sum of the probabilities equals 1.

Example 3.2

A newly married couple plans to have two children. Naturally, they are curious about whether their children will be boys or girls. Therefore, we consider the experiment of having two children. In order to find the sample space of this experiment, we let B denote that a child is a boy and G denote that a child is a girl. Then, it is useful to construct the tree diagram shown in Figure 3.1. This diagram pictures the experiment as a two-step process—having the first child, which could be either a boy or a girl (B or G), and then having the second child, which could also be either a boy or a girl (B or G). Each branch of the tree leads to a sample space outcome. These outcomes are listed at the right ends of the branches. We see that there are four sample space outcomes. Therefore, the sample space (that is, the set of all the sample space outcomes) is

$$BB \qquad BG \qquad GB \qquad GG$$

In order to consider the probabilities of these outcomes, suppose that boys and girls are equally likely each time a child is born. Intuitively, this says that each of the sample space outcomes is equally likely. That is, this implies that

$$P(BB) = P(BG) = P(GB) = P(GG) = \frac{1}{4}$$

This says that there is a 25 percent chance that each of these outcomes will occur. Again, notice that these probabilities sum to 1.

FIGURE 3.1 A Tree Diagram of the Genders of Two Children

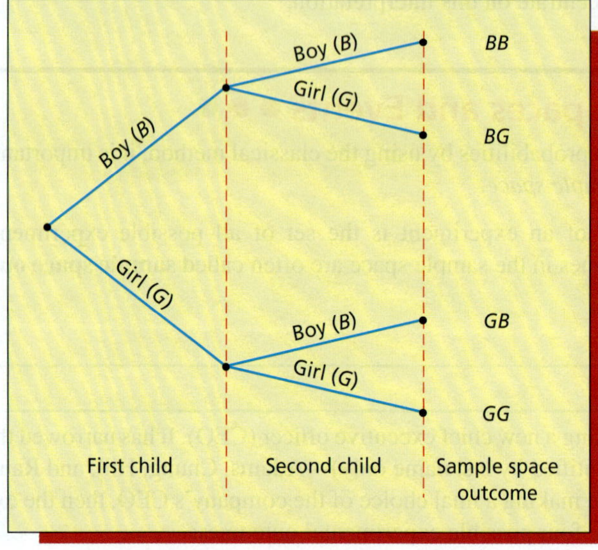

Example 3.3

A student takes a pop quiz that consists of three true–false questions. If we consider our experiment to be answering the three questions, each question can be answered correctly or incorrectly. We will let C denote answering a question correctly and I denote answering a question incorrectly. Then, Figure 3.2 depicts a tree diagram of the sample space outcomes for the experiment. The diagram portrays the experiment as a three-step process—answering the first question (correctly or incorrectly, that is, C or I), answering the second question, and answering the third question. The tree diagram has eight different branches, and the eight sample space outcomes are listed at the ends of the branches. We see that the sample space is

$$CCC \quad CCI \quad CIC \quad CII$$
$$ICC \quad ICI \quad IIC \quad III$$

Next, suppose that the student was totally unprepared for the quiz and had to blindly guess the answer to each question. That is, the student had a 50–50 chance (or .5 probability) of correctly answering each question. Intuitively, this would say that each of the eight sample space outcomes is equally likely to occur. That is,

$$P(CCC) = P(CCI) = \cdots = P(III) = \frac{1}{8}$$

Here, as in Examples 3.1 and 3.2, the sum of the probabilities of the sample space outcomes is equal to 1.

Events and finding probabilities by using sample spaces At the beginning of this chapter, we informally talked about events. We now give the formal definition of an event.

An **event** is a set (or collection) of sample space outcomes.

For instance, if we consider the couple planning to have two children, the event "the couple will have at least one girl" consists of the sample space outcomes BG, GB, and GG. That is, the event "the couple will have at least one girl" will occur if and only if one of the sample

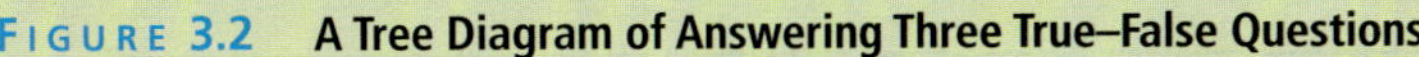

FIGURE 3.2 A Tree Diagram of Answering Three True–False Questions

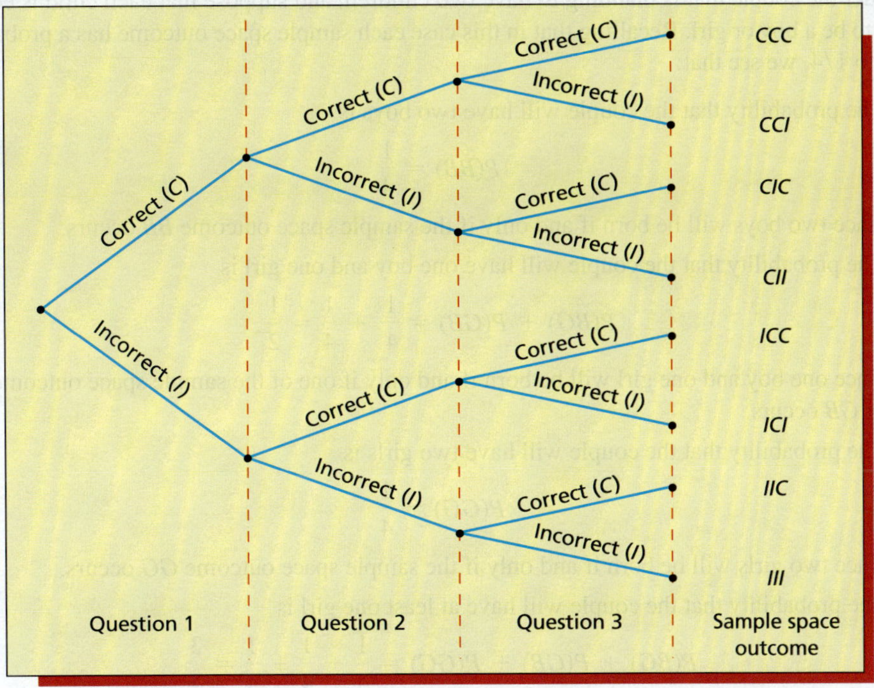

space outcomes *BG*, *GB*, or *GG* occurs. As another example, in the pop quiz situation, the event "the student will answer at least two out of three questions correctly" consists of the sample space outcomes *CCC*, *CCI*, *CIC*, and *ICC*, while the event "the student will answer all three questions correctly" consists of the sample space outcome *CCC*. In general, we see that the word description of an event determines the sample space outcomes that correspond to the event.

Suppose that we wish to find the probability that an event will occur. We can find such a probability as follows:

The **probability of an event** is the **sum of the probabilities of the sample space outcomes** that correspond to the event.

As an example, in the CEO situation, suppose only Adams and Hill are internal candidates (they already work for the company). Letting *INT* denote the event that "an internal candidate is selected for the CEO position," then *INT* consists of the sample space outcomes *A* and *H* (that is, *INT* will occur if and only if either of the sample space outcomes *A* or *H* occurs). It follows that $P(INT) = P(A) + P(H) = .1 + .5 = .6$. This says that the probability that an internal candidate will be chosen to be CEO is .6.

In general, we have seen that the probability of any sample space outcome (experimental outcome) is a number between 0 and 1, and we have also seen that the probabilities of all the sample space outcomes sum to 1. It follows that **the probability of an event** (that is, the probability of a set of sample space outcomes) **is a number between 0 and 1.** That is,

If *A* is an event, then $0 \leq P(A) \leq 1$.

Moreover:

1 If an event never occurs, then the probability of this event equals 0.

2 If an event is certain to occur, then the probability of this event equals 1.

Example 3.4

Consider the couple that is planning to have two children, and suppose that each child is equally likely to be a boy or girl. Recalling that in this case each sample space outcome has a probability equal to 1/4, we see that:

1 The probability that the couple will have two boys is

$$P(BB) = \frac{1}{4}$$

since two boys will be born if and only if the sample space outcome *BB* occurs.

2 The probability that the couple will have one boy and one girl is

$$P(BG) + P(GB) = \frac{1}{4} + \frac{1}{4} = \frac{1}{2}$$

since one boy and one girl will be born if and only if one of the sample space outcomes *BG* or *GB* occurs.

3 The probability that the couple will have two girls is

$$P(GG) = \frac{1}{4}$$

since two girls will be born if and only if the sample space outcome *GG* occurs.

4 The probability that the couple will have at least one girl is

$$P(BG) + P(GB) + P(GG) = \frac{1}{4} + \frac{1}{4} + \frac{1}{4} = \frac{3}{4}$$

since at least one girl will be born if and only if one of the sample space outcomes *BG*, *GB*, or *GG* occurs.

Example 3.5

Again consider the pop quiz consisting of three true–false questions, and suppose that the student blindly guesses the answers. Remembering that in this case each sample space outcome has a probability equal to 1/8, then:

1 The probability that the student will get all three questions correct is

$$P(CCC) = \frac{1}{8}$$

2 The probability that the student will get exactly two questions correct is

$$P(CCI) + P(CIC) + P(ICC) = \frac{1}{8} + \frac{1}{8} + \frac{1}{8} = \frac{3}{8}$$

since two questions will be answered correctly if and only if one of the sample space outcomes *CCI*, *CIC*, or *ICC* occurs.

3 The probability that the student will get exactly one question correct is

$$P(CII) + P(ICI) + P(IIC) = \frac{1}{8} + \frac{1}{8} + \frac{1}{8} = \frac{3}{8}$$

since one question will be answered correctly if and only if one of the sample space outcomes *CII*, *ICI*, or *IIC* occurs.

4 The probability that the student will get all three questions incorrect is

$$P(III) = \frac{1}{8}$$

5 The probability that the student will get at least two questions correct is

$$P(CCC) + P(CCI) + P(CIC) + P(ICC) = \frac{1}{8} + \frac{1}{8} + \frac{1}{8} + \frac{1}{8} = \frac{1}{2}$$

since the student will get at least two questions correct if and only if one of the sample space outcomes *CCC*, *CCI*, *CIC*, or *ICC* occurs.

Notice that in the true–false question situation we find that, for instance, the probability that the student will get exactly two questions correct equals the ratio

$$\frac{\text{the number of sample space outcomes resulting in two correct answers}}{\text{the total number of sample space outcomes}} = \frac{3}{8}$$

In general, when a sample space is finite we can use the following method for computing the probability of an event.

If all of the sample space outcomes are equally likely, then the probability that an event will occur is equal to the ratio

$$\frac{\text{the number of sample space outcomes that correspond to the event}}{\text{the total number of sample space outcomes}}$$

When we use this rule, we are using the *classical method* for computing probabilities. Furthermore, it is important to emphasize that we can use this rule only when all of the sample space outcomes are equally likely (as they are in the true–false question situation). For example, if we were to use this rule in the CEO situation, we would find that the probability of choosing an internal candidate as CEO is

$$P(INT) = \frac{\text{the number of internal candidates}}{\text{the total number of candidates}} = \frac{2}{4} = .5$$

This result is not equal to the correct value of $P(INT)$, which we previously found to be equal to .6. Here, this rule does not give us the correct answer because the sample space outcomes A, C, H, and R are not equally likely—recall that $P(A) = .1$, $P(C) = .2$, $P(H) = .5$, and $P(R) = .2$.

Example 3.6

Suppose that 650,000 of the 1,000,000 households in an eastern U.S. city subscribe to a newspaper called the *Atlantic Journal,* and consider randomly selecting one of the households in this city. That is, consider selecting one household by giving each and every household in the city the same chance of being selected. Let A be the event that the randomly selected household subscribes to the *Atlantic Journal.* Then, because the sample space of this experiment consists of 1,000,000 equally likely sample space outcomes (households), it follows that

$$\begin{aligned} P(A) &= \frac{\text{the number of households that subscribe to the \textit{Atlantic Journal}}}{\text{the total number of households in the city}} \\ &= \frac{650{,}000}{1{,}000{,}000} \\ &= .65 \end{aligned}$$

This says that the probability that the randomly selected household subscribes to the *Atlantic Journal* is .65.

Example 3.7 The AccuRatings Case

C

As discussed in the introduction to this chapter, AccuRatings is a radio ratings service provided by Strategic Radio Research, a media research firm in Chicago, Illinois. Figure 3.3 gives portions of an AccuRatings report on radio ratings in the Los Angeles market. This report, based on interviews with 5,528 randomly selected persons 12 years of age or older, gives estimates of the number and the percentage of Los Angeles residents who would name each of the top 10 radio stations in Los Angeles as the station they listen to most.

To better understand the estimates in Figure 3.3, we will consider how they were obtained. AccuRatings asked each of the 5,528 sampled residents to name which station (if any) he or

FIGURE 3.3 **Portions of an AccuRatings Report on Radio Ratings in the Los Angeles Market**

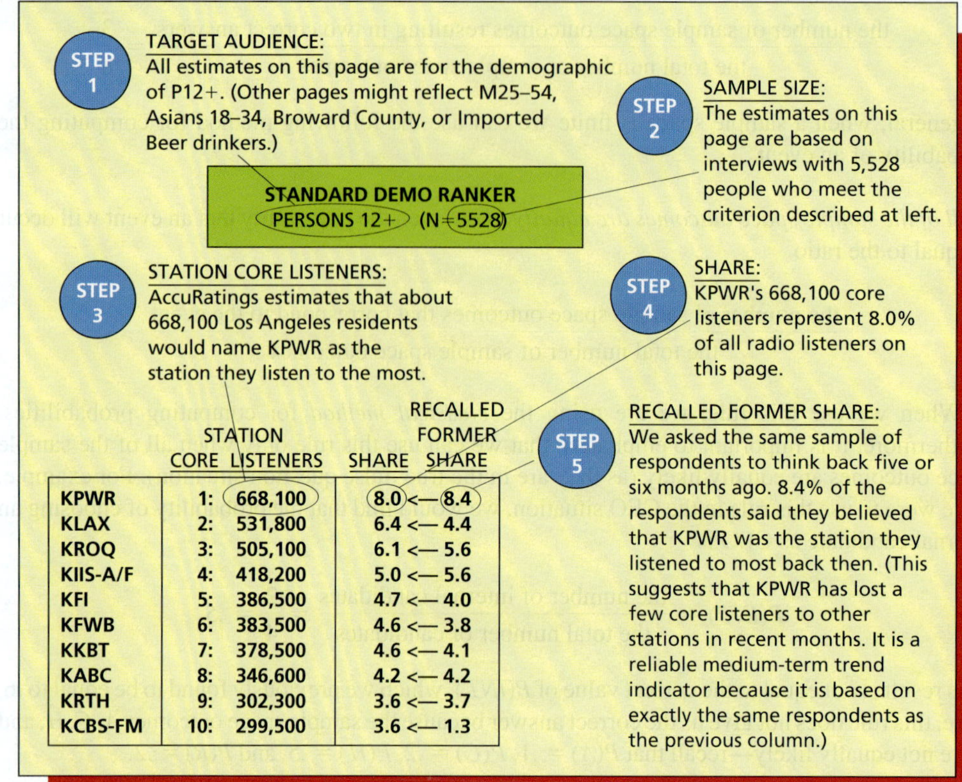

Source: Strategic Radio Research, *AccuRatings Introduction for Broadcasters.*

she listens to most. AccuRatings then used the responses of the sampled residents to calculate the proportion of these residents who favored each station. The sample proportion of the residents who favored a particular station is an estimate of the population proportion of all Los Angeles residents (12 years of age or older) who favor the station, or, equivalently, of the probability that a randomly selected Los Angeles resident would favor the station. For example, if 445 of the 5,528 sampled residents favored station KPWR, then $445/5{,}528 = .080499276$ is an estimate of $P(\text{KPWR})$, the probability that a randomly selected Los Angeles resident would favor station KPWR. Furthermore, assuming that there are 8,300,000 Los Angeles residents 12 years of age or older, an estimate of the number of these residents who favor station KPWR is

$$(8{,}300{,}000) \times (.080499276) = 668{,}143.99$$

Now, if we

1 Round the estimated number of residents favoring station KPWR to 668,100, and
2 Express the estimated probability $P(\text{KPWR})$ as the rounded percentage 8.0%,

we obtain what the AccuRatings report in Figure 3.3 states are (1) the estimated number of **core listeners** for station KPWR and (2) the estimated **share** of all listeners for station KPWR. These measures of listenership would be determined for other stations in a similar manner (see Figure 3.3).

To conclude this section, we note that in Appendix C (Part 1) on page 844 we discuss several *counting rules* that can be used to count the number of sample space outcomes in an experiment.

These rules are particularly useful when there are many sample space outcomes and thus these outcomes are difficult to list.

Exercises for Sections 3.1 and 3.2

CONCEPTS

3.1 Define the following terms: *experiment, event, probability, sample space.*

3.2 Explain the properties that must be satisfied by a probability.

METHODS AND APPLICATIONS

3.3 Two randomly selected grocery store patrons are each asked to take a blind taste test and to then state which of three diet colas (marked as *A*, *B*, or *C*) he or she prefers.

a Draw a tree diagram depicting the sample space outcomes for the test results.

b List the sample space outcomes that correspond to each of the following events:

(1) Both patrons prefer diet cola *A*.

(2) The two patrons prefer the same diet cola.

(3) The two patrons prefer different diet colas.

(4) Diet cola *A* is preferred by at least one of the two patrons.

(5) Neither of the patrons prefers diet cola *C*.

c Assuming that all sample space outcomes are equally likely, find the probability of each of the events given in part *b*.

3.4 Suppose that a couple will have three children. Letting *B* denote a boy and *G* denote a girl:

a Draw a tree diagram depicting the sample space outcomes for this experiment.

b List the sample space outcomes that correspond to each of the following events:

(1) All three children will have the same gender.

(2) Exactly two of the three children will be girls.

(3) Exactly one of the three children will be a girl.

(4) None of the three children will be a girl.

c Assuming that all sample space outcomes are equally likely, find the probability of each of the events given in part *b*.

3.5 Four people will enter an automobile showroom, and each will either purchase a car (*P*) or not purchase a car (*N*).

a Draw a tree diagram depicting the sample space of all possible purchase decisions that could potentially be made by the four people.

b List the sample space outcomes that correspond to each of the following events:

(1) Exactly three people will purchase a car.

(2) Two or fewer people will purchase a car.

(3) One or more people will purchase a car.

(4) All four people will make the same purchase decision.

c Assuming that all sample space outcomes are equally likely, find the probability of each of the events given in part *b*.

3.6 THE ACCURATINGS CASE

Using the information given in the AccuRatings report of Figure 3.3 (page 134), find estimates of each of the following:

a The probability that a randomly selected Los Angeles resident (12 years or older) would name station KLAX as the station that he or she listens to most.

b The probability that a randomly selected Los Angeles resident (12 years or older) would name station KABC as the station that he or she listens to most.

c The percentage of all Los Angeles residents (12 years or older) who would name KCBS-FM as the station that he or she listens to most.

d The number of the 5,528 sampled residents who named station KFI as the station he or she listens to most.

e The number of the 5,528 sampled residents who named station KROQ as the station he or she listens to most.

3.7 Let *A*, *B*, *C*, *D*, and *E* be sample space outcomes forming a sample space. Suppose that $P(A) = .2$, $P(B) = .15$, $P(C) = .3$, and $P(D) = .2$. What is $P(E)$? Explain how you got your answer.

3.3 Some Elementary Probability Rules

We can often calculate probabilities by using formulas called **probability rules.** We will begin by presenting the simplest probability rule: the *rule of complements.* To start, we define the complement of an event:

Given an event A, the **complement of** A is the event consisting of all sample space outcomes that do not correspond to the occurrence of A. The complement of A is denoted $\overline{A}$. Furthermore, $P(\overline{A})$ denotes **the probability that A will not occur.**

FIGURE 3.4 The Complement of an Event (the Shaded Region Is $\overline{A}$, the Complement of A)

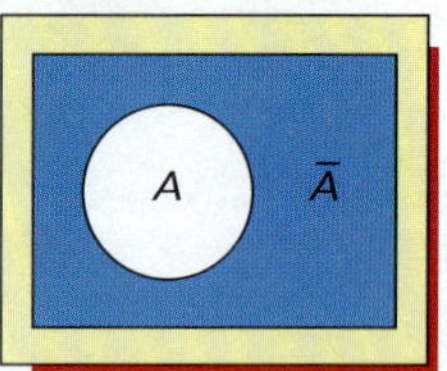

Figure 3.4 is a **Venn diagram** depicting the complement $\overline{A}$ of an event A. In any probability situation, either an event A or its complement $\overline{A}$ must occur. Therefore, we have

$$P(A) + P(\overline{A}) = 1$$

This implies the following result:

The Rule of Complements

Consider an event A. Then, **the probability that A *will not occur*** is

$$P(\overline{A}) = 1 - P(A)$$

Example 3.8

Recall from Example 3.6 that the probability that a randomly selected household in an eastern U.S. city subscribes to the *Atlantic Journal* is .65. It follows that the probability of the complement of this event (that is, the probability that a randomly selected household in the eastern U.S. city does not subscribe to the *Atlantic Journal*) is $1 - .65 = .35$.

Example 3.9

Consider Example 3.6, and recall that 650,000 of the 1,000,000 households in an eastern U.S. city subscribe to the *Atlantic Journal.* Also, suppose that 500,000 households in the city subscribe to a competing newspaper, the *Beacon News,* and further suppose that 250,000 households subscribe to both the *Atlantic Journal* and the *Beacon News.* As in Example 3.6, we consider randomly selecting one household in the city, and we define the following events.

$A \equiv$ the randomly selected household subscribes to the *Atlantic Journal.*

$\overline{A} \equiv$ the randomly selected household does not subscribe to the *Atlantic Journal.*

$B \equiv$ the randomly selected household subscribes to the *Beacon News.*

$\overline{B} \equiv$ the randomly selected household does not subscribe to the *Beacon News.*

Using the notation $A \cap B$ to denote *both A and B,* we also define

$A \cap B \equiv$ the randomly selected household subscribes to both the *Atlantic Journal* and the *Beacon News.*

Since 650,000 of the 1,000,000 households subscribe to the *Atlantic Journal* (that is, correspond to the event A occurring), then 350,000 households do not subscribe to the *Atlantic Journal* (that is, correspond to the event $\overline{A}$ occurring). Similarly, 500,000 households subscribe to the *Beacon News* (B), so 500,000 households do not subscribe to the *Beacon News* ($\overline{B}$). We summarize this information, as well as the 250,000 households that correspond to the event $A \cap B$ occurring, in Table 3.1.

TABLE 3.1 A Summary of the Number of Households Corresponding to the Events A, $\overline{A}$, B, $\overline{B}$, and $A \cap B$

Events	Subscribes to *Beacon News*, B	Does Not Subscribe to *Beacon News*, $\overline{B}$	Total
Subscribes to *Atlantic Journal, A*	250,000		650,000
Does Not Subscribe to *Atlantic Journal,* $\overline{A}$			350,000
Total	500,000	500,000	1,000,000

Next, consider the events

$A \cap \overline{B} \equiv$ the randomly selected household subscribes to the *Atlantic Journal* and does not subscribe to the *Beacon News*.

$\overline{A} \cap B \equiv$ the randomly selected household does not subscribe to the *Atlantic Journal* and does subscribe to the *Beacon News*.

$\overline{A} \cap \overline{B} \equiv$ the randomly selected household does not subscribe to the *Atlantic Journal* and does not subscribe to the *Beacon News*.

Since 650,000 households subscribe to the *Atlantic Journal* (A) and 250,000 households subscribe to both the *Atlantic Journal* and the *Beacon News* ($A \cap B$), it follows that 650,000 − 250,000 = 400,000 households subscribe to the *Atlantic Journal* but do not subscribe to the *Beacon News* ($A \cap \overline{B}$). This subtraction is illustrated in Table 3.2(a). By similar logic, it also follows that:

1 As illustrated in Table 3.2(b), 500,000 − 250,000 = 250,000 households do not subscribe to the *Atlantic Journal* but do subscribe to the *Beacon News* ($\overline{A} \cap B$).

2 As illustrated in Table 3.2(c), 350,000 − 250,000 = 100,000 households do not subscribe to the *Atlantic Journal* and do not subscribe to the *Beacon News* ($\overline{A} \cap \overline{B}$).

TABLE 3.2 Subtracting to Find the Number of Households Corresponding to the Events $A \cap \overline{B}$, $\overline{A} \cap B$, and $\overline{A} \cap \overline{B}$

(a) The Number of Households Corresponding to (A and $\overline{B}$)

Events	Subscribes to *Beacon News*, B	Does Not Subscribe to *Beacon News*, $\overline{B}$	Total
Subscribes to *Atlantic Journal, A*	250,000	650,000 − 250,000 = 400,000	650,000
Does Not Subscribe to *Atlantic Journal,* $\overline{A}$			350,000
Total	500,000	500,000	1,000,000

(b) The Number of Households Corresponding to ($\overline{A}$ and B)

Events	Subscribes to *Beacon News*, B	Does Not Subscribe to *Beacon News*, $\overline{B}$	Total
Subscribes to *Atlantic Journal, A*	250,000	650,000 − 250,000 = 400,000	650,000
Does Not Subscribe to *Atlantic Journal,* $\overline{A}$	500,000 − 250,000 = 250,000		350,000
Total	500,000	500,000	1,000,000

Table 3.2 (continued)

(c) The Number of Households Corresponding to ($\bar{A}$ and $\bar{B}$)

Events	Subscribes to *Beacon News,* *B*	Does Not Subscribe to *Beacon News,* $\bar{B}$	Total
Subscribes to *Atlantic Journal, A*	250,000	650,000 − 250,000 = 400,000	650,000
Does Not Subscribe to *Atlantic Journal,* $\bar{A}$	500,000 − 250,000 = 250,000	350,000 − 250,000 = 100,000	350,000
Total	500,000	500,000	1,000,000

Table 3.3 A Contingency Table Summarizing Subscription Data for the *Atlantic Journal* and the *Beacon News*

Events	Subscribes to *Beacon News,* *B*	Does Not Subscribe to *Beacon News,* $\bar{B}$	Total
Subscribes to *Atlantic Journal, A*	250,000	400,000	650,000
Does Not Subscribe to *Atlantic Journal,* $\bar{A}$	250,000	100,000	350,000
Total	500,000	500,000	1,000,000

We summarize all of these results in Table 3.3, which is called a **contingency table.** Because we will randomly select one household (making all of the households equally likely to be chosen), the probability of any of the previously defined events is the ratio of the number of households corresponding to the event's occurrence to the total number of households in the city. Therefore, for example,

$$P(A) = \frac{650{,}000}{1{,}000{,}000} = .65 \qquad P(B) = \frac{500{,}000}{1{,}000{,}000} = .5$$

$$P(A \cap B) = \frac{250{,}000}{1{,}000{,}000} = .25$$

This last probability says that the probability that the randomly selected household subscribes to both the *Atlantic Journal* and the *Beacon News* is .25.

Next, letting $A \cup B$ denote A or B (or both), we consider finding the probability of the event

$A \cup B \equiv$ the randomly selected household subscribes to the *Atlantic Journal* or the *Beacon News* (or both)—that is, subscribes to at least one of the two newspapers.

Looking at Table 3.3, we see that the households subscribing to the *Atlantic Journal* or the *Beacon News* are (1) the 400,000 households that subscribe to only the *Atlantic Journal,* $A \cap \bar{B}$, (2) the 250,000 households that subscribe to only the *Beacon News,* $\bar{A} \cap B$, and (3) the 250,000 households that subscribe to both the *Atlantic Journal* and the *Beacon News,* $A \cap B$. Therefore, since a total of 900,000 households subscribe to the *Atlantic Journal* or the *Beacon News,* it follows that

$$P(A \cup B) = \frac{900{,}000}{1{,}000{,}000} = .9$$

This says that the probability that the randomly selected household subscribes to the *Atlantic Journal* or the *Beacon News* is .90. That is, 90 percent of the households in the city subscribe to the *Atlantic Journal* or the *Beacon News.* Notice that $P(A \cup B) = .90$ does not equal

$$P(A) + P(B) = .65 + .5 = 1.15$$

Logically, the reason for this is that both $P(A) = .65$ and $P(B) = .5$ count the 25 percent of the households that subscribe to both newspapers. Therefore, the sum of $P(A)$ and $P(B)$ counts this

25 percent of the households once too often. It follows that if we subtract $P(A \cap B) = .25$ from the sum of $P(A)$ and $P(B)$, then we will obtain $P(A \cup B)$. That is,

$$P(A \cup B) = P(A) + P(B) - P(A \cap B)$$
$$= .65 + .5 - .25 = .90$$

In order to generalize the ideas in the previous example, we make the following definitions:

The Intersection and Union of Two Events

Given two events A and B,

1. The **intersection of A and B** is the event consisting of the sample space outcomes belonging to both A and B. The intersection is denoted by $A \cap B$. Furthermore, $P(A \cap B)$ denotes **the probability that *both A and B will simultaneously occur.***
2. The **union of A and B** is the event consisting of the sample space outcomes belonging to A or B (or both). The union is denoted $A \cup B$. Furthermore, $P(A \cup B)$ denotes **the probability that *A or B (or both) will occur.***

Noting that Figure 3.5 shows **Venn diagrams** depicting the events A, B, $A \cap B$, and $A \cup B$, we have the following general result:

The Addition Rule

Let A and B be events. Then, **the probability that *A or B (or both) will occur*** is

$$P(A \cup B) = P(A) + P(B) - P(A \cap B)$$

The reasoning behind this result has been illustrated at the end of Example 3.9. Similarly, the Venn diagrams in Figure 3.5 show that when we compute $P(A) + P(B)$, we are counting each of the sample space outcomes in $A \cap B$ twice. We correct for this by subtracting $P(A \cap B)$.

We next define the idea of *mutually exclusive events:*

Mutually Exclusive Events

Two events A and B are **mutually exclusive** if they have no sample space outcomes in common. In this case, the events A and B cannot occur simultaneously, and thus

$$P(A \cap B) = 0$$

Noting that Figure 3.6 is a Venn diagram depicting two mutually exclusive events, we consider the following example.

Example 3.10

Consider randomly selecting a card from a standard deck of 52 playing cards. We define the following events:

$J \equiv$ the randomly selected card is a jack.
$Q \equiv$ the randomly selected card is a queen.
$R \equiv$ the randomly selected card is a red card (that is, a diamond or a heart).

Because there is no card that is both a jack and a queen, the events J and Q are mutually exclusive. On the other hand, there are two cards that are both jacks and red cards—the jack of diamonds and the jack of hearts—so the events J and R are not mutually exclusive.

FIGURE 3.5 Venn Diagrams Depicting the Events A, B, $A \cap B$, and $A \cup B$

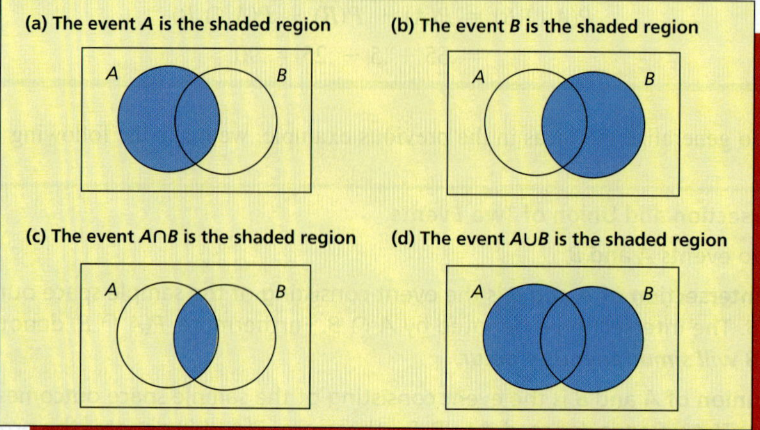

FIGURE 3.6 Two Mutually Exclusive Events

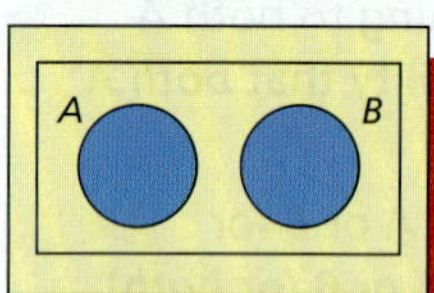

We have seen that for any two events A and B, the probability that A or B (or both) will occur is

$$P(A \cup B) = P(A) + P(B) - P(A \cap B)$$

Therefore, when calculating $P(A \cup B)$, we should always subtract $P(A \cap B)$ from the sum of $P(A)$ and $P(B)$. However, when A and B are mutually exclusive, $P(A \cap B)$ equals 0. Therefore, in this case—and only in this case—we have the following:

The Addition Rule for Two Mutually Exclusive Events

Let A and B be **mutually exclusive** events. Then, **the probability that *A or B will occur*** is

$$P(A \cup B) = P(A) + P(B)$$

Example 3.11

Again consider randomly selecting a card from a standard deck of 52 playing cards, and define the events

$J \equiv$ the randomly selected card is a jack.

$Q \equiv$ the randomly selected card is a queen.

$R \equiv$ the randomly selected card is a red card (a diamond or a heart).

Since there are four jacks, four queens, and 26 red cards, we have $P(J) = \frac{4}{52}$, $P(Q) = \frac{4}{52}$, and $P(R) = \frac{26}{52}$. Furthermore, since there is no card that is both a jack and a queen, the events J and Q are mutually exclusive and thus $P(J \cap Q) = 0$. It follows that the probability that the randomly selected card is a jack or a queen is

$$\begin{aligned} P(J \cup Q) &= P(J) + P(Q) \\ &= \frac{4}{52} + \frac{4}{52} = \frac{8}{52} = \frac{2}{13} \end{aligned}$$

Since there are two cards that are both jacks and red cards—the jack of diamonds and the jack of hearts—the events J and R are not mutually exclusive. Therefore, the probability that the randomly selected card is a jack or a red card is

$$\begin{aligned} P(J \cup R) &= P(J) + P(R) - P(J \cap R) \\ &= \frac{4}{52} + \frac{26}{52} - \frac{2}{52} = \frac{28}{52} = \frac{7}{13} \end{aligned}$$

We now consider an arbitrary group of events—$A_1, A_2, \ldots, A_N$. We will denote the probability that A_1 or A_2 or $\cdots$ or A_N occurs (that is, the probability that at least one of the events occurs) as $P(A_1 \cup A_2 \cup \cdots \cup A_N)$. Although there is a formula for this probability, it is quite complicated and we will not present it in this book. However, sometimes we can use sample spaces to reason out such a probability. For instance, in the playing card situation of Example 3.11, there are four jacks, four queens, and 22 red cards that are not jacks or queens (the 26 red cards minus the two red jacks and the two red queens). Therefore, because there are a total of 30 cards corresponding to the event $J \cup Q \cup R$, it follows that

$$P(J \cup Q \cup R) = \frac{30}{52} = \frac{15}{26}$$

Because some cards are both jacks and red cards, and because some cards are both queens and red cards, we say that the events J, Q, and R are not mutually exclusive. When, however, a group of events is mutually exclusive, there is a simple formula for the probability that at least one of the events will occur:

The Addition Rule for N Mutually Exclusive Events

The events $A_1, A_2, \ldots, A_N$ are mutually exclusive if no two of the events have any sample space outcomes in common. In this case, no two of the events can occur simultaneously, and

$$P(A_1 \cup A_2 \cup \cdots \cup A_N) = P(A_1) + P(A_2) + \cdots + P(A_N)$$

As an example of using this formula, again consider the playing card situation and the events J and Q. If we define the event

$$K \equiv \text{the randomly selected card is a king}$$

then the events J, Q, and K are mutually exclusive. Therefore,

$$P(J \cup Q \cup K) = P(J) + P(Q) + P(K) = \frac{4}{52} + \frac{4}{52} + \frac{4}{52} = \frac{12}{52} = \frac{3}{13}$$

Example 3.12 The AccuRatings Case

C

Recall that Figure 3.3 (page 134) gives the AccuRatings estimates of the number and the percentage of Los Angeles residents who favor each of the 10 top radio stations in Los Angeles. We will let the call letters of each station denote the event that a randomly selected Los Angeles resident would favor the station. Since the AccuRatings survey asked each resident to name the *single* station (if any) that he or she listens to most, the 10 events

KPWR	KLAX	KROQ	KIIS–A/F		KFI
KFWB	KKBT	KABC	KRTH	and	KCBS–FM

are mutually exclusive. Therefore, for example, the probability that a randomly selected Los Angeles resident would favor a station that is rated among the top 10

$$P(\text{KPWR} \cup \text{KLAX} \cup \cdots \cup \text{KCBS–FM})$$

is the sum of the 10 individual station probabilities

$$P(\text{KPWR}) + P(\text{KLAX}) + \cdots + P(\text{KCBS–FM})$$

Since we can estimate each individual station probability by dividing the share for the station in Figure 3.3 by 100, we estimate that the probability that a randomly selected Los Angeles resident would favor a station that is rated among the top 10 is

$$.08 + .064 + .061 + .050 + .047 + .046 + .046 + .042 + .036 + .036 = .508$$

Note that these probabilities sum to less than 1 because there are far more than 10 stations in Los Angeles.

Exercises for Section 3.3

CONCEPTS

3.8 Explain what it means for two events to be mutually exclusive; for *N* events.

3.9 If *A* and *B* are events, define $\overline{A}$, $A \cup B$, $A \cap B$, and $\overline{A} \cap \overline{B}$.

METHODS AND APPLICATIONS

3.10 Consider a standard deck of 52 playing cards, a randomly selected card from the deck, and the following events:

$$R = \text{red} \quad B = \text{black} \quad A = \text{ace} \quad N = \text{nine} \quad D = \text{diamond} \quad C = \text{club}$$

a Describe the sample space outcomes that correspond to each of these events.

b For each of the following pairs of events, indicate whether the events are mutually exclusive. In each case, if you think the events are mutually exclusive, explain why the events have no common sample space outcomes. If you think the events are not mutually exclusive, list the sample space outcomes that are common to both events.

(1) *R* and *A* (3) *A* and *N* (5) *D* and *C*
(2) *R* and *C* (4) *N* and *C*

3.11 Of 10,000 students at a college, 2,500 have a Mastercard (*M*), 4,000 have a VISA (*V*), and 1,000 have both.

a Find the probability that a randomly selected student
(1) Has a Mastercard.
(2) Has a VISA.
(3) Has both credit cards.

b Construct and fill in a contingency table summarizing the credit card data. Employ the following pairs of events: *M* and $\overline{M}$, *V* and $\overline{V}$.

c Use the contingency table to find the probability that a randomly selected student
(1) Has a Mastercard or a VISA.
(2) Has neither credit card.
(3) Has exactly one of the two credit cards.

3.12 The card game of Euchre employs a deck that consists of all four of each of the aces, kings, queens, jacks, tens, and nines (one of each suit—clubs, diamonds, spades, and hearts). Find the probability that a randomly selected card from a Euchre deck is

a A jack (*J*).
b A spade (*S*).
c A jack or an ace (*A*).
d A jack or a spade.
e Are the events *J* and *A* mutually exclusive? *J* and *S*? Why or why not?

3.13 Each month a brokerage house studies various companies and rates each company's stock as being either "low risk" or "moderate to high risk." In a recent report, the brokerage house summarized its findings about 15 aerospace companies and 25 food retailers in the following table:

Company Type	Low Risk	Moderate to High Risk
Aerospace company	6	9
Food retailer	15	10

If we randomly select one of the total of 40 companies, find

a The probability that the company is a food retailer.
b The probability that the company's stock is "low risk."
c The probability that the company's stock is "moderate to high risk."
d The probability that the company is a food retailer and has a stock that is "low risk."
e The probability that the company is a food retailer or has a stock that is "low risk."

3.14 In the book *Essentials of Marketing Research,* William R. Dillon, Thomas J. Madden, and Neil H. Firtle present the results of a concept study for a new wine cooler. Three hundred consumers between 21 and 49 years old were randomly selected. After sampling the new beverage, each was asked to rate the appeal of the phrase

> Not sweet like wine coolers, not filling like beer, and more refreshing than wine or mixed drinks

as it relates to the new wine cooler. The rating was made on a scale from 1 to 5, with 5 representing "extremely appealing" and with 1 representing "not at all appealing." The results obtained are given in Table 3.4. WineCooler

TABLE 3.4 Results of a Concept Study for a New Wine Cooler WineCooler

Rating	Total	Gender		Age Group		
		Male	Female	21–24	25–34	35–49
Extremely appealing (5)	151	68	83	48	66	37
(4)	91	51	40	36	36	19
(3)	36	21	15	9	12	15
(2)	13	7	6	4	6	3
Not at all appealing (1)	9	3	6	4	3	2

Source: W. R. Dillon, T. J. Madden, and N. H. Firtle, *Essentials of Marketing Research* (Burr Ridge, IL: Richard D. Irwin, Inc., 1993), p. 390.

Based on these results, estimate the probability that a randomly selected 21- to 49-year-old consumer

a Would give the phrase a rating of 5.
b Would give the phrase a rating of 3 or higher.
c Is in the 21–24 age group; the 25–34 age group; the 35–49 age group.
d Is a male who gives the phrase a rating of 4.
e Is a 35- to 49-year-old who gives the phrase a rating of 1.

3.15 THE ACCURATINGS CASE

Using the information in Figure 3.3 (page 134), find an estimate of the probability that a randomly selected Los Angeles resident (12 years or older) would

a Name one of the top three rated stations (KPWR, KLAX, or KROQ) as the station that he or she listens to most.
b Not name one of the top five rated stations as the station that he or she listens to most.
c Name a station that is not rated among the top seven stations as the station that he or she listens to most.
d Name a station that is not rated among the top three stations nor is rated lower than 10th as the station that he or she listens to most.

3.4 Conditional Probability and Independence

Conditional probability In Table 3.5 we repeat the contingency table summarizing the subscription data for the *Atlantic Journal* and the *Beacon News.* Suppose that we randomly select a household, and that the chosen household reports that it subscribes to the *Beacon News.* Given this new information, we wish to find the probability that the household subscribes to the *Atlantic Journal*. This new probability is called a **conditional probability.**

The **probability of the event A, given the condition that the event B *has occurred,*** is written as **$P(A \mid B)$**—pronounced "the probability of A given B." We often refer to such a probability as the **conditional probability of A given B.**

In order to find the conditional probability that a household subscribes to the *Atlantic Journal,* given that it subscribes to the *Beacon News,* notice that if we know that the randomly selected household subscribes to the *Beacon News,* we know that we are considering one of 500,000 households (see Table 3.5). That is, we are now considering what we might call a reduced sample space of 500,000 households. Since 250,000 of these 500,000 *Beacon News* subscribers also subscribe to the *Atlantic Journal,* we have

$$P(A \mid B) = \frac{250{,}000}{500{,}000} = .5$$

This says that the probability that the randomly selected household subscribes to the *Atlantic Journal,* given that the household subscribes to the *Beacon News,* is .5. That is, 50 percent of the *Beacon News* subscribers also subscribe to the *Atlantic Journal.*

Next, suppose that we randomly select another household from the community of 1,000,000 households, and suppose that this newly chosen household reports that it subscribes to the *Atlantic Journal.* We now wish to find the probability that this household subscribes to the

TABLE 3.5 A Contingency Table Summarizing Subscription Data for the *Atlantic Journal* and the *Beacon News*

Events	Subscribes to *Beacon News*, *B*	Does Not Subscribe to *Beacon News*, $\bar{B}$	Total
Subscribes to *Atlantic Journal, A*	250,000	400,000	650,000
Does Not Subscribe to *Atlantic Journal,* $\bar{A}$	250,000	100,000	350,000
Total	500,000	500,000	1,000,000

Beacon News. We write this new probability as $P(B|A)$. If we know that the randomly selected household subscribes to the *Atlantic Journal,* we know that we are considering a reduced sample space of 650,000 households (see Table 3.5). Since 250,000 of these 650,000 *Atlantic Journal* subscribers also subscribe to the *Beacon News,* we have

$$P(B|A) = \frac{250{,}000}{650{,}000} = .3846$$

This says that the probability that the randomly selected household subscribes to the *Beacon News,* given that the household subscribes to the *Atlantic Journal,* is .3846. That is, 38.46 percent of the *Atlantic Journal* subscribers also subscribe to the *Beacon News.*

If we divide both the numerator and denominator of each of the conditional probabilities $P(A \mid B)$ and $P(B \mid A)$ by 1,000,000, we obtain

$$P(A|B) = \frac{250{,}000}{500{,}000} = \frac{250{,}000/1{,}000{,}000}{500{,}000/1{,}000{,}000} = \frac{P(A \cap B)}{P(B)}$$

$$P(B|A) = \frac{250{,}000}{650{,}000} = \frac{250{,}000/1{,}000{,}000}{650{,}000/1{,}000{,}000} = \frac{P(A \cap B)}{P(A)}$$

We express these conditional probabilities in terms of $P(A)$, $P(B)$, and $P(A \cap B)$ in order to obtain a more general formula for a conditional probability. We need a more general formula because, although we can use the reduced sample space approach we have demonstrated to find conditional probabilities when all of the sample space outcomes are equally likely, this approach may not give correct results when the sample space outcomes are *not* equally likely. We now give expressions for conditional probability that are valid for any sample space.

Conditional Probability

1 The **conditional probability that *A* will occur given that *B* will occur** is written ***P*(*A* | *B*)** and is defined to be

$$P(A|B) = \frac{P(A \cap B)}{P(B)}$$

Here we assume that $P(B)$ is greater than 0.

2 The **conditional probability that *B* will occur given that *A* will occur** is written ***P*(*B* | *A*)** and is defined to be

$$P(B|A) = \frac{P(A \cap B)}{P(A)}$$

Here we assume that $P(A)$ is greater than 0.

If we multiply both sides of the equation

$$P(A \mid B) = \frac{P(A \cap B)}{P(B)}$$

by $P(B)$, we obtain the equation

$$P(A \cap B) = P(B)P(A \mid B)$$

Similarly, if we multiply both sides of the equation

$$P(B|A) = \frac{P(A \cap B)}{P(A)}$$

by $P(A)$, we obtain the equation

$$P(A \cap B) = P(A)P(B \mid A)$$

In summary, we now have two equations that can be used to calculate $P(A \cap B)$. These equations are often referred to as the **general multiplication rule** for probabilities.

The General Multiplication Rule—Two Ways to Calculate $P(A \cap B)$

Given any two events A and B,

$$P(A \cap B) = P(A)P(B|A)$$
$$= P(B)P(A|B)$$

Example 3.13

In a soft drink taste test, each of 1,000 consumers chose between two colas—Cola 1 and Cola 2—and stated whether they preferred their cola drinks *sweet* or *very sweet.* Unfortunately, some of the survey information was lost. The following information remains:

1 68.3 percent of the consumers (that is, 683 consumers) preferred Cola 1 to Cola 2.

2 62 percent of the consumers (that is, 620 consumers) preferred their cola *sweet* (rather than *very sweet*).

3 85 percent of the consumers who said that they liked their cola *sweet* preferred Cola 1 to Cola 2.

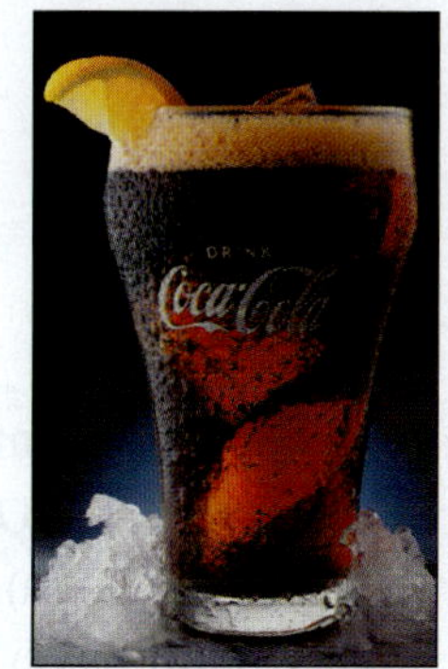

To recover all of the lost survey information, consider randomly selecting one of the 1,000 survey participants, and define the following events:

$C1 \equiv$ the randomly selected consumer prefers Cola 1.

$C2 \equiv$ the randomly selected consumer prefers Cola 2.

$S \equiv$ the randomly selected consumer prefers *sweet* cola drinks.

$V \equiv$ the randomly selected consumer prefers *very sweet* cola drinks.

From the survey information that remains, (1) says that $P(C1) = .683$, (2) says that $P(S) = .62$, and (3) says that $P(C1 \mid S) = .85$.

We will see that we can recover all of the lost survey information if we can find $P(C1 \cap S)$. The general multiplication rule says that

$$P(C1 \cap S) = P(C1)P(S \mid C1) = P(S)P(C1 \mid S)$$

Although we know that $P(C1) = .683$, we do not know $P(S \mid C1)$. Therefore, we cannot calculate $P(C1 \cap S)$ as $P(C1)P(S \mid C1)$. However, because we know that $P(S) = .62$ and that $P(C1 \mid S) = .85$, we can calculate

$$P(C1 \cap S) = P(S)P(C1 \mid S) = (.62)(.85) = .527$$

This implies that 527 consumers preferred Cola 1 and preferred their cola *sweet.* Since 683 consumers preferred Cola 1, and 620 consumers preferred *sweet* cola drinks, we can summarize the numbers of consumers corresponding to the events $C1$, $C2$, S, V, and $C1 \cap S$ as shown in Table 3.6. Furthermore, by performing subtractions as shown in Table 3.7, the numbers of consumers corresponding to the events $C1 \cap V$, $C2 \cap S$, and $C2 \cap V$ can be obtained. We summarize all of our results in Table 3.8. We will use these results in the next subsection to investigate the relationship between cola preference and sweetness preference.

Table 3.6 A Summary of the Number of Consumers Corresponding to the Events C1, C2, *S*, *V*, and C1 ∩ *S*

Events	*S* (Sweet)	*V* (Very Sweet)	Total
C1 (Cola 1)	527		683
C2 (Cola 2)			317
Total	620	380	1,000

Table 3.7 Subtractions to Obtain the Number of Consumers Corresponding to the Events C1 ∩ *V*, C2 ∩ *S*, and C2 ∩ *V*

Events	*S* (Sweet)	*V* (Very Sweet)	Total
C1 (Cola 1)	527	683 − 527 = 156	683
C2 (Cola 2)	620 − 527 = 93	380 − 156 = 224	317
Total	620	380	1,000

Table 3.8 A Contingency Table Summarizing the Cola Brand and Sweetness Preferences

Events	*S* (Sweet)	*V* (Very Sweet)	Total
C1 (Cola 1)	527	156	683
C2 (Cola 2)	93	224	317
Total	620	380	1,000

Independence We have seen in Example 3.13 that $P(C1) = .683$, while $P(C1 \mid S) = .85$. Because $P(C1 \mid S)$ is greater than $P(C1)$, the probability that a randomly selected consumer will prefer Cola 1 is higher if we know that the person prefers *sweet* cola than it is if we have no knowledge of the person's sweetness preference. Another way to see this is to use Table 3.8 to calculate

$$P(C1|V) = \frac{P(C1 \cap V)}{P(V)} = \frac{156/1{,}000}{380/1{,}000} = .4105$$

Since $P(C1|S) = .85$ is greater than $P(C1|V) = .4105$, the probability that a randomly selected consumer will prefer Cola 1 is higher if the consumer prefers *sweet* colas than it is if the consumer prefers *very sweet* colas. Since the probability of the event $C1$ is influenced by whether the event S occurs, we say that the events $C1$ and S are **dependent.** If $P(C1|S)$ were equal to $P(C1)$, then the probability of the event $C1$ would not be influenced by whether S occurs. In this case we would say that the events $C1$ and S are **independent.** This leads to the following definition of **independence:**

Independent Events

Two events *A* and *B* are **independent** if and only if

1 $P(A \mid B) = P(A)$ or, equivalently,

2 $P(B \mid A) = P(B)$

Here we assume that $P(A)$ and $P(B)$ are greater than 0.

When we say that conditions (1) and (2) are equivalent, we mean that condition (1) holds if and only if condition (2) holds. Although we will not prove this, we will demonstrate it in the next example.

Example 3.14

In the soft drink taste test of Example 3.13, we have seen that $P(C1 \mid S) = .85$ does not equal $P(C1) = .683$. This implies that $P(S \mid C1)$ does not equal $P(S)$. To demonstrate this, note from Table 3.8 that

$$P(S \mid C1) = \frac{P(C1 \cap S)}{P(C1)} = \frac{527/1{,}000}{683/1{,}000} = .7716$$

This probability is larger than $P(S) = 620/1{,}000 = .62$. In summary:

1 A comparison of $P(C1 \mid S) = .85$ and $P(C1) = .683$ says that a consumer is more likely to prefer Cola 1 if the consumer prefers *sweet* colas.

2 A comparison of $P(S \mid C1) = .7716$ and $P(S) = .62$ says that a consumer is more likely to prefer *sweet* colas if the consumer prefers Cola 1.

This suggests, but does not prove, that one reason Cola 1 is preferred to Cola 2 is that Cola 1 is *sweet* (as opposed to *very sweet*).

If the occurrences of the events A and B have nothing to do with each other, then we know that A and B are independent events. This implies that $P(A \mid B)$ equals $P(A)$ and that $P(B \mid A)$ equals $P(B)$. Recall that the general multiplication rule tells us that, for any two events A and B, we can say that

$$P(A \cap B) = P(A)P(B \mid A)$$

Therefore, if $P(B \mid A)$ equals $P(B)$, it follows that

$$P(A \cap B) = P(A)P(B)$$

which is called the **multiplication rule for independent events.** To summarize:

The Multiplication Rule for Two Independent Events

If A and B are **independent events,** then

$$P(A \cap B) = P(A)P(B)$$

As a simple example, define the events C and P as follows:

$C \equiv$ your favorite college football team wins its first game next season.

$P \equiv$ your favorite professional football team wins its first game next season.

Suppose you believe that for next season $P(C) = .6$ and $P(P) = .6$. Then, because the outcomes of a college football game and a professional football game would probably have nothing to do with each other, it is reasonable to assume that C and P are independent events. It follows that

$$P(C \cap P) = P(C)P(P) = (.6)(.6) = .36$$

This probability might be surprisingly low. That is, since you believe that each of your teams has a 60 percent chance of winning, you might feel reasonably confident that both your college and professional teams will win their first game. Yet, the chance of this happening is really only .36!

Next, consider a group of events $A_1, A_2, \ldots, A_N$. Intuitively, the events $A_1, A_2, \ldots, A_N$ are independent if the occurrences of these events have nothing to do with each other. Denoting the probability that A_1 and A_2 and ... and A_N will simultaneously occur as $P(A_1 \cap A_2 \cap \cdots \cap A_N)$, we have the following:

The Multiplication Rule for *N* Independent Events

If $A_1, A_2, \ldots, A_N$ are independent events, then

$$P(A_1 \cap A_2 \cap \cdots \cap A_N) = P(A_1)P(A_2) \cdots P(A_N)$$

This says that the multiplication rule for two independent events can be extended to any number of independent events.

Example 3.15

This example is based on a real situation encountered by a major producer and marketer of consumer products. The company assessed the service it provides by surveying the attitudes of its customers regarding 10 different aspects of customer service—order filled correctly, billing amount on invoice correct, delivery made on time, and so forth. When the survey results were analyzed, the company was dismayed to learn that only 59 percent of the survey participants indicated that they were satisfied with all 10 aspects of the company's service. Upon investigation, each of the 10 departments responsible for the aspects of service considered in the study insisted that it satisfied its customers 95 percent of the time. That is, each department claimed that its error rate was only 5 percent. Company executives were confused and felt that there was a substantial discrepancy between the survey results and the claims of the departments providing the services. However, a company statistician pointed out that there was no discrepancy. To understand this, consider randomly selecting a customer from among the survey participants, and define 10 events (corresponding to the 10 aspects of service studied):

$A_1 \equiv$ the customer is satisfied that the order is filled correctly (aspect 1).

$A_2 \equiv$ the customer is satisfied that the billing amount on the invoice is correct (aspect 2).

$\vdots$

$A_{10} \equiv$ the customer is satisfied that the delivery is made on time (aspect 10).

Also, define the event

$S \equiv$ the customer is satisfied with all 10 aspects of customer service.

Since 10 different departments are responsible for the 10 aspects of service being studied, it is reasonable to assume that all 10 aspects of service are independent of each other. For instance, billing amounts would be independent of delivery times. Therefore, $A_1, A_2, \ldots, A_{10}$ are independent events, and

$$\begin{aligned} P(S) &= P(A_1 \cap A_2 \cap \cdots \cap A_{10}) \\ &= P(A_1)P(A_2) \cdots P(A_{10}) \end{aligned}$$

If, as the departments claim, each department satisfies its customers 95 percent of the time, then the probability that the customer is satisfied with all 10 aspects is

$$P(S) = (.95)(.95) \cdots (.95) = (.95)^{10} = .5987$$

This result is almost identical to the 59 percent satisfaction rate reported by the survey participants.

If the company wants to increase the percentage of its customers who are satisfied with all 10 aspects of service, it must improve the quality of service provided by the 10 departments. For example, to satisfy 95 percent of its customers with all 10 aspects of service, the company must require each department to raise the fraction of the time it satisfies its customers to x, where

$$(x)^{10} = .95$$

It follows that

$$x = (.95)^{\frac{1}{10}} = .9949$$

and that each department must satisfy its customers 99.49 percent of the time (rather than the current 95 percent of the time).

A real-world application of conditional probability, independence, and dependence

Example 3.16 The AccuRatings Case: Estimating Radio Station Share by Daypart 

In addition to asking each of the 5,528 sampled Los Angeles residents to name which station (if any) he or she listens to most on an overall basis, AccuRatings asked each resident to name which station (if any) he or she listens to most during various parts of the day. The various parts of the day considered by AccuRatings and the results of the survey are given in Figure 3.7. To explain these results, suppose that 2,827 of the 5,528 sampled residents said that they listen to the radio during

FIGURE 3.7 Further Portions of an AccuRatings Report on Radio Ratings in the Los Angeles Market

STATION		CORE LISTENERS	SHARE		RECALLED FORMER SHARE
KPWR	1:	668,100	8.0	<—	8.4
KLAX	2:	531,800	6.4	<—	4.4
KROQ	3:	505,100	6.1	<—	5.6
KIIS-A/F	4:	418,200	5.0	<—	5.6
KFI	5:	386,500	4.7	<—	4.0
KFWB	6:	383,500	4.6	<—	3.8
KKBT	7:	378,500	4.6	<—	4.1
KABC	8:	346,600	4.2	<—	4.2
KRTH	9:	302,300	3.6	<—	3.7
KCBS-FM	10:	299,500	3.6	<—	1.3

'SHARE OF CORE LISTENERSHIP' BY DAYPART

6–10A	10A–3P	3–7P	7P–12M	WKEND
2: 6.9	1: 9.0	1: 10.0	1: 10.7	1: 10.4
6: 5.1	3: 6.1	3: 5.9	5: 5.6	3: 7.1
3: 5.4	4: 5.6	2: 6.8	2: 9.1	2: 7.5
1: 7.1	5: 4.9	4: 4.9	6: 3.5	5: 4.7
5: 5.2	2: 6.5	6: 3.7	10: 2.7	13: 2.9
etc.				

SHARE OF CORE LISTENERSHIP BY DAYPART:
KIIS's Rick Dees has the #1 morning show in the 6–10A daypart. Of people who listen to radio during that daypart, 7.1% say that their primary station during that daypart is KIIS.
Similarly, KFI is the #2 station during middays (which includes Rush Limbaugh's shift), with 6.5% of midday listeners saying that KFI is the station they listen to most during that daypart.

Source: Strategic Radio Research, *AccuRatings Introduction for Broadcasters.*

some portion of the 6–10 A.M. daypart. Furthermore, suppose that 201 of these 2,827 residents named station KIIS as the station that they listen to most during that daypart. It follows that

$$\frac{201}{2{,}827} = .071100106$$

is an estimate of $P(\text{KIIS} \mid 6\text{–}10 \text{ A.M.})$, the probability that a randomly selected Los Angeles resident who listens to the radio during the 6–10 A.M. daypart would name KIIS as his or her primary station during that daypart. Said equivalently, station KIIS has an estimated share of 7.1 percent of the 6–10 A.M. radio listeners. In general, Figure 3.7 gives the estimated shares during the various dayparts for the five stations that are rated best overall (KPWR, KLAX, KROQ, KIIS, and KFI). Examination of this figure seems to reveal that a station's share depends somewhat on the daypart being considered. For example, note that Figure 3.7 tells us that the estimate of $P(\text{KIIS} \mid 6\text{–}10 \text{ A.M.})$ is .071, whereas the estimate of $P(\text{KIIS} \mid 3\text{–}7 \text{ P.M.})$ is .049. This says that station KIIS's estimated share of the 6–10 A.M. radio listeners is higher than its estimated share of the 3–7 P.M. radio listeners.

Estimating Probabilities of Radio Station Listenership

AccuRatings provides the sort of estimates given in Figures 3.3 and 3.7 not only for the Los Angeles market but for other markets as well. In addition, AccuRatings provides (for a given market) hour-by-hour estimates of the probabilities of different stations being listened to in the market. How this is done is an excellent real-world application of the general multiplication rule. As an example, consider how AccuRatings might find an estimate of "the probability that a randomly selected Los Angeles resident will be listening to station KIIS at an average moment from 7 to 8 A.M." To estimate this probability, AccuRatings estimates

1. The probability that a randomly selected Los Angeles resident will be listening to the radio at an average moment from 7 to 8 A.M.

and multiplies this estimate by an estimate of

2. The probability that a randomly selected Los Angeles resident who is listening to the radio at an average moment from 7 to 8 A.M. will be listening to station KIIS at that average moment.

Because the hour of 7 to 8 A.M. is in the 6–10 A.M. daypart, it is reasonable to estimate the probability in (2) by using an estimate of $P(\text{KIIS} \mid 6\text{–}10 \text{ A.M.})$, which Figure 3.7 tells us is .071. To find an estimate of the probability in (1), AccuRatings uses a 2,000-person national study. Here, each person is interviewed to obtain a detailed, minute-by-minute reconstruction of the times that the person listened to the radio on the previous day (with no attempt to identify the specific stations listened to). Then, for each minute of the day the proportion of the 2,000 people who listened to the radio during that minute is determined. The average of the 60 such proportions for a particular hour is the estimate of the probability that a randomly selected person will listen to the radio at an average moment during that hour. Using a national study is reasonable because the detailed reconstruction made by AccuRatings would be extremely time-consuming to construct for individual markets and because AccuRatings' studies show very consistent hour-by-hour patterns of radio usage across markets, across seasons, and across demographics. This implies that the national study applies to individual markets (such as the Los Angeles market). Suppose, then, that the national study estimate of the 7 to 8 A.M. radio listening probability in (1) is .242. Since (as previously discussed) an estimate of the station KIIS conditional listening probability in (2) is .071, it follows than an estimate of the desired probability is $.242 \times .071 = .017182 \approx .017$. This says that we estimate that 1.7 percent of all Los Angeles residents will be listening to station KIIS at an average moment from 7 to 8 A.M. Assuming that there are 8,300,000 Los Angeles residents, we estimate that

$$(8{,}300{,}000) \times (.017) = 141{,}000$$

of these residents will be listening to station KIIS at an average moment from 7 to 8 A.M. Finally, note that in making its hour-by-hour radio station listening estimates, AccuRatings makes a separate set of estimates for the hours on a weekday, for the hours on Saturday, and for the hours on Sunday. The above 7 to 8 A.M. estimate is for the 7 to 8 A.M. hour on a weekday.

Estimating Song Ratings

In addition to providing AccuRatings reports to radio stations, Strategic Radio Research does music research for clients such as MTV. Figure 3.8 gives a portion of a *title-by-title analysis* for the song "Gangsta's Paradise" by Coolio. Listeners are surveyed and are asked to rate the song on a 1 to 5 rating scale with 1 being the lowest possible rating and 5 being the highest. Figure 3.8 gives a histogram of these ratings; notice that *UNFAM* indicates that the listener was not familiar with this particular song. The percentages above the bars of the histogram give the percentages of listeners rating the song 5, 4, 3, 2, 1, and *UNFAM*, respectively. If we let the symbol denoting

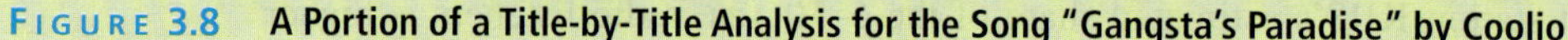

FIGURE 3.8 A Portion of a Title-by-Title Analysis for the Song "Gangsta's Paradise" by Coolio

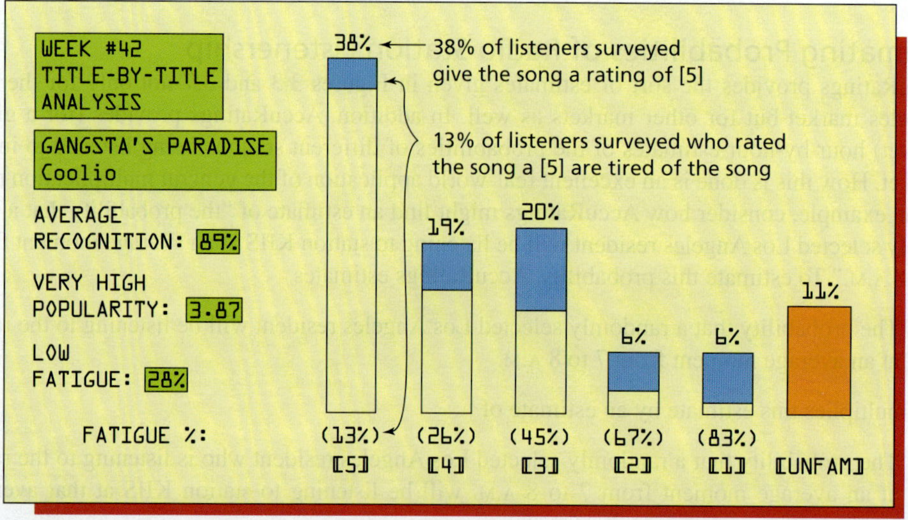

Source: Strategic Radio Research, Chicago, Illinois.

a particular rating also denote the event that a randomly selected listener would give the song the rating, it follows that we estimate that

$$P(5) = .38 \qquad P(4) = .19 \qquad P(3) = .20$$

$$P(2) = .06 \qquad P(1) = .06 \qquad P(UNFAM) = .11$$

The three boxes on the left of Figure 3.8 give *recognition, popularity,* and *fatigue* indexes for the song being analyzed. Although we will have to wait until Chapter 4 to learn the meaning of the popularity index, we now explain the meaning of the recognition and fatigue indexes. The recognition index estimates the probability that a randomly selected listener is familiar with the song. We have seen that the estimate of $P(UNFAM)$ is .11, so the recognition index is $1 - .11 = .89$, which is expressed as the 89 percent in Figure 3.8. This index says we estimate that 89 percent of all listeners are familiar with the song. The fatigue index, 28 percent, estimates the percentage of listeners who are tired of the song. That is, if T denotes the event that a randomly selected listener is tired of the song, we estimate that $P(T) = .28$. Finally, note that at the bottom of each histogram bar in Figure 3.8, and shaded in blue, is the fatigue percentage corresponding to the rating described by the bar. This percentage is an estimate of the conditional probability that a randomly selected listener giving the song that rating is tired of the song. Therefore, we estimate that $P(T \mid 1) = .83$, $P(T \mid 2) = .67$, $P(T \mid 3) = .45$, $P(T \mid 4) = .26$, and $P(T \mid 5) = .13$. From these conditional probabilities we might conclude that the higher the song is rated, the lower is its fatigue percentage.

Exercises for Section 3.4

CONCEPTS

3.16 Explain the concept of a conditional probability. Give an example of a conditional probability that would be of interest to a college student; to a business.

3.17 Explain what it means for two events to be independent.

METHODS AND APPLICATIONS

3.18 Recall from Exercise 3.11 (page 142) that of 10,000 students at a college, 2,500 have a Mastercard (M), 4,000 have a VISA (V), and 1,000 have both. Find

a The proportion of Mastercard holders who have VISA cards. Interpret and write this proportion as a conditional probability.

b The proportion of VISA cardholders who have Mastercards. Interpret and write this proportion as a conditional probability.

c Are the events *having a Mastercard* and *having a VISA* independent? Justify your answer.

3.19 Recall from Exercise 3.13 (page 142) that each month a brokerage house studies various companies and rates each company's stock as being either "low risk" or "moderate to high risk." In a recent report, the brokerage house summarized its findings about 15 aerospace companies and 25 food retailers in the following table:

Company Type	Low Risk	Moderate to High Risk
Aerospace company	6	9
Food retailer	15	10

If we randomly select one of the total of 40 companies, find

a The probability that the company's stock is moderate to high risk given that the firm is an aerospace company.

b The probability that the company's stock is moderate to high risk given that the firm is a food retailer.

c Determine if the *company type* is independent of the *level of risk* of the firm's stock.

3.20 John and Jane are married. The probability that John watches a certain television show is .4. The probability that Jane watches the show is .5. The probability that John watches the show, given that Jane does, is .7.

a Find the probability that both John and Jane watch the show.

b Find the probability that Jane watches the show, given that John does.

c Do John and Jane watch the show independently of each other? Justify your answer.

3.21 In Exercise 3.20, find the probability that either John or Jane watches the show.

3.22 In the July 29, 2001, issue of *The Journal News* (Hamilton, Ohio), Lynn Elber of the Associated Press reported that "while 40 percent of American families own a television set with a V-chip installed to block designated programs with sex and violence, only 17 percent of those parents use the device."[2]

a Use the report's results to find an estimate of the probability that a randomly selected American family has used a V-chip to block programs containing sex and violence.

b According to the report, more than 50 percent of parents have used the TV rating system (TV-14, etc.) to control their children's TV viewing. How does this compare to the percentage using the V-chip?

3.23 According to the Associated Press report (in Exercise 3.22), 47 percent of parents who have purchased TV sets after V-chips became standard equipment in January 2000 are aware that their sets have V-chips, and of those who are aware of the option, 36 percent have programmed their V-chips. Using these results, find an estimate of the probability that a randomly selected parent who has bought a TV set since January 2000 has programmed the V-chip.

3.24 Fifteen percent of the employees in a company have managerial positions, and 25 percent of the employees in the company have MBA degrees. Also, 60 percent of the managers have MBA degrees. Using the probability formulas,

a Find the proportion of employees who are managers and have MBA degrees.

b Find the proportion of MBAs who are managers.

c Are the events *being a manager* and *having an MBA* independent? Justify your answer.

3.25 In Exercise 3.24, find the proportion of employees who either have MBAs or are managers.

3.26 Consider Exercise 3.14 (page 142). Using the results in Table 3.4 (page 143), estimate the probability that a randomly selected 21- to 49-year-old consumer would

a Give the phrase a rating of 4 or 5 given that the consumer is male; give the phrase a rating of 4 or 5 given that the consumer is female. Based on these results, is the appeal of the phrase among males much different from the appeal of the phrase among females? Explain.

b Give the phrase a rating of 4 or 5, given that the consumer is in the 21–24 age group; given that the consumer is in the 25–34 age group; given that the consumer is in the 35–49 age group. Based on these results, which age group finds the phrase most appealing? Least appealing?

3.27 In a survey of 100 insurance claims, 40 are fire claims ($FIRE$), 16 of which are fraudulent ($FRAUD$). Also, there are a total of 40 fraudulent claims.

a Construct a contingency table summarizing the claims data. Use the pairs of events $FIRE$ and $\overline{FIRE}$, $FRAUD$ and $\overline{FRAUD}$.

b What proportion of the fire claims are fraudulent?

c Are the events *a claim is fraudulent* and *a claim is a fire claim* independent? Use your probability of part *b* to prove your answer.

3.28 Recall from Exercise 3.3 (page 135) that two randomly selected customers are each asked to take a blind taste test and then to state which of three diet colas (marked as *A*, *B*, or *C*) he or she prefers. Suppose that cola *A*'s distributor claims that 80 percent of all people prefer cola *A* and that only 10 percent prefer each of colas *B* and *C*.

a Assuming that the distributor's claim is true and that the two taste test participants make independent cola preference decisions, find the probability of each sample space outcome.

b Find the probability that neither taste test participant will prefer cola *A*.

c If, when the taste test is carried out, neither participant prefers cola *A*, use the probability you computed in part *b* to decide whether the distributor's claim seems valid. Explain.

3.29 A sprinkler system inside an office building has two types of activation devices, $D1$ and $D2$, which operate independently. When there is a fire, if either device operates correctly, the sprinkler system is turned on. In case of fire, the probability that $D1$ operates correctly is .95, and the probability that $D2$ operates correctly is .92. Find the probability that

a Both $D1$ and $D2$ will operate correctly.

b The sprinkler system will come on.

c The sprinkler system will fail.

3.30 A product is assembled using 10 different components, each of which must meet specifications for five different quality characteristics. Suppose that there is a .9973 probability that each individual specification will be met.

a Assuming that all 50 specifications are met independently, find the probability that the product meets all 50 specifications.

[2]Source: *The Journal News* (Hamilton, Ohio), July 29, 2001, p. C5.

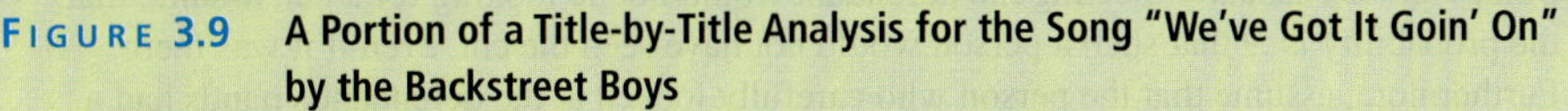

FIGURE 3.9 A Portion of a Title-by-Title Analysis for the Song "We've Got It Goin' On" by the Backstreet Boys

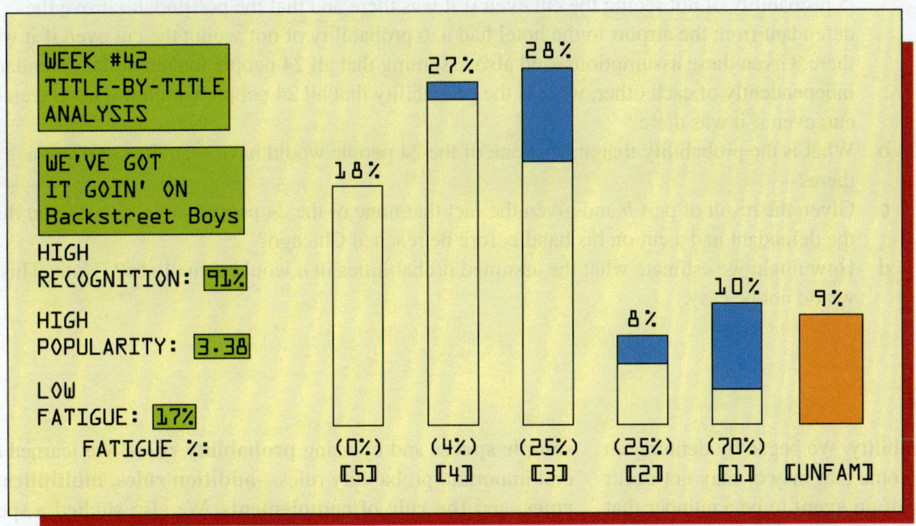

Source: Strategic Radio Research, Chicago, Illinois.

b Suppose that we wish to have a 99.73 percent chance that all 50 specifications will be met. If each specification will have the same chance of being met, how large must we make the probability of meeting each individual specification?

3.31 THE ACCURATINGS CASE

Consider the share of core listenership by daypart information given in Figure 3.7 (page 149).

a Find an estimate of $P(\text{KPWR} \mid 3\text{–}7\text{ P.M.})$, the probability that a randomly selected Los Angeles resident who listens to the radio during the 3–7 P.M. daypart would name KPWR as his or her primary station during that daypart.

b Find $P(\text{KLAX} \mid 3\text{–}7\text{ P.M.})$, $P(\text{KROQ} \mid 3\text{–}7\text{ P.M.})$, $P(\text{KIIS} \mid 3\text{–}7\text{ P.M.})$, and $P(\text{KFI} \mid 3\text{–}7\text{ P.M.})$.

c Suppose that the AccuRatings national survey estimates that the probability that a randomly selected Los Angeles resident will be listening to the radio at an average moment between 5 and 6 P.M. is .256. Use this survey result and the estimate in part *a* to estimate the probability that a randomly selected Los Angeles resident will be listening to station KPWR at an average moment between 5 and 6 P.M.

d Repeat part *c* for each of KLAX, KROQ, KIIS, and KFI.

e Find an estimate of the probability that a randomly selected Los Angeles resident will be listening to one of the five most highly rated stations in the Los Angeles market (KPWR, KLAX, KROQ, KIIS, or KFI) at an average moment between 5 and 6 P.M.

3.32 THE ACCURATINGS CASE

Figure 3.9 gives a portion of a title-by-title analysis for the song "We've Got It Goin' On" by the Backstreet Boys. The ratings information given in this figure is the same type given in Figure 3.8 (page 150) and explained in Example 3.16 (pages 150–151). Using the ratings information:

a Find an estimate of the probability that a randomly selected listener would give the song each of the ratings 5, 4, 3, 2, and 1.

b Find an estimate of the probability that a randomly selected listener is (1) familiar with the song; (2) tired of the song.

c Find estimates of each of $P(T \mid 5)$, $P(T \mid 4)$, $P(T \mid 3)$, $P(T \mid 2)$, and $P(T \mid 1)$, where T denotes the event that a listener is tired of the song.

3.33 In a murder trial in Los Angeles, the prosecution claims that the defendant was cut on the left middle finger at the murder scene, but the defendant claims the cut occurred in Chicago, the day after the murders had been committed. Because the defendant is a sports celebrity, many people noticed him before he reached Chicago. Twenty-two people saw him casually, one person on the plane to Chicago carefully studied his hands looking for a championship ring, and another person stood with him as he signed autographs and drove him from the airport to the hotel. None of these 24 people saw a cut on the defendant's finger. If in fact he was not cut at all, it would be extremely unlikely that he left blood at the murder scene.

a Since a person casually meeting the defendant would not be looking for a cut, assume that the probability is .9 that such a person would not have seen the cut, even if it was there. Furthermore, assume that the person who carefully looked at the defendant's hands had a .5 probability of not seeing the cut even if it was there and that the person who drove the defendant from the airport to the hotel had a .6 probability of not seeing the cut even if it was there. Given these assumptions, and also assuming that all 24 people looked at the defendant independently of each other, what is the probability that all 24 people would not have seen the cut, even if it was there?

b What is the probability that at least one of the 24 people would have seen the cut if it was there?

c Given the result of part *b* and given the fact that none of the 24 people saw a cut, do you think the defendant had a cut on his hand before he reached Chicago?

d How might we estimate what the assumed probabilities in *a* would actually be? (Note: This would not be easy.)

Chapter Summary

In this chapter we studied **probability.** We began by defining an **event** to be an experimental outcome that may or may not occur and by defining the **probability of an event** to be a number that measures the likelihood that the event will occur. We learned that a probability is often interpreted as a **long-run relative frequency,** and we saw that probabilities can be found by examining **sample spaces** and by using **probability rules.** We learned several important probability rules—**addition rules, multiplication rules,** and **the rule of complements.** We also studied a special kind of probability called a **conditional probability,** which is the probability that one event will occur given that another event occurs, and we used probabilities to define **independent events.**

Glossary of Terms

complement (of an event): If *A* is an event, the complement of *A* is the event that *A* will not occur. (page 136)

conditional probability: The probability that one event will occur given that we know that another event occurs. (page 143)

dependent events: When the probability of one event is influenced by whether another event occurs, the events are said to be dependent. (page 146)

event: A set of sample space outcomes. (page 130)

experiment: A process of observation that has an uncertain outcome. (page 127)

independent events: When the probability of one event is not influenced by whether another event occurs, the events are said to be independent. (page 146)

mutually exclusive events: Events that have no sample space outcomes in common, and, therefore, cannot occur simultaneously. (page 139)

probability (of an event): A number that measures the chance, or likelihood, that an event will occur when an experiment is carried out. (page 131)

sample space: The set of all possible experimental outcomes (sample space outcomes). (page 129)

sample space outcome: A distinct outcome of an experiment (that is, an element in the sample space). (page 129)

subjective probability: A probability assessment that is based on experience, intuitive judgment, or expertise. (page 128)

Important Formulas

Probabilities when all sample space outcomes are equally likely: page 133

The rule of complements: page 136

The addition rule for two events: page 139

The addition rule for two mutually exclusive events: page 140

The addition rule for *N* mutually exclusive events: page 141

Conditional probability: page 144

The general multiplication rule: page 145

Independence: page 146

The multiplication rule for two independent events: page 147

The multiplication rule for *N* independent events: page 147

Supplementary Exercises

Exercises 3.34 through 3.37 are based on the following situation: An investor holds two stocks, each of which can rise (*R*), remain unchanged (*U*), or decline (*D*) on any particular day.

3.34 Construct a tree diagram showing all possible combined movements for both stocks on a particular day (for instance, *RR*, *RD*, and so on, where the first letter denotes the movement of the first stock, and the second letter denotes the movement of the second stock).

3.35 If all outcomes are equally likely, find the probability that both stocks rise; that both stocks decline; that exactly one stock declines.

3.36 Find the probabilities you found in Exercise 3.35 by assuming that for each stock $P(R) = .6$, $P(U) = .1$, and $P(D) = .3$, and assuming that the two stocks move independently.

3.37 Assume that for the first stock (on a particular day)

$$P(R) = .4, \; P(U) = .2, \; P(D) = .4$$

and that for the second stock (on a particular day)

$$P(R) = .8, \; P(U) = .1, \; P(D) = .1$$

Assuming that these stocks move independently, find the probability that both stocks decline; the probability that exactly one stock rises; the probability that exactly one stock is unchanged; the probability that both stocks rise.

The Bureau of Labor Statistics reports on a variety of employment statistics. "College Enrollment and Work Activity of 2004 High School Graduates" provides information on high school graduates by gender, by race, and by labor force participation as of October 2004.[3] (All numbers are in thousands.) The following two tables provide information on the "Labor force status of persons 16 to 24 years old by educational attainment and gender, October 2004." Using the information contained in the tables, do Exercises 3.38 through 3.42. LabForce

Women, age 16 to 24	Civilian labor force Employed	Civilian labor force Unemployed	Not in labor force	Row total
< High School	662	205	759	1626
HS degree	2050	334	881	3265
Some college	1352	126	321	1799
Bachelors degree or more	921	55	105	1081
Column total	4985	720	2066	7771

Men, age 16 to 24	Civilian labor force Employed	Civilian labor force Unemployed	Not in labor force	Row total
< High School	1334	334	472	2140
HS degree	3110	429	438	3977
Some college	1425	106	126	1657
Bachelors degree or more	708	37	38	783
Column total	6577	906	1074	8557

3.38 Find the probability that a randomly selected female aged 16 to 24 is in the civilian labor force, if she has a high school degree. LabForce

3.39 Find the probability that a randomly selected female aged 16 to 24 is in the civilian labor force, if she has a bachelor's degree or more. LabForce

3.40 Find the probability that a randomly selected female aged 16 to 24 is employed, if she is in the civilian labor force and has a high school degree. LabForce

3.41 Find the probability that a randomly selected female aged 16 to 24 is employed, if she is in the civilian labor force and has a bachelors degree or more. LabForce

3.42 Repeat Exercises 3.38 through 3.41 for a randomly selected male aged 16 to 24. In general, do the above tables imply that labor force status and employment status depend upon educational attainment? Explain your answer. LabForce

Suppose that in a survey of 1,000 U.S. residents, 721 residents believed that the amount of violent television programming had increased over the past 10 years, 454 residents believed that the overall quality of television programming had decreased over the past 10 years, and 362 residents believed both. Use this information to do Exercises 3.43 through 3.49.

3.43 What proportion of the 1,000 U.S. residents believed that the amount of violent programming had increased over the past 10 years?

3.44 What proportion of the 1,000 U.S. residents believed that the overall quality of programming had decreased over the past 10 years?

3.45 What proportion of the 1,000 U.S. residents believed that both the amount of violent programming had increased and the overall quality of programming had decreased over the past 10 years?

3.46 What proportion of the 1,000 U.S. residents believed that either the amount of violent programming had increased or the overall quality of programming had decreased over the past 10 years?

3.47 What proportion of the U.S. residents who believed that the amount of violent programming had increased believed that the overall quality of programming had decreased?

3.48 What proportion of the U.S. residents who believed that the overall quality of programming had decreased believed that the amount of violent programming had increased?

[3]Source: www.bls.gov. College Enrollment and Work Activity of 2004 High School Graduates, Table 2. Labor force status of persons 16 to 24 years old by school enrollment, educational attainment, sex, race, and Hispanic or Latino ethnicity, October 2004.

3.49 What sort of dependence seems to exist between whether U.S. residents believed that the amount of violent programming had increased and whether U.S. residents believed that the overall quality of programming had decreased? Explain your answer.

3.50 Enterprise Industries has been running a television advertisement for Fresh liquid laundry detergent. When a survey was conducted, .21 of the individuals surveyed had purchased Fresh, .41 of the individuals surveyed had recalled seeing the advertisement, and .13 of the individuals surveyed had purchased Fresh and recalled seeing the advertisement.

a What proportion of the individuals surveyed who recalled seeing the advertisement had purchased Fresh?

b Based on your answer to part *a*, does the advertisement seem to have been effective? Explain.

3.51 A company employs 400 salespeople. Of these, 83 received a bonus last year, 100 attended a special sales training program at the beginning of last year, and 42 both attended the special sales training program and received a bonus. (Note: the bonus was based totally on sales performance.)

a What proportion of the 400 salespeople received a bonus last year?

b What proportion of the 400 salespeople attended the special sales training program at the beginning of last year?

c What proportion of the 400 salespeople both attended the special sales training program and received a bonus?

d What proportion of the salespeople who attended the special sales training program received a bonus?

e Based on your answers to parts *a* and *d*, does the special sales training program seem to have been effective? Explain your answer.

Exercises 3.52, 3.53, and 3.54 extend Exercise 3.32 (page 153). Recall that Figure 3.9 (page 153) gives an AccuRatings analysis for the song "We've Got It Goin' On" by the Backstreet Boys. Also recall that

1. Estimates of the probabilities that a randomly selected listener would give the song the ratings 5, 4, 3, 2, and 1 are $P(5) = .18$, $P(4) = .27$, $P(3) = .28$, $P(2) = .08$, and $P(1) = .10$.
2. An estimate of the probability that a randomly selected listener is tired of the song is $P(T) = .17$.
3. We estimate that $P(T \mid 5) = 0$, $P(T \mid 4) = .04$, $P(T \mid 3) = .25$, $P(T \mid 2) = .25$, and $P(T \mid 1) = .70$.
4. We estimate that the probability that a randomly selected listener is familiar with the song is $P(FAM) = .91$.

3.52 Find estimates of $P(5 \mid T)$, $P(4 \mid T)$, $P(3 \mid T)$, $P(2 \mid T)$, and $P(1 \mid T)$.

Hint:

$$P(1 \mid T) = \frac{P(1 \cap T)}{P(T)} = \frac{P(1)P(T \mid 1)}{P(T)}$$

and the other probabilities are calculated similarly.

3.53 Let NT denote the event that a randomly selected listener is not tired of the song. Because we estimate that $P(T) = .17$ and $P(T \mid 1) = .70$, we estimate that

$$P(NT) = 1 - P(T) = .83 \quad \text{and} \quad P(NT \mid 1) = 1 - P(T \mid 1) = .30$$

a Estimate $P(NT \mid 5)$, $P(NT \mid 4)$, $P(NT \mid 3)$, and $P(NT \mid 2)$.

b Estimate $P(5 \mid NT)$, $P(4 \mid NT)$, $P(3 \mid NT)$, $P(2 \mid NT)$, and $P(1 \mid NT)$.

Hint:

$$P(1 \mid NT) = \frac{P(1 \cap NT)}{P(NT)} = \frac{P(1)P(NT \mid 1)}{P(NT)}$$

and the other probabilities are calculated similarly.

c The reason that the probabilities in *b* do not sum to 1 (with rounding) is that, if a listener is not tired of the song, the listener could be unfamiliar ($UNFAM$) with the song. Using the facts that

$$P(UNFAM) = 1 - P(FAM) = .09 \quad \text{and} \quad P(NT \mid UNFAM) = 1$$

find $P(UNFAM \cap NT)$, $P(UNFAM \mid NT)$, and $P(UNFAM \cup NT)$.

3.54 In this exercise we estimate the proportions of listeners familiar with the song who would give the song each rating. Using the definition of conditional probability, we estimate that

$$P(5 \mid FAM) = \frac{P(5 \cap FAM)}{P(FAM)} = \frac{P(5)}{P(FAM)} = \frac{.18}{.91} = .1978$$

Note here that $P(5 \cap FAM)$ equals $P(5)$ because the event $5 \cap FAM$ and the event 5 are equivalent. That is, a randomly selected listener would give the song a rating of 5 if and only if the listener is familiar with the song and would give the song a rating of 5. By using similar reasoning, find $P(4 \mid FAM)$, $P(3 \mid FAM)$, $P(2 \mid FAM)$, and $P(1 \mid FAM)$.

3.55 Suppose that A and B are events and that $P(A)$ and $P(B)$ are both positive.

a If A and B are mutually exclusive, what is $P(A \cap B)$?

b If A and B are independent events, explain why $P(A \cap B)$ is positive.

c Can two mutually exclusive events, each having a positive probability of occurrence, also be independent? Prove your answer using your answers to parts *a* and *b*.

3.56 Below we give two contingency tables of data from reports submitted by airlines to the U.S. Department of Transportation. The data concern the numbers of on-time and delayed flights for Alaska Airlines and America West Airlines at five major airports. AirDelays

	Alaska Airlines		
	On Time	**Delayed**	**Total**
Los Angeles	497	62	559
Phoenix	221	12	233
San Diego	212	20	232
San Francisco	503	102	605
Seattle	1,841	305	2,146
Total	3,274	501	3,775

	America West		
	On Time	**Delayed**	**Total**
Los Angeles	694	117	811
Phoenix	4,840	415	5,255
San Diego	383	65	448
San Francisco	320	129	449
Seattle	201	61	262
Total	6,438	787	7,225

Source: A. Barnett, "How Numbers Can Trick You," *Technology Review,* October 1994, pp. 38–45.

a What percentage of all Alaska Airlines flights were delayed? That is, use the data to estimate the probability that an Alaska Airlines flight will be delayed. Do the same for America West Airlines. Which airline does best overall?

b For Alaska Airlines find the percentage of delayed flights at each airport. That is, use the data to estimate each of the probabilities $P(\text{delayed} \mid \text{Los Angeles})$, $P(\text{delayed} \mid \text{Phoenix})$, and so on. Then do the same for America West Airlines. Which airline does best at each individual airport?

c We find that America West Airlines does worse at every airport, yet America West does best overall. This seems impossible, but it is true! By looking carefully at the data, explain how this can happen. Hint: Consider the weather in Phoenix and Seattle. (This exercise is an example of what is called *Simpson's paradox.*)

3.57 Internet Exercise

What is the age, gender, and ethnic composition of U.S. college students? As background for its 1995 study of college students and their risk behaviors, the Centers for Disease Control and Prevention collects selected demographic data—age, gender, and ethnicity—about college students. A report on the 1995 National Health Risk Behavior Survey can be found at the CDC website [http://www.cdc.gov: Data & Statistics; Youth Risk Behavior Surveillance System: Data Products; 1995 National College Health Risk Behavior Survey or, directly, go to http://www.cdc.gov/nccdphp/dash/MMWRFile/ss4606.htm.] This report includes a large number of tables, the first of which summarizes the demographic information for the sample of $n = 4609$ college students. An excerpt of Table 1 is given on the right.

Using conditional probabilities, discuss (a) the dependence between age and gender and (b) the dependence between age and ethnicity for U.S. college students. CDCData

TABLE 1. Demographic Characteristics of Undergraduate College Students Aged >=18 Years, by Age Group – United States, National College Health Risk Behavior Survey, 1995

		Age Group (%)	
Category	Total (%)	18-24 Years	>=25 Years
Total	--	63.6	36.4
Sex			
Female	55.5	52.0	61.8
Male	44.5	48.0	38.2
Race/ethnicity			
White*	72.8	70.9	76.1
Black*	10.3	10.5	9.6
Hispanic	7.1	6.9	7.4
Other	9.9	11.7	6.9

CHAPTER 4

Discrete Random Variables

Chapter Outline

We often use what we call **random variables** to describe the important aspects of the outcomes of experiments. In this chapter we introduce two important types of random variables—**discrete random variables** and **continuous random variables**—and learn how to find probabilities concerning discrete random variables. As one application, we will see in the AccuRatings case how Strategic Radio Research determines the popularity index of each song it rates.

4.1 Two Types of Random Variables

We begin with the definition of a random variable:

A **random variable** is a variable that assumes numerical values that are determined by the outcome of an experiment, where one and only one numerical value is assigned to each experimental outcome.

Before an experiment is carried out, its outcome is uncertain. It follows that, since a random variable assigns a number to each experimental outcome, a random variable can be thought of as *representing an uncertain numerical outcome.*

To illustrate the idea of a random variable, suppose that Sound City sells and installs car stereo systems. One of Sound City's most popular stereo systems is the TrueSound-XL, a top-of-the-line stereo cassette car radio. Consider (the experiment of) selling the TrueSound-XL radio at the Sound City store during a particular week. If we let x denote the number of radios sold during the week, then x is a random variable. That is, looked at before the week, the number of radios x that will be sold is uncertain, and, therefore, x is a random variable.

Notice that x, the number of TrueSound-XL radios sold in a week, might be 0 or 1 or 2 or 3, and so forth. In general, when the possible values of a random variable can be counted or listed, we say that the random variable is a **discrete random variable.** That is, either a discrete random variable may assume a finite number of possible values or the possible values may take the form of a *countable* sequence or list such as 0, 1, 2, 3, 4, . . . (a *countably infinite* list).

CHAPTER 3

Some other examples of discrete random variables are

1 The number, x, of the next three customers entering a store who will make a purchase. Here x could be 0, 1, 2, or 3.

2 The number, x, of four patients taking a new antibiotic who experience gastrointestinal distress as a side effect. Here x could be 0, 1, 2, 3, or 4.

3 The number, x, of television sets in a sample of 8 five-year-old television sets that have not needed a single repair. Here x could be any of the values 0, 1, 2, 3, 4, 5, 6, 7, or 8.

4 The rating, x, on a 1 through 5 scale given to a song by a listener in an AccuRatings music survey. Here x could be 1, 2, 3, 4, or 5.

5 The number, x, of major fires in a large city during the last two months. Here x could be 0, 1, 2, 3, and so forth (there is no definite maximum number of fires).

6 The number, x, of dirt specks in a one-square-yard sheet of plastic wrap. Here x could be 0, 1, 2, 3, and so forth (there is no definite maximum number of dirt specks).

The values of the random variables described in examples 1, 2, 3, and 4 are countable and finite. In contrast, the values of the random variables described in 5 and 6 are countable and infinite (or countably infinite lists). For example, in theory there is no limit to the number of major fires that could occur in a city in two months.

Not all random variables have values that are countable. When a random variable may assume any numerical value in one or more intervals on the real number line, then we say that the random variable is a **continuous random variable.**

Example 4.1 The Car Mileage Case

Consider the car mileage situation that we have discussed in Chapters 1 and 2. The EPA combined city and highway mileage, x, of a randomly selected midsize car is a continuous random variable. This is because, although we have measured mileages to the nearest one-tenth of a mile per gallon, technically speaking, the potential mileages that might be obtained correspond (starting at, perhaps, 26 mpg) to an interval of numbers on the real line. We cannot count or list the numbers in such an interval because they are infinitesimally close together. That is, given any two numbers in an interval on the real line, there is always another number between them. To understand this, try listing the mileages starting with 26 mpg. Would the next mileage be 26.1 mpg? No, because we could obtain a mileage of 26.05 mpg. Would 26.05 mpg be the next mileage? No, because we could obtain a mileage of 26.025 mpg. We could continue this line of reasoning indefinitely. That is, whatever value we would try to list as the *next mileage,* there would always be another mileage between this *next mileage* and 26 mpg.

Some other examples of continuous random variables are

1 The temperature (in degrees Fahrenheit) of a cup of coffee served at a McDonald's restaurant.
2 The weight (in ounces) of strawberry preserves dispensed by an automatic filling machine into a 16-ounce jar.
3 The time (in minutes) that a customer in a store must wait to receive a credit card authorization.
4 The interest rate (in percent) charged for mortgage loans at a bank.

Exercises for Section 4.1

CONCEPTS

4.1 Explain the concept of a random variable.

4.2 Explain how the values of a discrete random variable differ from the values of a continuous random variable.

4.3 Classify each of the following random variables as discrete or continuous:
a x = the number of girls born to a couple who will have three children.
b x = the number of defects found on an automobile at final inspection.
c x = the weight (in ounces) of the sandwich meat placed on a submarine sandwich.
d x = the number of incorrect lab procedures conducted at a hospital during a particular week.
e x = the number of customers served during a given day at a drive-through window.
f x = the time needed by a clerk to complete a task.
g x = the temperature of a pizza oven at a particular time.

4.2 Discrete Probability Distributions

The value assumed by a discrete random variable depends on the outcome of an experiment. Because the outcome of the experiment will be uncertain, the value assumed by the random variable will also be uncertain. However, it is often useful to know the probabilities that are associated with the different values that the random variable can take on. That is, we often wish to know the random variable's **probability distribution.**

The **probability distribution** of a discrete random variable is a table, graph, or formula that gives the probability associated with each possible value that the random variable can assume.

We denote the probability distribution of the discrete random variable x as $p(x)$. As will be demonstrated in the following example, we can sometimes use the sample space of an experiment and probability rules to find the probability distribution of a random variable.

Example 4.2

Consider the pop quiz consisting of three true–false questions. Remember that the sample space when a student takes such a quiz consists of the outcomes

CCC *CCI* *CIC* *ICC*
CII *ICI* *IIC* *III*

We now define the random variable x to be the number of questions that the student answers correctly. Here x can assume the values 0, 1, 2, or 3. That is, the student could answer anywhere between 0 and 3 questions correctly. In Examples 3.3 and 3.5 we assumed that the

TABLE 4.1 Finding the Probability Distribution of x = the Number of Questions Answered Correctly When the Student Studies and Has a 90 Percent Chance of Answering Each Question Correctly

Value of x = the Number of Correct Answers	Sample Space Outcomes Corresponding to Value of x	Probability of Sample Space Outcome	$p(x)$ = Probability of the Value of x
$x = 0$ (no correct answers)	*III*	$(.1)(.1)(.1) = .001$	$p(0) = .001$
$x = 1$ (one correct answer)	*CII*	$(.9)(.1)(.1) = .009$	$p(1) = .009 + .009 + .009 = .027$
	ICI	$(.1)(.9)(.1) = .009$	
	IIC	$(.1)(.1)(.9) = .009$	
$x = 2$ (two correct answers)	*CCI*	$(.9)(.9)(.1) = .081$	$p(2) = .081 + .081 + .081 = .243$
	CIC	$(.9)(.1)(.9) = .081$	
	ICC	$(.1)(.9)(.9) = .081$	
$x = 3$ (three correct answers)	*CCC*	$(.9)(.9)(.9) = .729$	$p(3) = .729$

student is totally unprepared for the quiz and thus has only a .5 probability of answering each question correctly. We now assume that the student studies and has a .9 probability of answering each question correctly. Table 4.1 summarizes finding the probabilities associated with each of the values of x (0, 1, 2, and 3). As an example of the calculations, consider finding the probability that x equals 2. Two questions will be answered correctly if and only if we obtain one of the sample space outcomes

$$CCI \qquad CIC \qquad ICC$$

Assuming that the three questions will be answered independently, these sample space outcomes have probabilities

$$P(CCI) = (.9)(.9)(.1) = .081$$
$$P(CIC) = (.9)(.1)(.9) = .081$$
$$P(ICC) = (.1)(.9)(.9) = .081$$

Therefore,

$$\begin{aligned} P(x = 2) &= P(CCI) + P(CIC) + P(ICC) \\ &= .081 + .081 + .081 \\ &= .243 \end{aligned}$$

Similarly, we can obtain probabilities associated with $x = 0$, $x = 1$, and $x = 3$. The probability distribution of x is summarized as follows:

x, Number of Questions Answered Correctly	$p(x)$, Probability of x
0	$p(0) = P(x = 0) = .001$
1	$p(1) = P(x = 1) = .027$
2	$p(2) = P(x = 2) = .243$
3	$p(3) = P(x = 3) = .729$

Notice that the probabilities in this probability distribution sum to $.001 + .027 + .243 + .729 = 1$.

To show the advantage of studying, note that the above probability distribution says that if the student has a .9 probability of answering each question correctly, then the probability that the student will answer all three questions correctly is .729. Furthermore, the probability that the student will answer *at least* two out of three questions correctly is (since the events $x = 2$ and $x = 3$ are mutually exclusive)

$$\begin{aligned} P(x \geq 2) &= P(x = 2 \text{ or } x = 3) \\ &= P(x = 2) + P(x = 3) \\ &= .243 + .729 \\ &= .972 \end{aligned}$$

By contrast, we saw in Example 3.5 that if the student is totally unprepared and has only a .5 probability of answering each question correctly, then the probabilities that the student will answer zero, one, two, and three questions correctly are, respectively, 1/8, 3/8, 3/8, and 1/8. Therefore, the probability that the unprepared student will answer all three questions correctly is only 1/8, and the probability that this student will answer at least two out of three questions correctly is only (3/8 + 1/8) = .5.

In general, a discrete probability distribution $p(x)$ must satisfy two conditions:

Properties of a Discrete Probability Distribution $p(x)$

A **discrete probability distribution $p(x)$** must be such that

1 $p(x) \geq 0$ for each value of x

2 $\sum_{\text{All } x} p(x) = 1$

The first of these conditions says that each probability in a probability distribution must be zero or positive. The second condition says that the probabilities in a probability distribution must sum to 1. Looking at the probability distribution illustrated in Example 4.2, we can see that these properties are satisfied.

Often it is not possible to examine the entire sample space of an experiment. In such a case we sometimes collect data that will allow us to estimate the probabilities in a probability distribution.

Example 4.3

Recall that Sound City sells the TrueSound-XL car radio, and define the random variable x to be the number of such radios sold in a particular week. In order to know the true probabilities of the various values of x, we would have to observe sales during all of the (potentially infinite number of) weeks in which the TrueSound-XL radio could be sold. That is, if we consider an experiment in which we randomly select a week and observe sales of the TrueSound-XL, the sample space would consist of a potentially infinite number of equally likely weeks. Obviously, it is not possible to examine this entire sample space.

Suppose, however, that Sound City has kept historical records of TrueSound-XL sales during the last 100 weeks. These records tell us that

1 No radios have been sold in 3 (that is, 3/100 = .03) of the weeks.
2 One radio has been sold in 20 (that is, .20) of the weeks.
3 Two radios have been sold in 50 (that is, .50) of the weeks.
4 Three radios have been sold in 20 (that is, .20) of the weeks.
5 Four radios have been sold in 5 (that is, .05) of the weeks.
6 Five radios have been sold in 2 (that is, .02) of the weeks.
7 No more than five radios were sold in any of the past 100 weeks.

It follows that we might *estimate* that the probability distribution of x, the number of TrueSound-XL radios sold during a particular week at Sound City, is as shown in Table 4.2. A graph of this distribution is shown in Figure 4.1.

TABLE 4.2 An Estimate (Based on 100 Weeks of Historical Data) of the Probability Distribution of x, the Number of TrueSound-XL Radios Sold at Sound City in a Week

x, Number of Radios Sold	$p(x)$, the Probability of x
0	$p(0) = P(x = 0) = 3/100 = .03$
1	$p(1) = P(x = 1) = 20/100 = .20$
2	$p(2) = P(x = 2) = 50/100 = .50$
3	$p(3) = P(x = 3) = 20/100 = .20$
4	$p(4) = P(x = 4) = 5/100 = .05$
5	$p(5) = P(x = 5) = 2/100 = .02$

FIGURE 4.1 A Graph of the Probability Distribution of x, the Number of TrueSound-XL Radios Sold at Sound City in a Week

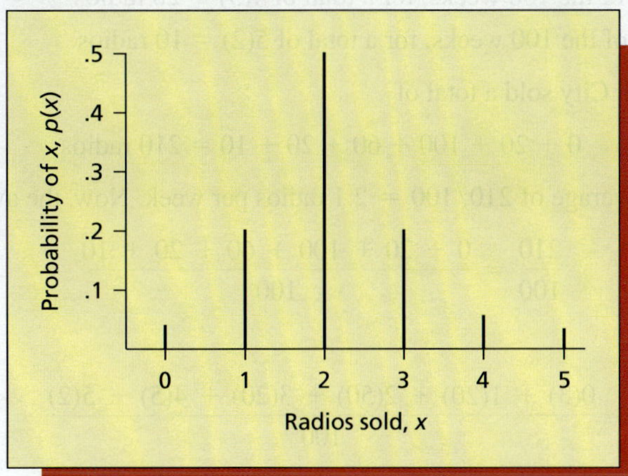

Finally, it is reasonable to use the historical sales data from the past 100 weeks to estimate the true probabilities associated with the various numbers of radios sold if the sales process remains stable over time and is not seasonal (that is, if radio sales are not higher at one time of the year than at others).

Suppose that the experiment described by a random variable x is repeated an indefinitely large number of times. If the values of the random variable x observed on the repetitions are recorded, we would obtain the population of all possible observed values of the random variable x. This population has a mean, which we denote as μ_x and which we sometimes call the **expected value of x.** In order to calculate μ_x, we multiply each value of x by its probability $p(x)$ and then sum the resulting products over all possible values of x.

The Mean or Expected Value of a Discrete Random Variable

The **mean,** or **expected value,** of a discrete random variable x is

$$\mu_x = \sum_{\text{All } x} xp(x)$$

In the next example we illustrate how to calculate μ_x, and we reason that the calculation really does give the mean of all possible observed values of the random variable x.

Example 4.4

Remember that Table 4.2 gives the probability distribution of x, the number of TrueSound-XL radios sold in a week at Sound City. Using this distribution, it follows that

$$\begin{aligned} \mu_x &= \sum_{\text{All } x} xp(x) \\ &= 0p(0) + 1p(1) + 2p(2) + 3p(3) + 4p(4) + 5p(5) \\ &= 0(.03) + 1(.20) + 2(.50) + 3(.20) + 4(.05) + 5(.02) \\ &= 2.1 \end{aligned}$$

To see that such a calculation gives the mean of all possible observed values of x, recall from Example 4.3 that the probability distribution in Table 4.2 was estimated from historical records of TrueSound-XL sales during the last 100 weeks. Also recall that these historical records tell us that during the last 100 weeks Sound City sold

1 Zero radios in 3 of the 100 weeks, for a total of $0(3) = 0$ radios
2 One radio in 20 of the 100 weeks, for a total of $1(20) = 20$ radios

3 Two radios in 50 of the 100 weeks, for a total of 2(50) = 100 radios
4 Three radios in 20 of the 100 weeks, for a total of 3(20) = 60 radios
5 Four radios in 5 of the 100 weeks, for a total of 4(5) = 20 radios
6 Five radios in 2 of the 100 weeks, for a total of 5(2) = 10 radios

In other words, Sound City sold a total of

$$0 + 20 + 100 + 60 + 20 + 10 = 210 \text{ radios}$$

in 100 weeks, or an average of 210/100 = 2.1 radios per week. Now, the average

$$\frac{210}{100} = \frac{0 + 20 + 100 + 60 + 20 + 10}{100}$$

can be written as

$$\frac{0(3) + 1(20) + 2(50) + 3(20) + 4(5) + 5(2)}{100}$$

which can be rewritten as

$$0\left(\frac{3}{100}\right) + 1\left(\frac{20}{100}\right) + 2\left(\frac{50}{100}\right) + 3\left(\frac{20}{100}\right) + 4\left(\frac{5}{100}\right) + 5\left(\frac{2}{100}\right)$$
$$= 0(.03) + 1(.20) + 2(.50) + 3(.20) + 4(.05) + 5(.02)$$

which equals $\mu_x = 2.1$. That is, if observed sales values occur with relative frequencies equal to those specified by the probability distribution in Table 4.2, then the average number of radios sold per week is equal to the expected value of x.

Of course, if we observe radio sales for another 100 weeks, the relative frequencies of the observed sales values would not (unless we are very lucky) be exactly as specified by the estimated probabilities in Table 4.2. Rather, the observed relative frequencies would differ somewhat from the estimated probabilities in Table 4.2, and the average number of radios sold per week would not exactly equal $\mu_x = 2.1$ (although the average would likely be close). However, the point is this: If the probability distribution in Table 4.2 were the true probability distribution of weekly radio sales, and if we were to observe radio sales for an indefinitely large number of weeks, then we would observe sales values with relative frequencies that are exactly equal to those specified by the probabilities in Table 4.2. In this case, when we calculate the expected value of x to be $\mu_x = 2.1$, we are saying that *in the long run* (that is, over an indefinitely large number of weeks) Sound City would average selling 2.1 TrueSound-XL radios per week.

As another example, again consider Example 4.2, and let the random variable x denote the number of the three true–false questions that the student who studies answers correctly. Using the probability distribution shown in Table 4.1, the expected value of x is

$$\mu_x = 0(.001) + 1(.027) + 2(.243) + 3(.729)$$
$$= 2.7$$

This expected value says that if a student takes a large number of three-question true–false quizzes and has a .9 probability of answering any single question correctly, then the student will average approximately 2.7 correct answers per quiz.

Example 4.5 The AccuRatings Case

In this example we will compute the *popularity* index for the song "Gangsta's Paradise" by Coolio. Recall from Example 3.16 (pages 148–151) that Strategic Radio Research had surveyed listeners rate this song as a 5, 4, 3, 2, 1, or *UNFAM*. Although not discussed in Example 3.16, Strategic Radio Research also estimated the proportions of listeners *familiar with the song* who would give the song ratings of 5, 4, 3, 2, and 1 to be, respectively, .43, .21, .22, .07, and .07. Now, it is reasonable to assign the numerical values 1 through 5 to the ratings 1 through 5 (this sort of thing is done when colleges assign the numerical values 4 through 0 to the grades A through F).

Table 4.3 An Estimate of the Probability Distribution of x, the Rating of the Song "Gangsta's Paradise" by a Randomly Selected Listener Who Is Familiar with This Song

x, Rating	p(x), Probability of x
1	$p(1) = .07$
2	$p(2) = .07$
3	$p(3) = .22$
4	$p(4) = .21$
5	$p(5) = .43$

Therefore, we can regard the song's rating, x, by a randomly selected listener who is familiar with the song to be a discrete random variable having the estimated probability distribution shown in Table 4.3. It follows that the expected value of this estimated probability distribution is

$$\mu_x = 1(.07) + 2(.07) + 3(.22) + 4(.21) + 5(.43)$$
$$= 3.86$$

This estimated expected value is reported as the *popularity* index in Figure 3.8 (page 150) (the difference between the 3.86 calculated here and the 3.87 in Figure 3.8 is due to rounding). It says that Strategic Radio Research estimates that the mean rating of the song that would be given by all listeners who are familiar with the song is 3.86. As indicated in Figure 3.8, Strategic Radio Research reports that the song has a "very high popularity" index, which is the highest (#1) of all the songs rated for the week.

Example 4.6

An insurance company sells a \$20,000 whole life insurance policy for an annual premium of \$300. Actuarial tables show that a person who would be sold such a policy with this premium has a .001 probability of death during a year. Let x be a random variable representing the insurance company's profit made on one of these policies during a year. The probability distribution of x is

x, Profit	p(x), Probability of x
\$300 (if the policyholder lives)	.999
\$300 − \$20,000 = −\$19,700 (a \$19,700 loss if the policyholder dies)	.001

The expected value of x (expected profit per year) is

$$\mu_x = \$300(.999) + (-\$19{,}700)(.001)$$
$$= \$280$$

This says that if the insurance company sells a very large number of these policies, it will average a profit of \$280 per policy per year. Since insurance companies actually do sell large numbers of policies, it is reasonable for these companies to make profitability decisions based on expected values.

Next, suppose that we wish to find the premium that the insurance company must charge for a \$20,000 policy if the company wishes the average profit per policy per year to be greater than \$0. If we let *prem* denote the premium the company will charge, then the probability distribution of the company's yearly profit x is

x, Profit	p(x), Probability of x
prem (if policyholder lives)	.999
prem − \$20,000 (if policyholder dies)	.001

The expected value of x (expected profit per year) is

$$\mu_x = prem(.999) + (prem - 20{,}000)(.001)$$
$$= prem - 20$$

In order for this expected profit to be greater than zero, the premium must be greater than \$20. If, as previously stated, the company charges \$300 for such a policy, the \$280 charged in excess of the needed \$20 compensates the company for commissions paid to salespeople, administrative costs, dividends paid to investors, and other expenses.

In general, it is reasonable to base decisions on an expected value if we perform the experiment related to the decision (for example, if we sell the life insurance policy) many times. If we do not (for instance, if we perform the experiment only once), then it may not be a good idea to base decisions on the expected value. For example, it might not be wise for you—as an individual—to sell one person a \$20,000 life insurance policy for a premium of \$300. To see this, again consider the probability distribution of yearly profit:

x, Profit	**p(x), Probability of x**
\$300 (if policyholder lives)	.999
\$300 − \$20,000 = −\$19,700 (if policyholder dies)	.001

and recall that the expected profit per year is \$280. However, since you are selling only one policy, you will not receive the \$280. You will either gain \$300 (with probability .999) or you will lose \$19,700 (with probability .001). Although the decision is personal, and although the chance of losing \$19,700 is very small, many people would not risk such a loss when the potential gain is only \$300.

Just as the population of all possible observed values of a discrete random variable x has a mean μ_x, this population also has a variance σ_x^2 and a standard deviation σ_x. Recall that the variance of a population is the average of the squared deviations of the different population values from the population mean. To find σ_x^2, we calculate $(x - \mu_x)^2$ for each value of x, multiply $(x - \mu_x)^2$ by the probability $p(x)$, and sum the resulting products over all possible values of x.

The Variance and Standard Deviation of a Discrete Random Variable

The **variance** of a discrete random variable x is

$$\sigma_x^2 = \sum_{\text{All } x} (x - \mu_x)^2 p(x)$$

The **standard deviation** of x is the positive square root of the variance of x. That is,

$$\sigma_x = \sqrt{\sigma_x^2}$$

Example 4.7

Table 4.2 gives the probability distribution of x, the number of TrueSound-XL radios sold in a week at Sound City. Remembering that we have calculated μ_x (in Example 4.4) to be 2.1, it follows that

$$\begin{aligned}\sigma_x^2 &= \sum_{\text{All } x} (x - \mu_x)^2 p(x)\\ &= (0 - 2.1)^2 p(0) + (1 - 2.1)^2 p(1) + (2 - 2.1)^2 p(2) + (3 - 2.1)^2 p(3)\\ &\quad + (4 - 2.1)^2 p(4) + (5 - 2.1)^2 p(5)\\ &= (4.41)(.03) + (1.21)(.20) + (.01)(.50) + (.81)(.20) + (3.61)(.05) + (8.41)(.02)\\ &= .89\end{aligned}$$

and that the standard deviation of x is $\sigma_x = \sqrt{.89} = .9434$

The variance σ_x^2 and the standard deviation σ_x measure the spread of the population of all possible observed values of the random variable. To see how to use σ_x, remember that Chebyshev's

Theorem (see Chapter 2, page 74) tells us that, for any value of k that is greater than 1, at least $100(1 - 1/k^2)\%$ of all possible observed values of the random variable x lie in the interval $[\mu_x \pm k\sigma_x]$. Stated in terms of a probability, we have

$$P(x \text{ falls in the interval } [\mu_x \pm k\sigma_x]) \geq 1 - 1/k^2$$

For example, consider the probability distribution (in Table 4.2) of x, the number of TrueSound-XL radios sold in a week at Sound City. If we set k equal to 2, and if we use $\mu_x = 2.1$ and $\sigma_x = .9434$ to calculate the interval

$$[\mu_x \pm 2\sigma_x] = [2.1 \pm 2(.9434)] = [.2132, \ 3.9868]$$

then Chebyshev's Theorem tells us that

$$P(x \text{ falls in the interval } [.2132, \ 3.9868]) \geq 1 - 1/2^2 = 3/4$$

This says that in at least 75 percent of all weeks, Sound City will sell between .2132 and 3.9868 TrueSound-XL radios. As illustrated in Figure 4.2, there are three values of x between .2132 and 3.9868—namely, $x = 1$, $x = 2$, and $x = 3$. Therefore, the exact probability that x will be in the interval $[\mu_x \pm 2\sigma_x]$ is

$$p(1) + p(2) + p(3) = .20 + .50 + .20 = .90$$

This illustrates that, although Chebyshev's Theorem guarantees us that at least $100(1 - 1/k^2)\%$ of all possible observed values of a random variable x fall in the interval $[\mu_x \pm k\sigma_x]$, often the percentage is considerably higher.

In some cases, the graph of the probability distribution of a discrete random variable has the symmetrical, bell-shaped appearance of a normal curve. For example, the graph in Figure 4.2 is roughly bell-shaped and symmetrical. In such a situation—and *under certain additional assumptions*—the probability distribution can sometimes be *approximated* by a normal curve. We will discuss the needed assumptions in Chapter 5. As an example of such assumptions, note that although the graph in Figure 4.2 is roughly bell-shaped and symmetrical, it can be shown that there are not enough values of x, and thus not enough probabilities $p(x)$, for us to approximate the probability distribution by using a normal curve. If, however, the probability distribution of a discrete random variable x can be approximated by a normal curve, then the **Empirical Rule** for normally distributed populations describes the population of all possible values of x. Specifically, we can say that approximately 68.26 percent, 95.44 percent, and 99.73 percent of all possible observed values of x fall in the intervals $[\mu_x \pm \sigma_x]$, $[\mu_x \pm 2\sigma_x]$, and $[\mu_x \pm 3\sigma_x]$.

FIGURE 4.2 The Interval $[\mu_x \pm 2\sigma_x]$ for the Probability Distribution Describing TrueSound-XL Radio Sales (see Table 4.2)

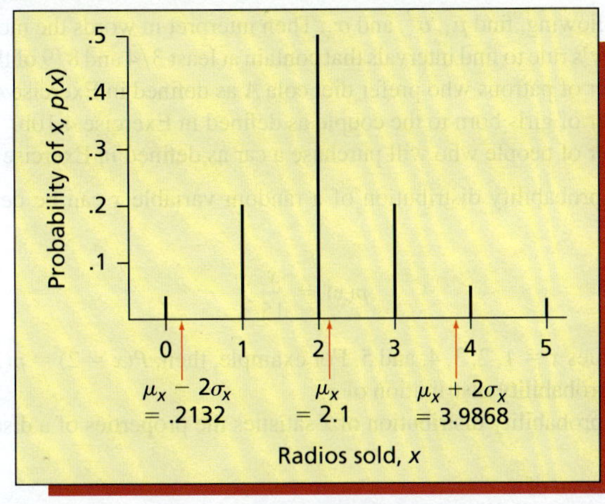

To summarize, the standard deviation σ_x of a discrete random variable measures the spread of the population of all possible observed values of x. When the probability distribution of x can be approximated by a normal curve, this spread can be characterized by the Empirical Rule. When this is not possible, we can use Chebyshev's Theorem to characterize the spread of x.

To conclude this section, note that in Appendix D (Part 2) on page 850 we discuss various theoretical properties of the means and variances of random variables. In this appendix we also discuss the idea of the **covariance** between two random variables.

Exercises for Section 4.2

CONCEPTS

4.4 What is a discrete probability distribution? Explain in your own words.

4.5 What conditions must be satisfied by the probabilities in a discrete probability distribution? Explain what these conditions mean.

4.6 Describe how to compute the mean (or expected value) of a discrete random variable, and interpret what this quantity tells us about the observed values of the random variable.

4.7 Describe how to compute the standard deviation of a discrete random variable, and interpret what this quantity tells us about the observed values of the random variable.

METHODS AND APPLICATIONS

4.8 Explain whether each of the following is a valid probability distribution. If the probability distribution is valid, show why. Otherwise, show which condition(s) of a probability distribution are not satisfied.

a

x	p(x)
−1	.2
0	.6
1	.2

b

x	p(x)
1/2	−1
3/4	0
1	2

c

x	p(x)
2	.25
4	.35
6	.3

d

x	p(x)
.1	2/7
.7	4/7
.9	1/7

4.9 Consider each of the following probability distributions.

a

x	p(x)
0	.2
1	.8

b

x	p(x)
0	.25
1	.45
2	.2
3	.1

c

x	p(x)
−2	.1
0	.3
2	.4
5	.2

Calculate μ_x and σ_x for each distribution. Then explain, using the probabilities, why μ_x is the mean of all possible observed values of x.

4.10 For each of the following, write out and graph the probability distribution of x. That is, list all the possible values of x and also list the corresponding probabilities. Then graph the distribution.

a Refer to Exercise 3.3 (page 135), and let x equal the number of patrons who prefer diet cola A.

b Refer to Exercise 3.4 (page 135), and let x equal the number of girls born to the couple.

c Refer to Exercise 3.5 (page 135), and let x equal the number of people who will purchase a car.

4.11 For each of the following, find μ_x, σ_x^2, and σ_x. Then interpret in words the meaning of μ_x, and employ Chebyshev's rule to find intervals that contain at least 3/4 and 8/9 of the observed values of x.

a x = the number of patrons who prefer diet cola A as defined in Exercise 4.10a.

b x = the number of girls born to the couple as defined in Exercise 4.10b.

c x = the number of people who will purchase a car as defined in Exercise 4.10c.

4.12 Suppose that the probability distribution of a random variable x can be described by the formula

$$p(x) = \frac{x}{15}$$

for each of the values $x = 1, 2, 3, 4,$ and 5. For example, then, $P(x = 2) = p(2) = 2/15$.

a Write out the probability distribution of x.

b Show that the probability distribution of x satisfies the properties of a discrete probability distribution.

c Calculate the mean of x.

d Calculate the variance, σ_x^2, and the standard deviation, σ_x.

4.13 The following table summarizes investment outcomes and corresponding probabilities for a particular oil well:

x = the outcome in \$	$p(x)$
−\$40,000 (no oil)	.25
10,000 (some oil)	.7
70,000 (much oil)	.05

a Graph $p(x)$; that is, graph the probability distribution of x.

b Find the expected monetary outcome. Mark this value on your graph of part *a*. Then interpret this value.

4.14 In the book *Foundations of Financial Management* (7th ed.), Stanley B. Block and Geoffrey A. Hirt discuss risk measurement for investments. Block and Hirt present an investment with the possible outcomes and associated probabilities given in Table 4.4. The authors go on to say that the probabilities

> may be based on past experience, industry ratios and trends, interviews with company executives, and sophisticated simulation techniques. The probability values may be easy to determine for the introduction of a mechanical stamping process in which the manufacturer has 10 years of past data, but difficult to assess for a new product in a foreign market.

a Use the probability distribution in Table 4.4 to calculate the expected value (mean) and the standard deviation of the investment outcomes. Interpret the expected value.

b Block and Hirt interpret the standard deviation of the investment outcomes as follows: "Generally, the larger the standard deviation (or spread of outcomes), the greater is the risk." Explain why this makes sense. Use Chebyshev's Theorem to illustrate your point.

c Block and Hirt compare three investments having the following means and standard deviations of the investment outcomes:

Investment 1	Investment 2	Investment 3
μ = \$600	μ = \$600	μ = \$600
σ = \$20	σ = \$190	σ = \$300

Which of these investments involves the most risk? The least risk? Explain why by using Chebyshev's Theorem to compute an interval for each investment that will contain at least 8/9 of the investment outcomes.

d Block and Hirt continue by comparing two more investments:

Investment *A*	Investment *B*
μ = \$6,000	μ = \$600
σ = \$600	σ = \$190

The authors explain that Investment *A*

> appears to have a high standard deviation, but not when related to the expected value of the distribution. A standard deviation of \$600 on an investment with an expected value of \$6,000 may indicate less risk than a standard deviation of \$190 on an investment with an expected value of only \$600.
>
> We can eliminate the size difficulty by developing a third measure, the **coefficient of variation** (V). This term calls for nothing more difficult than dividing the standard deviation of an investment by the expected value. Generally, the larger the coefficient of variation, the greater is the risk.
>
> $$\text{Coefficient of variation } (V) = \frac{\sigma}{\mu}$$

TABLE 4.4 Probability Distribution of Outcomes for an Investment

Outcome	Probability of Outcome	Assumptions
\$300	.2	Pessimistic
600	.6	Moderately successful
900	.2	Optimistic

Source: S. B. Block and G. A. Hirt, *Foundations of Financial Management*, 7th ed., p. 378. Copyright © 1994. Reprinted by permission of McGraw-Hill Companies, Inc.

Calculate the coefficient of variation for investments *A* and *B*. Which investment carries the greater risk?

e Calculate the coefficient of variation for investments 1, 2, and 3 in part *c*. Based on the coefficient of variation, which investment involves the most risk? The least risk? Do we obtain the same results as we did by comparing standard deviations (in part *c*)? Why?

4.15 An insurance company will insure a $50,000 diamond for its full value against theft at a premium of $400 per year. Suppose that the probability that the diamond will be stolen is .005, and let x denote the insurance company's profit.

a Set up the probability distribution of the random variable x.

b Calculate the insurance company's expected profit.

c Find the premium that the insurance company should charge if it wants its expected profit to be $1,000.

4.16 In the book *Foundations of Financial Management* (7th ed.), Stanley B. Block and Geoffrey A. Hirt discuss a semiconductor firm that is considering two choices: (1) expanding the production of semiconductors for sale to end users or (2) entering the highly competitive home computer market. The cost of both projects is $60 million, but the net present value of the cash flows from sales and the risks are different.

Figure 4.3 gives a tree diagram of the project choices. The tree diagram gives a probability distribution of expected sales for each project. It also gives the present value of cash flows from sales and the net present value (NPV = present value of cash flow from sales minus initial cost) corresponding to each sales alternative. Note that figures in parentheses denote losses.

a For each project choice, calculate the expected net present value.

b For each project choice, calculate the variance and standard deviation of the net present value.

c Calculate the coefficient of variation for each project choice. See Exercise 4.14*d* for a discussion of the coefficient of variation.

d Which project has the higher expected net present value?

e Which project carries the least risk? Explain.

f In your opinion, which project should be undertaken? Justify your answer.

4.17 Five thousand raffle tickets are to be sold at $10 each to benefit a local community group. The prizes, the number of each prize to be given away, and the dollar value of winnings for each prize are as follows:

Prize	Number to Be Given Away	Dollar Value
Automobile	1	$13,000
Entertainment center	2	3,000 each
VCR	5	400 each
Gift certificate	50	20 each

FIGURE 4.3 A Tree Diagram of Two Project Choices

	(1) Sales	(2) Probability	(3) Present Value of Cash Flow from Sales ($ millions)	(4) Initial Cost ($ millions)	(5) Net Present Value, NPV = (3) − (4) ($ millions)
A: Expand semiconductor capacity	High	.50	$100	$60	$40
	Moderate	.25	75	60	15
	Low	.25	40	60	(20)
B: Enter home computer market	High	.20	$200	$60	$140
	Moderate	.50	75	60	15
	Low	.30	25	60	(35)

Start

Source: S. B. Block and G. A. Hirt, *Foundations of Financial Management*, 7th ed., p. 387. Copyright © 1994. Reprinted by permission of McGraw-Hill Companies, Inc.

TABLE 4.5 Return Distributions for Companies *A*, *B*, and *C* and for Two Possible Acquisitions

Economic Condition	Probability	Company *A* Returns	Company *B* Returns	Company *C* Returns	Company *A* + *B* Returns	Company *A* + *C* Returns
1	.2	17%	19%	13%	18%	15%
2	.2	15	17	11	16	13
3	.2	13	15	15	14	14
4	.2	11	13	17	12	14
5	.2	9	11	19	10	14

If you buy one ticket, calculate your expected winnings. (Form the probability distribution of x = your dollar winnings, and remember to subtract the cost of your ticket.)

4.18 Company *A* is considering the acquisition of two separate but large companies, Company *B* and Company *C*, having sales and assets equal to its own. Table 4.5 gives the probabilities of returns for each of the three companies under various economic conditions. The table also gives the probabilities of returns for each possible combination: Company *A* plus Company *B*, and Company *A* plus Company *C*.

a For each of Companies *A*, *B*, and *C* find the mean return and the standard deviation of returns.

b Find the mean return and the standard deviation of returns for the combination of Company *A* plus Company *B*.

c Find the mean return and the standard deviation of returns for the combination of Company *A* plus Company *C*.

d Compare the mean returns for each of the two possible combinations—Company *A* plus Company *B* and Company *A* plus Company *C*. Is either mean higher? How do they compare to Company *A*'s mean return?

e Compare the standard deviations of the returns for each of the two possible combinations—Company *A* plus Company *B* and Company *A* plus Company *C*. Which standard deviation is smaller? Which possible combination involves less risk? How does the risk carried by this combination compare to the risk carried by Company *A* alone?

f Which acquisition would you recommend—Company *A* plus Company *B* or Company *A* plus Company *C*?

4.19 THE ACCURATINGS CASE

Again consider Exercise 3.31 (page 153) and the title-by-title analysis of the song "We've Got It Goin' On" by the Backstreet Boys. Although not discussed in Exercise 3.31, Strategic Radio Research estimated the proportions of listeners *familiar with the song* who would give the song ratings of 5, 4, 3, 2, and 1 to be, respectively, .1978, .2967, .3077, .0879, and .1099. Assign the numerical values 1 through 5 to the ratings 1 through 5.

a Find an estimate of the probability distribution of this song's rating, x, by a randomly selected listener who is familiar with the song.

b Find the *popularity* index for the song "We've Got It Goin' On" that would be reported by Strategic Radio Research. That is, find an estimate of the mean rating of this song that would be given by all listeners who are familiar with this song.

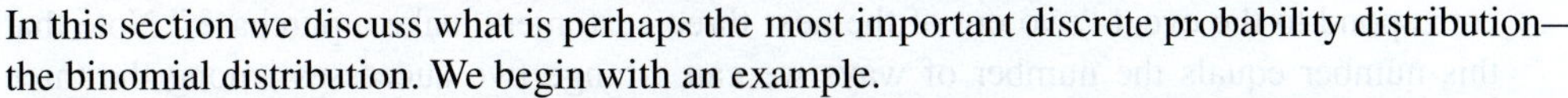

4.3 The Binomial Distribution

In this section we discuss what is perhaps the most important discrete probability distribution—the binomial distribution. We begin with an example.

Example 4.8

Suppose that historical sales records indicate that 40 percent of all customers who enter a discount department store make a purchase. What is the probability that two of the next three customers will make a purchase?

In order to find this probability, we first note that the experiment of observing three customers making a purchase decision has several distinguishing characteristics:

1 The experiment consists of three identical *trials;* each trial consists of a customer making a purchase decision.

2 Two outcomes are possible on each trial: the customer makes a purchase (which we call a *success* and denote as S), or the customer does not make a purchase (which we call a *failure* and denote as F).

3 Since 40 percent of all customers make a purchase, it is reasonable to assume that $P(S)$, the probability that a customer makes a purchase, is .4 and is constant for all customers. This implies that $P(F)$, the probability that a customer does not make a purchase, is .6 and is constant for all customers.

4 We assume that customers make independent purchase decisions. That is, we assume that the outcomes of the three trials are independent of each other.

It follows that the sample space of the experiment consists of the following eight sample space outcomes:

$$\begin{array}{cc} SSS & FFS \\ SSF & FSF \\ SFS & SFF \\ FSS & FFF \end{array}$$

Here the sample space outcome SSS represents all three customers making purchases. On the other hand, the sample space outcome SFS represents the first customer making a purchase, the second customer not making a purchase, and the third customer making a purchase.

Two out of three customers make a purchase if one of the sample space outcomes SSF, SFS, or FSS occurs. Furthermore, since the trials (purchase decisions) are independent, we can simply multiply the probabilities associated with the different trial outcomes (each of which is S or F) to find the probability of a sequence of outcomes:

$$P(SSF) = P(S)P(S)P(F) = (.4)(.4)(.6) = (.4)^2(.6)$$
$$P(SFS) = P(S)P(F)P(S) = (.4)(.6)(.4) = (.4)^2(.6)$$
$$P(FSS) = P(F)P(S)P(S) = (.6)(.4)(.4) = (.4)^2(.6)$$

It follows that the probability that two out of the next three customers make a purchase is

$$\begin{aligned} &P(SSF) + P(SFS) + P(FSS) \\ &= (.4)^2(.6) + (.4)^2(.6) + (.4)^2(.6) \\ &= 3(.4)^2(.6) = .288 \end{aligned}$$

We can now generalize the previous result and find the probability that x of the next n customers will make a purchase. Here we will assume that p is the probability that a customer makes a purchase, $q = 1 - p$ is the probability that a customer does not make a purchase, and purchase decisions (trials) are independent. To generalize the probability that two out of the next three customers make a purchase, which equals

$$3(.4)^2(.6)$$

we note that

1 The 3 in this expression is the number of sample space outcomes (SSF, SFS, and FSS) that correspond to the event "two out of the next three customers make a purchase." Note that this number equals the number of ways we can arrange two successes among the three trials.

2 The .4 is p, the probability that a customer makes a purchase.

3 The .6 is $q = 1 - p$, the probability that a customer does not make a purchase.

Therefore, the probability that two of the next three customers make a purchase is

$$\begin{pmatrix} \text{The number of ways} \\ \text{to arrange 2 successes} \\ \text{among 3 trials} \end{pmatrix} p^2 q^1$$

Now, notice that, although each of the sample space outcomes *SSF*, *SFS*, and *FSS* represents a different arrangement of the two successes among the three trials, each of these sample space outcomes consists of two successes and one failure. For this reason, the probability of each of these sample space outcomes equals $(.4)^2(.6)^1 = p^2q^1$. It follows that p is raised to a power that equals the number of successes (2) in the three trials, and q is raised to a power that equals the number of failures (1) in the three trials.

In general, each sample space outcome describing the occurrence of x successes (purchases) in n trials represents a different arrangement of x successes in n trials. However, each outcome consists of x successes and $n - x$ failures. Therefore, the probability of each sample space outcome is $p^x q^{n-x}$. It follows by analogy that the probability that x of the next n trials are successes (purchases) is

$$\begin{pmatrix}\text{The number of ways} \\ \text{to arrange } x \text{ successes} \\ \text{among } n \text{ trials}\end{pmatrix} p^x q^{n-x}$$

We can use the expression we have just arrived at to compute the probability of x successes in the next n trials if we can find a way to calculate the number of ways to arrange x successes among n trials. It can be shown that:

The number of ways to arrange x *successes among* n *trials* equals

$$\frac{n!}{x!\,(n-x)!}$$

where $n!$ is pronounced "n factorial" and is calculated as $n! = n(n-1)(n-2) \cdots (1)$ and where (by definition) $0! = 1$.

For instance, using this formula, we can see that the number of ways to arrange $x = 2$ successes among $n = 3$ trials equals

$$\frac{n!}{x!\,(n-x)!} = \frac{3!}{2!\,(3-2)!} = \frac{3!}{2!\,1!} = \frac{3 \cdot 2 \cdot 1}{2 \cdot 1 \cdot 1} = 3$$

Of course, we have previously seen that the three ways to arrange $x = 2$ successes among $n = 3$ trials are *SSF*, *SFS*, and *FSS*.

Using the preceding formula, we obtain the following general result:

The Binomial Distribution

A **binomial experiment** has the following characteristics:

1. The experiment consists of *n identical trials.*
2. Each trial results in a **success** or a **failure.**
3. The probability of a success on any trial is p and remains constant from trial to trial. This implies that the probability of failure, q, on any trial is $1 - p$ and remains constant from trial to trial.
4. The trials are **independent** (that is, the results of the trials have nothing to do with each other).

Furthermore, if we define the random variable

$x =$ the total number of successes in n trials of a binomial experiment

then we call x a **binomial random variable,** and the probability of obtaining x successes in n trials is

$$p(x) = \frac{n!}{x!\,(n-x)!} p^x q^{n-x}$$

Noting that we sometimes refer to the formula for $p(x)$ as the **binomial formula,** we illustrate the use of this formula in the following example.

Example 4.9

Consider the discount department store situation discussed in Example 4.8. In order to find the probability that three of the next five customers make purchases, we calculate

$$\begin{aligned} p(3) &= \frac{5!}{3!\,(5-3)!}(.4)^3(.6)^{5-3} = \frac{5!}{3!\,2!}(.4)^3(.6)^2 \\ &= \frac{5\cdot4\cdot3\cdot2\cdot1}{(3\cdot2\cdot1)(2\cdot1)}(.4)^3(.6)^2 \\ &= 10(.064)(.36) \\ &= .2304 \end{aligned}$$

Here we see that

1 $\frac{5!}{3!\,(5-3)!} = 10$ is the number of ways to arrange three successes among five trials. For instance, two ways to do this are described by the sample space outcomes *SSSFF* and *SFSSF.* There are eight other ways.

2 $(.4)^3(.6)^2$ is the probability of any sample space outcome consisting of three successes and two failures.

Thus far we have shown how to calculate binomial probabilities. We next give several examples that illustrate some practical applications of the binomial distribution. As we demonstrate in the first example, the term *success* does not necessarily refer to a *desirable* experimental outcome. Rather, it refers to an outcome that we wish to investigate.

Example 4.10

Antibiotics occasionally cause nausea as a side effect. A major drug company has developed a new antibiotic called Phe-Mycin. The company claims that, at most, 10 percent of all patients treated with Phe-Mycin would experience nausea as a side effect of taking the drug. Suppose that we randomly select $n = 4$ patients and treat them with Phe-Mycin. Each patient will either experience nausea (which we arbitrarily call a success) or will not experience nausea (a failure). We will assume that p, the true probability that a patient will experience nausea as a side effect, is .10, the maximum value of p claimed by the drug company. Furthermore, it is reasonable to assume that patients' reactions to the drug would be independent of each other. Let x denote the number of patients among the four who will experience nausea as a side effect. It follows that x is a binomial random variable, which can take on any of the potential values 0, 1, 2, 3, or 4. That is, anywhere between none of the patients and all four of the patients could potentially experience nausea as a side effect. Furthermore, we can calculate the probability associated with each possible value of x as shown in Table 4.6. For instance, the probability that none of the four randomly selected patients experience nausea is

$$\begin{aligned} p(0) = P(x=0) &= \frac{4!}{0!\,(4-0)!}(.1)^0(.9)^{4-0} \\ &= \frac{4!}{0!\,4!}(.1)^0(.9)^4 \\ &= \frac{4!}{(1)(4!)}(1)(.9)^4 \\ &= (.9)^4 = .6561 \end{aligned}$$

Because Table 4.6 lists each possible value of x and also gives the probability of each value, we say that this table gives the **binomial probability distribution of x.**

The binomial probabilities given in Table 4.6 need not be hand calculated. MINITAB, Excel, and MegaStat can be used to calculate binomial probabilities. For instance, Figure 4.4(a) gives

TABLE 4.6 The Binomial Probability Distribution of *x*, the Number of Four Randomly Selected Patients Who Will Experience Nausea as a Side Effect of Being Treated with Phe-Mycin

x (Number Who Experience Nausea)	$p(x) = \frac{n!}{x!\,(n-x)!}p^x(1-p)^{n-x}$
0	$p(0) = P(x=0) = \frac{4!}{0!\,(4-0)!}(.1)^0(.9)^{4-0} = .6561$
1	$p(1) = P(x=1) = \frac{4!}{1!\,(4-1)!}(.1)^1(.9)^{4-1} = .2916$
2	$p(2) = P(x=2) = \frac{4!}{2!\,(4-2)!}(.1)^2(.9)^{4-2} = .0486$
3	$p(3) = P(x=3) = \frac{4!}{3!\,(4-3)!}(.1)^3(.9)^{4-3} = .0036$
4	$p(4) = P(x=4) = \frac{4!}{4!\,(4-4)!}(.1)^4(.9)^{4-4} = .0001$

FIGURE 4.4 The Binomial Probability Distribution with $p = .10$ and $n = 4$

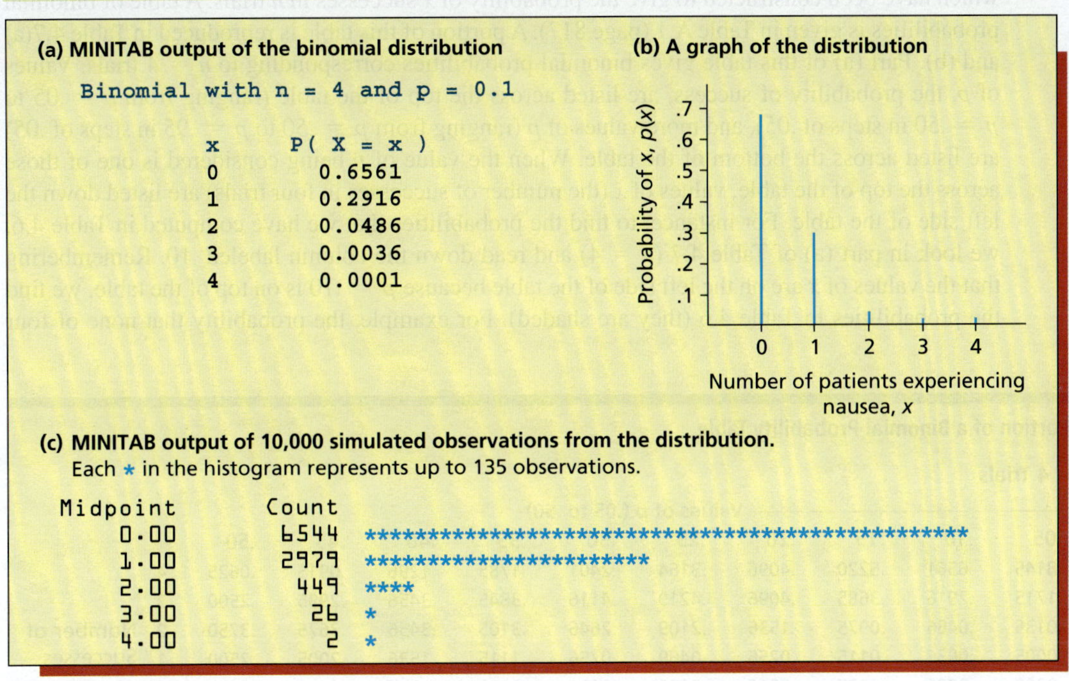

the MINITAB output of the binomial probability distribution listed in Table 4.6.[1] Figure 4.4(b) shows a graph of this distribution.

(a) MINITAB output of the binomial distribution
Binomial with n = 4 and p = 0.1
x P(X = x)
0 0.6561
1 0.2916
2 0.0486
3 0.0036
4 0.0001
(b) A graph of the distribution
Probability of x, p(x)
.7
.6
.5
.4
.3
.2
.1
0 1 2 3 4
Number of patients experiencing nausea, x
(c) MINITAB output of 10,000 simulated observations from the distribution.
Each * in the histogram represents up to 135 observations.
Midpoint Count
0.00 6544 **
1.00 2979 **********************
2.00 449 ****
3.00 26 *
4.00 2 *

In order to interpret these binomial probabilities, consider administering the antibiotic Phe-Mycin to all possible samples of four randomly selected patients. Then, for example,

$$P(x = 0) = 0.6561$$

says that none of the four sampled patients would experience nausea in 65.61 percent of all possible samples. Furthermore, as another example,

$$P(x = 3) = 0.0036$$

says that three out of the four sampled patients would experience nausea in only .36 percent of all possible samples.

[1] As we will see in this chapter's appendixes, we can use Excel or MegaStat to obtain output of the binomial distribution that is essentially identical to the output given by MINITAB.

To better understand these interpretations, we can use MINITAB to *simulate* giving the antibiotic to a large number of samples of four randomly selected patients. That is, we can use MINITAB to randomly select a large number of observations from the binomial distribution of Table 4.6. The MINITAB output of a simulation of 10,000 samples of four randomly selected patients is given in Figure 4.4(c). In other words, this figure gives the results obtained when MINITAB has randomly selected 10,000 observations from the binomial distribution with $p = .10$ and $n = 4$. Each observation (or simulated sample of four patients) results in either 0, 1, 2, 3, or 4 patients experiencing nausea. The MINITAB output presents the results in the form of a histogram that shows the number of simulated samples in which 0, 1, 2, 3, or 4 patients experienced nausea. For instance, none of the four patients experienced nausea in 6,544 (that is, in 65.44 percent) of the 10,000 samples, while 3 out of 4 patients experienced nausea in 26 (or in .26 percent) of the 10,000 samples. These simulated results are quite close to the percentages given by the probabilities in Table 4.6. If we could use MINITAB to simulate an indefinitely large number of samples of four patients, then the simulated percentages would be exactly equal to the percentages given by the binomial probabilities. Note, of course, that we cannot do this—we can simulate only some large number of samples (say, 10,000 samples).

Another way to avoid hand calculating binomial probabilities is to use **binomial tables,** which have been constructed to give the probability of x successes in n trials. A table of binomial probabilities is given in Table A.1 (page 817). A portion of this table is reproduced in Table 4.7(a) and (b). Part (a) of this table gives binomial probabilities corresponding to $n = 4$ trials. Values of p, the probability of success, are listed across the top of the table (ranging from $p = .05$ to $p = .50$ in steps of .05), and more values of p (ranging from $p = .50$ to $p = .95$ in steps of .05) are listed across the bottom of the table. When the value of p being considered is one of those across the top of the table, values of x (the number of successes in four trials) are listed down the left side of the table. For instance, to find the probabilities that we have computed in Table 4.6, we look in part (a) of Table 4.7 ($n = 4$) and read down the column labeled .10. Remembering that the values of x are on the left side of the table because $p = .10$ is on top of the table, we find the probabilities in Table 4.6 (they are shaded). For example, the probability that none of four

TABLE 4.7 A Portion of a Binomial Probability Table

(a) A Table for $n = 4$ Trials

Number of Successes ↓	Values of p (.05 to .50) ← .05	.10	.15	.20	.25	.30	.35	.40	.45	.50	Number of Successes
0	.8145	.6561	.5220	.4096	.3164	.2401	.1785	.1296	.0915	.0625	4
1	.1715	.2916	.3685	.4096	.4219	.4116	.3845	.3456	.2995	.2500	3
2	.0135	.0486	.0975	.1536	.2109	.2646	.3105	.3456	.3675	.3750	2
3	.0005	.0036	.0115	.0256	.0469	.0756	.1115	.1536	.2005	.2500	1
4	.0000	.0001	.0005	.0016	.0039	.0081	.0150	.0256	.0410	.0625	0
	.95	.90	.85	.80	.75	.70	.65	.60	.55	.50	↑ Values of p (.50 to .95) →

(b) A Table for $n = 8$ trials

Number of Successes ↓	Values of p (.05 to .50) ← .05	.10	.15	.20	.25	.30	.35	.40	.45	.50	Number of Successes
0	.6634	.4305	.2725	.1678	.1001	.0576	.0319	.0168	.0084	.0039	8
1	.2793	.3826	.3847	.3355	.2670	.1977	.1373	.0896	.0548	.0313	7
2	.0515	.1488	.2376	.2936	.3115	.2965	.2587	.2090	.1569	.1094	6
3	.0054	.0331	.0839	.1468	.2076	.2541	.2786	.2787	.2568	.2188	5
4	.0004	.0046	.0185	.0459	.0865	.1361	.1875	.2322	.2627	.2734	4
5	.0000	.0004	.0026	.0092	.0231	.0467	.0808	.1239	.1719	.2188	3
6	.0000	.0000	.0002	.0011	.0038	.0100	.0217	.0413	.0703	.1094	2
7	.0000	.0000	.0000	.0001	.0004	.0012	.0033	.0079	.0164	.0313	1
8	.0000	.0000	.0000	.0000	.0000	.0001	.0002	.0007	.0017	.0039	0
	.95	.90	.85	.80	.75	.70	.65	.60	.55	.50	↑ Values of p (.50 to .95) →

patients experience nausea is $p(0) = .6561$, the probability that one of the four patients experiences nausea is $p(1) = .2916$, and so forth. If the value of p is across the bottom of the table, then we read the values of x from the right side of the table. As an example, if p equals .60, then the probability of two successes in four trials is $p(2) = .3456$ (we have shaded this probability).

Example 4.11

Suppose that we wish to investigate whether p, the probability that a patient will experience nausea as a side effect of taking Phe-Mycin, is greater than .10, the maximum value of p claimed by the drug company. This assessment will be made by assuming, for the sake of argument, that p equals .10, and by using sample information to weigh the evidence against this assumption and in favor of the conclusion that p is greater than .10. Suppose that when a sample of $n = 4$ randomly selected patients is treated with Phe-Mycin, three of the four patients experience nausea. Since the fraction of patients in the sample that experience nausea is $3/4 = .75$, which is far greater than .10, we have some evidence contradicting the assumption that p equals .10. To evaluate the strength of this evidence, we calculate the probability that at least 3 out of 4 randomly selected patients would experience nausea as a side effect if, in fact, p equals .10. Using the binomial probabilities in Table 4.7(a), and realizing that the events $x = 3$ and $x = 4$ are mutually exclusive, we have

$$\begin{aligned} P(x \geq 3) &= P(x = 3 \text{ or } x = 4) \\ &= P(x = 3) + P(x = 4) \\ &= .0036 + .0001 \\ &= .0037 \end{aligned}$$

This probability says that, if p equals .10, then in only .37 percent of all possible samples of four randomly selected patients would at least three of the four patients experience nausea as a side effect. This implies that, if we are to believe that p equals .10, then we must believe that we have observed a sample result that is so rare that it can be described as a 37 in 10,000 chance. Because observing such a result is very unlikely, we have very strong evidence that p does not equal .10 and is, in fact, greater than .10.

Next, suppose that we consider what our conclusion would have been if only one of the four randomly selected patients had experienced nausea. Since the sample fraction of patients who experienced nausea is $1/4 = .25$, which is greater than .10, we would have some evidence to contradict the assumption that p equals .10. To evaluate the strength of this evidence, we calculate the probability that at least one out of four randomly selected patients would experience nausea as a side effect of being treated with Phe-Mycin if, in fact, p equals .10. Using the binomial probabilities in Table 4.7(a), we have

$$\begin{aligned} P(x \geq 1) &= P(x = 1 \text{ or } x = 2 \text{ or } x = 3 \text{ or } x = 4) \\ &= P(x = 1) + P(x = 2) + P(x = 3) + P(x = 4) \\ &= .2916 + .0486 + .0036 + .0001 \\ &= .3439 \end{aligned}$$

This probability says that, if p equals .10, then in 34.39 percent of all possible samples of four randomly selected patients, at least one of the four patients would experience nausea. Since it is not particularly difficult to believe that a 34.39 percent chance has occurred, we would not have much evidence against the claim that p equals .10.

Example 4.11 illustrates what is sometimes called the **rare event approach to making a statistical inference.** The idea of this approach is that if the probability of an observed sample result under a given assumption is *small,* then we have *strong evidence* that the assumption is false. Although there are no strict rules, many statisticians judge the probability of an observed sample result to be small if it is less than .05. The logic behind this will be explained more fully in Chapter 8.

Example 4.12

The manufacturer of the ColorSmart-5000 television set claims that 95 percent of its sets last at least five years without requiring a single repair. Suppose that we contact $n = 8$ randomly selected ColorSmart-5000 purchasers five years after they purchased their sets. Each purchaser's set will have needed no repairs (a success) or will have been repaired at least once (a failure). We will assume that p, the true probability that a purchaser's television set will require no repairs within five years, is .95, as claimed by the manufacturer. Furthermore, it is reasonable to believe that the repair records of the purchasers' sets are independent of each other. Let x denote the number of the $n = 8$ randomly selected sets that have lasted at least five years without a single repair. Then x is a binomial random variable that can take on any of the potential values 0, 1, 2, 3, 4, 5, 6, 7, or 8. The binomial distribution of x is listed in Table 4.8. Here we have obtained these probabilities from Table 4.7(b). To use the table, we look at the column corresponding to $p = .95$. Because $p = .95$ is listed at the bottom of the table, we read the values of x and their corresponding probabilities from bottom to top (we have shaded the probabilities). Notice that the values of x are listed on the right side of the table.

Figure 4.5(a) gives the MINITAB output of the binomial distribution with $p = .95$ and $n = 8$ (that is, the binomial distribution of Table 4.8). This binomial distribution is graphed in

TABLE 4.8 The Binomial Distribution of x, the Number of Eight ColorSmart-5000 Television Sets That Have Lasted at Least Five Years Without Needing a Single Repair, When $p = .95$

x, Number of Sets That Require No Repairs	$p(x) = \frac{8!}{x!\,(8-x)!}(.95)^x(.05)^{8-x}$
0	$p(0) = .0000$
1	$p(1) = .0000$
2	$p(2) = .0000$
3	$p(3) = .0000$
4	$p(4) = .0004$
5	$p(5) = .0054$
6	$p(6) = .0515$
7	$p(7) = .2793$
8	$p(8) = .6634$

FIGURE 4.5 The Binomial Probability Distribution with $p = .95$ and $n = 8$

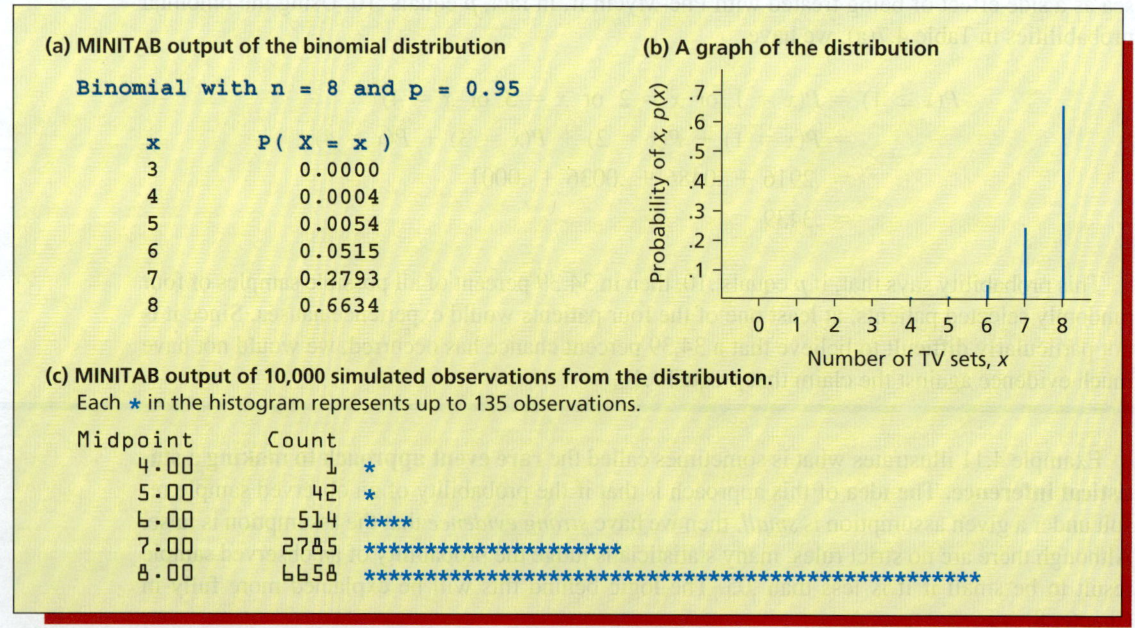

(a) MINITAB output of the binomial distribution
Binomial with n = 8 and p = 0.95
x P(X = x)
3 0.0000
4 0.0004
5 0.0054
6 0.0515
7 0.2793
8 0.6634
(b) A graph of the distribution
Probability of x, p(x)
.7
.6
.5
.4
.3
.2
.1
0 1 2 3 4 5 6 7 8
Number of TV sets, x
(c) MINITAB output of 10,000 simulated observations from the distribution.
Each * in the histogram represents up to 135 observations.
Midpoint Count
4.00 1 *
5.00 42 *
6.00 514 ****
7.00 2785 *********************
8.00 6658 **

Figure 4.5(b), and Figure 4.5(c) gives the MINITAB output of 10,000 simulated observations from this distribution. Looking at Figure 4.5(c), we see that, for example, seven out of eight sets have lasted at least five years without a single repair in 2,785 (27.85 percent) of the 10,000 simulated samples. This result is very close to the percentage (27.93 percent) given by the binomial distribution [see Figure 4.5(a)].

Next, suppose that when we actually contact eight randomly selected purchasers, we find that five out of the eight television sets owned by these purchasers have lasted at least five years without a single repair. Since the sample fraction, $5/8 = .625$, of television sets needing no repairs is less than .95, we have some evidence contradicting the manufacturer's claim that p equals .95. To evaluate the strength of this evidence, we will calculate the probability that five or fewer of the eight randomly selected televisions would last five years without a single repair if, in fact, p equals .95. Using the binomial probabilities in Table 4.8, we have

$$\begin{aligned} P(x \leq 5) &= P(x = 5 \text{ or } x = 4 \text{ or } x = 3 \text{ or } x = 2 \text{ or } x = 1 \text{ or } x = 0) \\ &= P(x = 5) + P(x = 4) + P(x = 3) + P(x = 2) + P(x = 1) + P(x = 0) \\ &= .0054 + .0004 + .0000 + .0000 + .0000 + .0000 \\ &= .0058 \end{aligned}$$

This probability says that, if p equals .95, then in only .58 percent of all possible samples of eight randomly selected ColorSmart-5000 televisions would five or fewer of the eight televisions last five years without a single repair. Therefore, if we are to believe that p equals .95, we must believe that a 58 in 10,000 chance has occurred. Since it is difficult to believe that such a small chance has occurred, we have strong evidence that p does not equal .95, and is, in fact, less than .95.

In Examples 4.10 and 4.12 we have illustrated binomial distributions with different values of n and p. The values of n and p are often called the **parameters** of the binomial distribution. Figure 4.6 shows several different binomial distributions. We see that, depending on the parameters, a binomial distribution can be skewed to the right, skewed to the left, or symmetrical.

We next consider calculating the mean, variance, and standard deviation of a binomial random variable. If we place the binomial probability formula into the expressions (given in Section 4.2) for the mean and variance of a discrete random variable, we can derive formulas that allow us to

FIGURE 4.6 Several Binomial Distributions

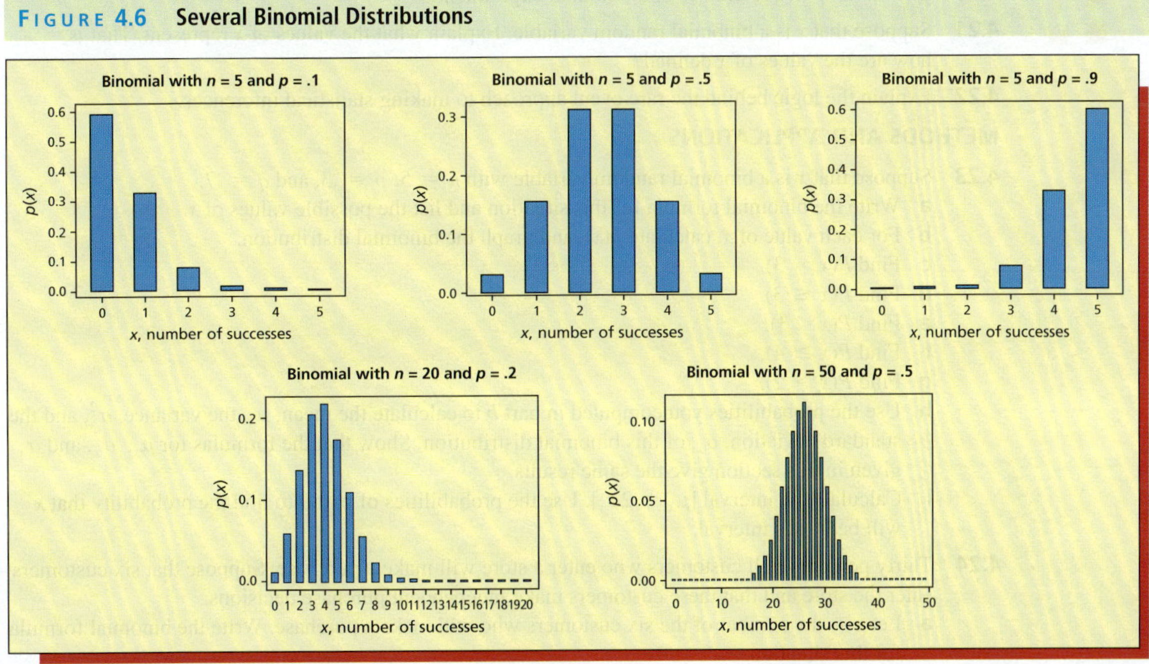

easily compute μ_x, σ_x^2, and σ_x for a binomial random variable. Omitting the details of the derivation, we have the following results:

The Mean, Variance, and Standard Deviation of a Binomial Random Variable

If x is a binomial random variable, then

$$\mu_x = np \qquad \sigma_x^2 = npq \qquad \sigma_x = \sqrt{npq}$$

where n is the number of trials, p is the probability of success on each trial, and $q = 1 - p$ is the probability of failure on each trial.

As a simple example, again consider the television manufacturer, and recall that x is the number of eight randomly selected ColorSmart-5000 televisions that last five years without a single repair. If the manufacturer's claim that p equals .95 is true (which implies that q equals $1 - p = 1 - .95 = .05$), it follows that

$$\mu_x = np = 8(.95) = 7.6$$
$$\sigma_x^2 = npq = 8(.95)(.05) = .38$$
$$\sigma_x = \sqrt{npq} = \sqrt{.38} = .6164$$

In order to interpret $\mu_x = 7.6$, suppose that we were to randomly select all possible samples of eight ColorSmart-5000 televisions and record the number of sets in each sample that last five years without a repair. If we averaged all of our results, we would find that the average number of sets per sample that last five years without a repair is equal to 7.6.

To conclude this section, note that in Appendix C (Part 2) on page 846 we discuss the **hypergeometric distribution.** This distribution is related to the binomial distribution. The main difference between the two distributions is that in the case of the hypergeometric distribution, the trials are not independent and the probabilities of success and failure change from trial to trial. This occurs when we sample without replacement from a finite population. However, when the finite population is large compared to the sample, the binomial distribution can be used to approximate the hypergeometric distribution. The details are explained in Appendix C (Part 2).

Exercises for Section 4.3

CONCEPTS

4.20 List the four characteristics of a binomial experiment.

4.21 Suppose that x is a binomial random variable. Explain what the values of x represent. That is, how are the values of x defined?

4.22 Explain the logic behind the rare event approach to making statistical inferences.

METHODS AND APPLICATIONS

4.23 Suppose that x is a binomial random variable with $n = 5$, $p = .3$, and $q = .7$.

- **a** Write the binomial formula for this situation and list the possible values of x.
- **b** For each value of x, calculate $p(x)$, and graph the binomial distribution.
- **c** Find $P(x = 3)$.
- **d** Find $P(x \leq 3)$.
- **e** Find $P(x < 3)$.
- **f** Find $P(x \geq 4)$.
- **g** Find $P(x > 2)$.
- **h** Use the probabilities you computed in part *b* to calculate the mean, μ_x, the variance, σ_x^2, and the standard deviation, σ_x, of this binomial distribution. Show that the formulas for μ_x, σ_x^2, and σ_x given in this section give the same results.
- **i** Calculate the interval $[\mu_x \pm 2\sigma_x]$. Use the probabilities of part *b* to find the probability that x will be in this interval.

4.24 Thirty percent of all customers who enter a store will make a purchase. Suppose that six customers enter the store and that these customers make independent purchase decisions.

- **a** Let x = the number of the six customers who will make a purchase. Write the binomial formula for this situation.

b Use the binomial formula to calculate
(1) The probability that exactly five customers make a purchase.
(2) The probability that at least three customers make a purchase.
(3) The probability that two or fewer customers make a purchase.
(4) The probability that at least one customer makes a purchase.

4.25 The customer service department for a wholesale electronics outlet claims that 90 percent of all customer complaints are resolved to the satisfaction of the customer. In order to test this claim, a random sample of 15 customers who have filed complaints is selected.

a Let x = the number of sampled customers whose complaints were resolved to the customer's satisfaction. Assuming the claim is true, write the binomial formula for this situation.

b Use the binomial tables (see Table A.1, page 817) to find each of the following if we assume that the claim is true:
(1) $P(x \leq 13)$.
(2) $P(x > 10)$.
(3) $P(x \geq 14)$.
(4) $P(9 \leq x \leq 12)$.
(5) $P(x \leq 9)$.

c Suppose that of the 15 customers selected, 9 have had their complaints resolved satisfactorily. Using part *b*, do you believe the claim of 90 percent satisfaction? Explain.

4.26 The United States Golf Association requires that the weight of a golf ball must not exceed 1.62 oz. The association periodically checks golf balls sold in the United States by sampling specific brands stocked by pro shops. Suppose that a manufacturer claims that no more than 1 percent of its brand of golf balls exceed 1.62 oz. in weight. Suppose that 24 of this manufacturer's golf balls are randomly selected, and let x denote the number of the 24 randomly selected golf balls that exceed 1.62 oz. Figure 4.7 gives part of a MegaStat output of the binomial distribution with $n = 24$, $p = .01$, and $q = .99$. (Note that, since $P(X = x) = .0000$ for values of x from 6 to 24, we omit these probabilities). Use this output to

a Find $P(x = 0)$, that is, find the probability that none of the randomly selected golf balls exceeds 1.62 oz. in weight.

b Find the probability that at least one of the randomly selected golf balls exceeds 1.62 oz. in weight.

c Find $P(x \leq 3)$.

d Find $P(x \geq 2)$.

e Suppose that 2 of the 24 randomly selected golf balls are found to exceed 1.62 oz. Using your result from part *d*, do you believe the claim that no more than 1 percent of this brand of golf balls exceed 1.62 oz. in weight?

FIGURE 4.7 **MegaStat Output of the Binomial Distribution with $n = 24$, $p = .01$, and $q = .99$**

Binomial with
$n = 24$; $p = .01$

X	$p(X)$
0	0.78568
1	0.19047
2	0.02213
3	0.00164
4	0.00009
5	0.00000

4.27 An industry representative claims that 50 percent of all satellite dish owners subscribe to at least one premium movie channel. In an attempt to justify this claim, the representative will poll a randomly selected sample of dish owners.

a Suppose that the representative's claim is true, and suppose that a sample of four dish owners is randomly selected. Assuming independence, use an appropriate formula to compute
(1) The probability that none of the dish owners in the sample subscribes to at least one premium movie channel.
(2) The probability that more than two dish owners in the sample subscribe to at least one premium movie channel.

b Suppose that the representative's claim is true, and suppose that a sample of 20 dish owners is randomly selected. Assuming independence, what is the probability that
(1) Nine or fewer dish owners in the sample subscribe to at least one premium movie channel?
(2) More than 11 dish owners in the sample subscribe to at least one premium movie channel?
(3) Fewer than five dish owners in the sample subscribe to at least one premium movie channel?

c Suppose that, when we survey 20 randomly selected dish owners, we find that 4 of the dish owners actually subscribe to at least one premium movie channel. Using a probability you found in this exercise as the basis for your answer, do you believe the industry representative's claim? Explain.

4.28 For each of the following, calculate μ_x, σ_x^2, and σ_x by using the formulas given in this section. Then (1) interpret the meaning of μ_x, and (2) find the probability that x falls in the interval $[\mu_x \pm 2\sigma_x]$.

a The situation of Exercise 4.24, where x = the number of the six customers who will make a purchase.

b The situation of Exercise 4.25, where x = the number of 15 sampled customers whose complaints were resolved to the customer's satisfaction.

c The situation of Exercise 4.26, where x = the number of the 24 randomly selected golf balls that exceed 1.62 oz. in weight.

4.29 The January 1986 mission of the Space Shuttle Challenger was the 25th such shuttle mission. It was unsuccessful due to an explosion caused by an O-ring seal failure.

a According to NASA, the probability of such a failure in a single mission was 1/60,000. Using this value of p and assuming all missions are independent, calculate the probability of no mission failures in 25 attempts. Then calculate the probability of at least one mission failure in 25 attempts.

b According to a study conducted for the Air Force, the probability of such a failure in a single mission was 1/35. Recalculate the probability of no mission failures in 25 attempts and the probability of at least one mission failure in 25 attempts.

c Based on your answers to parts *a* and *b*, which value of p seems more likely to be true? Explain.

d How small must p be made in order to ensure that the probability of no mission failures in 25 attempts is .999?

4.4 The Poisson Distribution (Optional)

CHAPTER 4

We now discuss a discrete random variable that describes the number of occurrences of an event over a specified interval of time or space. For instance, we might wish to describe (1) the number of customers who arrive at the checkout counters of a grocery store in one hour, or (2) the number of major fires in a city during the last two months, or (3) the number of dirt specks found in one square yard of plastic wrap.

Such a random variable can often be described by a **Poisson distribution.** We describe this distribution and give two assumptions needed for its use in the following box:

The Poisson Distribution

Consider the number of times an event occurs over an interval of time or space, and assume that

1 The probability of the event's occurrence is the same for any two intervals of equal length, and

2 Whether the event occurs in any interval is independent of whether the event occurs in any other nonoverlapping interval.

Then, the probability that the event will occur x times in a *specified interval* is

$$p(x) = \frac{e^{-\mu}\mu^x}{x!}$$

Here μ is the mean (or expected) number of occurrences of the event in the *specified interval,* and $e = 2.71828\ldots$ is the base of Napierian logarithms.

In theory, there is no limit to how large x might be. That is, theoretically speaking, the event under consideration could occur an indefinitely large number of times during any specified interval. This says that a **Poisson random variable** might take on any of the values 0, 1, 2, 3, . . . and so forth. We will now look at an example.

Example 4.13

In an article[2] in the August 15, 1998, edition of *The Journal News* (Hamilton, Ohio), the Associated Press reported that the Cleveland Air Route Traffic Control Center, the busiest in the nation for guiding planes on cross-country routes, had experienced an unusually high number of errors since the end of July. An error occurs when controllers direct flights either within five miles of each other horizontally, or within 2,000 feet vertically at a height of 18,000 feet or more (the standard is 1,000 feet vertically at heights less than 18,000 feet). The controllers' union blamed

[2] F. J. Frommer, "Errors on the Rise at Traffic Control Center in Ohio," *The Journal News,* August 15, 1998.

TABLE 4.9 A Portion of a Poisson Probability Table

x, Number of Occurrences	μ, Mean Number of Occurrences									
	.1	.2	.3	.4	.5	.6	.7	.8	.9	1.0
0	.9048	.8187	.7408	.6703	.6065	.5488	.4966	.4493	.4066	.3679
1	.0905	.1637	.2222	.2681	.3033	.3293	.3476	.3595	.3659	.3679
2	.0045	.0164	.0333	.0536	.0758	.0988	.1217	.1438	.1647	.1839
3	.0002	.0011	.0033	.0072	.0126	.0198	.0284	.0383	.0494	.0613
4	.0000	.0001	.0003	.0007	.0016	.0030	.0050	.0077	.0111	.0153
5	.0000	.0000	.0000	.0001	.0002	.0004	.0007	.0012	.0020	.0031
6	.0000	.0000	.0000	.0000	.0000	.0000	.0001	.0002	.0003	.0005

x, Number of Occurrences	μ, Mean Number of Occurrences									
	1.1	1.2	1.3	1.4	1.5	1.6	1.7	1.8	1.9	2.0
0	.3329	.3012	.2725	.2466	.2231	.2019	.1827	.1653	.1496	.1353
1	.3662	.3614	.3543	.3452	.3347	.3230	.3106	.2975	.2842	.2707
2	.2014	.2169	.2303	.2417	.2510	.2584	.2640	.2678	.2700	.2707
3	.0738	.0867	.0998	.1128	.1255	.1378	.1496	.1607	.1710	.1804
4	.0203	.0260	.0324	.0395	.0471	.0551	.0636	.0723	.0812	.0902
5	.0045	.0062	.0084	.0111	.0141	.0176	.0216	.0260	.0309	.0361
6	.0008	.0012	.0018	.0026	.0035	.0047	.0061	.0078	.0098	.0120
7	.0001	.0002	.0003	.0005	.0008	.0011	.0015	.0020	.0027	.0034
8	.0000	.0000	.0001	.0001	.0001	.0002	.0003	.0005	.0006	.0009

Source: From Brooks/Cole © 1991.

the errors on a staff shortage, whereas the Federal Aviation Administration (FAA) claimed that the cause was improved error reporting and an unusual number of thunderstorms.

Suppose that an air traffic control center has been averaging 20.8 errors per year and that the center experiences 3 errors in a week. The FAA must decide whether this occurrence is unusual enough to warrant an investigation as to the causes of the (possible) increase in errors. To investigate this possibility, we will find the probability distribution of x, the number of errors in a week, when we assume that the center is still averaging 20.8 errors per year.

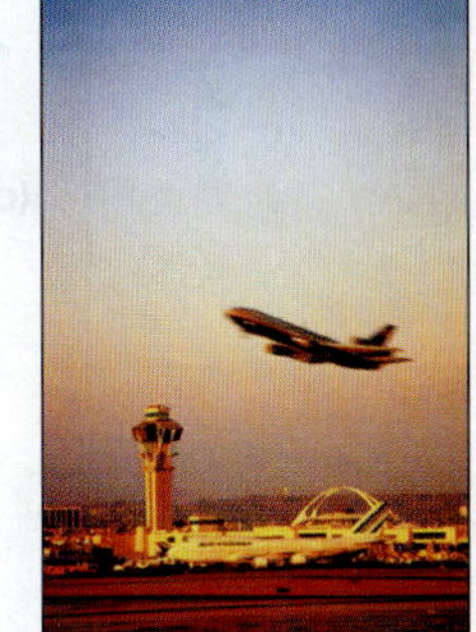

Arbitrarily choosing a time unit of one week, the average (or expected) number of errors per week is $20.8/52 = .4$. Therefore, we can use the Poisson formula (note that the Poisson assumptions are probably satisfied) to calculate the probability of no errors in a week to be

$$p(0) = P(x = 0) = \frac{e^{-\mu}\mu^0}{0!} = \frac{e^{-.4}(.4)^0}{1} = .6703$$

Similarly, the probability of three errors in a week is

$$p(3) = P(x = 3) = \frac{e^{-.4}(.4)^3}{3!} = \frac{e^{-.4}(.4)^3}{3 \cdot 2 \cdot 1} = .0072$$

As with the binomial distribution, tables have been constructed that give Poisson probabilities. A table of these probabilities is given in Table A.2 (page 821). A portion of this table is reproduced in Table 4.9. In this table, values of the mean number of occurrences, μ, are listed across the top of the table, and values of x (the number of occurrences) are listed down the left side of the table. In order to use the table in the traffic control situation, we look at the column in Table 4.9 corresponding to .4, and we find the probabilities of 0, 1, 2, 3, 4, 5, and 6 errors (we have shaded these probabilities). For instance, the probability of one error in a week is .2681. Also, note that the probability of any number of errors greater than 6 is so small that it is not listed in the table. Table 4.10 summarizes the Poisson distribution of x, the number of errors in a week. This table also shows how the probabilities associated with the different values of x are calculated.

Poisson probabilities can also be calculated by using MINITAB, Excel, and MegaStat. For instance, Figure 4.8(a) gives the MINITAB output of the Poisson distribution presented in Table 4.10.[3] This Poisson distribution is graphed in Figure 4.8(b), and Figure 4.8(c) gives the

[3] As we will show in the appendixes to this chapter, we can use Excel and MegaStat to obtain output of the Poisson distribution that is essentially identical to the output given by MINITAB.

TABLE 4.10 The Poisson Distribution of x, the Number of Errors at an Air Traffic Control Center in a Week, When $\mu = .4$

x, the Number of Errors in a Week	$p(x) = \dfrac{e^{-\mu}\mu^x}{x!}$
0	$p(0) = \dfrac{e^{-.4}(.4)^0}{0!} = .6703$
1	$p(1) = \dfrac{e^{-.4}(.4)^1}{1!} = .2681$
2	$p(2) = \dfrac{e^{-.4}(.4)^2}{2!} = .0536$
3	$p(3) = \dfrac{e^{-.4}(.4)^3}{3!} = .0072$
4	$p(4) = \dfrac{e^{-.4}(.4)^4}{4!} = .0007$
5	$p(5) = \dfrac{e^{-.4}(.4)^5}{5!} = .0001$
6	$p(6) = \dfrac{e^{-.4}(.4)^6}{6!} = .0000$

FIGURE 4.8 The Poisson Probability Distribution with $\mu = .4$

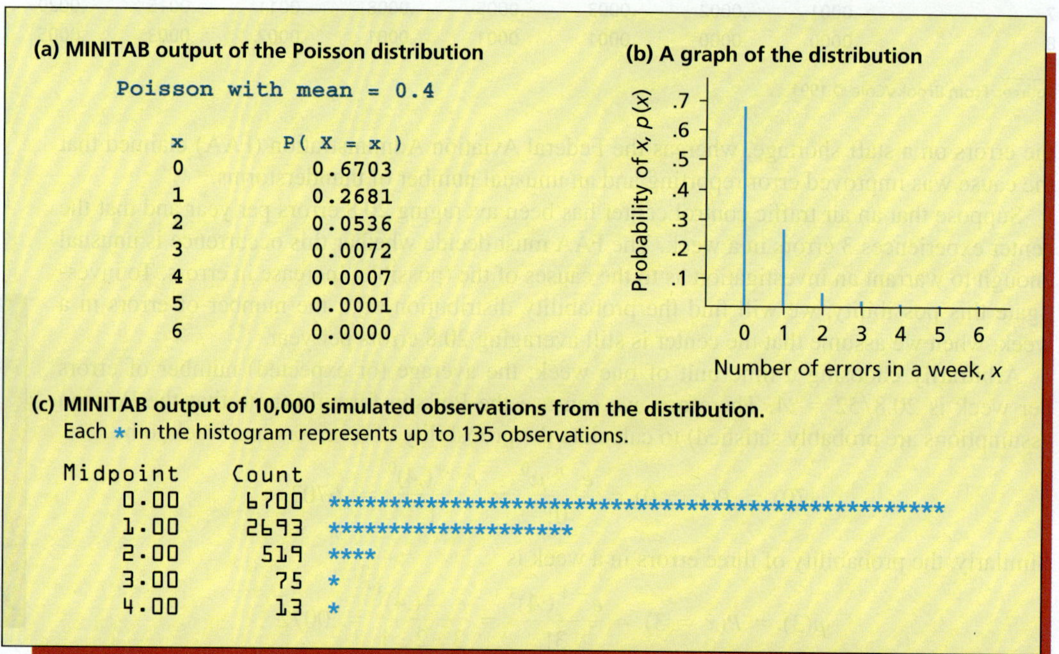
(a) MINITAB output of the Poisson distribution

```
Poisson with mean = 0.4

x    P( X = x )
0    0.6703
1    0.2681
2    0.0536
3    0.0072
4    0.0007
5    0.0001
6    0.0000
```


(c) MINITAB output of 10,000 simulated observations from the distribution. Each * in the histogram represents up to 135 observations.

```
Midpoint   Count
  0.00     6700  **************************************************
  1.00     2693  ********************
  2.00      519  ****
  3.00       75  *
  4.00       13  *
```

MINITAB output of a histogram of 10,000 simulated observations from this distribution. Looking at Figure 4.8(c), we see that, for example, three errors have occurred in 75 (.75 percent) of the 10,000 simulated weeks. This result is very close to the percentage (.72 percent) given by the Poisson distribution [see Figure 4.8(a)].

Next, recall that there have been three errors at the air traffic control center in the last week. This is considerably more errors than .4, the expected number of errors assuming the center is still averaging 20.8 errors per year. Therefore, we have some evidence to contradict this assumption. To evaluate the strength of this evidence, we calculate the probability that at least three errors will occur in a week if, in fact, μ equals .4. Using the Poisson probabilities in Table 4.10 (for $\mu = .4$), we obtain

$$P(x \geq 3) = p(3) + p(4) + p(5) + p(6) = .0072 + .0007 + .0001 + .0000 = .008$$

This probability says that, if the center is averaging 20.8 errors per year, then there would be three errors in a week in only .8 percent of all weeks. That is, if we are to believe that the control center is averaging 20.8 errors per year, then we must believe that an 8 in 1,000 chance has occurred. Since it is very difficult to believe that such a rare event has occurred, we have strong evidence that the average number of errors per week has increased. Therefore, an investigation by the FAA into the reasons for such an increase is probably justified.

Example 4.14

In the book *Modern Statistical Quality Control and Improvement,* Nicholas R. Farnum (1994) presents an example dealing with the quality of computer software. In the example, Farnum measures software quality by monitoring the number of errors per 1,000 lines of computer code.

Suppose that the number of errors per 1,000 lines of computer code is described by a Poisson distribution with a mean of four errors per 1,000 lines of code. If we wish to find the probability of obtaining eight errors in 2,500 lines of computer code, we must adjust the mean of the Poisson distribution. To do this, we arbitrarily choose a *space unit* of one line of code, and we note that a mean of four errors per 1,000 lines of code is equivalent to 4/1,000 of an error per line of code. Therefore, the mean number of errors per 2,500 lines of code is (4/1,000)(2,500) = 10. It follows that

$$p(8) = \frac{e^{-\mu}\,\mu^8}{8!} = \frac{e^{-10}\,10^8}{8!} = .1126$$

The mean, μ, is often called the *parameter* of the Poisson distribution. Figure 4.9 shows several Poisson distributions. We see that, depending on its parameter (mean), a Poisson distribution can be very skewed to the right or can be quite symmetrical.

Finally, if we place the Poisson probability formula into the general expressions (of Section 4.2) for μ_x, σ_x^2, and σ_x, we can derive formulas for calculating the mean, variance, and standard deviation of a Poisson distribution:

The Mean, Variance, and Standard Deviation of a Poisson Random Variable

Suppose that x is a **Poisson random variable.** If μ is the average number of occurrences of an event over the specified interval of time or space of interest, then

$$\mu_x = \mu \qquad \sigma_x^2 = \mu \qquad \sigma_x = \sqrt{\mu}$$

Here we see that both the mean and the variance of a Poisson random variable equal the average number of occurrences μ of the event of interest over the specified interval of time or space. For example, in the air traffic control situation, the Poisson distribution of x, the number of errors at the air traffic control center in a week, has a mean of $\mu_x = .4$ and a standard deviation of $\sigma_x = \sqrt{.4} = .6325$.

FIGURE 4.9 Several Poisson Distributions

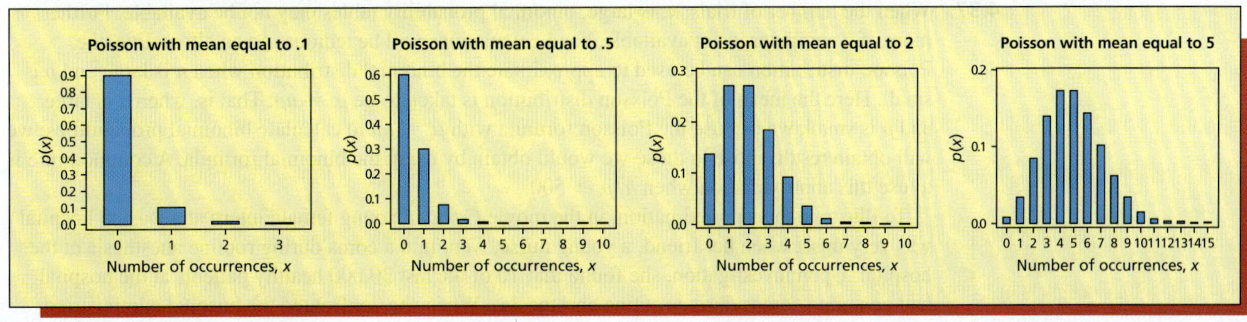

Exercises for Section 4.4

CONCEPTS

4.30 The values of a Poisson random variable are $x = 0, 1, 2, 3, \ldots$ Explain what these values represent.

4.31 Explain the assumptions that must be satisfied when a Poisson distribution adequately describes a random variable x.

METHODS AND APPLICATIONS

4.32 Suppose that x has a Poisson distribution with $\mu = 2$.

a Write the Poisson formula and describe the possible values of x.
b Starting with the smallest possible value of x, calculate $p(x)$ for each value of x until $p(x)$ becomes smaller than .001.
c Graph the Poisson distribution using your results of b.
d Find $P(x = 2)$. **e** Find $P(x \leq 4)$. **f** Find $P(x < 4)$.
g Find $P(x \geq 1)$ and $P(x > 2)$. **h** Find $P(1 \leq x \leq 4)$.
i Find $P(2 < x < 5)$. **j** Find $P(2 \leq x < 6)$.

4.33 Suppose that x has a Poisson distribution with $\mu = 2$.

a Use the formulas given in this section to compute the mean, μ_x, variance, σ_x^2, and standard deviation, σ_x.
b Calculate the intervals $[\mu_x \pm 2\sigma_x]$ and $[\mu_x \pm 3\sigma_x]$. Then use the probabilities you calculated in Exercise 4.32 to find the probability that x will be inside each of these intervals.

4.34 A bank manager wishes to provide prompt service for customers at the bank's drive-up window. The bank currently can serve up to 10 customers per 15-minute period without significant delay. The average arrival rate is 7 customers per 15-minute period. Let x denote the number of customers arriving per 15-minute period. Assuming x has a Poisson distribution:

a Find the probability that 10 customers will arrive in a particular 15-minute period.
b Find the probability that 10 or fewer customers will arrive in a particular 15-minute period.
c Find the probability that there will be a significant delay at the drive-up window. That is, find the probability that more than 10 customers will arrive during a particular 15-minute period.

4.35 A telephone company's goal is to have no more than five monthly line failures on any 100 miles of line. The company currently experiences an average of two monthly line failures per 50 miles of line. Let x denote the number of monthly line failures per 100 miles of line. Assuming x has a Poisson distribution:

a Find the probability that the company will meet its goal on a particular 100 miles of line.
b Find the probability that the company will not meet its goal on a particular 100 miles of line.
c Find the probability that the company will have no more than five monthly failures on a particular 200 miles of line.
d Find the probability that the company will have more than 12 monthly failures on a particular 150 miles of line.

4.36 A local law enforcement agency claims that the number of times that a patrol car passes through a particular neighborhood follows a Poisson process with a mean of three times per nightly shift. Let x denote the number of times that a patrol car passes through the neighborhood during a nightly shift.

a Calculate the probability that no patrol cars pass through the neighborhood during a nightly shift.
b Suppose that during a randomly selected night shift no patrol cars pass through the neighborhood. Based on your answer in part a, do you believe the agency's claim? Explain.
c Assuming that nightly shifts are independent and assuming that the agency's claim is correct, find the probability that exactly one patrol car will pass through the neighborhood on each of four consecutive nights.

4.37 When the number of trials, n, is large, binomial probability tables may not be available. Furthermore, if a computer is not available, hand calculations will be tedious. As an alternative, the Poisson distribution can be used to approximate the binomial distribution when n is large and p is small. Here the mean of the Poisson distribution is taken to be $\mu = np$. That is, when n is large and p is small, we can use the Poisson formula with $\mu = np$ to calculate binomial probabilities; we will obtain results close to those we would obtain by using the binomial formula. A common rule is to use this approximation when $n/p \geq 500$.

To illustrate this approximation, in the movie *Coma,* a young female intern at a Boston hospital was very upset when her friend, a young nurse, went into a coma during routine anesthesia at the hospital. Upon investigation, she found that 10 of the last 30,000 healthy patients at the hospital had gone into comas during routine anesthesias. When she confronted the hospital administrator with this fact and the fact that the national average was 6 out of 100,000 healthy patients going into comas during routine anesthesias, the administrator replied that 10 out of 30,000 was still quite small and thus not that unusual.

a Use the Poisson distribution to approximate the probability that 10 or more of 30,000 healthy patients would slip into comas during routine anesthesias, if in fact the true average at the hospital was 6 in 100,000. Hint: $\mu = np = 30{,}000(6/100{,}000) = 1.8$.

b Given the hospital's record and part *a*, what conclusion would you draw about the hospital's medical practices regarding anesthesia?

(Note: It turned out that the hospital administrator was part of a conspiracy to sell body parts and was purposely putting healthy adults into comas during routine anesthesias. If the intern had taken a statistics course, she could have avoided a great deal of danger.)

4.38 Suppose that an automobile parts wholesaler claims that .5 percent of the car batteries in a shipment are defective. A random sample of 200 batteries is taken, and four are found to be defective.

a Use the Poisson approximation discussed in Exercise 4.37 to find the probability that four or more car batteries in a random sample of 200 such batteries would be found to be defective, if we assume that the wholesaler's claim is true.

b Based on your answer to part *a*, do you believe the claim? Explain.

Chapter Summary

In this chapter we began our study of **random variables.** We learned that **a random variable represents an uncertain numerical outcome.** We also learned that a random variable whose values can be listed is called a **discrete random variable,** while the values of a **continuous random variable** correspond to one or more intervals on the real number line. We saw that a **probability distribution** of a discrete random variable is a table, graph, or formula that gives the probability associated with each of the random variable's possible values. We also discussed several descriptive measures of a discrete random variable—its **mean** (or **expected value**), its **variance,** and its **standard deviation.** We concluded this chapter by studying two important, commonly used discrete probability distributions—the **binomial distribution** and the **Poisson distribution**—and we demonstrated how these distributions can be used to make statistical inferences.

Glossary of Terms

binomial distribution: The probability distribution that describes a binomial random variable. (page 173)

binomial experiment: An experiment that consists of n independent, identical trials, each of which results in either a success or a failure and is such that the probability of success on any trial is the same. (page 173)

binomial random variable: A random variable that is defined to be the total number of successes in n trials of a binomial experiment. (page 173)

binomial tables: Tables in which we can look up binomial probabilities. (page 176)

continuous random variable: A random variable whose values correspond to one or more intervals of numbers on the real number line. (page 159)

discrete random variable: A random variable whose values can be counted or listed. (page 159)

expected value (of a random variable): The mean of the population of all possible observed values of a random variable. That is, the long-run average value obtained if values of a random variable are observed a (theoretically) infinite number of times. (page 163)

Poisson distribution: The probability distribution that describes a Poisson random variable. (page 182)

Poisson random variable: A discrete random variable that can often be used to describe the number of occurrences of an event over a specified interval of time or space. (page 182)

probability distribution (of a discrete random variable): A table, graph, or formula that gives the probability associated with each of the random variable's values. (page 160)

random variable: A variable that assumes numerical values that are determined by the outcome of an experiment. That is, a variable that represents an uncertain numerical outcome. (page 159)

standard deviation (of a random variable): The standard deviation of the population of all possible observed values of a random variable. It measures the spread of the population of all possible observed values of the random variable. (page 166)

variance (of a random variable): The variance of the population of all possible observed values of a random variable. It measures the spread of the population of all possible observed values of the random variable. (page 166)

Important Formulas

Properties of a discrete probability distribution: page 162

The mean (expected value) of a discrete random variable: page 163

Variance and standard deviation of a discrete random variable: page 166

Binomial probability formula: page 173

Mean, variance, and standard deviation of a binomial random variable: page 180

Poisson probability formula: page 182

Mean, variance, and standard deviation of a Poisson random variable: page 185

Supplementary Exercises

4.39 An investor holds two stocks, each of which can rise (R), remain unchanged (U), or decline (D) on any particular day. Let x equal the number of stocks that rise on a particular day.

a Write the probability distribution of x assuming that all outcomes are equally likely.

b Write the probability distribution of x assuming that for each stock $P(R) = .6$, $P(U) = .1$, and $P(D) = .3$ and assuming that movements of the two stocks are independent.

c Write the probability distribution of x assuming that for the first stock

$$P(R) = .4, \quad P(U) = .2, \quad P(D) = .4$$

and that for the second stock

$$P(R) = .8, \quad P(U) = .1, \quad P(D) = .1$$

and assuming that movements of the two stocks are independent.

4.40 Repeat Exercise 4.39, letting x equal the number of stocks that decline on the particular day.

4.41 Consider Exercise 4.39, and let x equal the number of stocks that rise on the particular day. Find μ_x and σ_x for

a The probability distribution of x in Exercise 4.39*a*.

b The probability distribution of x in Exercise 4.39*b*.

c The probability distribution of x in Exercise 4.39*c*.

d In which case is μ_x the largest? Interpret what this means in words.

e In which case is σ_x the largest? Interpret what this means in words.

4.42 Suppose that the probability distribution of a random variable x can be described by the formula

$$p(x) = \frac{(x - 3)^2}{55}$$

for each of the values $x = -2, -1, 0, 1,$ and 2.

a Write the probability distribution of x.

b Show that the probability distribution of x satisfies the properties of a discrete probability distribution.

c Calculate the mean of x.

d Calculate the variance and standard deviation of x.

4.43 A rock concert promoter has scheduled an outdoor concert on July 4th. If it does not rain, the promoter will make $30,000. If it does rain, the promoter will lose $15,000 in guarantees made to the band and other expenses. The probability of rain on the 4th is .4.

a What is the promoter's expected profit? Is the expected profit a reasonable decision criterion? Explain.

b How much should an insurance company charge to insure the promoter's full losses? Explain your answer.

4.44 The demand (in number of copies per day) for a city newspaper is listed below with corresponding probabilities:

x = Demand	$p(x)$
50,000	.1
70,000	.25
90,000	.4
110,000	.2
130,000	.05

a Graph the probability distribution of x.

b Find the expected demand. Interpret this value, and label it on the graph of part *a*.

c Using Chebyshev's Theorem, find the minimum percentage of all possible daily demand values that will fall in the interval $[\mu_x \pm 2\sigma_x]$.

d Calculate the interval $[\mu_x \pm 2\sigma_x]$. Illustrate this interval on the graph of part *a*. According to the probability distribution of demand x previously given, what percentage of all possible daily demand values fall in the interval $[\mu_x \pm 2\sigma_x]$?

4.45 United Medicine, Inc., claims that a drug, Viro, significantly relieves the symptoms of a certain viral infection for 80 percent of all patients. Suppose that this drug is given to eight randomly selected patients who have been diagnosed with the viral infection.

a Let x equal the number of the eight randomly selected patients whose symptoms are significantly relieved. What distribution describes the random variable x? Explain.

b Assuming that the company's claim is correct, find $P(x \leq 3)$.

c Suppose that of the eight randomly selected patients, three have had their symptoms significantly relieved by Viro. Based on the probability in part *b*, would you believe the claim of United Medicine, Inc.? Explain.

4.46 A consumer advocate claims that 80 percent of cable television subscribers are not satisfied with their cable service. In an attempt to justify this claim, a randomly selected sample of cable subscribers will be polled on this issue.

a Suppose that the advocate's claim is true, and suppose that a random sample of five cable subscribers is selected. Assuming independence, use an appropriate formula to compute the probability that four or more subscribers in the sample are not satisfied with their service.

b Suppose that the advocate's claim is true, and suppose that a random sample of 25 cable subscribers is selected. Assuming independence, find

(1) The probability that 15 or fewer subscribers in the sample are not satisfied with their service.

(2) The probability that more than 20 subscribers in the sample are not satisfied with their service.

(3) The probability that between 20 and 24 (inclusive) subscribers in the sample are not satisfied with their service.

(4) The probability that exactly 24 subscribers in the sample are not satisfied with their service.

c Suppose that when we survey 25 randomly selected cable television subscribers, we find that 15 are actually not satisfied with their service. Using a probability you found in this exercise as the basis for your answer, do you believe the consumer advocate's claim? Explain.

4.47 A retail store has implemented procedures aimed at reducing the number of bad checks cashed by its cashiers. The store's goal is to cash no more than eight bad checks per week. The average number of bad checks cashed is three per week. Let x denote the number of bad checks cashed per week. Assuming that x has a Poisson distribution:

a Find the probability that the store's cashiers will not cash any bad checks in a particular week.

b Find the probability that the store will meet its goal during a particular week.

c Find the probability that the store will not meet its goal during a particular week.

d Find the probability that the store's cashiers will cash no more than 10 bad checks per two-week period.

e Find the probability that the store's cashiers will cash no more than five bad checks per three-week period.

4.48 Suppose that the number of accidents occurring in an industrial plant is described by a Poisson process with an average of 1.5 accidents every three months. During the last three months, four accidents occurred.

a Find the probability that no accidents will occur during the current three-month period.

b Find the probability that fewer accidents will occur during the current three-month period than occurred during the last three-month period.

c Find the probability that no more than 12 accidents will occur during a particular year.

d Find the probability that no accidents will occur during a particular year.

4.49 A high-security government installation has installed four security systems to detect attempted break-ins. The four security systems operate independently of each other, and each has a .85 probability of detecting an attempted break-in. Assume an attempted break-in occurs. Use the binomial distribution to find the probability that at least one of the four security systems will detect it.

4.50 A new stain removal product claims to completely remove the stains on 90 percent of all stained garments. Assume that the product will be tested on 20 randomly selected stained garments, and let x denote the number of these garments from which the stains will be completely removed. Use the binomial distribution to find $P(x \leq 13)$ if the stain removal product's claim is correct. If x actually turns out to be 13, what do you think of the claim?

4.51 Consider Exercise 4.50, and find $P(x \leq 17)$ if the stain removal product's claim is correct. If x actually turns out to be 17, what do you think of the claim?

4.52 A state has averaged one small business failure per week over the past several years. Let x denote the number of small business failures in the next eight weeks. Use the Poisson distribution to find $P(x \geq 17)$ if the mean number of small business failures remains what it has been. If x actually turns out to be 17, what does this imply?

4.53 A candy company claims that its new chocolate almond bar averages 10 almonds per bar. Let x denote the number of almonds in the next bar that you buy. Use the Poisson distribution to find $P(x \leq 4)$ if the candy company's claim is correct. If x actually turns out to be 4, what do you think of the claim?

4.54 Consider Exercise 4.53, and find $P(x \leq 8)$ if the candy company's claim is true. If x actually turns out to be 8, what do you think of the claim?

Appendix 4.1 ■ Binomial and Poisson Probabilities Using MINITAB

Binomial probabilities in Figure 4.4(a) on page 175:

- In the data window, enter the values 0 through 4 into column C1 and name the column x.
- Select **Calc : Probability Distributions : Binomial.**
- In the Binomial Distribution dialog box, select the Probability option by clicking.
- In the "Number of trials" box, enter 4 for the value of n.
- In the "Probability of success" box, enter 0.1 for the value of p.
- Select the "Input column" option and enter the variable name x into the Input column box.
- Click OK in the Binomial Distribution dialog box.
- The binomial probabilities will be displayed in the Session window.

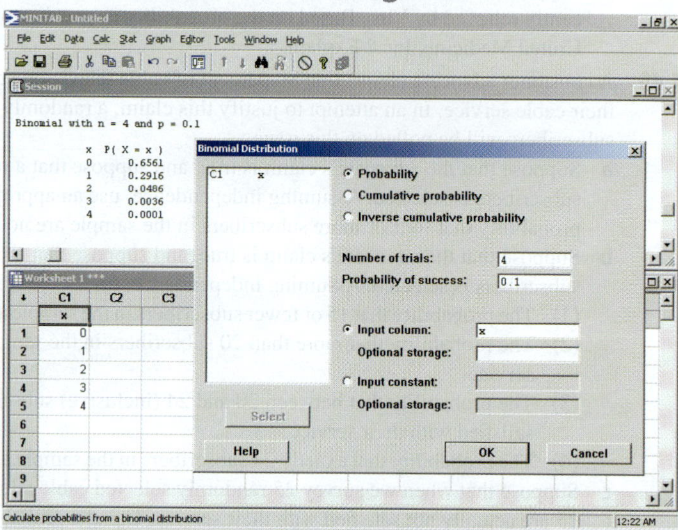

Poisson probabilities in Figure 4.8(a) on page 184:

- In the data window, enter the values 0 through 6 into column C1 and name the column x.
- Select **Calc : Probability Distributions : Poisson.**
- In the Poisson Distribution dialog box, select the Probability option by clicking.
- In the Mean box, enter 0.4.
- Select the "Input column" option and enter the variable name x into the Input column box.
- Click OK in Poisson Distribution dialog box.
- The Poisson probabilities will be displayed in the Session window.

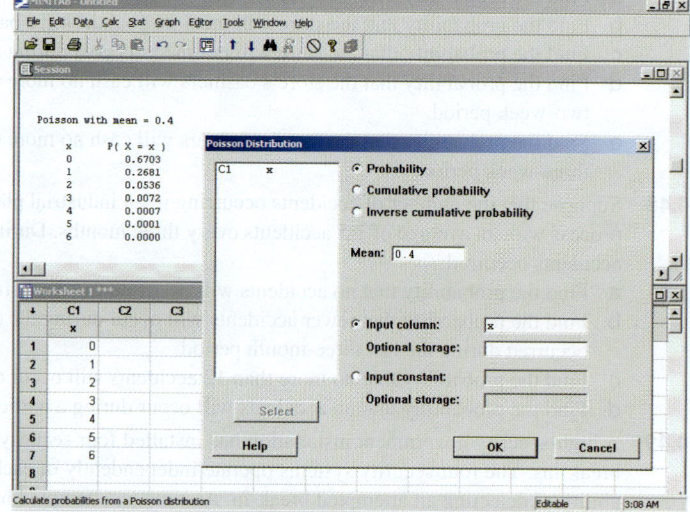

Appendix 4.2 ■ Binomial and Poisson Probabilities Using Excel

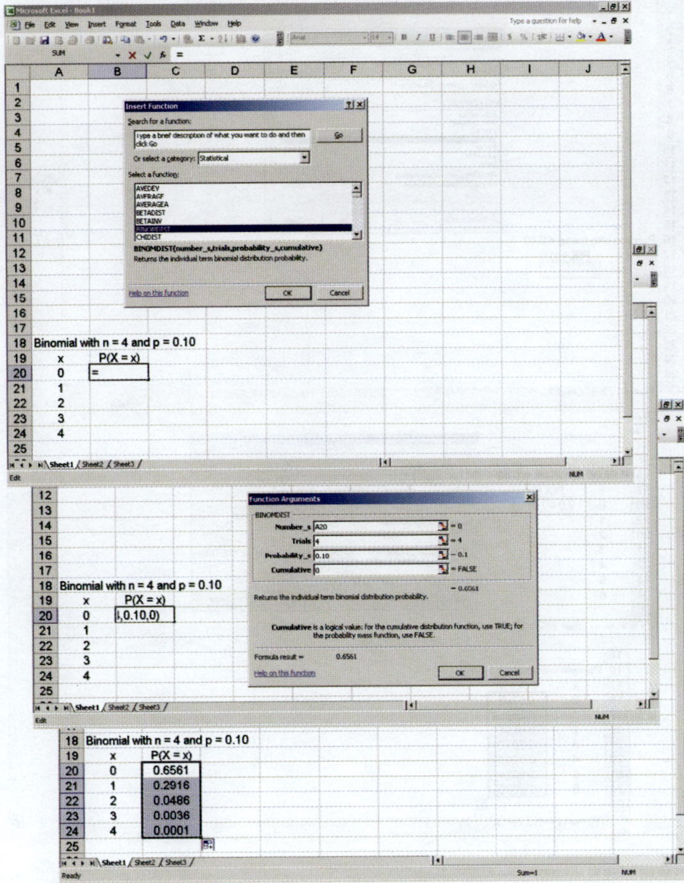

Binomial probabilities similar to Figure 4.4(a) on page 175:

- Enter the title, "Binomial with n = 4 and p = 0.10", in the location in which you wish to place the binomial results. Here we have placed the title beginning in cell A18 (any other choice will do).
- In cell A19, enter the heading, x.
- Enter the values 0 through 4 in cells A20 through A24.
- In cell B19, enter the heading P(X = x).
- Click in cell B20 (this is where the first binomial probability will be placed). Click on the Insert Function button f_x on the Excel toolbar.
- In the Insert Function dialog box, select Statistical from the "Or select a category:" menu, select BINOMDIST from the "Select a function:" menu, and click OK.
- In the BINOMDIST Function Arguments dialog box, enter the cell location A20 (this cell contains the value for which the first binomial probability will be calculated) in the "Number_s" box.
- Enter the value 4 in the Trials box.
- Enter the value 0.10 in the "Probability_s" box.
- Enter the value 0 in the Cumulative box.
- Click OK in the BINOMDIST Function Arguments dialog box.
- When you click OK, the calculated result (0.6561) will appear in cell B20. Double-click the drag handle (in the lower right corner) of cell B20 to automatically extend the cell formula in B20 through cell B24.
- The remaining probabilities will be placed in cells B21 through B24.

Poisson probabilities similar to Figure 4.8(a) on page 184:

- Enter the title "Poisson with mean = 0.40" in the location in which you wish to place the Poisson results. Here we have placed the title beginning in cell A16 (any other choice will do).
- In cell A17, enter the heading, x.
- Enter the values 0 through 6 in cells A18 through A24.
- In cell B17, enter the heading, P(X = x).
- Click in cell B18 (this is where the first Poisson probability will be placed). Click on the Insert Function button $\boxed{f_x}$ on the Excel toolbar.
- In the Insert Function dialog box, select Statistical from the "Or select a category" menu, select POISSON from the "Select a function" menu, and click OK.
- In the POISSON Function Arguments dialog box, enter the cell location A18 (this cell contains the value for which the first Poisson probability will be calculated) in the "X" box.
- Enter the value 0.40 in the Mean box.
- Enter the value 0 in the Cumulative box.
- Click OK in the POISSON Function Arguments dialog box.
- The calculated result for the probability of 0 events will appear in cell B18.
- Click on cell B18 and select **Format : Cells.**
- In the Format Cells dialog box, click on the Number tab, select Number from the Category menu, enter 4 in the Decimal places box, and click OK.
- The calculated result will now be rounded to 4 decimal places (0.6703). Double-click on the drag handle (in the lower right corner) of cell B18 to automatically extend the cell formula and formatting through cell B24.

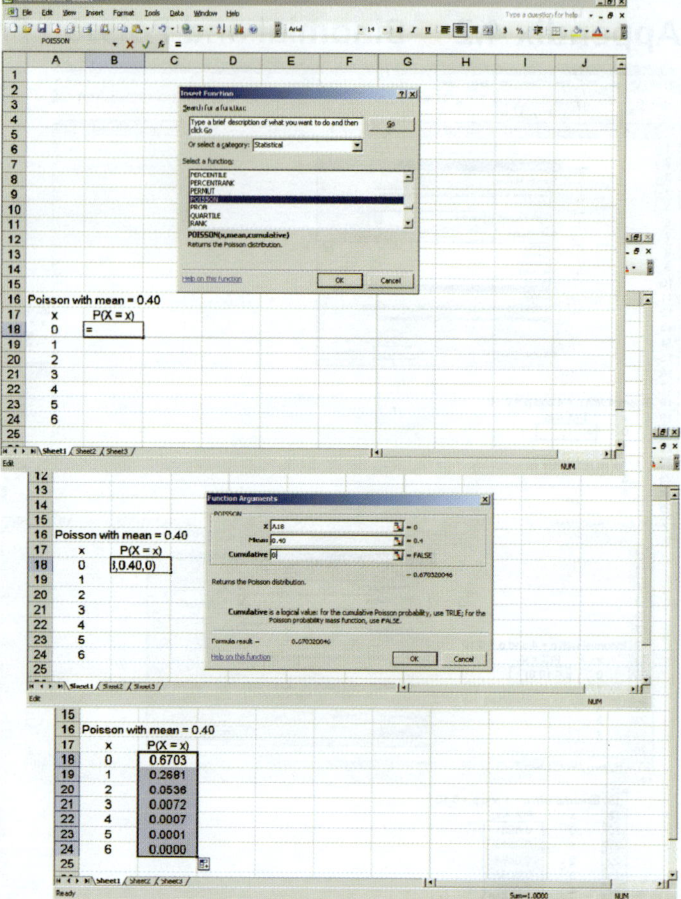

Appendix 4.3 ■ Binomial and Poisson Probabilities Using MegaStat

Microsoft Excel - Figure4-7.xls
File Edit View Insert Format Tools MegaStat Data Window Help
Discrete Probability Distributions
Binomial
Hypergeometric
Poisson
24
n, number of trials
.01
p, probability of occurence
display graph
OK
Clear
Cancel
Help
Binomial distribution
24 n
0.01 p
cumulative
X p(X) probability
0 0.78568 0.78568
1 0.19047 0.97615
2 0.02213 0.99827
3 0.00164 0.99991
4 0.00009 1.00000
5 0.00000 1.00000
6 0.00000 1.00000
7 0.00000 1.00000
8 0.00000 1.00000
9 0.00000 1.00000
Output
Sheet1
Sheet2
Sheet3
Ready
NUM

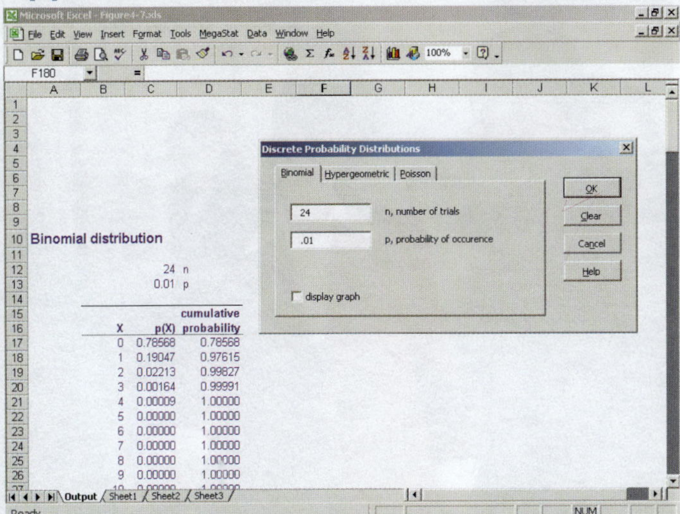

Binomial probabilities in Figure 4.7 on page 181.

- Select **MegaStat : Probability : Discrete Probability Distributions.**
- In the "Discrete Probability Distributions" dialog box, enter the number of trials (here equal to 24) and the probability of success p (here equal to .01) in the appropriate boxes.
- Click the Display Graph check box if a plot of the distribution is desired.
- Click OK in the "Discrete Probability Distributions" dialog box.

The binomial output is placed in an Output worksheet.

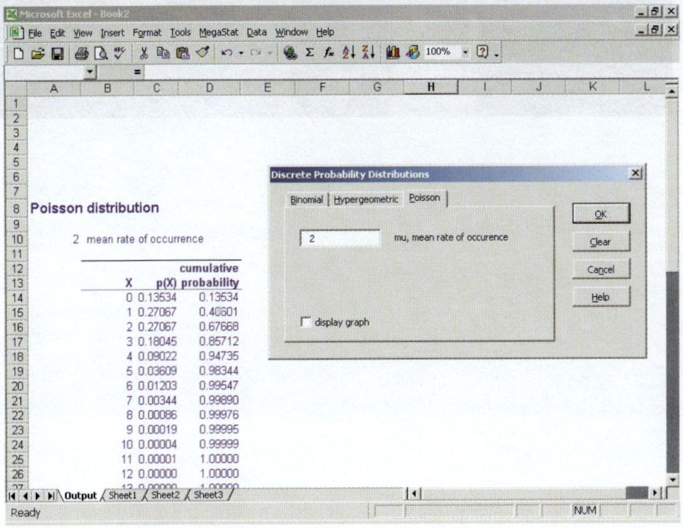

Microsoft Excel - Book2
File Edit View Insert Format Tools MegaStat Data Window Help
Discrete Probability Distributions
Binomial
Hypergeometric
Poisson
2
mu, mean rate of occurence
display graph
OK
Clear
Cancel
Help
Poisson distribution
2 mean rate of occurrence
cumulative
X p(X) probability
0 0.13534 0.13534
1 0.27067 0.40601
2 0.27067 0.67668
3 0.18045 0.85712
4 0.09022 0.94735
5 0.03609 0.98344
6 0.01203 0.99547
7 0.00344 0.99890
8 0.00086 0.99976
9 0.00019 0.99995
10 0.00004 0.99999
11 0.00001 1.00000
12 0.00000 1.00000
Output
Sheet1
Sheet2
Sheet3
Ready
NUM

To calculate **Poisson probabilities,** click on the Poisson tab and enter the mean of the Poisson distribution. Then click OK.

To calculate **Hypergeometric probabilities** (discussed in part (2) of Appendix C), click on the Hypergeometric tab. Then enter the population size, the number of successes in the population, and the sample size in the appropriate boxes and click OK.

CHAPTER 5

Continuous Random Variables

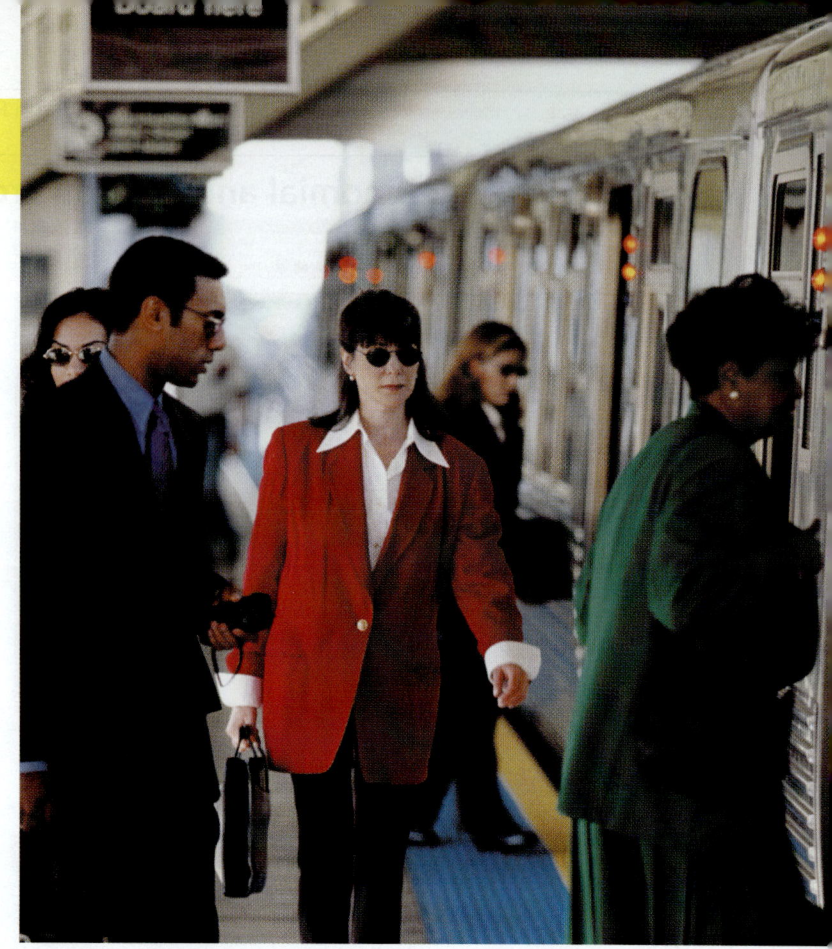

Chapter Outline

In Chapter 4 we defined discrete and continuous random variables. We also discussed discrete probability distributions, which are used to compute the probabilities of values of discrete random variables. In this chapter we discuss **continuous probability distributions.** These are used to find probabilities concerning continuous random variables. We begin by explaining the general idea behind a continuous probability distribution. Then we present three important continuous distributions—the **uniform, normal,** and **exponential distributions.** We also study when and how the normal distribution can be used to approximate the binomial distribution (which was discussed in Chapter 4).

In order to illustrate the concepts in this chapter, we continue two previously discussed cases, and we also introduce a new case:

The Car Mileage Case: A competitor claims that its midsize car gets better mileage than an automaker's new midsize model. The automaker uses sample information and a probability based on the normal distribution to provide strong evidence that the competitor's claim is false.

The Coffee Temperature Case: The fast-food restaurant uses the normal distribution to estimate the proportion of coffee it serves that has a temperature outside the range 153° to 167°, the customer requirement for best-tasting coffee.

The Cheese Spread Case: A food processing company markets a soft cheese spread that is sold in a plastic container. The company has developed a new spout for the container. However, the new spout will be used only if fewer than 10 percent of all current purchasers would no longer buy the cheese spread if the new spout were used. The company uses sample information and a probability based on approximating the binomial distribution by the normal distribution to provide very strong evidence that fewer than 10 percent of all current purchasers would stop buying the spread if the new spout were used. This implies that the company can use the new spout without alienating its current customers.

5.1 Continuous Probability Distributions

Remember (from Section 4.1) that the values of a continuous random variable correspond to one or more intervals on the real number line. We often wish to compute probabilities about the range of values that a continuous random variable x might attain. We do this by assigning probabilities to **intervals of values** by using what we call a **continuous probability distribution.** To understand this idea, suppose that $f(x)$ is a continuous function of the numbers on the real line, and consider the continuous curve that results when $f(x)$ is graphed. Such a curve is illustrated in Figure 5.1. Then:

Continuous Probability Distributions

The curve $f(x)$ is the **continuous probability distribution** of the random variable x if the probability that x will be in a specified interval of numbers is the area under the curve $f(x)$ corresponding to the interval. Sometimes we refer to a continuous probability distribution as a **probability curve** or as a **probability density function.**

An *area* under a continuous probability distribution (or probability curve) is a *probability.* For instance, consider the range of values on the number line from the number a to the number b—that is, the interval of numbers from a to b. If the continuous random variable x is described by the probability curve $f(x)$, then the area under $f(x)$ corresponding to the interval from a to b is the probability that x will attain a value between a and b. Such a probability is illustrated as the shaded area in Figure 5.1. We write this probability as $P(a \leq x \leq b)$. Since there is no area under a continuous curve at a single point, the probability that a continuous random variable x attains a single value is always equal to 0. It follows that in Figure 5.1 we have $P(x = a) = 0$ and $P(x = b) = 0$. Therefore, $P(a \leq x \leq b)$ equals $P(a < x < b)$ because each of the interval endpoints a and b has a probability that is equal to 0.

FIGURE 5.1 An Example of a Continuous Probability Distribution $f(x)$

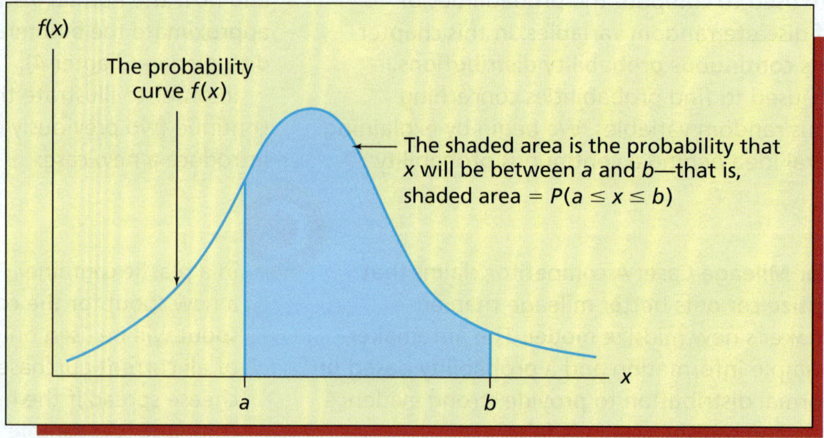

We know that any probability is 0 or positive, and we also know that the probability assigned to all possible values of x must be 1. It follows that, similar to the conditions required for a discrete probability distribution, a probability curve must satisfy the following properties:

Properties of a Continuous Probability Distribution

The **continuous probability distribution** (or **probability curve**) $f(x)$ of a random variable x must satisfy the following two conditions:

1 $f(x) \geq 0$ for any value of x.

2 The total area under the curve of $f(x)$ is equal to 1.

Any continuous curve $f(x)$ that satisfies these conditions is a valid continuous probability distribution. Such probability curves can have a variety of shapes—bell-shaped and symmetrical, skewed to the right, skewed to the left, or any other shape. In a practical problem, the shape of a probability curve would be estimated by looking at a frequency (or relative frequency) histogram of observed data (as we have done in Chapter 2). Later in this chapter, we study probability curves having several different shapes. For example, in the next section we introduce the *uniform distribution,* which has a rectangular shape.

It is important to point out that *the height of a probability curve $f(x)$ at a particular point is not a probability. In order to calculate a probability concerning a continuous random variable, we must compute an appropriate area under the curve $f(x)$.* In theory, such areas are calculated by calculus methods and/or numerical techniques. Because these methods are difficult, needed areas under commonly used probability curves have been compiled in statistical tables. As we need them, we show how to use the required statistical tables.

Finally, we wish to emphasize that a continuous (or discrete) probability distribution is used to represent a population. That is, if $f(x)$ is a continuous probability distribution for a random variable x, then the area under the curve $f(x)$ between a and b—that is, $P(a \leq x \leq b)$—is *the proportion of values in the population of all possible values of x that are between a and b.* For instance, suppose that the probability curve $f(x)$ describes the random variable x = the mileage obtained by a midsize car model. Then the area under the curve $f(x)$ between 31 mpg and 33 mpg is the proportion of mileages in the population of all possible midsize car mileages that are between 31 mpg and 33 mpg.

5.2 The Uniform Distribution

Suppose that over a period of several days the manager of a large hotel has recorded the waiting times of 1,000 people waiting for an elevator in the lobby at dinnertime (5:00 P.M. to 7:00 P.M.). The observed waiting times range from zero to four minutes. Furthermore, when the waiting times are arranged into a histogram, the bars making up the histogram have approximately equal heights, giving the histogram a rectangular appearance. This implies that the relative frequencies of all waiting times from zero to four minutes are about the same. Therefore, it is reasonable to use the *uniform distribution* to describe the random variable x, the amount of time a randomly selected hotel patron spends waiting for the elevator. In general, the equation that describes the uniform distribution is given in the following box, and this equation is graphed in Figure 5.2(a).

The Uniform Distribution

If c and d are numbers on the real line, the probability curve describing the **uniform distribution** is

$$f(x) = \begin{cases} \dfrac{1}{d - c} & \text{for } c \leq x \leq d \\ 0 & \text{otherwise} \end{cases}$$

Furthermore, the mean and the standard deviation of the population of all possible observed values of a random variable x that has a uniform distribution are

$$\mu_x = \frac{c + d}{2} \quad \text{and} \quad \sigma_x = \frac{d - c}{\sqrt{12}}$$

FIGURE 5.2 The Uniform Distribution

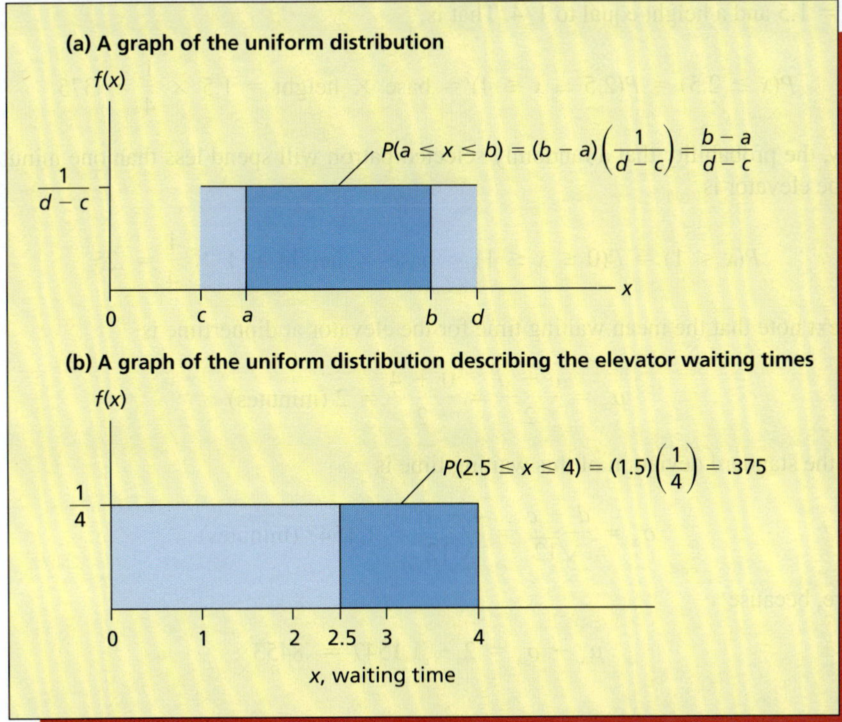

Notice that the total area under the uniform distribution is the area of a rectangle having a base equal to $(d - c)$ and a height equal to $1/(d - c)$. Therefore, the probability curve's total area is

$$\text{base} \times \text{height} = (d - c)\left(\frac{1}{d - c}\right) = 1$$

(remember that the total area under any continuous probability curve must equal 1). Furthermore, if a and b are numbers that are as illustrated in Figure 5.2(a), then the probability that x will be between a and b is the area of a rectangle with base $(b - a)$ and height $1/(d - c)$. That is,

$$\begin{aligned} P(a \leq x \leq b) &= \text{base} \times \text{height} \\ &= (b - a)\left(\frac{1}{d - c}\right) \\ &= \frac{b - a}{d - c} \end{aligned}$$

Example 5.1

In the introduction to this section we have said that the amount of time, x, that a randomly selected hotel patron spends waiting for the elevator at dinnertime is uniformly distributed between zero and four minutes. In this case, $c = 0$ and $d = 4$. Therefore,

$$f(x) = \begin{cases} \dfrac{1}{d - c} = \dfrac{1}{4 - 0} = \dfrac{1}{4} & \text{for } 0 \leq x \leq 4 \\ 0 & \text{otherwise} \end{cases}$$

Noting that this equation is graphed in Figure 5.2(b), suppose that the hotel manager wishes to find the probability that a randomly selected patron will spend at least 2.5 minutes waiting for the elevator. This probability is the area under the curve $f(x)$ that corresponds to the interval [2.5, 4]. As shown in Figure 5.2(b), this probability is the area of a rectangle having a base equal to $4 - 2.5 = 1.5$ and a height equal to $1/4$. That is,

$$P(x \geq 2.5) = P(2.5 \leq x \leq 4) = \text{base} \times \text{height} = 1.5 \times \frac{1}{4} = .375$$

Similarly, the probability that a randomly selected patron will spend less than one minute waiting for the elevator is

$$P(x < 1) = P(0 \leq x \leq 1) = \text{base} \times \text{height} = 1 \times \frac{1}{4} = .25$$

We next note that the mean waiting time for the elevator at dinnertime is

$$\mu_x = \frac{c + d}{2} = \frac{0 + 4}{2} = 2 \text{ (minutes)}$$

and that the standard deviation of this waiting time is

$$\sigma_x = \frac{d - c}{\sqrt{12}} = \frac{4 - 0}{\sqrt{12}} = 1.1547 \text{ (minutes)}$$

Therefore, because

$$\mu_x - \sigma_x = 2 - 1.1547 = .8453$$

and

$$\mu_x + \sigma_x = 2 + 1.1547 = 3.1547$$

the probability that the waiting time of a randomly selected patron will be within (plus or minus) one standard deviation of the mean waiting time is

$$P(.8453 \leq x \leq 3.1547) = (3.1547 - .8453) \times \frac{1}{4}$$
$$= .57735$$

Exercises for Sections 5.1 and 5.2

CONCEPTS

5.1 A discrete probability distribution assigns probabilities to individual values. To what are probabilities assigned by a continuous probability distribution?

5.2 How do we use the continuous probability distribution (or probability curve) of a random variable x to find probabilities? Explain.

5.3 What two properties must be satisfied by a continuous probability distribution (or probability curve)?

5.4 Explain the meaning of the height of a probability curve over a given point.

5.5 When is it appropriate to use the uniform distribution to describe a random variable x?

METHODS AND APPLICATIONS

5.6 Suppose that the random variable x has a uniform distribution with $c = 2$ and $d = 8$.

- **a** Write the formula for the probability curve of x, and write an interval that gives the possible values of x.
- **b** Graph the probability curve of x.
- **c** Find $P(3 \leq x \leq 5)$.
- **d** Find $P(1.5 \leq x \leq 6.5)$.
- **e** Calculate the mean μ_x, variance σ_x^2, and standard deviation σ_x.
- **f** Calculate the interval $[\mu_x \pm 2\sigma_x]$. What is the probability that x will be in this interval?

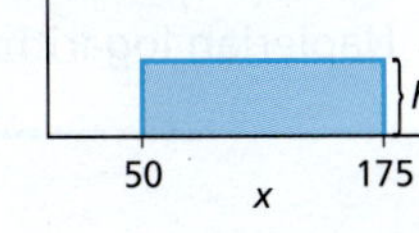

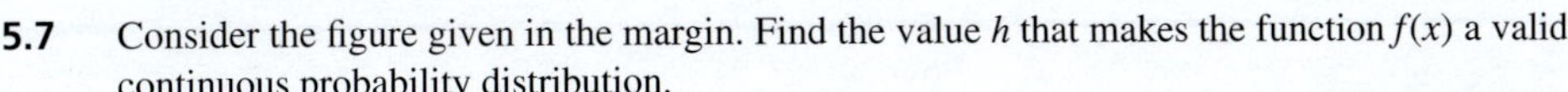

5.7 Consider the figure given in the margin. Find the value h that makes the function $f(x)$ a valid continuous probability distribution.

5.8 Assume that the waiting time x for an elevator is uniformly distributed between zero and six minutes.

- **a** Write the formula for the probability curve of x.
- **b** Graph the probability curve of x.
- **c** Find $P(2 \leq x \leq 4)$.
- **d** Find $P(3 \leq x \leq 6)$.
- **e** Find $P(\{0 \leq x \leq 2\} \text{ or } \{5 \leq x \leq 6\})$.

5.9 Refer to Exercise 5.8.

- **a** Calculate the mean, μ_x, the variance, σ_x^2, and the standard deviation, σ_x.
- **b** Find the probability that the waiting time of a randomly selected patron will be within one standard deviation of the mean.

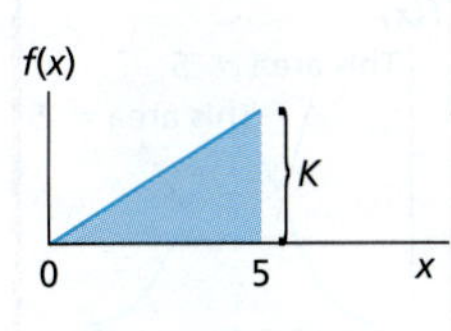

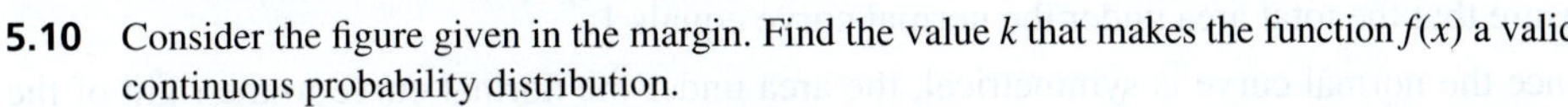

5.10 Consider the figure given in the margin. Find the value k that makes the function $f(x)$ a valid continuous probability distribution.

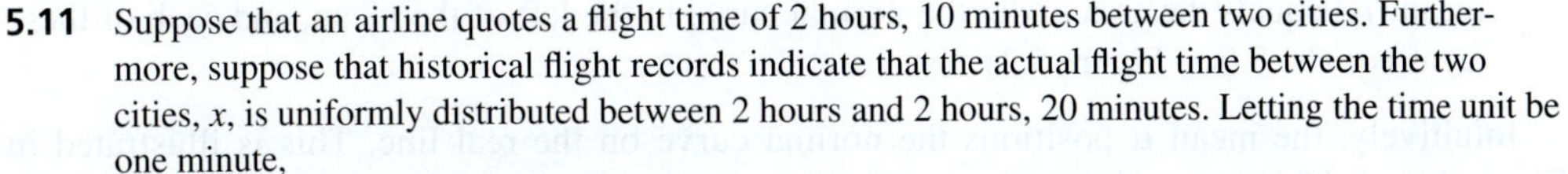

5.11 Suppose that an airline quotes a flight time of 2 hours, 10 minutes between two cities. Furthermore, suppose that historical flight records indicate that the actual flight time between the two cities, x, is uniformly distributed between 2 hours and 2 hours, 20 minutes. Letting the time unit be one minute,

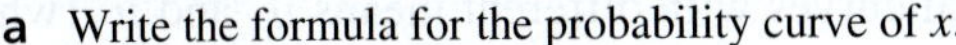

- **a** Write the formula for the probability curve of x.
- **b** Graph the probability curve of x.
- **c** Find $P(125 \leq x \leq 135)$
- **d** Find the probability that a randomly selected flight between the two cities will be at least five minutes late.

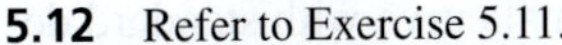

5.12 Refer to Exercise 5.11.

- **a** Calculate the mean flight time and the standard deviation of the flight time.
- **b** Find the probability that the flight time will be within one standard deviation of the mean.

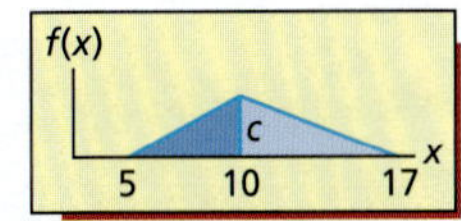

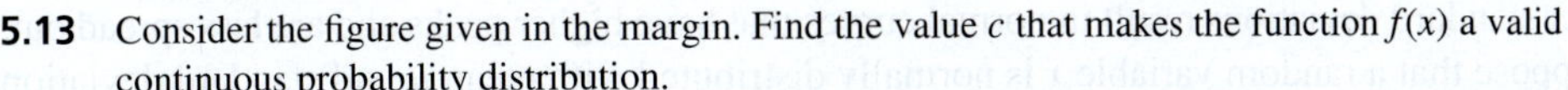

5.13 Consider the figure given in the margin. Find the value c that makes the function $f(x)$ a valid continuous probability distribution.

5.14 A weather forecaster predicts that the May rainfall in a local area will be between three and six inches but has no idea where within the interval the amount will be. Let x be the amount of May rainfall in the local area, and assume that x is uniformly distributed in the interval three to six inches.

a Write the formula for the probability curve of x.

b Graph the probability curve of x.

c What is the probability that May rainfall will be at least four inches? At least five inches? At most 4.5 inches?

5.15 Refer to Exercise 5.14.

a Calculate the expected May rainfall.

b What is the probability that the observed May rainfall will fall within two standard deviations of the mean? Within one standard deviation of the mean?

5.3 The Normal Probability Distribution

CHAPTER 5

The normal curve The bell-shaped appearance of the normal probability distribution is illustrated in Figure 5.3. The equation that defines this normal curve is given in the following box:

The Normal Probability Distribution

The **normal probability distribution** is defined by the equation

$$f(x) = \frac{1}{\sigma\sqrt{2\pi}} e^{-\frac{1}{2}\left(\frac{x-\mu}{\sigma}\right)^2} \quad \text{for all values of } x \text{ on the real line}$$

Here μ and σ are the mean and standard deviation of the population of all possible observed values of the random variable x under consideration. Furthermore, $\pi = 3.14159\ldots$, and $e = 2.71828\ldots$ is the base of Napierian logarithms.

FIGURE 5.3 The Normal Probability Curve

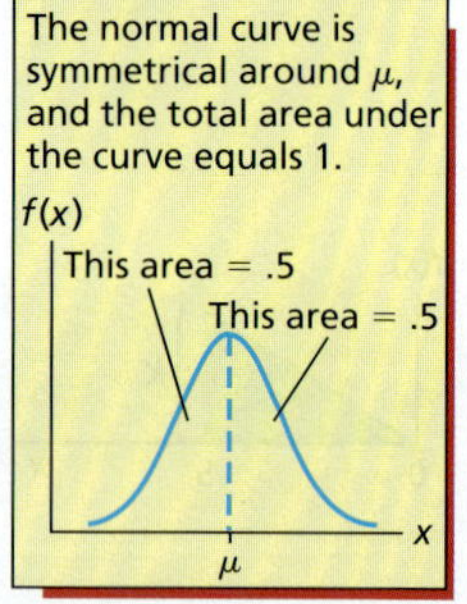
The normal curve is symmetrical around μ, and the total area under the curve equals 1.
f(x)
This area = .5
This area = .5
x
μ

The normal probability distribution has several important properties:

1 There is an entire family of normal probability distributions; the specific shape of each normal distribution is determined by its mean μ and its standard deviation σ.

2 The highest point on the normal curve is located at the mean, which is also the median and the mode of the distribution.

3 The normal distribution is symmetrical: The curve's shape to the left of the mean is the mirror image of its shape to the right of the mean.

4 The tails of the normal curve extend to infinity in both directions and never touch the horizontal axis. However, the tails get close enough to the horizontal axis quickly enough to ensure that the total area under the normal curve equals 1.

5 Since the normal curve is symmetrical, the area under the normal curve to the right of the mean (μ) equals the area under the normal curve to the left of the mean, and each of these areas equals .5 (see Figure 5.3).

Intuitively, the mean μ positions the normal curve on the real line. This is illustrated in Figure 5.4(a). This figure shows two normal curves with different means μ_1 and μ_2 (where μ_1 is greater than μ_2) and with equal standard deviations. We see that the normal curve with mean μ_1 is centered farther to the right.

The variance σ^2 (and the standard deviation σ) measure the spread of the normal curve. This is illustrated in Figure 5.4(b), which shows two normal curves with the same mean and two different standard deviations σ_1 and σ_2. Because σ_1 is greater than σ_2, the normal curve with standard deviation σ_1 is more spread out (flatter) than the normal curve with standard deviation σ_2. In general, larger standard deviations result in normal curves that are flatter and more spread out, while smaller standard deviations result in normal curves that have higher peaks and are less spread out.

Suppose that a random variable x is normally distributed with mean μ and standard deviation σ. If a and b are numbers on the real line, we consider the probability that x will attain a value

Figure 5.4 How the Mean μ and Standard Deviation σ Affect the Position and Shape of a Normal Probability Curve

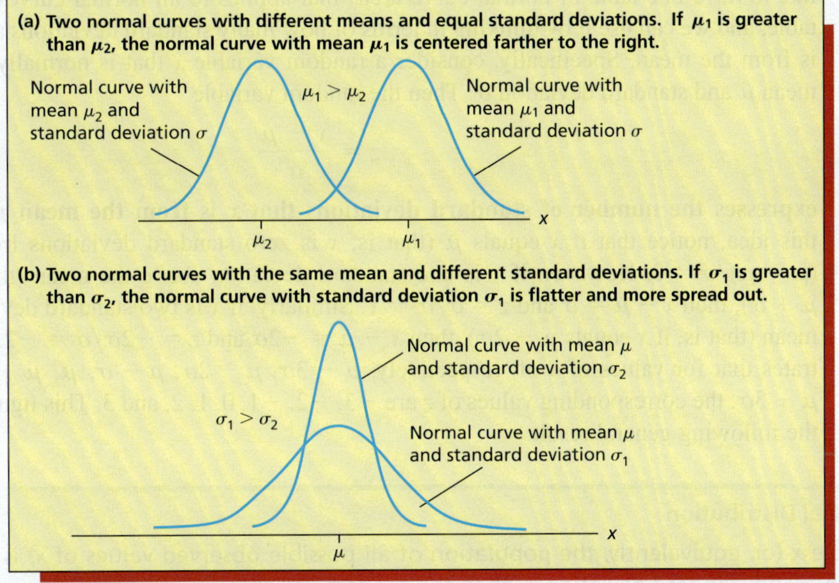
(a) Two normal curves with different means and equal standard deviations. If μ_1 is greater than μ_2, the normal curve with mean μ_1 is centered farther to the right.
Normal curve with mean μ_2 and standard deviation σ
$\mu_1 > \mu_2$
Normal curve with mean μ_1 and standard deviation σ
x
μ_2
μ_1
(b) Two normal curves with the same mean and different standard deviations. If σ_1 is greater than σ_2, the normal curve with standard deviation σ_1 is flatter and more spread out.
Normal curve with mean μ and standard deviation σ_2
$\sigma_1 > \sigma_2$
Normal curve with mean μ and standard deviation σ_1
x
μ

Figure 5.5 An Area under a Normal Curve Corresponding to the Interval [a, b]

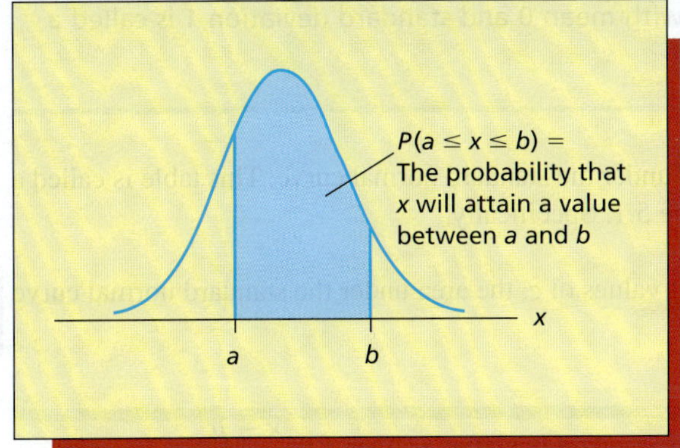
$P(a \le x \le b)$ = The probability that x will attain a value between a and b
x
a
b

Figure 5.6 Three Important Percentages Concerning a Normally Distributed Random Variable x with Mean μ and Standard Deviation σ

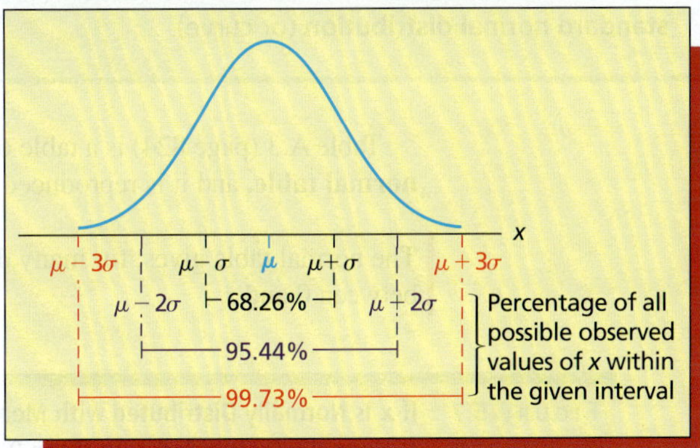
x
$\mu - 3\sigma$
$\mu - \sigma$
μ
$\mu + \sigma$
$\mu + 3\sigma$
$\mu - 2\sigma$
68.26%
$\mu + 2\sigma$
95.44%
99.73%
Percentage of all possible observed values of x within the given interval

between a and b. That is, we consider

$$P(a \le x \le b)$$

which equals the area under the normal curve with mean μ and standard deviation σ corresponding to the interval $[a, b]$. Such an area is depicted in Figure 5.5. We soon explain how to find such areas using a statistical table called a **normal table.** For now, we emphasize three important areas under a normal curve. These areas form the basis for the **Empirical Rule** for a normally distributed population (discussed on page 71). Specifically, if x is normally distributed with mean μ and standard deviation σ, it can be shown (using a normal table) that, as illustrated in Figure 5.6:

Three Important Areas under the Normal Curve

1. $P(\mu - \sigma \le x \le \mu + \sigma) = .6826$

   This means that 68.26 percent of all possible observed values of x are within (plus or minus) one standard deviation of μ.

2. $P(\mu - 2\sigma \le x \le \mu + 2\sigma) = .9544$

   This means that 95.44 percent of all possible observed values of x are within (plus or minus) two standard deviations of μ.

3. $P(\mu - 3\sigma \le x \le \mu + 3\sigma) = .9973$

   This means that 99.73 percent of all possible observed values of x are within (plus or minus) three standard deviations of μ.

Finding normal curve areas There is a unique normal curve for every combination of μ and σ. Since there are many (theoretically, an unlimited number of) such combinations, we would like to have one table of normal curve areas that applies to all normal curves. There is such a table, and we can use it by thinking in terms of how many standard deviations a value of interest is from the mean. Specifically, consider a random variable x that is normally distributed with mean μ and standard deviation σ. Then the random variable

$$z = \frac{x - \mu}{\sigma}$$

expresses the number of standard deviations that x is from the mean μ. To understand this idea, notice that if x equals μ (that is, x is zero standard deviations from μ), then $z = (\mu - \mu)/\sigma = 0$. However, if x is one standard deviation above the mean (that is, if x equals $\mu + \sigma$), then $x - \mu = \sigma$ and $z = \sigma/\sigma = 1$. Similarly, if x is two standard deviations below the mean (that is, if x equals $\mu - 2\sigma$), then $x - \mu = -2\sigma$ and $z = -2\sigma/\sigma = -2$. Figure 5.7 illustrates that for values of x of, respectively, $\mu - 3\sigma$, $\mu - 2\sigma$, $\mu - \sigma$, μ, $\mu + \sigma$, $\mu + 2\sigma$, and $\mu + 3\sigma$, the corresponding values of z are -3, -2, -1, 0, 1, 2, and 3. This figure also illustrates the following general result:

The Standard Normal Distribution

If a random variable x (or, equivalently, the population of all possible observed values of x) is normally distributed with mean μ and standard deviation σ, then the random variable

$$z = \frac{x - \mu}{\sigma}$$

(or, equivalently, the population of all possible observed values of z) is normally distributed with mean 0 and standard deviation 1. A normal distribution (or curve) with mean 0 and standard deviation 1 is called a **standard normal distribution** (or curve).

Table A.3 (page 824) is a table of areas under the standard normal curve. This table is called a **normal table,** and it is reproduced in Table 5.1. Specifically,

> The normal table gives, for many different values of z, the area under the standard normal curve between 0 and z.

FIGURE 5.7 If x Is Normally Distributed with Mean μ and Standard Deviation σ, Then $z = \frac{x - \mu}{\sigma}$ Is Normally Distributed with Mean 0 and Standard Deviation 1

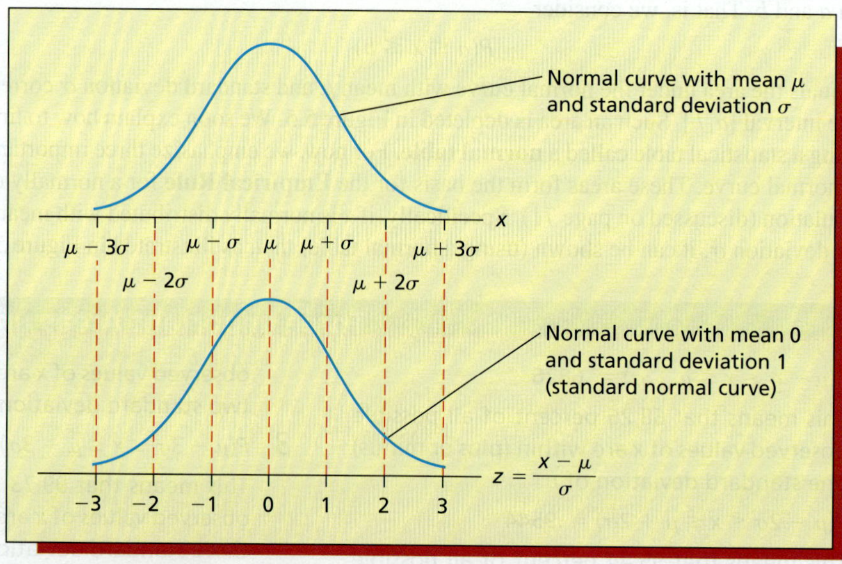

TABLE 5.1 A Table of Areas under the Standard Normal Curve

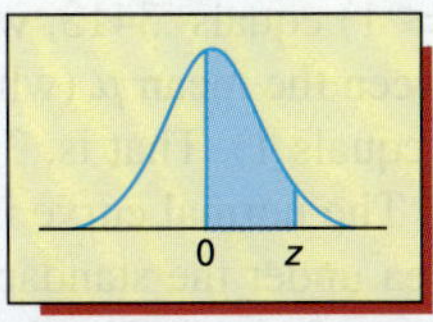

z	.00	.01	.02	.03	.04	.05	.06	.07	.08	.09
0.0	.0000	.0040	.0080	.0120	.0160	.0199	.0239	.0279	.0319	.0359
0.1	.0398	.0438	.0478	.0517	.0557	.0596	.0636	.0675	.0714	.0753
0.2	.0793	.0832	.0871	.0910	.0948	.0987	.1026	.1064	.1103	.1141
0.3	.1179	.1217	.1255	.1293	.1331	.1368	.1406	.1443	.1480	.1517
0.4	.1554	.1591	.1628	.1664	.1700	.1736	.1772	.1808	.1844	.1879
0.5	.1915	.1950	.1985	.2019	.2054	.2088	.2123	.2157	.2190	.2224
0.6	.2257	.2291	.2324	.2357	.2389	.2422	.2454	.2486	.2517	.2549
0.7	.2580	.2611	.2642	.2673	.2704	.2734	.2764	.2794	.2823	.2852
0.8	.2881	.2910	.2939	.2967	.2995	.3023	.3051	.3078	.3106	.3133
0.9	.3159	.3186	.3212	.3238	.3264	.3289	.3315	.3340	.3365	.3389
1.0	.3413	.3438	.3461	.3485	.3508	.3531	.3554	.3577	.3599	.3621
1.1	.3643	.3665	.3686	.3708	.3729	.3749	.3770	.3790	.3810	.3830
1.2	.3849	.3869	.3888	.3907	.3925	.3944	.3962	.3980	.3997	.4015
1.3	.4032	.4049	.4066	.4082	.4099	.4115	.4131	.4147	.4162	.4177
1.4	.4192	.4207	.4222	.4236	.4251	.4265	.4279	.4292	.4306	.4319
1.5	.4332	.4345	.4357	.4370	.4382	.4394	.4406	.4418	.4429	.4441
1.6	.4452	.4463	.4474	.4484	.4495	.4505	.4515	.4525	.4535	.4545
1.7	.4554	.4564	.4573	.4582	.4591	.4599	.4608	.4616	.4625	.4633
1.8	.4641	.4649	.4656	.4664	.4671	.4678	.4686	.4693	.4699	.4706
1.9	.4713	.4719	.4726	.4732	.4738	.4744	.4750	.4756	.4761	.4767
2.0	.4772	.4778	.4783	.4788	.4793	.4798	.4803	.4808	.4812	.4817
2.1	.4821	.4826	.4830	.4834	.4838	.4842	.4846	.4850	.4854	.4857
2.2	.4861	.4864	.4868	.4871	.4875	.4878	.4881	.4884	.4887	.4890
2.3	.4893	.4896	.4898	.4901	.4904	.4906	.4909	.4911	.4913	.4916
2.4	.4918	.4920	.4922	.4925	.4927	.4929	.4931	.4932	.4934	.4936
2.5	.4938	.4940	.4941	.4943	.4945	.4946	.4948	.4949	.4951	.4952
2.6	.4953	.4955	.4956	.4957	.4959	.4960	.4961	.4962	.4963	.4964
2.7	.4965	.4966	.4967	.4968	.4969	.4970	.4971	.4972	.4973	.4974
2.8	.4974	.4975	.4976	.4977	.4977	.4978	.4979	.4979	.4980	.4981
2.9	.4981	.4982	.4982	.4983	.4984	.4984	.4985	.4985	.4986	.4986
3.0	.4987	.4987	.4987	.4988	.4988	.4989	.4989	.4989	.4990	.4990

Such an area is the shaded area in the figure at the top of Table 5.1. The values of z in the table range from 0.00 to 3.09 in increments of .01. As can be seen from Table 5.1, values of z accurate to the nearest tenth (0.0, 0.1, 0.2, . . . , 2.9, 3.0) are given in the far left column (headed z) of the table. Further graduations to the nearest hundredth (.00, .01, .02, . . . , .09) are given across the top of the table. The areas under the normal curve are given in the body of the table, accurate to four decimal places.

As a first example, suppose that we wish to find the area under the standard normal curve between 0 and 1. In order to find this area, we must find the area in the normal table corresponding to a z value of 1.00. Looking at Table 5.1, we first scan down the far left column of the table (starting at the top) until we find the value 1.0. Having found this value, we now scan across the row in the table corresponding to the z value 1.0 until we find the column in the table corresponding to .00. The desired area is in the row corresponding to the z value 1.0 and in the column headed .00. We see that this area equals .3413 (we have shaded it), and we illustrate this area in Figure 5.8. The area under the standard normal curve between 0 and 1 is the probability that the random variable z will be between 0 and 1. That is, we have found that

$$P(0 \leq z \leq 1) = .3413$$

FIGURE 5.8 The Area under the Standard Normal Curve between 0 and 1 Equals .3413; That Is, $P(0 \leq z \leq 1) = .3413$

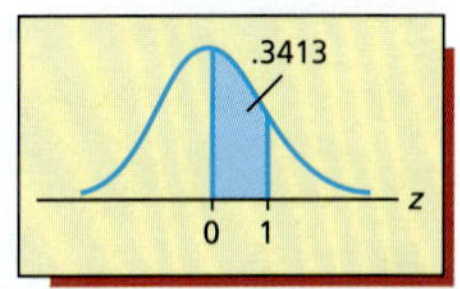

Next, suppose that a random variable x is normally distributed with mean μ and standard deviation σ, and remember that z is the number of standard deviations σ that x is from μ. It follows that, when we say that $P(0 \le z \le 1)$ equals .3413, we are saying that 34.13 percent of all possible observed values of x are between the mean μ (where z equals 0) and a point that is one standard deviation above μ (where z equals 1). That is, 34.13 percent of all possible observed values of x are between μ and $\mu + \sigma$. The normal curve in Figure 5.9(a) illustrates that, by the symmetry of the normal curve, the area under the standard normal curve between -1 and 0 is equal to the area under this curve between 0 and 1. That is,

$$P(-1 \le z \le 0) = P(0 \le z \le 1) = .3413$$

This says that 34.13 percent of all possible observed values of x are between $\mu - \sigma$ and μ. If we add the two areas in Figure 5.9(a), we have

$$P(-1 \le z \le 1) = .3413 + .3413 = .6826$$

That is, 68.26 percent of all possible observed values of x are within (plus or minus) one standard deviation of the mean μ. Similarly, if we look up the z value 2.00 in the normal table, we find that $P(0 \le z \le 2) = .4772$. This implies, as illustrated in Figure 5.9(b), that $P(-2 \le z \le 2) = .4772 + .4772 = .9544$. In other words, 95.44 percent of all possible observed values of x are within (plus or minus) two standard deviations of μ. Furthermore, if we look up the z value 3.00 in the normal table, we find that $P(0 \le z \le 3) = .4987$. This implies, as illustrated in Figure 5.9(c), that $P(-3 \le z \le 3) = .4987 + .4987 = .9974$. Actually, the probability .4987 in Table 5.1 is rounded slightly, and a more precise calculation shows that $P(-3 \le z \le 3)$ is actually closer to .9973. This says that 99.73 percent of all possible observed values of x are within (plus or minus) three standard deviations of the mean μ.

As a final example of this kind of area, consider finding the area under the standard normal curve between 0 and 2.53. There is nothing special about this area, but we want to demonstrate using the normal table when the needed z value does not end in .00. To look up this area, we locate the area in the normal table in the row corresponding to 2.5 and in the column headed by .03. This area is .4943 (we have shaded it in Table 5.1), which implies that $P(0 \le z \le 2.53) = .4943$. This

FIGURE 5.9 Some Areas under the Standard Normal Curve

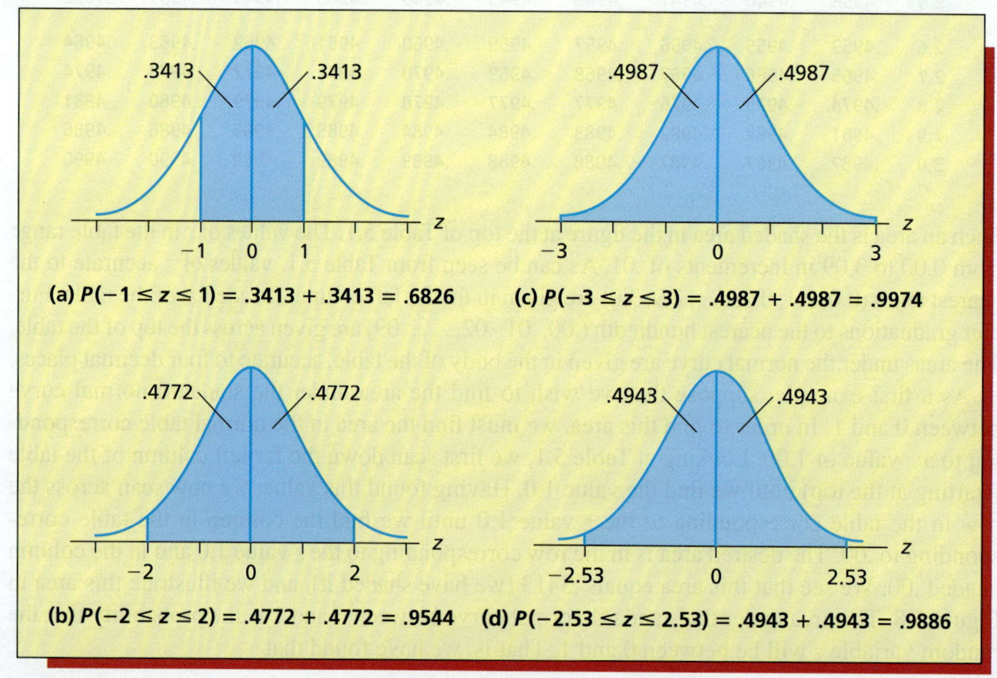

FIGURE 5.10 Calculating $P(z \leq 1)$

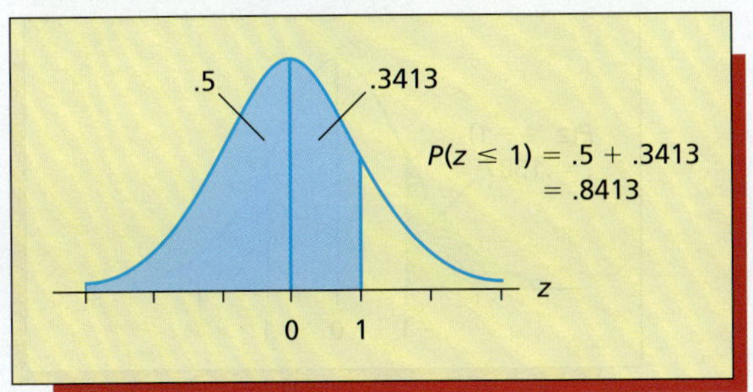

FIGURE 5.11 Calculating $P(z \geq -1)$

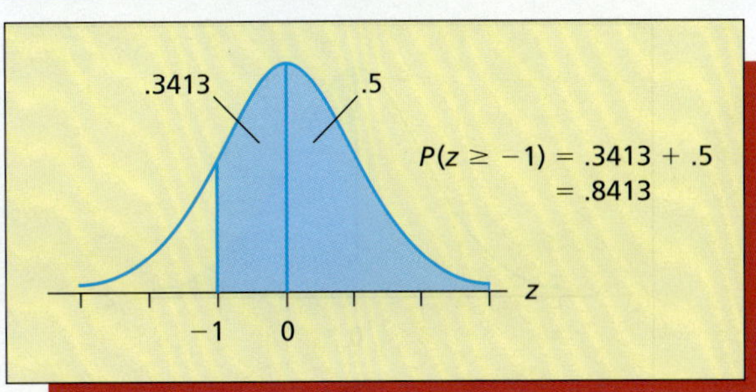

implies, as illustrated in Figure 5.9(d), that $P(-2.53 \leq z \leq 2.53) = .4943 + .4943 = .9886$. In other words, 98.86 percent of all possible observed values of x are within (plus or minus) 2.53 standard deviations of the mean μ.

Before continuing, recall that there is no area under a continuous probability curve at a single value of a random variable. Because the standard normal curve is a continuous probability curve, it follows, for example, that $P(-2.53 \leq z \leq 2.53)$ equals $P(-2.53 < z < 2.53)$. Keep this idea in mind as we continue through this section.

Thus far we have shown how to find **the area under the standard normal curve between 0 and a positive z value,** which, by the symmetry of the curve, **equals the area under the curve between 0 and the corresponding negative z value.** We now show how to find some other areas that will be important in later sections.

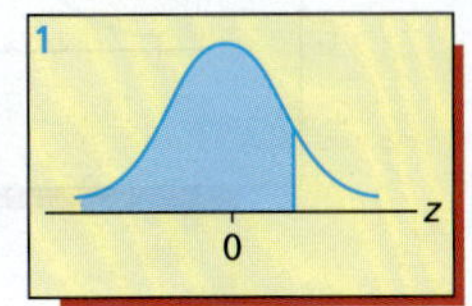

1 **The area under the standard normal curve to the left of a positive z value:** Suppose that we want to find the area under the standard normal curve to the left of the z value 1. As illustrated in Figure 5.10, this is the area under the curve between 0 and 1, which the normal table tells us is .3413, plus the area under the curve to the left of 0 (the mean), which is .5. Therefore, $P(z \leq 1) = .5 + .3413 = .8413$.

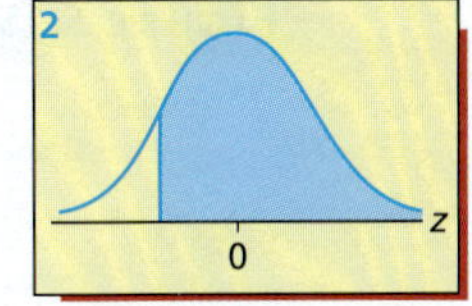

2 **The area under the standard normal curve to the right of a negative z value:** As illustrated in Figure 5.11, the area under the standard normal curve to the right of the z value -1 is $P(z \geq -1) = .3413 + .5 = .8413$.

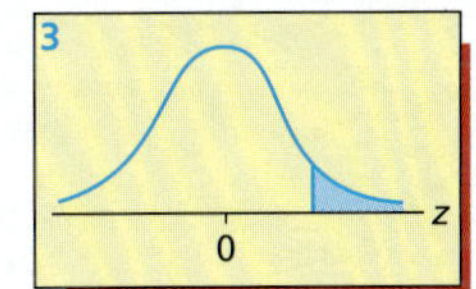

3 **The area under the standard normal curve to the right of a positive z value—a right-hand tail area:** Consider finding the area under the standard normal curve to the right of the z value 1. As illustrated in Figure 5.12, this is the area under the curve to the right of 0, which is .5, minus the area under the curve between 0 and 1, which the normal table tells us is .3413. Therefore, $P(z \geq 1) = .5 - .3413 = .1587$.

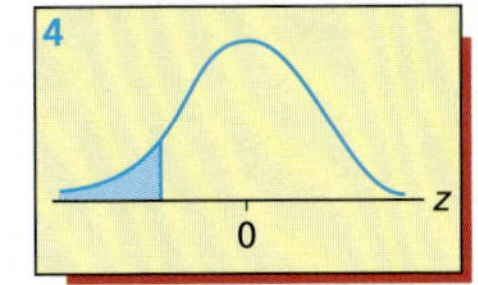

4 **The area under the standard normal curve to the left of a negative z value—a left-hand tail area:** As illustrated in Figure 5.13, the symmetry of the standard normal curve implies that the area under the standard normal curve to the left of the z value -1 equals the area under this curve to the right of the z value 1. That is, $P(z \leq -1)$ equals $P(z \geq 1)$. Therefore, $P(z \leq -1) = .5 - .3413 = .1587$.

5 **Right-hand tail areas corresponding to z values greater than 3.09, and left-hand tail areas corresponding to z values less than -3.09:** The largest z value in the normal table is 3.09. Because the area under the standard normal curve between 0 and 3.09 is .499, the area under this curve to the right of 3.09 is $.5 - .499 = .001$ (see Figure 5.14). Therefore, if we wish to find the area under the standard normal curve to the right of any z value greater than 3.09, the most we can say (without using a computer) is that this area is less than .001. Similarly, the area under the standard normal curve to the left of any z value less than -3.09 is also less than .001.

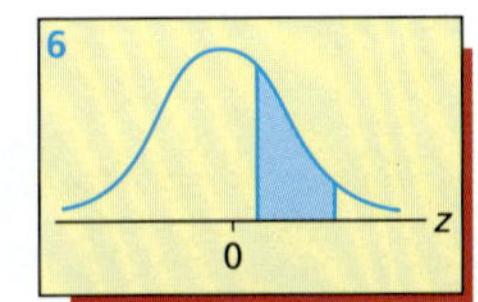

6 **The area under the standard normal curve between two positive z values:** Consider finding the area under the standard normal curve between 1 and 2. As illustrated in Figure 5.15(a), this area equals the area under the curve between 0 and 2, which the normal table tells us

FIGURE 5.12 Calculating $P(z \geq 1)$

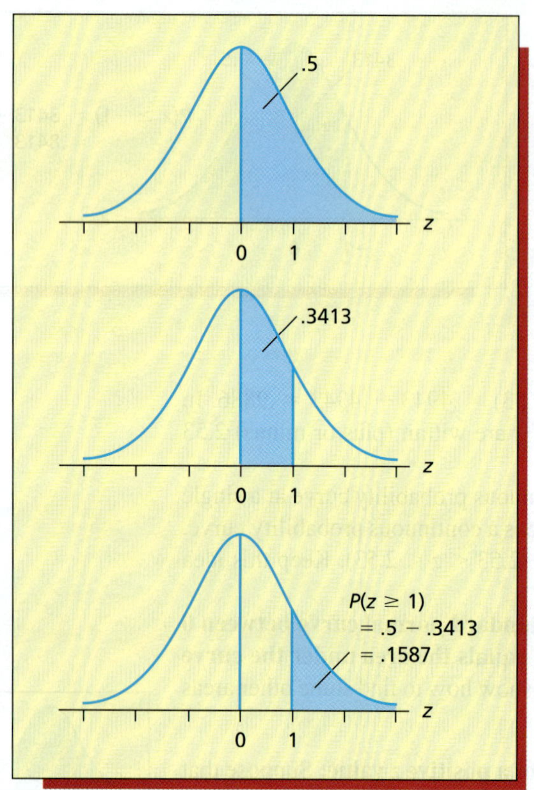

FIGURE 5.13 Calculating $P(z \leq -1)$

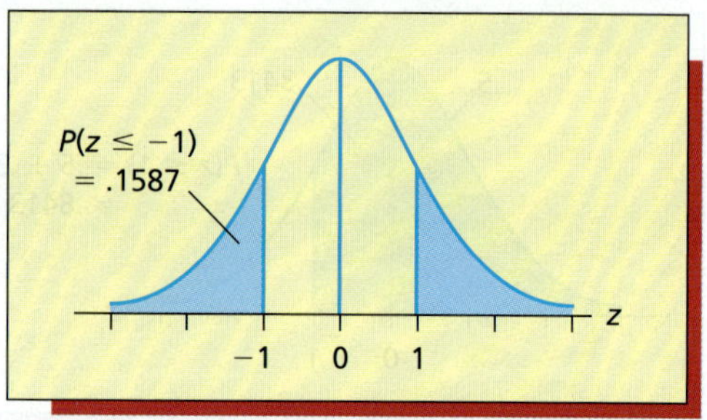

FIGURE 5.14 Calculating $P(z \geq 3.09)$

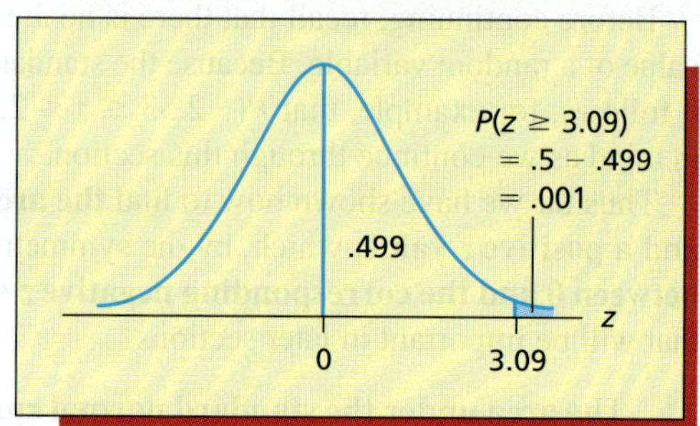

FIGURE 5.15 Calculating $P(1 \leq z \leq 2)$ and $P(-2 \leq z \leq -1)$

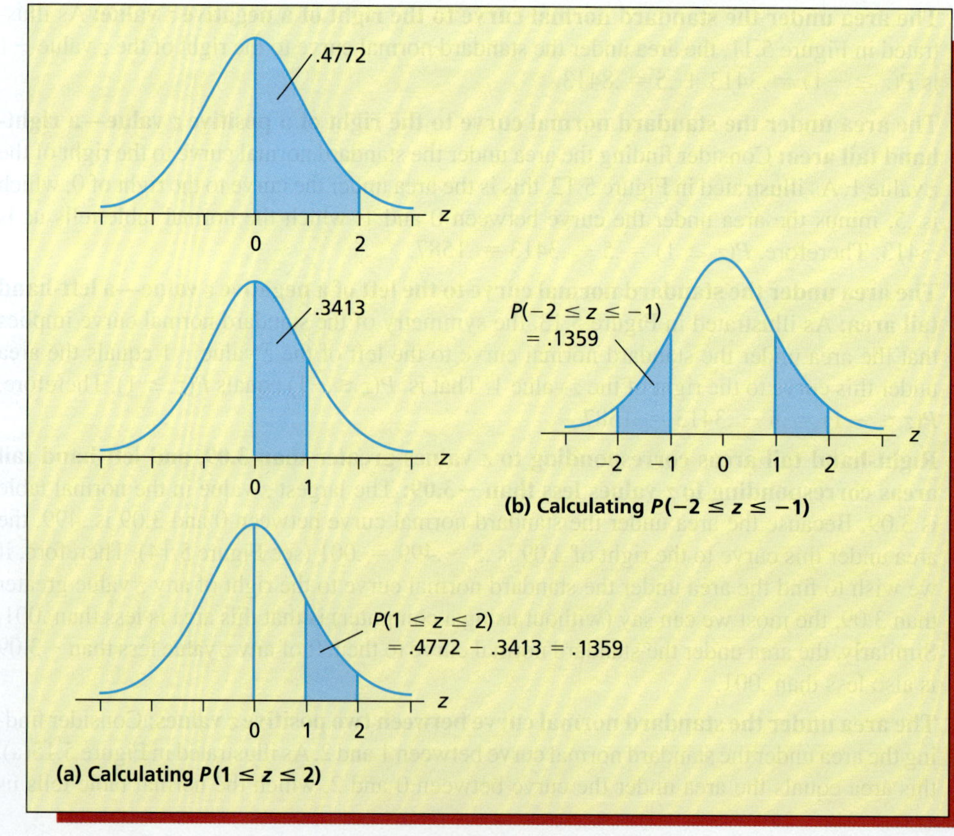

is .4772, minus the area under the curve between 0 and 1, which the normal table tells us is .3413. Therefore, $P(1 \le z \le 2) = .4772 - .3413 = .1359$.

7 **The area under the standard normal curve between two negative z values:** As illustrated in Figure 5.15(b), the symmetry of the normal curve implies that the area under the standard normal curve between -2 and -1 equals the area under this curve between 1 and 2. That is, $P(-2 \le z \le -1)$ equals $P(1 \le z \le 2)$. Therefore, $P(-2 \le z \le -1) = .4772 - .3413 = .1359$.

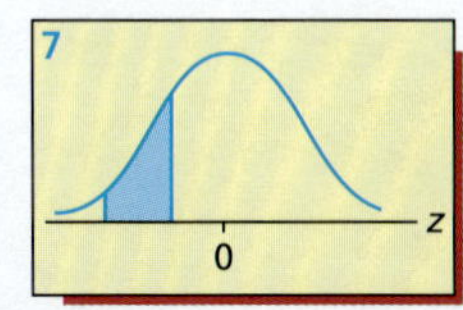

Some practical applications We have seen how to use z values and the normal table to find areas under the standard normal curve. However, most practical problems are not stated in such terms. We now consider an example in which we must restate the problem in terms of the standard normal random variable z before using the normal table.

Example 5.2 The Car Mileage Case

C

Recall from Chapters 1 and 2 that an automaker has recently introduced a new midsize model and that we have used the sample of 49 mileages to estimate that the population of mileages of all cars of this type is normally distributed with a mean mileage equal to 31.5531 mpg and a standard deviation equal to .7992 mpg. Suppose that a competing automaker produces a midsize model that is somewhat smaller and less powerful than the new midsize model. The competitor claims, however, that its midsize model gets better mileages. Specifically, the competitor claims that the mileages of all its midsize cars are normally distributed with a mean mileage μ equal to 33 mpg and a standard deviation σ equal to .7 mpg. In the next example we consider one way to investigate the validity of this claim. In this example we assume that the claim is true, and we calculate the probability that the mileage, x, of a randomly selected competing midsize car will be between 32 mpg and 35 mpg. That is, we wish to find $P(32 \le x \le 35)$. As illustrated in Figure 5.16(a), this probability is the area between 32 and 35 under the normal curve having mean $\mu = 33$ and standard deviation $\sigma = .7$. In order to use the normal table, we must restate the problem in terms of the standard normal random variable z. The z value corresponding to 32 is

$$z = \frac{x - \mu}{\sigma} = \frac{32 - 33}{.7} = \frac{-1}{.7} = -1.43$$

which says that the mileage 32 is 1.43 standard deviations below the mean $\mu = 33$. The z value corresponding to 35 is

$$z = \frac{x - \mu}{\sigma} = \frac{35 - 33}{.7} = \frac{2}{.7} = 2.86$$

which says that the mileage 35 is 2.86 standard deviations above the mean $\mu = 33$. Looking at Figure 5.16(a), we see that the area between 32 and 35 under the normal curve having mean $\mu = 33$ and standard deviation $\sigma = .7$ equals the area between -1.43 and 2.86 under the standard normal curve. This equals the area between -1.43 and 0 plus the area between 0 and 2.86. The normal table tells us that the area between -1.43 and 0, which equals the area between 0 and 1.43, is .4236. The normal table also tells us that the area between 0 and 2.86 is .4979. It follows that the probability we seek is $.4236 + .4979 = .9215$. We can summarize this result as follows:

$$\begin{aligned} P(32 \le x \le 35) &= P\left(\frac{32 - 33}{.7} \le \frac{x - \mu}{\sigma} \le \frac{35 - 33}{.7}\right) \\ &= P(-1.43 \le z \le 2.86) = .4236 + .4979 = .9215 \end{aligned}$$

This probability says that, if the competing automaker's claim is valid, then 92.15 percent of all of its midsize cars will get mileages between 32 mpg and 35 mpg.

In addition to using the normal table, we can find areas under the normal curve by using MINITAB, Excel, and MegaStat. We can also obtain simulated observations from a normal

FIGURE 5.16 **Illustrating the Results of Example 5.2**

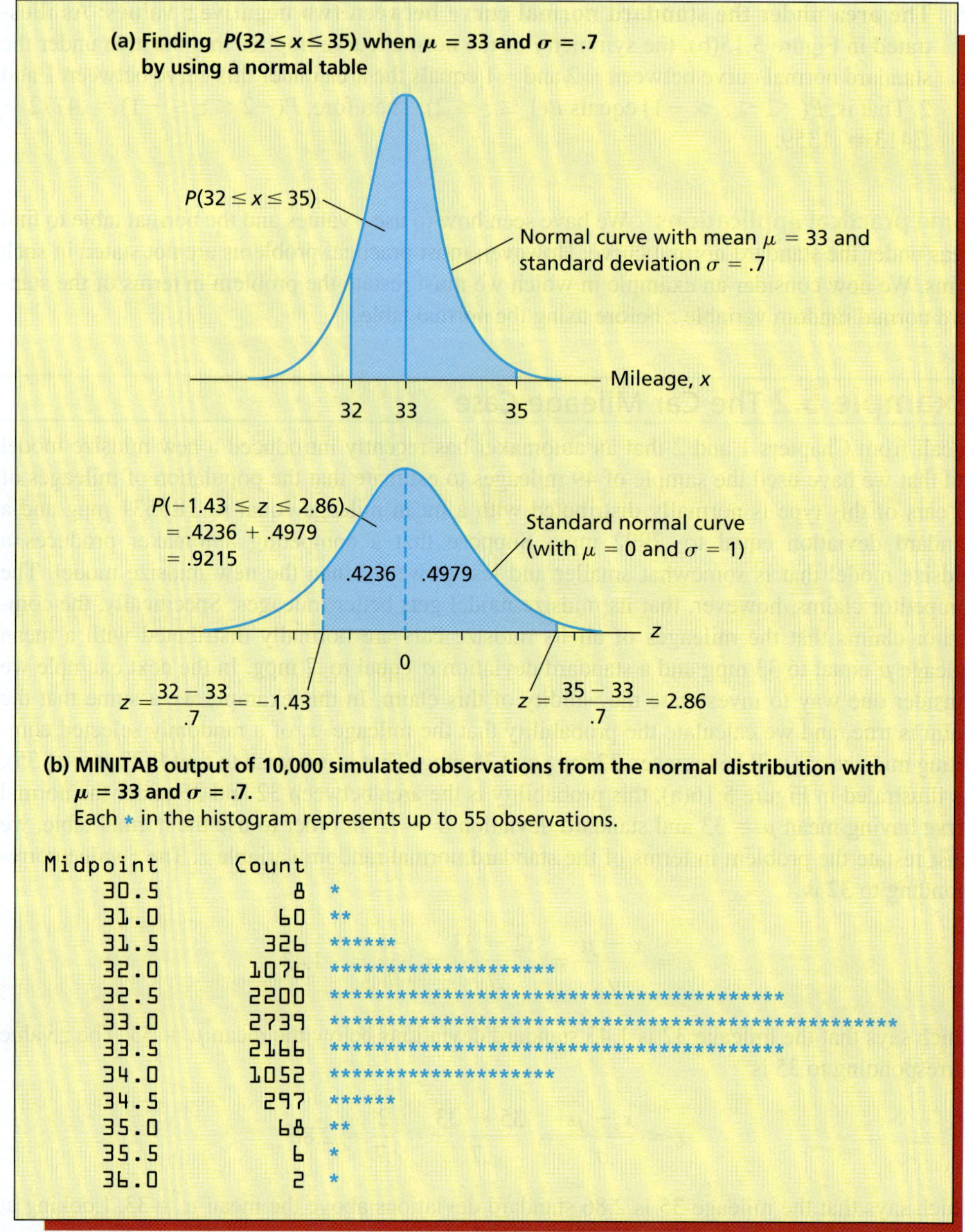


```
Midpoint    Count
    30.5        8  *
    31.0       60  **
    31.5      326  ******
    32.0     1076  ********************
    32.5     2200  ****************************************
    33.0     2739  **************************************************
    33.5     2166  ****************************************
    34.0     1052  ********************
    34.5      297  ******
    35.0       68  **
    35.5        6  *
    36.0        2  *
```

distribution. For instance, Figure 5.16(b) gives the MINITAB output of a histogram of 10,000 simulated mileages obtained from a normally distributed population of mileages having mean $\mu = 33$ mpg and standard deviation $\sigma = .7$ mpg. Looking at this figure, we see that, if we assume that 50 percent of the observed mileages in the class with midpoint 32.0 are above 32.0, and if we assume that 50 percent of the observed mileages in the class with midpoint 35.0 are below 35.0, then the fraction of simulated mileages between 32 mpg and 35 mpg is

$$(1{,}076/2 + 2{,}200 + 2{,}739 + 2{,}166 + 1{,}052 + 297 + 68/2) \div 10{,}000 = .9026$$

This fraction is quite close to the fraction (.9215) we calculated by using the normal table.

Example 5.2 illustrates the general procedure for finding a probability about a normally distributed random variable x. We summarize this procedure in the following box:

Finding Normal Probabilities

1. Formulate the problem in terms of the random variable x.
2. Calculate relevant z values and restate the problem in terms of the standard normal random variable

$$z = \frac{x - \mu}{\sigma}$$

3. Find the required area under the standard normal curve by using the normal table.
4. Note that it is always useful to draw a picture illustrating the needed area before using the normal table.

Example 5.3 The Car Mileage Case

C

Recall from Example 5.2 that the competing automaker claims that the population of mileages of all its midsize cars is normally distributed with mean $\mu = 33$ and standard deviation $\sigma = .7$. Suppose that an independent testing agency randomly selects one of these cars and finds that it gets a mileage of 31.2 mpg when tested as prescribed by the EPA. Because the sample mileage of 31.2 mpg is *less than* the claimed mean $\mu = 33$, we have some evidence that contradicts the competing automaker's claim. To evaluate the strength of this evidence, we will calculate the probability that the mileage, x, of a randomly selected midsize car would be *less than or equal to* 31.2 if, in fact, the competing automaker's claim is true. To calculate $P(x \leq 31.2)$ under the assumption that the claim is true, we find the area to the left of 31.2 under the normal curve with mean $\mu = 33$ and standard deviation $\sigma = .7$ (see Figure 5.17). In order to use the normal table, we must find the z value corresponding to 31.2. This z value is

$$z = \frac{x - \mu}{\sigma} = \frac{31.2 - 33}{.7} = -2.57$$

which says that the mileage 31.2 is 2.57 standard deviations below the mean mileage $\mu = 33$. Looking at Figure 5.17, we see that the area to the left of 31.2 under the normal curve having mean $\mu = 33$ and standard deviation $\sigma = .7$ equals the area to the left of -2.57 under the standard normal curve. This area under the standard normal curve is the area to the left of 0, which is .5, minus the area between -2.57 and 0, which the normal table tells us is .4949. It follows that the needed

FIGURE 5.17 Finding $P(x \leq 31.2)$ When $\mu = 33$ and $\sigma = .7$ by Using a Normal Table

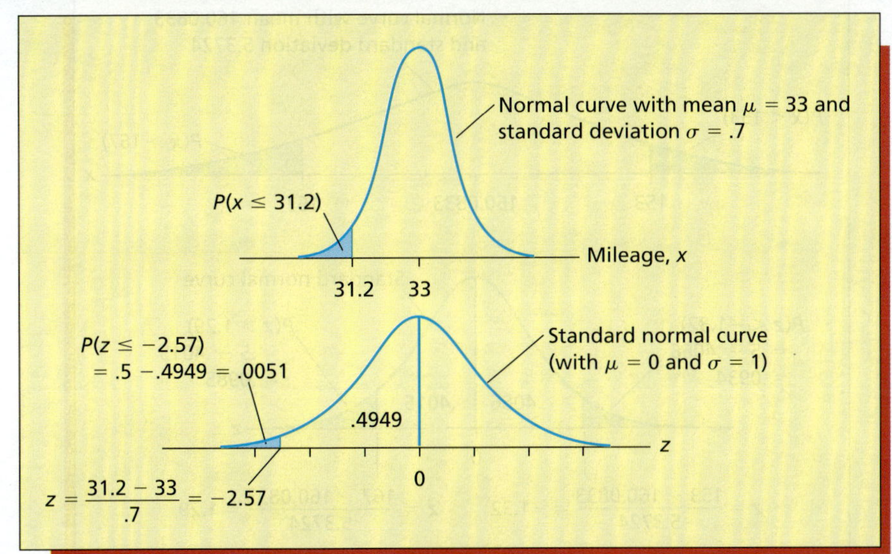

area equals $.5 - .4949 = .0051$. This is illustrated in Figure 5.17. We can summarize our calculations as follows:

$$P(x \leq 31.2) = P\left(\frac{x - \mu}{\sigma} \leq \frac{31.2 - 33}{.7}\right)$$
$$= P(z \leq -2.57) = .5 - .4949 = .0051$$

This probability says that, if the competing automaker's claim is valid, then only 51 in 10,000 cars would obtain a mileage of less than or equal to 31.2 mpg. Since it is very difficult to believe that a 51 in 10,000 chance has occurred, we have very strong evidence against the competing automaker's claim. It is probably true that μ is less than 33 and/or σ is greater than .7 and/or the population of all mileages is not normally distributed.

Example 5.4 The Coffee Temperature Case

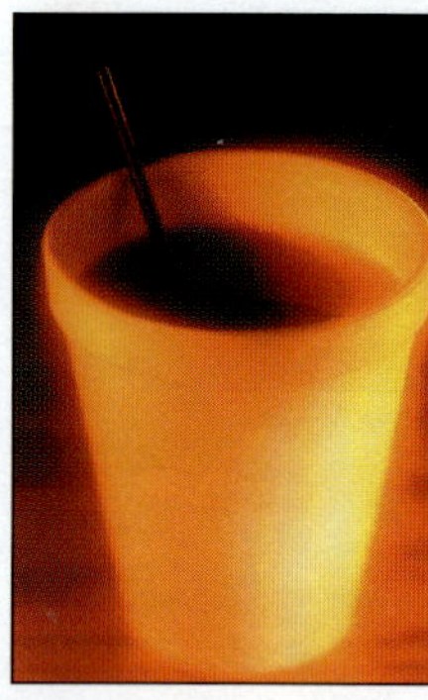

Recall that the runs plot and histogram of the sample of 24 coffee temperatures indicate that the coffee-making process is in statistical control and that the population of all coffee temperatures is normally distributed. Also recall that customer requirements state that each cup of coffee should have a temperature between 153° and 167°. The mean and standard deviation of the sample of 24 coffee temperatures are $\bar{x} = 160.0833$ and $s = 5.3724$. Using $\bar{x}$ and s as point estimates of the population mean μ and population standard deviation σ, we want to calculate the probability that x, the temperature of a randomly selected cup of coffee, is outside the requirements (that is, less than 153° or greater than 167°). In order to compute the probability $P(x < 153$ or $x > 167)$ we compute the z values

$$z = \frac{153 - 160.0833}{5.3724} = -1.32 \quad \text{and} \quad z = \frac{167 - 160.0833}{5.3724} = 1.29$$

Because the events $\{x < 153\}$ and $\{x > 167\}$ are mutually exclusive, we have

$$P(x < 153 \text{ or } x > 167) = P(x < 153) + P(x > 167)$$
$$= P(z < -1.32) + P(z > 1.29)$$
$$= (.5 - .4066) + (.5 - .4015)$$
$$= .0934 + .0985 = .1919$$

This calculation is illustrated in Figure 5.18. The probability of .1919 says that 19.19 percent of the coffee temperatures do not meet customer requirements. Therefore, if management believes that meeting this requirement is important, the coffee-making process must be improved.

FIGURE 5.18 Finding $P(x < 153$ or $x > 167)$ in the Coffee Temperature Case

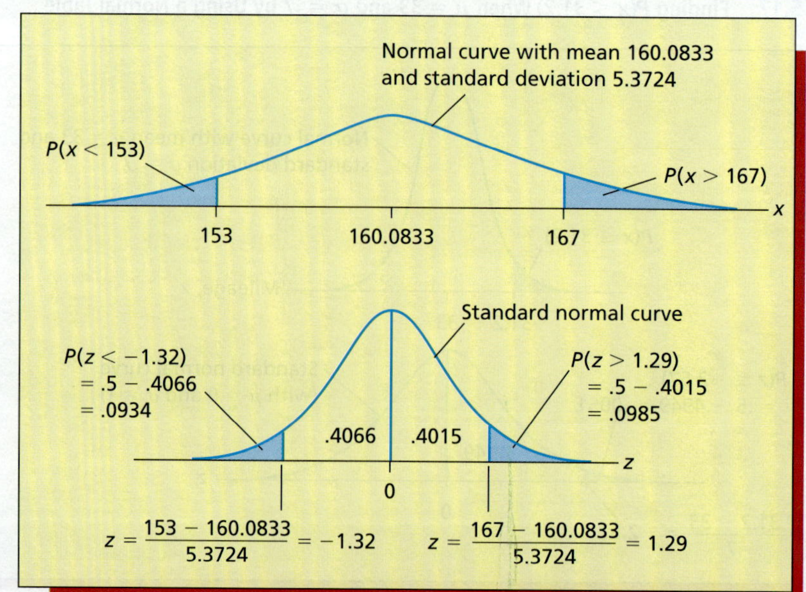

FIGURE 5.19 The Point $z_{.025} = 1.96$

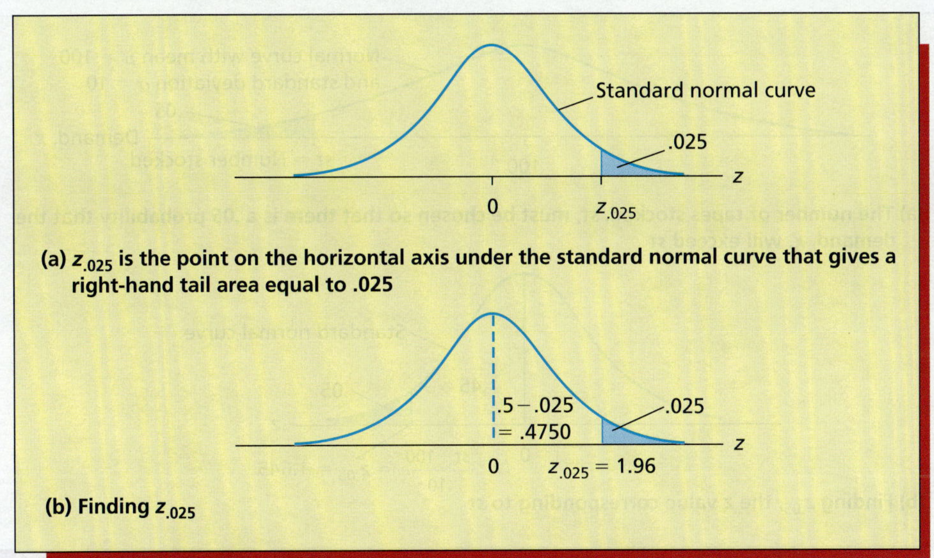
Standard normal curve
.025
z
0
z.025
(a) z.025 is the point on the horizontal axis under the standard normal curve that gives a right-hand tail area equal to .025
.5 − .025
= .4750
.025
z
0
z.025 = 1.96
(b) Finding z.025

Finding a point on the horizontal axis under a normal curve In order to use many of the formulas given in later chapters, we must be able to find the z value so that the tail area to the right of z under the standard normal curve is a particular value. For instance, we might need to find the z value so that the tail area to the right of z under the standard normal curve is .025. This z value is denoted $z_{.025}$, and we illustrate $z_{.025}$ in Figure 5.19(a). We refer to $z_{.025}$ as **the point on the horizontal axis under the standard normal curve that gives a right-hand tail area equal to .025.** It is easy to use a normal table to find such a z point. For instance, in order to find $z_{.025}$, we note from Figure 5.19(b) that the area under the standard normal curve between 0 and $z_{.025}$ equals $.5 - .025 = .4750$. Remembering that areas under the standard normal curve between 0 and z are the four-digit numbers given in the body of a normal table, we scan the body of the table and find the area .4750. We have shaded this area in Table 5.1 (page 203), and we note that the area .4750 is in the row corresponding to a z of 1.9 and the column headed by .06. It follows that the z value corresponding to .4750 is 1.96. Because this z value gives an area under the standard normal curve between 0 and z that equals .4750, it also gives a right-hand tail area equal to .025. Therefore, $z_{.025} = 1.96$.

In general, **we let z_α denote the point on the horizontal axis under the standard normal curve that gives a right-hand tail area equal to α.** With this definition in mind, we consider the following example.

Example 5.5

A large discount store sells HX-120 videocassette tapes and receives a shipment of these tapes every Monday. Historical sales records indicate that the weekly demand, x, for HX-120 tapes is normally distributed with a mean of $\mu = 100$ tapes and a standard deviation of $\sigma = 10$ tapes. How many tapes should be stocked at the beginning of a week so that there is only a 5 percent chance that the store will run short of tapes during the week?

If we let st equal the number of tapes that will be stocked, then st must be chosen to allow only a .05 probability that weekly demand, x, will exceed st. That is, st must be chosen so that

$$P(x > st) = .05$$

Figure 5.20(a) shows that the number of tapes stocked, st, is located under the right-hand tail of the normal curve having mean $\mu = 100$ and standard deviation $\sigma = 10$. In order to find st, we need to determine how many standard deviations st must be above the mean in order to give a right-hand tail area that is equal to .05.

The z value corresponding to st is

$$z = \frac{st - \mu}{\sigma} = \frac{st - 100}{10}$$

FIGURE 5.20 **Finding the Number of Tapes Stocked, *st*, so That $P(x > st) = .05$ When $\mu = 100$ and $\sigma = 10$**

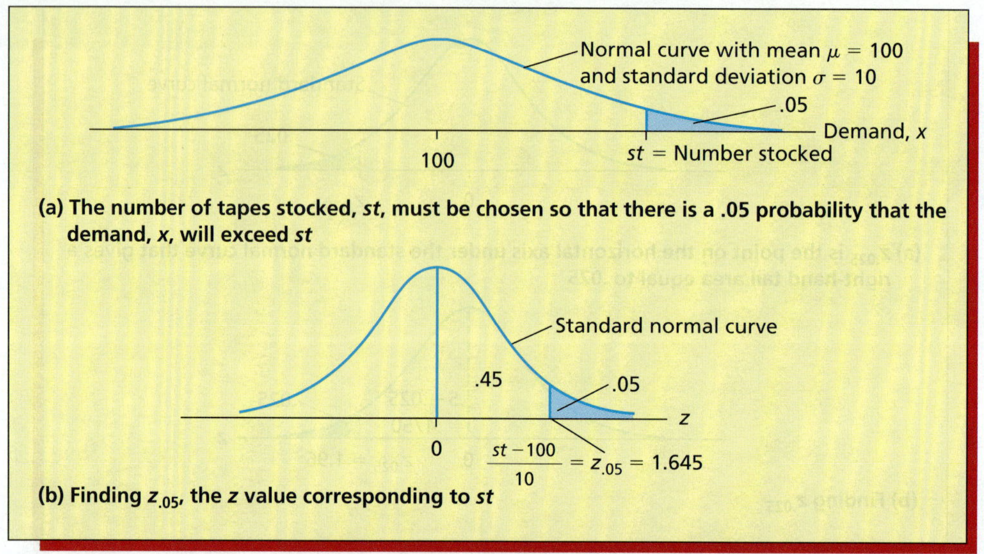

and this z value is the number of standard deviations that st is from μ. This z value is illustrated in Figure 5.20(b), and it is the point on the horizontal axis under the standard normal curve that gives a right-hand tail area equal to .05. That is, the z value corresponding to st is $z_{.05}$. Since the area under the standard normal curve between 0 and $z_{.05}$ is $.5 - .05 = .45$—see Figure 5.20(b)—we look for .45 in the body of the normal table. In Table 5.1, we see that the areas closest to .45 are .4495, which has a corresponding z value of 1.64, and .4505, which has a corresponding z value of 1.65. Although it would probably be sufficient to use either of these z values, we will (because it is easy to do so) interpolate halfway between them and assume that $z_{.05}$ equals 1.645. To find st, we solve the equation

$$\frac{st - 100}{10} = 1.645$$

for st. Doing this yields

$$st - 100 = 1.645(10)$$

or

$$st = 100 + 1.645(10) = 116.45$$

This last equation says that st is 1.645 standard deviations ($\sigma = 10$) above the mean ($\mu = 100$). Rounding $st = 116.45$ up so that the store's chances of running short of HX-120 tapes will be *no more* than 5 percent, the store should plan to stock 117 tapes at the beginning of each week.

Sometimes we need to find the point on the horizontal axis under the standard normal curve that gives a particular **left-hand tail area** (say, for instance, an area of .025). Looking at Figure 5.21, it

FIGURE 5.21 **The z Value $-z_{.025} = -1.96$ Gives a Left-Hand Tail Area of .025 under the Standard Normal Curve**

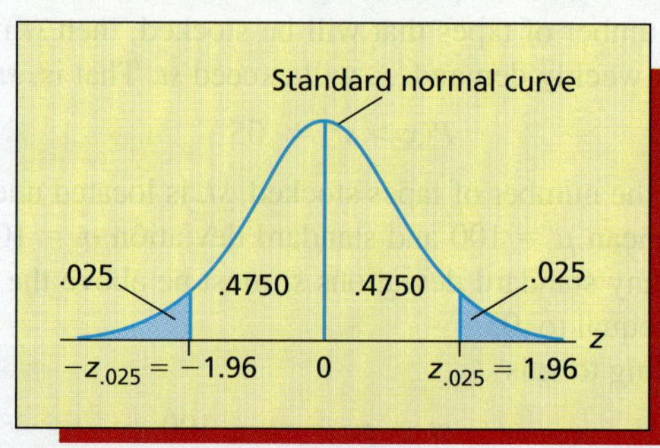

is easy to see that, if, for instance, we want a left-hand tail area of .025, the needed z value is $-z_{.025}$, where $z_{.025}$ gives a right-hand tail area equal to .025. Therefore, since $z_{.025} = 1.96$, it follows that $-z_{.025} = -1.96$ gives a left-hand tail area equal to .025. In general, **$-z_\alpha$ is the point on the horizontal axis under the standard normal curve that gives a left-hand tail area equal to α.**

Example 5.6

Extensive testing indicates that the lifetime of the Everlast automobile battery is normally distributed with a mean of $\mu = 60$ months and a standard deviation of $\sigma = 6$ months. The Everlast's manufacturer has decided to offer a free replacement battery to any purchaser whose Everlast battery does not last at least as long as the minimum lifetime specified in its guarantee. How can the manufacturer establish the guarantee period so that only 1 percent of the batteries will need to be replaced free of charge?

If the battery will be guaranteed to last l months, l must be chosen to allow only a .01 probability that the lifetime, x, of an Everlast battery will be less than l. That is, we must choose l so that

$$P(x < l) = .01$$

Figure 5.22(a) shows that the guarantee period, l, is located under the left-hand tail of the normal curve having mean $\mu = 60$ and standard deviation $\sigma = 6$. In order to find l, we need to determine how many standard deviations l must be below the mean in order to give a left-hand tail area that equals .01. The z value corresponding to l is

$$z = \frac{l - \mu}{\sigma} = \frac{l - 60}{6}$$

and this z value is the number of standard deviations that l is from μ. This z value is illustrated in Figure 5.22(b), and it is the point on the horizontal axis under the standard normal curve that gives a left-hand tail area equal to .01. That is, the z value corresponding to l is $-z_{.01}$. Since the area under the standard normal curve between 0 and $-z_{.01}$ is $.5 - .01 = .49$—see Figure 5.22(b)—we look for .49 in the body of the normal table. In Table 5.1 (page 203), we see that the area closest to .49 is .4901, which has a corresponding z value of 2.33. Therefore, $-z_{.01}$ is (roughly) -2.33. To find l, we solve the equation

$$\frac{l - 60}{6} = -2.33$$

for l. Doing this yields

$$l - 60 = -2.33(6)$$

or

$$l = 60 - 2.33(6) = 46.02$$

FIGURE 5.22 Finding the Guarantee Period, l, so That $P(x < l) = .01$ When $\mu = 60$ and $\sigma = 6$

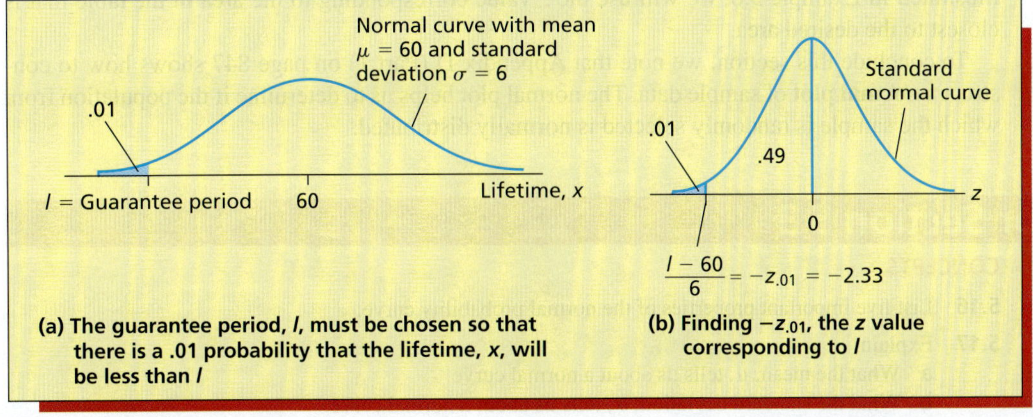

(a) The guarantee period, l, must be chosen so that there is a .01 probability that the lifetime, x, will be less than l

(b) Finding $-z_{.01}$, the z value corresponding to l

Note that this last equation says that l is 2.33 standard deviations ($\sigma = 6$) below the mean ($\mu = 60$). Rounding $l = 46.02$ down so that *no more* than 1 percent of the batteries will need to be replaced free of charge, it seems reasonable to guarantee the Everlast battery to last 46 months.

In Section 2.3 we saw that the intervals $[\mu \pm \sigma]$, $[\mu \pm 2\sigma]$, and $[\mu \pm 3\sigma]$ are **tolerance intervals** containing, respectively, 68.26 percent, 95.44 percent, and 99.73 percent of the measurements in a normally distributed population having mean μ and standard deviation σ. In the following example we demonstrate how to use the normal table to find the value k so that the interval $[\mu \pm k\sigma]$ contains any desired percentage of the measurements in a normally distributed population.

Example 5.7

Consider computing a tolerance interval $[\mu \pm k\sigma]$ that contains 99 percent of the measurements in a normally distributed population having mean μ and standard deviation σ. As illustrated in Figure 5.23, we must find the value k so that the area under the normal curve having mean μ and standard deviation σ between $(\mu - k\sigma)$ and $(\mu + k\sigma)$ is .99. As also shown in this figure, the area under this normal curve between μ and $(\mu + k\sigma)$ is equal to .495. Because the z value corresponding to a value of x tells us how many standard deviations x is from μ, the z value corresponding to $(\mu + k\sigma)$ is obviously k. It follows that k is the point on the horizontal axis under the standard normal curve so that the area under this curve between 0 and k is .495. Looking up .495 in the body of the normal table (Table 5.1 on page 203), we find that the values closest to .495 are .4949, which has a corresponding z value of 2.57, and .4951, which has a corresponding z value of 2.58. Although it would be sufficient to use either of these z values, we will interpolate halfway between them, and we will assume that k equals 2.575. It follows that the interval $[\mu \pm 2.575\sigma]$ contains 99 percent of the measurements in a normally distributed population having mean μ and standard deviation σ.

FIGURE 5.23 Finding a Tolerance Interval $[\mu \pm k\sigma]$ That Contains 99 Percent of the Measurements in a Normally Distributed Population

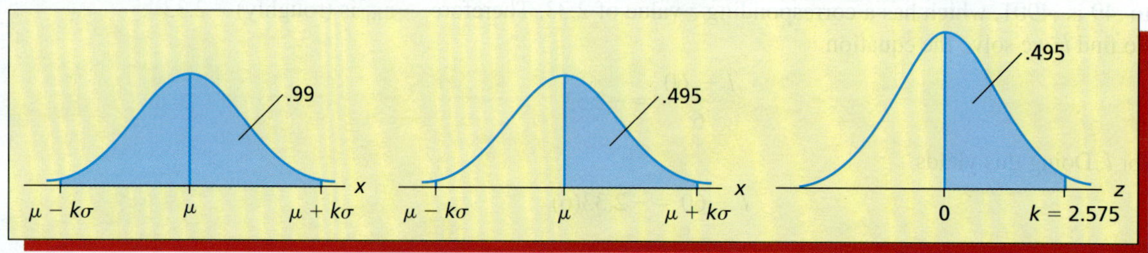

Whenever we use a normal table to find a z point corresponding to a particular normal curve area, we will use the *halfway interpolation* procedure illustrated in Examples 5.5 and 5.7 if the area we are looking for is exactly halfway between two areas in the table. Otherwise, as illustrated in Example 5.6, we will use the z value corresponding to the area in the table that is closest to the desired area.

To conclude this section, we note that Appendix D (Part 1) on page 847 shows how to construct a **normal plot** of sample data. The normal plot helps us to determine if the population from which the sample is randomly selected is normally distributed.

Exercises for Section 5.3

CONCEPTS

5.16 List five important properties of the normal probability curve.

5.17 Explain:

a What the mean, μ, tells us about a normal curve.

b What the standard deviation, σ, tells us about a normal curve.

5.18 If the random variable x is normally distributed, what percentage of all possible observed values of x will be

a Within one standard deviation of the mean?
b Within two standard deviations of the mean?
c Within three standard deviations of the mean?

5.19 Explain how to compute the z value corresponding to a value of a normally distributed random variable. What does the z value tell us about the value of the random variable?

5.20 Explain how x relates to the mean μ if the z value corresponding to x

a Equals zero.
b Is positive.
c Is negative.

5.21 Why do we compute z values when using the normal table? Explain.

METHODS AND APPLICATIONS

5.22 In each case, sketch the two specified normal curves on the same set of axes:

a A normal curve with $\mu = 20$ and $\sigma = 3$, and a normal curve with $\mu = 20$ and $\sigma = 6$.
b A normal curve with $\mu = 20$ and $\sigma = 3$, and a normal curve with $\mu = 30$ and $\sigma = 3$.
c A normal curve with $\mu = 100$ and $\sigma = 10$, and a normal curve with $\mu = 200$ and $\sigma = 20$.

5.23 Let x be a normally distributed random variable having mean $\mu = 30$ and standard deviation $\sigma = 5$. Find the z value for each of the following observed values of x:

a $x = 25$ **d** $x = 40$
b $x = 15$ **e** $x = 50$
c $x = 30$

In each case, explain what the z value tells us about how the observed value of x compares to the mean, μ.

5.24 If the random variable z has a standard normal distribution, sketch and find each of the following probabilities:

a $P(0 \leq z \leq 1.5)$ **d** $P(z \geq -1)$ **g** $P(-2.5 \leq z \leq .5)$
b $P(z \geq 2)$ **e** $P(z \leq -3)$ **h** $P(1.5 \leq z \leq 2)$
c $P(z \leq 1.5)$ **f** $P(-1 \leq z \leq 1)$ **i** $P(-2 \leq z \leq -.5)$

5.25 Suppose that the random variable z has a standard normal distribution. Sketch each of the following z points, and use the normal table to find each z point.

a $z_{.01}$ **d** $-z_{.01}$
b $z_{.05}$ **e** $-z_{.05}$
c $z_{.02}$ **f** $-z_{.10}$

5.26 Suppose that the random variable x is normally distributed with mean $\mu = 1{,}000$ and standard deviation $\sigma = 100$. Sketch and find each of the following probabilities:

a $P(1{,}000 \leq x \leq 1{,}200)$ **e** $P(x \leq 700)$
b $P(x > 1{,}257)$ **f** $P(812 \leq x \leq 913)$
c $P(x < 1{,}035)$ **g** $P(x > 891)$
d $P(857 \leq x \leq 1{,}183)$ **h** $P(1{,}050 \leq x \leq 1{,}250)$

5.27 Suppose that the random variable x is normally distributed with mean $\mu = 500$ and standard deviation $\sigma = 100$. For each of the following, use the normal table to find the needed value k. In each case, draw a sketch.

a $P(x \geq k) = .025$ **d** $P(x \leq k) = .015$ **g** $P(x \leq k) = .975$
b $P(x \geq k) = .05$ **e** $P(x < k) = .985$ **h** $P(x \geq k) = .0228$
c $P(x < k) = .025$ **f** $P(x > k) = .95$ **i** $P(x > k) = .9772$

5.28 Stanford–Binet IQ Test scores are normally distributed with a mean score of 100 and a standard deviation of 16.

a Sketch the distribution of Stanford–Binet IQ test scores.
b Write the equation that gives the z score corresponding to a Stanford–Binet IQ test score. Sketch the distribution of such z scores.
c Find the probability that a randomly selected person has an IQ test score
(1) Over 140.
(2) Under 88.
(3) Between 72 and 128.
(4) Within 1.5 standard deviations of the mean.
d Suppose you take the Stanford–Binet IQ Test and receive a score of 136. What percentage of people would receive a score higher than yours?

5.29 Weekly demand at a grocery store for a brand of breakfast cereal is normally distributed with a mean of 800 boxes and a standard deviation of 75 boxes.

a What is the probability that weekly demand is

(1) 959 boxes or less?

(2) More than 1,004 boxes?

(3) Less than 650 boxes or greater than 950 boxes?

b The store orders cereal from a distributor weekly. How many boxes should the store order for a week to have only a 2.5 percent chance of running short of this brand of cereal during the week?

5.30 The lifetimes of a particular brand of DVD player are normally distributed with a mean of eight years and a standard deviation of six months. Find each of the following probabilities where x denotes the lifetime in years. In each case, sketch the probability.

a $P(7 \leq x \leq 9)$

b $P(8.5 \leq x \leq 9.5)$

c $P(6.5 \leq x \leq 7.5)$

d $P(x \geq 8)$

e $P(x \leq 7)$

f $P(x \geq 7)$

g $P(x \leq 10)$

h $P(x > 10)$

5.31 United Motors claims that one of its cars, the Starbird 300, gets city driving mileages that are normally distributed with a mean of 30 mpg and a standard deviation of 1 mpg. Let x denote the city driving mileage of a randomly selected Starbird 300.

a Assuming that United Motors' claim is correct, find $P(x \leq 27)$.

b If you purchase (randomly select) a Starbird 300 and your car gets 27 mpg in city driving, what do you think of United Motors' claim? Explain your answer.

5.32 An investment broker reports that the yearly returns on common stocks are approximately normally distributed with a mean return of 12.4 percent and a standard deviation of 20.6 percent. On the other hand, the firm reports that the yearly returns on tax-free municipal bonds are approximately normally distributed with a mean return of 5.2 percent and a standard deviation of 8.6 percent. Find the probability that a randomly selected

a Common stock will give a positive yearly return.

b Tax-free municipal bond will give a positive yearly return.

c Common stock will give more than a 10 percent return.

d Tax-free municipal bond will give more than a 10 percent return.

e Common stock will give a loss of at least 10 percent.

f Tax-free municipal bond will give a loss of at least 10 percent.

5.33 A filling process is supposed to fill jars with 16 ounces of grape jelly. Specifications state that each jar must contain between 15.95 ounces and 16.05 ounces. A jar is selected from the process every half hour until a sample of 100 jars is obtained. When the fills of the jars are measured, it is found that $\bar{x} = 16.0024$ and $s = .02454$. Using $\bar{x}$ and s as point estimates of μ and σ, estimate the probability that a randomly selected jar will have a fill, x, that is out of specification. Assume that the process is in control and that the population of all jar fills is normally distributed.

5.34 A tire company has developed a new type of steel-belted radial tire. Extensive testing indicates the population of mileages obtained by all tires of this new type is normally distributed with a mean of 40,000 miles and a standard deviation of 4,000 miles. The company wishes to offer a guarantee providing a discount on a new set of tires if the original tires purchased do not exceed the mileage stated in the guarantee. What should the guaranteed mileage be if the tire company desires that no more than 2 percent of the tires will fail to meet the guaranteed mileage?

5.35 Recall from Exercise 5.32 that yearly returns on common stocks are normally distributed with a mean of 12.4 percent and a standard deviation of 20.6 percent.

a What percentage of yearly returns are at or below the 10th percentile of the distribution of yearly returns? What percentage are at or above the 10th percentile? Find the 10th percentile of the distribution of yearly returns.

b Find the first quartile, Q_1, and the third quartile, Q_3, of the distribution of yearly returns.

5.36 Two students take a college entrance exam known to have a normal distribution of scores. The students receive raw scores of 63 and 93, which correspond to z scores (often called the standardized scores) of -1 and 1.5, respectively. Find the mean and standard deviation of the distribution of raw exam scores.

5.37 THE TRASH BAG CASE TrashBag

Suppose that a population of measurements is normally distributed with mean μ and standard deviation σ.

a Write an expression (involving μ and σ) for a tolerance interval containing 98 percent of all the population measurements.

b Estimate a tolerance interval containing 98 percent of all the trash bag breaking strengths by using the fact that a random sample of 40 breaking strengths has a mean of $\bar{x} = 50.575$ and a standard deviation of $s = 1.6438$.

5.38 Consider the situation of Exercise 5.32.

a Use the investment broker's report to estimate the maximum yearly return that might be obtained by investing in tax-free municipal bonds.

b Find the probability that the yearly return obtained by investing in common stocks will be higher than the maximum yearly return that might be obtained by investing in tax-free municipal bonds.

5.39 In the book *Advanced Managerial Accounting,* Robert P. Magee discusses monitoring cost variances. A *cost variance* is the difference between a budgeted cost and an actual cost. Magee describes the following situation:

> Michael Bitner has responsibility for control of two manufacturing processes. Every week he receives a cost variance report for each of the two processes, broken down by labor costs, materials costs, and so on. One of the two processes, which we'll call process *A*, involves a stable, easily controlled production process with a little fluctuation in variances. Process *B* involves more random events: the equipment is more sensitive and prone to breakdown, the raw material prices fluctuate more, and so on.
>
> "It seems like I'm spending more of my time with process *B* than with process *A*," says Michael Bitner. "Yet I know that the probability of an inefficiency developing and the expected costs of inefficiencies are the same for the two processes. It's just the magnitude of random fluctuations that differs between the two, as you can see in the information below.
>
> At present, I investigate variances if they exceed $2,500, regardless of whether it was process *A* or *B*. I suspect that such a policy is not the most efficient. I should probably set a higher limit for process *B*."

The means and standard deviations of the cost variances of processes *A* and *B*, when these processes are in control, are as follows:

	Process *A*	Process *B*
Mean cost variance (in control)	$ 0	$ 0
Standard deviation of cost variance (in control)	$5,000	$10,000

Furthermore, the means and standard deviations of the cost variances of processes *A* and *B*, when these processes are out of control, are as follows:

	Process *A*	Process *B*
Mean cost variance (out of control)	$7,500	$ 7,500
Standard deviation of cost variance (out of control)	$5,000	$10,000

a Recall that the current policy is to investigate a cost variance if it exceeds $2,500 for either process. Assume that cost variances are normally distributed and that both Process *A* and Process *B* cost variances are in control. Find the probability that a cost variance for Process *A* will be investigated. Find the probability that a cost variance for Process *B* will be investigated. Which in-control process will be investigated more often?

b Assume that cost variances are normally distributed and that both Process *A* and Process *B* cost variances are out of control. Find the probability that a cost variance for Process *A* will be investigated. Find the probability that a cost variance for Process *B* will be investigated. Which out-of-control process will be investigated more often?

c If both Processes *A* and *B* are almost always in control, which process will be investigated more often?

d Suppose that we wish to reduce the probability that Process *B* will be investigated (when it is in control) to .3085. What cost variance investigation policy should be used? That is, how large a cost variance should trigger an investigation? Using this new policy, what is the probability that an out-of-control cost variance for Process *B* will be investigated?

5.40 Suppose that yearly health care expenses for a family of four are normally distributed with a mean expense equal to $3,000 and a standard deviation of $500. An insurance company has decided to offer a health insurance premium reduction if a policyholder's health care expenses do not exceed a specified dollar amount. What dollar amount should be established if the insurance company wants families having the lowest 33 percent of yearly health care expenses to be eligible for the premium reduction?

5.41 Suppose that the 33rd percentile of a normal distribution is equal to 656 and that the 97.5th percentile of this normal distribution is 896. Find the mean μ and the standard deviation σ of the normal distribution. Hint: Sketch these percentiles.

FIGURE 5.24 Several Binomial Distributions

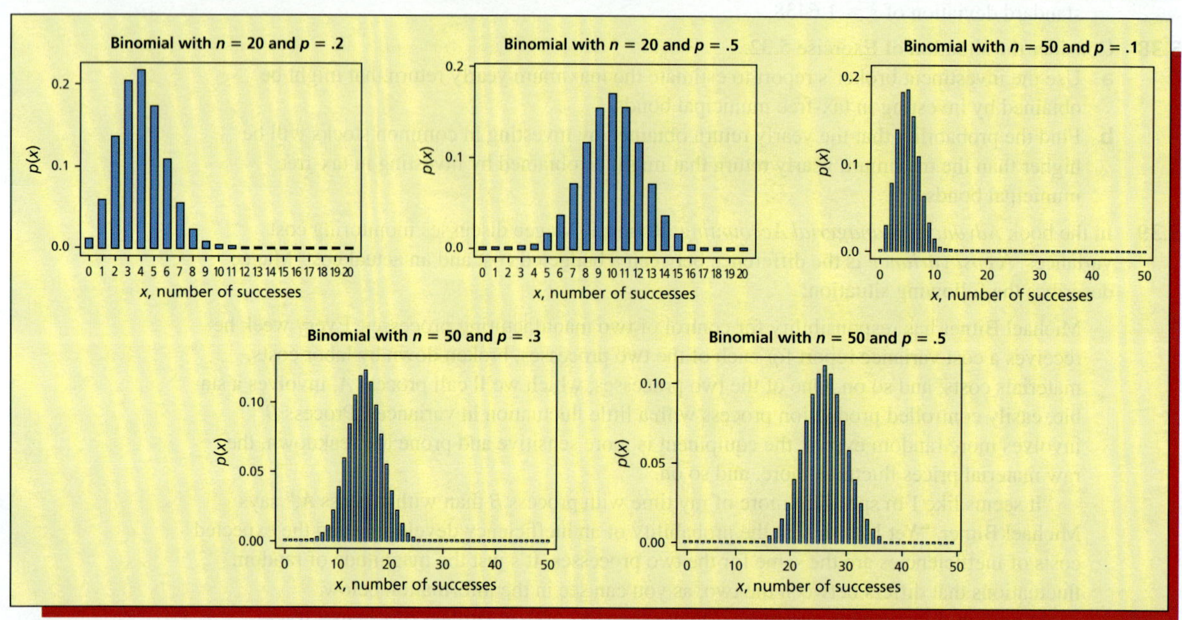

5.4 Approximating the Binomial Distribution by Using the Normal Distribution (Optional)

Figure 5.24 illustrates several binomial distributions. In general, we can see that as n gets larger and as p gets closer to .5, the graph of a binomial distribution tends to have the symmetrical, bell-shaped appearance of a normal curve. It follows that, under conditions given in the following box, we can approximate the binomial distribution by using a normal distribution.

The Normal Approximation of the Binomial Distribution

Consider a binomial random variable x, where n is the number of trials performed and p is the probability of success on each trial. If n and p have values so that $np \geq 5$ and $n(1 - p) \geq 5$, then x is approximately normally distributed with mean $\mu = np$ and standard deviation $\sigma = \sqrt{npq}$, where $q = 1 - p$.

This approximation is often useful because binomial tables for large values of n are often unavailable. The conditions $np \geq 5$ and $n(1 - p) \geq 5$ must be met in order for the approximation to be appropriate. Note that if p is near 0 or near 1, then n must be larger for a good approximation, while if p is near .5, then n need not be as large.[1]

CHAPTER 4

When we say that we can approximate the binomial distribution by using a normal distribution, we are saying that we can compute binomial probabilities by finding corresponding areas under a normal curve (rather than by using the binomial formula). We illustrate how to do this in the following example.

Example 5.8

Consider the binomial random variable x with $n = 50$ trials and probability of success $p = .5$. This binomial distribution is one of those illustrated in Figure 5.24. Suppose we want to use the normal approximation to this binomial distribution to compute the probability of 23 successes in the 50 trials. That is, we wish to compute $P(x = 23)$. Because $np = (50)(.5) = 25$ is at least 5,

[1]As an alternative to the rule that both np and $n(1 - p)$ must be at least 5, some statisticians suggest using the more conservative rule that both np and $n(1 - p)$ must be at least 10.

FIGURE 5.25 Approximating the Binomial Probability $P(x = 23)$ by Using the Normal Curve When $\mu = np = 25$ and $\sigma = \sqrt{npq} = 3.5355$

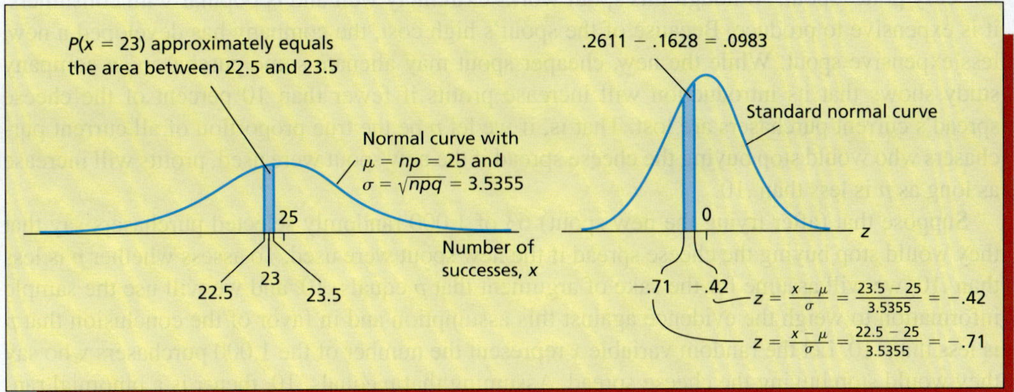

and $n(1 - p) = 50(1 - .5) = 25$ is also at least 5, we can appropriately use the approximation. Moreover, we can approximate the binomial distribution of x by using a normal distribution with mean $\mu = np = 50(.5) = 25$ and standard deviation $\sigma = \sqrt{npq} = \sqrt{50(.5)(1 - .5)} = 3.5355$.

In order to compute the needed probability, we must make a **continuity correction.** This is because a discrete distribution (the binomial) is being approximated by a continuous distribution (the normal). Because there is no area under a normal curve at the single point $x = 23$, we must assign an area under the normal curve to the binomial outcome $x = 23$. It is logical to assign the area corresponding to the interval from 22.5 to 23.5 to the integer outcome $x = 23$. That is, the area under the normal curve corresponding to all values within .5 units of the integer outcome $x = 23$ is assigned to the value $x = 23$. So we approximate the binomial probability $P(x = 23)$ by calculating the normal curve area $P(22.5 \le x \le 23.5)$. This area is illustrated in Figure 5.25. Calculating the z values

$$z = \frac{22.5 - 25}{3.5355} = -.71 \quad \text{and} \quad z = \frac{23.5 - 25}{3.5355} = -.42$$

we find that $P(22.5 \le x \le 23.5) = P(-.71 \le z \le -.42) = .2611 - .1628 = .0983$. Therefore, we estimate that the binomial probability $P(x = 23)$ is .0983.

Making the proper continuity correction can sometimes be tricky. A good way to approach this is to list the numbers of successes that are included in the event for which the binomial probability is being calculated. Then assign the appropriate area under the normal curve to each number of successes in the list. Putting these areas together gives the normal curve area that must be calculated. For example, again consider the binomial random variable x with $n = 50$ and $p = .5$. If we wish to find $P(27 \le x \le 29)$, then the event $27 \le x \le 29$ includes 27, 28, and 29 successes. Because we assign the areas under the normal curve corresponding to the intervals [26.5, 27.5], [27.5, 28.5], and [28.5, 29.5] to the values 27, 28, and 29, respectively, then the area to be found under the normal curve is $P(26.5 \le x \le 29.5)$. Table 5.2 gives several other examples.

TABLE 5.2 Several Examples of the Continuity Correction ($n = 50$)

Binomial Probability	Numbers of Successes Included in Event	Normal Curve Area (with Continuity Correction)
$P(25 < x \le 30)$	26, 27, 28, 29, 30	$P(25.5 \le x \le 30.5)$
$P(x \le 27)$	0, 1, 2, . . . , 26, 27	$P(x \le 27.5)$
$P(x > 30)$	31, 32, 33, . . . , 50	$P(x \ge 30.5)$
$P(27 < x < 31)$	28, 29, 30	$P(27.5 \le x \le 30.5)$

Example 5.9 The Cheese Spread Case

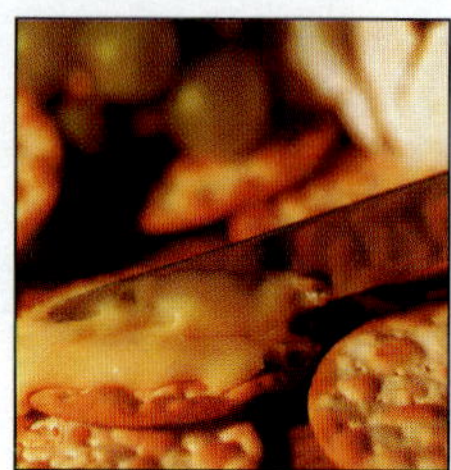

A food processing company markets a soft cheese spread that is sold in a plastic container with an "easy pour" spout. Although this spout works extremely well and is popular with consumers, it is expensive to produce. Because of the spout's high cost, the company has developed a new, less expensive spout. While the new, cheaper spout may alienate some purchasers, a company study shows that its introduction will increase profits if fewer than 10 percent of the cheese spread's current purchasers are lost. That is, if we let p be the true proportion of all current purchasers who would stop buying the cheese spread if the new spout were used, profits will increase as long as p is less than .10.

Suppose that (after trying the new spout) 63 of 1,000 randomly selected purchasers say that they would stop buying the cheese spread if the new spout were used. To assess whether p is less than .10, we will assume for the sake of argument that p equals .10, and we will use the sample information to weigh the evidence against this assumption and in favor of the conclusion that p is less than .10. Let the random variable x represent the number of the 1,000 purchasers who say they would stop buying the cheese spread. Assuming that p equals .10, then x is a binomial random variable with $n = 1{,}000$ and $p = .10$. Since the sample result of 63 is less than $\mu = np = 1{,}000(.1) = 100$, the expected value of x when p equals .10, we have some evidence to contradict the assumption that p equals .10. To evaluate the strength of this evidence, we calculate the probability that *63 or fewer* of the 1,000 randomly selected purchasers would say that they would stop buying the cheese spread if the new spout were used if, in fact, p equals .10.

Since both $np = 1{,}000(.10) = 100$ and $n(1 - p) = 1{,}000(1 - .10) = 900$ are at least 5, we can use the normal approximation to the binomial distribution to compute the needed probability. The appropriate normal curve has mean $\mu = np = 1{,}000(.10) = 100$ and standard deviation $\sigma = \sqrt{npq} = \sqrt{1{,}000(.10)(1 - .10)} = 9.4868$. In order to make the continuity correction, we note that the discrete value $x = 63$ is assigned the area under the normal curve corresponding to the interval from 62.5 to 63.5. It follows that the binomial probability $P(x \leq 63)$ is approximated by the normal probability $P(x \leq 63.5)$. This is illustrated in Figure 5.26. Calculating the z value for 63.5 to be

$$z = \frac{63.5 - 100}{9.4868} = -3.85$$

we find that

$$P(x \leq 63.5) = P(z \leq -3.85)$$

Because 3.85 is larger than 3.09, which is the largest z value in the normal table, the area under the standard normal curve to the left of -3.85 is less than $.5 - .499 = .001$. This says that, if p equals .10, then in fewer than 1 in 1,000 of all possible random samples of 1,000 purchasers would 63 or fewer say they would stop buying the cheese spread if the new spout were used. Since it is very difficult to believe that such a small chance (a smaller than 1 in 1,000 chance) has occurred, we have very strong evidence that p does not equal .10 and is, in fact, less than .10. Therefore, it seems that using the new spout will be profitable.

FIGURE 5.26 Approximating the Binomial Probability $P(x \leq 63)$ by Using the Normal Curve When $\mu = np = 100$ and $\sigma = \sqrt{npq} = 9.4868$

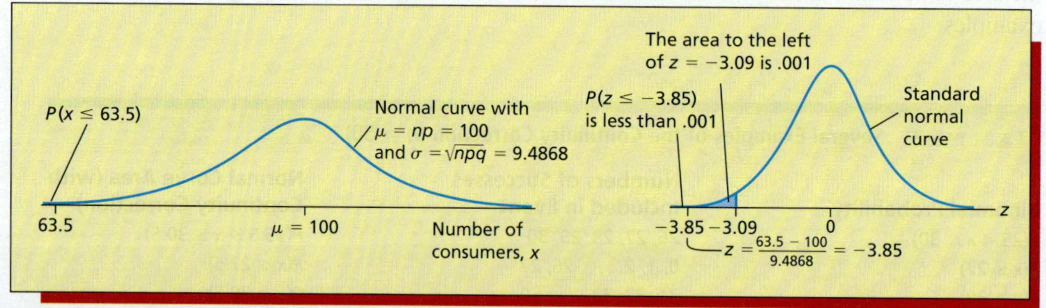

Exercises for Section 5.4

CONCEPTS

5.42 Explain why it might be convenient to approximate binomial probabilities by using areas under an appropriate normal curve.

5.43 Under what condition may we use the normal approximation to the binomial distribution?

5.44 Explain how we make a continuity correction. Why is a continuity correction needed when we approximate a binomial distribution by a normal distribution?

METHODS AND APPLICATIONS

5.45 Suppose that x has a binomial distribution with $n = 200$ and $p = .4$.

a Show that the normal approximation to the binomial can appropriately be used to calculate probabilities about x.

b Make continuity corrections for each of the following, and then use the normal approximation to the binomial to find each probability:

(1) $P(x = 80)$

(2) $P(x \leq 95)$

(3) $P(x < 65)$

(4) $P(x \geq 100)$

(5) $P(x > 100)$

5.46 Repeat Exercise 5.45 with $n = 200$ and $p = .5$.

5.47 An advertising agency conducted an ad campaign aimed at making consumers in an Eastern state aware of a new product. Upon completion of the campaign, the agency claimed that 20 percent of consumers in the state had become aware of the product. The product's distributor surveyed 1,000 consumers in the state and found that 150 were aware of the product.

a Assuming that the ad agency's claim is true:

(1) Verify that we may use the normal approximation to the binomial.

(2) Calculate the mean, μ, and the standard deviation, σ, we should use in the normal approximation.

(3) Find the probability that 150 or fewer consumers in a random sample of 1,000 consumers would be aware of the product.

b Should the distributor believe the ad agency's claim? Explain.

5.48 THE MARKETING ETHICS CASE

Recall that in Example 2.17 (page 89) we found that of the 205 randomly selected marketing researchers who participated in the survey, 117 said they disapprove of the actions taken in the ultraviolet ink scenario. Suppose that, before the survey was taken, a marketing manager claimed that at least 65 percent of all marketing researchers would disapprove of that scenario.

a Assuming that the manager's claim is correct, calculate the probability that 117 or fewer of 205 randomly selected marketing researchers would disapprove of the scenario. Use the normal approximation to the binomial.

b Based on your result of part *a*, do you believe the marketing manager's claim? Explain.

5.49 THE ELECTRONIC ARTICLE SURVEILLANCE CASE

Recall that in Example 2.18 (page 89) we found that based on a survey of 250 consumers, 40 said that if they were to set off an EAS alarm because store personnel failed to deactivate merchandise leaving the store, then they would never shop at that store again. A company marketing the alarm system claimed that no more than 5 percent of all consumers would say that they would never shop at that store again if they were subjected to a false alarm.

a Assuming that the company's claim is valid, use the normal approximation to the binomial to calculate the probability that at least 40 of the 250 randomly selected consumers would say that they would never shop at that store again if they were subjected to a false alarm.

b Do you believe the company's claim based on your answer to part *a*? Explain.

5.50 A department store will place a sale item in a special display for a one-day sale. Previous experience suggests that 20 percent of all customers who pass such a special display will purchase the item. If 2,000 customers will pass the display on the day of the sale, and if a one-item-per-customer limit is placed on the sale item, how many units of the sale item should the store stock in order to have at most a 1 percent chance of running short of the item on the day of the sale? Assume here that customers make independent purchase decisions.

FIGURE 5.27 A Graph of the Exponential Distribution $f(x) = \lambda e^{-\lambda x}$

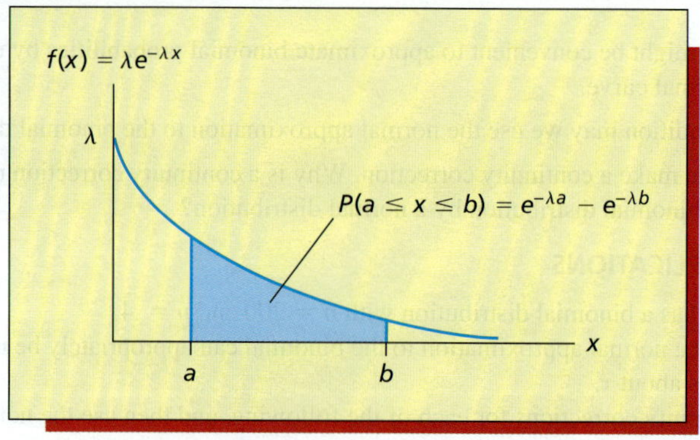

5.5 The Exponential Distribution (Optional)

Suppose that the number of times that a particular event occurs over an interval of time or space has a Poisson distribution. Furthermore, consider an arbitrary time or space unit (for example, minute, week, inch, square foot, or the like), and let x denote the number of time or space units between successive occurrences of the event. Then, it can be shown that x is described by an **exponential distribution** having parameter λ. Here, λ is the mean number of events that occur per time or space unit. Furthermore, the mean value of x can be proven to be $1/\lambda$. In words, $1/\lambda$ is *the mean number of time or space units between successive occurrences of the event.* In general, we can describe the exponential distribution as follows:

The Exponential Distribution

If λ is a positive number, then the equation describing the exponential distribution is

$$f(x) = \begin{cases} \lambda e^{-\lambda x} & \text{for } x \geq 0 \\ 0 & \text{otherwise} \end{cases}$$

Using this probability curve, it can be shown that:

$$P(a \leq x \leq b) = e^{-\lambda a} - e^{-\lambda b}$$

In particular, since $e^0 = 1$ and $e^{-\infty} = 0$, this implies that

$$P(x \leq c) = 1 - e^{-\lambda c} \quad \text{and} \quad P(x \geq c) = e^{-\lambda c}$$

Furthermore, the mean and the standard deviation of the population of all possible observed values of a random variable x that has an exponential distribution are

$$\mu_x = \frac{1}{\lambda} \quad \text{and} \quad \sigma_x = \frac{1}{\lambda}$$

The graph of the equation describing the exponential distribution and the probability $P(a \leq x \leq b)$ where x is described by this exponential distribution are illustrated in Figure 5.27.

We illustrate the use of the exponential distribution in the following examples.

Example 5.10

Recall from Example 4.13 (pages 182–185) that an air traffic control center is experiencing an average of 20.8 errors per year, and that it is reasonable to believe that the number of errors in a given time period is described by a Poisson distribution. If we consider x to be the number of weeks between successive errors, then x is described by an exponential distribution. Furthermore, since the air traffic control center is averaging 20.8 errors per year, it follows that λ, the average number of errors per week, is $20.8/52 = .4$. Therefore, the equation of the exponential distribution describing x is $f(x) = \lambda e^{-\lambda x} = .4e^{-.4x}$, and the mean number of weeks between successive errors is $1/\lambda = 1/.4 = 2.5$. For example, the probability that the time between successive errors will be between 1 and 2 weeks is

$$\begin{aligned} P(1 \le x \le 2) &= e^{-\lambda a} - e^{-\lambda b} = e^{-\lambda(1)} - e^{-\lambda(2)} \\ &= e^{-.4(1)} - e^{-.4(2)} = e^{-.4} - e^{-.8} \\ &= .6703 - .4493 = .221 \end{aligned}$$

Example 5.11

Suppose that the number of people who arrive at a hospital emergency room during a given time period has a Poisson distribution. It follows that the time, x, between successive arrivals of people to the emergency room has an exponential distribution. Furthermore, historical records indicate that the mean time between successive arrivals of people to the emergency room is seven minutes. Therefore, $\mu_x = 1/\lambda = 7$, which implies that $\lambda = 1/7 = .14286$. Noting that $\sigma_x = 1/\lambda = 7$, it follows that

$$\mu_x - \sigma_x = 7 - 7 = 0 \qquad \text{and} \qquad \mu_x + \sigma_x = 7 + 7 = 14$$

Therefore, the probability that the time between successive arrivals of people to the emergency room will be within (plus or minus) one standard deviation of the mean interarrival time is

$$\begin{aligned} P(0 \le x \le 14) &= e^{-\lambda a} - e^{-\lambda b} \\ &= e^{-(.14286)(0)} - e^{-(.14286)(14)} \\ &= 1 - .1353 \\ &= .8647 \end{aligned}$$

To conclude this section we note that the exponential and related Poisson distributions are useful in analyzing waiting lines, or **queues.** In general, **queueing theory** attempts to determine the number of servers (for example, doctors in an emergency room) that strikes an optimal balance between the time customers wait for service and the cost of providing service. The reader is referred to any textbook on management science or operations research for a discussion of queueing theory.

Exercises for Section 5.5

CONCEPTS

5.51 Give two examples of situations in which the exponential distribution might appropriately be used. In each case, define the random variable having an exponential distribution.

5.52 State the formula for the exponential probability curve. Define each symbol in the formula.

5.53 Explain the relationship between the Poisson and exponential distributions.

METHODS AND APPLICATIONS

5.54 Suppose that the random variable x has an exponential distribution with $\lambda = 2$.

- **a** Write the formula for the exponential probability curve of x. What are the possible values of x?
- **b** Sketch the probability curve.
- **c** Find $P(x \le 1)$.
- **d** Find $P(.25 \le x \le 1)$.
- **e** Find $P(x \ge 2)$.
- **f** Calculate the mean, μ_x, the variance, σ_x^2, and the standard deviation, σ_x, of the exponential distribution of x.
- **g** Find the probability that x will be in the interval $[\mu_x \pm 2\sigma_x]$.

5.55 Repeat Exercise 5.54 with $\lambda = 3$.

5.56 Recall in Exercise 4.34 (page 186) that the number of customer arrivals at a bank's drive-up window in a 15-minute period is Poisson distributed with a mean of seven customer arrivals per

15-minute period. Define the random variable x to be the time (in minutes) between successive customer arrivals at the bank's drive-up window.

a Write the formula for the exponential probability curve of x.

b Sketch the probability curve of x.

c Find the probability that the time between arrivals is

(1) Between one and two minutes.

(2) Less than one minute.

(3) More than three minutes.

(4) Between 1/2 and $3\frac{1}{2}$ minutes.

d Calculate μ_x, σ_x^2, and σ_x.

e Find the probability that the time between arrivals falls within one standard deviation of the mean; within two standard deviations of the mean.

5.57 The length of a particular telemarketing phone call, x, has an exponential distribution with mean equal to 1.5 minutes.

a Write the formula for the exponential probability curve of x.

b Sketch the probability curve of x.

c Find the probability that the length of a randomly selected call will be

(1) No more than three minutes.

(2) Between one and two minutes.

(3) More than four minutes.

(4) Less than 30 seconds.

5.58 The maintenance department in a factory claims that the number of breakdowns of a particular machine follows a Poisson distribution with a mean of two breakdowns every 500 hours. Let x denote the time (in hours) between successive breakdowns.

a Find λ and μ_x.

b Write the formula for the exponential probability curve of x.

c Sketch the probability curve.

d Assuming that the maintenance department's claim is true, find the probability that the time between successive breakdowns is at most five hours.

e Assuming that the maintenance department's claim is true, find the probability that the time between successive breakdowns is between 100 and 300 hours.

f Suppose that the machine breaks down five hours after its most recent breakdown. Based on your answer to part *d*, do you believe the maintenance department's claim? Explain.

5.59 Suppose that the number of accidents occurring in an industrial plant is described by a Poisson distribution with an average of one accident per month. Let x denote the time (in months) between successive accidents.

a Find the probability that the time between successive accidents is

(1) More than two months.

(2) Between one and two months.

(3) Less than one week (1/4 of a month).

b Suppose that an accident occurs less than one week after the plant's most recent accident. Would you consider this event unusual enough to warrant special investigation? Explain.

5.6 The Cumulative Normal Table (Optional)

(Note: Read pages 200–202 before reading this section)

Table A.19 (page 840) is a table of cumulative areas under the standard normal curve. This table is called a *cumulative normal table,* and it is reproduced in Table 5.3. Specifically,

The **cumulative normal table** gives, for many different values of z, the area under the standard normal curve at or below z.

Two such areas are shown in the figures to the right of Table 5.3—one with a negative z value and one with a positive z value. The values of z in the cumulative normal table range from -3.49 to 3.49 in increments of .01. As can be seen from Table 5.3, values of z accurate to the nearest tenth are given in the far left column (headed z) of the table. Further graduations to the nearest hundredth (.00, .01, .02, . . . , .09) are given across the top of the table. The areas under the normal curve are given in the body of the table, accurate to four decimal places.

TABLE 5.3 Cumulative Areas under the Standard Normal Curve

z	.00	.01	.02	.03	.04	.05	.06	.07	.08	.09
−3.4	.0003	.0003	.0003	.0003	.0003	.0003	.0003	.0003	.0003	.0002
−3.3	.0005	.0005	.0005	.0004	.0004	.0004	.0004	.0004	.0004	.0003
−3.2	.0007	.0007	.0006	.0006	.0006	.0006	.0006	.0005	.0005	.0005
−3.1	.0010	.0009	.0009	.0009	.0008	.0008	.0008	.0008	.0007	.0007
−3.0	.0013	.0013	.0013	.0012	.0012	.0011	.0011	.0011	.0010	.0010
−2.9	.0019	.0018	.0018	.0017	.0016	.0016	.0015	.0015	.0014	.0014
−2.8	.0026	.0025	.0024	.0023	.0023	.0022	.0021	.0021	.0020	.0019
−2.7	.0035	.0034	.0033	.0032	.0031	.0030	.0029	.0028	.0027	.0026
−2.6	.0047	.0045	.0044	.0043	.0041	.0040	.0039	.0038	.0037	.0036
−2.5	.0062	.0060	.0059	.0057	.0055	.0054	.0052	.0051	.0049	.0048
−2.4	.0082	.0080	.0078	.0075	.0073	.0071	.0069	.0068	.0066	.0064
−2.3	.0107	.0104	.0102	.0099	.0096	.0094	.0091	.0089	.0087	.0084
−2.2	.0139	.0136	.0132	.0129	.0125	.0122	.0119	.0116	.0113	.0110
−2.1	.0179	.0174	.0170	.0166	.0162	.0158	.0154	.0150	.0146	.0143
−2.0	.0228	.0222	.0217	.0212	.0207	.0202	.0197	.0192	.0188	.0183
−1.9	.0287	.0281	.0274	.0268	.0262	.0256	.0250	.0244	.0239	.0233
−1.8	.0359	.0351	.0344	.0336	.0329	.0322	.0314	.0307	.0301	.0294
−1.7	.0446	.0436	.0427	.0418	.0409	.0401	.0392	.0384	.0375	.0367
−1.6	.0548	.0537	.0526	.0516	.0505	.0495	.0485	.0475	.0465	.0455
−1.5	.0668	.0655	.0643	.0630	.0618	.0606	.0594	.0582	.0571	.0559
−1.4	.0808	.0793	.0778	.0764	.0749	.0735	.0721	.0708	.0694	.0681
−1.3	.0968	.0951	.0934	.0918	.0901	.0885	.0869	.0853	.0838	.0823
−1.2	.1151	.1131	.1112	.1093	.1075	.1056	.1038	.1020	.1003	.0985
−1.1	.1357	.1335	.1314	.1292	.1271	.1251	.1230	.1210	.1190	.1170
−1.0	.1587	.1562	.1539	.1515	.1492	.1469	.1446	.1423	.1401	.1379
−0.9	.1841	.1814	.1788	.1762	.1736	.1711	.1685	.1660	.1635	.1611
−0.8	.2119	.2090	.2061	.2033	.2005	.1977	.1949	.1922	.1894	.1867
−0.7	.2420	.2389	.2358	.2327	.2296	.2266	.2236	.2206	.2177	.2148
−0.6	.2743	.2709	.2676	.2643	.2611	.2578	.2546	.2514	.2483	.2451
−0.5	.3085	.3050	.3015	.2981	.2946	.2912	.2877	.2843	.2810	.2776
−0.4	.3446	.3409	.3372	.3336	.3300	.3264	.3228	.3192	.3156	.3121
−0.3	.3821	.3783	.3745	.3707	.3669	.3632	.3594	.3557	.3520	.3483
−0.2	.4207	.4168	.4129	.4090	.4052	.4013	.3974	.3936	.3897	.3859
−0.1	.4602	.4562	.4522	.4483	.4443	.4404	.4364	.4325	.4286	.4247
−0.0	.5000	.4960	.4920	.4880	.4840	.4801	.4761	.4721	.4681	.4641
0.0	.5000	.5040	.5080	.5120	.5160	.5199	.5239	.5279	.5319	.5359
0.1	.5398	.5438	.5478	.5517	.5557	.5596	.5636	.5675	.5714	.5753
0.2	.5793	.5832	.5871	.5910	.5948	.5987	.6026	.6064	.6103	.6141
0.3	.6179	.6217	.6255	.6293	.6331	.6368	.6406	.6443	.6480	.6517
0.4	.6554	.6591	.6628	.6664	.6700	.6736	.6772	.6808	.6844	.6879
0.5	.6915	.6950	.6985	.7019	.7054	.7088	.7123	.7157	.7190	.7224
0.6	.7257	.7291	.7324	.7357	.7389	.7422	.7454	.7486	.7517	.7549
0.7	.7580	.7611	.7642	.7673	.7704	.7734	.7764	.7794	.7823	.7852
0.8	.7881	.7910	.7939	.7967	.7995	.8023	.8051	.8078	.8106	.8133
0.9	.8159	.8186	.8212	.8238	.8264	.8289	.8315	.8340	.8365	.8389
1.0	.8413	.8438	.8461	.8485	.8508	.8531	.8554	.8577	.8599	.8621
1.1	.8643	.8665	.8686	.8708	.8729	.8749	.8770	.8790	.8810	.8830
1.2	.8849	.8869	.8888	.8907	.8925	.8944	.8962	.8980	.8997	.9015
1.3	.9032	.9049	.9066	.9082	.9099	.9115	.9131	.9147	.9162	.9177
1.4	.9192	.9207	.9222	.9236	.9251	.9265	.9279	.9292	.9306	.9319
1.5	.9332	.9345	.9357	.9370	.9382	.9394	.9406	.9418	.9429	.9441
1.6	.9452	.9463	.9474	.9484	.9495	.9505	.9515	.9525	.9535	.9545
1.7	.9554	.9564	.9573	.9582	.9591	.9599	.9608	.9616	.9625	.9633
1.8	.9641	.9649	.9656	.9664	.9671	.9678	.9686	.9693	.9699	.9706
1.9	.9713	.9719	.9726	.9732	.9738	.9744	.9750	.9756	.9761	.9767
2.0	.9772	.9778	.9783	.9788	.9793	.9798	.9803	.9808	.9812	.9817
2.1	.9821	.9826	.9830	.9834	.9838	.9842	.9846	.9850	.9854	.9857
2.2	.9861	.9864	.9868	.9871	.9875	.9878	.9881	.9884	.9887	.9890
2.3	.9893	.9896	.9898	.9901	.9904	.9906	.9909	.9911	.9913	.9916
2.4	.9918	.9920	.9922	.9925	.9927	.9929	.9931	.9932	.9934	.9936

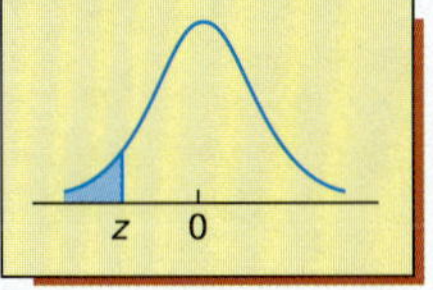

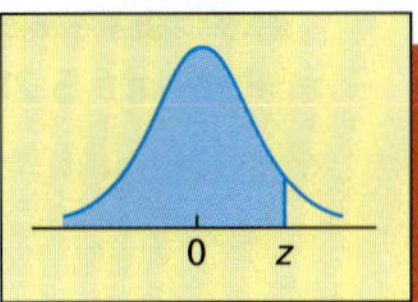

TABLE 5.3 (Continued)

z	.00	.01	.02	.03	.04	.05	.06	.07	.08	.09
2.5	.9938	.9940	.9941	.9943	.9945	.9946	.9948	.9949	.9951	.9952
2.6	.9953	.9955	.9956	.9957	.9959	.9960	.9961	.9962	.9963	.9964
2.7	.9965	.9966	.9967	.9968	.9969	.9970	.9971	.9972	.9973	.9974
2.8	.9974	.9975	.9976	.9977	.9977	.9978	.9979	.9979	.9980	.9981
2.9	.9981	.9982	.9982	.9983	.9984	.9984	.9985	.9985	.9986	.9986
3.0	.9987	.9987	.9987	.9988	.9988	.9989	.9989	.9989	.9990	.9990
3.1	.9990	.9991	.9991	.9991	.9992	.9992	.9992	.9992	.9993	.9993
3.2	.9993	.9993	.9994	.9994	.9994	.9994	.9994	.9995	.9995	.9995
3.3	.9995	.9995	.9995	.9996	.9996	.9996	.9996	.9996	.9996	.9997
3.4	.9997	.9997	.9997	.9997	.9997	.9997	.9997	.9997	.9997	.9998

As an example, suppose that we wish to find the area under the standard normal curve at or below a z value of 1.00. This area is illustrated in Figure 5.28. To find this area, we scan down the far left column of the table (starting at the top) until we find the value 1.0. We now scan across the row in the table corresponding to the z value 1.0 until we find the column corresponding to the heading .00. The desired area (which we have shaded blue) is in the row corresponding to the z value 1.0 and in the column headed .00. This area, which equals .8413, is the probability that the random variable z is less than or equal to 1.00. That is, we have found that $P(z \leq 1.00) =$ .8413. As another example, the area under the standard normal curve at or below the z value 2.53 is found in the row corresponding to 2.5 and in the column corresponding to .03. We find that this area is .9943—that is, $P(z \leq 2.53) = .9943$.

We now show how to use the cumulative normal table to find several other kinds of normal curve areas. First, suppose that we wish to find the area under the standard normal curve at or above a z value of 2—that is, we wish to find $P(z \geq 2)$. This area is illustrated in Figure 5.29 and is called a **right-hand tail area.** Since the total area under the normal curve equals 1, the area under the curve at or above 2 equals 1 minus the area under the curve at or below 2. That is, we find that $P(z \geq 2) = 1 - P(z \leq 2) = 1 - .9772 = .0228$.

Next, suppose that we wish to find the area under the standard normal curve at or below a z value of -1. That is, we wish to find $P(z \leq -1)$. This area is illustrated in Figure 5.30 and is called a **left-hand tail area.** The needed area is found in the row of the cumulative normal table corresponding to -1 and in the column headed by .00. We find that $P(z \leq -1) = .1587$. Notice that the area under the standard normal curve at or below -1 is equal to the area under this curve at or above 1. This is true because of the symmetry of the normal curve. Therefore, $P(z \geq 1) = .1587$.

Finally, suppose that we wish to find the area under the standard normal curve between the z values of -1 and 1. This area is illustrated in Figure 5.31, and we can see that this area equals the area under the curve at or below 1 minus the area under the curve at or below -1. Referring to Table 5.3, we see that $P(-1 \leq z \leq 1) = P(z \leq 1) - P(z \leq -1) = .8413 - .1587 = .6826$.

FIGURE 5.28 Finding $P(z \leq 1)$

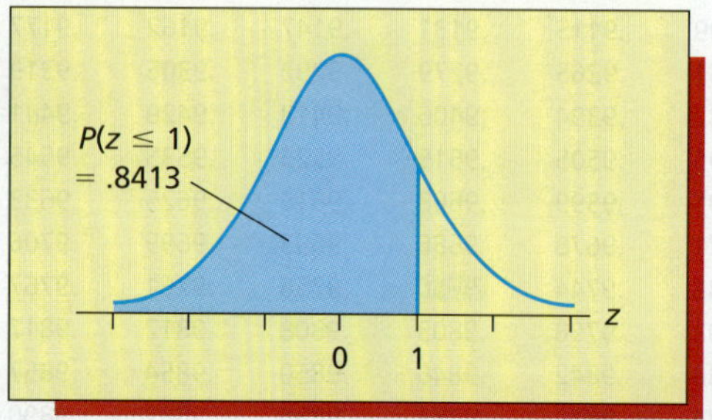

FIGURE 5.29 Finding $P(z \geq 2)$

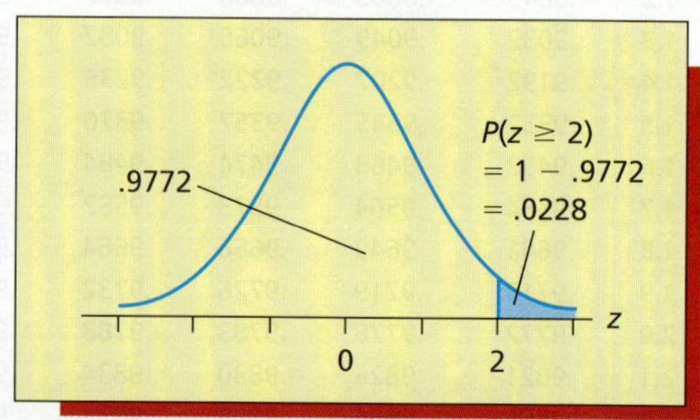

FIGURE 5.30 Finding $P(z \le -1)$

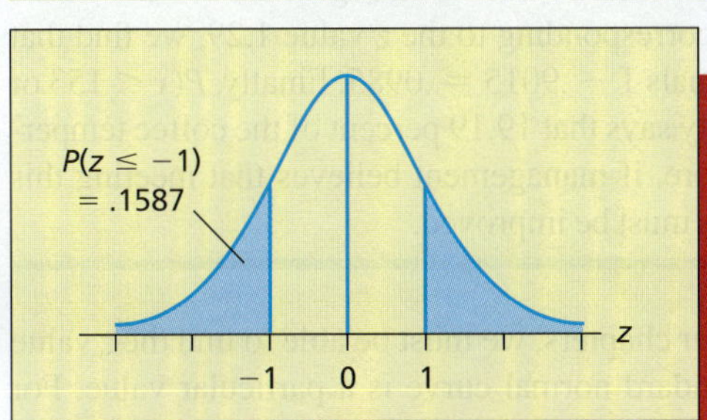

FIGURE 5.31 Finding $P(-1 \le z \le 1)$

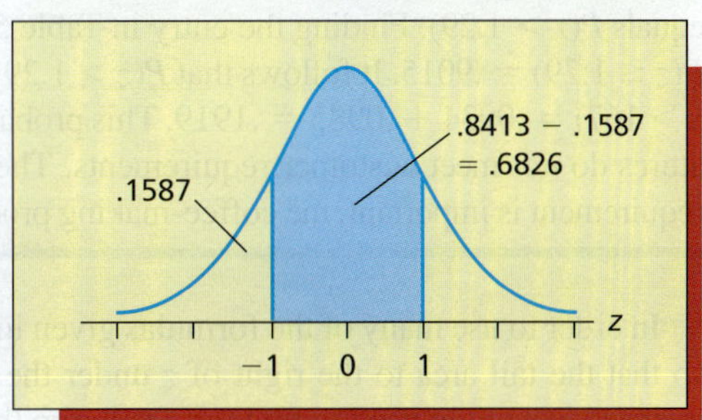

Example 5.12 The Coffee Temperature Case

Recall that the runs plot and histogram of the sample of 24 coffee temperatures indicate that the coffee-making process is in statistical control and that the population of all coffee temperatures is normally distributed. Also recall that customer requirements state that each cup of coffee should have a temperature between 153° and 167°. The mean and standard deviation of the sample of 24 coffee temperatures are $\bar{x} = 160.0833$ and $s = 5.3724$. Using $\bar{x}$ and s as point estimates of the population mean μ and population standard deviation σ, we want to calculate the probability that x, the temperature of a randomly selected cup of coffee, is outside the requirements (that is, less than 153° or greater than 167°). In order to compute the probability $P(x < 153$ or $x > 167)$ we compute the z values

$$z = \frac{153 - 160.0833}{5.3724} = -1.32 \quad \text{and} \quad z = \frac{167 - 160.0833}{5.3724} = 1.29$$

These z values tell us that 153° is 1.32 standard deviations below the mean and that 167° is 1.29 standard deviations above the mean. Because the events $\{x < 153\}$ and $\{x > 167\}$ are mutually exclusive, $P(x < 153$ or $x > 167)$ is the sum of $P(x < 153)$ and $P(x > 167)$. As shown in Figure 5.32,

FIGURE 5.32 Finding $P(x < 153$ or $x > 167)$ in the Coffee Temperature Case

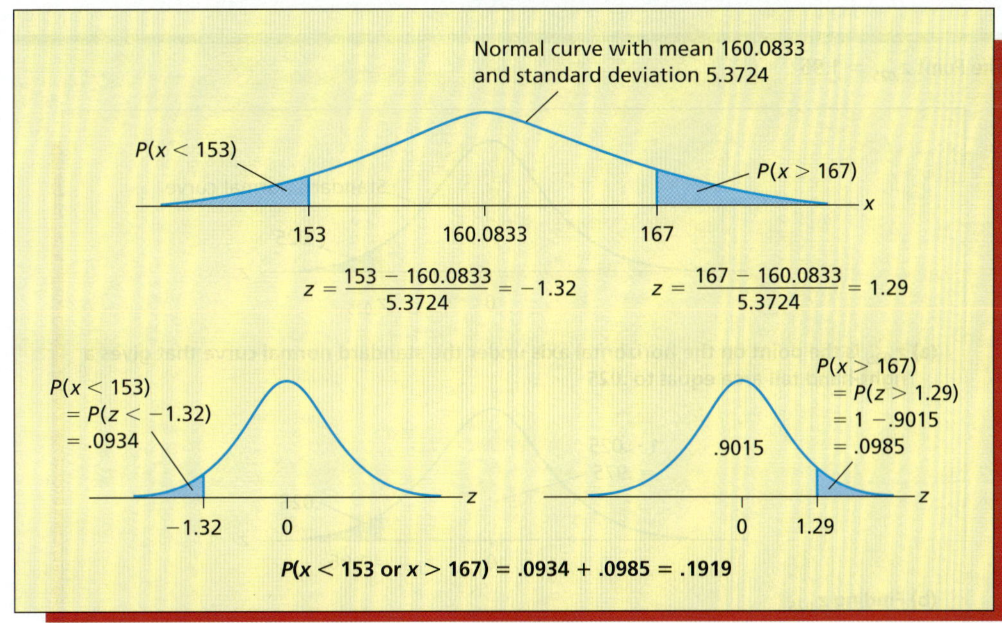

$P(x < 153)$ equals $P(z < -1.32)$. We obtain this probability by finding the entry in Table 5.3 corresponding to the z value -1.32, which is .0934. As also shown in Figure 5.32, $P(x > 167)$ equals $P(z > 1.29)$. Finding the entry in Table 5.3 corresponding to the z value 1.29, we find that $P(z \leq 1.29) = .9015$. It follows that $P(z > 1.29)$ equals $1 - .9015 = .0985$. Finally, $P(x < 153$ or $x > 167) = .0934 + .0985 = .1919$. This probability says that 19.19 percent of the coffee temperatures do not meet customer requirements. Therefore, if management believes that meeting this requirement is important, the coffee-making process must be improved.

In order to use many of the formulas given in later chapters, we must be able to find the z value so that the tail area to the right of z under the standard normal curve is a particular value. For instance, we might need to find the z value so that the tail area to the right of z under the standard normal curve is .025. This z value is denoted $z_{.025}$, and we illustrate $z_{.025}$ in Figure 5.33. We refer to $z_{.025}$ as **the point on the horizontal axis under the standard normal curve that gives a right-hand tail area equal to .025.** It is easy to use the cumulative normal table to find such a point. For instance, in order to find $z_{.025}$, we note from Figure 5.33 that the area under the standard normal curve at or below $z_{.025}$ equals .975. Remembering that areas under the standard normal curve at or below z are the four-digit numbers given in the body of Table 5.3, we scan the body of the table and find the area .9750. We have shaded this area in Table 5.3, and we note that the area .9750 is in the row corresponding to a z of 1.9 and in the column headed by .06. It follows that the z value corresponding to .9750 is 1.96. Because the z value 1.96 gives an area under the standard normal curve at or below z that equals .975, it also gives a right-hand tail area equal to .025. Therefore, $z_{.025} = 1.96$.

In Section 2.3 we saw that the intervals $[\mu \pm \sigma]$, $[\mu \pm 2\sigma]$, and $[\mu \pm 3\sigma]$ are **tolerance intervals** containing, respectively, 68.26 percent, 95.44 percent, and 99.73 percent of the measurements in a normally distributed population having mean μ and standard deviation σ. In the following example we demonstrate how to use the cumulative normal table to find the value k so that the interval $[\mu \pm k\sigma]$ contains any desired percentage of the measurements in a normally distributed population.

Example 5.13

Consider computing a tolerance interval $[\mu \pm k\sigma]$ that contains 99 percent of the measurements in a normally distributed population having mean μ and standard deviation σ. As illustrated in Figure 5.34, we must find the value k so that the area under the normal curve having mean μ and standard deviation σ between $(\mu - k\sigma)$ and $(\mu + k\sigma)$ is .99. As also shown in this figure, the

FIGURE 5.33 The Point $z_{.025} = 1.96$

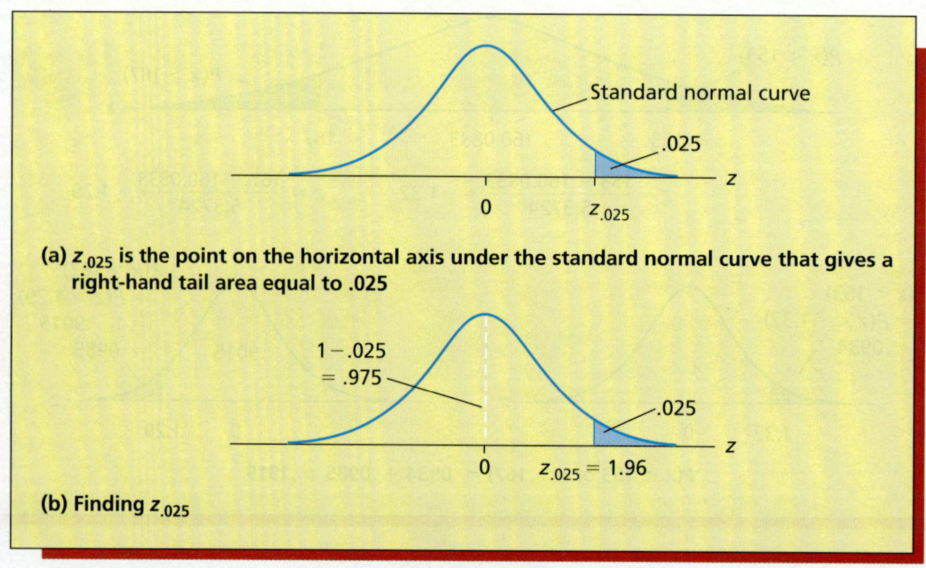
Standard normal curve
.025
z
0
$z_{.025}$
(a) $z_{.025}$ is the point on the horizontal axis under the standard normal curve that gives a right-hand tail area equal to .025
1 − .025
= .975
.025
z
0
$z_{.025}$ = 1.96
(b) Finding $z_{.025}$

FIGURE 5.34 Finding a Tolerance Interval $[\mu \pm k\sigma]$ That Contains 99 Percent of the Measurements in a Normally Distributed Population

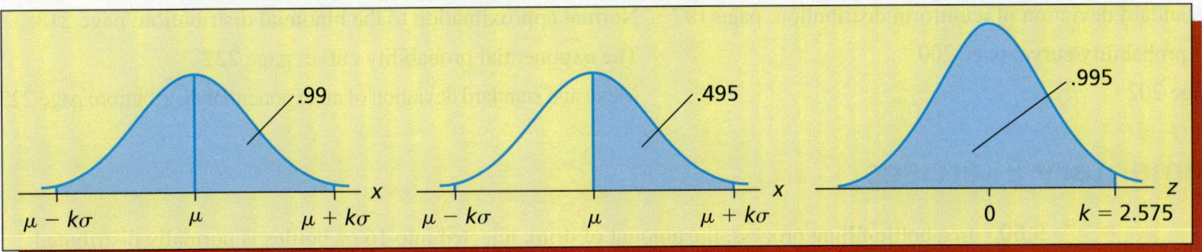

area under this normal curve between μ and $(\mu + k\sigma)$ is equal to .495. Because the z value corresponding to a value of x tells us how many standard deviations x is from μ, the z value corresponding to $(\mu + k\sigma)$ is obviously k. It follows that k is the point on the horizontal axis under the standard normal curve so that the area under this curve at or below k equals .995 (see Figure 5.34). Looking for .995 in the body of the cumulative normal table (Table 5.3, pages 225 and 226), we find that the values closest to .995 are .9949, which has a corresponding z value of 2.57, and .9951, which has a corresponding z value of 2.58. Although it would be sufficient to use either of these z values, we will interpolate halfway between them, and we will assume that k equals 2.575. It follows that the interval $[\mu \pm 2.575\sigma]$ contains 99 percent of the measurements in a normally distributed population having mean μ and standard deviation σ.

Exercises for Section 5.6

Work the exercises for Section 5.3 using the cumulative normal table on pages 225 and 226.

Chapter Summary

In this chapter we have discussed **continuous probability distributions.** We began by learning that **a continuous probability distribution is described by a continuous probability curve** and that in this context **probabilities are areas under the probability curve.** We next studied several important continuous probability distributions—**the uniform distribution, the normal distribution,** and **the exponential distribution.** In particular, we concentrated on the normal distribution, which is the most important continuous probability distribution. We learned about the properties of the normal curve, and we saw how to use a **normal table** to find various areas under a normal curve. We also saw that the normal curve can be employed to approximate binomial probabilities, and we demonstrated how we can use a normal curve probability to make a statistical inference. We concluded this chapter with an optional section that covers the **cumulative normal table.**

Glossary of Terms

continuous probability distribution (or **probability curve**): A curve that is defined so that the probability that a random variable will be in a specified interval of numbers is the area under the curve corresponding to the interval. (page 195)

exponential probability distribution: A probability distribution that describes the time or space between successive occurrences of an event when the number of times the event occurs over an interval of time or space is described by a Poisson distribution. (page 222)

normal probability distribution: The most important continuous probability distribution. Its probability curve is the *bell-shaped* normal curve. (page 200)

normal table: A table in which we can look up areas under the standard normal curve. (pages 202–203, 224–226)

queueing theory: A methodology that attempts to determine the number of servers that strikes an optimal balance between the time customers wait for service and the cost of providing service. (page 223)

standard normal distribution (or curve): A normal distribution (or curve) having mean 0 and standard deviation 1. (page 202)

uniform distribution: A continuous probability distribution having a rectangular shape that says the probability is distributed evenly (or uniformly) over an interval of numbers. (page 197)

z_α point: The point on the horizontal axis under the standard normal curve that gives a right-hand tail area equal to α. (page 211)

$-z_\alpha$ point: The point on the horizontal axis under the standard normal curve that gives a left-hand tail area equal to α. (page 213)

z value: A value that tells us the number of standard deviations that a value x is from the mean of a normal curve. If the z value is positive, then x is above the mean. If the z value is negative, then x is below the mean. (page 202)

Important Formulas

The uniform probability curve: page 197

Mean and standard deviation of a uniform distribution: page 197

The normal probability curve: page 200

z values: page 202

Finding normal probabilities: page 209

Normal approximation to the binomial distribution: page 218

The exponential probability curve: page 222

Mean and standard deviation of an exponential distribution: page 222

Supplementary Exercises

5.60 In a bottle-filling process, the amount of drink injected into 16 oz bottles is normally distributed with a mean of 16 oz and a standard deviation of .02 oz. Bottles containing less than 15.95 oz do not meet the bottler's quality standard. What percentage of filled bottles do not meet the standard?

5.61 In a murder trial in Los Angeles, a shoe expert stated that the range of heights of men with a size 12 shoe is 71 inches to 76 inches. Suppose the heights of all men wearing size 12 shoes are normally distributed with a mean of 73.5 inches and a standard deviation of 1 inch. What is the probability that a randomly selected man who wears a size 12 shoe

a Has a height outside the range 71 inches to 76 inches?

b Is 74 inches or taller?

c Is shorter than 70.5 inches?

5.62 In the movie *Forrest Gump,* the public school required an IQ of at least 80 for admittance.

a If IQ test scores are normally distributed with mean 100 and standard deviation 16, what percentage of people would qualify for admittance to the school?

b If the public school wishes 95 percent of all children to qualify for admittance, what minimum IQ test score should be required for admittance?

5.63 The amount of sales tax paid on a purchase is rounded to the nearest cent. Assume that the round-off error is uniformly distributed in the interval $-.5$ to $.5$ cents.

a Write the formula for the probability curve describing the round-off error.

b Graph the probability curve describing the round-off error.

c What is the probability that the round-off error exceeds .3 cents or is less than $-.3$ cents?

d What is the probability that the round-off error exceeds .1 cent or is less than $-.1$ cent?

e Find the mean and the standard deviation of the round-off error.

f Find the probability that the round-off error will be within one standard deviation of the mean.

5.64 A *consensus forecast* is the average of a large number of individual analysts' forecasts. Suppose the individual forecasts for a particular interest rate are normally distributed with a mean of 5.0 percent and a standard deviation of 1.2 percent. A single analyst is randomly selected. Find the probability that his/her forecast is

a At least 3.5 percent.

b At most 6 percent.

c Between 3.5 percent and 6 percent.

5.65 Recall from Exercise 5.64 that individual forecasts of a particular interest rate are normally distributed with a mean of 5 percent and a standard deviation of 1.2 percent.

a What percentage of individual forecasts are at or below the 10th percentile of the distribution of forecasts? What percentage are at or above the 10th percentile? Find the 10th percentile of the distribution of individual forecasts.

b Find the first quartile, Q_1, and the third quartile, Q_3, of the distribution of individual forecasts.

5.66 The scores on the entrance exam at a well-known, exclusive law school are normally distributed with a mean score of 200 and a standard deviation equal to 50. At what value should the lowest passing score be set if the school wishes only 2.5 percent of those taking the test to pass?

5.67 A machine is used to cut a metal automobile part to its desired length. The machine can be set so that the mean length of the part will be any value that is desired. The standard deviation of the lengths always runs at .02 inches. Where should the mean be set if we want only .4 percent of the parts cut by the machine to be shorter than 15 inches long?

5.68 A motel accepts 325 reservations for 300 rooms on July 1, expecting 10 percent no-shows on average from past records. Use the normal approximation to the binomial to find the probability that all guests who arrive on July 1 will receive a room.

5.69 Suppose a software company finds that the number of errors in its software per 1,000 lines of code is described by a Poisson distribution. Furthermore, it is found that there is an average of four errors per 1,000 lines of code. Letting x denote the number of lines of code between successive errors:

a Find the probability that there will be at least 400 lines of code between successive errors in the company's software.

b Find the probability that there will be no more than 100 lines of code between successive errors in the company's software.

5.70 THE INVESTMENT CASE InvestRet

For each investment class in Figure 2.57 and Table 2.15 (page 110), assume that future returns are normally distributed with the population mean and standard deviation given in Table 2.15. Based on this assumption:

a For each investment class, find the probability of a return that is less than zero (that is, find the probability of a loss). Is your answer reasonable for all investment classes? Explain.

b For each investment class, find the probability of a return that is

(1) Greater than 5 percent.
(2) Greater than 10 percent.
(3) Greater than 20 percent.
(4) Greater than 50 percent.

c For which investment classes is the probability of a return greater than 50 percent essentially zero? For which investment classes is the probability of such a return greater than 1 percent? Greater than 5 percent?

d For which investment classes is the probability of a loss essentially zero? For which investment classes is the probability of a loss greater than 1 percent? Greater than 10 percent? Greater than 20 percent?

5.71 The daily water consumption for an Ohio community is normally distributed with a mean consumption of 800,000 gallons and a standard deviation of 80,000 gallons. The community water system will experience a noticeable drop in water pressure when the daily water consumption exceeds 984,000 gallons. What is the probability of experiencing such a drop in water pressure?

5.72 Suppose the times required for a cable company to fix cable problems in its customers' homes are uniformly distributed between 10 minutes and 25 minutes. What is the probability that a randomly selected cable repair visit will take at least 15 minutes?

5.73 Suppose the waiting time to get food after placing an order at a fast-food restaurant is exponentially distributed with a mean of 60 seconds. If a randomly selected customer orders food at the restaurant, what is the probability that the customer will wait at least

a One minute, 30 seconds?

b Two minutes?

5.74 Net interest margin—often referred to as *spread*—is the difference between the rate banks pay on deposits and the rate they charge for loans. Suppose that the net interest margins for all U.S. banks are normally distributed with a mean of 4.15 percent and a standard deviation of .5 percent.

a Find the probability that a randomly selected U.S. bank will have a net interest margin that exceeds 5.40 percent.

b Find the probability that a randomly selected U.S. bank will have a net interest margin less than 4.40 percent.

c A bank wants its net interest margin to be less than the net interest margins of 95 percent of all U.S. banks. Where should the bank's net interest margin be set?

5.75 In an article in the November 11, 1991, issue of *Advertising Age,* Nancy Giges studies global spending patterns. Giges presents data concerning the percentage of adults in various countries who have purchased various consumer items (such as soft drinks, athletic footware, blue jeans, beer, and so on) in the past three months.

a Suppose we wish to justify the claim that fewer than 50 percent of adults in Germany have purchased blue jeans in the past three months. The survey reported by Giges found that 45 percent of the respondents in Germany had purchased blue jeans in the past three months.[2]

Assume that a random sample of 400 German adults was employed, and let p be the proportion of all German adults who have purchased blue jeans in the past three months. If, for the sake of argument, we assume that $p = .5$, use the normal approximation to the binomial distribution to calculate the probability that 45 percent or fewer of 400 randomly selected German adults would have purchased blue jeans in the past three months. Note: Because 45 percent of 400 is 180, you should calculate the probability that 180 or fewer of 400 randomly selected German adults would have purchased blue jeans in the past three months.

[2] Source: N. Giges, "Global Spending Patterns Emerge," *Advertising Age* (November 11, 1991), p. 64.

b Based on the probability you computed in part *a*, would you conclude that *p* is really less than .5? That is, would you conclude that fewer than 50 percent of adults in Germany have purchased blue jeans in the past three months? Explain.

5.76 Assume that the ages for first marriages are normally distributed with a mean of 26 years and a standard deviation of 4 years. What is the probability that a person getting married for the first time is in his or her twenties?

Appendix 5.1 ■ Normal Distribution Using MINITAB

Normal probability $P(X \leq 31.2)$ in Example 5.3 (pages 209–210):

- Select **Calc : Probability Distributions : Normal.**
- In the Normal Distribution dialog box, select the Cumulative probability option.
- In the Mean box, enter 33.
- In the Standard deviation box, enter 0.7.
- Click on the "Input constant" option and enter 31.2 in the "Input constant" box.
- Click OK in the Normal Distribution dialog box to see the desired probability in the Session window.

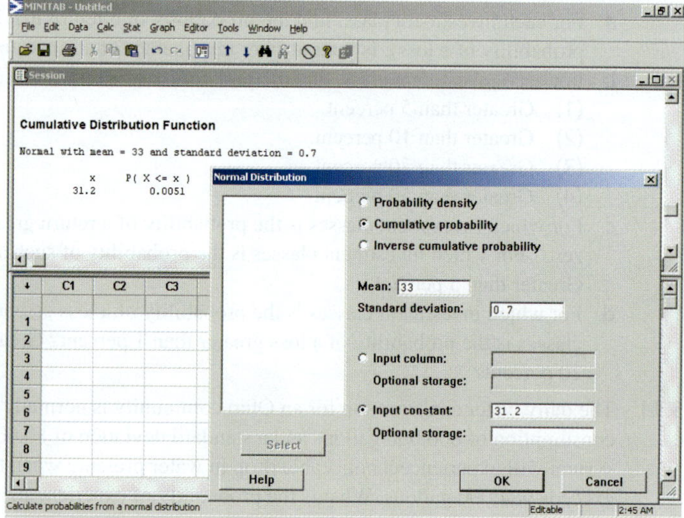

Normal probability $P(X < 153 \text{ or } X > 167)$ in Example 5.4 (page 210):

- In columns C1, C2, and C3, enter the variable names—x, $P(X < x)$, and $P(X > x)$.
- In column C1, enter the values 153 and 167.
- Select **Calc : Probability Distributions : Normal.**
- In the Normal Distribution dialog box, select the Cumulative probability option.
- In the Mean box, enter 160.0833.
- In the Standard deviation box, enter 5.3724.
- Click the "Input column" option, enter x in the "Input column" box, and enter 'P(X < x)' in the "Optional storage" box.
- Click OK in Normal Distribution dialog box.

- Select **Calc : Calculator.**
- In the Calculator dialog box, enter 'P(X > x)' in the "Store result in variable" box.
- Enter 1 − 'P(X < x)' in the Expression box.
- Click OK in the Calculator dialog box.

The desired probability is the sum of the lower tail probability for 153 and the upper tail probability for 167 or 0.093675 + 0.098969 = 0.192644. This value differs slightly from the value in Example 5.4 since Minitab carries out probability calculations to higher precision than can be achieved using normal probability tables.

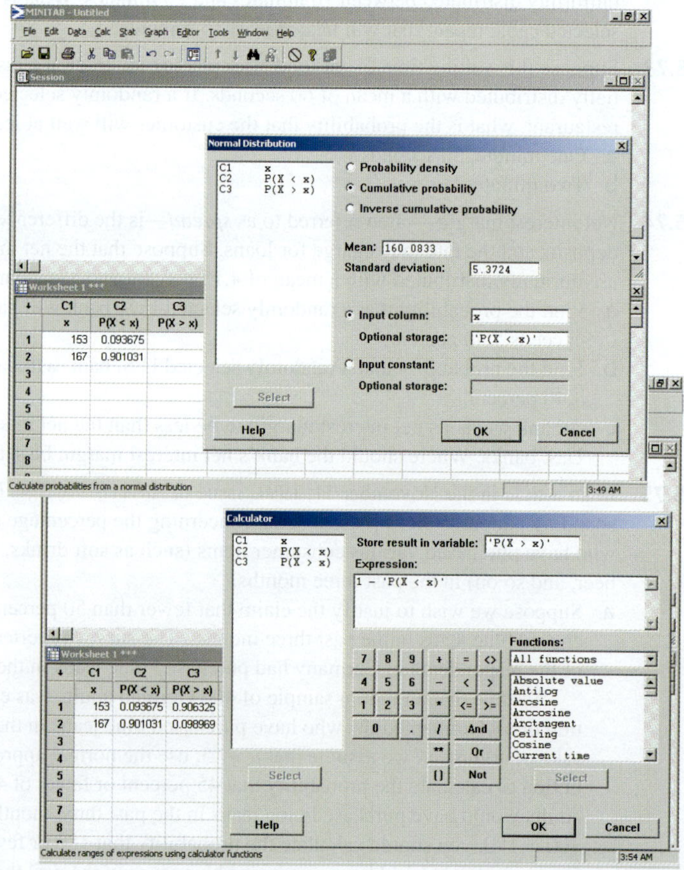

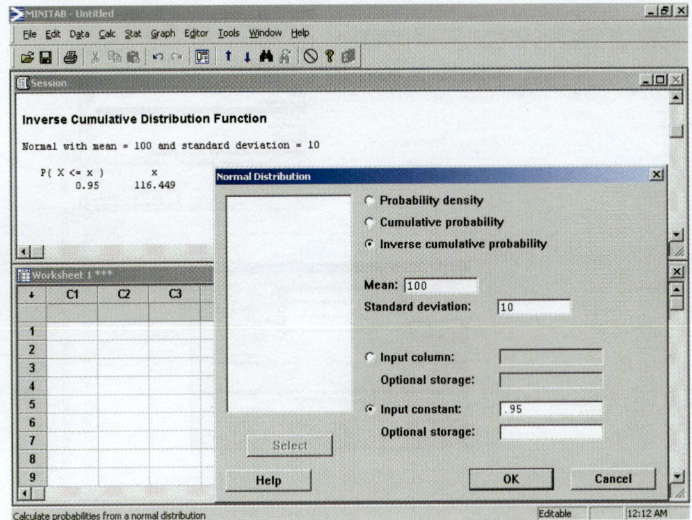

Inverse normal probability to find the number of units stocked, *st*, such that P(X > *st*) = 0.05 in Example 5.5 (pages 211–212):

- Select **Calc : Probability Distributions : Normal.**
- In the Normal Distribution dialog box, select the Inverse cumulative probability option.
- In the Mean box, enter 100.
- In the Standard deviation box, enter 10.
- Click the "Input constant" option and enter 0.95 in the "Input constant" box. That is, P(X ≤ *st*) = 0.95 when P(X > *st*) = 0.05.
- Click OK in Normal Distribution dialog box to see the desired value of *st* in the Session window.

Appendix 5.2 ■ Normal Distribution Using Excel

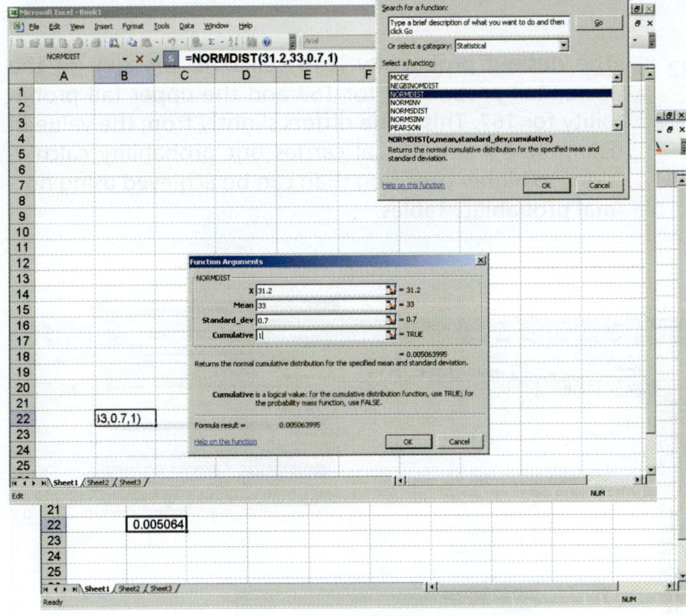

Normal probability P(X ≤ 31.2) in Example 5.3 (pages 209–210):

- Click in the cell where you wish to place the answer. Here we have clicked in cell B22. Then select the Insert Function button f_x from the Excel toolbar.
- In the Insert Function dialog box, select Statistical from the "Or select a category:" menu, select NORMDIST from the "Select a function:" menu, and click OK.
- In the NORMDIST Function Arguments dialog box, enter the value 31.2 in the X box.
- Enter the value 33 in the Mean box.
- Enter the value 0.7 in the Standard_dev box.
- Enter the value 1 in the Cumulative box.
- Click OK in the NORMDIST Function Arguments dialog box.
- When you click OK in this dialog box, the answer will be placed in cell B22.

Normal probability P(X < 153 or X > 167) in Example 5.4 (page 210):

- Enter the headings—x, P(X < x), P(X > x)—in the spreadsheet where you wish the results to be placed. Here we will enter these headings in cells A21, B21, and C21. The calculated results will be placed below the headings.
- In cells A22 and A23, enter the values 153 and 167.
- Click in cell B22 and select the Insert Function button f_x from the Excel toolbar.
- In the Insert Function dialog box, select Statistical from the "Or select a category:" menu, select NORMDIST from the "Select a function:" menu, and click OK.
- In the NORMDIST Function Arguments dialog box, enter the cell location A22 in the X box.
- Enter the value 160.0833 in the Mean box.
- Enter the value 5.3724 in the Standard_dev box.
- Enter the value 1 in the Cumulative box.
- Click OK in the NORMDIST Function Arguments dialog box.
- When you click OK, the result for P(X < 153) will be placed in cell B22. Double-click the drag- handle (in the lower right corner) of cell B22 to automatically extend the cell formula of B22 through cell B23.
- In cells C22 and C23, enter the formulas = 1 − B22 and = 1 − B23. The results for P(X > 153) and P(X > 167) will be placed in cells C22 and C23.
- In cell D24, enter the formula = B22 + C23.

(Continued in right column)

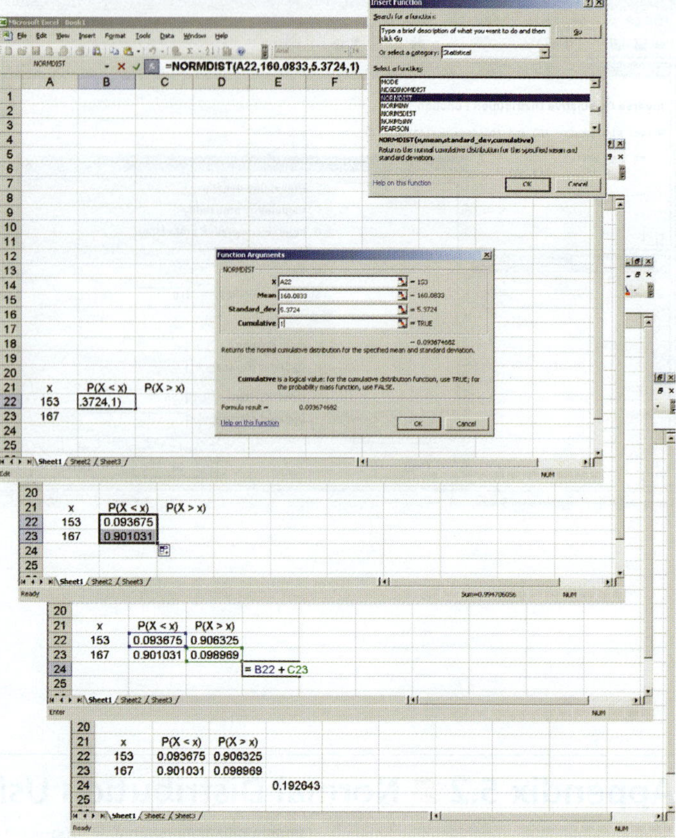

The desired probability is in cell D24, the sum of the lower tail probability for 153 and the upper tail probability for 167. This value differs slightly from the value in Example 5.4 since Excel carries out probability calculations to higher precision than can be achieved using normal probability tables.

Inverse normal probability *st* such that P(X > *st*) = 0.05 in Example 5.5 (pages 211–212):

- Click in the cell where you wish the answer to be placed. Here we will click in cell A21. Select the Insert Function button f_x from the Excel toolbar.
- In the Insert Function dialog box, select Statistical from the "Or select a category:" menu, select NORMINV from the "Select a function:" menu, and click OK.
- In the NORMINV Function Arguments dialog box, enter the value 0.95 in the Probability box, that is,

  [P(X ≤ *st*) = 0.95 when P(X > *st*) = 0.05.]
- Enter the value 100 in the Mean box.
- Enter the value 10 in the Standard_dev box.
- Click OK in the NORMINV Function Arguments dialog box.
- When you click OK, the answer is placed in cell A21.

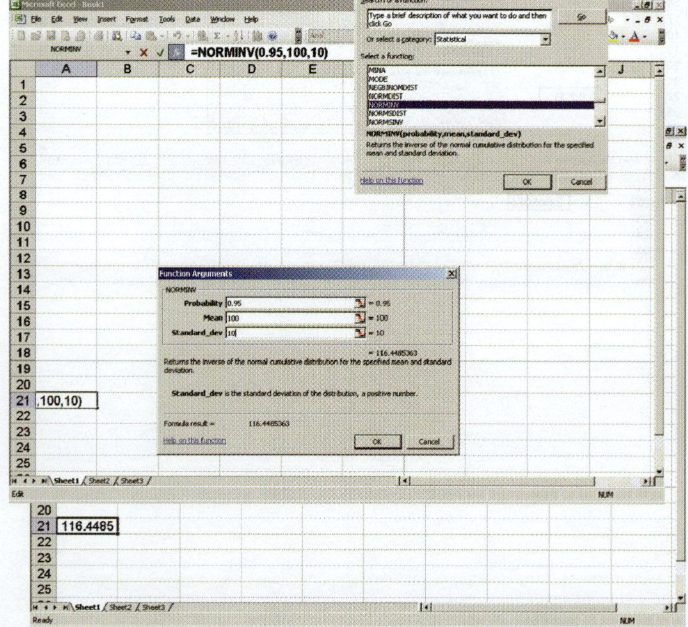

Appendix 5.3 ■ Normal Distribution Using MegaStat

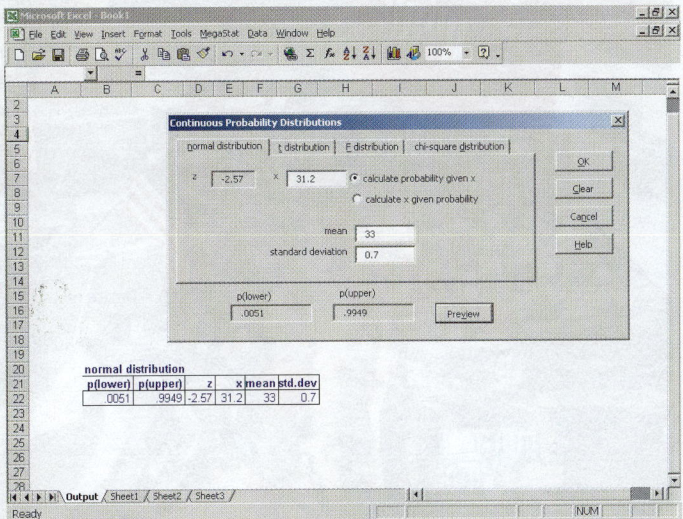

Normal probability $P(x \leq 31.2)$ in Example 5.3 (pages 209–210):

- Select **MegaStat : Probability : Continuous Probability Distributions.**
- In the "Continuous Probability Distributions" dialog box, enter the distribution mean (here equal to 33) and the distribution standard deviation (here equal to 0.7) in the appropriate boxes.
- Enter the value of *x* (here equal to 31.2) into the "Calculate probability given x" box.
- Click OK in the "Continuous Probability Distributions" dialog box.
- The output includes ***P*(lower),** which is the area under the specified normal curve below the given value of *x*, and ***P*(upper),** which is the area under the specified normal curve above the given value of *x*. The value of *z* corresponding to the specified value of *x* is also included. In this case, $P(x \leq 31.2)$ equals *P*(lower) = .0051.
- (Optional) Click on the Preview button to see the values of *P*(lower) and *P*(upper) before obtaining results in the Output worksheet.

Note that if a **standard normal distribution** is specified—0 is entered in the mean box and 1 is entered in the standard deviation box—the "calculate probability" box will read "calculate probability given z." In this case, when we enter a value of *z* in the "calculate probability given z" box, *P*(lower) and *P*(upper) are, respectively, the areas below and above the specified value of *z* under the standard normal curve.

Normal probability $P(x < 153 \text{ or } x > 167)$ in Example 5.4 on page 210. Enter 160.0833 into the mean box and enter 5.3724 into the standard deviation box. Find *P*(lower) corresponding to 153 and find *P*(upper) corresponding to 167. When these values are placed in the Output worksheet, use a simple Excel cell formula to add them together.

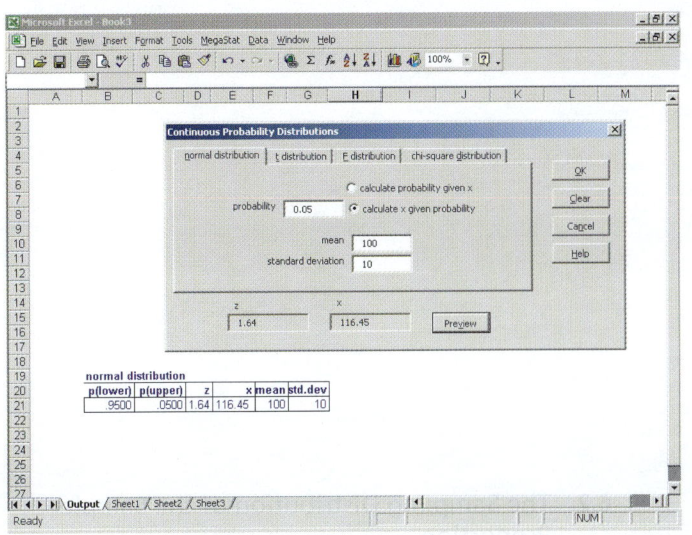

Inverse normal probability *st* such that $P(x > st) = 0.05$ in Example 5.5 on pages 211 to 212.

- Select **MegaStat : Probability : Continuous Probability Distributions.**
- Enter 100 into the mean box and enter 10 into the standard deviation box.
- Click the "Calculate x given probability" button.
- Enter 0.05 into the probability box. This is the area under the normal curve we want to have above *st* (that is, above the desired value of *x*).
- Click OK in the "Continuous Probability Distributions" dialog box.
- The output includes *P*(lower) and *P*(upper)—as defined above—as well as the desired value of *x* (in this case *x* equals 116.45).

CHAPTER 6

Sampling Distributions

Chapter Outline

6.1 The Sampling Distribution of the Sample Mean

6.2 The Sampling Distribution of the Sample Proportion

We have seen that the sample mean is the point estimate of the population mean and the sample proportion is the point estimate of the population proportion. In much of this book we use point estimates to make statistical inferences about populations and processes. As mentioned in Chapter 3, these inferences are based on calculating probabilities. To calculate these probabilities, we use a certain type of probability distribution called a **sampling distribution.**

In this chapter we discuss the properties of two important sampling distributions—the **sampling distribution of the sample mean** and the **sampling distribution of the sample proportion.** In order to help explain these sampling distributions, we consider three previously introduced cases:

The Car Mileage Case: The automaker uses the properties of the sampling distribution of the sample mean and its sample of 49 mileages to provide convincing evidence that the new midsize model's mean EPA combined city and highway mileage exceeds the tax credit standard of 31 mpg.

The Payment Time Case: The management consulting firm uses the properties of the sampling distribution of the sample mean and its sample of 65 payment times to provide strong evidence that the new electronic billing system has reduced the mean bill payment time by more than 50 percent.

The Cheese Spread Case: The food processing company uses the properties of the sampling distribution of the sample proportion and its survey results to provide extremely strong evidence that fewer than 10 percent of all current purchasers would stop buying the cheese spread if the new spout were used.

We also introduce a new case, the **Stock Return Case.**

6.1 The Sampling Distribution of the Sample Mean

Introductory ideas and basic properties Suppose that we are about to randomly select a sample of n measurements from a population of measurements having mean μ and standard deviation σ. *Before* we actually select the sample, there are many different samples of n measurements that we might potentially obtain. Because different samples generally have different sample means, there are many different sample means that we might potentially obtain. It follows that, *before we draw the sample, the sample mean $\bar{x}$ is a random variable.*

The **sampling distribution of the sample mean $\bar{x}$** is the probability distribution of the population of all possible sample means obtained from samples of size n.

Example 6.1 The Stock Return Case

To illustrate the sampling distribution of the sample mean, we consider the population of last year's percentage returns for six stocks (see Table 6.1). This population consists of the percentage returns 10 percent, 20 percent, 30 percent, 40 percent, 50 percent, and 60 percent (which we have arranged in increasing order). Table 6.1 and Figure 6.1(a) (on the next page) show the relative frequency distribution and the relative frequency histogram describing the population of six returns. The mean and the standard deviation of this population can be calculated to be 35 percent and 17.078 percent, respectively. Now consider randomly selecting without replacement a sample

TABLE 6.1 A Relative Frequency Distribution Describing the Population of Six Individual Stock Returns

Stock	Percentage Return	Frequency	Relative Frequency
Stock A	10	1	1/6
Stock B	20	1	1/6
Stock C	30	1	1/6
Stock D	40	1	1/6
Stock E	50	1	1/6
Stock F	60	1	1/6

FIGURE 6.1 A Comparison of Individual Stock Returns and Sample Mean Returns

(a) A relative frequency histogram describing the population of six individual stock returns

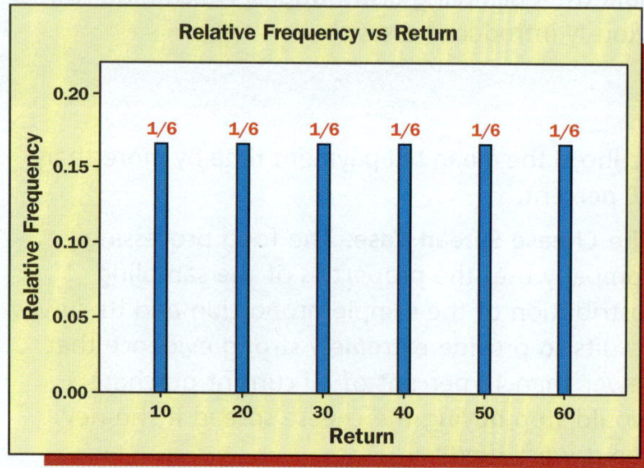

(b) A relative frequency histogram describing the population of 15 sample mean returns

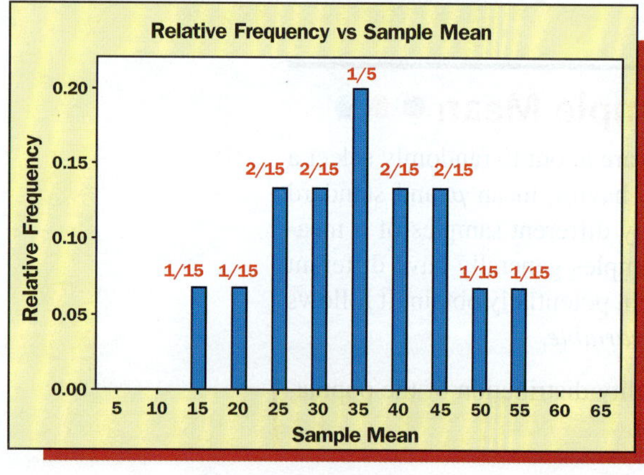

TABLE 6.2 The Population of Sample Means

(a) The population of the 15 samples of $n = 2$ returns and corresponding sample means

Sample	$n = 2$ Returns in Sample		Sample Mean
1	10	20	15
2	10	30	20
3	10	40	25
4	10	50	30
5	10	60	35
6	20	30	25
7	20	40	30
8	20	50	35
9	20	60	40
10	30	40	35
11	30	50	40
12	30	60	45
13	40	50	45
14	40	60	50
15	50	60	55

(b) A relative frequency distribution describing the population of 15 sample mean returns

Sample Mean	Frequency	Relative Frequency
15	1	1/15
20	1	1/15
25	2	2/15
30	2	2/15
35	3	3/15
40	2	2/15
45	2	2/15
50	1	1/15
55	1	1/15

of $n = 2$ returns from the population of six returns. Table 6.2(a) lists the 15 distinct samples of $n = 2$ returns that could be obtained and also shows the mean of each sample (note that each sample is specified only with respect to which two returns are contained in the sample, and not with respect to the different orders in which the returns could be randomly selected). To describe what the distribution of the population of 15 sample means looks like, we form the relative frequency distribution shown in Table 6.2(b) and the relative frequency histogram shown in Figure 6.1(b). Comparing Figures 6.1(a) and (b) we see that, although the histogram of six individual returns and the histogram of 15 sample mean returns seem to be centered over the same mean of 35 percent, the histogram of sample mean returns looks *more bell-shaped* and *less spread out* than the histogram of individual returns.

In general, there are several relationships between (1) a population of individual measurements and (2) the population of all possible sample means based on all samples of size n that can be randomly selected from the population of individual measurements. Before explaining these relationships, however, we consider another example. The year 1987 featured extreme volatility on the stock market, including a loss of over 20 percent of the market's value on a single day. Figure 6.2(a) shows the relative frequency histogram of the percentage returns for the entire year 1987 for the population of all 1,815 stocks listed on the New York Stock Exchange. The mean and the standard deviation of the population of percentage returns are -3.5 percent and 26 percent, respectively. Consider drawing a random sample of $n = 5$ stocks from the population of 1,815 stocks and calculating the mean return, $\bar{x}$, of the sampled stocks. If we use a computer, we

FIGURE 6.2 The New York Stock Exchange in 1987: A Comparison of Individual Stock Returns and Sample Mean Returns

(a) The relative frequency histogram describing the population of individual stock returns

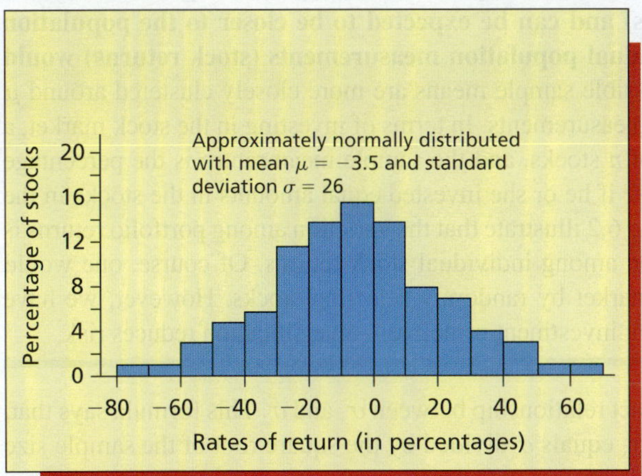

(b) The relative frequency histogram describing the population of all possible sample mean returns when $n = 5$

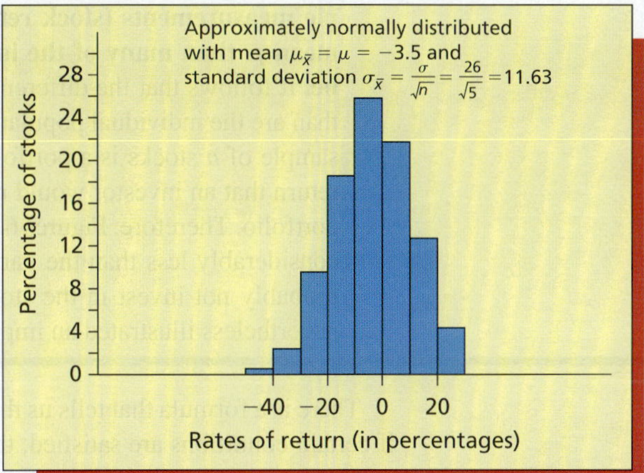

Figure 6.2 is adapted with permission from *The American Association of Individual Investors Journal,* by John K. Ford, "A Method for Grading 1987 Stock Recommendations," March 1988, pp. 16–17.

can generate all the different samples of five stocks that can be obtained (there are trillions of such samples) and calculate the corresponding sample mean returns. A relative frequency histogram describing the population of all possible sample mean returns is given in Figure 6.2(b). Comparing Figures 6.2(a) and (b), we see that, although the histogram of individual stock returns and the histogram of sample mean returns are both bell-shaped and seem to be centered over the same mean of −3.5 percent, the histogram of sample mean returns looks less spread out than the histogram of individual returns.

Thus far we have considered two stock return examples. Together, these examples illustrate several important facts about randomly selecting a sample of n individual measurements from a population of individual measurements having mean μ and standard deviation σ. Specifically, it can be shown that

1 **If the population of individual measurements is normally distributed, then the population of all possible sample means is also normally distributed.** This is illustrated in Figures 6.2(a) and (b): Because the population of individual stock returns is (approximately) normally distributed, the population of all possible sample mean returns is also (approximately) normally distributed.

2 **Even if the population of individual measurements is not normally distributed, there are circumstances when the population of all possible sample means is approximately normally distributed.** This result is based on a theorem called the **Central Limit Theorem** and is discussed more fully in the next subsection. For now, note that the result is intuitively illustrated in Figures 6.1(a) and (b): Although the population of six stock returns does not have a normal distribution (it has a uniform distribution), the population of 15 sample mean returns has a distribution that looks somewhat like a normal distribution.

3 **The mean, $\mu_{\bar{x}}$, of the population of all possible sample means equals μ, the mean of the population of individual measurements.** This is illustrated in both Figures 6.1 and 6.2. That is, in each stock return example, the histogram of individual stock returns and the histogram of all possible sample mean returns are centered over the same mean μ (note that μ equals 35 percent in Figure 6.1 and −3.5 percent in Figure 6.2). Furthermore, this implies that, although the sample mean return for a particular sample of n randomly selected stocks probably will not equal the population mean return μ, the mean of the population of all possible sample mean returns (based on all possible samples of n stocks) is equal to μ.

4 **The standard deviation, $\sigma_{\bar{x}}$, of the population of all possible sample means is less than σ, the standard deviation of the population of individual measurements.**[1] This is also illustrated in both Figures 6.1 and 6.2. That is, in each stock return example, the histogram of all possible sample mean returns is less spread out than the histogram of individual stock returns. Intuitively, $\sigma_{\bar{x}}$ is smaller than σ because each possible sample mean is an average of n measurements (stock returns). Thus, **each sample mean *averages out* high and low sample measurements (stock returns) and can be expected to be closer to the population mean μ than many of the individual population measurements (stock returns) would be.** It follows that the different possible sample means are more closely clustered around μ than are the individual population measurements. In terms of investing in the stock market, a sample of n stocks is a portfolio of n stocks, and the sample mean return is the percentage return that an investor would realize if he or she invested equal amounts in the stocks in the portfolio. Therefore, Figures 6.1 and 6.2 illustrate that the variation among portfolio returns is considerably less than the variation among individual stock returns. Of course, one would probably not invest in the stock market by randomly selecting stocks. However, we have nevertheless illustrated an important investment principle—diversification reduces risk.

There is a formula that tells us the exact relationship between $\sigma_{\bar{x}}$ and σ. This formula says that, if certain conditions are satisfied, then $\sigma_{\bar{x}}$ equals σ divided by the square root of the sample size n. That is,

$$\sigma_{\bar{x}} = \frac{\sigma}{\sqrt{n}}$$

It follows that $\sigma_{\bar{x}}$ is less than σ if the sample size n is greater than 1. Furthermore, this formula is valid if the sampled population is infinite and is approximately valid if the sampled population is finite and much larger than (say, at least 20 times) the size of the sample. For example, consider randomly selecting $n = 5$ stock returns from the 1987 population of 1,815 individual stock returns. Because the population size of 1,815 is more than 20 times the sample size ($20 \times 5 = 100$), and since we have previously seen that the population standard deviation σ is 26 percent, it follows that

$$\sigma_{\bar{x}} = \frac{\sigma}{\sqrt{n}} = \frac{26}{\sqrt{5}} = 11.63$$

Figures 6.2(a) and (b) illustrate the fact that $\sigma_{\bar{x}} = 11.63$ is smaller than $\sigma = 26$. Specifically, Figure 6.2(a) illustrates that the population of individual stock returns is approximately normally distributed with mean $\mu = -3.5$ percent and standard deviation $\sigma = 26$ percent. Therefore, for example, approximately 95.44 percent of all individual stock returns are in the interval $[-3.5 \pm 2(26)] = [-3.5 \pm 52]$—that is, are between -55.5 percent and 48.5 percent. Figure 6.2(b) illustrates that the population of all possible sample mean returns is approximately normally distributed with mean $\mu_{\bar{x}} = -3.5$ percent and standard deviation $\sigma_{\bar{x}} = 11.63$ percent. This implies that approximately 95.44 percent of all possible *sample mean returns* are in the interval $[-3.5 \pm 2(11.63)] = [-3.5 \pm 23.26]$—that is, are between -26.76 percent and 19.76 percent. In summary, because $\sigma_{\bar{x}} = 11.63$ is less than $\sigma = 26$, the variation among 95.44 percent of all possible sample mean returns is considerably less than the variation among 95.44 percent of all individual stock returns.

Before continuing, it is important to make two comments. First, the formula $\sigma_{\bar{x}} = \sigma/\sqrt{n}$ follows, in theory, from the formula for $\sigma^2_{\bar{x}}$, the variance of the population of all possible sample means. The formula for $\sigma^2_{\bar{x}}$ is $\sigma^2_{\bar{x}} = \sigma^2/n$. Second, the technical note at the end of this section gives a theoretically correct formula for $\sigma_{\bar{x}}$ when the sampled population is finite. As stated above, if the sampled population is finite and at least 20 times the size of the sample, the formula $\sigma_{\bar{x}} = \sigma/\sqrt{n}$ can be used to approximate the theoretically correct formula. However, if the sampled population is finite and smaller than 20 times the size of the sample, then the theoretically correct formula at the end of this section must be used to compute $\sigma_{\bar{x}}$. We will see how the theoretically correct formula can be used in Section 7.5. With the exception of Section 7.5, all of the

[1]We will see that this is true if the sample size is greater than 1.

sampled populations in this book will be either infinite or much larger than the samples that we take (and thus $\sigma_{\bar{x}} = \sigma/\sqrt{n}$ is either exactly or approximately correct).

We now summarize what we have learned about the sampling distribution of $\bar{x}$.

The Sampling Distribution of $\bar{x}$

Assume that the population from which we will randomly select a sample of n measurements has mean μ and standard deviation σ. Then, the population of all possible sample means

1 Has a normal distribution, if the sampled population has a normal distribution.

2 Has mean $\mu_{\bar{x}} = \mu$.

3 Has variance $\sigma^2_{\bar{x}} = \dfrac{\sigma^2}{n}$ and standard deviation $\sigma_{\bar{x}} = \dfrac{\sigma}{\sqrt{n}}$.

The formulas for $\sigma^2_{\bar{x}}$ and $\sigma_{\bar{x}}$ in (3) hold exactly if the sampled population is infinite and hold approximately if the sampled population is finite and much larger than (say, at least 20 times) the size of the sample.

Stated equivalently, the sampling distribution of $\bar{x}$ has mean $\mu_{\bar{x}} = \mu$, has standard deviation $\sigma_{\bar{x}} = \sigma/\sqrt{n}$ [under the conditions described above], and is a normal distribution (if the sampled population has a normal distribution).[2]

In the stock return case, we know the values of the mean μ and the standard deviation σ of the sampled population of 1,815 individual stock returns. In most situations, however, we randomly select a sample from a population in order to estimate the unknown mean μ and the unknown standard deviation σ of the population. We have seen that the sample mean $\bar{x}$ is the point estimate of μ and the sample standard deviation s is the point estimate of σ. Furthermore, a larger sample is more likely to give a more accurate point estimate $\bar{x}$ of μ and a more accurate point estimate s of σ. This is certainly intuitive. Furthermore, we can use the formula $\sigma_{\bar{x}} = \sigma/\sqrt{n}$ to demonstrate why a larger sample is more likely to give a more accurate point estimate $\bar{x}$ of μ. Notice that the sample size n is in the denominator of the formula $\sigma_{\bar{x}} = \sigma/\sqrt{n}$. This implies that the larger the sample size n is, the smaller is $\sigma_{\bar{x}}$. This is logical because, the larger the sample size is, the better is the chance that the high and low measurements in the sample will cancel each other out to give a sample mean near μ (because more measurements are being averaged). Therefore, when the sample size is large, the possible sample means will be more closely clustered around μ than when the sample size is smaller. This implies that the sample mean calculated from the actual sample that we select is more likely to be near μ. In the following example we illustrate this idea and also show how the sampling distribution of $\bar{x}$ can help us to make a statistically based conclusion about a population mean μ.

Example 6.2 The Car Mileage Case

C

Recall that the federal government will give a tax credit to any automaker selling a midsize model equipped with an automatic transmission that achieves a mean EPA combined city and highway mileage μ of at least 31 mpg. Also recall that we have considered an automaker that has introduced a new midsize car, and consider the population of all mileages that would be obtained by all individual cars of this type. If this population is normally distributed with mean μ and standard deviation σ [see Figure 6.3(a)], and if the automaker will randomly select a sample of n cars and test them as prescribed by the EPA, then the population of all possible sample means is normally distributed with mean $\mu_{\bar{x}} = \mu$ and standard deviation $\sigma_{\bar{x}} = \sigma/\sqrt{n}$. In order to show that a larger sample is more likely to give a more accurate point estimate $\bar{x}$ of μ, compare taking a sample of size $n = 5$ with taking a sample of size $n = 49$. If $n = 5$, then $\sigma_{\bar{x}} = \sigma/\sqrt{5}$, whereas if $n = 49$, then $\sigma_{\bar{x}} = \sigma/\sqrt{49}$. Therefore, if $n = 49$, the different possible sample means that the automaker might obtain will be more closely clustered around μ than they will be if $n = 5$ (see Figures 6.3(b) and (c)). This implies that the larger sample of size $n = 49$ is more likely to give a sample mean $\bar{x}$ that is near μ.

[2]In Appendix D (Part 3) on page 853 we derive the formulas $\mu_{\bar{x}} = \mu$ and $\sigma^2_{\bar{x}} = \sigma^2/n$.

FIGURE 6.3 A Comparison of (1) the Population of All Individual Car Mileages, (2) the Sampling Distribution of the Sample Mean $\bar{x}$ When $n = 5$, and (3) the Sampling Distribution of the Sample Mean $\bar{x}$ When $n = 49$

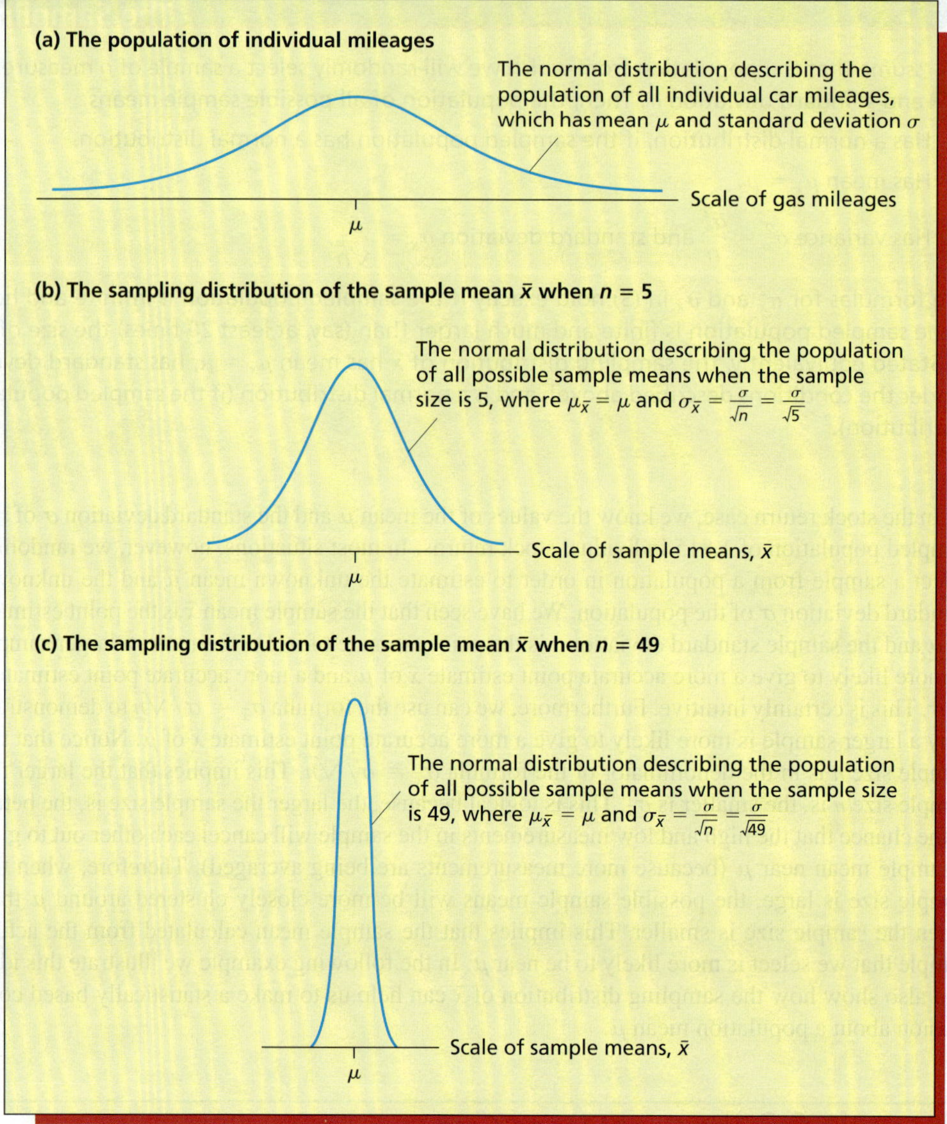
(a) The population of individual mileages
The normal distribution describing the population of all individual car mileages, which has mean μ and standard deviation σ
Scale of gas mileages
μ
(b) The sampling distribution of the sample mean $\bar{x}$ when $n = 5$
The normal distribution describing the population of all possible sample means when the sample size is 5, where $\mu_{\bar{x}} = \mu$ and $\sigma_{\bar{x}} = \frac{\sigma}{\sqrt{n}} = \frac{\sigma}{\sqrt{5}}$
Scale of sample means, $\bar{x}$
μ
(c) The sampling distribution of the sample mean $\bar{x}$ when $n = 49$
The normal distribution describing the population of all possible sample means when the sample size is 49, where $\mu_{\bar{x}} = \mu$ and $\sigma_{\bar{x}} = \frac{\sigma}{\sqrt{n}} = \frac{\sigma}{\sqrt{49}}$
Scale of sample means, $\bar{x}$
μ

Recall from Chapter 2 that the automaker has randomly selected a sample of $n = 49$ mileages, which has mean $\bar{x} = 31.5531$. We now wish to determine whether this sample information provides strong statistical evidence that the population mean mileage μ is greater than 31 mpg (and, therefore, is at least 31 mpg). This will be done by assuming (for the sake of argument) that μ equals 31 and using the sample information to reject this assumption in favor of the conclusion that μ is greater than 31. Since the sample mean $\bar{x} = 31.5531$ is greater than 31, we have some evidence against the assumption that μ equals 31. To evaluate the strength of this evidence, we calculate the probability of observing a sample mean that is greater than or equal to 31.5531 if, in fact, μ equals 31. To do this, recall from Chapter 2 that a stem-and-leaf display and a histogram of the 49 mileages in Table 2.1 indicate that the population of all individual mileages is normally distributed. Assuming that the population standard deviation is known to be $\sigma = .8$ mpg, it follows that the sampling distribution of the sample mean $\bar{x}$ is a normal distribution, with

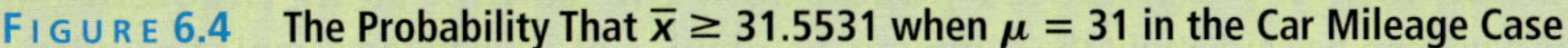

FIGURE 6.4 The Probability That $\bar{x} \geq 31.5531$ when $\mu = 31$ in the Car Mileage Case

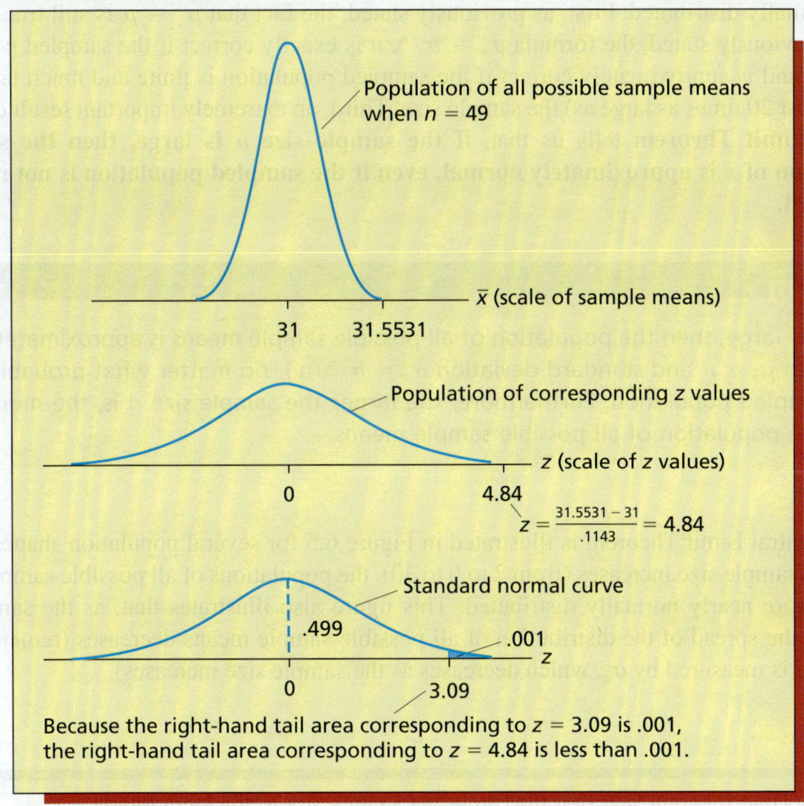

mean $\mu_{\bar{x}} = \mu$ and standard deviation $\sigma_{\bar{x}} = \sigma/\sqrt{n} = .8/\sqrt{49} = .8/7 = .1143$. Therefore,

$$P(\bar{x} \geq 31.5531 \text{ if } \mu = 31) = P\left(z \geq \frac{31.5531 - \mu_{\bar{x}}}{\sigma_{\bar{x}}}\right) = P\left(z \geq \frac{31.5531 - 31}{.1143}\right)$$

$$= P(z \geq 4.84)$$

To find $P(z \geq 4.84)$, notice that the largest z value given in Table A.3 (page 824) is 3.09, which gives a right-hand tail area of .001. Therefore, since

$$P(z \geq 3.09) = .5 - .499 = .001$$

it follows that $P(z \geq 4.84)$ is less than .001 (see Figure 6.4). The fact that this probability is less than .001 says that, if μ equals 31, then fewer than 1 in 1,000 of all possible sample means are at least as large as the sample mean $\bar{x} = 31.5531$ that we have actually observed. Therefore, if we are to believe that μ equals 31, then we must believe that we have observed a sample mean that can be described as a smaller than 1 in 1,000 chance. Since it is extremely difficult to believe that such a small chance would occur, we have extremely strong evidence that μ does not equal 31 and that μ is, in fact, larger than 31. This evidence would probably convince the federal government that the midsize model's mean mileage exceeds 31 mpg.

In the preceding example, we assumed that the population standard deviation σ is known to be equal to .8 mpg. Of course, in almost all real-world situations the value of σ is not known. In Chapters 7 and 8 we will see how to make statistical inferences when σ is unknown. For now, we will assume that through extensive experience with the population or process under consideration, we know the value of σ.

Sampling a nonnormally distributed population: the Central Limit Theorem We now consider what can be said about the sampling distribution of $\bar{x}$ when the sampled population is not normally distributed. First, as previously stated, the fact that $\mu_{\bar{x}} = \mu$ is still true. Second, as also previously stated, the formula $\sigma_{\bar{x}} = \sigma/\sqrt{n}$ is exactly correct if the sampled population is infinite and is approximately correct if the sampled population is finite and much larger than (say, at least 20 times as large as) the sample size. Third, an extremely important result called the **Central Limit Theorem** tells us that, **if the sample size n is large, then the sampling distribution of $\bar{x}$ is approximately normal, even if the sampled population is not normally distributed.**

The Central Limit Theorem

If the sample size n is sufficiently large, then the population of all possible sample means is approximately normally distributed (with mean $\mu_{\bar{x}} = \mu$ and standard deviation $\sigma_{\bar{x}} = \sigma/\sqrt{n}$), no matter what probability distribution describes the sampled population. Furthermore, the larger the sample size n is, the more nearly normally distributed is the population of all possible sample means.

CHAPTERS 7 AND 8

The Central Limit Theorem is illustrated in Figure 6.5 for several population shapes. Notice that as the sample size increases (from 2 to 6 to 30), the populations of all possible sample means become more nearly normally distributed. This figure also illustrates that, as the sample size increases, the spread of the distribution of all possible sample means decreases (remember that this spread is measured by $\sigma_{\bar{x}}$, which decreases as the sample size increases).

FIGURE 6.5 **The Central Limit Theorem Says that the Larger the Sample Size Is, the More Nearly Normally Distributed Is the Population of All Possible Sample Means**

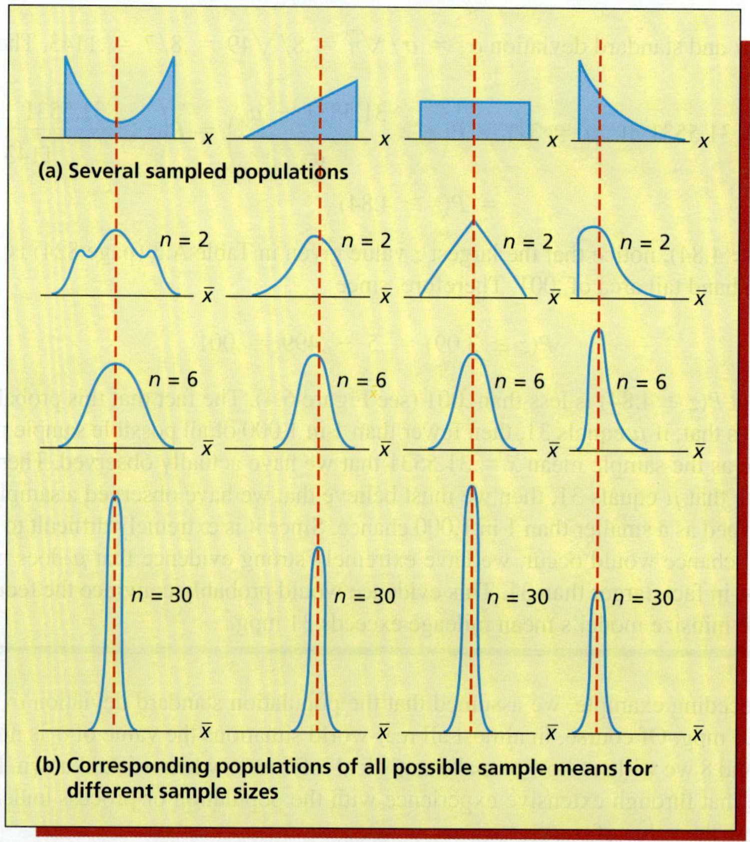

(a) Several sampled populations

(b) Corresponding populations of all possible sample means for different sample sizes

How large must the sample size be for the sampling distribution of $\bar{x}$ to be approximately normal? In general, the more skewed the probability distribution of the sampled population, the larger the sample size must be for the population of all possible sample means to be approximately normally distributed. For some sampled populations, particularly those described by symmetric distributions, the population of all possible sample means is approximately normally distributed for a fairly small sample size. In addition, studies indicate that, **if the sample size is at least 30, then for most sampled populations the population of all possible sample means is approximately normally distributed.** In this book, whenever the sample size n is at least 30, we will assume that the sampling distribution of $\bar{x}$ is approximately a normal distribution. Of course, if the sampled population is exactly normally distributed, the sampling distribution of $\bar{x}$ is exactly normal for any sample size.

We can see the shapes of sampling distributions such as those illustrated in Figure 6.5 by using computer simulation. Specifically, for a population having a particular probability distribution, we can have the computer draw a given number of samples of n observations, compute the mean of each sample, and arrange the sample means into a histogram. To illustrate this, consider Figure 6.6(a), which shows the exponential distribution describing the hospital emergency room interarrival times discussed in Example 5.11 (page 223). Figure 6.6(b) gives the results of a simulation in which MINITAB randomly selected 1,000 samples of five interarrival times from this exponential distribution, calculated the mean of each sample, and arranged the 1,000 sample means into a histogram. Figure 6.6(c) gives the results of a simulation in which MINITAB randomly selected 1,000 samples of 30 interarrival times from the exponential distribution, calculated the mean of each sample, and arranged the 1,000 sample means into a histogram. Note that, whereas the histogram in Figure 6.6(b) is somewhat skewed to the right, the histogram in Figure 6.6(c) appears approximately bell-shaped. Therefore, we might conclude that when we randomly select a sample of n observations from an exponential distribution, the sampling distribution of the sample mean is somewhat skewed to the right when $n = 5$ and is approximately normal when $n = 30$.

FIGURE 6.6 Simulating the Sampling Distribution of the Sample Mean When Sampling from an Exponential Distribution

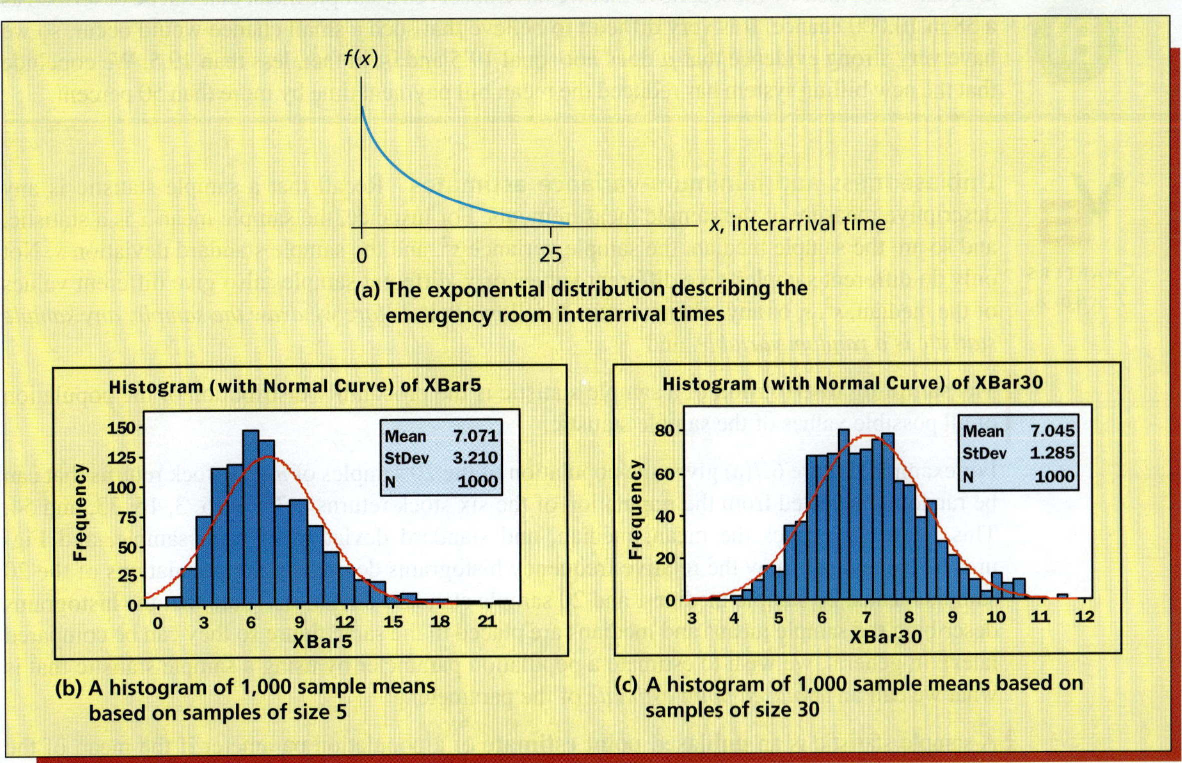

(a) The exponential distribution describing the emergency room interarrival times

(b) A histogram of 1,000 sample means based on samples of size 5

(c) A histogram of 1,000 sample means based on samples of size 30

Example 6.3 The Payment Time Case

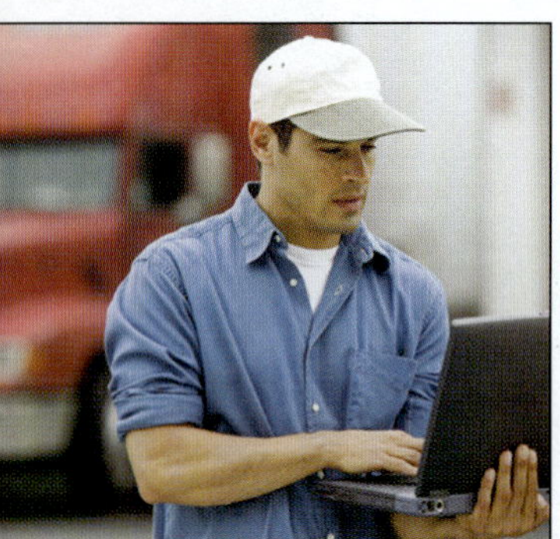

Recall from Example 2.2 (page 45) that a management consulting firm has installed a new computer-based billing system in a Hamilton, Ohio, trucking company. Because of the previously discussed advantages of the new billing system, and because the trucking company's clients are receptive to using this system, the management consulting firm believes that the new system will reduce the mean bill payment time by more than 50 percent. The mean payment time using the old billing system was approximately equal to, but no less than, 39 days. Therefore, if μ denotes the new mean payment time, the consulting firm believes that μ will be less than 19.5 days. To assess whether μ is less than 19.5, we will assume for the sake of argument that μ equals 19.5 and use the sample of $n = 65$ payment times to weigh the evidence against this assumption and in favor of the conclusion that μ is less than 19.5. The mean of the 65 payment times is $\bar{x} = 18.1077$, and because this sample mean is less than 19.5, we have some evidence contradicting the assumption that μ equals 19.5. To evaluate the strength of this evidence, we calculate the probability of observing a sample mean that is less than or equal to 18.1077 if, in fact, μ equals 19.5. To do this, recall from Chapter 2 that a stem-and-leaf display of the 65 payment times indicates that the population of all payment times is skewed with a tail to the right. However, the Central Limit Theorem tells us that, because the sample size $n = 65$ is large, the sampling distribution of $\bar{x}$ is approximately a normal distribution with mean $\mu_{\bar{x}} = \mu$ and standard deviation $\sigma_{\bar{x}} = \sigma/\sqrt{n}$. Assuming that the population standard deviation σ is known to be 4.2 days, $\sigma_{\bar{x}}$ equals $4.2/\sqrt{65} = .5209$. It follows that

$$\begin{aligned} P(\bar{x} \le 18.1077 \text{ if } \mu = 19.5) &= P\left(z \le \frac{18.1077 - 19.5}{.5209}\right) \\ &= P(z \le -2.67) \end{aligned}$$

The normal table tells us that the area under the standard normal curve from -2.67 to 0 is .4962. It follows that the tail area under this curve to the left of -2.67 is $.5 - .4962 = .0038$. Therefore,

$$P(\bar{x} \le 18.1077 \text{ if } \mu = 19.5) = .0038$$

This probability says that, if μ equals 19.5, then only .0038 of all possible sample means are at least as small as the sample mean $\bar{x} = 18.1077$ that we have actually observed. If we are to believe that μ equals 19.5, then we must believe that we have observed a sample mean that can be described as a 38 in 10,000 chance. It is very difficult to believe that such a small chance would occur, so we have very strong evidence that μ does not equal 19.5 and is, in fact, less than 19.5. We conclude that the new billing system has reduced the mean bill payment time by more than 50 percent.

CHAPTERS 7 AND 8

Unbiasedness and minimum-variance estimates Recall that a sample statistic is any descriptive measure of the sample measurements. For instance, the sample mean $\bar{x}$ is a statistic, and so are the sample median, the sample variance s^2, and the sample standard deviation s. Not only do different samples give different values of $\bar{x}$, different samples also give different values of the median, s^2, s, or any other statistic. It follows that, *before we draw the sample, any sample statistic is a random variable,* and

The **sampling distribution** of a sample statistic is the probability distribution of the population of all possible values of the sample statistic.

For example, Figure 6.7(a) gives the population of the 20 samples of $n = 3$ stock returns that can be randomly selected from the population of the six stock returns -36, -15, 3, 15, 33, and 54. This figure also gives the mean, median, and standard deviation of each sample, and Figures 6.7(b) and (c) show the relative frequency histograms describing the populations of the 20 sample means, 20 sample medians, and 20 sample standard deviations (note that the histograms describing the sample means and medians are placed in the same figure so they can be compared later). In general, we wish to estimate a population parameter by using a sample statistic that is what we call an *unbiased point estimate* of the parameter.

A sample statistic is an **unbiased point estimate** of a population parameter if the mean of the population of all possible values of the sample statistic equals the population parameter.

FIGURE 6.7 **Populations of Sample Means, Medians, and Standard Deviations**

(a) The population of the 20 samples of $n = 3$ returns and corresponding populations of sample means, medians, and standard deviations

Sample	$n = 3$ Returns in Sample			Sample Statistics Mean	Median	Std. Dev.
1	−36	−15	3	−16.00	−15.00	19.52
2	−36	−15	15	−12.00	−15.00	25.63
3	−36	−15	33	−6.00	−15.00	35.37
4	−36	−15	54	1.00	−15.00	47.09
5	−36	3	15	−6.00	3.00	26.66
6	−36	3	33	0.00	3.00	34.60
7	−36	3	54	7.00	3.00	45.13
8	−36	15	33	4.00	15.00	35.79
9	−36	15	54	11.00	15.00	45.13
10	−36	33	54	17.00	33.00	47.09
11	−15	3	15	1.00	3.00	15.10
12	−15	3	33	7.00	3.00	24.25
13	−15	3	54	14.00	3.00	35.79
14	−15	15	33	11.00	15.00	24.25
15	−15	15	54	18.00	15.00	34.60
16	−15	33	54	24.00	33.00	35.37
17	3	15	33	17.00	15.00	15.10
18	3	15	54	24.00	15.00	26.66
19	3	33	54	30.00	33.00	25.63
20	15	33	54	34.00	33.00	19.52

Summary of sample means and medians
Mean of the 20 sample means = 9
Mean of the 20 sample medians = 9
Standard deviation of the 20 sample means = 13.26
Standard deviation of the 20 sample medians = 15.88

(b) The relative frequency histograms describing the populations of sample means and medians

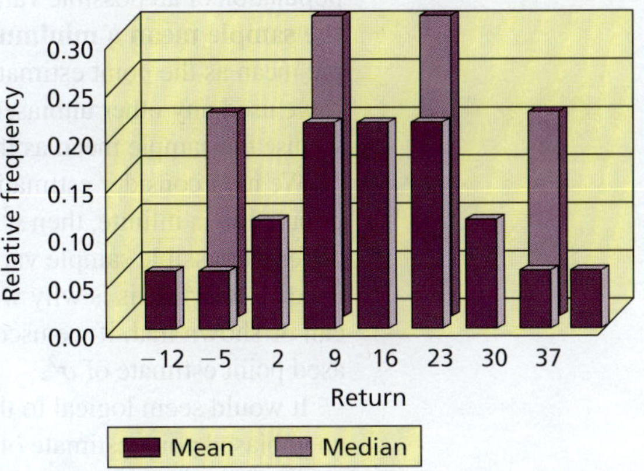

(c) The relative frequency histogram describing the population of sample standard deviations

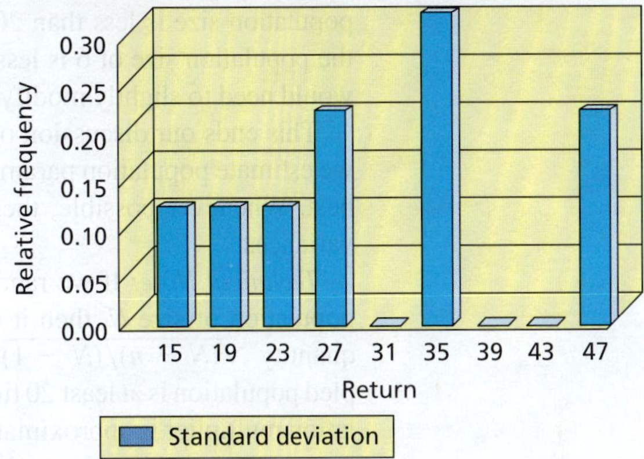

We use the sample mean $\bar{x}$ as the point estimate of the population mean μ because **$\bar{x}$ is an unbiased point estimate of μ.** That is, $\mu_{\bar{x}} = \mu$. In words, the average of all the different possible sample means (that we could obtain from all the different possible samples) equals μ. For example, consider the summary of sample means and medians given at the bottom of Figure 6.7(a). Doing this, we see that (1) the mean of the population of 20 sample means and (2) the mean of the population of 20 sample medians are both equal to 9, which is the mean of the sampled population of six stock returns (−36, −15, 3, 15, 33, and 54). Thus, in this situation both the sample mean and the sample median are unbiased estimates of the population mean. In general, as we have said, the sample mean is always an unbiased estimate of the population mean. However, the sample median is *not always* an unbiased estimate of the population mean.

Although we want a sample statistic to be an unbiased point estimate of the population parameter of interest, we also want the statistic to have a small standard deviation (and variance). That is, we wish the different possible values of the sample statistic to be closely clustered around the population parameter. If this is the case, when we actually randomly select one sample and compute the sample statistic, its value is likely to be close to the value of the population parameter. For example, note from the bottom of Figure 6.7(a) that, although both the sample mean and the sample median are unbiased estimates of the population mean in this situation, the standard deviation of the population of 20 sample means, which is 13.26, is less than the standard deviation of the population of 20 sample medians, which is 15.88. This says, as is illustrated in Figure 6.7(b), that the 20 sample means are more closely clustered around the population mean than are the 20 sample medians. Therefore, the sample mean is the preferred point estimate of the population mean. Furthermore, although the sampled population of six stock returns is not normally distributed, some general results apply to estimating the mean μ of a normally distributed population. In this situation, it can be shown that both the sample mean and the sample median are unbiased point estimates of μ. In fact, there are many unbiased point estimates of μ. However, it can be shown that the variance of the population of all possible sample means is smaller than the variance of the population of all possible values of any other unbiased point estimate of μ. For this reason, **we call the sample mean a minimum-variance unbiased point estimate of μ.** When we use the sample mean as the point estimate of μ, we are more likely to obtain a point estimate close to μ than if we used any other unbiased sample statistic as the point estimate of μ. This is one reason why we use the sample mean as the point estimate of the population mean.

We next consider estimating the population variance σ^2. It can be shown that if the sampled population is infinite, then **s^2 is an unbiased point estimate of σ^2.** That is, the average of all the different possible sample variances that we could obtain (from all the different possible samples) is equal to σ^2. This is why we use a divisor equal to $n - 1$ rather than n when we estimate σ^2. It can be shown that, if we used n as the divisor when estimating σ^2, we would not obtain an unbiased point estimate of σ^2.

It would seem logical to think that, because s^2 is an unbiased point estimate of σ^2, s should be an unbiased point estimate of σ. This seems plausible, but it is not the case. There is no easy way to calculate an unbiased point estimate of σ. Because of this, the usual practice is to use s as the point estimate of σ (even though it is not an unbiased estimate).

In Section 7.5 we discuss a slight modification of s^2 that is an unbiased estimate of σ^2 when the sampled population is finite. In practice, this modification is not used (and s^2 is used) unless the population size is less than 20 times the sample size. In the stock return example of Figure 6.7, the population size of 6 is less than 20 times the sample size of 3. Therefore, in this situation we would need to slightly modify s^2 and s to obtain appropriate point estimates of σ^2 and σ.

This ends our discussion of the theory of point estimation. It suffices to say that in this book we estimate population parameters by using sample statistics that statisticians generally agree are best. Whenever possible, these sample statistics are unbiased point estimates and have small variances.

Technical Note: If we randomly select a sample of size n without replacement from a finite population of size N, then it can be shown that $\sigma_{\bar{x}} = (\sigma/\sqrt{n})\sqrt{(N - n)/(N - 1)}$, where the quantity $\sqrt{(N - n)/(N - 1)}$ is called the *finite population multiplier*. If the size of the sampled population is at least 20 times the size of the sample (that is, if $N \geq 20n$), then the finite population multiplier is approximately equal to one, and $\sigma_{\bar{x}}$ approximately equals $\sigma/\sqrt{n}$. However, if the population size N is smaller than 20 times the size of the sample, then the finite population multiplier is substantially less than one, and we must include this multiplier in the calculation of $\sigma_{\bar{x}}$. For instance, in our initial stock return example on page 237 (where $N = 6$ is only three times $n = 2$), we have

$$\sigma_{\bar{x}} = \frac{\sigma}{\sqrt{n}}\sqrt{\frac{N-n}{N-1}} = \left(\frac{17.078}{\sqrt{2}}\right)\sqrt{\frac{6-2}{6-1}} = 12.076(.8944) = 10.8$$

We will see how this formula can be used to make statistical inferences in Section 7.5.

Exercises for Section 6.1

CONCEPTS

6.1 Suppose that we will randomly select a sample of four measurements from a larger population of measurements. The sampling distribution of the sample mean $\bar{x}$ is the probability distribution of a population. In your own words, describe the units in this population.

6.2 Suppose that we will randomly select a sample of n measurements from a normally distributed population of measurements having mean μ and standard deviation σ. If we consider the sampling distribution of $\bar{x}$ (that is, if we consider the population of all possible sample means):

a Describe the shape of the population of all possible sample means.

b Write formulas that express the central tendency and the variability of the population of all possible sample means. Explain what these formulas say in your own words.

6.3 Explain how the central tendency of the population of all possible sample means compares to the central tendency of the individual measurements in the population from which the sample will be taken.

6.4 Explain how the variability of the population of all possible sample means compares to the variability of the individual measurements in the population from which the sample will be taken. Assume here that the sample size is greater than 1. Intuitively explain why this is true.

6.5 What does the Central Limit Theorem tell us about the sampling distribution of the sample mean?

6.6 In your own words, explain each of the following terms:

a Unbiased point estimate. **b** Minimum-variance unbiased point estimate.

METHODS AND APPLICATIONS

6.7 Suppose that we will take a random sample of size n from a population having mean μ and standard deviation σ. For each of the following situations, find the mean, variance, and standard deviation of the sampling distribution of the sample mean $\bar{x}$:

a $\mu = 10$, $\sigma = 2$, $n = 25$ **c** $\mu = 3$, $\sigma = .1$, $n = 4$

b $\mu = 500$, $\sigma = .5$, $n = 100$ **d** $\mu = 100$, $\sigma = 1$, $n = 1{,}600$

6.8 For each situation in Exercise 6.7, find an interval that contains (approximately or exactly) 99.73 percent of all the possible sample means. In which cases must we assume that the population is normally distributed? Why?

6.9 Suppose that we will randomly select a sample of 64 measurements from a population having a mean equal to 20 and a standard deviation equal to 4.

a Describe the shape of the sampling distribution of the sample mean $\bar{x}$. Do we need to make any assumptions about the shape of the population? Why or why not?

b Find the mean and the standard deviation of the sampling distribution of the sample mean $\bar{x}$.

c Calculate the probability that we will obtain a sample mean greater than 21; that is, calculate $P(\bar{x} > 21)$. Hint: Find the z value corresponding to 21 by using $\mu_{\bar{x}}$ and $\sigma_{\bar{x}}$ because we wish to calculate a probability about $\bar{x}$. Then sketch the sampling distribution and the probability.

d Calculate the probability that we will obtain a sample mean less than 19.385; that is, calculate $P(\bar{x} < 19.385)$.

6.10 Suppose that the percentage returns for a given year for all stocks listed on the New York Stock Exchange are approximately normally distributed with a mean of 12.4 percent and a standard deviation of 20.6 percent. Consider drawing a random sample of $n = 5$ stocks from the population of all stocks and calculating the mean return, $\bar{x}$, of the sampled stocks. Find the mean and the standard deviation of the sampling distribution of $\bar{x}$, and find an interval containing 95.44 percent of all possible sample mean returns.

6.11 THE BANK CUSTOMER WAITING TIME CASE WaitTime

Recall that the bank manager wants to show that the new system reduces typical customer waiting times to less than six minutes. One way to do this is to demonstrate that the mean of the population of all customer waiting times is less than 6. Letting this mean be μ, in this exercise we wish to investigate whether the sample of 100 waiting times provides evidence to support the claim that μ is less than 6.

For the sake of argument, we will begin by assuming that μ equals 6, and we will then attempt to use the sample to contradict this assumption in favor of the conclusion that μ is less than 6. Recall that the mean of the sample of 100 waiting times is $\bar{x} = 5.46$ and assume that σ, the standard deviation of the population of all customer waiting times, is known to be 2.47.

a Consider the population of all possible sample means obtained from random samples of 100 waiting times. What is the shape of this population of sample means? That is, what is the shape of the sampling distribution of $\bar{x}$? Why is this true?

b Find the mean and standard deviation of the population of all possible sample means when we assume that μ equals 6.

c The sample mean that we have actually observed is $\bar{x} = 5.46$. Assuming that μ equals 6, find the probability of observing a sample mean that is less than or equal to $\bar{x} = 5.46$.

d If μ equals 6, what percentage of all possible sample means are less than or equal to 5.46? Since we have actually observed a sample mean of $\bar{x} = 5.46$, is it more reasonable to believe that (1) μ equals 6 and we have observed one of the sample means that is less than or equal to 5.46 when μ equals 6, or (2) that we have observed a sample mean less than or equal to 5.46 because μ is less than 6? Explain. What do you conclude about whether the new system has reduced the typical customer waiting time to less than six minutes?

6.12 THE VIDEO GAME SATISFACTION RATING CASE VideoGame

Recall that a customer is considered to be very satisfied with his or her XYZ Box video game system if the customer's composite score on the survey instrument of Figure 1.2 (page 10) is at least 42. One way to show that customers are typically very satisfied is to show that the mean of the population of all satisfaction ratings is at least 42. Letting this mean be μ, in this exercise we wish to investigate whether the sample of 65 satisfaction ratings provides evidence to support the claim that μ exceeds 42 (and, therefore, is at least 42).

For the sake of argument, we begin by assuming that μ equals 42, and we then attempt to use the sample to contradict this assumption in favor of the conclusion that μ exceeds 42. Recall that the mean of the sample of 65 satisfaction ratings is $\bar{x} = 42.95$, and assume that σ, the standard deviation of the population of all satisfaction ratings, is known to be 2.64.

a Consider the sampling distribution of $\bar{x}$ for random samples of 65 customer satisfaction ratings. Use the properties of this sampling distribution to find the probability of observing a sample mean greater than or equal to 42.95 when we assume that μ equals 42.

b If μ equals 42, what percentage of all possible sample means are greater than or equal to 42.95? Since we have actually observed a sample mean of $\bar{x} = 42.95$, is it more reasonable to believe that (1) μ equals 42 and we have observed a sample mean that is greater than or equal to 42.95 when μ equals 42, or (2) that we have observed a sample mean that is greater than or equal to 42.95 because μ is greater than 42? Explain. What do you conclude about whether customers are typically very satisfied with the XYZ Box video game system?

6.13 In an article in the *Journal of Management,* Joseph Martocchio studied and estimated the costs of employee absences. Based on a sample of 176 blue-collar workers, Martocchio estimated that the mean amount of paid time lost during a three-month period was 1.4 days per employee with a standard deviation of 1.3 days. Martocchio also estimated that the mean amount of unpaid time lost during a three-month period was 1.0 day per employee with a standard deviation of 1.8 days.

Suppose we randomly select a sample of 100 blue-collar workers. Based on Martocchio's estimates:

a What is the probability that the average amount of paid time lost during a three-month period for the 100 blue-collar workers will exceed 1.5 days?

b What is the probability that the average amount of unpaid time lost during a three-month period for the 100 blue-collar workers will exceed 1.5 days?

c Suppose we randomly select a sample of 100 blue-collar workers, and suppose the sample mean amount of unpaid time lost during a three-month period actually exceeds 1.5 days. Would it be reasonable to conclude that the mean amount of unpaid time lost has increased above the previously estimated 1.0 days? Explain.

6.14 When a pizza restaurant's delivery process is operating effectively, pizzas are delivered in an average of 45 minutes with a standard deviation of 6 minutes. To monitor its delivery process, the restaurant randomly selects five pizzas each night and records their delivery times.

a For the sake of argument, assume that the population of all delivery times on a given evening is normally distributed with a mean of $\mu = 45$ minutes and a standard deviation of $\sigma = 6$ minutes. (That is, we assume that the delivery process is operating effectively.)

(1) Describe the shape of the population of all possible sample means. How do you know what the shape is?

(2) Find the mean of the population of all possible sample means.

(3) Find the standard deviation of the population of all possible sample means.

(4) Calculate an interval containing 99.73 percent of all possible sample means.

b Suppose that the mean of the five sampled delivery times on a particular evening is $\bar{x} = 55$ minutes. Using the interval that you calculated in *a*(4), what would you conclude about whether the restaurant's delivery process is operating effectively? Why?

6.2 The Sampling Distribution of the Sample Proportion

A food processing company markets a soft cheese spread that is sold in a plastic container with an "easy pour" spout. Although this spout works extremely well and is popular with consumers, it is expensive to produce. Because of the spout's high cost, the company has developed a new, less expensive spout. While the new, cheaper spout may alienate some purchasers, a company study shows that its introduction will increase profits if fewer than 10 percent of the cheese spread's current purchasers are lost. That is, if we let p be the true proportion of all current purchasers who would stop buying the cheese spread if the new spout were used, profits will increase as long as p is less than .10.

Suppose that (after trying the new spout) 63 of 1,000 randomly selected purchasers say that they would stop buying the cheese spread if the new spout were used. The point estimate of the population proportion p is the sample proportion $\hat{p} = 63/1{,}000 = .063$. This sample proportion says that we estimate that 6.3 percent of all current purchasers would stop buying the cheese spread if the new spout were used. Since $\hat{p}$ equals .063, we have some evidence that the population proportion p is less than .10. In order to determine the strength of this evidence, we need to consider the sampling distribution of $\hat{p}$. In general, assume that we will randomly select a sample of n units from a population, and assume that a proportion p of all the units in the population fall into a particular category (for instance, the category of consumers who would stop buying the cheese spread). Before we actually select the sample, there are many different samples of n units that we might potentially obtain. The number of units that fall into the category in question will vary from sample to sample, so the sample proportion of units falling into the category will also vary from sample to sample. Therefore, we might potentially obtain many different sample proportions. It follows that, before we draw the sample, the sample proportion $\hat{p}$ is a random variable. In the following box we give the properties of the probability distribution of this random variable, which is called **the sampling distribution of the sample proportion $\hat{p}$.**

The Sampling Distribution of the Sample Proportion $\hat{p}$

The population of all possible sample proportions

1 Approximately has a normal distribution, if the sample size n is large.

2 Has mean $\mu_{\hat{p}} = p$.

3 Has variance $\sigma^2_{\hat{p}} = \dfrac{p(1-p)}{n}$ and standard deviation $\sigma_{\hat{p}} = \sqrt{\dfrac{p(1-p)}{n}}$.

Stated equivalently, the sampling distribution of $\hat{p}$ has mean $\mu_{\hat{p}} = p$, has standard deviation $\sigma_{\hat{p}} = \sqrt{p(1-p)/n}$, and is approximately a normal distribution (if the sample size n is large).[3]

Property 1 in the box says that, if n is large, then the population of all possible sample proportions approximately has a normal distribution. Here, it can be shown that **n should be considered large if both np and $n(1-p)$ are at least 5.**[4] Property 2, which says that $\mu_{\hat{p}} = p$, is valid for any sample size and tells us that $\hat{p}$ is an unbiased estimate of p. That is, although the sample proportion $\hat{p}$ that we calculate probably does not equal p, the average of all the different sample proportions that we could have calculated (from all the different possible samples) is equal to p. Property 3, which says that

$$\sigma^2_{\hat{p}} = \frac{p(1-p)}{n} \quad \text{and} \quad \sigma_{\hat{p}} = \sqrt{\frac{p(1-p)}{n}}$$

is exactly correct if the sampled population is infinite and is approximately correct if the sampled population is finite and much larger than (say, at least 20 times as large as) the sample size. Property 3 tells us that the variance and the standard deviation of the population of all possible sample proportions decrease as the sample size increases. That is, the larger n is, the more closely clustered are all the different sample proportions around the true population proportion.

Example 6.4 The Cheese Spread Case

C

In the cheese spread situation, the food processing company must decide whether p, the proportion of all current purchasers who would stop buying the cheese spread if the new spout were used, is less than .10. In order to do this, we (for the sake of argument) assume that p equals .10. Then we use the sample information to weigh the evidence against this assumption and in favor of the conclusion that p is less than .10. Remember that when 1,000 purchasers of the cheese spread are randomly selected, 63 of these purchasers say they would stop buying the cheese spread if the new spout were used. Because the sample proportion $\hat{p} = .063$ is less than .10, we have some evidence contradicting the assumption that p equals .10. To evaluate the strength of

[3] In Appendix D (Part 3) on page 853 we derive the formulas for $\mu_{\hat{p}}$ and $\sigma^2_{\hat{p}}$.

[4] Some statisticians suggest using the more conservative rule that both np and $n(1-p)$ must be at least 10.

this evidence, we calculate the probability of observing a sample proportion that is less than or equal to .063 if, in fact, p equals .10.

If p equals .10, we can assume that the sampling distribution of $\hat{p}$ is approximately a normal distribution because both $np = 1{,}000(.10) = 100$ and $n(1 - p) = 1{,}000(1 - .10) = 900$ are at least 5. Furthermore, the mean and standard deviation of the sampling distribution of $\hat{p}$ are $\mu_{\hat{p}} = p = .10$ and

$$\sigma_{\hat{p}} = \sqrt{\frac{p(1-p)}{n}} = \sqrt{\frac{(.10)(.90)}{1{,}000}} = .0094868$$

Therefore,

$$P(\hat{p} \leq .063 \text{ if } p = .10) = P\left(z \leq \frac{.063 - \mu_{\hat{p}}}{\sigma_{\hat{p}}}\right) = P\left(z \leq \frac{.063 - .10}{.0094868}\right)$$
$$= P(z \leq -3.90)$$

Because the tail area under the normal curve to the left of -3.90 is smaller than the tail area to the left of -3.09, this probability is less than .001. It says that, if p equals .10, fewer than 1 in 1,000 of all possible sample proportions are at least as small as the sample proportion $\hat{p} = .063$ that we have actually observed. If we are to believe that p equals .10, then we must believe that we have observed a sample proportion that can be described as less than a 1 in 1,000 chance. Therefore, we have extremely strong evidence that p does not equal .10 and is, in fact, less than .10. That is, we conclude that we have extremely strong evidence that fewer than 10 percent of current purchasers would stop buying the cheese spread if the new spout were used. Therefore, we have extremely strong evidence that introducing the new spout will be profitable.

Exercises for Section 6.2

CONCEPTS

6.15 What population is described by the sampling distribution of $\hat{p}$?

6.16 Suppose that we will randomly select a sample of n units from a population and that we will compute the sample proportion $\hat{p}$ of these units that fall into a category of interest. If we consider the sampling distribution of $\hat{p}$:

a If the sample size n is large, the sampling distribution of $\hat{p}$ is approximately a normal distribution. What condition must be satisfied to guarantee that n is large enough to say that $\hat{p}$ is normally distributed?

b Write formulas that express the central tendency and variability of the population of all possible sample proportions. Explain what each of these formulas means in your own words.

6.17 Describe the effect of increasing the sample size on the population of all possible sample proportions.

METHODS AND APPLICATIONS

6.18 In each of the following cases, determine whether the sample size n is large enough to say that the sampling distribution of $\hat{p}$ is a normal distribution.

a $p = .4,\ n = 100$ **d** $p = .8,\ n = 400$
b $p = .1,\ n = 10$ **e** $p = .98,\ n = 1{,}000$
c $p = .1,\ n = 50$ **f** $p = .99,\ n = 400$

6.19 In each of the following cases, find the mean, variance, and standard deviation of the sampling distribution of the sample proportion $\hat{p}$.

a $p = .5,\ n = 250$ **c** $p = .8,\ n = 400$
b $p = .1,\ n = 100$ **d** $p = .98,\ n = 1{,}000$

6.20 For each situation in Exercise 6.19, find an interval that contains approximately 95.44 percent of all the possible sample proportions.

6.21 Suppose that we will randomly select a sample of $n = 100$ units from a population and that we will compute the sample proportion $\hat{p}$ of these units that fall into a category of interest. If the true population proportion p equals .9:

a Describe the shape of the sampling distribution of $\hat{p}$. Why can we validly describe the shape?

b Find the mean and the standard deviation of the sampling distribution of $\hat{p}$.

c Calculate the following probabilities about the sample proportion $\hat{p}$. In each case sketch the sampling distribution and the probability.
(1) $P(\hat{p} \geq .96)$
(2) $P(.855 \leq \hat{p} \leq .945)$
(3) $P(\hat{p} \leq .915)$

6.22 In the July 29, 2001, issue of *The Journal News* (Hamilton, Ohio) Lynn Elber of the Associated Press reported on a study conducted by the Kaiser Family Foundation regarding parents' use of television set V-chips for controlling their childrens' TV viewing. The study asked parents who own TVs equipped with V-chips whether they use the devices to block programs with objectionable content.

a Suppose that we wish to use the study results to justify the claim that fewer than 20 percent of parents who own TV sets with V-chips use the devices. The study actually found that 17 percent of the parents polled used their V-chips.[5] If the poll surveyed 1,000 parents, and if for the sake of argument we assume that 20 percent of parents who own V-chips actually use the devices (that is, $p = .2$), calculate the probability of observing a sample proportion of .17 or less. That is, calculate $P(\hat{p} \leq .17)$.

b Based on the probability you computed in part *a*, would you conclude that fewer than 20 percent of parents who own TV sets equipped with V-chips actually use the devices? Explain.

6.23 On February 8, 2002, the Gallup Organization released the results of a poll concerning American attitudes toward the 19th Winter Olympic Games in Salt Lake City, Utah. The poll results were based on telephone interviews with a randomly selected national sample of 1,011 adults, 18 years and older, conducted February 4–6, 2002.

a Suppose we wish to use the poll's results to justify the claim that more than 30 percent of Americans (18 years or older) say that figure skating is their favorite Winter Olympic event. The poll actually found that 32 percent of respondents reported that figure skating was their favorite event.[6] If, for the sake of argument, we assume that 30 percent of Americans (18 years or older) say figure skating is their favorite event (that is, $p = .3$), calculate the probability of observing a sample proportion of .32 or more; that is, calculate $P(\hat{p} \geq .32)$.

b Based on the probability you computed in *a*, would you conclude that more than 30 percent of Americans (18 years or older) say that figure skating is their favorite Winter Olympic event?

6.24 *Quality Progress*, February 2005, reports on improvements in customer satisfaction and loyalty made by Bank of America. A key measure of customer satisfaction is the response (on a scale from 1 to 10) to the question: "Considering all the business you do with Bank of America, what is your overall satisfaction with Bank of America?" Here, a response of 9 or 10 represents "customer delight."

a Historically, the percentage of Bank of America customers expressing customer delight has been 48%. Suppose that we wish to use the results of a survey of 350 Bank of America customers to justify the claim that more than 48% of all current Bank of America customers would express customer delight. The survey finds that 189 of 350 randomly selected Bank of America customers express customer delight. If, for the sake of argument, we assume that the proportion of customer delight is $p = .48$, calculate the probability of observing a sample proportion greater than or equal to $189/350 = .54$. That is, calculate $P(\hat{p} \geq .54)$.

b Based on the probability you computed in part (a), would you conclude that more than 48 percent of current Bank of America customers express customer delight? Explain.

6.25 Again consider the survey of 350 Bank of America customers discussed in Exercise 6.24.

a Assume that 48% of Bank of America customers would currently express customer delight. That is, assume $p = .48$. Find:
(1) The probability that the sample proportion obtained from the sample of 350 Bank of America customers would be within three percentage points of the population proportion. That is, find $P(.45 \leq \hat{p} \leq .51)$.
(2) The probability that the sample proportion obtained from the sample of 350 Bank of America customers would be within six percentage points of the population proportion. That is, find $P(.42 \leq \hat{p} \leq .54)$.

b Based on your results of part (a), would it be reasonable to state that the survey's "margin of error" is ± 3 percentage points? ± 6 percentage points? Explain.

6.26 THE MARKETING ETHICS CASE: CONFLICT OF INTEREST

a Consider the Marketing Ethics Case (of Exercise 2.55, page 92) and remember that 111 of 205 randomly selected marketing researchers disapproved of the actions taken in the conflict of

[5]Source: L. Elber, "Study: Parents Make Scant Use of TV V-Chip", *The Journal News* (Hamilton, Ohio), July 29, 2001, p. c5.
[6]Source: World Wide Web, http://www.gallup.com/poll/releases/, The Gallup Organization, February 13, 2002.

interest scenario. Suppose that we wish to justify the claim that a majority (more than 50 percent) of all marketing researchers disapprove of these actions. If, for the sake of argument, we assume that p, the proportion of all marketing researchers who disapprove of the actions taken, equals .5, calculate a probability that expresses the amount of doubt cast by the sample result on the assumption that p equals .5.

b Based on the probability you computed in part *a*, would you conclude that p is really greater than .5? That is, would you conclude that a majority of marketing researchers disapprove of the actions taken in the conflict of interest scenario? Explain.

6.27 A special advertising section in the July 20, 1998, issue of *Fortune* magazine discusses "outsourcing." According to the article, outsourcing is "the assignment of critical, but noncore, business functions to outside specialists." This allows a company to immediately bring operations up to best-in-world standards while avoiding huge capital investments. The article includes the results of a poll of business executives addressing the benefits of outsourcing.

a Suppose we wish to use the poll's results to justify the claim that fewer than 26 percent of business executives feel that the benefits of outsourcing are either "less or much less than expected." The poll actually found that 15 percent of the respondents felt that the benefits of outsourcing were either "less or much less than expected."[7] If 1,000 randomly selected business executives were polled, and if for the sake of argument, we assume that 20 percent of all business executives feel that the benefits of outsourcing are either less or much less than expected (that is, $p = .20$), calculate the probability of observing a sample proportion of .15 or less. That is, calculate $P(\hat{p} \leq .15)$.

b Based on the probability you computed in part *a*, would you conclude that fewer than 20 percent of business executives feel that the benefits of outsourcing are either "less or much less than expected"? Explain.

6.28 The July 20, 1998, issue of *Fortune* magazine reported the results of a survey on executive training that was conducted by the Association of Executive Search Consultants. The survey showed that 75 percent of 300 polled CEOs believe that companies should have "fast-track training programs" for developing managerial talent.[8]

a Suppose we wish to use the results of this survey to justify the claim that more than 70 percent of CEOs believe that companies should have fast-track training programs. Assuming that the 300 surveyed CEOs were randomly selected, and assuming, for the sake of argument, that 70 percent of CEOs believe that companies should have fast-track training programs (that is, $p = .70$), calculate the probability of observing a sample proportion of .75 or more. That is, calculate $P(\hat{p} \geq .75)$.

b Based on the probability you computed in part *a*, would you conclude that more than 70 percent of CEOs believe that companies should have fast-track training programs? Explain.

Chapter Summary

A **sampling distribution** is the probability distribution that describes the population of all possible values of a sample statistic. In this chapter we studied the properties of two important sampling distributions—the sampling distribution of the sample mean, $\bar{x}$, and the sampling distribution of the sample proportion, $\hat{p}$.

Because different samples that can be randomly selected from a population give different sample means, there is a population of sample means corresponding to a particular sample size. The probability distribution describing the population of all possible sample means is called the **sampling distribution of the sample mean, $\bar{x}$.** We studied the properties of this sampling distribution when the sampled population is and is not normally distributed. We found that, when the sampled population has a normal distribution, then the sampling distribution of the sample mean is a normal distribution. Furthermore, the **Central Limit Theorem** tells us that, if the sampled population is not normally distributed, then the sampling distribution of the sample mean is approximately a normal distribution when the sample size is large (at least 30). We also saw that the mean of the sampling distribution of $\bar{x}$ always equals the mean of the sampled population, and we presented formulas for the variance and the standard deviation of this sampling distribution. Finally, we explained that the sample mean is a **minimum-variance unbiased point estimate** of the mean of a normally distributed population.

We also studied the properties of the **sampling distribution of the sample proportion $\hat{p}$.** We found that, if the sample size is large, then this sampling distribution is approximately a normal distribution, and we gave a rule for determining whether the sample size is large. We found that the mean of the sampling distribution of $\hat{p}$ is the population proportion p, and we gave formulas for the variance and the standard deviation of this sampling distribution.

Finally, we demonstrated that knowing the properties of sampling distributions can help us make statistical inferences about population parameters. In fact, we will see that the properties of various sampling distributions provide the foundation for most of the techniques to be discussed in future chapters.

[7]Source: M. R. Ozanne and M. F. Corbette, "Outsourcing 98," *Fortune* (July 20, 1998), p. 510.

[8]Source: E. P. Gunn, "The Fast Track Is Where to Be, If You Can Find It," *Fortune* (July 20, 1998), p. 152.

Glossary of Terms

Central Limit Theorem: A theorem telling us that when the sample size n is sufficiently large, then the population of all possible sample means is approximately normally distributed no matter what probability distribution describes the sampled population. (page 244)

minimum-variance unbiased point estimate: An unbiased point estimate of a population parameter having a variance that is smaller than the variance of any other unbiased point estimate of the parameter. (page 248)

sampling distribution of a sample statistic: The probability distribution of the population of all possible values of the sample statistic. (page 246)

sampling distribution of the sample mean $\bar{x}$: The probability distribution of the population of all possible sample means obtained from samples of a particular size n. (page 237)
when a population is normally distributed (page 241)
Central Limit Theorem (page 244)

sampling distribution of the sample proportion $\hat{p}$: The probability distribution of the population of all possible sample proportions obtained from samples of a particular size n. (page 251)

unbiased point estimate: A sample statistic is an unbiased point estimate of a population parameter if the mean of the population of all possible values of the sample statistic equals the population parameter. (page 246)

Important Formulas

The sampling distribution of the sample mean: pages 241 and 244

The sampling distribution of the sample proportion: page 251

Supplementary Exercises

6.29 A chain of audio/video equipment discount stores employs 36 salespeople. Daily dollar sales for individual sellers employed by the chain have a mound-shaped distribution with a mean of $2,000 and a standard deviation equal to $300.

a Suppose that the chain's management decides to implement an incentive program that awards a daily bonus to any salesperson who achieves daily sales over $2,150. Calculate the probability that an individual salesperson will earn the bonus on any particular day.

b Suppose that (as an alternative) the chain's management decides to award a daily bonus to the entire sales force if all 36 achieve an *average* daily sales figure that exceeds $2,150. Calculate the probability that average daily sales for the entire sales force will exceed $2,150 on any particular day.

c Intuitively, do you think it would be more difficult for an individual salesperson to achieve a daily sales figure that exceeds $2,150 or for the entire sales force of 36 to achieve an *average* sales figure that exceeds $2,150? Are the probabilities you computed in parts *a* and *b* consistent with your intuition? Explain.

d Sketch the distribution of individual daily sales figures and the probability you computed in part *a*. Place values that are three standard deviations above and below the mean in the tails of the distribution. Also sketch the distribution of all possible sample means (the sampling distribution of $\bar{x}$) and the probability you computed in part *b*. Place values that are three standard deviations of $\bar{x}$ above and below the mean in the tails of the sampling distribution. Compare the sketches. Do you see why the results in parts *a* and *b* turned out the way they did? Explain why.

6.30 In the book *Essentials of Marketing Research,* William R. Dillon, Thomas J. Madden, and Neil H. Firtle discuss an advertising study for a new suntan lotion. In this study, each respondent is assigned to a group whose members will evaluate an ad for the new lotion. Each respondent is asked to rate the ad on six items:

High quality/low quality	Persuasive/nonpersuasive
Informative/uninformative	Artful/artless
Good/bad	Refined/vulgar

The rating for each item is made using a seven-point scale, where, for example, a rating of 1 on the informative/uninformative dimension indicates that the ad is extremely uninformative, and a rating of 7 says that the ad is extremely informative.

Suppose experience shows that a "very informative" ad is typically rated by a large group of respondents according to the probability distribution given in the right page margin.

Rating	Probability
1	0
2	.05
3	.05
4	.10
5	.20
6	.40
7	.20

a Calculate the mean, variance, and standard deviation of the ratings for a typical "very informative" ad.

b Suppose that a group of 36 randomly selected respondents rates a typical "very informative" ad, and consider the sample mean $\bar{x}$ of the 36 ratings. Find the mean and standard deviation of the population of all possible sample means. What is the shape of the population of all possible sample means? How do you know?

c Draw a sketch of the sampling distribution of the sample mean $\bar{x}$ and compare it to a sketch of the distribution of individual ratings.

d Suppose that a randomly selected group of 36 respondents rates a typical "very informative" ad. Find the probability that the respondents give the ad a sample mean rating less than 5.

e Suppose that 36 randomly selected respondents are exposed to a new ad in order to determine whether the ad is "very informative," and suppose that the sample mean rating is less than 5. In light of the probability you computed in part *d*, what would you conclude about whether the new ad is "very informative"? Explain.

6.31 The April 21, 2005, issue of *Sports Illustrated* reported the results of a poll of 757 Division I student athletes from 59 schools and all 36 NCAA championship sports. The athletes were asked 20 questions relating to college sports and college life. One of the questions asked was: "Have you ever received preferential treatment from a professor because of your status as an athlete?"

a Suppose that we wish to justify the claim that more than 25 percent of Division I student athletes have received preferential treatment from a professor. The poll actually found that 29.7 percent of the 757 surveyed athletes had received preferential treatment from a professor. If, for the sake of argument, we assume that 25 percent of all Division I student athletes have received preferential treatment from a professor (that is, $p = .25$), and if we assume that the 757 sampled student athletes were randomly selected, calculate the probability of observing a sample proportion greater than or equal to .297. That is, calculate $P(\hat{p} \geq .297)$.

b Based on the probability you computed in part (a), would you conclude that more than 25 percent of Division I student athletes have received preferential treatment from a professor? Explain.

6.32 Suppose that we randomly select a sample of size 100.

a What is the probability of obtaining a sample mean greater than 50.2 when the sampled population has mean 50 and standard deviation 1? Must we assume that the population is normally distributed in order to answer this question? Why or why not?

b Rework part *a* of this exercise with a sample size of 225. Compare your answer here with that of part *a*. Why are they different?

6.33 Each day a manufacturing plant receives a large shipment of drums of Chemical ZX-900. These drums are supposed to have a mean fill of 50 gallons, while the fills have a standard deviation known to be .6 gallon.

a Suppose that the mean fill for the shipment is actually 50 gallons. If we draw a random sample of 100 drums from the shipment, what is the probability that the average fill for the 100 drums is between 49.88 gallons and 50.12 gallons?

b The plant manager is worried that the drums of Chemical ZX-900 are underfilled. Because of this, she decides to draw a sample of 100 drums from each daily shipment and will reject the shipment (send it back to the supplier) if the average fill for the 100 drums is less than 49.85 gallons. Suppose that a shipment that actually has a mean fill of 50 gallons is received. What is the probability that this shipment will be rejected and sent back to the supplier?

6.34 In its October 12, 1992, issue, *The Milwaukee Journal* published the results of an Ogilvy, Adams, and Rinehart poll of 1,250 American investors that was conducted in early October 1992. The poll investigated the stock market's appeal to investors five years after the market suffered its biggest one-day decline (in 1987).

Assume that 50 percent of all American investors in 1992 found the stock market less attractive than it was in 1987 (that is, $p = .5$). Find the probability that the sample proportion obtained from the sample of 1,250 investors would be

a Within 4 percentage points of the population proportion—that is, find $P(.46 \leq \hat{p} \leq .54)$.

b Within 2 percentage points of the population proportion.

c Within 1 percentage point of the population proportion.

d Based on these probabilities, would it be reasonable to claim a ± 2 percentage point margin of error? A ± 1 percentage point margin of error? Explain.

6.35 Again consider the stock market poll discussed in Exercise 6.34.

a Suppose we wish to use the poll's results to justify the claim that fewer than 50 percent of American investors in 1992 found the stock market less attractive than in 1987. The poll actually found that 41 percent of the respondents said the stock market was less attractive than in 1987. If, for the sake of argument, we assume that $p = .5$, calculate the probability of observing a sample proportion of .41 or less. That is, calculate $P(\hat{p} \leq .41)$.

b Based on the probability you computed in part *b*, would you conclude that fewer than 50 percent of American investors in 1992 found the stock market to be less attractive than in 1987? Explain.

6.36 Aamco Heating and Cooling, Inc., advertises that any customer buying an air conditioner during the first 16 days of July will receive a 25 percent discount if the average high temperature for this 16-day period is more than five degrees above normal.

a If daily high temperatures in July are normally distributed with a mean of 84 degrees and a standard deviation of 8 degrees, what is the probability that Aamco Heating and Cooling will have to give its customers the 25 percent discount?

b Based on the probability you computed in part *a*, do you think that Aamco's promotion is ethical? Write a paragraph justifying your opinion.

6.37 THE TRASH BAG CASE TrashBag

Recall that the trash bag manufacturer has concluded that its new 30-gallon bag will be the strongest such bag on the market if its mean breaking strength is at least 50 pounds. In order to provide statistical evidence that the mean breaking strength of the new bag is at least 50 pounds, the manufacturer randomly selects a sample of *n* bags and calculates the mean $\bar{x}$ of the breaking strengths of these bags. If the sample mean so obtained is at least 50 pounds, this provides some evidence that the mean breaking strength of all new bags is at least 50 pounds.

Suppose that (unknown to the manufacturer) the breaking strengths of the new 30-gallon bag are normally distributed with a mean of $\mu = 50.6$ pounds and a standard deviation of $\sigma = 1.62$ pounds.

a Find an interval containing 95.44 percent of all possible sample means if the sample size employed is $n = 5$.

b Find an interval containing 95.44 percent of all possible sample means if the sample size employed is $n = 40$.

c If the trash bag manufacturer hopes to obtain a sample mean that is at least 50 pounds (so that it can provide evidence that the population mean breaking strength of the new bags is at least 50), which sample size ($n = 5$ or $n = 40$) would be best? Explain why.

6.38 A computer supply house receives a large shipment of floppy disks each week. Past experience has shown that the number of flaws per disk can be described by the following probability distribution:

Number of Flaws per Floppy Disk	Probability
0	.65
1	.2
2	.1
3	.05

a Calculate the mean and standard deviation of the number of flaws per floppy disk.

b Suppose that we randomly select a sample of 100 floppy disks. Describe the shape of the sampling distribution of the sample mean $\bar{x}$. Then compute the mean and the standard deviation of the sampling distribution of $\bar{x}$.

c Sketch the sampling distribution of the sample mean $\bar{x}$ and compare it to the distribution describing the number of flaws on a single floppy disk.

d The supply house's managers are worried that the floppy disks being received have an excessive number of flaws. Because of this, a random sample of 100 disks is drawn from each shipment and the shipment is rejected (sent back to the supplier) if the average number of flaws per disk for the 100 sample disks is greater than .75. Suppose that the mean number of flaws per disk for this week's entire shipment is actually .55. What is the probability that this shipment will be rejected and sent back to the supplier?

6.39 On January 4, 2000, the Gallup Organization released the results of a poll concerning public skepticism about the extent of Y2K computer problems. The poll results were based on a randomly selected national sample of 622 adults, 18 years and older, conducted December 28, 1999. One question asked if the respondent felt that media warnings about possible Y2K computer problems were "necessary precautions."

a Suppose that we want to justify the claim that a majority of U.S. adults believe that media warnings about possible Y2K computer problems were necessary precautions. The poll actually found that 59 percent of the respondents felt this way.[9] If, for the sake of argument, we assume that 50 percent of U.S. adults believe that the media warnings were necessary precautions (that is, $p = .5$), calculate the probability of observing a sample proportion of .59 or more. That is, calculate $P(\hat{p} \geq .59)$.

b Based on the probability you computed in part *a*, would you conclude that a majority of U.S. adults believe that the media warnings were necessary precautions? Explain.

6.40 On January 7, 2000, the Gallup Organization released the results of a poll comparing lifestyles of today with those of yesteryear. The poll results were based on telephone interviews with a randomly selected national sample of 1,031 adults, 18 years and older, conducted December 20–21, 1999. One question asked if the respondent had vacationed for six days or longer within the last 12 months.

a Suppose that we will attempt to use the poll's results to justify the claim that more than 40 percent of U.S. adults have vacationed for six days or longer within the last 12 months. The poll actually found that 42 percent of the respondents had done so.[10] If, for the sake of argument, we assume that 40 percent of U.S. adults have vacationed for six days or longer within the last 12 months (that is, $p = .4$), calculate the probability of observing a sample proportion of .42 or more; that is, calculate $P(\hat{p} \geq .42)$.

b Based on the probability you computed in *a*, would you conclude that more than 40 percent of U.S. adults have vacationed for six days or longer within the last 12 months? Explain.

6.41 THE INTERNATIONAL BUSINESS TRAVEL EXPENSE CASE

Suppose that the large international corporation wants to assess whether the mean, μ, of all one-day travel expenses in Moscow exceeds \$500. Recall that the mean of a random sample of 35 one-day travel expenses is $\bar{x} = \$538$, and assume that σ is known to equal \$40.

a Assuming that μ equals \$500 and the sample size is 35, what is the probability of observing a sample mean that is greater than or equal to \$538?

b Based on your answer to *a*, do you think that the mean of all one-day travel expenses in Moscow exceeds \$500? Explain.

6.42 THE UNITED KINGDOM INSURANCE CASE

Suppose that we wish to assess whether more than 60 percent of all United Kingdom households spent on life insurance in 1993. That is, we wish to assess whether the proportion, p, of all United Kingdom households that spent on life insurance in 1993 exceeds .60. Assume here that the U.K. insurance survey is based on 1,000 randomly selected households and that 640 of these households spent on life insurance in 1993.

a Assuming that p equals .60 and the sample size is 1,000, what is the probability of observing a sample proportion that is at least .64?

b Based on your answer in *a*, do you think more than 60 percent of all United Kingdom households spent on life insurance in 1993? Explain.

6.43 Internet Exercise

The best way to observe, first-hand, the concepts of sampling distributions is to conduct sampling experiments with real data. However, sampling experiments can be prohibitively time consuming and tedious. An excellent alternative is to conduct computer-assisted sampling experiments or simulations. *Visual Statistics* by Doane, Mathieson, and Tracy (Irwin/McGraw-Hill) includes a simulation module to illustrate sampling distributions and the Central Limit Theorem. In this exercise, we will download and install the Central Limit Theorem demonstration module from *Visual Statistics* and use the software to demonstrate the Central Limit Theorem.

From the Irwin/McGraw-Hill Business Statistics Center (http://www.mhhe.com/business/opsci/bstat/), select in turn—"Visual Statistics and Other Data Visualization Tools" : "Visual Statistics by Doane" : "Free Stuff"—and download both the CLT module and the Worktext. When the download is complete, install the CLT module by double-clicking the installation file (vs_setup.exe). Study the overview and orientation sections of the work text and work through the first four learning exercises on the Width of Car Hood example.

[9]Source: World Wide Web, http://www.gallup.com/poll/releases/, The Gallup Organization, January 7, 2000.

[10]Source: World Wide Web, http://www.gallup.com/poll/releases/, The Gallup Organization, January 4, 2000.

Appendix 6.1 ■ Simulating Sampling Distributions Using MINITAB

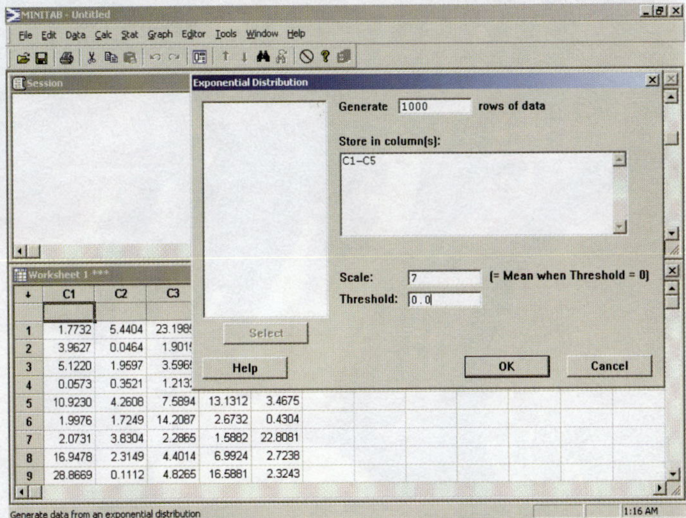

Histogram of sample means from an exponential distribution similar to Figure 6.6(b) on page 245:

In this example we construct a histogram of 1000 sample means from exponential samples of size 5.

- Select **Calc : Random Data : Exponential.**
- In the Exponential Distribution dialog box, enter 1000 in the "Generate … rows of data" box.
- Enter C1-C5 in the "Store in column(s):" window to request 1000 values per column in columns C1 to C5.
- Be sure that 0.0 is the entry in the Threshold box.
- Enter 7 in the Scale box. This specifies the mean of the exponential distribution when Threshold equals 0.
- Click OK in the Exponential Distribution dialog box. The 1000 exponential samples of size 5 will be generated in rows 1 through 1000.

- Select **Calc : Row Statistics.**
- In the Row Statistics dialog box, under "Statistic" select the Mean option.
- Enter C1-C5 in the "Input variables" window.
- Enter XBar5 in the "Store result in" box.
- Click OK in the Row Statistics dialog box to compute the means for the 1000 samples of size 5.

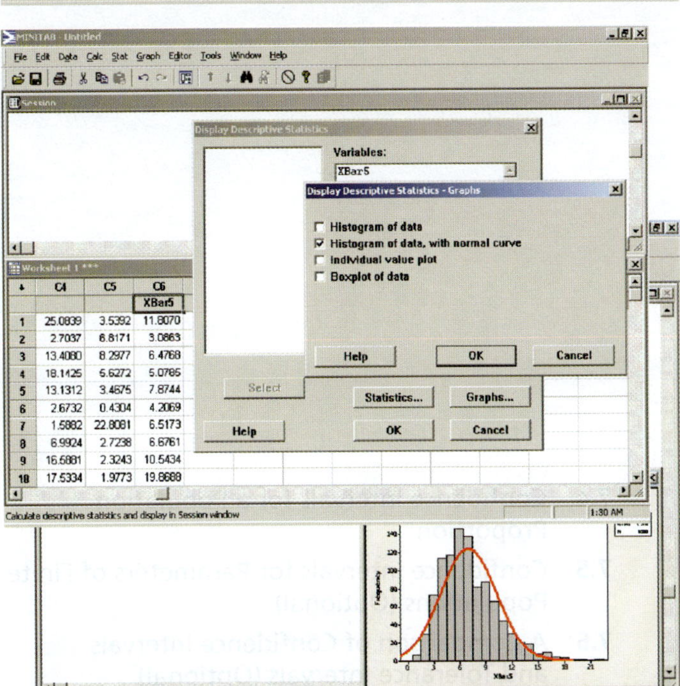

- Select **Stat : Basic Statistics : Display Descriptive Statistics**
- In the Display Descriptive Statistics dialog box, enter XBar5 in the Variables window.
- Click on the Graphs button.
- In the "Display Descriptive Statistics—Graphs" dialog box, check the "Histogram of data, with normal curve" check box.
- Click OK in the "Display Descriptive Statistics—Graphs" dialog box.
- Click OK in the Display Descriptive Statistics dialog box.
- The histogram will appear in a graphics window and can be printed or can be copied and pasted into a word processor document.

CHAPTER 7

Confidence Intervals

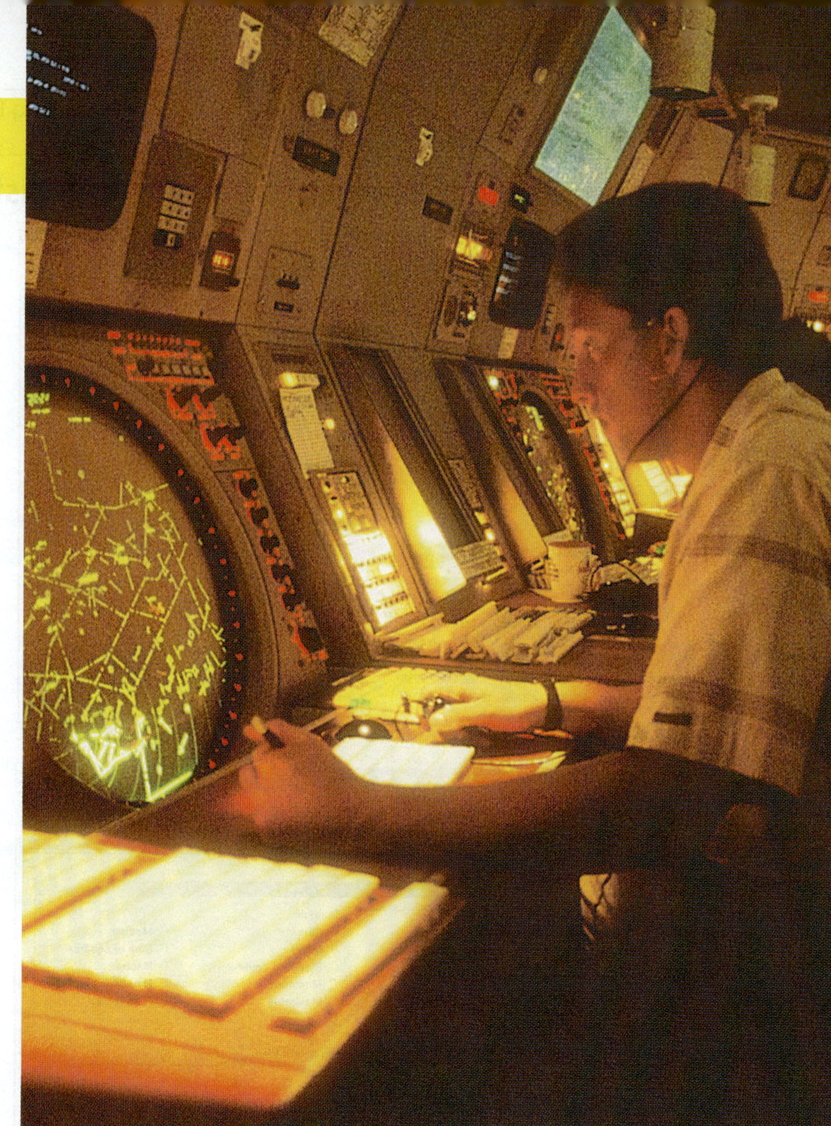

Chapter Outline

We have seen that we obtain a point estimate of a population mean by computing the mean of a sample that has been randomly selected from the population, and we have seen that we obtain a point estimate of a population proportion by computing a sample proportion. In general, we often compute a point estimate of a population parameter (mean, proportion, or the like) in order to make an inference about a population. Unfortunately, a point estimate seldom gives us all the information we need because the point estimate provides no information about its distance from the population parameter.

In this chapter we study how to use a **confidence interval** to estimate a population parameter. A confidence interval for a population parameter is an interval, or range of numbers, constructed around the point estimate so that we are very sure, or confident, that the population parameter is inside the interval. By computing such an interval, we estimate how far the point estimate might be from the parameter.

As we illustrate by revisiting several cases we have introduced in earlier chapters, confidence intervals often help in business decision making and in assessing the need for and the results obtained from process improvement efforts. Specifically,

In the **Car Mileage Case,** we use a confidence interval to provide strong evidence that the mean EPA combined city and highway mileage for the automaker's new midsize model meets the tax credit standard of 31 mpg.

In the **Payment Time Case,** we use a confidence interval to more completely assess the reduction in mean payment time that was achieved by the new billing system.

In the **Marketing Research Case,** we use a confidence interval to provide strong evidence that the mean rating of the new bottle design exceeds the minimum standard for a successful design.

In the **Cheese Spread Case,** we use a confidence interval to provide strong evidence that fewer than 10 percent of all current purchasers will stop buying the cheese spread if the new spout is used, and, therefore, that it is reasonable to use the new spout.

In the **Marketing Ethics Case,** we use a confidence interval to provide strong evidence that more than half of all marketing researchers disapprove of the actions taken in the ultraviolet ink scenario.

Sections 7.1 through 7.4 present confidence intervals for population means and proportions. These intervals are appropriate when the sampled population is either infinite or finite and *much larger* than (say, at least 20 times as large as) the size of the sample. The appropriate procedures to use when the population is not large compared to the sample are explained in optional Section 7.5. Finally, optional Section 7.6 compares confidence intervals and tolerance intervals.

7.1 *z*-Based Confidence Intervals for a Population Mean: σ Known

CHAPTER 9

An example of calculating and interpreting a confidence interval for μ We have seen that we use the sample mean as the point estimate of the population mean. A **confidence interval** for the population mean is an interval constructed around the sample mean so that we are reasonably sure, or confident, that this interval contains the population mean. For example, suppose in the car mileage case we wish to calculate a confidence interval for the mean μ of the population of all EPA combined city and highway mileages that would be obtained by the new midsize model. To do this, we use the random sample of $n = 49$ mileages given in Table 2.1 (page 44). Before using this sample, however, we first consider calculating a confidence interval for μ by using a smaller sample of $n = 5$ mileages. We do this because it is somewhat simpler to explain the meaning of confidence intervals in terms of smaller samples. Assume, then, that we randomly select a sample of five cars and calculate the mean $\bar{x}$ of the mileages that the cars obtain when tested as prescribed by the EPA. We have seen in Chapter 6 that, if the population of all individual car mileages is normally distributed with mean μ and standard deviation σ, then the sampling distribution of $\bar{x}$ is normal with mean $\mu_{\bar{x}} = \mu$ and standard deviation

TABLE 7.1 The Sample Mean $\bar{x}$ and the Interval $[\bar{x} \pm .7155]$ Given by Each of Three Samples

Sample	Sample	Sample
$x_1 = 30.8$	$x_1 = 32.4$	$x_1 = 32.7$
$x_2 = 31.9$	$x_2 = 30.8$	$x_2 = 31.6$
$x_3 = 30.3$	$x_3 = 31.9$	$x_3 = 33.3$
$x_4 = 32.1$	$x_4 = 31.5$	$x_4 = 32.3$
$x_5 = 31.4$	$x_5 = 32.0$	$x_5 = 32.6$
$\bar{x} = 31.3$	$\bar{x} = 31.72$	$\bar{x} = 32.5$
$[\bar{x} \pm .7155] = [31.3 \pm .7155]$	$[\bar{x} \pm .7155] = [31.72 \pm .7155]$	$[\bar{x} \pm .7155] = [32.5 \pm .7155]$
$= [30.5845, 32.0155]$	$= [31.0045, 32.4355]$	$= [31.7845, 33.2155]$
$= [30.6, 32.0]$	$= [31.0, 32.4]$	$= [31.8, 33.2]$

$\sigma_{\bar{x}} = \sigma/\sqrt{n}$. To obtain a confidence interval for μ, consider using $\bar{x}$ and $\sigma_{\bar{x}}$ to calculate the interval

$$[\bar{x} \pm 2\sigma_{\bar{x}}] = \left[\bar{x} \pm 2\frac{\sigma}{\sqrt{n}}\right]$$

$$= \left[\bar{x} - 2\frac{\sigma}{\sqrt{5}},\quad \bar{x} + 2\frac{\sigma}{\sqrt{5}}\right]$$

In order to interpret this interval, we find the probability that it contains μ. To do this, we assume that, although we do not know the true value of μ, we do know that the true value of σ is .8 mpg. This is unrealistic, but it simplifies our initial presentation of confidence intervals. Later in this chapter, we will see that we can calculate a confidence interval without knowing σ. Assuming that σ is .8, we will calculate the interval

$$\left[\bar{x} \pm 2\frac{.8}{\sqrt{5}}\right] = [\bar{x} \pm .7155]$$

Clearly, the interval that we calculate—and whether it contains μ—depends on the sample mean $\bar{x}$ that we obtain. For example, Table 7.1 gives three samples of five mileages that might be randomly selected from the population of all mileages. This table also presents the sample mean $\bar{x}$ and the interval $[\bar{x} \pm .7155]$ that would be given by each sample. In order to see that some intervals contain μ and some do not, suppose that the true value of μ is 31.5 (of course, no human being would know this true value). We then see that the interval given by the leftmost sample in Table 7.1—[30.6, 32.0]—contains μ. Furthermore, the interval given by the middle sample—[31.0, 32.4]—contains μ. However, the interval given by the rightmost sample—[31.8, 33.2]—does not contain μ. Therefore, two out of the three intervals in Table 7.1 contain μ.

In general, there are an infinite number of samples of five mileages that we might randomly select from the population of all mileages. It follows that there are an infinite number of sample means and thus intervals that we might calculate from the samples. To find the probability that such an interval will contain μ, we use the fact that the sampling distribution of the sample mean is normal with mean $\mu_{\bar{x}} = \mu$ and standard deviation $\sigma_{\bar{x}} = \sigma/\sqrt{n}$, and we reason as follows:

1 The Empirical Rule for a normally distributed population implies that the probability is .9544 that $\bar{x}$ will be within plus or minus

$$2\sigma_{\bar{x}} = 2\frac{\sigma}{\sqrt{n}} = 2\frac{(.8)}{\sqrt{5}} = .7155$$

of μ. This is illustrated in Figure 7.1.

2 Saying

$\bar{x}$ will be within plus or minus .7155 of μ

is the same as saying

$\bar{x}$ will be such that the interval $[\bar{x} \pm .7155]$ contains μ.

To see this, consider Figure 7.1, which illustrates the sample means and intervals given by the three samples in Table 7.1. Note that, because $\bar{x} = 31.3$ is within .7155 of $\mu = 31.5$, the interval $[31.3 \pm .7155] = [30.6, 32.0]$ contains μ. Similarly, since $\bar{x} = 31.72$ is within

FIGURE 7.1 **Three 95.44 Percent Confidence Intervals for μ**

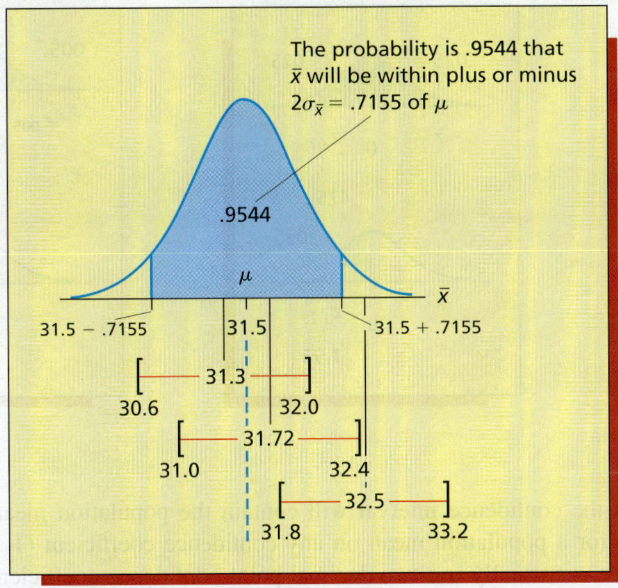

.7155 of $\mu = 31.5$, the interval $[31.72 \pm .7155] = [31.0, 32.4]$ contains μ. However, because $\bar{x} = 32.5$ is not within .7155 of $\mu = 31.5$, the interval $[32.5 \pm .7155] = [31.8, 33.2]$ does not contain μ.

3 Combining 1 and 2, we see that there is a .9544 probability that $\bar{x}$ will be such that the interval $[\bar{x} \pm .7155]$ contains μ.

Statement 3 says that, **before we randomly select the sample,** there is a .9544 probability that we will obtain an interval $[\bar{x} \pm .7155]$ that contains μ. In other words, 95.44 percent of all intervals that we might obtain contain μ, and 4.56 percent of these intervals do not contain μ. For this reason, we call the interval $[\bar{x} \pm .7155]$ a **95.44 percent confidence interval for μ.** To better understand this interval, we must realize that, **when we actually select the sample,** we will observe one particular sample from the infinite number of possible samples. Therefore, we will obtain one particular confidence interval from the infinite number of possible confidence intervals. For example, suppose that when we actually select the sample of five cars and record their mileages, we obtain the leftmost sample of mileages in Table 7.1. Since the mean of our sample is $\bar{x} = 31.3$, the 95.44 percent confidence interval for μ that it gives is

$$[\bar{x} \pm .7155] = [31.3 \pm .7155] = [30.6, 32.0]$$

Because we do not know the true value of μ, we do not know for sure whether μ is contained in our interval. However, we are 95.44 percent confident that μ is contained in this interval. That is, we are 95.44 percent confident that μ is between 30.6 mpg and 32.0 mpg. What we mean by this is that we hope that the interval [30.6, 32.0] is one of the 95.44 percent of all intervals that contain μ and not one of the 4.56 percent of all intervals that do not contain μ.

A general confidence interval formula Later in this section we will see how to make practical use of confidence intervals. First, however, we present a general formula for finding a confidence interval. To do this, recall from the previous example that, before we randomly select the sample, the probability that the confidence interval

$$[\bar{x} \pm 2\sigma_{\bar{x}}] = \left[\bar{x} \pm 2\frac{\sigma}{\sqrt{n}}\right]$$

will contain the population mean is .9544. It follows that the probability that this confidence interval will not contain the population mean is .0456. In general, we denote the probability that a confidence interval for a population mean will *not* contain the population mean by the symbol **α (pronounced alpha).** This implies that **$(1 - \alpha)$, which we call the confidence coefficient,** is

FIGURE 7.2 The Point $z_{\alpha/2}$

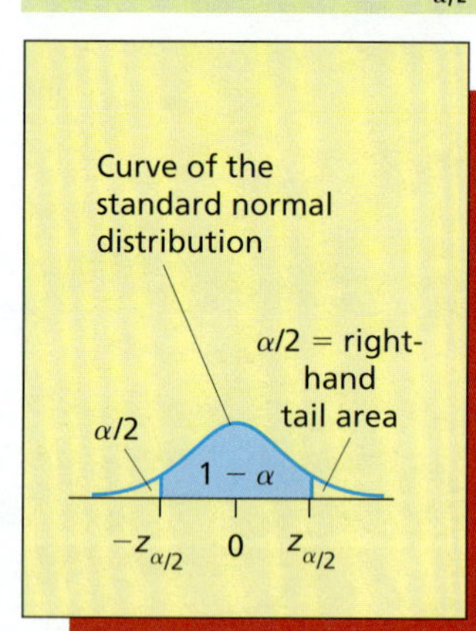

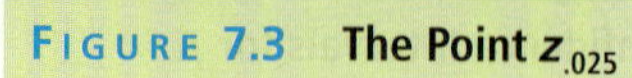

FIGURE 7.3 The Point $z_{.025}$

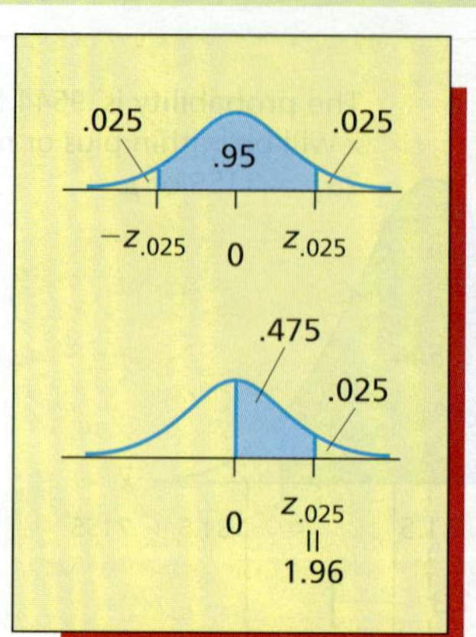

FIGURE 7.4 The Point $z_{.005}$

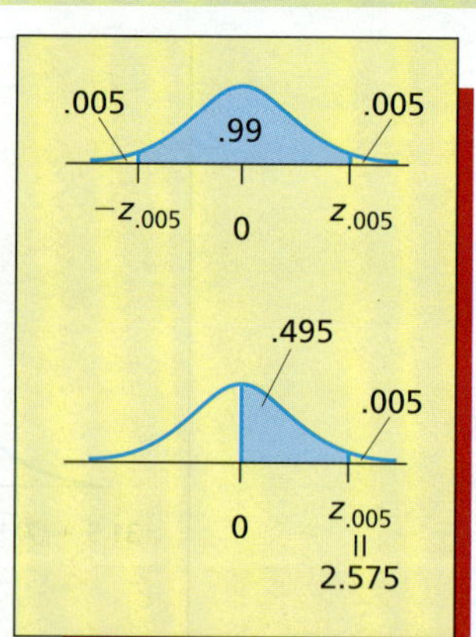

the probability that the confidence interval will contain the population mean. We can base a confidence interval for a population mean on any confidence coefficient $(1 - \alpha)$ less than 1. However, in practice, we usually use two decimal point confidence coefficients, such as .95 or .99. To find a general formula for a confidence interval for a population mean μ, we assume that the sampled population is normally distributed, or the sample size n is large. Under these conditions, the sampling distribution of the sample mean $\bar{x}$ is exactly (or approximately, by the Central Limit Theorem) a normal distribution with mean $\mu_{\bar{x}} = \mu$ and standard deviation $\sigma_{\bar{x}} = \sigma/\sqrt{n}$. Then, in order to obtain a confidence interval that has a $(1 - \alpha)$ probability of containing μ, we find the normal point $z_{\alpha/2}$ that gives a right-hand tail area under the standard normal curve equal to $\alpha/2$, and we find the normal point $-z_{\alpha/2}$ that gives a left-hand tail area under this curve equal to $\alpha/2$ (see Figure 7.2). Noting from Figure 7.2 that the area under the standard normal curve between $-z_{\alpha/2}$ and $z_{\alpha/2}$ is $(1 - \alpha)$, it can be shown that the probability is $(1 - \alpha)$ that the sample mean $\bar{x}$ will be within plus or minus $z_{\alpha/2}\sigma_{\bar{x}}$ units of the population mean μ. The quantity $z_{\alpha/2}\sigma_{\bar{x}}$ is called the **margin of error** when estimating μ by $\bar{x}$. If this margin of error is added to and subtracted from $\bar{x}$ to form the interval

$$[\bar{x} \pm z_{\alpha/2}\sigma_{\bar{x}}] = \left[\bar{x} \pm z_{\alpha/2}\frac{\sigma}{\sqrt{n}}\right]$$

then this interval will contain the population mean with probability $(1 - \alpha)$. In other words, this interval is a confidence interval for μ based on a confidence coefficient of $(1 - \alpha)$, and hence we call this interval a **100(1 − α) percent confidence interval for the population mean.** Here, **100(1 − α) percent** is called the **confidence level** associated with the confidence interval. This confidence level is the percentage of the time that the confidence interval would contain the population mean if all possible samples were used to calculate this interval. (Note that we will formally justify the confidence interval formula at the end of this section.)

For example, suppose we wish to find a 95 percent confidence interval for the population mean. Since the confidence level is 95 percent, we have $100(1 - \alpha) = 95$. This implies that the confidence coefficient is $(1 - \alpha) = .95$, which implies that $\alpha = .05$ and $\alpha/2 = .025$. Therefore, we need to find the normal point $z_{.025}$. As shown in Figure 7.3, the area under the standard normal curve between $-z_{.025}$ and $z_{.025}$ is .95, and the area under this curve between 0 and $z_{.025}$ is .475. Looking up the area .475 in Table A.3 (page 824), we find that $z_{.025} = 1.96$. It follows that the interval

$$[\bar{x} \pm z_{.025}\sigma_{\bar{x}}] = \left[\bar{x} \pm 1.96\frac{\sigma}{\sqrt{n}}\right]$$

is a 95 percent confidence interval for the population mean μ. This means that if all possible samples were used to calculate this interval, 95 percent of the resulting intervals would contain μ.

As another example, consider a 99 percent confidence interval for the population mean. Because the confidence level is 99 percent, we have $100(1 - \alpha) = 99$, and the confidence coefficient is $(1 - \alpha) = .99$. This implies that $\alpha = .01$ and $\alpha/2 = .005$. Therefore, we need to find the

TABLE 7.2 The Normal Point $z_{\alpha/2}$ for Various Levels of Confidence

$100(1-\alpha)$ percent	α	$\alpha/2$	Normal Point $z_{\alpha/2}$
$90\% = 100(1-.10)\%$	.10	.05	$z_{.05} = 1.645$
$95\% = 100(1-.05)\%$	.05	.025	$z_{.025} = 1.96$
$98\% = 100(1-.02)\%$	.02	.01	$z_{.01} = 2.33$
$99\% = 100(1-.01)\%$	.01	.005	$z_{.005} = 2.575$

normal point $z_{.005}$. As shown in Figure 7.4, the area under the standard normal curve between $-z_{.005}$ and $z_{.005}$ is .99, and the area under this curve between 0 and $z_{.005}$ is .495. Looking up the area .495 in Table A.3, we find that $z_{.005} = 2.575$. It follows that the interval

$$[\bar{x} \pm z_{.005}\sigma_{\bar{x}}] = \left[\bar{x} \pm 2.575\frac{\sigma}{\sqrt{n}}\right]$$

is a 99 percent confidence interval for the population mean μ. This means that if all possible samples were used to calculate this interval, 99 percent of the resulting intervals would contain μ.

To compare the 95 percent and 99 percent confidence intervals, notice that the margin of error $2.575(\sigma/\sqrt{n})$ used to compute the 99 percent interval is larger than the margin of error $1.96(\sigma/\sqrt{n})$ used to compute the 95 percent interval. Therefore, the 99 percent interval is the longer of these intervals. In general, increasing the confidence level (1) has the advantage of making us more confident that μ is contained in the confidence interval, but (2) has the disadvantage of increasing the margin of error and thus providing a less precise estimate of the true value of μ. Frequently, 95 percent confidence intervals are used to make conclusions. If conclusions based on stronger evidence are desired, 99 percent intervals are sometimes used.

Table 7.2 shows the confidence levels 95 percent and 99 percent, as well as two other confidence levels—90 percent and 98 percent—that are sometimes used to calculate confidence intervals. In addition, this table gives the values of α, $\alpha/2$, and $z_{\alpha/2}$ that correspond to these confidence levels. The following box summarizes the formula used in calculating a $100(1-\alpha)$ percent confidence interval for a population mean μ.

A Confidence Interval for a Population Mean μ: σ Known

Suppose that the sampled population is normally distributed. Then a **$100(1-\alpha)$ percent confidence interval for μ** is

$$\left[\bar{x} \pm z_{\alpha/2}\frac{\sigma}{\sqrt{n}}\right] = \left[\bar{x} - z_{\alpha/2}\frac{\sigma}{\sqrt{n}}, \bar{x} + z_{\alpha/2}\frac{\sigma}{\sqrt{n}}\right]$$

This interval is also approximately correct for non-normal populations if the sample size is large (at least 30).

This confidence interval is based on the normal distribution and requires that the true value of the population standard deviation σ is known. Of course, in almost all real-world situations this value is not known. However, the concepts and calculations related to confidence intervals are most easily illustrated using the normal distribution. Therefore, in this section we will assume that through extensive experience with the population or process under consideration, we know σ. When σ is unknown, we construct a confidence interval for μ by using the t distribution. In Section 7.2 we study t-based confidence intervals for μ, and we will revisit the examples of this section assuming that σ is unknown.

Example 7.1 The Car Mileage Case

C

Recall that the federal government will give a tax credit to any automaker selling a midsize model equipped with an automatic transmission that has an EPA combined city and highway mileage estimate of at least 31 mpg. Furthermore, to ensure that it does not overestimate a car model's mileage, the EPA will obtain the model's mileage estimate by rounding down—to the nearest mile per gallon—the lower limit of a 95 percent confidence interval for the model's mean mileage μ. That is, the model's mileage estimate is an estimate of the smallest that μ might reasonably be. Suppose the automaker conducts mileage tests on a sample of 49 of its new midsize cars and obtains the sample of 49 mileages in Table 2.1, which has mean $\bar{x} = 31.5531$. As illustrated in Figure 7.3, in order to compute a 95 percent interval we use the normal point $z_{\alpha/2} = z_{.05/2} = z_{.025} = 1.96$. Assuming that σ is known to equal .8, it follows that the 95 percent confidence interval for μ is

$$\left[\bar{x} \pm z_{.025}\frac{\sigma}{\sqrt{n}}\right] = \left[31.5531 \pm 1.96\frac{.8}{\sqrt{49}}\right]$$
$$= [31.5531 \pm .224]$$
$$= [31.33, 31.78]$$

This interval says we are 95 percent confident that the model's mean mileage μ is between 31.33 mpg and 31.78 mpg. Based on this interval, the model's EPA mileage estimate is 31 mpg, and the automaker will receive the tax credit.

If we wish to compute a 99 percent confidence interval for μ, then, as illustrated in Figure 7.4, we use the normal point $z_{\alpha/2} = z_{.01/2} = z_{.005} = 2.575$. We obtain

$$\left[\bar{x} \pm z_{.005}\frac{\sigma}{\sqrt{n}}\right] = \left[31.5531 \pm 2.575\frac{.8}{\sqrt{49}}\right]$$
$$= [31.5531 \pm .294]$$
$$= [31.26, 31.85]$$

This interval says we are 99 percent confident that the model's mean mileage μ is between 31.26 mpg and 31.85 mpg. Note that increasing the level of confidence to 99 percent has increased the margin of error from .224 to .294, which makes the 99 percent interval longer than the 95 percent interval.

Example 7.2 The Payment Time Case

Recall that a management consulting firm has installed a new computer-based, electronic billing system in a Hamilton, Ohio, trucking company. The mean payment time using the trucking company's old billing system was approximately equal to, but no less than, 39 days. In order to assess whether the mean payment time, μ, using the new billing system is substantially less than 39 days, the consulting firm will use the sample of $n = 65$ payment times in Table 2.2 to find a 95 percent confidence interval for μ. The mean of the 65 payment times is $\bar{x} = 18.1077$. Using the normal point $z_{\alpha/2} = z_{.025} = 1.96$, and assuming that σ is known to equal 4.2, it follows that the 95 percent confidence interval for μ is

$$\left[\bar{x} \pm z_{.025}\frac{\sigma}{\sqrt{n}}\right] = \left[18.1077 \pm 1.96\frac{4.2}{\sqrt{65}}\right]$$
$$= [18.1077 \pm 1.021]$$
$$= [17.1, 19.1]$$

Recalling that the mean payment time using the old billing system is 39 days, the point estimate $\bar{x} = 18.1$ says we estimate that the new billing system reduces the mean payment time by 20.9 days. Because the interval says that we are 95 percent confident that the mean payment time using the new billing system is between 17.1 days and 19.1 days, we are 95 percent confident that the new billing system reduces the mean payment time by at most 21.9 days and by at least 19.9 days.

Example 7.3 The Marketing Research Case

Recall that a brand group is considering a new bottle design for a popular soft drink and that Table 1.3 (page 8) gives a random sample of $n = 60$ consumer ratings of this new bottle design. Let μ denote the mean rating of the new bottle design that would be given by all consumers. In order to assess whether μ exceeds the minimum standard composite score of 25 for a successful bottle design, the brand group will calculate a 95 percent confidence interval for μ. The mean of the bottle design ratings is $\bar{x} = 30.35$. Using the normal point $z_{\alpha/2} = z_{.025} = 1.96$, and assuming that σ is known to equal 2.8, the 95 percent confidence interval for μ is

$$\left[\bar{x} \pm z_{.025}\frac{\sigma}{\sqrt{n}}\right] = \left[30.35 \pm 1.96\frac{2.8}{\sqrt{60}}\right]$$
$$= [30.35 \pm .7085]$$
$$= [29.6, 31.1]$$

The point estimate $\bar{x} = 30.35$ says we estimate that the mean rating of the new bottle design is 5.35 points higher than the minimum standard of 25 for a successful bottle design. Since the interval says we are 95 percent confident that the mean rating of the new bottle design is between 29.6 and 31.1, we are 95 percent confident that this mean rating exceeds the minimum standard of 25 by at least 4.6 points and by at most 6.1 points.

Justifying the confidence interval formula To show why the interval

$$\left[\bar{x} \pm z_{\alpha/2}\frac{\sigma}{\sqrt{n}}\right]$$

is a $100(1 - \alpha)$ percent confidence interval for μ, recall that if the sampled population is normally distributed or the sample size n is large, then the sampling distribution of $\bar{x}$ is (exactly or approximately) a normal distribution with mean $\mu_{\bar{x}} = \mu$ and standard deviation $\sigma_{\bar{x}} = \sigma/\sqrt{n}$. It follows that the sampling distribution of

$$z = \frac{\bar{x} - \mu}{\sigma/\sqrt{n}}$$

is (exactly or approximately) a standard normal distribution. Therefore, the probability that we will obtain a sample mean $\bar{x}$ such that z is between $-z_{\alpha/2}$ and $z_{\alpha/2}$ is $1 - \alpha$ (see Figure 7.5). That is, we can say that the probability that

$$-z_{\alpha/2} \le \frac{\bar{x} - \mu}{\sigma/\sqrt{n}} \le z_{\alpha/2}$$

equals $1 - \alpha$. Using some algebraic manipulations, we can show that this is equivalent to saying that the probability that

$$\bar{x} - z_{\alpha/2}\frac{\sigma}{\sqrt{n}} \le \mu \le \bar{x} + z_{\alpha/2}\frac{\sigma}{\sqrt{n}}$$

equals $1 - \alpha$. This probability statement says that the probability is $1 - \alpha$ (for example, .95) that we will obtain a sample mean $\bar{x}$ such that the interval

$$\left[\bar{x} \pm z_{\alpha/2}\frac{\sigma}{\sqrt{n}}\right]$$

contains μ. In other words, this interval is a $100(1 - \alpha)$ percent confidence interval for μ.

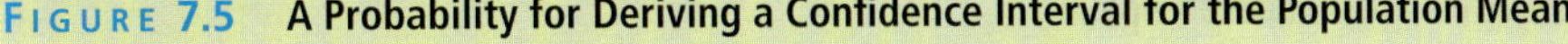

FIGURE 7.5 A Probability for Deriving a Confidence Interval for the Population Mean

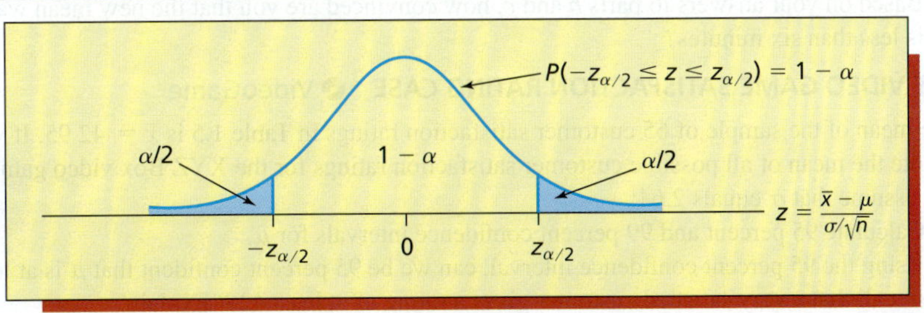

Exercises for Section 7.1

CONCEPTS

7.1 Explain why it is important to calculate a confidence interval in addition to calculating a point estimate of a population parameter.

7.2 Write a paragraph explaining exactly what the term "95 percent confidence" means in the context of calculating a 95 percent confidence interval for a population mean.

7.3 For each of the following changes, indicate whether a confidence interval for μ will have a larger or smaller margin of error:

a An increase in the level of confidence.
b An increase in the sample size.
c A decrease in the level of confidence.
d A decrease in the sample size.

METHODS AND APPLICATIONS

7.4 For each of the following confidence levels, $100(1 - \alpha)$ percent, find the $z_{\alpha/2}$ point needed to compute a confidence interval for μ:

a 95% **c** 99.73% **e** 97%
b 99% **d** 80% **f** 92%

7.5 Suppose that, for a sample of size $n = 100$ measurements, we find that $\bar{x} = 50$. Assuming that σ equals 2, calculate confidence intervals for the population mean μ with the following confidence levels:

a 95% **b** 99% **c** 97% **d** 80% **e** 99.73%

7.6 THE TRASH BAG CASE TrashBag

Consider the trash bag problem. Suppose that an independent laboratory has tested trash bags and has found that no 30-gallon bags that are currently on the market have a mean breaking strength of 50 pounds or more. On the basis of these results, the producer of the new, improved trash bag feels sure that its 30-gallon bag will be the strongest such bag on the market if the new trash bag's mean breaking strength can be shown to be at least 50 pounds. The mean of the sample of 40 trash bag breaking strengths in Table 1.10 is $\bar{x} = 50.575$. If we let μ denote the mean of the breaking strengths of all possible trash bags of the new type and assume that σ equals 1.65:

a Calculate 95 percent and 99 percent confidence intervals for μ.
b Using the 95 percent confidence interval, can we be 95 percent confident that μ is at least 50 pounds? Explain.
c Using the 99 percent confidence interval, can we be 99 percent confident that μ is at least 50 pounds? Explain.
d Based on your answers to parts *b* and *c*, how convinced are you that the new 30-gallon trash bag is the strongest such bag on the market?

7.7 THE BANK CUSTOMER WAITING TIME CASE WaitTime

Recall that a bank manager has developed a new system to reduce the time customers spend waiting to be served by tellers during peak business hours. The mean waiting time during peak business hours under the current system is roughly 9 to 10 minutes. The bank manager hopes that the new system will have a mean waiting time that is less than six minutes. The mean of the sample of 100 bank customer waiting times in Table 1.6 is $\bar{x} = 5.46$. If we let μ denote the mean of all possible bank customer waiting times using the new system and assume that σ equals 2.47:

a Calculate 95 percent and 99 percent confidence intervals for μ.
b Using the 95 percent confidence interval, can the bank manager be 95 percent confident that μ is less than six minutes? Explain.
c Using the 99 percent confidence interval, can the bank manager be 99 percent confident that μ is less than six minutes? Explain.
d Based on your answers to parts *b* and *c*, how convinced are you that the new mean waiting time is less than six minutes?

7.8 THE VIDEO GAME SATISFACTION RATING CASE VideoGame

The mean of the sample of 65 customer satisfaction ratings in Table 1.5 is $\bar{x} = 42.95$. If we let μ denote the mean of all possible customer satisfaction ratings for the XYZ Box video game system, and assume that σ equals 2.64:

a Calculate 95 percent and 99 percent confidence intervals for μ.
b Using the 95 percent confidence interval, can we be 95 percent confident that μ is at least 42 (recall that a very satisfied customer gives a rating of at least 42)? Explain.

c Using the 99 percent confidence interval, can we be 99 percent confident that μ is at least 42? Explain.

d Based on your answers to parts *b* and *c*, how convinced are you that the mean satisfaction rating is at least 42?

7.9 In an article in the *Journal of Management,* Morris, Avila, and Allen studied innovation by surveying firms to find (among other things) the number of new products introduced by the firms. Suppose a random sample of 100 California-based firms is selected and each firm is asked to report the number of new products it has introduced during the last year. The sample mean is found to be $\bar{x} = 5.68$. Assuming σ equals 8.70:

a Calculate a 98 percent confidence interval for the population mean number of new products introduced in the last year.

b Based on your confidence interval, find a reasonable estimate for the smallest value that the mean number of new products might be. Explain.

7.10 In an article in *Marketing Science,* Silk and Berndt investigate the output of advertising agencies. They describe ad agency output by finding the shares of dollar billing volume coming from various media categories such as network television, spot television, newspapers, radio, and so forth.

a Suppose that a random sample of 400 U.S. advertising agencies gives an average percentage share of billing volume from network television equal to 7.46 percent, and assume that σ equals 1.42 percent. Calculate a 95 percent confidence interval for the mean percentage share of billing volume from network television for the population of all U.S. advertising agencies.

b Suppose that a random sample of 400 U.S. advertising agencies gives an average percentage share of billing volume from spot television commercials equal to 12.44 percent, and assume that σ equals 1.55 percent. Calculate a 95 percent confidence interval for the mean percentage share of billing volume from spot television commercials for the population of all U.S. advertising agencies.

c Compare the confidence intervals in parts *a* and *b*. Does it appear that the mean percentage share of billing volume from spot television commercials for U.S. advertising agencies is greater than the mean percentage share of billing volume from network television? Explain.

7.11 In an article in *Accounting and Business Research,* Carslaw and Kaplan investigate factors that influence "audit delay" for firms in New Zealand. Audit delay, which is defined to be the length of time (in days) from a company's financial year-end to the date of the auditor's report, has been found to affect the market reaction to the report. This is because late reports seem to often be associated with lower returns and early reports seem to often be associated with higher returns.

Carslaw and Kaplan investigated audit delay for two kinds of public companies—owner-controlled and manager-controlled companies. Here a company is considered to be owner controlled if 30 percent or more of the common stock is controlled by a single outside investor (an investor not part of the management group or board of directors). Otherwise, a company is considered manager controlled. It was felt that the type of control influences audit delay. To quote Carslaw and Kaplan:

> Large external investors, having an acute need for timely information, may be expected to pressure the company and auditor to start and to complete the audit as rapidly as practicable.

a Suppose that a random sample of 100 public owner-controlled companies in New Zealand is found to give a mean audit delay of $\bar{x} = 82.6$ days, and assume that σ equals 33 days. Calculate a 95 percent confidence interval for the population mean audit delay for all public owner-controlled companies in New Zealand.

b Suppose that a random sample of 100 public manager-controlled companies in New Zealand is found to give a mean audit delay of $\bar{x} = 93$ days, and assume that σ equals 37 days. Calculate a 95 percent confidence interval for the population mean audit delay for all public manager-controlled companies in New Zealand.

c Use the confidence intervals you computed in parts *a* and *b* to compare the mean audit delay for all public owner-controlled companies versus that of all public manager-controlled companies. How do the means compare? Explain.

7.12 In an article in the *Journal of Marketing,* Bayus studied the differences between "early replacement buyers" and "late replacement buyers" in making consumer durable good replacement purchases. Early replacement buyers are consumers who replace a product during the early part of its lifetime, while late replacement buyers make replacement purchases late in the product's lifetime. In particular, Bayus studied automobile replacement purchases. Consumers who traded in cars with ages of zero to three years and mileages of no more than 35,000 miles were classified as early replacement buyers. Consumers who traded in cars with ages of seven or more years and mileages of more than 73,000 miles were classified as late replacement buyers. Bayus compared the two groups of buyers with respect to demographic variables such as income, education, age, and so forth. He also compared the two groups with respect to the amount of search activity in the replacement purchase process. Variables compared included the number of dealers visited, the time spent gathering information, and the time spent visiting dealers.

a Suppose that a random sample of 800 early replacement buyers yields a mean number of dealers visited of $\bar{x} = 3.3$, and assume that σ equals .71. Calculate a 99 percent confidence interval for the population mean number of dealers visited by early replacement buyers.

b Suppose that a random sample of 500 late replacement buyers yields a mean number of dealers visited of $\bar{x} = 4.3$, and assume that σ equals .66. Calculate a 99 percent confidence interval for the population mean number of dealers visited by late replacement buyers.

c Use the confidence intervals you computed in parts *a* and *b* to compare the mean number of dealers visited by early replacement buyers with the mean number of dealers visited by late replacement buyers. How do the means compare? Explain.

7.2 *t*-Based Confidence Intervals for a Population Mean: σ Unknown

If we do not know σ (which is usually the case), we can use the sample standard deviation s to help construct a confidence interval for μ. The interval is based on the sampling distribution of

$$t = \frac{\bar{x} - \mu}{s/\sqrt{n}}$$

CHAPTER 5

If the sampled population is normally distributed, then for any sample size n this sampling distribution is what is called a ***t* distribution.**

The curve of the t distribution has a shape similar to that of the standard normal curve. Two t curves and a standard normal curve are illustrated in Figure 7.6. A t curve is symmetrical about zero, which is the mean of any t distribution. However, the t distribution is more spread out, or variable, than the standard normal distribution. Since the above t statistic is a function of two random variables, $\bar{x}$ and s, it is logical that the sampling distribution of this statistic is more variable than the sampling distribution of the z statistic, which is a function of only one random variable, $\bar{x}$. The exact spread, or standard deviation, of the t distribution depends on a parameter that is called the **number of degrees of freedom (denoted *df*).** The degrees of freedom *df* varies depending on the problem. In the present situation the sampling distribution of t has a number of degrees of freedom that equals the sample size minus 1. We say that this sampling distribution is a ***t* distribution with $n - 1$ degrees of freedom.** As the sample size n (and thus the number of degrees of freedom) increases, the spread of the t distribution decreases (see Figure 7.6). Furthermore, as the number of degrees of freedom approaches infinity, the curve of the t distribution approaches (that is, becomes shaped more and more like) the curve of the standard normal distribution. In fact, when the sample size n is at least 30 and thus the number of degrees of freedom $n - 1$ is at least 29, the curve of the t distribution is very similar to the standard normal curve.

In order to use the t distribution, we employ a **t point that is denoted t_α.** As illustrated in Figure 7.7, **t_α is the point on the horizontal axis under the curve of the t distribution that gives a right-hand tail area equal to α.** The value of t_α in a particular situation depends upon the right-hand tail area α and the number of degrees of freedom of the t distribution. Values of t_α are tabulated in a ***t* table.** Such a table is given in Table A.4 of Appendix A (page 825) and a portion of Table A.4 is reproduced in this chapter as Table 7.3. In this t table, the rows correspond to the different numbers of degrees of freedom (which are denoted as *df*). The values of *df* are listed down the left side of the table, while the columns designate the right-hand tail area α. For example, suppose we wish to find the t point that gives a right-hand tail area of .025 under a t curve having $df = 14$ degrees of freedom. To do this, we look in Table 7.3 at the row labeled 14 and the column labeled $t_{.025}$. We find that this $t_{.025}$ point is 2.145 (also see Figure 7.8). Similarly, when there are $df = 14$ degrees of freedom, we find that $t_{.005} = 2.977$ (see Table 7.3 and Figure 7.9).

FIGURE 7.6 As the Number of Degrees of Freedom Increases, the Spread of the *t* Distribution Decreases and the *t* Curve Approaches the Standard Normal Curve

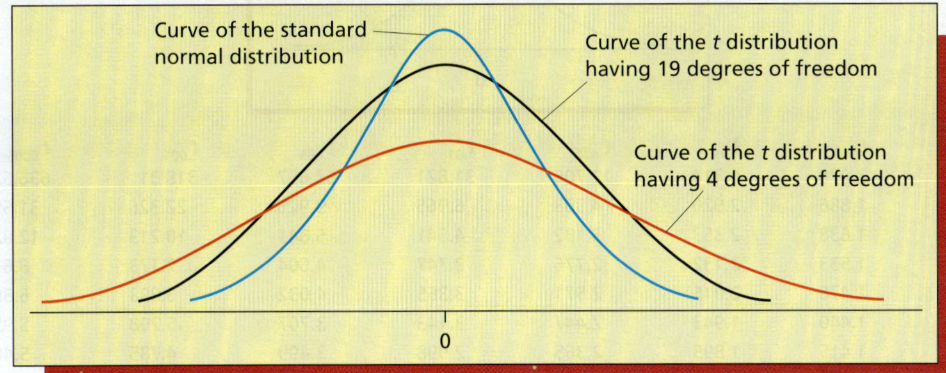

FIGURE 7.7 An Example of a *t* Point Giving a Specified Right-Hand Tail Area (This *t* Point Gives a Right-Hand Tail Area Equal to α).

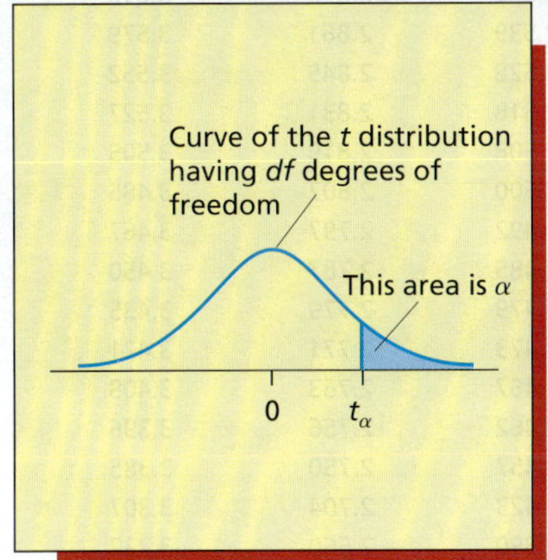

FIGURE 7.8 The *t* Point Giving a Right-Hand Tail Area of .025 under the *t* Curve Having 14 Degrees of Freedom: $t_{.025} = 2.145$

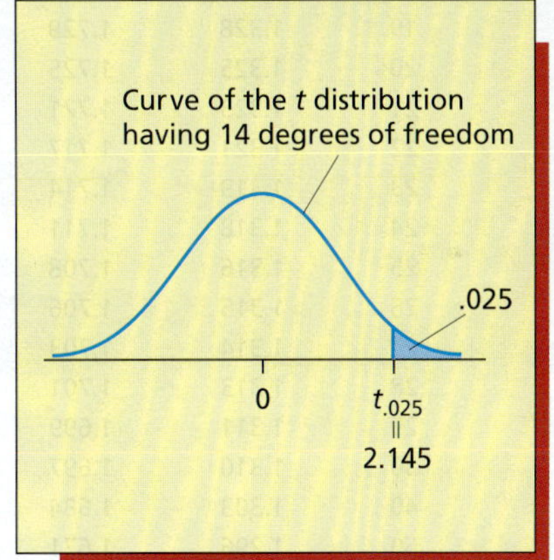

Table 7.3 gives t points for degrees of freedom df from 1 to 30. The table also gives t points for 40, 60, 120, and an infinite number of degrees of freedom. Looking at this table, it is useful to realize that the normal points giving the various right-hand tail areas are listed in the row of the t table corresponding to an infinite (∞) number of degrees of freedom. Looking at the row corresponding to ∞, we see that, for example, $z_{.025} = 1.96$ and $z_{.005} = 2.576$. Therefore, we can use this row in the t table as an alternative to using the normal table when we need to find normal points (such as $z_{\alpha/2}$ in Section 7.1).

Table A.4 of Appendix A (page 825) gives t points for values of df from 1 to 100. We can use a computer to find t points based on values of df greater than 100. Alternatively, because a t curve based on more than 100 degrees of freedom is approximately the shape of the standard normal curve, t points based on values of df greater than 100 can be approximated by their corresponding z points. That is, when performing hand calculations, it is reasonable to approximate values of t_α by z_α when df is greater than 100.

TABLE 7.3 A *t* Table

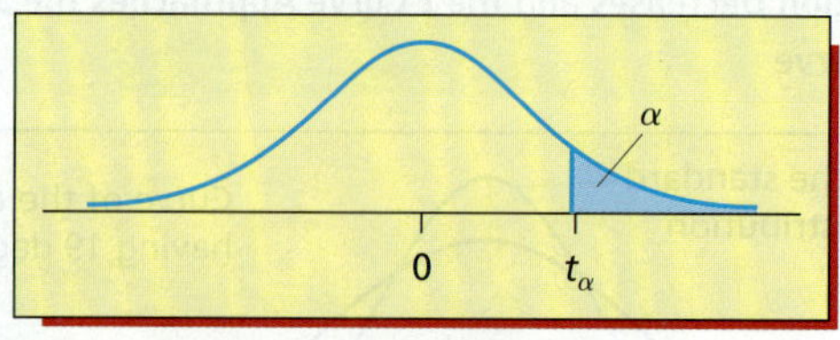

df	$t_{.100}$	$t_{.050}$	$t_{.025}$	$t_{.01}$	$t_{.005}$	$t_{.001}$	$t_{.0005}$
1	3.078	6.314	12.706	31.821	63.657	318.31	636.62
2	1.886	2.920	4.303	6.965	9.925	22.326	31.598
3	1.638	2.353	3.182	4.541	5.841	10.213	12.924
4	1.533	2.132	2.776	3.747	4.604	7.173	8.610
5	1.476	2.015	2.571	3.365	4.032	5.893	6.869
6	1.440	1.943	2.447	3.143	3.707	5.208	5.959
7	1.415	1.895	2.365	2.998	3.499	4.785	5.408
8	1.397	1.860	2.306	2.896	3.355	4.501	5.041
9	1.383	1.833	2.262	2.821	3.250	4.297	4.781
10	1.372	1.812	2.228	2.764	3.169	4.144	4.587
11	1.363	1.796	2.201	2.718	3.106	4.025	4.437
12	1.356	1.782	2.179	2.681	3.055	3.930	4.318
13	1.350	1.771	2.160	2.650	3.012	3.852	4.221
14	1.345	1.761	2.145	2.624	2.977	3.787	4.140
15	1.341	1.753	2.131	2.602	2.947	3.733	4.073
16	1.337	1.746	2.120	2.583	2.921	3.686	4.015
17	1.333	1.740	2.110	2.567	2.898	3.646	3.965
18	1.330	1.734	2.101	2.552	2.878	3.610	3.922
19	1.328	1.729	2.093	2.539	2.861	3.579	3.883
20	1.325	1.725	2.086	2.528	2.845	3.552	3.850
21	1.323	1.721	2.080	2.518	2.831	3.527	3.819
22	1.321	1.717	2.074	2.508	2.819	3.505	3.792
23	1.319	1.714	2.069	2.500	2.807	3.485	3.767
24	1.318	1.711	2.064	2.492	2.797	3.467	3.745
25	1.316	1.708	2.060	2.485	2.787	3.450	3.725
26	1.315	1.706	2.056	2.479	2.779	3.435	3.707
27	1.314	1.703	2.052	2.473	2.771	3.421	3.690
28	1.313	1.701	2.048	2.467	2.763	3.408	3.674
29	1.311	1.699	2.045	2.462	2.756	3.396	3.659
30	1.310	1.697	2.042	2.457	2.750	3.385	3.646
40	1.303	1.684	2.021	2.423	2.704	3.307	3.551
60	1.296	1.671	2.000	2.390	2.660	3.232	3.460
120	1.289	1.658	1.980	2.358	2.617	3.160	3.373
∞	1.282	1.645	1.960	2.326	2.576	3.090	3.291

Source: E. S. Pearson and H. O. Hartley eds., *The Biometrika Tables for Statisticians* 1, 3d ed. (Biometrika, 1966). Reproduced by permission of Oxford University Press Biometrika Trustees.

We now present the formula for a $100(1 - \alpha)$ percent confidence interval for a population mean μ based on the t distribution.

A *t*-Based $100(1 - \alpha)$ percent Confidence Interval for a Population Mean μ: σ Unknown

If the sampled population is normally distributed with mean μ, then a **$100(1 - \alpha)$ percent confidence interval for μ** is

$$\left[\bar{x} \pm t_{\alpha/2}\frac{s}{\sqrt{n}}\right]$$

Here s is the sample standard deviation, $t_{\alpha/2}$ is the t point giving a right-hand tail area of $\alpha/2$ under the t curve having $n - 1$ degrees of freedom, and n is the sample size.

CHAPTER 9

FIGURE 7.9 The t Point Giving a Right-Hand Tail Area of .005 under the t Curve Having 14 Degrees of Freedom: $t_{.005} = 2.977$

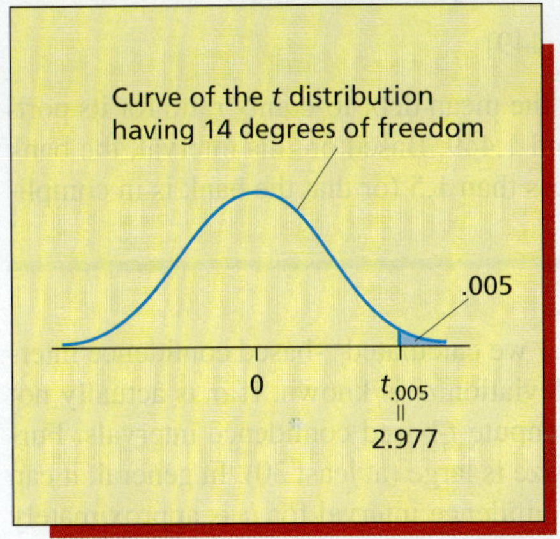

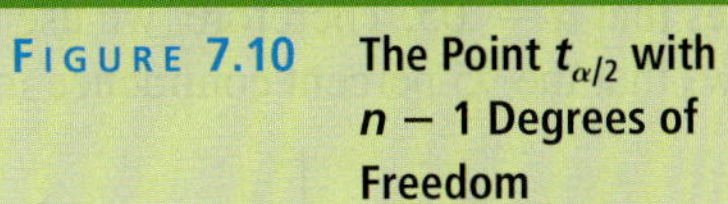

FIGURE 7.10 The Point $t_{\alpha/2}$ with $n - 1$ Degrees of Freedom

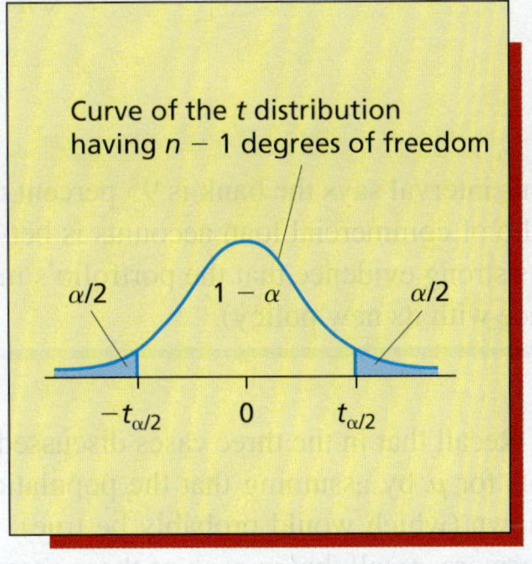

Before presenting an example, we need to make a few comments. First, it has been shown that this confidence interval is approximately valid for many populations that are not exactly normally distributed. In particular, this interval is approximately valid for a mound-shaped, or single-peaked, population, even if the population is somewhat skewed to the right or left. Second, this interval employs the point $t_{\alpha/2}$, which as shown in Figure 7.10, gives a right-hand tail area equal to $\alpha/2$ under the t curve having $n - 1$ degrees of freedom. Here $\alpha/2$ is determined from the desired confidence level $100(1 - \alpha)$ percent.

Example 7.4

One measure of a company's financial health is its *debt-to-equity ratio.* This quantity is defined to be the ratio of the company's corporate debt to the company's equity. If this ratio is too high, it is one indication of financial instability. For obvious reasons, banks often monitor the financial health of companies to which they have extended commercial loans. Suppose that, in order to reduce risk, a large bank has decided to initiate a policy limiting the mean debt-to-equity ratio for its portfolio of commercial loans to 1.5. In order to estimate the mean debt-to-equity ratio of its loan portfolio, the bank randomly selects a sample of 15 of its commercial loan accounts. Audits of these companies result in the following debt-to-equity ratios:

1.31	1.05	1.45	1.21	1.19
1.78	1.37	1.41	1.22	1.11
1.46	1.33	1.29	1.32	1.65

Stem	Leaf
1.0	5
1.1	1 9
1.2	1 2 9
1.3	1 2 3 7
1.4	1 5 6
1.5	
1.6	5
1.7	8

DebtEq

A stem-and-leaf display of these ratios is given on the page margin, and a box plot of the ratios is given below. The stem-and-leaf display looks reasonably mound-shaped, and both the stem-and-leaf display and the box plot look reasonably symmetrical. Furthermore, the sample mean and standard deviation of the ratios can be calculated to be $\bar{x} = 1.343$ and $s = .192$.

1.0 1.1 1.2 1.3 1.4 1.5 1.6 1.7 1.8
Ratio

Suppose the bank wishes to calculate a 95 percent confidence interval for the loan portfolio's mean debt-to-equity ratio, μ. Because the bank has taken a sample of size $n = 15$, we have $n - 1 = 15 - 1 = 14$ degrees of freedom, and the level of confidence $100(1 - \alpha)\% = 95\%$

implies that $\alpha = .05$. Therefore, we use the t point $t_{\alpha/2} = t_{.05/2} = t_{.025} = 2.145$ (see Table 7.3). It follows that the 95 percent confidence interval for μ is

$$\left[\bar{x} \pm t_{.025}\frac{s}{\sqrt{n}}\right] = \left[1.343 \pm 2.145\frac{.192}{\sqrt{15}}\right]$$

$$= [1.343 \pm 0.106]$$

$$= [1.237, 1.449]$$

This interval says the bank is 95 percent confident that the mean debt-to-equity ratio for its portfolio of commercial loan accounts is between 1.237 and 1.449. Based on this interval, the bank has strong evidence that the portfolio's mean ratio is less than 1.5 (or that the bank is in compliance with its new policy).

Recall that in the three cases discussed in Section 7.1 we calculated z-based confidence intervals for μ by assuming that the population standard deviation σ is known. If σ is actually not known (which would probably be true), we should compute t-based confidence intervals. Furthermore, recall that in each of these cases the sample size is large (at least 30). In general, it can be shown that if the sample size is large, the t-based confidence interval for μ is approximately valid even if the sampled population is not normally distributed (or mound shaped). Therefore, consider the gas mileage case and the sample of 49 mileages in Table 2.1, which has mean $\bar{x} = 31.5531$ and standard deviation $s = .7992$. The 95 percent t-based confidence interval for the population mean mileage μ is

$$\left[\bar{x} \pm t_{.025}\frac{s}{\sqrt{n}}\right] = \left[31.5531 \pm 2.011\frac{.7992}{\sqrt{49}}\right] = [31.32, 31.78]$$

where $t_{.025} = 2.011$ is based on $n - 1 = 49 - 1 = 48$ degrees of freedom—see Table A.4 (page 825). This interval is very close to the 95 percent z-based interval [31.33, 31.78] computed in Example 7.1 (page 265).

As another example, the sample of 65 payment times in Table 2.2 has mean $\bar{x} = 18.1077$ and standard deviation $s = 3.9612$. The 95 percent t-based confidence interval for the population mean payment time μ is $[18.1077 \pm 1.998(3.9612/\sqrt{65})] = [17.1, 19.1]$, where $t_{.025} = 1.998$ is based on $n - 1 = 65 - 1 = 64$ degrees of freedom—see Table A.4. This interval is (within rounding) the same as the 95 percent z-based interval computed in Example 7.2 (page 266). As a third example, the sample of 60 bottle design ratings in Table 1.3 has mean $\bar{x} = 30.35$ and standard deviation $s = 3.1073$. The 95 percent t-based confidence interval for the population mean bottle design rating μ is $[30.35 \pm 2.001(3.1073/\sqrt{60})] = [29.5, 31.2]$, where $t_{.025} = 2.001$ is based on $n - 1 = 60 - 1 = 59$ degrees of freedom—see Table A.4. This interval is very close to the 95 percent z-based interval [29.6, 31.1] computed in Example 7.3 (page 266).

In summary, the t-based 95 percent confidence intervals computed using $\bar{x}$ and s for the samples of mileages, payment times, and bottle design ratings do not differ by much from the z-based intervals computed in Section 7.1. Therefore, the practical conclusions reached in Section 7.1 using z-based intervals would also be reached using the t-based intervals discussed here.

Confidence intervals for μ can be computed using MINITAB, Excel, and MegaStat. For example, Figure 7.11(a) gives the Excel output of the sample mean $\bar{x} = 31.5531$ (see "Mean") and the margin of error $t_{.025}(s/\sqrt{n}) = .22957$ (see "Confidence Level (95%)") of the t-based 95 percent confidence interval for μ in the car mileage case. The interval, which must be hand calculated, is $[31.5531 \pm .22957] = [31.32, 31.78]$, as shown above. Figure 7.11(b) gives the Excel output of the sample mean and the margin of error for the t-based 95 percent confidence interval for μ computed using the sample of $n = 15$ debt-to-equity ratios in Example 7.4. Figure 7.12(a) gives the MINITAB output of the t-based 95 percent confidence interval for the mean debt-to-equity ratio, which (as hand calculated in Example 7.4) is [1.2369, 1.4497]. The MINITAB output also gives the sample mean $\bar{x}$, as well as the sample standard deviation s and the quantity $s/\sqrt{n}$, which is called the **standard error of the estimate $\bar{x}$** and denoted "SE Mean" on the MINITAB output (note that $s/\sqrt{n}$ is given on the Excel output as "Standard Error"). Finally, the MINITAB output gives a box plot of the sample of 15 debt-to-equity ratios and graphically

FIGURE 7.11 Excel and MINITAB Outputs for the Car Mileage Case, the Debt-to-Equity Ratio Example, and the Payment Time Case

(a) Excel output in the car mileage case

STATISTICS	
Mean	31.55306
Standard Error	0.114178
Median	31.6
Mode	31.7
Standard Deviation	0.799245
Sample Variance	0.638793
Kurtosis	−0.57098
Skewness	−0.10602
Range	3.5
Minimum	29.8
Maximum	33.3
Sum	1546.1
Count	49
Confidence Level(95.0%)	0.22957

(b) Excel output in the debt-to-equity ratio example

STATISTICS	
Mean	1.343333
Standard Error	0.049595
Median	1.32
Mode	#N/A
Standard Deviation	0.192081
Sample Variance	0.036895
Kurtosis	0.833414
Skewness	0.805013
Range	0.73
Minimum	1.05
Maximum	1.78
Sum	20.15
Count	15
Confidence Level(95.0%)	0.106371

(c) MINITAB output of the payment time case

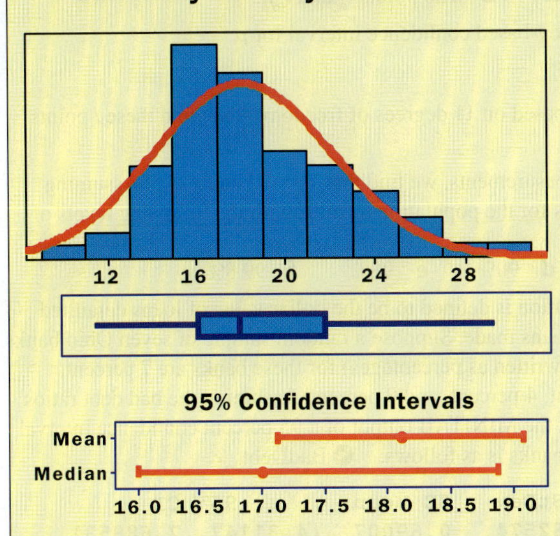

Anderson-Darling Normality Test	
A-Squared	0.92
P-Value	0.018
Mean	18.108
StDev	3.961
Variance	15.691
Skewness	0.600799
Kurtosis	0.033812
N	65
Minimum	10.000
1st Quartile	15.000
Median	17.000
3rd Quartile	21.000
Maximum	29.000
95% Confidence Interval for Mean	
17.126	19.089
95% Confidence Interval for Median	
16.000	18.879
95% Confidence Interval for StDev	
3.378	4.790

FIGURE 7.12 MINITAB and MegaStat Outputs of a t-Based 95 Percent Confidence Interval for the Mean Debt-to-Equity Ratio

(a) The MINITAB output

Variable	N	Mean	StDev	SE Mean	95% CI
Ratio	15	1.3433	0.1921	0.0496	(1.2370, 1.4497)

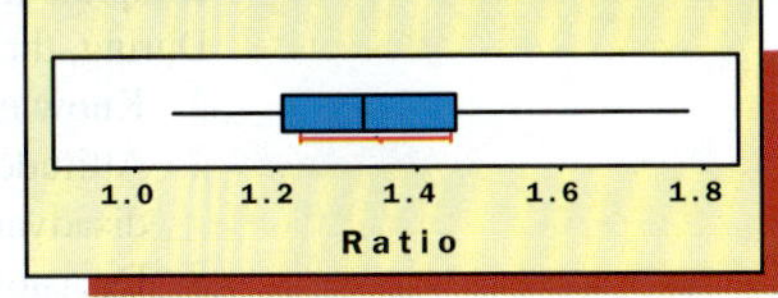

(b) The MegaStat output

Confidence interval - mean

1.3433 mean	15 n	1.4497 upper confidence limit
0.1921 std. dev	2.145 t (df = 14)	1.2369 lower confidence limit

illustrates under the box plot the 95 percent confidence interval for the mean debt-to-equity ratio. Figure 7.12(b) gives the MegaStat output of the 95 percent confidence interval for the mean debt-to-equity ratio.

To conclude this section, we note that if the sample size n is small and the sampled population is not mound-shaped or is highly skewed, then the t-based confidence interval for the population mean might not be valid. In this case we can use a **nonparametric method**—a method that makes no assumption about the shape of the sampled population and is valid for any sample size—to find a confidence interval for the **population median.** For example, Figure 7.11(c) gives the MINITAB output of a 95 percent confidence interval for the population *median* payment time using the new electronic billing system. This figure also shows the 95 percent t-based confidence interval for the population mean and a 95 percent confidence interval for the population standard deviation (in Section 8.8 we discuss how this latter interval is calculated). Because the histogram of payment times is mound-shaped and not highly skewed to the right, both the population mean and the population median are reasonable measures of central tendency. The confidence interval for the population median is particularly useful if the sampled population is highly skewed and is valid even if the sample size is small. In Chapter 15 we further discuss nonparametric methods.

Exercises for Section 7.2

CONCEPTS

7.13 Explain how each of the following changes as *the number of degrees of freedom* describing a t curve *increases:*

a The standard deviation of the t curve. **b** The points t_α and $t_{\alpha/2}$.

7.14 Discuss when it is appropriate to use the t-based confidence interval for μ.

METHODS AND APPLICATIONS

7.15 Using Table 7.3, find $t_{.10}$, $t_{.025}$, and $t_{.001}$ based on 11 degrees of freedom. Also, find these t points based on 6 degrees of freedom.

7.16 Suppose that for a sample of $n = 11$ measurements, we find that $\bar{x} = 72$ and $s = 5$. Assuming normality, compute confidence intervals for the population mean μ with the following levels of confidence:

a 95% **b** 99% **c** 80% **d** 90% **e** 98% **f** 99.8%

7.17 The *bad debt ratio* for a financial institution is defined to be the dollar value of loans defaulted divided by the total dollar value of all loans made. Suppose a random sample of seven Ohio banks is selected and that the bad debt ratios (written as percentages) for these banks are 7 percent, 4 percent, 6 percent, 7 percent, 5 percent, 4 percent, and 9 percent. Assuming the bad debt ratios are approximately normally distributed, the MINITAB output of a 95 percent confidence interval for the mean bad debt ratio of all Ohio banks is as follows: BadDebt

```
Variable  N      Mean      StDev   SE Mean       95% CI
D-Ratio   7   6.00000   1.82574   0.69007   (4.31147, 7.68853)
```

a Using the $\bar{x}$ and s on the MINITAB output, verify the calculation of the 95 percent confidence interval, and calculate a 99 percent confidence interval for the mean debt-to-equity ratio.

b Banking officials claim the mean bad debt ratio for all banks in the Midwest region is 3.5 percent and that the mean bad debt ratio for Ohio banks is higher. Using the 95 percent confidence interval, can we be 95 percent confident that this claim is true? Using the 99 percent confidence interval, can we be 99 percent confident that this claim is true?

7.18 In an article in *Quality Progress,* Blauw and During study how long it takes Dutch companies to complete five stages in the adoption of total quality control (TQC). According to Blauw and During, the adoption of TQC can be divided into five stages as follows: TQC

1 Knowledge: the organization has heard of TQC.
2 Attitude formation: the organization seeks information and compares advantages and disadvantages.
3 Decision making: the organization decides to implement TQC.
4 Implementation: the organization implements TQC.
5 Confirmation: the organization decides to apply TQC as a normal business activity.

Suppose a random sample of five Dutch firms that have adopted TQC is selected. Each firm is asked to report how long it took to complete the implementation stage. The firms report the following durations (in years) for this stage: 2.5, 1.5, 1.25, 3.5, and 1.25. Assuming that the durations are approximately normally distributed, the MegaStat output of a 95 percent confidence interval for the mean duration of the implementation stage for Dutch firms is as follows:

Confidence interval - mean		
2 mean	5 n	3.222 upper confidence limit
0.984 std. dev.	2.776 t (df = 4)	0.778 lower confidence limit

Based on the 95 percent confidence interval, is there conclusive evidence that the mean duration of the implementation stage exceeds one year? Explain. What is one possible reason for the lack of conclusive evidence?

7.19 A federal agency wishes to assess the effectiveness of a new air traffic control display panel. The mean time required for air traffic controllers to stabilize an air traffic emergency in which two aircraft have been assigned to the same air space is known to be roughly equal to, but no less than, 17 seconds when the current display panel is used. In order to test the new display panel, 20 air traffic controllers are randomly selected and each is trained to use the new panel. When each randomly selected controller uses the new display panel to stabilize a simulated emergency in which two aircraft have been assigned to the same air space, the mean and standard deviation of the 20 stabilization times so obtained are $\bar{x} = 13.8$ seconds and $s = 1.57$ seconds.

a Assuming that stabilization times are approximately normally distributed, find a 95 percent confidence interval for the true mean time required to stabilize the emergency situation using the new display panel.

b Are we 95 percent confident that the mean stabilization time using the new display panel is less than the 17 seconds for the current display panel? Explain.

7.20 Whole Foods is an all-natural grocery chain that has 50,000 square foot stores, up from the industry average of 34,000 square feet. Sales per square foot of supermarkets average just under \$400 per square foot, as reported by *USA Today* in an article on "A whole new ballgame in grocery shopping." Suppose that sales per square foot in the most recent fiscal year are recorded for a random sample of 10 Whole Foods supermarkets. The data (sales dollars per square foot) are as follows: 854, 858, 801, 892, 849, 807, 894, 863, 829, 815. Using the fact that $\bar{x} = 846.2$ and $s = 32.866$, find a 95 percent confidence interval for the true mean sales dollars per square foot for all Whole Foods supermarkets during the most recent fiscal year. Are we 95 percent confident that this mean is greater than \$800, the historical average for Whole Foods? WholeFoods

7.21 A production supervisor at a major chemical company wishes to determine whether a new catalyst, catalyst XA-100, increases the mean hourly yield of a chemical process beyond the current mean hourly yield, which is known to be roughly equal to, but no more than, 750 pounds per hour. To test the new catalyst, five trial runs using catalyst XA-100 are made. The resulting yields for the trial runs (in pounds per hour) are 801, 814, 784, 836, and 820. Assuming that all factors affecting yields of the process have been held as constant as possible during the test runs, it is reasonable to regard the five yields obtained using the new catalyst as a random sample from the population of all possible yields that would be obtained by using the new catalyst. Furthermore, we will assume that this population is approximately normally distributed. ChemYield

a Using the Excel output in Figure 7.13, find a 95 percent confidence interval for the mean of all possible yields obtained using catalyst XA-100.

b Based on the confidence interval, can we be 95 percent confident that the mean yield using catalyst XA-100 exceeds 750 pounds per hour? Explain.

7.22 THE TRASH BAG CASE TrashBag

The mean and the standard deviation of the sample of 40 trash bag breaking strengths in Table 1.10 are $\bar{x} = 50.575$ and $s = 1.6438$. Calculate a t-based 95 percent confidence interval for μ, the mean of the breaking strengths of all possible trash bags of the new type. Also, find this interval using the Excel output in Figure 7.14. Are we 95 percent confident that μ is at least 50 pounds?

7.23 THE BANK CUSTOMER WAITING TIME CASE WaitTime

The mean and the standard deviation of the sample of 100 bank customer waiting times in Table 1.6 are $\bar{x} = 5.46$ and $s = 2.475$. Calculate a t-based 95 percent confidence interval for μ, the mean of all possible bank customer waiting times using the new system. Also, find this interval using the MINITAB output in Figure 7.15. Are we 95 percent confident that μ is less than six minutes?

7.24 THE VIDEO GAME SATISFACTION RATING CASE VideoGame

The mean and the standard deviation of the sample of $n = 65$ customer satisfaction ratings in Table 1.5 are $\bar{x} = 42.95$ and $s = 2.6424$. Calculate a t-based 95 percent confidence interval for μ, the mean of all possible customer satisfaction ratings for the XYZ Box video game system. Are we 95 percent confident that μ is at least 42, the minimal rating given by a very satisfied customer?

FIGURE 7.13 Excel Output for Exercise 7.21

STATISTICS	
Mean	811
Standard Error	8.786353
Median	814
Mode	#N/A
Standard Deviation	19.64688
Sample Variance	386
Kurtosis	−0.12472
Skewness	−0.23636
Range	52
Minimum	784
Maximum	836
Sum	4055
Count	5
Confidence Level(95.0%)	24.39488

FIGURE 7.14 Excel Output for Exercise 7.22

STATISTICS	
Mean	50.575
Standard Error	0.2599
Median	50.65
Mode	50.9
Standard Deviation	1.643753
Sample Variance	2.701923
Kurtosis	−0.2151
Skewness	−0.05493
Range	7.2
Minimum	46.8
Maximum	54
Sum	2023
Count	40
Confidence Level(95.0%)	0.525697

FIGURE 7.15 MINITAB Output for Exercise 7.23

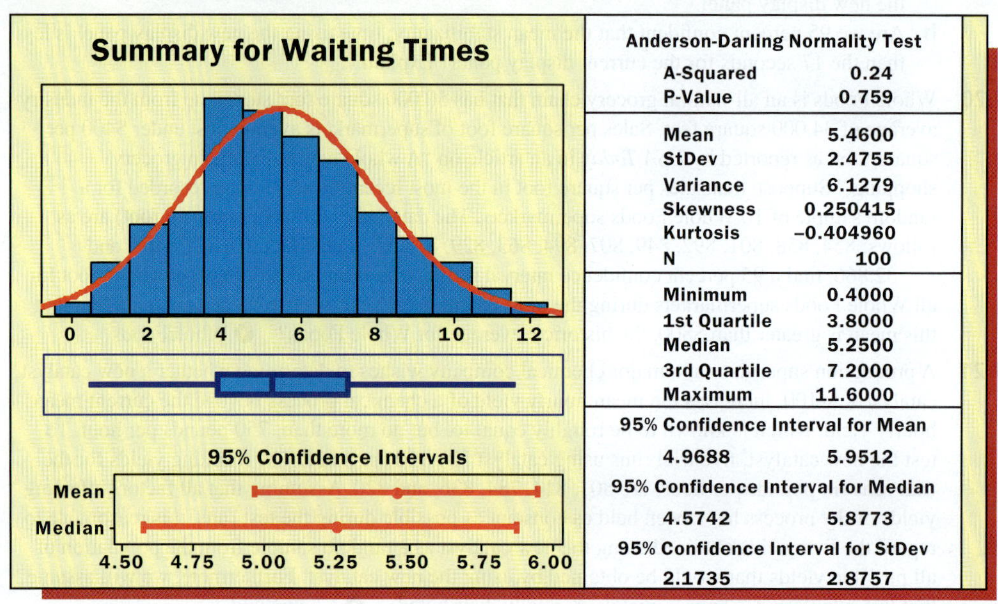

7.3 Sample Size Determination

In Example 7.1 we used a sample of 49 mileages to construct a 95 percent confidence interval for the midsize model's mean mileage μ. The size of this sample was not arbitrary—it was planned. To understand this, suppose that before the automaker selected the random sample of 49 mileages, it randomly selected the small sample of five mileages that is shown as the leftmost sample in Table 7.1. This sample consists of the mileages

30.8 31.9 30.3 32.1 31.4

and has mean $\bar{x} = 31.3$ and standard deviation $s = .7517$. Assuming that the population of all mileages is mound-shaped, we can calculate a confidence interval for the population mean mileage μ by using the t distribution with $n - 1 = 5 - 1 = 4$ degrees of freedom. It follows that a 95 percent confidence interval for μ is

$$\left[\bar{x} \pm t_{.025}\frac{s}{\sqrt{n}}\right] = \left[31.3 \pm 2.776\frac{.7517}{\sqrt{5}}\right]$$
$$= [31.3 \pm .9333]$$
$$= [30.4, 32.2]$$

Although the sample mean $\bar{x} = 31.3$ is at least 31, the lower limit of the 95 percent confidence interval for μ is less than 31. Therefore, the midsize model's EPA mileage estimate would be 30 mpg, and the automaker would not receive its tax credit. One reason that the lower limit of this 95 percent interval is less than 31 is that the sample size of 5 is not large enough to make the margin of error in the interval

$$t_{.025}\frac{s}{\sqrt{n}} = 2.776\frac{.7515}{\sqrt{5}} = .9333$$

small enough. We can attempt to make the margin of error in the interval smaller by increasing the sample size. If we feel that the mean $\bar{x}$ of the larger sample will be at least 31.3 mpg (the mean of the small sample we have already taken), then the lower limit of a $100(1 - \alpha)$ percent confidence interval for μ will be at least 31 if the margin of error is .3 or less.

We will now explain how to find the size of the sample that will be needed to make the margin of error in a confidence interval for μ as small as we wish. In order to develop a formula for the needed sample size, we will initially assume that we know σ. Then, if the population is normally distributed or the sample size is large, the z-based $100(1 - \alpha)$ percent confidence interval for μ is

$$\left[\bar{x} \pm z_{\alpha/2}\frac{\sigma}{\sqrt{n}}\right]$$

To find the needed sample size, we set $z_{\alpha/2}(\sigma/\sqrt{n})$ equal to the desired margin of error and solve for n. Letting E denote the desired margin of error, we obtain

$$z_{\alpha/2}\frac{\sigma}{\sqrt{n}} = E$$

Multiplying both sides of this equation by $\sqrt{n}$ and dividing both sides by E, we obtain

$$\sqrt{n} = \frac{z_{\alpha/2}\sigma}{E}$$

Squaring both sides of this result gives us the formula for n.

Determining the Sample Size for a Confidence Interval for μ: σ Known

A sample of size

$$n = \left(\frac{z_{\alpha/2}\sigma}{E}\right)^2$$

makes the margin of error in a $100(1 - \alpha)$ percent confidence interval for μ equal to E. That is, this sample size makes us $100(1 - \alpha)$ percent confident that $\bar{x}$ is within E units of μ. If the calculated value of n is not a whole number, round this value up to the next whole number (so that the margin of error is at least as small as desired).

If we consider the formula for the sample size n, it intuitively follows that the value E is the farthest that the user is willing to allow $\bar{x}$ to be from μ at a given level of confidence, and the normal point $z_{\alpha/2}$ follows directly from the given level of confidence. Furthermore, because the population standard deviation σ is in the numerator of the formula for n, it follows that the more variable that the individual population measurements are, the larger is the sample size needed to estimate μ with a specified accuracy.

In order to use this formula for n, we must either know σ (which is unlikely) or we must compute an estimate of σ. Often we estimate σ by using a **preliminary sample.** In this case we modify the above formula for n by replacing σ by the standard deviation s of the preliminary sample and by replacing $z_{\alpha/2}$ by $t_{\alpha/2}$. Thus we obtain

$$n = \left(\frac{t_{\alpha/2}\, s}{E}\right)^2$$

where the number of degrees of freedom for the $t_{\alpha/2}$ point is the size of the preliminary sample minus 1. Intuitively, using $t_{\alpha/2}$ compensates for the fact that the preliminary sample's value of s might underestimate σ.

Example 7.5 The Car Mileage Case

Suppose that in the car mileage situation we wish to find the sample size that is needed to make the margin of error in a 95 percent confidence interval for μ equal to .3. Assuming we do not know σ, we regard the previously discussed sample of five mileages as a preliminary sample. Therefore, we replace σ by the standard deviation of the preliminary sample (recall that s = .7517 for this sample), and we replace $z_{\alpha/2} = z_{.025} = 1.96$ by $t_{.025} = 2.776$, which is based on $n - 1 = 4$ degrees of freedom. We find that the appropriate sample size is

$$n = \left(\frac{t_{.025}\, s}{E}\right)^2 = \left(\frac{2.776(.7517)}{.3}\right)^2 = 48.38$$

Rounding up, we employ a sample of size 49.

When we make the margin of error in our 95 percent confidence interval for μ equal to .3, we can say we are 95 percent confident that the sample mean $\bar{x}$ is within .3 of μ. To understand this, suppose the true value of μ is 31.5. Recalling that the mean of the sample of 49 mileages is $\bar{x}$ = 31.5531, we see that this sample mean is within .3 of μ (in fact, it is 31.5531 − 31.5 = .0531 mpg from μ = 31.5). Other samples of 49 mileages would give different sample means that would be different distances from μ. When we say that our sample of 49 mileages makes us 95 percent confident that $\bar{x}$ is within .3 of μ, we mean that **95 percent of all possible sample means based on 49 mileages are within .3 of μ** and 5 percent of such sample means are not. Therefore, when we randomly select one sample of size 49 and compute its sample mean $\bar{x}$ = 31.5531, we can be 95 percent confident that this sample mean is within .3 of μ.

In general, the purpose behind replacing $z_{\alpha/2}$ by $t_{\alpha/2}$ when we are using a preliminary sample to obtain an estimate of σ is to be **conservative,** so that we compute a sample size that is **at least as large as needed.** Because of this, as we illustrate in the next example, we often obtain a margin of error that is even smaller than we have requested.

Example 7.6 The Car Mileage Case

To see that the sample of 49 mileages has actually produced a 95 percent confidence interval with a margin of error that is as small as we requested, recall that the 49 mileages have mean $\bar{x}$ = 31.5531 and standard deviation s = .7992. Therefore, the t-based 95 percent confidence interval for μ is

$$\left[\bar{x} \pm t_{.025}\frac{s}{\sqrt{n}}\right] = \left[31.5531 \pm 2.011\frac{.7992}{\sqrt{49}}\right]$$
$$= [31.5531 \pm .2296]$$
$$= [31.32, 31.78]$$

where $t_{.025}$ = 2.011 is based on $n - 1 = 49 - 1 = 48$ degrees of freedom—see Table A.4 (page 825). We see that the margin of error in this interval is .2296, which is smaller than the .3 we asked for. Furthermore, as the automaker had hoped, the sample mean $\bar{x}$ = 31.5531 of the sample of 49 mileages turned out to be at least 31.3. Therefore, since the margin of error is less than .3, the lower limit of the 95 percent confidence interval is higher than 31 mpg, and the midsize model's EPA mileage estimate is 31 mpg. Because of this, the automaker will receive its tax credit.

Finally, sometimes we do not have a preliminary sample that can be used to estimate σ. In this case we have two alternatives. First, we might estimate σ by using our knowledge about a similar population or process. For instance, the automaker might believe that the standard deviation of the mileages for this year's midsize model is about the same as the standard deviation of the mileages for last year's model. Thus, it might be reasonable to use the best available estimate of σ for last year's model as a preliminary estimate of σ for this year's model. Second, it can be shown that, if we can make a reasonable guess of the range of the population being studied, then a conservatively large estimate of σ is this estimated range divided by 4. For example, if the automaker's design engineers feel that almost all of its midsize cars should get mileages within a range of 5 mpg, then a conservatively large estimate of σ is $5/4 = 1.25$ mpg. When employing such an estimate of σ, it is sufficient to use the z-based sample size formula $n = (z_{\alpha/2}\sigma/E)^2$, because a conservatively large estimate of σ will give us a conservatively large sample size.

Exercises for Section 7.3

CONCEPTS

7.25 Explain what is meant by the margin of error for a confidence interval. What error are we talking about in the context of an interval for μ?

7.26 Explain exactly what we mean when we say that a sample of size n makes us 99 percent confident that $\bar{x}$ is within E units of μ.

7.27 Why do we usually need to take a preliminary sample when determining the size of the sample needed to make the margin of error of a confidence interval equal to E?

METHODS AND APPLICATIONS

7.28 Consider a population having a standard deviation equal to 10. We wish to estimate the mean of this population.

a How large a random sample is needed to construct a 95.44 percent confidence interval for the mean of this population with a margin of error equal to 1?

b Suppose that we now take a random sample of the size we have determined in part *a*. If we obtain a sample mean equal to 295, calculate the 95.44 percent confidence interval for the population mean. What is the interval's margin of error?

7.29 Referring to Exercise 7.11*a*, regard the sample of 100 public owner controlled companies for which $s = 32.83$ as a preliminary sample. How large a random sample of public owner-controlled companies is needed to make us

a 95 percent confident that $\bar{x}$, the sample mean audit delay, is within a margin of error of four days of μ, the true mean audit delay?

b 99 percent confident that $\bar{x}$ is within a margin of error of four days of μ?

7.30 Referring to Exercise 7.12*b*, regard the sample of 500 late replacement buyers for which $s = .68$ as a preliminary sample. How large a sample of late replacement buyers is needed to make us

a 99 percent confident that $\bar{x}$, the sample mean number of dealers visited, is within a margin of error of .04 of μ, the true mean number of dealers visited? Note: $t_{.005} = 2.59$ when $df = 499$.

b 99.73 percent confident that $\bar{x}$ is within a margin of error of .05 of μ? Note: $t_{.00135} = 3.02$ when $df = 499$.

7.31 Referring to Exercise 7.21, regard the sample of five trial runs for which $s = 19.65$ as a preliminary sample. Determine the number of trial runs of the chemical process needed to make us

a 95 percent confident that $\bar{x}$, the sample mean hourly yield, is within a margin of error of eight pounds of the true mean hourly yield μ when catalyst XA-100 is used.

b 99 percent confident that $\bar{x}$ is within a margin of error of five pounds of μ. ChemYield

7.32 Referring to Exercise 7.20, regard the sample of 10 sales figures for which $s = 32.866$ as a preliminary sample. How large a sample of sales figures is needed to make us 95 percent confident that $\bar{x}$, the sample mean sales dollars per square foot, is within a margin of error of \$10 of μ, the true mean sales dollars per square foot for all Whole Foods supermarkets.

7.33 Referring to Exercise 7.19, regard the sample of 20 stabilization times for which $s = 1.57$ as a preliminary sample. Determine the sample size needed to make us 95 percent confident that $\bar{x}$, the sample mean time required to stabilize the emergency situation, is within a margin of error of .5 seconds of μ, the true mean time required to stabilize the emergency situation using the new display panel.

7.4 Confidence Intervals for a Population Proportion

In Chapter 6, the soft cheese spread producer decided to replace its current spout with the new spout if p, the true proportion of all current purchasers who would stop buying the cheese spread if the new spout were used, is less than .10. Suppose that when 1,000 current purchasers are randomly selected and are asked to try the new spout, 63 say they would stop buying the spread if the new spout were used. The point estimate of the population proportion p is the sample proportion $\hat{p} = 63/1{,}000 = .063$. This sample proportion says we estimate that 6.3 percent of all current purchasers would stop buying the cheese spread if the new spout were used. Since $\hat{p}$ equals .063, we have some evidence that p is less than .10.

In order to see if there is strong evidence that p is less than .10, we can calculate a confidence interval for p. As explained in Chapter 6, if the sample size n is large, then the sampling distribution of the sample proportion $\hat{p}$ is approximately a normal distribution with mean $\mu_{\hat{p}} = p$ and standard deviation $\sigma_{\hat{p}} = \sqrt{p(1-p)/n}$. By using the same logic we used in developing confidence intervals for μ, it follows that a $100(1-\alpha)$ percent confidence interval for p is

$$\left[\hat{p} \pm z_{\alpha/2}\sqrt{\frac{p(1-p)}{n}}\right]$$

Estimating $p(1-p)$ by $\hat{p}(1-\hat{p})$, it follows that a $100(1-\alpha)$ percent confidence interval for p can be calculated as summarized below.

A Large Sample $100(1-\alpha)$ percent Confidence Interval for a Population Proportion p

If the sample size n is large, a **$100(1-\alpha)$ percent confidence interval for the population proportion p** is

$$\left[\hat{p} \pm z_{\alpha/2}\sqrt{\frac{\hat{p}(1-\hat{p})}{n}}\right]$$

Here n should be considered large if both $n\hat{p}$ and $n(1-\hat{p})$ are at least 5.[1]

Example 7.7 The Cheese Spread Case

In the cheese spread situation, consider calculating a confidence interval for p, the population proportion of purchasers who would stop buying the cheese spread if the new spout were used. In order to see whether the sample size $n = 1{,}000$ is large enough to enable us to use the confidence interval formula just given, recall that the point estimate of p is $\hat{p} = 63/1{,}000 = .063$. Therefore, because $n\hat{p} = 1{,}000(.063) = 63$ and $n(1-\hat{p}) = 1{,}000(.937) = 937$ are both greater

[1]Some statisticians suggest using the more conservative rule that both $n\hat{p}$ and $n(1-\hat{p})$ must be at least 10. Furthermore, because $\hat{p}(1-\hat{p})/(n-1)$ is an unbiased point estimate of $p(1-p)/n$, a more correct $100(1-\alpha)$ percent confidence interval for p is $[\hat{p} \pm z_{\alpha/2}\sqrt{\hat{p}(1-\hat{p})/(n-1)}]$. However, because n is large, there is little difference between intervals obtained by using this formula and those obtained by using the formula in the above box.

than 5, we can use the confidence interval formula. For example, a 95 percent confidence interval for p is

$$\left[\hat{p} \pm z_{.025}\sqrt{\frac{\hat{p}(1-\hat{p})}{n}}\right] = \left[.063 \pm 1.96\sqrt{\frac{(.063)(.937)}{1000}}\right]$$
$$= [.063 \pm .0151]$$
$$= [.0479, .0781]$$

This interval says that we are 95 percent confident that between 4.79 percent and 7.81 percent of all current purchasers would stop buying the cheese spread if the new spout were used. Below we give the MegaStat output of this interval.

Confidence interval - proportion

1000 n	95% confidence level	**0.078 upper confidence limit**
1.960 z	0.063 proportion	**0.048 lower confidence limit**

A 99 percent confidence interval for p is

$$\left[\hat{p} \pm z_{.005}\sqrt{\frac{\hat{p}(1-\hat{p})}{n}}\right] = \left[.063 \pm 2.575\sqrt{\frac{(.063)(.937)}{1000}}\right]$$
$$= [.063 \pm .0198]$$
$$= [.0432, .0828]$$

The upper limits of both the 95 percent and 99 percent intervals are less than .10. Therefore, we have very strong evidence that the true proportion p of all current purchasers who would stop buying the cheese spread is less than .10. Based on this result, it seems reasonable to use the new spout.

In the cheese spread example, a sample of 1,000 purchasers gives us a 95 percent confidence interval for p—[.063 ± .0151]—with a reasonably small margin of error of .0151. Generally speaking, quite a large sample is needed in order to make the margin of error in a confidence interval for p reasonably small. The next two examples demonstrate that a sample size of 200, which most people would consider quite large, does not necessarily give a 95 percent confidence interval for p with a small margin of error.

Example 7.8

Antibiotics occasionally cause nausea as a side effect. Scientists working for a major drug company have developed a new antibiotic called Phe-Mycin. The company wishes to estimate p, the proportion of all patients who would experience nausea as a side effect when being treated with Phe-Mycin. Suppose that a sample of 200 patients is randomly selected. When these patients are treated with Phe-Mycin, 35 patients experience nausea. The point estimate of the population proportion p is the sample proportion $\hat{p} = 35/200 = .175$. This sample proportion says that we estimate that 17.5 percent of all patients would experience nausea as a side effect of taking Phe-Mycin. Furthermore, because $n\hat{p} = 200(.175) = 35$ and $n(1-\hat{p}) = 200(.825) = 165$ are both at least 5, we can use the previously given formula to calculate a confidence interval for p. Doing this, we find that a 95 percent confidence interval for p is

$$\left[\hat{p} \pm z_{.025}\sqrt{\frac{\hat{p}(1-\hat{p})}{n}}\right] = \left[.175 \pm 1.96\sqrt{\frac{(.175)(.825)}{200}}\right]$$
$$= [.175 \pm .053]$$
$$= [.122, .228]$$

This interval says we are 95 percent confident that between 12.2 percent and 22.8 percent of all patients would experience nausea as a side effect of taking Phe-Mycin. Notice that the margin of error (.053) in this interval is rather large. Therefore, this interval is fairly long, and it does not provide a very precise estimate of p.

Example 7.9 The Marketing Ethics Case

Recall from Example 2.17 (page 89) that we wish to estimate the proportion, p, of all marketing researchers who disapprove of the actions taken in the ultraviolet ink scenario. Also recall that since 117 of the 205 surveyed marketing researchers said that they disapproved, the point estimate of p is the sample proportion $\hat{p} = 117/205 = .5707$. Because $n\hat{p} = 205(.5707) = 117$ and $n(1 - \hat{p}) = 205(.4293) = 88$ are both at least 5, it follows that a 95 percent confidence interval for p is

$$\left[\hat{p} \pm z_{.025}\sqrt{\frac{\hat{p}(1-\hat{p})}{n}}\right] = \left[.5707 \pm 1.96\sqrt{\frac{(.5707)(.4293)}{205}}\right]$$
$$= [.5707 \pm .0678]$$
$$= [.5029, .6385]$$

This interval says we are 95 percent confident that between 50.29 percent and 63.85 percent of all marketing researchers disapprove of the actions taken in the ultraviolet ink scenario. Notice that since the margin of error (.0678) in this interval is rather large, this interval does not provide a very precise estimate of p. Below we show the MINITAB output of this interval.

CI for One Proportion

X	N	Sample p	95% CI
117	205	0.570732	(0.502975, 0.638488)

In order to find the size of the sample needed to estimate a population proportion, we consider the theoretically correct interval

$$\left[\hat{p} \pm z_{\alpha/2}\sqrt{\frac{p(1-p)}{n}}\right]$$

To obtain the sample size needed to make the margin of error in this interval equal to E, we set

$$z_{\alpha/2}\sqrt{\frac{p(1-p)}{n}} = E$$

and solve for n. When we do this, we get the following result:

Determining the Sample Size for a Confidence Interval for p

A sample of size

$$n = p(1-p)\left(\frac{z_{\alpha/2}}{E}\right)^2$$

makes the margin of error in a $100(1 - \alpha)$ percent confidence interval for p equal to E. That is, this sample size makes us $100(1 - \alpha)$ percent confident that $\hat{p}$ is within E units of p. If the calculated value of n is not a whole number, round this value up to the next whole number.

Looking at this formula, we see that, the larger $p(1 - p)$ is, the larger n will be. To make sure n is large enough, consider Figure 7.16, which is a graph of $p(1 - p)$ versus p. This figure shows that $p(1 - p)$ equals .25 when p equals .5. Furthermore, $p(1 - p)$ is never larger than .25. Therefore, if the true value of p could be near .5, we should set $p(1 - p)$ equal to .25. This will ensure that n is as large as needed to make the margin of error as small as desired. For example, suppose we wish to estimate the proportion p of all registered voters who currently favor a particular candidate for President of the United States. If this candidate is the nominee of a major political party, or if the candidate enjoys broad popularity for some other reason, then p could be near .5. Furthermore, suppose we wish to make the margin of error in a 95 percent confidence interval for

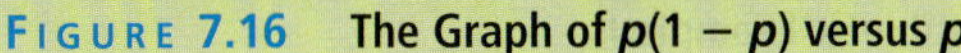

FIGURE 7.16 The Graph of $p(1-p)$ versus p

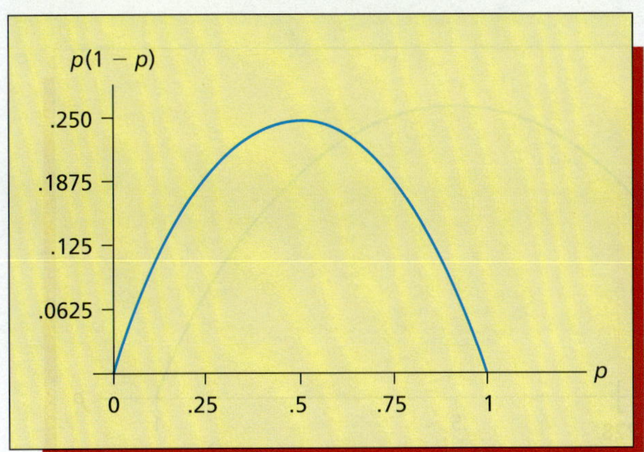

FIGURE 7.17 MegaStat Output of a Sample Size Calculation

Sample size - proportion	
0.02	E, error tolerance
0.5	estimated population proportion
95%	confidence level
1.960	z
2400.905	sample size
2401	rounded up

p equal to .02. If the sample to be taken is random, it should consist of

$$n = p(1-p)\left(\frac{z_{\alpha/2}}{E}\right)^2 = .25\left(\frac{1.96}{.02}\right)^2 = 2{,}401$$

registered voters. The MegaStat output of the results of this calculation is shown in Figure 7.17. In reality, a list of all registered voters in the United States is not available to polling organizations. Therefore, it is not feasible to take a (technically correct) random sample of registered voters. For this reason, polling organizations actually employ other (more complicated) kinds of samples. We have explained some of the basic ideas behind these more complex samples in optional Section 1.5. For now, we consider the samples taken by polling organizations to be approximately random. Suppose, then, that when the sample of voters is actually taken, the proportion $\hat{p}$ of sampled voters who favor the candidate turns out to be greater than .52. It follows, because the sample is large enough to make the margin of error in a 95 percent confidence interval for p equal to .02, that the lower limit of such an interval is greater than .50. This says we have strong evidence that a majority of all registered voters favor the candidate. For instance, if the sample proportion $\hat{p}$ equals .53, we are 95 percent confident that the proportion of all registered voters who favor the candidate is between .51 and .55.

Major polling organizations conduct public opinion polls concerning many kinds of issues. Whereas making the margin of error in a 95 percent confidence interval for p equal to .02 requires a sample size of 2,401, making the margin of error in such an interval equal to .03 requires a sample size of only

$$n = p(1-p)\left(\frac{z_{\alpha/2}}{E}\right)^2 = .25\left(\frac{1.96}{.03}\right)^2 = 1{,}067.1$$

or 1,068 (rounding up). Of course, these calculations assume that the proportion p being estimated could be near .5. However, for any value of p, increasing the margin of error from .02 to .03 substantially decreases the needed sample size and thus saves considerable time and money. For this reason, although the most accurate public opinion polls use a margin of error of .02, the vast majority of public opinion polls use a margin of error of .03 or larger.

When the news media report the results of a public opinion poll, they express the margin of error in a 95 percent confidence interval for p **in percentage points.** For instance, if the margin of error is .03, the media would say the poll's margin of error is 3 percentage points. The media seldom report the level of confidence, but almost all polling results are based on 95 percent confidence. Sometimes the media make a vague reference to the level of confidence. For instance, if the margin of error is 3 percentage points, the media might say that "the sample result will be within 3 percentage points of the population value in 19 out of 20 samples." Here the "19 out of 20 samples" is a reference to the level of confidence, which is $100(19/20) = 100(.95) = 95$ percent.

As an example, suppose a news report says a recent poll finds that 34 percent of the public favors military intervention in an international crisis, and suppose the poll's margin of error is reported to be 3 percentage points. This means the sample taken is large enough to make us

FIGURE 7.18 The Largest Reasonable Value for $p(1 - p)$ in the Antibiotic Example Is $(.228)(1 - .228) = .1760$

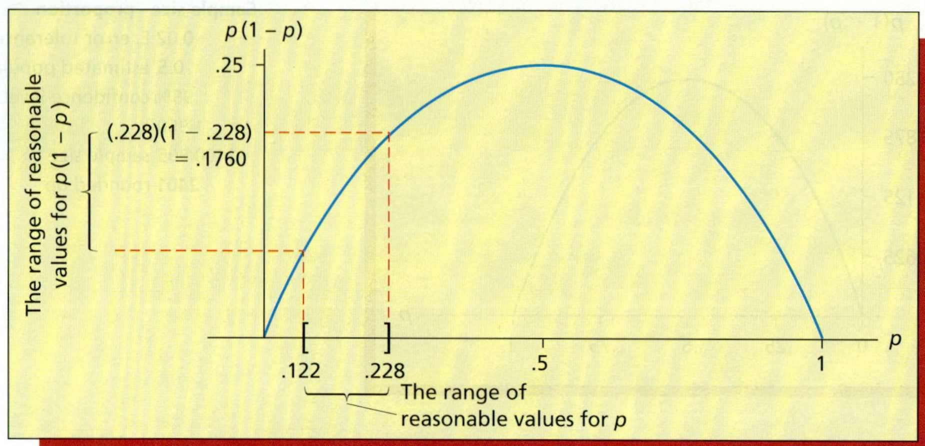

95 percent confident that the sample proportion $\hat{p} = .34$ is within .03 (that is, 3 percentage points) of the true proportion p of the entire public that favors military intervention. That is, we are 95 percent confident that p is between .31 and .37.

If the population proportion we are estimating is substantially different from .5, setting p equal to .5 will give a sample size that is much larger than is needed. In this case, we should use our intuition or previous sample information—along with Figure 7.16—to determine the largest reasonable value for $p(1 - p)$. Figure 7.16 implies that for any range of reasonable values of p that does not contain .5, the quantity $p(1 - p)$ is maximized by the reasonable value of p that is closest to .5. Therefore, **when we are estimating a proportion that is substantially different from .5, we use the reasonable value of p that is closest to .5 to calculate the sample size needed to obtain a specified margin of error.**

Example 7.10

Again consider estimating the proportion of all patients who would experience nausea as a side effect of taking the new antibiotic Phe-Mycin. Suppose the drug company wishes to find the size of the random sample that is needed in order to obtain a 2 percent margin of error with 95 percent confidence. In Example 7.8 we employed a sample of 200 patients to compute a 95 percent confidence interval for p. This interval, which is [.122, .228], makes us very confident that p is between .122 and .228. As shown in Figure 7.18, because .228 is the reasonable value of p that is closest to .5, the largest reasonable value of $p(1 - p)$ is $.228(1 - .228) = .1760$, and thus the drug company should take a sample of

$$n = p(1 - p)\left(\frac{z_{\alpha/2}}{B}\right)^2 = .1760\left(\frac{1.96}{.02}\right)^2 = 1{,}691 \text{ (rounded up)}$$

patients.

Finally, as a last example of choosing p for sample size calculations, suppose that experience indicates that a population proportion p is at least .75. Then, .75 is the reasonable value of p that is closest to .5, and we would use the largest reasonable value of $p(1 - p)$, which is $.75(1 - .75) = .1875$.

Exercises for Section 7.4

CONCEPTS

7.34 **a** What does a population proportion tell us about the population?

b Explain the difference between p and $\hat{p}$.

c What is meant when a public opinion poll's *margin of error* is 3 percent?

7.35 Suppose we are using the sample size formula in the box on page 284 to find the sample size needed to make the margin of error in a confidence interval for p equal to E. In each of the following situations, explain what value of p would be used in the formula for finding n:

a We have no idea what value p is—it could be any value between 0 and 1.

b Past experience tells us that p is no more than .3.

c Past experience tells us that p is at least .8.

METHODS AND APPLICATIONS

7.36 In each of the following cases, determine whether the sample size n is large enough to use the large sample formula presented in the box on page 282 to compute a confidence interval for p.

a $\hat{p} = .1, \quad n = 30$ **d** $\hat{p} = .8, \quad n = 400$

b $\hat{p} = .1, \quad n = 100$ **e** $\hat{p} = .9, \quad n = 30$

c $\hat{p} = .5, \quad n = 50$ **f** $\hat{p} = .99, \quad n = 200$

7.37 In each of the following cases, compute 95 percent, 98 percent, and 99 percent confidence intervals for the population proportion p.

a $\hat{p} = .4$ and $n = 100$ **c** $\hat{p} = .9$ and $n = 100$

b $\hat{p} = .1$ and $n = 300$ **d** $\hat{p} = .6$ and $n = 50$

7.38 *Quality Progress,* February 2005, reports on the results achieved by Bank of America in improving customer satisfaction and customer loyalty by listening to the 'voice of the customer.' A key measure of customer satisfaction is the response on a scale from 1 to 10 to the question: "Considering all the business you do with Bank of America, what is your overall satisfaction with Bank of America?"[2] Suppose that a random sample of 350 current customers results in 195 customers with a response of 9 or 10 representing 'customer delight.' Find a 95 percent confidence interval for the true proportion of all current Bank of America customers who would respond with a 9 or 10. Are we 95 percent confident that this proportion exceeds .48, the historical proportion of customer delight for Bank of America?

7.39 THE MARKETING ETHICS CASE: CONFLICT OF INTEREST

Recall that a conflict of interest scenario was presented to a sample of 205 marketing researchers and that 111 of these researchers disapproved of the actions taken in the scenario.

a Assuming that the sample of 205 marketing researchers was randomly selected, use this sample information to show that the 95 percent confidence interval for the proportion of all marketing researchers who disapprove of the actions taken in the conflict of interest scenario is as given in the MINITAB output below. Interpret this interval.

CI for One Proportion

```
  X    N    Sample p         95% CI
111  205    0.541463    (0.473254, 0.609673)
```

b On the basis of this interval, is there convincing evidence that a majority of all marketing researchers disapprove of the actions taken in the conflict of interest scenario? Explain.

7.40 In a news story distributed by the *Washington Post,* Lew Sichelman reports that a substantial fraction of mortgage loans that go into default within the first year of the mortgage were approved on the basis of falsified applications. For instance, loan applicants often exaggerate their income or fail to declare debts. Suppose that a random sample of 1,000 mortgage loans that were defaulted within the first year reveals that 410 of these loans were approved on the basis of falsified applications.

a Find a point estimate of and a 95 percent confidence interval for p, the proportion of all first-year defaults that are approved on the basis of falsified applications.

b Based on your interval, what is a reasonable estimate of the minimum percentage of first-year defaults that are approved on the basis of falsified applications?

7.41 On January 7, 2000, the Gallup Organization released the results of a poll comparing the lifestyles of today with yesteryear. The survey results were based on telephone interviews with a randomly selected national sample of 1,031 adults,18 years and older, conducted December 20–21, 1999.[3]

a The Gallup poll found that 42 percent of the respondents said that they spend less than three hours watching TV on an average weekday. Based on this finding, calculate a 99 percent confidence interval for the proportion of U.S. adults who say that they spend less than three hours watching TV on an average weekday. Based on this interval, is it reasonable to conclude that more than 40 percent of U.S. adults say they spend less than three hours watching TV on an average weekday?

[2]Source: "Driving Organic Growth at Bank of America" *Quality Progress* (February 2005), pp. 23–27.

[3]Source: World Wide Web, http://www.gallup.com/poll/releases/, The Gallup Organization, January 7, 2000.

b The Gallup poll found that 60 percent of the respondents said they took part in some form of daily activity (outside of work, including housework) to keep physically fit. Based on this finding, find a 95 percent confidence interval for the proportion of U.S. adults who say they take part in some form of daily activity to keep physically fit. Based on this interval, is it reasonable to conclude that more than 50 percent of U.S. adults say they take part in some form of daily activity to keep physically fit?

c In explaining its survey methods, Gallup states the following: "For results based on this sample, one can say with 95 percent confidence that the maximum error attributable to sampling and other random effects is plus or minus 3 percentage points." Explain how your calculations for part *b* verify that this statement is true.

7.42 In an article in the *Journal of Advertising,* Weinberger and Spotts compare the use of humor in television ads in the United States and the United Kingdom. They found that a substantially greater percentage of U.K. ads use humor.

a Suppose that a random sample of 400 television ads in the United Kingdom reveals that 142 of these ads use humor. Show that the point estimate and 95 percent confidence interval for the proportion of all U.K. television ads that use humor are as given in the MegaStat output below.

Confidence interval - proportion

400 n	95% confidence level	**0.402 upper confidence limit**
1.960 z	0.355 proportion	**0.308 lower confidence limit**

b Suppose a random sample of 500 television ads in the United States reveals that 122 of these ads use humor. Find a point estimate of and a 95 percent confidence interval for the proportion of all U.S. television ads that use humor.

c Do the confidence intervals you computed in parts *a* and *b* suggest that a greater percentage of U.K. ads use humor? Explain. How might an ad agency use this information?

7.43 In an article in *CA Magazine,* Neil Fitzgerald surveyed Scottish business customers concerning their satisfaction with aspects of their banking relationships. Fitzgerald reports that, in 418 telephone interviews conducted by George Street Research, 67 percent of the respondents gave their banks a high rating for overall satisfaction.

a Assuming that the sample is randomly selected, calculate a 99 percent confidence interval for the proportion of Scottish business customers who give their banks a high rating for overall satisfaction.

b Based on this interval, can we be 99 percent confident that more than 60 percent of Scottish business customers give their banks a high rating for overall satisfaction?

7.44 In the March 16, 1998, issue of *Fortune* magazine, the results of a survey of 2,221 MBA students from across the United States conducted by the Stockholm-based academic consulting firm Universum showed that only 20 percent of MBA students expect to stay at their first job five years or more.[4] Assuming that a random sample was employed, find a 95 percent confidence interval for the proportion of all U.S. MBA students who expect to stay at their first job five years or more. Based on this interval, is there strong evidence that fewer than one-fourth of all U.S. MBA students expect to stay?

7.45 *Consumer Reports* (January 2005) indicates that profit margins on extended warranties are much greater than on the purchase of most products.[5] In this exercise we consider a major electronics retailer that wishes to increase the proportion of customers who buy extended warranties on digital cameras. Historically, 20 percent of digital camera customers have purchased the retailer's extended warranty. To increase this percentage, the retailer has decided to offer a new warranty that is less expensive and more comprehensive. Suppose that three months after starting to offer the new warranty, a random sample of 500 customer sales invoices shows that 152 out of 500 digital camera customers purchased the new warranty. Find a 95 percent confidence interval for the proportion of all digital camera customers who have purchased the new warranty. Are we 95 percent confident that this proportion exceeds .20?

7.46 The manufacturer of the ColorSmart-5000 television set claims 95 percent of its sets last at least five years without needing a single repair. In order to test this claim, a consumer group randomly selects 400 consumers who have owned a ColorSmart-5000 television set for five years. Of these 400 consumers, 316 say their ColorSmart-5000 television sets did not need a repair, whereas 84 say their ColorSmart-5000 television sets did need at least one repair.

a Find a 99 percent confidence interval for the proportion of all ColorSmart-5000 television sets that have lasted at least five years without needing a single repair.

[4] **Source:** Shelly Branch, "MBAs: What Do They Really Want," *Fortune* (March 16, 1998), p. 167.

[5] *Consumer Reports,* January 2005, page 51.

b Does this confidence interval provide strong evidence that the percentage of ColorSmart-5000 television sets that last at least five years without a single repair is less than the 95 percent claimed by the manufacturer? Explain.

7.47 In the book *Cases in Finance,* Nunnally and Plath present a case in which the estimated percentage of uncollectible accounts varies with the age of the account. Here the age of an unpaid account is the number of days elapsed since the invoice date.

Suppose an accountant believes the percentage of accounts that will be uncollectible increases as the ages of the accounts increase. To test this theory, the accountant randomly selects 500 accounts with ages between 31 and 60 days from the accounts receivable ledger dated one year ago. The accountant also randomly selects 500 accounts with ages between 61 and 90 days from the accounts receivable ledger dated one year ago.

a If 10 of the 500 accounts with ages between 31 and 60 days were eventually classified as uncollectible, find a point estimate of and a 95 percent confidence interval for the proportion of all accounts with ages between 31 and 60 days that will be uncollectible.

b If 27 of the 500 accounts with ages between 61 and 90 days were eventually classified as uncollectible, find a point estimate of and a 95 percent confidence interval for the proportion of all accounts with ages between 61 and 90 days that will be uncollectible.

c Based on these intervals, is there strong evidence that the percentage of accounts aged between 61 and 90 days that will be uncollectible is higher than the percentage of accounts aged between 31 and 60 days that will be uncollectible? Explain.

7.48 Consider Exercise 7.41*b* and suppose we wish to find the sample size n needed in order to be 95 percent confident that $\hat{p}$, the sample proportion of respondents who said they took part in some sort of daily activity to keep physically fit, is within a margin of error of .02 of p, the true proportion of all U.S. adults who say that they take part in such activity. In order to find an appropriate value for $p(1 - p)$, note that the 95 percent confidence interval for p that you calculated in Exercise 7.41*b* was [.57, .63]. This indicates that the reasonable value for p that is closest to .5 is .57, and thus the largest reasonable value for $p(1 - p)$ is $.57(1 - .57) = .2451$. Calculate the required sample size n.

7.49 Referring to Exercise 7.46, determine the sample size needed in order to be 99 percent confident that $\hat{p}$, the sample proportion of ColorSmart-5000 television sets that last at least five years without a single repair, is within a margin of error of .03 of p, the true proportion of sets that last at least five years without a single repair.

7.50 Suppose we conduct a poll to estimate the proportion of voters who favor a major presidential candidate. Assuming that 50 percent of the electorate could be in favor of the candidate, determine the sample size needed so that we are 95 percent confident that $\hat{p}$, the sample proportion of voters who favor the candidate, is within a margin of error of .01 of p, the true proportion of all voters who are in favor of the candidate.

7.5 Confidence Intervals for Parameters of Finite Populations (Optional)

It is best to use the confidence intervals presented in Sections 7.1 through 7.4 when the sampled population is either infinite or finite and *much larger than* (say, at least 20 times as large as) the sample. Although these previously discussed intervals are sometimes used when a finite population is not much larger than the sample, better methods exist for handling such situations. We present these methods in this section.

As we have explained, we often wish to estimate a population mean. Sometimes we also wish to estimate a *population total.*

A **population total** is the sum of the values of all the population measurements.

For example, companies in financial trouble have sometimes falsified their accounts receivable invoices in order to mislead stockholders. For this reason, independent auditors are often asked to estimate a company's true total sales for a given period. The auditor randomly selects a sample of invoices from the population of all invoices, and then independently determines the actual amount of each sale by contacting the purchasers. The sample results are used to estimate the company's total sales, and this estimate can then be compared with the total sales reported by the company.

In order to estimate **a population total, which we denote as τ (pronounced "tau"),** we note that the population mean μ is the population total divided by the number, N, of population measurements. That is, we have $\mu = \tau/N$, which implies that $\tau = N\mu$. It follows, because a point estimate of the population mean μ is the sample mean $\bar{x}$, that

A point estimate of a population total τ is $N\bar{x}$, where N is the size of the population.

Example 7.11

A company sells and installs satellite dishes and receivers for both private individuals and commercial establishments (bars, restaurants, and so forth). The company accumulated 2,418 sales invoices during last year. The total of the sales amounts listed on these invoices (that is, the total sales claimed by the company) is \$5,127,492.17. In order to estimate the true total sales, τ, for last year, an independent auditor randomly selects 242 of the invoices and determines the actual sales amounts by contacting the purchasers. When the sales amounts are averaged, the mean of the actual sales amounts for the 242 sampled invoices is $\bar{x}$ = \$1,843.93. This says that a point estimate of the true total sales τ is

$$N\bar{x} = 2{,}418(\$1{,}843.93) = \$4{,}458{,}622.70$$

This point estimate is considerably lower than the claimed total sales of \$5,127,492.17. However, we cannot expect the point estimate of τ to exactly equal the true total sales, so we need to calculate a confidence interval for τ before drawing any unwarranted conclusions.

In order to find a confidence interval for the mean and total of a finite population, we consider the sampling distribution of the sample mean $\bar{x}$. It can be shown that, if we randomly select a large sample of n measurements without replacement from a finite population of N measurements, then the sampling distribution of $\bar{x}$ is approximately normal with mean $\mu_{\bar{x}} = \mu$ and standard deviation

$$\sigma_{\bar{x}} = \frac{\sigma}{\sqrt{n}}\sqrt{\frac{N-n}{N-1}}$$

It can also be shown that the appropriate point estimate of $\sigma_{\bar{x}}$ is $(s/\sqrt{n})(\sqrt{(N-n)/N})$, where s is the sample standard deviation. This point estimate of $\sigma_{\bar{x}}$ is used in the confidence intervals for μ and τ, which we summarize as follows:

Confidence Intervals for the Population Mean and Population Total for a Finite Population

Suppose we randomly select a sample of n measurements **without replacement from a finite population of N measurements.** Then, if n is large (say, at least 30)

1 **A 100(1 − α) percent confidence interval for the population mean μ is**

$$\left[\bar{x} \pm z_{\alpha/2}\frac{s}{\sqrt{n}}\sqrt{\frac{N-n}{N}}\right]$$

2 **A 100(1 − α) percent confidence interval for the population total τ** is found by multiplying the lower and upper limits of the 100(1 − α) percent confidence interval for μ by N.

The quantity $\sqrt{(N-n)/N}$ in the confidence intervals for μ and τ is called the **finite population correction.** If the population size N is much larger than (say, at least 20 times as large as) the sample size n, then the finite population correction is approximately equal to 1. For example, if we randomly select (without replacement) a sample of 1,000 from a population of 1 million, then the finite population correction is $\sqrt{(1{,}000{,}000 - 1{,}000)/1{,}000{,}000} = .9995$. In such a case, many people believe it is not necessary to include the finite population correction in the confidence interval calculations. This is because the correction is not far enough below 1 to meaningfully shorten the confidence intervals for μ and τ. However, **if the population size N**

is not much larger than the sample size n (say, if n is more than 5 percent of N), then the finite population correction is substantially less than 1 and should be included in the confidence interval calculations.

Example 7.12

Recall that the satellite dish dealer claims that its total sales τ for last year were \$5,127,492.17. Since the company accumulated 2,418 invoices during last year, the company is claiming that μ, the mean sales amount per invoice, is \$5,127,492.17/2,418 = \$2,120.55. Suppose when the independent auditor randomly selects a sample of n = 242 invoices, the mean and standard deviation of the actual sales amounts for these invoices are $\bar{x}$ = 1,843.93 and s = 516.42. Here the sample size n = 242 is (242/2,418)100 = 10.008 percent of the population size N = 2,418. Because n is more than 5 percent of N, we should include the finite population correction in our confidence interval calculations. It follows that a 95 percent confidence interval for the mean sales amount μ per invoice is

$$\left[\bar{x} \pm z_{.025}\frac{s}{\sqrt{n}}\sqrt{\frac{N-n}{N}}\right] = \left[1{,}843.93 \pm 1.96\frac{516.42}{\sqrt{242}}\sqrt{\frac{2{,}418-242}{2{,}418}}\right]$$

$$= [1{,}843.93 \pm 61.723812]$$

$$= [1{,}782.21, 1{,}905.65]$$

The upper limit of this interval is less than the mean amount of \$2,120.55 claimed by the company, so we have strong evidence that the company is overstating its mean sales per invoice for last year. A 95 percent confidence interval for the total sales τ last year is found by multiplying the lower and upper limits of the 95 percent confidence interval for μ by N = 2,418. Therefore, this interval is [1,782.21(2,418), 1,905.65(2,418)], or [4,309,383.8, 4,607,861.7]. Because the upper limit of this interval is more than \$500,000 below the total sales amount of \$5,127,492.17 claimed by the company, we have strong evidence that the satellite dealer is substantially overstating its total sales for last year.

We sometimes estimate the total number, τ, of population units that fall into a particular category. For instance, the auditor of Examples 7.11 and 7.12 might wish to estimate the total number of the 2,418 invoices having incorrect sales amounts. Here the proportion, p, of the population units that fall into a particular category is the total number, τ, of population units that fall into the category divided by the number, N, of population units. That is, $p = \tau/N$, which implies that $\tau = Np$. Therefore, since a point estimate of the population proportion p is the sample proportion $\hat{p}$, a point estimate of the population total τ is $N\hat{p}$. For example, suppose that 34 of the 242 sampled invoices have incorrect sales amounts. Because the sample proportion is $\hat{p} = 34/242 = .1405$, a point estimate of the total number of the 2,418 invoices that have incorrect sales amounts is

$$N\hat{p} = 2{,}418(.1405) = 339.729$$

We now summarize how to find confidence intervals for p and τ.

Confidence Intervals for the Proportion of and Total Number of Units in a Category When Sampling a Finite Population

Suppose that we randomly select a sample of n units **without replacement from a finite population of N units.** Then, if n is large

1 **A 100(1 − α) percent confidence interval for the population proportion p is**

$$\left[\hat{p} \pm z_{\alpha/2}\sqrt{\frac{\hat{p}(1-\hat{p})}{n-1}\left(\frac{N-n}{N}\right)}\right]$$

2 **A 100(1 − α) percent confidence interval for the population total τ** is found by multiplying the lower and upper limits of the 100(1 − α) percent confidence interval for p by N.

Example 7.13

Recall that in Examples 7.11 and 7.12 we found that 34 of the 242 sampled invoices have incorrect sales amounts. Since $\hat{p} = 34/242 = .1405$, a 95 percent confidence interval for the proportion of the 2,418 invoices that have incorrect sales amounts is

$$\left[\hat{p} \pm z_{.025}\sqrt{\frac{\hat{p}(1-\hat{p})}{n-1}\left(\frac{N-n}{N}\right)}\right] = \left[.1405 \pm 1.96\sqrt{\frac{(.1405)(.8595)}{241}\left(\frac{2{,}418-242}{2{,}418}\right)}\right]$$
$$= [.1405 \pm .0416208]$$
$$= [.0989, \ .1821]$$

This interval says we are 95 percent confident that between 9.89 percent and 18.21 percent of the invoices have incorrect sales amounts. A 95 percent confidence interval for the total number of the 2,418 invoices that have incorrect sales amounts is found by multiplying the lower and upper limits of the 95 percent confidence interval for p by $N = 2{,}418$. Therefore, this interval is [.0989(2,418), .1821(2,418)], or [239.14, 440.32], and we are 95 percent confident that between (roughly) 239 and 440 of the 2,418 invoices have incorrect sales amounts.

Finally, we can determine the sample size that is needed to make the margin of error in a confidence interval for μ, p, or τ equal to a desired size E by setting the appropriate margin of error formula equal to E and by solving the resulting equation for the sample size n. We will not carry out the details in this book, but the procedure is the same as illustrated in Sections 7.3 and 7.4. Exercise 7.57 gives the reader an opportunity to use the sample size formulas that are obtained.

Exercises for Section 7.5

CONCEPTS

7.51 Define a population total. Give an example of a population total that will interest you in your career when you graduate from college.

7.52 Explain why the finite population correction $\sqrt{(N-n)/N}$ is unnecessary when the population is at least 20 times as large as the sample. Give an example using numbers.

METHODS AND APPLICATIONS

7.53 A retailer that sells home entertainment systems accumulated 10,451 sales invoices during the previous year. The total of the sales amounts listed on these invoices (that is, the total sales claimed by the company) is $6,384,675. In order to estimate the true total sales for last year, an independent auditor randomly selects 350 of the invoices and determines the actual sales amounts by contacting the purchasers. The mean and the standard deviation of the 350 sampled sales amounts are $\bar{x} = \$532$ and $s = \$168$.

a Find a 95 percent confidence interval for μ, the true mean sales amount per invoice on the 10,451 invoices.

b Find a point estimate of and a 95 percent confidence interval for τ, the true total sales for the previous year.

c What does this interval say about the company's claim that the true total sales were $6,384,675? Explain.

7.54 A company's manager is considering simplification of a travel voucher form. In order to assess the costs associated with erroneous travel vouchers, the manager must estimate the total number of such vouchers that were filled out incorrectly in the last month. In a random sample of 100 vouchers drawn without replacement from the 1,323 travel vouchers submitted in the last month, 31 vouchers were filled out incorrectly.

a Find a point estimate of and a 95 percent confidence interval for the true proportion of travel vouchers that were filled out incorrectly in the last month.

b Find a point estimate of and a 95 percent confidence interval for the total number of travel vouchers that were filled out incorrectly in the last month.

c If it costs the company $10 to correct an erroneous travel voucher, find a reasonable estimate of the minimum cost of correcting all of last month's erroneous travel vouchers. Would it be worthwhile to spend $5,000 to design a simplified travel voucher that could be used for at least a year?

7.55 A personnel manager is estimating the total number of person-days lost to unexcused absences by hourly workers in the last year. In a random sample of 50 employees drawn without replacement from the 687 hourly workers at the company, records show that the 50 sampled workers had an average of $\bar{x} = 4.3$ days of unexcused absences over the past year with a standard deviation of $s = 1.26$.

a Find a point estimate of and a 95 percent confidence interval for the total number of unexcused absences by hourly workers in the last year.

b Can the personnel manager be 95 percent confident that more than 2,500 person-days were lost to unexcused absences last year? Can the manager be 95 percent confident that more than 3,000 person-days were lost to unexcused absences last year? Explain.

7.56 An auditor randomly samples 32 accounts receivable without replacement from a firm's 600 accounts and checks to verify that all documents for the accounts comply with company procedures. Ten of the 32 accounts are found to have documents not in compliance. Find a point estimate of and a 95 percent confidence interval for the total number of accounts having documents that do not comply with company procedures.

7.57 SAMPLE SIZES WHEN SAMPLING FINITE POPULATIONS

a *Estimating μ and τ*

Consider randomly selecting a sample of n measurements without replacement from a finite population consisting of N measurements and having variance σ^2. Also consider the sample size given by the formula

$$n = \frac{N\sigma^2}{(N-1)D + \sigma^2}$$

Then, it can be shown that this sample size makes the margin of error in a $100(1-\alpha)$ percent confidence interval for μ equal to E if we set D equal to $(E/z_{\alpha/2})^2$. It can also be shown that this sample size makes the margin of error in a $100(1-\alpha)$ percent confidence interval for τ equal to E if we set D equal to $[E/(z_{\alpha/2}N)]^2$. Now consider Exercise 7.55. Using $s^2 = (1.26)^2$, or 1.5876, as an estimate of σ^2, determine the sample size that makes the margin of error in a 95 percent confidence interval for the *total number* of person-days lost to unexcused absences last year equal to 100 days.

b *Estimating p and τ*

Consider randomly selecting a sample of n units without replacement from a finite population consisting of N units and having a proportion p of these units fall into a particular category. Also, consider the sample size given by the formula

$$n = \frac{Np(1-p)}{(N-1)D + p(1-p)}$$

It can be shown that this sample size makes the margin of error in a $100(1-\alpha)$ percent confidence interval for p equal to E if we set D equal to $(E/z_{\alpha/2})^2$. It can also be shown that this sample size makes the margin of error in a $100(1-\alpha)$ percent confidence interval for τ equal to E if we set D equal to $[E/(z_{\alpha/2}N)]^2$. Now consider Exercise 7.54. Using $\hat{p} = .31$ as an estimate of p, determine the sample size that makes the margin of error in a 95 percent confidence interval for the *proportion* of the 1,323 vouchers that were filled out incorrectly equal to .04.

7.6 A Comparison of Confidence Intervals and Tolerance Intervals (Optional)

In this section we compare confidence intervals with tolerance intervals. We saw in Chapter 2 (page 72) that a tolerance interval is an interval that is meant to contain a specified percentage (often 68.26 percent, 95.44 percent, or 99.73 percent) of the **individual** population measurements. By contrast, a confidence interval for the population mean μ is an interval that is meant to contain one thing—the population mean μ—and the confidence level associated with the confidence interval expresses how sure we are that this interval contains μ. Often we choose the confidence level to be 95 percent or 99 percent because such a confidence level is usually considered high enough to provide convincing evidence about the true value of μ.

Example 7.14 The Car Mileage Case

C

Recall in the car mileage case that the mean and the standard deviation of the sample of 49 mileages are $\bar{x} = 31.5531$ and $s = .7992$. Also, recall that we have concluded in Example 2.14 (page 72) that the estimated tolerance intervals $[\bar{x} \pm s] = [30.8, 32.4]$, $[\bar{x} \pm 2s] = [30.0, 33.2]$,

FIGURE 7.19 A Comparison of Confidence Intervals and Tolerance Intervals

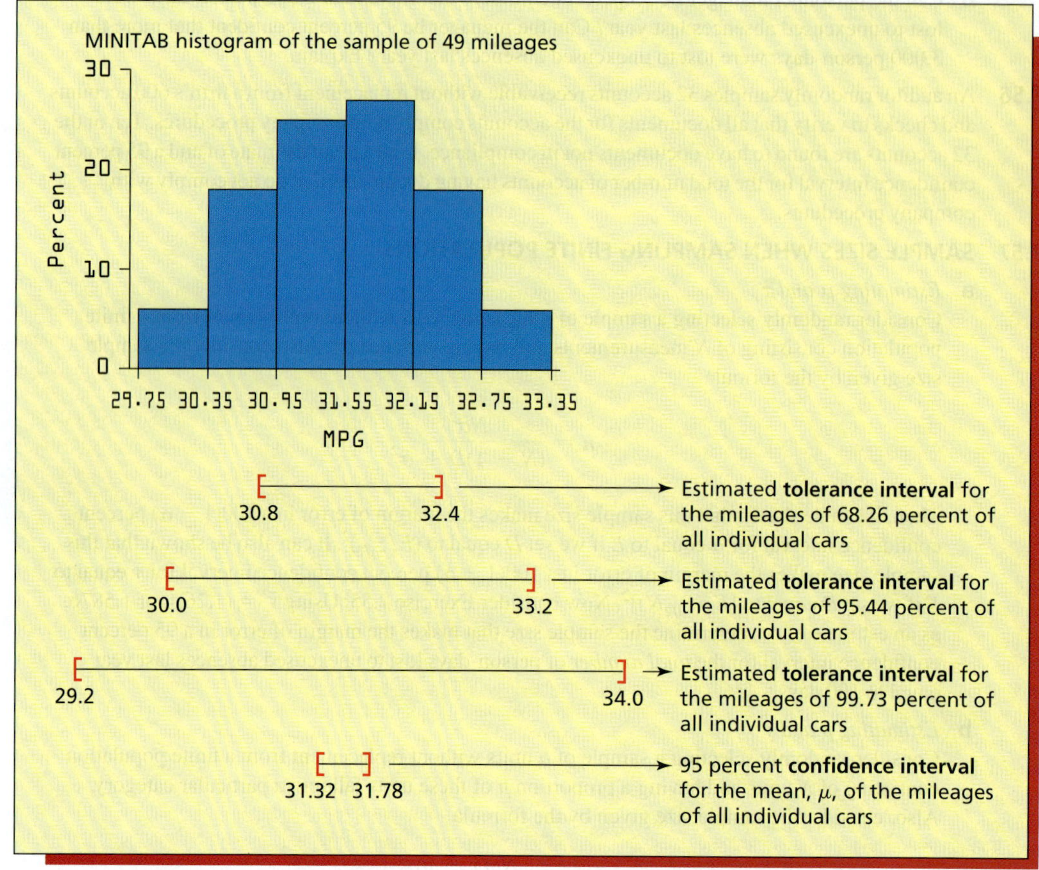

and $[\bar{x} \pm 3s] = [29.2, 34.0]$ imply that approximately (1) 68.26 percent of all individual cars will obtain mileages between 30.8 mpg and 32.4 mpg; (2) 95.44 percent of all individual cars will obtain mileages between 30.0 mpg and 33.2 mpg; and (3) 99.73 percent of all individual cars will obtain mileages between 29.2 mpg and 34.0 mpg. By contrast, we have seen in Section 7.2 (page 274) that a 95 percent *t*-based confidence interval for the mean, μ, of the mileages of all individual cars is $[\bar{x} \pm 2.011\ (s/\sqrt{49})] = [31.32, 31.78]$. This interval says that we are 95 percent confident that μ is between 31.32 mpg and 31.78 mpg. Figure 7.19 graphically depicts the three estimated tolerance intervals and the 95 percent confidence interval, which are shown below a MINITAB histogram of the 49 mileages. Note that the estimated tolerance intervals, which are meant to contain the *many* mileages that comprise specified percentages of all individual cars, are longer than the 95 percent confidence interval, which is meant to contain the *single* population mean μ.

Exercises for Section 7.6

CONCEPTS

7.58 What is a tolerance interval meant to contain?

7.59 What is a confidence interval for the population mean meant to contain?

7.60 Intuitively, why is a tolerance interval longer than a confidence interval?

METHODS AND APPLICATIONS

In Exercises 7.61 through 7.63 we give the mean and the standard deviation of a sample that has been randomly selected from a population. For each exercise, find estimated tolerance intervals that contain approximately 68.26 percent, 95.44 percent, and 99.73 percent of the individual population measurements.

FIGURE 7.20 Computing an Appropriate Confidence Interval for a Population Mean

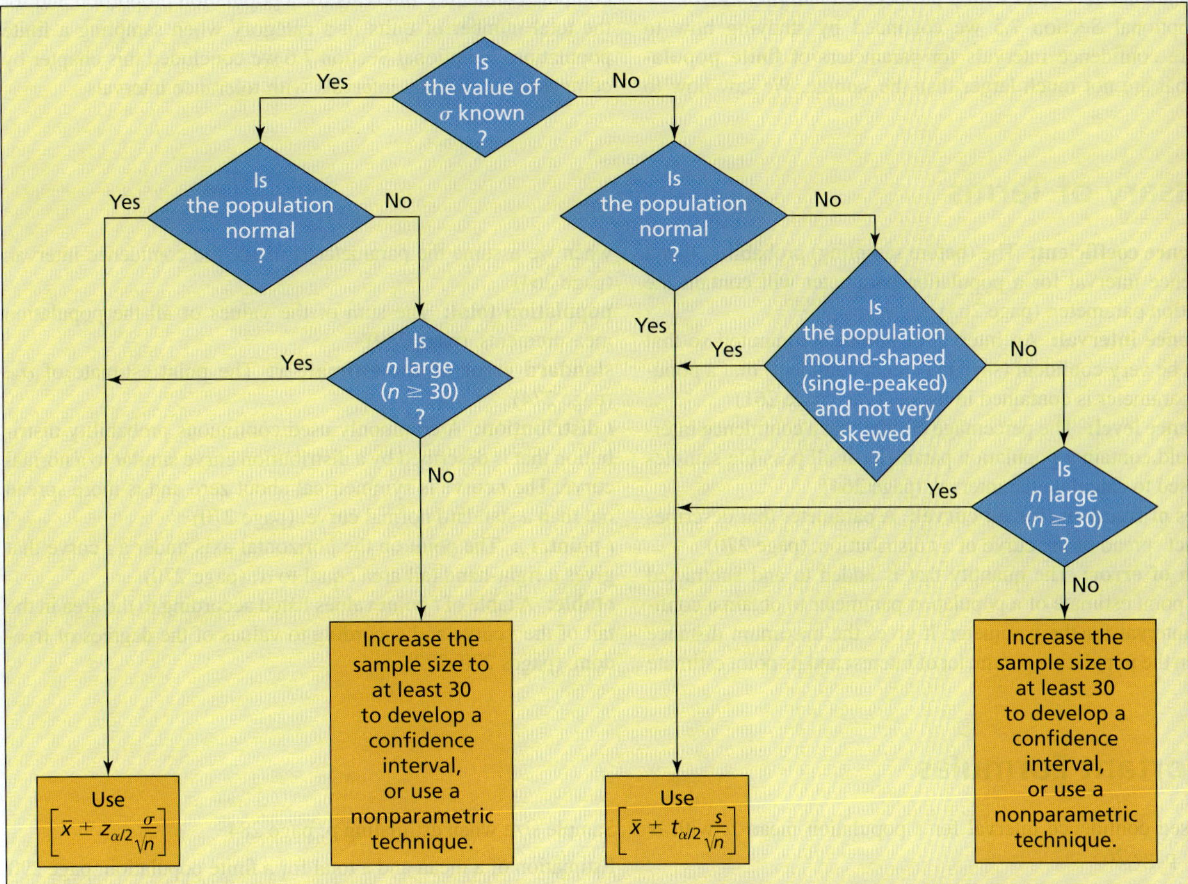

Also, find a 95 percent confidence interval for the population mean. Interpret the estimated tolerance intervals and the confidence interval in the context of the situation related to the exercise.

7.61 THE TRASH BAG CASE TrashBag

The mean and the standard deviation of the sample of 40 trash bag breaking strengths are $\bar{x} = 50.575$ and $s = 1.6438$.

7.62 THE BANK CUSTOMER WAITING TIME CASE WaitTime

The mean and the standard deviation of the sample of 100 bank customer waiting times are $\bar{x} = 5.46$ and $s = 2.475$.

7.63 THE VIDEO GAME SATISFACTION RATING CASE VideoGame

The mean and the standard deviation of the sample of 65 customer satisfaction ratings are $\bar{x} = 42.95$ and $s = 2.6424$.

Chapter Summary

In this chapter we discussed **confidence intervals** for population **means, proportions,** and **totals.** We began by assuming that the population is either infinite or much larger than (say, at least 20 times as large as) the sample. First, we studied how to compute a confidence interval for a **population mean.** We saw that when the population standard deviation σ is known, we can use the **normal distribution** to compute a confidence interval for a population mean. When σ is not known, if the population is normally distributed (or at least mound-shaped) or if the sample size n is large, we use the **t distribution** to compute this interval. We also studied how to find the size of the sample needed if we wish to compute a confidence interval for a mean with a prespecified *confidence level* and with a prespecified *margin of error.* Figure 7.20 is a flowchart summarizing our discussions concerning how to compute an appropriate confidence interval for a population mean.

Next we saw that we are often interested in estimating the proportion of population units falling into a category of interest. We showed how to compute a large sample confidence interval for a **population proportion,** and we saw how to find the sample size needed to estimate a population proportion with a prespecified *confidence level* and with a prespecified *margin of error.*

In optional Section 7.5 we continued by studying how to compute confidence intervals for parameters of **finite populations** that are not much larger than the sample. We saw how to compute confidence intervals for a population mean and total when we are sampling *without replacement.* We also saw how to compute confidence intervals for a population proportion and for the total number of units in a category when sampling a finite population. In optional Section 7.6 we concluded this chapter by comparing confidence intervals with tolerance intervals.

Glossary of Terms

confidence coefficient: The (before sampling) probability that a confidence interval for a population parameter will contain the population parameter. (page 263)

confidence interval: An interval of numbers computed so that we can be very confident (say, 95 percent confident) that a population parameter is contained in the interval. (page 261)

confidence level: The percentage of time that a confidence interval would contain a population parameter if all possible samples were used to calculate the interval. (page 264)

degrees of freedom (for a *t* curve): A parameter that describes the exact spread of the curve of a *t* distribution. (page 270)

margin of error: The quantity that is added to and subtracted from a point estimate of a population parameter to obtain a confidence interval for the parameter. It gives the maximum distance between the population parameter of interest and its point estimate when we assume the parameter is inside the confidence interval. (page 264)

population total: The sum of the values of all the population measurements. (page 289)

standard error of the estimate $\bar{x}$: The point estimate of $\sigma_{\bar{x}}$. (page 274)

***t* distribution:** A commonly used continuous probability distribution that is described by a distribution curve similar to a normal curve. The *t* curve is symmetrical about zero and is more spread out than a standard normal curve. (page 270)

***t* point, t_α:** The point on the horizontal axis under a *t* curve that gives a right-hand tail area equal to α. (page 270)

***t* table:** A table of *t* point values listed according to the area in the tail of the *t* curve and according to values of the degrees of freedom. (pages 270–272)

Important Formulas

A *z*-based confidence interval for a population mean μ with σ known: page 265

A *t*-based confidence interval for a population mean μ with σ unknown: page 272

Sample size when estimating μ: page 279

A large sample confidence interval for a population proportion *p*: page 282

Sample size when estimating *p*: page 284

Estimation of a mean and a total for a finite population: page 290

Estimation of a proportion and a total for a finite population: page 291

Supplementary Exercises

7.64 In an article in the *Journal of Accounting Research,* Ashton, Willingham, and Elliott studied audit delay (the length of time from a company's fiscal year-end to the date of the auditor's report) for industrial and financial companies. In the study, a random sample of 250 industrial companies yielded a mean audit delay of 68.04 days with a standard deviation of 35.72 days, while a random sample of 238 financial companies yielded a mean audit delay of 56.74 days with a standard deviation of 34.87 days. Use these sample results to do the following:

a Calculate a 95 percent confidence interval for the mean audit delay for all industrial companies. Note: $t_{.025} = 1.97$ when $df = 249$.

b Calculate a 95 percent confidence interval for the mean audit delay for all financial companies. Note: $t_{.025} = 1.97$ when $df = 237$.

c By comparing the 95 percent confidence intervals you calculated in parts *a* and *b*, is there strong evidence that the mean audit delay for financial companies is shorter than the mean audit delay for industrial companies? Explain.

7.65 In an article in *Accounting and Business Research,* Beattie and Jones investigate the use and abuse of graphic presentations in the annual reports of United Kingdom firms. The authors found that 65 percent of the sampled companies graph at least one key financial variable, but that 30 percent of the graphics are materially distorted (nonzero vertical axis, exaggerated trend, or the like). Results for U.S. firms have been found to be similar.

a Suppose that in a random sample of 465 graphics from the annual reports of United Kingdom firms, 142 of the graphics are found to be distorted. Find a point estimate of and a 95 percent confidence interval for the proportion of U.K. annual report graphics that are distorted.

b Based on this interval, can we be 95 percent confident that more than 25 percent of all graphics appearing in the annual reports of U.K. firms are distorted? Explain. Does this suggest that auditors should understand proper graphing methods?

c Determine the sample size needed in order to be 95 percent confident that $\hat{p}$, the sample proportion of U.K. annual report graphics that are distorted, is within a margin of error of .03 of p, the true proportion of U.K. annual report graphics that are distorted.

7.66 On January 4, 2000, the Gallup Organization released the results of a poll dealing with the likelihood of computer-related Y2K problems and the possibility of terrorist attacks during the New Year's holiday at the turn of the century.[6] The survey results were based on telephone interviews with a randomly selected national sample of 622 adults, 18 years and older, conducted December 28, 1999.

a The Gallup poll found that 61 percent of the respondents believed that one or more terrorist attacks were likely to happen on the New Year's holiday. Based on this finding, calculate a 95 percent confidence interval for the proportion of all U.S. adults who believed that one or more terrorist attacks were likely to happen on the 2000 New Year's holiday. Based on this interval, is it reasonable to conclude that fewer than two-thirds of all U.S. adults believed that one or more terrorist attacks were likely?

b In explaining its survey methods, Gallup states the following: "For results based on this sample, one can say with 95 percent confidence that the maximum error attributable to sampling and other random effects is plus or minus 4 percentage points." Explain how your calculations for part *a* verify that this statement is true.

7.67 The manager of a chain of discount department stores wishes to estimate the total number of erroneous discounts allowed by sales clerks during the last month. A random sample of 200 of the chain's 57,532 transactions for the last month reveals that erroneous discounts were allowed on eight of the transactions. Use this sample information to find a point estimate of and a 95 percent confidence interval for the total number of erroneous discounts allowed during the last month.

7.68 National Motors has equipped the ZX-900 with a new disk brake system. We define the stopping distance for a ZX-900 to be the distance (in feet) required to bring the automobile to a complete stop from a speed of 35 mph under normal driving conditions using this new brake system. In addition, we define μ to be the mean stopping distance of all ZX-900s. One of the ZX-900's major competitors is advertised to achieve a mean stopping distance of 60 feet. National Motors would like to claim in a new advertising campaign that the ZX-900 achieves a shorter mean stopping distance.

Suppose that National Motors randomly selects a sample of $n = 81$ ZX-900s. The company records the stopping distance of each automobile and calculates the mean and standard deviation of the sample of $n = 81$ stopping distances to be $\bar{x} = 57.8$ ft and $s = 6.02$ ft.

a Calculate a 95 percent confidence interval for μ. Can National Motors be 95 percent confident that μ is less than 60 ft? Explain.

b Using the sample of $n = 81$ stopping distances as a preliminary sample, find the sample size necessary to make National Motors 95 percent confident that $\bar{x}$ is within a margin of error of one foot of μ.

7.69 A large construction contractor is building 257 homes, which are in various stages of completion. For tax purposes, the contractor needs to estimate the total dollar value of its inventory due to construction in progress. The contractor randomly selects (without replacement) a sample of 40 of the 257 houses and determines the accumulated costs (the amount of money tied up in inventory) for each sampled house. The contractor finds that the sample mean accumulated cost is $\bar{x} = \$75{,}162.70$ and that the sample standard deviation is $s = \$28{,}865.04$.

a Find a point estimate of and a 99 percent confidence interval for the total accumulated costs (total amount of money tied up in inventory) for all 257 homes that are under construction.

b Using the confidence interval as the basis for your answer, find a reasonable estimate of the largest possible total dollar value of the contractor's inventory due to construction in progress.

[6] Source: World Wide Web, http://www.gallup.com/poll/releases/, The Gallup Organization, January 4, 2000.

7.70 In an article in the *Journal of Retailing,* J. G. Blodgett, D. H. Granbois, and R. G. Walters investigated negative word-of-mouth consumer behavior. In a random sample of 201 consumers, 150 reported that they engaged in negative word-of-mouth behavior (for instance, they vowed never to patronize a retailer again). In addition, the 150 respondents who engaged in such behavior, on average, told 4.88 people about their dissatisfying experience (with a standard deviation equal to 6.11).

a Use these sample results to compute a 95 percent confidence interval for the proportion of all consumers who engage in negative word-of-mouth behavior. On the basis of this interval, would it be reasonable to claim that more than 70 percent of all consumers engage in such behavior? Explain.

b Use the sample results to compute a 95 percent confidence interval for the mean number of people who are told about a dissatisfying experience by consumers who engage in negative word-of-mouth behavior. On the basis of this interval, would it be reasonable to claim that these dissatisfied consumers tell, on average, at least three people about their bad experience? Explain. Note: $t_{.025} = 1.98$ when $df = 149$.

7.71 A random sample of 50 perceived age estimates for a model in a cigarette advertisement showed that $\bar{x} = 26.22$ years and that $s = 3.7432$ years. ModelAge

a Use this sample to calculate a 95 percent confidence interval for the population mean age estimate for all viewers of the ad.

b Remembering that the cigarette industry requires that models must appear at least 25 years old, does the confidence interval make us 95 percent confident that the mean perceived age estimate is at least 25? Is the mean perceived age estimate much more than 25? Explain.

7.72 In an article in the *Journal of Management Information Systems,* Mahmood and Mann investigate how information technology (IT) investment relates to company performance. In particular, Mahmood and Mann obtain sample data concerning IT investment for companies that effectively use information systems. Among the variables studied are the company's IT budget as a percentage of company revenue, percentages of the IT budget spent on staff and training, and number of PCs and terminals as a percentage of total employees.

a Suppose a random sample of 15 companies considered to effectively use information systems yields a sample mean IT budget as a percentage of company revenue of $\bar{x} = 2.73$ with a standard deviation of $s = 1.64$. Assuming that IT budget percentages are approximately normally distributed, calculate a 99 percent confidence interval for the mean IT budget as a percentage of company revenue for all firms that effectively use information systems. Does this interval provide evidence that a firm can successfully use information systems with an IT budget that is less than 5 percent of company revenue? Explain.

b Suppose a random sample of 15 companies considered to effectively use information systems yields a sample mean number of PCs and terminals as a percentage of total employees of $\bar{x} = 34.76$ with a standard deviation of $s = 25.37$. Assuming approximate normality, calculate a 99 percent confidence interval for the mean number of PCs and terminals as a percentage of total employees for all firms that effectively use information systems. Why is this interval so wide? What can we do to obtain a narrower (more useful) confidence interval?

7.73 THE INVESTMENT CASE InvestRet

Suppose that random samples of 50 returns for each of the following investment classes give the indicated sample mean and sample standard deviation:

Fixed annuities: $\bar{x} = 7.83\%$, $s = .51\%$

Domestic large cap stocks: $\bar{x} = 13.42\%$, $s = 15.17\%$

Domestic midcap stocks: $\bar{x} = 15.03\%$, $s = 18.44\%$

Domestic small cap stocks: $\bar{x} = 22.51\%$, $s = 21.75\%$

a For each investment class, compute a 95 percent confidence interval for the population mean return.

b Do these intervals suggest that the current mean return for each investment class differs from the historical (1970 to 1994) mean return given in Table 2.15 (page 110)? Explain.

7.74 THE INTERNATIONAL BUSINESS TRAVEL EXPENSE CASE

Recall that the mean and the standard deviation of a random sample of 35 one-day travel expenses in Moscow are $\bar{x} = \$538$ and $s = \$41$. Find a 95 percent confidence interval for the mean, μ, of all one-day travel expenses in Moscow.

7.75 THE UNITED KINGDOM INSURANCE CASE

Assume that the U.K. insurance survey is based on 1,000 randomly selected U.K. households and that 640 of these households spent on life insurance in 1993. Find a 95 percent confidence interval for the proportion, p, of all U.K. households that spent on life insurance in 1993.

7.76 How safe are child car seats? *Consumer Reports* (May 2005) tested the safety of child car seats in 30 mph crashes. They found "slim safety margins" for some child car seats. Suppose that Consumer Reports simulates the safety of the market-leading child car seat. Their test consists of placing the maximum claimed weight in the car seat and simulating crashes at higher and higher miles per hour until a problem occurs. The following data identifies the speed at which a problem with the car seat first appeared; such as the strap breaking, seat shell cracked, strap adjuster broke, detached from the base, etc.: 31.0, 29.4, 30.4, 28.9, 29.7, 30.1, 32.3, 31.7, 35.4, 29.1, 31.2, 30.2. Using the fact that $\bar{x} = 30.7833$ and $s = 1.7862$, find a 95 percent confidence interval for the true mean speed at which a problem with the car seat first appears. Are we 95 percent confident that this mean is at least 30 mph? CarSeat

7.77 In Exercise 2.11 (page 57), we briefly described a series of international quality standards called ISO 9000. In the results of a Quality Systems Update/Deloitte & Touche survey of ISO 9000 registered companies published by CEEM Information Systems, 515 of 620 companies surveyed reported that they are encouraging their suppliers to pursue ISO 9000 registration.[7]

a Using these survey results, compute a 95.44 percent confidence interval for the proportion of all ISO 9000 registered companies that encourage their suppliers to pursue ISO 9000 registration. Assume here that the survey participants have been randomly selected.

b Based on this interval, is there conclusive evidence that more than 75 percent of all ISO 9000 registered companies encourage their suppliers to pursue ISO 9000 registration?

7.78 Internet Exercise

What is the average selling price of a home? The Data and Story Library (DASL) contains data, including the sale price, for a random sample of 117 homes sold in Albuquerque, New Mexico. Go to the DASL website (http://lib.stat.cmu.edu/DASL/) and retrieve the home price data set (http://lib.stat.cmu.edu/DASL/Datafiles/homedat.html.) Use MINITAB, Excel, or MegaStat to produce appropriate graphical (histogram, stem-and-leaf, box plot) and numerical summaries of the price data. Identify, from your numerical summaries, the sample mean and standard deviation. Use these summaries to construct a 99% confidence interval for μ, the mean sale price. Use statistical software (MINITAB, Excel, or MegaStat) to compute a 99% confidence interval for μ. Do the results of your hand calculations agree with those from your statistical software?

Technical note: There are many ways to capture the home price data from the DASL site. One simple way is to select just the rows containing the data values (and not the labels), copy, paste directly into an Excel or MINITAB worksheet, add your own variable labels, and save the resulting worksheet. It is possible to copy the variable labels from DASL as well, but the differences in alignment and the intervening blank line add to the difficulty. AlbHome

Appendix 7.1 ■ Confidence Intervals Using MINITAB

The instruction blocks in this section each begin by describing the entry of data into the MINITAB data window. Alternatively, the data may be loaded directly from the data disk included with the text. The appropriate data file name is given at the top of each instruction block. Please refer to Appendix 1.1 for further information about entering data, saving data, and printing results.

[7]Source: *Is ISO 9000 for You?* (Fairfax, VA: CEEM Information Services).

Confidence interval for a population mean in Figure 7.12(a) on page 275 (data file: DebtEq.mtw):

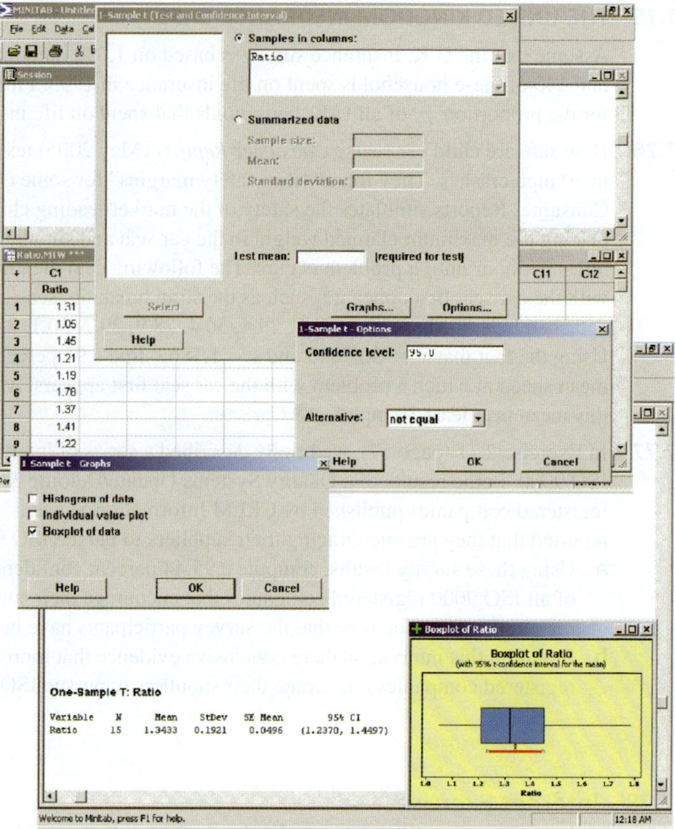

- In the Data window, enter the debt-to-equity ratio data from Example 7.4 (page 273) into a single column with variable name Ratio.
- Select **Stat : Basic Statistics : 1-Sample t.**
- In the "1-Sample t (Test and Confidence Interval)" dialog box, select "Samples in columns."
- Select the variable name Ratio into the "Samples in columns" window.
- Click the Options... button.
- In the "1-Sample t - Options" dialog box, enter the desired level of confidence (here 95.0) into the "Confidence level" box.
- Select "not equal" from the Alternative drop-down menu, and click OK in the "1-Sample t - Options" dialog box.
- To produce a box plot of the data with a graphical representation of the confidence interval—click the Graphs ... button, check the "Boxplot of data" check box, and click OK in the "1-Sample t - Graphs" dialog box.
- Click OK in "1-Sample t (Test and Confidence Interval)" dialog box.
- The confidence interval is given in the Session window, and the boxplot appears in a graphics window.

A "1-Sample Z" interval is also available in MINITAB under Basic Statistics. It requires a user-specified value of the population standard deviation, which is rarely known.

Confidence interval for a population proportion in the marketing ethics situation of Example 7.9 on page 284.

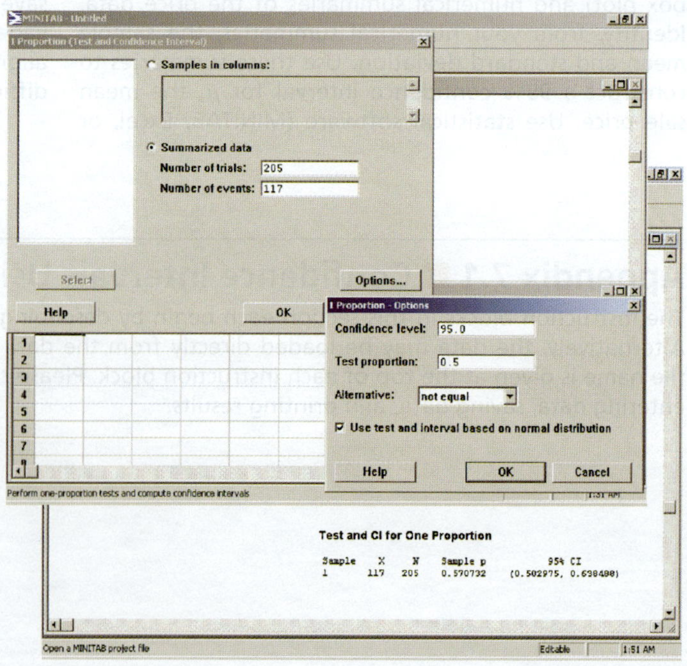

- Select **Stat : Basic Statistics : 1 Proportion**
- In the "1 Proportion (Test and Confidence Interval)" dialog box, select "Summarized data".
- Enter the number of trials (here equal to 205) and the number of successes—or events—(here equal to 117) into the appropriate boxes.
- Click on the Options... button.
- In the "1 Proportion—Options" dialog box, enter the desired level of confidence (here 95.0) into the "Confidence level" box.
- Select "not equal" from the Alternative drop-down menu.
- Check the "Use test and interval based on normal distribution" checkbox.
- Click OK in the "1 Proportion – Options" dialog box.
- Click OK in the "1 Proportion (Test and Confidence Interval)" dialog box.
- The confidence interval will be displayed in the Session window.

Appendix 7.2 ■ Confidence Intervals Using Excel

The instruction block in this section begins by describing the entry of data into an Excel spreadsheet. Alternatively, the data may be loaded directly from the data disk included with the text. The appropriate data file name is given at the top of the instruction block. Please refer to Appendix 1.2 for further information about entering data, saving data, and printing results.

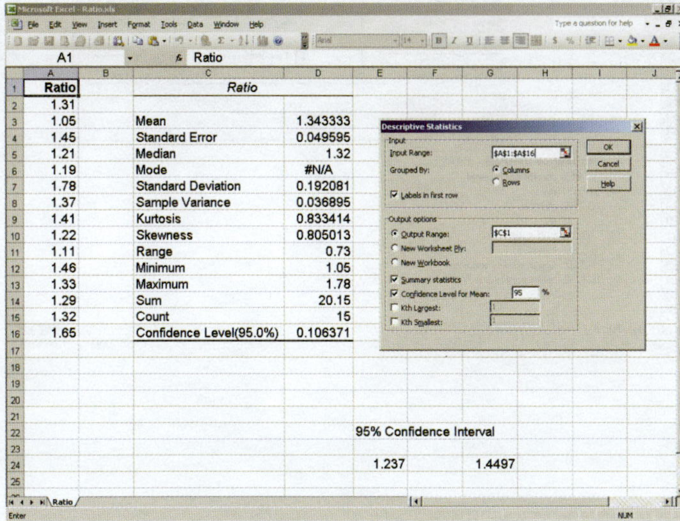

Confidence interval for a population mean in Figure 7.11(b) on page 275 (data file: DebtEq.xls):

- Enter the debt-to-equity ratio data from Example 7.4 (page 273) into cells A2 to A16 with the label Ratio in cell A1.
- Select **Tools : Data Analysis : Descriptive Statistics.**
- Click OK in the Data Analysis dialog box.
- In the Descriptive Statistics dialog box, enter A1.A16 into the Input Range box.
- Place a checkmark in the "Labels in first row" check box.
- Select the Output Range option and enter C1 into the Output Range box.
- Place checkmarks in the Summary Statistics and "Confidence Level for Mean" check boxes. This produces a t–based error bound for a confidence interval for both large (>=30) and small (<30) samples.
- Type 95 in the "Confidence Level for Mean" box.
- Click OK in the Descriptive Statistics dialog box.
- A descriptive statistics summary will appear in cells C3 through D16. Drag the Column C border to reveal complete labels for all of the descriptive statistics.
- Type the heading "95% Confidence Interval" into cells E22 to G22.
- Compute the lower bound of the interval by typing the formula = D3 − D16 into cell E24. This subtracts the error bound of the interval (labeled "Confidence Level (95%)") from the sample mean.
- Compute the upper bound of the interval by typing the formula = D3 + D16 into cell G24.

Appendix 7.3 ■ Confidence Intervals Using MegaStat

Confidence interval for the population mean gas mileage similar to the output in Figure 7.11(a) on page 275.

- Select **MegaStat : Confidence Intervals / Sample Size.**
- In the "Confidence Intervals / Sample Size" dialog box, click on the "Confidence Interval—mean" tab.
- Enter the sample mean (here equal to 31.5531) into the Mean box.
- Enter the sample standard deviation (here equal to .7992) into the "Std Dev" box.
- Enter the sample size (here equal to 49) into the "n" box.
- Select a level of confidence from the pull-down menu or type a desired percentage.
- Select a *t*-based or *z*-based interval by clicking on "t" or "z". Here we request a *t*-based interval.
- Click OK in the "Confidence Intervals / Sample Size" dialog box.

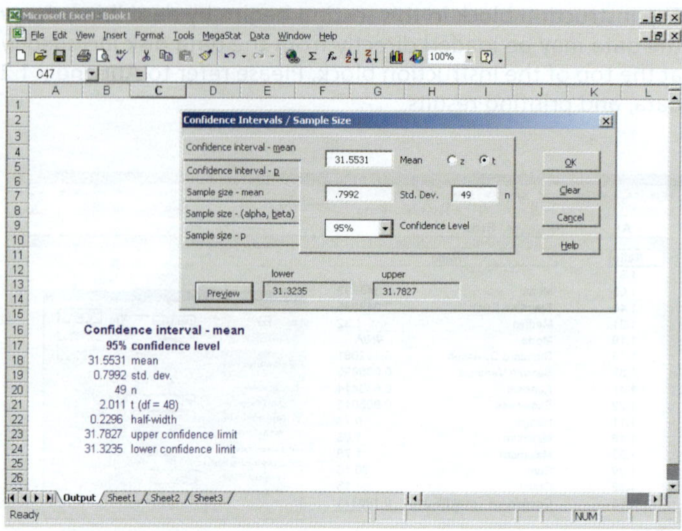

If we wish to use raw data, a *t*-based confidence interval for a population mean can be obtained by using the Descriptive Statistics dialog box—see page 124.

Confidence interval for a population proportion in the cheese spread situation of Example 7.7 on pages 282–283.

- In the "Confidence Intervals / Sample Size" dialog box, click on the "Confidence Interval—p" tab.
- Enter the sample proportion (here equal to .063) into the "p" box.
- Enter the sample size (here equal to 1,000) into the "n" box.
- Select a level of confidence from the pull-down menu or type a desired percentage.
- Click OK in the "Confidence Intervals / Sample Size" dialog box.

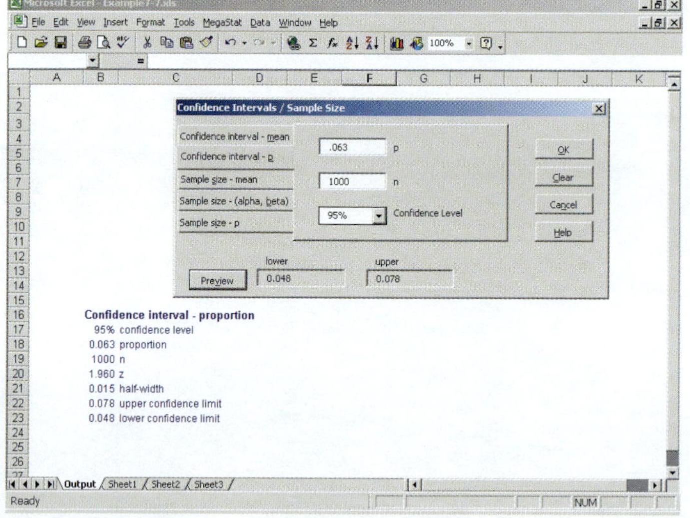

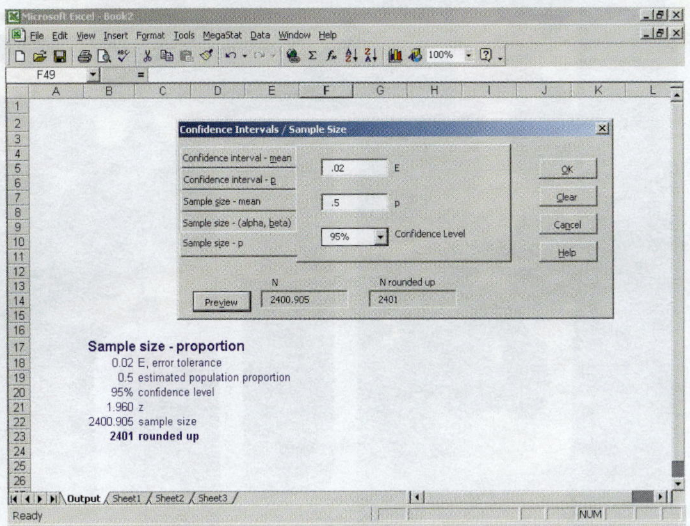

Sample size determination for a population proportion in Figure 7.17 on page 285.

- In the "Confidence Intervals / Sample Size" dialog box, click on the "Sample size—p" tab.
- Enter the desired margin of error (here equal to 0.02) into the "E" box and enter an estimate of the population proportion into the "p" box.
- Select a level of confidence from the pull-down menu or type a desired percentage.
- Click OK in the "Confidence Intervals / Sample Size" dialog box.

Sample size determination for a population mean problem is done by clicking on the "Sample Size—mean" tab. Then enter a desired margin of error, an estimate of the population standard deviation, and the desired level of confidence. Click OK.

CHAPTER 8

Hypothesis Testing

Chapter Outline

8.1 The Null and Alternative Hypotheses and Errors in Hypothesis Testing

8.2 *z* Tests about a Population Mean (σ Known): One-Sided Alternatives

8.3 *z* Tests about a Population Mean (σ Known): Two-Sided Alternatives

8.4 *t* Tests about a Population Mean (σ Unknown)

8.5 *z* Tests about a Population Proportion

8.6 Type II Error Probabilities and Sample Size Determination (Optional)

8.7 The Chi-Square Distribution (Optional)

8.8 Statistical Inference for a Population Variance (Optional)

Hypothesis testing is a statistical procedure used to provide evidence in favor of some statement (called a *hypothesis*). For instance, hypothesis testing might be used to assess whether a population parameter, such as a population mean, differs from a specified standard or previous value. In this chapter we discuss testing hypotheses about population means, proportions, and variances.

In order to illustrate how hypothesis testing works, we revisit several cases introduced in previous chapters:

The Payment Time Case: The consulting firm uses hypothesis testing to provide strong evidence that the new electronic billing system has reduced the mean payment time by more than 50 percent.

The Cheese Spread Case: The cheese spread producer uses hypothesis testing to supply extremely strong evidence that fewer than 10 percent of all current purchasers would stop buying the cheese spread if the new spout were used.

The Electronic Article Surveillance Case: A company that sells and installs EAS systems claims that no more than 5 percent of all consumers would say they would never shop in a store again if the store subjected them to a false EAS alarm. A store considering the purchase of such a system uses hypothesis testing to provide extremely strong evidence that this claim is not true.

In addition, we introduce two new cases that illustrate how to test a hypothesis:

The Trash Bag Case: A marketer of trash bags uses hypothesis testing to support its claim that the mean breaking strength of its new trash bag is greater than 50 pounds. As a result, a television network approves use of this claim in a commercial.

The Camshaft Case: An automobile manufacturer uses hypothesis testing to study an important quality characteristic affecting V6 engine camshafts. It finds that the mean "hardness depth" differs from its desired target value and that this problem is one reason why some of the hardness depths fail to meet specifications.

8.1 The Null and Alternative Hypotheses and Errors in Hypothesis Testing

One of the authors' former students is employed by a major television network in the standards and practices division. One of the division's responsibilities is to reduce the chances that advertisers will make false claims in commercials run on the network. Our former student reports that the network uses a statistical methodology called **hypothesis testing** to do this.

CHAPTER 9

To see how this might be done, suppose that a company wishes to advertise a claim, and suppose that the network has reason to doubt that this claim is true. The network assumes for the sake of argument that **the claim is not valid.** This assumption is called the **null hypothesis.** The statement that **the claim is valid** is called the **alternative, or research, hypothesis.** The network will run the commercial only if the company making the claim provides **sufficient sample evidence** to reject the null hypothesis that the claim is not valid in favor of the alternative hypothesis that the claim is valid. Explaining the exact meaning of *sufficient sample evidence* is quite involved and will be discussed in the next section.

The Null Hypothesis and the Alternative Hypothesis

In hypothesis testing:

1. The **null hypothesis,** denoted H_0, is the statement being tested. Usually this statement represents the *status quo* and is not rejected unless there is convincing sample evidence that it is false.
2. The **alternative,** or **research, hypothesis,** denoted H_a, is a statement that will be accepted only if there is convincing sample evidence that it is true.

Setting up the null and alternative hypotheses in a practical situation can be tricky. In some situations there is a condition for which we need to attempt to find supportive evidence. We then formulate (1) the alternative hypothesis to be the statement that this condition exists and (2) the null hypothesis to be the statement that this condition does not exist. To illustrate this, we consider the following case study.

Example 8.1 The Trash Bag Case[1]

A leading manufacturer of trash bags produces the strongest trash bags on the market. The company has developed a new 30-gallon bag using a specially formulated plastic that is stronger and more biodegradable than other plastics. This plastic's increased strength allows the bag's thickness to be reduced, and the resulting cost savings will enable the company to lower its bag price by 25 percent. The company also believes the new bag is stronger than its current 30-gallon bag.

The manufacturer wants to advertise the new bag on a major television network. In addition to promoting its price reduction, the company also wants to claim the new bag is better for the environment and stronger than its current bag. The network is convinced of the bag's environmental advantages on scientific grounds. However, the network questions the company's claim of increased strength and requires statistical evidence to justify this claim. Although there are various measures of bag strength, the manufacturer and the network agree to employ "breaking strength." A bag's breaking strength is the amount of a representative trash mix (in pounds) that, when loaded into a bag suspended in the air, will cause the bag to rip or tear. Tests show that the current bag has a mean breaking strength that is very close to (but does not exceed) 50 pounds. The new bag's mean breaking strength μ is unknown and in question. The alternative hypothesis H_a is the statement for which we wish to find supportive evidence. Because we hope the new bags are stronger than the current bags, H_a says that μ is greater than 50. The null hypothesis states that H_a is false. Therefore, H_0 says that μ is less than or equal to 50. We summarize these hypotheses by stating that we are testing

$$H_0: \mu \leq 50 \quad \text{versus} \quad H_a: \mu > 50$$

The network will run the manufacturer's commercial if a random sample of n new bags provides sufficient evidence to reject $H_0: \mu \leq 50$ in favor of $H_a: \mu > 50$.

In the trash bag example, the decision to run the commercial is based solely on whether H_0 will be rejected in favor of H_a. In many situations, however, the result of a hypothesis test is used as input into a more complex decision-making process, and the hypothesis test is not the sole basis for the decision that will be made. This is true in the next two cases.

Example 8.2 The Payment Time Case

Recall that a management consulting firm has installed a new computer-based, electronic billing system in a Hamilton, Ohio, trucking company. Because of the system's advantages, and because the trucking company's clients are receptive to using this system, the management consulting firm believes that the new system will reduce the mean bill payment time by more than 50 percent. The mean payment time using the old billing system was approximately equal to, but no less than, 39 days. Therefore, if μ denotes the mean payment time using the new system, the consulting firm believes that μ will be less than 19.5 days. Because it is hoped that the new billing system *reduces* mean payment time, we formulate the alternative hypothesis as $H_a: \mu < 19.5$ and the null hypothesis as $H_0: \mu \geq 19.5$. The consulting firm will randomly select a sample of n invoices and determine how much evidence their payment times provide to reject H_0 in favor of H_a. The firm will use the results of the hypothesis test to demonstrate the benefits of the new billing system both to the Hamilton company and to other trucking companies that are considering using such a system. Note, however, that a potential user will decide whether to install the new system by considering factors beyond the results of the hypothesis test. For example, the cost of the new billing system and the receptiveness of the company's clients to using the new system are among other factors that must be considered. In complex business and industrial situations such as this,

[1]This case is based on conversations by the authors with several employees working for a leading producer of trash bags. For purposes of confidentiality, we have agreed to withhold the company's name.

hypothesis testing is used to accumulate knowledge about and understand the problem at hand. The ultimate decision (such as whether to adopt the new billing system) is made on the basis of nonstatistical considerations, intuition, and the results of one or more hypothesis tests.

Example 8.3 The Camshaft Case

C

On March 8, 1999, Coltec Industries of Charlotte, North Carolina, made an alarming discovery. A Coltec quality control study revealed that the company had supplied Consolidated Edison–Indian Point 2 nuclear power plant with inadequately hardened engine camshafts. The suspect camshafts were a significant safety hazard because they could cause failure of FM-ALCO 251 engines, which the power plant used to run emergency standby power generators. Although Coltec was not aware of any engine failures in nuclear power plants, such failures had occurred in commercial applications after approximately 200 hours of operation. Coltec immediately reported its conclusions to the U.S. Nuclear Regulatory Commission, and a crisis was averted at the Consolidated Edison plant. Coltec also substantially improved its camshaft inspection process so that the problem would not occur again. (Source: www.nrc.gov/reading-rm/doc-collections/event-status/part21/1999/1999161.html).

BI

In general, an engine camshaft is an important engine part used in a variety of commercial and industrial applications. For example, the camshaft of a V6 automobile engine is illustrated in Figure 8.1. Positioned on this (or any) camshaft are metal disks called *eccentrics.* As the camshaft turns, these eccentrics repeatedly make contact with *engine lifters* and thus must have the appropriate hardness to wear properly. To harden the eccentrics, the camshaft is heat treated, and a hardened layer is produced on the surface of the camshaft. The depth of this layer is called the **hardness depth** of the camshaft. If the hardness depth of a camshaft is within given specifications, the camshaft will wear properly, resulting in long engine life.

FIGURE 8.1 A Camshaft and Related Parts

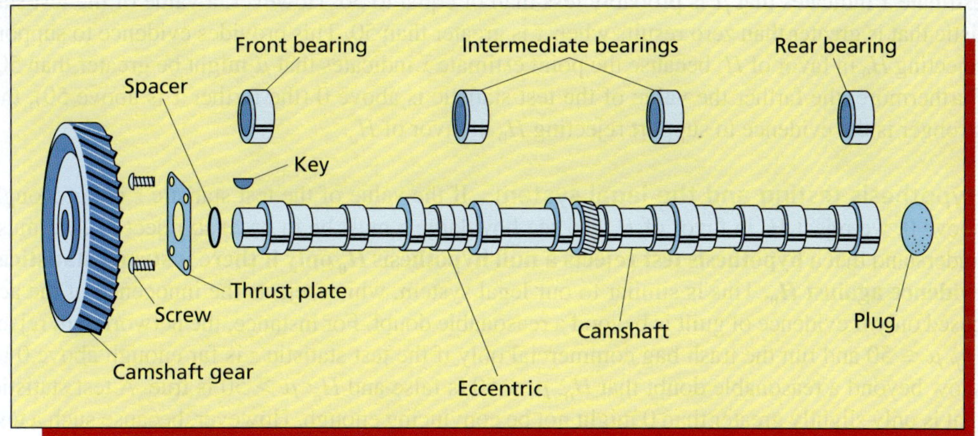

To illustrate how we might use a hypothesis test to study camshaft hardness, we consider an automobile manufacturer that is having problems properly hardening the camshaft of a V6 automobile engine. The *optimal,* or *target,* hardness depth of this camshaft is 4.5 mm, and specifications state that, in order for the camshaft to wear properly, the hardness depth of the camshaft must be between 3.0 mm and 6.0 mm. Unfortunately, however, the hardening process has been producing too many out-of-specification camshafts. To investigate why this is so, a quality control analyst randomly selects n camshafts from the population of all camshafts produced on a particular day and measures the hardness depth of each sampled camshaft. Then, letting μ denote the population mean hardness depth of all camshafts produced that day, the analyst will evaluate whether μ differs from the target value of 4.5 mm by testing the null hypothesis H_0: $\mu = 4.5$ versus the alternative hypothesis H_a: $\mu \neq 4.5$. Of course, μ differing from 4.5 is not the only reason why the hardness depths of the camshafts produced on the particular day might be out of specification. Another reason is that the variation of the hardness depths might be too large.

We next summarize the sets of null and alternative hypotheses that we have thus far considered.

$H_0: \mu \leq 50$	$H_0: \mu \geq 19.5$	$H_0: \mu = 4.5$
versus	versus	versus
$H_a: \mu > 50$	$H_a: \mu < 19.5$	$H_a: \mu \neq 4.5$

The alternative hypothesis H_a: $\mu > 50$ is called a **one-sided, greater than** alternative hypothesis, whereas H_a: $\mu < 19.5$ is called a **one-sided, less than** alternative hypothesis, and H_a: $\mu \neq 4.5$ is called a **two-sided, not equal to** alternative hypothesis. Many of the alternative hypotheses we consider in this book are one of these three types. Also, note that each null hypothesis we have considered involves an **equality.** For example, the null hypothesis H_0: $\mu \leq 50$ says that μ is either less than or **equal to** 50. We will see that, in general, the approach we use to test a null hypothesis versus an alternative hypothesis requires that the null hypothesis involve an equality.

The idea of a test statistic Suppose that in the trash bag case the manufacturer randomly selects a sample of $n = 40$ new trash bags. Each of these bags is tested for breaking strength, and the sample mean $\bar{x}$ of the 40 breaking strengths is calculated. In order to test H_0: $\mu \leq 50$ versus H_a: $\mu > 50$, we utilize the **test statistic**

$$z = \frac{\bar{x} - 50}{\sigma_{\bar{x}}} = \frac{\bar{x} - 50}{\sigma / \sqrt{n}}$$

The test statistic z measures the distance between $\bar{x}$ and 50. The division by $\sigma_{\bar{x}}$ says that this distance is measured in units of the standard deviation of all possible sample means. For example, a value of z equal to, say, 2.4 would tell us that $\bar{x}$ is 2.4 such standard deviations above 50. In general, a value of the test statistic that is less than or equal to zero results when $\bar{x}$ is less than or equal to 50. This provides no evidence to support rejecting H_0 in favor of H_a because the point estimate $\bar{x}$ indicates that μ is probably less than or equal to 50. However, a value of the test statistic that is greater than zero results when $\bar{x}$ is greater than 50. This provides evidence to support rejecting H_0 in favor of H_a because the point estimate $\bar{x}$ indicates that μ might be greater than 50. Furthermore, the farther the value of the test statistic is above 0 (the farther $\bar{x}$ is above 50), the stronger is the evidence to support rejecting H_0 in favor of H_a.

Hypothesis testing and the legal system If the value of the test statistic z is far enough above 0, we reject H_0 in favor of H_a. To see how large z must be in order to reject H_0, we must understand that **a hypothesis test rejects a null hypothesis H_0 only if there is strong statistical evidence against H_0.** This is similar to our legal system, which rejects the innocence of the accused only if evidence of guilt is beyond a reasonable doubt. For instance, the network will reject H_0: $\mu \leq 50$ and run the trash bag commercial only if the test statistic z is far enough above 0 to show beyond a reasonable doubt that H_0: $\mu \leq 50$ is false and H_a: $\mu > 50$ is true. A test statistic that is only slightly greater than 0 might not be convincing enough. However, because such a test statistic would result from a sample mean $\bar{x}$ that is slightly greater than 50, it would provide some evidence to support rejecting H_0: $\mu \leq 50$, and it certainly would not provide strong evidence supporting H_0: $\mu \leq 50$. Therefore, if the value of the test statistic is not large enough to convince us to reject H_0, **we do not say that we accept H_0. Rather we say that we do not reject H_0** because the evidence against H_0 is not strong enough. Again, this is similar to our legal system, where the lack of evidence of guilt beyond a reasonable doubt results in a verdict of **not guilty,** but does not prove that the accused is innocent.

Type I and Type II errors and their probabilities To determine exactly how much statistical evidence is required to reject H_0, we consider the errors and the correct decisions that can be made in hypothesis testing. These errors and correct decisions, as well as their implications in the trash bag advertising example, are summarized in Tables 8.1 and 8.2. Across the top of each table are listed the two possible "states of nature." Either H_0: $\mu \leq 50$ is true, which says the manufacturer's claim that μ is greater than 50 is false, or H_0 is false, which says the claim is true. Down the left side of each table are listed the two possible decisions we can make in the hypothesis test.

TABLE 8.1 Type I and Type II Errors

	State of Nature	
Decision	**H_0 True**	**H_0 False**
Reject H_0	Type I error	Correct decision
Do not reject H_0	Correct decision	Type II error

TABLE 8.2 The Implications of Type I and Type II Errors in the Trash Bag Example

	State of Nature	
Decision	**Claim False**	**Claim True**
Advertise the claim	Advertise a false claim	Advertise a true claim
Do not advertise the claim	Do not advertise a false claim	Do not advertise a true claim

Using the sample data, we will either reject H_0: $\mu \leq 50$, which implies that the claim will be advertised, or we will not reject H_0, which implies that the claim will not be advertised.

In general, the two types of errors that can be made in hypothesis testing are defined here:

> **Type I and Type II Errors**
>
> If we reject H_0 when it is true, this is a **Type I error.**
> If we do not reject H_0 when it is false, this is a **Type II error.**

As can be seen by comparing Tables 8.1 and 8.2, if we commit a Type I error, we will advertise a false claim. If we commit a Type II error, we will fail to advertise a true claim.

We now let the symbol α (pronounced **alpha**) **denote the probability of a Type I error,** and we let β (pronounced **beta**) **denote the probability of a Type II error.** Obviously, we would like both α and β to be small. A common (but not the only) procedure is to base a hypothesis test on taking a sample of a fixed size (for example, $n = 40$ trash bags) and on setting α equal to a small prespecified value. Setting α low means there is only a small chance of rejecting H_0 when it is true. This implies that we are requiring strong evidence against H_0 before we reject it.

We sometimes choose α as high as .10, but we usually choose α between .05 and .01. A frequent choice for α is .05. In fact, our former student tells us that the network often tests advertising claims by setting the probability of a Type I error equal to .05. That is, the network will run a commercial making a claim if the sample evidence allows it to reject a null hypothesis that says the claim is not valid in favor of an alternative hypothesis that says the claim is valid with α set equal to .05. Since a Type I error is deciding that the claim is valid when it is not, the policy of setting α equal to .05 says that, in the long run, the network will advertise only 5 percent of all invalid claims made by advertisers.

One might wonder why the network does not set α lower—say at .01. One reason is that **it can be shown that, for a fixed sample size, the lower we set α, the higher is β, and the higher we set α, the lower is β.** Setting α at .05 means that β, the probability of failing to advertise a true claim (a Type II error), will be smaller than it would be if α were set at .01. As long as (1) the claim to be advertised is plausible and (2) the consequences of advertising the claim even if it is false are not terribly serious, then it is reasonable to set α equal to .05. However, if either (1) or (2) is not true, then we might set α lower than .05. For example, suppose a pharmaceutical company wishes to advertise that it has developed an effective treatment for a disease that has formerly been very resistant to treatment. Such a claim is (perhaps) difficult to believe. Moreover, if the claim is false, patients suffering from the disease would be subjected to false hope and needless expense. In such a case, it might be reasonable for the network to set α at .01 because this would lower the chance of advertising the claim if it is false. We usually do not set α lower than .01 because doing so often leads to an unacceptably large value of β. We explain some methods for computing the probability of a Type II error in optional Section 8.6. However, β can be difficult or impossible to calculate in many situations, and we often must rely on our intuition when deciding how to set α.

Exercises for Section 8.1

CONCEPTS

8.1 Which hypothesis (the null hypothesis, H_0, or the alternative hypothesis, H_a) is the "status quo" hypothesis (that is, the hypothesis that states that things are remaining "as is")? Which hypothesis is the hypothesis that says that a "hoped for" or "suspected" condition exists?

8.2 Which hypothesis (H_0 or H_a) is not rejected unless there is convincing sample evidence that it is false? Which hypothesis (H_0 or H_a) will be accepted only if there is convincing sample evidence that it is true?

8.3 Define each of the following:

a Type I error
b Type II error
c α
d β

8.4 For each of the following situations, indicate whether an error has occurred and, if so, indicate what kind of error (Type I or Type II) has occurred.

a We do not reject H_0 and H_0 is true.
b We reject H_0 and H_0 is true.
c We do not reject H_0 and H_0 is false.
d We reject H_0 and H_0 is false.

8.5 If we reject H_0, what is the only type of error that we could be making? Explain.

8.6 If we do not reject H_0, what is the only type of error that we could be making? Explain.

8.7 When testing a hypothesis, why don't we set the probability of a Type I error to be extremely small? Explain.

METHODS AND APPLICATIONS

8.8 THE VIDEO GAME SATISFACTION RATING CASE VideoGame

Recall that "very satisfied" customers give the XYZ-Box video game system a rating that is at least 42. Suppose that the manufacturer of the XYZ-Box wishes to use the 65 satisfaction ratings to provide evidence supporting the claim that the mean composite satisfaction rating for the XYZ-Box exceeds 42.

a Letting μ represent the mean composite satisfaction rating for the XYZ-Box, set up the null and alternative hypotheses needed if we wish to attempt to provide evidence supporting the claim that μ exceeds 42.
b In the context of this situation, interpret making a Type I error; interpret making a Type II error.

8.9 THE BANK CUSTOMER WAITING TIME CASE WaitTime

Recall that a bank manager has developed a new system to reduce the time customers spend waiting for teller service during peak hours. The manager hopes the new system will reduce waiting times from the current 9 to 10 minutes to less than 6 minutes.

Suppose the manager wishes to use the 100 waiting times to support the claim that the mean waiting time under the new system is shorter than six minutes.

a Letting μ represent the mean waiting time under the new system, set up the null and alternative hypotheses needed if we wish to attempt to provide evidence supporting the claim that μ is shorter than six minutes.
b In the context of this situation, interpret making a Type I error; interpret making a Type II error.

8.10 An automobile parts supplier owns a machine that produces a cylindrical engine part. This part is supposed to have an outside diameter of three inches. Parts with diameters that are too small or too large do not meet customer requirements and must be rejected. Lately, the company has experienced problems meeting customer requirements. The technical staff feels that the mean diameter produced by the machine is off target. In order to verify this, a special study will randomly sample 100 parts produced by the machine. The 100 sampled parts will be measured, and if the results obtained cast a substantial amount of doubt on the hypothesis that the mean diameter equals the target value of three inches, the company will assign a problem-solving team to intensively search for the causes of the problem.

a The parts supplier wishes to set up a hypothesis test so that the problem-solving team will be assigned when the null hypothesis is rejected. Set up the null and alternative hypotheses for this situation.
b In the context of this situation, interpret making a Type I error; interpret making a Type II error.
c Suppose it costs the company $3,000 a day to assign the problem-solving team to a project. Is this $3,000 figure the daily cost of a Type I error or a Type II error? Explain.

8.11 The Crown Bottling Company has just installed a new bottling process that will fill 16-ounce bottles of the popular Crown Classic Cola soft drink. Both overfilling and underfilling bottles are undesirable: Underfilling leads to customer complaints and overfilling costs the company considerable money. In order to verify that the filler is set up correctly, the company wishes to see whether the mean bottle fill, μ, is close to the target fill of 16 ounces. To this end, a random sample of 36 filled bottles is selected from the output of a test filler run. If the sample results cast a substantial amount of doubt on the hypothesis that the mean bottle fill is the desired 16 ounces, then the filler's initial setup will be readjusted.

a The bottling company wants to set up a hypothesis test so that the filler will be readjusted if the null hypothesis is rejected. Set up the null and alternative hypotheses for this hypothesis test.

b In the context of this situation, interpret making a Type I error; interpret making a Type II error.

8.12 Consolidated Power, a large electric power utility, has just built a modern nuclear power plant. This plant discharges waste water that is allowed to flow into the Atlantic Ocean. The Environmental Protection Agency (EPA) has ordered that the waste water may not be excessively warm so that thermal pollution of the marine environment near the plant can be avoided. Because of this order, the waste water is allowed to cool in specially constructed ponds and is then released into the ocean. This cooling system works properly if the mean temperature of waste water discharged is 60°F or cooler. Consolidated Power is required to monitor the temperature of the waste water. A sample of 100 temperature readings will be obtained each day, and if the sample results cast a substantial amount of doubt on the hypothesis that the cooling system is working properly (the mean temperature of waste water discharged is 60°F or cooler), then the plant must be shut down and appropriate actions must be taken to correct the problem.

a Consolidated Power wishes to set up a hypothesis test so that the power plant will be shut down when the null hypothesis is rejected. Set up the null and alternative hypotheses that should be used.

b In the context of this situation, interpret making a Type I error; interpret making a Type II error.

c The EPA periodically conducts spot checks to determine whether the waste water being discharged is too warm. Suppose the EPA has the power to impose very severe penalties (for example, very heavy fines) when the waste water is excessively warm. Other things being equal, should Consolidated Power set the probability of a Type I error equal to $\alpha = .01$ or $\alpha = .05$? Explain.

d Suppose Consolidated Power has been experiencing technical problems with the cooling system. Because the system has been unreliable, the company feels it must take precautions to avoid failing to shut down the plant when its waste water is too warm. Other things being equal, should Consolidated Power set the probability of a Type I error equal to $\alpha = .01$ or $\alpha = .05$? Explain.

8.13 THE DISK BRAKE CASE

National Motors has equipped the ZX-900 with a new disk brake system. We define the stopping distance for a ZX-900 as the distance (in feet) required to bring the automobile to a complete stop from a speed of 35 mph under normal driving conditions using this new brake system. In addition, we define μ to be the mean stopping distance of all ZX-900s. One of the ZX-900's major competitors is advertised to achieve a mean stopping distance of 60 ft. National Motors would like to claim in a new television commercial that the ZX-900 achieves a shorter mean stopping distance. The standards and practices division of a major television network will permit National Motors to run the commercial if H_0: $\mu \geq 60$ can be rejected in favor of H_a: $\mu < 60$ by setting $\alpha = .05$. Interpret what it means to set α at .05.

8.2 z Tests about a Population Mean (σ Known): One-Sided Alternatives

CHAPTER 9

In this (and the next) section we discuss hypothesis tests about a population mean that are *based on the normal distribution*. These tests are called *z* **tests,** and they require that the *true value of the population standard deviation σ is known.* Of course, in almost all real-world situations the true value of σ is not known. However, the concepts and calculations of hypothesis testing are most easily illustrated using the normal distribution. Therefore, in this (and the next) section we will assume that, through extensive experience with the population or process under consideration, we know σ. When σ is unknown, we test hypotheses about a population mean by using the *t distribution.* In Section 8.4 we study ***t* tests,** and we will revisit the examples of this (and the next) section assuming that σ is unknown.

Testing a "greater than" alternative hypothesis by using a rejection point rule In Section 8.1 we explained how to set up appropriate null and alternative hypotheses. We also discussed how to specify a value for α, the probability of a Type I error (also called the **level of significance**) of the hypothesis test, and we introduced the idea of a test statistic. We can use these concepts to begin developing a seven step hypothesis testing procedure. We will introduce these steps in the context of the trash bag case and testing a "greater than" alternative hypothesis.

Step 1: State the null hypothesis H_0 and the alternative hypothesis H_a. In the trash bag case, we will test H_0: $\mu \leq 50$ versus H_a: $\mu > 50$. Here, μ is the mean breaking strength of the new trash bag.

Step 2: Specify the level of significance α. The television network will run the commercial stating that the new trash bag is stronger than the former bag if we can reject H_0: $\mu \leq 50$ in favor of H_a: $\mu > 50$ by setting α equal to .05.

Step 3: Select the test statistic. In order to test H_0: $\mu \leq 50$ versus H_a: $\mu > 50$, we will test the modified null hypothesis H_0: $\mu = 50$ versus H_a: $\mu > 50$. The idea here is that if there is sufficient evidence to reject the hypothesis that μ equals 50 in favor of $\mu > 50$, then there is certainly also sufficient evidence to reject the hypothesis that μ is less than or equal to 50. In order to test H_0: $\mu = 50$ versus H_a: $\mu > 50$, we will randomly select a sample of $n = 40$ new trash bags and calculate the mean $\bar{x}$ of the breaking strengths of these bags. We will then utilize the **test statistic**

$$z = \frac{\bar{x} - 50}{\sigma_{\bar{x}}} = \frac{\bar{x} - 50}{\sigma/\sqrt{n}}$$

A positive value of this test statistic results from an $\bar{x}$ that is greater than 50 and thus provides evidence against H_0: $\mu = 50$ and in favor of H_a: $\mu > 50$.

Step 4: Determine the rejection point rule for deciding whether to reject H_0. To decide how large the test statistic must be to reject H_0 in favor of H_a by setting the probability of a Type I error equal to α, we do the following:

- Place the probability of a Type I error, α, in the right-hand tail of the standard normal curve and use the normal table (see Table A.3, page 824) to find the normal point z_α. Here z_α, which we call a **rejection point** (or **critical point**), is the point on the horizontal axis under the standard normal curve that gives a right-hand tail area equal to α.
- **Reject H_0: $\mu = 50$ in favor of H_a: $\mu > 50$ if and only if the test statistic z is greater than the rejection point z_α.** (This is the **rejection point rule.**)

Figure 8.2 illustrates that since we have set α equal to .05, we should use the rejection point $z_\alpha = z_{.05} = 1.645$ (see Table A.3). This says that we should reject H_0 if $z > 1.645$ and we should not reject H_0 if $z \leq 1.645$.

To more fully explain what it means to set α equal to .05 and to use the rejection point rule, we consider the sampling distribution of the test statistic z. Because the sample size $n = 40$ is large, the Central Limit Theorem tells us that the sampling distribution of $(\bar{x} - \mu)/\sigma_{\bar{x}}$ is (approximately) a standard normal distribution. It follows that if the null hypothesis H_0: $\mu = 50$ is true, then the sampling distribution of the test statistic $z = (\bar{x} - 50)/\sigma_{\bar{x}}$ is (approximately) a standard normal distribution. Therefore, examining the standard normal curve in Figure 8.2, we can see that the areas under this curve imply the following:

- If H_0: $\mu = 50$ is true, 95 percent of all possible values of the test statistic z are less than or equal to $z_{.05} = 1.645$ and thus would tell us to not reject H_0: $\mu = 50$—a correct decision.
- If H_0: $\mu = 50$ is true, 5 percent of all possible values of the test statistic z are greater than $z_{.05} = 1.645$ and thus would tell us to reject H_0: $\mu = 50$: a Type I error.

FIGURE 8.2 **The Rejection Point for Testing H_0: $\mu = 50$ versus H_a: $\mu > 50$ by Setting $\alpha = .05$**

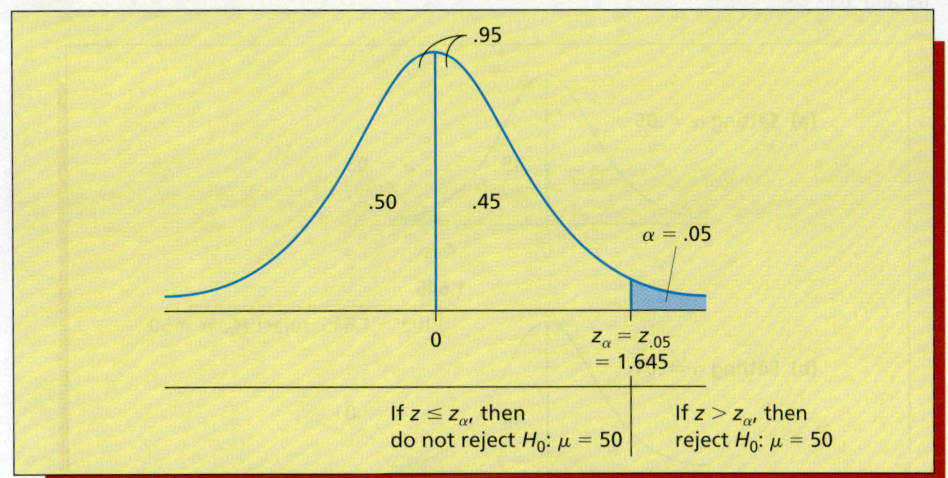

These two statements explain what it means to set α equal to .05 and to use the rejection point rule.

Step 5: Collect the sample data and compute the value of the test statistic. When the sample of $n = 40$ new trash bags is randomly selected, the mean of the breaking strengths is calculated to be $\bar{x} = 50.575$. Assuming that σ is known to equal 1.65, the value of the test statistic is

$$z = \frac{\bar{x} - 50}{\sigma/\sqrt{n}} = \frac{50.575 - 50}{1.65/\sqrt{40}} = 2.20$$

Step 6: Decide whether to reject H_0 by using the test statistic value and the rejection point rule. Since the test statistic value $z = 2.20$ is greater than the rejection point $z_{.05} = 1.645$, we can reject H_0: $\mu = 50$ in favor of H_a: $\mu > 50$ by setting α equal to .05. Furthermore, we can be intuitively confident that H_0: $\mu = 50$ is false and H_a: $\mu > 50$ is true. This is because, since we have rejected H_0 by setting α equal to .05, we have rejected H_0 by using a test that allows only a 5 percent chance of wrongly rejecting H_0. In general, if we can reject a null hypothesis in favor of an alternative hypothesis by setting the probability of a Type I error equal to α, we say that we have **statistical significance at the α level.**

Step 7: Interpret the statistical results in managerial (real-world) terms and assess their practical importance. Since we have rejected H_0: $\mu = 50$ in favor of H_a: $\mu > 50$ by setting α equal to .05, we conclude (at an α of .05) that the mean breaking strength of the new trash bag exceeds 50 pounds. Furthermore, this conclusion has practical importance to the trash bag manufacturer because it means that the television network will approve running commercials claiming that the new trash bag is stronger than the former bag. Note, however, that the point estimate of μ, $\bar{x} = 50.575$, indicates that μ is not much larger than 50. Therefore, the trash bag manufacturer can claim only that its new bag is slightly stronger than its former bag. Of course, this might be practically important to consumers who feel that, because the new bag is 25 percent less expensive and is more environmentally sound, it is definitely worth purchasing if it has any strength advantage. However, to customers who are looking only for a substantial increase in bag strength, the statistical results would not be practically important. This illustrates that, in general, a finding of statistical significance (that is, concluding that the alternative hypothesis is true) can be practically important to some people but not to others. Notice that the point estimate of the parameter involved in a hypothesis test can help us to assess practical importance. We can also use confidence intervals to help assess practical importance as will be illustrated in Section 8.3.

BI

Considerations in setting α We have reasoned in Section 8.1 that the television network has set α equal to .05 rather than .01 because doing so means that β, the probability of failing to advertise a true claim (a Type II error), will be smaller than it would be if α were set at .01. It is

FIGURE 8.3 **The Rejection Points for Testing H_0: $\mu = 50$ versus H_a: $\mu > 50$ by Setting $\alpha = .05$ and .01**

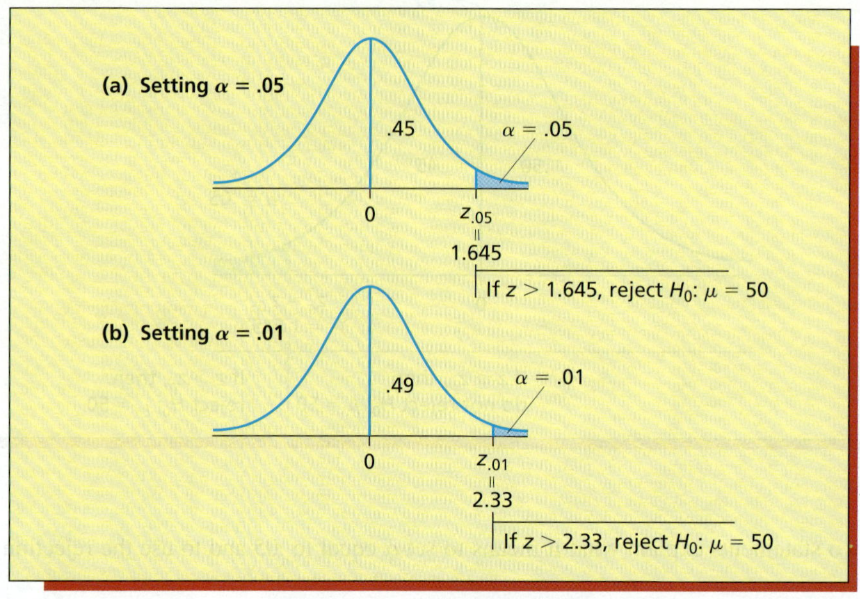

informative, however, to see what would have happened if the network had set α equal to .01. Figure 8.3 illustrates that as we decrease α from .05 to .01, the rejection point z_α increases from $z_{.05} = 1.645$ to $z_{.01} = 2.33$. Because the test statistic value $z = 2.20$ is less than $z_{.01} = 2.33$, we cannot reject H_0: $\mu = 50$ in favor of H_a: $\mu > 50$ by setting α equal to .01. This illustrates the point that, the smaller we set α, the larger is the rejection point, and thus the stronger is the statistical evidence that we are requiring to reject the null hypothesis H_0. Some statisticians have concluded (somewhat subjectively) that (1) **if we set α equal to .05, then we are requiring strong evidence to reject H_0**; and (2) **if we set α equal to .01, then we are requiring very strong evidence to reject H_0.**

A *p*-value for testing a "greater than" alternative hypothesis To decide whether to reject the null hypothesis H_0 at level of significance α, steps 4, 5, and 6 of the seven-step hypothesis testing procedure compare the test statistic value with a rejection point. Another way to make this decision is to calculate a ***p*-value,** which measures the likelihood of the sample results if the null hypothesis H_0 is true. Sample results that are not likely if H_0 is true are evidence that H_0 is not true. To test H_0 by using a *p*-value, we use the following steps 4, 5, and 6:

Step 4: Collect the sample data and compute the value of the test statistic. In the trash bag case, we have computed the value of the test statistic to be $z = 2.20$.

Step 5: Calculate the *p*-value by using the test statistic value. The *p*-value for testing H_0: $\mu = 50$ versus H_a: $\mu > 50$ in the trash bag case is the area under the standard normal curve to the right of the test statistic value $z = 2.20$. As illustrated in Figure 8.4(b), this area is $.5 - .4861 = .0139$. The *p*-value is the probability, computed assuming that H_0: $\mu = 50$ is true, of observing a value of the test statistic that is greater than or equal to the value $z = 2.20$ that we have actually computed from the sample data. The *p*-value of .0139 says that, if H_0: $\mu = 50$ is true, then only 139 in 10,000 of all possible test statistic values are at least as large, or extreme, as the value $z = 2.20$. That is, if we are to believe that H_0 is true, we must believe that we have observed a test statistic value that can be described as a 139 in 10,000 chance. Because it is difficult to believe that we have observed a 139 in 10,000 chance, we intuitively have strong evidence that H_0: $\mu = 50$ is false and H_a: $\mu > 50$ is true.

FIGURE 8.4 Testing H_0: $\mu = 50$ versus H_a: $\mu > 50$ by Using Rejection Points and the p-Value

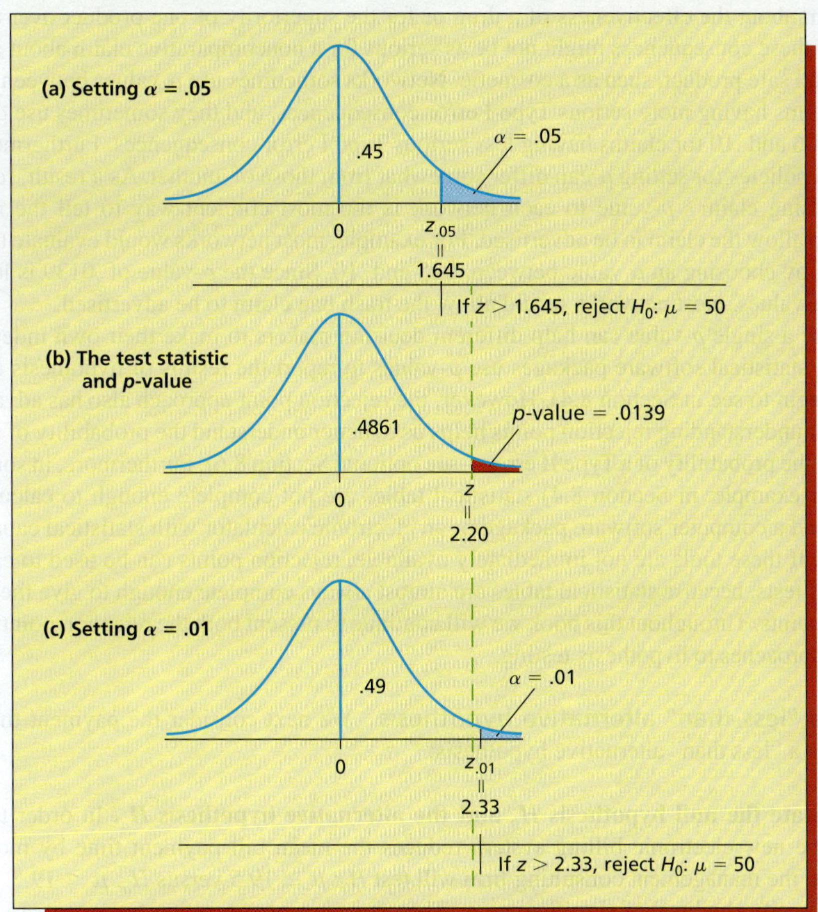

Step 6: Reject H_0 if the p-value is less than α. Recall that the television network has set α equal to .05. **The p-value of .0139 is less than the α of .05.** Comparing the two normal curves in Figures 8.4(a) and (b), we see that this implies that the test statistic value $z = 2.20$ is greater than the rejection point $z_{.05} = 1.645$. Therefore, **we can reject H_0 by setting α equal to .05.** As another example, suppose that the television network had set α equal to .01. **The p-value of .0139 is greater than the α of .01.** Comparing the two normal curves in Figures 8.4(b) and (c), we see that this implies that the test statistic value $z = 2.20$ is less than the rejection point $z_{.01} = 2.33$. Therefore, **we cannot reject H_0 by setting α equal to .01.** Generalizing these examples, we conclude that the value of the test statistic z will be greater than the rejection point z_α if and only if the p-value is less than α. That is, we can reject H_0 in favor of H_a at level of significance α if and only if the p-value is less than α.

Comparing the rejection point and p-value methods Thus far we have considered two methods for testing H_0: $\mu = 50$ versus H_a: $\mu > 50$ at the .05 and .01 values of α. Using the first method, we determine if the test statistic value $z = 2.20$ is greater than the rejection points $z_{.05} = 1.645$ and $z_{.01} = 2.33$. Using the second method, we determine if the p-value of .0139 is less than .05 and .01. Whereas the rejection point method requires that we look up a different rejection point for each different α value, the p-value method requires only that we calculate a single p-value and compare it directly with the different α values. It follows that the p-value method is the most efficient way to test a hypothesis at different α values. This can be useful when there are different decision makers who might use different α values. For example, television networks do not always evaluate advertising claims by setting α equal to .05. The reason is

© NBC, Inc. Used with permission.

Note: This logo appears on an NBC advertising standards booklet. This booklet, along with other information provided by NBC and CBS, forms the basis for much of the discussion in the paragraph to the right.

that the consequences of a Type I error (advertising a false claim) are more serious for some claims than for others. For example, the consequences of a Type I error would be fairly serious for a claim about the effectiveness of a drug or for the superiority of one product over another. However, these consequences might not be as serious for a noncomparative claim about an inexpensive and safe product, such as a cosmetic. Networks sometimes use α values between .01 and .04 for claims having more serious Type I error consequences, and they sometimes use α values between .06 and .10 for claims having less serious Type I error consequences. Furthermore, one network's policies for setting α can differ somewhat from those of another. As a result, reporting an advertising claim's p-value to each network is the most efficient way to tell the network whether to allow the claim to be advertised. For example, most networks would evaluate the trash bag claim by choosing an α value between .025 and .10. Since the p-value of .0139 is less than all these α values, most networks would allow the trash bag claim to be advertised.

Because a single p-value can help different decision makers to make their own independent decisions, statistical software packages use p-values to report the results of hypothesis tests (as we will begin to see in Section 8.4). However, the rejection point approach also has advantages. One is that understanding rejection points helps us to better understand the probability of a Type I error (and the probability of a Type II error—see optional Section 8.6). Furthermore, in some situations (for example, in Section 8.4) statistical tables are not complete enough to calculate the p-value, and a computer software package or an electronic calculator with statistical capabilities is needed. If these tools are not immediately available, rejection points can be used to carry out hypothesis tests, because statistical tables are almost always complete enough to give the needed rejection points. Throughout this book we will continue to present both the rejection point and the p-value approaches to hypothesis testing.

Testing a "less than" alternative hypothesis We next consider the payment time case and testing a "less than" alternative hypothesis:

Step 1: State the null hypothesis H_0 and the alternative hypothesis H_a. In order to study whether the new electronic billing system reduces the mean bill payment time by more than 50 percent, the management consulting firm will test H_0: $\mu \geq 19.5$ versus H_a: $\mu < 19.5$.

Step 2: Specify the level of significance α. The management consulting firm wants to be very sure that it truthfully describes the benefits of the new system both to the company in which it has been installed and to other companies that are considering installing such a system. Therefore, the firm will require very strong evidence to conclude that μ is less than 19.5, which implies that it will test H_0: $\mu \geq 19.5$ versus H_a: $\mu < 19.5$ by setting α equal to .01.

Step 3: Select the test statistic. In order to test H_0: $\mu \geq 19.5$ versus H_a: $\mu < 19.5$, we will test the modified null hypothesis H_0: $\mu = 19.5$ versus H_a: $\mu < 19.5$. The idea here is that if there is sufficient evidence to reject the hypothesis that μ equals 19.5 in favor of $\mu < 19.5$, then there is certainly also sufficient evidence to reject the hypothesis that μ is greater than or equal to 19.5. In order to test H_0: $\mu = 19.5$ versus H_a: $\mu < 19.5$, we will randomly select a sample of $n = 65$ invoices paid using the billing system and calculate the mean $\bar{x}$ of the payment times of these invoices. Since the sample size is large, the Central Limit Theorem applies, and we will utilize the test statistic

$$z = \frac{\bar{x} - 19.5}{\sigma / \sqrt{n}}$$

A value of the test statistic z that is less than zero results when $\bar{x}$ is less than 19.5. This provides evidence to support rejecting H_0 in favor of H_a because the point estimate $\bar{x}$ indicates that μ might be less than 19.5.

Step 4: Determine a rejection point rule for deciding whether to reject H_0. To decide how much less than zero the test statistic must be to reject H_0 in favor of H_a by setting the probability of a Type I error equal to α, we do the following:

- Place the probability of a Type I error, α, in the left-hand tail of the standard normal curve and use the normal table to find the rejection point $-z_\alpha$. Here $-z_\alpha$ is the negative of the normal point z_α. That is, $-z_\alpha$ is the point on the horizontal axis under the standard normal curve that gives a left-hand tail area equal to α.

FIGURE 8.5 Testing H_0: $\mu = 19.5$ versus H_a: $\mu < 19.5$ by Using Rejection Points and the *p*-Value

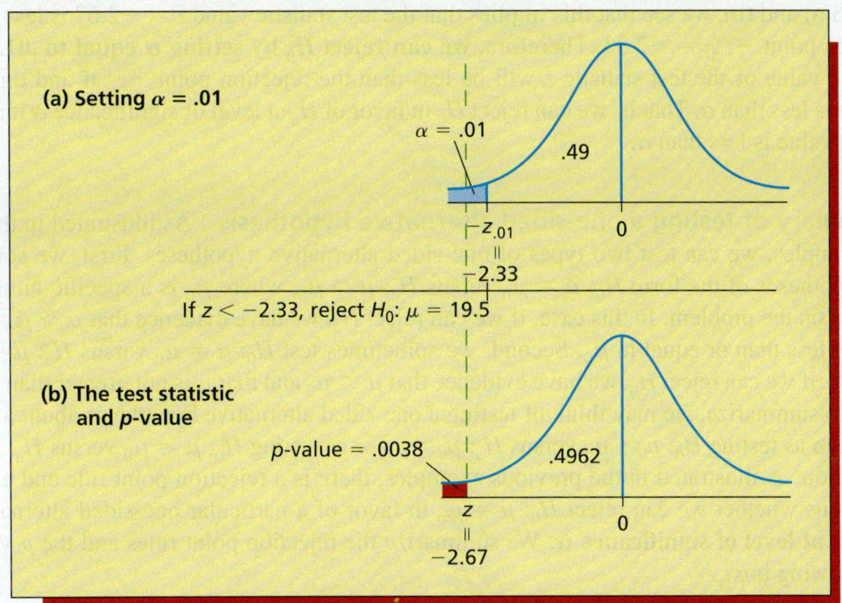

- **Reject H_0: $\mu = 19.5$ in favor of H_a: $\mu < 19.5$ if and only if the test statistic z is less than the rejection point $-z_\alpha$.** Because α equals .01, the rejection point $-z_\alpha$ is $-z_{.01} = -2.33$ (see Figure 8.5(a)).

Step 5: Collect the sample data and compute the value of the test statistic. When the sample of $n = 65$ invoices is randomly selected, the mean of the payment times of these invoices is calculated to be $\bar{x} = 18.1077$. Assuming that σ is known to equal 4.2, the value of the test statistic is

$$z = \frac{\bar{x} - 19.5}{\sigma/\sqrt{n}} = \frac{18.1077 - 19.5}{4.2/\sqrt{65}} = -2.67$$

Step 6: Decide whether to reject H_0 by using the test statistic value and the rejection point rule. Since the test statistic value $z = -2.67$ is less than the rejection point $-z_{.01} = -2.33$, we can reject H_0: $\mu = 19.5$ in favor of H_a: $\mu < 19.5$ by setting α equal to .01.

Step 7: Interpret the statistical results in managerial (real-world) terms and assess their practical importance. We conclude (at an α of .01) that the mean payment time for the new electronic billing system is less than 19.5 days. This, along with the fact that the sample mean $\bar{x} = 18.1077$ is slightly less than 19.5, implies that it is reasonable for the management consulting firm to conclude that the new electronic billing system has reduced the mean payment time by slightly more than 50 percent (a substantial improvement over the old system). BI

A *p*-value for testing a "less than" alternative hypothesis To test H_0: $\mu = 19.5$ versus H_a: $\mu < 19.5$ in the payment time case by using a *p*-value, we use the following steps 4, 5, and 6:

Step 4: Collect the sample data and compute the value of the test statistic. We have computed the value of the test statistic in the payment time case to be $z = -2.67$.

Step 5: Calculate the *p*-value by using the test statistic value. The *p*-value for testing H_0: $\mu = 19.5$ versus H_a: $\mu < 19.5$ is the area under the standard normal curve to the left of the test statistic value $z = -2.67$. As illustrated in Figure 8.5(b), this area is $.5 - .4962 = .0038$. The *p*-value is the probability, computed assuming that H_0: $\mu = 19.5$ is true, of observing a value of the test statistic that is less than or equal to the value $z = -2.67$ that we have actually computed from the sample data. The *p*-value of .0038 says that, if H_0: $\mu = 19.5$ is true, then only 38 in 10,000 of all possible test statistic values are at least as negative, or extreme, as the value $z = -2.67$. That is, if we are to believe that H_0 is true, we must believe that we have observed a test statistic value that can be described as a 38 in 10,000 chance.

Step 6: Reject H_0 if the p-value is less than α. The management consulting firm has set α equal to .01. **The p-value of .0038 is less than the α of .01.** Comparing the two normal curves in Figures 8.5(a) and (b), we see that this implies that the test statistic value $z = -2.67$ is less than the rejection point $-z_{.01} = -2.33$. Therefore, **we can reject H_0 by setting α equal to .01.** In general, the value of the test statistic z will be less than the rejection point $-z_\alpha$ if and only if the p-value is less than α. That is, we can reject H_0 in favor of H_a at level of significance α if and only if the p-value is less than α.

A summary of testing a one-sided alternative hypothesis As illustrated in the previous examples, we can test two types of one-sided alternative hypotheses. First, we sometimes test hypotheses of the form H_0: $\mu = \mu_0$ versus H_a: $\mu > \mu_0$, where μ_0 is a specific number that depends on the problem. In this case, if we can reject H_0, we have evidence that $\mu > \mu_0$ and that μ is not less than or equal to μ_0. Second, we sometimes test H_0: $\mu = \mu_0$ versus H_a: $\mu < \mu_0$. In this case, if we can reject H_0, we have evidence that $\mu < \mu_0$ and that μ is not greater than or equal to μ_0. To summarize, we may think of testing a one-sided alternative hypothesis about a population mean as testing H_0: $\mu = \mu_0$ versus H_a: $\mu > \mu_0$ or as testing H_0: $\mu = \mu_0$ versus H_a: $\mu < \mu_0$. In addition, as illustrated in the previous examples, there is a rejection point rule and a p-value that tell us whether we can reject H_0: $\mu = \mu_0$ in favor of a particular one-sided alternative hypothesis **at level of significance α.** We summarize the rejection point rules and the p-values in the following box.

A Hypothesis Test about a Population Mean: Testing H_0: $\mu = \mu_0$ versus a One-Sided Alternative Hypothesis when σ Is Known

Define the test statistic

$$z = \frac{\bar{x} - \mu_0}{\sigma/\sqrt{n}}$$

and assume that the population sampled is normally distributed, or that the sample size n is large. We can test H_0: $\mu = \mu_0$ versus a particular alternative hypothesis at level of significance α by using the appropriate rejection point rule, or, equivalently, the corresponding p-value.

Alternative Hypothesis	Rejection Point Rule: Reject H_0 if	p-Value (reject H_0 if p-value $< \alpha$)
H_a: $\mu > \mu_0$	$z > z_\alpha$	The area under the standard normal curve to the right of z
H_a: $\mu < \mu_0$	$z < -z_\alpha$	The area under the standard normal curve to the left of z

When using this summary box, it is vital to understand that the **alternative hypothesis** being tested **determines the rejection point rule and the p-value** that should be used to perform the hypothesis test. For example, consider the trash bag case and testing H_0: $\mu = 50$ versus H_a: $\mu > 50$ at level of significance α. Since the alternative hypothesis H_a: $\mu > 50$ is of the form H_a: $\mu > \mu_0$ (that is, is a "greater than" alternative hypothesis), the summary box tells us that (1) we should reject H_0 if $z > z_\alpha$ and (2) the p-value is the area under the standard normal curve to the right of z. When we tested H_0: $\mu = 50$ versus H_a: $\mu > 50$, we illustrated using this rejection point rule and this p-value. As another example, consider the payment time case and testing H_0: $\mu = 19.5$ versus H_a: $\mu < 19.5$ at level of significance α. Since the alternative hypothesis H_a: $\mu < 19.5$ is of the form H_a: $\mu < \mu_0$ (that is, is a "less than" alternative hypothesis), the summary box tells us that (1) we should reject H_0 if $z < -z_\alpha$ and (2) the p-value is the area under the standard normal curve to the left of z. When we tested H_0: $\mu = 19.5$ versus H_a: $\mu < 19.5$, we illustrated using this rejection point rule and this p-value. For most future hypothesis tests that we will consider, we will present hypothesis testing summary boxes. Therefore, we now present the seven step hypothesis testing procedure in a way that emphasizes using a summary box to determine an appropriate rejection point rule and an appropriate p-value.

The Seven Steps of Hypothesis Testing

1. State the null hypothesis H_0 and the alternative hypothesis H_a.
2. Specify the level of significance α.
3. Select the test statistic.

Using a rejection point rule:

4. Use the summary box to find the rejection point rule corresponding to the alternative hypothesis. Use the specified value of α to find the rejection point given in the rejection point rule.
5. Collect the sample data and compute the value of the test statistic.
6. Decide whether to reject H_0 by using the test statistic value and the rejection point rule.

Using a *p*-value:

4. Collect the sample data and compute the value of the test statistic.
5. Use the summary box to find the *p*-value corresponding to the alternative hypothesis. Calculate the *p*-value by using the test statistic value.
6. Reject H_0 at level of significance α if the *p*-value is less than α.

7. Interpret your statistical results in managerial (real-world) terms and assess their practical importance.

Measuring the weight of evidence against the null hypothesis In general, the decision to take an action (for example, run the trash bag commercial) is sometimes based solely on whether there is sufficient sample evidence to reject a null hypothesis (H_0: $\mu = 50$) by setting α equal to a single, prespecified value (.05). In such situations, it is often also useful to know all of the information—called the **weight of evidence**—that the hypothesis test provides against the null hypothesis and in favor of the alternative hypothesis. For example, the trash bag manufacturer would almost certainly wish to know *how much* evidence there is that its new bag is stronger than its former bag. Furthermore, although we tested a hypothesis in the payment time case by setting α equal to a single, prespecified value, the hypothesis test did not immediately lead to a decision as to whether to take an action. In a situation such as this, when hypothesis testing is used more as a way to achieve evolving understanding of an industrial or scientific process, it is particularly important to know the weight of evidence against the null hypothesis and in favor of the alternative hypothesis.

The most informative way to measure the weight of evidence is to use the *p*-value. For every hypothesis test considered in this book we can interpret the *p*-value to be the **probability, computed assuming that the null hypothesis H_0 is true, of observing a value of the test statistic that is at least as extreme as the value actually computed from the sample data. The smaller the *p*-value is, the less likely are the sample results if the null hypothesis H_0 is true.** Therefore, the stronger is the evidence that H_0 is false and that the alternative hypothesis H_a is true. We can use the *p*-value to test H_0 versus H_a at level of significance α as follows:

We reject H_0 in favor of H_a at level of significance α if and only if the *p*-value is less than α.

Experience with hypothesis testing has resulted in statisticians making the following (somewhat subjective) conclusions:

Interpreting the Weight of Evidence against the Null Hypothesis

If the *p*-value for testing H_0 is less than

- .10, we have **some evidence** that H_0 is false.
- .05, we have **strong evidence** that H_0 is false.
- .01, we have **very strong evidence** that H_0 is false.
- .001, we have **extremely strong evidence** that H_0 is false.

For example, recall that the p-value for testing H_0: $\mu = 50$ versus H_a: $\mu > 50$ in the trash bag case is .0139. This p-value is less than .05 but not less than .01. Therefore, we have strong evidence, but not very strong evidence, that H_0: $\mu = 50$ is false and H_a: $\mu > 50$ is true. That is, we have strong evidence that the mean breaking strength of the new trash bag exceeds 50 pounds. As another example, the p-value for testing H_0: $\mu = 19.5$ versus H_a: $\mu < 19.5$ in the payment time case is .0038. This p-value is less than .01 but not less than .001. Therefore, we have very strong evidence, but not extremely strong evidence, that H_0: $\mu = 19.5$ is false and H_a: $\mu < 19.5$ is true. That is, we have very strong evidence that the new billing system has reduced the mean payment time to less than 19.5 days.

To conclude this section we note that, while many statisticians believe in assessing the weight of evidence, other statisticians do not. Those who do not might be called **decision theorists.** They contend that measuring the weight of evidence lets the results of a single sample bias our view too much as to the relative validity of H_0 and H_a. Decision theorists feel that, even in establishing your own personal belief, you should make a choice between H_0 and H_a by setting α equal to a single value that is prespecified before the sample is taken. Even for decision theorists, however, the p-value has the advantage of being the most efficient way to report the results of a hypothesis test to different decision makers who might use different prespecified values of α. In this book we will continue to assess the weight of evidence, and the decision theorist can regard the p-value as simply an efficient way to report the results of a hypothesis test.

Exercises for Section 8.2

CONCEPTS

8.14 Explain what a rejection point is, and explain how it is used to test a hypothesis.

8.15 Explain what a p-value is, and explain how it is used to test a hypothesis.

METHODS AND APPLICATIONS

In Exercises 8.16 through 8.22 we consider using a random sample of 100 measurements to test H_0: $\mu = 80$ versus H_a: $\mu > 80$.

8.16 If $\bar{x} = 85$ and $\sigma = 20$, calculate the value of the test statistic z.

8.17 Use a rejection point to test H_0 versus H_a by setting α equal to .10.

8.18 Use a rejection point to test H_0 versus H_a by setting α equal to .05.

8.19 Use a rejection point to test H_0 versus H_a by setting α equal to .01.

8.20 Use a rejection point to test H_0 versus H_a by setting α equal to .001.

8.21 Calculate the p-value and use it to test H_0 versus H_a at each of $\alpha = .10, .05, .01$, and .001.

8.22 How much evidence is there that H_0: $\mu = 80$ is false and H_a: $\mu > 80$ is true?

In Exercises 8.23 through 8.29 we consider using a random sample of 49 measurements to test H_0: $\mu = 20$ versus H_a: $\mu < 20$.

8.23 If $\bar{x} = 18$ and $\sigma = 7$, calculate the value of the test statistic z.

8.24 Use a rejection point to test H_0 versus H_a by setting α equal to .10.

8.25 Use a rejection point to test H_0 versus H_a by setting α equal to .05.

8.26 Use a rejection point to test H_0 versus H_a by setting α equal to .01.

8.27 Use a rejection point to test H_0 versus H_a by setting α equal to .001.

8.28 Calculate the p-value and use it to test H_0 versus H_a at each of $\alpha = .10, .05, .01$, and .001.

8.29 How much evidence is there that H_0: $\mu = 20$ is false and H_a: $\mu < 20$ is true?

8.30 THE VIDEO GAME SATISFACTION RATING CASE VideoGame

Recall that "very satisfied" customers give the XYZ-Box video game system a rating that is at least 42. Letting μ be the mean composite satisfaction rating for the XYZ-Box, we found in Exercise 8.8 that we should test H_0: $\mu \leq 42$ versus H_a: $\mu > 42$ in order to attempt to provide evidence supporting the claim that μ exceeds 42. The random sample of 65 satisfaction ratings yields a sample mean of $\bar{x} = 42.954$. Assuming that σ equals 2.64:

a Use rejection points to test H_0 versus H_a at each of $\alpha = .10, .05, .01$, and .001.

FIGURE 8.6 MINITAB Output of the Test of H_0: $\mu = 6$ versus H_a: $\mu < 6$ in the Bank Customer Waiting Time Case

```
Test of mu = 6 vs < 6.  The assumed standard deviation = 2.47
Variable    N     Mean    StDev  SE Mean      Z      P
WaitTime  100  5.46000  2.47546  0.24700  -2.19  0.014
```

Note: Because the test statistic z has a denominator $\sigma/\sqrt{n}$ that uses the population standard deviation σ, MINITAB makes the user specify an assumed value for σ.

b Calculate the p-value and use it to test H_0 versus H_a at each of $\alpha = .10, .05, .01$, and $.001$.

c How much evidence is there that the mean composite satisfaction rating exceeds 42?

8.31 THE BANK CUSTOMER WAITING TIME CASE WaitTime

Letting μ be the mean waiting time under the new system, we found in Exercise 8.9 that we should test H_0: $\mu \geq 6$ versus H_a: $\mu < 6$ in order to attempt to provide evidence that μ is less than six minutes. The random sample of 100 waiting times yields a sample mean of $\bar{x} = 5.46$ minutes. Moreover, Figure 8.6 gives the MINITAB output obtained when we use the waiting time data to test H_0: $\mu = 6$ versus H_a: $\mu < 6$. On this output the label "SE Mean," which stands for "the standard error of the mean," denotes the quantity $\sigma/\sqrt{n}$, and the label "Z" denotes the calculated test statistic. Assuming that σ equals 2.47:

a Use rejection points to test H_0 versus H_a at each of $\alpha = .10, .05, .01$, and $.001$.

b Calculate the p-value and verify that it equals .014, as shown on the MINITAB output. Use the p-value to test H_0 versus H_a at each of $\alpha = .10, .05, .01$, and $.001$.

c How much evidence is there that the new system has reduced the mean waiting time to below six minutes?

8.32 Again consider the audit delay situation of Exercise 7.11. Letting μ be the mean audit delay for all public owner-controlled companies in New Zealand, formulate the null hypothesis H_0 and the alternative hypothesis H_a that would be used to attempt to provide evidence supporting the claim that μ is less than 90 days. Suppose that a random sample of 100 public owner-controlled companies in New Zealand is found to give a mean audit delay of $\bar{x} = 86.6$ days. Assuming that σ equals 32.83, calculate the p-value for testing H_0 versus H_a and determine how much evidence there is that the mean audit delay for all public-owner controlled companies in New Zealand is less than 90 days.

8.33 THE CAR MILEAGE CASE GasMiles

Suppose the federal government proposes to give a substantial tax break to automakers producing midsize cars that get a mean mileage exceeding 31 mpg. Letting μ be a midsize car's mean mileage, the government will award the tax credit if an automaker is able to reject H_0: $\mu \leq 31$ in favor of H_a: $\mu > 31$ at the .05 level of significance. Recall that the sample of 49 mileages has mean $\bar{x} = 31.5531$. Assuming that σ equals .8, use these sample results and a rejection point to test H_0 versus H_a at the .05 level of significance. Will the automaker be awarded the tax break? Calculate the p-value. Would the tax break have been awarded if the federal government had set α equal to .01? Justify your answer.

8.34 Consider the Consolidated Power waste water situation and recall that the power plant will be shut down and corrective action will be taken on the cooling system if the null hypothesis H_0: $\mu \leq 60$ is rejected in favor of H_a: $\mu > 60$. Suppose Consolidated Power decides to use a level of significance of $\alpha = .05$, and suppose a random sample of 100 temperature readings is obtained. For each of the following sample results, determine whether the power plant should be shut down and the cooling system repaired. In each case, assume that $\sigma = 2$.

a $\bar{x} = 60.482$ **b** $\bar{x} = 60.262$ **c** $\bar{x} = 60.618$

8.35 THE DISK BRAKE CASE

Recall that the television network will permit National Motors to claim that the ZX-900 achieves a shorter mean stopping distance than a competitor if H_0: $\mu \geq 60$ can be rejected in favor of H_a: $\mu < 60$ by setting α equal to .05. If the stopping distances of a random sample of $n = 81$ ZX-900s have a mean of $\bar{x} = 57.8$ ft, will National Motors be allowed to run the commercial? Assume here that $\sigma = 6.02$. Calculate a 95 percent confidence interval for μ. Do the point estimate of μ and confidence interval for μ indicate that μ might be far enough below 60 feet to suggest that we have a practically important result?

8.3 z Tests about a Population Mean (σ Known): Two-Sided Alternatives

Testing a "not equal to" alternative hypothesis We next consider the camshaft case and testing a "not equal to" alternative hypothesis.

Step 1: State the null hypothesis H_0 and the alternative hypothesis H_a. The quality control analyst will test H_0: $\mu = 4.5$ versus H_a: $\mu \neq 4.5$. Here, μ is the mean of the population of the hardness depths of all camshafts produced on a particular day.

Step 2: Specify the level of significance α. The quality control analyst will set α equal to .05. To understand this choice of α, recall that the camshaft hardening process has not been meeting specifications. For this reason, the analyst has decided that it is very important to avoid committing a Type II error. That is, it is very important to avoid failing to reject H_0: $\mu = 4.5$ if μ for the day's production does differ from 4.5 mm. Setting α equal to .05 rather than .01 makes the probability of this Type II error smaller than it would be if α were set at .01.

Step 3: Select the test statistic. The quality control analyst will randomly select $n = 35$ camshafts from the day's production of camshafts and calculate the mean $\bar{x}$ of the hardness depths of these camshafts. Since the sample size is large, the Central Limit Theorem applies, and we will utilize the test statistic

$$z = \frac{\bar{x} - 4.5}{\sigma/\sqrt{n}}$$

A value of the test statistic that is greater than 0 results when $\bar{x}$ is greater than 4.5. This provides evidence to support rejecting H_0 in favor of H_a because the point estimate $\bar{x}$ indicates that μ might be greater than 4.5. Similarly, a value of the test statistic that is less than 0 results when $\bar{x}$ is less than 4.5. This also provides evidence to support rejecting H_0 in favor of H_a because the point estimate $\bar{x}$ indicates that μ might be less than 4.5.

Step 4: Determine a rejection point rule for deciding whether to reject H_0. To decide how different from zero (positive or negative) the test statistic must be in order to reject H_0 in favor of H_a by setting the probability of a Type I error equal to α, we do the following:

- Divide the probability of a Type I error, α, into two equal parts, and place the area $\alpha/2$ in the right-hand tail of the standard normal curve and the area $\alpha/2$ in the left-hand tail of the standard normal curve. Then use the normal table to find the rejection points $z_{\alpha/2}$ and $-z_{\alpha/2}$. Here $z_{\alpha/2}$ is the point on the horizontal axis under the standard normal curve that gives a right-hand tail area equal to $\alpha/2$, and $-z_{\alpha/2}$ is the point giving a left-hand tail area equal to $\alpha/2$.
- **Reject H_0: $\mu = 4.5$ in favor of H_a: $\mu \neq 4.5$ if and only if the test statistic z is greater than the rejection point $z_{\alpha/2}$ or less than the rejection point $-z_{\alpha/2}$.** Note that this is equivalent to saying that we should **reject H_0 if and only if the absolute value of the test statistic, $|z|$, is greater than the rejection point $z_{\alpha/2}$.** Because α equals .05, the rejection points are [see Figure 8.7(a)]

$$z_{\alpha/2} = z_{.05/2} = z_{.025} = 1.96 \quad \text{and} \quad -z_{\alpha/2} = -z_{.025} = -1.96$$

Step 5: Collect the sample data and compute the value of the test statistic. When the sample of $n = 35$ camshafts is randomly selected, the mean of the hardness depths of these camshafts is calculated to be $\bar{x} = 4.26$. Assuming that σ is known to equal .47, the value of the test statistic is

$$z = \frac{\bar{x} - 4.5}{\sigma/\sqrt{n}} = \frac{4.26 - 4.5}{.47/\sqrt{35}} = -3.02$$

Step 6: Decide whether to reject H_0 by using the test statistic value and the rejection point rule. Since the test statistic value $z = -3.02$ is less than $-z_{.025} = -1.96$ (or, equivalently, since $|z| = 3.02$ is greater than $z_{.025} = 1.96$), we can reject H_0: $\mu = 4.5$ in favor of H_a: $\mu \neq 4.5$ by setting α equal to .05.

Step 7: Interpret the statistical results in managerial (real-world) terms and assess their practical importance. We conclude (at an α of .05) that the mean camshaft hardness depth μ differs from 4.5 mm. To help determine whether the difference between μ and 4.5 mm is practically

FIGURE 8.7 Testing H_0: $\mu = 4.5$ versus H_a: $\mu \neq 4.5$ by Using Rejection Points and the p-Value

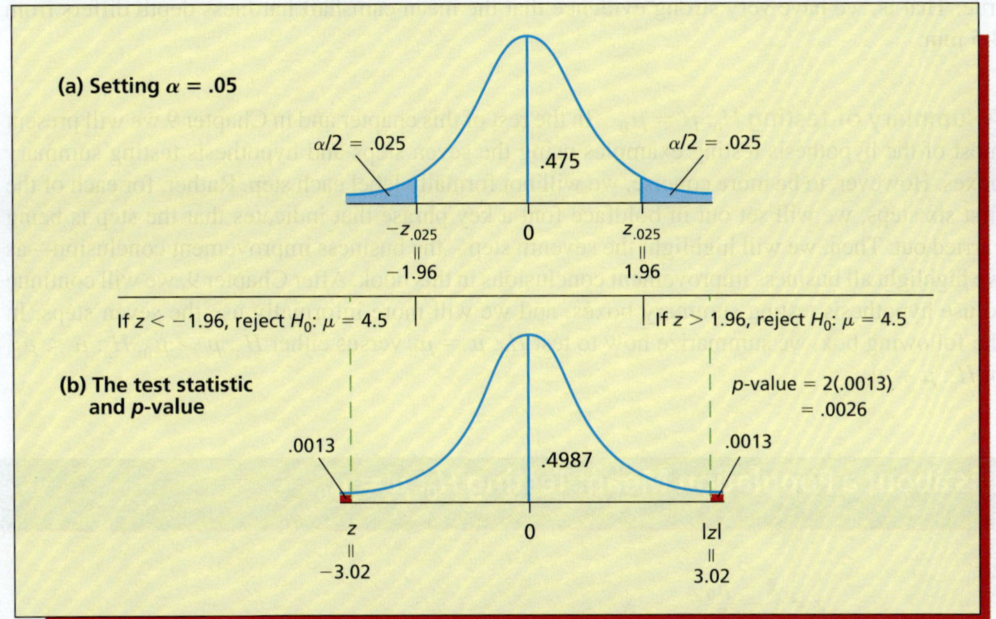

important, recall that specifications state that each individual camshaft hardness depth should be between 3 mm and 6 mm. Using $\bar{x} = 4.26$ and $\sigma = .47$, we estimate that 99.73 percent of all individual camshaft hardness depths are in the interval $[\bar{x} \pm 3\sigma] = [4.26 \pm 3(.47)] = [2.85, 5.67]$. This estimated tolerance interval says that, because of a somewhat small $\bar{x}$ of 4.26, we estimate that we are producing some hardness depths that are below the lower specification limit of 3 mm. This is a practically important result. Clearly, the automobile manufacturer must modify the camshaft heat treatment process so that it produces hardness depths with an average value nearer the 4.5 mm target. In Chapter 14 we will learn how to use **statistical process control** to do this. BI

A p-value for testing a "not equal to" alternative hypothesis To test H_0: $\mu = 4.5$ versus H_a: $\mu \neq 4.5$ in the camshaft case by using a p-value, we use the following steps 4, 5, and 6:

Step 4: Collect the sample data and compute the value of the test statistic. We have computed the value of the test statistic in the camshaft case to be $z = -3.02$.

Step 5: Calculate the p-value by using the test statistic value. Note from Figure 8.7(b) that the area under the standard normal curve to the right of $|z| = 3.02$ is .0013. Twice this area—that is, $2(.0013) = .0026$—is the p-value for testing H_0: $\mu = 4.5$ versus H_a: $\mu \neq 4.5$. To interpret the p-value as a probability, note that the symmetry of the standard normal curve implies that twice the area under the curve to the right of $|z| = 3.02$ equals the area under this curve to the right of 3.02 plus the area under the curve to the left of -3.02 [see Figure 8.7(b)]. Also, note that since both positive and negative test statistic values count against H_0: $\mu = 4.5$, a test statistic value that is either greater than or equal to 3.02 or less than or equal to -3.02 is at least as extreme as the observed test statistic value $z = -3.02$. It follows that the p-value of .0026 says that, if H_0: $\mu = 4.5$ is true, then only 26 in 10,000 of all possible test statistic values are at least as extreme as $z = -3.02$. That is, if we are to believe that H_0 is true, we must believe that we have observed a test statistic value that can be described as a 26 in 10,000 chance.

Step 6: Reject H_0 if the p-value is less than α. The quality control analyst has set α equal to .05. Since **the p-value of .0026 is less than the α of .05,** one-half the p-value $= .0013$ is less than $\alpha/2 = .025$. Comparing the two normal curves in Figures 8.7(a) and (b), we see that this implies that $|z| = 3.02$ is greater than the rejection point $z_{.025} = 1.96$. Therefore, **we can reject H_0 by setting α equal to .05.** In general, the absolute value of the test statistic z will be greater than the rejection point $z_{\alpha/2}$ if and only if the p-value is less than α. That is, we can reject H_0 in favor of H_a at level of significance α if and only if the p-value is less than α. For example, the

p-value of .0026 is less than an α of .01 but not less than an α of .001. It follows that we have very strong evidence, but not extremely strong evidence, that H_0: $\mu = 4.5$ is false and H_a: $\mu \neq 4.5$ is true. That is, we have very strong evidence that the mean camshaft hardness depth differs from 4.5 mm.

A summary of testing H_0: $\mu = \mu_0$ In the rest of this chapter and in Chapter 9 we will present most of the hypothesis testing examples using the seven steps and hypothesis testing summary boxes. However, to be more concise, we will not formally label each step. Rather, for each of the first six steps, we will set out in boldface font a key phrase that indicates that the step is being carried out. Then, we will highlight the seventh step—the business improvement conclusion—as we highlight all business improvement conclusions in this book. After Chapter 9, we will continue to use hypothesis testing summary boxes, and we will more informally use the seven steps. In the following box, we summarize how to test H_0: $\mu = \mu_0$ versus either H_a: $\mu > \mu_0$, H_a: $\mu < \mu_0$, or H_a: $\mu \neq \mu_0$:

Testing a Hypothesis about a Population Mean: Testing H_0: $\mu = \mu_0$ when σ Is Known

Define the test statistic

$$z = \frac{\bar{x} - \mu_0}{\sigma/\sqrt{n}}$$

and assume that the population sampled is normally distributed, or that the sample size n is large. We can test H_0: $\mu = \mu_0$ versus a particular alternative hypothesis at level of significance α by using the appropriate rejection point rule, or, equivalently, the corresponding p-value.

Alternative Hypothesis	Rejection Point Rule: Reject H_0 if	p-Value (reject H_0 if p-value $< \alpha$)
H_a: $\mu > \mu_0$	$z > z_\alpha$	The area under the standard normal curve to the right of z
H_a: $\mu < \mu_0$	$z < -z_\alpha$	The area under the standard normal curve to the left of z
H_a: $\mu \neq \mu_0$	$\lvert z\rvert > z_{\alpha/2}$—that is, $z > z_{\alpha/2}$ or $z < -z_{\alpha/2}$	Twice the area under the standard normal curve to the right of $\lvert z\rvert$

In many future examples, we will first use a rejection point rule to test the hypotheses under consideration at a fixed value of α, and we will then use a p-value to assess the weight of evidence against the null hypothesis. For example, suppose that airline flights from the New York/Boston corridor to midwestern metropolitan airports have routinely experienced delays for the last several years. Last year, these delayed flights were an average of 35 minutes late. A consumer advocacy group wishes to assess whether this average has changed. To do this, the consumer group will test a hypothesis about the mean delay time, μ, of New York/Boston flights that were delayed over the last two months. **The null hypothesis to be tested is H_0: $\mu = 35$, and the alternative hypothesis is H_a: $\mu \neq 35$.** If H_0 can be rejected in favor of H_a at the **.05 level of significance,** the consumer group will conclude that the mean delay time over the last two months differs from last year's 35 minute mean delay time. To perform the hypothesis test, we will randomly select $n = 36$ flights that were delayed over the last two months and use their delay times to calculate the value of the **test statistic z in the summary box.** Then, since H_a: $\mu \neq 35$ is of the form H_a: $\mu \neq \mu_0$, we will **reject H_0: $\mu = 35$ if the absolute value of z is greater than $z_{\alpha/2} = z_{.025} = 1.96$.** Suppose that when the sample is randomly selected, the mean of the delay times of the $n = 36$ flights is calculated to be $\bar{x} = 33$ minutes. Assuming that σ is known to equal 12, the **value of the test statistic** is

$$z = \frac{\bar{x} - 35}{\sigma/\sqrt{n}} = \frac{33 - 35}{12/\sqrt{36}} = -1$$

Since $|z| = 1$ is less than $z_{.025} = 1.96$, we cannot reject H_0: $\mu = 35$ in favor of H_a: $\mu \neq 35$. That is, we cannot conclude (at an α of .05) that the mean delay time over the last two months differs from last year's 35 minute mean delay time. The p-value for testing H_0: $\mu = 35$ versus H_a: $\mu \neq 35$ is twice the area under the standard normal curve to the right of $|z| = 1$. Using Table A.3 (page 824), we find that this p-value equals $2(.5 - .3413) = 2(.1587) = .3174$. Since the p-value of .3174 is greater than any reasonable value of α, we have little evidence against H_0: $\mu = 35$ and in favor of H_a: $\mu \neq 35$. That is, we have little evidence that the mean delay time over the last two months differs from last year's 35-minute mean delay time.

BI

Using confidence intervals to test hypotheses Confidence intervals can be used to test hypotheses. Specifically, it can be proven that we can reject H_0: $\mu = \mu_0$ in favor of H_a: $\mu \neq \mu_0$ by setting the probability of a Type I error equal to α if and only if the $100(1 - \alpha)$ percent confidence interval for μ does not contain μ_0. For example, consider the camshaft case and testing H_0: $\mu = 4.5$ versus H_a: $\mu \neq 4.5$ by setting α equal to .05. To do this, we use the mean $\bar{x} = 4.26$ of the sample of $n = 35$ camshafts to calculate the 95 percent confidence interval for μ to be

$$\left[\bar{x} \pm z_{\alpha/2}\frac{\sigma}{\sqrt{n}}\right] = \left[4.26 \pm 1.96\frac{.47}{\sqrt{35}}\right] = [4.10, 4.42]$$

Because this interval does not contain 4.5, we can reject H_0: $\mu = 4.5$ in favor of H_a: $\mu \neq 4.5$ by setting α equal to .05.

Whereas we can use the **two-sided** confidence intervals of this book to test "not equal to" alternative hypotheses, we must use **one-sided** confidence intervals to test "greater than" or "less than" alternative hypotheses. We will not study one-sided confidence intervals in this book. However, it should be emphasized that we do not need to use confidence intervals (one-sided or two-sided) to test hypotheses. We can test hypotheses by using test statistics and rejection points or p-values. Furthermore, confidence intervals can help us to evaluate practical importance after we have established statistical significance by using a hypothesis test. This is illustrated in the next subsection.

The effect of sample size If we can reject a null hypothesis by setting the probability of a Type I error equal to α, we say that we have **statistical significance at the α level.** Whether we have statistical significance at a given level often depends greatly on the size of the sample we have selected. To see this, recall that the trash bag manufacturer wishes to test H_0: $\mu \leq 50$ versus H_a: $\mu > 50$ and has obtained the sample mean $\bar{x} = 50.575$ based on a sample of $n = 40$ trash bags. Assuming that σ is known to equal 1.65, the p-value associated with

$$z = \frac{\bar{x} - 50}{\sigma/\sqrt{n}} = \frac{50.575 - 50}{1.65/\sqrt{40}} = \frac{.575}{.26089} = 2.20$$

is .0139. It follows that we have statistical significance at the .05 level but not at the .01 level. However, suppose that the manufacturer had obtained the same $\bar{x}$ based on a larger sample of $n = 100$ new bags. The test statistic value is then

$$z = \frac{\bar{x} - 50}{\sigma/\sqrt{n}} = \frac{50.575 - 50}{1.65/\sqrt{100}} = \frac{.575}{.165} = 3.48$$

and the p-value is the area under the standard normal curve to the right of $z = 3.48$. Looking at the normal table (see Table A.3, page 824), we see that the area to the right of 3.09 is $.5 - .4990 = .001$. Therefore, because 3.48 is greater than 3.09, the p-value is less than .001, and we have statistical significance at the .001 level. What has happened here is that the numerator of the test statistic has remained the same, while the larger sample size makes the denominator of the test statistic smaller. This results in a larger and more statistically significant value of the test statistic. Understand, however, that the highly statistically significant test statistic value means only that we have extremely strong evidence that μ is greater than 50. It does not necessarily mean that the difference between μ and 50 is large enough to be practically important to consumers who desire a substantially stronger trash bag. In fact, the sample mean $\bar{x} = 50.575$

indicates that μ is not much larger than 50. A difference of about .575 pounds would not represent a large increase in bag strength to potential buyers.

To conclude this section, suppose that the manufacturer further improves the trash bag by better sealing and thus strengthening the bottom of the bag. A random sample of $n = 40$ of the improved bags yields $\bar{x} = 58.213$. Assuming σ equals 1.65, the reader can verify that the value of the test statistic z for testing $H_0: \mu \leq 50$ versus $H_a: \mu > 50$ is 31.48. The associated p-value is less than .001, which implies that we have extremely strong evidence that μ exceeds 50 pounds. Furthermore, the point estimate of μ is $\bar{x} = 58.213$ and a 95 percent confidence interval for μ is $[58.213 \pm 1.96(1.65/\sqrt{40})] = [57.702, 58.724]$. The increase in mean breaking strength implied by these estimates would probably represent an important increase in strength to many consumers.

Exercises for Section 8.3

CONCEPTS

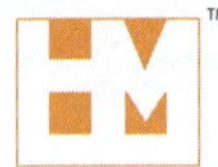

8.36 When carrying out a two-sided hypothesis test about a population mean:

a Give the rejection point rule for rejecting $H_0: \mu = \mu_0$.

b Explain how the p-value and α tell us whether $H_0: \mu = \mu_0$ should be rejected.

8.37 Discuss how we assess the practical importance of a statistically significant result.

METHODS AND APPLICATIONS

In Exercises 8.38 through 8.44 we consider using a random sample of $n = 81$ measurements to test $H_0: \mu = 40$ versus $H_a: \mu \neq 40$. If $\bar{x} = 34$ and $\sigma = 18$:

8.38 Calculate the value of the test statistic z.

8.39 Use rejection points to test H_0 versus H_a by setting α equal to .10.

8.40 Use rejection points to test H_0 versus H_a by setting α equal to .05.

8.41 Use rejection points to test H_0 versus H_a by setting α equal to .01.

8.42 Use rejection points to test H_0 versus H_a by setting α equal to .001.
Hint: $z_{.0005}$ can be shown to equal 3.29.

8.43 Calculate the p-value and use it to test H_0 versus H_a at each of $\alpha = .10, .05, .01$, and .001.

8.44 How much evidence is there that $H_0: \mu = 40$ is false and $H_a: \mu \neq 40$ is true?

8.45 Consider the automobile parts supplier in Exercise 8.10. Suppose that a problem-solving team will be assigned to rectify the process producing cylindrical engine parts if the null hypothesis H_0: $\mu = 3$ can be rejected in favor of $H_a: \mu \neq 3$ by setting α equal to .05.

a A sample of 40 parts yields a sample mean diameter of $\bar{x} = 3.006$ inches. Assuming σ equals .016, use rejection points and a p-value to test H_0 versus H_a by setting α equal to .05. Should the problem-solving team be assigned?

b Suppose that product specifications state that each and every part must have a diameter between 2.95 and 3.05 inches—that is, the specifications are 3" ± .05". Use the sample information given in part *a* to estimate an interval that contains almost all (99.73 percent) of the diameters. Compare this estimated interval with the specification limits. Are the specification limits being met, or are some diameters outside the specification limits? Explain.

8.46 Consider the Crown Bottling Company fill process in Exercise 8.11. Recall that the initial setup of the filler will be readjusted if the null hypothesis $H_0: \mu = 16$ is rejected in favor of $H_a: \mu \neq 16$. Suppose that Crown Bottling Company decides to use a level of significance of $\alpha = .01$, and suppose a random sample of 36 bottle fills is obtained from a test run of the filler. For each of the following sample results, determine whether the filler's initial setup should be readjusted. In each case, use a rejection point and a p-value, and assume that σ equals .1.

a $\bar{x} = 16.05$ **b** $\bar{x} = 15.96$ **c** $\bar{x} = 16.02$

8.47 Use the sample information in part (a) of Exercise 8.46 and a confidence interval to test $H_0: \mu = 16$ versus $H_a: \mu \neq 16$ by setting α equal to .05. What considerations would help you to decide whether the result has practical importance?

8.48 Recall from Exercise 7.12 that Bayus (1991) studied the mean numbers of auto dealers visited by early and late replacement buyers.

a Letting μ be the mean number of dealers visited by early replacement buyers, suppose that we wish to test $H_0: \mu = 4$ versus $H_a: \mu \neq 4$. A random sample of 800 early replacement buyers yields a mean number of dealers visited of $\bar{x} = 3.3$. Assuming σ equals .71, calculate the p-value and test H_0 versus H_a. Do we estimate that μ is less than 4 or greater than 4?

b Letting μ be the mean number of dealers visited by late replacement buyers, suppose that we wish to test H_0: $\mu = 4$ versus H_a: $\mu \neq 4$. A random sample of 500 late replacement buyers yields a mean number of dealers visited of $\bar{x} = 4.3$. Assuming σ equals .66, calculate the p-value and test H_0 versus H_a. Do we estimate that μ is less than 4 or greater than 4?

8.4 *t* Tests about a Population Mean (σ Unknown)

If we do not know σ (which is usually the case), we can base a hypothesis test about μ on the sampling distribution of

$$\frac{\bar{x} - \mu}{s/\sqrt{n}}$$

If the sampled population is normally distributed, then this sampling distribution is a ***t* distribution having $n - 1$ degrees of freedom.** This leads to the following results:

A *t* Test about a Population Mean: Testing H_0: $\mu = \mu_0$ when σ Is Unknown

Define the test statistic

$$t = \frac{\bar{x} - \mu_0}{s/\sqrt{n}}$$

and assume that the population sampled is normally distributed. We can test H_0: $\mu = \mu_0$ versus a particular alternative hypothesis at level of significance α by using the appropriate rejection point rule, or, equivalently, the corresponding p-value.

Alternative Hypothesis	Rejection Point Rule: Reject H_0 if	p-Value (reject H_0 if p-value $< \alpha$)
H_a: $\mu > \mu_0$	$t > t_\alpha$	The area under the t distribution curve to the right of t
H_a: $\mu < \mu_0$	$t < -t_\alpha$	The area under the t distribution curve to the left of t
H_a: $\mu \neq \mu_0$	$\|t\| > t_{\alpha/2}$—that is, $t > t_{\alpha/2}$ or $t < -t_{\alpha/2}$	Twice the area under the t distribution curve to the right of $\|t\|$

Here t_α, $t_{\alpha/2}$, and the p-values are based on $n - 1$ degrees of freedom.

Example 8.4

In 1991 the average interest rate charged by U.S. credit card issuers was 18.8 percent. Since that time, there has been a proliferation of new credit cards affiliated with retail stores, oil companies, alumni associations, professional sports teams, and so on. A financial officer wishes to study whether the increased competition in the credit card business has reduced interest rates. To do this, the officer will test a hypothesis about the current mean interest rate, μ, charged by U.S. credit card issuers. **The null hypothesis to be tested is H_0: $\mu = 18.8\%$, and the alternative hypothesis is H_a: $\mu < 18.8\%$.** If H_0 can be rejected in favor of H_a at the **.05 level of significance,** the officer will conclude that the current mean interest rate is less than the 18.8% mean interest rate charged in 1991. To perform the hypothesis test, suppose that we randomly select $n = 15$ credit cards and determine their current interest rates. The interest rates for the 15 sampled cards are given in Table 8.3. A stem-and-leaf display and MINITAB box plot are given in Figure 8.8. The stem-and-leaf display looks reasonably mound-shaped, and both the stem-and-leaf display and the box plot look reasonably symmetrical. It follows that it is appropriate to calculate the value of the **test statistic *t* in the summary box.** Furthermore, since H_a: $\mu < 18.8\%$ is of the form H_a: $\mu < \mu_0$, we should **reject H_0: $\mu = 18.8\%$ if the value of *t* is less than the rejection point $-t_\alpha = -t_{.05} = -1.761$.** Here, $-t_{.05} = -1.761$ is based on $n - 1 = 15 - 1 = 14$ degrees of freedom and this rejection point is illustrated in Figure 8.9(a). The mean and the standard deviation of the $n = 15$ interest rates in Table 8.3 are $\bar{x} = 16.827$ and $s = 1.538$. This implies that the **value of the test statistic** is

$$t = \frac{\bar{x} - 18.8}{s/\sqrt{n}} = \frac{16.827 - 18.8}{1.538/\sqrt{15}} = -4.97$$

TABLE 8.3 Interest Rates Charged by 15 Randomly Selected Credit Cards CreditCd

15.6%	15.3%	19.2%
17.8	16.4	15.8
14.6	18.4	18.1
17.3	17.6	16.6
18.7	14.0	17.0

FIGURE 8.8 Stem-and-Leaf Display and Box Plot of the Interest Rates

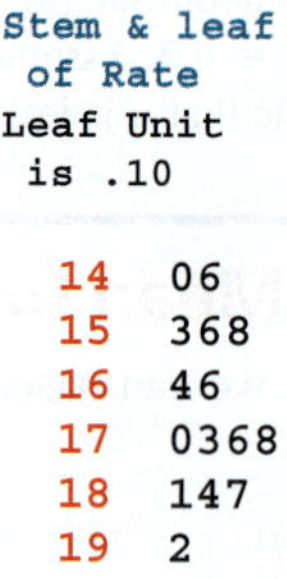

Stem & leaf
of Rate
Leaf Unit
is .10
14 06
15 368
16 46
17 0368
18 147
19 2

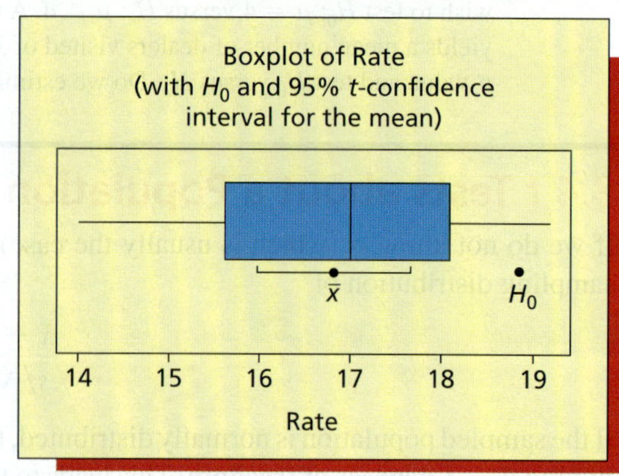

FIGURE 8.9 Testing H_0: μ = 18.8% versus H_a: μ < 18.8% by Using a Rejection Point and a p-Value

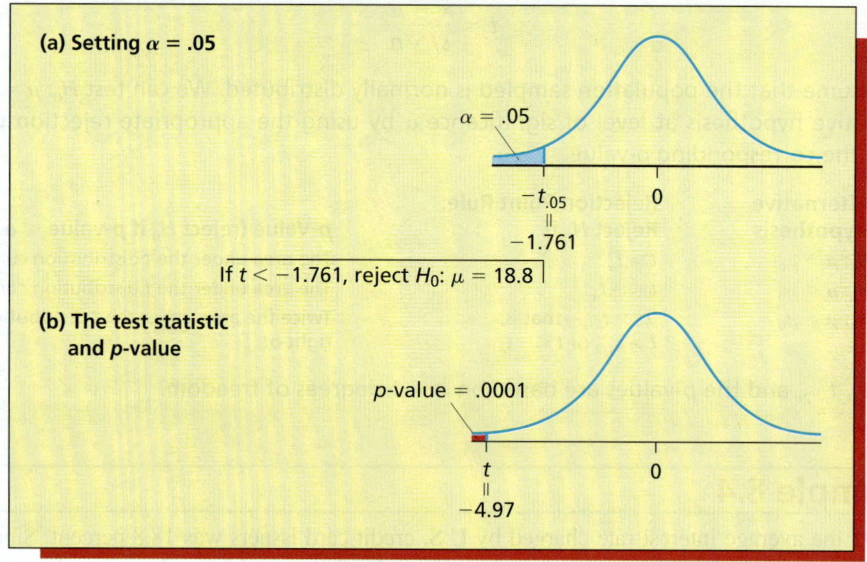

Since $t = -4.97$ is less than $-t_{.05} = -1.761$, we reject H_0: μ = 18.8% in favor of H_a: μ < 18.8%. That is, we conclude (at an α of .05) that the current mean credit card interest rate is lower than 18.8%, the mean interest rate in 1991. Furthermore, the sample mean $\bar{x}$ = 16.827 says that we estimate the mean interest rate is 18.8% − 16.827% = 1.973% lower than it was in 1991.

The p-value for testing H_0: μ = 18.8% versus H_a: μ < 18.8% is the area under the curve of the t distribution having 14 degrees of freedom to the left of $t = -4.97$. Tables of t points (such as Table A.4, page 825) are not complete enough to give such areas for most t statistic values, so we use computer software packages to calculate p-values that are based on the t distribution. For example, the MINITAB output in Figure 8.10(a) and the MegaStat output in Figure 8.11 tell us that the p-value for testing H_0: μ = 18.8% versus H_a: μ < 18.8% is .0001. Notice that both MINITAB and MegaStat round p-values to three or four decimal places. The Excel output in Figure 8.10(b) gives the slightly more accurate value of 0.000103 for the p-value. Because this p-value is less than .05, .01, and .001, we can reject H_0 at the .05, .01, and .001 levels of significance. Also note that the p-value of .0001 on the MegaStat output is shaded dark yellow. This indicates that we can reject H_0 at the .01 level of significance (light yellow shading would indicate significance at the .05 level, but not at the .01 level). As a probability, the p-value of .0001 says that if we are to believe that H_0: μ = 18.8% is true, we must believe that we have observed

FIGURE 8.10 The MINITAB and Excel Outputs for Testing H_0: $\mu = 18.8\%$ versus H_a: $\mu < 18.8\%$

(a) The MINITAB output

```
Test of mu = 18.8 vs < 18.8

Variable     N      Mean    StDev    SE Mean       T       P
Rate        15   16.8267   1.5378     0.3971   -4.97   0.000
```

(b) The Excel output

t-statistic
−4.97
p-value
0.000103

FIGURE 8.11 The MegaStat Output for Testing H_0: $\mu = 18.8\%$ versus H_a: $\mu < 18.8\%$

Hypothesis Test: Mean vs. Hypothesized Value

18.8000 hypothesized value	1.5378 std. dev.	15 n	−4.97 t
16.8267 mean Rate	0.3971 std. error	14 df	.0001 p-value (one-tailed, lower)

= Significant at .05 level   = Significant at .01 level

a t statistic value ($t = -4.97$) that can be described as a 1 in 10,000 chance. In summary, we have extremely strong evidence that H_0: $\mu = 18.8\%$ is false and H_a: $\mu < 18.8\%$ is true. That is, we have extremely strong evidence that the current mean credit card interest rate is less than 18.8%.

Recall that in three cases discussed in Sections 8.2 and 8.3 we tested hypotheses by assuming that the population standard deviation σ is known and by using z tests. If σ is actually not known in these cases (which would probably be true), we should test the hypotheses under consideration by using t tests. Furthermore, recall that in each case the sample size is large (at least 30). In general, it can be shown that if the sample size is large, the t test is approximately valid even if the sampled population is not normally distributed (or mound shaped). Therefore, consider the camshaft case and testing **H_0: $\mu = 4.5$ versus H_a: $\mu \neq 4.5$ at the .05 level of significance.** To perform the hypothesis test, assume that we will randomly select $n = 35$ camshafts and use their hardness depths to calculate the value of the **test statistic t in the summary box.** Then, since the alternative hypothesis H_a: $\mu \neq 4.5$ is of the form H_a: $\mu \neq \mu_0$, we will **reject H_0: $\mu = 4.5$ if the absolute value of t is greater than $t_{\alpha/2} = t_{.025} = 2.032$ (based on $n - 1 = 34$ degrees of freedom).** Suppose that when the sample is randomly selected, the mean and the standard deviation of the hardness depths of the $n = 35$ camshafts are calculated to be $\bar{x} = 4.26$ and $s = .49$. The **value of the test statistic** is

$$t = \frac{\bar{x} - 4.5}{s/\sqrt{n}} = \frac{4.26 - 4.5}{.49/\sqrt{35}} = -2.8977$$

Since $|t| = 2.8977$ is greater than $t_{.025} = 2.032$, we can reject H_0: $\mu = 4.5$ by setting α equal to .05. The p-value for the hypothesis test is twice the area under the t distribution curve having 34 degrees of freedom to the right of $|t| = 2.8977$. Using a computer, we find that this p-value is .0066.

As another example, consider the trash bag case and note that the sample of $n = 40$ trash bag breaking strengths in Table 1.10 (page 19) has mean $\bar{x} = 50.575$ and standard deviation $s = 1.6438$. The p-value for testing H_0: $\mu = 50$ versus H_a: $\mu > 50$ is the area under the t distribution curve having $n - 1 = 39$ degrees of freedom to the right of $t = (50.575 - 50)/(1.6438/\sqrt{40}) = 2.2123$. Using a computer, we find that this p-value is .0164. As a third example, consider the payment time case and note that the sample of $n = 65$ payment times in Table 2.2 (page 46) has mean $\bar{x} = 18.1077$ and standard deviation $s = 3.9612$. The p-value for testing H_0: $\mu = 19.5$ versus H_a: $\mu < 19.5$ is the area under the t distribution curve having $n - 1 = 64$ degrees of freedom to the left of $t = (18.1077 - 19.5)/(3.9612/\sqrt{65}) = -2.8338$. Using a computer, we find that this p-value is .0031. In summary, the p-values obtained for the three cases using t tests are .0066, .0164, and .0031. These p-values do not differ by much from the corresponding p-values using z tests—.0026, .0139, and .0038 (see Sections 8.2 and 8.3). Therefore, the practical conclusions reached in Sections 8.2 and 8.3 using z tests would also be reached using the t tests discussed here. Finally, if the sample size is small (<30) and the sampled population is not mound-shaped, or if the sampled population is highly skewed, then it might be appropriate to use a **nonparametric test about the population median.** Such a test is discussed in Chapter 15.

Exercises for Section 8.4

CONCEPTS

8.49 What assumptions must be met in order to carry out the test about a population mean based on the t distribution?

8.50 How do we decide whether to use a z test or a t test when testing a hypothesis about a population mean?

METHODS AND APPLICATIONS

8.51 Suppose that a random sample of 16 measurements from a normally distributed population gives a sample mean of $\bar{x} = 13.5$ and a sample standard deviation of $s = 6$. Use rejection points to test $H_0: \mu \leq 10$ versus $H_a: \mu > 10$ using levels of significance $\alpha = .10$, $\alpha = .05$, $\alpha = .01$, and $\alpha = .001$. What do you conclude at each value of α?

8.52 Suppose that a random sample of nine measurements from a normally distributed population gives a sample mean of $\bar{x} = 2.57$ and a sample standard deviation of $s = .3$. Use rejection points to test $H_0: \mu = 3$ versus $H_a: \mu \neq 3$ using levels of significance $\alpha = .10$, $\alpha = .05$, $\alpha = .01$, and $\alpha = .001$. What do you conclude at each value of α?

8.53 The *bad debt ratio* for a financial institution is defined to be the dollar value of loans defaulted divided by the total dollar value of all loans made. Suppose that a random sample of seven Ohio banks is selected and that the bad debt ratios (written as percentages) for these banks are 7%, 4%, 6%, 7%, 5%, 4%, and 9%. BadDebt

a Banking officials claim that the mean bad debt ratio for all Midwestern banks is 3.5 percent and that the mean bad debt ratio for Ohio banks is higher. Set up the null and alternative hypotheses needed to attempt to provide evidence supporting the claim that the mean bad debt ratio for Ohio banks exceeds 3.5 percent.

b Assuming that bad debt ratios for Ohio banks are approximately normally distributed, use rejection points and the given sample information to test the hypotheses you set up in part *a* by setting α equal to .10, .05, .01, and .001. How much evidence is there that the mean bad debt ratio for Ohio banks exceeds 3.5 percent? What does this say about the banking official's claim?

c Are you qualified to decide whether we have a practically important result? Who would be? How might practical importance be defined in this situation?

8.54 Consider Exercise 8.53. Below we give the MINITAB output of the test statistic and p-value for testing $H_0: \mu = 3.5$ versus $H_a: \mu > 3.5$. BadDebt

```
Test of mu = 3.5 vs > 3.5
Variable   N    Mean     StDev    SE Mean      T      P
d-ratio    7   6.000   1.82574    0.69007   3.62  0.006
```

a Use the p-value to test H_0 versus H_a by setting α equal to .10, .05, .01, and .001. What do you conclude at each value of α?

b How much evidence is there that the mean bad debt ratio for Ohio banks exceeds 3.5 percent?

8.55 In the book *Business Research Methods,* Donald R. Cooper and C. William Emory (1995) discuss using hypothesis testing to study receivables outstanding. To quote Cooper and Emory:

> . . . the controller of a large retail chain may be concerned about a possible slowdown in payments by the company's customers. She measures the rate of payment in terms of the average number of days receivables outstanding. Generally, the company has maintained an average of about 50 days with a standard deviation of 10 days. Since it would be too expensive to analyze all of a company's receivables frequently, we normally resort to sampling.

a Set up the null and alternative hypotheses needed to attempt to show that there has been a slowdown in payments by the company's customers (there has been a slowdown if the average days outstanding exceeds 50).

b Assume approximate normality and suppose that a random sample of 25 accounts gives an average days outstanding of $\bar{x} = 54$ with a standard deviation of $s = 8$. Use rejection points to test the hypotheses you set up in part *a* at levels of significance $\alpha = .10$, $\alpha = .05$, $\alpha = .01$, and $\alpha = .001$. How much evidence is there of a slowdown in payments?

c Are you qualified to decide whether this result has practical importance? Who would be?

8.56 Consider a chemical company that wishes to determine whether a new catalyst, catalyst XA-100, changes the mean hourly yield of its chemical process from the historical process mean of 750 pounds per hour. When five trial runs are made using the new catalyst, the following yields (in pounds per hour) are recorded: 801, 814, 784, 836, and 820. ChemYield

a Let μ be the mean of all possible yields using the new catalyst. Assuming that chemical yields are approximately normally distributed, the MegaStat output of the test statistic and p-value, and the Excel output of the p-value, for testing H_0: $\mu = 750$ versus H_a: $\mu \neq 750$ are as follows:

Hypothesis Test: Mean vs. Hypothesized Value

750.000 hypothesized value	19.647 std. dev.	5 n	6.94 t
811.000 mean Hourly Yield	8.786 std. error	4 df	.0023 p-value (two-tailed)

t-statistic
6.942585
p-value
0.002261

(Here we had Excel calculate twice the area under the t distribution curve having 4 degrees of freedom to the right of 6.942585.) Use the sample data to verify that the values of $\bar{x}$, s, and t given on the output are correct.

b Use the test statistic and rejection points to test H_0 versus H_a by setting α equal to .10, .05, .01, and .001.

8.57 Consider Exercise 8.56. Use the p-value to test H_0: $\mu = 750$ versus H_a: $\mu \neq 750$ by setting α equal to .10, .05, .01, and .001. How much evidence is there that the new catalyst changes the mean hourly yield?

8.58 Whole Foods is an all-natural grocery chain that has 50,000 square foot stores, up from the industry average of 34,000 square feet. Sales per square foot of supermarkets average just under \$400 per square foot, as reported by *USA Today* in an article on "A whole new ballgame in grocery shopping." Suppose that sales per square foot in the most recent fiscal year are recorded for a random sample of 10 Whole Foods supermarkets. The data (sales dollars per square foot) are as follows: 854, 858, 801, 892, 849, 807, 894, 863, 829, 815. Let μ denote the mean sales dollars per square foot for all Whole Foods supermarkets during the most recent fiscal year, and note that the historical mean sales dollars per square foot for Whole Foods supermarkets in previous years has been \$800. Below we present the MINITAB output obtained by using the sample data to test H_0: $\mu = 800$ versus H_a: $\mu > 800$. WholeFoods

```
Test of mu = 800 vs > 800

Variable    N     Mean    StDev  SE Mean     T      P
SqFtSales  10  846.200   32.866   10.393  4.45  0.001
```

a Use the p-value to test H_0 versus H_a by setting α equal to .10, .05, .01, and .001.

b How much evidence is there that μ exceeds \$800?

8.59 Consider Exercise 8.58. Do you think that the difference between the sample mean of \$846.20 and the historical average of \$800 has practical importance?

8.60 THE VIDEO GAME SATISFACTION RATING CASE VideoGame

The mean and the standard deviation of the sample of $n = 65$ customer satisfaction ratings in Table 1.5 are $\bar{x} = 42.95$ and $s = 2.6424$. Let μ denote the mean of all possible customer satisfaction ratings for the XYZ-Box video game system, and consider testing H_0: $\mu = 42$ versus H_a: $\mu > 42$. Perform a t test of these hypotheses by setting α equal to .05 and using a rejection point. Also, interpret the p-value of .0025 for the hypothesis test.

8.61 THE BANK CUSTOMER WAITING TIME CASE WaitTime

The mean and the standard deviation of the sample of 100 bank customer waiting times in Table 1.6 are $\bar{x} = 5.46$ and $s = 2.475$. Let μ denote the mean of all possible bank customer waiting times using the new system and consider testing H_0: $\mu = 6$ versus H_a: $\mu < 6$. Perform a t test of these hypotheses by setting α equal to .05 and using a rejection point. Also, interpret the p-value of .0158 for the hypothesis test.

8.62 THE CAR MILEAGE CASE GasMiles

The mean and the standard deviation of the sample of 49 mileages in Table 2.1 are $\bar{x} = 31.5531$ and $s = .7992$. Let μ denote the population mean mileage of the new midsize car and consider testing H_0: $\mu = 31$ versus H_a: $\mu > 31$. Perform a t test of these hypotheses by setting α equal to .05 and using a rejection point. Also, interpret the p-value of .00000683 for the hypothesis test.

8.5 z Tests about a Population Proportion

In this section we study a large sample hypothesis test about a population proportion (that is, about the fraction of population units that possess some qualitative characteristic). We begin with an example.

Example 8.5 The Cheese Spread Case

Recall that the soft cheese spread producer has decided that replacing the current spout with the new spout is profitable only if p, the true proportion of all current purchasers who would stop buying the cheese spread if the new spout were used, is less than .10. The producer feels that it is unwise to change the spout unless it has very strong evidence that p is less than .10. Therefore, the spout will be changed if and only if the null hypothesis H_0: $p = .10$ can be rejected in favor of the alternative hypothesis H_a: $p < .10$ at the .01 level of significance.

In order to see how to test this kind of hypothesis, remember that when n is large, the sampling distribution of

$$\frac{\hat{p} - p}{\sqrt{\frac{p(1-p)}{n}}}$$

is approximately a standard normal distribution. Let p_0 denote a specified value between 0 and 1 (its exact value will depend on the problem), and consider testing the null hypothesis H_0: $p = p_0$. We then have the following result:

A Large Sample Test about a Population Proportion: Testing H_0: $p = p_0$

Define the test statistic

$$z = \frac{\hat{p} - p_0}{\sqrt{\frac{p_0(1-p_0)}{n}}}$$

If the sample size n is large, we can test H_0: $p = p_0$ versus a particular alternative hypothesis at level of significance α by using the appropriate rejection point rule, or, equivalently, the corresponding p-value.

Alternative Hypothesis	Rejection Point Rule: Reject H_0 if	p-Value (reject H_0 if p-value $< \alpha$)
H_a: $p > p_0$	$z > z_\alpha$	The area under the standard normal curve to the right of z
H_a: $p < p_0$	$z < -z_\alpha$	The area under the standard normal curve to the left of z
H_a: $p \neq p_0$	$\lvert z\rvert > z_{\alpha/2}$—that is, $z > z_{\alpha/2}$ or $z < -z_{\alpha/2}$	Twice the area under the standard normal curve to the right of $\lvert z\rvert$

Here n should be considered large if both np_0 and $n(1 - p_0)$ are at least 5.[2]

Example 8.6 The Cheese Spread Case

We have seen that the cheese spread producer wishes to test H_0: $p = .10$ versus H_a: $p < .10$, where p is the proportion of all current purchasers who would stop buying the cheese spread if the new spout were used. The producer will use the new spout if H_0 can be rejected in favor of H_a at the **.01 level of significance.** To perform the hypothesis test, we will randomly select n = 1,000 current purchasers of the cheese spread, find the proportion ($\hat{p}$) of these purchasers who would stop buying the cheese spread if the new spout were used, and calculate the value of the **test statistic z in the summary box.** Then, since the alternative hypothesis H_a: $p < .10$ is of the

[2]Some statisticians suggest using the more conservative rule that both np_0 and $n(1 - p_0)$ must be at least 10.

form $H_a: p < p_0$, we will **reject $H_0: p = .10$ if the value of z is less than $-z_\alpha = -z_{.01} = -2.33$.** (Note that using this procedure is valid because $np_0 = 1{,}000(.10) = 100$ and $n(1 - p_0) = 1{,}000(1 - .10) = 900$ are both at least 5.) Suppose that when the sample is randomly selected, we find that 63 of the 1,000 current purchasers say they would stop buying the cheese spread if the new spout were used. Since $\hat{p} = 63/1{,}000 = .063$, the **value of the test statistic** is

$$z = \frac{\hat{p} - p_0}{\sqrt{\dfrac{p_0(1 - p_0)}{n}}} = \frac{.063 - .10}{\sqrt{\dfrac{.10(1 - .10)}{1{,}000}}} = -3.90$$

Because $z = -3.90$ is less than $-z_{.01} = -2.33$, we reject $H_0: p = .10$ in favor of $H_a: p < .10$. That is, we conclude (at an α of .01) that the proportion of current purchasers who would stop buying the cheese spread if the new spout were used is less than .10. It follows that the company will use the new spout. Furthermore, the point estimate $\hat{p} = .063$ says we estimate that 6.3 percent of all current customers would stop buying the cheese spread if the new spout were used.

Although the cheese spread producer has made its decision by setting α equal to a single, prechosen value (.01), it would probably also wish to know the weight of evidence against H_0 and in favor of H_a. The p-value is the area under the standard normal curve to the left of $z = -3.90$. Since Table A.3 (page 824) tells us that the area to the left of -3.09 is .001, and since -3.90 is less than -3.09, the p-value is less than .001. Therefore, we have extremely strong evidence that $H_a: p < .10$ is true. That is, we have extremely strong evidence that fewer than 10 percent of current purchasers would stop buying the cheese spread if the new spout were used.

Example 8.7

Recent medical research has sought to develop drugs that lessen the severity and duration of viral infections. Virol, a relatively new drug, has been shown to provide relief for 70 percent of all patients suffering from viral upper respiratory infections. A major drug company is developing a competing drug called Phantol. The drug company wishes to investigate whether Phantol is more effective than Virol. To do this, the drug company will test a hypothesis about the true proportion, p, of all patients whose symptoms would be relieved by Phantol. **The null hypothesis to be tested is $H_0: p = .70$, and the alternative hypothesis is $H_a: p > .70$.** If H_0 can be rejected in favor of H_a at the **.05 level of significance,** the drug company will conclude that Phantol helps more than the 70 percent of patients helped by Virol. To perform the hypothesis test, we will randomly select $n = 300$ patients having viral upper respiratory infections, find the proportion ($\hat{p}$) of these patients whose symptoms are relieved by Phantol and calculate the value of the **test statistic z in the summary box.** Then, since the alternative hypothesis $H_a: p > .70$ is of the form $H_a: p > p_0$, we will **reject $H_0: p = .70$ if the value of z is greater than $z_\alpha = z_{.05} = 1.645$.** (Note that using this procedure is valid because $np_0 = 300(.70) = 210$ and $n(1 - p_0) = 300(1 - .70) = 90$ are both at least 5.) Suppose that when the sample is randomly selected, we find that Phantol provides relief for 231 of the 300 patients. Since $\hat{p} = 231/300 = .77$, the **value of the test statistic** is

$$z = \frac{\hat{p} - p_0}{\sqrt{\dfrac{p_0(1 - p_0)}{n}}} = \frac{.77 - .70}{\sqrt{\dfrac{(.70)(1 - .70)}{300}}} = 2.65$$

Because $z = 2.65$ is greater than $z_{.05} = 1.645$, we reject $H_0: p = .70$ in favor of $H_a: p > .70$. That is, we conclude (at an α of .05) that Phantol will provide relief for more than 70 percent of all patients suffering from viral upper respiratory infections. More specifically, the point estimate $\hat{p} = .77$ of p says that we estimate that Phantol will provide relief for 77 percent of all such patients. Comparing this estimate to the 70 percent of patients whose symptoms are relieved by Virol, we conclude that Phantol is somewhat more effective.

The p-value for testing $H_0: p = .70$ versus $H_a: p > .70$ is the area under the standard normal curve to the right of $z = 2.65$. This p-value is $(.5 - .4960) = .004$ (see Table A.3, page 824), and it provides very strong evidence against $H_0: p = .70$ and in favor of $H_a: p > .70$. That is, we have very strong evidence that Phantol will provide relief for more than 70 percent of all patients suffering from viral upper respiratory infections.

Example 8.8 The Electronic Article Surveillance Case

Suppose that a company selling electronic article surveillance devices claims that the proportion, p, of all consumers who would say they would never shop in a store again if the store subjected them to a false alarm is no more than .05. A store considering installing such a device is concerned that p is greater than .05 and wishes to test $\boldsymbol{H_0: p = .05}$ **versus** $\boldsymbol{H_a: p > .05}$. To perform the hypothesis test, the store will calculate a p-value and use it to measure the **weight of evidence** against H_0 and in favor of H_a. Recall that 40 out of 250 consumers in a systematic sample said they would never shop in a store again if the store subjected them to a false alarm. Therefore, the sample proportion of lost consumers is $\hat{p} = 40/250 = .16$. Since $np_0 = 250(.05) = 12.5$ and $n(1 - p_0) = 250(1 - .05) = 237.5$ are both at least 5, we can use the **test statistic z in the summary box.** The **value of the test statistic** is

$$z = \frac{\hat{p} - p_0}{\sqrt{\frac{p_0(1 - p_0)}{n}}} = \frac{.16 - .05}{\sqrt{\frac{(.05)(.95)}{250}}} = 7.98$$

Noting that $H_a: p > .05$ is of the form $H_a: p > p_0$, **the p-value is the area under the standard normal curve to the right of $z = 7.98$. The normal table tells us that the area under the standard normal curve to the right of 3.09 is .001. Therefore, the p-value is less than .001** and provides **extremely strong evidence against $H_0: p = .05$ and in favor of $H_a: p > .05$.** That is, we have extremely strong evidence that the proportion of all consumers who say they would never shop in a store again if the store subjected them to a false alarm is greater than .05. Furthermore, the point estimate $\hat{p} = .16$ says we estimate that the percentage of such consumers is 11 percent more than the 5 percent maximum claimed by the company selling the electronic article surveillance devices. A 95 percent confidence interval for p is

BI

$$\left[\hat{p} \pm z_{.025}\sqrt{\frac{\hat{p}(1 - \hat{p})}{n}}\right] = \left[.16 \pm 1.96\sqrt{\frac{(.16)(.84)}{250}}\right] = [.1146, .2054]$$

This interval says we are 95 percent confident that the percentage of consumers who would say they would never shop in a store again if the store subjected them to a false alarm is between 6.46 percent and 15.54 percent more than the 5 percent maximum claimed by the company selling the electronic article surveillance devices. The rather large increases over the claimed 5 percent maximum implied by the point estimate and the confidence interval would mean substantially more lost customers and thus are practically important. Figure 8.12 gives the MegaStat output for testing H_0: $p = .05$ versus H_a: $p > .05$. Note that this output includes a 95 percent confidence interval for p. Also notice that MegaStat expresses the p-value for this test in scientific notation. In general, when a p-value is less than .0001, MegaStat (and also Excel) express the p-value in scientific notation. Here the p-value of 7.77 E-16 says that we must move the decimal point 16 places to the left to obtain the decimal equivalent. That is, the p-value is .000000000000000777.

FIGURE 8.12 The MegaStat Output for Testing H_0: $p = .05$ versus H_a: $p > .05$

Hypothesis test for proportion vs hypothesized value

Observed	*Hypothesized*		
0.16	0.05 p (as decimal)	0.0138 std. error	0.1146 confidence interval 95.% lower
40/250	13/250 p (as fraction)	7.98 z	0.2054 confidence interval 95.% upper
40.	12.5 X	7.77E-16 p-value	0.0454 half-width
250	250 n	(one-tailed upper)	

Exercises for Section 8.5

CONCEPTS

8.63 If we test a hypothesis to provide evidence supporting the claim that a majority of voters prefer a political candidate, explain the difference between p and $\hat{p}$.

8.64 If we test a hypothesis to provide evidence supporting the claim that more than 30 percent of all consumers prefer a particular brand of beer, explain the difference between p and $\hat{p}$.

8.65 If we test a hypothesis to provide evidence supporting the claim that fewer than 5 percent of the units produced by a process are defective, explain the difference between p and $\hat{p}$.

8.66 What condition must be satisfied in order to appropriately use the methods of this section?

METHODS AND APPLICATIONS

8.67 For each of the following sample sizes and hypothesized values of the population proportion p, determine whether the sample size is large enough to use the large sample test about p given in this section:

a $n = 400$ and $p_0 = .5$.
b $n = 100$ and $p_0 = .01$.
c $n = 10{,}000$ and $p_0 = .01$.
d $n = 100$ and $p_0 = .2$.
e $n = 256$ and $p_0 = .7$.
f $n = 200$ and $p_0 = .98$.
g $n = 1{,}000$ and $p_0 = .98$.
h $n = 25$ and $p_0 = .4$.

8.68 Suppose we wish to test H_0: $p \leq .8$ versus H_a: $p > .8$ and that a random sample of $n = 400$ gives a sample proportion $\hat{p} = .86$.

a Test H_0 versus H_a at the .05 level of significance by using a rejection point. What do you conclude?
b Find the p-value for this test.
c Use the p-value to test H_0 versus H_a by setting α equal to .10, .05, .01, and .001. What do you conclude at each value of α?

8.69 Suppose we test H_0: $p = .3$ versus H_a: $p \neq .3$ and that a random sample of $n = 100$ gives a sample proportion $\hat{p} = .20$.

a Test H_0 versus H_a at the .01 level of significance by using a rejection point. What do you conclude?
b Find the p-value for this test.
c Use the p-value to test H_0 versus H_a by setting α equal to .10, .05, .01, and .001. What do you conclude at each value of α?

8.70 Suppose we are testing H_0: $p \leq .5$ versus H_a: $p > .5$, where p is the proportion of all beer drinkers who have tried at least one brand of "cold-filtered beer." If a random sample of 500 beer drinkers has been taken and if $\hat{p}$ equals .57, how many beer drinkers in the sample have tried at least one brand of "cold-filtered beer"?

8.71 **THE MARKETING ETHICS CASE: CONFLICT OF INTEREST**

Recall that a conflict of interest scenario was presented to a sample of 205 marketing researchers and that 111 of these researchers disapproved of the actions taken.

a Let p be the proportion of all marketing researchers who disapprove of the actions taken in the conflict of interest scenario. Set up the null and alternative hypotheses needed to attempt to provide evidence supporting the claim that a majority (more than 50 percent) of all marketing researchers disapprove of the actions taken.
b Assuming that the sample of 205 marketing researchers has been randomly selected, use rejection points and the previously given sample information to test the hypotheses you set up in part *a* at the .10, .05, .01, and .001 levels of significance. How much evidence is there that a majority of all marketing researchers disapprove of the actions taken?
c Suppose a random sample of 1,000 marketing researchers reveals that 540 of the researchers disapprove of the actions taken in the conflict of interest scenario. Use rejection points to determine how much evidence there is that a majority of all marketing researchers disapprove of the actions taken.
d Note that in parts *b* and *c* the sample proportion $\hat{p}$ is (essentially) the same. Explain why the results of the hypothesis tests in parts *b* and *c* differ.

8.72 Last year, television station WXYZ's share of the 11 P.M. news audience was approximately equal to, but no greater than, 25 percent. The station's management believes that the current audience share is higher than last year's 25 percent share. In an attempt to substantiate this belief, the station surveyed a random sample of 400 11 P.M. news viewers and found that 146 watched WXYZ.

a Let p be the current proportion of all 11 P.M. news viewers who watch WXYZ. Set up the null and alternative hypotheses needed to attempt to provide evidence supporting the claim that the current audience share for WXYZ is higher than last year's 25 percent share.

b Use rejection points and the following MINITAB output to test the hypotheses you set up in part a at the .10, .05, .01, and .001 levels of significance. How much evidence is there that the current audience share is higher than last year's 25 percent share?

```
Test of p = 0.25 vs p > 0.25

Sample    X    N   Sample p   Z-Value   P-Value
1       146  400   0.365000      5.31     0.000
```

c Calculate the p-value for the hypothesis test in part b. Use the p-value to carry out the test by setting α equal to .10, .05, .01, and .001. Interpret your results.

d Do you think that the result of the station's survey has practical importance? Why or why not?

8.73 In the book *Essentials of Marketing Research,* William R. Dillon, Thomas J. Madden, and Neil H. Firtle discuss a marketing research proposal to study day-after recall for a brand of mouthwash. To quote the authors:

> The ad agency has developed a TV ad for the introduction of the mouthwash. The objective of the ad is to create awareness of the brand. The objective of this research is to evaluate the awareness generated by the ad measured by aided- and unaided-recall scores.
>
> A minimum of 200 respondents who claim to have watched the TV show in which the ad was aired the night before will be contacted by telephone in 20 cities.
>
> The study will provide information on the incidence of unaided and aided recall.

Suppose a random sample of 200 respondents shows that 46 of the people interviewed were able to recall the commercial without any prompting (unaided recall).

a In order for the ad to be considered successful, the percentage of unaided recall must be above the category norm for a TV commercial for the product class. If this norm is 18 percent, set up the null and alternative hypotheses needed to attempt to provide evidence that the ad is successful.

b Use the previously given sample information to compute the p-value for the hypothesis test you set up in part a. Use the p-value to carry out the test by setting α equal to .10, .05, .01, and .001. How much evidence is there that the TV commercial is successful?

c Do you think the result of the ad agency's survey has practical importance? Explain your opinion.

8.74 *Quality Progress,* February 2005, reports on the results achieved by Bank of America in improving customer satisfaction and customer loyalty by listening to the 'voice of the customer'. A key measure of customer satisfaction is the response on a scale from 1 to 10 to the question: "Considering all the business you do with Bank of America, what is your overall satisfaction with Bank of America?"[3] Suppose that a random sample of 350 current customers results in 195 customers with a response of 9 or 10 representing 'customer delight.'

a Let p denote the true proportion of all current Bank of America customers who would respond with a 9 or 10, and note that the historical proportion of customer delight for Bank of America has been .48. Calculate the p-value for testing H_0: $p = .48$ versus H_a: $p > .48$. How much evidence is there that p exceeds .48?

b Bank of America has a base of nearly 30 million customers. Do you think that the sample results have practical importance? Explain your opinion.

8.75 The manufacturer of the ColorSmart-5000 television set claims that 95 percent of its sets last at least five years without needing a single repair. In order to test this claim, a consumer group randomly selects 400 consumers who have owned a ColorSmart-5000 television set for five years. Of these 400 consumers, 316 say that their ColorSmart-5000 television sets did not need repair, while 84 say that their ColorSmart-5000 television sets did need at least one repair.

a Letting p be the proportion of ColorSmart-5000 television sets that last five years without a single repair, set up the null and alternative hypotheses that the consumer group should use to attempt to show that the manufacturer's claim is false.

b Use rejection points and the previously given sample information to test the hypotheses you set up in part a by setting α equal to .10, .05, .01, and .001. How much evidence is there that the manufacturer's claim is false?

c Do you think the results of the consumer group's survey have practical importance? Explain your opinion.

[3]Source: "Driving Organic Growth at Bank of America" *Quality Progress* (February 2005), pp. 23–27.

8.6 Type II Error Probabilities and Sample Size Determination (Optional)

As we have seen, we usually take action (for example, advertise a claim) on the basis of having rejected the null hypothesis. In this case, we know the chances that the action has been taken erroneously because we have prespecified α, the probability of rejecting a true null hypothesis. However, sometimes we must act (for example, use a day's production of camshafts to make V6 engines) on the basis of *not* rejecting the null hypothesis. If we must do this, it is best to know the probability of not rejecting a false null hypothesis (a Type II error). If this probability is not small enough, we may change the hypothesis testing procedure. In order to discuss this further, we must first see how to compute the probability of a Type II error.

CHAPTERS 9 AND 11

As an example, the Federal Trade Commission (FTC) often tests claims that companies make about their products. Suppose coffee is being sold in cans that are labeled as containing three pounds, and also suppose that the FTC wishes to determine if the mean amount of coffee μ in all such cans is at least three pounds. To do this, the FTC tests H_0: $\mu \geq 3$ (or $\mu = 3$) versus H_a: $\mu < 3$ by setting $\alpha = .05$. Suppose that a sample of 35 coffee cans yields $\bar{x} = 2.9973$. Assuming that σ equals .0147, we see that because

$$z = \frac{2.9973 - 3}{.0147/\sqrt{35}} = -1.08$$

is not less than $-z_{.05} = -1.645$, we cannot reject H_0: $\mu \geq 3$ by setting $\alpha = .05$. Since we cannot reject H_0, we cannot have committed a Type I error, which is the error of rejecting a true H_0. However, we might have committed a Type II error, which is the error of not rejecting a false H_0. Therefore, before we make a final conclusion about μ, we should calculate the probability of a Type II error.

A Type II error is not rejecting H_0: $\mu \geq 3$ when H_0 is false. Because any value of μ that is less than 3 makes H_0 false, there is a different Type II error (and, therefore, a different Type II error probability) associated with each value of μ that is less than 3. In order to demonstrate how to calculate these probabilities, we will calculate the probability of not rejecting H_0: $\mu \geq 3$ when in fact μ equals 2.995. This is the probability of failing to detect an average underfill of .005 pounds. For a fixed sample size (for example, $n = 35$ coffee can fills), the value of β, the probability of a Type II error, depends upon how we set α, the probability of a Type I error. Since we have set $\alpha = .05$, we reject H_0 if

$$\frac{\bar{x} - 3}{\sigma/\sqrt{n}} < -z_{.05}$$

or, equivalently, if

$$\bar{x} < 3 - z_{.05}\frac{\sigma}{\sqrt{n}} = 3 - 1.645\frac{.0147}{\sqrt{35}} = 2.9959126$$

Therefore, we do not reject H_0 if $\bar{x} \geq 2.9959126$. It follows that β, the probability of not rejecting H_0: $\mu \geq 3$ when μ equals 2.995, is

$$\begin{aligned}\beta &= P(\bar{x} \geq 2.9959126 \text{ when } \mu = 2.995)\\ &= P\left(z \geq \frac{2.9959126 - 2.995}{.0147/\sqrt{35}}\right)\\ &= P(z \geq .37) = .5 - .1443 = .3557\end{aligned}$$

This calculation is illustrated in Figure 8.13. Similarly, it follows that β, the probability of not rejecting H_0: $\mu \geq 3$ when μ equals 2.99, is

$$\begin{aligned}\beta &= P(\bar{x} \geq 2.9959126 \text{ when } \mu = 2.99)\\ &= P\left(z \geq \frac{2.9959126 - 2.99}{.0147/\sqrt{35}}\right)\\ &= P(z \geq 2.38) = .5 - .4913 = .0087\end{aligned}$$

FIGURE 8.13 Calculating β When μ Equals 2.995

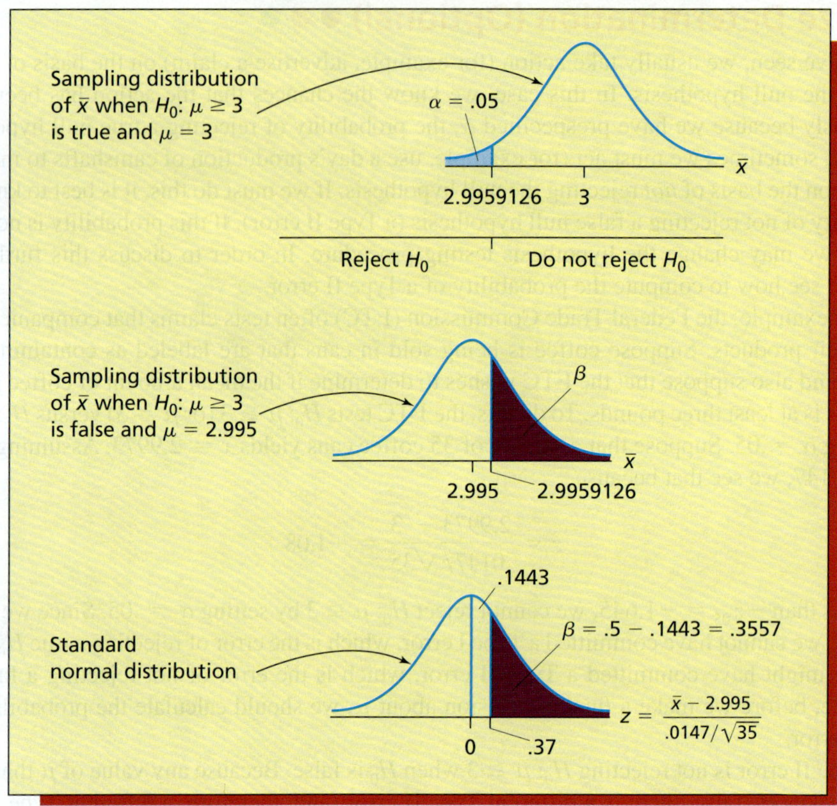

It also follows that β, the probability of not rejecting H_0: $\mu \geq 3$ when μ equals 2.985, is

$$\beta = P(\bar{x} \geq 2.9959126 \text{ when } \mu = 2.985)$$

$$= P\left(z \geq \frac{2.9959126 - 2.985}{.0147/\sqrt{35}}\right)$$

$$= P(z \geq 4.39)$$

This probability is less than .001 (because z is greater than 3.09).

In Figure 8.14 we illustrate the values of β that we have calculated. Notice that the closer an alternative value of μ is to 3 (the value specified by H_0: $\mu = 3$), the larger is the associated value of β. Although alternative values of μ that are closer to 3 have larger associated probabilities of Type II errors, these values of μ have associated Type II errors with less serious consequences. For example, we are more likely to not reject H_0: $\mu = 3$ when $\mu = 2.995$ ($\beta = .3557$) than we are to not reject H_0: $\mu = 3$ when $\mu = 2.99$ ($\beta = .0087$). However, not rejecting H_0: $\mu = 3$ when $\mu = 2.995$, which means that we are failing to detect an average underfill of .005 pounds, is less serious than not rejecting H_0: $\mu = 3$ when $\mu = 2.99$, which means that we are failing to detect a larger average underfill of .01 pounds. In order to decide whether a particular hypothesis test adequately controls the probability of a Type II error, we must determine which Type II errors are serious, and then we must decide whether the probabilities of these errors are small enough. For example, suppose that the FTC and the coffee producer agree that failing to reject H_0: $\mu = 3$ when μ equals 2.99 is a serious error, but that failing to reject H_0: $\mu = 3$ when μ equals 2.995 is not a particularly serious error. Then, since the probability of not rejecting H_0: $\mu = 3$ when μ equals 2.99, which is .0087, is quite small, we might decide that the hypothesis test adequately controls the probability of a Type II error. To understand the implication of this, recall that the sample of 35 coffee cans, which has $\bar{x} = 2.9973$, does not provide enough evidence to reject H_0: $\mu \geq 3$ by setting $\alpha = .05$. We have just shown that the probability that we have failed to detect a serious underfill is quite small (.0087), so the FTC might decide that no action should be taken

FIGURE 8.14 How β Changes as the Alternative Value of μ Changes

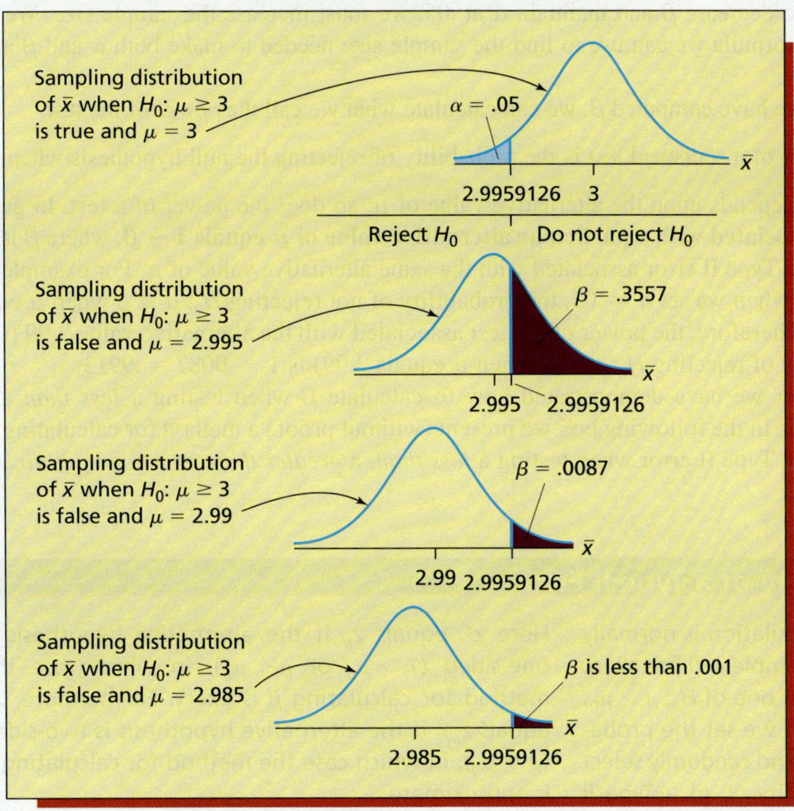

against the coffee producer. Of course, this decision should also be based on the variability of the fills of the individual cans. Because $\bar{x} = 2.9973$ and $\sigma = .0147$, we estimate that 99.73 percent of all individual coffee can fills are contained in the interval $[\bar{x} \pm 3\sigma] = [2.9973 \pm 3(.0147)] = [2.9532, 3.0414]$. If the FTC believes it is reasonable to accept fills as low as (but no lower than) 2.9532 pounds, this evidence also suggests that no action against the coffee producer is needed.

Suppose, instead, that the FTC and the coffee producer had agreed that failing to reject H_0: $\mu \geq 3$ when μ equals 2.995 is a serious mistake. The probability of this Type II error, which is .3557, is large. Therefore, we might conclude that the hypothesis test is not adequately controlling the probability of a serious Type II error. In this case, we have two possible courses of action. First, we have previously said that, for a fixed sample size, the lower we set α, the higher is β, and the higher we set α, the lower is β. Therefore, if we keep the sample size fixed at $n = 35$ coffee cans, we can reduce β by increasing α. To demonstrate this, suppose we increase α to .10. In this case we reject H_0 if

$$\frac{\bar{x} - 3}{\sigma/\sqrt{n}} < -z_{.10}$$

or, equivalently, if

$$\bar{x} < 3 - z_{.10}\frac{\sigma}{\sqrt{n}} = 3 - 1.282\frac{.0147}{\sqrt{35}} = 2.9968145$$

Therefore, we do not reject H_0 if $\bar{x} \geq 2.9968145$. It follows that β, the probability of not rejecting H_0: $\mu \geq 3$ when μ equals 2.995, is

$$\begin{aligned}\beta &= P(\bar{x} \geq 2.9968145 \text{ when } \mu = 2.995) \\ &= P\left(z \geq \frac{2.9968145 - 2.995}{.0147/\sqrt{35}}\right) \\ &= P(z \geq .73) = .5 - .2673 = .2327\end{aligned}$$

We thus see that increasing α from .05 to .10 reduces β from .3557 to .2327. However, β is still too large, and, besides, we might not be comfortable making α larger than .05. Therefore, if we wish to decrease β and maintain α at .05, we must increase the sample size. We will soon present a formula we can use to find the sample size needed to make both α and β as small as we wish.

Once we have computed β, we can calculate what we call the *power* of the test.

The **power** of a statistical test is the probability of rejecting the null hypothesis when it is false.

Just as β depends upon the alternative value of μ, so does the power of a test. In general, **the power associated with a particular alternative value of μ equals $1 - \beta$,** where β is the probability of a Type II error associated with the same alternative value of μ. For example, we have seen that, when we set $\alpha = .05$, the probability of not rejecting H_0: $\mu \geq 3$ when μ equals 2.99 is .0087. Therefore, the power of the test associated with the alternative value 2.99 (that is, the probability of rejecting H_0: $\mu \geq 3$ when μ equals 2.99) is $1 - .0087 = .9913$.

Thus far we have demonstrated how to calculate β when testing a *less than* alternative hypothesis. In the following box we present (without proof) a method for calculating the probability of a Type II error when testing a *less than,* a *greater than,* or a *not equal to* alternative hypothesis:

Calculating the Probability of a Type II Error

Assume that the sampled population is normally distributed, or that a large sample will be taken. Consider testing H_0: $\mu = \mu_0$ versus one of H_a: $\mu > \mu_0$, H_a: $\mu < \mu_0$, or H_a: $\mu \neq \mu_0$. Then, if we set the probability of a Type I error equal to α and randomly select a sample of size *n,* the probability, β, of a Type II error corresponding to the alternative value μ_a of μ is (exactly or approximately) equal to the area under the standard normal curve to the left of

$$z^* - \frac{|\mu_0 - \mu_a|}{\sigma/\sqrt{n}}$$

Here z^* equals z_α if the alternative hypothesis is one-sided ($\mu > \mu_0$ or $\mu < \mu_0$), in which case the method for calculating β is exact. Furthermore, z^* equals $z_{\alpha/2}$ if the alternative hypothesis is two-sided ($\mu \neq \mu_0$), in which case the method for calculating β is approximate.

Example 8.9 The Camshaft Case

C

Reconsider the camshaft situation and testing H_0: $\mu = 4.5$ versus H_a: $\mu \neq 4.5$ by setting $\alpha = .05$. Assume that a random sample of 35 camshafts that has been selected from a day's production yields $\bar{x} = 4.5716$. Assuming that σ equals .47, we see that because

$$z = \frac{4.5716 - 4.5}{.47/\sqrt{35}} = .90$$

is between $-z_{.025} = -1.96$ and $z_{.025} = 1.96$, we cannot reject H_0: $\mu = 4.5$ by setting $\alpha = .05$. Since we cannot reject H_0, we might have committed a Type II error. Suppose that an automobile assembly plant that is considering using the camshafts decides that failing to reject H_0: $\mu = 4.5$ when μ differs from 4.5 by as much as .3 mm (that is, when μ is 4.2 or 4.8) is a serious Type II error. Because we have set α equal to .05, β for the alternative value $\mu_a = 4.8$ (that is, the probability of not rejecting H_0: $\mu = 4.5$ when μ equals 4.8) is the area under the standard normal curve to the left of

$$\begin{aligned} z^* - \frac{|\mu_0 - \mu_a|}{\sigma/\sqrt{n}} &= z_{.025} - \frac{|\mu_0 - \mu_a|}{\sigma/\sqrt{n}} \\ &= 1.96 - \frac{|4.5 - 4.8|}{.47/\sqrt{35}} \\ &= -1.82 \end{aligned}$$

Here $z^* = z_{\alpha/2} = z_{.05/2} = z_{.025}$ since the alternative hypothesis ($\mu \neq 4.5$) is two-sided. The area under the standard normal curve to the left of -1.82 is $.5 - .4656 = .0344$. Therefore, β for the alternative value $\mu_a = 4.8$ is .0344. Similarly, it can be verified that β for the alternative value $\mu_a = 4.2$ is .0344. It follows, since we cannot reject H_0: $\mu = 4.5$ by setting $\alpha = .05$, and since we have just shown that there is a reasonably small (.0344) probability that we have failed to detect a serious (that is, a .3 mm) deviation of μ from 4.5, that the assembly plant might decide to use the day's production of camshafts. Of course, this decision should also be based on knowing the variability of the hardness depths of the individual camshafts. Because $\bar{x} = 4.5716$ and $\sigma = .47$, we estimate that 99.73 percent of all individual hardness depths are contained in the interval $[\bar{x} \pm 3\sigma] = [4.5716 \pm 3(.47)] = [3.16, 5.98]$. The limits of this interval are within the specification limits of 3.00 mm to 6.00 mm, so the assembly plant has further evidence that it should use the camshafts.

In the following box we present (without proof) a formula that tells us the sample size needed to make both the probability of a Type I error and the probability of a Type II error as small as we wish:

Calculating the Sample Size Needed to Achieve Specified Values of α and β

Assume that the sampled population is normally distributed, or that a large sample will be taken. Consider testing H_0: $\mu = \mu_0$ versus one of H_a: $\mu > \mu_0$, H_a: $\mu < \mu_0$, or H_a: $\mu \neq \mu_0$. Then, in order to make the probability of a Type I error equal to α and the probability of a Type II error corresponding to the alternative value μ_a of μ equal to β, we should take a sample of size

$$n = \frac{(z^* + z_\beta)^2\sigma^2}{(\mu_0 - \mu_a)^2}$$

Here z^* equals z_α if the alternative hypothesis is one-sided ($\mu > \mu_0$ or $\mu < \mu_0$), and z^* equals $z_{\alpha/2}$ if the alternative hypothesis is two-sided ($\mu \neq \mu_0$). Also, z_β is the point on the scale of the standard normal curve that gives a right-hand tail area equal to β.

Example 8.10

Again consider the coffee fill example and suppose we wish to test H_0: $\mu \geq 3$ (or $\mu = 3$) versus H_a: $\mu < 3$. If we wish α to be .05 and β for the alternative value $\mu_a = 2.995$ of μ to be .05, we should take a sample of size

$$\begin{aligned} n &= \frac{(z^* + z_\beta)^2\sigma^2}{(\mu_0 - \mu_a)^2} = \frac{(z_\alpha + z_\beta)^2\sigma^2}{(\mu_0 - \mu_a)^2} \\ &= \frac{(z_{.05} + z_{.05})^2\sigma^2}{(\mu_0 - \mu_a)^2} \\ &= \frac{(1.645 + 1.645)^2(.0147)^2}{(3 - 2.995)^2} \\ &= 93.5592 = 94 \text{ (rounding up)} \end{aligned}$$

Here, $z^* = z_\alpha = z_{.05} = 1.645$ because the alternative hypothesis ($\mu < 3$) is one-sided, and $z_\beta = z_{.05} = 1.645$.

Although we have set both α and β equal to the same value in the coffee fill situation, it is not necessary for α and β to be equal. As an example, again consider the camshaft situation in which we are testing H_0: $\mu = 4.5$ versus H_a: $\mu \neq 4.5$. Suppose that the assembly plant decides that failing to reject H_0: $\mu = 4.5$ when μ differs from 4.5 by as much as .2 mm (that is, when μ is 4.3 or 4.7) is a serious Type II error. Furthermore, suppose that it is also decided that this Type II error is more serious than a Type I error. Therefore, α will be set equal to .05 and β for the alternative value $\mu_a = 4.7$ (or $\mu_a = 4.3$) of μ will be set equal to .01. It follows that the assembly plant should take a sample of size

$$n = \frac{(z^* + z_\beta)^2\sigma^2}{(\mu_0 - \mu_a)^2} = \frac{(z_{\alpha/2} + z_\beta)^2\sigma^2}{(\mu_0 - \mu_a)^2}$$

$$= \frac{(z_{.025} + z_{.01})^2\sigma^2}{(\mu_0 - \mu_a)^2}$$

$$= \frac{(1.96 + 2.326)^2(.47)^2}{(4.5 - 4.7)^2}$$

$$= 101.45 = 102 \text{ (rounding up)}$$

Here, $z^* = z_{\alpha/2} = z_{.05/2} = z_{.025} = 1.96$ since the alternative hypothesis ($\mu \neq 4.5$) is two-sided, and $z_\beta = z_{.01} = 2.326$ (see the bottom row of the t table on page 272).

To conclude this section, we point out that the methods we have presented for calculating the probability of a Type II error and determining sample size can be extended to other hypothesis tests that utilize the normal distribution. We will not, however, present the extensions in this book.

Exercises for Section 8.6

CONCEPTS

8.76 We usually take action on the basis of having rejected the null hypothesis. When we do this, we know the chances that the action has been taken erroneously because we have prespecified α, the probability of rejecting a true null hypothesis. Here, it is obviously important to know (prespecify) α, the probability of a Type I error. When is it important to know the probability of a Type II error? Explain why.

8.77 Explain why we are able to compute many different values of β, the probability of a Type II error, for a single hypothesis test.

8.78 Explain what is meant by

a A serious Type II error.

b The power of a statistical test.

In general, do we want the power corresponding to a serious Type II error to be near 0 or near 1? Explain.

METHODS AND APPLICATIONS

8.79 Again consider the Consolidated Power waste water situation. Remember that the power plant will be shut down and corrective action will be taken on the cooling system if the null hypothesis H_0: $\mu \leq 60$ is rejected in favor of H_a: $\mu > 60$. In this exercise we calculate probabilities of various Type II errors in the context of this situation.

a Recall that Consolidated Power's hypothesis test is based on a sample of $n = 100$ temperature readings and assume that σ equals 2. If the power company sets $\alpha = .025$, calculate the probability of a Type II error for each of the following alternative values of μ: 60.1, 60.2, 60.3, 60.4, 60.5, 60.6, 60.7, 60.8, 60.9, 61.

b If we want the probability of making a Type II error when μ equals 60.5 to be very small, is Consolidated Power's hypothesis test adequate? Explain why or why not. If not, and if we wish to maintain the value of α at .025, what must be done?

c The **power curve** for a statistical test is a plot of the power $= 1 - \beta$ on the vertical axis versus values of μ that make the null hypothesis false on the horizontal axis. Plot the power curve for Consolidated Power's test of H_0: $\mu \leq 60$ versus H_a: $\mu > 60$ by plotting power $= 1 - \beta$ for each of the alternative values of μ in part a. What happens to the power of the test as the alternative value of μ moves away from 60?

8.80 Again consider the automobile parts supplier situation. Remember that a problem-solving team will be assigned to rectify the process producing the cylindrical engine parts if the null hypothesis H_0: $\mu = 3$ is rejected in favor of H_a: $\mu \neq 3$. In this exercise we calculate probabilities of various Type II errors in the context of this situation.

a Suppose that the parts supplier's hypothesis test is based on a sample of $n = 100$ diameters and that σ equals .023. If the parts supplier sets $\alpha = .05$, calculate the probability of a Type II error for each of the following alternative values of μ: 2.990, 2.995, 3.005, 3.010.

b If we want the probabilities of making a Type II error when μ equals 2.995 and when μ equals 3.005 to both be very small, is the parts supplier's hypothesis test adequate? Explain why or why not. If not, and if we wish to maintain the value of α at .05, what must be done?

c Plot the power of the test versus the alternative values of μ in part *a*. What happens to the power of the test as the alternative value of μ moves away from 3?

8.81 In the Consolidated Power hypothesis test of H_0: $\mu \leq 60$ versus H_a: $\mu > 60$ (as discussed in Exercise 8.79) find the sample size needed to make the probability of a Type I error equal to .025 and the probability of a Type II error corresponding to the alternative value $\mu_a = 60.5$ equal to .025. Here, assume σ equals 2.

8.82 In the automobile parts supplier's hypothesis test of H_0: $\mu = 3$ versus H_a: $\mu \neq 3$ (as discussed in Exercise 8.80) find the sample size needed to make the probability of a Type I error equal to .05 and the probability of a Type II error corresponding to the alternative value $\mu_a = 3.005$ equal to .05. Here, assume σ equals .023.

8.7 The Chi-Square Distribution (Optional)

Sometimes we can make statistical inferences by using the **chi-square distribution.** The probability curve of the χ^2 (pronounced *chi-square*) distribution is skewed to the right. Moreover, the exact shape of this probability curve depends on a parameter that is called the **number of degrees of freedom** (denoted *df*). Figure 8.15 illustrates chi-square distributions having 1, 5, and 10 degrees of freedom.

CHAPTER 5

In order to use the chi-square distribution, we employ a **chi-square point,** which is denoted χ^2_α. As illustrated in the upper portion of Figure 8.16, χ^2_α is the point on the horizontal axis under the curve of the chi-square distribution that gives a right-hand tail area equal to α. The value of χ^2_α in a particular situation depends on the right-hand tail area α and the number of degrees of freedom (*df*) of the chi-square distribution. Values of χ^2_α are tabulated in a **chi-square table.** Such a table is given in Table A.17 of Appendix A (page 838); a portion of this table is reproduced as Table 8.4. Looking at the chi-square table, the rows correspond to the appropriate number of degrees of freedom (values of which are listed down the right side of the table), while the columns designate the right-hand tail area α. For example, suppose we wish to find the chi-square

FIGURE 8.15 Chi-Square Distributions with 1, 5, and 10 Degrees of Freedom

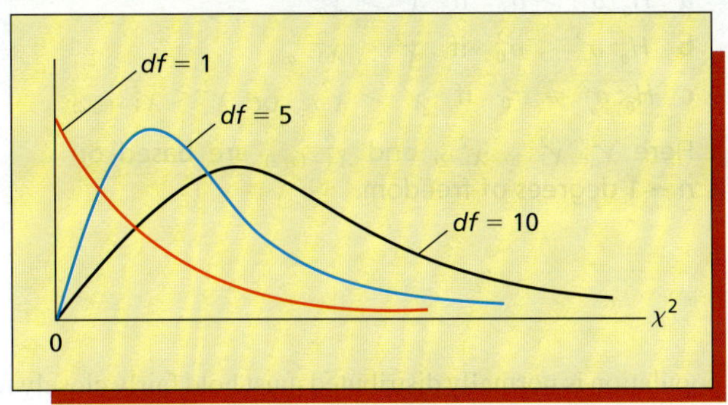

FIGURE 8.16 Chi-Square Points

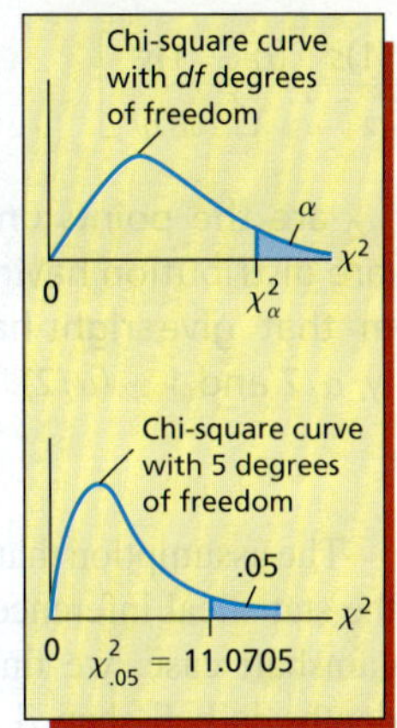

TABLE 8.4 A Portion of the Chi-Square Table

$\chi^2_{.10}$	$\chi^2_{.05}$	$\chi^2_{.025}$	$\chi^2_{.01}$	$\chi^2_{.005}$	Degrees of Freedom (df)
2.70554	3.84146	5.02389	6.63490	7.87944	1
4.60517	5.99147	7.37776	9.21034	10.5966	2
6.25139	7.81473	9.34840	11.3449	12.8381	3
7.77944	9.48773	11.1433	13.2767	14.8602	4
9.23635	11.0705	12.8325	15.0863	16.7496	5
10.6446	12.5916	14.4494	16.8119	18.5476	6
12.0170	14.0671	16.0123	18.4753	20.2777	7
13.3616	15.5073	17.5346	20.0902	21.9550	8
14.6837	16.9190	19.0228	21.6660	23.5893	9
15.9871	18.3070	20.4831	23.2093	25.1882	10

point that gives a right-hand tail area of .05 under a chi-square curve having 5 degrees of freedom. To do this, we look in Table 8.4 at the row labeled 5 and the column labeled $\chi^2_{.05}$. We find that this $\chi^2_{.05}$ point is 11.0705 (see the lower portion of Figure 8.16).

8.8 Statistical Inference for a Population Variance (Optional)

CHAPTER 9

Consider the camshaft case, and suppose the automobile manufacturer has determined that the variance of the population of all camshaft hardness depths produced by the current hardening process is approximately equal to, but no less than, $(.47)^2 = .2209$. To reduce this variance, a new electrical coil is designed, and a random sample of $n = 30$ camshaft hardness depths produced by using this new coil has a mean of $\bar{x} = 4.60$ and a variance of $s^2 = .0885$. In order to attempt to show that the variance, σ^2, of the population of all camshaft hardness depths that would be produced by using the new coil is less than .2209, we can use the following result:

Statistical Inference for a Population Variance

Suppose that s^2 is the variance of a sample of n measurements randomly selected from a normally distributed population having variance σ^2. The sampling distribution of the statistic $(n-1)s^2/\sigma^2$ is a chi-square distribution having $n-1$ degrees of freedom. This implies that

1 **A $100(1-\alpha)$ percent confidence interval for σ^2 is**

$$\left[\frac{(n-1)s^2}{\chi^2_{\alpha/2}}, \frac{(n-1)s^2}{\chi^2_{1-(\alpha/2)}}\right]$$

Here $\chi^2_{\alpha/2}$ and $\chi^2_{1-(\alpha/2)}$ are the points under the curve of the chi-square distribution having $n-1$ degrees of freedom that give right-hand tail areas of, respectively, $\alpha/2$ and $1-(\alpha/2)$.

2 We can test $H_0\colon \sigma^2 = \sigma_0^2$ by using the test statistic

$$\chi^2 = \frac{(n-1)s^2}{\sigma_0^2}$$

Specifically, if we set the probability of a Type I error equal to α, then we can reject H_0 in favor of

a $H_a\colon \sigma^2 > \sigma_0^2$ if $\chi^2 > \chi^2_\alpha$

b $H_a\colon \sigma^2 < \sigma_0^2$ if $\chi^2 < \chi^2_{1-\alpha}$

c $H_a\colon \sigma^2 \neq \sigma_0^2$ if $\chi^2 > \chi^2_{\alpha/2}$ or $\chi^2 < \chi^2_{1-(\alpha/2)}$

Here χ^2_α, $\chi^2_{1-\alpha}$, $\chi^2_{\alpha/2}$, and $\chi^2_{1-(\alpha/2)}$ are based on $n-1$ degrees of freedom.

The assumption that the sampled population is normally distributed must hold fairly closely for the statistical inferences just given about σ^2 to be valid. When we check this assumption in the camshaft case, we find that a histogram (not given here) of the sample of $n = 30$ hardness depths is bell-shaped and symmetrical. In order to compute a 95 percent confidence interval for σ^2, we note that $\chi^2_{\alpha/2}$ is $\chi^2_{.025}$ and $\chi^2_{1-(\alpha/2)}$ is $\chi^2_{.975}$. Table A.17 (page 838) tells us that these

FIGURE 8.17 The Chi-Square Points $\chi^2_{.025}$ and $\chi^2_{.975}$

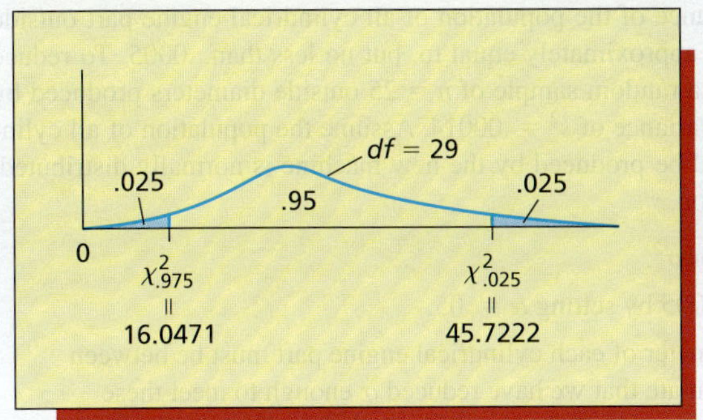

FIGURE 8.18 Testing H_0: $\sigma^2 = .2209$ versus H_a: $\sigma^2 < .2209$ by Setting $\alpha = .05$

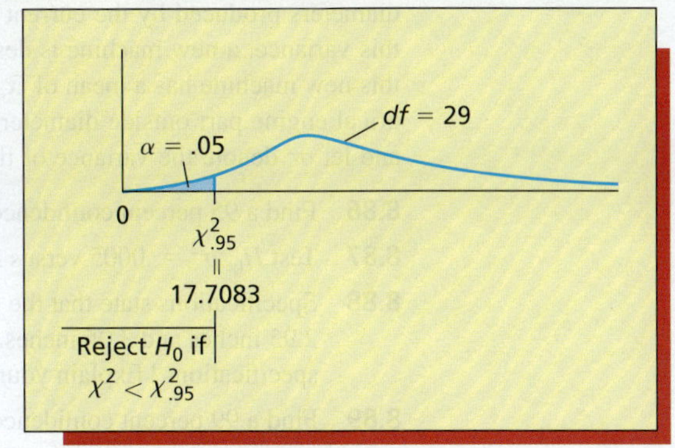

points—based on $n - 1 = 29$ degrees of freedom—are $\chi^2_{.025} = 45.7222$ and $\chi^2_{.975} = 16.0471$ (see Figure 8.17). It follows that a 95 percent confidence interval for σ^2 is

$$\left[\frac{(n-1)s^2}{\chi^2_{\alpha/2}}, \frac{(n-1)s^2}{\chi^2_{1-(\alpha/2)}}\right] = \left[\frac{(29)(.0885)}{45.7222}, \frac{(29)(.0885)}{16.0471}\right] = [.0561, .1599]$$

This interval provides strong evidence that σ^2 is less than .2209.

If we wish to use a hypothesis test, we test **the null hypothesis H_0: $\sigma^2 = .2209$ versus the alternative hypothesis H_a: $\sigma^2 < .2209$.** If H_0 can be rejected in favor of H_a at the **.05 level of significance,** we will conclude that the new coil has reduced the variance of the camshaft hardness depths. Since the histogram of the sample of $n = 30$ hardness depths is bell shaped and symmetrical, **the appropriate test statistic is given in the summary box.** Furthermore, since H_a: $\sigma^2 < .2209$ is of the form H_a: $\sigma^2 < \sigma_0^2$, we should **reject H_0: $\sigma^2 = .2209$ if the value of χ^2 is less than the rejection point $\chi^2_{1-\alpha} = \chi^2_{.95} = 17.7083$.** Here $\chi^2_{.95} = 17.7083$ is based on $n - 1 = 30 - 1 = 29$ degrees of freedom, and this rejection point is illustrated in Figure 8.18. Since the sample variance is $s^2 = .0885$, the **value of the test statistic** is

$$\chi^2 = \frac{(n-1)s^2}{\sigma_0^2} = \frac{(29)(.0885)}{.2209} = 11.6184$$

Since $\chi^2 = 11.6184$ is less than $\chi^2_{.95} = 17.7083$, we reject H_0: $\sigma^2 = .2209$ in favor of H_a: $\sigma^2 < .2209$. That is, we conclude (at an α of .05) that the new coil has reduced the variance of the camshaft hardness depths.

To see if there has been a practically important decrease in σ^2, note that $s^2 = .0885$ implies that $s = .2975$. It follows, since $\bar{x} = 4.6$, that we estimate that 99.73 percent of all individual camshaft hardness depths are in the interval $[\bar{x} \pm 3s] = [4.6 \pm 3(.2975)] = [3.71, 5.49]$ and are, therefore, within specifications (recall that hardness depth specifications are [3, 6]). This was not the case with the original σ^2 of .2209 (or σ of .47), because $[4.6 \pm 3(.47)] = [3.19, 6.01]$ is not within the specifications of [3, 6]. Therefore, reducing σ^2 from .2209 to an estimated value of .0885 seems to have practical importance. In Appendix 8.3 we show a MegaStat output of the above confidence interval for σ^2 and of the test of H_0: $\sigma^2 = .2209$ versus H_a: $\sigma^2 < .2209$.

Exercises for Sections 8.7 and 8.8

CONCEPTS

8.83 What assumption must hold to use the chi-square distribution to make statistical inferences about a population variance?

8.84 Define the meaning of the chi-square points $\chi^2_{\alpha/2}$ and $\chi^2_{1-(\alpha/2)}$.

8.85 Give an example of a situation in which we might wish to compute a confidence interval for σ^2.

METHODS AND APPLICATIONS

Exercises 8.86 through 8.90 relate to the following situation: Consider an engine parts supplier and suppose the supplier has determined that the variance of the population of all cylindrical engine part outside diameters produced by the current machine is approximately equal to, but no less than, .0005. To reduce this variance, a new machine is designed, and a random sample of $n = 25$ outside diameters produced by this new machine has a mean of $\bar{x} = 3$ and a variance of $s^2 = .00014$. Assume the population of all cylindrical engine part outside diameters that would be produced by the new machine is normally distributed, and let σ^2 denote the variance of this population.

8.86 Find a 95 percent confidence interval for σ^2.

8.87 Test H_0: $\sigma^2 = .0005$ versus H_a: $\sigma^2 < .0005$ by setting $\alpha = .05$.

8.88 Specifications state that the outside diameter of each cylindrical engine part must be between 2.95 inches and 3.05 inches. Do we estimate that we have reduced σ enough to meet these specifications? Explain your answer.

8.89 Find a 99 percent confidence interval for σ^2.

8.90 Test H_0: $\sigma^2 = .0005$ versus H_a: $\sigma^2 \neq .0005$ by setting $\alpha = .01$.

Chapter Summary

We began this chapter by learning about the two hypotheses that make up the structure of a hypothesis test. The **null hypothesis** is the statement being tested. Usually it represents the *status quo* and it is not rejected unless there is convincing sample evidence that it is false. The **alternative, or, research, hypothesis** is a statement that is accepted only if there is convincing sample evidence that it is true and that the null hypothesis is false. In some situations, the alternative hypothesis is a condition for which we need to attempt to find supportive evidence. We also learned that two types of errors can be made in a hypothesis test. A **Type I error** occurs when we reject a true null hypothesis, and a **Type II error** occurs when we do not reject a false null hypothesis.

We studied two commonly used ways to conduct a hypothesis test. The first involves comparing the value of a test statistic with what is called a **rejection point,** and the second employs what is called a ***p*-value.** The *p*-value measures the weight of evidence against the null hypothesis. The smaller the *p*-value, the more we doubt the null hypothesis. We learned that, if we can reject the null hypothesis with the probability of a Type I error equal to α, then we say that the test result has **statistical significance at the α level.** However, we also learned that, even if the result of a hypothesis test tells us that statistical significance exists, we must carefully assess whether the result is practically important. One good way to do this is to use a point estimate and confidence interval for the parameter of interest.

The specific hypothesis tests we covered in this chapter all dealt with a hypothesis about one population parameter. First, we studied a test about a **population mean** that is based on the assumption that the population standard deviation **σ is known.** This test employs the **normal distribution.** Second, we studied a test about a population mean that assumes that **σ is unknown.** We learned that this test is based on the ***t* distribution.** Figure 8.19 presents a flowchart summarizing how to select an appropriate test statistic to test a hypothesis about a population mean. Then we presented a test about a **population proportion** that is based on the **normal distribution.** Next (in optional Section 8.6) we studied Type II error probabilities, and we showed how we can find the sample size needed to make both the probability of a Type I error and the probability of a serious Type II error as small as we wish. We concluded this chapter by discussing (in optional Sections 8.7 and 8.8) the **chi-square distribution** and its use in making statistical inferences about a population variance.

Glossary of Terms

alternative (research) hypothesis: A statement that will be accepted only if there is convincing sample evidence that it is true. Sometimes it is a condition for which we need to attempt to find supportive evidence. (page 305)

chi-square distribution: A useful continuous probability distribution. Its probability curve is skewed to the right, and the exact shape of the probability curve depends on the number of degrees of freedom associated with the curve. (page 343)

greater than alternative: An alternative hypothesis that is stated as a *greater than* (>) inequality. (page 308)

less than alternative: An alternative hypothesis that is stated as a *less than* (<) inequality. (page 308)

not equal to alternative: An alternative hypothesis that is stated as a *not equal to* (≠) inequality. (page 308)

null hypothesis: The statement being tested in a hypothesis test. It usually represents the status quo and it is not rejected unless there is convincing sample evidence that it is false. (page 305)

one-sided alternative hypothesis: An alternative hypothesis that is stated as either a *greater than* (>) or a *less than* (<) inequality. (page 308)

power (of a statistical test): The probability of rejecting the null hypothesis when it is false. (page 340)

***p*-value (probability value):** The probability, computed assuming that the null hypothesis is true, of observing a value of the test statistic that is at least as extreme as the value actually computed from the sample data. The *p*-value measures how much doubt is cast on the null hypothesis by the sample data. The

FIGURE 8.19 Selecting an Appropriate Test Statistic to Test a Hypothesis about a Population Mean

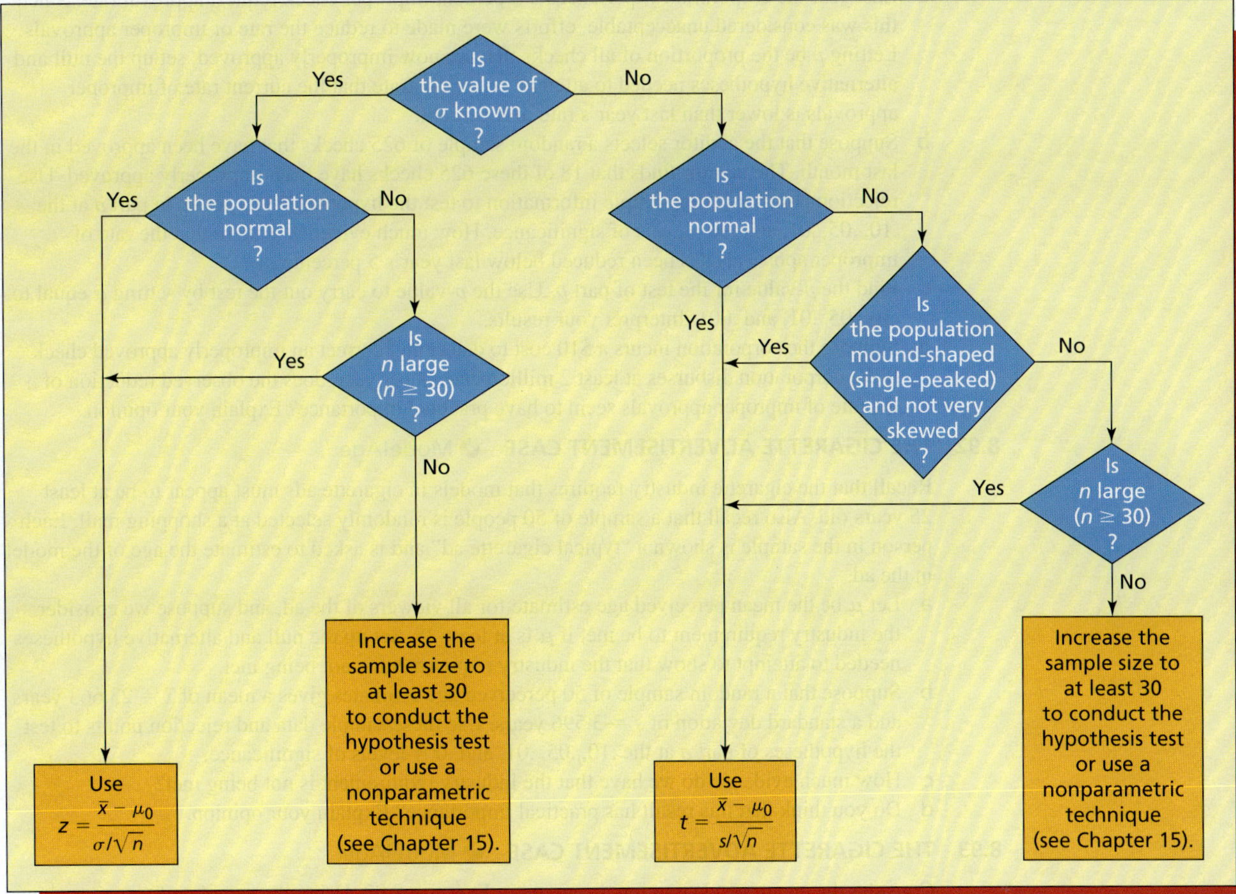

smaller the *p*-value, the more we doubt the null hypothesis. (pages 314, 317, 319, 323)

rejection point (or **critical point**)**:** The value of the test statistic is compared with a rejection point in order to decide whether the null hypothesis can be rejected. (pages 312, 316, 322)

statistical significance at the α level: When we can reject the null hypothesis by setting the probability of a Type I error equal to α. (pages 313, 325)

test statistic: A statistic computed from sample data in a hypothesis test. It is either compared with a rejection point or used to compute a *p*-value. (page 308)

two-sided alternative hypothesis: An alternative hypothesis that is stated as a *not equal to* ($\neq$) inequality. (page 308)

Type I error: Rejecting a true null hypothesis. (page 309)

Type II error: Failing to reject a false null hypothesis. (page 309)

Important Formulas and Tests

A hypothesis test about a population mean (σ known): page 324

A hypothesis test about a population mean (σ unknown): page 327

A large sample hypothesis test about a population proportion: page 332

Hypothesis Testing steps: page 319

Calculating the probability of a Type II error: page 340

Sample size determination to achieve specified values of α and β: page 341

Statistical inference about a population variance: page 344

Supplementary Exercises

8.91 The auditor for a large corporation routinely monitors cash disbursements. As part of this process, the auditor examines check request forms to determine whether they have been properly approved. Improper approval can occur in several ways. For instance, the check may have no approval, the

check request might be missing, the approval might be written by an unauthorized person, or the dollar limit of the authorizing person might be exceeded.

a Last year the corporation experienced a 5 percent improper check request approval rate. Since this was considered unacceptable, efforts were made to reduce the rate of improper approvals. Letting p be the proportion of all checks that are now improperly approved, set up the null and alternative hypotheses needed to attempt to demonstrate that the current rate of improper approvals is lower than last year's rate of 5 percent.

b Suppose that the auditor selects a random sample of 625 checks that have been approved in the last month. The auditor finds that 18 of these 625 checks have been improperly approved. Use rejection points and this sample information to test the hypotheses you set up in part *a* at the .10, .05, .01, and .001 levels of significance. How much evidence is there that the rate of improper approvals has been reduced below last year's 5 percent rate?

c Find the p-value for the test of part *b*. Use the p-value to carry out the test by setting α equal to .10, .05, .01, and .001. Interpret your results.

d Suppose the corporation incurs a $10 cost to detect and correct an improperly approved check. If the corporation disburses at least 2 million checks per year, does the observed reduction of the rate of improper approvals seem to have practical importance? Explain your opinion.

8.92 THE CIGARETTE ADVERTISEMENT CASE ModelAge

Recall that the cigarette industry requires that models in cigarette ads must appear to be at least 25 years old. Also recall that a sample of 50 people is randomly selected at a shopping mall. Each person in the sample is shown a "typical cigarette ad" and is asked to estimate the age of the model in the ad.

a Let μ be the mean perceived age estimate for all viewers of the ad, and suppose we consider the industry requirement to be met if μ is at least 25. Set up the null and alternative hypotheses needed to attempt to show that the industry requirement is not being met.

b Suppose that a random sample of 50 perceived age estimates gives a mean of $\bar{x} = 23.663$ years and a standard deviation of $s = 3.596$ years. Use these sample data and rejection points to test the hypotheses of part *a* at the .10, .05, .01, and .001 levels of significance.

c How much evidence do we have that the industry requirement is not being met?

d Do you think that this result has practical importance? Explain your opinion.

8.93 THE CIGARETTE ADVERTISEMENT CASE ModelAge

Consider the cigarette ad situation discussed in Exercise 8.92. Using the sample information given in that exercise, the p-value for testing H_0 versus H_a can be calculated to be .0057.

a Determine whether H_0 would be rejected at each of $\alpha = .10$, $\alpha = .05$, $\alpha = .01$, and $\alpha = .001$.

b Describe how much evidence we have that the industry requirement is not being met.

8.94 In an article in the *Journal of Retailing,* Kumar, Kerwin, and Pereira study factors affecting merger and acquisition activity in retailing. As part of the study, the authors compare the characteristics of "target firms" (firms targeted for acquisition) and "bidder firms" (firms attempting to make acquisitions). Among the variables studied in the comparison were earnings per share, debt-to-equity ratio, growth rate of sales, market share, and extent of diversification.

a Let μ be the mean growth rate of sales for all target firms (firms that have been targeted for acquisition in the last five years and that have not bid on other firms), and assume growth rates are approximately normally distributed. Furthermore, suppose a random sample of 25 target firms yields a sample mean sales growth rate of $\bar{x} = 0.16$ with a standard deviation of $s = 0.12$. Use rejection points and this sample information to test H_0: $\mu \leq .10$ versus H_a: $\mu > .10$ by setting α equal to .10, .05, .01, and .001. How much evidence is there that the mean growth rate of sales for target firms exceeds .10 (that is, exceeds 10 percent)?

b Now let μ be the mean growth rate of sales for all firms that are bidders (firms that have bid to acquire at least one other firm in the last five years), and again assume growth rates are approximately normally distributed. Furthermore, suppose a random sample of 25 bidders yields a sample mean sales growth rate of $\bar{x} = 0.12$ with a standard deviation of $s = 0.09$. Use rejection points and this sample information to test H_0: $\mu \leq .10$ versus H_a: $\mu > .10$ by setting α equal to .10, .05, .01, and .001. How much evidence is there that the mean growth rate of sales for bidders exceeds .10 (that is, exceeds 10 percent)?

8.95 A consumer electronics firm has developed a new type of remote control button that is designed to operate longer before becoming intermittent. A random sample of 35 of the new buttons is selected and each is tested in continuous operation until becoming intermittent. The resulting lifetimes are found to have a sample mean of $\bar{x} = 1{,}241.2$ hours and a sample standard deviation of $s = 110.8$.

a Independent tests reveal that the mean lifetime (in continuous operation) of the best remote control button on the market is 1,200 hours. Letting μ be the mean lifetime of the population of all new remote control buttons that will or could potentially be produced, set up the null and alternative hypotheses needed to attempt to provide evidence that the new button's mean lifetime exceeds the mean lifetime of the best remote button currently on the market.

b Using the previously given sample results, use rejection points to test the hypotheses you set up in part *a* by setting α equal to .10, .05, .01, and .001. What do you conclude for each value of α?

c Suppose that $\bar{x} = 1{,}241.2$ and $s = 110.8$ had been obtained by testing a sample of 100 buttons. Use rejection points to test the hypotheses you set up in part *a* by setting α equal to .10, .05, .01, and .001. Which sample (the sample of 35 or the sample of 100) gives a more statistically significant result? That is, which sample provides stronger evidence that H_a is true?

d If we define practical importance to mean that μ exceeds 1,200 by an amount that would be clearly noticeable to most consumers, do you think that the result has practical importance? Explain why the samples of 35 and 100 both indicate the same degree of practical importance.

e Suppose that further research and development effort improves the new remote control button and that a random sample of 35 buttons gives $\bar{x} = 1{,}524.6$ hours and $s = 102.8$ hours. Test your hypotheses of part *a* by setting α equal to .10, .05, .01, and .001.

(1) Do we have a highly statistically significant result? Explain.

(2) Do you think we have a practically important result? Explain.

8.96 Again consider the remote control button lifetime situation discussed in Exercise 8.95. Using the sample information given in the introduction to Exercise 8.95, the *p*-value for testing H_0 versus H_a can be calculated to be .0174.

a Determine whether H_0 would be rejected at each of $\alpha = .10$, $\alpha = .05$, $\alpha = .01$, and $\alpha = .001$.

b Describe how much evidence we have that the new button's mean lifetime exceeds the mean lifetime of the best remote button currently on the market.

8.97 Calculate and use an appropriate 95 percent confidence interval to help evaluate practical importance as it relates to the hypothesis test in each of the following situations discussed in previous review exercises. Explain what you think each confidence interval says about practical importance.

a The check approval situation of Exercise 8.91.

b The cigarette ad situation of Exercise 8.92.

c The remote control button situation of Exercise 8.95*a*, *c*, and *e*.

8.98 Several industries located along the Ohio River discharge a toxic substance called carbon tetrachloride into the river. The state Environmental Protection Agency monitors the amount of carbon tetrachloride pollution in the river. Specifically, the agency requires that the carbon tetrachloride contamination must average no more than 10 parts per million. In order to monitor the carbon tetrachloride contamination in the river, the agency takes a daily sample of 100 pollution readings at a specified location. If the mean carbon tetrachloride reading for this sample casts substantial doubt on the hypothesis that the average amount of carbon tetrachloride contamination in the river is at most 10 parts per million, the agency must issue a shutdown order. In the event of such a shutdown order, industrial plants along the river must be closed until the carbon tetrachloride contamination is reduced to a more acceptable level. Assume that the state Environmental Protection Agency decides to issue a shutdown order if a sample of 100 pollution readings implies that H_0: $\mu \leq 10$ can be rejected in favor of H_a: $\mu > 10$ by setting $\alpha = .01$. If σ equals 2, calculate the probability of a Type II error for each of the following alternative values of μ: 10.1, 10.2, 10.3, 10.4, 10.5, 10.6, 10.7, 10.8, 10.9, and 11.0.

8.99 THE INVESTMENT CASE InvestRet

Suppose that random samples of 50 returns for each of the following investment classes give the indicated sample mean and sample standard deviation:

Fixed annuities: $\bar{x} = 7.83\%$, $s = .51\%$
Domestic large-cap stocks: $\bar{x} = 13.42\%$, $s = 15.17\%$
Domestic midcap stocks: $\bar{x} = 15.03\%$, $s = 18.44\%$
Domestic small-cap stocks: $\bar{x} = 22.51\%$, $s = 21.75\%$

a For each investment class, set up the null and alternative hypotheses needed to test whether the current mean return differs from the historical (1970 to 1994) mean return given in Table 2.15 (page 110).

b Test each hypothesis you set up in part *a* at the .05 level of significance. What do you conclude? For which investment classes does the current mean return differ from the historical mean?

8.100 THE UNITED KINGDOM INSURANCE CASE

Assume that the U.K. insurance survey is based on 1,000 randomly selected United Kingdom households and that 640 of these households spent on life insurance in 1993.

a If p denotes the proportion of all U.K. households that spent on life insurance in 1993, set up the null and alternative hypotheses needed to attempt to justify the claim that more than 60 percent of U.K. households spent on life insurance in 1993.

b Test the hypotheses you set up in part *a* by setting $\alpha = .10, .05, .01$, and .001. How much evidence is there that more than 60 percent of U.K. households spent on life insurance in 1993?

8.101 How safe are child car seats? *Consumer Reports* (May 2005) tested the safety of child car seats in 30 mph crashes. They found "slim safety margins" for some child car seats. Suppose that Consumer Reports simulates the safety of the market-leading child car seat. Their test consists of placing the maximum claimed weight in the car seat and simulating crashes at higher and higher miles per hour until a problem occurs. The following data identify the speed at which a problem with the car seat first appeared; such as the strap breaking, seat shell cracked, strap adjuster broke, detached from the base, etc.: 31.0, 29.4, 30.4, 28.9, 29.7, 30.1, 32.3, 31.7, 35.4, 29.1, 31.2, 30.2. Let μ denote the true mean speed at which a problem with the car seat first appears. The following MINITAB output gives the results of using the sample data to test H_0: $\mu = 30$ versus H_a: $\mu > 30$. CarSeat

```
Test of mu = 30 vs > 30
Variable   N     Mean   StDev  SE Mean     T      P
mph       12  30.7833  1.7862   0.5156  1.52  0.078
```

How much evidence is there that μ exceeds 30 mph?

8.102 *Consumer Reports* (January 2005) indicates that profit margins on extended warranties are much greater than on the purchase of most products.[4] In this exercise we consider a major electronics retailer that wishes to increase the proportion of customers who buy extended warranties on digital cameras. Historically, 20 percent of digital camera customers have purchased the retailer's extended warranty. To increase this percentage, the retailer has decided to offer a new warranty that is less expensive and more comprehensive. Suppose that three months after starting to offer the new warranty, a random sample of 500 customer sales invoices shows that 152 out of 500 digital camera customers purchased the new warranty. Letting p denote the proportion of all digital camera customers who have purchased the new warranty, calculate the p-value for testing H_0: $p = .20$ versus H_a: $p > .20$. How much evidence is there that p exceeds .20? Does the difference between $\hat{p}$ and .2 seem to be practically important? Explain your opinion.

8.103 *Fortune* magazine has periodically reported on the rise of fees and expenses charged by stock funds.

a Suppose that 10 years ago the average annual expense for stock funds was 1.19 percent. Let μ be the current mean annual expense for all stock funds, and assume that stock fund annual expenses are approximately normally distributed. If a random sample of 12 stock funds gives a sample mean annual expense of $\bar{x} = 1.63\%$ with a standard deviation of $s = .31\%$, use rejection points and this sample information to test H_0: $\mu \leq 1.19\%$ versus H_a: $\mu > 1.19\%$ by setting α equal to .10, .05, .01, and .001. How much evidence is there that the current mean annual expense for stock funds exceeds the average of 10 years ago?

b Do you think that the result in part *a* has practical importance? Explain your opinion.

8.104 Internet Exercise

Are American consumers comfortable using their credit cards to make purchases over the Internet? Suppose that a noted authority suggests that credit cards will be firmly established on the Internet once the 80 percent barrier is broken; that is, as soon as more than 80 percent of those who make purchases over the Internet are willing to use a credit card to pay for their transactions. A recent Gallup Poll (story, survey results, and analysis can be found at http://www.gallup.com/poll/releases/pr000223.asp) found that, out of $n = 302$ Internet purchasers surveyed, 267 have paid for Internet purchases using a credit card. Based on the results of the Gallup survey, is there sufficient evidence to conclude that the proportion of Internet purchasers willing to use a credit card now exceeds 0.80? Set up the appropriate null and alternative hypotheses, test at the 0.05 and

[4] *Consumer Reports*, January 2005, page 51.

0.01 levels of significance, and calculate a p-value for your test.

Go to the Gallup Organization website (http://www.gallup.com) and find the index of recent poll results (http://www.gallup.com/poll/index.asp). Select an interesting current poll and prepare a brief written summary of the poll or some aspect thereof. Include a statistical test for the significance of a proportion (you may have to make up your own value for the hypothesized proportion p_0) as part of your report. For example, you might select a political poll and test whether a particular candidate is preferred by a majority of voters ($p > 0.50$).

Appendix 8.1 ■ One-Sample Hypothesis Testing Using MINITAB

The first instruction block in this section begins by describing the entry of data into the MINITAB data window. Alternatively, the data may be loaded directly from the data disk included with the text. The appropriate data file name is given at the top of the instruction block. Please refer to Appendix 1.1 for further information about entering data, saving data, and printing results.

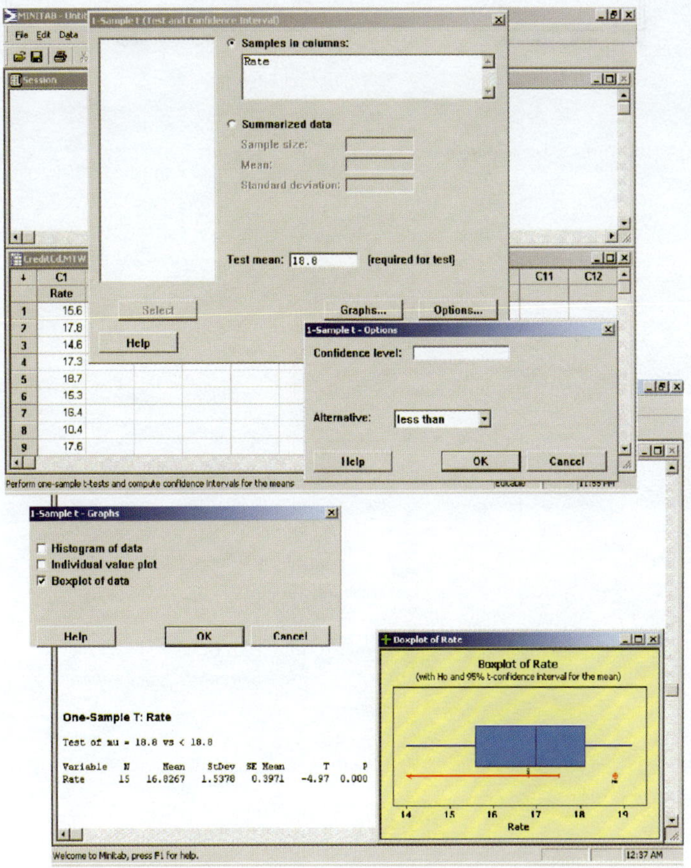

Hypothesis test for a population mean in Figure 8.10(a) on page 329 (data file: CreditCd.mtw):

- In the Data window, enter the interest rate data from Table 8.3 (page 328) into a single column with variable name Rate.
- Select **Stat : Basic Statistics : 1-Sample t.**
- In the "1-Sample t (Test and Confidence Interval)" dialog box, select the "Samples in columns" option.
- Select the variable Rate into the "Samples in columns" window.
- Enter the hypothesized mean (here 18.8) into the "Test mean" box.
- Click the Options... button, select the desired alternative (in this case "less than") from the Alternative drop-down menu, and click OK in the "1-Sample t -Options" dialog box.
- To produce a box plot of the data with a graphical representation of the hypothesis test—click the Graphs... button in the "1-Sample t (Test and Confidence Interval)" dialog box, check the "Boxplot of data" checkbox, and click OK in the "1-Sample t—Graphs" dialog box.
- Click OK in the "1-Sample t (Test and Confidence Interval)" dialog box.
- The confidence interval is given in the Session window, and the box plot appears in a graphics window.

A "1-Sample Z" test is also available in MINITAB under Basic Statistics. It requires a user-specified value of the population standard deviation, which is rarely known.

Hypothesis test for a population proportion in Exercise 8.72 on page 335:

- Select **Stat : Basic Statistics : 1 Proportion.**
- In the "1 Proportion (Test and Confidence Interval)" dialog box, select the "Summarized data" option.
- Enter the sample size (here equal to 400) into the "Number of Trials" box.
- Enter the sample number of successes (here equal to 146) into the "Number of events" box.
- Click on the Options... button.
- In the "1 Proportion—Options" dialog box, enter the hypothesized proportion (here equal to 0.25) into the "Test proportion" box.
- Select the desired alternative (in this case "greater than") from the Alternative drop-down menu.
- Check the "Use test and interval based on normal distribution" checkbox.
- Click OK in the "1 Proportion—Options" dialog box and click OK in the "1 Proportion (Test and Confidence Interval)" dialog box.
- The hypothesis test results are given in the Session window.

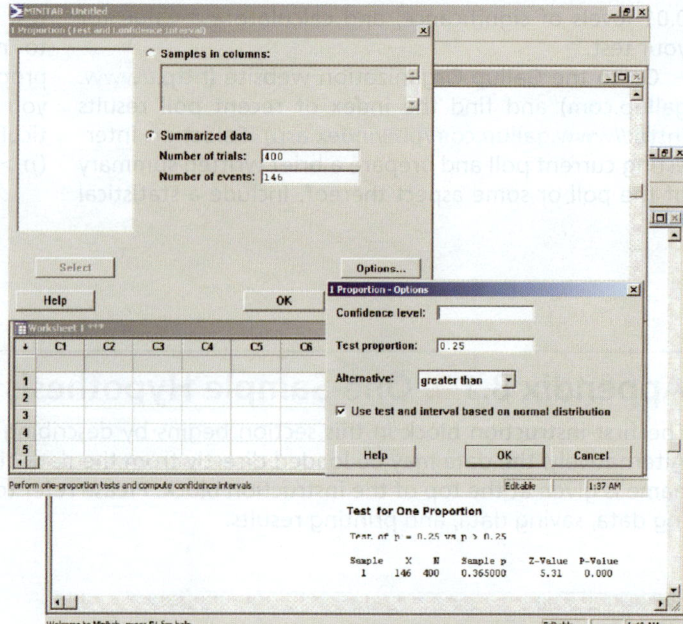

Appendix 8.2 ■ One-Sample Hypothesis Testing Using Excel

The instruction block in this section begins by describing the entry of data into an Excel spreadsheet. Alternatively, the data may be loaded directly from the data disk included with the text. The appropriate data file name is given at the top of the instruction block. Please refer to Appendix 1.2 for further information about entering data, saving data, and printing results.

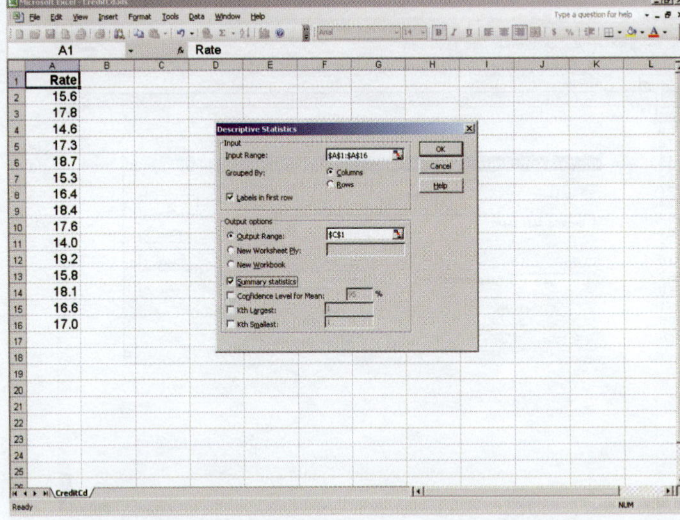

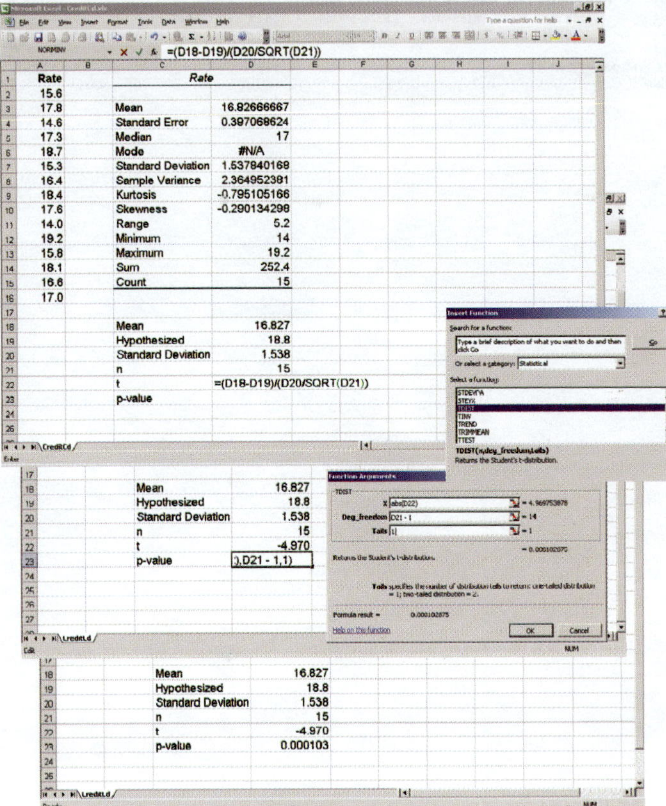

Hypothesis test for a population mean in Figure 8.10(b) on page 329 (data file: CreditCd.xls):

The Data Analysis ToolPak in Excel does not explicitly provide for one-sample tests of hypotheses. A one-sample test can be conducted using the Descriptive Statistics component of the Analysis ToolPak and a few additional computations using Excel.

Descriptive statistics:

- Enter the interest rate data from Table 8.3 (page 328) into cells A2.A16 with the label Rate in cell A1.
- Select **Tools : Data Analysis : Descriptive Statistics.**
- Click OK in the Data Analysis dialog box.
- In the Descriptive Statistics dialog box, enter A1.A16 into the Input Range box.
- Place a checkmark in the "Labels in first row" check box.
- Select the Output Range option and enter C1 into the Output Range box.
- Place a checkmark in the Summary Statistics check box.
- Click OK in the Descriptive Statistics dialog box.

The resulting block of descriptive statistics is displayed in the range C1.D15 and the values needed to carry out the test computations have been entered into the range C18.D21.

Computation of the test statistic and p-value:

- In cell D22, use the formula

  = (D18 − D19)/(D20/SQRT(D21)) to compute the test statistic t.
- Click on cell D23 and then select the Insert Function button f_x on the Excel toolbar.
- In the Insert Function dialog box, select Statistical from the "Or select a category:" menu, select TDIST from the "Select a function:" menu, and click OK in the Insert Function dialog box.
- In the TDIST Function Arguments dialog box, enter abs(D22) in the X box.
- Enter D21 – 1 in the Deg_freedom box.
- Enter 1 in the Tails box to select a one-tailed test.
- Click OK in the TDIST Function Arguments dialog box.
- The p-value related to the test will be placed in cell D23.

Appendix 8.3 ■ One-Sample Hypothesis Testing Using MegaStat

The instructions in this section begin by describing the entry of data into an Excel worksheet. Alternatively, the data may be loaded directly from the data disk included with the text. The appropriate data file name is given at the top of each instruction block. Please refer to Appendix 1.2 for further information about entering data and saving and printing results in Excel. Please refer to Appendix 1.3 for more information about using MegaStat.

Hypothesis test for a population mean in Figure 8.11 on page 329 (data file: CreditCd.xls):

- Enter the interest rate data from Table 8.3 (page 328) into cells A2.A16 with the label Rate in cell A1.
- Select **MegaStat : Hypothesis Tests : Mean vs. Hypothesized Value**
- In the "Hypothesis Test: Mean vs. Hypothesized Value" dialog box, click on "data input" and use the autoexpand feature to enter the range A1.A16 into the Input Range box.
- Enter the hypothesized value (here equal to 18.8) into the Hypothesized Mean box.
- Select the desired alternative (here "less than") from the drop-down menu in the Alternative box.
- Click on t-test and click OK in the "Hypothesis Test: Mean vs. Hypothesized Value" dialog box.
- A hypothesis test employing summary data can be carried out by clicking on "summary data", and by entering a range into the Input Range box that contains the following—label; sample mean; sample standard deviation; sample size n.

A z test can be carried out for large samples (or in the unlikely event that the population standard deviation is known) by clicking on "z-test".

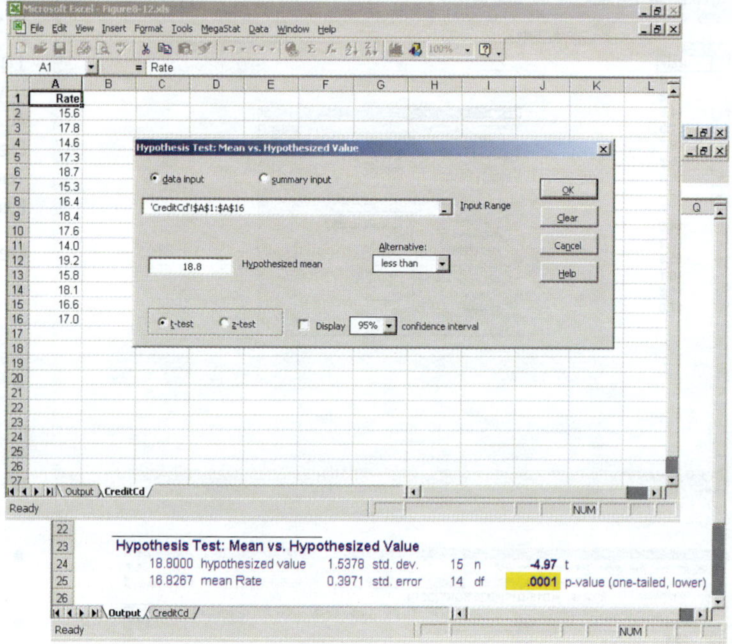

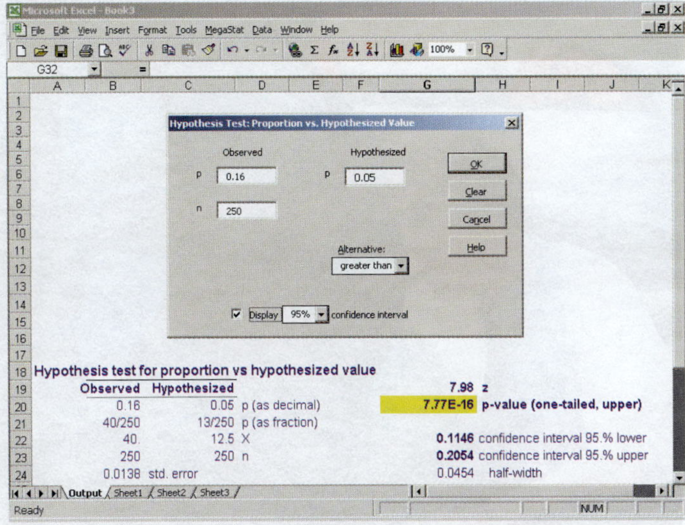

Hypothesis test for a population proportion shown in Figure 8.12 in the electronic article surveillance situation on page 334:

- Select **MegaStat : Hypothesis Tests : Proportion vs. Hypothesized Value**
- In the "Hypothesis Test: Proportion vs. Hypothesized Value" dialog box, enter the hypothesized value (here equal to 0.05) into the "Hypothesized p" box.
- Enter the observed sample proportion (here equal to 0.16) into the "Observed p" box.
- Enter the sample size (here equal to 250) into the "n" box.
- Select the desired alternative (here "greater than") from the drop-down menu in the Alternative box.
- Check the "Display confidence interval" checkbox (if desired), and select or type the appropriate level of confidence.
- Click OK in the "Hypothesis Test: Proportion vs. Hypothesized Value" dialog box.

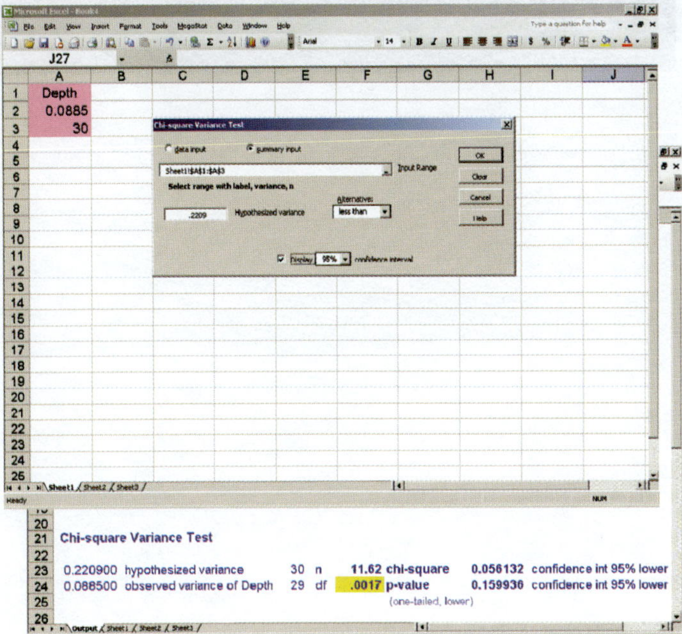

Hypothesis test for a population variance in the camshaft situation of Section 8.8 on page 345:

- Enter a label (in this case Depth) into cell A1, the sample variance (here equal to .0885) into cell A2, and the sample size (here equal to 30) into cell A3.
- Select **MegaStat : Hypothesis Tests : Chi-square Variance Test**
- Click on "summary input".
- Enter the range A1.A3 into the Input Range box—that is, enter the range containing the data label, the sample variance, and the sample size.
- Enter the hypothesized value (here equal to 0.2209) into the "Hypothesized variance" box.
- Select the desired alternative (in this case "less than") from the drop-down menu in the Alternative box.
- Check the "Display confidence interval" checkbox (if desired) and select or type the appropriate level of confidence.
- Click OK in the "Chi-square Variance Test" dialog box.
- A chi-square variance test may be carried out using **data input** by entering the observed sample values into a column in the Excel worksheet, and by then using the autoexpand feature to enter the range containing the label and sample values into the Input Range box.

CHAPTER 9

Statistical Inferences Based on Two Samples

Chapter Outline

9.1 Comparing Two Population Means by Using Independent Samples: Variances Known

9.2 Comparing Two Population Means by Using Independent Samples: Variances Unknown

9.3 Paired Difference Experiments

9.4 Comparing Two Population Proportions by Using Large, Independent Samples

9.5 Comparing Two Population Variances by Using Independent Samples

Business improvement often requires making comparisons. For example, to increase consumer awareness of a product or service, it might be necessary to compare different types of advertising campaigns. Or to offer more profitable investments to its customers, an investment firm might compare the profitability of different investment portfolios. As a third example, a manufacturer might compare different production methods in order to minimize or eliminate out-of-specification product.

In this chapter we discuss using confidence intervals and hypothesis tests to **compare two populations.** Specifically, we compare two population means, two population variances, and two population proportions. We make these comparisons by studying **differences** and **ratios.** For instance, to compare two population means, say μ_1 and μ_2, we consider the difference between these means, $\mu_1 - \mu_2$. If, for example, we use a confidence interval or hypothesis test to conclude that $\mu_1 - \mu_2$ is a positive number, then we conclude that μ_1 is greater than μ_2. On the other hand, if a confidence interval or hypothesis test shows that $\mu_1 - \mu_2$ is a negative number, then we conclude that μ_1 is less than μ_2. As another example, if we compare two population variances, say σ_1^2 and σ_2^2, we might consider the ratio σ_1^2/σ_2^2. If this ratio exceeds 1, then we can conclude that σ_1^2 is greater than σ_2^2.

We explain many of this chapter's methods in the context of three new cases:

C

The Catalyst Comparison Case: The production supervisor at a chemical plant uses confidence intervals and hypothesis tests for the difference between two population means to determine which of two catalysts maximizes the hourly yield of a chemical process. By maximizing yield, the plant increases its productivity and improves its profitability.

The Repair Cost Comparison Case: In order to reduce the costs of automobile accident claims, an insurance company uses confidence intervals and hypothesis tests for the difference between two population means to compare repair cost estimates for damaged cars at two different garages.

The Advertising Media Case: An advertising agency is test marketing a new product by using one advertising campaign in Des Moines, Iowa, and a different campaign in Toledo, Ohio. The agency uses confidence intervals and hypothesis tests for the difference between two population proportions to compare the effectiveness of the two advertising campaigns.

9.1 Comparing Two Population Means by Using Independent Samples: Variances Known

VS CHAPTER 10

A bank manager has developed a new system to reduce the time customers spend waiting to be served by tellers during peak business hours. We let μ_1 denote the mean customer waiting time during peak business hours under the current system. To estimate μ_1, the manager randomly selects $n_1 = 100$ customers and records the length of time each customer spends waiting for service. The manager finds that the sample mean waiting time for these 100 customers is $\bar{x}_1 = 8.79$ minutes. We let μ_2 denote the mean customer waiting time during peak business hours for the new system. During a trial run, the manager finds that the mean waiting time for a random sample of $n_2 = 100$ customers is $\bar{x}_2 = 5.14$ minutes.

In order to compare μ_1 and μ_2, the manager estimates $\mu_1 - \mu_2$, the difference between μ_1 and μ_2. Intuitively, a logical point estimate of $\mu_1 - \mu_2$ is the difference between the sample means

$$\bar{x}_1 - \bar{x}_2 = 8.79 - 5.14 = 3.65 \text{ minutes}$$

This says we estimate that the current mean waiting time is 3.65 minutes longer than the mean waiting time under the new system. That is, we estimate that the new system reduces the mean waiting time by 3.65 minutes.

To compute a confidence interval for $\mu_1 - \mu_2$ (or to test a hypothesis about $\mu_1 - \mu_2$), we need to know the properties of the sampling distribution of $\bar{x}_1 - \bar{x}_2$. To understand this sampling distribution, consider randomly selecting a sample[1] of n_1 measurements from a population having mean μ_1 and variance σ_1^2. Let $\bar{x}_1$ be the mean of this sample. Also consider randomly selecting a

[1] Each sample in this chapter is a *random* sample. As has been our practice throughout this book, for brevity we sometimes refer to "random samples" as "samples."

FIGURE 9.1 The Sampling Distribution of $\bar{x}_1 - \bar{x}_2$ Has Mean $\mu_1 - \mu_2$ and Standard Deviation $\sigma_{\bar{x}_1-\bar{x}_2}$

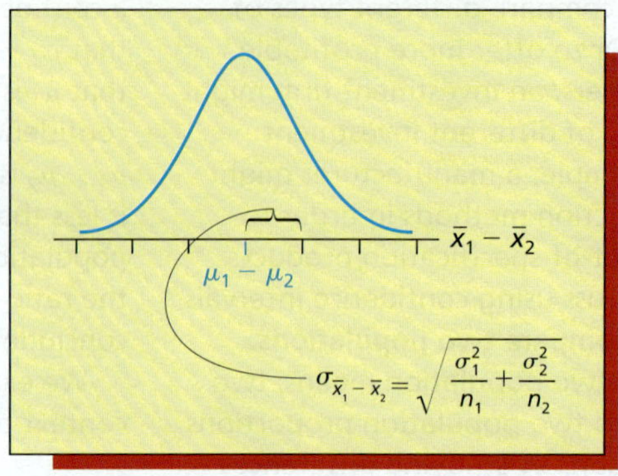

sample of n_2 measurements from another population having mean μ_2 and variance σ_2^2. Let $\bar{x}_2$ be the mean of this sample. Different samples from the first population would give different values of $\bar{x}_1$, and different samples from the second population would give different values of $\bar{x}_2$—so different pairs of samples from the two populations would give different values of $\bar{x}_1 - \bar{x}_2$. In the following box we describe the sampling distribution of $\bar{x}_1 - \bar{x}_2$, which is the probability distribution of all possible values of $\bar{x}_1 - \bar{x}_2$:

The Sampling Distribution of $\bar{x}_1 - \bar{x}_2$

If the randomly selected samples are **independent** of each other,[2] then the population of all possible values of $\bar{x}_1 - \bar{x}_2$

1 Has a normal distribution if each sampled population has a normal distribution, or has approximately a normal distribution if the sampled populations are not normally distributed and each of the sample sizes n_1 and n_2 is large.

2 Has mean $\mu_{\bar{x}_1-\bar{x}_2} = \mu_1 - \mu_2$

3 Has standard deviation $\sigma_{\bar{x}_1-\bar{x}_2} = \sqrt{\frac{\sigma_1^2}{n_1} + \frac{\sigma_2^2}{n_2}}$

Figure 9.1 illustrates the sampling distribution of $\bar{x}_1 - \bar{x}_2$. Using this sampling distribution, we can find a confidence interval for and test a hypothesis about $\mu_1 - \mu_2$. Although the interval and test assume that the true values of the population variances σ_1^2 and σ_2^2 are known, we believe that they are worth presenting because they provide a simple introduction to the basic idea of comparing two population means. Readers who wish to proceed more quickly to the more practical *t*-based procedures of the next section may skip the rest of this section without loss of continuity.

A *z*-Based Confidence Interval for $\mu_1 - \mu_2$, the Difference between Two Population Means, when σ_1 and σ_2 are Known

Let $\bar{x}_1$ be the mean of a sample of size n_1 that has been randomly selected from a population with mean μ_1 and standard deviation σ_1, and let $\bar{x}_2$ be the mean of a sample of size n_2 that has been randomly selected from a population with mean μ_2 and standard deviation σ_2. Furthermore, suppose that each sampled population is normally distributed, or that each of the sample sizes n_1 and n_2 is large. Then, if the samples are independent of each other, a **100(1 − α) percent confidence interval for $\mu_1 - \mu_2$** is

$$\left[(\bar{x}_1 - \bar{x}_2) \pm z_{\alpha/2}\sqrt{\frac{\sigma_1^2}{n_1} + \frac{\sigma_2^2}{n_2}}\right]$$

[2]This means that there is no relationship between the measurements in one sample and the measurements in the other sample.

Example 9.1 The Bank Customer Waiting Time Case 

Suppose the random sample of $n_1 = 100$ waiting times observed under the current system gives a sample mean $\bar{x}_1 = 8.79$ and the random sample of $n_2 = 100$ waiting times observed during the trial run of the new system yields a sample mean $\bar{x}_2 = 5.14$. Assuming that σ_1^2 is known to equal 4.7 and σ_2^2 is known to equal 1.9, and noting that each sample is large, a 95 percent confidence interval for $\mu_1 - \mu_2$ is

$$\left[(\bar{x}_1 - \bar{x}_2) \pm z_{.025}\sqrt{\frac{\sigma_1^2}{n_1} + \frac{\sigma_2^2}{n_2}}\right] = \left[(8.79 - 5.14) \pm 1.96\sqrt{\frac{4.7}{100} + \frac{1.9}{100}}\right]$$
$$= [3.65 \pm .5035]$$
$$= [3.15,\ 4.15]$$

This interval says we are 95 percent confident that the new system reduces the mean waiting time by between 3.15 minutes and 4.15 minutes.

Suppose we wish to test a hypothesis about $\mu_1 - \mu_2$. In the following box we describe how this can be done. Here we test the null hypothesis H_0: $\mu_1 - \mu_2 = D_0$, where D_0 is a number whose value varies depending on the situation.

A z Test about the Difference between Two Population Means: Testing H_0: $\mu_1 - \mu_2 = D_0$ when σ_1 and σ_2 Are Known

Let all notation be as defined in the preceding box, and define the test statistic

$$z = \frac{(\bar{x}_1 - \bar{x}_2) - D_0}{\sqrt{\frac{\sigma_1^2}{n_1} + \frac{\sigma_2^2}{n_2}}}$$

Assume that each sampled population is normally distributed, or that each of the sample sizes n_1 and n_2 is large. Then, if the samples are independent of each other, we can test H_0: $\mu_1 - \mu_2 = D_0$ versus a particular alternative hypothesis at level of significance α by using the appropriate rejection point rule, or, equivalently, the corresponding p-value.

Alternative Hypothesis	Rejection Point Rule: Reject H_0 if	p-Value (reject H_0 if p-value $< \alpha$)
H_a: $\mu_1 - \mu_2 > D_0$	$z > z_\alpha$	The area under the standard normal curve to the right of z
H_a: $\mu_1 - \mu_2 < D_0$	$z < -z_\alpha$	The area under the standard normal curve to the left of z
H_a: $\mu_1 - \mu_2 \neq D_0$	$\lvert z \rvert > z_{\alpha/2}$—that is, $z > z_{\alpha/2}$ or $z < -z_{\alpha/2}$	Twice the area under the standard normal curve to the right of $\lvert z \rvert$

Often D_0 will be the number 0. In such a case, the null hypothesis H_0: $\mu_1 - \mu_2 = 0$ says there is **no difference** between the population means μ_1 and μ_2. For example, in the bank customer waiting time situation, the null hypothesis H_0: $\mu_1 - \mu_2 = 0$ says there is no difference between the mean customer waiting times under the current and new systems. When D_0 is 0, each alternative hypothesis in the box implies that the population means μ_1 and μ_2 differ. For instance, in the bank waiting time situation, the alternative hypothesis H_a: $\mu_1 - \mu_2 > 0$ says that the current mean customer waiting time is longer than the new mean customer waiting time. That is, this alternative hypothesis says that the new system reduces the mean customer waiting time.

Example 9.2 The Bank Customer Waiting Time Case 

To attempt to provide evidence supporting the claim that the new system reduces the mean bank customer waiting time, we will test $\boldsymbol{H_0: \mu_1 - \mu_2 = 0}$ **versus** $\boldsymbol{H_a: \mu_1 - \mu_2 > 0}$ **at the .05 level of significance.** To perform the hypothesis test, we will use the sample information in Example 9.1 to calculate the value of the **test statistic** z **in the summary box.** Then, since $H_a: \mu_1 - \mu_2 > 0$ is of the form $H_a: \mu_1 - \mu_2 > D_0$, we will **reject** $\boldsymbol{H_0: \mu_1 - \mu_2 = 0}$ **if the value of** z **is greater than** $\boldsymbol{z_\alpha = z_{.05} = 1.645}$. Assuming that $\sigma_1^2 = 4.7$ and $\sigma_2^2 = 1.9$, the **value of the test statistic is**

$$z = \frac{(\bar{x}_1 - \bar{x}_2) - D_0}{\sqrt{\dfrac{\sigma_1^2}{n_1} + \dfrac{\sigma_2^2}{n_2}}} = \frac{(8.79 - 5.14) - 0}{\sqrt{\dfrac{4.7}{100} + \dfrac{1.9}{100}}} = \frac{3.65}{.2569} = 14.21$$

Because $\boldsymbol{z = 14.21}$ **is greater than** $\boldsymbol{z_{.05} = 1.645}$**, we reject** $\boldsymbol{H_0: \mu_1 - \mu_2 = 0}$ **in favor of** $\boldsymbol{H_a: \mu_1 - \mu_2 > 0}$**.** We conclude (at an α of .05) that $\mu_1 - \mu_2$ is greater than 0 and, therefore, that the new system reduces the mean customer waiting time. Furthermore, the point estimate $\bar{x}_1 - \bar{x}_2 = 3.65$ says we estimate that the new system reduces mean waiting time by 3.65 minutes. The p-value for the test is the area under the standard normal curve to the right of $z = 14.21$. Since this p-value is less than .001, it provides extremely strong evidence that H_0 is false and that H_a is true. That is, we have extremely strong evidence that $\mu_1 - \mu_2$ is greater than 0 and, therefore, that the new system reduces the mean customer waiting time.

Next, suppose that because of cost considerations, the bank manager wants to implement the new system only if it reduces mean waiting time by more than three minutes. In order to demonstrate that $\mu_1 - \mu_2$ is greater than 3, the manager (setting D_0 equal to 3) will attempt to reject the null hypothesis $H_0: \mu_1 - \mu_2 = 3$ in favor of the alternative hypothesis $H_a: \mu_1 - \mu_2 > 3$ at the .05 level of significance. To perform the hypothesis test, we compute

$$z = \frac{(\bar{x}_1 - \bar{x}_2) - 3}{\sqrt{\dfrac{\sigma_1^2}{n_1} + \dfrac{\sigma_2^2}{n_2}}} = \frac{(8.79 - 5.14) - 3}{\sqrt{\dfrac{4.7}{100} + \dfrac{1.9}{100}}} = \frac{.65}{.2569} = 2.53$$

Because $z = 2.53$ is greater than $z_{.05} = 1.645$, we can reject $H_0: \mu_1 - \mu_2 = 3$ in favor of $H_a: \mu_1 - \mu_2 > 3$. The p-value for the test is the area under the standard normal curve to the right of $z = 2.53$. Table A.3 (page 824) tells us that this area is $.5 - .4943 = .0057$. Therefore, we have very strong evidence against $H_0: \mu_1 - \mu_2 = 3$ and in favor of $H_a: \mu_1 - \mu_2 > 3$. In other words, we have very strong evidence that the new system reduces mean waiting time by more than three minutes.

Exercises for Section 9.1

CONCEPTS

9.1 Suppose we compare two population means, μ_1 and μ_2, and consider the difference $\mu_1 - \mu_2$. In each case, indicate how μ_1 relates to μ_2 (that is, is μ_1 greater than, less than, equal to, or not equal to μ_2)?

a $\mu_1 - \mu_2 < 0$
b $\mu_1 - \mu_2 = 0$
c $\mu_1 - \mu_2 < -10$
d $\mu_1 - \mu_2 > 0$
e $\mu_1 - \mu_2 > 20$
f $\mu_1 - \mu_2 \neq 0$

9.2 Suppose we compute a 95 percent confidence interval for $\mu_1 - \mu_2$. If the interval is

a [3, 5], can we be 95 percent confident that μ_1 is greater than μ_2? Why or why not?
b [3, 5], can we be 95 percent confident that μ_1 is not equal to μ_2? Why or why not?
c [−20, −10], can we be 95 percent confident that μ_1 is not equal to μ_2? Why or why not?
d [−20, −10], can we be 95 percent confident that μ_1 is greater than μ_2? Why or why not?
e [−3, 2], can we be 95 percent confident that μ_1 is not equal to μ_2? Why or why not?
f [−10, 10], can we be 95 percent confident that μ_1 is less than μ_2? Why or why not?
g [−10, 10], can we be 95 percent confident that μ_1 is greater than μ_2? Why or why not?

9.3 In order to employ the formulas and tests of this section, the samples that have been randomly selected from the populations being compared must be independent of each other. In such a case, we say that we are performing an **independent samples experiment.** In your own words, explain what it means when we say that samples are independent of each other.

9.4 Describe the assumptions that must be met in order to validly use the methods of Section 9.1.

METHODS AND APPLICATIONS

9.5 Suppose we randomly select two independent samples from populations having means μ_1 and μ_2. If $\bar{x}_1 = 25$, $\bar{x}_2 = 20$, $\sigma_1 = 3$, $\sigma_2 = 4$, $n_1 = 100$, and $n_2 = 100$:

a Calculate a 95 percent confidence interval for $\mu_1 - \mu_2$. Can we be 95 percent confident that μ_1 is greater than μ_2? Explain.

b Test the null hypothesis H_0: $\mu_1 - \mu_2 = 0$ versus H_a: $\mu_1 - \mu_2 > 0$ by setting $\alpha = .05$. What do you conclude about how μ_1 compares to μ_2?

c Find the *p*-value for testing H_0: $\mu_1 - \mu_2 = 4$ versus H_a: $\mu_1 - \mu_2 > 4$. Use the *p*-value to test these hypotheses by setting α equal to .10, .05, .01, and .001.

9.6 Suppose we select two independent random samples from populations having means μ_1 and μ_2. If $\bar{x}_1 = 151$, $\bar{x}_2 = 162$, $\sigma_1 = 6$, $\sigma_2 = 8$, $n_1 = 625$, and $n_2 = 625$:

a Calculate a 95 percent confidence interval for $\mu_1 - \mu_2$. Can we be 95 percent confident that μ_2 is greater than μ_1? By how much? Explain.

b Test the null hypothesis H_0: $\mu_1 - \mu_2 = -10$ versus H_a: $\mu_1 - \mu_2 < -10$ by setting $\alpha = .05$. What do you conclude?

c Test the null hypothesis H_0: $\mu_1 - \mu_2 = -10$ versus H_a: $\mu_1 - \mu_2 \neq -10$ by setting α equal to .01. What do you conclude?

d Find the *p*-value for testing H_0: $\mu_1 - \mu_2 = -10$ versus H_a: $\mu_1 - \mu_2 \neq -10$. Use the *p*-value to test these hypotheses by setting α equal to .10, .05, .01, and .001.

9.7 In an article in *Accounting and Business Research,* Carslaw and Kaplan study the effect of control (owner versus manager control) on audit delay (the length of time from a company's financial year-end to the date of the auditor's report) for public companies in New Zealand. Suppose a random sample of 100 public owner-controlled companies in New Zealand gives a mean audit delay of $\bar{x}_1 = 82.6$ days, while a random sample of 100 public manager-controlled companies in New Zealand gives a mean audit delay of $\bar{x}_2 = 93$ days. Assuming the samples are independent and that $\sigma_1 = 32.83$ and $\sigma_2 = 37.18$:

a Let μ_1 be the mean audit delay for all public owner-controlled companies in New Zealand, and let μ_2 be the mean audit delay for all public manager-controlled companies in New Zealand. Calculate a 95 percent confidence interval for $\mu_1 - \mu_2$. Based on this interval, can we be 95 percent confident that the mean audit delay for all public owner-controlled companies in New Zealand is less than that for all public manager-controlled companies in New Zealand? If so, by how much?

b Consider testing the null hypothesis H_0: $\mu_1 - \mu_2 = 0$ versus H_a: $\mu_1 - \mu_2 < 0$. Interpret (in writing) the meaning (in practical terms) of each of H_0 and H_a.

c Use a rejection point to test the null hypothesis H_0: $\mu_1 - \mu_2 = 0$ versus H_a: $\mu_1 - \mu_2 < 0$ at the .05 level of significance. Based on this test, what do you conclude about how μ_1 and μ_2 compare? Write your conclusion in practical terms.

d Find the *p*-value for testing H_0: $\mu_1 - \mu_2 = 0$ versus H_a: $\mu_1 - \mu_2 < 0$. Use the *p*-value to test H_0 versus H_a by setting α equal to .10, .05, .025, .01, and .001. How much evidence is there that μ_1 is less than μ_2?

9.8 In an article in the *Journal of Management,* Wright and Bonett study the relationship between voluntary organizational turnover and such factors as work performance, work satisfaction, and company tenure. As part of the study, the authors compare work performance ratings for "stayers" (employees who stay in their organization) and "leavers" (employees who voluntarily quit their jobs). Suppose that a random sample of 175 stayers has a mean performance rating (on a 20-point scale) of $\bar{x}_1 = 12.8$, and that a random sample of 140 leavers has a mean performance rating of $\bar{x}_2 = 14.7$. Assuming these random samples are independent and that $\sigma_1 = 3.7$ and $\sigma_2 = 4.5$:

a Let μ_1 be the mean performance rating for stayers, and let μ_2 be the mean performance rating for leavers. Use the sample information to calculate a 99 percent confidence interval for $\mu_1 - \mu_2$. Based on this interval, can we be 99 percent confident that the mean performance rating for leavers is greater than the mean performance rating for stayers? What are the managerial implications of this result?

b Set up the null and alternative hypotheses needed to try to establish that the mean performance rating for leavers is higher than the mean performance rating for stayers.

c Use rejection points to test the hypotheses you set up in part *b* by setting α equal to .10, .05, .01, and .001. How much evidence is there that leavers have a higher mean performance rating than do stayers?

9.9 An Ohio university wishes to demonstrate that car ownership is detrimental to academic achievement. A random sample of 100 students who do not own cars had a mean grade point average (GPA) of 2.68, while a random sample of 100 students who own cars had a mean GPA of 2.55.

a Assuming that the independence assumption holds, and letting μ_1 = the mean GPA for all students who do not own cars, and μ_2 = the mean GPA for all students who own cars, use the above data to compute a 95 percent confidence interval for $\mu_1 - \mu_2$. Assume here that $\sigma_1 = .7$ and $\sigma_2 = .6$.

b On the basis of the interval calculated in part *a*, can the university statistically justify that car ownership harms academic achievement? That is, can the university justify that μ_1 is greater than μ_2? Explain.

c Set up the null and alternative hypotheses that should be used to attempt to justify that the mean GPA for non–car owners is higher than the mean GPA for car owners.

d Test the hypotheses that you set up in part *c* with $\alpha = .05$. Again assume that $\sigma_1 = .7$ and $\sigma_2 = .6$. Interpret the results of this test. That is, what do your results say about whether the university can statistically justify that car ownership hurts academic achievement?

9.10 In the *Journal of Marketing,* Bayus studied differences between "early replacement buyers" and "late replacement buyers." Suppose that a random sample of 800 early replacement buyers yields a mean number of dealers visited of $\bar{x}_1 = 3.3$, and that a random sample of 500 late replacement buyers yields a mean number of dealers visited of $\bar{x}_2 = 4.5$. Assuming that these samples are independent:

a Let μ_1 be the mean number of dealers visited by early replacement buyers, and let μ_2 be the mean number of dealers visited by late replacement buyers. Calculate a 95 percent confidence interval for $\mu_2 - \mu_1$. Assume here that $\sigma_1 = .71$ and $\sigma_2 = .66$. Based on this interval, can we be 95 percent confident that on average late replacement buyers visit more dealers than do early replacement buyers?

b Set up the null and alternative hypotheses needed to attempt to show that the mean number of dealers visited by late replacement buyers exceeds the mean number of dealers visited by early replacement buyers by more than 1.

c Test the hypotheses you set up in part *b* by using rejection points and by setting α equal to .10, .05, .01, and .001. How much evidence is there that H_0 should be rejected?

d Find the *p*-value for testing the hypotheses you set up in part *b*. Use the *p*-value to test these hypotheses with α equal to .10, .05, .01, and .001. How much evidence is there that H_0 should be rejected? Explain your conclusion in practical terms.

e Do you think that the results of the hypothesis tests in parts *c* and *d* have practical significance? Explain and justify your answer.

9.11 In the book *Essentials of Marketing Research,* William R. Dillon, Thomas J. Madden, and Neil H. Firtle discuss a corporate image study designed to find out whether perceptions of technical support services vary depending on the position of the respondent in the organization. The management of a company that supplies telephone cable to telephone companies commissioned a media campaign primarily designed to

> (1) increase awareness of the company and (2) create favorable perceptions of the company's technical support. The campaign was targeted to purchasing managers and technical managers at independent telephone companies with greater than 10,000 trunk lines.

Perceptual ratings were measured with a nine-point agree–disagree scale. Suppose the results of a telephone survey of 175 technical managers and 125 purchasing managers reveal that the mean perception score for technical managers is 7.3 and that the mean perception score for purchasing managers is 8.2.

a Let μ_1 be the mean perception score for all purchasing managers, and let μ_2 be the mean perception score for all technical managers. Set up the null and alternative hypotheses needed to establish whether the mean perception scores for purchasing managers and technical managers differ. Hint: If μ_1 and μ_2 do not differ, what does $\mu_1 - \mu_2$ equal?

b Assuming that the samples of 175 technical managers and 125 purchasing managers are independent random samples, test the hypotheses you set up in part *a* by using a rejection point with $\alpha = .05$. Assume here that $\sigma_1 = 1.6$ and $\sigma_2 = 1.4$. What do you conclude about whether the mean perception scores for purchasing managers and technical managers differ?

c Find the *p*-value for testing the hypotheses you set up in part *a*. Use the *p*-value to test these hypotheses by setting α equal to .10, .05, .01, and .001. How much evidence is there that the mean perception scores for purchasing managers and technical managers differ?

d Calculate a 99 percent confidence interval for $\mu_1 - \mu_2$. Interpret this interval.

9.2 Comparing Two Population Means by Using Independent Samples: Variances Unknown

CHAPTER 10

Suppose that (as is usually the case) the true values of the population variances σ_1^2 and σ_2^2 are not known. We then estimate σ_1^2 and σ_2^2 by using s_1^2 and s_2^2, the variances of the samples randomly selected from the populations being compared. There are two approaches to doing this. The first approach assumes that the population variances σ_1^2 and σ_2^2 are equal. Denoting the common value of these variances as σ^2, it follows that

$$\sigma_{\bar{x}_1-\bar{x}_2} = \sqrt{\frac{\sigma_1^2}{n_1} + \frac{\sigma_2^2}{n_2}} = \sqrt{\frac{\sigma^2}{n_1} + \frac{\sigma^2}{n_2}} = \sqrt{\sigma^2\left(\frac{1}{n_1} + \frac{1}{n_2}\right)}$$

Because we are assuming that $\sigma_1^2 = \sigma_2^2 = \sigma^2$, we do not need separate estimates of σ_1^2 and σ_2^2. Instead, we combine the results of the two independent random samples to compute a single estimate of σ^2. This estimate is called the **pooled estimate** of σ^2, and it is a weighted average of the two sample variances s_1^2 and s_2^2. Denoting the pooled estimate as s_p^2, it is computed using the formula

$$s_p^2 = \frac{(n_1 - 1)s_1^2 + (n_2 - 1)s_2^2}{n_1 + n_2 - 2}$$

Using s_p^2, the estimate of $\sigma_{\bar{x}_1-\bar{x}_2}$ is

$$\sqrt{s_p^2\left(\frac{1}{n_1} + \frac{1}{n_2}\right)}$$

and we form the statistic

$$\frac{(\bar{x}_1 - \bar{x}_2) - (\mu_1 - \mu_2)}{\sqrt{s_p^2\left(\frac{1}{n_1} + \frac{1}{n_2}\right)}}$$

It can be shown that, if we have randomly selected independent samples from two normally distributed populations having equal variances, then the sampling distribution of this statistic is a t distribution having $(n_1 + n_2 - 2)$ degrees of freedom. Therefore, we can obtain the following confidence interval for $\mu_1 - \mu_2$:

A *t*-Based Confidence Interval for $\mu_1 - \mu_2$, the Difference between Two Population Means, when $\sigma_1^2 = \sigma_2^2$

Suppose we have randomly selected independent samples from two normally distributed populations having equal variances. Then, a **100(1 − α) percent confidence interval for $\mu_1 - \mu_2$** is

$$\left[(\bar{x}_1 - \bar{x}_2) \pm t_{\alpha/2}\sqrt{s_p^2\left(\frac{1}{n_1} + \frac{1}{n_2}\right)}\right] \quad \text{where} \quad s_p^2 = \frac{(n_1 - 1)s_1^2 + (n_2 - 1)s_2^2}{n_1 + n_2 - 2}$$

and $t_{\alpha/2}$ is based on $(n_1 + n_2 - 2)$ degrees of freedom.

Example 9.3 The Catalyst Comparison Case

C

A production supervisor at a major chemical company must determine which of two catalysts, catalyst XA-100 or catalyst ZB-200, maximizes the hourly yield of a chemical process. In order to compare the mean hourly yields obtained by using the two catalysts, the supervisor runs the process using each catalyst for five one-hour periods. The resulting yields (in pounds per hour)

TABLE 9.1 Yields of a Chemical Process Obtained Using Two Catalysts Catalyst

Catalyst XA-100	Catalyst ZB-200
801	752
814	718
784	776
836	742
820	763
$\bar{x}_1 = 811$	$\bar{x}_2 = 750.2$
$s_1^2 = 386$	$s_2^2 = 484.2$

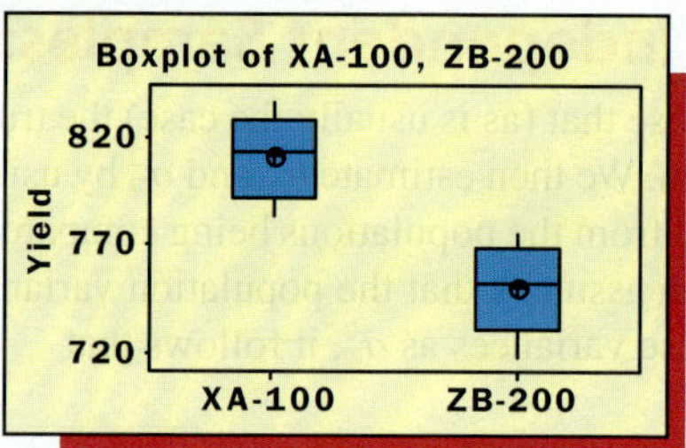

for each catalyst, along with the means, variances, and box plots[3] of the yields, are given in Table 9.1. Assuming that all other factors affecting yields of the process have been held as constant as possible during the test runs, it seems reasonable to regard the five observed yields for each catalyst as a random sample from the population of all possible hourly yields for the catalyst. Furthermore, since the sample variances $s_1^2 = 386$ and $s_2^2 = 484.2$ do not differ substantially (notice that $s_1 = 19.65$ and $s_2 = 22.00$ differ by even less), it might be reasonable to conclude that the population variances are approximately equal.[4] It follows that the pooled estimate

$$s_p^2 = \frac{(n_1 - 1)s_1^2 + (n_2 - 1)s_2^2}{n_1 + n_2 - 2}$$

$$= \frac{(5 - 1)(386) + (5 - 1)(484.2)}{5 + 5 - 2} = 435.1$$

is a point estimate of the common variance σ^2.

We define μ_1 as the mean hourly yield obtained by using catalyst XA-100, and we define μ_2 as the mean hourly yield obtained by using catalyst ZB-200. If the populations of all possible hourly yields for the catalysts are normally distributed, then a 95 percent confidence interval for $\mu_1 - \mu_2$ is

$$\left[(\bar{x}_1 - \bar{x}_2) \pm t_{.025}\sqrt{s_p^2\left(\frac{1}{n_1} + \frac{1}{n_2}\right)}\right]$$

$$= \left[(811 - 750.2) \pm 2.306\sqrt{435.1\left(\frac{1}{5} + \frac{1}{5}\right)}\right]$$

$$= [60.8 \pm 30.4217]$$

$$= [30.38,\ 91.22]$$

Here $t_{.025} = 2.306$ is based on $n_1 + n_2 - 2 = 5 + 5 - 2 = 8$ degrees of freedom. This interval tells us that we are 95 percent confident that the mean hourly yield obtained by using catalyst XA-100 is between 30.38 and 91.22 pounds higher than the mean hourly yield obtained by using catalyst ZB-200.

Suppose we wish to test a hypothesis about $\mu_1 - \mu_2$. In the following box we describe how this can be done. Here we test the null hypothesis $H_0: \mu_1 - \mu_2 = D_0$, where D_0 is a number whose value varies depending on the situation. Often D_0 will be the number 0. In such a case, the null hypothesis $H_0: \mu_1 - \mu_2 = 0$ says there is **no difference** between the population means μ_1 and μ_2. In this case, each alternative hypothesis in the box implies that the population means μ_1 and μ_2 differ in a particular way.

[3]All of the box plots presented in this chapter and in Chapter 10 have been obtained using MINITAB.

[4]We describe how to test the equality of two variances in Section 9.5 (although, as we will explain, this test has drawbacks).

A t Test about the Difference between Two Population Means: Testing $H_0: \mu_1 - \mu_2 = D_0$ when $\sigma_1^2 = \sigma_2^2$

Define the test statistic

$$t = \frac{(\bar{x}_1 - \bar{x}_2) - D_0}{\sqrt{s_p^2\left(\frac{1}{n_1} + \frac{1}{n_2}\right)}}$$

and assume that the sampled populations are normally distributed with equal variances. Then, if the samples are independent of each other, we can test $H_0: \mu_1 - \mu_2 = D_0$ versus a particular alternative hypothesis at level of significance α by using the appropriate rejection point rule, or, equivalently, the corresponding p-value.

Alternative Hypothesis	Rejection Point Rule: Reject H_0 if	p-Value (reject H_0 if p-value $< \alpha$)
$H_a: \mu_1 - \mu_2 > D_0$	$t > t_\alpha$	The area under the t distribution curve to the right of t
$H_a: \mu_1 - \mu_2 < D_0$	$t < -t_\alpha$	The area under the t distribution curve to the left of t
$H_a: \mu_1 - \mu_2 \neq D_0$	$\lvert t\rvert > t_{\alpha/2}$—that is, $t > t_{\alpha/2}$ or $t < -t_{\alpha/2}$	Twice the area under the t distribution curve to the right of $\lvert t\rvert$.

Here t_α, $t_{\alpha/2}$, and the p-values are based on $n_1 + n_2 - 2$ degrees of freedom.

Example 9.4 The Catalyst Comparison Case

C

In order to compare the mean hourly yields obtained by using catalysts XA-100 and ZB-200, we will test $\boldsymbol{H_0: \mu_1 - \mu_2 = 0}$ **versus** $\boldsymbol{H_a: \mu_1 - \mu_2 \neq 0}$ **at the .05 level of significance.** To perform the hypothesis test, we will use the sample information in Table 9.1 to calculate the value of the **test statistic t in the summary box.** Then, since $H_a: \mu_1 - \mu_2 \neq 0$ is of the form $H_a: \mu_1 - \mu_2 \neq D_0$, we will **reject $H_0: \mu_1 - \mu_2 = 0$ if the absolute value of t is greater than $t_{\alpha/2} = t_{.025} = 2.306$.** Here the $t_{\alpha/2}$ point is based on $n_1 + n_2 - 2 = 5 + 5 - 2 = 8$ degrees of freedom. Using the data in Table 9.1, the **value of the test statistic** is

$$t = \frac{(\bar{x}_1 - \bar{x}_2) - D_0}{\sqrt{s_p^2\left(\frac{1}{n_1} + \frac{1}{n_2}\right)}} = \frac{(811 - 750.2) - 0}{\sqrt{435.1\left(\frac{1}{5} + \frac{1}{5}\right)}} = 4.6087$$

Because $\lvert t\rvert = 4.6087$ is greater than $t_{.025} = 2.306$, we can reject $H_0: \mu_1 - \mu_2 = 0$ in favor of $H_a: \mu_1 - \mu_2 \neq 0$. We conclude (at an α of .05) that the mean hourly yields obtained by using the two catalysts differ. Furthermore, the point estimate $\bar{x}_1 - \bar{x}_2 = 811 - 750.2 = 60.8$ says we estimate that the mean hourly yield obtained by using catalyst XA-100 is 60.8 pounds higher than the mean hourly yield obtained by using catalyst ZB-200.

BI

Figures 9.2(a) and (b) give the MegaStat and Excel outputs for testing H_0 versus H_a. The outputs tell us that $t = 4.61$ and that the associated p-value is .001736 (rounded to .0017 on the MegaStat output). The very small p-value tells us that we have very strong evidence against $H_0: \mu_1 - \mu_2 = 0$ and in favor of $H_a: \mu_1 - \mu_2 \neq 0$. In other words, we have very strong evidence that the mean hourly yields obtained by using the two catalysts differ. Finally, notice that the MegaStat output gives the 95 percent confidence interval for $\mu_1 - \mu_2$, which is [30.378, 91.222].

FIGURE 9.2 MegaStat and Excel Outputs for Testing the Equality of Means in the Catalyst Comparison Case Assuming Equal Variances

(a) The MegaStat Output

Hypothesis Test: Independent Groups (t-test, pooled variance)

XA-100	ZB-200			
811.00	750.20	mean	4.61	t
19.65	22.00	std. dev.	.0017	p-value (two-tailed)
5	5	n	30.378	confidence interval 95% lower
			91.222	confidence interval 95% upper

8	df
60.800	difference (XA-100 - ZB-200)
435.100	pooled variance
20.859	pooled std. dev.
13.192	standard error of difference
0	hypothesized difference

F-test for equality of variance

484.20	variance: ZB-200
386.00	variance: XA-100
1.25	F
.8314	p-value

(b) The Excel Output

t-Test: Two-Sample Assuming Equal Variances

	XA-100	ZB-200
Mean	811	750.2
Variance	386	484.2
Observations	5	5
Pooled Variance	435.1	
Hypothesized Mean Diff	0	
df	8	
t Stat	4.608706	
P(T<=t) one-tail	0.000868	
t Critical one-tail	1.859548	
P(T<=t) two-tail	0.001736	
t Critical two-tail	2.306004	

When the sampled populations are normally distributed and the population variances σ_1^2 and σ_2^2 differ, the following can be shown.

t-Based Confidence Intervals for $\mu_1 - \mu_2$, and t Tests of H_0: $\mu_1 - \mu_2 = D_0$ when $\sigma_1^2 \neq \sigma_2^2$

1 When the sample sizes n_1 and n_2 are equal, the "equal variances" t-based confidence interval and hypothesis test given in the preceding two boxes are approximately valid even if the population variances σ_1^2 and σ_2^2 differ substantially. As a rough rule of thumb, if the larger sample variance is not more than three times the smaller sample variance when the sample sizes are equal, we can use the equal variances interval and test.

2 Suppose that the larger sample variance is more than three times the smaller sample variance when the sample sizes are equal or, suppose that both the sample sizes and the sample variances differ substantially. Then, we can use an approximate procedure that is sometimes called an "unequal variances" procedure. This procedure says that an **approximate 100(1 − α) percent confidence interval for $\mu_1 - \mu_2$** is

$$\left[(\bar{x}_1 - \bar{x}_2) \pm t_{\alpha/2}\sqrt{\frac{s_1^2}{n_1} + \frac{s_2^2}{n_2}}\right]$$

Furthermore, we can test H_0: $\mu_1 - \mu_2 = D_0$ by using the test statistic

$$t = \frac{(\bar{x}_1 - \bar{x}_2) - D_0}{\sqrt{\frac{s_1^2}{n_1} + \frac{s_2^2}{n_2}}}$$

and by using the previously given rejection point and p-value conditions.

For both the interval and the test, the degrees of freedom are equal to

$$df = \frac{(s_1^2/n_1 + s_2^2/n_2)^2}{\frac{(s_1^2/n_1)^2}{n_1 - 1} + \frac{(s_2^2/n_2)^2}{n_2 - 1}}$$

Here, if df is not a whole number, we can round df down to the next smallest whole number.

In general, both the "equal variances" and the "unequal variances" procedures have been shown to be approximately valid when the sampled populations are only approximately normally distributed (say, if they are mound-shaped). Furthermore, although the above summary box might seem to imply that we should use the unequal variances procedure only if we cannot use the equal variances procedure, this is not necessarily true. In fact, since the unequal variances procedure can be shown to be a very accurate approximation whether or not the population variances are equal and for most sample sizes (here, both n_1 and n_2 should be at least 5), **many statisticians believe that it is best to use the unequal variances procedure in almost every situation.** If each of n_1 and n_2 is large (at least 30), both the equal variances procedure and the unequal variances procedure are approximately valid, no matter what probability distributions describe the sampled populations.

To illustrate the unequal variances procedure, consider the bank customer waiting time situation, and recall that $\mu_1 - \mu_2$ is the difference between the mean customer waiting time under the current system and the mean customer waiting time under the new system. Because of cost considerations, the bank manager wants to implement the new system only if it reduces the mean waiting time by more than three minutes. Therefore, the manager will test the **null hypothesis H_0: $\mu_1 - \mu_2 = 3$ versus the alternative hypothesis H_a: $\mu_1 - \mu_2 > 3$.** If H_0 can be rejected in favor of H_a at the **.05 level of significance,** the manager will implement the new system. Suppose that a random sample of $n_1 = 100$ waiting times observed under the current system gives a sample mean $\bar{x}_1 = 8.79$ and a sample variance $s_1^2 = 4.8237$. Further, suppose a random sample of $n_2 = 100$ waiting times observed during the trial run of the new system yields a sample mean $\bar{x}_2 = 5.14$ and a sample variance $s_2^2 = 1.7927$. Since each sample is large, we can use the **unequal variances test statistic *t* in the summary box.** The degrees of freedom for this statistic are

$$df = \frac{(s_1^2/n_1 + s_2^2/n_2)^2}{\dfrac{(s_1^2/n_1)^2}{n_1 - 1} + \dfrac{(s_2^2/n_2)^2}{n_2 - 1}}$$

$$= \frac{[(4.8237/100) + (1.7927/100)]^2}{\dfrac{(4.8237/100)^2}{99} + \dfrac{(1.7927/100)^2}{99}}$$

$$= 163.657$$

which we will round down to 163. Therefore, since H_a: $\mu_1 - \mu_2 > 3$ is of the form H_a: $\mu_1 - \mu_2 > D_0$, we will **reject H_0: $\mu_1 - \mu_2 = 3$ if the value of the test statistic *t* is greater than $t_\alpha = t_{.05} =$ 1.65** (which is based on 163 degrees of freedom and has been found using a computer). Using the sample data, the **value of the test statistic** is

$$t = \frac{(\bar{x}_1 - \bar{x}_2) - 3}{\sqrt{\dfrac{s_1^2}{n_1} + \dfrac{s_2^2}{n_2}}} = \frac{(8.79 - 5.14) - 3}{\sqrt{\dfrac{4.8237}{100} + \dfrac{1.7927}{100}}} = \frac{.65}{.25722} = 2.53$$

Because $t = 2.53$ is greater than $t_{.05} = 1.65$, we reject H_0: $\mu_1 - \mu_2 = 3$ in favor of H_a: $\mu_1 - \mu_2 > 3$. We conclude (at an α of .05) that $\mu_1 - \mu_2$ is greater than 3 and, therefore, that the new system reduces the mean customer waiting time by more than 3 minutes. Therefore, the bank manager will implement the new system. Furthermore, the point estimate $\bar{x}_1 - \bar{x}_2 = 3.65$ says that we estimate that the new system reduces mean waiting time by 3.65 minutes.

BI

Figure 9.3 gives the MegaStat output of using the unequal variances procedure to test H_0: $\mu_1 - \mu_2 = 3$ versus H_a: $\mu_1 - \mu_2 > 3$. The output tells us that $t = 2.53$ and that the associated *p*-value is .0062. The very small *p*-value tells us that we have very strong evidence against H_0: $\mu_1 - \mu_2 = 3$ and in favor of H_a: $\mu_1 - \mu_2 > 3$. That is, we have very strong evidence that $\mu_1 - \mu_2$ is greater than 3 and, therefore, that the new system reduces the mean customer waiting time by more than 3 minutes. To find a 95 percent confidence interval for $\mu_1 - \mu_2$, note that we can use a computer to find that $t_{.025}$ based on 163 degrees of freedom is 1.97. It follows that the 95 percent confidence interval for $\mu_1 - \mu_2$ is

$$\left[(\bar{x}_1 - \bar{x}_2) \pm t_{.025}\sqrt{\frac{s_1^2}{n_1} + \frac{s_2^2}{n_2}}\right] = \left[(8.79 - 5.14) \pm 1.97\sqrt{\frac{4.8237}{100} + \frac{1.7927}{100}}\right]$$

$$= [3.65 \pm .50792]$$

$$= [3.14, 4.16]$$

This interval is given on the MegaStat output and says that we are 95 percent confident that the new system reduces the mean customer waiting time by between 3.14 minutes and 4.16 minutes.

FIGURE 9.3 MegaStat Output of the Unequal Variances Procedure for the Bank Customer Waiting Time Situation

Hypothesis Test: Independent Groups (t-test, unequal variance)

Current	New	
8.79	5.14	mean
2.1963	1.3389	std. dev.
100	100	n

163	df
3.65000	difference (Current - New)
0.25722	standard error of difference
3	hypothesized difference
2.53	t
.0062	p-value (one-tailed, upper)
3.14208	confidence interval 95.% lower
4.15792	confidence interval 95.% upper
0.50792	half-width

F-test for equality of variance

2.69 F

1.46E-06 p-value

FIGURE 9.4 MINITAB Output of the Unequal Variances Procedure for the Catalyst Comparison Case

```
Two-Sample T-Test and CI: XA-100, ZB-200
          N     Mean    StDev   SE Mean
XA-100    5    811.0     19.6       8.8
ZB-200    5    750.2     22.0       9.8
Difference = mu (XA-100) - mu (ZB-200)
Estimate for difference:    60.8000
95% CI for difference:  (29.6049, 91.9951)
T-Test of difference = 0 (vs not =):
  T-Value = 4.61     P-Value = 0.002   DF = 7
```

In general, the degrees of freedom for the unequal variances procedure will always be less than or equal to $n_1 + n_2 - 2$, the degrees of freedom for the equal variances procedure. For example, if we use the unequal variances procedure to analyze the catalyst comparison data in Table 9.1, we can calculate *df* to be 7.9. This is slightly less than $n_1 + n_2 - 2 = 5 + 5 - 2 = 8$, the degrees of freedom for the equal variances procedure. Figure 9.4 gives the MINITAB output of the unequal variances analysis of the catalyst comparison data. Note that MINITAB rounds *df* down to 7 and finds that a 95 percent confidence interval for $\mu_1 - \mu_2$ is [29.6049, 91.9951]. MINITAB also finds that the test statistic for testing $H_0: \mu_1 - \mu_2 = 0$ versus $H_a: \mu_1 - \mu_2 \neq 0$ is $t = 4.61$ and that the associated *p*-value is .002. These results do not differ by much from the results given by the equal variances procedure (see Figure 9.2).

To conclude this section, it is important to point out that if the sample sizes n_1 and n_2 are not large (at least 30), and if we fear that the sampled populations might be far from normally distributed, we can use a **nonparametric method.** One nonparametric method for comparing populations when using independent samples is the **Wilcoxon rank sum test.** This test is discussed in Section 15.2 (pages 740–744).

Exercises for Section 9.2

CONCEPTS

For each of the formulas described below, list all of the assumptions that must be satisfied in order to validly use the formula.

9.12 The confidence interval formula in the formula box on page 363.

9.13 The confidence interval formula in the formula box on page 366.

9.14 The hypothesis test described in the formula box on page 365.

9.15 The hypothesis test described in the formula box on page 366.

METHODS AND APPLICATIONS

Suppose we have taken independent, random samples of sizes $n_1 = 7$ and $n_2 = 7$ from two normally distributed populations having means μ_1 and μ_2, and suppose we obtain $\bar{x}_1 = 240$, $\bar{x}_2 = 210$, $s_1 = 5$, and $s_2 = 6$. Using the equal variances procedure do Exercises 9.16, 9.17, and 9.18.

9.16 Calculate a 95 percent confidence interval for $\mu_1 - \mu_2$. Can we be 95 percent confident that $\mu_1 - \mu_2$ is greater than 20? Explain why we can use the equal variances procedure here.

9.17 Use rejection points to test the null hypothesis $H_0: \mu_1 - \mu_2 \leq 20$ versus the alternative hypothesis $H_a: \mu_1 - \mu_2 > 20$ by setting α equal to .10, .05, .01, and .001. How much evidence is there that the difference between μ_1 and μ_2 exceeds 20?

9.18 Use rejection points to test the null hypothesis $H_0: \mu_1 - \mu_2 = 20$ versus the alternative hypothesis $H_a: \mu_1 - \mu_2 \neq 20$ by setting α equal to .10, .05, .01, and .001. How much evidence is there that the difference between μ_1 and μ_2 is not equal to 20?

9.19 Repeat Exercises 9.16 through 9.18 using the unequal variances procedure. Compare your results to those obtained using the equal variances procedure.

9.20 The October 7, 1991, issue of *Fortune* magazine reported on the rapid rise of fees and expenses charged by mutual funds. Assuming that stock fund expenses and municipal bond fund expenses are each approximately normally distributed, suppose a random sample of 12 stock funds gives a mean annual expense of 1.63 percent with a standard deviation of .31 percent, and an independent random sample of 12 municipal bond funds gives a mean annual expense of 0.89 percent with a standard deviation of .23 percent. Let μ_1 be the mean annual expense for stock funds, and let μ_2 be the mean annual expense for municipal bond funds. Do parts (a), (b), and (c) by using the equal variances procedure. Then repeat (a), (b), and (c) using the unequal variances procedure. Compare your results.

a Set up the null and alternative hypotheses needed to attempt to establish that the mean annual expense for stock funds is larger than the mean annual expense for municipal bond funds. Test these hypotheses at the .05 level of significance. What do you conclude?

b Set up the null and alternative hypotheses needed to attempt to establish that the mean annual expense for stock funds exceeds the mean annual expense for municipal bond funds by more than .5 percent. Test these hypotheses at the .05 level of significance. What do you conclude?

c Calculate a 95 percent confidence interval for the difference between the mean annual expenses for stock funds and municipal bond funds. Can we be 95 percent confident that the mean annual expense for stock funds exceeds that for municipal bond funds by more than .5 percent? Explain.

9.21 In the book *Business Research Methods,* Donald R. Cooper and C. William Emory (1995) discuss a manager who wishes to compare the effectiveness of two methods for training new salespeople. The authors describe the situation as follows:

> The company selects 22 sales trainees who are randomly divided into two experimental groups—one receives type *A* and the other type *B* training. The salespeople are then assigned and managed without regard to the training they have received. At the year's end, the manager reviews the performances of salespeople in these groups and finds the following results:

	A Group	B Group
Average Weekly Sales	$\bar{x}_1 = \$1,500$	$\bar{x}_2 = \$1,300$
Standard Deviation	$s_1 = 225$	$s_2 = 251$

a Set up the null and alternative hypotheses needed to attempt to establish that type *A* training results in higher mean weekly sales than does type *B* training.

b Because different sales trainees are assigned to the two experimental groups, it is reasonable to believe that the two samples are independent. Assuming that the normality assumption holds, and using the equal variances procedure, test the hypotheses you set up in part *a* at levels of significance .10, .05, .01, and .001. How much evidence is there that type *A* training produces results that are superior to those of type *B*?

c Use the equal variances procedure to calculate a 95 percent confidence interval for the difference between the mean weekly sales obtained when type *A* training is used and the mean weekly sales obtained when type *B* training is used. Interpret this interval.

9.22 A marketing research firm wishes to compare the prices charged by two supermarket chains—Miller's and Albert's. The research firm, using a standardized one-week shopping plan (grocery list), makes identical purchases at 10 of each chain's stores. The stores for each chain are randomly selected, and all purchases are made during a single week.

The shopping expenses obtained at the two chains, along with box plots of the expenses, are as follows: ShopExp

Miller's

\$119.25	\$121.32	\$122.34	\$120.14	\$122.19
\$123.71	\$121.72	\$122.42	\$123.63	\$122.44

Albert's

\$111.99	\$114.88	\$115.11	\$117.02	\$116.89
\$116.62	\$115.38	\$114.40	\$113.91	\$111.87

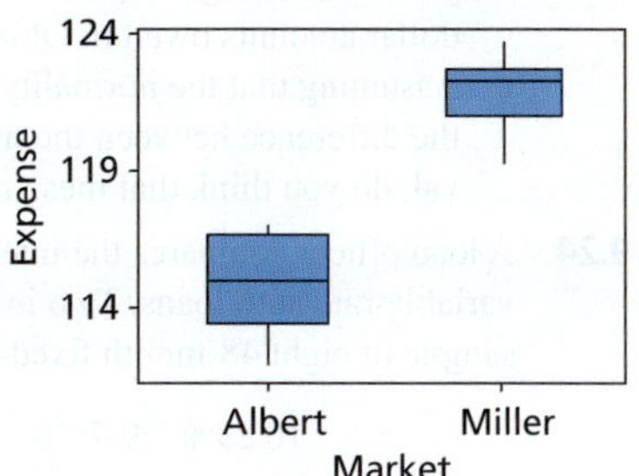

Because the stores in each sample are different stores in different chains, it is reasonable to assume that the samples are independent, and we assume that weekly expenses at each chain are normally distributed.

a Letting μ_M be the mean weekly expense for the shopping plan at Miller's, and letting μ_A be the mean weekly expense for the shopping plan at Albert's, Figure 9.5 gives the MINITAB output of the test of H_0: $\mu_M - \mu_A = 0$ (that is, there is no difference between μ_M and μ_A) versus H_a: $\mu_M - \mu_A \neq 0$ (that is, μ_M and μ_A differ). Note that MINITAB has employed the

FIGURE 9.5 MINITAB Output of Testing the Equality of Mean Weekly Expenses at Miller's and Albert's Supermarket Chains

```
Two-sample T for Millers vs Alberts
           N      Mean    StDev   SE Mean
Millers   10    121.92     1.40      0.44
Alberts   10    114.81     1.84      0.58

Difference = mu(Millers)- mu(Alberts)    Estimate for difference: 7.10900
95% CI for difference:   (5.57350, 8.64450)
T-Test of diff = 0 (vs not =): T-Value = 9.73   P-Value = 0.000  DF = 18
Both use Pooled StDev = 1.6343
```

equal variances procedure. Use the sample data to show that $\bar{x}_M = 121.92$, $s_M = 1.40$, $\bar{x}_A = 114.81$, $s_A = 1.84$, and $t = 9.73$.

b Using the t statistic given on the output and rejection points, test H_0 versus H_a by setting α equal to .10, .05, .01, and .001. How much evidence is there that the mean weekly expenses at Miller's and Albert's differ?

c Figure 9.5 gives the p-value for testing H_0: $\mu_M - \mu_A = 0$ versus H_a: $\mu_M - \mu_A \neq 0$. Use the p-value to test H_0 versus H_a by setting α equal to .10, .05, .01, and .001. How much evidence is there that the mean weekly expenses at Miller's and Albert's differ?

d Figure 9.5 gives a 95 percent confidence interval for $\mu_M - \mu_A$. Use this confidence interval to describe the size of the difference between the mean weekly expenses at Miller's and Albert's. Do you think that these means differ in a practically important way?

e Set up the null and alternative hypotheses needed to attempt to establish that the mean weekly expense for the shopping plan at Miller's exceeds the mean weekly expense at Albert's by more than $5. Test the hypotheses at the .10, .05, .01, and .001 levels of significance. How much evidence is there that the mean weekly expense at Miller's exceeds that at Albert's by more than $5?

9.23 A large discount chain compares the performance of its credit managers in Ohio and Illinois by comparing the mean dollar amounts owed by customers with delinquent charge accounts in these two states. Here a small mean dollar amount owed is desirable because it indicates that bad credit risks are not being extended large amounts of credit. Two independent, random samples of delinquent accounts are selected from the populations of delinquent accounts in Ohio and Illinois, respectively. The first sample, which consists of 10 randomly selected delinquent accounts in Ohio, gives a mean dollar amount of $524 with a standard deviation of $68. The second sample, which consists of 20 randomly selected delinquent accounts in Illinois, gives a mean dollar amount of $473 with a standard deviation of $22.

a Set up the null and alternative hypotheses needed to test whether there is a difference between the population mean dollar amounts owed by customers with delinquent charge accounts in Ohio and Illinois.

b Figure 9.6 gives the MegaStat output of using the unequal variances procedure to test the equality of mean dollar amounts owed by customers with delinquent charge accounts in Ohio and Illinois. Assuming that the normality assumption holds, test the hypotheses you set up in part a by setting α equal to .10, .05, .01, and .001. How much evidence is there that the mean dollar amounts owed in Ohio and Illinois differ?

c Assuming that the normality assumption holds, calculate a 95 percent confidence interval for the difference between the mean dollar amounts owed in Ohio and Illinois. Based on this interval, do you think that these mean dollar amounts differ in a practically important way?

9.24 A loan officer compares the interest rates for 48-month fixed-rate auto loans and 48-month variable-rate auto loans. Two independent, random samples of auto loan rates are selected. A sample of eight 48-month fixed-rate auto loans had the following loan rates: AutoLoan

10.29% 9.75% 9.50% 9.99% 9.75% 9.99% 11.40% 10.00%

while a sample of five 48-month variable-rate auto loans had loan rates as follows:

9.59% 8.75% 8.99% 8.50% 9.00%

a Set up the null and alternative hypotheses needed to determine whether the mean rates for 48-month fixed-rate and variable-rate auto loans differ.

b Figure 9.7 gives the MegaStat output of using the equal variances procedure to test the hypotheses you set up in part a. Assuming that the normality and equal variances assumptions hold, use the MegaStat output and rejection points to test these hypotheses by setting α equal to

FIGURE 9.6 MegaStat Output of Testing the Equality of Mean Dollar Amounts Owed for Ohio and Illinois

Hypothesis Test: Independent Groups (t-test, unequal variance)

Ohio	Illinois	
524	473	mean
68	22	std. dev.
10	20	n

9	df
51.000	difference (Ohio - Illinois)
22.059	standard error of difference
0	hypothesized difference
2.31	t
.0461	p-value (two-tailed)

FIGURE 9.7 MegaStat Output of Testing the Equality of Mean Loan Rates for Fixed and Variable 48-Month Auto Loans

Hypothesis Test: Independent Groups (t-test, pooled variance)

Fixed	Variable	
10.0838	8.9660	mean
0.5810	0.4046	std. dev.
8	5	n

F-test for equality of variance

0.3376	variance: Fixed
0.1637	variance: Variable
2.06	F
.5052	p-value

11	df
1.11775	difference (Fixed - Variable)
0.27437	pooled variance
0.52381	pooled std. dev.
0.29862	standard error of difference
0	hypothesized difference
3.74	t
.0032	p-value (two-tailed)

.10, .05, .01, and .001. How much evidence is there that the mean rates for 48-month fixed- and variable-rate auto loans differ?

c Figure 9.7 gives the p-value for testing the hypotheses you set up in part a. Use the p-value to test these hypotheses by setting α equal to .10, .05, .01, and .001. How much evidence is there that the mean rates for 48-month fixed- and variable-rate auto loans differ?

d Calculate a 95 percent confidence interval for the difference between the mean rates for fixed- and variable-rate 48-month auto loans. Can we be 95 percent confident that the difference between these means is .4 percent or more? Explain.

e Use a hypothesis test to establish that the difference between the mean rates for fixed- and variable-rate 48-month auto loans exceeds .4 percent. Use α equal to .05.

9.3 Paired Difference Experiments

Example 9.5 The Repair Cost Comparison Case

C

Home State Casualty, specializing in automobile insurance, wishes to compare the repair costs of moderately damaged cars (repair costs between \$700 and \$1,400) at two garages. One way to study these costs would be to take two independent samples (here we arbitrarily assume that each sample is of size $n = 7$). First we would randomly select seven moderately damaged cars that have recently been in accidents. Each of these cars would be taken to the first garage (garage 1), and repair cost estimates would be obtained. Then we would randomly select seven *different* moderately damaged cars, and repair cost estimates for these cars would be obtained at the second garage (garage 2). This sampling procedure would give us independent samples because the cars taken to garage 1 differ from those taken to garage 2. However, because the repair costs for moderately damaged cars can range from \$700 to \$1,400, there can be substantial differences in damages to moderately damaged cars. These differences might tend to conceal any real differences between repair costs at the two garages. For example, suppose the repair cost estimates for the cars taken to garage 1 are higher than those for the cars taken to garage 2. This difference might exist because garage 1 charges customers more for repair work than does garage 2. However, the difference could also arise because the cars taken to garage 1 are more severely damaged than the cars taken to garage 2.

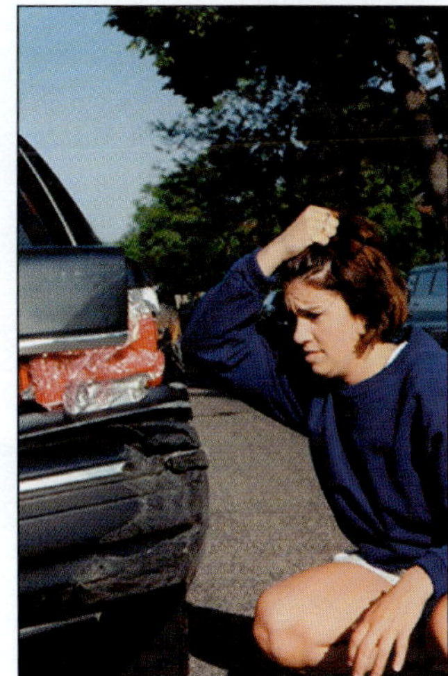

To overcome this difficulty, we can perform a **paired difference experiment.** Here we could randomly select one sample of $n = 7$ moderately damaged cars. The cars in this sample would be taken to both garages, and a repair cost estimate for each car would be obtained at each garage. The advantage of the paired difference experiment is that the repair cost estimates at the two garages are obtained for the same cars. Thus, any true differences in the repair cost estimates would not be concealed by possible differences in the severity of damages to the cars.

Suppose that when we perform the paired difference experiment, we obtain the repair cost estimates in Table 9.2 (these estimates are given in units of \$100). To analyze these data, we calculate the difference between the repair cost estimates at the two garages for each car. The resulting **paired differences** are given in the last column of Table 9.2. The mean of the sample of

TABLE 9.2 A Sample of $n = 7$ Paired Differences of the Repair Cost Estimates at Garages 1 and 2 (Cost Estimates in Hundreds of Dollars) Repair

Sample of $n = 7$ Damaged Cars	Repair Cost Estimates at Garage 1	Repair Cost Estimates at Garage 2	Sample of $n = 7$ Paired Differences
Car 1	\$ 7.1	\$ 7.9	$d_1 = -.8$
Car 2	9.0	10.1	$d_2 = -1.1$
Car 3	11.0	12.2	$d_3 = -1.2$
Car 4	8.9	8.8	$d_4 = .1$
Car 5	9.9	10.4	$d_5 = -.5$
Car 6	9.1	9.8	$d_6 = -.7$
Car 7	10.3	11.7	$d_7 = -1.4$
	$\bar{x}_1 = 9.329$	$\bar{x}_2 = 10.129$	$\bar{d} = -.8 = \bar{x}_1 - \bar{x}_2$ $s_d^2 = .2533$ $s_d = .5033$

$n = 7$ paired differences is

$$\bar{d} = \frac{-.8 + (-1.1) + (-1.2) + \cdots + (-1.4)}{7} = -.8$$

which equals the difference between the sample means of the repair cost estimates at the two garages

$$\bar{x}_1 - \bar{x}_2 = 9.329 - 10.129 = -.8$$

Furthermore, $\bar{d} = -.8$ (that is, $-\$80$) is the point estimate of

$$\mu_d = \mu_1 - \mu_2$$

the mean of the population of all possible paired differences of the repair cost estimates (for all possible moderately damaged cars) at garages 1 and 2—which is equivalent to μ_1, the mean of all possible repair cost estimates at garage 1, minus μ_2, the mean of all possible repair cost estimates at garage 2. This says we estimate that the mean of all possible repair cost estimates at garage 1 is \$80 less than the mean of all possible repair cost estimates at garage 2.

In addition, the variance and standard deviation of the sample of $n = 7$ paired differences

$$s_d^2 = \frac{\sum_{i=1}^{7} (d_i - \bar{d})^2}{7 - 1} = .2533$$

and

$$s_d = \sqrt{.2533} = .5033$$

are the point estimates of σ_d^2 and σ_d, the variance and standard deviation of the population of all possible paired differences.

In general, suppose we wish to compare two population means, μ_1 and μ_2. Also suppose that we have obtained two different measurements (for example, repair cost estimates) on the same n units (for example, cars), and suppose we have calculated the n paired differences between these measurements. Let $\bar{d}$ and s_d be the mean and the standard deviation of these n paired differences. If it is reasonable to assume that the paired differences have been randomly selected from a normally distributed (or at least mound-shaped) population of paired differences with mean μ_d and standard deviation σ_d, then the sampling distribution of

$$\frac{\bar{d} - \mu_d}{s_d/\sqrt{n}}$$

is a t distribution having $n - 1$ degrees of freedom. This implies that we have the following confidence interval for μ_d:

A Confidence Interval for the Mean, μ_d, of a Population of Paired Differences

Let μ_d be the mean of a **normally distributed population of paired differences,** and let $\bar{d}$ and s_d be the mean and standard deviation of a sample of n paired differences that have been randomly selected from the population. Then, a **100(1 − α) percent confidence interval for $\mu_d = \mu_1 - \mu_2$** is

$$\left[\bar{d} \pm t_{\alpha/2}\frac{s_d}{\sqrt{n}}\right]$$

Here $t_{\alpha/2}$ is based on $(n - 1)$ degrees of freedom.

Example 9.6 The Repair Cost Comparison Case

Using the data in Table 9.2, and assuming that the population of paired repair cost differences is normally distributed, a 95 percent confidence interval for $\mu_d = \mu_1 - \mu_2$ is

$$\left[\bar{d} \pm t_{.025}\frac{s_d}{\sqrt{n}}\right] = \left[-.8 \pm 2.447\frac{.5033}{\sqrt{7}}\right]$$
$$= [-.8 \pm .4654]$$
$$= [-1.2654, -.3346]$$

Here $t_{.025} = 2.447$ is based on $n - 1 = 7 - 1 = 6$ degrees of freedom. This interval says that Home State Casualty can be 95 percent confident that μ_d, the mean of all possible paired differences of the repair cost estimates at garages 1 and 2, is between −\$126.54 and −\$33.46. That is, we are 95 percent confident that μ_1, the mean of all possible repair cost estimates at garage 1, is between \$126.54 and \$33.46 less than μ_2, the mean of all possible repair cost estimates at garage 2.

We can also test a hypothesis about μ_d, the mean of a population of paired differences. We show how to test the null hypothesis

$$H_0: \mu_d = D_0$$

in the following box. Here the value of the constant D_0 depends on the particular problem. Often D_0 equals 0, and the null hypothesis $H_0: \mu_d = 0$ says that μ_1 and μ_2 do not differ.

Testing a Hypothesis about the Mean, μ_d, of a Population of Paired Differences: Testing $H_0: \mu_d = D_0$

Let μ_d, $\bar{d}$, and s_d be defined as in the preceding box. Also, assume that the population of paired differences is normally distributed, and consider testing

$$H_0: \mu_d = D_0$$

by using the test statistic

$$t = \frac{\bar{d} - D_0}{s_d/\sqrt{n}}$$

We can test $H_0: \mu_d = D_0$ versus a particular alternative hypothesis at level of significance α by using the appropriate rejection point rule, or, equivalently, the corresponding p-value.

Alternative Hypothesis	Rejection Point Rule: Reject H_0 if	p-Value (reject H_0 if p-value $< \alpha$)
$H_a: \mu_d > D_0$	$t > t_\alpha$	The area under the t distribution curve to the right of t
$H_a: \mu_d < D_0$	$t < -t_\alpha$	The area under the t distribution curve to the left of t
$H_a: \mu_d \neq D_0$	$\lvert t\rvert > t_{\alpha/2}$—that is, $t > t_{\alpha/2}$ or $t < -t_{\alpha/2}$	Twice the area under the t distribution curve to the right of $\lvert t\rvert$

Here t_α, $t_{\alpha/2}$, and the p-values are based on $n - 1$ degrees of freedom.

Example 9.7 The Repair Cost Comparison Case

Home State Casualty currently contracts to have moderately damaged cars repaired at garage 2. However, a local insurance agent suggests that garage 1 provides less expensive repair service that is of equal quality. Because it has done business with garage 2 for years, Home State has decided to give some of its repair business to garage 1 only if it has very strong evidence that μ_1, the mean repair cost estimate at garage 1, is smaller than μ_2, the mean repair cost estimate at garage 2—that is, if $\mu_d = \mu_1 - \mu_2$ is less than zero. Therefore, we will test **H_0: $\mu_d = 0$ or, equivalently, H_0: $\mu_1 - \mu_2 = 0$, versus H_a: $\mu_d < 0$ or, equivalently, H_a: $\mu_1 - \mu_2 < 0$,** at the **.01 level of significance.** To perform the hypothesis test, we will use the sample data in Table 9.2 to calculate the value of the **test statistic *t* in the summary box.** Since H_a: $\mu_d < 0$ is of the form H_a: $\mu_d < D_0$, we will **reject H_0: $\mu_d = 0$ if the value of *t* is less than $-t_\alpha = -t_{.01} = -3.143$.** Here the t_α point is based on $n - 1 = 7 - 1 = 6$ degrees of freedom. Using the data in Table 9.2, the **value of the test statistic** is

$$t = \frac{\bar{d} - D_0}{s_d/\sqrt{n}} = \frac{-.8 - 0}{.5033/\sqrt{7}} = -4.2053$$

Because $t = -4.2053$ is less than $-t_{.01} = -3.143$, we can reject H_0: $\mu_d = 0$ in favor of H_a: $\mu_d < 0$. We conclude (at an α of .01) that μ_1, the mean repair cost estimate at garage 1, is less than μ_2, the mean repair cost estimate at garage 2. As a result, Home State will give some of its repair business to garage 1. Furthermore, Figure 9.8(a), which gives the MINITAB output of this hypothesis test, shows us that the *p*-value for the test is .003. Since this *p*-value is very small, we have very strong evidence that H_0 should be rejected and that μ_1 is less than μ_2.

To demonstrate testing a "not equal to" alternative hypothesis, Figure 9.8(b) gives the MegaStat output of testing H_0: $\mu_d = 0$ versus H_a: $\mu_d \neq 0$. The output shows that the *p*-value for this two-tailed test is .0057. MegaStat will, of course, also perform the test of H_0: $\mu_d = 0$ versus H_a: $\mu_d < 0$. For this test (output not shown), MegaStat finds that the *p*-value is .0028 (or .003

FIGURE 9.8 MINITAB and MegaStat Outputs of Testing H_0: $\mu_d = 0$

(a) MINITAB output of testing H_0: $\mu_d = 0$ versus H_a: $\mu_d < 0$

```
Paired T for Garage1 - Garage2

              N       Mean      StDev    SE Mean
Garage1       7     9.3286     1.2500     0.4724
Garage2       7    10.1286     1.5097     0.5706
Difference    7  -0.800000   0.503322   0.190238

T-Test of mean difference = 0 (vs < 0):
                 T-Value = -4.21      P-Value = 0.003
```

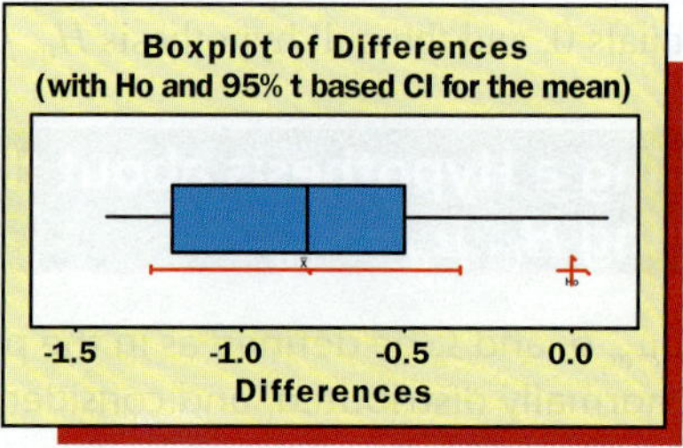

(b) MegaStat output of testing H_0: $\mu_d = 0$ versus H_a: $\mu_d \neq 0$

Hypothesis Test: Paired Observations

0.0000	hypothesized value
9.3286	mean Garage1
10.1286	mean Garage2
−0.8000	mean difference (Garage1 - Garage2)
0.5033	std. dev.
0.1902	std. error
7	n
6	df
−4.21	t
.0057	p-value (two-tailed)

FIGURE 9.9 Excel Output of Testing H_0: $\mu_d = 0$

t-Test: Paired Two Sample for Means

	Garage1	*Garage2*
Mean	9.328571	10.12857
Variance	1.562381	2.279048
Observations	7	7
Pearson Correlation	0.950744	
Hypothesized Mean	0	
df	6	
t Stat	−4.20526	
P(T<=t) one-tail	0.002826	
t Critical one-tail	1.943181	
P(T<=t) two-tail	0.005653	
t Critical two-tail	2.446914	

rounded). Finally, Figure 9.9 gives the Excel output of both the one- and two-tailed tests. The small p-value related to the one-tailed test tells us that Home State has very strong evidence that the mean repair cost at garage 1 is less than the mean repair cost at garage 2.

In general, an experiment in which we have obtained two different measurements on the same n units is called a **paired difference experiment.** The idea of this type of experiment is to remove the variability due to the variable (for example, the amount of damage to a car) on which the observations are paired. In many situations, a paired difference experiment will provide more information than an independent samples experiment. As another example, suppose that we wish to assess which of two different machines produces a higher hourly output. If we randomly select 10 machine operators and randomly assign 5 of these operators to test machine 1 and the others to test machine 2, we would be performing an independent samples experiment. This is because different machine operators test machines 1 and 2. However, any difference in machine outputs could be obscured by differences in the abilities of the machine operators. For instance, if the observed hourly outputs are higher for machine 1 than for machine 2, we might not be able to tell whether this is due to (1) the superiority of machine 1 or (2) the possible higher skill level of the operators who tested machine 1. Because of this, it might be better to randomly select five machine operators, thoroughly train each operator to use both machines, and have each operator test both machines. We would then be **pairing on the machine operator,** and this would remove the variability due to the differing abilities of the operators.

The formulas we have given for analyzing a paired difference experiment are based on the t distribution. These formulas assume that the population of all possible paired differences is normally distributed (or at least mound-shaped). If the sample size is large (say, at least 30), the t based interval and tests of this section are approximately valid no matter what the shape of the population of all possible paired differences. If the sample size is small, and if we fear that the population of all paired differences might be far from normally distributed, we can use a nonparametric method. One nonparametric method for comparing two populations when using a paired difference experiment is the **Wilcoxon signed ranks test,** discussed in Section 15.3.

Exercises for Section 9.3

CONCEPTS

9.25 Explain how a paired difference experiment differs from an independent samples experiment in terms of how the data for these experiments are collected.

9.26 Why is a paired difference experiment sometimes more informative than an independent samples experiment? Give an example of a situation in which a paired difference experiment might be advantageous.

9.27 What assumptions must be satisfied to appropriately carry out a paired difference experiment? When can we carry out a paired difference experiment no matter what the shape of the population of all paired differences might be?

9.28 Suppose a company wishes to compare the hourly output of its employees before and after vacations. Explain how you would collect data for a paired difference experiment to make this comparison.

METHODS AND APPLICATIONS

9.29 Suppose a sample of 11 paired differences that has been randomly selected from a normally distributed population of paired differences yields a sample mean of $\bar{d} = 103.5$ and a sample standard deviation of $s_d = 5$.

a Calculate 95 percent and 99 percent confidence intervals for $\mu_d = \mu_1 - \mu_2$. Can we be 95 percent confident that the difference between μ_1 and μ_2 exceeds 100? Can we be 99 percent confident?

b Test the null hypothesis H_0: $\mu_d \leq 100$ versus H_a: $\mu_d > 100$ by setting α equal to .05 and .01. How much evidence is there that $\mu_d = \mu_1 - \mu_2$ exceeds 100?

c Test the null hypothesis H_0: $\mu_d \geq 110$ versus H_a: $\mu_d < 110$ by setting α equal to .05 and .01. How much evidence is there that $\mu_d = \mu_1 - \mu_2$ is less than 110?

9.30 Suppose a sample of 49 paired differences that have been randomly selected from a normally distributed population of paired differences yields a sample mean of $\bar{d} = 5$ and a sample standard deviation of $s_d = 7$.

a Calculate a 95 percent confidence interval for $\mu_d = \mu_1 - \mu_2$. Can we be 95 percent confident that the difference between μ_1 and μ_2 is greater than 0?

b Test the null hypothesis H_0: $\mu_d = 0$ versus the alternative hypothesis H_a: $\mu_d \neq 0$ by setting α equal to .10, .05, .01, and .001. How much evidence is there that μ_d differs from 0? What does this say about how μ_1 and μ_2 compare?

c Find the p-value for testing H_0: $\mu_d \leq 3$ versus H_a: $\mu_d > 3$. Use the p-value to test these hypotheses with α equal to .10, .05, .01, and .001. How much evidence is there that μ_d exceeds 3? What does this say about the size of the difference between μ_1 and μ_2?

9.31 On its website, the *Statesman Journal* newspaper (Salem, Oregon, 1999) reports mortgage loan interest rates for 30-year and 15-year fixed-rate mortgage loans for a number of Willamette Valley lending institutions. Of interest is whether there is any systematic difference between 30-year rates and 15-year rates (expressed as annual percentage rate or APR) and, if there is, what is the size of that difference. Table 9.3 displays mortgage loan rates and the difference between 30-year and 15-year rates for nine randomly selected lending institutions. Assuming that the population of paired differences is normally distributed: Mortgage99

a Set up the null and alternative hypotheses needed to determine whether there is a difference between mean 30-year rates and mean 15-year rates.

b Figure 9.10 gives the MINITAB output for testing the hypotheses that you set up in part *a*. Use the output and rejection points to test these hypotheses by setting α equal to .10, .05, .01, and .001. How much evidence is there that mean mortgage loan rates for 30-year and 15-year terms differ?

TABLE 9.3 1999 Mortgage Loan Interest Rates for Nine Randomly Selected Willamette Valley Lending Institutions Mortgage99

Lending Institution	Annual Percentage Rate 30-Year	15-Year	Difference
American Mortgage N.W. Inc.	6.715	6.599	0.116
City and Country Mortgage	6.648	6.367	0.281
Commercial Bank	6.740	6.550	0.190
Landmark Mortgage Co.	6.597	6.362	0.235
Liberty Mortgage, Inc.	6.425	6.162	0.263
MaPS Credit Union	6.880	6.583	0.297
Mortgage Brokers, Inc.	6.900	6.800	0.100
Mortgage First Corp.	6.675	6.394	0.281
Silver Eagle Mortgage	6.790	6.540	0.250

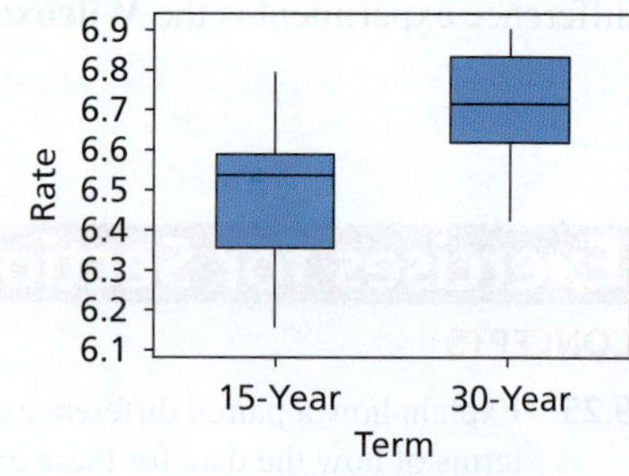

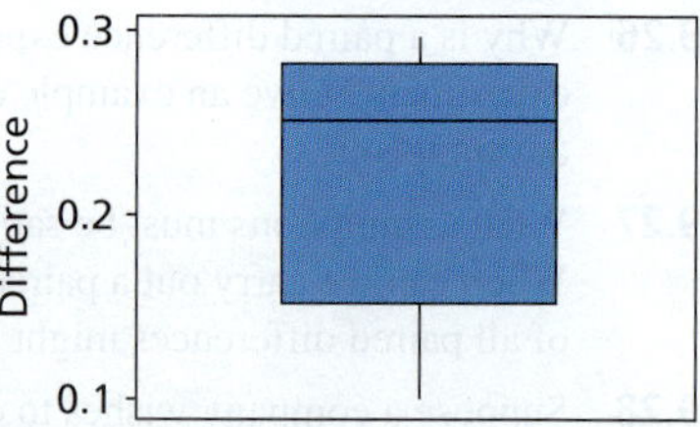

Source: World Wide Web, Salem Homeplace Mortgage Rates Directory, http://www.salemhomeplace.com/pages/finance/, *Statesman Journal Newspaper*, Salem, Oregon January 4, 1999.

FIGURE 9.10 MINITAB Paired Difference *t* Test of the Mortgage Loan Rate Data for Exercise 9.31

```
Paired T for 30-Year - 15-Year

              N       Mean        StDev       SE Mean
30-Year       9     6.70778     0.14635      0.04878
15-Year       9     6.48411     0.18396      0.06132
Difference    9    0.223667    0.072750     0.024250

95% CI for mean difference: (0.167746, 0.279587)
T-Test of mean difference = 0 (vs not = 0):
                                 T-Value = 9.22  P-Value = 0.000
```

c Figure 9.10 gives the *p*-value for testing the hypotheses that you set up in part *a*. Use the *p*-value to test these hypotheses by setting α equal to .10, .05, .01, and .001. How much evidence is there that mean mortgage loan rates for 30-year and 15-year terms differ?

d Calculate a 95 percent confidence interval for the difference between mean mortgage loan rates for 30-year rates versus 15-year rates. Interpret this interval.

9.32 In the book *Essentials of Marketing Research,* William R. Dillon, Thomas J. Madden, and Neil H. Firtle (1993) present preexposure and postexposure attitude scores from an advertising study involving 10 respondents. The data for the experiment are given in Table 9.4. Assuming that the differences between pairs of postexposure and preexposure scores are normally distributed: AdStudy

a Set up the null and alternative hypotheses needed to attempt to establish that the advertisement increases the mean attitude score (that is, that the mean postexposure attitude score is higher than the mean preexposure attitude score).

b Test the hypotheses you set up in part *a* at the .10, .05, .01, and .001 levels of significance. How much evidence is there that the advertisement increases the mean attitude score?

c Estimate the minimum difference between the mean postexposure attitude score and the mean preexposure attitude score. Justify your answer.

9.33 National Paper Company must purchase a new machine for producing cardboard boxes. The company must choose between two machines. The machines produce boxes of equal quality, so the company will choose the machine that produces (on average) the most boxes. It is known that there are substantial differences in the abilities of the company's machine operators. Therefore National Paper has decided to compare the machines using a paired difference experiment. Suppose that eight randomly selected machine operators produce boxes for one hour using machine 1 and for one hour using machine 2, with the following results: BoxYield

	Machine Operator							
	1	2	3	4	5	6	7	8
Machine 1	53	60	58	48	46	54	62	49
Machine 2	50	55	56	44	45	50	57	47

a Assuming normality, perform a hypothesis test to determine whether there is a difference between the mean hourly outputs of the two machines. Use $\alpha = .05$.

b Estimate the minimum and maximum differences between the mean outputs of the two machines. Justify your answer.

9.34 During 2004 a company implemented a number of policies aimed at reducing the ages of its customers' accounts. In order to assess the effectiveness of these measures, the company randomly selects 10 customer accounts. The average age of each account is determined for the years 2003 and 2004. These data are given in Table 9.5. Assuming that the population of paired differences between the average ages in 2004 and 2003 is normally distributed: AcctAge

a Set up the null and alternative hypotheses needed to establish that the mean average account age has been reduced by the company's new policies.

TABLE 9.4 Preexposure and Postexposure Attitude Scores for Exercise 9.32 AdStudy

Subject	Preexposure Attitudes (A_1)	Postexposure Attitudes (A_2)	Attitude Change (d_i)
1	50	53	3
2	25	27	2
3	30	38	8
4	50	55	5
5	60	61	1
6	80	85	5
7	45	45	0
8	30	31	1
9	65	72	7
10	70	78	8

Source: W. R. Dillon, T. J. Madden, and N. H. Firtle, *Essentials of Marketing Research* (Burr Ridge, IL: Richard D. Irwin, 1993), p. 435. Copyright © 1993. Reprinted by permission of McGraw-Hill Companies, Inc.

TABLE 9.5 Average Account Ages in 2003 and 2004 for 10 Randomly Selected Accounts AcctAge

Account	Average Age of Account in 2004 (Days)	Average Age of Account in 2003 (Days)
1	27	35
2	19	24
3	40	47
4	30	28
5	33	41
6	25	33
7	31	35
8	29	51
9	15	18
10	21	28

FIGURE 9.11 MegaStat and Excel Outputs of a Paired Difference Analysis of the Account Age Data (for Exercise 9.34)

(a) The MegaStat Output

Hypothesis Test: Paired Observations

0.000	hypothesized value
27.000	mean Average age of account in 2004 (days)
34.000	mean Average age of account in 2003 (days)
−7.000	mean difference (2004 Average - 2003 Average)
6.128	std. dev.
1.938	std. error
10	n
9	df
−3.61	t
.0028	p-value (one-tailed, lower)

(b) The Excel Output

t-Test: Paired Two Sample for Means

	04 Age	03 Age
Mean	27	34
Variance	53.55556	104.2222
Observations	10	10
Pearson Correlation	0.804586	
Hypothesized Mean	0	
df	9	
t Stat	−3.61211	
P(T<=t) one-tail	0.00282	
t Critical one-tail	1.833114	
P(T<=t) Two-tail	0.005641	
t Critical two-tail	2.262159	

TABLE 9.6 Weekly Study Time Data for Students Who Perform Well on the MidTerm StudyTime

Students	1	2	3	4	5	6	7	8
Before	15	14	17	17	19	14	13	16
After	9	9	11	10	19	10	14	10

b Figure 9.11 gives the MegaStat and Excel outputs needed to test the hypotheses of part *a*. Use rejection points to test these hypotheses by setting α equal to .10, .05, .01, and .001. How much evidence is there that the mean average account age has been reduced?

c Figure 9.11 gives the *p*-value for testing the hypotheses of part *a*. Use the *p*-value to test these hypotheses by setting α equal to .10, .05, .01, and .001. How much evidence is there that the mean average account age has been reduced?

d Calculate a 95 percent confidence interval for the mean difference in the average account ages between 2004 and 2003. Estimate the minimum reduction in the mean average account ages from 2003 to 2004.

9.35 Do students reduce study time in classes where they achieve a higher midterm score? In a *Journal of Economic Education* article (Winter 2005), Gregory Krohn and Catherine O'Connor studied student effort and performance in a class over a semester. In an intermediate macroeconomics course, they found that "students respond to higher midterm scores by reducing the number of hours they subsequently allocate to studying for the course."* Suppose that a random sample of $n = 8$ students who performed well on the midterm exam was taken and weekly study time before and after the exam were compared. The resulting data are given in Table 9.6. Assume that the population of all possible paired differences is normally distributed.

a Set up the null and alternative hypotheses to test whether there is a difference in the true mean study time before and after the midterm exam.

b Below we present the MINITAB output for the paired differences test. Use the output and rejection points to test the hypotheses at the .10, .05 and .01 levels of significance. Has the true mean study time changed?

Paired T-Test and CI: StudyBefore, StudyAfter

```
Paired T for StudyBefore - StudyAfter
              N      Mean     StDev   SE Mean
StudyBefore   8   15.6250    1.9955    0.7055
StudyAfter    8   11.5000    3.4226    1.2101
Difference    8   4.12500   2.99702   1.05961

95% CI for mean difference: (1.61943, 6.63057)
T-Test of mean difference = 0 (vs not = 0): T-Value = 3.89  P-Value = 0.006
```

c Use the *p*-value to test the hypotheses at the .10, .05, and .01 levels of significance. How much evidence is there against the null hypothesis?

*Source: "Student Effort and Performance over the Semester," *Journal of Economic Education,* Winter 2005, pages 3–28.

9.4 Comparing Two Population Proportions by Using Large, Independent Samples

Example 9.8 The Advertising Media Case

Suppose a new product was test marketed in the Des Moines, Iowa, and Toledo, Ohio, metropolitan areas. Equal amounts of money were spent on advertising in the two areas. However, different advertising media were employed in the two areas. Advertising in the Des Moines area was done entirely on television, while advertising in the Toledo area consisted of a mixture of television, radio, newspaper, and magazine ads. Two months after the advertising campaigns commenced, surveys were taken to estimate consumer awareness of the product. In the Des Moines area, 631 out of 1,000 randomly selected consumers were aware of the product, whereas in the Toledo area 798 out of 1,000 randomly selected consumers were aware of the product. We define p_1 to be the true proportion of consumers in the Des Moines area who are aware of the product and p_2 to be the true proportion of consumers in the Toledo area who are aware of the product. It follows that, since the sample proportions of consumers who are aware of the product in the Des Moines and Toledo areas are

$$\hat{p}_1 = \frac{631}{1,000} = .631$$

and

$$\hat{p}_2 = \frac{798}{1,000} = .798$$

then a point estimate of $p_1 - p_2$ is

$$\hat{p}_1 - \hat{p}_2 = .631 - .798 = -.167$$

This says we estimate that p_1 is .167 less than p_2. That is, we estimate that the percentage of consumers who are aware of the product in the Toledo area is 16.7 percentage points higher than the percentage in the Des Moines area.

In order to find a confidence interval for and to carry out a hypothesis test about $p_1 - p_2$, we need to know the properties of the sampling distribution of $\hat{p}_1 - \hat{p}_2$. In general, therefore, consider randomly selecting n_1 units from a population, and assume that a proportion p_1 of all the units in the population fall into a particular category. Let $\hat{p}_1$ denote the proportion of units in the sample that fall into the category. Also, consider randomly selecting a sample of n_2 units from a second population, and assume that a proportion p_2 of all the units in this population fall into the particular category. Let $\hat{p}_2$ denote the proportion of units in the second sample that fall into the category.

The Sampling Distribution of $\hat{p}_1 - \hat{p}_2$

If the randomly selected samples are independent of each other, then the population of all possible values of $\hat{p}_1 - \hat{p}_2$:

1 Approximately has a normal distribution if each of the sample sizes n_1 and n_2 is large. Here n_1 and n_2 are large enough if n_1p_1, $n_1(1 - p_1)$, n_2p_2, and $n_2(1 - p_2)$ are all at least 5.

2 Has mean $\mu_{\hat{p}_1 - \hat{p}_2} = p_1 - p_2$

3 Has standard deviation $\sigma_{\hat{p}_1 - \hat{p}_2} = \sqrt{\frac{p_1(1 - p_1)}{n_1} + \frac{p_2(1 - p_2)}{n_2}}$

If we estimate p_1 by $\hat{p}_1$ and p_2 by $\hat{p}_2$ in the expression for $\sigma_{\hat{p}_1 - \hat{p}_2}$, then the sampling distribution of $\hat{p}_1 - \hat{p}_2$ implies the following $100(1 - \alpha)$ percent confidence interval for $p_1 - p_2$.

A Large Sample Confidence Interval for $p_1 - p_2$, the Difference between Two Population Proportions[†]

Suppose we randomly select a sample of size n_1 from a population, and let $\hat{p}_1$ denote the proportion of units in this sample that fall into a category of interest. Also suppose we randomly select a sample of size n_2 from another population, and let $\hat{p}_2$ denote the proportion of units in this second sample that fall into the category of interest. Then, if each of the sample sizes n_1 and n_2 is large ($n_1\hat{p}_1$, $n_1(1 - \hat{p}_1)$, $n_2\hat{p}_2$, and $n_2(1 - \hat{p}_2)$ must all be at least 5), and if the random samples are independent of each other, a **100(1 − α) percent confidence interval for $p_1 - p_2$** is

$$\left[(\hat{p}_1 - \hat{p}_2) \pm z_{\alpha/2}\sqrt{\frac{\hat{p}_1(1 - \hat{p}_1)}{n_1} + \frac{\hat{p}_2(1 - \hat{p}_2)}{n_2}}\right]$$

Example 9.9 The Advertising Media Case

Recall that in the advertising media situation described at the beginning of this section, 631 of 1,000 randomly selected consumers in Des Moines were aware of the new product, while 798 of 1,000 randomly selected consumers in Toledo were aware of the new product. Also recall that

$$\hat{p}_1 = \frac{631}{1{,}000} = .631$$

and

$$\hat{p}_2 = \frac{798}{1{,}000} = .798$$

Because $n_1\hat{p}_1 = 1{,}000(.631) = 631$, $n_1(1 - \hat{p}_1) = 1{,}000(1 - .631) = 369$, $n_2\hat{p}_2 = 1{,}000(.798) = 798$, and $n_2(1 - \hat{p}_2) = 1{,}000(1 - .798) = 202$ are all at least 5, both n_1 and n_2 can be considered large. It follows that a 95 percent confidence interval for $p_1 - p_2$ is

$$\begin{aligned}&\left[(\hat{p}_1 - \hat{p}_2) \pm z_{.025}\sqrt{\frac{\hat{p}_1(1 - \hat{p}_1)}{n_1} + \frac{\hat{p}_2(1 - \hat{p}_2)}{n_2}}\right]\\ &= \left[(.631 - .798) \pm 1.96\sqrt{\frac{(.631)(.369)}{1{,}000} + \frac{(.798)(.202)}{1{,}000}}\right]\\ &= [-.167 \pm .0389]\\ &= [-.2059, \ -.1281]\end{aligned}$$

This interval says we are 95 percent confident that p_1, the proportion of all consumers in the Des Moines area who are aware of the product, is between .2059 and .1281 less than p_2, the proportion of all consumers in the Toledo area who are aware of the product. Thus, we have substantial evidence that advertising the new product by using a mixture of television, radio, newspaper, and magazine ads (as in Toledo) is more effective than spending an equal amount of money on television commercials only.

[†]More correctly, because $\hat{p}_1(1 - \hat{p}_1)/(n_1 - 1)$ and $\hat{p}_2(1 - \hat{p}_2)/(n_2 - 1)$ are unbiased point estimates of $p_1(1 - p_1)/n_1$ and $p_2(1 - p_2)/n_2$, a point estimate of $\sigma_{\hat{p}_1 - \hat{p}_2}$ is

$$s_{\hat{p}_1 - \hat{p}_2} = \sqrt{\frac{\hat{p}_1(1 - \hat{p}_1)}{n_1 - 1} + \frac{\hat{p}_2(1 - \hat{p}_2)}{n_2 - 1}}$$

and a 100(1 − α) percent confidence interval for $p_1 - p_2$ is $[(\hat{p}_1 - \hat{p}_2) \pm z_{\alpha/2}s_{\hat{p}_1 - \hat{p}_2}]$. Because both n_1 and n_2 are large, there is little difference between the interval obtained by using this formula and those obtained by using the formula in the box above.

To test the null hypothesis H_0: $p_1 - p_2 = D_0$, we use the test statistic

$$z = \frac{(\hat{p}_1 - \hat{p}_2) - D_0}{\sigma_{\hat{p}_1 - \hat{p}_2}}$$

A commonly employed special case of this hypothesis test is obtained by setting D_0 equal to 0. In this case, the null hypothesis H_0: $p_1 - p_2 = 0$ says there is **no difference** between the population proportions p_1 and p_2. When $D_0 = 0$, the best estimate of the common population proportion $p = p_1 = p_2$ is obtained by computing

$$\hat{p} = \frac{\text{the total number of units in the two samples that fall into the category of interest}}{\text{the total number of units in the two samples}}$$

Therefore, the point estimate of $\sigma_{\hat{p}_1 - \hat{p}_2}$ is

$$s_{\hat{p}_1 - \hat{p}_2} = \sqrt{\frac{\hat{p}(1 - \hat{p})}{n_1} + \frac{\hat{p}(1 - \hat{p})}{n_2}}$$

$$= \sqrt{\hat{p}(1 - \hat{p})\left(\frac{1}{n_1} + \frac{1}{n_2}\right)}$$

For the case where $D_0 \neq 0$, the point estimate of $\sigma_{\hat{p}_1 - \hat{p}_2}$ is obtained by estimating p_1 by $\hat{p}_1$ and p_2 by $\hat{p}_2$. With these facts in mind, we present the following procedure for testing H_0: $p_1 - p_2 = D_0$:

A Hypothesis Test about the Difference between Two Population Proportions: Testing H_0: $p_1 - p_2 = D_0$

Let $\hat{p}$ be as just defined, and let $\hat{p}_1$, $\hat{p}_2$, n_1, and n_2 be as defined in the preceding box. Furthermore, define the test statistic

$$z = \frac{(\hat{p}_1 - \hat{p}_2) - D_0}{\sigma_{\hat{p}_1 - \hat{p}_2}}$$

and assume that each of the sample sizes n_1 and n_2 is large. Then, if the samples are independent of each other, we can test H_0: $p_1 - p_2 = D_0$ versus a particular alternative hypothesis at level of significance α by using the appropriate rejection point rule, or, equivalently, the corresponding p-value.

Alternative Hypothesis	Rejection Point Rule: Reject H_0 if	p-Value (reject H_0 if p-value $< \alpha$)
H_a: $p_1 - p_2 > D_0$	$z > z_\alpha$	The area under the standard normal curve to the right of z
H_a: $p_1 - p_2 < D_0$	$z < -z_\alpha$	The area under the standard normal curve to the left of z
H_a: $p_1 - p_2 \neq D_0$	$\lvert z\rvert > z_{\alpha/2}$—that is, $z > z_{\alpha/2}$ or $z < -z_{\alpha/2}$	Twice the area under the standard normal curve to the right of $\lvert z\rvert$

Note:

1 If $D_0 = 0$, we estimate $\sigma_{\hat{p}_1 - \hat{p}_2}$ by

$$s_{\hat{p}_1 - \hat{p}_2} = \sqrt{\hat{p}(1 - \hat{p})\left(\frac{1}{n_1} + \frac{1}{n_2}\right)}$$

2 If $D_0 \neq 0$, we estimate $\sigma_{\hat{p}_1 - \hat{p}_2}$ by

$$s_{\hat{p}_1 - \hat{p}_2} = \sqrt{\frac{\hat{p}_1(1 - \hat{p}_1)}{n_1} + \frac{\hat{p}_2(1 - \hat{p}_2)}{n_2}}$$

Example 9.10 The Advertising Media Case

Recall that p_1 is the proportion of all consumers in the Des Moines area who are aware of the new product and that p_2 is the proportion of all consumers in the Toledo area who are aware of the new product. To test for the equality of these proportions, we will test H_0: $p_1 - p_2 = 0$ **versus** H_a: $p_1 - p_2 \neq 0$ **at the .05 level of significance.** Because both of the Des Moines and Toledo samples are large (see Example 9.9), we will calculate the value of the **test statistic** z **in the summary box** (where $D_0 = 0$). Since H_a: $p_1 - p_2 \neq 0$ is of the form H_a: $p_1 - p_2 \neq D_0$, we will **reject** H_0: $p_1 - p_2 = 0$ **if the absolute value of** z **is greater than** $z_{\alpha/2} = z_{.05/2} = z_{.025} = 1.96$**.** Because 631 out of 1,000 randomly selected Des Moines residents were aware of the product and 798 out of 1,000 randomly selected Toledo residents were aware of the product, the estimate of $p = p_1 = p_2$ is

$$\hat{p} = \frac{631 + 798}{1{,}000 + 1{,}000} = \frac{1{,}429}{2{,}000} = .7145$$

and the **value of the test statistic is**

$$z = \frac{(\hat{p}_1 - \hat{p}_2) - D_0}{\sqrt{\hat{p}(1-\hat{p})\left(\frac{1}{n_1} + \frac{1}{n_2}\right)}} = \frac{(.631 - .798) - 0}{\sqrt{(.7145)(.2855)\left(\frac{1}{1{,}000} + \frac{1}{1{,}000}\right)}} = \frac{-.167}{.0202} = -8.2673$$

Because $|z| = 8.2673$ **is greater than 1.96, we can reject** H_0: $p_1 - p_2 = 0$ **in favor of** H_a: $p_1 - p_2 \neq 0$**.** We conclude (at an α of .05) that the proportions of consumers who are aware of the product in Des Moines and Toledo differ. Furthermore, the point estimate $\hat{p}_1 - \hat{p}_2 = .631 - .798 = -.167$ says we estimate that the percentage of consumers who are aware of the product in Toledo is 16.7 percentage points higher than the percentage of consumers who are aware of the product in Des Moines. The p-value for this test is twice the area under the standard normal curve to the right of $|z| = 8.2673$. Since the area under the standard normal curve to the right of 3.29 is .0005, the p-value for testing H_0 is less than $2(.0005) = .001$. It follows that we have extremely strong evidence that H_0: $p_1 - p_2 = 0$ should be rejected in favor of H_a: $p_1 - p_2 \neq 0$. That is, this small p-value provides extremely strong evidence that p_1 and p_2 differ. Figure 9.12 presents the MegaStat output of the hypothesis test of H_0: $p_1 - p_2 = 0$ versus H_a: $p_1 - p_2 \neq 0$ and of a 95 percent confidence interval for $p_1 - p_2$. A MINITAB output of the test and confidence interval is given in Appendix 9.1 on page 397.

FIGURE 9.12 MegaStat Output of Statistical Inference in the Advertising Media Case

(a) Testing H_0: $p_1 - p_2 = 0$ versus H_a: $p_1 - p_2 \neq 0$

Hypothesis test for two independent proportions

p1	p2	pc		
			−0.167	difference
0.631	0.798	0.7145	0.	hypothesized difference
631/1000	798/1000	1429/2000	0.0202	std. error
631.	798.	1429. X	**−8.27**	z
1000	1000	2000 n	0.00E+00	p-value (two-tailed)

(b) 95 percent confidence interval for $p_1 - p_2$

Confidence Interval for $p_1 - p_2$

−0.2059	confidence interval 95.% lower
−0.1281	confidence interval 95.% upper
0.0389	half-width

Exercises for Section 9.4

CONCEPTS

9.36 Explain what population is described by the sampling distribution of $\hat{p}_1 - \hat{p}_2$.

9.37 What assumptions must be satisfied in order to use the methods presented in this section?

METHODS AND APPLICATIONS

In Exercises 9.38 through 9.40 we assume that we have selected two independent random samples from populations having proportions p_1 and p_2 and that $\hat{p}_1 = 800/1{,}000 = .8$ and $\hat{p}_2 = 950/1{,}000 = .95$.

9.38 Calculate a 95 percent confidence interval for $p_1 - p_2$. Interpret this interval. Can we be 95 percent confident that $p_1 - p_2$ is less than 0? That is, can we be 95 percent confident that p_1 is less than p_2? Explain.

9.39 Test H_0: $p_1 - p_2 = 0$ versus H_a: $p_1 - p_2 \neq 0$ by using rejection points and by setting α equal to .10, .05, .01, and .001. How much evidence is there that p_1 and p_2 differ? Explain. Hint: $z_{.0005} = 3.29$.

9.40 Test H_0: $p_1 - p_2 \geq -.12$ versus H_a: $p_1 - p_2 < -.12$ by using a p-value and by setting α equal to .10, .05, .01, and .001. How much evidence is there that p_2 exceeds p_1 by more than .12? Explain.

9.41 In an article in the *Journal of Advertising,* Weinberger and Spotts compare the use of humor in television ads in the United States and in the United Kingdom. Suppose that independent random samples of television ads are taken in the two countries. A random sample of 400 television ads in the United Kingdom reveals that 142 use humor, while a random sample of 500 television ads in the United States reveals that 122 use humor.

a Set up the null and alternative hypotheses needed to determine whether the proportion of ads using humor in the United Kingdom differs from the proportion of ads using humor in the United States.

b Test the hypotheses you set up in part *a* by using rejection points and by setting α equal to .10, .05, .01, and .001. How much evidence is there that the proportions of U.K. and U.S. ads using humor are different? Hint: $z_{.0005} = 3.29$.

c Set up the hypotheses needed to attempt to establish that the difference between the proportions of U.K. and U.S. ads using humor is more than .05 (five percentage points). Test these hypotheses by using a p-value and by setting α equal to .10, .05, .01, and .001. How much evidence is there that the difference between the proportions exceeds .05?

d Calculate a 95 percent confidence interval for the difference between the proportion of U.K. ads using humor and the proportion of U.S. ads using humor. Interpret this interval. Can we be 95 percent confident that the proportion of U.K. ads using humor is greater than the proportion of U.S. ads using humor?

9.42 In the book *Essentials of Marketing Research,* William R. Dillon, Thomas J. Madden, and Neil H. Firtle discuss a research proposal in which a telephone company wants to determine whether the appeal of a new security system varies between homeowners and renters. Independent samples of 140 homeowners and 60 renters are randomly selected. Each respondent views a TV pilot in which a test ad for the new security system is embedded twice. Afterward, each respondent is interviewed to find out whether he or she would purchase the security system.

Results show that 25 out of the 140 homeowners definitely would buy the security system, while 9 out of the 60 renters definitely would buy the system.

a Letting p_1 be the proportion of homeowners who would buy the security system, and letting p_2 be the proportion of renters who would buy the security system, set up the null and alternative hypotheses needed to determine whether the proportion of homeowners who would buy the security system differs from the proportion of renters who would buy the security system.

b Find the test statistic z and the p-value for testing the hypotheses of part *a*. Use the p-value to test the hypotheses with α equal to .10, .05, .01, and .001. How much evidence is there that the proportions of homeowners and renters differ?

c Calculate a 95 percent confidence interval for the difference between the proportions of homeowners and renters who would buy the security system. On the basis of this interval, can we be 95 percent confident that these proportions differ? Explain.

Note: A MegaStat output of the hypothesis test and confidence interval in parts *b* and *c* is given in Appendix 9.3 on page 401.

9.43 In the book *Cases in Finance,* Nunnally and Plath (1995) present a case in which the estimated percentage of uncollectible accounts varies with the age of the account. Here the age of an unpaid account is the number of days elapsed since the invoice date.

An accountant believes that the percentage of accounts that will be uncollectible increases as the ages of the accounts increase. To test this theory, the accountant randomly selects independent samples of 500 accounts with ages between 31 and 60 days and 500 accounts with ages between 61 and 90 days from the accounts receivable ledger dated one year ago. When the sampled accounts are examined, it is found that 10 of the 500 accounts with ages between 31 and 60 days were eventually classified as uncollectible, while 27 of the 500 accounts with ages between 61 and 90 days were eventually classified as uncollectible. Let p_1 be the proportion of accounts with ages between 31 and 60 days that will be uncollectible, and let p_2 be the proportion of accounts with ages between 61 and 90 days that will be uncollectible. Use the MINITAB output on the next page to determine how much evidence there is that we should reject H_0: $p_1 - p_2 = 0$ in favor of H_a: $p_1 - p_2 \neq 0$. Also, identify a 95 percent confidence interval for $p_1 - p_2$, and estimate the smallest that the difference between p_1 and p_2 might be.

Test and CI for Two Proportions

```
Sample               X    N     Sample p
1 (31 to 60 days)    10   500   0.020000       Difference = p(1) - p(2)
2 (61 to 90 days     27   500   0.054000       Estimate for difference:  -0.034

95% CI for difference:  (-0.0573036, -0.0106964)
Test for difference = 0 (vs not = 0):  Z = -2.85   P-Value = 0.004
```

9.44 On January 7, 2000, the Gallup Organization released the results of a poll comparing the lifestyles of today with yesteryear. The survey results were based on telephone interviews with a randomly selected national sample of 1,031 adults, 18 years and older, conducted December 20–21, 1999. The poll asked several questions and compared the 1999 responses with the responses given in polls taken in previous years. Below we summarize some of the poll's results.[5]

Percentage of respondents who

1	Had taken a vacation lasting six days or more within the last 12 months:	December 1999 42%	December 1968 62%
2	Took part in some sort of daily activity to keep physically fit:	December 1999 60%	September 1977 48%
3	Watched TV more than four hours on an average weekday:	December 1999 28%	April 1981 25%
4	Drove a car or truck to work:	December 1999 87%	April 1971 81%

Assuming that each poll was based on a randomly selected national sample of 1,031 adults and that the samples in different years are independent:

a Let p_1 be the December 1999 population proportion of U.S. adults who had taken a vacation lasting six days or more within the last 12 months, and let p_2 be the December 1968 population proportion who had taken such a vacation. Calculate a 99 percent confidence interval for the difference between p_1 and p_2. Interpret what this interval says about how these population proportions differ.

b Let p_1 be the December 1999 population proportion of U.S. adults who took part in some sort of daily activity to keep physically fit, and let p_2 be the September 1977 population proportion who did the same. Carry out a hypothesis test to attempt to justify that the proportion who took part in such daily activity increased from September 1977 to December 1999. Use $\alpha = .05$ and explain your result.

c Let p_1 be the December 1999 population proportion of U.S. adults who watched TV more than four hours on an average weekday, and let p_2 be the April 1981 population proportion who did the same. Carry out a hypothesis test to determine whether these population proportions differ. Use $\alpha = .05$ and interpret the result of your test.

d Let p_1 be the December 1999 population proportion of U.S. adults who drove a car or truck to work, and let p_2 be the April 1971 population proportion who did the same. Calculate a 95 percent confidence interval for the difference between p_1 and p_2. On the basis of this interval, can it be concluded that the 1999 and 1971 population proportions differ?

9.45 In the book *International Marketing,* Philip R. Cateora reports the results of an MTV-commissioned study of the lifestyles and spending habits of the 14–34 age group in six countries. The survey results are given in Table 9.7. PurchPct

a As shown in Table 9.7, 96 percent of the 14- to 34-year-olds surveyed in the United States had purchased soft drinks in the last three months, while 90 percent of the 14- to 34-year-olds

[5]Source: World Wide Web, http://www.gallup.com/poll/releases/, PR991230.ASP. The Gallup Poll, December 30, 1999.

TABLE 9.7 Results of an MTV-Commissioned Survey of the Lifestyles and Spending Habits of the 14–34 Age Group in Six Countries PurchPct

Which of the Following Have You Purchased in the Past Three Months?

Product	Percentage in United States	Percentage in Australia	Percentage in Brazil	Percentage in Germany	Percentage in Japan	Percentage in United Kingdom
Soft drinks	96%	90%	93%	83%	91%	94%
Fast food	94	94	91	70	86	85
Athletic footwear	59	40	54	33	30	49
Blue jeans	56	39	62	45	42	44
Beer*	46	50	60	46	57	57
Cigarettes*	24	33	30	38	39	40

*Among adults 18+. Source: Yankelovich Clancy Shulman.

Source: Philip R. Cateora, *International Marketing*, 9th ed. (Burr Ridge, IL: Richard D. Irwin, 1993), p. 262. Copyright © 1993. Reprinted by permission of McGraw-Hill Companies, Inc.

surveyed in Australia had done the same. Assuming that these results were obtained from independent random samples of 500 respondents in each country, carry out a hypothesis test that tests the equality of the population proportions of 14- to 34-year-olds in the United States and in Australia who have purchased soft drinks in the last three months. Also, calculate a 95 percent confidence interval for the difference between these two population proportions, and use this interval to estimate the largest and smallest values that the difference between these proportions might be. Based on your confidence interval, do you feel that this result has practical importance?

b Again as shown in Table 9.7, 40 percent of the 14- to 34-year-olds surveyed in Australia had purchased athletic footwear in the last three months, while 54 percent of the 14- to 34-year-olds surveyed in Brazil had done the same. Assuming that these results were obtained from independent random samples of 500 respondents in each country, carry out a hypothesis test that tests the equality of the population proportions of 14- to 34-year-olds in Australia and in Brazil who have purchased athletic footwear in the last three months. Also, calculate a 95 percent confidence interval for the difference between these two population proportions, and use this interval to estimate the largest and smallest values that the difference between these proportions might be. Based on your confidence interval, do you feel that this result has practical importance?

9.5 Comparing Two Population Variances by Using Independent Samples

We have seen (in Sections 9.1 and 9.2) that we often wish to compare two population means. In addition, it is often useful to compare two population variances. For example, in the bank waiting time situation of Example 9.1, we might compare the variance of the waiting times experienced under the current and new systems. Or, as another example, we might wish to compare the variance of the chemical yields obtained when using Catalyst XA-100 with that obtained when using Catalyst ZB-200. Here the catalyst that produces yields with the smaller variance is giving more consistent (or predictable) results.

CHAPTER 10

If σ_1^2 and σ_2^2 are the population variances that we wish to compare, one approach is to test the null hypothesis

$$H_0\colon\ \sigma_1^2 = \sigma_2^2$$

We might test H_0 versus an alternative hypothesis of, for instance,

$$H_a\colon\ \sigma_1^2 > \sigma_2^2$$

Dividing by σ_2^2, we see that testing these hypotheses is equivalent to testing

$$H_0\colon\ \frac{\sigma_1^2}{\sigma_2^2} = 1 \quad \text{versus} \quad H_a\colon\ \frac{\sigma_1^2}{\sigma_2^2} > 1$$

FIGURE 9.13 F Distribution Curves and F Points

(a) The point F_α corresponding to df_1 and df_2 degrees of freedom

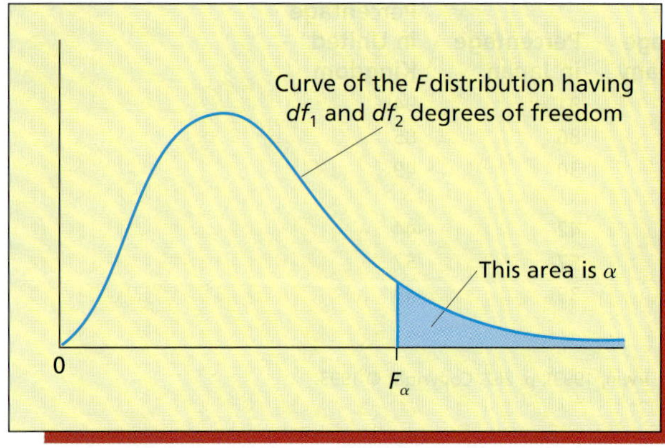

(b) The point $F_{.05}$ corresponding to 4 and 7 degrees of freedom

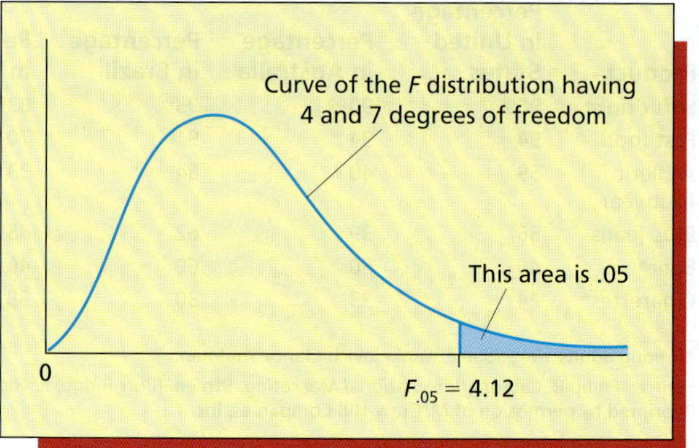

Intuitively, we would reject H_0 in favor of H_a if s_1^2/s_2^2 is significantly larger than 1. Here s_1^2 is the variance of a random sample of n_1 observations from the population with variance σ_1^2, and s_2^2 is the variance of a random sample of n_2 observations from the population with variance σ_2^2. To decide exactly how large s_1^2/s_2^2 must be in order to reject H_0, we need to consider the sampling distribution of s_1^2/s_2^2.[6]

It can be shown that, if the null hypothesis H_0: $\sigma_1^2/\sigma_2^2 = 1$ is true, then the population of all possible values of s_1^2/s_2^2 is described by what is called an ***F* distribution.** In general, as illustrated in Figure 9.13, the curve of the *F* distribution is skewed to the right. Moreover, the exact shape of this curve depends on two parameters that are called the **numerator degrees of freedom (denoted df_1)** and the **denominator degrees of freedom (denoted df_2).** The values of df_1 and df_2 that describe the sampling distribution of s_1^2/s_2^2 are given in the following result:

The Sampling Distribution of s_1^2/s_2^2

Suppose we randomly select independent samples from two normally distributed populations having variances σ_1^2 and σ_2^2. Then, if the null hypothesis H_0: $\sigma_1^2/\sigma_2^2 = 1$ is true, the population of all possible values of s_1^2/s_2^2 has an ***F* distribution** with **$df_1 = (n_1 - 1)$ numerator degrees of freedom** and with **$df_2 = (n_2 - 1)$ denominator degrees of freedom.**

In order to use the *F* distribution, we employ an ***F* point,** which is denoted F_α. As illustrated in Figure 9.13(a), **F_α is the point on the horizontal axis under the curve of the *F* distribution that gives a right-hand tail area equal to α.** The value of F_α in a particular situation depends on the size of the right-hand tail area (the size of α) and on the numerator degrees of freedom (df_1) and the denominator degrees of freedom (df_2). Values of F_α are given in an ***F* table.** Tables A.5, A.6, A.7, and A.8 (pages 827–830) give values of $F_{.10}$, $F_{.05}$, $F_{.025}$, and $F_{.01}$, respectively. Each table tabulates values of F_α according to the appropriate numerator degrees of freedom (values listed across the top of the table) and the appropriate denominator degrees of freedom (values listed down the left side of the table). A portion of Table A.6, which gives values of $F_{.05}$, is reproduced in this chapter as Table 9.8. For instance, suppose we wish to find the *F* point that gives a right-hand tail area of .05 under the curve of the *F* distribution having 4 numerator and 7 denominator degrees of freedom. To do this, we scan across the top of Table 9.8 until we find

[6]Note that we divide by σ_2^2 to form a null hypothesis of the form H_0: $\frac{\sigma_1^2}{\sigma_2^2} = 1$ rather than subtracting σ_2^2 to form a null hypothesis of the form H_0: $\sigma_1^2 - \sigma_2^2 = 0$. This is because the population of all possible values of $s_1^2 - s_2^2$ has no known sampling distribution.

TABLE 9.8 A Portion of an F Table: Values of $F_{.05}$

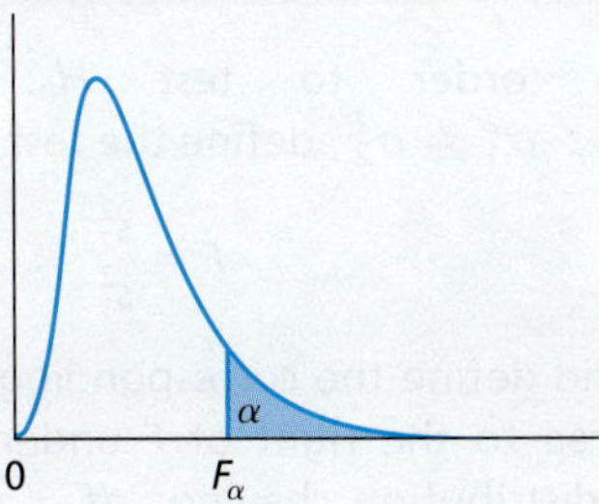

Denominator Degrees of Freedom, df_2 \ Numerator Degrees of Freedom, df_1	1	2	3	4	5	6	7	8	9
1	161.4	199.5	215.7	224.6	230.2	234.0	236.8	238.9	240.5
2	18.51	19.00	19.16	19.25	19.30	19.33	19.35	19.37	19.38
3	10.13	9.55	9.28	9.12	9.01	8.94	8.89	8.85	8.81
4	7.71	6.94	6.59	6.39	6.26	6.16	6.09	6.04	6.00
5	6.61	5.79	5.41	5.19	5.05	4.95	4.88	4.82	4.77
6	5.99	5.14	4.76	4.53	4.39	4.28	4.21	4.15	4.10
7	5.59	4.71	4.25	4.12	3.97	3.87	3.79	3.73	3.68
8	5.32	4.46	4.07	3.84	3.69	3.58	3.50	3.44	3.39
9	5.12	4.26	3.86	3.63	3.48	3.37	3.29	3.23	3.18
10	4.96	4.10	3.71	3.48	3.33	3.22	3.14	3.07	3.02
11	4.84	3.98	3.59	3.36	3.20	3.09	3.01	2.95	2.90
12	4.75	3.89	3.49	3.26	3.11	3.00	2.91	2.85	2.80
13	4.67	3.81	3.41	3.18	3.03	2.92	2.83	2.77	2.71
14	4.60	3.74	3.34	3.11	2.96	2.85	2.76	2.70	2.65
15	4.54	3.68	3.29	3.06	2.90	2.79	2.71	2.64	2.59
16	4.49	3.63	3.24	3.01	2.85	2.74	2.66	2.59	2.54
17	4.45	3.59	3.20	2.96	2.81	2.70	2.61	2.55	2.49
18	4.41	3.55	3.16	2.93	2.77	2.66	2.58	2.51	2.46
19	4.38	3.52	3.13	2.90	2.74	2.63	2.54	2.48	2.42
20	4.35	3.49	3.10	2.87	2.71	2.60	2.51	2.45	2.39
21	4.32	3.47	3.07	2.84	2.68	2.57	2.49	2.42	2.37
22	4.30	3.44	3.05	2.82	2.66	2.55	2.46	2.40	2.34
23	4.28	3.42	3.03	2.80	2.64	2.53	2.44	2.37	2.32
24	4.26	3.40	3.01	2.78	2.62	2.51	2.42	2.36	2.30
25	4.24	3.39	2.99	2.76	2.60	2.49	2.40	2.34	2.28
26	4.23	3.37	2.98	2.74	2.59	2.47	2.39	2.32	2.27
27	4.21	3.35	2.96	2.73	2.57	2.46	2.37	2.31	2.25
28	4.20	3.34	2.95	2.71	2.56	2.45	2.36	2.29	2.24
29	4.18	3.33	2.93	2.70	2.55	2.43	2.35	2.28	2.22
30	4.17	3.32	2.92	2.69	2.53	2.42	2.33	2.27	2.21
40	4.08	3.23	2.84	2.61	2.45	2.34	2.25	2.18	2.12
60	4.00	3.15	2.76	2.53	2.37	2.25	2.17	2.10	2.04
120	3.92	3.07	2.68	2.45	2.29	2.17	2.09	2.02	1.96
∞	3.84	3.00	2.60	2.37	2.21	2.10	2.01	1.94	1.88

Source: M. Merrington and C. M. Thompson, "Tables of Percentage Points of the Inverted Beta (*F*) Distribution," *Biometrika*, Vol. 33 (1943), pp. 73–88. Reproduced by permission of Oxford University Press and *Biometrika* trustees.

the column corresponding to 4 numerator degrees of freedom, and we scan down the left side of the table until we find the row corresponding to 7 denominator degrees of freedom. The table entry in this column and row is the desired *F* point. We find that the $F_{.05}$ point is 4.12 [see Figure 9.13(b)].

We now present the procedure for testing the equality of two population variances when the alternative hypothesis is one-tailed.

Testing the Equality of Population Variances: Testing H_0: $\sigma_1^2 = \sigma_2^2$ versus a One-Tailed Alternative Hypothesis

Suppose we randomly select independent samples from two normally distributed populations—populations 1 and 2. Let s_1^2 be the variance of the random sample of n_1 observations from population 1, and let s_2^2 be the variance of the random sample of n_2 observations from population 2.

1 In order to test H_0: $\sigma_1^2 = \sigma_2^2$ versus H_a: $\sigma_1^2 > \sigma_2^2$, define the test statistic

$$F = \frac{s_1^2}{s_2^2}$$

and define the corresponding p-value to be the area to the right of F under the curve of the F distribution having $df_1 = n_1 - 1$ numerator degrees of freedom and $df_2 = n_2 - 1$ denominator degrees of freedom. We can reject H_0 at level of significance α if and only if

a $F > F_\alpha$ or, equivalently,

b p-value $< \alpha$.

Here F_α is based on $df_1 = n_1 - 1$ and $df_2 = n_2 - 1$ degrees of freedom.

2 In order to test H_0: $\sigma_1^2 = \sigma_2^2$ versus H_a: $\sigma_1^2 < \sigma_2^2$, define the test statistic

$$F = \frac{s_2^2}{s_1^2}$$

and define the corresponding p-value to be the area to the right of F under the curve of the F distribution having $df_1 = n_2 - 1$ numerator degrees of freedom and $df_2 = n_1 - 1$ denominator degrees of freedom. We can reject H_0 at level of significance α if and only if

a $F > F_\alpha$ or, equivalently,

b p-value $< \alpha$.

Here F_α is based on $df_1 = n_2 - 1$ and $df_2 = n_1 - 1$ degrees of freedom.

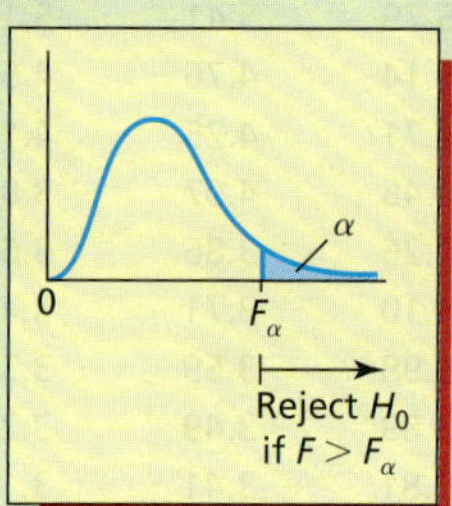

Example 9.11 The Catalyst Comparison Case

Again consider the catalyst comparison situation of Example 9.3, and suppose the production supervisor wishes to use the sample data in Table 9.1 to determine whether σ_1^2, the variance of the chemical yields obtained by using Catalyst XA-100, is smaller than σ_2^2, the variance of the chemical yields obtained by using Catalyst ZB-200. To do this, the supervisor will test the null hypothesis

$$H_0\text{: } \sigma_1^2 = \sigma_2^2$$

which says the catalysts produce yields having the same amount of variability, versus the alternative hypothesis

$$H_a\text{: } \sigma_1^2 < \sigma_2^2 \quad \text{or, equivalently,} \quad H_a\text{: } \sigma_2^2 > \sigma_1^2$$

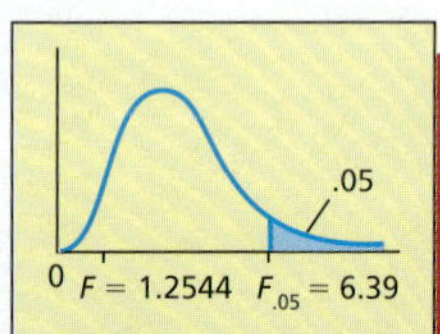

which says Catalyst XA-100 produces yields that are less variable (that is, more consistent) than the yields produced by Catalyst ZB-200. Recall from Table 9.1 that $n_1 = n_2 = 5$, $s_1^2 = 386$, and $s_2^2 = 484.2$. In order to test H_0 versus H_a, we compute the test statistic

$$F = \frac{s_2^2}{s_1^2} = \frac{484.2}{386} = 1.2544$$

and we compare this value with F_α based on $df_1 = n_2 - 1 = 5 - 1 = 4$ numerator degrees of freedom and $df_2 = n_1 - 1 = 5 - 1 = 4$ denominator degrees of freedom. If we test H_0 versus H_a at the .05 level of significance, then Table 9.8 tells us that when $df_1 = 4$ and $df_2 = 4$, we have $F_{.05} = 6.39$. Because $F = 1.2544$ is not greater than $F_{.05} = 6.39$, we cannot reject H_0 at the .05 level of significance. That is, at the .05 level of significance we cannot conclude that σ_1^2 is less than σ_2^2. This says that there is little evidence that Catalyst XA-100 produces yields that are more consistent than the yields produced by Catalyst ZB-200.

FIGURE 9.14 Excel and MINITAB Outputs for Testing H_0: $\sigma_1^2 = \sigma_2^2$ in the Catalyst Comparison Case

(a) Excel output of testing H_0: $\sigma_1^2 = \sigma_2^2$ versus H_a: $\sigma_1^2 < \sigma_2^2$

F-Test Two-Sample for Variances

	ZB-200	XA-100
Mean	750.2	811
Variance	484.2	386
Observations	5	5
df	4	4
F	1.254404	
P(F<=f) one-tail	0.415724	
F Critical one-tail	6.388234	

(b) MINITAB output of testing H_0: $\sigma_1^2 = \sigma_2^2$ versus H_a: $\sigma_1^2 \neq \sigma_2^2$

```
F-Test
Test Statistic: 0.797
P-Value       : 0.831
```

The p-value for testing H_0 versus H_a is the area to the right of $F = 1.2544$ under the curve of the F distribution having 4 numerator degrees of freedom and 4 denominator degrees of freedom. The Excel output in Figure 9.14(a) tells us that this p-value equals 0.415724. Since this p-value is large, we have little evidence to support rejecting H_0 in favor of H_a. That is, there is little evidence that Catalyst XA-100 produces yields that are more consistent than the yields produced by Catalyst ZB-200.

Again considering the catalyst comparison case, suppose we wish to test

$$H_0\text{: } \sigma_1^2 = \sigma_2^2 \quad \text{versus} \quad H_a\text{: } \sigma_1^2 \neq \sigma_2^2$$

One way to carry out this test is to compute

$$F = \frac{s_1^2}{s_2^2} = \frac{386}{484.2} = .797$$

As illustrated in Figure 9.15, if we set $\alpha = .10$, we compare F with the rejection points $F_{.95}$ and $F_{.05}$ under the curve of the F distribution having $n_1 - 1 = 4$ numerator and $n_2 - 1 = 4$ denominator degrees of freedom. We see that we can easily find the appropriate upper-tail rejection point to be $F_{.05} = 6.39$. In order to find the lower-tail rejection point, $F_{.95}$, we use the following relationship:

$$F_{(1-\alpha)} \text{ with } df_1 \text{ numerator and } df_2 \text{ denominator degrees of freedom}$$

$$= \frac{1}{F_\alpha \text{ with } df_2 \text{ numerator and } df_1 \text{ denominator degrees of freedom}}$$

FIGURE 9.15 Rejection Points for Testing H_0: $\sigma_1^2 = \sigma_2^2$ versus H_a: $\sigma_1^2 \neq \sigma_2^2$ with $\alpha = .10$

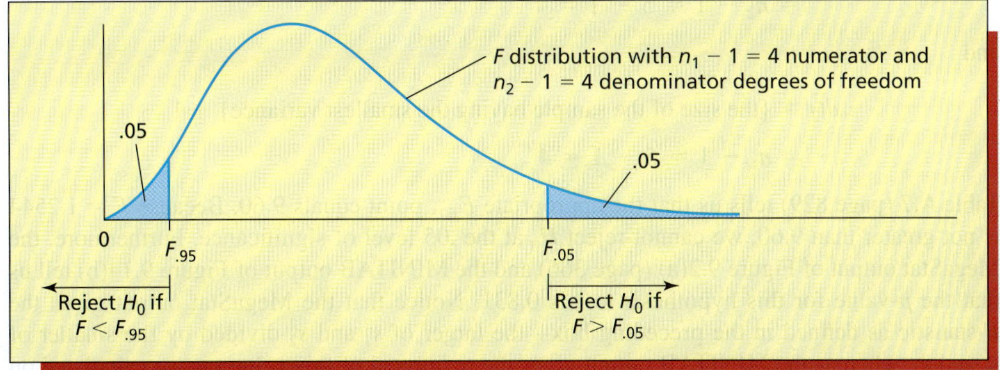

This says that for the F curve with 4 numerator and 4 denominator degrees of freedom, $F_{(1-.05)} = F_{.95} = 1/F_{.05} = 1/6.39 = .1565$. Therefore, because $F = .797$ is not greater than $F_{.05} = 6.39$ and since $F = .797$ is not less than $F_{.95} = .1565$, we cannot reject H_0 in favor of H_a at the .10 level of significance.

Although we can calculate the lower-tail rejection point for this hypothesis test as just illustrated, it is common practice to compute the test statistic F so that its value is always greater than 1. This means that we will always compare F with the upper-tail rejection point when carrying out the test. This can be done by always calculating F to be the larger of s_1^2 and s_2^2 divided by the smaller of s_1^2 and s_2^2. We obtain the following result:

Testing the Equality of Population Variances: Testing H_0: $\sigma_1^2 = \sigma_2^2$ versus H_a: $\sigma_1^2 \neq \sigma_2^2$

Suppose we randomly select independent samples from two normally distributed populations and define all notation as in the previous box. Then, in order to test H_0: $\sigma_1^2 = \sigma_2^2$ versus H_a: $\sigma_1^2 \neq \sigma_2^2$, define the test statistic

$$F = \frac{\text{the larger of } s_1^2 \text{ and } s_2^2}{\text{the smaller of } s_1^2 \text{ and } s_2^2}$$

and let

df_1 = {the size of the sample having the largest variance} − 1

df_2 = {the size of the sample having the smallest variance} − 1

Also, define the corresponding p-value to be twice the area to the right of F under the curve of the F distribution having df_1 numerator degrees of freedom and df_2 denominator degrees of freedom. We can reject H_0 at level of significance α if and only if

1. $F > F_{\alpha/2}$ or, equivalently,
2. p-value $< \alpha$.

Here $F_{\alpha/2}$ is based on df_1 and df_2 degrees of freedom.

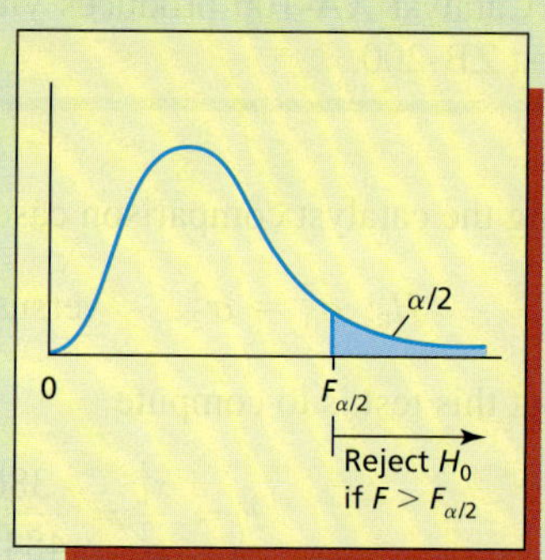

Example 9.12 The Catalyst Comparison Case

C

In the catalyst comparison situation, we can reject H_0: $\sigma_1^2 = \sigma_2^2$ in favor of H_a: $\sigma_1^2 \neq \sigma_2^2$ at the .05 level of significance if

$$F = \frac{\text{the larger of } s_1^2 \text{ and } s_2^2}{\text{the smaller of } s_1^2 \text{ and } s_2^2} = \frac{484.2}{386} = 1.2544$$

is greater than $F_{\alpha/2} = F_{.05/2} = F_{.025}$. Here the degrees of freedom are

$$df_1 = \{\text{the size of the sample having the largest variance}\} - 1$$
$$= n_2 - 1 = 5 - 1 = 4$$

and

$$df_2 = \{\text{the size of the sample having the smallest variance}\} - 1$$
$$= n_1 - 1 = 5 - 1 = 4$$

Table A.7 (page 829) tells us that the appropriate $F_{.025}$ point equals 9.60. Because $F = 1.2544$ is not greater than 9.60, we cannot reject H_0 at the .05 level of significance. Furthermore, the MegaStat output of Figure 9.2(a) (page 366) and the MINITAB output of Figure 9.14(b) tell us that the p-value for this hypothesis test is 0.831. Notice that the MegaStat output gives the F-statistic as defined in the preceding box—the larger of s_1^2 and s_2^2 divided by the smaller of s_1^2 and s_2^2, whereas the MINITAB output gives the reciprocal of this value (as we calculated on

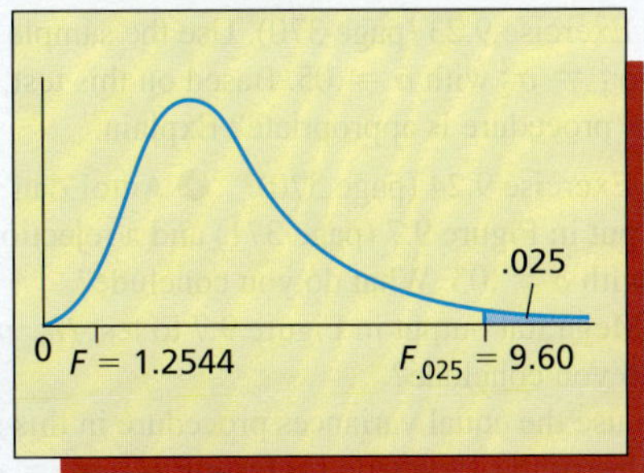

page 389). Since the p-value is large, we have little evidence that the consistencies of the yields produced by Catalysts XA-100 and ZB-200 differ.

It has been suggested that the F test of H_0: $\sigma_1^2 = \sigma_2^2$ be used to choose between the equal variances and unequal variances t based procedures when comparing two means (as described in Section 9.2). Certainly the F test is one approach to making this choice. However, studies have shown that the validity of the F test is very sensitive to violations of the normality assumption—much more sensitive, in fact, than the equal variances procedure is to violations of the equal variances assumption. While opinions vary, some statisticians believe that this is a serious problem and that the F test should never be used to choose between the equal variances and unequal variances procedures. Others feel that performing the test for this purpose is reasonable if the test's limitations are kept in mind.

As an example for those who believe that using the F test is reasonable, we found in Example 9.12 that we do not reject H_0: $\sigma_1^2 = \sigma_2^2$ at the .05 level of significance in the context of the catalyst comparison situation. Further, the p-value related to the F test, which equals 0.831, tells us that there is little evidence to suggest that the population variances differ. It follows that it might be reasonable to compare the mean yields of the catalysts by using the equal variances procedures (as we have done in Examples 9.3 and 9.4).

Exercises for Section 9.5

CONCEPTS

9.46 Explain what population is described by the sampling distribution of s_1^2/s_2^2.

9.47 Intuitively explain why a value of s_1^2/s_2^2 that is substantially greater than 1 provides evidence that σ_1^2 is not equal to σ_2^2.

METHODS AND APPLICATIONS

9.48 Use Table 9.8 to find the $F_{.05}$ point for each of the following:

a $df_1 = 3$ numerator degrees of freedom and $df_2 = 14$ denominator degrees of freedom.
b $df_1 = 6$ and $df_2 = 10$.
c $df_1 = 2$ and $df_2 = 22$.
d $df_1 = 7$ and $df_2 = 5$.

9.49 Use Tables A.5, A.6, A.7, and A.8 (pages 827–830) to find the following F_α points:

a $F_{.10}$ with $df_1 = 4$ numerator degrees of freedom and $df_2 = 7$ denominator degrees of freedom.
b $F_{.01}$ with $df_1 = 3$ and $df_2 = 25$.
c $F_{.025}$ with $df_1 = 7$ and $df_2 = 17$.
d $F_{.05}$ with $df_1 = 9$ and $df_2 = 3$.

9.50 Suppose two independent random samples of sizes $n_1 = 9$ and $n_2 = 7$ that have been taken from two normally distributed populations having variances σ_1^2 and σ_2^2 give sample variances of $s_1^2 = 100$ and $s_2^2 = 20$.

a Test H_0: $\sigma_1^2 = \sigma_2^2$ versus H_a: $\sigma_1^2 \neq \sigma_2^2$ with $\alpha = .05$. What do you conclude?
b Test H_0: $\sigma_1^2 \leq \sigma_2^2$ versus H_a: $\sigma_1^2 > \sigma_2^2$ with $\alpha = .05$. What do you conclude?

9.51 Suppose two independent random samples of sizes $n_1 = 5$ and $n_2 = 16$ that have been taken from two normally distributed populations having variances σ_1^2 and σ_2^2 give sample standard deviations of $s_1 = 5$ and $s_2 = 9$.

a Test H_0: $\sigma_1^2 = \sigma_2^2$ versus H_a: $\sigma_1^2 \neq \sigma_2^2$ with $\alpha = .05$. What do you conclude?
b Test H_0: $\sigma_1^2 \geq \sigma_2^2$ versus H_a: $\sigma_1^2 < \sigma_2^2$ with $\alpha = .01$. What do you conclude?

9.52 Consider the situation of Exercise 9.23 (page 370). Use the sample information to test H_0: $\sigma_1^2 = \sigma_2^2$ versus H_a: $\sigma_1^2 \neq \sigma_2^2$ with $\alpha = .05$. Based on this test, does it make sense to believe that the unequal variances procedure is appropriate? Explain.

9.53 Consider the situation of Exercise 9.24 (page 370). AutoLoan

a Use the MegaStat output in Figure 9.7 (page 371) and a rejection point to test H_0: $\sigma_1^2 = \sigma_2^2$ versus H_a: $\sigma_1^2 \neq \sigma_2^2$ with $\alpha = .05$. What do you conclude?

b Use a p-value on the MegaStat output in Figure 9.7 to test H_0: $\sigma_1^2 = \sigma_2^2$ versus H_a: $\sigma_1^2 \neq \sigma_2^2$ with $\alpha = .05$. What do you conclude?

c Does it make sense to use the equal variances procedure in this situation?

d Hand calculate the value of the F statistic for testing H_0: $\sigma_1^2 = \sigma_2^2$. Show that your result turns out to be the same as the F statistic given in Figure 9.7.

Chapter Summary

This chapter has explained **how to compare two populations** by using confidence intervals and hypothesis tests. First we discussed how to compare **two population means** by using **independent samples.** Here the measurements in one sample are not related to the measurements in the other sample. We saw that in the unlikely event that the population variances are known, a **z-based** inference can be made. When these variances are unknown, ***t*-based** inferences are appropriate if the populations are normally distributed or the sample sizes are large. Both **equal variances and unequal variances *t*-based procedures** exist. We learned that, because it can be difficult to compare the population variances, many statisticians believe that it is almost always best to use the unequal variances procedure.

Sometimes samples are not independent. We learned that one such case is what is called a **paired difference experiment.** Here we obtain two different measurements on the same sample units, and we can compare two population means by using a confidence interval or by conducting a hypothesis test that employs the differences between the pairs of measurements. We next explained how to compare **two population proportions** by using **large, independent samples.** Finally, we concluded this chapter by discussing how to compare **two population variances** by using independent samples, and we learned that this comparison is done by using a test based on the ***F* distribution.**

Glossary of Terms

***F* distribution:** A continuous probability curve having a shape that depends on two parameters—the numerator degrees of freedom, df_1, and the denominator degrees of freedom, df_2. (pages 386–387)

independent samples experiment: An experiment in which there is no relationship between the measurements in the different samples. (pages 358, 361)

paired difference experiment: An experiment in which two different measurements are taken on the same units and inferences are made using the differences between the pairs of measurements. (pages 371, 375)

sampling distribution of $\hat{p}_1 - \hat{p}_2$: The probability distribution that describes the population of all possible values of $\hat{p}_1 - \hat{p}_2$, where $\hat{p}_1$ is the sample proportion for a random sample taken from one population and $\hat{p}_2$ is the sample proportion for a random sample taken from a second population. (page 379)

sampling distribution of s_1^2/s_2^2: The probability distribution that describes the population of all possible values of s_1^2/s_2^2, where s_1^2 is the sample variance of a random sample taken from one population and s_2^2 is the sample variance of a random sample taken from a second population. (page 386)

sampling distribution of $\bar{x}_1 - \bar{x}_2$: The probability distribution that describes the population of all possible values of $\bar{x}_1 - \bar{x}_2$, where $\bar{x}_1$ is the sample mean of a random sample taken from one population and $\bar{x}_2$ is the sample mean of a random sample taken from a second population. (page 358)

Important Formulas and Tests

Sampling distribution of $\bar{x}_1 - \bar{x}_2$ (independent random samples): page 358

z-based confidence interval for $\mu_1 - \mu_2$: page 358

z test about $\mu_1 - \mu_2$: page 359

t-based confidence interval for $\mu_1 - \mu_2$ when $\sigma_1^2 = \sigma_2^2$: page 363

t-based confidence interval for $\mu_1 - \mu_2$ when $\sigma_1^2 \neq \sigma_2^2$: page 366

t test about $\mu_1 - \mu_2$ when $\sigma_1^2 = \sigma_2^2$: page 365

t test about $\mu_1 - \mu_2$ when $\sigma_1^2 \neq \sigma_2^2$: page 366

Confidence interval for μ_d: page 373

A hypothesis test about μ_d: page 373

Sampling distribution of $\hat{p}_1 - \hat{p}_2$ (independent random samples): page 379

Large sample confidence interval for $p_1 - p_2$: page 380

Large sample hypothesis test about $p_1 - p_2$: page 381

Sampling distribution of s_1^2/s_2^2 (independent random samples): page 386

A hypothesis test about the equality of σ_1^2 and σ_2^2: pages 388 and 390

Supplementary Exercises

9.54 In its February 2, 1998, issue, *Fortune* magazine published the results of a Yankelovich Partners survey of 600 adults that investigated their ideas about marriage, divorce, and the contributions of the corporate wife. The survey results are shown in Figure 9.16. For each statement in the figure, the proportions of men and women who agreed with the statement are given. Assuming that the survey results were obtained from independent random samples of 300 men and 300 women:

a For each statement, carry out a hypothesis test that tests the equality of the population proportions of men and women who agree with the statement. Use α equal to .10, .05, .01, and .001. How much evidence is there that the population proportions of men and women who agree with each statement differ?

b For each statement, calculate a 95 percent confidence interval for the difference between the population proportion of men who agree with the statement and the population proportion of women who agree with the statement. Use the interval to help assess whether you feel that the difference between population proportions has practical significance.

Exercises 9.55 and 9.56 deal with the following situation:

In an article in the *Journal of Retailing,* Kumar, Kerwin, and Pereira study factors affecting merger and acquisition activity in retailing by comparing "target firms" and "bidder firms" with respect to several financial and marketing-related variables. If we consider two of the financial variables included in the study, suppose a random sample of 36 "target firms" gives a mean earnings per share of $1.52 with a standard deviation of $0.92, and that this sample gives a mean debt-to-equity ratio of 1.66 with a standard deviation of 0.82. Furthermore, an independent random sample of 36 "bidder firms" gives a mean earnings per share of $1.20 with a standard deviation of $0.84, and this sample gives a mean debt-to-equity ratio of 1.58 with a standard deviation of 0.81.

9.55 **a** Set up the null and alternative hypotheses needed to test whether the mean earnings per share for all "target firms" differs from the mean earnings per share for all "bidder firms." Test these hypotheses at the .10, .05, .01, and .001 levels of significance. How much evidence is there that these means differ? Explain.

b Calculate a 95 percent confidence interval for the difference between the mean earnings per share for "target firms" and "bidder firms." Interpret the interval.

FIGURE 9.16 The Results of a Yankelovich Partners Survey of 600 Adults on Marriage, Divorce, and the Contributions of the Corporate Wife (All Respondents with Income $50,000 or More)

People were magnanimous on the general proposition:

- In a divorce in a long-term marriage where the husband works outside the home and the wife is not employed for pay, the wife should be entitled to half the assets accumulated during the marriage.
  93% of women agree
  85% of men agree

But when we got to the goodies, a gender gap began to appear . . .

- The pension accumulated during the marriage should be split evenly.
  80% of women agree
  68% of men agree
- Stock options granted during the marriage should be split evenly.
  77% of women agree
  62% of men agree

. . . and turned into a chasm over the issue of how important a stay-at-home wife is to a husband's success.

- Managing the household and child rearing are extremely important to a husband's success.
  57% of women agree
  41% of men agree
- A corporate wife who also must travel, entertain, and act as a sounding board is extremely important to the success of a high-level business executive.
  51% of women agree
  28% of men agree
- The lifestyle of a corporate wife is more of a job than a luxury.
  73% of women agree
  57% of men agree

Source: Reprinted from the February 2, 1998, issue of *Fortune*. Copyright 1998 Time, Inc. Reprinted by permission.

9.56 **a** Set up the null and alternative hypotheses needed to test whether the mean debt-to-equity ratio for all "target firms" differs from the mean debt-to-equity ratio for all "bidder firms." Test these hypotheses at the .10, .05, .01, and .001 levels of significance. How much evidence is there that these means differ? Explain.

b Calculate a 95 percent confidence interval for the difference between the mean debt-to-equity ratios for "target firms" and "bidder firms." Interpret the interval.

c Based on the results of this exercise and Exercise 9.55, does a firm's earnings per share or the firm's debt-to-equity ratio seem to have the most influence on whether a firm will be a "target" or a "bidder"? Explain.

9.57 What impact did the September 11 terrorist attack have on U.S. airline demand? An analysis was conducted by Ito and Lee, "Assessing the impact of the September 11 terrorist attacks on U.S. airline demand", in the *Journal of Economics and Business* (January-February 2005). They found a negative short-term effect of over 30% and an ongoing negative impact of over 7%. Suppose that we wish to test the impact by taking a random sample of 12 airline routes before and after 9/11. Passenger miles (millions of passenger miles) for the same routes were tracked for the 12 months prior to and the 12 months immediately following 9/11. Assume that the population of all possible paired differences is normally distributed.

a Set up the null and alternative hypotheses needed to determine whether there was a reduction in mean airline passenger demand.

b Below we present the MINITAB output for the paired differences test. Use the output and rejection points to test the hypotheses at the .10, .05, and .01 levels of significance. Has the true mean airline demand been reduced?

Paired T-Test and CI: Before911, After911

```
Paired T for Before911 - After911
              N      Mean     StDev  SE Mean
Before911    12   117.333    26.976    7.787
After911     12    87.583    25.518    7.366
Difference   12   29.7500   10.3056   2.9750
T-Test of mean difference = 0 (vs > 0): T-Value = 10.00  P-Value = 0.000
```

c Use the *p*-value to test the hypotheses at the .10, .05, and .01 levels of significance. How much evidence is there against the null hypothesis?

9.58 In the book *Essentials of Marketing Research,* William R. Dillon, Thomas J. Madden, and Neil H. Firtle discuss evaluating the effectiveness of a test coupon. Samples of 500 test coupons and 500 control coupons were randomly delivered to shoppers. The results indicated that 35 of the 500 control coupons were redeemed, while 50 of the 500 test coupons were redeemed.

a In order to consider the test coupon for use, the marketing research organization required that the proportion of all shoppers who would redeem the test coupon be statistically shown to be greater than the proportion of all shoppers who would redeem the control coupon. Assuming that the two samples of shoppers are independent, carry out a hypothesis test at the .01 level of significance that will show whether this requirement is met by the test coupon. Explain your conclusion.

b Use the sample data to find a point estimate and a 95 percent interval estimate of the difference between the proportions of all shoppers who would redeem the test coupon and the control coupon. What does this interval say about whether the test coupon should be considered for use? Explain.

c Carry out the test of part *a* at the .10 level of significance. What do you conclude? Is your result statistically significant? Compute a 90 percent interval estimate instead of the 95 percent interval estimate of part *b*. Based on the interval estimate, do you feel that this result is practically important? Explain.

9.59 A marketing manager wishes to compare the mean prices charged for two brands of CD players. The manager conducts a random survey of retail outlets and obtains independent random samples of prices with the following results:

	Onkyo	JVC
Sample mean, $\bar{x}$	\$189	\$145
Sample standard deviation, *s*	\$ 12	\$ 10
Sample size	6	12

Assuming normality and equal variances:

a Use an appropriate hypothesis test to determine whether the mean prices for the two brands differ. How much evidence is there that the mean prices differ?

b Use an appropriate 95 percent confidence interval to estimate the difference between the mean prices of the two brands of CD players. Do you think that the difference has practical importance?

c Use an appropriate hypothesis test to provide evidence supporting the claim that the mean price of the Onkyo CD player is more than $30 higher than the mean price for the JVC CD player. Set α equal to .05.

9.60 Consider the situation of Exercise 9.59. Use the sample information to test H_0: $\sigma_1^2 = \sigma_2^2$ versus H_a: $\sigma_1^2 \neq \sigma_2^2$ with $\alpha = .05$. Based on this test, does it make sense to use the equal variances procedure? Explain.

9.61 Internet Exercise

a A prominent issue of the 2000 U.S. presidential campaign was campaign finance reform. A *Washington Post*/ABC News poll (reported April 4, 2000) found that 63 percent of 1,083 American adults surveyed believed that stricter campaign finance laws would be effective (a lot or somewhat) in reducing the influence of money in politics. Was this view uniformly held or did it vary by gender, race, or political party affiliation? A summary of survey responses, broken down by gender, is given in the table below.

Summary of Responses	Male	Female	All
Believe reduce influence, p	59%	66%	63%
Number surveyed, n	520	563	1,083

[Source: *Washington Post* website: http://www.washingtonpost.com/wp-srv/politics/polls/vault/vault.htm. Click on the data link under *Gore Seen More Able to Reform Education, April 4, 2000,* then click again on the date link, *04/04/2000,* to the right of the campaign finance question. For a gender breakdown, select *sex* in the *Results By:* box and click *Go.* Note that the survey report does not include numbers of males and females questioned. These values were estimated using 1990 U.S. Census figures showing that males made up 48 percent of the U.S. adult population.]

Is there sufficient evidence in this survey to conclude that the proportion of individuals who believed that campaign finance laws can reduce the influence of money in politics differs between females and males? Set up the appropriate null and alternative hypotheses. Conduct your test at the .05 and .01 levels of significance and calculate the p-value for your test. Make sure your conclusion is clearly stated.

b Search the World Wide Web for an interesting recent political poll dealing with an issue or political candidates, where responses are broken down by gender or some other two-category classification. (A list of high-potential websites is given below.) Use a difference in proportions test to determine whether political preference differs by gender or other two-level grouping.

Political polls on the World Wide Web:

ABC News:	http://www.abcnews.go.com/sections/politics/PollVault/PollVault.html
Washington Post:	http://www.washingtonpost.com/wp-srv/politics/polls/vault/vault.htm
Gallup:	http://www.gallup.com/poll/index.asp
L. A. Times:	http://www.latimes.com/news/timespoll/
CBS News:	http://cbsnews.cbs.com/now/section/0,1636,215-412,00.shtml
Newsweek:	http://www.newsweek.com/nw-srv/web/special/campaign2000/pollsurveys_front.htm
Polling report:	http://www.pollingreport.com/

Appendix 9.1 ■ Two-Sample Hypothesis Testing Using MINITAB

The instruction blocks in this section each begin by describing the entry of data into the Minitab data window. Alternatively, the data may be loaded directly from the data disk included with the text. The appropriate data file name is given at the top of each instruction block. Please refer to Appendix 1.1 for further information about entering data, saving data, and printing results.

Test for the difference between means, unequal variances, in Figure 9.4 on page 368 (data file: Catalyst.mtw):

- In the data window, enter the data from Table 9.1 (page 364) into two columns with variable names XA-100 and ZB-200.
- Select **Stat : Basic Statistics : 2-Sample t.**
- In the "2-Sample t (Test and Confidence Interval)" dialog box, select the "Samples in different columns" option.
- Select the XA-100 variable into the First box.
- Select the ZB-200 variable into the Second box.
- Click on the Options... button, enter the desired level of confidence (here, 95.0) in the "Confidence level" box, enter 0.0 in the "Test difference" box, and select "not equal" from the Alternative pull-down menu. Click OK in the "2-Sample t—Options" dialog box.
- To produce yield by catalyst type box plots, click the Graphs... button, check the "Boxplots of data" check box, and click OK in the "2-Sample t—Graphs" dialog box.
- Click OK in the "2-Sample t (Test and Confidence Interval)" dialog box.
- The results of the two-sample t test (including the t statistic and p-value) and the confidence interval for the difference between means appear in the Session window, while the box plots appear in a graphics window.
- A test for the difference between two means when the **variances are equal** can be performed by placing a checkmark in the "Assume Equal Variances" checkbox in the "2-Sample t (Test and Confidence Interval)" dialog box.

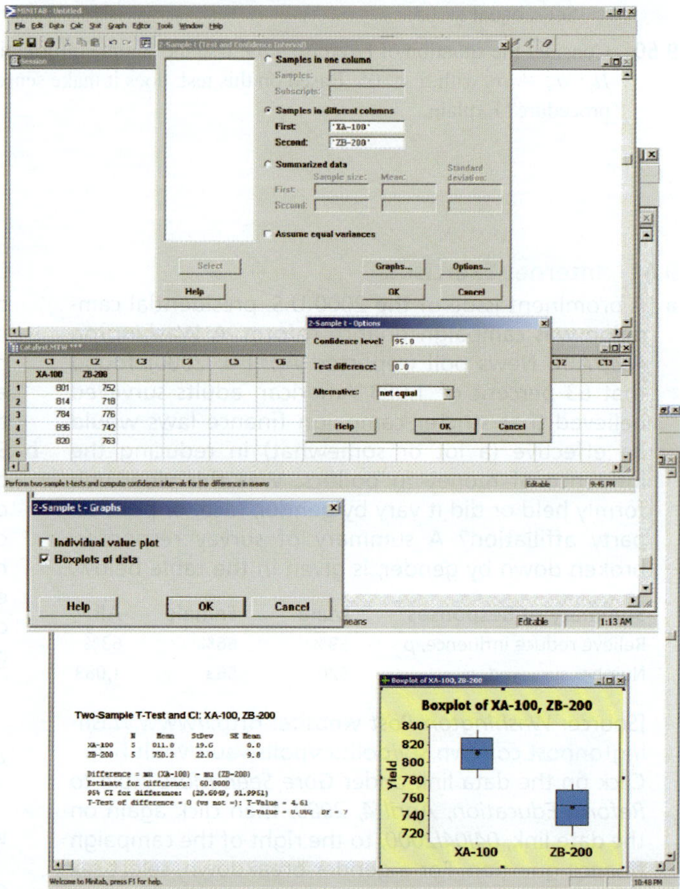

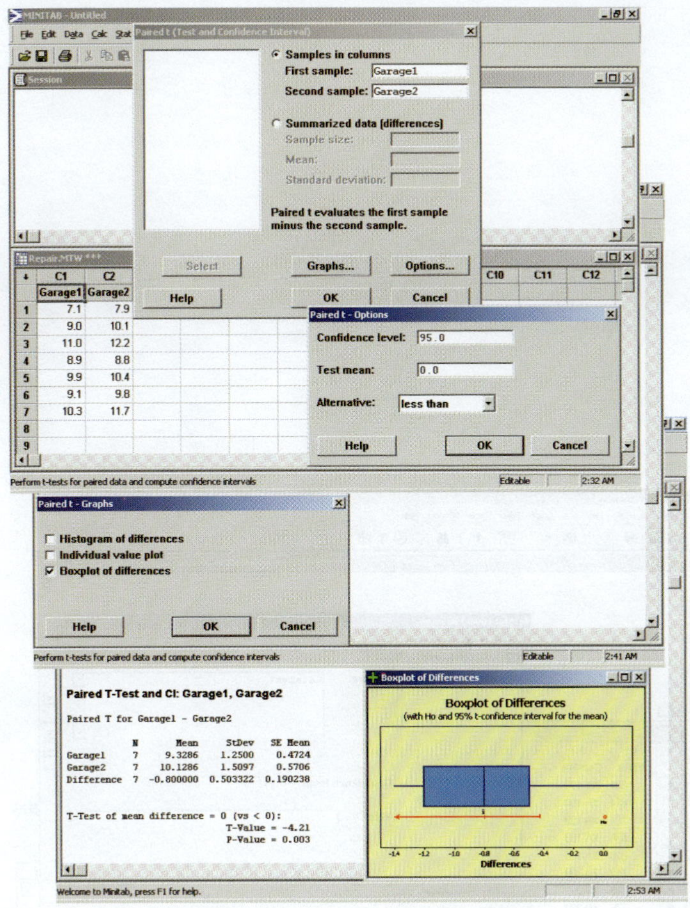

Test for paired differences in Figure 9.8(a) on page 374 (data file: Repair.mtw):

- In the Data window, enter the data from Table 9.2 (page 372) into two columns with variable names Garage1 and Garage2.
- Select **Stat : Basic Statistics : Paired t.**
- In the "Paired t (Test and Confidence Interval)" dialog box, select the "Samples in columns" option.
- Select Garage1 into the "First sample" box and Garage2 into the "Second sample" box.
- Click the Options... button.
- In the "Paired t—Options" dialog box, enter the desired level of confidence (here, 95.0) in the "Confidence level" box, enter 0.0 in the "Test mean" box, select "less than" from the Alternative pull-down menu, and click OK.
- To produce a boxplot of differences with a graphical summary of the test, click the Graphs... button, check the "Boxplot of differences" checkbox, and click OK in the "Paired t—Graphs" dialog box.
- Click OK in the "Paired t (Test and Confidence Interval)" dialog box.

The results of the paired t-test are given in the Session window, and graphical output appears in a graphics window.

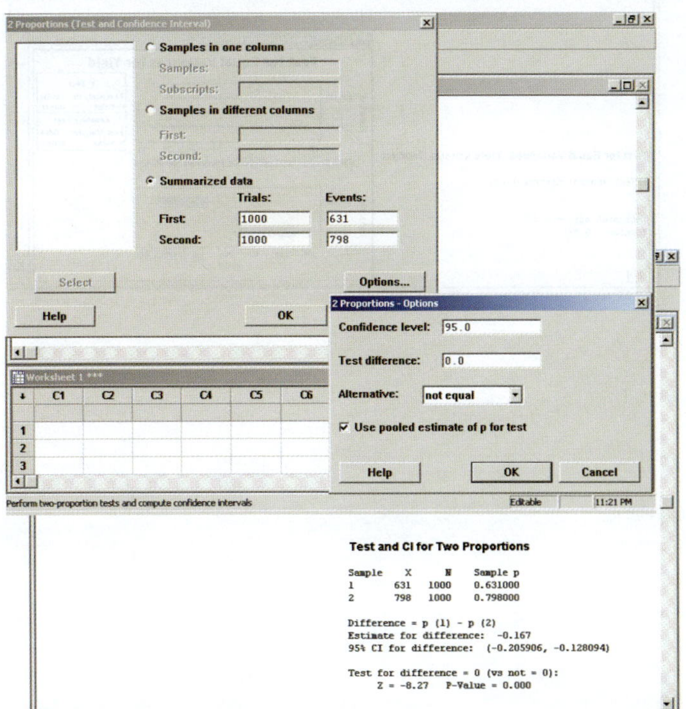

Hypothesis test and confidence interval for two independent proportions in the advertising media situation of Examples 9.9 and 9.10 on pages 380 to 382:

- Select **Stat : Basic Statistics : 2 Proportions**
- In the "2 Proportions (Test and Confidence Interval)" dialog box, select the "Summarized data" option.
- Enter the sample size for Des Moines (equal to 1000) into the "First—Trials" box, and enter the number of successes for Des Moines (equal to 631) into the "First—Events" box.
- Enter the sample size for Toledo (equal to 1000) into the "Second—Trials" box, and enter the number of successes for Toledo (equal to 798) into the "Second—Events" box.
- Click on the Options… button.
- In the "2 Proportions—Options" dialog box, enter the desired level of confidence (here 95.0) in the "Confidence level" box.
- Enter 0 into the "Test difference" box since we are testing that the difference between two proportions equals zero.

- Select the desired alternative hypothesis (here "not equal") from the Alternative drop-down menu.
- Check the "Use pooled estimate of p for test" checkbox since "Test difference" equals zero. Do not check this box in cases where "Test difference" does not equal zero.
- Click OK in the "2 Proportions—Options" dialog box.
- Click OK in the "2 Proportions (Test and Confidence Interval)" dialog box to obtain results for the test in the Session window.

Test for equality of variances in Figure 9.14(b) on page 389 (data file: Catalyst.mtw):

- The MINITAB equality of variance test requires that the yield data be entered in a single column with sample identifiers in a second column.
- In the Data window, enter the yield data from Table 9.1 (page 364) into a single column with variable name Yield. In a second column with variable name Catalyst, enter the corresponding identifying tag, XA-100 or ZB-200, for each yield figure.
- Select **Stat : ANOVA : Test for Equal Variances**
- In the "Test for Equal Variances" dialog box, select the Yield variable into the Response box.
- Select the Catalyst variable into the Factors box.
- Enter the desired level of confidence (here, 95.0) in the Confidence Level box.
- Click OK in the "Test for Equal Variances" dialog box.
- The reciprocal of the F-statistic (as described in the text) and the p-value will be displayed in the session window (along with additional output that we do not describe in this book). A graphical summary of the test is shown in a graphics window.

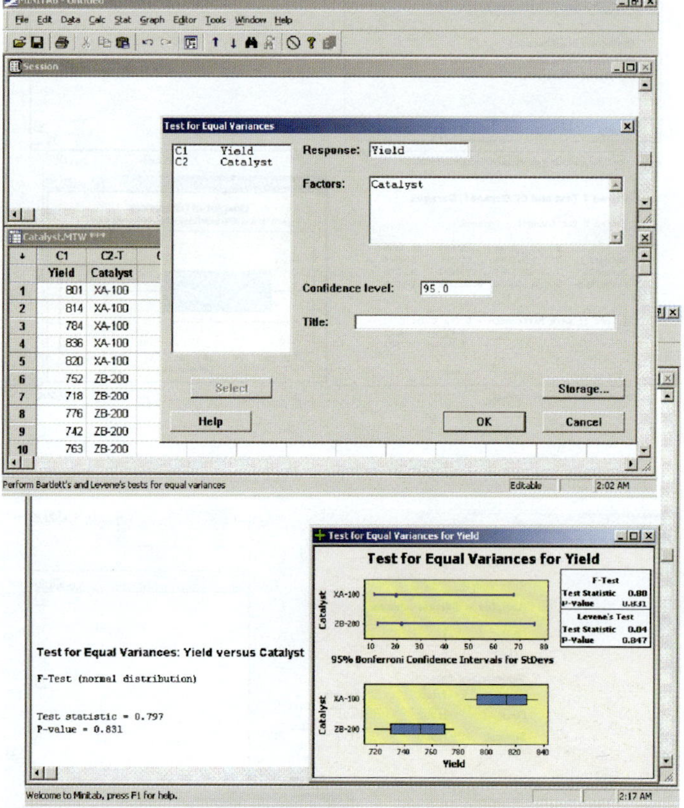

Appendix 9.2 ■ Two-Sample Hypothesis Testing Using Excel

The instruction blocks in this section each begin by describing the entry of data into an Excel spreadsheet. Alternatively, the data may be loaded directly from the data disk included with the text. The appropriate data file name is given at the top of each instruction block. Please refer to Appendix 1.2 for further information about entering data, saving data, and printing results.

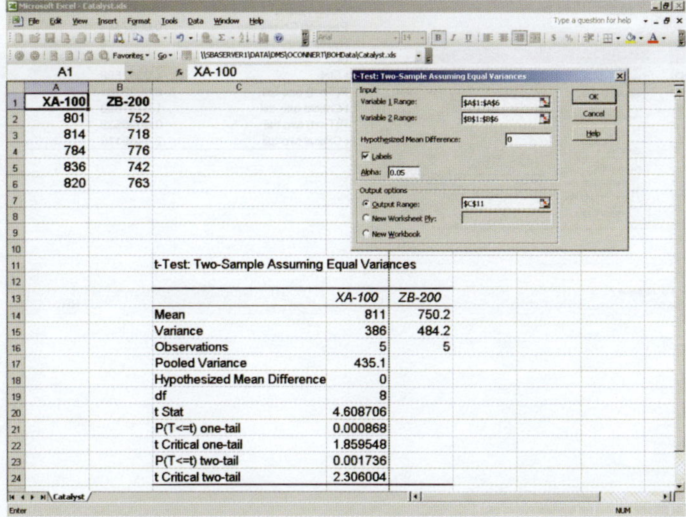

Test for the difference between means, equal variances, in Figure 9.2(b) on page 366 (data file: Catalyst.xls):

- Enter the data from Table 9.1 (page 364) into two columns: yields for catalyst XA-100 in column A and yields for catalyst ZB-200 in column B, with labels XA-100 and ZB-200.
- Select **Tools : Data Analysis : t-Test: Two-Sample Assuming Equal Variances** and click OK in the Data Analysis dialog box.
- In the t-Test dialog box, enter A1.A6 in the "Variable 1 Range" box.
- Enter B1.B6 in the "Variable 2 Range" box.
- Enter 0 (zero) in the "Hypothesized Mean Difference" box.
- Place a checkmark in the Labels check box.
- Enter 0.05 into the Alpha box.
- Select the Output Range option and enter C11 into the Output Range box.
- Click OK in the t-Test dialog box.
- The output will appear beginning in cell C11. Drag the column C border to uncover complete labels for all statistics.

Test for equality of variances similar to Figure 9.14(a) on page 389 (data file: Catalyst.xls):

- Enter the data from Table 9.1 (page 364) into two columns: yields for catalyst XA-100 in column A and yields for catalyst ZB-200 in column B, with labels XA-100 and ZB-200.
- Select **Tools: Data Analysis : F-Test Two-Sample for Variances** and click OK in the Data Analysis dialog box.
- In the F-Test dialog box, enter A1.A6 in the "Variable 1 Range" box.
- Enter B1.B6 in the "Variable 2 Range" box.
- Place a checkmark in the Labels check box.
- Enter 0.05 into the Alpha box.
- Select the Output Range option and enter F3 into the Output Range box.
- Click OK in the F-Test dialog box.
- The output will appear beginning in cell F3. Drag the column F border to uncover complete labels for all statistics.

Test for paired differences in Figure 9.9 on page 374 (data file: Repair.xls):

- Enter the data from Table 9.2 (page 372) into two columns: costs for Garage 1 in column A and costs for Garage 2 in column B, with labels Garage 1 and Garage 2.
- Select **Tools : Data Analysis : t-Test: Paired Two Sample for Means** and click OK in the Data Analysis dialog box.
- In the t-Test dialog box, enter A1.A8 into the "Variable 1 Range" box.
- Enter B1.B8 into the "Variable 2 Range" box.
- Enter 0 (zero) in the "Hypothesized Mean Difference" box.
- Place a checkmark in the Labels check box.
- Enter 0.05 into the Alpha box.
- Select the Output Range option and enter F3 into the Output Range box.
- Click OK in the t-Test dialog box.
- The output will appear beginning in cell F3. Drag the column F border to uncover complete labels for all statistics.

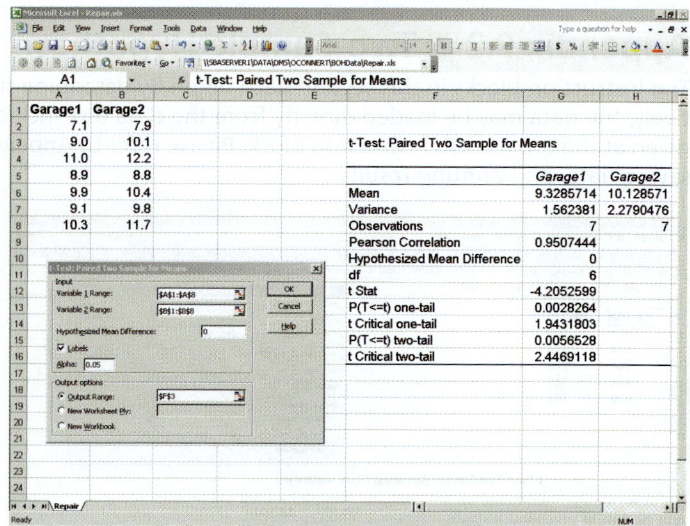

Appendix 9.3 ■ Two-Sample Hypothesis Testing Using MegaStat

The instructions in this section begin by describing the entry of data into an Excel worksheet. Alternatively, the data may be loaded directly from the data disk included with the text. The appropriate data file name is given at the top of each instruction block. Please refer to Appendix 1.2 for further information about entering data and saving and printing results in Excel. Please refer to Appendix 1.3 for more information about using MegaStat.

Test for the difference between means, equal variances, in Figure 9.2(a) on page 366 (data file: Catalyst.xls):

- Enter the data from Table 9.1 (page 364) into two columns: yields for catalyst XA-100 in column A and yields for catalyst ZB-200 in column B, with labels XA-100 and ZB-200.
- Select **MegaStat : Hypothesis Tests : Compare Two Independent Groups**
- In the "Hypothesis Test: Compare Two Independent Groups" dialog box, click on "data input".
- Click in the Group 1 box to make it active, and use the autoexpand feature to enter the range A1.A6.
- Click in the Group 2 box to make it active, and use the autoexpand feature to enter the range B1.B6.
- Enter the Hypothesized Difference (here equal to 0) into the so labeled box.
- Select an Alternative (here "not equal") from the drop-down menu in the Alternative box.

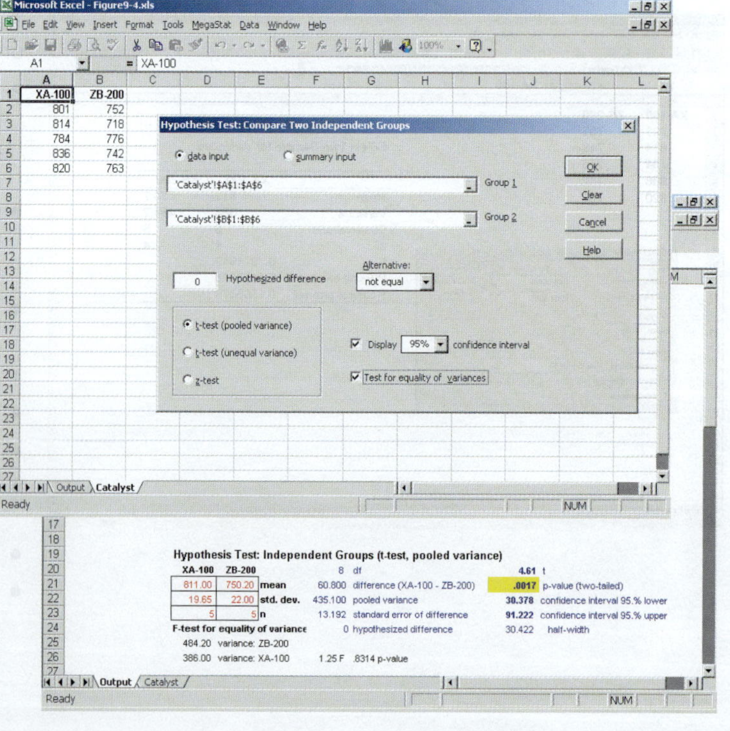

- Click on "t-test (pooled variance)" to request the equal variances test described on page 365.
- Check the "Display confidence interval" checkbox, and select or type a desired level of confidence.
- Check the "Test for equality of variances" checkbox to request the F test described on page 388.
- Click OK in the "Hypothesis Test: Compare Two Independent Groups" dialog box.
- The t test assuming unequal variances described on page 366 can be done by clicking "t-test (unequal variances)".

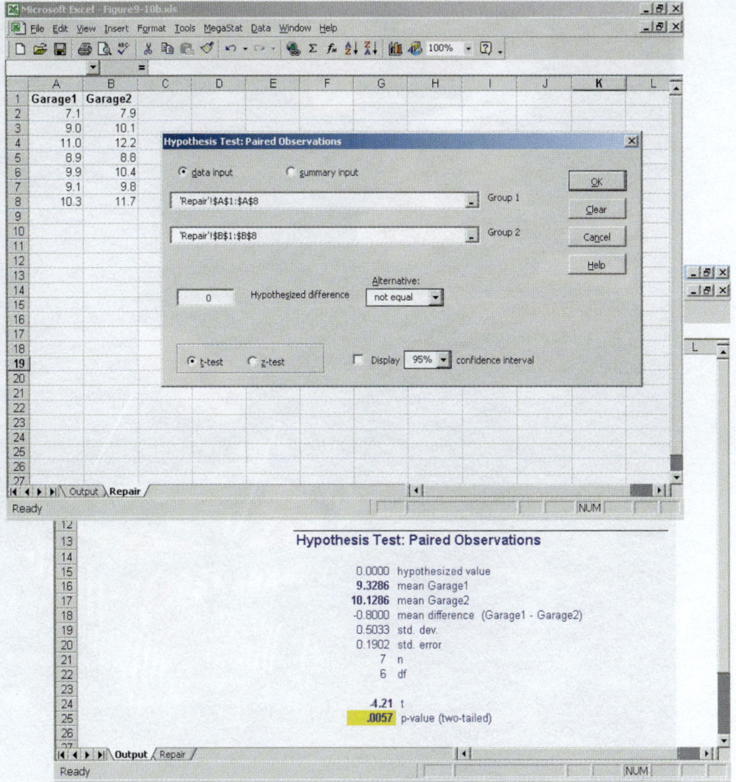

Test for paired differences in Figure 9.8(b) on page 374 (data file: Repair.xls):

- Enter the data from Table 9.2 (page 372) into two columns: costs for Garage 1 in column A and costs for Garage 2 in column B, with labels Garage1 and Garage2.
- Select **MegaStat : Hypothesis Tests : Paired Observations**
- In the "Hypothesis Test: Paired Observations" dialog box, click on "data input".
- Click in the Group 1 box to make it active, and use the autoexpand feature to enter the range A1.A8.
- Click in the Group 2 box to make it active, and use the autoexpand feature to enter the range B1.B8.
- Enter the Hypothesized difference (here equal to 0) into the so labeled box.
- Select an Alternative (here "not equal") from the drop-down menu in the Alternative box.
- Click on "t-test".
- Click OK in the "Hypothesis Test: Paired Observations" dialog box.
- If the sample sizes are large, a test based on the normal distribution can be done by clicking on "z-test".

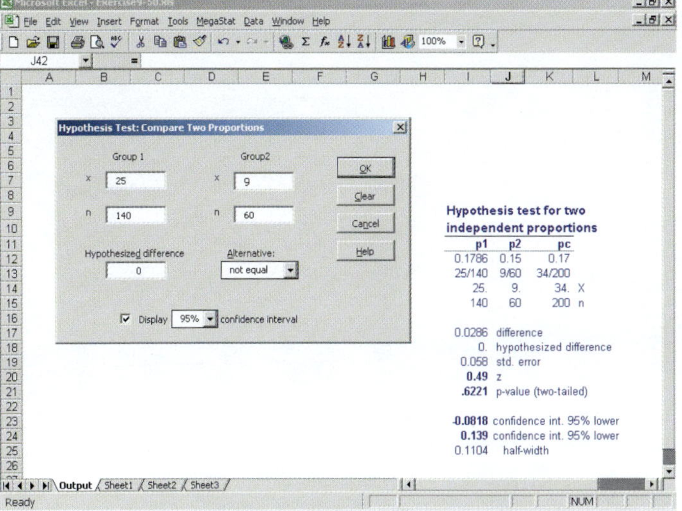

Hypothesis Test and Confidence Interval for Two Independent Proportions in Exercise 9.42 on page 383:

- Select **MegaStat : Hypothesis Tests : Compare Two Independent Proportions**
- In the "Hypothesis Test: Compare Two Proportions" dialog box, enter the number of successes x (here equal to 25) and the sample size n (here equal to 140) for homeowners in the "x" and "n" boxes for Group 1.
- Enter the number of successes x (here equal to 9) and the sample size n (here equal to 60) for renters in the "x" and "n" boxes for Group 2.
- Enter the Hypothesized difference (here equal to 0) into the so labeled box.
- Select an Alternative (here "not equal") from the drop-down menu in the Alternative box.
- Check the "Display confidence interval" checkbox, and select or type a desired level of confidence (here equal to 95%).
- Click OK in the "Hypothesis Test: Compare Two Proportions" dialog box.

CHAPTER 10

Experimental Design and Analysis of Variance

Chapter Outline

In Chapter 9 we learned that business improvement often involves making **comparisons.** In that chapter we presented several confidence intervals and several hypothesis testing procedures for comparing two population means. However, business improvement often requires that we compare more than two population means. For instance, we might compare the mean sales obtained by using three different advertising campaigns in order to improve a company's marketing process. Or, we might compare the mean production output obtained by using four different manufacturing process designs to improve productivity.

In this chapter we extend the methods presented in Chapter 9 by considering statistical procedures for **comparing two or more population means.** Each of the methods we discuss is called an **analysis of variance (ANOVA)** procedure. We also present some basic concepts of **experimental design,** which involves deciding how to collect data in a way that allows us to most effectively compare population means.

We explain the methods of this chapter in the context of four cases:

C

The Gasoline Mileage Case: An oil company wishes to develop a reasonably priced gasoline that will deliver improved mileages. The company uses **one-way analysis of variance** to compare the effects of three types of gasoline on mileage in order to find the gasoline type that delivers the highest mean mileage.

The Commercial Response Case: Firms that run commercials on television want to make the best use of their advertising dollars. In this case, researchers use **one-way analysis of variance** to compare the effects of varying program content on a viewer's ability to recall brand names after watching TV commercials.

The Defective Cardboard Box Case: A paper company performs an experiment to investigate the effects of four production methods on the number of defective cardboard boxes produced in an hour. The company uses a **randomized block ANOVA** to determine which production method yields the smallest mean number of defective boxes.

The Shelf Display Case: A commercial bakery supplies many supermarkets. In order to improve the effectiveness of its supermarket shelf displays, the company wishes to compare the effects of shelf display height (bottom, middle, or top) and width (regular or wide) on monthly demand. The bakery employs **two-way analysis of variance** to find the display height and width combination that produces the highest monthly demand.

10.1 Basic Concepts of Experimental Design

In many statistical studies a variable of interest, called the **response variable** (or **dependent variable**), is identified. Then data are collected that tell us about how one or more **factors** (or **independent variables**) influence the variable of interest. If we cannot control the factor(s) being studied, we say that the data obtained are **observational.** For example, suppose that in order to study how the size of a home relates to the sales price of the home, a real estate agent randomly selects 50 recently sold homes and records the square footages and sales prices of these homes. Because the real estate agent cannot control the sizes of the randomly selected homes, we say that the data are observational.

If we can control the factors being studied, we say that the data are **experimental.** Furthermore, in this case the values, or **levels,** of the factor (or combination of factors) are called **treatments.** The purpose of most experiments is **to compare and estimate the effects of the different treatments on the response variable.** For example, suppose that an oil company wishes to study how three different gasoline types (A, B, and C) affect the mileage obtained by a popular midsized automobile model. Here the response variable is gasoline mileage, and the company will study a single factor—gasoline type. Since the oil company can control which gasoline type is used in the midsized automobile, the data that the oil company will collect are experimental. Furthermore, the treatments—the levels of the factor gasoline type—are gasoline types A, B, and C.

In order to collect data in an experiment, the different treatments are assigned to objects (people, cars, animals, or the like) that are called **experimental units.** For example, in the gasoline mileage situation, gasoline types A, B, and C will be compared by conducting mileage tests using a midsized automobile. The automobiles used in the tests are the experimental units.

In general, when a treatment is applied to more than one experimental unit, it is said to be **replicated.** Furthermore, when the analyst controls the treatments employed and how they are applied to the experimental units, a **designed experiment** is being carried out. A commonly used, simple experimental design is called the **completely randomized experimental design.**

In a **completely randomized experimental design,** independent random samples of experimental units are assigned to the treatments.

Suppose we assign three experimental units to each of five treatments. We can achieve a completely randomized experimental design by assigning experimental units to treatments as follows. First, randomly select three experimental units and assign them to the first treatment. Next, randomly select three **different** experimental units from those remaining and assign them to the second treatment. That is, select these units from those not assigned to the first treatment. Third, randomly select three **different** experimental units from those not assigned to either the first or second treatment. Assign these experimental units to the third treatment. Continue this procedure until the required number of experimental units have been assigned to each treatment.

Once experimental units have been assigned to treatments, a value of the response variable is observed for each experimental unit. Thus we obtain a **sample** of values of the response variable for each treatment. When we employ a completely randomized experimental design, we assume that each sample has been randomly selected from the population of all values of the response variable that could potentially be observed when using its particular treatment. We also assume that the different samples of response variable values are **independent** of each other. This is usually reasonable because the completely randomized design ensures that each different sample results from **different measurements** being taken on **different experimental units.** Thus we sometimes say that we are conducting an **independent samples experiment.**

Example 10.1 The Gasoline Mileage Case

North American Oil Company is attempting to develop a reasonably priced gasoline that will deliver improved gasoline mileages. As part of its development process, the company would like to compare the effects of three types of gasoline (*A*, *B*, and *C*) on gasoline mileage. For testing purposes, North American Oil will compare the effects of gasoline types *A*, *B*, and *C* on the gasoline mileage obtained by a popular midsized model called the Fire-Hawk. Suppose the company has access to 1,000 Fire-Hawks that are representative of the population of all Fire-Hawks, and suppose the company will utilize a completely randomized experimental design that employs samples of size five. In order to accomplish this, five Fire-Hawks will be randomly selected from the 1,000 available Fire-Hawks. These autos will be assigned to gasoline type *A*. Next, five **different** Fire-Hawks will be randomly selected from the remaining 995 available Fire-Hawks. These autos will be assigned to gasoline type *B*. Finally, five **different** Fire-Hawks will be randomly selected from the remaining 990 available Fire-Hawks. These autos will be assigned to gasoline type *C*.

Each randomly selected Fire-Hawk is test driven using the appropriate gasoline type (treatment) under normal conditions for a specified distance, and the gasoline mileage for each test drive is measured. We let x_{ij} denote the jth mileage obtained when using gasoline type *i*. The mileage data obtained are given in Table 10.1. Here we assume that the set of gasoline mileage observations obtained by using a particular gasoline type is a sample randomly selected from the infinite population of all Fire-Hawk mileages that could be obtained using that gasoline type.

TABLE 10.1 The Gasoline Mileage Data GasMile2

Gasoline Type *A*	Gasoline Type *B*	Gasoline Type *C*
$x_{A1} = 34.0$	$x_{B1} = 35.3$	$x_{C1} = 33.3$
$x_{A2} = 35.0$	$x_{B2} = 36.5$	$x_{C2} = 34.0$
$x_{A3} = 34.3$	$x_{B3} = 36.4$	$x_{C3} = 34.7$
$x_{A4} = 35.5$	$x_{B4} = 37.0$	$x_{C4} = 33.0$
$x_{A5} = 35.8$	$x_{B5} = 37.6$	$x_{C5} = 34.9$

Examining the box plots shown next to the mileage data, we see some evidence that gasoline type *B* yields the highest gasoline mileages.[1]

Example 10.2 The Shelf Display Case

The Tastee Bakery Company supplies a bakery product to many supermarkets in a metropolitan area. The company wishes to study the effect of the shelf display height employed by the supermarkets on monthly sales (measured in cases of 10 units each) for this product. Shelf display height, the factor to be studied, has three levels—bottom (B), middle (M), and top (T)—which are the treatments. To compare these treatments, the bakery uses a completely randomized experimental design. For each shelf height, six supermarkets (the experimental units) of equal sales potential are randomly selected, and each supermarket displays the product using its assigned shelf height for a month. At the end of the month, sales of the bakery product (the response variable) at the 18 participating stores are recorded, giving the data in Table 10.2. Here we assume that the set of sales amounts for each display height is a sample randomly selected from the population of all sales amounts that could be obtained (at supermarkets of the given sales potential) at that display height. Examining the box plots that are shown next to the sales data, we seem to have evidence that a middle display height gives the highest bakery product sales.

TABLE 10.2 The Bakery Product Sales Data BakeSale

	Shelf Display Height	
Bottom (B)	**Middle (M)**	**Top (T)**
58.2	73.0	52.4
53.7	78.1	49.7
55.8	75.4	50.9
55.7	76.2	54.0
52.5	78.4	52.1
58.9	82.1	49.9

Example 10.3 The Commercial Response Case

Advertising research indicates that when a television program is involving (such as the 2002 Super Bowl between the St. Louis Rams and New England Patriots, which was very exciting), individuals exposed to commercials tend to have difficulty recalling the names of the products advertised. Therefore, in order for companies to make the best use of their advertising dollars, it is important to show their most original and memorable commercials during involving programs.

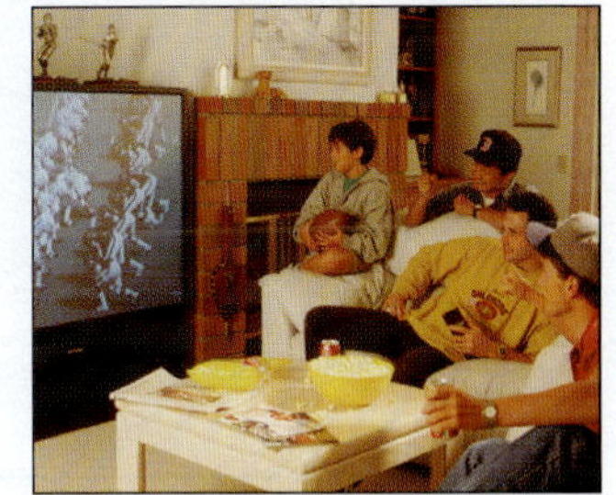

In an article in the *Journal of Advertising Research,* Soldow and Principe (1981) studied the effect of program content on the response to commercials. Program content, the factor studied, has three levels—more involving programs, less involving programs, and no program (that is, commercials only)—which are the treatments. To compare these treatments, Soldow and Principe employed a completely randomized experimental design. For each program content level, 29 subjects were randomly selected and exposed to commercials in that program content level. Then a brand recall score (measured on a continuous scale) was obtained for each subject. The 29 brand recall scores for each program content level are assumed to be a sample randomly selected from the population of all brand recall scores for that program content level. Although we do not give the results in this example, the reader will analyze summary statistics describing these results in the exercises of Section 10.2.

Exercises for Section 10.1

CONCEPTS

10.1 Define the meaning of the terms *response variable, factor, treatments,* and *experimental units.*

10.2 What is a completely randomized experimental design?

[1] All of the box plots presented in this chapter have been obtained using MINITAB.

TABLE 10.3 Display Panel Study Data Display

Display Panel		
A	*B*	*C*
21	24	40
27	21	36
24	18	35
26	19	32

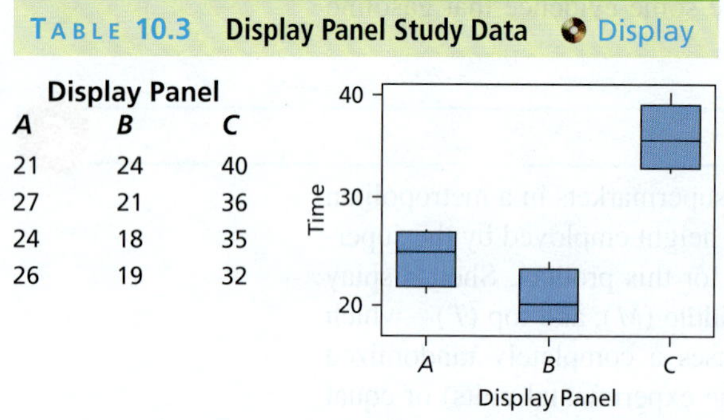

TABLE 10.4 Bottle Design Study Data BottleDes

Bottle Design		
A	*B*	*C*
16	33	23
18	31	27
19	37	21
17	29	28
13	34	25

METHODS AND APPLICATIONS

10.3 A study compared three different display panels for use by air traffic controllers. Each display panel was tested in a simulated emergency condition; 12 highly trained air traffic controllers took part in the study. Four controllers were randomly assigned to each display panel. The time (in seconds) needed to stabilize the emergency condition was recorded. The results of the study are given in Table 10.3. For this situation, identify the response variable, factor of interest, treatments, and experimental units. Display

10.4 A consumer preference study compares the effects of three different bottle designs (*A*, *B*, and *C*) on sales of a popular fabric softener. A completely randomized design is employed. Specifically, 15 supermarkets of equal sales potential are selected, and 5 of these supermarkets are randomly assigned to each bottle design. The number of bottles sold in 24 hours at each supermarket is recorded. The data obtained are displayed in Table 10.4. For this situation, identify the response variable, factor of interest, treatments, and experimental units. BottleDes

10.2 One-Way Analysis of Variance

CHAPTER 12

Suppose we wish to study the effects of p **treatments** (treatments 1, 2, . . . , p) on a **response variable.** For any particular treatment, say treatment i, we define μ_i and σ_i to be the mean and standard deviation of the population of all possible values of the response variable that could potentially be observed when using treatment i. Here we refer to μ_i as **treatment mean *i*.** The goal of **one-way analysis of variance** (often called **one-way ANOVA**) is to estimate and compare the effects of the different treatments on the response variable. We do this by **estimating and comparing the treatment means** $\mu_1, \mu_2, \ldots, \mu_p$. Here we assume that a sample has been randomly selected for each of the p treatments by employing a completely randomized experimental design. We let n_i denote the size of the sample that has been randomly selected for treatment i, and we let x_{ij} denote the jth value of the response variable that is observed when using treatment i. It then follows that the point estimate of μ_i is $\bar{x}_i$, the average of the sample of n_i values of the response variable observed when using treatment i. It further follows that the point estimate of σ_i is s_i, the standard deviation of the sample of n_i values of the response variable observed when using treatment i.

Example 10.4 The Gasoline Mileage Case

Consider the gasoline mileage situation. We let μ_A, μ_B, and μ_C denote the means and σ_A, σ_B, and σ_C denote the standard deviations of the populations of all possible gasoline mileages using gasoline types *A*, *B*, and *C*. To estimate these means and standard deviations, North American Oil has employed a completely randomized experimental design and has obtained the samples of mileages in Table 10.1. The means of these samples—$\bar{x}_A = 34.92$, $\bar{x}_B = 36.56$, and $\bar{x}_C = 33.98$—are the point estimates of μ_A, μ_B, and μ_C. The standard deviations of these samples—$s_A = .7662$, $s_B = .8503$, and $s_C = .8349$—are the point estimates of σ_A, σ_B, and σ_C. Using these point estimates, we will (later in this section) test to see whether there are any statistically significant differences between the treatment means μ_A, μ_B, and μ_C. If such differences exist, we will estimate the magnitudes of these differences. This will allow North American Oil to judge whether these differences have practical importance.

The one-way ANOVA formulas allow us to test for significant differences between treatment means and allow us to estimate differences between treatment means. The validity of these formulas requires that the following assumptions hold:

Assumptions for One-Way Analysis of Variance

1 **Constant variance**—the p populations of values of the response variable associated with the treatments have equal variances.

2 **Normality**—the p populations of values of the response variable associated with the treatments all have normal distributions.

3 **Independence**—the samples of experimental units associated with the treatments are randomly selected, independent samples.

The one-way ANOVA results are not very sensitive to violations of the equal variances assumption. Studies have shown that this is particularly true when the sample sizes employed are equal (or nearly equal). Therefore, a good way to make sure that unequal variances will not be a problem is to take samples that are the same size. In addition, it is useful to compare the sample standard deviations $s_1, s_2, \ldots, s_p$ to see if they are reasonably equal. As a general rule, *the one-way ANOVA results will be approximately correct if the largest sample standard deviation is no more than twice the smallest sample standard deviation.* The variations of the samples can also be compared by constructing a box plot for each sample (as we have done for the gasoline mileage data in Table 10.1). Several statistical texts also employ the sample variances to test the equality of the population variances [see Bowerman and O'Connell (1990) for two of these tests]. However, these tests have some drawbacks—in particular, their results are very sensitive to violations of the normality assumption. Because of this, there is controversy as to whether these tests should be performed.

The normality assumption says that each of the p populations is normally distributed. This assumption is not crucial. It has been shown that the one-way ANOVA results are approximately valid for mound-shaped distributions. It is useful to construct a box plot and/or a stem-and-leaf display for each sample. If the distributions are reasonably symmetric, and if there are no outliers, the ANOVA results can be trusted for sample sizes as small as 4 or 5. As an example, consider the gasoline mileage study of Examples 10.1 and 10.4. The box plots of Table 10.1 suggest that the variability of the mileages in each of the three samples is roughly the same. Furthermore, the sample standard deviations $s_A = .7662$, $s_B = .8503$, and $s_C = .8349$ are reasonably equal (the largest is not even close to twice the smallest). Therefore, it is reasonable to believe that the constant variance assumption is satisfied. Moreover, because the sample sizes are the same, unequal variances would probably not be a serious problem anyway. Many small, independent factors influence gasoline mileage, so the distributions of mileages for gasoline types A, B, and C are probably mound-shaped. In addition, the box plots of Table 10.1 indicate that each distribution is roughly symmetric with no outliers. Thus, the normality assumption probably approximately holds. Finally, because North American Oil has employed a completely randomized design, the independence assumption probably holds. This is because the gasoline mileages in the different samples were obtained for *different* Fire-Hawks.

Testing for significant differences between treatment means As a preliminary step in one-way ANOVA, we wish to determine whether there are any statistically significant differences between the treatment means $\mu_1, \mu_2, \ldots, \mu_p$. To do this, we test the null hypothesis

$$H_0: \mu_1 = \mu_2 = \cdots = \mu_p$$

This hypothesis says that all the treatments have the same effect on the mean response. We test H_0 versus the alternative hypothesis

$$H_a\text{: At least two of } \mu_1, \mu_2, \ldots, \mu_p \text{ differ}$$

This alternative says that at least two treatments have different effects on the mean response.

FIGURE 10.1 Comparing Between-Treatment Variability and Within-Treatment Variability

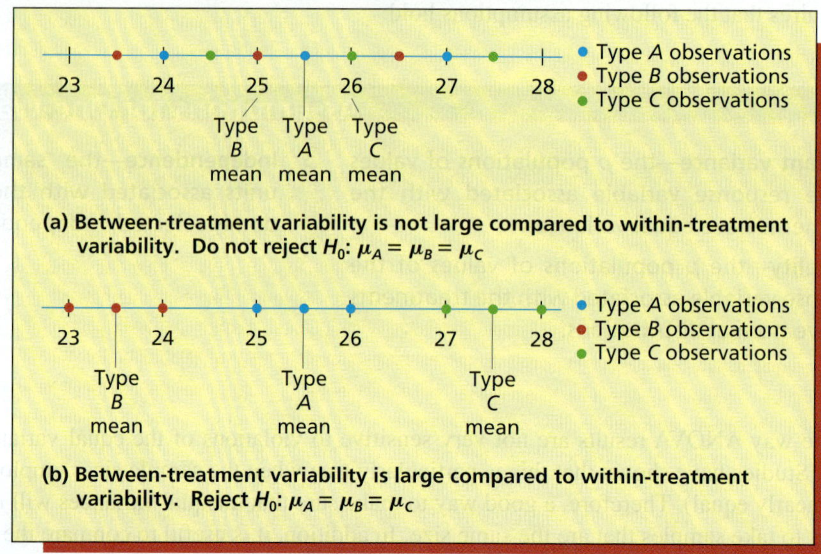

(a) Between-treatment variability is not large compared to within-treatment variability. Do not reject H_0: $\mu_A = \mu_B = \mu_C$

(b) Between-treatment variability is large compared to within-treatment variability. Reject H_0: $\mu_A = \mu_B = \mu_C$

To carry out such a test, we compare what we call the **between-treatment variability** to the **within-treatment variability.** For instance, suppose we wish to study the effects of three gasoline types (*A*, *B*, and *C*) on mean gasoline mileage, and consider Figure 10.1(a). This figure depicts three independent random samples of gasoline mileages obtained using gasoline types *A*, *B*, and *C*. Observations obtained using gasoline type *A* are plotted as blue dots (●), observations obtained using gasoline type *B* are plotted as red dots (●), and observations obtained using gasoline type *C* are plotted as green dots (●). Furthermore, the sample treatment means are labeled as "type *A* mean," "type *B* mean," and "type *C* mean." We see that the variability of the sample treatment means—that is, the **between-treatment variability**—is not large compared to the variability within each sample (the **within-treatment variability**). In this case, the differences between the sample treatment means could quite easily be the result of sampling variation. Thus we would not have sufficient evidence to reject

$$H_0: \mu_A = \mu_B = \mu_C$$

Next look at Figure 10.1(b), which depicts a different set of three independent random samples of gasoline mileages. Here the variability of the sample treatment means (the between-treatment variability) is large compared to the variability within each sample. This would probably provide enough evidence to tell us to reject

$$H_0: \mu_A = \mu_B = \mu_C$$

in favor of

$$H_a\text{: At least two of } \mu_A, \mu_B, \text{ and } \mu_C \text{ differ}$$

We would conclude that at least two of gasoline types *A*, *B*, and *C* have different effects on mean mileage.

In order to numerically compare the between-treatment and within-treatment variability, we can define several **sums of squares** and **mean squares.** To begin, we define n to be the total number of experimental units employed in the one-way ANOVA, and we define $\bar{x}$ to be the overall mean of all observed values of the response variable. Then we define the following:

The **treatment sum of squares** is

$$SST = \sum_{i=1}^{p} n_i(\bar{x}_i - \bar{x})^2$$

In order to compute SST, we calculate the difference between each sample treatment mean $\bar{x}_i$ and the overall mean $\bar{x}$, we square each of these differences, we multiply each squared difference by the number of observations for that treatment, and we sum over all treatments. The SST

measures the variability of the sample treatment means. For instance, if all the sample treatment means ($\bar{x}_i$ values) were equal, then the treatment sum of squares would be equal to 0. The more the $\bar{x}_i$ values vary, the larger will be SST. In other words, the **treatment sum of squares** measures the amount of **between-treatment variability.**

As an example, consider the gasoline mileage data in Table 10.1. In this experiment we employ a total of

$$n = n_A + n_B + n_C = 5 + 5 + 5 = 15$$

experimental units. Furthermore, the overall mean of the 15 observed gasoline mileages is

$$\bar{x} = \frac{34.0 + 35.0 + \cdots + 34.9}{15} = \frac{527.3}{15} = 35.153$$

Then

$$\begin{aligned} SST &= \sum_{i=A,B,C} n_i(\bar{x}_i - \bar{x})^2 \\ &= n_A(\bar{x}_A - \bar{x})^2 + n_B(\bar{x}_B - \bar{x})^2 + n_C(\bar{x}_C - \bar{x})^2 \\ &= 5(34.92 - 35.153)^2 + 5(36.56 - 35.153)^2 + 5(33.98 - 35.153)^2 \\ &= 17.0493 \end{aligned}$$

In order to measure the within-treatment variability, we define the following quantity:

The **error sum of squares** is

$$SSE = \sum_{j=1}^{n_1} (x_{1j} - \bar{x}_1)^2 + \sum_{j=1}^{n_2} (x_{2j} - \bar{x}_2)^2 + \cdots + \sum_{j=1}^{n_p} (x_{pj} - \bar{x}_p)^2$$

Here x_{1j} is the jth observed value of the response in the first sample, x_{2j} is the jth observed value of the response in the second sample, and so forth. The formula above says that we compute SSE by calculating the squared difference between each observed value of the response and its corresponding treatment mean and by summing these squared differences over all the observations in the experiment.

The SSE measures the variability of the observed values of the response variable around their respective treatment means. For example, if there were no variability within each sample, the error sum of squares would be equal to 0. The more the values within the samples vary, the larger will be SSE.

As an example, in the gasoline mileage study, the sample treatment means are $\bar{x}_A = 34.92$, $\bar{x}_B = 36.56$, and $\bar{x}_C = 33.98$. It follows that

$$\begin{aligned} SSE &= \sum_{j=1}^{n_A} (x_{Aj} - \bar{x}_A)^2 + \sum_{j=1}^{n_B} (x_{Bj} - \bar{x}_B)^2 + \sum_{j=1}^{n_C} (x_{Cj} - \bar{x}_C)^2 \\ &= [(34.0 - 34.92)^2 + (35.0 - 34.92)^2 + (34.3 - 34.92)^2 + (35.5 - 34.92)^2 + (35.8 - 34.92)^2] \\ &\quad + [(35.3 - 36.56)^2 + (36.5 - 36.56)^2 + (36.4 - 36.56)^2 + (37.0 - 36.56)^2 + (37.6 - 36.56)^2] \\ &\quad + [(33.3 - 33.98)^2 + (34.0 - 33.98)^2 + (34.7 - 33.98)^2 + (33.0 - 33.98)^2 + (34.9 - 33.98)^2] \\ &= 8.028 \end{aligned}$$

Finally, we define a sum of squares that measures the total amount of variability in the observed values of the response:

The **total sum of squares** is

$$SSTO = SST + SSE$$

The variability in the observed values of the response must come from one of two sources—the between-treatment variability or the within-treatment variability. It follows that the total sum of squares equals the sum of the treatment sum of squares and the error sum of squares. Therefore, the ***SST* and *SSE* are said to partition the total sum of squares.**

In the gasoline mileage study, we see that

$$SSTO = SST + SSE = 17.0493 + 8.028 = 25.0773$$

Using the treatment and error sums of squares, we next define two **mean squares:**

The **treatment mean square** is

$$MST = \frac{SST}{p - 1}$$

The **error mean square** is

$$MSE = \frac{SSE}{n - p}$$

In order to decide whether there are any statistically significant differences between the treatment means, it makes sense to compare the amount of between-treatment variability to the amount of within-treatment variability. This comparison suggests the following F test:

An F Test for Differences between Treatment Means

Suppose that we wish to compare p treatment means $\mu_1, \mu_2, \ldots, \mu_p$ and consider testing

$H_0: \mu_1 = \mu_2 = \cdots = \mu_p$ (all treatment means are equal) versus H_a: At least two of $\mu_1, \mu_2, \ldots, \mu_p$ differ (at least two treatment means differ)

Define the F statistic

$$F = \frac{MST}{MSE} = \frac{SST/(p - 1)}{SSE/(n - p)}$$

and its p-value to be the area under the F curve with $p - 1$ and $n - p$ degrees of freedom to the right of F. We can reject H_0 in favor of H_a at level of significance α if either of the following equivalent conditions holds:

1 $F > F_\alpha$

2 p-value $< \alpha$

Here the F_α point is based on $p - 1$ numerator and $n - p$ denominator degrees of freedom.

A large value of F results when SST, which measures the between-treatment variability, is large compared to SSE, which measures the within-treatment variability. If F is large enough, this implies that H_0 should be rejected. The rejection point F_α tells us when F is large enough to allow us to reject H_0 at level of significance α. When F is large, the associated p-value is small. If this p-value is less than α, we can reject H_0 at level of significance α.

Example 10.5 The Gasoline Mileage Case

Consider the North American Oil Company data in Table 10.1. The company wishes to determine whether any of gasoline types A, B, and C have different effects on mean Fire-Hawk gasoline mileage. That is, we wish to see whether there are any statistically significant differences between μ_A, μ_B, and μ_C. To do this, we test the null hypothesis

$$H_0: \mu_A = \mu_B = \mu_C$$

which says that gasoline types A, B, and C have the same effects on mean gasoline mileage. We test H_0 versus the alternative

$$H_a\text{: At least two of } \mu_A, \mu_B, \text{ and } \mu_C \text{ differ}$$

which says that at least two of gasoline types A, B, and C have different effects on mean gasoline mileage.

Since we have previously computed SST to be 17.0493 and SSE to be 8.028, and because we are comparing $p = 3$ treatment means, we have

$$MST = \frac{SST}{p - 1} = \frac{17.0493}{3 - 1} = 8.525$$

FIGURE 10.2 MINITAB and Excel Output of an Analysis of Variance of the Gasoline Mileage Data in Table 10.1

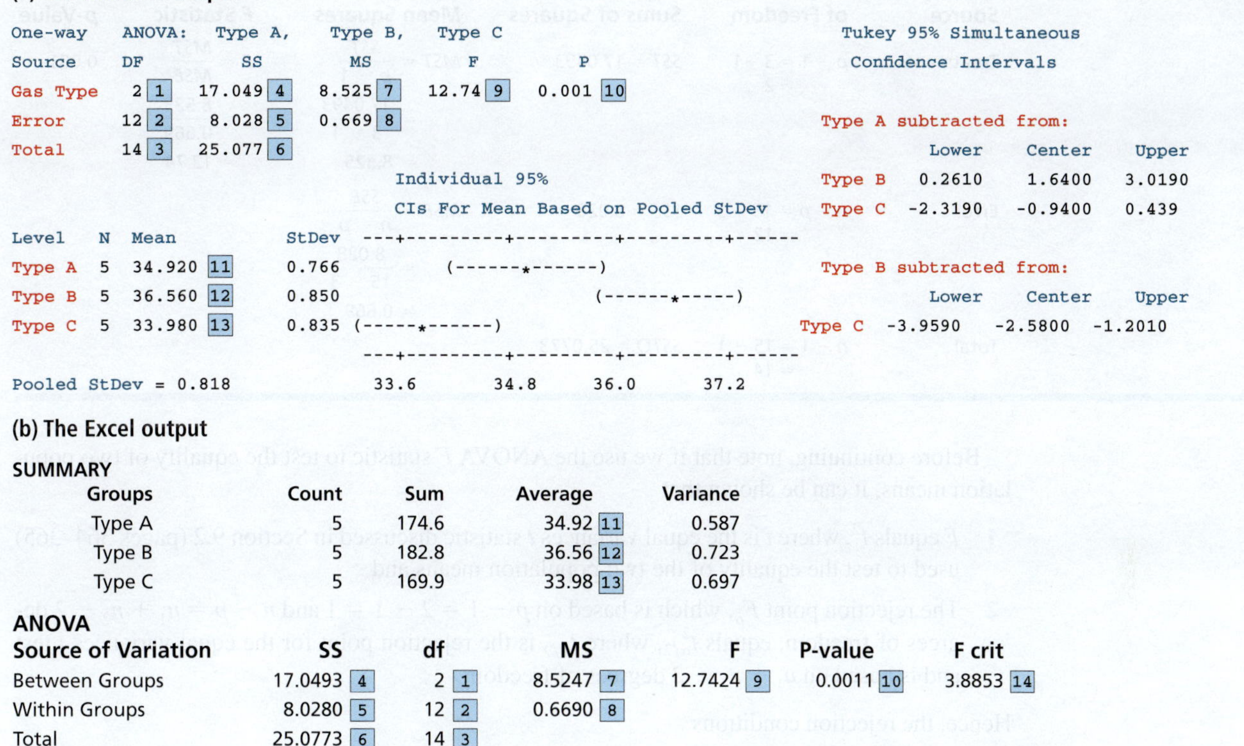

(a) The MINITAB output

```
One-way  ANOVA:  Type A,    Type B,   Type C                Tukey 95% Simultaneous
Source   DF        SS         MS        F          P          Confidence Intervals
Gas Type  2 [1]  17.049 [4]  8.525 [7]  12.74 [9]  0.001 [10]
Error    12 [2]   8.028 [5]  0.669 [8]                      Type A subtracted from:
Total    14 [3]  25.077 [6]                                          Lower    Center    Upper
                             Individual 95%                 Type B   0.2610   1.6400   3.0190
                             CIs For Mean Based on Pooled StDev  Type C  -2.3190  -0.9400   0.439
Level    N  Mean         StDev  ---+---------+---------+---------+------
Type A   5  34.920 [11]  0.766         (------*------)       Type B subtracted from:
Type B   5  36.560 [12]  0.850                     (------*-----)      Lower    Center    Upper
Type C   5  33.980 [13]  0.835  (-----*------)               Type C  -3.9590  -2.5800  -1.2010
                                ---+---------+---------+---------+------
Pooled StDev = 0.818               33.6      34.8      36.0      37.2
```

(b) The Excel output

SUMMARY

Groups	Count	Sum	Average	Variance
Type A	5	174.6	34.92 [11]	0.587
Type B	5	182.8	36.56 [12]	0.723
Type C	5	169.9	33.98 [13]	0.697

ANOVA

Source of Variation	SS	df	MS	F	P-value	F crit
Between Groups	17.0493 [4]	2 [1]	8.5247 [7]	12.7424 [9]	0.0011 [10]	3.8853 [14]
Within Groups	8.0280 [5]	12 [2]	0.6690 [8]			
Total	25.0773 [6]	14 [3]				

[1] p-1 [2] n-p [3] n-1 [4] SST [5] SSE [6] $SSTO$ [7] MST [8] MSE [9] Fstatistic [10] p-value related to F [11] $\bar{x}_A$ [12] $\bar{x}_B$ [13] $\bar{x}_C$ [14] $F_{.05}$

and

$$MSE = \frac{SSE}{n - p} = \frac{8.028}{15 - 3} = 0.669$$

It follows that

$$F = \frac{MST}{MSE} = \frac{8.525}{0.669} = 12.74$$

In order to test H_0 at the .05 level of significance, we use $F_{.05}$ with $p - 1 = 3 - 1 = 2$ numerator and $n - p = 15 - 3 = 12$ denominator degrees of freedom. Table A.6 (page 828) tells us that this F point equals 3.89, so we have

$$F = 12.74 > F_{.05} = 3.89$$

Therefore, we reject H_0 at the .05 level of significance. This says we have strong evidence that at least two of the treatment means μ_A, μ_B, and μ_C differ. In other words, we conclude that at least two of gasoline types A, B, and C have different effects on mean gasoline mileage.

Figure 10.2 gives the MINITAB and Excel output of an analysis of variance of the gasoline mileage data. Note that each output gives the value $F = 12.74$ and the related p-value, which equals .001(rounded). Since this p-value is less than .05, we reject H_0 at the .05 level of significance.

The results of an analysis of variance are often summarized in what is called an **analysis of variance table.** This table gives the sums of squares (SST, SSE, $SSTO$), the mean squares (MST and MSE), and the F statistic and its related p-value for the ANOVA. The table also gives the degrees of freedom associated with each source of variation—treatments, error, and total. Table 10.5 gives the ANOVA table for the gasoline mileage problem. Notice that in the column labeled "Sums of Squares," the values of SST and SSE sum to $SSTO$. Also notice that the upper portion of the MINITAB output and the lower portion of the Excel output give the ANOVA table of Table 10.5.

TABLE 10.5 Analysis of Variance Table for Testing $H_0: \mu_A = \mu_B = \mu_C$ in the Gasoline Mileage Problem ($p = 3$ Gasoline Types, $n = 15$ Observations)

Source	Degrees of Freedom	Sums of Squares	Mean Squares	F Statistic	p-Value
Treatments	$p - 1 = 3 - 1 = 2$	$SST = 17.0493$	$MST = \frac{SST}{p-1} = \frac{17.0493}{3-1} = 8.525$	$F = \frac{MST}{MSE} = \frac{8.525}{0.669} = 12.74$	0.001
Error	$n - p = 15 - 3 = 12$	$SSE = 8.028$	$MSE = \frac{SSE}{n-p} = \frac{8.028}{15-3} = 0.669$		
Total	$n - 1 = 15 - 1 = 14$	$SSTO = 25.0773$			

Before continuing, note that if we use the ANOVA F statistic to test the equality of two population means, it can be shown that

1 F equals t^2, where t is the equal variances t statistic discussed in Section 9.2 (pages 364–365) used to test the equality of the two population means and

2 The rejection point F_α, which is based on $p - 1 = 2 - 1 = 1$ and $n - p = n_1 + n_2 - 2$ degrees of freedom, equals $t^2_{\alpha/2}$, where $t_{\alpha/2}$ is the rejection point for the equal variances t test and is based on $n_1 + n_2 - 2$ degrees of freedom.

Hence, the rejection conditions

$$F > F_\alpha \qquad \text{and} \qquad |t| > t_{\alpha/2}$$

are equivalent. It can also be shown that in this case the p-value related to F equals the p-value related to t. Therefore, the ANOVA F test of the equality of p treatment means can be regarded as a generalization of the equal variances t test of the equality of two treatment means.

Pairwise comparisons If the one-way ANOVA F test says that at least two treatment means differ, then we investigate which treatment means differ and we estimate how large the differences are. We do this by making what we call **pairwise comparisons** (that is, we compare treatment means **two at a time**). One way to make these comparisons is to compute point estimates of and confidence intervals for **pairwise differences.** For example, in the gasoline mileage case we might estimate the pairwise differences $\mu_A - \mu_B$, $\mu_A - \mu_C$, and $\mu_B - \mu_C$. Here, for instance, the pairwise difference $\mu_A - \mu_B$ can be interpreted as the change in mean mileage achieved by changing from using gasoline type B to using gasoline type A.

There are two approaches to calculating confidence intervals for pairwise differences. The first involves computing the usual, or **individual,** confidence interval for each pairwise difference. Here, if we are computing $100(1 - \alpha)$ percent confidence intervals, we are $100(1 - \alpha)$ percent confident that each individual pairwise difference is contained in its respective interval. That is, the confidence level associated with each (individual) comparison is $100(1 - \alpha)$ percent, and we refer to α as the **comparisonwise error rate.** However, we are less than $100(1 - \alpha)$ percent confident that all of the pairwise differences are simultaneously contained in their respective intervals. A more conservative approach is to compute **simultaneous** confidence intervals. Such intervals make us $100(1 - \alpha)$ percent confident that all of the pairwise differences are simultaneously contained in their respective intervals. That is, when we compute simultaneous intervals, the overall confidence level associated with all the comparisons being made in the experiment is $100(1 - \alpha)$ percent, and we refer to α as the **experimentwise error rate.**

Several kinds of simultaneous confidence intervals can be computed. In this book we present what is called the **Tukey formula** for simultaneous intervals. We do this because, *if we are interested in studying all pairwise differences between treatment means, the Tukey formula yields the most precise (shortest) simultaneous confidence intervals.* In general, a Tukey simultaneous

$100(1 - \alpha)$ percent confidence interval is longer than the corresponding individual $100(1 - \alpha)$ percent confidence interval. Thus, intuitively, we are paying a penalty for simultaneous confidence by obtaining longer intervals. One pragmatic approach to comparing treatment means is to first determine if we can use the more conservative Tukey intervals to make meaningful pairwise comparisons. If we cannot, then we might see what the individual intervals tell us. In the following box we present both individual and Tukey simultaneous confidence intervals for pairwise differences. We also present the formula for a confidence interval for a single treatment mean, which we might use after we have used pairwise comparisons to determine the "best" treatment.

Estimation in One-Way ANOVA

1 Consider the **pairwise difference** $\mu_i - \mu_h$, which can be interpreted to be the change in the mean value of the response variable associated with changing from using treatment h to using treatment i. Then, a **point estimate of the difference** $\mu_i - \mu_h$ **is** $\bar{x}_i - \bar{x}_h$, where $\bar{x}_i$ and $\bar{x}_h$ are the sample treatment means associated with treatments i and h.

2 **An individual** $100(1 - \alpha)$ **percent confidence interval for** $\mu_i - \mu_h$ is

$$\left[(\bar{x}_i - \bar{x}_h) \pm t_{\alpha/2}\sqrt{MSE\left(\frac{1}{n_i} + \frac{1}{n_h}\right)}\right]$$

Here the $t_{\alpha/2}$ point is based on $n - p$ degrees of freedom, and MSE is the previously defined error mean square found in the ANOVA table.

3 **A Tukey simultaneous** $100(1 - \alpha)$ **percent confidence interval for** $\mu_i - \mu_h$ is

$$\left[(\bar{x}_i - \bar{x}_h) \pm q_\alpha\sqrt{\frac{MSE}{m}}\right]$$

Here the value q_α is obtained from Table A.9 (page 831), which is a **table of percentage points of the studentized range.** In this table q_α is listed corresponding to values of p and $n - p$. Furthermore, we assume that the sample sizes n_i and n_h are equal to the same value, which we denote as m. If n_i and n_h are not equal, we replace $q_\alpha\sqrt{MSE/m}$ by $(q_\alpha/\sqrt{2})\sqrt{MSE[(1/n_i) + (1/n_h)]}$.

4 **A point estimate of the treatment mean** μ_i **is** $\bar{x}_i$ and an **individual** $100(1 - \alpha)$ **percent confidence interval for** μ_i is

$$\left[\bar{x}_i \pm t_{\alpha/2}\sqrt{\frac{MSE}{n_i}}\right]$$

Here the $t_{\alpha/2}$ point is based on $n - p$ degrees of freedom.

Example 10.6 The Gasoline Mileage Case

In the gasoline mileage study, we are comparing $p = 3$ treatment means (μ_A, μ_B, and μ_C). Furthermore, each sample is of size $m = 5$, there are a total of $n = 15$ observed gas mileages, and the MSE found in Table 10.5 is .669. Because $q_{.05} = 3.77$ is the entry found in Table A.9 (page 831) corresponding to $p = 3$ and $n - p = 12$, a Tukey simultaneous 95 percent confidence interval for $\mu_B - \mu_A$ is

$$\left[(\bar{x}_B - \bar{x}_A) \pm q_{.05}\sqrt{\frac{MSE}{m}}\right] = \left[(36.56 - 34.92) \pm 3.77\sqrt{\frac{.669}{5}}\right]$$
$$= [1.64 \pm 1.379]$$
$$= [.261, 3.019]$$

Similarly, Tukey simultaneous 95 percent confidence intervals for $\mu_A - \mu_C$ and $\mu_B - \mu_C$ are, respectively,

$$[(\bar{x}_A - \bar{x}_C) \pm 1.379] \quad \text{and} \quad [(\bar{x}_B - \bar{x}_C) \pm 1.379]$$
$$= [(34.92 - 33.98) \pm 1.379] \quad = [(36.56 - 33.98) \pm 1.379]$$
$$= [-0.439, 2.319] \quad = [1.201, 3.959]$$

These intervals make us simultaneously 95 percent confident that (1) changing from gasoline type A to gasoline type B increases mean mileage by between .261 and 3.019 mpg, (2) changing from gasoline type C to gasoline type A might decrease mean mileage by as much as .439 mpg or might increase mean mileage by as much as 2.319 mpg, *and* (3) changing from gasoline type C to gasoline type B increases mean mileage by between 1.201 and 3.959 mpg. The first and third of these intervals make us 95 percent confident that μ_B is at least .261 mpg greater than μ_A and at

least 1.201 mpg greater than μ_C. Therefore, we have strong evidence that gasoline type B yields the highest mean mileage of the gasoline types tested. Furthermore, noting that $t_{.025}$ based on $n - p = 12$ degrees of freedom is 2.179, it follows that an individual 95 percent confidence interval for μ_B is

$$\left[\bar{x}_B \pm t_{.025}\sqrt{\frac{MSE}{n_B}}\right] = \left[36.56 \pm 2.179\sqrt{\frac{.669}{5}}\right] = [35.763, 37.357]$$

This interval says we can be 95 percent confident that the mean mileage obtained by using gasoline type B is between 35.763 and 37.357 mpg. Notice that this confidence interval is graphed on the MINITAB output of Figure 10.2. This output also shows the 95 percent confidence intervals for μ_A and μ_C and gives Tukey simultaneous 95 percent intervals. For example, consider finding the Tukey interval for $\mu_B - \mu_A$ on the MINITAB output. To do this, we look in the table corresponding to "Type A subtracted from" and find the row in this table labeled "Type B." This row gives the interval for "Type A subtracted from Type B"—that is, the interval for $\mu_B - \mu_A$. This interval is [.261, 3.109], as calculated above. Finally, note that the half-length of the individual 95 percent confidence interval for a pairwise comparison is (because $n_A = n_B = n_C = 5$)

$$t_{.025}\sqrt{MSE\left(\frac{1}{n_i} + \frac{1}{n_h}\right)} = 2.179\sqrt{.669\left(\frac{1}{5} + \frac{1}{5}\right)} = 1.127$$

This half-length implies that the individual intervals are shorter than the previously constructed Tukey intervals, which have a half-length of 1.379. Recall, however, that the Tukey intervals are short enough to allow us to conclude with 95 percent confidence that μ_B is greater than μ_A and μ_C.

We next consider testing H_0: $\mu_i - \mu_h = 0$ versus H_a: $\mu_i - \mu_h \neq 0$. The test statistic t for performing this test is calculated by dividing $\bar{x}_i - \bar{x}_h$ by $\sqrt{MSE\,[(1/n_i) + (1/n_h)]}$. For example, consider testing H_0: $\mu_B - \mu_A = 0$ versus H_a: $\mu_B - \mu_A \neq 0$. Since $\bar{x}_B - \bar{x}_A = 34.92 - 36.56 = 1.64$ and $\sqrt{MSE\,[(1/n_B) + (1/n_A)]} = \sqrt{.669[(1/5) + (1/5)]} = .5173$, the test statistic t equals $1.64/.5173 = 3.17$. This test statistic value is given in the leftmost table of the following MegaStat output, as is the test statistic value for testing H_0: $\mu_B - \mu_C = 0$ ($t = 4.99$) and the test statistic value for testing H_0: $\mu_A - \mu_C = 0$ ($t = 1.82$):

Tukey simultaneous comparison t-values (d.f. = 12)

		Type C	Type A	Type B
		33.98	34.92	36.56
Type C	33.98			
Type A	34.92	1.82		
Type B	36.56	4.99	3.17	

critical values for experimentwise error rate:

0.05	2.67
0.01	3.56

p-values for pairwise t-tests

		Type C	Type A	Type B
		33.98	34.92	36.56
Type C	33.98			
Type A	34.92	.0942		
Type B	36.56	.0003	.0081	

= Significant at .05 level
= Significant at .01 level
= Significant at .01 level

If we wish to use the Tukey simultaneous comparison procedure having an experimentwise error rate of α, we reject H_0: $\mu_i - \mu_h = 0$ in favor of H_a: $\mu_i - \mu_h \neq 0$ if the absolute value of t is greater than the rejection point $q_\alpha/\sqrt{2}$. Table A.9 tells us that $q_{.05}$ is 3.77 and $q_{.01}$ is 5.04. Therefore, the rejection points for experimentwise error rates of .05 and .01 are, respectively, $3.77/\sqrt{2} = 2.67$ and $5.04/\sqrt{2} = 3.56$ (see the MegaStat output). Suppose we set α equal to .05. Then, since the test statistic value for testing H_0: $\mu_B - \mu_A = 0$ ($t = 3.17$) and the test statistic value for testing H_0: $\mu_B - \mu_C = 0$ ($t = 4.99$) are greater than the rejection point 2.67, we reject both null hypotheses. This, along with the fact that $\bar{x}_B = 36.56$ is greater than $\bar{x}_A = 34.92$ and $\bar{x}_C = 33.98$, leads us to conclude that gasoline type B yields the highest mean mileage of the gasoline types tested (note that the MegaStat output conveniently arranges the sample means in increasing order). Finally, note that the rightmost table of the MegaStat output gives the p-values for individual (rather than simultaneous) pairwise hypothesis tests. For example, the individual p-value for testing H_0: $\mu_B - \mu_C = 0$ is .0003, and the individual p-value for testing H_0: $\mu_B - \mu_A = 0$ is .0081.

In general, when we use a completely randomized experimental design, it is important to compare the treatments by using experimental units that are essentially the same with respect to the characteristic under study. For example, in the gasoline mileage case we have used cars of the same type (Fire-Hawks) to compare the different gasoline types, and in the shelf display case we have used grocery stores of the same sales potential for the bakery product to compare the shelf display heights (the reader will analyze the data for this case in the exercises). Sometimes, however, it is not possible to use experimental units that are essentially the same with respect to the characteristic under study. For example, suppose a chain of stores that sells audio and video equipment wishes to compare the effects of street, mall, and downtown locations on the sales volume of its stores. The experimental units in this situation are the areas where the stores are located, but these areas are not of the same sales potential because each area is populated by a different number of households. In such a situation we must explicitly account for the differences in the experimental units. One way to do this is to use **regression analysis,** which is discussed in Chapters 11 and 12. When we use regression analysis to explicitly account for a variable (such as the number of households in the store's area) that causes differences in the experimental units, we call the variable a **covariate.** Furthermore, we say that we are performing an **analysis of covariance.** Finally, another way to deal with differing experimental units is to employ a **randomized block design.** This experimental design is discussed in Section 10.3.

To conclude this section, we note that if we fear that the normality and/or equal variances assumptions for one-way analysis of variance do not hold, we can use a nonparametric approach to compare several populations. One such approach is the Kruskal–Wallis H test, which is discussed in Section 15.4.

Exercises for Section 10.2

CONCEPTS

10.5 Explain the assumptions that must be satisfied in order to validly use the one-way ANOVA formulas.

10.6 Explain the difference between the between-treatment variability and the within-treatment variability when performing a one-way ANOVA.

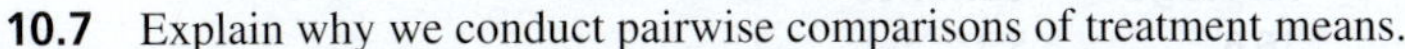

10.7 Explain why we conduct pairwise comparisons of treatment means.

10.8 Explain the difference between individual and simultaneous confidence intervals for a set of several pairwise differences.

METHODS AND APPLICATIONS

10.9 THE SHELF DISPLAY CASE BakeSale

Consider Example 10.2, and let μ_B, μ_M, and μ_T represent the mean monthly sales when using the bottom, middle, and top shelf display heights, respectively. Figure 10.3 gives the MINITAB output of a one-way ANOVA of the bakery sales study data in Table 10.2 (page 405).

a Test the null hypothesis that μ_B, μ_M, and μ_T are equal by setting $\alpha = .05$. On the basis of this test, can we conclude that the bottom, middle, and top shelf display heights have different effects on mean monthly sales?

b Consider the pairwise differences $\mu_M - \mu_B$, $\mu_T - \mu_B$, and $\mu_T - \mu_M$. Find a point estimate of and a Tukey simultaneous 95 percent confidence interval for each pairwise difference. Interpret the meaning of each interval in practical terms. Which display height maximizes mean sales?

c Find an individual 95 percent confidence interval for each pairwise difference in part *b*. Interpret each interval.

d Find 95 percent confidence intervals for μ_B, μ_M, and μ_T. Interpret each interval.

10.10 Consider the display panel situation in Exercise 10.3, and let μ_A, μ_B, and μ_C represent the mean times to stabilize the emergency condition when using display panels A, B, and C, respectively. Figure 10.4 gives the MINITAB output of a one-way ANOVA of the display panel data in Table 10.3 (page 406). Display

a Test the null hypothesis that μ_A, μ_B, and μ_C are equal by setting $\alpha = .05$. On the basis of this test, can we conclude that display panels A, B, and C have different effects on the mean time to stabilize the emergency condition?

b Consider the pairwise differences $\mu_B - \mu_A$, $\mu_C - \mu_A$, and $\mu_C - \mu_B$. Find a point estimate of and a Tukey simultaneous 95 percent confidence interval for each pairwise difference. Interpret the results by describing the effects of changing from using each display panel to

FIGURE 10.3 MINITAB Output of a One-Way ANOVA of the Bakery Sales Study Data in Table 10.2

```
One-way ANOVA: Bakery Sales versus Display Height
                                                           Tukey 95% Simultaneous
Source          DF       SS       MS       F      P         Confidence Intervals
Display Height   2  2273.88  1136.94  184.57  0.000
Error           15    92.40     6.16                       Bottom subtracted from:
Total           17  2366.28                                        Lower   Center   Upper
                               Individual 95%              Middle 17.681   21.400  25.119
                               CIs For Mean Based on Pooled StDev   Top   -8.019   -4.300  -0.581
Level    N    Mean  StDev  ---------+---------+---------+---------+-
Bottom   6  55.800  2.477           (--*-)                         Middle subtracted from:
Middle   6  77.200  3.103                               (--*-)             Lower   Center   Upper
Top      6  51.500  1.648  (-*--)                                  Top   -29.419  -25.700  -21.981
                           ---------+---------+---------+---------+-
  Pooled StDev = 2.482           56.0      64.0      72.0      80.0
```

FIGURE 10.4 MINITAB Output of a One-Way ANOVA of the Display Panel Study Data in Table 10.3

```
One-way ANOVA: Time versus Display                          Tukey 95% Simultaneous
                                                             Confidence Intervals
Source   DF      SS      MS      F      P
Display   2  500.17  250.08  30.11  0.000                   A subtracted from:
Error     9   74.75    8.31                                     Lower   Center   Upper
Total    11  574.92                                         B  -9.692   -4.000   1.692
                          Individual 95%                    C   5.558   11.250  16.942
                          CIs For Mean Based on Pooled StDev
Level  N    Mean  StDev  -+---------+---------+---------+-------
A      4  24.500  2.646          (-----*----)                B subtracted from:
B      4  20.500  2.646   (----*-----)                          Lower   Center   Upper
C      4  35.750  3.304                    (-----*----)      C   9.558   15.250  20.942
                         -+---------+---------+---------+-------
Pooled StDev = 2.882    18.0      24.0      30.0      36.0
```

FIGURE 10.5 Excel Output of a One-Way ANOVA of the Bottle Design Study Data in Table 10.4

SUMMARY

Groups	Count	Sum	Average	Variance
DESIGN A	5	83	16.6	5.3
DESIGN B	5	164	32.8	9.2
DESIGN C	5	124	24.8	8.2

ANOVA

Source of Variation	SS	df	MS	F	P-Value	F crit
Between Groups	656.1333	2	328.0667	43.35683	3.23E-06	3.88529
Within Groups	90.8	12	7.566667			
Total	746.9333	14				

using each of the other panels. Which display panel minimizes the time required to stabilize the emergency condition?

c Find an individual 95 percent confidence interval for each pairwise difference in part *b*. Interpret the results.

10.11 Consider the bottle design study situation in Exercise 10.4, and let μ_A, μ_B, and μ_C represent mean daily sales using bottle designs *A*, *B*, and *C*, respectively. Figure 10.5 gives the Excel output of a one-way ANOVA of the bottle design study data in Table 10.4 (page 406). BottleDes

a Test the null hypothesis that μ_A, μ_B, and μ_C are equal by setting $\alpha = .05$. That is, test for statistically significant differences between these treatment means at the .05 level of significance. Based on this test, can we conclude that bottle designs *A*, *B*, and *C* have different effects on mean daily sales?

b Consider the pairwise differences $\mu_B - \mu_A$, $\mu_C - \mu_A$, and $\mu_C - \mu_B$. Find a point estimate of and a Tukey simultaneous 95 percent confidence interval for each pairwise difference. Interpret the results in practical terms. Which bottle design maximizes mean daily sales?

c Find an individual 95 percent confidence interval for each pairwise difference in part *b*. Interpret the results in practical terms.

d Find a 95 percent confidence interval for each of the treatment means μ_A, μ_B, and μ_C. Interpret these intervals.

10.12 In order to compare the durability of four different brands of golf balls (ALPHA, BEST, CENTURY, and DIVOT), the National Golf Association randomly selects five balls of each brand

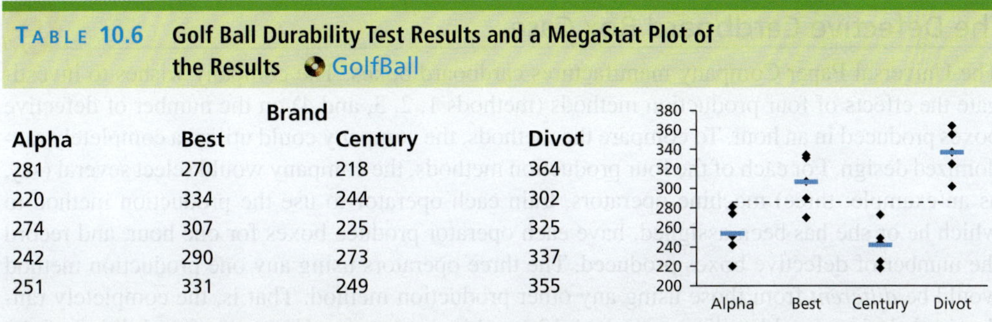

TABLE 10.6 Golf Ball Durability Test Results and a MegaStat Plot of the Results GolfBall

Brand			
Alpha	**Best**	**Century**	**Divot**
281	270	218	364
220	334	244	302
274	307	225	325
242	290	273	337
251	331	249	355

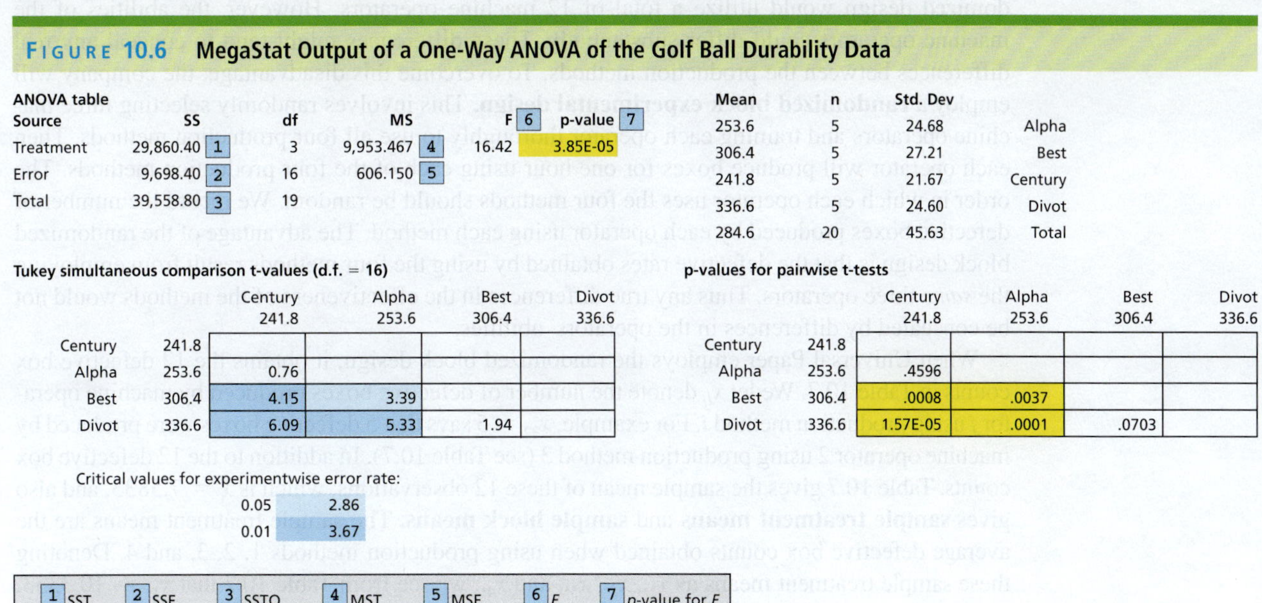

FIGURE 10.6 MegaStat Output of a One-Way ANOVA of the Golf Ball Durability Data

ANOVA table

Source	SS	df	MS	F [6]	p-value [7]
Treatment	29,860.40 [1]	3	9,953.467 [4]	16.42	3.85E-05
Error	9,698.40 [2]	16	606.150 [5]		
Total	39,558.80 [3]	19			

	Mean	n	Std. Dev
Alpha	253.6	5	24.68
Best	306.4	5	27.21
Century	241.8	5	21.67
Divot	336.6	5	24.60
Total	284.6	20	45.63

Tukey simultaneous comparison t-values (d.f. = 16)

		Century 241.8	Alpha 253.6	Best 306.4	Divot 336.6
Century	241.8				
Alpha	253.6	0.76			
Best	306.4	4.15	3.39		
Divot	336.6	6.09	5.33	1.94	

Critical values for experimentwise error rate:

0.05	2.86
0.01	3.67

p-values for pairwise t-tests

		Century 241.8	Alpha 253.6	Best 306.4	Divot 336.6
Century	241.8				
Alpha	253.6	.4596			
Best	306.4	.0008	.0037		
Divot	336.6	1.57E-05	.0001	.0703	

[1] SST [2] SSE [3] SSTO [4] MST [5] MSE [6] F [7] p-value for F

and places each ball into a machine that exerts the force produced by a 250-yard drive. The number of simulated drives needed to crack or chip each ball is recorded. The results are given in Table 10.6. The MegaStat output of a one-way ANOVA of this data is shown in Figure 10.6. Test for statistically significant differences between the treatment means μ_{ALPHA}, μ_{BEST}, $\mu_{CENTURY}$, and μ_{DIVOT}. Set $\alpha = .05$. GolfBall

10.13 Perform pairwise comparisons of the treatment means in Exercise 10.12. Which brand(s) are most durable? Find a 95 percent confidence interval for each of the treatment means.

10.14 THE COMMERCIAL RESPONSE CASE

Recall from Example 10.3 that (1) 29 randomly selected subjects were exposed to commercials shown in more involving programs, (2) 29 randomly selected subjects were exposed to commercials shown in less involving programs, and (3) 29 randomly selected subjects watched commercials only (note: this is called the **control group**). The mean brand recall scores for these three groups were, respectively, $\bar{x}_1 = 1.21$, $\bar{x}_2 = 2.24$, and $\bar{x}_3 = 2.28$. Furthermore, a one-way ANOVA of the data shows that $SST = 21.40$ and $SSE = 85.56$.

a Define appropriate treatment means μ_1, μ_2, and μ_3. Then test for statistically significant differences between these treatment means. Set $\alpha = .05$.

b Perform pairwise comparisons of the treatment means by computing a Tukey simultaneous 95 percent confidence interval for each of the pairwise differences $\mu_1 - \mu_2$, $\mu_1 - \mu_3$, and $\mu_2 - \mu_3$. Which type of program content results in the worst mean brand recall score?

10.3 The Randomized Block Design

Not all experiments employ a completely randomized design. For instance, suppose that when we employ a completely randomized design, we fail to reject the null hypothesis of equality of treatment means because the within-treatment variability (which is measured by the *SSE*) is large. This could happen because differences between the experimental units are concealing true differences between the treatments. We can often remedy this by using what is called a **randomized block design.**

Example 10.7 The Defective Cardboard Box Case

The Universal Paper Company manufactures cardboard boxes. The company wishes to investigate the effects of four production methods (methods 1, 2, 3, and 4) on the number of defective boxes produced in an hour. To compare the methods, the company could utilize a completely randomized design. For each of the four production methods, the company would select several (say, as an example, three) machine operators, train each operator to use the production method to which he or she has been assigned, have each operator produce boxes for one hour, and record the number of defective boxes produced. The three operators using any one production method would be *different* from those using any other production method. That is, the completely randomized design would utilize a total of 12 machine operators. However, the abilities of the machine operators could differ substantially. These differences might tend to conceal any real differences between the production methods. To overcome this disadvantage, the company will employ a **randomized block experimental design.** This involves randomly selecting three machine operators and training each operator thoroughly to use all four production methods. Then each operator will produce boxes for one hour using each of the four production methods. The order in which each operator uses the four methods should be random. We record the number of defective boxes produced by each operator using each method. The advantage of the randomized block design is that the defective rates obtained by using the four methods result from employing the *same* three operators. Thus any true differences in the effectiveness of the methods would not be concealed by differences in the operators' abilities.

When Universal Paper employs the randomized block design, it obtains the 12 defective box counts in Table 10.7. We let x_{ij} denote the number of defective boxes produced by machine operator j using production method i. For example, $x_{32} = 5$ says that 5 defective boxes were produced by machine operator 2 using production method 3 (see Table 10.7). In addition to the 12 defective box counts, Table 10.7 gives the sample mean of these 12 observations, which is $\bar{x} = 7.5833$, and also gives **sample treatment means** and **sample block means.** The sample treatment means are the average defective box counts obtained when using production methods 1, 2, 3, and 4. Denoting these sample treatment means as $\bar{x}_{1\bullet}$, $\bar{x}_{2\bullet}$, $\bar{x}_{3\bullet}$, and $\bar{x}_{4\bullet}$, we see from Table 10.7 that $\bar{x}_{1\bullet} = 10.3333$, $\bar{x}_{2\bullet} = 10.3333$, $\bar{x}_{3\bullet} = 5.0$, and $\bar{x}_{4\bullet} = 4.6667$. Because $\bar{x}_{3\bullet}$ and $\bar{x}_{4\bullet}$ are less than $\bar{x}_{1\bullet}$ and $\bar{x}_{2\bullet}$, we estimate that the mean number of defective boxes produced per hour by production method 3 or 4 is less than the mean number of defective boxes produced per hour by production method 1 or 2. The sample block means are the average defective box counts obtained by machine operators 1, 2, and 3. Denoting these sample block means as $\bar{x}_{\bullet 1}$, $\bar{x}_{\bullet 2}$, and $\bar{x}_{\bullet 3}$, we see from Table 10.7 that $\bar{x}_{\bullet 1} = 6.0$, $\bar{x}_{\bullet 2} = 7.75$, and $\bar{x}_{\bullet 3} = 9.0$. Because $\bar{x}_{\bullet 1}$, $\bar{x}_{\bullet 2}$, and $\bar{x}_{\bullet 3}$ differ, we have evidence that the abilities of the machine operators differ and thus that using the machine operators as blocks is reasonable.

TABLE 10.7 Numbers of Defective Cardboard Boxes Obtained by Production Methods 1, 2, 3, and 4 and Machine Operators 1, 2, and 3 CardBox

Treatment (Production Method)	Block (Machine Operator) 1	2	3	Sample Treatment Mean
1	9	10	12	10.3333
2	8	11	12	10.3333
3	3	5	7	5.0
4	4	5	5	4.6667
Sample Block Mean	6.0	7.75	9.0	$\bar{x} = 7.5833$

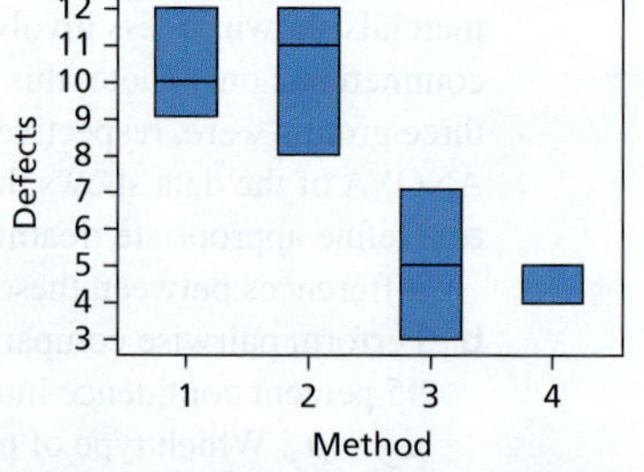

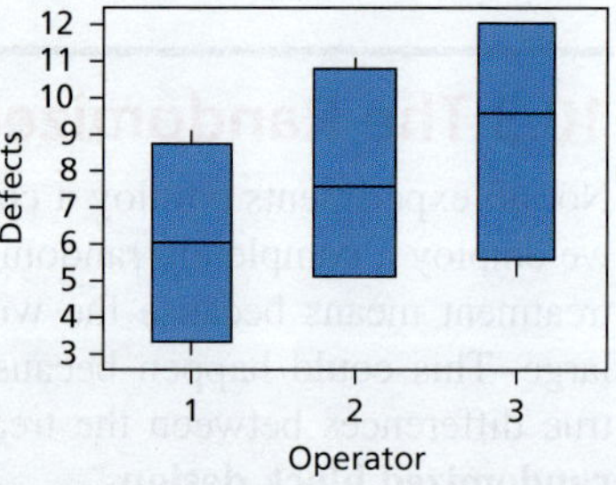

In general, a **randomized block design** compares p treatments (for example, production methods) by using b blocks (for example, machine operators). Each block is used exactly once to measure the effect of each and every treatment. The advantage of the randomized block design over the completely randomized design is that we are comparing the treatments by using the *same* experimental units. Thus any true differences in the treatments will not be concealed by differences in the experimental units.

In some experiments a block consists of **similar or matched sets of experimental units.** For example, suppose we wish to compare the performance of business majors, science majors, and fine arts majors on a graduate school admissions test. Here the blocks might be matched sets of students. Each matched set (block) would consist of a business major, a science major, and a fine arts major selected so that each is in his or her senior year, attends the same university, and has the same grade point average. By selecting blocks in this fashion, any true differences between majors would not be concealed by differences between college classes, universities, or grade point averages.

In order to analyze the data obtained in a randomized block design, we define

x_{ij} = the value of the response variable observed when block j uses treatment i

$\bar{x}_{i\cdot}$ = the mean of the b values of the response variable observed when using treatment i

$\bar{x}_{\cdot j}$ = the mean of the p values of the response variable observed when using block j

$\bar{x}$ = the mean of the total of the bp values of the response variable that we have observed in the experiment

The ANOVA procedure for a randomized block design partitions the **total sum of squares (*SSTO*)** into three components: the **treatment sum of squares (*SST*),** the **block sum of squares (*SSB*),** and the **error sum of squares (*SSE*).** The formula for this partitioning is

$$SSTO = SST + SSB + SSE$$

The steps for calculating these sums of squares, as well as what is measured by the sums of squares, can be summarized as follows:

Step 1: Calculate *SST*, which measures the amount of between-treatment variability:

$$SST = b\sum_{i=1}^{p}(\bar{x}_{i\cdot} - \bar{x})^2$$

Step 2: Calculate *SSB*, which measures the amount of variability due to the blocks:

$$SSB = p\sum_{j=1}^{b}(\bar{x}_{\cdot j} - \bar{x})^2$$

Step 3: Calculate *SSTO*, which measures the total amount of variability:

$$SSTO = \sum_{i=1}^{p}\sum_{j=1}^{b}(x_{ij} - \bar{x})^2$$

Step 4: Calculate *SSE*, which measures the amount of variability due to the error:

$$SSE = SSTO - SST - SSB$$

These sums of squares are shown in Table 10.8, which is the ANOVA table for a randomized block design. This table also gives the degrees of freedom associated with each source of variation—treatments, blocks, error, and total—as well as the mean squares and F statistics used to test the hypotheses of interest in a randomized block experiment.

Before discussing these hypotheses, we will illustrate how the entries in the ANOVA table are calculated. The sums of squares in the defective cardboard box case are calculated as follows (note that $p = 4$ and $b = 3$):

Step 1:
$$\begin{aligned} SST &= 3[(\bar{x}_{1\cdot} - \bar{x})^2 + (\bar{x}_{2\cdot} - \bar{x})^2 + (\bar{x}_{3\cdot} - \bar{x})^2 + (\bar{x}_{4\cdot} - \bar{x})^2] \\ &= 3[(10.3333 - 7.5833)^2 + (10.3333 - 7.5833)^2 \\ &\quad + (5.0 - 7.5833)^2 + (4.6667 - 7.5833)^2] \\ &= 90.9167 \end{aligned}$$

TABLE 10.8 ANOVA Table for the Randomized Block Design with *p* Treatments and *b* Blocks

Source of Variation	Degrees of Freedom	Sum of Squares	Mean Square	F
Treatments	$p - 1$	SST	$MST = \frac{SST}{p-1}$	$F(\text{treatments}) = \frac{MST}{MSE}$
Blocks	$b - 1$	SSB	$MSB = \frac{SSB}{b-1}$	$F(\text{blocks}) = \frac{MSB}{MSE}$
Error	$(p-1)(b-1)$	SSE	$MSE = \frac{SSE}{(p-1)(b-1)}$	
Total	$pb - 1$	$SSTO$		

Step 2:
$$\begin{aligned} SSB &= 4[(\bar{x}_{\cdot 1} - \bar{x})^2 + (\bar{x}_{\cdot 2} - \bar{x})^2 + (\bar{x}_{\cdot 3} - \bar{x})^2] \\ &= 4[(6.0 - 7.5833)^2 + (7.75 - 7.5833)^2 + (9.0 - 7.5833)^2] \\ &= 18.1667 \end{aligned}$$

Step 3:
$$\begin{aligned} SSTO &= (9 - 7.5833)^2 + (10 - 7.5833)^2 + (12 - 7.5833)^2 \\ &\quad + (8 - 7.5833)^2 + (11 - 7.5833)^2 + (12 - 7.5833)^2 \\ &\quad + (3 - 7.5833)^2 + (5 - 7.5833)^2 + (7 - 7.5833)^2 \\ &\quad + (4 - 7.5833)^2 + (5 - 7.5833)^2 + (5 - 7.5833)^2 \\ &= 112.9167 \end{aligned}$$

Step 4:
$$\begin{aligned} SSE &= SSTO - SST - SSB \\ &= 112.9167 - 90.9167 - 18.1667 \\ &= 3.8333 \end{aligned}$$

Figure 10.7 gives the MINITAB output of a randomized block ANOVA of the defective box data. This figure shows the above calculated sums of squares, as well as the degrees of freedom (recall that $p = 4$ and $b = 3$), the mean squares, and the F statistics (and associated p-values) used to test the hypotheses of interest.

Of main interest is the test of the null hypothesis H_0 that **no differences exist between the treatment effects** on the mean value of the response variable versus the alternative hypothesis H_a that **at least two treatment effects differ.** We can reject H_0 in favor of H_a at level of

FIGURE 10.7 MINITAB Output of a Randomized Block ANOVA of the Defective Box Data

```
Rows: Method    Columns: Operator
          1          2          3        All
1     9.000     10.000     12.000     10.333
2     8.000     11.000     12.000     10.333
3     3.000      5.000      7.000      5.000
4     4.000      5.000      5.000      4.667
All   6.000      7.750      9.000      7.583

Two-way ANOVA: Rejects versus Method, Operator
Source      DF        SS           MS            F          P
Method       3    90.917 1    30.3056 5    47.43 8    0.000 9
Operator     2    18.167 2     9.0833 6    14.22 10   0.005 11
Error        6     3.833 3     0.6389 7
Total       11   112.917 4

Method    Mean          Operator    Mean
1      10.3333 12       1          6.00 16
2      10.3333 13       2          7.75 17
3       5.0000 14       3          9.00 18
4       4.6667 15
```

1 SST 2 SSB 3 SSE 4 SSTO 5 MST 6 MSB 7 MSE 8 F(treatments) 9 p-value for F(treatments) 10 F(blocks) 11 p-value for F(blocks) 12 $\bar{x}_{1\cdot}$ 13 $\bar{x}_{2\cdot}$ 14 $\bar{x}_{3\cdot}$ 15 $\bar{x}_{4\cdot}$ 16 $\bar{x}_{\cdot 1}$ 17 $\bar{x}_{\cdot 2}$ 18 $\bar{x}_{\cdot 3}$

significance α if

$$F(\text{treatments}) = \frac{MST}{MSE}$$

is greater than the F_α point based on $p - 1$ numerator and $(p - 1)(b - 1)$ denominator degrees of freedom. In the defective cardboard box case, $F_{.05}$ based on $p - 1 = 3$ numerator and $(p - 1)(b - 1) = 6$ denominator degrees of freedom is 4.76 (see Table A.6, page 828). Because

$$F(\text{treatments}) = \frac{MST}{MSE} = \frac{30.306}{.639} = 47.43$$

is greater than $F_{.05} = 4.76$, we reject H_0 at the .05 level of significance. Therefore, we have strong evidence that at least two production methods have different effects on the mean number of defective boxes produced per hour. Alternatively, we can reject H_0 in favor of H_a at level of significance α if the p-value is less than α. Here the p-value is the area under the curve of the F distribution [having $p - 1$ and $(p - 1)(b - 1)$ degrees of freedom] to the right of F(treatments). The MINITAB output in Figure 10.7 tells us that this p-value is 0.000 (that is, less than .001) for the defective box data. Therefore, we have extremely strong evidence that at least two production methods have different effects on the mean number of defective boxes produced per hour.

It is also of interest to test the null hypothesis H_0 that **no differences exist between the block effects** on the mean value of the response variable versus the alternative hypothesis H_a that **at least two block effects differ.** We can reject H_0 in favor of H_a at level of significance α if

$$F(\text{blocks}) = \frac{MSB}{MSE}$$

is greater than the F_α point based on $b - 1$ numerator and $(p - 1)(b - 1)$ denominator degrees of freedom. In the defective cardboard box case, $F_{.05}$ based on $b - 1 = 2$ numerator and $(p - 1)(b - 1) = 6$ denominator degrees of freedom is 5.14 (see Table A.6, page 828). Because

$$F(\text{blocks}) = \frac{MSB}{MSE} = \frac{9.083}{.639} = 14.22$$

is greater than $F_{.05} = 5.14$, we reject H_0 at the .05 level of significance. Therefore, we have strong evidence that at least two machine operators have different effects on the mean number of defective boxes produced per hour. Alternatively, we can reject H_0 in favor of H_a at level of significance α if the p-value is less than α. Here the p-value is the area under the curve of the F distribution [having $b - 1$ and $(p - 1)(b - 1)$ degrees of freedom] to the right of F(blocks). The MINITAB output tells us that this p-value is .005 for the defective box data. Therefore, we have very strong evidence that at least two machine operators have different effects on the mean number of defective boxes produced per hour. This implies that using the machine operators as blocks is reasonable.

If, in a randomized block design, we conclude that at least two treatment effects differ, we can perform pairwise comparisons to determine how they differ.

Point Estimates and Confidence Intervals in a Randomized Block ANOVA

Consider the **difference between the effects of treatments *i* and *h* on the mean value of the response variable.** Then:

1. A **point estimate** of this difference is $\bar{x}_{i\cdot} - \bar{x}_{h\cdot}$.
2. An **individual 100(1 − α) percent confidence interval** for this difference is

$$\left[(\bar{x}_{i\cdot} - \bar{x}_{h\cdot}) \pm t_{\alpha/2}\, s\sqrt{\frac{2}{b}}\right]$$

Here $t_{\alpha/2}$ is based on $(p - 1)(b - 1)$ degrees of freedom, and s is the square root of the *MSE* found in the randomized block ANOVA table.

3. A **Tukey simultaneous 100(1 − α) percent confidence interval** for this difference is

$$\left[(\bar{x}_{i\cdot} - \bar{x}_{h\cdot}) \pm q_\alpha \frac{s}{\sqrt{b}}\right]$$

Here the value q_α is obtained from Table A.9 (page 831), which is a table of percentage points of the studentized range. In this table q_α is listed corresponding to values of p and $(p - 1)(b - 1)$.

Example 10.8 The Defective Cardboard Box Case

We have previously concluded that we have extremely strong evidence that at least two production methods have different effects on the mean number of defective boxes produced per hour. We have also seen that the sample treatment means are $\bar{x}_{1\cdot} = 10.3333$, $\bar{x}_{2\cdot} = 10.3333$, $\bar{x}_{3\cdot} = 5.0$, and $\bar{x}_{4\cdot} = 4.6667$. Since $\bar{x}_{4\cdot}$ is the smallest sample treatment mean, we will use Tukey simultaneous 95 percent confidence intervals to compare the effect of production method 4 with the effects of production methods 1, 2, and 3. To compute these intervals, we first note that $q_{.05} = 4.90$ is the entry in Table A.9 (page 831) corresponding to $p = 4$ and $(p - 1)(b - 1) = 6$. Also, note that the *MSE* found in the randomized block ANOVA table is .639 (see Figure 10.7), which implies that $s = \sqrt{.639} = .7994$. It follows that a Tukey simultaneous 95 percent confidence interval for the difference between the effects of production methods 4 and 1 on the mean number of defective boxes produced per hour is

$$\left[(\bar{x}_{4\cdot} - \bar{x}_{1\cdot}) \pm q_{.05}\frac{s}{\sqrt{b}}\right] = \left[(4.6667 - 10.3333) \pm 4.90\left(\frac{.7994}{\sqrt{3}}\right)\right]$$
$$= [-5.6666 \pm 2.2615]$$
$$= [-7.9281, -3.4051]$$

Furthermore, it can be verified that a Tukey simultaneous 95 percent confidence interval for the difference between the effects of production methods 4 and 2 on the mean number of defective boxes produced per hour is also $[-7.9281, -3.4051]$. Therefore, we can be 95 percent confident that changing from production method 1 or 2 to production method 4 decreases the mean number of defective boxes produced per hour by a machine operator by between 3.4051 and 7.9281 boxes.

A Tukey simultaneous 95 percent confidence interval for the difference between the effects of production methods 4 and 3 on the mean number of defective boxes produced per hour is

$$[(\bar{x}_{4\cdot} - \bar{x}_{3\cdot}) \pm 2.2615] = [(4.6667 - 5) \pm 2.2615]$$
$$= [-2.5948, 1.9282]$$

This interval tells us (with 95 percent confidence) that changing from production method 3 to production method 4 might decrease the mean number of defective boxes produced per hour by as many as 2.5948 boxes or might increase this mean by as many as 1.9282 boxes. In other words, because this interval contains 0, we cannot conclude that the effects of production methods 4 and 3 differ.

Exercises for Section 10.3

CONCEPTS

10.15 In your own words, explain why we sometimes employ the randomized block design.

10.16 How can we test to determine if the blocks we have chosen are reasonable?

METHODS AND APPLICATIONS

10.17 A marketing organization wishes to study the effects of four sales methods on weekly sales of a product. The organization employs a randomized block design in which three salesman use each sales method. The results obtained are given in Table 10.9. Figure 10.8 gives the Excel output of a randomized block ANOVA of the sales method data. SaleMeth

TABLE 10.9 Results of a Sales Method Experiment Employing a Randomized Block Design SaleMeth

Sales Method, *i*	Salesman, *j* A	B	C
1	32	29	30
2	32	30	28
3	28	25	23
4	25	24	23

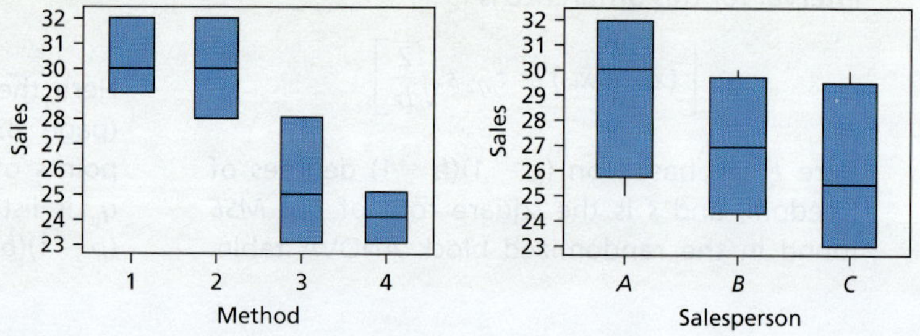

Sales (23–32) by Method (1, 2, 3, 4); Sales (23–32) by Salesperson (A, B, C)

FIGURE 10.8 Excel Output of a Randomized Block ANOVA of the Sales Method Data Given in Table 10.9

Anova: Two-Factor Without Replication

SUMMARY	Count	Sum	Average	Variance
Method 1	3	91	30.3333 [12]	2.3333
Method 2	3	90	30 [13]	4
Method 3	3	76	25.3333 [14]	6.3333
Method 4	3	72	24 [15]	1
Salesman A	4	117	29.25 [16]	11.5833
Salesman B	4	108	27 [17]	8.6667
Salesman C	4	104	26 [18]	12.6667

ANOVA

Source of Variation	SS	df	MS	F	P-value	F crit
Rows	93.5833 [1]	3	31.1944 [5]	36.2258 [8]	0.0003 [9]	4.7571
Columns	22.1667 [2]	2	11.0833 [6]	12.8710 [10]	0.0068 [11]	5.1433
Error	5.1667 [3]	6	0.8611 [7]			
Total	120.9167 [4]	11				

[1] SST [2] SSB [3] SSE [4] SSTO [5] MST [6] MSB [7] MSE [8] F(treatments) [9] p-value for F(treatments) [10] F(blocks) [11] p-value for F(blocks) [12] $\bar{x}_{1\cdot}$ [13] $\bar{x}_{2\cdot}$ [14] $\bar{x}_{3\cdot}$ [15] $\bar{x}_{4\cdot}$ [16] $\bar{x}_{\cdot 1}$ [17] $\bar{x}_{\cdot 2}$ [18] $\bar{x}_{\cdot 3}$

a Test the null hypothesis H_0 that no differences exist between the effects of the sales methods (treatments) on mean weekly sales. Set $\alpha = .05$. Can we conclude that the different sales methods have different effects on mean weekly sales?

b Test the null hypothesis H_0 that no differences exist between the effects of the salesmen (blocks) on mean weekly sales. Set $\alpha = .05$. Can we conclude that the different salesmen have different effects on mean weekly sales?

c Use Tukey simultaneous 95 percent confidence intervals to make pairwise comparisons of the sales method effects on mean weekly sales. Which sales method(s) maximize mean weekly sales?

10.18 A consumer preference study involving three different bottle designs (A, B, and C) for the jumbo size of a new liquid laundry detergent was carried out using a randomized block experimental design, with supermarkets as blocks. Specifically, four supermarkets were supplied with all three bottle designs, which were priced the same. Table 10.10 gives the number of bottles of each design sold in a 24-hour period at each supermarket. If we use these data, SST, SSB, and SSE can be calculated to be 586.1667, 421.6667, and 1.8333, respectively. BottleDes2

a Test the null hypothesis H_0 that no differences exist between the effects of the bottle designs on mean daily sales. Set $\alpha = .05$. Can we conclude that the different bottle designs have different effects on mean sales?

b Test the null hypothesis H_0 that no differences exist between the effects of the supermarkets on mean daily sales. Set $\alpha = .05$. Can we conclude that the different supermarkets have different effects on mean sales?

c Use Tukey simultaneous 95 percent confidence intervals to make pairwise comparisons of the bottle design effects on mean daily sales. Which bottle design(s) maximize mean sales?

10.19 To compare three brands of computer keyboards, four data entry specialists were randomly selected. Each specialist used all three keyboards to enter the same kind of text material for 10 minutes, and the number of words entered per minute was recorded. The data obtained are given in Table 10.11. If we use these data, SST, SSB, and SSE can be calculated to be 392.6667, 143.5833, and 2.6667, respectively. Keyboard

TABLE 10.10 Results of a Bottle Design Experiment BottleDes2

	Supermarket, j			
Bottle Design, i	**1**	**2**	**3**	**4**
A	16	14	1	6
B	33	30	19	23
C	23	21	8	12

TABLE 10.11 Results of a Keyboard Experiment Keyboard

	Keyboard Brand		
Data Entry Specialist	**A**	**B**	**C**
1	77	67	63
2	71	62	59
3	74	63	59
4	67	57	54

a Test the null hypothesis H_0 that no differences exist between the effects of the keyboard brands on the mean number of words entered per minute. Set $\alpha = .05$.

b Test the null hypothesis H_0 that no differences exist between the effects of the data entry specialists on the mean number of words entered per minute. Set $\alpha = .05$.

c Use Tukey simultaneous 95 percent confidence intervals to make pairwise comparisons of the keyboard brand effects on the mean number of words entered per minute. Which keyboard brand maximizes the mean number of words entered per minute?

10.20 In an advertisement in a local newspaper, Best Food supermarket attempted to convince consumers that it offered them the lowest total food bill. To do this, Best Food presented the following comparison of the prices of 60 grocery items purchased at three supermarkets—Best Food, Public, and Cash' N Carry—on a single day. BestFood

Item	Best Food	Public	Cash N' Carry
Big Thirst Towel	1.21	1.49	1.59
Camp Crm/Broccoli	.55	.67	.67
Royal Oak Charcoal	2.99	3.59	3.39
Combo Chdr/Chz Snk	1.29	1.29	1.39
Sure Sak Trash Bag	1.29	1.79	1.89
Dow Handi Wrap	1.59	2.39	2.29
White Rain Shampoo	.96	.97	1.39
Post Golden Crisp	2.78	2.99	3.35
Surf Detergent	2.29	1.89	1.89
Sacramento T/Juice	.79	.89	.99
SS Prune Juice	1.36	1.61	1.48
V-8 Cocktail	1.18	1.29	1.28
Rodd Kosher Dill	1.39	1.79	1.79
Bisquick	2.09	2.19	2.09
Kraft Italian Drs	.99	1.19	1.00
BC Hamburger Helper	1.46	1.75	1.75
Comstock Chrry Pie	1.29	1.69	1.69
Dawn Liquid King	2.59	2.29	2.58
DelMonte Ketchup	1.05	1.25	.59
Silver Floss Kraut	.77	.81	.69
Trop Twist Beverag	1.74	2.15	2.25
Purina Kitten Chow	1.09	1.05	1.29
Niag Spray Starch	.89	.99	1.39
Soft Soap Country	.97	1.19	1.19
Northwood Syrup	1.13	1.37	1.37
Bumble Bee Tuna	.58	.65	.65
Mueller Elbow/Mac	2.09	2.69	2.69
Kell Nut Honey Crn	2.95	3.25	3.23
Cutter Spray	3.09	3.95	3.69
Lawry Season Salt	2.28	2.97	2.85

Item	Best Food	Public	Cash N' Carry
Keb Graham Crust	.79	1.29	1.28
Spiffits Glass	1.98	2.19	2.59
Prog Lentil Soup	.79	1.13	1.12
Lipton Tea Bags	2.07	2.17	2.17
Carnation Hot Coco	1.59	1.89	1.99
Crystal Hot Sauce	.70	.87	.89
C/F/N/ Coffee Bag	1.17	1.15	1.55
Soup Start Bf Veg	1.39	2.03	1.94
Camp Pork & Beans	.44	.49	.58
Sunsweet Pit Prune	.98	1.33	1.10
DM Vgcls Grdn Duet	1.07	1.13	1.29
Argo Corn Starch	.69	.89	.79
Sno Drop Bowl Clnr	.53	1.15	.99
Cadbury Milk Choc	.79	1.29	1.28
Andes Crm/De Ment	1.09	1.30	1.09
Combat Ant & Roach	2.33	2.39	2.79
Joan/Arc Kid Bean	.45	.56	.38
La Vic Salsa Pican	1.22	1.75	1.49
Moist N Beef/Chz	2.39	3.19	2.99
Ortega Taco Shells	1.08	1.33	1.09
Fresh Step Cat Lit	3.58	3.79	3.81
Field Trial Dg/Fd	3.49	3.79	3.49
Tylenol Tablets	5.98	5.29	5.98
Rolaids Tablets	1.88	2.20	2.49
Plax Rinse	2.88	3.14	2.53
Correctol Laxative	3.44	3.98	3.59
Tch Scnt Potpourri	1.50	1.89	1.89
Chld Enema 2.250	.98	1.15	1.19
Gillette Atra Plus	5.00	5.24	5.59
Colgate Shave	.94	1.10	1.19

If we use these data to compare the mean prices of grocery items at the three supermarkets, then we have a randomized block design where the treatments are the three supermarkets and the blocks are the 60 grocery items. Figure 10.9 gives the MegaStat output of a randomized block ANOVA of the supermarket data.

a Test the null hypothesis H_0 that no differences exist between the mean prices of grocery items at the three supermarkets. Do the three supermarkets differ with respect to mean grocery prices?

b Make pairwise comparisons of the mean prices of grocery items at the three supermarkets. Which supermarket has the lowest mean prices?

10.21 The Coca-Cola Company introduced new Coke in 1985. Within three months of this introduction, negative consumer reaction forced Coca-Cola to reintroduce the original formula of Coke as Coca-Cola classic. Suppose that two years later, in 1987, a marketing research firm in Chicago compared the sales of Coca-Cola classic, new Coke, and Pepsi in public building vending machines. To do this, the marketing research firm randomly selected 10 public buildings in Chicago

FIGURE 10.9 MegaStat Output of a Randomized Block ANOVA of the Supermarket Data for Exercise 10.20

ANOVA table

Source	SS	df	MS	F	p-value
Treatments	2.6413 [1]	2	1.3206 [5]	39.2281 [8]	8.68E-14 [9]
Blocks	215.5949 [2]	59	3.6542 [6]	108.5428 [10]	8.13E-81 [11]
Error	3.9725 [3]	118	0.0337 [7]		
Total	222.2087 [4]	179			

Tukey simultaneous comparison t-values (d.f. = 118)

		BEST FOOD 1.66550	PUBLIC 1.91950	CASH N' CARRY 1.92533
BEST FOOD	1.66550			
PUBLIC	1.91950	7.58		
CASH N' CARRY	1.92533	7.76	0.17	

critical values for experimentwise error rate:

0.05	2.38
0.01	2.97

p-values for pairwise t-tests

		BEST FOOD 1.66550	PUBLIC 1.91950	CASH N' CARRY 1.92533
BEST FOOD	1.66550			
PUBLIC	1.91950	8.52E-12		
CASH N' CARRY	1.92533	3.44E-12	.8621	

[1] SST [2] SSB [3] SSE [4] SSTO [5] MST [6] MSB [7] MSE [8] F(treatments) [9] p-value for F(treatments) [10] F(blocks) [11] p-value for F(blocks)

Exercise 10.21 (continued)

having both a Coke machine (selling Coke classic and new Coke) and a Pepsi machine. The data—in number of cans sold over a given period of time—and a MegaStat randomized block ANOVA of the data are as follows: Coke

Building	1	2	3	4	5	6	7	8	9	10
Coke Classic	45	136	134	41	146	33	71	224	111	87
New Coke	6	114	56	14	39	20	42	156	61	140
Pepsi	24	90	100	43	51	42	68	131	74	107

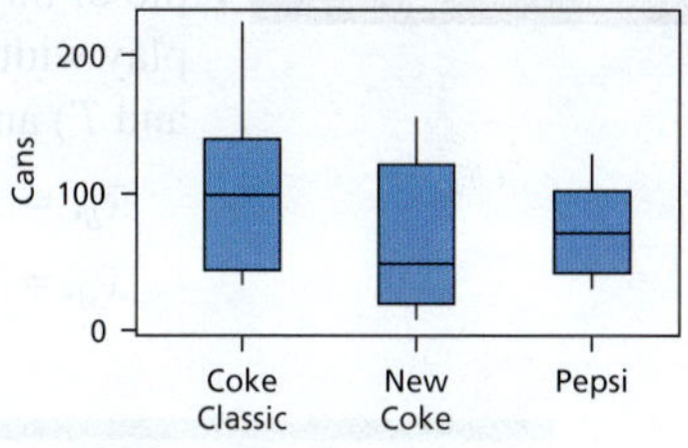

ANOVA table

Source	SS	df	MS	F	p-value
Treatments	7,997.60	2	3,998.800	5.78	.0115
Blocks	55,573.47	9	6,174.830	8.93	4.97E-05
Error	12,443.73	18	691.319		
Total	76,014.80	29			

Tukey simultaneous comparison t-values (d.f. = 18)

		New Coke 64.800	Pepsi 73.000	Coke Classic 102.800
New Coke	64.800			
Pepsi	73.000	0.70		
Coke Classic	102.800	3.23	2.53	

critical values for experimentwise error rate:

0.05	2.55
0.01	3.32

p-values for pairwise t-tests

		New Coke 64.800	Pepsi 73.000	Coke Classic 102.800
New Coke	64.800			
Pepsi	73.000	.4945		
Coke Classic	102.800	.0046	.0208	

a Test the null hypothesis H_0 that no differences exist between the mean sales of Coca-Cola classic, new Coke, and Pepsi in Chicago public building vending machines. Set $\alpha = .05$.

b Make pairwise comparisons of the mean sales of Coca-Cola classic, new Coke, and Pepsi in Chicago public building vending machines.

c By the mid-1990s the Coca-Cola Company had discontinued making new Coke and had returned to making only its original product. Is there evidence in the 1987 study that this might happen? Explain your answer.

10.4 Two-Way Analysis of Variance

Many response variables are affected by more than one factor. Because of this we must often conduct experiments in which we study the effects of several factors on the response. In this section we consider studying the effects of **two factors** on a response variable. To begin, recall that in Example 10.2 we discussed an experiment in which the Tastee Bakery Company investigated the effect of shelf display height on monthly demand for one of its bakery products. This one-factor experiment is actually a simplification of a two-factor experiment carried out by the Tastee Bakery Company. We discuss this two-factor experiment in the following example.

Example 10.9 The Shelf Display Case

C

The Tastee Bakery Company supplies a bakery product to many metropolitan supermarkets. The company wishes to study the effects of two factors—**shelf display height** and **shelf display width**—on **monthly demand** (measured in cases of 10 units each) for this product. The factor "display height" is defined to have three levels: *B* (bottom), *M* (middle), and *T* (top). The factor "display width" is defined to have two levels: *R* (regular) and *W* (wide). The **treatments** in this experiment are **display height and display width combinations.** These treatments are

$$BR \quad BW \quad MR \quad MW \quad TR \quad TW$$

Here, for example, the notation *BR* denotes the treatment "bottom display height and regular display width." For each display height and width combination the company randomly selects a sample of $m = 3$ metropolitan area supermarkets (all supermarkets used in the study will be of equal sales potential). Each supermarket sells the product for one month using its assigned display height and width combination, and the month's demand for the product is recorded. The six samples obtained in this experiment are given in Table 10.12. We let $x_{ij,k}$ denote the monthly demand obtained at the *k*th supermarket that used display height *i* and display width *j*. For example, $x_{MW,2} = 78.4$ is the monthly demand obtained at the second supermarket that used a middle display height and a wide display.

In addition to giving the six samples, Table 10.12 gives the **sample treatment mean** for each display height and display width combination. For example, $\bar{x}_{BR} = 55.9$ is the mean of the sample of three demands observed at supermarkets using a bottom display height and a regular display width. The table also gives the sample mean demand for each level of display height (*B*, *M*, and *T*) and for each level of display width (*R* and *W*). Specifically,

$\bar{x}_{B\bullet} = 55.8$ = the mean of the six demands observed when using a bottom display height

$\bar{x}_{M\bullet} = 77.2$ = the mean of the six demands observed when using a middle display height

TABLE 10.12 Six Samples of Monthly Demands for a Bakery Product BakeSale2

Display Height	Display Width *R*	*W*	
B	58.2	55.7	
	53.7	52.5	
	55.8	58.9	
	$\bar{x}_{BR} = 55.9$	$\bar{x}_{BW} = 55.7$	$\bar{x}_{B\bullet} = 55.8$
M	73.0	76.2	
	78.1	78.4	
	75.4	82.1	
	$\bar{x}_{MR} = 75.5$	$\bar{x}_{MW} = 78.9$	$\bar{x}_{M\bullet} = 77.2$
T	52.4	54.0	
	49.7	52.1	
	50.9	49.9	
	$\bar{x}_{TR} = 51.0$	$\bar{x}_{TW} = 52.0$	$\bar{x}_{T\bullet} = 51.5$
	$\bar{x}_{\bullet R} = 60.8$	$\bar{x}_{\bullet W} = 62.2$	$\bar{x} = 61.5$

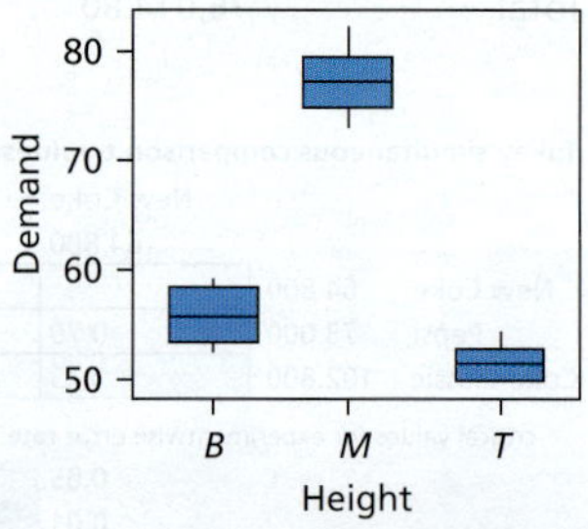

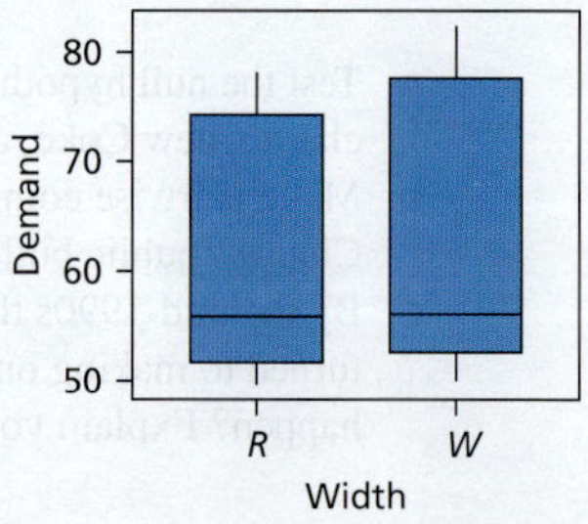

FIGURE 10.10 Graphical Analysis of the Bakery Demand Data

(a) Plotting the treatment means

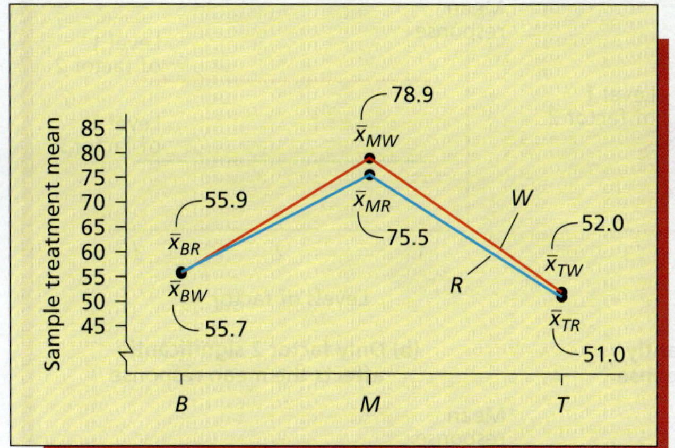

(b) A MINITAB output of the graphical analysis

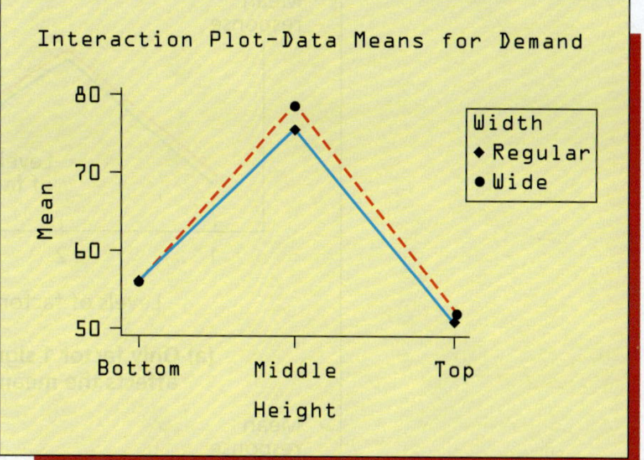

$\bar{x}_{T\bullet} = 51.5$ = the mean of the six demands observed when using a top display height

$\bar{x}_{\bullet R} = 60.8$ = the mean of the nine demands observed when using a regular display width

$\bar{x}_{\bullet W} = 62.2$ = the mean of the nine demands observed when using a wide display

Finally, Table 10.12 gives $\bar{x} = 61.5$, which is the overall mean of the total of 18 demands observed in the experiment. Because $\bar{x}_{M\bullet} = 77.2$ is considerably larger than $\bar{x}_{B\bullet} = 55.8$ and $\bar{x}_{T\bullet} = 51.5$, we estimate that mean monthly demand is highest when using a middle display height. Since $\bar{x}_{\bullet R} = 60.8$ and $\bar{x}_{\bullet W} = 62.2$ do not differ by very much, we estimate there is little difference between the effects of a regular display width and a wide display on mean monthly demand.

Figure 10.10 presents a graphical analysis of the bakery demand data. In this figure we plot, for each display width (R and W), the change in the sample treatment mean demand associated with changing the display height from bottom (B) to middle (M) to top (T). Note that, for either a regular display width (R) or a wide display (W), the middle display height (M) gives the highest mean monthly demand. Also, note that, for either a bottom, middle, or top display height, there is little difference between the effects of a regular display width and a wide display on mean monthly demand. This sort of graphical analysis is useful in determining whether a condition called **interaction** exists. We explain the meaning of interaction in the following discussion.

In general, suppose we wish to study the effects of two factors on a response variable. We assume that the first factor, which we refer to as **factor 1,** has ***a* levels** (levels 1, 2, . . . , a). Further, we assume that the second factor, which we will refer to as **factor 2,** has ***b* levels** (levels 1, 2, . . . , b). Here a **treatment** is considered to be a **combination of a level of factor 1 and a level of factor 2.** It follows that there are a total of ab treatments, and we assume that we will employ a *completely randomized experimental design* in which we will assign m experimental units to each treatment. This procedure results in our observing m values of the response variable for each of the ab treatments, and in this case we say that we are performing a **two-factor factorial experiment.**

The method we will explain for analyzing the results of a two-factor factorial experiment is called **two-way analysis of variance** or **two-way ANOVA.** This method assumes that we have obtained a random sample corresponding to each and every treatment, and that the sample sizes are equal (as described above). Further, we can assume that the samples are independent because we have employed a completely randomized experimental design. In addition, we assume that the populations of values of the response variable associated with the treatments have normal distributions with equal variances.

In order to understand the various ways in which factor 1 and factor 2 might affect the mean response, consider Figure 10.11. It is possible that only factor 1 significantly affects the mean response [see Figure 10.11(a)]. On the other hand, it is possible that only factor 2 significantly affects the mean response [see Figure 10.11(b)]. It is also possible that both factors 1 and 2

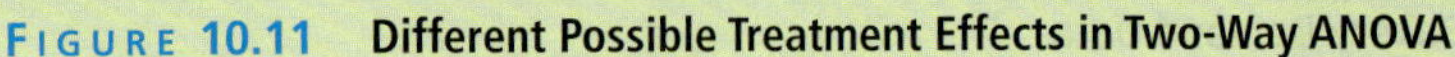

FIGURE 10.11 Different Possible Treatment Effects in Two-Way ANOVA

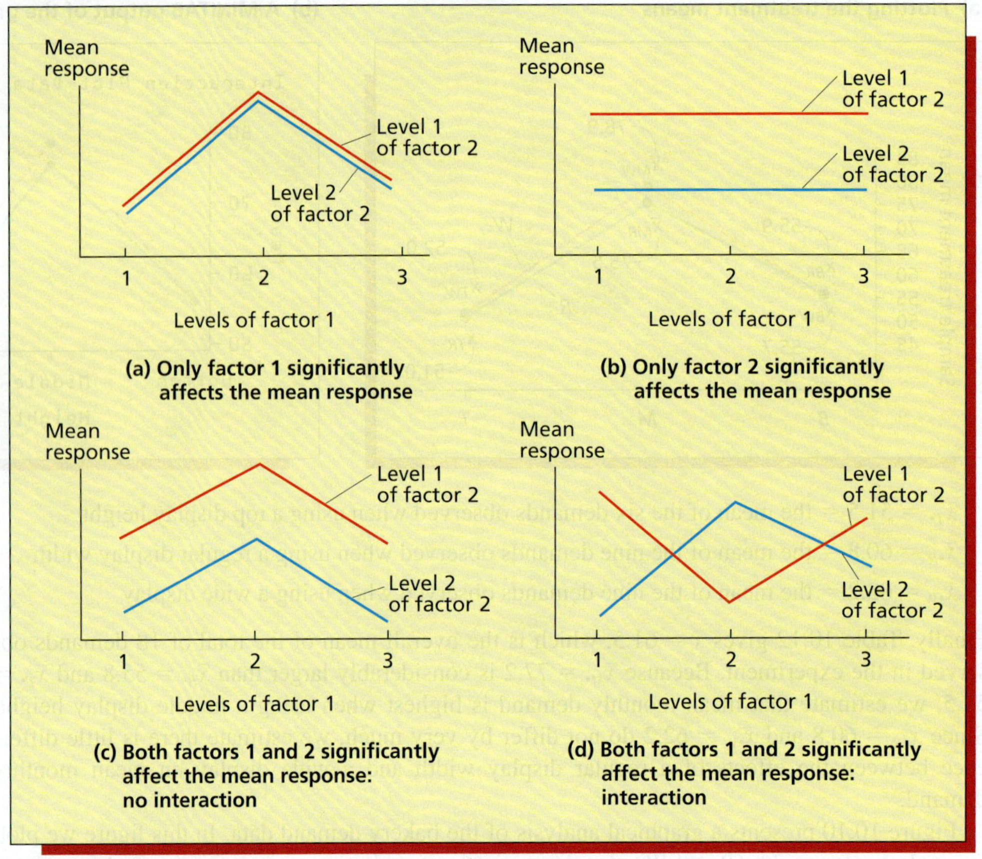

significantly affect the mean response. If this is so, these factors might affect the mean response independently [see Figure 10.11(c)], or these factors might **interact** as they affect the mean response [see Figure 10.11(d)]. In general, we say that *there is* **interaction** *between factors 1 and 2 if the relationship between the mean response and one of the factors depends upon the level of the other factor.* This is clearly true in Figure 10.11(d). Note here that at levels 1 and 3 of factor 1, level 1 of factor 2 gives the highest mean response, whereas at level 2 of factor 1, level 2 of factor 2 gives the highest mean response. On the other hand, the **parallel** line plots in Figure 10.11(a), (b), and (c) indicate a lack of interaction between factors 1 and 2. To graphically check for interaction, we can plot the sample treatment means, as we have done in Figure 10.10. If we obtain essentially parallel line plots, then it might be reasonable to conclude that there is little or no interaction between factors 1 and 2 (this is true in Figure 10.10). On the other hand, if the line plots are not parallel, then it might be reasonable to conclude that factors 1 and 2 interact.

In addition to graphical analysis, analysis of variance is a useful tool for analyzing the data from a two-factor factorial experiment. To explain the ANOVA approach for analyzing such an experiment, we define

$x_{ij,k}$ = the kth value of the response variable observed when using level i of factor 1 and level j of factor 2

$\bar{x}_{ij}$ = the mean of the m values observed when using the ith level of factor 1 and the jth level of factor 2

$\bar{x}_{i\cdot}$ = the mean of the bm values observed when using the ith level of factor 1

$\bar{x}_{\cdot j}$ = the mean of the am values observed when using the jth level of factor 2

$\bar{x}$ = the mean of the total of abm values that we have observed in the experiment

TABLE 10.13 Two-Way ANOVA Table

Source of Variation	Degrees of Freedom	Sum of Squares	Mean Square	F
Factor 1	$a - 1$	$SS(1)$	$MS(1) = \frac{SS(1)}{a - 1}$	$F(1) = \frac{MS(1)}{MSE}$
Factor 2	$b - 1$	$SS(2)$	$MS(2) = \frac{SS(2)}{b - 1}$	$F(2) = \frac{MS(2)}{MSE}$
Interaction	$(a - 1)(b - 1)$	$SS(\text{int})$	$MS(\text{int}) = \frac{SS(\text{int})}{(a - 1)(b - 1)}$	$F(\text{int}) = \frac{MS(\text{int})}{MSE}$
Error	$ab(m - 1)$	SSE	$MSE = \frac{SSE}{ab(m - 1)}$	
Total	$abm - 1$	$SSTO$		

The ANOVA procedure for a two-factor factorial experiment partitions the **total sum of squares ($SSTO$)** into four components: the **factor 1 sum of squares-$SS(1)$,** the **factor 2 sum of squares-$SS(2)$,** the **interaction sum of squares-$SS(\text{int})$,** and the **error sum of squares-SSE.** The formula for this partitioning is as follows:

$$SSTO = SS(1) + SS(2) + SS(\text{int}) + SSE$$

The steps for calculating these sums of squares, as well as what is measured by the sums of squares, can be summarized as follows:

Step 1: Calculate $SSTO$, which measures the total amount of variability:

$$SSTO = \sum_{i=1}^{a}\sum_{j=1}^{b}\sum_{k=1}^{m}(x_{ij,k} - \bar{x})^2$$

Step 2: Calculate $SS(1)$, which measures the amount of variability due to the different levels of factor 1:

$$SS(1) = bm\sum_{i=1}^{a}(\bar{x}_{i\bullet} - \bar{x})^2$$

Step 3: Calculate $SS(2)$, which measures the amount of variability due to the different levels of factor 2:

$$SS(2) = am\sum_{j=1}^{b}(\bar{x}_{\bullet j} - \bar{x})^2$$

Step 4: Calculate $SS(\text{interaction})$, which measures the amount of variability due to the interaction between factors 1 and 2:

$$SS(\text{int}) = m\sum_{i=1}^{a}\sum_{j=1}^{b}(\bar{x}_{ij} - \bar{x}_{i\bullet} - \bar{x}_{\bullet j} + \bar{x})^2$$

Step 5: Calculate SSE, which measures the amount of variability due to the error:

$$SSE = SSTO - SS(1) - SS(2) - SS(\text{int})$$

These sums of squares are shown in Table 10.13, which is called a **two-way analysis of variance (ANOVA) table.** This table also gives the degrees of freedom associated with each source of variation—factor 1, factor 2, interaction, error, and total—as well as the mean squares and F statistics used to test the hypotheses of interest in a two-factor factorial experiment.

Before discussing these hypotheses, we will illustrate how the entries in the ANOVA table are calculated. The sums of squares in the shelf display case are calculated as follows (note that $a = 3$, $b = 2$, and $m = 3$):

Step 1:

$$\begin{aligned} SSTO &= (58.2 - 61.5)^2 + (53.7 - 61.5)^2 + (55.8 - 61.5)^2 \\ &\quad + (55.7 - 61.5)^2 + \cdots + (49.9 - 61.5)^2 \\ &= 2{,}366.28 \end{aligned}$$

Step 2: $SS(1) = 2 \cdot 3[(\bar{x}_{B\bullet} - \bar{x})^2 + (\bar{x}_{M\bullet} - \bar{x})^2 + (\bar{x}_{T\bullet} - \bar{x})^2]$

$$= 6[(55.8 - 61.5)^2 + (77.2 - 61.5)^2 + (51.5 - 61.5)^2]$$
$$= 6[32.49 + 246.49 + 100]$$
$$= 2{,}273.88$$

Step 3: $SS(2) = 3 \cdot 3[(\bar{x}_{\bullet R} - \bar{x})^2 + (\bar{x}_{\bullet W} - \bar{x})^2]$

$$= 9[(60.8 - 61.5)^2 + (62.2 - 61.5)^2]$$
$$= 9[.49 + .49]$$
$$= 8.82$$

Step 4: $SS(\text{int}) = 3[(\bar{x}_{BR} - \bar{x}_{B\bullet} - \bar{x}_{\bullet R} + \bar{x})^2 + (\bar{x}_{BW} - \bar{x}_{B\bullet} - \bar{x}_{\bullet W} + \bar{x})^2$

$$+ (\bar{x}_{MR} - \bar{x}_{M\bullet} - \bar{x}_{\bullet R} + \bar{x})^2 + (\bar{x}_{MW} - \bar{x}_{M\bullet} - \bar{x}_{\bullet W} + \bar{x})^2$$
$$+ (\bar{x}_{TR} - \bar{x}_{T\bullet} - \bar{x}_{\bullet R} + \bar{x})^2 + (\bar{x}_{TW} - \bar{x}_{T\bullet} - \bar{x}_{\bullet W} + \bar{x})^2]$$
$$= 3[(55.9 - 55.8 - 60.8 + 61.5)^2 + (55.7 - 55.8 - 62.2 + 61.5)^2$$
$$+ (75.5 - 77.2 - 60.8 + 61.5)^2 + (78.9 - 77.2 - 62.2 + 61.5)^2$$
$$+ (51.0 - 51.5 - 60.8 + 61.5)^2 + (52.0 - 51.5 - 62.2 + 61.5)^2]$$
$$= 3(3.36) = 10.08$$

Step 5: $SSE = SSTO - SS(1) - SS(2) - SS(\text{int})$

$$= 2{,}366.28 - 2{,}273.88 - 8.82 - 10.08$$
$$= 73.50$$

Figure 10.12 gives the MINITAB output of a two-way ANOVA for the shelf display data. This figure shows the above calculated sums of squares, as well as the degrees of freedom (recall that $a = 3$, $b = 2$, and $m = 3$), mean squares, and F statistics used to test the hypotheses of interest.

We first test the null hypothesis H_0 that **no interaction exists between factors 1 and 2** versus the alternative hypothesis H_a that **interaction does exist.** We can reject H_0 in favor of H_a at level of significance α if

$$F(\text{int}) = \frac{MS(\text{int})}{MSE}$$

FIGURE 10.12 MINITAB Output of a Two-Way ANOVA of the Shelf Display Data

```
Rows : Height      Columns : Width      Cell Contents : Demand : Mean

             Regular      Wide        All
   Bottom     55.90      55.70      55.80
   Middle     75.50      78.90      77.20
   Top        51.00      52.00      51.50
   All        60.80      62.20      61.50

Two-way ANOVA: Demand versus Height, Width

Source        DF        SS           MS            F            P
Height         2    2273.88 [1]  1136.94 [6]  185.62 [10]  0.000 [11]
Width          1       8.82 [2]     8.82 [7]    1.44 [12]  0.253 [13]
Interaction    2      10.08 [3]     5.04 [8]    0.82 [14]  0.462 [15]
Error         12      73.50 [4]     6.12 [9]
Total         17    2366.28 [5]

Height     Mean         Width      Mean
Bottom     55.8 [16]    Regular    60.8 [19]
Middle     77.2 [17]    Wide       62.2 [20]
Top        51.5 [18]
```

[1] SS(1) [2] SS(2) [3] SS(int) [4] SSE [5] SSTO [6] MS(1) [7] MS(2) [8] MS(int) [9] MSE [10] $F(1)$ [11] p-value for $F(1)$ [12] $F(2)$ [13] p-value for $F(2)$ [14] $F(\text{int})$ [15] p-value for $F(\text{int})$ [16] $\bar{x}_{B\bullet}$ [17] $\bar{x}_{M\bullet}$ [18] $\bar{x}_{T\bullet}$ [19] $\bar{x}_{\bullet R}$ [20] $\bar{x}_{\bullet W}$

is greater than the F_α point based on $(a - 1)(b - 1)$ numerator and $ab(m - 1)$ denominator degrees of freedom. In the shelf display case, $F_{.05}$ based on $(a - 1)(b - 1) = 2$ numerator and $ab(m - 1) = 12$ denominator degrees of freedom is 3.89 (see Table A.6, page 828). Because

$$F(\text{int}) = \frac{MS(\text{int})}{MSE} = \frac{5.04}{6.12} = .82$$

is less than $F_{.05} = 3.89$, we cannot reject H_0 at the .05 level of significance. We conclude that little or no interaction exists between shelf display height and shelf display width. That is, we conclude that the relationship between mean demand for the bakery product and shelf display height depends little (or not at all) on the shelf display width. Further, we conclude that the relationship between mean demand and shelf display width depends little (or not at all) on the shelf display height. Notice that these conclusions are suggested by the previously given plots of Figure 10.10 (page 427).

In general, when we conclude that little or no interaction exists between factors 1 and 2, we can (separately) test the significance of each of factors 1 and 2. We call this **testing the significance of the main effects** (what we do if we conclude that interaction does exist between factors 1 and 2 will be discussed at the end of this section).

To test the significance of factor 1, we test the null hypothesis $\boldsymbol{H_0}$ **that no differences exist between the effects of the different levels of factor 1** on the mean response versus the alternative hypothesis $\boldsymbol{H_a}$ **that at least two levels of factor 1 have different effects.** We can reject H_0 in favor of H_a at level of significance α if

$$F(1) = \frac{MS(1)}{MSE}$$

is greater than the F_α point based on $a - 1$ numerator and $ab(m - 1)$ denominator degrees of freedom. In the shelf display case, $F_{.05}$ based on $a - 1 = 2$ numerator and $ab(m - 1) = 12$ denominator degrees of freedom is 3.89. Because

$$F(1) = \frac{MS(1)}{MSE} = \frac{1{,}136.94}{6.12} = 185.77$$

is greater than $F_{.05} = 3.89$, we can reject H_0 at the .05 level of significance. Therefore, we have strong evidence that at least two of the bottom, middle, and top display heights have different effects on mean monthly demand.

To test the significance of factor 2, we test the null hypothesis $\boldsymbol{H_0}$ **that no differences exist between the effects of the different levels of factor 2** on the mean response versus the alternative hypothesis $\boldsymbol{H_a}$ **that at least two levels of factor 2 have different effects.** We can reject H_0 in favor of H_a at level of significance α if

$$F(2) = \frac{MS(2)}{MSE}$$

is greater than the F_α point based on $b - 1$ numerator and $ab(m - 1)$ denominator degrees of freedom. In the shelf display case, $F_{.05}$ based on $b - 1 = 1$ numerator and $ab(m - 1) = 12$ denominator degrees of freedom is 4.75. Because

$$F(2) = \frac{MS(2)}{MSE} = \frac{8.82}{6.12} = 1.44$$

is less than $F_{.05} = 4.75$, we cannot reject H_0 at the .05 level of significance. Therefore, we do not have strong evidence that the regular display width and the wide display have different effects on mean monthly demand.

If, in a two-factor factorial experiment, we conclude that at least two levels of factor 1 have different effects or at least two levels of factor 2 have different effects, we can make pairwise comparisons to determine how the effects differ.

Point Estimates and Confidence Intervals in Two-Way ANOVA

1 Consider the **difference between the effects of levels i and i' of factor 1 on the mean value of the response variable.**

a A **point estimate** of this difference is $\bar{x}_{i\cdot} - \bar{x}_{i'\cdot}$

b An **individual 100(1 − α) percent confidence interval** for this difference is

$$\left[(\bar{x}_{i\cdot} - \bar{x}_{i'\cdot}) \pm t_{\alpha/2}\sqrt{MSE\left(\frac{2}{bm}\right)}\right]$$

where the $t_{\alpha/2}$ point is based on $ab(m-1)$ degrees of freedom, and MSE is the error mean square found in the two-way ANOVA table.

c A **Tukey simultaneous 100(1 − α) percent confidence interval** for this difference (in the set of all possible paired differences between the effects of the different levels of factor 1) is

$$\left[(\bar{x}_{i\cdot} - \bar{x}_{i'\cdot}) \pm q_{\alpha}\sqrt{MSE\left(\frac{1}{bm}\right)}\right]$$

where q_α is obtained from Table A.9 (page 831), which is a table of percentage points of the studentized range. Here q_α is listed corresponding to values of a and $ab(m-1)$.

2 Consider the **difference between the effects of levels j and j' of factor 2 on the mean value of the response variable.**

a A **point estimate** of this difference is $\bar{x}_{\cdot j} - \bar{x}_{\cdot j'}$

b An **individual 100(1 − α) percent confidence interval** for this difference is

$$\left[(\bar{x}_{\cdot j} - \bar{x}_{\cdot j'}) \pm t_{\alpha/2}\sqrt{MSE\left(\frac{2}{am}\right)}\right]$$

where the $t_{\alpha/2}$ point is based on $ab(m-1)$ degrees of freedom.

c A **Tukey simultaneous 100(1 − α) percent confidence interval** for this difference (in the set of all possible paired differences between the effects of the different levels of factor 2) is

$$\left[(\bar{x}_{\cdot j} - \bar{x}_{\cdot j'}) \pm q_{\alpha}\sqrt{MSE\left(\frac{1}{am}\right)}\right]$$

where q_α is obtained from Table A.9 and is listed corresponding to values of b and $ab(m-1)$.

3 Let μ_{ij} denote the **mean value of the response variable obtained when using level i of factor 1 and level j of factor 2. A point estimate of μ_{ij} is** $\bar{x}_{ij}$, and an **individual 100(1 − α) percent confidence interval** for μ_{ij} is

$$\left[\bar{x}_{ij} \pm t_{\alpha/2}\sqrt{\frac{MSE}{m}}\right]$$

where the $t_{\alpha/2}$ point is based on $ab(m-1)$ degrees of freedom.

Example 10.10 The Shelf Display Case

We have previously concluded that at least two of the bottom, middle, and top display heights have different effects on mean monthly demand. Since $\bar{x}_{M\cdot} = 77.2$ is greater than $\bar{x}_{B\cdot} = 55.8$ and $\bar{x}_{T\cdot} = 51.5$, we will use Tukey simultaneous 95 percent confidence intervals to compare the effect of a middle display height with the effects of the bottom and top display heights. To compute these intervals, we first note that $q_{.05} = 3.77$ is the entry in Table A.9 (page 831) corresponding to $a = 3$ and $ab(m-1) = 12$. Also note that the MSE found in the two-way ANOVA table is 6.12 (see Figure 10.12). It follows that a Tukey simultaneous 95 percent confidence interval for the difference between the effects of a middle and bottom display height on mean monthly demand is

$$\left[(\bar{x}_{M\cdot} - \bar{x}_{B\cdot}) \pm q_{.05}\sqrt{MSE\left(\frac{1}{bm}\right)}\right] = \left[(77.2 - 55.8) \pm 3.77\sqrt{6.12\left(\frac{1}{2(3)}\right)}\right]$$
$$= [21.4 \pm 3.8075]$$
$$= [17.5925, 25.2075]$$

This interval says we are 95 percent confident that changing from a bottom display height to a middle display height will increase the mean demand for the bakery product by between 17.5925 and 25.2075 cases per month. Similarly, a Tukey simultaneous 95 percent confidence interval for the difference between the effects of a middle and top display height on mean monthly demand is

$$[(\bar{x}_{M\cdot} - \bar{x}_{T\cdot}) \pm 3.8075] = [(77.2 - 51.5) \pm 3.8075]$$
$$= [21.8925, 29.5075]$$

This interval says we are 95 percent confident that changing from a top display height to a middle display height will increase mean demand for the bakery product by between 21.8925 and 29.5075 cases per month. Together, these intervals make us 95 percent confident that a middle shelf display height is, on average, at least 17.5925 cases sold per month better than a bottom shelf display height and at least 21.8925 cases sold per month better than a top shelf display height.

BI

Next, recall that previously conducted F tests suggest that there is little or no interaction between display height and display width and that there is little difference between using a regular display width and a wide display. However, intuitive and graphical analysis should always be used to supplement the results of hypothesis testing. In this case, note from Table 10.12 (page 426) that $\bar{x}_{MR} = 75.5$ and $\bar{x}_{MW} = 78.9$. This implies that we estimate that, when we use a middle display height, changing from a regular display width to a wide display increases mean monthly demand by 3.4 cases (or 34 units). This slight increase can be seen in Figure 10.10 (page 427) and suggests that it might be best (depending on what supermarkets charge for different display heights and widths) for the bakery to use a wide display with a middle display height. Since $t_{.025}$ based on $ab(m - 1) = 12$ degrees of freedom is 2.179, an individual 95 percent confidence interval for μ_{MW}, the mean demand obtained when using a middle display height and a wide display, is

$$\left[\bar{x}_{MW} \pm t_{.025}\sqrt{\frac{MSE}{m}}\right] = \left[78.9 \pm 2.179\sqrt{\frac{6.12}{3}}\right]$$
$$= [75.7878, 82.0122]$$

This interval says that, when we use a middle display height and a wide display, we can be 95 percent confident that mean demand for the bakery product will be between 75.7878 and 82.0122 cases per month.

If we conclude that (substantial) interaction exists between factors 1 and 2, the effects of changing the level of one factor will depend on the level of the other factor. In this case, we cannot separate the analysis of the effects of the levels of the two factors. One simple alternative procedure is to use one-way ANOVA (see Section 10.2) to compare all of the treatment means (the μ_{ij}'s) with the possible purpose of finding the best combination of levels of factors 1 and 2. For example, if there had been (substantial) interaction in the shelf display case, we could have used one-way ANOVA to compare the six treatment means—μ_{BR}, μ_{BW}, μ_{MR}, μ_{MW}, μ_{TR}, and μ_{TW}—to find the best combination of display height and width. Alternatively, we could study the effects of the different levels of one factor at a specified level of the other factor. This is what we did at the end of the shelf display case, when we noticed that at a middle display height, a wide display seemed slightly more effective than a regular display width.

Finally, we might wish to study the effects of more than two factors on a response variable of interest. The ideas involved in such a study are an extension of those involved in a two-way ANOVA. Although studying more than two factors is beyond the scope of this text, a good reference is Neter, Kutner, Nachtsheim, and Wasserman (1996).

Exercises for Section 10.4

CONCEPTS

10.22 What is a treatment in the context of a two-factor factorial experiment?

10.23 Explain what we mean when we say that

a Interaction exists between factor 1 and factor 2.

b No interaction exists between the factors.

METHODS AND APPLICATIONS

10.24 An experiment is conducted to study the effects of two sales approaches—high-pressure (H) and low-pressure (L)—and to study the effects of two sales pitches (1 and 2) on the weekly sales of a product. The data in Table 10.14 are obtained by using a completely randomized

TABLE 10.14 Results of the Sales Approach Experiment SaleMeth2

Sales Pressure	Sales Pitch 1	Sales Pitch 2
H	32	32
	29	30
	30	28
L	28	25
	25	24
	23	23

FIGURE 10.13 Excel Output of a Two-Way ANOVA of the Sales Approach Data

Anova: Two-Factor With Replication

SUMMARY	Pitch 1	Pitch 2	Total
High Pressure			
Count	3	3	6
Sum	91	90	181
Average	30.3333	30	30.1667 [16]
Variance	2.3333	4	2.5667
Low Pressure			
Count	3	3	6
Sum	76	72	148
Average	25.3333	24	24.6667 [17]
Variance	6.3333	1	3.4667
Total			
Count	6	6	
Sum	167	162	
Average	27.8333 [18]	27 [19]	
Variance	10.9667	12.8	

ANOVA

Source of Variation	SS	df	MS	F	P-value	F crit
Pressure	90.75 [1]	1	90.75 [6]	26.5610 [10]	0.0009 [11]	5.3177
Pitch	2.0833 [2]	1	2.0833 [7]	0.6098 [12]	0.4574 [13]	5.3177
Interaction	0.75 [3]	1	0.75 [8]	0.2195 [14]	0.6519 [15]	5.3177
Within	27.3333 [4]	8	3.4167 [9]			
Total	120.917 [5]	11				

[1] SS(1) [2] SS(2) [3] SS(int) [4] SSE [5] SSTO
[6] MS(1) [7] MS(2) [8] MS(int) [9] MSE
[10] $F(1)$ [11] p-value for $F(1)$ [12] $F(2)$ [13] p-value for $F(2)$
[14] $F(\text{int})$ [15] p-value for $F(\text{int})$ [16] $\bar{x}_{H\cdot}$ [17] $\bar{x}_{L\cdot}$ [18] $\bar{x}_{\cdot 1}$ [19] $\bar{x}_{\cdot 2}$

TABLE 10.15 Results of a Two-Factor Display Panel Experiment Display2

Display Panel	Emergency Condition 1	2	3	4
A	17	25	31	14
	14	24	34	13
B	15	22	28	9
	12	19	31	10
C	21	29	32	15
	24	28	37	19

design, and Figure 10.13 gives the Excel output of a two-way ANOVA of the sales experiment data. SaleMeth2

a Perform graphical analysis to check for interaction between sales pressure and sales pitch.
b Test for interaction by setting $\alpha = .05$.
c Test for differences in the effects of the levels of sales pressure by setting $\alpha = .05$. That is, test the significance of sales pressure effects with $\alpha = .05$.
d Calculate and interpret a 95 percent individual confidence interval for $\mu_{H\cdot} - \mu_{L\cdot}$.
e Test for differences in the effects of the levels of sales pitch by setting $\alpha = .05$. That is, test the significance of sales pitch effects with $\alpha = .05$.
f Calculate and interpret a 95 percent individual confidence interval for $\mu_{\cdot 1} - \mu_{\cdot 2}$.
g Calculate a 95 percent (individual) confidence interval for mean sales when using high sales pressure and sales pitch 1. Interpret this interval.

10.25 A study compared three display panels used by air traffic controllers. Each display panel was tested for four different simulated emergency conditions. Twenty-four highly trained air traffic controllers were used in the study. Two controllers were randomly assigned to each display panel–emergency condition combination. The time (in seconds) required to stabilize the emergency condition was recorded. The data in Table 10.15 were observed. Figure 10.14 presents the MegaStat output of a two-way ANOVA of the display panel data. Display2

a Interpret the MegaStat interaction plot in Figure 10.14. Then test for interaction with $\alpha = .05$.
b Test the significance of display panel effects with $\alpha = .05$.
c Test the significance of emergency condition effects with $\alpha = .05$.
d Make pairwise comparisons of display panels *A*, *B*, and *C*.
e Make pairwise comparisons of emergency conditions 1, 2, 3, and 4.
f Which display panel minimizes the time required to stabilize an emergency condition? Does your answer depend on the emergency condition? Why?
g Calculate a 95 percent (individual) confidence interval for the mean time required to stabilize emergency condition 4 using display panel *B*.

FIGURE 10.14 MegaStat Output of a Two-Way ANOVA of the Display Panel Data

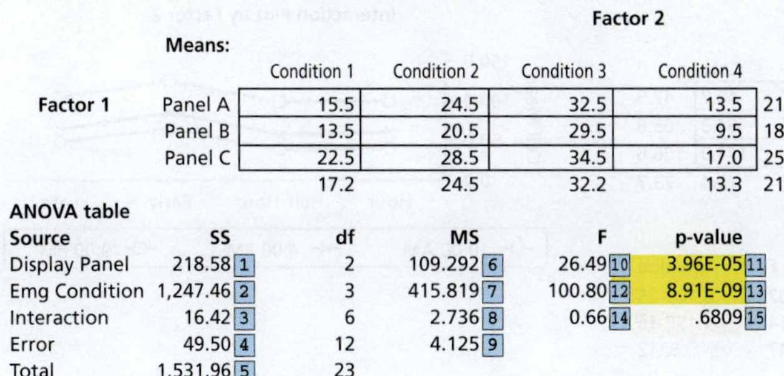

Means:

		Factor 2				
		Condition 1	Condition 2	Condition 3	Condition 4	
Factor 1	Panel A	15.5	24.5	32.5	13.5	21.5
	Panel B	13.5	20.5	29.5	9.5	18.3
	Panel C	22.5	28.5	34.5	17.0	25.6
		17.2	24.5	32.2	13.3	21.8

ANOVA table

Source	SS	df	MS	F	p-value
Display Panel	218.58 [1]	2	109.292 [6]	26.49 [10]	3.96E-05 [11]
Emg Condition	1,247.46 [2]	3	415.819 [7]	100.80 [12]	8.91E-09 [13]
Interaction	16.42 [3]	6	2.736 [8]	0.66 [14]	.6809 [15]
Error	49.50 [4]	12	4.125 [9]		
Total	1,531.96 [5]	23			

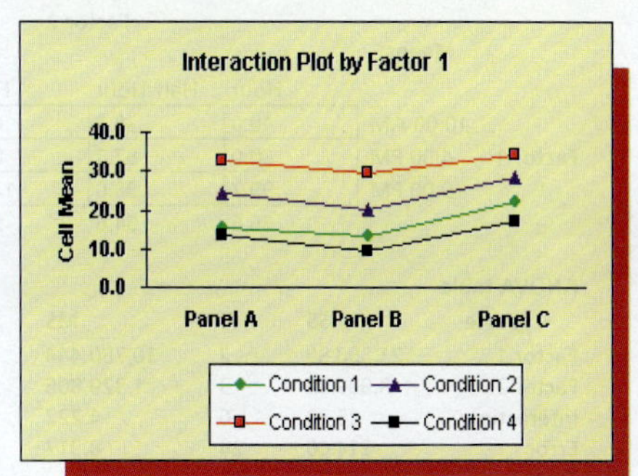

Post hoc analysis for Factor 1
Tukey simultaneous comparison t-values (d.f. = 12)

		Panel B	Panel A	Panel C
		18.3	21.5	25.6
Panel B	18.3			
Panel A	21.5	3.20		
Panel C	25.6	7.26	4.06	

critical values for experimentwise error rate:

0.05	2.67
0.01	3.56

Post hoc analysis for Factor 2
Tukey simultaneous comparison t-values (d.f. = 12)

		Condition 4	Condition 1	Condition 2	Condition 3
		13.3	17.2	24.5	32.2
Condition 4	13.3				
Condition 1	17.2	3.27			
Condition 2	24.5	9.52	6.25		
Condition 3	32.2	16.06	12.79	6.54	

critical values for experimentwise error rate:

0.05	2.97
0.01	3.89

p-values for pairwise t-tests

		Panel B	Panel A	Panel C
		18.3	21.5	25.6
Panel B	18.3			
Panel A	21.5	.0076		
Panel C	25.6	9.98E-06	.0016	

p-values for pairwise t-tests

		Condition 4	Condition 1	Condition 2	Condition 3
		13.3	17.2	24.5	32.2
Condition 4	13.3				
Condition 1	17.2	.0067			
Condition 2	24.5	6.06E-07	4.23E-05		
Condition 3	32.2	1.77E-09	2.36E-08	2.78E-05	

[1] SS(1) [2] SS(2) [3] SS(int) [4] SSE [5] SSTO [6] MS(1) [7] MS(2) [8] MS(int)
[9] MSE [10] $F(1)$ [11] p-value for $F(1)$ [12] $F(2)$ [13] p-value for $F(2)$ [14] $F(\text{int})$ [15] p-value for $F(\text{int})$

TABLE 10.16 Results of a Two-Factor Telemarketing Response Experiment TelMktResp

	Position of Advertisement			
Time of Day	**On the Hour**	**On the Half-Hour**	**Early in Program**	**Late in Program**
10:00 morning	42	36	62	51
	37	41	68	47
	41	38	64	48
4:00 afternoon	62	57	88	67
	60	60	85	60
	58	55	81	66
9:00 evening	100	97	127	105
	96	96	120	101
	103	101	126	107

10.26 A telemarketing firm has studied the effects of two factors on the response to its television advertisements. The first factor is the time of day at which the ad is run, while the second is the position of the ad within the hour. The data in Table 10.16, which were obtained by using a completely randomized experimental design, give the number of calls placed to an 800 number following a sample broadcast of the advertisement. If we use MegaStat to analyze these data, we obtain the output in Figure 10.15. TelMktResp

a Perform graphical analysis to check for interaction between time of day and position of advertisement. Explain your conclusion. Then test for interaction with $\alpha = .05$.

b Test the significance of time of day effects with $\alpha = .05$.

FIGURE 10.15 MegaStat Output of a Two-Way ANOVA of the Telemarketing Data

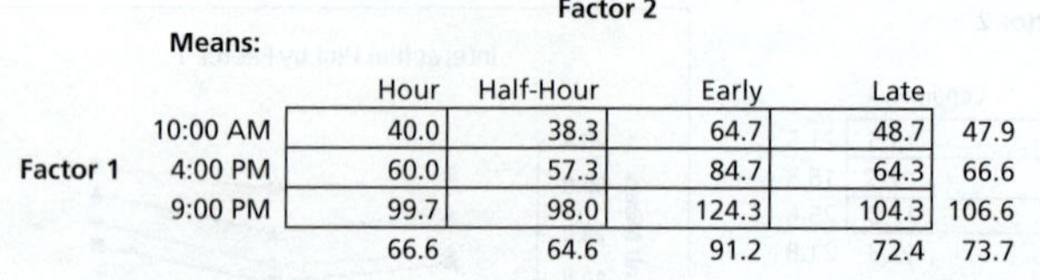

Means:

		Factor 2				
		Hour	Half-Hour	Early	Late	
Factor 1	10:00 AM	40.0	38.3	64.7	48.7	47.9
	4:00 PM	60.0	57.3	84.7	64.3	66.6
	9:00 PM	99.7	98.0	124.3	104.3	106.6
		66.6	64.6	91.2	72.4	73.7

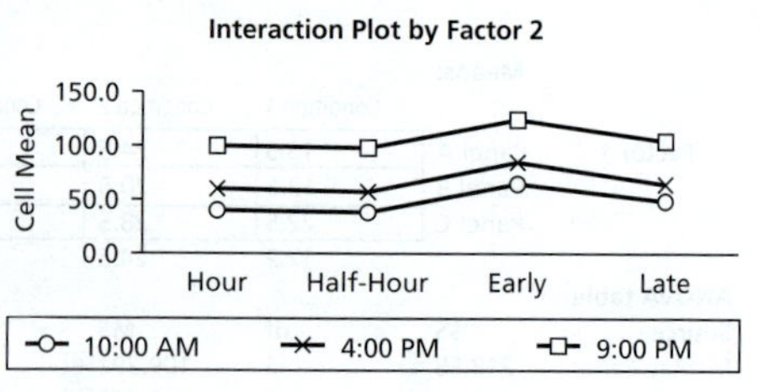

ANOVA table

Source	SS	df	MS	F	p-value
Factor 1	21,560.89	2	10,780.444	1209.02	8.12E-25
Factor 2	3,989.42	3	1,329.806	149.14	1.19E-15
Interaction	25.33	6	4.222	0.47	.8212
Error	214.00	24	8.917		
Total	25,789.64	35			

Post hoc analysis for Factor 1

Tukey simultaneous comparison t-values (d.f. = 24)

		10:00 AM	4:00 PM	9:00 PM
		47.9	66.6	106.6
10:00 AM	47.9			
4:00 PM	66.6	15.31		
9:00 PM	106.6	48.12	32.81	

critical values for experimentwise error rate:

0.05	2.50
0.01	3.21

p-values for pairwise t-tests

		10:00 AM	4:00 PM	9:00 PM
		47.9	66.6	106.6
10:00 AM	47.9			
4:00 PM	66.6	6.93E-14		
9:00 PM	106.6	2.19E-25	1.88E-21	

Post hoc analysis for Factor 2

Tukey simultaneous comparison t-values (d.f. = 24)

		Half-Hour	Hour	Late	Early
		64.6	66.6	72.4	91.2
Half-Hour	64.6				
Hour	66.6	1.42			
Late	72.4	5.60	4.18		
Early	91.2	18.94	17.52	13.34	

critical values for experimentwise error rate:

0.05	2.76
0.01	3.47

p-values for pairwise t-tests

		Half-Hour	Hour	Late	Early
		64.6	66.6	72.4	91.2
Half-Hour	64.6				
Hour	66.6	.1682			
Late	72.4	9.08E-06	.0003		
Early	91.2	6.11E-16	3.52E-15	1.36E-12	

c Test the significance of position of advertisement effects with $\alpha = .05$.

d Make pairwise comparisons of the morning, afternoon, and evening times.

e Make pairwise comparisons of the four ad positions.

f Which time of day and advertisement position maximizes consumer response? Compute a 95 percent (individual) confidence interval for the mean number of calls placed for this time of day/ad position combination.

10.27 A small builder of speculative homes builds three basic house designs and employs two foremen. The builder has used each foreman to build two houses of each design and has obtained the profits given in Table 10.17 (the profits are given in thousands of dollars). Figure 10.16 presents the MINITAB output of a two-way ANOVA of the house profitability data. HouseProf

a Interpret the MINITAB interaction plot in Figure 10.16. Then test for interaction with $\alpha = .05$. Can we (separately) test for the significance of house design and foreman effects? Explain why or why not.

b Which house design/foreman combination gets the highest profit? When we analyze the six house design/foreman combinations using one-way ANOVA, we obtain $MSE = .390$. Compute a 95 percent (individual) confidence interval for mean profit when the best house design/foreman combination is employed.

10.28 In the article "Humor in American, British, and German ads" (*Industrial Marketing Management,* vol. 22, 1993), L. S. McCullough and R. K. Taylor study humor in trade magazine advertisements. A sample of 665 ads were categorized according to two factors: nationality (American, British, or German) and industry (29 levels, ranging from accounting to travel). A panel of judges ranked the degree of humor in each ad on a five-point scale. When the resulting data were analyzed using two-way ANOVA, the p-values for testing the significance of nationality, industry, and the interaction between nationality and industry were, respectively, .087, .000, and .046. Discuss why these p-values agree with the following verbal conclusions of the authors: "British ads were more likely to be humorous than German or American ads in the graphics industry. German ads were least humorous in the grocery and mining industries, but funnier than American ads in the medical industry and funnier than British ads in the packaging industry."

FIGURE 10.16 MINITAB Output of a Two-Way ANOVA of the House Profitability Data

```
Rows: Foreman   Columns: Design

          A       B       C     All
1     10.65   11.95   18.80   13.80
2     10.25   11.80   13.15   11.73
All   10.45   11.88   15.98   12.77

Cell Contents: Profit : Mean
```

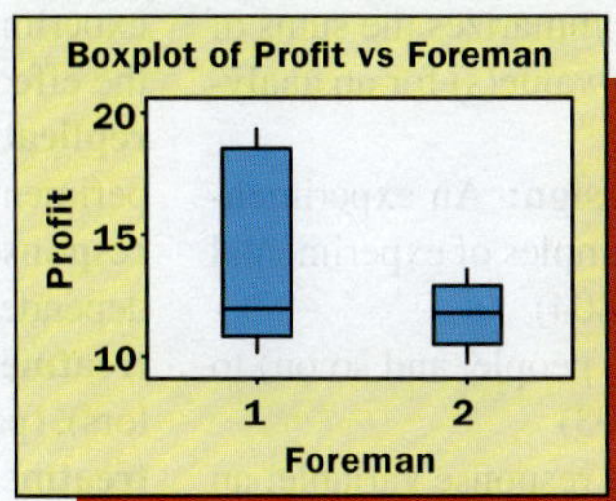

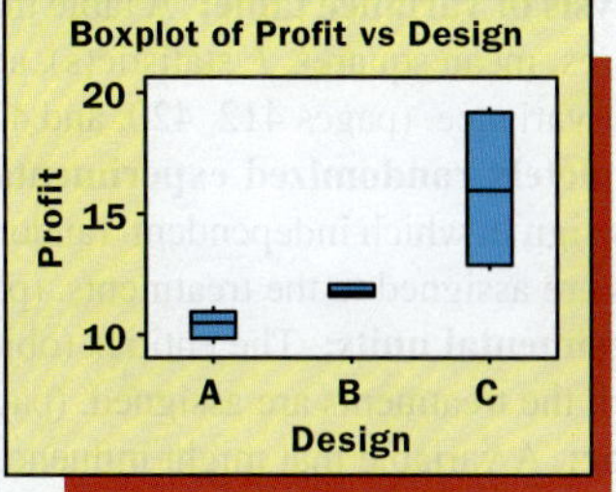

Two-way ANOVA: Profit versus Foreman, Design

```
Source        DF       SS        MS       F       P
Foreman        1   12.813   12.8133   32.85   0.001
Design         2   65.822   32.9108   84.39   0.000
Interaction    2   19.292    9.6458   24.73   0.001
Error          6    2.340    0.3900
Total         11  100.267

Foreman      Mean        Design     Mean
1         13.8000        A        10.450
2         11.7333        B        11.875
                         C        15.975
```

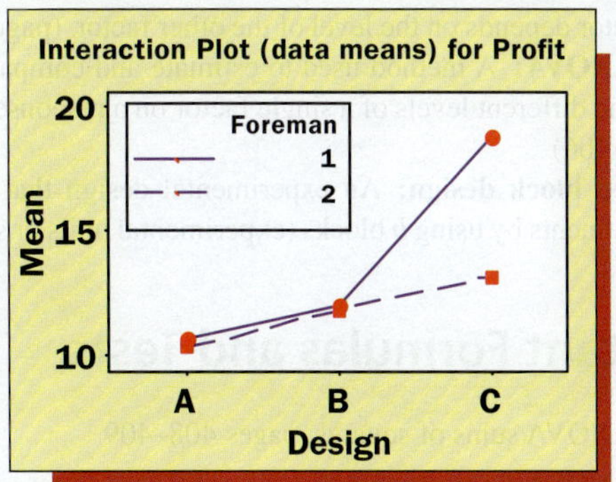

TABLE 10.17 Results of the House Profitability Study HouseProf

	House Design		
Foreman	*A*	*B*	*C*
1	10.2	12.2	19.4
	11.1	11.7	18.2
2	9.7	11.6	13.6
	10.8	12.0	12.7

Chapter Summary

We began this chapter by introducing some basic concepts of **experimental design.** We saw that we carry out an experiment by setting the values of one or more **factors** before the values of the **response variable** are observed. The different values (or levels) of a factor are called **treatments,** and the purpose of most experiments is to compare and estimate the effects of the various treatments on the response variable. We saw that the different treatments are assigned to **experimental units,** and we discussed the **completely randomized experimental design.** This design assigns independent, random samples of experimental units to the treatments.

We began studying how to analyze experimental data by discussing **one-way analysis of variance (one-way ANOVA).** Here we study how one factor (having p levels) affects the response variable. In particular, we learned how to use this methodology to test for differences between the **treatment means** and to estimate the size of pairwise differences between the treatment means.

Sometimes, even if we randomly select the experimental units, differences between the experimental units conceal differences between the treatments. In such a case, we learned that we can employ a **randomized block design.** Each **block** (experimental unit or set of experimental units) is used exactly once to measure the effect of each and every treatment. Because we are comparing the treatments by using the same experimental units, any true differences between the treatments will not be concealed by differences between the experimental units.

The last technique we studied in this chapter was **two-way analysis of variance (two-way ANOVA).** Here we study the effects of two factors by carrying out a **two-factor factorial experiment.** If there is little or no interaction between the two factors, then we are able to separately study the significance of each of the two factors. On the other hand, if substantial interaction exists between the two factors, we study the nature of the differences between the treatment means.

Glossary of Terms

analysis of variance table: A table that summarizes the sums of squares, mean squares, F statistic(s), and p-value(s) for an analysis of variance. (pages 412, 420, and 429)
completely randomized experimental design: An experimental design in which independent, random samples of experimental units are assigned to the treatments. (page 404)
experimental units: The entities (objects, people, and so on) to which the treatments are assigned. (page 403)
factor: A variable that might influence the response variable; an independent variable. (page 403)
interaction: When the relationship between the mean response and one factor depends on the level of the other factor. (page 428)
one-way ANOVA: A method used to estimate and compare the effects of the different levels of a single factor on a response variable. (page 406)
randomized block design: An experimental design that compares p treatments by using b blocks (experimental units or sets of experimental units). Each block is used exactly once to measure the effect of each and every treatment. (page 417)
replication: When a treatment is applied to more than one experimental unit. (page 404)
response variable: The variable of interest in an experiment; the dependent variable. (page 403)
treatment: A value (or level) of a factor (or combination of factors). (page 403)
treatment mean: The mean value of the response variable obtained by using a particular treatment. (page 406)
two-factor factorial experiment: An experiment in which we randomly assign m experimental units to each combination of levels of two factors. (page 427)
two-way ANOVA: A method used to study the effects of two factors on a response variable. (page 427)

Important Formulas and Tests

One-way ANOVA sums of squares: pages 408–409
One-way ANOVA F test: page 410
One-way ANOVA table: page 412
Estimation in one-way ANOVA: page 413
Randomized block sums of squares: page 419
Randomized block ANOVA table: page 420
Estimation in a randomized block experiment: page 421
Two-way ANOVA sums of squares: page 429
Two-way ANOVA table: page 429
Estimation in two-way ANOVA: page 432

Supplementary Exercises

10.29 A drug company wishes to compare the effects of three different drugs (X, Y, and Z) that are being developed to reduce cholesterol levels. Each drug is administered to six patients at the recommended dosage for six months. At the end of this period the reduction in cholesterol level is recorded for each patient. The results are given in Table 10.18. Completely analyze these data using one-way ANOVA. Use the MegaStat output in Figure 10.17. CholRed

TABLE 10.18 Reduction of Cholesterol Levels CholRed

	Drug	
X	Y	Z
22	40	15
31	35	9
19	47	14
27	41	11
25	39	21
18	33	5

10.30 In an article in *Accounting and Finance* (the journal of the Accounting Association of Australia and New Zealand), Church and Schneider (1993) report on a study concerning auditor objectivity. A sample of 45 auditors was randomly divided into three groups: (1) the 15 auditors in group 1 designed an audit program for accounts receivable and evaluated an audit program for accounts payable designed by somebody else; (2) the 15 auditors in group 2 did the reverse; (3) the 15 auditors in group 3 (the control group) evaluated the audit programs for both accounts. All 45 auditors were then instructed to spend an additional 15 hours investigating suspected irregularities in either or both of the audit programs. The mean additional number of hours allocated to the accounts receivable audit program by the auditors in groups 1, 2, and 3 were $\bar{x}_1 = 6.7$, $\bar{x}_2 = 9.7$, and $\bar{x}_3 = 7.6$. Furthermore, a one-way ANOVA of the data shows that $SST = 71.51$ and $SSE = 321.3$.

a Define appropriate treatment means μ_1, μ_2, and μ_3. Then test for statistically significant differences between these treatment means. Set $\alpha = .05$. Can we conclude that the different auditor groups have different effects on the mean additional time allocated to investigating the accounts receivable audit program?

b Perform pairwise comparisons of the treatment means by computing a Tukey simultaneous 95 percent confidence interval for each of the pairwise differences $\mu_1 - \mu_2$, $\mu_1 - \mu_3$, and $\mu_2 - \mu_3$. Interpret the results. What do your results imply about the objectivity of auditors? What are the practical implications of this result?

10.31 The loan officers at a large bank can use three different methods for evaluating loan applications. Loan decisions can be based on (1) the applicant's balance sheet (B), (2) examination of key financial ratios (F), or (3) use of a new decision support system (D). In order to compare these three methods, four of the bank's loan officers are randomly selected. Each officer employs each of the evaluation methods for one month (the methods are employed in randomly selected orders). After a year has passed, the percentage of bad loans for each loan officer and evaluation

FIGURE 10.17 MegaStat Output of an ANOVA of the Cholesterol Reduction Data

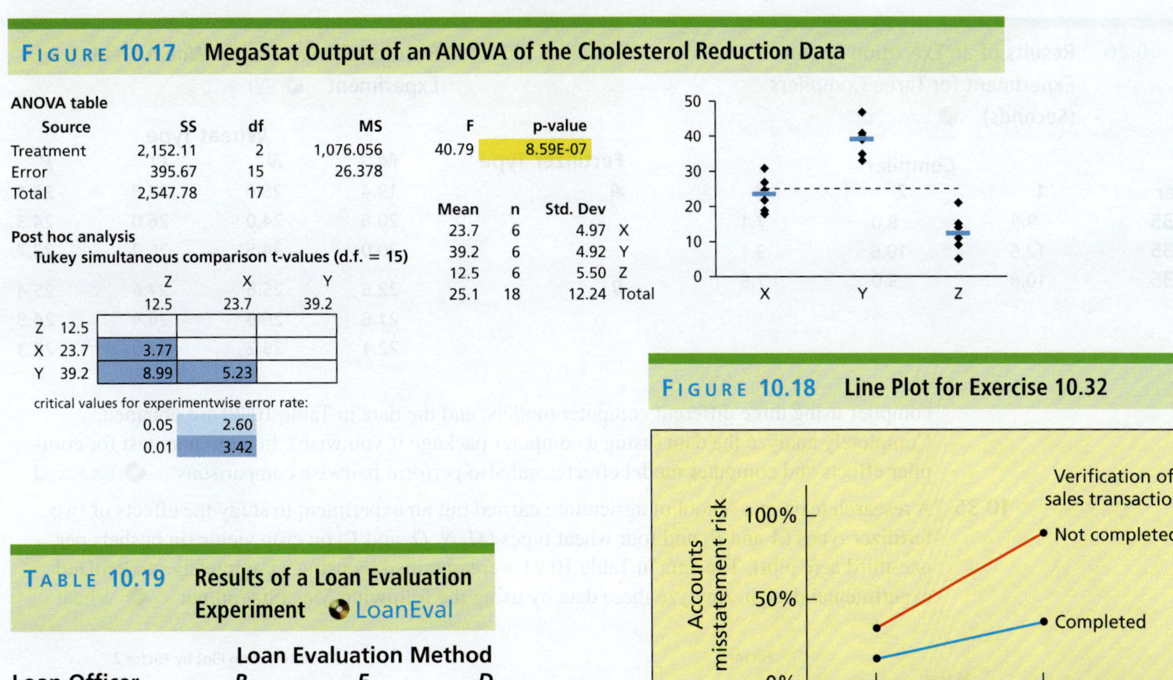

ANOVA table

Source	SS	df	MS	F	p-value
Treatment	2,152.11	2	1,076.056	40.79	8.59E-07
Error	395.67	15	26.378		
Total	2,547.78	17			

Mean	n	Std. Dev	
23.7	6	4.97	X
39.2	6	4.92	Y
12.5	6	5.50	Z
25.1	18	12.24	Total

Post hoc analysis

Tukey simultaneous comparison t-values (d.f. = 15)

		Z	X	Y
		12.5	23.7	39.2
Z	12.5			
X	23.7	3.77		
Y	39.2	8.99	5.23	

critical values for experimentwise error rate:

0.05	2.60
0.01	3.42

FIGURE 10.18 Line Plot for Exercise 10.32

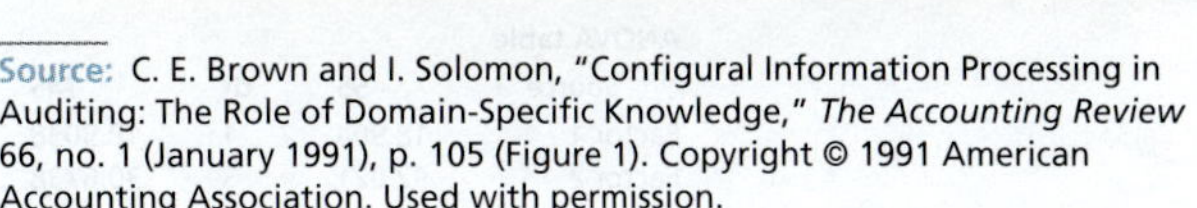

Source: C. E. Brown and I. Solomon, "Configural Information Processing in Auditing: The Role of Domain-Specific Knowledge," *The Accounting Review* 66, no. 1 (January 1991), p. 105 (Figure 1). Copyright © 1991 American Accounting Association. Used with permission.

TABLE 10.19 Results of a Loan Evaluation Experiment LoanEval

Loan Officer	Loan Evaluation Method *B*	*F*	*D*
1	8	5	4
2	6	4	3
3	5	2	1
4	4	1	0

method is determined. The data obtained by using this randomized block design are given in Table 10.19. Completely analyze the data using randomized block ANOVA. LoanEval

10.32 In an article in the *Accounting Review* (1991), Brown and Solomon study the effects of two factors—confirmation of accounts receivable and verification of sales transactions—on account misstatement risk by auditors. Both factors had two levels—completed or not completed—and a line plot of the treatment mean misstatement risks is shown in Figure 10.18. This line plot makes it appear that interaction exists between the two factors. In your own words, explain what the nature of the interaction means in practical terms.

10.33 In an article in the *Academy of Management Journal* (1987), W. D. Hicks and R. J. Klimoski studied the effects of two factors—degree of attendance choice and prior information—on managers' evaluation of a two-day workshop concerning performance reviews. Degree of attendance choice had two levels: high (little pressure from supervisors to attend) and low (mandatory attendance). Prior information also had two levels: realistic preview and traditional announcement. Twenty-one managers were randomly assigned to the four treatment combinations. At the end of the program, each manager was asked to rate the workshop on a seven-point scale (1 = no satisfaction, 7 = extreme satisfaction). The following sample treatment means were obtained:

Degree of Attendance Choice	Prior Information: Realistic Preview	Traditional Announcement
High	6.20	6.06
Low	5.33	4.82

Source: W. D. Hicks and R. J. Klimoski, "Entry into Training Programs and Its Effects on Training Outcomes: A Field Experiment," *Academy of Management Journal* 30, no. 3 (September 1987), p. 548.

In addition, *SS*(1), *SS*(2), *SS*(int), and *SSE* were calculated to be, respectively, 22.26, 1.55, .61, and 114.4. Here factor 1 is degree of choice and factor 2 is prior information. Completely analyze this situation using two-way ANOVA.

10.34 An information systems manager wishes to compare the execution speed (in seconds) for a standard statistical software package using three different compilers. The manager tests each

TABLE 10.20 Results of an Execution Speed Experiment for Three Compilers (Seconds) ExecSpd

Computer	Compiler 1	Compiler 2	Compiler 3
Model 235	9.9	8.0	7.1
Model 335	12.5	10.6	9.1
Model 435	10.8	9.0	7.8

TABLE 10.21 Results of a Two-Factor Wheat Yield Experiment Wheat

Fertilizer Type	Wheat Type *M*	*N*	*O*	*P*
A	19.4	25.0	24.8	23.1
	20.6	24.0	26.0	24.3
	20.0	24.5	25.4	23.7
B	22.6	25.6	27.6	25.4
	21.6	26.8	26.4	24.5
	22.1	26.2	27.0	26.3

compiler using three different computer models, and the data in Table 10.20 are obtained. Completely analyze the data (using a computer package if you wish). In particular, test for compiler effects and computer model effects, and also perform pairwise comparisons. ExecSpd

10.35 A research team at a school of agriculture carried out an experiment to study the effects of two fertilizer types (*A* and *B*) and four wheat types (*M*, *N*, *O*, and *P*) on crop yields (in bushels per one-third acre plot). The data in Table 10.21 were obtained by using a completely randomized experimental design. Analyze these data by using the following MegaStat output: Wheat

Means:

		Factor 2 M	N	O	P	
Factor 1	A	20.00	24.50	25.40	23.70	23.40
	B	22.10	26.20	27.00	25.40	25.18
		21.05	25.35	26.20	24.55	24.29

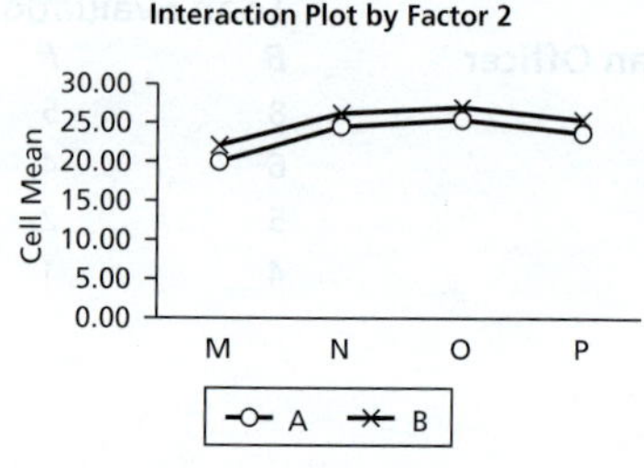

ANOVA table

Source	SS	df	MS	F	p-value
Factor 1	18.904	1	18.9038	48.63	3.14E-06
Factor 2	92.021	3	30.6738	78.90	8.37E-10
Interaction	0.221	3	0.0737	0.19	.9019
Error	6.220	16	0.3888		
Total	117.366	23			

Post hoc analysis for Factor 1

Tukey simultaneous comparison t-values (d.f. = 16)

	A 23.40	B 25.18
A 23.40		
B 25.18	6.97	

critical values for experimentwise error rate:

0.05	2.12
0.01	2.92

p-values for pairwise t-tests

	A 23.40	B 25.18
A 23.40		
B 25.18	3.14E-06	

Post hoc analysis for Factor 2

Tukey simultaneous comparison t-values (d.f. = 16)

	M 21.05	P 24.55	N 25.35	O 26.20
M 21.05				
P 24.55	9.72			
N 25.35	11.95	2.22		
O 26.20	14.31	4.58	2.36	

critical values for experimentwise error rate:

0.05	2.86
0.01	3.67

p-values for pairwise t-tests

	M 21.05	P 24.55	N 25.35	O 26.20
M 21.05				
P 24.55	4.06E-08			
N 25.35	2.20E-09	.0410		
O 26.20	1.55E-10	.0003	.0312	

10.36 Internet Exercise

In an article from the *Journal of Statistics Education,* Robin Lock describes a rich set of interesting data on selected attributes for a sample of 1993-model new cars. These data support a wide range of analyses. Indeed, the analysis possibilities are the subject of Lock's article. Here our interest is in comparing mean highway gas mileage figures among the six identified vehicle types—compact, small, midsize, large, sporty, and van.

Go to the *Journal of Statistics Education* Web archive and retrieve the 1993-cars data set and related documentation: http://www.amstat.org/publications/jse/archive.htm. Click on *93cars.dat* for data, 93cars.txt for documentation, and *article associated with this data set* for a full text of the article. Excel and MINITAB data files are also included on the CD-ROM (93Cars). Construct box plots of *Highway MPG* by *Vehicle Type* (if MINITAB or other suitable statistical software is available). Describe any apparent differences in gas mileage by vehicle type. Conduct an analysis of variance to test for differences in mean gas mileage by vehicle type. Prepare a brief report of your analysis and conclusions.

Appendix 10.1 ■ Experimental Design and Analysis of Variance Using MINITAB

The instruction blocks in this section each begin by describing the entry of data into the MINITAB data window. Alternatively, the data may be loaded directly from the data disk included with the text. The appropriate data file name is given at the top of each instruction block. Please refer to Appendix 1.1 for further information about entering data, saving data, and printing results.

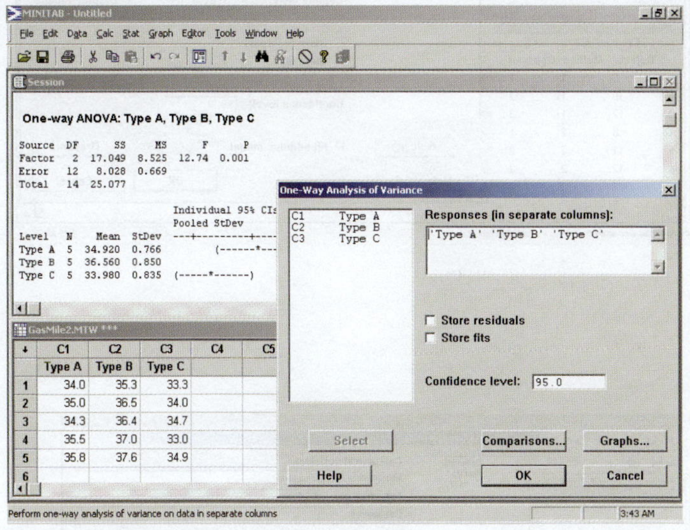

- **One-way ANOVA** in Figure 10.2(a) on page 411 (data file: GasMile2.mtw):
- In the Data window, enter the data from Table 10.1 (page 404) into three columns with variable names Type A, Type B, and Type C.
- Select **Stat : ANOVA : One-way [Unstacked]**
- In the "One-Way Analysis of Variance" dialog box, select 'Type A' 'Type B' 'Type C' into the "Responses [in separate columns]" window. (The single quotes are necessary because of the blank spaces in the variable names. The quotes will be added automatically if the names are selected from the variable list or if they are selected by double clicking.)
- Click OK in the "One-Way Analysis of Variance" dialog box.

To produce **mileage by gasoline type boxplots** similar to those shown in Table 10.1 (page 404):

- Click the Graphs . . . button in the "One-Way Analysis of Variance" dialog box.
- Check the "Boxplots of data" checkbox and click OK in the "One-Way Analysis of Variance—Graphs" dialog box.
- Click OK in the "One-Way Analysis of Variance" dialog box.

To produce **Tukey pairwise comparisons:**

- Click on the Comparisons . . . button in the "One-Way Analysis of Variance" dialog box.
- Check the "Tukey's family error rate" checkbox.
- In the "Tukey's family error rate" box, enter the desired experimentwise error rate (here we have entered 5, which denotes 5%—alternatively, we could enter the decimal fraction .05).
- Click OK in the "One-Way Multiple Comparisons" dialog box.
- Click OK in the "One-Way Analysis of Variance" dialog box.
- The one-way ANOVA output and the Tukey multiple comparisons will be given in the Session window, and the box plots will appear in a graphics window.

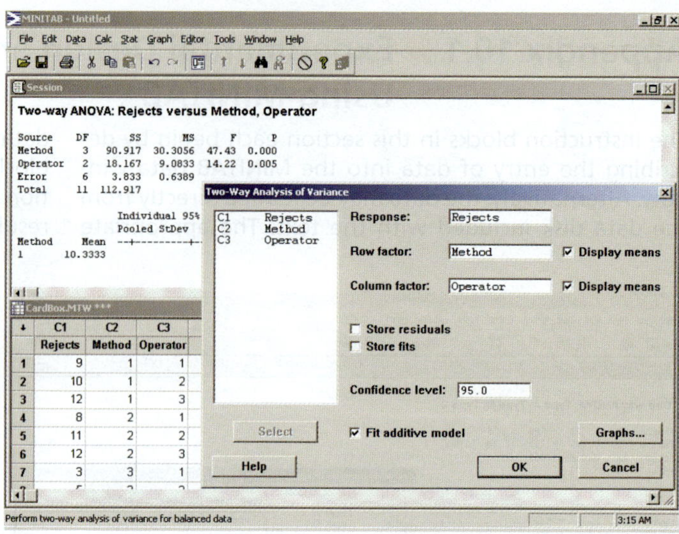

- **Randomized Block ANOVA** in Figure 10.7 on page 420 (data File: CardBox.mtw):
- In the data window, enter the observed number of defective boxes from Table 10.7 (page 418) into column C1 with variable name Rejects; enter the corresponding production method (1,2,3,or 4) into column C2 with variable name Method; and enter the corresponding machine operator (1,2,or 3) into column C3 with variable name Operator.
- Select **Stat : ANOVA : Two-way**
- In the "Two-way Analysis of Variance" dialog box, select Rejects into the Response box.
- Select Method into the Row Factor box and check the "Display Means" checkbox.
- Select Operator into the Column Factor box and check the "Display Means" checkbox.
- Check the "Fit additive model" checkbox.
- Click OK in the "Two-way Analysis of Variance" dialog box to display the randomized block ANOVA in the Session window.

Table of row, column, and cell means in Figure 10.12 on page 430 (data file: BakeSale2.mtw):

- In the data window, enter the observed demands from Table 10.12 (page 426) into column C1 with variable name Demand, enter the corresponding shelf display heights (Bottom, Middle, or Top) into column C2 with variable name Height, and enter the corresponding shelf display widths (Regular or Wide) into column C3 with variable name Width.
- Select **Stat : Tables : Descriptive Statistics**
- In the "Table of Descriptive Statistics" dialog box, select Height into the "Categorical variables: For rows" box and select Width into the "Categorical variables: For columns" box.
- Click on the "Display summaries for Associated Variables..." button.
- In the "Descriptive Statistics—Summaries for Associated Variables" dialog box, select Demand into the "Associated variables" window, check the "Display Means" checkbox, and click OK.
- If cell frequencies are desired in addition to the row, column, and cell means, click OK in the "Table of Descriptive Statistics" dialog box.
- If cell frequencies are not desired, click on the "Display summaries for Categorical Variables . . ." button, uncheck the "Display Counts" checkbox, and click OK in the "Descriptive Statistics—Summaries for Categorical Variables" dialog box. Then, click OK in the "Table of Descriptive Statistics" dialog box.
- The row, column, and cell means are displayed in the Session window.

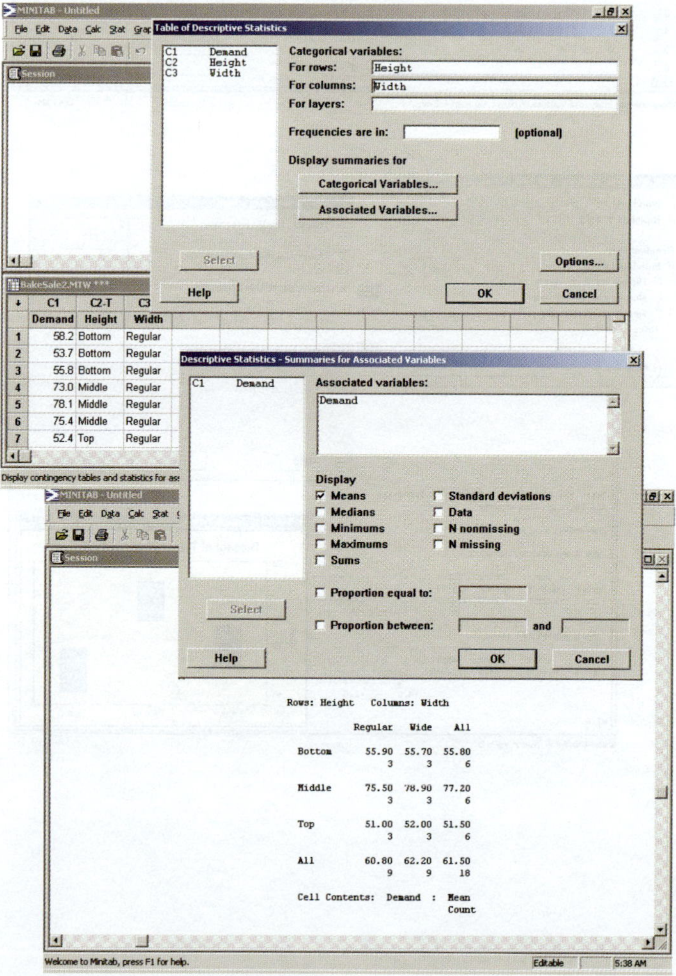

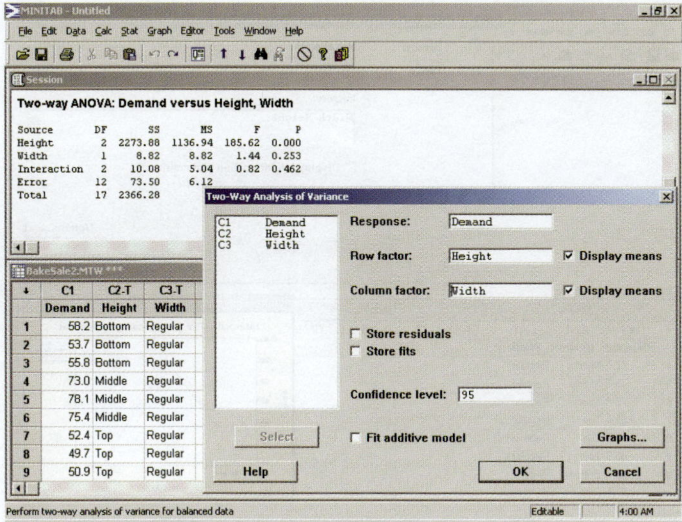

- **Two-way ANOVA** in Figure 10.12 on page 430 (data file: BakeSale2.mtw):
- In the data window, enter the observed demands from Table 10.12 (page 426) into column C1 with variable name Demand; enter the corresponding shelf display heights (Bottom, Middle, or Top) into column C2 with variable name Height; and enter the corresponding shelf display widths (Regular or Wide) into column C3 with variable name Width.
- Select **Stat : ANOVA : Two-Way**
- In the "Two-Way Analysis of Variance" dialog box, select Demand into the Response box.
- Select Height into the "Row Factor" box.
- Select Width into the "Column Factor" box.
- To produce tables of means by Height and Width, check the "Display means" checkboxes next to the "Row factor" and "Column factor" boxes. This will also produce individual confidence intervals for each level of the row factor and each level of the column factor—these intervals are not shown in Figure 10.12.
- Enter the desired level of confidence for the individual confidence intervals in the "Confidence level" box.
- Click OK in the "Two-Way Analysis of Variance" dialog box.

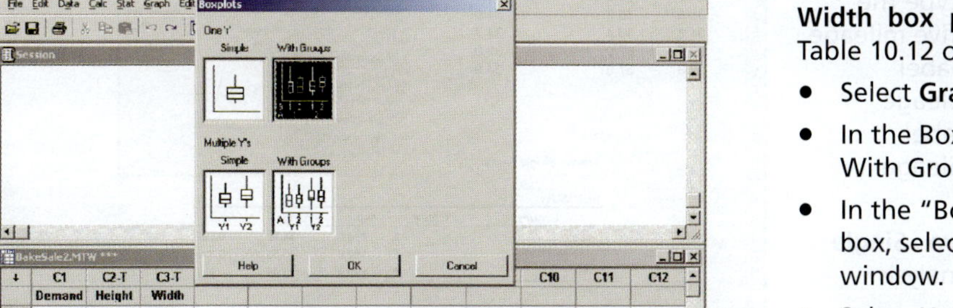

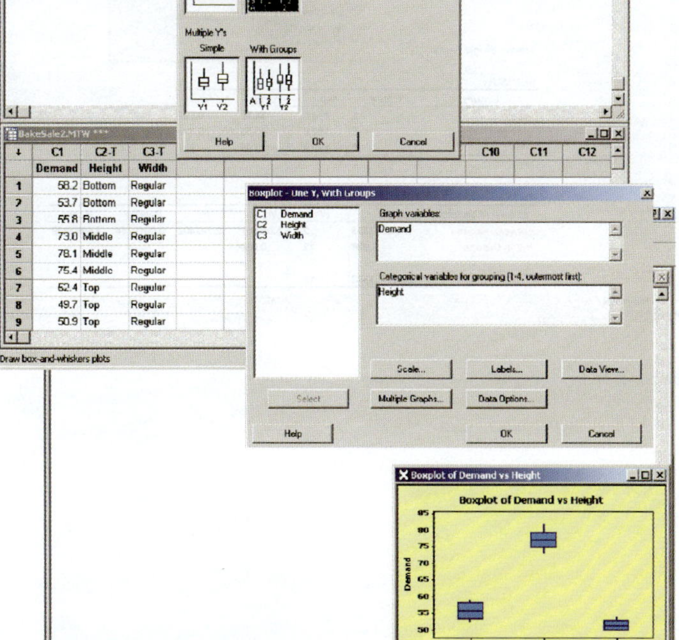

To produce **Demand by Height and Demand by Width box plots** similar to those displayed in Table 10.12 on page 426:

- Select **Graph : Boxplot**
- In the Boxplots dialog box, select "One Y With Groups" and click OK.
- In the "Boxplot—One Y, With Groups" dialog box, select Demand into the Graph variables window.
- Select Height into the "Categorical variables for grouping" window.
- Click OK in the "Boxplot—One Y, With Groups" dialog box to obtain boxplots of demand by levels of height in a graphics window.
- Repeat the steps above using Width as the "Categorical variable for grouping" to obtain boxplots of demand by levels of width in a separate graphics window.

To produce an **interaction plot** similar to that displayed in Figure 10.10 (b) on page 427:

- Select **Stat : ANOVA : Interactions plot**
- In the Interactions Plot dialog box, select Demand into the Responses box.
- Select Width and Height into the Factors box.
- Click OK in the Interactions Plot dialog box to obtain the plot in a graphics window.

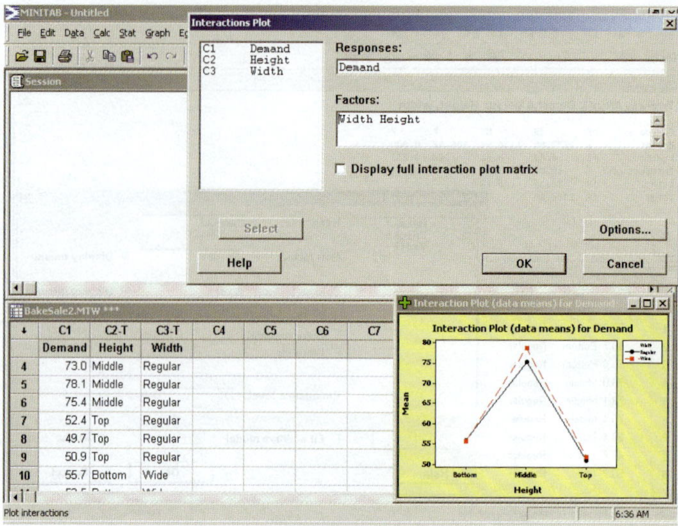

Appendix 10.2 ■ Experimental Design and Analysis of Variance Using Excel

The instruction blocks in this section each begin by describing the entry of data into an Excel spreadsheet. Alternatively, the data may be loaded directly from the data disk included with the text. The appropriate data file name is given at the top of each instruction block. Please refer to Appendix 1.2 for further information about entering data, saving data, and printing results.

One-way ANOVA in Figure 10.2(b) on page 411 (data file: GasMile2.xls):

- Enter the gasoline mileage data from Table 10.1 (page 404) as follows: type the label "Type A" in cell A1 with its five mileage values in cells A2 to A6; type the label "Type B" in cell B1 with its five mileage values in cells B2 to B6; type the label "Type C" in cell C1 with its five mileage values in cells C2 to C6.
- Select **Tools : Data Analysis : Anova : Single Factor** and click OK in the Data Analysis dialog box.
- In the "Anova: Single Factor" dialog box, enter A1.C6 into the "Input Range" box.
- Select the "Grouped by: Columns" option.
- Place a checkmark in the "Labels in first row" check box.
- Enter 0.05 into the Alpha box.
- Select the "Output Range" option and enter a cell location for the upper left-hand corner of the output (here, cell C11) into the Output Range box.
- Click OK in the "Anova: Single Factor" dialog box.
- Drag the border of column C to reveal complete labels for the ANOVA output.

Type A	Type B	Type C
34.0	35.3	33.3
35.0	36.5	34.0
34.3	36.4	34.7
35.5	37.0	33.0
35.8	37.6	34.9

Anova: Single Factor

SUMMARY

Groups	Count	Sum	Average	Variance
Type A	5	174.6	34.92	0.587
Type B	5	182.8	36.56	0.723
Type C	5	169.9	33.98	0.697

ANOVA

Source of Variation	SS	df	MS	F	P-value	F crit
Between Groups	17.04933333	2	8.5246667	12.742402	0.0010764	3.8852938
Within Groups	8.028	12	0.669			
Total	25.07733333	14				

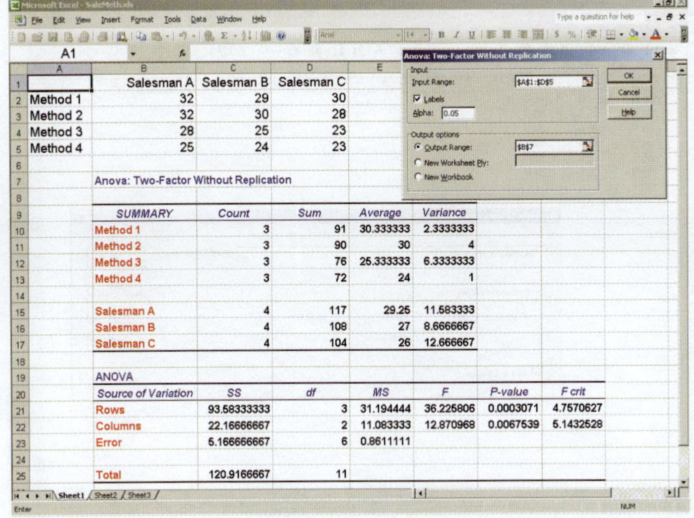

- Place a checkmark in the "Labels" check box.
- Enter 0.05 in the Alpha box.
- Select the "Output Range" option, and enter a cell location for the upper left-hand corner of the output (here, cell B7) into the "Output Range" box.

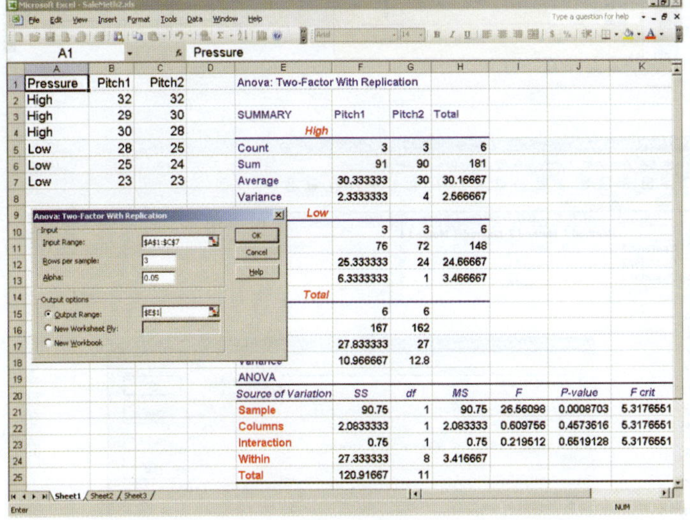

- Enter 0.05 in the Alpha box.
- Select the "Output Range" option, and enter a cell location for the upper left-hand corner of the output (here, cell E1) into the "Output Range" box.

Randomized block ANOVA in Figure 10.8 on page 423 (data file: SaleMeth.xls):

- Enter the sales methods data from Table 10.9 (page 422) as follows: Type the blocks (Salesman A, Salesman B, and Salesman C) into cells B1, C1, and D1, respectively; type the levels of sales method (Method 1, Method 2, Method 3, and Method 4) into cells A2, A3, A4, and A5, respectively; and type the sales results data in the same arrangement as in Table 10.9. Drag the borders of columns A, B, C, and D to make space for the appropriate cell entries.
- Select **Tools : Data Analysis : Anova: Two-Factor Without Replication** and click OK in the Data Analysis dialog box.
- In the "Anova : Two Factor Without Replication" dialog box, enter A1.D5 into the "Input Range" box. (*Continues in left column*)
- Click OK in the "Anova: Two Factor Without Replication" dialog box.
- Drag the border of column B to reveal complete labels for the ANOVA output.

Two-way ANOVA in Figure 10.13 on page 434 (data file: SaleMeth2.xls):

- Enter the sales approach experiment data from Table 10.14 (page 434) as follows: type the levels of sales pitch (Pitch1 and Pitch2) into cells B1 and C1, respectively; type the levels of pressure (High and Low) into cells A2.A4 and A5.A7, respectively; and type the sales data in the same arrangement as in Table 10.14.
- Select **Tools : Data Analysis : Anova : Two-Factor With Replication** and click OK in the Data Analysis dialog box.
- In the "Anova: Two Factor With Replication" dialog box, enter A1.C7 into the "Input Range" box.
- Enter the value 3 into the "Rows per Sample" box (this indicates the number of replications). (*Continues in left column*)
- Click OK in the "Anova: Two Factor With Replication" dialog box.
- Drag the border of column E to reveal complete labels for the ANOVA output.

Appendix 10.3 ■ Experimental Design and Analysis of Variance Using MegaStat

The instructions in this section begin by describing the entry of data into an Excel worksheet. Alternatively, the data may be loaded directly from the data disk included with the text. The appropriate data file name is given at the top of each instruction block. Please refer to Appendix 1.2 for further information about entering data and saving and printing results in Excel. Please refer to Appendix 1.3 for more information about using MegaStat.

One-way ANOVA similar to Figure 10.2(b) on page 411 (data file: GasMile2.xls):

- Enter the gas mileage data in Table 10.1 (page 404) into columns A, B, and C—Type A mileages in column A (with label Type A), Type B mileages in column B (with label Type B), and Type C mileages in column C (with label Type C). Note that the input columns for the different groups must be side by side. However, the number of observations in each group can be different.
- Select **MegaStat : Analysis of Variance : One-Factor ANOVA.**
- In the One-Factor ANOVA dialog box, use the AutoExpand feature to enter the range A1.C6 into the Input range box.
- If desired, request "Post-Hoc Analysis" to obtain Tukey simultaneous comparisons and pairwise *t* tests. Select from the options "Never," "Always," or "When p < .05." The option "When p < .05" gives post hoc analysis when the *p*-value for the *F* statistic is less than .05.
- Check the Plot Data check box to obtain a plot comparing the groups.
- Click OK in the One-Factor ANOVA dialog box.

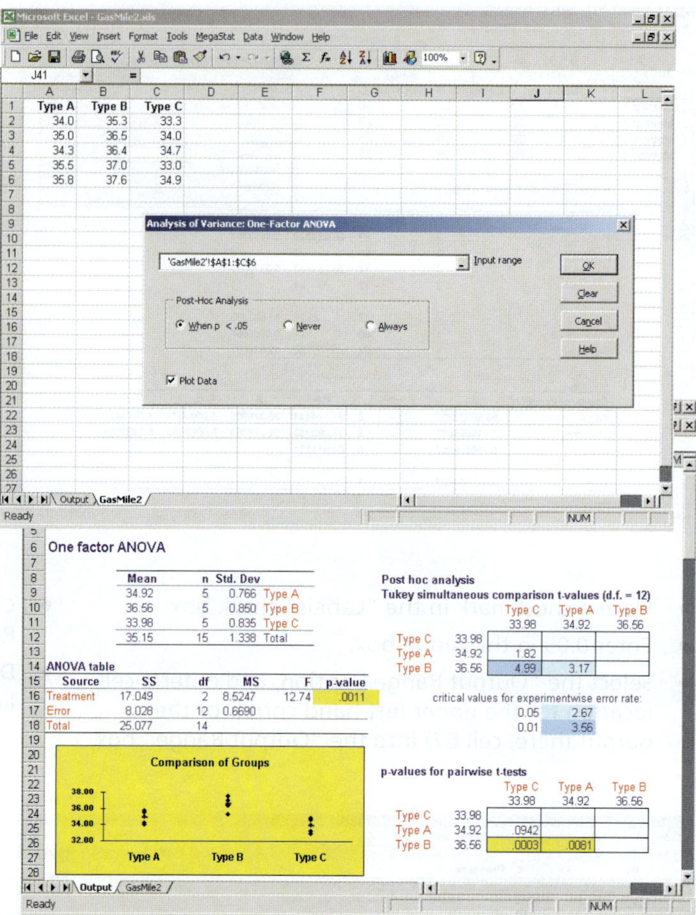

Randomized block ANOVA similar to Figure 10.7 on page 420 (data file: CardBox.xls):

- Enter the cardboard box data in Table 10.7 (page 418) in the arrangement shown in the screenshot. Here each column corresponds to a **treatment** (in this case, a production method), and each row corresponds to a **block** (in this case, a machine operator). Identify the production methods using the labels Method 1, Method 2, Method 3, and Method 4 in cells B1, C1, D1, and E1. Identify the blocks using the labels Operator 1, Operator 2, and Operator 3 in cells A2, A3, and A4.
- Select **MegaStat : Analysis of Variance : Randomized Blocks ANOVA.**
- In the Randomized Blocks ANOVA dialog box, click in the Input range box and enter the range A1.E4.
- If desired, request "Post-Hoc Analysis" to obtain Tukey simultaneous comparisons and pairwise *t* tests. Select from the options "Never," "Always," or "When p < .05." The option "When p < .05" gives post hoc analysis when the *p*-value related to the *F* statistic for the treatments is less than .05.
- Check the Plot Data check box to obtain a plot comparing the treatments.
- Click OK in the Randomized Blocks ANOVA dialog box.

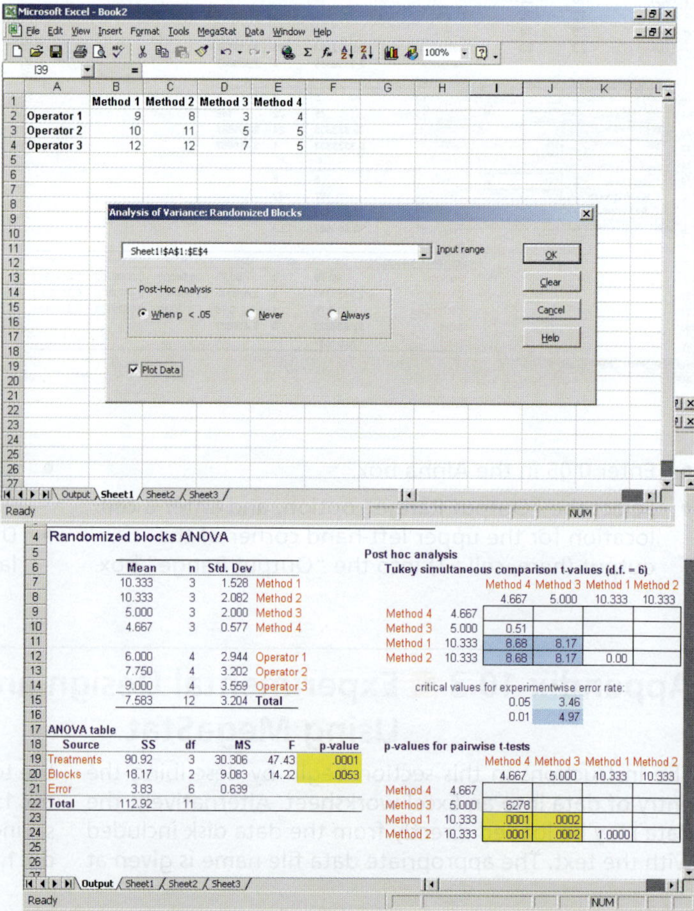

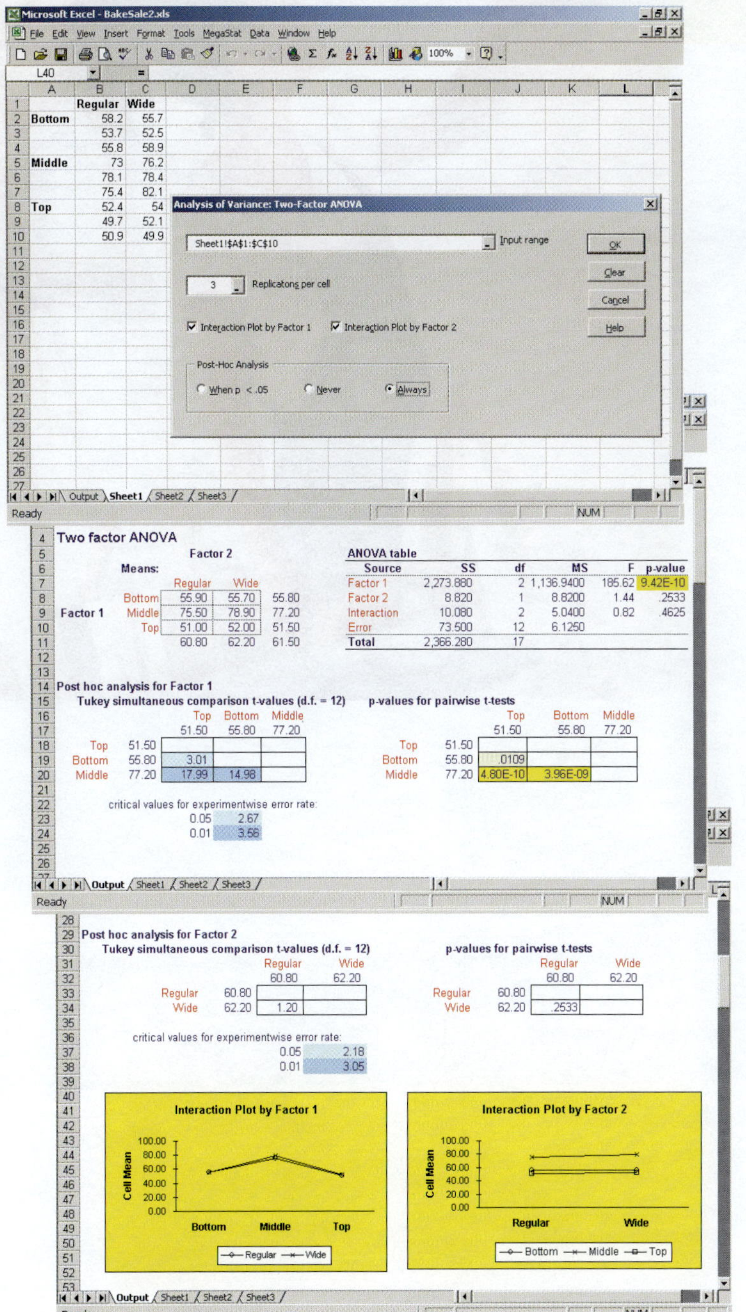

Two-way ANOVA similar to Figure 10.12 on page 430 (data file: BakeSale2.xls):

- Enter the bakery demand data in Table 10.12 (page 426) in the arrangement shown in the screenshot. Here the row labels Bottom, Middle, and Top are the levels of factor 1 (in this case, shelf display height), and the column labels Regular and Wide are the levels of factor 2 (in this case, shelf display width). The arrangement of the data is as laid out in Table 10.12.
- Select **MegaStat : Analysis of Variance : Two-Factor ANOVA.**
- In the Two-Factor ANOVA dialog box, enter the range A1.C10 into the Input range box.
- Type 3 into the "Replications per cell" box.
- Check the "Interaction Plot by Factor 1" and "Interaction Plot by Factor 2" check boxes to obtain interaction plots.
- If desired, request "Post-Hoc Analysis" to obtain Tukey simultaneous comparisons and pairwise *t* tests. Select from the options "Never," "Always," and "When p < .05." The option "When p < .05" gives post hoc analysis when the *p*-value related to the *F* statistic for a factor is less than .05. Here we have selected "Always."
- Click OK in the Two-Factor ANOVA dialog box.

CHAPTER 11

Simple Linear Regression Analysis

Chapter Outline

Managers often make decisions by studying the relationships between variables, and process improvements can often be made by understanding how changes in one or more variables affect the process output. **Regression analysis** is a statistical technique in which we use observed data to relate a variable of interest, which is called the **dependent** (or **response**) **variable,** to one or more **independent** (or **predictor**) **variables.** The objective is to build a **regression model,** or **prediction equation,** that can be used to **describe, predict,** and **control** the dependent variable on the basis of the independent variables. For example, a company might wish to improve its marketing process. After collecting data concerning the demand for a product, the product's price, and the advertising expenditures made to promote the product, the company might use regression analysis to develop an equation to predict demand on the basis of price and advertising expenditure. Predictions of demand for various price–advertising expenditure combinations can then be used to evaluate potential changes in the company's marketing strategies. As another example, a manufacturer might use regression analysis to describe the relationship between several input variables and an important output variable. Understanding the relationships between these variables would allow the manufacturer to identify *control variables* that can be used to improve the process performance.

In the next two chapters we give a thorough presentation of regression analysis. We begin in this chapter by presenting simple linear regression analysis. Using this technique is appropriate when we are relating a dependent variable to a single independent variable and when *a straight-line model* describes the relationship between these two variables. We explain many of the methods of this chapter in the context of two new cases:

C

The Fuel Consumption Case: A management consulting firm uses simple linear regression analysis to predict the weekly amount of fuel (in millions of cubic feet of natural gas) that will be required to heat the homes and businesses in a small city on the basis of the week's average hourly temperature. A natural gas company uses these predictions to improve its gas ordering process. One of the gas company's objectives is to reduce the fines imposed by its pipeline transmission system when the company places inaccurate natural gas orders.

The QHIC Case: The marketing department at Quality Home Improvement Center (QHIC) uses simple linear regression analysis to predict home upkeep expenditure on the basis of home value. Predictions of home upkeep expenditures are used to help determine which homes should be sent advertising brochures promoting QHIC's products and services.

11.1 The Simple Linear Regression Model

CHAPTER 14

The **simple linear regression model** assumes that the relationship between the **dependent variable, which is denoted y,** and the **independent variable, denoted x,** can be approximated by a straight line. We can tentatively decide whether there is an approximate straight-line relationship between y and x by making a **scatter diagram,** or **scatter plot,** of y versus x. First, data concerning the two variables are observed in pairs. To construct the scatter plot, each value of y is plotted against its corresponding value of x. If the y values tend to increase or decrease in a straight-line fashion as the x values increase, and if there is a scattering of the (x, y) points around the straight line, then it is reasonable to describe the relationship between y and x by using the simple linear regression model. We illustrate this in the following case study, which shows how regression analysis can help a natural gas company improve its ordering process.

Example 11.1 The Fuel Consumption Case: Reducing Natural Gas Transmission Fines

C

Part 1: The natural gas transmission problem When the natural gas industry was deregulated in 1993, natural gas companies became responsible for acquiring the natural gas needed to heat the homes and businesses in the cities they serve. To do this, natural gas companies purchase natural gas from marketers (usually through long-term contracts) and periodically (daily, weekly, monthly, or the like) place orders for natural gas to be transmitted by pipeline transmission systems to their cities. There are hundreds of pipeline transmission systems in the United States, and

FIGURE 11.1 The Columbia Gas System

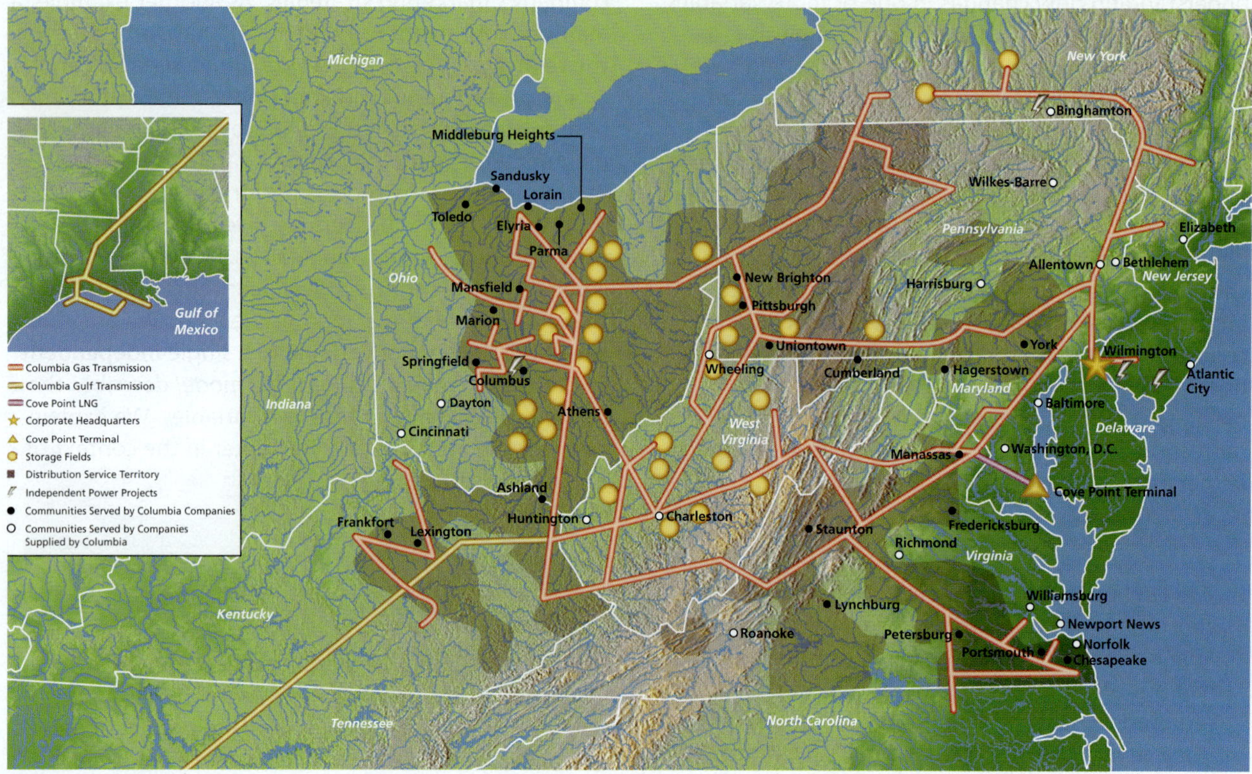

Source: Columbia Gas System 1995 Annual Report.

many of these systems supply a large number of cities. For instance, the map in Figure 11.1 illustrates the pipelines of and the cities served by the Columbia Gas System.

To place an order (called a *nomination*) for an amount of natural gas to be transmitted to its city over a period of time (day, week, month), a natural gas company makes its best prediction of the city's natural gas needs for that period. The natural gas company then instructs its marketer(s) to deliver this amount of gas to its pipeline transmission system. If most of the natural gas companies being supplied by the transmission system can predict their cities' natural gas needs with reasonable accuracy, then the overnominations of some companies will tend to cancel the undernominations of other companies. As a result, the transmission system will probably have enough natural gas to efficiently meet the needs of the cities it supplies.

In order to encourage natural gas companies to make accurate transmission nominations and to help control costs, pipeline transmission systems charge, in addition to their usual fees, transmission fines. A natural gas company is charged a transmission fine if it substantially undernominates natural gas, which can lead to an excessive number of unplanned transmissions, or if it substantially overnominates natural gas, which can lead to excessive storage of unused gas. Typically, pipeline transmission systems allow a certain percentage nomination error before they impose a fine. For example, some systems do not impose a fine unless the actual amount of natural gas used by a city differs from the nomination by more than 10 percent. Beyond the allowed percentage nomination error, fines are charged on a sliding scale—the larger the nomination error, the larger the transmission fine.

Part 2: The fuel consumption data Suppose we are analysts in a management consulting firm. The natural gas company serving a small city has hired the consulting firm to develop an accurate way to predict the amount of fuel (in millions of cubic feet—MMcf—of natural gas) that will be required to heat the city. Because the pipeline transmission system supplying the city

TABLE 11.1 The Fuel Consumption Data FuelCon1

Week	Average Hourly Temperature, *x* (°F)	Weekly Fuel Consumption, *y* (MMcf)
1	28.0	12.4
2	28.0	11.7
3	32.5	12.4
4	39.0	10.8
5	45.9	9.4
6	57.8	9.5
7	58.1	8.0
8	62.5	7.5

FIGURE 11.2 Excel Output of a Scatter Plot of *y* versus *x*

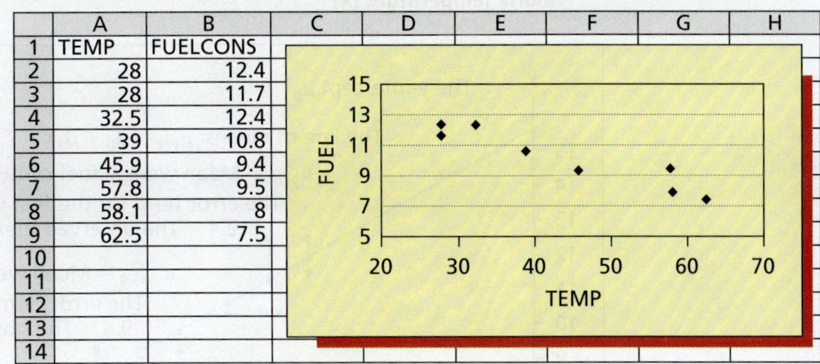

	A	B
1	TEMP	FUELCONS
2	28	12.4
3	28	11.7
4	32.5	12.4
5	39	10.8
6	45.9	9.4
7	57.8	9.5
8	58.1	8
9	62.5	7.5
10		
11		
12		
13		
14		

evaluates nomination errors and assesses fines weekly, the natural gas company wants predictions of future weekly fuel consumptions. Moreover, since the pipeline transmission system allows a 10 percent nomination error before assessing a fine, the natural gas company would like the actual and predicted weekly fuel consumptions to differ by no more than 10 percent. Our experience suggests that weekly fuel consumption substantially depends on the average hourly temperature (in degrees Fahrenheit) measured in the city during the week. Therefore, we will try to predict the **dependent (response) variable** weekly fuel consumption (y) on the basis of the **independent (predictor) variable** average hourly temperature (x) during the week. To this end, we observe values of y and x for eight weeks. The data are given in Table 11.1. In Figure 11.2 we give an Excel output of a scatter plot of y versus x. This plot shows

1 A tendency for the fuel consumption to decrease in a straight-line fashion as the temperatures increase.

2 A scattering of points around the straight line.

A **regression model** describing the relationship between y and x must represent these two characteristics. We now develop such a model.[1]

Part 3: The line of means Consider a specific average hourly temperature x. For example, consider the average hourly temperature 28°F, which was observed in week 1, or consider the average hourly temperature 45.9°F, which was observed in week 5 (there is nothing special about these two average hourly temperatures, but we will use them throughout this example to help explain the idea of a regression model). For the specific average hourly temperature x that we consider, there are, in theory, many weeks that could have this temperature. However, although these weeks each have the same average hourly temperature, other factors that affect fuel consumption could vary from week to week. For example, these weeks might have different average hourly wind velocities, different amounts of cloud cover, and so forth. Therefore, the weeks could have different fuel consumptions. It follows that there is a population of weekly fuel consumptions that could be observed when the average hourly temperature is x. Furthermore, this population has a mean, which we denote as $\boldsymbol{\mu_{y|x}}$ (pronounced **mu of *y* given *x***).

We can represent the straight-line tendency we observe in Figure 11.2 by assuming that $\mu_{y|x}$ is related to x by the equation

$$\mu_{y|x} = \beta_0 + \beta_1 x$$

This equation is the equation of a straight line with **y-intercept** $\boldsymbol{\beta_0}$ (pronounced **beta zero**) and **slope** $\boldsymbol{\beta_1}$ (pronounced **beta one**). To better understand the straight line and the meanings of β_0 and β_1, we first emphasize that the values of β_0 and β_1 determine the value of the mean weekly

[1]Generally, the larger the sample size is—that is, the more combinations of values of y and x that we have observed—the more accurately we can describe the relationship between y and x. Therefore, as the natural gas company observes values of y and x in future weeks, the new data should be added to the data in Table 11.1.

FIGURE 11.3 The Simple Linear Regression Model Relating Weekly Fuel Consumption (y) to Average Hourly Temperature (x)

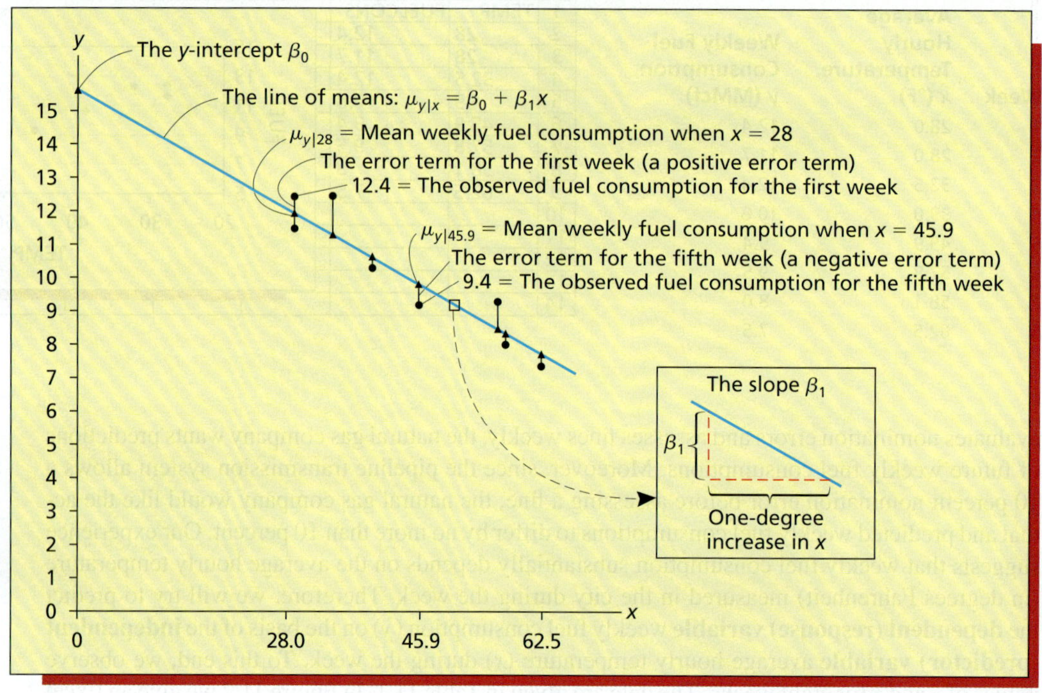

fuel consumption $\mu_{y|x}$ that corresponds to a given value of the average hourly temperature x. For example, the mean of the population of all weekly fuel consumptions that could be observed when x equals 28°F is

$$\mu_{y|28} = \beta_0 + \beta_1(28)$$

As another example, the mean of the population of all weekly fuel consumptions that could be observed when x equals 45.9°F is

$$\mu_{y|45.9} = \beta_0 + \beta_1(45.9)$$

Because we do not know the true values of β_0 and β_1, we cannot actually calculate these mean weekly fuel consumptions. However, when we learn (in the next section) how to estimate β_0 and β_1, we will be able to estimate these means. For now, when we say that $\mu_{y|x}$ is related to x by a straight-line equation, we mean that the different mean weekly fuel consumptions that correspond to different average hourly temperatures lie exactly on a straight line. For example, consider the eight mean weekly fuel consumptions that correspond to the eight average hourly temperatures in Table 11.1. In Figure 11.3 we depict these mean weekly fuel consumptions as triangles that lie exactly on the straight line defined by the equation $\mu_{y|x} = \beta_0 + \beta_1 x$. Furthermore, in this figure we specifically identify the triangles that represent the previously defined means $\mu_{y|28}$ and $\mu_{y|45.9}$. In general, in simple linear regression we sometimes refer to the straight line defined by the equation $\mu_{y|x} = \beta_0 + \beta_1 x$ as the **line of means.**

In order to interpret the slope β_1 of the line of means, consider two different weeks. Suppose that for the first week the average hourly temperature is c. The mean weekly fuel consumption for all such weeks is $\beta_0 + \beta_1(c)$. For the second week, suppose that the average hourly temperature is $(c + 1)$. The mean weekly fuel consumption for all such weeks is $\beta_0 + \beta_1(c + 1)$. It is easy to see that the difference between these mean weekly fuel consumptions is β_1. Thus, as illustrated in Figure 11.3, the slope β_1 is the change in mean weekly fuel consumption that is associated with a one-degree increase in average hourly temperature. To interpret the meaning of the y-intercept β_0, consider a week having an average hourly temperature of 0°F. The mean weekly fuel consumption for all such weeks is $\beta_0 + \beta_1(0) = \beta_0$. Therefore, as illustrated in Figure 11.3, the

y-intercept β_0 is the mean weekly fuel consumption when the average hourly temperature is 0°F. However, because we have not observed any weeks with temperatures near 0, we have no data to tell us what the relationship between mean weekly fuel consumption and average hourly temperature looks like for temperatures near 0. Therefore, the interpretation of β_0 is of dubious practical value. More will be said about this later.

Part 4: The simple linear regression model Recall that the observed weekly fuel consumptions are not exactly on a straight line. Rather, they are scattered around a straight line. To represent this phenomenon, we use the **simple linear regression model**

$$\begin{aligned} y &= \mu_{y|x} + \varepsilon \\ &= \beta_0 + \beta_1 x + \varepsilon \end{aligned}$$

This model says that the weekly fuel consumption y observed when the average hourly temperature is x differs from the mean weekly fuel consumption $\mu_{y|x}$ by an amount equal to ε (pronounced **epsilon**). Here **ε is called an error term.** The error term describes the effect on y of all factors other than the average hourly temperature. Such factors would include the average hourly wind velocity and the amount of cloud cover in the city. For example, Figure 11.3 shows that the error term for the first week is positive. Therefore, the observed fuel consumption $y = 12.4$ in the first week was above the corresponding mean weekly fuel consumption for all weeks when $x = 28$. As another example, Figure 11.3 also shows that the error term for the fifth week was negative. Therefore, the observed fuel consumption $y = 9.4$ in the fifth week was below the corresponding mean weekly fuel consumption for all weeks when $x = 45.9$. More generally, Figure 11.3 illustrates that the simple linear regression model says that the eight observed fuel consumptions (the dots in the figure) deviate from the eight mean fuel consumptions (the triangles in the figure) by amounts equal to the error terms (the line segments in the figure). Of course, since we do not know the true values of β_0 and β_1, the relative positions of the quantities pictured in the figure are only hypothetical.

With the fuel consumption example as background, we are ready to define the **simple linear regression model relating the dependent variable y to the independent variable x.** We suppose that we have gathered n observations—each observation consists of an observed value of x and its corresponding value of y. Then:

The Simple Linear Regression Model

The **simple linear (or straight line) regression model** is: $y = \mu_{y|x} + \varepsilon = \beta_0 + \beta_1 x + \varepsilon$
Here

1 $\mu_{y|x} = \beta_0 + \beta_1 x$ is the **mean value** of the dependent variable y when the value of the independent variable is x.

2 β_0 is the ***y*-intercept.** β_0 is the mean value of y when x equals zero.[2]

3 β_1 is the **slope.** β_1 is the change (amount of increase or decrease) in the mean value of y associated with a one-unit increase in x. If β_1 is positive, the mean value of y increases as x increases. If β_1 is negative, the mean value of y decreases as x increases.

4 ε is an error term that describes the effects on y of all factors other than the value of the independent variable x.

This model is illustrated in Figure 11.4 (note that x_0 in this figure denotes a specific value of the independent variable x). The y-intercept β_0 and the slope β_1 are called **regression parameters.** Because we do not know the true values of these parameters, we must use the sample data to estimate these values. We see how this is done in the next section. In later sections we show how to use these estimates to predict y.

[2]As implied by the discussion of Example 11.1, if we have not observed any values of x near 0, this interpretation is of dubious practical value.

FIGURE 11.4 **The Simple Linear Regression Model (Here the Slope β_1 Is Positive)**

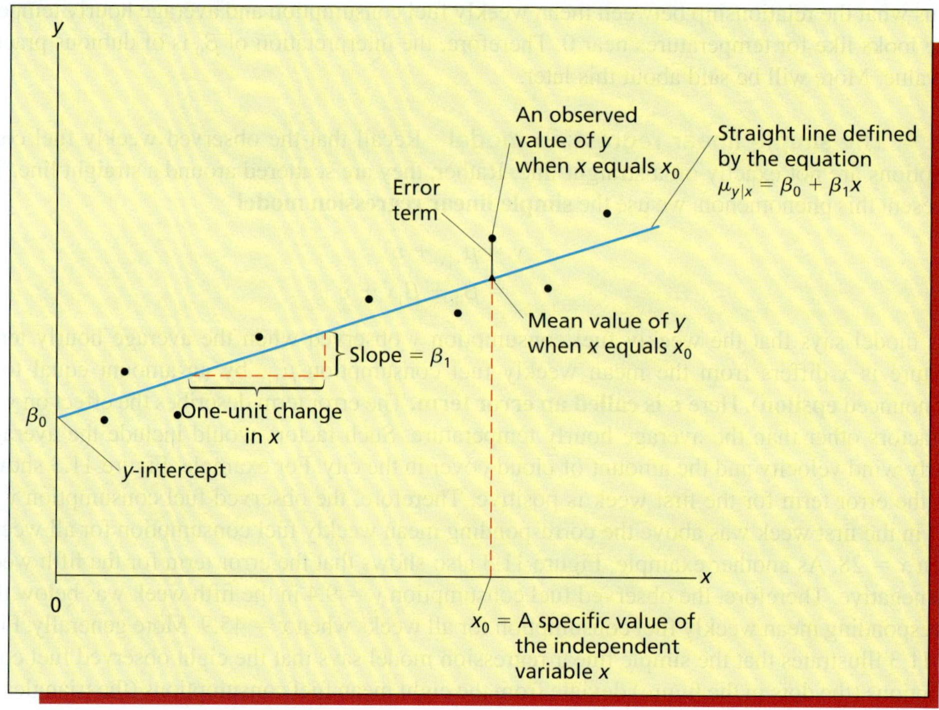

The fuel consumption data in Table 11.1 were observed sequentially over time (in eight consecutive weeks). When data are observed in time sequence, the data are called **time series data.** Many applications of regression utilize such data. Another frequently used type of data is called **cross-sectional data.** This kind of data is observed at a single point in time.

Example 11.2 The QHIC Case

Quality Home Improvement Center (QHIC) operates five stores in a large metropolitan area. The marketing department at QHIC wishes to study the relationship between x, home value (in thousands of dollars), and y, yearly expenditure on home upkeep (in dollars). A random sample of 40 homeowners is taken and asked to estimate their expenditures during the previous year on the types of home upkeep products and services offered by QHIC. Public records of the county auditor are used to obtain the previous year's assessed values of the homeowner's homes. The resulting x and y values are given in Table 11.2(a). Because the 40 observations are for the same year (for different homes), *these data are cross-sectional.*

The MINITAB output of a scatter plot of y versus x is given in Table 11.2(b). We see that the observed values of y tend to increase in a straight-line (or slightly curved) fashion as x increases. Assuming that $\mu_{y|x}$ and x have a straight-line relationship, it is reasonable to relate y to x by using the simple linear regression model having a positive slope ($\beta_1 > 0$)

$$y = \beta_0 + \beta_1 x + \varepsilon$$

The slope β_1 is the change (increase) in mean dollar yearly upkeep expenditure that is associated with each \$1,000 increase in home value. In later examples the marketing department at QHIC will use predictions given by this simple linear regression model to help determine which homes should be sent advertising brochures promoting QHIC's products and services.

We have interpreted the slope β_1 of the simple linear regression model to be the change in the mean value of y associated with a one-unit increase in x. We sometimes refer to this change as *the effect of the independent variable x on the dependent variable y*. However, we cannot prove that

TABLE 11.2 The QHIC Upkeep Expenditure Data QHIC

(a) The data

Home	Value of Home, x (Thousands of Dollars)	Upkeep Expenditure, y (Dollars)	Home	Value of Home, x (Thousands of Dollars)	Upkeep Expenditure, y (Dollars)
1	237.00	1,412.08	21	153.04	849.14
2	153.08	797.20	22	232.18	1,313.84
3	184.86	872.48	23	125.44	602.06
4	222.06	1,003.42	24	169.82	642.14
5	160.68	852.90	25	177.28	1,038.80
6	99.68	288.48	26	162.82	697.00
7	229.04	1,288.46	27	120.44	324.34
8	101.78	423.08	28	191.10	965.10
9	257.86	1,351.74	29	158.78	920.14
10	96.28	378.04	30	178.50	950.90
11	171.00	918.08	31	272.20	1,670.32
12	231.02	1,627.24	32	48.90	125.40
13	228.32	1,204.76	33	104.56	479.78
14	205.90	857.04	34	286.18	2,010.64
15	185.72	775.00	35	83.72	368.36
16	168.78	869.26	36	86.20	425.60
17	247.06	1,396.00	37	133.58	626.90
18	155.54	711.50	38	212.86	1,316.94
19	224.20	1,475.18	39	122.02	390.16
20	202.04	1,413.32	40	198.02	1,090.84

(b) MINITAB Plot of Upkeep Expenditure versus Value of Home

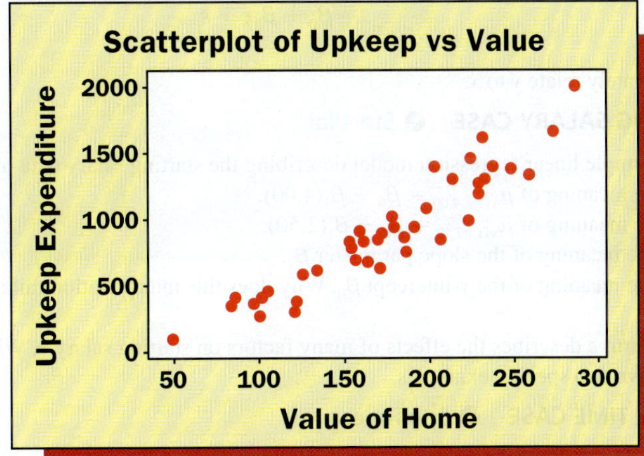

a *change in an independent variable causes a change in the dependent variable.* Rather, regression can be used only to establish that the two variables move together and that the independent variable contributes information for predicting the dependent variable. For instance, regression analysis might be used to establish that as liquor sales have increased over the years, college professors' salaries have also increased. However, this does not prove that increases in liquor sales cause increases in college professors' salaries. Rather, both variables are influenced by a third variable—long-run growth in the national economy.

Exercises for Section 11.1

CONCEPTS

11.1 When does the scatter plot of the values of a dependent variable y versus the values of an independent variable x suggest that the simple linear regression model

$$y = \mu_{y|x} + \varepsilon$$
$$= \beta_0 + \beta_1 x + \varepsilon$$

might appropriately relate y to x?

11.2 In the simple linear regression model, what are y, $\mu_{y|x}$, and ε?

11.3 In the simple linear regression model, define the meanings of the slope β_1 and the y-intercept β_0.

11.4 What is the difference between time series data and cross-sectional data?

METHODS AND APPLICATIONS

11.5 THE STARTING SALARY CASE StartSal

The chairman of the marketing department at a large state university undertakes a study to relate starting salary (y) after graduation for marketing majors to grade point average (GPA) in major courses. To do this, records of seven recent marketing graduates are randomly selected.

Marketing Graduate	GPA, x	Starting Salary, y (Thousands of Dollars)
1	3.26	33.8
2	2.60	29.8
3	3.35	33.5
4	2.86	30.4
5	3.82	36.4
6	2.21	27.6
7	3.47	35.3

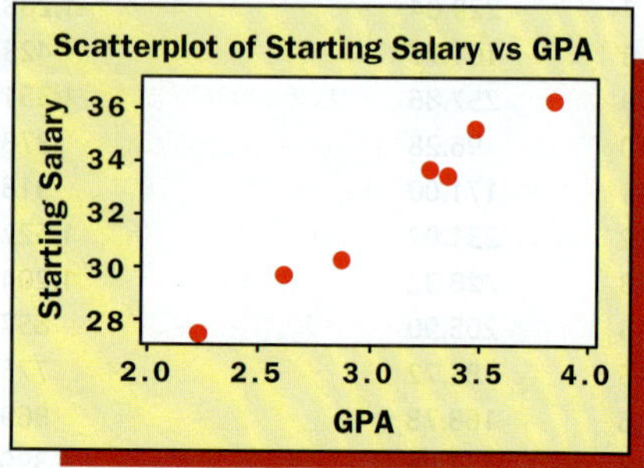

Using the scatter plot (from MINITAB) of y versus x, explain why the simple linear regression model

$$y = \mu_{y|x} + \varepsilon$$
$$= \beta_0 + \beta_1 x + \varepsilon$$

might appropriately relate y to x.

11.6 THE STARTING SALARY CASE StartSal

Consider the simple linear regression model describing the starting salary data of Exercise 11.5.

a Explain the meaning of $\mu_{y|x=4.00} = \beta_0 + \beta_1(4.00)$.

b Explain the meaning of $\mu_{y|x=2.50} = \beta_0 + \beta_1(2.50)$.

c Interpret the meaning of the slope parameter β_1.

d Interpret the meaning of the y-intercept β_0. Why does this interpretation fail to make practical sense?

e The error term ε describes the effects of many factors on starting salary y. What are these factors? Give two specific examples.

11.7 THE SERVICE TIME CASE SrvcTime

Accu-Copiers, Inc., sells and services the Accu-500 copying machine. As part of its standard service contract, the company agrees to perform routine service on this copier. To obtain information about the time it takes to perform routine service, Accu-Copiers has collected data for 11 service calls. The data are as follows:

Service Call	Number of Copiers Serviced, x	Number of Minutes Required, y
1	4	109
2	2	58
3	5	138
4	7	189
5	1	37
6	3	82
7	4	103
8	5	134
9	2	68
10	4	112
11	6	154

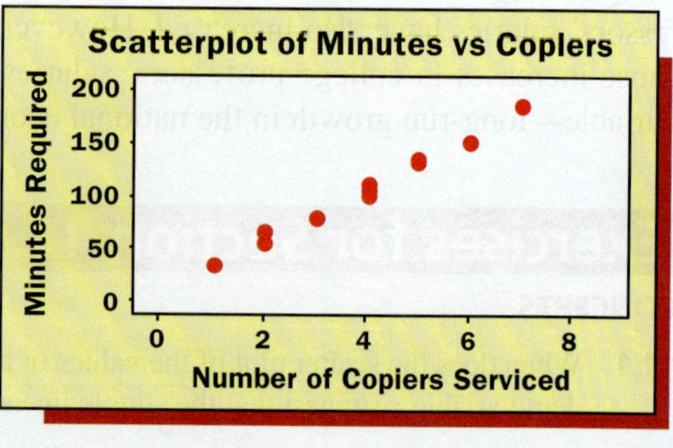

Using the scatter plot (from MINITAB) of y versus x, discuss why the simple linear regression model might appropriately relate y to x.

11.8 THE SERVICE TIME CASE SrvcTime

Consider the simple linear regression model describing the service time data in Exercise 11.7.

a Explain the meaning of $\mu_{y|x=4} = \beta_0 + \beta_1(4)$.

b Explain the meaning of $\mu_{y|x=6} = \beta_0 + \beta_1(6)$.

c Interpret the meaning of the slope parameter β_1.

d Interpret the meaning of the y-intercept β_0. Does this interpretation make practical sense?

e The error term ε describes the effects of many factors on service time. What are these factors? Give two specific examples.

11.9 THE FRESH DETERGENT CASE Fresh

Enterprise Industries produces Fresh, a brand of liquid laundry detergent. In order to study the relationship between price and demand for the large bottle of Fresh, the company has gathered data concerning demand for Fresh over the last 30 sales periods (each sales period is four weeks). Here, for each sales period,

y = demand for the large bottle of Fresh (in hundreds of thousands of bottles) in the sales period, and

x = the difference between the average industry price (in dollars) of competitors' similar detergents and the price (in dollars) of Fresh as offered by Enterprise Industries in the sales period.

Referring to the variable x as the "price difference" for brevity's sake, the data are as follows.

Fresh Detergent Demand Data

Sales Period	y	x	Sales Period	y	x
1	7.38	−.05	16	8.87	.30
2	8.51	.25	17	9.26	.50
3	9.52	.60	18	9.00	.50
4	7.50	0	19	8.75	.40
5	9.33	.25	20	7.95	−.05
6	8.28	.20	21	7.65	−.05
7	8.75	.15	22	7.27	−.10
8	7.87	.05	23	8.00	.20
9	7.10	−.15	24	8.50	.10
10	8.00	.15	25	8.75	.50
11	7.89	.20	26	9.21	.60
12	8.15	.10	27	8.27	−.05
13	9.10	.40	28	7.67	0
14	8.86	.45	29	7.93	.05
15	8.90	.35	30	9.26	.55

Using the scatter plot (from MINITAB) of y versus x shown below, discuss why the simple linear regression model might appropriately relate y to x.

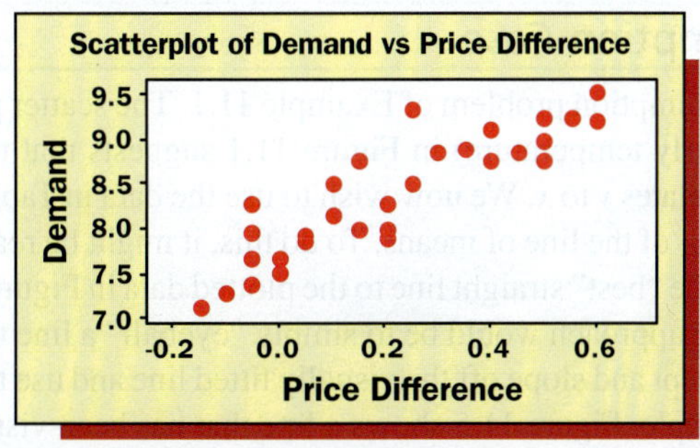

Direct Labor Cost Data DirLab

Direct Labor Cost, y ($100s)	Batch Size, x
71	5
663	62
381	35
138	12
861	83
145	14
493	46
548	52
251	23
1024	100
435	41
772	75

11.10 THE FRESH DETERGENT CASE Fresh

Consider the simple linear regression model relating demand, y, to the price difference, x, and the Fresh demand data of Exercise 11.9.

a Explain the meaning of $\mu_{y|x=.10} = \beta_0 + \beta_1(.10)$.
b Explain the meaning of $\mu_{y|x=-.05} = \beta_0 + \beta_1(-.05)$.
c Explain the meaning of the slope parameter β_1.
d Explain the meaning of the intercept β_0. Does this explanation make practical sense?
e What factors are represented by the error term in this model? Give two specific examples.

11.11 THE DIRECT LABOR COST CASE DirLab

An accountant wishes to predict direct labor cost (y) on the basis of the batch size (x) of a product produced in a job shop. Data for 12 production runs are given in the table in the margin.

a Construct a scatter plot of y versus x.
b Discuss whether the scatter plot suggests that a simple linear regression model might appropriately relate y to x.

11.12 THE DIRECT LABOR COST CASE DirLab

Consider the simple linear regression model describing the direct labor cost data of Exercise 11.11.

a Explain the meaning of $\mu_{y|x=60} = \beta_0 + \beta_1(60)$.
b Explain the meaning of $\mu_{y|x=30} = \beta_0 + \beta_1(30)$.
c Explain the meaning of the slope parameter β_1.
d Explain the meaning of the intercept β_0. Does this explanation make practical sense?
e What factors are represented by the error term in this model? Give two specific examples of these factors.

Real Estate Sales Price Data RealEst

Sales Price (y)	Home Size (x)
180	23
98.1	11
173.1	20
136.5	17
141	15
165.9	21
193.5	24
127.8	13
163.5	19
172.5	25

Source: Reprinted with permission from *The Real Estate Appraiser and Analyst* Spring 1986 issue. Copyright 1986 by the Appraisal Institute, Chicago, Illinois.

11.13 THE REAL ESTATE SALES PRICE CASE RealEst

A real estate agency collects data concerning y = the sales price of a house (in thousands of dollars), and x = the home size (in hundreds of square feet). The data are given in the margin.

a Construct a scatter plot of y versus x.
b Discuss whether the scatter plot suggests that a simple linear regression model might appropriately relate y to x.

11.14 THE REAL ESTATE SALES PRICE CASE RealEst

Consider the simple linear regression model describing the sales price data of Exercise 11.13.

a Explain the meaning of $\mu_{y|x=20} = \beta_0 + \beta_1(20)$.
b Explain the meaning of $\mu_{y|x=18} = \beta_0 + \beta_1(18)$.
c Explain the meaning of the slope parameter β_1.
d Explain the meaning of the intercept β_0. Does this explanation make practical sense?
e What factors are represented by the error term in this model? Give two specific examples.

11.2 The Least Squares Estimates, and Point Estimation and Prediction

CHAPTER 15

The true values of the y-intercept (β_0) and slope (β_1) in the simple linear regression model are unknown. Therefore, it is necessary to use observed data to compute estimates of these regression parameters. To see how this is done, we begin with a simple example.

Example 11.3 The Fuel Consumption Case

Consider the fuel consumption problem of Example 11.1. The scatter plot of y (fuel consumption) versus x (average hourly temperature) in Figure 11.1 suggests that the simple linear regression model appropriately relates y to x. We now wish to use the data in Table 11.1 to estimate the intercept β_0 and the slope β_1 of the line of means. To do this, it might be reasonable to estimate the line of means by "fitting" the "best" straight line to the plotted data in Figure 11.1. But how do we fit the best straight line? One approach would be to simply "eyeball" a line through the points. Then we could read the y-intercept and slope off the visually fitted line and use these values as the estimates of β_0 and β_1. For example, Figure 11.5 shows a line that has been visually fitted to the plot of the

FIGURE 11.5 **Visually Fitting a Line to the Fuel Consumption Data**

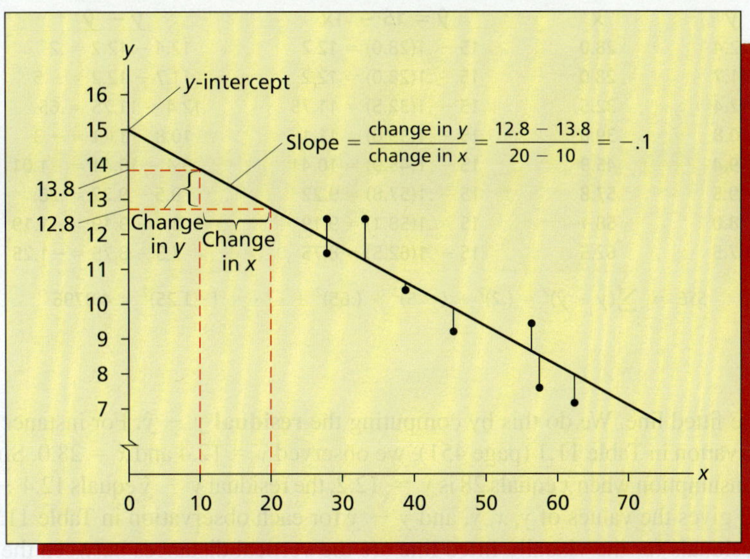

FIGURE 11.6 **Using the Visually Fitted Line to Predict When x = 28**

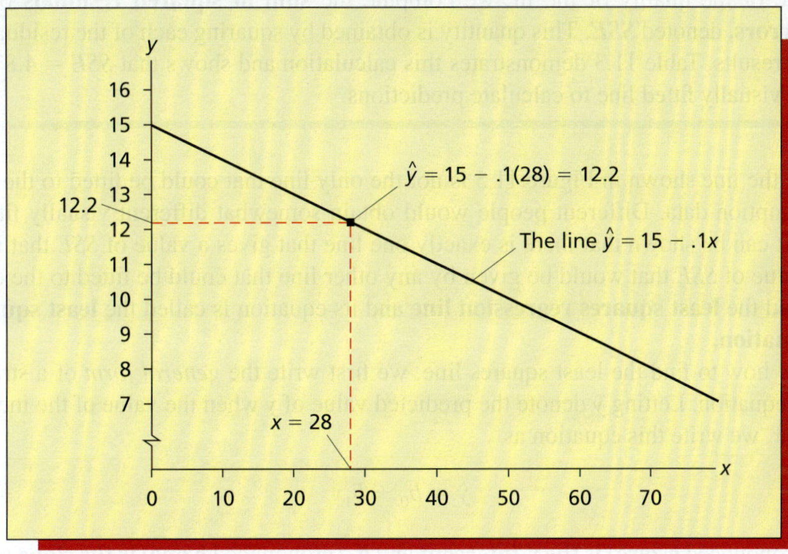

fuel consumption data. We see that this line intersects the y axis at $y = 15$. Therefore, the ***y*-intercept** of the line is 15. In addition, the figure shows that the **slope** of the line is

$$\frac{\text{change in } y}{\text{change in } x} = \frac{12.8 - 13.8}{20 - 10} = \frac{-1}{10} = -.1$$

Therefore, based on the visually fitted line, we estimate that β_0 is 15 and that β_1 is $-.1$.

In order to evaluate how "good" our point estimates of β_0 and β_1 are, consider using the visually fitted line to predict weekly fuel consumption. Denoting such a **prediction** as $\hat{y}$ (pronounced ***y* hat**), a reasonable prediction of y when average hourly temperature is x is simply the point on the visually fitted line corresponding to x. For instance, when temperature is 28°F, predicted fuel consumption is

$$\hat{y} = 15 - .1x = 15 - .1(28) = 12.2$$

as shown in Figure 11.6. We can evaluate how well the visually determined line fits the points on the scatter plot by comparing each observed value of y with the corresponding predicted value of

TABLE 11.3 Calculation of *SSE* for a Line Visually Fitted to the Fuel Consumption Data

y	x	$\hat{y} = 15 - .1x$	$y - \hat{y}$
12.4	28.0	15 − .1(28.0) = 12.2	12.4 − 12.2 = .2
11.7	28.0	15 − .1(28.0) = 12.2	11.7 − 12.2 = −.5
12.4	32.5	15 − .1(32.5) = 11.75	12.4 − 11.75 = .65
10.8	39.0	15 − .1(39.0) = 11.1	10.8 − 11.1 = −.3
9.4	45.9	15 − .1(45.9) = 10.41	9.4 − 10.41 = −1.01
9.5	57.8	15 − .1(57.8) = 9.22	9.5 − 9.22 = .28
8.0	58.1	15 − .1(58.1) = 9.19	8.0 − 9.19 = −1.19
7.5	62.5	15 − .1(62.5) = 8.75	7.5 − 8.75 = −1.25

$$SSE = \sum(y - \hat{y})^2 = (.2)^2 + (-.5)^2 + (.65)^2 + \cdots + (-1.25)^2 = 4.8796$$

y given by the fitted line. We do this by computing the **residual $y - \hat{y}$.** For instance, looking at the first observation in Table 11.1 (page 451), we observed $y = 12.4$ and $x = 28.0$. Since the predicted fuel consumption when x equals 28 is $\hat{y} = 12.2$, the residual $y - \hat{y}$ equals $12.4 - 12.2 = .2$.

Table 11.3 gives the values of y, x, $\hat{y}$, and $y - \hat{y}$ for each observation in Table 11.1. Geometrically, the residuals for the visually fitted line are the vertical distances between the observed y values and the predictions obtained using the fitted line, which are depicted as the eight line segments in Figure 11.5.

If the visually determined line fits the data well, the residuals will be small. To obtain an overall measure of the quality of the fit, we compute the **sum of squared residuals** or **sum of squared errors,** denoted ***SSE.*** This quantity is obtained by squaring each of the residuals and by adding the results. Table 11.3 demonstrates this calculation and shows that $SSE = 4.8796$ when we use the visually fitted line to calculate predictions.

Clearly, the line shown in Figure 11.5 is not the only line that could be fitted to the observed fuel consumption data. Different people would obtain somewhat different visually fitted lines. However, it can be shown that there is exactly one line that gives a value of *SSE* that is smaller than the value of *SSE* that would be given by any other line that could be fitted to the data. This line is called the **least squares regression line** and its equation is called the **least squares prediction equation.**

To show how to find the least squares line, we first write the *general form* of a straight-line prediction equation. Letting $\hat{y}$ denote the predicted value of y when the value of the independent variable is x, we write this equation as

$$\hat{y} = b_0 + b_1 x$$

Here **b_0** (pronounced ***b* zero**) **is the *y*-intercept** and **b_1** (pronounced ***b* one**) **is the slope** of the line. Now suppose we have collected n observations $(x_1, y_1), (x_2, y_2), \ldots, (x_n, y_n)$ and consider a particular observation (x_i, y_i). The predicted value of y_i is

$$\hat{y}_i = b_0 + b_1 x_i$$

and the residual for this observation is

$$e_i = y_i - \hat{y}_i = y_i - (b_0 + b_1 x_i)$$

Then the **least squares line** is the line that *minimizes the sum of squared residuals*

$$SSE = \sum_{i=1}^{n} (y_i - (b_0 + b_1 x_i))^2$$

To find this line, we find the values of the y-intercept b_0 and the slope b_1 that minimize *SSE*. These values of b_0 and b_1 are called the **least squares point estimates** of β_0 and β_1. Using calculus, it can be shown that these estimates are calculated as follows:[3]

The Least Squares Point Estimates

For the simple linear regression model:

1 The **least squares point estimate of the slope β_1** is $b_1 = \frac{SS_{xy}}{SS_{xx}}$ where

$$SS_{xy} = \sum(x_i - \bar{x})(y_i - \bar{y}) = \sum x_i y_i - \frac{\left(\sum x_i\right)\left(\sum y_i\right)}{n} \quad \text{and} \quad SS_{xx} = \sum(x_i - \bar{x})^2 = \sum x_i^2 - \frac{\left(\sum x_i\right)^2}{n}$$

2 The **least squares point estimate of the y-intercept β_0** is $b_0 = \bar{y} - b_1\bar{x}$ where

$$\bar{y} = \frac{\sum y_i}{n} \quad \text{and} \quad \bar{x} = \frac{\sum x_i}{n}$$

Here n is the number of observations (an observation is an observed value of x and its corresponding value of y).

The following example illustrates how to calculate these point estimates and how to use these point estimates to estimate mean values and predict individual values of the dependent variable. Note that the quantities SS_{xy} and SS_{xx} used to calculate the least squares point estimates are also used throughout this chapter to perform other important calculations.

Example 11.4 The Fuel Consumption Case

C

Part 1: Calculating the least squares point estimates Again consider the fuel consumption problem. To compute the least squares point estimates of the regression parameters β_0 and β_1 we first calculate the following preliminary summations:

y_i	x_i	x_i^2	$x_i y_i$
12.4	28.0	$(28.0)^2 = 784$	$(28.0)(12.4) = 347.2$
11.7	28.0	$(28.0)^2 = 784$	$(28.0)(11.7) = 327.6$
12.4	32.5	$(32.5)^2 = 1{,}056.25$	$(32.5)(12.4) = 403$
10.8	39.0	$(39.0)^2 = 1{,}521$	$(39.0)(10.8) = 421.2$
9.4	45.9	$(45.9)^2 = 2{,}106.81$	$(45.9)(9.4) = 431.46$
9.5	57.8	$(57.8)^2 = 3{,}340.84$	$(57.8)(9.5) = 549.1$
8.0	58.1	$(58.1)^2 = 3{,}375.61$	$(58.1)(8.0) = 464.8$
7.5	62.5	$(62.5)^2 = 3{,}906.25$	$(62.5)(7.5) = 468.75$
$\sum y_i = 81.7$	$\sum x_i = 351.8$	$\sum x_i^2 = 16{,}874.76$	$\sum x_i y_i = 3{,}413.11$

Using these summations, we calculate SS_{xy} and SS_{xx} as follows.

$$SS_{xy} = \sum x_i y_i - \frac{\left(\sum x_i\right)\left(\sum y_i\right)}{n}$$

$$= 3{,}413.11 - \frac{(351.8)(81.7)}{8} = -179.6475$$

$$SS_{xx} = \sum x_i^2 - \frac{\left(\sum x_i\right)^2}{n}$$

$$= 16{,}874.76 - \frac{(351.8)^2}{8} = 1{,}404.355$$

[3]In order to simplify notation, we will often drop the limits on summations in this and subsequent chapters. That is, instead of using the summation $\sum_{i=1}^{n}$ we will simply write $\sum$.

TABLE 11.4 Calculation of *SSE* Obtained by Using the Least Squares Point Estimates

y_i	x_i	$\hat{y}_i = 15.84 - .1279x_i$	$y_i - \hat{y}_i$ = residual
12.4	28.0	15.84 − .1279(28.0) = 12.2588	12.4 − 12.2588 = .1412
11.7	28.0	15.84 − .1279(28.0) = 12.2588	11.7 − 12.2588 = −.5588
12.4	32.5	15.84 − .1279(32.5) = 11.68325	12.4 − 11.68325 = .71675
10.8	39.0	15.84 − .1279(39.0) = 10.8519	10.8 − 10.8519 = −.0519
9.4	45.9	15.84 − .1279(45.9) = 9.96939	9.4 − 9.96939 = −.56939
9.5	57.8	15.84 − .1279(57.8) = 8.44738	9.5 − 8.44738 = 1.05262
8.0	58.1	15.84 − .1279(58.1) = 8.40901	8.0 − 8.40901 = −.40901
7.5	62.5	15.84 − .1279(62.5) = 7.84625	7.5 − 7.84625 = −.34625

$$SSE = \sum (y_i - \hat{y}_i)^2 = (.1412)^2 + (-.5588)^2 + \cdots + (-.34625)^2 = 2.568$$

It follows that the least squares point estimate of the slope β_1 is

$$b_1 = \frac{SS_{xy}}{SS_{xx}} = \frac{-179.6475}{1{,}404.355} = -.1279$$

Furthermore, because

$$\bar{y} = \frac{\sum y_i}{8} = \frac{81.7}{8} = 10.2125 \quad \text{and} \quad \bar{x} = \frac{\sum x_i}{8} = \frac{351.8}{8} = 43.98$$

the least squares point estimate of the y-intercept β_0 is

$$b_0 = \bar{y} - b_1\bar{x} = 10.2125 - (-.1279)(43.98) = 15.84$$

Since $b_1 = -.1279$, we estimate that mean weekly fuel consumption decreases (since b_1 is negative) by .1279 MMcf of natural gas when average hourly temperature increases by 1 degree. Since $b_0 = 15.84$, we estimate that mean weekly fuel consumption is 15.84 MMcf of natural gas when average hourly temperature is 0°F. However, we have not observed any weeks with temperatures near 0, so making this interpretation of b_0 might be dangerous. We discuss this point more fully after this example.

Table 11.4 gives predictions of fuel consumption for each observed week obtained by using the least squares line (or prediction equation)

$$\hat{y} = b_0 + b_1 x = 15.84 - .1279x$$

The table also gives each of the residuals and the sum of squared residuals ($SSE = 2.568$) obtained by using this prediction equation. Notice that the *SSE* here, which was obtained using the least squares point estimates, is smaller than the *SSE* of Table 11.3, which was obtained using the visually fitted line $\hat{y} = 15 - .1x$. In general, it can be shown that the *SSE* obtained by using the least squares point estimates is smaller than the value of *SSE* that would be obtained by using any other estimates of β_0 and β_1. Figure 11.7(a) illustrates the eight observed fuel consumptions (the dots in the figure) and the eight predicted fuel consumptions (the squares in the figure) given by the least squares line. The distances between the observed and predicted fuel consumptions are the residuals. Therefore, when we say that the least squares point estimates minimize *SSE*, we are saying that these estimates position the least squares line so as to minimize the sum of the squared distances between the observed and predicted fuel consumptions. In this sense, the least squares line is the best straight line that can be fitted to the eight observed fuel consumptions. Figure 11.7(b) gives the MINITAB output of this best fit line. Note that this output gives the least squares estimates $b_0 = 15.84$ and $b_1 = -0.1279$. In general, we will rely on MINITAB, Excel, and MegaStat to compute the least squares estimates (and to perform many other regression calculations).

Part 2: Estimating a mean fuel consumption and predicting an individual fuel consumption We define the **experimental region** to be the range of the previously observed values of the average hourly temperature x. Referring to Table 11.4, we see that the experimental region consists of the range of average hourly temperatures from 28°F to 62.5°F. The simple linear regression model relates weekly fuel consumption y to average hourly temperature x for

FIGURE 11.7 **The Least Squares Line for the Fuel Consumption Data**

(a) The observed and predicted fuel consumptions

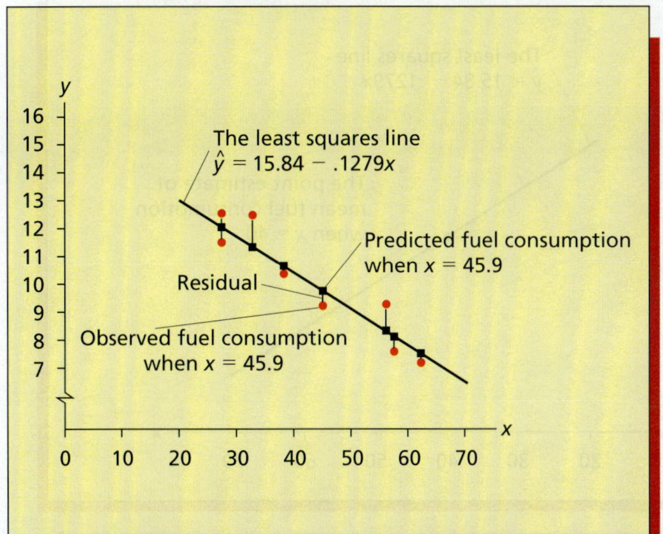

(b) The MINITAB output of the least squares line

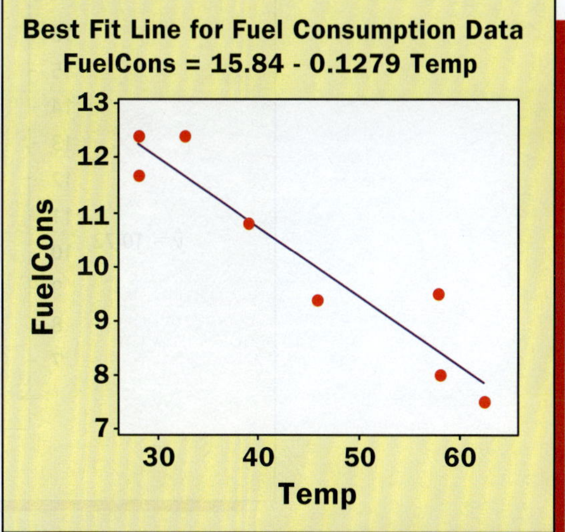

values of x that are in the experimental region. For such values of x, the least squares line is the estimate of the line of means.

We now consider finding a point estimate of

$$\mu_{y|x} = \beta_0 + \beta_1 x$$

which is the mean of all of the weekly fuel consumptions that could be observed when the average hourly temperature is x. Because the least squares line is the estimate of the line of means, the point estimate of $\mu_{y|x}$ is the point on the least squares line that corresponds to the average hourly temperature x:

$$\hat{y} = b_0 + b_1 x$$
$$= 15.84 - .1279x$$

This point estimate is intuitively logical because it is obtained by replacing the unknown parameters β_0 and β_1 in the expression for $\mu_{y|x}$ by their least squares estimates b_0 and b_1.

The quantity $\hat{y}$ is also the point prediction of the individual value

$$y = \beta_0 + \beta_1 x + \varepsilon$$

which is the amount of fuel consumed in a single week when average hourly temperature equals x. To understand why $\hat{y}$ is the point prediction of y, note that y is the sum of the mean $\beta_0 + \beta_1 x$ and the error term ε. We have already seen that $\hat{y} = b_0 + b_1 x$ is the point estimate of $\beta_0 + \beta_1 x$. We will now reason that **we should predict the error term ε to be 0,** which implies that $\hat{y}$ is also the point prediction of y. To see why we should predict the error term to be 0, note that in the next section we discuss several assumptions concerning the simple linear regression model. One implication of these assumptions is that the error term has a 50 percent chance of being positive and a 50 percent chance of being negative. Therefore, it is reasonable to predict the error term to be 0 and to use $\hat{y}$ as the point prediction of a single value of y when the average hourly temperature equals x.

Now suppose a weather forecasting service predicts that the average hourly temperature in the next week will be 40°F. Because 40°F is in the experimental region

$$\hat{y} = 15.84 - .1279(40)$$
$$= 10.72 \text{ MMcf of natural gas}$$

is (1) the point estimate of the mean weekly fuel consumption when the average hourly temperature is 40°F and (2) the point prediction of an individual weekly fuel consumption when the

FIGURE 11.8 Point Estimation and Point Prediction in the Fuel Consumption Problem

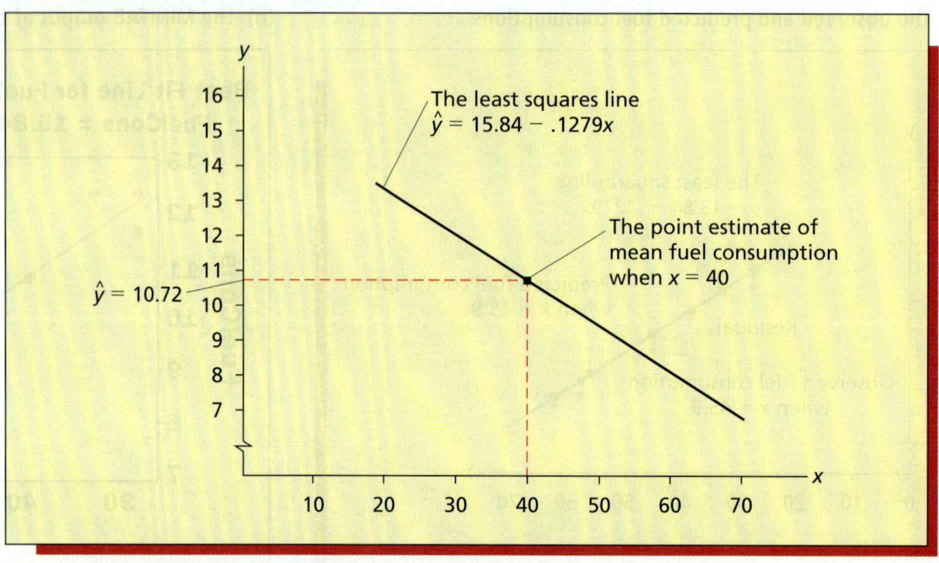

FIGURE 11.9 The Danger of Extrapolation Outside the Experimental Region

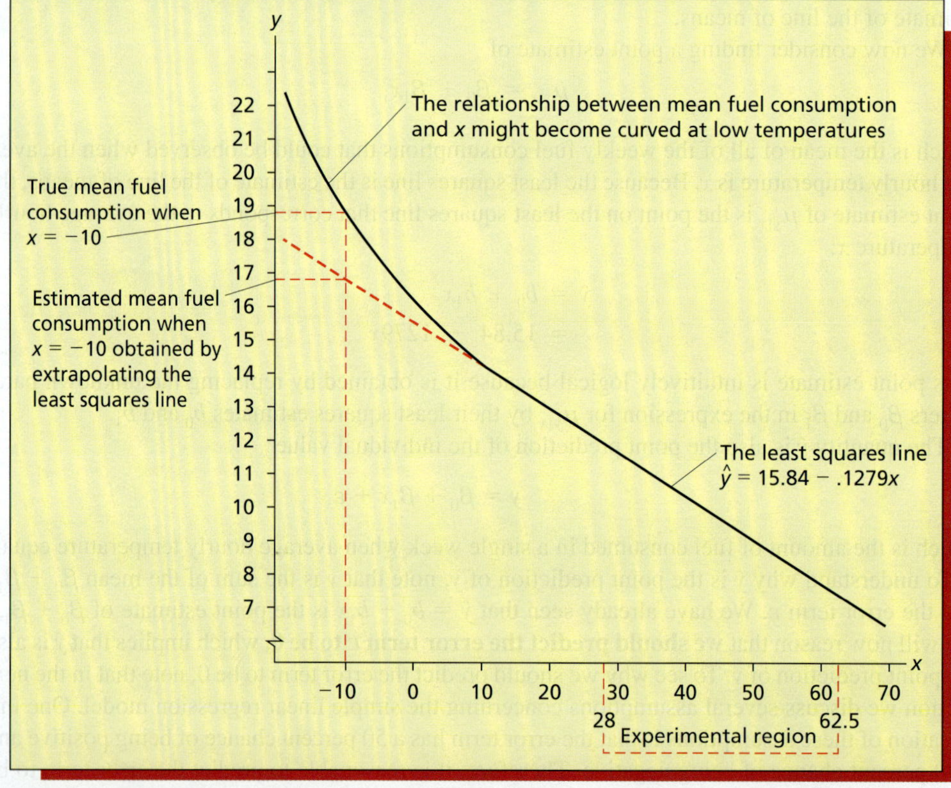

average hourly temperature is 40°F. This says that (1) we estimate that the average of all weekly fuel consumptions that could be observed when the average hourly temperature is 40°F equals 10.72 MMcf of natural gas, and (2) we predict that the fuel consumption in a single week when the average hourly temperature is 40°F will be 10.72 MMcf of natural gas. Note that Figure 11.8 illustrates $\hat{y} = 10.72$ as a square on the least squares line.

To conclude this example, note that Figure 11.9 illustrates the potential danger of using the least squares line to predict outside the experimental region. In the figure, we extrapolate the least squares line far beyond the experimental region to obtain a prediction for a temperature of

$-10°F$. As shown in Figure 11.2 (page 451) for values of x in the experimental region the observed values of y tend to decrease in a straight-line fashion as the values of x increase. However, for temperatures lower than 28°F the relationship between y and x might become curved. If it does, extrapolating the straight-line prediction equation to obtain a prediction for $x = -10$ might badly underestimate mean weekly fuel consumption (see Figure 11.9).

The previous example illustrates that when we are using a least squares regression line, we should not estimate a mean value or predict an individual value unless the corresponding value of x is in the **experimental region**—the range of the previously observed values of x. Often the value $x = 0$ is not in the experimental region. In such a situation, it would not be appropriate to interpret the y-intercept b_0 as the estimate of the mean value of y when x equals 0. For example, consider the fuel consumption problem. Figure 11.9 illustrates that the average hourly temperature 0°F is not in the experimental region. Therefore, it would not be appropriate to use $b_0 = 15.84$ as the point estimate of the mean weekly fuel consumption when average hourly temperature is 0. Because it is not meaningful to interpret the y-intercept in many regression situations, we often omit such interpretations.

We now present a general procedure for estimating a mean value and predicting an individual value:

Point Estimation and Point Prediction in Simple Linear Regression

Let b_0 and b_1 be the least squares point estimates of the y-intercept β_0 and the slope β_1 in the simple linear regression model, and suppose that x_0, a specified value of the independent variable x, is inside the experimental region. Then

$$\hat{y} = b_0 + b_1 x_0$$

1. is the **point estimate** of the **mean value of the dependent variable** when the value of the independent variable is x_0.
2. is the **point prediction** of an **individual value of the dependent variable** when the value of the independent variable is x_0. Here we predict the error term to be 0.

Example 11.5 The QHIC Case

C

Consider the simple linear regression model relating yearly home upkeep expenditure, y, to home value, x. Using the data in Table 11.2 (page 455), we can calculate the least squares point estimates of the y-intercept β_0 and the slope β_1 to be $b_0 = -348.3921$ and $b_1 = 7.2583$. Since $b_1 = 7.2583$, we estimate that mean yearly upkeep expenditure increases by \$7.26 for each additional \$1,000 increase in home value. Consider a home worth \$220,000, and note that $x_0 = 220$ is in the range of previously observed values of x: 48.9 to 286.18 (see Table 11.2 on page 455). It follows that

$$\begin{aligned}\hat{y} &= b_0 + b_1 x_0 \\ &= -348.3921 + 7.2583(220) \\ &= 1{,}248.43 \text{ (or \$1,248.43)}\end{aligned}$$

is the point estimate of the mean yearly upkeep expenditure for all homes worth \$220,000 and is the point prediction of a yearly upkeep expenditure for an individual home worth \$220,000.

The marketing department at QHIC wishes to determine which homes should be sent advertising brochures promoting QHIC's products and services. The prediction equation $\hat{y} = b_0 + b_1 x$ implies that the home value x corresponding to a predicted upkeep expenditure of $\hat{y}$ is

$$x = \frac{\hat{y} - b_0}{b_1} = \frac{\hat{y} - (-348.3921)}{7.2583} = \frac{\hat{y} + 348.3921}{7.2583}$$

For instance, if we set predicted upkeep expenditure $\hat{y}$ equal to \$500, we have

$$x = \frac{\hat{y} + 348.3921}{7.2583} = \frac{500 + 348.3921}{7.2583} = 116.886 \text{ (\$116,886)}$$

Therefore, if QHIC wishes to send an advertising brochure to any home that has a predicted upkeep expenditure of at least \$500, then QHIC should send this brochure to any home that has a value of at least \$116,886.

Exercises for Section 11.2

CONCEPTS

11.15 What does *SSE* measure?

11.16 What is the least squares regression line, and what are the least squares point estimates?

11.17 How do we obtain a point estimate of the mean value of the dependent variable and a point prediction of an individual value of the dependent variable?

11.18 Why is it dangerous to extrapolate outside the experimental region?

METHODS AND APPLICATIONS

11.19 THE STARTING SALARY CASE StartSal

The following output is obtained when MINITAB is used to fit a least squares line to the starting salary data given in Exercise 11.5 (page 456).

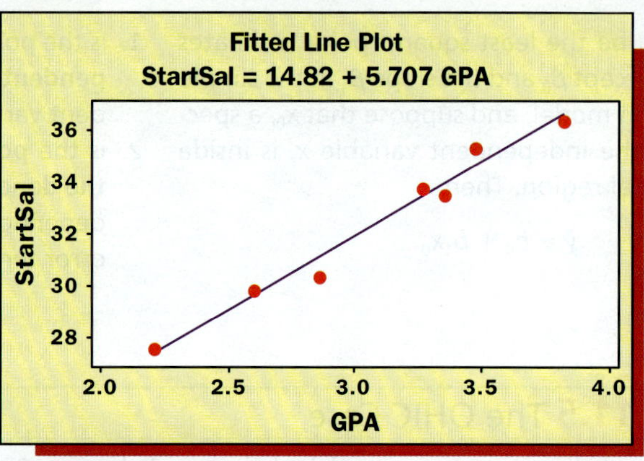

a Find the least squares point estimates b_0 and b_1 on the computer output and report their values. Interpret b_0 and b_1. Does the interpretation of b_0 make practical sense?

b Use the least squares line to compute a point estimate of the mean starting salary for all marketing graduates having a grade point average of 3.25 and a point prediction of the starting salary for an individual marketing graduate having a grade point average of 3.25.

11.20 THE SERVICE TIME CASE SrvcTime

The following output is obtained when Excel is used to fit a least squares line to the service time data given in Exercise 11.7 (page 456).

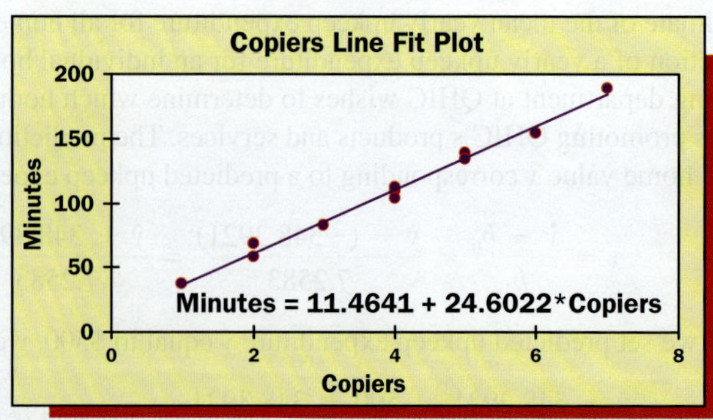

a Find the least squares point estimates b_0 and b_1 on the computer output and report their values. Interpret b_0 and b_1. Does the interpretation of b_0 make practical sense?

b Use the least squares line to compute a point estimate of the mean time to service four copiers and a point prediction of the time to service four copiers on a single call.

11.21 THE FRESH DETERGENT CASE Fresh

The following output is obtained when MINITAB is used to fit a least squares line to the Fresh detergent demand data given in Exercise 11.9 (page 457).

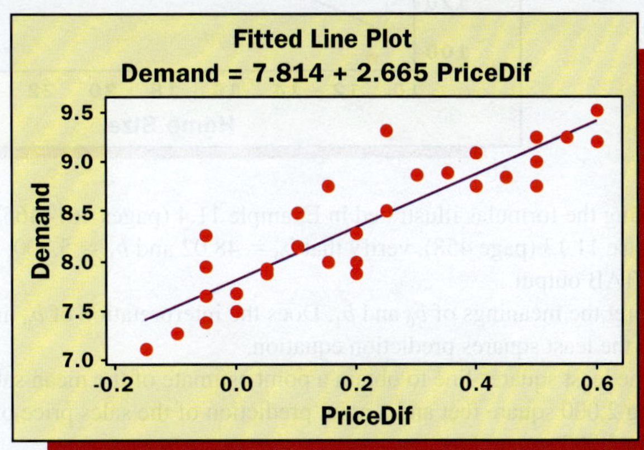

a Find the least squares point estimates b_0 and b_1 on the computer output and report their values. Interpret b_0 and b_1. Does the interpretation of b_0 make practical sense?

b Use the least squares line to compute a point estimate of the mean demand in all sales periods when the price difference is .10 and a point prediction of the actual demand in an individual sales period when the price difference is .10.

c If Enterprise Industries wishes to maintain a price difference that corresponds to a predicted demand of 850,000 bottles (that is, $\hat{y} = 8.5$), what should this price difference be?

11.22 THE DIRECT LABOR COST CASE DirLab

The following output is obtained when Excel is used to fit a least squares line to the direct labor cost data given in Exercise 11.11 (page 458).

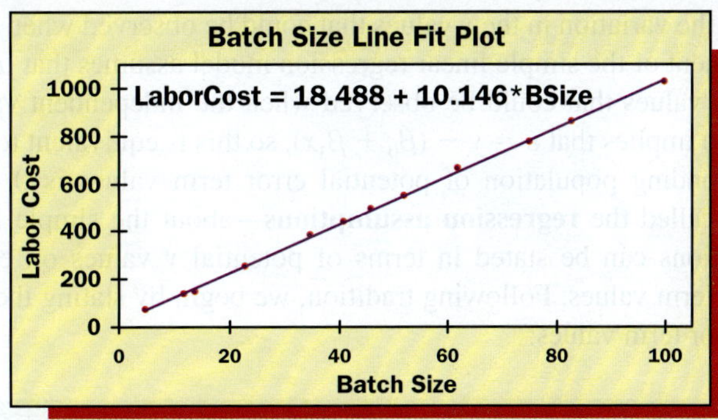

a By using the formulas illustrated in Example 11.4 (pages 461–465) and the data of Exercise 11.11 (page 458), verify that $b_0 = 18.488$ and $b_1 = 10.146$, as shown on the Excel output.

b Interpret the meanings of b_0 and b_1. Does the interpretation of b_0 make practical sense?

c Write the least squares prediction equation.

d Use the least squares line to obtain a point estimate of the mean direct labor cost for all batches of size 60 and a point prediction of the direct labor cost for an individual batch of size 60.

11.23 THE REAL ESTATE SALES PRICE CASE RealEst

The following output is obtained when MINITAB is used to fit a least squares line to the real estate sales price data given in Exercise 11.13 (page 458).

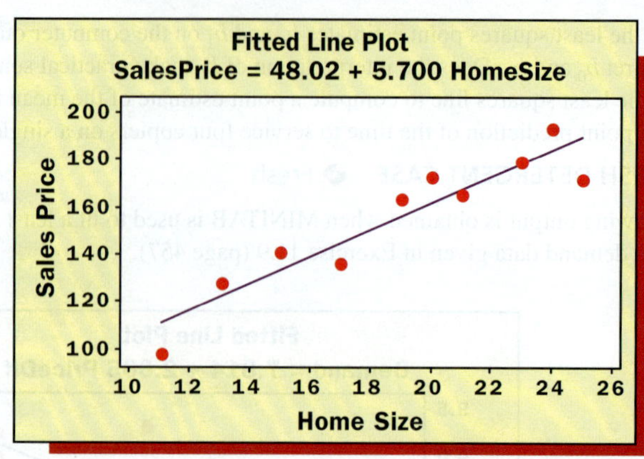

a By using the formulas illustrated in Example 11.4 (pages 461–465) and the data of Exercise 11.13 (page 458), verify that $b_0 = 48.02$ and $b_1 = 5.700$, as shown on the MINITAB output.

b Interpret the meanings of b_0 and b_1. Does the interpretation of b_0 make practical sense?

c Write the least squares prediction equation.

d Use the least squares line to obtain a point estimate of the mean sales price of all houses having 2,000 square feet and a point prediction of the sales price of an individual house having 2,000 square feet.

11.3 Model Assumptions and the Standard Error

Model assumptions In order to perform hypothesis tests and set up various types of intervals when using the simple linear regression model

$$y = \mu_{y|x} + \varepsilon$$
$$= \beta_0 + \beta_1 x + \varepsilon$$

we need to make certain assumptions about the error term ε. At any given value of x, there is a population of error term values that could potentially occur. These error term values describe the different potential effects on y of all factors other than the value of x. Therefore, these error term values explain the variation in the y values that could be observed when the independent variable is x. Our statement of the simple linear regression model assumes that $\mu_{y|x}$, the mean of the population of all y values that could be observed when the independent variable is x, is $\beta_0 + \beta_1 x$. This model also implies that $\varepsilon = y - (\beta_0 + \beta_1 x)$, so this is equivalent to assuming that the mean of the corresponding population of potential error term values is 0. In total, we make four assumptions—called the **regression assumptions**—about the simple linear regression model. These assumptions can be stated in terms of potential y values or, equivalently, in terms of potential error term values. Following tradition, we begin by stating these assumptions in terms of potential error term values:

The Regression Assumptions

1 At any given value of x, the population of potential error term values has a **mean equal to 0.**

2 **Constant Variance Assumption**
At any given value of x, the population of potential error term values has a variance that does not depend on the value of x. That is, the different populations of potential error term values corresponding to different values of x have **equal variances.** We denote the **constant variance as σ^2.**

3 **Normality Assumption**
At any given value of x, the population of potential error term values has a **normal distribution.**

4 **Independence Assumption**
Any one value of the error term ε is **statistically independent** of any other value of ε. That is, the value of the error term ε corresponding to an observed value of y is statistically independent of the value of the error term corresponding to any other observed value of y.

FIGURE 11.10 **An Illustration of the Model Assumptions**

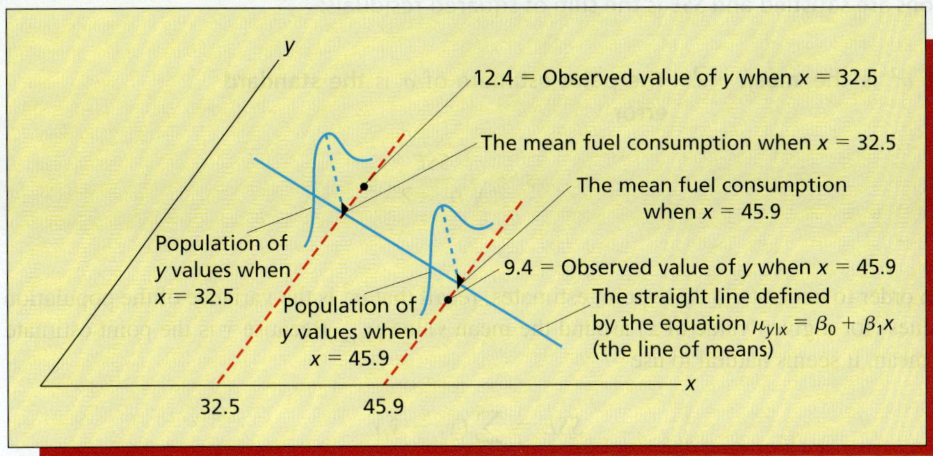

Taken together, the first three assumptions say that, at any given value of x, the population of potential error term values is **normally distributed** with **mean zero** and a **variance σ^2 that does not depend on the value of x.** Because the potential error term values cause the variation in the potential y values, these assumptions imply that the population of all y values that could be observed when the independent variable is x is **normally distributed** with **mean $\beta_0 + \beta_1 x$** and **a variance σ^2 that does not depend on x.** These three assumptions are illustrated in Figure 11.10 in the context of the fuel consumption problem. Specifically, this figure depicts the populations of weekly fuel consumptions corresponding to two values of average hourly temperature—32.5 and 45.9. Note that these populations are shown to be normally distributed with different means (each of which is on the line of means) and with the same variance (or spread).

The independence assumption is most likely to be violated when time series data are being utilized in a regression study. Intuitively, this assumption says that there is no pattern of positive error terms being followed (in time) by other positive error terms, and there is no pattern of positive error terms being followed by negative error terms. That is, there is no pattern of higher-than-average y values being followed by other higher-than-average y values, and there is no pattern of higher-than-average y values being followed by lower-than-average y values.

It is important to point out that the regression assumptions very seldom, if ever, hold exactly in any practical regression problem. However, it has been found that regression results are not extremely sensitive to mild departures from these assumptions. In practice, only pronounced departures from these assumptions require attention. In optional Section 11.8 we show how to check the regression assumptions. Prior to doing this, we will suppose that the assumptions are valid in our examples.

In Section 11.2 we stated that, when we predict an individual value of the dependent variable, we predict the error term to be 0. To see why we do this, note that the regression assumptions state that, at any given value of the independent variable, the population of all error term values that can potentially occur is normally distributed with a mean equal to 0. Since we also assume that successive error terms (observed over time) are statistically independent, each error term has a 50 percent chance of being positive and a 50 percent chance of being negative. Therefore, it is reasonable to predict any particular error term value to be 0.

The mean square error and the standard error To present statistical inference formulas in later sections, we need to be able to compute point estimates of σ^2 and σ, the constant variance and standard deviation of the error term populations. The point estimate of σ^2 is called the **mean square error** and the point estimate of σ is called the **standard error.** In the following box, we show how to compute these estimates:

The Mean Square Error and the Standard Error

If the regression assumptions are satisfied and *SSE* is the sum of squared residuals:

1 The point estimate of σ^2 is the **mean square error**

$$s^2 = \frac{SSE}{n-2}$$

2 The point estimate of σ is the **standard error**

$$s = \sqrt{\frac{SSE}{n-2}}$$

In order to understand these point estimates, recall that σ^2 is the variance of the population of y values (for a given value of x) around the mean value $\mu_{y|x}$. Because $\hat{y}$ is the point estimate of this mean, it seems natural to use

$$SSE = \sum (y_i - \hat{y}_i)^2$$

to help construct a point estimate of σ^2. We divide *SSE* by $n - 2$ because it can be proven that doing so makes the resulting s^2 an unbiased point estimate of σ^2. Here we call $n - 2$ the **number of degrees of freedom** associated with *SSE*.

Example 11.6 The Fuel Consumption Case

Consider the fuel consumption situation, and recall that in Table 11.4 (page 462) we have calculated the sum of squared residuals to be $SSE = 2.568$. It follows, because we have observed $n = 8$ fuel consumptions, that the point estimate of σ^2 is the mean square error

$$s^2 = \frac{SSE}{n-2} = \frac{2.568}{8-2} = .428$$

This implies that the point estimate of σ is the standard error

$$s = \sqrt{s^2} = \sqrt{.428} = .6542$$

As another example, it can be verified that the standard error for the simple linear regression model describing the QHIC data is $s = 146.8970$.

To conclude this section, note that in optional Section 11.10 we present a shortcut formula for calculating *SSE*. The reader may study Section 11.10 now or at any later point.

Exercises for Section 11.3

CONCEPTS

11.24 What four assumptions do we make about the simple linear regression model?

11.25 What is estimated by the mean square error, and what is estimated by the standard error?

METHODS AND APPLICATIONS

11.26 THE STARTING SALARY CASE StartSal

When a least squares line is fit to the 7 observations in the starting salary data, we obtain $SSE = 1.438$. Calculate s^2 and s.

11.27 THE SERVICE TIME CASE SrvcTime

When a least squares line is fit to the 11 observations in the service time data, we obtain $SSE = 191.7017$. Calculate s^2 and s.

11.28 THE FRESH DETERGENT CASE Fresh

When a least squares line is fit to the 30 observations in the Fresh detergent data, we obtain $SSE = 2.806$. Calculate s^2 and s.

11.29 THE DIRECT LABOR COST CASE DirLab

When a least squares line is fit to the 12 observations in the labor cost data, we obtain $SSE = 746.7624$. Calculate s^2 and s.

11.30 THE REAL ESTATE SALES PRICE CASE RealEst

When a least squares line is fit to the 10 observations in the real estate sales price data, we obtain $SSE = 896.8$. Calculate s^2 and s.

11.31 Ten sales regions of equal sales potential for a company were randomly selected. The advertising expenditures (in units of \$10,000) in these 10 sales regions were purposely set during July of last year at, respectively, 5, 6, 7, 8, 9, 10, 11, 12, 13 and 14. The sales volumes (in units of \$10,000) were then recorded for the 10 sales regions and found to be, respectively, 89, 87, 98, 110, 103, 114, 116, 110, 126, and 130. Assuming that the simple linear regression model is appropriate, it can be shown that $b_0 = 66.2121$, $b_1 = 4.4303$, and $SSE = 222.8242$. Calculate s^2 and s. SalesVol

11.4 Testing the Significance of the Slope and y Intercept

Testing the significance of the slope A simple linear regression model is not likely to be useful unless there is a **significant relationship between y and x.** In order to judge the significance of the relationship between y and x, we test the null hypothesis

$$H_0: \beta_1 = 0$$

which says that there is no change in the mean value of y associated with an increase in x, versus the alternative hypothesis

$$H_a: \beta_1 \neq 0$$

which says that there is a (positive or negative) change in the mean value of y associated with an increase in x. It would be reasonable to conclude that x is significantly related to y if we can be quite certain that we should reject H_0 in favor of H_a.

In order to test these hypotheses, recall that we compute the least squares point estimate b_1 of the true slope β_1 by using a sample of n observed values of the dependent variable y. Different samples of n observed y values would yield different values of the least squares point estimate b_1. It can be shown that, if the regression assumptions hold, then the population of all possible values of b_1 is normally distributed with a mean of β_1 and with a standard deviation of

$$\sigma_{b_1} = \frac{\sigma}{\sqrt{SS_{xx}}}$$

The standard error s is the point estimate of σ, so it follows that a point estimate of σ_{b_1} is

$$s_{b_1} = \frac{s}{\sqrt{SS_{xx}}}$$

which is called the **standard error of the estimate b_1.** Furthermore, if the regression assumptions hold, then the population of all values of

$$\frac{b_1 - \beta_1}{s_{b_1}}$$

has a t distribution with $n - 2$ degrees of freedom. It follows that, if the null hypothesis H_0: $\beta_1 = 0$ is true, then the population of all possible values of the test statistic

$$t = \frac{b_1}{s_{b_1}}$$

has a t distribution with $n - 2$ degrees of freedom. Therefore, we can test the significance of the regression relationship as follows:

Testing the Significance of the Regression Relationship: Testing the Significance of the Slope

Define the test statistic

$$t = \frac{b_1}{s_{b_1}} \quad \text{where} \quad s_{b_1} = \frac{s}{\sqrt{SS_{xx}}}$$

and suppose that the regression assumptions hold. Then we can test H_0: $\beta_1 = 0$ versus a particular alternative hypothesis at significance level α (that is, by setting the probability of a Type I error equal to α) by using the appropriate rejection point rule, or, equivalently, the corresponding p-value.

Alternative Hypothesis	Rejection Point Condition: Reject H_0 if	p-Value (reject H_0 if p-value $< \alpha$)
H_a: $\beta_1 \neq 0$	$\lvert t \rvert > t_{\alpha/2}$	Twice the area under the t curve to the right of $\lvert t \rvert$
H_a: $\beta_1 > 0$	$t > t_\alpha$	The area under the t curve to the right of t
H_a: $\beta_1 < 0$	$t < -t_\alpha$	The area under the t curve to the left of t

Here $t_{\alpha/2}$, t_α, and all p-values are based on $n - 2$ degrees of freedom. **If we can reject H_0: $\beta_1 = 0$ at a given value of α, then we conclude that the slope (or, equivalently, the regression relationship) is significant at the α level.**

We usually use the two-sided alternative H_a: $\beta_1 \neq 0$ for this test of significance. However, sometimes a one-sided alternative is appropriate. For example, in the fuel consumption problem we can say that if the slope β_1 is not 0, then it must be negative. A negative β_1 would say that mean fuel consumption decreases as temperature x increases. Because of this, it would be appropriate to decide that x is significantly related to y if we can reject H_0: $\beta_1 = 0$ in favor of the one-sided alternative H_a: $\beta_1 < 0$. Although this test would be slightly more effective than the usual two-sided test, there is little practical difference between using the one-sided or two-sided alternative. Furthermore, computer packages (such as MINITAB and Excel) present results for testing a two-sided alternative hypothesis. For these reasons we will emphasize the two-sided test.

It should also be noted that

1. **If we can decide that the slope is significant at the .05 significance level,** then we have concluded that x is significantly related to y by using a test that allows only a .05 probability of concluding that x is significantly related to y when it is not. **This is usually regarded as strong evidence that the regression relationship is significant.**
2. **If we can decide that the slope is significant at the .01 significance level, this is usually regarded as very strong evidence that the regression relationship is significant.**
3. The smaller the significance level α at which H_0 can be rejected, the stronger is the evidence that the regression relationship is significant.

Example 11.7 The Fuel Consumption Case

C

Again consider the fuel consumption model

$$y = \beta_0 + \beta_1 x + \varepsilon$$

For this model $SS_{xx} = 1{,}404.355$, $b_1 = -.1279$, and $s = .6542$ [see Examples 11.4 (pages 461–462) and 11.6 (page 470)]. Therefore

$$s_{b_1} = \frac{s}{\sqrt{SS_{xx}}} = \frac{.6542}{\sqrt{1{,}404.355}} = .01746$$

and

$$t = \frac{b_1}{s_{b_1}} = \frac{-.1279}{.01746} = -7.33$$

FIGURE 11.11 MINITAB and Excel Output of a Simple Linear Regression Analysis of the Fuel Consumption Data

(a) The MINITAB Output

```
The regression equation is
FuelCons = 15.8 - 0.128 Temp

Predictor          Coef          SE Coef           T         P [7]
Constant        15.8379 [1]     0.8018 [3]     19.75 [5]   0.000
Temp           -0.12792 [2]    0.01746 [4]     -7.33 [6]   0.000

S = 0.654209 [8]    R-Sq = 89.9% [9]     R-Sq(adj) = 88.3%

Analysis of Variance
Source            DF          SS           MS           F          P
Regression         1     22.981 [10]   22.981     53.69 [13]   0.000 [14]
Residual Error     6      2.568 [11]    0.428
Total              7     25.549 [12]

Values of Predictors for New Obs    Predicted Values for New Observations
New Obs   Temp                      New Obs    Fit [15]  SE Fit [16]     95% CI [17]         95% PI [18]
      1   40.0                            1    10.721     0.241     (10.130, 11.312)   (9.015, 12.427)
```

(b) The Excel Output

Regression Statistics	
Multiple R	0.9484
R Square	0.8995 [9]
Adjusted R Square	0.8827
Standard Error	0.6542 [8]
Observations	8

ANOVA

	df	SS	MS	F	Significance F
Regression	1	22.9808 [10]	22.9808	53.6949 [13]	0.0003 [14]
Residual	6	2.5679 [11]	0.4280		
Total	7	25.5488 [12]			

	Coefficients	Standard Error	t Stat	P-value [7]	Lower 95%	Upper 95%
Intercept	15.8379 [1]	0.8018 [3]	19.7535 [5]	1.09E-06	13.8760	17.7997
TEMP	-0.1279 [2]	0.0175 [4]	-7.3277 [6]	0.0003	-0.1706 [19]	-0.0852 [19]

[1] b_0 = point estimate of the y-intercept [2] b_1 = point estimate of the slope [3] s_{b_0} = standard error of the estimate b_0 [4] s_{b_1} = standard error of the estimate b_1 [5] t for testing significance of the y-intercept [6] t for testing significance of the slope [7] p-values for t statistics [8] s = standard error [9] r^2 [10] Explained variation [11] SSE = Unexplained variation [12] Total variation [13] F(model) statistic [14] p-value for F(model) [15] $\hat{y}$ = point prediction when $x = 40$ [16] $s_{\hat{y}}$ = standard error of the estimate $\hat{y}$ [17] 95% confidence interval when $x = 40$ [18] 95% prediction interval when $x = 40$ [19] 95% confidence interval for the slope β_1

To test the significance of the slope we compare $|t|$ with $t_{\alpha/2}$ based on $n - 2 = 8 - 2 = 6$ degrees of freedom. Because

$$|t| = 7.33 > t_{.025} = 2.447$$

we can reject H_0: $\beta_1 = 0$ in favor of H_a: $\beta_1 \neq 0$ and conclude that the slope (regression relationship) is significant at the .05 level.

The p-value for testing H_0 versus H_a is twice the area to the right of $|t| = 7.33$ under the curve of the t distribution having $n - 2 = 6$ degrees of freedom. Since this p-value can be shown to be .0003, we can reject H_0 in favor of H_a at level of significance .05, .01, or .001. We therefore have extremely strong evidence that x is significantly related to y and that the regression relationship is significant.

Figure 11.11 presents the MINITAB and Excel outputs of a simple linear regression analysis of the fuel consumption data. Note that b_0 (labeled as [1] on the outputs), b_1 (labeled [2]), s (labeled [8]), s_{b_1} (labeled [4]), and t (labeled [6]) are given on each of these outputs. Also note that each output gives the p-value related to $t = -7.33$ (labeled [7]). Excel tells us that this p-value equals 0.0003, while MINITAB has rounded this p-value to 0.000 (which means less than .001). Other quantities on the MINITAB and Excel outputs will be discussed later.

In addition to testing the significance of the slope, it is often useful to calculate a confidence interval for β_1. We show how this is done in the following box:

A Confidence Interval for the Slope

If the regression assumptions hold, a $100(1 - \alpha)$ percent confidence interval for the true slope β_1 is $[b_1 \pm t_{\alpha/2} s_{b_1}]$. Here $t_{\alpha/2}$ is based on $n - 2$ degrees of freedom.

Example 11.8 The Fuel Consumption Case

The MINITAB output in Figure 11.11(a) tells us that $b_1 = -.12792$ and $s_{b_1} = .01746$. Thus, for instance, because $t_{.025}$ based on $n - 2 = 8 - 2 = 6$ degrees of freedom equals 2.447, a 95 percent confidence interval for β_1 is

$$[b_1 \pm t_{.025} s_{b_1}] = [-.12792 \pm 2.447(.01746)]$$
$$= [-.1706, -.0852]$$

This interval says we are 95 percent confident that, if average hourly temperature increases by one degree, then mean weekly fuel consumption will decrease (because both the lower bound and the upper bound of the interval are negative) by at least .0852 MMcf of natural gas and by at most .1706 MMcf of natural gas. Also, because the 95 percent confidence interval for β_1 does not contain 0, we can reject H_0: $\beta_1 = 0$ in favor of H_a: $\beta_1 \neq 0$ at level of significance .05. Note that the 95 percent confidence interval for β_1 is given on the Excel output but not on the MINITAB output (see Figure 11.11).

Example 11.9 The QHIC Case

Figure 11.12 presents the MegaStat output of a simple linear regression analysis of the QHIC data. We summarize some important quantities from the output as follows (we discuss the other quantities later): $b_0 = -348.3921$, $b_1 = 7.2583$, $s = 146.897$, $s_{b_1} = .4156$, and $t = b_1/s_{b_1} = 17.466$. Since the p-value related to $t = 17.466$ is less than .001 (see the MegaStat output), we can reject H_0: $\beta_1 = 0$ in favor of H_a: $\beta_1 \neq 0$ at the .001 level of significance. It follows that we have extremely strong evidence that the regression relationship is significant. The MegaStat output also tells us that a 95 percent confidence interval for the true slope β_1 is [6.4170, 8.0995]. This interval says we are 95 percent confident that mean yearly upkeep expenditure increases by between \$6.42 and \$8.10 for each additional \$1,000 increase in home value.

Testing the significance of the y-intercept We can also test the significance of the y-intercept β_0. We do this by testing the null hypothesis H_0: $\beta_0 = 0$ versus the alternative hypothesis H_a: $\beta_0 \neq 0$. **If we can reject H_0 in favor of H_a by setting the probability of a Type I error equal to α, we conclude that the intercept β_0 is significant at the α level.** To carry out the hypothesis test, we use the test statistic

$$t = \frac{b_0}{s_{b_0}} \quad \text{where} \quad s_{b_0} = s\sqrt{\frac{1}{n} + \frac{\bar{x}^2}{SS_{xx}}}$$

Here the rejection point and p-value conditions for rejecting H_0 are the same as those given previously for testing the significance of the slope, except that t is calculated as b_0/s_{b_0}. For example, if we consider the fuel consumption problem and the MINITAB output in Figure 11.11, we see that $b_0 = 15.8379$, $s_{b_0} = .8018$, $t = 19.75$, and p-value $= .000$. Because $t = 19.75 > t_{.025} = 2.447$ and p-value $< .05$, we can reject H_0: $\beta_0 = 0$ in favor of H_a: $\beta_0 \neq 0$ at the .05 level of significance. In fact, since the p-value $< .001$, we can also reject H_0 at the .001 level of significance. This

FIGURE 11.12 MegaStat Output of a Simple Linear Regression Analysis of the QHIC Data

Regression Analysis		
r^2 0.889 [9]	n 40	
r 0.943	k 1	
Std. Error 146.897 [8]	Dep. Var. Upkeep	

ANOVA table

Source	SS	df	MS	F [13]	p-value [14]
Regression	6,582,759.6972 [10]	1	6,582,759.6972	305.06	9.49E-20
Residual	819,995.5427 [11]	38	21,578.8301		
Total	7,402,755.2399 [12]	39			

Regression output

variables	coefficients	std. error	t (df=38)	p-value [7]	95% lower	95% upper
					confidence interval	
Intercept	-348.3921 [1]	76.1410 [3]	-4.576 [5]	4.95E-05	-502.5314	-194.2527
Value	7.2583 [2]	0.4156 [4]	17.466 [6]	9.49E-20	6.4170 [19]	8.0995 [19]

Predicted values for: Upkeep

Value	Predicted [15]	95% Confidence Interval [16] lower	upper	95% Prediction Interval [17] lower	upper	Leverage [18]
220	1,248.42597	1,187.78944	1,309.06251	944.92879	1,551.92315	0.042

[1] b_0 = point estimate of the y-intercept [2] b_1 = point estimate of the slope [3] s_{b_0} = standard error of the estimate b_0 [4] s_{b_1} = standard error of the estimate b_1 [5] t for testing significance of the y-intercept [6] t for testing significance of the slope [7] p-values for t statistics [8] s = standard error [9] r^2 [10] Explained variation [11] SSE = Unexplained variation [12] Total variation [13] F(model) statistic [14] p-value for F(model) [15] $\hat{y}$ = point prediction when x = 220 [16] 95% confidence interval when x = 220 [17] 95% prediction interval when x = 220 [18] distance value [19] 95% confidence interval for the slope β_1

provides extremely strong evidence that the y-intercept β_0 does not equal 0 and thus is significant. Therefore, we should include β_0 in the fuel consumption model.

In general, if we fail to conclude that the intercept is significant at a level of significance of .05, it might be reasonable to drop the y-intercept from the model. However, remember that β_0 equals the mean value of y when x equals 0. If, logically speaking, the mean value of y would not equal 0 when x equals 0 (for example, in the fuel consumption problem, mean fuel consumption would not equal 0 when the average hourly temperature is 0), it is common practice to include the y-intercept whether or not H_0: $\beta_0 = 0$ is rejected. In fact, experience suggests that it is definitely safest, when in doubt, to include the intercept β_0.

Exercises for Section 11.4

CONCEPTS

11.32 What do we conclude if we can reject H_0: $\beta_1 = 0$ in favor of H_a: $\beta_1 \neq 0$ by setting
a α equal to .05? **b** α equal to .01?

11.33 Give an example of a practical application of the confidence interval for β_1.

METHODS AND APPLICATIONS

In Exercises 11.34 through 11.38, we refer to MINITAB, MegaStat, and Excel output of simple linear regression analyses of the data sets related to the five case studies introduced in the exercises for Section 11.1. Using the appropriate output for each case study,

a Find the least squares point estimates b_0 and b_1 of β_0 and β_1 on the output and report their values.
b Find SSE and s on the computer output and report their values.
c Find s_{b_1} and the t statistic for testing the significance of the slope on the output and report their values. Show how t has been calculated by using b_1 and s_{b_1} from the computer output.
d Using the t statistic and appropriate rejection point, test H_0: $\beta_1 = 0$ versus H_a: $\beta_1 \neq 0$ by setting α equal to .05. Is the slope (regression relationship) significant at the .05 level?
e Using the t statistic and appropriate rejection point, test H_0: $\beta_1 = 0$ versus H_a: $\beta_1 \neq 0$ by setting α equal to .01. Is the slope (regression relationship) significant at the .01 level?
f Find the p-value for testing H_0: $\beta_1 = 0$ versus H_a: $\beta_1 \neq 0$ on the output and report its value. Using the p-value, determine whether we can reject H_0 by setting α equal to .10, .05, .01, and .001. How much evidence is there that the slope (regression relationship) is significant?
g Calculate the 95 percent confidence interval for β_1 using numbers on the output. Interpret the interval.

h Calculate the 99 percent confidence interval for β_1 using numbers on the output.

i Find s_{b_0} and the t statistic for testing the significance of the y intercept on the output and report their values. Show how t has been calculated by using b_0 and s_{b_0} from the computer output.

j Find the p-value for testing H_0: $\beta_0 = 0$ versus H_a: $\beta_0 \neq 0$. Using the p-value, determine whether we can reject H_0 by setting α equal to .10, .05, .01, and .001. What do you conclude?

k Using the appropriate data set and s from the computer output, hand calculate SS_{xx}, s_{b_0}, and s_{b_1}.

11.34 THE STARTING SALARY CASE StartSal

The MINITAB output of a simple linear regression analysis of the data set for this case (see Exercise 11.5 on page 456) is given in Figure 11.13. Recall that a labeled MINITAB regression output is on page 473.

11.35 THE SERVICE TIME CASE SrvcTime

The MegaStat output of a simple linear regression analysis of the data set for this case (see Exercise 11.7 on page 456) is given in Figure 11.14. Recall that a labeled MegaStat regression output is on page 475.

FIGURE 11.13 MINITAB Output of a Simple Linear Regression Analysis of the Starting Salary Data

```
The regression equation is
StartSal = 14.8 + 5.71 GPA

Predictor     Coef   SE Coef      T      P
Constant    14.816     1.235  12.00  0.000
GPA         5.7066    0.3953  14.44  0.000

S = 0.536321   R-Sq = 97.7%   R-Sq(adj) = 97.2%

Analysis of Variance
Source          DF      SS      MS       F      P
Regression       1  59.942  59.942  208.39  0.000
Residual Error   5   1.438   0.288
Total            6  61.380

Values of Predictors for New Obs    Predicted Values for New Observations
New Obs   GPA                       New Obs     Fit  SE Fit         95% CI             95% PI
      1  3.25                             1  33.362   0.213  (32.813, 33.911)  (31.878, 34.846)
```

FIGURE 11.14 MegaStat Output of a Simple Linear Regression Analysis of the Service Time Data

Regression Analysis

r^2 0.990 n 11
r 0.995 k 1
Std. Error 4.615 Dep. Var. Minutes (y)

ANOVA table

Source	SS	df	MS	F	p-value
Regression	19,918.8438	1	19,918.8438	935.15	2.09E-10
Residual	191.7017	9	21.3002		
Total	20,110.5455	10			

Regression output

variables	coefficients	std. error	t (df=9)	p-value	confidence interval 95% lower	95% upper
Intercept	11.4641	3.4390	3.334	0.0087	3.6845	19.2437
Copiers (x)	24.6022	0.8045	30.580	2.09E-10	22.7823	26.4221

Predicted values for: Minutes (y)

Copiers (x)	Predicted	95% Confidence Intervals lower	upper	95% Prediction Intervals lower	upper	Leverage
1	36.066	29.907	42.226	23.944	48.188	0.348
2	60.669	55.980	65.357	49.224	72.113	0.202
3	85.271	81.715	88.827	74.241	96.300	0.116
4	109.873	106.721	113.025	98.967	120.779	0.091
5	134.475	130.753	138.197	123.391	145.559	0.127
6	159.077	154.139	164.016	147.528	170.627	0.224
7	183.680	177.233	190.126	171.410	195.950	0.381

FIGURE 11.15 MINITAB Output of a Simple Linear Regression Analysis of the Fresh Detergent Demand Data

```
The regression equation is
Demand = 7.81 + 2.67 PriceDif

Predictor      Coef   SE Coef      T      P
Constant    7.81409   0.07988  97.82  0.000
PriceDif     2.6652    0.2585  10.31  0.000

S = 0.316561    R-Sq = 79.2%    R-Sq(adj) = 78.4%

Analysis of Variance
Source          DF      SS      MS       F      P
Regression       1  10.653  10.653  106.30  0.000
Residual Error  28   2.806   0.100
Total           29  13.459

Values of Predictors for New Obs    Predicted Values for New Observations
New Obs  PriceDif                   New Obs     Fit  SE Fit        95% CI              95% PI
      1     0.100                         1  8.0806  0.0648  (7.9479, 8.2133)  (7.4187, 8.7425)
      2     0.250                         2  8.4804  0.0586  (8.3604, 8.6004)  (7.8209, 9.1398)
```

FIGURE 11.16 Excel and MegaStat Output of a Simple Linear Regression Analysis of the Direct Labor Cost Data

(a) The Excel Output

Regression Statistics	
Multiple R	0.9996
R Square	0.9993
Adjusted R Square	0.9992
Standard Error	8.6415
Observations	12

ANOVA	df	SS	MS	F	Significance F
Regression	1	1024592.9043	1024592.9043	13720.4677	5.04E-17
Residual	10	746.7624	74.6762		
Total	11	1025339.6667			

	Coefficients	Standard Error	t Stat	P-value	Lower 95%	Upper 95%
Intercept	18.4875	4.6766	3.9532	0.0027	8.0674	28.9076
BatchSize (x)	10.1463	0.0866	117.1344	5.04E-17	9.9533	10.3393

(b) Prediction Using MegaStat

Predicted values for: LaborCost (y)

		95% Confidence Interval		95% Prediction Interval		
BatchSize (x)	Predicted	lower	upper	lower	upper	Leverage
60	627.263	621.054	633.472	607.032	647.494	0.104

11.36 THE FRESH DETERGENT CASE Fresh

The MINITAB output of a simple linear regression analysis of the data set for this case (see Exercise 11.9 on page 457) is given in Figure 11.15. Recall that a labeled MINITAB regression output is on page 473.

11.37 THE DIRECT LABOR COST CASE DirLab

The Excel and MegaStat output of a simple linear regression analysis of the data set for this case (see Exercise 11.11 on page 458) is given in Figure 11.16. Recall that labeled Excel and MegaStat regression outputs are on pages 473 and 475.

11.38 THE REAL ESTATE SALES PRICE CASE RealEst

The MINITAB output of a simple linear regression analysis of the data set for this case (see Exercise 11.13 on page 458) is given in Figure 11.17 on page 478. Recall that a labeled MINITAB regression output is on page 473.

11.39 Find and interpret a 95 percent confidence interval for the slope β_1 of the simple linear regression model describing the sales volume data in Exercise 11.31 (page 471). SalesVol

FIGURE 11.17 MINITAB Output of a Simple Linear Regression Analysis of the Real Estate Sales Price Data

```
The regression equation is
SPrice = 48.0 + 5.70 HomeSize

Predictor    Coef  SE Coef     T      P
Constant    48.02    14.41  3.33  0.010
HomeSize   5.7003   0.7457  7.64  0.000

S = 10.5880     R-Sq = 88.0%     R-Sq(adj) = 86.5%

Analysis of Variance
Source          DF      SS      MS      F      P
Regression       1  6550.7  6550.7  58.43  0.000
Residual Error   8   896.8   112.1
Total            9  7447.5

Values of Predictors for New Obs    Predicted Values for New Observations
New Obs  HomeSize                   New Obs     Fit  SE Fit          95% CI              95% PI
      1      20.0                         1  162.03    3.47  (154.04, 170.02)  (136.34, 187.72)
```

FIGURE 11.18 Excel Output of a Simple Linear Regression Analysis of the Fast-Food Restaurant Rating Data

Regression Statistics	
Multiple R	0.9873
R Square	0.9747
Adjusted R Square	0.9684
Standard Error	0.1833
Observations	6

ANOVA	df	SS	MS	F	Significance F
Regression	1	5.1817	5.1817	154.2792	0.0002
Residual	4	0.1343	0.0336		
Total	5	5.3160			

	Coefficients	Standard Error	t Stat	P-value	Lower 95%	Upper 95%
Intercept	-0.1602	0.3029	-0.5289	0.6248	-1.0011	0.6807
MeanTaste (x)	1.2731	0.1025	12.4209	0.0002	0.9885	1.5577

11.40 THE FAST-FOOD RESTAURANT RATING CASE FastFood

In the early 1990s researchers at The Ohio State University studied consumer ratings of six fast-food restaurants: Borden Burger, Hardee's, Burger King, McDonald's, Wendy's, and White Castle. Each of 406 randomly selected individuals gave each restaurant a rating of 1, 2, 3, 4, 5, or 6 on the basis of taste, and then ranked the restaurants from 1 through 6 on the basis of overall preference. In each case, 1 is the best rating and 6 the worst. The mean ratings given by the 406 individuals are given in the following table:

Restaurant	Mean Taste	Mean Preference
Borden Burger	3.5659	4.2552
Hardee's	3.329	4.0911
Burger King	2.4231	3.0052
McDonald's	2.0895	2.2429
Wendy's	1.9661	2.5351
White Castle	3.8061	4.7812

Figure 11.18 gives the Excel output of a simple linear regression analysis of this data. Here, mean preference is the dependent variable and mean taste is the independent variable. Recall that a labeled Excel regression output is given on page 473.

a Find the least squares point estimates b_0 and b_1 of β_0 and β_1 on the computer output and report their values.

b Find SSE, s, and s_{b_1} on the computer output and report their values.

c Find the t statistic and related p-value for testing the significance of the slope (regression relationship) on the computer output and report their values.

d Use the p-value to test the significance of the regression relationship with $\alpha = .05$, $\alpha = .01$, and $\alpha = .001$. Is the regression significant at these levels?

e Find the 95 percent confidence interval for β_1 on the output. Report and interpret the interval.

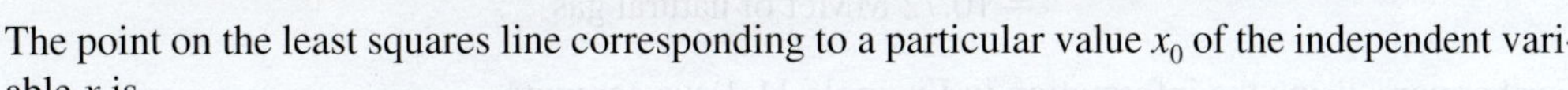

11.5 Confidence and Prediction Intervals

CHAPTER 15

The point on the least squares line corresponding to a particular value x_0 of the independent variable x is

$$\hat{y} = b_0 + b_1 x_0$$

Unless we are very lucky, $\hat{y}$ will not exactly equal either the mean value of y when x equals x_0 or a particular individual value of y when x equals x_0. Therefore, we need to place bounds on how far $\hat{y}$ might be from these values. We can do this by calculating a **confidence interval for the mean value of *y*** and a **prediction interval for an individual value of *y*.**

Both of these intervals employ a quantity called the **distance value.** For simple linear regression this quantity is calculated as follows:

The Distance Value for Simple Linear Regression

In simple linear regression the **distance value** for a particular value x_0 of x is

$$\text{Distance value} = \frac{1}{n} + \frac{(x_0 - \bar{x})^2}{SS_{xx}}$$

This quantity is given its name because it is a measure of the distance between the value x_0 of x and $\bar{x}$, the average of the previously observed values of x. Notice from the above formula that the farther x_0 is from $\bar{x}$, which can be regarded as the center of the experimental region, the larger is the distance value. The significance of this fact will become apparent shortly.

We now consider establishing a confidence interval for the mean value of y when x equals a particular value x_0 (for later reference, we call this mean value $\mu_{y|x_0}$). Because each possible sample of n values of the dependent variable gives values of b_0 and b_1 that differ from the values given by other samples, different samples give different values of the point estimate

$$\hat{y} = b_0 + b_1 x_0$$

It can be shown that, if the regression assumptions hold, then the population of all possible values of $\hat{y}$ is normally distributed with mean $\mu_{y|x_0}$ and standard deviation

$$\sigma_{\hat{y}} = \sigma\sqrt{\text{Distance value}}$$

The point estimate of $\sigma_{\hat{y}}$ is

$$s_{\hat{y}} = s\sqrt{\text{Distance value}}$$

which is called the **standard error of the estimate $\hat{y}$.** Using this standard error, we form a confidence interval as follows:

A Confidence Interval for a Mean Value of y

If the regression assumptions hold, a **100(1 − α) percent confidence interval for the mean value of *y*** when the value of the independent variable is x_0 is

$$[\hat{y} \pm t_{\alpha/2}\, s\sqrt{\text{Distance value}}]$$

Here $t_{\alpha/2}$ is based on $n - 2$ degrees of freedom.

Example 11.10 The Fuel Consumption Case

In the fuel consumption problem, suppose we wish to compute a 95 percent confidence interval for the mean value of weekly fuel consumption when the average hourly temperature is $x_0 = 40°F$. From Example 11.4 (pages 463 and 464), the point estimate of this mean is

$$\begin{aligned}\hat{y} &= b_0 + b_1x_0 \\ &= 15.84 - .1279(40) \\ &= 10.72 \text{ MMcf of natural gas}\end{aligned}$$

Furthermore, using the information in Example 11.4, we compute

$$\begin{aligned}\text{Distance value} &= \frac{1}{n} + \frac{(x_0 - \bar{x})^2}{SS_{xx}} \\ &= \frac{1}{8} + \frac{(40 - 43.98)^2}{1{,}404.355} \\ &= .1363\end{aligned}$$

Since $s = .6542$ (see Example 11.6 on page 470) and since $t_{\alpha/2} = t_{.025}$ based on $n - 2 = 8 - 2 = 6$ degrees of freedom equals 2.447, it follows that the desired 95 percent confidence interval is

$$\begin{aligned}&[\hat{y} \pm t_{\alpha/2}s\sqrt{\text{Distance value}}] \\ &= [10.72 \pm 2.447(.6542)\sqrt{.1363}] \\ &= [10.72 \pm .59] \\ &= [10.13, 11.31]\end{aligned}$$

This interval says we are 95 percent confident that the mean (or average) of all the weekly fuel consumptions that would be observed in all weeks having an average hourly temperature of 40°F is between 10.13 MMcf of natural gas and 11.31 MMcf of natural gas.

We develop an interval for an individual value of y when x equals a particular value x_0 by considering the **prediction error $y - \hat{y}$**. After observing each possible sample and calculating the point prediction based on that sample, we could observe any one of an infinite number of different individual values of y (because of different possible error terms). Therefore, there are an infinite number of different prediction errors that could be observed. If the regression assumptions hold, it can be shown that the population of all possible prediction errors is normally distributed with mean 0 and standard deviation

$$\sigma_{(y-\hat{y})} = \sigma\sqrt{1 + \text{Distance value}}$$

The point estimate of $\sigma_{(y-\hat{y})}$ is

$$s_{(y-\hat{y})} = s\sqrt{1 + \text{Distance value}}$$

which is called the **standard error of the prediction error.** Using this quantity we obtain a **prediction interval** as follows:

A Prediction Interval for an Individual Value of y

If the regression assumptions hold, a **100(1 − α) percent prediction interval for an individual value of y** when the value of the independent variable is x_0 is

$$[\hat{y} \pm t_{\alpha/2}s\sqrt{1 + \text{Distance value}}]$$

Here $t_{\alpha/2}$ is based on $n - 2$ degrees of freedom.

Example 11.11 The Fuel Consumption Case

C

In the fuel consumption problem, suppose we wish to compute a 95 percent prediction interval for an individual weekly fuel consumption when average hourly temperature equals 40°F. Recalling that $\hat{y} = 10.72$ when $x_0 = 40$, the desired interval is

$$\begin{aligned}
&[\hat{y} \pm t_{\alpha/2} s\sqrt{1 + \text{Distance value}}] \\
&= [10.72 \pm 2.447(.6542)\sqrt{1.1363}] \\
&= [10.72 \pm 1.71] \\
&= [9.01, 12.43]
\end{aligned}$$

Here $t_{\alpha/2} = t_{.025}$ is again based on $n - 2 = 6$ degrees of freedom. This interval says we are 95 percent confident that the individual fuel consumption in a future single week having an average hourly temperature of 40°F will be between 9.01 MMcf of natural gas and 12.43 MMcf of natural gas. Because the weather forecasting service has predicted that the average hourly temperature in the next week will be 40°F, we can use the prediction interval to evaluate how well our regression model is likely to predict next week's fuel consumption and to evaluate whether the natural gas company will be assessed a transmission fine. First, recall that the point prediction $\hat{y} = 10.72$ given by our model is the natural gas company's transmission nomination for next week. Also, note that the half-length of the 95 percent prediction interval given by our model is 1.71, which is $(1.71/10.72)100\% = 15.91\%$ of the transmission nomination. It follows that we are 95 percent confident that the actual amount of natural gas that will be used by the city next week will differ from the natural gas company's transmission nomination by no more than 15.91 percent. That is, we are 95 percent confident that the natural gas company's percentage nomination error will be less than or equal to 15.91 percent. Although this does not imply that the natural gas company is likely to make a terribly inaccurate nomination, we are not confident that the company's percentage nomination error will be within the 10 percent allowance granted by the pipeline transmission system. Therefore, the natural gas company may be assessed a transmission fine. In Chapter 12 we use a *multiple regression model* to substantially reduce the natural gas company's percentage nomination errors. BI

Below we repeat the bottom of the MINITAB output in Figure 11.11(a). This output gives the point estimate and prediction $\hat{y} = 10.72$, the 95 percent confidence interval for the mean value of y when x equals 40, and the 95 percent prediction interval for an individual value of y when x equals 40.

```
Predicted Values for New Observations
New Obs     Fit    SE Fit        95% CI              95% PI
      1  10.721     0.241  (10.130, 11.312)  (9.015, 12.427)
```

Although the MINITAB output does not directly give the distance value, it does give $s_{\hat{y}} = s\sqrt{\text{Distance value}}$ under the heading "SE Fit". A little algebra shows that this implies that the distance value equals $(s_{\hat{y}}/s)^2$. Specifically, because $s_{\hat{y}} = .241$ and $s = .6542$ [see the MINITAB output in Figure 11.11(a) on page 473], it follows that the distance value equals $(.241/.6542)^2 = .1357$. This distance value is (within rounding) equal to the distance value that we hand calculated in Example 11.10.

Figure 11.19 illustrates and compares the 95 percent confidence interval for the mean value of y when x equals 40 and the 95 percent prediction interval for an individual value of y when x equals 40. We see that both intervals are centered at $\hat{y} = 10.72$. However, the prediction interval is longer than the confidence interval. This is because the formula for the prediction interval has an "extra 1 under the radical," which accounts for the added uncertainty introduced by our not knowing the value of the error term (which we nevertheless predict to be 0, while it probably will not equal 0).

To conclude this example, note that Figure 11.20 illustrates the MINITAB output of the 95 percent confidence and prediction intervals corresponding to all values of x in the experimental region.

FIGURE 11.19 A Comparison of a Confidence Interval for the Mean Value of *y* When *x* Equals 40 and a Prediction Interval for an Individual Value of *y* When *x* Equals 40

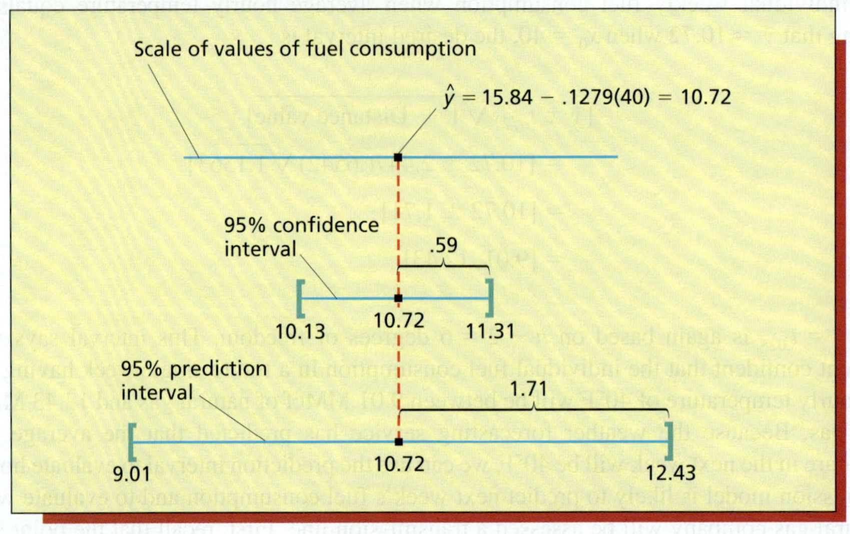

FIGURE 11.20 MINITAB Output of 95% Confidence and Prediction Intervals for the Fuel Consumption Case

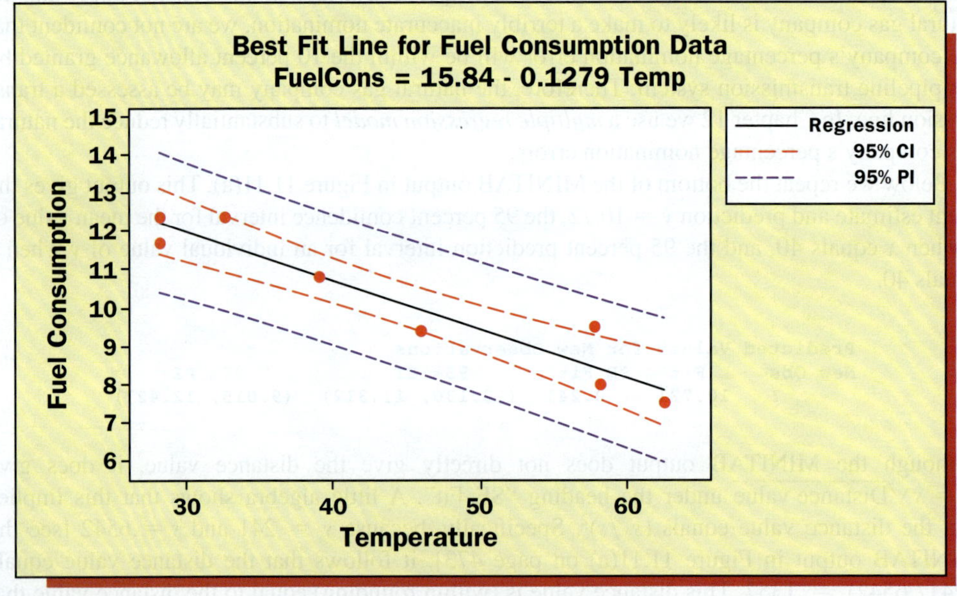

Here $\bar{x} = 43.98$ can be regarded as the center of the experimental region. Notice that the farther x is from $\bar{x} = 43.98$, the larger is the distance value and, therefore, the longer are the 95 percent confidence and prediction intervals. These longer intervals are undesirable because they give us less information about mean and individual values of y.

In general, the prediction interval is useful if, as in the fuel consumption problem, it is important to predict an individual value of the dependent variable. A confidence interval is useful if it is important to estimate the mean value. Although it is not important to estimate a mean value in the fuel consumption problem, it is important to estimate a mean value in other situations. To understand this, recall that the mean value is the average of all the values of the dependent variable that could potentially be observed when the independent variable equals a particular value. Therefore, it might be important to estimate the mean value if we will observe and are affected by a very large number of values of the dependent variable when the independent variable equals a particular value. We illustrate this in the following example.

Example 11.12 The QHIC Case

C

Consider a home worth \$220,000. We have seen that the predicted yearly upkeep expenditure for such a home is

$$\begin{aligned}\hat{y} &= b_0 + b_1x_0 \\ &= -348.3921 + 7.2583(220) \\ &= 1{,}248.43 \text{ (that is, \$1,248.43)}\end{aligned}$$

This predicted value is given at the bottom of the MegaStat output in Figure 11.12, which we repeat here:

Predicted values for: Upkeep

		95% Confidence Interval		95% Prediction Interval		
Value	**Predicted**	**lower**	**upper**	**lower**	**upper**	**Leverage**
220	1,248.42597	1,187.78944	1,309.06251	944.92879	1,551.92315	0.042

In addition to giving $\hat{y} = 1{,}248.43$, the MegaStat output also tells us that the distance value, which is given under the heading "Leverage" on the output, equals .042. Therefore, since s equals 146.897 (see Figure 11.12 on page 475), it follows that a 95 percent prediction interval for the yearly upkeep expenditure of an individual home worth \$220,000 is calculated as follows:

$$\begin{aligned}&[\hat{y} \pm t_{.025}s\sqrt{1 + \text{Distance value}}] \\ &= [1{,}248.43 \pm 2.024(146.897)\sqrt{1.042}] \\ &= [944.93, 1551.93]\end{aligned}$$

Here $t_{.025}$ is based on $n - 2 = 40 - 2 = 38$ degrees of freedom. Note that this interval is given on the MegaStat output.

Because there are many homes worth roughly \$220,000 in the metropolitan area, QHIC is more interested in the mean upkeep expenditure for all such homes than in the individual upkeep expenditure for one such home. The MegaStat output tells us that a 95 percent confidence interval for this mean upkeep expenditure is [1187.79, 1309.06]. This interval says that QHIC is 95 percent confident that the mean upkeep expenditure for all homes worth \$220,000 is at least \$1,187.79 and is no more than \$1,309.06.

Exercises for Section 11.5

CONCEPTS

11.41 What does the distance value measure?

11.42 What is the difference between a confidence interval and a prediction interval?

11.43 Discuss how the distance value affects the length of a confidence interval and a prediction interval.

METHODS AND APPLICATIONS

11.44 THE STARTING SALARY CASE StartSal

The following partial MINITAB regression output for the starting salary data relates to predicting the starting salary of a marketing graduate having a grade point average of 3.25.

```
Predicted Values for New Observations
New Obs      Fit    SE Fit          95% CI                95% PI
      1   33.362     0.213   (32.813, 33.911)   (31.878, 34.846)
```

a Report (as shown on the computer output) a point estimate of and a 95 percent confidence interval for the mean starting salary of all marketing graduates having a grade point average of 3.25.

b Report (as shown on the computer output) a point prediction of and a 95 percent prediction interval for the starting salary of an individual marketing graduate having a grade point average of 3.25.

c Remembering that $s = .536321$ and that the distance value equals $(s_{\hat{y}}/s)^2$, use $s_{\hat{y}}$ from the computer output to hand calculate the distance value when $x = 3.25$.

d Remembering that for the starting salary data $n = 7$, $b_0 = 14.816$, and $b_1 = 5.7066$, hand calculate (within rounding) the confidence interval of part (a) and the prediction interval of part (b).

11.45 THE SERVICE TIME CASE SrvcTime

The following partial MegaStat regression output for the service time data relates to predicting service times for 1, 2, 3, 4, 5, 6, and 7 copiers.

Predicted values for: Minutes (y)

		95% Confidence Intervals		95% Prediction Intervals		
Copiers (x)	Predicted	lower	upper	lower	upper	Leverage
1	36.066	29.907	42.226	23.944	48.188	0.348
2	60.669	55.980	65.357	49.224	72.113	0.202
3	85.271	81.715	88.827	74.241	96.300	0.116
4	109.873	106.721	113.025	98.967	120.779	0.091
5	134.475	130.753	138.197	123.391	145.559	0.127
6	159.077	154.139	164.016	147.528	170.627	0.224
7	183.680	177.233	190.126	171.410	195.950	0.381

a Report (as shown on the computer output) a point estimate of and a 95 percent confidence interval for the mean time to service four copiers.

b Report (as shown on the computer output) a point prediction of and a 95 percent prediction interval for the time to service four copiers on a single call.

c For this case: $n = 11$, $b_0 = 11.4641$, $b_1 = 24.6022$, and $s = 4.615$. Using this information and a distance value from the MegaStat output, hand calculate (within rounding) the confidence interval of part (a) and the prediction interval of part (b).

d If we examine the service time data, we see that there was at least one call on which Accu-Copiers serviced each of 1, 2, 3, 4, 5, 6, and 7 copiers. The 95 percent confidence intervals for the mean service times on these calls might be used to schedule future service calls. To understand this, note that a person making service calls will (in, say, a year or more) make a very large number of service calls. Some of the person's individual service times will be below, and some will be above, the corresponding mean service times. However, since the very large number of individual service times will average out to the mean service times, it seems fair to both the efficiency of the company and to the person making service calls to schedule service calls by using estimates of the mean service times. Therefore, suppose we wish to schedule a call to service five copiers. Examining the MegaStat output, we see that a 95 percent confidence interval for the mean time to service five copiers is [130.753, 138.197]. Since the mean time might be 138.197 minutes, it would seem fair to allow 138 minutes to make the service call. Now suppose we wish to schedule a call to service four copiers. Determine how many minutes to allow for the service call.

11.46 THE FRESH DETERGENT CASE Fresh

The following partial MINITAB regression output for the Fresh detergent data relates to predicting demand for future sales periods in which the price difference will be .10 (see New Obs 1) and .25 (see New Obs2).

```
Predicted Values for New Observations
New Obs     Fit   SE Fit          95% CI               95% PI
      1  8.0806   0.0648  (7.9479, 8.2133)   (7.4187, 8.7425)
      2  8.4804   0.0586  (8.3604, 8.6004)   (7.8209, 9.1398)
```

a Report (as shown on the computer output) a point estimate of and a 95 percent confidence interval for the mean demand for Fresh in all sales periods when the price difference is .10.

b Report (as shown on the computer output) a point prediction of and a 95 percent prediction interval for the actual demand for Fresh in an individual sales period when the price difference is .10.

c Remembering that $s = .316561$ and that the distance value equals $(s_{\hat{y}}/s)^2$, use $s_{\hat{y}}$ from the computer output to hand calculate the distance value when $x = .10$.

d For this case: $n = 30$, $b_0 = 7.81409$, $b_1 = 2.6652$, and $s = .316561$. Using this information, and your result from part (c), find 99 percent confidence and prediction intervals for mean and individual demands when $x = .10$.

e Repeat parts (a), (b), (c), and (d) when $x = .25$.

11.47 THE DIRECT LABOR COST CASE DirLab

The following partial MegaStat regression output for the direct labor cost data relates to predicting direct labor cost when the batch size is 60.

Predicted values for: LaborCost (y)

		95% Confidence Interval		95% Prediction Interval		
BatchSize (x)	**Predicted**	**lower**	**upper**	**lower**	**upper**	**Leverage**
60	627.263	621.054	633.472	607.032	647.494	0.104

a Report (as shown on the MegaStat output) a point estimate of and a 95 percent confidence interval for the mean direct labor cost of all batches of size 60.

b Report (as shown on the MegaStat output) a point prediction of and a 95 percent prediction interval for the actual direct labor cost of an individual batch of size 60.

c For this case: $n = 12$, $b_0 = 18.4875$, $b_1 = 10.1463$, and $s = 8.6415$. Use this information and the distance value from the MegaStat output to compute 99 percent confidence and prediction intervals for the mean and individual labor costs when $x = 60$.

11.48 THE REAL ESTATE SALES PRICE CASE RealEst

The following partial MINITAB regression output for the real estate sales price data relates to predicting the sales price of a home having 2,000 square feet.

```
Predicted Values for New Observations
New Obs    Fit  SE Fit       95% CI              95% PI
      1 162.03    3.47  (154.04, 170.02)   (136.34, 187.72)
```

a Report (as shown on the MINITAB output) a point estimate of and a 95 percent confidence interval for the mean sales price of all houses having 2,000 square feet.

b Report (as shown on the MINITAB output) a point prediction of and a 95 percent prediction interval for the sales price of an individual house having 2,000 square feet.

c If you were purchasing a home having 2,000 square feet, which of the above intervals would you find to be most useful? Explain.

FIGURE 11.21 MINITAB Output of a Simple Linear Regression Analysis of the Fast-Food Restaurant Rating Data

```
The regression equation is
MeanPref = - 0.160 + 1.27 MeanTaste

Predictor      Coef  SE Coef      T      P
Constant    -0.1602   0.3029  -0.53  0.625
MeanTaste    1.2731   0.1025  12.42  0.000

S = 0.183266     R-Sq = 97.5%     R-Sq(adj) = 96.8%

Analysis of Variance
Source          DF      SS      MS       F      P
Regression       1  5.1817  5.1817  154.28  0.000
Residual Error   4  0.1343  0.0336
Total            5  5.3160

Values of Predictors for New Obs      Predicted Values for New Observations
New Obs  MeanTaste                    New Obs     Fit  SE Fit          95% CI            95% PI
      1     1.9661                          1  2.3429  0.1186  (2.0137, 2.6720)  (1.7369, 2.9489)
```

11.49 THE FAST-FOOD RESTAURANT RATING CASE FastFood

Figure 11.21 gives the MINITAB output of a simple linear regression analysis of the fast-food restaurant rating data in Exercise 11.40 (page 478). The information at the bottom of the output relates to a fast-food restaurant that has a mean taste rating of 1.9661. Use the computer output to find and report a point prediction of and a 95 percent prediction interval for the mean preference ranking (given by 406 randomly selected individuals) of the restaurant.

11.50 Ott (1987) presents a study of the amount of heat loss for a certain brand of thermal pane window. Three different windows were randomly assigned to each of three different outdoor temperatures. For each trial the indoor window temperature was controlled at 68°F and 50 percent relative humidity. The heat losses at the outdoor temperatures of 20°F, 40°F, and 60°F are given in Table 11.5.

TABLE 11.5 The Heat Loss Data HeatLoss

Temperature	20	20	20	40	40	40	60	60	60
Heat Loss	86	80	77	78	84	75	33	38	43

Use the simple linear regression model to find a point prediction of and a 95 percent prediction interval for the heat loss of an individual window when the outdoor temperature is

a 20°F **b** 30°F **c** 40°F **d** 50°F **e** 60°F

11.51 Using the sales volume data in Exercise 11.31 (page 471), find a point prediction of and a 95 percent prediction interval for sales volume when advertising expenditure is 11 (that is, $110,000). SalesVol

11.6 Simple Coefficients of Determination and Correlation

CHAPTER 15

The simple coefficient of determination The **simple coefficient of determination** is a measure of the usefulness of a simple linear regression model. To introduce this quantity, which is denoted r^2 (pronounced ***r* squared**), suppose we have observed n values of the dependent variable y. However, we choose to predict y without using a predictor (independent) variable x. In such a case the only reasonable prediction of a specific value of y, say y_i, would be $\bar{y}$, which is simply the average of the n observed values $y_1, y_2, \ldots, y_n$. Here the error of prediction in predicting y_i would be $y_i - \bar{y}$. For example, Figure 11.22(a) illustrates the prediction errors obtained for the fuel consumption data when we do not use the information provided by the independent variable x, average hourly temperature.

FIGURE 11.22 The Reduction in the Prediction Errors Accomplished by Employing the Predictor Variable *x*

(a) Prediction errors for the fuel consumption problem when we do not use the information contributed by *x*

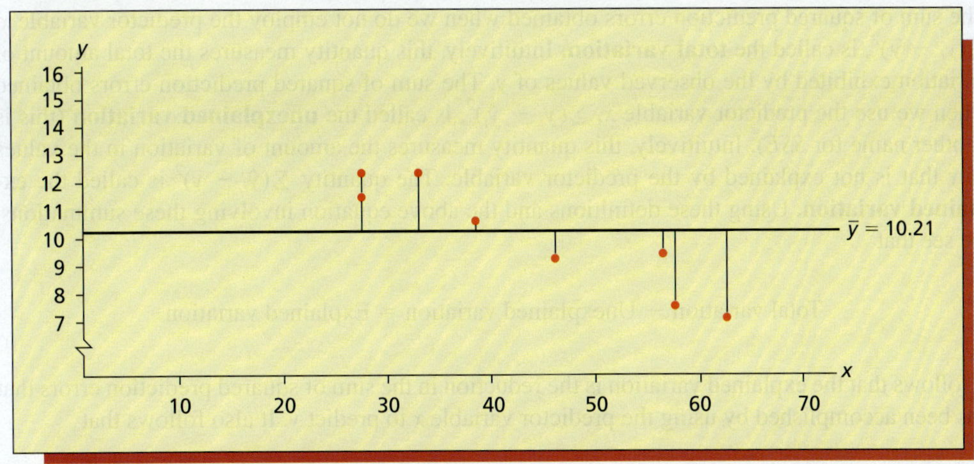

(b) Prediction errors for the fuel consumption problem when we use the information contributed by *x* by using the least squares line

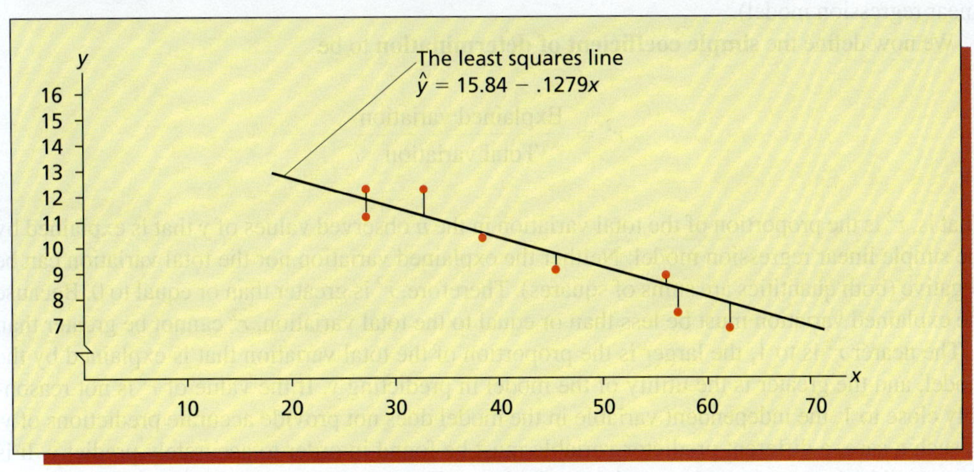

Next, suppose we decide to employ the predictor variable x and observe the values $x_1, x_2, \ldots, x_n$ corresponding to the observed values of y. In this case the prediction of y_i is

$$\hat{y}_i = b_0 + b_1 x_i$$

and the error of prediction is $y_i - \hat{y}_i$. For example, Figure 11.22(b) illustrates the prediction errors obtained in the fuel consumption problem when we use the predictor variable x. Together, Figures 11.22(a) and (b) show the reduction in the prediction errors accomplished by employing the predictor variable x (and the least squares line).

Using the predictor variable x decreases the prediction error in predicting y_i from $(y_i - \bar{y})$ to $(y_i - \hat{y}_i)$, or by an amount equal to

$$(y_i - \bar{y}) - (y_i - \hat{y}_i) = (\hat{y}_i - \bar{y})$$

It can be shown that in general

$$\sum (y_i - \bar{y})^2 - \sum (y_i - \hat{y}_i)^2 = \sum (\hat{y}_i - \bar{y})^2$$

The sum of squared prediction errors obtained when we do not employ the predictor variable x, $\Sigma(y_i - \bar{y})^2$, is called the **total variation.** Intuitively, this quantity measures the total amount of variation exhibited by the observed values of y. The sum of squared prediction errors obtained when we use the predictor variable x, $\Sigma(y_i - \hat{y}_i)^2$, is called the **unexplained variation** (this is another name for *SSE*). Intuitively, this quantity measures the amount of variation in the values of y that is not explained by the predictor variable. The quantity $\Sigma(\hat{y}_i - \bar{y})^2$ is called the **explained variation.** Using these definitions and the above equation involving these summations, we see that

$$\text{Total variation} - \text{Unexplained variation} = \text{Explained variation}$$

It follows that the explained variation is the reduction in the sum of squared prediction errors that has been accomplished by using the predictor variable x to predict y. It also follows that

$$\text{Total variation} = \text{Explained variation} + \text{Unexplained variation}$$

Intuitively, this equation implies that the explained variation represents the amount of the total variation in the observed values of y that is explained by the predictor variable x (and the simple linear regression model).

We now define the **simple coefficient of determination** to be

$$r^2 = \frac{\text{Explained variation}}{\text{Total variation}}$$

That is, r^2 is the proportion of the total variation in the n observed values of y that is explained by the simple linear regression model. Neither the explained variation nor the total variation can be negative (both quantities are sums of squares). Therefore, r^2 is greater than or equal to 0. Because the explained variation must be less than or equal to the total variation, r^2 cannot be greater than 1. The nearer r^2 is to 1, the larger is the proportion of the total variation that is explained by the model, and the greater is the utility of the model in predicting y. If the value of r^2 is not reasonably close to 1, the independent variable in the model does not provide accurate predictions of y. In such a case, a different predictor variable must be found in order to accurately predict y. It is also possible that no regression model employing a single predictor variable will accurately predict y. In this case the model must be improved by including more than one independent variable. We see how to do this in Chapter 12.

In the following box we summarize the results of this section:

The Simple Coefficient of Determination, r^2

For the simple linear regression model

1. **Total variation** $= \sum (y_i - \bar{y})^2$
2. **Explained variation** $= \sum (\hat{y}_i - \bar{y})^2$
3. **Unexplained variation** $= \sum (y_i - \hat{y}_i)^2$
4. **Total variation** $=$ **Explained variation** $+$ **Unexplained variation**
5. **The simple coefficient of determination is**

$$r^2 = \frac{\text{Explained variation}}{\text{Total variation}}$$

6. r^2 is the proportion of the total variation in the n observed values of the dependent variable that is explained by the simple linear regression model.

Example 11.13 The Fuel Consumption Case

For the fuel consumption data (see Table 11.1 on page 451) we have seen that $\bar{y} = (12.4 + 11.7 + \cdots + 7.5)/8 = 81.7/8 = 10.2125$. It follows that the total variation is

$$\sum (y_i - \bar{y})^2 = (12.4 - 10.2125)^2 + (11.7 - 10.2125)^2 + \cdots + (7.5 - 10.2125)^2$$
$$= 25.549$$

Furthermore, we found in Table 11.4 (page 462) that the unexplained variation is $SSE = 2.568$. Therefore, we can compute the explained variation and r^2 as follows:

$$\text{Explained variation} = \text{Total variation} - \text{Unexplained variation}$$
$$= 25.549 - 2.568 = 22.981$$
$$r^2 = \frac{\text{Explained variation}}{\text{Total variation}} = \frac{22.981}{25.549} = .899$$

This value of r^2 says that the regression model explains 89.9 percent of the total variation in the eight observed fuel consumptions.

Example 11.14 The QHIC Case

In the QHIC case, it can be shown that: Total variation = 7,402,755.2399; Explained variation = 6,582,759.6972; SSE = Unexplained variation = 819,995.5427; and

$$r^2 = \frac{\text{Explained variation}}{\text{Total variation}} = \frac{6{,}582{,}759.6972}{7{,}402{,}755.2399} = 0.889$$

This value of r^2 says that the simple linear regression model that employs home value as a predictor variable explains 88.9 percent of the total variation in the 40 observed home upkeep expenditures.

In optional Section 11.10 we present some shortcut formulas for calculating the total, explained, and unexplained variations. Finally, for those who have already read Section 11.4, r^2, the explained variation, the unexplained variation, and the total variation are calculated by MINITAB, Excel, and MegaStat. These quantities are identified on the MINITAB and Excel outputs of Figure 11.11 (page 473) and on the MegaStat output of Figure 11.12 (page 475) by, respectively, the labels 9, 10, 11, and 12. These outputs also give an "adjusted r^2." We explain the meaning of this quantity in Chapter 12.

The simple correlation coefficient, r People often claim that two variables are correlated. For example, a college admissions officer might feel that the academic performance of college students (measured by grade point average) is correlated with the students' scores on a standardized college entrance examination. This means that college students' grade point averages are related to their college entrance exam scores. One measure of the relationship between two variables y and x is the **simple correlation coefficient.** We define this quantity as follows:

The Simple Correlation Coefficient

The **simple correlation coefficient between y and x,** denoted by r, is

$$r = +\sqrt{r^2} \quad \text{if } b_1 \text{ is positive} \qquad \text{and} \qquad r = -\sqrt{r^2} \quad \text{if } b_1 \text{ is negative}$$

where b_1 is the slope of the least squares line relating y to x. This correlation coefficient **measures the strength of the linear relationship between y and x.**

FIGURE 11.23 An Illustration of Different Values of the Simple Correlation Coefficient

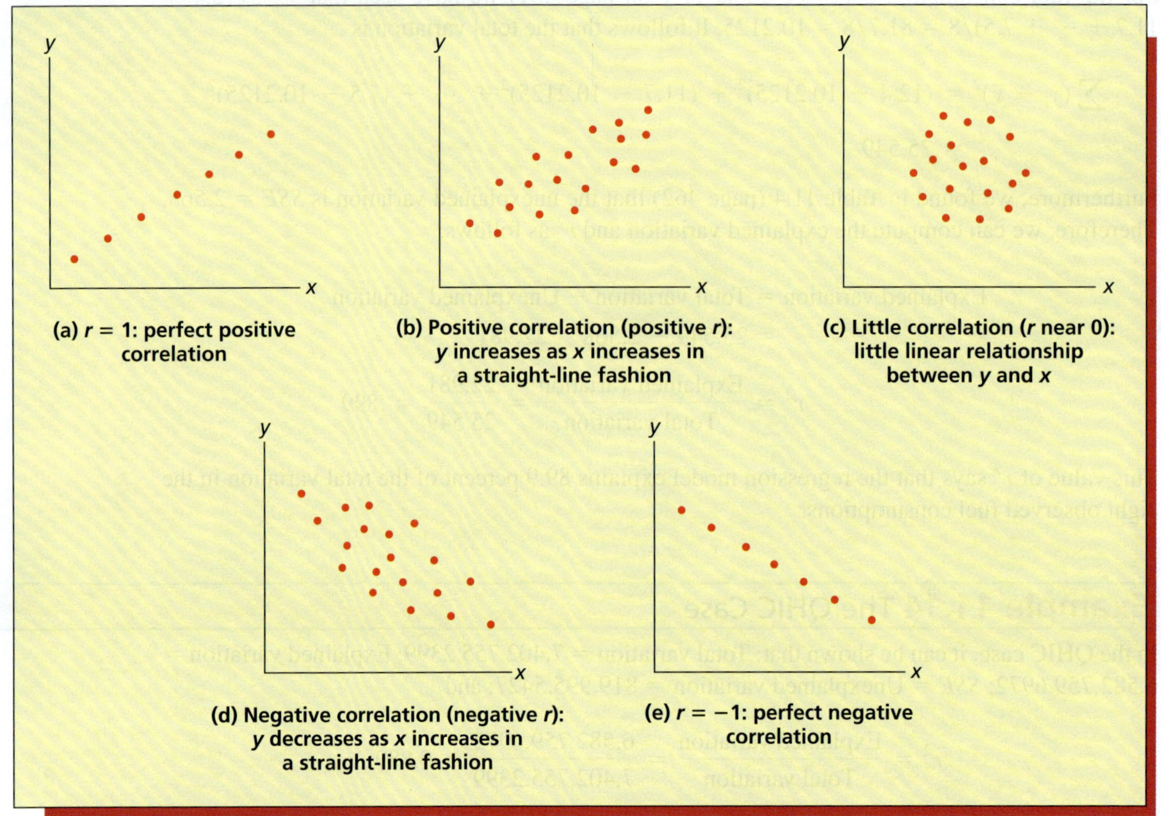
y
x
(a) r = 1: perfect positive correlation
y
x
(b) Positive correlation (positive r): y increases as x increases in a straight-line fashion
y
x
(c) Little correlation (r near 0): little linear relationship between y and x
y
x
(d) Negative correlation (negative r): y decreases as x increases in a straight-line fashion
y
x
(e) r = −1: perfect negative correlation

Because r^2 is always between 0 and 1, the correlation coefficient r is between -1 and 1. A value of r near 0 implies little linear relationship between y and x. A value of r close to 1 says that y and x have a strong tendency to move together in a straight-line fashion with a positive slope and, therefore, that y and x are highly related and **positively correlated.** A value of r close to -1 says that y and x have a strong tendency to move together in a straight-line fashion with a negative slope and, therefore, that y and x are highly related and **negatively correlated.** Figure 11.23 illustrates these relationships. Notice that when $r = 1$, y and x have a perfect linear relationship with a positive slope, whereas when $r = -1$, y and x have a perfect linear relationship with a negative slope.

Example 11.15 The Fuel Consumption Case

C

In the fuel consumption problem we have previously found that $b_1 = -.1279$ and $r^2 = .899$. It follows that the simple correlation coefficient between y (weekly fuel consumption) and x (average hourly temperature) is

$$r = -\sqrt{r^2} = -\sqrt{.899} = -.948$$

This simple correlation coefficient says that x and y have a strong tendency to move together in a linear fashion with a negative slope. We have seen this tendency in Figure 11.2 (page 451), which indicates that y and x are negatively correlated.

If we have computed the least squares slope b_1 and r^2, the method given in the previous box provides the easiest way to calculate r. The simple correlation coefficient can also be calculated using the formula

$$r = \frac{SS_{xy}}{\sqrt{SS_{xx}SS_{yy}}}$$

Here SS_{xy} and SS_{xx} have been defined in Section 11.2 on page 461, and SS_{yy} denotes the total variation, which has been defined in this section. Furthermore, this formula for r automatically gives r the correct (+ or −) sign. For instance, in the fuel consumption problem, $SS_{xy} = -179.6475$, $SS_{xx} = 1{,}404.355$, and $SS_{yy} = 25.549$ (see Examples 11.4 on page 461 and 11.13 on page 489). Therefore

$$r = \frac{SS_{xy}}{\sqrt{SS_{xx}SS_{yy}}} = \frac{-179.6475}{\sqrt{(1{,}404.355)(25.549)}} = -.948$$

It is important to make two points. First, **the value of the simple correlation coefficient is not the slope of the least squares line.** If we wish to find this slope, we should use the previously given formula for b_1.[4] Second, **high correlation does not imply that a cause-and-effect relationship exists.** When r indicates that y and x are highly correlated, this says that y and x have a strong tendency to move together in a straight-line fashion. The correlation does not mean that changes in x cause changes in y. Instead, some other variable (or variables) could be causing the apparent relationship between y and x. For example, suppose that college students' grade point averages and college entrance exam scores are highly positively correlated. This does not mean that earning a high score on a college entrance exam causes students to receive a high grade point average. Rather, other factors such as intellectual ability, study habits, and attitude probably determine both a student's score on a college entrance exam and a student's college grade point average. In general, while the simple correlation coefficient can show that variables tend to move together in a straight-line fashion, scientific theory must be used to establish cause-and-effect relationships.

Exercises for Section 11.6

CONCEPTS

11.52 Discuss the meanings of the total variation, the unexplained variation, and the explained variation.

11.53 What does the simple coefficient of determination measure?

METHODS AND APPLICATIONS

In Exercises 11.54 through 11.58, we give the total variation, the unexplained variation (*SSE*), and the least squares point estimate b_1 that are obtained when simple linear regression is used to analyze the data set related to each of five previously discussed case studies. Using the information given in each exercise, find the explained variation, the simple coefficient of determination (r^2), and the simple correlation coefficient (r). Interpret r^2.

11.54 THE STARTING SALARY CASE StartSal

Total variation = 61.380; $SSE = 1.438$; $b_1 = 5.7066$

11.55 THE SERVICE TIME CASE SrvcTime

Total variation = 20,110.5455; $SSE = 191.7017$; $b_1 = 24.6022$

11.56 THE FRESH DETERGENT CASE Fresh

Total variation = 13.459; $SSE = 2.806$; $b_1 = 2.6652$

11.57 THE DIRECT LABOR COST CASE DirLab

Total variation = 1,025,339.6667; $SSE = 746.7624$; $b_1 = 10.1463$

11.58 THE REAL ESTATE SALES PRICE CASE RealEst

Total variation = 7447.5; $SSE = 896.8$; $b_1 = 5.7003$

11.59 THE FAST-FOOD RESTAURANT RATING CASE FastFood

Note: This exercise is only for those who have previously read Section 11.4. Use the Excel output of Figure 11.18 (page 478) or the MINITAB output of Figure 11.21 (page 486) to find and report each of the following: explained variation, unexplained variation, total variation, r^2. Interpret r^2.

[4]Essentially, the difference between r and b_1 is a change of scale. It can be shown that b_1 and r are related by the equation $b_1 = (SS_{yy}/SS_{xx})^{1/2}\, r$.

11.7 Testing the Significance of the Population Correlation Coefficient (Optional)

We have seen that the simple correlation coefficient measures the linear relationship between the observed values of x and the observed values of y that make up the sample. A similar coefficient of linear correlation can be defined for the population of *all possible combinations of observed values of x and y.* We call this coefficient the **population correlation coefficient** and denote it by the symbol $\boldsymbol{\rho}$ (pronounced **rho**). We use r as the point estimate of ρ. In addition, we can carry out a hypothesis test. Here we test the null hypothesis **H_0: $\rho = 0$, which says there is no linear relationship between x and y,** against the alternative **H_a: $\rho \neq 0$, which says there is a positive or negative linear relationship between x and y.** This test employs the test statistic

$$t = \frac{r\sqrt{n-2}}{\sqrt{1-r^2}}$$

and is based on the assumption that the population of all possible observed combinations of values of x and y has a **bivariate normal probability distribution.** See Wonnacott and Wonnacott (1981) for a discussion of this distribution. It can be shown that the preceding test statistic t and the p-value used to test H_0: $\rho = 0$ versus H_a: $\rho \neq 0$ are equal to, respectively, the test statistic $t = b_1/s_{b_1}$ and the p-value used to test H_0: $\beta_1 = 0$ versus H_a: $\beta_1 \neq 0$, where β_1 is the slope in the simple linear regression model. Keep in mind, however, that although the mechanics involved in these hypothesis tests are the same, these tests are based on different assumptions (remember that the test for significance of the slope is based on the regression assumptions). If the bivariate normal distribution assumption for the test concerning ρ is badly violated, we can use a nonparametric approach to correlation. One such approach is **Spearman's rank correlation coefficient.** This approach is discussed in optional Section 15.5.

Example 11.16 The Fuel Consumption Case

Again consider testing the significance of the slope in the fuel consumption problem. Recall that in Example 11.7 (page 472) we found that $t = -7.33$ and that the p-value related to this t statistic is .0003. We therefore (if the regression assumptions hold) can reject H_0: $\beta_1 = 0$ at level of significance .05, .01, or .001, and we have extremely strong evidence that x is significantly related to y. This also implies (if the population of all possible observed combinations of x and y has a bivariate normal probability distribution) that we can reject H_0: $\rho = 0$ in favor of H_a: $\rho \neq 0$ at level of significance .05, .01, or .001. It follows that we have extremely strong evidence of a linear relationship, or correlation, between x and y. Furthermore, because we have previously calculated r to be $-.9482$, we estimate that x and y are negatively correlated.

Exercises for Section 11.7

CONCEPTS

11.60 Explain what is meant by the population correlation coefficient ρ.

11.61 Explain how we test H_0: $\rho = 0$ versus H_a: $\rho \neq 0$. What do we conclude if we reject H_0: $\rho = 0$?

METHODS AND APPLICATIONS

11.62 THE STARTING SALARY CASE StartSal

Consider testing H_0: $\beta_1 = 0$ versus H_a: $\beta_1 \neq 0$. Figure 11.13 (page 476) tells us that $t = 14.44$ and that the related p-value is less than .001. Assuming that the bivariate normal probability distribution assumption holds, test H_0: $\rho = 0$ versus H_a: $\rho \neq 0$ by setting α equal to .05, .01, and .001. What do you conclude about how x and y are related?

11.63 THE SERVICE TIME CASE SrvcTime

Consider testing H_0: $\beta_1 = 0$ versus H_a: $\beta_1 \neq 0$. Figure 11.14 (page 476) tells us that $t = 30.580$ and that the related p-value is less than .001. Assuming that the bivariate normal probability distribution assumption holds, test H_0: $\rho = 0$ versus H_a: $\rho \neq 0$ by setting α equal to .05, .01, and .001. What do you conclude about how x and y are related?

11.8 An F Test for the Model

In this section we discuss an F test that can be used to test the significance of the regression relationship between x and y. Sometimes people refer to this as testing the significance of the simple linear regression model. For simple linear regression, this test is another way to test the null hypothesis H_0: $\beta_1 = 0$ (the relationship between x and y is not significant) versus H_a: $\beta_1 \neq 0$ (the relationship between x and y is significant). If we can reject H_0 at level of significance α, we often say that **the simple linear regression model is significant at level of significance α.**

An F Test for the Simple Linear Regression Model

Suppose that the regression assumptions hold, and define the **overall F statistic** to be

$$F(\text{model}) = \frac{\text{Explained variation}}{(\text{Unexplained variation})/(n-2)}$$

Also define the p-value related to F(model) to be the area under the curve of the F distribution (having 1 numerator and $n - 2$ denominator degrees of freedom) to the right of F(model)—see Figure 11.24(b).

We can reject H_0: $\beta_1 = 0$ in favor of H_a: $\beta_1 \neq 0$ at level of significance α if either of the following equivalent conditions hold:

1. $F(\text{model}) > F_\alpha$
2. $p\text{-value} < \alpha$

Here the point F_α is based on 1 numerator and $n - 2$ denominator degrees of freedom.

The first condition in the box says we should reject H_0: $\beta_1 = 0$ (and conclude that the relationship between x and y is significant) when F(model) is large. This is intuitive because a large overall F statistic would be obtained when the explained variation is large compared to the unexplained variation. This would occur if x is significantly related to y, which would imply that the slope β_1 is not equal to 0. Figure 11.24(a) illustrates that we reject H_0 when F(model) is greater

FIGURE 11.24 An F Test for the Simple Linear Regression Model

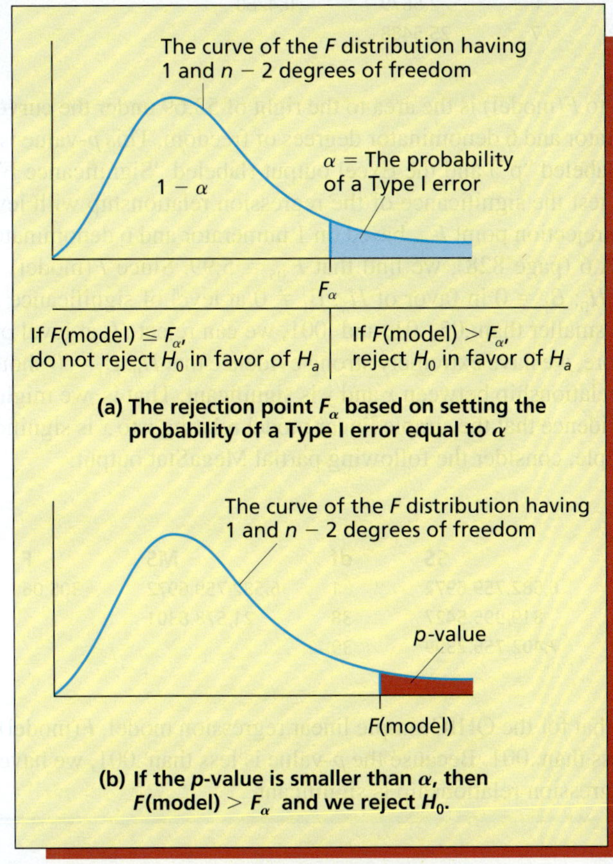

(a) The rejection point F_α based on setting the probability of a Type I error equal to α

(b) If the p-value is smaller than α, then $F(\text{model}) > F_\alpha$ and we reject H_0.

than F_α. As can be seen in Figure 11.24(b), when F(model) is large, the related p-value is small. When the p-value is small enough [resulting from an F(model) statistic that is large enough], we reject H_0. Figure 11.24(b) illustrates that the second condition in the box (p-value $< \alpha$) is an equivalent way to carry out this test.

Example 11.17 The Fuel Consumption Case

Consider the fuel consumption problem and the following partial MINITAB output of the simple linear regression analysis relating weekly fuel consumption y to average hourly temperature x:

```
Analysis of Variance
Source            DF        SS          MS         F        P
Regression         1    22.981      22.981     53.69    0.000
Residual Error     6     2.568       0.428
Total              7    25.549
```

Looking at this output, we see that the explained variation is 22.981 and the unexplained variation is 2.568. It follows that

$$F(\text{model}) = \frac{\text{Explained variation}}{(\text{Unexplained variation})/(n-2)}$$

$$= \frac{22.981}{2.568/(8-2)} = \frac{22.981}{.428}$$

$$= 53.69$$

Note that this overall F statistic is given on the MINITAB output and is also given on the following partial Excel output:

ANOVA	df	SS	MS	F	Significance F
Regression	1	22.9808	22.9808	53.6949	0.0003
Residual	6	2.5679	0.4280		
Total	7	25.5488			

The p-value related to F(model) is the area to the right of 53.69 under the curve of the F distribution having 1 numerator and 6 denominator degrees of freedom. This p-value is given on both the MINITAB output (labeled "p") and the Excel output (labeled "Significance F") and is less than .001. If we wish to test the significance of the regression relationship with level of significance $\alpha = .05$, we use the rejection point $F_{.05}$ based on 1 numerator and 6 denominator degrees of freedom. Using Table A.6 (page 828), we find that $F_{.05} = 5.99$. Since $F(\text{model}) = 53.69 > F_{.05} = 5.99$, we can reject H_0: $\beta_1 = 0$ in favor of H_a: $\beta_1 \neq 0$ at level of significance .05. Alternatively, since the p-value is smaller than .05, .01, and .001, we can reject H_0 at level of significance .05, .01, or .001. Therefore, we have extremely strong evidence that H_0: $\beta_1 = 0$ should be rejected and that the regression relationship between x and y is significant. That is, we might say that we have extremely strong evidence that the simple linear model relating y to x is significant.

As another example, consider the following partial MegaStat output:

ANOVA table Source	SS	df	MS	F	p-value
Regression	6,582,759.6972	1	6,582,759.6972	305.06	9.49E-20
Residual	819,995.5427	38	21,578.8301		
Total	7,402,755.2399	39			

This output tells us that for the QHIC simple linear regression model, F(model) is 305.06 and the related p-value is less than .001. Because the p-value is less than .001, we have extremely strong evidence that the regression relationship is significant.

Testing the significance of the regression relationship between y and x by using the overall F statistic and its related p-value is equivalent to doing this test by using the t statistic and its related p-value. Specifically, it can be shown that $(t)^2 = F(\text{model})$ and that $(t_{\alpha/2})^2$ based on $n - 2$ degrees of freedom equals F_α based on 1 numerator and $n - 2$ denominator degrees of freedom. It follows that the rejection point conditions

$$|t| > t_{\alpha/2} \quad \text{and} \quad F(\text{model}) > F_\alpha$$

are equivalent. Furthermore, the p-values related to t and F(model) can be shown to be equal. Because these tests are equivalent, it would be logical to ask why we have presented the F test. There are two reasons. First, most standard regression computer packages include the results of the F test as a part of the regression output. Second, the F test has a useful generalization in multiple regression analysis (where we employ more than one predictor variable). The F test in multiple regression is not equivalent to a t test. This is further explained in Chapter 12.

Exercises for Section 11.7

CONCEPTS

11.64 What are the null and alternative hypotheses for the F test in simple linear regression?

11.65 The F test in simple linear regression is equivalent to what other test?

METHODS AND APPLICATIONS

In Exercises 11.66 through 11.71, we give MINITAB, MegaStat, and Excel outputs of simple linear regression analyses of the data sets related to six previously discussed case studies. Using the appropriate computer output,

a Use the explained variation and the unexplained variation as given on the computer output to calculate the F(model) statistic.

b Utilize the F(model) statistic and the appropriate rejection point to test H_0: $\beta_1 = 0$ versus H_a: $\beta_1 \neq 0$ by setting α equal to .05. What do you conclude about the regression relationship between y and x?

c Utilize the F(model) statistic and the appropriate rejection point to test H_0: $\beta_1 = 0$ versus H_a: $\beta_1 \neq 0$ by setting α equal to .01. What do you conclude about the regression relationship between y and x?

d Find the p-value related to F(model) on the computer output and report its value. Using the p-value, test the significance of the regression model at the .10, .05, .01, and .001 levels of significance. What do you conclude?

e Show that the F(model) statistic is (within rounding) the square of the t statistic for testing H_0: $\beta_1 = 0$ versus H_a: $\beta_1 \neq 0$. Also, show that the $F_{.05}$ rejection point is the square of the $t_{.025}$ rejection point.

Note that in the lower right hand corner of each output we give (in parentheses) the number of observations, n, used to perform the regression analysis and the t statistic for testing H_0: $\beta_1 = 0$ versus H_a: $\beta_1 \neq 0$.

11.66 THE STARTING SALARY CASE StartSal

```
Analysis of Variance
Source           DF      SS      MS       F       P
Regression        1  59.942  59.942  208.39   0.000
Residual Error    5   1.438   0.288
Total             6  61.380          (n=7; t=14.44)
```

11.67 THE SERVICE TIME CASE SrvcTime

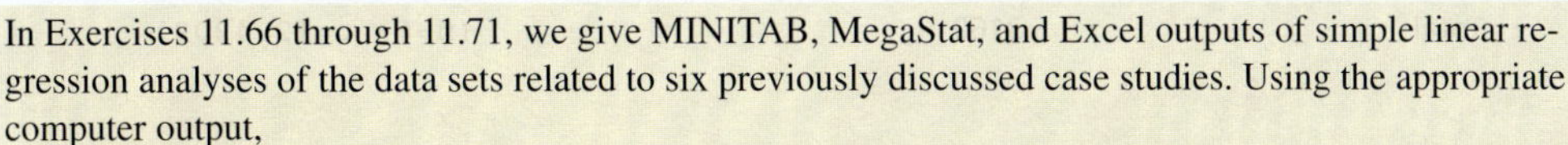

ANOVA table

Source	SS	df	MS	F	p-value
Regression	19,918.8438	1	19,918.8438	935.15	2.09E-10
Residual	191.7017	9	21.3002		
Total	20,110.5455	10		(n=11; t=30.580)	

11.68 THE FRESH DETERGENT CASE Fresh

Analysis of Variance

Source	DF	SS	MS	F	P
Regression	1	10.653	10.653	106.30	0.000
Residual Error	28	2.806	0.100		
Total	29	13.459		(n=30; t=10.31)	

11.69 THE DIRECT LABOR COST CASE DirLab

ANOVA	df	SS	MS	F	Significance F
Regression	1	1024592.9043	1024592.9043	13720.4677	5.04E-17
Residual	10	746.7624	74.6762		
Total	11	1025339.6667		(n=12; t=117.1344)	

11.70 THE REAL ESTATE SALES PRICE CASE RealEst

Analysis of Variance

Source	DF	SS	MS	F	P
Regression	1	6550.7	6550.7	58.43	0.000
Residual Error	8	896.8	112.1		
Total	9	7447.5		(n=10; t=7.64)	

11.71 THE FAST-FOOD RESTAURANT RATING CASE FastFood

ANOVA	df	SS	MS	F	Significance F
Regression	1	5.1817	5.1817	154.2792	0.0002
Residual	4	0.1343	0.0336		
Total	5	5.3160		(n=6; t=12.4209)	

11.9 Residual Analysis (Optional)

CHAPTER 16

In this section we explain how to check the validity of the regression assumptions. The required checks are carried out by analyzing the **regression residuals.** The residuals are defined as follows:

For any particular observed value of y, the corresponding **residual** is

$$e = y - \hat{y} = (\text{observed value of } y - \text{predicted value of } y)$$

where the predicted value of y is calculated using the **least squares prediction equation**

$$\hat{y} = b_0 + b_1 x$$

The linear regression model $y = \beta_0 + \beta_1 x + \varepsilon$ implies that the error term ε is given by the equation $\varepsilon = y - (\beta_0 + \beta_1 x)$. Since $\hat{y}$ in the previous box is clearly the point estimate of $\beta_0 + \beta_1 x$, we see that the residual $e = y - \hat{y}$ is the point estimate of the error term ε. If the regression assumptions are valid, then, for any given value of the independent variable, the population of potential error term values will be normally distributed with mean 0 and variance σ^2 (see the regression assumptions in Section 11.3 on page 468). Furthermore, the different error terms will be statistically independent. Because the residuals provide point estimates of the error terms, it follows that

If the regression assumptions hold, the residuals should look like they have been randomly and independently selected from normally distributed populations having mean 0 and variance σ^2.

In any real regression problem, the regression assumptions will not hold exactly. In fact, it is important to point out that mild departures from the regression assumptions do not seriously hinder our ability to use a regression model to make statistical inferences. Therefore, we are looking for pronounced, rather than subtle, departures from the regression assumptions. Because of this, we will require that the residuals only approximately fit the description just given.

FIGURE 11.25 The QHIC Upkeep Expenditure Data and a Scatterplot of the Data QHIC

Home	Value of Home, x (Thousands of Dollars)	Upkeep Expenditure, y (Dollars)	Home	Value of Home, x (Thousands of Dollars)	Upkeep Expenditure, y (Dollars)
1	237.00	1,412.08	21	153.04	849.14
2	153.08	797.20	22	232.18	1,313.84
3	184.86	872.48	23	125.44	602.06
4	222.06	1,003.42	24	169.82	642.14
5	160.68	852.90	25	177.28	1,038.80
6	99.68	288.48	26	162.82	697.00
7	229.04	1,288.46	27	120.44	324.34
8	101.78	423.08	28	191.10	965.10
9	257.86	1,351.74	29	158.78	920.14
10	96.28	378.04	30	178.50	950.90
11	171.00	918.08	31	272.20	1,670.32
12	231.02	1,627.24	32	48.90	125.40
13	228.32	1,204.76	33	104.56	479.78
14	205.90	857.04	34	286.18	2,010.64
15	185.72	775.00	35	83.72	368.36
16	168.78	869.26	36	86.20	425.60
17	247.06	1,396.00	37	133.58	626.90
18	155.54	711.50	38	212.86	1,316.94
19	224.20	1,475.18	39	122.02	390.16
20	202.04	1,413.32	40	198.02	1,090.84

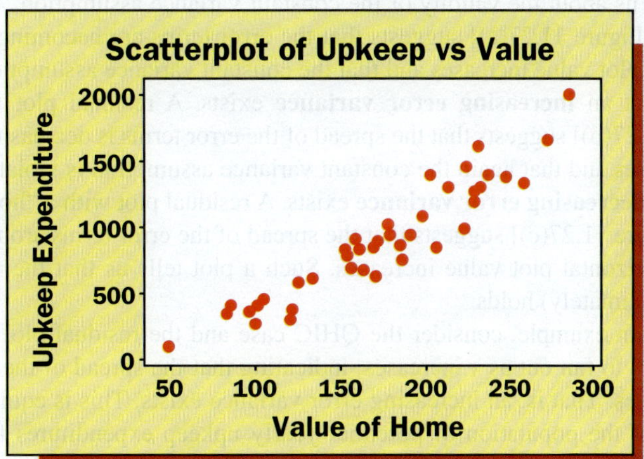

Residual plots One useful way to analyze residuals is to plot them versus various criteria. The resulting plots are called **residual plots.** To construct a residual plot, we compute the residual for each observed y value. The calculated residuals are then plotted versus some criterion. To validate the regression assumptions, we make residual plots against (1) values of the independent variable x; (2) values of $\hat{y}$, the predicted value of the dependent variable; and (3) the time order in which the data have been observed (if the regression data are time series data).

We next look at an example of constructing residual plots. Then we explain how to use these plots to check the regression assumptions.

Example 11.18 The QHIC Case

Figure 11.25 gives the QHIC upkeep expenditure data and a scatterplot of the data. If we use a simple linear regression model to describe the QHIC data, we find that the least squares point estimates of β_0 and β_1 are $b_0 = -348.3921$ and $b_1 = 7.2583$. The MegaStat output in Figure 11.26(a) presents the predicted home upkeep expenditures and residuals that are given by the simple linear regression model. Here each residual is computed as

$$e = y - \hat{y} = y - (b_0 + b_1x) = y - (-348.3921 + 7.2583x)$$

For instance, for the first observation (home) when $y = 1{,}412.08$ and $x = 237.00$ (see Figure 11.25), the residual is

$$e = 1{,}412.08 - (-348.3921 + 7.2583(237))$$
$$= 1{,}412.08 - 1{,}371.816 = 40.264$$

The MINITAB output in Figure 11.26(b) and (c) gives plots of the residuals for the QHIC simple linear regression model against values of x and $\hat{y}$. To understand how these plots are constructed, recall that for the first observation (home) $y = 1{,}412.08$, $x = 237.00$, $\hat{y} = 1{,}371.816$, and the residual is 40.264. It follows that the point plotted in Figure 11.26(b) corresponding to the first observation has a horizontal axis coordinate of the x value 237.00 and a vertical axis coordinate of the residual 40.264. It also follows that the point plotted in Figure 11.26(c) corresponding to the first observation has a horizontal axis coordinate of the $\hat{y}$ value 1,371.816, and a vertical axis coordinate of the residual 40.264. Finally, note that the QHIC data are cross-sectional data, not time series data. Therefore, we cannot make a residual plot versus time.

The constant variance assumption To check the validity of the constant variance assumption, we examine plots of the residuals against values of x, $\hat{y}$, and time (if the regression data are time series data). When we look at these plots, the pattern of the residuals' fluctuation around 0 tells us about the validity of the constant variance assumption. A residual plot that "fans out" [as in Figure 11.27(a)] suggests that the error terms are becoming more spread out as the horizontal plot value increases and that the constant variance assumption is violated. Here we would say that an **increasing error variance** exists. A residual plot that "funnels in" [as in Figure 11.27(b)] suggests that the spread of the error terms is decreasing as the horizontal plot value increases and that again the constant variance assumption is violated. In this case we would say that a **decreasing error variance** exists. A residual plot with a "horizontal band appearance" [as in Figure 11.27(c)] suggests that the spread of the error terms around 0 is not changing much as the horizontal plot value increases. Such a plot tells us that the constant variance assumption (approximately) holds.

As an example, consider the QHIC case and the residual plot in Figure 11.26(b). This plot appears to fan out as x increases, indicating that the spread of the error terms is increasing as x increases. That is, an increasing error variance exists. This is equivalent to saying that the variance of the population of potential yearly upkeep expenditures for houses worth x (thousand dollars) appears to increase as x increases. The reason is that the model $y = \beta_0 + \beta_1x + \varepsilon$ says that the variation of y is the same as the variation of ε. For example, the variance of the population of potential yearly upkeep expenditures for houses worth \$200,000 would be larger than the variance of the population of potential yearly upkeep expenditures for houses worth \$100,000. Increasing variance makes some intuitive sense because people with more expensive homes generally have more discretionary income. These people can choose to spend either a substantial amount or a much smaller amount on home upkeep, thus causing a relatively large variation in upkeep expenditures.

Another residual plot showing the increasing error variance in the QHIC case is Figure 11.26(c). This plot tells us that the residuals appear to fan out as $\hat{y}$ (predicted y) increases, which is logical because $\hat{y}$ is an increasing function of x. Also, note that the scatter plot of y versus x in Figure 11.25 shows the increasing error variance—the y values appear to fan out as x increases. In fact, one might ask why we need to consider residual plots when we can simply look at scatter plots of y versus x. One answer is that, in general, because of possible differences in scaling between residual plots and scatter plots of y versus x, one of these types of plots might be more informative in a particular situation. Therefore, we should always consider both types of plots.

When the constant variance assumption is violated, we cannot use the formulas of this chapter to make statistical inferences. Later in this section we discuss how we can make statistical inferences when a nonconstant error variance exists.

FIGURE 11.26 MegaStat and MINITAB Output of the Residuals and Residual Plots for the QHIC Simple Linear Regression Model

(a) MegaStat output of the residuals

Observation	Upkeep	Predicted	Residual	Observation	Upkeep	Predicted	Residual
1	1,412.080	1,371.816	40.264	21	849.140	762.413	86.727
2	797.200	762.703	34.497	22	1,313.840	1,336.832	−22.992
3	872.480	993.371	−120.891	23	602.060	562.085	39.975
4	1,003.420	1,263.378	−259.958	24	642.140	884.206	−242.066
5	852.900	817.866	35.034	25	1,038.800	938.353	100.447
6	288.480	375.112	−86.632	26	697.000	833.398	−136.398
7	1,288.460	1,314.041	−25.581	27	324.340	525.793	−201.453
8	423.080	390.354	32.726	28	965.100	1,038.662	−73.562
9	1,351.740	1,523.224	−171.484	29	920.140	804.075	116.065
10	378.040	350.434	27.606	30	950.900	947.208	3.692
11	918.080	892.771	25.309	31	1,670.320	1,627.307	43.013
12	1,627.240	1,328.412	298.828	32	125.400	6.537	118.863
13	1,204.760	1,308.815	−104.055	33	479.780	410.532	69.248
14	857.040	1,146.084	−289.044	34	2,010.640	1,728.778	281.862
15	775.000	999.613	−224.613	35	368.360	259.270	109.090
16	869.260	876.658	−7.398	36	425.600	277.270	148.330
17	1,396.000	1,444.835	−48.835	37	626.900	621.167	5.733
18	711.500	780.558	−69.058	38	1,316.940	1,196.602	120.338
19	1,475.180	1,278.911	196.269	39	390.160	537.261	−147.101
20	1,413.320	1,118.068	295.252	40	1,090.840	1,088.889	1.951

(b) MINITAB output of residual plot versus *x*

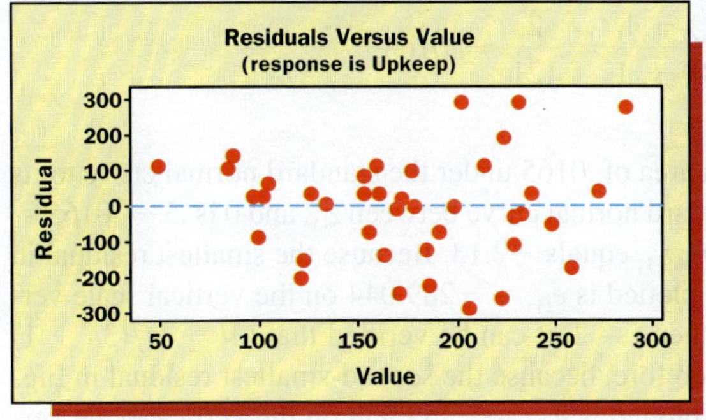

(c) MINITAB output of residual plot versus $\hat{y}$

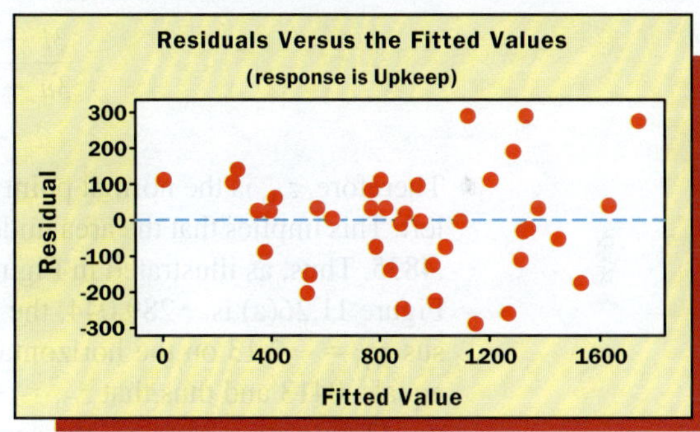

FIGURE 11.27 Residual Plots and the Constant Variance Assumption

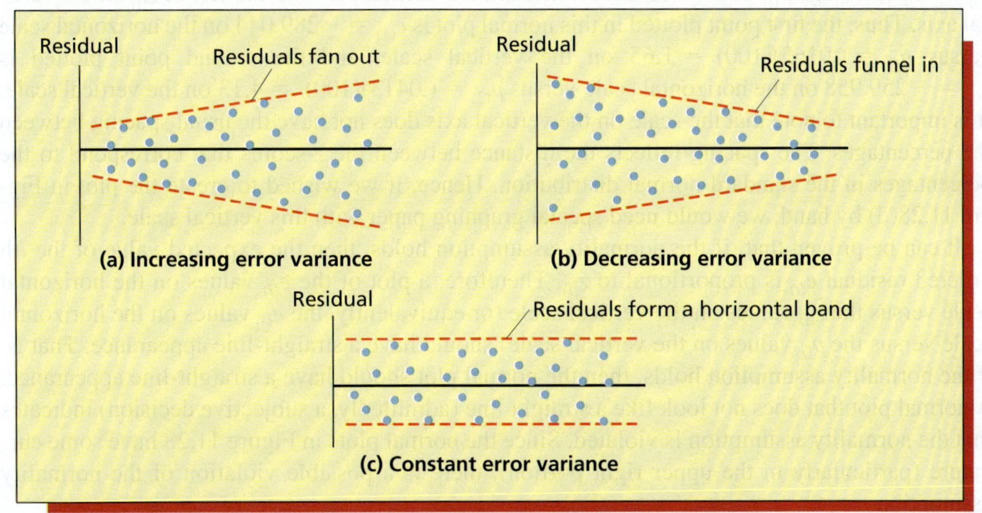

The assumption of correct functional form If the functional form of a regression model is incorrect, the residual plots constructed by using the model often display a pattern suggesting the form of a more appropriate model. For instance, if we use a simple linear regression model when the true relationship between y and x is curved, the residual plot will have a curved appearance. For example, the scatter plot of upkeep expenditure, y, versus home value, x, in Figure 11.25 (page 497) has either a straight-line or slightly curved appearance. We used a simple linear regression model to describe the relationship between y and x, but note that there is a "dip," or slightly curved appearance, in the upper left portion of each residual plot in Figure 11.26. Therefore, both the scatter plot and residual plots indicate that there might be a slightly curved relationship between y and x. Later in this section we discuss one way to model curved relationships.

The normality assumption If the normality assumption holds, a histogram and/or stem-and-leaf display of the residuals should look reasonably bell-shaped and reasonably symmetric about 0. Figure 11.28(a) gives the MINITAB output of a stem-and-leaf display of the residuals from the simple linear regression model describing the QHIC data. The stem-and-leaf display looks fairly bell-shaped and symmetric about 0. However, the tails of the display look somewhat long and "heavy" or "thick," indicating a possible violation of the normality assumption.

Another way to check the normality assumption is to construct a **normal plot** of the residuals. To make a normal plot, we first arrange the residuals in order from smallest to largest. Letting the ordered residuals be denoted as $e_{(1)}, e_{(2)}, \ldots, e_{(n)}$ we denote the ith residual in the ordered listing as $e_{(i)}$. We plot $e_{(i)}$ on the vertical axis against a point called $z_{(i)}$ on the horizontal axis. Here $z_{(i)}$ is defined to be the point on the horizontal axis under the standard normal curve so that the area under this curve to the left of $z_{(i)}$ is $(3i - 1)/(3n + 1)$. For example, recall in the QHIC case that there are $n = 40$ residuals given in Figure 11.26(a). It follows that, when $i = 1$, then

$$\frac{3i - 1}{3n + 1} = \frac{3(1) - 1}{3(40) + 1} = \frac{2}{121} = .0165$$

Therefore, $z_{(1)}$ is the normal point having an area of .0165 under the standard normal curve to its left. This implies that the area under the standard normal curve between $z_{(1)}$ and 0 is $.5 - .0165 = .4835$. Thus, as illustrated in Figure 11.28(b), $z_{(1)}$ equals -2.13. Because the smallest residual in Figure 11.26(a) is -289.044, the first point plotted is $e_{(1)} = -289.044$ on the vertical scale versus $z_{(1)} = -2.13$ on the horizontal scale. When $i = 2$, it can be verified that $(3i - 1)/(3n + 1)$ equals .0413 and thus that $z_{(2)} = -1.74$. Therefore, because the second-smallest residual in Figure 11.26(a) is -259.958, the second point plotted is $e_{(2)} = -259.958$ on the vertical scale versus $z_{(2)} = -1.74$ on the horizontal scale. This process is continued until the entire normal plot is constructed. The MegaStat output of this plot is given in Figure 11.28(c).

An equivalent plot is shown in Figure 11.28(d), which is a MINITAB output. In this figure, we plot the percentage $p_{(i)}$ of the area under the standard normal curve to the left of $z_{(i)}$ on the vertical axis. Thus, the first point plotted in this normal plot is $e_{(1)} = -289.044$ on the horizontal scale versus $p_{(1)} = (.0165)(100) = 1.65$ on the vertical scale, and the second point plotted is $e_{(2)} = -259.958$ on the horizontal scale versus $p_{(2)} = (.0413)(100) = 4.13$ on the vertical scale. It is important to note that the scale on the vertical axis does not have the usual spacing between the percentages. The spacing reflects the distance between the z-scores that correspond to the percentages in the standard normal distribution. Hence, if we wished to create the plot in Figure 11.28(d) by hand, we would need special graphing paper with this vertical scale.

It can be proven that, if the normality assumption holds, then the expected value of the ith ordered residual $e_{(i)}$ is proportional to $z_{(i)}$. Therefore, a plot of the $e_{(i)}$ values on the horizontal scale versus the $z_{(i)}$ values on the vertical scale (or equivalently, the $e_{(i)}$ values on the horizontal scale versus the $p_{(i)}$ values on the vertical scale) should have a straight-line appearance. That is, if the normality assumption holds, then the normal plot should have a straight-line appearance. A normal plot that does not look like a straight line (admittedly, a subjective decision) indicates that the normality assumption is violated. Since the normal plots in Figure 11.28 have some curvature (particularly in the upper right portion), there is a possible violation of the normality assumption.

FIGURE 11.28 Stem-and-Leaf Display and Normal Plots of the Residuals from the Simple Linear Regression Model Describing the QHIC Data

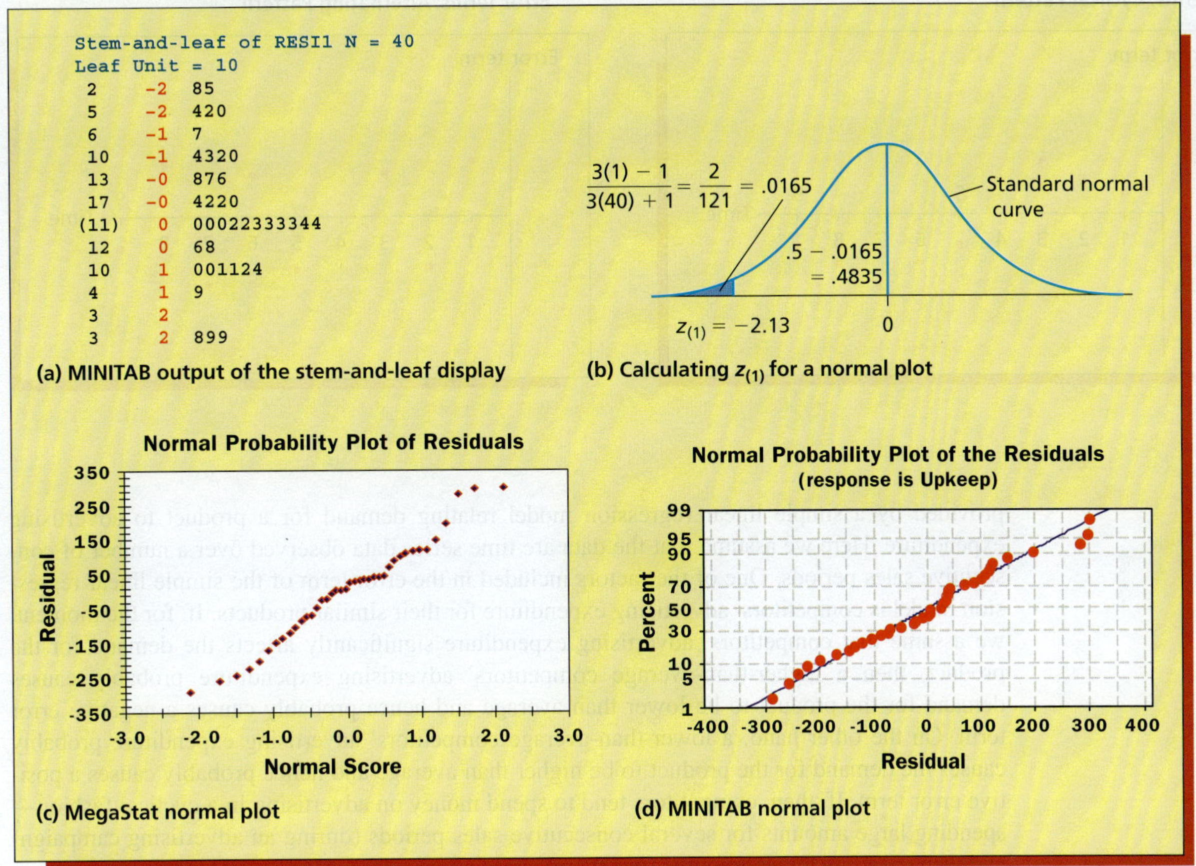

It is important to realize that violations of the constant variance and correct functional form assumptions can often cause a histogram and/or stem-and-leaf display of the residuals to look nonnormal and can cause the normal plot to have a curved appearance. Because of this, it is usually a good idea to use residual plots to check for nonconstant variance and incorrect functional form before making any final conclusions about the normality assumption. Later in this section we discuss a procedure that sometimes remedies simultaneous violations of the constant variance, correct functional form, and normality assumptions.

The independence assumption The independence assumption is most likely to be violated when the regression data are **time series data**—that is, data that have been collected in a time sequence. For such data the time-ordered error terms can be **autocorrelated.** Intuitively, we say that error terms occurring over time have **positive autocorrelation** if a positive error term in time period i tends to produce, or be followed by, another positive error term in time period $i + k$ (some later time period) and if a negative error term in time period i tends to produce, or be followed by, another negative error term in time period $i + k$. In other words, positive autocorrelation exists when positive error terms tend to be followed over time by positive error terms and when negative error terms tend to be followed over time by negative error terms. Positive autocorrelation in the error terms is depicted in Figure 11.29(a), which illustrates that **positive autocorrelation can produce a cyclical error term pattern over time.** The simple linear regression model implies that a positive error term produces a greater-than-average value of y and a negative error term produces a smaller-than-average value of y. It follows that positive autocorrelation in the error terms means that greater-than-average values of y tend to be followed by greater-than-average values of y, and smaller-than-average values of y tend to be followed by smaller-than-average values of y. An example of positive autocorrelation could hypothetically be

FIGURE 11.29 Positive and Negative Autocorrelation

(a) Positive Autocorrelation in the Error Terms: Cyclical Pattern

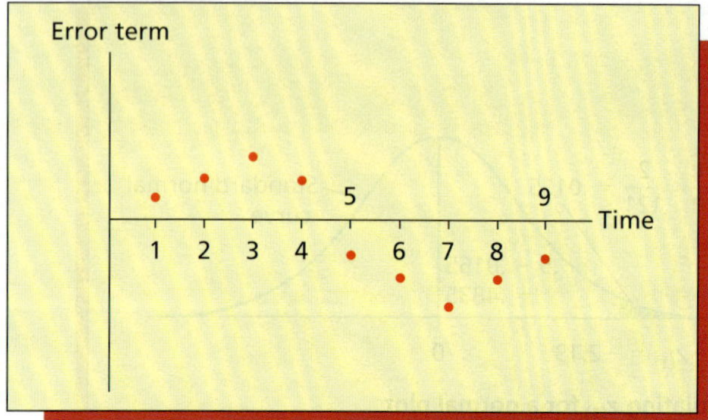

(b) Negative Autocorrelation in the Error Terms: Alternating Pattern

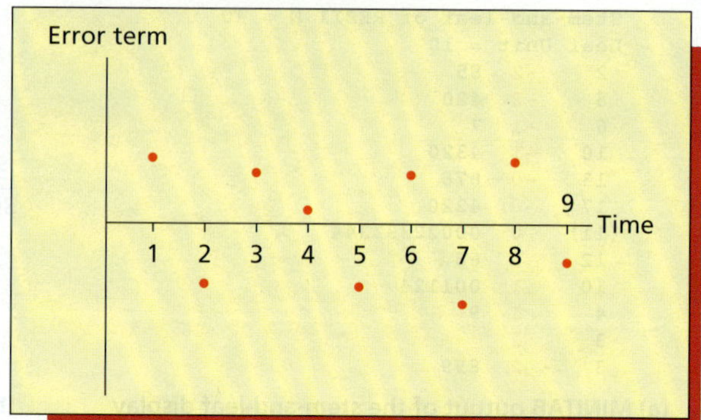

provided by a simple linear regression model relating demand for a product to advertising expenditure. Here we assume that the data are time series data observed over a number of consecutive sales periods. One of the factors included in the error term of the simple linear regression model is competitors' advertising expenditure for their similar products. If, for the moment, we assume that competitors' advertising expenditure significantly affects the demand for the product, then a higher-than-average competitors' advertising expenditure probably causes demand for the product to be lower than average and hence probably causes a negative error term. On the other hand, a lower-than-average competitors' advertising expenditure probably causes the demand for the product to be higher than average and hence probably causes a positive error term. If, then, competitors tend to spend money on advertising in a cyclical fashion—spending large amounts for several consecutive sales periods (during an advertising campaign) and then spending lesser amounts for several consecutive sales periods—a negative error term in one sales period will tend to be followed by a negative error term in the next sales period, and a positive error term in one sales period will tend to be followed by a positive error term in the next sales period. In this case the error terms would display positive autocorrelation, and thus these error terms would not be statistically independent.

Intuitively, error terms occurring over time have **negative autocorrelation** if a positive error term in time period i tends to produce, or be followed by, a negative error term in time period $i + k$ and if a negative error term in time period i tends to produce, or be followed by, a positive error term in time period $i + k$. In other words, negative autocorrelation exists when positive error terms tend to be followed over time by negative error terms and negative error terms tend to be followed over time by positive error terms. An example of negative autocorrelation in the error terms is depicted in Figure 11.29(b), which illustrates that **negative autocorrelation in the error terms can produce an alternating pattern over time.** It follows that negative autocorrelation in the error terms means that greater-than-average values of y tend to be followed by smaller-than-average values of y and smaller-than-average values of y tend to be followed by greater-than-average values of y. An example of negative autocorrelation might be provided by a retailer's weekly stock orders. Here a larger-than-average stock order one week might result in an oversupply and hence a smaller-than-average order the next week.

The **independence assumption** basically says that the time-ordered error terms display no positive or negative autocorrelation. This says that **the error terms occur in a random pattern over time.** Such a random pattern would imply that the error terms (and their corresponding y values) are statistically independent.

Because the residuals are point estimates of the error terms, a residual plot versus time is used to check the independence assumption. If a residual plot versus the data's time sequence has a cyclical appearance, the error terms are positively autocorrelated, and the independence assumption is violated. If a plot of the time-ordered residuals has an alternating pattern, the error terms are negatively autocorrelated, and again the independence assumption is violated.

However, if a plot of the time-ordered residuals displays a random pattern, the error terms have little or no autocorrelation. In such a case, it is reasonable to conclude that the independence assumption holds.

Example 11.19

Figure 11.30(a) presents data concerning weekly sales at Pages' Bookstore (Sales), Pages' weekly advertising expenditure (Adver), and the weekly advertising expenditure of Pages' main competitor (Compadv). Here the sales values are expressed in thousands of dollars, and the advertising expenditure values are expressed in hundreds of dollars. Figure 11.30(a) also gives the residuals that are obtained when MegaStat is used to perform a simple linear regression analysis relating Pages' sales to Pages' advertising expenditure. These residuals are plotted versus time in Figure 11.30(b). We see that the residual plot has a cyclical pattern. This tells us that the error terms for the model are positively autocorrelated and the independence assumption is violated. Furthermore, there tend to be positive residuals when the competitor's advertising expenditure is lower (in weeks 1 through 8 and weeks 14, 15, and 16) and negative residuals when the competitor's advertising expenditure is higher (in weeks 9 through 13). Therefore, the competitor's advertising expenditure seems to be causing the positive autocorrelation.

FIGURE 11.30 Pages' Bookstore Sales and Advertising Data, and Residual Analysis

(a) The data and the MegaStat output of the residuals from a simple linear regression relating Pages' sales to Pages' advertising expenditure BookSales

Observation	Adver	Compadv	Sales	Predicted	Residual
1	18	10	22	18.7	3.3
2	20	10	27	23.0	4.0
3	20	15	23	23.0	−0.0
4	25	15	31	33.9	−2.9
5	28	15	45	40.4	4.6
6	29	20	47	42.6	4.4
7	29	20	45	42.6	2.4
8	28	25	42	40.4	1.6
9	30	35	37	44.7	−7.7
10	31	35	39	46.9	−7.9
11	34	35	45	53.4	−8.4
12	35	30	52	55.6	−3.6
13	36	30	57	57.8	−0.8
14	38	25	62	62.1	−0.1
15	41	20	73	68.6	4.4
16	45	20	84	77.3	6.7

Durbin-Watson = 0.65

(b) MegaStat output of a plot of the residuals in Figure 11.30(a) versus time

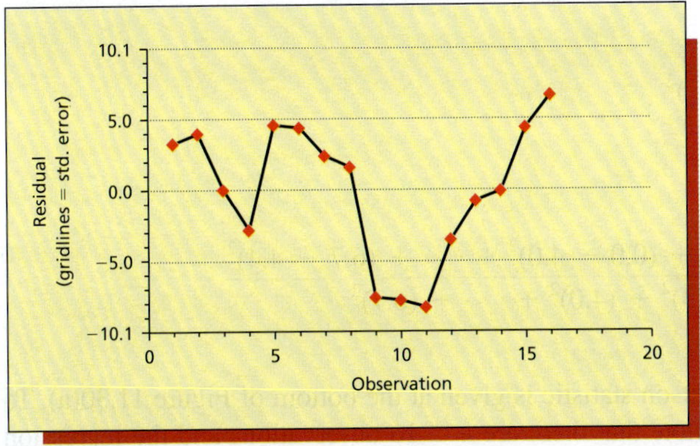

To conclude this example, note that the simple linear regression model relating Pages' sales to Pages' advertising expenditure has a standard error, s, of 5.038. The MegaStat residual plot in Figure 11.30(b) includes grid lines that are placed one and two standard errors above and below the residual mean of 0. All MegaStat residual plots use such grid lines to help better diagnose potential violations of the regression assumptions.

When the independence assumption is violated, various remedies can be employed. One approach is to identify which independent variable left in the error term (for example, competitors' advertising expenditure) is causing the error terms to be autocorrelated. We can then remove this independent variable from the error term and insert it directly into the regression model, forming a **multiple regression model.** (Multiple regression models are discussed in Chapter 12.)

CHAPTER 16

The Durbin–Watson test One type of positive or negative autocorrelation is called **first-order autocorrelation.** It says that ε_t, the error term in time period t, is related to ε_{t-1}, the error term in time period $t - 1$. To check for first-order autocorrelation, we can use the **Durbin–Watson statistic**

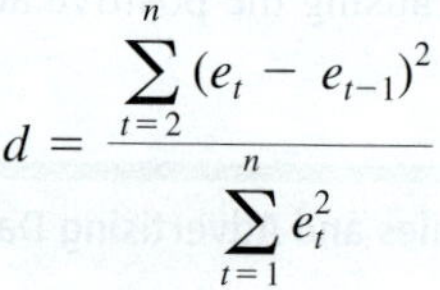

$$d = \frac{\sum_{t=2}^{n} (e_t - e_{t-1})^2}{\sum_{t=1}^{n} e_t^2}$$

where $e_1, e_2, \ldots, e_n$ are the time-ordered residuals.

Intuitively, small values of d lead us to conclude that there is positive autocorrelation. This is because, if d is small, the differences $(e_t - e_{t-1})$ are small. This indicates that the adjacent residuals e_t and e_{t-1} are of the same magnitude, which in turn says that the adjacent error terms ε_t and ε_{t-1} are positively correlated. Consider testing the null hypothesis H_0 **that the error terms are not autocorrelated** versus the alternative hypothesis H_a **that the error terms are positively autocorrelated.** Durbin and Watson have shown that there are points (denoted $d_{L,\alpha}$ and $d_{U,\alpha}$) such that, if α is the probability of a Type I error, then

1 If $d < d_{L,\alpha}$, we reject H_0.

2 If $d > d_{U,\alpha}$, we do not reject H_0.

3 If $d_{L,\alpha} \le d \le d_{U,\alpha}$, the test is inconclusive.

So that the Durbin–Watson test may be easily done, tables containing the points $d_{L,\alpha}$ and $d_{U,\alpha}$ have been constructed. These tables give the appropriate $d_{L,\alpha}$ and $d_{U,\alpha}$ points for various values of α; k, the number of independent variables used by the regression model; and n, the number of observations. Tables A.10, A.11, and A.12 (pages 834–835) give these points for $\alpha = .05$, $\alpha = .025$, and $\alpha = .01$. A portion of Table A.10 is given in Table 11.6. Note that when we are considering a simple linear regression model, which uses *one* independent variable, we look up the points $d_{L,\alpha}$ and $d_{U,\alpha}$ under the heading "$k = 1$." Other values of k are used when we study multiple regression models in Chapter 12. Using the residuals in Figure 11.30(a), the Durbin–Watson statistic for the simple linear regression model relating Pages' sales to Pages' advertising expenditure is calculated to be

$$\begin{aligned} d &= \frac{\sum_{t=2}^{16} (e_t - e_{t-1})^2}{\sum_{t=1}^{16} e_t^2} \\ &= \frac{(4.0 - 3.3)^2 + (0.0 - 4.0)^2 + \cdots + (6.7 - 4.4)^2}{(3.3)^2 + (4.0)^2 + \cdots + (6.7)^2} \\ &= .65 \end{aligned}$$

A MegaStat output of the Durbin–Watson statistic is given at the bottom of Figure 11.30(a). To test for positive autocorrelation, we note that there are $n = 16$ observations and the regression

TABLE 11.6 Critical Values for the Durbin–Watson *d* Statistic ($\alpha = .05$)

	$k = 1$		$k = 2$		$k = 3$		$k = 4$	
n	$d_{L,.05}$	$d_{U,.05}$	$d_{L,.05}$	$d_{U,.05}$	$d_{L,.05}$	$d_{U,.05}$	$d_{L,.05}$	$d_{U,.05}$
15	1.08	1.36	0.95	1.54	0.82	1.75	0.69	1.97
16	1.10	1.37	0.98	1.54	0.86	1.73	0.74	1.93
17	1.13	1.38	1.02	1.54	0.90	1.71	0.78	1.90
18	1.16	1.39	1.05	1.53	0.93	1.69	0.82	1.87
19	1.18	1.40	1.08	1.53	0.97	1.68	0.86	1.85
20	1.20	1.41	1.10	1.54	1.00	1.68	0.90	1.83

model uses $k = 1$ independent variable. Therefore, if we set $\alpha = .05$, Table 11.6 tells us that $d_{L,.05} = 1.10$ and $d_{U,.05} = 1.37$. Since $d = .65$ is less than $d_{L,.05} = 1.10$, we reject the null hypothesis of no autocorrelation. That is, we conclude (at an α of .05) that there is positive (first-order) autocorrelation.

It can be shown that the Durbin–Watson statistic d is always between 0 and 4. Large values of d (and hence small values of $4 - d$) lead us to conclude that there is negative autocorrelation because if d is large, this indicates that the differences $(e_t - e_{t-1})$ are large. This says that the adjacent error terms ε_t and ε_{t-1} are negatively autocorrelated. Consider testing the null hypothesis ***H*₀ that the error terms are not autocorrelated** versus the alternative hypothesis ***Hₐ* that the error terms are negatively autocorrelated.** Durbin and Watson have shown that based on setting the probability of a Type I error equal to α, the points $d_{L,\alpha}$ and $d_{U,\alpha}$ are such that

1 If $(4 - d) < d_{L,\alpha}$, we reject H_0.
2 If $(4 - d) > d_{U,\alpha}$, we do not reject H_0.
3 If $d_{L,\alpha} \le (4 - d) \le d_{U,\alpha}$, the test is inconclusive.

As an example, for the Pages' sales simple linear regression model, we see that

$$(4 - d) = (4 - .65) = 3.35 > d_{U,.05} = 1.37$$

Therefore, on the basis of setting α equal to .05, we do not reject the null hypothesis of no autocorrelation. That is, there is no evidence of negative (first-order) autocorrelation.

We can also use the Durbin–Watson statistic to test for positive or negative autocorrelation. Specifically, consider testing the null hypothesis ***H*₀ that the error terms are not autocorrelated** versus the alternative hypothesis ***Hₐ* that the error terms are positively or negatively autocorrelated.** Durbin and Watson have shown that, based on setting the probability of a Type I error equal to α,

1 If $d < d_{L,\alpha/2}$ or if $(4 - d) < d_{L,\alpha/2}$, we reject H_0.
2 If $d > d_{U,\alpha/2}$ and if $(4 - d) > d_{U,\alpha/2}$, we do not reject H_0.
3 If $d_{L,\alpha/2} \le d \le d_{U,\alpha/2}$ or if $d_{L,\alpha/2} \le (4 - d) \le d_{U,\alpha/2}$, the test is inconclusive.

For example, consider testing for positive or negative autocorrelation in the Pages' sales model. If we set α equal to .05, then $\alpha/2 = .025$, and we need to find the points $d_{L,.025}$ and $d_{U,.025}$ when $n = 16$ and $k = 1$. Looking up these points in Table A.11 (page 834), we find that $d_{L,.025} = .98$ and $d_{U,.025} = 1.24$. Since $d = .65$ is less than $d_{L,.025} = .98$, we reject the null hypothesis of no autocorrelation. That is, we conclude (at an α of .05) that there is first-order autocorrelation.

Although we have used the Pages' sales model in these examples to demonstrate the Durbin–Watson tests for (1) positive autocorrelation, (2) negative autocorrelation, and (3) positive or negative autocorrelation, we must in practice choose one of these Durbin–Watson tests in a particular situation. Since positive autocorrelation is more common in real time series data than negative autocorrelation, the Durbin–Watson test for positive autocorrelation is used more often than the other two tests. Also, note that each Durbin–Watson test assumes that the population of all possible residuals at any time t has a normal distribution.

Transforming the dependent variable: A possible remedy for violations of the constant variance, correct functional form, and normality assumptions In general, if a data or residual plot indicates that the error variance of a regression model increases as an independent variable or the predicted value of the dependent variable increases, then we can sometimes remedy the situation by transforming the dependent variable. One transformation that works well is to take each y value to a fractional power. As an example, we might use a transformation in which we take the square root (or one-half power) of each y value. Letting y^* denote the value obtained when the transformation is applied to y, we would write the **square root transformation** as

$$y^* = \sqrt{y} = y^{.5}$$

Another commonly used transformation is the **quartic root transformation.** Here we take each y value to the one-fourth power. That is,

$$y^* = y^{.25}$$

If we consider a transformation that takes each y value to a fractional power (such as .5, .25, or the like), as the power approaches 0, the transformed value y^* approaches the natural logarithm of y (commonly written lny). In fact, we sometimes use the **logarithmic transformation**

$$y^* = lny$$

which takes the natural logarithm of each y value. In general, when we take a fractional power (including the natural logarithm) of the dependent variable, the transformation not only tends to equalize the error variance but also tends to "straighten out" certain types of nonlinear data plots. Specifically, if a data plot indicates that the dependent variable is increasing at an increasing rate (as in Figure 11.25 on page 497), then a fractional power transformation tends to straighten out the data plot. A fractional power transformation can also help to remedy a violation of the normality assumption. Because we cannot know which fractional power to use before we actually take the transformation, we recommend taking all of the square root, quartic root, and natural logarithm transformations and seeing which one best equalizes the error variance and (possibly) straightens out a nonlinear data plot.

Example 11.20 The QHIC Case

C

Consider the QHIC upkeep expenditures. In Figures 11.31, 11.32, and 11.33 we show the plots that result when we take the square root, quartic root, and natural logarithmic transformations of the upkeep expenditures and plot the transformed values versus the home values. The square root transformation seems to best equalize the error variance and straighten out the curved data plot in Figure 11.25. Note that the natural logarithm transformation seems to "overtransform" the data—the error variance tends to decrease as the home value increases and the data plot seems to

FIGURE 11.31 MINITAB Plot of the Square Roots of the Upkeep Expenditures versus the Home Values

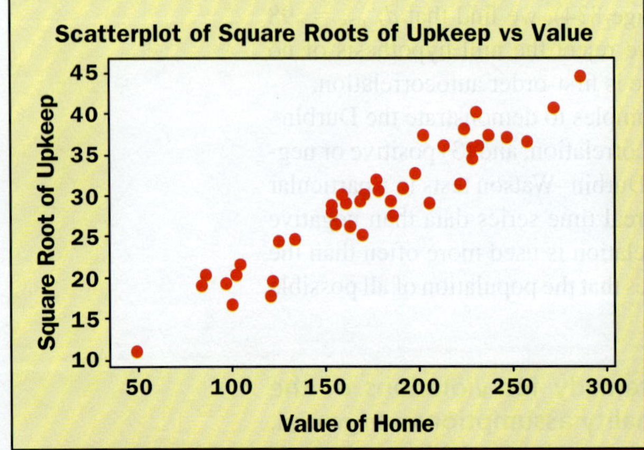

FIGURE 11.32 MINITAB Plot of the Quartic Roots of the Upkeep Expenditures versus the Home Values

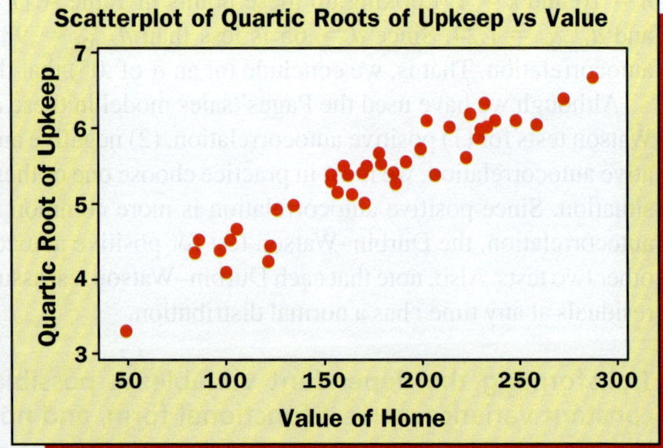

FIGURE 11.33 MINITAB Plot of the Natural Logarithms of the Upkeep Expenditures versus the Home Values

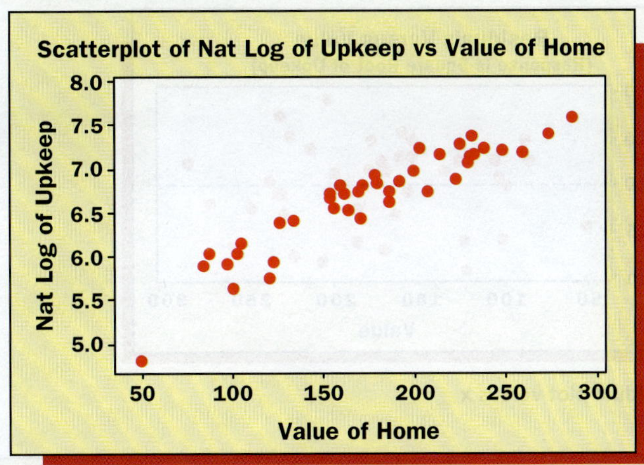

FIGURE 11.34 MINITAB Output of a Regression Analysis of the Upkeep Expenditure Data by Using the Model $y^* = \beta_0 + \beta_1 x + \varepsilon$ where $y^* = y^{.5}$

```
The regression equation is
SqRtUpkeep = 7.20 + 0.127 Value

Predictor        Coef   SE Coef      T      P
Constant        7.201     1.205   5.98  0.000
Value        0.127047  0.006577  19.32  0.000

S = 2.32479   R-Sq = 90.8%   R-Sq(adj) = 90.5%

Analysis of Variance
Source          DF      SS      MS       F      P
Regression       1  2016.8  2016.8  373.17  0.000
Residual Error  38   205.4     5.4
Total           39  2222.2

Values of Predictors for New Obs   Predicted Values for New Observations
New Obs  Value                     New Obs     Fit  SE Fit          95% CI              95% PI
      1    220                           1  35.151   0.474  (34.191, 36.111)  (30.348, 39.954)
```

"bend down." The plot of the quartic roots indicates that the quartic root transformation also seems to overtransform the data (but not by as much as the logarithmic transformation). In general, as the fractional power gets smaller, the transformation gets stronger. Different fractional powers are best in different situations.

Since the plot in Figure 11.31 of the square roots of the upkeep expenditures versus the home values has a straight-line appearance, we consider the model

$$y^* = \beta_0 + \beta_1 x + \varepsilon \quad \text{where } y^* = y^{.5}$$

The MINITAB output of a regression analysis using this transformed model is given in Figure 11.34, and the MINITAB output of an analysis of the model's residuals is given in Figure 11.35. Note that the residual plot versus x for the transformed model in Figure 11.35(a) has a horizontal band appearance. It can also be verified that the transformed model's residual plot versus $\hat{y}$, which we do not give here, has a similar horizontal band appearance. Therefore, we conclude that the constant variance and the correct functional form assumptions approximately hold for the transformed model. Next, note that the histogram of the transformed model's residuals in

FIGURE 11.35 MINITAB Output of Residual Analysis for the Upkeep Expenditure Model $y^* = \beta_0 + \beta_1 x + \varepsilon$ where $y^* = y^{.5}$

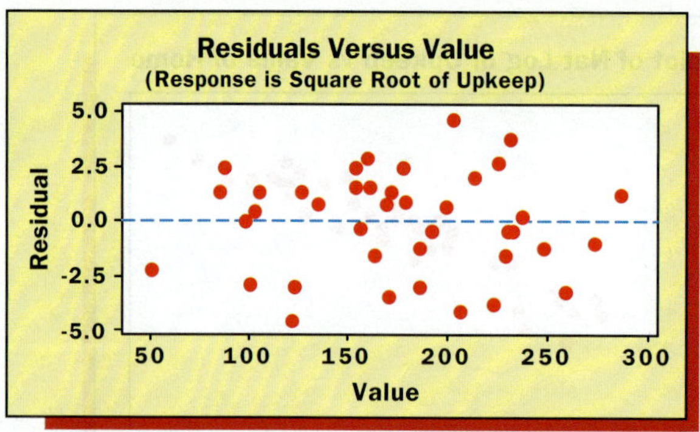

(a) Residual plot versus x

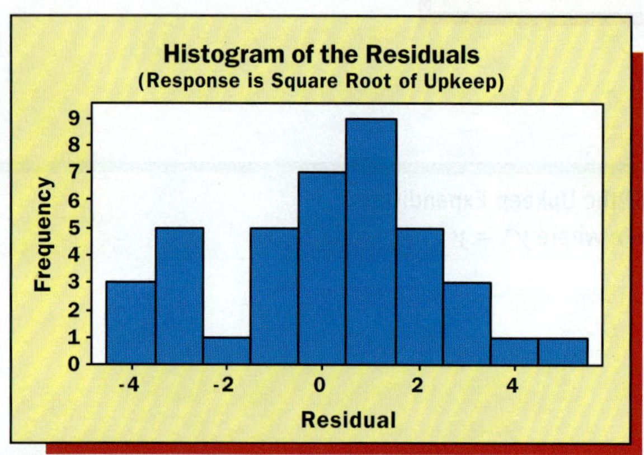

(b) Histogram of the residuals

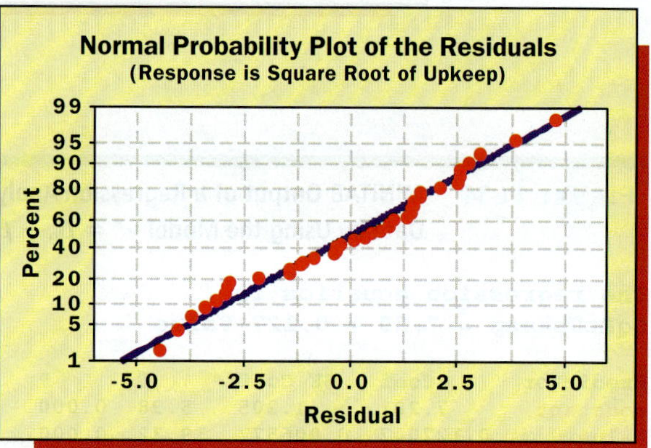

(c) Normal plot of the residuals

Figure 11.35(b) looks reasonably bell-shaped and symmetric, and note that the normal plot of these residuals in Figure 11.35(c) looks straighter than the normal plot for the untransformed model (see Figure 11.28 on page 501). Therefore, we also conclude that the normality assumption approximately holds for the transformed model.

Because the regression assumptions approximately hold for the transformed regression model, we can use this model to make statistical inferences. Consider a home worth \$220,000. Using the least squares point estimates on the MINITAB output in Figure11.34, it follows that a point prediction of y^* for such a home is

$$\begin{aligned}\hat{y}^* &= 7.201 + .127047(220)\\ &= 35.151\end{aligned}$$

This point prediction is given at the bottom of the MINITAB output, as is the 95 percent prediction interval for y^*, which is [30.348, 39.954]. It follows that a point prediction of the upkeep expenditure for a home worth \$220,000 is $(35.151)^2 = \$1{,}235.59$ and that a 95 percent prediction interval for this upkeep expenditure is $[(30.348)^2, (39.954)^2] = [\$921.00, \$1596.32]$. Suppose that QHIC wishes to send an advertising brochure to any home that has a predicted upkeep expenditure of at least \$500. Solving the prediction equation $\hat{y}^* = b_0 + b_1x$ for x, and noting that a predicted upkeep expenditure of \$500 corresponds to a $\hat{y}^*$ of $\sqrt{500} = 22.36068$, we obtain

$$x = \frac{\hat{y}^* - b_0}{b_1} = \frac{22.36068 - 7.201}{.127047} = 119.3234 \text{ (or \$119,323)}$$

It follows that QHIC should send the advertising brochure to any home that has a value of at least \$119,323.

Recall that because there are many homes of a particular value in the metropolitan area, QHIC is interested in estimating the mean upkeep expenditure corresponding to this value. Consider all homes worth, for example, $220,000. The MINITAB output in Figure 11.34 tells us that a point estimate of the mean of the square roots of the upkeep expenditures for all such homes is 35.151 and that a 95 percent confidence interval for this mean is [34.191, 36.111]. Unfortunately, because it can be shown that the mean of the square root is not the square root of the mean, we cannot transform the results for the mean of the square roots back into a result for the mean of the original upkeep expenditures. This is a major drawback to transforming the dependent variable and one reason why many statisticians avoid transforming the dependent variable unless the regression assumptions are badly violated. In Chapter 12 we discuss other remedies for violations of the regression assumptions that do not have some of the drawbacks of transforming the dependent variable. Some of these remedies involve transforming the independent variable—a procedure introduced in Exercise 11.82 of this section. Furthermore, if we reconsider the residual analysis of the original, untransformed QHIC model in Figures 11.26 (page 499) and 11.28 (page 501), we might conclude that the regression assumptions are not badly violated for the untransformed model. Also, note that the point prediction, 95 percent prediction interval, and value of x obtained here using the transformed model are not very different from the results obtained in Examples 11.5 (page 465) and 11.12 (page 483) using the untransformed model. This implies that it might be reasonable to rely on the results obtained using the untransformed model, or to at least rely on the results for the mean upkeep expenditures obtained using the untransformed model.

In this section we have concentrated on analyzing the residuals for the QHIC simple linear regression model. If we analyze the residuals in Table 11.4 (page 462) for the fuel consumption simple linear regression model (recall that the fuel consumption data are time series data), we conclude that the regression assumptions approximately hold for this model.

Exercises for Section 11.9

CONCEPTS

11.72 In a regression analysis, what variables should the residuals be plotted against? What types of patterns in residual plots indicate violations of the regression assumptions?

11.73 In regression analysis, how do we check the normality assumption?

11.74 What is one possible remedy for violations of the constant variance, correct functional form, and normality assumptions?

METHODS AND APPLICATIONS

11.75 THE FUEL CONSUMPTION CASE FuelCon1

Recall that Table 11.4 gives the residuals from the simple linear regression model relating weekly fuel consumption to average hourly temperature. Figure 11.36(a) gives the Excel output of a plot of these residuals versus average hourly temperature. Describe the appearance of this plot. Does the plot indicate any violations of the regression assumptions?

11.76 THE FRESH DETERGENT CASE Fresh

Figure 11.36(b) gives the MINITAB output of residual diagnostics that are obtained when the simple linear regression model is fit to the Fresh detergent demand data. Interpret the diagnostics and determine if they indicate any violations of the regression assumptions.

11.77 THE SERVICE TIME CASE SrvcTime

The MegaStat output of the residuals given by the service time model is given in Figure 11.37, and MegaStat output of residual plots versus x and $\hat{y}$ is given in Figure 11.38(a) and (b). Do the plots indicate any violations of the regression assumptions?

11.78 THE SERVICE TIME CASE SrvcTime

Figure 11.37 gives the MegaStat output of the residuals from the simple linear regression model describing the service time-data in Exercise 11.7.

FIGURE 11.36 Residual Diagnostics for Exercises 11.75 and 11.76

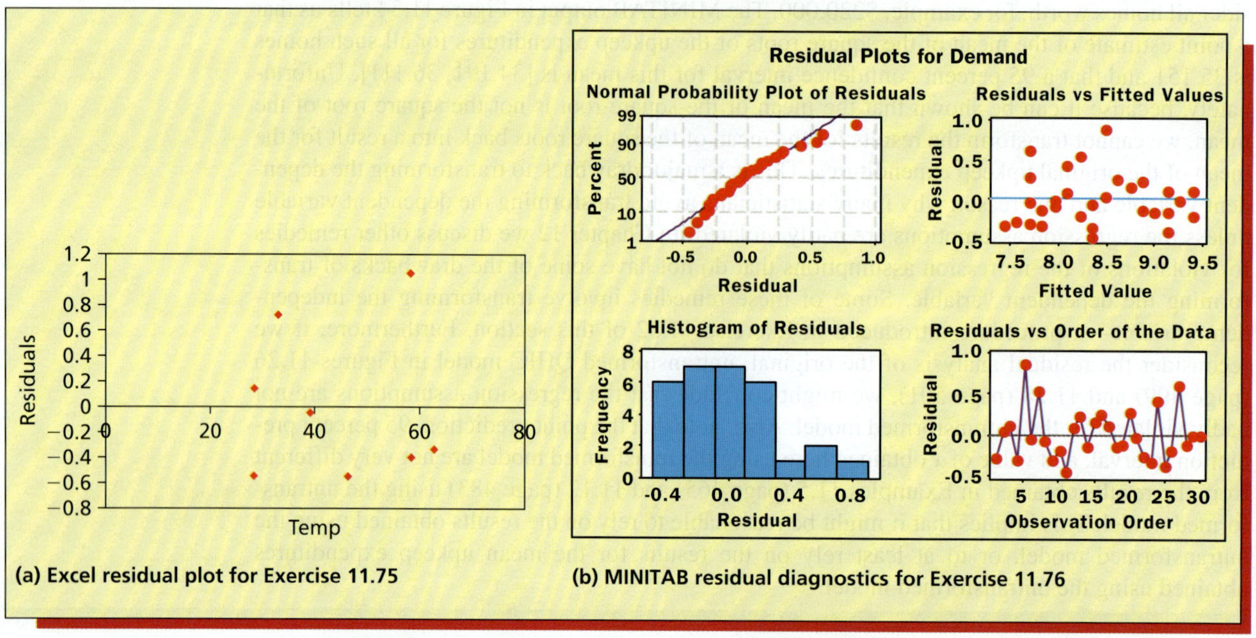

(a) Excel residual plot for Exercise 11.75

(b) MINITAB residual diagnostics for Exercise 11.76

FIGURE 11.37 MegaStat Output of the Residuals for the Service Time Model

Observation	Minutes	Predicted	Residual
1	109.0	109.9	−0.9
2	58.0	60.7	−2.7
3	138.0	134.5	3.5
4	189.0	183.7	5.3
5	37.0	36.1	0.9
6	82.0	85.3	−3.3
7	103.0	109.9	−6.9
8	134.0	134.5	−0.5
9	68.0	60.7	7.3
10	112.0	109.9	2.1
11	154.0	159.1	−5.1

TABLE 11.7 Ordered Residuals and Normal Plot Calculations

i	Ordered Residual, $e_{(i)}$	$\frac{3i-1}{3n+1}$	$z_{(i)}$
1	−6.9	.0588	−1.565
2	−5.1	.1470	−1.05
3	−3.3	.2353	−.72
4	−2.7	.3235	−.46
5	−0.9	.4118	−.22
6	−0.5	.5000	0
7	0.9	.5882	.22
8	2.1	.6765	.46
9	3.5	.7647	.72
10	5.3	.8529	1.05
11	7.3	.9412	1.565

a In this exercise we construct a normal plot of the residuals from the simple linear regression model. To construct this plot, we must first arrange the residuals in order from smallest to largest. These ordered residuals are given in Table 11.7. Denoting the ith ordered residual as $e_{(i)}$ $(i = 1, 2, \ldots, 11)$, we next compute for each value of i the point $z_{(i)}$. These computations are summarized in Table 11.7. Show how $z_{(4)} = -.46$ and $z_{(10)} = 1.05$ have been obtained.

b The ordered residuals (the $e_{(i)}$'s) are plotted against the $z_{(i)}$'s on the MegaStat output of Figure 11.38(c). Does this figure indicate a violation of the normality assumption?

11.79 A simple linear regression model is employed to analyze the 24 monthly observations given in Table 11.8. Residuals are computed and are plotted versus time. The resulting residual plot is shown in Figure 11.39 (on page 512). Discuss why the residual plot suggests the existence of positive autocorrelation. The Durbin–Watson statistic d can be calculated to be .473. Test for positive (first-order) autocorrelation at $\alpha = .05$, and test for negative (first-order) autocorrelation at $\alpha = .05$. SalesAdv

11.80 USING A NATURAL LOGARITHM TRANSFORMATION WestStk

Western Steakhouses, a fast-food chain, opened 15 years ago. Each year since then the number of steakhouses in operation, y, was recorded. An analyst for the firm wishes to use these data to

FIGURE 11.38 MegaStat Residual Plots for the Service Time Model

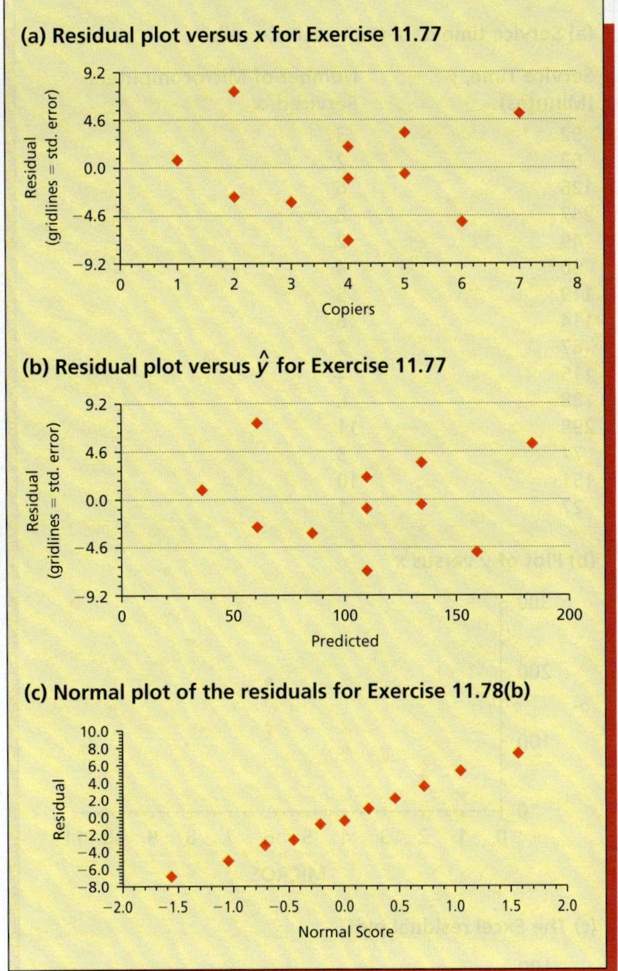

TABLE 11.8 Sales and Advertising Data for Exercise 11.79 SalesAdv

Month	Monthly Total Sales, *y*	Advertising Expenditures, *x*
1	202.66	116.44
2	232.91	119.58
3	272.07	125.74
4	290.97	124.55
5	299.09	122.35
6	296.95	120.44
7	279.49	123.24
8	255.75	127.55
9	242.78	121.19
10	255.34	118.00
11	271.58	121.81
12	268.27	126.54
13	260.51	129.85
14	266.34	122.65
15	281.24	121.64
16	286.19	127.24
17	271.97	132.35
18	265.01	130.86
19	274.44	122.90
20	291.81	117.15
21	290.91	109.47
22	264.95	114.34
23	228.40	123.72
24	209.33	130.33

Source: *Forecasting Methods and Applications*, "Sales and Advertising Data," by S. Makridakis, S. C. Wheelwright, and V. E. McGee, *Forecasting: Methods and Applications* (Copyright © 1983 John Wiley & Sons, Inc.). Reprinted by permission of John Wiley & Sons, Inc.

predict the number of steakhouses that will be in operation next year. The data are given in Figure 11.40(a) on page 512, and a plot of the data is given in Figure 11.40(b). Examining the data plot, we see that the number of steakhouse openings has increased over time at an increasing rate and with increasing variation. A plot of the natural logarithms of the steakhouse values versus time (see Figure 11.40(c)) has a straight-line appearance with constant variation. Therefore, we consider the model

$$\ln y_t = \beta_0 + \beta_1 t + \varepsilon_t$$

If we use MINITAB, we find that the least squares point estimates of β_0 and β_1 are $b_0 = 2.07012$ and $b_1 = .256880$. We also find that a point prediction of and a 95 percent prediction interval for the natural logarithm of the number of steakhouses in operation next year (year 16) are 6.1802 and [5.9945, 6.3659]. See the MINITAB output in Figure 11.43 on page 513.

a Use the least squares point estimates to verify the point prediction.

b By exponentiating the point prediction and prediction interval—that is, by calculating $e^{6.1802}$ and $[e^{5.9945}, e^{6.3659}]$—find a point prediction of and a 95 percent prediction interval for the number of steakhouses in operation next year.

c Use the Durbin-Watson statistic on the MINITAB output to test for positive autocorrelation at the .05 level of significance.

d The model $\ln y_t = \beta_0 + \beta_1 t + \varepsilon_t$ is called a **growth curve model** because it implies that

$$y_t = e^{(\beta_0 + \beta_1 t + \varepsilon_t)} = (e^{\beta_0})(e^{\beta_1 t})(e^{\varepsilon_t}) = \alpha_0 \alpha_1^t \eta_t$$

FIGURE 11.39 Residual Plot for Exercise 11.79

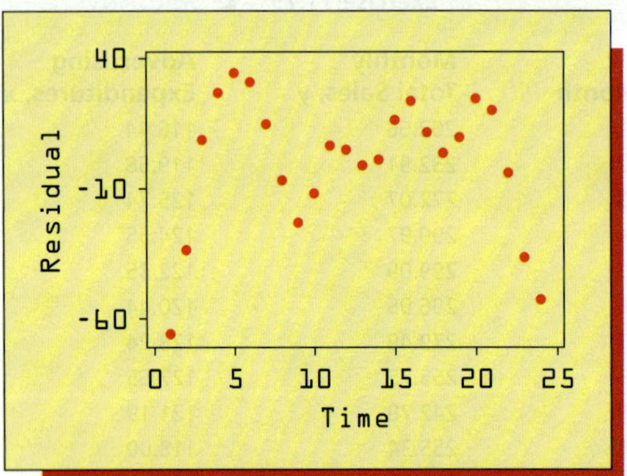

FIGURE 11.40 The Data and Data Plots for Exercise 11.80 WestStk

(a) Western Steakhouse Openings for the Last 15 Years

Year, t	Steakhouse Openings, y
1	11
2	14
3	16
4	22
5	28
6	36
7	46
8	67
9	82
10	99
11	119
12	156
13	257
14	284
15	403

(b) Time Series Plot of y versus t

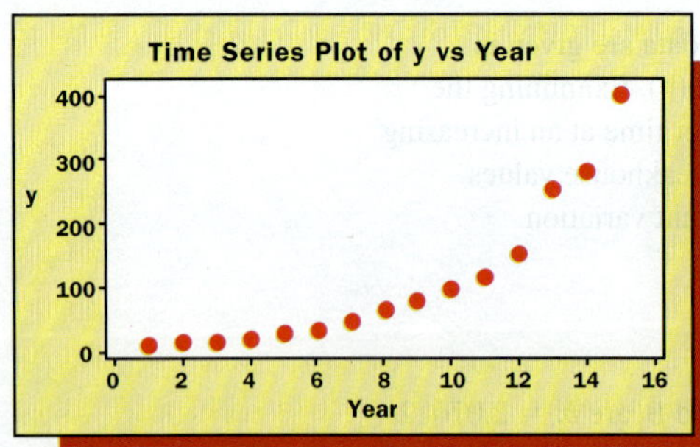

(c) Time Series Plot of Natural Logarithm of y versus t

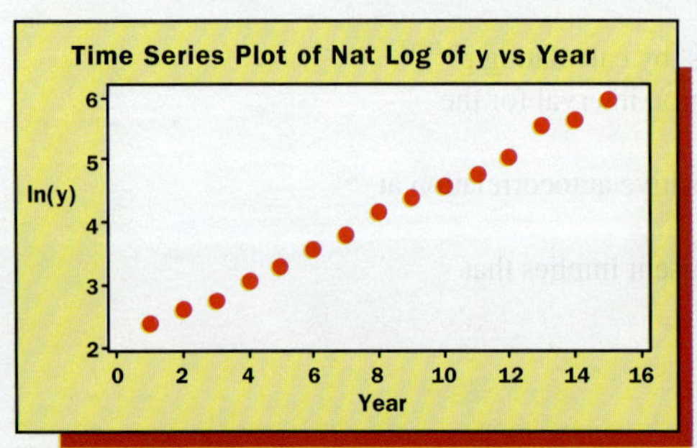

FIGURE 11.41 The Data, Data Plot, and Residual Plot for Exercise 11.81 SrvcTime2

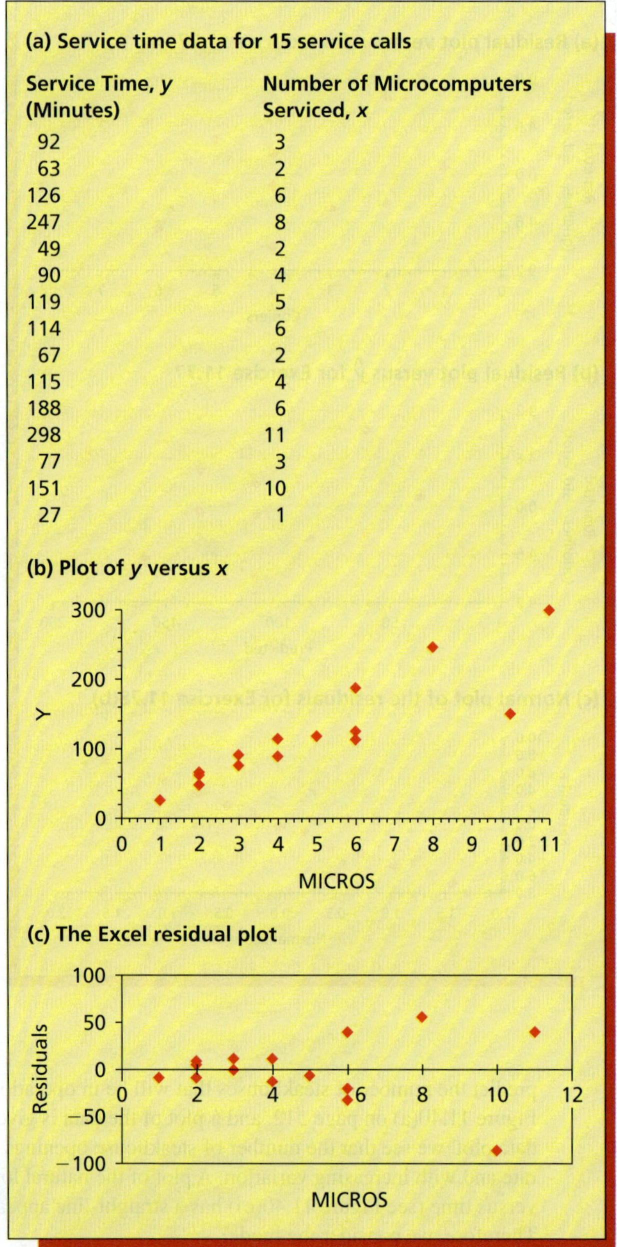

(a) Service time data for 15 service calls

Service Time, y (Minutes)	Number of Microcomputers Serviced, x
92	3
63	2
126	6
247	8
49	2
90	4
119	5
114	6
67	2
115	4
188	6
298	11
77	3
151	10
27	1

(b) Plot of y versus x

(c) The Excel residual plot

FIGURE 11.42 MegaStat Residual Plot for Exercise 11.82

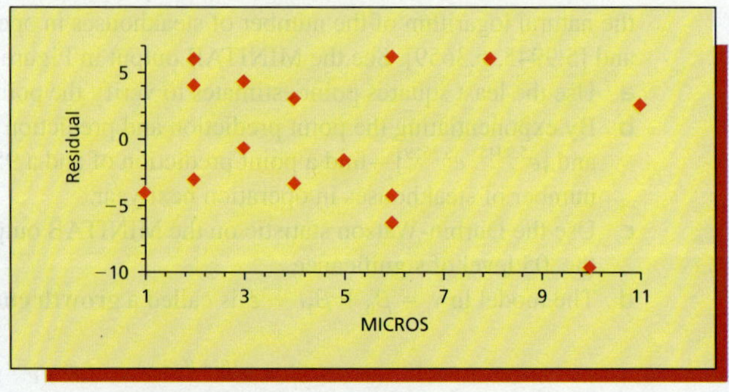

where $\alpha_0 = e^{\beta_0}$, $\alpha_1 = e^{\beta_1}$, and $\eta_t = e^{\varepsilon_t}$. Here $\alpha_1 = e^{\beta_1}$ is called the **growth rate** of the y values. Noting that the least squares point estimate of β_1 is $b_1 = .256880$, estimate the growth rate α_1. Also, interpret this growth rate by using the fact that $y_t = \alpha_0 \alpha_1^t \eta_t = (\alpha_0 \alpha_1^{t-1})\alpha_1 \eta_t \approx (y_{t-1})\alpha\eta_t$. This says that y_t is expected to be approximately α_1 times y_{t-1}.

11.81 THE UNEQUAL VARIANCES SERVICE TIME CASE SrvcTime2

Figure 11.41(a) presents data concerning the time, y, required to perform service and the number of microcomputers serviced, x, for 15 service calls. Figure 11.41(b) gives a plot of y versus x, and Figure 11.41(c) gives the Excel output of a plot of the residuals versus x for a simple linear regression model. What regression assumption appears to be violated?

11.82 THE UNEQUAL VARIANCES SERVICE TIME CASE SrvcTime2

Consider the simple linear regression model describing the service time data in Figure 11.41(a). Figure 11.41(c) shows that the residual plot versus x for this model fans out, indicating that the error term ε tends to become larger in magnitude as x increases. To remedy this violation of the

FIGURE 11.43 MINITAB Output of a Regression Analysis of the Steakhouse Data Using the Model $y^* = \beta_0 + \beta_1 x + \varepsilon$ where $y^* = ln y$

```
The regression equation is
ln(y) = 2.07 + 0.257 Year

Predictor      Coef     SE Coef       T       P
Constant    2.07012     0.04103   50.45   0.000
Year       0.256880    0.004513   56.92   0.000

S = 0.0755161   R-Sq = 99.6%   R-Sq(adj) = 99.6%   Durbin-Watson statistic = 1.87643

Analysis of Variance
Source          DF      SS      MS        F       P
Regression       1  18.477  18.477  3239.97   0.000
Residual Error  13   0.074   0.006
Total           14  18.551

Values of Predictors for New Obs      Predicted Values for New Observations
New Obs  Year                         Obs     Fit  SE Fit          95% CI            95% PI
      1    16                           1  6.1802  0.0410  (6.0916, 6.2689)  (5.9945, 6.3659)
```

FIGURE 11.44 MegaStat Output of a Regression Analysis of the Service Time Data Using the Model $y/x = \beta_0 + \beta_1(1/x) + \varepsilon/x$

Regression Analysis

r^2	0.095	n	15
r	0.308	k	1
Std. Error	5.158	Dep. Var.	**Y/X**

ANOVA table

Source	SS	df	MS	F	p-value
Regression	36.2685	1	36.2685	1.36	.2640
Residual	345.8857	13	26.6066		
Total	382.1542	14			

Regression output					confidence interval	
variables	coefficients	std. error	t (df = 13)	p-value	95% lower	95% upper
Intercept	24.0406	2.2461	10.703	8.13E-08	19.1883	28.8929
1/X	6.7642	5.7936	1.168	.2640	−5.7521	19.2804

Predicted values for: Y/X

		95% Confidence Intervals		95% Prediction Intervals		
1/X	Predicted	lower	upper	lower	upper	Leverage
0.1429	25.0069	21.4335	28.5803	13.3044	36.7094	0.103

constant variance assumption, we divide all terms in the simple linear regression model by x. This gives the transformed model

$$\frac{y}{x} = \beta_0\left(\frac{1}{x}\right) + \beta_1 + \frac{\varepsilon}{x} \quad \text{or, equivalently,} \quad \frac{y}{x} = \beta_0 + \beta_1\left(\frac{1}{x}\right) + \frac{\varepsilon}{x}$$

Figure 11.44 and Figure 11.42 give a regression output and a residual plot versus x for this model.

a Does the residual plot indicate that the constant variance assumption holds for the transformed model?

b Consider a future service call on which seven microcomputers will be serviced. Let μ_0 represent the mean service time for all service calls on which seven microcomputers will be serviced, and let y_0 represent the actual service time for an individual service call on which seven microcomputers will be serviced. The bottom of the MegaStat output in Figure 11.44 tells us that

$$\frac{\hat{y}}{7} = 24.0406 + 6.7642\left(\frac{1}{7}\right) = 25.0069$$

is a point estimate of $\mu_0/7$ and a point prediction of $y_0/7$. Multiply this result by 7 to obtain $\hat{y}$. Multiply the ends of the confidence interval and prediction interval shown on the MegaStat output by 7. This will give a 95 percent confidence interval for μ_0 and a 95 percent prediction interval for y_0. If the number of minutes we will allow for the future service call is the upper limit of the 95 percent confidence interval for μ_0, how many minutes will we allow?

11.10 Some Shortcut Formulas (Optional)

Calculating the sum of squared residuals A shortcut formula for the sum of squared residuals is

$$SSE = SS_{yy} - \frac{SS_{xy}^2}{SS_{xx}}$$

where

$$SS_{yy} = \sum (y_i - \bar{y})^2 = \sum y_i^2 - \frac{\left(\sum y_i\right)^2}{n}$$

For example, consider the fuel consumption case. If we square each of the eight observed fuel consumptions in Table 11.1 (page 451) and add up the resulting squared values, we find that $\Sigma y_i^2 = 859.91$. We have also found in Example 11.4 (page 461) that $\Sigma y_i = 81.7$, $SS_{xy} = -179.6475$, and $SS_{xx} = 1{,}404.355$. It follows that

$$SS_{yy} = \sum y_i^2 - \frac{\left(\sum y_i\right)^2}{n}$$

$$= 859.91 - \frac{(81.7)^2}{8} = 25.549$$

and

$$SSE = SS_{yy} - \frac{SS_{xy}^2}{SS_{xx}} = 25.549 - \frac{(-179.6475)^2}{1{,}404.355}$$

$$= 25.549 - 22.981 = 2.568$$

Finally, note that SS_{xy}^2/SS_{xx} equals $b_1 SS_{xy}$. However, we recommend using the first of these expressions, because doing so usually gives less round-off error.

Calculating the total, explained, and unexplained variations The **unexplained variation** is *SSE*, and thus the shortcut formula for *SSE* is a shortcut formula for the unexplained variation. The quantity SS_{yy} defined on page 514 is the **total variation,** and thus the shortcut formula for SS_{yy} is a shortcut formula for the total variation. Lastly, it can be shown that the expression SS_{xy}^2/SS_{xx} equals the **explained variation** and thus is a shortcut formula for this quantity.

Chapter Summary

This chapter has discussed **simple linear regression analysis,** which relates a **dependent variable** to a single **independent** (predictor) **variable.** We began by considering the **simple linear regression model,** which employs two parameters: the **slope** and ***y* intercept.** We next discussed how to compute the **least squares point estimates** of these parameters and how to use these estimates to calculate a **point estimate of the mean value of the dependent variable** and a **point prediction of an individual value** of the dependent variable. Then, after considering the assumptions behind the simple linear regression model, we discussed **testing the significance of the regression relationship (slope),** calculating a **confidence interval** for the mean value of the dependent variable, and calculating a **prediction interval** for an individual value of the dependent variable. We next explained several measures of the utility of the simple linear regression model. These include the **simple coefficient of determination** and an ***F* test for the simple linear model.** We concluded this chapter by giving an optional discussion of using **residual analysis** to detect violations of the regression assumptions. We learned that we can sometimes remedy violations of these assumptions by **transforming** the dependent variable.

Glossary of Terms

cross-sectional data: Data that are observed at a single point in time. (page 454)

dependent variable: The variable that is being described, predicted, or controlled. (page 449)

distance value: A measure of the distance between a particular value x_0 of the independent variable x and $\bar{x}$, the average of the previously observed values of x (the center of the experimental region). (page 479)

error term: The difference between an individual value of the dependent variable and the corresponding mean value of the dependent variable. (page 453)

experimental region: The range of the previously observed values of the independent variable. (page 462)

independent variable: A variable used to describe, predict, and control the dependent variable. (page 449)

least squares point estimates: The point estimates of the slope and *y* intercept of the simple linear regression model that minimize the sum of squared residuals. (pages 460–461)

negative autocorrelation: The situation in which positive error terms tend to be followed over time by negative error terms and negative error terms tend to be followed over time by positive error terms. (page 502)

normal plot: A residual plot that is used to check the normality assumption. (page 500)

positive autocorrelation: The situation in which positive error terms tend to be followed over time by positive error terms and negative error terms tend to be followed over time by negative error terms. (page 501)

residual: The difference between the observed value of the dependent variable and the corresponding predicted value of the dependent variable. (pages 460, 496)

residual plot: A plot of the residuals against some criterion. The plot is used to check the validity of one or more regression assumptions. (page 497)

simple coefficient of determination: The proportion of the total variation in the observed values of the dependent variable that is explained by the simple linear regression model. (page 486)

simple correlation coefficient: A measure of the linear association between two variables. (page 489)

simple linear regression model: An equation that describes the straight-line relationship between a dependent variable and an independent variable. (page 453)

slope (of the simple linear regression model): The change in the mean value of the dependent variable that is associated with a one-unit increase in the value of the independent variable. (page 453)

time series data: Data that are observed in time sequence. (page 454)

***y* intercept (of the simple linear regression model):** The mean value of the dependent variable when the value of the independent variable is 0. (page 453)

Important Formulas and Tests

Simple linear regression model: page 453
Least squares point estimates of β_0 and β_1: pages 460–461
Least squares line (prediction equation): page 460
The predicted value of y_i: page 460
The residual: pages 460 and 496
Sum of squared residuals: pages 460 and 514
Mean square error: page 470
Standard error: page 470
Sampling distribution of b_1: page 471
Standard error of the estimate b_1: page 471
Testing the significance of the slope: page 472
Testing the significance of the *y*-intercept: page 474

Supplementary Exercises

11.83 Consider the following data concerning the demand (y) and price (x) of a consumer product. Demand

Demand, y	252	244	241	234	230	223
Price, x	\$2.00	\$2.20	\$2.40	\$2.60	\$2.80	\$3.00

a Plot y versus x. Does it seem reasonable to use the simple linear regression model to relate y to x?
b Calculate the least squares point estimates of the parameters in the simple linear regression model.
c Write the least squares prediction equation. Graph this equation on the plot of y versus x.
d Test the significance of the regression relationship between y and x.
e Find a point prediction of and a 95 percent prediction interval for the demand corresponding to each of the prices \$2.10, \$2.75, and \$3.10.

11.84 In an article in *Public Roads* (1983), Bissell, Pilkington, Mason, and Woods study bridge safety (measured in accident rates per 100 million vehicles) and the **difference** between the width of the bridge and the width of the roadway approach (road plus shoulder):[5] AutoAcc

WidthDiff.	−6	−4	−2	0	2	4	6	8	10	12
Accident	120	103	87	72	58	44	31	20	12	7

The MINITAB output of a simple linear regression analysis relating accident to width difference is as follows:

```
The regression equation is
Accident Rate = 74.7 - 6.44 WidthDif

Predictor      Coef     SE Coef        T        P
Constant     74.727       1.904    39.25    0.000
WidthDif    -6.4424      0.2938   -21.93    0.000

S = 5.33627   R-Sq = 98.4%    R-Sq(adj) = 98.2%

Analysis of Variance
Source            DF        SS       MS        F        P
Regression         1     13697    13697   480.99    0.000
Residual Error     8       228       28
Total              9     13924
```

Using the MINITAB output
a Identify and interpret the least squares point estimate of the slope of the simple linear regression model.
b Identify and interpret the p-value for testing H_0: $\beta_1 = 0$ versus H_a: $\beta_1 \neq 0$.
c Identify and interpret r^2.

11.85 The data in Table 11.9 concerning the relationship between smoking and lung cancer death are presented in a course of The Open University, *Statistics in Society*, Unit C4, The Open University Press, Milton Keynes, England, 1983. The original source of the data is *Occupational Mortality: The Registrar General's Decennial Supplement for England and Wales, 1970–1972,* Her Majesty's Stationery Office, London, 1978. In the table, a smoking index greater (less) than 100 indicates that men in the occupational group smoke more (less) than average when compared to all men of the same age. Similarly, a lung cancer death index greater (less) than 100 indicates that men in the occupational group have a greater (less) than average lung cancer death rate when compared to all men of the same age. In Figure 11.45 we present a portion of a MINITAB output of a simple linear regression analysis relating the lung cancer death index to the smoking index. In Figure 11.46 we present a plot of the lung cancer death index versus the smoking index. Smoking

[5]Source: H. H. Bissell, G. B. Pilkington II, J. M. Mason, and D. L. Woods, "Roadway Cross Section and Alignment," *Public Roads* 46 (March 1983), pp. 132–41

TABLE 11.9 The Smoking and Lung Cancer Death Data Smoking

Occupational Group	Smoking Index	Lung Cancer Death Index
Farmers, foresters, and fisherman	77	84
Miners and quarrymen	137	116
Gas, coke, and chemical makers	117	123
Glass and ceramics makers	94	128
Furnace, forge, foundry, and rolling mill workers	116	155
Electrical and electronics workers	102	101
Engineering and allied trades	111	118
Woodworkers	93	113
Leather workers	88	104
Textile workers	102	88
Clothing workers	91	104
Food, drink, and tobacco workers	104	129
Paper and printing workers	107	86
Makers of other products	112	96
Construction workers	113	144
Painters and decorators	110	139
Drivers of stationary engines, cranes, etc.	125	113
Laborers not included elsewhere	133	146
Transport and communications workers	115	128
Warehousemen, storekeepers, packers, and bottlers	105	115
Clerical workers	87	79
Sales workers	91	85
Service, sport, and recreation workers	100	120
Administrators and managers	76	60
Professionals, technical workers, and artists	66	51

FIGURE 11.45 MINITAB Output of a Simple Linear Regression Analysis of the Data in Table 11.9

```
The regression equation is
Death Index = - 2.9 + 1.09 Smoking Index

Predictor        Coef    SE Coef       T       P
Constant        -2.89      23.03   -0.13   0.901
Smoking Index  1.0875     0.2209    4.92    0.00

S = 18.6154    R-Sq = 51.3%    R-Sq(adj) = 49.2%
```

FIGURE 11.46 A Plot of the Lung Cancer Death Index versus the Smoking Index

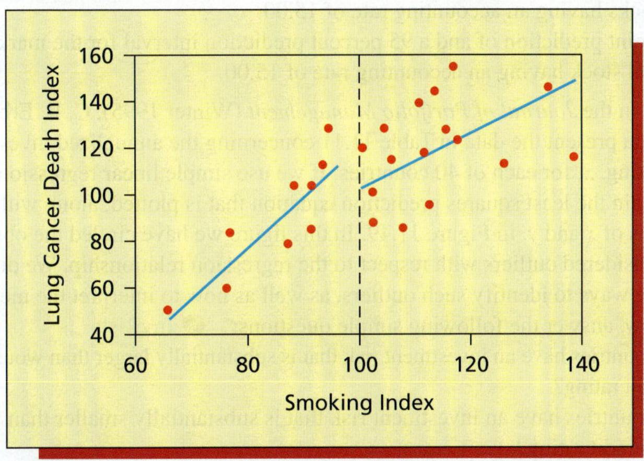

FIGURE 11.47 A Data Plot Based on Seven Launches

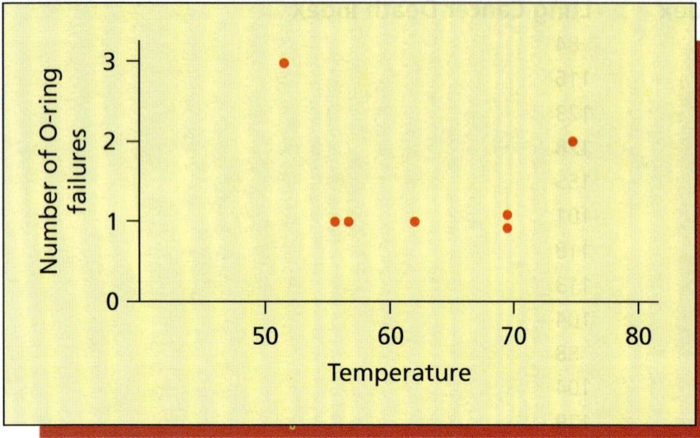

FIGURE 11.48 A Data Plot Based on All 24 Launches

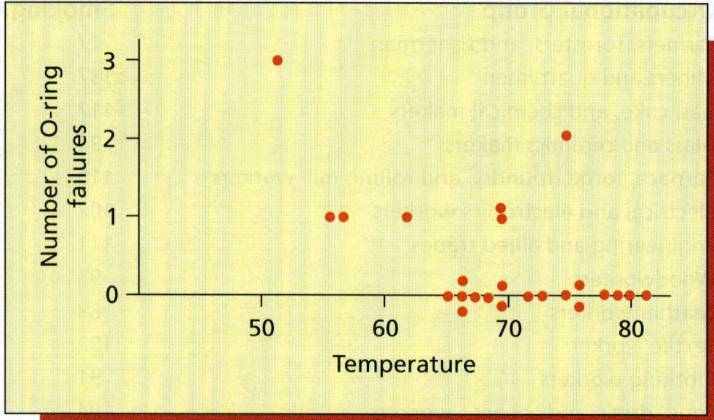

a Although the data do not prove that smoking increases your chance of getting lung cancer, can you think of a third factor that would cause the two indexes to move together?

b Does the slope of the hypothetical line relating the two indexes when the smoking index is less than 100 seem to equal the slope of the hypothetical line relating the two indexes when the smoking index is greater than 100? If you wish, use simple linear regression to make a more precise determination. What practical conclusion might you make?

11.86 On January 28, 1986, the space shuttle Challenger exploded soon after takeoff, killing all eight astronauts aboard. The temperature at the Kennedy Space Center at liftoff was 31°F. Before the launch, several scientists argued that the launch should be delayed because the shuttle's O-rings might harden in the cold and leak. Other scientists used the data plot in Figure 11.47 to argue that there was no relationship between temperature and O-ring failure. On the basis of this figure and other considerations, Challenger was launched to its disastrous, last flight.

Scientists using the data plot in Figure 11.47 made a horrible mistake. They relied on a data plot that was created by using only the seven previous launches where there was at least one O-ring failure. A plot based on all 24 previous launches—17 of which had no O-ring failures—is given in Figure 11.48.

a Intuitively, do you think that Figure 11.48 indicates that there is a relationship between temperature and O-ring failure? Use simple linear regression to justify your answer.

b Even though the figure using only seven launches is incomplete, what about it should have cautioned the scientists not to make the launch?

11.87 In an article in the *Journal of Accounting Research,* Benzion Barlev and Haim Levy consider relating accounting rates on stocks and market returns. Fifty-four companies were selected. For each company the authors recorded values of x, the mean yearly accounting rate for the period 1959 to 1974, and y, the mean yearly market return rate for the period 1959 to 1974. The data in Table 11.10 were obtained. Here the accounting rate can be interpreted to represent input into investment and therefore is a logical predictor of market return. Use the simple linear regression model and a computer to AcctRet

a Find a point estimate of and a 95 percent confidence interval for the mean market return rate of all stocks having an accounting rate of 15.00.

b Find a point prediction of and a 95 percent prediction interval for the market return rate of an individual stock having an accounting rate of 15.00.

11.88 In an article in the *Journal of Portfolio Management* (Winter 1995), C. B. Erb, C. R. Harvey, and T. E. Viskanta present the data in Table 11.11 concerning the annualized investment risk, y, and the credit rating, x, for each of 40 countries. If we use simple linear regression to analyze these data, we obtain the least squares prediction equation that is plotted, along with the observed combinations of x and y, in Figure 11.49. In this figure we have circled the observations that might be considered outliers with respect to the regression relationship. We discuss in Chapter 12 more precise ways to identify such outliers, as well as how to interpret the meanings of the outliers. For now, answer the following simple questions: InvRisk

a Which countries have an investment risk that is substantially larger than would be suggested by their credit rating?

b Which countries have an investment risk that is substantially smaller than would be suggested by their credit rating?

TABLE 11.10 Accounting Rates on Stocks and Market Returns for 54 Companies AcctRet

Company	Market Rate	Accounting Rate	Company	Market Rate	Accounting Rate
McDonnell Douglas	17.73	17.96	FMC	5.71	13.30
NCR	4.54	8.11	Caterpillar Tractor	13.38	17.66
Honeywell	3.96	12.46	Georgia Pacific	13.43	14.59
TRW	8.12	14.70	Minnesota Mining & Manufacturing	10.00	20.94
Raytheon	6.78	11.90	Standard Oil (Ohio)	16.66	9.62
W. R. Grace	9.69	9.67	American Brands	9.40	16.32
Ford Motors	12.37	13.35	Aluminum Company of America	.24	8.19
Textron	15.88	16.11	General Electric	4.37	15.74
Lockheed Aircraft	−1.34	6.78	General Tire	3.11	12.02
Getty Oil	18.09	9.41	Borden	6.63	11.44
Atlantic Richfield	17.17	8.96	American Home Products	14.73	32.58
Radio Corporation of America	6.78	14.17	Standard Oil (California)	6.15	11.89
Westinghouse Electric	4.74	9.12	International Paper	5.96	10.06
Johnson & Johnson	23.02	14.23	National Steel	6.30	9.60
Champion International	7.68	10.43	Republic Steel	.68	7.41
R. J. Reynolds	14.32	19.74	Warner Lambert	12.22	19.88
General Dynamics	−1.63	6.42	U.S. Steel	.90	6.97
Colgate-Palmolive	16.51	12.16	Bethlehem Steel	2.35	7.90
Coca-Cola	17.53	23.19	Armco Steel	5.03	9.34
International Business Machines	12.69	19.20	Texaco	6.13	15.40
Allied Chemical	4.66	10.76	Shell Oil	6.58	11.95
Uniroyal	3.67	8.49	Standard Oil (Indiana)	14.26	9.56
Greyhound	10.49	17.70	Owens Illinois	2.60	10.05
Cities Service	10.00	9.10	Gulf Oil	4.97	12.11
Philip Morris	21.90	17.47	Tenneco	6.65	11.53
General Motors	5.86	18.45	Inland Steel	4.25	9.92
Philips Petroleum	10.81	10.06	Kraft	7.30	12.27

Source: Reprinted by permission from Benzion Barlev and Haim Levy, "On the Variability of Accounting Income Numbers," *Journal of Accounting Research* (Autumn 1979), pp. 305–315. Copyright © 1979. Used with permission of Blackwell Publishers.

TABLE 11.11 Annualized Investment Risk and Credit Rating for 40 Countries InvRisk

Country	Annualized Investment Risk	Credit Rating	Country	Annualized Investment Risk	Credit Rating
Argentina	87.0	31.8	Malaysia	26.7	64.4
Australia	26.9	78.2	Mexico	46.3	43.3
Austria	26.3	83.8	Netherlands	18.5	87.6
Belgium	22.0	78.4	New Zealand	26.3	68.9
Brazil	64.8	36.2	Nigeria	41.4	30.6
Canada	19.2	87.1	Norway	28.3	83.0
Chile	31.6	38.6	Pakistan	24.4	26.4
Colombia	31.5	44.4	Philippines	38.4	29.6
Denmark	20.6	72.6	Portugal	47.5	56.7
Finland	26.1	76.0	Singapore	26.4	77.6
France	23.8	85.3	Spain	24.8	70.8
Germany	23.0	93.4	Sweden	24.5	79.5
Greece	39.6	51.9	Switzerland	19.6	94.7
Hong Kong	34.3	69.6	Taiwan	53.7	72.9
India	30.0	46.6	Thailand	27.0	55.8
Ireland	23.4	66.4	Turkey	74.1	32.6
Italy	28.0	75.5	United Kingdom	21.8	87.6
Japan	25.7	94.5	United States	15.4	93.4
Jordan	17.6	33.6	Venezuela	46.0	45.0
Korea	30.7	62.2	Zimbabwe	35.6	24.5

Source: C. B. Erb, C. R. Harvey, and T. E. Viskanta, "Country Risk and Global Equity Selection," *Journal of Portfolio Management* Vol. 21, No. 2, p. 76. This copyrighted material is reprinted with permission from *The Journal of Portfolio Management*, a publication of Institutional Investor, Inc., 488 Madison Ave., New York, NY 10022.

FIGURE 11.49 Plot of the Least Squares Prediction Equation for the Investment Risk Data

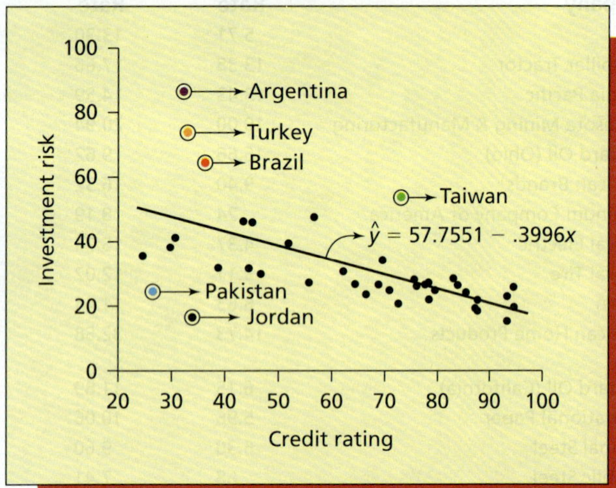

TABLE 11.12 The New Jersey Bank Data
NJBank

County	Percentage of Minority Population, x	Number of Residents Per Bank Branch, y
Atlantic	23.3	3,073
Bergen	13.0	2,095
Burlington	17.8	2,905
Camden	23.4	3,330
Cape May	7.3	1,321
Cumberland	26.5	2,557
Essex	48.8	3,474
Gloucester	10.7	3,068
Hudson	33.2	3,683
Hunterdon	3.7	1,998
Mercer	24.9	2,607
Middlesex	18.1	3,154
Monmouth	12.6	2,609
Morris	8.2	2,253
Ocean	4.7	2,317
Passaic	28.1	3,307
Salem	16.7	2,511
Somerset	12.0	2,333
Sussex	2.4	2,568
Union	25.6	3,048
Warren	2.8	2,349

Source: P. D'Ambrosio and S. Chambers, "No Checks and Balances," *Asbury Park Press,* September 10, 1995. Copyright © 1995 Asbury Park Press. Used with permission.

FIGURE 11.50 Excel Output of a Simple Linear Regression Analysis of the New Jersey Bank Data

Regression Statistics	
Multiple R	0.7256
R Square	0.5265
Adjusted R Square	0.5016
Standard Error	400.2546
Observations	21

ANOVA	df	SS	MS	F	Significance F
Regression	1	3385090.234	3385090	21.1299	0.0002
Residual	19	3043870.432	160203.7		
Total	20	6428960.667			

	Coefficients	Standard Error	t Stat	P-value	Lower 95%	Upper 95%
Intercept	2082.0153	159.1070	13.0856	5.92E-11	1749.0005	2415.0301
% Minority Pop (x)	35.2877	7.6767	4.5967	0.0002	19.2202	51.3553

11.89 In New Jersey, banks have been charged with withdrawing from counties having a high percentage of minorities. To substantiate this charge, P. D'Ambrosio and S. Chambers (1995) present the data in Table 11.12 concerning the percentage, x, of minority population and the number of county residents, y, per bank branch in each of New Jersey's 21 counties. If we use Excel to perform a simple linear regression analysis of this data, we obtain the output given in Figure 11.50. NJBank

a Determine if there is a significant relationship between x and y.

b Describe the exact nature of any relationship that exists between x and y. (Hint: Estimate β_1 by a point estimate and a confidence interval.)

11.90 In analyzing the stock market, we sometimes use the model $y = \beta_0 + \beta_1 x + \varepsilon$ to relate y, the rate of return on a particular stock, to x, the rate of return on the overall stock market. When using the preceding model, we can interpret β_1 to be the percentage point change in the mean (or expected) rate of return on the particular stock that is associated with an increase of one percentage point in the rate of return on the overall stock market.

If regression analysis can be used to conclude (at a high level of confidence) that β_1 is greater than 1 (for example, if the 95 percent confidence interval for β_1 were [1.1826, 1.4723]), this indicates that the mean rate of return on the particular stock changes more quickly than the rate of return on the overall stock market. Such a stock is called an *aggressive stock* because gains for such a stock tend to be greater than overall market gains (which occur when the market is bullish). However, losses for such a stock tend to be greater than overall market losses (which occur when the market is bearish). Aggressive stocks should be purchased if you expect the market to rise and avoided if you expect the market to fall.

If regression analysis can be used to conclude (at a high level of confidence) that β_1 is less than 1 (for example, if the 95 percent confidence interval for β_1 were [.4729, .7861]), this indicates that the mean rate of return on the particular stock changes more slowly than the rate of return on the overall stock market. Such a stock is called a *defensive stock.* Losses for such a stock tend to be less than overall market losses, whereas gains for such a stock tend to be less than overall market gains. Defensive stocks should be held if you expect the market to fall and sold off if you expect the market to rise.

If the least squares point estimate b_1 of β_1 is nearly equal to 1, and if the 95 percent confidence interval for β_1 contains 1, this might indicate that the mean rate of return on the particular stock changes at roughly the same rate as the rate of return on the overall stock market. Such a stock is called a *neutral stock.*

In a 1984 article in *Financial Analysts Journal,* Haim Levy considers how a stock's value of β_1 depends on the length of time for which the rate of return is calculated. Levy calculated estimated values of β_1 for return length times varying from 1 to 30 months for each of 38 aggressive stocks, 38 defensive stocks, and 68 neutral stocks. Each estimated value was based on data from 1946 to 1975. In the following table we present the average estimate of β_1 for each stock type for different return length times:

Average Estimate of β_1 Beta

Return Length Time	Aggressive Stocks	Defensive Stocks	Neutral Stocks
1	1.37	.50	.98
3	1.42	.44	.95
6	1.53	.41	.94
9	1.69	.39	1.00
12	1.83	.40	.98
15	1.67	.38	1.00
18	1.78	.39	1.02
24	1.86	.35	1.14
30	1.83	.33	1.22

Source: Reprinted by permission from H. Levy, "Measuring Risk and Performance over Alternative Investment Horizons," *Financial Analysts Journal* (March–April 1984), pp. 61–68. Copyright © 1984, CFA Institute. Reproduced and modified from Financial Analysts Journal with permission of CFA Institute.

Let y = average estimate of β_1 and x = return length time, and consider relating y to x for each stock type by using the simple linear regression model

$$y = \beta_0^* + \beta_1^* x + \varepsilon$$

Here β_0^* and β_1^* are regression parameters relating y to x. We use the asterisks to indicate that these regression parameters are different from β_0 and β_1. Calculate a 95 percent confidence interval for β_1^* for each stock type. Carefully interpret the meaning of each interval.

11.91 The State Department of Taxation wishes to investigate the effect of experience, x, on the amount of time, y, required to fill out Form ST 1040AVG, the state income-averaging form. In order to do this, nine people whose financial status makes income averaging advantageous are chosen at random. Each is asked to fill out Form ST 1040AVG and to report (1) the time y (in hours) required to complete the form and (2) the number of times x (including this one) that he or she has filled out this form. The following data are obtained: TaxTime

FIGURE 11.51 Plot of y versus x in Exercise 11.91

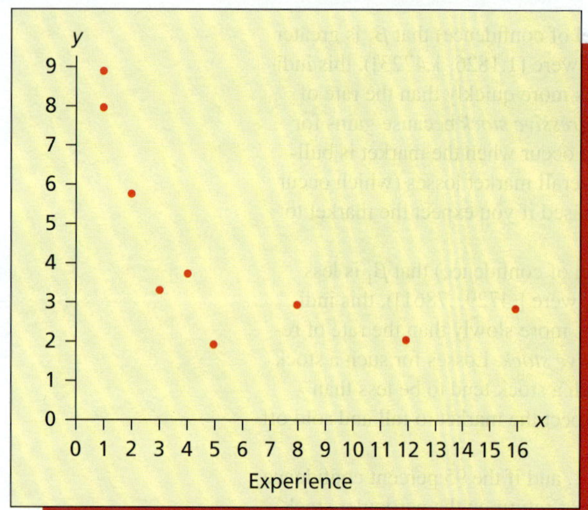

FIGURE 11.52 Plot of y versus $1/x$ in Exercise 11.91

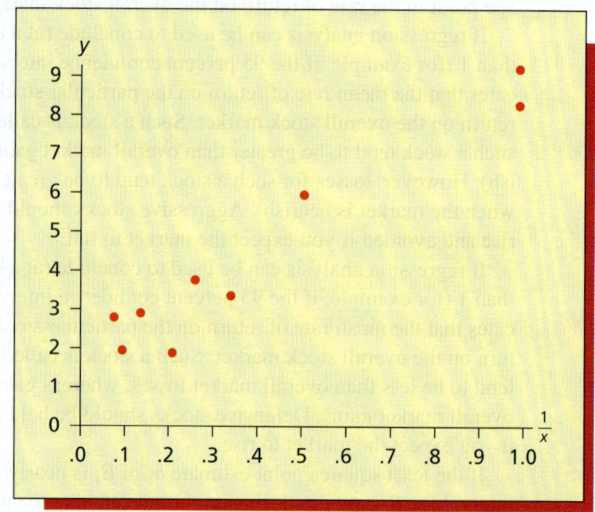

Completion time, y (in Hours)	8.0	4.7	3.7	2.8	8.9	5.8	2.0	1.9	3.3
Experience, x	1	8	4	16	1	2	12	5	3

A plot of these data is given in Figure 11.51 and indicates that the model

$$y = \mu_{y|x} + \varepsilon = \beta_0 + \beta_1\left(\frac{1}{x}\right) + \varepsilon$$

might appropriately relate y to x. To understand this model, note that as x increases, $1/x$ decreases and thus $\mu_{y|x}$ decreases. This seems to be what the data plot indicates is happening. To further understand this model, note that a plot of the values of y versus the values of $1/x$ in Figure 11.52 has a straight-line appearance. This indicates that a simple linear regression model having y as the dependent variable and $1/x$ as the independent variable—that is, the model we are considering—might be appropriate. Using the formulas of simple linear regression analysis, the least squares point estimates of β_0 and β_1 can be calculated to be $b_0 = 2.0572$ and $b_1 = 6.3545$. Furthermore, consider the completion time of an individual filling out the form for the fifth time (that is, $x = 5$). Then, it can be verified that a point prediction of and a 95 percent prediction interval for this completion time are, respectively, 3.3281 and [.7225, 5.9337]. Show how the point prediction has been calculated.

11.92 Internet Exercise US News

Graduate business schools use a variety of factors to guide the selection of applicants for admission to MBA programs. Among the key indicators are undergraduate GPA and Graduate Management Admissions Test (GMAT) score. Is there a statistically significant relationship between the average GMAT score and the average undergraduate GPA for admitted MBA program applicants? Can we develop a statistical model describing the relationship? How reliable are the predictions of the model? The U.S. News website ranks the top MBA programs and provides some interesting data on these questions—the average undergraduate GPA and the average GMAT score of admitted applicants for its 50 top-ranked MBA programs. Note that the data are somewhat limited in scope in that they reflect only the experience of top 50 programs.

Go to the U.S. News website and retrieve the data for the 50 top-ranked MBA programs, http://www.usnews.com. Click on (in turn) *.edu : Business : Top Business Schools* or go directly to http://www.usnews.com/usnews/edu/beyond/gradrank/mba/gdmbat1.htm. To capture the data—select the entire data table, copy and paste it into Excel or MINITAB, add your own variable labels, and clean up the data as necessary. Excel and MINITAB data files are also included on the CD-ROM (USNews.xls and USNews.mtw). Construct a scatter plot of *GMAT* versus *GPA*. Describe any apparent relationship between the two variables. Develop a simple linear regression model expressing *GMAT* as a linear function of *GPA*. Identify and interpret the key summary measures—R^2, the standard error, and the F-statistic from the ANOVA table. Identify and interpret the estimated regression coefficients. Suppose that the average undergraduate GPA for a particular program is 3.50. Use your regression model to predict the average GMAT score for the program. Prepare a brief report summarizing your analysis and conclusions.

Appendix 11.1 ■ Simple Linear Regression Analysis Using MINITAB

The instruction blocks in this section each begin by describing the entry of data into the MINITAB data window. Alternatively, the data may be loaded directly from the data disk included with the text. The appropriate data file name is given at the top of each instruction block. Please refer to Appendix 1.1 for further information about entering data, saving data, and printing results.

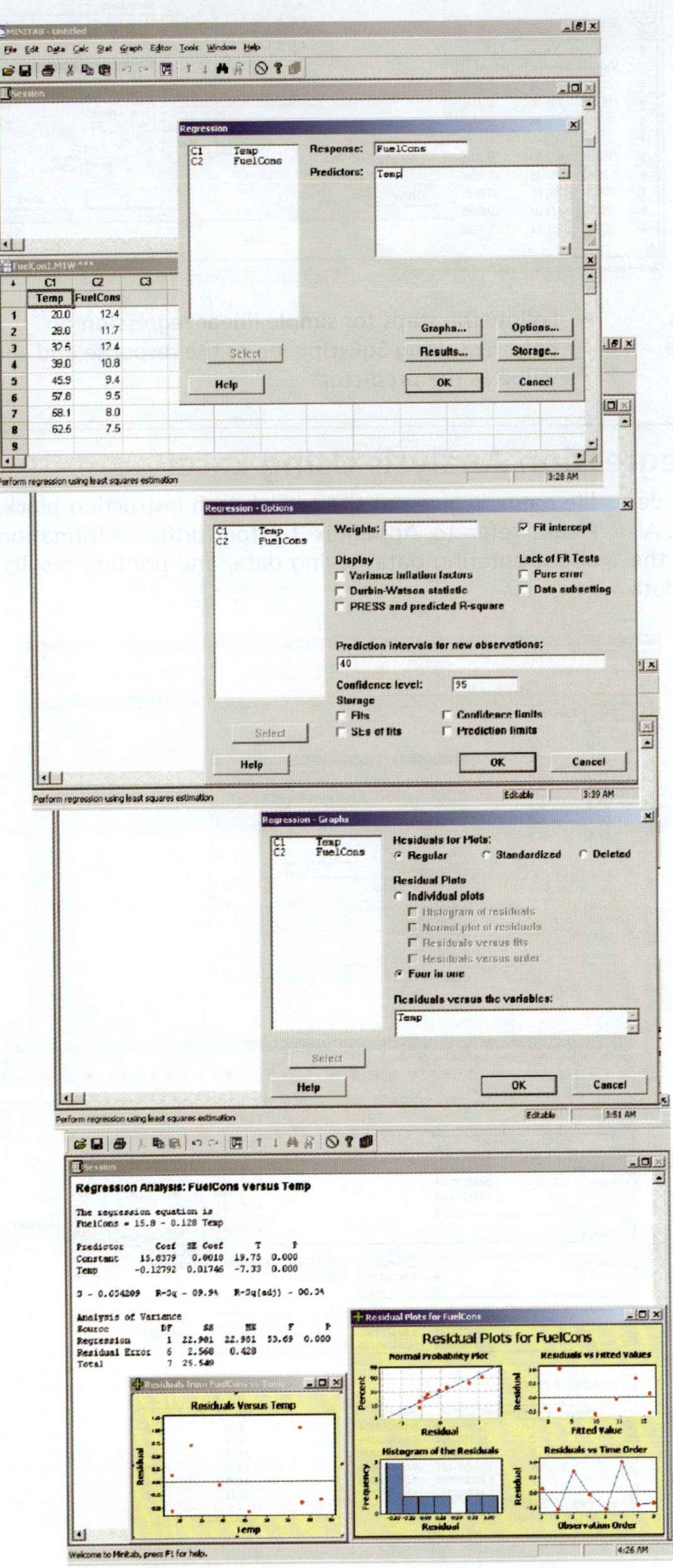

Simple linear regression of the fuel consumption data in Figure 11.11(a) on page 473 (data file: FuelCon1.mtw):

- In the Data window, enter the fuel consumption data from Table 11.1 on page 451—average hourly temperatures in column C1 with variable name Temp and weekly fuel consumptions in column C2 with variable name FuelCons.
- Select **Stat : Regression : Regression.**
- In the Regression dialog box, select FuelCons into the Response box.
- Select Temp into the Predictors window.

To compute a **prediction** for fuel consumption when temperature is 40°F:

- In the Regression dialog box, click on the Options... button.
- In the Regression—Options dialog box, type 40 in the "Prediction intervals for new observations" box.
- Click OK in the Regression—Options dialog box.

To produce **residual analysis** similar to Figure 11.36 on page 510:

- In the Regression dialog box, click on the Graphs... button.
- In the Regression—Graphs dialog box, select the "Residuals for Plots: Regular" option.
- To obtain a histogram and normal plot of the residuals, a plot of the residuals versus the fitted values, and a plot of the residuals versus time order, select "Four in one" in the list of options under Residual Plots. (Note that the plot versus time order is generally informative only if the data are in time sequence order.)
- Enter Temp in the "Residuals versus the variables" box to obtain a plot of the residuals versus the values of average hourly temperature.
- Click OK in the Regression—Graphs dialog box.
- To see the regression results in the Session window and high-resolution graphs in two graphics windows, click OK in the Regression dialog box.

Simple linear regression with a transformed response in Figure 11.34 on page 507 (data file: QHIC.mtw):

- In the Data window, enter the QHIC upkeep expenditure data from Table 11.2 (page 455) – home values in column C1 with variable name Value and upkeep expenditures in column C2 with variable name Upkeep.
- Select **Calc : Calculator.**
- In the Calculator dialog box, enter SqRtUpkeep in the "Store result in variable" box.
- From the Functions menu list, double-click on "Square root" giving SQRT(number) in the Expression window.
- Replace "number" in the Expression window with Upkeep by double-clicking Upkeep in the variables list.
- Click OK in the Calculator dialog box to obtain a new column, SqRtUpkeep, containing the square roots of the Upkeep values.

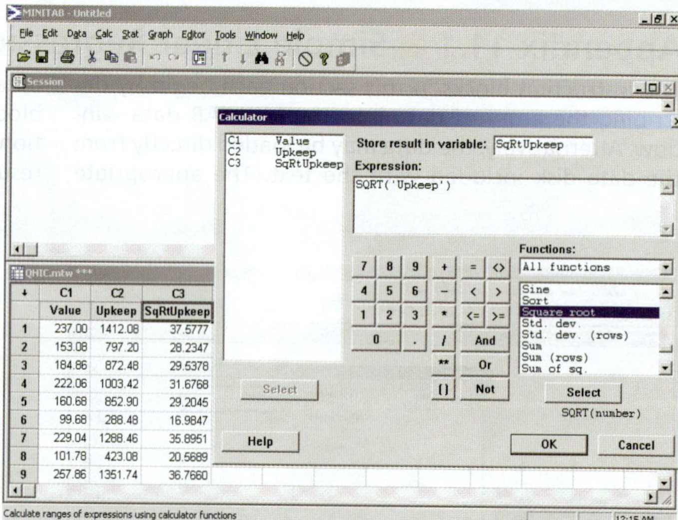

- Follow the steps for **simple linear regression** on page 523 using SqRtUpkeep as the response and Value as the predictor.

Appendix 11.2 ■ Simple Linear Regression Analysis Using Excel

The instruction blocks in this section each begin by describing the entry of data into an Excel spreadsheet. Alternatively, the data may be loaded directly from the data disk included with the text. The appropriate data file name is given at the top of each instruction block. Please refer to Appendix 1.2 for further information about entering data, saving data, and printing results.

Simple linear regression in Figure 11.11(b) on page 473 (data file: FuelCon1.xls):

- Enter the fuel consumption data from Table 11.1 (page 451) with the temperatures in column A (with label Temp) and the fuel consumptions in column B (with label FuelCons).
- Select **Tools : Data Analysis : Regression** and click OK in the Data Analysis dialog box.
- In the Regression dialog box:
  Enter B1.B9 into the "Input Y Range" box.
  Enter A1.A9 into the "Input X Range" box.
- Place a checkmark in the Labels check box.
- Be sure that the "Constant is Zero" check box is NOT checked.
- Select the "New Worksheet Ply" option.
- Click OK in the Regression dialog box to obtain the regression results in a new worksheet.

To produce residual plots similar to Figures 11.26 (page 499) and 11.28 (page 501):

- In the Regression dialog box, place a checkmark in the Residuals check box to request predicted values and residuals.
- Place a checkmark in the Residual Plots check box.
- Place a checkmark in the Normal Probability Plots check box.
- Click OK in the Regression dialog box.
- Resize the plots, as necessary, for effective viewing. Additional residual plots—residuals versus predicted values and residuals versus time—can be produced using the Excel Chart Wizard.

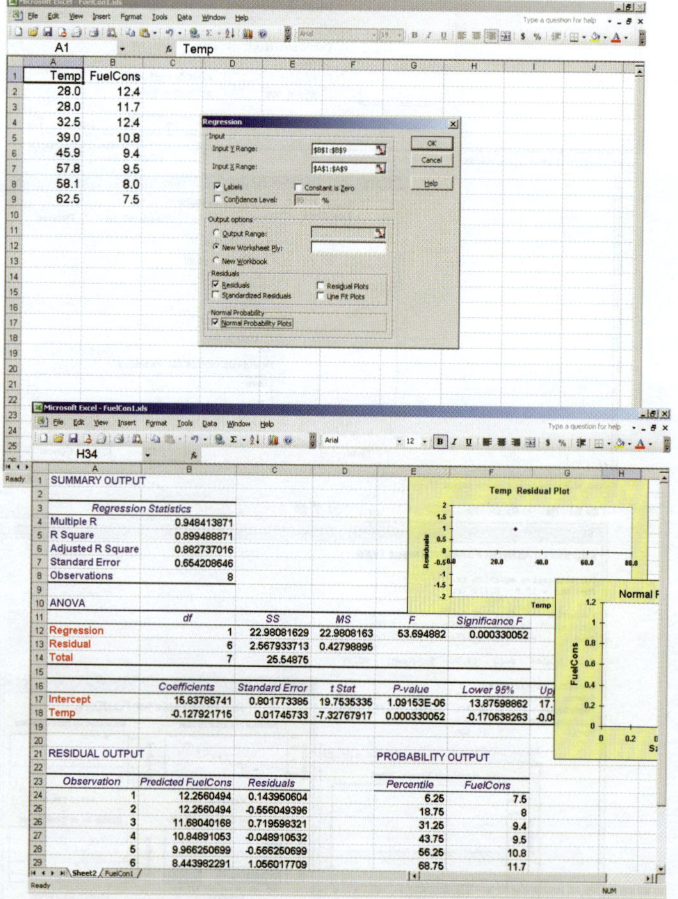

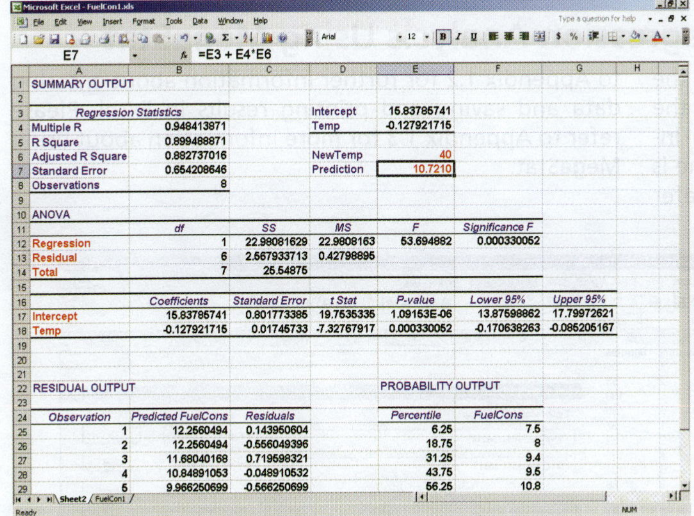

To compute a point prediction for fuel consumption when the temperature is 40°F (data file: FuelCon1.xls):

- The Excel Analysis ToolPak does not provide an option for computing point or interval predictions. A point prediction can be computed from the regression results using Excel cell formulas.
- In the regression output, the estimated intercept and slope parameters from cells A17.B18 have been copied to cells D3.E4 and the predictor value 40 has been placed in cell E6.
- In cell E7, enter the Excel formula =E3+E4*E6 (=10.7210) to compute the prediction.

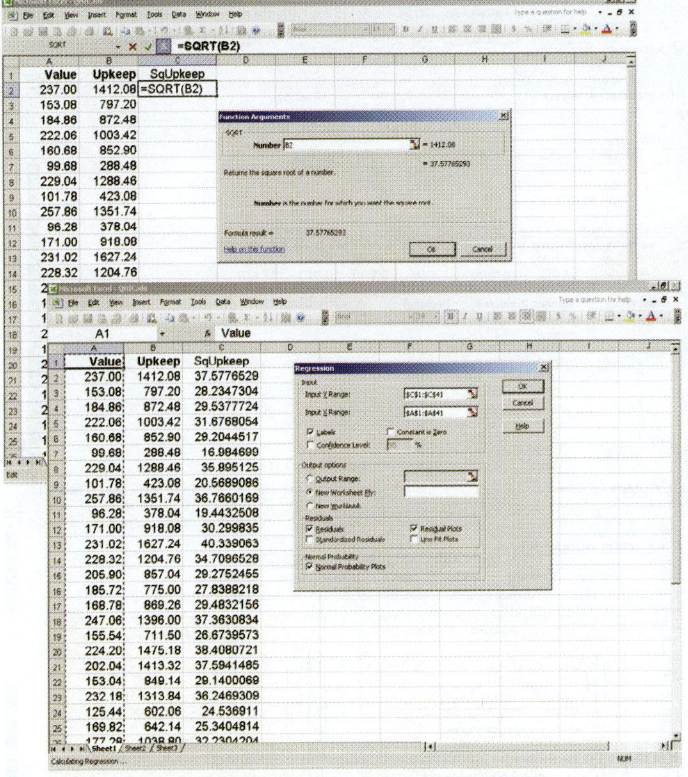

Simple linear regression with a transformed response similar to Figure 11.34 on page 507 (data file: QHIC.xls):

- Enter the QHIC upkeep expenditure data from Table 11.2 (page 455). Enter the label Value in cell A1 with the home values in cells A2 to A41 and enter the label Upkeep in cell B1 with the upkeep expenditures in cells B2 to B41.
- Enter the label SqUpkeep in cell C1.
- Click on cell C2 and then select the Insert Function button f_x on the Excel toolbar.
- Select **Math & Trig** from the "Or select a category:" menu, select **SQRT** from the "Select a function:" menu, and click OK in the Insert Function dialog box.
- In the "SQRT Function Arguments" dialog box, enter B2 in the Number box and click OK to compute the square root of the value in B2.
- Copy the cell formula of C2 through cell C41 by double-clicking the drag handle (in the lower right corner) of cell C2 to compute the square roots of the remaining upkeep values.
- Follow the steps for **simple linear regression** (on page 524) using cells C1.C41 as the response (Input Y Range) and cells A1.A41 as the predictor (Input X Range).

Appendix 11.3 ■ Simple Linear Regression Analysis Using MegaStat

The instructions in this section begin by describing the entry of data into an Excel worksheet. Alternatively, the data may be loaded directly from the data disk included with the text. The appropriate data file name is given at the top of each instruction block. Please refer to Appendix 1.2 for further information about entering data and saving and printing results in Excel. Please refer to Appendix 1.3 for more information about using MegaStat.

Simple linear regression for the service time data in Figure 11.14 on page 476 (data file: SrvcTime.xls):

- Enter the service time data (page 456) with the numbers of copiers serviced in column A (with label Copiers) and the service times in column B (with label Minutes).
- Select **MegaStat : Correlation/Regression : Regression Analysis.**
- In the Regression Analysis dialog box, click in the "Independent variables" box and use the AutoExpand feature to enter the range A1.A12.
- Click in the "Dependent variable" box and use the AutoExpand feature to enter the range B1.B12.
- Check the appropriate Options and Residuals check boxes as follows:
  1. Check "Test Intercept" to include a y-intercept and to test its significance.
  2. Check "Output Residuals" to obtain a list of the model residuals.
  3. Check "Plot Residuals by Observation" and "Plot Residuals by Predicted Y and X" to obtain residual plots versus time, versus the predicted values of y, and versus the values of the independent variable.
  4. Check "Normal Probability Plot of Residuals" to obtain a normal plot.
  5. Check "Durbin-Watson" to obtain the Durbin–Watson statistic.

To obtain a **point prediction** of *y* when four computers will be serviced (as well as a confidence interval and prediction interval):

- Click on the drop-down menu above the Predictor Values box and select "Type in predictor values."
- Type the value of the independent variable for which a prediction is desired (here equal to 4) into the "predictor values" box.
- Select a desired level of confidence (here 95%) from the Confidence Level drop-down menu or type in a value.
- Click OK in the Regression Analysis dialog box.

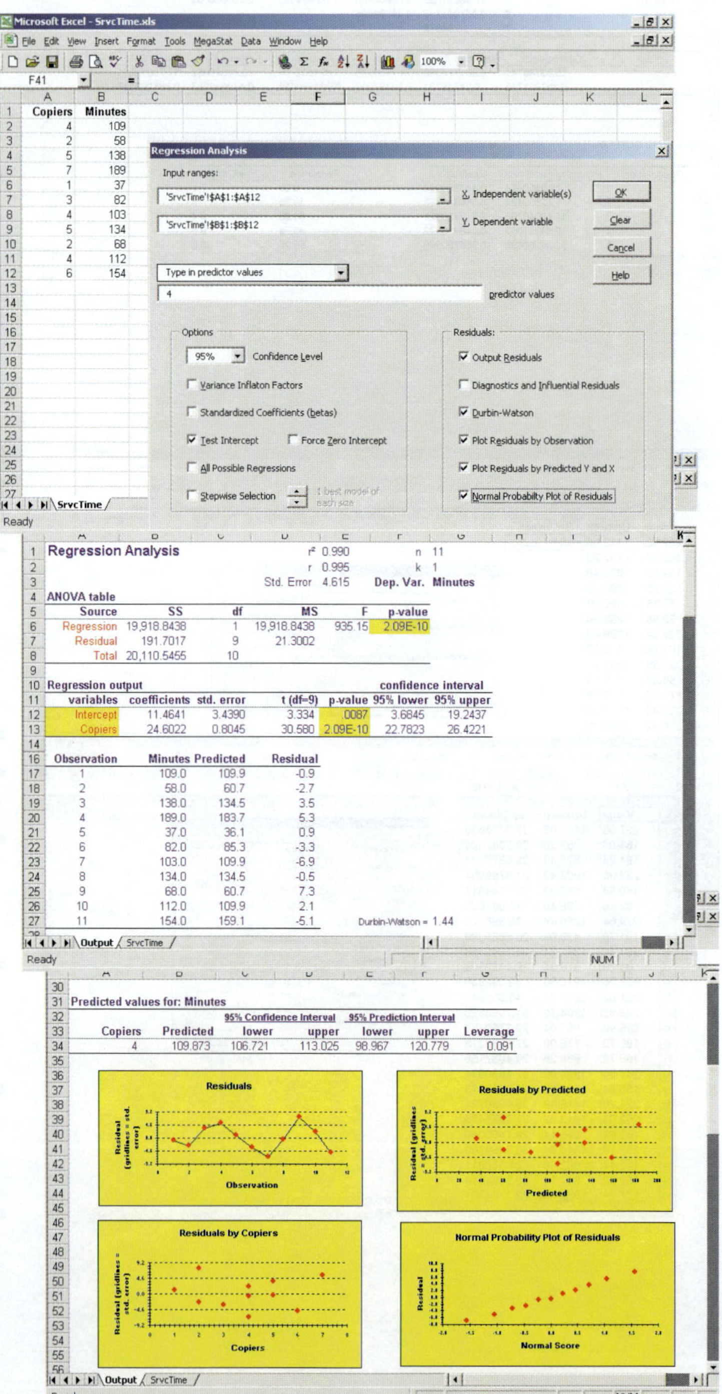

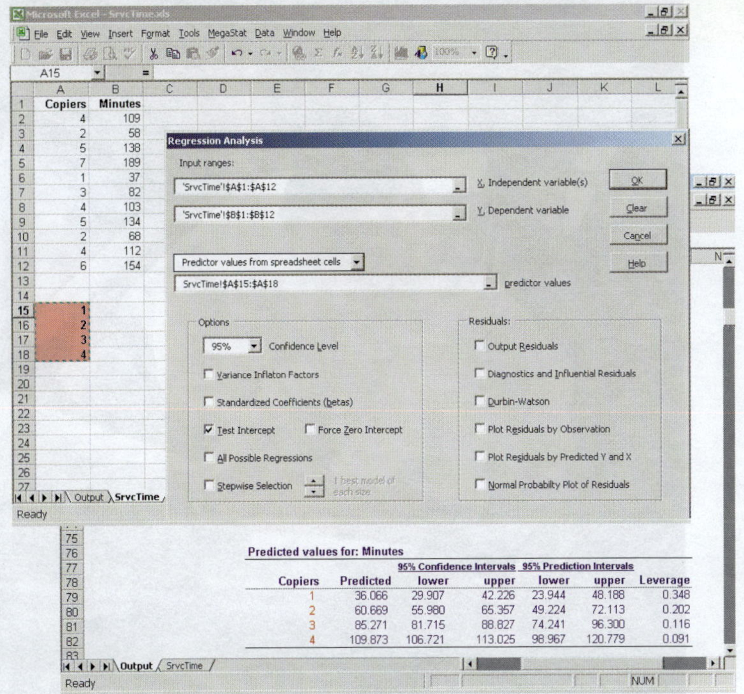

To compute **several point predictions** of *y*—say, when 1, 2, 3, and 4 computers will be serviced—(and corresponding confidence and prediction intervals):

- Enter the values of *x* for which predictions are desired into a column in the spreadsheet—these values can be in any column. Here we have entered the values 1, 2, 3, and 4 into cells A15 through A18.
- Click on the drop-down menu above the "predictor values" box and select "Predictor values from spreadsheet cells."
- Enter the range A15.A18 into the "predictor values" box.
- Click OK in the Regression Analysis dialog box.

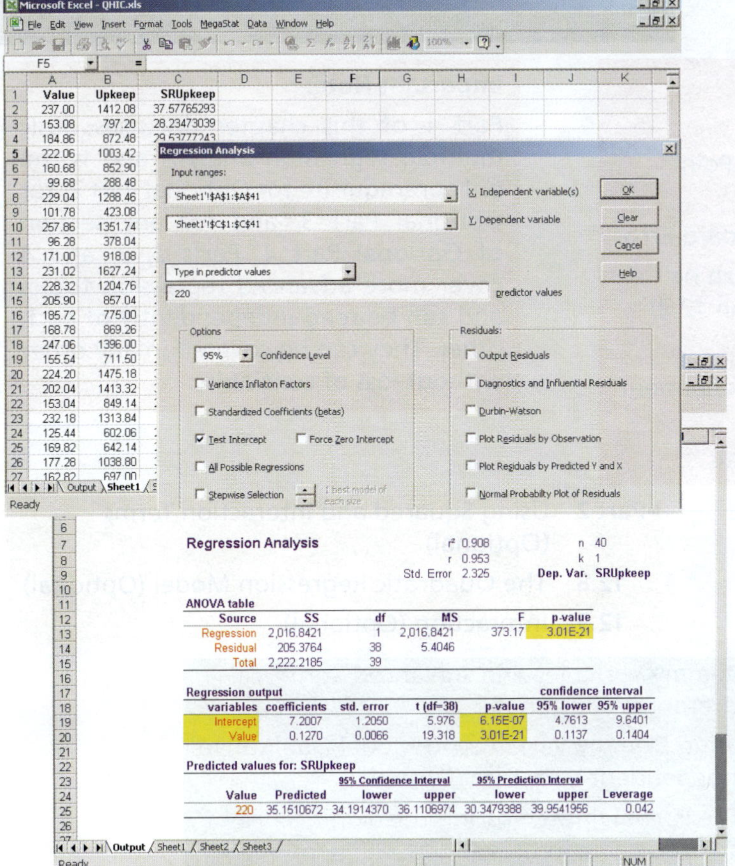

Regression Analysis
Input ranges:
'Sheet1'!$A$1:$A$41
X, Independent variable(s)
'Sheet1'!$C$1:$C$41
Y, Dependent variable
Type in predictor values
220
predictor values
Regression Analysis
r² 0.908 n 40
r 0.953 k 1
Std. Error 2.325 Dep. Var. SRUpkeep
ANOVA table
Source SS df MS F p-value
Regression 2,016.8421 1 2,016.8421 373.17 3.01E-21
Residual 205.3764 38 5.4046
Total 2,222.2185 39
Regression output
confidence interval
variables coefficients std. error t (df=38) p-value 95% lower 95% upper
Intercept 7.2007 1.2050 5.976 6.15E-07 4.7613 9.6401
Value 0.1270 0.0066 19.318 3.01E-21 0.1137 0.1404
Predicted values for: SRUpkeep
95% Confidence Interval
95% Prediction Interval
Value Predicted lower upper lower upper Leverage
220 35.1510672 34.1914370 36.1106974 30.3479388 39.9541956 0.042

Simple linear regression with a transformed response similar to Figure 11.34 on page 507 (data file: QHIC.xls):

- Enter the QHIC data from Table 11.2 (page 455)—the home values in column A (with label Value) and the upkeep expenditures in column B (with label Upkeep).
- Follow the instructions on page 525 in Appendix 11.2 to calculate the square roots of the upkeep expenditures in column C (with label SRUpkeep).
- Select **MegaStat : Correlation/Regression : Regression Analysis.**
- In the Regression Analysis dialog box, click in the "Independent variables" box, and use the AutoExpand feature to enter the range A1.A41.
- Click in the "Dependent variable" box, and use the AutoExpand feature to enter the range C1.C41.
- Check the "Test Intercept" check box to include a *y*-intercept and test its significance.

To compute a **point prediction of the square root of *y*** (as well as a confidence interval and prediction interval) for a house having a value of $220,000:

- Select "Type in predictor values" from the drop-down menu above the "predictor values" box.
- Type 220 into the "predictor values" box.
- Select a desired level of confidence (here 95%) from the drop-down menu in the Confidence Level box or type in a value.
- Click OK in the Regression Analysis dialog box.

CHAPTER 12

Multiple Regression and Model Building

Chapter Outline

Part 1 Basic Multiple Regression

- 12.1 The Multiple Regression Model
- 12.2 The Least Squares Estimates, and Point Estimation and Prediction
- 12.3 Model Assumptions and the Standard Error
- 12.4 R^2 and Adjusted R^2 (This section can be read anytime after reading Section 12.2)
- 12.5 The Overall F Test
- 12.6 Testing the Significance of an Independent Variable
- 12.7 Confidence and Prediction Intervals

Part 2 Using Squared and Interaction Terms (Optional)

- 12.8 The Quadratic Regression Model (Optional)
- 12.9 Interaction (Optional)

Part 3 Dummy Variables and Advanced Statistical Inferences (Optional)

- 12.10 Using Dummy Variables to Model Qualitative Independent Variables (Optional)
- 12.11 The Partial F Test: Testing the Significance of a Portion of a Regression Model (Optional)

Part 4 Model Building and Model Diagnostics (Optional)

- 12.12 Model Building, and the Effects of Multicollinearity (Optional)
- 12.13 Residual Analysis in Multiple Regression (Optional)
- 12.14 Diagnostics for Detecting Outlying and Influential Observations (Optional)
- 12.15 Logistic Regression (Optional)

Important Note:

Part 1 of this chapter discusses basic multiple regression analysis and is the only prerequisite for Optional Part 2, for Optional Part 3, and for any section of Optional Part 4. Parts 2, 3, and 4 cover more advanced regression topics and can be read independently of each other. They can be covered in any order without loss of continuity.

Often we can more accurately describe, predict, and control a dependent variable by using a regression model that employs more than one independent variable. Such a model is called a **multiple regression model,** which is the subject of this chapter.

In order to explain the ideas of this chapter, we consider the following cases:

C

The Fuel Consumption Case: The management consulting firm more accurately predicts the city's future weekly fuel consumptions by using a multiple regression model that employs as independent variables the average hourly temperature and the "chill index." The chill index measures weather-related factors such as the wind velocity and the cloud cover. The more accurate predictions given by the multiple regression model are likely to produce percentage nomination errors within the 10 percent allowance granted by the pipeline transmission system.

The Sales Territory Performance Case: A sales manager evaluates the performance of sales representatives by using a multiple regression model that predicts sales performance on the basis of five independent variables. Salespeople whose actual performance is far worse than predicted performance will get extra training to help improve their sales techniques.

The Fresh Detergent Case: Enterprise Industries predicts future demand for Fresh liquid laundry detergent by using a multiple regression model that employs as independent variables the advertising expenditures used to promote Fresh and the difference between the price of Fresh and the average price of competing detergents.

12.1 The Multiple Regression Model

PART 1
Basic Multiple Regression

Regression models that employ more than one independent variable are called **multiple regression models.** We begin our study of these models by considering the following example.

Example 12.1 The Fuel Consumption Case

C

Part 1: The data and a regression model Consider the fuel consumption problem in which the natural gas company wishes to predict weekly fuel consumption for its city. In Chapter 11 we used the single predictor variable x, average hourly temperature, to predict y, weekly fuel consumption. We now consider predicting y on the basis of average hourly temperature and a second predictor variable—the chill index. The chill index for a given average hourly temperature expresses the combined effects of all other major weather-related factors that influence fuel consumption, such as wind velocity, cloud cover, and the passage of weather fronts. The chill index is expressed as a whole number between 0 and 30. A weekly chill index near 0 indicates that, given the average hourly temperature during the week, all other major weather-related factors will only slightly increase weekly fuel consumption. A weekly chill index near 30 indicates that, given the average hourly temperature during the week, other weather-related factors will greatly increase weekly fuel consumption.

CHAPTER 17

The company has collected data concerning weekly fuel consumption (y), average hourly temperature (x_1), and the chill index (x_2) for the last eight weeks. These data are given in Table 12.1. Figure 12.1 presents a scatter plot of y versus x_1. This plot shows that y tends to decrease in a straight-line fashion as x_1 increases. This suggests that, if we wish to predict y on the basis of x_1 only, the simple linear regression model (having a negative slope)

$$y = \beta_0 + \beta_1 x_1 + \varepsilon$$

relates y to x_1. Figure 12.2 presents a scatter plot of y versus x_2. This plot shows that y tends to increase in a straight-line fashion as x_2 increases. This suggests that, if we wish to predict y on the basis of x_2 only, the simple linear regression model (having a positive slope)

$$y = \beta_0 + \beta_1 x_2 + \varepsilon$$

relates y to x_2. Since we wish to predict y on the basis of both x_1 and x_2, it seems reasonable to combine these models to form the model

$$y = \beta_0 + \beta_1 x_1 + \beta_2 x_2 + \varepsilon$$

TABLE 12.1 Fuel Consumption Data FuelCon2

Week	Average Hourly Temperature, x_1 (°F)	Chill Index, x_2	Fuel Consumption, y (MMcf)
1	28.0	18	12.4
2	28.0	14	11.7
3	32.5	24	12.4
4	39.0	22	10.8
5	45.9	8	9.4
6	57.8	16	9.5
7	58.1	1	8.0
8	62.5	0	7.5

FIGURE 12.1 Plot of y (Weekly Fuel Consumption) versus x_1 (Average Hourly Temperature)

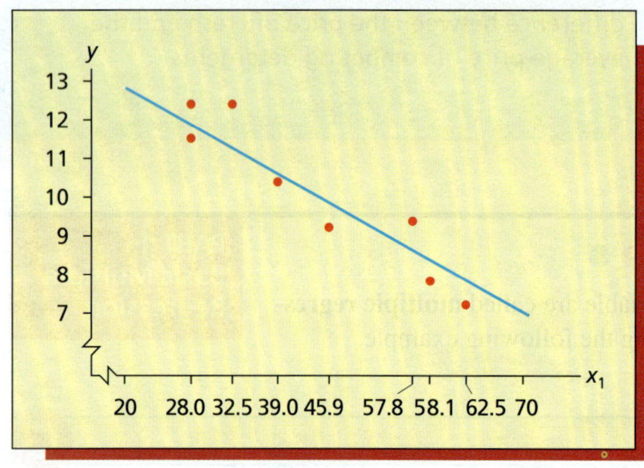

FIGURE 12.2 Plot of y (Weekly Fuel Consumption) versus x_2 (the Chill Index)

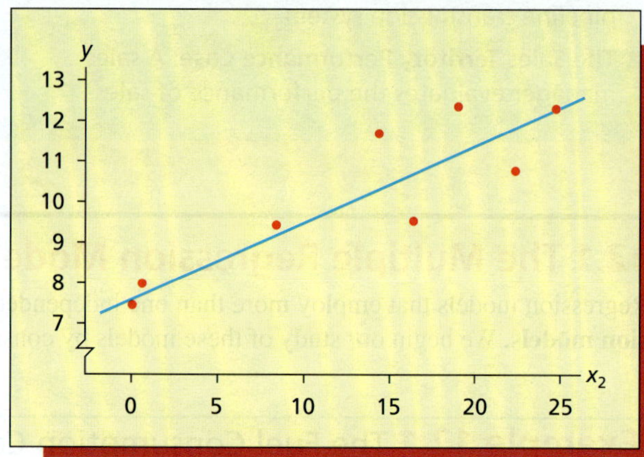

to relate y to x_1 and x_2. Here we have arbitrarily placed the $\beta_1 x_1$ term first and the $\beta_2 x_2$ term second, and we have renumbered β_1 and β_2 to be consistent with the subscripts on x_1 and x_2. This regression model says that

1 $\beta_0 + \beta_1 x_1 + \beta_2 x_2$ is the mean value of y when the average hourly temperature is x_1 and the chill index is x_2. For instance,

$$\beta_0 + \beta_1(45.9) + \beta_2(8)$$

is the average fuel consumption for all weeks having an average hourly temperature equal to 45.9 and a chill index equal to 8.

2 β_0, β_1, and β_2 are regression parameters relating the mean value of y to x_1 and x_2.

3 ε is an error term that describes the effects on y of all factors other than x_1 and x_2.

Part 2: Interpreting the regression parameters β_0, β_1, and β_2 The exact interpretations of the parameters β_0, β_1, and β_2 are quite simple. First, suppose that $x_1 = 0$ and $x_2 = 0$. Then

$$\beta_0 + \beta_1 x_1 + \beta_2 x_2$$
$$= \beta_0 + \beta_1(0) + \beta_2(0) = \beta_0$$

So β_0 is the mean weekly fuel consumption for all weeks having an average hourly temperature of 0°F and a chill index of 0. The parameter β_0 is called the **intercept** in the regression model. One might wonder whether β_0 has any practical interpretation, since it is unlikely that a week having an average hourly temperature of 0°F would also have a chill index of 0. Indeed, sometimes the parameter β_0 and other parameters in a regression analysis do not have practical interpretations because the situations related to the interpretations would not be likely to occur in practice. In fact, sometimes each parameter does not, by itself, have much practical importance.

FIGURE 12.3 The Experimental Region

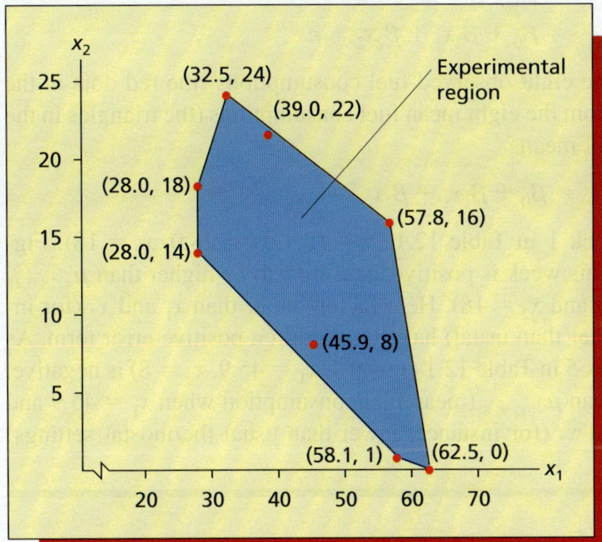

FIGURE 12.4 A Geometrical Interpretation of the Regression Model Relating y to x_1 and x_2

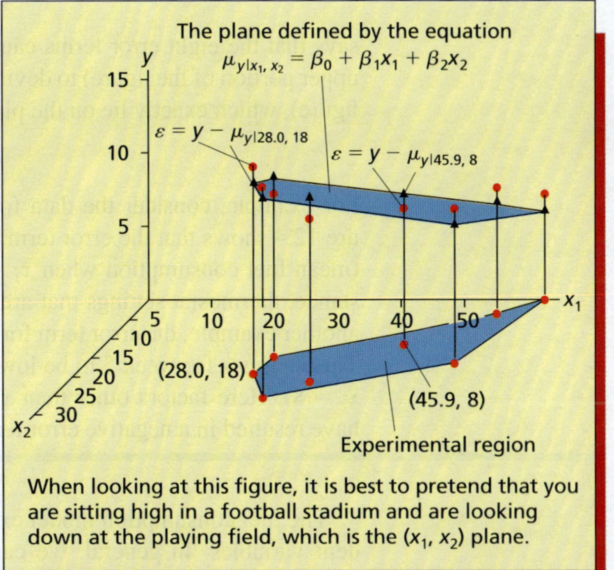

Rather, the parameters relate the mean of the dependent variable to the independent variables in an overall sense.

We next interpret the individual meanings of β_1 and β_2. To examine the interpretation of β_1, consider two different weeks. Suppose that for the first week the average hourly temperature is c and the chill index is d. The mean weekly fuel consumption for all such weeks is

$$\beta_0 + \beta_1(c) + \beta_2(d)$$

For the second week, suppose that the average hourly temperature is $c + 1$ and the chill index is d. The mean weekly fuel consumption for all such weeks is

$$\beta_0 + \beta_1(c + 1) + \beta_2(d)$$

It is easy to see that the difference between these mean fuel consumptions is β_1. Since weeks 1 and 2 differ only in that the average hourly temperature during week 2 is one degree higher than the average hourly temperature during week 1, we can interpret the parameter β_1 as the change in mean weekly fuel consumption that is associated with a one-degree increase in average hourly temperature when the chill index does not change.

The interpretation of β_2 can be established similarly. We can interpret β_2 as the change in mean weekly fuel consumption that is associated with a one-unit increase in the chill index when the average hourly temperature does not change.

Part 3: A geometric interpretation of the regression model We now interpret our fuel consumption model geometrically. We begin by defining the **experimental region** to be the range of the combinations of the observed values of x_1 and x_2. From the data in Table 12.1, it is reasonable to depict the experimental region as the shaded region in Figure 12.3. Here the combinations of x_1 and x_2 values are the ordered pairs in the figure.

We next write the mean value of y when average hourly temperature is x_1 and the chill index is x_2 as $\mu_{y|x_1, x_2}$ (pronounced **mu of y given x_1 and x_2**) and consider the equation

$$\mu_{y|x_1, x_2} = \beta_0 + \beta_1 x_1 + \beta_2 x_2$$

which relates mean fuel consumption to x_1 and x_2. Since this is a linear equation in two variables, geometry tells us that this equation is the equation of a plane in three-dimensional space. We sometimes refer to this plane as the **plane of means,** and we illustrate the portion of this plane corresponding to the (x_1, x_2) combinations in the experimental region in Figure 12.4. As illustrated in this figure, the model

$$y = \mu_{y|x_1, x_2} + \varepsilon$$
$$= \beta_0 + \beta_1 x_1 + \beta_2 x_2 + \varepsilon$$

says that the eight error terms cause the eight observed fuel consumptions (the red dots in the upper portion of the figure) to deviate from the eight mean fuel consumptions (the triangles in the figure), which exactly lie on the plane of means

$$\mu_{y|x_1, x_2} = \beta_0 + \beta_1 x_1 + \beta_2 x_2$$

For example, consider the data for week 1 in Table 12.1 ($y = 12.4$, $x_1 = 28.0$, $x_2 = 18$). Figure 12.4 shows that the error term for this week is positive, causing y to be higher than $\mu_{y|28.0, 18}$ (mean fuel consumption when $x_1 = 28$ and $x_2 = 18$). Here factors other than x_1 and x_2 (for instance, thermostat settings that are higher than usual) have resulted in a positive error term. As another example, the error term for week 5 in Table 12.1 ($y = 9.4$, $x_1 = 45.9$, $x_2 = 8$) is negative. This causes y for week 5 to be lower than $\mu_{y|45.9, 8}$ (mean fuel consumption when $x_1 = 45.9$ and $x_2 = 8$). Here factors other than x_1 and x_2 (for instance, lower-than-usual thermostat settings) have resulted in a negative error term.

The fuel consumption model expresses the dependent variable as a function of two independent variables. In general, we can use a multiple regression model to express a dependent variable as a function of any number of independent variables. For example, the Cincinnati Gas and Electric Company predicts daily natural gas consumption as a function of four independent variables—average temperature, average wind velocity, average sunlight, and change in average temperature from the previous day. The general form of a multiple regression model expresses the dependent variable y as a function of k independent variables $x_1, x_2, \ldots, x_k$. We express this general form in the following box. Here we assume that we have obtained n observations, with each observation consisting of an observed value of y and corresponding observed values of $x_1, x_2, \ldots, x_k$.

The Multiple Regression Model

The **multiple regression model relating y to $x_1, x_2, \ldots, x_k$** is

$$y = \mu_{y|x_1, x_2, \ldots, x_k} + \varepsilon = \beta_0 + \beta_1 x_1 + \beta_2 x_2 + \cdots + \beta_k x_k + \varepsilon$$

Here

1 $\mu_{y|x_1, x_2, \ldots, x_k} = \beta_0 + \beta_1 x_1 + \beta_2 x_2 + \cdots + \beta_k x_k$ is the mean value of the dependent variable y when the values of the independent variables are $x_1, x_2, \ldots, x_k$.

2 $\beta_0, \beta_1, \beta_2, \ldots, \beta_k$ are (unknown) **regression parameters** relating the mean value of y to $x_1, x_2, \ldots, x_k$.

3 ε is an **error term** that describes the effects on y of all factors other than the values of the independent variables $x_1, x_2, \ldots, x_k$.

Example 12.2 The Sales Territory Performance Case

Suppose the sales manager of a company wishes to evaluate the performance of the company's sales representatives. Each sales representative is solely responsible for one sales territory, and the manager decides that it is reasonable to measure the performance, y, of a sales representative by using the yearly sales of the company's product in the representative's sales territory. The manager feels that sales performance y substantially depends on five independent variables:

x_1 = number of months the representative has been employed by the company
x_2 = sales of the company's product and competing products in the sales territory
x_3 = dollar advertising expenditure in the territory

TABLE 12.2 Sales Territory Performance Study Data SalePerf

Sales, y	Time with Company, x_1	Market Potential, x_2	Advertising, x_3	Market Share, x_4	Market Share Change, x_5
3,669.88	43.10	74,065.11	4,582.88	2.51	0.34
3,473.95	108.13	58,117.30	5,539.78	5.51	0.15
2,295.10	13.82	21,118.49	2,950.38	10.91	−0.72
4,675.56	186.18	68,521.27	2,243.07	8.27	0.17
6,125.96	161.79	57,805.11	7,747.08	9.15	0.50
2,134.94	8.94	37,806.94	402.44	5.51	0.15
5,031.66	365.04	50,935.26	3,140.62	8.54	0.55
3,367.45	220.32	35,602.08	2,086.16	7.07	−0.49
6,519.45	127.64	46,176.77	8,846.25	12.54	1.24
4,876.37	105.69	42,053.24	5,673.11	8.85	0.31
2,468.27	57.72	36,829.71	2,761.76	5.38	0.37
2,533.31	23.58	33,612.67	1,991.85	5.43	−0.65
2,408.11	13.82	21,412.79	1,971.52	8.48	0.64
2,337.38	13.82	20,416.87	1,737.38	7.80	1.01
4,586.95	86.99	36,272.00	10,694.20	10.34	0.11
2,729.24	165.85	23,093.26	8,618.61	5.15	0.04
3,289.40	116.26	26,878.59	7,747.89	6.64	0.68
2,800.78	42.28	39,571.96	4,565.81	5.45	0.66
3,264.20	52.84	51,866.15	6,022.70	6.31	−0.10
3,453.62	165.04	58,749.82	3,721.10	6.35	−0.03
1,741.45	10.57	23,990.82	860.97	7.37	−1.63
2,035.75	13.82	25,694.86	3,571.51	8.39	−0.43
1,578.00	8.13	23,736.35	2,845.50	5.15	0.04
4,167.44	58.54	34,314.29	5,060.11	12.88	0.22
2,799.97	21.14	22,809.53	3,552.00	9.14	−0.74

Source: This data set is from a research study published in "An Analytical Approach for Evaluation of Sales Territory Performance," *Journal of Marketing*, January 1972, 31–37 (authors are David W. Cravens, Robert B. Woodruff, and Joseph C. Stamper). We have updated the situation in our case study to be more modern.

x_4 = weighted average of the company's market share in the territory for the previous four years

x_5 = change in the company's market share in the territory over the previous four years

In Table 12.2 we present values of y and x_1 through x_5 for 25 randomly selected sales representatives. To understand the values of y and x_2 in the table, note that sales of the company's product or any competing product are measured in hundreds of units of the product sold. Therefore, for example, the first sales figure of 3,669.88 in Table 12.2 means that the first randomly selected sales representative sold 366,988 units of the company's product during the year.

Plots of y versus x_1 through x_5 are given on the page margin next to Table 12.2. Since each plot has an approximate straight-line appearance, it is reasonable to relate y to x_1 through x_5 by using the regression model

$$y = \beta_0 + \beta_1 x_1 + \beta_2 x_2 + \beta_3 x_3 + \beta_4 x_4 + \beta_5 x_5 + \varepsilon$$

Here, $\mu_{y|x_1, x_2, \ldots, x_5} = \beta_0 + \beta_1 x_1 + \beta_2 x_2 + \beta_3 x_3 + \beta_4 x_4 + \beta_5 x_5$ is, intuitively, the mean sales in all sales territories where the values of the previously described five independent variables are x_1, x_2, x_3, x_4, and x_5. Furthermore, for example, the parameter β_3 equals the increase in mean sales that is associated with a \$1 increase in advertising expenditure (x_3) when the other four independent variables do not change. The main objective of the regression analysis is to help the sales manager evaluate sales performance by comparing actual performance to predicted performance. The manager has randomly selected the 25 representatives from all the representatives the company considers to be effective and wishes to use a regression model based on effective representatives to evaluate questionable representatives.

Exercises for Section 12.1

CONCEPTS

For Exercises 12.1 through 12.5, consider the multiple regression model

$$y = \mu_{y|x_1, x_2, \ldots, x_k} + \varepsilon$$
$$= \beta_0 + \beta_1 x_1 + \beta_2 x_2 + \cdots + \beta_k x_k + \varepsilon$$

12.1 What is y? What are $x_1, x_2, \ldots, x_k$?

12.2 Discuss the meaning of $\mu_{y|x_1, x_2, \ldots, x_k}$.

12.3 What are $\beta_0, \beta_1, \beta_2, \ldots, \beta_k$?

12.4 What does the error term ε describe?

12.5 In your own words, interpret β_0, β_1, and β_2.

METHODS AND APPLICATIONS

TABLE 12.3 The Real Estate Sales Price Data RealEst2

Sales Price (y)	Home Size (x_1)	Rating (x_2)
180	23	5
98.1	11	2
173.1	20	9
136.5	17	3
141	15	8
165.9	21	4
193.5	24	7
127.8	13	6
163.5	19	7
172.5	25	2

Source: R. L. Andrews and J. T. Ferguson, "Integrating Judgement with a Regression Appraisal," *The Real Estate Appraiser and Analyst* 52, no. 2 (1986). Reprinted by permission.

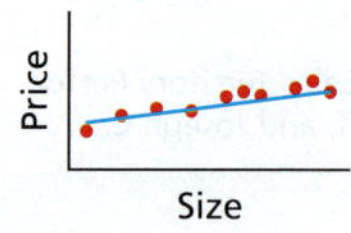

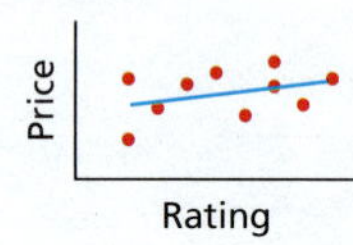

12.6 THE REAL ESTATE SALES PRICE CASE RealEst2

A real estate agency collects the data in Table 12.3 concerning

y = sales price of a house (in thousands of dollars)

x_1 = home size (in hundreds of square feet)

x_2 = rating (an overall "niceness rating" for the house expressed on a scale from 1 [worst] to 10 [best], and provided by the real estate agency)

The agency wishes to develop a regression model that can be used to predict the sales prices of future houses it will list. Consider relating y to x_1 and x_2 by using the model

$$y = \mu_{y|x_1,x_2} + \varepsilon$$
$$= \beta_0 + \beta_1 x_1 + \beta_2 x_2 + \varepsilon$$

a Discuss why the data plots given on the page margin under Table 12.3 indicate that this model might be reasonable.

b Explain the meaning of

$$\mu_{y|x_1=20,\, x_2=9} = \beta_0 + \beta_1(20) + \beta_2(9)$$

c Explain the meanings of β_0, β_1, and β_2.

d What factors are represented by the error term in this model? Give a specific example of these factors.

12.7 THE FRESH DETERGENT CASE Fresh2

Enterprise Industries produces Fresh, a brand of liquid laundry detergent. In order to more effectively manage its inventory and make revenue projections, the company would like to better predict demand for Fresh. To develop a prediction model, the company has gathered data concerning demand for Fresh over the last 30 sales periods (each sales period is defined to be a four-week period). The demand data are presented in Table 12.4. Here, for each sales period,

y = the demand for the large size bottle of Fresh (in hundreds of thousands of bottles) in the sales period

x_1 = the price (in dollars) of Fresh as offered by Enterprise Industries in the sales period

x_2 = the average industry price (in dollars) of competitors' similar detergents in the sales period

x_3 = Enterprise Industries' advertising expenditure (in hundreds of thousands of dollars) to promote Fresh in the sales period

$x_4 = x_2 - x_1$ = the "price difference" in the sales period

Consider relating y to x_1, x_2, and x_3 by using the model

$$y = \beta_0 + \beta_1 x_1 + \beta_2 x_2 + \beta_3 x_3 + \varepsilon$$

a Discuss why the data plots given under Table 12.4 indicate that this model might be reasonable.

TABLE 12.4 Historical Data Concerning Demand for Fresh Detergent Fresh2

Sales Period	Price for Fresh, x_1	Average Industry Price, x_2	Price Difference, $x_4 = x_2 - x_1$	Advertising Expenditure for Fresh, x_3	Demand for Fresh, y
1	3.85	3.80	.05	5.50	7.38
2	3.75	4.00	.25	6.75	8.51
3	3.70	4.30	.60	7.25	9.52
4	3.70	3.70	0	5.50	7.50
5	3.60	3.85	.25	7.00	9.33
6	3.60	3.80	.20	6.50	8.28
7	3.60	3.75	.15	6.75	8.75
8	3.80	3.85	.05	5.25	7.87
9	3.80	3.65	−.15	5.25	7.10
10	3.85	4.00	.15	6.00	8.00
11	3.90	4.10	.20	6.50	7.89
12	3.90	4.00	.10	6.25	8.15
13	3.70	4.10	.40	7.00	9.10
14	3.75	4.20	.45	6.90	8.86
15	3.75	4.10	.35	6.80	8.90
16	3.80	4.10	.30	6.80	8.87
17	3.70	4.20	.50	7.10	9.26
18	3.80	4.30	.50	7.00	9.00
19	3.70	4.10	.40	6.80	8.75
20	3.80	3.75	−.05	6.50	7.95
21	3.80	3.75	−.05	6.25	7.65
22	3.75	3.65	−.10	6.00	7.27
23	3.70	3.90	.20	6.50	8.00
24	3.55	3.65	.10	7.00	8.50
25	3.60	4.10	.50	6.80	8.75
26	3.65	4.25	.60	6.80	9.21
27	3.70	3.65	−.05	6.50	8.27
28	3.75	3.75	0	5.75	7.67
29	3.80	3.85	.05	5.80	7.93
30	3.70	4.25	.55	6.80	9.26

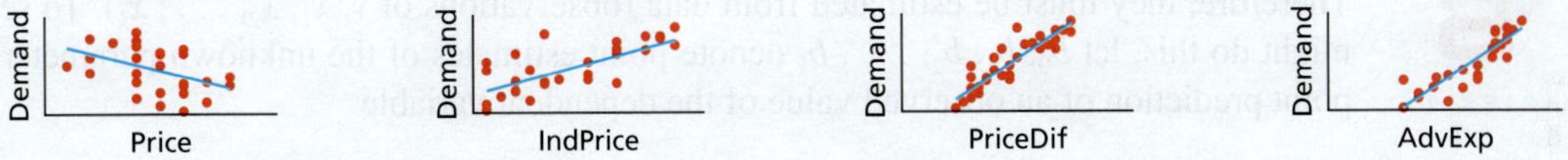

TABLE 12.5 Hospital Labor Needs Data HospLab

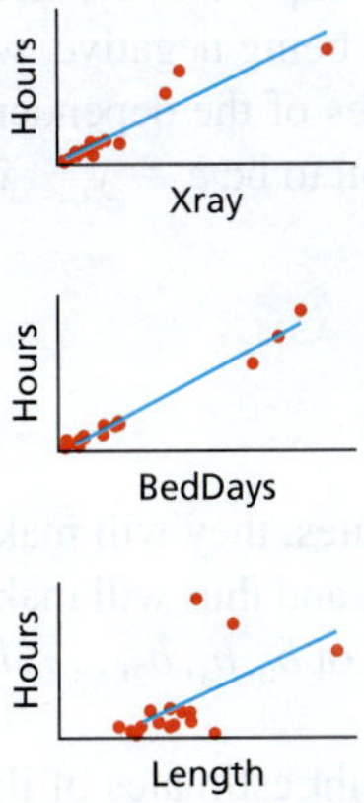

Hospital	Monthly X-Ray Exposures, x_1	Monthly Occupied Bed Days, x_2	Average Length of Stay, x_3	Monthly Labor Hours Required, y
1	2,463	472.92	4.45	566.52
2	2,048	1,339.75	6.92	696.82
3	3,940	620.25	4.28	1,033.15
4	6,505	568.33	3.90	1,603.62
5	5,723	1,497.60	5.50	1,611.37
6	11,520	1,365.83	4.60	1,613.27
7	5,779	1,687.00	5.62	1,854.17
8	5,969	1,639.92	5.15	2,160.55
9	8,461	2,872.33	6.18	2,305.58
10	20,106	3,655.08	6.15	3,503.93
11	13,313	2,912.00	5.88	3,571.89
12	10,771	3,921.00	4.88	3,741.40
13	15,543	3,865.67	5.50	4,026.52
14	34,703	12,446.33	10.78	11,732.17
15	39,204	14,098.40	7.05	15,414.94
16	86,533	15,524.00	6.35	18,854.45

Source: *Procedures and Analysis for Staffing Standards Development Regression Analysis Handbook* (San Diego, CA: Navy Manpower and Material Analysis Center, 1979).

b Explain the meaning of

$$\mu_{y|x_1=3.70,\, x_2=3.90,\, x_3=6.50} = \beta_0 + \beta_1(3.70) + \beta_2(3.90) + \beta_3(6.50)$$

c Explain the meaning of β_0, β_1, β_2, β_3, and ε in the model.

d Discuss why the data plots given under Table 12.4 indicate that it might be reasonable to use the following alternative model

$$y = \beta_0 + \beta_1 x_4 + \beta_2 x_3 + \varepsilon$$

12.8 THE HOSPITAL LABOR NEEDS CASE HospLab

Table 12.5 presents data concerning the need for labor in 16 U.S. Navy hospitals. Here

y = monthly labor hours required

x_1 = monthly X-ray exposures

x_2 = monthly occupied bed days (a hospital has one occupied bed day if one bed is occupied for an entire day)

x_3 = average length of patients' stay (in days)

The main objective of the regression analysis is to help the navy evaluate the performance of its hospitals in terms of how many labor hours are used relative to how many labor hours are needed. The navy selected hospitals 1 through 16 from hospitals that it thought were efficiently run and wishes to use a regression model based on efficiently run hospitals to evaluate the efficiency of questionable hospitals. Consider relating y to x_1, x_2, and x_3 by using the model

$$y = \beta_0 + \beta_1 x_1 + \beta_2 x_2 + \beta_3 x_3 + \varepsilon$$

Discuss why the data plots given on the page margin next to Table 12.5 indicate that this model might be reasonable. Explain the meanings of β_0, β_1, β_2, β_3, and ε in this model.

12.2 The Least Squares Estimates, and Point Estimation and Prediction

CHAPTER 17

The regression parameters $\beta_0, \beta_1, \beta_2, \ldots, \beta_k$ in the multiple regression model are unknown. Therefore, they must be estimated from data (observations of $y, x_1, x_2, \ldots, x_k$). To see how we might do this, let $b_0, b_1, b_2, \ldots, b_k$ denote point estimates of the unknown parameters. Then, a point prediction of an observed value of the dependent variable

$$y = \beta_0 + \beta_1 x_1 + \beta_2 x_2 + \cdots + \beta_k x_k + \varepsilon$$

is

$$\hat{y} = b_0 + b_1 x_1 + b_2 x_2 + \cdots + b_k x_k$$

Here, since the regression assumptions (to be fully discussed in Section 12.3) imply that the error term ε has a 50 percent chance of being positive and a 50 percent chance of being negative, we predict ε to be 0. Next, let y_i and $\hat{y}_i$ denote the observed and predicted values of the dependent variable for the ith observation, and define the **residual** for the ith observation to be $e_i = y_i - \hat{y}_i$. We then consider the **sum of squared residuals**

$$SSE = \sum_{i=1}^{n} (y_i - \hat{y}_i)^2$$

Intuitively, if any particular values of $b_0, b_1, b_2, \ldots, b_k$ are good point estimates, they will make (for $i = 1, 2, \ldots, n$) the predicted value $\hat{y}_i$ fairly close to the observed value y_i and thus will make SSE fairly small. We define the **least squares point estimates** to be the values of $b_0, b_1, b_2, \ldots, b_k$ that minimize SSE.

It can be shown that a formula exists for computing the least squares point estimates of the parameters in the multiple regression model. This formula is written using a branch of mathematics called **matrix algebra** and is presented in Appendix G of the CD-ROM included with this book. In practice, the least squares point estimates can be easily computed using many standard statistical computer packages. In our discussion of multiple regression here, we will rely on MINITAB, Excel, and MegaStat to compute the needed estimates.

Example 12.3 The Fuel Consumption Case

Part 1: The least squares point estimates Consider the fuel consumption model of Example 12.1:

$$y = \beta_0 + \beta_1 x_1 + \beta_2 x_2 + \varepsilon$$

The MINITAB and Excel output in Figure 12.5 tells us that if we use the data in Table 12.1 to calculate the least squares point estimates of the parameters β_0, β_1, and β_2, we obtain $b_0 = 13.1087$, $b_1 = -0.09001$, and $b_2 = 0.08249$.

FIGURE 12.5 MINITAB and Excel Output of a Regression Analysis of the Fuel Consumption Data in Table 12.1 Using the Model $y = \beta_0 + \beta_1 x_1 + \beta_2 x_2 + \varepsilon$

(a) The MINITAB output

```
The regression equation is
FuelCons = 13.1 - 0.0900 Temp + 0.0825 Chill

Predictor          Coef        SE Coef [4]        T [5]        P [6]
Constant       13.1087 [1]     0.8557         15.32        0.000
Temp          -0.09001 [2]     0.01408        -6.39        0.001
Chill          0.08249 [3]     0.02200         3.75        0.013

s = 0.367078 [7]     R-Sq = 97.4% [8]     R-Sq(adj) = 96.3% [9]

Analysis of Variance
Source            DF         SS            MS          F             P
Regression         2     24.875 [10]    12.438     92.30 [13]    0.000 [14]
Residual Error     5      0.674 [11]     0.135
Total              7     25.549 [12]

Values of Predictors for New Obs     Predicted Values for New Observations
New Obs  Temp  Chill                 New Obs   Fit [15]   SE Fit [16]   95% CI [17]         95% PI [18]
      1  40.0   10.0                       1   10.333     0.170         (9.895, 10.771)     (9.293, 11.374)
```

(b) The Excel output

Regression Statistics	
Multiple R	0.9867
R Square	0.9736 [8]
Adjusted R Square	0.9631 [9]
Standard Error	0.3671 [7]
Observations	8

ANOVA

	df	SS	MS	F	Significance F
Regression	2	24.8750 [10]	12.4375	92.3031 [13]	0.0001 [14]
Residual	5	0.6737 [11]	0.1347		
Total	7	25.5488 [12]			

	Coefficients	Standard Error [4]	t Stat [5]	P-value [6]	Lower 95% [19]	Upper 95% [19]
Intercept	13.1087 [1]	0.8557	15.3193	2.15E-05	10.9091	15.3084
TEMP	-0.0900 [2]	0.0141	-6.3942	0.0014	-0.1262	-0.0538
CHILL	0.0825 [3]	0.0220	3.7493	0.0133	0.0259	0.1391

[1] b_0 [2] b_1 [3] b_2 [4] s_{b_j} = standard error of the estimate b_j [5] t statistics [6] p-values for t statistics [7] s = standard error [8] R^2 [9] Adjusted R^2 [10] Explained variation [11] SSE = Unexplained variation [12] Total variation [13] F(model) statistic [14] p-value for F(model) [15] $\hat{y}$ = point prediction when $x_1 = 40$ and $x_2 = 10$ [16] $s_{\hat{y}}$ = standard error of the estimate $\hat{y}$ [17] 95% confidence interval when $x_1 = 40$ and $x_2 = 10$ [18] 95% prediction interval when $x_1 = 40$ and $x_2 = 10$ [19] 95% confidence interval for β_j

The point estimate $b_1 = -.09001$ of β_1 says we estimate that mean weekly fuel consumption decreases (since b_1 is negative) by .09001 MMcf of natural gas when average hourly temperature increases by one degree and the chill index does not change. The point estimate $b_2 = .08249$ of β_2 says we estimate that mean weekly fuel consumption increases (since b_2 is positive) by .08249 MMcf of natural gas when there is a one-unit increase in the chill index and average hourly temperature does not change.

The equation

$$\begin{aligned}\hat{y} &= b_0 + b_1x_1 + b_2x_2 \\ &= 13.1087 - 0.09001x_1 + 0.08249x_2\end{aligned}$$

is called the **least squares prediction equation.** It is obtained by replacing β_0, β_1, and β_2 by their estimates b_0, b_1, and b_2 and by predicting the error term to be 0. This equation is given on the MINITAB output (labeled as the "regression equation"—note that b_0, b_1, and b_2 have been rounded to 13.1, −0.0900, and 0.0825). We can use this equation to compute a prediction for any

TABLE 12.6 The Point Predictions and Residuals Using the Least Squares Point Estimates, $b_0 = 13.1$, $b_1 = -.0900$, and $b_2 = .0825$

Week	Average Hourly Temperature, x_1 (°F)	Chill Index, x_2	Observed Fuel Consumption, y (MMcf)	Predicted Fuel Consumption, $\hat{y} = b_0 + b_1x_1 + b_2x_2 = 13.1 - .0900x_1 + .0825x_2$	Residual, $e = y - \hat{y}$
1	28.0	18	12.4	12.0733	.3267
2	28.0	14	11.7	11.7433	−.0433
3	32.5	24	12.4	12.1632	.2368
4	39.0	22	10.8	11.4131	−.6131
5	45.9	8	9.4	9.6371	−.2371
6	57.8	16	9.5	9.2259	.2741
7	58.1	1	8.0	7.9614	.0386
8	62.5	0	7.5	7.4829	.0171

$$SSE = (.3267)^2 + (-.0433)^2 + \cdots + (.0171)^2 = .674$$

FIGURE 12.6 A Geometrical Interpretation of the Prediction Equation Relating $\hat{y}$ to x_1 and x_2

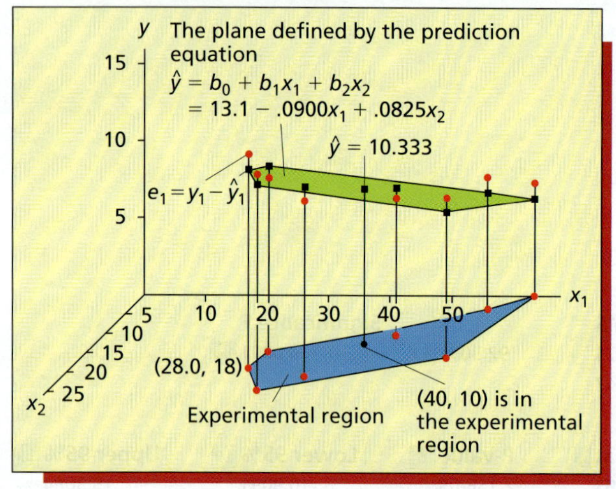

FIGURE 12.7 The MINITAB Output of the Least Squares Plane

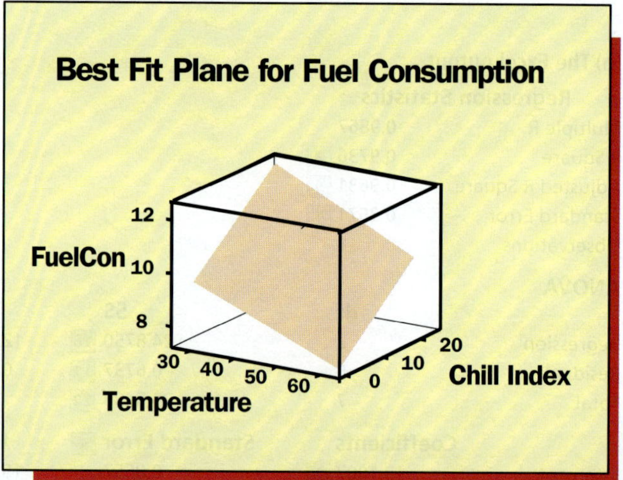

observed value of y. For instance, a point prediction of $y_1 = 12.4$ (when $x_1 = 28.0$ and $x_2 = 18$) is

$$\hat{y}_1 = 13.1087 - 0.09001(28.0) + 0.08249(18) = 12.0733$$

This results in a residual equal to

$$e_1 = y_1 - \hat{y}_1 = 12.4 - 12.0733 = .3267$$

Table 12.6 gives the point prediction obtained using the least squares prediction equation and the residual for each of the eight observed fuel consumption values. In addition, this table tells us that the sum of squared residuals (SSE) equals .674.

The least squares prediction equation is the equation of a plane, which we sometimes call the **least squares plane.** Figure 12.6 illustrates a portion of this plane—the portion that corresponds to the (x_1, x_2) combinations in the experimental region. Figure 12.6 also shows the residuals for the eight weeks. These residuals are depicted as line segments drawn between the observed fuel consumptions (the dots scattered around the least squares plane) and the predicted fuel consumptions (the squares on the least squares plane). Since the least squares point estimates minimize the sum of squared residuals, we can interpret them as positioning the planar prediction equation in three-dimensional space so as to minimize the sum of squared distances between the observed and predicted fuel consumptions. In this sense we can say that the plane defined by the least squares point estimates is the best plane that can be positioned between the observed fuel consumptions. The MINITAB output of the least squares plane is given in Figure 12.7.

Part 2: Estimating means and predicting individual values For combinations of values of x_1 and x_2 that are in the experimental region, the **least squares plane** (see Figure 12.6) is the estimate of the **plane of means** (see Figure 12.4 on page 531). This implies that the point on the least squares plane corresponding to the average hourly temperature x_1 and the chill index x_2

$$\begin{aligned}\hat{y} &= b_0 + b_1x_1 + b_2x_2 \\ &= 13.1087 - .09001x_1 + .08249x_2\end{aligned}$$

is the point estimate of $\mu_{y|x_1, x_2}$, the mean of all the weekly fuel consumptions that could be observed when the average hourly temperature is x_1 and the chill index is x_2. In addition, since we predict the error term to be 0, $\hat{y}$ is also the point prediction of $y = \mu_{y|x_1, x_2} + \varepsilon$, which is the amount of fuel consumed in a single week when the average hourly temperature is x_1 and the chill index is x_2.

For example, suppose a weather forecasting service predicts that in the next week the average hourly temperature will be 40°F and the chill index will be 10. Since this combination is inside the experimental region (see Figure 12.6), we see that

$$\begin{aligned}\hat{y} &= 13.1087 - .09001(40) + .08249(10) \\ &= 10.333 \text{ MMcf of natural gas}\end{aligned}$$

is

1 The point estimate of the mean weekly fuel consumption when the average hourly temperature is 40°F and the chill index is 10, and

2 The point prediction of the amount of fuel consumed in a single week when the average hourly temperature is 40°F and the chill index is 10.

Notice that $\hat{y} = 10.333$ is given at the bottom of the MINITAB output in Figure 12.5. In addition, Figure 12.6 illustrates this point estimate and prediction.

Generalizing the previous example, we obtain the following:

Point Estimation and Point Prediction in Multiple Regression

Let $b_0, b_1, b_2, \ldots, b_k$ be the least squares point estimates of the parameters $\beta_0, \beta_1, \beta_2, \ldots, \beta_k$ in the multiple regression model, and suppose that $x_{01}, x_{02}, \ldots, x_{0k}$ are specified values of the independent variables $x_1, x_2, \ldots, x_k$. If the combination of specified values is inside the experimental region, then

$$\hat{y} = b_0 + b_1x_{01} + b_2x_{02} + \cdots + b_kx_{0k}$$

is the **point estimate** of the **mean value of the dependent variable** when the values of the independent variables are $x_{01}, x_{02}, \ldots, x_{0k}$. In addition, $\hat{y}$ is the **point prediction** of an **individual value of the dependent variable** when the values of the independent variables are $x_{01}, x_{02}, \ldots, x_{0k}$. Here we predict the error term to be 0.

Example 12.4 The Sales Territory Performance Case

C

Figure 12.8 presents the MegaStat output of a regression analysis of the data in Table 12.2 using the model

$$y = \beta_0 + \beta_1x_1 + \beta_2x_2 + \beta_3x_3 + \beta_4x_4 + \beta_5x_5 + \varepsilon$$

On this output x_1, x_2, x_3, x_4, and x_5 are denoted as Time, MktPoten, Adver, MktShare, and Change, respectively. The MegaStat output tells us that the least squares point estimates of the model parameters are $b_0 = -1{,}113.7879$, $b_1 = 3.6121$, $b_2 = .0421$, $b_3 = .1289$, $b_4 = 256.9555$, and $b_5 = 324.5334$. These estimates give the least squares prediction equation

$$\hat{y} = -1{,}113.7879 + 3.6121x_1 + .0421x_2 + .1289x_3 + 256.9555x_4 + 324.5334x_5$$

Recalling that the sales values in Table 12.2 are measured in hundreds of units of the product sold, the point estimate $b_3 = .1289$ says we estimate that mean sales increase by .1289 hundreds of units—that is, by 12.89 units—for each dollar increase in advertising expenditure when the

FIGURE 12.8 MegaStat Output of the Sales Territory Performance Data Using the Model $y = \beta_0 + \beta_1 x_1 + \beta_2 x_2 + \beta_3 x_3 + \beta_4 x_4 + \beta_5 x_5 + \varepsilon$

Regression Analysis

R^2 0.915 [6]
Adjusted R^2 0.893 [7]
R 0.957
Std. Error 430.232 [8]

n 25
k 5
Dep. Var. Sales

= significant at .05 level
= significant at .01 level

ANOVA table

Source	SS	df	MS	F	p-value
Regression	37,862,658.9002 [1]	5	7,572,531.7800	40.91 [4]	1.59E-09 [5]
Residual	3,516,890.0266 [2]	19	185,099.4751		
Total	41,379,548.9269 [3]	24			

Regression output

variables	coefficients [9]	std. error [10]	t(df=19) [11]	p-value [12]	confidence interval [17] 95% lower	95% upper
Intercept	-1,113.7879	419.8869	-2.653	0.0157	-1,992.6213	-234.9545
Time	3.6121	1.1817	3.057	0.0065	1.1388	6.0854
MktPoten	0.0421	0.0067	6.253	5.27E-06	0.0280	0.0562
Adver	0.1289	0.0370	3.479	0.0025	0.0513	0.2064
MktShare	256.9555	39.1361	6.566	2.76E-06	175.0428	338.8683
Change	324.5334	157.2831	2.063	0.0530	-4.6638	653.7307

Predicted values for: Sales

Predicted [13]	95% Confidence Interval [14] lower	upper	95% Prediction Interval [15] lower	upper	Leverage [16]
4,181.74333	3,884.90651	4,478.58015	3,233.59431	5,129.89235	0.109

[1] Explained variation [2] SSE = Unexplained variation [3] Total variation [4] F(model) [5] p-value for F(model)
[6] R^2 [7] Adjusted R^2 [8] s = standard error [9] b_j = least squares estimate of β_j [10] s_{b_j} = standard error of the estimate b_j
[11] t statistics for testing significance of independent variables [12] p-values for t statistics [13] $\hat{y}$ = point prediction
[14] 95% confidence interval [15] 95% prediction interval [16] distance value [17] 95% confidence interval for β_j

other four independent variables do not change. If the company sells each unit for $1.10, this implies that we estimate that mean sales revenue increases by ($1.10)(12.89) = $14.18 for each dollar increase in advertising expenditure when the other four independent variables do not change. The other β values in the model can be interpreted similarly.

Consider a questionable sales representative for whom Time = 85.42, MktPoten = 35,182.73, Adver = 7,281.65, MktShare = 9.64, and Change = .28. The point prediction of the sales corresponding to this combination of values of the independent variables is

$$\begin{aligned}\hat{y} &= -1{,}113.7879 + 3.6121(85.42) + .0421(35{,}182.73) \\ &\quad + .1289(7{,}281.65) + 256.9555(9.64) + 324.5334(.28) \\ &= 4{,}181.74 \text{ (that is, 418,174 units)}\end{aligned}$$

which is given on the MegaStat output. The actual sales for the questionable sales representative were 3,087.52. This sales figure is 1,094.22 less than the point prediction $\hat{y}$ = 4,181.74. However, we will have to wait until we study prediction intervals in multiple regression (see Section 12.6) to determine whether there is strong evidence that this sales figure is unusually low.

Exercises for Section 12.2

CONCEPTS

12.9 In the multiple regression model, what sum of squared deviations do the least squares point estimates minimize?

12.10 When using the multiple regression model, how do we obtain a point estimate of the mean value of the dependent variable and a point prediction of an individual value of the dependent variable?

FIGURE 12.9 MINITAB Output of a Regression Analysis of the Real Estate Sales Price Data Using the Model $y = \beta_0 + \beta_1 x_1 + \beta_2 x_2 + \varepsilon$

```
The regression equation is
SalesPrice = 29.3 + 5.61 HomeSize + 3.83 Rating

Predictor     Coef   SE Coef      T      P
Constant    29.347     4.891   6.00  0.001
HomeSize    5.6128    0.2285  24.56  0.000
Rating      3.8344    0.4332   8.85  0.000

S = 3.24164    R-Sq = 99.0%    R-Sq(adj) = 98.7%

Analysis of Variance
Source          DF      SS      MS       F      P
Regression       2  7374.0  3687.0  350.87  0.000
Residual Error   7    73.6    10.5
Total            9  7447.5

Values of Predictors for New Obs    Predicted Values for New Observations
New Obs  HomeSize  Rating           New Obs     Fit  SE Fit          95% CI              95% PI
      1      20.0    8.00                 1  172.28    1.57  (168.56, 175.99)  (163.76, 180.80)
```

FIGURE 12.10 Excel Output of a Regression Analysis of the Real Estate Sales Price Data Using the Model $y = \beta_0 + \beta_1 x_1 + \beta_2 x_2 + \varepsilon$

Regression Statistics	
Multiple R	0.9950
R Square	0.9901
Adjusted R Square	0.9873
Standard Error	3.2416
Observations	10

ANOVA	df	SS	MS	F	Significance F
Regression	2	7373.9516	3686.9758	350.8665	9.58E-08
Residual	7	73.5574	10.5082		
Total	9	7447.5090			

	Coefficients	Standard Error	t Stat	P-value	Lower 95%	Upper 95%
Intercept	29.3468	4.8914	5.9996	0.0005	17.7804	40.9132
Home Size (x1)	5.6128	0.2285	24.5615	4.73E-08	5.0724	6.1532
Rating (x2)	3.8344	0.4332	8.8514	4.75E-05	2.8101	4.8588

METHODS AND APPLICATIONS

12.11 THE REAL ESTATE SALES PRICE CASE RealEst2

Figures 12.9 and 12.10 give the MINITAB and Excel output of a regression analysis of the real estate sales price data in Table 12.3 (page 534) using the model

$$y = \beta_0 + \beta_1 x_1 + \beta_2 x_2 + \varepsilon$$

a Using the MINITAB or Excel output, find (on the output) and report the values of b_0, b_1, and b_2, the least squares point estimates of β_0, β_1, and β_2. Interpret b_0, b_1, and b_2.

b Calculate a point estimate of the mean sales price of all houses having 2,000 square feet and a rating of 8, and a point prediction of the sales price of an individual house having 2,000 square feet and a rating of 8. Find this point estimate (prediction), which is given at the bottom of the MINITAB output.

12.12 THE FRESH DETERGENT CASE Fresh2

Figure 12.11 gives the MegaStat output of a regression analysis of the Fresh Detergent demand data in Table 12.4 (page 535) using the model

$$y = \beta_0 + \beta_1 x_1 + \beta_2 x_2 + \beta_3 x_3 + \varepsilon$$

FIGURE 12.11 MegaStat Output of a Regression Analysis of the Fresh Detergent Demand Data Using the Model $y = \beta_0 + \beta_1x_1 + \beta_2x_2 + \beta_3x_3 + \varepsilon$

Regression Analysis

	R^2 0.894		
	Adjusted R^2 0.881		n 30
R 0.945		k 3	
	Std. Error 0.235		Dep. Var. **Demand (y)**

ANOVA table

Source	SS	df	MS	F	p-value
Regression	12.0268	3	4.0089	72.80	8.88E-13
Residual	1.4318	26	0.0551		
Total	13.4586	29			

Regression output

variables	coefficients	std. error	t (df = 26)	p-value	confidence interval 95% lower	95% upper
Intercept	7.5891	2.4450	3.104	0.0046	2.5633	12.6149
Price (x1)	-2.3577	0.6379	-3.696	0.0010	-3.6690	-1.0464
IndPrice (x2)	1.6122	0.2954	5.459	1.01E-05	1.0051	2.2193
AdvExp (x3)	0.5012	0.1259	3.981	0.0005	0.2424	0.7599

Predicted values for: Demand (y)

Price (x1)	IndPrice (x2)	AdvExp (x3)	Predicted	95% Confidence Interval lower	upper	95% Prediction Interval lower	upper	Leverage
3.7	3.9	6.5	8.4107	8.3143	8.5070	7.9188	8.9025	0.040

FIGURE 12.12 Excel and MegaStat Output of a Regression Analysis of the Hospital Labor Needs Data Using the Model $y = \beta_0 + \beta_1x_1 + \beta_2x_2 + \beta_3x_3 + \varepsilon$

(a) The Excel output

Regression Statistics

Multiple R	0.9981
R Square	0.9961
Adjusted R Square	0.9952
Standard Error	387.1598
Observations	16

ANOVA

	df	SS	MS	F	Significance F
Regression	3	462327889.4	154109296.5	1028.1309	9.92E-15
Residual	12	1798712.2	149892.7		
Total	15	464126601.6			

	Coefficients	Standard Error	t Stat	P-value	Lower 95%	Upper 95%
Intercept	1946.8020	504.1819	3.8613	0.0023	848.2840	3045.3201
XRay (x1)	0.0386	0.0130	2.9579	0.0120	0.0102	0.0670
BedDays (x2)	1.0394	0.0676	15.3857	2.91E-09	0.8922	1.1866
LengthStay (x3)	-413.7578	98.5983	-4.1964	0.0012	-628.5850	-198.9306

(b) Prediction using MegaStat

Predicted values for: LaborHours

XRay (x1)	BedDays (x2)	LengthStay (x3)	Predicted	95% Confidence Interval lower	upper	95% Prediction Interval lower	upper	Leverage
56194	14077.88	6.89	15,896.2473	15,378.0313	16,414.4632	14,906.2361	16,886.2584	0.3774

a Find (on the output) and report the values of b_0, b_1, b_2, and b_3, the least squares point estimates of β_0, β_1, β_2, and β_3. Interpret b_0, b_1, b_2, and b_3.

b Consider the demand for Fresh Detergent in a future sales period when Enterprise Industries' price for Fresh will be $x_1 = 3.70$, the average price of competitors' similar detergents will be $x_2 = 3.90$ and Enterprise Industries' advertising expenditure for Fresh will be $x_3 = 6.50$. The point prediction of this demand is given at the bottom of the MegaStat output. Report this point prediction and show how it has been calculated.

c Using the price for Fresh ($3.70), make a point prediction of the sales revenue from Fresh in the future sales period.

12.13 THE HOSPITAL LABOR NEEDS CASE HospLab

Figure 12.12 gives the Excel and MegaStat output of a regression analysis of the hospital labor needs data in Table 12.5 (page 535) using the model

$$y = \beta_0 + \beta_1 x_1 + \beta_2 x_2 + \beta_3 x_3 + \varepsilon$$

Note that the variables x_1, x_2, and x_3 are denoted as XRay, BedDays, and LengthStay on the output.

a Find (on the output) and interpret b_0, b_1, b_2, and b_3, the least squares point estimates of β_0, β_1, β_2, and β_3.

b Consider a questionable hospital for which XRay = 56,194, BedDays = 14,077.88, and LengthStay = 6.89. A point prediction of the labor hours corresponding to this combination of values of the independent variables is given on the MegaStat output. Report this point prediction and show how it has been calculated.

c If the actual number of labor hours used by the questionable hospital was $y = 17{,}207.31$, how does this y value compare with the point prediction?

12.3 Model Assumptions and the Standard Error

CHAPTER 17

Model assumptions In order to perform hypothesis tests and set up various types of intervals when using the multiple regression model

$$y = \beta_0 + \beta_1 x_1 + \beta_2 x_2 + \cdots + \beta_k x_k + \varepsilon$$

we need to make certain assumptions about the error term ε. At any given combination of values of $x_1, x_2, \ldots, x_k$, there is a population of error term values that could potentially occur. These error term values describe the different potential effects on y of all factors other than the combination of values of $x_1, x_2, \ldots, x_k$. Therefore, these error term values explain the variation in the y values that could be observed at the combination of values of $x_1, x_2, \ldots, x_k$. We make the following four assumptions about the potential error term values.

Assumptions for the Multiple Regression Model

1 At any given combination of values of $x_1, x_2, \ldots, x_k$, the population of potential error term values has a mean equal to 0.

2 **Constant variance assumption:** At any given combination of values of $x_1, x_2, \ldots, x_k$, the population of potential error term values has a variance that does not depend on the combination of values of $x_1, x_2, \ldots, x_k$. That is, the different populations of potential error term values corresponding to different combinations of values of $x_1, x_2, \ldots, x_k$ have equal variances. We denote the constant variance as σ^2.

3 **Normality assumption:** At any given combination of values of $x_1, x_2, \ldots, x_k$, the population of potential error term values has a **normal distribution.**

4 **Independence assumption:** Any one value of the error term ε is **statistically independent** of any other value of ε. That is, the value of the error term ε corresponding to an observed value of y is statistically independent of the error term corresponding to any other observed value of y.

Taken together, the first three assumptions say that, at any given combination of values of $x_1, x_2, \ldots, x_k$, the population of potential error term values is normally distributed with mean 0 and a variance σ^2 that does not depend on the combination of values of $x_1, x_2, \ldots, x_k$. Because the potential error term values cause the variation in the potential y values, the first three assumptions imply that, at any given combination of values of $x_1, x_2, \ldots, x_k$, the population of y values that could be observed is normally distributed with mean $\beta_0 + \beta_1 x_1 + \beta_2 x_2 + \cdots + \beta_k x_k$ and a variance σ^2 that does not depend on the combination of values of $x_1, x_2, \ldots, x_k$. Furthermore, the independence assumption says that, when time series data are utilized in a regression study, there are no patterns in the error term values. In Section 12.13 we show how to check the validity of the regression assumptions. That section can be read at any time after Section 12.7. As in simple linear regression, only pronounced departures from the assumptions must be remedied.

The mean square error and the standard error To present statistical inference formulas in later sections, we need to be able to compute point estimates of σ^2 and σ (the constant variance and standard deviation of the different error term populations). We show how to do this in the following box:

The Mean Square Error and the Standard Error

Suppose that the multiple regression model

$$y = \beta_0 + \beta_1 x_1 + \beta_2 x_2 + \cdots + \beta_k x_k + \varepsilon$$

utilizes k independent variables and thus has $(k + 1)$ parameters $\beta_0, \beta_1, \beta_2, \ldots, \beta_k$. Then, if the regression assumptions are satisfied, and if SSE denotes the sum of squared residuals for the model:

1 A point estimate of σ^2 is the **mean square error**

$$s^2 = \frac{SSE}{n - (k + 1)}$$

2 A point estimate of σ is the **standard error**

$$s = \sqrt{\frac{SSE}{n - (k + 1)}}$$

In order to explain these point estimates, recall that σ^2 is the variance of the population of y values (for given values of $x_1, x_2, \ldots, x_k$) around the mean value $\mu_{y|x_1, x_2, \ldots, x_k}$. Since $\hat{y}$ is the point estimate of this mean, it seems natural to use $SSE = \Sigma (y_i - \hat{y}_i)^2$ to help construct a point estimate of σ^2. We divide SSE by $n - (k + 1)$ because it can be proven that doing so makes the resulting s^2 an unbiased point estimate of σ^2. We call $n - (k + 1)$ the **number of degrees of freedom** associated with SSE.

We will see in Section 12.7 that if a particular regression model gives a small standard error, then the model will give short prediction intervals and thus accurate predictions of individual y values. For example, Table 12.6 (page 538) shows that SSE for the fuel consumption model

$$y = \beta_0 + \beta_1 x_1 + \beta_2 x_2 + \varepsilon$$

is .674. Since this model utilizes $k = 2$ independent variables and thus has $k + 1 = 3$ parameters (β_0, β_1, and β_2), a point estimate of σ^2 is the mean square error

$$s^2 = \frac{SSE}{n - (k + 1)} = \frac{.674}{8 - 3} = \frac{.674}{5} = .1348$$

and a point estimate of σ is the standard error $s = \sqrt{.1348} = .3671$. Note that $SSE = .674$, $s^2 = .1348 \approx .135$, and $s = .3671$ are given on the MINITAB and Excel outputs in Figure 12.5 (page 537). Also note that the s of .3671 for the two independent variable model is less than the s of .6542 for the simple linear regression model that uses only the average hourly temperature to predict weekly fuel consumption (see Example 11.6, page 470).

As another example, the SSE for the sales territory performance model

$$y = \beta_0 + \beta_1 x_1 + \beta_2 x_2 + \beta_3 x_3 + \beta_4 x_4 + \beta_5 x_5 + \varepsilon$$

is 3,516,890.0266. Since this model utilizes $k = 5$ independent variables and thus has $k + 1 = 6$ parameters, a point estimate of σ^2 is the mean square error

$$s^2 = \frac{SSE}{n - (k + 1)} = \frac{3,516,890.0266}{25 - 6} = 185,099.4751$$

and a point estimate of σ is the standard error $s = \sqrt{185,099.4751} = 430.232$. Note that these values of SSE, s^2, and s are given on the MegaStat output in Figure 12.8 (page 540).

12.4 R^2 and Adjusted R^2

The multiple coefficient of determination, R^2 In this section we discuss several ways to assess the utility of a multiple regression model. We first discuss a quantity called the **multiple coefficient of determination,** which is denoted R^2. The formulas for R^2 and several other related quantities are given in the following box:

The Multiple Coefficient of Determination, R^2

For the multiple regression model:

1. **Total variation** $= \sum (y_i - \bar{y})^2$
2. **Explained variation** $= \sum (\hat{y}_i - \bar{y})^2$
3. **Unexplained variation** $= \sum (y_i - \hat{y}_i)^2$
4. **Total variation** = **Explained variation** + **Unexplained variation**
5. The **multiple coefficient of determination** is
$$R^2 = \frac{\text{Explained variation}}{\text{Total variation}}$$
6. R^2 is the proportion of the total variation in the n observed values of the dependent variable that is explained by the overall regression model.
7. **Multiple correlation coefficient** $= R = \sqrt{R^2}$

As an example, consider the fuel consumption model

$$y = \beta_0 + \beta_1 x_1 + \beta_2 x_2 + \varepsilon$$

and the following MINITAB output:

```
S = 0.367078    R-Sq = 97.4%    R-Sq(adj) = 96.3%

Analysis of Variance
Source           DF      SS      MS      F      P
Regression        2  24.875  12.438  92.30  0.000
Residual Error    5   0.674   0.135
Total             7  25.549
```

This output tells us that the total variation (SS Total), explained variation (SS Regression), and unexplained variation (SS Residual Error) for the model are, respectively, 25.549, 24.875, and .674. The output also tells us that the multiple coefficient of determination is

$$R^2 = \frac{\text{Explained variation}}{\text{Total variation}} = \frac{24.875}{25.549} = .974 \text{ (97.4\% on the output)}$$

which implies that the multiple correlation coefficient is $R = \sqrt{.974} = .9869$. The value of $R^2 = .974$ says that the two independent variable fuel consumption model explains 97.4 percent of the total variation in the eight observed fuel consumptions. Note this R^2 value is larger than the r^2 of .899 for the simple linear regression model that uses only the average hourly temperature to predict weekly fuel consumption. Also note that the quantities given on the MINITAB output are given on the following Excel output.

Regression Statistics	
Multiple R	0.9867
R Square	0.9736
Adjusted R Square	0.9631
Standard Error	0.3671
Observations	8

ANOVA	df	SS	MS	F	Significance F
Regression	2	24.8750	12.4375	92.3031	0.0001
Residual	5	0.6737	0.1347		
Total	7	25.5488			

As another example, consider the sales territory performance model

$$y = \beta_0 + \beta_1 x_1 + \beta_2 x_2 + \beta_3 x_3 + \beta_4 x_4 + \beta_5 x_5 + \varepsilon$$

and the following MegaStat output

Regression Analysis

R²	0.915		
Adjusted R²	0.893	n	25
R	0.957	k	5
Std. Error	430.232	Dep. Var.	**Sales**

ANOVA table

Source	SS	df	MS	F	p-value
Regression	37,862,658.9002	5	7,572,531.7800	40.91	1.59E-09
Residual	3,516,890.0266	19	185,099.4751		
Total	41,379,548.9269	24			

This output tells us that the total, explained, and unexplained variations for the model are, respectively, 41,379,548.9269, 37,862,658.9002, and 3,516,890.0266. The MegaStat output also tells us that R^2 equals .915.

Adjusted R^2 Even if the independent variables in a regression model are unrelated to the dependent variable, they will make R^2 somewhat greater than 0. To avoid overestimating the importance of the independent variables, many analysts recommend calculating an *adjusted* multiple coefficient of determination.

Adjusted R^2

The **adjusted multiple coefficient of determination (adjusted R^2)** is

$$\overline{R}^2 = \left(R^2 - \frac{k}{n-1}\right)\left(\frac{n-1}{n-(k+1)}\right)$$

where R^2 is the multiple coefficient of determination, n is the number of observations, and k is the number of independent variables in the model under consideration.

To briefly explain this formula, note that it can be shown that subtracting $k/(n-1)$ from R^2 helps avoid overestimating the importance of the k independent variables. Furthermore, multiplying $[R^2 - (k/(n-1))]$ by $(n-1)/(n-(k+1))$ makes $\overline{R}^2$ equal to 1 when R^2 equals 1.

As an example, consider the fuel consumption model

$$y = \beta_0 + \beta_1 x_1 + \beta_2 x_2 + \varepsilon$$

Since we have seen that $R^2 = .974$, it follows that

$$\begin{aligned}\overline{R}^2 &= \left(R^2 - \frac{k}{n-1}\right)\left(\frac{n-1}{n-(k+1)}\right)\\ &= \left(.974 - \frac{2}{8-1}\right)\left(\frac{8-1}{8-(2+1)}\right)\\ &= .963\end{aligned}$$

which is given on the MINITAB and Excel outputs. Similarly, in addition to telling us that $R^2 =$ .915 for the five independent variable sales territory performance model, the MegaStat output tells us that $\overline{R}^2 = .893$ for this model.

If R^2 is less than $k/(n-1)$ (which can happen), then $\overline{R}^2$ will be negative. In this case, statistical software systems set $\overline{R}^2$ equal to 0. Historically, R^2 and $\overline{R}^2$ have been popular measures of model utility—possibly because they are unitless and between 0 and 1. In general, we desire R^2 and $\overline{R}^2$ to be near 1. However, sometimes even if a regression model has an R^2 and an $\overline{R}^2$ that are near 1, the model is still not able to predict accurately. We will discuss assessing a model's ability to predict accurately, as well as using R^2 and $\overline{R}^2$ to help choose a regression model, as we proceed through this chapter.

12.5 The Overall F Test

Another way to assess the utility of a regression model is to test the significance of the regression relationship between y and $x_1, x_2, \ldots, x_k$. For the multiple regression model, we test the null hypothesis H_0: $\beta_1 = \beta_2 = \cdots = \beta_k = 0$, which says that **none of the independent variables $x_1, x_2, \ldots, x_k$ is significantly related to y (the regression relationship is not significant),** versus the alternative hypothesis H_a: At least one of $\beta_1, \beta_2, \ldots, \beta_k$ does not equal 0, which says that **at least one of the independent variables is significantly related to y (the regression relationship is significant).** If we can reject H_0 at level of significance α, we say that **the multiple regression model is significant at level of significance α.** We carry out the test as follows:

An F Test for the Multiple Regression Model

Suppose that the regression assumptions hold and that the multiple regression model has $(k + 1)$ parameters, and consider testing

$$H_0: \beta_1 = \beta_2 = \cdots = \beta_k = 0$$

versus

H_a: At least one of $\beta_1, \beta_2, \ldots, \beta_k$ does not equal 0.

We define the **overall F statistic** to be

$$F(\text{model}) = \frac{(\text{Explained variation})/k}{(\text{Unexplained variation})/[n - (k + 1)]}$$

Also define the p-value related to F(model) to be the area under the curve of the F distribution (having k and $[n - (k + 1)]$ degrees of freedom) to the right of F(model). Then, we can reject H_0 in favor of H_a at level of significance α if either of the following equivalent conditions holds:

1 $F(\text{model}) > F_\alpha$

2 $p\text{-value} < \alpha$

Here the point F_α is based on k numerator and $n - (k + 1)$ denominator degrees of freedom.

Condition 1 is intuitively reasonable because a large value of F(model) would be caused by an explained variation that is large relative to the unexplained variation. This would occur if at least one independent variable in the regression model significantly affects y, which would imply that H_0 is false and H_a is true.

Example 12.5 The Fuel Consumption Case

C

Consider the fuel consumption model

$$y = \beta_0 + \beta_1 x_1 + \beta_2 x_2 + \varepsilon$$

and the following MINITAB output

```
Analysis of Variance
Source          DF      SS      MS      F      P
Regression       2  24.875  12.438  92.30  0.000
Residual Error   5   0.674   0.135
Total            7  25.549
```

This output tells us that the explained and unexplained variations for this model are, respectively, 24.875 and .674. It follows, since there are $k = 2$ independent variables, that

$$\begin{aligned} F(\text{model}) &= \frac{(\text{Explained variation})/k}{(\text{Unexplained variation})/[n - (k + 1)]} \\ &= \frac{24.875/2}{.674/[8 - (2 + 1)]} = \frac{12.438}{.135} \\ &= 92.30 \end{aligned}$$

Note that this overall F statistic is given on the MINITAB output and is also given on the following Excel output:

ANOVA	df	SS	MS	F	Significance F
Regression	2	24.8750	12.4375	92.3031	0.0001
Residual	5	0.6737	0.1347		
Total	7	25.5488			

The p-value related to F(model) is the area to the right of 92.30 under the curve of the F distribution having $k = 2$ numerator and $n - (k + 1) = 8 - 3 = 5$ denominator degrees of freedom. Both the MINITAB and Excel output say this p-value is less than .001.

If we wish to test the significance of the regression model at level of significance $\alpha = .05$, we use the rejection point $F_{.05}$ based on 2 numerator and 5 denominator degrees of freedom. Using Table A.6 (page 828), we find that $F_{.05} = 5.79$. Since $F(\text{model}) = 92.30 > F_{.05} = 5.79$, we can reject H_0 in favor of H_a at level of significance .05. Alternatively, since the p-value is smaller than .05, .01, and .001, we can reject H_0 at level of significance .05, .01, and .001. Therefore, we have extremely strong evidence that the fuel consumption model is significant. That is, we have extremely strong evidence that at least one of the independent variables x_1 and x_2 in the model is significantly related to y.

Similarly, consider the following MegaStat output:

ANOVA table

Source	SS	df	MS	F	p-value
Regression	37,862,658.9002	5	7,572,531.7800	40.91	1.59E-09
Residual	3,516,890.0266	19	185,099.4751		
Total	41,379,548.9269	24			

This output tells us that $F(\text{model}) = 40.91$ for the five independent variable sales territory performance model. Furthermore, since the MegaStat output also tells us that the p-value related to F(model) is less than .001, we have extremely strong evidence that at least one of the five independent variables in this model is significantly related to sales territory performance.

If the overall F test tells us that at least one independent variable in a regression model is significant, we next attempt to decide which independent variables are significant. In the next section we discuss one way to do this.

Exercises for Sections 12.3, 12.4, and 12.5

CONCEPTS

12.14 What is estimated by the mean square error, and what is estimated by the standard error?

12.15 **a** What do R^2 and $\bar{R}^2$ measure? **b** How do R^2 and $\bar{R}^2$ differ?

12.16 What is the purpose of the overall F test?

METHODS AND APPLICATIONS

In Exercises 12.17 to 12.19 we give MINITAB, MegaStat, and Excel outputs of regression analyses of the data sets related to three case studies introduced in Section 12.1. Above each output we give the regression model and the number of observations, n, used to perform the regression analysis under consideration. Using the appropriate model, sample size n, and output:

1 Report SSE, s^2, and s as shown on the output. Calculate s^2 from SSE and other numbers.

2 Report the total variation, unexplained variation, and explained variation as shown on the output.

3 Report R^2 and $\bar{R}^2$ as shown on the output. Interpret R^2 and $\bar{R}^2$. Show how $\bar{R}^2$ has been calculated from R^2 and other numbers.

4 Calculate the F(model) statistic by using the explained variation, the unexplained variation, and other relevant quantities. Find F(model) on the output to check your answer.

5 Use the F(model) statistic and the appropriate rejection point to test the significance of the linear regression model under consideration by setting α equal to .05.

6 Use the F(model) statistic and the appropriate rejection point to test the significance of the linear regression model under consideration by setting α equal to .01.

7 Find the p-value related to F(model) on the output. Using the p-value, test the significance of the linear regression model by setting α = .10, .05, .01, and .001. What do you conclude?

12.17 THE REAL ESTATE SALES PRICE CASE RealEst2

Model: $y = \beta_0 + \beta_1 x_1 + \beta_2 x_2 + \varepsilon$ Sample size: $n = 10$

```
S = 3.24164    R-Sq = 99.0%    R-Sq(adj) = 98.7%

Analysis of Variance
Source           DF      SS       MS       F       P
Regression        2  7374.0   3687.0  350.87   0.000
Residual Error    7    73.6     10.5
Total             9  7447.5
```

12.18 THE FRESH DETERGENT CASE Fresh2

Model: $y = \beta_0 + \beta_1 x_1 + \beta_2 x_2 + \beta_3 x_3 + \varepsilon$ Sample size: $n = 30$

Regression Analysis

R^2	0.894		
Adjusted R^2	0.881	n	30
R	0.945	k	3
Std. Error	0.235	Dep. Var.	**Demand (y)**

ANOVA table

Source	SS	df	MS	F	p-value
Regression	12.0268	3	4.0089	72.80	8.88E-13
Residual	1.4318	26	0.0551		
Total	13.4586	29			

12.19 THE HOSPITAL LABOR NEEDS CASE HospLab

Model: $y = \beta_0 + \beta_1 x_1 + \beta_2 x_2 + \beta_3 x_3 + \varepsilon$ Sample size: $n = 16$

Regression Statistics

Multiple R	0.9981
R Square	0.9961
Adjusted R Square	0.9952
Standard Error	387.1598
Observations	16

ANOVA	df	SS	MS	F	Significance F
Regression	3	462327889.4	154109296.5	1028.1309	9.92E-15
Residual	12	1798712.2	149892.7		
Total	15	464126601.6			

12.6 Testing the Significance of an Independent Variable

Consider the multiple regression model

$$y = \beta_0 + \beta_1 x_1 + \beta_2 x_2 + \cdots + \beta_k x_k + \varepsilon$$

CHAPTER 17

In order to gain information about which independent variables significantly affect y, we can test the significance of a single independent variable. We arbitrarily refer to this variable as x_j and assume that it is multiplied by the parameter β_j. For example, if $j = 1$, we are testing the significance of x_1, which is multiplied by β_1; if $j = 2$, we are testing the significance of x_2, which is multiplied by β_2. To test the significance of x_j, we test the null hypothesis H_0: $\beta_j = 0$. We usually test H_0 versus the alternative hypothesis H_a: $\beta_j \neq 0$. **It is reasonable to conclude that x_j is significantly related to y in the regression model under consideration if H_0 can be rejected in favor of H_a at a small level of significance.** Here the phrase *in the regression model under consideration* is very important. This is because it can be shown that whether x_j is significantly related to y in a particular regression model can depend on what other independent variables are included in the model. This issue will be discussed in detail in Section 12.12.

Testing the significance of x_j in a multiple regression model is similar to testing the significance of the slope in the simple linear regression model (recall we test H_0: $\beta_1 = 0$ in simple regression). It can be proved that, if the regression assumptions hold, the population of all possible values of the least squares point estimate b_j is normally distributed with mean β_j and standard deviation σ_{b_j}. The point estimate of σ_{b_j} is called the **standard error of the estimate b_j** and is denoted s_{b_j}. The formula for s_{b_j} involves matrix algebra and is discussed in Appendix G of the CD-ROM included with this book. In our discussion here, we will rely on MINITAB, MegaStat, and Excel to compute s_{b_j}. It can be shown that, if the regression assumptions hold, then the population of all possible values of

$$\frac{b_j - \beta_j}{s_{b_j}}$$

has a t distribution with $n - (k + 1)$ degrees of freedom. It follows that, if the null hypothesis H_0: $\beta_j = 0$ is true, then the population of all possible values of the test statistic

$$t = \frac{b_j}{s_{b_j}}$$

has a t distribution with $n - (k + 1)$ degrees of freedom. Therefore, we can test the significance of x_j as follows:

Testing the Significance of the Independent Variable x_j

Define the test statistic

$$t = \frac{b_j}{s_{b_j}}$$

and suppose that the regression assumptions hold. Then we can test H_0: $\beta_j = 0$ versus a particular alternative hypothesis at significance level α by using the appropriate rejection point rule, or, equivalently, the corresponding p-value.

Alternative Hypothesis	Rejection Point Rule: Reject H_0 if	p-Value (reject H_0 if p-value $< \alpha$)
H_a: $\beta_j \neq 0$	$\lvert t \rvert > t_{\alpha/2}$	Twice the area under the t curve to the right of $\lvert t \rvert$
H_a: $\beta_j > 0$	$t > t_\alpha$	The area under the t curve to the right of t
H_a: $\beta_j < 0$	$t < -t_\alpha$	The area under the t curve to the left of t

Here $t_{\alpha/2}$, t_α, and all p-values are based on $n - (k + 1)$ degrees of freedom.

As in testing H_0: $\beta_1 = 0$ in simple linear regression, we usually use the two-sided alternative hypothesis H_a: $\beta_j \neq 0$ unless we have theoretical reasons to believe that β_j has a particular (plus or minus) sign. Moreover, MINITAB, MegaStat, and Excel present the results for the two-sided test.

It is customary to test the significance of each and every independent variable in a regression model. Generally speaking,

1 If we can reject H_0: $\beta_j = 0$ at the .05 level of significance, we have strong evidence that the independent variable x_j is significantly related to y in the regression model.

2 If we can reject H_0: $\beta_j = 0$ at the .01 level of significance, we have very strong evidence that x_j is significantly related to y in the regression model.

3 The smaller the significance level α at which H_0 can be rejected, the stronger is the evidence that x_j is significantly related to y in the regression model.

TABLE 12.7 ***t* Statistics and *p*-Values for Testing the Significance of the Intercept, x_1, and x_2 in the Fuel Consumption Model $y = \beta_0 + \beta_1 x_1 + \beta_2 x_2 + \varepsilon$**

(a) Calculation of the *t* statistics

Independent Variable	Null Hypothesis	b_j	s_{b_j}	$t = \frac{b_j}{s_{b_j}}$	*p*-Value
Intercept	$H_0: \beta_0 = 0$	$b_0 = 13.1087$	$s_{b_0} = .8557$	$t = \frac{b_0}{s_{b_0}} = \frac{13.1087}{.8557} = 15.32$	.000
x_1	$H_0: \beta_1 = 0$	$b_1 = -0.09001$	$s_{b_1} = .01408$	$t = \frac{b_1}{s_{b_1}} = \frac{-.09001}{.01408} = -6.39$	.001
x_2	$H_0: \beta_2 = 0$	$b_2 = 0.08249$	$s_{b_2} = .02200$	$t = \frac{b_2}{s_{b_2}} = \frac{.08249}{.02200} = 3.75$	.013

(b) The MINITAB output

```
Predictor      Coef     SE Coef      T       P
Constant     13.1087    0.8557    15.32   0.000
Temp        -0.09001    0.01408   -6.39   0.001
Chill        0.08249    0.02200    3.75   0.013
```

(c) The Excel output

	Coefficients	Standard Error	t Stat	P-value	Lower 95%	Upper 95%
Intercept	13.1087	0.8557	15.3193	2.15E-05	10.9091	15.3084
TEMP	-0.0900	0.0141	-6.3942	0.0014	-0.1262	-0.0538
CHILL	0.0825	0.0220	3.7493	0.0133	0.0259	0.1391

Example 12.6 The Fuel Consumption Case

Again consider the fuel consumption model

$$y = \beta_0 + \beta_1 x_1 + \beta_2 x_2 + \varepsilon$$

Table 12.7(a) summarizes the calculation of the *t* statistics and related *p*-values for testing the significance of the intercept and each of the independent variables x_1 and x_2. Here the values of b_j, s_{b_j}, t, and the *p*-value have been obtained from the MINITAB and Excel outputs of Table 12.7(b) and (c). If we wish to carry out tests at the .05 level of significance, we use the rejection point $t_{.05/2} = t_{.025} = 2.571$, which is based on $n - (k + 1) = 8 - 3 = 5$ degrees of freedom. Looking at Table 12.7 (a), we see that

1. For the intercept, $|t| = 15.32 > 2.571$.
2. For x_1, $|t| = 6.39 > 2.571$.
3. For x_2, $|t| = 3.75 > 2.571$.

Since in each case $|t| > t_{.025}$, we reject each of the null hypotheses in Table 12.7(a) at the .05 level of significance. Furthermore, since the *p*-values related to the intercept and x_1 are each less than .01, we can reject H_0: $\beta_0 = 0$ and H_0: $\beta_1 = 0$ at the .01 level of significance. Since the *p*-value related to x_2 is less than .05 but not less than .01, we can reject H_0: $\beta_2 = 0$ at the .05 level of significance, but not at the .01 level of significance. On the basis of these results, we have very strong evidence that in the above model the intercept β_0 is significant and x_1 (average hourly temperature) is significantly related to *y*. We also have strong evidence that in this model x_2 (the chill index) is significantly related to *y*.

Example 12.7 The Sales Territory Performance Case

Consider the sales territory performance model

$$y = \beta_0 + \beta_1 x_1 + \beta_2 x_2 + \beta_3 x_3 + \beta_4 x_4 + \beta_5 x_5 + \varepsilon$$

Since the MegaStat output in Figure 12.13 tells us that the *p*-values associated with Time, MktPoten, Adver, and MktShare are all less than .01, we have very strong evidence that these

FIGURE 12.13 MegaStat Output of t Statistics and p-Values for the Sales Territory Performance Model

Regression output variables	coefficients	std. error	t (df=19)	p-value	confidence interval 95% lower	95% upper
Intercept	-1,113.7879	419.8869	-2.653	0.0157	-1,992.6213	-234.9545
Time	3.6121	1.1817	3.057	0.0065	1.1388	6.0854
MktPoten	0.0421	0.0067	6.253	5.27E-06	0.0280	0.0562
Adver	0.1289	0.0370	3.479	0.0025	0.0513	0.2064
MktShare	256.9555	39.1361	6.566	2.76E-06	175.0428	338.8683
Change	324.5334	157.2831	2.063	0.0530	-4.6638	653.7307

variables are significantly related to y and, thus, are important in this model. Since the p-value associated with Change is .0530, we have close to strong evidence that this variable is also important.

We next consider how to calculate a confidence interval for a regression parameter.

A Confidence Interval for the Regression Parameter β_j

If the regression assumptions hold, a **100(1 − α) percent confidence interval for β_j** is

$$[b_j \pm t_{\alpha/2} s_{b_j}]$$

Here $t_{\alpha/2}$ is based on $n - (k + 1)$ degrees of freedom.

Example 12.8 The Fuel Consumption Case

Consider the fuel consumption model

$$y = \beta_0 + \beta_1 x_1 + \beta_2 x_2 + \varepsilon$$

The MINITAB and Excel output in Table 12.7 tells us that $b_1 = -.09001$ and $s_{b_1} = .01408$. It follows, since $t_{.025}$ based on $n - (k + 1) = 8 - 3 = 5$ degrees of freedom equals 2.571, that a 95 percent confidence interval for β_1 is (see the Excel output)

$$[b_1 \pm t_{.025} s_{b_1}] = [-.09001 \pm 2.571(.01408)]$$
$$= [-.1262, -.0538]$$

This interval says we are 95 percent confident that, if average hourly temperature increases by one degree and the chill index does not change, then mean weekly fuel consumption will decrease by at least .0538 MMcf of natural gas and by at most .1262 MMcf of natural gas. Furthermore, since this 95 percent confidence interval does not contain 0, we can reject H_0: $\beta_1 = 0$ in favor of H_a: $\beta_1 \neq 0$ at the .05 level of significance.

Exercises for Section 12.6

CONCEPTS

12.20 What do we conclude about x_j if we can reject H_0: $\beta_j = 0$ in favor of H_a: $\beta_j \neq 0$ by setting

a α equal to .05?

b α equal to .01?

12.21 Give an example of a practical application of the confidence interval for β_j.

METHODS AND APPLICATIONS

In Exercises 12.22 through 12.24 we refer to MINITAB, MegaStat, and Excel outputs of regression analyses of the data sets related to three case studies introduced in Section 12.1. The outputs are given in Figure 12.14. Using the appropriate output, do the following for **each parameter** β_j in the model under consideration:

FIGURE 12.14 *t* Statistics and *p*-Values for Three Case Studies

(a) MINITAB output for the real estate sales price case (sample size: $n = 10$)

Predictor	Coef	SE Coef	T	P
Constant	29.347	4.891	6.00	0.001
HomeSize	5.6128	0.2285	24.56	0.000
Rating	3.8344	0.4332	8.85	0.000

(b) MegaStat output for the Fresh detergent case (sample size: $n = 30$)

Regression output					confidence interval	
variables	coefficients	std. error	t (df=26)	p-value	95% lower	95% upper
Intercept	7.5891	2.4450	3.104	0.0046	2.5633	12.6149
Price (x1)	-2.3577	0.6379	-3.696	0.0010	-3.6690	-1.0464
IndPrice (x2)	1.6122	0.2954	5.459	1.01E-05	1.0051	2.2193
AdvExp (x3)	0.5012	0.1259	3.981	0.0005	0.2424	0.7599

(c) Excel output for the hospital labor needs case (sample size: $n = 16$)

	Coefficients	Standard Error	t Stat	P-value	Lower 95%	Upper 95%
Intercept	1946.8020	504.1819	3.8613	0.0023	848.2840	3045.3201
XRay (x1)	0.0386	0.0130	2.9579	0.0120	0.0102	0.0670
BedDays (x2)	1.0394	0.0676	15.3857	2.91E-09	0.8922	1.1866
LengthStay (x3)	-413.7578	98.5983	-4.1964	0.0012	-628.5850	-198.9306

1 Find b_j, s_{b_j}, and the t statistic for testing H_0: $\beta_j = 0$ on the output and report their values. Show how t has been calculated by using b_j and s_{b_j}.

2 Using the t statistic and appropriate rejection points, test H_0: $\beta_j = 0$ versus H_a: $\beta_j \neq 0$ by setting α equal to .05. Which independent variables are significantly related to y in the model with $\alpha = .05$?

3 Using the t statistic and appropriate rejection points, test H_0: $\beta_j = 0$ versus H_a: $\beta_j \neq 0$ by setting α equal to .01. Which independent variables are significantly related to y in the model with $\alpha = .01$?

4 Find the p-value for testing H_0: $\beta_j = 0$ versus H_a: $\beta_j \neq 0$ on the output. Using the p-value, determine whether we can reject H_0 by setting α equal to .10, .05, .01, and .001. What do you conclude about the significance of the independent variables in the model?

5 Calculate the 95 percent confidence interval for β_j. Discuss one practical application of this interval.

6 Calculate the 99 percent confidence interval for β_j. Discuss one practical application of this interval.

12.22 THE REAL ESTATE SALES PRICE CASE RealEst2

Use the MINITAB output in Figure 12.14(a) to do (1) through (6) for each of β_0, β_1, and β_2.

12.23 THE FRESH DETERGENT CASE Fresh2

Use the MegaStat output in Figure 12.14(b) to do (1) through (6) for each of β_0, β_1, β_2, and β_3.

12.24 THE HOSPITAL LABOR NEEDS CASE HospLab

Use the Excel output in Figure 12.14(c) to do (1) through (6) for each of β_0, β_1, β_2, and β_3.

12.7 Confidence and Prediction Intervals

In this section we show how to use the multiple regression model to find a **confidence interval for a mean value of *y*** and a **prediction interval for an individual value of *y*.** We first present two examples of these intervals, and we then discuss the logic behind and formulas used to compute the intervals.

Example 12.9 The Fuel Consumption Case

C

In the fuel consumption problem, recall that the weather forecasting service has predicted that in the next week the average hourly temperature will be $x_{01} = 40°$F and the chill index will be

$x_{02} = 10$. Also, recall from Example 12.3 that

$$\begin{aligned}\hat{y} &= 13.1087 - .09001x_{01} + .08249x_{02} \\ &= 13.1087 - .09001(40) + .08249(10) \\ &= 10.333 \text{ MMcf of natural gas}\end{aligned}$$

is the point estimate of mean weekly fuel consumption when x_1 equals 40 and x_2 equals 10, and is the point prediction of fuel consumption in a single week when x_1 equals 40 and x_2 equals 10. This point estimate and prediction are given at the bottom of the MINITAB output in Figure 12.5, which we repeat here as follows:

```
New Obs     Fit   SE Fit        95% CI              95% PI
      1  10.333    0.170  (9.895, 10.771)  (9.293, 11.374)
```

In addition to giving $\hat{y} = 10.333$, the MINITAB output tells us that a 95 percent confidence interval for mean weekly fuel consumption when x_1 equals 40 and x_2 equals 10 is [9.895, 10.771]. This interval says we are 95 percent confident that mean weekly fuel consumption for all weeks having an average hourly temperature of 40°F and a chill index of 10 is between 9.895 MMcf of natural gas and 10.771 MMcf of natural gas. The MINITAB output also tells us that a 95 percent prediction interval for fuel consumption in a single week when x_1 equals 40 and x_2 equals 10 is [9.293, 11.374]. This interval says we are 95 percent confident that the amount of fuel consumed next week will be between 9.293 MMcf of natural gas and 11.374 MMcf of natural gas.

Recall from Example 11.11 (page 481) that the simple linear regression model, which predicts next week's fuel consumption on the basis of the average hourly temperature being 40°F, makes us 95 percent confident that the natural gas company's percentage nomination error will be no more than 15.91 percent. We now wish to determine if our new model, which predicts next week's fuel consumption on the basis of the average hourly temperature being 40°F and the chill index being 10, is likely to produce a percentage nomination error that is within the 10 percent allowance granted by the pipeline transmission system. First, recall that the point prediction $\hat{y} = 10.333$ given by our new model would be the natural gas company's transmission nomination for next week. Also note that $\hat{y} = 10.333$ is the midpoint of the 95 percent prediction interval, [9.293, 11.374], for next week's fuel consumption. The half-length of this interval is $(11.374 - 9.293)/2 = 1.041$, which implies that the interval can be expressed as $[10.333 \pm 1.041]$. Therefore, since 1.041 is $(1.041/10.333)100\% = 10.07\%$ of the transmission nomination of 10.333, the model makes us 95 percent confident that the actual amount of natural gas that will be used by the city next week will differ from the natural gas company's transmission nomination by no more than 10.07 percent. That is, we are 95 percent confident that the natural gas company's percentage nomination error will be less than or equal to 10.07 percent. Therefore, this error will probably be within the 10 percent allowance granted by the pipeline transmission system, and it is unlikely that the natural gas company will be required to pay a transmission fine.

Example 12.10 The Sales Territory Performance Case

Consider a questionable sales representative for whom TIME = 85.42, MktPoten = 35,182.73, Adver = 7,281.65, MktShare = 9.64, and Change = .28. We have seen in Example 12.4 that the point prediction of the sales corresponding to this combination of values of the independent variables is

$$\begin{aligned}\hat{y} &= -1{,}113.7879 + 3.6121(85.42) + .0421(35{,}182.73) \\ &\quad + .1289(7{,}281.65) + 256.9555(9.64) + 324.5334(.28) \\ &= 4{,}181.74 \text{ (that is, 418,174 units)}\end{aligned}$$

This point prediction is given at the bottom of the MegaStat output in Figure 12.8, which we repeat here:

Predicted values for: Sales

	95% Confidence Interval		95% Prediction Interval		
Predicted	**lower**	**upper**	**lower**	**upper**	**Leverage**
4,181.74333	3,884.90651	4,478.58015	3,233.59431	5,129.89235	0.109

In addition to giving $\hat{y} = 4{,}181.74$, the MegaStat output tells us that a 95 percent prediction interval for y is [3233.59, 5129.89]. Furthermore, the actual sales y for the questionable representative were 3,087.52. This actual sales figure is less than the point prediction $\hat{y} = 4{,}181.74$ and is less than the lower bound of the 95 percent prediction interval for y, [3233.59, 5129.89]. Therefore, we conclude that there is strong evidence that the actual performance of the questionable representative is less than predicted performance. We should investigate the reason for this. Perhaps the questionable representative needs special training.

In general

$$\hat{y} = b_0 + b_1x_{01} + \cdots + b_kx_{0k}$$

is the point estimate of the mean value of y when the values of the independent variables are $x_{01}, x_{02}, \ldots, x_{0k}$. Calling this mean value $\mu_{y|x_{01}, x_{02}, \ldots, x_{0k}}$, it can be proved that, if the regression assumptions hold, then the population of all possible values of $\hat{y}$ is normally distributed with mean $\mu_{y|x_{01}, x_{02}, \ldots, x_{0k}}$ and standard deviation

$$\sigma_{\hat{y}} = \sigma\sqrt{\text{Distance value}}$$

The formula for the distance value involves matrix algebra and is given in Appendix G of the CD-ROM included with this book. We will soon see how to use MINITAB or MegaStat output to find the distance value. It can be shown that the farther the values $x_{01}, x_{02}, \ldots, x_{0k}$ are from the center of the experimental region, the larger is the distance value. We regard the center of the experimental region to be the point $(\bar{x}_1, \bar{x}_2, \ldots, \bar{x}_k)$, where $\bar{x}_1$ is the average of the observed x_1 values, $\bar{x}_2$ is the average of the observed x_2 values, and so forth. Since s is the point estimate of σ, the point estimate of $\sigma_{\hat{y}}$ is

$$s_{\hat{y}} = s\sqrt{\text{Distance value}}$$

which is called the **standard error of the estimate $\hat{y}$.** Using this standard error, we can form a confidence interval.

A Confidence Interval for a Mean Value of y

If the regression assumptions hold, a **100(1 − α) percent confidence interval for the mean value of y** when the values of the independent variables are $x_{01}, x_{02}, \ldots, x_{0k}$ is

$$[\hat{y} \pm t_{\alpha/2}\, s\sqrt{\text{Distance value}}]$$

Here $t_{\alpha/2}$ is based on $n - (k + 1)$ degrees of freedom.

To develop an interval for an individual value of y, we consider the prediction error $y - \hat{y}$. It can be proved that, if the regression assumptions hold, then the population of all possible prediction errors is normally distributed with mean 0 and standard deviation

$$\sigma_{(y-\hat{y})} = \sigma\sqrt{1 + \text{Distance value}}$$

The point estimate of $\sigma_{(y-\hat{y})}$ is

$$s_{(y-\hat{y})} = s\sqrt{1 + \text{Distance value}}$$

which is called the **standard error of the prediction error.** Using this standard error, we can form a prediction interval.

A Prediction Interval for an Individual Value of y

If the regression assumptions hold, a **100(1 − α) percent prediction interval for an individual value of y** when the values of the independent variables are $x_{01}, x_{02}, \ldots, x_{0k}$ is

$$[\hat{y} \pm t_{\alpha/2}\, s\sqrt{1 + \text{Distance value}}]$$

Here $t_{\alpha/2}$ is based on $n - (k + 1)$ degrees of freedom.

Recall that the farther the values $x_{01}, x_{02}, \ldots, x_{0k}$ are from the center of the experimental region, the larger is the distance value. It follows that the farther the values $x_{01}, x_{02}, \ldots, x_{0k}$ are from the center of the experimental region, the longer (less precise) are the confidence intervals and prediction intervals provided by a regression model.

MINITAB gives $s_{\hat{y}} = s\sqrt{\text{Distance value}}$ under the heading "SE Fit." Since the MINITAB output also gives s, the distance value can be found by calculating $(s_{\hat{y}}/s)^2$. For example, the MINITAB output in Example 12.9 (page 553) tells us that $\hat{y} = 10.333$ (see "Fit") and $s_{\hat{y}} = .170$ (see "SE Fit"). Therefore, since s for the two variable fuel consumption model equals .3671, the distance value equals $(.170/.3671)^2 = .2144515$. It follows that the 95 percent confidence and prediction intervals given on the MINITAB output of Example 12.9 have been calculated as follows:

$$\begin{aligned}&[\hat{y} \pm t_{.025}\, s\sqrt{\text{Distance value}}]\\ &= [10.333 \pm 2.571(.3671)\sqrt{.2144515}]\\ &= [10.333 \pm .438]\\ &= [9.895, 10.771]\end{aligned}
\qquad
\begin{aligned}&[\hat{y} \pm t_{.025}\, s\sqrt{1 + \text{Distance value}}]\\ &= [10.333 \pm 2.571(.3671)\sqrt{1 + .2144515}]\\ &= [10.333 \pm 1.041]\\ &= [9.292, 11.374]\end{aligned}$$

Here $t_{\alpha/2} = t_{.025} = 2.571$ is based on $n - (k + 1) = 8 - 3 = 5$ degrees of freedom.

As another example, the MegaStat output in Example 12.10 (page 554) tells us that $\hat{y} = 4{,}181.74$. This output also tells us that the distance value, which is given under the heading "Leverage" on the output, equals .109. Therefore, since s for the five variable sales territory performance model equals 430.232, it follows that the 95 percent prediction interval given on the MegaStat output of Example 12.10 has been calculated as follows:

$$\begin{aligned}&[\hat{y} \pm t_{.025}\, s\sqrt{1 + \text{Distance value}}]\\ &= [4{,}181.74 \pm 2.093(430.232)\sqrt{1 + .109}]\\ &= [3233.59, 5129.89]\end{aligned}$$

Here $t_{.025} = 2.093$ is based on $n - (k + 1) = 25 - 6 = 19$ degrees of freedom.

Exercises for Section 12.7

CONCEPTS

12.25 What does the distance value measure?

12.26 How do we obtain the distance value from MINITAB output and MegaStat output?

METHODS AND APPLICATIONS

12.27 THE REAL ESTATE SALES PRICE CASE RealEst2

The following MINITAB output relates to a house having 2,000 square feet and a rating of 8.

```
New Obs     Fit   SE Fit        95% CI               95% PI
      1  172.28     1.57  (168.56, 175.99)   (163.76, 180.80)
```

a Report (as shown on the output) a point estimate of and a 95 percent confidence interval for the mean sales price of all houses having 2,000 square feet and a rating of 8.

b Report (as shown on the output) a point prediction of and a 95 percent prediction interval for the actual sales price of an individual house having 2,000 square feet and a rating of 8.

c Find 99 percent confidence and prediction intervals for the mean and actual sales prices referred to in parts *a* and *b*. Hint: $n = 10$ and $s = 3.24164$.

12.28 THE FRESH DETERGENT CASE Fresh2

Consider the demand for Fresh Detergent in a future sales period when Enterprise Industries' price for Fresh will be $x_1 = 3.70$, the average price of competitors' similar detergents will be $x_2 = 3.90$, and Enterprise Industries' advertising expenditure for Fresh will be $x_3 = 6.50$. A 95 percent prediction interval for this demand is given on the following MegaStat output:

	95% Confidence Interval		95% Prediction Interval		
Predicted	lower	upper	lower	upper	Leverage
8.4107	8.3143	8.5070	7.9188	8.9025	0.040

a Find and report the 95 percent prediction interval on the output. If Enterprise Industries plans to have in inventory the number of bottles implied by the upper limit of this interval, it can be very confident that it will have enough bottles to meet demand for Fresh in the future sales period. How many bottles is this? If we multiply the number of bottles implied by the lower limit of the prediction interval by the price of Fresh ($3.70), we can be very confident that the resulting dollar amount will be the minimal revenue from Fresh in the future sales period. What is this dollar amount?

b Calculate a 99 percent prediction interval for the demand for Fresh in the future sales period. Hint: $n = 30$.

c Recall that the data plots given at the bottom of Table 12.4 (page 535) suggest that the model $y = \beta_0 + \beta_1 x_4 + \beta_2 x_3 + \varepsilon$ might appropriately relate demand for Fresh (y) to the price difference ($x_4 = x_2 - x_1$) and advertising expenditure (x_3). The 95 percent prediction interval given by this model for the demand for Fresh in the future sales period is [7.89034, 8.88523]. Is this interval shorter or longer than the interval of part *a*? What does this imply about which model might best predict y?

12.29 THE HOSPITAL LABOR NEEDS CASE HospLab

Consider a questionable hospital for which XRay = 56,194, BedDays = 14,077.88, and LengthStay = 6.89. A 95 percent prediction interval for the labor hours corresponding to this combination of values of the independent variables is given on the following MegaStat output:

	95% Confidence Interval		95% Prediction Interval		
Predicted	lower	upper	lower	upper	Leverage
15,896.2473	15,378.0313	16,414.4632	14,906.2361	16,886.2584	0.3774

Find and report the prediction interval on the output. Then, use this interval to determine if the actual number of labor hours used by the questionable hospital ($y = 17{,}207.31$) is unusually low or high.

12.8 The Quadratic Regression Model (Optional)

PART 2 Using Squared and Interaction Terms (Optional)

One useful form of the multiple regression model is what we call the **quadratic regression model.** Assuming that we have obtained n observations—each consisting of an observed value of y and a corresponding value of x—the model is as follows:

The Quadratic Regression Model

The **quadratic regression model** relating y to x is

$$y = \beta_0 + \beta_1 x + \beta_2 x^2 + \varepsilon$$

where

1. $\beta_0 + \beta_1 x + \beta_2 x^2$ is $\mu_{y|x}$, the mean value of the dependent variable y when the value of the independent variable is x.
2. β_0, β_1, and β_2 are (unknown) **regression parameters** relating the mean value of y to x.
3. ε is an error term that describes the effects on y of all factors other than x and x^2.

The quadratic equation $\mu_{y|x} = \beta_0 + \beta_1 x + \beta_2 x^2$ that relates $\mu_{y|x}$ to x is the equation of a **parabola.** Two parabolas are shown in Figure 12.15(a) and (b) and help to explain the meanings of the parameters β_0, β_1, and β_2. Here β_0 is the **y-intercept** of the parabola (the value of $\mu_{y|x}$ when $x = 0$). Furthermore, β_1 is the **shift parameter** of the parabola: the value of β_1 shifts the parabola to the left or right. Specifically, increasing the value of β_1 shifts the parabola to the left. Lastly, β_2 is the **rate of curvature** of the parabola. If β_2 is greater than 0, the parabola opens upward [see Figure 12.15(a)]. If β_2 is less than 0, the parabola opens downward [see Figure 12.15(b)]. If a scatter plot of y versus x shows points scattered around a parabola, or a part of a parabola [some typical parts are shown in Figure 12.15(c), (d), (e), and (f)], then the quadratic regression model might appropriately relate y to x.

CHAPTER 18

FIGURE 12.15 The Mean Value of the Dependent Variable Changing in a Quadratic Fashion as x Increases ($\mu_{y|x} = \beta_0 + \beta_1 x + \beta_2 x^2$)

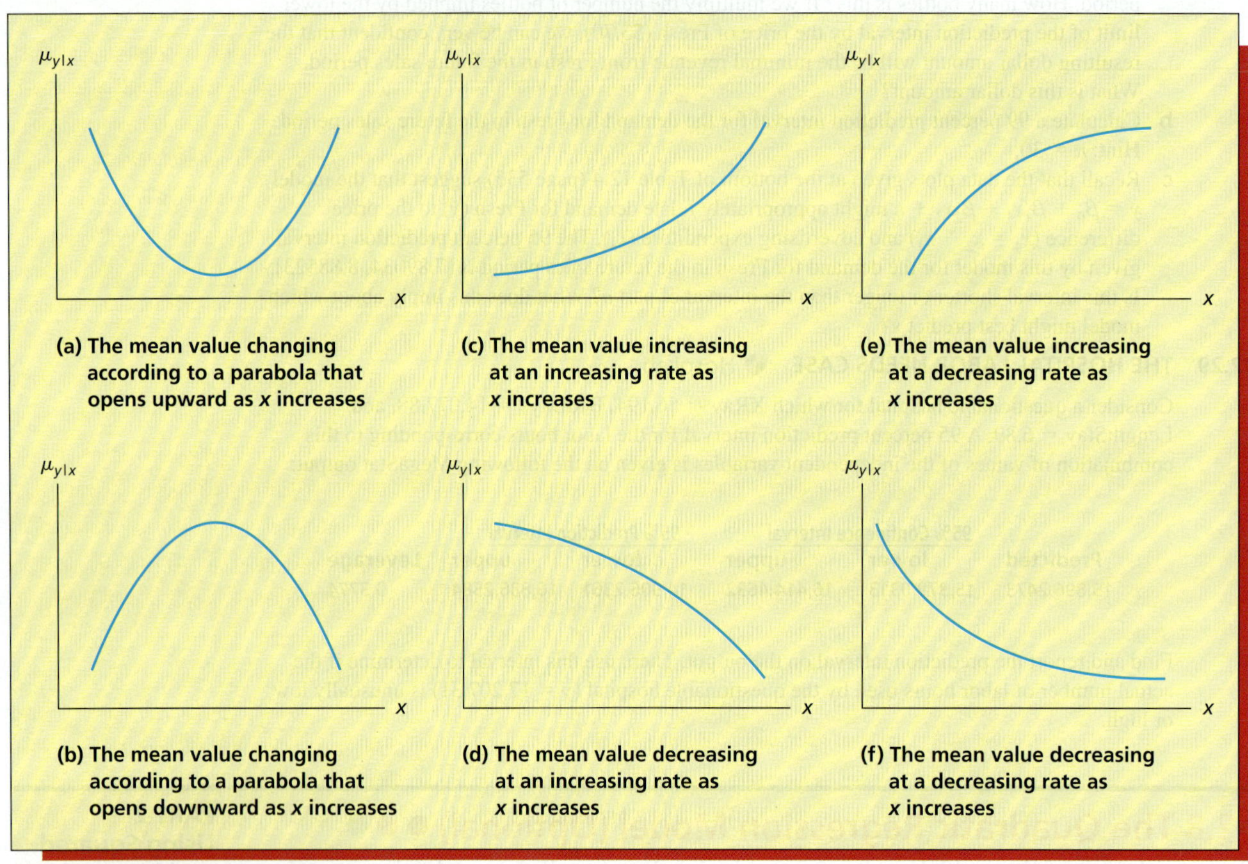

$\mu_{y|x}$
x
(a) The mean value changing according to a parabola that opens upward as x increases
(c) The mean value increasing at an increasing rate as x increases
(e) The mean value increasing at a decreasing rate as x increases
(b) The mean value changing according to a parabola that opens downward as x increases
(d) The mean value decreasing at an increasing rate as x increases
(f) The mean value decreasing at a decreasing rate as x increases

Example 12.11 The Gasoline Additive Case

An oil company wishes to improve the gasoline mileage obtained by cars that use its premium unleaded gasoline. Company chemists suggest that an additive, ST-3000, be blended with the gasoline. In order to study the effects of this additive, mileage tests are carried out in a laboratory using test equipment that simulates driving under prescribed conditions. The amount of additive ST-3000 blended with the gasoline is varied, and the gasoline mileage for each test run is recorded. Table 12.8(a) gives the results of the test runs. Here the dependent variable y is gasoline mileage (in miles per gallon) and the independent variable x is the amount of additive ST-3000 used (measured as the number of units of additive added to each gallon of gasoline). One of the study's goals is to determine the number of units of additive that should be blended with the gasoline to maximize gasoline mileage. The company would also like to predict the maximum mileage that can be achieved using additive ST-3000.

Table 12.8(b) gives a scatter plot of y versus x. Since the scatter plot has the appearance of a quadratic curve (that is, part of a parabola), it seems reasonable to relate y to x by using the quadratic model

$$y = \beta_0 + \beta_1 x + \beta_2 x^2 + \varepsilon$$

Figure 12.16 gives the MINITAB output of a regression analysis of the data using this quadratic model. Here the squared term x^2 is denoted as UnitsSq on the output. The MINITAB output tells us that the least squares point estimates of the model parameters are $b_0 = 25.7152$,

TABLE 12.8 The Gasoline Mileage Study Data, and a Scatter Plot of the Data GasAdd

(a) The Data

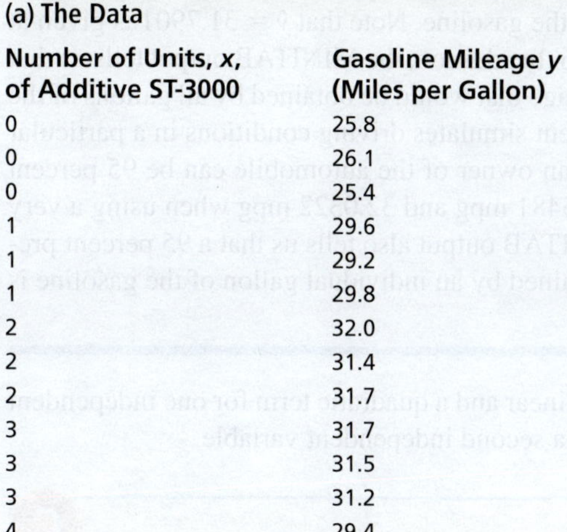

Number of Units, x, of Additive ST-3000	Gasoline Mileage y (Miles per Gallon)
0	25.8
0	26.1
0	25.4
1	29.6
1	29.2
1	29.8
2	32.0
2	31.4
2	31.7
3	31.7
3	31.5
3	31.2
4	29.4
4	29.0
4	29.5

(b) Scatter plot of y versus x

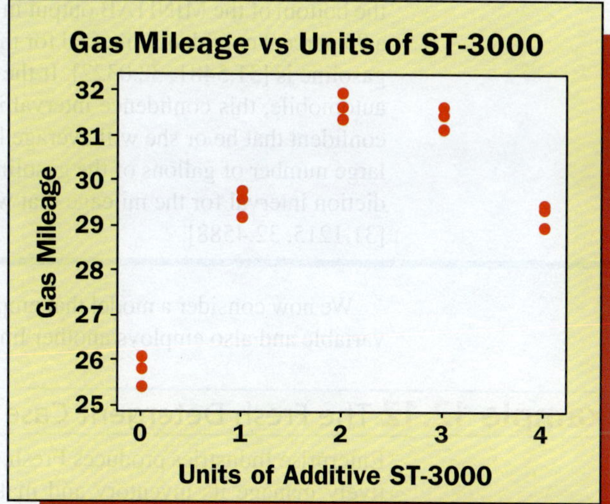

FIGURE 12.16 MINITAB Output of a Regression Analysis of the Gasoline Mileage Data Using the Quadratic Model

```
The regression equation is
Mileage = 25.7 + 4.98 Units - 1.02 UnitsSq

Predictor      Coef    SE Coef       T      P
Constant    25.7152     0.1554  165.43  0.000
Units        4.9762     0.1841   27.02  0.000
UnitsSq    -1.01905    0.04414  -23.09  0.000

S = 0.286079    R-Sq = 98.6%    R-Sq(adj) = 98.3%

Analysis of Variance
Source          DF      SS      MS       F      P
Regression       2  67.915  33.958  414.92  0.000
Residual Error  12   0.982   0.082
Total           14  68.897

Values of Predictors for New Obs    Predicted Values for New Observations
New Obs  Unit  UnitsSq              New Obs      Fit  SE Fit       95% CI              95% PI
      1  2.44   5.9536                    1  31.7901  0.1111  (31.5481, 32.0322)  (31.1215, 32.4588)
```

$b_1 = 4.9762$, and $b_2 = -1.01905$. These estimates give us the least squares prediction equation

$$\hat{y} = 25.7152 + 4.9762x - 1.01905x^2$$

Intuitively, this is the equation of the best quadratic curve that can be fitted to the data plotted in Table 12.8(b). The MINITAB output also tells us that the p-values related to x and x^2 are less than .001. This implies that we have very strong evidence that each of these model components is significant. The fact that x^2 seems significant confirms the graphical evidence that there is a quadratic relationship between y and x. Once we have such confirmation, we usually retain the linear term x in the model no matter what the size of its p-value. The reason is that geometrical considerations indicate that it is best to use both x and x^2 to model a quadratic relationship.

The oil company wishes to find the value of x that results in the highest predicted mileage. Using calculus, it can be shown that the value $x = 2.44$ maximizes predicted gas mileage. Therefore, the oil company can maximize predicted mileage by blending 2.44 units of additive ST-3000 with each gallon of gasoline. This will result in a predicted gas mileage equal to

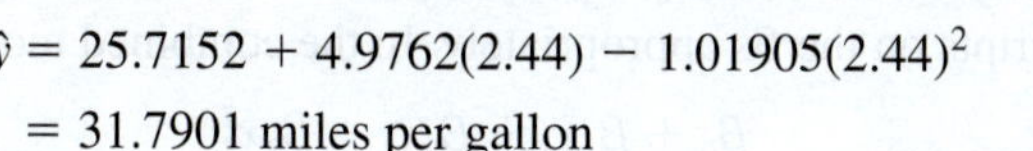

$$\hat{y} = 25.7152 + 4.9762(2.44) - 1.01905(2.44)^2$$
$$= 31.7901 \text{ miles per gallon}$$

This predicted mileage is the point estimate of the mean mileage that would be obtained by all gallons of the gasoline (when blended as just described) and is the point prediction of the mileage that would be obtained by an individual gallon of the gasoline. Note that $\hat{y} = 31.7901$ is given at the bottom of the MINITAB output in Figure 12.16. In addition, the MINITAB output tells us that a 95 percent confidence interval for the mean mileage that would be obtained by all gallons of the gasoline is [31.5481, 32.0322]. If the test equipment simulates driving conditions in a particular automobile, this confidence interval implies that an owner of the automobile can be 95 percent confident that he or she will average between 31.5481 mpg and 32.0322 mpg when using a very large number of gallons of the gasoline. The MINITAB output also tells us that a 95 percent prediction interval for the mileage that would be obtained by an individual gallon of the gasoline is [31.1215, 32.4588].

We now consider a model that employs both a linear and a quadratic term for one independent variable and also employs another linear term for a second independent variable.

Example 12.12 The Fresh Detergent Case

Enterprise Industries produces Fresh, a brand of liquid laundry detergent. In order to more effectively manage its inventory and make revenue projections, the company would like to better predict demand for Fresh. To develop a prediction model, the company has gathered data concerning demand for Fresh over the last 30 sales periods (each sales period is defined to be a four-week period). The demand data are presented in Table 12.9. Here, for each sales period,

y = the demand for the large size bottle of Fresh (in hundreds of thousands of bottles) in the sales period

x_1 = the price (in dollars) of Fresh as offered by Enterprise Industries in the sales period

x_2 = the average industry price (in dollars) of competitors' similar detergents in the sales period

x_3 = Enterprise Industries' advertising expenditure (in hundreds of thousands of dollars) to promote Fresh in the sales period

$x_4 = x_2 - x_1$ = the "price difference" in the sales period

To begin our analysis, suppose that Enterprise Industries believes on theoretical grounds that the single independent variable x_4 adequately describes the effects of x_1 and x_2 on y. That is, perhaps demand for Fresh depends more on how the price for Fresh compares to competitors' prices than it does on the absolute levels of the prices for Fresh and other competing detergents. This makes sense since most consumers must buy a certain amount of detergent no matter what the price might be. We will examine the validity of using x_4 to predict y more fully in Exercise 12.33 on page 563. For now, we will build a prediction model utilizing x_3 and x_4.

Figure 12.17 presents scatter plots of y versus x_4 and y versus x_3. The plot in Figure 12.17(a) indicates that y tends to increase in a straight-line fashion as x_4 increases. This suggests that the simple linear model

$$y = \beta_0 + \beta_1 x_4 + \varepsilon$$

might appropriately relate y to x_4. The plot in Figure 12.17(b) indicates that y tends to increase in a curved fashion as x_3 increases. Since this curve appears to have the shape of Figure 12.15(c), this suggests that the quadratic model

$$y = \beta_0 + \beta_1 x_3 + \beta_2 x_3^2 + \varepsilon$$

might appropriately relate y to x_3.

To construct a prediction model based on both x_3 and x_4, it seems reasonable to combine these two models to form the regression model

$$y = \beta_0 + \beta_1 x_4 + \beta_2 x_3 + \beta_3 x_3^2 + \varepsilon$$

Here we have arbitrarily ordered the x_4, x_3, and x_3^2 terms in the combined model, and we have renumbered the subscripts on the βs appropriately. In the combined model

$$\beta_0 + \beta_1 x_4 + \beta_2 x_3 + \beta_3 x_3^2$$

TABLE 12.9 Historical Data, Including Price Differences, Concerning Demand for Fresh Detergent Fresh2

Sales Period	Price for Fresh, x_1 (Dollars)	Average Industry Price, x_2 (Dollars)	Price Difference, $x_4 = x_2 - x_1$ (Dollars)	Advertising Expenditure for Fresh, x_3 (Hundreds of Thousands of Dollars)	Demand for Fresh, y (Hundreds of Thousands of Bottles)
1	3.85	3.80	−.05	5.50	7.38
2	3.75	4.00	.25	6.75	8.51
3	3.70	4.30	.60	7.25	9.52
4	3.70	3.70	0	5.50	7.50
5	3.60	3.85	.25	7.00	9.33
6	3.60	3.80	.20	6.50	8.28
7	3.60	3.75	.15	6.75	8.75
8	3.80	3.85	.05	5.25	7.87
9	3.80	3.65	−.15	5.25	7.10
10	3.85	4.00	.15	6.00	8.00
11	3.90	4.10	.20	6.50	7.89
12	3.90	4.00	.10	6.25	8.15
13	3.70	4.10	.40	7.00	9.10
14	3.75	4.20	.45	6.90	8.86
15	3.75	4.10	.35	6.80	8.90
16	3.80	4.10	.30	6.80	8.87
17	3.70	4.20	.50	7.10	9.26
18	3.80	4.30	.50	7.00	9.00
19	3.70	4.10	.40	6.80	8.75
20	3.80	3.75	−.05	6.50	7.95
21	3.80	3.75	−.05	6.25	7.65
22	3.75	3.65	−.10	6.00	7.27
23	3.70	3.90	.20	6.50	8.00
24	3.55	3.65	.10	7.00	8.50
25	3.60	4.10	.50	6.80	8.75
26	3.65	4.25	.60	6.80	9.21
27	3.70	3.65	−.05	6.50	8.27
28	3.75	3.75	0	5.75	7.67
29	3.80	3.85	.05	5.80	7.93
30	3.70	4.25	.55	6.80	9.26

FIGURE 12.17 Scatter Plots of the Fresh Demand Data

(a) Plot of y (Demand for Fresh Detergent) versus x_4 (Price Difference)

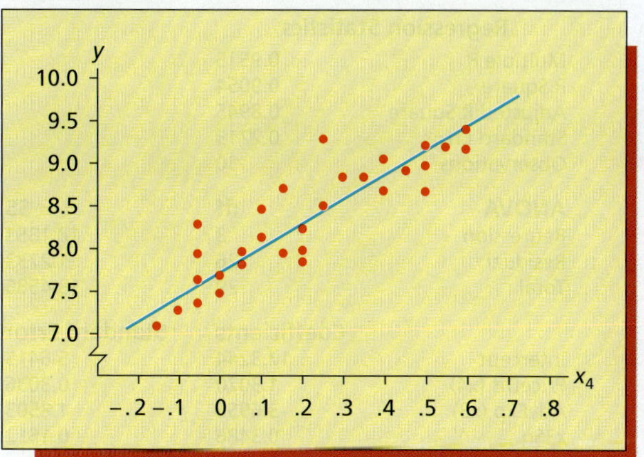

(b) Plot of y (Demand for Fresh Detergent) versus x_3 (Advertising Expenditure for Fresh)

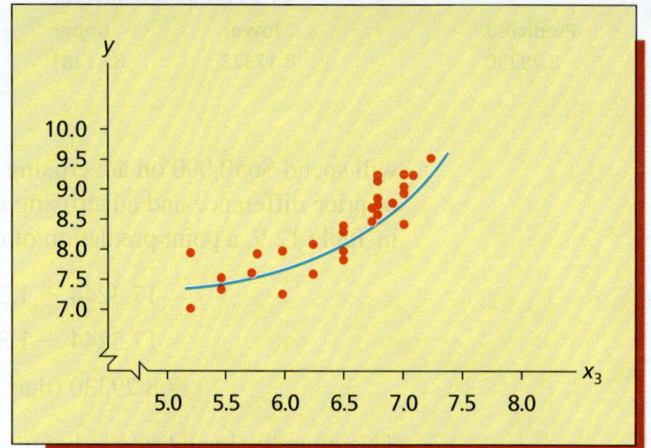

is the mean demand for Fresh when the price difference is x_4 and the advertising expenditure is x_3. The error term describes the effects on demand of all factors other than x_4 and x_3.

Figure 12.18(a) presents the Excel output of a regression analysis of the Fresh demand data using the combined model. The output tells us that the least squares point estimates of the model parameters are $b_0 = 17.3244$, $b_1 = 1.3070$, $b_2 = -3.6956$, and $b_3 = .3486$. The output also tells us that the p-values related to x_4, x_3, and x_3^2 are .0002, .0564, and .0293. Therefore, we have strong evidence that each of the model components x_4 and x_3^2 is significant. Furthermore, although the p-value related to x_3 is slightly greater than .05, we will (as discussed in Example 12.11) retain x_3 in the model because x_3^2 is significant.

In order to predict demand in a future sales period, Enterprise Industries must determine future values of x_3 and $x_4 = x_2 - x_1$. Of course, the company can set x_1 (its price for Fresh) and x_3 (its advertising expenditure). Also, it feels that by examining the prices of competitors' similar products immediately prior to a future period, it can very accurately predict x_2 (the average industry price for competitors' similar detergents). Furthermore, the company can react to any change in competitors' price to maintain any desired price difference $x_4 = x_2 - x_1$. This is an advantage of predicting on the basis of x_4 rather than on the basis of x_1 and x_2 (which the company cannot control). Therefore, suppose that the company will maintain a price difference of \$.20 ($x_{04} = .20$) and

FIGURE 12.18 Excel and MegaStat Output of a Regression Analysis of the Fresh Demand Data in Table 12.9 Using the Model $y = \beta_0 + \beta_1 x_4 + \beta_2 x_3 + \beta_3 x_3^2 + \varepsilon$

(a) The Excel output

Regression Statistics	
Multiple R	0.9515
R Square	0.9054
Adjusted R Square	0.8945
Standard Error	0.2213
Observations	30

ANOVA	df	SS	MS	F	Significance F
Regression	3	12.1853	4.0618	82.9409	1.94E-13
Residual	26	1.2733	0.0490		
Total	29	13.4586			

	Coefficients	Standard Error	t Stat	P-value	Lower 95%	Upper 95%
Intercept	17.3244	5.6415	3.0709	0.0050	5.7282	28.9206
PriceDif (x4)	1.3070	0.3036	4.3048	0.0002	0.6829	1.9311
AdvExp (x3)	-3.6956	1.8503	-1.9973	0.0564	-7.4989	0.1077
x3Sq	0.3486	0.1512	2.3060	0.0293	0.0379	0.6594

(b) Prediction using MegaStat

Predicted values for: Y

	95% Confidence Interval		95% Prediction Interval		
Predicted	lower	upper	lower	upper	Leverage
8.29330	8.17378	8.41281	7.82298	8.76362	0.069

will spend \$650,000 on advertising ($x_{03} = 6.50$) in a future sales period. Since this combination of price difference and advertising expenditure is in the experimental region defined by the data in Table 12.9, a point prediction of demand in the future sales period is

$$\begin{aligned}\hat{y} &= 17.3244 + 1.3070x_{04} - 3.6956x_{03} + .3486x_{03}^2 \\ &= 17.3244 + 1.3070(.20) - 3.6956(6.50) + .3486(6.50)^2 \\ &= 8.29330 \text{ (that is, 829,330 bottles)}\end{aligned}$$

This quantity, in addition to being the point prediction of demand in a single sales period when the price difference is \$.20 and the advertising expenditure is \$650,000, is also the point estimate of the mean of all possible demands when $x_4 = .20$ and $x_3 = 6.50$. Note that $\hat{y} = 8.29330$ is given on the MegaStat output of Figure 12.18(b). The output also gives a 95 percent confidence interval for mean demand when x_4 equals .20 and x_3 equals 6.50, which is [8.17378, 8.41281], and a 95 percent prediction interval for an individual demand when x_4 equals .20 and x_3 equals 6.50, which is [7.82298, 8.76362]. This latter interval says we are 95 percent confident that the actual demand in the future sales period will be between 782,298 bottles and 876,362 bottles. The upper limit of this interval can be used for inventory control. It says that if Enterprise Industries plans to have 876,362 bottles on hand to meet demand in the future sales period, then the company can be very confident that it will have enough bottles. The lower limit of the interval can be used to better understand Enterprise Industries' cash flow situation. It says the company can be very confident that it will sell at least 782,298 bottles in the future sales period. Therefore, for example, if the average competitors' price is \$3.90 and thus Enterprise Industries' price is \$3.70, the company can be very confident that its minimum revenue from the large size bottle of Fresh in the future period will be at least 782,298 × \$3.70 = \$2,894,502.60.

Exercises for Section 12.8

CONCEPTS

12.30 When does a scatter plot suggest the use of the quadratic regression model?

12.31 In the quadratic regression model, what are y, $(\beta_0 + \beta_1 x + \beta_2 x^2)$, and ε?

FIGURE 12.19 MINITAB Output of a Regression Analysis of the Real Estate Sales Price Data Using the Model $y = \beta_0 + \beta_1 x_1 + \beta_2 x_2 + \beta_3 x_2^2 + \varepsilon$

```
The regression equation is
SalesPrice = 19.1 + 5.56 x1 + 9.22 x2 - 0.513 x2sq

Predictor      Coef   SE Coef      T      P
Constant     19.074     3.632   5.25  0.002
x1           5.5596    0.1255  44.29  0.000
x2            9.223     1.312   7.03  0.000
x2sq        -0.5129    0.1228  -4.18  0.006

S = 1.77128    R-Sq = 99.7%    R-Sq(adj) = 99.6%

Analysis of Variance
Source          DF      SS      MS       F      P
Regression       3  7428.7  2476.2  789.25  0.000
Residual Error   6    18.8     3.1
Total            9  7447.5

Values of Predictors for New Obs    Predicted Values for New Observations
New Obs    x1     x2  x2sq          New Obs      Fit  SE Fit          95% CI               95% PI
      1  20.0   8.00  64.0                1  171.222   0.895  (169.033, 173.411)  (166.367, 176.078)
```

METHODS AND APPLICATIONS

12.32 THE REAL ESTATE SALES PRICE CASE RealEst2

Figure 12.19 presents the MINITAB output of a regression analysis of the real estate sales price data (see the page margin) using the model

$$y = \beta_0 + \beta_1 x_1 + \beta_2 x_2 + \beta_3 x_2^2 + \varepsilon$$

a Discuss why the plots of y versus x_1 and y versus x_2 in the page margin below the data indicate that this model might appropriately relate y to x_1 and x_2.

b Do the p-values for the independent variables in this model indicate that these independent variables are significant? Explain your answer.

c Report and interpret a point prediction of and a 95 percent prediction interval for the sales price of an individual house having 2,000 square feet and a rating of 8 (see the bottom of the MINITAB output in Figure 12.19).

The Real Estate Sales Price Data RealEst2

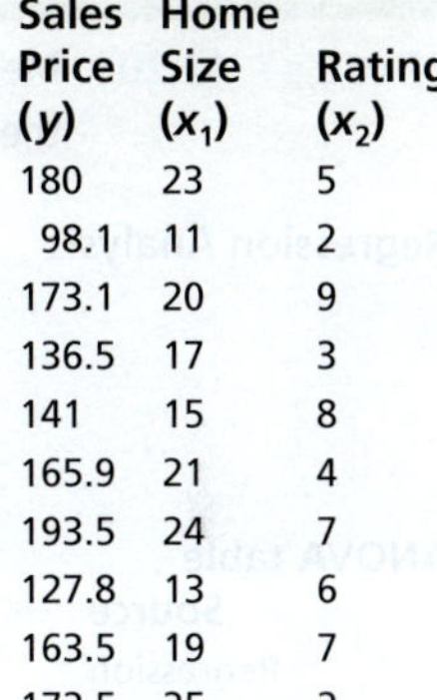

Sales Price (y)	Home Size (x_1)	Rating (x_2)
180	23	5
98.1	11	2
173.1	20	9
136.5	17	3
141	15	8
165.9	21	4
193.5	24	7
127.8	13	6
163.5	19	7
172.5	25	2

Source: R. L. Andrews and J. T. Ferguson, "Integrating Judgement with a Regression Appraisal," *The Real Estate Appraiser and Analyst* 52, no. 2 (1986). Reprinted by permission.

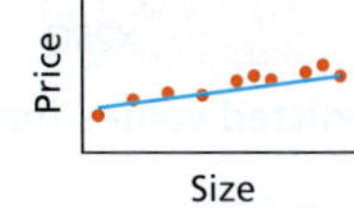

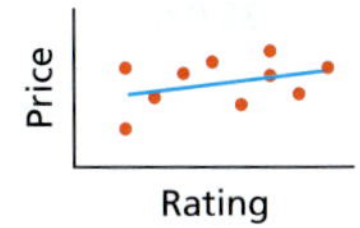

12.33 THE FRESH DETERGENT CASE Fresh2

Consider the demand for Fresh Detergent in a future sales period when Enterprise Industries' price for Fresh will be $x_1 = 3.70$, the average price of competitors' similar detergents will be $x_2 = 3.90$, the price difference $x_4 = x_2 - x_1$ will be .20, and Enterprise Industries' advertising expenditure for Fresh will be $x_3 = 6.50$. We have seen in Example 12.12 that the 95 percent prediction interval for this demand given by the model

$$y = \beta_0 + \beta_1 x_4 + \beta_2 x_3 + \beta_3 x_3^2 + \varepsilon$$

is [7.82298, 8.76362]. The 95 percent prediction interval for this demand given by the model

$$y = \beta_0 + \beta_1 x_1 + \beta_2 x_2 + \beta_3 x_3 + \beta_4 x_3^2 + \varepsilon$$

is [7.84139, 8.79357]. Which interval is shorter? Based on this, which model seems better?

12.34 United Oil Company is attempting to develop a reasonably priced unleaded gasoline that will deliver higher gasoline mileages than can be achieved by its current unleaded gasolines. As part of its development process, United Oil wishes to study the effect of two independent variables—x_1, amount of gasoline additive RST (0, 1, or 2 units), and x_2, amount of gasoline additive XST (0, 1, 2, or 3 units), on gasoline mileage y. Mileage tests are carried out using equipment that simulates driving under prescribed conditions. The combinations of x_1 and x_2 used in the experiment, along with the corresponding values of y, are given in Table 12.10.

a Discuss why the data plots given to the right of Table 12.10 indicate that the model UnitedOil

$$y = \beta_0 + \beta_1 x_1 + \beta_2 x_1^2 + \beta_3 x_2 + \beta_4 x_2^2 + \varepsilon$$

might appropriately relate y to x_1 and x_2.

b If we use MegaStat to analyze the data in Table 12.10 by using the model in part *a*, we obtain the output in Figure 12.20. Noting from Table 12.10 that the combination of one unit of

TABLE 12.10 United Oil Company Unleaded Gasoline Mileage Data UnitedOil

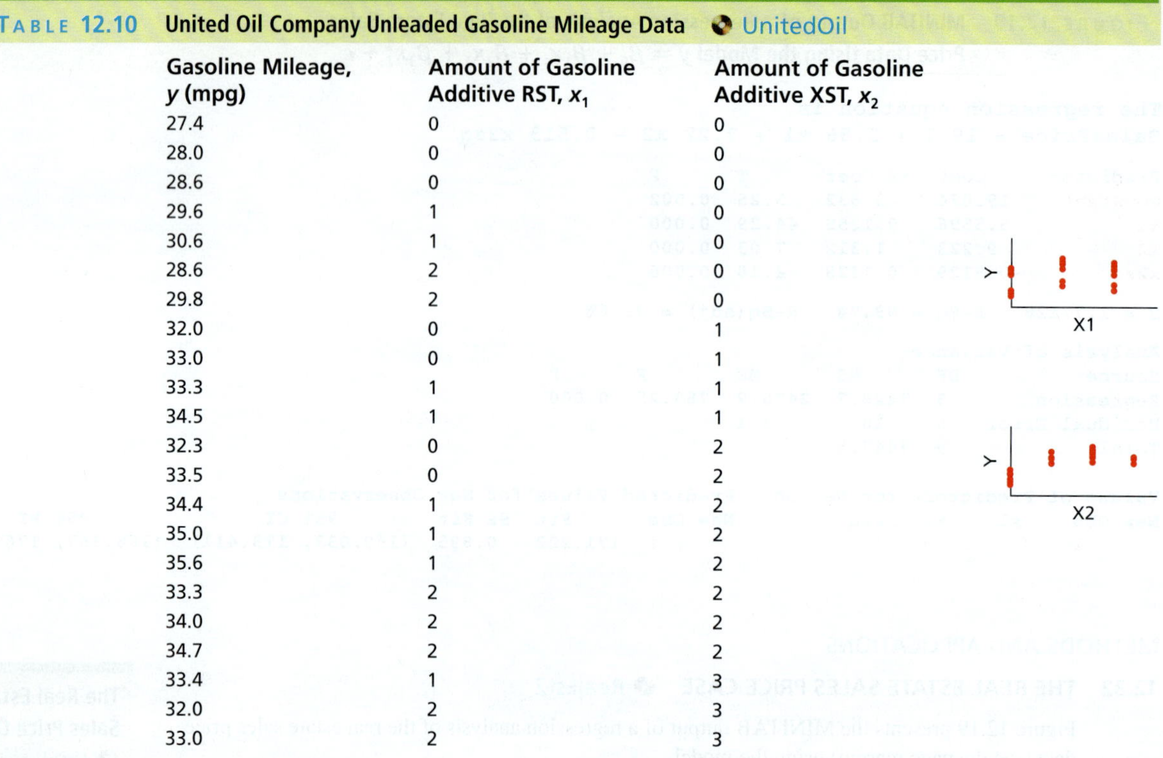

Gasoline Mileage, y (mpg)	Amount of Gasoline Additive RST, x_1	Amount of Gasoline Additive XST, x_2
27.4	0	0
28.0	0	0
28.6	0	0
29.6	1	0
30.6	1	0
28.6	2	0
29.8	2	0
32.0	0	1
33.0	0	1
33.3	1	1
34.5	1	1
32.3	0	2
33.5	0	2
34.4	1	2
35.0	1	2
35.6	1	2
33.3	2	2
34.0	2	2
34.7	2	2
33.4	1	3
32.0	2	3
33.0	2	3

FIGURE 12.20 MegaStat Output of a Regression Analysis of the United Oil Company Data Using the Model $y = \beta_0 + \beta_1 x_1 + \beta_2 x_1^2 + \beta_3 x_2 + \beta_4 x_2^2 + \varepsilon$

Regression Analysis

R^2	0.947		
Adjusted R^2	0.935	n	22
R	0.973	k	4
Std. Error	0.631	Dep. Var.	Y

ANOVA table

Source	SS	df	MS	F	p-value
Regression	120.7137	4	30.1784	75.90	1.30E-10
Residual	6.7590	17	0.3976		
Total	127.4727	21			

Regression output

variables	coefficients	std. error	t (df = 17)	p-value	confidence interval 95% lower	95% upper
Intercept	28.1589	0.2902	97.040	9.01E-25	27.5467	28.7711
X1	3.3133	0.5896	5.619	3.07E-05	2.0693	4.5573
X1SQ	−1.4111	0.2816	−5.012	.0001	−2.0051	−0.8170
X2	5.2752	0.4129	12.776	3.83E-10	4.4041	6.1463
X2SQ	−1.3964	0.1509	−9.257	4.74E-08	−1.7146	−1.0781

Predicted values for: Y

Predicted	95% Confidence Interval lower	upper	95% Prediction Interval lower	upper	Leverage
35.0261	34.4997	35.5525	33.5954	36.4568	0.157

gasoline additive RST and two units of gasoline additive XST seems to maximize gasoline mileage, assume that United Oil Company will use this combination to make its unleaded gasoline. The estimation and prediction results at the bottom of the MegaStat output are for the combination $x_1 = 1$ and $x_2 = 2$.

(1) Use the computer output to find and report a point estimate of and a 95 percent confidence interval for the mean mileage obtained by all gallons of the gasoline when it is made using one unit of RST and two units of XST.

(2) Use the computer output to find and report a point prediction of and a 95 percent prediction interval for the mileage that would be obtained by an individual gallon of the gasoline when it is made using one unit of RST and two units of XST.

12.9 Interaction (Optional)

Multiple regression models often contain **interaction variables.** We form an interaction variable by multiplying two independent variables together. For instance, if a regression model includes the independent variables x_1 and x_2, then we can form the interaction variable x_1x_2. It is appropriate to employ an interaction variable if the relationship between the mean value of the dependent variable y and one of the independent variables is dependent on (that is, is different depending on) the value of the other independent variable. We explain the concept of interaction in the following example.

Example 12.13

Part 1: The data and data plots Bonner Frozen Foods, Inc., has designed an experiment to study the effects of two types of advertising expenditures on sales of one of its lines of frozen foods. Twenty-five sales regions of equal sales potential were selected. Different combinations of x_1 = radio and television expenditures (measured in units of \$1,000) and x_2 = print expenditures (measured in units of \$1,000) were specified and randomly assigned to the sales regions. Table 12.11 shows the expenditure combinations along with the associated values of sales volume, measured in units of \$10,000 and denoted y, for the sales regions during August of last year.

To help decide whether interaction exists between x_1 and x_2, we can plot the data in Table 12.11. To do this, we first plot y versus x_1. In constructing this plot, we make the plot character for each point the corresponding value of x_2 (x_2 = 1, 2, 3, 4, 5). The resulting plot (shown in Figure 12.21) is called a **plot of y versus x_1 for the different "levels" of x_2.** Looking at this plot, we see that the straight line relating y to x_1 when x_2 equals 5 appears to have a smaller slope than does the line relating y to x_1 when x_2 equals 1. That is, the rate of increase of the line corresponding to $x_2 = 5$ is less steep than the rate of increase of the line corresponding to $x_2 = 1$. Examining the entire data plot, Figure 12.21 might suggest that the larger x_2 is, the smaller is the slope of the straight line relating y to x_1.

In Figure 12.22 we plot y versus x_2 for the different levels of x_1 (x_1 = 1, 2, 3, 4, 5). Here the plot character for each point is the corresponding value of x_1. We see that the straight line relating y to x_2 when x_1 equals 5 appears to have a smaller slope than does the straight line relating y to x_2 when x_1 equals 1. Looking at the entire data plot, Figure 12.22 might suggest that the larger x_1 is, the smaller is the slope of the straight line relating y to x_2.

TABLE 12.11 Bonner Frozen Foods, Inc., Sales Volume Data Bonner

Sales Region	Radio and Television Expenditures, x_1	Print Expenditures, x_2	Sales Volume, y	Sales Region	Radio and Television Expenditures, x_1	Print Expenditures, x_2	Sales Volume, y
1	1	1	3.27	14	3	4	17.99
2	1	2	8.38	15	3	5	19.85
3	1	3	11.28	16	4	1	9.46
4	1	4	14.50	17	4	2	12.61
5	1	5	19.63	18	4	3	15.50
6	2	1	5.84	19	4	4	17.68
7	2	2	10.01	20	4	5	21.02
8	2	3	12.46	21	5	1	12.23
9	2	4	16.67	22	5	2	13.58
10	2	5	19.83	23	5	3	16.77
11	3	1	8.51	24	5	4	20.56
12	3	2	10.14	25	5	5	21.05
13	3	3	14.75				

FIGURE 12.21 **Plot of y versus x_1 (Plot Character Is the Corresponding Value of x_2): The Larger x_2 Is, the Smaller Is the Slope of the Straight Line Relating y to x_1**

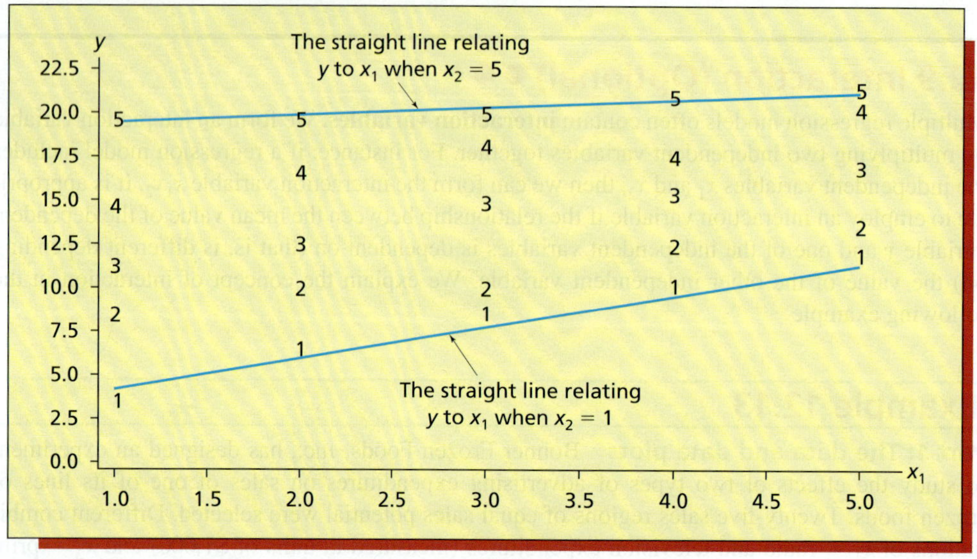

FIGURE 12.22 **Plot of y versus x_2 (Plot Character Is the Corresponding Value of x_1): The Larger x_1 Is, the Smaller Is the Slope of the Straight Line Relating y to x_2**

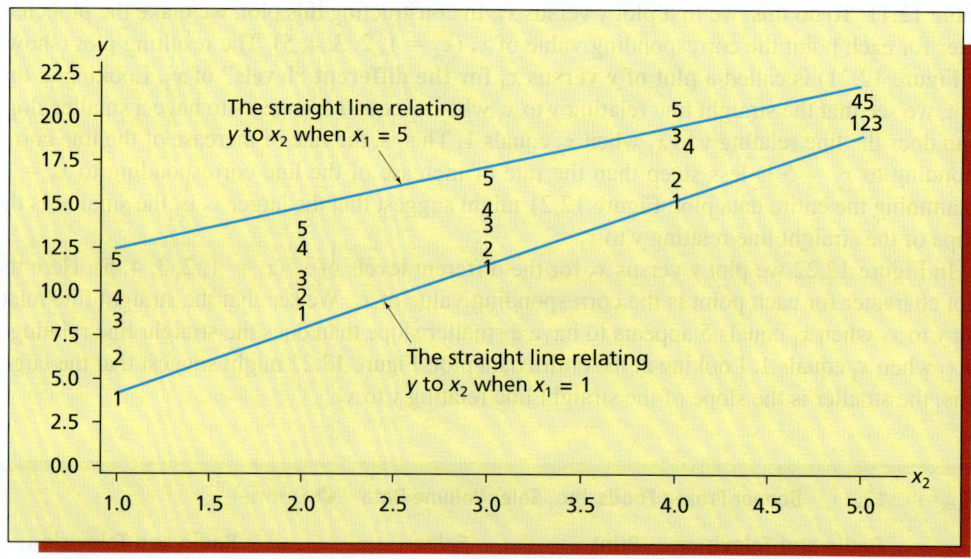

In summary, Figures 12.21 and 12.22 seem to imply that the more money spent on one type of advertising, the smaller is the slope of the straight line relating sales volume to the amount spent on the other type of advertising. This says that there is interaction between x_1 and x_2 because

1 The relationship between y and x_1 (the slope of the line relating y to x_1) is different for different values of x_2.

2 The relationship between y and x_2 (the slope of the line relating y to x_2) is different for different values of x_1.

Intuitively, interaction between x_1 and x_2 makes sense because as Bonner Frozen Foods spends more money on one type of advertising, increases in spending on the other type of advertising might become less effective.

Part 2: Modeling the interaction between x_1 and x_2 The regression model

$$y = \beta_0 + \beta_1 x_1 + \beta_2 x_2 + \varepsilon$$

cannot describe the interaction between x_1 and x_2 because this model says that mean sales volume equals

$$\beta_0 + \beta_1 x_1 + \beta_2 x_2 = (\beta_0 + \beta_1 x_1) + \beta_2 x_2$$

This implies that for any particular value of x_1, the slope of the straight line relating the mean value of y to x_2 will always be β_2. That is, no matter what the value of x_1 is, the slope of the line relating mean y to x_2 is always the same. This rules out the possibility of describing the relationships illustrated in Figure 12.22 by using the above model. The model also says that mean sales volume equals

$$\beta_0 + \beta_1 x_1 + \beta_2 x_2 = (\beta_0 + \beta_2 x_2) + \beta_1 x_1$$

This implies that, no matter what the value of x_2 is, the slope of the line relating mean y to x_1 is always the same (here the slope equals β_1). This rules out the possibility of describing the relationships illustrated in Figure 12.21 by using the above model. In short, we say that the above model assumes **no interaction** between x_1 and x_2.

In order to model the interaction between x_1 and x_2 we can use the **cross-product term** or **interaction term** x_1x_2. Therefore, we consider the model

$$y = \beta_0 + \beta_1 x_1 + \beta_2 x_2 + \beta_3 x_1 x_2 + \varepsilon$$

This model says that mean sales volume equals

$$\beta_0 + \beta_1 x_1 + \beta_2 x_2 + \beta_3 x_1 x_2$$

which can be rewritten as $(\beta_0 + \beta_1 x_1) + (\beta_2 + \beta_3 x_1)x_2$. **This implies that the slope of the line relating mean y to x_2, which is $(\beta_2 + \beta_3 x_1)$, will be different for different values of x_1.** This allows the **interaction model** to describe relationships such as those illustrated in Figure 12.22. Furthermore, for this model the mean sales volume

$$\beta_0 + \beta_1 x_1 + \beta_2 x_2 + \beta_3 x_1 x_2$$

can also be rewritten as $(\beta_0 + \beta_2 x_2) + (\beta_1 + \beta_3 x_2)x_1$. **This implies that the slope of the line relating mean y to x_1, which is $(\beta_1 + \beta_3 x_2)$, will be different for different values of x_2.** This allows the interaction model to describe relationships such as those illustrated in Figure 12.21. In short, we say that the model employing the term x_1x_2 assumes that **interaction exists** between x_1 and x_2.

Part 3: Statistical inference Figure 12.23 gives the MINITAB output of a regression analysis of the data in Table 12.11 by using the model

$$y = \beta_0 + \beta_1 x_1 + \beta_2 x_2 + \beta_3 x_1 x_2 + \varepsilon$$

Note that x_1x_2 is denoted as Interaction on the output. Since all of the p-values related to the intercept and the independent variables are less than .01, we have very strong evidence that each of β_0, x_1, x_2, and x_1x_2 is significant in the above model. In particular, the very small p-value related to x_1x_2 confirms that interaction exists between x_1 and x_2 as was originally suggested by the plots in Figures 12.21 and 12.22 (if there were little or no interaction between x_1 and x_2, the term x_1x_2 would be insignificant since it would not help us to model the data).

Next, suppose that Bonner Frozen Foods will spend $2,000 on radio and television advertising ($x_1 = 2$) and will spend $5,000 on print advertising ($x_2 = 5$) in a future month in a particular sales region. If there are no trend, seasonal, or other time-related influences affecting monthly sales volume, then it is reasonable to believe that the regression relationship between y and x_1 and x_2 that we have developed probably applies to the future month and particular sales region. It follows that

$$\begin{aligned}\hat{y} &= -2.3497 + 2.3611(2) + 4.1831(5) - 0.3489(2)(5) \\ &= 19.799 \text{ (that is, \$197,990)}\end{aligned}$$

is a point estimate of mean sales volume when $2,000 is spent on radio and television advertising and $5,000 is spent on print advertising. In addition, $\hat{y}$ is a point prediction of the individual

FIGURE 12.23 MINITAB Output of a Regression Analysis of the Sales Volume Data in Table 12.11 by Using the Model $y = \beta_0 + \beta_1 x_1 + \beta_2 x_2 + \beta_3 x_1 x_2 + \varepsilon$

```
The regression equation is
SalesVol = - 2.35 + 2.36 RadioTV + 4.18 Print - 0.349 Interaction

Predictor          Coef     SE Coef        T        P
Constant        -2.3497      0.6883    -3.41    0.003
RadioTV          2.3611      0.2075    11.38    0.000
Print            4.1831      0.2075    20.16    0.000
Interaction    -0.34890     0.06257    -5.58    0.000

S = 0.6257         R-Sq = 98.6%        R-Sq(adj) = 98.4%

Analysis of Variance
Source            DF        SS        MS         F        P
Regression         3    590.41    196.80    502.67    0.000
Residual Error    21      8.22      0.39
Total             24    598.63

Values of Predictors for New Obs    Predicted Values for New Observations
New Obs  RadioTV  Print  Interaction  New Obs     Fit  SE Fit        95% CI             95% PI
      1     2.00   5.00         10.0        1  19.799   0.265  (19.247, 20.351)  (18.385, 21.213)
```

sales volume that will be observed in the future month in the particular sales region. Besides giving $\hat{y} = 19.799$, the MINITAB output in Figure 12.23 tells us that the 95 percent confidence interval for mean sales volume is [19.247, 20.351] and that the 95 percent prediction interval for an individual sales volume is [18.385, 21.213]. This prediction interval says we are 95 percent confident that the individual sales volume in the future month in the particular sales region will be between $183,850 and $212,130. In Exercise 12.37 we will continue this example.

It is easy to construct data plots to check for interaction in the Bonner Frozen Foods example because the company has carried out a designed experiment. In many regression problems, however, we do not carry out a designed experiment, and the data are "unstructured." In such a case, it may not be possible to construct the data plots needed to detect interaction between independent variables. For example, if we consider the Fresh demand data in Table 12.9, we might suspect that there is interaction between x_3 (advertising expenditure) and x_4 (the price difference). That is, we might suspect that the relationship between mean demand for Fresh and advertising expenditure is different for different levels of the price difference. For instance, increases in advertising expenditures might be more effective at some price differences than at others. To detect such interaction, we would like to construct plots of demand versus x_3 for different levels of x_4. However, examination of the Fresh demand data reveals that there are only a few observations at any one level of the price difference, and therefore the needed data plots cannot easily be made. In such a case we can use t statistics and p-values related to potential interaction terms to try to assess the importance of interaction. We illustrate this in the following example.

Example 12.14 The Fresh Detergent Case

Part 1: An interaction model and statistical inference In Example 12.12 we considered the Fresh demand model

$$y = \beta_0 + \beta_1 x_4 + \beta_2 x_3 + \beta_3 x_3^2 + \varepsilon$$

Since we might logically suspect that there is interaction between x_4 and x_3, we add the interaction term $x_4 x_3$ to this model and form the model

$$y = \beta_0 + \beta_1 x_4 + \beta_2 x_3 + \beta_3 x_3^2 + \beta_4 x_4 x_3 + \varepsilon$$

Figure 12.24(a) presents the Excel output obtained by using this model to perform a regression analysis of the Fresh demand data. This output shows that each of the p-values for testing the significance of the intercept and the independent variables is less than .05. Therefore, we have strong evidence that the intercept and each of x_4, x_3, x_3^2, and $x_4 x_3$ are significant. In particular,

FIGURE 12.24 **Excel and MegaStat Output of a Regression Analysis of the Fresh Demand Data by Using the Interaction Model $y = \beta_0 + \beta_1 x_4 + \beta_2 x_3 + \beta_3 x_3^2 + \beta_4 x_4 x_3 + \varepsilon$**

(a) The Excel output

Regression Statistics	
Multiple R	0.9596
R Square	0.9209
Adjusted R Square	0.9083
Standard Error	0.2063
Observations	30

ANOVA	df	SS	MS	F	Significance F
Regression	4	12.3942	3.0985	72.7771	2.11E-13
Residual	25	1.0644	0.0426		
Total	29	13.4586			

	Coefficients	Standard Error	t Stat	P-value	Lower 95%	Upper 95%
Intercept	29.1133	7.4832	3.8905	0.0007	13.7013	44.5252
PriceDif (x4)	11.1342	4.4459	2.5044	0.0192	1.9778	20.2906
AdvExp (x3)	-7.6080	2.4691	-3.0813	0.0050	-12.6932	-2.5228
x3sq	0.6712	0.2027	3.3115	0.0028	0.2538	1.0887
x4x3	-1.4777	0.6672	-2.2149	0.0361	-2.8518	-0.1037

(b) Prediction using MegaStat

Predicted values for: Y

	95% Confidence Interval		95% Prediction Interval		
Predicted	lower	upper	lower	upper	Leverage
8.32725	8.21121	8.44329	7.88673	8.76777	0.075

since the p-value related to x_4x_3 is .0361, we have strong evidence that the interaction variable x_4x_3 is important. This confirms that the interaction between x_3 and x_4 that we suspected really does exist.

Suppose again that Enterprise Industries wishes to predict demand for Fresh in a future sales period when the price difference will be \$.20 ($x_4 = .20$) and when the advertising expenditure for Fresh will be \$650,000 ($x_3 = 6.50$). Using the least squares point estimates in Figure 12.24, the needed point prediction is

$$\begin{aligned}\hat{y} &= 29.1133 + 11.1342(.20) - 7.6080(6.50) + 0.6712(6.50)^2 \\ &\quad - 1.4777(.20)(6.50) \\ &= 8.32725 (832{,}725 \text{ bottles})\end{aligned}$$

This point prediction is given on the MegaStat output of Figure 12.24(b), which also tells us that the 95 percent confidence interval for mean demand when x_4 equals .20 and x_3 equals 6.50 is [8.21121, 8.44329] and that the 95 percent prediction interval for an individual demand when x_4 equals .20 and x_3 equals 6.50 is [7.88673, 8.76777]. Notice that this prediction interval is shorter than the 95 percent prediction interval—[7.82298, 8.76362]—obtained using the model that omits the interaction term x_4x_3 and predicts y on the basis of x_4, x_3, and x_3^2. This is another indication that it is useful to include the interaction variable x_4x_3 in the model.

Part 2: The nature of interaction between x_3 and x_4 To understand the exact nature of the interaction between x_3 and x_4, consider the prediction equation

$$\hat{y} = 29.1133 + 11.1342x_4 - 7.6080x_3 + .6712x_3^2 - 1.4777x_4x_3$$

obtained by using the Fresh demand interaction model. If we set x_4 equal to .10 and place this value of x_4 into the prediction equation, we obtain

$$\begin{aligned}\hat{y} &= 29.1133 + 11.1342x_4 - 7.6080x_3 + .6712x_3^2 - 1.4777x_4x_3 \\ &= 29.1133 + 11.1342(.10) - 7.6080x_3 + .6712x_3^2 - 1.4777(.10)x_3 \\ &= 30.2267 - 7.7558x_3 + .6712x_3^2\end{aligned}$$

FIGURE 12.25 Interaction between x_4 and x_3 in the Fresh Detergent Case

(a) Calculating values of predicted demand when x_4 equals .10

x_3	$\hat{y} = 30.2267 - 7.7558x_3 + .6712x_3^2$
6.0	$\hat{y} = 30.2267 - 7.7558(6.0) + .6712(6.0)^2 = 7.86$
6.4	$\hat{y} = 30.2267 - 7.7558(6.4) + .6712(6.4)^2 = 8.08$
6.8	$\hat{y} = 30.2267 - 7.7558(6.8) + .6712(6.8)^2 = 8.52$

(b) Calculating values of predicted demand when x_4 equals .30

x_3	$\hat{y} = 32.4535 - 8.0513x_3 + .6712x_3^2$
6.0	$\hat{y} = 32.4535 - 8.0513(6.0) + .6712(6.0)^2 = 8.31$
6.4	$\hat{y} = 32.4535 - 8.0513(6.4) + .6712(6.4)^2 = 8.42$
6.8	$\hat{y} = 32.4535 - 8.0513(6.8) + .6712(6.8)^2 = 8.74$

(c) Illustrating the interaction

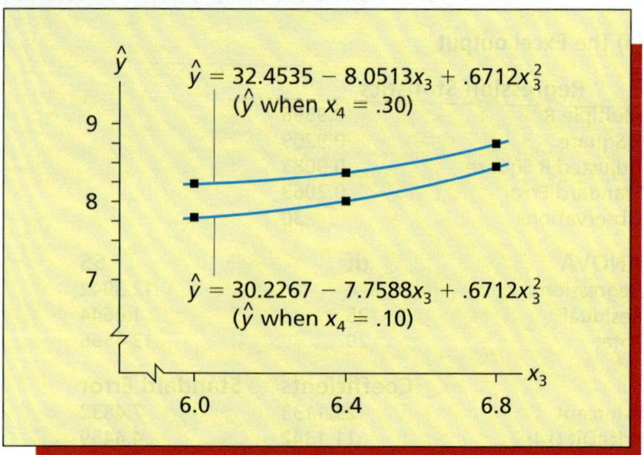

This quadratic equation shows us how predicted demand changes as advertising expenditure x_3 increases when the price difference is .10. Next we set x_4 equal to .30. If we place this value of x_4 into the Fresh prediction equation, we obtain

$$\begin{aligned}\hat{y} &= 29.1133 + 11.1342x_4 - 7.6080x_3 + .6712x_3^2 - 1.4777x_4x_3 \\ &= 29.1133 + 11.1342(.30) - 7.6080x_3 + .6712x_3^2 - 1.4777(.30)x_3 \\ &= 32.4535 - 8.0513x_3 + .6712x_3^2\end{aligned}$$

This quadratic equation shows us how predicted demand changes as advertising expenditure x_3 increases when the price difference is .30.

In Figure 12.25(a) and (b) we calculate three points (predicted demands) on each of these quadratic curves. Figure 12.25(c) shows graphs of the two quadratic curves with the predicted demands plotted on these graphs. Comparing these graphs, we see that predicted demand is higher when x_4 equals .30 than when x_4 equals .10. This makes sense—predicted demand should be higher when Enterprise Industries has a larger price advantage. Furthermore, for each curve we see that predicted demand increases at an increasing rate as x_3 increases. However, the rate of increase in predicted demand is slower when x_4 equals .30 than when x_4 equals .10—this is the effect of the interaction between x_3 and x_4.

This type of interaction is logical because when the price difference is large (the price for Fresh is low relative to the average industry price), the mean demand for Fresh will be high (assuming the quality of Fresh is comparable to competing brands). Thus with mean demand already high because many consumers are buying Fresh on the basis of price, there may be little opportunity for increased advertising expenditure to increase mean demand. However, when the price difference is smaller, there may be more potential consumers who are not buying Fresh who can be convinced to do so by increased advertising. Thus when the price difference is smaller, increased advertising expenditure is more effective than it is when the price difference is larger.

It should be noted that this type of interaction between x_4 and x_3 was estimated from the observed Fresh demand data in Table 12.9. This is because we obtained the least squares point estimates using these data. We are not hypothesizing the existence of the interaction; the importance of the x_4x_3 term and the least squares point estimates tell us that this type of interaction exists. However, we can only hypothesize the reasons behind the interaction. We should also point out that this type of interaction can be assumed to exist only for values of x_4 and x_3 inside the experimental region. Examination of the Fresh demand data shows that Fresh was being sold at either a price advantage (when the price of Fresh is lower than the average industry price) or at a slight price disadvantage (when the price of Fresh is slightly higher than the average industry price). However, if Fresh were sometimes sold at a large price disadvantage, the type of interaction that exists between x_4 and x_3 might be different. In such a case, increases in advertising expenditure might be very ineffective because most consumers will not wish to buy a product with a much higher price.

As another example, if we perform a regression analysis of the fuel consumption data by using the model

$$y = \beta_0 + \beta_1x_1 + \beta_2x_2 + \beta_3x_1x_2 + \varepsilon$$

we find that the p-value for testing H_0: $\beta_3 = 0$ is .787. Therefore, we conclude that the interaction term x_1x_2 is not needed and that there is little or no interaction between the average hourly temperature and the chill index.

A final comment is in order. If a p-value indicates that an interaction term (say, x_1x_2) is important, then it is usual practice to retain the corresponding linear terms (x_1 and x_2) in the model no matter what the size of their p-values. The reason is that doing so can be shown to give a model that will better describe the interaction between x_1 and x_2.

Exercises for Section 12.9

CONCEPTS

12.35 If a regression model utilizes the independent variables x_1 and x_2, how do we form an interaction variable involving x_1 and x_2?

12.36 What is meant when we say that interaction exists between two independent variables?

METHODS AND APPLICATIONS

12.37 Consider the Bonner Frozen Foods, Inc., sales volume model Bonner

$$y = \beta_0 + \beta_1x_1 + \beta_2x_2 + \beta_3x_1x_2 + \varepsilon$$

a We have seen in Example 12.13 that $\beta_1 + \beta_3x_2$ is the slope of the line relating mean y to x_1 at a given value of x_2. This slope is the increase in mean sales volume (in units of \$10,000) obtained by increasing radio and TV advertising by \$1000 when print advertising is x_2 thousand dollars. Using $b_1 = 2.3611$ and $b_3 = -.3489$ from the MINITAB output in Figure 12.23 (page 568), a point estimate of the slope $\beta_1 + \beta_3x_2$ is $2.3611 - .3489x_2$. Calculate this point estimate for each of the values 1, 2, 3, 4, and 5 of x_2. Interpret the five point estimates.

b We have seen in Example 12.13 that $\beta_2 + \beta_3x_1$ is the slope of the line relating mean y to x_2 at a given value of x_1. This slope is the increase in mean sales volume (in units of \$10,000) obtained by increasing print advertising by \$1000 when radio and TV advertising is x_1 thousand dollars. Using $b_2 = 4.1831$ and $b_3 = -.3489$ from the MINITAB output in Figure 12.23, a point estimate of the slope $\beta_2 + \beta_3x_1$ is $4.1831 - .3489x_1$. Calculate this point estimate for each of the values 1, 2, 3, 4, and 5 of x_1. Interpret the five point estimates.

c By comparing the five point estimates calculated in part (b) with the five point estimates calculated in part (a), discuss why it is reasonable to conclude that increasing print advertising expenditures is more effective than increasing radio and TV advertising expenditures.

12.38 THE REAL ESTATE SALES PRICE CASE RealEst2

We concluded in Exercise 12.32 (page 563) that the model

$$y = \beta_0 + \beta_1x_1 + \beta_2x_2 + \beta_3x_2^2 + \varepsilon$$

might appropriately relate y to x_1 and x_2. To investigate whether interaction exists between x_1 and x_2, we consider the model

$$y = \beta_0 + \beta_1x_1 + \beta_2x_2 + \beta_3x_2^2 + \beta_4x_1x_2 + \varepsilon$$

Figure 12.26 presents the MINITAB output of a regression analysis of the real estate sales price data using this model.

a Does the p-value for x_1x_2 indicate that this interaction variable is important? Do the p-values for the other independent variables in the model indicate that these variables are important? Explain your answer.

FIGURE 12.26 MINITAB Output of a Regression Analysis of the Real Estate Sales Price Data Using the Model $y = \beta_0 + \beta_1 x_1 + \beta_2 x_2 + \beta_3 x_2^2 + \beta_4 x_1 x_2 + \varepsilon$

```
The regression equation is
SalesPrice = 27.4 + 5.08 x1 + 7.29 x2 - 0.531 x2sq + 0.115 x1x2

Predictor      Coef   SE Coef      T      P
Constant     27.438     3.059   8.97  0.000
x1           5.0813    0.1476  34.42  0.000
x2           7.2899    0.9089   8.02  0.000
x2sq       -0.53110   0.06978  -7.61  0.001
x1x2        0.11473   0.03103   3.70  0.014

S = 1.00404    R-Sq = 99.9%    R-Sq(adj) = 99.9%

Analysis of Variance
Source          DF      SS      MS        F      P
Regression       4  7442.5  1860.6  1845.66  0.000
Residual Error   5     5.0     1.0
Total            9  7447.5

Values of Predictors for New Obs    Predicted Values for New Observations
New Obs    x1     x2  x2sq  x1x2    New Obs      Fit  SE Fit          95% CI                 95% PI
      1  20.0   8.00  64.0   160          1  171.751   0.527 (170.396, 173.105) (168.836, 174.665)
```

b Report and interpret a point prediction of and a 95 percent prediction interval for the sales price of an individual house having 2,000 square feet and a rating of 8 (see the bottom of the MINITAB output in Figure 12.26). Is the 95 percent prediction interval given by the model

$$y = \beta_0 + \beta_1 x_1 + \beta_2 x_2 + \beta_3 x_2^2 + \beta_4 x_1 x_2 + \varepsilon$$

shorter than the 95 percent prediction interval given by the model

$$y = \beta_0 + \beta_1 x_1 + \beta_2 x_2 + \beta_3 x_2^2 + \varepsilon$$

(see the MINITAB output in Figure 12.19 on page 563). If so, what does this mean?

12.39 THE REAL ESTATE SALES PRICE CASE RealEst2

In this exercise we study the nature of the interaction between x_1, square footage, and x_2, rating.

a Consider all houses with a rating of 2. In this case, predicted sales price is (using the least squares point estimates in Figure 12.26)

$$\hat{y} = b_0 + b_1 x_1 + b_2 x_2 + b_3 x_2^2 + b_4 x_1 x_2$$
$$= 27.438 + 5.0813x_1 + 7.2899(2) - .5311(2)^2 + .11473x_1(2)$$

Calculate $\hat{y}$ when $x_1 = 13$ and 22. Plot $\hat{y}$ versus x_1, for $x_1 = 13$ and 22.

b Consider all houses with a rating of 8. In this case, predicted sales are (using the least squares point estimates in Figure 12.26)

$$\hat{y} = b_0 + b_1 x_1 + b_2 x_2 + b_3 x_2^2 + b_4 x_1 x_2$$
$$= 27.438 + 5.0813x_1 + 7.2899(8) - .5311(8)^2 + .11473x_1(8)$$

Calculate $\hat{y}$ when $x_1 = 13$ and 22. Plot $\hat{y}$ versus x_1, for $x_1 = 13$ and 22.

c By comparing the plots you made in *a* and *b*, discuss the nature of the interaction between x_1 and x_2.

PART 3 Dummy Variables and Advanced Statistical Inferences (Optional)

12.10 Using Dummy Variables to Model Qualitative Independent Variables (Optional)

While the levels (or values) of a quantitative independent variable are numerical, the levels of a **qualitative** independent variable are defined by describing them. For instance, the type of sales technique used by a door-to-door salesperson is a qualitative independent variable. Here we might define three different levels—high pressure, medium pressure, and low pressure.

TABLE 12.12 The Electronics World Sales Volume Data Electronics1

Store	Number of Households, x	Location	Sales Volume, y
1	161	Street	157.27
2	99	Street	93.28
3	135	Street	136.81
4	120	Street	123.79
5	164	Street	153.51
6	221	Mall	241.74
7	179	Mall	201.54
8	204	Mall	206.71
9	214	Mall	229.78
10	101	Mall	135.22

FIGURE 12.27 Plot of the Sales Volume Data and a Geometrical Interpretation of the Model $y = \beta_0 + \beta_1 x + \beta_2 D_M + \varepsilon$

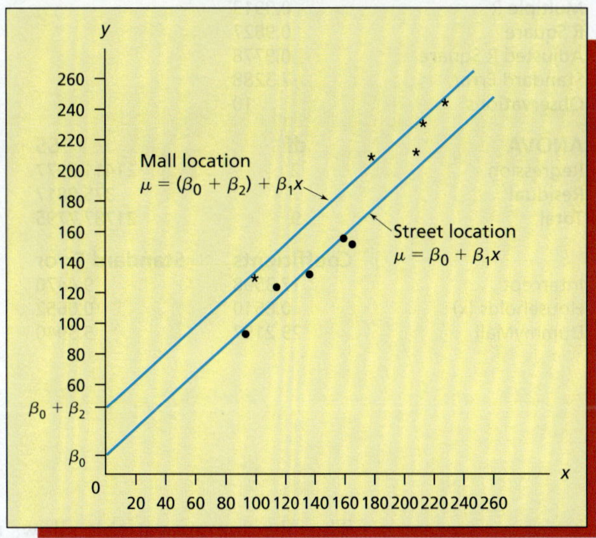

We can model the effects of the different levels of a qualitative independent variable by using what we call **dummy variables** (also called **indicator variables**). Such variables are usually defined so that they take on two values—either 0 or 1. To see how we use dummy variables, we begin with an example.

CHAPTER 19

Example 12.15

Part 1: The data and data plots Suppose that Electronics World, a chain of stores that sells audio and video equipment, has gathered the data in Table 12.12. These data concern store sales volume in July of last year (y, measured in thousands of dollars), the number of households in the store's area (x, measured in thousands), and the location of the store (on a suburban street or in a suburban shopping mall—a qualitative independent variable). Figure 12.27 gives a data plot of y versus x. Stores having a street location are plotted as solid dots, while stores having a mall location are plotted as asterisks. Notice that the line relating y to x for mall locations has a higher y-intercept than does the line relating y to x for street locations.

Part 2: A dummy variable model In order to model the effects of the street and shopping mall locations, we define a dummy variable denoted D_M as follows:

$$D_M = \begin{cases} 1 & \text{if a store is in a mall location} \\ 0 & \text{otherwise} \end{cases}$$

Using this dummy variable, we consider the regression model

$$y = \beta_0 + \beta_1 x + \beta_2 D_M + \varepsilon$$

This model and the definition of D_M imply that

1 For a street location, mean sales volume equals

$$\begin{aligned}\beta_0 + \beta_1 x + \beta_2 D_M &= \beta_0 + \beta_1 x + \beta_2(0) \\ &= \beta_0 + \beta_1 x\end{aligned}$$

2 For a mall location, mean sales volume equals

$$\begin{aligned}\beta_0 + \beta_1 x + \beta_2 D_M &= \beta_0 + \beta_1 x + \beta_2(1) \\ &= (\beta_0 + \beta_2) + \beta_1 x\end{aligned}$$

FIGURE 12.28 Excel Output of a Regression Analysis of the Sales Volume Data Using the Model $y = \beta_0 + \beta_1 x + \beta_2 D_M + \varepsilon$

Regression Statistics	
Multiple R	0.9913
R Square	0.9827
Adjusted R Square	0.9778
Standard Error	7.3288
Observations	10

ANOVA	df	SS	MS	F	Significance F
Regression	2	21411.7977	10705.8989	199.3216	6.75E-07
Residual	7	375.9817	53.7117		
Total	9	21787.7795			

	Coefficients	Standard Error	t Stat	P-value	Lower 95%	Upper 95%
Intercept	17.3598	9.4470	1.8376	0.1087	-4.9788	39.6985
Households (x)	0.8510	0.0652	13.0439	3.63E-06	0.6968	1.0053
DummyMall	29.2157	5.5940	5.2227	0.0012	15.9881	42.4434

Thus the dummy variable allows us to model the situation illustrated in Figure 12.27. Here, the lines relating mean sales volume to x for street and mall locations have different y intercepts—β_0 and $(\beta_0 + \beta_2)$—and the same slope β_1. Note that β_2 is the difference between the mean monthly sales volume for stores in mall locations and the mean monthly sales volume for stores in street locations, when all these stores have the same number of households in their areas. That is, we can say that β_2 represents the effect on mean sales of a mall location compared to a street location. The Excel output in Figure 12.28 tells us that the least squares point estimate of β_2 is $b_2 = 29.2157$. This says that for any given number of households in a store's area, we estimate that the mean monthly sales volume in a mall location is \$29,215.70 greater than the mean monthly sales volume in a street location.

Part 3: A dummy variable model for comparing three locations In addition to the data concerning street and mall locations in Figure 12.12, Electronics World has also collected data concerning downtown locations. The complete data set is given in Table 12.13 and plotted in Figure 12.29. Here stores having a downtown location are plotted as open circles. A model describing these data is

$$y = \beta_0 + \beta_1 x + \beta_2 D_M + \beta_3 D_D + \varepsilon$$

Here the dummy variable D_M is as previously defined and the dummy variable D_D is defined as follows

$$D_D = \begin{cases} 1 & \text{if a store is in a downtown location} \\ 0 & \text{otherwise} \end{cases}$$

It follows that

1 For a street location, mean sales volume equals

$$\begin{aligned} \beta_0 + \beta_1 x + \beta_2 D_M + \beta_3 D_D &= \beta_0 + \beta_1 x + \beta_2(0) + \beta_3(0) \\ &= \beta_0 + \beta_1 x \end{aligned}$$

2 For a mall location, mean sales volume equals

$$\begin{aligned} \beta_0 + \beta_1 x + \beta_2 D_M + \beta_3 D_D &= \beta_0 + \beta_1 x + \beta_2(1) + \beta_3(0) \\ &= (\beta_0 + \beta_2) + \beta_1 x \end{aligned}$$

TABLE 12.13 The Complete Electronics World Sales Volume Data Electronics2

Store	Number of Households, x	Location	Sales Volume, y
1	161	Street	157.27
2	99	Street	93.28
3	135	Street	136.81
4	120	Street	123.79
5	164	Street	153.51
6	221	Mall	241.74
7	179	Mall	201.54
8	204	Mall	206.71
9	214	Mall	229.78
10	101	Mall	135.22
11	231	Downtown	224.71
12	206	Downtown	195.29
13	248	Downtown	242.16
14	107	Downtown	115.21
15	205	Downtown	197.82

FIGURE 12.29 Plot of the Complete Electronics World Sales Volume Data and a Geometrical Interpretation of the Model $y = \beta_0 + \beta_1 x + \beta_2 D_M + \beta_3 D_D + \varepsilon$

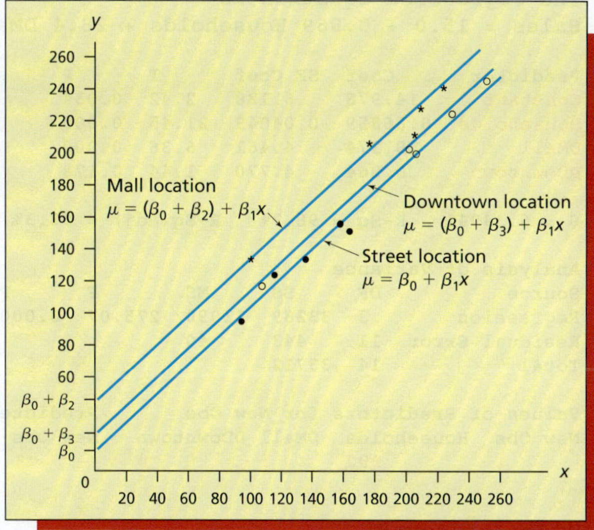

3 For a downtown location, mean sales volume equals

$$\beta_0 + \beta_1 x + \beta_2 D_M + \beta_3 D_D = \beta_0 + \beta_1 x + \beta_2(0) + \beta_3(1)$$
$$= (\beta_0 + \beta_3) + \beta_1 x$$

Thus the dummy variables allow us to model the situation illustrated in Figure 12.29. Here the lines relating mean sales volume to x for street, mall, and downtown locations have different y-intercepts—β_0, $(\beta_0 + \beta_2)$, and $(\beta_0 + \beta_3)$—and the same slope β_1. Note that β_2 represents the effect on mean sales of a mall location compared to a street location, and β_3 represents the effect on mean sales of a downtown location compared to a street location. Furthermore, the difference between β_2 and β_3, $\beta_2 - \beta_3$, represents the effect on mean sales of a mall location compared to a downtown location.

Part 4: Comparing the three locations Figure 12.30 gives the MINITAB and Excel output of a regression analysis of the sales volume data using the dummy variable model. The output tells us that the least squares point estimate of β_2 is $b_2 = 28.374$. This says that for any given number of households in a store's area, we estimate that the mean monthly sales volume in a mall location is \$28,374 greater than the mean monthly sales volume in a street location. Furthermore, since the Excel output tells us that a 95 percent confidence interval for β_2 is [18.5545, 38.193], we are 95 percent confident that for any given number of households in a store's area, the mean monthly sales volume in a mall location is between \$18,554.50 and \$38,193 greater than the mean monthly sales volume in a street location. The MINITAB and Excel output also shows that the t statistic for testing H_0: $\beta_2 = 0$ versus H_a: $\beta_2 \neq 0$ equals 6.36 and that the related p-value is less than .001. Therefore, we have very strong evidence that there is a difference between the mean monthly sales volumes in mall and street locations.

We next note that the output in Figure 12.30 shows that the least squares point estimate of β_3 is $b_3 = 6.864$. Therefore, we estimate that for any given number of households in a store's area, the mean monthly sales volume in a downtown location is \$6,864 greater than the mean monthly sales volume in a street location. Furthermore, the Excel output shows that a 95 percent confidence interval for β_3 is [−3.636, 17.3635]. This says we are 95 percent confident that for any given number of households in a store's area, the mean monthly sales volume in a downtown

FIGURE 12.30 MINITAB and Excel Output of a Regression Analysis of the Sales Volume Data Using the Model $y = \beta_0 + \beta_1 x + \beta_2 D_M + \beta_3 D_D + \varepsilon$

(a) The MINITAB output

```
The regression equation is
Sales = 15.0 + 0.869 Households + 28.4 DMall + 6.86 DDowntown

Predictor        Coef   SE Coef      T      P
Constant       14.978     6.188   2.42  0.034
Households    0.86859   0.04049  21.45  0.000
DMall          28.374     4.461   6.36  0.000
DDowntown       6.864     4.770   1.44  0.178

S = 6.34941    R-Sq = 98.7%    R-Sq(adj) = 98.3%

Analysis of Variance
Source          DF      SS      MS       F      P
Regression       3   33269   11090  275.07  0.000
Residual Error  11     443      40
Total           14   33712

Values of Predictors for New Obs        Predicted Values for New Observations
New Obs  Households  DMall DDowntown    New Obs     Fit  SE Fit         95% CI             95% PI
      1         200      1         0          1  217.07    2.91  (210.65, 223.48)  (201.69, 232.45)
```

(b) The Excel output

Regression Statistics	
Multiple R	0.9934
R Square	0.9868
Adjusted R Square	0.9833
Standard Error	6.3494
Observations	15

ANOVA	df	SS	MS	F	Significance F
Regression	3	33268.6953	11089.5651	275.0729	1.27E-10
Residual	11	443.4650	40.3150		
Total	14	33712.1603			

	Coefficients	Standard Error	t Stat	P-value	Lower 95%	Upper 95%
Intercept	14.9777	6.1884	2.4203	0.0340	1.3570	28.5984
Households (x)	0.8686	0.0405	21.4520	2.52E-10	0.7795	0.9577
DummyMall	28.3738	4.4613	6.3600	5.37E-05	18.5545	38.1930
DummyDtown	6.8638	4.7705	1.4388	0.1780	-3.6360	17.3635

location is between \$3,636 less than and \$17,363.50 greater than the mean monthly sales volume in a street location. The MINITAB and Excel output also show that the t statistic and p-value for testing H_0: $\beta_3 = 0$ versus H_a: $\beta_3 \neq 0$ are $t = 1.44$ and p-value $= .178$. Therefore, we do not have strong evidence that there is a difference between the mean monthly sales volumes in downtown and street locations.

Finally, note that, since $b_2 = 28.374$ and $b_3 = 6.864$, the point estimate of $\beta_2 - \beta_3$ is $b_2 - b_3 = 28.374 - 6.864 = 21.51$. Therefore, we estimate that mean monthly sales volume in a mall location is \$21,510 higher than mean monthly sales volume in a downtown location. Near the end of this section we show how to compare the mall and downtown locations by using a confidence interval and a hypothesis test. We will find that there is very strong evidence that the mean monthly sales volume in a mall location is higher than the mean monthly sales volume in a downtown location. In summary, the mall location seems to give a higher mean monthly sales volume than either the street or downtown location.

Part 5: Predicting a future sales volume Suppose that Electronics World wishes to predict the sales volume in a future month for an individual store that has 200,000 households in its area

FIGURE 12.31 Geometrical Interpretation of the Sales Volume Model $y = \beta_0 + \beta_1 x + \beta_2 D_M + \beta_3 x D_M + \varepsilon$

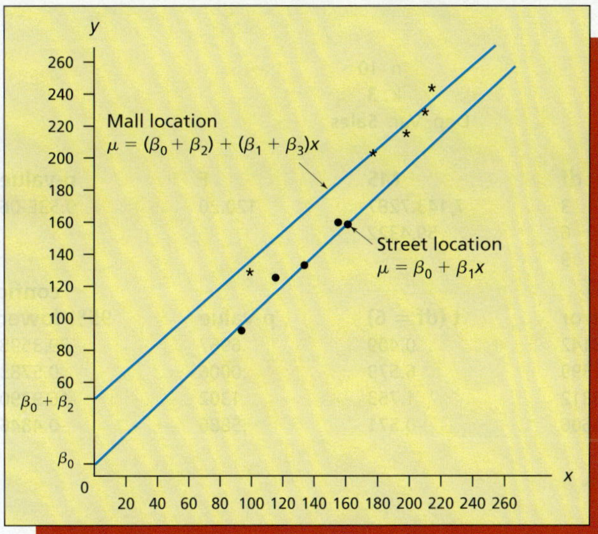

and is located in a shopping mall. The point prediction of this sales volume is (since $D_M = 1$ and $D_D = 0$ when a store is in a shopping mall)

$$\begin{aligned}\hat{y} &= b_0 + b_1(200) + b_2(1) + b_3(0)\\ &= 14.978 + .8686(200) + 28.374(1)\\ &= 217.07\end{aligned}$$

This point prediction is given at the bottom of the MINITAB output in Figure 12.30(a). The corresponding 95 percent prediction interval, which is [201.69, 232.45], says we are 95 percent confident that the sales volume in a future sales period for an individual mall store that has 200,000 households in its area will be between \$201,690 and \$232,450.

Part 6: Interaction models Consider the Electronics World data for street and mall locations given in Table 12.12 (page 573) and the model

$$y = \beta_0 + \beta_1 x + \beta_2 D_M + \beta_3 x D_M + \varepsilon$$

This model uses the *cross-product,* or *interaction, term* xD_M and implies that

1 For a street location, mean sales volume equals (since $D_M = 0$)

$$\beta_0 + \beta_1 x + \beta_2(0) + \beta_3 x(0) = \beta_0 + \beta_1 x$$

2 For a mall location, mean sales volume equals (since $D_M = 1$)

$$\beta_0 + \beta_1 x + \beta_2(1) + \beta_3 x(1) = (\beta_0 + \beta_2) + (\beta_1 + \beta_3)x$$

As illustrated in Figure 12.31, if we use this model, then the straight lines relating mean sales volume to x for street and mall locations have *different y-intercepts* and *different slopes.* Therefore, we say that this model assumes *interaction* between x and store location. Such a model is appropriate if the relationship between mean sales volume and x depends on (that is, is different for) the street and mall store locations. In general, **interaction** exists between two independent variables if the relationship between (for example, the slope of the line relating) the mean value of the dependent variable and one of the independent variables depends upon the value (or level) of the other independent variable. Figure 12.32 gives the MegaStat output of a regression analysis of the sales volume data using the interaction model. Here D_M and xD_M are labeled as DM and XDM, respectively, on the output. The MegaStat output tells us that the p-value related to the significance of xD_M is .5886. This large p-value tells us that the interaction term is not important. It follows that the no-interaction model on page 573 seems best.

FIGURE 12.32 MegaStat Output Using the Interaction Model $y = \beta_0 + \beta_1 x + \beta_2 D_M + \beta_3 x D_M + \varepsilon$

Regression Analysis

R^2	0.984		
Adjusted R^2	0.975	n	10
R	0.992	k	3
Std. Error	7.709	Dep. Var.	**Sales**

ANOVA table

Source	SS	df	MS	F	p-value
Regression	21,431.1861	3	7,143.7287	120.20	9.53E-06
Residual	356.5933	6	59.4322		
Total	21,787.7795	9			

Regression output

variables	coefficients	std. error	t (df = 6)	p-value	confidence interval 95% lower	95% upper
Intercept	7.9004	19.3142	0.409	.6967	-39.3598	55.1607
X	0.9207	0.1399	6.579	.0006	0.5783	1.2631
DM	42.7297	24.3812	1.753	.1302	-16.9290	102.3885
XDM	-0.0917	0.1606	-0.571	.5886	-0.4846	0.3012

Next, consider the Electronics World data for street, mall, and downtown locations given in Table 12.13 (page 575). In modeling these data, if we believe that interaction exists between the number of households in a store's area and store location, we might consider using the model

$$y = \beta_0 + \beta_1 x + \beta_2 D_M + \beta_3 D_D + \beta_4 x D_M + \beta_5 x D_D + \varepsilon$$

Similar to Figure 12.31, this model implies that the straight lines relating mean sales volume to x for the street, mall, and downtown locations have *different y-intercepts* and *different slopes.* If we perform a regression analysis of the sales volume data using this interaction model, we find that the p-values related to the significance of xD_M and xD_D are large $-.5334$ and $.8132$, respectively. Since these interaction terms are not significant, it seems best to employ the no-interaction model on page 574.

In general, if we wish to model the effect of a qualitative independent variable having a levels, we use $a - 1$ dummy variables. The parameter multiplied by a particular dummy variable expresses the effect of the level represented by that dummy variable with respect to the effect of the level that is not represented by a dummy variable. For example, if we wish to compare the effects on sales, y, of four different types of advertising campaigns—television (T), radio (R), magazine (M), and mailed coupons (C)—we might employ the model

$$y = \beta_0 + \beta_1 D_T + \beta_2 D_R + \beta_3 D_M + \varepsilon$$

Since this model does not use a dummy variable to represent the mailed coupon advertising campaign, the parameter β_1 is the difference between mean sales when a television advertising campaign is used and mean sales when a mailed coupon advertising campaign is used. The interpretations of β_2 and β_3 follow similarly. As another example, if we wish to employ a confidence interval and a hypothesis test to compare the mall and downtown locations in the Electronics World example, we can use the model

$$y = \beta_0 + \beta_1 x + \beta_2 D_S + \beta_3 D_M + \varepsilon$$

Here the dummy variable D_M is as previously defined, and

$$D_S = \begin{cases} 1 & \text{if a store is in a street location} \\ 0 & \text{otherwise} \end{cases}$$

Since this model does not use a dummy variable to represent the downtown location, the parameter β_2 expresses the effect on mean sales of a street location compared to a downtown location, and the parameter β_3 expresses the effect on mean sales of a mall location compared to a downtown location.

The Excel output of the least squares point estimates of the parameters of this model is as follows:

	Coefficients	Standard Error	t Stat	P-value	Lower 95%	Upper 95%
Intercept	21.8415	8.5585	2.5520	0.0269	3.0044	40.6785
Households (x)	0.8686	0.0405	21.4520	2.52E-10	0.7795	0.9577
DummyStreet	-6.8638	4.7705	-1.4388	0.1780	-17.3635	3.6360
DummyMall	21.5100	4.0651	5.2914	0.0003	12.5628	30.4572

Since the least squares point estimate of β_3 is $b_3 = 21.51$, we estimate that for any given number of households in a store's area, the mean monthly sales volume in a mall location is \$21,510 higher than the mean monthly sales volume in a downtown location. The Excel output tells us that a 95 percent confidence interval for β_3 is [12.5628, 30.4572]. Therefore, we are 95 percent confident that for any given number of households in a store's area, the mean monthly sales volume in a mall location is between \$12,562.80 and \$30,457.20 greater than the mean monthly sales volume in a downtown location. The Excel output also shows that the t statistic and p-value for testing H_0: $\beta_3 = 0$ versus H_a: $\beta_3 \neq 0$ in this model are, respectively, 5.2914 and .0003. Therefore, we have very strong evidence that there is a difference between the mean monthly sales volumes in mall and downtown locations.

In some situations dummy variables represent the effects of unusual events or occurrences that may have an important impact on the dependent variable. For instance, suppose we wish to build a regression model relating quarterly sales of automobiles (y) to automobile prices (x_1), fuel prices (x_2), and personal income (x_3). If an autoworkers' strike occurred in a particular quarter that had a major impact on automobile sales, then we might define a dummy variable D_S to be equal to 1 if an autoworkers' strike occurs and to be equal to 0 otherwise. The least squares point estimate of the regression parameter multiplied by D_S would estimate the effect of the strike on mean auto sales. Finally, dummy variables can be used to model the impact of regularly occuring *seasonal* influences on time series data—for example, the impact of the hot summer months on soft drink sales. This is discussed in Chapter 13.

Exercises for Section 12.10

CONCEPTS

12.40 What is a qualitative independent variable?

12.41 How do we use dummy variables to model the effects of a qualitative independent variable?

12.42 What does the parameter multiplied by a dummy variable express?

METHODS AND APPLICATIONS

12.43 Neter, Kutner, Nachtsheim, and Wasserman (1996) relate the speed, y, with which a particular insurance innovation is adopted to the size of the insurance firm, x, and the type of firm. The dependent variable y is measured by the number of months elapsed between the time the first firm adopted the innovation and the time the firm being considered adopted the innovation. The size of the firm, x, is measured by the total assets of the firm, and the type of firm—a qualitative independent variable—is either a mutual company or a stock company. The data in Table 12.14 are observed.

a Discuss why the data plot in the page margin indicates that the model

$$y = \beta_0 + \beta_1 x + \beta_2 D_S + \varepsilon$$

might appropriately describe the observed data. Here D_S equals 1 if the firm is a stock company and 0 if the firm is a mutual company.

b The model of part (a) implies that the mean adoption time of an insurance innovation by mutual companies having an asset size x equals

$$\beta_0 + \beta_1 x + \beta_2(0) = \beta_0 + \beta_1 x$$

and that the mean adoption time by stock companies having an asset size x equals

$$\beta_0 + \beta_1 x + \beta_2(1) = \beta_0 + \beta_1 x + \beta_2$$

Plot of the Insurance Innovation Data

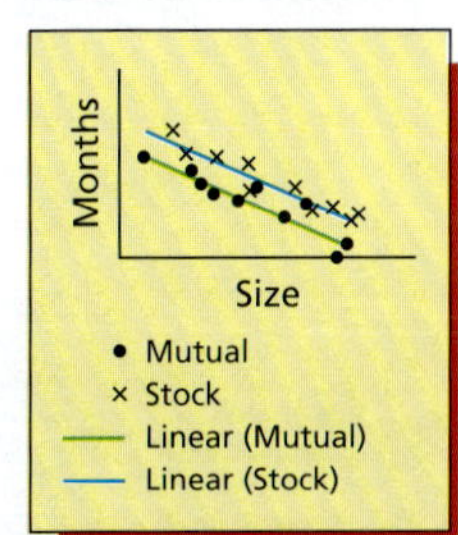

TABLE 12.14 The Insurance Innovation Data InsInnov

Firm	Number of Months Elapsed, y	Size of Firm (Millions of Dollars), x	Type of Firm	Firm	Number of Months Elapsed, y	Size of Firm (Millions of Dollars), x	Type of Firm
1	17	151	Mutual	11	28	164	Stock
2	26	92	Mutual	12	15	272	Stock
3	21	175	Mutual	13	11	295	Stock
4	30	31	Mutual	14	38	68	Stock
5	22	104	Mutual	15	31	85	Stock
6	0	277	Mutual	16	21	224	Stock
7	12	210	Mutual	17	20	166	Stock
8	19	120	Mutual	18	13	305	Stock
9	4	290	Mutual	19	30	124	Stock
10	16	238	Mutual	20	14	246	Stock

FIGURE 12.33 Excel Output of a Regression Analysis of the Insurance Innovation Data Using the Model $y = \beta_0 + \beta_1 x + \beta_2 D_S + \varepsilon$

Regression Statistics	
Multiple R	0.9461
R Square	0.8951
Adjusted R Square	0.8827
Standard Error	3.2211
Observations	20

ANOVA	df	SS	MS	F	Significance F
Regression	2	1,504.4133	752.2067	72.4971	4.77E-09
Residual	17	176.3867	10.3757		
Total	19	1,680.8			

	Coefficients	Standard Error	t Stat	P-value	Lower 95%	Upper 95%
Intercept	33.8741	1.8139	18.6751	9.15E-13	30.0472	37.7010
Size of Firm (x)	-0.1017	0.0089	-11.4430	2.07E-09	-0.1205	-0.0830
DummyStock	8.0555	1.4591	5.5208	3.74E-05	4.9770	11.1339

The difference between these two means equals the model parameter β_2. In your own words, interpret the practical meaning of β_2.

c Figure 12.33 presents the Excel output of a regression analysis of the insurance innovation data using the model of part *a*. Using the output, test H_0: $\beta_2 = 0$ versus H_a: $\beta_2 \neq 0$ by setting $\alpha = .05$ and .01. Interpret the practical meaning of the result of this test. Also, use the computer output to find, report, and interpret a 95 percent confidence interval for β_2.

d If we add the interaction term xD_S to the model of part *a*, we find that the *p*-value related to this term is .9821. What does this imply?

12.44 THE FLORIDA POOL HOME CASE PooL

Table 2.17 (page 112) gives the selling price (Price, expressed in thousands of dollars), the square footage (SqrFt), the number of bathrooms (Bathrms), and the niceness rating (Niceness, expressed as an integer from 1 to 7) of 80 homes randomly selected from all homes sold in a Florida city during the last six months. (The random selections were made from homes having between 2,000 and 3,500 square feet.) Table 2.17 also gives values of the dummy variable Pool?, which equals 1 if a home has a pool and 0 otherwise. Figure 12.34 presents the MegaStat output of a regression analysis of these data using the model

$$\text{Price} = \beta_0 + \beta_1 \cdot \text{SqrFt} + \beta_2 \cdot \text{Bathrms} + \beta_3 \cdot \text{Niceness} + \beta_4 \cdot \text{Pool?} + \varepsilon$$

a Noting that β_4 is the effect on mean sales price of a home having a pool, find (on the output) a point estimate of this effect. If the average current selling price of the pools in the sample is \$32,500, find a point estimate of the percentage of a pool's cost that a customer buying a pool can expect to recoup when selling his (or her) home.

FIGURE 12.34 MegaStat Output of a Regression Analysis of the Florida Pool Home Data Using the Model Price = $\beta_0 + \beta_1 \cdot$ SqrFt + $\beta_2 \cdot$ Bathrms + $\beta_3 \cdot$ Niceness + $\beta_4 \cdot$ Pool? + ε

Regression Analysis

R^2	0.874		
Adjusted R^2	0.868	n	80
R	0.935	k	4
Std. Error	13.532	Dep. Var.	Price

ANOVA table

Source	SS	df	MS	F	p-value
Regression	95,665.2412	4	23,916.3103	130.61	5.41E-33
Residual	13,733.7327	75	183.1164		
Total	109,398.9739	79			

Regression output

variables	coefficients	std. error	t (df=75)	p-value	confidence interval 95% lower	95% upper
Intercept	24.9760	16.6267	1.502	.1373	-8.1460	58.0980
SqrFt	0.0526	0.0066	7.982	1.29E-11	0.0395	0.0658
Bathrms	10.0430	3.7287	2.693	.0087	2.6151	17.4710
Niceness	10.0420	0.7915	12.687	2.38E-20	8.4653	11.6188
Pool?	25.8623	3.5747	7.235	3.36E-10	18.7411	32.9835

b If we add various combinations of the interaction terms SqrFt · Pool?, Bathrooms · Pool?, and Niceness · Pool? to the above model, we find that the p-values related to these terms are greater than .05. What does this imply?

12.45 THE SHELF DISPLAY CASE BakeSale

The Tastee Bakery Company supplies a bakery product to many supermarkets in a metropolitan area. The company wishes to study the effect of the height of the shelf display employed by the supermarkets on monthly sales, y (measured in cases of 10 units each), for this product. Shelf display height has three levels—bottom (B), middle (M), and top (T). For each shelf display height, six supermarkets of equal sales potential will be randomly selected, and each supermarket will display the product using its assigned shelf height for a month. At the end of the month, sales of the bakery product at the 18 participating stores will be recorded. When the experiment is carried out, the data in Table 12.15 are obtained. Here we assume that the set of sales amounts for each display height is a sample that has been randomly selected from the population of all sales amounts that could be obtained (at supermarkets of the given sales potential) when using that display height. To compare the population mean sales amounts μ_B, μ_M, and μ_T that would be obtained by using the bottom, middle, and top display heights, we use the following dummy variable regression model:

$$y = \beta_B + \beta_M D_M + \beta_T D_T + \varepsilon$$

Here D_M equals 1 if a middle display height is used and 0 otherwise; D_T equals 1 if a top display height is used and 0 otherwise. Figure 12.35 presents the MINITAB output of a regression analysis of the bakery sales study data using this model.[1]

a By using the definitions of the dummy variables, show that

$$\mu_B = \beta_B \qquad \mu_M = \beta_B + \beta_M \qquad \mu_T = \beta_B + \beta_T$$

b Use the overall F statistic to test H_0: $\beta_M = \beta_T = 0$, or, equivalently, H_0: $\mu_B = \mu_M = \mu_T$. Interpret the practical meaning of the result of this test.

c Show that your results in part a, imply that

$$\mu_M - \mu_B = \beta_M \qquad \mu_T - \mu_B = \beta_T \qquad \mu_M - \mu_T = \beta_M - \beta_T$$

TABLE 12.15 Bakery Sales Study Data (Sales in Cases) BakeSale

Shelf Display Height		
Bottom (B)	Middle (M)	Top (T)
58.2	73.0	52.4
53.7	78.1	49.7
55.8	75.4	50.9
55.7	76.2	54.0
52.5	78.4	52.1
58.9	82.1	49.9

[1]In general, the regression approach of this exercise produces the same comparisons of several population means that are produced by **one-way analysis of variance** (see Section 10.2). In Appendix H of the CD-ROM included with this book we discuss the regression approach to **two-way analysis of variance** (see Section 10.4).

FIGURE 12.35 MINITAB Output of a Dummy Variable Regression Analysis of the Bakery Sales Data in Table 12.15

```
The regression equation is
Bakery Sales = 55.8 + 21.4 DMiddle - 4.30 DTop

Predictor     Coef   SE Coef      T      P
Constant    55.800     1.013  55.07  0.000
DMiddle     21.400     1.433  14.93  0.000
DTop        -4.300     1.433  -3.00  0.009

S = 2.48193    R-Sq = 96.1%    R-Sq(adj) = 95.6%

Analysis of Variance
Source          DF      SS      MS       F      P
Regression       2  2273.9  1136.9  184.57  0.000
Residual Error  15    92.4     6.2
Total           17  2366.3

Values of Predictors for New Obs     Predicted Values for New Observations
New Obs  DMiddle  DTop               New Obs     Fit  SE Fit          95% CI              95% PI
      1        1     0                     1  77.200   1.013  (75.040, 79.360)  (71.486, 82.914)
```

Then use the least squares point estimates of the model parameters to find a point estimate of each of the three differences in means. Also, find a 95 percent confidence interval for and test the significance of each of the first two differences in means. Interpret your results.

d Find a point estimate of mean sales when using a middle display height, a 95 percent confidence interval for mean sales when using a middle display height, and a 95 percent prediction interval for sales at an individual supermarket that employs a middle display height (see the bottom of the MINITAB output in Figure 12.35).

e Consider the following alternative model

$$y = \beta_T + \beta_B D_B + \beta_M D_M + \varepsilon$$

Here D_B equals 1 if a bottom display height is used and 0 otherwise. The MINITAB output of the least squares point estimates of the parameters of this model is as follows:

```
Predictor      Coef   SE Coef       T       P
Constant     51.500     1.013   50.83   0.000
DBottom       4.300     1.433    3.00   0.009
DMiddle      25.700     1.433   17.94   0.000
```

Since β_M expresses the effect of the middle display height with respect to the effect of the top display height, β_M equals $\mu_M - \mu_T$. Use the MINITAB output to calculate a 95 percent confidence interval for and test the significance of $\mu_M - \mu_T$. Interpret your results.

TABLE 12.16 Advertising Campaigns Used by Enterprise Industries Fresh3

Sales Period	Advertising Campaign
1	*B*
2	*B*
3	*B*
4	*A*
5	*C*
6	*A*
7	*C*
8	*C*
9	*B*
10	*C*
11	*A*
12	*C*
13	*C*
14	*A*
15	*B*
16	*B*
17	*B*
18	*A*
19	*B*
20	*B*
21	*C*
22	*A*
23	*A*
24	*A*
25	*A*
26	*B*
27	*C*
28	*B*
29	*C*
30	*C*

12.46 THE FRESH DETERGENT CASE Fresh3

Recall from Exercise 12.7 that Enterprise Industries has observed the historical data in Table 12.4 (page 535) concerning y (demand for Fresh liquid laundry detergent), x_1 (the price of Fresh), x_2 (the average industry price of competitors' similar detergents), and x_3 (Enterprise Industries' advertising expenditure for Fresh). To ultimately increase the demand for Fresh, Enterprise Industries' marketing department is comparing the effectiveness of three different advertising campaigns. These campaigns are denoted as campaigns *A*, *B*, and *C*. Campaign *A* consists entirely of television commercials, campaign *B* consists of a balanced mixture of television and radio commercials, and campaign *C* consists of a balanced mixture of television, radio, newspaper, and magazine ads. To conduct the study, Enterprise Industries has randomly selected one advertising campaign to be used in each of the 30 sales periods in Table 12.4. Although logic would indicate that each of campaigns *A*, *B*, and *C* should be used in 10 of the 30 sales periods, Enterprise Industries has made previous commitments to the advertising media involved in the study. As a result, campaigns *A*, *B*, and *C* were randomly assigned to, respectively, 9, 11, and 10 sales periods. Furthermore, advertising was done in only the first three weeks of each sales period, so that the carryover effect of the campaign used in a sales period to the next sales period would be minimized. Table 12.16 lists the campaigns used in the sales periods.

To compare the effectiveness of advertising campaigns *A*, *B*, and *C*, we define two dummy variables. Specifically, we define the dummy variable D_B to equal 1 if campaign *B* is used in a

FIGURE 12.36 MegaStat Output of a Dummy Variable Regression Model Analysis of the Fresh Demand Data

Regression Analysis

R^2	0.960		
Adjusted R^2	0.951	n	30
R	0.980	k	5
Std. Error	0.150	Dep. Var.	Demand

ANOVA table

Source	SS	df	MS	F	p-value
Regression	12.9166	5	2.5833	114.39	6.24E-16
Residual	0.5420	24	0.0226		
Total	13.4586	29			

Regression output

variables	coefficients	std. error	t (df = 24)	p-value	confidence interval 95% lower	95% upper
Intercept	8.7154	1.5849	5.499	1.18E-05	5.4443	11.9866
X1	−2.7680	0.4144	−6.679	6.58E-07	−3.6234	−1.9127
X2	1.6667	0.1913	8.711	6.77E-09	1.2718	2.0616
X3	0.4927	0.0806	6.110	2.60E-06	0.3263	0.6592
DB	0.2695	0.0695	3.880	.0007	0.1262	0.4128
DC	0.4396	0.0703	6.250	1.85E-06	0.2944	0.5847

Predicted values for: Demand

Predicted	95% Confidence Interval lower	upper	95% Prediction Interval lower	upper	Leverage
8.61621	8.51380	8.71862	8.28958	8.94285	0.109

sales period and 0 otherwise. Furthermore, we define the dummy variable D_C to equal 1 if campaign C is used in a sales period and 0 otherwise. Figure 12.36 presents the MegaStat output of a regression analysis of the Fresh demand data by using the model

$$y = \beta_0 + \beta_1 x_1 + \beta_2 x_2 + \beta_3 x_3 + \beta_4 D_B + \beta_5 D_C + \varepsilon$$

a In this model the parameter β_4 represents the effect on mean demand of advertising campaign B compared to advertising campaign A, and the parameter β_5 represents the effect on mean demand of advertising campaign C compared to advertising campaign A. Use the regression output to find and report a point estimate of each of the above effects and to test the significance of each of the above effects. Also, find and report a 95 percent confidence interval for each of the above effects. Interpret your results.

b The prediction results at the bottom of the MegaStat output correspond to a future period when the price of Fresh will be $x_1 = 3.70$, the competitor's average price of similar detergents will be $x_2 = 3.90$, the advertising expenditure for Fresh will be $x_3 = 6.50$, and advertising campaign C will be used. Show how $\hat{y} = 8.61621$ is calculated. Then find, report, and interpret a 95 percent confidence interval for mean demand and a 95 percent prediction interval for an individual demand when $x_1 = 3.70$, $x_2 = 3.90$, $x_3 = 6.50$, and campaign C is used.

c Consider the alternative model

$$y = \beta_0 + \beta_1 x_1 + \beta_2 x_2 + \beta_3 x_3 + \beta_4 D_A + \beta_5 D_C + \varepsilon$$

Here D_A equals 1 if advertising campaign A is used and equals 0 otherwise. Describe the effect represented by the regression parameter β_5.

d The MegaStat output of the least squares point estimates of the parameters of the model of part (c) is as follows.

Regression output

variables	coefficients	std. error	t (df = 23)	p-value	confidence interval 95% lower	95% upper
Intercept	8.9849	1.5971	5.626	8.61E-06	5.6888	12.2811
X1	−2.7680	0.4144	−6.679	6.58E-07	−3.6234	−1.9127
X2	1.6667	0.1913	8.711	6.77E-09	1.2718	2.0616
X3	0.4927	0.0806	6.110	2.60E-06	0.3263	0.6592
DA	−0.2695	0.0695	−3.880	.0007	−0.4128	−0.1262
DC	0.1701	0.0669	2.543	.0179	0.0320	0.3081

FIGURE 12.37 MegaStat Output of a Regression Analysis of the Fresh Demand Data Using the Model $y = \beta_0 + \beta_1x_1 + \beta_2x_2 + \beta_3x_3 + \beta_4D_B + \beta_5D_C + \beta_6x_3D_B + \beta_7x_3D_C + \varepsilon$

Regression output

variables	coefficients	std. error	t (df = 22)	p-value	confidence interval 95% lower	95% upper
Intercept	8.7619	1.7071	5.133	3.82E-05	5.2216	12.3021
X1	−2.7895	0.4339	−6.428	1.81E-06	−3.6894	−1.8895
X2	1.6365	0.2062	7.938	6.72E-08	1.2089	2.0641
X3	0.5160	0.1288	4.007	.0006	0.2489	0.7831
DB	0.2539	0.8722	0.291	.7737	−1.5550	2.0628
DC	0.8435	0.9739	0.866	.3958	−1.1762	2.8631
X3DB	0.0030	0.1334	0.023	.9822	−0.2736	0.2797
X3DC	−0.0629	0.1502	−0.419	.6794	−0.3744	0.2486

Predicted values for: Demand

Predicted	95% Confidence Interval lower	95% Confidence Interval upper	95% Prediction Interval lower	95% Prediction Interval upper	Leverage
8.61178	8.50372	8.71984	8.27089	8.95266	0.112

R^2 0.960
Adjusted R^2 0.948
R 0.980
Std. Error 0.156

Use the MegaStat output to test the significance of the effect represented by β_5 and find a 95 percent confidence interval for β_5. Interpret your results.

12.47 THE FRESH DETERGENT CASE Fresh3

Figure 12.37 presents the MegaStat output of a regression analysis of the Fresh demand data using the model

$$y = \beta_0 + \beta_1x_1 + \beta_2x_2 + \beta_3x_3 + \beta_4D_B + \beta_5D_C + \beta_6x_3D_B + \beta_7x_3D_C + \varepsilon$$

where the dummy variables D_B and D_C are defined as in Exercise 12.46.

a This model assumes that there is interaction between advertising expenditure x_3 and type of advertising campaign. What do the p-values related to the significance of the cross-product terms x_3D_B and x_3D_C say about the need for these interaction terms and about whether there is interaction between x_3 and type of advertising campaign?

b The prediction results at the bottom of Figure 12.37 are for a future sales period in which $x_1 = 3.70$, $x_2 = 3.90$, $x_3 = 6.50$, and advertising campaign C will be used. Use the output to find and report a point prediction of and a 95 percent prediction interval for Fresh demand in such a sales period. Is the 95 percent prediction interval given by this model shorter or longer than the 95 percent prediction interval given by the model that utilizes D_B and D_C in Exercise 12.46? What are the implications of this comparison?

12.11 The Partial *F* Test: Testing the Significance of a Portion of a Regression Model (Optional)

We now present a **partial *F* test** that allows us to test the significance of a set of independent variables in a regression model. That is, we can use this F test to test the significance of a **portion** of a regression model. For example, in the Electronics World situation, we employed the dummy variable model

$$y = \beta_0 + \beta_1x + \beta_2D_M + \beta_3D_D + \varepsilon$$

It might be useful to test the significance of the dummy variables D_M and D_D. We can do this by testing the null hypothesis

$$H_0: \beta_2 = \beta_3 = 0$$

which says that neither dummy variable significantly affects y, versus the alternative hypothesis

$$H_a: \text{At least one of } \beta_2 \text{ and } \beta_3 \text{ does not equal } 0$$

which says at least one of the dummy variables significantly affects y. Intuitively, since β_2 and β_3 represent the effects of the mall and downtown locations with respect to the street location, the null hypothesis says that the effects of the mall, downtown, and street locations on mean sales volume do not differ (insignificant dummy variables). The alternative hypothesis says that at least two locations have different effects on mean sales volume (at least one significant dummy variable).

In general, consider the regression model

$$y = \beta_0 + \beta_1 x_1 + \cdots + \beta_g x_g + \beta_{g+1} x_{g+1} + \cdots + \beta_k x_k + \varepsilon$$

Suppose we wish to test the null hypothesis

$$H_0: \beta_{g+1} = \beta_{g+2} = \cdots = \beta_k = 0$$

which says that none of the independent variables $x_{g+1}, x_{g+2}, \ldots, x_k$ affect y, versus the alternative hypothesis

$$H_a: \text{At least one of } \beta_{g+1}, \beta_{g+2}, \ldots, \beta_k \text{ does not equal } 0$$

which says that at least one of the independent variables $x_{g+1}, x_{g+2}, \ldots, x_k$ affects y. If we can reject H_0 in favor of H_a by specifying a *small* probability of a Type I error, then it is reasonable to conclude that at least one of $x_{g+1}, x_{g+2}, \ldots, x_k$ *significantly* affects y. In this case we should use t statistics and other techniques to determine which of $x_{g+1}, x_{g+2}, \ldots, x_k$ significantly affect y. To test H_0 versus H_a, consider the following two models:

Complete model: $y = \beta_0 + \beta_1 x_1 + \cdots + \beta_g x_g + \beta_{g+1} x_{g+1} + \cdots + \beta_k x_k + \varepsilon$

Reduced model: $y = \beta_0 + \beta_1 x_1 + \cdots + \beta_g x_g + \varepsilon$

Here the complete model is assumed to have k independent variables, the reduced model is the complete model under the assumption that H_0 is true, and $(k - g)$ denotes the number of regression parameters we have set equal to 0 in the statement of H_0.

To carry out this test, we calculate **SSE_C, the unexplained variation for the complete model,** and **SSE_R, the unexplained variation for the reduced model.** The appropriate test statistic is based on the difference

$$SSE_R - SSE_C$$

which is called **the drop in the unexplained variation attributable to the independent variables $x_{g+1}, x_{g+2}, \ldots, x_k$**. In the following box we give the formula for the test statistic and show how to carry out the test:

The Partial F Test: An F Test for a Portion of a Regression Model

Suppose that the regression assumptions hold and consider testing

$$H_0: \beta_{g+1} = \beta_{g+2} = \cdots = \beta_k = 0$$

versus

H_a: At least one of $\beta_{g+1}, \beta_{g+2}, \ldots, \beta_k$ does not equal 0

We define the **partial F statistic** to be

$$F = \frac{(SSE_R - SSE_C)/(k - g)}{SSE_C/[n - (k + 1)]}$$

Also define the p-value related to F to be the area under the curve of the F distribution [having $k - g$ and $n - (k + 1)$ degrees of freedom] to the right of F. Then, we can reject H_0 in favor of H_a at level of significance α if either of the following equivalent conditions holds:

1 $F > F_\alpha$

2 p-value $< \alpha$

Here the point F_α is based on $k - g$ numerator and $n - (k + 1)$ denominator degrees of freedom.

It can be shown that the "extra" independent variables $x_{g+1}, x_{g+2}, \ldots, x_k$ will always explain some of the variation in the observed y values and, therefore, will always make SSE_C somewhat smaller than SSE_R. Condition 1 says that we should reject H_0 if

$$F = \frac{(SSE_R - SSE_C)/(k - g)}{SSE_C/[n - (k + 1)]}$$

is large. This is reasonable because a large value of F would result from a large value of $(SSE_R - SSE_C)$, which would be obtained if at least one of the independent variables $x_{g+1}, x_{g+2}, \ldots, x_k$ makes SSE_C substantially smaller than SSE_R. This would suggest that H_0 is false and that H_a is true.

Before looking at an example, we should point out that testing the significance of a single independent variable by using a partial F test is equivalent[2] to carrying out this test by using the previously discussed t test (see Section 12.6).

Example 12.16

In Example 12.15 (pages 573–578) we used the dummy variable model

$$y = \beta_0 + \beta_1 x + \beta_2 D_M + \beta_3 D_D + \varepsilon$$

to make pairwise comparisons of the street, mall, and downtown store locations by carrying out a t test for each of the parameters β_2, β_3, and $\beta_2 - \beta_3$. There is a theoretical problem with this because, although we can set the probability of a Type I error equal to .05 for each individual test, it is possible to show that the probability of falsely rejecting H_0 in **at least one** of these tests is greater than .05. Because of this problem, some people feel that before making pairwise comparisons we should test for overall differences between the effects of the locations by testing the null hypothesis

$$H_0: \beta_2 = \beta_3 = 0$$

which says that the street, mall, and downtown locations have the same effects on mean sales volume (no differences between locations), versus the alternative hypothesis

$$H_a\text{: At least one of } \beta_2 \text{ and } \beta_3 \text{ does not equal } 0$$

which says that at least two locations have different effects on mean sales volume.

To carry out this test we consider the following:

Complete model: $y = \beta_0 + \beta_1 x + \beta_2 D_M + \beta_3 D_D + \varepsilon$

For this complete model (which has $k = 3$ independent variables), we obtain an unexplained variation equal to $SSE_C = 443.4650$. The reduced model is the complete model when H_0 is true. Therefore, we obtain

Reduced model: $y = \beta_0 + \beta_1 x + \varepsilon$

For this model the unexplained variation is $SSE_R = 2{,}467.8067$. Noting that two parameters (β_2 and β_3) are set equal to 0 in the statement of H_0, we have $k - g = 2$. Therefore, the needed

[2]It can be shown that when we test $H_0: \beta_j = 0$ versus $H_a: \beta_j \neq 0$ using a partial F test,

$$F = t^2 \quad \text{and} \quad F_\alpha = (t_{\alpha/2})^2$$

Here $t_{\alpha/2}$ is based on $n - (k + 1)$ degrees of freedom, and F_α is based on 1 numerator and $n - (k + 1)$ denominator degrees of freedom. Hence the rejection conditions

$$|t| > t_{\alpha/2} \quad \text{and} \quad F > F_\alpha$$

are equivalent. It can also be shown that in this case the p-value related to t equals the p-value related to F.

partial F statistic is

$$F = \frac{(SSE_R - SSE_C)/(k - g)}{SSE_C/[n - (k + 1)]}$$

$$= \frac{(2{,}467.8067 - 443.4650)/2}{443.4650/[15 - 4]}$$

$$= 25.1066$$

We compare F with $F_{.01} = 7.21$, which is based on $k - g = 2$ numerator and $n - (k + 1) = 15 - 4 = 11$ denominator degrees of freedom. Since

$$F = 25.1066 > 7.21$$

we can reject H_0 at the .01 level of significance, and we have very strong statistical evidence that at least two locations have different effects on mean sales volume. Having reached this conclusion, it makes sense to compare the effects of specific pairs of locations. We have already done this in Example 12.15. It should also be noted that even if H_0 were not rejected, some practitioners feel that pairwise comparisons should still be made. This is because there is always a possibility that we have erroneously decided to not reject H_0.

Exercises for Section 12.11

CONCEPTS

12.48 When we perform a partial F test, what are the complete and reduced models?

12.49 When we perform a partial F test, what is $(k - g)$? What is $n - (k + 1)$?

METHODS AND APPLICATIONS

THE FRESH DETERGENT CASE Fresh3

In Exercises 12.50 through 12.52, you will perform partial F tests by using the following three Fresh detergent models:

Model 1: $y = \beta_0 + \beta_1x_1 + \beta_2x_2 + \beta_3x_3 + \varepsilon$

Model 2: $y = \beta_0 + \beta_1x_1 + \beta_2x_2 + \beta_3x_3 + \beta_4D_B + \beta_5D_C + \varepsilon$

Model 3: $y = \beta_0 + \beta_1x_1 + \beta_2x_2 + \beta_3x_3 + \beta_4D_B + \beta_5D_C + \beta_6x_3D_B + \beta_7x_3D_C + \varepsilon$

The values of SSE for models 1, 2, and 3 are, respectively, 1.4318, .5420, and .5347.

12.50 In Model 2, test H_0: $\beta_4 = \beta_5 = 0$ by setting α equal to .05 and .01. Interpret your results.

12.51 In Model 3, test H_0: $\beta_4 = \beta_5 = \beta_6 = \beta_7 = 0$ by setting α equal to .05 and .01. Interpret.

12.52 In Model 3, test H_0: $\beta_6 = \beta_7 = 0$ by setting α equal to .05 and .01. Interpret your results.

12.12 Model Building, and the Effects of Multicollinearity (Optional)

PART 4 Model Building and Model Diagnostics (Optional)

CHAPTER 17

Multicollinearity Recall the sales territory performance data in Table 12.2 (page 533). These data consist of values of the dependent variable y (SALES) and of the independent variables x_1 (TIME), x_2 (MKTPOTEN), x_3 (ADVER), x_4 (MKTSHARE), and x_5 (CHANGE). The complete sales territory performance data analyzed by Cravens, Woodruff, and Stomper (1972) consist of the data presented in Table 12.2 and data concerning three additional independent variables. These three additional variables are defined as follows:

x_6 = number of accounts handled by the representative (we will sometimes denote this variable as ACCTS)

x_7 = average workload per account, measured by using a weighting based on the sizes of the orders by the accounts and other workload-related criteria (we will sometimes denote this variable as WKLOAD)

FIGURE 12.38 MINITAB Output of a Correlation Matrix for the Sales Territory Performance Data

	Sales	Time	MktPoten	Adver	MktShare	Change	Accts	WkLoad
Time	0.623 0.001							
MktPoten	0.598 0.002	0.454 0.023						
Adver	0.596 0.002	0.249 0.230	0.174 0.405					
MktShare	0.484 0.014	0.106 0.613	-0.211 0.312	0.264 0.201				
Change	0.489 0.013	0.251 0.225	0.268 0.195	0.377 0.064	0.085 0.685			
Accts	0.754 0.000	0.758 0.000	0.479 0.016	0.200 0.338	0.403 0.046	0.327 0.110		
WkLoad	-0.117 0.577	-0.179 0.391	-0.259 0.212	-0.272 0.188	0.349 0.087	-0.288 0.163	-0.199 0.341	
Rating	0.402 0.046	0.101 0.631	0.359 0.078	0.411 0.041	-0.024 0.911	0.549 0.004	0.229 0.272	-0.277 0.180

Cell Contents: Pearson correlation
P-Value

x_8 = an aggregate rating on eight dimensions of the representative's performance, made by a sales manager and expressed on a 1–7 scale (we will sometimes denote this variable as RATING)

TABLE 12.17 Values of ACCTS, WKLOAD, and RATING
SalePerf2

Accounts, x_6	Work-load, x_7	Rating, x_8
74.86	15.05	4.9
107.32	19.97	5.1
96.75	17.34	2.9
195.12	13.40	3.4
180.44	17.64	4.6
104.88	16.22	4.5
256.10	18.80	4.6
126.83	19.86	2.3
203.25	17.42	4.9
119.51	21.41	2.8
116.26	16.32	3.1
142.28	14.51	4.2
89.43	19.35	4.3
84.55	20.02	4.2
119.51	15.26	5.5
80.49	15.87	3.6
136.58	7.81	3.4
78.86	16.00	4.2
136.58	17.44	3.6
138.21	17.98	3.1
75.61	20.99	1.6
102.44	21.66	3.4
76.42	21.46	2.7
136.58	24.78	2.8
88.62	24.96	3.9

Table 12.17 gives the observed values of x_6, x_7, and x_8, and Figure 12.38 presents the MINITAB output of a **correlation matrix** for the sales territory performance data. Examining the first column of this matrix, we see that the simple correlation coefficient between SALES and WKLOAD is $-.117$ and that the p-value for testing the significance of the relationship between SALES and WKLOAD is .577. This indicates that there is little or no relationship between SALES and WKLOAD. However, the simple correlation coefficients between SALES and the other seven independent variables range from .402 to .754, with associated p-values ranging from .046 to .000. This indicates the existence of potentially useful relationships between SALES and these seven independent variables.

While simple correlation coefficients (and scatter plots) give us a preliminary understanding of the data, they cannot be relied upon alone to tell us which independent variables are significantly related to the dependent variable. One reason for this is a condition called *multicollinearity.* **Multicollinearity** is said to exist among the independent variables in a regression situation if these independent variables are related to or dependent upon each other. One way to investigate multicollinearity is to examine the correlation matrix. To understand this, note that all of the simple correlation coefficients not located in the first column of this matrix measure the **simple correlations between the independent variables.** For example, the simple correlation coefficient between ACCTS and TIME is .758, which says that the ACCTS values increase as the TIME values increase. Such a relationship makes sense because it is logical that the longer a sales representative has been with the company, the more accounts he or she handles. Statisticians often regard multicollinearity in a data set to be severe if at least one simple correlation coefficient between the independent variables is at least .9. Since the largest such simple correlation coefficient in Figure 12.38 is .758, this is not true for the sales territory performance data. Note, however, that even moderate multicollinearity can be a potential problem. This will be demonstrated later using the sales territory performance data.

Another way to measure multicollinearity is to use **variance inflation factors.** Consider a regression model relating a dependent variable y to a set of independent variables $x_1, \ldots, x_{j-1}, x_j, x_{j+1}, \ldots, x_k$. The **variance inflation factor VIF_j** for the independent variable x_j in this set is denoted VIF_j and is defined by the equation

$$VIF_j = \frac{1}{1 - R_j^2}$$

where R_j^2 is the multiple coefficient of determination for the regression model that relates x_j to all the other independent variables $x_1, \ldots, x_{j-1}, x_{j+1}, \ldots, x_k$ in the set. For example, Figure 12.39 gives the MegaStat output of the t statistics, p-values, and variance inflation factors

FIGURE 12.39 MegaStat Output of the *t* Statistics, *p*-Values, and Variance Inflation Factors for the Sales Territory Performance Model
$$y = \beta_0 + \beta_1x_1 + \beta_2x_2 + \beta_3x_3 + \beta_4x_4 + \beta_5x_5 + \beta_6x_6 + \beta_7x_7 + \beta_8x_8 + \varepsilon$$

Regression output					confidence interval		
variables	coefficients	std. error	t (df = 16)	p-value	95% lower	95% upper	VIF
Intercept	−1,507.8137	778.6349	−1.936	.0707	−3,158.4457	142.8182	
Time	2.0096	1.9307	1.041	.3134	−2.0832	6.1024	3.343
MktPoten	0.0372	0.0082	4.536	.0003	0.0198	0.0546	1.978
Adver	0.1510	0.0471	3.205	.0055	0.0511	0.2509	1.910
MktShare	199.0235	67.0279	2.969	.0090	56.9307	341.1164	3.236
Change	290.8551	186.7820	1.557	.1390	−105.1049	686.8152	1.602
Accts	5.5510	4.7755	1.162	.2621	−4.5728	15.6747	5.639
WkLoad	19.7939	33.6767	0.588	.5649	−51.5975	91.1853	1.818
Rating	8.1893	128.5056	0.064	.9500	−264.2304	280.6090	1.809
							2.667 mean VIF

for the sales territory performance model that relates y to all eight independent variables. The largest variance inflation factor is $VIF_6 = 5.639$. To calculate VIF_6, MegaStat first calculates the multiple coefficient of determination for the regression model that relates x_6 to x_1, x_2, x_3, x_4, x_5, x_7, and x_8 to be $R_6^2 = .822673$. It then follows that

$$VIF_6 = \frac{1}{1 - R_6^2} = \frac{1}{1 - .822673} = 5.639$$

In general, if $R_j^2 = 0$, which says that x_j is not related to the other independent variables, then the variance inflation factor VIF_j equals 1. On the other hand, if $R_j^2 > 0$, which says that x_j is related to the other independent variables, then $(1 - R_j^2)$ is less than 1, making VIF_j greater than 1. Both the largest variance inflation factor among the independent variables and the mean VIF of the variance inflation factors for the independent variables indicate the severity of multicollinearity. Generally, the multicollinearity between independent variables is considered severe if

1 The largest variance inflation factor is greater than 10 (which means that the largest R_j^2 is greater than .9).

2 The mean VIF of the variance inflation factors is substantially greater than 1.

The largest variance inflation factor in Figure 12.39 is not greater than 10, and the average of the variance inflation factors, which is 2.667, would probably not be considered substantially greater than 1. Therefore, we would probably not consider the multicollinearity among the eight independent variables to be severe.

The reason that VIF_j is called the variance inflation factor is that it can be shown that, when VIF_j is greater than 1, then the standard deviation σ_{b_j} of the population of all possible values of the least squares point estimate b_j is likely to be inflated beyond its value when $R_j^2 = 0$. If σ_{b_j} is greatly inflated, two slightly different samples of values of the dependent variable can yield two substantially different values of b_j. To intuitively understand why strong multicollinearity can significantly affect the least squares point estimates, consider the so-called "picket fence" display on the page margin. This figure depicts two independent variables (x_1 and x_2) exhibiting strong multicollinearity (note that as x_1 increases, x_2 increases). The heights of the pickets on the fence represent the y observations. If we assume that the model

The picket fence display

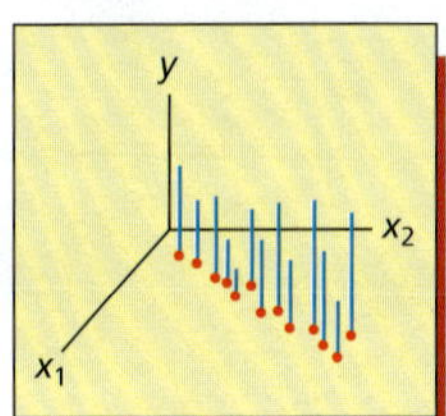

$$y = \beta_0 + \beta_1x_1 + \beta_2x_2 + \varepsilon$$

adequately describes this data, then calculating the least squares point estimates amounts to fitting a plane to the points on the top of the picket fence. Clearly, this plane would be quite unstable. That is, a slightly different height of one of the pickets (a slightly different y value) could cause the slant of the fitted plane (and the least squares point estimates that determine this slant) to radically change. It follows that, when strong multicollinearity exists, sampling variation can result in least squares point estimates that differ substantially from the true values of the regression parameters. In fact, some of the least squares point estimates may have a sign (positive or negative) that differs from the sign of the true value of the parameter (we will see an example of this in the exercises). Therefore, when strong multicollinearity exists, it is dangerous to individually interpret the least squares point estimates.

The most important problem caused by multicollinearity is that, even when multicollinearity is not severe, it can hinder our ability to use the *t* statistics and related *p*-values to assess the importance of the independent variables. Recall that we can reject H_0: $\beta_j = 0$ in favor of H_a: $\beta_j \neq 0$ at level of significance α if and only if the absolute value of the corresponding *t* statistic is greater than $t_{\alpha/2}$ based on $n - (k + 1)$ degrees of freedom, or, equivalently, if and only if the related *p*-value is less than α. Thus the larger (in absolute value) the *t* statistic is and the smaller the *p*-value is, the stronger is the evidence that we should reject H_0: $\beta_j = 0$ and the stronger is the evidence that the independent variable x_j is significant. When multicollinearity exists, the sizes of the *t* statistic and of the related *p*-value **measure the additional importance of the independent variable x_j over the combined importance of the other independent variables in the regression model.** Since two or more correlated independent variables contribute redundant information, multicollinearity often causes the *t* statistics obtained by relating a dependent variable to a set of correlated independent variables to be smaller (in absolute value) than the *t* statistics that would be obtained if separate regression analyses were run, where each separate regression analysis relates the dependent variable to a smaller set (for example, only one) of the correlated independent variables. Thus multicollinearity can cause some of the correlated independent variables to appear less important—in terms of having small absolute *t* statistics and large *p*-values—than they really are. Another way to understand this is to note that since multicollinearity inflates σ_{b_j}, it inflates the point estimate s_{b_j} of σ_{b_j}. Since $t = b_j/s_{b_j}$, an inflated value of s_{b_j} can (depending on the size of b_j) cause *t* to be small (and the related *p*-value to be large). This would suggest that x_j is not significant even though x_j may really be important.

For example, Figure 12.39 tells us that when we perform a regression analysis of the sales territory performance data using a model that relates *y* to all eight independent variables, the *p*-values related to TIME, MKTPOTEN, ADVER, MKTSHARE, CHANGE, ACCTS, WKLOAD, and RATING are, respectively, .3134, .0003, .0055, .0090, .1390, .2621, .5650, and .9500. By contrast, recall from Figure 12.8 (page 537) that when we perform a regression analysis of the sales territory performance data using a model that relates *y* to the first five independent variables, the *p*-values related to TIME, MKTPOTEN, ADVER, MKTSHARE, and CHANGE are, respectively, .0065, .0001, .0025, .0001, and .0530. Note that TIME (*p*-value = .0065) seems *highly significant* and CHANGE (*p*-value = .0530) seems *somewhat significant* in the five independent variable model. However, when we consider the model that uses all eight independent variables, TIME (*p*-value = .3134) seems *insignificant* and CHANGE (*p*-value = .1390) seems *somewhat insignificant.* The reason that TIME and CHANGE seem more significant in the five independent variable model is that, since this model uses fewer variables, TIME and CHANGE contribute less overlapping information and thus have more additional importance in this model.

Comparing regression models on the basis of R^2, *s*, adjusted R^2, prediction interval length, and the C statistic We have seen that when multicollinearity exists in a model, the *p*-value associated with an independent variable in the model measures the additional importance of the variable over the combined importance of the other variables in the model. Therefore, it can be difficult to use the *p*-values to determine which variables to retain in and which variables to remove from a model. The implication of this is that we need to evaluate more than the *additional importance* of each independent variable in a regression model. We also need to evaluate how well the independent variables *work together* to accurately describe, predict, and control the dependent variable. One way to do this is to determine if the *overall* model gives a high R^2 and $\bar{R}^2$, a small *s*, and short prediction intervals.

It can be proved that **adding any independent variable to a regression model, even an unimportant independent variable, will decrease the unexplained variation and will increase the explained variation.** Therefore, since the total variation $\Sigma(y_i - \bar{y})^2$ depends only on the observed *y* values and thus remains unchanged when we add an independent variable to a regression model, it follows that **adding any independent variable to a regression model will increase**

$$R^2 = \frac{\textbf{Explained variation}}{\textbf{Total variation}}$$

This implies that R^2 cannot tell us (by decreasing) that adding an independent variable is undesirable. That is, although we wish to obtain a model with a large R^2, there are better criteria than R^2 that can be used to *compare* regression models.

One better criterion is the standard error

$$s = \sqrt{\frac{SSE}{n - (k + 1)}}$$

When we add an independent variable to a regression model, the number of model parameters $(k + 1)$ increases by one, and thus the number of degrees of freedom $n - (k + 1)$ decreases by one. If the decrease in $n - (k + 1)$, which is used in the denominator to calculate s, is proportionally more than the decrease in SSE (the unexplained variation) that is caused by adding the independent variable to the model, then s will increase. **If s increases, this tells us that we should not add the independent variable to the model.** To see one reason why, consider the formula for the prediction interval for y

$$[\hat{y} \pm t_{\alpha/2} s\sqrt{1 + \text{Distance value}}]$$

Since *adding an independent variable* to a model decreases the number of degrees of freedom, adding the variable will increase the $t_{\alpha/2}$ point used to calculate the prediction interval. To understand this, look at any column of the t table in Table A.4 (page 825) and scan from the bottom of the column to the top—you can see that the t points increase as the degrees of freedom decrease. It can also be shown that adding any independent variable to a regression model will not decrease (and usually increases) the distance value. Therefore, since adding an independent variable increases $t_{\alpha/2}$ and does not decrease the distance value, **if s increases, the length of the prediction interval for y will increase.** This means the model will predict less accurately and thus we should not add the independent variable.

On the other hand, if adding an independent variable to a regression model **decreases s,** the length of a prediction interval for y will decrease if and only if the decrease in s is enough to offset the increase in $t_{\alpha/2}$ and the (possible) increase in the distance value. Therefore, **an independent variable should not be included in a final regression model unless it reduces s enough to reduce the length of the desired prediction interval for y.** However, we must balance the length of the prediction interval, or in general, the "goodness" of any criterion, against the difficulty and expense of using the model. For instance, predicting y requires knowing the corresponding values of the independent variables. So we must decide whether including an independent variable reduces s and prediction interval lengths enough to offset the potential errors caused by possible inaccurate determination of values of the independent variables, or the possible expense of determining these values. If adding an independent variable provides prediction intervals that are only slightly shorter while making the model more difficult and/or more expensive to use, we might decide that including the variable is not desirable.

Since a key factor is the length of the prediction intervals provided by the model, one might wonder why we do not simply make direct comparisons of prediction interval lengths (without looking at s). It is useful to compare interval lengths, but these lengths depend on the distance value, which depends on how far the values of the independent variables we wish to predict for are from the center of the experimental region. We often wish to compute prediction intervals for several different combinations of values of the independent variables (and thus for several different values of the distance value). Thus we would compute prediction intervals having slightly different lengths. However, the standard error s is a constant factor with respect to the length of prediction intervals (as long as we are considering the same regression model). Thus it is common practice to compare regression models on the basis of s (and s^2). Finally, note that it can be shown that the standard error s decreases if and only if $\bar{R}^2$ (adjusted R^2) increases. It follows that, if we are comparing regression models, the model that gives the smallest s gives the largest $\bar{R}^2$.

Example 12.17 The Sales Territory Performance Case 

Figure 12.40 gives MINITAB and MegaStat output resulting from calculating R^2, $\bar{R}^2$, and s for **all possible regression models** based on all possible combinations of the eight independent variables in the sales territory performance situation (the values of C_p on the output will be explained after we complete this example). The MINITAB output gives the two best models of

FIGURE 12.40 MINITAB and MegaStat Output of Some of the Best Sales Territory Performance Regression Models

(a) The MINITAB output of the two best models of each size

Vars	R-Sq	R-Sq(adj)	Mallows C-p	S	Time	MktPoten	Adver	MktShare	Change	Accts	WkLoad	Rating
1	56.8	55.0	67.6	881.09						X		
1	38.8	36.1	104.6	1049.3	X							
2	77.5	75.5	27.2	650.39			X			X		
2	74.6	72.3	33.1	691.10		X		X				
3	84.9	82.7	14.0	545.51		X	X	X				
3	82.8	80.3	18.4	582.64		X	X			X		
4	90.0	88.1	5.4	453.84		X	X	X		X		
4	89.6	87.5	6.4	463.95	X	X	X	X				
5	91.5	89.3	4.4	430.23	X	X	X	X	X			
5	91.2	88.9	5.0	436.75		X	X	X	X	X		
6	92.0	89.4	5.4	428.00	X	X	X	X	X	X		
6	91.6	88.9	6.1	438.20		X	X	X	X	X	X	
7	92.2	89.0	7.0	435.67	X	X	X	X	X	X	X	
7	92.0	88.8	7.3	440.30	X	X	X	X	X	X		X
8	92.2	88.3	9.0	449.03	X	X	X	X	X	X	X	X

(b) The MegaStat output of the best single model of each size

Nvar	Time	MktPoten	Adver	MktShare	Change	Accts	WkLoad	Rating	s	Adj R^2	R^2	Cp	p-value
1						.0000			881.093	.550	.568	67.558	1.35E-05
2			.0002			.0000			650.392	.755	.775	27.156	7.45E-08
3		.0000	.0011	.0000					545.515	.827	.849	13.995	8.43E-09
4		.0001	.0001	.0011		.0043			453.836	.881	.900	5.431	9.56E-10
5	.0065	.0000	.0025	.0000	.0530				430.232	.893	.915	4.443	1.59E-09
6	.1983	.0001	.0018	.0004	.0927	.2881			428.004	.894	.920	5.354	6.14E-09
7	.2868	.0002	.0027	.0066	.0897	.2339	.5501		435.674	.890	.922	7.004	3.21E-08
8	.3134	.0003	.0055	.0090	.1390	.2621	.5649	.9500	449.026	.883	.922	9.000	1.82E-07

(c) The MegaStat output of the best eight models

Nvar	Time	MktPoten	Adver	MktShare	Change	Accts	WkLoad	Rating	s	Adj R^2	R^2	Cp	p-value
6	.1983	.0001	.0018	.0004	.0927	.2881			428.004	.894	.920	5.354	6.14E-09
5	.0065	.0000	.0025	.0000	.0530				430.232	.893	.915	4.443	1.59E-09
7	.2868	.0002	.0027	.0066	.0897	.2339	.5501		435.674	.890	.922	7.004	3.21E-08
5		.0001	.0006	.0006	.1236	.0089			436.746	.889	.912	4.975	2.10E-09
6		.0002	.0006	.0098	.1035	.0070	.3621		438.197	.889	.916	6.142	9.31E-09
7	.2204	.0002	.0040	.0006	.1449	.3194		.9258	440.297	.888	.920	7.345	3.82E-08
6	.0081	.0000	.0054	.0000	.1143			.7692	440.936	.887	.915	6.357	1.04E-08
6	.0083	.0000	.0044	.0000	.0629		.9474		441.966	.887	.915	6.438	1.08E-08

each size in terms of s and $\bar{R}^2$—the two best one-variable models, the two best two-variable models, the two best three-variable models, and so on. The first MegaStat output gives the best single model of each size, and the second MegaStat output gives the eight best models of any size, in terms of s and $\bar{R}^2$. The MegaStat output also gives the p-values for the variables in each model. Examining the output, we see that the three models having the smallest values of s and largest values of $\bar{R}^2$ are

1 The six-variable model that contains

TIME, MKTPOTEN, ADVER, MKTSHARE, CHANGE, ACCTS

and has $s = 428.004$ and $\bar{R}^2 = 89.4$; we refer to this model as Model 1.

2 The five-variable model that contains

TIME, MKTPOTEN, ADVER, MKTSHARE, CHANGE

and has $s = 430.232$ and $\bar{R}^2 = 89.3$; we refer to this model as Model 2.

3 The seven-variable model that contains

TIME, MKTPOTEN, ADVER, MKTSHARE, CHANGE, ACCTS, WKLOAD

and has $s = 435.674$ and $\bar{R}^2 = 89.0$; we refer to this model as Model 3.

To see that s can increase when we add an independent variable to a regression model, note that s increases from 428.004 to 435.674 when we add WKLOAD to Model 1 to form Model 3. In this case, although it can be verified that adding WKLOAD decreases the unexplained variation from 3,297,279.3342 to 3,226,756.2751, this decrease has not been enough to offset the change in the denominator of

$$s^2 = \frac{SSE}{n - (k + 1)}$$

which decreases from $25 - 7 = 18$ to $25 - 8 = 17$. To see that prediction interval lengths might increase even though s decreases, consider adding ACCTS to Model 2 to form Model 1. This decreases s from 430.232 to 428.004. However, consider a questionable sales representative for whom TIME = 85.42, MKTPOTEN = 35,182.73, ADVER = 7,281.65, MKTSHARE = 9.64, CHANGE = .28, and ACCTS = 120.61. The 95 percent prediction interval given by Model 2 for sales corresponding to this combination of values of the independent variables is [3,233.59, 5,129.89] and has length 5,129.89 − 3,233.59 = 1896.3. The 95 percent prediction interval given by Model 1 for such sales is [3,193.86, 5,093.14] and has length 5,093.14 − 3,193.86 = 1,899.28. In other words, the slight decrease in s accomplished by adding ACCTS to Model 2 to form Model 1 is not enough to offset the increases in $t_{\alpha/2}$ and the distance value (which can be shown to increase from .109 to .115), and thus the length of the prediction interval given by Model 1 increases. In addition, the extra independent variable ACCTS in Model 1 has a p-value of .2881. Therefore, we conclude that Model 2 is better than Model 1 and is, in fact, the "best" sales territory performance model (using only linear terms).

Another quantity that can be used for comparing regression models is called the **C statistic** (also often called the **C_p statistic**). To show how to calculate the C statistic, suppose that we wish to choose an appropriate set of independent variables from p potential independent variables. We first calculate the mean square error, which we denote as s_p^2, for the model using all p potential independent variables. Then, if SSE denotes the unexplained variation for another particular model that has k independent variables, it follows that the C statistic for this model is

$$C = \frac{SSE}{s_p^2} - [n - 2(k + 1)]$$

For example, consider the sales territory performance case. It can be verified that the mean square error for the model using all $p = 8$ independent variables is 201,621.21 and that the SSE for the model using the first $k = 5$ independent variables (Model 2 in the previous example) is 3,516,812.7933. It follows that the C statistic for this latter model is

$$C = \frac{3{,}516{,}812.7933}{201{,}621.21} - [25 - 2(5 + 1)] = 4.4$$

Since the C statistic for a given model is a function of the model's SSE, and since we want SSE to be small, **we want C to be small.** Although adding an unimportant independent variable to a regression model will decrease SSE, adding such a variable can increase C. This can happen when the decrease in SSE caused by the addition of the extra independent variable is not enough to offset the decrease in $n - 2(k + 1)$ caused by the addition of the extra independent variable (which increases k by 1). It should be noted that although adding an unimportant independent variable to a regression model can increase both s^2 and C, there is no exact relationship between s^2 and C.

While we want C to be small, it can be shown from the theory behind the C statistic that **we also wish to find a model for which the C statistic roughly equals $k + 1$,** the number of parameters in the model. **If a model has a C statistic substantially greater than $k + 1$, it can be shown that this model has substantial *bias* and is undesirable.** Thus, although we want to find a model for which C is as small as possible, if C for such a model is substantially greater than $k + 1$, we may prefer to choose a different model for which C is slightly larger and more nearly equal to the number of parameters in that (different) model. **If a particular model has a small value of C and C for this model is less than $k + 1$, then the model should be considered desirable.** Finally, it should be noted that for the model that includes all p potential independent variables (and thus utilizes $p + 1$ parameters), it can be shown that $C = p + 1$.

If we examine Figure 12.40, we see that Model 2 of the previous example has the smallest C statistic. The C statistic for this model equals 4.4. Since $C = 4.4$ is less than $k + 1 = 6$, the model is not biased. Therefore, this model should be considered best with respect to the C statistic.

Thus far we have considered how to find the best model using linear independent variables. In supplementary Exercise 12.74 we illustrate, using the sales territory performance case, a systematic procedure for deciding which squared and interaction terms (see Sections 12.8 and 12.9) to include in a regression model. We have found that this systematic procedure often identifies important squared and interaction terms that are not identified by simply using scatter and residual plots. After finding one or more potential final regression models, we use the techniques of Sections 11.9 and 12.13 to check the regression assumptions and the techniques of Section 12.14 to identify outlying and influential observations. Based on this analysis, we make needed improvements and eventually find one or more final regression models that can be used to describe, predict, and control the dependent variable.

Stepwise regression and backward elimination In some situations it is useful to employ an **iterative model selection procedure,** where at each step a single independent variable is added to or deleted from a regression model, and a new regression model is evaluated. We discuss here two such procedures—**stepwise regression** and **backward elimination.**

There are slight variations in the way different computer packages carry out **stepwise regression.** Assuming that y is the dependent variable and $x_1, x_2, \ldots, x_p$ are the p potential independent variables (where p will generally be large), we explain how most of the computer packages perform stepwise regression. Stepwise regression uses t statistics (and related p-values) to determine the significance of the independent variables in various regression models. In this context we say that **the t statistic indicates that the independent variable x_j is significant at the α level if and only if the related p-value is less than α.** Then stepwise regression is carried out as follows.

Choice of α_{entry} and α_{stay} Before beginning the stepwise procedure we choose a value of α_{entry}, which we call *the probability of a Type I error related to entering an independent variable into the regression model.* We also choose a value of α_{stay}, which we call *the probability of a Type I error related to retaining an independent variable that was previously entered into the model.* Although there are many considerations in choosing these values, it is common practice to set both α_{entry} and α_{stay} equal to .05 or .10.

Step 1 The stepwise procedure considers the p possible one-independent-variable regression models of the form

$$y = \beta_0 + \beta_1 x_j + \varepsilon$$

Each different model includes a different potential independent variable. For each model the t statistic (and p-value) related to testing H_0: $\beta_1 = 0$ versus H_a: $\beta_1 \neq 0$ is calculated. Denoting the independent variable giving the largest absolute value of the t statistic (and the smallest p-value) by the symbol $x_{[1]}$, we consider the model

$$y = \beta_0 + \beta_1 x_{[1]} + \varepsilon$$

If the t statistic does not indicate that $x_{[1]}$ is significant at the α_{entry} level, then the stepwise procedure terminates by concluding that none of the independent variables are significant at the α_{entry} level. If the t statistic indicates that the independent variable $x_{[1]}$ is significant at the α_{entry} level, then $x_{[1]}$ is retained for use in Step 2.

Step 2 The stepwise procedure considers the $p - 1$ possible two-independent-variable regression models of the form

$$y = \beta_0 + \beta_1 x_{[1]} + \beta_2 x_j + \varepsilon$$

Each different model includes $x_{[1]}$, the independent variable chosen in Step 1, and a different potential independent variable chosen from the remaining $p - 1$ independent variables that were not chosen in Step 1. For each model the t statistic (and p-value) related to testing H_0: $\beta_2 = 0$ versus H_a: $\beta_2 \neq 0$ is calculated. Denoting the independent variable giving the largest absolute value of the t statistic (and the smallest p-value) by the symbol $x_{[2]}$, we consider the model

$$y = \beta_0 + \beta_1 x_{[1]} + \beta_2 x_{[2]} + \varepsilon$$

If the t statistic indicates that $x_{[2]}$ is significant at the α_{entry} level, then $x_{[2]}$ is retained in this model, and the stepwise procedure checks to see whether $x_{[1]}$ should be allowed to stay in the model. This check should be made because multicollinearity will probably cause the t statistic related to the importance of $x_{[1]}$ to change when $x_{[2]}$ is added to the model. If the t statistic does not indicate that $x_{[1]}$ is significant at the α_{stay} level, then the stepwise procedure returns to the beginning of Step 2. Starting with a new one-independent-variable model that uses the new significant independent variable $x_{[2]}$, the stepwise procedure attempts to find a new two-independent-variable model

$$y = \beta_0 + \beta_1 x_{[2]} + \beta_2 x_j + \varepsilon$$

If the t statistic indicates that $x_{[1]}$ is significant at the α_{stay} level in the model

$$y = \beta_0 + \beta_1 x_{[1]} + \beta_2 x_{[2]} + \varepsilon$$

then both the independent variables $x_{[1]}$ and $x_{[2]}$ are retained for use in further steps.

Further steps The stepwise procedure continues by adding independent variables one at a time to the model. At each step an independent variable is added to the model if it has the largest (in absolute value) t statistic of the independent variables not in the model and if its t statistic indicates that it is significant at the α_{entry} level. After adding an independent variable the stepwise procedure checks all the independent variables already included in the model and removes an independent variable if it has the smallest (in absolute value) t statistic of the independent variables already included in the model and if its t statistic indicates that it is not significant at the α_{stay} level. This removal procedure is sequentially continued, and only after the necessary removals are made does the stepwise procedure attempt to add another independent variable to the model. The stepwise procedure terminates when all the independent variables not in the model are insignificant at the α_{entry} level or when the variable to be added to the model is the one just removed from it.

For example, again consider the sales territory performance data. We let $x_1, x_2, x_3, x_4, x_5, x_6, x_7$, and x_8 be the eight potential independent variables employed in the stepwise procedure. Figure 12.41(a) gives the MINITAB output of the stepwise regression employing these independent variables where both α_{entry} and α_{stay} have been set equal to .10. The stepwise procedure

1 Adds ACCTS (x_6) on the first step.
2 Adds ADVER (x_3) and retains ACCTS on the second step.
3 Adds MKTPOTEN (x_2) and retains ACCTS and ADVER on the third step.
4 Adds MKTSHARE (x_4) and retains ACCTS, ADVER, and MKTPOTEN on the fourth step.

The procedure terminates after step 4 when no more independent variables can be added. Therefore, the stepwise procedure arrives at the model that utilizes x_2, x_3, x_4, and x_6.

To carry out **backward elimination,** we perform a regression analysis by using a regression model containing all the p potential independent variables. Then the independent variable having the smallest (in absolute value) t statistic is chosen. If the t statistic indicates that this independent variable is significant at the α_{stay} level (α_{stay} is chosen prior to the beginning of the procedure), then the procedure terminates by choosing the regression model containing all p independent variables. If this independent variable is not significant at the α_{stay} level, then it is removed from the model, and a regression analysis is performed by using a regression model containing all the remaining independent variables. The procedure continues by removing independent variables one at a time from the model. At each step an independent variable is removed from the model if it has the smallest (in absolute value) t statistic of the independent variables remaining in the model and if it is not significant at the α_{stay} level. The procedure terminates when no independent variable remaining in the model can be removed. Backward elimination is generally considered a reasonable procedure, especially for analysts who like to start with all possible independent variables in the model so that they will not "miss any important variables."

FIGURE 12.41 The MINITAB Output of Stepwise Regression and Backward Elimination for the Sales Territory Performance Problem

(a) Stepwise regression ($\alpha_{entry} = \alpha_{stay} = .10$)

```
Alpha-to-Enter: 0.1  Alpha-to-Remove: 0.1
Response is Sales on 8 predictors, with N = 25

Step              1        2        3         4
Constant     709.32    50.30  -327.23  -1441.94

Accts          21.7     19.0     15.6       9.2
T-Value        5.50     6.41     5.19      3.22
P-Value       0.000    0.000    0.000     0.004

Adver                  0.227    0.216     0.175
T-Value                 4.50     4.77      4.74
P-Value                0.000    0.000     0.000

MktPoten                       0.0219    0.0382
T-Value                          2.53      4.79
P-Value                         0.019     0.000

MktShare                                    190
T-Value                                    3.82
P-Value                                   0.001

S               881      650      583       454
R-Sq          56.85    77.51    82.77     90.04
R-Sq(adj)     54.97    75.47    80.31     88.05
Mallows C-p    67.6     27.2     18.4       5.4
```

(b) Backward elimination ($\alpha_{stay} = .05$)

```
Backward elimination.  Alpha-to-Remove: 0.05
Response is Sales on 8 predictors, with N = 25

Step            1        2        3        4        5
Constant    -1508    -1486    -1165    -1114    -1312

Time          2.0      2.0      2.3      3.6      3.8
T-Value      1.04     1.10     1.34     3.06     3.01
P-Value     0.313    0.287    0.198    0.006    0.007

MktPoten   0.0372   0.0373   0.0383   0.0421   0.0444
T-Value      4.54     4.75     5.07     6.25     6.20
P-Value     0.000    0.000    0.000    0.000    0.000

Adver       0.151    0.152    0.141    0.129    0.152
T-Value      3.21     3.51     3.66     3.48     4.01
P-Value     0.006    0.003    0.002    0.003    0.001

MktShare      199      198      222      257      259
T-Value      2.97     3.09     4.38     6.57     6.15
P-Value     0.009    0.007    0.000    0.000    0.000

Change        291      296      285      325
T-Value      1.56     1.80     1.78     2.06
P-Value     0.139    0.090    0.093    0.053

Accts         5.6      5.6      4.4
T-Value      1.16     1.23     1.09
P-Value     0.262    0.234    0.288

WkLoad         20       20
T-Value      0.59     0.61
P-Value     0.565    0.550

Rating          8
T-Value      0.06
P-Value     0.950

S             449      436      428      430      464
R-Sq        92.20    92.20    92.03    91.50    89.60
R-Sq(adj)   88.31    88.99    89.38    89.26    87.52
Mallows C-p   9.0      7.0      5.4      4.4      6.4
```

To illustrate backward elimination, we first note that choosing the independent variable that has the smallest (in absolute value) *t* statistic in a model is equivalent to choosing the independent variable that has the largest *p*-value in the model. With this in mind, Figure 12.41(b) gives the MINITAB output of a backward elimination of the sales territory performance data. Here the backward elimination uses $\alpha_{stay} = .05$, begins with the model using all eight independent variables, and removes (in order) RATING (x_8), then WKLOAD (x_7), then ACCTS (x_6), and finally CHANGE (x_5). The procedure terminates when no independent variable remaining can be removed—that is, when no independent variable has a related *p*-value greater than $\alpha_{stay} = .05$—and arrives at a model that uses TIME (x_1), MKTPOTEN (x_2), ADVER (x_3), and MKTSHARE (x_4). This model has an *s* of 464 and an $\bar{R}^2$ of .8752 and is inferior to the model arrived at by stepwise regression, which has an *s* of 454 and an $\bar{R}^2$ of .8805 [see Figure 12.41(a)]. However, the backward elimination process allows us to find a model that is better than either of these. If we look at the model considered by backward elimination after RATING (x_8), WKLOAD (x_7), and ACCTS (x_6) have been removed, we have the model using x_1, x_2, x_3, x_4, and x_5. This model has an *s* of 430 and an $\bar{R}^2$ of .8926, and in Example 12.17 we reasoned that this model is perhaps the best sales territory performance model. Interestingly, this is the model that backward elimination would arrive at if we were to set α_{stay} equal to .10 rather than .05—note that this model has no *p*-values greater than .10.

The sales territory performance example brings home two important points. First, the models obtained by backward elimination and stepwise regression depend on the choices of α_{entry} and α_{stay} (whichever is appropriate). Second, it is best not to think of these methods as "automatic model-building procedures." Rather, they should be regarded as processes that allow us to find and evaluate a variety of model choices.

Exercises for Section 12.12

CONCEPTS

12.53 What is multicollinearity? What problems can be caused by multicollinearity?

12.54 Discuss how we compare regression models.

METHODS AND APPLICATIONS

12.55 THE HOSPITAL LABOR NEEDS CASE HospLab2

Recall that Table 12.5 (page 535) presents data concerning the need for labor in 16 U.S. Navy hospitals. This table gives values of the dependent variable Hours (monthly labor hours) and of the independent variables Xray (monthly X-ray exposures), BedDays (monthly occupied bed days—a hospital has one occupied bed day if one bed is occupied for an entire day), and Length (average length of patients' stay, in days). The data in Table 12.5 are part of a larger data set analyzed by the navy. The complete data set consists of two additional independent variables—Load (average daily patient load) and Pop (eligible population in the area, in thousands)—values of which are given on the page margin. Figure 12.42 gives MINITAB and MegaStat output of multicollinearity analysis and model building for the complete hospital labor needs data set.

a Find the three largest simple correlation coefficients between the independent variables in Figure 12.42(a). Also, find the three largest variance inflation factors in Figure 12.42(b).

b Based on your answers to part *a*, which independent variables are most strongly involved in multicollinearity?

c Do any least squares point estimates have a sign (positive or negative) that is different from what we would intuitively expect—another indication of multicollinearity?

Load	Pop
15.57	18.0
44.02	9.5
20.42	12.8
18.74	36.7
49.20	35.7
44.92	24.0
55.48	43.3
59.28	46.7
94.39	78.7
128.02	180.5
96.00	60.9
131.42	103.7
127.21	126.8
409.20	169.4
463.70	331.4
510.22	371.6

FIGURE 12.42 MINITAB and MegaStat Output of Multicollinearity Analysis and Model Building for the Hospital Labor Needs Data

(a) The MegaStat output of a correlation matrix

	Load	Xray	BedDays	Pop	Length	Hours
Load	1.0000					
Xray	.9051	1.0000				
BedDays	.9999	.9048	1.0000			
Pop	.9353	.9121	.9328	1.0000		
Length	.6610	.4243	.6609	.4515	1.0000	
Hours	.9886	.9425	.9889	.9465	.5603	1.0000

16 sample size

±.497 critical value .05 (two-tail)

±.623 critical value .01 (two-tail)

(b) The MINITAB output of the variance inflation factors

Predictor	Coef	SE Coef	T	P	VIF
Constant	2270.4	670.8	3.38	0.007	
Load	-9.30	60.81	-0.15	0.882	9334.5
XRay	0.04112	0.01368	3.01	0.013	8.1
BedDays	1.413	1.925	0.73	0.480	8684.2
Pop	-3.223	4.474	-0.72	0.488	23.0
Length	-467.9	131.6	-3.55	0.005	4.2

(c) The MegaStat output of the best single model of each size

Nvar	Load	Xray	BedDays	Pop	Length	s	Adj R^2	R^2	Cp	p-value
1			.0000			856.707	.976	.978	52.313	5.51E-13
2			.0000		.0001	489.126	.992	.993	9.467	7.41E-15
3		.0120	.0000		.0012	387.160	.995	.996	3.258	9.92E-15
4		.0091	.0000	.2690	.0013	381.555	.995	.997	4.023	1.86E-13
5	.8815	.0132	.4799	.4878	.0052	399.712	.995	.997	6.000	5.65E-12

(d) The MegaStat output of the best five models

Nvar	Load	Xray	BedDays	Pop	Length	s	Adj R^2	R^2	Cp	p-value
4		.0091	.0000	.2690	.0013	381.555	.995	.997	4.023	1.86E-13
3		.0120	.0000		.0012	387.160	.995	.996	3.258	9.92E-15
4	.3981	.0121	.1381		.0018	390.876	.995	.996	4.519	2.43E-13
4	.0000	.0097		.1398	.0011	391.236	.995	.996	4.538	2.45E-13
5	.8815	.0132	.4799	.4878	.0052	399.712	.995	.997	6.000	5.65E-12

FIGURE 12.43 MINITAB Output of a Stepwise Regression and a Backward Elimination of the Hospital Labor Needs Data

(a) Stepwise regression ($\alpha_{entry} = \alpha_{stay} = .10$)

```
Step              1         2         3
Constant     -70.23   2741.24   1946.80

BedDays       1.101     1.223     1.039
T-Value       24.87     36.30     15.39
P-Value       0.000     0.000     0.000

Length                   -572      -414
T-Value                 -5.47     -4.20
P-Value                 0.000     0.001

XRay                              0.039
T-Value                            2.96
P-Value                           0.012

S               857       489       387
R-Sq          97.79     99.33     99.61
```

(b) Backward elimination ($\alpha_{stay} = .05$)

```
Step           1        2        3
Constant    2270     2311     1947

Load          -9
T-Value    -0.15
P-Value    0.882

XRay       0.041    0.041    0.039
T-Value     3.01     3.16     2.96
P-Value    0.013    0.009    0.012

BedDays    1.413    1.119    1.039
T-Value     0.73    11.74    15.39
P-Value    0.480    0.000    0.000

Pop         -3.2     -3.7
T-Value    -0.72    -1.16
P-Value    0.488    0.269

Length      -468     -477     -414
T-Value    -3.55    -4.28    -4.20
P-Value    0.005    0.001    0.001

S            400      382      387
R-Sq       99.66    99.65    99.61
```

d The *p*-value associated with *F*(model) for the model in Figure 12.42(b) is less than .0001. In general, if the *p*-value associated with *F*(model) is much smaller than any of the *p*-values associated with the independent variables, this is another indication of multicollinearity. Is this true in this situation?

e Figure 12.42(c) and (d) indicate that the two best hospital labor needs models are the model using Xray, BedDays, Pop, and Length, which we will call Model 1, and the model using Xray, BedDays, and Length, which we will call Model 2. Which model gives the smallest value of s and the largest value of $\bar{R}^2$? Which model gives the smallest value of C? Consider a questionable hospital for which Xray = 56,194, BedDays = 14,077.88, Pop = 329.7, and Length = 6.89. The 95 percent prediction intervals given by Models 1 and 2 for labor hours corresponding to this combination of values of the independent variables are, respectively, [14,888.43, 16,861.30] and [14,906.24, 16,886.26]. Which model gives the shortest prediction interval?

TABLE 12.18 Prescription Sales Data PreSales

Pharmacy	Sales, y	Floor Space, x_1	Prescription Percentage, x_2	Parking, x_3	Income, x_4	Shopping Center, x_5
1	22	4,900	9	40	18	1
2	19	5,800	10	50	20	1
3	24	5,000	11	55	17	1
4	28	4,400	12	30	19	0
5	18	3,850	13	42	10	0
6	21	5,300	15	20	22	1
7	29	4,100	20	25	8	0
8	15	4,700	22	60	15	1
9	12	5,600	24	45	16	1
10	14	4,900	27	82	14	1
11	18	3,700	28	56	12	0
12	19	3,800	31	38	8	0
13	15	2,400	36	35	6	0
14	22	1,800	37	28	4	0
15	13	3,100	40	43	6	0
16	16	2,300	41	20	5	0
17	8	4,400	42	46	7	1
18	6	3,300	42	15	4	0
19	7	2,900	45	30	9	1
20	17	2,400	46	16	3	0

FIGURE 12.44 The MegaStat Output of the Single Best Model of Each Size for the Prescription Sales Data

Nvar	FloorSpace	Presc.Pct	Parking	Income	ShopCntr?	s	Adj R^2	R^2	Cp	p-value
1		.0014				4.835	.408	.439	10.171	.0014
2	.0035	.0000				3.842	.626	.666	1.606	.0001
3	.1523	.0002			.2716	3.809	.633	.691	2.436	.0002
4	.1997	.0003	.5371		.3424	3.883	.618	.699	4.062	.0008
5	.2095	.0087	.5819	.8066	.3564	4.010	.593	.700	6.000	.0025

f Consider Figure 12.43. Which model is chosen by both stepwise regression and backward elimination? Overall, which model seems best?

12.56 Market Planning, Inc., a marketing research firm, has obtained the prescription sales data in Table 12.18 for $n = 20$ independent pharmacies.[3] In this table y is the average weekly prescription sales over the past year (in units of \$1,000), x_1 is the floor space (in square feet), x_2 is the percentage of floor space allocated to the prescription department, x_3 is the number of parking spaces available to the store, x_4 is the weekly per capita income for the surrounding community (in units of \$100), and x_5 is a **dummy variable** that equals 1 if the pharmacy is located in a shopping center and 0 otherwise. Use the MegaStat output in Figure 12.44 to discuss why the model using FloorSpace and Pres.Pct might be the best model describing prescription sales. The least squares point estimates of the parameters of this model can be calculated to be $b_0 = 48.2909$, $b_1 = -.003842$, and $b_2 = -.5819$. Discuss what b_1 and b_2 say about obtaining high prescription sales. PreSales

12.13 Residual Analysis in Multiple Regression (Optional)

CHAPTER 17

In Section 11.9 we showed how to use residual analysis to check the regression assumptions for a simple linear regression model. In multiple regression we proceed similarly. Specifically, for a multiple regression model we plot the residuals given by the model against (1) values of each independent variable, (2) values of the predicted value of the dependent variable, and (3) the time order in which the data have been observed (if the regression data are time series data). A fanning-out pattern on a residual plot indicates an increasing error variance; a funneling-in pattern indicates a decreasing error variance. Both violate the constant variance assumption. A curved pattern on a residual plot indicates that the functional form of the regression model is incorrect. If the regression data are time series data, a cyclical pattern on the residual plot versus time suggests positive autocorrelation, while an alternating pattern suggests negative autocorrelation. Both violate the independence assumption. On the other hand, if all residual plots have (at least approximately) a horizontal band appearance, then it is reasonable to believe that the constant variance, correct functional form, and independence assumptions approximately hold. To check the normality assumption, we can construct a histogram, stem-and-leaf display, and normal plot of the residuals. The histogram and stem-and-leaf display should look bell-shaped and symmetric about 0; the normal plot should have a straight-line appearance.

To illustrate these ideas, consider the sales territory performance data in Table 12.2 (page 533). Figure 12.8 (page 540) gives the MegaStat output of a regression analysis of these data using the model

$$y = \beta_0 + \beta_1 x_1 + \beta_2 x_2 + \beta_3 x_3 + \beta_4 x_4 + \beta_5 x_5 + \varepsilon$$

The least squares point estimates on the output give the prediction equation

$$\hat{y} = -1{,}113.7879 + 3.6121x_1 + .0421x_2 + .1289x_3 + 256.9555x_4 + 324.5334x_5$$

Using this prediction equation, we can calculate the predicted sales values and residuals given on the MegaStat output of Figure 12.45. For example, observation 10 on this output corresponds to a sales representative for whom $x_1 = 105.69$, $x_2 = 42{,}053.24$, $x_3 = 5{,}673.11$, $x_4 = 8.85$, and $x_5 = .31$. If we insert these values into the prediction equation, we obtain a predicted sales value of $\hat{y}_{10} = 4{,}143.597$. Since the actual sales for the sales representative are $y_{10} = 4{,}876.370$, the residual e_{10} equals the difference between $y_{10} = 4{,}876.370$ and $\hat{y}_{10} = 4{,}143.597$, which is 732.773. The

[3] This problem is taken from an example in L. Ott, *An Introduction to Statistical Methods and Data Analysis*, 2nd ed. (Boston: PWS-KENT Publishing Company, 1987). Used with permission.

FIGURE 12.45 MegaStat Output of the Sales Territory Performance Model Residuals

Observation	Sales	Predicted	Residual
1	3,669.880	3,504.990	164.890
2	3,473.950	3,901.180	−427.230
3	2,295.100	2,774.866	−479.766
4	4,675.560	4,911.872	−236.312
5	6,125.960	5,415.196	710.764
6	2,134.940	2,026.090	108.850
7	5,031.660	5,126.127	−94.467
8	3,367.450	3,106.925	260.525
9	6,519.450	6,055.297	464.153
10	4,876.370	4,143.597	732.773
11	2,468.270	2,503.165	−34.895
12	2,533.310	1,827.065	706.245
13	2,408.110	2,478.083	−69.973
14	2,337.380	2,351.344	−13.964
15	4,586.950	4,797.688	−210.738
16	2,729.240	2,904.099	−174.859
17	3,289.400	3,362.660	−73.260
18	2,800.780	2,907.376	−106.596
19	3,264.200	3,625.026	−360.826
20	3,453.620	4,056.443	−602.823
21	1,741.450	1,409.835	331.615
22	2,035.750	2,494.101	−458.351
23	1,578.000	1,617.561	−39.561
24	4,167.440	4,574.903	−407.463
25	2,799.970	2,488.700	311.270

FIGURE 12.46 MegaStat Residual Plots for the Sales Territory Performance Model

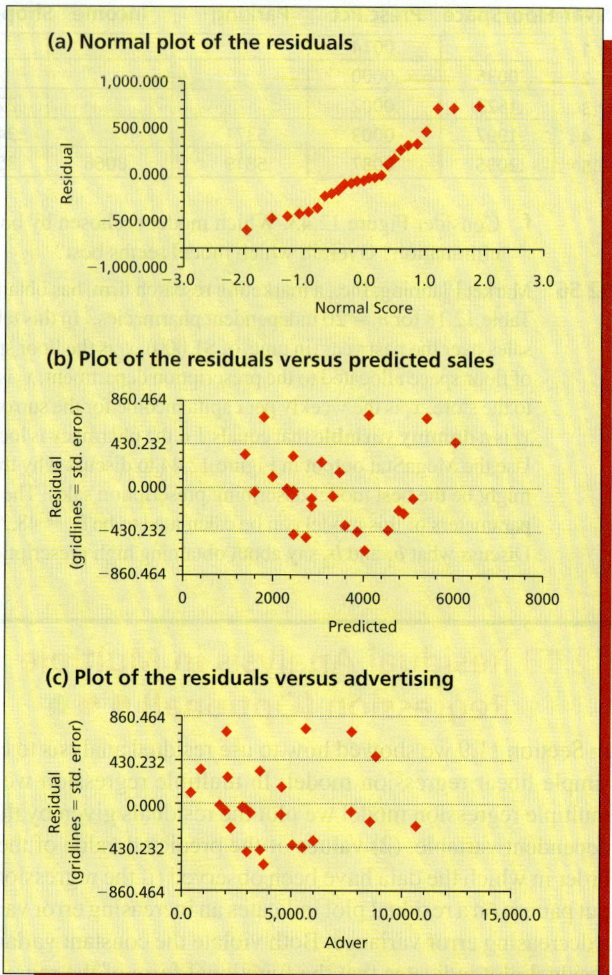

FIGURE 12.47 MINITAB Plot of the Quadratic QHIC Model Residuals Versus x

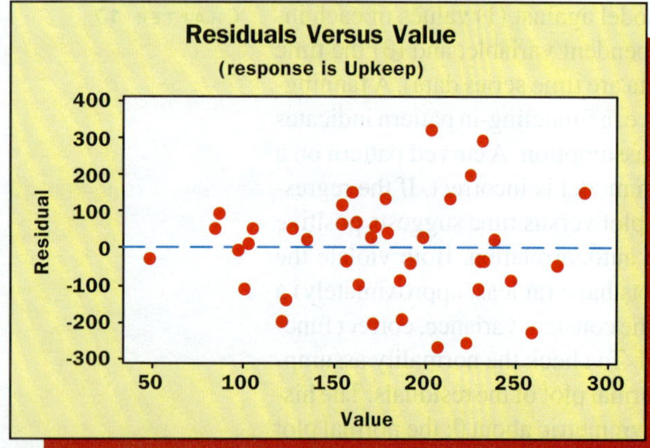

normal plot of the residuals in Figure 12.46(a) has a straight-line appearance. The plot of the residuals versus predicted sales in Figure 12.46(b) has a horizontal band appearance, as do the plots of the residuals versus the independent variables [the plot versus x_3, advertising, is shown in Figure 12.46(c)]. We conclude that the regression assumptions approximately hold for the sales territory performance model (note that since the data are cross-sectional, a residual plot versus time is not appropriate).

We next consider the QHIC data in Table 11.2 (page 455). When we performed a regression analysis of these data by using the simple linear regression model, plots of the model's residuals versus x (home value) and $\hat{y}$ (predicted upkeep expenditure) both fanned out and had a "dip," or slightly curved appearance (see Figure 11.26, page 499). In order to remedy the indicated violations of the constant variance and correct functional form assumptions, we transformed the dependent variable by taking the square roots of the upkeep expenditures. An alternative approach consists of two steps. First, the slightly curved appearance of the residual plots implies that it is reasonable to add the squared term x^2 to the simple linear regression model. This gives the

quadratic regression model

$$y = \beta_0 + \beta_1 x + \beta_2 x^2 + \varepsilon$$

The MINITAB output in Figure 12.47 shows that the plot of this model's residuals versus x fans out, indicating a violation of the constant variance assumption. The second step of the alternative approach remedies this violation by **dividing through the model by x.** How this is done is discussed in Exercise 12.61. We will see that the final model obtained will allow us to do what the square root transformation of Chapter 11 would not allow us to do—make statistical inferences about **mean** upkeep expenditures.

To conclude this section, we consider the **Durbin–Watson test** for first-order autocorrelation. This test is carried out for a multiple regression model exactly as it is for a simple linear regression model (see Section 11.9), except that we consider k, the number of independent variables used by the model, when looking up the critical values $d_{L,\alpha}$ and $d_{U,\alpha}$. For example, recall that Figure 11.30 (page 503) gives $n = 16$ weekly values of Pages' Bookstore sales (y), Pages' advertising expenditure (x_1), and competitor's advertising expenditure (x_2). The Durbin–Watson statistic for the model

$$y = \beta_0 + \beta_1 x_1 + \beta_2 x_2 + \varepsilon$$

is $d = 1.63$. If we set α equal to .05, then we use Table A.10 (page 834)—a portion of which is shown on the page margin. Since $n = 16$ and $k = 2$, the appropriate critical values for a test for first-order positive autocorrelation are $d_{L,.05} = .98$ and $d_{U,.05} = 1.54$. Since $d = 1.63$ is greater than $d_{U,.05}$, we conclude that there is no first-order positive autocorrelation. The Durbin–Watson test carried out in Section 11.9 indicates that this autocorrelation does exist for the model relating y to x_1. Therefore, adding x_2 to this model seems to have removed the autocorrelation.

	$k = 2$	
n	$d_{L,.05}$	$d_{U,.05}$
15	0.95	1.54
16	0.98	1.54
17	1.02	1.54
18	1.05	1.53

Exercises for Section 12.13

CONCEPTS

12.57 Discuss how we use the residuals to check the regression assumptions for a multiple regression model.

12.58 Discuss how we carry out the Durbin–Watson test for a multiple regression model.

FIGURE 12.48 MegaStat and Excel Residual Analysis for the Hospital Labor Needs Model (for Exercise 12.59)

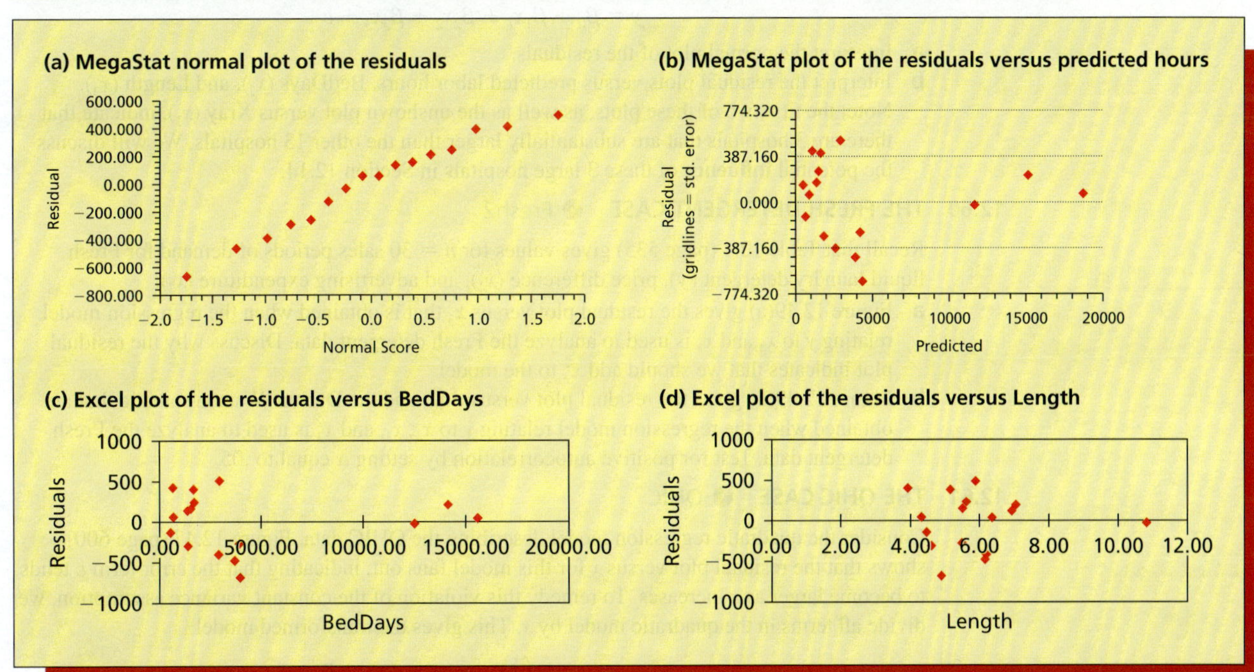

FIGURE 12.49 MegaStat and MINITAB Outputs for Exercises 12.60 and 12.61

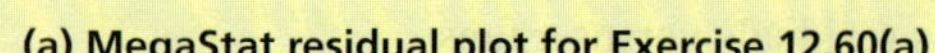

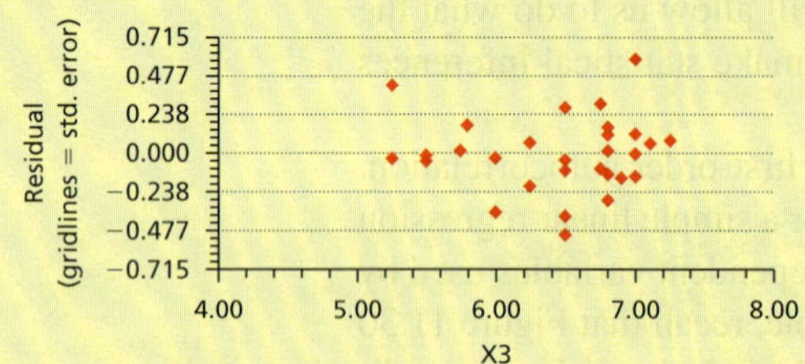

(b) MINITAB output for Exercise 12.60(b)

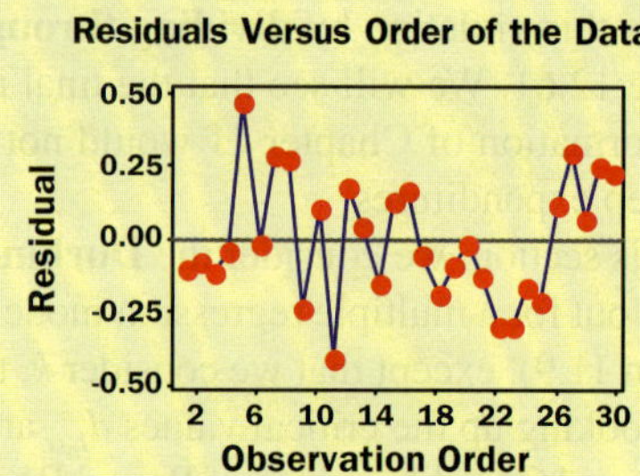

Durbin - Watson Statistic = 1.62

(c) MINITAB regression output for Exercise 12.61(b)

```
Predictor       Coef      SE Coef      T       P
Noconstant
1/Value       -53.50       83.20   -0.64   0.524
One            3.409       1.321    2.58   0.014
Value       0.011224    0.004627    2.43   0.020

Predicted Values for New Observations
     Fit          95% CI               95% PI
   5.635    (5.306, 5.964)    (3.994, 7.276)
```

$$\frac{\hat{y}}{220} = \frac{-53.50}{220} + 3.409 + .011224(220) = 5.635$$

(d) MINITAB residual plot for Exercise 12.61(a)

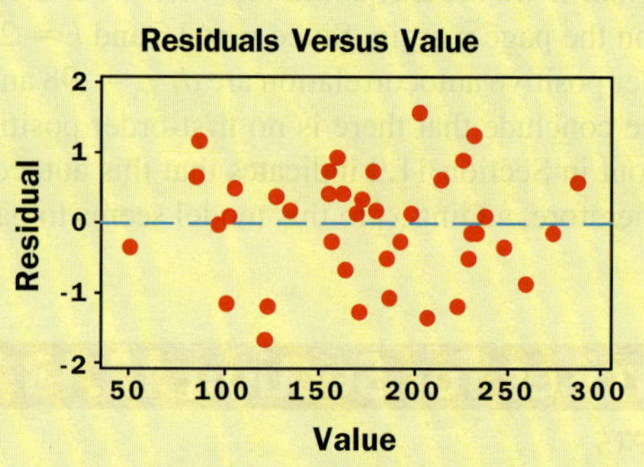

METHODS AND APPLICATIONS

12.59 THE HOSPITAL LABOR NEEDS CASE HospLab

Consider the hospital labor needs data in Table 12.5 (page 535). Figure 12.48 gives residual plots that are obtained when we perform a regression analysis of these data by using the model

$$y = \beta_0 + \beta_1 x_1 + \beta_2 x_2 + \beta_3 x_3 + \varepsilon$$

a Interpret the normal plot of the residuals.

b Interpret the residual plots versus predicted labor hours, BedDays (x_2), and Length (x_3). Note: the first two of these plots, as well as the unshown plot versus Xray (x_1), indicate that there are 3 hospitals that are substantially larger than the other 13 hospitals. We will discuss the potential **influence** of these 3 large hospitals in Section 12.14.

12.60 THE FRESH DETERGENT CASE Fresh2

Recall that Table 12.4 (page 535) gives values for $n = 30$ sales periods of demand for Fresh liquid laundry detergent (y), price difference (x_4), and advertising expenditure (x_3).

a Figure 12.49(a) gives the residual plot versus x_3 that is obtained when the regression model relating y to x_4 and x_3 is used to analyze the Fresh detergent data. Discuss why the residual plot indicates that we should add x_3^2 to the model.

b Figure 12.49(b) gives the residual plot versus time and the Durbin–Watson statistic that are obtained when the regression model relating y to x_4, x_3, and x_3^2 is used to analyze the Fresh detergent data. Test for positive autocorrelation by setting α equal to .05.

12.61 THE QHIC CASE QHIC

Consider the quadratic regression model describing the QHIC data. Figure 12.47 (page 600) shows that the residual plot versus x for this model fans out, indicating that the error term ε tends to become larger as x increases. To remedy this violation of the constant variance assumption, we divide all terms in the quadratic model by x. This gives the transformed model

$$\frac{y}{x} = \beta_0\left(\frac{1}{x}\right) + \beta_1 + \beta_2 x + \frac{\varepsilon}{x}$$

Figures 12.49(c) and (d) give a regression output and a residual plot versus x for this model.

a Does the residual plot indicate the constant variance assumption holds for the transformed model?

b Consider a home worth \$220,000. We let μ_0 represent the mean yearly upkeep expenditure for all homes worth \$220,000, and we let y_0 represent the yearly upkeep expenditure for an individual home worth \$220,000. The bottom of the MINITAB output in Figure 12.49(c) tells us that $\hat{y}/220 = 5.635$ is a point estimate of $\mu_0/220$ and a point prediction of $y_0/220$. Multiply this result by 220 to obtain $\hat{y}$. Multiply the ends of the confidence interval and prediction interval shown on the MINITAB output by 220. This will give a 95 percent confidence interval for μ_0 and a 95 percent prediction interval for y_0.

12.14 Diagnostics for Detecting Outlying and Influential Observations (Optional)

Introduction An observation that is well separated from the rest of the data is called an **outlier.** An observation that would cause some important aspect of the regression analysis (for example, the least squares point estimates or the standard error s) to substantially change if it were removed from the data set is called **influential.** An observation may be an outlier with respect to its y value and/or its x values, but an outlier may or may not be influential. We illustrate these ideas by considering Figure 12.50, which is a hypothetical plot of the values of a dependent variable y against an independent variable x. Observation 1 in this figure is outlying with respect to its y value. However, it is not outlying with respect to its x value, since its x value is near the middle of the other x values. Moreover, observation 1 may not be influential because there are several observations with similar x values and nonoutlying y values, which will keep the least squares point estimates from being excessively influenced by observation 1. Observation 2 in Figure 12.50 is outlying with respect to its x value, but since its y value is consistent with the regression relationship displayed by the nonoutlying observations, it is probably not influential. Observation 3, however, is probably influential, because it is outlying with respect to its x value and because its y value is not consistent with the regression relationship displayed by the other observations.

In addition to using data plots (such as Figure 12.50), we can use more sophisticated procedures to detect outlying and influential observations. These procedures are particularly important when we are performing a multiple regression analysis and thus simple data plots are unlikely to tell us what we need to know. To illustrate, we consider the data in Table 12.19, which concerns the need

FIGURE 12.50 Data Plot Illustrating Outlying and Influential Observations

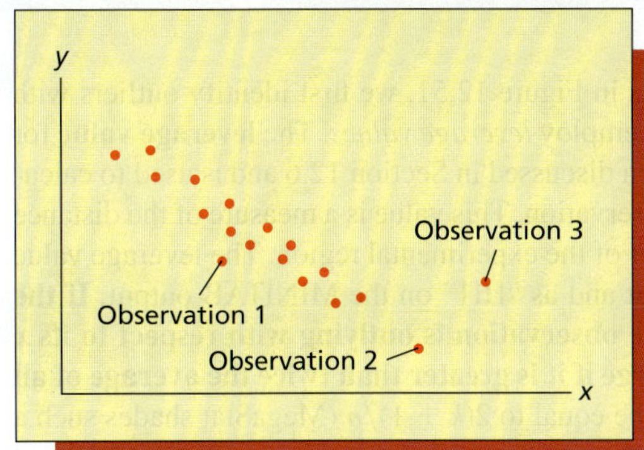

TABLE 12.19 Hospital Labor Needs Data HospLab3

Hospital	Hours y	Xray x_1	BedDays x_2	Length x_3
1	566.52	2463	472.92	4.45
2	696.82	2048	1339.75	6.92
3	1033.15	3940	620.25	4.28
4	1603.62	6505	568.33	3.90
5	1611.37	5723	1497.60	5.50
6	1613.27	11520	1365.83	4.60
7	1854.17	5779	1687.00	5.62
8	2160.55	5969	1639.92	5.15
9	2305.58	8461	2872.33	6.18
10	3503.93	20106	3655.08	6.15
11	3571.89	13313	2912.00	5.88
12	3741.40	10771	3921.00	4.88
13	4026.52	15543	3865.67	5.50
14	10343.81	36194	7684.10	7.00
15	11732.17	34703	12446.33	10.78
16	15414.94	39204	14098.40	7.05
17	18854.45	86533	15524.00	6.35

Source: *Procedures and Analysis for Staffing Standards Development: Regression Analysis Handbook* (San Diego, CA: Navy Manpower and Material Analysis Center, 1979).

FIGURE 12.51 The MegaStat and MINITAB Output of Outlying and Influential Observation Diagnostics for Model I

Observation	Hours	Predicted	Residual	Leverage	Studentized Residual	Studentized Deleted Residual	Cook's D	TRES1	HI1	COOK1
1	566.520	688.409	-121.889	0.121	-0.211	-0.203	0.002	-0.2035	0.120749	0.00153
2	696.820	721.848	-25.028	0.226	-0.046	-0.044	0.000	-0.04447	0.226128	0.00016
3	1,033.150	965.393	67.757	0.130	0.118	0.114	0.001	0.11356	0.129664	0.00052
4	1,603.620	1,172.464	431.156	0.159	0.765	0.752	0.028	0.75174	0.158762	0.02759
5	1,611.370	1,526.780	84.590	0.085	0.144	0.138	0.000	0.1383	0.084914	0.00048
6	1,613.270	1,993.869	-380.599	0.112	-0.657	-0.642	0.014	-0.64194	0.112011	0.01361
7	1,854.170	1,676.558	177.612	0.084	0.302	0.291	0.002	0.29105	0.084078	0.00209
8	2,160.550	1,791.405	369.145	0.083	0.627	0.612	0.009	0.61176	0.083005	0.0089
9	2,305.580	2,798.761	-493.181	0.085	-0.838	-0.828	0.016	-0.82827	0.084596	0.01624
10	3,503.930	4,191.333	-687.403	0.120	-1.192	-1.214	0.049	-1.21359	0.120262	0.04857
11	3,571.890	3,190.957	380.933	0.077	0.645	0.630	0.009	0.62993	0.077335	0.00872
12	3,741.400	4,364.502	-623.102	0.177	-1.117	-1.129	0.067	-1.129	0.177058	0.06714
13	4,026.520	4,364.229	-337.709	0.064	-0.568	-0.553	0.006	-0.55255	0.064498	0.00556
14	10,343.810	8,713.307	1,630.503	0.146	2.871	4.558	0.353	4.55845	0.146451	0.35349
15	11,732.170	12,080.864	-348.694	0.682	-1.005	-1.006	0.541	-1.00588	0.681763	0.5414
16	15,414.940	15,133.026	281.914	0.785	0.990	0.989	0.897	0.98925	0.78548	0.89729
17	18,854.450	19,260.453	-406.003	0.863	-1.786	-1.975	5.033	-1.97506	0.863247	5.03294

for labor in 17 U.S. Navy hospitals. Specifically, this table gives values of the dependent variable Hours (y, monthly labor hours required) and of the independent variables Xray (x_1, monthly X-ray exposures), BedDays (x_2, monthly occupied bed days—a hospital has one occupied bed day if one bed is occupied for an entire day), and Length (x_3, average length of patients' stay, in days). When we perform a regression analysis of these data using the model

$$y = \beta_0 + \beta_1 x_1 + \beta_2 x_2 + \beta_3 x_3 + \varepsilon$$

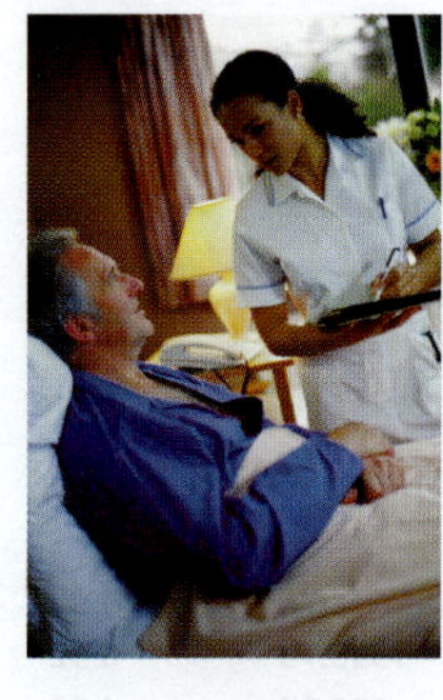

we find that the least squares point estimates of the model parameters and their associated p-values (given in parentheses) are $b_0 = 1{,}523.3892(.0749)$, $b_1 = .0530(.0205)$, $b_2 = .9785(<.0001)$ and $b_3 = -320.9508(.0563)$. In addition, Figure 12.51 gives the MegaStat and MINITAB output of outlying and influential observation diagnostics for the model, which we will sometimes refer to as Model I. Note that the MINITAB output is the output that uses grid lines. The main objective of the regression analysis is to help the navy evaluate the performance of its hospitals in terms of how many labor hours are used relative to how many labor hours are needed. The navy selected hospitals 1 through 17 from hospitals that it thought were efficiently run and wishes to use a regression model based on efficiently run hospitals to evaluate the efficiency of questionable hospitals.

Leverage values To interpret the diagnostics in Figure 12.51, we first identify outliers with respect to their x values. One way to do this is to employ *leverage values.* The **leverage value** for an observation is the **distance value** that has been discussed in Section 12.6 and is used to calculate a prediction interval for the y value of the observation. This value is a measure of the distance between the observation's x values and the center of the experimental region. The leverage value is labeled as "Leverage" on the MegaStat output and as "HI1" on the MINITAB output. **If the leverage value for an observation is large, the observation is outlying with respect to its x values. A leverage value is considered to be large if it is greater than twice the average of all of the leverage values,** which can be shown to be equal to $2(k + 1)/n$ (MegaStat shades such a leverage value in dark blue). For example, since there are $n = 17$ observations in Table 12.19 and since the model

$$y = \beta_0 + \beta_1 x_1 + \beta_2 x_2 + \beta_3 x_3 + \varepsilon$$

utilizes $k = 3$ independent variables, twice the average leverage value is $2(k + 1)/n = 2(3 + 1)/17 = .4706$. Looking at Figure 12.51, we see that the leverage values for hospitals 15, 16, and 17 are, respectively, .682, .785, and .863. Since these leverage values are greater than .4706, we conclude that **hospitals 15, 16, and 17 are outliers with respect to their *x* values.** Intuitively, this is because Table 12.19 indicates that x_1 (monthly X-ray exposures) and x_2 (monthly occupied bed days) are substantially larger for hospitals 15, 16, and 17 than for hospitals 1 through 14. In other words, hospitals 15, 16, and 17 are substantially larger hospitals than hospitals 1 through 14.

Residuals and studentized residuals To identify outliers with respect to their *y* values, we can use residuals. Any residual that is substantially different from the others is suspect. For example, note from Table 12.19 that hospital 14's values of Xray, BedDays, and Length are 36,194, 7,684.1, and 7. Using the least squares point estimates for Model I, it follows that the point prediction of labor hours for hospital 14 is

$$\begin{aligned}\hat{y}_{14} &= 1{,}523.3892 + .0530(36{,}194) + .9785(7{,}684.1) - 320.9508(7)\\ &= 8{,}713.307\end{aligned}$$

Since the actual number of labor hours for hospital 14 is $y_{14} = 10{,}343.810$, the residual e_{14} for hospital 14 is the difference between $y_{14} = 10{,}343.810$ and $\hat{y}_{14} = 8{,}713.307$, which is 1,630.503. Figure 12.51 shows the residuals for all 17 hospitals. Since $e_{14} = 1{,}630.503$ is much larger than the other residuals, it seems that hospital 14 used a number of labor hours that is much larger than predicted by the regression model. To obtain a somewhat more precise idea about whether an observation is an outlier with respect to its *y* value, we can calculate the *studentized residual* for the observation. The **studentized residual** for an observation is the observation's residual divided by the residual's standard error.[4] As a very rough rule of thumb, if the studentized residual for an observation is greater than 2 in absolute value, we have some evidence that the observation is an outlier with respect to its *y* value. For example, since Figure 12.51 tells us that the studentized residual (see "Studentized Residual" on the MegaStat output) for hospital 14 is 2.871, we have some evidence that hospital 14 is an outlier with respect to its *y* value.[5]

Deleted residuals and studentized deleted residuals Many statisticians feel that an excellent way to identify an outlier with respect to its *y* value is to use the **PRESS, or deleted, residual.** To calculate the deleted residual for observation *i*, we subtract from y_i the point prediction $\hat{y}_{(i)}$ computed using least squares point estimates based on all *n* observations except for observation *i*. We do this because, if observation *i* is an outlier with respect to its *y* value, using this observation to compute the usual least squares point estimates might "draw" the usual point prediction $\hat{y}_i$ toward y_i and thus cause the resulting usual residual to be small. This would falsely imply that observation *i* is not an outlier with respect to its *y* value. For example, consider using observation 3 in Figure 12.50 (page 603) to determine the least squares line. Doing this might draw the least squares line toward observation 3, causing the point prediction $\hat{y}_3$ given by the line to be near y_3 and thus the usual residual $y_3 - \hat{y}_3$ to be small. This would falsely imply that observation 3 is not an outlier with respect to its *y* value. To illustrate more precisely the concept of the deleted residual, recall that hospital 14's values of Xray, BedDays, and Length are 36,194, 7,684.1, and 7. Furthermore, let $b_0^{(14)}$, $b_1^{(14)}$, $b_2^{(14)}$, and $b_3^{(14)}$ denote the least squares point estimates of $\beta_0, \beta_1, \beta_2$, and β_3 that are calculated by using all 17 observations in Table 12.19 except for observation 14. Then, it can be shown that the point prediction of y_{14} using these least squares point estimates

$$\hat{y}_{(14)} = b_0^{(14)} + b_1^{(14)}(36{,}194) + b_2^{(14)}(7{,}684.1) + b_3^{(14)}(7)$$

equals 8,433.43. It follows that the deleted residual for hospital 14 is the difference between $y_{14} = 10{,}343.810$ and $\hat{y}_{(14)} = 8{,}433.43$, which is 1,910.38. Standard statistical software packages calculate the deleted residual for each observation and divide this residual by its standard error to form the **studentized deleted residual.** The studentized deleted residual is labeled as "Studentized Deleted Residual" on the MegaStat output and as "TRES1" on the MINITAB output. Examining Figure 12.51, we see that the studentized deleted residual for hospital 14 is 4.558.

To evaluate the studentized deleted residual for an observation, we compare this quantity with two *t* distribution points—$t_{.025}$ and $t_{.005}$—based on $n - k - 2$ degrees of freedom. Specifically, if the studentized deleted residual is greater in absolute value than $t_{.025}$ (and thus is shaded in light

[4]The formula for the residual's standard error, as well as the formulas for the other outlying and influential observation diagnostics discussed in this section, will be given in an optional technical note at the end of this section.

[5]Both MegaStat and MINITAB give all of the diagnostics discussed in this section.

blue on the MegaStat output), then there is *some evidence* that the observation is an outlier with respect to its y value. If the studentized deleted residual is greater in absolute value than $t_{.005}$ (and thus is shaded in dark blue on the MegaStat output), then there is *strong evidence* that the observation is an outlier with respect to its y value. The data analysis experience of the authors leads us to suggest that one should not be overly concerned that an observation is an outlier with respect to its y value unless the studentized deleted residual is greater in absolute value than $t_{.005}$. For the hospital labor needs model, $n - k - 2 = 17 - 3 - 2 = 12$, and therefore $t_{.025} = 2.179$ and $t_{.005} = 3.055$. The studentized deleted residual for hospital 14, which equals 4.558, is greater in absolute value than both $t_{.025} = 2.179$ and $t_{.005} = 3.055$. Therefore, we should be very concerned that **hospital 14 is an outlier with respect to its y value.**

Cook's distance measure One way to determine if an observation is influential is to calculate **Cook's distance measure,** which we sometimes refer to as **Cook's D,** or simply **D.** Cook's D is labeled as "Cook's D" on the MegaStat output and as "Cook1" on the MINITAB output. It can be shown that, if Cook's D for observation i is large, then the least squares point estimates calculated by using all n observations differ substantially (*as a group*) from the least squares point estimates calculated by using all n observations except for observation i. This would say that observation i is influential. To determine whether D is large, we compare D with two F distribution points—$F_{.80}$, the 20th percentile of the F distribution, and $F_{.50}$, the 50th percentile of the F distribution—based on $(k + 1)$ numerator and $[n - (k + 1)]$ denominator degrees of freedom. If D is less than $F_{.80}$, the observation should not be considered influential. If D is greater than $F_{.50}$ (and thus is shaded in dark blue on the MegaStat output), the observation should be considered influential. If D is between $F_{.80}$ and $F_{.50}$ (and thus is shaded in light blue on the MegaStat output), then the nearer D is to $F_{.50}$, the greater the influence of the observation. Examining Figure 12.51, we see that for observation 17 Cook's D is 5.033 and is the largest value of Cook's D on the output. This value of Cook's D is greater than $F_{.05} = 3.18$, which is based on $k + 1 = 4$ numerator and $n - (k + 1) = 17 - 4 = 13$ denominator degrees of freedom. Since $F_{.05}$ is itself greater than $F_{.50}$, Cook's D for observation 17 is greater than $F_{.50}$, which says that **removing hospital 17 from the data set would substantially change (as a group) the least squares point estimates** of the parameters β_0, β_1, β_2, and β_3. Therefore, hospital 17 is **influential,** as is hospital 16—note that the values of Cook's D for both hospitals are shaded in dark blue on the MegaStat output.

In general, if we decide (by using Cook's D) that removing observation i from the data set would substantially change (as a group) the least squares point estimates, we might wish to determine whether the point estimate of a particular parameter β_j would change substantially. We might also wish to determine if the point prediction of y_i would change substantially. We discuss in the supplementary exercises how to make such determinations.

What to do about outlying and influential observations To illustrate how we deal with outlying and influential observations, we summarize what we have learned in the hospital labor needs case:

1 Hospitals 15, 16, and 17, outliers with respect to their x values, are larger than the other hospitals. Hospitals 16 and 17 are influential in that removing either from the data set would substantially change (as a group) the least squares point estimates of the parameters β_0, β_1, β_2, and β_3.

2 Hospital 14 is an outlier with respect to its y value. Furthermore, hospital 14 is influential in that, since its residual ($e_{14} = 1{,}630.5$) is large, the sum of squared residuals and thus the standard error s (which equals 614.779) are larger than they would be if hospital 14 were removed from the data set.

We recommend first dealing with outliers with respect to their y values, because they affect the overall fit of the model. Often when we decide what to do with such outliers, other problems become much less important or disappear. In general, we should first check to see if the y value in question was recorded correctly. If it was recorded incorrectly, it should be corrected and the regression should be rerun. If it cannot be corrected, the corresponding observation should be discarded and the regression should be rerun. We will assume that the labor hours for hospital 14 ($y_{14} = 10{,}343.8$) were recorded correctly.

FIGURE 12.52 MegaStat Outlying and Influential Observation Diagnostics and Residual Plots

(a) Model I diagnostics without hospital 14

Obs	Residual	Leverage	Studentized Residual	Studentized Deleted Residual	Cook's D
1	−125.624	0.121	−0.346	−0.333	0.004
2	141.691	0.235	0.418	0.404	0.013
3	60.555	0.130	0.168	0.161	0.001
4	428.812	0.159	1.208	1.234	0.069
5	162.866	0.087	0.440	0.425	0.005
6	−294.287	0.114	−0.808	−0.795	0.021
7	256.296	0.086	0.692	0.677	0.011
8	409.814	0.084	1.106	1.117	0.028
9	−396.076	0.088	−1.071	−1.078	0.028
10	−472.953	0.135	−1.313	−1.359	0.067
11	517.698	0.083	1.397	1.461	0.044
12	−677.234	0.178	−1.929	−2.224	0.202
13	−262.164	0.066	−0.701	−0.685	0.009
14	−29.679	0.714	−0.143	−0.137	0.013
15	218.990	0.787	1.225	1.254	1.384
16	61.298	0.933	0.613	0.597	1.317

(b) Model II diagnostics

Obs	Residual	Leverage	Studentized Residual	Studentized Deleted Residual	Cook's D
1	−461.012	0.155	−1.379	−1.439	0.070
2	77.456	0.229	0.242	0.233	0.003
3	−254.577	0.161	−0.764	−0.750	0.022
4	68.769	0.198	0.211	0.202	0.002
5	77.192	0.085	0.222	0.213	0.001
6	−485.910	0.115	−1.420	−1.490	0.053
7	220.635	0.085	0.634	0.617	0.007
8	351.558	0.083	1.009	1.010	0.018
9	−144.646	0.121	−0.424	−0.409	0.005
10	−134.015	0.212	−0.415	−0.400	0.009
11	727.155	0.113	2.122	2.571	0.115
12	−204.698	0.230	−0.641	−0.624	0.025
13	162.093	0.140	0.480	0.464	0.007
14	266.801	0.706	1.352	1.406	0.877
15	−373.625	0.682	−1.821	−2.049	1.422
16	183.743	0.788	1.098	1.108	0.898
17	−76.920	0.896	−0.655	−0.639	0.738

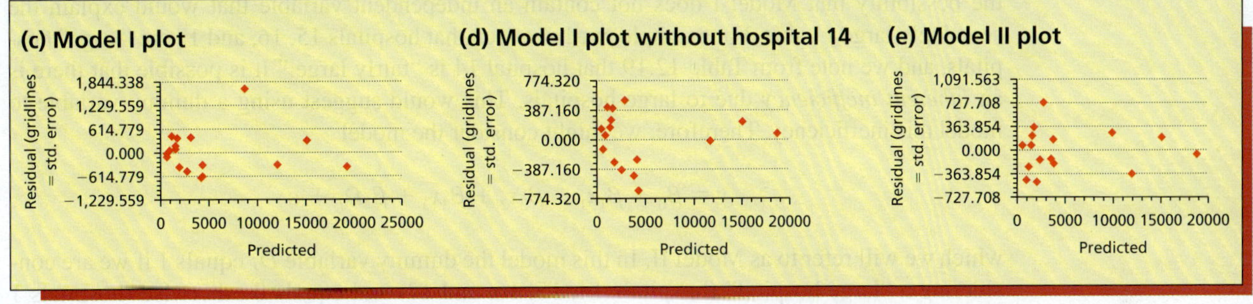

If the y value has been recorded correctly, we must search for a reason for it. The y value could have resulted from a situation that we do not wish the regression model to describe. For example, the fact that $y_{14} = 10{,}343.8$ is substantially greater than the point prediction $\hat{y}_{14} = 8{,}713.3$ might have resulted from a one-time disaster at the naval base—such as a fire on a ship—that we are not building a model to describe. We will assume there was no such disaster at the naval base. In this case—and in the absence of any other reason—we might conclude that $y_{14} = 10{,}343.8$ resulted from the fact that hospital 14 was run significantly more inefficiently than any other hospital. We should then talk to the administrative staff at hospital 14 and try to correct the problem. From the point of view of the regression model—and using it to predict and evaluate labor needs for other hospitals—we would remove hospital 14 from the data set. This is because we do not wish the model to be based on a hospital that is run inefficiently. If we remove hospital 14 from the data set and use Model I to carry out a regression analysis of the remaining 16 hospitals, we find that the least squares point estimates of the model parameters and their associated p-values (given in parentheses) are $b_0 = 1{,}946.8020(.0023)$, $b_1 = .0386(.0120)$, $b_2 = 1.0394(<.0001)$, and $b_4 = -413.7578(.0012)$. Furthermore, the standard error s for Model I with hospital 14 removed is 387.160, which is considerably less than the s of 614.779 for Model I using all 17 hospitals. Figure 12.52(a) gives the MegaStat output of outlying and influential observation diagnostics for Model I with hospital 14 removed. Note that hospitals 14, 15, and 16 on this output are the original hospitals 15, 16, and 17. In the exercises the reader will use the output to verify that removing hospital 14 has made the original hospital 17 considerably less influential and the original hospital 16 only slightly more influential.

FIGURE 12.53 MegaStat Model Building for the Hospital Labor Needs Data

(a) Using all 17 hospitals

Nvar	Load	Xray	BedDays	Pop	Length	s	Adj R^2	R^2	Cp	p-value
3		.0205	.0000		.0563	614.779	.988	.990	2.918	2.89E-13
4		.0175	.0000	.3441	.0400	615.489	.988	.991	4.026	4.18E-12
4	.0000	.0173		.2377	.0337	622.094	.987	.991	4.264	4.75E-12

(b) With hospital 14 removed

Nvar	Load	Xray	BedDays	Pop	Length	s	Adj R^2	R^2	Cp	p-value
4		.0091	.0000	.2690	.0013	381.555	.995	.997	4.023	1.86E-13
3		.0120	.0000		.0012	387.160	.995	.996	3.258	9.92E-15
4	.3981	.0121	.1381		.0018	390.876	.995	.996	4.519	2.43E-13

(c) Using all 17 hospitals (with the dummy variable Large)

Nvar	Load	Xray	BedDays	Pop	Length	Large	s	Adj R^2	R^2	Cp	p-value
4		.0016	.0000		.0006	.0003	363.854	.996	.997	3.533	7.66E-15
4	.0000	.0019			.0005	.0002	365.057	.996	.997	3.602	7.97E-15
5		.0034	.0001	.5004	.0035	.0007	371.914	.996	.997	5.087	2.00E-13

Before deciding, however, that hospital 14 has been run inefficiently, we should consider the possibility that Model I does not contain an independent variable that would explain the seemingly large y value. For example, we have seen that hospitals 15, 16, and 17 are "large" hospitals, and we note from Table 12.19 that hospital 14 is "fairly large." It is possible that there is an *inherent inefficiency* due to large hospitals. This would suggest using a dummy variable to model this inefficiency. Therefore, we might consider the model

$$y = \beta_0 + \beta_1 x_1 + \beta_2 x_2 + \beta_3 x_3 + \beta_4 D_L + \varepsilon$$

which we will refer to as Model II. In this model the dummy variable D_L equals 1 if we are considering a "large hospital" (hospitals 14, 15, 16, and 17) and equals 0 otherwise (hospitals 1 through 13). It follows that β_4 is an extra expected number of labor hours that is associated with the inefficiency of large hospitals. If we use Model II to perform a regression analysis of the data in Table 12.19, we find that the least squares point estimates of the model parameters and their associated p-values (given in parentheses) are $b_0 = 2{,}462.21(.0004)$, $b_1 = .0482(.0016)$, $b_2 = .7843(<.0001)$, $b_3 = -432.4095(.0006)$, and $b_4 = 2{,}871.7828(.0003)$. Furthermore, the standard error s for Model II is 363.854, which is less than even the s of 387.160 for Model I with hospital 14 removed. Figure 12.52(b) gives the MegaStat output of outlying and influential observation diagnostics for Model II. In the exercises the reader will use this output to verify that Model II has made hospital 17 considerably less influential, hospital 15 slightly more influential, and **hospital 14 no longer an outlier with respect to its y value.** In addition, consider the residual plots versus predicted labor given in Figure 12.52(c), (d), and (e). The residual plot for Model II in Figure 12.52(e) has the most "horizontal band" appearance. This implies that Model II has done the best at making the residuals for small, medium, and large hospitals more of the same size. Finally, consider a questionable large hospital ($D_L = 1$) for which Xray = 56,194, BedDays = 14,077.88, and Length = 6.89. Also, consider the labor needs in an efficiently run large hospital described by this combination of values of the independent variables. The 95 percent prediction intervals for these labor needs given by Model I using all 17 hospitals, Model I with hospital 14 removed, and Model II are, respectively, [14,510.96, 17,618.15], [14,906.24, 16,886.26], and [15,175.04, 17,030.01]. The reader can verify that Model II has given the shortest interval and Model I with hospital 14 removed has given a slightly longer interval. It is probably reasonable to use either model to evaluate the labor needs of the questionable hospital.

We next note that the hospital labor needs data in Table 12.19 are part of a larger data set analyzed by the navy. The complete data set consists of two additional variables—Load (average daily patient load) and Pop (eligible population in the area)—values of which are given on the page margin. The additional variables imply that the transition from Model I using all 17 hospitals to either Model I with hospital 14 removed or Model II is part of a larger model-building process. Figure 12.53 gives MegaStat outputs summarizing this process. Figure 12.53(a) shows that, if we use all 17 hospitals and the five potential independent variables listed across the top of the output, then Model I (the model using Xray, BedDays, and Length) is the best model. This model has the smallest values of s and C (Section 12.12 discusses C). We have seen that for Model I hospital 14 is an outlier with respect to its y value. Figure 12.53(b) shows that, if we remove hospital 14 from the data set and use the same five potential independent variables, then Model I is still the best model. Note that, although the model that uses Pop has a slightly smaller s than Model I, Model I has a smaller value of C. Figure 12.53(c) shows that, if we use all 17 hospitals and add the previously discussed dummy variable D_L (referred to as Large on the output) as a potential independent variable, then Model II (the model using Xray, BedDays, Length, and Large) is the best model. This model has the smallest values of s and C.

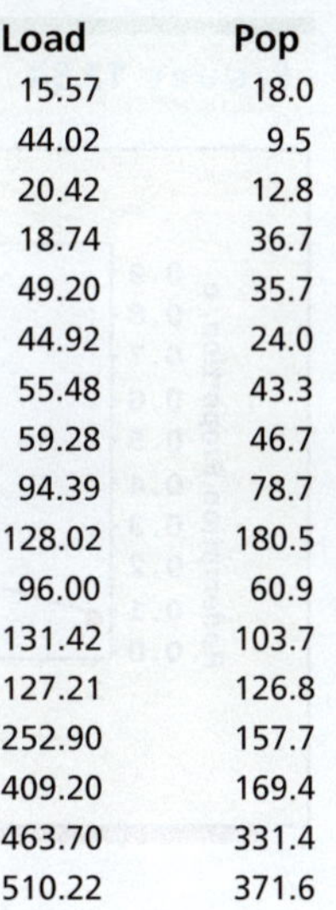

Load	Pop
15.57	18.0
44.02	9.5
20.42	12.8
18.74	36.7
49.20	35.7
44.92	24.0
55.48	43.3
59.28	46.7
94.39	78.7
128.02	180.5
96.00	60.9
131.42	103.7
127.21	126.8
252.90	157.7
409.20	169.4
463.70	331.4
510.22	371.6

A technical note (optional) Suppose we perform a regression analysis of n observations by using a regression model that utilizes k independent variables. Let SSE and s denote the unexplained variation and the standard error for the regression model. Also, let h_i and $e_i = y_i - \hat{y}_i$ denote the leverage value and the usual residual for observation i. Then, the standard error of the residual e_i can be proven to equal $s\sqrt{1 - h_i}$. This implies that the **studentized residual** for observation i equals $e_i/(s\sqrt{1 - h_i})$. Furthermore, let $d_i = y_i - \hat{y}_{(i)}$ denote the **deleted residual** for observation i, and let s_{d_i} denote the standard error of d_i. Then, it can be shown that the **deleted residual d_i** and the **studentized deleted residual d_i/s_{d_i}** can be calculated by using the equations

$$d_i = \frac{e_i}{1 - h_i} \quad \text{and} \quad \frac{d_i}{s_{d_i}} = e_i\left[\frac{n - k - 2}{SSE(1 - h_i) - e_i^2}\right]^{1/2}$$

Finally, if D_i denotes the value of Cook's D statistic for observation i, it can be proven that

$$D_i = \frac{e_i^2}{(k + 1)s^2}\left[\frac{h_i}{(1 - h_i)^2}\right]$$

Exercises for Section 12.14

CONCEPTS

12.62 What do leverage values identify? What do studentized deleted residuals identify?

12.63 What does Cook's distance measure identify?

METHODS AND APPLICATIONS

12.64 Use Figure 12.52(a) to explain why Model I without hospital 14 has made the original hospital 17 considerably less influential and the original hospital 16 only slightly more influential.

12.65 Use Figure 12.52(b) to explain why Model II has made hospital 17 considerably less influential, hospital 15 slightly more influential, and hospital 14 no longer an outlier with respect to its y value.

12.15 Logistic Regression (Optional)

Suppose that in a study of the effectiveness of offering a price reduction on a given product, 300 households having similar incomes were selected. A coupon offering a price reduction, x, on the product, as well as advertising material for the product, was sent to each household. The coupons offered different price reductions (10, 20, 30, 40, 50, and 60 dollars), and 50 homes were assigned at random to each price-reduction. The following table summarizes the number, y, and proportion, $\hat{p}$, of households redeeming coupons for each price reduction, x (expressed

FIGURE 12.54 **MINITAB Output of a Logistic Regression of the Price Reduction Data**

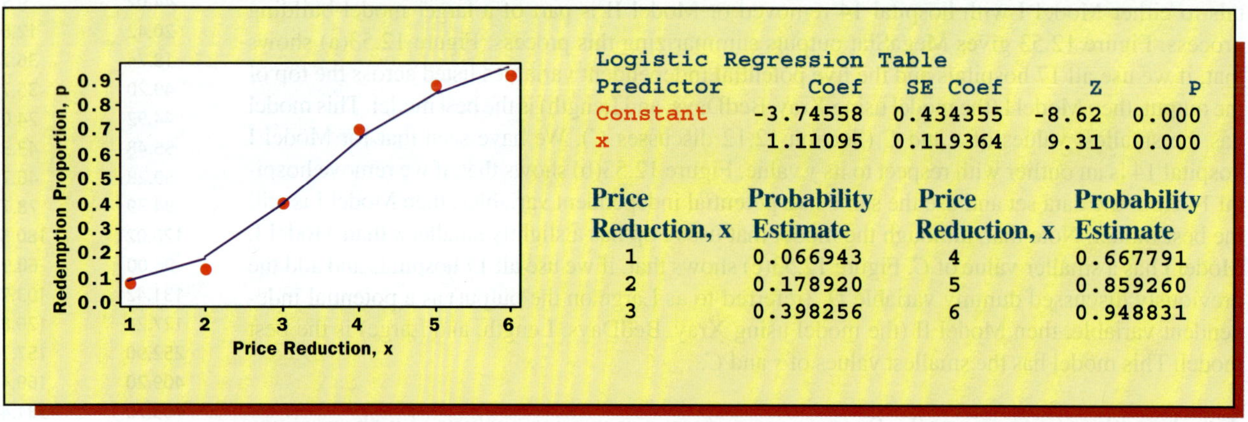

Logistic Regression Table

Predictor	Coef	SE Coef	Z	P
Constant	-3.74558	0.434355	-8.62	0.000
x	1.11095	0.119364	9.31	0.000

Price Reduction, x	Probability Estimate	Price Reduction, x	Probability Estimate
1	0.066943	4	0.667791
2	0.178920	5	0.859260
3	0.398256	6	0.948831

in units of \$10): PrcRed

x	1	2	3	4	5	6
y	4	7	20	35	44	46
$\hat{p}$	.08	.14	.40	.70	.88	.92

On the left side of Figure 12.54 we plot the $\hat{p}$ values versus the x values and draw a hypothetical curve through the plotted points. A theoretical curve having the shape of the curve in Figure 12.54 is the **logistic curve**

$$p(x) = \frac{e^{(\beta_0 + \beta_1 x)}}{1 + e^{(\beta_0 + \beta_1 x)}}$$

where $p(x)$ denotes the probability that a household receiving a coupon having a price reduction of x will redeem the coupon. The MINITAB output in Figure 12.54 tells us that the point estimates of β_0 and β_1 are $b_0 = -3.7456$ and $b_1 = 1.1109$. (The point estimates in logistic regression are usually obtained by an advanced statistical procedure called *maximum likelihood estimation.*) Using these estimates, it follows that, for example

$$\hat{p}(5) = \frac{e^{(-3.7456 + 1.1109(5))}}{1 + e^{(-3.7456 + 1.1109(5))}} = \frac{6.1037}{1 + 6.1037} = .8593$$

That is, $\hat{p}(5) = .8593$ is the point estimate of the probability that a household receiving a coupon having a price reduction of \$50 will redeem the coupon. The MINITAB output in Figure 12.54 gives the values of $\hat{p}(x)$ for $x = 1, 2, 3, 4, 5,$ and 6.

The **general logistic regression model** relates the probability that an event (such as redeeming a coupon) will occur to k independent variables $x_1, x_2, \ldots, x_k$. This general model is

$$p(x_1, x_2, \ldots, x_k) = \frac{e^{(\beta_0 + \beta_1 x_1 + \beta_2 x_2 + \cdots + \beta_k x_k)}}{1 + e^{(\beta_0 + \beta_1 x_1 + \beta_2 x_2 + \cdots + \beta_k x_k)}}$$

where $p(x_1, x_2, \ldots, x_k)$ is the probability that the event will occur when the values of the independent variables are $x_1, x_2, \ldots, x_k$. In order to estimate $\beta_0, \beta_1, \beta_2, \ldots, \beta_k$ we obtain n observations, with each observation consisting of observed values of $x_1, x_2, \ldots, x_k$ and of a dependent variable y. Here, y is a **dummy variable** that equals 1 if the event has occurred and 0 otherwise.

For example, suppose that the personnel director of a firm has developed two tests to help determine whether potential employees would perform successfully in a particular position. To help

FIGURE 12.55 MINITAB Output of a Logistic Regression of the Performance Data

```
Response Information

Variable   Value   Count
Group      1          23   (Event)
           0          20
           Total      43
Logistic Regression Table
                                                 Odds      95% CI
Predictor      Coef      SE Coef      Z       P  Ratio   Lower   Upper
Constant   -56.1704     17.4516   -3.22   0.001
Test 1     0.483314    0.157779    3.06   0.002   1.62    1.19    2.21
Test 2     0.165218    0.102070    1.62   0.106   1.18    0.97    1.44

Log-Likelihood = -13.959
Test that all slopes are zero: G = 31.483, DF = 2, P-Value = 0.000
```

estimate the usefulness of the tests, the director gives both tests to 43 employees that currently hold the position. Table 12.20 gives the scores of each employee on both tests and indicates whether the employee is currently performing successfully or unsuccessfully in the position. If the employee is performing successfully, we set the dummy variable *Group* equal to 1; if the employee is performing unsuccessfully, we set *Group* equal to 0. Let x_1 and x_2 denote the scores of a potential employee on tests 1 and 2, and let $p(x_1, x_2)$ denote the probability that a potential employee having the scores x_1 and x_2 will perform successfully in the position. We can estimate the relationship between $p(x_1, x_2)$ and x_1 and x_2 by using the logistic regression model

$$p(x_1, x_2) = \frac{e^{(\beta_0 + \beta_1 x_1 + \beta_2 x_2)}}{1 + e^{(\beta_0 + \beta_1 x_1 + \beta_2 x_2)}}$$

The MINITAB output in Figure 12.55 tells us that the point estimates of β_0, β_1, and β_2 are $b_0 = -56.17$, $b_1 = .4833$, and $b_2 = .1652$. Consider, therefore, a potential employee who scores a 93 on test 1 and an 84 on test 2. It follows that a point estimate of the probability that the potential employee will perform successfully in the position is

$$\hat{p}(93, 84) = \frac{e^{(-56.17 + .4833(93) + .1652(84))}}{1 + e^{(-56.17 + .4833(93) + .1652(84))}} = \frac{14.206506}{15.206506} = .9342$$

If we **classify** a potential employee into *group 1* ("will perform successfully"), as opposed to *group 2* ("will not perform successfully"), if and only if $\hat{p}(x_1, x_2)$ is greater than .5, this potential employee is classified into group 1.

To further analyze the logistic regression output, we consider several hypothesis tests that are based on the chi-square distribution (see Section 8.7, page 343). We first consider testing H_0: $\beta_1 = \beta_2 = 0$ versus H_a: At least one of β_1 or β_2 does not equal 0. The *p*-value for this test is the area under the chi-square curve having $k = 2$ degrees of freedom to the right of the test statistic value $G = 31.483$. Although the calculation of G is too complicated to demonstrate in this book, the MINITAB output gives the value of G and the related *p*-value, which is less than .001. This *p*-value implies that we have extremely strong evidence that at least one of β_1 or β_2 does not equal zero. The *p*-value for testing H_0: $\beta_1 = 0$ versus H_a: $\beta_1 \neq 0$ is the area under the chi-square curve having one degree of freedom to the right of the square of $z = (b_1/s_{b_1}) = (.4833/.1578) = 3.06$. The MINITAB output tells us that this *p*-value is .002, which implies that we have very strong evidence that the score on test 1 is related to the probability of a potential employee's success. The *p*-value for testing H_0: $\beta_2 = 0$ versus H_a: $\beta_2 \neq 0$ is the area under the chi-square curve having one degree of freedom to the right of the square of $z = (b_2/s_{b_2}) = (.1652/.1021) = 1.62$. The MINITAB output tells us that this *p*-value is .106, which implies that we do not have strong evidence that the score on test 2 is related to the probability of a potential employee's success. In Exercise 12.68 we will consider a logistic regression model that uses only the score on test 1 to estimate the probability of a potential employee's success.

TABLE 12.20 The Performance Data PerfTest

Group	Test 1	Test 2
1	96	85
1	96	88
1	91	81
1	95	78
1	92	85
1	93	87
1	98	84
1	92	82
1	97	89
1	95	96
1	99	93
1	89	90
1	94	90
1	92	94
1	94	84
1	90	92
1	91	70
1	90	81
1	86	81
1	90	76
1	91	79
1	88	83
1	87	82
0	93	74
0	90	84
0	91	81
0	91	78
0	88	78
0	86	86
0	79	81
0	83	84
0	79	77
0	88	75
0	81	85
0	85	83
0	82	72
0	82	81
0	81	77
0	86	76
0	81	84
0	85	78
0	83	77
0	81	71

Source: T. Dielman, *Applied Regression Analysis for Business and Economics*, second edition.

The **odds** of success for a potential employee is defined to be the probability of success divided by the probability of failure for the employee. That is,

$$\text{odds} = \frac{p(x_1, x_2)}{1 - p(x_1, x_2)}$$

For the potential employee who scores a 93 on test 1 and an 84 on test 2, we estimate that the odds of success are $.9342/(1 - .9342) = 14.22$. That is, we estimate that the odds of success for the potential employee are about 14 to 1. It can be shown that $e^{b_1} = e^{.4833} = 1.62$ is a point estimate of the **odds ratio for x_1**, which is the proportional change in the odds (for any potential employee) that is associated with an increase of one in x_1 when x_2 stays constant. This point estimate of the odds ratio for x_1 is shown on the MINITAB output and says that, for every one point increase in the score on test 1 when the score on test 2 stays constant, we estimate that a potential employee's odds of success increase by 62 percent. Furthermore, the 95 percent confidence interval for the odds ratio for x_1—[1.19, 2.21]—does not contain 1. Therefore, as with the (equivalent) chi-square test of H_0: $\beta_1 = 0$, we conclude that there is strong evidence that the score on test 1 is related to the probability of success for a potential employee. Similarly, it can be shown that $e^{b_2} = e^{.1652} = 1.18$ is a point estimate of the **odds ratio for x_2**, which is the proportional change in the odds (for any potential employee) that is associated with an increase of one in x_2 when x_1 stays constant. This point estimate of the odds ratio for x_2 is shown on the MINITAB output and says that, for every one point increase in the score on test 2 when the score on test 1 stays constant, we estimate that a potential employee's odds of success increases by 18 percent. However, the 95 percent confidence interval for the odds ratio for x_2—[.97, 1.44]—contains 1. Therefore, as with the equivalent chi-square test of H_0: $\beta_2 = 0$, we cannot conclude that there is strong evidence that the score on test 2 is related to the probability of success for a potential employee.

To conclude this section, consider the general logistic regression model

$$p(x_1, x_2, \ldots, x_k) = \frac{e^{(\beta_0 + \beta_1 x_1 + \beta_2 x_2 + \cdots + \beta_k x_k)}}{1 + e^{(\beta_0 + \beta_1 x_1 + \beta_2 x_2 + \cdots + \beta_k x_k)}}$$

where $p(x_1, x_2, \ldots, x_k)$ is the probability that the event under consideration will occur when the values of the independent variables are $x_1, x_2, \ldots, x_k$. The **odds** of the event occurring is defined to be $p(x_1, x_2, \ldots, x_k)/(1 - p(x_1, x_2, \ldots, x_k))$, which is the probability that the event will occur divided by the probability that the event will not occur. It can be shown that the odds equals $e^{(\beta_0 + \beta_1 x_1 + \beta_2 x_2 + \cdots + \beta_k x_k)}$. The natural logarithm of the odds is $(\beta_0 + \beta_1 x_1 + \beta_2 x_2 + \cdots + \beta_k x_k)$, which is called the **logit.** If $b_0, b_1, b_2, \ldots, b_k$ are the point estimates of $\beta_0, \beta_1, \beta_2, \ldots, \beta_k$, the point estimate of the logit, denoted $\widehat{\ell g}$, is $(b_0 + b_1 x_1 + b_2 x_2 + \cdots + b_k x_k)$. It follows that the point estimate of the probability that the event will occur is

$$\hat{p}(x_1, x_2, \ldots, x_k) = \frac{e^{\widehat{\ell g}}}{1 + e^{\widehat{\ell g}}} = \frac{e^{(b_0 + b_1 x_1 + b_2 x_2 + \cdots + b_k x_k)}}{1 + e^{(b_0 + b_1 x_1 + b_2 x_2 + \cdots + b_k x_k)}}$$

Finally, consider an arbitrary independent variable x_j. It can be shown that e^{b_j} is the point estimate of the **odds ratio for x_j**, which is the proportional change in the odds that is associated with a one unit increase in x_j when the other independent variables stay constant.

Exercises for Section 12.15

CONCEPTS

12.66 What two values does the dependent variable equal in logistic regression? What do these values represent?

12.67 What is the odds? What is the odds ratio?

METHODS AND APPLICATIONS

12.68 If we use the logistic regression model

$$p(x_1) = \frac{e^{(\beta_0 + \beta_1 x_1)}}{1 + e^{(\beta_0 + \beta_1 x_1)}}$$

to analyze the performance data in Table 12.20, we find that the point estimates of the model parameters and their associated p-values (given in parentheses) are $b_0 = -43.37(.001)$ and

$b_1 = .4897(.001)$. Find a point estimate of the probability of success for a potential employee who scores a 93 on test 1. Using $b_1 = .4897$, find a point estimate of the odds ratio for x_1. Interpret this point estimate.

12.69 Mendenhall and Sincich (1993) present data that can be used to investigate allegations of gender discrimination in the hiring practices of a particular firm. These data are as follows: Gender

Hiring Status y	Education x_1, years	Experience x_2, years	Gender x_3	Hiring Status y	Education x_1, years	Experience x_2, years	Gender x_3
0	6	2	0	1	4	5	1
0	4	0	1	0	6	4	0
1	6	6	1	0	8	0	1
1	6	3	1	1	6	1	1
0	4	1	0	0	4	7	0
1	8	3	0	0	4	1	1
0	4	2	1	0	4	5	0
0	4	4	0	0	6	0	1
0	6	1	0	1	8	5	1
1	8	10	0	0	4	9	0
0	4	2	1	0	8	1	0
0	8	5	0	0	6	1	1
0	4	2	0	1	4	10	1
0	6	7	0	1	6	12	0

Source: William Mendenhall and Terry Sincich, *A Second Course in Business Statistics: Regression Analysis*, Fourth edition, © 1993. Reprinted with permission of Prentice Hall.

In this table, y is a dummy variable that equals 1 if a potential employee was hired and 0 otherwise; x_1 is the number of years of education of the potential employee; x_2 is the number of years of experience of the potential employee; and x_3 is a dummy variable that equals 1 if the potential employee was a male and 0 if the potential employee was a female. If we use the logistic regression model

$$p(x_1, x_2, x_3) = \frac{e^{(\beta_0 + \beta_1 x_1 + \beta_2 x_2 + \beta_3 x_3)}}{1 + e^{(\beta_0 + \beta_1 x_1 + \beta_2 x_2 + \beta_3 x_3)}}$$

to analyze these data, we find that the point estimates of the model parameters and their associated p-values (given in parentheses) are $b_0 = -14.2483(.0191)$, $b_1 = 1.1549(.0552)$, $b_2 = .9098\ (.0341)$, and $b_3 = 5.6037(.0313)$.

a. Consider a potential employee having 4 years of education and 5 years of experience. Find a point estimate of the probability that the potential employee will be hired if the potential employee is a male, and find a point estimate of the probability that the potential employee will be hired if the potential employee is a female.

b. Using $b_3 = 5.6037$, find a point estimate of the odds ratio for x_3. Interpret this odds ratio. Using the p-value describing the importance of x_3, can we conclude that there is strong evidence that gender is related to the probability that a potential employee will be hired?

Chapter Summary

This chapter has discussed **multiple regression analysis.** We began by considering the **multiple regression model.** We next discussed the **least squares point estimates** of the model parameters, the assumptions behind the model, and some ways to judge **overall model utility**—the **standard error,** the **multiple coefficient of determination,** the **adjusted multiple coefficient of determination,** and the **overall *F* test.** Then we considered testing the significance of a single independent variable in a multiple regression model, calculating a **confidence interval** for the mean value of the dependent variable, and calculating a **prediction interval** for an individual value of the dependent variable. We continued this chapter by discussing using **squared terms** to model **quadratic** relationships, using **cross-product terms** to model **interaction,** and using **dummy variables** to model **qualitative** independent variables. We then considered how to use the **partial *F* test** to evaluate a portion of a regression model. We next discussed **multicollinearity,** which can adversely affect the ability of the t statistics and associated p-values to assess the importance of the independent variables in a regression model. For this reason, we need to determine if the overall model gives a **high R^2,** a **small s,** a **high adjusted R^2, short prediction intervals,** and a **small C.** We considered how to compare regression models on the basis of these criteria, and we also showed how to use **stepwise regression** and **backward elimination** to help select a regression model. We concluded this chapter by showing (1) how to use residual analysis to check the regression assumptions for multiple regression models, (2) how to use various diagnostics to detect **outlying** and **influential** observations, and (3) how to use **logistic regression** to estimate the probability that an event will occur.

Glossary of Terms

dummy variable: A variable that takes on the values 0 or 1 and is used to describe the effects of the different levels of a qualitative independent variable in a regression model. (page 573)

experimental region: The range of the previously observed combinations of values of the independent variables. (page 531)

influential observation: An observation that causes the least squares point estimates (or other aspects of the regression analysis) to be substantially different from what they would be if the observation were removed from the data. (page 603)

interaction: The situation in which the relationship between the mean value of the dependent variable and an independent variable is dependent on the value of another independent variable. (page 565)

multicolinearity: The situation in which the independent variables used in a regression analysis are related to each other. (page 588)

multiple regression model: An equation that describes the relationship between a dependent variable and more than one independent variable. (page 532)

outlier: An observation that is well separated from the rest of the data with respect to its y value and/or its x values. (page 603)

Important Formulas and Tests

The multiple regression model: page 532
The least squares point estimates: page 536
Mean square error: page 544
Standard error: page 544
Total variation: page 545
Explained variation: page 545
Unexplained variation: page 545
Multiple coefficient of determination: page 545
Multiple correlation coefficient: page 545
Adjusted multiple coefficient of determination: page 546
An F test for the linear regression model: page 547
Sampling distribution of b_j: page 550
Testing the significance of an independent variable: page 550
Confidence interval for β_j: page 552
Point estimate of a mean value of y: page 539
Point prediction of an individual value of y: page 539
Sampling distribution of $\hat{y}$ (and the distance value): page 555
Confidence interval for a mean value of y: page 555
Prediction interval for an individual value of y: page 555
The quadratic regression model: page 557
The partial F test: page 585
Variance inflation factor: page 588
C statistic: page 593
The Durbin–Watson test: page 601
Leverage value: page 604
Studentized residual: pages 605, 609
PRESS (deleted) residual: pages 605, 609
The studentized deleted residual: pages 605, 609
Cook's distance measure: pages 606, 609
The logistic regression model: page 610
Odds: page 612

Supplementary Exercises

12.70 In a September 1982 article in *Business Economics,* C. I. Allmon related y = Crest toothpaste sales in a given year (in thousands of dollars) to x_1 = Crest advertising budget in the year (in thousands of dollars), x_2 = ratio of Crest's advertising budget to Colgate's advertising budget in the year, and x_3 = U.S. personal disposable income in the year (in billions of dollars). The data analyzed are given in Table 12.21. When we perform a regression analysis of these data using the model

$$y = \beta_0 + \beta_1 x_1 + \beta_2 x_2 + \beta_3 x_3 + \varepsilon$$

we find that the least squares point estimates of the model parameters and their associated p-values (given in parentheses) are $b_0 = 30{,}626(.156)$, $b_1 = 3.893(.094)$, $b_2 = -29{,}607(.245)$, and $b_3 = 86.52(<.001)$. Suppose it was estimated at the end of 1979 that in 1980 the advertising budget for Crest would be 28,000; the ratio of Crest's advertising budget to Colgate's advertising budget would be 1.56; and the U.S. personal disposable income would be 1,821.7. Using the model, a point prediction of and a 95 percent prediction interval for Crest sales in 1980 are 251,059 and [221,988, 280,130]. Show how the point prediction has been calculated. Crest

12.71 The trend in home building in recent years has been to emphasize open spaces and great rooms, rather than smaller living rooms and family rooms. A builder of speculative homes in the college community of Oxford, Ohio, had been building such homes, but his homes had been taking many months to sell and selling for substantially less than the asking price. In order to determine what types of homes would attract residents of the community, the builder contacted a statistician at a local college. The statistician went to a local real estate agency and obtained the data in Table 12.22. This table presents the sales price y, square footage x_1, number of rooms x_2, number

TABLE 12.21 Crest Toothpaste Sales Data Crest

Year	Crest Sales, y	Crest Budget, x_1	Ratio, x_2	U.S. Personal Disposable Income, x_3
1967	105,000	16,300	1.25	547.9
1968	105,000	15,800	1.34	593.4
1969	121,600	16,000	1.22	638.9
1970	113,750	14,200	1.00	695.3
1971	113,750	15,000	1.15	751.8
1972	128,925	14,000	1.13	810.3
1973	142,500	15,400	1.05	914.5
1974	126,000	18,250	1.27	998.3
1975	162,000	17,300	1.07	1,096.1
1976	191,625	23,000	1.17	1,194.4
1977	189,000	19,300	1.07	1,311.5
1978	210,000	23,056	1.54	1,462.9
1979	224,250	26,000	1.59	1,641.7

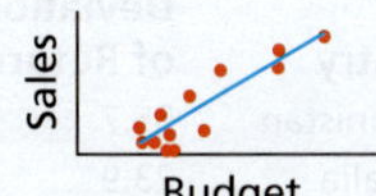

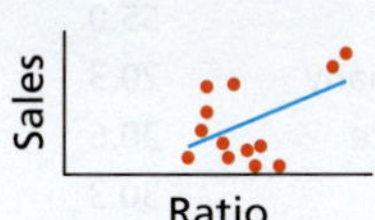

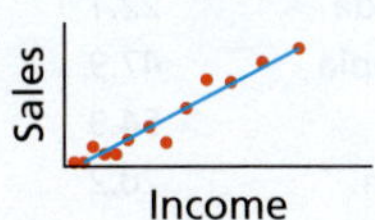

Source: C. I. Allmon, "Advertising and Sales Relationships for Toothpaste: Another Look," *Business Economics* (September 1982), pp. 17, 58. Reprinted by permission.

TABLE 12.22 Measurements Taken on 63 Single-Family Residences OxHome

Residence	Sales Price, y (× \$1,000)	Square Feet, x_1	Rooms, x_2	Bedrooms, x_3	Age, x_4
1	53.5	1,008	5	2	35
2	49.0	1,290	6	3	36
3	50.5	860	8	2	36
4	49.9	912	5	3	41
5	52.0	1,204	6	3	40
6	55.0	1,204	5	3	10
7	80.5	1,764	8	4	64
8	86.0	1,600	7	3	19
9	69.0	1,255	5	3	16
10	149.0	3,600	10	5	17
11	46.0	864	5	3	37
12	38.0	720	4	2	41
13	49.5	1,008	6	3	35
14	105.0	1,950	8	3	52
15	152.5	2,086	7	3	12
16	85.0	2,011	9	4	76
17	60.0	1,465	6	3	102
18	58.5	1,232	5	2	69
19	101.0	1,736	7	3	67
20	79.4	1,296	6	3	11
21	125.0	1,996	7	3	9
22	87.9	1,874	5	2	14
23	80.0	1,580	5	3	11
24	94.0	1,920	5	3	14
25	74.0	1,430	9	3	16
26	69.0	1,486	6	3	27
27	63.0	1,008	5	2	35
28	67.5	1,282	5	3	20
29	35.0	1,134	5	2	74
30	142.5	2,400	9	4	15
31	92.2	1,701	5	3	15
32	56.0	1,020	6	3	16
33	63.0	1,053	5	2	24
34	60.0	1,728	6	3	26
35	34.0	416	3	1	42
36	52.0	1,040	5	2	9
37	75.0	1,496	6	3	30
38	93.0	1,936	8	4	39
39	60.0	1,904	7	4	32
40	73.0	1,080	5	2	24
41	71.0	1,768	8	4	74
42	83.0	1,503	6	3	14
43	90.0	1,736	7	3	16
44	83.0	1,695	6	3	12
45	115.0	2,186	8	4	12
46	50.0	888	5	2	34
47	55.2	1,120	6	3	29
48	61.0	1,400	5	3	33
49	147.0	2,165	7	3	2
50	210.0	2,353	8	4	15
51	60.0	1,536	6	3	36
52	100.0	1,972	8	3	37
53	44.5	1,120	5	3	27
54	55.0	1,664	7	3	79
55	53.4	925	5	3	20
56	65.0	1,288	5	3	2
57	73.0	1,400	5	3	2
58	40.0	1,376	6	3	103
59	141.0	2,038	12	4	62
60	68.0	1,572	6	3	29
61	139.0	1,545	6	3	9
62	140.0	1,993	6	3	4
63	55.0	1,130	5	2	21

TABLE 12.23 The Stock Market Return Volatility Data InvRisk2

Country	Standard Deviation of Return, y	Credit Rating, x_1	Developing or Emerging	Country	Standard Deviation of Return, y	Credit Rating, x_1	Developing or Emerging
Afghanistan	55.7	8.3	E	New Zealand	24.3	69.4	D
Australia	23.9	71.2	D	Nigeria	46.2	15.8	E
China	27.2	57.0	E	Oman	28.6	51.8	D
Cuba	55.0	8.7	E	Panama	38.6	26.4	E
Germany	20.3	90.9	D	Spain	23.4	73.7	D
France	20.6	89.1	D	Sudan	60.5	6.0	E
India	30.3	46.1	E	Taiwan	22.2	79.9	D
Belgium	22.3	79.2	D	Norway	21.4	84.6	D
Canada	22.1	80.3	D	Sweden	23.3	74.1	D
Ethiopia	47.9	14.1	E	Togo	45.1	17.0	E
Haiti	54.9	8.8	E	Ukraine	46.3	15.7	E
Japan	20.2	91.6	D	United Kingdom	20.8	87.8	D
Libya	36.7	30.0	E	United States	20.3	90.7	D
Malaysia	24.3	69.1	E	Vietnam	36.9	29.5	E
Mexico	31.8	41.8	E	Zimbabwe	36.2	31.0	E

Source: C. B. Erb, C. R. Harvey, and T. E. Viskanta, "Expected Returns and Volatility in 135 Countries." *Journal of Portfolio Management,* Vol. 22, no. 3, Spring 1996, pp. 54–55 (Exhibit 6). This copyrighted material is reprinted with permission from the *Journal of Portfolio Management,* a publication of Institutional Investor, Inc., 488 Madison Ave., New York, NY 10022.

of bedrooms x_3, and age x_4 for each of 63 single-family residences recently sold in the community. When we perform a regression analysis of these data using the model

$$y = \beta_0 + \beta_1 x_1 + \beta_2 x_2 + \beta_3 x_3 + \beta_4 x_4 + \varepsilon$$

we find that the least squares point estimates of the model parameters and their associated p-values (given in parentheses) are $b_0 = 10.3676(.3710)$, $b_1 = .0500(<.001)$, $b_2 = 6.3218(.0152)$, $b_3 = -11.1032(.0635)$, and $b_4 = -.4319(.0002)$. Discuss why the estimates $b_2 = 6.3218$ and $b_3 = -11.1032$ suggest that it might be more profitable when building a house of a specified square footage (1) to include both a (smaller) living room and family room rather than a (larger) great room and (2) to not increase the number of bedrooms (at the cost of another type of room) that would normally be included in a house of the specified square footage. OxHome

Note: Based on the statistical results, the builder realized that there are many families with children in a college town and that the parents in such families would rather have one living area for the children (the family room) and a separate living area for themselves (the living room). The builder started modifying his open-space homes accordingly and greatly increased his profits.

12.72 Recall from Exercise 11.88 (page 518) that C. B. Erb, C. R. Harvey, and T. E. Viskanta studied the relationship between credit rating and investment risk for 40 countries. In a more recent article (*Journal of Portfolio Management,* Spring 1996), these authors studied the volatility of a country's stock market returns by considering the standard deviation of these returns. They used the model InvRisk2

$$y = \beta_0 + \beta_1 x_1 + \beta_2 x_2 + \beta_3 x_1 x_2 + \varepsilon$$

to relate y, the standard deviation of a country's stock returns, to x_1, the country's credit rating, and x_2, a dummy variable that equals 1 if the country is a developing country and 0 if the country is an emerging country. When regression analysis is used to fit this model to the data in Table 12.23, we find that the least squares point estimates of the model parameters and their associated p-values (given in parentheses) are $b_0 = 56.9171(<.001)$, $b_1 = -.5574(<.001)$, $b_2 = -18.2934(.0026)$, and $b_3 = .3537(<.001)$. Using the least squares point estimates, show that the equation $\hat{y} = 56.9171 - .5574x_1$ estimates the relationship between stock market return volatility and credit rating for emerging countries, and that the equation $\hat{y} = 38.6237 - .2037x_1$ estimates the relationship between stock market return volatility and credit rating for developing countries. Then use these equations to discuss the nature of the interaction between x_1 and x_2.

12.73 In the article "The Effect of Promotion Timing on Major League Baseball Attendance" (*Sport Marketing Quarterly,* December 1999), T. C. Boyd and T. C. Krehbiel use data from six major league baseball teams having outdoor stadiums to study the effect of promotion timing on major league baseball attendance. One of their regression models describes game attendance in 1996 as follows (p-values less than .10 are shown in parentheses under the appropriate independent variables):

$$\text{Attendance} = 2{,}521 + 106.5\,\textit{Temperature} + 12.33\,\textit{Winning \%} + .2248\,\textit{OpWin \%}$$
$$(<.001) \qquad (<.001) \qquad (<.001)$$
$$-\ 424.2\,\textit{DayGame} + 4{,}845\,\textit{Weekend} + 1{,}192\,\textit{Rival} + 4{,}745\,\textit{Promotion}$$
$$(<.001) \qquad (<.10) \qquad (<.001)$$
$$+\ 5{,}059\,\textit{Promo*DayGame} - 4{,}690\,\textit{Promo*Weekend} + 696.5\,\textit{Promo*Rival}$$
$$(<.001) \qquad (<.001)$$

In this model, *Temperature* is the high temperature recorded in the city on game day; *Winning %* is the home team's winning percentage at the start of the game; *OpWin %* is a dummy variable that equals 1 if the opponent's winning percentage was .500 or higher and 0 otherwise; *DayGame* is a dummy variable that equals 1 if the game was a day game and 0 otherwise; *Weekend* is a dummy variable that equals 1 if the game was on a Friday, Saturday, or Sunday and 0 otherwise; *Rival* is a dummy variable that equals 1 if the opponent was a rival and 0 otherwise; *Promotion* is a dummy variable that equals 1 if the home team ran a promotion during the game and 0 otherwise. Using the model, which is based on 475 games and has on R^2 of .6221, Boyd and Krehbiel conclude that "promotions run during day games and on weekdays are likely to result in greater attendance increases." Explain these conclusions by using the least squares point estimates 5,059 and −4,690, which are multiplied by the interaction terms *Promo*DayGame,* and *Promo*Weekend.* Given that major league baseball teams tend to run promotions during night games and on weekends, what are the practical consequences of the authors' conclusions?

12.74 MODEL BUILDING WITH SQUARED AND INTERACTION TERMS

Recall from Example 12.17 (page 591) that we have concluded that perhaps the best sales territory performance model using only linear terms is the model using TIME, MKTPOTEN, ADVER, MKTSHARE, and CHANGE. For this model, $s = 430.23$ and $\bar{R}^2 = .893$. To decide which squared and pairwise interaction terms should be added to this model, we consider all possible squares and pairwise interactions of the five linear independent variables in this model. So that we can better understand a MINITAB output to follow, the MINITAB notation for these squares and pairwise interactions is as follows:

SQT = TIME*TIME		TC = TIME*CHANGE	
SQMP = MKTPOTEN*MKTPOTEN		MPA = MKTPOTEN*ADVER	
SQA = ADVER*ADVER		MPMS = MKTPOTEN*MKTSHARE	
SQMS = MKTSHARE*MKTSHARE		MPC = MKTPOTEN*CHANGE	
SQC = CHANGE*CHANGE		AMS = ADVER*MKTSHARE	
TMP = TIME*MKTPOTEN		AC = ADVER*CHANGE	
TA = TIME*ADVER		MSC = MKTSHARE*CHANGE	
TMS = TIME*MKTSHARE			

Consider having MINITAB evaluate all possible models involving these squared and pairwise interaction terms, where the five linear terms TIME, MKTPOTEN, ADVER, MKTSHARE, and CHANGE are included in each possible model. If we have MINITAB do this and find the best single model of each size, we obtain the following output:

The following variables are included in all models: Time MktPoten Adver MktShare Change

Vars	R-Sq	R-Sq(adj)	Mallows C-p	S	SQT	SQMP	SQA	SQMS	SQC	TMP	TA	TMS	TC	MPA	MPMS	MPC	AMS	AC	MSC
1	94.2	92.2	43.2	365.87								X							
2	95.8	94.1	29.7	318.19	X							X							
3	96.5	94.7	25.8	301.61	X							X		X					
4	97.0	95.3	22.5	285.54	X						X	X			X				
5	97.5	95.7	20.3	272.05	X						X	X			X		X		
6	98.1	96.5	16.4	244.00	X		X				X	X			X			X	
7	98.7	97.4	13.0	210.70	X	X					X	X			X		X	X	
8	99.0	97.8	12.3	193.95	X	X			X		X	X			X		X	X	
9	99.2	98.0	12.7	185.45	X	X		X			X	X			X		X	X	X
10	99.3	98.2	13.3	175.70	X	X		X			X	X			X	X	X	X	X
11	99.4	98.2	14.6	177.09	X	X		X		X	X	X			X	X	X	X	X
12	99.5	98.2	15.8	174.60	X	X		X	X	X	X	X			X	X	X	X	X
13	99.5	98.1	17.5	183.22	X	X	X		X	X	X	X	X		X	X	X	X	X
14	99.6	97.9	19.1	189.77	X	X		X	X	X	X	X	X	X	X	X	X	X	X
15	99.6	97.4	21.0	210.78	X	X	X	X	X	X	X	X	X	X	X	X	X	X	X

The model using 12 squared and pairwise interaction terms has the smallest s. However, if we desire a somewhat simpler model, note that s does not increase substantially until we move from a model having seven squared and pairwise interaction terms to a model having six such terms. It can also be verified that the model having seven squared and pairwise interaction terms is the largest model for which all of the independent variables have p-values less than .05. Therefore, we might consider this model to have an optimal mix of a small s and simplicity. Identify s and $\bar{R}^2$ for this model. How do the s and $\bar{R}^2$ you have identified compare with the s and $\bar{R}^2$ for the model using only the linear terms TIME, MKTPOTEN, ADVER, MKTSHARE, and CHANGE?

12.75 THE FRESH DETERGENT CASE Fresh3

Recall from Exercise 12.46 (page 582) that Enterprise Industries has advertised Fresh liquid laundry detergent by using three different advertising campaigns—advertising campaign A (television commercials), advertising campaign B (a balanced mixture of television and radio commercials) and advertising campaign C (a balanced mixture of television, radio, newspaper, and magazine ads). To compare the effectiveness of these advertising campaigns, consider the model

$$y = \beta_0 + \beta_1 x_4 + \beta_2 x_3 + \beta_3 x_3^2 + \beta_4 x_4 x_3 + \beta_5 D_B + \beta_6 D_C + \varepsilon$$

Here, y is demand for Fresh; x_4 is the price difference; x_3 is Enterprise Industries' advertising expenditure for Fresh; D_B equals 1 if advertising campaign B is used in a sales period and 0 otherwise; and D_C equals 1 if advertising campaign C is used in a sales period and 0 otherwise. If we use this model to perform a regression analysis of the data in Tables 12.4 and 12.16, we obtain the following partial MegaStat output:

Regression output

variables	coefficients	std. error	t (df = 23)	p-value	confidence interval 95% lower	confidence interval 95% upper
Intercept	25.6127	4.7938	5.343	2.00E-05	15.6960	35.5294
X4	9.0587	3.0317	2.988	.0066	2.7871	15.3302
X3	−6.5377	1.5814	−4.134	.0004	−9.8090	−3.2664
X3SQ	0.5844	0.1299	4.500	.0002	0.3158	0.8531
X43	−1.1565	0.4557	−2.538	.0184	−2.0992	−0.2137
DB	0.2137	0.0622	3.438	.0022	0.0851	0.3423
DC	0.3818	0.0613	6.233	2.33E-06	0.2551	0.5085

Predicted values for: Y

Predicted	95% Confidence Interval lower	95% Confidence Interval upper	95% Prediction Interval lower	95% Prediction Interval upper	Leverage
8.50068	8.40370	8.59765	8.21322	8.78813	0.128

R^2 0.971
Adjusted R^2 0.963
R 0.985
Std. Error 0.131

a In the above model the parameter β_5 represents the effect on mean demand of advertising campaign B compared to advertising campaign A, and the parameter β_6 represents the effect on mean demand of advertising campaign C compared to advertising campaign A. Use the regression output to find a point estimate of each of the above effects and to test the significance of each of the above effects. Also, find a 95 percent confidence interval for each of the above effects. Interpret your results.

b Consider the alternative model

$$y = \beta_0 + \beta_1 x_4 + \beta_2 x_3 + \beta_3 x_3^2 + \beta_4 x_4 x_3 + \beta_5 D_A + \beta_6 D_C + \varepsilon$$

Here D_A equals 1 if advertising campaign A is used and 0 otherwise. The MegaStat output of the least squares point estimates of the parameters of this model is as follows:

Regression output

variables	coefficients	std. error	t (df = 23)	p-value	confidence interval 95% lower	confidence interval 95% upper
Intercept	25.8264	4.7946	5.387	1.80E-05	15.9081	35.7447
X4	9.0587	3.0317	2.988	.0066	2.7871	15.3302
X3	−6.5377	1.5814	−4.134	.0004	−9.8090	−3.2664
X3SQ	0.5844	0.1299	4.500	.0002	0.3158	0.8531
X43	−1.1565	0.4557	−2.538	.0184	−2.0992	−0.2137
DA	−0.2137	0.0622	−3.438	.0022	−0.3423	−0.0851
DC	0.1681	0.0637	2.638	.0147	0.0363	0.2999

Noting that β_6 represents the effect on mean demand of advertising campaign C compared to advertising campaign B, find a point estimate of and a 95 percent confidence interval for this effect. Also, test the significance of this effect. Interpret your results.

c Consider the alternative model

$$y = \beta_0 + \beta_1 x_4 + \beta_2 x_3 + \beta_3 x_3^2 + \beta_4 x_4 x_3 + \beta_5 D_B + \beta_6 D_C + \beta_7 x_3 D_B + \beta_8 x_3 D_C + \varepsilon$$

The MegaStat output of the least squares point estimates of the parameters of this model is as follows:

Regression output

variables	coefficients	std. error	t (df = 21)	p-value	confidence interval 95% lower	95% upper
Intercept	28.6873	5.1285	5.594	1.50E-05	18.0221	39.3526
X4	10.8253	3.2988	3.282	.0036	3.9651	17.6855
X3	−7.4115	1.6617	−4.460	.0002	−10.8671	−3.9558
X3SQ	0.6458	0.1346	4.798	.0001	0.3659	0.9257
X43	−1.4156	0.4929	−2.872	.0091	−2.4406	−0.3907
DB	−0.4807	0.7309	−0.658	.5179	−2.0007	1.0393
DC	−0.9351	0.8357	−1.119	.2758	−2.6731	0.8029
X3DB	0.1072	0.1117	0.960	.3480	−0.1251	0.3395
X3DC	0.2035	0.1288	1.580	.1291	−0.0644	0.4714

R^2	0.974
Adjusted R^2	0.964
R	0.987
Std. Error	0.129
n	30
k	8
Dep. Var.	Y

Predicted values for: Y

Predicted	95% Confidence Interval lower	upper	95% Prediction Interval lower	upper	Leverage
8.51183	8.41229	8.61136	8.22486	8.79879	0.137

Let $\mu_{[d,a,A]}$, $\mu_{[d,a,B]}$, and $\mu_{[d,a,C]}$ denote the mean demands for Fresh when the price difference is d, the advertising expenditure is a, and we use advertising campaigns A, B, and C, respectively. The model of this part implies that

$$\mu_{[d,a,A]} = \beta_0 + \beta_1 d + \beta_2 a + \beta_3 a^2 + \beta_4 da + \beta_5(0) + \beta_6(0) + \beta_7 a(0) + \beta_8 a(0)$$
$$\mu_{[d,a,B]} = \beta_0 + \beta_1 d + \beta_2 a + \beta_3 a^2 + \beta_4 da + \beta_5(1) + \beta_6(0) + \beta_7 a(1) + \beta_8 a(0)$$
$$\mu_{[d,a,C]} = \beta_0 + \beta_1 d + \beta_2 a + \beta_3 a^2 + \beta_4 da + \beta_5(0) + \beta_6(1) + \beta_7 a(0) + \beta_8 a(1)$$

Using these equations, verify that $\mu_{[d,a,C]} - \mu_{[d,a,A]}$ equals $\beta_6 + \beta_8 a$. Then, using the least squares point estimates, show that a point estimate of $\mu_{[d,a,C]} - \mu_{[d,a,A]}$ equals .3266 when $a = 6.2$ and equals .4080 when $a = 6.6$. Also, verify that $\mu_{[d,a,C]} - \mu_{[d,a,B]}$ equals $\beta_6 - \beta_5 + \beta_8 a - \beta_7 a$. Using the least squares point estimates, show that a point estimate of $\mu_{[d,a,C]} - \mu_{[d,a,B]}$ equals .14266 when $a = 6.2$ and equals .18118 when $a = 6.6$. Discuss why these results imply that the larger that advertising expenditure a is, then the larger is the improvement in mean sales that is obtained by using advertising campaign C rather than advertising campaign A or B.

d The prediction results given at the bottom of the first and third MegaStat outputs of this exercise correspond to a future period when the price difference will be $x_4 = .20$, the advertising expenditure will be $x_3 = 6.50$, and campaign C will be used. Which model—the first model or the third model of this exercise—gives the shortest 95 percent prediction interval for Fresh demand? Using all of the results in this exercise, discuss why there might be a small amount of interaction between advertising expenditure and advertising campaign.

12.76 THE DIFFERENCE IN ESTIMATE OF β_j STATISTIC

Consider the difference between the least squares point estimate b_j of β_j, computed using all n observations, and the least squares point estimate $b_j^{(i)}$ of β_j, computed using all n observations except for observation i. SAS (an advanced software system) calculates this difference for each observation and divides the difference by its standard error to form the **difference in estimate of β_j statistic.** If the absolute value of this statistic is greater than 2 (a sometimes-used critical value for this statistic), then removing observation i from the data set would substantially change the least squares point estimate of β_j. For example, consider the hospital labor needs model of Section 12.14 that uses all 17 observations to relate y to x_1, x_2, and x_3. Also consider the columns labeled "Dfbetas" in Figure 12.56. Notice that there are four such columns—one for each model parameter—which are labeled INTERCEP, X1, X2, and X3. Each of these columns contains the **difference in estimate of β_j statistic** related to the column's parameter label for each observation.

FIGURE 12.56 Difference in Estimate of β_j Statistics

Obs	INTERCEP Dfbetas	X1 Dfbetas	X2 Dfbetas	X3 Dfbetas
1	-0.0477	0.0157	-0.0083	0.0309
2	0.0138	-0.0050	0.0119	-0.0183
3	0.0307	-0.0084	0.0060	-0.0216
4	0.2416	-0.0217	0.0251	-0.1821
5	0.0035	0.0014	-0.0099	0.0074
6	-0.0881	-0.0703	0.0724	0.0401
7	0.0045	-0.0008	-0.0180	0.0179
8	0.0764	-0.0319	0.0063	-0.0314
9	0.0309	0.0243	0.0304	-0.0873
10	0.1787	-0.2924	0.3163	-0.2544
11	-0.0265	0.0560	-0.0792	0.0680
12	-0.4387	0.3549	-0.3782	0.3864
13	-0.0671	0.0230	-0.0243	0.0390
14	-0.8544	1.1389	-0.9198	0.9620
15	0.9616	0.1324	-0.0133	-0.9561
16	0.9880	-1.4289	1.7339	-1.1029
17	0.0294	-3.0114	1.2688	0.3155

We see that for observation 17 "INTERCEP Dfbetas" (=.0294), "X2 Dfbetas" (=1.2688), and "X3 Dfbetas" (=.3155) are all less than 2 in absolute value. This says that the least squares point estimates of β_0, β_2, and β_3 probably would not change substantially if hospital 17 were removed from the data set. However, for observation 17 "X1 Dfbetas" (= −3.0114) is greater than 2 in absolute value. What does this say?

Note: If we remove hospital 14 from the data set or use a dummy variable to model the inefficiency of large hospitals (see Section 12.14), then hospital 17 becomes much less influential with respect to the difference in estimate of β_j statistic.

Note: The formula for the difference in estimate of β_j statistic involves a fairly complicated matrix algebra expression and will not be given in this book. The interested reader is referred to Bowerman and O'Connell (1990). MINITAB and MegaStat do not give this statistic.

12.77 THE DIFFERENCE IN FITS STATISTIC

Consider the difference between the point prediction $\hat{y}_i$ of y_i computed using least squares point estimates based on all n observations and the point prediction $\hat{y}_{(i)}$ of y_i computed using least squares point estimates based on all n observations except for observation i. Some statistical software packages calculate this difference for each observation and divide the difference by its standard error to form the **difference in fits statistic.** If the absolute value of this statistic is greater than 2 (a sometimes-used critical value for this statistic), then removing observation i from the data set would substantially change the point prediction of y_i. For example, consider the hospital labor needs model of Section 12.14 that uses all 17 observations to relate y to x_1, x_2, and x_3. Also consider the MINITAB output of the column labeled "Dffits" on the page margin. This column contains the **difference in fits statistic** for each observation. The value of this statistic for observation 17 is −4.9623. What does this say?

Difference in Fits Statistics

Hosp	Dffits
1	−0.07541
2	−0.02404
3	0.04383
4	0.32657
5	0.04213
6	−0.22799
7	0.08818
8	0.18406
9	−0.25179
10	−0.44871
11	0.18237
12	−0.52368
13	−0.14509
14	1.88820
15	−1.47227
16	1.89295
17	−4.96226

Note: If we remove hospital 14 from the data set or use a dummy variable to model the inefficiency of large hospitals (see Section 12.14), then hospital 17 becomes much less influential with respect to the difference in fits statistic.

Note: The formula for the difference in fits statistic for observation i is found by multiplying the formula for the studentized deleted residual for observation i by $[h_i/(1 - h_i)]^{1/2}$. Here h_i is the leverage value for observation i.

12.78 DISCRIMINATE ANALYSIS PerfTest

Consider the performance data in Table 12.20 (page 611). In Section 12.15 we used logistic regression to classify a potential employee into group 1 ("will perform successfully") or group 0 ("will not perform successfully"). Another way to make the classification is to use **discriminant analysis.** For example, Figure 12.57 presents the MINITAB output of a discriminant analysis

FIGURE 12.57 **MINITAB Output of a Discriminant Analysis of the Performance Data**

```
Linear Discriminant Function for Groups
                0          1
Constant   -298.27   -351.65
Test 1        5.20      5.68
Test 2        1.97      2.10
```

of the performance data. This figure gives a **discriminant equation for group 0** and a **discriminant equation for group 1.** Denoting these equations as $\hat{y}_{(0)}$ and $\hat{y}_{(1)}$, the MINITAB output tells us that

$$\hat{y}_{(0)} = -298.27 + 5.20x_1 + 1.97x_2 \quad \text{and} \quad \hat{y}_{(1)} = -351.65 + 5.68x_1 + 2.10x_2$$

A prospective employee is classified into group 1 if and only if $\hat{y}_{(1)}$ is greater than $\hat{y}_{(0)}$. For example, consider a prospective employee who scores a 93 on test 1 and an 84 on test 2. For this prospective employee, $\hat{y}_{(0)} = 350.81$ and $\hat{y}_{(1)} = 352.99$. Since $\hat{y}_{(1)}$ is greater than $\hat{y}_{(0)}$, the prospective employee is classified into group 1. Calculate $\hat{y}_{(0)}$ and $\hat{y}_{(1)}$ for a prospective employee who scores an 85 on test 1 and an 82 on test 2. Then, classify this employee into group 0 or group 1. Interpret what your classification means.

Note: Discriminant analysis is a **multivariate statistical technique.** In Appendix I on the CD-ROM included with this book we discuss three other multivariate techniques—factor analysis, cluster analysis, and multidimensional scaling.

12.79 Internet Exercise AlbHome

How do home prices vary with square footage, age, and a variety of other factors? The Data and Story Library (DASL) contains data, including the sale price, for a random sample of 117 homes sold in Albuquerque, New Mexico. Go to the DASL website (http://lib.stat.cmu.edu/DASL/) and retrieve the home price data set (http://lib.stat.cmu.edu/DASL/Datafiles/homedat.html). There are a number of ways to capture the home price data from the DASL site. One simple way is to select just the rows containing the data values (and not the labels), copy, paste directly into an Excel or MINITAB worksheet, add your own variable labels, and save the resulting worksheet. It is possible to copy the variable labels from DASL as well, but the differences in alignment and the intervening blank line add to the difficulty (data sets: AlbHome.xls, AlbHome.mtw).

a Construct plots of PRICE versus SQFT and PRICE versus AGE. Describe the nature and apparent strength of the relationships between PRICE and the variables SQFT and AGE. Construct box plots of PRICE versus each of the qualitative/dummy variables NE (northeast location), CUST (custom built), and COR (corner location). What do the box plots suggest about the effect of these features on home prices?

b Using MINITAB, Excel, MegaStat, or other available statistical software, develop a multiple regression model of the dependent variable PRICE versus independent variables SQFT, AGE, NE, CUST, and COR. Report and interpret the key summary measures $-R^2$, the standard error, and the F-statistic from the ANOVA table. Report and interpret the p-values for the estimated regression coefficients. Which of the independent variables appear to be most important for predicting Albuquerque home prices? Compute and interpret a point prediction and a 95 percent prediction interval for a five-year-old, 2,500 square foot, custom-built home located in the northeast sector of the city (not on a corner lot). Prepare a brief summary of your observations.

c Using MINITAB, Excel, MegaStat, or other available statistical software, develop a multiple regression model of the dependent variable PRICE versus independent variables SQFT, NE, and SQFT*NE (an interaction variable formed as the product of SQFT and NE). Report and interpret the estimated regression coefficients to describe how the relationship between PRICE and SQFT varies by location (NE sector or not). You may find it helpful to construct a scatter plot of PRICE versus SQFT using two different plot symbols depending on whether the home is in the northeast sector.

Appendix 12.1 ■ Multiple Linear Regression Analysis Using MINITAB

The instruction blocks in this section each begin by describing the entry of data into the MINITAB Data window. Alternatively, the data may be loaded directly from the data disk included with the text. The appropriate data file name is given at the top of each instruction block. Please refer to Appendix 1.1 for further information about entering data, saving data, and printing results.

Multiple linear regression in Figure 12.5(a) on page 537 (data file: FuelCon2.mtw):

- In the Data window, enter the fuel consumption data from Table 12.1 (page 530)—the average hourly temperatures in column C1 with variable name Temp, the chill indices in column C2 with variable name Chill, and the weekly fuel consumptions in column C3 with variable name FuelCons.
- Select **Stat : Regression : Regression.**
- In the Regression dialog box, select FuelCons into the Response box.
- Select Temp and Chill into the Predictors window.

To compute a **prediction** for fuel consumption when the temperature is 40° F and the chill index 10:

- In the Regression dialog box, click on the Options... button.
- Type 40 and 10 in the "Prediction intervals for new observations" box. [The number and order of values in this box must match the Predictors list in the Regression dialog box.]
- Click OK in the Regression—Options dialog box.

To obtain **residual plots:**

- Click on the Graphs... button and check the desired plots (see Appendix 11.1).
- Click OK in the Regression—Graphs dialog box.

To see the regression results in the Session window and the high-resolution graphs:

- Click OK in the Regression dialog box.

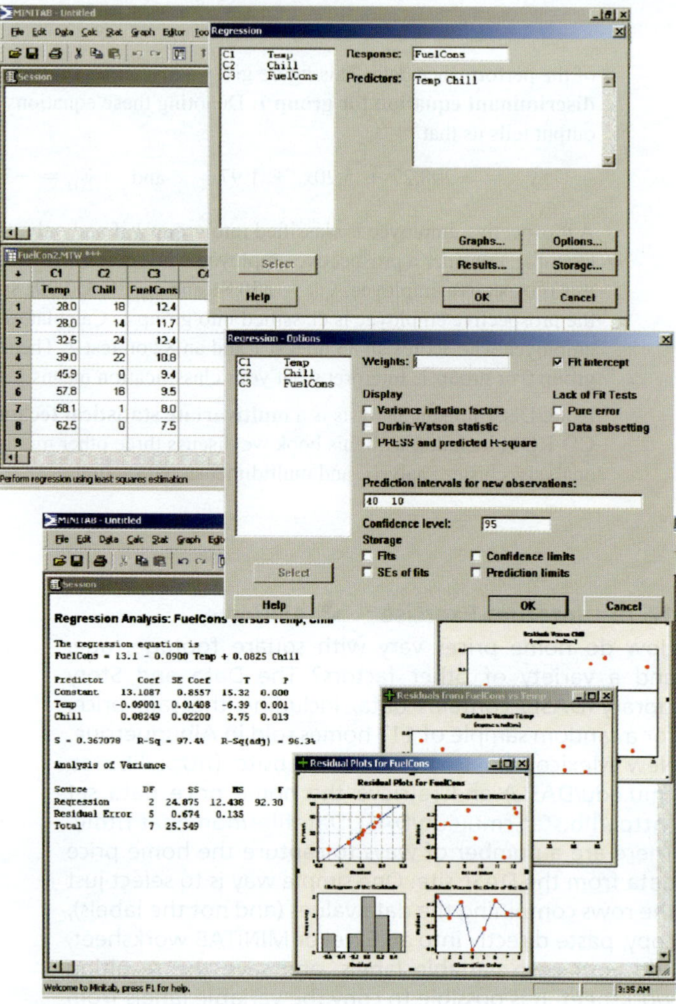

Multiple linear regression with a quadratic term in Figure 12.16 on page 559 (data file: GasAdd.mtw):

- In the Data window, enter the gasoline mileage data from Table 12.8 (page 559)—mileages in column C1 with variable name Mileage and units of additive in column C2 with variable name Units.

To compute the **quadratic predictor,** Units squared:

- Select **Calc : Calculator.**
- In the Calculator dialog box, enter UnitsSq in the "Store result in variable" box.
- Enter Units*Units in the Expression box.
- Click OK in the Calculator dialog box to obtain the squared values in column C3 with variable name UnitsSq.

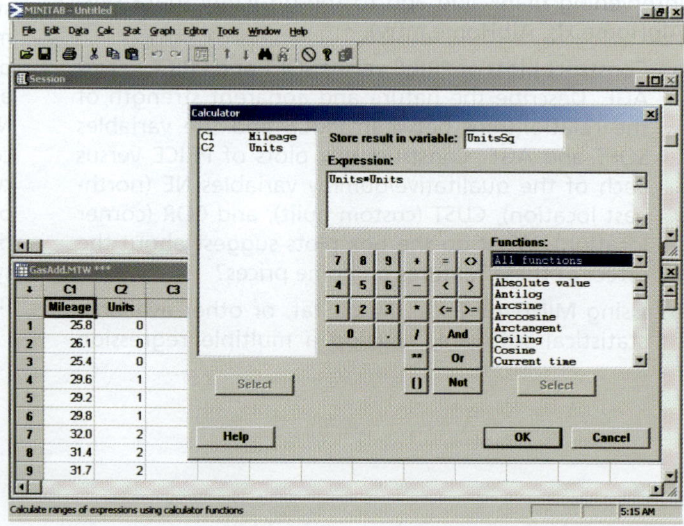

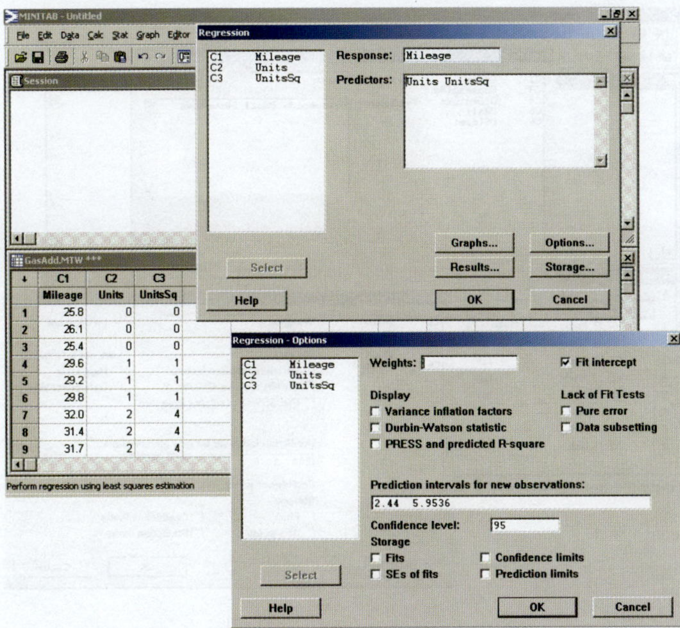

To **fit the quadratic regression** model:

- Select **Stat : Regression : Regression**
- In the Regression dialog box, select Mileage into the Response box.
- Select Units and UnitsSq into the Predictors window.
- Click OK in the Regression dialog box.

To compute a **prediction** for mileage when 2.44 units of additive are used:

- Click on the Options... button.
- In the Regression – Options dialog box, type 2.44 and 5.9536 into the "Prediction intervals for new observations" box. [$(2.44)^2 = 5.9536$ must first be calculated by hand.]
- Click OK in the Regression—Options dialog box.
- Click OK in the Regression dialog box.

Logistic regression in Figure 12.55 on page 611: In the Data window, enter the performance data in Table 12.20 on page 611—Group (either 1 or 0) in column C1 with variable name Group, the score on test 1 in column C2 with variable name Test 1, and the score on test 2 in column C3 with variable name Test 2. Select **Stat : Regression : Binary Logistic Regression.** In the "Binary Logistic Regression" dialog box, enter Group into the Response box, and enter Test 1 and Test 2 into the Model box. Click OK.

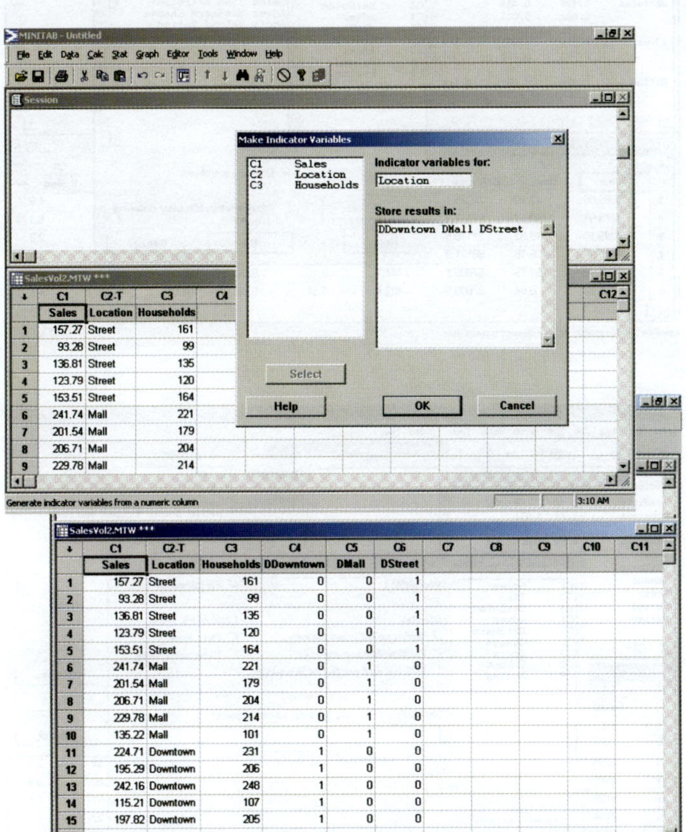

Multiple linear regression with indicator (dummy) variables in Figure 12.30(a) on page 576 (data file: Electronics2.mtw):

- In the Data window, enter the sales volume data from Table 12.13 on page 575 with sales volume in column C1 with variable name Sales, location in column C2 with variable name Location, and number of households in column C3 with variable name Households.

To **create indicator/dummy variable predictors:**

- Select **Calc : Make Indicator Variables.**
- In the "Make Indicator Variables" dialog box, enter Location into the "Indicator variables for" box.
- Enter DDowntown DMall DStreet in the "Store results in" window.

Indicator variables will be defined so that the first variable listed in the "Store results in" box (here DDowntown) is assigned the value 1 for each row containing the first (alphabetically ordered) distinct value (here Downtown) stored in the variable listed in the "Indicator variables for" box (here Location), with the value 0 assigned to all other rows. The second indicator variable (DMall) is assigned the value 1 for each row containing the next (alphabetically ordered) value (Mall) stored in Location. The last indicator variable (DStreet) is assigned the value 1 for each row containing the last (alphabetically ordered) value (Street) stored in Location.

- Click OK in the "Make Indicator Variables" dialog box.

To **fit the multiple regression** model:

- Select **Stat : Regression : Regression**
- In the Regression dialog box, select Sales into the Response box.
- Select Households DMall DDowntown into the Predictors window.

To compute a **prediction** of sales volume for 200,000 households and a mall location:

- Click on the Options… button.
- In the Regression—Options dialog box, type 200 1 0 in the "Prediction intervals for new observations" box.
- Click OK in the Regression—Options dialog box.
- Click OK in the Regression dialog box.

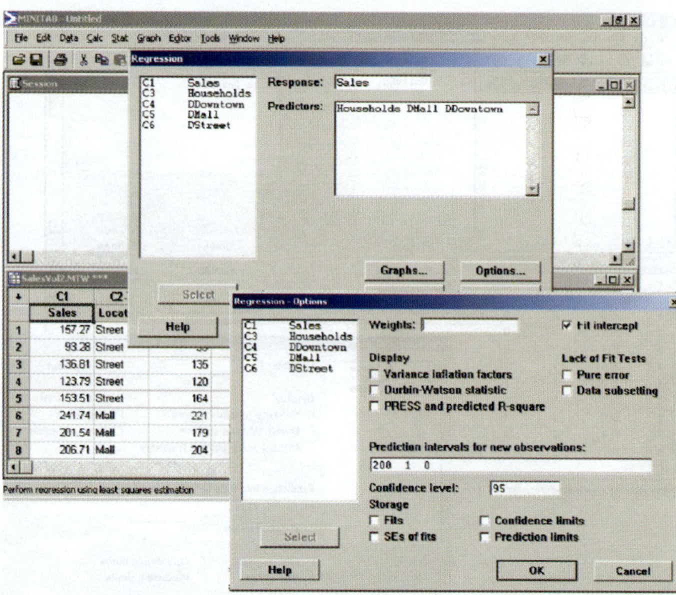

Correlation matrix in Figure 12.38 on page 588 (data file: SalePerf2.mtw):

- In the Data window, enter the sales territory performance data from Tables 12.2 (page 533) and 12.17 (page 588) into columns C1 – C9 with variable names Sales, Time, MktPoten, Adver, MktShare, Change, Accts, WkLoad, and Rating.
- Select **Stat : Basic Statistics : Correlation.**
- In the Correlation dialog box, enter all variable names into the Variables window.
- If p-values are desired, make sure that the "Display p-values" checkbox is checked.
- Click OK in the Correlation dialog box.

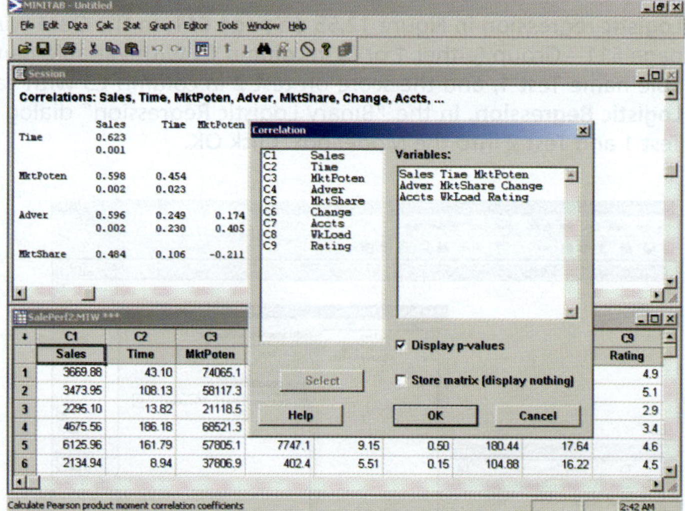

Variance inflation factors (VIF) similar to Figure 12.39 on page 589 (data file: SalePerf2.mtw):

- In the Data window, enter the sales territory performance data from Tables 12.2 (page 533) and 12.17 (page 588) into columns C1 – C9 with variable names Sales, Time, MktPoten, Adver, MktShare, Change, Accts, WkLoad, and Rating.
- Select **Stat : Regression : Regression.**
- In the Regression dialog box, enter Sales into the Response box and the remaining variables Time—Rating into the Predictors window.
- Click the Options… button.
- In the Regression—Options dialog box, click the "Variance inflation factors" checkbox.
- Click OK in the Regression—Options dialog box.
- Click OK in the Regression dialog box.

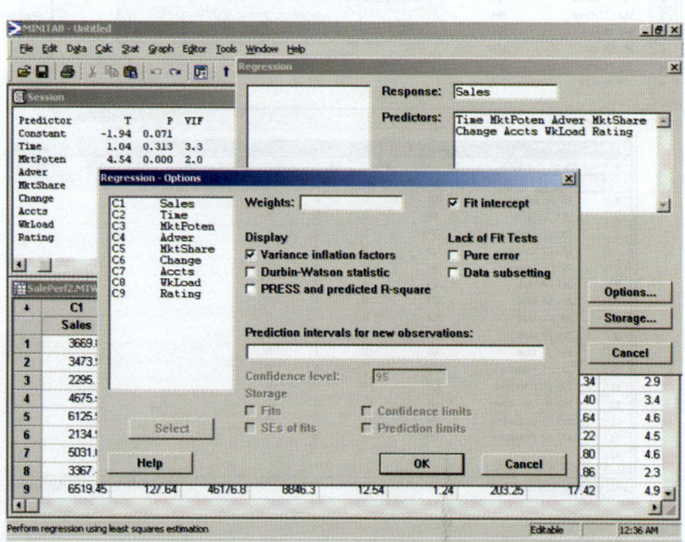

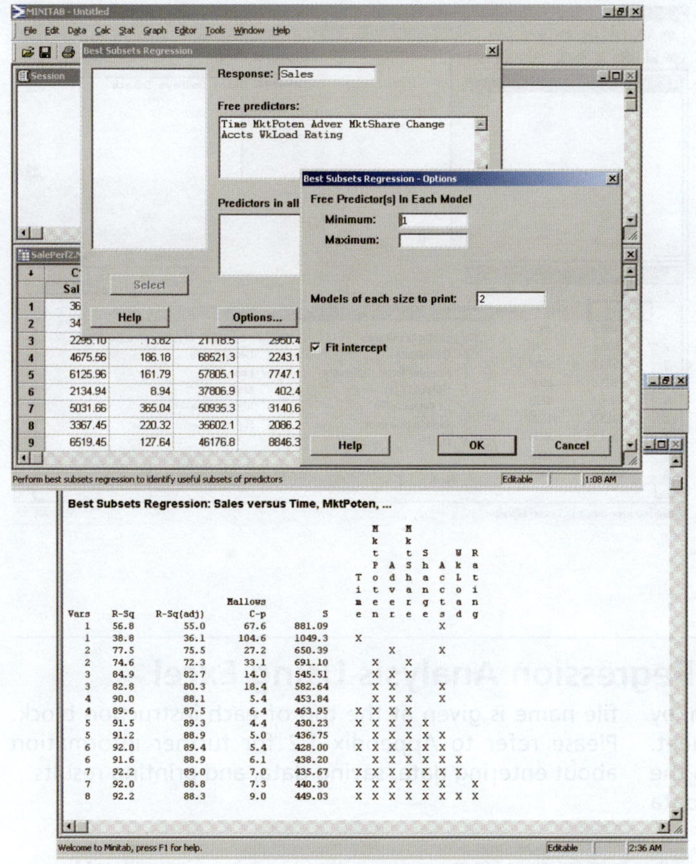

Best subsets regression in Figure 12.40(a) on page 592 (data file: SalePerf2.mtw):

- In the Data window, enter the sales territory performance data from Tables 12.2 (page 533) and 12.17 (page 588) into columns C1 – C9 with variable names Sales, Time, MktPoten, Adver, MktShare, Change, Accts, WkLoad, and Rating.
- Select **Stat : Regression : Best Subsets.**
- In the Best Subsets Regression dialog box, enter Sales into the Response box.
- Enter the remaining variable names into the "Free predictors" window.
- Click on the Options… button.
- In the "Best Subsets Regression—Options" dialog box, enter 2 in the "Models of each size to print" box.
- Click OK in the "Best Subsets Regression—Options" dialog box.
- Click OK in the Best Subsets Regression dialog box.

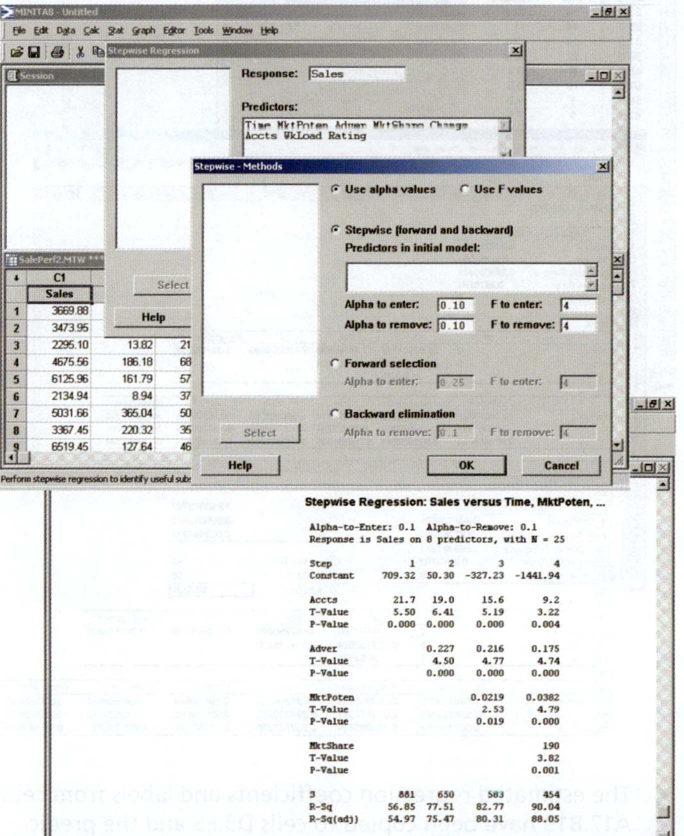

Stepwise regression in Figure 12.41(a) on page 596 (data file: SalePerf2.mtw):

- In the Data window, enter the sales territory performance data from Tables 12.2 (page 533) and 12.17 (page 588) into columns C1 – C9 with variable names Sales, Time, MktPoten, Adver, MktShare, Change, Accts, WkLoad, and Rating.
- Select **Stat : Regression : Stepwise.**
- In the Stepwise Regression dialog box, enter Sales into the Response box.
- Enter the remaining variable names into the Predictors window.
- Click on the Methods… button.
- In the Stepwise—Methods dialog box, select the "Use alpha values" option.
- Select the "Stepwise (Forward and Backward)" option.
- Enter 0.10 in the "Alpha to enter" and "Alpha to remove" boxes.
- Click OK in the Stepwise—Methods dialog box.
- Click OK in the Stepwise Regression dialog box.
- The results of the stepwise regression are given in the Session window.
- Note that **backward elimination** may be performed by clicking on the appropriate selections in the Stepwise—Methods dialog box.

Diagnostic measures for outlying and influential observations in Figure 12.51 on page 604 (data file: HospLab3.mtw):

- In the Data window, enter the hospital labor needs data from Table 12.19 on page 603 with variable names Hours, XRay, BedDays, and Length.
- Select **Stat : Regression : Regression.**
- In the Regression dialog box, select Hours into the Response box and select Xray, BedDays, and Length into the Predictors box. Click the Storage button.
- In the Regression—Storage dialog box, click the following checkboxes: Fits (for predicted values), Residuals, Deleted t residuals (for studentized deleted residuals), Hi (leverages), and Cook's distance. Then click OK.
- Click OK in the Regression dialog box to view the diagnostics in the data window.

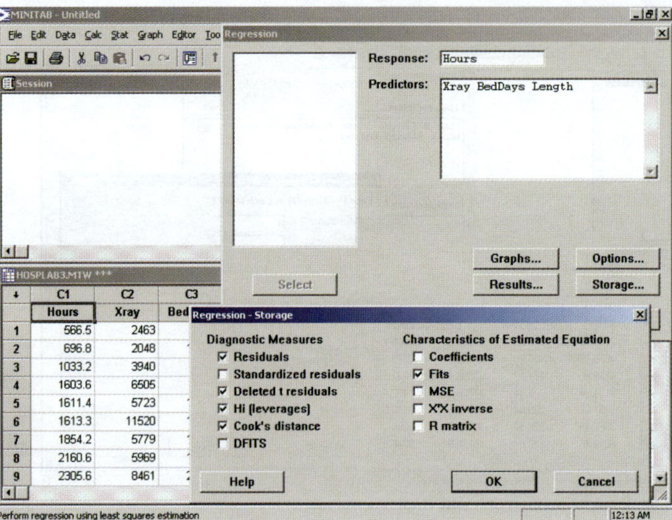

Appendix 12.2 ■ Multiple Linear Regression Analysis Using Excel

The instruction blocks in this section each begin by describing the entry of data into an Excel spreadsheet. Alternatively, the data may be loaded directly from the data disk included with the text. The appropriate data file name is given at the top of each instruction block. Please refer to Appendix 1.2 for further information about entering data, saving data, and printing results.

Multiple linear regression in Figure 12.5(b) on page 537 (data file: FuelCon2.xls):

- Enter the fuel consumption data from Table 12.1 (page 530)—temperatures (with label Temp) in column A, chill indexes (with label Chill) in column B, and fuel consumptions (with label FuelCons) in column C.
- Select **Tools : Data Analysis : Regression** and click OK in Data Analysis dialog box.
- In the Regression dialog box:
  Enter C1.C9 into the "Input Y Range" box.
  Enter A1.B9 into the "Input X Range" box.
- Place a checkmark in the Labels check box.
- Be sure that the "Constant is Zero" check box is NOT checked.
- Select the "New Worksheet Ply" Output option.
- Click OK in the Regression dialog box to obtain the regression output in a new worksheet.

Note: The independent variables must be in adjacent columns because the "Input X Range" must span the range of the values for all of the independent variables.

To compute a point prediction for fuel consumption when temperature is 40° F and the chill index is 10:

- The Excel Analysis ToolPak does not provide an option for computing point or interval predictions. A point prediction can be computed from the regression results using Excel cell formulas as follows.

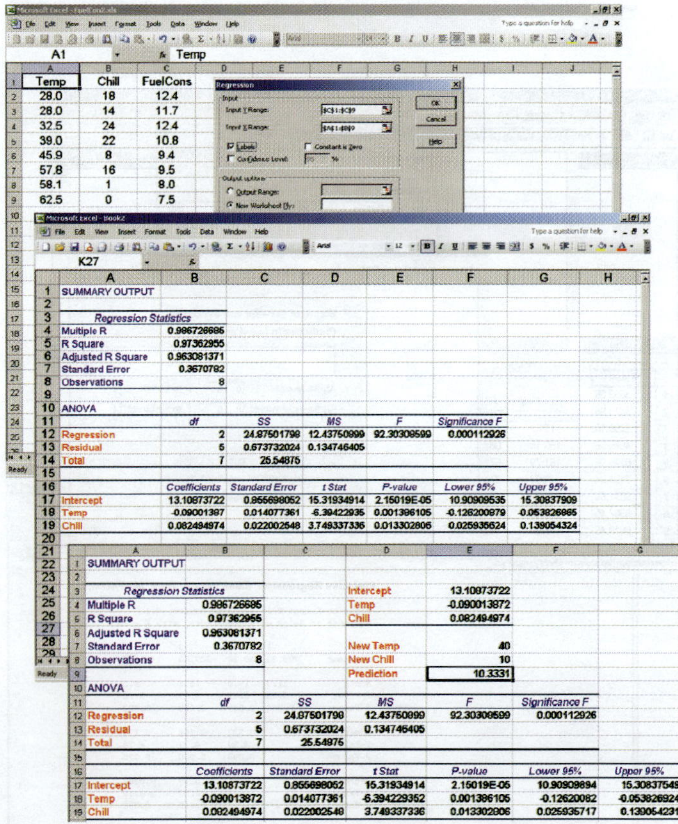

- The estimated regression coefficients and labels from cells A17.B19 have been copied to cells D3.E5 and the predictor values 40 and 10 have been placed in cells E7 and E8.
- In cell E9, enter the Excel formula =E3+E4*E7+E5*E8 (=10.3331) to compute the point prediction.

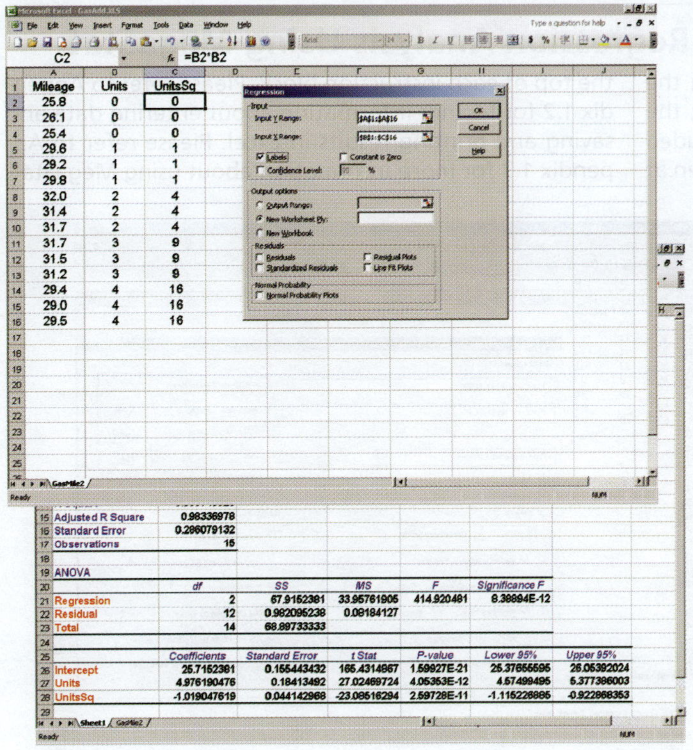

	Mileage	Units	UnitsSq
2	25.8	0	0
3	26.1	0	0
4	25.4	0	0
5	29.6	1	1
6	29.2	1	1
7	29.8	1	1
8	32.0	2	4
9	31.4	2	4
10	31.7	2	4
11	31.7	3	9
12	31.5	3	9
13	31.2	3	9
14	29.4	4	16
15	29.0	4	16
16	29.5	4	16

Adjusted R Square	0.98336978					
Standard Error	0.286079132					
Observations	15					
ANOVA						
	df	SS	MS	F	Significance F	
Regression	2	67.9152381	33.95761905	414.920481	8.38894E-12	
Residual	12	0.982095238	0.08184127			
Total	14	68.89733333				
	Coefficients	Standard Error	t Stat	P-value	Lower 95%	Upper 95%
Intercept	25.7152381	0.155443432	165.4314867	1.59927E-21	25.37655595	26.05392024
Units	4.976190476	0.18413492	27.02469724	4.05353E-12	4.57499495	5.377386003
UnitsSq	-1.019047619	0.044142968	-23.08516294	2.59728E-11	-1.115226865	-0.922866353

Multiple linear regression with a quadratic term similar to Figure 12.16 on page 559 (data file: GasAdd.xls):

- Enter the gas mileage data from Table 12.8 (page 559)—mileages (with label Mileage) in column A and units of additive (with label Units) in column B. (Units are listed second in order to be adjacent to the squared units predictor.)
- Enter UnitsSq into cell C1.
- Click on cell C2, and enter the formula =B2*B2. Press "Enter" to compute the squared value of Units for the first observation.
- Copy the cell formula of C2 through cell C16 (by double-clicking the drag handle in the lower right corner of cell C2) to compute the squared units for the remaining observations.
- Select **Tools : Data Analysis : Regression** and click OK in Data Analysis dialog box.
- In the Regression dialog box:

  Enter A1.A16 into the "Input Y Range" box.

  Enter B1.C16 into the "Input X Range" box.
- Place a checkmark in the Labels check box.
- Select the "New Worksheet Ply" Output option.
- Click OK in the Regression dialog box to obtain the regression output in a new worksheet.

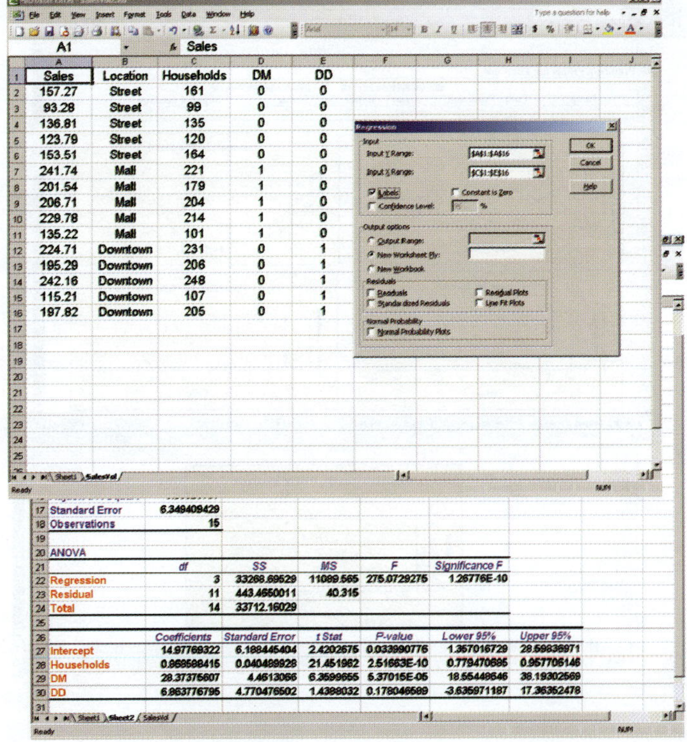

	Sales	Location	Households	DM	DD
2	157.27	Street	161	0	0
3	93.28	Street	99	0	0
4	136.81	Street	135	0	0
5	123.79	Street	120	0	0
6	153.51	Street	164	0	0
7	241.74	Mall	221	1	0
8	201.54	Mall	179	1	0
9	206.71	Mall	204	1	0
10	229.78	Mall	214	1	0
11	135.22	Mall	101	1	0
12	224.71	Downtown	231	0	1
13	195.29	Downtown	206	0	1
14	242.16	Downtown	248	0	1
15	115.21	Downtown	107	0	1
16	197.82	Downtown	205	0	1

Standard Error	6.349409429					
Observations	15					
ANOVA						
	df	SS	MS	F	Significance F	
Regression	3	33268.69529	11089.565	275.0729276	1.26776E-10	
Residual	11	443.4650011	40.315			
Total	14	33712.16029				
	Coefficients	Standard Error	t Stat	P-value	Lower 95%	Upper 95%
Intercept	14.97769322	6.188445404	2.4202676	0.033990776	1.357016729	28.59838971
Households	0.868588415	0.040489928	21.451962	2.51663E-10	0.779470685	0.957705146
DM	28.37376607	4.4613066	6.3599655	5.37015E-05	18.55449546	38.19302569
DD	6.863776795	4.7704765	1.4388032	0.178046589	-3.635971187	17.36352478

Multiple linear regression with indicator (dummy) variables in Figure 12.30(b) on page 576 (data file: Electronics2.xls):

- Enter the sales volume data from Table 12.13 (page 575) – sales volumes (with label Sales) in column A, store locations (with label Location) in column B, and number of households (with label Households) in column C. (The order of the columns is chosen to arrange for an adjacent block of predictor variables.)
- Enter the labels DM and DD in cells D1 and E1.
- Following the definition of the dummy variables DM and DD in Example 12.15 (pages 573 and 574), enter the appropriate values of 0 and 1 for these two variables into columns D and E.
- Select **Tools : Data Analysis : Regression** and click OK in the Data Analysis dialog box.
- In the Regression dialog box:

  Enter A1.A16 into the "Input Y Range" box.

  Enter C1.E16 into the "Input X Range" box.
- Place a checkmark in the Labels check box.
- Select the "New Worksheet Ply" Output option.
- Click OK in the Regression dialog box to obtain the regression results in a new worksheet.

Appendix 12.3 ■ Multiple Linear Regression Analysis Using MegaStat

The instructions in this section begin by describing the entry of data into an Excel worksheet. Alternatively, the data may be loaded directly from the data disk included with the text. The appropriate data file name is given at the top of each instruction block. Please refer to Appendix 1.2 for further information about entering data and saving and printing results in Excel. Please refer to Appendix 1.3 for more information about using MegaStat.

Multiple linear regression similar to Figure 12.5 on page 537 (data file: FuelCon2.xls):

- Enter the fuel consumption data in Table 12.1 (page 530) as shown—temperature (with label Temp) in column A, chill index (with label Chill) in column B, and fuel consumption (with label FuelCons) in column C. Note that Temp and Chill are contiguous columns (that is, they are next to each other). This is not necessary but makes selection of the independent variables (as described below) easiest.
- Select **MegaStat : Correlation/Regression : Regression Analysis.**
- In the Regression Analysis dialog box, click in the "Independent variables" box and use the AutoExpand feature to enter the range A1.B9. Note that if the independent variables are not next to each other, hold the CTRL key down while making selections and then AutoExpand.
- Click in the "Dependent variable" box and enter the range C1.C9.
- Check the appropriate Options and Residuals check boxes as follows:
  1. Check "Test Intercept" to include a y-intercept and to test its significance.
  2. Check "Output Residuals" to obtain a list of the model residuals, and check "Diagnostics and Influential Residuals" to obtain diagnostics (see Section 12.14).
  3. Check "Plot Residuals by Observation" and "Plot Residuals by Predicted Y and X" to obtain residual plots versus time, versus the predicted values of y, and versus the values of each independent variable (see Section 12.13).
  4. Check "Normal Probability Plot of Residuals" to obtain a normal plot (see Section 12.13).
  5. Check "Durbin-Watson" to obtain the Durbin–Watson statistic (see Section 12.13), and check "Variance Inflation Factors" (see Section 12.12).

To obtain a **point prediction** of y when temperature equals 40 and chill index equals 10 (as well as a confidence interval and prediction interval):

- Click on the drop-down menu above the Predictor Values box and select "Type in predictor values."
- Type 40 and 10 (separated by at least one blank space) into the Predictor Values box.

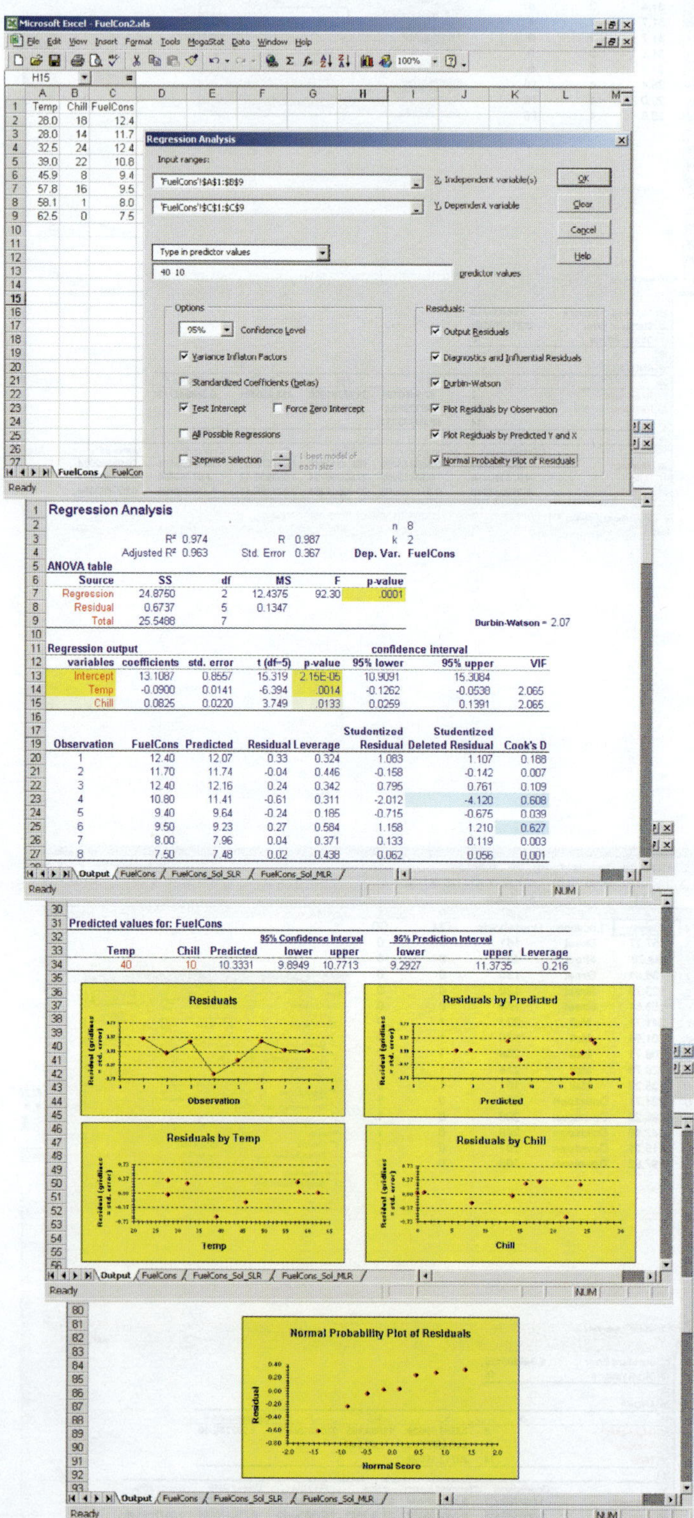

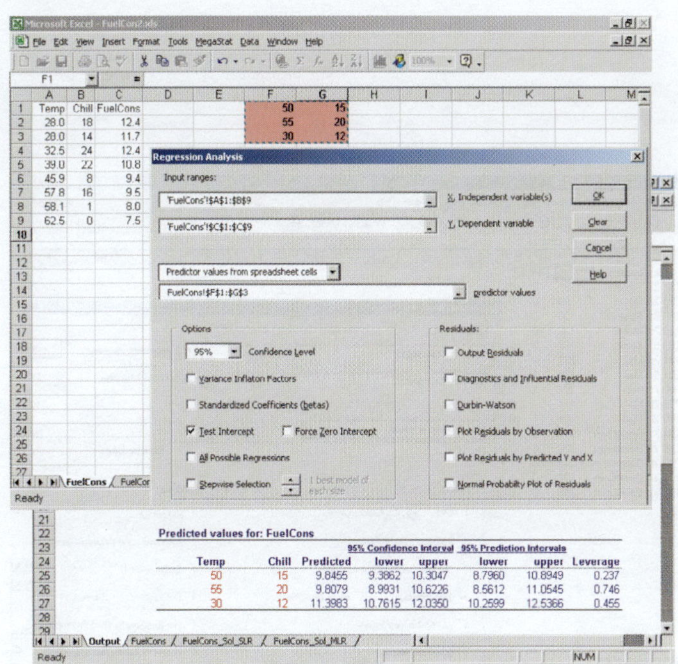

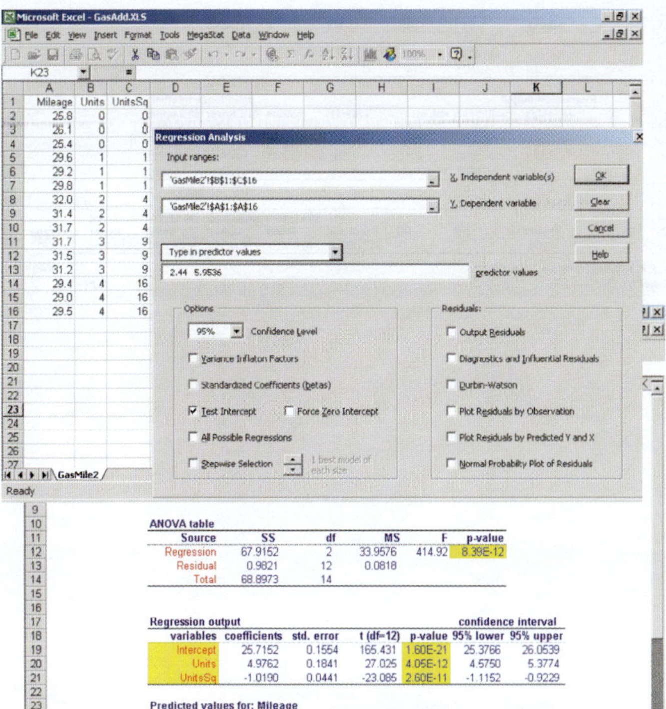

- Select a desired level of confidence (here 95%) from the Confidence Level drop-down menu or type in a value.
- Click OK in the Regression Analysis dialog box.

Predictions can also be obtained by placing the values of the predictor variables into spreadsheet cells. For example, suppose we wish to compute predictions of *y* for each of the following three temperature—chill index combinations: 50 and 15; 55 and 20; 30 and 12. To do this:

- Enter the values for which predictions are desired in spreadsheet cells as illustrated in the screenshot—here temperatures are entered in column F and chill indexes are entered in column G. However, the values could be entered in any contiguous columns.
- In the drop-down menu above the Predictor Values box, select "Predictor values from spreadsheet cells."
- Select the range of cells containing the predictor values (here F1.G3) into the Predictor Values box.
- Select a desired level of confidence from the Confidence Level drop-down menu or type in a value.
- Click OK in the Regression Analysis dialog box.

Multiple linear regression with a quadratic term similar to Figure 12.16 on page 559 (data file: GasAdd.xls):

- Enter the gasoline additive data from Table 12.8 (page 559)—mileages (with label Mileage) in column A and units of additive (with label Units) in column B.
- Enter the label UnitsSq in cell C1.
- Click on cell C2 and type the cell formula =B2*B2. Press enter to compute the squared value of Units for the first observation.
- Copy the cell formula of C2 through cell C16 (by double-clicking the drag handle in the lower right corner of cell C2) to compute the squared units for the remaining observations.
- Select **MegaStat : Correlation/Regression : Regression Analysis.**
- In the Regression Analysis dialog box, click in the "Independent variables" box and use the AutoExpand feature to enter the range B1.C16.
- Click in the "Dependent variable" box and enter the range A1.A16.

To compute a prediction for mileage when Units equals 2.44:

- Select "Type in predictor values" from the drop-down menu above the Predictor Values box.

- Type 2.44 5.9536 in the Predictor Values box. Note that (2.44)**2=5.9536 must first be hand calculated.
- Select or type the desired level of confidence (here 95%) in the Confidence Level box.
- Click the Options and Residuals check boxes as shown (or as desired).
- Click OK in the Regression Analysis dialog box.

Multiple linear regression with indicator (dummy) variables similar to Figure 12.30 on page 576 (data file: Electronics2.xls):

- Enter the sales volume data from Table 12.13 (page 575)—sales volume (with label Sales) in column A, store location (with label Location) in column B, and number of households (with label Hholds) in column C. Again note that the order of the variables is chosen to allow for a contiguous block of predictor variables.
- Enter the labels DM and DD into cells D1 and E1.
- Following the definitions of the dummy variables DM and DD in Example 12.15 (pages 573 and 574), enter the appropriate values of 0 and 1 for these two variables into columns D and E as shown in the screenshot.
- Select **MegaStat : Correlation/Regression : Regression Analysis.**
- In the Regression Analysis dialog box, click in the "Independent variables" box and use the AutoExpand feature to enter the range C1.E16.
- Click in the "Dependent variable" box and enter the range A1.A16.

To compute a prediction of sales volume for 200,000 households and a mall location:

- Select "Type in predictor values" from the drop-down menu above the Predictor Values box.
- Type 200 1 0 into the Predictor Values box.
- Select or type a desired level of confidence (here 95%) in the Confidence Level box.
- Click the Options and Residuals check boxes as shown (or as desired).
- Click OK in the Regression Analysis dialog box.

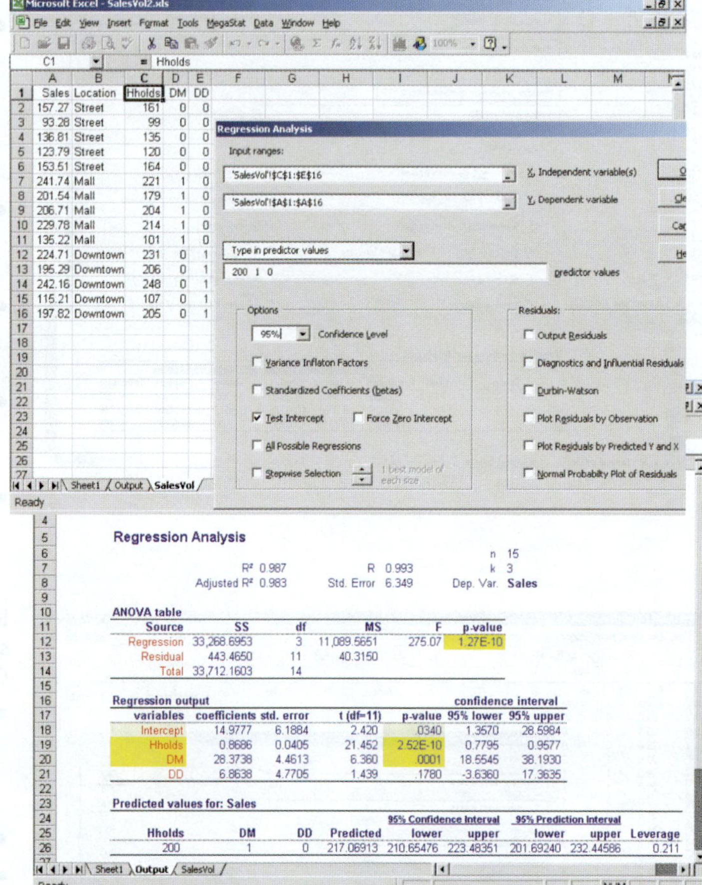

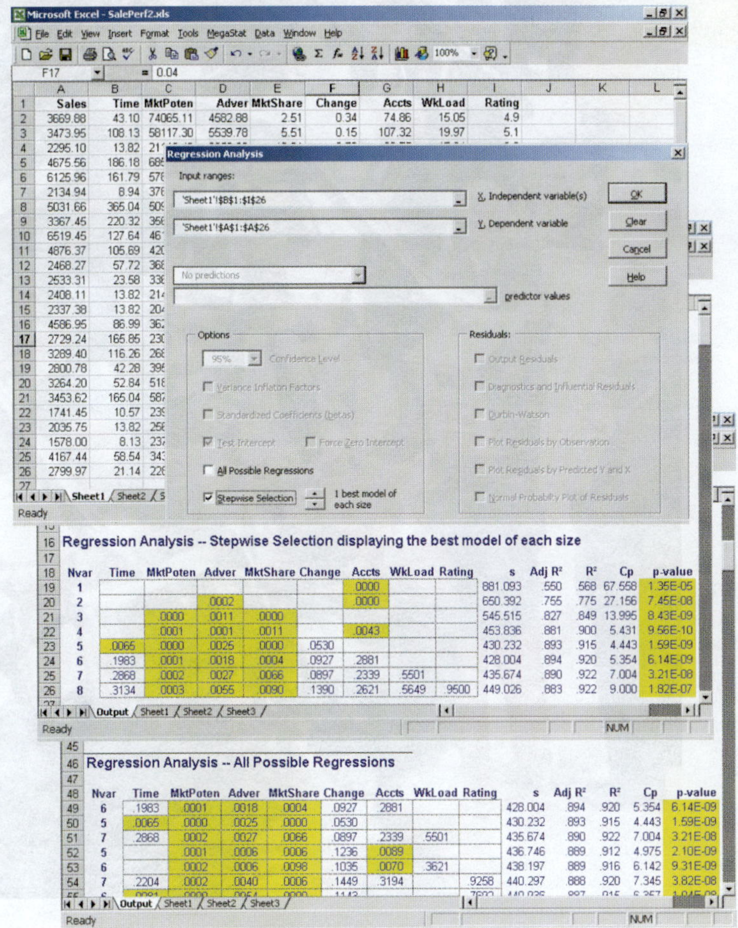

Stepwise selection in Figure 12.40(b) on page 592 and **all possible regressions** in Figure 12.40(c) on page 592 (data file: SalePerf2.xls):

- Enter the sales performance data in Tables 12.2 (page 533) and 12.17 (page 588) into columns A through I with labels as shown in the screenshot.
- Select **MegaStat : Correlation/Regression : Regression Analysis.**
- In the Regression Analysis dialog box, click in the "Independent variables" box and use the AutoExpand feature to enter the range B1.I26.
- Click in the "Dependent variable" box and use the AutoExpand feature to enter the range A1.A26.
- Check the "Stepwise Selection" check box.
- Click OK in the Regression Analysis dialog box.

Stepwise selection will give the best model of each size (1, 2, 3 etc. independent variables). The default gives one model of each size. For more models, use the arrow buttons to request the desired number of models of each size.

- Check the "All Possible Regressions" check box to obtain the results for all possible regressions. This option will handle up to 12 independent variables.

CHAPTER 13

Time Series Forecasting

Chapter Outline

13.1 Time Series Components and Models

13.2 Time Series Regression: Basic Models

13.3 Time Series Regression: More Advanced Models (Optional)

13.4 Multiplicative Decomposition

13.5 Exponential Smoothing

13.6 Forecast Error Comparisons

13.7 Index Numbers

A **time series** is a set of observations on a variable of interest that has been collected in **time order.** In this chapter we discuss developing and using **univariate time series models,** which forecast future values of a time series **solely on the basis of past values of the time series.** Often univariate time series models forecast future time series values by extrapolating the **trend** and/or **seasonal patterns** exhibited by the past values of the time series. To illustrate these ideas, we consider several cases in this chapter, including:

The Calculator Sales Case: By extrapolating an upward trend in past sales of the Bismark X-12 electronic calculator, Smith's Department Stores, Inc., forecasts future sales of this calculator. The forecasts help the department store chain to better implement its inventory and financial policies.

The Traveler's Rest Case: By extrapolating an upward trend and the seasonal behavior of its past hotel room occupancies, Traveler's Rest, Inc., forecasts future hotel room occupancies. The forecasts help the hotel chain to more effectively hire help and acquire supplies.

13.1 Time Series Components and Models

In order to identify patterns in time series data, it is often convenient to think of such data as consisting of several components: **trend, cycle, seasonal variations,** and **irregular fluctuations. Trend** refers to the upward or downward movement that characterizes a time series over time. Thus trend reflects the long-run growth or decline in the time series. Trend movements can represent a variety of factors. For example, long-run movements in the sales of a particular industry might be determined by changes in consumer tastes, increases in total population, and increases in per capita income. **Cycle** refers to recurring up-and-down movements around trend levels. These fluctuations can last from 2 to 10 years or even longer measured from peak to peak or trough to trough. One of the common cyclical fluctuations found in time series data is the *business cycle,* which is represented by fluctuations in the time series caused by recurrent periods of prosperity and recession. **Seasonal variations** are periodic patterns in a time series that complete themselves within a calendar year or less and then are repeated on a regular basis. Often seasonal variations occur yearly. For example, soft drink sales and hotel room occupancies are annually higher in the summer months, while department store sales are annually higher during the winter holiday season. Seasonal variations can also last less than one year. For example, daily restaurant patronage might exhibit within-week seasonal variation, with daily patronage higher on Fridays and Saturdays. **Irregular fluctuations** are erratic time series movements that follow no recognizable or regular pattern. Such movements represent what is "left over" in a time series after trend, cycle, and seasonal variations have been accounted for.

Time series that exhibit trend, seasonal, and cyclical components are illustrated in Figure 13.1. In Figure 13.1(a) a time series of sales observations that has an essentially straight-line or linear trend is plotted. Figure 13.1(b) portrays a time series of sales observations that contains a

FIGURE 13.1 Time Series Exhibiting Trend, Seasonal, and Cyclical Components

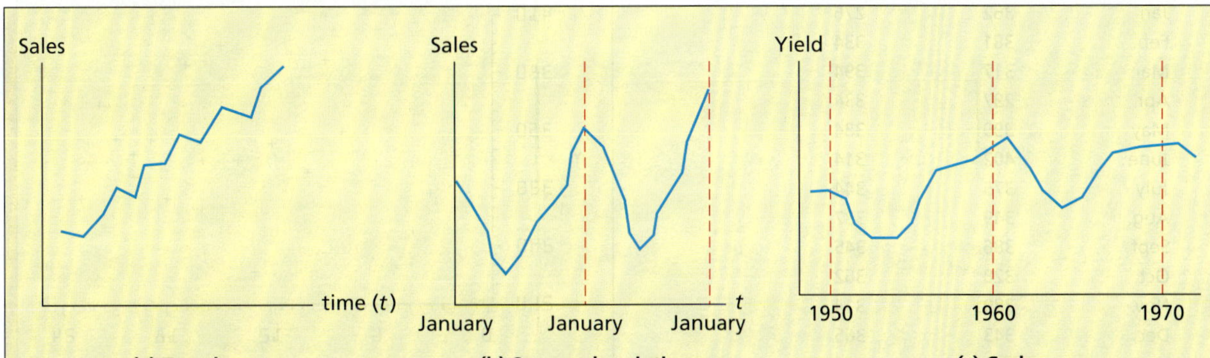

seasonal pattern that repeats annually. Figure 13.1(c) exhibits a time series of agricultural yields that is cyclical, repeating a cycle about once every 10 years.

Time series models attempt to identify significant patterns in the components of a time series. Then, assuming that these patterns will continue into the future, time series models extrapolate these patterns to forecast future time series values. In Section 13.2 and optional Section 13.3 we discuss forecasting by **time series regression models,** and in Section 13.4 we discuss forecasting by using an intuitive method called **multiplicative decomposition.** Both of these approaches assume that the time series components remain essentially constant over time. If the time series components might be changing slowly over time, it is appropriate to forecast by using **exponential smoothing.** This approach is discussed in Section 13.5. If the time series components might be changing fairly quickly over time, it is appropriate to forecast by using the **Box–Jenkins methodology.** This advanced approach is discussed in Appendix J of the CD-ROM included with this book.

CHAPTER 20

13.2 Time Series Regression: Basic Models

Modeling trend components We begin this section with two examples.

Example 13.1 The Cod Catch Case

The Bay City Seafood Company owns a fleet of fishing trawlers and operates a fish processing plant. In order to forecast its minimum and maximum possible revenues from cod sales and plan the operations of its fish processing plant, the company desires to make both point forecasts and prediction interval forecasts of its monthly cod catch (measured in tons). The company has recorded monthly cod catch for the previous two years (years 1 and 2). The cod history is given in Table 13.1. A runs plot (or time series plot) shows that the cod catches appear to randomly fluctuate around a constant average level (see the plot in Figure 13.2). Since the company subjectively believes that this data pattern will continue in the future, it seems reasonable to use the **"no trend"** regression model

$$y_t = \beta_0 + \varepsilon_t$$

to forecast cod catch in future months. It can be shown that for the no trend regression model the least squares point estimate b_0 of β_0 is $\bar{y}$, the average of the n observed time series values. Since the average $\bar{y}$ of the $n = 24$ observed cod catches is 351.29, it follows that $\hat{y}_t = b_0 = 351.29$ is the point prediction of the cod catch (y_t) in any future month. Furthermore, it can be shown that a $100(1 - \alpha)$ percent prediction interval for any future y_t value described by the no trend model is $[\hat{y}_t \pm t_{\alpha/2}\, s\sqrt{1 + (1/n)}]$. Here s is the sample standard deviation of the n observed time series values, and $t_{\alpha/2}$ is based on $n - 1$ degrees of freedom. For example, since s can be calculated to be

TABLE 13.1 Cod Catch (in Tons) CodCatch

Month	Year 1	Year 2
Jan.	362	276
Feb.	381	334
Mar.	317	394
Apr.	297	334
May	399	384
June	402	314
July	375	344
Aug.	349	337
Sept.	386	345
Oct.	328	362
Nov.	389	314
Dec.	343	365

FIGURE 13.2 Plot of Cod Catch versus Time

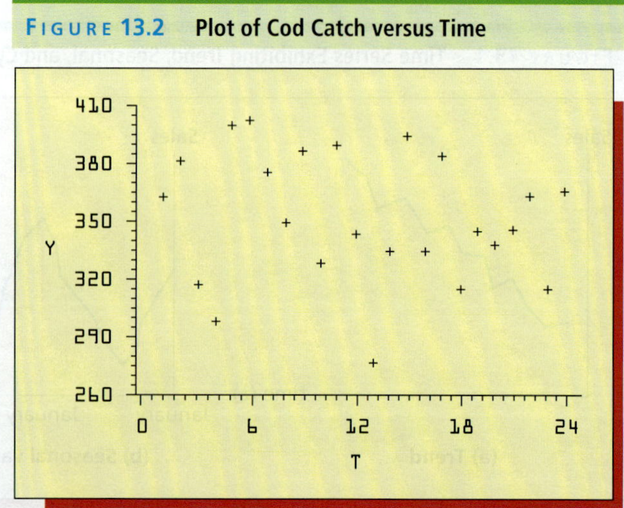

33.82 for the $n = 24$ cod catches, and since $t_{.025}$ based on $n - 1 = 23$ degrees of freedom is 2.069, it follows that a 95 percent prediction interval for the cod catch in any future month is $[351.29 \pm 2.069(33.82)\sqrt{1 + (1/24)}]$, or [279.92, 422.66].

Example 13.2 The Calculator Sales Case

C

For the last two years Smith's Department Stores, Inc., has carried a new type of electronic calculator called the Bismark X-12. Sales of this calculator have generally increased over these two years. Smith's inventory policy attempts to ensure that stores will have enough Bismark X-12 calculators to meet practically all demand for the Bismark X-12, while at the same time ensuring that Smith's does not needlessly tie up its money by ordering many more calculators than can be sold. In order to implement this inventory policy in future months, Smith's requires both point predictions and prediction intervals for total monthly Bismark X-12 demand.

The monthly calculator demand data for the last two years are given in Table 13.2. A runs plot of the demand data is shown in Figure 13.3. The demands appear to randomly fluctuate around an average level that increases over time in a linear fashion. Furthermore, Smith's believes that this trend will continue for at least the next year. Thus it is reasonable to use the **"linear trend"** regression model

$$y_t = \beta_0 + \beta_1 t + \varepsilon_t$$

to forecast calculator sales in future months. Notice that this model is just a simple linear regression model where the time period t plays the role of the independent variable. The least squares point estimates of β_0 and β_1 can be calculated to be $b_0 = 198.028986$ and $b_1 = 8.074348$. Therefore, for example, point forecasts of Bismark X-12 demand in January and February of year 3 (time periods 25 and 26) are, respectively

$$\hat{y}_{25} = 198.028986 + 8.074348(25) = 399.9 \quad \text{and}$$

$$\hat{y}_{26} = 198.028986 + 8.074348(26) = 408.0$$

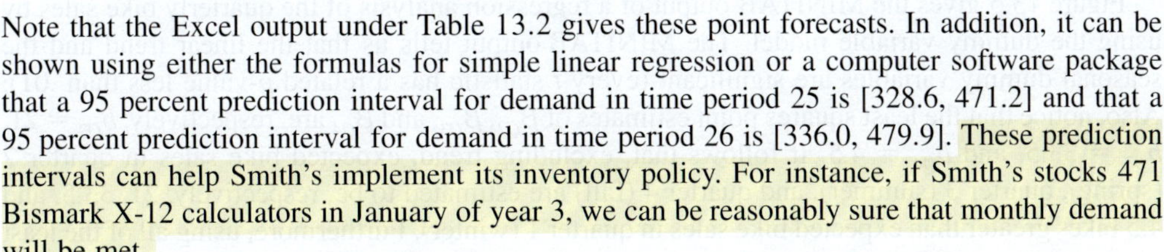

Note that the Excel output under Table 13.2 gives these point forecasts. In addition, it can be shown using either the formulas for simple linear regression or a computer software package that a 95 percent prediction interval for demand in time period 25 is [328.6, 471.2] and that a 95 percent prediction interval for demand in time period 26 is [336.0, 479.9]. These prediction intervals can help Smith's implement its inventory policy. For instance, if Smith's stocks 471 Bismark X-12 calculators in January of year 3, we can be reasonably sure that monthly demand will be met.

TABLE 13.2 Calculator Sales Data CalcSale

Month	Year 1	Year 2
Jan.	197	296
Feb.	211	276
Mar.	203	305
Apr.	247	308
May	239	356
June	269	393
July	308	363
Aug.	262	386
Sept.	258	443
Oct.	256	308
Nov.	261	358
Dec.	288	384

A	B	C	D
358	23		
384	24		
399.8877	25	USING TREND	
407.962	26		

FIGURE 13.3 Plot of Calculator Sales versus Time

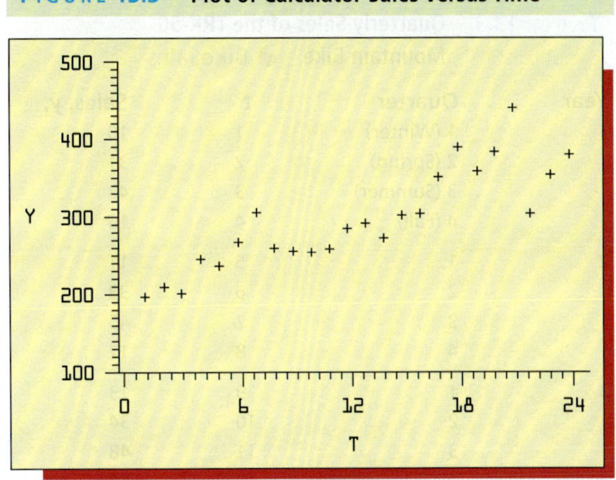

Example 13.1 illustrates that the intercept β_0 can be used to model a lack of trend over time, and Example 13.2 illustrates that the expression $(\beta_0 + \beta_1 t)$ can model a linear trend over time. In addition, as will be illustrated in the exercises, the expression $(\beta_0 + \beta_1 t + \beta_2 t^2)$ can model a quadratic trend over time.

Modeling seasonal components We next consider how to forecast time series described by trend and seasonal components.

Example 13.3 The Bike Sales Case

Table 13.3 presents quarterly sales of the TRK-50 mountain bike for the previous four years at a bicycle shop in Switzerland. The MINITAB plot in Figure 13.4 shows that the bike sales exhibit a linear trend and a strong seasonal pattern, with bike sales being higher in the spring and summer quarters than in the winter and fall quarters. If we let y_t denote the number of TRK-50 mountain bikes sold in time period t at the Swiss bike shop, then a regression model describing y_t is

$$y_t = \beta_0 + \beta_1 t + \beta_{Q2}Q_2 + \beta_{Q3}Q_3 + \beta_{Q4}Q_4 + \varepsilon_t$$

CHAPTER 19

Here the expression $(\beta_0 + \beta_1 t)$ models the linear trend evident in Figure 13.4. Q_2, Q_3, and Q_4 are dummy variables defined for quarters 2, 3, and 4. Specifically, Q_2 equals 1 if quarterly bike sales were observed in quarter 2 (spring) and 0 otherwise; Q_3 equals 1 if quarterly bike sales were observed in quarter 3 (summer) and 0 otherwise; Q_4 equals 1 if quarterly bike sales were observed in quarter 4 (fall) and 0 otherwise. Note that we have not defined a dummy variable for quarter 1 (winter). It follows that the regression parameters β_{Q2}, β_{Q3}, and β_{Q4} compare quarters 2, 3, and 4 with quarter 1. Intuitively, for example, β_{Q4} is the difference, excluding trend, between the level of the time series (y_t) in quarter 4 (fall) and the level of the time series in quarter 1 (winter). A positive β_{Q4} would imply that, excluding trend, bike sales in the fall can be expected to be higher than bike sales in the winter. A negative β_{Q4} would imply that, excluding trend, bike sales in the fall can be expected to be lower than bike sales in the winter.

Figure 13.5 gives the MINITAB output of a regression analysis of the quarterly bike sales by using the dummy variable model. The MINITAB output tells us that the linear trend and the seasonal dummy variables are significant (every t statistic has a related p-value less than .01). Also, notice that the least squares point estimates of β_{Q2}, β_{Q3}, and β_{Q4} are, respectively, $b_{Q2} = 21$, $b_{Q3} = 33.5$, and $b_{Q4} = 4.5$. It follows that, excluding trend, expected bike sales in quarter 2 (spring), quarter 3 (summer), and quarter 4 (fall) are estimated to be, respectively, 21, 33.5, and 4.5 bikes greater than expected bike sales in quarter 1 (winter). Furthermore, using all of the least squares point estimates in Figure 13.5, we can compute point forecasts of bike sales in quarters

TABLE 13.3 Quarterly Sales of the TRK-50 Mountain Bike BikeSales

Year	Quarter	t	Sales, y_t
1	1 (Winter)	1	10
	2 (Spring)	2	31
	3 (Summer)	3	43
	4 (Fall)	4	16
2	1	5	11
	2	6	33
	3	7	45
	4	8	17
3	1	9	13
	2	10	34
	3	11	48
	4	12	19
4	1	13	15
	2	14	37
	3	15	51
	4	16	21

FIGURE 13.4 MINITAB Plot of TRK-50 Bike Sales

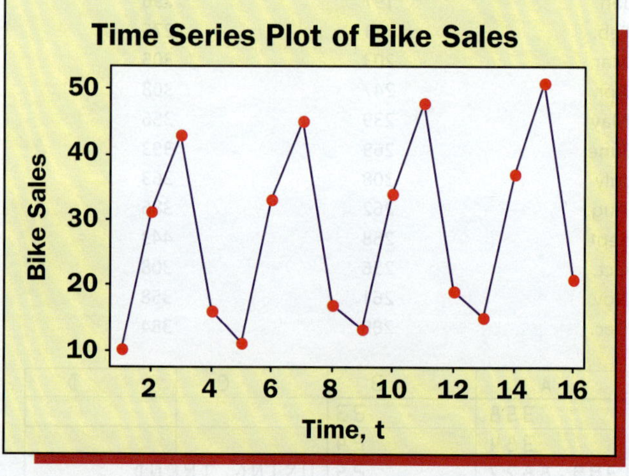

FIGURE 13.5 MINITAB Output of an Analysis of the Quarterly Bike Sales by Using Dummy Variable Regression

```
The regression equation is
BikeSales = 8.75 + 0.500 Time + 21.0 Q2 + 33.5 Q3 + 4.50 Q4

Predictor      Coef   SE Coef       T      P
Constant     8.7500    0.4281   20.44  0.000
Time        0.50000   0.03769   13.27  0.000
Q2          21.0000    0.4782   43.91  0.000
Q3          33.5000    0.4827   69.41  0.000
Q4           4.5000    0.4900    9.18  0.000

S = 0.674200    R-Sq = 99.8%    R-Sq(adj) = 99.8%

Values of Predictors for New Obs      Predicted Values for New Observations
New Obs   Time    Q2    Q3    Q4      New Obs     Fit   SE Fit        95% CI               95% PI
      1   17.0     0     0     0            1  17.250    0.506  (16.137, 18.363)   (15.395, 19.105)
      2   18.0     1     0     0            2  38.750    0.506  (37.637, 39.863)   (36.895, 40.605)
      3   19.0     0     1     0            3  51.750    0.506  (50.637, 52.863)   (49.895, 53.605)
      4   20.0     0     0     1            4  23.250    0.506  (22.137, 24.363)   (21.395, 25.105)
```

1 through 4 of next year (periods 17 through 20) as follows:

$$\hat{y}_{17} = b_0 + b_1(17) + b_{Q2}(0) + b_{Q3}(0) + b_{Q4}(0) = 8.75 + .5(17) = 17.250$$
$$\hat{y}_{18} = b_0 + b_1(18) + b_{Q2}(1) + b_{Q3}(0) + b_{Q4}(0) = 8.75 + .5(18) + 21 = 38.750$$
$$\hat{y}_{19} = b_0 + b_1(19) + b_{Q2}(0) + b_{Q3}(1) + b_{Q4}(0) = 8.75 + .5(19) + 33.5 = 51.750$$
$$\hat{y}_{20} = b_0 + b_1(20) + b_{Q2}(0) + b_{Q3}(0) + b_{Q4}(1) = 8.75 + .5(20) + 4.5 = 23.250$$

These point forecasts are given at the bottom of the MINITAB output, as are 95 percent prediction intervals for y_{17}, y_{18}, y_{19}, and y_{20}. The upper limits of these prediction intervals suggest that the bicycle shop can be reasonably sure that it will meet demand for the TRK-50 mountain bike if the numbers of bikes it stocks in quarters 1 through 4 are, respectively, 19, 41, 54, and 25 bikes.

We next consider Table 13.4, which presents a time series of hotel room occupancies observed by Traveler's Rest, Inc., a corporation that operates four hotels in a midwestern city. The analysts in the operating division of the corporation were asked to develop a model that could be used to obtain short-term forecasts (up to one year) of the number of occupied rooms in the hotels. These forecasts were needed by various personnel to assist in hiring additional help during the summer months, ordering materials that have long delivery lead times, budgeting of local advertising expenditures, and so on. The available historical data consisted of the number of occupied rooms during each day for the previous 14 years. Because it was desired to obtain monthly forecasts, these data were reduced to monthly averages by dividing each monthly total by the number of days in the month. The monthly room averages for the previous 14 years are the time series values given in Table 13.4. A runs plot of these values in Figure 13.6 shows that the monthly room averages follow a strong trend and have a seasonal pattern with one major and several minor peaks during the year. Note that the major peak each year occurs during the high summer travel months of June, July, and August.

Although the quarterly bike sales and monthly hotel room averages both exhibit seasonal variation, they exhibit different kinds of seasonal variation. The quarterly bike sales plotted in Figure 13.4 exhibit *constant seasonal variation.* In general, **constant seasonal variation** is seasonal variation where the magnitude of the seasonal swing does not depend on the level of the time series. On the other hand, **increasing seasonal variation** is seasonal variation where the magnitude of the seasonal swing increases as the level of the time series increases. Figure 13.6 shows that the monthly hotel room averages exhibit increasing seasonal variation. We have illustrated in the bike sales case that we can use **dummy variables** to model *constant seasonal variation.* The number of dummy variables that we use is, in general, the number of seasons minus 1. For example, if we model quarterly data, we use three dummy variables (as in the bike sales case). If we model monthly data, we use 11 dummy variables (this will be illustrated in optional

TABLE 13.4 Monthly Hotel Room Averages TravRest

t	y_t	t	y_t	t	y_t	t	y_t	t	y_t	t	y_t	t	y_t	t	y_t
1	501.	22	587.	43	785.	64	657.	85	645.	106	759.	127	1067.	148	827.
2	488.	23	497.	44	830.	65	680.	86	602.	107	643.	128	1038.	149	788.
3	504.	24	558.	45	645.	66	759.	87	601.	108	728.	129	812.	150	937.
4	578.	25	555.	46	643.	67	878.	88	709.	109	691.	130	790.	151	1,076.
5	545.	26	523.	47	551.	68	881.	89	706.	110	649.	131	692.	152	1,125.
6	632.	27	532.	48	606.	69	705.	90	817.	111	656.	132	782.	153	840.
7	728.	28	623.	49	585.	70	684.	91	930.	112	735.	133	758.	154	864.
8	725.	29	598.	50	553.	71	577.	92	983.	113	748.	134	709.	155	717.
9	585.	30	683.	51	576.	72	656.	93	745.	114	837.	135	715.	156	813.
10	542.	31	774.	52	665.	73	645.	94	735.	115	995.	136	788.	157	811.
11	480.	32	780.	53	656.	74	593.	95	620.	116	1,040.	137	794.	158	732.
12	530.	33	609.	54	720.	75	617.	96	698.	117	809.	138	893.	159	745.
13	518.	34	604.	55	826.	76	686.	97	665.	118	793.	139	1046.	160	844.
14	489.	35	531.	56	838.	77	679.	98	626.	119	692.	140	1075.	161	833.
15	528.	36	592.	57	652.	78	773.	99	649.	120	763.	141	812.	162	935.
16	599.	37	578.	58	661.	79	906.	100	740.	121	723.	142	822.	163	1,110.
17	572.	38	543.	59	584.	80	934.	101	729.	122	655.	143	714.	164	1,124.
18	659.	39	565.	60	644.	81	713.	102	824.	123	658.	144	802.	165	868.
19	739.	40	648.	61	623.	82	710.	103	937.	124	761.	145	748.	166	860.
20	758.	41	615.	62	553.	83	600.	104	994.	125	768.	146	731.	167	762.
21	602.	42	697.	63	599.	84	676.	105	781.	126	885.	147	748.	168	877.

FIGURE 13.6 Plot of the Monthly Hotel Room Averages versus Time

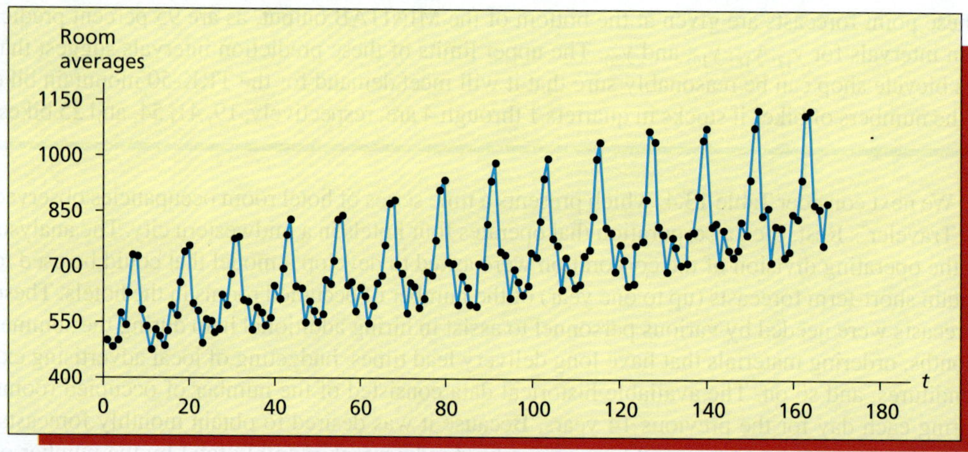

Section 13.3). If a time series exhibits increasing seasonal variation, one approach is to first use a **fractional power transformation** (see Section 11.9) that produces a transformed time series exhibiting constant seasonal variation. Then, as will be shown in Section 13.3, we use dummy variables to model the constant seasonal variation. A second approach to modeling increasing seasonal variation is to use a **multiplicative model** and a technique called **multiplicative decomposition.** This approach, which is intuitive, is discussed in Section 13.4.

Exercises for Section 13.2

CONCEPTS

13.1 Discuss how we model no trend and a linear trend.

13.2 Discuss the difference between constant seasonal variation and increasing seasonal variation.

13.3 Discuss how we use dummy variables to model constant seasonal variation.

TABLE 13.5 Annual Total U.S. Lumber Production (Millions of Board Feet)* LumberProd

35,404	36,762	32,901	38,902	37,515
37,462	36,742	36,356	37,858	38,629
32,901	33,385	37,166	32,926	32,019
33,178	34,171	35,733	35,697	35,710
34,449	36,124	35,791	34,548	36,693
38,044	38,658	34,592	32,087	37,153

*Table reads from left to right.

TABLE 13.6 Watch Sales Values WatchSale

Month	Sales	Month	Sales
1	298	11	356
2	302	12	371
3	301	13	399
4	351	14	392
5	336	15	425
6	361	16	411
7	407	17	455
8	351	18	457
9	357	19	465
10	346	20	481

A	B	C	D
465	19		
481	20		
472.1105	21	USING TREND	

METHODS AND APPLICATIONS

13.4 THE LUMBER PRODUCTION CASE LumberProd

In this problem we consider annual U.S. lumber production over 30 years. The data were obtained from the U.S. Department of Commerce *Survey of Current Business* and are presented in Table 13.5.

a Plot the lumber production values versus time and discuss why the plot indicates that the model

$$y_t = \beta_0 + \varepsilon_t$$

might appropriately describe these values.

b The mean and the standard deviation of the lumber production values can be calculated to be $\bar{y} = 35{,}651.9$ and $s = 2{,}037.3599$. Find a point forecast of and a 95 percent prediction interval for any future lumber production value.

13.5 THE WATCH SALES CASE WatchSale

The past 20 monthly sales figures for a new type of watch sold at Lambert's Discount Stores are given in Table 13.6.

a Plot the watch sales values versus time and discuss why the plot indicates that the model

$$y_t = \beta_0 + \beta_1 t + \varepsilon_t$$

might appropriately describe these values.

b The least squares point estimates of β_0 and β_1 can be calculated to be $b_0 = 290.089474$ and $b_1 = 8.667669$. Use b_0 and b_1 to show that a point forecast of watch sales in period 21 is $\hat{y}_{21} = 472.1$ (see the Excel output in Table 13.6). Use the formulas of simple linear regression analysis or a computer software package to show that a 95 percent prediction interval for watch sales in period 21 is [421.5, 522.7].

13.6 THE AIR CONDITIONER SALES CASE ACSales

Bargain Department Stores, Inc., is a chain of department stores in the Midwest. Quarterly sales of the "Bargain 8000-Btu Air Conditioner" over the past three years are as given in Table 13.7.

a Plot sales versus time and discuss why the plot indicates that the model

$$y_t = \beta_0 + \beta_1 t + \beta_2 t^2 + \beta_{Q2} Q_2 + \beta_{Q3} Q_3 + \beta_{Q4} Q_4 + \varepsilon_t$$

might appropriately describe the sales values. In this model Q_2, Q_3, and Q_4 are appropriately defined dummy variables for quarters 2, 3, and 4.

To the right of Table 13.7 is the MINITAB output of a regression analysis of the air conditioner sales data using this model.

b Define the dummy variables Q_2, Q_3, and Q_4. Then use the MINITAB output to find, report, and interpret the least squares point estimates of β_{Q2}, β_{Q3}, and β_{Q4}.

c At the bottom of the MINITAB output are point and prediction interval forecasts of air conditioner sales in the four quarters of year 4. Find and report these forecasts and show how the point forecasts have been calculated.

TABLE 13.7 Air Conditioner Sales ACSales

Year	Quarter	Sales
1	1	2,915
	2	8,032
	3	10,411
	4	2,427
2	1	4,381
	2	9,138
	3	11,386
	4	3,382
3	1	5,105
	2	9,894
	3	12,300
	4	4,013

```
The regression equation is
Sales = 2625 + 383 T - 11.4 TSq + 4630 Q2 + 6739 Q3 - 1565 Q4

Predictor      Coef   SE Coef       T       P
Constant     2624.5     100.4   26.15   0.000     S = 92.4244
T            382.82     34.03   11.25   0.000     R-Sq = 100.0%
TSq         -11.354     2.541   -4.47   0.004     R-Sq(adj)= 99.9%
Q2          4629.74     76.08   60.86   0.000
Q3          6738.85     77.38   87.09   0.000
Q4         -1565.32     79.34  -19.73   0.000

Time      Fit   SE Fit         95% CI                  95% PI
 13    5682.4    112.6   ( 5406.9,  5957.9)   ( 5325.9,  6038.8)
 14   10388.4    142.8   (10039.0, 10737.8)   ( 9972.2, 10804.6)
 15   12551.0    177.2   (12117.4, 12984.7)   (12061.9, 13040.2)
 16    4277.7    213.9   ( 3754.4,  4801.1)   ( 3707.6,  4847.8)
```

13.3 Time Series Regression: More Advanced Models (Optional)

Example 13.4 The Traveler's Rest Case

Consider taking the square roots, quartic roots, and natural logarithms of the monthly hotel room averages in Table 13.4. If we do this and plot the resulting three sets of transformed values versus time, we find that the quartic root transformation best equalizes the seasonal variation. Figure 13.7 presents a plot of the quartic roots of the monthly hotel room averages versus time. Letting y_t denote the hotel room average observed in time period t, it follows that a regression model describing the quartic root of y_t is

$$y_t^{.25} = \beta_0 + \beta_1 t + \beta_{M1}M_1 + \beta_{M2}M_2 + \cdots + \beta_{M11}M_{11} + \varepsilon_t$$

The expression $(\beta_0 + \beta_1 t)$ models the linear trend evident in Figure 13.7. Furthermore, M_1, $M_2, \ldots, M_{11}$ are dummy variables defined for months January (month 1) through November (month 11). For example, M_1 equals 1 if a monthly room average was observed in January, and 0 otherwise; M_2 equals 1 if a monthly room average was observed in February, and 0 otherwise. Note that we have not defined a dummy variable for December (month 12). It follows that the regression parameters $\beta_{M1}, \beta_{M2}, \ldots, \beta_{M11}$ compare January through November with December. Intuitively, for example, β_{M1} is the difference, excluding trend, between the level of the time series ($y_t^{.25}$) in January and the level of the time series in December. A positive β_{M1} would imply that, excluding trend, the value of the time series in January can be expected to be greater than the value in December. A negative β_{M1} would imply that, excluding trend, the value of the time series in January can be expected to be smaller than the value in December.

FIGURE 13.7 Plot of the Quartic Roots of the Monthly Hotel Room Averages versus Time

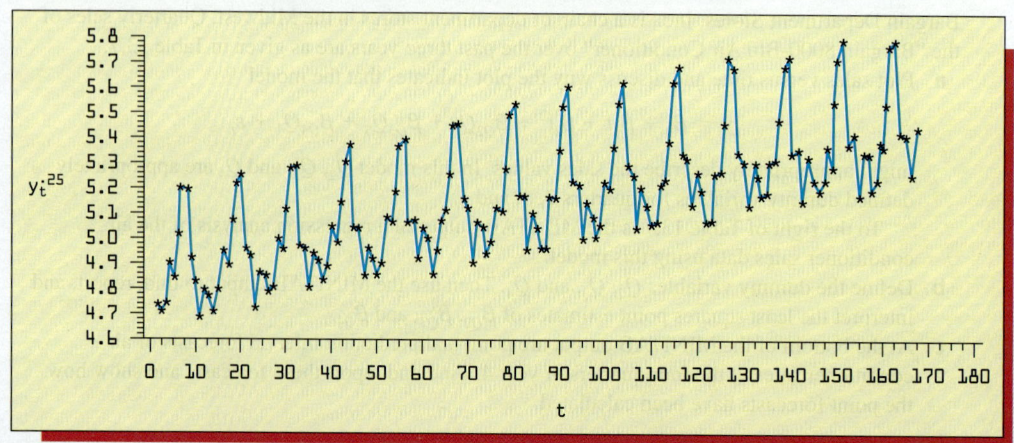

FIGURE 13.8 MegaStat Output of an Analysis of the Quartic Roots of the Room Averages Using Dummy Variable Regression (TFY2 = $y_t^{.25}$)

Regression output

variables	coefficients	std. error	t (df = 155)	p-value	95% lower	95% upper
Intercept	4.807318	0.00846255	568.070	4.06E-259	4.7906	4.8240
t	0.003515	0.00004449	79.009	3.95E-127	0.0034	0.0036
M1	−0.052467	0.01055475	−4.971	1.75E-06	−0.0733	−0.0316
M2	−0.140790	0.01055278	−13.342	1.59E-27	−0.1616	−0.1199
M3	−0.107103	0.01055100	−10.151	7.02E-19	−0.1279	−0.0863
M4	0.049882	0.01054940	4.728	5.05E-06	0.0290	0.0707
M5	0.025417	0.01054800	2.410	.0171	0.0046	0.0463
M6	0.190170	0.01054678	18.031	6.85E-40	0.1693	0.2110
M7	0.382455	0.01054575	36.266	1.28E-77	0.3616	0.4033
M8	0.413370	0.01054490	39.201	2.41E-82	0.3925	0.4342
M9	0.071417	0.01054424	6.773	2.47E-10	0.0506	0.0922
M10	0.050641	0.01054377	4.803	3.66E-06	0.0298	0.0715
M11	−0.141943	0.01054349	−13.463	7.47E-28	−0.1628	−0.1211

(confidence interval: 95% lower, 95% upper)

Durbin-Watson = 1.26

Predicted values for: TFY2

t	Predicted	95% Confidence Intervals lower	95% Confidence Intervals upper	95% Prediction Intervals lower	95% Prediction Intervals upper	Leverage
169	5.3489	5.3322	5.3656	5.2913	5.4065	0.092
170	5.2641	5.2474	5.2808	5.2065	5.3217	0.092
171	5.3013	5.2846	5.3180	5.2437	5.3589	0.092
172	5.4618	5.4451	5.4785	5.4042	5.5194	0.092
173	5.4409	5.4241	5.4576	5.3833	5.4984	0.092
174	5.6091	5.5924	5.6258	5.5515	5.6667	0.092
175	5.8049	5.7882	5.8216	5.7473	5.8625	0.092
176	5.8394	5.8226	5.8561	5.7818	5.8969	0.092
177	5.5009	5.4842	5.5176	5.4433	5.5585	0.092
178	5.4837	5.4669	5.5004	5.4261	5.5412	0.092
179	5.2946	5.2779	5.3113	5.2370	5.3522	0.092
180	5.4400	5.4233	5.4568	5.3825	5.4976	0.092

Figure 13.8 gives relevant portions of the MegaStat output of a regression analysis of the hotel room data using the quartic root dummy variable model. The MegaStat output tells us that the linear trend and the seasonal dummy variables are significant (every t statistic has a related p-value less than .05). In addition, although not shown on the output, $R^2 = .988$. Now consider time period 169, which is January of next year and which therefore implies that $M_1 = 1$ and that all the other dummy variables equal 0. Using the least squares point estimates in Figure 13.8, we compute a point forecast of $y_{169}^{.25}$ to be

$$b_0 + b_1(169) + b_{M1}(1) = 4.807318 + 0.003515(169) + (-0.052467)(1)$$
$$= 5.3489$$

Note that this point forecast is given in Figure 13.8 (see time period 169). It follows that a point forecast of y_{169} is

$$(5.3489)^4 = 818.57$$

Furthermore, the MegaStat output shows that a 95 percent prediction interval for $y_{169}^{.25}$ is [5.2913, 5.4065]. It follows that a 95 percent prediction interval for y_{169} is

$$[(5.2913)^4, (5.4065)^4] = [783.88, 854.41]$$

This interval says that Traveler's Rest, Inc., can be 95 percent confident that the monthly hotel room average in period 169 will be no less than 783.88 rooms per day and no more than 854.41 rooms per day. Lastly, note that the MegaStat output also gives point forecasts of and 95 percent prediction intervals for the quartic roots of the hotel room averages in February through December of next year (time periods 170 through 180).

The validity of the regression methods just illustrated requires that the independence assumption be satisfied. However, when time series data are analyzed, this assumption is often violated. It is quite common for the time-ordered error terms to exhibit **positive or negative autocorrelation.** In Section 11.9 we discussed positive and negative autocorrelation, and we saw that we can use residual plots to check for these kinds of autocorrelation.

One type of positive or negative autocorrelation is called **first-order autocorrelation.** It says that ε_t, the error term in time period t, is related to ε_{t-1}, the error term in time period $t - 1$, by the equation

$$\varepsilon_t = \phi\varepsilon_{t-1} + a_t$$

Here we assume that **ϕ (pronounced "phi")** is the correlation coefficient that measures the relationship between error terms separated by one time period, and a_t is an error term (often called a **random shock**) that satisfies the usual regression assumptions. To check for positive or negative first-order autocorrelation, we can use the **Durbin–Watson statistic d,** which was discussed in Sections 11.9 and 12.13. For example, it can be verified that this statistic shows no evidence of positive or negative first-order autocorrelation in the error terms of the calculator sales model or in the error terms of the bike sales model. However, note from the the MegaStat output in Figure 13.8 that the Durbin–Watson statistic for the dummy variable regression model describing the quartic roots of the hotel room averages is $d = 1.26$. Since the dummy variable regression model uses $k = 12$ independent variables, and since Tables A.10, A.11, and A.12 (pages 834–835) do not give the **Durbin–Watson critical points** corresponding to $k = 12$, we cannot test for autocorrelation using these tables. However, it can be shown that $d = 1.26$ is quite small and indicates **positive autocorrelation** in the error terms. One approach to dealing with first-order autocorrelation in the error terms is to predict future values of the error terms by using the model $\varepsilon_t = \phi\varepsilon_{t-1} + a_t$. Of course, the error term ε_t could be related to more than just the previous error term ε_{t-1}. It could be related to any number of previous error terms. The **autoregressive error term model of order q**

$$\varepsilon_t = \phi_1\varepsilon_{t-1} + \phi_2\varepsilon_{t-2} + \cdots + \phi_q\varepsilon_{t-q} + a_t$$

relates ε_t, the error term in time period t, to the previous error terms $\varepsilon_{t-1}, \varepsilon_{t-2}, \ldots, \varepsilon_{t-q}$. Here $\phi_1, \phi_2, \ldots, \phi_q$ are unknown parameters, and a_t is an error term (random shock) with mean 0 that satisfies the regression assumptions. The **Box–Jenkins methodology** can be used to systematically identify an autoregressive error term model that relates ε_t to an appropriate number of past error terms. More generally, the Box–Jenkins methodology can be employed to predict future time series values (y_t) by using a procedure that combines the autoregressive error term model of order q with the model

$$y_t = \beta_0 + \beta_1 y_{t-1} + \beta_2 y_{t-2} + \cdots + \beta_p y_{t-p} + \varepsilon_t$$

This latter model, which is called the **autoregressive observation model of order p,** expresses the observation y_t in terms of the previous observations $y_{t-1}, y_{t-2}, \ldots, y_{t-p}$ and an error term ε_t. The Box–Jenkins methodology, which is discussed in Appendix J of the CD-ROM included with this book, identifies which previous observations and which previous error terms describe y_t.

Although sophisticated techniques such as the Box–Jenkins methodology can be quite useful, studies show that the regression techniques discussed in Section 13.2 and in this section often provide accurate forecasts, even if we ignore the autocorrelation in the error terms. In fact, whenever we observe time series data we should determine whether trend and/or seasonal effects exist. For example, recall that the Fresh demand data in Table 12.9 (page 561) are time series data observed over 30 consecutive four-week sales periods. Although we predicted demand for Fresh detergent on the basis of price difference and advertising expenditure, it is also possible that this demand is affected by a linear or quadratic trend over time and/or by seasonal effects (for example, more laundry detergent might be sold in summer sales periods when children are home from school). If we try using trend equations and dummy variables to search for trend and seasonal effects, we find that these effects do not exist in the Fresh demand data. However, in the supplemental exercises (see Exercise 13.38) we present a situation where we use trend equations and seasonal dummy variables, as well as **causal variables** such as price difference and advertising expenditure, to predict demand for a fishing lure.

Exercises for Section 13.3

CONCEPTS

13.7 What transformations can be used to transform a time series exhibiting increasing seasonal variation into a time series exhibiting constant seasonal variation?

13.8 What is the purpose of an autoregressive error term model?

METHODS AND APPLICATIONS

13.9 Table 13.8 gives the monthly international passenger totals over the last 11 years for an airline company. A plot of these passenger totals reveals an upward trend with increasing seasonal variation, and the natural logarithmic transformation is found to best equalize the seasonal variation (see Figure 13.9(a) and (b)). Figure 13.9(c) gives the MINITAB output of a regression analysis of the monthly international passenger totals by using the model

$$\ln y_t = \beta_0 + \beta_1 t + \beta_{M1}M_1 + \beta_{M2}M_2 + \cdots + \beta_{M11}M_{11} + \varepsilon_t$$

Here $M_1, M_2, \ldots, M_{11}$ are appropriately defined dummy variables for January (month 1) through November (month 11). Let y_{133} denote the international passenger totals in month 133 (January of next year). The MINITAB output tells us that a point forecast of and a 95 percent prediction interval for $\ln y_{133}$ are, respectively, 6.08610 and [5.96593, 6.20627]. Using the least squares point estimates on the MINITAB output, show how the point forecast has been calculated. Then, by calculating $e^{6.08610}$ and $[e^{5.96593}, e^{6.20627}]$, find a point forecast of and a 95 percent prediction interval for y_{133}. AirPass

13.10 Use the Durbin–Watson statistic given at the bottom of the MINITAB output in Figure 13.9(c) to test for positive autocorrelation.

TABLE 13.8 Monthly International Passenger Totals (Thousands of Passengers) AirPass

Year	Jan.	Feb.	Mar.	Apr.	May	June	July	Aug.	Sept.	Oct.	Nov.	Dec.
1	112	118	132	129	121	135	148	148	136	119	104	118
2	115	126	141	135	125	149	170	170	158	133	114	140
3	145	150	178	163	172	178	199	199	184	162	146	166
4	171	180	193	181	183	218	230	242	209	191	172	194
5	196	196	236	235	229	243	264	272	237	211	180	201
6	204	188	235	227	234	264	302	293	259	229	203	229
7	242	233	267	269	270	315	364	347	312	274	237	278
8	284	277	317	313	318	374	413	405	355	306	271	306
9	315	301	356	348	355	422	465	467	404	347	305	336
10	340	318	362	348	363	435	491	505	404	359	310	337
11	360	342	406	396	420	472	548	559	463	407	362	405

Source: *FAA Statistical Handbook of Civil Aviation* (several annual issues). These data were originally presented by Box and Jenkins (1976). We have updated the situation in this exercise to be more modern.

FIGURE 13.9 Analysis of the Monthly International Passenger Totals

(a) Plot of the passenger totals

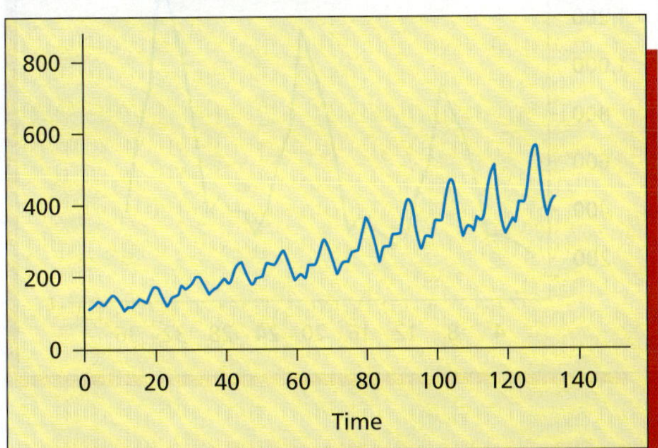

(b) Plot of the natural logarithms of the passenger totals

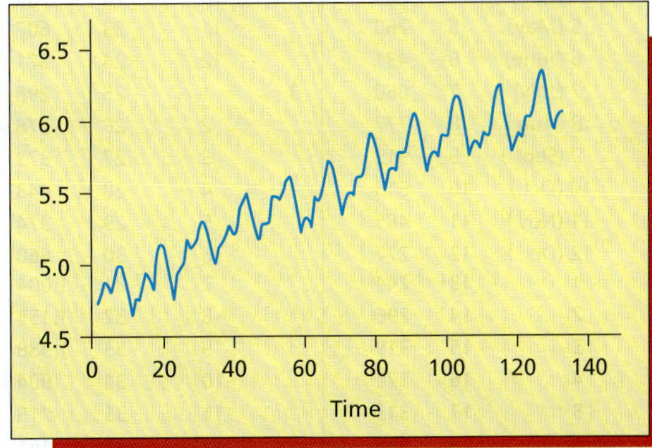

FIGURE 13.9 Analysis of the Monthly International Passenger Totals (*continued*)

(c) MINITAB Output of a Regression Analysis of the Monthly International Passenger Totals Using the Dummy Variable Model

Predictor	Coef	SE Coef	T	P
Constant	4.69618	0.01973	238.02	0.000
Time	0.0103075	0.0001316	78.30	0.000
Jan	0.01903	0.02451	0.78	0.439
Feb	0.00150	0.02451	0.06	0.951
March	0.13795	0.02450	5.63	0.000
April	0.09583	0.02449	3.91	0.000
May	0.09178	0.02449	3.75	0.000
June	0.21432	0.02448	8.75	0.000
July	0.31469	0.02448	12.85	0.000
Aug	0.30759	0.02448	12.57	0.000
Sept	0.16652	0.02448	6.80	0.000
Oct	0.02531	0.02447	1.03	0.303
Nov	-0.11559	0.02447	-4.72	0.000

Predicted Values for New Observations

Time	Fit	SE Fit	95% PI
133	6.08610	0.01973	(5.96593, 6.20627)
134	6.07888	0.01973	(5.95871, 6.19905)
135	6.22564	0.01973	(6.10547, 6.34581)
136	6.19383	0.01973	(6.07366, 6.31400)
137	6.20008	0.01973	(6.07991, 6.32025)
138	6.33292	0.01973	(6.21276, 6.45309)
139	6.44360	0.01973	(6.32343, 6.56377)
140	6.44682	0.01973	(6.32665, 6.56699)
141	6.31605	0.01973	(6.19588, 6.43622)
142	6.18515	0.01973	(6.06498, 6.30531)
143	6.05455	0.01973	(5.93438, 6.17472)
144	6.18045	0.01973	(6.06028, 6.30062)

S = 0.0573917 R-Sq = 98.3% R-Sq(adj) = 98.1% Durbin-Watson statistic = 0.420944

CHAPTER 20

13.4 Multiplicative Decomposition

When a time series exhibits increasing (or decreasing) seasonal variation, we can use the **multiplicative decomposition method** to decompose the time series into its **trend, seasonal, cyclical,** and **irregular** components. This is illustrated in the following example.

Example 13.5 The Tasty Cola Case

The Discount Soda Shop, Inc., owns and operates 10 drive-in soft drink stores. Discount Soda has been selling Tasty Cola, a soft drink introduced just three years ago and gaining in popularity. Periodically, Discount Soda orders Tasty Cola from the regional distributor. To better implement its inventory policy, Discount Soda needs to forecast monthly Tasty Cola sales (in hundreds of cases).

Discount Soda has recorded monthly Tasty Cola sales for the previous three years. This time series is given in Table 13.9 and plotted in Figure 13.10. Notice that, in addition to having a linear trend, the Tasty Cola sales time series possesses seasonal variation, with sales of the soft drink

TABLE 13.9 Monthly Sales of Tasty Cola (in Hundreds of Cases) TastyCola

Year	Month	t	Sales, y_t	Year	Month	t	Sales, y_t
1	1 (Jan.)	1	189	2	7	19	831
	2 (Feb.)	2	229		8	20	960
	3 (Mar.)	3	249		9	21	1,152
	4 (Apr.)	4	289		10	22	759
	5 (May)	5	260		11	23	607
	6 (June)	6	431		12	24	371
	7 (July)	7	660	3	1	25	298
	8 (Aug.)	8	777		2	26	378
	9 (Sept.)	9	915		3	27	373
	10 (Oct.)	10	613		4	28	443
	11 (Nov.)	11	485		5	29	374
	12 (Dec.)	12	277		6	30	660
2	1	13	244		7	31	1,004
	2	14	296		8	32	1,153
	3	15	319		9	33	1,388
	4	16	370		10	34	904
	5	17	313		11	35	715
	6	18	556		12	36	441

FIGURE 13.10 Monthly Sales of Tasty Cola (in Hundreds of Cases)

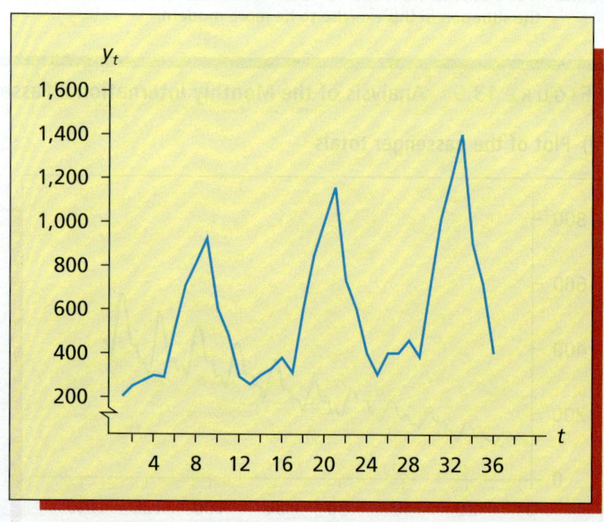

greatest in the summer and early fall months and lowest in the winter months. Since, furthermore, the seasonal variation seems to be increasing, we will see as we progress through this example that it might be reasonable to conclude that y_t, the sales of Tasty Cola in period t, is described by the **multiplicative model**

$$y_t = TR_t \times SN_t \times CL_t \times IR_t$$

Here TR_t, SN_t, CL_t, and IR_t represent the trend, seasonal, cyclical, and irregular components of the time series in time period t.

Table 13.10 summarizes the calculations needed to find estimates—denoted tr_t, sn_t, cl_t, and ir_t—of TR_t, SN_t, CL_t, and IR_t. As shown in the table, we begin by calculating **moving averages** and **centered moving averages.** The purpose behind computing these averages is to eliminate seasonal variations and irregular fluctuations from the data. The first moving average of the first 12 Tasty Cola sales values is

$$\frac{189 + 229 + 249 + 289 + 260 + 431 + 660 + 777 + 915 + 613 + 485 + 277}{12}$$

$$= 447.833$$

TABLE 13.10 Tasty Cola Sales and the Multiplicative Decomposition Method TastyCola

t Time Period	y_t Tasty Cola Sales	First Step 12-Period Moving Average	$tr_t \times cl_t$ Centered Moving Average	$sn_t \times ir_t$ $\frac{y_t}{tr_t \times cl_t}$	sn_t Table 13.11	d_t $\frac{y_t}{sn_t}$	tr_t 380.163 +9.489t	$tr_t \times sn_t$ Multiply tr_t by sn_t	$cl_t \times ir_t$ $\frac{y_t}{tr_t \times sn_t}$	cl_t 3-Period Moving Average	ir_t $\frac{cl_t \times ir_t}{cl_t}$
1 (Jan)	189				.493	383.37	389.652	192.10	.9839		
2	229				.596	384.23	399.141	237.89	.9626	.9902	.9721
3	249				.595	418.49	408.630	243.13	1.0241	1.0010	1.0231
4	289				.680	425	418.119	284.32	1.0165	1.0396	.9778
5	260				.564	460.99	427.608	241.17	1.0781	1.0315	1.0452
6	431	447.833			.986	437.12	437.097	430.98	1.0000	1.0285	.9723
7	660	452.417	450.125	1.466	1.467	449.9	446.586	655.14	1.0074	1.0046	1.0028
8	777	458	455.2085	1.707	1.693	458.95	456.075	772.13	1.0063	1.0004	1.0059
9	915	563.833	460.9165	1.985	1.990	459.79	465.564	926.47	.9876	.9937	.9939
10	613	470.583	467.208	1.312	1.307	469.01	475.053	620.89	.9873	.9825	1.0049
11	485	475	472.7915	1.026	1.029	471.33	489.542	498.59	.9727	.9648	1.0082
12	277	485.417	480.2085	.577	.600	461.67	494.031	296.42	.9345	.9634	.9700
13 (Jan)	244	499.667	492.542	.495	.493	494.97	503.520	248.24	.9829	.9618	1.0219
14	296	514.917	507.292	.583	.596	496.64	513.009	305.75	.9681	.9924	.9755
15	319	534.667	524.792	.608	.595	536.13	522.498	310.89	1.0261	1.0057	1.0203
16	370	546.833	540.75	.684	.680	544.12	531.987	361.75	1.0228	1.0246	.9982
17	313	557	551.9165	.567	.564	554.97	541.476	305.39	1.0249	1.0237	1.0012
18	556	564.833	560.9165	.991	.986	563.89	550.965	543.25	1.0235	1.0197	1.0037
19	831	569.333	567.083	1.465	1.467	566.46	560.454	822.19	1.0107	1.0097	1.0010
20	960	576.167	572.75	1.676	1.693	567.04	569.943	964.91	.9949	1.0016	.9933
21	1,152	580.667	578.417	1.992	1.990	578.89	579.432	1,153.07	.9991	.9934	1.0057
22	759	586.75	583.7085	1.300	1.307	580.72	588.921	769.72	.9861	.9903	.9958
23	607	591.833	589.2915	1.030	1.029	589.89	598.410	615.76	.9858	.9964	.9894
24	371	600.5	596.1665	.622	.600	618.33	607.899	364.74	1.0172	.9940	1.0233
25 (Jan)	298	614.917	607.7085	.490	.493	604.46	617.388	304.37	.9791	1.0027	.9765
26	378	631	622.9585	.607	.596	634.23	626.877	373.62	1.0117	.9920	1.0199
27	373	650.667	640.8335	.582	.595	626.89	636.366	378.64	.9851	1.0018	.9833
28	443	662.75	656.7085	.675	.680	651.47	645.855	439.18	1.0087	1.0030	1.0057
29	374	671.75	667.25	.561	.564	663.12	655.344	369.61	1.0119	1.0091	1.0028
30	660	677.583	674.6665	.978	.986	669.37	664.833	655.53	1.0068	1.0112	.9956
31	1,004				1.467	684.39	674.322	989.23	1.0149	1.0059	1.0089
32	1,153				1.693	681.04	683.811	1,157.69	.9959	1.0053	.9906
33	1,388				1.990	697.49	693.300	1,379.67	1.0060	.9954	1.0106
34	904				1.307	691.66	702.789	918.55	.9842	.9886	.9955
35	715				1.029	694.85	712.278	732.93	.9755	.9927	.9827
36	441				.600	735	721.707	433.06	1.0183		

Here we use a "12-period moving average" because the Tasty Cola time series data are monthly (12 time periods or "seasons" per year). If the data were quarterly, we would compute a "4-period moving average." The second moving average is obtained by dropping the first sales value (y_1) from the average and by including the next sales value (y_{13}) in the average. Thus we obtain

$$\frac{229 + 249 + 289 + 260 + 431 + 660 + 777 + 915 + 613 + 485 + 277 + 244}{12}$$
$$= 452.417$$

The third moving average is obtained by dropping y_2 from the average and by including y_{14} in the average. We obtain

$$\frac{249 + 289 + 260 + 431 + 660 + 777 + 915 + 613 + 485 + 277 + 244 + 296}{12}$$
$$= 458$$

Successive moving averages are computed similarly until we include y_{36} in the last moving average. Note that we use the term "*moving average*" here because, as we calculate these averages, we move along by dropping the most remote observation in the previous average and by including the "next" observation in the new average.

The first moving average corresponds to a time that is midway between periods 6 and 7, the second moving average corresponds to a time that is midway between periods 7 and 8, and so forth. In order to obtain averages corresponding to time periods in the original Tasty Cola time series, we calculate **centered moving averages.** The centered moving averages are two-period moving averages of the previously computed 12-period moving averages. Thus the first centered moving average is

$$\frac{447.833 + 452.417}{2} = 450.125$$

The second centered moving average is

$$\frac{452.417 + 458}{2} = 455.2085$$

Successive centered moving averages are calculated similarly. The 12-period moving averages and centered moving averages for the Tasty Cola sales time series are given in Table 13.10.

If the original moving averages had been computed using an odd number of time series values, the centering procedure would not have been necessary. For example, if we had three seasons per year, we would compute three-period moving averages. Then, the first moving average would correspond to period 2, the second moving average would correspond to period 3, and so on. However, most seasonal time series are quarterly, monthly, or weekly, so the centering procedure is necessary.

The centered moving average in time period t is considered to equal $tr_t \times cl_t$, the estimate of $TR_t \times CL_t$, because the averaging procedure is assumed to have removed seasonal variations (note that each moving average is computed using exactly one observation from each season) and (short-term) irregular fluctuations. The (longer-term) trend effects and cyclical effects—that is, $tr_t \times cl_t$—remain.

Since the model

$$y_t = TR_t \times SN_t \times CL_t \times IR_t$$

implies that

$$SN_t \times IR_t = \frac{y_t}{TR_t \times CL_t}$$

it follows that the estimate $sn_t \times ir_t$ of $SN_t \times IR_t$ is

$$sn_t \times ir_t = \frac{y_t}{tr_t \times cl_t}$$

TABLE 13.11 Estimation of the Seasonal Factors TastyCola

		$sn_t \times ir_t = y_t/(tr_t \times cl_t)$ Year 1	Year 2	$\overline{sn}_t$	$sn_t = 1.0008758(\overline{sn}_t)$
1	Jan.	.495	.490	.4925	.493
2	Feb.	.583	.607	.595	.596
3	Mar.	.608	.582	.595	.595
4	Apr.	.684	.675	.6795	.680
5	May	.567	.561	.564	.564
6	June	.991	.978	.9845	.986
7	July	1.466	1.465	1.4655	1.467
8	Aug.	1.707	1.676	1.6915	1.693
9	Sep.	1.985	1.992	1.9885	1.990
10	Oct.	1.312	1.300	1.306	1.307
11	Nov.	1.026	1.030	1.028	1.029
12	Dec.	.577	.622	.5995	.600

FIGURE 13.11 Plot of Tasty Cola Sales and Deseasonalized Sales

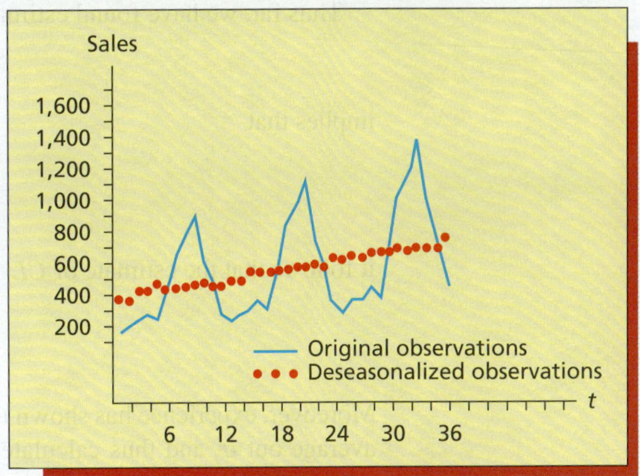

Noting that the values of $sn_t \times ir_t$ are calculated in Table 13.10, we can find sn_t by grouping the values of $sn_t \times ir_t$ by months and calculating an average, $\overline{sn}_t$, for each month. These monthly averages are given for the Tasty Cola data in Table 13.11. The monthly averages are then normalized so that they sum to the number of time periods in a year. Denoting the number of time periods in a year by L (for instance, $L = 4$ for quarterly data, $L = 12$ for monthly data), we accomplish the normalization by multiplying each value of $\overline{sn}_t$ by the quantity

$$\frac{L}{\sum \overline{sn}_t} = \frac{12}{.4925 + .595 + \cdots + .5995}$$

$$= \frac{12}{11.9895} = 1.0008758$$

This normalization process results in the estimate $sn_t = 1.0008758(\overline{sn}_t)$, which is the estimate of SN_t. These calculations are summarized in Table 13.11.

Having calculated the values of sn_t and placed them in Table 13.10, we next define the **deseasonalized observation** in time period t to be

$$d_t = \frac{y_t}{sn_t}$$

Deseasonalized observations are computed to better estimate the trend component TR_t. Dividing y_t by the estimated seasonal factor removes the seasonality from the data and allows us to better understand the nature of the trend. The deseasonalized observations are calculated in Table 13.10 and are plotted in Figure 13.11. Since the deseasonalized observations have a straight-line appearance, it seems reasonable to assume a linear trend

$$TR_t = \beta_0 + \beta_1 t$$

We estimate TR_t by fitting a straight line to the deseasonalized observations. That is, we compute the least squares point estimates of the parameters in the simple linear regression model relating the dependent variable d_t to the independent variable t:

$$d_t = \beta_0 + \beta_1 t + \varepsilon_t$$

We obtain $b_0 = 380.163$ and $b_1 = 9.489$. It follows that the estimate of TR_t is

$$tr_t = b_0 + b_1 t = 380.163 + 9.489t$$

The values of tr_t are calculated in Table 13.10. Note that, for example, although $y_{22} = 759$, Tasty Cola sales in period 22 (October of year 2), are larger than $tr_{22} = 588.921$ (the estimated trend in period 22), $d_{22} = 580.72$ is smaller than $tr_{22} = 588.921$. This implies that, on a deseasonalized basis, Tasty Cola sales were slightly down in October of year 2. This might have been caused by a slightly colder October than usual.

Thus far, we have found estimates sn_t and tr_t of SN_t and TR_t. Since the model

$$y_t = TR_t \times SN_t \times CL_t \times IR_t$$

implies that

$$CL_t \times IR_t = \frac{y_t}{TR_t \times SN_t}$$

it follows that the estimate of $CL_t \times IR_t$ is

$$cl_t \times ir_t = \frac{y_t}{tr_t \times sn_t}$$

Moreover, experience has shown that, when considering either monthly or quarterly data, we can average out ir_t and thus calculate the estimate cl_t of CL_t by computing a three-period moving average of the $cl_t \times ir_t$ values.

Finally, we calculate the estimate ir_t of IR_t by using the equation

$$ir_t = \frac{cl_t \times ir_t}{cl_t}$$

The calculations of the values cl_t and ir_t for the Tasty Cola data are summarized in Table 13.10. Since there are only three years of data, and since most of the values of cl_t are near 1, we cannot discern a well-defined cycle. Furthermore, examining the values of ir_t, we cannot detect a pattern in the estimates of the irregular factors.

Traditionally, the estimates tr_t, sn_t, cl_t, and ir_t obtained by using the multiplicative decomposition method are used to describe the time series. However, we can also use these estimates to forecast future values of the time series. If there is no pattern in the irregular component, we predict IR_t to equal 1. Therefore, the point forecast of y_t is

$$\hat{y}_t = tr_t \times sn_t \times cl_t$$

if a well-defined cycle exists and can be predicted. The point forecast is

$$\hat{y}_t = tr_t \times sn_t$$

if a well-defined cycle does not exist or if CL_t cannot be predicted, as in the Tasty Cola example. Since values of $tr_t \times sn_t$ have been calculated in column 9 of Table 13.10, these values are the point forecasts of the $n = 36$ historical Tasty Cola sales values. Furthermore, we present in Table 13.12 point forecasts of future Tasty Cola sales in the 12 months of year 4. Recalling that

TABLE 13.12 Forecasts of Future Values of Tasty Cola Sales Calculated Using the Multiplicative Decomposition Method TastyCola

t	sn_t	$tr_t = 380.163 + 9.489t$	Point Prediction, $\hat{y}_t = tr_t \times sn_t$	Approximate 95% Prediction Interval	y_t
37	.493	731.273	360.52	[333.72, 387.32]	352
38	.596	740.762	441.48	[414.56, 468.40]	445
39	.595	750.252	446.40	[419.36, 473.44]	453
40	.680	759.741	516.62	[489.45, 543.79]	541
41	.564	769.231	433.85	[406.55, 461.15]	457
42	.986	778.720	767.82	[740.38, 795.26]	762
43	1.467	788.209	1,156.30	[1,128.71, 1,183.89]	1,194
44	1.693	797.699	1,350.50	[1,322.76, 1,378.24]	1,361
45	1.990	807.188	1,606.30	[1,578.41, 1,634.19]	1,615
46	1.307	816.678	1,067.40	[1,039.35, 1,095.45]	1,059
47	1.029	826.167	850.12	[821.90, 878.34]	824
48	.600	835.657	501.39	[473, 529.78]	495

the estimated trend equation is $tr_t = 380.163 + 9.489t$ and that the estimated seasonal factor for August is 1.693 (see Table 13.11), it follows, for example, that the point forecast of Tasty Cola sales in period 44 (August of year 4) is

$$\begin{aligned}\hat{y}_{44} &= tr_{44} \times sn_{44} \\ &= (380.163 + 9.489(44))(1.693) \\ &= 797.699(1.693) \\ &= 1{,}350.50\end{aligned}$$

Although there is no theoretically correct prediction interval for y_t, a **fairly accurate approximate 100(1 − α) percent prediction interval for y_t** is obtained by computing an interval that is centered at $\hat{y}_t$ and that has a length equal to the length of the 100(1 − α) percent prediction interval for the **deseasonalized observation d_t.** Here the interval for d_t is obtained by using the model

$$\begin{aligned}d_t &= TR_t + \varepsilon_t \\ &= \beta_0 + \beta_1 t + \varepsilon_t\end{aligned}$$

For instance, using MINITAB to predict d_t on the basis of this model, we find that a 95 percent prediction interval for d_{44} is [769.959, 825.439]. Since this interval has a length equal to 825.439 − 769.959 = 55.48, it follows that an approximate 95 percent prediction interval for y_{44} is

$$\begin{aligned}\left[\hat{y}_{44} \pm \frac{55.48}{2}\right] &= [1{,}350.50 \pm 27.74] \\ &= [1{,}322.76, 1{,}378.24]\end{aligned}$$

In Table 13.12 we give the approximate 95 percent prediction intervals (calculated by the above method) for Tasty Cola sales in the 12 months of year 4.

Next, suppose we actually observe Tasty Cola sales in year 4, and these sales are as given in Table 13.12. In Figure 13.12 we plot the observed and forecast sales for all 48 sales periods. In practice, the comparison of the observed and forecast sales in years 1 through 3 would be used by the analyst to determine whether the forecasting equation adequately fits the historical data. An adequate fit (as indicated by Figure 13.12, for example) might prompt an analyst to use this equation to calculate forecasts for future time periods. One reason that the Tasty Cola forecasting equation

$$\begin{aligned}\hat{y}_t &= tr_t \times sn_t \\ &= (380.163 + 9.489t)sn_t\end{aligned}$$

FIGURE 13.12 A Plot of the Observed and Forecast Tasty Cola Sales Values

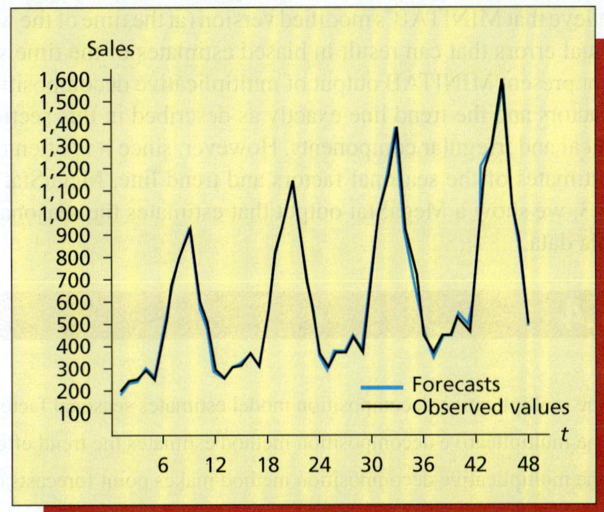

provides reasonable forecasts is that this equation multiplies tr_t by sn_t. Therefore, as the average level of the time series (determined by the trend) increases, the seasonal swing of the time series increases, which is consistent with the data plots in Figures 13.10 and 13.12. For example, note from Table 13.11 that the estimated seasonal factor for August is 1.693. The forecasting equation yields a prediction of Tasty Cola sales in August of year 1 equal to

$$\begin{aligned}\hat{y}_8 &= [380.163 + 9.489(8)]1.693 \\ &= (456.075)(1.693) \\ &= 772.13\end{aligned}$$

This implies a seasonal swing of 772.13 − 456.075 = 316.055 (hundreds of cases) above 456.075, the estimated trend level. The forecasting equation yields a prediction of Tasty Cola sales in August of year 2 equal to

$$\begin{aligned}\hat{y}_{20} &= [380.163 + 9.489(20)]1.693 \\ &= (569.943)(1.693) \\ &= 964.91\end{aligned}$$

which implies an increased seasonal swing of 964.91 − 569.943 = 394.967 (hundreds of cases) above 569.943, the estimated trend level. In general, then, the forecasting equation is appropriate for forecasting a time series with a seasonal swing that is proportional to the average level of the time series as determined by the trend—that is, a time series exhibiting increasing seasonal variation.

We next note that the U.S. Bureau of the Census has developed the **Census II method,** which is a sophisticated version of the multiplicative decomposition method discussed in this section. The initial version of Census II was primarily developed by Julius Shiskin in the late 1950s when a computer program was written to perform the rather complex calculations. Several modifications have been made to the first version of the method over the years. Census II continues to be widely used by a variety of businesses and government agencies.

Census II first adjusts the original data for "trading day variations." That is, the data are adjusted to account for the fact that, for example, different months or quarters will consist of different numbers of business days or "trading days." The method then uses an iterative procedure to obtain estimates of the seasonal component (SN_t), the trading day component, the so-called trend-cycle component ($TR_t \times CL_t$), and the irregular component (IR_t). The iterative procedure makes extensive use of moving averages and a method for identifying and replacing extreme values in order to eliminate randomness. For a good explanation of the details involved here and in the Census II method as a whole, see Makridakis, Wheelwright, and McGee (1983). After carrying out a number of tests to check the correctness of the estimates, the method estimates the trend-cycle, seasonal, and irregular components.

MINITAB carries out a modified version of the multiplicative decomposition method discussed in this section. We believe that MINITAB's modified version (at the time of the writing of this book) makes some conceptual errors that can result in biased estimates of the time series components. Therefore, we will not present MINITAB output of multiplicative decomposition. MegaStat estimates the seasonal factors and the trend line exactly as described in this section. MegaStat does not estimate the cyclical and irregular components. However, since it is often reasonable to make forecasts by using estimates of the seasonal factors and trend line, MegaStat can be used to do this. In Appendix 13.3, we show a MegaStat output that estimates the seasonal factors and trend line for the Tasty Cola data.

Exercises for Section 13.4

CONCEPTS

13.11 Explain how the multiplicative decomposition model estimates seasonal factors.

13.12 Explain how the multiplicative decomposition method estimates the trend effect.

13.13 Discuss how the multiplicative decomposition method makes point forecasts of future time series values.

METHODS AND APPLICATIONS

Exercises 13.14 through 13.18 are based on the following situation: International Machinery, Inc., produces a tractor and wishes to use **quarterly** tractor sales data observed in the last four years to predict quarterly tractor sales next year. The following MegaStat output gives the tractor sales data and the estimates of the seasonal factors and trend line for the data: IntMach

t	Year	Quarter	Sales, y	Centered Moving Average	Ratio to CMA	Seasonal Indexes	Sales, y Deseasonalized
1	1	1	293			1.191	245.9
2	1	2	392			1.521	257.7
3	1	3	221	275.125	0.803	0.804	275.0
4	1	4	147	302.000	0.487	0.484	303.9
5	2	1	388	325.250	1.193	1.191	325.7
6	2	2	512	338.125	1.514	1.521	336.6
7	2	3	287	354.125	0.810	0.804	357.1
8	2	4	184	381.500	0.482	0.484	380.4
9	3	1	479	405.000	1.183	1.191	402.0
10	3	2	640	417.375	1.533	1.521	420.7
11	3	3	347	435.000	0.798	0.804	431.8
12	3	4	223	462.125	0.483	0.484	461.0
13	4	1	581	484.375	1.199	1.191	487.7
14	4	2	755	497.625	1.517	1.521	496.3
15	4	3	410			0.804	510.2
16	4	4	266			0.484	549.9

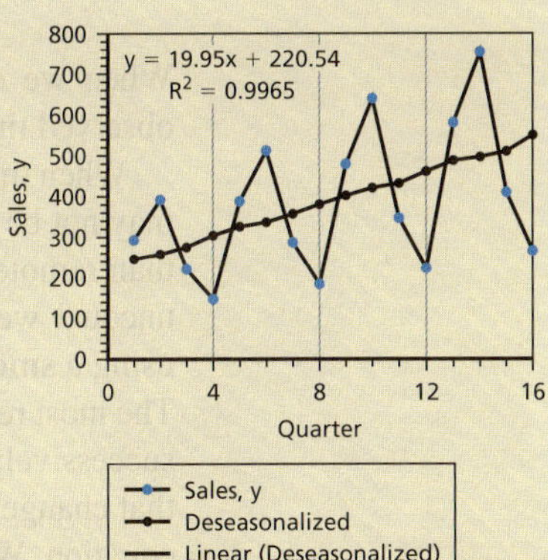

Calculation of Seasonal Indexes

	1	2	3	4	
1			0.803	0.487	
2	1.193	1.514	0.810	0.482	
3	1.183	1.533	0.798	0.483	
4	1.199	1.517			
mean:	1.192	1.522	0.804	0.484	4.001
adjusted:	1.191	1.521	0.804	0.484	4.000

13.14 Find and identify the four seasonal factors for quarters 1, 2, 3, and 4.

13.15 What type of trend is indicated by the plot of the deseasonalized data?

13.16 What is the equation of the estimated trend that has been calculated using the deseasonalized data?

13.17 Compute a point forecast of tractor sales (based on trend and seasonal factors) for each of the quarters next year.

13.18 Compute an approximate 95 percent prediction interval forecast of tractor sales for each of the quarters next year. Use the fact that the half-lengths of 95 percent prediction intervals for the deseasonalized sales values in the four quarters of next year are, respectively, 14, 14.4, 14.6, and 15.

13.19 If we use the multiplicative decomposition method to analyze the quarterly bicycle sales data given in Table 13.3 (page 636), we find that the quarterly seasonal factors are .46, 1.22, 1.68, and .64. Furthermore, if we use a statistical software package to fit a straight line to the deseasonalized sales values, we find that the estimate of the trend is BikeSales

$$tr_t = 22.61 + .59t$$

In addition, we find that the half-lengths of 95 percent prediction intervals for the deseasonalized sales values in the four quarters of the next year are, respectively, 2.80, 2.85, 2.92, and 2.98.

a Calculate point predictions of bicycle sales in the four quarters of the next year.

b Calculate approximate 95 percent prediction intervals for bicycle sales in the four quarters of the next year.

13.5 Exponential Smoothing

In ongoing forecasting systems, forecasts of future time series values are made each period for succeeding periods. At the end of each period the estimates of the time series parameters and the forecasting equation need to be updated to account for the most recent observation. This updating accounts for possible changes in the parameters that may occur over time. In addition, such changes may imply that unequal weights should be applied to the time series observations when the estimates of the parameters are updated.

Simple exponential smoothing We begin by assuming that a time series is appropriately described by the no trend equation

$$y_t = \beta_0 + \varepsilon_t$$

When the parameter β_0 remains constant over time, we have seen that it is reasonable to forecast future values of y_t by using regression analysis (see Example 13.1). In such a case the least squares point estimate of β_0 is

$$b_0 = \bar{y} = \text{the average of the observed time series values}$$

When we compute the point estimate b_0 we are **equally weighting** each of the previously observed time series values $y_1, y_2, \ldots, y_n$.

When the value of the parameter β_0 is slowly changing over time, the equal weighting scheme may not be appropriate. Instead, it may be desirable to weight recent observations more heavily than remote observations. **Simple exponential smoothing** is a forecasting method that applies unequal weights to the time series observations. This unequal weighting is accomplished by using a **smoothing constant** that determines how much weight is attached to each observation. The most recent observation is given the most weight. More distantly past observations are given successively smaller weights. The procedure allows the forecaster to update the estimate of β_0 so that changes in the value of this parameter can be detected and incorporated into the forecasting equation. We illustrate simple exponential smoothing in the following example.

Example 13.6 The Cod Catch Case

Consider the cod catch data of Example 13.1, which are given in Table 13.1 (page 634). The plot of these data (in Figure 13.2 on page 634) suggests that the no trend model

$$y_t = \beta_0 + \varepsilon_t$$

may appropriately describe the cod catch series. It is also possible that the parameter β_0 could be slowly changing over time.

We begin the simple exponential smoothing procedure by calculating an initial estimate of the average level β_0 of the series. This estimate is denoted S_0 and is computed by averaging the first six time series values. We obtain

$$S_0 = \frac{\sum_{t=1}^{6} y_t}{6} = \frac{362 + 381 + \cdots + 402}{6} = 359.67$$

Note that, since simple exponential smoothing attempts to track changes over time in the average level β_0 by using newly observed values to update the estimates of β_0, we use only six of the $n = 24$ time series observations to calculate the initial estimate of β_0. If we do this, then 18 observations remain to tell us how β_0 may be changing over time. Experience has shown that, in general, it is reasonable to calculate initial estimates in exponential smoothing procedures by using half of the historical data. However, it can be shown that, in simple exponential smoothing, using six observations is reasonable (it would not, however, be reasonable to use a very small number of observations because doing so might make the initial estimate so different from the true value of β_0 that the exponential smoothing procedure would be adversely affected).

Next, assume that at the end of time period $T - 1$ we have an estimate S_{T-1} of β_0. Then, assuming that in time period T we obtain a new observation y_T, we can update S_{T-1} to S_T, which is an estimate made in period T of β_0. We compute the updated estimate by using the so-called **smoothing equation**

$$S_T = \alpha y_T + (1 - \alpha)S_{T-1}$$

Here α is a smoothing constant between 0 and 1 (α will be discussed in more detail later). The updating equation says that S_T, the estimate made in time period T of β_0, equals a fraction α (for example, .1) of the newly observed time series observation y_T plus a fraction $(1 - \alpha)$ (for example, .9) of S_{T-1}, the estimate made in time period $T - 1$ of β_0. The more the average level of the process is changing, the more a newly observed time series value should influence our estimate, and thus the larger the smoothing constant α should be set. We will soon see how to use historical data to determine an appropriate value of α.

TABLE 13.13 One-Period-Ahead Forecasting of the Historical Cod Catch Time Series Using Simple Exponential Smoothing with $\alpha = .02$ CodCatch

Year	Month	Actual Cod Catch, y_T	Smoothed Estimate, S_T ($S_0 = 359.67$)	Forecast Made Last Period	Forecast Error	Squared Forecast Error
1	Jan.	362	359.72	360	2	4
	Feb.	381	360.14	360	21	441
	Mar.	317	359.28	360	−43	1,849
	Apr.	297	358.03	359	−62	3,844
	May	399	358.85	358	41	1,681
	June	402	359.71	359	43	1,849
	July	375	360.02	360	15	225
	Aug.	349	359.80	360	−11	121
	Sept.	386	360.32	360	26	676
	Oct.	328	359.68	360	−32	1,024
	Nov.	389	360.26	360	29	841
	Dec.	343	359.92	360	−17	289
2	Jan.	276	358.24	360	−84	7,056
	Feb.	334	357.75	358	−24	576
	Mar.	394	358.48	358	36	1,296
	Apr.	334	357.99	358	−24	576
	May	384	358.51	358	26	676
	June	314	357.62	359	−45	2,025
	July	344	357.35	358	−14	196
	Aug.	337	356.94	357	−20	400
	Sept.	345	356.70	357	−12	144
	Oct.	362	356.81	357	5	25
	Nov.	314	355.95	357	−43	1,849
	Dec.	365	356.13	356	9	81

We will now begin with the initial estimate $S_0 = 359.67$ and update this initial estimate by applying the smoothing equation to the 24 observed cod catches. To do this, we arbitrarily set α equal to .02, and to judge the appropriateness of this choice of α we calculate "one-period-ahead" forecasts of the historical cod catches as we carry out the smoothing procedure. Since the initial estimate of β_0 is $S_0 = 359.67$, it follows that 360 is the rounded forecast made at time 0 for y_1, the value of the time series in period 1. Since we see from Table 13.13 that $y_1 = 362$, we have a forecast error of $362 - 360 = 2$. Using $y_1 = 362$, we can update S_0 to S_1, an estimate made in period 1 of the average level of the time series, by using the equation

$$S_1 = \alpha y_1 + (1 - \alpha)S_0$$
$$= .02(362) + .98(359.67) = 359.72$$

Since this implies that 360 is the rounded forecast made in period 1 for y_2, and since we see from Table 13.13 that $y_2 = 381$, we have a forecast error of $381 - 360 = 21$. Using $y_2 = 381$, we can update S_1 to S_2, an estimate made in period 2 of β_0, by using the equation

$$S_2 = \alpha y_2 + (1 - \alpha)S_1$$
$$= .02(381) + .98(359.72) = 360.14$$

Since this implies that 360 is the rounded forecast made in period 2 for y_3, and since we see from Table 13.13 that $y_3 = 317$, we have a forecast error of $317 - 360 = -43$. This procedure is continued through the entire 24 periods of historical data. The results are summarized in Table 13.13. Using the results in this table, we find that, for $\alpha = .02$, the sum of squared forecast errors is 27,744. To find a "good" value of α, we evaluate the sum of squared forecast errors for values of α ranging from .02 to .30 in increments of .02 (in most exponential smoothing applications, the value of the smoothing constant used is between .01 and .30). When we do this, we find that $\alpha = .02$ minimizes the sum of squared forecast errors. Since this minimizing value of α is small, it appears to be best to apply small weights to new observations, which tells us that the level of the time series is not changing very much.

In general, simple exponential smoothing is carried out as follows:

Simple Exponential Smoothing

1 Suppose that the time series $y_1, \ldots, y_n$ is described by the equation

$$y_t = \beta_0 + \varepsilon_t$$

where the average level β_0 of the process may be slowly changing over time. Then the estimate S_T of β_0 made in time period T is given by the **smoothing equation**

$$S_T = \alpha y_T + (1 - \alpha)S_{T-1}$$

where α is a smoothing constant between 0 and 1 and S_{T-1} is the estimate of β_0 made in time period $T - 1$.

2 A point forecast made in time period T for any future value of the time series is S_T.

3 If we observe y_{T+1} in time period $T + 1$, we can update S_T to S_{T+1} by using the equation

$$S_{T+1} = \alpha y_{T+1} + (1 - \alpha)S_T$$

and a point forecast made in time period $T + 1$ for any future value of the time series is S_{T+1}.

Example 13.7 The Cod Catch Case

C

In Example 13.6 we saw that $\alpha = .02$ is a "good" value of the smoothing constant when forecasting the 24 observed cod catches in Table 13.13. Therefore, we will use simple exponential smoothing with $\alpha = .02$ to forecast future monthly cod catches. From Table 13.13 we see that $S_{24} = 356.13$ is the estimate made in month 24 of the average level β_0 of the monthly cod catches. It follows that the point forecast made in month 24 of any future monthly cod catch is 356.13 tons of cod. Now, assuming that we observe a cod catch in January of year 3 of $y_{25} = 384$, we can update S_{24} to S_{25} by using the equation

$$\begin{aligned} S_{25} &= \alpha y_{25} + (1 - \alpha)S_{24} \\ &= .02(384) + .98(356.13) \\ &= 356.69 \end{aligned}$$

This implies that the point forecast made in month 25 of any future monthly cod catch is 356.69 tons of cod.

By using the smoothing equation

$$S_T = \alpha y_T + (1 - \alpha)S_{T-1}$$

it can be shown that S_T, the estimate made in time period T of the average level β_0 of the time series, can be expressed as

$$\begin{aligned} S_T = {} & \alpha y_T + \alpha(1 - \alpha)y_{T-1} + \alpha(1 - \alpha)^2 y_{T-2} \\ & + \cdots + \alpha(1 - \alpha)^{T-1} y_1 + (1 - \alpha)^T S_0 \end{aligned}$$

The coefficients measuring the contributions of the observations $y_T, y_{T-1}, y_{T-2}, \ldots, y_1$—that is, $\alpha, \alpha(1 - \alpha), \alpha(1 - \alpha)^2, \ldots, \alpha(1 - \alpha)^{T-1}$—decrease **exponentially** with age. For this reason we refer to this procedure as simple **exponential** smoothing.

Since the coefficients measuring the contributions of $y_T, y_{T-1}, y_{T-2}, \ldots, y_1$ are decreasing exponentially, the most recent observation y_T makes the largest contribution to the current estimate of β_0. Older observations make smaller and smaller contributions to this estimate. Thus remote observations are "dampened out" of the current estimate of β_0 as time advances. The rate at which remote observations are dampened out depends on the smoothing constant α. For values of α near 1, remote observations are dampened out quickly. For example, if $\alpha = .9$ we obtain coefficients .9, .09, .009, .0009, ... For values of α near 0, remote observations are dampened out more slowly (if $\alpha = .1$, we obtain coefficients .1, .09, .081, .0729, . . .). The choice of a smoothing constant α is usually made by simulated forecasting of a historical data set as illustrated in Example 13.6.

Computer software packages can be used to implement exponential smoothing. These packages choose the smoothing constant (or constants) in different ways and also compute approximate prediction intervals in different ways. Optimally, the user should carefully investigate how the computer software package implements exponential smoothing. At a minimum, the user should not trust the forecasts given by the software package if they seem illogical.

Figure 13.13 gives the MINITAB output of using simple exponential smoothing to forecast in month 24 the cod catches in future months. Note that MINITAB has selected the smoothing constant $\alpha = .0703909$ and tells us that the point forecast and the 95 percent prediction interval forecast of the cod catch in any future month are, respectively, 348.168 and [276.976, 419.360]. Looking at Figure 13.13(a), these forecasts seem intuitively reasonable. A MegaStat output of simple exponential smoothing for the cod catch data is given in Appendix 13.3.

Holt–Winters' models Various extensions of simple exponential smoothing can be used to forecast time series that are described by models different from the model

$$y_t = \beta_0 + \varepsilon_t$$

For example, **Holt–Winters' double exponential smoothing** can forecast time series that are described by the linear trend model

$$y_t = \beta_0 + \beta_1 t + \varepsilon_t$$

Here we assume that β_0 and β_1 (and thus the linear trend) may be changing slowly over time. To implement Holt–Winters' double exponential smoothing, we find initial estimates of β_0 and β_1 and then use updating equations to track changes in these estimates. The updating equation for the estimate of β_0 uses a smoothing constant that MINITAB calls **alpha,** and the updating equation for the estimate of β_1 uses a smoothing constant that MINITAB calls **gamma.** Although we will not

FIGURE 13.13 MINITAB Output of Using Simple Exponential Smoothing to Forecast the Cod Catches

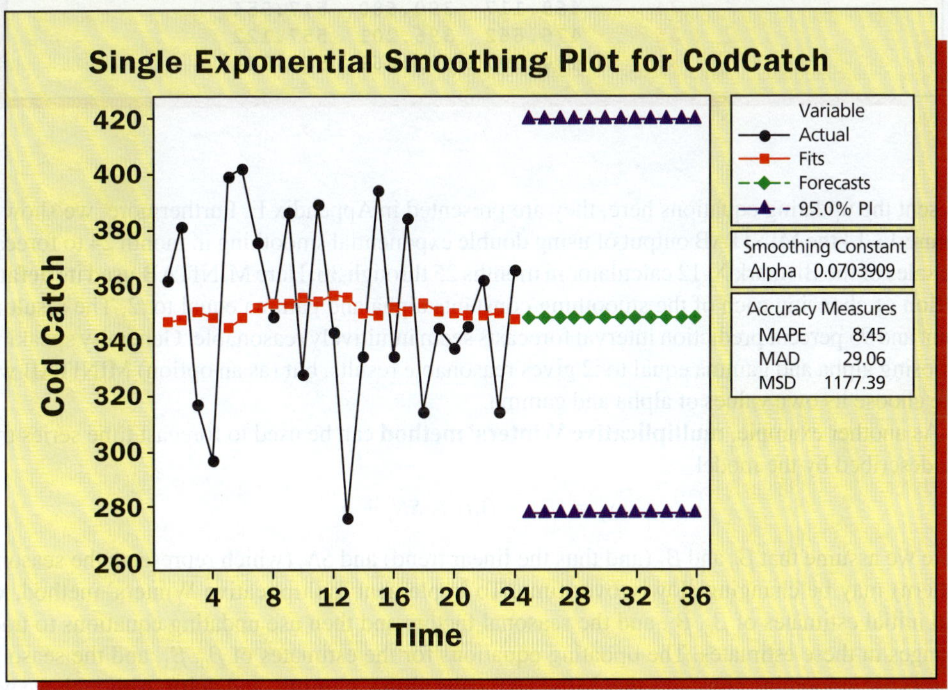

(a) The graphical forecasts

```
Forecasts
Period  Forecast    Lower    Upper
25       348.168  276.976  419.360
```

(b) The numerical forecasts of the cod catch in month 25 (and any other future month)

FIGURE 13.14 MINITAB Output of Using Double Exponential Smoothing to Forecast Calculator Sales

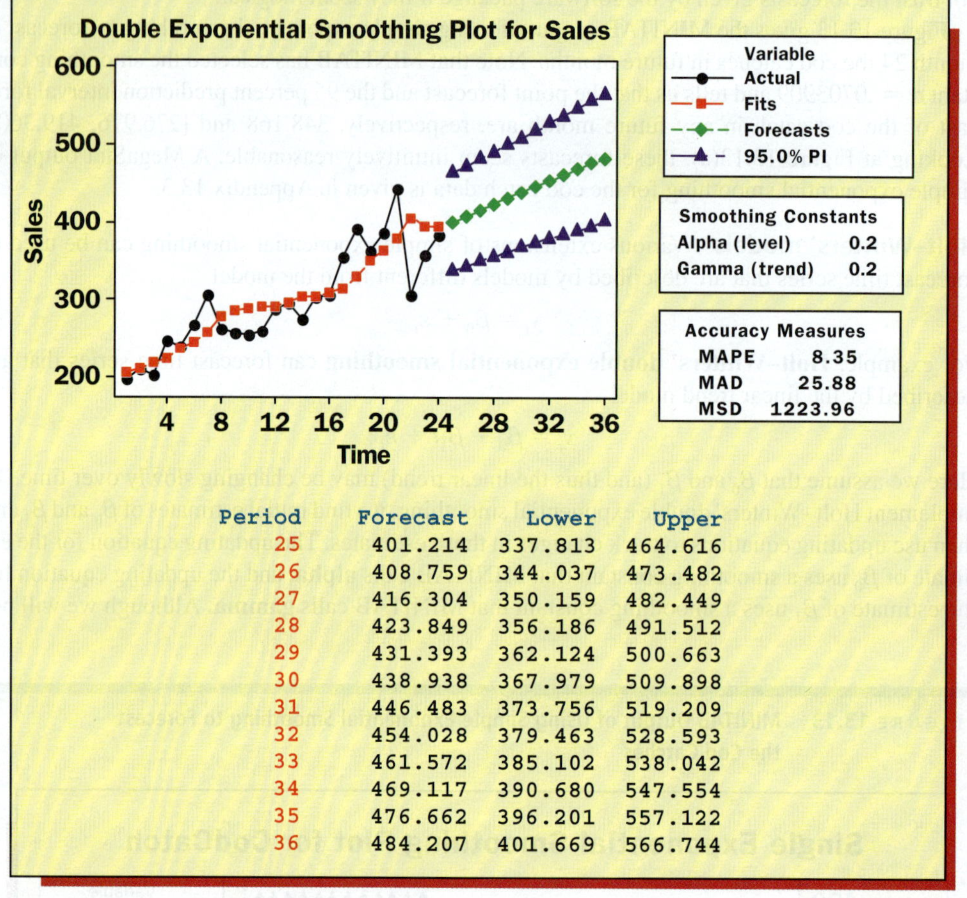

Period	Forecast	Lower	Upper
25	401.214	337.813	464.616
26	408.759	344.037	473.482
27	416.304	350.159	482.449
28	423.849	356.186	491.512
29	431.393	362.124	500.663
30	438.938	367.979	509.898
31	446.483	373.756	519.209
32	454.028	379.463	528.593
33	461.572	385.102	538.042
34	469.117	390.680	547.554
35	476.662	396.201	557.122
36	484.207	401.669	566.744

present the updating equations here, they are presented in Appendix E. Furthermore, we show in Figure 13.14 the MINITAB output of using double exponential smoothing in month 24 to forecast the sales of the Bismark X-12 calculator in months 25 through 36. Here MINITAB used its **default option** of choosing each of the smoothing constants alpha and gamma equal to .2. The resulting point and 95 percent prediction interval forecasts seem intuitively reasonable. Generally speaking, choosing alpha and gamma equal to .2 gives reasonable results, but (as an option) MINITAB will also choose its own values of alpha and gamma.

As another example, **multiplicative Winters' method** can be used to forecast time series that are described by the model

$$y_t = (\beta_0 + \beta_1 t) \times SN_t + \varepsilon_t$$

Here we assume that β_0 and β_1 (and thus the linear trend) and SN_t (which represents the seasonal pattern) may be changing slowly over time. To implement multiplicative Winters' method, we find initial estimates of β_0, β_1, and the seasonal factors and then use updating equations to track changes in these estimates. The updating equations for the estimates of β_0, β_1, and the seasonal factors use smoothing constants that MINITAB calls **alpha, gamma,** and **delta.** Although we will not present these updating equations here, they are presented in Appendix E. Furthermore, we present in Figure 13.15 the MINITAB output of using Winters' method in month 36 to forecast the sales of Tasty Cola in months 37 through 48. Here MINITAB used its default option of choosing each of the smoothing constants alpha, gamma, and delta to be .2. The resulting point forecasts seem intuitively reasonable, but the 95 percent prediction intervals seem very wide. This is further discussed in Appendix E. We show in this appendix that the wide prediction intervals result from a combination of a short historical series (36 sales values) and MINITAB obtaining inaccurate initial estimates of the model parameters. We also show how the prediction intervals can be appropriately adjusted. When the historical series is long (for example, see Exercise 13.27),

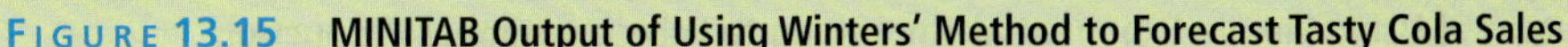

FIGURE 13.15 MINITAB Output of Using Winters' Method to Forecast Tasty Cola Sales

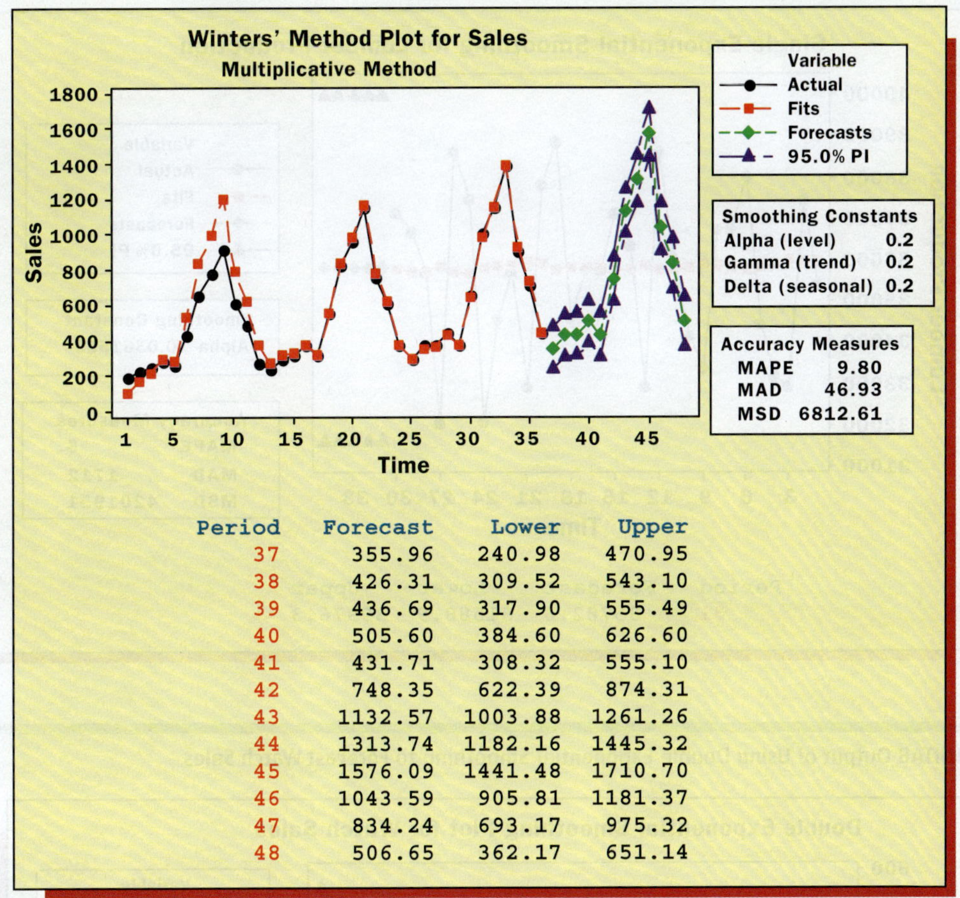

Period	Forecast	Lower	Upper
37	355.96	240.98	470.95
38	426.31	309.52	543.10
39	436.69	317.90	555.49
40	505.60	384.60	626.60
41	431.71	308.32	555.10
42	748.35	622.39	874.31
43	1132.57	1003.88	1261.26
44	1313.74	1182.16	1445.32
45	1576.09	1441.48	1710.70
46	1043.59	905.81	1181.37
47	834.24	693.17	975.32
48	506.65	362.17	651.14

MINITAB usually obtains reasonable prediction intervals. Finally, note that MINITAB will not choose its own values of alpha, gamma, and delta. However, the user can simply experiment with different combinations of values of these smoothing constants until a combination is found that produces adequate results.

Exercises for Section 13.5

CONCEPTS

13.20 In general, when it is appropriate to use exponential smoothing?

13.21 What is the purpose of a smoothing constant in exponential smoothing?

13.22 What are the differences between the types of time series forecast by simple exponential smoothing, double exponential smoothing, and Winters' method?

METHODS AND APPLICATIONS

13.23 THE COD CATCH CASE CodCatch

Consider Table 13.13 (page 653). Verify that S_3, an estimate made in period 3 of β_0, is 359.28. Also verify that the one-period-ahead forecast error for period 4 is -62, as shown in Table 13.13.

13.24 THE COD CATCH CASE CodCatch

Consider Example 13.7 (page 654). Suppose that we observe a cod catch in February of year 3 of $y_{26} = 328$. Update $S_{25} = 356.69$ to S_{26}, a point forecast made in month 26 of any future monthly cod catch. Use $\alpha = .02$ as in Example 13.7.

13.25 THE LUMBER PRODUCTION CASE LumberProd

Figure 13.16 gives the MINITAB output of using simple exponential smoothing to forecast yearly U.S. lumber production. Here MINITAB has estimated the smoothing constant alpha to be .0361553. Use the MINITAB output to find and report the point prediction of and the 95 percent prediction interval for the total U.S. lumber production in a future year.

FIGURE 13.16 MINITAB Output of Using Simple Exponential Smoothing to Forecast Lumber Production

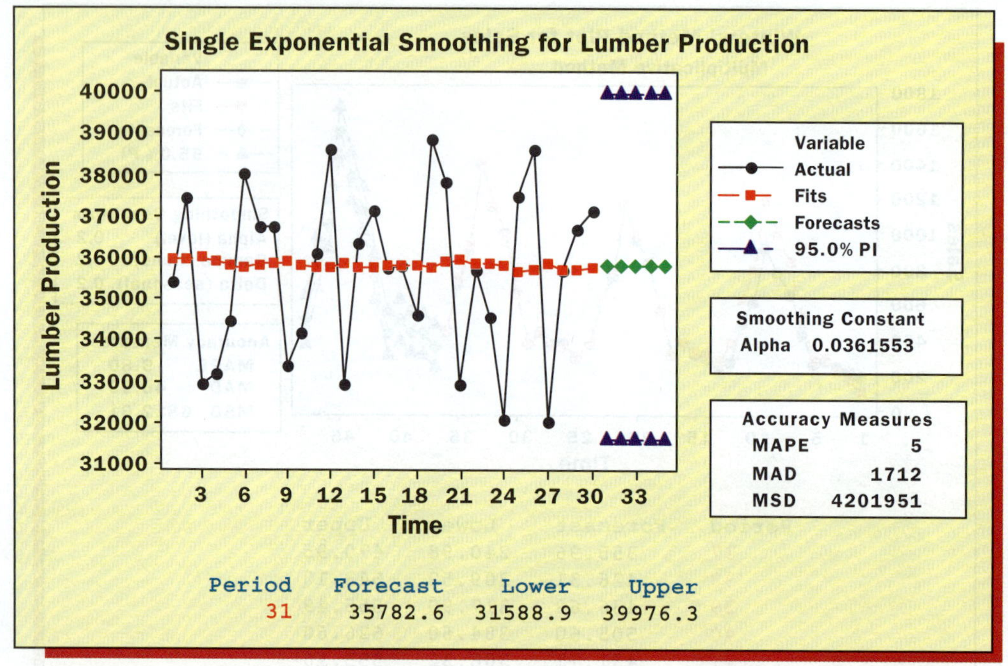

FIGURE 13.17 MINITAB Output of Using Double Exponential Smoothing to Forecast Watch Sales

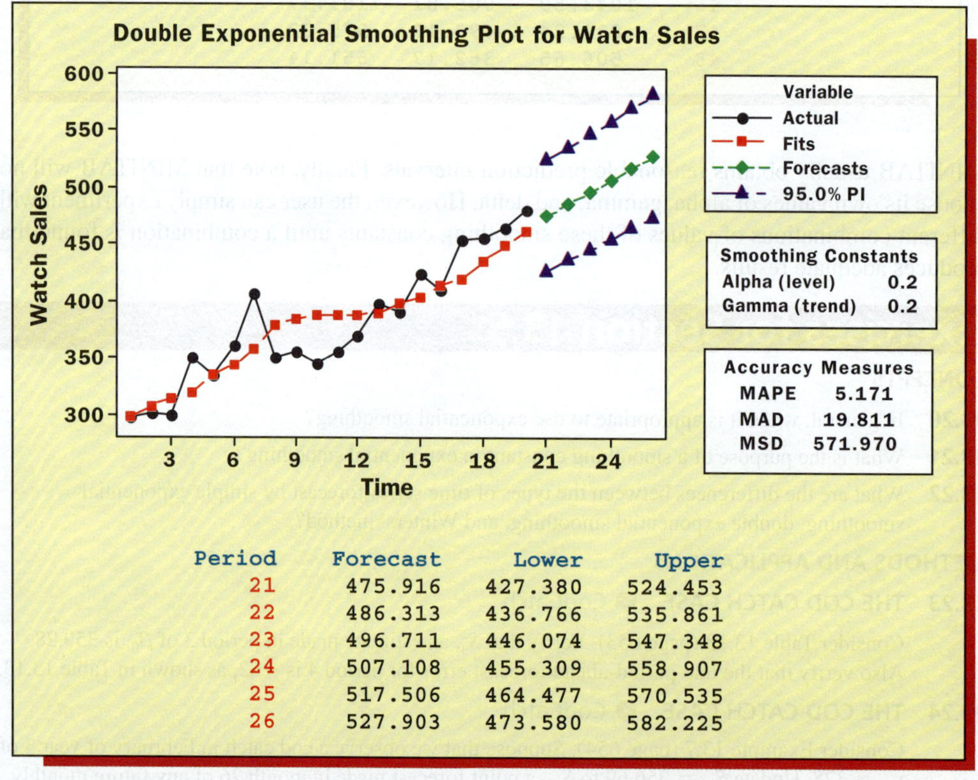

13.26 THE WATCH SALES CASE WatchSale

Figure 13.17 gives the MINITAB output of using double exponential smoothing in month 20 to forecast watch sales in months 21 through 26. Here we have used MINITAB's default option that sets each of the smoothing constants alpha and gamma equal to .2. Find and report the point prediction of and a 95 percent prediction interval for watch sales in month 21.

FIGURE 13.18 MINITAB Output of Using Winters' Method to Forecast the Monthly Hotel Room Averages

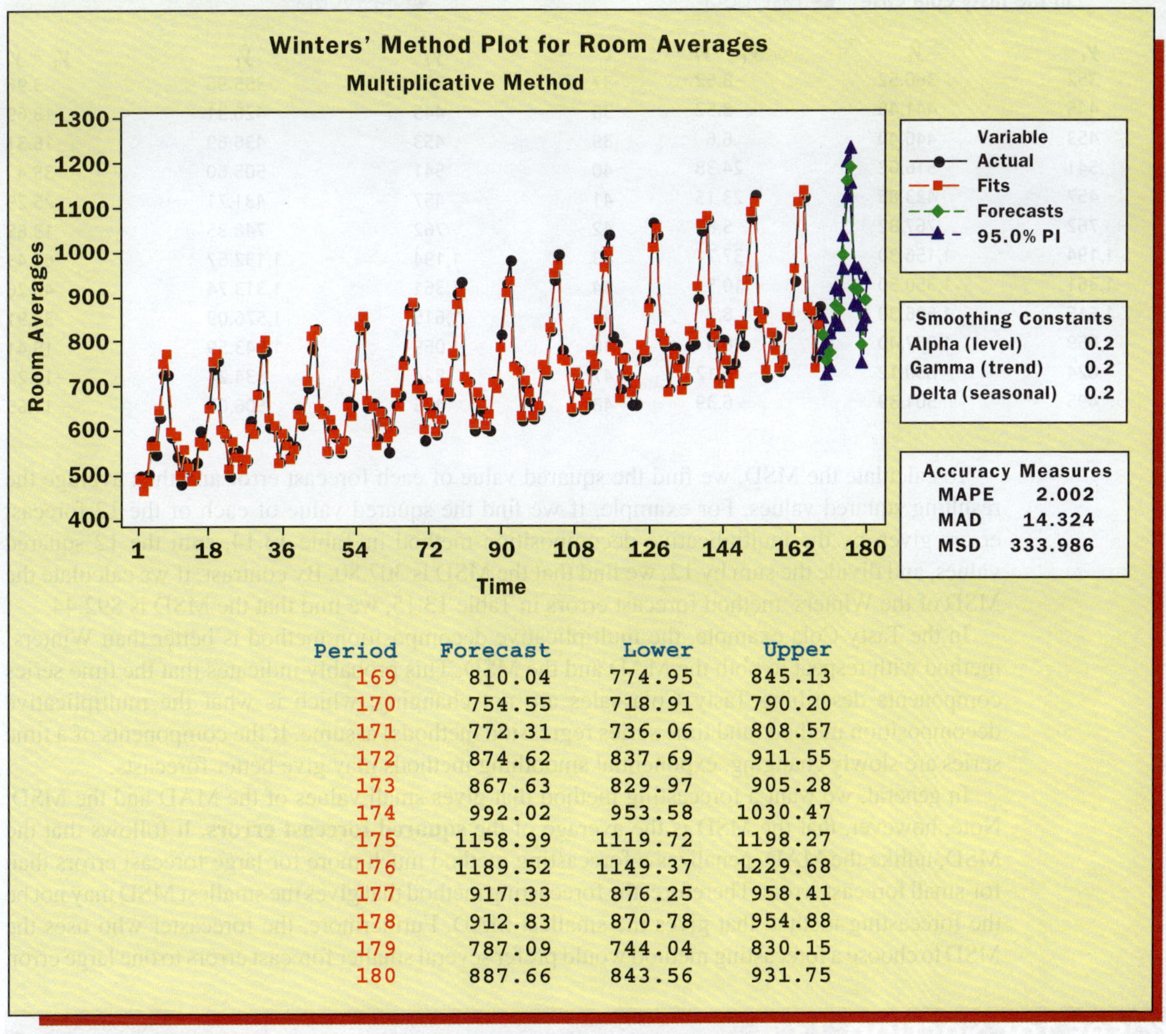

Period	Forecast	Lower	Upper
169	810.04	774.95	845.13
170	754.55	718.91	790.20
171	772.31	736.06	808.57
172	874.62	837.69	911.55
173	867.63	829.97	905.28
174	992.02	953.58	1030.47
175	1158.99	1119.72	1198.27
176	1189.52	1149.37	1229.68
177	917.33	876.25	958.41
178	912.83	870.78	954.88
179	787.09	744.04	830.15
180	887.66	843.56	931.75

13.27 THE TRAVELER'S REST CASE TravRest

Figure 13.18 gives the MINITAB output of using Winters' method in month 168 to forecast the monthly hotel room averages in months 169 through 180. Here we have used MINITAB's default option that sets each of the smoothing constants alpha, gamma, and delta equal to .2. Use the MINITAB output to find and report the point prediction of and a 95 percent prediction interval for the monthly hotel room average in period 169.

13.6 Forecast Error Comparisons

Table 13.14 gives the actual values of Tasty Cola sales (y_t) in periods 37 through 48 and the multiplicative decomposition method point forecasts ($\hat{y}_t$) of these actual values. Consider the *differences* between the actual values and the point forecasts, which are called **forecast errors** and are also given in Table 13.14. We can use these forecast errors to compare the point forecasts given by the multiplicative decomposition method with the point forecasts given by other techniques, such as Winters' method. Two criteria by which to compare forecasting methods are the **mean absolute deviation (MAD)** and the **mean squared deviation (MSD).**

To calculate the MAD, we find the absolute value of each forecast error and then average the resulting absolute values. For example, if we find the absolute value of each of the 12 forecast errors given by the multiplicative decomposition method in Table 13.14, sum the 12 absolute values, and divide the sum by 12, we find that the MAD is 14.15. By contrast, if we calculate the MAD of the Winters' method forecast errors in Table 13.15, we find that the MAD is 25.6.

TABLE 13.14 Forecast Errors Given by the Multiplicative Decomposition Method in the Tasty Cola Case TastyCola

t	y_t	$\hat{y}_t$	$y_t - \hat{y}_t$
37	352	360.52	−8.52
38	445	441.48	3.52
39	453	446.40	6.6
40	541	516.62	24.38
41	457	433.85	23.15
42	762	767.82	−5.82
43	1,194	1,156.30	37.7
44	1,361	1,350.50	10.5
45	1,615	1,606.30	8.7
46	1,059	1,067.40	−8.4
47	824	850.12	−26.12
48	495	501.39	−6.39

TABLE 13.15 Forecast Errors Given by Winters' Method in the Tasty Cola Case TastyCola

t	y_t	$\hat{y}_t$	$y_t - \hat{y}_t$
37	352	355.96	−3.96
38	445	426.31	18.69
39	453	436.69	16.31
40	541	505.60	35.4
41	457	431.71	25.29
42	762	748.35	13.65
43	1,194	1,132.57	61.43
44	1,361	1,313.74	47.26
45	1,615	1,576.09	38.91
46	1,059	1,043.59	15.41
47	824	834.24	−10.24
48	495	506.65	−11.65

To calculate the MSD, we find the squared value of each forecast error and then average the resulting squared values. For example, if we find the squared value of each of the 12 forecast errors given by the multiplicative decomposition method in Table 13.14, sum the 12 squared values, and divide the sum by 12, we find that the MSD is 307.80. By contrast, if we calculate the MSD of the Winters' method forecast errors in Table 13.15, we find that the MSD is 892.44.

In the Tasty Cola example, the multiplicative decomposition method is better than Winters' method with respect to both the MAD and the MSD. This probably indicates that the time series components describing Tasty Cola sales are not changing, which is what the multiplicative decomposition method (and time series regression methods) assume. If the components of a time series are slowly changing, exponential smoothing methods may give better forecasts.

In general, we want a forecasting method that gives small values of the MAD and the MSD. Note, however, that the MSD is the average of the **squared forecast errors.** It follows that the MSD, unlike the MAD, penalizes a forecasting method much more for large forecast errors than for small forecast errors. Therefore, the forecasting method that gives the smallest MSD may not be the forecasting method that gives the smallest MAD. Furthermore, the forecaster who uses the MSD to choose a forecasting method would prefer several smaller forecast errors to one large error.

Exercises for Section 13.6

CONCEPTS

13.28 What is the MAD? What is the MSD? How do we use these quantities?

13.29 Why does the MSD penalize a forecasting method much more for large forecast errors than for small forecast errors?

METHODS AND APPLICATIONS

Exercises 13.30 and 13.31 compare two forecasting methods—method A and method B. Suppose that method A gives the point forecasts 57, 61, and 70 of three future time series values. Method B gives the point forecasts 59, 65, and 73 of these three future values. The three future values turn out to be 60, 64, and 67.

13.30 Calculate the MAD and MSD for method A. Calculate the MAD and MSD for method B.

13.31 Which method—method A or method B—gives the smallest MAD? The smallest MSD?

13.7 Index Numbers

We often wish to compare a value of a time series relative to another value of the time series. For instance, according to the U.S. Bureau of Labor Statistics, energy prices increased by 4.7 percent from 1995 to 1996, while apparel prices decreased by .2 percent from 1995 to 1996. In order to make such comparisons, we must describe the time series. We have seen (in Section 13.4) that time series decomposition can be employed to describe a time series. Another way to describe time-related data is to use *index numbers.*

TABLE 13.16 Installment Credit Outstanding (in Billions of Dollars): 1990 to 1996
InstCred

	1990	1991	1992	1993	1994	1995	1996
Installment Credit Outstanding	796.4	781.1	784.9	844.1	966.5	1,103.3	1,194.6
Index (Base Year = 1990)	100.0	98.08	98.56	105.99	121.36	138.54	150.0

Source: U.S. Bureau of the Census, *Statistical Abstract of the United States*, 1997, p. 520.

When we compare time series values to the same previous value, we say that the previous value is in the **base time period,** and successive comparisons of time series values to the value in the base period form a sequence of **index numbers.** More formally, a **simple index number** (or **simple index**) is defined as follows:

A **simple index** is obtained by dividing the current value of a time series by the value of the time series in the base time period and by multiplying this ratio by 100. That is, if y_t denotes the current value and if y_0 denotes the value in the base time period, then the **simple index number** is

$$\frac{y_t}{y_0} \times 100$$

The time series values used to construct an index are often *quantities* or *prices*. For instance, in Table 13.16 we give the total amount of consumer installment credit outstanding in the United States (in billions of dollars) for the years 1990 through 1996. If we consider 1990 the base year, we compute an index for each succeeding year by dividing the installment credit outstanding for each year by 796.4 (the installment credit outstanding for the base year 1990) and by multiplying by 100. For example, for 1991 the simple index is

$$(781.1/796.4) \times 100 = 98.08$$

while the simple index for 1996 is

$$(1{,}194.6/796.4) \times 100 = 150.0$$

Table 13.16 gives the remaining index values for 1990 through 1996. Notice that (by definition) the index for the base year will always equal 100.0 (as it does here).

Although the simple index is not written with a percentage sign, comparisons of the index with the base year are percentage comparisons. For instance, the index of 150.0 for 1996 tells us that installment credit outstanding in 1996 was up 50 percent compared to the 1990 base year. The index of 98.08 for 1991 tells us that installment credit outstanding in 1991 was down 1.92 percent compared to 1990. In general, *if we are comparing the index to the base year,* the difference between the index and 100 gives the percentage change from the base year. It is important to point out that other period-to-period percentage comparisons cannot be made by subtracting indexes. For instance, the percentage difference between installment credit outstanding in 1996 and 1995 is *not* 150.0 − 138.54 = 11.46 percent. Rather, the percentage difference is

$$\frac{150.0 - 138.54}{138.54} \times 100 = 8.27$$

This says that installment credit outstanding in 1996 was up 8.27 percent relative to 1995.

Since the installment credit values are quantities, the time series of index values that we obtain is called a **quantity index.** As mentioned previously, often the original time series values are prices, in which case the index is referred to as a **price index.** Our next example will be a price index.

A simple index is computed by using the values of one time series. Often, however, we compute an index based on the accumulated values of more than one time series. Such an index is called an **aggregate index.** As an example, food prices are often compared with an aggregate index based on a "market basket" of commonly bought grocery items. For instance, consider a market basket consisting of six items—a five-pound bag of apples, a one-pound loaf of bread, a six-ounce can of tuna fish, one gallon of 2% milk, an 18-ounce jar of peanut butter, and a 16-ounce can of green beans. Table 13.17 gives 1992 and 1997 prices for each item in this market basket.

One way to compare prices would be to compute a simple index for each individual item in the market basket. However, we can create an aggregate price index by totaling the prices for each year and by then computing a simple index of the yearly price totals. Using the data in Table 13.17 we obtain

$$(10.74/8.54) \times 100 = 125.76$$

This index tells us that prices of the market basket grocery items in 1997 have increased by 25.76 percent over the prices of these items in the base year 1992. Notice that this percentage increase does not necessarily apply to each individual grocery item, nor does this index necessarily apply to any of the individual grocery items. It applies only to the aggregate of grocery items in the market basket.

In general, we compute an aggregate price index as follows:

An **aggregate price index** is

$$\left(\frac{\sum p_t}{\sum p_0}\right) \times 100$$

where Σp_t is the sum of the prices in the current time period and Σp_0 is the sum of the prices in the base year.

A disadvantage of this aggregate price index is that it does not take into account the fact that some items in the market basket are purchased more frequently than others. To remedy this deficiency, we can weight each price by the quantity of that item purchased in a given period (say yearly). Then we can total the weighted prices for each year and compute a simple index of the weighted price totals. To illustrate, Table 13.18 gives the 1992 and 1997 prices of the market basket items and also gives estimates of the quantity of each item purchased in a year by a typical family. The table also gives the price multiplied by the quantity for each item, which is simply the total yearly cost of purchasing the item. These costs are totaled for each year. Looking at Table 13.18, we see that a typical family in 1992 spent $458.77 purchasing the market basket items during the year, while the family spent $578.37 purchasing the market basket items during 1997. We now compute a simple index of the total costs, which is

$$(578.37/458.77) \times 100 = 126.07$$

This type of index is called a **weighted aggregate price index.** Two versions of this kind of index are commonly used. The first version is called a **Laspeyres index.** Here the quantities that

TABLE 13.17 1992 and 1997 Prices for a Market Basket of Grocery Items MkBskt

Grocery Item	1992 Price	1997 Price
5 lb. bag of apples	$2.99	$3.69
1 lb. loaf of bread	$.99	$1.29
6 oz. can of tuna fish	$.69	$.79
1 gal. of 2% milk	$1.29	$1.59
18 oz. jar of peanut butter	$1.99	$2.59
16 oz. can of green beans	$.59	$.79
Totals	$8.54	$10.74

TABLE 13.18 1992 and 1997 Prices and Quantities for a Market Basket of Grocery Items MkBskt

	1992 (Base Year)			1997		
Grocery Item	Price, p_0	Quantity, q	$p_0 \times q$ = cost	Price, p_t	Quantity, q	$p_t \times q$ = cost
5 lb. bag of apples	$2.99	26	$77.74	$3.69	26	$95.94
1 lb. loaf of bread	$.99	156	$154.44	$1.29	156	$201.24
6 oz. can of tuna fish	$.69	52	$35.88	$.79	52	$41.08
1 gal. of 2% milk	$1.29	104	$134.16	$1.59	104	$165.36
18 oz. jar of peanut butter	$1.99	13	$25.87	$2.59	13	$33.67
16 oz. can of green beans	$.59	52	$30.68	$.79	52	$41.08
Totals	$8.54		$458.77	$10.74		$578.37

are specified for the base year are also employed for all succeeding time periods. This is the assumption we have made in Table 13.18. Notice that the quantities for 1997 are the same as those specified for 1992. In general,

A **Laspeyres index** is

$$\frac{\sum p_t q_0}{\sum p_0 q_0} \times 100$$

where p_0 represents a base period price, q_0 represents a base period quantity, and p_t represents a current period price.

Because the Laspeyres index employs the base period quantities in all succeeding time periods, this index allows for ready comparison of prices for identical quantities of goods purchased. Such an index is useful as long as the base quantities provide a reasonable representation of consumption patterns in succeeding time periods. However, sometimes purchasing patterns can change drastically as consumer preferences change or as dramatic price changes occur. If consumption patterns in the current period are very different from the quantities specified in the base period, then a Laspeyres index can be misleading because it relates to quantities of goods that few people would purchase.

A second version of the weighted aggregate price index is called a **Paasche index.** Here we update the quantities so that they reflect consumption patterns in the current time period.

A **Paasche index** is

$$\frac{\sum p_t q_t}{\sum p_0 q_t} \times 100$$

where p_0 represents a base period price, p_t represents a current period price, and q_t represents a current period quantity.

As an example, Table 13.19 presents revised quantities for the grocery items in our previously discussed market basket. These quantities reflect increased consumption of apples, green beans, and tuna fish and somewhat decreased consumption of milk and peanut butter in 1997. We calculate a 1992 cost of $590.26 for the items in the market basket and a 1997 cost of $743.26 for the items in the market basket. Therefore, we obtain a Paasche index equal to

$$(\$743.26/\$590.26) \times 100 = 125.92$$

Because the Paasche index uses quantities from the current period, it reflects current buying habits. However, the Paasche index requires quantity data for each year, which can be difficult to obtain. Furthermore, although each period is compared to the base period, it is difficult to compare the index at other points in time. This is because different quantities are used in different periods, and thus changes in the index are affected by changes in both prices and quantities.

Economic indexes Several commonly quoted economic indexes are compiled monthly by the U.S. Bureau of Labor Statistics. Two important indexes are the **Consumer Price Index** (the **CPI**) and the **Producer Price Index** (the **PPI**). These are both *Laspeyres indexes.* The CPI monitors the price of a market basket of goods and services that would be purchased by typical

TABLE 13.19 1992 and 1997 Prices and 1997 Quantities for a Market Basket of Grocery Items MkBsktR

Grocery Item	1992 Price, p_0	1997 Quantity, q_t	$p_0 \times q_t$ = cost	1997 Price, p_t	1997 Quantity, q_t	$p_t \times q_t$ = cost
5 lb. bag of apples	$2.99	52	$155.48	$3.69	52	$191.88
1 lb. loaf of bread	$.99	156	$154.44	$1.29	156	$201.24
6 oz. can of tuna fish	$.69	104	$71.76	$.79	104	$82.16
1 gal. of 2% milk	$1.29	78	$100.62	$1.59	78	$124.02
18 oz. jar of peanut butter	$1.99	8	$15.92	$2.59	8	$20.72
16 oz. can of green beans	$.59	156	$92.04	$.79	156	$123.24
Totals	$8.54	Total	$590.26	$10.74	Total	$743.26

FIGURE 13.19 Excel Plot of the Annual Average CPI-U (1980–1996)

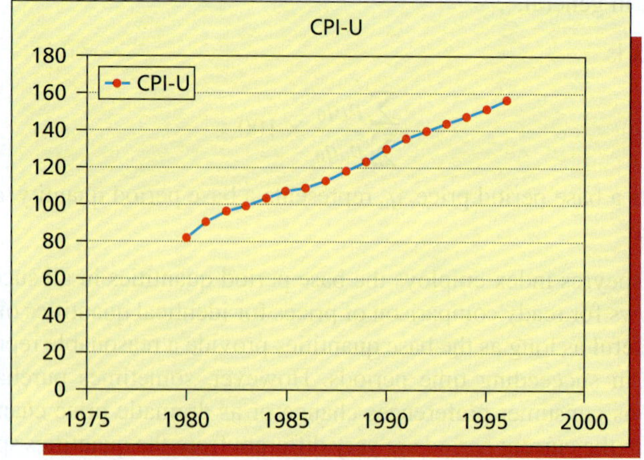

Source: U.S. Bureau of the Census, *Statistical Abstract of the United States*, 1997, p. 487.

nonfarm consumers. Actually, there are two Consumer Price Indexes. The CPI-U, the Consumer Price Index for all Urban Workers, is often reported by the press as an indicator of price changes. Figure 13.19, which gives an Excel plot of the annual average CPI-U from 1980 to 1996, shows the general increasing trend in prices over this period. The CPI-W, the Consumer Price Index for Urban Wage Earners and Clerical Workers, is often used to determine wage increases that are written into labor contracts. The PPI tracks the prices of goods sold by wholesalers. An increase in the PPI is often regarded as an indication that retail prices will soon rise.

Exercises for Section 13.7

CONCEPTS

13.32 Explain the difference between a simple index and an aggregate index.

13.33 Explain the difference between a Laspeyres index and a Paasche index.

METHODS AND APPLICATIONS

13.34 Below we present new retail passenger car sales in the United States for each of the years 1990 to 1996: PassCar

Year	1990	1991	1992	1993	1994	1995	1996
Sales (1,000s)	9,300	8,175	8,213	8,518	8,991	8,635	8,527

Source: American Automobile Manufacturers Association, *Motor Vehicle Facts and Figures* (Detroit, MI: annual), as presented in *Statistical Abstract of the United States*, 1997, p. 770.

a By using the year 1990 as the base year, construct a simple index for the passenger car sales data.

b Interpret the meaning of the index in each of the years 1993 and 1996.

13.35 In the following table we present the average prices of three precious metals—gold, silver, and platinum—for the years 1988 through 1996: Metals

Year	1988	1989	1990	1991	1992	1993	1994	1995	1996
Gold Price ($/Fine Oz.)	438	383	385	363	345	361	385	368	390
Silver Price ($/Fine Oz.)	6.53	5.50	4.82	4.04	3.94	4.30	5.29	5.15	5.30
Platinum Price ($/Troy Oz.)	523	507	467	371	360	374	411	425	410

Source: Through 1994, U.S. Bureau of Mines; thereafter, U.S. Geological Survey, *Minerals Yearbook* and *Mineral Commodities Summaries*, as presented in *Statistical Abstract of the United States*, 1997, p. 701.

a By using the year 1988 as the base year, construct a simple index for each of gold, silver, and platinum.

b Using the three indexes you constructed in part *a*, describe price trends for gold, silver, and platinum from 1988 to 1996.

c By using the year 1988 as the base year, construct an aggregate price index for these precious metals. Using the aggregate price index, describe trends for precious metals prices from 1988 to 1996.

d By using the year 1990 as the base year, construct an aggregate price index for these precious metals.

13.36 In the following table we present prices for three commonly used sources of energy—motor gasoline, natural gas, and electricity—for the years 1990 through 1996: Energy

Year	1990	1991	1992	1993	1994	1995	1996
Motor Gasoline Price ($ per Gal.)	$1.22	$1.20	$1.19	$1.17	$1.17	$1.21	$1.29
Natural Gas Price ($ per mcf)	$1.71	$1.64	$1.74	$2.04	$1.85	$1.55	$2.25
Electricity ($ per Kilowatt-Hr.)	$.066	$.067	$.068	$.069	$.069	$.069	$.069

Source: U.S. Energy Information Administration, *Annual Energy Review,* as presented in *Statistical Abstract of the United States,* 1997, pp. 588, 701.

a Consider a family that consumes 1,850 gallons of gasoline, 150 mcf of natural gas, and 17,000 kilowatt-hours of electricity every year. Construct the Laspeyres index for these energy products using 1990 as the base year. Then describe how energy prices have changed for this family over this period.

b Consider a family having the following energy consumption pattern from 1990 to 1996:

Year	1990	1991	1992	1993	1994	1995	1996
Motor Gasoline (Gallons)	2,200	2,100	2,000	1,950	1,950	1,900	1,750
Natural Gas (mcf)	150	150	150	150	150	150	150
Electricity (Kilowatt-Hr.)	15,000	16,000	17,000	18,000	20,000	21,000	22,500

Construct the Paasche index for these energy products using 1990 as the base year. How does the Paasche index compare to the Laspeyres index you constructed in part *a*?

Chapter Summary

In this chapter we have discussed using **univariate time series** models to forecast future time series values. We began by seeing that it can be useful to think of a time series as consisting of **trend, seasonal, cyclical, and irregular components.** If these components remain *constant* over time, then it is appropriate to describe and forecast the time series by using a **time series regression model.** We discussed using such models to describe **no trend,** a **linear trend,** a **quadratic trend,** and **constant seasonal variation** (by utilizing dummy variables). We also considered various transformations that transform **increasing seasonal variation** into constant seasonal variation, and we saw that we can use the Durbin–Watson test to check for **first-order autocorrelations.** As an alternative to using a transformation and dummy variables to model increasing seasonal variation, we can use the **multiplicative decomposition method.** We discussed this intuitive method and saw how to calculate approximate prediction intervals when using it. We then turned to a consideration of **exponential smoothing,** which is appropriate to use if the components of a time series may be *changing slowly* over time. Specifically, we discussed **simple exponential smoothing, Holt–Winters' double exponential smoothing, and multiplicative Winters' method.** We next considered how to compare forecasting methods by using the **mean absolute deviation (MAD)** and the **mean squared deviation (MSD).** We concluded this chapter by showing how to use **index numbers** to describe time-related data.

Glossary of Terms

cyclical variation: Recurring up-and-down movements of a time series around trend levels that last more than one calendar year (often 2 to 10 years) from peak to peak or trough to trough. (page 633)

deseasonalized time series: A time series that has had the effect of seasonal variation removed. (page 647)

exponential smoothing: A forecasting method that weights recent observations more heavily than remote observations. (page 634)

index number: A number that compares a value of a time series relative to another value of the time series. (pages 661–663)

irregular component: What is "left over" in a time series after trend, cycle, and seasonal variations have been accounted for. (page 633)

moving averages: Averages of successive groups of time series observations. (page 645)

seasonal variation: Periodic patterns in a time series that repeat themselves within a calendar year and are then repeated yearly. (page 633)

smoothing constant: A number that determines how much weight is attached to each observation when using exponential smoothing. (page 652)

time series: A set of observations that has been collected in time order. (page 633)

trend: The long-run upward or downward movement that characterizes a time series over a period of time. (page 633)

univariate time series model: A model that predicts future values of a time series solely on the basis of past values of the time series. (page 633)

Important Formulas and Tests

No trend: page 634
Linear trend: page 635
Quadratic trend: page 636
Modeling constant seasonal variation by using dummy variables: pages 636–637
The multiplicative decomposition model: pages 644–650
Simple exponential smoothing: pages 652–655
Double exponential smoothing: page 655
Winters' method: page 656
Mean absolute deviation (MAD): page 659
Mean squared deviation (MSD): page 659
Simple index: page 661
Aggregate price index: page 662
Laspeyres index: page 663
Paasche index: page 663

Supplementary Exercises

13.37 The State University Credit Union, a savings institution open to the faculty and staff of State University, handles savings accounts and makes loans to members. In order to plan its investment strategies, the credit union requires both point and prediction interval forecasts of monthly loan requests (in thousands of dollars) to be made by the faculty and staff in future months. The credit union has recorded monthly loan requests for its past two years of operation. These loan requests are given in the page margin. If we use MINITAB to fit the model

$$y_t = \beta_0 + \beta_1 t + \beta_2 t^2 + \varepsilon_t$$

to these data, we obtain the following partial MINITAB output.

Loan Requests (in $1000s) Loans

Year 1	Year 2
297	808
249	809
340	867
406	855
464	965
481	921
549	956
553	990
556	1019
642	1021
670	1033
712	1127

```
The regression equation is
Y = 200 + 50.9 Time - 0.568 TimeSQ

Predictor      Coef     SE Coef       T        P
Constant     199.62      20.85      9.58    0.000
Time         50.937      3.842     13.26    0.000
TimeSQ      -0.5677     0.1492     -3.80    0.001

S = 31.2469   R-Sq = 98.7%   R-Sq(adj) = 98.6%

Predicted Values for New Observations
New Obs  Time  TimeSQ      Fit   SE Fit          95% CI                95% PI
   1     25.0    625   1118.21    20.85  (1074.85, 1161.56)  (1040.09, 1196.32)
   2     26.0    676   1140.19    24.44  (1089.37, 1191.01)  (1057.70, 1222.68)
```

a Does the quadratic term t^2 seem important in the model? Justify your answer.

b At the bottom of the MINITAB output are point and prediction interval forecasts of loan requests in months 25 and 26. Find and report these forecasts. Then show how the point forecasts have been calculated.

13.38 Alluring Tackle, Inc., a manufacturer of fishing equipment, makes the Bass Grabber, a type of fishing lure. The company would like to develop a prediction model that can be used to obtain point forecasts and prediction interval forecasts of the sales of the Bass Grabber. The sales (in tens of thousands of lures) of the Bass Grabber in sales period t, where each sales period is defined to last four weeks, are denoted by the symbol y_t and are believed to be partially determined by one or more of the independent variables x_1 = the price in period t of the Bass Grabber as offered by Alluring Tackle (in dollars); x_2 = the average industry price in period t of

TABLE 13.20 Sales of the Bass Grabber (in Tens of Thousands of Lures) BassGrab

Period, t	Sales, y_t	Price, x_1	Average Industry Price, x_2	Advertising Expenditure, x_3
1	4.797	3.85	3.80	5.50
2	6.297	3.75	4.00	6.75
3	8.010	3.70	4.30	7.25
4	7.800	3.70	3.70	5.50
5	9.690	3.60	3.85	7.00
6	10.871	3.60	3.80	6.50
7	12.425	3.60	3.75	6.75
8	10.310	3.80	3.85	5.25
9	8.307	3.80	3.65	5.25
10	8.960	3.85	4.00	6.00
11	7.969	3.90	4.10	6.50
12	6.276	3.90	4.00	6.25
13	4.580	3.70	4.10	7.00
14	5.759	3.75	4.20	6.90
15	6.586	3.75	4.10	6.80
16	8.199	3.80	4.10	6.80
17	9.630	3.70	4.20	7.10
18	9.810	3.80	4.30	7.00
19	11.913	3.70	4.10	6.80
20	12.879	3.80	3.75	6.50
21	12.065	3.80	3.75	6.25
22	10.530	3.75	3.65	6.00
23	9.845	3.70	3.90	6.50
24	9.524	3.55	3.65	7.00
25	7.354	3.60	4.10	6.80
26	4.697	3.65	4.25	6.80
27	6.052	3.70	3.65	6.50
28	6.416	3.75	3.75	5.75
29	8.253	3.80	3.85	5.80
30	10.057	3.70	4.25	6.80

competitors' similar lures (in dollars); and x_3 = the advertising expenditure in period t of Alluring Tackle to promote the Bass Grabber (in tens of thousands of dollars). The data in Table 13.20 have been observed over the past 30 sales periods, and a plot of these data indicates that sales of the Bass Grabber have been increasing in a linear fashion over time and have been seasonal, with sales of the lure being largest in the spring and summer, when most recreational fishing takes place. Alluring Tackle believes that this pattern will continue in the future. Hence, remembering that each year consists of 13, four-week seasons, a possible regression model for predicting y_t would relate y_t to x_1, x_2, x_3, t, and the seasonal dummy variables $S_2, S_3, \ldots, S_{13}$. Here, for example, S_2 equals 1 if sales period t is the second four-week season, and 0 otherwise. As another example, S_{13} equals 1 if sales period t is the 13th four-week season, and 0 otherwise. If we calculate the least squares point estimates of the parameters of the model, we obtain the following prediction equation (the t statistic for the importance of each independent variable is given in parentheses under the independent variable): BassGrab

$$\hat{y}_t = .1776 + .4071x_1 - .7837x_2 + .9934x_3 + .0435t$$
$$(0.05) \quad (0.42) \quad (-1.51) \quad (4.89) \quad (6.49)$$
$$+ .7800S_2 + 2.373S_3 + 3.488S_4 + 3.805S_5$$
$$(3.16) \quad (9.28) \quad (12.88) \quad (13.01)$$
$$+ 5.673S_6 + 6.738S_7 + 6.097S_8 + 4.301S_9$$
$$(19.41) \quad (23.23) \quad (21.47) \quad (14.80)$$
$$+ 3.856S_{10} + 2.621S_{11} + .9969S_{12} - 1.467S_{13}$$
$$(13.89) \quad (9.24) \quad (3.50) \quad (-4.70)$$

a For sales period 31, which is the fifth season of the year, x_1 will be 3.80, x_2 will be 3.90, and x_3 will be 6.80. Using these values, it can be shown that a point prediction and a 95 percent prediction interval for sales of the Bass Grabber are, respectively, 10.578 and [9.683, 11.473]. Using the given prediction equation, verify that the point prediction is 10.578.

b Some t statistics indicate that some of the independent variables might not be important. Using the regression techniques of Chapter 12, try to find a better model for predicting sales of the Bass Grabber.

13.39 The following table gives information concerning finance rates (in percent) for consumer installment loans from 1990 to 1996: InstLoan

	Finance Rates (Percent)						
	1990	1991	1992	1993	1994	1995	1996
Commercial Banks:							
New Automobiles	11.78	11.13	9.28	8.08	8.13	9.57	9.05
Other Consumer Loans	15.46	15.17	14.04	13.46	13.20	13.94	13.53
Credit Card Plans	18.17	18.23	17.77	16.81	15.69	16.02	15.63
Finance Companies:							
New Automobiles	12.54	12.41	9.93	9.47	9.80	11.19	9.89
Used Automobiles	15.99	15.59	13.80	12.78	13.51	14.47	13.54

Source: Board of Governors of the Federal Reserve System, *Federal Reserve Bulletin*, monthly; and *Annual Statistical Digest* as presented in *Statistical Abstract of the United States*, 1997, p. 520.

a Using 1990 as the base year, construct an aggregate index of finance rates charged by commercial banks.

b Using 1993 as the base year, construct an aggregate index of finance rates charged by finance companies for automobile loans.

c Suppose that in 1990 commercial banks extended \$50 billion worth of new automobile loans, \$125 billion worth of other consumer loans, and \$225 billion worth of credit card loans. Construct a Laspeyres index of finance rates charged by commercial banks.

d Suppose that the amounts of credit extended for automobile loans by finance companies from 1990 to 1996 are as follows:

	1990	1991	1992	1993	1994	1995	1996
New Automobiles (\$ Billion)	75	85	97	103	117	121	135
Used Automobiles (\$ Billion)	75	79	81	85	86	90	93

Construct a Paasche index of finance rates charged by finance companies for auto loans.

13.40 Internet Exercise ISOReg

In an article in the March/April 2000 issue of the periodical *Business Standards*, Stewart Anderson discusses the growth of ISO 9000 registrations in North America from 1990 to 1999. ISO 9000 is a series of international standards for quality assurance management systems. Companies meeting the standards are "ISO 9000 registered." Figure 13.20 reproduces a time series plot of registrations from the article.

a Go to the *Business Standards* website (http://www.businessstandards.com), and by clicking on *back issues,* find the March/April 2000 issue. Then find the article "North American Registrations Rising" and verify that ISO 9000 registrations from 1990 to 1999 are as given in Figure 13.20. Use a quadratic trend model $y = \beta_0 + \beta_1 t + \beta_2 t^2 + \varepsilon$ to forecast ISO 9000 registrations for future years. Also try using simple exponential smoothing (with a smoothing constant equal to .10) to forecast future ISO 9000 registrations. How do the forecasts obtained using the two methods compare? Try using a smoothing constant equal to .30. How do the resulting forecasts compare to the others?

b Search the *Business Standards* website for ISO 9000 registrations in North America for years beyond 1999. Which forecasts in part *a* were the most accurate? Use the 1990 to 1999 data plus any new data you find for years beyond 1999 to forecast ISO 9000 registrations in future years by using an appropriate model.

FIGURE 13.20 North American ISO 9000 Registrations

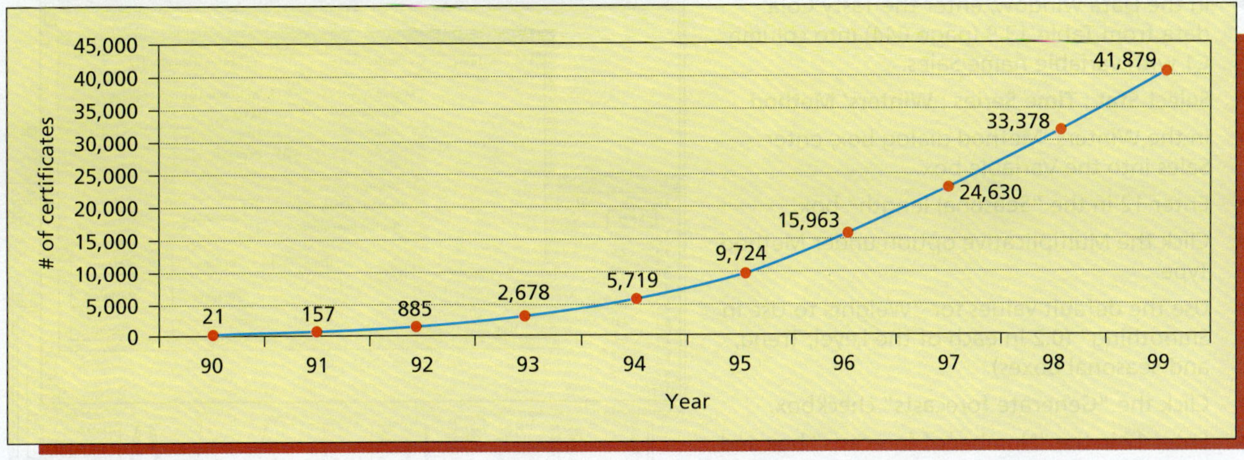

Source: *Business Standards* (www.businessstandards.com), North American Edition, Volume 2, Issue 2, March/April 2000, published by BSI, Inc., page 23.

Appendix 13.1 ■ Time Series Analysis Using MINITAB

The instruction blocks in this section each begin by describing the entry of data into the MINITAB data window. Alternatively, the data may be loaded directly from the data disk included with the text. The appropriate data file name is given at the top of each instruction block. Please refer to Appendix 1.1 for further information about entering data, saving data, and printing results.

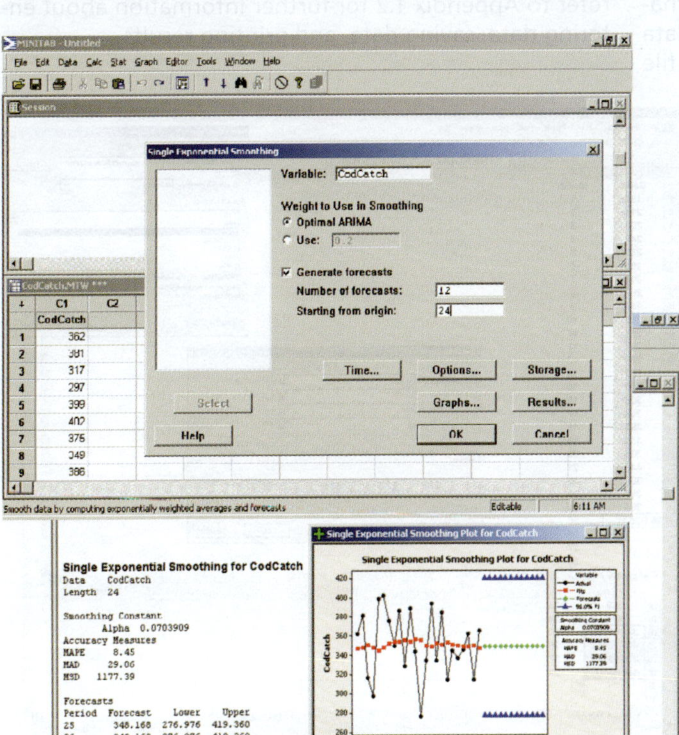

Simple exponential smoothing in Figure 13.13 on page 655 (data file: CodCatch.mtw):

- In the Data window, enter the cod catch data from Table 13.1 (page 634) into column C1 with variable name CodCatch.
- Select **Stat : Time Series : Single Exp Smoothing.**
- In the Single Exponential Smoothing dialog box, enter CodCatch in the Variable box.
- To request that MINITAB select the smoothing constant, select the "Optimal ARIMA" option under "Weight to Use in Smoothing". To choose your own smoothing constant, select the "Use" option and enter the desired smoothing constant in the box.
- Place a checkmark in the "Generate forecasts" checkbox.
- Enter 12 in the "Number of forecasts" box and enter 24 in the "Starting from origin" box.
- Click OK in the Single Exponential Smoothing dialog box to see the forecast results in the Session window and a graphical summary in a high-resolution graphics window.

Double exponential smoothing can be performed by choosing **Double Exp Smoothing** from the Time Series menu and by following the remainder of the preceding steps.

Multiplicative Winters' method in Figure 13.15 on page 657 (data file: TastyCola.mtw):

- In the Data window, enter the Tasty Cola data from Table 13.9 (page 644) into column C1 with variable name Sales.
- Select **Stat : Time Series : Winters' Method**
- In the Winters' Method dialog box, enter Sales into the Variable box.
- Enter 12 in the "Seasonal length" box.
- Click the Multiplicative option under Method Type.
- Use the default values for "Weights to Use in Smoothing" (0.2 in each of the Level, Trend, and Seasonal boxes).
- Click the "Generate forecasts" checkbox.
- Enter 12 in the "Number of forecasts" box and enter 36 in the "Starting from origin" box.
- Click OK in the Winters' Method dialog box to obtain the forecast results in the Session window and a graphical summary in a high-resolution graphics window.

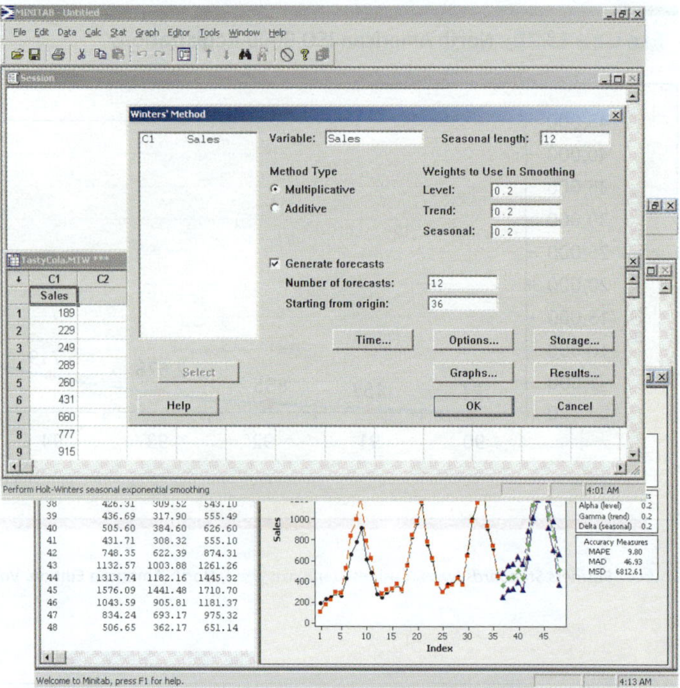

Appendix 13.2 ■ Time Series Analysis Using Excel

The instruction block in this section begins by describing the entry of data into an Excel spreadsheet. Alternatively, the data may be loaded directly from the data disk included with the text. The appropriate data file name is given at the top of the instruction block. Please refer to Appendix 1.2 for further information about entering data, saving data, and printing results.

Point forecasts from a linear trend line for the calculator sales data in Table 13.2 on page 635 (data file: CalcSale.xls):

- Enter the calculator sales data from Table 13.2 with the label Sales in cell A1 and the values of sales in cells A2 through A25.
- Enter the label Month in cell B1 and the values 1 to 28 in cells B2 through B29.
- Click on cell A26.
- Click the Insert Function button f_x on the Excel toolbar.
- In the Insert Function dialog box, select Statistical from the "Or select a category:" menu and select TREND from the "Select a function:" menu. Then click OK in the Insert Function dialog box.
- In the "TREND Function Arguments" dialog box, enter A2.A25 into the "Known_ y's" box.
- Enter B2.B25 into the "Known_ x's" box.
- Enter B26 into the "New_x's" box.
- Enter the value 1 into the Const box.
- Click OK in the "TREND Function Arguments" dialog box to produce the point forecast for time period 25.
- Double-click on the drag handle in cell A26 to extend the forecasts through time period 28.

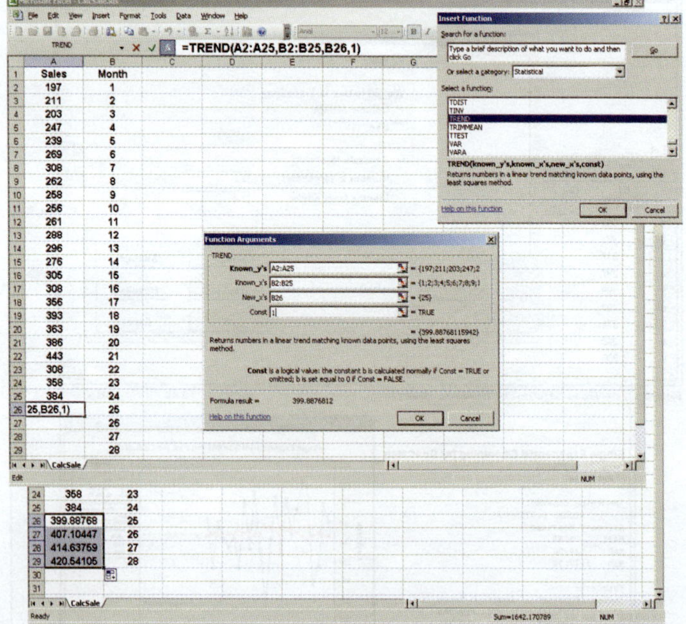

Appendix 13.3 ■ Time Series Analysis Using MegaStat

The instructions in this section begin by describing the entry of data into an Excel worksheet. Alternatively, the data may be loaded directly from the data disk included with the text. The appropriate data file name is given at the top of each instruction block. Please refer to Appendix 1.2 for further information about entering data and saving and printing results in Excel. Please refer to Appendix 1.3 for more information about using MegaStat.

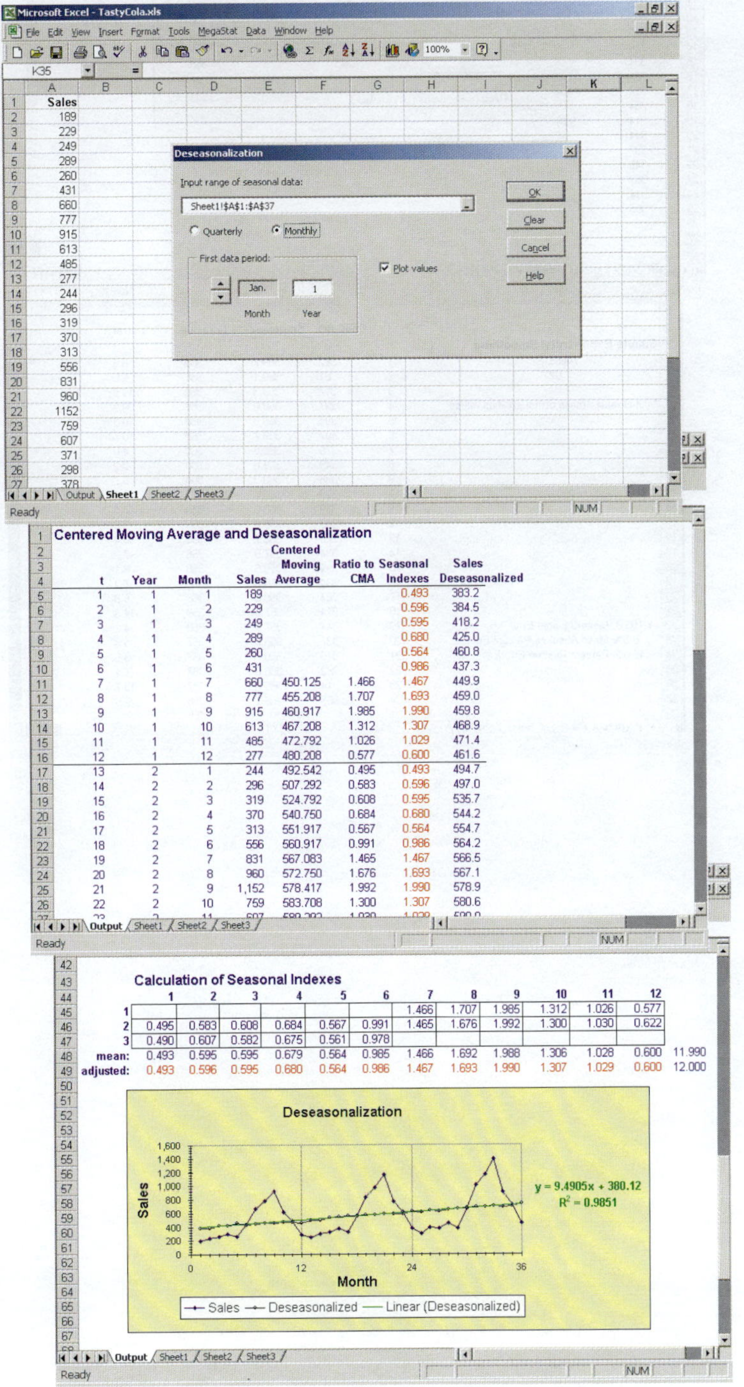

Centered Moving Average and Deseasonalization

t	Year	Month	Sales	Centered Moving Average	Ratio to CMA	Seasonal Indexes	Sales Deseasonalized
1	1	1	189			0.493	383.2
2	1	2	229			0.596	384.5
3	1	3	249			0.595	418.2
4	1	4	289			0.680	425.0
5	1	5	260			0.564	460.8
6	1	6	431			0.986	437.3
7	1	7	660	450.125	1.466	1.467	449.9
8	1	8	777	455.208	1.707	1.693	459.0
9	1	9	915	460.917	1.985	1.990	459.8
10	1	10	613	467.208	1.312	1.307	468.9
11	1	11	485	472.792	1.026	1.029	471.4
12	1	12	277	480.208	0.577	0.600	461.6
13	2	1	244	492.542	0.495	0.493	494.7
14	2	2	296	507.292	0.583	0.596	497.0
15	2	3	319	524.792	0.608	0.595	535.7
16	2	4	370	540.750	0.684	0.680	544.2
17	2	5	313	551.917	0.567	0.564	554.7
18	2	6	556	560.917	0.991	0.986	564.2
19	2	7	831	567.083	1.465	1.467	566.5
20	2	8	960	572.750	1.676	1.693	567.1
21	2	9	1,152	578.417	1.992	1.990	578.9
22	2	10	759	583.708	1.300	1.307	580.6

Calculation of Seasonal Indexes

	1	2	3	4	5	6	7	8	9	10	11	12	
1							1.466	1.707	1.985	1.312	1.026	0.577	
2	0.495	0.583	0.608	0.684	0.567	0.991	1.465	1.676	1.992	1.300	1.030	0.622	
3	0.490	0.607	0.582	0.675	0.561	0.978							
mean:	0.493	0.595	0.595	0.679	0.564	0.985	1.466	1.692	1.988	1.306	1.028	0.600	11.990
adjusted:	0.493	0.596	0.595	0.680	0.564	0.986	1.467	1.693	1.990	1.307	1.029	0.600	12.000

Calculation of seasonal factors and deseasonalization similar to Table 13.10, Table 13.11, and Figure 13.11 on pages 645 and 647 (data file: TastyCola.xls):

- Enter the Tasty Cola data in Table 13.9 (page 644) into column A (with label Sales). Only the sales values in Table 13.9 need to be entered—the year, month, and time period need not be entered.
- Select **MegaStat : Time Series / Forecasting : Deseasonalization.**
- In the Deseasonalization dialog box, enter the range A1.A37 into the "Input Range of Seasonal Data" box. This range can be entered by dragging with the mouse—the AutoExpand feature cannot be used in this dialog box.
- Select the type of seasonal data—quarterly or monthly—by clicking. Here we have selected "Monthly" because the Tasty Cola data consist of monthly sales values.
- In the "First data period" box, specify the month (in this case January) in which the first time series value was observed by using the up or down arrow buttons.
- In the "First data period" box, enter the year in which the first time series value was observed (here equal to 1) into the Year box.
- Check the "Plot values" check box to obtain plots of the seasonal observations, the deseasonalized data, and a trend line fit to the deseasonalized data.
- Click OK in the Deseasonalization dialog box.
- The seasonal factors are displayed in the "Seasonal Indexes" column of the "Centered Moving Average and Deseasonalization" table in the Output worksheet. They are also given in the "adjusted" row at the bottom of the "Calculation of Seasonal Indexes" table in the Output worksheet.

Simple exponential smoothing similar to Table 13.13 on page 653 (data file: CodCatch.xls):

- Enter the cod catch data in Table 13.1 (page 634) into column A (with label CodCatch).
- Select **MegaStat : Time Series / Forecasting : Exponential Smoothing : Simple Exponential Smoothing.**
- In the Simple Exponential Smoothing dialog box, enter the range A1.A25 into the "Input range for data" box. Enter this range by dragging with the mouse—the AutoExpand feature cannot be used in this dialog box.
- Type the value of the smoothing constant (here equal to .02) into the Alpha box.
- Leave the "Initial value" box blank if you wish to use an initial value equal to the average of the first six time series observations. If another initial value is desired, type it into the "Initial value" box.
- Click OK in the Simple Exponential Smoothing dialog box.
- The forecast for a future value of the time series is found at the bottom of the "Forecast" column in the Output worksheet.

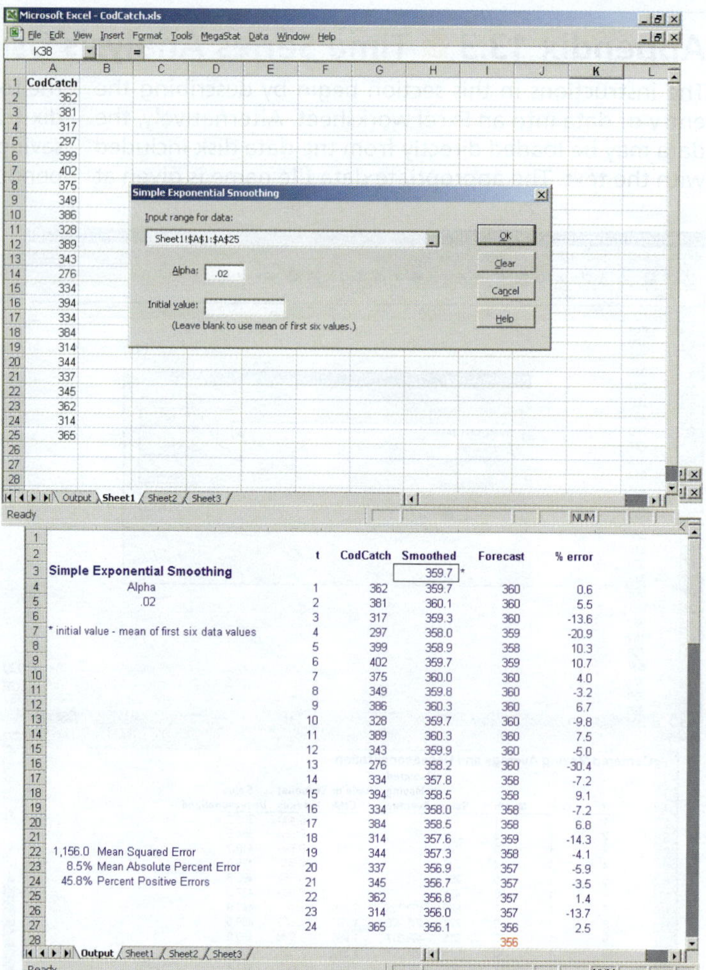

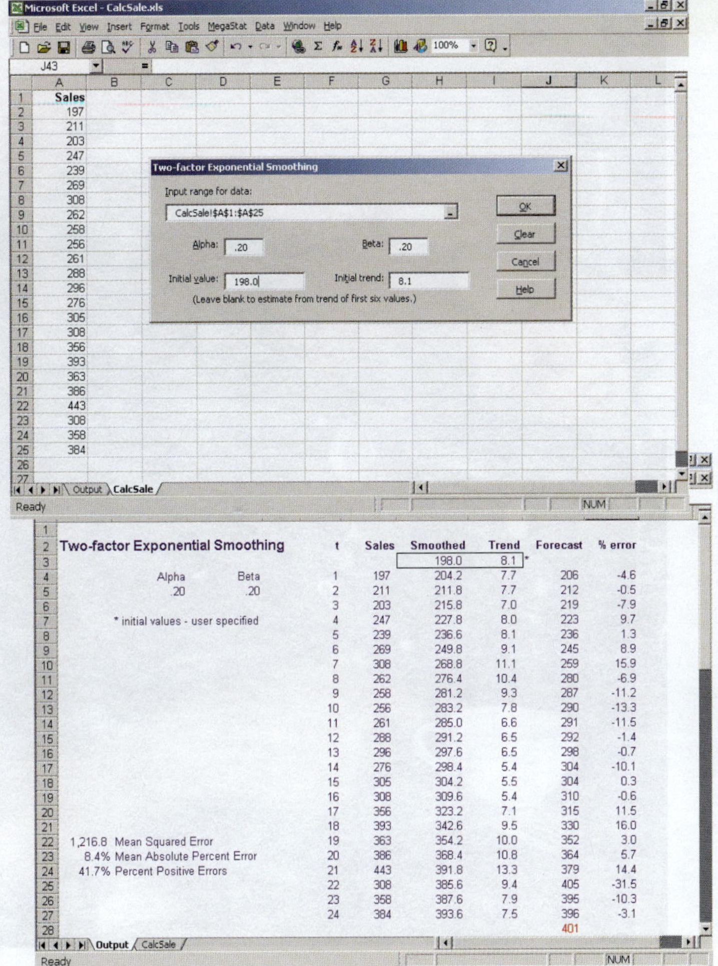

Two-factor Exponential Smoothing

		t	Sales	Smoothed	Trend	Forecast	% error
				198.0	8.1*		
Alpha	Beta	1	197	204.2	7.7	206	-4.6
.20	.20	2	211	211.8	7.7	212	-0.5
		3	203	215.8	7.0	219	-7.9
* initial values - user specified		4	247	227.8	8.0	223	9.7
		5	239	236.6	8.1	236	1.3
		6	269	249.8	9.1	245	8.9
		7	308	268.8	11.1	259	15.9
		8	262	276.4	10.4	280	-6.9
		9	258	281.2	9.3	287	-11.2
		10	256	283.2	7.8	290	-13.3
		11	261	285.0	6.6	291	-11.5
		12	288	291.2	6.5	292	-1.4
		13	296	297.6	6.5	298	-0.7
		14	276	298.4	5.4	304	-10.1
		15	305	304.2	5.5	304	0.3
		16	308	309.6	5.4	310	-0.6
		17	356	323.2	7.1	315	11.5
		18	393	342.6	9.5	330	16.0
1,216.8	Mean Squared Error	19	363	354.2	10.0	352	3.0
8.4%	Mean Absolute Percent Error	20	386	368.4	10.8	364	5.7
41.7%	Percent Positive Errors	21	443	391.8	13.3	379	14.4
		22	308	385.6	9.4	405	-31.5
		23	358	387.6	7.9	395	-10.3
		24	384	393.6	7.5	396	-3.1
						401	

Double exponential smoothing similar to Figure 13.14 on page 656 (data file: CalcSale.xls):

- Enter the calculator sales data in Table 13.2 on page 635 into column A (with label Sales).
- Select **MegaStat : Time Series / Forecasting : Exponential Smoothing : Two-factor Exponential Smoothing.**
- In the Two-Factor Exponential Smoothing dialog box, enter the range A1.A25 into the "Input range for data" box. Enter this range by dragging with the mouse—the AutoExpand feature cannot be used in this dialog box.
- Type the desired values of the smoothing constants (here both are set equal to .20) into the Alpha and Beta boxes.
- Leave the "Initial value" and "Initial trend" boxes blank if you wish to use initial values that are estimated by the computer using the first six time series observations. If you wish to supply initial values, type an initial value of the intercept into the "Initial value" box and type an initial value of the slope into the "Initial trend" box. Here we have supplied the values 198.0 and 8.1.
- Click OK in the Two-Factor Exponential Smoothing dialog box.
- The forecast for the next time series value is found at the bottom of the Forecast column in the Output worksheet.

CHAPTER 14

Process Improvement Using Control Charts

Chapter Outline

This chapter explains how to use **control charts** to improve business processes. Basically, a control chart is a graphical device that helps us determine when a process is "out of control." The information provided by a control chart helps us discover the causes of unusual process variations. When such causes have been identified, we attempt to remove them in order to reduce the amount of process variation. By doing so, we improve the process.

We begin this chapter by tracing the history of the U.S. quality movement. Then we study control charts for monitoring the level and variability of a process and for monitoring the fraction of nonconforming (or defective) units produced. We also discuss how to evaluate the process capability. That is, we show how to assess a process's ability to produce individual items that meet customer requirements (specifications). In particular, we explain the concept of six sigma capability, which was introduced by Motorola Inc. In an optional section we discuss cause-and-effect diagrams.

In order to demonstrate the ideas of this chapter, we employ three case studies:

C

The Hole Location Case: A manufacturer of automobile air conditioner compressors uses control charts to reduce variation in the locations of a hose connection hole that is punched in the outer housing (or shell) of the compressor.

The Hot Chocolate Temperature Case: The food service staff at a university dining hall wishes to avoid possible litigation by making sure that it does not serve excessively hot beverages. The staff uses control charts to find and eliminate causes of unusual variations in hot chocolate temperatures.

The Camshaft Case: An automobile manufacturer wishes to improve the process it uses to harden a part in a camshaft assembly. The manufacturer uses control charts and process capability studies to reduce the sources of process variation that are responsible for a 12 percent rework rate and a 9 percent scrap rate. After the process variation is reduced, virtually all of the hardened parts meet specifications (note: this case is included in the supplementary exercises).

14.1 Quality: Its Meaning and a Historical Perspective

What is quality? It is not easy to define quality, and a number of different definitions have been proposed. One definition that makes sense is **fitness for use.** Here the user of a product or service can be an individual, a manufacturer, a retailer, or the like. For instance, an individual who purchases a television set or a videocassette recorder expects the unit to be defect free and to provide years of reliable, high-performance service. If the TV or VCR performs as desired, it is fit for use. Another definition of quality that makes sense says that **quality is the extent to which customers feel that a product or service exceeds their needs and expectations.** For instance, if the VCR purchaser believes the unit exceeds all the needs and expectations he or she had for the VCR when it was purchased, then the customer is satisfied with the unit's quality.

Three types of quality can be considered: **quality of design, quality of conformance,** and **quality of performance. Quality of design** has to do with intentional differences between goods and services with the same basic purpose. For instance, all VCRs are built to perform the same function—record and play back videocassette tapes. However, VCRs differ with respect to various design characteristics—picture sharpness, monophonic or stereo audio, digital effects, ease of use, and so forth. A given level of design quality may satisfy some consumers and may not satisfy others. The product design will specify a set of **tolerances (specifications)** that must be met. For example, the design of a VCR sets forth many specifications regarding electronic and physical characteristics that must be met if the unit is to operate acceptably. **Quality of conformance** is the ability of a process to meet the specifications set forth by the design. **Quality of performance** is how well the product or service actually performs in the marketplace. Companies must find out how well customers' needs are met and how reliable products are by conducting after-sales research.

The marketing research arm of a company must determine what the customer seeks in each of these dimensions. Consumer research is used to develop a product or service concept—a combination of design characteristics that exceeds the expectations of a large number of consumers. This concept is translated into a design. The design includes specifications that, if met, will satisfy consumer wants and needs. A production process is then developed to meet the design specifications. In order to do this, variables that can control the process must be identified, and the relationships between input variables and final quality characteristics must be understood. The manufacturer expresses quality characteristics as measurable variables that can be tracked and used to monitor and improve the performance of the process. Service call analysis often leads to product or service redesigns in order to improve the product or service concept. It is extremely important that the initial design be a good one so that excessive redesigns and customer dissatisfaction may be avoided.

History of the quality movement In the 1700s and 1800s, master craftsmen and their apprentices were responsible for designing and building products. Quantities of goods produced were small, and product quality was controlled by expert workmanship. Master craftsmen had a great deal of pride in their work, and quality was not a problem. However, the introduction of mass production in the late 1800s and early 1900s changed things. Production processes became very complex, with many workers (rather than one skilled craftsman) responsible for the final product. Inevitably, product quality characteristics displayed variation. In particular, Henry Ford developed the moving assembly line at Ford Motor Company. As assembly line manufacturing spread, quality became a problem. Production managers were rewarded for meeting production quotas, and quality suffered. To make mass-produced products more consistent, inspectors were hired to check product quality. However, 100 percent inspection proved to be costly, and people started to look for alternatives.

Much of the early work in quality control was done at Bell Telephone (now known as American Telephone and Telegraph or AT&T). The Bell System and Western Electric, the manufacturing arm of Bell Telephone, formed the Inspection Engineering Department to deal with quality problems. In 1924 Walter Shewhart of Bell Telephone Laboratories introduced the concept of statistical quality control—controlling quality of mass-produced goods. Shewhart believed that variation always exists in manufactured products, and that the variation can be studied, monitored, and controlled using statistics. In particular, Shewhart developed a statistical tool called the **control chart.** Such a chart is a graph that can tell a company when a process needs to be adjusted and when the process should be left alone. In the late 1920s Harold F. Dodge and Harold G. Romig, also of Bell Telephone Laboratories, introduced **statistical acceptance sampling,** a statistical sampling technique that enables a company to accept or reject a quantity of goods (called a **lot**) without inspecting the entire lot. By the mid-1930s, Western Electric was heavily using **statistical quality control (SQC)** to improve quality, increase productivity, and reduce inspection costs. However, these statistical methods were not widely adopted outside Bell Telephone.

During World War II statistical quality control became widespread. Faced with the task of producing large quantities of high-quality war matériel, industry turned to statistical methods, failure analysis, vendor certification, and early product design. The U.S. War Department required that suppliers of war matériel employ acceptance sampling, and its use became commonplace. Statistical control charts were also used, although not as widely as acceptance sampling.

In 1946 the **American Society for Quality Control (ASQC)** was established to encourage the use of quality improvement methods. The organization sponsors training programs, seminars, and publications dealing with quality issues. In spite of the efforts of the ASQC, however, interest in quality in American industry diminished after the war. American business had little competition in the world market—Europe and Japan were rebuilding their shattered economies. Tremendous emphasis was placed on increased production because firms were often unable to meet the demand for their products. Profits were high, and the concern for quality became unimportant. As a result, postwar American managers did not understand the importance of quality and process improvement, and they were not informed about quality improvement techniques.

However, events in Japan took a different turn. After the war, Japanese industrial capacity was crippled. Productivity was very low, and products were of notoriously bad quality. In those days, products stamped "Made in Japan" were generally considered to be "cheap junk." The man credited with turning this situation around is W. Edwards Deming. Deming, born in 1900, earned a Ph.D. in mathematical physics from Yale University in 1927. He then went to work in a Department of Agriculture–affiliated laboratory. Deming, who had learned statistics while studying physics, applied statistics to experiments conducted at the laboratory. Through this work, Deming was introduced to Walter Shewhart, who explained his theories about using statistical control charts to improve quality and productivity. During World War II, Deming was largely responsible for teaching 35,000 American engineers and technical people how to use statistics to improve the quality of war matériel. After the war, the Allied command sent a group of these engineers to Japan. Their mission was to improve the Japanese communication system. In doing so, the engineers employed the statistical methods they had learned, and Deming's work was brought to the attention of the **Union of Japanese Scientists and Engineers (JUSE).** Deming, who had started his own consulting firm in 1946, was asked by the JUSE to help increase Japanese productivity. In July 1950 Deming traveled to Japan and gave a series of lectures titled "Elementary Principles of the Statistical Control of Quality" to a group of 230 Japanese managers. Deming taught the Japanese how to use statistics to determine how well a system can perform, and taught them how to design process improvements to make the system operate better and more efficiently. He also taught the Japanese that the more quality a producer builds into a product, the less it costs. Realizing the serious nature of their economic crisis, the Japanese adopted Deming's ideas as a philosophy of doing business. Through Deming, the Japanese found that by listening to the wants and needs of consumers and by using statistical methods for process improvement in production, they could export high-quality products to the world market.

Although American business was making only feeble attempts to improve product quality in the 1950s and 1960s, it was able to maintain a dominant competitive position. Many U.S. companies focused more on marketing and financial strategies than on product and production. But the Japanese and other foreign competitors were making inroads. By the 1970s, the quality of many Japanese and European products (for instance, automobiles, television sets, and electronic equipment) became far superior to their American-made counterparts. Also, rising prices made consumers more quality conscious—people expected high quality if they were going to pay high prices. As a result, the market shares of U.S. firms rapidly decreased. Many U.S. firms were severely injured or went out of business.

Meanwhile, Deming continued teaching and preaching quality improvement. While Deming was famous in Japan, he was relatively unknown in the United States until 1980. In June 1980 Deming was featured in an NBC television documentary titled "If Japan Can, Why Can't We?" This program, written and narrated by then–NBC correspondent Lloyd Dobyns, compared Japanese and American industrial productivity and credited Deming for Japan's success. Within days, demand for Deming's consulting services skyrocketed. Deming has since consulted with many major U.S. firms. Among these firms are The Ford Motor Company, General Motors Corporation, and The Procter & Gamble Company. Ford, for instance, began consulting with Deming in 1981. Donald Petersen, who was Ford's chairman and chief executive officer at the time, became a Deming disciple. By following the Deming philosophy, Ford, which was losing 2 billion dollars yearly in 1980, attempted to create a quality culture. Quality of Ford products was greatly improved, and the company again became profitable. The 1980s saw many U.S. companies adopt a philosophy of continuous improvement of quality and productivity in all areas of their businesses—manufacturing, accounting, sales, finance, personnel, marketing, customer service, maintenance, and so forth. This overall approach of applying quality principles to all company activities is called **total quality management (TQM)** or **total quality control (TQC).** It is becoming an important management strategy in American business. Dr. Deming taught seminars on quality improvement for managers and statisticians until his death on December 20, 1993. Deming's work resulted in widespread changes in both the structure of the world economy and the ways in which American businesses are managed.

The fundamental ideas behind Deming's approach to quality and productivity improvement are contained in his **"14 points."** These are a set of managerial principles that, if followed, Deming believed would enable a company to improve quality and productivity, reduce costs, and compete effectively in the world market. We briefly summarize the 14 points in Table 14.1. For more complete discussions of these points, see Bowerman and O'Connell (1996), Deming (1986), Walton (1986), Scherkenbach (1987), or Gitlow, Gitlow, Oppenheim, and Oppenheim (1989). Deming stressed that implementation of the 14 points requires both changes in management philosophy and the use of statistical methods. In addition, Deming believed that it is necessary to follow all of the points, not just some of them.

In 1988 the first **Malcolm Baldrige National Quality Awards** were presented. These awards, presented by the U.S. Commerce Department, are named for the late Malcolm Baldrige, who was Commerce Secretary during the Reagan administration. The awards were established to promote

Table 14.1 W. Edwards Deming's 14 Points

1 **Create constancy of purpose toward improvement of product and service with a plan to become competitive, stay in business, and provide jobs.**
Devise a plan for the long-term success of the company based on quality improvement.

2 **Adopt a new philosophy.**
Do not tolerate commonly accepted mistakes, delays, defective materials, and defective workmanship.

3 **Cease dependence on mass inspection.**
Quality cannot be inspected into a product. It must be built into the product through process improvement.

4 **End the practice of awarding business on the basis of price tag.**
Do not buy from the lowest bidder without taking the quality of goods purchased into account. Purchasing should be based on lowest total cost (including the cost of bad quality).

5 **Improve constantly and forever the system of production and service to improve quality and productivity, and thus constantly decrease costs.**
Constantly seek to improve every aspect of the business.

6 **Institute training.**
Workers should know how to do their jobs and should know how their jobs affect quality and the success of the company.

7 **Institute leadership.**
The job of management is leadership, not mere supervision. Leadership involves understanding the work that needs to be done and fostering process improvement.

8 **Drive out fear, so that everyone may work more effectively for the company.**
Workers should not be afraid to express ideas, to ask questions, or to take appropriate action.

9 **Break down organizational barriers.**
Barriers that damage the company performance (such as competition between staff areas, poor communication, disputes between labor and management, and so on) must be removed so that everyone can work for the good of the company.

10 **Eliminate slogans, exhortations, and arbitrary numerical goals and targets for the workforce that urge the workers to achieve new levels of productivity and quality without providing methods.**
Slogans and numerical goals (such as production quotas) are counterproductive unless management provides methods for achieving them.

11 **Eliminate work standards and numerical quotas.**
Work standards and numerical quotas that specify the quantity of goods to be produced while quality is ignored are counterproductive and should be eliminated.

12 **Remove barriers that rob employees of their pride of workmanship.**
While workers want to do a good job and have pride in their work, bad management practices often rob workers of their pride. Barriers that rob workers of pride (such as inadequate instructions, cheap materials, poor maintenance, and so on) must be removed.

13 **Institute a vigorous program of education and self-improvement.**
Education and training are necessary for everyone if continuous improvement is to be achieved.

14 **Take action to accomplish the transformation.**
A management structure that is committed to continuous improvement must be put in place.

Source: W. Edwards Deming, "Deming's 14 Points, condensed version" from *Out of Crisis.*

quality awareness, to recognize quality achievements by U.S. companies, and to publicize successful quality strategies. The Malcolm Baldrige National Quality Award Consortium, formed by the ASQC (now known as the ASQ) and the American Productivity and Quality Center, administers the award. The Baldrige award has become one of the most prestigious honors in American business. Annual awards are given in three categories—manufacturing, service, and small business. Winners include companies such as Motorola Inc., Xerox Corporation Business Products and Systems, the Commercial Nuclear Fuel Division of Westinghouse Electric Corporation, Milliken and Company, Cadillac Division, General Motors Corporation, Ritz Carlton Hotels, and AT&T Consumer Communications.

Finally, the 1990s saw the adoption of an international quality standards system called **ISO 9000.** More than 90 countries around the globe have adopted the ISO 9000 standards for their companies, as have many multinational corporations (including AT&T, 3M, IBM, Motorola, and DuPont). As a brief introduction to ISO 9000, we quote "Is ISO 9000 for You?" published by CEEM Information Systems:

> **What Is ISO 9000?**
>
> ISO 9000 is a series of international standards for quality assurance management systems. It establishes the organizational structure and processes for assuring that the production of goods or services meets a consistent and agreed-upon level of quality for a company's customers.
>
> The ISO 9000 series is unique in that it applies to a very wide range of organizations and industries encompassing both the manufacturing and service sectors.

Why Is ISO 9000 Important?
ISO 9000 is important for two reasons. First . . . the discipline imposed by the standard for processes influencing your quality management systems can enhance your company's quality consistency. Whether or not you decide to register your company to ISO 9000 standards, your implementing such discipline can achieve greater efficiency in your quality control systems.

Second . . . more and more companies, both here at home and internationally, are requiring their suppliers to be ISO 9000 registered. To achieve your full market potential in such industries, registration is becoming essential. Those companies who become registered have a distinct competitive advantage, and sales growth in today's demanding market climate requires every advantage you can muster.[1]

Clearly, quality has finally become a crucially important issue in American business. The quality revolution now affects every area in business. But the Japanese continue to mount new challenges. For years, the Japanese have used **designed statistical experiments** to develop new processes, find and remedy process problems, improve product performance, and improve process efficiency. Much of this work is based on the insights of Genichi Taguchi, a Japanese engineer. His methods of experimental design, the so-called **Taguchi methods,** have been heavily used in Japan since the 1960s. Although Taguchi's methodology is controversial in statistical circles, the use of experimental design gives the Japanese a considerable advantage over U.S. competitors because it enables them to design a high level of quality into a product before production begins. Some U.S. manufacturers have begun to use experimental design techniques to design quality into their products. It will be necessary for many more U.S. companies to do so in order to remain competitive in the future—a challenge for the 21st century.

14.2 Statistical Process Control and Causes of Process Variation

Statistical process control In Chapter 1 we learned that **statistical process control (SPC)** is a systematic method for analyzing process data (quality characteristics) in which we monitor and study the **process variation.** The goal is to stabilize the process and to reduce the amount of process variation. The ultimate goal is **continuous process improvement.** We often use SPC to monitor and improve manufacturing processes. However, SPC is also commonly used to improve service quality. For instance, we might use SPC to reduce the time it takes to process a loan application, or to improve the accuracy of an order entry system.

Before the widespread use of SPC, quality control was based on an **inspection** approach. Here the product is first made, and then the final product is inspected to eliminate defective items. This is called **action on the output** of the process. The emphasis here is on detecting defective product that has already been produced. This is costly and wasteful because, if defective product is produced, the bad items must be (1) **scrapped,** (2) **reworked or reprocessed** (that is, fixed), or (3) **downgraded** (sold off at a lower price). In fact, the cost of bad quality (scrap, rework, and so on) can be tremendously high. It is not unusual for this cost to be as high as 10 to 30 percent or more of a company's dollar sales.

In contrast to the inspection approach, SPC emphasizes integrating quality improvement into the process. Here the goal is **preventing bad quality by taking appropriate action on the process.** In order to accomplish this goal, we must decide when actions on the process are needed. The focus of much of this chapter is to show how such decisions can be made.

Causes of process variation In order to understand SPC methodology, we must realize that the variations we observe in quality characteristics are caused by different sources. These sources include factors such as equipment (machines or the like), materials, people, methods and procedures, the environment, and so forth. Here we must distinguish between **usual process variation** and **unusual process variation.** Usual process variation results from what we call **common causes of process variation.**

Common causes are sources of variation that have the potential to influence all process observations. That is, these sources of variation are inherent to the current process design.

[1]Source: CEEM Information Services, "Is ISO 9000 for You?" 1993.

Common cause variation can be substantial. For instance, obsolete or poorly maintained equipment, a poorly designed process, and inadequate instructions for workers are examples of common causes that might significantly influence all process output. As an example, suppose that we are filling 16-ounce jars with grape jelly. A 25-year-old, obsolete filler machine might be a common cause of process variation that influences all the jar fills. While (in theory) it might be possible to replace the filler machine with a new model, we might have chosen not to do so, and the obsolete filler causes all the jar fills to exhibit substantial variation.

Common causes also include small influences that would cause slight variation even if all conditions are held as constant as humanly possible. For example, in the jar fill situation, small variations in the speed at which jars move under the filler valves, slight floor vibrations, and small differences between filler valve settings would always influence the jar fills even when conditions are held as constant as possible. Sometimes these small variations are described as being due to "chance."

Together, the important and unimportant common causes of variation determine the **usual process variability.** That is, these causes determine the amount of variation that exists when the process is operating routinely. We can reduce the amount of common cause variation by removing some of the important common causes. **Reducing common cause variation is usually a management responsibility.** For instance, replacing obsolete equipment, redesigning a plant or process, or improving plant maintenance would require management action.

In addition to common cause variation, processes are affected by a different kind of variation called **assignable cause variation** (sometimes also called **special cause** or **specific cause variation).**

Assignable causes are sources of **unusual process variation.** These are intermittent or permanent changes in the process that are not common to all process observations and that may cause important process variation. Assignable causes are usually of short duration, but they can be persistent or recurring conditions.

For example, in the jar filling situation, one of the filler valves may become clogged so that some jars are being substantially underfilled (or perhaps are not filled at all). Or a relief operator might incorrectly set the filler so that all jars are being substantially overfilled for a short period of time. As another example, suppose that a bank wishes to study the length of time customers must wait before being served by a teller. If a customer fills out a banking form incorrectly, this might cause a temporary delay that increases the waiting time for other customers. Notice that **assignable causes** such as these can often be remedied by local supervision—for instance, by a production line foreman, a machine operator, a head bank teller, or the like. **One objective of SPC is to detect and eliminate assignable causes of process variation.** By doing this, we reduce the amount of process variation. This results in improved quality.

It is important to point out that an assignable cause could be beneficial—that is, it could be an unusual process variation resulting in unusually good process performance. In such a situation, we wish to discover the root cause of the variation, and then we wish to incorporate this condition into the process if possible. For instance, suppose we find that a process performs unusually well when a raw material purchased from a particular supplier is used. It might be desirable to purchase as much of the raw material as possible from this supplier.

When a process exhibits only common cause variation, it will operate in a stable fashion. That is, in the absence of any unusual process variations, the process will display a constant amount of variation around a constant mean. On the other hand, if assignable causes are affecting the process, then the process will not be stable—unusual variations will cause the process mean or variability to change over time. It follows that

1 When a process is influenced only by **common cause variation, the process will be in statistical control.**

2 When a process is influenced by **one or more assignable causes, the process will not be in statistical control.**

In general, in order to bring a process into statistical control, we must find and eliminate undesirable assignable causes of process variation, and we should (if feasible) build desirable assignable causes into the process. When we have done these things, the process is what we call a **stable, common cause system.** This means that the process operates in a **consistent** fashion and is **predictable.** Since there are no unusual process variations, the process (as currently configured) is doing all it can be expected to do.

When a process is in statistical control, management can estimate the **process capability.** That is, it is possible to determine whether the process performs well enough to produce output that meets **customer requirements.** If it does not, action by local supervision will not remedy the situation—remember, the assignable causes (the sources of process variation that can be dealt with by local supervision) have already been removed. Rather, some fundamental change will be needed in order to reduce common cause variation. For instance, perhaps a new, more modern filler machine must be purchased and installed. This will require action by management.

Finally, the SPC approach is really a philosophy of doing business. It is an entire firm or organization that is focused on a single goal: continuous quality and productivity improvement. The impetus for this philosophy must come from management. Unless management is supportive and directly involved in the ongoing quality improvement process, the SPC approach will not be successful.

Exercises for Sections 14.1 and 14.2

CONCEPTS

14.1 Write an essay comparing the management philosophy that Dr. Deming advocated in his 14 points to the management styles you have been exposed to in your personal work experiences. Do you think Dr. Deming's philosophy is preferable to the management styles you have seen in practice? Which of the 14 points do you agree with? Which do you disagree with?

14.2 Write a paragraph explaining how common causes of process variation differ from assignable causes of process variation.

METHODS AND APPLICATIONS

14.3 In this exercise we consider several familiar processes. In each case, describe several common causes and several assignable causes that might result in variation in the given quality characteristic.

a Process: getting ready for school or work in the morning.
Quality characteristic: the time it takes to get ready.

b Process: driving, walking, or otherwise commuting from your home or apartment to school or work.
Quality characteristic: the time it takes to commute.

c Process: studying for and taking a statistics exam.
Quality characteristic: the score received on the exam.

d Process: starting your car in the morning.
Quality characteristic: the time it takes to start your car.

14.4 Form a group of three or four students in your class. As a group project, select a familiar process and determine a variable that measures the quality of some aspect of the output of this process. Then list some common causes and assignable causes that might result in variation of the variable you have selected for the process. Discuss your lists in class.

14.3 Sampling a Process, Rational Subgrouping, and Control Charts

In order to find and eliminate assignable causes of process variation, we sample output from the process. To do this, we first decide which **process variables**—that is, which process characteristics—will be studied. Several graphical techniques (sometimes called *prestatistical tools*) are used here. Pareto charts (see Section 2.5) help identify problem areas and opportunities for improvement. Cause-and-effect diagrams (see optional Section 14.8) help uncover sources of process variation and potentially important process variables. The goal is to identify process variables that can be studied in order to decrease the gap between customer expectations and process performance.

Whenever possible and economical, it is best to study a **quantitative,** rather than a **categorical,** process variable. For example, suppose we are filling 16-ounce jars with grape jelly, and suppose specifications state that each jar should contain between 15.95 and 16.05 ounces of jelly. If we record the fill of each sampled jar by simply noting that the jar either "meets specifications" (the fill is between 15.95 and 16.05 ounces) or "does not meet the specifications," then we are studying a **categorical process variable.** However, if we measure and record the amount of grape jelly contained in the jar (say, to the nearest one-hundredth of an ounce), then we are studying a **quantitative process variable.** Actually measuring the fill is best because this tells us **how close** we are to the specification limits and thus provides more information. As we will soon see, this additional information often allows us to decide whether to take action on a process by using a relatively small number of measurements.

When we study a quantitative process variable, we say that we are employing **measurement data.** To analyze such data, we take a series of samples (usually called **subgroups**) over time. Each subgroup consists of a set of several measurements; subgroup sizes between 2 and 6 are often used. Summary statistics (for example, means and ranges) for each subgroup are calculated and are plotted versus time. By comparing plot points, we hope to discover when unusual process variations are taking place.

Each subgroup is typically observed over a short period of time—a period of time in which the process operating characteristics do not change much. That is, we employ **rational subgroups.**

Rational Subgroups

Rational subgroups are selected so that, **if process changes of practical importance exist, the chance that these changes will occur between subgroups is maximized and the chance that these changes will occur within subgroups is minimized.**

In order to obtain rational subgroups, we must determine the frequency with which subgroups will be selected. For example, we might select a subgroup once every 15 minutes, once an hour, or once a day. In general, we should observe subgroups often enough to detect important process changes. For instance, suppose we wish to study a process, and suppose we feel that workers' shift changes (that take place every eight hours) may be an important source of process variation. In this case, rational subgroups can be obtained by selecting a subgroup during each eight-hour shift. Here shift changes will occur **between** subgroups. Therefore, if shift changes are an important source of variation, the rational subgroups will enable us to observe the effects of these changes by comparing plot points for different subgroups (shifts). However, in addition, suppose hourly machine resets are made, and we feel that these resets may also be an important source of process variation. In this case, rational subgroups can be obtained by selecting a subgroup during each hour. Here machine resets will occur **between** subgroups, and we will be able to observe their effects by comparing plot points for different subgroups (hours). If in this situation we selected one subgroup each eight-hour shift, we would not obtain rational subgroups. This is because hourly machine resets would occur **within** subgroups, and we would not be able to observe the effects of these resets by comparing plot points for different shifts. In general, it is very important to try to identify important sources of variation (potential assignable causes such as shift changes, resets, and so on) before deciding how subgroups will be selected. As previously stated, constructing a cause-and-effect diagram helps uncover these sources of variation (see optional Section 14.8).

Once we determine the sampling frequency, we need to determine the **subgroup size**—that is, the number of measurements that will be included in each subgroup—and how we will actually select the measurements in each subgroup. It is recommended that the **subgroup size be held constant.** Denoting this constant subgroup size as n, we typically choose n to be from 2 to 6, with $n = 4$ or 5 being a frequent choice. To illustrate how we can actually select the subgroup measurements, suppose we select a subgroup of 5 units every hour from the output of a machine that produces 100 units per hour. We can select these units by using a **consecutive, periodic,** or **random** sampling process. If we employ consecutive sampling, we would select 5 consecutive units produced by the machine at the beginning of (or at some time during) each hour. Here **production conditions**—machine operator, machine setting, raw material batch, and the like—**will be as constant as possible within the subgroup.** Such a subgroup provides a "freeze-frame picture" of the process at a particular point in time. Thus the **chance of variations occurring within the subgroups is minimized.** If we use periodic sampling, we would select 5 units periodically through each hour. For example, since the machine produces 100 units per hour, we could select the 1st, 21st, 41st, 61st, and 81st units produced. If we use random sampling, we would use a random number table to randomly select 5 of the 100 units produced during each hour. If production conditions are really held fairly constant during each hour, then consecutive, periodic, and random sampling will each provide a similar representation of the process. If production conditions vary considerably during each hour, and if we are able to recognize this variation by using a periodic or random sampling procedure, this would tell us that we should be sampling the process more often than once an hour. Of course, if we are using periodic or random sampling every hour, we might not realize that the process operates with considerably less variation during shorter periods (perhaps because we have not used a consecutive sampling procedure). We therefore might not recognize the extent of the hourly variation.

Lastly, it is important to point out that we **must also take subgroups for a period of time that is long enough to give potential sources of variation a chance to show up.** If, for instance, different batches of raw materials are suspected to be a significant source of process variation, and if we receive new batches every few days, we may need to collect subgroups for several weeks in order to assess the effects of the batch-to-batch variation. **A statistical rule of thumb says that we require at least 20 subgroups of size 4 or 5 in order to judge statistical control and in order to obtain reasonable estimates of the process mean and variability.** However, practical considerations may require the collection of much more data.

We now look at two more concrete examples of subgrouped data.

Example 14.1 The Hole Location Case[2]

C

A manufacturer produces automobile air conditioner compressor shells. The compressor shell is basically the outer metal housing of the compressor. Several holes of various sizes must be punched into the shell to accommodate hose connections that must be made to the compressor. If any one of these holes is punched in the wrong location, the compressor shell becomes a piece of scrap metal (at considerable cost to the manufacturer). Figure 14.1(a) illustrates a compressor shell (note the holes that have been punched in the housing). Experience with the hole-punching process suggests that substantial changes (machine resets, equipment lubrication, and the like)

FIGURE 14.1 The Compressor Shell and the Hole Location Data HoleLoc

(a) Holes punched in a compressor shell for hose connections

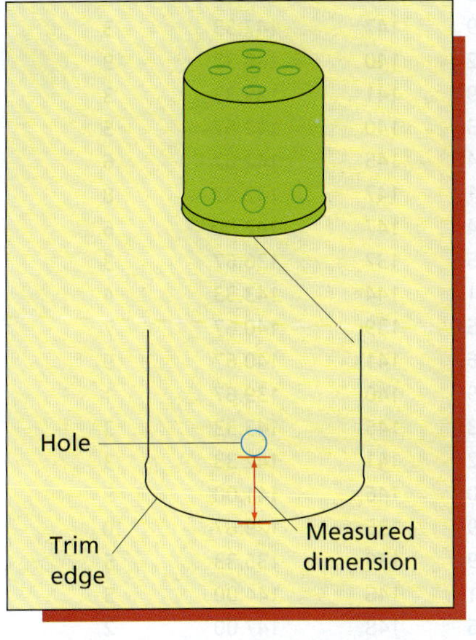

(b) Twenty subgroups of 5 hole location measurements (measurement from trim edge to the bottom of hole; target value is 3.00 inches)

		Measurement						
Time	Subgroup	1	2	3	4	5	Mean	Range
8:00 AM	1	3.05	3.02	3.04	3.09	3.05	3.05	0.07
8:20 AM	2	3.00	3.04	2.98	2.99	2.99	3.00	0.06
8:40 AM	3	3.07	3.06	2.94	2.97	3.01	3.01	0.13
9:00 AM	4	3.02	2.96	3.01	2.98	3.02	2.998	0.06
9:20 AM	5	3.01	2.98	3.04	3.01	3.01	3.01	0.06
9:40 AM	6	3.01	3.02	2.99	2.97	2.96	2.99	0.06
10:00 AM	7	3.03	2.98	2.92	3.17	2.96	3.012	0.25
10:20 AM	8	3.05	3.03	2.96	3.01	2.97	3.004	0.09
10:40 AM	9	2.99	2.96	3.01	3.00	2.95	2.982	0.06
11:00 AM	10	3.02	3.02	2.98	3.03	3.02	3.014	0.05
11:20 AM	11	2.97	2.96	2.96	3.00	3.04	2.986	0.08
11:40 AM	12	3.06	3.04	3.02	3.10	3.05	3.054	0.08
12:00 PM	13	2.99	3.00	3.04	2.96	3.02	3.002	0.08
12:20 PM	14	3.00	3.01	2.99	3.00	3.01	3.002	0.02
12:40 PM	15	3.02	2.96	3.04	2.95	2.97	2.988	0.09
1:00 PM	16	3.02	3.02	3.04	2.98	3.03	3.018	0.06
1:20 PM	17	3.01	2.87	3.09	3.02	3.00	2.998	0.22
1:40 PM	18	3.05	2.96	3.01	2.97	2.98	2.994	0.09
2:00 PM	19	3.02	2.99	3.00	2.98	3.00	2.998	0.04
2:20 PM	20	3.00	3.00	3.01	3.05	3.01	3.014	0.05

[2]The data for this case were obtained from a metal fabrication plant located in the Cincinnati, Ohio, area. For confidentiality, we have agreed to withhold the company's name.

can occur quite frequently—as often as two or three times an hour. Because we wish to observe the impact of these changes if and when they occur, rational subgroups are obtained by selecting a subgroup every 20 minutes or so. Specifically, about every 20 minutes five compressor shells are consecutively selected from the process output. For each shell selected, a measurement that helps to specify the location of a particular hole in the compressor shell is made. The measurement is taken by measuring from one of the edges of the compressor shell (called the trim edge) to the bottom of the hole [see Figure 14.1(a)]. Obviously, it is not possible to measure to the center of the hole because you cannot tell where it is! The target value for the measured dimension is 3.00 inches. Of course, the manufacturer would like as little variation around the target as possible. Figure 14.1(b) gives the measurements obtained for 20 subgroups that were selected between 8 A.M. and 2:20 P.M. on a particular day. Here a subgroup consists of the five measurements labeled 1 through 5 in a single row in the table. Notice that Figure 14.1(b) also gives the mean, $\bar{x}$, and the range, R, of the measurements in each subgroup. In the next section we will see how to use the subgroup means and ranges to detect when unusual process variations have taken place.

Example 14.2 The Hot Chocolate Temperature Case[3]

Since 1994 a number of consumers have filed and won large claims against national fast-food chains as a result of being scalded by excessively hot beverages such as coffee, tea, and hot chocolate. Because of such litigation, the food service staff at a university dining hall wishes to study the temperature of the hot chocolate dispensed by its hot chocolate machine. The dining hall staff believes that there might be substantial variations in hot chocolate temperatures from meal to meal. Therefore, it is decided that at least one subgroup of hot chocolate temperatures will be observed during each meal—breakfast (6:30 A.M. to 10 A.M.), lunch (11 A.M. to 1:30 P.M.), and dinner (5 P.M. to 7:30 P.M.). In addition, since the hot chocolate machine is heavily used during most meals, the dining hall staff also believes that hot chocolate temperatures might vary

TABLE 14.2 24 Subgroups of Three Hot Chocolate Temperatures (Measurements to the Nearest Degree Fahrenheit) HotChoc

			Temperature			Subgroup	Subgroup
Day	Meal	Subgroup	1	2	3	Mean, $\bar{x}$	Range, R
Monday	Breakfast	1	142°	140°	139°	140.33°	3°
		2	141	138	140	139.67	3
	Lunch	3	143	146	147	145.33	4
		4	146	149	147	147.33	3
	Dinner	5	133	142	140	138.33	9
		6	138	139	141	139.33	3
Tuesday	Breakfast	7	145	143	140	142.67	5
		8	139	144	145	142.67	6
	Lunch	9	139	141	147	142.33	8
		10	150	144	147	147.00	6
	Dinner	11	138	135	137	136.67	3
		12	145	141	144	143.33	4
Wednesday	Breakfast	13	138	145	139	140.67	7
		14	145	136	141	140.67	9
	Lunch	15	140	139	140	139.67	1
		16	142	143	145	143.33	3
	Dinner	17	144	142	141	142.33	3
		18	137	140	146	141.00	9
Thursday	Breakfast	19	125	129	135	129.67	10
		20	134	139	136	136.33	5
	Lunch	21	145	141	146	144.00	5
		22	147	146	148	147.00	2
	Dinner	23	140	143	139	140.67	4
		24	139	139	143	140.33	4

[3]The data for this case were collected for a student's term project with the cooperation of the Food Service at Miami University, Oxford, Ohio.

substantially from the beginning to the end of a single meal. It follows that the staff will obtain rational subgroups by selecting a subgroup a half hour after the beginning of each meal and by selecting another subgroup a half hour prior to the end of each meal. Specifically, each subgroup will be selected by pouring three cups of hot chocolate over a 10-minute time span using periodic sampling (the second cup will be poured 5 minutes after the first, and the third cup will be poured 5 minutes after the second). The temperature of the hot chocolate will be measured by a candy thermometer (to the nearest degree Fahrenheit) immediately after each cup is poured.

Table 14.2 gives the results for 24 subgroups of three hot chocolate temperatures taken at each meal served at the dining hall over a four-day period. Here a subgroup consists of the three temperatures labeled 1 through 3 in a single row in the table. The table also gives the mean, $\bar{x}$, and the range, R, of the temperatures in each subgroup. In the next section we will use the subgroup means and ranges to detect unusual process variations (that is, to detect assignable causes).

Subgrouped data are used to determine when assignable causes of process variation exist. Typically, we analyze subgrouped data by plotting summary statistics for the subgroups versus time. The resulting plots are often called **graphs of process performance.** For example, the subgroup means and the subgroup ranges of the hole location measurements in Figure 14.1(b) are plotted in time order on graphs of process performance in the Excel output of Figure 14.2. The subgroup means ($\bar{x}$ values) and ranges (R values) are plotted on the vertical axis, while the time sequence (in this case, the subgroup number) is plotted on the horizontal axis. The $\bar{x}$ values and R values for corresponding subgroups are lined up vertically. The plot points on each graph are connected by line segments as a visual aid. However, the lines between the plot points do not really say anything about the process performance between the observed subgroups. Notice that the subgroup means and ranges vary over time.

If we consider the plot of subgroup means, very high and very low points are undesirable—they represent large deviations from the target hole location dimension (3 inches). If we consider the plot of subgroup ranges, very high points are undesirable (high variation in the hole location dimensions), while very low points are desirable (little variation in the hole location dimensions).

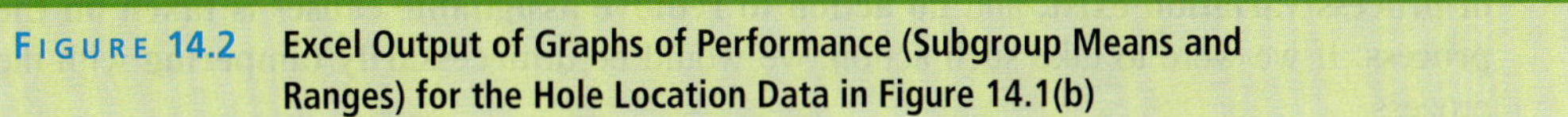

FIGURE 14.2 Excel Output of Graphs of Performance (Subgroup Means and Ranges) for the Hole Location Data in Figure 14.1(b)

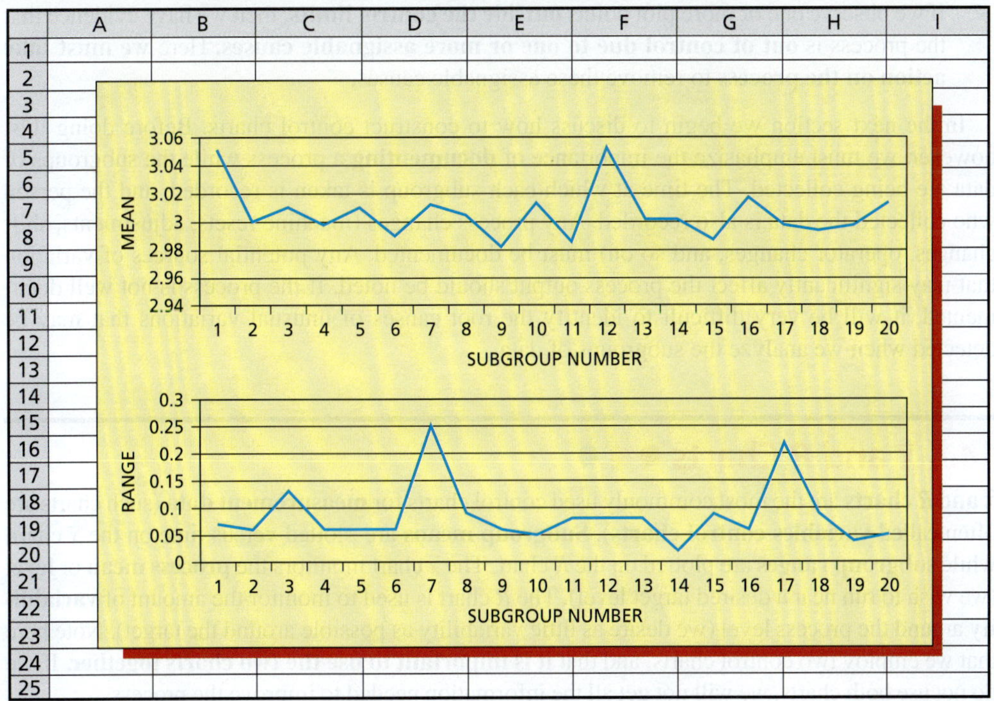

We now wish to answer a very basic question. **Is the variation that we see on the graphs of performance due to the usual process variation (that is, due to common causes), or is the variation due to one or more assignable causes (unusual variations)?** It is possible that unusual variations have occurred and that action should be taken to reduce the variation in production conditions. It is also possible that the variation in the plot points is caused by common causes and that (given the current configuration of the process) production conditions have been held as constant as possible. For example, do the high points on the $\bar{x}$ plot in Figure 14.2 suggest that one or more assignable causes have increased the hole location dimensions enough to warrant corrective action? As another example, do the high points on the R plot suggest that excess variability in the hole location dimensions exists and that corrective action is needed? Or does the lowest point on the R plot indicate that an improvement in process performance (reduction in variation) has occurred due to an assignable cause?

We can answer these questions by converting the graphs of performance shown in Figure 14.2 into **control charts.** In general, by converting graphs of performance into control charts, we can (with only a small chance of being wrong) determine whether observed process variations are unusual (due to assignable causes). That is, the purpose of a control chart is to monitor a process so we can take corrective action in response to assignable causes when it is needed. This is called **statistical process monitoring.** The use of "seat of the pants intuition" has not been found to be a particularly effective way to decide whether observed process performance is unusual. By using a control chart, we can reduce our chances of making two possible errors—(1) taking action when none is needed and (2) not taking action when action is needed.

A control chart employs a **center line** (denoted **CNL**) and two control limits—an **upper control limit** (denoted **UCL**) and a **lower control limit** (denoted **LCL**). The center line represents the average performance of the process when it is in a state of statistical control—that is, when only common cause variation exists. The upper and lower control limits are horizontal lines situated above and below the center line. These control limits are established so that, when the process is in control, almost all plot points will be between the upper and lower limits. In practice, the control limits are used as follows:

1. If all observed plot points are **between the LCL and UCL** (and if no unusual patterns of points exist—this will be explained later), we have no evidence that assignable causes exist and we assume that the process is in **statistical control.** In this case, **only common causes of process variation exist,** and **no action to remove assignable causes is taken on the process.** If we were to take such action, we would be **unnecessarily tampering** with the process.
2. If we observe one or more plot points **outside the control limits,** then we have evidence that the process is **out of control due to one or more assignable causes.** Here **we must take action on the process** to remove these assignable causes.

In the next section we begin to discuss how to construct control charts. Before doing this, however, we must emphasize the importance of **documenting** a process while the subgroups of data are being collected. The time at which each subgroup is taken is recorded, and the person who collected the data is also recorded. Any process changes (machine resets, adjustments, shift changes, operator changes, and so on) must be documented. Any potential sources of variation that may significantly affect the process output should be noted. If the process is not well documented, it will be very difficult to identify the root causes of unusual variations that may be detected when we analyze the subgroups of data.

14.4 $\bar{x}$ and R Charts

CHAPTER 21

$\bar{x}$ and R charts are the most commonly used control charts for **measurement data** (such charts are often called **variables control charts**). **Subgroup means** are plotted versus time on the $\bar{x}$ chart, while **subgroup ranges** are plotted on the R chart. The $\bar{x}$ chart monitors the **process mean** or **level** (we wish to run near a desired target level). The R chart is used to monitor the amount of **variability** around the process level (we desire as little variability as possible around the target). Note here that we employ two control charts, and that **it is important to use the two charts together.** If we do not use both charts, we will not get all the information needed to improve the process.

Before seeing how to construct $\bar{x}$ and R charts, we should mention that it is also possible to monitor the process variability by using a chart for **subgroup standard deviations.** Such a chart is called an ***s* chart.** However, the overwhelming majority of practitioners use R charts rather than s charts. This is partly due to historical reasons. When control charts were developed, electronic calculators and computers did not exist. It was, therefore, much easier to compute a subgroup range than it was to compute a subgroup standard deviation. For this reason, the use of R charts has persisted. Some people also feel that it is easier for factory personnel (some of whom may have little mathematical background) to understand and relate to the subgroup range. In addition, while the standard deviation (which is computed using all the measurements in a subgroup) is a better measure of variability than the range (which is computed using only two measurements), the R chart usually suffices. This is because $\bar{x}$ and R charts usually employ small subgroups—as mentioned previously, subgroup sizes are often between 2 and 6. For such subgroup sizes, it can be shown that using subgroup ranges is almost as effective as using subgroup standard deviations.

To construct $\bar{x}$ and R charts, suppose we have observed rational subgroups of n measurements over successive time periods (hours, shifts, days, or the like). We first calculate the mean $\bar{x}$ and range R for each subgroup, and we construct graphs of performance for the $\bar{x}$ values and for the R values (as in Figure 14.2). In order to calculate center lines and control limits, let $\bar{x}$ denote the mean of the subgroup of n measurements that is selected in a particular time period. Furthermore, assume that the population of all process measurements that could be observed in any time period is normally distributed with mean μ and standard deviation σ, and also assume successive process measurements are statistically independent.[4] Then, if μ and σ stay constant over time, the sampling distribution of subgroup means in any time period is normally distributed with mean μ and standard deviation $\sigma/\sqrt{n}$. It follows that (in any time period) 99.73 percent of all possible values of the subgroup mean $\bar{x}$ are in the interval

$$[\mu - 3(\sigma/\sqrt{n}),\ \mu + 3(\sigma/\sqrt{n})]$$

This fact is illustrated in Figure 14.3. It follows that we can set a center line and control limits for the $\bar{x}$ chart as

$$\begin{aligned} \text{Center line} &= \mu \\ \text{Upper control limit} &= \text{UCL}_{\bar{x}} = \mu + 3(\sigma/\sqrt{n}) \\ \text{Lower control limit} &= \text{LCL}_{\bar{x}} = \mu - 3(\sigma/\sqrt{n}) \end{aligned}$$

If an observed subgroup mean is inside these control limits, we have no evidence to suggest that the process is out of control. However, if the subgroup mean is outside these limits, we conclude that μ and/or σ have changed, and that the process is out of control. The $\bar{x}$ chart limits are illustrated in Figure 14.3.

If the process is in control, and thus μ and σ stay constant over time, it follows that μ and σ are the mean and standard deviation of all possible process measurements. For this reason, we call μ the **process mean** and σ the **process standard deviation.** Since in most real situations we do not know the true values of μ and σ, we must estimate these values. If the process is in control, an appropriate estimate of the process mean μ is

$$\bar{\bar{x}} = \text{the mean of all observed subgroup means}$$

($\bar{\bar{x}}$ is **pronounced "x double bar"**). It follows that the center line for the $\bar{x}$ chart is

$$\text{Center line}_{\bar{x}} = \bar{\bar{x}}$$

To obtain control limits for the $\bar{x}$ chart, we compute

$$\bar{R} = \text{the mean of all observed subgroup ranges}$$

It can be shown that an appropriate estimate of the process standard deviation σ is $(\bar{R}/d_2)$, where d_2 is a constant that depends on the subgroup size n. Although we do not present a development of d_2 here, it intuitively makes sense that, for a given subgroup size, our best estimate of the process standard deviation should be related to the average of the subgroup ranges $(\bar{R})$. The

[4]Basically, *statistical independence* here means that successive process measurements do not display any kind of pattern over time.

FIGURE 14.3 An Illustration of $\bar{x}$ Chart Control Limits with the Process Mean μ and Process Standard Deviation σ Known

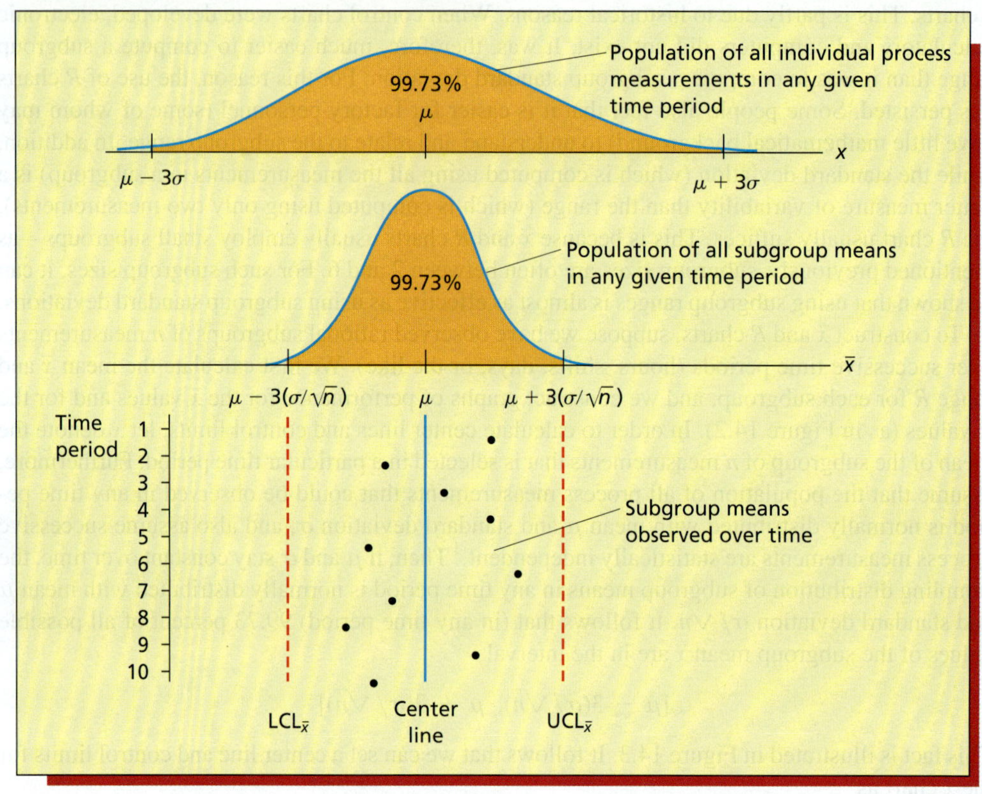

number d_2 relates these quantities. Values of d_2 are given in Table 14.3 for subgroup sizes $n = 2$ through $n = 25$. At the end of this section we further discuss why we use $\bar{R}/d_2$ to estimate the process standard deviation.

Substituting the estimate $\bar{\bar{x}}$ of μ and the estimate $\bar{R}/d_2$ of σ into the limits

$$\mu + 3(\sigma/\sqrt{n}) \quad \text{and} \quad \mu - 3(\sigma/\sqrt{n})$$

we obtain

$$\text{UCL}_{\bar{x}} = \bar{\bar{x}} + 3\left(\frac{\bar{R}/d_2}{\sqrt{n}}\right) = \bar{\bar{x}} + \left(\frac{3}{d_2\sqrt{n}}\right)\bar{R}$$

$$\text{LCL}_{\bar{x}} = \bar{\bar{x}} - 3\left(\frac{\bar{R}/d_2}{\sqrt{n}}\right) = \bar{\bar{x}} - \left(\frac{3}{d_2\sqrt{n}}\right)\bar{R}$$

Finally, we define

$$A_2 = \frac{3}{d_2\sqrt{n}}$$

and rewrite the control limits as

$$\text{UCL}_{\bar{x}} = \bar{\bar{x}} + A_2\bar{R} \quad \text{and} \quad \text{LCL}_{\bar{x}} = \bar{\bar{x}} - A_2\bar{R}$$

Here we call A_2 a **control chart constant.** As the formula for A_2 implies, this control chart constant depends on the subgroup size n. Values of A_2 are given in Table 14.3 for subgroup sizes $n = 2$ through $n = 25$.

The center line for the R chart is

$$\text{Center line}_R = \bar{R}$$

Furthermore, assuming normality, it can be shown that there are control chart constants D_4 and D_3 so that

$$\text{UCL}_R = D_4\bar{R} \quad \text{and} \quad \text{LCL}_R = D_3\bar{R}$$

TABLE 14.3 Control Chart Constants for $\bar{x}$ and R Charts

	Chart for Averages (x)	Chart for Ranges (R)		
Subgroup Size, n	Factor for Control Limits, A_2	Divisor for Estimate of Standard Deviation, d_2	Factors for Control Limits D_3	D_4
2	1.880	1.128	—	3.267
3	1.023	1.693	—	2.574
4	0.729	2.059	—	2.282
5	0.577	2.326	—	2.114
6	0.483	2.534	—	2.004
7	0.419	2.704	0.076	1.924
8	0.373	2.847	0.136	1.864
9	0.337	2.970	0.184	1.816
10	0.308	3.078	0.223	1.777
11	0.285	3.173	0.256	1.744
12	0.266	3.258	0.283	1.717
13	0.249	3.336	0.307	1.693
14	0.235	3.407	0.328	1.672
15	0.223	3.472	0.347	1.653
16	0.212	3.532	0.363	1.637
17	0.203	3.588	0.378	1.622
18	0.194	3.640	0.391	1.608
19	0.187	3.689	0.403	1.597
20	0.180	3.735	0.415	1.585
21	0.173	3.778	0.425	1.575
22	0.167	3.819	0.434	1.566
23	0.162	3.858	0.443	1.557
24	0.157	3.895	0.451	1.548
25	0.153	3.931	0.459	1.541

Here the control chart constants D_4 and D_3 also depend on the subgroup size n. Values of D_4 and D_3 are given in Table 14.3 for subgroup sizes $n = 2$ through $n = 25$. We summarize the center lines and control limits for $\bar{x}$ and R charts in the following box:

$\bar{x}$ and R Chart Center Lines and Control Limits

$$\text{Center line}_{\bar{x}} = \bar{\bar{x}} \qquad \text{Center line}_R = \bar{R}$$

$$UCL_{\bar{x}} = \bar{\bar{x}} + A_2\bar{R} \qquad UCL_R = D_4\bar{R}$$

$$LCL_{\bar{x}} = \bar{\bar{x}} - A_2\bar{R} \qquad LCL_R = D_3\bar{R}$$

where $\bar{\bar{x}}$ = the mean of all subgroup means
$\bar{R}$ = the mean of all subgroup ranges

and A_2, D_4, and D_3 are control chart constants that depend on the subgroup size (see Table 14.3). When D_3 is not listed, the R chart does not have a lower control limit.[5]

Example 14.3 The Hole Location Case

Consider the hole location data for air conditioner compressor shells that is given in Figure 14.1 (page 683). In order to calculate $\bar{x}$ and R chart control limits for this data, we compute

$$\bar{\bar{x}} = \text{the average of the 20 subgroup means}$$

$$= \frac{3.05 + 3.00 + \cdots + 3.014}{20} = 3.0062$$

[5]When D_3 is not listed, the theoretical lower control limit for the R chart is negative. In this case, some practitioners prefer to say that the LCL_R equals 0. Others prefer to say that the LCL_R does not exist because a range R equal to 0 does not indicate that an assignable cause exists and because it is impossible to observe a negative range below LCL_R. We prefer the second alternative. In practice, it makes no difference.

FIGURE 14.4 MINITAB Output of $\bar{x}$ and R Charts for the Hole Location Data

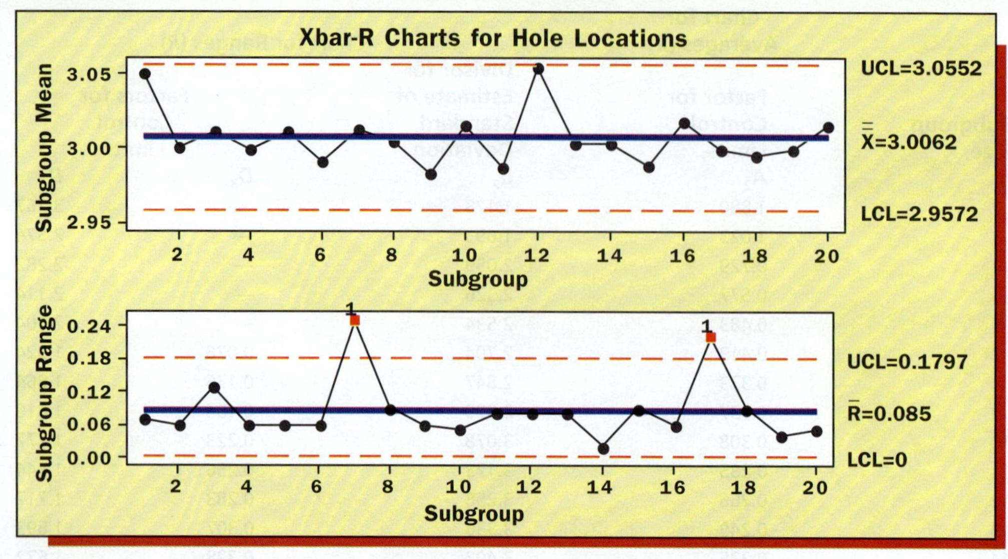

$$\bar{R} = \text{the average of the 20 subgroup ranges}$$

$$= \frac{.07 + .06 + \cdots + .05}{20} = 0.085$$

Looking at Table 14.3, we see that when the subgroup size is $n = 5$, the control chart constants needed for $\bar{x}$ and R charts are $A_2 = .577$ and $D_4 = 2.114$. It follows that center lines and control limits are

$$\text{Center line}_{\bar{x}} = \bar{\bar{x}} = 3.0062$$

$$\text{UCL}_{\bar{x}} = \bar{\bar{x}} + A_2\bar{R} = 3.0062 + .577(0.085) = 3.0552$$

$$\text{LCL}_{\bar{x}} = \bar{\bar{x}} - A_2\bar{R} = 3.0062 - .577(0.085) = 2.9572$$

$$\text{Center line}_R = \bar{R} = .085$$

$$\text{UCL}_R = D_4\bar{R} = 2.114(.085) = 0.1797$$

Since D_3 is not listed in Table 14.3 for a subgroup size of $n = 5$, the R chart does not have a lower control limit. Figure 14.4 presents the MINITAB output of the $\bar{x}$ and R charts for the hole location data. Note that the center lines and control limits that we have just calculated are shown on the $\bar{x}$ and R charts.

Control limits such as those computed in Example 14.3 are called **trial control limits.** Theoretically, control limits are supposed to be computed using subgroups collected while the process is in statistical control. However, it is impossible to know whether the process is in control until we have constructed the control charts. If, after we have set up the $\bar{x}$ and R charts, we find that the process is in control, we can use the charts to monitor the process.

If the charts show that the process is not in statistical control (for example, there are plot points outside the control limits), we must find and eliminate the assignable causes before we can calculate control limits for monitoring the process. In order to understand how to find and eliminate assignable causes, we must understand how changes in the process mean and the process variation show up on $\bar{x}$ and R charts. To do this, consider Figures 14.5 and 14.6. These figures illustrate that, whereas a change in the process mean shows up only on the $\bar{x}$ chart, a change in the process variation shows up on both the $\bar{x}$ and R charts. Specifically, Figure 14.5 shows that, when the process mean increases, the sample means plotted on the $\bar{x}$ chart increase and go out of control. Figure 14.6 shows that, when the process variation (standard

FIGURE 14.5 A Shift of the Process Mean Shows Up on the $\bar{x}$ Chart

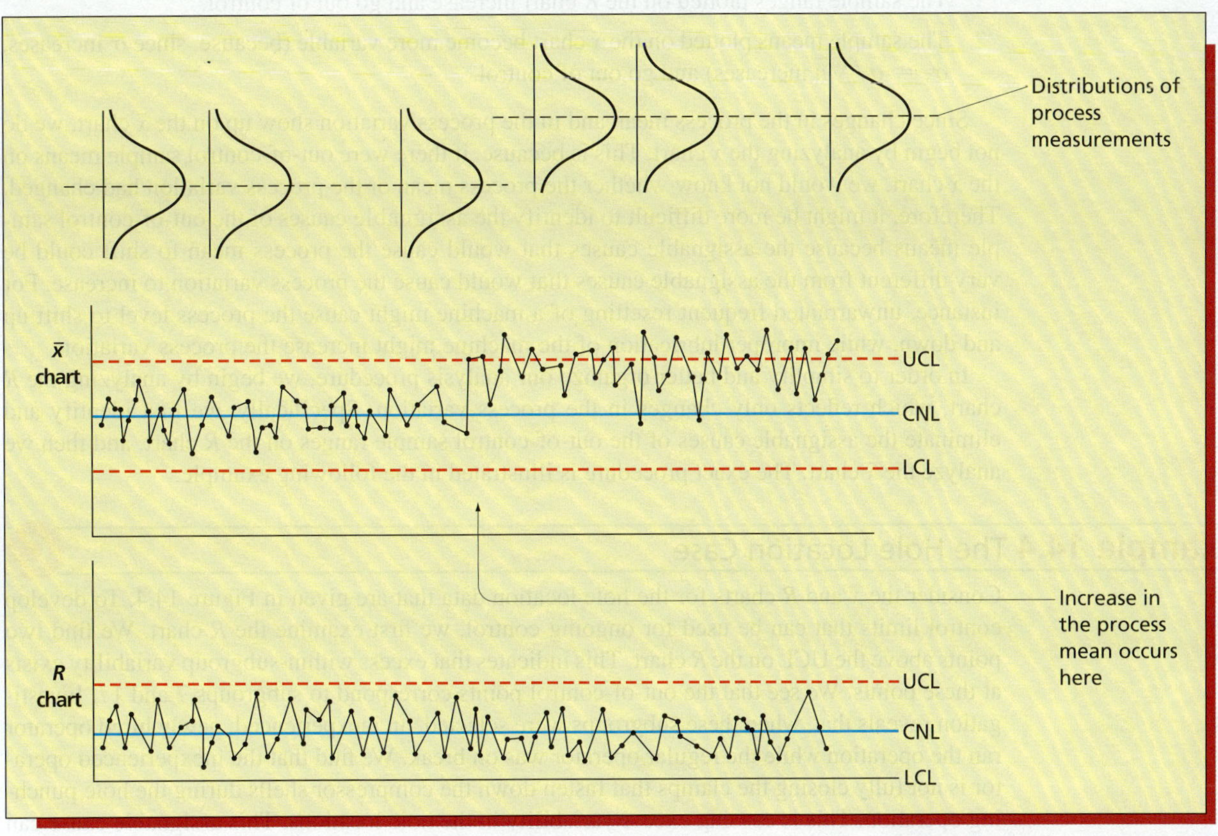

FIGURE 14.6 An Increase in the Process Variation Shows Up on Both the $\bar{x}$ and R Charts

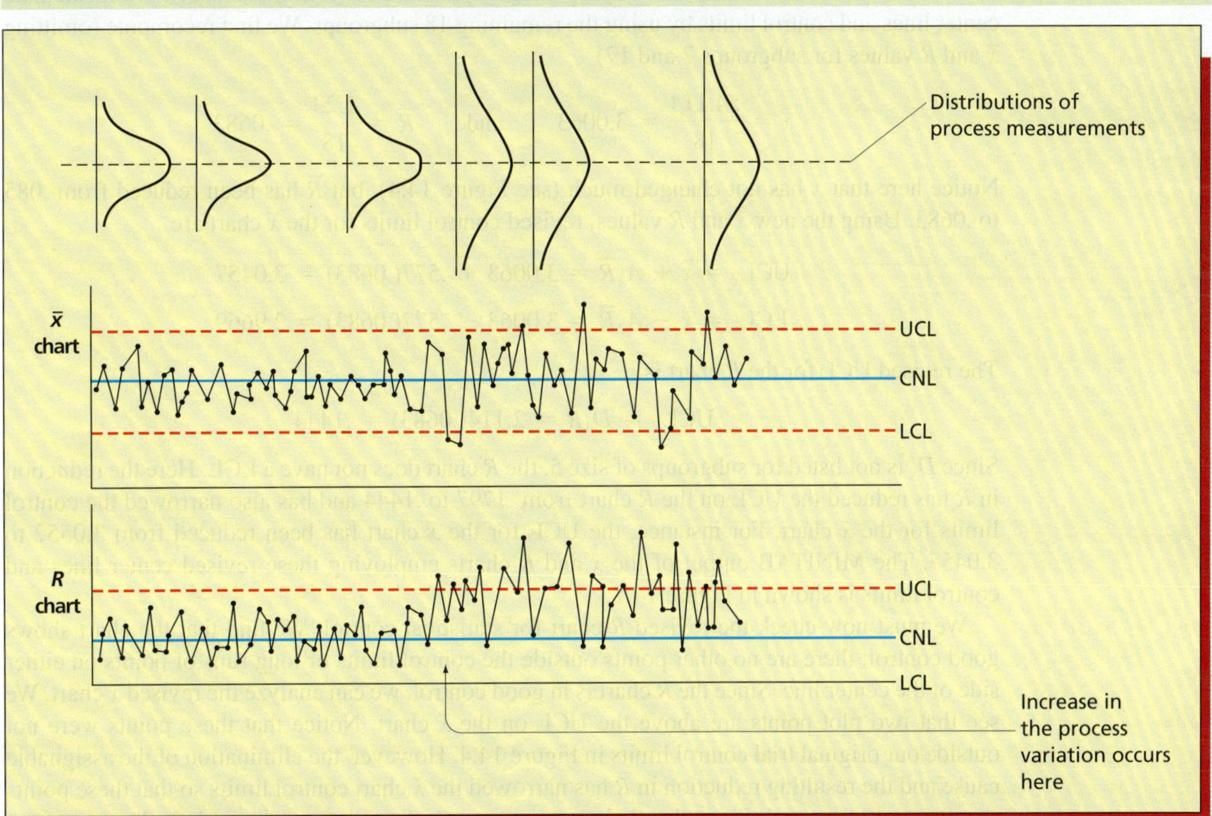

deviation, σ) increases,

1 The sample ranges plotted on the R chart increase and go out of control.

2 The sample means plotted on the $\bar{x}$ chart become more variable (because, since σ increases, $\sigma_{\bar{x}} = \sigma/\sqrt{n}$ increases) and go out of control.

Since changes in the process mean and in the process variation show up on the $\bar{x}$ chart, we do not begin by analyzing the $\bar{x}$ chart. This is because, if there were out-of-control sample means on the $\bar{x}$ chart, we would not know whether the process mean or the process variation had changed. Therefore, it might be more difficult to identify the assignable causes of the out-of-control sample means because the assignable causes that would cause the process mean to shift could be very different from the assignable causes that would cause the process variation to increase. For instance, unwarranted frequent resetting of a machine might cause the process level to shift up and down, while improper lubrication of the machine might increase the process variation.

In order to simplify and better organize our analysis procedure, we begin by analyzing the R chart, which reflects only changes in the process variation. Specifically, we first identify and eliminate the assignable causes of the out-of-control sample ranges on the R chart, and then we analyze the $\bar{x}$ chart. The exact procedure is illustrated in the following example.

Example 14.4 The Hole Location Case

Consider the $\bar{x}$ and R charts for the hole location data that are given in Figure 14.4. To develop control limits that can be used for ongoing control, we first examine the R chart. We find two points above the UCL on the R chart. This indicates that excess within-subgroup variability exists at these points. We see that the out-of-control points correspond to subgroups 7 and 17. Investigation reveals that, when these subgroups were selected, an inexperienced, newly hired operator ran the operation while the regular operator was on break. We find that the inexperienced operator is not fully closing the clamps that fasten down the compressor shells during the hole punching operation. This is causing excess variability in the hole locations. This assignable cause can be eliminated by thoroughly retraining the newly hired operator.

Since we have identified and corrected the assignable cause associated with the points that are out of control on the R chart, we can drop subgroups 7 and 17 from the data set. We recalculate center lines and control limits by using the remaining 18 subgroups. We first recompute (omitting $\bar{x}$ and R values for subgroups 7 and 17)

$$\bar{\bar{x}} = \frac{54.114}{18} = 3.0063 \quad \text{and} \quad \bar{R} = \frac{1.23}{18} = .0683$$

Notice here that $\bar{\bar{x}}$ has not changed much (see Figure 14.4), but $\bar{R}$ has been reduced from .085 to .0683. Using the new $\bar{\bar{x}}$ and $\bar{R}$ values, revised control limits for the $\bar{x}$ chart are

$$\text{UCL}_{\bar{x}} = \bar{\bar{x}} + A_2\bar{R} = 3.0063 + .577(.0683) = 3.0457$$

$$\text{LCL}_{\bar{x}} = \bar{\bar{x}} - A_2\bar{R} = 3.0063 - .577(.0683) = 2.9669$$

The revised UCL for the R chart is

$$\text{UCL}_R = D_4\bar{R} = 2.114(.0683) = .1444$$

Since D_3 is not listed for subgroups of size 5, the R chart does not have a LCL. Here the reduction in $\bar{R}$ has reduced the UCL on the R chart from .1797 to .1444 and has also narrowed the control limits for the $\bar{x}$ chart. For instance, the UCL for the $\bar{x}$ chart has been reduced from 3.0552 to 3.0457. The MINITAB output of the $\bar{x}$ and R charts employing these revised center lines and control limits is shown in Figure 14.7.

We must now check the revised R chart for statistical control. We find that the chart shows good control: there are no other points outside the control limits or long runs of points on either side of the center line. Since the R chart is in good control, we can analyze the revised $\bar{x}$ chart. We see that two plot points are above the UCL on the $\bar{x}$ chart. Notice that these points were not outside our original trial control limits in Figure 14.4. However, the elimination of the assignable cause and the resulting reduction in $\bar{R}$ has narrowed the $\bar{x}$ chart control limits so that these points are now out of control. Since the R chart is in control, the points on the $\bar{x}$ chart that are out of

FIGURE 14.7 MINITAB Output of $\bar{x}$ and R Charts for the Hole Location Data: Subgroups 7 and 17 Omitted

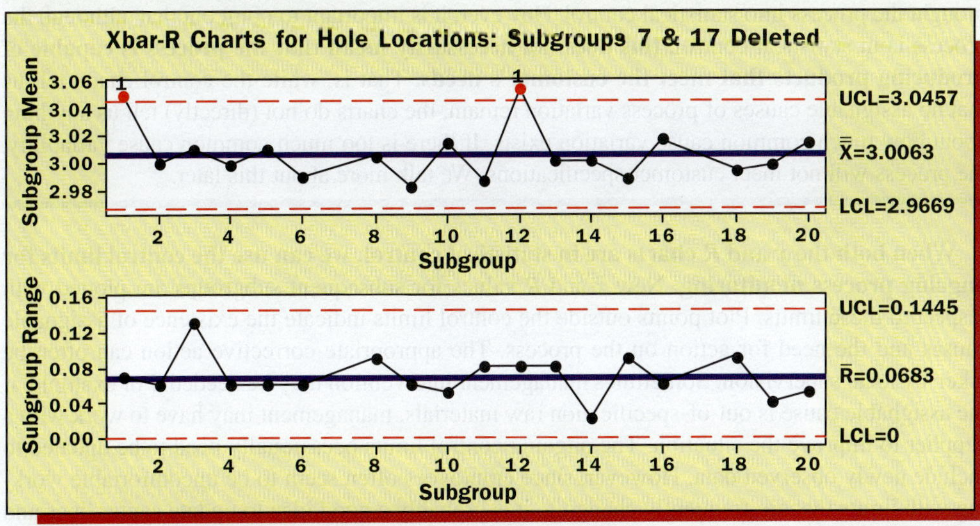

FIGURE 14.8 MINITAB Output of $\bar{x}$ and R Charts for the Hole Location Data: Subgroups 1, 7, 12, and 17 Omitted. The Charts Show Good Control.

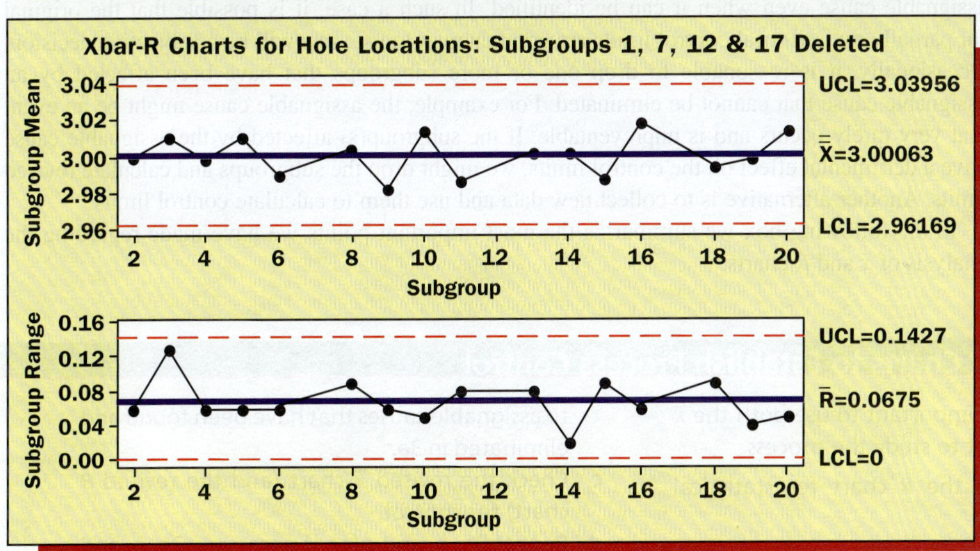

control suggest that the process level has shifted when subgroups 1 and 12 were taken. Investigation reveals that these subgroups were observed immediately after start-up at the beginning of the day and immediately after start-up following the lunch break. We find that, if we allow a five-minute machine warm-up period, we can eliminate the process level problem.

Since we have again found and eliminated an assignable cause, we must compute newly revised center lines and control limits. Dropping subgroups 1 and 12 from the data set, we recompute

$$\bar{\bar{x}} = \frac{48.01}{16} = 3.0006 \quad \text{and} \quad \bar{R} = \frac{1.08}{16} = .0675$$

Using the newest $\bar{\bar{x}}$ and $\bar{R}$ values, we compute newly revised control limits as follows:

$$UCL_{\bar{x}} = \bar{\bar{x}} + A_2\bar{R} = 3.0006 + .577(.0675) = 3.0396$$

$$LCL_{\bar{x}} = \bar{\bar{x}} - A_2\bar{R} = 3.0006 - .577(.0675) = 2.9617$$

$$UCL_R = D_4\bar{R} = 2.114(.0675) = .1427$$

Again, the R chart does not have a LCL. We obtain the newly revised $\bar{x}$ and R charts that are shown in the MINITAB output of Figure 14.8. We see that all the points on each chart are inside their respective control limits. This says that the actions taken to remove assignable causes have brought the process into statistical control. However, it is important to point out that, although the process is in statistical control, **this does not necessarily mean that the process is capable of producing products that meet the customer's needs.** That is, while the control charts tell us that no assignable causes of process variation remain, the charts do not (directly) tell us anything about how much common cause variation exists. If there is too much common cause variability, the process will not meet customer specifications. We talk more about this later.

When both the $\bar{x}$ and R charts are in statistical control, we can use the control limits for ongoing process monitoring. New $\bar{x}$ and R values for subsequent subgroups are plotted with respect to these limits. Plot points outside the control limits indicate the existence of assignable causes and the need for action on the process. The appropriate corrective action can often be taken by local supervision. Sometimes management intervention may be needed. For example, if the assignable cause is out-of-specification raw materials, management may have to work with a supplier to improve the situation. The ongoing control limits occasionally need to be updated to include newly observed data. However, since employees often seem to be uncomfortable working with limits that are frequently changing, it is probably a good idea to update center lines and control limits only when the new data would substantially change the limits. Of course, if an important process change is implemented, new data must be collected, and we may need to develop new center lines and control limits from scratch.

Sometimes it is not possible to find an assignable cause, or it is not possible to eliminate the assignable cause even when it can be identified. In such a case, it is possible that the original (or partially revised) trial control limits are good enough to use; this will be a subjective decision. Occasionally, it is reasonable to drop one or more subgroups that have been affected by an assignable cause that cannot be eliminated. For example, the assignable cause might be an event that very rarely occurs and is unpreventable. If the subgroup(s) affected by the assignable cause have a detrimental effect on the control limits, we might drop the subgroups and calculate revised limits. Another alternative is to collect new data and use them to calculate control limits.

In the following box we summarize the most important points we have made regarding the analysis of $\bar{x}$ and R charts:

Analyzing $\bar{x}$ and R Charts to Establish Process Control

1. Remember that it is important to use both the $\bar{x}$ chart and the R chart to study the process.
2. Begin by analyzing the R chart for statistical control.
   a. Find and eliminate assignable causes that are indicated by the R chart.
   b. Revise both the $\bar{x}$ and R chart control limits, dropping data for subgroups corresponding to assignable causes that have been found and eliminated in 2*a*.
   c. Check the revised R chart for control.
   d. Repeat 2*a*, *b*, and *c* as necessary until the R chart shows statistical control.
3. When the R chart is in statistical control, the $\bar{x}$ chart can be properly analyzed.
   a. Find and eliminate assignable causes that are indicated by the $\bar{x}$ chart.
   b. Revise both the $\bar{x}$ and R chart control limits, dropping data for subgroups corresponding to assignable causes that have been found and eliminated in 3*a*.
   c. Check the revised $\bar{x}$ chart (and the revised R chart) for control.
   d. Repeat 3*a*, *b*, and *c* (or, if necessary, 2*a*, *b*, and *c* and 3*a*, *b*, and *c*) as needed until both the $\bar{x}$ and R charts show statistical control.
4. When both the $\bar{x}$ and R charts are in control, use the control limits for process monitoring.
   a. Plot $\bar{x}$ and R points for newly observed subgroups with respect to the established limits.
   b. If either the $\bar{x}$ chart or the R chart indicates a lack of control, take corrective action on the process.
5. Periodically update the $\bar{x}$ and R control limits using all relevant data (data that describe the process as it now operates).
6. When a major process change is made, develop new control limits if necessary.

Example 14.5 The Hole Location Case

C

We consider the hole location problem and the revised $\bar{x}$ and R charts shown in Figure 14.8. Since the process has been brought into statistical control, we may use the control limits in Figure 14.8 to monitor the process. This would assume that we have used an appropriate subgrouping scheme and have observed enough subgroups to give potential assignable causes a chance to show up. In reality, we probably want to collect considerably more than 20 subgroups before setting control limits for ongoing control of the process.

We assume for this example that the control limits in Figure 14.8 are reasonable. Table 14.4 gives four subsequently observed subgroups of five hole location dimensions. The subgroup means and ranges for these data are plotted with respect to the ongoing control limits in the MINITAB output of Figure 14.9. We see that the R chart remains in control, while the mean for subgroup 24 is above the UCL on the $\bar{x}$ chart. This tells us that an assignable cause has increased the process mean. Therefore, action is needed to reduce the process mean.

TABLE 14.4 Four Subgroups of Five Hole Location Dimensions Observed after Developing Control Limits for Ongoing Process Monitoring

	Measurement (Inches)					Mean,	Range,
Subgroup	1	2	3	4	5	$\bar{x}$	R
21	2.98	3.00	2.97	2.99	2.98	2.984	.03
22	3.02	3.06	3.01	2.97	3.03	3.018	.09
23	3.03	3.08	3.01	2.99	3.02	3.026	.09
24	3.05	3.00	3.11	3.07	3.06	3.058	.11

FIGURE 14.9 MINITAB Output of $\bar{x}$ and R Charts for the Hole Location Data: Ongoing Control

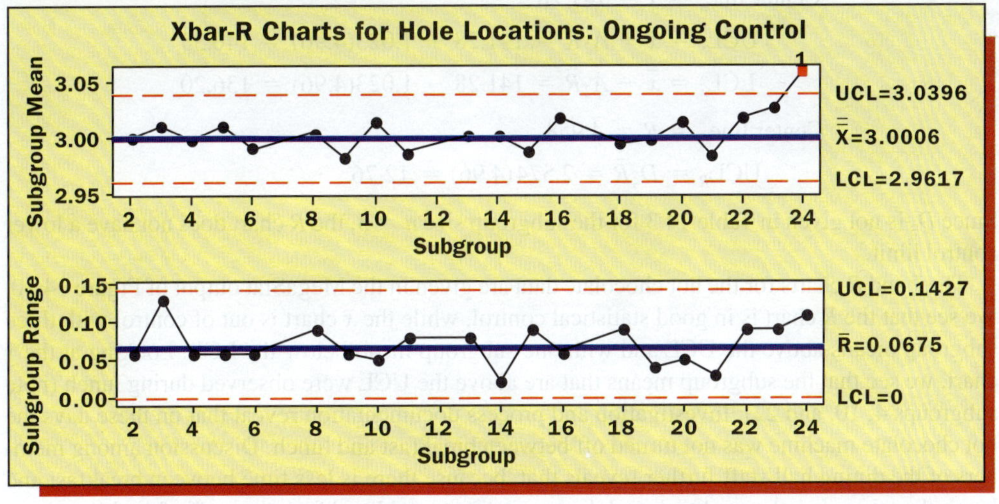

Example 14.6 The Hot Chocolate Temperature Case

C

Consider the hot chocolate data given in Table 14.2 (page 684). In order to set up $\bar{x}$ and R charts for these data, we compute

$$\bar{\bar{x}} = \text{the average of the 24 subgroup means}$$

$$= \frac{140.33 + 139.67 + \cdots + 140.33}{24}$$

$$= 141.28$$

FIGURE 14.10 MegaStat Output of $\bar{x}$ and R Charts for the Hot Chocolate Temperature Data

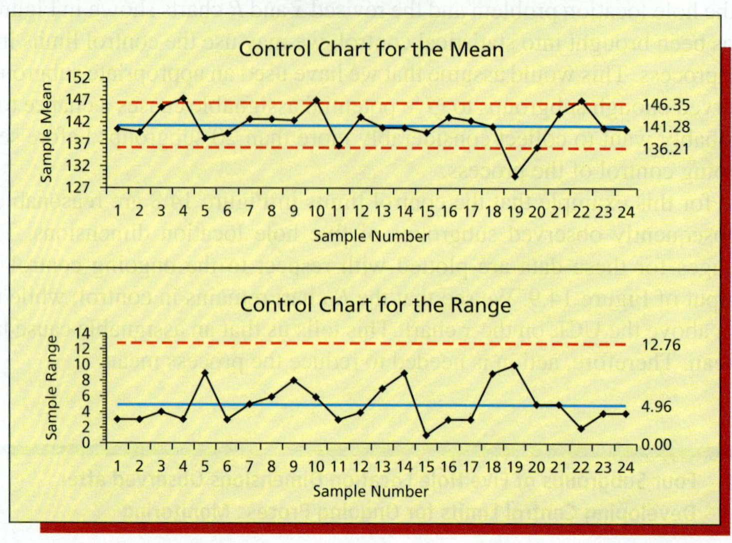

and

$$\bar{R} = \text{the average of the 24 subgroup ranges}$$
$$= \frac{3 + 3 + \cdots + 4}{24} = 4.96$$

Looking at Table 14.3 (page 689), we see that the $\bar{x}$ and R control chart constants for the subgroup size $n = 3$ are $A_2 = 1.023$ and $D_4 = 2.574$. It follows that we calculate center lines and control limits as follows:

$$\text{Center line}_{\bar{x}} = \bar{\bar{x}} = 141.28$$
$$\text{UCL}_{\bar{x}} = \bar{\bar{x}} + A_2\bar{R} = 141.28 + 1.023(4.96) = 146.35$$
$$\text{LCL}_{\bar{x}} = \bar{\bar{x}} - A_2\bar{R} = 141.28 - 1.023(4.96) = 136.20$$
$$\text{Center line}_R = \bar{R} = 4.958$$
$$\text{UCL}_R = D_4\bar{R} = 2.574(4.96) = 12.76$$

Since D_3 is not given in Table 14.3 for the subgroup size $n = 3$, the R chart does not have a lower control limit.

The $\bar{x}$ and R charts for the hot chocolate data are given in the MegaStat output of Figure 14.10. We see that the R chart is in good statistical control, while the $\bar{x}$ chart is out of control with three subgroup means above the UCL and with one subgroup mean below the LCL. Looking at the $\bar{x}$ chart, we see that the subgroup means that are above the UCL were observed during lunch (note subgroups 4, 10, and 22). Investigation and process documentation reveal that on these days the hot chocolate machine was not turned off between breakfast and lunch. Discussion among members of the dining hall staff further reveals that, because there is less time between breakfast and lunch than there is between lunch and dinner or dinner and breakfast, the staff often fails to turn off the hot chocolate machine between breakfast and lunch. Apparently, this is the reason behind the higher hot chocolate temperatures observed during lunch. Investigation also shows that the dining hall staff failed to turn on the hot chocolate machine before breakfast on Thursday (see subgroup 19)—in fact, a student had to ask that the machine be turned on. This caused the subgroup mean for subgroup 19 to be far below the $\bar{x}$ chart LCL. The dining hall staff concludes that the hot chocolate machine needs to be turned off after breakfast and then turned back on 15 minutes before lunch (prior experience suggests that it takes the machine 15 minutes to warm up). The staff also concludes that the machine should be turned on 15 minutes before each meal. In order to ensure that these actions are taken, an automatic timer is purchased to turn on the hot chocolate machine at the appropriate times. This brings the process into statistical control. Figure 14.11 shows $\bar{x}$ and R charts with revised control limits calculated using the subgroups that remain after

FIGURE 14.11 MegaStat Output of Revised $\bar{x}$ and R Charts for the Hot Chocolate Temperature Data. The Process Is Now in Control.

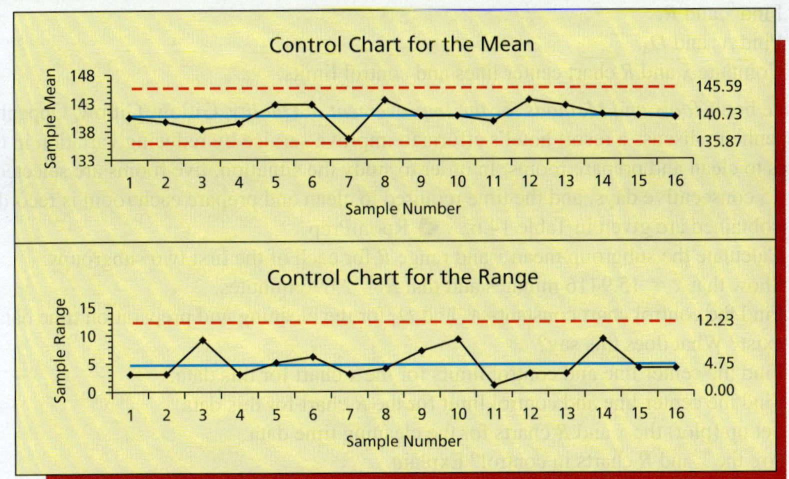

the subgroups for the out-of-control lunches (subgroups 3, 4, 9, 10, 21, and 22) and the out-of-control breakfast (subgroups 19 and 20) are eliminated from the data set. We see that these revised control charts are in statistical control.

Having seen how to interpret $\bar{x}$ and R charts, we are now better prepared to understand why we estimate the process standard deviation σ by $\bar{R}/d_2$. Recall that when μ and σ are known, the $\bar{x}$ chart control limits are $[\mu \pm 3(\sigma/\sqrt{n})]$. The standard deviation σ in these limits is the process standard deviation **when the process is in control.** When this standard deviation is unknown, **we estimate σ as if the process is in control, even though the process might not be in control.** The quantity $\bar{R}/d_2$ is an appropriate estimate of σ because $\bar{R}$ **is the average of individual ranges computed from rational subgroups—subgroups selected so that the chances that important process changes occur within a subgroup are minimized.** Thus each subgroup range, and therefore $\bar{R}/d_2$, estimates the process variation as if the process were in control. Of course, we could also compute the standard deviation of the measurements in each subgroup, and employ the average of the subgroup standard deviations to estimate σ. The key is not whether we use ranges or standard deviations to measure the variation within the subgroups. Rather, the key is that we must calculate a measure of variation for each subgroup and then must average the separate measures of subgroup variation in order to estimate the process variation as if the process is in control. In Exercise 14.16 we show why we do not compute a single value of process variation by combining the subgrouped observations into a single sample, and in Exercise 14.17 we show what can go wrong if we do not select **rational subgroups.**

Exercises for Sections 14.3 and 14.4

CONCEPTS

14.5 Explain (1) the purpose of an $\bar{x}$ chart, (2) the purpose of an R chart, (3) why both charts are needed.

14.6 Explain why the initial control limits calculated for a set of subgrouped data are called "trial control limits."

14.7 Explain why a change in process variability shows up on both the $\bar{x}$ and R charts.

14.8 In each of the following situations, what conclusions (if any) can be made about whether the process mean is changing? Explain your logic.

a R chart out of control.

b R chart in control, $\bar{x}$ chart out of control.

c Both $\bar{x}$ and R charts in control.

METHODS AND APPLICATIONS

14.9 Table 14.5 gives five subgroups of measurement data. Use these data to

a Find $\bar{x}$ and R for each subgroup. Measure1

b Find $\bar{\bar{x}}$ and $\bar{R}$.

c Find A_2 and D_4.

d Compute $\bar{x}$ and R chart center lines and control limits.

14.10 In the book *Tools and Methods for the Improvement of Quality,* Gitlow, Gitlow, Oppenheim, and Oppenheim discuss a resort hotel's efforts to improve service by reducing variation in the time it takes to clean and prepare rooms. In order to study the situation, five rooms are selected each day for 25 consecutive days, and the time required to clean and prepare each room is recorded. The data obtained are given in Table 14.6. RoomPrep

a Calculate the subgroup mean $\bar{x}$ and range R for each of the first two subgroups.

b Show that $\bar{\bar{x}} = 15.9416$ minutes and that $\bar{R} = 2.696$ minutes.

c Find the control chart constants A_2 and D_4 for the cleaning and preparation time data. Does D_3 exist? What does this say?

d Find the center line and control limits for the $\bar{x}$ chart for this data.

e Find the center line and control limit for the R chart for this data.

f Set up (plot) the $\bar{x}$ and R charts for the cleaning time data.

g Are the $\bar{x}$ and R charts in control? Explain.

14.11 A pizza restaurant monitors the size (measured by the diameter) of the 10-inch pizzas that it prepares. Pizza crusts are made from doughs that are prepared and prepackaged in boxes of 15 by a supplier. Doughs are thawed and pressed in a pressing machine. The toppings are added, and the pizzas are baked. The wetness of the doughs varies from box to box, and if the dough is too wet or greasy, it is difficult to press, resulting in a crust that is too small. The first shift of workers begins work at 4 P.M., and a new shift takes over at 9 P.M. and works until closing. The pressing machine is readjusted at the beginning of each shift.

TABLE 14.5 Five Subgroups of Measurement Data Measure1

Subgroup	Measurement 1	2	3
1	4	5	6
2	9	7	5
3	4	8	6
4	2	4	3
5	5	6	10

TABLE 14.6 25 Daily Samples of Five Room Cleaning and Preparation Times RoomPrep

Sample (Day)	Cleaning and Preparation Time (Minutes) 1	2	3	4	5	Mean, $\bar{x}$	Range, R
1	15.6	14.3	17.7	14.3	15.0	—	—
2	15.0	14.8	16.8	16.9	17.4	—	—
3	16.4	15.1	15.7	17.3	16.6	16.22	2.2
4	14.2	14.8	17.3	15.0	16.4	15.54	3.1
5	16.4	16.3	17.6	17.9	14.9	16.62	3.0
6	14.9	17.2	17.2	15.3	14.1	15.74	3.1
7	17.9	17.9	14.7	17.0	14.5	16.40	3.4
8	14.0	17.7	16.9	14.0	14.9	15.50	3.7
9	17.6	16.5	15.3	14.5	15.1	15.80	3.1
10	14.6	14.0	14.7	16.9	14.2	14.88	2.9
11	14.6	15.5	15.9	14.8	14.2	15.00	1.7
12	15.3	15.3	15.9	15.0	17.8	15.86	2.8
13	17.4	14.9	17.7	16.6	14.7	16.26	3.0
14	15.3	16.9	17.9	17.2	17.5	16.96	2.6
15	14.8	15.1	16.6	16.3	14.5	15.46	2.1
16	16.1	14.6	17.5	16.9	17.7	16.56	3.1
17	14.2	14.7	15.3	15.7	14.3	14.84	1.5
18	14.6	17.2	16.0	16.7	16.3	16.16	2.6
19	15.9	16.5	16.1	15.0	17.8	16.26	2.8
20	16.2	14.8	14.8	15.0	15.3	15.22	1.4
21	16.3	15.3	14.0	17.4	14.5	15.50	3.4
22	15.0	17.6	14.5	17.5	17.8	16.48	3.3
23	16.4	15.9	16.7	15.7	16.9	16.32	1.2
24	16.6	15.1	14.1	17.4	17.8	16.20	3.7
25	17.0	17.5	17.4	16.2	17.9	17.20	1.7

Source: H. Gitlow, S. Gitlow, A. Oppenheim, and R. Oppenheim, *Tools and Methods for the Improvement of Quality*, pp. 333–34.

The restaurant takes subgroups of five consecutive pizzas prepared at the beginning of each hour from opening to closing on a particular day. The diameter of each baked pizza in the subgroups is measured, and the pizza crust diameters obtained are given here: PizzaDiam

Subgroup	Time	Pizza Crust Diameter (Inches) 1	2	3	4	5	Mean, $\bar{x}$	Range, R
1	4 P.M.	9.8	9.0	9.0	9.2	9.2	9.24	0.8
2	5 P.M.	9.5	10.3	10.2	10.0	10.0	10.00	0.8
3	6 P.M.	10.5	10.3	9.8	10.0	10.3	10.18	0.7
4	7 P.M.	10.7	9.5	9.8	10.0	10.0	10.00	1.2
5	8 P.M.	10.0	10.5	10.0	10.5	10.5	10.30	0.5
6	9 P.M.	10.0	9.0	9.0	9.2	9.3	9.30	1.0
7	10 P.M.	11.0	10.0	10.3	10.3	10.0	10.32	1.0
8	11 P.M.	10.0	10.2	10.1	10.3	11.0	10.32	1.0
9	12 A.M.	10.0	10.4	10.4	10.5	10.0	10.26	0.5
10	1 A.M.	11.0	10.5	10.1	10.2	10.2	10.40	0.9

New shift at 9 P.M., pressing machine adjusted at the start of each shift (4 P.M. and 9 P.M.).

Use the pizza crust diameter data to do the following:

a Show that $\bar{\bar{x}} = 10.032$ and $\bar{R} = .84$.

b Find the center lines and control limits for the $\bar{x}$ and R charts for the pizza crust data.

c Set up the $\bar{x}$ and R charts for the pizza crust data.

d Is the R chart for the pizza crust data in statistical control? Explain.

e Is the $\bar{x}$ chart for the pizza crust data in statistical control? If not, use the $\bar{x}$ chart and the information given with the data to try to identify any assignable causes that might exist.

f Suppose that, based on the $\bar{x}$ chart, the manager of the restaurant decides that the employees do not know how to properly adjust the dough pressing machine. Because of this, the manager thoroughly trains the employees in the use of this equipment. Because an assignable cause (incorrect adjustment of the pressing machine) has been found and eliminated, we can remove the subgroups affected by this unusual process variation from the data set. We therefore drop subgroups 1 and 6 from the data. Use the remaining eight subgroups to show that we obtain revised center lines of $\bar{\bar{x}} = 10.2225$ and $\bar{R} = .825$.

g Use the revised values of $\bar{\bar{x}}$ and $\bar{R}$ to compute revised $\bar{x}$ and R chart control limits for the pizza crust diameter data. Set up $\bar{x}$ and R charts using these revised limits. Be sure to omit subgroup means and ranges for subgroups 1 and 6 when setting up these charts.

h Has removing the assignable cause brought the process into statistical control? Explain.

14.12 A chemical company has collected 15 daily subgroups of measurements of an important chemical property called "acid value" for one of its products. Each subgroup consists of six acid value readings: a single reading was taken every four hours during the day, and the readings for a day are taken as a subgroup. The 15 daily subgroups are given in Table 14.7. AcidVal

TABLE 14.7 15 Subgroups of Acid Value Measurements for a Chemical Process AcidVal

Subgroup (Day)	Acid Value Measurements 1	2	3	4	5	6	Mean, $\bar{x}$	Range, R
1	202.1	201.2	196.2	201.6	201.6	201.6	200.717	5.9
2	201.6	201.2	201.2	200.8	201.2	201.2	201.2	.8
3	200.4	200.0	200.8	200.1	198.7	200.4	200.067	2.1
4	200.4	200.4	200.4	200.8	200.4	201.2	200.6	.8
5	200.0	201.6	202.9	201.6	201.2	201.2	201.417	2.9
6	200.0	200.4	200.8	200.8	199.5	200.4	200.317	1.3
7	200.4	200.0	200.4	200.4	200.4	200.4	200.333	.4
8	200.0	200.8	200.0	200.4	200.0	200.0	200.2	.8
9	199.1	200.4	200.4	200.4	200.4	200.0	200.117	1.3
10	201.2	195.3	197.4	201.2	200.0	201.6	199.45	6.3
11	201.6	200.8	200.4	201.2	200.4	199.5	200.65	2.1
12	200.0	199.5	200.4	200.8	200.4	200.8	200.317	1.3
13	201.6	201.6	200.8	201.2	200.8	200.8	201.133	.8
14	200.4	200.0	202.5	200.4	201.2	201.2	200.95	2.5
15	200.0	200.0	201.6	200.8	200.4	200.0	200.467	1.6

a Show that for these data $\bar{\bar{x}} = 200.529$ and $\bar{R} = 2.06$.

b Set up $\bar{x}$ and R charts for the acid value data. Are these charts in statistical control?

c On the basis of these charts, is it possible to draw proper conclusions about whether the mean acid value is changing? Explain why or why not.

d Suppose that investigation reveals that the out-of-control points on the R chart (the ranges for subgroups 1 and 10) were caused by an equipment malfunction that can be remedied by redesigning a mechanical part. Since the assignable cause that is responsible for the large ranges for subgroups 1 and 10 has been found and eliminated, we can remove subgroups 1 and 10 from the data set. Show that using the remaining 13 subgroups gives revised center lines of $\bar{\bar{x}} = 200.5975$ and $\bar{R} = 1.4385$.

e Use the revised values of $\bar{\bar{x}}$ and $\bar{R}$ to compute revised $\bar{x}$ and R chart control limits for the acid value data. Set up the revised $\bar{x}$ and R charts, making sure to omit subgroup means and ranges for subgroups 1 and 10.

f Are the revised $\bar{x}$ and R charts for the remaining 13 subgroups in statistical control? Explain. What does this result tell us to do?

14.13 The data in Table 14.8 consist of 30 subgroups of measurements that specify the location of a "tube hole" in an air conditioner compressor shell. Each subgroup contains the tube hole dimension measurement for five consecutive compressor shells selected from the production line. The first 15 subgroups were observed on March 21, and the second 15 subgroups were observed on March 22. As indicated in Table 14.8, the die press used in the hole punching operation was changed after subgroup 5 was observed, and a die repair was made after subgroup 25 was observed. TubeHole

a Show that for the first 15 subgroups (observed on March 21) we have $\bar{\bar{x}} = 15.8$ and $\bar{R} = 6.1333$.

b Set up $\bar{x}$ and R charts for the 15 subgroups that were observed on March 21 (do not use any of the March 22 data). Do these $\bar{x}$ and R charts show statistical control?

TABLE 14.8 **30 Subgroups of Tube Hole Location Dimensions for Air Conditioner Compressor Shells** TubeHole

	Subgroup	Tube Hole Location Measurements 1	2	3	4	5	Mean, $\bar{x}$	Range, R
March 21	1	15	15	16	15	13	14.8	3
	2	15	20	15	17	19	17.2	5
	3	19	16	15	18	17	17.0	4
	4	17	20	18	18	15	17.6	5
Changed to →	5	20	16	15	9	16	15.2	11
Die Press	6	13	16	20	17	22	17.6	9
#628 Here	7	15	13	9	17	13	13.4	8
	8	13	14	18	17	14	15.2	5
	9	19	12	16	13	15	15.0	7
	10	19	14	12	13	13	14.2	7
	11	17	22	15	14	16	16.8	8
	12	19	17	17	15	9	15.4	10
	13	17	13	14	17	15	15.2	4
	14	15	17	17	17	16	16.4	2
	15	14	16	18	16	16	16.0	4
March 22	16	18	10	14	16	18	15.2	8
	17	12	16	15	18	17	15.6	6
	18	15	19	19	17	17	17.4	4
	19	21	16	17	19	17	18.0	5
	20	20	22	25	18	19	20.8	7
	21	18	18	17	17	19	17.8	2
	22	19	20	19	18	18	18.8	2
	23	13	16	15	17	16	15.4	4
	24	16	15	16	17	17	16.2	2
Die Repair →	25	17	20	13	16	16	16.4	7
Made Here	26	25	23	21	24	21	22.8	4
	27	22	25	21	22	25	23.0	4
	28	26	29	25	26	23	25.8	6
	29	24	25	22	22	27	24.0	5
	30	26	21	27	25	26	25.0	6

c Using the control limits you computed by using the 15 subgroups observed on March 21, set up $\bar{x}$ and R charts for all 30 subgroups. That is, add the subgroup means and ranges for March 22 to your $\bar{x}$ and R charts, but use the limits you computed from the March 21 data.

d Do the $\bar{x}$ and R charts obtained in part *c* show statistical control? Explain.

e Does it appear that changing to die press #628 is an assignable cause? Explain. (Note that the die press is the machine that is used to punch the tube hole.)

f Does it appear that making a die repair is an assignable cause? Explain.

14.14 A company packages a bulk product in bags with a 50-pound label weight. During a typical day's operation of the fill process, 22 subgroups of five bag fills are observed. Using the observed data, $\bar{\bar{x}}$ and $\bar{R}$ are calculated to be 52.9364 pounds and 1.6818 pounds, respectively. When the 22 $\bar{x}$'s and 22 R's are plotted with respect to the appropriate control limits, the first 6 subgroups are found to be out of control. This is traced to a mechanical start-up problem, which is remedied. Using the remaining 16 subgroups, $\bar{\bar{x}}$ and $\bar{R}$ are calculated to be 52.5875 pounds and 1.2937 pounds, respectively.

a Calculate appropriate revised $\bar{x}$ and R chart control limits.

b When the remaining 16 $\bar{x}$'s and 16 R's are plotted with respect to the appropriate revised control limits, they are found to be within these limits. What does this imply?

14.15 In the book *Tools and Methods for the Improvement of Quality,* Gitlow, Gitlow, Oppenheim, and Oppenheim discuss an example of using $\bar{x}$ and R charts to study tuning knob diameters. In their problem description the authors say this:

> A manufacturer of high-end audio components buys metal tuning knobs to be used in the assembly of its products. The knobs are produced automatically by a subcontractor using a single machine that is supposed to produce them with a constant diameter. Nevertheless, because of persistent final assembly problems with the knobs, management has decided to examine this process output by requesting that the subcontractor keep an *x*-bar and *R* chart for knob diameter.

On a particular day the subcontractor selects four knobs every half hour and carefully measures their diameters. Twenty-five subgroups are obtained, and these subgroups (along with their subgroup means and ranges) are given in Table 14.9. KnobDiam

a For these data show that $\bar{\bar{x}} = 841.45$ and $\bar{R} = 5.16$. Then use these values to calculate control limits and to set up $\bar{x}$ and R charts for the 25 subgroups of tuning knob diameters. Do these $\bar{x}$ and R charts indicate the existence of any assignable causes? Explain.

b An investigation is carried out to find out what caused the large range for subgroup 23. The investigation reveals that a water pipe burst at 7:25 P.M. and that the mishap resulted in water leaking under the machinery used in the tuning knob production process. The resulting disruption is the apparent cause for the out-of-control range for subgroup 23. The water pipe is mended, and since this fix is reasonably permanent, we are justified in removing subgroup 23 from the data set. Using the remaining 24 subgroups, show that revised center lines are $\bar{\bar{x}} = 841.40$ and $\bar{R} = 4.88$.

c Use the revised values of $\bar{\bar{x}}$ and $\bar{R}$ to set up revised $\bar{x}$ and R charts for the remaining 24 subgroups of diameters. Be sure to omit the mean and range for subgroup 23.

d Looking at the revised R chart, is this chart now in statistical control? What does your answer say about whether we can use the $\bar{x}$ chart to decide if the process mean is changing?

e Looking at the revised $\bar{x}$ chart, is this chart in statistical control? What does your answer tell us about the process mean?

f An investigation is now undertaken to find the cause of the very high $\bar{x}$ values for subgroups 10, 11, 12, and 13. We again quote Gitlow, Gitlow, Oppenheim, and Oppenheim:

> The investigation leads to the discovery that . . . a keyway wedge had cracked and needed to be replaced on the machine. The mechanic who normally makes this repair was out to lunch, so the machine operator made the repair. This individual had not been properly trained for the repair; for this reason, the wedge was not properly aligned in the keyway, and the subsequent points were out of control. Both the operator and the mechanic agree that the need for this repair was not unusual. To correct this problem it is decided to train the machine operator and provide the appropriate tools for making this repair in the mechanic's absence. Furthermore, the maintenance and engineering staffs agree to search for a replacement part for the wedge that will not be so prone to cracking.

Since the assignable causes responsible for the very high $\bar{x}$ values for subgroups 10, 11, 12, and 13 have been found and eliminated, we remove these subgroups from the data set. Show that removing subgroups 10, 11, 12, and 13 (in addition to the previously removed subgroup 23) results in the revised center lines $\bar{\bar{x}} = 840.46$ and $\bar{R} = 5.25$. Then use these revised values to set up revised $\bar{x}$ and R charts for the remaining 20 subgroups.

TABLE 14.9 25 Subgroups of Tuning Knob Diameters KnobDiam

Time	Subgroup Number	Diameter Measurement 1	2	3	4	Average, $\bar{x}$	Range, R
8:30 A.M.	1	836	846	840	839	840.25	10
9:00	2	842	836	839	837	838.50	6
9:30	3	839	841	839	844	840.75	5
10:00	4	840	836	837	839	838.00	4
10:30	5	838	844	838	842	840.50	6
11:00	6	838	842	837	843	840.00	6
11:30	7	842	839	840	842	840.75	3
12:00	8	840	842	844	836	840.50	8
12:30 P.M.	9	842	841	837	837	839.25	5
1:00	10	846	846	846	845	845.75	1
1:30	11	849	846	848	844	846.75	5
2:00	12	845	844	848	846	845.75	4
2:30	13	847	845	846	846	846.00	2
3:00	14	839	840	841	838	839.50	3
3:30	15	840	839	839	840	839.50	1
4:00	16	842	839	841	837	839.75	5
4:30	17	841	845	839	839	841.00	6
5:00	18	841	841	836	843	840.25	7
5:30	19	845	842	837	840	841.00	8
6:00	20	839	841	842	840	840.50	3
6:30	21	840	840	842	836	839.50	6
7:00	22	844	845	841	843	843.25	4
7:30	23	848	843	844	836	842.75	12
8:00	24	840	844	841	845	842.50	5
8:30	25	843	845	846	842	844.00	4

Source: H. Gitlow, S. Gitlow, A. Oppenheim, and R. Oppenheim, *Tools and Methods for the Improvement of Quality*, p. 301.

g Are all of the subgroup means and ranges for these newly revised $\bar{x}$ and R charts inside their respective control limits?

Note: While we might wish to use these newest control limits for ongoing process monitoring, the last few plot points on the chart might suggest future trouble. We will explain indications such as this in the next section, which discusses *pattern analysis*.

14.16 In an article titled "Charts Done Right" in the May 1994 issue of *Quality Progress*, Donald J. Wheeler illustrates why $\bar{x}$ chart control limits are calculated by using the formula $[\bar{\bar{x}} \pm A_2\bar{R}]$ rather than by using several (incorrect) formulas that employ s, the sample standard deviation of all the observed individual measurements. In order to demonstrate his point, Wheeler presents the three subgroups of data in Table 14.10. Measure2

a For the three subgroups in Table 14.10, calculate $\bar{x}$ and R. Then use these values and the (correct) formula $[\bar{\bar{x}} \pm A_2\bar{R}]$ to compute the control limits for an $\bar{x}$ chart for these data.

b Plot the three subgroup means on an $\bar{x}$ chart that employs the control limits you calculated in part *a*. Is the $\bar{x}$ chart in control or out of control?

TABLE 14.10 Three Subgroups of Data Presented in the Article "Charts Done Right" Measure2

Subgroup	Measurement 1	2	3	4	5	6	7	8	Mean, $\bar{x}$	Range, R
1	4	5	5	4	8	4	3	7	5	5
2	0	2	1	5	3	2	0	3	2	5
3	6	9	9	7	8	7	9	9	8	3

Source: D. J. Wheeler, "Charts Done Right," *Quality Progress* (May 1994), pp. 65–68.

c Show that when we calculate s, the sample standard deviation for the 24 individual measurements in Table 14.10, we obtain $s = 2.904$. Then use the (incorrect) formula $[\bar{\bar{x}} \pm 3(s/\sqrt{n})]$ to compute control limits for an $\bar{x}$ chart for this data.

d Plot the three subgroup means on an $\bar{x}$ chart that employs the control limits you calculated in part *c*. Is the $\bar{x}$ chart in control or out of control?

e Which set of control limits—those calculated using $\bar{R}$ or those calculated using s—are narrower?

f As Wheeler states in his article, "the objective is to detect a lack of control when it exists." This being the case, explain why $\bar{x}$ chart control limits calculated by the formula $[\bar{\bar{x}} \pm A_2\bar{R}]$ are preferred over control limits calculated using s.

14.17 A filling process is supposed to fill jars with 16 ounces of grape jelly. A subgroup of six filled jars is taken every hour from the process. In order to obtain an hourly subgroup, jars are selected at 10-minute intervals—on the hour and 10 minutes after, 20 minutes after, 30 minutes after, 40 minutes after, and 50 minutes after the hour. The fill of each jar is measured, and these six measurements form a subgroup. In order to simplify the calculations, we consider two such subgroups:

Fill Measurements JarFill

Subgroup	On The Hour	10 Minutes After	20 Minutes After	30 Minutes After	40 Minutes After	50 Minutes After	Mean, $\bar{x}$	Range, R
1	15.88	15.90	15.93	16.10	16.09	16.13		
2	15.87	15.91	15.89	16.07	16.10	16.11		

a Calculate $\bar{x}$ and R for each subgroup and then compute the control limits and center lines for $\bar{x}$ and R charts for these two subgroups.

b Do the two R values that you calculated indicate that the R chart is in control? Explain.

c Do the two $\bar{x}$ values that you calculated indicate that the $\bar{x}$ chart is in control? Explain.

d If we look at the individual jar fills in subgroups 1 and 2, we see evidence that the subgroups were not taken frequently enough. Explain why this is true.

e Re-subgroup the data into a larger number of subgroups (subgroups that are more rational). When doing this, keep in mind that we still wish to plot the subgroups so that the data are in time order.

f Calculate new subgroup means and ranges for the new subgroups you obtained in part *e*. Then calculate control limits for the new $\bar{x}$ and R charts for the re-subgrouped data.

g Are the new R and $\bar{x}$ charts in control? What do you conclude?

14.5 Pattern Analysis

When we observe a plot point outside the control limits on a control chart, we have strong evidence that an assignable cause exists. In addition, several other data patterns indicate the presence of assignable causes. Precise description of these patterns is often made easier by **dividing the control band into zones—designated *A*, *B*, and *C*.** Zone boundaries are set at points that are one and two standard deviations (of the plotted statistic) on either side of the center line. We obtain six zones—each zone being one standard deviation wide—with three zones on each side of the center line. The zones that stretch one standard deviation above and below the center line are designated as ***C* zones.** The zones that extend from one to two standard deviations away from the center line are designated as ***B* zones.** The zones that extend from two to three standard deviations away from the center line are designated as ***A* zones.** Figure 14.12(a) illustrates a control chart with the six zones, and Figure 14.12(b) shows how the zone boundaries for an $\bar{x}$ chart and an R chart are calculated. Part (b) of this figure also shows the values of the zone boundaries for the hole location $\bar{x}$ and R charts shown in Figure 14.9 (page 695). In calculating these boundaries, we use $\bar{\bar{x}} = 3.0006$ and $\bar{R} = .0675$, which we computed from subgroups 1 through 20 with subgroups 1, 7, 12, and 17 removed from the data set; that is, we are using $\bar{\bar{x}}$ and $\bar{R}$ when the process is in control. For example, the upper A–B boundary for the $\bar{x}$ chart has been calculated as follows:

CHAPTER 21

$$\bar{\bar{x}} + \frac{2}{3}(A_2\bar{R}) = 3.0006 + \frac{2}{3}(.577(.0675)) = 3.0266$$

FIGURE 14.12 Zone Boundaries

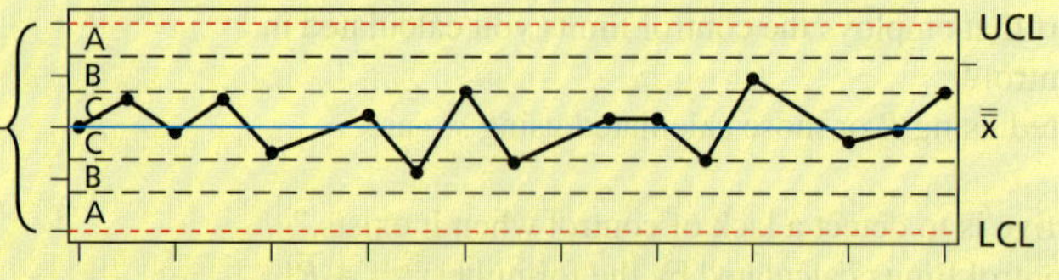

A, B, C, C, B, A — UCL, $\bar{\bar{x}}$, LCL

(a) A control chart with *A*, *B*, and *C* zones

Zone	Zone Boundaries	$\bar{x}$ Chart	*R* Chart
(.135%)			
	Upper Control Limit:	$\bar{\bar{x}} + A_2\bar{R} = 3.0396$	$D_4\bar{R} = .1427$
Zone *A* (2.145%)			
	Upper *A–B* Boundary:	$\bar{\bar{x}} + \frac{2}{3}(A_2\bar{R}) = 3.0266$	$\bar{R} + \frac{2}{3}(D_4\bar{R} - \bar{R}) = .1176$
Zone *B* (13.59%)			
	Upper *B–C* Boundary:	$\bar{\bar{x}} + \frac{1}{3}(A_2\bar{R}) = 3.0136$	$\bar{R} + \frac{1}{3}(D_4\bar{R} - \bar{R}) = .0926$
Zone *C* (34.13%)			
	Center Line:	$\bar{\bar{x}} = 3.0006$	$\bar{R} = .0675$
Zone *C* (34.13%)			
	Lower *B–C* Boundary:*	$\bar{\bar{x}} - \frac{1}{3}(A_2\bar{R}) = 2.9876$	$\bar{R} - \frac{1}{3}(D_4\bar{R} - \bar{R}) = .0424$
Zone *B* (13.59%)			
	Lower *A–B* Boundary:*	$\bar{\bar{x}} - \frac{2}{3}(A_2\bar{R})$ 2.9746	$\bar{R} - \frac{2}{3}(D_4\bar{R} - \bar{R}) = .0174$
Zone *A* (2.145%)			
	Lower Control Limit:*	$\bar{\bar{x}} - A_2\bar{R} = 2.9617$	$D_3\bar{R}$ = does not exist
(.135%)			

(b) Calculating zone boundaries for $\bar{x}$ and *R* charts in the hole location case

*When the *R* chart does not have a lower control limit ($n < 7$), the lower *B–C* and *A–B* boundaries should still be computed as long as they are 0 or positive.

Finally, Figure 14.12(b) shows (based on a normal distribution of plot points) the percentages of points that we would expect to observe in each zone when the process is in statistical control. For instance, we would expect to observe 34.13 percent of the plot points in the upper portion of zone *C*.

For an $\bar{x}$ chart, if the distribution of process measurements is reasonably normal, then the distribution of subgroup means will be approximately normal, and the percentages shown in Figure 14.12 apply. That is, the plotted subgroup means for an "in control" $\bar{x}$ chart should look as if they have been randomly selected from a normal distribution. Any distribution of plot points that looks very different from the expected percentages will suggest the existence of an assignable cause.

FIGURE 14.13 A Plot Point outside the Control Limits

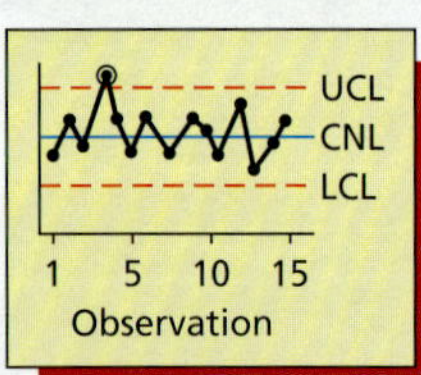

Various companies (for example, Western Electric [AT&T] and Ford Motor Company) have established sets of rules for identifying assignable causes; use of such rules is called **pattern analysis.** We now summarize some commonly accepted rules. Note that many of these rules are illustrated in Figures 14.13, 14.14, 14.15, and 14.16, which show several common out-of-control patterns.

FIGURE 14.14 Two Out of Three Consecutive Plot Points in Zone *A* (or beyond)

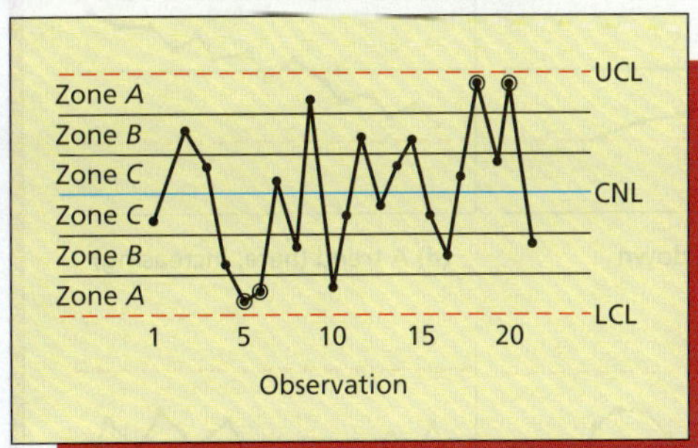

FIGURE 14.15 Four Out of Five Consecutive Plot Points in Zone *B* (or beyond)

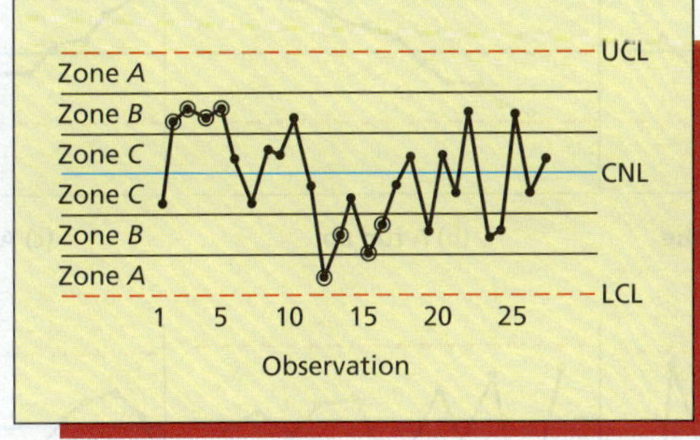

Source: H. Gitlow, S. Gitlow, A. Oppenheim, and R. Oppenheim, *Tools and Methods for the Improvement of Quality*, pp. 191–93, 209–11. Copyright © 1989. Reprinted by permission of McGraw-Hill Companies, Inc.

Pattern Analysis for $\bar{x}$ and *R* Charts

If one or more of the following conditions exist, it is reasonable to conclude that one or more assignable causes are present:

1 One plot point beyond zone *A* (that is, outside the three standard deviation control limits)—see Figure 14.13.

2 Two out of three consecutive plot points in zone *A* (or beyond) on one side of the center line of the control chart. Sometimes a zone boundary that separates zones *A* and *B* is called a **two standard deviation warning limit.** It can be shown that, if the process is in control, then the likelihood of observing two out of three plot points beyond this warning limit (even when no points are outside the control limits) is very small. Therefore, such a pattern signals an assignable cause. Figure 14.14 illustrates this pattern. Specifically, note that plot points 5 and 6 are two consecutive plot points in zone *A* and that plot points 19 and 21 are two out of three consecutive plot points in zone *A*.

3 Four out of five consecutive plot points in zone *B* (or beyond) on one side of the center line of the control chart. Figure 14.15 illustrates this pattern. Specifically, note that plot points 2, 3, 4, and 5 are four consecutive plot points in zone *B* and that plot points 12, 13, 15, and 16 are four out of five consecutive plot points in zone *B* (or beyond).

4 **A run of at least eight plot points.** Here we define a **run** to be **a sequence of plot points of the same type.** For example, we can have a run of points on one side of (above or below) the center line. Such a run is illustrated in part (a) of Figure 14.16, which shows a run above the center line. We might also observe a run of steadily increasing plot points (a **run up**) or a run of steadily decreasing plot points (a **run down**). These patterns are illustrated in parts (b) and (c) of Figure 14.16. Any of the above types of runs consisting of at least eight points is an out-of-control signal.

5 A **nonrandom pattern** of plot points. Such a pattern might be an **increasing** or **decreasing trend, a fanning-out or funneling-in pattern, a cycle, an alternating pattern,** or any other pattern that is very inconsistent with the percentages given in Figure 14.12 (see parts (d) through (h) of Figure 14.16).

If none of the patterns or conditions in 1 through 5 exists, then the process shows **good statistical control**—or is said to be **"in control." A process that is in control should not be tampered with.** On the other hand, **if one or more of the patterns in 1 through 5 exist, action must be taken to find the cause of the out-of-control pattern(s)** (which should be eliminated if the assignable cause is undesirable).

It is tempting to use many rules to decide when an assignable cause exists. However, if we use too many rules we can end up with an unacceptably high chance of a **false out-of-control signal** (that is, an out-of-control signal when there is no assignable cause present). For most control charts, the use of the rules just described will yield an overall probability of a false signal in the range of 1 to 2 percent.

FIGURE 14.16 Other Out-of-Control Patterns

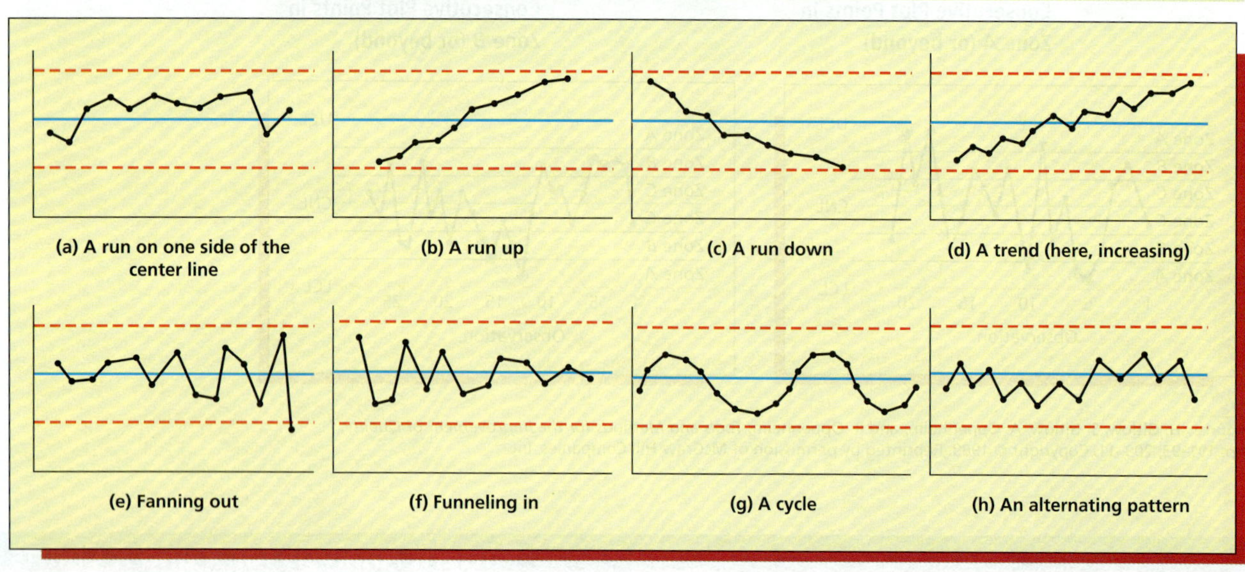

Example 14.7 The Hole Location Case

Figure 14.17 shows ongoing $\bar{x}$ and R charts for the hole location problem. Here the $\bar{x}$ chart includes zone boundaries with zones A, B, and C labeled. Notice that the first out-of-control condition (one plot point beyond zone A) exists. Looking at the last five plot points on the $\bar{x}$ chart, we see that the third out-of-control condition (four out of five consecutive plot points in zone B or beyond) also exists.

FIGURE 14.17 Ongoing $\bar{x}$ and R Charts for the Hole Location Data—Zones A, B, and C Included

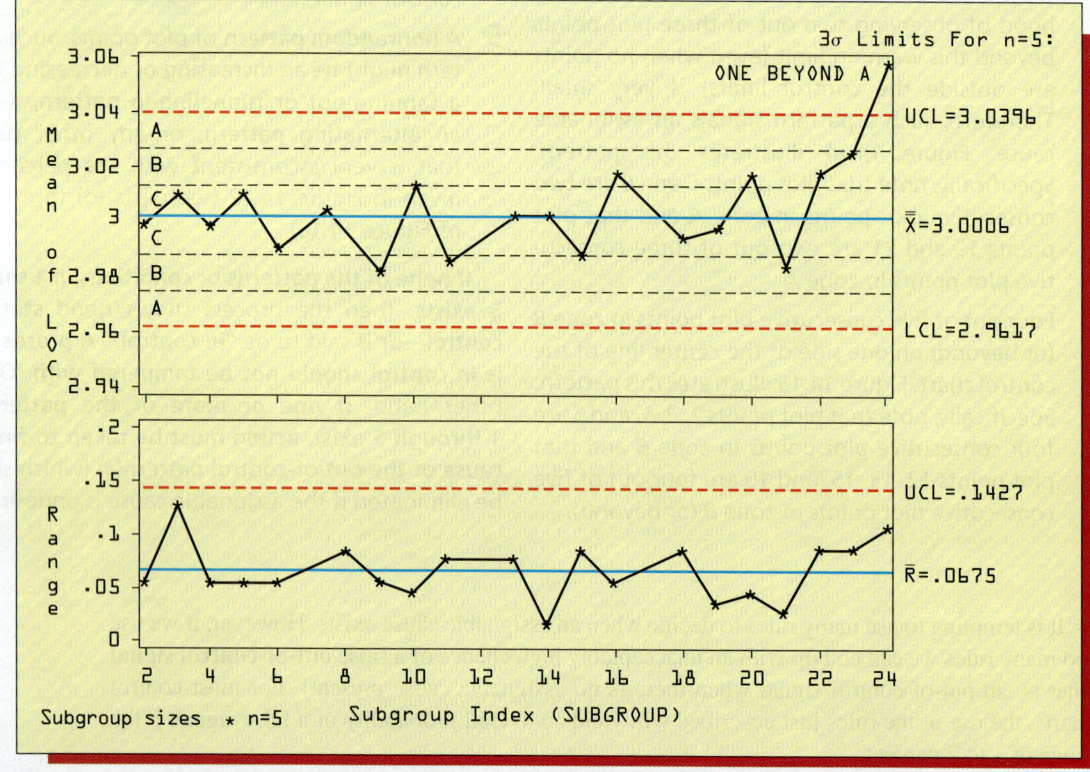

Exercises for Section 14.5

CONCEPTS

14.18 When a process is in statistical control:

a What percentage of the plot points on an $\bar{x}$ chart will be found in the C zones (that is, in the middle 1/3 of the chart's "control band")?

b What percentage of the plot points on an $\bar{x}$ chart will be found in either the C zones or the B zones (that is, in the middle 2/3 of the chart's "control band")?

c What percentage of the plot points on an $\bar{x}$ chart will be found in the C zones, the B zones, or the A zones (that is, in the chart's "control band")?

14.19 For each of the following process changes, write a paragraph that summarizes how the process change would show up on an $\bar{x}$ chart.

a A sudden increase in the process mean.

b A sudden decrease in the process mean.

c A steady increase in the process mean.

d A steady decrease in the process mean.

14.20 Explain what we mean by a "false out-of-control signal."

METHODS AND APPLICATIONS

14.21 In the June 1991 issue of *Quality Progress,* Gunter presents several control charts. Four of these charts are reproduced in Figure 14.18. For each chart, find any evidence of a lack of statistical control (that is, for each chart identify any evidence of the existence of one or more assignable causes). In each case, if such evidence exists, clearly explain why the plot points indicate that the process is not in control.

14.22 In the book *Tools and Methods for the Improvement of Quality,* Gitlow, Gitlow, Oppenheim, and Oppenheim present several control charts in a discussion and exercises dealing with pattern analysis. These control charts, which include appropriate A, B, and C zones, are reproduced in Figure 14.19. For each chart, identify any evidence of a lack of statistical control (that is, for each chart identify any evidence suggesting the existence of one or more assignable causes). In each case, if such evidence exists, clearly explain why the plot points indicate that the process is not in control.

FIGURE 14.18 Charts for Exercise 14.21

(a)

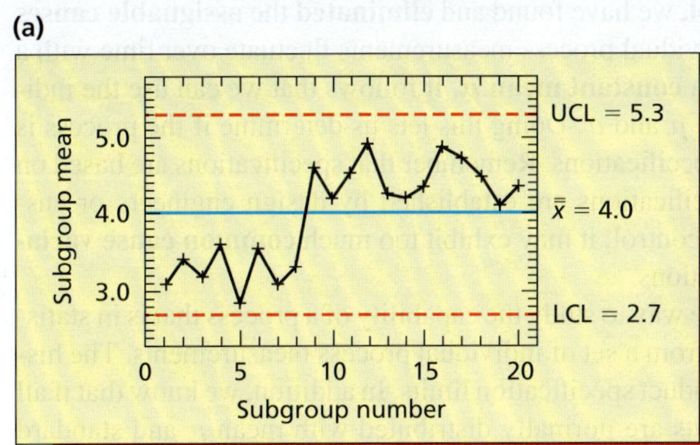

(b)

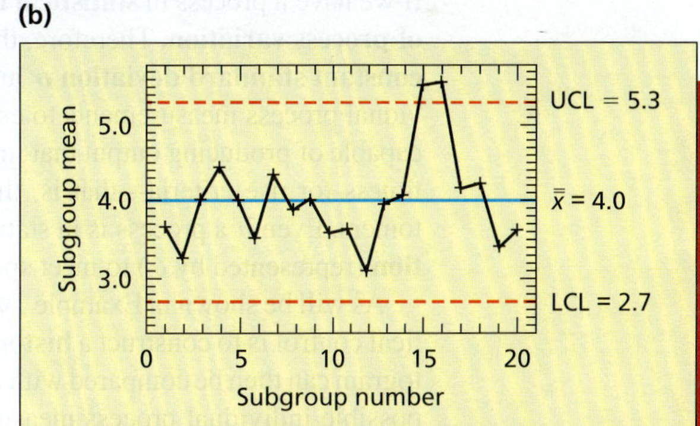

(c)

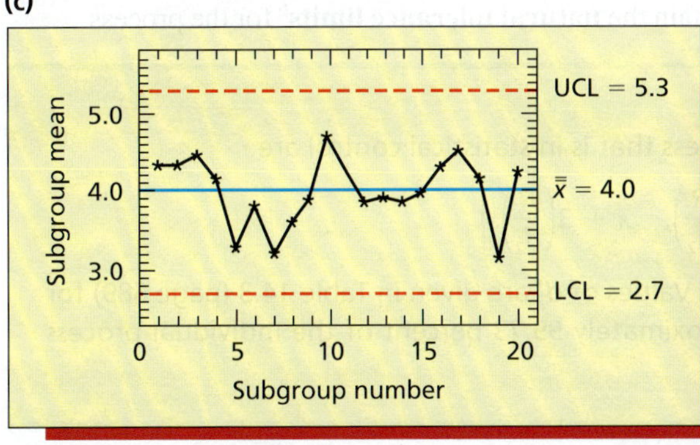

(d)

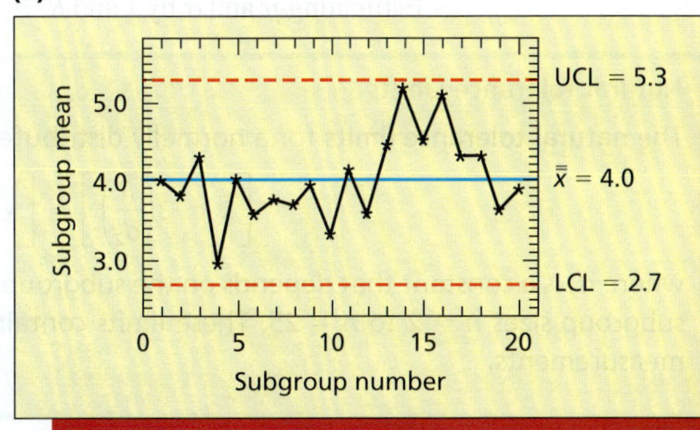

Source: B. Gunter, "Process Capability Studies Part 3: The Tale of the Charts," *Quality Progress* (June 1991), pp. 77–82.

FIGURE 14.19 Charts for Exercise 14.22

(a)

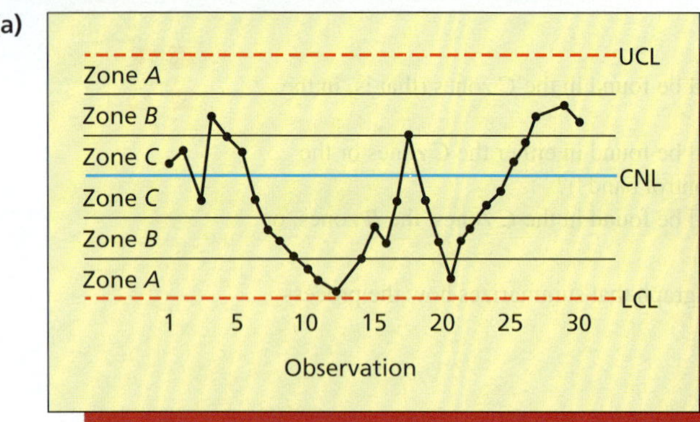

(b)

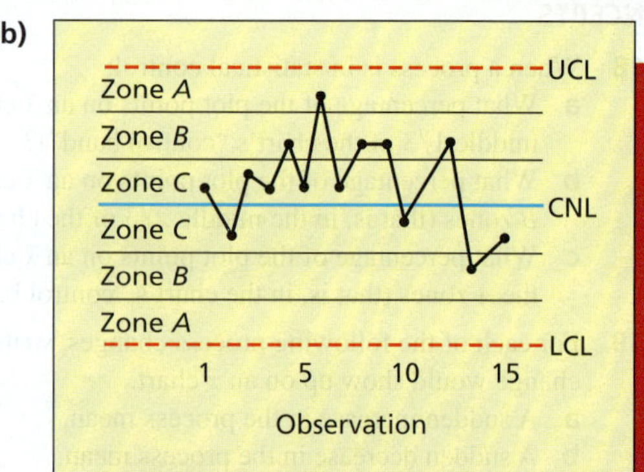

Source: H. Gitlow, S. Gitlow, A. Oppenheim, and R. Oppenheim, *Tools and Methods for the Improvement of Quality*, pp. 191–93, 209–11. Copyright © 1989. Reprinted by permission of McGraw-Hill Companies, Inc.

14.23 Consider the tuning knob diameter data given in Table 14.9 (page 702). Recalling that the subgroup size is $n = 4$ and that $\bar{\bar{x}} = 841.45$ and $\bar{R} = 5.16$ for these data, KnobDiam

a Calculate all of the zone boundaries for the $\bar{x}$ chart.

b Calculate all of the R chart zone boundaries that are either 0 or positive.

14.24 Given what you now know about pattern analysis, examine each of the following $\bar{x}$ and R charts for evidence of lack of statistical control. In each case, explain any evidence indicating the existence of one or more assignable causes.

a The pizza crust diameter $\bar{x}$ and R charts of Exercise 14.11 (page 698). PizzaDiam

b The acid value $\bar{x}$ and R charts of Exercise 14.12 (page 699). AcidVal

c The tube hole location $\bar{x}$ and R charts of Exercise 14.13 (page 700). TubeHole

14.6 Comparison of a Process with Specifications: Capability Studies

If we have a process in **statistical control,** we have found and **eliminated** the **assignable causes of process variation.** Therefore, the individual process measurements fluctuate over time with a **constant standard deviation σ** around a **constant mean μ.** It follows that we can use the individual process measurements to estimate μ and σ. Doing this lets us determine if the process is capable of producing output that meets specifications. Remember that specifications are based on fitness for use criteria—that is, the specifications are established by design engineers or customers. Even if a process is in statistical control, it may exhibit too much **common cause variation** (represented by σ) to meet specifications.

As will be shown in Example 14.9, one way to study the capability of a process that is in statistical control is to construct a **histogram** from a set of individual process measurements. The histogram can then be compared with the product specification limits. In addition, we know that if all possible individual process measurements are normally distributed with mean μ and standard deviation σ, then 99.73 percent of these measurements will be in the interval $[\mu - 3\sigma, \mu + 3\sigma]$. Estimating μ and σ by $\bar{\bar{x}}$ and $\bar{R}/d_2$, we obtain the **natural tolerance limits**[6] for the process.

Natural Tolerance Limits

The **natural tolerance limits** for a normally distributed process that is in statistical control are

$$\left[\bar{\bar{x}} \pm 3\left(\frac{\bar{R}}{d_2}\right)\right] = \left[\bar{\bar{x}} - 3\left(\frac{\bar{R}}{d_2}\right),\ \ \bar{\bar{x}} + 3\left(\frac{\bar{R}}{d_2}\right)\right]$$

where d_2 is a constant that depends on the subgroup size n. Values of d_2 are given in Table 14.3 (page 689) for subgroup sizes $n = 2$ to $n = 25$. These limits contain approximately 99.73 percent of the individual process measurements.

[6]There are a number of alternative formulas for the natural tolerance limits. Here we give the version that is the most clearly related to using $\bar{\bar{x}}$ and R charts. At the end of this section we present an alternative formula.

If the natural tolerance limits are inside the specification limits, then almost all (99.73 percent) of the individual process measurements are produced within the specification limits. In this case we say that the process is **capable** of meeting specifications. Furthermore, if we use $\bar{x}$ and R charts to monitor the process, then as long as the process remains in statistical control, the process will continue to meet the specifications. If the natural tolerance limits are wider than the specification limits, we say that the process is **not capable.** Here some individual process measurements are outside the specification limits.

Example 14.8 The Hot Chocolate Temperature Case

Consider the $\bar{x}$ and R chart analysis of the hot chocolate temperature data. Suppose the dining hall staff has determined that all of the hot chocolate it serves should have a temperature between 130°F and 150°F. Recalling that the $\bar{x}$ and R charts of Figure 14.11 (page 697) show that the process has been brought into control with $\bar{\bar{x}} = 140.73$ and with $\bar{R} = 4.75$, we find that $\bar{\bar{x}} = 140.73$ is an estimate of the mean hot chocolate temperature, and that $\bar{R}/d_2 = 4.75/1.693 = 2.81$ is an estimate of the standard deviation of all the hot chocolate temperatures. Here $d_2 = 1.693$ is obtained from Table 14.3 (page 689) corresponding to the subgroup size $n = 3$. Assuming that the temperatures are approximately normally distributed, the natural tolerance limits

$$[\bar{\bar{x}} \pm 3(\bar{R}/d_2)] = [140.73 \pm 3(4.75/1.693)]$$
$$= [140.73 \pm 8.42] = [132.31, 149.15]$$

tell us that approximately 99.73 percent of the individual hot chocolate temperatures will be between 132.31°F and 149.15°F. Since these natural tolerance limits are inside the specification limits (130°F to 150°F), almost all the temperatures are within the specifications. Therefore, the hot chocolate–making process is capable of meeting the required temperature specifications. Furthermore, if the process remains in control on its $\bar{x}$ and R charts, it will continue to meet specifications.

Example 14.9 The Hole Location Case

Again consider the hole punching process for air conditioner compressor shells. Recall that we were able to get this process into a state of statistical control with $\bar{\bar{x}} = 3.0006$ and $\bar{R} = .0675$ by removing several assignable causes of process variation.

Figure 14.20 gives a relative frequency histogram of the 80 individual hole location measurements used to construct the $\bar{x}$ and R charts of Figure 14.8 (page 693). This histogram

FIGURE 14.20 A Relative Frequency Histogram of the Hole Location Data (Based on the Data with Subgroups 1, 7, 12, and 17 Omitted)

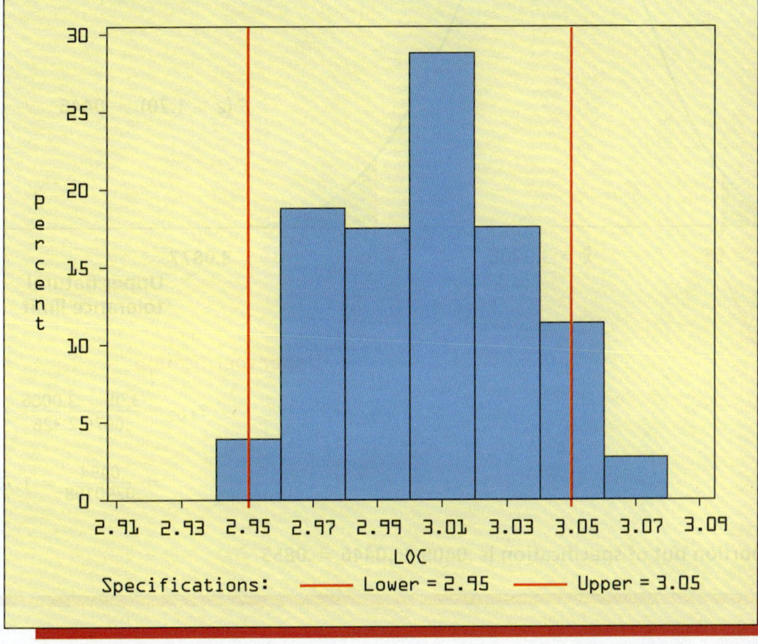

suggests that the population of all individual hole location dimensions is approximately normally distributed.

Since the process is in statistical control, $\bar{\bar{x}} = 3.0006$ is an estimate of the process mean, and $\bar{R}/d_2 = .0675/2.326 = .0290198$ is an estimate of the process standard deviation. Here $d_2 = 2.326$ is obtained from Table 14.3 (page 689) corresponding to the subgroup size $n = 5$. Furthermore, the natural tolerance limits

$$\left[\bar{\bar{x}} \pm 3\left(\frac{\bar{R}}{d_2}\right)\right] = \left[3.0006 \pm 3\left(\frac{.0675}{2.326}\right)\right]$$
$$= [3.0006 \pm .0871]$$
$$= [2.9135, 3.0877]$$

tell us that almost all (approximately 99.73 percent) of the individual hole location dimensions produced by the hole punching process are between 2.9135 inches and 3.0877 inches.

Suppose a major customer requires that the hole location dimension must meet specifications of 3.00 ± .05 inches. That is, the customer requires that every individual hole location dimension must be between 2.95 inches and 3.05 inches. The natural tolerance limits, [2.9135, 3.0877], which contain almost all individual hole location dimensions, are wider than the specification limits [2.95, 3.05]. This says that some of the hole location dimensions are outside the specification limits. Therefore, the process is not capable of meeting the specifications. Note that the histogram in Figure 14.20 also shows that some of the hole location dimensions are outside the specification limits.

Figure 14.21 illustrates the situation, assuming that the individual hole location dimensions are normally distributed. The figure shows that the natural tolerance limits are wider than the

FIGURE 14.21 Calculating the Fraction out of Specification for the Hole Location Data. Specifications Are 3.00 ± .05.

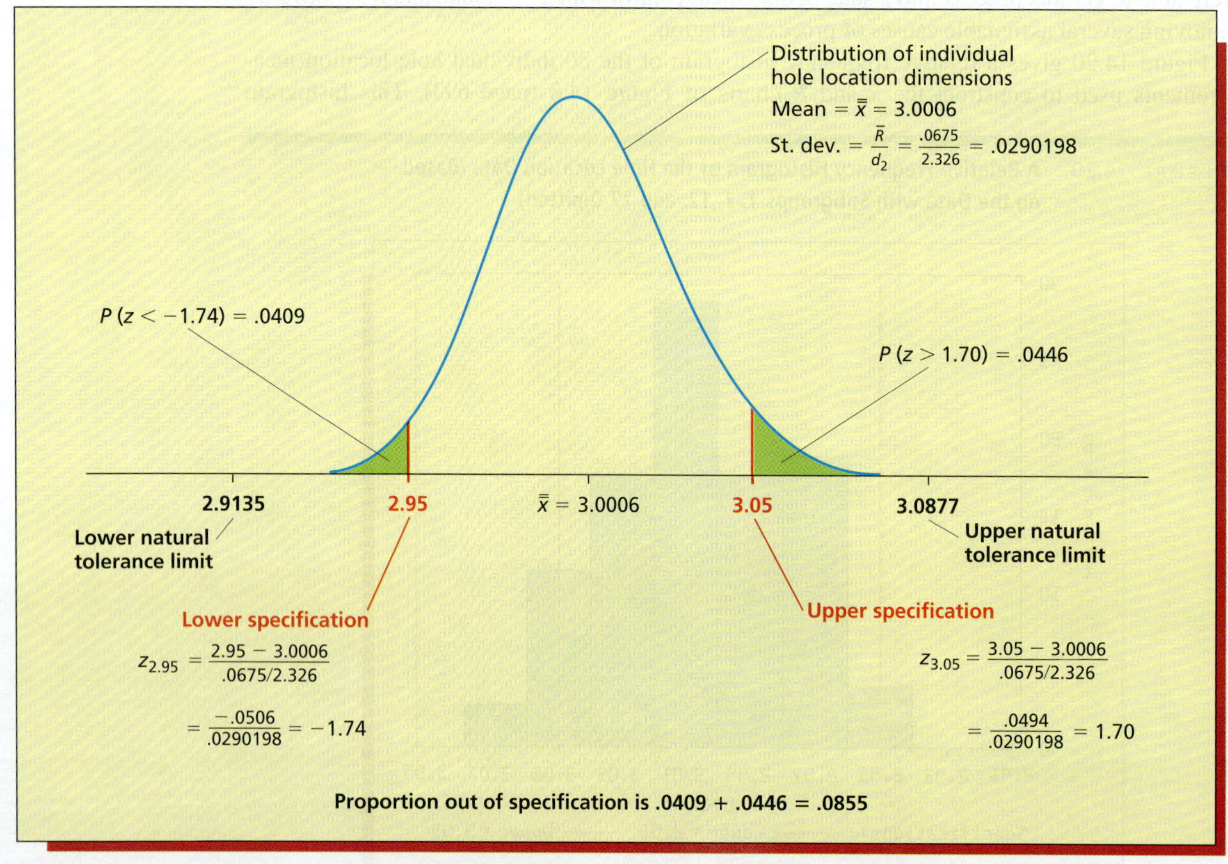

specification limits. The shaded areas under the normal curve make up the fraction of product that is outside the specification limits. Figure 14.21 also shows the calculation of the estimated fraction of hole location dimensions that are out of specification. We estimate that 8.55 percent of the dimensions do not meet the specifications.

Since the process is not capable of meeting specifications, it must be improved by removing common cause variation. This is management's responsibility. Suppose engineering and management conclude that the excessive variation in the hole locations can be reduced by redesigning the machine that punches the holes in the compressor shells. Also suppose that after a research and development program is carried out to do this, the process is run using the new machine and 20 new subgroups of $n = 5$ hole location measurements are obtained. The resulting $\bar{x}$ and R charts (not given here) indicate that the process is in control with $\bar{\bar{x}} = 3.0002$ and $\bar{R} = .0348$. Furthermore, a histogram of the 100 hole location dimensions used to construct the $\bar{x}$ and R charts indicates that all possible hole location measurements are approximately normally distributed. It follows that we estimate that almost all individual hole location dimensions are contained within the new natural tolerance limits

$$\left[\bar{\bar{x}} \pm 3\left(\frac{\bar{R}}{d_2}\right)\right] = \left[3.0002 \pm 3\left(\frac{.0348}{2.326}\right)\right]$$
$$= [3.0002 \pm .0449]$$
$$= [2.9553, 3.0451]$$

As illustrated in Figure 14.22, these tolerance limits are within the specification limits 3.00 ± .05. Therefore, the new process is now capable of producing almost all hole location dimensions inside the specifications. The new process is capable because the estimated process standard deviation has been substantially reduced (from $\bar{R}/d_2 = .0675/2.326 = .0290$ for the old process to $\bar{R}/d_2 = .0348/2.326 = .0149613$ for the redesigned process).

BI

Next, note that (for the improved process) the z value corresponding to the lower specification limit (2.95) is

$$z_{2.95} = \frac{2.95 - 3.0002}{.0149613} = -3.36$$

This says that the lower specification limit is 3.36 estimated process standard deviations below $\bar{\bar{x}}$. Since the lower natural tolerance limit is 3 estimated process standard deviations below $\bar{\bar{x}}$, there is a **leeway** of .36 estimated process standard deviations between the lower natural tolerance limit and the lower specification limit (see Figure 14.22). Also, note that the z value corresponding to

FIGURE 14.22 A Capable Process: The Natural Tolerance Limits Are within the Specification Limits

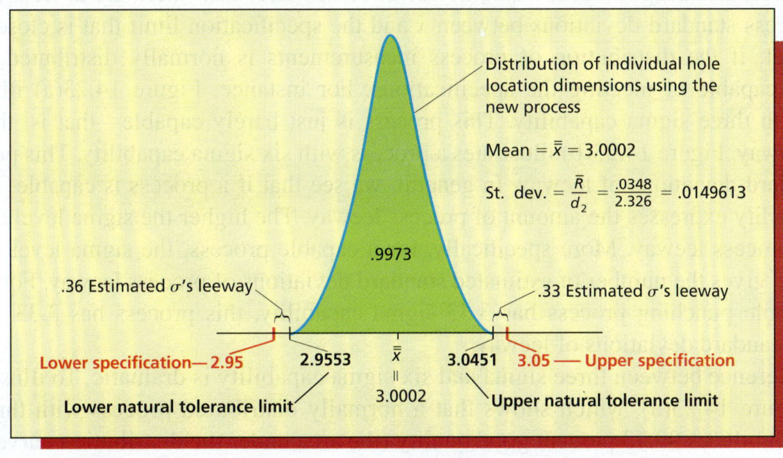

the upper specification limit (3.05) is

$$z_{3.05} = \frac{3.05 - 3.0002}{.0149613} = 3.33$$

This says that the upper specification limit is 3.33 estimated process standard deviations above $\bar{\bar{x}}$. Since the upper natural tolerance limit is 3 estimated process standard deviations above $\bar{\bar{x}}$, there is a **leeway** of .33 estimated process standard deviations between the upper natural tolerance limit and the upper specification limit (see Figure 14.22). Because some leeway exists between the natural tolerance limits and the specification limits, the distribution of process measurements (that is, the curve in Figure 14.22) can shift slightly to the right or left (or can become slightly more spread out) without violating the specifications. Obviously, the more leeway, the better.

To understand why process leeway is important, recall that a process must be in statistical control before we can assess the capability of the process. In fact:

In order to demonstrate that a company's product meets customer requirements, the company must present

1 $\bar{x}$ and R charts that are in statistical control.

2 Natural tolerance limits that are within the specification limits.

However, even if a capable process shows good statistical control, the process mean and/or the process variation will occasionally change (due to new assignable causes or unexpected recurring problems). If the process mean shifts and/or the process variation increases, a process will need some leeway between the natural tolerance limits and the specification limits in order to avoid producing out-of-specification product. We can determine the amount of process leeway (if any exists) by defining what we call the **sigma level capability** of the process.

Sigma Level Capability

The **sigma level capability** of a process is the number of estimated process standard deviations between the estimated process mean, $\bar{\bar{x}}$, and the specification limit that is closest to $\bar{\bar{x}}$.

For instance, in the previous example the lower specification limit (2.95) is 3.36 estimated standard deviations below the estimated process mean, $\bar{\bar{x}}$, and the upper specification limit (3.05) is 3.33 estimated process standard deviations above $\bar{\bar{x}}$. It follows that the upper specification limit is closest to the estimated process mean $\bar{\bar{x}}$, and because this specification limit is 3.33 estimated process standard deviations from $\bar{\bar{x}}$, we say that the hole punching process has 3.33 sigma capability.

If a process has a sigma level capability of three or more, then there are at least three estimated process standard deviations between $\bar{\bar{x}}$ and the specification limit that is closest to $\bar{\bar{x}}$. It follows that, if the distribution of process measurements is normally distributed, then the process is capable of meeting the specifications. For instance, Figure 14.23(a) illustrates a process with three sigma capability. This process is just barely capable—that is, there is no process leeway. Figure 14.23(b) illustrates a process with six sigma capability. This process has three standard deviations of leeway. In general, we see that if a process is capable, the sigma level capability expresses the amount of process leeway. The higher the sigma level capability, the more process leeway. More specifically, for a capable process, the sigma level capability minus three gives the number of estimated standard deviations of process leeway. For example, since the hole punching process has 3.33 sigma capability, this process has 3.33 − 3 = .33 estimated standard deviations of leeway.

The difference between three sigma and six sigma capability is dramatic. To illustrate this, look at Figure 14.23(a), which shows that a normally distributed process with three sigma capability produces 99.73 percent good quality (the area under the distribution curve between

FIGURE 14.23 **Sigma Level Capability and Process Leeway**

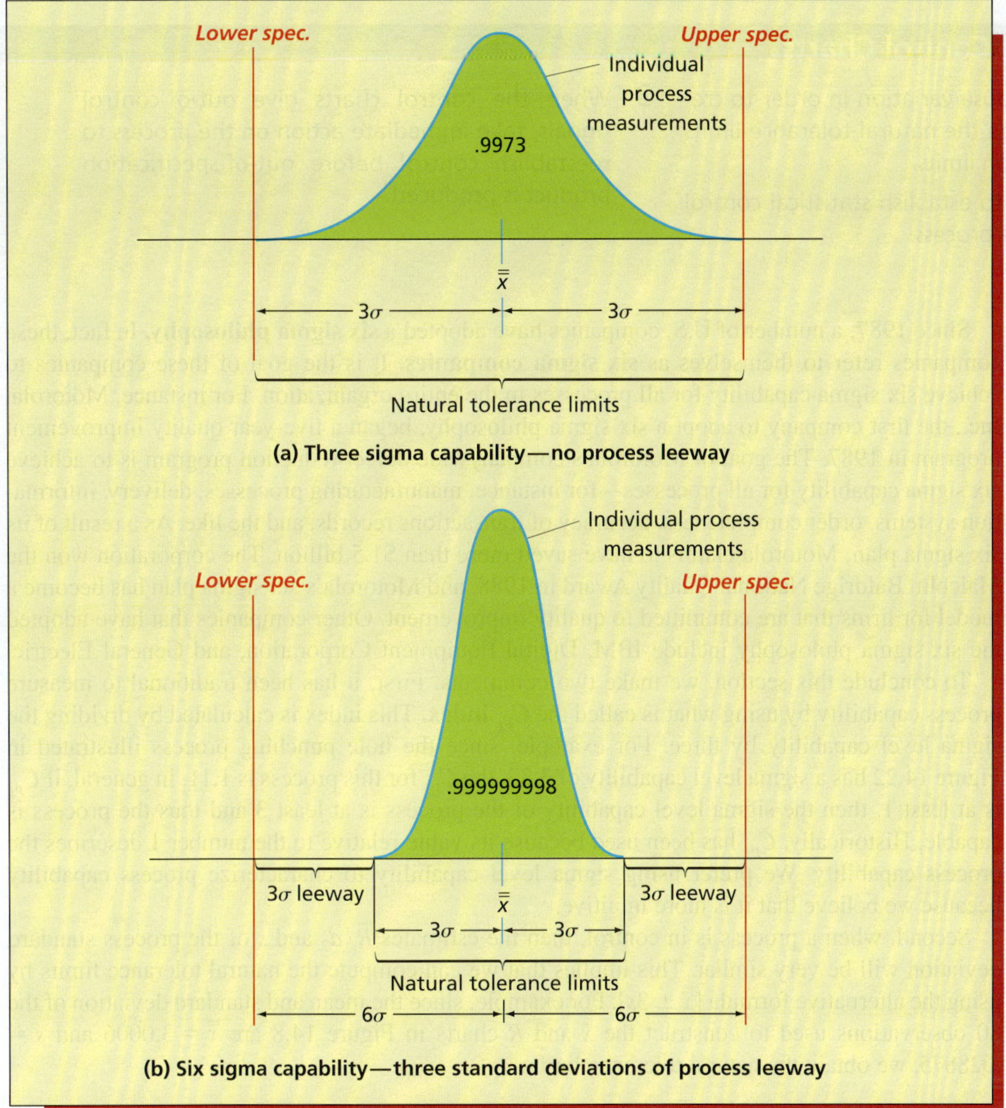

the specification limits is .9973). On the other hand, Figure 14.23(b) shows that a normally distributed process with six sigma capability produces 99.9999998 percent good quality. Said another way, if the process mean is centered between the specifications, and if we produce large quantities of product, then a normally distributed process with three sigma capability will produce an average of 2,700 defective products per million, while a normally distributed process with six sigma capability will produce an average of only .002 defective products per million.

In the long run, however, process shifts due to assignable causes are likely to occur. It can be shown that, if we monitor the process by using an $\bar{x}$ chart that employs a typical subgroup size of 4 to 6, the largest sustained shift of the process mean that might remain undetected by the $\bar{x}$ chart is a shift of 1.5 process standard deviations. In this worst case, it can be shown that a normally distributed three sigma capable process will produce an average of 66,800 defective products per million (clearly unacceptable), while a normally distributed six sigma capable process will produce an average of only 3.4 defective products per million. Therefore, if a six sigma capable process is monitored by $\bar{x}$ and R charts, then, when a process shift occurs, we can detect the shift (by using the control charts), and we can take immediate corrective action before a substantial number of defective products are produced.

This is, in fact, how control charts are supposed to be used to prevent the production of defective product. That is, our strategy is

Prevention Using Control Charts

1. Reduce common cause variation in order to create leeway between the natural tolerance limits and the specification limits.
2. Use control charts to establish statistical control and to monitor the process.
3. When the control charts give out-of-control signals, take immediate action on the process to reestablish control before out-of-specification product is produced.

Since 1987, a number of U.S. companies have adopted a **six sigma philosophy.** In fact, these companies refer to themselves as **six sigma companies.** It is the goal of these companies to achieve six sigma capability for all processes in the entire organization. For instance, Motorola, Inc., the first company to adopt a six sigma philosophy, began a five-year quality improvement program in 1987. The goal of Motorola's companywide defect reduction program is to achieve six sigma capability for all processes—for instance, manufacturing processes, delivery, information systems, order completeness, accuracy of transactions records, and the like. As a result of its six sigma plan, Motorola claims to have saved more than \$1.5 billion. The corporation won the Malcolm Baldrige National Quality Award in 1988, and Motorola's six sigma plan has become a model for firms that are committed to quality improvement. Other companies that have adopted the six sigma philosophy include IBM, Digital Equipment Corporation, and General Electric.

To conclude this section, we make two comments. First, it has been traditional to measure process capability by using what is called the $\boldsymbol{C_{p_k}}$ **index.** This index is calculated by dividing the sigma level capability by three. For example, since the hole punching process illustrated in Figure 14.22 has a sigma level capability of 3.33, the C_{p_k} for this process is 1.11. In general, if C_{p_k} is at least 1, then the sigma level capability of the process is at least 3 and thus the process is capable. Historically, C_{p_k} has been used because its value relative to the number 1 describes the process capability. We prefer using sigma level capability to characterize process capability because we believe that it is more intuitive.

Second, when a process is in control, then the estimates $\bar{R}/d_2$ and s of the process standard deviation will be very similar. This implies that we can compute the natural tolerance limits by using the alternative formula $[\bar{\bar{x}} \pm 3s]$. For example, since the mean and standard deviation of the 80 observations used to construct the $\bar{x}$ and R charts in Figure 14.8 are $\bar{\bar{x}} = 3.0006$ and $s = .028875$, we obtain the natural tolerance limits

$$[\bar{\bar{x}} \pm 3s] = [3.0006 \pm 3(.028875)]$$
$$= [2.9140,\ 3.0872]$$

These limits are very close to those obtained in Example 14.9, [2.9135, 3.0877], which were computed by using the estimate $\bar{R}/d_2 = .0290198$ of the process standard deviation. Use of the alternative formula $[\bar{\bar{x}} \pm 3s]$ is particularly appropriate when there are long-run process variations that are not measured by the subgroup ranges (in which case $\bar{R}/d_2$ underestimates the process standard deviation). Since statistical control in any real application of SPC will not be perfect, some people believe that this version of the natural tolerance limits is the most appropriate.

Exercises for Section 14.6

CONCEPTS

14.25 Write a short paragraph explaining why a process that is in statistical control is not necessarily capable of meeting customer requirements (specifications).

14.26 Explain the interpretation of the natural tolerance limits for a process. What assumptions must be made in order to properly make this interpretation? How do we check these assumptions?

14.27 Explain how the natural tolerance limits compare to the specification limits when

a A process is capable of meeting specifications.

b A process is not capable of meeting specifications.

14.28 For each of the following, explain

a Why it is important to have leeway between the natural tolerance limits and the specification limits.

b What is meant by the sigma level capability for a process.

c Two reasons why it is important to achieve six sigma capability.

METHODS AND APPLICATIONS

14.29 Consider the room cleaning and preparation time situation in Exercise 14.10 (page 698). We found that $\bar{x}$ and R charts based on subgroups of size 5 for this data are in statistical control with $\bar{\bar{x}} = 15.9416$ minutes and $\bar{R} = 2.696$ minutes. RoomPrep

a Assuming that the cleaning and preparation times are approximately normally distributed, calculate a range of values that contains almost all (approximately 99.73 percent) of the individual cleaning and preparation times.

b Find reasonable estimates of the maximum and minimum times needed to clean and prepare an individual room.

c Suppose the resort hotel wishes to specify that every individual room should be cleaned and prepared in 20 minutes or less. Is this upper specification being met? Explain. Note here that there is no lower specification, since we would like cleaning times to be as short as possible (as long as the job is done properly).

d If the upper specification for room cleaning and preparation times is 20 minutes, find the sigma level capability of the process. If the upper specification is 30 minutes, find the sigma level capability.

14.30 Suppose that $\bar{x}$ and R charts based on subgroups of size 3 are used to monitor the moisture content of a type of paper. The $\bar{x}$ and R charts are found to be in statistical control with $\bar{\bar{x}} = 6.0$ percent and $\bar{R} = .4$ percent. Further, a histogram of the individual moisture content readings suggests that these measurements are approximately normally distributed.

a Compute the natural tolerance limits (limits that contain almost all the individual moisture content readings) for this process.

b If moisture content specifications are 6.0 percent $\pm$ .5 percent, is this process capable of meeting the specifications? Why or why not?

c Estimate the fraction of paper that is out of specification.

d Find the sigma level capability of the process.

14.31 A grocer has a contract with a produce wholesaler that specifies that the wholesaler will supply the grocer with grapefruit that weigh at least .75 pounds each. In order to monitor the grapefruit weights, the grocer randomly selects three grapefruit from each of 25 different crates of grapefruit received from the wholesaler. Each grapefruit's weight is determined and, therefore, 25 subgroups of three grapefruit weights are obtained. When $\bar{x}$ and R charts based on these subgroups are constructed, we find that these charts are in statistical control with $\bar{\bar{x}} = .8467$ and $\bar{R} = .11$. Further, a histogram of the individual grapefruit weights indicates that these measurements are approximately normally distributed.

a Calculate a range of values that contains almost all (approximately 99.73 percent) of the individual grapefruit weights.

b Find a reasonable estimate of the maximum weight of a grapefruit that the grocer is likely to sell.

c Suppose that the grocer's contract with its produce supplier specifies that grapefruits are to weigh a minimum of .75 lb. Is this lower specification being met? Explain. Note here that there is no upper specification, since we would like grapefruits to be as large as possible.

d If the lower specification of .75 lb. is not being met, estimate the fraction of grapefruits that weigh less than .75 lb. Hint: Find an estimate of the standard deviation of the individual grapefruit weights.

14.32 Consider the pizza crust diameters for 10-inch pizzas given Exercise 14.11 (pages 698–699). We found that, by removing an assignable cause, we were able to bring the process into statistical control with $\bar{\bar{x}} = 10.2225$ and $\bar{R} = .825$. PizzaDiam

a Recalling that the subgroup size for the pizza crust $\bar{x}$ and R charts is 5, and assuming that the pizza crust diameters are approximately normally distributed, calculate the natural tolerance limits for the diameters.

b Using the natural tolerance limits, estimate the largest diameter likely to be sold by the restaurant as a 10-inch pizza.

c Using the natural tolerance limits, estimate the smallest diameter likely to be sold by the restaurant as a 10-inch pizza.

d Are all 10-inch pizzas sold by this restaurant really at least 10 inches in diameter? If not, estimate the fraction of pizzas that are not at least 10 inches in diameter.

14.33 Consider the bag fill situation in Exercise 14.14 (page 701). We found that the elimination of a start-up problem brought the filling process into statistical control with $\bar{\bar{x}} = 52.5875$ and $\bar{R} = 1.2937$.

a Recalling that the fill weight $\bar{x}$ and R charts are based on subgroups of size 5, and assuming that the fill weights are approximately normally distributed, calculate the natural tolerance limits for the process.

b Suppose that management wishes to reduce the mean fill weight in order to save money by "giving away" less product. However, since customers expect each bag to contain at least 50 pounds of product, management wishes to leave some process leeway. Therefore, after the mean fill weight is reduced, the lower natural tolerance limit is to be no less than 50.5 lb. Based on the natural tolerance limits, how much can the mean fill weight be reduced? If the product costs \$2 per pound, and if 1 million bags are sold per year, what is the yearly cost reduction achieved by lowering the mean fill weight?

14.34 Suppose that a normally distributed process (centered at target) has three sigma capability. If the process shifts 1.5 sigmas to the right, show that the process will produce defective products at a rate of 66,800 per million.

14.35 Suppose that a product is assembled using 10 different components, each of which must meet specifications for five different quality characteristics. Therefore, we have 50 different specifications that potentially could be violated. Further suppose that each component possesses three sigma capability (process centered at target) for each quality characteristic. Then, if we assume normality and independence, find the probability that all 50 specifications will be met.

14.7 Charts for Fraction Nonconforming

Sometimes, rather than collecting measurement data, we inspect items and simply decide whether each item conforms to some desired criterion (or set of criteria). For example, a fuel tank does or does not leak, an order is correctly or incorrectly processed, a batch of chemical product is acceptable or must be reprocessed, or plastic wrap appears clear or too hazy. When an inspected unit does not meet the desired criteria, it is said to be **nonconforming** (or **defective**). When an inspected unit meets the desired criteria, it is said to be **conforming** (or **nondefective**). Traditionally, the terms *defective* and *nondefective* have been employed. Lately, the terms *nonconforming* and *conforming* have become popular.

The control chart that we set up for this type of data is called a ***p* chart.** To construct this chart, we observe subgroups of n units over time. We inspect or test the n units in each subgroup and determine the number d of these units that are nonconforming. We then calculate for each subgroup

$$\hat{p} = d/n = \text{the fraction of nonconforming units in the subgroup}$$

and we plot the $\hat{p}$ values versus time on the p chart. If the process being studied is in statistical control and producing a fraction p of nonconforming units, and if the units inspected are independent, then the number of nonconforming units d in a subgroup of n units inspected can be described by a binomial distribution. If, in addition, n is large enough so that np is greater than 2,[7] then both d and the fraction $\hat{p}$ of nonconforming units are approximately described by normal distributions. Furthermore, the population of all possible $\hat{p}$ values has mean $\mu_{\hat{p}} = p$ and standard deviation

$$\sigma_{\hat{p}} = \sqrt{\frac{p(1-p)}{n}}$$

Therefore, if p is known we can compute three standard deviation control limits for values of $\hat{p}$ by setting

$$\text{UCL} = p + 3\sqrt{\frac{p(1-p)}{n}} \quad \text{and} \quad \text{LCL} = p - 3\sqrt{\frac{p(1-p)}{n}}$$

However, since it is unlikely that p will be known, we usually must estimate p from process data. The estimate of p is

$$\bar{p} = \frac{\text{Total number of nonconforming units in all subgroups}}{\text{Total number inspected in all subgroups}}$$

[7] Some statisticians believe that this condition should be $np > 5$. However, for p charts many think $np > 2$ is sufficient.

Substituting $\bar{p}$ for p, we obtain the following:

Center Line and Control Limits for a p Chart

$$\text{Center line} = \bar{p}$$

$$UCL = \bar{p} + 3\sqrt{\frac{\bar{p}(1-\bar{p})}{n}}$$

$$LCL = \bar{p} - 3\sqrt{\frac{\bar{p}(1-\bar{p})}{n}}$$

Note that if the LCL calculates negative, there is no lower control limit for the p chart.

The control limits calculated using these formulas are considered to be **trial control limits.** Plot points above the upper control limit suggest that one or more assignable causes have increased the process fraction nonconforming. Plot points below the lower control limit may suggest that an improvement in the process performance has been observed. However, plot points below the lower control limit may also tell us that an inspection problem exists. Perhaps defective items are still being produced, but for some reason the inspection procedure is not finding them. If the chart shows a lack of control, assignable causes must be found and eliminated and the trial control limits must be revised. Here data for subgroups associated with assignable causes that have been eliminated will be dropped, and data for newly observed subgroups will be added when calculating the revised limits. This procedure is carried out until the process is in statistical control. When control is achieved, the limits can be used to monitor process performance. **The process capability for a process that is in statistical control is expressed using $\bar{p}$, the estimated process fraction nonconforming.** When the process is in control and $\bar{p}$ is too high to meet internal or customer requirements, common causes of process variation must be removed in order to reduce $\bar{p}$. This is a management responsibility.

Example 14.10

To improve customer service, a corporation wishes to study the fraction of incorrect sales invoices that are sent to its customers. Every week a random sample of 100 sales invoices sent during the week is selected, and the number of sales invoices containing at least one error is determined. The data for the last 30 weeks are given in Table 14.11. To construct a p chart for these data, we plot the fraction of incorrect invoices versus time. Since the true overall fraction p of incorrect invoices is unknown, we estimate p by (see Table 14.11)

$$\bar{p} = \frac{1 + 5 + 4 + \cdots + 0}{3{,}000} = \frac{69}{3{,}000} = .023$$

Since $n\bar{p} = 100(.023) = 2.3$ is greater than 2, the population of all possible $\hat{p}$ values approximately has a normal distribution if the process is in statistical control. Therefore, we calculate the center line and control limits for the p chart as follows:

$$\text{Center line} = \bar{p} = .023$$

$$\begin{aligned} UCL = \bar{p} + 3\sqrt{\frac{\bar{p}(1-\bar{p})}{n}} &= .023 + 3\sqrt{\frac{.023(1-.023)}{100}} \\ &= .023 + .04497 \\ &= .06797 \end{aligned}$$

$$\begin{aligned} LCL = \bar{p} - 3\sqrt{\frac{\bar{p}(1-\bar{p})}{n}} &= .023 - .04497 \\ &= -.02197 \end{aligned}$$

Since the LCL calculates negative, there is no lower control limit for this p chart. The MegaStat output of the p chart for these data is shown in Figure 14.24. We note that none of the plot points are outside the control limits, and we fail to see any nonrandom patterns of points.

TABLE 14.11 Sales Invoice Data—100 Invoices Sampled Weekly Invoice

Week	Number of Incorrect Sales Invoices (d)	Fraction of Incorrect Sales Invoices ($\hat{p} = d/100$)	Week	Number of Incorrect Sales Invoices (d)	Fraction of Incorrect Sales Invoices ($\hat{p} = d/100$)
1	1	.01	16	3	.03
2	5	.05	17	3	.03
3	4	.04	18	2	.02
4	0	.00	19	1	.01
5	3	.03	20	0	.00
6	2	.02	21	4	.04
7	1	.01	22	2	.02
8	3	.03	23	1	.01
9	0	.00	24	2	.02
10	6	.06	25	5	.05
11	4	.04	26	2	.02
12	3	.03	27	3	.03
13	2	.02	28	4	.04
14	0	.00	29	1	.01
15	2	.02	30	0	.00

FIGURE 14.24 MegaStat Output of a *p* Chart for the Sales Invoice Data

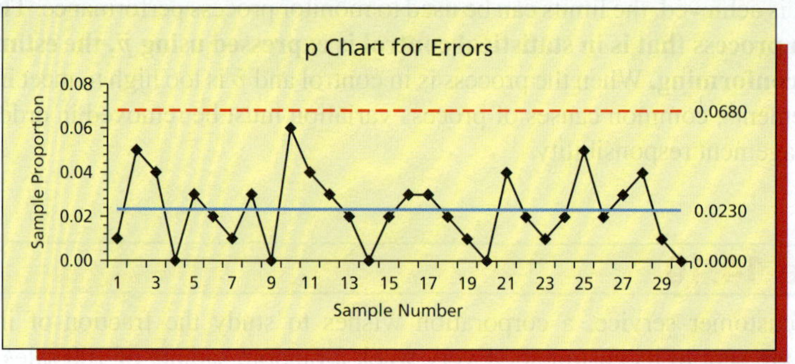

BI

We conclude that the process is in statistical control with a relatively constant process fraction nonconforming of $\bar{p} = .023$. That is, the process is stable with an average of approximately 2.3 incorrect invoices per each 100 invoices processed. Since no assignable causes are present, there is no reason to believe that any of the plot points have been affected by unusual process variations. That is, it will not be worthwhile to look for unusual circumstances that have changed the average number of incorrect invoices per 100 invoices processed. If an average of 2.3 incorrect invoices per each 100 invoices is not acceptable, then management must act to remove common causes of process variation. For example, perhaps sales personnel need additional training or perhaps the invoice itself needs to be redesigned.

In the previous example, subgroups of 100 invoices were randomly selected each week for 30 weeks. In general, subgroups must be taken often enough to detect possible sources of variation in the process fraction nonconforming. For example, if we believe that shift changes may significantly influence the process performance, then we must observe at least one subgroup per shift in order to study the shift-to-shift variation. Subgroups must also be taken long enough to allow the major sources of process variation to show up. As a general rule, at least 25 subgroups will be needed to estimate the process performance and to test for process control.

We have said that the size n of each subgroup should be large enough so that np (which is usually estimated by $n\bar{p}$) is greater than 2 (some practitioners prefer np to be greater than 5). Since we often monitor a p that is quite small (.05 or .01 or less), n must often be quite large. Subgroup sizes of 50 to 200 or more are common. Another suggestion is to choose a subgroup size that is large enough to give a positive lower control limit (often, when employing a p chart, smaller subgroup sizes give a calculated lower control limit that is negative). A positive LCL is desirable because it allows us to detect opportunities for process improvement. Such an opportunity exists when we observe a plot point below the LCL. If there is no LCL, it would obviously be impossible to obtain a plot point below the LCL. It can be shown that

A condition that guarantees that the subgroup size is large enough to yield a **positive lower control limit for a p chart is**

$$n > \frac{9(1 - p_0)}{p_0}$$

where **p_0 is an initial estimate of the fraction nonconforming** produced by the process. This condition is appropriate when **three standard deviation control limits** are employed.

For instance, suppose experience suggests that a process produces 2 percent nonconforming items. Then, in order to construct a p chart with a positive lower control limit, the subgroup size employed must be greater than

$$\frac{9(1 - p_0)}{p_0} = \frac{9(1 - .02)}{.02} = 441$$

As can be seen from this example, for small values of p_0 the above condition may require very large subgroup sizes. For this reason, it is not crucial that the lower control limit be positive.

We have thus far discussed how often—that is, over what specified periods of time (each hour, shift, day, week, or the like)—we should select subgroups. We have also discussed how large each subgroup should be. We next consider how we actually choose the items in a subgroup. One common procedure—which often yields large subgroup sizes—is to include in a subgroup **all (that is, 100 percent) of the units produced in a specified period of time.** For instance, a subgroup might consist of all the units produced during a particular hour. When employing this kind of scheme, we must carefully consider the independence assumption. The binomial distribution assumes that successive units are produced independently. It follows that a p chart would not be appropriate if the likelihood of a unit being defective depends on whether other units produced in close proximity are defective. Another procedure is to **randomly select the units in a subgroup from all the units produced in a specified period of time.** This was the procedure used in Example 14.10 to obtain the subgroups of sales invoices. As long as the subgroup size is small relative to the total number of units produced in the specified period, the units in the randomly selected subgroup should probably be **independent.** However, if the rate of production is low, it could be difficult to obtain a large enough subgroup when using this method. In fact, even if we inspect 100 percent of the process output over a specified period, and even if the production rate is quite high, it might still be difficult to obtain a large enough subgroup. This is because (as previously discussed) we must select subgroups often enough to detect possible assignable causes of variation. If we must select subgroups fairly often, the production rate may not be high enough to yield the needed subgroup size in the time in which the subgroup must be selected.

In general, the large subgroup sizes that are required can make it difficult to set up useful p charts. For this reason, we sometimes (especially when we are monitoring a very small p) relax the requirement that np be greater than 2. Practice shows that even if np is somewhat smaller than 2, we can still use the three standard deviation p chart control limits. In such a case, we detect assignable causes by looking for points outside the control limits and by looking for runs of points on the same side of the center line. In order for the distribution of all possible $\hat{p}$ values to be sufficiently normal to use the pattern analysis rules we presented for $\bar{x}$ charts, $n\bar{p}$ must be greater than 2. In this case we carry out pattern analysis for a p chart as we do for an $\bar{x}$ chart (see Section 14.5), and we use the following zone boundaries:

Upper A–B boundary: $\bar{p} + 2\sqrt{\frac{\bar{p}(1 - \bar{p})}{n}}$ Lower B–C boundary: $\bar{p} - \sqrt{\frac{\bar{p}(1 - \bar{p})}{n}}$

Upper B–C boundary: $\bar{p} + \sqrt{\frac{\bar{p}(1 - \bar{p})}{n}}$ Lower A–B boundary: $\bar{p} - 2\sqrt{\frac{\bar{p}(1 - \bar{p})}{n}}$

Here, when the LCL calculates negative, it should not be placed on the control chart. Zone boundaries, however, can still be placed on the control chart as long as they are not negative.

Exercises for Section 14.7

CONCEPTS

14.36 In your own words, define a *nonconforming unit.*

14.37 Describe two situations in your personal life in which you might wish to plot a control chart for fraction nonconforming.

14.38 Explain why it can sometimes be difficult to obtain rational subgroups when using a control chart for fraction nonconforming.

METHODS AND APPLICATIONS

14.39 Suppose that $\bar{p} = .1$ and $n = 100$. Calculate the upper and lower control limits, UCL and LCL, of the corresponding p chart.

14.40 Suppose that $\bar{p} = .04$ and $n = 400$. Calculate the upper and lower control limits, UCL and LCL, of the corresponding p chart.

14.41 In the July 1989 issue of *Quality Progress,* William J. McCabe discusses using a p chart to study a company's order entry system. The company was experiencing problems meeting the promised 60-day delivery schedule. An investigation found that the order entry system frequently lacked all the information needed to correctly process orders. Figure 14.25 gives a p chart analysis of the percentage of orders having missing information.

a From Figure 14.25 we see that $\bar{p} = .527$. If the subgroup size for this p chart is $n = 250$, calculate the upper and lower control limits, UCL and LCL.

b Is the p chart of Figure 14.25 in statistical control? That is, are there any assignable causes affecting the fraction of orders having missing information?

c On the basis of the p chart in Figure 14.25, McCabe says,

> The process was stable and one could conclude that the cause of the problem was built into the system. The major cause of missing information was salespeople not paying attention to detail, combined with management not paying attention to this problem. Having sold the product, entering the order into the system was generally left to clerical people while the salespeople continued selling.

Can you suggest possible improvements to the order entry system?

14.42 In the book *Tools and Methods for the Improvement of Quality,* Gitlow, Gitlow, Oppenheim, and Oppenheim discuss a data entry operation that makes a large number of entries every day. Over a 24-day period, daily samples of 200 data entries are inspected. Table 14.12 gives the number of erroneous entries per 200 that were inspected each day. DataErr

a Use the data in Table 14.12 to compute $\bar{p}$. Then use this value of $\bar{p}$ to calculate the control limits for a p chart of the data entry operation, and set up the p chart. Include zone boundaries on the chart.

FIGURE 14.25 A *p* Chart for the Fraction of Orders with Missing Information

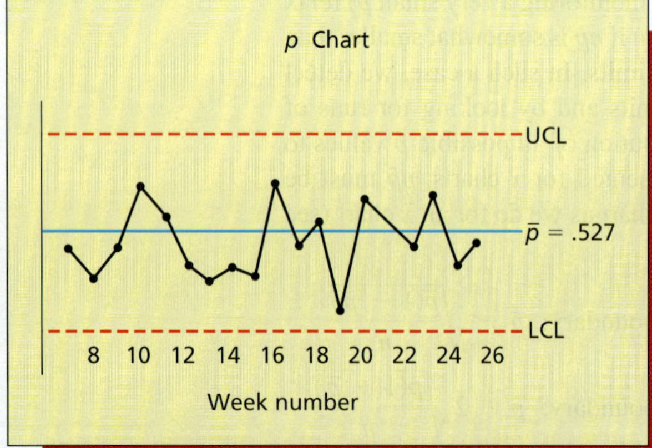

Source: W. J. McCabe, "Examining Processes Improves Operations," *Quality Progress* (July 1989), pp. 26–32. Copyright © 1989 American Society for Quality. Used with permission.

TABLE 14.12 The Number of Erroneous Entries for 24 Daily Samples of 200 Data Entries DataErr

Day	Number of Erroneous Entries	Day	Number of Erroneous Entries
1	6	13	2
2	6	14	4
3	6	15	7
4	5	16	1
5	0	17	3
6	0	18	1
7	6	19	4
8	14	20	0
9	4	21	4
10	0	22	15
11	1	23	4
12	8	24	1

Source: H. Gitlow, S. Gitlow, A. Oppenheim, and R. Oppenheim, *Tools and Methods for the Improvement of Quality*, pp. 168–72. Copyright © 1989. Reprinted by permission of McGraw-Hill Companies, Inc.

b Is the data entry process in statistical control, or are assignable causes affecting the process? Explain.

c Investigation of the data entry process is described by Gitlow, Gitlow, Oppenheim, and Oppenheim as follows:

> In our example, to bring the process under control, management investigated the observations which were out of control (days 8 and 22) in an effort to discover and remove the special causes of variation in the process. In this case, management found that on day 8 a new operator had been added to the workforce without any training. The logical conclusion was that the new environment probably caused the unusually high number of errors. To ensure that this special cause would not recur, the company added a one-day training program in which data entry operators would be acclimated to the work environment.
>
> A team of managers and workers conducted an investigation of the circumstances occurring on day 22. Their work revealed that on the previous night one of the data entry consoles malfunctioned and was replaced with a standby unit. The standby unit was older and slightly different from the ones currently used in the department. The repairs on the regular console were not expected to be completed until the morning of day 23. To correct this special source of variation, the team recommended purchasing a spare console that would match the existing equipment and disposing of the outdated model presently being used as the backup. Management then implemented the suggestion.

Since the assignable causes on days 8 and 22 have been found and eliminated, we can remove the data for these days from the data set. Remove the data and calculate the new value of $\bar{p}$. Then set up a revised p chart for the remaining 22 subgroups.

d Did the actions taken bring the process into statistical control? Explain.

14.43 In the July 1989 issue of *Quality Progress,* William J. McCabe discusses using a p chart to study the percentage of errors made by 21 buyers processing purchase requisitions. The p chart presented by McCabe is shown in Figure 14.26. In his explanation of this chart, McCabe says,

> The causes of the errors . . . could include out-of-date procedures, unreliable office equipment, or the perceived level of management concern with errors. These causes are all associated with the system and are all under management control.
>
> Focusing on the 21 buyers, weekly error rates were calculated for a 30-week period (the data existed, but weren't being used). A *p*-chart was set up for the weekly department error rate. It showed a 5.2 percent average rate for the department. In week 31, the manager called the buyers together and made two statements: "I care about errors because they affect our costs and delivery schedules," and "I am going to start to count errors by individual buyers so I can understand the causes." The *p*-chart . . . shows an almost immediate drop from 5.2 percent to 3.1 percent.
>
> The explanation is that the common cause system (supervision, in this case) had changed; the improvement resulted from eliminating buyer sloppiness in the execution of orders. The *p*-chart indicates that buyer errors are now stable at 3.1 percent. The error rate will stay there until the common cause system is changed again.

FIGURE 14.26 ***p* Chart for the Weekly Department Error Rate for 21 Buyers Processing Purchase Requisitions**

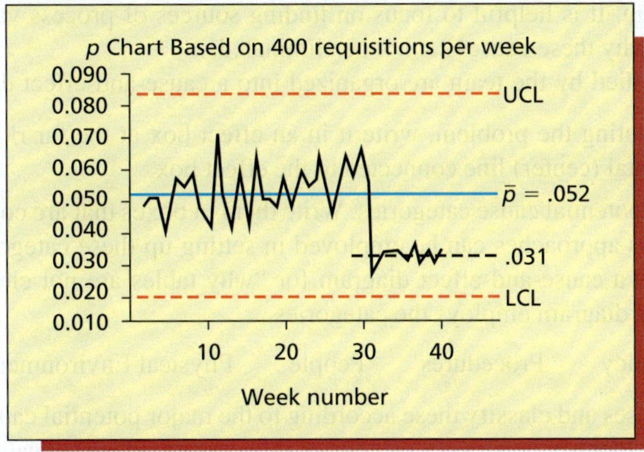

Source: W. J. McCabe, "Examining Processes Improves Operations," *Quality Progress* (July 1989), pp. 26–32. Copyright © 1989 American Society for Quality. Used with permission.

a The p chart in Figure 14.26 shows that $\bar{p} = .052$ for weeks 1 through 30. Noting that the subgroup size for this chart is $n = 400$, calculate the control limits UCL and LCL for the p chart during weeks 1 through 30.

b The p chart in Figure 14.26 shows that after week 30 the value of $\bar{p}$ is reduced to .031. Assuming that the process has been permanently changed after week 30, calculate new control limits based on $\bar{p} = .031$. If we use these new control limits after week 30, is the improved process in statistical control? Explain.

14.44 The customer service manager of a discount store monitors customer complaints. Each day a random sample of 100 customer transactions is selected. These transactions are monitored, and the number of complaints received concerning these transactions during the next 30 days is recorded. The numbers of complaints received for 20 consecutive daily samples of 100 transactions are, respectively, 2, 5, 10, 1, 5, 6, 9, 4, 1, 7, 1, 5, 7, 4, 5, 4, 6, 3, 10, and 5. Complaints

a Use the data to compute $\bar{p}$. Then use this value of $\bar{p}$ to calculate the control limits for a p chart of the complaints data. Set up the p chart.

b Are the customer complaints for this 20-day period in statistical control? That is, have any unusual problems caused an excessive number of complaints during this period? Explain why or why not.

c Suppose the discount store receives 13 complaints in the next 30 days for the 100 transactions that have been randomly selected on day 21. Should the situation be investigated? Explain why or why not.

14.8 Cause-and-Effect and Defect Concentration Diagrams (Optional)

We saw in Chapter 2 that Pareto charts are often used to identify quality problems that require attention. When an opportunity for improvement has been identified, it is necessary to examine potential causes of the problem or defect (the undesirable **effect**). Because many processes are complex, there are often a very large number of possible **causes,** and it may be difficult to focus on the important ones. In this section we discuss two diagrams that can be employed to help uncover potential causes of process variation that are resulting in the undesirable effect.

The **cause-and-effect diagram** was initially developed by Japanese quality expert **Professor Kaoru Ishikawa.** In fact, these diagrams are often called **Ishikawa diagrams;** they are also called **fishbone charts** for reasons that will become obvious when we look at an example. Cause-and-effect diagrams are usually constructed by a quality team. For example, the team might consist of product designers and engineers, production workers, inspectors, supervisors and foremen, quality engineers, managers, sales representatives, and maintenance personnel. The team will set up the cause-and-effect diagram during a **brainstorming session.** After the problem (effect) is clearly stated, the team attempts to identify as many potential causes (sources of process variation) as possible. None of the potential causes suggested by team members should be criticized or rejected. The goal is to identify as many potential causes as possible. No attempt is made to actually develop solutions to the problem at this point. After beginning to brainstorm potential causes, it may be useful to observe the process in operation for a period of time before finishing the diagram. It is helpful to focus on finding sources of process variation rather than discussing reasons why these causes cannot be eliminated.

The causes identified by the team are organized into a cause-and-effect diagram as follows:

1. After clearly stating the problem, write it in an effect box at the far right of the diagram. Draw a horizontal (center) line connected to the effect box.
2. Identify major potential cause categories. Write them in boxes that are connected to the center line. Various approaches can be employed in setting up these categories. For example, Figure 14.27 is a cause-and-effect diagram for "why tables are not cleared quickly" in a restaurant. This diagram employs the categories

   Policy   Procedures   People   Physical Environment

3. Identify subcauses and classify these according to the major potential cause categories identified in step 2. Identify new major categories if necessary. Place subcauses on the diagram as branches. See Figure 14.27.

FIGURE 14.27 A Cause-and-Effect Diagram for "Why Tables Are Not Cleared Quickly" in a Restaurant

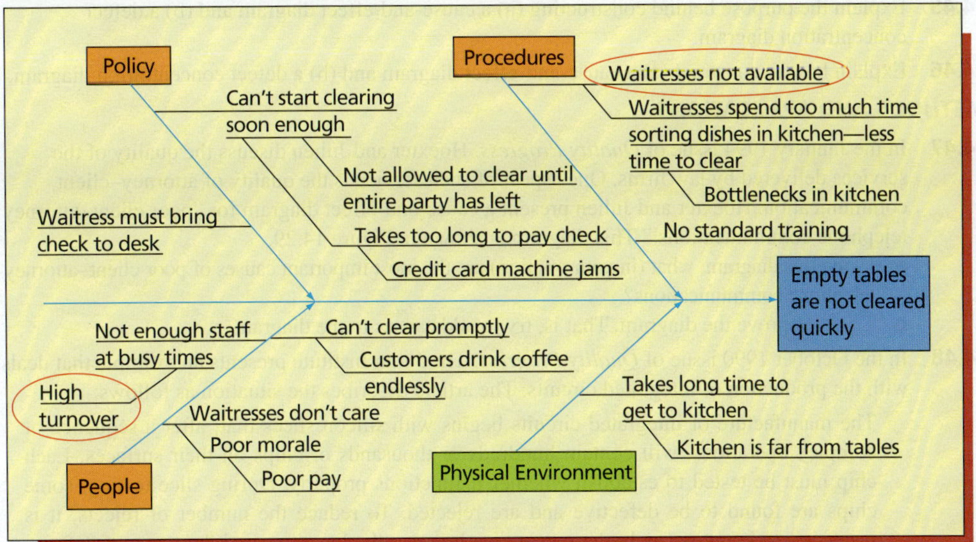

Source: M. Gaudard, R. Coates, and L. Freeman, "Accelerating Improvement," *Quality Progress* (October 1991), pp. 81–88. Copyright © 1991. American Society for Quality. Used with permission.

4 Try to decide which causes are most likely causing the problem or defect. Circle the most likely causes. See Figure 14.27.

After the cause-and-effect diagram has been constructed, the most likely causes of the problem or defect need to be studied. It is usually necessary to collect and analyze data in order to find out if there is a relationship between likely causes and the effect. We have studied various statistical methods (for instance, control charts, scatter plots, ANOVA, and regression) that help in this determination.

A **defect concentration diagram** is a picture of the product. It depicts all views—for example, front, back, sides, bottom, top, and so on. The various kinds of defects are then illustrated on the diagram. Often, by examining the locations of the defects, we can discern information concerning the causes of the defects. For example, in the October 1990 issue of *Quality Progress,* The Juran Institute presents a defect concentration diagram that plots the locations of chips in the enamel finish of a kitchen range. This diagram is shown in Figure 14.28. If the manufacturer of this range plans to use protective packaging to prevent chipping, it appears that the protective packaging should be placed on the corners, edges, and burners of the range.

FIGURE 14.28 Defect Concentration Diagram Showing the Locations of Enamel Chips on Kitchen Ranges

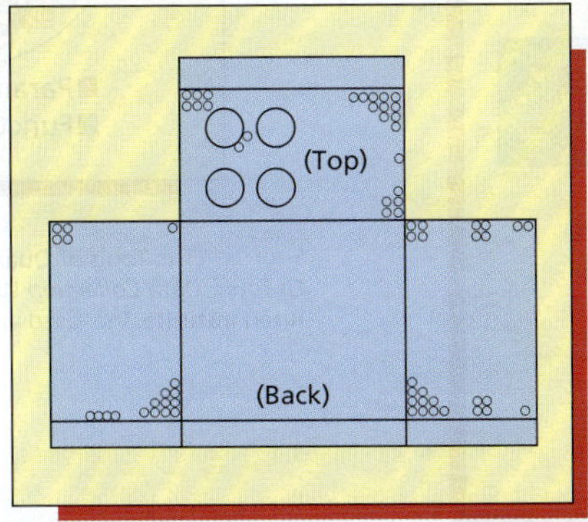

Source: "The Tools of Quality Part V: Check Sheets," from *QI Tools: Data Collection Workbook,* p. 11. Copyright © 1989. Juran Institute, Inc. Reprinted with permission from Juran Institute, Inc.

Exercises for Section 14.8

CONCEPTS

14.45 Explain the purpose behind constructing (a) a cause-and-effect diagram and (b) a defect concentration diagram.

14.46 Explain how to construct (a) a cause-and-effect diagram and (b) a defect concentration diagram.

METHODS AND APPLICATIONS

14.47 In the January 1994 issue of *Quality Progress,* Hoexter and Julien discuss the quality of the services delivered by law firms. One aspect of such service is the quality of attorney–client communication. Hoexter and Julien present a cause-and-effect diagram for "poor client–attorney telephone communications." This diagram is shown in Figure 14.29.

a Using this diagram, what (in your opinion) are the most important causes of poor client–attorney telephone communications?

b Try to improve the diagram. That is, try to add causes to the diagram.

14.48 In the October 1990 issue of *Quality Progress,* The Juran Institute presents an example that deals with the production of integrated circuits. The article describes the situation as follows:

> The manufacture of integrated circuits begins with silicon slices that, after a sequence of complex operations, will contain hundreds or thousands of chips on their surfaces. Each chip must be tested to establish whether it functions properly. During slice testing, some chips are found to be defective and are rejected. To reduce the number of rejects, it is necessary to know not only the percentage but also the locations and the types of defects. There are normally two major types of defects: functional and parametric. A functional reject occurs when a chip does not perform one of its functions. A parametric reject occurs when the circuit functions properly, but a parameter of the chip, such as speed or power consumption, is not correct.

Figure 14.30 gives a defect concentration diagram showing the locations of rejected chips within the integrated circuit. Only those chips that had five or more defects during the testing of 1,000 integrated circuits are shaded. Describe where parametric rejects tend to be, and describe where functional rejects tend to be.

FIGURE 14.29 A Cause-and-Effect Diagram for "Poor Client–Attorney Telephone Communications"

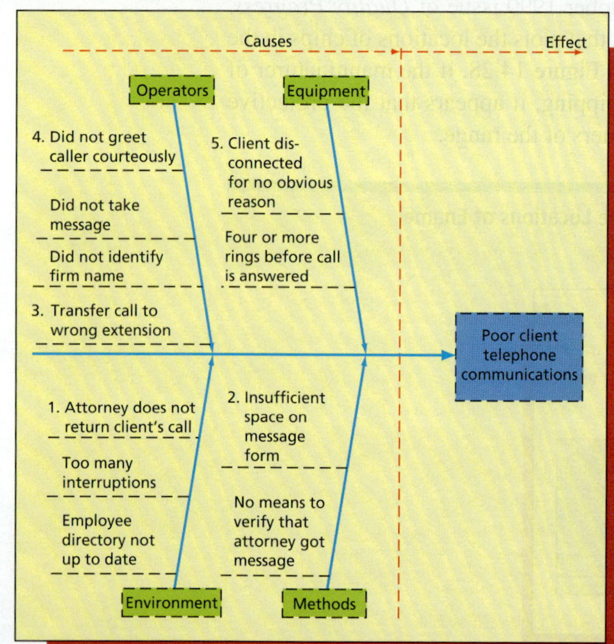

Source: R. Hoexter and M. Julien, "Legal Eagles Become Quality Hawks," *Quality Progress* (January 1994), pp. 31–33. Copyright © 1994 American Society for Quality. Used with permission.

FIGURE 14.30 Defect Concentration Diagram Showing the Locations of Rejected Chips on Integrated Circuits

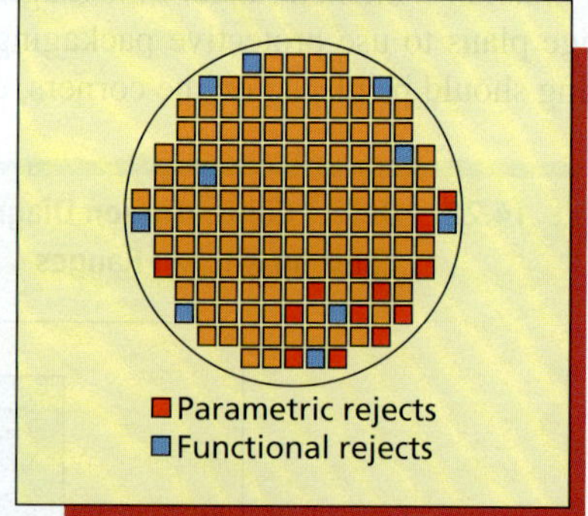

Source: "The Tools of Quality Part V: Check Sheets," from *QI Tools: Data Collection Workbook*, p. 12. Copyright © 1989 Juran Institute, Inc. Used with permission.

FIGURE 14.31 A Cause-and-Effect Diagram on the "Lack of Quality in Schools"

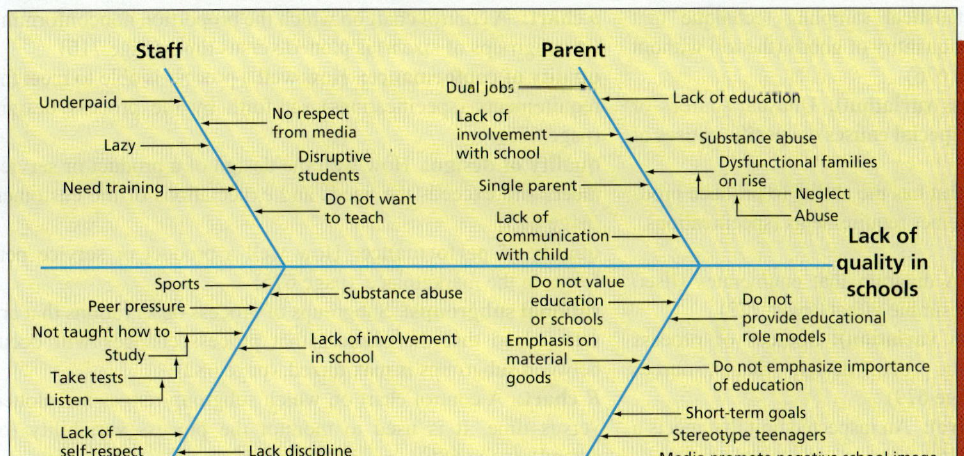

Source: F. P. Schargel, "Teaching TQM in an Inner City High School," *Quality Progress* (September 1994), pp. 87–90. Copyright © 1994 American Society for Quality. Used with permission.

14.49 In the September 1994 issue of *Quality Progress,* Franklin P. Schargel presents a cause-and-effect diagram for the "lack of quality in schools." We present this diagram in Figure 14.31.

a Identify and circle the causes that you feel contribute the most to the "lack of quality in schools."

b Try to improve the diagram. That is, see if you can add causes to the diagram.

Chapter Summary

In this chapter we studied how to improve business processes by using **control charts.** We began by considering several meanings of quality, and we discussed the history of the quality movement in the United States. We saw that Walter Shewhart introduced statistical quality control while working at Bell Telephone Laboratories during the 1920s and 30s, and we also saw that W. Edwards Deming taught the Japanese how to use statistical methods to improve product quality following World War II. When the quality of Japanese products surpassed that of American-made goods, and when, as a result, U.S. manufacturers lost substantial shares of their markets, Dr. Deming consulted and lectured extensively in the United States. This sparked an American reemphasis on quality that continues to this day. We also briefly presented **Deming's 14 Points,** a set of management principles that, if followed, Deming believed would enable a company to improve quality and productivity, reduce costs, and gain competitive advantage.

We next learned that processes are influenced by **common cause variation** (inherent variation) and by **assignable cause variation** (unusual variation), and we saw that a control chart signals when assignable causes exist. Then we discussed how to sample a process. In particular, we explained that effective control charting requires **rational subgrouping.** Such subgroups minimize the chances that important process variations will occur within subgroups, and they maximize the chances that such variations will occur between subgroups.

Next we studied **$\bar{x}$ and *R* charts** in detail. We saw that $\bar{x}$ charts are used to monitor and stabilize the process mean (level), and that *R* charts are used to monitor and stabilize the process variability. In particular, we studied how to construct $\bar{x}$ and *R* charts by using **control chart constants,** how to recognize out-of-control conditions by employing **zone boundaries** and **pattern analysis,** and how to use $\bar{x}$ and *R* charts to get a process into statistical control.

While it is important to bring a process into statistical control, we learned that it is also necessary to meet the **customer's requirements** (or **specifications**). Since statistical control does not guarantee that the process output meets specifications, we must carry out a **capability study** after the process has been brought into control. We studied how this is done by computing **natural tolerance limits,** which are limits that contain almost all the individual process measurements. We saw that, if the natural tolerance limits are inside the specification limits, then the process is **capable** of meeting the specifications. We also saw that we can measure how capable a process is by using **sigma level capability,** and we learned that a number of major businesses now orient their management philosophy around the concept of **six sigma capability.** In particular, we learned that, if a process is in statistical control and if the process has six sigma or better capability, then the defective rate will be very low (3.4 per million or less).

We continued by studying ***p* charts,** which are charts for fraction nonconforming. Such charts are useful when it is not possible (or when it is very expensive) to measure the quality characteristic of interest.

We concluded this chapter with an optional section on how to construct **cause-and-effect diagrams** and **defect concentration diagrams.** These diagrams are used to identify opportunities for process improvement and to discover sources of process variation.

It should be noted that two useful types of control charts not discussed in this chapter are **individuals charts** and ***c* charts.** These charts are discussed in Appendix L of the CD-ROM included with this book.

Glossary of Terms

acceptance sampling: A statistical sampling technique that enables us to accept or reject a quantity of goods (the lot) without inspecting the entire lot. (page 676)

assignable causes (of process variation): Unusual sources of process variation. Also called **special causes** or **specific causes** of process variation. (page 680)

capable process: A process that has the ability to produce products or services that meet customer requirements (specifications). (page 681)

cause-and-effect diagram: A diagram that enumerates (lists) the potential causes of an undesirable effect. (page 722)

common causes (of process variation): Sources of process variation that are inherent to the process design—that is, sources of usual process variation. (page 679)

conforming unit (nondefective): An inspected unit that meets a set of desired criteria. (page 716)

control chart: A graph of process performance that includes a center line and two control limits—an upper control limit, UCL, and a lower control limit, LCL. Its purpose is to detect assignable causes. (page 686)

C_{pk} index: A process's sigma level capability divided by 3. (page 714)

defect concentration diagram: An illustration of a product that depicts the locations of defects that have been observed. (page 723)

ISO 9000: A series of international standards for quality assurance management systems. (page 678)

natural tolerance limits: Assuming a process is in statistical control and assuming process measurements are normally distributed, limits that contain almost all (approximately 99.73 percent) of the individual process measurements. (page 708)

nonconforming unit (defective): An inspected unit that does not meet a set of desired criteria. (page 716)

pattern analysis: Looking for patterns of plot points on a control chart in order to find evidence of assignable causes. (page 703)

***p* chart:** A control chart on which the proportion nonconforming (in subgroups of size n) is plotted versus time. (page 716)

quality of conformance: How well a process is able to meet the requirements (specifications) set forth by the process design. (page 675)

quality of design: How well the design of a product or service meets and exceeds the needs and expectations of the customer. (page 675)

quality of performance: How well a product or service performs in the marketplace. (page 675)

rational subgroups: Subgroups of process observations that are selected so that the chances that process changes will occur between subgroups is maximized. (page 682)

***R* chart:** A control chart on which subgroup ranges are plotted versus time. It is used to monitor the process variability (or spread). (page 686)

run: A sequence of plot points on a control chart that are of the same type—for instance, a sequence of plot points above the center line. (page 705)

sigma level capability: The number of estimated process standard deviations between the estimated process mean, $\bar{\bar{x}}$, and the specification limit that is closest to $\bar{\bar{x}}$. (page 712)

statistical process control (SPC): A systematic method for analyzing process data in which we monitor and study the process variation. The goal is continuous process improvement. (page 679)

subgroup: A set of process observations that are grouped together for purposes of control charting. (page 682)

total quality management (TQM): Applying quality principles to all company activities. (page 677)

variables control charts: Control charts constructed by using measurement data. (page 686)

$\bar{x}$ chart (x-bar chart): A control chart on which subgroup means are plotted versus time. It is used to monitor the process mean (or level). (page 686)

Important Formulas

Center line and control limits for an $\bar{x}$ chart: page 689

Center line and control limits for an R chart: page 689

Zone boundaries for an $\bar{x}$ chart: page 704

Zone boundaries for an R chart: page 704

Natural tolerance limits for normally distributed process measurements: page 708

Sigma level capability: page 712

C_{pk} index: page 714

Center line and control limits for a p chart: page 717

Zone boundaries for a p chart: page 719

Supplementary Exercises

Exercises 14.50 through 14.53 are based on a case study adapted from an example presented in the paper "Managing with Statistical Models" by James C. Seigel (1982). Seigel's example concerned a problem encountered by Ford Motor Company.

The Camshaft Case Camshaft

An automobile manufacturer produces the parts for its vehicles in many different locations and transports them to assembly plants. In order to keep the assembly operations running efficiently, it is vital that all parts be within specification limits. One important part used in the assembly of V6 engines is the engine camshaft, and one important quality characteristic of this camshaft is the case hardness depth of its eccentrics. A camshaft eccentric is a metal disk positioned on the camshaft so that as the camshaft turns, the eccentric drives a lifter that opens and closes an engine valve. The V6 engine camshaft and its

FIGURE 14.32 A Camshaft and Related Parts

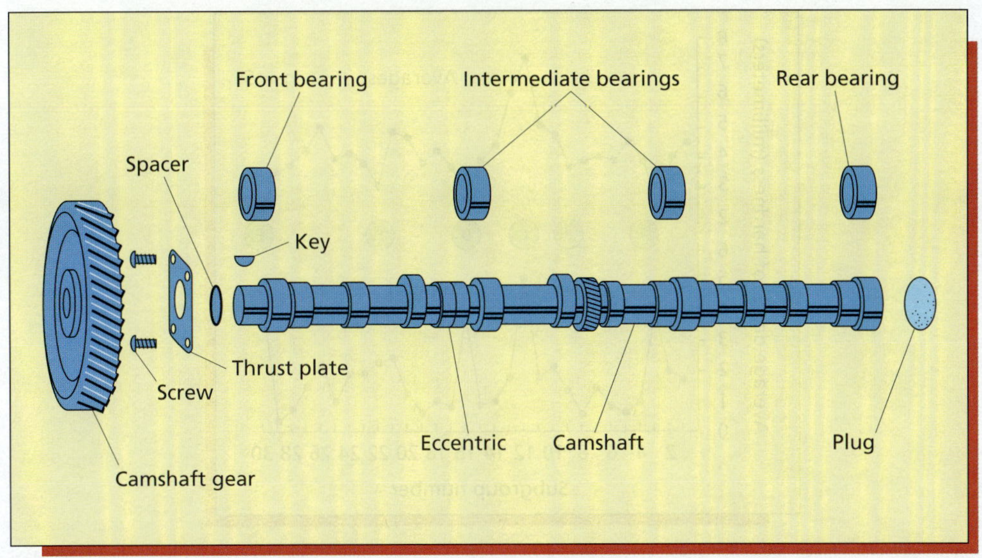

TABLE 14.13 Hardness Depth Data for Camshafts (Coil #1) Camshaft

Date	6/7	8	9	10	11	14	15	16	17	18	21	22	23	24	25
Readings 1	3.7	5.5	4.0	4.5	4.7	4.3	5.1	4.3	4.0	3.7	4.4	5.0	7.2	4.9	4.7
2	4.3	4.0	3.8	4.1	4.7	4.5	4.4	4.1	4.5	4.2	4.6	5.9	6.9	5.1	4.0
3	5.5	4.3	3.0	3.5	5.0	3.6	4.0	3.7	4.1	4.9	5.4	6.5	6.0	4.5	3.9
4	4.6	3.5	1.7	4.2	4.3	3.8	3.6	3.9	3.5	5.5	5.5	9.4	5.4	4.0	4.2
5	4.9	3.6	0	3.9	4.4	4.1	3.7	4.0	3.0	5.9	6.3	10.1	5.5	4.2	3.7
Subgroup Mean $\bar{x}$	4.6	4.2	2.5	4.0	4.6	4.1	4.2	4	3.8	4.8	5.2	7.4	6.2	4.5	4.1
Subgroup Range R	1.8	2.0	4.0	1.0	0.7	0.9	1.5	0.6	1.5	2.2	1.9	5.1	1.8	1.1	1.0

Date	28	29	30	7/1	2	5	6	7	8	9	12	13	14	15	16
Readings 1	3.7	3.5	4.7	4.0	5.0	5.8	3.6	4.0	3.5	4.1	6.2	5.5	4.4	4.0	3.9
2	3.9	3.8	5.0	3.7	4.1	6.3	3.9	3.6	5.5	4.8	5.1	5.0	4.0	3.6	3.5
3	3.4	3.6	4.1	3.9	4.2	3.8	4.1	3.5	5.0	3.8	5.4	3.9	3.7	3.7	3.3
4	3.0	4.1	3.9	4.4	5.2	5.2	3.0	5.5	4.0	3.9	3.9	4.2	3.9	3.5	1.7
5	0	4.4	4.3	4.2	5.5	3.9	1.7	3.5	3.5	4.4	4.7	4.4	3.6	3.7	0
Subgroup Mean $\bar{x}$	2.8	3.9	4.4	4	4.8	5	3.3	4	4.3	4.2	5.1	4.6	3.9	3.7	2.5
Subgroup Range R	3.9	0.9	1.1	0.7	1.4	2.5	2.4	2.0	2.0	1.0	2.3	1.6	0.8	0.5	3.9

eccentrics are illustrated in Figure 14.32. These eccentrics are hardened by a process that passes the camshaft through an electrical coil that "cooks" or "bakes" the camshaft. Studies indicate that the hardness depth of the eccentric pointed out in Figure 14.32 is representative of the hardness depth of all the eccentrics on the camshaft. Therefore, the hardness depth of this representative eccentric is measured at a specific location and is regarded to be the **hardness depth of the camshaft.** The optimal or target hardness depth for a camshaft is 4.5 mm. In addition, specifications state that, in order for the camshaft to wear properly, the hardness depth of a camshaft must be between 3.0 mm and 6.0 mm.

The automobile manufacturer was having serious problems with the process used to harden the camshaft. This problem was resulting in 12 percent rework and 9 percent scrap, or a total of 21 percent out-of-specification camshafts. The hardening process was automated. However, adjustments could be made to the electrical coil employed in the process. To begin study of the process, a problem-solving team selected 30 daily subgroups of $n = 5$ hardened camshafts and measured the hardness depth of each camshaft. For each subgroup, the team calculated the mean $\bar{x}$ and range R of the $n = 5$ hardness depth readings. The 30 subgroups are given in Table 14.13. The subgroup means and ranges are plotted in Figure 14.33. These means and ranges seem to exhibit substantial variability, which suggests that the hardening process was not in statistical control; we will compute control limits shortly.

FIGURE 14.33 **Graphs of Performance ($\bar{x}$ and R) for Hardness Depth Data (Using Coil #1)**

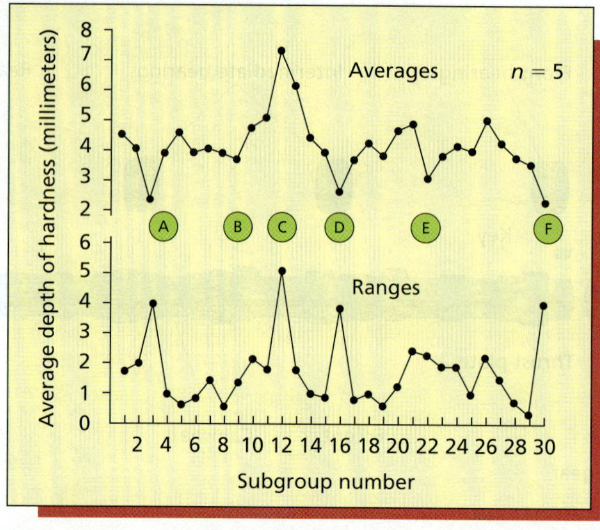

Although control limits had not yet been established, the problem-solving team took several actions to try to stabilize the process while the 30 subgroups were being collected:

1. At point *A*, which corresponds to a low average and a high range, the power on the coil was increased from 8.2 to 9.2.
2. At point *B* the problem-solving team found a bent coil. The coil was straightened, although at point *B* the subgroup mean and range do not suggest that any problem exists.
3. At point *C*, which corresponds to a high average and a high range, the power on the coil was decreased to 8.8.
4. At point *D*, which corresponds to a low average and a high range, the coil shorted out. The coil was straightened, and the team designed a gauge that could be used to check the coil spacing to the camshaft.
5. At point *E*, which corresponds to a low average, the spacing between the coil and the camshaft was decreased.
6. At point *F*, which corresponds to a low average and a high range, the first coil (Coil #1) was replaced. Its replacement (Coil #2) was a coil of the same type.

14.50 Using the data in Table 14.13: Camshaft

a Calculate $\bar{\bar{x}}$ and $\bar{R}$ and then find the center lines and control limits for $\bar{x}$ and R charts for the camshaft hardness depths.

b Set up the $\bar{x}$ and R charts for the camshaft hardness depth data.

c Are the $\bar{x}$ and R charts in statistical control? Explain.

Examining the actions taken at points *A* through *E* (in Figure 14.33), the problem-solving team learned that the power on the coil should be roughly 8.8 and that it is important to monitor the spacing between the camshaft and the coil. It also learned that it may be important to check for bent coils. The problem-solving team then (after replacing Coil #1 with Coil #2) attempted to control the hardening process by using this knowledge. Thirty new daily subgroups of $n = 5$ hardness depths were collected. The $\bar{x}$ and R charts for these subgroups are given in Figure 14.34.

14.51 Using the values of $\bar{\bar{x}}$ and $\bar{R}$ in Figure 14.34: Camshaft

a Calculate the control limits for the $\bar{x}$ chart in Figure 14.34.

b Calculate the upper control limit for the R chart in Figure 14.34.

c Are the $\bar{x}$ and R charts for the 30 new subgroups using Coil #2 (which we recall was of the same type as Coil #1) in statistical control? Explain.

14.52 Consider the $\bar{x}$ and R charts in Figure 14.34. Camshaft

a Calculate the natural tolerance limits for the improved process.

b Recalling that specifications state that the hardness depth of each camshaft must be between 3.0 mm. and 6.0 mm., is the improved process capable of meeting these specifications? Explain.

c Use $\bar{\bar{x}}$ and $\bar{R}$ to estimate the fraction of hardness depths that are out of specification for the improved process.

FIGURE 14.34 $\bar{x}$ **and** R **Charts for Hardness Depth Data Using Coil #2 (Same Type as Coil #1)**

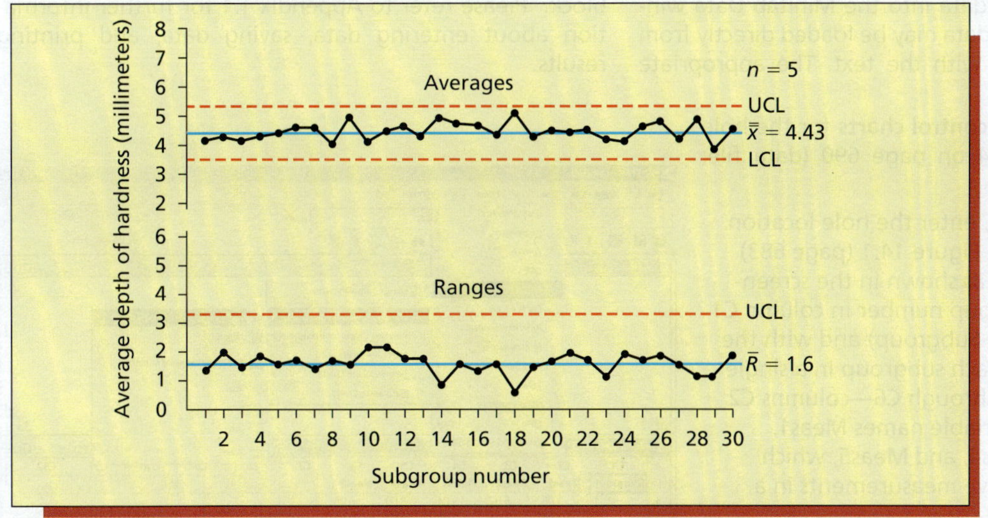

FIGURE 14.35 $\bar{x}$ **and** R **Charts for Hardness Depth Data Using a Redesigned Coil**

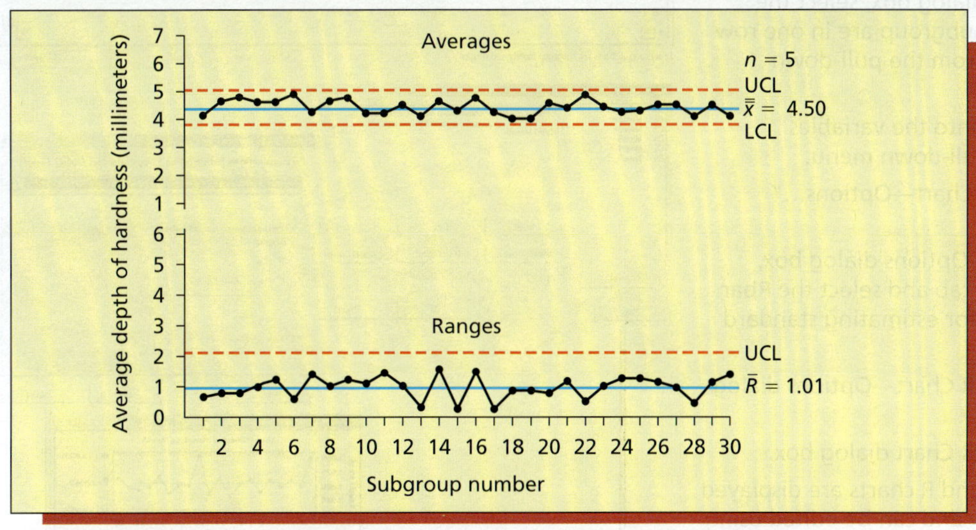

Since the hardening process shown in Figure 14.34 was not capable, the problem-solving team redesigned the coil to reduce the common cause variability of the process. Thirty new daily subgroups of $n = 5$ hardness depths were collected using the redesigned coil, and the resulting $\bar{x}$ and R charts are given in Figure 14.35.

14.53 Using the values of $\bar{\bar{x}}$ and $\bar{R}$ given in Figure 14.35: Camshaft

- **a** Calculate the control limits for the $\bar{x}$ and R charts in Figure 14.35.
- **b** Is the process (using the redesigned coil) in statistical control? Explain.
- **c** Calculate the natural tolerance limits for the process (using the redesigned coil).
- **d** Is the process (using the redesigned coil) capable of meeting specifications of 3.0 mm. to 6.0 mm.? Explain. Also find and interpret the sigma level capability.

14.54 A bank officer wishes to study how many credit cardholders attempt to exceed their established credit limits. To accomplish this, the officer randomly selects a weekly sample of 100 of the cardholders that have been issued credit cards by the bank, and the number of cardholders who have attempted to exceed their credit limit during the week is recorded. The numbers of cardholders who exceeded their credit limit in 20 consecutive weekly samples of 100 cardholders are, respectively, 1, 4, 9, 0, 4, 6, 0, 3, 8, 5, 3, 5, 2, 9, 4, 4, 3, 6, 4, and 0. Construct a control chart for the data and determine if the data are in statistical control. If 12 cardholders in next week's sample of 100 cardholders attempt to exceed their credit limit, should the bank regard this as unusual variation in the process? CredLim

Appendix 14.1 ■ Control Charts Using MINITAB

The instruction blocks in this section each begin by describing the entry of data into the Minitab Data window. Alternatively, the data may be loaded directly from the data disk included with the text. The appropriate data file name is given at the top of each instruction block. Please refer to Appendix 1.1 for further information about entering data, saving data, and printing results.

Combined X-bar and R control charts for the hole locations in Figure 14.4 on page 690 (data file: HoleLoc.mtw):

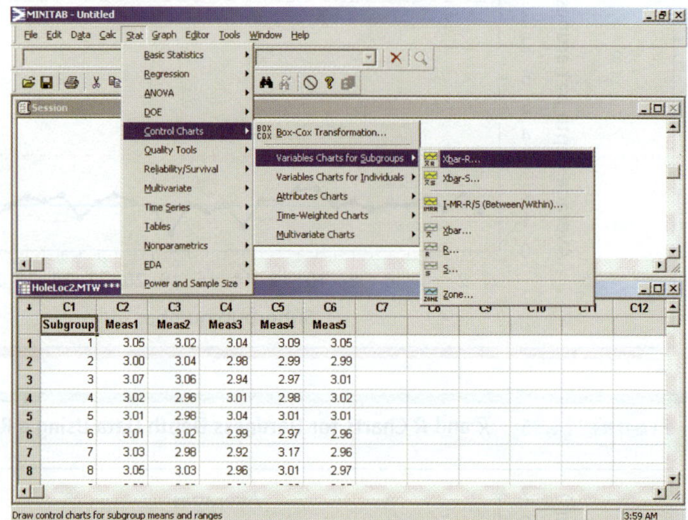

- In the Data window, enter the hole location measurements from Figure 14.1 (page 683) into columns C1–C6 as shown in the screenshot with the subgroup number in column C1 (with variable name Subgroup) and with the measurements for each subgroup in a single row of columns C2 through C6—columns C2 through C6 have variable names Meas1, Meas2, Meas3, Meas4, and Meas5, which correspond to the five measurements in a single subgroup.
- Select **Stat : Control Charts : Variables Charts for Subgroups : Xbar-R.**
- In the Xbar-R Chart dialog box, select the "Observations for a subgroup are in one row of columns" option from the pull-down menu.
- Select Meas1-Meas5 into the variables window below the pull-down menu.
- Click on the "Xbar-R Chart—Options..." button.
- In the Xbar-R Chart—Options dialog box, click on the Estimate tab and select the Rbar option for "Method for estimating standard deviation".
- Click OK in the Xbar-R Chart—Options dialog box.
- Click OK in the Xbar-R Chart dialog box.
- The combined Xbar and R charts are displayed in a graphics window and can be edited using the usual MINITAB editing features.

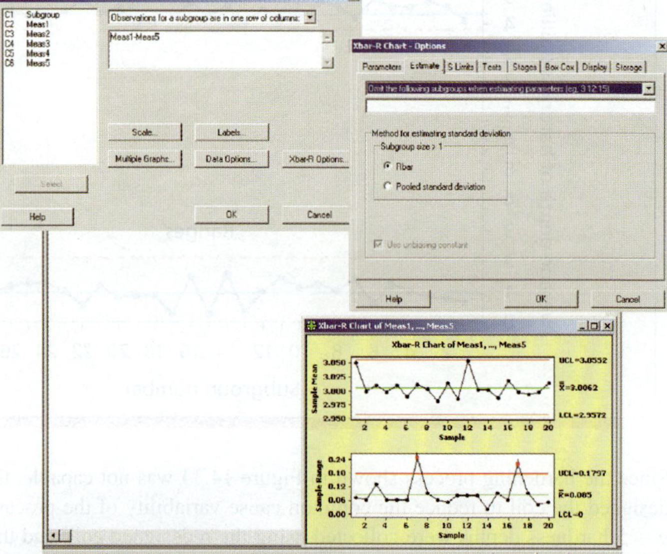

To delete subgroups of data from the control chart (as in Figure 14.7 on page 693):

- In the Xbar-R Chart dialog box, click on the Data Options... button.
- Select the "Specify which rows to exclude" option under "Include or Exclude".
- Under "Specify Which Rows To Exclude", select the "Row numbers" option.
- In the Row numbers window, enter the subgroups that are to be deleted—subgroups 7 and 17 in the case of Figure 14.7.
- Follow the previously given steps to construct the Xbar and R charts.

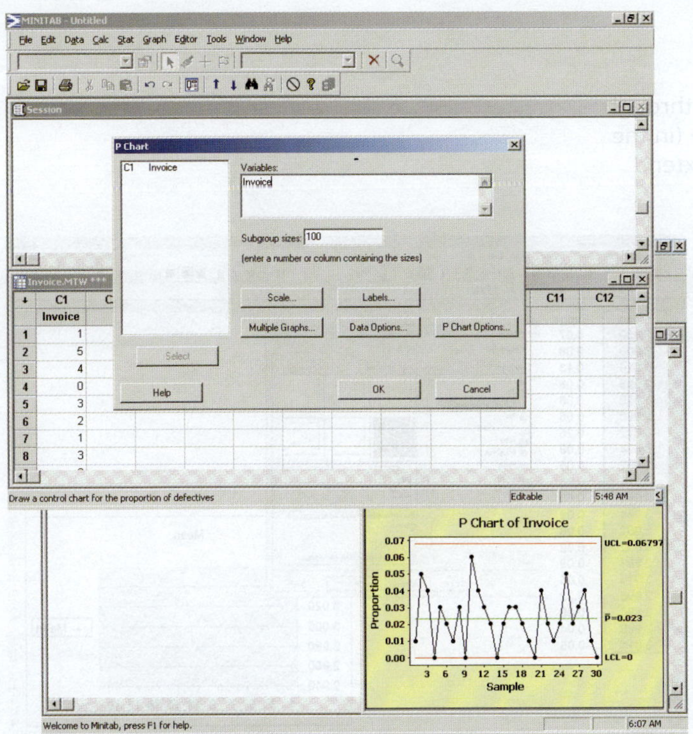

p control chart similar to Figure 14.24 on page 718 (data file: Invoice.mtw):

- In the Data window, enter the 30 weekly error counts from Table 14.11 (page 718) into column C1 with variable name Invoice.
- Select **Stat : Control Charts : Attributes Charts : p**
- In the p Chart dialog box, enter Invoice into the Variables box.
- Enter 100 in the "Subgroup size" box to indicate that each error count is based on a sample of 100 invoices.
- Click OK in the p Chart dialog box.
- The p control chart will be displayed in a graphics window.

Appendix 14.2 ■ Control Charts Using Excel

The instruction blocks in this section each begin by describing the entry of data into an Excel spreadsheet. Alternatively, the data may be loaded directly from the data disk included with the text. The appropriate data file name is given at the top of each instruction block. Please refer to Appendix 1.2 for further information about entering data, saving data, and printing results.

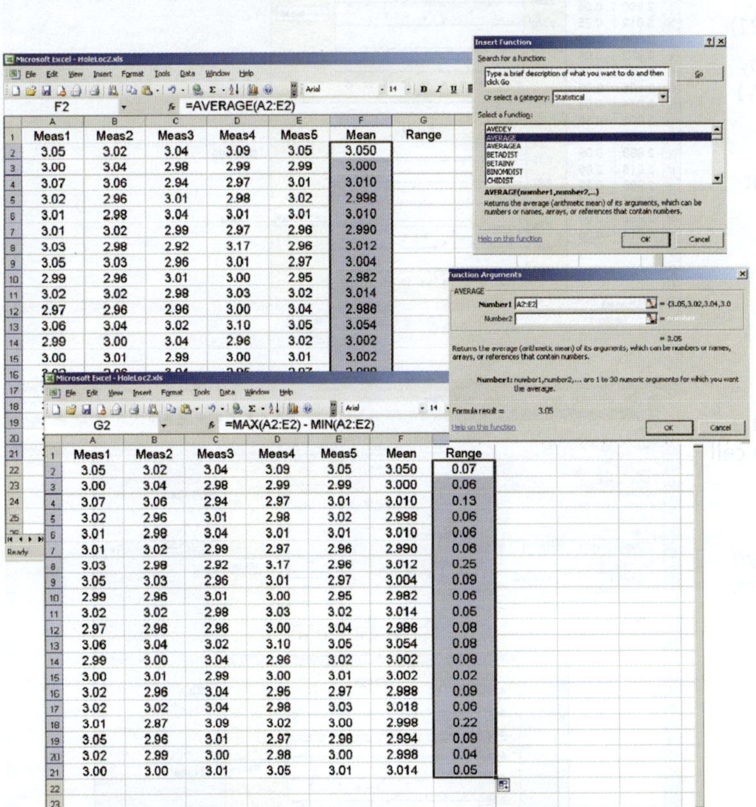

G2 =MAX(A2:E2) - MIN(A2:E2)

	Meas1	Meas2	Meas3	Meas4	Meas5	Mean	Range
2	3.05	3.02	3.04	3.09	3.05	3.050	0.07
3	3.00	3.04	2.98	2.99	2.99	3.000	0.06
4	3.07	3.06	2.94	2.97	3.01	3.010	0.13
5	3.02	2.96	3.01	2.98	3.02	2.998	0.06
6	3.01	2.98	3.04	3.01	3.01	3.010	0.06
7	3.01	3.02	2.99	2.97	2.96	2.990	0.06
8	3.03	2.98	2.92	3.17	2.96	3.012	0.25
9	3.05	3.03	2.96	3.01	2.97	3.004	0.09
10	2.99	2.96	3.01	3.00	2.95	2.982	0.06
11	3.02	3.02	2.98	3.03	3.02	3.014	0.05
12	2.97	2.96	2.96	3.00	3.04	2.986	0.08
13	3.06	3.04	3.02	3.10	3.05	3.054	0.08
14	2.99	3.00	3.04	2.96	3.02	3.002	0.08
15	3.00	3.01	2.99	3.00	3.01	3.002	0.02
16	3.02	2.96	3.04	2.95	2.97	2.988	0.09
17	3.02	3.02	3.04	2.98	3.03	3.018	0.06
18	3.01	2.87	3.09	3.02	3.00	2.998	0.22
19	3.05	2.96	3.01	2.97	2.98	2.994	0.09
20	3.02	2.99	3.00	2.98	3.00	2.998	0.04
21	3.00	3.00	3.01	3.05	3.01	3.014	0.05

X-bar and R charts similar to Figure 14.2 on page 685 (data file: HoleLoc.xls):

- In cells A1to E1, enter the column labels Meas1, Meas2, Meas3, Meas4, and Meas5.
- In columns A through E, enter the hole location data as 20 rows of 5 measurements, as laid out in Figure 14.1(b) on page 683.

Compute means and ranges for plotting:

- In cells F1 and G1, enter the column labels Mean and Range.
- Click in cell F2 and select the Insert Function button f_x from the Excel toolbar.
- In the Insert Function dialog box, select Statistical from the "Or select a category:" menu, select AVERAGE from the "Select a function:" menu, and click OK.
- In the "AVERAGE Function Arguments" dialog box, enter A2.E2 in the box labeled "Number 1" and click OK to obtain the mean for cells A2 through E2 in cell F2.
- Double-click the drag handle (in the lower right corner) of cell F2 to automatically extend the mean calculation through cell F21.

- In cell G2, enter the cell formula

  = Max(A2.E2) – Min(A2.E2)

  and press Enter to obtain the range for cells A2 through E2 in cell G2. Then, double-click the drag handle (in the lower right corner) of cell G2 to automatically extend the range calculation through cell G21.

Produce means and ranges charts:

- Use the mouse to select the range F1.F21 and select the Chart Wizard from the Excel toolbar.
- In the "Chart Wizard—Step 1 of 4—Chart Type" dialog box, select the Line option from the "Chart type" menu, and click Finish.
- Use the mouse to select the range G1.G21 and select the Chart Wizard from the Excel toolbar.
- In the "Chart Wizard—Step 1 of 4—Chart Type" dialog box, select the Line option from the "Chart type" menu, and click Finish.
- Use the mouse to reposition and resize the charts as desired. Chart attributes—gridlines, titles, legends, fonts, colors—can be changed by right-clicking on the corresponding areas of the chart.

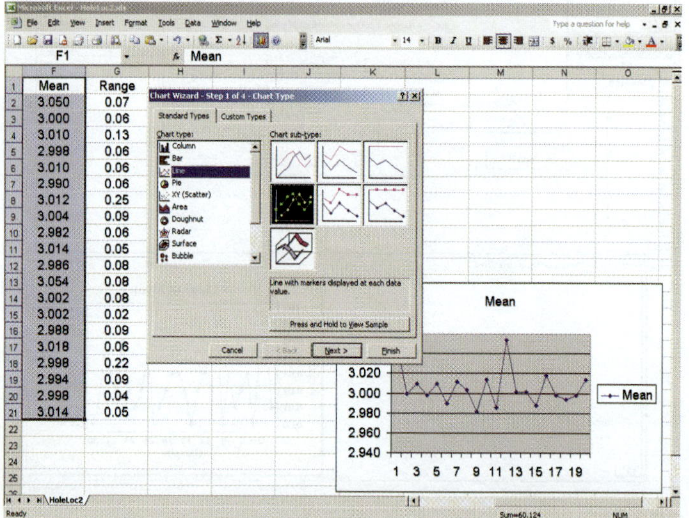

Calculate control limits and draw them on the charts:

- Control limits can be calculated by using cell formulas. For instance, the upper control limit for the X-bar chart (which is calculated in cell M3) is obtained by using the cell formula:

  =Average(F2.F21) + .577*Average(G2.G21)

- Control limits can be drawn on the charts by clicking on the "straight line autoshape" (\ ) and by using the mouse to click and draw straight lines in the appropriate locations. The control limits can be formatted by right-clicking on them and using the dialog box that appears.

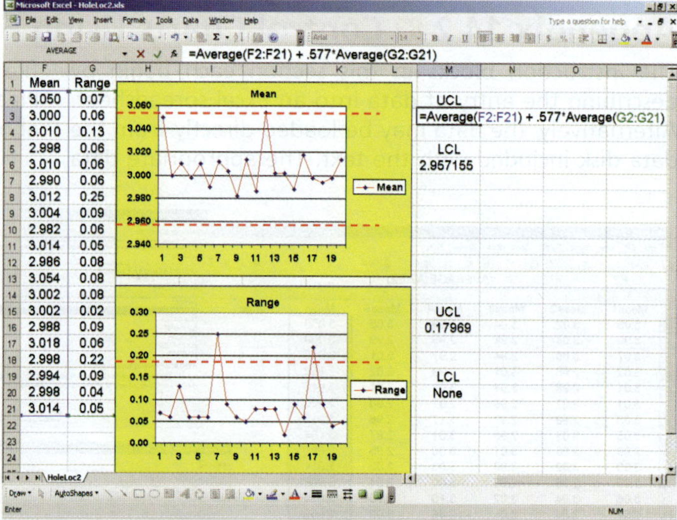

To print the two charts together:

- Reposition the charts in an open area of the spreadsheet and use the mouse to select a cell range that includes the charts.
- Select **File : Print**.
- In the Print dialog box, choose the Selection option in the "Print what" section, and click OK.

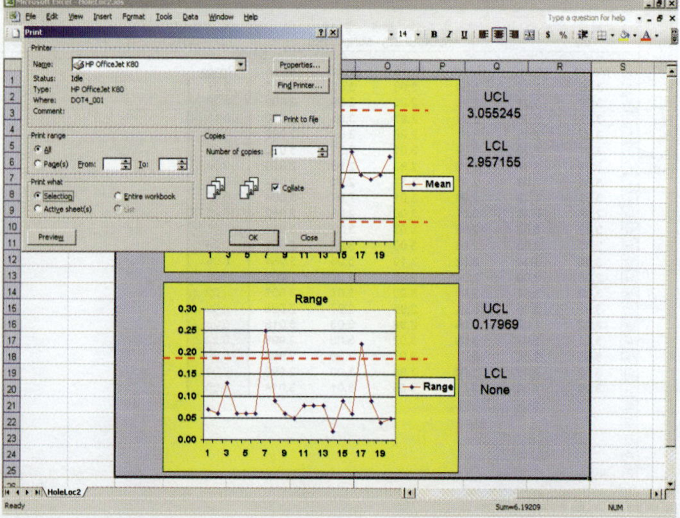

Appendix 14.3 ■ Control Charts Using MegaStat

The instructions in this section begin by describing the entry of data into an Excel worksheet. Alternatively, the data may be loaded directly from the data disk included with the text. The appropriate data file name is given at the top of each instruction block. Please refer to Appendix 1.2 for further information about entering data and saving and printing results in Excel. Please refer to Appendix 1.3 for more information about using MegaStat.

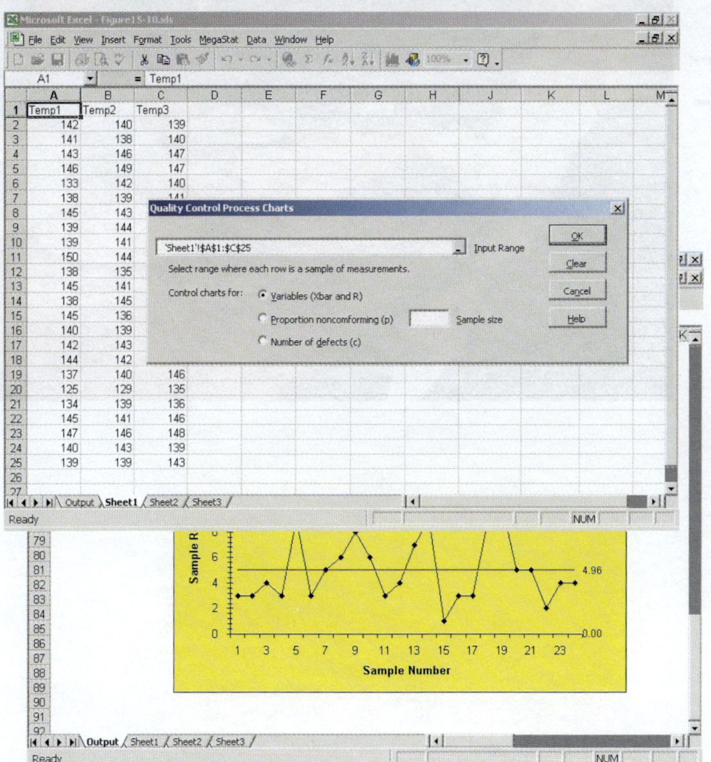

***x*-bar and *R* charts** in Figure 14.10 on page 696 (data file: HotChoc.xls):

- In cells A1–A3, enter the column labels Temp1, Temp2, and Temp3.
- In columns A, B, and C, enter the hot chocolate temperature data as 24 rows of 3 measurements, as laid out in the columns headed 1, 2, and 3 in Table 14.2 on page 684. When entered in this way, each row is a subgroup (sample) of three temperatures. Calculated means and ranges (as in Table 14.2) need not be entered – only the raw data is needed.
- Select **MegaStat : Quality Control Process Charts.**
- In the "Quality Control Process Charts" dialog box, click on "Variables (Xbar and R)."
- Use the AutoExpand feature to select the range A1.C25 into the Input Range box. Here each row in the selected range is a subgroup (sample) of measurements.
- Click OK in the "Quality Control Process Charts" dialog box.
- The requested control charts are placed in an output file and may be edited using standard Excel editing features. See Appendix 1.3 (page 39) for additional information about editing Excel graphics.

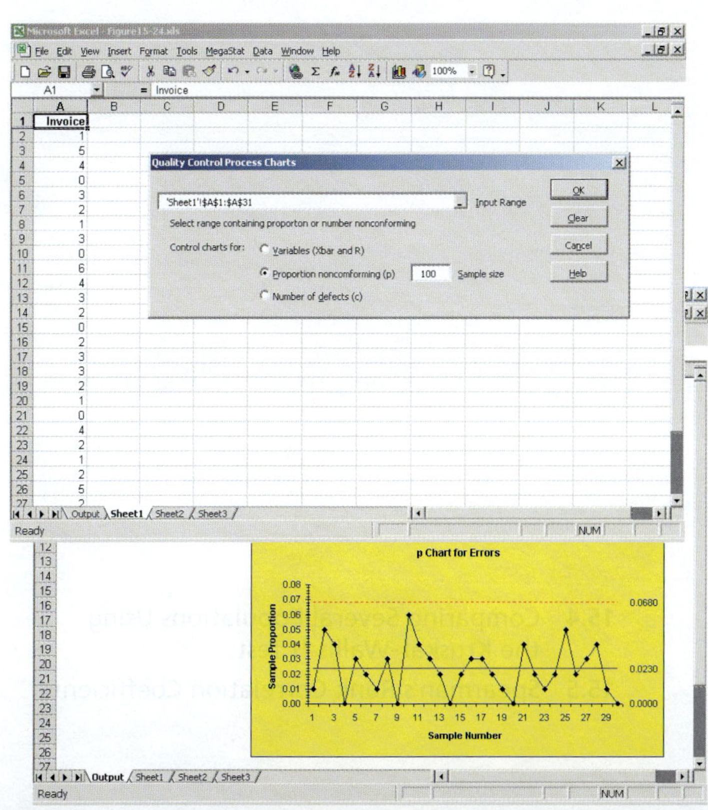

***p* control chart** in Figure 14.24 on page 718 (data file: Invoice.xls):

- Enter the 30 weekly error counts from Table 14.11 (page 718) into Column A with the label Invoice in cell A1.
- Select **MegaStat : Quality Control Process Charts.**
- In the "Quality Control Process Charts" dialog box, click on "Proportion nonconforming (p)."
- Use the AutoExpand feature to enter the range A1.A31 into the input Range box.
- Enter the subgroup (sample) size (here equal to 100) into the Sample size box.
- Click OK in the "Quality Control Process Charts" dialog box.

A c chart for nonconformities (discussed in Appendix L on this book's CD-ROM) can be obtained by entering data as for the *p* chart and by clicking on "Number of defects (c)."

CHAPTER 15

Nonparametric Methods

Chapter Outline

Recall from Chapter 2 that the manufacturer of a DVD recorder has randomly selected a sample of 20 purchasers who have owned the recorder for one year. Each purchaser in the sample is asked to rank his or her satisfaction with the recorder along the following 10-point scale:

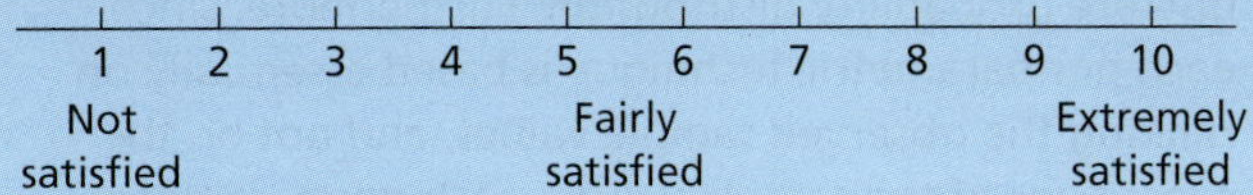

The stem-and-leaf display below gives the 20 ratings obtained.

```
 1  0
 2
 3  0
 4
 5  00
 6
 7  0
 8  000000
 9  00000
10  0000
```

Let μ denote the mean rating that would be given by all purchasers who have owned the DVD recorder for one year, and suppose we wish to show that μ exceeds 7. To do this, we will test H_0: $\mu \leq 7$ versus H_a: $\mu > 7$. The mean and the standard deviation of the sample of 20 ratings are $\bar{x} = 7.7$ and $s = 2.4301$, and the test statistic t is

$$t = \frac{\bar{x} - 7}{s/\sqrt{n}} = \frac{7.7 - 7}{2.4301/\sqrt{20}} = 1.2882$$

Since $t = 1.2882$ is less than $t_{.10} = 1.328$ (based on 19 degrees of freedom), we cannot reject H_0: $\mu \leq 7$ by setting α equal to .10. That is, the t test does not provide even mildly strong evidence that μ exceeds 7. But how appropriate is the t test in this situation? The t test is, in fact, not appropriate for two reasons:

1 The t test assumes that, when the sample size n is small (less than 30), the sampled population is normally distributed (or, at least, mound-shaped and not highly skewed to the right or left). The stem-and-leaf display of the ratings indicates the population of all DVD recorder ratings might be highly skewed to the left.

2 The rating of 1 in the stem-and-leaf display is an extreme **outlier** (see Figure 2.34 on page 81). This outlier, along with the other small ratings of 3, 5, and 5 in the tail of the stem-and-leaf display, affects both the sample mean and the sample standard deviation. First, the sample mean of 7.7 is "pulled down" by the low ratings and thus is smaller than the sample median, which is 8. Although there is not much difference here between the mean and the median, the outlier and overall skewness indicate that the median might be a better measure of central tendency. More important, however, is the fact that the low ratings inflate the sample standard deviation s. As a result, although the sample mean of 7.7 is greater than 7, the inflated s of 2.4301 makes the denominator of the t statistic large enough to cause us to not reject H_0: $\mu \leq 7$. Intuitively, therefore, even if the population mean DVD recorder rating really does exceed 7, the t test is not **powerful enough** to tell us that this is true.

In addition, some statisticians would consider the t test to be inappropriate for a third reason. The variable DVD recorder rating is an *ordinal variable.* Recall from Section 1.4 that an **ordinal variable** is a **qualitative variable** with a meaningful **ordering,** or **ranking,** of the categories. In general, when the measurements of an ordinal variable are numerical, statisticians debate whether the ordinal variable is "somewhat quantitative." Statisticians who argue that DVD recorder rating is not somewhat quantitative would reason, for instance, that the difference between 10 ("extremely satisfied") and 6 ("fairly satisfied") may not be the same as the difference between 5 ("fairly satisfied") and 1 ("not satisfied"). In other words, although each difference is four rating points, the two differences may not be the same qualitatively. Other statisticians would argue that as soon as respondents see equally spaced numbers (even though the numbers are described by words), their responses are influenced enough to make the ordinal variable somewhat quantitative. In general, the choice of words associated with the numbers probably substantially affects whether an ordinal variable may be considered somewhat quantitative. However, in practice numerical ordinal ratings are often analyzed as though they are quantitative. For example, although a teacher's effectiveness rating given by a student and a student's course grade are both ordinal variables with the possible measurements 4 ("excellent"), 3 ("good"), 2 ("average"), 1 ("poor"), and 0 ("unsatisfactory"), a teacher's effectiveness **average** and a student's grade point **average** are calculated. Furthermore, some statisticians would argue that when there are "fairly many" numerical ordinal ratings (for example, the 10 ratings in the DVD recorder example), it is even more reasonable to consider the ratings somewhat quantitative and thus to analyze means and variances. However, for statisticians who feel that numerical ordinal ratings should never be considered quantitative, analyzing the means and standard deviations of these ratings—and thus performing t tests—would always be considered inappropriate.

In general, consider the one-sample t test (see Section 8.4), the two independent sample t tests (see Section 9.2), the paired difference t test (see Section 9.3), and the one-way analysis of variance F test (see Section 10.2). All of these procedures assume that the sampled populations are normally distributed (or mound-shaped and not highly skewed to the right or left). When this assumption is not satisfied, we can use techniques that do not require assumptions about the shapes of the probability distributions of the sampled populations. These techniques are often called **nonparametric methods,** and we discuss several of these methods in this chapter. Specifically, we consider four nonparametric tests that can be used in place of the previously mentioned *t* and *F* tests. These four nonparametric tests are the **sign test,** the **Wilcoxon rank sum test,** the **Wilcoxon signed rank test,** and the **Kruskal–Wallis *H* test.** These tests require no assumptions about the shapes of the sampled populations. In addition, these nonparametric tests are usually better than the *t* and *F* tests at correctly finding statistically significant differences in the presence of outliers and extreme skewness. Therefore, we say that the nonparametric tests can be **more powerful** than the *t* and *F* tests. For example, we will find in Section 15.1 that, although the *t* test does not allow us to conclude that the population **mean** DVD recorder rating exceeds 7, the nonparametric sign test does allow us to conclude that the population **median** DVD recorder rating exceeds 7.

Each nonparametric test discussed in this chapter theoretically assumes that each sampled population under consideration is described by a continuous probability distribution. However, in most situations, each nonparametric technique is slightly **statistically conservative** if the sampled population is described by a discrete probability distribution. This means, for example, that a nonparametric hypothesis test has a slightly smaller chance of falsely rejecting the null hypothesis than the specified α value would seem to indicate, if the sampled population is described by a discrete probability distribution. Furthermore, since each nonparametric technique is based essentially on **ranking** the observed sample values, and not on the exact sizes of the sample values, each nonparametric technique can be used to analyze any type of data that can be ranked. This includes ordinal data (for example, teaching effectiveness ratings and DVD recorder ratings) in addition to quantitative data.

To conclude this introduction, we note that *t* and *F* tests are more powerful (better at correctly finding statistically significant differences) than nonparametric tests when the sampled populations are normally distributed (or mound-shaped and not highly skewed to the right or left). In addition, nonparametric tests are largely limited to simple settings. For example, there is a nonparametric measure of correlation between two variables—**Spearman's rank correlation coefficient**—which is discussed at the end of this chapter. However, nonparametric tests do not extend easily to multiple regression and complex experimental designs. This is one reason why we have stressed *t* and *F* procedures in this book. These procedures can be extended to more advanced statistical methods.

15.1 The Sign Test: A Hypothesis Test about the Median

If a population is highly skewed to the right or left, then the population median might be a better measure of central tendency than the population mean. Furthermore, if the sample size is small and the population is highly skewed or clearly non–mound-shaped, then the *t* test for the population mean that we have presented in Section 8.4 might not be valid. For these reasons, when we have taken a small sample and when we believe that the sampled population might be far from being normally distributed, it is sometimes useful to use a hypothesis test about the population median. This test, called the **sign test,** is valid for any sample size and population shape. To illustrate the sign test, we consider the following example.

Example 15.1

The leading compact disc player is advertised to have a median lifetime (or time to failure) of 6,000 hours of continuous play. The developer of a new compact disc player wishes to show that the median lifetime of the new player exceeds 6,000 hours of continuous play. To this end, the developer randomly selects 20 new players and tests them in continuous play until each fails. Figure 15.1(a) presents the 20 lifetimes obtained (expressed in hours and arranged in increasing order), and Figure 15.1(b) shows a stem-and-leaf display of these lifetimes. The stem-and-leaf display and the three low lifetimes of 5, 947, and 2,142 suggest that the population of all lifetimes might be highly skewed to the left. In addition, the sample size is small. Therefore, it might be reasonable to use the sign test.

FIGURE 15.1 The Compact Disc Player Lifetime Data and Associated Statistical Analyses

(a) The compact disc player lifetime data CompDisc

5	947	2,142	4,867	5,840	6,085	6,238	6,411	6,507	6,687
6,827	6,985	7,082	7,176	7,285	7,410	7,563	7,668	7,724	7,846

(b) A stem-and-leaf display

```
0  005
0  947
1
1
2  142
2
3
3
4
4  867
5
5  840
6  085 238 411
6  507 687 827 985
7  082 176 285 410
7  563 668 724 846
```

(c) MINITAB output of the sign test of H_0: M_d = 6,000 versus H_a: $M_d > 6{,}000$

```
Sign test of median = 6000 versus > 6000
            N   Below   Equal   Above        P    Median
LifeTime   20       5       0      15   0.0207      6757
```

(d) MegaStat output of the sign test of H_0: M_d = 6,000 versus H_a: $M_d > 6{,}000$

Sign Test

6000 hypothesized value	5 below	binomial
6757 median Life Time	0 equal	.0207 p-value (one-tailed, upper)
20 n	15 above	

In order to show that the population median lifetime, M_d, of the new compact disc player exceeds 6,000 (hours), recall that this median divides the population of ordered lifetimes into two equal parts. It follows that, if more than half of the individual population lifetimes exceed 6,000, then the population median, M_d, exceeds 6,000. Let p denote the proportion of the individual population lifetimes that exceed 6,000. Then, we can reject H_0: $M_d = 6{,}000$ in favor of H_a: $M_d > 6{,}000$ if we can reject H_0: $p = .5$ in favor of H_a: $p > .5$. Let x denote the total number of lifetimes that exceed 6,000 in a random sample of 20 lifetimes. If H_0: $p = .5$ is true, then x is a binomial random variable where $n = 20$ and $p = .5$. This says that if H_0: $p = .5$ is true, then we would expect $\mu_x = np = 20(.5) = 10$ of the 20 lifetimes to exceed 6,000. Considering the 20 lifetimes we have actually observed, we note that 15 of these 20 lifetimes exceed 6,000. The p-value for testing H_0: $p = .5$ versus H_a: $p > .5$ is the probability, computed assuming that H_0: $p = .5$ is true, of observing a sample result that is at least as contradictory to H_0 as the sample result we have actually observed. Since any number of lifetimes out of 20 lifetimes that is greater than or equal to 15 is at least this contradictory, we have

$$p\text{-value} = P(x \geq 15) = \sum_{x=15}^{20} \frac{20!}{x!(20-x)!}(.5)^x(.5)^{20-x}$$

Using the binomial distribution table in Table A.1 (page 817), we find that

$$\begin{aligned} p\text{-value} &= P(x \geq 15) \\ &= P(x = 15) + P(x = 16) + P(x = 17) + P(x = 18) \\ &\quad + P(x = 19) + P(x = 20) \\ &= .0148 + .0046 + .0011 + .0002 + .0000 + .0000 \\ &= .0207 \end{aligned}$$

This says that if H_0: $p = .5$ is true, then the probability that at least 15 out of 20 lifetimes would exceed 6,000 is only .0207. Since it is difficult to believe that such a small chance would occur, we have strong evidence against H_0: $p = .5$ and in favor of H_a: $p > .5$. That is, we have strong evidence that H_0: $M_d = 6{,}000$ is false and H_a: $M_d > 6{,}000$ is true. This implies that it is reasonable to conclude that the median lifetime of the new compact disc player exceeds the advertised median lifetime of the market's leading compact disc player. Figure 15.1(c) and (d) present the MINITAB and MegaStat output of the sign test of H_0: $M_d = 6{,}000$ versus H_a: $M_d > 6{,}000$. In addition, the output tells us that a point estimate of the population median lifetime is the sample median of 6,757 hours. Recall that in Figure 7.11 (page 275) we showed that MINITAB can also be used to find a confidence interval for a population median.

BI

We summarize how to carry out the sign test in the following box:

The Sign Test for a Population Median

Suppose we have randomly selected a sample of size n from a population, and suppose we wish to test the null hypothesis H_0: $M_d = M_0$ versus one of H_a: $M_d < M_0$, H_a: $M_d > M_0$, or H_a: $M_d \neq M_0$ where M_d denotes the population median. Define the test statistic S as follows:

If the alternative is H_a: $M_d < M_0$, then S = the number of sample measurements less than M_0.

If the alternative is H_a: $M_d > M_0$, then S = the number of sample measurements greater than M_0.

If the alternative is H_a: $M_d \neq M_0$, then S = the larger of S_1 and S_2

where S_1 = the number of sample measurements less than M_0, and

S_2 = the number of sample measurements greater than M_0.

Furthermore, define x to be a binomial variable with parameters n and $p = .5$. Then, we can test H_0: $M_d = M_0$ versus a particular alternative hypothesis at level of significance α by using the appropriate p-value.

Alternative Hypothesis	p-Value (reject H_0 if p-value $< \alpha$)
H_a: $M_d > M_0$	The probability that x is greater than or equal to S
H_a: $M_d < M_0$	The probability that x is greater than or equal to S
H_a: $M_d \neq M_0$	Twice the probability that x is greater than or equal to S

Here we can use Table A.1 (page 817) to find the p-value.

We next point out that, when we take a large sample, we can use the normal approximation to the binomial distribution to implement the sign test. Here, when the null hypothesis H_0: $M_d = M_0$ (or H_0: $p = .5$) is true, the binomial variable x is approximately normally distributed with mean $np = n(.5) = .5n$ and standard deviation $\sqrt{np(1-p)} = \sqrt{n(.5)(1-.5)} = .5\sqrt{n}$. The test is based on the test statistic

$$z = \frac{(S - .5) - .5n}{.5\sqrt{n}}$$

where S is as defined in the previous box and where we subtract .5 from S as a correction for continuity. This motivates the following test:

The Large Sample Sign Test for a Population Median

Suppose we have taken a large sample (for this test, $n \geq 10$ will suffice). Define S as in the previous box, and define the test statistic

$$z = \frac{(S - .5) - .5n}{.5\sqrt{n}}$$

We can test H_0: $M_d = M_0$ versus a particular alternative hypothesis at level of significance α by using the appropriate rejection point rule, or, equivalently, the corresponding p-value.

Alternative Hypothesis	Rejection Point Rule: Reject H_0 if	p-Value (reject H_0 if p-value $< \alpha$)
H_a: $M_d > M_0$	$z > z_\alpha$	The area under the standard normal curve to the right of z
H_a: $M_d < M_0$	$z > z_\alpha$	The area under the standard normal curve to the right of z
H_a: $M_d \neq M_0$	$z > z_{\alpha/2}$	Twice the area under the standard normal curve to the right of z

Example 15.2

Consider Example 15.1. Since the sample size $n = 20$ is greater than 10, we can use the large sample sign test to test H_0: $M_d = 6{,}000$ versus H_a: $M_d > 6{,}000$. Since $S = 15$ is the number of compact disc player lifetimes that exceed $M_0 = 6{,}000$, the test statistic z is

$$z = \frac{(S - .5) - .5n}{.5\sqrt{n}} = \frac{(15 - .5) - .5(20)}{.5\sqrt{20}} = 2.01$$

The p-value for the test is the area under the standard normal curve to the right of $z = 2.01$, which is $.5 - .4778 = .0222$. Since this p-value is less than .05, we have strong evidence that H_a: $M_d > 6{,}000$ is true. Also, note that the large sample, approximate p-value of .0222 given by the normal distribution is fairly close to the exact p-value of .0207 given by the binomial distribution [see Figure 15.1(c)].

To conclude this section, we consider the DVD recorder rating example discussed in the chapter introduction, and we let M_d denote the median rating that would be given by all purchasers who have owned the DVD recorder for one year. Below we present the MINITAB output of the sign test of H_0: $M_d = 7.5$ versus H_a: $M_d > 7.5$:

```
Sign test of median = 7.500 versus > 7.500
               N   Below  Equal   Above       P   Median
DVD Rating    20       5      0      15  0.0207    8.000
```

Since the p-value of .0207 is less than .05, we have strong evidence that the population median rating exceeds 7.5. Furthermore, note that the sign test has reached this conclusion by showing that **more than 50 percent** of all DVD recorder ratings exceed 7.5. It follows, since a rating exceeding 7.5 is the same as a rating being at least 8 (because of the discrete nature of the ratings), that we have strong evidence that the population median rating is at least 8.

Exercises for Section 15.1

CONCEPTS

15.1 What is a nonparametric test? Why would such a test be particularly useful when we must take a small sample?

15.2 When we perform the sign test, we use the sample data to compute a p-value. What probability distribution is used to compute the p-value? Explain why.

METHODS AND APPLICATIONS

15.3 Consider the following sample of five chemical yields: ChemYield

801 814 784 836 820

a Use this sample to test H_0: $M_d = 800$ versus H_a: $M_d \neq 800$ by setting $\alpha = .01$.

b Use this sample to test H_0: $M_d = 750$ versus H_a: $M_d > 750$ by setting $\alpha = .05$.

15.4 Consider the following sample of seven bad debt ratios: BadDebt

7% 4% 6% 7% 5% 4% 9%

Use this sample and the following MINITAB output to test the null hypothesis that the median bad debt ratio equals 3.5 percent versus the alternative hypothesis that the median bad debt ratio exceeds 3.5 percent by setting α equal to .05.

```
Sign test of median = 3.500 versus > 3.500
          N   Below  Equal   Above       P   Median
Ratio     7       0      0       7  0.0078    6.000
```

15.5 A local newspaper randomly selects 20 patrons of the Springwood Restaurant on a given Saturday night and has each patron rate the quality of his or her meal as 5 (excellent), 4 (good), 3 (average), 2 (poor), or 1 (unsatisfactory). When the results are summarized, it is found that there are 16 ratings of 5, 3 ratings of 4, and 1 rating of 3. Let M_d denote the population median rating that would be given by all possible patrons of the restaurant on the Saturday night.

a Test H_0: $M_d = 4.5$ versus H_a: $M_d > 4.5$ by setting $\alpha = .05$.

b Reason that your conclusion in part *a* implies that we have very strong evidence that the median rating that would be given by all possible patrons is 5.

15.6 Suppose that a particular type of plant has a median growing height of 20 inches in a specified time period when the best plant food currently on the market is used as directed. A developer of a new plant food wishes to show that the new plant food increases the median growing height. If a stem-and-leaf display indicates that the population of all growing heights using the new plant food is markedly nonnormal, it would be appropriate to use the sign test to test H_0: $M_d = 20$ versus H_a: $M_d > 20$. Here M_d denotes the population median growing height when the new plant food is

TABLE 15.1 Results of a Taste Test of Coke versus Pepsi CokePep

Customer	Preference (Coke or Pepsi)	Value (Sign)
1	Coke	+1
2	Pepsi	−1
3	Pepsi	−1
4	Coke	+1
5	Coke	+1
6	Pepsi	−1
7	Coke	+1
8	Coke	+1
9	Pepsi	−1

Sign Test				
	0 hypothesized value	4 below		binomial
9 n	1 median Value (sign)	0 equal	1.0000	p-value (two-tailed)
		5 above		

used. Suppose that 13 out of 15 sample plants grown using the new plant food reach a height of more than 20 inches. Test H_0: $M_d = 20$ versus H_a: $M_d > 20$ by using the large sample sign test.

15.7 A common application of the sign test deals with analyzing consumer preferences. For instance, suppose that a blind taste test is administered to nine randomly selected convenience store customers. Each participant is asked to express a preference for either Coke or Pepsi after tasting unidentified samples of each soft drink. The sample results are expressed by recording a +1 for each consumer who prefers Coke and a −1 for each consumer who prefers Pepsi. Note that sometimes, rather than recording either a +1 or a −1, we simply record the sign + or −, hence the name "sign test." A 0 is recorded if a consumer is unable to rank the two brands, and these observations are eliminated from the analysis.

The null hypothesis in this application says that there is no difference in preferences for Coke and Pepsi. If this null hypothesis is true, then the number of +1 values in the population of all preferences should equal the number of −1 values, which implies that the median preference $M_d = 0$ (and that the proportion p of +1 values equals .5). The alternative hypothesis says that there is a significant difference in preferences (or that there is a significant difference in the number of +1 values and −1 values in the population of all preferences). This implies that the median preference does not equal 0 (and that the proportion p of +1 values does not equal .5). CokePep

a Table 15.1 gives the results of the taste test administered to the nine randomly selected consumers. If we consider testing H_0: $M_d = 0$ versus H_a: $M_d \neq 0$ where M_d is the median of the (+1 and −1) preference rankings, determine the values of S_1, S_2, and S for the sign test needed to test H_0 versus H_a. Identify the value of S on the MegaStat output.

b Use the value of S to find the p-value for testing H_0: $M_d = 0$ versus H_a: $M_d \neq 0$. Then use the p-value to test H_0 versus H_a by setting α equal to .10, .05, .01, and .001. How much evidence is there of a difference in the preferences for Coke and Pepsi? What do you conclude?

15.2 The Wilcoxon Rank Sum Test

Recall that in Section 9.2 we presented t tests for comparing two population means in an independent samples experiment. If the sampled populations are far from normally distributed and the sample sizes are small, these tests are not valid. In such a case, a nonparametric method should be used to compare the populations.

We have seen that the mean of a population measures the **central tendency,** or **location,** of the probability distribution describing the population. Thus, for instance, if a t test provides strong evidence that μ_1 is greater than μ_2, we might conclude that the probability distribution of population 1 is *shifted to the right* of the probability distribution of population 2. The nonparametric test for comparing the locations of two populations is not (necessarily) a test about the difference between population means. Rather, it is a more general test to detect whether the probability distribution of population 1 is shifted to the right (or left) of the probability distribution of population 2.[1] Furthermore, **the nonparametric test is valid for any shapes that might describe the sampled populations.**

[1]To be precise, we say that the probability distribution of population 1 is shifted to the right (left) of the probability distribution of population 2 if there is more than a 50 percent chance that a randomly selected observation from population 1 will be greater than (less than) a randomly selected observation from population 2.

In this section we present the **Wilcoxon rank sum test** (also called the **Mann–Whitney test**), which is used to compare the locations of two populations when **independent samples** are selected. To perform this test, we first combine all of the observations in both samples into a single set, and we rank these observations from smallest to largest, with the smallest observation receiving rank 1, the next smallest observation receiving rank 2, and so forth. The sum of the ranks of the observations in each sample is then calculated. If the probability distributions of the two populations are identical, we would expect the sum of the ranks for sample 1 to roughly equal the sum of the ranks for sample 2. However, if, for example, the sum of the ranks for sample 1 is substantially larger than the sum of the ranks for sample 2, this would suggest that the probability distribution of population 1 is shifted to the right of the probability distribution of population 2. We explain how to carry out the Wilcoxon rank sum test in the following box:

The Wilcoxon Rank Sum Test

Let D_1 and D_2 denote the probability distributions of populations 1 and 2, and assume that we randomly select independent samples of sizes n_1 and n_2 from populations 1 and 2. Rank the $n_1 + n_2$ observations in the two samples from the smallest (rank 1) to the largest (rank $n_1 + n_2$). Here, if two or more observations are equal, we assign to each "tied" observation a rank equal to the average of the consecutive ranks that would otherwise be assigned to the tied observations. Let T_1 denote the sum of the ranks of the observations in sample 1, and let T_2 denote the sum of the ranks of the observations in sample 2. Furthermore, define the **test statistic T** to be T_1 if $n_1 \leq n_2$ and to be T_2 if $n_1 > n_2$. Then, we can test

$$H_0\text{: } D_1 \text{ and } D_2 \text{ are identical probability distributions}$$

versus a particular alternative hypothesis at level of significance α by using the appropriate rejection point rule.

Alternative Hypothesis	**Rejection Point Rule: Reject H_0 if**
H_a: D_1 is shifted to the right of D_2	$T \geq T_U$ if $n_1 \leq n_2$ $T \leq T_L$ if $n_1 > n_2$
H_a: D_1 is shifted to the left of D_2	$T \leq T_L$ if $n_1 \leq n_2$ $T \geq T_U$ if $n_1 > n_2$
H_a: D_1 is shifted to the right or left of D_2	$T \leq T_L$ or $T \geq T_U$

The first two alternative hypotheses above are **one-sided,** while the third alternative hypothesis is **two-sided.** Values of the rejection points T_U and T_L are given in Table A.15 (page 836) for values of n_1 and n_2 from 3 to 10.

Table 15.2 repeats a portion of Table A.15. This table gives the rejection point (T_U or T_L) for testing a one-sided alternative hypothesis at level of significance $\alpha = .05$ and also gives the rejection points (T_U and T_L) for testing a two-sided alternative hypothesis at level of significance $\alpha = .10$. The rejection points are tabulated according to n_1 and n_2, the sizes of the samples taken from populations 1 and 2, respectively. For instance, as shown in Table 15.2, if we have taken a sample of size $n_1 = 10$ from population 1, and if we have taken a sample of size $n_2 = 7$ from

TABLE 15.2 A Portion of the Wilcoxon Rank Sum Table Rejection Points for $\alpha = .05$ (One-Sided); $\alpha = .10$ (Two-Sided)

n_2 \ n_1	3		4		5		6		7		8		9		10	
	T_L	T_U	T_L	T_U	T_L	T_U	T_L	T_U	T_L	T_U	T_L	T_U	T_L	T_U	T_L	T_U
3	6	15	7	17	7	20	8	22	9	24	9	27	10	29	11	31
4	7	17	12	24	13	27	14	30	15	33	16	36	17	39	18	42
5	7	20	13	27	19	36	20	40	22	43	24	46	25	50	26	54
6	8	22	14	30	20	40	28	50	30	54	32	58	33	63	35	67
7	9	24	15	33	22	43	30	54	39	66	41	71	43	76	46	80
8	9	27	16	36	24	46	32	58	41	71	52	84	54	90	57	95
9	10	29	17	39	25	50	33	63	43	76	54	90	66	105	69	111
10	11	31	18	42	26	54	35	67	46	80	57	95	69	111	83	127

$\alpha = .05$ one-sided; $\alpha = .10$ two-sided

population 2, then for a one-sided test with $\alpha = .05$, we use $T_U = 80$ or $T_L = 46$. Similarly, if $n_1 = 10$ and $n_2 = 7$, we use $T_U = 80$ and $T_L = 46$ for a two-sided test with $\alpha = .10$.

Example 15.3

The State Court Administrator for the State of Oregon commissioned a study of two circuit court jurisdictions within the state to examine the effect of administrative rule differences on litigation processing time. The two jurisdictions of interest are Coos County and Lane County. Samples of 10 cases were selected at random from each jurisdiction. However, records for three of the cases selected from Lane County were incomplete, and the cases had to be discarded from the analysis, leaving $n_1 = 10$ cases for Coos County and $n_2 = 7$ cases for Lane County. Each selected case was examined to determine the total elapsed time (in days) required for processing the case, from filing to completion. The processing times are given in Figure 15.2(a). Since the corresponding box plots indicate that the population of all possible processing times for each county might be skewed to the right, we will perform the Wilcoxon rank sum test. It was theorized before the samples were taken that the administrative rules in Lane County were somewhat inefficient. Therefore, we will test

H_0: the probability distributions of all possible processing times for Coos County and Lane County are identical

versus

H_a: the probability distribution of all possible processing times for Coos County is shifted to the left of the probability distribution of all possible processing times for Lane County (note that this alternative hypothesis intuitively implies that the Coos County processing times are "systematically less than" the Lane County processing times)

To perform the test, we rank the $n_1 + n_2 = 10 + 7 = 17$ processing times in the two samples as shown in Figure 15.2(a). Note that, since there are two processing times of 145 that are tied as the sixth and seventh smallest processing times, we assign each of these an average rank of 6.5. The sum of the ranks of the processing times in sample 1 (Coos County) is $T_1 = 72.5$, and the sum of the ranks of the processing times in sample 2 (Lane County) is $T_2 = 80.5$. Since $n_1 = 10$ is

FIGURE 15.2 Analysis of the Coos County and Lane County Litigation Processing Times

(a) The Coos County and Lane County litigation processing times Court

Coos County Time	Coos County Rank	Lane County Time	Lane County Rank
48	1	109	4
97	2	145	6.5
103	3	196	10
117	5	273	13
145	6.5	289	14
151	8	417	16
179	9	505	17
220	11		$T_2 = 80.5$
257	12		
294	15		
	$T_1 = 72.5$		

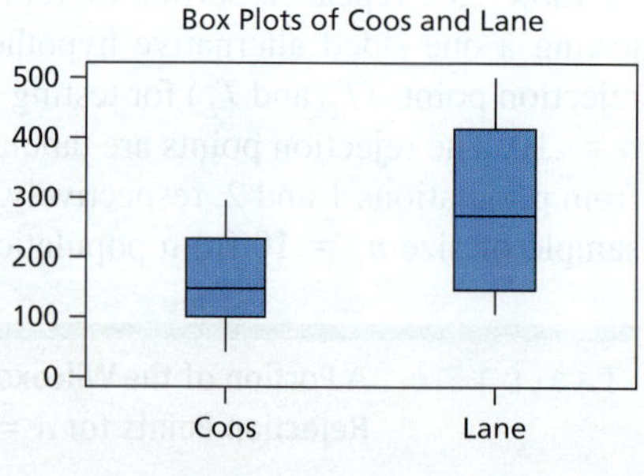

Box Plots of Coos and Lane

500
400
300
200
100
0
Coos
Lane

(b) MINITAB output of the Wilcoxon rank sum test for the litigation processing times

```
Coos    N = 10    Median = 148.0
Lane    N =  7    Median = 273.0
Point estimate for ETA1-ETA2 is -98.0
95.5 Percent CI for ETA1-ETA2 is (-248.0,7.9)
W = 72.5
Test of ETA1 = ETA2 vs ETA1 < ETA2 is significant at 0.0486
The test is significant at 0.0485 (adjusted for ties)
```

greater than $n_2 = 7$, the summary box tells us that the test statistic T is $T_2 = 80.5$. Since we are testing a "shifted left" alternative hypothesis, and since n_1 is greater than n_2, the summary box also tells us that we can reject H_0 in favor of H_a at the .05 level of significance if T is greater than or equal to T_U. Since $T = 80.5$ is greater than $T_U = 80$ (see Table 15.2), we conclude at the .05 level of significance that the Coos County processing times are shifted to the left of, and thus are "systematically less than," the Lane County processing times. This supports the theory that the Lane County administrative rules are somewhat inefficient.

BI

Figure 15.2(b) presents the MINITAB output of the Wilcoxon rank sum test for the litigation processing times. In general, MINITAB gives T_1, the sum of the ranks of the observations in sample 1, as the test statistic, which MINITAB denotes as W. If, as in the present example, n_1 is greater than n_2 and thus the correct test statistic is T_2, **we can obtain T_2 by subtracting T_1 from $(n_1 + n_2)(n_1 + n_2 + 1)/2$.** This last quantity can be proven to equal the sum of the ranks of the $(n_1 + n_2)$ observations in both samples. In the present example, this quantity equals $(10 + 7)(10 + 7 + 1)/2 = (17)(18)/2$, or 153. Therefore, since the MINITAB output tells us that $T_1 = 72.5$, the correct test statistic T_2 is $(153 - 72.5) = 80.5$. In addition to giving T_1, MINITAB gives two p-values related to the hypothesis test. The first p-value—.0486—is calculated assuming that there are no ties. Since there is a tie, the second p-value—.0485—is adjusted accordingly and is more correct (although there is little difference in this situation).

In general, the Wilcoxon rank sum test tests the equality of the population medians if the distributions of the sampled populations have the same shapes and equal variances. MINITAB tells us that under these assumptions a point estimate of the difference in the population medians is −98.0 (days), and a 95.5 percent confidence interval for the difference in the population medians is [−248.0, 7.9]. Note that the point estimate of the difference in the population medians, which is −98.0, is not equal to the difference in the sample medians, which is $148.0 - 273.0 = -125.0$. In the present example, the box plots in Figure 15.2 indicate that the variances of the two populations are not equal. In fact, in most situations it is a bit too much to ask that the sampled populations have exactly the same shapes and equal variances (although we will see in Exercise 15.12 that this might be approximately true in some situations).

As another example, suppose that on a given Saturday night a local newspaper randomly selects 20 patrons from each of two restaurants and has each patron rate the quality of his or her meal as 5 (excellent), 4 (good), 3 (average), 2 (poor), or 1 (unsatisfactory). The following results are obtained:

Rating	Restaurant 1 Patrons	Restaurant 2 Patrons	Total Patrons	Ranks Involved	Average Rank	Restaurant 1 Rank Sum	Restaurant 2 Rank Sum
5	15	5	20	21–40	30.5	(15)(30.5) = 457.5	(5)(30.5) = 152.5
4	4	11	15	6–20	13	(4)(13) = 52	(11)(13) = 143
3	1	2	3	3, 4, 5	4	(1)(4) = 4	(2)(4) = 8
2	0	1	1	2	2	(0)(2) = 0	(1)(2) = 2
1	0	1	1	1	1	(0)(1) = 0	(1)(1) = 1
						$T_1 = 513.5$	$T_2 = 306.5$

Suppose that we wish to test

H_0: The probability distributions of all possible Saturday night meal ratings for restaurants 1 and 2 are identical

versus

H_a: The probability distribution of all possible Saturday night meal ratings for restaurant 1 is shifted to the right or left of the probability distribution of all possible Saturday night meal ratings for restaurant 2.

Since there are only five numerical ordinal ratings, there are many ties. The above table shows how we determine the sum of the ranks for each sample. Since $n_1 = 20$ and $n_2 = 20$, we cannot obtain rejection points by using Table A.15 (which gives rejection points for sample sizes up to $n_1 = 10$ and $n_2 = 10$). However, we can use a large sample, normal approximation, which is valid if both n_1 and n_2 are at least 10. The normal approximation involves making two modifications. First, we replace the test statistic T in the previously given summary box by a standardized value of the test statistic. This standardized value, denoted z, is calculated by subtracting the mean

$\mu_T = n_i(n_1 + n_2 + 1)/2$ from the test statistic T and by then dividing the resulting difference by the standard deviation $\sigma_T = \sqrt{n_1 n_2(n_1 + n_2 + 1)/12}$. Here n_i in the expression for μ_T equals n_1 if the test statistic T is T_1 and equals n_2 if T is T_2. Second, when testing a one-sided alternative hypothesis, we replace the rejection points T_U and T_L by the normal points z_α and $-z_\alpha$. When testing a two-sided alternative hypothesis, we replace T_U and T_L by $z_{\alpha/2}$ and $-z_{\alpha/2}$. For the current example, $n_1 = n_2$, and thus the test statistic T is $T_1 = 513.5$. Furthermore,

$$\mu_T = \frac{n_1(n_1 + n_2 + 1)}{2} = \frac{20(20 + 20 + 1)}{2} = 410$$

$$\sigma_T = \sqrt{\frac{n_1 n_2(n_1 + n_2 + 1)}{12}} = \sqrt{\frac{20(20)(41)}{12}} = 36.968455$$

and

$$z = \frac{T - \mu_T}{\sigma_T} = \frac{513.5 - 410}{36.968455} = 2.7997$$

Since we are testing a "shifted right or left" (that is, a two-sided) alternative hypothesis, the summary box tells us that we reject the null hypothesis if $T \leq T_L$ or $T \geq T_U$. Stated in terms of standardized values, we reject the null hypothesis if $z < -z_{\alpha/2}$ or $z > z_{\alpha/2}$ (here we use strict inequalities to be consistent with other normal distribution rejection point conditions). If we set $\alpha = .01$, we use the rejection points $-z_{.005} = -2.575$ and $z_{.005} = 2.575$. Since $z = 2.7997$ is greater than $z_{.005} = 2.575$, we reject the null hypothesis at the .01 level of significance. Therefore, we have very strong evidence that there is a systematic difference between the Saturday night meal ratings at restaurants 1 and 2. Looking at the original data, we would estimate that Saturday night meal ratings are higher at restaurant 1.

To conclude this section, we make two comments. First, when there are ties, there is an adjusted formula for σ_T that takes into account the ties.[2] If (as in the restaurant example) we ignore the formula, the results we obtain are statistically conservative. Therefore, if we reject the null hypothesis by using the unadjusted formula, we would reject the null hypothesis by using the adjusted formula. Second, MINITAB calculates p-values by using the large sample, normal approximation (and a *continuity correction*), even if the sample sizes n_1 and n_2 are small (less than 10). This will be illustrated in Exercise 15.12.

Exercises for Section 15.2

CONCEPTS

15.8 Explain the circumstances in which we use the Wilcoxon rank sum test.

15.9 Identify the parametric test corresponding to the Wilcoxon rank sum test. What assumption is needed for the validity of this parametric test (and not needed for the Wilcoxon rank sum test)?

METHODS AND APPLICATIONS

15.10 A loan officer at a bank wishes to compare the mortgage rates charged at banks in Texas with the mortgage rates of Texas savings and loans. Two independent random samples of bank mortgage rates and savings and loan mortgage rates in Texas are obtained with the following results:

Bank Rates:	11.25	10.50	11.50	11.00	10.00	9.75	11.50	10.25
S&L Rates:	9.25	10.25	8.75	11.00	9.50	9.00	9.10	8.50

Because both samples are small, the bank officer is uncertain about the shape of the distributions of bank and savings and loan mortgage rates. Therefore, the Wilcoxon rank sum test will be used to compare the two types of mortgage rates. TexMort

a Let D_1 be the distribution of bank mortgage rates and let D_2 be the distribution of savings and loan mortgage rates. Carry out the Wilcoxon rank sum test to determine whether D_1 and D_2 are identical versus the alternative that D_1 is shifted to the right or left of D_2. Use $\alpha = .05$.

b Carry out the Wilcoxon rank sum test to determine whether D_1 is shifted to the right of D_2. Use $\alpha = .025$. What do you conclude?

[2] The adjusted formula is quite complicated.

15.11 A company collected employee absenteeism data (in hours per year) at two of its manufacturing plants. The data were obtained by randomly selecting a sample from all of the employees at the first plant, and by randomly selecting another independent sample from all of the employees at the second plant. For each randomly selected employee, absenteeism records were used to determine the exact number of hours the employee has been absent during the past year. The following results were obtained: Absent

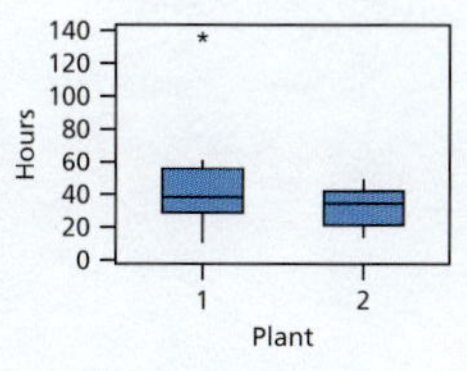

Plant 1:	10	131	53	37	59	29	45	26	39	36
Plant 2:	21	46	33	31	49	33	39	19	12	35

Use a Wilcoxon rank sum test and the following MINITAB output to determine whether absenteeism is different at the two plants. Use $\alpha = .05$.

```
          N   Median
Plant 1   10   38.00
Plant 2   10   33.00
Point estimate for ETA1-ETA2 is 7.00
95.5 Percent CI for ETA1-ETA2 is (-6.99,24.01)
W = 120.5
Test of ETA1 = ETA2 vs ETA1 not = ETA2 is significant at 0.2568
The test is significant at 0.2565 (adjusted for ties)
```

15.12 THE CATALYST COMPARISON CASE

The following table presents samples of hourly yields for catalysts XA-100 and ZB-200. We analyzed these data using a two independent sample t test in Example 9.4 (page 365). Catalyst

Catalyst XA-100	Catalyst ZB-200
801	752
814	718
784	776
836	742
820	763

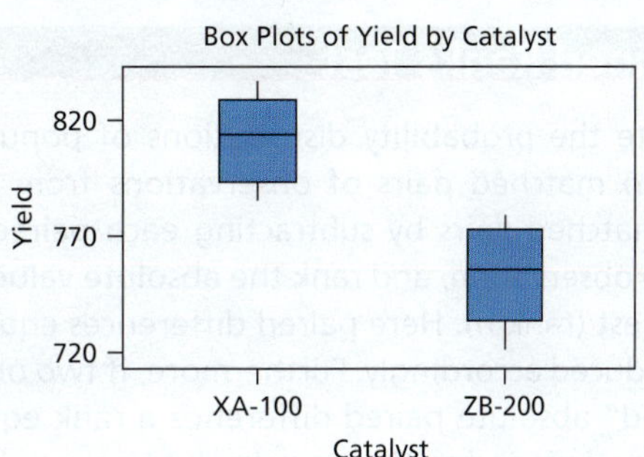

Wilcoxon-Mann/Whitney Test

n	sum of ranks				
5	40	XA-100	27.50 expected value	2.51	z
5	15	ZB-200	4.79 standard deviation	.0122	p-value (two-tailed)
10	55	total			

a Use a Wilcoxon rank sum test and the MegaStat output to test for systematic differences in the yields of the two catalysts. Use $\alpha = .05$.

b The p-value on the MegaStat output has been calculated by finding twice the area under the standard normal curve to the right of

$$z = \frac{39.5 - \mu_T}{\sigma_T} = \frac{39.5 - 27.5}{4.79} = 2.51$$

Here we have used a continuity correction and changed $T_1 = 40$ to 39.5. Verify the calculations of μ_T, σ_T, and the p-value.

c Assume that the second yield for catalyst ZB-200 in the above table is invalid. Use the remaining data to determine if we can conclude that the XA-100 yields are systematically higher than the ZB-200 yields. Set $\alpha = .05$.

15.13 Moore (2000) reports on a study by Boo (1997), who asked 303 randomly selected people at fairs:

How often do you think people become sick because of food they consume prepared at outdoor fairs and festivals?

The possible responses were 5 (always), 4 (often), 3 (more often than not), 2 (once in a while), and 1 (very rarely). The following data were obtained:

Response	Females	Males	Total
5	2	1	3
4	23	5	28
3	50	22	72
2	108	57	165
1	13	22	35

Gender	N	Sum of Scores
Female	196	31996.5
Male	107	14059.5

T = 14059.5 z = −3.33353
Test significant at 0.0009

Source: H. C. Boo, "Consumers' Perceptions and Concerns about Safety and Healthfulness of Food Served at Fairs and Festivals," M. S. thesis, Purdue University, 1997.

The computer output at the right of the data presents the results of a Wilcoxon rank sum test that attempts to determine if men and women systematically differ in their responses. Here the normal approximation has been used to calculate the p-value of .0009. What do you conclude?

15.3 The Wilcoxon Signed Ranks Test

In Section 9.3 we presented a t test for comparing two population means in a paired difference experiment. If the sample size is small and the population of paired differences is far from normally distributed, this test is not valid and we should use a nonparametric test. In this section we present the **Wilcoxon signed ranks test,** which is a nonparametric test for comparing two populations when a **paired difference experiment** has been carried out.

The Wilcoxon Signed Ranks Test

Let D_1 and D_2 denote the probability distributions of populations 1 and 2, and assume that we have randomly selected n matched pairs of observations from populations 1 and 2. Calculate the paired differences of the n matched pairs by subtracting each paired population 2 observation from the corresponding population 1 observation, and rank the absolute values of the n paired differences from the smallest (rank 1) to the largest (rank n). Here paired differences equal to 0 are eliminated, and the number n of paired differences is reduced accordingly. Furthermore, if two or more absolute paired differences are equal, we assign to each "tied" absolute paired difference a rank equal to the average of the consecutive ranks that would otherwise be assigned to the tied absolute paired differences. Let

$$T^- = \text{the sum of the ranks associated with the negative paired differences}$$

and

$$T^+ = \text{the sum of the ranks associated with the positive paired differences}$$

We can test

$$H_0\text{: } D_1 \text{ and } D_2 \text{ are identical probability distributions}$$

versus a particular alternative hypothesis at level of significance α by using the appropriate test statistic and the corresponding rejection point rule.

Alternative Hypothesis	Test Statistic	Rejection Point Rule: Reject H_0 if
H_a: D_1 is shifted to the right of D_2	T^-	$T^- \leq T_0$
H_a: D_1 is shifted to the left of D_2	T^+	$T^+ \leq T_0$
H_a: D_1 is shifted to the right or left of D_2	T = the smaller of T^- and T^+	$T \leq T_0$

The first two alternative hypotheses above are **one-sided,** while the third alternative hypothesis is **two-sided.** Values of the rejection point T_0 are given in Table A.16 (page 837) for values of n from 5 to 50.

Table 15.3 repeats a portion of Table A.16. This table gives the rejection point T_0 for testing one-sided and two-sided alternative hypotheses at several different values of α. The rejection points are tabulated according to n, the number of paired differences. For instance, Table 15.3

TABLE 15.3 A Portion of the Wilcoxon Signed Ranks Table

One-Sided	Two-Sided	$n = 5$	$n = 6$	$n = 7$	$n = 8$	$n = 9$	$n = 10$
$\alpha = .05$	$\alpha = .10$	1	2	4	6	8	11
$\alpha = .025$	$\alpha = .05$		1	2	4	6	8
$\alpha = .01$	$\alpha = .02$			0	2	3	5
$\alpha = .005$	$\alpha = .01$				0	2	3
		$n = 11$	$n = 12$	$n = 13$	$n = 14$	$n = 15$	$n = 16$
$\alpha = .05$	$\alpha = .10$	14	17	21	26	30	36
$\alpha = .025$	$\alpha = .05$	11	14	17	21	25	30
$\alpha = .01$	$\alpha = .02$	7	10	13	16	20	24
$\alpha = .005$	$\alpha = .01$	5	7	10	13	16	19

shows that, if we are analyzing 10 paired differences, then the rejection point for testing a one-sided alternative hypothesis at the .01 level of significance is equal to $T_0 = 5$. This table also shows that we would use the rejection point $T_0 = 5$ for testing a two-sided alternative hypothesis at level of significance $\alpha = .02$.

Example 15.4 The Repair Cost Comparison Case

C

Again consider the automobile repair cost data, which are given in Figure 15.3(a). We analyzed these data using a paired sample t test in Example 9.7 (page 374). If we fear that the population of all possible paired differences of repair cost estimates at garages 1 and 2 may be far from normally distributed, we can perform the Wilcoxon signed ranks test. Here we test

H_0: the probability distributions of the populations of all possible repair cost estimates at garages 1 and 2 are identical

versus

H_a: the probability distribution of repair cost estimates at garage 1 is shifted to the left of the probability distribution of repair cost estimates at garage 2

To perform this test, we find the absolute value of each paired difference, and we assign ranks to the absolute differences [see Figure 15.3(a)]. Because of the form of the alternative hypothesis (see the preceding summary box), we use the test statistic

$$T^+ = \text{the sum of the ranks associated with the positive paired differences}$$

FIGURE 15.3 Analysis of the Repair Cost Estimates at Two Garages

(a) Sample of $n = 7$ Paired Differences of the Repair Cost Estimates at Garages 1 and 2 (Cost Estimates in Hundreds of Dollars) Repair

Sample of $n = 7$ Damaged Cars	Repair Cost Estimates at Garage 1	Repair Cost Estimates at Garage 2	Sample of $n = 7$ Paired Differences	Absolute Paired Differences	Ranks
Car 1	\$ 7.1	\$ 7.9	$d_1 = -.8$	.8	4
Car 2	9.0	10.1	$d_2 = -1.1$	1.1	5
Car 3	11.0	12.2	$d_3 = -1.2$	1.2	6
Car 4	8.9	8.8	$d_4 = .1$	.1	1
Car 5	9.9	10.4	$d_5 = -.5$	.5	2
Car 6	9.1	9.8	$d_6 = -.7$	.7	3
Car 7	10.3	11.7	$d_7 = -1.4$	1.4	7

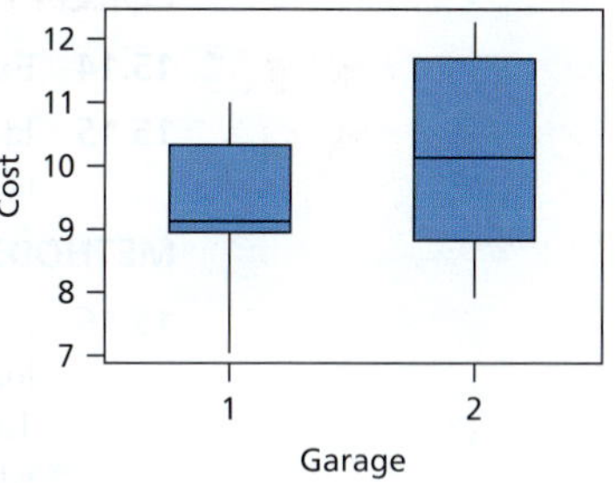

(b) MINITAB output of the Wilcoxon signed ranks test

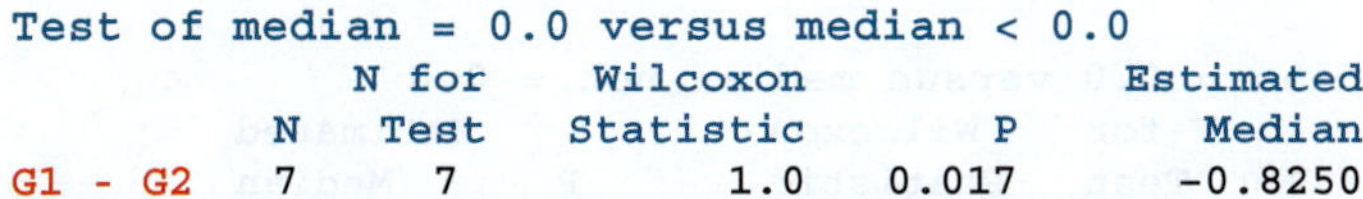

```
Test of median = 0.0 versus median < 0.0
          N for    Wilcoxon              Estimated
      N   Test    Statistic       P       Median
G1 - G2  7    7          1.0   0.017     -0.8250
```

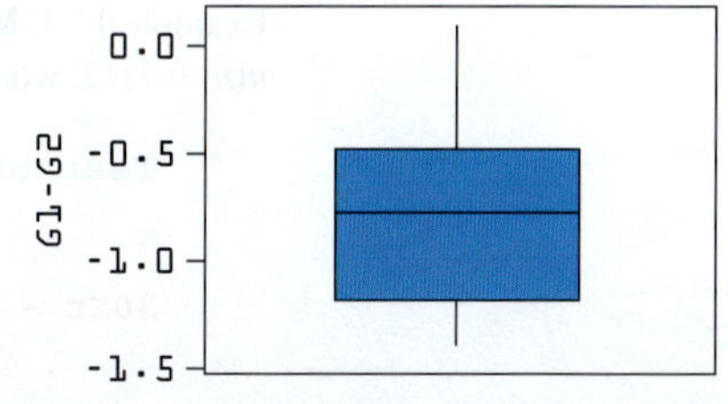

Since .1 is the only positive paired difference, and since the rank associated with this difference equals 1, we find that $T^+ = 1$. The alternative hypothesis is one-sided, and we are analyzing $n = 7$ paired differences. Therefore, Table 15.3 tells us that we can test H_0 versus H_a at the .05, .025, and .01 levels of significance by setting the rejection point T_0 equal to 4, 2, and 0, respectively. The rejection point condition is $T^+ \leq T_0$. It follows that, since $T^+ = 1$ is less than or equal to 4 and 2, but is not less than or equal to 0, we can reject H_0 in favor of H_a at the .05 and .025 levels of significance, but not at the .01 level of significance. Therefore, we have strong

evidence that the probability distribution of repair cost estimates at garage 1 is shifted to the left of the probability distribution of repair cost estimates at garage 2. That is, the repair cost estimates at garage 1 seem to be systematically lower than the repair cost estimates at garage 2. Figure 15.3(b) presents the MINITAB output of the Wilcoxon signed ranks test for this repair cost comparison. In general, MINITAB gives T^+ as the "Wilcoxon statistic," even if T^- is the appropriate test statistic. It can be shown that **T^- can be obtained by subtracting T^+ from $n(n + 1)/2$,** where n is the total number of paired differences being analyzed.

Notice that in Example 15.4 the nonparametric Wilcoxon signed ranks test would not allow us to reject H_0 in favor of H_a at the .01 level of significance. On the other hand, the *parametric* paired difference t test performed in Example 9.7 did allow us to reject H_0: $\mu_1 - \mu_2 = 0$ in favor of H_a: $\mu_1 - \mu_2 < 0$ at the .01 level of significance. In general, **a parametric test is often *more powerful*** than the analogous nonparametric test. That is, the parametric test often allows us to reject H_0 at smaller values of α. Therefore, if the assumptions for the parametric test are satisfied—for example, if, when we are using small samples, the sampled populations are approximately normally distributed—it is preferable to use the parametric test. **The advantage of nonparametric tests is that they can be used without assuming that the sampled populations have the shapes of any particular probability distributions.** As an example, this can be important when reporting statistical conclusions to U.S. federal agencies. Federal guidelines specify that, when reporting statistical conclusions, the validity of the assumptions behind the statistical methods used must be fully justified. If, for instance, there are insufficient data to justify the assumption that the sampled populations are approximately normally distributed, then we must use a nonparametric method to make conclusions.

Finally, if the sample size n is at least 25, we can use a large sample approximation of the Wilcoxon signed ranks test. This is done by making two modifications. First, we replace the test statistic (T^- or T^+) by a standardized value of the test statistic. This standardized value is calculated by subtracting the mean $n(n + 1)/4$ from the test statistic (T^- or T^+) and then dividing the resulting difference by the standard deviation $\sqrt{n(n + 1)(2n + 1)/24}$. Second, when testing a one-sided alternative hypothesis, we replace the rejection point T_0 by the normal point $-z_\alpha$. When testing a two-sided alternative hypothesis, we replace T_0 by $-z_{\alpha/2}$.

Exercises for Section 15.3

CONCEPTS

15.14 Explain the circumstances in which we use the Wilcoxon signed ranks test.

15.15 Identify the parametric test corresponding to the Wilcoxon signed ranks test. What assumption is needed for the validity of the parametric test (and not needed for the Wilcoxon signed ranks test)?

METHODS AND APPLICATIONS

15.16 Recall that in Exercise 9.31 (page 376) we compared 30-year and 15-year fixed rate mortgage loans for a number of Willamette Valley lending institutions. The results obtained are shown in Table 15.4. Use the Wilcoxon signed ranks test and the following MINITAB output to determine whether, for Willamette Valley lending institutions, the distribution of 30-year rates is shifted to the right or left of the distribution of 15-year rates. Use $\alpha = .01$. Hint: As discussed in Example 15.4, MINITAB gives T^+ as the Wilcoxon statistic. Find T^- by subtracting T^+ from $n(n + 1)/2$, where $n = 9$. Mortgage99

```
Test of median = 0.0 versus median not = 0.0
                 N for   Wilcoxon              Estimated
              N   Test   Statistic        P       Median
30Yr - 15Yr   9      9        45.0    0.009       0.2355
```

TABLE 15.4 1999 Mortgage Loan Interest Rates for Nine Randomly Selected Willamette Valley Lending Institutions Mortgage99

	Annual Percentage Rate		
Lending Institution	**30-Year**	**15-Year**	**Difference**
American Mortgage N.W. Inc.	6.715	6.599	0.116
City and Country Mortgage	6.648	6.367	0.281
Commercial Bank	6.740	6.550	0.190
Landmark Mortgage Co.	6.597	6.362	0.235
Liberty Mortgage, Inc.	6.425	6.162	0.263
MaPS Credit Union	6.880	6.583	0.297
Mortgage Brokers, Inc.	6.900	6.800	0.100
Mortgage First Corp.	6.675	6.394	0.281
Silver Eagle Mortgage	6.790	6.540	0.250

Source: Via World Wide Web, Salem Homeplace Mortgage Rates Directory http://www.salemhomeplace.com/pages/finance/, January 4, 1999. Reproduced by permission of the Statesman Journal Newspaper, Salem, Oregon.

TABLE 15.5 Pretest and Posttest Leadership Scores Leader

Manager	Pretest Score	Posttest Score	Difference
1	35	54	−19
2	27	43	−16
3	51	53	−2
4	38	50	−12
5	32	42	−10
6	44	58	−14
7	33	35	−2
8	26	39	−13
9	40	47	−7
10	50	48	2
11	36	41	−5
12	31	37	−6

15.17 A consumer advocacy group is concerned about the ability of tax preparation firms to correctly prepare complex returns. To test the performance of tax preparers in two different tax preparation firms—Quick Tax and Discount Tax—the group designed a tax case for a family with a gross annual income of $150,000 involving several thorny tax issues. In a "tax-off" competition, the advocacy group randomly selected independent samples of 10 preparers from each firm and asked each preparer to compute the tax liability for the test case. The preparers' returns were collected, and the group computed the difference between each preparer's computed tax and the actual tax that should have been computed. The data below consist of the resulting two sets of tax computation errors, one for preparers from Quick Tax and the other for preparers from Discount Tax. Fully interpret the following MINITAB output of a Wilcoxon signed ranks test analysis of this data. TaxErr

Quick Tax Errors	Discount Tax Errors	Difference
857	156	701
920	200	720
1,090	202	888
1,594	390	1,204
1,820	526	1,294
1,943	749	1,194
1,987	911	1,076
2,008	920	1,088
2,083	2,145	−62
2,439	2,602	−163

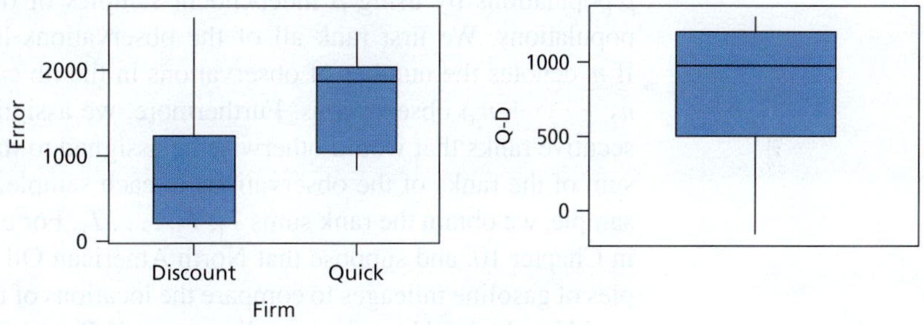

```
Test of median = 0.0 versus median not = 0.0
      N   N for Test   Wilcoxon Statistic       P   Estimated Median
Q-D  10           10                 52.0   0.014              898.0
```

15.18 A human resources director wishes to assess the benefits of sending a company's managers to an innovative management course. Twelve of the company's managers are randomly selected to attend the course, and a psychologist interviews each participating manager before and after taking the course. Based on these interviews, the psychologist rates the manager's leadership ability on a 1-to-100 scale. The pretest and posttest leadership scores for each of the 12 managers are given in Table 15.5. Leader

a Let D_1 be the distribution of leadership scores before taking the course, and let D_2 be the distribution of leadership scores after taking the course. Carry out the Wilcoxon signed ranks test to test whether D_1 and D_2 are identical (that is, the course has no effect on leadership scores) versus the alternative that D_2 is shifted to the right or left of D_1 (that is, the course affects leadership scores). Use $\alpha = .05$.

b Carry out the Wilcoxon signed ranks test to determine whether D_2 is shifted to the right of D_1. Use $\alpha = .05$. What do you conclude?

15.19 Recall that in Exercise 9.32 (page 377) we compared preexposure and postexposure attitude scores for an advertising study by using a paired difference t test. The data obtained and related MegaStat output are shown in Table 15.6. Use the Wilcoxon signed ranks test and the MegaStat output to determine whether the distributions of preexposure and postexposure attitude scores are different. Use $\alpha = .05$. AdStudy

TABLE 15.6 Preexposure and Postexposure Attitude Scores for an Advertising Study
AdStudy

Subject	Preexposure Attitudes (A_1)	Postexposure Attitudes (A_2)	Attitude Change (d_i)
1	50	53	3
2	25	27	2
3	30	38	8
4	50	55	5
5	60	61	1
6	80	85	5
7	45	45	0
8	30	31	1
9	65	72	7
10	70	78	8

Wilcoxon Signed Rank Test

variables: Pre. Attitudes(A1) - Post. Attitudes(A2)

0	sum of positive ranks
45	sum of negative ranks
9	n
22.50	expected value
7.89	standard deviation
−2.85	z, corrected for ties
.0043	p-value (two-tailed)

Source: W. R. Dillon, T. J. Madden, and N. H. Firtle, *Essentials of Marketing Research* (Burr Ridge, IL: Richard D. Irwin, 1993), p. 435. Copyright © 1993. Reprinted by permission of McGraw-Hill Companies, Inc.

15.4 Comparing Several Populations Using the Kruskal–Wallis *H* Test

If we fear that the normality and/or equal variances assumptions for one-way ANOVA do not hold, we can use a nonparametric approach to compare several populations. One such approach is the **Kruskal–Wallis *H* test,** which compares the locations of three or more populations by using independent random samples and a completely randomized experimental design.

In general, suppose we wish to use the Kruskal–Wallis H test to compare the locations of p populations by using p independent samples of observations randomly selected from these populations. We first rank all of the observations in the p samples from smallest to largest. If n_i denotes the number of observations in the ith sample, we are ranking a total of $n = (n_1 + n_2 + \cdots + n_p)$ observations. Furthermore, we assign tied observations the average of the consecutive ranks that would otherwise be assigned to the tied observations. Next, we calculate the sum of the ranks of the observations in each sample. Letting T_i denote the rank sum for the ith sample, we obtain the rank sums $T_1, T_2, \ldots, T_p$. For example, consider the gasoline mileage case in Chapter 10, and suppose that North American Oil wishes to use the $p = 3$ independent samples of gasoline mileages to compare the locations of the populations of all gasoline mileages that could be obtained by using gasoline types A, B, and C. The gasoline mileage data are repeated in Table 15.7, along with the ranking (given in parentheses) of each observation in each sample. If we sum the ranks in each sample, we find that $T_1 = 37.5$, $T_2 = 63$, and $T_3 = 19.5$. Note that, although the box plots in Table 15.7 do not indicate any serious violations of the normality or equal variances assumptions, the samples are quite small, and thus we cannot be sure that these assumptions approximately hold. Therefore, it is reasonable to compare gasoline types A, B, and C by using the Kruskal–Wallis H test.

The Kruskal–Wallis *H* Test

Consider testing the null hypothesis H_0 that the p populations under consideration are identical versus the alternative hypothesis H_a that at least two populations differ in location (that is, are shifted either to the left or to the right of one another). We can reject H_0 in favor of H_a at level of significance α if the **Kruskal–Wallis *H* statistic**

$$H = \frac{12}{n(n+1)} \sum_{i=1}^{p} \frac{T_i^2}{n_i} - 3(n+1)$$

is greater than the χ^2_α point based on $p - 1$ degrees of freedom. Here, for this test to be valid, there should be five or more observations in each sample. Furthermore, the number of ties should be small relative to the total number of observations. Values of χ^2_α are given in Table A.17 (page 838).

TABLE 15.7 The Gasoline Mileage Samples and Rank Sums GasMile2

Gasoline Type *A*	Gasoline Type *B*	Gasoline Type *C*
34.0 (3.5)	35.3 (9)	33.3 (2)
35.0 (8)	36.5 (13)	34.0 (3.5)
34.3 (5)	36.4 (12)	34.7 (6)
35.5 (10)	37.0 (14)	33.0 (1)
35.8 (11)	37.6 (15)	34.9 (7)
$T_1 = 37.5$	$T_2 = 63$	$T_3 = 19.5$

FIGURE 15.4 MINITAB Output of the Kruskal–Wallis *H* Test in the Gasoline Mileage Case

```
Kruskal-Wallis Test on Mileage
Type        N    Median    Ave Rank        Z
A           5     35.00         7.5    -0.31
B           5     36.50        12.6     2.82
C           5     34.00         3.9    -2.51
Overall    15                   8.0

H = 9.56    DF = 2    P = 0.008
H = 9.57    DF = 2    P = 0.008  (adjusted for ties)
```

In the gasoline mileage case, $\chi^2_{.05}$ based on $p - 1 = 2$ degrees of freedom is 5.99147 (see Table A.17). Furthermore, since $n = n_1 + n_2 + n_3 = 15$, the Kruskal–Wallis H statistic is

$$H = \frac{12}{15(15+1)}\left[\frac{(37.5)^2}{5} + \frac{(63)^2}{5} + \frac{(19.5)^2}{5}\right] - 3(15+1)$$

$$= \frac{12}{240}\left[\frac{1{,}406.25}{5} + \frac{3{,}969}{5} + \frac{380.25}{5}\right] - 48 = 9.555$$

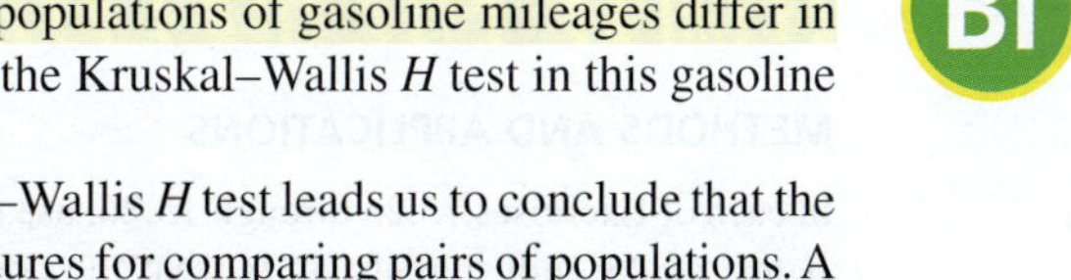

Since $H = 9.555 > \chi^2_{.05} = 5.99147$, we can reject H_0 at the .05 level of significance. Therefore, we have strong evidence that at least two of the three populations of gasoline mileages differ in location. Figure 15.4 presents the MINITAB output of the Kruskal–Wallis H test in this gasoline mileage case.

To conclude this section, we note that, if the Kruskal–Wallis H test leads us to conclude that the p populations differ in location, there are various procedures for comparing pairs of populations. A simple procedure is to use the Wilcoxon rank sum test to compare pairs of populations. For example, if we use this test to make separate, **two-sided** comparisons of (1) gasoline types A and B, (2) gasoline types A and C, and (3) gasoline types B and C, and if we set α equal to .05 for each comparison, we find that the mileages given by gasoline type B differ systematically from the mileages given by gasoline types A and C. Examining the mileages in Table 15.7, we would estimate that gasoline type B gives the highest mileages. One problem, however, with using the Wilcoxon rank sum test to make pairwise comparisons is that it is difficult to know how to set α for each comparison. Therefore, some practitioners prefer to make **simultaneous** pairwise comparisons (such as given by the Tukey simultaneous confidence intervals discussed in Chapter 10). Gibbons (1985) discusses a nonparametric approach for making simultaneous pairwise comparisons.

Exercises for Section 15.4

CONCEPTS

15.20 Explain the circumstances in which we use the Kruskal–Wallis H test.

15.21 Identify the parametric test corresponding to the Kruskal–Wallis H test.

15.22 What are the assumptions needed for the validity of the parametric test identified in Exercise 15.21 that are not needed for the Kruskal–Wallis H test?

TABLE 15.8 Display Panel Study Data (Time, in Seconds, Required to Stabilize Air Traffic Emergency Condition) Display3

Display Panel		
A	*B*	*C*
21	24	40
27	21	36
24	18	35
26	19	32
25	20	37

TABLE 15.9 Bottle Design Study Data (Sales during a 24-Hour Period) BottleDes

Bottle Design		
A	*B*	*C*
16	33	23
18	31	27
19	37	21
17	29	28
13	34	25

TABLE 15.10 Bakery Sales Study Data (Sales in Cases) BakeSale

Shelf Display Height		
Bottom (*B*)	Middle (*M*)	Top (*T*)
58.2	73.0	52.4
53.7	78.1	49.7
55.8	75.4	50.9
55.7	76.2	54.0
52.5	78.4	52.1
58.9	82.1	49.9

FIGURE 15.5 MINITAB Output of the Kruskal–Wallis *H* Test for the Bakery Sales Data

```
Kruskal-Wallis Test on Bakery Sales

Display   N    Median    Ave Rank       Z
Bottom    6     55.75       9.2     -0.19
Middle    6     77.15      15.5      3.37
Top       6     51.50       3.8     -3.18
Overall  18                 9.5
H = 14.36      DF = 2      P = 0.001
```

TABLE 15.11 Golf Ball Durability Test Results GolfBall

Brand			
Alpha	Best	Century	Divot
281	270	218	364
220	334	244	302
274	307	225	325
242	290	273	337
251	331	249	355

Kruskal-Wallis Test

Median	n	Avg. Rank	
251.00	5	6.80	Alpha
307.00	5	13.40	Best
244.00	5	4.80	Century
337.00	5	17.00	Divot
277.50	20		Total

13.834	H
3	d.f.
.0031	p-value

METHODS AND APPLICATIONS

In each of Exercises 15.23 through 15.26, use the given independent samples to perform the Kruskal–Wallis H test of the null hypothesis H_0 that the corresponding populations are identical versus the alternative hypothesis H_a that at least two populations differ in location. Note that we analyzed each of these data sets using the one-way ANOVA F test in the exercises of Chapter 10.

15.23 Use the Kruskal–Wallis H test to compare display panels A, B, and C using the data in Table 15.8. Use $\alpha = .05$. Display3

15.24 Use the Kruskal–Wallis H test to compare bottle designs A, B, and C using the data in Table 15.9. Use $\alpha = .01$. BottleDes

15.25 Use the Kruskal–Wallis H test and the MINITAB output in Figure 15.5 to compare the bottom (B), middle (M), and top (T) display heights using the data in Table 15.10. Use $\alpha = .05$. Then, repeat the analysis if the first sales value for the middle display height is found to be incorrect and must be removed from the data set. BakeSale

15.26 Use the Kruskal–Wallis H test to compare golf ball brands Alpha, Best, Century, and Divot using the data in Table 15.11. Use $\alpha = .01$ and the MegaStat output to the right of Table 15.11. GolfBall

15.5 Spearman's Rank Correlation Coefficient

In Section 11.7 (page 492) we showed how to test the significance of a population correlation coefficient. This test is based on the assumption that the population of all possible combinations of values of x and y has a bivariate normal probability distribution. If we fear that this assumption

TABLE 15.12 Electronics World Sales Volume Data and Ranks for 15 Stores
Electronics

Store	Number of Households, x	Sales Volume, y	x-Rank	y-Rank	Difference, d	d^2
1	161	157.27	6	7	−1	1
2	99	93.28	1	1	0	0
3	135	136.81	5	5	0	0
4	120	123.79	4	3	1	1
5	164	153.51	7	6	1	1
6	221	241.74	13	14	−1	1
7	179	201.54	8	10	−2	4
8	204	206.71	9	11	−2	4
9	214	229.78	12	13	−1	1
10	101	135.22	2	4	−2	4
11	231	224.71	14	12	2	4
12	206	195.29	11	8	3	9
13	248	242.16	15	15	0	0
14	107	115.21	3	2	1	1
15	205	197.82	10	9	1	1
						$\Sigma d_i^2 = 32$

is badly violated, we can use a nonparametric approach. One such approach is **Spearman's rank correlation coefficient,** which is denoted r_s.

To illustrate, suppose that Electronics World, a chain of stores that sells audio and video equipment, has gathered the data in Table 15.12. The company wishes to study the relationship between store sales volume in July of last year (y, measured in thousands of dollars) and the number of households in the store's area (x, measured in thousands). Spearman's rank correlation coefficient is found by first ranking the values of x and y separately (ties are treated by averaging the tied ranks). To calculate r_s, we use the formula given in Section 11.6 (page 489) for r and replace the x and y values in that formula by their ranks. If there are no ties in the ranks, this formula can be calculated by the simple equation

$$r_s = 1 - \frac{6\Sigma d_i^2}{n(n^2 - 1)}$$

where d_i is the difference between the x-rank and the y-rank for the ith observation (if there are few ties in the ranks, this formula is approximately valid). For example, Table 15.12 gives the ranks of x and y, the difference between the ranks, and the squared difference for each of the $n = 15$ stores in the Electronics World example. Since the sum of the squared differences is 32, we calculate r_s to be

$$r_s = 1 - \frac{6(32)}{15(225 - 1)} = .9429$$

Equivalently, if we have MINITAB (1) find the ranks of the x (household) values (which we call the *HRanks*) and the ranks of the y (sales) values (which we call the *SRanks*) and (2) use the formula given in Section 11.6 (page 489) for r to calculate the correlation coefficient between the *HRanks* and *SRanks,* we obtain the following output:

```
Pearson correlation of HRank and SRank = 0.943
```

This large positive value of r_s says that there is a strong positive rank correlation between the numbers of households and sales volumes in the sample.

In general, let ρ_s denote the **population rank correlation coefficient**—the rank correlation coefficient for the population of all possible (x, y) values. We can test the significance of ρ_s by using **Spearman's rank correlation test.**

Spearman's Rank Correlation Test

Let r_s denote Spearman's rank correlation coefficient. Then, we can test H_0: $\rho_s = 0$ versus a particular alternative hypothesis at level of significance α by using the appropriate rejection point rule.

Alternative Hypothesis	Rejection Point Rule: Reject H_0 if
H_a: $\rho_s > 0$	$r_s > r_\alpha$
H_a: $\rho_s < 0$	$r_s < -r_\alpha$
H_a: $\rho_s \neq 0$	$\lvert r_s \rvert > r_{\alpha/2}$

Table A.18 (page 839) gives values of the rejection points r_α, $-r_\alpha$, and $r_{\alpha/2}$ for values of n from 5 to 30. Note that for this test to be valid the number of ties encountered in ranking the observations should be small relative to the number of observations.

A portion of Table A.18 is reproduced here as Table 15.13. To illustrate using this table, suppose in the Electronics World example that we wish to test H_0: $\rho_s = 0$ versus H_a: $\rho_s > 0$ by setting $\alpha = .05$. Since there are $n = 15$ stores, Table 15.13 tells us that we use the rejection point $r_{.05} = .441$. Since $r_s = .9429$ is greater than this rejection point, we can reject H_0: $\rho_s = 0$ in favor of H_a: $\rho_s > 0$ by setting $\alpha = .05$. Therefore, we have strong evidence that in July of last year the sales volume of an Electronics World store was positively correlated with the number of households in the store's area.

BI

To illustrate testing a two-sided alternative hypothesis, consider Table 15.14. This table presents the rankings of $n = 12$ midsize cars given by two automobile magazines. Here each magazine has ranked the cars from 1 (best) to 12 (worst) on the basis of overall ride. Since the two magazines sometimes have differing views, we cannot theorize about whether their rankings would be positively or negatively correlated. Therefore, we will test H_0: $\rho_s = 0$ versus H_a: $\rho_s \neq 0$. The summary box tells us that to perform this test at level of significance α, we use the rejection point $r_{\alpha/2}$. To look up $r_{\alpha/2}$ in Table A.18 (or Table 15.13), we replace the symbol α by the symbol $\alpha/2$. For example, consider setting $\alpha = .05$. Then, since $\alpha/2 = .025$, we look in Table 15.13 for the value .025. Since there are $n = 12$ cars, we find that $r_{.025} = .591$. Spearman's rank correlation coefficient for the car ranking data can be calculated to be .8951. Since $r_s = .8951$ is greater than $r_{.025} = .591$, we reject H_0 at the .05 level of significance. Therefore, we conclude that the midsize car ride rankings given by the two magazines are correlated. Furthermore, since $r_s = .8951$, we estimate that these rankings are positively correlated.

BI

To conclude this section, we make two comments. First, the car ranking example illustrates that Spearman's rank correlation coefficient and test can be used when the raw measurements of the x and/or y variables are themselves **ranks.** Ranks are measurements of an ordinal variable,

TABLE 15.13 Critical Values for Spearman's Rank Correlation Coefficient

n	$\alpha = .05$	$\alpha = .025$	$\alpha = .01$	$\alpha = .005$
10	.564	.648	.745	.794
11	.523	.623	.736	.818
12	.497	.591	.703	.780
13	.475	.566	.673	.745
14	.457	.545	.646	.716
15	.441	.525	.623	.689
16	.425	.507	.601	.666
17	.412	.490	.582	.645
18	.399	.476	.564	.625
19	.388	.462	.549	.608
20	.377	.450	.534	.591

TABLE 15.14 Rankings of 12 Midsize Cars by Two Automobile Magazines

CarRank

Car	Magazine 1 Ranking	Magazine 2 Ranking
1	5	7
2	1	1
3	4	5
4	7	4
5	6	6
6	8	10
7	9	8
8	12	11
9	2	3
10	3	2
11	10	12
12	11	9

and Spearman's nonparametric approach applies to ordinal variables. Second, it can be shown that if the sample size n is at least 10, then we can carry out an approximation to Spearman's rank correlation test by replacing r_s by the t statistic

$$t = \frac{r_s\sqrt{n-2}}{\sqrt{1-r_s^2}}$$

and by replacing the rejection points r_α, $-r_\alpha$, and $r_{\alpha/2}$ by the t points t_α, $-t_\alpha$, and $t_{\alpha/2}$ (with $n-2$ degrees of freedom). Since Table A.18 gives r_α points for sample sizes up to $n = 30$, this approximate procedure is particularly useful if the sample size exceeds 30. In this case, we can use the z points z_α, $-z_\alpha$, and $z_{\alpha/2}$ in place of the corresponding t points.

Exercises for Section 15.5

CONCEPTS

15.27 Explain the circumstances in which we use Spearman's rank correlation coefficient.

15.28 Write the formula that we use to compute Spearman's rank correlation coefficient when

a There are no (or few) ties in the ranks of the x and y values.

b There are many ties in the ranks of the x and y values.

METHODS AND APPLICATIONS

15.29 A sales manager ranks 10 people at the end of their training on the basis of their sales potential. A year later, the number of units sold by each person is determined. The following data and MegaStat output are obtained. Note that the manager's ranking of 1 is "best." SalesRank

Person	1	2	3	4	5	6	7	8	9	10
Manager's Ranking, x	7	4	2	6	1	10	3	5	9	8
Units Sold, y	770	630	820	580	720	440	690	810	560	470

	MgrRank, x	UnitSold, y
MgrRank, x	1.000	
UnitSold, y	−.721	1.000

10 sample size

±.632 critical value .05 (two-tail)
±.765 critical value .01 (two-tail)

a Find r_s on the MegaStat output and use Table 15.13 to find the critical value for testing H_0: $\rho_s = 0$ versus H_a: $\rho_s \neq 0$ at the .05 level of significance. Do we reject H_0?

b The MegaStat output gives approximate critical values for $\alpha = .05$ and $\alpha = .01$. Do these approximate critical values, which are based on the t distribution, differ by much from the exact critical values in Table 15.13 (recall that $n = 10$)?

15.30 Use the following MINITAB output to find r_s, and then test H_0: $\rho_s = 0$ versus H_a: $\rho_s > 0$ for the service time data below. CopyServ

Copiers Serviced, x	4	2	5	7	1	3	4	5	2	4	6
Minutes Required, y	109	58	138	189	37	82	103	134	68	112	154

```
Pearson correlation of CRank and MRank = 0.986
```

15.31 Compute r_s and test H_0: $\rho_s = 0$ versus H_a: $\rho_s > 0$ for the direct labor cost data below. DirLab

Batch Size, x	5	62	35	12	83	14	46	52	23	100	41	75
Direct Labor Cost, y	71	663	381	138	861	145	493	548	251	1,024	435	772

Chapter Summary

The validity of many of the inference procedures presented in this book requires that various assumptions be met. Often, for instance, a normality assumption is required. In this chapter we have learned that, when the needed assumptions are not met, we must employ a **nonparametric method.** Such a method does not require any assumptions about the shape(s) of the distribution(s) of the sampled population(s).

We first presented the **sign test,** which is a hypothesis test about a population median. This test is useful when we have taken a sample from a population that may not be normally distributed. We next presented two nonparametric tests for comparing the locations of two populations. The first such test, the **Wilcoxon rank sum test,** is appropriate when an **independent samples experiment** has been carried out. The second, the **Wilcoxon signed**

ranks test, is appropriate when a **paired difference experiment** has been carried out. Both of these tests can be used without assuming that the sampled populations have the shapes of any particular probability distributions. We then discussed the **Kruskal–Wallis *H* test,** which is a nonparametric test for comparing the locations of several populations by using independent samples. This test, which employs the chi-square distribution, can be used when the normality and/or equal variances assumptions for one-way analysis of variance do not hold. Finally, we presented a nonparametric approach for testing the significance of a population correlation coefficient. Here we saw how to compute **Spearman's rank correlation coefficient,** and we discussed how to use this quantity to test the significance of the population correlation coefficient.

Glossary of Terms

Kruskal–Wallis *H* test: A nonparametric test for comparing the locations of three or more populations by using independent random samples. (page 750)

nonparametric test: A hypothesis test that requires no assumptions about the distribution(s) of the sampled population(s). (page 736)

sign test: A hypothesis test about a population median that requires no assumptions about the sampled population. (page 736)

Spearman's rank correlation coefficient: A correlation coefficient computed using the ranks of the observed values of two variables x and y. (page 752)

Wilcoxon rank sum test: A nonparametric test for comparing the locations of two populations when an independent samples experiment has been carried out. (page 740)

Wilcoxon signed ranks test: A nonparametric test for comparing the locations of two populations when a paired difference experiment has been carried out. (page 746)

Important Formulas and Tests

Sign test for a population median: page 738
Large sample sign test: page 738
Wilcoxon rank sum test: page 741
Wilcoxon rank sum test (large sample approximation): pages 743–744
Kruskal–Wallis *H* statistic: page 750
Kruskal–Wallis *H* test: page 750
Wilcoxon signed ranks test: page 746
Wilcoxon signed ranks test (large sample approximation): page 748
Spearman's rank correlation coefficient: page 753
Spearman's rank correlation test: page 754

Supplementary Exercises

15.32 Again consider the price comparison situation in which weekly expenses were compared at two chains—Miller's and Albert's. Recall that independent random samples at the two chains yielded the following weekly expenses: ShopExp

Miller's

$119.25	$121.32	$122.34	$120.14	$122.19
$123.71	$121.72	$122.42	$123.63	$122.44

Albert's

$111.99	$114.88	$115.11	$117.02	$116.89
$116.62	$115.38	$114.40	$113.91	$111.87

Since the sample sizes are small, there might be reason to doubt that the populations of expenses at the two chains are normally distributed. Therefore, use a Wilcoxon rank sum test to determine whether expenses at Miller's and at Albert's differ. Use $\alpha = .05$.

15.33 A drug company wishes to compare the effects of three different drugs (X, Y, and Z) that are being developed to reduce cholesterol levels. Each drug is administered to six patients at the recommended dosage for six months. At the end of this period the reduction in cholesterol level is recorded for each patient. The results are given in Table 15.15. Assuming that the three samples are independent, use a nonparametric test to see whether the effects of the three drugs differ. Use $\alpha = .05$. CholRed

15.34 In an article published in *The Journal News* (Hamilton, Ohio) on February 21, 1993, Lew Sichelman (United Features Syndication) wrote the following:

> Despite a relatively weak market, housing prices moved slightly higher last year.

Table 15.16 gives the average 1991 and 1992 prices for new and used homes (in thousands of dollars) for six randomly selected U.S. housing markets. Use a nonparametric test to attempt to show that housing prices increased from 1991 to 1992. Use $\alpha = .05$ and explain your conclusion. HomePrice

TABLE 15.15 Reduction of Cholesterol Levels Using Three Drugs CholRed

	Drug	
X	Y	Z
22	40	15
31	35	9
19	47	14
27	41	11
25	39	21
18	33	5

TABLE 15.16 1991 and 1992 Average Prices for New and Used Homes (in Thousands of Dollars) for Six Randomly Selected Housing Markets HomePrice

Housing Market	1991 Average Price	1992 Average Price
Minneapolis, Minn.	$134.2	$126.3
St. Louis, Mo.	125.4	159.2
Columbus, Ohio	127.7	126.6
Baltimore, Md.	164.6	166.0
Pittsburgh, Pa.	95.8	110.1
Seattle, Wash.	168.3	179.2

Source: L. Sichelman, "Housing Prices See Slight Rise through 1992," *The Journal News* (Hamilton, Ohio), February 21, 1993.

TABLE 15.17 Average Account Ages in 1999 and 2000 for 10 Randomly Selected Accounts AcctAge

Account	Average Age of Account in 1999 (Days)	Average Age of Account in 2000 (Days)
1	35	27
2	24	19
3	47	40
4	28	30
5	41	33
6	33	25
7	35	31
8	51	29
9	18	15
10	28	21

15.35 During 2000 a company implemented a number of policies aimed at reducing the ages of its customers' accounts. In order to assess the effectiveness of these measures, the company randomly selects 10 customer accounts. The average age of each account is determined for each of the years 1999 and 2000. These data are given in Table 15.17. Use a nonparametric technique to attempt to show that average account ages have decreased from 1999 to 2000. Use $\alpha = .05$. AcctAge

15.36 The following data concern the divorce rate (y) per 1,000 women and the percentage of the female population in the labor force (x): Divorce

Year	1890	1900	1910	1920	1930	1940	1950	1960	1970
Divorce Rate, y	3.0	4.1	4.7	8.0	7.5	8.8	10.3	9.2	14.9
% of Females in Labor Force, x^*	18.9	20.6	25.4	23.7	24.8	27.4	31.4	34.8	42.6

*15 years old and over 1890–1930; 14 and over 1940–1960; 16 and over thereafter.

Source: U.S. Department of Commerce, Bureau of the Census, *Bicentennial Statistics*, Washington, D.C., 1976.

Use a nonparametric technique to attempt to show that x and y are positively correlated. Use $\alpha = .05$.

15.37 A loan officer wishes to compare the interest rates being charged for 48-month fixed-rate auto loans and 48-month variable-rate auto loans. Two independent, random samples of auto loan rates are selected. A sample of eight *48-month fixed-rate* auto loans had the following loan rates: AutoLoan

10.29% 9.75% 9.50% 9.99% 9.75% 9.99% 11.40% 10.00%

while a sample of five *48-month variable-rate* auto loans had loan rates as follows:

9.59% 8.75% 8.99% 8.50% 9.00%

Perform a nonparametric test to determine whether loan rates for 48-month fixed-rate auto loans differ from loan rates for 48-month variable-rate auto loans. Use $\alpha = .05$. Explain your conclusion.

15.38 A large bank wishes to limit the median debt-to-equity ratio for its portfolio of commercial loans to 1.5. The bank randomly selects 15 of its commercial loan accounts. Audits result in the following debt-to-equity ratios: DebtEq

1.31	1.05	1.45	1.21	1.19
1.78	1.37	1.41	1.22	1.11
1.46	1.33	1.29	1.32	1.65

Can it be concluded that the median debt-to-equity ratio is less than 1.5 at the .05 level of significance? Explain.

15.39 Internet Exercise LaborFrc

Did labor force participation rates (LFPR) for women increase between 1968 and 1972? The Data and Story Library (DASL) contains LFPR figures for 1968 and 1972, for each of 19 cities. Go to the DASL website (http://lib.stat.cmu.edu/DASL/) and retrieve the Women in the Labor Force data set (http://lib.stat.cmu.edu/DASL/Datafiles/LaborForce.html). Produce appropriate graphical (histogram, stem-and-leaf, box plot) and numerical summaries of the LFPR data and conduct the following nonparametric statistical analyses (data sets: LaborFrc.xls, LaborFrc.mtw):

a Do the data provide sufficient evidence to conclude that the LFPR for women *increased* between 1968 and 1972? Conduct a nonparametric, two-sample, independent samples Wilcoxon rank sum test at the 0.01 level of significance. Clearly state the hypotheses and your conclusion. Report the *p*-value (observed level of significance) for your test.

b Consider, as an alternative to the foregoing independent sample analysis, a paired sample procedure, the nonparametric Wilcoxon signed ranks test. Test once more the hypothesis of part *a*, this time using the Wilcoxon signed ranks test applied to the differences in LFPRs [1972−1968]. Again, clearly state your conclusion and *p*-value.

c Between the two tests of parts *a* and *b*, which is the more appropriate for the current data situation? Why?

Appendix 15.1 ■ Nonparametric Methods Using MINITAB

The instruction blocks in this section each begin by describing the entry of data into the MINITAB data window. Alternatively, the data may be loaded directly from the data disk included with the text. The appropriate data file name is given at the top of each instruction block. Please refer to Appendix 1.1 for further information about entering data, saving data, and printing results.

Sign test for the median in Figure 15.1(c) on page 737 (data file: CompDisc.mtw):

- Enter the compact disc data from Figure 15.1(a) on page 737 into column C1 with variable name LifeTime.
- Select **Stat : Nonparametrics : 1-Sample Sign**
- In the 1-Sample Sign dialog box, enter LifeTime into the Variables window.
- Click on "Test median", and enter the number 6000 into the Test median box.
- Click on the "Alternative" arrow button, and select "greater than" from the pull-down menu.
- Click OK in the 1-Sample Sign dialog box to obtain the sign test results in the Session window.

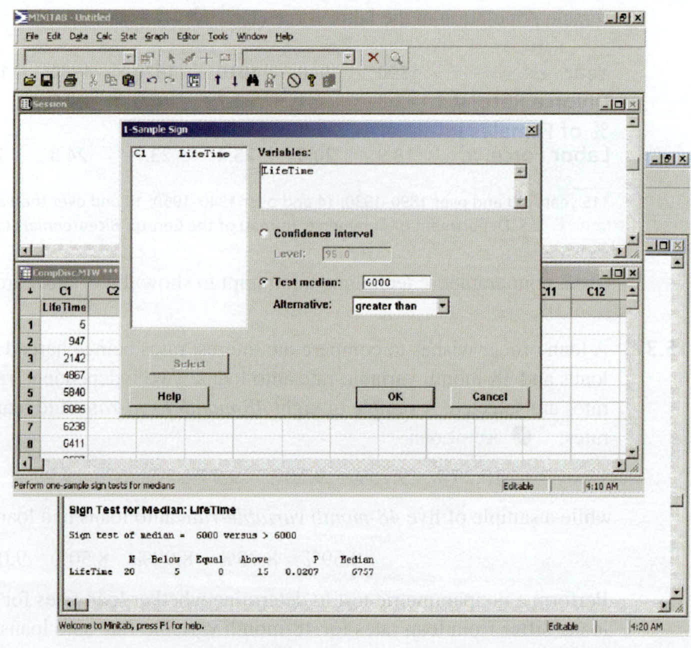

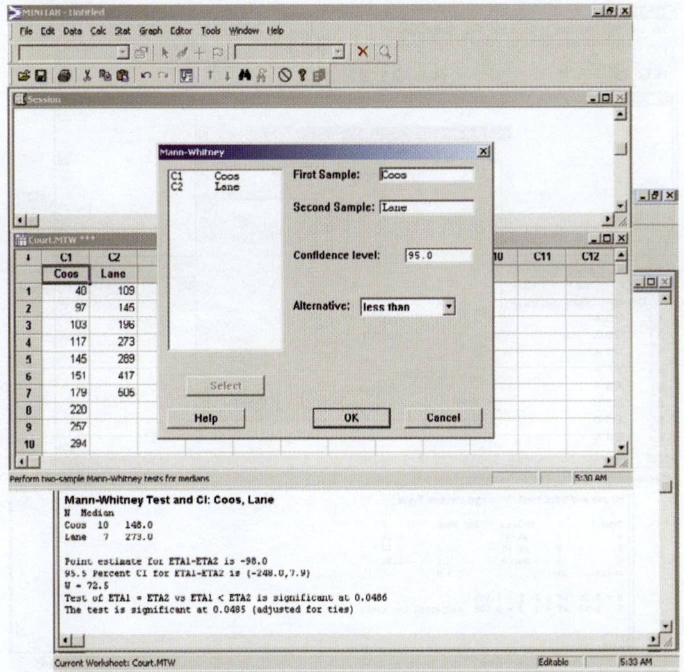

Wilcoxon (also known as Mann–Whitney) rank sum test for two independent samples in Figure 15.2(b) on page 742 (data file: Court.mtw):

- Enter the litigation data from Figure 15.2(a) on page 742 into two columns—Coos County data in column C1 with variable name Coos and Lane County data in column C2 with variable name Lane.
- Select **Stat : Nonparametrics : Mann–Whitney**
- In the Mann-Whitney dialog box, enter Coos into the First Sample box and enter Lane into the Second Sample box.
- Type 95 in the Confidence level box.
- Click on the "Alternative" arrow button and select "less than" from the pull-down menu.
- Click OK in the Mann–Whitney dialog box to obtain test results in the Session window.

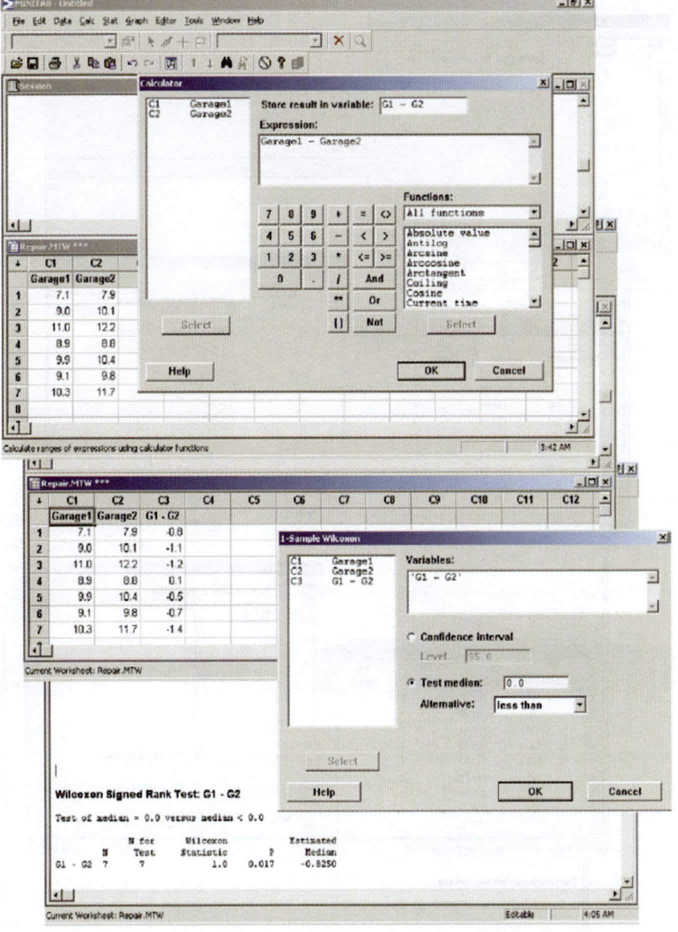

Wilcoxon signed ranks test for paired differences in Figure 15.3(b) on page 747 (data file: Repair.mtw):

- Enter the garage repair data from Figure 15.3(a) on page 747 into two columns—garage 1 cost estimates in column C1 with variable name Garage1 and garage 2 cost estimates in column C2 with variable name Garage2.
- Select **Calc : Calculator.**
- In the Calculator dialog box, enter G1 − G2 into the "Store result in variable" box.
- Enter Garage1 − Garage2 into the Expression window.
- In the Calculator dialog box, click OK to store the repair cost differences in column G1 − G2.
- Select **Stat : Nonparametrics : 1-Sample Wilcoxon.**
- In the 1-Sample Wilcoxon dialog box, enter 'G1 − G2' into the Variables window by selecting G1 − G2 from the variables list.
- In the 1-Sample Wilcoxon dialog box, click "Test median" and enter the number 0 into the Test median box.
- Click the "Alternative" arrow button, and select "less than" from the pull-down menu.
- Click OK in the 1-Sample Wilcoxon dialog box to obtain test results in the Session window.

Kruskal–Wallis *H* test for comparing several populations in Figure 15.4 on page 751 (data file: GasMile2.mtw):

- Enter the gas mileage data from Table 15.7 (page 751) into two columns—gas mileages in column C1 with variable name Mileage and gasoline type (A, B, or C) in column C2 with variable name Type.
- Select **Stat : Nonparametrics : Kruskal–Wallis.**
- In the Kruskal–Wallis dialog box, enter Mileage into the Response box and enter Type into the Factor box.
- Click OK in the Kruskal–Wallis dialog box to obtain test results in the Session window.

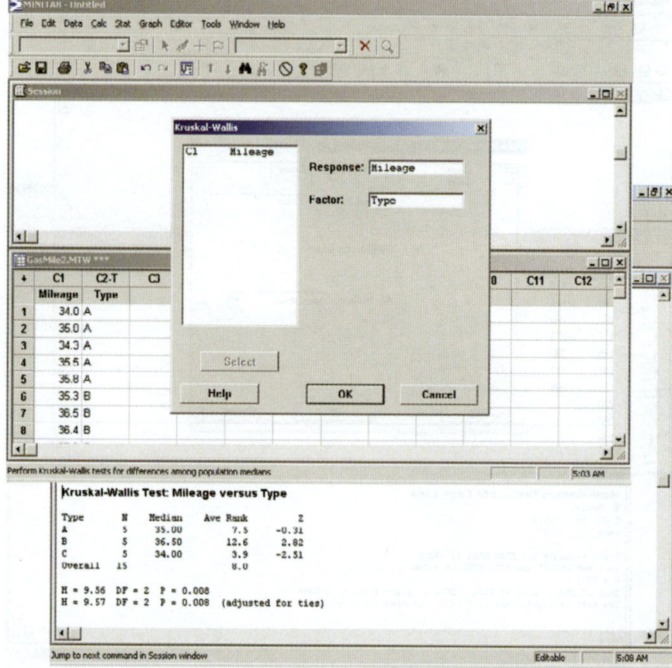

Spearman's rank correlation coefficient in Section 15.5 on page 753 (data file: Electronics.mtw):

- Enter the electronics sales data from Table 15.12 (page 753) into two columns—number of households in column C1 with variable name Households and sales volumes in column C2 with variable name Sales.
- Select **Data : Rank.**
- In the Rank dialog box, enter Households into the "Rank data in" box and enter HRank into the "Store ranks in" box.
- Click OK in the Rank dialog box to obtain column C3 with variable name HRank containing ranks for the Households observations.
- Select **Data : Rank.**
- In the Rank dialog box, enter Sales into the "Rank data in" box and enter SRank into the "Store ranks in" box.
- Click OK in the Rank dialog box to obtain column C4 with variable name SRank containing ranks for the Sales observations.
- Select **Stat : Basic Statistics : Correlation.**
- In the Correlation dialog box, enter HRank and SRank into the Variables window.
- Click on "Display p-values" to uncheck this option (or leave it checked, if desired).
- Click OK in the Correlation dialog box to obtain the rank correlation coefficient in the Session window.

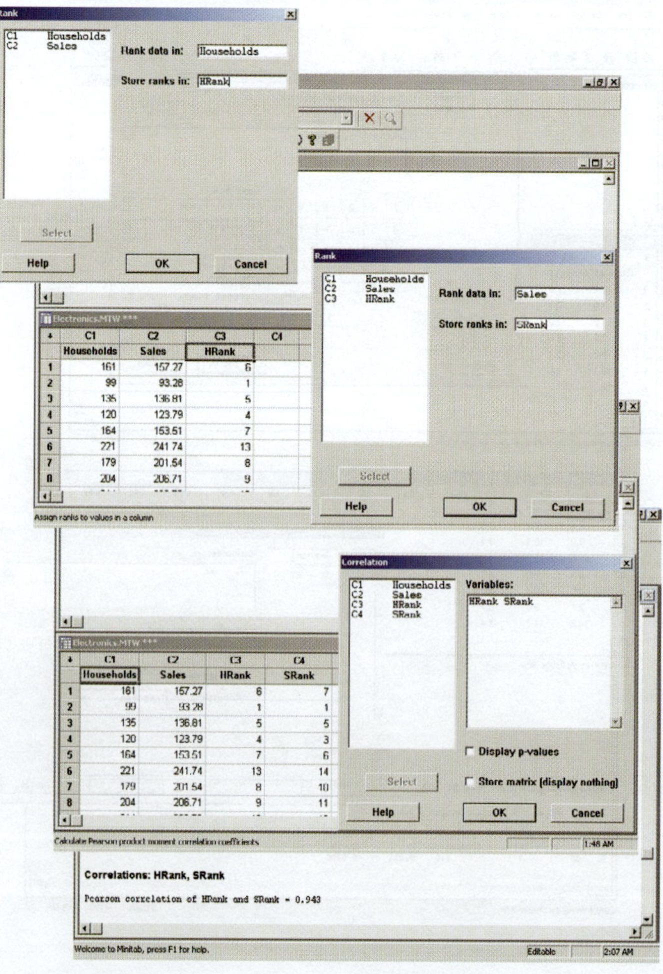

Appendix 15.2 ■ Nonparametric Methods Using MegaStat

The instructions in this section begin by describing the entry of data into an Excel worksheet. Alternatively, the data may be loaded directly from the data disk included with the text. The appropriate data file name is given at the top of each instruction block. Please refer to Appendix 1.2 for further information about entering data and saving and printing results in Excel. Please refer to Appendix 1.3 for more information about using MegaStat.

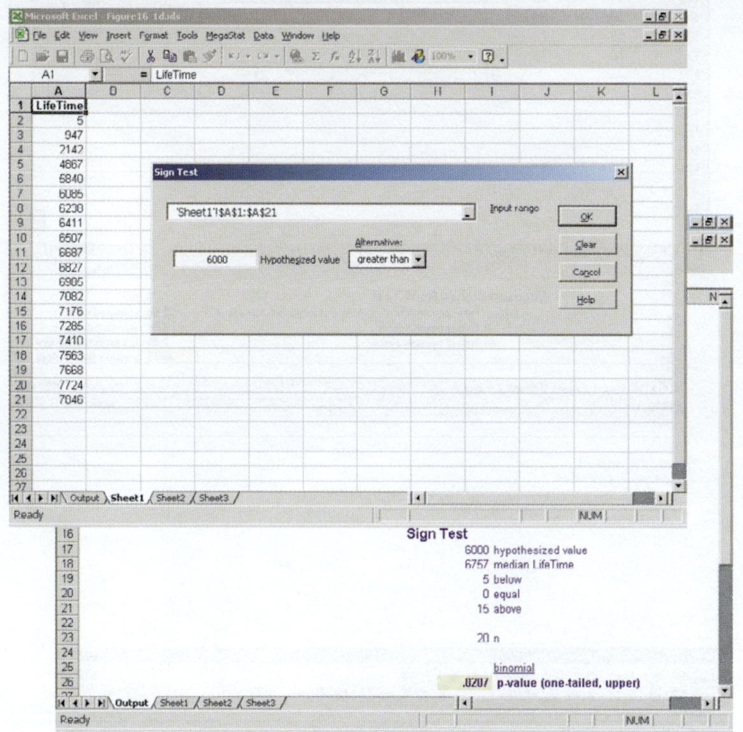

Sign test for the median in Figure 15.1(d) on page 737 (data file: CompDisc.xls):

- Enter the compact disc data from Figure 15.1(a) on page 737 into column A with the label LifeTime in cell A1.
- Select **MegaStat : Nonparametric Tests : Sign Test.**
- In the Sign Test dialog box, use the AutoExpand feature to enter the range A1.A21 into the Input range box.
- Enter the hypothesized median (here equal to 6000) into the "Hypothesized value" box.
- Select the desired alternative (in this case "greater than") from the drop-down menu in the Alternative box.
- Click OK in the Sign Test dialog box.

Wilcoxon (also known as Mann–Whitney) rank sum test for independent samples in Exercise 15.12 on page 745 (data file: Catalyst.xls):

- Enter the data for Catalyst XA-100 into column A with label XA-100 in cell A1, and enter the data for Catalyst ZB-200 into column B with label ZB-200 in cell B1.
- Select **MegaStat : Nonparametric Tests : Wilcoxon–Mann/Whitney Test.**
- In the "Wilcoxon–Mann/Whitney Test" dialog box, click in the Group 1 box to make it active and use the AutoExpand feature to enter the range A1.A6 into the Group 1 box.
- Click in the Group 2 box to make it active, and use the AutoExpand feature to enter the range B1.B6 into the Group 2 Box.
- Select the desired alternative (in this case "not equal") from the drop-down menu in the Alternative box.
- Check the "Correct for ties" check box.
- Click OK in the "Wilcoxon–Mann/Whitney Test" dialog box.

Wilcoxon signed ranks test for paired differences in Table 15.6 on page 750 (data file: AdStudy.xls):

- Enter the advertising study data in Table 15.6. Enter the preexposure scores in column A with label PreAttitude, and enter the postexposure scores in column B with label PostAttitude.
- Select **MegaStat : Nonparametric Tests : Wilcoxon Signed Ranks Test.**
- In the "Wilcoxon Signed Ranks Test" dialog box, click in the Group 1 box to make it active, and use the AutoExpand feature to enter the range A1.A11 into the Group 1 box.
- Click in the Group 2 box to make it active, and use the AutoExpand feature to enter the range B1.B11 into the Group 2 box.
- Select the desired alternative (in this case "not equal") from the drop-down menu in the Alternative box.
- Check the "Correct for ties" check box.
- Click OK in the "Wilcoxon Signed Ranks Test" dialog box.

Kruskal–Wallis *H* test for comparing several populations in Table 15.11 on page 752 (data file: GolfBall.xls):

- Enter the golf ball durability data into columns A, B, C, and D as shown in the screenshot with labels Alpha, Best, Century, and Divot.
- Select **MegaStat : Nonparametric Tests : Kruskal–Wallis Test.**
- In the "Kruskal–Wallis Test" dialog box, enter (by dragging with the mouse) the range A1.D6. Each column in the selected range will be considered by MegaStat as a group to be compared to the other groups.
- Check the "Correct for ties" check box.
- Click OK in the "Kruskal–Wallis Test" dialog box.

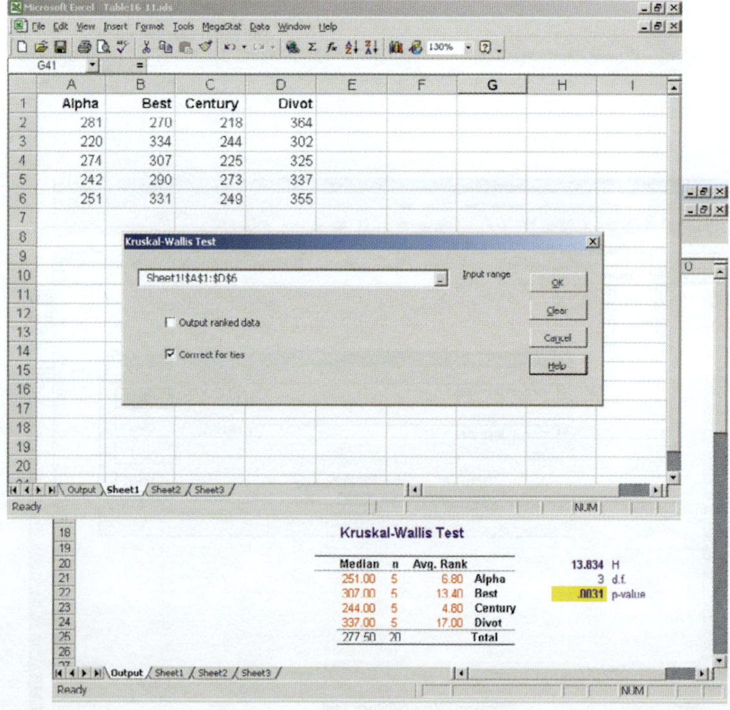

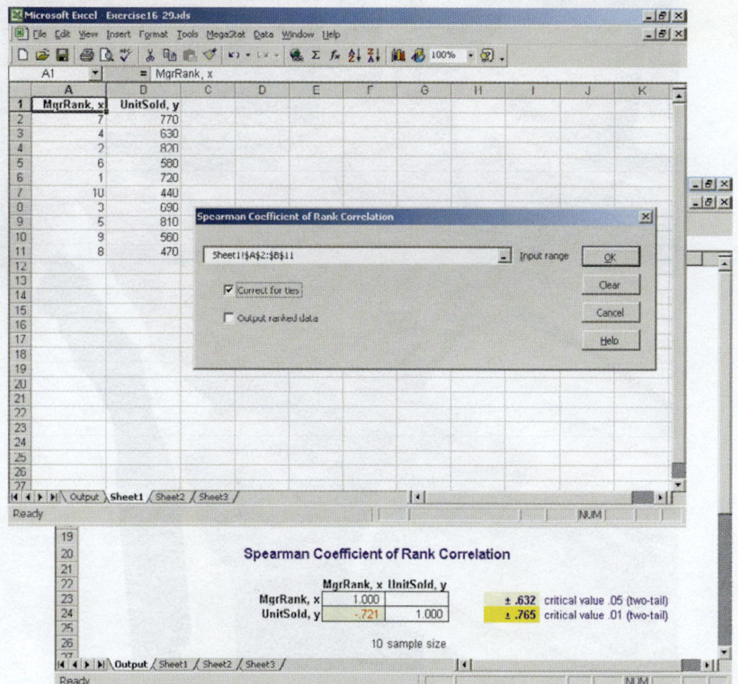

Spearman's rank correlation coefficient in Exercise 15.29 on page 755 (data file: SalesRank.xls):

- Enter the sales data in Exercise 15.29 into columns A and B. Enter the manager's rankings into column A with label "MgrRank, x" in cell A1, and enter the units sold into column B with label "UnitsSold, y" in cell B1.
- Select **MegaStat : Nonparametric Tests : Spearman Coefficient of Rank Correlation.**
- In the "Spearman Coefficient of Rank Correlation" dialog box, enter (by dragging with the mouse) the range A1.B11. Here each column in the selected range will be considered by MegaStat to be a separate variable.
- Check the "Correct for ties" check box.
- Click OK in the "Spearman Coefficient of Rank Correlation" dialog box.

CHAPTER 16

Chi-Square Tests

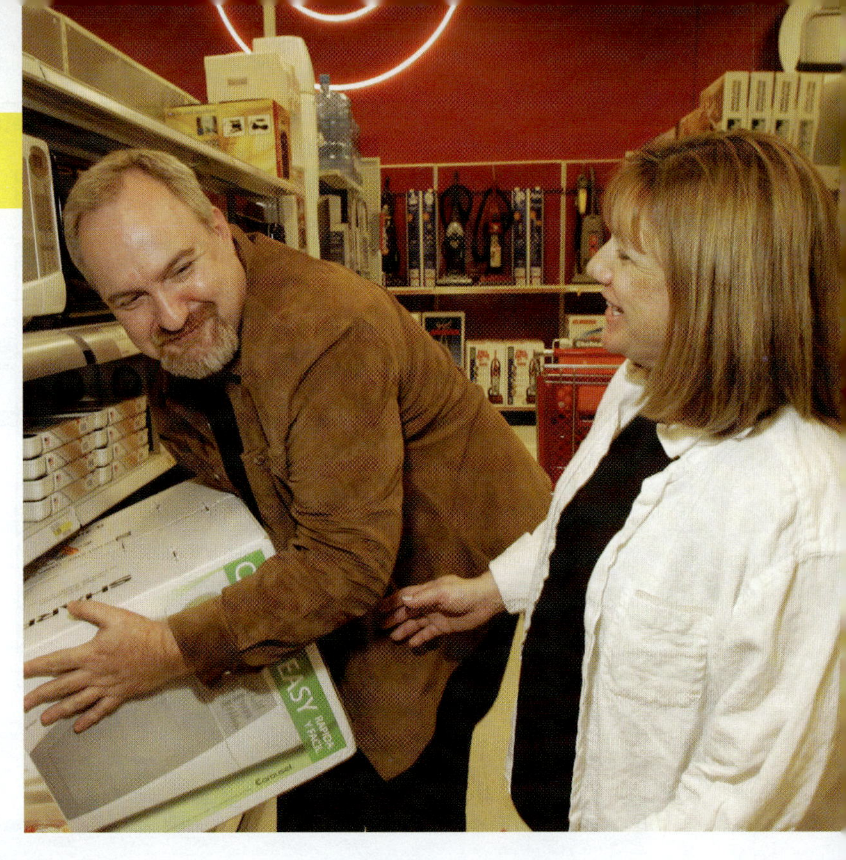

Chapter Outline

In this chapter we present two useful hypothesis tests based on the **chi-square distribution** (we have discussed the chi-square distribution in Section 8.7). First, we consider the **chi-square test of goodness of fit.** This test evaluates whether data falling into several categories do so with a hypothesized set of probabilities. Second, we discuss the **chi-square test for independence.** Here data are classified on two dimensions and are summarized in a **contingency table.** The test for independence then evaluates whether the cross-classified variables are independent of each other. If we conclude that the variables are not independent, then we have established that the variables in question are related, and we must then investigate the nature of the relationship.

16.1 Chi-Square Goodness of Fit Tests

Multinomial probabilities Sometimes we collect count data in order to study how the counts are distributed among several **categories** or **cells.** As an example, we might study consumer preferences for four different brands of a product. To do this, we select a random sample of consumers, and we ask each survey participant to indicate a brand preference. We then count the number of consumers who prefer each of the four brands. Here we have four categories (brands), and we study the distribution of the counts in each category in order to see which brands are preferred.

CHAPTER 13

We often use categorical data to carry out a statistical inference. For instance, suppose that a major wholesaler in Cleveland, Ohio, carries four different brands of microwave ovens. Historically, consumer behavior in Cleveland has resulted in the market shares shown in Table 16.1. The wholesaler plans to begin doing business in a new territory—Milwaukee, Wisconsin. To study whether its policies for stocking the four brands of ovens in Cleveland can also be used in Milwaukee, the wholesaler compares consumer preferences for the four ovens in Milwaukee with the historical market shares observed in Cleveland. A random sample of 400 consumers in Milwaukee gives the preferences shown in Table 16.2.

To compare consumer preferences in Cleveland and Milwaukee, we must consider a **multinomial experiment.** This is similar to the binomial experiment. However, a binomial experiment concerns count data that can be classified into two categories, while a multinomial experiment concerns count data that are classified into more than two categories. Specifically, the assumptions for the multinomial experiment are as follows:

The Multinomial Experiment

1 We perform an experiment in which we carry out n identical trials and in which there are k possible outcomes on each trial.

2 The probabilities of the k outcomes are denoted $p_1, p_2, \ldots, p_k$ where $p_1 + p_2 + \cdots + p_k = 1$. These probabilities stay the same from trial to trial.

3 The trials in the experiment are independent.

4 The results of the experiment are observed frequencies (counts) of the number of trials that result in each of the k possible outcomes. The frequencies are denoted $f_1, f_2, \ldots, f_k$. That is, f_1 is the number of trials resulting in the first possible outcome, f_2 is the number of trials resulting in the second possible outcome, and so forth.

TABLE 16.1 Market Shares for Four Microwave Oven Brands in Cleveland, Ohio MicroWav

Brand	Market Share
1	20%
2	35%
3	30%
4	15%

TABLE 16.2 Brand Preferences for Four Microwave Ovens in Milwaukee, Wisconsin MicroWav

Brand	Observed Frequency (Number of Consumers Sampled Who Prefer the Brand)
1	102
2	121
3	120
4	57

Notice that the scenario that defines a multinomial experiment is similar to that which defines a binomial experiment. In fact, a binomial experiment is simply a multinomial experiment where k equals 2 (there are two possible outcomes on each trial).

In general, the probabilities $p_1, p_2, \ldots, p_k$ are unknown, and we estimate their values. Or, we compare estimates of these probabilities with a set of specified values. We now look at such an example.

Example 16.1 The Microwave Oven Preference Case

Suppose the microwave oven wholesaler wishes to compare consumer preferences in Milwaukee with the historical market shares in Cleveland. If the consumer preferences in Milwaukee are substantially different, the wholesaler will consider changing its policies for stocking the ovens. Here we will define

p_1 = the proportion of Milwaukee consumers who prefer brand 1

p_2 = the proportion of Milwaukee consumers who prefer brand 2

p_3 = the proportion of Milwaukee consumers who prefer brand 3

p_4 = the proportion of Milwaukee consumers who prefer brand 4

Remembering that the historical market shares for brands 1, 2, 3, and 4 in Cleveland are 20 percent, 35 percent, 30 percent, and 15 percent, we test the null hypothesis

$$H_0\colon p_1 = .20, \quad p_2 = .35, \quad p_3 = .30, \quad \text{and} \quad p_4 = .15$$

which says that consumer preferences in Milwaukee are consistent with the historical market shares in Cleveland. We test H_0 versus

$$H_a\colon \text{the previously stated null hypothesis is not true}$$

To test H_0 we must compare the "observed frequencies" given in Table 16.2 with the "expected frequencies" for the brands calculated on the assumption that H_0 is true. For instance, if H_0 is true, we would expect $400(.20) = 80$ of the 400 Milwaukee consumers surveyed to prefer brand 1. Denoting this expected frequency for brand 1 as E_1, the expected frequencies for brands 2, 3, and 4 when H_0 is true are $E_2 = 400(.35) = 140$, $E_3 = 400(.30) = 120$, and $E_4 = 400(.15) = 60$. Recalling that Table 16.2 gives the observed frequency for each brand, we have $f_1 = 102$, $f_2 = 121$, $f_3 = 120$, and $f_4 = 57$. We now compare the observed and expected frequencies by computing a **chi-square statistic** as follows:

$$\chi^2 = \sum_{i=1}^{k=4} \frac{(f_i - E_i)^2}{E_i}$$

$$= \frac{(102 - 80)^2}{80} + \frac{(121 - 140)^2}{140} + \frac{(120 - 120)^2}{120} + \frac{(57 - 60)^2}{60}$$

$$= \frac{484}{80} + \frac{361}{140} + \frac{0}{120} + \frac{9}{60} = 8.7786$$

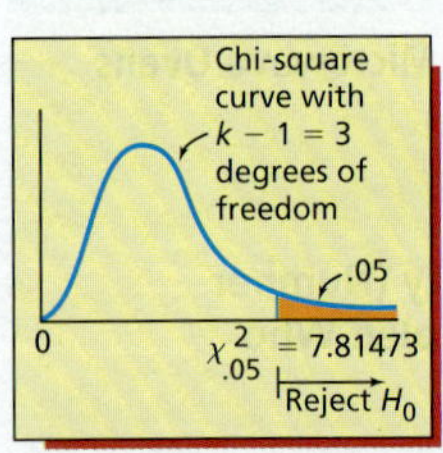

Clearly, the more the observed frequencies differ from the expected frequencies, the larger χ^2 will be and the more doubt will be cast on the null hypothesis. If the chi-square statistic is large enough (beyond a rejection point), then we reject H_0.

To find an appropriate rejection point, it can be shown that, when the null hypothesis is true, the sampling distribution of χ^2 is approximately a χ^2 distribution with $k - 1 = 4 - 1 = 3$ degrees of freedom. If we wish to test H_0 at the .05 level of significance, we reject H_0 if and only if

$$\chi^2 > \chi^2_{.05}$$

FIGURE 16.1 Output of a MINITAB Session That Computes the Chi-Square Statistic and Its Related *p*-Value for the Oven Wholesaler Example

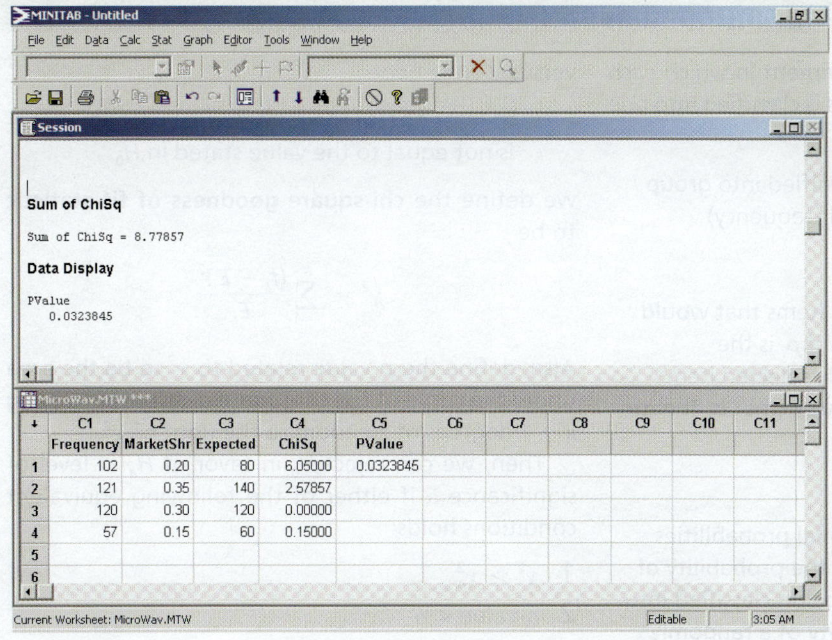

Since Table A.17 (pages 838–839) tells us that the $\chi^2_{.05}$ point corresponding to $k - 1 = 3$ degrees of freedom equals 7.81473, we find that

$$\chi^2 = 8.7786 > \chi^2_{.05} = 7.81473$$

and we reject H_0 at the .05 level of significance. Alternatively, the *p*-value for this hypothesis test is the area under the curve of the chi-square distribution having 3 degrees of freedom to the right of $\chi^2 = 8.7786$. This *p*-value can be calculated to be .0323845. Since this *p*-value is less than .05, we can reject H_0 at the .05 level of significance. Although there is no single MINITAB dialog box that produces a chi-square goodness of fit test, Figure 16.1 shows the output of a MINITAB session that computes the chi-square statistic and its related *p*-value for the oven wholesaler problem.

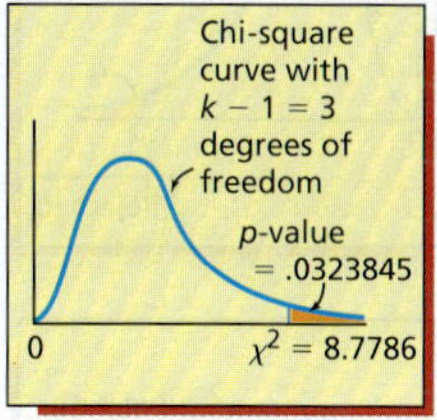

We conclude that consumer preferences in Milwaukee for the four brands of ovens are not consistent with the historical market shares in Cleveland. Based on this conclusion, the wholesaler should consider changing its stocking policies for microwave ovens when it enters the Milwaukee market. To study how to change its policies, the wholesaler might compute a 95 percent confidence interval for, say, the proportion of consumers in Milwaukee who prefer brand 2. Since $\hat{p}_2 = 121/400 = .3025$, this interval is (see Section 7.4, page 282)

$$\left[\hat{p}_2 \pm z_{.025}\sqrt{\frac{\hat{p}_2(1-\hat{p}_2)}{n_2}}\right] = \left[.3025 \pm 1.96\sqrt{\frac{.3025(1-.3025)}{400}}\right]$$
$$= [.2575, .3475]$$

Since this entire interval is below .35, it suggests that (1) the market share for brand 2 ovens in Milwaukee will be smaller than the 35 percent market share that this brand commands in Cleveland, and (2) fewer brand 2 ovens (on a percentage basis) should be stocked in Milwaukee. Notice here that by restricting our attention to one particular brand (brand 2), we are essentially combining the other brands into a single group. It follows that we now have two possible outcomes—"brand 2" and "all other brands." Therefore, we have a binomial experiment, and we can employ the methods of Section 7.4, which are based on the binomial distribution.

In the following box we give a general chi-square goodness of fit test for multinomial probabilities:

A Goodness of Fit Test for Multinomial Probabilities

Consider a **multinomial experiment** in which each of n randomly selected items is classified into one of k groups. We let

f_i = the number of items classified into group i (that is, the ith observed frequency)

$E_i = np_i$

= the expected number of items that would be classified into group i if p_i is the probability of a randomly selected item being classified into group i (that is, the ith expected frequency)

If we wish to test

H_0: the values of the multinomial probabilities are $p_1, p_2, \ldots, p_k$—that is, the probability of a randomly selected item being classified into group 1 is p_1, the probability of a randomly selected item being classified into group 2 is p_2, and so forth

versus

H_a: at least one of the multinomial probabilities is not equal to the value stated in H_0

we define the **chi-square goodness of fit statistic** to be

$$\chi^2 = \sum_{i=1}^{k} \frac{(f_i - E_i)^2}{E_i}$$

Also, define the p-value related to χ^2 to be the area under the curve of the chi-square distribution having $k - 1$ degrees of freedom to the right of χ^2.

Then, we can reject H_0 in favor of H_a at level of significance α if either of the following equivalent conditions holds:

1 $\chi^2 > \chi^2_\alpha$

2 p-value $< \alpha$

Here the χ^2_α point is based on $k - 1$ degrees of freedom.

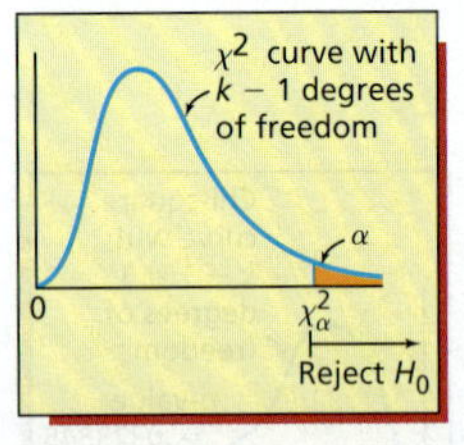

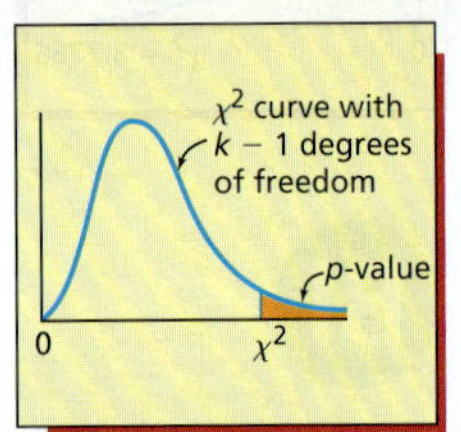

This test is based on the fact that it can be shown that, when H_0 is true, the sampling distribution of χ^2 is approximately a chi-square distribution with $k - 1$ degrees of freedom, if the sample size n is large. **It is generally agreed that n should be considered large if all of the "expected cell frequencies" (E_i values) are at least 5.** Furthermore, recent research implies that this condition on the E_i values can be somewhat relaxed. For example, Moore and McCabe (1993) indicate that **it is reasonable to use the chi-square approximation if the number of groups (k) exceeds 4, the average of the E_i values is at least 5, and the smallest E_i value is at least 1.** Notice that in Example 16.1 all of the E_i values are much larger than 5. Therefore, the chi-square test is valid.

A special version of the chi-square goodness of fit test for multinomial probabilities is called a **test for homogeneity.** This involves testing the null hypothesis that all of the multinomial probabilities are equal. For instance, in the microwave oven situation we would test

$$H_0: p_1 = p_2 = p_3 = p_4 = .25$$

which would say that no single brand of microwave oven is preferred to any of the other brands (equal preferences). If this null hypothesis is rejected in favor of

$$H_a: \text{At least one of } p_1, p_2, p_3, \text{ and } p_4 \text{ exceeds } .25$$

we would conclude that there is a preference for one or more of the brands. Here each of the expected cell frequencies equals .25(400) = 100. Remembering that the observed cell frequencies are $f_1 = 102, f_2 = 121, f_3 = 120$, and $f_4 = 57$, the chi-square statistic is

$$\begin{aligned}\chi^2 &= \sum_{i=1}^{4} \frac{(f_i - E_i)^2}{E_i} \\ &= \frac{(102 - 100)^2}{100} + \frac{(121 - 100)^2}{100} + \frac{(120 - 100)^2}{100} + \frac{(57 - 100)^2}{100} \\ &= .04 + 4.41 + 4 + 18.49 = 26.94\end{aligned}$$

Since $\chi^2 = 26.94$ is greater than $\chi^2_{.05} = 7.81473$ (see Table A.17 on pages 838 and 839 with $k - 1 = 4 - 1 = 3$ degrees of freedom), we reject H_0 at level of significance .05. We conclude that preferences for the four brands are not equal and that at least one brand is preferred to the others.

Normal distributions We have seen that many statistical methods are based on the assumption that a random sample has been selected from a normally distributed population. We can check the validity of the normality assumption by using frequency distributions, stem-and-leaf displays, histograms, and normal plots. Another approach is to use a chi-square goodness of fit test to check the normality assumption. We show how this can be done in the following example.

Example 16.2 The Car Mileage Case

C

Consider the sample of 49 gas mileages given in Table 2.1 (page 44). A histogram of these mileages (see Figure 2.4, page 49) is symmetrical and bell-shaped. This suggests that the sample of mileages has been randomly selected from a normally distributed population. In this example we use a chi-square goodness of fit test to check the normality of the mileages.

To perform this test, we first divide the number line into intervals (or categories). One way to do this is to use the class boundaries of the histogram in Figure 2.4. Table 16.3 gives these intervals and also gives observed frequencies (counts of the number of mileages in each interval), which have been obtained from the histogram of Figure 2.4. The chi-square test is done by comparing these observed frequencies with the expected frequencies in the rightmost column of Table 16.3. To explain how the expected frequencies are calculated, we first use the sample mean $\bar{x} = 31.55$ and the sample standard deviation $s = .8$ of the 49 mileages as point estimates of the population mean μ and population standard deviation σ. Then, for example, consider p_1, the probability that a randomly selected mileage will be in the first interval (less than 30.35) in Table 16.3, if the population of all mileages is normally distributed. We estimate p_1 to be

$$\begin{aligned} p_1 &= P(\text{mileage} < 30.35) = P\left(z < \frac{30.35 - 31.55}{.8}\right) \\ &= P(z < -1.5) = .5 - .4332 = .0668 \end{aligned}$$

It follows that $E_1 = 49p_1 = 49(.0668) = 3.2732$ is the expected frequency for the first interval under the normality assumption. Next, if we consider p_2, the probability that a randomly selected mileage will be in the second interval in Table 16.3 if the population of all mileages is normally distributed, we estimate p_2 to be

$$\begin{aligned} p_2 &= P(30.35 < \text{mileage} < 30.95) = P\left(\frac{30.35 - 31.55}{.8} < z < \frac{30.95 - 31.55}{.8}\right) \\ &= P(-1.5 < z < -.75) = .4332 - .2734 = .1598 \end{aligned}$$

It follows that $E_2 = 49p_2 = 49(.1598) = 7.8302$ is the expected frequency for the second interval under the normality assumption. The other expected frequencies are computed similarly. In general, p_i is the probability that a randomly selected mileage will be in interval i if the population of all possible mileages is normally distributed with mean 31.55 and standard deviation .8, and E_i is the expected number of the 49 mileages that would be in interval i if the population of all possible mileages has this normal distribution.

It seems reasonable to reject the null hypothesis

H_0: the population of all mileages is normally distributed

in favor of the alternative hypothesis

H_a: the population of all mileages is not normally distributed

TABLE 16.3 Observed and Expected Cell Frequencies for a Chi-Square Goodness of Fit Test for Testing the Normality of the 49 Gasoline Mileages in Table 2.1 GasMiles

Interval	Observed Frequency (f_i)	p_i If the Population of Mileages Is Normally Distributed	Expected Frequency, $E_i = np_i = 49p_i$
Less than 30.35	3	$p_1 = P(\text{mileage} < 30.35) = .0668$	$E_1 = 49(.0668) = 3.2732$
30.35 < 30.95	9	$p_2 = P(30.35 < \text{mileage} < 30.95) = .1598$	$E_2 = 49(.1598) = 7.8302$
30.95 < 31.55	12	$p_3 = P(30.95 < \text{mileage} < 31.55) = .2734$	$E_3 = 49(.2734) = 13.3966$
31.55 < 32.15	13	$p_4 = P(31.55 < \text{mileage} < 32.15) = .2734$	$E_4 = 49(.2734) = 13.3966$
32.15 < 32.75	9	$p_5 = P(32.15 < \text{mileage} < 32.75) = .1598$	$E_5 = 49(.1598) = 7.8302$
Greater than 32.75	3	$p_6 = P(\text{mileage} > 32.75) = .0668$	$E_6 = 49(.0668) = 3.2732$

if the observed frequencies in Table 16.3 differ substantially from the corresponding expected frequencies in Table 16.3. We compare the observed frequencies with the expected frequencies under the normality assumption by computing the chi-square statistic

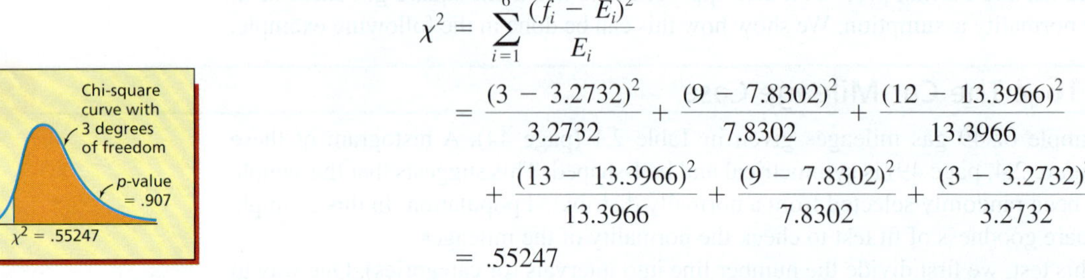

$$\chi^2 = \sum_{i=1}^{6} \frac{(f_i - E_i)^2}{E_i}$$

$$= \frac{(3 - 3.2732)^2}{3.2732} + \frac{(9 - 7.8302)^2}{7.8302} + \frac{(12 - 13.3966)^2}{13.3966}$$

$$+ \frac{(13 - 13.3966)^2}{13.3966} + \frac{(9 - 7.8302)^2}{7.8302} + \frac{(3 - 3.2732)^2}{3.2732}$$

$$= .55247$$

Since we have estimated $m = 2$ parameters (μ and σ) in computing the expected frequencies (E_i values), it can be shown that the sampling distribution of χ^2 is approximately a chi-square distribution with $k - 1 - m = 6 - 1 - 2 = 3$ degrees of freedom. Therefore, we can reject H_0 at level of significance α if

$$\chi^2 > \chi^2_\alpha$$

where the χ^2_α point is based on $k - 1 - m = 6 - 1 - 2 = 3$ degrees of freedom. If we wish to test H_0 at the .05 level of significance, Table A.17 tells us that $\chi^2_{.05} = 7.81473$. Therefore, since

$$\chi^2 = .55247 < \chi^2_{.05} = 7.81473$$

we cannot reject H_0 at the .05 level of significance, and we cannot reject the hypothesis that the population of all mileages is normally distributed. Therefore, for practical purposes it is probably reasonable to assume that the population of all mileages is approximately normally distributed and that inferences based on this assumption are valid. Finally, the p-value for this test, which is the area under the chi-square curve having 3 degrees of freedom to the right of $\chi^2 = .55247$, can be shown to equal .907. Since this p-value is large (much greater than .05), we have little evidence to support rejecting the null hypothesis (normality).

Note that although some of the expected cell frequencies in Table 16.3 are not at least 5, the number of classes (groups) is 6 (which exceeds 4), the average of the expected cell frequencies is at least 5, and the smallest expected cell frequency is at least 1. Therefore, it is probably reasonable to consider the result of this chi-square test valid. If we choose to base the chi-square test on the more restrictive assumption that all of the expected cell frequencies are at least 5, then we can combine adjacent cell frequencies as follows:

Original f_i Values	Original p_i Values	Original E_i Values	Combined E_i Values	Combined p_i Values	Combined f_i Values
3	.0668	3.2732	11.1034	.2266	12
9	.1598	7.8302			
12	.2734	13.3966	13.3966	.2734	12
13	.2734	13.3966	13.3966	.2734	13
9	.1598	7.8302	11.1034	.2266	12
3	.0668	3.2732			

When we use these combined cell frequencies, the chi-square approximation is based on $k - 1 - m = 4 - 1 - 2 = 1$ degree of freedom. We find that $\chi^2 = .30214$ and that p-value $=$ .582545. Since this p-value is much greater than .05, we cannot reject the hypothesis of normality at the .05 level of significance.

In Example 16.2 we based the intervals employed in the chi-square goodness of fit test on the class boundaries of a histogram for the observed mileages. Another way to establish intervals for such a test is to compute the sample mean $\bar{x}$ and the sample standard deviation s and to use intervals based on the Empirical Rule as follows:

Interval 1: less than $\bar{x} - 2s$

Interval 2: $\bar{x} - 2s < \bar{x} - s$

Interval 3: $\bar{x} - s < \bar{x}$

Interval 4: $\bar{x} < \bar{x} + s$

Interval 5: $\bar{x} + s < \bar{x} + 2s$

Interval 6: greater than $\bar{x} + 2s$

However, care must be taken to ensure that each of the expected frequencies is large enough (using the previously discussed criteria).

No matter how the intervals are established, we use $\bar{x}$ as an estimate of the population mean μ and we use s as an estimate of the population standard deviation σ when we calculate the expected frequencies (E_i values). Since we are estimating $m = 2$ population parameters, the rejection point χ^2_α is based on $k - 1 - m = k - 1 - 2 = k - 3$ degrees of freedom, where k is the number of intervals employed.

In the following box we summarize how to carry out this chi-square test:

A Goodness of Fit Test for a Normal Distribution

1. We will test the following null and alternative hypotheses:

   H_0: the population has a normal distribution

   H_a: the population does not have a normal distribution

2. Select a random sample of size n and compute the sample mean $\bar{x}$ and sample standard deviation s.

3. Define k intervals for the test. Two reasonable ways to do this are to use the classes of a histogram of the data or to use intervals based on the Empirical Rule.

4. Record the observed frequency (f_i) for each interval.

5. Calculate the expected frequency (E_i) for each interval under the normality assumption. Do this by computing the probability that a normal variable having mean $\bar{x}$ and standard deviation s is within the interval and by multiplying this probability by n. Make sure that each expected frequency is large enough. If necessary, combine intervals to make the expected frequencies large enough.

6. Calculate the chi-square statistic

$$\chi^2 = \sum_{i=1}^{k} \frac{(f_i - E_i)^2}{E_i}$$

   and define the p-value for the test to be the area under the curve of the chi-square distribution having $k - 3$ degrees of freedom to the right of χ^2.

7. Reject H_0 in favor of H_a at level of significance α if either of the following equivalent conditions holds:

   a $\chi^2 > \chi^2_\alpha$ **b** p-value $< \alpha$

   Here the χ^2_α point is based on $k - 3$ degrees of freedom.

While chi-square goodness of fit tests are often used to verify that it is reasonable to assume that a random sample has been selected from a normally distributed population, such tests can also check other distribution forms. For instance, we might verify that it is reasonable to assume that a random sample has been selected from a Poisson distribution. In general, **the number of degrees of freedom for the chi-square goodness of fit test will equal $k - 1 - m$,** where k is the number of intervals or categories employed in the test and m is the number of population parameters that must be estimated to calculate the needed expected frequencies.

Exercises for Section 16.1

CONCEPTS

16.1 Describe the characteristics that define a multinomial experiment.

16.2 Give the conditions that the expected cell frequencies must meet in order to validly carry out a chi-square goodness of fit test.

16.3 Explain the purpose of a goodness of fit test.

16.4 When performing a chi-square goodness of fit test, explain why a large value of the chi-square statistic provides evidence that H_0 should be rejected.

16.5 Explain two ways to obtain intervals for a goodness of fit test of normality.

METHODS AND APPLICATIONS

16.6 The shares of the U.S. automobile market held in 1990 by General Motors, Japanese manufacturers, Ford, Chrysler, and other manufacturers were, respectively, 36%, 26%, 21%, 9%, and 8%. Suppose that a new survey of 1,000 new-car buyers shows the following purchase frequencies:

GM	Japanese	Ford	Chrysler	Other
391	202	275	53	79

a Show that it is appropriate to carry out a chi-square test using these data. AutoMkt

b Test to determine whether the current market shares differ from those of 1990. Use $\alpha = .05$.

16.7 Last rating period, the percentages of viewers watching several channels between 11 P.M. and 11:30 P.M. in a major TV market were as follows: TVRate

WDUX (News)	WWTY (News)	WACO (*Cheers* Reruns)	WTJW (News)	Others
15%	19%	22%	16%	28%

Suppose that in the current rating period, a survey of 2,000 viewers gives the following frequencies:

WDUX (News)	WWTY (News)	WACO (*Cheers* Reruns)	WTJW (News)	Others
182	536	354	151	777

a Show that it is appropriate to carry out a chi-square test using these data.

b Test to determine whether the viewing shares in the current rating period differ from those in the last rating period at the .10 level of significance. What do you conclude?

16.8 In the *Journal of Marketing Research* (November 1996), Gupta studied the extent to which the purchase behavior of **scanner panels** is representative of overall brand preferences. A scanner panel is a sample of households whose purchase data are recorded when a magnetic identification card is presented at a store checkout. The table below gives peanut butter purchase data collected by the A. C. Nielson Company using a panel of 2,500 households in Sioux Falls, South Dakota. The data were collected over 102 weeks. The table also gives the market shares obtained by recording all peanut butter purchases at the same stores during the same period. ScanPan

a Show that it is appropriate to carry out a chi-square test.

b Test to determine whether the purchase behavior of the panel of 2,500 households is consistent with the purchase behavior of the population of all peanut butter purchasers. Assume here that purchase decisions by panel members are reasonably independent, and set $\alpha = .05$.

Brand	Size	Number of Purchases by Household Panel	Market Shares
Jif	18 oz.	3,165	20.10%
Jif	28	1,892	10.10
Jif	40	726	5.42
Peter Pan	10	4,079	16.01
Skippy	18	6,206	28.56
Skippy	28	1,627	12.33
Skippy	40	1,420	7.48
Total		19,115	

Source: Reprinted with permission from *The Journal of Marketing Research*, published by the American Marketing Association, S. Gupta et al., Vol. 33, "Do Household Scanner Data Provide Representative Inferences from Brand Choices? A Comparison with Store Data," p. 393 (Table 6).

Goodness of Fit Test

obs	expected	O − E	(O − E)²/E	% of chisq
3165	3842.115	−677.115	119.331	13.56
1892	1930.615	−38.615	0.772	0.09
726	1036.033	−310.033	92.777	10.54
4079	3060.312	1018.689	339.092	38.52
6206	5459.244	746.756	102.147	11.60
1627	2356.880	−729.880	226.029	25.68
1420	1429.802	−9.802	0.067	0.01
19115	19115.000	0.000	880.216	100.00

880.22 chisquare 6 df 7.10E-187 p-value

16.9 The purchase frequencies for six different brands of videotape are observed at a video store over one month: VidTape

Brand	Memorex	Scotch	Kodak	TDK	BASF	Sony
Purchase Frequency	131	273	119	301	176	200

a Carry out a test of homogeneity for this data with $\alpha = .025$.

b Interpret the result of your test.

16.10 A wholesaler has recently developed a computerized sales invoicing system. Prior to implementing this system, a manual system was used. The distribution of the number of errors per invoice for the manual system is as follows: Invoice2

Errors per Invoice	0	1	2	3	More Than 3
Percentage of Invoices	87%	8%	3%	1%	1%

After implementation of the computerized system, a random sample of 500 invoices gives the following error distribution:

Errors per Invoice	0	1	2	3	More Than 3
Number of Invoices	479	10	8	2	1

a Show that it is appropriate to carry out a chi-square test using these data.

b Use the following Excel output to determine whether the error percentages for the computerized system differ from those for the manual system at the .05 level of significance. What do you conclude?

pi	Ei	fi	(f-E)^2/E	
0.87	435	479	4.4506	
0.08	40	10	22.5000	
0.03	15	8	3.2667	
0.01	5	2	1.8000	
0.01	5	1	3.2000	
		Chi-Square	35.21724	p-value 0.000000196

16.11 Consider the sample of 65 payment times given in Table 2.2 (page 46). Use these data to carry out a chi-square goodness of fit test to test whether the population of all payment times is normally distributed by doing the following: PayTime

a It can be shown that $\bar{x} = 18.1077$ and that $s = 3.9612$ for the payment time data. Use these values to compute the intervals

(1) Less than $\bar{x} - 2s$

(2) $\bar{x} - 2s < \bar{x} - s$

(3) $\bar{x} - s < \bar{x}$

(4) $\bar{x} < \bar{x} + s$

(5) $\bar{x} + s < \bar{x} + 2s$

(6) Greater than $\bar{x} + 2s$

b Assuming that the population of all payment times is normally distributed, find the probability that a randomly selected payment time will be contained in each of the intervals found in part *a*. Use these probabilities to compute the expected frequency under the normality assumption for each interval.

c Verify that the average of the expected frequencies is at least 5 and that the smallest expected frequency is at least 1. What does this tell us?

d Formulate the null and alternative hypotheses for the chi-square test of normality.

e For each interval given in part *a*, find the observed frequency. Then calculate the chi-square statistic needed for the chi-square test of normality.

f Use the chi-square statistic to test normality at the .05 level of significance. What do you conclude?

16.12 Consider the sample of 60 bottle design ratings given in Table 1.3 (page 8). Use these data to carry out a chi-square goodness of fit test to determine whether the population of all bottle design ratings is normally distributed. Use $\alpha = .05$, and note that $\bar{x} = 30.35$ and $s = 3.1073$ for the 60 bottle design ratings. Design

16.13 THE BANK CUSTOMER WAITING TIME CASE

Consider the sample of 100 waiting times given in Table 1.6 (page 11). Use these data to carry out a chi-square goodness of fit test to determine whether the population of all waiting times is normally distributed. Use $\alpha = .10$, and note that $\bar{x} = 5.46$ and $s = 2.475$ for the 100 waiting times. WaitTime

16.14 The table on the next page gives a frequency distribution describing the number of errors found in 30 1,000-line samples of computer code. Suppose that we wish to determine whether the number of errors can be described by a Poisson distribution with mean $\mu = 4.5$. Using the Poisson probability tables, fill in the table. Then perform an appropriate chi-square goodness of fit test at the .05 level of significance. What do you conclude about whether the number of errors can be described by a Poisson distribution with $\mu = 4.5$? Explain. CodeErr

Number of Errors	Observed Frequency	Probability Assuming Errors Are Poisson Distributed with $\mu = 4.5$	Expected Frequency
0–1	6		
2–3	5		
4–5	7		
6–7	8		
8 or more	4		

16.2 A Chi-Square Test for Independence

We have spent considerable time in previous chapters studying relationships between variables. One way to study the relationship between two variables is to classify multinomial count data on two scales (or dimensions) by setting up a *contingency table*.

Example 16.3 The Client Satisfaction Case

A financial institution sells several kinds of investment products—a stock fund, a bond fund, and a tax-deferred annuity. The company is examining whether customer satisfaction depends on the type of investment product purchased. To do this, 100 clients are randomly selected from the population of clients who have purchased shares in exactly one of the funds. The company records the fund type purchased by these clients and asks each sampled client to rate his or her level of satisfaction with the fund as high, medium, or low. Table 16.4 on page 776 gives the survey results.

We can look at the data in Table 16.4 in an organized way by constructing a **contingency table** (also called a **two-way cross-classification table**). Such a table classifies the data on two dimensions—type of fund and degree of client satisfaction. Figure 16.2 gives MegaStat and MINITAB output of a contingency table of fund type versus level of satisfaction. This table consists of a row for each fund type and a column for each level of satisfaction. Together, the rows and columns form a "cell" for each fund type–satisfaction level combination. That is, there is a cell for each "contingency" with respect to fund type and satisfaction level. Both the MegaStat and MINITAB output give a **cell frequency** for each cell, which is the top number given in the cell. This is a count (observed frequency) of the number of surveyed clients with the cell's fund type–satisfaction level combination. For instance, 15 of the surveyed clients invest in the bond fund and report high satisfaction, while 24 of the surveyed clients invest in the tax-deferred annuity and report medium satisfaction. In addition to the cell frequencies, each output also gives

Row totals (at the far right of each table): These are counts of the numbers of clients who invest in each fund type. These row totals tell us that

1. 30 clients invest in the bond fund.
2. 30 clients invest in the stock fund.
3. 40 clients invest in the tax-deferred annuity.

Column totals (at the bottom of each table): These are counts of the numbers of clients who report high, medium, and low satisfaction. These column totals tell us that

1. 40 clients report high satisfaction.
2. 40 clients report medium satisfaction.
3. 20 clients report low satisfaction.

Overall total (the bottom-right entry in each table): This tells us that a total of 100 clients were surveyed.

Besides the row and column totals, both outputs give **row and total percentages** (directly below the row and column totals). For example, 30.00 percent of the surveyed clients invest in the bond fund, and 20.00 percent of the surveyed clients report low satisfaction. Furthermore, in addition to a cell frequency, the MegaStat output gives a **row percentage,** a **column percentage,** and a **cell percentage** for each cell (these are below the cell frequency in each cell). For instance,

FIGURE 16.2 MegaStat and MINITAB Output of a Contingency Table of Fund Type versus Level of Client Satisfaction (See the Survey Results in Table 16.4) Invest

(a) The MegaStat output

Crosstabulation

Fund Type		Satisfaction Rating HIGH	MED	LOW	Total
BOND	Observed	15	12	3	30
	% of row	50.0%	40.0%	10.0%	100.5%
	% of column	37.5%	30.0%	15.0%	30.0%
	% of total	15.0%	12.0%	3.0%	30.0%
STOCK	Observed	24	4	2	30
	% of row	80.0%	13.3%	6.7%	100.0%
	% of column	60.0%	10.0%	10.0%	30.0%
	% of total	24.0%	4.0%	2.0%	30.0%
TAXDEF	Observed	1	24	15	40
	% of row	2.5%	60.0%	37.5%	100.0%
	% of column	2.5%	60.0%	75.0%	40.0%
	% of total	1.0%	24.0%	15.0%	40.0%
Total	Observed	40	40	20	100
	% of row	40.0%	40.0%	20.0%	100.0%
	% of column	100.0%	100.0%	100.0%	100.0%
	% of total	40.0%	40.0%	20.0%	100.0%

46.44[a]	chi-square
4	df
2.00E-09[b]	p-value

[a]Chi-square statistic.
[b]p-value for chi-square.

(b) The MINITAB output

```
Rows: FundType     Columns: SatRating

              High      Med      Low      All

Bond            15       12        3       30
             50.00    40.00    10.00   100.00
             37.50    30.00    15.00    30.00
                12       12        6       30

Stock           24        4        2       30
             80.00    13.33     6.67   100.00
             60.00    10.00    10.00    30.00
                12       12        6       30

TaxDef           1       24       15       40
              2.50    60.00    37.50   100.00
              2.50    60.00    75.00    40.00
                16       16        8       40

All             40       40       20      100
             40.00    40.00    20.00   100.00
            100.00   100.00   100.00   100.00
                40       40       20      100

Pearson Chi-Square = 46.438, DF = 4
       P-Value = 0.000

Cell Contents:        Count
                      % of Row
                      % of Column
                      Expected count
```

looking at the "bond fund–high satisfaction cell," we see that the 15 clients in this cell make up 50.0 percent of the 30 clients who invest in the bond fund, and they make up 37.5 percent of the 40 clients who report high satisfaction. In addition, these 15 clients make up 15.0 percent of the 100 clients surveyed. The MINITAB output gives a row percentage and a column percentage, but not a cell percentage, for each cell. We will explain the last number that appears in each cell of the MINITAB output later in this section.

Looking at the contingency tables, it appears that the level of client satisfaction may be related to the fund type. We see that higher satisfaction ratings seem to be reported by stock and bond fund investors, while holders of tax-deferred annuities report lower satisfaction ratings. To carry out a formal statistical test we can test the null hypothesis

H_0: fund type and level of client satisfaction are independent

versus

H_a: fund type and level of client satisfaction are dependent

In order to perform this test, we compare the counts (or **observed cell frequencies**) in the contingency table with the counts that would appear in the contingency table if we assume that fund type and level of satisfaction are independent. Because these latter counts are computed by assuming independence, we call them the **expected cell frequencies under the independence assumption.** We illustrate how to calculate these expected cell frequencies by considering the cell corresponding to the bond fund and high client satisfaction. We first use the data in the contingency table to compute an estimate of the probability that a randomly selected client invests in the bond fund. Denoting this probability as p_B, we estimate p_B by dividing the row total for the bond fund by the total number of clients surveyed. That is, denoting the row total for the bond fund as r_B and letting n denote the total number of clients surveyed, the estimate of p_B is $r_B/n = 30/100 = .3$. Next we compute an estimate of the probability that a randomly selected client will report high satisfaction. Denoting this probability as p_H, we estimate p_H by dividing the column

TABLE 16.4 Results of a Customer Satisfaction Survey Given to 100 Randomly Selected Clients Who Invest in One of Three Fund Types—a Bond Fund, a Stock Fund, or a Tax-Deferred Annuity Invest

Client	Fund Type	Level of Satisfaction	Client	Fund Type	Level of Satisfaction	Client	Fund Type	Level of Satisfaction
1	BOND	HIGH	35	STOCK	HIGH	69	BOND	MED
2	STOCK	HIGH	36	BOND	MED	70	TAXDEF	MED
3	TAXDEF	MED	37	TAXDEF	MED	71	TAXDEF	MED
4	TAXDEF	MED	38	TAXDEF	LOW	72	BOND	HIGH
5	STOCK	LOW	39	STOCK	HIGH	73	TAXDEF	MED
6	STOCK	HIGH	40	TAXDEF	MED	74	TAXDEF	LOW
7	STOCK	HIGH	41	BOND	HIGH	75	STOCK	HIGH
8	BOND	MED	42	BOND	HIGH	76	BOND	HIGH
9	TAXDEF	LOW	43	BOND	LOW	77	TAXDEF	LOW
10	TAXDEF	LOW	44	TAXDEF	LOW	78	BOND	MED
11	STOCK	MED	45	STOCK	HIGH	79	STOCK	HIGH
12	BOND	LOW	46	BOND	HIGH	80	STOCK	HIGH
13	STOCK	HIGH	47	BOND	MED	81	BOND	MED
14	TAXDEF	MED	48	STOCK	HIGH	82	TAXDEF	MED
15	TAXDEF	MED	49	TAXDEF	MED	83	BOND	HIGH
16	TAXDEF	LOW	50	TAXDEF	MED	84	STOCK	MED
17	STOCK	HIGH	51	STOCK	HIGH	85	STOCK	HIGH
18	BOND	HIGH	52	TAXDEF	MED	86	BOND	MED
19	BOND	MED	53	STOCK	HIGH	87	TAXDEF	MED
20	TAXDEF	MED	54	TAXDEF	MED	88	TAXDEF	LOW
21	TAXDEF	MED	55	STOCK	LOW	89	STOCK	HIGH
22	BOND	HIGH	56	BOND	HIGH	90	TAXDEF	MED
23	TAXDEF	MED	57	STOCK	HIGH	91	BOND	HIGH
24	TAXDEF	LOW	58	BOND	MED	92	TAXDEF	HIGH
25	STOCK	HIGH	59	TAXDEF	LOW	93	TAXDEF	LOW
26	BOND	HIGH	60	TAXDEF	LOW	94	TAXDEF	LOW
27	TAXDEF	LOW	61	STOCK	MED	95	STOCK	HIGH
28	BOND	MED	62	BOND	LOW	96	BOND	HIGH
29	STOCK	HIGH	63	STOCK	HIGH	97	BOND	MED
30	STOCK	HIGH	64	TAXDEF	MED	98	STOCK	HIGH
31	BOND	MED	65	TAXDEF	MED	99	TAXDEF	MED
32	TAXDEF	MED	66	TAXDEF	LOW	100	TAXDEF	MED
33	BOND	HIGH	67	STOCK	HIGH			
34	STOCK	MED	68	BOND	HIGH			

total for high satisfaction by the total number of clients surveyed. That is, denoting the column total for high satisfaction as c_H, the estimate of p_H is $c_H/n = 40/100 = .4$. Next, assuming that investing in the bond fund and reporting high satisfaction are **independent,** we compute an estimate of the probability that a randomly selected client invests in the bond fund and reports high satisfaction. Denoting this probability as p_{BH}, we can compute its estimate by recalling from Section 3.4 that if two events A and B are statistically independent, then $P(A \cap B)$ equals $P(A)P(B)$. It follows that, if we assume that investing in the bond fund and reporting high satisfaction are independent, we can compute an estimate of p_{BH} by multiplying the estimate of p_B by the estimate of p_H. That is, the estimate of p_{BH} is $(r_B/n)(c_H/n) = (.3)(.4) = .12$. Finally, we compute an estimate of the expected cell frequency under the independence assumption. Denoting the expected cell frequency as E_{BH}, the estimate of E_{BH} is

$$\hat{E}_{BH} = n\left(\frac{r_B}{n}\right)\left(\frac{c_H}{n}\right) = 100(.3)(.4) = 12$$

This estimated expected cell frequency is given in the MINITAB output of Figure 16.2(b) as the last number under the observed cell frequency for the bond fund–high satisfaction cell.

Noting that the expression for $\hat{E}_{BH}$ can be written as

$$\hat{E}_{BH} = n\left(\frac{r_B}{n}\right)\left(\frac{c_H}{n}\right) = \frac{r_B c_H}{n}$$

we can generalize to obtain a formula for the estimated expected cell frequency for any cell in the contingency table. Letting $\hat{E}_{ij}$ denote the estimated expected cell frequency corresponding to row i and column j in the contingency table, we see that

$$\hat{E}_{ij} = \frac{r_i c_j}{n}$$

where r_i is the row total for row i and c_j is the column total for column j. For example, for the fund type–satisfaction level contingency table, we obtain

$$\hat{E}_{SL} = \frac{r_S c_L}{n} = \frac{30(20)}{100} = \frac{600}{100} = 6$$

and

$$\hat{E}_{TM} = \frac{r_T c_M}{n} = \frac{40(40)}{100} = \frac{1{,}600}{100} = 16$$

These (and the other estimated expected cell frequencies under the independence assumption) are the last numbers below the observed cell frequencies in the MINITAB output of Figure 16.2(b). Intuitively, these estimated expected cell frequencies tell us what the contingency table looks like if fund type and level of client satisfaction are independent.

To test the null hypothesis of independence, we will compute a chi-square statistic that compares the observed cell frequencies with the estimated expected cell frequencies calculated assuming independence. Letting f_{ij} denote the observed cell frequency for cell ij, we compute

$$\begin{aligned}\chi^2 &= \sum_{\text{all cells}} \frac{(f_{ij} - \hat{E}_{ij})^2}{\hat{E}_{ij}} \\ &= \frac{(f_{BH} - \hat{E}_{BH})^2}{\hat{E}_{BH}} + \frac{(f_{BM} - \hat{E}_{BM})^2}{\hat{E}_{BM}} + \cdots + \frac{(f_{TL} - \hat{E}_{TL})^2}{\hat{E}_{TL}} \\ &= \frac{(15-12)^2}{12} + \frac{(12-12)^2}{12} + \frac{(3-6)^2}{6} + \frac{(24-12)^2}{12} + \frac{(4-12)^2}{12} \\ &\quad + \frac{(2-6)^2}{6} + \frac{(1-16)^2}{16} + \frac{(24-16)^2}{16} + \frac{(15-8)^2}{8} \\ &= 46.4375\end{aligned}$$

If the value of the chi-square statistic is large, this indicates that the observed cell frequencies differ substantially from the expected cell frequencies calculated by assuming independence. Therefore, the larger the value of chi-square, the more doubt is cast on the null hypothesis of independence.

To find an appropriate rejection point, we let r denote the number of rows in the contingency table and we let c denote the number of columns. Then, it can be shown that, when the null hypothesis of independence is true, the sampling distribution of χ^2 is approximately a χ^2 distribution with $(r-1)(c-1) = (3-1)(3-1) = 4$ degrees of freedom. If we test H_0 at the .05 level of significance, we reject H_0 if and only if

$$\chi^2 > \chi^2_{.05}$$

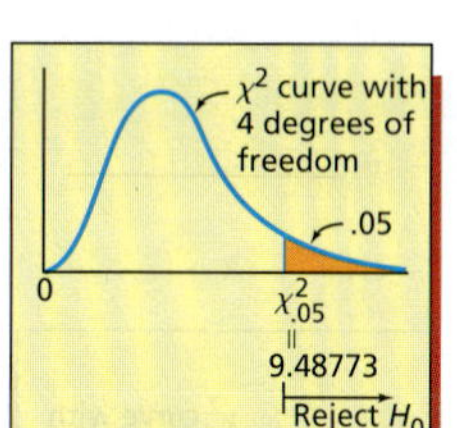

Since Table A.17 (pages 838 and 839) tells us that the $\chi^2_{.05}$ point corresponding to $(r-1)(c-1) =$ 4 degrees of freedom equals 9.48773, we have

$$\chi^2 = 46.4375 > \chi^2_{.05} = 9.48773$$

and we reject H_0 at the .05 level of significance. We conclude that fund type and level of client satisfaction are not independent.

In the following box we summarize how to carry out a chi-square test for independence:

A Chi-Square Test for Independence

Suppose that each of n randomly selected elements is classified on two dimensions, and suppose that the result of the two-way classification is a **contingency table having r rows and c columns.** Let

f_{ij} = the cell frequency corresponding to row i and column j of the contingency table (that is, the number of elements classified in row i and column j)

r_i = the row total for row i in the contingency table

c_j = the column total for column j in the contingency table

$\hat{E}_{ij} = \dfrac{r_i c_j}{n}$

= the estimated expected number of elements that would be classified in row i and column j of the contingency table if the two classifications are statistically independent

If we wish to test

H_0: the two classifications are statistically independent

versus

H_a: the two classifications are statistically dependent

we define the test statistic

$$\chi^2 = \sum_{\text{all cells}} \frac{(f_{ij} - \hat{E}_{ij})^2}{\hat{E}_{ij}}$$

Also, define the p-value related to χ^2 to be the area under the curve of the chi-square distribution having $(r - 1)(c - 1)$ degrees of freedom to the right of χ^2.

Then, we can reject H_0 in favor of H_a at level of significance α if either of the following equivalent conditions holds:

1 $\chi^2 > \chi^2_\alpha$

2 p-value $< \alpha$

Here the χ^2_α point is based on $(r - 1)(c - 1)$ degrees of freedom.

This test is based on the fact that it can be shown that, when the null hypothesis of independence is true, the sampling distribution of χ^2 is approximately a chi-square distribution with $(r - 1)(c - 1)$ degrees of freedom, if the sample size n is large. **It is generally agreed that n should be considered large if all of the estimated expected cell frequencies ($\hat{E}_{ij}$ values) are at least 5.** Moore and McCabe (1993) indicate that **it is reasonable to use the chi-square approximation if the number of cells (rc) exceeds 4, the average of the $\hat{E}_{ij}$ values is at least 5, and the smallest $\hat{E}_{ij}$ value is at least 1.** Notice that in Figure 16.2(b) all of the estimated expected cell frequencies are greater than 5.

Example 16.4 The Client Satisfaction Case

Again consider the MegaStat and MINITAB outputs of Figure 16.2, which give the contingency table of fund type versus level of client satisfaction. Both outputs give the chi-square statistic (= 46.438) for testing the null hypothesis of independence, as well as the related p-value. We see that this p-value is less than .001. It follows, for example, that we can reject

H_0: fund type and level of client satisfaction are independent

at the .05 level of significance, since the p-value is less than .05.

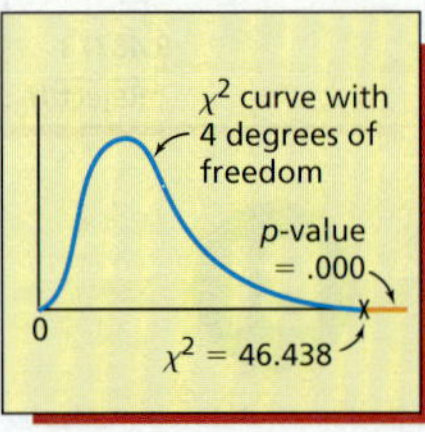

In order to study the nature of the dependency between the classifications in a contingency table, it is often useful to plot the row and/or column percentages. As an example, Figure 16.3 gives plots of the row percentages in the contingency table of Figure 16.2(a). For instance, looking at the column in this contingency table corresponding to a high level of satisfaction, the contingency table tells us that 40.00 percent of the surveyed clients report a high level of satisfaction. If fund type and level of satisfaction really are independent, then we would expect roughly 40 percent of the clients in each of the three categories—bond fund participants, stock fund participants, and tax-deferred annuity holders—to report a high level of satisfaction. That is, we would expect the row percentages in the "high satisfaction" column to be roughly 40 percent in each row.

FIGURE 16.3 Plots of Row Percentages versus Investment Type for the Contingency Table in Figure 16.2(a)

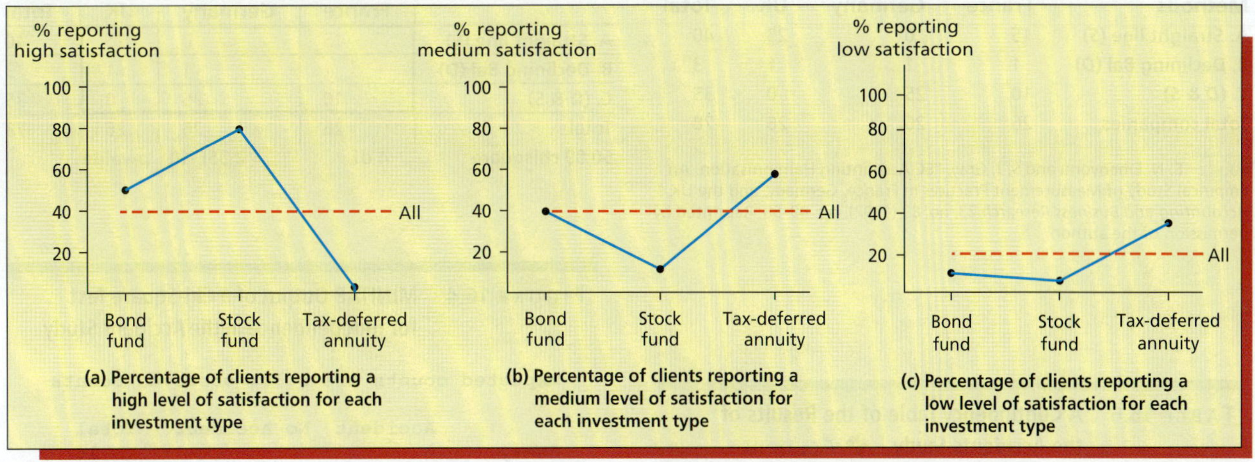

(a) Percentage of clients reporting a high level of satisfaction for each investment type

(b) Percentage of clients reporting a medium level of satisfaction for each investment type

(c) Percentage of clients reporting a low level of satisfaction for each investment type

However, Figure 16.3(a) gives a plot of the percentages of clients reporting a high level of satisfaction for each investment type (that is, the figure plots the three row percentages in the column corresponding to "high satisfaction"). We see that these percentages vary considerably. Noting that the dashed line in the figure is the 40 percent reporting a high level of satisfaction for the overall group, we see that the percentage of stock fund participants reporting high satisfaction is 80 percent. This is far above the 40 percent we would expect if independence exists. On the other hand, the percentage of tax-deferred annuity holders reporting high satisfaction is only 2.5 percent—way below the expected 40 percent if independence exists. In a similar fashion, Figures 16.3(b) and (c) plot the row percentages for the medium and low satisfaction columns in the contingency table. These plots indicate that stock fund participants report medium and low levels of satisfaction less frequently than the overall group of clients, and that tax-deferred annuity participants report medium and low levels of satisfaction more frequently than the overall group of clients.

BI

To conclude this section, we note that the chi-square test for independence can be used to test the equality of several population proportions. We will show how this is done in Exercise 16.21.

Exercises for Section 16.2

CONCEPTS

16.15 What is the purpose behind summarizing data in the form of a two-way contingency table?

16.16 When performing a chi-square test for independence, explain how the "cell frequencies under the independence assumption" are calculated. For what purpose are these frequencies calculated?

METHODS AND APPLICATIONS

16.17 A marketing research firm wishes to study the relationship between wine consumption and whether a person likes to watch professional tennis on television. One hundred randomly selected people are asked whether they drink wine and whether they watch tennis. The following results are obtained: WineCons

	Watch Tennis	Do Not Watch Tennis	Totals
Drink Wine	16	24	40
Do Not Drink Wine	4	56	60
Totals	20	80	100

a For each row and column total, calculate the corresponding row or column percentage.

b For each cell, calculate the corresponding cell, row, and column percentages.

TABLE 16.5 Depreciation Methods Used by a Sample of 78 Firms DeprMeth

Depreciation Methods	France	Germany	UK	Total
A. Straight line (*S*)	15	0	25	40
B. Declining Bal (*D*)	1	1	1	3
C. (*D* & *S*)	10	25	0	35
Total companies	26	26	26	78

Source: E. N. Emenyonu and S. J. Gray, "EC Accounting Harmonisation: An Empirical Study of Measurement Practices in France, Germany, and the UK," *Accounting and Business Research* 23, no. 89 (1992), pp. 49–58. Reprinted by permission of the author.

Chi-Square Test for Independence

	France	Germany	UK	Total
A. Straight line (S)	15	0	25	40
B. Declining Bal (D)	1	1	1	3
C. (D & S)	10	25	0	35
Total	26	26	26	78
50.89 chisquare	4 df	2.35E-10	p-value	

FIGURE 16.4 MINITAB Output of a Chi-Square Test for Independence in the Accident Study

```
Expected counts are below observed counts

           Accident  No Accident   Total
Heavy            12            4      16
               8.24         7.76

Moderate          9            6      15
               7.73         7.27

Nonsmoker        13           22      35
              18.03        16.97

Total            34           32      66

Chi-Sq = 6.860, DF = 2, P-Value = 0.032
```

TABLE 16.6 A Contingency Table of the Results of the Accidents Study Accident

Smoker	On-the-Job Accident Yes	No	Row Total
Heavy	12	4	16
Moderate	9	6	15
Nonsmoker	13	22	35
Column total	34	32	66

Source: D. R. Cooper and C. W. Emory, *Business Research Methods* (5th ed.) (Burr Ridge, IL: Richard D. Irwin, 1995), p. 451.

c Test the hypothesis that whether people drink wine is independent of whether people watch tennis. Set $\alpha = .05$.

d Given the results of the chi-square test, does it make sense to advertise wine during a televised tennis match (assuming that the ratings for the tennis match are high enough)? Explain.

16.18 In recent years major efforts have been made to standardize accounting practices in different countries; this is called *harmonization*. In an article in *Accounting and Business Research,* Emmanuel N. Emenyonu and Sidney J. Gray (1992) studied the extent to which accounting practices in France, Germany, and the UK are harmonized. DeprMeth

a Depreciation method is one of the accounting practices studied by Emenyonu and Gray. Three methods were considered—the straight-line method (S), the declining balance method (D), and a combination of D & S (sometimes European firms start with the declining balance method and then switch over to the straight-line method when the figure derived from straight line exceeds that from declining balance). The data in Table 16.5 summarize the depreciation methods used by a sample of 78 French, German, and U.K. firms. Use these data and the MegaStat output to test the hypothesis that depreciation method is independent of a firm's location (country) at the .05 level of significance.

b Perform a graphical analysis to study the relationship between depreciation method and country. What conclusions can be made about the nature of the relationship?

16.19 In the book *Business Research Methods* (5th ed.), Donald R. Cooper and C. William Emory discuss studying the relationship between on-the-job accidents and smoking. Cooper and Emory describe the study as follows: Accident

> Suppose a manager implementing a smoke-free workplace policy is interested in whether smoking affects worker accidents. Since the company has complete reports of on-the-job accidents, she draws a sample of names of workers who were involved in accidents during the last year. A similar sample from among workers who had no reported accidents in the last year is drawn. She interviews members of both groups to determine if they are smokers or not.

The sample results are given in Table 16.6.

a For each row and column total in Table 16.6, find the corresponding row/column percentage.

b For each cell in Table 16.6, find the corresponding cell, row, and column percentages.

TABLE 16.7 A Contingency Table Relating Delivery Time and Computer-Assisted Ordering DelTime

Computer-Assisted Ordering	Delivery Time: Below Industry Average	Equal to Industry Average	Above Industry Average	Row Total
No	4	12	8	24
Yes	10	4	2	16
Column total	14	16	10	40

TABLE 16.8 A Summary of the Results of a TV Viewership Study TVView

Watch 11 P.M. News?	Age Group: 18 or Less	19 to 35	36 to 54	55 or Older	Total
Yes	37	48	56	73	214
No	213	202	194	177	786
Total	250	250	250	250	1,000

c Use the MINITAB output in Figure 16.4 to test the hypothesis that the incidence of on-the-job accidents is independent of smoking habits. Set $\alpha = .01$.

d Is there a difference in on-the-job accident occurrences between smokers and nonsmokers? Explain.

16.20 In the book *Essentials of Marketing Research,* William R. Dillon, Thomas J. Madden, and Neil A. Firtle discuss the relationship between delivery time and computer-assisted ordering. A sample of 40 firms shows that 16 use computer-assisted ordering, while 24 do not. Furthermore, past data are used to categorize each firm's delivery times as below the industry average, equal to the industry average, or above the industry average. The results obtained are given in Table 16.7.

a Test the hypothesis that delivery time performance is independent of whether computer-assisted ordering is used. What do you conclude by setting $\alpha = .05$? DelTime

b Verify that a chi-square test is appropriate.

c Is there a difference between delivery-time performance between firms using computer-assisted ordering and those not using computer-assisted ordering?

d Carry out graphical analysis to investigate the relationship between delivery-time performance and computer-assisted ordering. Describe the relationship.

16.21 A television station wishes to study the relationship between viewership of its 11 P.M. news program and viewer age (18 years or less, 19 to 35, 36 to 54, 55 or older). A sample of 250 television viewers in each age group is randomly selected, and the number who watch the station's 11 P.M. news is found for each sample. The results are given in Table 16.8. TVView

a Let p_1, p_2, p_3, and p_4 be the proportions of all viewers in each age group who watch the station's 11 P.M. news. If these proportions are equal, then whether a viewer watches the station's 11 P.M. news is independent of the viewer's age group. Therefore, we can test the null hypothesis H_0 that p_1, p_2, p_3, and p_4 are equal by carrying out a chi-square test for independence. Perform this test by setting $\alpha = .05$.

b Compute a 95 percent confidence interval for the difference between p_1 and p_4.

Chapter Summary

In this chapter we presented two hypothesis tests that employ the **chi-square distribution.** In Section 16.1 we discussed a **chi-square test of goodness of fit.** Here we considered a situation in which we study how count data are distributed among various categories. In particular, we considered a **multinomial experiment** in which randomly selected items are classified into several groups, and we saw how to perform a goodness of fit test for the multinomial probabilities associated with these groups. We also explained how to perform a goodness of fit test for normality. In Section 16.2 we presented a **chi-square test for independence.** Here we classify count data on two dimensions, and we summarize the cross-classification in the form of a **contingency table.** We use the cross-classified data to test whether the two classifications are **statistically independent,** which is really a way to see whether the classifications are related. We also learned that we can use graphical analysis to investigate the nature of the relationship between the classifications.

Glossary of Terms

chi-square test for independence: A test to determine whether two classifications are independent. (page 778)
contingency table: A table that summarizes data that have been classified on two dimensions or scales. (page 774)
goodness of fit test for multinomial probabilities: A test to determine whether multinomial probabilities are equal to a specific set of values. (page 768)
goodness of fit test for normality: A test to determine if a sample has been randomly selected from a normally distributed population. (page 771)
homogeneity (test for): A test of the null hypothesis that all multinomial probabilities are equal. (page 768)
multinomial experiment: An experiment that concerns count data that are classified into more than two categories. (page 765)

Important Formulas and Tests

A goodness of fit test for multinomial probabilities: page 768
A goodness of fit test for a normal distribution: page 771
A test for homogeneity: page 768
A chi-square test for independence: page 778

Supplementary Exercises

16.22 A large supermarket conducted a consumer preference study by recording the brand of wheat bread purchased by customers in its stores. The supermarket carries four brands of wheat bread, and the brand preferences of a random sample of 200 purchasers are given in the following table: BreadPref

Brand			
A	*B*	*C*	*D*
51	82	27	40

Test the null hypothesis that the four brands are equally preferred by setting α equal to .05. Find a 95 percent confidence interval for the proportion of all purchasers who prefer Brand *B*.

16.23 An occupant traffic study was carried out to aid in the remodeling of a large building on a university campus. The building has five entrances, and the choice of entrance was recorded for a random sample of 300 persons entering the building. The results obtained are given in the following table: EntrPref

Entrance				
I	II	III	IV	V
30	91	97	40	42

Test the null hypothesis that the five entrances are equally used by setting α equal to .05. Find a 95 percent confidence interval for the proportion of all people who use Entrance III.

16.24 In a 1993 article in *Accounting and Business Research,* Meier, Alam, and Pearson studied auditor lobbying on several proposed U.S. accounting standards that affect banks and savings and loan associations. As part of this study, the authors investigated auditors' positions regarding proposed changes in accounting standards that would increase client firms' reported earnings. It was hypothesized that auditors would favor such proposed changes because their clients' managers would receive higher compensation (salary, bonuses, and so on) when client earnings were reported to be higher. Table 16.9 summarizes auditor and client positions (in favor or opposed) regarding proposed changes in accounting standards that would increase client firms' reported earnings. Here the auditor and client positions are cross-classified versus the size of the client firm. AuditPos

a Test to determine whether auditor positions regarding earnings-increasing changes in accounting standards depend on the size of the client firm. Use $\alpha = .05$.

b Test to determine whether client positions regarding earnings-increasing changes in accounting standards depend on the size of the client firm. Use $\alpha = .05$.

c Carry out a graphical analysis to investigate a possible relationship between (1) auditor positions and the size of the client firm and (2) client positions and the size of the client firm.

TABLE 16.9 Auditor and Client Positions Regarding Earnings-Increasing Changes in Accounting Standards AuditPos

(a) Auditor Positions

	Large Firms	Small Firms	Total
In Favor	13	130	143
Opposed	10	24	34
Total	23	154	177

(b) Client Positions

	Large Firms	Small Firms	Total
In Favor	12	120	132
Opposed	11	34	45
Total	23	154	177

Source: Heidi Hylton Meier, Pervaiz Alam, and Michael A. Pearson, "Auditor Lobbying for Accounting Standards: The Case of Banks and Savings and Loan Associations," *Accounting and Business Research* 23, no. 92 (1993), pp. 477–487.

TABLE 16.10 Auditor Positions Regarding Earnings-Decreasing Changes in Accounting Standards AuditPos2

	Large Firms	Small Firms	Total
In Favor	27	152	179
Opposed	29	154	183
Total	56	306	362

Source: Heidi Hylton Meier, Pervaiz Alam, and Michael A. Pearson, "Auditor Lobbying for Accounting Standards: The Case of Banks and Savings and Loan Associations," *Accounting and Business Research* 23, no. 92 (1993), pp. 477–487.

TABLE 16.11 Results of the Coupon Redemption Study Coupon

Coupon Redemption Level	Store Location Midtown	North Side	South Side	Total
High	69	97	52	218
Medium	101	93	76	270
Low	30	10	72	112
Total	200	200	200	600

d Does the relationship between position and the size of the client firm seem to be similar for both auditors and clients? Explain.

16.25 In the book *Business Research Methods* (5th ed.), Donald R. Cooper and C. William Emory discuss a market researcher for an automaker who is studying consumer preferences for styling features of larger sedans. Buyers, who were classified as "first-time" buyers or "repeat" buyers, were asked to express their preference for one of two types of styling—European styling or Japanese styling. Of 40 first-time buyers, 8 preferred European styling and 32 preferred Japanese styling. Of 60 repeat buyers, 40 preferred European styling, and 20 preferred Japanese styling.

a Set up a contingency table for these data.

b Test the hypothesis that buyer status (repeat versus first-time) and styling preference are independent at the .05 level of significance. What do you conclude?

c Carry out a graphical analysis to investigate the nature of any relationship between buyer status and styling preference. Describe the relationship.

16.26 Again consider the situation of Exercise 16.24. Table 16.10 summarizes auditor positions regarding proposed changes in accounting standards that would decrease client firms' reported earnings. Determine whether the relationship between auditor position and the size of the client firm is the same for earnings-decreasing changes in accounting standards as it is for earnings-increasing changes in accounting standards. Justify your answer using both a statistical test and a graphical analysis. AuditPos2

16.27 The manager of a chain of three discount drug stores wishes to investigate the level of discount coupon redemption at its stores. All three stores have the same sales volume. Therefore, the manager will randomly sample 200 customers at each store with regard to coupon usage. The survey results are given in Table 16.11. Test the hypothesis that redemption level and location are independent with $\alpha = .01$. Use the MINITAB output in Figure 16.5. Coupon

16.28 THE VIDEO GAME SATISFACTION RATING CASE

Consider the sample of 65 customer satisfaction ratings given in Table 16.12. Carry out a chi-square goodness of fit test of normality for the population of all customer satisfaction ratings. Recall that we previously calculated $\bar{x} = 42.95$ and $s = 2.6424$ for the 65 ratings. VideoGame

FIGURE 16.5 MINITAB Output of a Chi-Square Test for Independence in the Coupon Redemption Study

```
Expected counts are below observed counts

         Midtown    North    South   Total
High          69       97       52     218
           72.67    72.67    72.67

Medium       101       93       76     270
           90.00    90.00    90.00

Low           30       10       72     112
           37.33    37.33    37.33

Total        200      200      200     600

Chi-Sq = 71.476, DF = 4, P-Value = 0.000
```

TABLE 16.12 A Sample of 65 Customer Satisfaction Ratings VideoGame

39	46	42	40	45	44	44	44	45
45	44	46	46	46	41	46	46	
38	40	40	41	43	38	48	39	
42	39	47	43	47	43	44	41	
42	40	44	39	43	36	41	44	
41	42	43	43	41	44	45	42	
38	45	45	46	40	44	44	47	
42	44	45	45	43	45	44	43	

16.29 Internet Exercise

A report on the 1995 National Health Risk Behavior Survey, conducted by the Centers for Disease Control and Prevention, can be found at the CDC website [http://www.cdc.gov: Data & Statistics : Youth Risk Behavior Surveillance System : Data Products : 1995 National College Health Risk Behavior Survey or, directly, go to http://www.cdc.gov/nocdphp/dash/MMWRFile/ss4606.htm]. Among the issues addressed in the survey was whether the subjects had, in the prior 30 days, ridden with a driver who had been drinking alcohol. Does the proportion of students exhibiting this selected risk behavior vary by ethnic group? The report includes tables summarizing the "Ridden Drinking" risk behavior by ethnic group (Table 3) and the ethnic composition (Table 1) for a sample of $n = 4{,}609$ college students. The "Ridden Drinking" and ethnic group information is extracted from Tables 1 and 3 and is displayed as proportions or probabilities in the leftmost panel of the table below. Note that the values in the body of the leftmost panel are given as conditional probabilities, the probabilities of exhibiting the "Ridden Drinking" risk behavior, given ethnic group. These conditional probabilities can be multiplied by the appropriate marginal probabilities to compute the joint probabilities for all the risk behavior by ethnic group combinations to obtain the summaries in the center panel. Finally, the joint probabilities are multiplied by the sample size to obtain projected counts for the number of students in each "Ridden Drinking" by ethnic group combination. The "Other" ethnic group was omitted from the Table 3 summaries and is thus not included in this analysis.

Is there sufficient evidence to conclude that the proportion of college students exhibiting the "Ridden Drinking" behavior varies by ethnic group? Conduct a chi-square test for independence using the projected count data provided in the rightmost panel of the summary table. (Data are available in MINITAB and Excel files, YouthRisk.mtw and YouthRisk.xls.) Test at the 0.01 level of significance and report an approximate *p*-value for your test. Be sure to clearly state your hypotheses and conclusion. YouthRisk

	Conditional Probabilities [Table 3: P(R|E). Table 1: P(E)]			Joint Probabilities [P(ER) = P(R|E)P(E)]			Projected Counts [n = 4609] [n(ER) = P(ER) × 4609]		
	Ridden Drinking?			Ridden Drinking?			Ridden Drinking?		
Ethnic	**%Y|Eth**	**%N|Eth**	**% Ethnic**	**Yes**	**No**	**Total**	**Yes**	**No**	**Total**
White	0.383	0.617	0.728	0.2788	0.4492	0.7280	1,285	2,070	3,355
Black	0.275	0.725	0.103	0.0283	0.0747	0.1030	131	344	475
Hispanic	0.307	0.693	0.071	0.0218	0.0492	0.0710	100	227	327

Appendix 16.1 ■ Chi-Square Tests Using MINITAB

The instruction blocks in this section each begin by describing the entry of data into the MINITAB Data window. Alternatively, the data may be loaded directly from the data disk included with the text. The appropriate data file name is given at the top of each instruction block. Please refer to Appendix 1.1 for further information about entering data, saving data, and printing results.

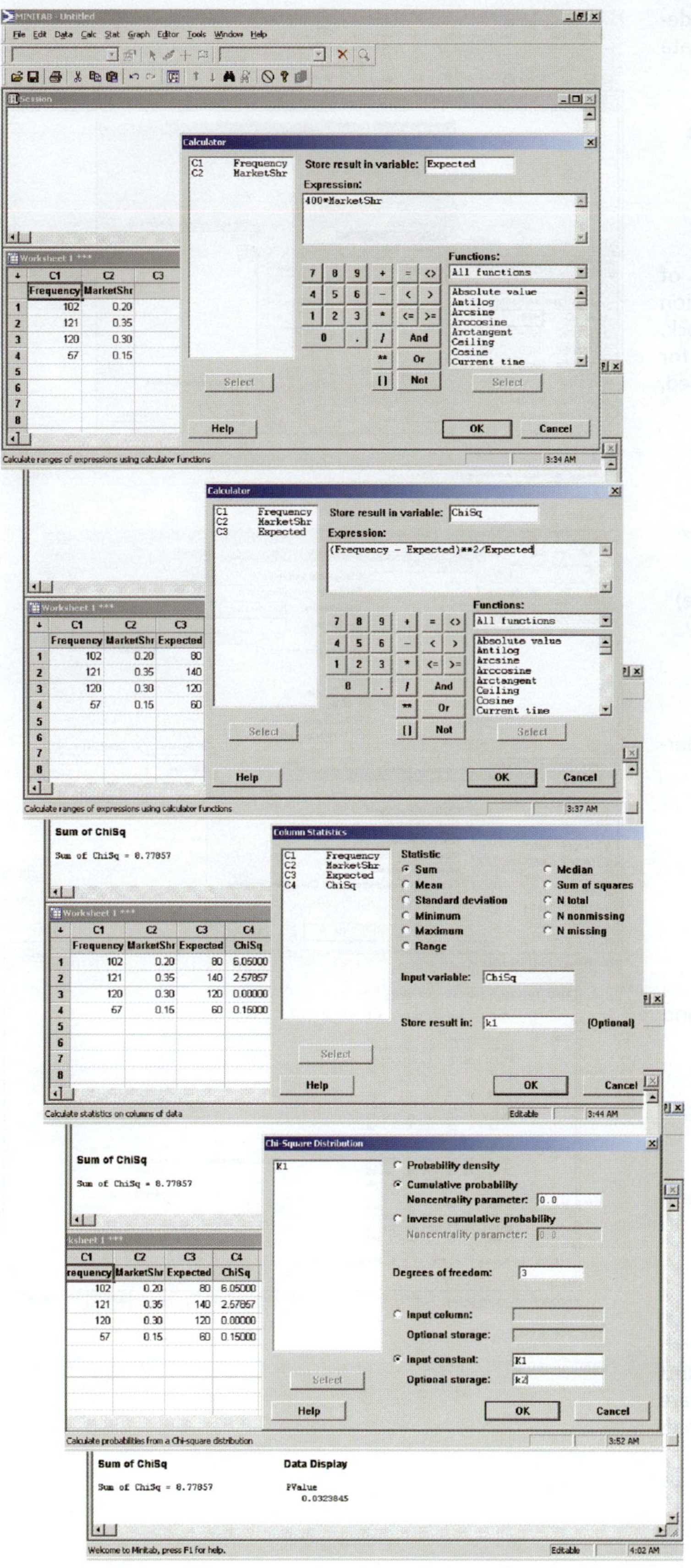

Chi-square test for goodness of fit in Figure 16.1 on page 767 (data file: MicroWav.mtw):

- Enter the microwave oven data from Tables 16.1 and 16.2 on page 765—observed frequencies in column C1 with variable name Frequency and market shares (entered as decimal fractions) in column C2 with variable name MarketShr.
- Select **Calc : Calculator.**
- In the Calculator dialog box, enter Expected into the "Store result in variable" box.
- In the Expression window, enter 400*MarketShr and click OK to compute the expected values.
- Select **Calc : Calculator.**
- Enter ChiSq into the "Store result in variable" box.
- In the Expression window enter the formula (Frequency − Expected)**2/Expected and click OK to compute the cell Chi-square contributions.
- Select **Calc : Column Statistics.**
- In the Column Statistics dialog box, click on Sum.
- Enter ChiSq in the "Input variable" box.
- Enter k1 in the "Store result in" box and click OK to compute the Chi-square statistic and to store it as the constant k1.
- Select **Calc : Probability Distributions : Chi-Square.**
- In the Chi-Square Distribution dialog box, click on "Cumulative probability".
- Enter 3 in the "Degrees of freedom" box.
- Click the "Input constant" option and enter k1 into the corresponding box.
- Enter k2 into the "Optional storage" box.
- Click OK in the Chi-Square Distribution dialog box.
- Select **Calc : Calculator.**
- In the Calculator dialog box, enter PValue into the "Store result in variable" box.
- In the Expression window, enter the formula 1 − k2, and click OK to compute the p-value related to the chi-square statistic.
- Select **Data : Display Data.**
- Enter PValue in the "Columns, constants, and matrices to display" window and click OK.

Sum of ChiSq (=8.77857) is the chi-square statistic, and PValue (=0.0323845) is the corresponding p-value.

Contingency table and chi-square test for independence in Figure 16.2 (b) on page 775 (data file: Invest.mtw):

- In the Data window, enter the investment customer satisfaction data from Table 16.4 (page 776)—fund type in column C1 with variable name FundType and level of satisfaction in column C2 with variable name SatRating.

The default ordering for the different levels of each categorical variable in the cross tabulation table will be alphabetical—that is, Bond, Stock, TaxDef for FundType and High, Low, Med for SatRating. **To change the ordering to High, Med, Low** for SatRating:

- Click on any cell in column C2 (SatRating).
- Select **Editor : Column : Value order**
- In the "Value Order for C2 (SatRating)" dialog box, click the "User specified order" option.
- In the "Define an order (one value per line)" window, specify the order High, Med, Low.
- Click OK in the "Value Order for C2 (SatRating)" dialog box.

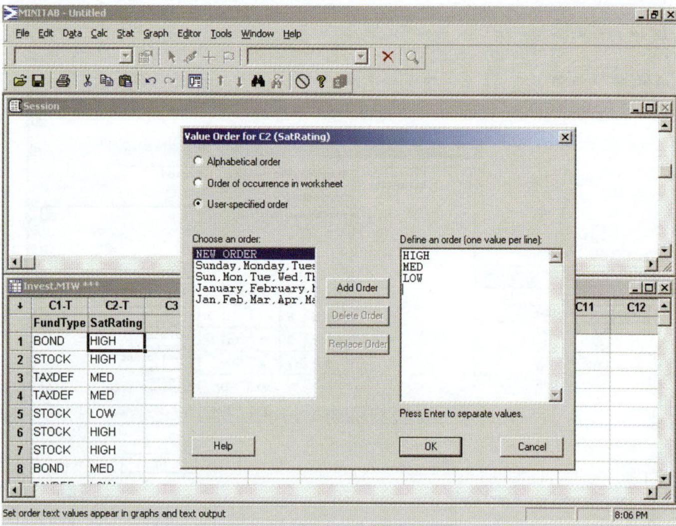

To construct the cross tabulation table and perform a chi-square test:

- Select **Stat : Tables : Cross Tabulation and Chi-Square**
- In the Cross Tabulation and Chi-Square dialog box, enter FundType into the "Categorical variables: For rows" box.
- Enter SatRating into the "Categorical variables: For columns" box.
- Check the Display Counts, Row percents, and Column percents check boxes.
- Click on the Chi-Square... button.
- In the Cross Tabulation—Chi-Square dialog box, check the "Chi-Square analysis" and "Expected cell counts" check boxes.
- Click OK in the Cross Tabulation—Chi-Square dialog box.
- Click OK in the Cross Tabulation and Chi-Square dialog box to obtain results in the Session window.

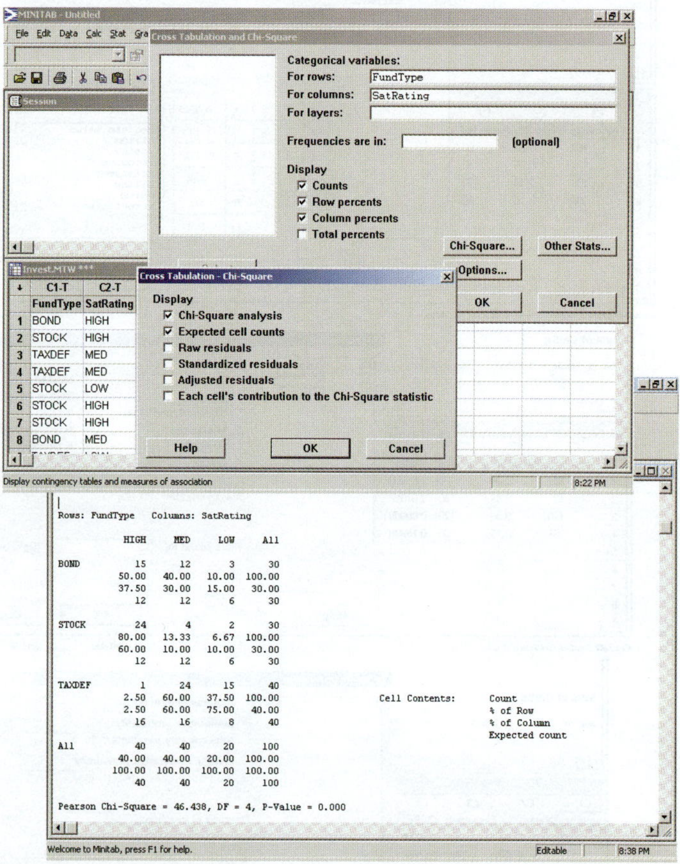

	HIGH	MED	LOW	All
BOND	15	12	3	30
	50.00	40.00	10.00	100.00
	37.50	30.00	15.00	30.00
	12	12	6	30
STOCK	24	4	2	30
	80.00	13.33	6.67	100.00
	60.00	10.00	10.00	30.00
	12	12	6	30
TAXDEF	1	24	15	40
	2.50	60.00	37.50	100.00
	2.50	60.00	75.00	40.00
	16	16	8	40
All	40	40	20	100
	40.00	40.00	20.00	100.00
	100.00	100.00	100.00	100.00
	40	40	20	100

The chi-square statistic can also be calculated from summary data by entering the cell counts from Table 16.2(b) and by selecting "Chi-Square Test (Table in Worksheet)" from the Stat : Tables sub-menu.

Appendix 16.2 ■ Chi-Square Tests Using Excel

The instruction blocks in this section each begin by describing the entry of data into an Excel spreadsheet. Alternatively, the data may be loaded directly from the data disk included with the text. The appropriate data file name is given at the top of each instruction block. Please refer to Appendix 1.2 for further information about entering data, saving data, and printing results.

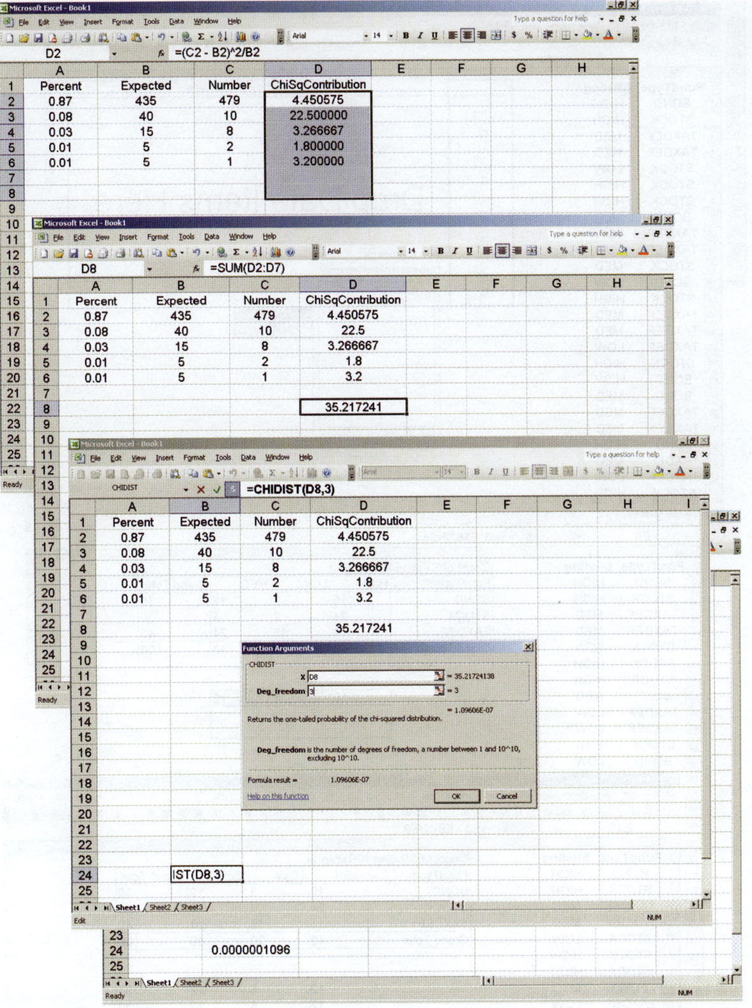

Chi-square goodness of fit test in Exercise 16.10 on page 773 (data file: Invoice.xls):

- In the first row of the spreadsheet, enter the following column headings in order—Percent, Expected, Number, ChiSqContribution.
- Beginning in cell A2, enter the "percentage of invoice figures" from Exercise 16.10 as decimal fractions into column A.
- Compute expected values. Enter the formula =500*A2 into cell B2 and press enter. Copy this formula through cell B6 by double-clicking the drag handle (in the lower right corner) of cell B2.
- Enter the "number of invoice figures" from Exercise 16.10 into cells C2 through C6.
- Compute cell Chi-square contributions. In cell D2, enter the formula =(C2 − B2)^2/B2 and press enter. Copy this formula through cell D6 by double-clicking the drag handle (in the lower right corner) of cell D2.
- Compute the Chi-square statistic in cell D8. Use the mouse to select the range of cells D2.D8 and click the $\sum$ button on the Excel tool bar.
- Click on an empty cell, say cell B24, and select the Insert Function button f_x on the Excel toolbar.
- In the Insert Function dialog box, select Statistical from the "Or select a category:" menu, select CHIDIST from the "Select a function:" menu, and click OK.
- In the "CHIDIST Function Arguments" dialog box, enter D8 into the "X" box and 3 into the "Deg_freedom" box.
- Click OK in the "CHIDIST Function Arguments" dialog box to produce the p-value related to the chi-square statistic in cell B24.

Contingency table and chi-square test for independence similar to Figure 16.2(b) on page 775 (data file: Invest.xls):

- Enter the investment customer satisfaction data from Table 16.4 (page 776) with the fund type in column A (with label FundType), and the level of satisfaction in column B (with label SRating).

To build a contingency table (using the PivotTable and PivotChart Wizard):

- Click on cell A1.
- Select **Data : PivotTable and PivotChart Report.**
- In the "PivotTable and PivotChart Wizard—Step 1 of 3" dialog box, select the "Microsoft Office Excel list or database" option and then click Next >.
- In the "PivotTable and PivotChart Wizard—Step 2 of 3" dialog box, the range A1.B101 should already be selected (if not, select it) and click Next >.
- Select the "Existing worksheet" option in the "PivotTable and PivotChart Wizard—Step 3 of 3" dialog box, enter D1 in the box, and click Finish.
- Now use the mouse to drag items in the "Pivot Table Field List" to the Pivot Table Report. Drag FundType to the "Drop Row Fields Here" area, and drag SRating to the "Drop Column Fields Here" area. Then also drag SRating to the "Drop Data Items Here" area.

To compute a table of expected values:

- In cell E9, type the formula =$H3*E$6/$H$6 (be very careful to include the $ in all the correct places) and press the enter key (to obtain the expected value 12 in cell E9).
- Click on cell E9 and use the mouse to point the cursor to the drag handle (in the lower right corner) of the cell. The cursor will change to a black cross. Using the black cross, drag the handle right to cell G9 and release the mouse button to fill cells F9.G9. With E9.G9 still selected, use the black cross to drag the handle down to cell G11. Release the mouse button to fill cells E10.G11.
- To add marginal totals, select the range E9.H12 and click the $\sum$ button on the Excel toolbar.

To compute the Chi-square statistic:

- In cell E15, type the formula =(E3 – E9)^2/E9 and press the enter key to obtain the cell contribution 0.75 in E15.

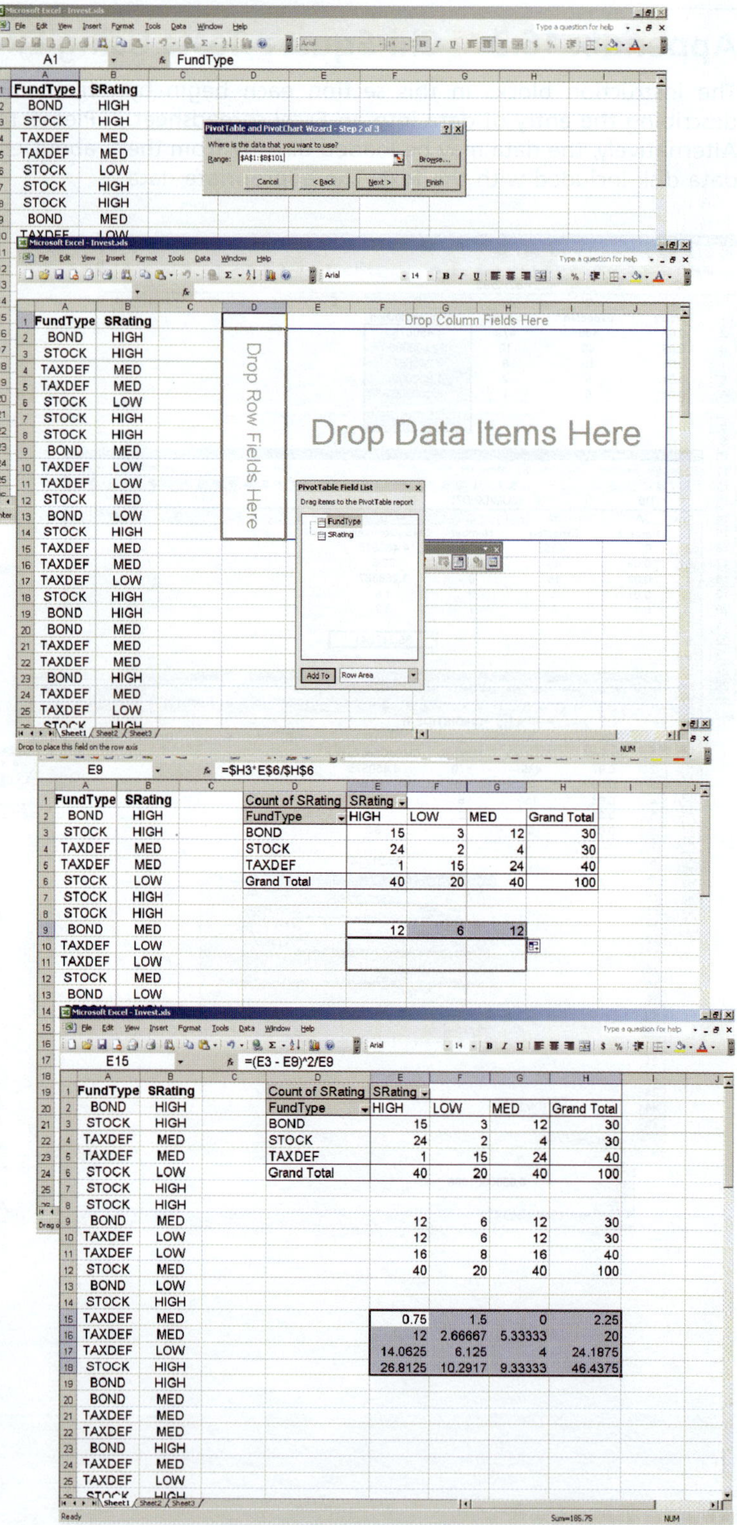

- Click on cell E15 and (using the procedure described above) use the "black cross cursor" to drag the cell handle right to cell G15 and then down to cell G17 (obtaining the cell contributions in cells E15.G17).
- To add marginal totals, select the range E15.H18 and click the $\sum$ button on the Excel toolbar.
- The Chi-square statistic is in cell H18 (=46.4375).

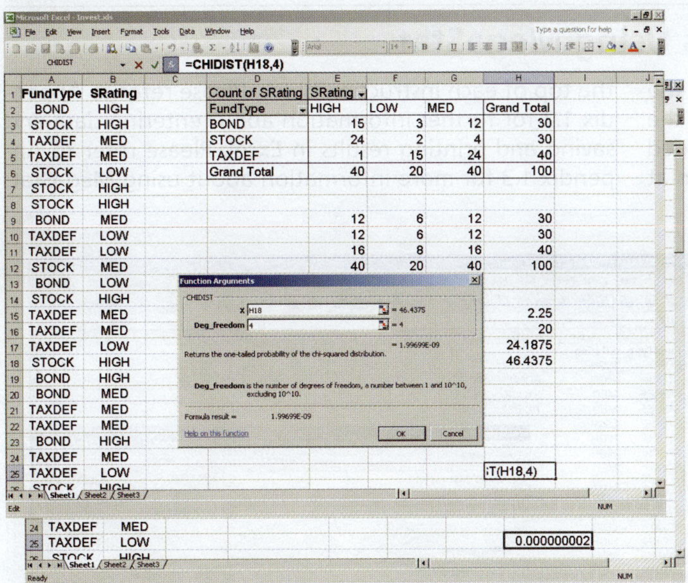

To compute the p-value for the Chi-square test of independence:

- Click on an empty cell, say H25.
- Select the Insert Function button f_x on the Excel toolbar.
- In the Insert Function dialog box, select Statistical from the "Or select a category:" menu, select CHIDIST from the "Select a function:" menu, and click OK.
- In the "CHIDIST Function Arguments" dialog box, enter H18 into the "X" box and 4 into the "Deg_freedom" box.
- Click OK in the "CHIDIST Function Arguments" dialog box to produce the p-value related to the chi-square statistic in cell H25.

Appendix 16.3 ■ Chi-Square Tests Using MegaStat

The instructions in this section begin by describing the entry of data into an Excel worksheet. Alternatively, the data may be loaded directly from the data disk included with the text. The appropriate data file name is given at the top of each instruction block. Please refer to Appendix 1.2 for further information about entering data and saving and printing results in Excel. Please refer to Appendix 1.3 for more information about using MegaStat.

Contingency table and chi-square test for independence in Figure 16.2(a) on page 775 (data file: Invest.xls):

- Enter the investment satisfaction survey data in Table 16.4 (page 776) with the type of investment fund in column A (with label FundType) and the level of customer satisfaction in column B (with label SRating).
- Type the labels BOND, STOCK, and TAXDEF into cells C3, C4, and C5. These labels will specify the row categories in the contingency table.
- Type the labels HIGH, MED, and LOW into cells D3, D4, and D5. These labels will specify the column categories in the contingency table.
- Select **MegaStat : Chi-Square/Crosstab : Crosstabulation.**
- In the Crosstabulation dialog box, click in the "Row variable data range" box and use the AutoExpand feature to enter the range A1.A101. This defines the variable FundType to be the **row variable** in the contingency table.
- Click in the "Row variable specification range" box and drag the mouse to enter the range C3.C5. The labels in this range specify the categories for the row variable FundType in the contingency table.
- Click in the "Column variable data range" box and use the AutoExpand feature to enter the range B1.B101. This defines the variable SRating to be the **column variable** in the contingency table.
- Click in the "Column variable specification range" box and drag the mouse to enter the range D3.D5. The labels in this range specify the categories for the column variable SRating in the contingency table.
- In the list of Output Options, check the Chi-square check box to obtain results of the chi-square test for independence.
- In the list of Output Options, check the following check boxes: "% of row," "% of column," and "% of total."
- Click OK in the Crosstabulation dialog box.

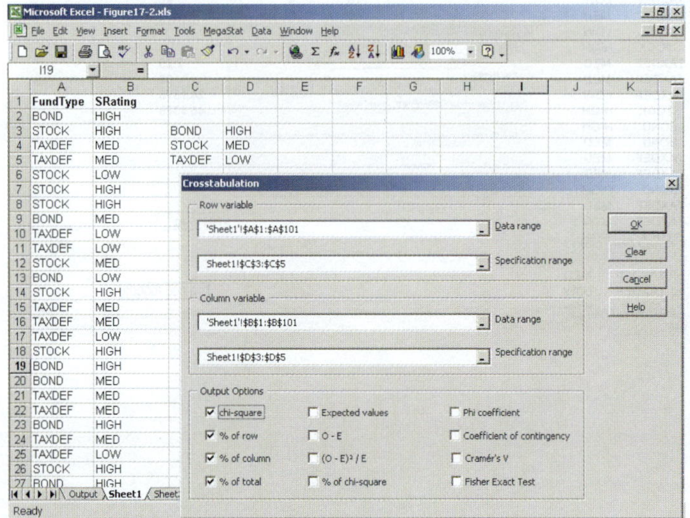

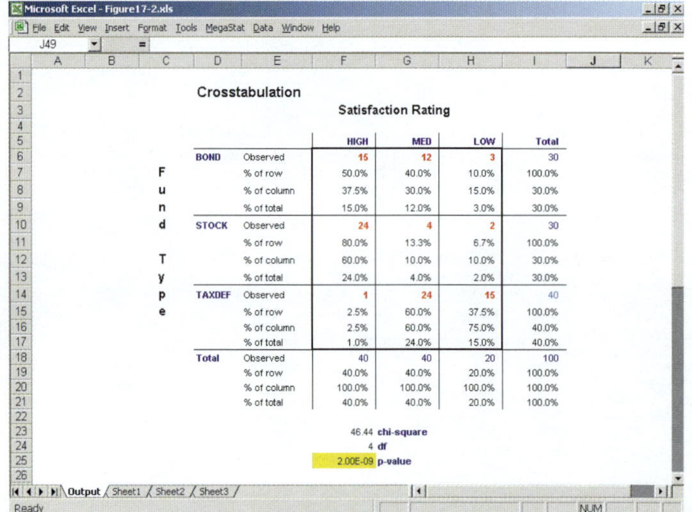

		HIGH	MED	LOW	Total
BOND	Observed	15	12	3	30
	% of row	50.0%	40.0%	10.0%	100.0%
	% of column	37.5%	30.0%	15.0%	30.0%
	% of total	15.0%	12.0%	3.0%	30.0%
STOCK	Observed	24	4	2	30
	% of row	80.0%	13.3%	6.7%	100.0%
	% of column	60.0%	10.0%	10.0%	30.0%
	% of total	24.0%	4.0%	2.0%	30.0%
TAXDEF	Observed	1	24	15	40
	% of row	2.5%	60.0%	37.5%	100.0%
	% of column	2.5%	60.0%	75.0%	40.0%
	% of total	1.0%	24.0%	15.0%	40.0%
Total	Observed	40	40	20	100
	% of row	40.0%	40.0%	20.0%	100.0%
	% of column	100.0%	100.0%	100.0%	100.0%
	% of total	40.0%	40.0%	20.0%	100.0%

46.44 chi-square
4 df
2.00E-09 p-value

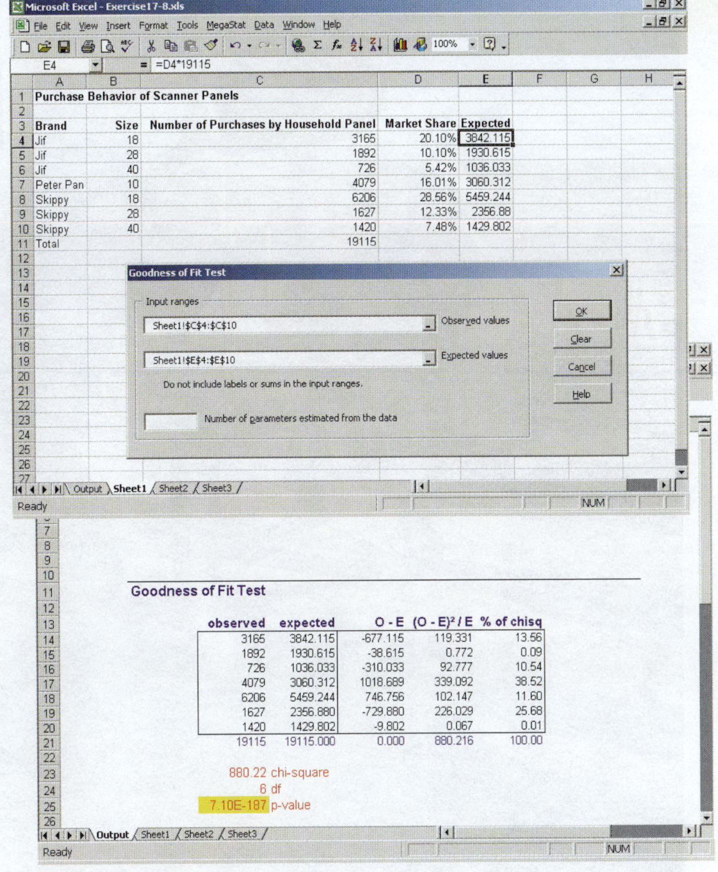

Chi-square goodness of fit test for the scanner panel data in Exercise 16.8 on page 772 (data file: ScanPan.xls):

- Enter the scanner panel data in Exercise 16.8 (page 772) as shown in the screenshot with the number of purchases for each brand in column C and with the market share for each brand (expressed as a percentage) in column D. Note that the total number of purchases for all brands equals 19,115 (which is in cell C11).
- In cell E4, type the cell formula =D4*19115 and press enter to compute the expected frequency for the Jif—18 ounce brand/size combination. Copy this cell formula (by double-clicking the drag handle in the lower right corner of cell E4) to compute the expected frequencies for each of the other brand/size combinations in cells E5 through E10.
- Select **MegaStat : Chi-square/Crosstab : Goodness of Fit Test.**
- In the "Goodness of Fit Test" dialog box, click in the "Observed values input range" box and enter the range C4.C10. Enter this range by dragging with the mouse—the AutoExpand feature cannot be used in the "Goodness of Fit Test" dialog box.
- Click in the "Expected values input range" box, and enter the range E4.E10. Again, enter this range by dragging with the mouse.
- Click OK in the "Goodness of Fit Test" dialog box.

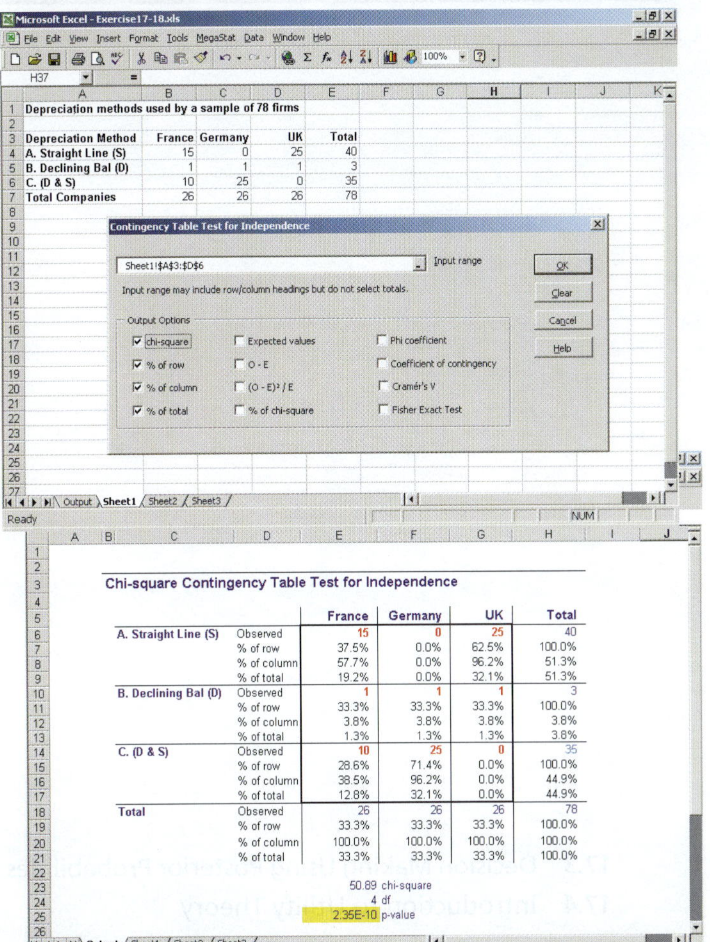

Chi-square test for independence with contingency table input data in the depreciation situation of Exercise 16.18 on page 780 (data file: DeprMeth.xls):

- Enter the depreciation method contingency table data in Table 16.5 on page 780 as shown in the screenshot—depreciation methods in rows and countries in columns.
- Select **MegaStat : Chi-square/Crosstab : Contingency Table.**
- In the "Contingency Table Test for Independence" dialog box, click in the "Input range" box and (by dragging the mouse) enter the range A3.D6. Note that the entered range may contain row and column labels, but the range should not include the "total row" or "total column."
- In the list of Output Options, check the Chi-square check box to obtain the results of the chi-square test for independence.
- In the list of Output Options, check the following check boxes: "% of row," "% of column," and "% of total."
- Click OK in the "Contingency Table Test for Independence" dialog box.

CHAPTER 17

Decision Theory

Chapter Outline

Every day businesses and the people who run them face a myriad of decisions. For instance, a manufacturer might need to decide where to locate a new factory and might also need to decide how large the new facility should be. Or, an investor might decide where to invest money from among several possible investment choices. In this chapter we study some probabilistic methods that can help a decision maker to make intelligent decisions. In Section 17.1 we present **Bayes' theorem,** which is useful for updating probabilities on the basis of newly obtained information that may help in making a decision. In Section 17.2 we formally introduce **decision theory.** We discuss the elements of a decision problem, and we present strategies for making decisions when we face various levels of uncertainty. We also show how to construct a **decision tree,** which is a diagram that can help us analyze a decision problem, and we show how the concept of **expected value** can help us make decisions. In Section 17.3 we show how to use **sample information** to help make decisions, and we demonstrate how to assess the worth of sample information in order to decide whether the sample information should be obtained. We conclude this chapter with Section 17.4, which introduces using **utility theory** to help make decisions.

Many of this chapter's concepts are presented in the context of

C

The Oil Drilling Case: An oil company uses decision theory to help to decide whether to drill for oil on a particular site. The company can perform a seismic experiment at the site to obtain information about the site's potential, and the company uses decision theory to decide whether to drill based on the various possible survey results. In addition, decision theory is employed to determine whether the seismic experiment should be carried out.

17.1 Bayes' Theorem

Sometimes we have an initial or **prior** probability that an event will occur. Then, based on new information, we revise the prior probability to what is called a **posterior** probability. This revision can be done by using a theorem called **Bayes' theorem.**

Example 17.1

To illustrate Bayes' theorem, consider the event that a randomly selected American has the deadly disease AIDS. We let *AIDS* represent this event, and we let $\overline{AIDS}$ represent the event that the randomly selected American does not have AIDS. Since it is estimated that .6 percent of the American population has AIDS,

$$P(AIDS) = .006 \qquad \text{and} \qquad P(\overline{AIDS}) = .994$$

A diagnostic test is used to attempt to detect whether a person has AIDS. According to historical data, 99.9 percent of people with AIDS receive a positive (*POS*) result when this test is administered, while 1 percent of people who do not have AIDS receive a positive result. That is,

$$P(POS \mid AIDS) = .999 \qquad \text{and} \qquad P(POS \mid \overline{AIDS}) = .01$$

If we administer the test to a randomly selected American (who may or may not have AIDS) and the person receives a positive test result, what is the probability that the person actually has AIDS? This probability is

$$P(AIDS \mid POS) = \frac{P(AIDS \cap POS)}{P(POS)}$$

The idea behind Bayes' theorem is that we can find $P(AIDS \mid POS)$ by thinking as follows. A person will receive a positive result (*POS*) if the person receives a positive result and actually has AIDS—that is, $(AIDS \cap POS)$—or if the person receives a positive result and actually does not have AIDS—that is, $(\overline{AIDS} \cap POS)$. Therefore,

$$P(POS) = P(AIDS \cap POS) + P(\overline{AIDS} \cap POS)$$

This implies that

$$P(AIDS \mid POS) = \frac{P(AIDS \cap POS)}{P(POS)}$$

$$= \frac{P(AIDS \cap POS)}{P(AIDS \cap POS) + P(\overline{AIDS} \cap POS)}$$

$$= \frac{P(AIDS)P(POS \mid AIDS)}{P(AIDS)P(POS \mid AIDS) + P(\overline{AIDS})P(POS \mid \overline{AIDS})}$$

$$= \frac{.006(.999)}{.006(.999) + (.994)(.01)} = .38$$

This probability says that, if all Americans were given an AIDS test, only 38 percent of the people who would react positively to the test would actually have AIDS. That is, 62 percent of Americans identified as having AIDS would actually be free of the disease! The reason for this rather surprising result is that, since so few people actually have AIDS, the majority of people who would receive a positive result are people who are free of AIDS and who erroneously test positive. This is why statisticians have frequently spoken against proposals for mandatory AIDS testing.

In the preceding example, there were two *states of nature*—*AIDS* and $\overline{AIDS}$—and two outcomes of the diagnostic test—*POS* and $\overline{POS}$. In general, there might be any number of states of nature and any number of experimental outcomes. This leads to a general statement of Bayes' theorem.

Bayes' Theorem

Let $S_1, S_2, \ldots, S_k$ be k mutually exclusive states of nature, one of which must be true, and suppose that $P(S_1), P(S_2), \ldots, P(S_k)$ are the prior probabilities of these states of nature. Also, let E be a particular outcome of an experiment designed to help determine which state of nature is really true. Then, the **posterior probability** of a particular state of nature, say S_i, given the experimental outcome E, is

$$P(S_i \mid E) = \frac{P(S_i \cap E)}{P(E)} = \frac{P(S_i)P(E \mid S_i)}{P(E)}$$

where

$$P(E) = P(S_1 \cap E) + P(S_2 \cap E) + \cdots + P(S_k \cap E)$$
$$= P(S_1)P(E \mid S_1) + P(S_2)P(E \mid S_2) + \cdots + P(S_k)P(E \mid S_k)$$

We illustrate Bayes' theorem in the following case.

Example 17.2 The Oil Drilling Case

An oil company is attempting to decide whether to drill for oil on a particular site. There are three possible states of nature:

1 No oil (state of nature S_1, which we will denote as *none*)
2 Some oil (state of nature S_2, which we will denote as *some*)
3 Much oil (state of nature S_3, which we will denote as *much*)

Based on experience and knowledge concerning the site's geological characteristics, the oil company feels that the prior probabilities of these states of nature are as follows:

$$P(S_1 \equiv \text{none}) = .7 \qquad P(S_2 \equiv \text{some}) = .2 \qquad P(S_3 \equiv \text{much}) = .1$$

In order to obtain more information about the potential drilling site, the oil company can perform a seismic experiment, which has three readings—low, medium, and high. Moreover, information exists concerning the accuracy of the seismic experiment. The company's historical records tell us that

1 Of 100 past sites that were drilled and produced no oil, 4 sites gave a high reading. Therefore,

$$P(\text{high} \mid \text{none}) = \frac{4}{100} = .04$$

2 Of 400 past sites that were drilled and produced some oil, 8 sites gave a high reading. Therefore,

$$P(\text{high} \mid \text{some}) = \frac{8}{400} = .02$$

3 Of 300 past sites that were drilled and produced much oil, 288 sites gave a high reading. Therefore,

$$P(\text{high} \mid \text{much}) = \frac{288}{300} = .96$$

Intuitively, these conditional probabilities tell us that sites that produce no oil or some oil seldom give a high reading, while sites that produce much oil often give a high reading. Figure 17.1(a) shows a tree diagram that illustrates the prior probabilities of no, some, and much oil and the above conditional probabilities. This figure also gives the conditional probabilities for medium and low readings of the seismic experiment given each of the states of nature (none, some, or much).

Now, suppose that when the company performs the seismic experiment on the site in question, it obtains a high reading. The previously given conditional probabilities suggest that, given this new information, the company might feel that the likelihood of much oil is higher than its prior probability $P(\text{much}) = .1$, and that the likelihoods of some oil and no oil are lower than the prior probabilities $P(\text{some}) = .2$ and $P(\text{none}) = .7$. To be more specific, we wish to *revise the prior probabilities* of no, some, and much oil to what we call *posterior probabilities.* We can do this by using Bayes' theorem as follows.

If we wish to compute $P(\text{none} \mid \text{high})$, we first calculate

$$\begin{aligned} P(\text{high}) &= P(\text{none} \cap \text{high}) + P(\text{some} \cap \text{high}) + P(\text{much} \cap \text{high}) \\ &= P(\text{none})P(\text{high} \mid \text{none}) + P(\text{some})P(\text{high} \mid \text{some}) + P(\text{much})P(\text{high} \mid \text{much}) \\ &= (.7)(.04) + (.2)(.02) + (.1)(.96) = .128 \end{aligned}$$

Then Bayes' theorem says that

$$\begin{aligned} P(\text{none} \mid \text{high}) &= \frac{P(\text{none} \cap \text{high})}{P(\text{high})} = \frac{P(\text{none})P(\text{high} \mid \text{none})}{P(\text{high})} \\ &= \frac{.7(.04)}{.128} = \frac{.028}{.128} = .21875 \end{aligned}$$

These calculations are summarized in part (b) of Figure 17.1. This table, which is called a **probability revision table,** also contains the calculations of the revised probabilities $P(\text{some} \mid \text{high}) = .03125$ and $P(\text{much} \mid \text{high}) = .75$. The revised probabilities in part (b) of Figure 17.1 tell us that, given that the seismic experiment gives a high reading, the revised probabilities of no, some, and much oil are .21875, .03125, and .75, respectively.

Since the posterior probability of much oil is .75, we might conclude that we should drill on the oil site. However, this decision should also be based on economic considerations, and we will see in Section 17.3 how to combine Bayesian posterior probabilities with economic considerations to arrive at reasonable decisions.

In this section we have only introduced Bayes' theorem. There is an entire subject called **Bayesian statistics,** which uses Bayes' theorem to update prior belief about a probability or population parameter to posterior belief. The use of Bayesian statistics is controversial in the case where the prior belief is largely based on subjective considerations, because many statisticians do not believe that we should base decisions on subjective considerations. Realistically, however, we all do this in our daily lives. For example, how each of us viewed the evidence in the O. J. Simpson trial had a great deal to do with our prior beliefs about both O. J. Simpson and the police.

FIGURE 17.1 A Tree Diagram and Probability Revision Tables for Bayes' Theorem in the Oil Drilling Example

(a) A tree diagram illustrating the prior and conditional probabilities

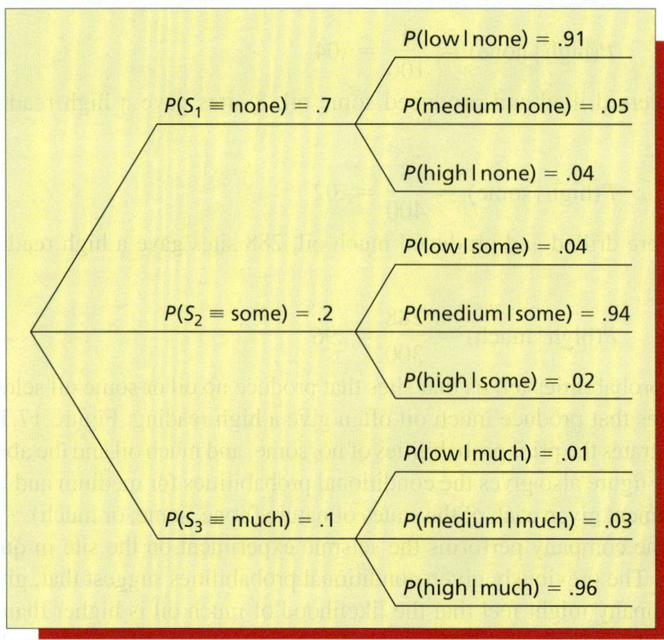

(b) A probability revision table for calculating the probability of a high reading and the posterior probabilities of no oil (S_1), some oil (S_2), and much oil (S_3) given a high reading

S_j	$P(S_j)$	$P(\text{high} \mid S_j)$	$P(S_j \cap \text{high}) = P(S_j)P(\text{high} \mid S_j)$	$P(S_j \mid \text{high}) = P(S_j \cap \text{high})/P(\text{high})$
$S_1 \equiv$ none	$P(\text{none}) = .7$	$P(\text{high} \mid \text{none}) = .04$	$P(\text{none} \cap \text{high}) = .7(.04) = .028$	$P(\text{none} \mid \text{high}) = .028/.128 = .21875$
$S_2 \equiv$ some	$P(\text{some}) = .2$	$P(\text{high} \mid \text{some}) = .02$	$P(\text{some} \cap \text{high}) = .2(.02) = .004$	$P(\text{some} \mid \text{high}) = .004/.128 = .03125$
$S_3 \equiv$ much	$P(\text{much}) = .1$	$P(\text{high} \mid \text{much}) = .96$	$P(\text{much} \cap \text{high}) = .1(.96) = .096$	$P(\text{much} \mid \text{high}) = .096/.128 = .75$
Total	1		$P(\text{high}) = .028 + .004 + .096 = .128$	1

(c) A probability revision table for calculating the probability of a medium reading and the posterior probabilities of no oil (S_1), some oil (S_2), and much oil (S_3) given a medium reading

S_j	$P(S_j)$	$P(\text{medium} \mid S_j)$	$P(S_j \cap \text{medium}) = P(S_j)P(\text{medium} \mid S_j)$	$P(S_j \mid \text{medium}) = P(S_j \cap \text{medium})/P(\text{medium})$
$S_1 \equiv$ none	$P(\text{none}) = .7$	$P(\text{medium} \mid \text{none}) = .05$	$P(\text{none} \cap \text{medium}) = .7(.05) = .035$	$P(\text{none} \mid \text{medium}) = .035/.226 = .15487$
$S_2 \equiv$ some	$P(\text{some}) = .2$	$P(\text{medium} \mid \text{some}) = .94$	$P(\text{some} \cap \text{medium}) = .2(.94) = .188$	$P(\text{some} \mid \text{medium}) = .188/.226 = .83186$
$S_3 \equiv$ much	$P(\text{much}) = .1$	$P(\text{medium} \mid \text{much}) = .03$	$P(\text{much} \cap \text{medium}) = .1(.03) = .003$	$P(\text{much} \mid \text{medium}) = .003/.226 = .01327$
Total	1		$P(\text{medium}) = .035 + .188 + .003 = .226$	1

(d) A probability revision table for calculating the probability of a low reading and the posterior probabilities of no oil (S_1), some oil (S_2) and much oil (S_3) given a low reading

S_j	$P(S_j)$	$P(\text{low} \mid S_j)$	$P(S_j \cap \text{low}) = P(S_j)P(\text{low} \mid S_j)$	$P(S_j \mid \text{low}) = P(S_j \cap \text{low})/P(\text{low})$
$S_1 \equiv$ none	$P(\text{none}) = .7$	$P(\text{low} \mid \text{none}) = .91$	$P(\text{none} \cap \text{low}) = .7(.91) = .637$	$P(\text{none} \mid \text{low}) = .637/.646 = .98607$
$S_2 \equiv$ some	$P(\text{some}) = .2$	$P(\text{low} \mid \text{some}) = .04$	$P(\text{some} \cap \text{low}) = .2(.04) = .008$	$P(\text{some} \mid \text{low}) = .008/.646 = .01238$
$S_3 \equiv$ much	$P(\text{much}) = .1$	$P(\text{low} \mid \text{much}) = .01$	$P(\text{much} \cap \text{low}) = .1(.01) = .001$	$P(\text{much} \mid \text{low}) = .001/.646 = .00155$
Total	1		$P(\text{low}) = .637 + .008 + .001 = .646$	1

Exercises for Section 17.1

CONCEPTS

17.1 What is a prior probability? What is a posterior probability?

17.2 Explain the purpose behind using Bayes' theorem.

METHODS AND APPLICATIONS

17.3 Suppose that A_1, A_2, and B are events where A_1 and A_2 are mutually exclusive and

$$P(A_1) = .8 \qquad P(B \mid A_1) = .1$$
$$P(A_2) = .2 \qquad P(B \mid A_2) = .3$$

Use this information to find $P(A_1 \mid B)$ and $P(A_2 \mid B)$.

17.4 Suppose that A_1, A_2, A_3, and B are events where A_1, A_2, and A_3 are mutually exclusive and

$$P(A_1) = .2 \qquad P(A_2) = .5 \qquad P(A_3) = .3$$
$$P(B \mid A_1) = .02 \qquad P(B \mid A_2) = .05 \qquad P(B \mid A_3) = .04$$

Use this information to find $P(A_1 \mid B)$, $P(A_2 \mid B)$ and $P(A_3 \mid B)$.

17.5 Again consider the diagnostic test for AIDS discussed in Example 17.1 (page 793) and recall that $P(POS \mid AIDS) = .999$ and $P(POS \mid \overline{AIDS}) = .01$, where POS denotes a positive test result. Assuming that the percentage of people who have AIDS is 1 percent, recalculate the probability that a randomly selected person has the AIDS virus, given that his or her test result is positive.

17.6 A department store is considering a new credit policy to try to reduce the number of customers defaulting on payments. A suggestion is made to discontinue credit to any customer who has been one week or more late with his/her payment at least twice. Past records show 95 percent of defaults were late at least twice. Also, 3 percent of all customers default, and 30 percent of those who have not defaulted have had at least two late payments.

a Find the probability that a customer with at least two late payments will default.

b Based on part *a*, should the policy be adopted? Explain.

17.7 A company administers an "aptitude test for managers" to aid in selecting new management trainees. Prior experience suggests that 60 percent of all applicants for management trainee positions would be successful if they were hired. Furthermore, past experience with the aptitude test indicates that 85 percent of applicants who turn out to be successful managers pass the test and 90 percent of applicants who turn out not to be successful managers fail the test.

a If an applicant passes the "aptitude test for managers," what is the probability that the applicant will succeed in a management position?

b Based on your answer to part *a*, do you think that the "aptitude test for managers" is a valuable way to screen applicants for management trainee positions? Explain.

17.8 Three data entry specialists enter requisitions into a computer. Specialist 1 processes 30 percent of the requisitions, specialist 2 processes 45 percent, and specialist 3 processes 25 percent. The proportions of incorrectly entered requisitions by data entry specialists 1, 2, and 3 are .03, .05, and .02, respectively. Suppose that a random requisition is found to have been incorrectly entered. What is the probability that it was processed by data entry specialist 1? By data entry specialist 2? By data entry specialist 3?

17.9 A truth serum given to a suspect is known to be 90 percent reliable when the person is guilty and 99 percent reliable when the person is innocent. In other words, 10 percent of the guilty are judged innocent by the serum and 1 percent of the innocent are judged guilty. If the suspect was selected from a group of suspects of which only 5 percent are guilty of having committed a crime, and the serum indicates that the suspect is guilty of having committed a crime, what is the probability that the suspect is innocent?

17.10 A firm designs and builds automatic electronic control devices and installs them in customers' plants. In shipment, a device has a prior probability of .10 of getting out of alignment. Before a control device is installed, test equipment is used to check the device's alignment. The test equipment has two readings, "in" or "out" of alignment. If the control device is in alignment, there is a .8 probability that the test equipment will read "in." If the control device is not in alignment, there is a .9 probability that the test equipment will read "out."

a Draw a tree diagram illustrating the prior and conditional probabilities for this situation.

b Construct a probability revision table for calculating the probability that the test equipment reads "in," and for calculating the posterior probabilities of the control device being in alignment and out of alignment given that the test equipment reads "in." What is $P(\text{in} \mid \text{reads "in"})$? What is $P(\text{out} \mid \text{reads "in"})$?

c Construct a probability revision table for calculating the probability that the test equipment reads "out," and for calculating the posterior probabilities of the control device being in alignment and out of alignment given that the test equipment reads "out." What is $P(\text{in} \mid \text{reads "out"})$? What is $P(\text{out} \mid \text{reads "out"})$?

17.2 Introduction to Decision Theory

Suppose that a real estate developer is proposing the development of a condominium complex on an exclusive parcel of lakefront property. The developer wishes to choose between three possible options—building a large complex, building a medium-sized complex, and building a small complex. The profitability of each option depends on the level of demand for condominium units after the complex has been built. For simplicity, the developer considers only two possible levels of demand—high or low; the developer must choose whether to build a large, medium, or small complex based on her beliefs about whether demand for condominium units will be high or low.

The real estate developer's situation requires a decision. **Decision theory** is a general approach that helps decision makers make intelligent choices. A decision theory problem typically involves the following elements:

1 **States of nature:** a set of potential future conditions that affects the results of the decision. For instance, the level of demand (high or low) for condominium units will affect profits after the developer chooses to build a large, medium, or small complex. Thus, we have two states of nature—high demand and low demand.

2 **Alternatives:** several alternative actions for the decision maker to choose from. For example, the real estate developer can choose between building a large, medium, or small condominium complex. Therefore, the developer has three alternatives—large, medium, and small.

3 **Payoffs:** a payoff for each alternative under each potential state of nature. The payoffs are often summarized in a **payoff table.** For instance, Table 17.1 gives a payoff table for the condominium complex situation. This table gives the profit[1] for each alternative under the different states of nature. For example, the payoff table tells us that, if the developer builds a large complex and if demand for units turns out to be high, a profit of $22 million will be realized. However, if the developer builds a large complex and if demand for units turns out to be low, a loss of $11 million will be suffered.

Once the states of nature have been identified, the alternatives have been listed, and the payoffs have been determined, we evaluate the alternatives by using a **decision criterion.** How this is done depends on the **degree of uncertainty** associated with the states of nature. Here there are three possibilities:

1 **Certainty:** we know for certain which state of nature will actually occur.

2 **Uncertainty:** we have no information about the likelihoods of the various states of nature.

3 **Risk:** the likelihood (probability) of each state of nature can be estimated.

Decision making under certainty In the unlikely event that we know for certain which state of nature will actually occur, we simply choose the alternative that gives the best payoff for that state of nature. For instance, in the condominium complex situation, if we know that demand for units will be high, then the payoff table (see Table 17.1) tells us that the best alternative is to build a large complex and that this choice will yield a profit of $22 million. On the other hand, if we know that demand for units will be low, then the payoff table tells us that the best alternative is to build a small complex and that this choice will yield a profit of $8 million.

Of course, we rarely (if ever) know for certain which state of nature will actually occur. However, analyzing the payoff table in this way often provides insight into the nature of the problem. For instance, examining the payoff table tells us that, if we know that demand for units will be

TABLE 17.1 A Payoff Table for the Condominium Complex Situation

	States of Nature	
Alternatives	**Low Demand**	**High Demand**
Small complex	$8 million	$8 million
Medium complex	$5 million	$15 million
Large complex	−$11 million	$22 million

[1]Here profits are really present values representing current dollar values of expected future income minus costs.

low, then building either a small complex or a medium complex will be far superior to building a large complex (which would yield an $11 million loss).

Decision making under uncertainty This is the exact opposite of certainty. Here we have no information about how likely the different states of nature are. That is, we have no idea how to assign probabilities to the different states of nature.

In such a case, several approaches are possible; we will discuss two commonly used methods. The first is called the **maximin criterion.**

Maximin: Find the worst possible payoff for each alternative, and then choose the alternative that yields the maximum worst possible payoff.

For instance, to apply the maximin criterion to the condominium complex situation, we proceed as follows (see Table 17.1):

1 If a small complex is built, the worst possible payoff is $8 million.
2 If a medium complex is built, the worst possible payoff is $5 million.
3 If a large complex is built, the worst possible payoff is −$11 million.

Since the maximum of these worst possible payoffs is $8 million, the developer should choose to build a small complex.

The maximin criterion is a *pessimistic approach* because it considers the worst possible payoff for each alternative. When an alternative is chosen using the maximin criterion, the actual payoff obtained may be higher than the maximum worst possible payoff. However, using the maximin criterion assures a "guaranteed minimum" payoff.

A second approach is called the **maximax criterion.**

Maximax: Find the best possible payoff for each alternative, and then choose the alternative that yields the maximum best possible payoff.

To apply the maximax criterion to the condominium complex situation, we proceed as follows (see Table 17.1):

1 If a small complex is built, the best possible payoff is $8 million.
2 If a medium complex is built, the best possible payoff is $15 million.
3 If a large complex is built, the best possible payoff is $22 million.

Since the maximum of these best possible payoffs is $22 million, the developer should choose to build a large complex.

The maximax criterion is an *optimistic approach* because we always choose the alternative that yields the highest possible payoff. This is a "go for broke" strategy, and the actual payoff obtained may be far less than the highest possible payoff. For example, in the condominium complex situation, if a large complex is built and demand for units turns out to be low, an $11 million loss will be suffered (instead of a $22 million profit).

Decision making under risk In this case we can estimate the probability of occurrence for each state of nature. Thus, we have a situation in which we have more information about the states of nature than in the case of uncertainty and less information than in the case of certainty. Here a commonly used approach is to use the **expected monetary value criterion.** This involves computing the expected monetary payoff for each alternative and choosing the alternative with the largest expected payoff.

The expected value criterion can be employed by using *prior probabilities.* As an example, suppose that in the condominium complex situation the developer assigns prior probabilities of .7 and .3 to high and low demands, respectively. We find the expected monetary value for each alternative by multiplying the probability of occurrence for each state of nature by the payoff associated with the state of nature and by summing these products. Referring to the payoff table in Table 17.1, the expected monetary values are as follows:

Small complex: Expected value = .3($8 million) + .7($8 million) = $8 million
Medium complex: Expected value = .3($5 million) + .7($15 million) = $12 million
Large complex: Expected value = .3(−$11 million) + .7($22 million) = $12.1 million

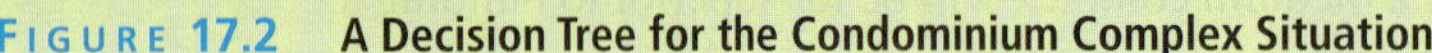

FIGURE 17.2 A Decision Tree for the Condominium Complex Situation

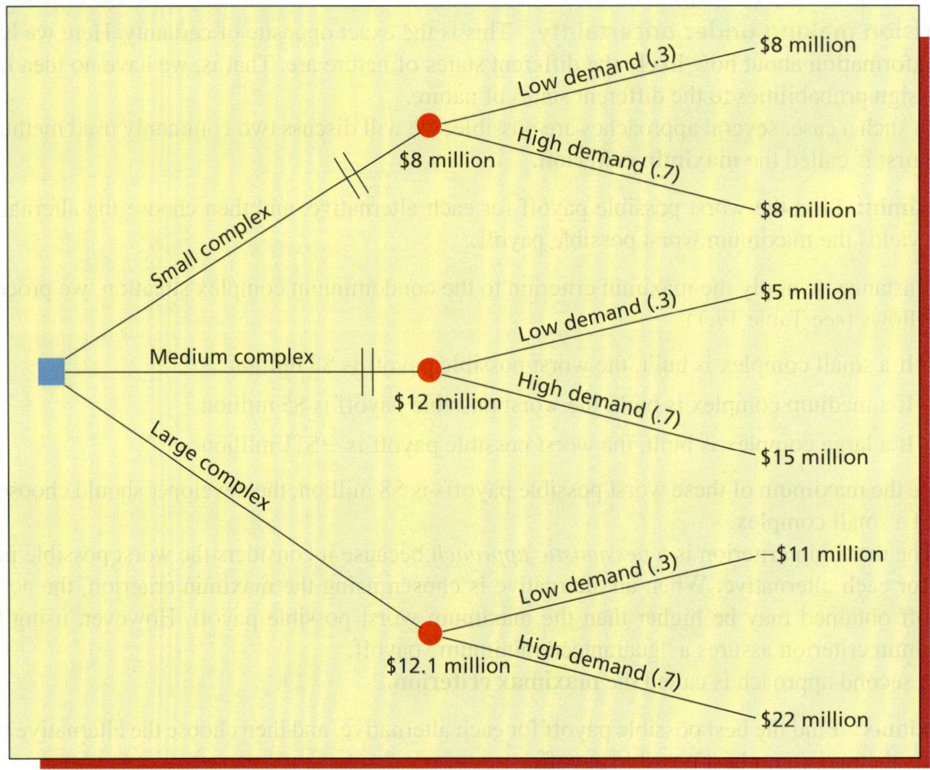

Choosing the alternative with the highest expected monetary value, the developer would choose to build a large complex.

Remember that the expected payoff is not necessarily equal to the actual payoff that will be realized. Rather, the expected payoff is the long-run average payoff that would be realized if many identical decisions were made. For instance, the expected monetary payoff of $12.1 million for a large complex is the average payoff that would be obtained if many large condominium complexes were built. Thus, the expected monetary value criterion is best used when many similar decisions will be made.

Using a decision tree It is often convenient to depict the alternatives, states of nature, payoffs, and probabilities (in the case of risk) in the form of a **decision tree** or **tree diagram.** The diagram is made up of **nodes** and **branches.** We use square nodes to denote decision points and circular nodes to denote chance events. The branches emanating from a decision point represent alternatives, and the branches emanating from a circular node represent the possible states of nature. Figure 17.2 presents a decision tree for the condominium complex situation (in the case of risk as described previously). Notice that the payoffs are shown at the rightmost end of each branch and that the probabilities associated with the various states of nature are given in parentheses corresponding to each branch emanating from a chance node. The expected monetary values for the alternatives are shown below the chance nodes. The double slashes placed through the small complex and medium complex branches indicate that these alternatives would not be chosen (because of their lower expected payoffs) and that the large complex alternative would be selected.

A decision tree is particularly useful when a problem involves a sequence of decisions. For instance, in the condominium complex situation, if demand turns out to be small, it might be possible to improve payoffs by selling the condominiums at lower prices. Figure 17.3 shows a decision tree in which, after a decision to build a small, medium, or large condominium complex is made, the developer can choose to either keep the same prices or charge lower prices for condominium units. In order to analyze the decision tree, we start with the last (rightmost) decision to be made. For each decision we choose the alternative that gives the highest payoff. For instance, if the developer builds a large complex and demand turns out to be low, the developer should lower prices (as indicated by the double slash through the alternative of same prices). If decisions

FIGURE 17.3 A Decision Tree with Sequential Decisions

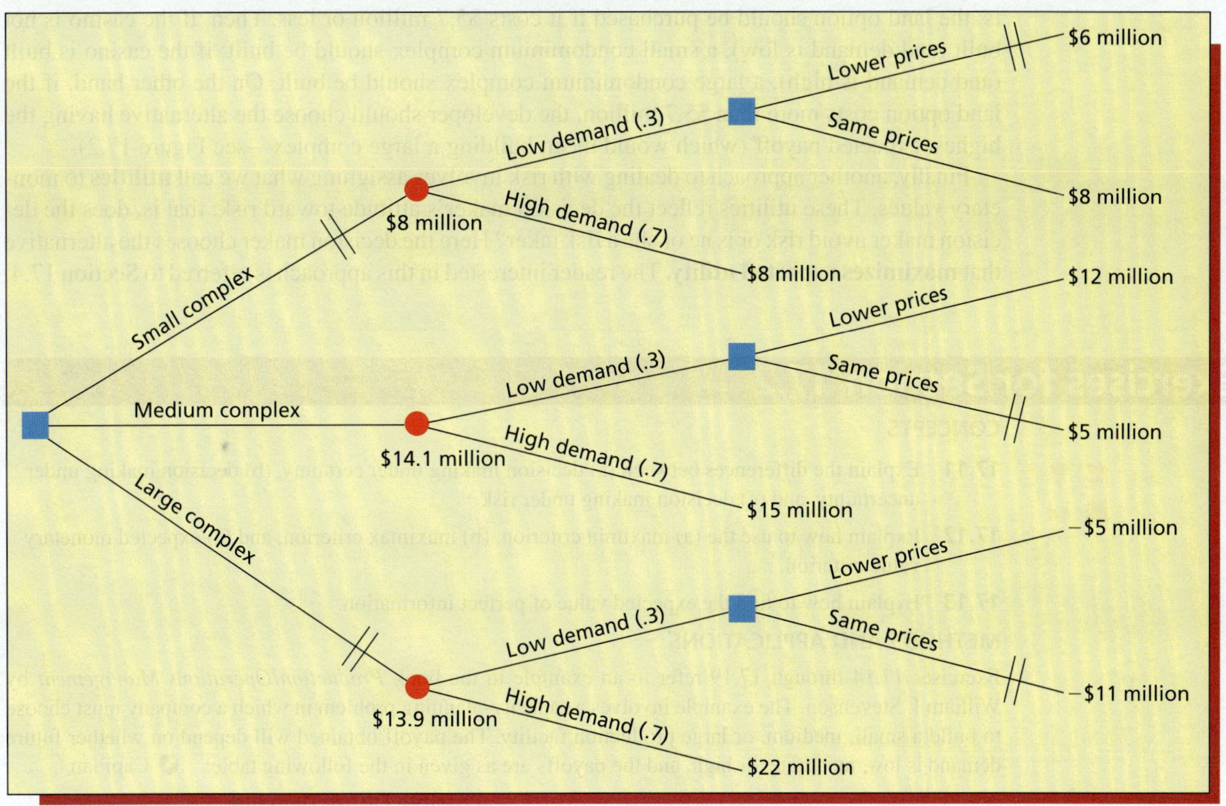

are followed by chance events, we choose the alternative that gives the highest expected monetary value. For example, again looking at Figure 17.3, we see that a medium complex should now be built because of its highest expected monetary value ($14.1 million). This is indicated by the double slashes drawn through the small and large complex alternatives. Looking at the entire decision tree in Figure 17.3, we see that the developer should build a medium complex and should sell condominium units at lower prices if demand turns out to be low.

Sometimes it is possible to determine exactly which state of nature will occur in the future. For example, in the condominium complex situation, the level of demand for units might depend on whether a new resort casino is built in the area. While the developer may have prior probabilities concerning whether the casino will be built, it might be feasible to postpone a decision about the size of the condominium complex until a final decision about the resort casino has been made.

If we can find out exactly which state of nature will occur, we say we have obtained **perfect information.** There is usually a cost involved in obtaining this information (if it can be obtained at all). For instance, we might have to acquire an option on the lakefront property on which the condominium complex is to be built in order to postpone a decision about the size of the complex. Or perfect information might be acquired by conducting some sort of research that must be paid for. A question that arises here is whether it is worth the cost to obtain perfect information. We can answer this question by computing the **expected value of perfect information,** which we denote as the **EVPI.** The EVPI is defined as follows:

EVPI = Expected payoff under certainty − Expected payoff under risk

For instance, if we consider the condominium complex situation depicted in the decision tree of Figure 17.2, we found that the expected payoff under risk is $12.1 million (which is the expected payoff associated with building a large complex). To find the expected payoff under certainty, we find the highest payoff under each state of nature. Referring to Table 17.1, we see that if demand is low, the highest payoff is $8 million (when we build a small complex); we see that if demand is high, the highest payoff is $22 million (when we build a large complex). Since the prior probabilities of high and low demand are, respectively, .7 and .3, the expected payoff under certainty is .7($22 million) + .3($8 million) = $17.8 million. Therefore, the expected value of perfect information is \$17.8 million − \$12.1 million = \$5.7 million. This is the maximum amount of money that the developer should be willing to pay to obtain perfect information. That is, the land option should be purchased if it costs \$5.7 million or less. Then, if the casino is not built (and demand is low), a small condominium complex should be built; if the casino is built (and demand is high), a large condominium complex should be built. On the other hand, if the land option costs more than \$5.7 million, the developer should choose the alternative having the highest expected payoff (which would mean building a large complex—see Figure 17.2).

Finally, another approach to dealing with risk involves assigning what we call **utilities** to monetary values. These utilities reflect the decision maker's attitude toward risk: that is, does the decision maker avoid risk or is he or she a risk taker? Here the decision maker chooses the alternative that **maximizes expected utility.** The reader interested in this approach is referred to Section 17.4.

Exercises for Section 17.2

CONCEPTS

17.11 Explain the differences between (a) decision making under certainty, (b) decision making under uncertainty, and (c) decision making under risk.

17.12 Explain how to use the (a) maximin criterion, (b) maximax criterion, and (c) expected monetary value criterion.

17.13 Explain how to find the expected value of perfect information.

METHODS AND APPLICATIONS

Exercises 17.14 through 17.19 refer to an example in the book *Production/Operations Management* by William J. Stevenson. The example involves a capacity-planning problem in which a company must choose to build a small, medium, or large production facility. The payoff obtained will depend on whether future demand is low, moderate, or high, and the payoffs are as given in the following table: CapPlan

	Possible Future Demand		
Alternatives	**Low**	**Moderate**	**High**
Small facility	\$10*	\$10	\$10
Medium facility	7	12	12
Large facility	−4	2	16

*Present value in \$ millions.

Source: W. J. Stevenson, *Production/Operations Management*, 5th ed. (Burr Ridge, IL: Richard D. Irwin, 1996), p. 73.

17.14 Find the best alternative (and the resulting payoff) in the given payoff table if it is known with certainty that demand will be

a Low. **b** Medium. **c** High.

17.15 Given the payoff table, find the alternative that would be chosen using the maximin criterion.

17.16 Given the payoff table, find the alternative that would be chosen using the maximax criterion.

17.17 Suppose that the company assigns prior probabilities of .3, .5, and .2 to low, moderate, and high demands, respectively.

a Find the expected monetary value for each alternative (small, medium, and large).

b What is the best alternative if we use the expected monetary value criterion?

17.18 Construct a decision tree for the information in the payoff table assuming that the prior probabilities of low, moderate, and high demands are, respectively, .3, .5, and .2.

17.19 For the information in the payoff table find

a The expected payoff under certainty.

b The expected value of perfect information, EVPI.

17.20 A firm wishes to choose the location for a new factory. Profits obtained will depend on whether a new railroad spur is constructed to serve the town in which the new factory will be located. The following payoff table summarizes the relevant information: FactLoc

Alternatives	**New Railroad Spur Built**	**No New Railroad Spur**
Location *A*	\$1*	\$14
Location *B*	2	10
Location *C*	4	6

*Profits in \$ millions.

Determine the location that should be chosen if the firm uses

a The maximin criterion.

b The maximax criterion.

17.21 Refer to the information given in Exercise 17.20. Using the probabilities of .60 for a new railroad spur and .40 for no new railroad spur FactLoc

a Compute the expected monetary value for each location.

b Find the location that should be selected using the expected monetary value criterion.

c Compute the EVPI, expected value of perfect information.

17.22 Construct a decision tree for the information given in Exercises 17.20 and 17.21. FactLoc

17.23 Figure 17.4 gives a decision tree presented in the book *Production/Operations Management* by William J. Stevenson. Use this tree diagram to do the following:

a Find the expected monetary value for each of the alternatives (subcontract, expand, and build).

b Determine the alternative that should be selected in order to maximize the expected monetary value.

FIGURE 17.4 Decision Tree for Exercise 17.23

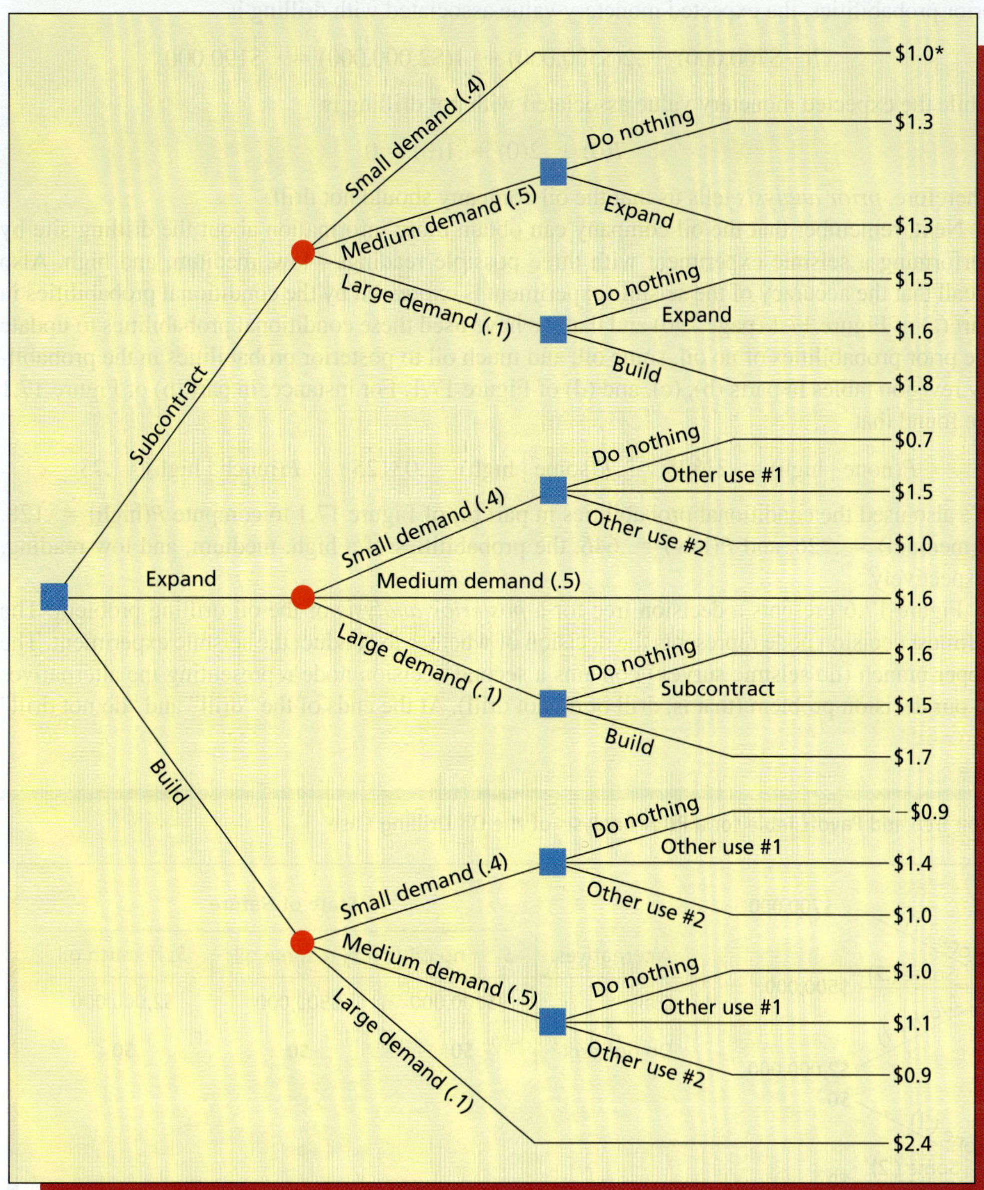

*Net present value in millions.

Source: Reprinted with permission from W. J. Stevenson, *Production/Operations Management*, 6th ed., p. 228. © 1999 by The McGraw-Hill Companies, Inc.

17.3 Decision Making Using Posterior Probabilities

We have seen that the *expected monetary value criterion* tells us to choose the alternative having the highest expected payoff. In Section 17.2 we computed expected payoffs by using *prior probabilities.* When we use the expected monetary value criterion to choose the best alternative based on expected values computed using prior probabilities, we call this **prior decision analysis.** Often, however, sample information can be obtained to help us make decisions. In such a case, we compute expected values by using *posterior probabilities,* and we call the analysis **posterior decision analysis.** In the following example we demonstrate how to carry out posterior analysis.

Example 17.3 The Oil Drilling Case

Recall from Example 17.2 that an oil company wishes to decide whether to drill for oil on a particular site, and recall that the company has assigned prior probabilities to the states of nature $S_1 \equiv$ no oil, $S_2 \equiv$ some oil, and $S_3 \equiv$ much oil of .7, .2, and .1, respectively. Figure 17.5 gives a decision tree and payoff table for a *prior analysis* of the oil drilling situation. Here, using the prior probabilities, the expected monetary value associated with drilling is

$$.7(-\$700{,}000) + .2(\$500{,}000) + .1(\$2{,}000{,}000) = -\$190{,}000$$

while the expected monetary value associated with not drilling is

$$.7(0) + .2(0) + .1(0) = 0$$

Therefore, *prior analysis* tells us that the oil company should not drill.

Next, remember that the oil company can obtain more information about the drilling site by performing a seismic experiment with three possible readings—low, medium, and high. Also recall that the accuracy of the seismic experiment is expressed by the conditional probabilities in part (a) of Figure 17.1 (page 796) and that we have used these conditional probabilities to update the prior probabilities of no oil, some oil, and much oil to posterior probabilities in the probability revision tables in parts (b), (c), and (d) of Figure 17.1. For instance, in part (b) of Figure 17.1 we found that

$$P(\text{none} \mid \text{high}) = .21875 \qquad P(\text{some} \mid \text{high}) = .03125 \qquad P(\text{much} \mid \text{high}) = .75$$

We also used the conditional probabilities in part (a) of Figure 17.1 to compute $P(\text{high}) = .128$, $P(\text{medium}) = .226$, and $P(\text{low}) = .646$, the probabilities of a high, medium, and low reading, respectively.

Figure 17.6 presents a decision tree for a *posterior analysis* of the oil drilling problem. The leftmost decision node represents the decision of whether to conduct the seismic experiment. The upper branch (no seismic survey) contains a second decision node representing the alternatives in our decision problem (that is, drill or do not drill). At the ends of the "drill" and "do not drill"

FIGURE 17.5 A Decision Tree and Payoff Table for a Prior Analysis of the Oil Drilling Case

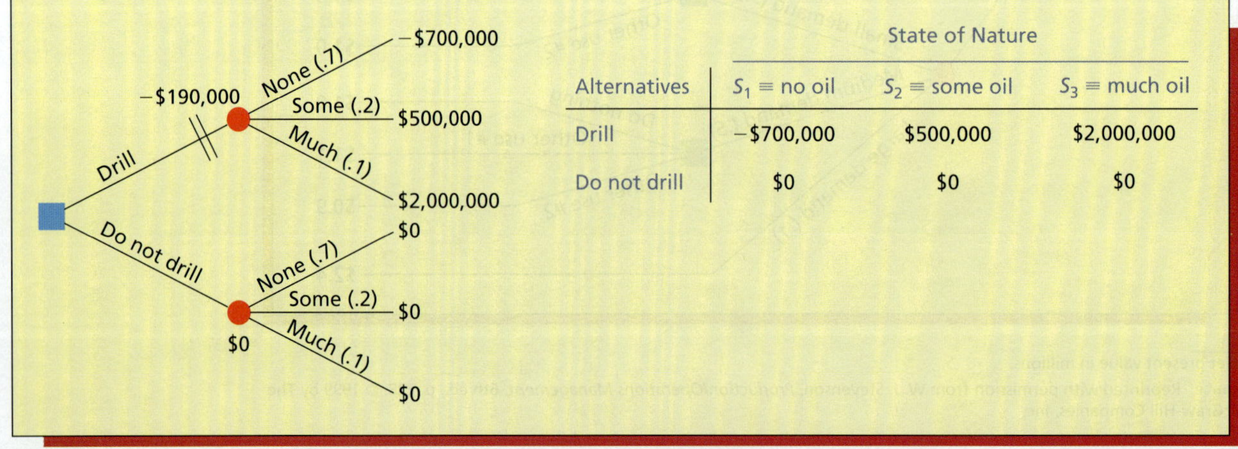

	State of Nature		
Alternatives	$S_1 \equiv$ no oil	$S_2 \equiv$ some oil	$S_3 \equiv$ much oil
Drill	−$700,000	$500,000	$2,000,000
Do not drill	$0	$0	$0

FIGURE 17.6 A Decision Tree for a Posterior Analysis of the Oil Drilling Case

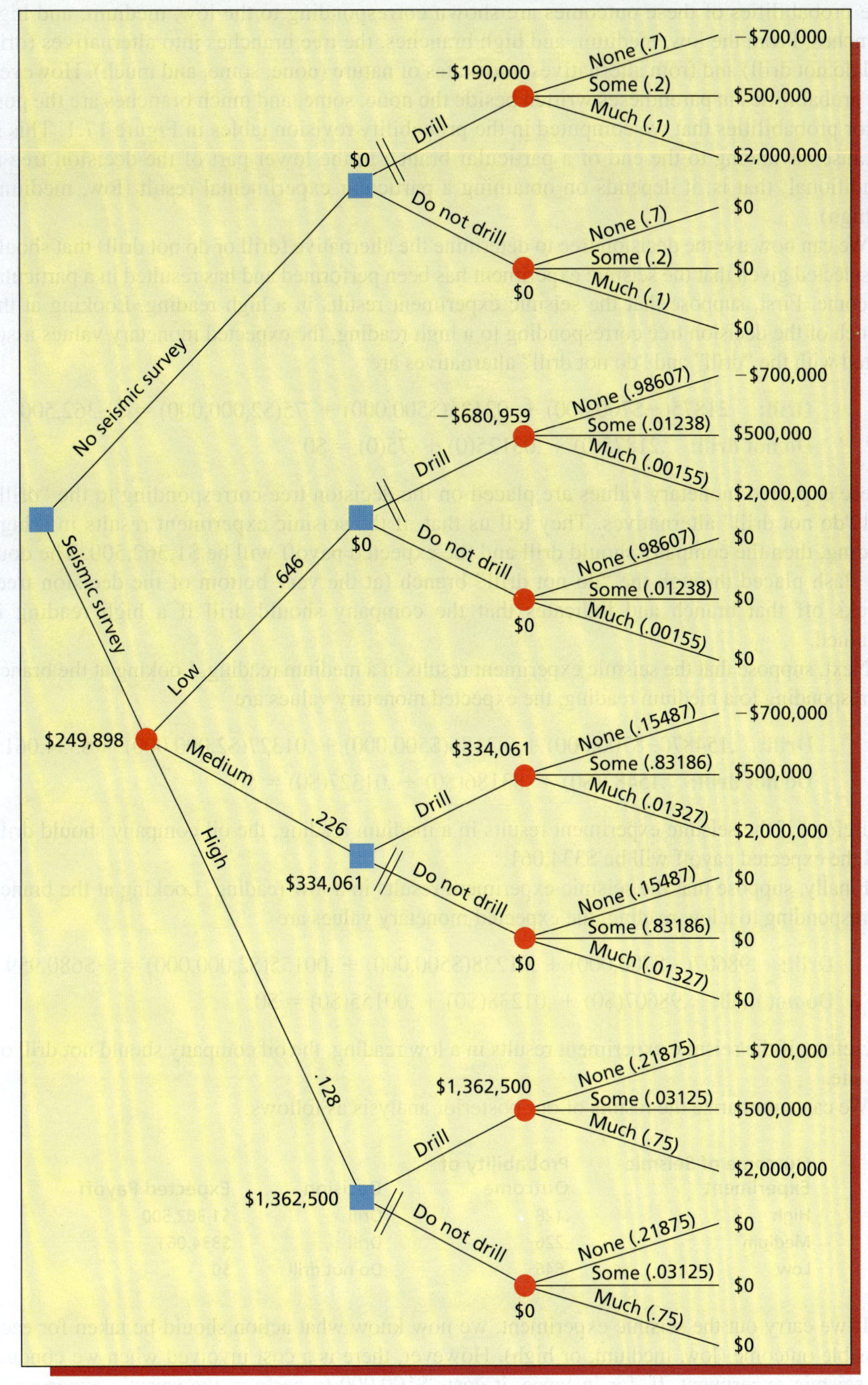

branches we have chance nodes that branch into the three states of nature—no oil (none), some oil (some), and much oil (much). The appropriate payoff is placed at the rightmost end of each branch, and since this uppermost branch corresponds to "no seismic survey," the probabilities in parentheses for the states of nature are the prior probabilities. The expected payoff associated with drilling (which we found to be −$190,000) is shown at the chance node for the "drill" branch, and the expected payoff associated with not drilling (which we found to be $0) is shown at the chance node for the "do not drill" branch.

The lower branch of the decision tree (seismic survey) has an extra chance node that branches into the three possible outcomes of the seismic experiment—low, medium, and high. The probabilities of these outcomes are shown corresponding to the low, medium, and high branches. From the low, medium, and high branches, the tree branches into alternatives (drill and do not drill) and from alternatives into states of nature (none, some, and much). However, the probabilities in parentheses written beside the none, some, and much branches are the posterior probabilities that we computed in the probability revision tables in Figure 17.1. This is because advancing to the end of a particular branch in the lower part of the decision tree is conditional; that is, it depends on obtaining a particular experimental result (low, medium, or high).

We can now use the decision tree to determine the alternative (drill or do not drill) that should be selected given that the seismic experiment has been performed and has resulted in a particular outcome. First, suppose that the seismic experiment results in a high reading. Looking at the branch of the decision tree corresponding to a high reading, the expected monetary values associated with the "drill" and "do not drill" alternatives are

Drill: .21875(−\$700,000) + .03125(\$500,000) + .75(\$2,000,000) = \$1,362,500
Do not drill: .21875(0) + .03125(0) + .75(0) = \$0

BI These expected monetary values are placed on the decision tree corresponding to the "drill" and "do not drill" alternatives. They tell us that, if the seismic experiment results in a high reading, then the company should drill and the expected payoff will be \$1,362,500. The double slash placed through the "do not drill" branch (at the very bottom of the decision tree) blocks off that branch and indicates that the company should drill if a high reading is obtained.

Next, suppose that the seismic experiment results in a medium reading. Looking at the branch corresponding to a medium reading, the expected monetary values are

Drill: .15487(−\$700,000) + .83186(\$500,000) + .01327(\$2,000,000) = \$334,061
Do not drill: .15487(\$0) + .83186(\$0) + .01327(\$0) = \$0

BI Therefore, if the seismic experiment results in a medium reading, the oil company should drill, and the expected payoff will be \$334,061.

Finally, suppose that the seismic experiment results in a low reading. Looking at the branch corresponding to a low reading, the expected monetary values are

Drill: .98607(−\$700,000) + .01238(\$500,000) + .00155(\$2,000,000) = −\$680,959
Do not drill: .98607(\$0) + .01238(\$0) + .00155(\$0) = \$0

BI Therefore, if the seismic experiment results in a low reading, the oil company should not drill on the site.

We can summarize the results of our posterior analysis as follows:

Outcome of Seismic Experiment	Probability of Outcome	Decision	Expected Payoff
High	.128	Drill	\$1,362,500
Medium	.226	Drill	\$334,061
Low	.646	Do not drill	\$0

If we carry out the seismic experiment, we now know what action should be taken for each possible outcome (low, medium, or high). However, there is a cost involved when we conduct the seismic experiment. If, for instance, it costs \$100,000 to perform the seismic experiment, we need to investigate whether it is worth it to perform the experiment. This will depend on the expected worth of the information provided by the experiment. Naturally, we must decide whether the experiment is worth it *before* our posterior analysis is actually done. Therefore, when we assess the worth of the sample information, we say that we are performing a **preposterior analysis.**

In order to assess the worth of the sample information, we compute the **expected payoff of sampling.** To calculate this result, we find the expected payoff and the probability of each sample outcome (that is, at each possible outcome of the seismic experiment). Looking at the decision tree in Figure 17.6, we find the following:

Experimental Outcome	Expected Payoff	Probability
Low	\$0	.646
Medium	\$334,061	.226
High	\$1,362,500	.128

Therefore, the **expected payoff of sampling,** which is denoted **EPS,** is

$$EPS = .646(\$0) + .226(\$334{,}061) + .128(\$1{,}362{,}500) = \$249{,}898$$

To find the worth of the sample information, we compare the expected payoff of sampling to the **expected payoff of no sampling,** which is denoted **EPNS.** The EPNS is the expected payoff of the alternative that we would choose by using the expected monetary value criterion with the prior probabilities. Recalling that we summarized our prior analysis in the tree diagram of Figure 17.5, we found that (based on the prior probabilities) we should choose not to drill and that the expected payoff of this action is \$0. Therefore, EPNS = \$0.

We compare the EPS and the EPNS by computing the **expected value of sample information,** which is denoted **EVSI** and is defined to be the expected payoff of sampling minus the expected payoff of no sampling. Therefore,

$$EVSI = EPS - EPNS = \$249{,}898 - \$0 = \$249{,}898$$

The EVSI is the expected gain from conducting the seismic experiment, and the oil company should pay no more than this amount to carry out the seismic experiment. If the experiment costs \$100,000, then it is worth the expense to conduct the experiment. Moreover, the difference between the EVSI and the cost of sampling is called the **expected net gain of sampling,** which is denoted **ENGS.** Here

$$ENGS = EVSI - \$100{,}000 = \$249{,}898 - \$100{,}000 = \$149{,}898$$

As long as the ENGS is greater than \$0, it is worth it to carry out the seismic experiment. That is, the oil company should carry out the seismic experiment before it chooses whether or not to drill. Then, as discussed earlier, our posterior analysis says that if the experiment gives a medium or high reading, the oil company should drill, and if the experiment gives a low reading, the oil company should not drill.

Exercises for Section 17.3

CONCEPTS

17.24 Explain what is meant by each of the following and describe the purpose of each:
a Prior analysis. **b** Posterior analysis. **c** Preposterior analysis.

17.25 Define and interpret each of the following:
- **a** Expected payoff of sampling, EPS.
- **b** Expected payoff of no sampling, EPNS.
- **c** Expected value of sample information, EVSI.
- **d** Expected net gain of sampling, ENGS.

METHODS AND APPLICATIONS

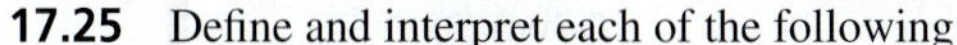

Exercises 17.26 through 17.31 refer to the following situation.

In the book *Making Hard Decisions: An Introduction to Decision Analysis* (2nd ed.), Robert T. Clemen presents an example in which an investor wishes to choose between investing money in (1) a high-risk stock, (2) a low-risk stock, or (3) a savings account. The payoffs received from the two stocks will depend on the behavior of the stock market—that is, whether the market goes up, stays the same, or goes down over the investment period. In addition, in order to obtain more information about the market behavior that might be anticipated during the investment period, the investor can hire an economist as a consultant who will predict the future market behavior. The results of the consultation will be one of the following three possibilities: (1) "economist says up," (2) "economist says flat" (the same), or (3) "economist says down." The conditional probabilities that express the ability of the economist to accurately forecast market behavior are given in the following table:

Economist's Prediction	True Market State Up	Flat	Down
"Economist says up"	.80	.15	.20
"Economist says flat"	.10	.70	.20
"Economist says down"	.10	.15	.60

InvDec

For instance, using this table we see that P("economist says up" | market up) = .80. Figure 17.7 gives an incomplete decision tree for the investor's situation. Notice that this decision tree gives all relevant payoffs and also gives the prior probabilities of up, flat, and down, which are, respectively, 0.5, 0.3, and 0.2.

FIGURE 17.7 An Incomplete Decision Tree for the Investor's Decision Problem of Exercises 17.26 through 17.31

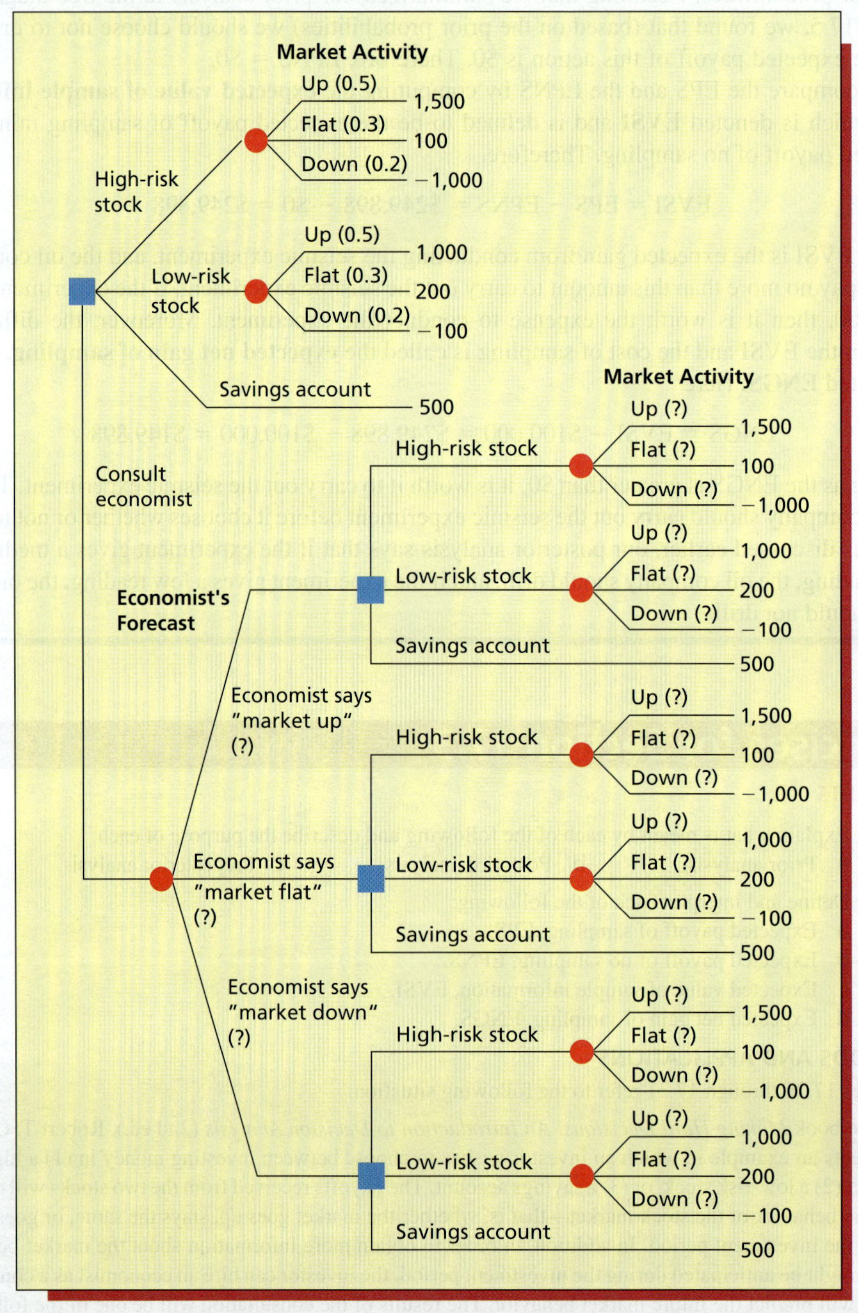

Source: From *Making Hard Decisions: An Introduction to Decision Analysis,* 2nd ed., by R. T. Clemen, © 1996. Reprinted with permission of Brooks/Cole, an imprint of the Wadsworth Group, a division of Thomson Learning. Fax 800-730-2215.

Using the information provided here, and any needed information on the decision tree of Figure 17.7, do the following:

17.26 Identify and list each of the following for the investor's decision problem:
- **a** The investor's alternative actions.
- **b** The states of nature.
- **c** The possible results of sampling (that is, of information gathering).

17.27 Write out the payoff table for the investor's decision problem.

17.28 Carry out a prior analysis of the investor's decision problem. That is, determine the investment choice that should be made and find the expected monetary value of that choice assuming that the investor does not consult the economist about future stock market behavior.

17.29 Set up probability revision tables to
- **a** Find the probability that the "economist says up" and find the posterior probabilities of market up, market flat, and market down given that the "economist says up."
- **b** Find the probability that the "economist says flat," and find the posterior probabilities of market up, market flat, and market down given that the "economist says flat."
- **c** Find the probability that the "economist says down," and find the posterior probabilities of market up, market flat, and market down given that the "economist says down."
- **d** Reproduce the decision tree of Figure 17.7 and insert the probabilities you found in parts *a*, *b*, and *c* in their appropriate locations.

17.30 Carry out a posterior analysis of the investor's decision problem. That is, determine the investment choice that should be made and find the expected monetary value of that choice assuming
- **a** The economist says "market up."
- **b** The economist says "market flat."
- **c** The economist says "market down."

17.31 Carry out a preposterior analysis of the investor's decision problem by finding
- **a** The expected monetary value associated with consulting the economist; that is, find the EPS.
- **b** The expected monetary value associated with not consulting the economist; that is, find the EPNS.
- **c** The expected value of sample information, EVSI.
- **d** The maximum amount the investor should be willing to pay for the economist's consulting advice.

Exercises 17.32 through 17.38 refer to the following situation.

A firm designs and manufactures automatic electronic control devices that are installed at customers' plant sites. The control devices are shipped by truck to customers' sites; while in transit, the devices sometimes get out of alignment. More specifically, a device has a prior probability of .10 of getting out of alignment during shipment. When a control device is delivered to the customer's plant site, the customer can install the device. If the customer installs the device, and if the device is in alignment, the manufacturer of the control device will realize a profit of $15,000. If the customer installs the device, and if the device is out of alignment, the manufacturer must dismantle, realign, and reinstall the device for the customer. This procedure costs $3,000, and therefore the manufacturer will realize a profit of $12,000. As an alternative to customer installation, the manufacturer can send two engineers to the customer's plant site to check the alignment of the control device, to realign the device if necessary before installation, and to supervise the installation. Since it is less costly to realign the device before it is installed, sending the engineers costs $500. Therefore, if the engineers are sent to assist with the installation, the manufacturer realizes a profit of $14,500 (this is true whether or not the engineers must realign the device at the site).

Before a control device is installed, a piece of test equipment can be used by the customer to check the device's alignment. The test equipment has two readings, "in" or "out" of alignment. Given that the control device is in alignment, there is a .8 probability that the test equipment will read "in." Given that the control device is out of alignment, there is a .9 probability that the test equipment will read "out."

17.32 Identify and list each of the following for the control device situation:
- **a** The firm's alternative actions.
- **b** The states of nature.
- **c** The possible results of sampling (that is, of information gathering).

17.33 Write out the payoff table for the control device situation.

17.34 Construct a decision tree for a prior analysis of the control device situation. Then determine whether the engineers should be sent assuming that the piece of test equipment is not employed to check the device's alignment. Also find the expected monetary value associated with the best alternative action.

17.35 Set up probability revision tables to
a Find the probability that the test equipment "reads in," and find the posterior probabilities of in alignment and out of alignment given that the test equipment "reads in."
b Find the probability that the test equipment "reads out," and find the posterior probabilities of in alignment and out of alignment given that the test equipment "reads out."

17.36 Construct a decision tree for a posterior and preposterior analysis of the control device situation.

17.37 Carry out a posterior analysis of the control device problem. That is, decide whether the engineers should be sent, and find the expected monetary value associated with either sending or not sending (depending on which is best) the engineers assuming
a The test equipment "reads in."
b The test equipment "reads out."

17.38 Carry out a preposterior analysis of the control device problem by finding
a The expected monetary value associated with using the test equipment; that is, find the EPS.
b The expected monetary value associated with not using the test equipment; that is, find the EPNS.
c The expected value of sample information, EVSI.
d The maximum amount that should be paid for using the test equipment.

17.4 Introduction to Utility Theory

Suppose that a decision maker is trying to decide whether to invest in one of two opportunities—Investment 1 or Investment 2—or to not invest in either of these opportunities. As shown in Table 17.2(a), (b), and (c), the expected profits associated with Investment 1, Investment 2, and no investment are \$32,000, \$28,000, and \$0. Thus, if the decision maker uses expected profit as a decision criterion, and decides to choose no more than one investment, the decision maker should choose Investment 1. However, as discussed earlier, the expected profit for an investment is the long-run average profit that would be realized if many identical investments could be made. If the decision maker will make only a limited number of investments (perhaps because of limited capital), he or she will not realize the expected profit. For example, a single undertaking of

TABLE 17.2 Three Possible Investments and Their Expected Utilities

(a) Investment 1 Profits

Profit	Probability
\$50,000	.7
\$10,000	.1
−\$20,000	.2

Expected profit = 50,000(.7) + 10,000(.1) + (−20,000)(.2) = 32,000

(b) Investment 2 Profits

Profit	Probability
\$40,000	.6
\$30,000	.2
−\$10,000	.2

Expected profit = 40,000(.6) + 30,000(.2) + (−10,000)(.2) = 28,000

(c) No Investment Profit

Profit	Probability
\$0	1

Expected profit = 0(1) = 0

(d) Utilities

Profit	Utility
\$50,000	1
\$40,000	.95
\$30,000	.90
\$10,000	.75
\$0	.60
−\$10,000	.45
−\$20,000	0

(e) A Utility Curve

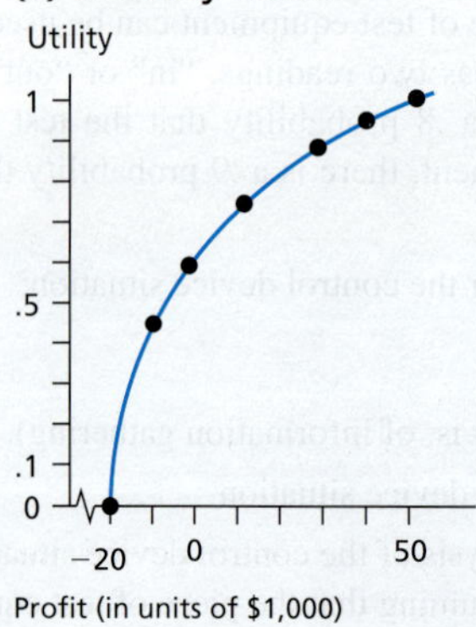

(f) Investment 1 Utilities

Utility	Probability
1	.7
.75	.1
0	.2

Expected utility = 1(.7) + .75(.1) + 0(.2) = .775

(g) Investment 2 Utilities

Utility	Probability
.95	.6
.90	.2
.45	.2

Expected utility = .95(.6) + .90(.2) + .45(.2) = .84

(h) No Investment Utility

Utility	Probability
.60	1

Expected utility = .60(1) = .60

Investment 1 will result in either a profit of $50,000, a profit of $10,000, or a loss of $20,000. Some decision makers might prefer a single undertaking of Investment 2, because the potential loss is only $10,000. Other decision makers might be unwilling to risk $10,000 and would choose no investment.

A risk averter's curve:

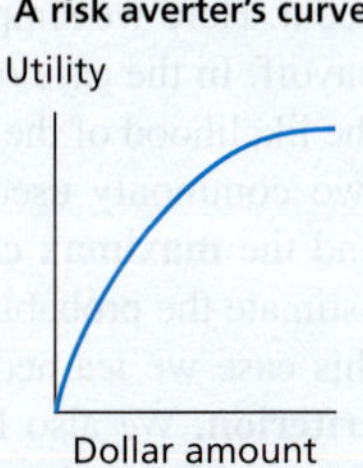

There is a way to combine the various profits, probabilities, and the decision maker's individual attitude toward risk to make a decision that is best for the decision maker. The method is based on a theory of utility discussed by J. Von Neumann and O. Morgenstern in *Theory of Games and Economic Behavior* (Princeton University Press, Princeton, N. J., 1st ed., 1944, 2nd ed., 1947). This theory says that if a decision maker agrees with certain assumptions about rational behavior (we will not discuss the assumptions here), then the decision maker should replace the profits in the various investments by **utilities** and choose the investment that gives the **highest expected utility.** To find the utility of a particular profit, we first arrange the profits from largest to smallest. The utility of the largest profit is 1 and the utility of the smallest profit is 0. The utility of any particular intermediate profit is the probability, call it u, such that the decision maker is **indifferent** between (1) getting the particular intermediate profit with certainty and (2) playing a lottery (or game) in which the probability is u of getting the highest profit and the probability is $1 - u$ of getting the smallest profit. Table 17.2(d) arranges the profits in Table 17.2(a), (b), and (c) in increasing order and gives a specific decision maker's utility for each profit. The utility of .95 for $40,000 means that the decision maker is indifferent between (1) getting $40,000 with certainty and (2) playing a lottery in which the probability is .95 of getting $50,000 and the probability is .05 of losing $20,000. The utilities for the other profits are interpreted similarly. Table 17.2(f), (g), and (h) show the investments with profits replaced by utilities. Since Investment 2 has the highest expected utility, the decision maker should choose Investment 2.

A risk seeker's curve:

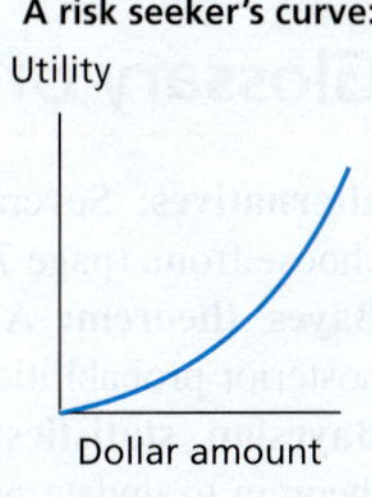

Table 17.2(e) shows a plot of the specific decision maker's utilities versus the profits. The curve connecting the plot points is the **utility curve** for the decision maker. This curve is an example of a **risk averter's curve.** In general, a risk averter's curve portrays a rapid increase in utility for initial amounts of money followed by a gradual leveling off for larger amounts of money. This curve is appropriate for many individuals or businesses because the marginal value of each additional dollar is not as great once a large amount of money has been earned. A risk averter's curve is shown on the page margin, as are a **risk seeker's curve** and a **risk neutral's curve.** The risk seeker's curve represents an individual who is willing to take large risks to have the opportunity to make large profits. The risk neutral curve represents an individual for whom each additional dollar has the same value. It can be shown that this individual should choose the investment having the highest expected profit.

A risk neutral's curve:

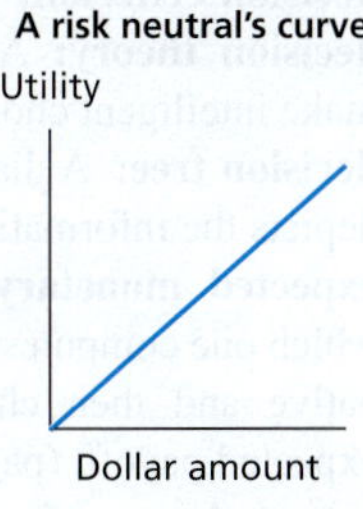

Exercises for Section 17.4

CONCEPTS

17.39 What is a utility?

17.40 What is a risk averter? A risk seeker? A risk neutral?

METHODS AND APPLICATIONS

17.41 Suppose that a decision maker has the opportunity to invest in an oil well drilling operation that has a .3 chance of yielding a profit of $1,000,000, a .4 chance of yielding a profit of $400,000, and a .3 chance of yielding a profit of −$100,000. Also, suppose that the decision maker's utilities for $400,000 and $0 are .9 and .7. Explain the meanings of these utilities.

17.42 Consider Exercise 17.41. Find the expected utility of the oil well drilling operation. Find the expected utility of not investing. What should the decision maker do if he/she wishes to maximize expected utility?

Chapter Summary

We began this chapter by discussing **Bayes' theorem.** We learned that this theorem is used to revise **prior probabilities** to **posterior probabilities,** which are revised probabilities based on new information. We also saw how to use a **probability revision table** (and Bayes' theorem) to update probabilities in a decision problem.

In Section 17.2 we presented an introduction to decision theory. We saw that a decision problem involves **states of nature, alternatives, payoffs,** and **decision criteria,** and we considered three degrees of uncertainty—**certainty, uncertainty,** and **risk.** In the case of *certainty,* we know which state of nature will actually occur. Here we simply choose the alternative that gives the best payoff. In the case of *uncertainty,* we have no information about the likelihood of the different states of nature. Here we discussed two commonly used decision criteria—the **maximin criterion** and the **maximax criterion.** In the case of *risk,* we are able to estimate the probability of occurrence for each state of nature. In this case we learned how to use the **expected monetary value criterion.** We also learned how to construct a **decision tree** in Section 17.2, and we saw how to use such a tree to analyze a decision problem. In Section 17.3 we learned how to make decisions by using posterior probabilities. We explained how to perform a **posterior analysis** to determine the best alternative for each of several sampling results. Then we showed how to carry out a **preposterior analysis,** which allows us to assess the worth of sample information. In particular, we saw how to obtain the **expected value of sample information.** This quantity is the expected gain from sampling, which tells us the maximum amount we should be willing to pay for sample information. We concluded this chapter with Section 17.4, which introduced using **utility theory** to help make decisions.

Glossary of Terms

alternatives: Several alternative actions for a decision maker to choose from. (page 798)

Bayes' theorem: A theorem (formula) that is used to compute posterior probabilities by revising prior probabilities. (page 793)

Bayesian statistics: An area of statistics that uses Bayes' theorem to update prior belief about a probability or population parameter to posterior belief. (page 795)

certainty: When we know for certain which state of nature will actually occur. (page 798)

decision criterion: A rule used to make a decision. (page 798)

decision theory: An approach that helps decision makers to make intelligent choices. (page 798)

decision tree: A diagram consisting of nodes and branches that depicts the information for a decision problem. (page 800)

expected monetary value criterion: A decision criterion in which one computes the expected monetary payoff for each alternative and then chooses the alternative yielding the largest expected payoff. (page 799)

expected net gain of sampling: The difference between the expected value of sample information and the cost of sampling. If this quantity is positive, it is worth it to perform sampling. (page 807)

expected value of perfect information: The difference between the expected payoff under certainty and the expected payoff under risk. (page 801)

expected value of sample information: The difference between the expected payoff of sampling and the expected payoff of no sampling. This measures the expected gain from sampling. (page 807)

maximax criterion: A decision criterion in which one finds the best possible payoff for each alternative and then chooses the alternative that yields the maximum best possible payoff. (page 799)

maximin criterion: A decision criterion in which one finds the worst possible payoff for each alternative and then chooses the alternative that yields the maximum worst possible payoff. (page 799)

payoff table: A tabular summary of the payoffs in a decision problem. (page 798)

perfect information: Information that tells us exactly which state of nature will occur. (page 801)

posterior decision analysis: Using a decision criterion based on posterior probabilities to choose the best alternative in a decision problem. (page 804)

posterior probability: A revised probability obtained by updating a prior probability after receiving new information. (page 794)

preposterior analysis: When we assess the worth of sample information before performing a posterior decision analysis. (page 806)

prior decision analysis: Using a decision criterion based on prior probabilities to choose the best alternative in a decision problem. (page 804)

prior probability: The initial probability that an event will occur. (page 793)

risk: When the likelihood (probability) of each state of nature can be estimated. (page 798)

states of nature: A set of potential future conditions that will affect the results of a decision. (page 798)

uncertainty: When we have no information about the likelihoods of the various states of nature. (page 798)

utility: A measure of monetary value based on an individual's attitude toward risk. (page 811)

Important Formulas

Bayes' theorem: page 794

Probability revision table: page 795

Maximin criterion: page 799

Maximax criterion: page 799

Expected monetary value criterion: page 799

Decision tree: page 800

Expected value of perfect information: page 801

Expected payoff of sampling: page 807

Expected payoff of no sampling: page 807

Expected value of sample information: page 807

Expected net gain of sampling: page 807

Expected utility: page 811

Supplementary Exercises

17.43 In the book *Making Hard Decisions: An Introduction to Decision Analysis,* Robert T. Clemen presents a decision tree for a research and development decision (note that payoffs are given in millions of dollars, which is denoted by M). Based on this decision tree (shown in Figure 17.8), answer the following:

a Should development of the research project be continued or stopped? Justify your answer by using relevant calculations, and explain your reasoning.

b If development is continued and if a patent is awarded, should the new technology be licensed, or should the company develop production and marketing to sell the product directly? Justify your answer by using relevant calculations and explain your reasoning.

17.44 On any given day, the probability that the Ohio River at Cincinnati is polluted by a carbon tetrachloride spill is .10. Each day, a test is conducted to determine whether the river is polluted by carbon tetrachloride. This test has proved correct 80 percent of the time. Suppose that on a particular day the test indicates carbon tetrachloride pollution. What is the probability that such pollution actually exists?

17.45 In the book *Production/Operations Management,* William J. Stevenson presents a decision tree concerning a firm's decision about the size of a production facility. This decision tree is given in Figure 17.9 (payoffs are given in millions of dollars). Use the decision tree to determine which alternative (build small or build large) should be chosen in order to maximize the expected monetary payoff. What is the expected monetary payoff associated with the best alternative?

17.46 Consider the decision tree in Figure 17.9 and the situation described in Exercise 17.45. Suppose that a marketing research study can be done to obtain more information about whether demand will be high or low. The marketing research study will result in one of two outcomes: "favorable" (indicating that demand will be high) or "unfavorable" (indicating that demand will be low). The accuracy of marketing research studies like the one to be carried out can be expressed by the conditional probabilities in the following table:

	True Demand	
Study Outcome	**High**	**Low**
Favorable	.9	.2
Unfavorable	.1	.8

For instance, $P(\text{favorable} \mid \text{high}) = .9$ and $P(\text{unfavorable} \mid \text{low}) = .8$. Given the prior probabilities and payoffs in Figure 17.9, do the following:

a Carry out a posterior analysis. Find the best alternative (build small or build large) for each possible study result (favorable or unfavorable), and find the associated expected payoffs.

b Carry out a preposterior analysis. Determine the maximum amount that should be paid for the marketing research study.

FIGURE 17.8 A Decision Tree for a Research and Development Decision

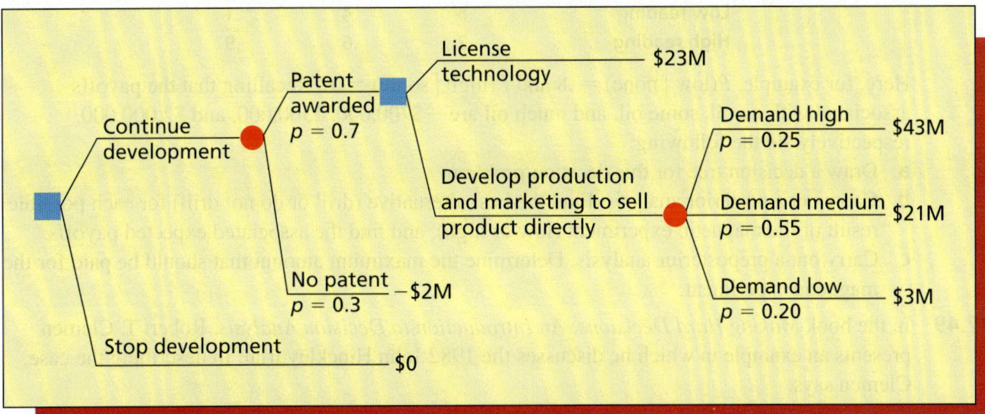

Source: From *Making Hard Decisions: An Introduction to Decision Analysis,* 2nd ed., by R. T. Clemen, © 1996. Reprinted with permission of Brooks/Cole, an imprint of the Wadsworth Group, a division of Thomson Learning. Fax 800-730-2215.

FIGURE 17.9 A Decision Tree for a Production Facility Decision

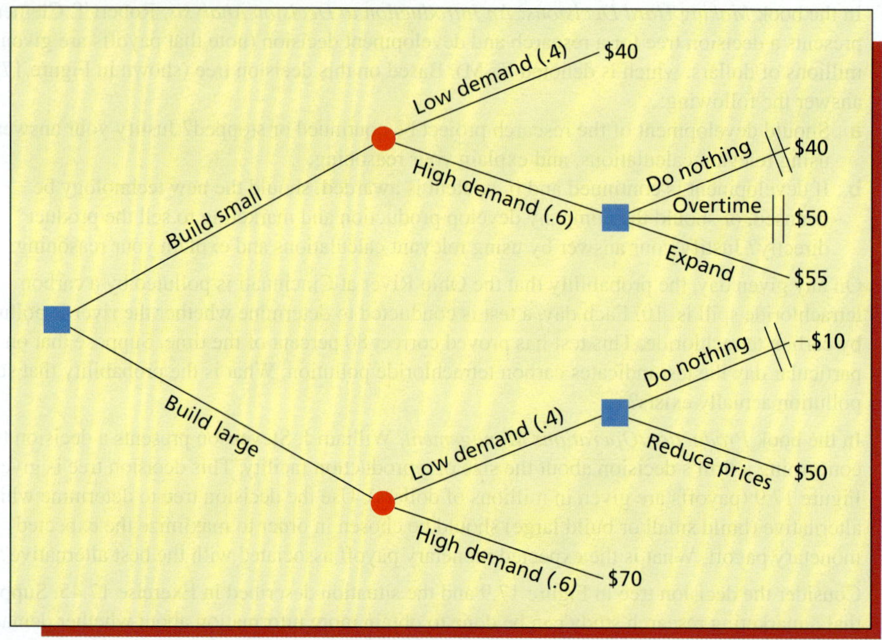

Source: Reprinted with permission from W. J. Stevenson, *Production/Operations Management,* 6th ed., p. 70. © 1999 by The McGraw-Hill Companies, Inc.

17.47 A marketing major will interview for an internship with a major consumer products manufacturer/distributor. Before the interview, the marketing major feels that the chances of being offered an internship are 40 percent. Suppose that of the students who have been offered internships with this company, 90 percent had good interviews, and that of the students who have not been offered internships, 50 percent had good interviews. If the marketing major has a good interview, what is the probability that he or she will be offered an internship?

17.48 THE OIL DRILLING CASE DrillTst

Again consider the oil drilling case that was described in Examples 17.2 and 17.3. Recall that the oil company wishes to decide whether to drill and that the prior probabilities of no oil, some oil, and much oil are $P(\text{none}) = .7$, $P(\text{some}) = .2$, and $P(\text{much}) = .1$. Suppose that, instead of performing the seismic survey to obtain more information about the site, the oil company can perform a cheaper magnetic experiment having two possible results: a high reading and a low reading. The past performance of the magnetic experiment can be summarized as follows:

Magnetic Experiment Result	State of Nature None	Some	Much
Low reading	.8	.4	.1
High reading	.2	.6	.9

Here, for example, $P(\text{low} \mid \text{none}) = .8$ and $P(\text{high} \mid \text{some}) = .6$. Recalling that the payoffs associated with no oil, some oil, and much oil are −$700,000, $500,000, and $2,000,000, respectively, do the following:

a Draw a decision tree for this decision problem.

b Carry out a posterior analysis. Find the best alternative (drill or do not drill) for each possible result of the magnetic experiment (low or high), and find the associated expected payoffs.

c Carry out a preposterior analysis. Determine the maximum amount that should be paid for the magnetic experiment.

17.49 In the book *Making Hard Decisions: An Introduction to Decision Analysis,* Robert T. Clemen presents an example in which he discusses the 1982 John Hinckley trial. In describing the case, Clemen says:

> In 1982 John Hinckley was on trial, accused of having attempted to kill President Reagan. During Hinckley's trial, Dr. Daniel R. Weinberger told the court that when individuals diagnosed as schizophrenics were given computerized axial tomography (CAT) scans, the scans

showed brain atrophy in 30% of the cases compared with only 2% of the scans done on normal people. Hinckley's defense attorney wanted to introduce as evidence Hinckley's CAT scan, which showed brain atrophy. The defense argued that the presence of atrophy strengthened the case that Hinckley suffered from mental illness.

a Approximately 1.5 percent of the people in the United States suffer from schizophrenia. If we consider the prior probability of schizophrenia to be .015, use the information given to find the probability that a person has schizophrenia given that a person's CAT scan shows brain atrophy.

b John Hinckleys CAT scan showed brain atrophy. Discuss whether your answer to part *a* helps or hurts the case that Hinckley suffered from mental illness.

c It can be argued that .015 is not a reasonable prior probability of schizophrenia. This is because .015 is the probability that a randomly selected U.S. citizen has schizophrenia. However, John Hinckley is not a randomly selected U.S. citizen. Rather, he was accused of attempting to assassinate the president. Therefore, it might be reasonable to assess a higher prior probability of schizophrenia. Suppose you are a juror who believes there is only a 10 percent chance that Hinckley suffers from schizophrenia. Using .10 as the prior probability of schizophrenia, find the probability that a person has schizophrenia given that a person's CAT scan shows brain atrophy.

d If you are a juror with a prior probability of .10 that John Hinckley suffers from schizophrenia and given your answer to part *c*, does the fact that Hinckley's CAT scan showed brain atrophy help the case that Hinckley suffered from mental illness?

e If you are a juror with a prior probability of .25 that Hinckley suffers from schizophrenia, find the probability of schizophrenia given that Hinckley's CAT scan showed brain atrophy. In this situation, how strong is the case that Hinckley suffered from mental illness?

17.50 In an exercise in the book *Production/Operations Management,* 5th ed. (1996), William J. Stevenson considers a theme park whose lease is about to expire. The theme park's management wishes to decide whether to renew its lease for another 10 years or relocate near the site of a new motel complex. The town planning board is debating whether to approve the motel complex. A consultant estimates the payoffs of the theme park's alternatives under each state of nature as shown in the following payoff table:

Theme Park Options	Motel Approved	Motel Rejected
Renew lease	$500,000	$4,000,000
Relocate	$5,000,000	$100,000

a What alternative should the theme park choose if it uses the maximax criterion? What is the resulting payoff of this choice?

b What alternative should the theme park choose if it uses the maximin criterion? What is the resulting payoff of this choice?

17.51 Again consider the situation described in Exercise 17.50, and suppose that management believes there is a .35 probability that the motel complex will be approved.

a Draw a decision tree for the theme park's decision problem.

b Which alternative should be chosen if the theme park uses the maximum expected monetary value criterion? What is the expected monetary payoff for this choice?

c Suppose that management is offered the option of a temporary lease while the planning board decides whether to approve the motel complex. If the lease costs $100,000, should the theme park's management sign the lease? Justify your answer.

Appendix A

Statistical Tables

Table A.1 A Binomial Probability Table: Binomial Probabilities (*n* between 2 and 6)

$n = 2$

x↓	.05	.10	.15	.20	.25	.30	.35	.40	.45	.50	
0	.9025	.8100	.7225	.6400	.5625	.4900	.4225	.3600	.3025	.2500	2
1	.0950	.1800	.2550	.3200	.3750	.4200	.4550	.4800	.4950	.5000	1
2	.0025	.0100	.0225	.0400	.0625	.0900	.1225	.1600	.2025	.2500	0
	.95	.90	.85	.80	.75	.70	.65	.60	.55	.50	x↑

$n = 3$

x↓	.05	.10	.15	.20	.25	.30	.35	.40	.45	.50	
0	.8574	.7290	.6141	.5120	.4219	.3430	.2746	.2160	.1664	.1250	3
1	.1354	.2430	.3251	.3840	.4219	.4410	.4436	.4320	.4084	.3750	2
2	.0071	.0270	.0574	.0960	.1406	.1890	.2389	.2880	.3341	.3750	1
3	.0001	.0010	.0034	.0080	.0156	.0270	.0429	.0640	.0911	.1250	0
	.95	.90	.85	.80	.75	.70	.65	.60	.55	.50	x↑

$n = 4$

x↓	.05	.10	.15	.20	.25	.30	.35	.40	.45	.50	
0	.8145	.6561	.5220	.4096	.3164	.2401	.1785	.1296	.0915	.0625	4
1	.1715	.2916	.3685	.4096	.4219	.4116	.3845	.3456	.2995	.2500	3
2	.0135	.0486	.0975	.1536	.2109	.2646	.3105	.3456	.3675	.3750	2
3	.0005	.0036	.0115	.0256	.0469	.0756	.1115	.1536	.2005	.2500	1
4	.0000	.0001	.0005	.0016	.0039	.0081	.0150	.0256	.0410	.0625	0
	.95	.90	.85	.80	.75	.70	.65	.60	.55	.50	x↑

$n = 5$

x↓	.05	.10	.15	.20	.25	.30	.35	.40	.45	.50	
0	.7738	.5905	.4437	.3277	.2373	.1681	.1160	.0778	.0503	.0313	5
1	.2036	.3281	.3915	.4096	.3955	.3602	.3124	.2592	.2059	.1563	4
2	.0214	.0729	.1382	.2048	.2637	.3087	.3364	.3456	.3369	.3125	3
3	.0011	.0081	.0244	.0512	.0879	.1323	.1811	.2304	.2757	.3125	2
4	.0000	.0005	.0022	.0064	.0146	.0284	.0488	.0768	.1128	.1563	1
5	.0000	.0000	.0001	.0003	.0010	.0024	.0053	.0102	.0185	.0313	0
	.95	.90	.85	.80	.75	.70	.65	.60	.55	.50	x↑

$n = 6$

x↓	.05	.10	.15	.20	.25	.30	.35	.40	.45	.50	
0	.7351	.5314	.3771	.2621	.1780	.1176	.0754	.0467	.0277	.0156	6
1	.2321	.3543	.3993	.3932	.3560	.3025	.2437	.1866	.1359	.0938	5
2	.0305	.0984	.1762	.2458	.2966	.3241	.3280	.3110	.2780	.2344	4
3	.0021	.0146	.0415	.0819	.1318	.1852	.2355	.2765	.3032	.3125	3
4	.0001	.0012	.0055	.0154	.0330	.0595	.0951	.1382	.1861	.2344	2
5	.0000	.0001	.0004	.0015	.0044	.0102	.0205	.0369	.0609	.0938	1
6	.0000	.0000	.0000	.0001	.0002	.0007	.0018	.0041	.0083	.0156	0
	.95	.90	.85	.80	.75	.70	.65	.60	.55	.50	x↑

(table continued)

TABLE A.1 *(continued)*
Binomial Probabilities (*n* between 7 and 10)

n = 7

x↓	.05	.10	.15	.20	.25	.30	.35	.40	.45	.50	
0	.6983	.4783	.3206	.2097	.1335	.0824	.0490	.0280	.0152	.0078	7
1	.2573	.3720	.3960	.3670	.3115	.2471	.1848	.1306	.0872	.0547	6
2	.0406	.1240	.2097	.2753	.3115	.3177	.2985	.2613	.2140	.1641	5
3	.0036	.0230	.0617	.1147	.1730	.2269	.2679	.2903	.2918	.2734	4
4	.0002	.0026	.0109	.0287	.0577	.0972	.1442	.1935	.2388	.2734	3
5	.0000	.0002	.0012	.0043	.0115	.0250	.0466	.0774	.1172	.1641	2
6	.0000	.0000	.0001	.0004	.0013	.0036	.0084	.0172	.0320	.0547	1
7	.0000	.0000	.0000	.0000	.0001	.0002	.0006	.0016	.0037	.0078	0
	.95	.90	.85	.80	.75	.70	.65	.60	.55	.50	*x*↑

n = 8

x↓	.05	.10	.15	.20	.25	.30	.35	.40	.45	.50	
0	.6634	.4305	.2725	.1678	.1001	.0576	.0319	.0168	.0084	.0039	8
1	.2793	.3826	.3847	.3355	.2670	.1977	.1373	.0896	.0548	.0313	7
2	.0515	.1488	.2376	.2936	.3115	.2965	.2587	.2090	.1569	.1094	6
3	.0054	.0331	.0839	.1468	.2076	.2541	.2786	.2787	.2568	.2188	5
4	.0004	.0046	.0185	.0459	.0865	.1361	.1875	.2322	.2627	.2734	4
5	.0000	.0004	.0026	.0092	.0231	.0467	.0808	.1239	.1719	.2188	3
6	.0000	.0000	.0002	.0011	.0038	.0100	.0217	.0413	.0703	.1094	2
7	.0000	.0000	.0000	.0001	.0004	.0012	.0033	.0079	.0164	.0313	1
8	.0000	.0000	.0000	.0000	.0000	.0001	.0002	.0007	.0017	.0039	0
	.95	.90	.85	.80	.75	.70	.65	.60	.55	.50	*x*↑

n = 9

x↓	.05	.10	.15	.20	.25	.30	.35	.40	.45	.50	
0	.6302	.3874	.2316	.1342	.0751	.0404	.0207	.0101	.0046	.0020	9
1	.2985	.3874	.3679	.3020	.2253	.1556	.1004	.0605	.0339	.0176	8
2	.0629	.1722	.2597	.3020	.3003	.2668	.2162	.1612	.1110	.0703	7
3	.0077	.0446	.1069	.1762	.2336	.2668	.2716	.2508	.2119	.1641	6
4	.0006	.0074	.0283	.0661	.1168	.1715	.2194	.2508	.2600	.2461	5
5	.0000	.0008	.0050	.0165	.0389	.0735	.1181	.1672	.2128	.2461	4
6	.0000	.0001	.0006	.0028	.0087	.0210	.0424	.0743	.1160	.1641	3
7	.0000	.0000	.0000	.0003	.0012	.0039	.0098	.0212	.0407	.0703	2
8	.0000	.0000	.0000	.0000	.0001	.0004	.0013	.0035	.0083	.0176	1
9	.0000	.0000	.0000	.0000	.0000	.0000	.0001	.0003	.0008	.0020	0
	.95	.90	.85	.80	.75	.70	.65	.60	.55	.50	*x*↑

n = 10

x↓	.05	.10	.15	.20	.25	.30	.35	.40	.45	.50	
0	.5987	.3487	.1969	.1074	.0563	.0282	.0135	.0060	.0025	.0010	10
1	.3151	.3874	.3474	.2684	.1877	.1211	.0725	.0403	.0207	.0098	9
2	.0746	.1937	.2759	.3020	.2816	.2335	.1757	.1209	.0763	.0439	8
3	.0105	.0574	.1298	.2013	.2503	.2668	.2522	.2150	.1665	.1172	7
4	.0010	.0112	.0401	.0881	.1460	.2001	.2377	.2508	.2384	.2051	6
5	.0001	.0015	.0085	.0264	.0584	.1029	.1536	.2007	.2340	.2461	5
6	.0000	.0001	.0012	.0055	.0162	.0368	.0689	.1115	.1596	.2051	4
7	.0000	.0000	.0001	.0008	.0031	.0090	.0212	.0425	.0746	.1172	3
8	.0000	.0000	.0000	.0001	.0004	.0014	.0043	.0106	.0229	.0439	2
9	.0000	.0000	.0000	.0000	.0000	.0001	.0005	.0016	.0042	.0098	1
10	.0000	.0000	.0000	.0000	.0000	.0000	.0000	.0001	.0003	.0010	0
	.95	.90	.85	.80	.75	.70	.65	.60	.55	.50	*x*↑

Table A.1 *(continued)*
Binomial Probabilities (*n* equal to 12, 14, and 15)

n = 12 *p*

x↓	.05	.10	.15	.20	.25	.30	.35	.40	.45	.50	
0	.5404	.2824	.1422	.0687	.0317	.0138	.0057	.0022	.0008	.0002	12
1	.3413	.3766	.3012	.2062	.1267	.0712	.0368	.0174	.0075	.0029	11
2	.0988	.2301	.2924	.2835	.2323	.1678	.1088	.0639	.0339	.0161	10
3	.0173	.0852	.1720	.2362	.2581	.2397	.1954	.1419	.0923	.0537	9
4	.0021	.0213	.0683	.1329	.1936	.2311	.2367	.2128	.1700	.1208	8
5	.0002	.0038	.0193	.0532	.1032	.1585	.2039	.2270	.2225	.1934	7
6	.0000	.0005	.0040	.0155	.0401	.0792	.1281	.1766	.2124	.2256	6
7	.0000	.0000	.0006	.0033	.0115	.0291	.0591	.1009	.1489	.1934	5
8	.0000	.0000	.0001	.0005	.0024	.0078	.0199	.0420	.0762	.1208	4
9	.0000	.0000	.0000	.0001	.0004	.0015	.0048	.0125	.0277	.0537	3
10	.0000	.0000	.0000	.0000	.0000	.0002	.0008	.0025	.0068	.0161	2
11	.0000	.0000	.0000	.0000	.0000	.0000	.0001	.0003	.0010	.0029	1
12	.0000	.0000	.0000	.0000	.0000	.0000	.0000	.0000	.0001	.0002	0
	.95	.90	.85	.80	.75	.70	.65	.60	.55	.50	x↑

n = 14 *p*

x↓	.05	.10	.15	.20	.25	.30	.35	.40	.45	.50	
0	.4877	.2288	.1028	.0440	.0178	.0068	.0024	.0008	.0002	.0001	14
1	.3593	.3559	.2539	.1539	.0832	.0407	.0181	.0073	.0027	.0009	13
2	.1229	.2570	.2912	.2501	.1802	.1134	.0634	.0317	.0141	.0056	12
3	.0259	.1142	.2056	.2501	.2402	.1943	.1366	.0845	.0462	.0222	11
4	.0037	.0349	.0998	.1720	.2202	.2290	.2022	.1549	.1040	.0611	10
5	.0004	.0078	.0352	.0860	.1468	.1963	.2178	.2066	.1701	.1222	9
6	.0000	.0013	.0093	.0322	.0734	.1262	.1759	.2066	.2088	.1833	8
7	.0000	.0002	.0019	.0092	.0280	.0618	.1082	.1574	.1952	.2095	7
8	.0000	.0000	.0003	.0020	.0082	.0232	.0510	.0918	.1398	.1833	6
9	.0000	.0000	.0000	.0003	.0018	.0066	.0183	.0408	.0762	.1222	5
10	.0000	.0000	.0000	.0000	.0003	.0014	.0049	.0136	.0312	.0611	4
11	.0000	.0000	.0000	.0000	.0000	.0002	.0010	.0033	.0093	.0222	3
12	.0000	.0000	.0000	.0000	.0000	.0000	.0001	.0005	.0019	.0056	2
13	.0000	.0000	.0000	.0000	.0000	.0000	.0000	.0001	.0002	.0009	1
14	.0000	.0000	.0000	.0000	.0000	.0000	.0000	.0000	.0000	.0001	0
	.95	.90	.85	.80	.75	.70	.65	.60	.55	.50	x↑

n = 15 *p*

x↓	.05	.10	.15	.20	.25	.30	.35	.40	.45	.50	
0	.4633	.2059	.0874	.0352	.0134	.0047	.0016	.0005	.0001	.0000	15
1	.3658	.3432	.2312	.1319	.0668	.0305	.0126	.0047	.0016	.0005	14
2	.1348	.2669	.2856	.2309	.1559	.0916	.0476	.0219	.0090	.0032	13
3	.0307	.1285	.2184	.2501	.2252	.1700	.1110	.0634	.0318	.0139	12
4	.0049	.0428	.1156	.1876	.2252	.2186	.1792	.1268	.0780	.0417	11
5	.0006	.0105	.0449	.1032	.1651	.2061	.2123	.1859	.1404	.0916	10
6	.0000	.0019	.0132	.0430	.0917	.1472	.1906	.2066	.1914	.1527	9
7	.0000	.0003	.0030	.0138	.0393	.0811	.1319	.1771	.2013	.1964	8
8	.0000	.0000	.0005	.0035	.0131	.0348	.0710	.1181	.1647	.1964	7
9	.0000	.0000	.0001	.0007	.0034	.0116	.0298	.0612	.1048	.1527	6
10	.0000	.0000	.0000	.0001	.0007	.0030	.0096	.0245	.0515	.0916	5
11	.0000	.0000	.0000	.0000	.0001	.0006	.0024	.0074	.0191	.0417	4
12	.0000	.0000	.0000	.0000	.0000	.0001	.0004	.0016	.0052	.0139	3
13	.0000	.0000	.0000	.0000	.0000	.0000	.0001	.0003	.0010	.0032	2
14	.0000	.0000	.0000	.0000	.0000	.0000	.0000	.0000	.0001	.0005	1
15	.0000	.0000	.0000	.0000	.0000	.0000	.0000	.0000	.0000	.0000	0
	.95	.90	.85	.80	.75	.70	.65	.60	.55	.50	x↑

(table continued)

TABLE A.1 ***(continued)***
Binomial Probabilities (*n* equal to 16 and 18)

n = 16 *p*

x↓	.05	.10	.15	.20	.25	.30	.35	.40	.45	.50	
0	.4401	.1853	.0743	.0281	.0100	.0033	.0010	.0003	.0001	.0000	16
1	.3706	.3294	.2097	.1126	.0535	.0228	.0087	.0030	.0009	.0002	15
2	.1463	.2745	.2775	.2111	.1336	.0732	.0353	.0150	.0056	.0018	14
3	.0359	.1423	.2285	.2463	.2079	.1465	.0888	.0468	.0215	.0085	13
4	.0061	.0514	.1311	.2001	.2252	.2040	.1553	.1014	.0572	.0278	12
5	.0008	.0137	.0555	.1201	.1802	.2099	.2008	.1623	.1123	.0667	11
6	.0001	.0028	.0180	.0550	.1101	.1649	.1982	.1983	.1684	.1222	10
7	.0000	.0004	.0045	.0197	.0524	.1010	.1524	.1889	.1969	.1746	9
8	.0000	.0001	.0009	.0055	.0197	.0487	.0923	.1417	.1812	.1964	8
9	.0000	.0000	.0001	.0012	.0058	.0185	.0442	.0840	.1318	.1746	7
10	.0000	.0000	.0000	.0002	.0014	.0056	.0167	.0392	.0755	.1222	6
11	.0000	.0000	.0000	.0000	.0002	.0013	.0049	.0142	.0337	.0667	5
12	.0000	.0000	.0000	.0000	.0000	.0002	.0011	.0040	.0115	.0278	4
13	.0000	.0000	.0000	.0000	.0000	.0000	.0002	.0008	.0029	.0085	3
14	.0000	.0000	.0000	.0000	.0000	.0000	.0000	.0001	.0005	.0018	2
15	.0000	.0000	.0000	.0000	.0000	.0000	.0000	.0000	.0001	.0002	1
	.95	.90	.85	.80	.75	.70	.65	.60	.55	.50	x↑

n = 18 *p*

x↓	.05	.10	.15	.20	.25	.30	.35	.40	.45	.50	
0	.3972	.1501	.0536	.0180	.0056	.0016	.0004	.0001	.0000	.0000	18
1	.3763	.3002	.1704	.0811	.0338	.0126	.0042	.0012	.0003	.0001	17
2	.1683	.2835	.2556	.1723	.0958	.0458	.0190	.0069	.0022	.0006	16
3	.0473	.1680	.2406	.2297	.1704	.1046	.0547	.0246	.0095	.0031	15
4	.0093	.0700	.1592	.2153	.2130	.1681	.1104	.0614	.0291	.0117	14
5	.0014	.0218	.0787	.1507	.1988	.2017	.1664	.1146	.0666	.0327	13
6	.0002	.0052	.0301	.0816	.1436	.1873	.1941	.1655	.1181	.0708	12
7	.0000	.0010	.0091	.0350	.0820	.1376	.1792	.1892	.1657	.1214	11
8	.0000	.0002	.0022	.0120	.0376	.0811	.1327	.1734	.1864	.1669	10
9	.0000	.0000	.0004	.0033	.0139	.0386	.0794	.1284	.1694	.1855	9
10	.0000	.0000	.0001	.0008	.0042	.0149	.0385	.0771	.1248	.1669	8
11	.0000	.0000	.0000	.0001	.0010	.0046	.0151	.0374	.0742	.1214	7
12	.0000	.0000	.0000	.0000	.0002	.0012	.0047	.0145	.0354	.0708	6
13	.0000	.0000	.0000	.0000	.0000	.0002	.0012	.0045	.0134	.0327	5
14	.0000	.0000	.0000	.0000	.0000	.0000	.0002	.0011	.0039	.0117	4
15	.0000	.0000	.0000	.0000	.0000	.0000	.0000	.0002	.0009	.0031	3
16	.0000	.0000	.0000	.0000	.0000	.0000	.0000	.0000	.0001	.0006	2
17	.0000	.0000	.0000	.0000	.0000	.0000	.0000	.0000	.0000	.0001	1
	.95	.90	.85	.80	.75	.70	.65	.60	.55	.50	x↑

TABLE A.1 *(concluded)*
Binomial Probabilities (*n* equal to 20)

n = 20						*p*					
x↓	**.05**	**.10**	**.15**	**.20**	**.25**	**.30**	**.35**	**.40**	**.45**	**.50**	
0	.3585	.1216	.0388	.0115	.0032	.0008	.0002	.0000	.0000	.0000	20
1	.3774	.2702	.1368	.0576	.0211	.0068	.0020	.0005	.0001	.0000	19
2	.1887	.2852	.2293	.1369	.0669	.0278	.0100	.0031	.0008	.0002	18
3	.0596	.1901	.2428	.2054	.1339	.0716	.0323	.0123	.0040	.0011	17
4	.0133	.0898	.1821	.2182	.1897	.1304	.0738	.0350	.0139	.0046	16
5	.0022	.0319	.1028	.1746	.2023	.1789	.1272	.0746	.0365	.0148	15
6	.0003	.0089	.0454	.1091	.1686	.1916	.1712	.1244	.0746	.0370	14
7	.0000	.0020	.0160	.0545	.1124	.1643	.1844	.1659	.1221	.0739	13
8	.0000	.0004	.0046	.0222	.0609	.1144	.1614	.1797	.1623	.1201	12
9	.0000	.0001	.0011	.0074	.0271	.0654	.1158	.1597	.1771	.1602	11
10	.0000	.0000	.0002	.0020	.0099	.0308	.0686	.1171	.1593	.1762	10
11	.0000	.0000	.0000	.0005	.0030	.0120	.0336	.0710	.1185	.1602	9
12	.0000	.0000	.0000	.0001	.0008	.0039	.0136	.0355	.0727	.1201	8
13	.0000	.0000	.0000	.0000	.0002	.0010	.0045	.0146	.0366	.0739	7
14	.0000	.0000	.0000	.0000	.0000	.0002	.0012	.0049	.0150	.0370	6
15	.0000	.0000	.0000	.0000	.0000	.0000	.0003	.0013	.0049	.0148	5
16	.0000	.0000	.0000	.0000	.0000	.0000	.0000	.0003	.0013	.0046	4
17	.0000	.0000	.0000	.0000	.0000	.0000	.0000	.0000	.0002	.0011	3
18	.0000	.0000	.0000	.0000	.0000	.0000	.0000	.0000	.0000	.0002	2
	.95	**.90**	**.85**	**.80**	**.75**	**.70**	**.65**	**.60**	**.55**	**.50**	**x↑**

Source: Computed by D. K. Hildebrand. Found in D. K. Hildebrand and L. Ott, *Statistical Thinking for Managers*, 3rd ed. (Boston, MA: PWS-KENT Publishing Company, 1991).

TABLE A.2 A Poisson Probability Table
Poisson Probabilities (μ between .1 and 2.0)

					μ					
x	**.1**	**.2**	**.3**	**.4**	**.5**	**.6**	**.7**	**.8**	**.9**	**1.0**
0	.9048	.8187	.7408	.6703	.6065	.5488	.4966	.4493	.4066	.3679
1	.0905	.1637	.2222	.2681	.3033	.3293	.3476	.3595	.3659	.3679
2	.0045	.0164	.0333	.0536	.0758	.0988	.1217	.1438	.1647	.1839
3	.0002	.0011	.0033	.0072	.0126	.0198	.0284	.0383	.0494	.0613
4	.0000	.0001	.0003	.0007	.0016	.0030	.0050	.0077	.0111	.0153
5	.0000	.0000	.0000	.0001	.0002	.0004	.0007	.0012	.0020	.0031
6	.0000	.0000	.0000	.0000	.0000	.0000	.0001	.0002	.0003	.0005

					μ					
x	**1.1**	**1.2**	**1.3**	**1.4**	**1.5**	**1.6**	**1.7**	**1.8**	**1.9**	**2.0**
0	.3329	.3012	.2725	.2466	.2231	.2019	.1827	.1653	.1496	.1353
1	.3662	.3614	.3543	.3452	.3347	.3230	.3106	.2975	.2842	.2707
2	.2014	.2169	.2303	.2417	.2510	.2584	.2640	.2678	.2700	.2707
3	.0738	.0867	.0998	.1128	.1255	.1378	.1496	.1607	.1710	.1804
4	.0203	.0260	.0324	.0395	.0471	.0551	.0636	.0723	.0812	.0902
5	.0045	.0062	.0084	.0111	.0141	.0176	.0216	.0260	.0309	.0361
6	.0008	.0012	.0018	.0026	.0035	.0047	.0061	.0078	.0098	.0120
7	.0001	.0002	.0003	.0005	.0008	.0011	.0015	.0020	.0027	.0034
8	.0000	.0000	.0001	.0001	.0001	.0002	.0003	.0005	.0006	.0009

(table continued)

TABLE A.2 ***(continued)***
Poisson Probabilities (μ between 2.1 and 5.0)

x	2.1	2.2	2.3	2.4	2.5	2.6	2.7	2.8	2.9	3.0
0	.1225	.1108	.1003	.0907	.0821	.0743	.0672	.0608	.0550	.0498
1	.2572	.2438	.2306	.2177	.2052	.1931	.1815	.1703	.1596	.1494
2	.2700	.2681	.2652	.2613	.2565	.2510	.2450	.2384	.2314	.2240
3	.1890	.1966	.2033	.2090	.2138	.2176	.2205	.2225	.2237	.2240
4	.0992	.1082	.1169	.1254	.1336	.1414	.1488	.1557	.1622	.1680
5	.0417	.0476	.0538	.0602	.0668	.0735	.0804	.0872	.0940	.1008
6	.0146	.0174	.0206	.0241	.0278	.0319	.0362	.0407	.0455	.0504
7	.0044	.0055	.0068	.0083	.0099	.0118	.0139	.0163	.0188	.0216
8	.0011	.0015	.0019	.0025	.0031	.0038	.0047	.0057	.0068	.0081
9	.0003	.0004	.0005	.0007	.0009	.0011	.0014	.0018	.0022	.0027
10	.0001	.0001	.0001	.0002	.0002	.0003	.0004	.0005	.0006	.0008
11	.0000	.0000	.0000	.0000	.0000	.0001	.0001	.0001	.0002	.0002

x	3.1	3.2	3.3	3.4	3.5	3.6	3.7	3.8	3.9	4.0
0	.0450	.0408	.0369	.0334	.0302	.0273	.0247	.0224	.0202	.0183
1	.1397	.1304	.1217	.1135	.1057	.0984	.0915	.0850	.0789	.0733
2	.2165	.2087	.2008	.1929	.1850	.1771	.1692	.1615	.1539	.1465
3	.2237	.2226	.2209	.2186	.2158	.2125	.2087	.2046	.2001	.1954
4	.1733	.1781	.1823	.1858	.1888	.1912	.1931	.1944	.1951	.1954
5	.1075	.1140	.1203	.1264	.1322	.1377	.1429	.1477	.1522	.1563
6	.0555	.0608	.0662	.0716	.0771	.0826	.0881	.0936	.0989	.1042
7	.0246	.0278	.0312	.0348	.0385	.0425	.0466	.0508	.0551	.0595
8	.0095	.0111	.0129	.0148	.0169	.0191	.0215	.0241	.0269	.0298
9	.0033	.0040	.0047	.0056	.0066	.0076	.0089	.0102	.0116	.0132
10	.0010	.0013	.0016	.0019	.0023	.0028	.0033	.0039	.0045	.0053
11	.0003	.0004	.0005	.0006	.0007	.0009	.0011	.0013	.0016	.0019
12	.0001	.0001	.0001	.0002	.0002	.0003	.0003	.0004	.0005	.0006
13	.0000	.0000	.0000	.0000	.0001	.0001	.0001	.0001	.0002	.0002

x	4.1	4.2	4.3	4.4	4.5	4.6	4.7	4.8	4.9	5.0
0	.0166	.0150	.0136	.0123	.0111	.0101	.0091	.0082	.0074	.0067
1	.0679	.0630	.0583	.0540	.0500	.0462	.0427	.0395	.0365	.0337
2	.1393	.1323	.1254	.1188	.1125	.1063	.1005	.0948	.0894	.0842
3	.1904	.1852	.1798	.1743	.1687	.1631	.1574	.1517	.1460	.1404
4	.1951	.1944	.1933	.1917	.1898	.1875	.1849	.1820	.1789	.1755
5	.1600	.1633	.1662	.1687	.1708	.1725	.1738	.1747	.1753	.1755
6	.1093	.1143	.1191	.1237	.1281	.1323	.1362	.1398	.1432	.1462
7	.0640	.0686	.0732	.0778	.0824	.0869	.0914	.0959	.1002	.1044
8	.0328	.0360	.0393	.0428	.0463	.0500	.0537	.0575	.0614	.0653
9	.0150	.0168	.0188	.0209	.0232	.0255	.0281	.0307	.0334	.0363
10	.0061	.0071	.0081	.0092	.0104	.0118	.0132	.0147	.0164	.0181
11	.0023	.0027	.0032	.0037	.0043	.0049	.0056	.0064	.0073	.0082
12	.0008	.0009	.0011	.0013	.0016	.0019	.0022	.0026	.0030	.0034
13	.0002	.0003	.0004	.0005	.0006	.0007	.0008	.0009	.0011	.0013
14	.0001	.0001	.0001	.0001	.0002	.0002	.0003	.0003	.0004	.0005
15	.0000	.0000	.0000	.0000	.0001	.0001	.0001	.0001	.0001	.0002

Table A.2 *(concluded)*
Poisson Probabilities (μ between 5.5 and 20.0)

	μ									
x	**5.5**	**6.0**	**6.5**	**7.0**	**7.5**	**8.0**	**8.5**	**9.0**	**9.5**	**10.0**
0	.0041	.0025	.0015	.0009	.0006	.0003	.0002	.0001	.0001	.0000
1	.0225	.0149	.0098	.0064	.0041	.0027	.0017	.0011	.0007	.0005
2	.0618	.0446	.0318	.0223	.0156	.0107	.0074	.0050	.0034	.0023
3	.1133	.0892	.0688	.0521	.0389	.0286	.0208	.0150	.0107	.0076
4	.1558	.1339	.1118	.0912	.0729	.0573	.0443	.0337	.0254	.0189
5	.1714	.1606	.1454	.1277	.1094	.0916	.0752	.0607	.0483	.0378
6	.1571	.1606	.1575	.1490	.1367	.1221	.1066	.0911	.0764	.0631
7	.1234	.1377	.1462	.1490	.1465	.1396	.1294	.1171	.1037	.0901
8	.0849	.1033	.1188	.1304	.1373	.1396	.1375	.1318	.1232	.1126
9	.0519	.0688	.0858	.1014	.1144	.1241	.1299	.1318	.1300	.1251
10	.0285	.0413	.0558	.0710	.0858	.0993	.1104	.1186	.1235	.1251
11	.0143	.0225	.0330	.0452	.0585	.0722	.0853	.0970	.1067	.1137
12	.0065	.0113	.0179	.0263	.0366	.0481	.0604	.0728	.0844	.0948
13	.0028	.0052	.0089	.0142	.0211	.0296	.0395	.0504	.0617	.0729
14	.0011	.0022	.0041	.0071	.0113	.0169	.0240	.0324	.0419	.0521
15	.0004	.0009	.0018	.0033	.0057	.0090	.0136	.0194	.0265	.0347
16	.0001	.0003	.0007	.0014	.0026	.0045	.0072	.0109	.0157	.0217
17	.0000	.0001	.0003	.0006	.0012	.0021	.0036	.0058	.0088	.0128
18	.0000	.0000	.0001	.0002	.0005	.0009	.0017	.0029	.0046	.0071
19	.0000	.0000	.0000	.0001	.0002	.0004	.0008	.0014	.0023	.0037
20	.0000	.0000	.0000	.0000	.0001	.0002	.0003	.0006	.0011	.0019
21	.0000	.0000	.0000	.0000	.0000	.0001	.0001	.0003	.0005	.0009
22	.0000	.0000	.0000	.0000	.0000	.0000	.0001	.0001	.0002	.0004
23	.0000	.0000	.0000	.0000	.0000	.0000	.0000	.0000	.0001	.0002

	μ									
x	**11.0**	**12.0**	**13.0**	**14.0**	**15.0**	**16.0**	**17.0**	**18.0**	**19.0**	**20.0**
0	.0000	.0000	.0000	.0000	.0000	.0000	.0000	.0000	.0000	.0000
1	.0002	.0001	.0000	.0000	.0000	.0000	.0000	.0000	.0000	.0000
2	.0010	.0004	.0002	.0001	.0000	.0000	.0000	.0000	.0000	.0000
3	.0037	.0018	.0008	.0004	.0002	.0001	.0000	.0000	.0000	.0000
4	.0102	.0053	.0027	.0013	.0006	.0003	.0001	.0001	.0000	.0000
5	.0224	.0127	.0070	.0037	.0019	.0010	.0005	.0002	.0001	.0001
6	.0411	.0255	.0152	.0087	.0048	.0026	.0014	.0007	.0004	.0002
7	.0646	.0437	.0281	.0174	.0104	.0060	.0034	.0019	.0010	.0005
8	.0888	.0655	.0457	.0304	.0194	.0120	.0072	.0042	.0024	.0013
9	.1085	.0874	.0661	.0473	.0324	.0213	.0135	.0083	.0050	.0029
10	.1194	.1048	.0859	.0663	.0486	.0341	.0230	.0150	.0095	.0058
11	.1194	.1144	.1015	.0844	.0663	.0496	.0355	.0245	.0164	.0106
12	.1094	.1144	.1099	.0984	.0829	.0661	.0504	.0368	.0259	.0176
13	.0926	.1056	.1099	.1060	.0956	.0814	.0658	.0509	.0378	.0271
14	.0728	.0905	.1021	.1060	.1024	.0930	.0800	.0655	.0514	.0387
15	.0534	.0724	.0885	.0989	.1024	.0992	.0906	.0786	.0650	.0516
16	.0367	.0543	.0719	.0866	.0960	.0992	.0963	.0884	.0772	.0646
17	.0237	.0383	.0550	.0713	.0847	.0934	.0963	.0936	.0863	.0760
18	.0145	.0255	.0397	.0554	.0706	.0830	.0909	.0936	.0911	.0844
19	.0084	.0161	.0272	.0409	.0557	.0699	.0814	.0887	.0911	.0888
20	.0046	.0097	.0177	.0286	.0418	.0559	.0692	.0798	.0866	.0888
21	.0024	.0055	.0109	.0191	.0299	.0426	.0560	.0684	.0783	.0846
22	.0012	.0030	.0065	.0121	.0204	.0310	.0433	.0560	.0676	.0769
23	.0006	.0016	.0037	.0074	.0133	.0216	.0320	.0438	.0559	.0669
24	.0003	.0008	.0020	.0043	.0083	.0144	.0226	.0328	.0442	.0557
25	.0001	.0004	.0010	.0024	.0050	.0092	.0154	.0237	.0336	.0446
26	.0000	.0002	.0005	.0013	.0029	.0057	.0101	.0164	.0246	.0343
27	.0000	.0001	.0002	.0007	.0016	.0034	.0063	.0109	.0173	.0254
28	.0000	.0000	.0001	.0003	.0009	.0019	.0038	.0070	.0117	.0181
29	.0000	.0000	.0001	.0002	.0004	.0011	.0023	.0044	.0077	.0125
30	.0000	.0000	.0000	.0001	.0002	.0006	.0013	.0026	.0049	.0083
31	.0000	.0000	.0000	.0000	.0001	.0003	.0007	.0015	.0030	.0054
32	.0000	.0000	.0000	.0000	.0001	.0001	.0004	.0009	.0018	.0034
33	.0000	.0000	.0000	.0000	.0000	.0001	.0002	.0005	.0010	.0020

Source: Computed by D. K. Hildebrand. Found in D. K. Hildebrand and L. Ott, *Statistical Thinking for Managers*, 3rd ed. (Boston, MA: PWS-KENT Publishing Company, 1991).

TABLE A.3 A Table of Areas under the Standard Normal Curve

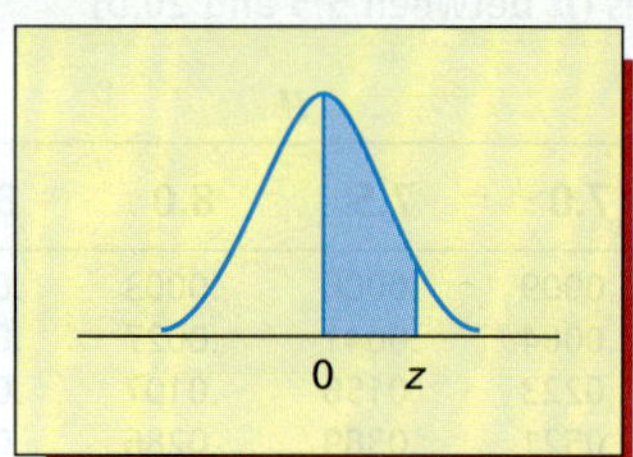

z	.00	.01	.02	.03	.04	.05	.06	.07	.08	.09
0.0	.0000	.0040	.0080	.0120	.0160	.0199	.0239	.0279	.0319	.0359
0.1	.0398	.0438	.0478	.0517	.0557	.0596	.0636	.0675	.0714	.0753
0.2	.0793	.0832	.0871	.0910	.0948	.0987	.1026	.1064	.1103	.1141
0.3	.1179	.1217	.1255	.1293	.1331	.1368	.1406	.1443	.1480	.1517
0.4	.1554	.1591	.1628	.1664	.1700	.1736	.1772	.1808	.1844	.1879
0.5	.1915	.1950	.1985	.2019	.2054	.2088	.2123	.2157	.2190	.2224
0.6	.2257	.2291	.2324	.2357	.2389	.2422	.2454	.2486	.2517	.2549
0.7	.2580	.2611	.2642	.2673	.2704	.2734	.2764	.2794	.2823	.2852
0.8	.2881	.2910	.2939	.2967	.2995	.3023	.3051	.3078	.3106	.3133
0.9	.3159	.3186	.3212	.3238	.3264	.3289	.3315	.3340	.3365	.3389
1.0	.3413	.3438	.3461	.3485	.3508	.3531	.3554	.3577	.3599	.3621
1.1	.3643	.3665	.3686	.3708	.3729	.3749	.3770	.3790	.3810	.3830
1.2	.3849	.3869	.3888	.3907	.3925	.3944	.3962	.3980	.3997	.4015
1.3	.4032	.4049	.4066	.4082	.4099	.4115	.4131	.4147	.4162	.4177
1.4	.4192	.4207	.4222	.4236	.4251	.4265	.4279	.4292	.4306	.4319
1.5	.4332	.4345	.4357	.4370	.4382	.4394	.4406	.4418	.4429	.4441
1.6	.4452	.4463	.4474	.4484	.4495	.4505	.4515	.4525	.4535	.4545
1.7	.4554	.4564	.4573	.4582	.4591	.4599	.4608	.4616	.4625	.4633
1.8	.4641	.4649	.4656	.4664	.4671	.4678	.4686	.4693	.4699	.4706
1.9	.4713	.4719	.4726	.4732	.4738	.4744	.4750	.4756	.4761	.4767
2.0	.4772	.4778	.4783	.4788	.4793	.4798	.4803	.4808	.4812	.4817
2.1	.4821	.4826	.4830	.4834	.4838	.4842	.4846	.4850	.4854	.4857
2.2	.4861	.4864	.4868	.4871	.4875	.4878	.4881	.4884	.4887	.4890
2.3	.4893	.4896	.4898	.4901	.4904	.4906	.4909	.4911	.4913	.4916
2.4	.4918	.4920	.4922	.4925	.4927	.4929	.4931	.4932	.4934	.4936
2.5	.4938	.4940	.4941	.4943	.4945	.4946	.4948	.4949	.4951	.4952
2.6	.4953	.4955	.4956	.4957	.4959	.4960	.4961	.4962	.4963	.4964
2.7	.4965	.4966	.4967	.4968	.4969	.4970	.4971	.4972	.4973	.4974
2.8	.4974	.4975	.4976	.4977	.4977	.4978	.4979	.4979	.4980	.4981
2.9	.4981	.4982	.4982	.4983	.4984	.4984	.4985	.4985	.4986	.4986
3.0	.4987	.4987	.4987	.4988	.4988	.4989	.4989	.4989	.4990	.4990

Source: A. Hald, *Statistical Tables and Formulas* (New York: Wiley, 1952), abridged from Table 1. Reproduced by permission of the publisher.

TABLE A.4 A t Table: Values of t_α for df = 1 through 48

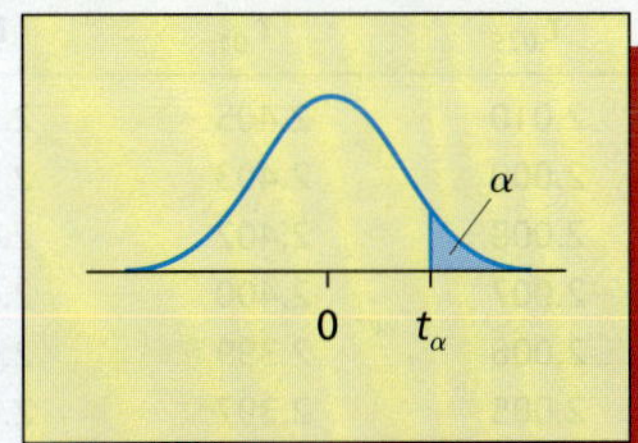

df	$t_{.100}$	$t_{.05}$	$t_{.025}$	$t_{.01}$	$t_{.005}$	$t_{.001}$	$t_{.0005}$
1	3.078	6.314	12.706	31.821	63.657	318.309	636.619
2	1.886	2.920	4.303	6.965	9.925	22.327	31.599
3	1.638	2.353	3.182	4.541	5.841	10.215	12.924
4	1.533	2.132	2.776	3.747	4.604	7.173	8.610
5	1.476	2.015	2.571	3.365	4.032	5.893	6.869
6	1.440	1.943	2.447	3.143	3.707	5.208	5.959
7	1.415	1.895	2.365	2.998	3.499	4.785	5.408
8	1.397	1.860	2.306	2.896	3.355	4.501	5.041
9	1.383	1.833	2.262	2.821	3.250	4.297	4.781
10	1.372	1.812	2.228	2.764	3.169	4.144	4.587
11	1.363	1.796	2.201	2.718	3.106	4.025	4.437
12	1.356	1.782	2.179	2.681	3.055	3.930	4.318
13	1.350	1.771	2.160	2.650	3.012	3.852	4.221
14	1.345	1.761	2.145	2.624	2.977	3.787	4.140
15	1.341	1.753	2.131	2.602	2.947	3.733	4.073
16	1.337	1.746	2.120	2.583	2.921	3.686	4.015
17	1.333	1.740	2.110	2.567	2.898	3.646	3.965
18	1.330	1.734	2.101	2.552	2.878	3.610	3.922
19	1.328	1.729	2.093	2.539	2.861	3.579	3.883
20	1.325	1.725	2.086	2.528	2.845	3.552	3.850
21	1.323	1.721	2.080	2.518	2.831	3.527	3.819
22	1.321	1.717	2.074	2.508	2.819	3.505	3.792
23	1.319	1.714	2.069	2.500	2.807	3.485	3.768
24	1.318	1.711	2.064	2.492	2.797	3.467	3.745
25	1.316	1.708	2.060	2.485	2.787	3.450	3.725
26	1.315	1.706	2.056	2.479	2.779	3.435	3.707
27	1.314	1.703	2.052	2.473	2.771	3.421	3.690
28	1.313	1.701	2.048	2.467	2.763	3.408	3.674
29	1.311	1.699	2.045	2.462	2.756	3.396	3.659
30	1.310	1.697	2.042	2.457	2.750	3.385	3.646
31	1.309	1.696	2.040	2.453	2.744	3.375	3.633
32	1.309	1.694	2.037	2.449	2.738	3.365	3.622
33	1.308	1.692	2.035	2.445	2.733	3.356	3.611
34	1.307	1.691	2.032	2.441	2.728	3.348	3.601
35	1.306	1.690	2.030	2.438	2.724	3.340	3.591
36	1.306	1.688	2.028	2.434	2.719	3.333	3.582
37	1.305	1.687	2.026	2.431	2.715	3.326	3.574
38	1.304	1.686	2.024	2.429	2.712	3.319	3.566
39	1.304	1.685	2.023	2.426	2.708	3.313	3.558
40	1.303	1.684	2.021	2.423	2.704	3.307	3.551
41	1.303	1.683	2.020	2.421	2.701	3.301	3.544
42	1.302	1.682	2.018	2.418	2.698	3.296	3.538
43	1.302	1.681	2.017	2.416	2.695	3.291	3.532
44	1.301	1.680	2.015	2.414	2.692	3.286	3.526
45	1.301	1.679	2.014	2.412	2.690	3.281	3.520
46	1.300	1.679	2.013	2.410	2.687	3.277	3.515
47	1.300	1.678	2.012	2.408	2.685	3.273	3.510
48	1.299	1.677	2.011	2.407	2.682	3.269	3.505

(table continued)

TABLE A.4 *(concluded)* A t Table: Values of t_α for df = 49 through 100, 120, and ∞

df	$t_{.100}$	$t_{.05}$	$t_{.025}$	$t_{.01}$	$t_{.005}$	$t_{.001}$	$t_{.0005}$
49	1.299	1.677	2.010	2.405	2.680	3.265	3.500
50	1.299	1.676	2.009	2.403	2.678	3.261	3.496
51	1.298	1.675	2.008	2.402	2.676	3.258	3.492
52	1.298	1.675	2.007	2.400	2.674	3.255	3.488
53	1.298	1.674	2.006	2.399	2.672	3.251	3.484
54	1.297	1.674	2.005	2.397	2.670	3.248	3.480
55	1.297	1.673	2.004	2.396	2.668	3.245	3.476
56	1.297	1.673	2.003	2.395	2.667	3.242	3.473
57	1.297	1.672	2.002	2.394	2.665	3.239	3.470
58	1.296	1.672	2.002	2.392	2.663	3.237	3.466
59	1.296	1.671	2.001	2.391	2.662	3.234	3.463
60	1.296	1.671	2.000	2.390	2.660	3.232	3.460
61	1.296	1.670	2.000	2.389	2.659	3.229	3.457
62	1.295	1.670	1.999	2.388	2.657	3.227	3.454
63	1.295	1.669	1.998	2.387	2.656	3.225	3.452
64	1.295	1.669	1.998	2.386	2.655	3.223	3.449
65	1.295	1.669	1.997	2.385	2.654	3.220	3.447
66	1.295	1.668	1.997	2.384	2.652	3.218	3.444
67	1.294	1.668	1.996	2.383	2.651	3.216	3.442
68	1.294	1.668	1.995	2.382	2.650	3.214	3.439
69	1.294	1.667	1.995	2.382	2.649	3.213	3.437
70	1.294	1.667	1.994	2.381	2.648	3.211	3.435
71	1.294	1.667	1.994	2.380	2.647	3.209	3.433
72	1.293	1.666	1.993	2.379	2.646	3.207	3.431
73	1.293	1.666	1.993	2.379	2.645	3.206	3.429
74	1.293	1.666	1.993	2.378	2.644	3.204	3.427
75	1.293	1.665	1.992	2.377	2.643	3.202	3.425
76	1.293	1.665	1.992	2.376	2.642	3.201	3.423
77	1.293	1.665	1.991	2.376	2.641	3.199	3.421
78	1.292	1.665	1.991	2.375	2.640	3.198	3.420
79	1.292	1.664	1.990	2.374	2.640	3.197	3.418
80	1.292	1.664	1.990	2.374	2.639	3.195	3.416
81	1.292	1.664	1.990	2.373	2.638	3.194	3.415
82	1.292	1.664	1.989	2.373	2.637	3.193	3.413
83	1.292	1.663	1.989	2.372	2.636	3.191	3.412
84	1.292	1.663	1.989	2.372	2.636	3.190	3.410
85	1.292	1.663	1.988	2.371	2.635	3.189	3.409
86	1.291	1.663	1.988	2.370	2.634	3.188	3.407
87	1.291	1.663	1.988	2.370	2.634	3.187	3.406
88	1.291	1.662	1.987	2.369	2.633	3.185	3.405
89	1.291	1.662	1.987	2.369	2.632	3.184	3.403
90	1.291	1.662	1.987	2.368	2.632	3.183	3.402
91	1.291	1.662	1.986	2.368	2.631	3.182	3.401
92	1.291	1.662	1.986	2.368	2.630	3.181	3.399
93	1.291	1.661	1.986	2.367	2.630	3.180	3.398
94	1.291	1.661	1.986	2.367	2.629	3.179	3.397
95	1.291	1.661	1.985	2.366	2.629	3.178	3.396
96	1.290	1.661	1.985	2.366	2.628	3.177	3.395
97	1.290	1.661	1.985	2.365	2.627	3.176	3.394
98	1.290	1.661	1.984	2.365	2.627	3.175	3.393
99	1.290	1.660	1.984	2.365	2.626	3.175	3.392
100	1.290	1.660	1.984	2.364	2.626	3.174	3.390
120	1.289	1.658	1.980	2.358	2.617	3.160	3.373
∞	1.282	1.645	1.960	2.326	2.576	3.090	3.291

Source: Provided by J. B. Orris using Excel.

TABLE A.5 An F Table: Values of $F_{.10}$

df_2 \ df_1	1	2	3	4	5	6	7	8	9	10	12	15	20	24	30	40	60	120	∞
1	39.86	49.50	53.59	55.83	57.24	58.20	58.91	59.44	59.86	60.19	60.71	61.22	61.74	62.00	62.26	62.53	62.79	63.06	63.33
2	8.53	9.00	9.16	9.24	9.29	9.33	9.35	9.37	9.38	9.39	9.41	9.42	9.44	9.45	9.46	9.47	9.47	9.48	9.49
3	5.54	5.46	5.39	5.34	5.31	5.28	5.27	5.25	5.24	5.23	5.22	5.20	5.18	5.18	5.17	5.16	5.15	5.14	5.13
4	4.54	4.32	4.19	4.11	4.05	4.01	3.98	3.95	3.94	3.92	3.90	3.87	3.84	3.83	3.82	3.80	3.79	3.78	3.76
5	4.06	3.78	3.62	3.52	3.45	3.40	3.37	3.34	3.32	3.30	3.27	3.24	3.21	3.19	3.17	3.16	3.14	3.12	3.10
6	3.78	3.46	3.29	3.18	3.11	3.05	3.01	2.98	2.96	2.94	2.90	2.87	2.84	2.82	2.80	2.78	2.76	2.74	2.72
7	3.59	3.26	3.07	2.96	2.88	2.83	2.78	2.75	2.72	2.70	2.67	2.63	2.59	2.58	2.56	2.54	2.51	2.49	2.47
8	3.46	3.11	2.92	2.81	2.73	2.67	2.62	2.59	2.56	2.54	2.50	2.46	2.42	2.40	2.38	2.36	2.34	2.32	2.29
9	3.36	3.01	2.81	2.69	2.61	2.55	2.51	2.47	2.44	2.42	2.38	2.34	2.30	2.28	2.25	2.23	2.21	2.18	2.16
10	3.29	2.92	2.73	2.61	2.52	2.46	2.41	2.38	2.35	2.32	2.28	2.24	2.20	2.18	2.16	2.13	2.11	2.08	2.06
11	3.23	2.86	2.66	2.54	2.45	2.39	2.34	2.30	2.27	2.25	2.21	2.17	2.12	2.10	2.08	2.05	2.03	2.00	1.97
12	3.18	2.81	2.61	2.48	2.39	2.33	2.28	2.24	2.21	2.19	2.15	2.10	2.06	2.04	2.01	1.99	1.96	1.93	1.90
13	3.14	2.76	2.56	2.43	2.35	2.28	2.23	2.20	2.16	2.14	2.10	2.05	2.01	1.98	1.96	1.93	1.90	1.88	1.85
14	3.10	2.73	2.52	2.39	2.31	2.24	2.19	2.15	2.12	2.10	2.05	2.01	1.96	1.94	1.91	1.89	1.86	1.83	1.80
15	3.07	2.70	2.49	2.36	2.27	2.21	2.16	2.12	2.09	2.06	2.02	1.97	1.92	1.90	1.87	1.85	1.82	1.79	1.76
16	3.05	2.67	2.46	2.33	2.24	2.18	2.13	2.09	2.06	2.03	1.99	1.94	1.89	1.87	1.84	1.81	1.78	1.75	1.72
17	3.03	2.64	2.44	2.31	2.22	2.15	2.10	2.06	2.03	2.00	1.96	1.91	1.86	1.84	1.81	1.78	1.75	1.72	1.69
18	3.01	2.62	2.42	2.29	2.20	2.13	2.08	2.04	2.00	1.98	1.93	1.89	1.84	1.81	1.78	1.75	1.72	1.69	1.66
19	2.99	2.61	2.40	2.27	2.18	2.11	2.06	2.02	1.98	1.96	1.91	1.86	1.81	1.79	1.76	1.73	1.70	1.67	1.63
20	2.97	2.59	2.38	2.25	2.16	2.09	2.04	2.00	1.96	1.94	1.89	1.84	1.79	1.77	1.74	1.71	1.68	1.64	1.61
21	2.96	2.57	2.36	2.23	2.14	2.08	2.02	1.98	1.95	1.92	1.87	1.83	1.78	1.75	1.72	1.69	1.66	1.62	1.59
22	2.95	2.56	2.35	2.22	2.13	2.06	2.01	1.97	1.93	1.90	1.86	1.81	1.76	1.73	1.70	1.67	1.64	1.60	1.57
23	2.94	2.55	2.34	2.21	2.11	2.05	1.99	1.95	1.92	1.89	1.84	1.80	1.74	1.72	1.69	1.66	1.62	1.59	1.55
24	2.93	2.54	2.33	2.19	2.10	2.04	1.98	1.94	1.91	1.88	1.83	1.78	1.73	1.70	1.67	1.64	1.61	1.57	1.53
25	2.92	2.53	2.32	2.18	2.09	2.02	1.97	1.93	1.89	1.87	1.82	1.77	1.72	1.69	1.66	1.63	1.59	1.56	1.52
26	2.91	2.52	2.31	2.17	2.08	2.01	1.96	1.92	1.88	1.86	1.81	1.76	1.71	1.68	1.65	1.61	1.58	1.54	1.50
27	2.90	2.51	2.30	2.17	2.07	2.00	1.95	1.91	1.87	1.85	1.80	1.75	1.70	1.67	1.64	1.60	1.57	1.53	1.49
28	2.89	2.50	2.29	2.16	2.06	2.00	1.94	1.90	1.87	1.84	1.79	1.74	1.69	1.66	1.63	1.59	1.56	1.52	1.48
29	2.89	2.50	2.28	2.15	2.06	1.99	1.93	1.89	1.86	1.83	1.78	1.73	1.68	1.65	1.62	1.58	1.55	1.51	1.47
30	2.88	2.49	2.28	2.14	2.05	1.98	1.93	1.88	1.85	1.82	1.77	1.72	1.67	1.64	1.61	1.57	1.54	1.50	1.46
40	2.84	2.44	2.23	2.09	2.00	1.93	1.87	1.83	1.79	1.76	1.71	1.66	1.61	1.57	1.54	1.51	1.47	1.42	1.38
60	2.79	2.39	2.18	2.04	1.95	1.87	1.82	1.77	1.74	1.71	1.66	1.60	1.54	1.51	1.48	1.44	1.40	1.35	1.29
120	2.75	2.35	2.13	1.99	1.90	1.82	1.77	1.72	1.68	1.65	1.60	1.55	1.48	1.45	1.41	1.37	1.32	1.26	1.19
∞	2.71	2.30	2.08	1.94	1.85	1.77	1.72	1.67	1.63	1.60	1.55	1.49	1.42	1.38	1.34	1.30	1.24	1.17	1.00

Numerator Degrees of Freedom (df_1); Denominator Degrees of Freedom (df_2)

Source: M. Merrington and C. M. Thompson, "Tables of Percentage Points of the Inverted Beta (F)-Distribution," *Biometrika* 33 (1943), pp. 73–88. Reproduced by permission of the Biometrika Trustees.

TABLE A.6 An F Table: Values of $F_{.05}$

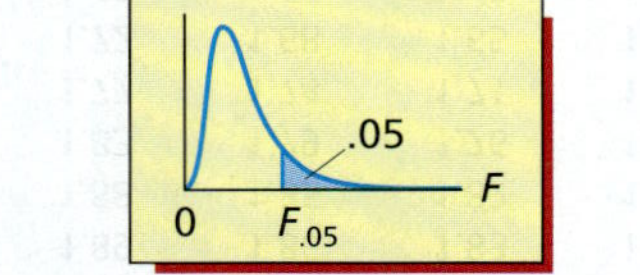

df_2 \ df_1	1	2	3	4	5	6	7	8	9	10	12	15	20	24	30	40	60	120	∞
1	161.4	199.5	215.7	224.6	230.2	234.0	236.8	238.9	240.5	241.9	243.9	245.9	248.0	249.1	250.1	251.1	252.2	253.3	254.3
2	18.51	19.00	19.16	19.25	19.30	19.33	19.35	19.37	19.38	19.40	19.41	19.43	19.45	19.45	19.46	19.47	19.48	19.49	19.50
3	10.13	9.55	9.28	9.12	9.01	8.94	8.89	8.85	8.81	8.79	8.74	8.70	8.66	8.64	8.62	8.59	8.57	8.55	8.53
4	7.71	6.94	6.59	6.39	6.26	6.16	6.09	6.04	6.00	5.96	5.91	5.86	5.80	5.77	5.75	5.72	5.69	5.66	5.63
5	6.61	5.79	5.41	5.19	5.05	4.95	4.88	4.82	4.77	4.74	4.68	4.62	4.56	4.53	4.50	4.46	4.43	4.40	4.36
6	5.99	5.14	4.76	4.53	4.39	4.28	4.21	4.15	4.10	4.06	4.00	3.94	3.87	3.84	3.81	3.77	3.74	3.70	3.67
7	5.59	4.74	4.35	4.12	3.97	3.87	3.79	3.73	3.68	3.64	3.57	3.51	3.44	3.41	3.38	3.34	3.30	3.27	3.23
8	5.32	4.46	4.07	3.84	3.69	3.58	3.50	3.44	3.39	3.35	3.28	3.22	3.15	3.12	3.08	3.04	3.01	2.97	2.93
9	5.12	4.26	3.86	3.63	3.48	3.37	3.29	3.23	3.18	3.14	3.07	3.01	2.94	2.90	2.86	2.83	2.79	2.75	2.71
10	4.96	4.10	3.71	3.48	3.33	3.22	3.14	3.07	3.02	2.98	2.91	2.85	2.77	2.74	2.70	2.66	2.62	2.58	2.54
11	4.84	3.98	3.59	3.36	3.20	3.09	3.01	2.95	2.90	2.85	2.79	2.72	2.65	2.61	2.57	2.53	2.49	2.45	2.40
12	4.75	3.89	3.49	3.26	3.11	3.00	2.91	2.85	2.80	2.75	2.69	2.62	2.54	2.51	2.47	2.43	2.38	2.34	2.30
13	4.67	3.81	3.41	3.18	3.03	2.92	2.83	2.77	2.71	2.67	2.60	2.53	2.46	2.42	2.38	2.34	2.30	2.25	2.21
14	4.60	3.74	3.34	3.11	2.96	2.85	2.76	2.70	2.65	2.60	2.53	2.46	2.39	2.35	2.31	2.27	2.22	2.18	2.13
15	4.54	3.68	3.29	3.06	2.90	2.79	2.71	2.64	2.59	2.54	2.48	2.40	2.33	2.29	2.25	2.20	2.16	2.11	2.07
16	4.49	3.63	3.24	3.01	2.85	2.74	2.66	2.59	2.54	2.49	2.42	2.35	2.28	2.24	2.19	2.15	2.11	2.06	2.01
17	4.45	3.59	3.20	2.96	2.81	2.70	2.61	2.55	2.49	2.45	2.38	2.31	2.23	2.19	2.15	2.10	2.06	2.01	1.96
18	4.41	3.55	3.16	2.93	2.77	2.66	2.58	2.51	2.46	2.41	2.34	2.27	2.19	2.15	2.11	2.06	2.02	1.97	1.92
19	4.38	3.52	3.13	2.90	2.74	2.63	2.54	2.48	2.42	2.38	2.31	2.23	2.16	2.11	2.07	2.03	1.98	1.93	1.88
20	4.35	3.49	3.10	2.87	2.71	2.60	2.51	2.45	2.39	2.35	2.28	2.20	2.12	2.08	2.04	1.99	1.95	1.90	1.84
21	4.32	3.47	3.07	2.84	2.68	2.57	2.49	2.42	2.37	2.32	2.25	2.18	2.10	2.05	2.01	1.96	1.92	1.87	1.81
22	4.30	3.44	3.05	2.82	2.66	2.55	2.46	2.40	2.34	2.30	2.23	2.15	2.07	2.03	1.98	1.94	1.89	1.84	1.78
23	4.28	3.42	3.03	2.80	2.64	2.53	2.44	2.37	2.32	2.27	2.20	2.13	2.05	2.01	1.96	1.91	1.86	1.81	1.76
24	4.26	3.40	3.01	2.78	2.62	2.51	2.42	2.36	2.30	2.25	2.18	2.11	2.03	1.98	1.94	1.89	1.84	1.79	1.73
25	4.24	3.39	2.99	2.76	2.60	2.49	2.40	2.34	2.28	2.24	2.16	2.09	2.01	1.96	1.92	1.87	1.82	1.77	1.71
26	4.23	3.37	2.98	2.74	2.59	2.47	2.39	2.32	2.27	2.22	2.15	2.07	1.99	1.95	1.90	1.85	1.80	1.75	1.69
27	4.21	3.35	2.96	2.73	2.57	2.46	2.37	2.31	2.25	2.20	2.13	2.06	1.97	1.93	1.88	1.84	1.79	1.73	1.67
28	4.20	3.34	2.95	2.71	2.56	2.45	2.36	2.29	2.24	2.19	2.12	2.04	1.96	1.91	1.87	1.82	1.77	1.71	1.65
29	4.18	3.33	2.93	2.70	2.55	2.43	2.35	2.28	2.22	2.18	2.10	2.03	1.94	1.90	1.85	1.81	1.75	1.70	1.64
30	4.17	3.32	2.92	2.69	2.53	2.42	2.33	2.27	2.21	2.16	2.09	2.01	1.93	1.89	1.84	1.79	1.74	1.68	1.62
40	4.08	3.23	2.84	2.61	2.45	2.34	2.25	2.18	2.12	2.08	2.00	1.92	1.84	1.79	1.74	1.69	1.64	1.58	1.51
60	4.00	3.15	2.76	2.53	2.37	2.25	2.17	2.10	2.04	1.99	1.92	1.84	1.75	1.70	1.65	1.59	1.53	1.47	1.39
120	3.92	3.07	2.68	2.45	2.29	2.17	2.09	2.02	1.96	1.91	1.83	1.75	1.66	1.61	1.55	1.50	1.43	1.35	1.25
∞	3.84	3.00	2.60	2.37	2.21	2.10	2.01	1.94	1.88	1.83	1.75	1.67	1.57	1.52	1.46	1.39	1.32	1.22	1.00

Column headings: Numerator Degrees of Freedom (df_1); row headings: Denominator Degrees of Freedom (df_2)

Source: M. Merrington and C. M. Thompson, "Tables of Percentage Points of the Inverted Beta (F)-Distribution," *Biometrika* 33 (1943), pp. 73–88. Reproduced by permission of the Biometrika Trustees.

TABLE A.7 An *F* Table: Values of $F_{.025}$

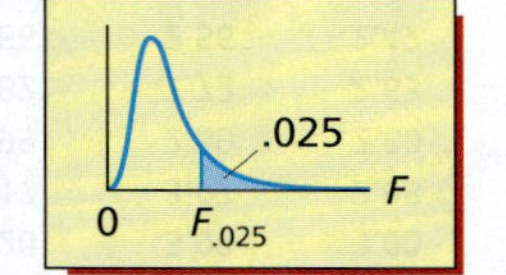

df_2 \ df_1	1	2	3	4	5	6	7	8	9	10	12	15	20	24	30	40	60	120	∞
	Numerator Degrees of Freedom (df_1)																		
Denominator Degrees of Freedom (df_2)																			
1	647.8	799.5	864.2	899.6	921.8	937.1	948.2	956.7	963.3	968.6	976.7	984.9	993.1	997.2	1,001	1,006	1,010	1,014	1,018
2	38.51	39.00	39.17	39.25	39.30	39.33	39.36	39.37	39.39	39.40	39.41	39.43	39.45	39.46	39.46	39.47	39.48	39.49	39.50
3	17.44	16.04	15.44	15.10	14.88	14.73	14.62	14.54	14.47	14.42	14.34	14.25	14.17	14.12	14.08	14.04	13.99	13.95	13.90
4	12.22	10.65	9.98	9.60	9.36	9.20	9.07	8.98	8.90	8.84	8.75	8.66	8.56	8.51	8.46	8.41	8.36	8.31	8.26
5	10.01	8.43	7.76	7.39	7.15	6.98	6.85	6.76	6.68	6.62	6.52	6.43	6.33	6.28	6.23	6.18	6.12	6.07	6.02
6	8.81	7.26	6.60	6.23	5.99	5.82	5.70	5.60	5.52	5.46	5.37	5.27	5.17	5.12	5.07	5.01	4.96	4.90	4.85
7	8.07	6.54	5.89	5.52	5.29	5.12	4.99	4.90	4.82	4.76	4.67	4.57	4.47	4.42	4.36	4.31	4.25	4.20	4.14
8	7.57	6.06	5.42	5.05	4.82	4.65	4.53	4.43	4.36	4.30	4.20	4.10	4.00	3.95	3.89	3.84	3.78	3.73	3.67
9	7.21	5.71	5.08	4.72	4.48	4.32	4.20	4.10	4.03	3.96	3.87	3.77	3.67	3.61	3.56	3.51	3.45	3.39	3.33
10	6.94	5.46	4.83	4.47	4.24	4.07	3.95	3.85	3.78	3.72	3.62	3.52	3.42	3.37	3.31	3.26	3.20	3.14	3.08
11	6.72	5.26	4.63	4.28	4.04	3.88	3.76	3.66	3.59	3.53	3.43	3.33	3.23	3.17	3.12	3.06	3.00	2.94	2.88
12	6.55	5.10	4.47	4.12	3.89	3.73	3.61	3.51	3.44	3.37	3.28	3.18	3.07	3.02	2.96	2.91	2.85	2.79	2.72
13	6.41	4.97	4.35	4.00	3.77	3.60	3.48	3.39	3.31	3.25	3.15	3.05	2.95	2.89	2.84	2.78	2.72	2.66	2.60
14	6.30	4.86	4.24	3.89	3.66	3.50	3.38	3.29	3.21	3.15	3.05	2.95	2.84	2.79	2.73	2.67	2.61	2.55	2.49
15	6.20	4.77	4.15	3.80	3.58	3.41	3.29	3.20	3.12	3.06	2.96	2.86	2.76	2.70	2.64	2.59	2.52	2.46	2.40
16	6.12	4.69	4.08	3.73	3.50	3.34	3.22	3.12	3.05	2.99	2.89	2.79	2.68	2.63	2.57	2.51	2.45	2.38	2.32
17	6.04	4.62	4.01	3.66	3.44	3.28	3.16	3.06	2.98	2.92	2.82	2.72	2.62	2.56	2.50	2.44	2.38	2.32	2.25
18	5.98	4.56	3.95	3.61	3.38	3.22	3.10	3.01	2.93	2.87	2.77	2.67	2.56	2.50	2.44	2.38	2.32	2.26	2.19
19	5.92	4.51	3.90	3.56	3.33	3.17	3.05	2.96	2.88	2.82	2.72	2.62	2.51	2.45	2.39	2.33	2.27	2.20	2.13
20	5.87	4.46	3.86	3.51	3.29	3.13	3.01	2.91	2.84	2.77	2.68	2.57	2.46	2.41	2.35	2.29	2.22	2.16	2.09
21	5.83	4.42	3.82	3.48	3.25	3.09	2.97	2.87	2.80	2.73	2.64	2.53	2.42	2.37	2.31	2.25	2.18	2.11	2.04
22	5.79	4.38	3.78	3.44	3.22	3.05	2.93	2.84	2.76	2.70	2.60	2.50	2.39	2.33	2.27	2.21	2.14	2.08	2.00
23	5.75	4.35	3.75	3.41	3.18	3.02	2.90	2.81	2.73	2.67	2.57	2.47	2.36	2.30	2.24	2.18	2.11	2.04	1.97
24	5.72	4.32	3.72	3.38	3.15	2.99	2.87	2.78	2.70	2.64	2.54	2.44	2.33	2.27	2.21	2.15	2.08	2.01	1.94
25	5.69	4.29	3.69	3.35	3.13	2.97	2.85	2.75	2.68	2.61	2.51	2.41	2.30	2.24	2.18	2.12	2.05	1.98	1.91
26	5.66	4.27	3.67	3.33	3.10	2.94	2.82	2.73	2.65	2.59	2.49	2.39	2.28	2.22	2.16	2.09	2.03	1.95	1.88
27	5.63	4.24	3.65	3.31	3.08	2.92	2.80	2.71	2.63	2.57	2.47	2.36	2.25	2.19	2.13	2.07	2.00	1.93	1.85
28	5.61	4.22	3.63	3.29	3.06	2.90	2.78	2.69	2.61	2.55	2.45	2.34	2.23	2.17	2.11	2.05	1.98	1.91	1.83
29	5.59	4.20	3.61	3.27	3.04	2.88	2.76	2.67	2.59	2.53	2.43	2.32	2.21	2.15	2.09	2.03	1.96	1.89	1.81
30	5.57	4.18	3.59	3.25	3.03	2.87	2.75	2.65	2.57	2.51	2.41	2.31	2.20	2.14	2.07	2.01	1.94	1.87	1.79
40	5.42	4.05	3.46	3.13	2.90	2.74	2.62	2.53	2.45	2.39	2.29	2.18	2.07	2.01	1.94	1.88	1.80	1.72	1.64
60	5.29	3.93	3.34	3.01	2.79	2.63	2.51	2.41	2.33	2.27	2.17	2.06	1.94	1.88	1.82	1.74	1.67	1.58	1.48
120	5.15	3.80	3.23	2.89	2.67	2.52	2.39	2.30	2.22	2.16	2.05	1.94	1.82	1.76	1.69	1.61	1.53	1.43	1.31
∞	5.02	3.69	3.12	2.79	2.57	2.41	2.29	2.19	2.11	2.05	1.94	1.83	1.71	1.64	1.57	1.48	1.39	1.27	1.00

Source: M. Merrington and C. M. Thompson, "Tables of Percentage Points of the Inverted Beta (*F*)-Distribution," *Biometrika* 33 (1943), pp. 73–88. Reproduced by permission of the Biometrika Trustees.

TABLE A.8 An F Table: Values of $F_{.01}$

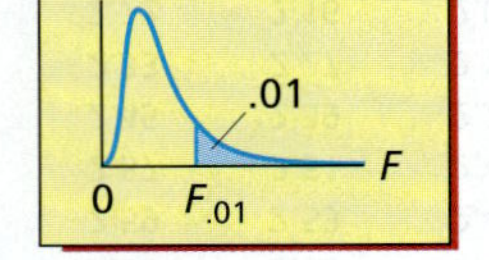

df_2 \ df_1	1	2	3	4	5	6	7	8	9	10	12	15	20	24	30	40	60	120	∞
	Numerator Degrees of Freedom (df_1)																		
Denominator Degrees of Freedom (df_2)																			
1	4,052	4,999.5	5,403	5,625	5,764	5,859	5,928	5,982	6,022	6,056	6,106	6,157	6,209	6,235	6,261	6,287	6,313	6,339	6,366
2	98.50	99.00	99.17	99.25	99.30	99.33	99.36	99.37	99.39	99.40	99.42	99.43	99.45	99.46	99.47	99.47	99.48	99.49	99.50
3	34.12	30.82	29.46	28.71	28.24	27.91	27.67	27.49	27.35	27.23	27.05	26.87	26.69	26.60	26.50	26.41	26.32	26.22	26.13
4	21.20	18.00	16.69	15.98	15.52	15.21	14.98	14.80	14.66	14.55	14.37	14.20	14.02	13.93	13.84	13.75	13.65	13.56	13.46
5	16.26	13.27	12.06	11.39	10.97	10.67	10.46	10.29	10.16	10.05	9.89	9.72	9.55	9.47	9.38	9.29	9.20	9.11	9.02
6	13.75	10.92	9.78	9.15	8.75	8.47	8.26	8.10	7.98	7.87	7.72	7.56	7.40	7.31	7.23	7.14	7.06	6.97	6.88
7	12.25	9.55	8.45	7.85	7.46	7.19	6.99	6.84	6.72	6.62	6.47	6.31	6.16	6.07	5.99	5.91	5.82	5.74	5.65
8	11.26	8.65	7.59	7.01	6.63	6.37	6.18	6.03	5.91	5.81	5.67	5.52	5.36	5.28	5.20	5.12	5.03	4.95	4.86
9	10.56	8.02	6.99	6.42	6.06	5.80	5.61	5.47	5.35	5.26	5.11	4.96	4.81	4.73	4.65	4.57	4.48	4.40	4.31
10	10.04	7.56	6.55	5.99	5.64	5.39	5.20	5.06	4.94	4.85	4.71	4.56	4.41	4.33	4.25	4.17	4.08	4.00	3.91
11	9.65	7.21	6.22	5.67	5.32	5.07	4.89	4.74	4.63	4.54	4.40	4.25	4.10	4.02	3.94	3.86	3.78	3.69	3.60
12	9.33	6.93	5.95	5.41	5.06	4.82	4.64	4.50	4.39	4.30	4.16	4.01	3.86	3.78	3.70	3.62	3.54	3.45	3.36
13	9.07	6.70	5.74	5.21	4.86	4.62	4.44	4.30	4.19	4.10	3.96	3.82	3.66	3.59	3.51	3.43	3.34	3.25	3.17
14	8.86	6.51	5.56	5.04	4.69	4.46	4.28	4.14	4.03	3.94	3.80	3.66	3.51	3.43	3.35	3.27	3.18	3.09	3.00
15	8.68	6.36	5.42	4.89	4.56	4.32	4.14	4.00	3.89	3.80	3.67	3.52	3.37	3.29	3.21	3.13	3.05	2.96	2.87
16	8.53	6.23	5.29	4.77	4.44	4.20	4.03	3.89	3.78	3.69	3.55	3.41	3.26	3.18	3.10	3.02	2.93	2.84	2.75
17	8.40	6.11	5.18	4.67	4.34	4.10	3.93	3.79	3.68	3.59	3.46	3.31	3.16	3.08	3.00	2.92	2.83	2.75	2.65
18	8.29	6.01	5.09	4.58	4.25	4.01	3.84	3.71	3.60	3.51	3.37	3.23	3.08	3.00	2.92	2.84	2.75	2.66	2.57
19	8.18	5.93	5.01	4.50	4.17	3.94	3.77	3.63	3.52	3.43	3.30	3.15	3.00	2.92	2.84	2.76	2.67	2.58	2.49
20	8.10	5.85	4.94	4.43	4.10	3.87	3.70	3.56	3.46	3.37	3.23	3.09	2.94	2.86	2.78	2.69	2.61	2.52	2.42
21	8.02	5.78	4.87	4.37	4.04	3.81	3.64	3.51	3.40	3.31	3.17	3.03	2.88	2.80	2.72	2.64	2.55	2.46	2.36
22	7.95	5.72	4.82	4.31	3.99	3.76	3.59	3.45	3.35	3.26	3.12	2.98	2.83	2.75	2.67	2.58	2.50	2.40	2.31
23	7.88	5.66	4.76	4.26	3.94	3.71	3.54	3.41	3.30	3.21	3.07	2.93	2.78	2.70	2.62	2.54	2.45	2.35	2.26
24	7.82	5.61	4.72	4.22	3.90	3.67	3.50	3.36	3.26	3.17	3.03	2.89	2.74	2.66	2.58	2.49	2.40	2.31	2.21
25	7.77	5.57	4.68	4.18	3.85	3.63	3.46	3.32	3.22	3.13	2.99	2.85	2.70	2.62	2.54	2.45	2.36	2.27	2.17
26	7.72	5.53	4.64	4.14	3.82	3.59	3.42	3.29	3.18	3.09	2.96	2.81	2.66	2.58	2.50	2.42	2.33	2.23	2.13
27	7.68	5.49	4.60	4.11	3.78	3.56	3.39	3.26	3.15	3.06	2.93	2.78	2.63	2.55	2.47	2.38	2.29	2.20	2.10
28	7.64	5.45	4.57	4.07	3.75	3.53	3.36	3.23	3.12	3.03	2.90	2.75	2.60	2.52	2.44	2.35	2.26	2.17	2.06
29	7.60	5.42	4.54	4.04	3.73	3.50	3.33	3.20	3.09	3.00	2.87	2.73	2.57	2.49	2.41	2.33	2.23	2.14	2.03
30	7.56	5.39	4.51	4.02	3.70	3.47	3.30	3.17	3.07	2.98	2.84	2.70	2.55	2.47	2.39	2.30	2.21	2.11	2.01
40	7.31	5.18	4.31	3.83	3.51	3.29	3.12	2.99	2.89	2.80	2.66	2.52	2.37	2.29	2.20	2.11	2.02	1.92	1.80
60	7.08	4.98	4.13	3.65	3.34	3.12	2.95	2.82	2.72	2.63	2.50	2.35	2.20	2.12	2.03	1.94	1.84	1.73	1.60
120	6.85	4.79	3.95	3.48	3.17	2.96	2.79	2.66	2.56	2.47	2.34	2.19	2.03	1.95	1.86	1.76	1.66	1.53	1.38
∞	6.63	4.61	3.78	3.32	3.02	2.80	2.64	2.51	2.41	2.32	2.18	2.04	1.88	1.79	1.70	1.59	1.47	1.32	1.00

Source: M. Merrington and C. M. Thompson, "Tables of Percentage Points of the Inverted Beta (F)-Distribution," *Biometrika* 33 (1943), pp. 73–88. Reproduced by permission of the Biometrika Trustees.

TABLE A.9 Percentage Points of the Studentized Range
(Note: r is the "first value" and v is the "second value" referred to in Chapter 10.)

Entry is $q_{.10}$

v \ r	2	3	4	5	6	7	8	9	10	11	12	13	14	15	16	17	18	19	20
1	8.93	13.4	16.4	18.5	20.2	21.5	22.6	23.6	24.5	25.2	25.9	26.5	27.1	27.6	28.1	28.5	29.0	29.3	29.7
2	4.13	5.73	6.77	7.54	8.14	8.63	9.05	9.41	9.72	10.0	10.3	10.5	10.7	10.9	11.1	11.2	11.4	11.5	11.7
3	3.33	4.47	5.20	5.74	6.16	6.51	6.81	7.06	7.29	7.49	7.67	7.83	7.98	8.12	8.25	8.37	8.48	8.58	8.68
4	3.01	3.98	4.59	5.03	5.39	5.68	5.93	6.14	6.33	6.49	6.65	6.78	6.91	7.02	7.13	7.23	7.33	7.41	7.50
5	2.85	3.72	4.26	4.66	4.98	5.24	5.46	5.65	5.82	5.97	6.10	6.22	6.34	6.44	6.54	6.63	6.71	6.79	6.86
6	2.75	3.56	4.07	4.44	4.73	4.97	5.17	5.34	5.50	5.64	5.76	5.87	5.98	6.07	6.16	6.25	6.32	6.40	6.47
7	2.68	3.45	3.93	4.28	4.55	4.78	4.97	5.14	5.28	5.41	5.53	5.64	5.74	5.83	5.91	5.99	6.06	6.13	6.19
8	2.63	3.37	3.83	4.17	4.43	4.65	4.83	4.99	5.13	5.25	5.36	5.46	5.56	5.64	5.72	5.80	5.87	5.93	6.00
9	2.59	3.32	3.76	4.08	4.34	4.54	4.72	4.87	5.01	5.13	5.23	5.33	5.42	5.51	5.58	5.66	5.72	5.79	5.85
10	2.56	3.27	3.70	4.02	4.26	4.47	4.64	4.78	4.91	5.03	5.13	5.23	5.32	5.40	5.47	5.54	5.61	5.67	5.73
11	2.54	3.23	3.66	3.96	4.20	4.40	4.57	4.71	4.84	4.95	5.05	5.15	5.23	5.31	5.38	5.45	5.51	5.57	5.63
12	2.52	3.20	3.62	3.92	4.16	4.35	4.51	4.65	4.78	4.89	4.99	5.08	5.16	5.24	5.31	5.37	5.44	5.49	5.55
13	2.50	3.18	3.59	3.88	4.12	4.30	4.46	4.60	4.72	4.83	4.93	5.02	5.10	5.18	5.25	5.31	5.37	5.43	5.48
14	2.49	3.16	3.56	3.85	4.08	4.27	4.42	4.56	4.68	4.79	4.88	4.97	5.05	5.12	5.19	5.26	5.32	5.37	5.43
15	2.48	3.14	3.54	3.83	4.05	4.23	4.39	4.52	4.64	4.75	4.84	4.93	5.01	5.08	5.15	5.21	5.27	5.32	5.38
16	2.47	3.12	3.52	3.80	4.03	4.21	4.36	4.49	4.61	4.71	4.81	4.89	4.97	5.04	5.11	5.17	5.23	5.28	5.33
17	2.46	3.11	3.50	3.78	4.00	4.18	4.33	4.46	4.58	4.68	4.77	4.86	4.93	5.01	5.07	5.13	5.19	5.24	5.30
18	2.45	3.10	3.49	3.77	3.98	4.16	4.31	4.44	4.55	4.65	4.75	4.83	4.90	4.98	5.04	5.10	5.16	5.21	5.26
19	2.45	3.09	3.47	3.75	3.97	4.14	4.29	4.42	4.53	4.63	4.72	4.80	4.88	4.95	5.01	5.07	5.13	5.18	5.23
20	2.44	3.08	3.46	3.74	3.95	4.12	4.27	4.40	4.51	4.61	4.70	4.78	4.85	4.92	4.99	5.05	5.10	5.16	5.20
24	2.42	3.05	3.42	3.69	3.90	4.07	4.21	4.34	4.44	4.54	4.63	4.71	4.78	4.85	4.91	4.97	5.02	5.07	5.12
30	2.40	3.02	3.39	3.65	3.85	4.02	4.16	4.28	4.38	4.47	4.56	4.64	4.71	4.77	4.83	4.89	4.94	4.99	5.03
40	2.38	2.99	3.35	3.60	3.80	3.96	4.10	4.21	4.32	4.41	4.49	4.56	4.63	4.69	4.75	4.81	4.86	4.90	4.95
60	2.36	2.96	3.31	3.56	3.75	3.91	4.04	4.16	4.25	4.34	4.42	4.49	4.56	4.62	4.67	4.73	4.78	4.82	4.86
120	2.34	2.93	3.28	3.52	3.71	3.86	3.99	4.10	4.19	4.28	4.35	4.42	4.48	4.54	4.60	4.65	4.69	4.74	4.78
∞	2.33	2.90	3.24	3.48	3.66	3.81	3.93	4.04	4.13	4.21	4.28	4.35	4.41	4.47	4.52	4.57	4.61	4.65	4.69

(table continued)

Table A.9 *(continued)*

Entry is $q_{.05}$

v	2	3	4	5	6	7	8	9	10	11	12	13	14	15	16	17	18	19	20
1	18.0	27.0	32.8	37.1	40.4	43.1	45.4	47.4	49.1	50.6	52.0	53.2	54.3	55.4	56.3	57.2	58.0	58.8	59.6
2	6.08	8.33	9.80	10.9	11.7	12.4	13.0	13.5	14.0	14.4	14.7	15.1	15.4	15.7	15.9	16.1	16.4	16.6	16.8
3	4.50	5.91	6.82	7.50	8.04	8.48	8.85	9.18	9.46	9.72	9.95	10.2	10.3	10.5	10.7	10.8	11.0	11.1	11.2
4	3.93	5.04	5.76	6.29	6.71	7.05	7.35	7.60	7.83	8.03	8.21	8.37	8.52	8.66	8.79	8.91	9.03	9.13	9.23
5	3.64	4.60	5.22	5.67	6.03	6.33	6.58	6.80	6.99	7.17	7.32	7.47	7.60	7.72	7.83	7.93	8.03	8.12	8.21
6	3.46	4.34	4.90	5.30	5.63	5.90	6.12	6.32	6.49	6.65	6.79	6.92	7.03	7.14	7.24	7.34	7.43	7.51	7.59
7	3.34	4.16	4.68	5.06	5.36	5.61	5.82	6.00	6.16	6.30	6.43	6.55	6.66	6.76	6.85	6.94	7.02	7.10	7.17
8	3.26	4.04	4.53	4.89	5.17	5.40	5.60	5.77	5.92	6.05	6.18	6.29	6.39	6.48	6.57	6.65	6.73	6.80	6.87
9	3.20	3.95	4.41	4.76	5.02	5.24	5.43	5.59	5.74	5.87	5.98	6.09	6.19	6.28	6.36	6.44	6.51	6.58	6.64
10	3.15	3.88	4.33	4.65	4.91	5.12	5.30	5.46	5.60	5.72	5.83	5.93	6.03	6.11	6.19	6.27	6.34	6.40	6.47
11	3.11	3.82	4.26	4.57	4.82	5.03	5.20	5.35	5.49	5.61	5.71	5.81	5.90	5.98	6.06	6.13	6.20	6.27	6.33
12	3.08	3.77	4.20	4.51	4.75	4.95	5.12	5.27	5.39	5.51	5.61	5.71	5.80	5.88	5.95	6.02	6.09	6.15	6.21
13	3.06	3.73	4.15	4.45	4.69	4.88	5.05	5.19	5.32	5.43	5.53	5.63	5.71	5.79	5.86	5.93	5.99	6.05	6.11
14	3.03	3.70	4.11	4.41	4.64	4.83	4.99	5.13	5.25	5.36	5.46	5.55	5.64	5.71	5.79	5.85	5.91	5.97	6.03
15	3.01	3.67	4.08	4.37	4.59	4.78	4.94	5.08	5.20	5.31	5.40	5.49	5.57	5.65	5.72	5.78	5.85	5.90	5.96
16	3.00	3.65	4.05	4.33	4.56	4.74	4.90	5.03	5.15	5.26	5.35	5.44	5.52	5.59	5.66	5.73	5.79	5.84	5.90
17	2.98	3.63	4.02	4.30	4.52	4.70	4.86	4.99	5.11	5.21	5.31	5.39	5.47	5.54	5.61	5.67	5.73	5.79	5.84
18	2.97	3.61	4.00	4.28	4.49	4.67	4.82	4.96	5.07	5.17	5.27	5.35	5.43	5.50	5.57	5.63	5.69	5.74	5.79
19	2.96	3.59	3.98	4.25	4.47	4.65	4.79	4.92	5.04	5.14	5.23	5.31	5.39	5.46	5.53	5.59	5.65	5.70	5.75
20	2.95	3.58	3.96	4.23	4.45	4.62	4.77	4.90	5.01	5.11	5.20	5.28	5.36	5.43	5.49	5.55	5.61	5.66	5.71
24	2.92	3.53	3.90	4.17	4.37	4.54	4.68	4.81	4.92	5.01	5.10	5.18	5.25	5.32	5.38	5.44	5.49	5.55	5.59
30	2.89	3.49	3.85	4.10	4.30	4.46	4.60	4.72	4.82	4.92	5.00	5.08	5.15	5.21	5.27	5.33	5.38	5.43	5.47
40	2.86	3.44	3.79	4.04	4.23	4.39	4.52	4.63	4.73	4.82	4.90	4.98	5.04	5.11	5.16	5.22	5.27	5.31	5.36
60	2.83	3.40	3.74	3.98	4.16	4.31	4.44	4.55	4.65	4.73	4.81	4.88	4.94	5.00	5.06	5.11	5.15	5.20	5.24
120	2.80	3.36	3.68	3.92	4.10	4.24	4.36	4.47	4.56	4.64	4.71	4.78	4.84	4.90	4.95	5.00	5.04	5.09	5.13
∞	2.77	3.31	3.63	3.86	4.03	4.17	4.29	4.39	4.47	4.55	4.62	4.68	4.74	4.80	4.85	4.89	4.93	4.97	5.01

Column headings 2–20 are values of r.

TABLE A.9 ***(concluded)***

Entry is $q_{.01}$

v	r: 2	3	4	5	6	7	8	9	10	11	12	13	14	15	16	17	18	19	20
1	90.0	135	164	186	202	216	227	237	246	253	260	266	272	277	282	286	290	294	298
2	14.0	19.0	22.3	24.7	26.6	28.2	29.5	30.7	31.7	32.6	33.4	34.1	34.8	35.4	36.0	36.5	37.0	37.5	37.9
3	8.26	10.6	12.2	13.3	14.2	15.0	15.6	16.2	16.7	17.1	17.5	17.9	18.2	18.5	18.8	19.1	19.3	19.5	19.8
4	6.51	8.12	9.17	9.96	10.6	11.1	11.5	11.9	12.3	12.6	12.8	13.1	13.3	13.5	13.7	13.9	14.1	14.2	14.4
5	5.70	6.97	7.80	8.42	8.91	9.32	9.67	9.97	10.2	10.5	10.7	10.9	11.1	11.2	11.4	11.6	11.7	11.8	11.9
6	5.24	6.33	7.03	7.56	7.97	8.32	8.61	8.87	9.10	9.30	9.49	9.65	9.81	9.95	10.1	10.2	10.3	10.4	10.5
7	4.95	5.92	6.54	7.01	7.37	7.68	7.94	8.17	8.37	8.55	8.71	8.86	9.00	9.12	9.24	9.35	9.46	9.55	9.65
8	4.74	5.63	6.20	6.63	6.96	7.24	7.47	7.68	7.87	8.03	8.18	8.31	8.44	8.55	8.66	8.76	8.85	8.94	9.03
9	4.60	5.43	5.96	6.35	6.66	6.91	7.13	7.32	7.49	7.65	7.78	7.91	8.03	8.13	8.23	8.32	8.41	8.49	8.57
10	4.48	5.27	5.77	6.14	6.43	6.67	6.87	7.05	7.21	7.36	7.48	7.60	7.71	7.81	7.91	7.99	8.07	8.15	8.22
11	4.39	5.14	5.62	5.97	6.25	6.48	6.67	6.84	6.99	7.13	7.25	7.36	7.46	7.56	7.65	7.73	7.81	7.88	7.95
12	4.32	5.04	5.50	5.84	6.10	6.32	6.51	6.67	6.81	6.94	7.06	7.17	7.26	7.36	7.44	7.52	7.59	7.66	7.73
13	4.26	4.96	5.40	5.73	5.98	6.19	6.37	6.53	6.67	6.79	6.90	7.01	7.10	7.19	7.27	7.34	7.42	7.48	7.55
14	4.21	4.89	5.32	5.63	5.88	6.08	6.26	6.41	6.54	6.66	6.77	6.87	6.96	7.05	7.12	7.20	7.27	7.33	7.39
15	4.17	4.83	5.25	5.56	5.80	5.99	6.16	6.31	6.44	6.55	6.66	6.76	6.84	6.93	7.00	7.07	7.14	7.20	7.26
16	4.13	4.78	5.19	5.49	5.72	5.92	6.08	6.22	6.35	6.46	6.56	6.66	6.74	6.82	6.90	6.97	7.03	7.09	7.15
17	4.10	4.74	5.14	5.43	5.66	5.85	6.01	6.15	6.27	6.38	6.48	6.57	6.66	6.73	6.80	6.87	6.94	7.00	7.05
18	4.07	4.70	5.09	5.38	5.60	5.79	5.94	6.08	6.20	6.31	6.41	6.50	6.58	6.65	6.72	6.79	6.85	6.91	6.96
19	4.05	4.67	5.05	5.33	5.55	5.73	5.89	6.02	6.14	6.25	6.34	6.43	6.51	6.58	6.65	6.72	6.78	6.84	6.89
20	4.02	4.64	5.02	5.29	5.51	5.69	5.84	5.97	6.09	6.19	6.29	6.37	6.45	6.52	6.59	6.65	6.71	6.76	6.82
24	3.96	4.54	4.91	5.17	5.37	5.54	5.69	5.81	5.92	6.02	6.11	6.19	6.26	6.33	6.39	6.45	6.51	6.56	6.61
30	3.89	4.45	4.80	5.05	5.24	5.40	5.54	5.65	5.76	5.85	5.93	6.01	6.08	6.14	6.20	6.26	6.31	6.36	6.41
40	3.82	4.37	4.70	4.93	5.11	5.27	5.39	5.50	5.60	5.69	5.77	5.84	5.90	5.96	6.02	6.07	6.12	6.17	6.21
60	3.76	4.28	4.60	4.82	4.99	5.13	5.25	5.36	5.45	5.53	5.60	5.67	5.73	5.79	5.84	5.89	5.93	5.98	6.02
120	3.70	4.20	4.50	4.71	4.87	5.01	5.12	5.21	5.30	5.38	5.44	5.51	5.56	5.61	5.66	5.71	5.75	5.79	5.83
∞	3.64	4.12	4.40	4.60	4.76	4.88	4.99	5.08	5.16	5.23	5.29	5.35	5.40	5.45	5.49	5.54	5.57	5.61	5.65

Source: *The Analysis of Variance,* pp. 414–16, by Henry Scheffe, ©1959 by John Wiley & Sons, Inc. Reprinted by permission of John Wiley & Sons, Inc.

TABLE A.10 Critical Values for the Durbin–Watson d Statistic ($\alpha = .05$)

	$k = 1$		$k = 2$		$k = 3$		$k = 4$		$k = 5$	
n	$d_{L,.05}$	$d_{U,.05}$	$d_{L,.05}$	$d_{U,.05}$	$d_{L,.05}$	$d_{U,.05}$	$d_{L,.05}$	$d_{U,.05}$	$d_{L,.05}$	$d_{U,.05}$
15	1.08	1.36	0.95	1.54	0.82	1.75	0.69	1.97	0.56	2.21
16	1.10	1.37	0.98	1.54	0.86	1.73	0.74	1.93	0.62	2.15
17	1.13	1.38	1.02	1.54	0.90	1.71	0.78	1.90	0.67	2.10
18	1.16	1.39	1.05	1.53	0.93	1.69	0.82	1.87	0.71	2.06
19	1.18	1.40	1.08	1.53	0.97	1.68	0.86	1.85	0.75	2.02
20	1.20	1.41	1.10	1.54	1.00	1.68	0.90	1.83	0.79	1.99
21	1.22	1.42	1.13	1.54	1.03	1.67	0.93	1.81	0.83	1.96
22	1.24	1.43	1.15	1.54	1.05	1.66	0.96	1.80	0.86	1.94
23	1.26	1.44	1.17	1.54	1.08	1.66	0.99	1.79	0.90	1.92
24	1.27	1.45	1.19	1.55	1.10	1.66	1.01	1.78	0.93	1.90
25	1.29	1.45	1.21	1.55	1.12	1.66	1.04	1.77	0.95	1.89
26	1.30	1.46	1.22	1.55	1.14	1.65	1.06	1.76	0.98	1.88
27	1.32	1.47	1.24	1.56	1.16	1.65	1.08	1.76	1.01	1.86
28	1.33	1.48	1.26	1.56	1.18	1.65	1.10	1.75	1.03	1.85
29	1.34	1.48	1.27	1.56	1.20	1.65	1.12	1.74	1.05	1.84
30	1.35	1.49	1.28	1.57	1.21	1.65	1.14	1.74	1.07	1.83
31	1.36	1.50	1.30	1.57	1.23	1.65	1.16	1.74	1.09	1.83
32	1.37	1.50	1.31	1.57	1.24	1.65	1.18	1.73	1.11	1.82
33	1.38	1.51	1.32	1.58	1.26	1.65	1.19	1.73	1.13	1.81
34	1.39	1.51	1.33	1.58	1.27	1.65	1.21	1.73	1.15	1.81
35	1.40	1.52	1.34	1.58	1.28	1.65	1.22	1.73	1.16	1.80
36	1.41	1.52	1.35	1.59	1.29	1.65	1.24	1.73	1.18	1.80
37	1.42	1.53	1.36	1.59	1.31	1.66	1.25	1.72	1.19	1.80
38	1.43	1.54	1.37	1.59	1.32	1.66	1.26	1.72	1.21	1.79
39	1.43	1.54	1.38	1.60	1.33	1.66	1.27	1.72	1.22	1.79
40	1.44	1.54	1.39	1.60	1.34	1.66	1.29	1.72	1.23	1.79
45	1.48	1.57	1.43	1.62	1.38	1.67	1.34	1.72	1.29	1.78
50	1.50	1.59	1.46	1.63	1.42	1.67	1.38	1.72	1.34	1.77
55	1.53	1.60	1.49	1.64	1.45	1.68	1.41	1.72	1.38	1.77
60	1.55	1.62	1.51	1.65	1.48	1.69	1.44	1.73	1.41	1.77
65	1.57	1.63	1.54	1.66	1.50	1.70	1.47	1.73	1.44	1.77
70	1.58	1.64	1.55	1.67	1.52	1.70	1.49	1.74	1.46	1.77
75	1.60	1.65	1.57	1.68	1.54	1.71	1.51	1.74	1.49	1.77
80	1.61	1.66	1.59	1.69	1.56	1.72	1.53	1.74	1.51	1.77
85	1.62	1.67	1.60	1.70	1.57	1.72	1.55	1.75	1.52	1.77
90	1.63	1.68	1.61	1.70	1.59	1.73	1.57	1.75	1.54	1.78
95	1.64	1.69	1.62	1.71	1.60	1.73	1.58	1.75	1.56	1.78
100	1.65	1.69	1.63	1.72	1.61	1.74	1.59	1.76	1.57	1.78

Source: J. Durbin and G. S. Watson, "Testing for Serial Correlation in Least Squares Regression, II," *Biometrika* 30 (1951), pp. 159–78. Reproduced by permission of the Biometrika Trustees.

TABLE A.11 Critical Values for the Durbin–Watson d Statistic ($\alpha = .025$)

	$k = 1$		$k = 2$		$k = 3$		$k = 4$		$k = 5$	
n	$d_{L,.025}$	$d_{U,.025}$	$d_{L,.025}$	$d_{U,.025}$	$d_{L,.025}$	$d_{U,.025}$	$d_{L,.025}$	$d_{U,.025}$	$d_{L,.025}$	$d_{U,.025}$
15	0.95	1.23	0.83	1.40	0.71	1.61	0.59	1.84	0.48	2.09
16	0.98	1.24	0.86	1.40	0.75	1.59	0.64	1.80	0.53	2.03
17	1.01	1.25	0.90	1.40	0.79	1.58	0.68	1.77	0.57	1.98
18	1.03	1.26	0.93	1.40	0.82	1.56	0.72	1.74	0.62	1.93
19	1.06	1.28	0.96	1.41	0.86	1.55	0.76	1.72	0.66	1.90
20	1.08	1.28	0.99	1.41	0.89	1.55	0.79	1.70	0.70	1.87
21	1.10	1.30	1.01	1.41	0.92	1.54	0.83	1.69	0.73	1.84
22	1.12	1.31	1.04	1.42	0.95	1.54	0.86	1.68	0.77	1.82
23	1.14	1.32	1.06	1.42	0.97	1.54	0.89	1.67	0.80	1.80
24	1.16	1.33	1.08	1.43	1.00	1.54	0.91	1.66	0.83	1.79
25	1.18	1.34	1.10	1.43	1.02	1.54	0.94	1.65	0.86	1.77
26	1.19	1.35	1.12	1.44	1.04	1.54	0.96	1.65	0.88	1.76
27	1.21	1.36	1.13	1.44	1.06	1.54	0.99	1.64	0.91	1.75
28	1.22	1.37	1.15	1.45	1.08	1.54	1.01	1.64	0.93	1.74
29	1.24	1.38	1.17	1.45	1.10	1.54	1.03	1.63	0.96	1.73
30	1.25	1.38	1.18	1.46	1.12	1.54	1.05	1.63	0.98	1.73
31	1.26	1.39	1.20	1.47	1.13	1.55	1.07	1.63	1.00	1.72
32	1.27	1.40	1.21	1.47	1.15	1.55	1.08	1.63	1.02	1.71
33	1.28	1.41	1.22	1.48	1.16	1.55	1.10	1.63	1.04	1.71
34	1.29	1.41	1.24	1.48	1.17	1.55	1.12	1.63	1.06	1.70
35	1.30	1.42	1.25	1.48	1.19	1.55	1.13	1.63	1.07	1.70
36	1.31	1.43	1.26	1.49	1.20	1.56	1.15	1.63	1.09	1.70
37	1.32	1.43	1.27	1.49	1.21	1.56	1.16	1.62	1.10	1.70
38	1.33	1.44	1.28	1.50	1.23	1.56	1.17	1.62	1.12	1.70
39	1.34	1.44	1.29	1.50	1.24	1.56	1.19	1.63	1.13	1.69
40	1.35	1.45	1.30	1.51	1.25	1.57	1.20	1.63	1.15	1.69
45	1.39	1.48	1.34	1.53	1.30	1.58	1.25	1.63	1.21	1.69
50	1.42	1.50	1.38	1.54	1.34	1.59	1.30	1.64	1.26	1.69
55	1.45	1.52	1.41	1.56	1.37	1.60	1.33	1.64	1.30	1.69
60	1.47	1.54	1.44	1.57	1.40	1.61	1.37	1.65	1.33	1.69
65	1.49	1.55	1.46	1.59	1.43	1.62	1.40	1.66	1.36	1.69
70	1.51	1.57	1.48	1.60	1.45	1.63	1.42	1.66	1.39	1.70
75	1.53	1.58	1.50	1.61	1.47	1.64	1.45	1.67	1.42	1.70
80	1.54	1.59	1.52	1.62	1.49	1.65	1.47	1.67	1.44	1.70
85	1.56	1.60	1.53	1.63	1.51	1.65	1.49	1.68	1.46	1.71
90	1.57	1.61	1.55	1.64	1.53	1.66	1.50	1.69	1.48	1.71
95	1.58	1.62	1.56	1.65	1.54	1.67	1.52	1.69	1.50	1.71
100	1.59	1.63	1.57	1.65	1.55	1.67	1.53	1.70	1.51	1.72

Source: J. Durbin and G. S. Watson, "Testing for Serial Correlation in Least Squares Regression, II," *Biometrika* 30 (1951), pp. 159–78. Reproduced by permission of the Biometrika Trustees.

TABLE A.12 Critical Values for the Durbin–Watson *d* Statistic ($\alpha = .01$)

	$k = 1$		$k = 2$		$k = 3$		$k = 4$		$k = 5$	
n	$d_{L,.01}$	$d_{U,.01}$	$d_{L,.01}$	$d_{U,.01}$	$d_{L,.01}$	$d_{U,.01}$	$d_{L,.01}$	$d_{U,.01}$	$d_{L,.01}$	$d_{U,.01}$
15	0.81	1.07	0.70	1.25	0.59	1.46	0.49	1.70	0.39	1.96
16	0.84	1.09	0.74	1.25	0.63	1.44	0.53	1.66	0.44	1.90
17	0.87	1.10	0.77	1.25	0.67	1.43	0.57	1.63	0.48	1.85
18	0.90	1.12	0.80	1.26	0.71	1.42	0.61	1.60	0.52	1.80
19	0.93	1.13	0.83	1.26	0.74	1.41	0.65	1.58	0.56	1.77
20	0.95	1.15	0.86	1.27	0.77	1.41	0.68	1.57	0.60	1.74
21	0.97	1.16	0.89	1.27	0.80	1.41	0.72	1.55	0.63	1.71
22	1.00	1.17	0.91	1.28	0.83	1.40	0.75	1.54	0.66	1.69
23	1.02	1.19	0.94	1.29	0.86	1.40	0.77	1.53	0.70	1.67
24	1.04	1.20	0.96	1.30	0.88	1.41	0.80	1.53	0.72	1.66
25	1.05	1.21	0.98	1.30	0.90	1.41	0.83	1.52	0.75	1.65
26	1.07	1.22	1.00	1.31	0.93	1.41	0.85	1.52	0.78	1.64
27	1.09	1.23	1.02	1.32	0.95	1.41	0.88	1.51	0.81	1.63
28	1.10	1.24	1.04	1.32	0.97	1.41	0.90	1.51	0.83	1.62
29	1.12	1.25	1.05	1.33	0.99	1.42	0.92	1.51	0.85	1.61
30	1.13	1.26	1.07	1.34	1.01	1.42	0.94	1.51	0.88	1.61
31	1.15	1.27	1.08	1.34	1.02	1.42	0.96	1.51	0.90	1.60
32	1.16	1.28	1.10	1.35	1.04	1.43	0.98	1.51	0.92	1.60
33	1.17	1.29	1.11	1.36	1.05	1.43	1.00	1.51	0.94	1.59
34	1.18	1.30	1.13	1.36	1.07	1.43	1.01	1.51	0.95	1.59
35	1.19	1.31	1.14	1.37	1.08	1.44	1.03	1.51	0.97	1.59
36	1.21	1.32	1.15	1.38	1.10	1.44	1.04	1.51	0.99	1.59
37	1.22	1.32	1.16	1.38	1.11	1.45	1.06	1.51	1.00	1.59
38	1.23	1.33	1.18	1.39	1.12	1.45	1.07	1.52	1.02	1.58
39	1.24	1.34	1.19	1.39	1.14	1.45	1.09	1.52	1.03	1.58
40	1.25	1.34	1.20	1.40	1.15	1.46	1.10	1.52	1.05	1.58
45	1.29	1.38	1.24	1.42	1.20	1.48	1.16	1.53	1.11	1.58
50	1.32	1.40	1.28	1.45	1.24	1.49	1.20	1.54	1.16	1.59
55	1.36	1.43	1.32	1.47	1.28	1.51	1.25	1.55	1.21	1.59
60	1.38	1.45	1.35	1.48	1.32	1.52	1.28	1.56	1.25	1.60
65	1.41	1.47	1.38	1.50	1.35	1.53	1.31	1.57	1.28	1.61
70	1.43	1.49	1.40	1.52	1.37	1.55	1.34	1.58	1.31	1.61
75	1.45	1.50	1.42	1.53	1.39	1.56	1.37	1.59	1.34	1.62
80	1.47	1.52	1.44	1.54	1.42	1.57	1.39	1.60	1.36	1.62
85	1.48	1.53	1.46	1.55	1.43	1.58	1.41	1.60	1.39	1.63
90	1.50	1.54	1.47	1.56	1.45	1.59	1.43	1.61	1.41	1.64
95	1.51	1.55	1.49	1.57	1.47	1.60	1.45	1.62	1.42	1.64
100	1.52	1.56	1.50	1.58	1.48	1.60	1.46	1.63	1.44	1.65

Source: J. Durbin and G. S. Watson, "Testing for Serial Correlation in Least Squares Regression, II," *Biometrika* 30 (1951), pp. 159–78. Reproduced by permission of the Biometrika Trustees.

TABLE A.13 Control Chart Constants for $\bar{x}$ and *R* Charts

	Chart for Averages ($\bar{x}$)	Chart for Ranges (*R*)		
Subgroup Size n	Factor for Control Limits A_2	Divisor for Estimate of Standard Deviation d_2	Factors for Control Limits D_3	D_4
2	1.880	1.128	—	3.267
3	1.023	1.693	—	2.574
4	0.729	2.059	—	2.282
5	0.577	2.326	—	2.114
6	0.483	2.534	—	2.004
7	0.419	2.704	0.076	1.924
8	0.373	2.847	0.136	1.864
9	0.337	2.970	0.184	1.816
10	0.308	3.078	0.223	1.777
11	0.285	3.173	0.256	1.744
12	0.266	3.258	0.283	1.717
13	0.249	3.336	0.307	1.693
14	0.235	3.407	0.328	1.672
15	0.223	3.472	0.347	1.653
16	0.212	3.532	0.363	1.637
17	0.203	3.588	0.378	1.622
18	0.194	3.640	0.391	1.608
19	0.187	3.689	0.403	1.597
20	0.180	3.735	0.415	1.585
21	0.173	3.778	0.425	1.575
22	0.167	3.819	0.434	1.566
23	0.162	3.858	0.443	1.557
24	0.157	3.895	0.451	1.548
25	0.153	3.931	0.459	1.541

Table A.14 Control Chart Constants for x (Individuals) and Moving R Charts

Size of Moving R	Chart for Individuals (x) E_2	Chart for Moving Ranges (MR) D_3	D_4
2	2.660	—	3.267
3	1.772	—	2.574
4	1.457	—	2.282
5	1.290	—	2.114
6	1.184	—	2.004
7	1.109	0.076	1.924
8	1.054	0.136	1.864
9	1.010	0.184	1.816
10	0.975	0.223	1.777

Table A.15 A Wilcoxon Rank Sum Table: Values of T_L and T_U

(a) $\alpha = .025$ One-Sided; $\alpha = .05$ Two-Sided

n_2 \ n_1	3		4		5		6		7		8		9		10	
	T_L	T_U	T_L	T_U	T_L	T_U	T_L	T_U	T_L	T_U	T_L	T_U	T_L	T_U	T_L	T_U
3	5	16	6	18	6	21	7	23	7	26	8	28	8	31	9	33
4	6	18	11	25	12	28	12	32	13	35	14	38	15	41	16	44
5	6	21	12	28	18	37	19	41	20	45	21	49	22	53	24	56
6	7	23	12	32	19	41	26	52	28	56	29	61	31	65	32	70
7	7	26	13	35	20	45	28	56	37	68	39	73	41	78	43	83
8	8	28	14	38	21	49	29	61	39	73	49	87	51	93	54	98
9	8	31	15	41	22	53	31	65	41	78	51	93	63	108	66	114
10	9	33	16	44	24	56	32	70	43	83	54	98	66	114	79	131

(b) $\alpha = .05$ One-Sided; $\alpha = .10$ Two-Sided

n_2 \ n_1	3		4		5		6		7		8		9		10	
	T_L	T_U	T_L	T_U	T_L	T_U	T_L	T_U	T_L	T_U	T_L	T_U	T_L	T_U	T_L	T_U
3	6	15	7	17	7	20	8	22	9	24	9	27	10	29	11	31
4	7	17	12	24	13	27	14	30	15	33	16	36	17	39	18	42
5	7	20	13	27	19	36	20	40	22	43	24	46	25	50	26	54
6	8	22	14	30	20	40	28	50	30	54	32	58	33	63	35	67
7	9	24	15	33	22	43	30	54	39	66	41	71	43	76	46	80
8	9	27	16	36	24	46	32	58	41	71	52	84	54	90	57	95
9	10	29	17	39	25	50	33	63	43	76	54	90	66	105	69	111
10	11	31	18	42	26	54	35	67	46	80	57	95	69	111	83	127

Source: F. Wilcoxon and R. A. Wilcox, "Some Rapid Approximate Statistical Procedures" (New York: American Cyanamid Company, 1964), pp. 20–23. Reproduced with the permission of American Cyanamid Company.

TABLE A.16 A Wilcoxon Signed Ranks Table: Values of T_0

One-Sided	Two-Sided	$n = 5$	$n = 6$	$n = 7$	$n = 8$	$n = 9$	$n = 10$
$\alpha = .05$	$\alpha = .10$	1	2	4	6	8	11
$\alpha = .025$	$\alpha = .05$		1	2	4	6	8
$\alpha = .01$	$\alpha = .02$			0	2	3	5
$\alpha = .005$	$\alpha = .01$				0	2	3
		$n = 11$	$n = 12$	$n = 13$	$n = 14$	$n = 15$	$n = 16$
$\alpha = .05$	$\alpha = .10$	14	17	21	26	30	36
$\alpha = .025$	$\alpha = .05$	11	14	17	21	25	30
$\alpha = .01$	$\alpha = .02$	7	10	13	16	20	24
$\alpha = .005$	$\alpha = .01$	5	7	10	13	16	19
		$n = 17$	$n = 18$	$n = 19$	$n = 20$	$n = 21$	$n = 22$
$\alpha = .05$	$\alpha = .10$	41	47	54	60	68	75
$\alpha = .025$	$\alpha = .05$	35	40	46	52	59	66
$\alpha = .01$	$\alpha = .02$	28	33	38	43	49	56
$\alpha = .005$	$\alpha = .01$	23	28	32	37	43	49
		$n = 23$	$n = 24$	$n = 25$	$n = 26$	$n = 27$	$n = 28$
$\alpha = .05$	$\alpha = .10$	83	92	101	110	120	130
$\alpha = .025$	$\alpha = .05$	73	81	90	98	107	117
$\alpha = .01$	$\alpha = .02$	62	69	77	85	93	102
$\alpha = .005$	$\alpha = .01$	55	61	68	76	84	92
		$n = 29$	$n = 30$	$n = 31$	$n = 32$	$n = 33$	$n = 34$
$\alpha = .05$	$\alpha = .10$	141	152	163	175	188	201
$\alpha = .025$	$\alpha = .05$	127	137	148	159	171	183
$\alpha = .01$	$\alpha = .02$	111	120	130	141	151	162
$\alpha = .005$	$\alpha = .01$	100	109	118	128	138	149
		$n = 35$	$n = 36$	$n = 37$	$n = 38$	$n = 39$	
$\alpha = .05$	$\alpha = .10$	214	228	242	256	271	
$\alpha = .025$	$\alpha = .05$	195	208	222	235	250	
$\alpha = .01$	$\alpha = .02$	174	186	198	211	224	
$\alpha = .005$	$\alpha = .01$	160	171	183	195	208	
		$n = 40$	$n = 41$	$n = 42$	$n = 43$	$n = 44$	$n = 45$
$\alpha = .05$	$\alpha = .10$	287	303	319	336	353	371
$\alpha = .025$	$\alpha = .05$	264	279	295	311	327	344
$\alpha = .01$	$\alpha = .02$	238	252	267	281	297	313
$\alpha = .005$	$\alpha = .01$	221	234	248	262	277	292
		$n = 46$	$n = 47$	$n = 48$	$n = 49$	$n = 50$	
$\alpha = .05$	$\alpha = .10$	389	408	427	446	466	
$\alpha = .025$	$\alpha = .05$	361	379	397	415	434	
$\alpha = .01$	$\alpha = .02$	329	345	362	380	398	
$\alpha = .005$	$\alpha = .01$	307	323	339	356	373	

Source: F. Wilcoxon and R. A. Wilcox, "Some Rapid Approximate Statistical Procedures" (New York: American Cyanamid Company, 1964), p. 28. Reproduced with the permission of American Cyanamid Company.

TABLE A.17 A Chi-Square Table: Values of χ^2_α

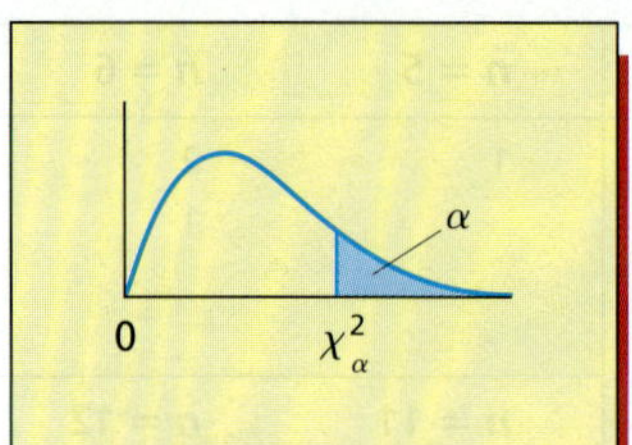

df	$\chi^2_{.995}$	$\chi^2_{.99}$	$\chi^2_{.975}$	$\chi^2_{.95}$	$\chi^2_{.90}$
1	.0000393	.0001571	.0009821	.0039321	.0157908
2	.0100251	.0201007	.0506356	.102587	.210720
3	.0717212	.114832	.215795	.341846	.584375
4	.206990	.297110	.484419	.710721	.063623
5	.411740	.554300	.831211	1.145476	1.61031
6	.675727	.872085	1.237347	1.63539	2.20413
7	.989265	1.239043	1.68987	2.16735	2.83311
8	1.344419	1.646482	2.17973	2.73264	3.48954
9	1.734926	2.087912	2.70039	3.32511	4.16816
10	2.15585	2.55821	3.24697	3.94030	4.86518
11	2.60321	3.05347	3.81575	4.57481	5.57779
12	3.07382	3.57056	4.40379	5.22603	6.30380
13	3.56503	4.10691	5.00874	5.89186	7.04150
14	4.07468	4.66043	5.62872	6.57063	7.78953
15	4.60094	5.22935	6.26214	7.26094	8.54675
16	5.14224	5.81221	6.90766	7.96164	9.31223
17	5.69724	6.40776	7.56418	8.67176	10.0852
18	6.26481	7.01491	8.23075	9.39046	10.8649
19	6.84398	7.63273	8.90655	10.1170	11.6509
20	7.43386	8.26040	9.59083	10.8508	12.4426
21	8.03366	8.89720	10.28293	11.5913	13.2396
22	8.64272	9.54249	10.9823	12.3380	14.0415
23	9.26042	10.19567	11.6885	13.0905	14.8479
24	9.88623	10.8564	12.4011	13.8484	15.6587
25	10.5197	11.5240	13.1197	14.6114	16.4734
26	11.1603	12.1981	13.8439	15.3791	17.2919
27	11.8076	12.8786	14.5733	16.1513	18.1138
28	12.4613	13.5648	15.3079	16.9279	18.9392
29	13.1211	14.2565	16.0471	17.7083	19.7677
30	13.7867	14.9535	16.7908	18.4926	20.5992
40	20.7065	22.1643	24.4331	26.5093	29.0505
50	27.9907	29.7067	32.3574	34.7642	37.6886
60	35.5346	37.4848	40.4817	43.1879	46.4589
70	43.2752	45.4418	48.7576	51.7393	55.3290
80	51.1720	53.5400	57.1532	60.3915	64.2778
90	59.1963	61.7541	65.6466	69.1260	73.2912
100	67.3276	70.0648	74.2219	77.9295	82.3581

(table continued)

TABLE A.17 A Chi-Square Table: Values of χ^2_α *(concluded)*

df	$\chi^2_{.10}$	$\chi^2_{.05}$	$\chi^2_{.025}$	$\chi^2_{.01}$	$\chi^2_{.005}$
1	2.70554	3.84146	5.02389	6.63490	7.87944
2	4.60517	5.99147	7.37776	9.21034	10.5966
3	6.25139	7.81473	9.34840	11.3449	12.8381
4	7.77944	9.48773	11.1433	13.2767	14.8602
5	9.23635	11.0705	12.8325	15.0863	16.7496
6	10.6446	12.5916	14.4494	16.8119	18.5476
7	12.0170	14.0671	16.0128	18.4753	20.2777
8	13.3616	15.5073	17.5346	20.0902	21.9550
9	14.6837	16.9190	19.0228	21.6660	23.5893
10	15.9871	18.3070	20.4831	23.2093	25.1882
11	17.2750	19.6751	21.9200	24.7250	26.7569
12	18.5494	21.0261	23.3367	26.2170	28.2995
13	19.8119	22.3621	24.7356	27.6883	29.8194
14	21.0642	23.6848	26.1190	29.1413	31.3193
15	22.3072	24.9958	27.4884	30.5779	32.8013
16	23.5418	26.2962	28.8454	31.9999	34.2672
17	24.7690	27.5871	30.1910	33.4087	35.7185
18	25.9894	28.8693	31.5264	34.8053	37.1564
19	27.2036	30.1435	32.8523	36.1908	38.5822
20	28.4120	31.4104	34.1696	37.5662	39.9968
21	29.6151	32.6705	35.4789	38.9321	41.4010
22	30.8133	33.9244	36.7807	40.2894	42.7956
23	32.0069	35.1725	38.0757	41.6384	44.1813
24	33.1963	36.4151	39.3641	42.9798	45.5585
25	34.3816	37.6525	40.6465	44.3141	46.9278
26	35.5631	38.8852	41.9232	45.6417	48.2899
27	36.7412	40.1133	43.1944	46.9630	49.6449
28	37.9159	41.3372	44.4607	48.2782	50.9933
29	39.0875	42.5569	45.7222	49.5879	52.3356
30	40.2560	43.7729	46.9792	50.8922	53.6720
40	51.8050	55.7585	59.3417	63.6907	66.7659
50	63.1671	67.5048	71.4202	76.1539	79.4900
60	74.3970	79.0819	83.2976	88.3794	91.9517
70	85.5271	90.5312	95.0231	100.425	104.215
80	96.5782	101.879	106.629	112.329	116.321
90	107.565	113.145	118.136	124.116	128.299
100	118.498	124.342	129.561	135.807	140.169

Source: C. M. Thompson, "Tables of the Percentage Points of the χ^2 Distribution," *Biometrika* 32 (1941), pp. 188–89. Reproduced by permission of the Biometrika Trustees.

TABLE A.18 Critical Values for Spearman's Rank Correlation Coefficient

n	$\alpha = .05$	$\alpha = .025$	$\alpha = .01$	$\alpha = .005$	*n*	$\alpha = .05$	$\alpha = .025$	$\alpha = .01$	$\alpha = .005$
5	.900	—	—	—	18	.399	.476	.564	.625
6	.829	.886	.943	—	19	.388	.462	.549	.608
7	.714	.786	.893	—	20	.377	.450	.534	.591
8	.643	.738	.833	.881	21	.368	.438	.521	.576
9	.600	.683	.783	.833	22	.359	.428	.508	.562
10	.564	.648	.745	.794	23	.351	.418	.496	.549
11	.523	.623	.736	.818	24	.343	.409	.485	.537
12	.497	.591	.703	.780	25	.336	.400	.475	.526
13	.475	.566	.673	.745	26	.329	.392	.465	.515
14	.457	.545	.646	.716	27	.323	.385	.456	.505
15	.441	.525	.623	.689	28	.317	.377	.448	.496
16	.425	.507	.601	.666	29	.311	.370	.440	.487
17	.412	.490	.582	.645	30	.305	.364	.432	.478

Source: E. G. Olds, "Distribution of Sums of Squares of Rank Differences for Small Samples," *Annals of Mathematical Statistics,* 1938, 9. Reproduced with the permission of the editor, *Annals of Mathematical Statistics.*

TABLE A.19 Cumulative Areas under the Standard Normal Curve

z	.00	.01	.02	.03	.04	.05	.06	.07	.08	.09
−3.4	.0003	.0003	.0003	.0003	.0003	.0003	.0003	.0003	.0003	.0002
−3.3	.0005	.0005	.0005	.0004	.0004	.0004	.0004	.0004	.0004	.0003
−3.2	.0007	.0007	.0006	.0006	.0006	.0006	.0006	.0005	.0005	.0005
−3.1	.0010	.0009	.0009	.0009	.0008	.0008	.0008	.0008	.0007	.0007
−3.0	.0013	.0013	.0013	.0012	.0012	.0011	.0011	.0011	.0010	.0010
−2.9	.0019	.0018	.0018	.0017	.0016	.0016	.0015	.0015	.0014	.0014
−2.8	.0026	.0025	.0024	.0023	.0023	.0022	.0021	.0021	.0020	.0019
−2.7	.0035	.0034	.0033	.0032	.0031	.0030	.0029	.0028	.0027	.0026
−2.6	.0047	.0045	.0044	.0043	.0041	.0040	.0039	.0038	.0037	.0036
−2.5	.0062	.0060	.0059	.0057	.0055	.0054	.0052	.0051	.0049	.0048
−2.4	.0082	.0080	.0078	.0075	.0073	.0071	.0069	.0068	.0066	.0064
−2.3	.0107	.0104	.0102	.0099	.0096	.0094	.0091	.0089	.0087	.0084
−2.2	.0139	.0136	.0132	.0129	.0125	.0122	.0119	.0116	.0113	.0110
−2.1	.0179	.0174	.0170	.0166	.0162	.0158	.0154	.0150	.0146	.0143
−2.0	.0228	.0222	.0217	.0212	.0207	.0202	.0197	.0192	.0188	.0183
−1.9	.0287	.0281	.0274	.0268	.0262	.0256	.0250	.0244	.0239	.0233
−1.8	.0359	.0351	.0344	.0336	.0329	.0322	.0314	.0307	.0301	.0294
−1.7	.0446	.0436	.0427	.0418	.0409	.0401	.0392	.0384	.0375	.0367
−1.6	.0548	.0537	.0526	.0516	.0505	.0495	.0485	.0475	.0465	.0455
−1.5	.0668	.0655	.0643	.0630	.0618	.0606	.0594	.0582	.0571	.0559
−1.4	.0808	.0793	.0778	.0764	.0749	.0735	.0721	.0708	.0694	.0681
−1.3	.0968	.0951	.0934	.0918	.0901	.0885	.0869	.0853	.0838	.0823
−1.2	.1151	.1131	.1112	.1093	.1075	.1056	.1038	.1020	.1003	.0985
−1.1	.1357	.1335	.1314	.1292	.1271	.1251	.1230	.1210	.1190	.1170
−1.0	.1587	.1562	.1539	.1515	.1492	.1469	.1446	.1423	.1401	.1379
−0.9	.1841	.1814	.1788	.1762	.1736	.1711	.1685	.1660	.1635	.1611
−0.8	.2119	.2090	.2061	.2033	.2005	.1977	.1949	.1922	.1894	.1867
−0.7	.2420	.2389	.2358	.2327	.2296	.2266	.2236	.2206	.2177	.2148
−0.6	.2743	.2709	.2676	.2643	.2611	.2578	.2546	.2514	.2483	.2451
−0.5	.3085	.3050	.3015	.2981	.2946	.2912	.2877	.2843	.2810	.2776
−0.4	.3446	.3409	.3372	.3336	.3300	.3264	.3228	.3192	.3156	.3121
−0.3	.3821	.3783	.3745	.3707	.3669	.3632	.3594	.3557	.3520	.3483
−0.2	.4207	.4168	.4129	.4090	.4052	.4013	.3974	.3936	.3897	.3859
−0.1	.4602	.4562	.4522	.4483	.4443	.4404	.4364	.4325	.4286	.4247
−0.0	.5000	.4960	.4920	.4880	.4840	.4801	.4761	.4721	.4681	.4641
0.0	.5000	.5040	.5080	.5120	.5160	.5199	.5239	.5279	.5319	.5359
0.1	.5398	.5438	.5478	.5517	.5557	.5596	.5636	.5675	.5714	.5753
0.2	.5793	.5832	.5871	.5910	.5948	.5987	.6026	.6064	.6103	.6141
0.3	.6179	.6217	.6255	.6293	.6331	.6368	.6406	.6443	.6480	.6517
0.4	.6554	.6591	.6628	.6664	.6700	.6736	.6772	.6808	.6844	.6879
0.5	.6915	.6950	.6985	.7019	.7054	.7088	.7123	.7157	.7190	.7224
0.6	.7257	.7291	.7324	.7357	.7389	.7422	.7454	.7486	.7517	.7549
0.7	.7580	.7611	.7642	.7673	.7704	.7734	.7764	.7794	.7823	.7852
0.8	.7881	.7910	.7939	.7967	.7995	.8023	.8051	.8078	.8106	.8133
0.9	.8159	.8186	.8212	.8238	.8264	.8289	.8315	.8340	.8365	.8389
1.0	.8413	.8438	.8461	.8485	.8508	.8531	.8554	.8577	.8599	.8621
1.1	.8643	.8665	.8686	.8708	.8729	.8749	.8770	.8790	.8810	.8830
1.2	.8849	.8869	.8888	.8907	.8925	.8944	.8962	.8980	.8997	.9015
1.3	.9032	.9049	.9066	.9082	.9099	.9115	.9131	.9147	.9162	.9177
1.4	.9192	.9207	.9222	.9236	.9251	.9265	.9279	.9292	.9306	.9319
1.5	.9332	.9345	.9357	.9370	.9382	.9394	.9406	.9418	.9429	.9441
1.6	.9452	.9463	.9474	.9484	.9495	.9505	.9515	.9525	.9535	.9545
1.7	.9554	.9564	.9573	.9582	.9591	.9599	.9608	.9616	.9625	.9633
1.8	.9641	.9649	.9656	.9664	.9671	.9678	.9686	.9693	.9699	.9706
1.9	.9713	.9719	.9726	.9732	.9738	.9744	.9750	.9756	.9761	.9767
2.0	.9772	.9778	.9783	.9788	.9793	.9798	.9803	.9808	.9812	.9817
2.1	.9821	.9826	.9830	.9834	.9838	.9842	.9846	.9850	.9854	.9857
2.2	.9861	.9864	.9868	.9871	.9875	.9878	.9881	.9884	.9887	.9890
2.3	.9893	.9896	.9898	.9901	.9904	.9906	.9909	.9911	.9913	.9916
2.4	.9918	.9920	.9922	.9925	.9927	.9929	.9931	.9932	.9934	.9936
2.5	.9938	.9940	.9941	.9943	.9945	.9946	.9948	.9949	.9951	.9952
2.6	.9953	.9955	.9956	.9957	.9959	.9960	.9961	.9962	.9963	.9964
2.7	.9965	.9966	.9967	.9968	.9969	.9970	.9971	.9972	.9973	.9974
2.8	.9974	.9975	.9976	.9977	.9977	.9978	.9979	.9979	.9980	.9981
2.9	.9981	.9982	.9982	.9983	.9984	.9984	.9985	.9985	.9986	.9986
3.0	.9987	.9987	.9987	.9988	.9988	.9989	.9989	.9989	.9990	.9990
3.1	.9990	.9991	.9991	.9991	.9992	.9992	.9992	.9992	.9993	.9993
3.2	.9993	.9993	.9994	.9994	.9994	.9994	.9994	.9995	.9995	.9995
3.3	.9995	.9995	.9995	.9996	.9996	.9996	.9996	.9996	.9996	.9997
3.4	.9997	.9997	.9997	.9997	.9997	.9997	.9997	.9997	.9997	.9998

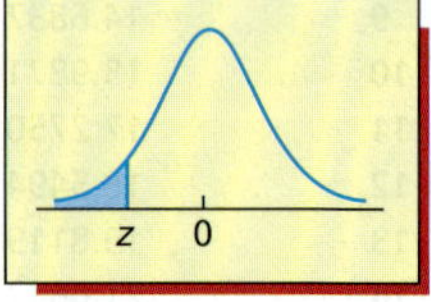

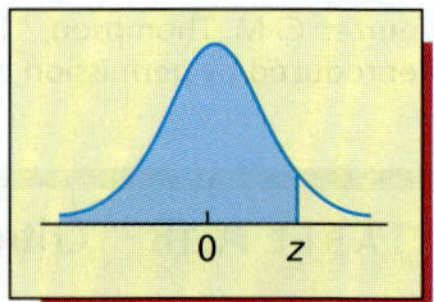

Appendix B: Covariance and Correlation

In Section 2.6 we discussed how to use a scatter plot to explore the relationship between a dependent variable y and an independent variable x. To construct a scatter plot, a sample of n pairs of values of x and y—$(x_1, y_1), (x_2, y_2), \ldots, (x_n, y_n)$—is collected. Then, each value of y is plotted against the corresponding value of x. If the plot points seem to fluctuate around a straight line, we say that there is a **linear relationship** between x and y. For example, suppose that 10 sales regions of equal sales potential for a company were randomly selected. The advertising expenditures (in units of \$10,000) in these 10 sales regions were purposely set in July of last year at the values given in the second column of Table B.1. The sales volumes (in units of \$10,000) were then recorded for the 10 sales regions and found to be as given in the third column of Table B.1. A scatter plot of sales volume, y, versus advertising expenditure, x, is given in Figure B.1 and shows a linear relationship between x and y.

A measure of the **strength of the linear relationship** between x and y is the **covariance.** The **sample covariance** is calculated by using the sample of n pairs of observed values and x and y. This sample covariance is denoted as s_{xy} and is defined as follows:

$$s_{xy} = \frac{\sum_{i=1}^{n} (x_i - \bar{x})(y_i - \bar{y})}{n - 1}$$

To use this formula, we first find the mean $\bar{x}$ of the n observed values of x and the mean $\bar{y}$ of the n observed values of y. For each observed (x_i, y_i) combination, we then multiply the deviation of x_i from $\bar{x}$ by the deviation of y_i from $\bar{y}$ to form the product $(x_i - \bar{x})(y_i - \bar{y})$. Finally we add together the n products $(x_1 - \bar{x})(y_1 - \bar{y}), (x_2 - \bar{x})(y_2 - \bar{y}), \ldots, (x_n - \bar{x})(y_n - \bar{y})$ and divide the resulting sum by $n - 1$. For example, the mean of the 10 advertising expenditures in Table B.1 is $\bar{x} = 9.5$, and the mean of the 10 sales volumes in Table B.1 is $\bar{y} = 108.3$. It follows that the numerator of s_{xy} is the sum of the values of $(x_i - \bar{x})(y_i - \bar{y}) = (x_i - 9.5)(y_i - 108.3)$. Table B.2 shows that this sum equals 365.50, which implies that the sample covariance is

$$s_{xy} = \frac{\sum (x_i - \bar{x})(y_i - \bar{y})}{n - 1} = \frac{365.50}{9} = 40.61111$$

To interpret the covariance, consider Figure B.2(a). This figure shows the scatter plot of Figure B.1 with a vertical blue line drawn at $\bar{x} = 9.5$ and a horizontal red line drawn at $\bar{y} = 108.3$. The lines divide the scatter plot into four quadrants. Points in quadrant I correspond to x_i greater than $\bar{x}$ and y_i greater than $\bar{y}$ and thus give a value of $(x_i - \bar{x})(y_i - \bar{y})$ greater than 0. Points in quadrant III correspond to x_i less than $\bar{x}$ and y_i less than $\bar{y}$ and thus also give a value of $(x_i - \bar{x})(y_i - \bar{y})$ greater than 0. It follows that if s_{xy} is positive, the points having the greatest influence on $\Sigma(x_i - \bar{x})(y_i - \bar{y})$ and thus on s_{xy} must be in quadrants I and III. Therefore, a positive value of s_{xy} (as in the sales volume example) indicates a positive linear relationship between x and y. That is, as x increases, y increases.

If we further consider Figure B.2, we see that points in quadrant II correspond to x_i less than $\bar{x}$ and y_i greater than $\bar{y}$ and thus give a value of $(x_i - \bar{x})(y_i - \bar{y})$ less than 0. Points in quadrant IV correspond to x_i greater than $\bar{x}$ and y_i less than $\bar{y}$ and thus also give a value of $(x_i - \bar{x})(y_i - \bar{y})$ less than 0. It follows that if s_{xy} is negative, the points having the greatest influence on $\Sigma(x_i - \bar{x})(y_i - \bar{y})$

TABLE B.1 The Sales Volume Data

Sales Region	Advertising Expenditure, x	Sales Volume, y
1	5	89
2	6	87
3	7	98
4	8	110
5	9	103
6	10	114
7	11	116
8	12	110
9	13	126
10	14	130

FIGURE B.1 A Scatter Plot of Sales Volume versus Advertising Expenditure

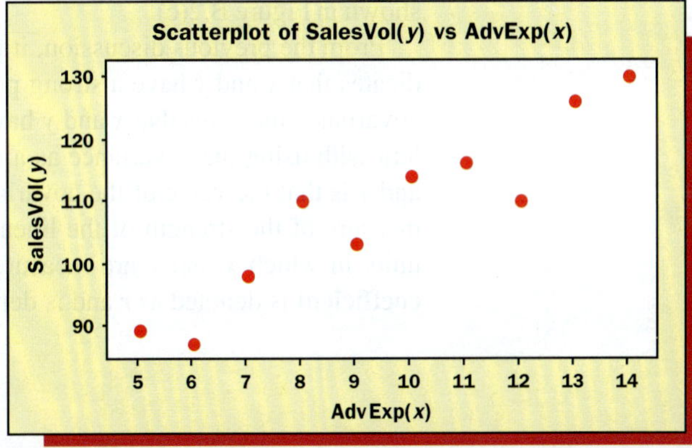

TABLE B.2 The Calculation of the Numerator of s_{xy}

	x_i	y_i	$(x_i - 9.5)$	$(y_i - 108.3)$	$(x_i - 9.5)(y_i - 108.3)$
	5	89	−4.5	−19.3	86.85
	6	87	−3.5	−21.3	74.55
	7	98	−2.5	−10.3	25.75
	8	110	−1.5	1.7	−2.55
	9	103	−0.5	−5.3	2.65
	10	114	0.5	5.7	2.85
	11	116	1.5	7.7	11.55
	12	110	2.5	1.7	4.25
	13	126	3.5	17.7	61.95
	14	130	4.5	21.7	97.65
Totals	95	1083	0	0	365.50

FIGURE B.2 Interpretation of the Sample Covariance

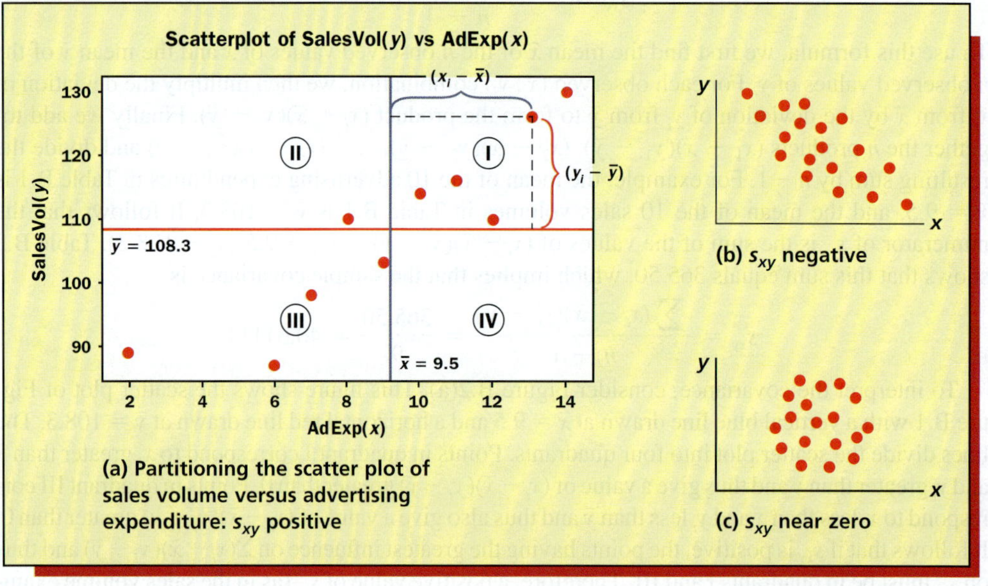

and thus on s_{xy} must be in quadrants II and IV. Therefore, a negative value of s_{xy} indicates a negative linear relationship between x and y. That is, as x increases, y decreases, as shown in Figure B.2(b). For example, a negative linear relationship might exist between average hourly outdoor temperature (x) in a city during a week and the city's natural gas consumption (y) during the week. That is, as the average hourly outdoor temperature increases, the city's natural gas consumption would decrease. Finally, note that if s_{xy} is near zero, the (x_i, y_i) points would be fairly evenly distributed across all four quadrants. This would indicate little or no linear relationship between x and y, as shown in Figure B.2(c).

From the previous discussion, it might seem that a large positive value for the covariance indicates that x and y have a strong positive linear relationship and a large negative value for the covariance indicates that x and y have a strong negative linear relationship. However, one problem with using the covariance as a measure of the strength of the linear relationship between x and y is that the value of the covariance depends on the units in which x and y are measured. A measure of the strength of the linear relationship between x and y that does not depend on the units in which x and y are measured is the **correlation coefficient.** The **sample correlation coefficient** is denoted as r and is defined as follows:

$$r = \frac{s_{xy}}{s_x s_y}$$

Here, s_{xy} is the previously defined sample covariance, s_x is the sample standard deviation of the sample of x values, and s_y is the sample standard deviation of the sample of y values. For the sales volume data,

$$s_x = \sqrt{\frac{\sum_{i=1}^{10} (x_i - \bar{x})^2}{9}} = 3.02765 \quad \text{and} \quad s_y = \sqrt{\frac{\sum_{i=1}^{10} (y_i - \bar{y})^2}{9}} = 14.30656$$

Therefore, the sample correlation coefficient is

$$r = \frac{s_{xy}}{s_x s_y} = \frac{40.61111}{(3.02765)(14.30656)} = .93757$$

It can be shown that the sample correlation coefficient r is always between -1 and 1. A value of r near 0 implies little linear relationship between x and y. A value of r close to 1 says that x and y have a strong tendency to move together in a straight-line fashion with a positive slope and, therefore, that x and y are highly related and **positively correlated.** A value of r close to -1 says that x and y have a strong tendency to move together in a straight-line fashion with a negative slope and, therefore, that x and y are highly related and **negatively correlated.** Note that if $r = 1$, the (x, y) points fall exactly on a positively sloped straight line, and, if $r = -1$, the (x, y) points fall exactly on a negatively sloped straight line. For example, since $r = .93757$ in the sales volume example, we conclude that advertising expenditure (x) and sales volume (y) have a strong tendency to move together in a straight line fashion with a positive slope. That is, x and y have a strong positive linear relationship. In general, however, note that a strong positive or a strong negative linear relationship between an independent variable x and a dependent variable y does not necessarily mean that we can accurately **predict** y on the basis of x. We consider predicting y on the basis of x in Chapter 11.

In conclusion, note that the sample covariance s_{xy} is the point estimate of the **population covariance,** which we denote as σ_{xy}, and the sample correlation coefficient r is the point estimate of the **population correlation coefficient,** which we denote as ρ. To define σ_{xy} and ρ, let μ_x and σ_x denote the mean and the standard deviation of the population of all possible x values, and let μ_y and σ_y denote the mean and the standard deviation of the population of all possible y values. Then, σ_{xy} is the average of all possible values of $(x - \mu_x)(y - \mu_y)$, and ρ equals $\sigma_{xy}/(\sigma_x\sigma_y)$. Similar to r, ρ is always between -1 and 1.

Exercises for Appendix B

B.1 Recall from Example 2.19 (page 94) that chemical XB-135 is used in the production of a chemical product, and chemists feel that the amount of chemical XB-135 may be related to the viscosity of the chemical product. Also, recall that to verify and quantify this relationship, 24 batches of the product are produced. The amount (x) of chemical XB-135 (in pounds) is varied from batch to batch, and the viscosity (y) obtained for each batch is measured. Table 2.11 (page 95) gives (in time order) the values of x and the corresponding values of y for the 24 batches. Using the facts that

$$\sum_{i=1}^{24} (x_i - \bar{x})(y_i - \bar{y}) = 10.2281 \qquad s_x = .7053 \qquad s_y = .6515$$

calculate the sample covariance s_{xy} and the sample correlation coefficient r. Interpret r. What can we say about the strength of the linear relationship between x and y?

B.2 The following table gives the average hourly outdoor temperature (x) in a city during a week and the city's natural gas consumption (y) during the week for each of the previous eight weeks (the temperature readings are expressed in degrees Fahrenheit and the natural gas consumptions are expressed in millions of cubic feet of natural gas):

Week	1	2	3	4	5	6	7	8
Temperature, x	28.0	28.0	32.5	39.0	45.9	57.8	58.1	62.5
Natural Gas Consumption, y	12.4	11.7	12.4	10.8	9.4	9.5	8.0	7.5

For these data, perform calculations to show that the sample correlation coefficient r equals $-.948$. Interpret r. What can we say about the strength of the linear relationship between x and y? Note: In Chapter 11 we use temperature to predict natural gas consumption.

Appendix C (Part 1): Counting Rules

Consider the situation in Example 3.3 (page 130) in which a student takes a pop quiz that consists of three true–false questions. If we consider our experiment to be answering the three questions, each question can be answered correctly or incorrectly. We will let *C* denote answering a question correctly and *I* denote answering a question incorrectly. Figure C.1 depicts a tree diagram of the sample space outcomes for the experiment. The diagram portrays the experiment as a three-step process—answering the first question (correctly or incorrectly, that is, *C* or *I*), answering the second question (correctly or incorrectly, that is, *C* or *I*), and answering the third question (correctly or incorrectly, that is, *C* or *I*). The tree diagram has eight different branches, and the eight distinct sample space outcomes are listed at the ends of the branches.

In general, a rule that is helpful in determining the number of experimental outcomes in a multiple-step experiment is as follows:

A Counting Rule for Multiple-Step Experiments

If an experiment can be described as a sequence of k steps in which there are n_1 possible outcomes on the first step, n_2 possible outcomes on the second step, and so on, then the total number of experimental outcomes is given by $(n_1)(n_2) \cdots (n_k)$.

For example, the pop quiz example consists of three steps in which there are $n_1 = 2$ possible outcomes on the first step, $n_2 = 2$ possible outcomes on the second step, and $n_3 = 2$ possible outcomes on the third step. Therefore, the total number of experimental outcomes is $(n_1)(n_2)(n_3) = (2)(2)(2) = 8$, as is shown in Figure C.1. Now suppose the student takes a pop quiz consisting of five true–false questions. Then, there are $(n_1)(n_2)(n_3)(n_4)(n_5) = (2)(2)(2)(2)(2) = 32$ experimental outcomes. If the student is totally unprepared for the quiz and has to blindly guess the answer

FIGURE C.1 A Tree Diagram of Answering Three True–False Questions

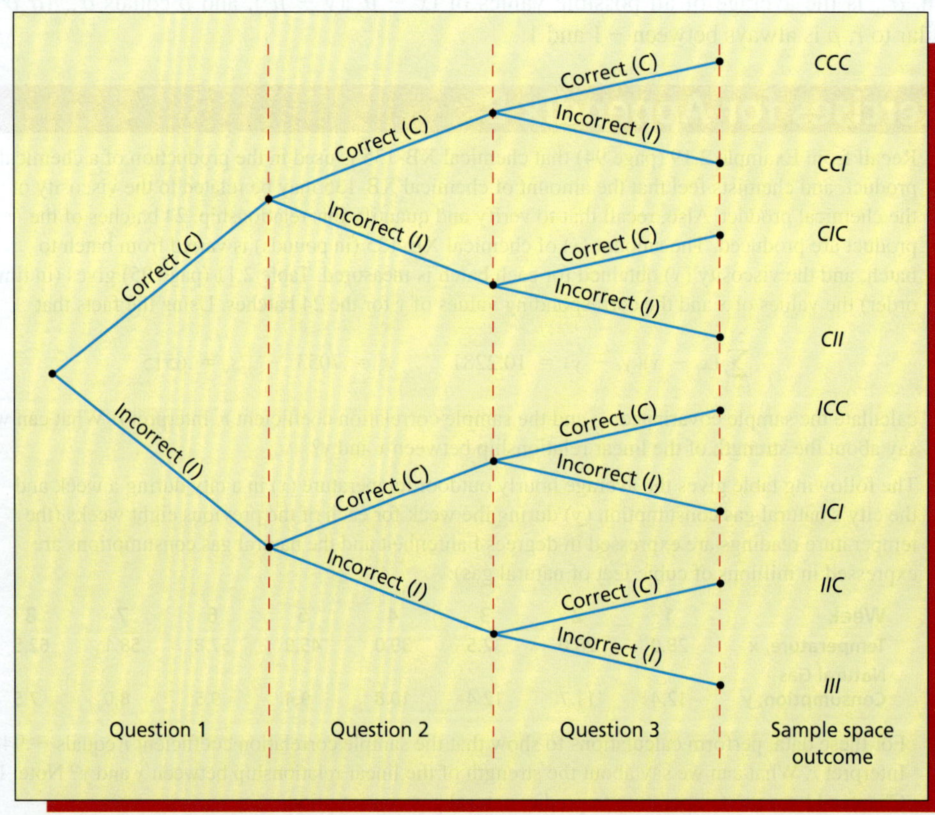

to each question, the 32 experimental outcomes might be considered to be equally likely. Therefore, since only one of these outcomes corresponds to all five questions being answered correctly, the probability that the student will answer all five questions correctly is 1/32.

As another example, suppose a bank has three branches; each branch has two departments, and each department has four employees. One employee is to be randomly selected to go to a convention. Since there are $(n_1)(n_2)(n_3) = (3)(2)(4) = 24$ employees, the probability that a particular one will be randomly selected is 1/24.

Next, consider the population of the percentage returns for last year of six high-risk stocks. This population consists of the percentage returns −36, −15, 3, 15, 33, and 54 (which we have arranged in increasing order). Now consider randomly selecting without replacement a sample of $n = 3$ stock returns from the population of six stock returns. Below we list the 20 distinct samples of $n = 3$ returns that can be obtained:

Sample	$n = 3$ Returns in Sample	Sample	$n = 3$ Returns in Sample
1	−36, −15, 3	11	−15, 3, 15
2	−36, −15, 15	12	−15, 3, 33
3	−36, −15, 33	13	−15, 3, 54
4	−36, −15, 54	14	−15, 15, 33
5	−36, 3, 15	15	−15, 15, 54
6	−36, 3, 33	16	−15, 33, 54
7	−36, 3, 54	17	3, 15, 33
8	−36, 15, 33	18	3, 15, 54
9	−36, 15, 54	19	3, 33, 54
10	−36, 33, 54	20	15, 33, 54

Since each sample is specified only with respect to what returns are contained in the sample, and therefore not with respect to the different orders in which the returns can be randomly selected, each sample is called a **combination of $n = 3$ stock returns selected from $N = 6$ stock returns.** In general, the following result can be proven:

A Counting Rule for Combinations

The number of combinations of n items that can be selected from N items is

$$\binom{N}{n} = \frac{N!}{n!\,(N-n)!}$$

where

$$N! = N(N-1)(N-2)\cdots 1$$

$$n! = n(n-1)(n-2)\cdots 1$$

Note: 0! is defined to be 1.

For example, the number of combinations of $n = 3$ stock returns that can be selected from the six previously discussed stock returns is

$$\binom{6}{3} = \frac{6!}{3!(6-3)!} = \frac{6!}{3!\,3!} = \frac{6\cdot 5\cdot 4\,\cancel{(3\cdot 2\cdot 1)}}{(3\cdot 2\cdot 1)\,\cancel{(3\cdot 2\cdot 1)}} = 20$$

The 20 combinations are listed above. As another example, the Ohio lottery system uses the random selection of 6 numbers from a group of 47 numbers to determine each week's lottery winner. There are

$$\binom{47}{6} = \frac{47!}{6!\,(47-6)!} = \frac{47\cdot 46\cdot 45\cdot 44\cdot 43\cdot 42\,\cancel{(41!)}}{6\cdot 5\cdot 4\cdot 3\cdot 2\cdot 1\,\cancel{(41!)}} = 10{,}737{,}573$$

combinations of 6 numbers that can be selected from 47 numbers. Therefore, if you buy a lottery ticket and pick six numbers, the probability that this ticket will win the lottery is 1/10,737,573.

Exercises for Appendix C (Part 1)

C.1 A credit union has two branches; each branch has two departments, and each department has four employees. How many total people does the credit union employ? If you work for the credit union, and one employee is randomly selected to go to a convention, what is the probability that you will be chosen?

C.2 How many combinations of two high-risk stocks could you randomly select from eight high-risk stocks? If you did this, what is the probability that you would obtain the two highest-returning stocks?

Appendix C (Part 2): The Hypergeometric Distribution

Suppose a population consists of N items (for example, stocks); r of these items are "successes" (for example, stocks with positive returns for a year), and $(N - r)$ of these items are "failures" (for example, stocks with zero or negative returns for the year). If we randomly select n of the N items without replacement, it can be shown that the probability that x of the n randomly selected items will be successes is given by the **hypergeometric distribution**

$$p(x) = \frac{\binom{r}{x}\binom{N-r}{n-x}}{\binom{N}{n}}$$

For example, recall from Appendix C (Part 1) that $N = 6$ high-risk stocks gave the following returns last year: -36, -15, 3, 15, 33, and 54. Note that $r = 4$ of these returns are positive, and $N - r = 2$ of these returns are negative. Suppose you randomly selected $n = 3$ of the six stocks to invest in at the beginning of last year, and let x denote the number of the three stocks that gave positive returns. It follows that the probability that x is at least 2 (that is, the probability that x is either 2 or 3) is

$$p(2) + p(3) = \frac{\binom{4}{2}\binom{2}{1}}{\binom{6}{3}} + \frac{\binom{4}{3}\binom{2}{0}}{\binom{6}{3}} = \frac{\left(\frac{4!}{2!\,2!}\right)\left(\frac{2!}{1!\,1!}\right)}{\frac{6!}{3!\,3!}} + \frac{\left(\frac{4!}{3!\,1!}\right)\left(\frac{2!}{0!\,2!}\right)}{\frac{6!}{3!\,3!}}$$

$$= \frac{(6)(2)}{20} + \frac{(4)(1)}{20} = .8$$

Note that, on the first random selection from the population of N items, the probability of a success is r/N. Since we are making selections **without replacement,** the probability of a success changes as we continue to make selections. However, if the population size N is "much larger" than the sample size n (say, at least 20 times as large), then making the selections will not substantially change the probability of a success. In this case, we can assume that the probability of a success stays essentially constant from selection to selection, and the different selections are essentially independent of each other. Therefore, we can approximate the hypergeometric distribution by the easier-to-compute binomial distribution:

$$p(x) = \frac{n!}{x!\,(n-x)!}p^x(1-p)^{n-x} = \frac{n!}{x!\,(n-x)!}\left(\frac{r}{N}\right)^x\left(1 - \frac{r}{N}\right)^{n-x}$$

The reader will use this approximation in Exercise C.4.

Exercises for Appendix C (Part 2)

C.3 Suppose that you purchase (randomly select) 3 TV sets from a production run of 10 TV sets. Of the 10 TV sets, 9 are destined to last at least five years without needing a single repair. What is the probability that all three of your TV sets will last at least five years without needing a single repair?

C.4 Suppose that you own an electronics store and purchase (randomly select) 15 TV sets from a production run of 500 TV sets. Of the 500 TV sets, 450 are destined to last at least five years without needing a single repair. Set up an expression using the hypergeometric distribution for the probability that at least 14 of your 15 TV sets will last at least five years without needing a single repair. Then, using the binomial tables, approximate this probability by using the binomial distribution. What justifies the approximation? Hint: $p = r/N = 450/500 = .9$.

Appendix D (Part 1): The Normal Probability Plot

The **normal probability plot** is a graphic that is used to visually check to see whether sample data come from a normal distribution. In order to illustrate the construction and interpretation of a normal probability plot, consider the payment time case and suppose that the trucking company operates in three regions of the country—the north, central, and south regions. In each region, 24 invoices are randomly selected and the payment time for each sampled invoice is found. The payment times obtained in each region are given in Table D.1, along with MINITAB side-by-side box plots of the data. Examination of the data and box plots indicates that the payment times for the central region are skewed to the left, while the payment times for the south region are skewed to the right. The box plot of the payment times for the north region, along with the MegaStat dot plot of these payment times in Figure D.1, indicate that the payment times for the north region are approximately normally distributed.

We will begin by constructing a normal probability plot for the payment times from the north region. We first arrange the payment times in order from smallest to largest. The ordered payment times are shown in column (1) of Table D.2. Next, for each ordered payment time we compute the quantity $i/(n + 1)$, where i denotes the observation's position in the ordered list of data and n denotes the sample size. For instance, for the first and second ordered payment times, we compute $1/(24 + 1) = 1/25 = .04$ and $2/(24 + 1) = 2/25 = .08$. Similarly, for the last (24th) ordered payment time, we compute $24/(24 + 1) = 24/25 = .96$. The positions ($i$ values) of all 24 payment times are given in column (2) of Table D.2, and the corresponding values of $i/(n + 1)$ are given in column (3) of this table. We continue by computing what is called the **standardized normal quantile value** for each ordered payment time. This value (denoted O_i) is the z value that gives an area of $i/(n + 1)$ to its left under the standard normal curve. Figure D.2 illustrates finding O_1, O_2, and O_{24}. For instance, O_1—the standardized normal quantile value corresponding to

TABLE D.1 Twenty-four Randomly Selected Payment Times for Each of Three Geographical Regions in the United States

North Region	Central Region	South Region
26	26	28
27	28	31
21	21	21
22	22	23
22	23	23
23	24	24
27	27	29
20	19	20
22	22	22
29	29	36
18	15	19
24	25	25
28	28	33
26	26	27
21	20	21
32	29	44
23	24	24
24	25	26
25	25	27
15	7	19
17	12	19
19	18	20
34	29	50
30	29	39

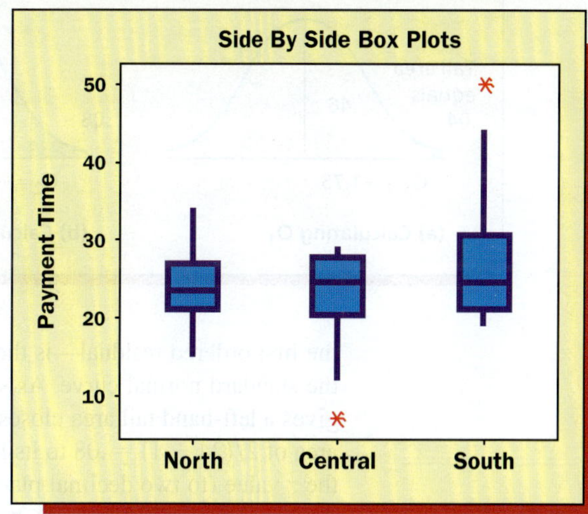

FIGURE D.1 Dot Plot of the Payment Times for the North Region

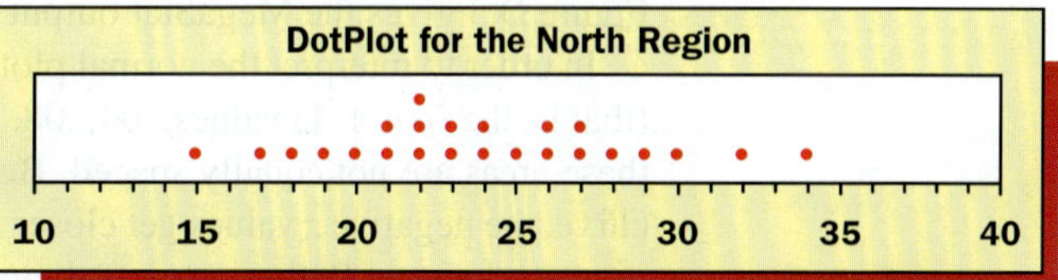

TABLE D.2 Calculations for Normal Probability Plots in the Payment Time Example

Ordered North Region Payment Times Column (1)	Observation Number (i) Column (2)	Area $i/(n+1)$ Column (3)	z value O_i Column (4)	Ordered Central Region Payment Times Column (5)	Ordered South Region Payment Times Column (6)
15	1	0.04	−1.75	7	19
17	2	0.08	−1.41	12	19
18	3	0.12	−1.18	15	19
19	4	0.16	−0.99	18	20
20	5	0.2	−0.84	19	20
21	6	0.24	−0.71	20	21
21	7	0.28	−0.58	21	21
22	8	0.32	−0.47	22	22
22	9	0.36	−0.36	22	23
22	10	0.4	−0.25	23	23
23	11	0.44	−0.15	24	24
23	12	0.48	−0.05	24	24
24	13	0.52	0.05	25	25
24	14	0.56	0.15	25	26
25	15	0.6	0.25	25	27
26	16	0.64	0.36	26	27
26	17	0.68	0.47	26	28
27	18	0.72	0.58	27	29
27	19	0.76	0.71	28	31
28	20	0.8	0.84	28	33
29	21	0.84	0.99	29	36
30	22	0.88	1.18	29	39
32	23	0.92	1.41	29	44
34	24	0.96	1.75	29	50

FIGURE D.2 Calculating Standardized Normal Quantile Values

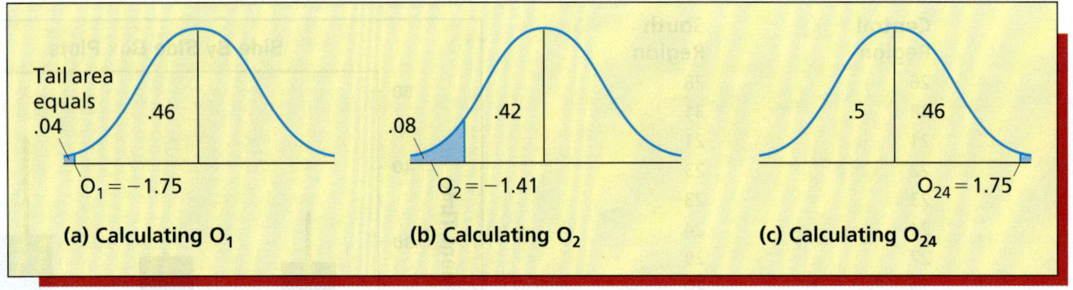

the first ordered residual—is the z value that gives an area of $1/(24 + 1) = .04$ to its left under the standard normal curve. As shown in Figure D.2(a), the z value (to two decimal places) that gives a left-hand tail area closest to .04 is $O_1 = -1.75$. Similarly, O_2 is the z value that gives an area of $2/(24 + 1) = .08$ to its left under the standard normal curve. As shown in Figure D.2(b), the z value (to two decimal places) that gives a left-hand tail area closest to .08 is $O_2 = -1.41$. As a final example, Figure D.2(c) shows that O_{24}, the z value that gives an area of $24/(24 + 1) = .96$ to its left under the standard normal curve, is 1.75. The standardized normal quantile values corresponding to the 24 ordered payment times are given in column (4) of Table D.2. Finally, we obtain the **normal probability plot** by plotting the 24 ordered payment times on the vertical axis versus the corresponding standardized normal quantile values (O_i values) on the horizontal axis. Figure D.3 gives the MegaStat output of this normal probability plot.

In order to interpret the normal plot, notice that, although the areas in column (3) of Table D.2 (that is, the $i/(n + 1)$ values: .04, .08, .12, etc.) are equally spaced, the z values corresponding to these areas are not equally spaced. Because of the mound-shaped nature of the standard normal curve, the negative z values get closer together as they get closer to the mean ($z = 0$) and the positive z values get farther apart as they get farther from the mean (more positive). If the distances

FIGURE D.3 MegaStat Normal Probability Plot for the North Region: Approximate Normality

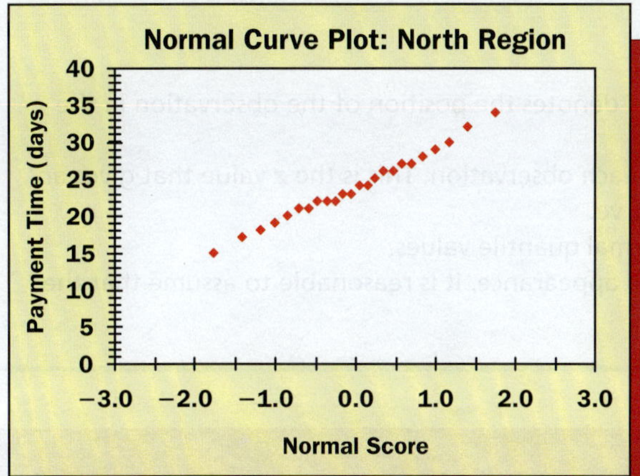

FIGURE D.4 MegaStat Normal Probability Plot for the Central Region: Data Skewed to the Left

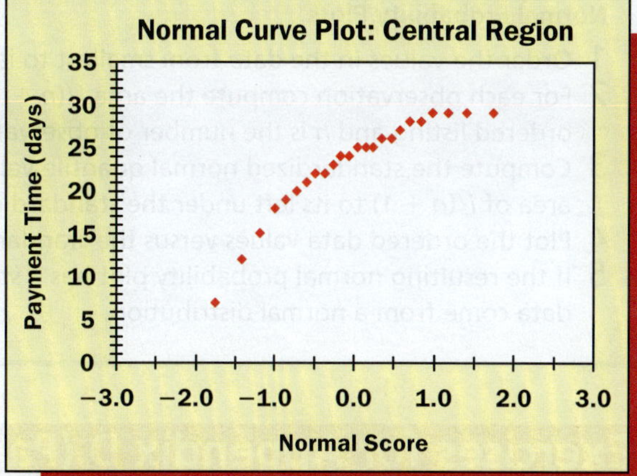

FIGURE D.5 MegaStat Normal Probability Plot for the South Region: Data Skewed to the Right

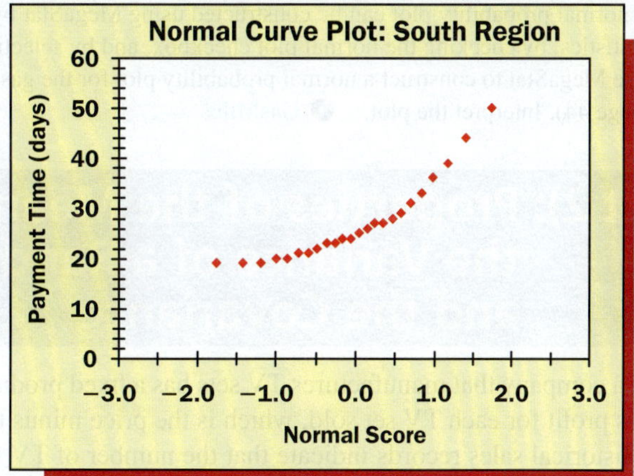

between the payment times behave the same way as the distances between the z values—that is, if the distances between the payment times are proportional to the distances between the z values—then the normal probability plot will be a straight line. This would suggest that the payment times are normally distributed. Examining Figure D.3, the normal probability plot for the payment times from the north region is approximately a straight line and, therefore, it is reasonable to assume that these payment times are approximately normally distributed.

Column (5) of Table D.2 gives the ordered payment times for the central region, and Figure D.4 plots these values versus the standardized normal quantile values in column (4). The resulting normal probability plot for the central region has a nonlinear appearance. The plot points rise more steeply at first and then continue to increase at a decreasing rate. This pattern indicates that the payment times for the central region are skewed to the left. Here the rapidly rising points at the beginning of the plot are due to the payment times being farther apart in the left tail of the distribution. Column (6) of Table D.2 gives the ordered payment times for the south region, and Figure D.5 gives the normal probability plot for this region. This plot also has a nonlinear appearance. The points rise slowly at first and then increase at an increasing rate. This pattern indicates that the payment times for the south region are skewed to the right. Here the rapidly rising points on the right side of the plot are due to the payment times being farther apart in the right tail of the distribution.

In the following box, we summarize how to construct and interpret a normal probability plot.

Normal Probability Plots

1. Order the values in the data from smallest to largest.
2. For each observation compute the area $i/(n + 1)$, where i denotes the position of the observation in the ordered listing and n is the number of observations.
3. Compute the standardized normal quantile value O_i for each observation. This is the z value that gives an area of $i/(n + 1)$ to its left under the standard normal curve.
4. Plot the ordered data values versus the standardized normal quantile values.
5. If the resulting normal probability plot has a straight line appearance, it is reasonable to assume that the data come from a normal distribution.

Exercises for Appendix D (Part 1)

D.1 Consider the sample of 13 internist's salaries given in Example 2.6 (page 61).

a Sort the salary data from smallest to largest, and compute $i/(n + 1)$ for each observation.

b Compute the standardized normal quantile value O_i for each observation.

c Graph the normal probability plot for the salary data and interpret this plot. Does the plot indicate that the data is skewed? Explain. DrSalary

D.2 Consider the 20 DVD satisfaction ratings given in Example 2.7 (page 61). Construct a normal probability plot for this data and interpret the plot. DVDSat

D.3 A normal probability plot can be constructed using MegaStat by selecting MegaStat: Descriptive Statistics, by checking the normal plot checkbox, and by selecting the data into the Input window. Use MegaStat to construct a normal probability plot for the gas mileage data in Table 2.1 (page 44). Interpret the plot. GasMiles

Appendix D (Part 2): Properties of the Mean and the Variance of a Random Variable, and the Covariance

Suppose a company that manufactures TV sets has a fixed production cost of \$2 million per year. The gross profit for each TV set sold, which is the price minus the unit variable production cost, is \$50. Historical sales records indicate that the number of TV sets sold per year, x, is a random variable with a mean of $\mu_x = 100{,}000$ and a standard deviation of $\sigma_x = 10{,}000$. Let y denote the company's annual profit from selling the TV set. Since this profit equals the gross profit associated with selling x TV sets, which is $50x$, minus the fixed cost of \$2,000,000, it follows that

$$y = -2{,}000{,}000 + 50x$$

In order to find the mean, variance, and standard deviation of y, we can use the following result:

If x is a random variable and a and b are fixed numbers, then

$$\mu_{(a+bx)} = a + b\mu_x \quad \text{and} \quad \sigma^2_{(a+bx)} = b^2\sigma^2_x$$

In the TV set manufacturing example, we have seen that the company's annual profit is

$$y = -2{,}000{,}000 + 50x$$

We have also seen that $\mu_x = 100{,}000$ and $\sigma_x = 10{,}000$. Therefore,

$$\mu_y = \mu_{(-2{,}000{,}000+50x)} = -2{,}000{,}000 + 50\mu_x = -2{,}000{,}000 + 50(100{,}000)$$
$$= 3{,}000{,}000$$

and

$$\sigma_y^2 = \sigma^2_{(-2{,}000{,}000 + 50x)} = (50)^2\sigma_x^2 = 2{,}500(10{,}000)^2 = 250{,}000{,}000{,}000$$

$$\sigma_y = \sqrt{\sigma_y^2} = \sqrt{250{,}000{,}000{,}000} = 500{,}000$$

Chebyshev's Theorem tells us that the probability is at least 3/4 that the annual profit from selling the TV set will be between $\mu_y - 2\sigma_y = \$2{,}000{,}000$ and $\mu_y + 2\sigma_y = \$4{,}000{,}000$.

We next consider a result concerning the mean and variance of a sum of random variables.

Let $x_1, x_2, \ldots, x_n$ be n random variables. Then:

1 $\mu_{(x_1+x_2+\cdots+x_n)} = \mu_{x_1} + \mu_{x_2} + \cdots + \mu_{x_n}$

2 If $x_1, x_2, \ldots, x_n$ are statistically independent (that is, the value taken by any one of these random variables is in no way associated with the value taken by any other of these random variables), then

$$\sigma^2_{(x_1+x_2+\cdots+x_n)} = \sigma^2_{x_1} + \sigma^2_{x_2} + \cdots + \sigma^2_{x_n}$$

For example, the time to set up a new production system in a particular company is denoted by the random variable y and is the sum of the following three random variables:

1 x_1, the time to purchase the production equipment and have it delivered, which has mean $\mu_{x_1} = 30$ days and standard deviation $\sigma_{x_1} = 3$ days.

2 x_2, the time to assemble the equipment, which has mean $\mu_{x_2} = 20$ days and standard deviation $\sigma_{x_2} = 2$ days.

3 x_3, the time to train the factory workers to use the equipment, which has mean $\mu_{x_3} = 14$ days and standard deviation $\sigma_{x_3} = 2$ days.

It follows that

$$\mu_y = \mu_{(x_1+x_2+x_3)} = \mu_{x_1} + \mu_{x_2} + \mu_{x_3} = 30 + 20 + 14 = 64 \text{ days}$$

Furthermore, although we cannot train the factory workers until we assemble the equipment, and although we cannot assemble the equipment until the equipment is purchased and delivered, it is reasonable that the times to do these tasks (x_1, x_2, and x_3) are statistically independent. Therefore,

$$\sigma_y^2 = \sigma^2_{(x_1+x_2+x_3)} = \sigma^2_{x_1} + \sigma^2_{x_2} + \sigma^2_{x_3} = (3)^2 + (2)^2 + (2)^2 = 9 + 4 + 4 = 17$$

and

$$\sigma_y = \sqrt{\sigma_y^2} = \sqrt{17} = 4.1231 \text{ (days)}$$

Chebyshev's Theorem tells us that the probability is at least 3/4 that the time to set up the production system will be between $\mu_y - 2\sigma_y = 55.75$ days and $\mu_y + 2\sigma_y = 72.25$ days.

To conclude this appendix, we note that sometimes random variables are not independent, and we can measure their dependence by using the **covariance.** For example, below we present (1) the probability distribution of x, the yearly proportional return for stock A, (2) the probability distribution of y, the yearly proportional return for stock B, and (3) the **joint probability distribution of (x, y),** the joint yearly proportional returns for stocks A and B [note that we have obtained the data below from Pfaffenberger and Patterson (1987)].

x	$p(x)$
−0.10	0.400
0.05	0.125
0.15	0.100
0.38	0.375

$\mu_x = .124$
$\sigma_x^2 = .0454$
$\sigma_x = .2131$

y	$p(y)$
−0.15	0.300
−0.05	0.200
0.12	0.150
0.46	0.350

$\mu_y = .124$
$\sigma_y^2 = .0681$
$\sigma_y = .2610$

Joint Distribution of (*x*, *y*)

Stock *B* Return, *y*	**Stock *A* Return, *x*** −0.10	0.05	0.15	0.38
−0.15	0.025	0.025	0.025	0.225
−0.05	0.075	0.025	0.025	0.075
0.12	0.050	0.025	0.025	0.050
0.46	0.250	0.050	0.025	0.025

To explain the joint probability distribution, note that the probability of .250 enclosed in the rectangle is the probability that in a given year the return for stock *A* will be −.10 and the return for stock *B* will be .46. The probability of .225 enclosed in the oval is the probability that in a given year the return for stock *A* will be .38 and the return for stock *B* will be −.15. Intuitively, these two rather large probabilities say that (1) a negative return *x* for stock *A* tends to be associated with a highly positive return *y* for stock *B*, and (2) a highly positive return *x* for stock *A* tends to be associated with a negative return *y* for stock *B*. To further measure the association between *x* and *y*, we can calculate the **covariance** between *x* and *y*. To do this, we calculate $(x - \mu_x)(y - \mu_y) = (x - .124)(y - .124)$ for each combination of values of *x* and *y*. Then, we multiply each $(x - \mu_x)(y - \mu_y)$ value by the probability $p(x, y)$ of the (x, y) combination of values and add up the quantities that we obtain. The resulting number is the covariance, denoted σ_{xy}. For example, for the combination of values $x = -.10$ and $y = .46$, we calculate

$$(x - \mu_x)(y - \mu_y)\, p(x, y) = (-.10 - .124)(.46 - .124)(.250) = -.0188$$

Doing this for all combinations of (x, y) values and adding up the resulting quantities, we find that the covariance is −.0318. **In general, a negative covariance says that as *x* increases, *y* tends to decrease in a linear fashion. A positive covariance says that as *x* increases, *y* tends to increase in a linear fashion.**

The covariance helps us in this situation to understand the importance of investment diversification. If we invest all of our money in stock *A*, we have seen that $\mu_x = .124$ and $\sigma_x = .2131$. If we invest all of our money in stock *B*, we have seen that $\mu_y = .124$ and $\sigma_y = .2610$. If we invest half of our money in stock *A* and half of our money in stock *B*, the return for the portfolio is $P = .5x + .5y$. The expected value of the portfolio return is

$$\mu_P = \mu_{(.5x+.5y)} = \mu_{.5x} + \mu_{.5y} = .5\mu_x + .5\mu_y = .5(.124) + .5(.124) = .124$$

To find the variance of the portfolio return, we must use a new rule. In general, if *x* and *y* have a nonzero covariance σ_{xy}, and *a* and *b* are constants, then

$$\sigma^2_{(ax+by)} = a^2\sigma^2_x + b^2\sigma^2_y + 2ab\sigma_{xy}$$

Therefore

$$\begin{aligned}\sigma^2_P = \sigma^2_{(.5x+.5y)} &= (.5)^2\sigma^2_x + (.5)^2\sigma^2_y + 2(.5)(.5)\sigma_{xy} \\ &= (.5)^2(.0454) + (.5)^2(.0681) + 2(.5)(.5)(-.0318) = .012475\end{aligned}$$

and

$$\sigma_P = \sqrt{.012475} = .1117$$

Note that, since $\mu_P = .124$ equals $\mu_x = .124$ and $\mu_y = .124$, the portfolio has the same expected return as either stock *A* or *B*. However, since $\sigma_P = .1117$ is less than $\sigma_x = .2131$ and $\sigma_y = .2610$, the portfolio is a less risky investment. In other words, diversification can reduce risk. Note, however, that **the reason that σ_P is less than σ_x and σ_y is that $\sigma_{xy} = -.0318$ is negative.** Intuitively, this says that the two stocks tend to balance each other's returns. However, if the covariance between the returns of two stocks is positive, σ_P can be larger than σ_x and/or σ_y. The reader will demonstrate this in Exercise D.6.

Finally, note that a measure of linear association between *x* and *y* that is unitless and always between −1 and 1 is the **correlation coefficient,** denoted ρ. We define ρ to be σ_{xy} divided by $(\sigma_x)(\sigma_y)$. For the stock return example, ρ equals $(-.0318)/((.2131)(.2610)) = -.5717$.

Exercises for Appendix D (Part 2)

D.4 The gross profit (price minus unit variable cost) for each computer sold by a company is $500. The company's fixed cost is $5,000,000 per year. The number of computers sold per year is a random variable having mean 15,000 and standard deviation 2,000. Let *y* denote the company's annual profit. Find μ_y and σ_y. Then, use Chebyshev's Theorem to find an interval containing at least 75 percent of the annual profits that might be obtained.

D.5 A product is manufactured on three different assembly lines that operate independently. The mean and standard deviation of the hourly production (in units produced) for each assembly line are as follows: (1) for assembly line 1, $\mu_1 = 35$ and $\sigma_1 = 4$; (2) for assembly line 2, $\mu_2 = 25$ and $\sigma_2 = 2$;

(3) for assembly line 3, $\mu_3 = 40$ and $\sigma_3 = 4$. Let T denote the total hourly production on all three assembly lines.

a Find μ_T and σ_T.

b Assuming that total hourly production is normally distributed, find an interval that contains 99.73 percent of the possible hourly production totals.

c Each unit of the product requires two 3/4" bolts for assembly. Use your result of part *b* to estimate the hourly supply of bolts needed in order to be very certain that the assembly lines will not run short of bolts during the hour.

D.6 Let x be the yearly proportional return for stock C, and let y be the yearly proportional return for stock D. If $\mu_x = .11$, $\mu_y = .09$, $\sigma_x = .17$, $\sigma_y = .17$, and $\sigma_{xy} = .0412$, find the mean and standard deviation of the portfolio return $P = .5x + .5y$. Discuss the risk of the portfolio.

D.7 Below we give what is called a **joint probability table** for two utility bonds where the random variable x represents the percentage return for bond 1 and the random variable y represents the percentage return for bond 2.

	x					
y	**8**	**9**	**10**	**11**	**12**	**p(y)**
8	.03	.04	.03	.00	.00	.10
9	.04	.06	.06	.04	.00	.20
10	.02	.08	.20	.08	.02	.40
11	.00	.04	.06	.06	.04	.20
12	.00	.00	.03	.04	.03	.10
p(x)	.09	.22	.38	.22	.09	

Source: David K. Hildebrand and Lyman Ott, *Statistical Thinking for Managers*, 2nd edition (Boston, Ma: Duxbury Press, 1987), p. 101.

In this table, probabilities associated with values of x are given in the row labeled $p(x)$ and probabilities associated with values of y are given in the column labeled $p(y)$. For example, $P(x = 9) = .22$ and $P(y = 11) = .20$. The entries inside the body of the table are joint probabilities—for instance, the probability that x equals 9 and y equals 10 is .08. Use the table to do the following:

a Calculate μ_x, σ_x, μ_y, and σ_y.

b Calculate σ_{xy}, the covariance between x and y.

c Calculate the variance and standard deviation of a portfolio in which 50 percent of the money is used to buy bond 1 and 50 percent is used to buy bond 2. That is, find σ_P^2 and σ_P, where $P = .5x + .5y$. How does the portfolio's risk compare to the risk associated with investing only in bond 1? Only in bond 2?

Appendix D (Part 3): Derivations of the Mean and Variance of $\bar{x}$ and $\hat{p}$

Derivation of the mean and the variance of the sample mean Before we randomly select the sample values $x_1, x_2, \ldots, x_n$ from a population having mean μ and variance σ^2, we note that, for $i = 1, 2, \ldots, n$, the ith sample value x_i is a random variable that can potentially be any of the values in the population. Moreover, it can be proven (and is intuitive) that

1 The mean (or expected value) of x_i, denoted μ_{x_i}, is μ, the mean of the population from which x_i will be randomly selected.

2 The variance of x_i, denoted $\sigma^2_{x_i}$, is σ^2, the variance of the population from which x_i will be randomly selected.

That is, for $i = 1, 2, \ldots, n$

$$\mu_{x_i} = \mu \quad \text{(or, equivalently, } \mu_{x_1} = \mu_{x_2} = \cdots = \mu_{x_n} = \mu)$$

and

$$\sigma^2_{x_i} = \sigma^2 \quad \text{(or, equivalently, } \sigma^2_{x_1} = \sigma^2_{x_2} = \cdots = \sigma^2_{x_n} = \sigma^2\text{)}$$

In Appendix D (Part 2) we studied properties of the mean and the variance of a random variable. We summarize these properties for later reference as follows:

Property 1: If b is a fixed number, $\mu_{bx} = b\mu_x$

Property 2: If b is a fixed number, $\sigma^2_{bx} = b^2\sigma^2_x$

Property 3: $\mu_{(x_1+x_2+\cdots+x_n)} = \mu_{x_1} + \mu_{x_2} + \cdots + \mu_{x_n}$

Property 4: If $x_1, x_2, \ldots, x_n$ are statistically independent, $\sigma^2_{(x_1+x_2+\cdots+x_n)} = \sigma^2_{x_1} + \sigma^2_{x_2} + \cdots + \sigma^2_{x_n}$

We now use these properties to prove that if we randomly select the sample of values $x_1, x_2, \ldots, x_n$ from an infinite population having mean μ and variance σ^2, and if we consider the sample mean $\bar{x} = \sum_{i=1}^{n} x_i/n$, then $\mu_{\bar{x}} = \mu$ and $\sigma^2_{\bar{x}} = \sigma^2/n$.

The first proof is as follows and is valid even if the population is not infinitely large:

$$\begin{aligned}
\mu_{\bar{x}} &= \mu_{\left(\sum_{i=1}^{n} x_i/n\right)} \\
&= \frac{1}{n}\mu_{\left(\sum_{i=1}^{n} x_i\right)} && \text{(see Property 1)} \\
&= \frac{1}{n}\mu_{(x_1+x_2+\cdots+x_n)} \\
&= \frac{1}{n}(\mu_{x_1} + \mu_{x_2} + \cdots + \mu_{x_n}) && \text{(see Property 3)} \\
&= \frac{1}{n}(\mu + \mu + \cdots + \mu) = \frac{n\mu}{n} = \mu
\end{aligned}$$

The second proof is as follows:

$$\begin{aligned}
\sigma^2_{\bar{x}} &= \sigma^2_{\left(\sum_{i=1}^{n} x_i/n\right)} = \left(\frac{1}{n}\right)^2 \sigma^2_{\left(\sum_{i=1}^{n} x_i\right)} && \text{(see Property 2)} \\
&= \frac{1}{n^2}\sigma^2_{(x_1+x_2+\cdots+x_n)} \\
&= \frac{1}{n^2}(\sigma^2_{x_1} + \sigma^2_{x_2} + \cdots + \sigma^2_{x_n}) && \text{(see Property 4)} \\
&= \frac{1}{n^2}(\sigma^2 + \sigma^2 + \cdots + \sigma^2) = \frac{n\sigma^2}{n^2} = \frac{\sigma^2}{n}
\end{aligned}$$

Note that we can use Property 4 because $x_1, x_2, \ldots, x_n$ are independent random variables. The reason that $x_1, x_2, \ldots, x_n$ are independent is that we are drawing these sample values from an infinite population. When we select a sample from an infinite population, a population value obtained on one selection can also be obtained on any other selection. This is because, since the population is infinite, there are an infinite number of repetitions of each population value. Therefore, since a value obtained on one selection is not precluded from being obtained on any other selection, the selections and thus $x_1, x_2, \ldots, x_n$ are statistically independent. Furthermore, this statistical independence approximately holds if the population size is much larger than (say, at least 20 times as large as) the sample size. Therefore, in this case it is approximately true that $\sigma^2_{\bar{x}} = \sigma^2/n$.

Derivation of the mean and the variance of the sample proportion We next assume that we randomly select a sample of n units from an infinite population, and we assume that a proportion p of all the units in the population fall into a particular category. Each population unit that falls into the category is 1 unit that falls into the category, and each population unit that does not fall into the category is 0 units that fall into the category. Therefore, the population can be considered a population of 1s and 0s. Furthermore, the mean and the variance of the population are the mean and the variance of the random variable, x_i, that describes the value (0 or 1) of the ith unit randomly selected from the population. Since a proportion p of the population values are 1, the probability that x_i will equal 1 is p, and the probability that x_i will equal 0 is $1 - p$. That is, the probability distribution of x_i is

x_i	$p(x_i)$
0	$1 - p$
1	p

Therefore,

$$\mu_{x_i} = 0(1 - p) + (1)p = p \quad \text{and} \quad \sigma^2_{x_i} = (0 - p)^2(1 - p) + (1 - p)^2 p = p(1 - p)$$

This says that the mean, μ, and the variance, σ^2, of the population of 1s and 0s are p and $p(1 - p)$. Furthermore, the mean of the sample randomly selected from this population is

$$\begin{aligned}\bar{x} &= \frac{x_1 + x_2 + \ldots + x_n}{n} \\ &= \frac{\text{the total number of 1s in the sample}}{\text{the total number of units in the sample}} \\ &= \text{the proportion of 1s in the sample} \\ &= \text{the proportion of units in the sample that fall into the category} \\ &= \hat{p}\end{aligned}$$

where we have previously referred to $\hat{p}$ as the sample proportion. To summarize, if we randomly select a sample of n values $x_1, x_2, \ldots, x_n$ from an infinite population that contains a proportion p of 1s and a proportion $1 - p$ of 0s, then

$$\mu = p \qquad \sigma^2 = p(1 - p) \qquad \text{and} \qquad \bar{x} = \hat{p}$$

Therefore, the previously proven result $\mu_{\bar{x}} = \mu$ implies (substituting $\hat{p}$ for $\bar{x}$ and p for μ) that $\mu_{\hat{p}} = p$. Furthermore, the previously proven result $\sigma^2_{\bar{x}} = \sigma^2/n$ implies (substituting $\hat{p}$ for $\bar{x}$ and $p(1 - p)$ for σ^2) that $\sigma^2_{\hat{p}} = p(1 - p)/n$. It follows that we have derived the mean and the variance of the sample proportion.

Appendix E: Holt–Winters' Models

Holt–Winters' double exponential smoothing Various extensions of simple exponential smoothing can be used to forecast time series that are described by models that are different from the model

$$y_t = \beta_0 + \varepsilon_t$$

For example, **Holt–Winters' double exponential smoothing** can be used to forecast time series that are described by the linear trend model

$$y_t = \beta_0 + \beta_1 t + \varepsilon_t$$

Here we assume that β_0 and β_1 (and thus the linear trend) may be changing slowly over time. To implement Holt–Winters' double exponential smoothing, we let ℓ_{T-1} denote the estimate of the level $\beta_0 + \beta_1(T - 1)$ of the time series in time period $T - 1$, and we let b_{T-1} denote the estimate of the slope β_1 of the time series in time period $T - 1$. Then, if we observe a new time series value y_T in time period T, the estimate of the level $\beta_0 + \beta_1 T$ of the time series in time period T uses the **smoothing constant** $\boldsymbol{\alpha}$ and is

$$\ell_T = \alpha y_T + (1 - \alpha)\,[\ell_{T-1} + b_{T-1}]$$

This equation says that ℓ_T equals a fraction α of the newly observed time series value y_T plus a fraction $(1 - \alpha)$ of $[\ell_{T-1} + b_{T-1}]$, which is the estimate of the level of the time series in time period T, as calculated using the estimates ℓ_{T-1} and b_{T-1} computed in time period $T-1$. Furthermore, the estimate of the slope β_1 of the time series in time period T uses the **smoothing constant** γ and is

$$b_T = \gamma[\ell_T - \ell_{T-1}] + (1-\gamma)b_{T-1}$$

This equation says that b_T equals a fraction γ of $[\ell_T - \ell_{T-1}]$, which is an estimate of the difference between the levels of the time series in periods T and $T-1$, plus a fraction $(1-\gamma)$ of b_{T-1}, the estimate of the slope made in time period $T-1$.

To use the updating equations, we first obtain initial estimates ℓ_0 and b_0 of the level and the slope of the time series in time period 0. One way to do this is to fit a least squares trend line to part (say, one-half) of the historical data and let the y-intercept and slope of the trend line be ℓ_0 and b_0. For example, consider the 24 observed calculator sales values in Table 13.2 (page 635). If we fit a least squares trend line to the first 12 of those values, we obtain

$$\hat{y}_t = 204.803 + 6.9406t$$

This would imply that $\ell_0 = 204.803$ and $b_0 = 6.9406$. MINITAB uses a more complicated method to find initial estimates and obtains $\ell_0 = 198.0290$ and $b_0 = 8.0743$. Starting with ℓ_0 and b_0, we calculate a point forecast of y_1 from time origin 0 to be

$$\hat{y}_1(0) = \ell_0 + b_0 = 198.0290 + 8.0743 = 206.103$$

This point forecast is shown on the MINITAB output of Figure E.1(a) [it is the first number under the column headed $\hat{y}_T(T-1)$]. Also shown on the output are the actual calculator sales value $y_1 = 197$ and the forecast error, which is

$$y_1 - \hat{y}_1(0) = 197 - 206.103 = -9.103$$

FIGURE E.1 The MINITAB Output of Double Exponential Smoothing for the Calculator Sales Data

(a) The updated level and slope estimates when $\alpha = .2$ and $\gamma = .2$

$\ell_0 = 198.0290$ $b_0 = 8.0743$

Time T	Sales y_T	Level ℓ_T	Slope b_T	Forecast $\hat{y}_T(T-1)$	Error $y_T - \hat{y}_T(T-1)$
1	197	204.283	7.7102	206.103	-9.1033
2	211	211.794	7.6705	211.993	-0.9929
3	203	216.172	7.0119	219.465	-16.4648
4	247	227.947	7.9646	223.184	23.8162
5	239	236.529	8.0881	235.912	3.0884
6	269	249.494	9.0634	244.617	24.3827
7	308	268.446	11.0411	258.557	49.4427
8	262	275.990	10.3416	279.487	-17.4869
9	258	280.665	9.2084	286.331	-28.3312
10	256	283.099	7.8535	289.873	-33.8733
11	261	284.962	6.6554	290.952	-29.9521
12	288	290.894	6.5107	291.617	-3.6171
13	296	297.123	6.4545	297.404	-1.4043
14	276	298.062	5.3514	303.578	-27.5780
15	305	303.731	5.4148	303.414	1.5862
16	308	308.917	5.3690	309.146	-1.1459
17	356	322.629	7.0376	314.286	41.7143
18	393	342.333	9.5709	329.666	63.3339
19	363	354.123	10.0148	351.904	11.0962
20	386	368.510	10.8893	364.138	21.8621
21	443	392.120	13.4333	379.400	63.6004
22	308	386.042	9.5312	405.553	-97.5529
23	358	388.059	8.0282	395.574	-37.5735
24	384	393.670	7.5447	396.087	-12.0870

(b) Point and 95 percent prediction interval forecasts when $\alpha = .2$ and $\gamma = .2$

Period	Forecast	Lower	Upper
25	401.214	337.812	464.617
26	408.759	344.036	473.483
27	416.304	350.158	482.450
28	423.849	356.185	491.513
29	431.393	362.122	500.665
30	438.938	367.977	509.899
31	446.483	373.755	519.211
32	454.028	379.461	528.594
33	461.572	385.101	538.044
34	469.117	390.679	547.555
35	476.662	396.200	557.124
36	484.207	401.668	566.746

(c) Point and 95 percent prediction interval forecasts when $\alpha = .496$ and $\gamma = .142$

Period	Forecast	Lower	Upper
25	383.677	319.133	448.221
26	389.121	316.065	462.178
27	394.565	312.107	477.024
28	400.010	307.532	492.487
29	405.454	302.519	508.388
30	410.898	297.189	524.606
31	416.342	291.624	541.059
32	421.786	285.882	557.690
33	427.230	280.002	574.458
34	432.674	274.015	591.333
35	438.118	267.941	608.295
36	443.562	261.798	625.327

We next choose values of the smoothing constants α and γ. A reasonable choice (and the default option of MINITAB) is to let each of α and γ be .2. Then, using $y_1 = 197$ and the equation for ℓ_T, it follows that the estimate of the level of the time series in time period 1 is

$$\begin{aligned} \ell_1 &= \alpha y_1 + (1 - \alpha)[\ell_0 + b_0] \\ &= .2(197) + .8[198.0290 + 8.0743] \\ &= 204.283 \end{aligned}$$

Furthermore, using the equation for b_T, the estimate of the slope of the time series in time period 1 is

$$\begin{aligned} b_1 &= \gamma[\ell_1 - \ell_0] + (1 - \gamma)b_0 \\ &= .2[204.283 - 198.0290] + .8(8.0743) \\ &= 7.7102 \end{aligned}$$

It follows that a point forecast made in time period 1 of y_2 is

$$\hat{y}_2(1) = \ell_1 + b_1 = 204.283 + 7.7102 = 211.993$$

Since the actual calculator sales value in period 2 is $y_2 = 211$, the forecast error is

$$y_2 - \hat{y}_2(1) = 211 - 211.933 = -.993$$

The MINITAB output in Figure E.1(a) shows the entire process of using the double exponential smoothing updating equations to find new period-by-period estimates of the level and slope of the time series. The output also shows the one-period-ahead forecasts and forecast errors, which are utilized to evaluate the effectiveness of the double exponential smoothing procedure. At the end of the updating process, MINITAB uses $\ell_{24} = 393.670$ and $b_{24} = 7.5447$ to calculate point forecasts of future calculator sales values. For example, point forecasts of y_{25} and y_{26} made from time origin 24 are

$$\hat{y}_{25}(24) = \ell_{24} + b_{24} = 393.670 + 7.5447 = 401.214$$

and

$$\hat{y}_{26}(24) = \ell_{24} + 2b_{24} = 393.670 + 2(7.5447) = 408.759$$

These point forecasts, as well as point forecasts of y_{27} through y_{36}, are shown on the MINITAB output in Figure E.1(b). Also shown are 95 percent prediction interval forecasts of y_{25} through y_{36}.

Figure E.2 shows a MINITAB output that graphically illustrates the forecasts when $\alpha = .2$ and $\gamma = .2$. Generally speaking, choosing $\alpha = .2$ and $\gamma = .2$ gives reasonable results, but MINITAB will choose its own values of α and γ. If we have MINITAB do this, it chooses $\alpha = .496$ and $\gamma = .142$. The forecasts given by this choice of α and γ are given in Figure E.1(c)

FIGURE E.2 The MINITAB Graphical Forecasts When $\alpha = .2$ and $\gamma = .2$

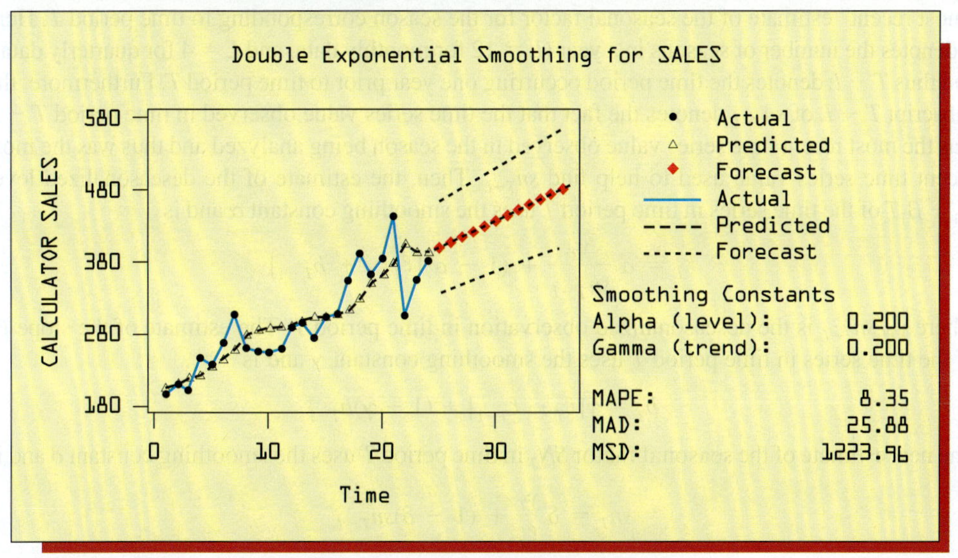

FIGURE E.3 **The MINITAB Graphical Forecasts When $\alpha = .496$ and $\gamma = .142$**

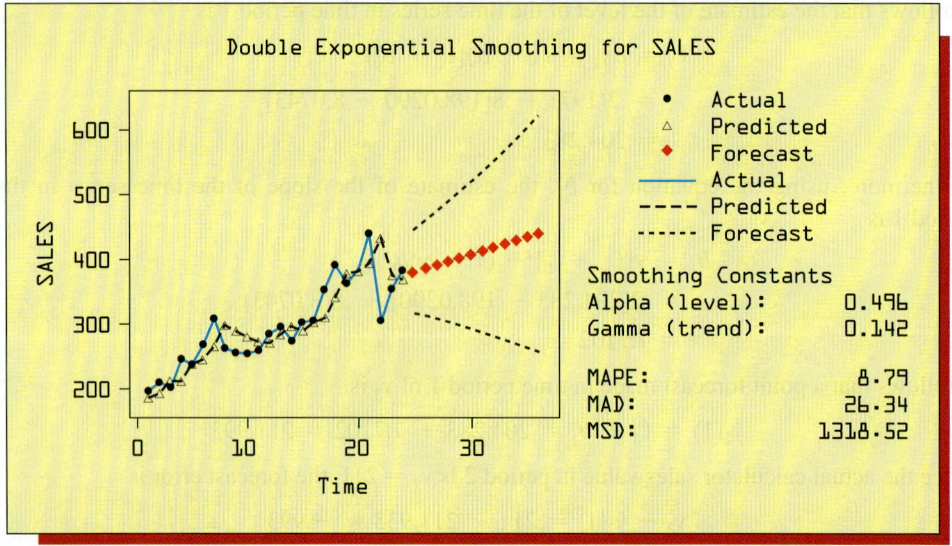

and graphically illustrated in Figure E.3. To evaluate the choice of a particular set of values for α and γ, MINITAB gives the mean of the absolute forecast errors (the MAD) and the mean of the squared forecast errors (the MSD) for the 24 historical calculator sales values. Comparing Figures E.2 and E.3, we see that $\alpha = .2$ and $\gamma = .2$ give a smaller MAD and MSD than do $\alpha = .496$ and $\gamma = .142$. Therefore, we might conclude that we should use the forecasts of y_{25} through y_{36} based on $\alpha = .2$ and $\gamma = .2$. On the other hand, we might believe that the lower sales values at the end of the observed data signal that the sales values will not continue to increase as fast as they have. In this case, we might use the lower forecasts given by $\alpha = .496$ and $\gamma = .142$ (see Figure E.3).

Multiplicative Winters' method **Multiplicative Winters' method** can be used to forecast time series that are described by the model

$$y_t = (\beta_0 + \beta_1 t) \times SN_t + \varepsilon_t$$

Here we assume that β_0 and β_1 (and thus the linear trend) and SN_t (which represents the seasonal pattern) may be changing slowly over time. To implement multiplicative Winters' method, we let ℓ_{T-1} denote the estimate of the deseasonalized level $\beta_0 + \beta_1(T-1)$ of the time series in time period $T-1$, and we let b_{T-1} denote the estimate of the slope β_1 of the time series in time period $T-1$. Then, suppose that we observe a new time series value y_T in time period T, and let sn_{T-L} denote the "most recent" estimate of the seasonal factor for the season corresponding to time period T. Here L denotes the number of seasons in a year ($L = 12$ for monthly data, and $L = 4$ for quarterly data), and thus $T - L$ denotes the time period occurring one year prior to time period T. Furthermore, the subscript $T - L$ of sn_{T-L} denotes the fact that the time series value observed in time period $T - L$ was the most recent time series value observed in the season being analyzed and thus was the most recent time series value used to help find sn_{T-L}. Then, the estimate of the deseasonalized level $\beta_0 + \beta_1 T$ of the time series in time period T uses the smoothing constant α and is

$$\ell_T = \alpha \frac{y_T}{sn_{T-L}} + (1 - \alpha)[\ell_{T-1} + b_{T-1}]$$

where y_T/sn_{T-L} is the deseasonalized observation in time period T. The estimate of the slope β_1 of the time series in time period T uses the smoothing constant γ and is

$$b_T = \gamma[\ell_T - \ell_{T-1}] + (1 - \gamma)b_{T-1}$$

The new estimate of the seasonal factor SN_T in time period T uses the smoothing constant δ and is

$$sn_T = \delta \frac{y_T}{\ell_T} + (1 - \delta)sn_{T-L}$$

where y_T/ℓ_T is an estimate of the newly observed seasonal variation.

To use the updating equations, we first obtain initial estimates ℓ_0, b_0, and sn_0 of the deseasonalized level, slope, and seasonal factors of the time series in time period 0. One way to do this is to use the multiplicative decomposition method (see Section 13.4) to analyze part (say, one-half) of the historical data. Here, if there are less than five years of historical data, it is probably best to base the initial estimates on all of the historical data. Then, we regard the y-intercept and slope of the trend line fit to the deseasonalized data as the initial estimates ℓ_0 and b_0. Furthermore, we regard the multiplicative decomposition method's seasonal factors as the initial estimates of the seasonal factors in time period 0. For example, consider the 36 Tasty Cola sales values in Table 13.9 (page 644). Using the multiplicative decomposition method results summarized in Tables 13.10 and 13.11, we obtain the initial estimates $\ell_0 = 380.163$ and $b_0 = 9.489$ and the following seasonal factor estimates:

Month	sn_0	Month	sn_0
Jan.	.493	July	1.467
Feb.	.596	Aug.	1.693
Mar.	.595	Sept.	1.990
Apr.	.680	Oct.	1.307
May	.564	Nov.	1.029
June	.986	Dec.	.600

Starting with these initial estimates, we calculate a point forecast of y_1 from time origin 0 to be

$$\begin{aligned}\hat{y}_1(0) &= (\ell_0 + b_0)sn_0 \\ &= (380.163 + 9.489)(.493) \\ &= 192.098\end{aligned}$$

Here we have used the initial January seasonal factor estimate $sn_0 = .493$ because y_1 is Tasty Cola sales in January of year 1. The actual value of y_1 is 189, so the forecast error is

$$y_1 - \hat{y}_1(0) = 189 - 192.098 = -3.098$$

We next choose values of the smoothing constants α, γ, and δ. A reasonable choice (and the default option of MINITAB) is to let each of α, γ, and δ be .2. Then, using $y_1 = 189$ and the equation for ℓ_T, it follows that the estimate of the deseasonalized level of the time series in time period 1 is

$$\begin{aligned}\ell_1 &= \alpha\frac{y_1}{sn_0} + (1 - \alpha)[\ell_0 + b_0] \\ &= .2\left[\frac{189}{.493}\right] + .8[380.163 + 9.489] \\ &= 388.395\end{aligned}$$

Here we have used the initial January seasonal factor estimate $sn_0 = .493$ as the most recent Winters' method estimate of the January seasonal factor. Using the equation for b_T, the estimate of the slope of the time series in time period 1 is

$$\begin{aligned}b_1 &= \gamma[\ell_1 - \ell_0] + (1 - \gamma)b_0 \\ &= .2[388.395 - 380.163] + .8(9.489) \\ &= 9.238\end{aligned}$$

Using the equation for sn_T, the new estimate of the January seasonal factor in time period 1 is

$$\begin{aligned}sn_1 &= \delta\frac{y_1}{\ell_1} + (1 - \delta)sn_0 \\ &= .2\left[\frac{189}{388.395}\right] + .8(.493) \\ &= .492\end{aligned}$$

It follows that a point forecast made in period 1 of y_2 is

$$\begin{aligned}\hat{y}_2(1) &= (\ell_1 + b_1)\, sn_0 \\ &= (388.395 + 9.238)(.596) \\ &= 236.989\end{aligned}$$

Here we have used the initial February seasonal factor estimate $sn_0 = .596$ because y_2 is the Tasty Cola sales in February of year 1. The actual value of y_2 is 229, so the forecast error is

$$y_2 - \hat{y}_2(1) = 229 - 236.989 = -7.989$$

The MINITAB output in Figure E.4(a) shows the entire process of using the Winters' method updating equations to find new period-by-period estimates of the level, slope, and seasonal factors of the time series. The output also shows the one-period-ahead forecasts and forecast errors, which are utilized to evaluate the effectiveness of the Winters' method procedure. MINITAB does not find initial estimates by using the multiplicative decomposition method. We will not discuss how MINITAB obtains initial estimates, but note from Figure E.4(a) that the values of ℓ_1 and b_1 obtained by MINITAB ($\ell_1 = 278.768$ and $b_1 = 44.9736$) are very different from the values that we obtained by hand calculation ($\ell_1 = 388.395$ and $b_1 = 9.238$). In addition, the one-period-ahead forecast errors obtained by MINITAB are generally quite large in periods 1 through 12 but then become reasonably small for periods 13 through 36. To further illustrate the Winters' method updating equations, note from Figure E.4(a) that $\ell_{35} = 725.603$ and $b_{35} = 8.9026$. Since the most recent estimate of the December seasonal factor is $sn_{24} = .60767$, the point forecast made in period 35 of y_{36} (sales in December of year 3) is

$$\begin{aligned}\hat{y}_{36}(35) &= (\ell_{35} + b_{35})sn_{24} \\ &= (725.603 + 8.9026)(.60767) \\ &= 446.34\end{aligned}$$

The actual sales value in period 36 is $y_{36} = 441$, so the forecast error is

$$y_{36} - \hat{y}_{36}(35) = 441 - 446.34 = -5.34$$

The updated estimates ℓ_{36}, b_{36}, and sn_{36} are calculated as follows:

$$\begin{aligned}\ell_{36} &= \alpha\frac{y_{36}}{sn_{24}} + (1 - \alpha)[\ell_{35} + b_{35}] \\ &= .2\left[\frac{441}{.60767}\right] + .8[725.603 + 8.9026] \\ &= 732.75\end{aligned}$$

$$\begin{aligned}b_{36} &= \gamma[\ell_{36} - \ell_{35}] + (1 - \gamma)b_{35} \\ &= .2[732.75 - 725.603] + .8(8.9026) \\ &= 8.5514\end{aligned}$$

and

$$\begin{aligned}sn_{36} &= \delta\frac{y_{36}}{\ell_{36}} + (1 - \delta)sn_{24} \\ &= .2\left[\frac{441}{732.75}\right] + .8(.60767) \\ &= .6065\end{aligned}$$

We are now at the end of the historical data, so we can forecast future Tasty Cola sales values. Figure E.4(b) gives the point and 95 percent prediction interval forecasts of future sales values in periods 37 through 48, and Figure E.5 graphically portrays the forecasts. To see how the point forecasts are calculated, note that, for example, the most recent estimates of the January and July seasonal factors are $sn_{25} = .48019$ and $sn_{31} = 1.42891$. Therefore, point forecasts made in period 36 of Tasty Cola sales in periods 37 and 43 (January and July of year 4) are

$$\begin{aligned}\hat{y}_{37}(36) &= (\ell_{36} + b_{36})sn_{25} \\ &= (732.75 + 8.5514)(.48019) \\ &= 355.96\end{aligned}$$

and

$$\begin{aligned}\hat{y}_{43}(36) &= (\ell_{36} + 7b_{36})sn_{31} \\ &= [732.75 + 7(8.5514)](1.42891) \\ &= 1{,}132.57\end{aligned}$$

FIGURE E.4 The MINITAB Output of Winters' Method for the Tasty Cola Sales Data, When $\alpha = .2$, $\gamma = .2$, and $\delta = .2$

(a) The updated level, slope, and seasonal factor estimates

Time T	Sales y_T	Level ℓ_T	Slope b_T	Seasonal sn_T	Forecast $\hat{y}_T(T-1)$	Error $y_T - \hat{y}_T(T-1)$
1	189	278.768	44.9736	0.48896	106.67	82.334
2	229	343.270	48.8794	0.56818	175.93	53.065
3	249	401.836	50.8167	0.57606	221.63	27.371
4	289	449.774	50.2409	0.65605	298.49	-9.492
5	260	492.009	48.6398	0.55787	282.62	-22.624
6	431	520.567	44.6235	0.94880	529.30	-98.301
7	660	541.448	39.8750	1.42638	835.48	-175.485
8	777	556.089	34.8280	1.64516	992.39	-215.395
9	915	562.722	29.1891	1.95207	1201.68	-286.680
10	613	565.315	23.8699	1.28544	790.62	-177.623
11	485	563.116	18.6561	1.01787	622.78	-137.777
12	277	552.752	12.8521	0.60770	369.04	-92.044
13	244	552.287	10.1887	0.47953	276.56	-32.557
14	296	554.174	8.5282	0.56137	319.59	-23.586
15	319	560.914	8.1706	0.57459	324.15	-5.151
16	370	568.063	7.9664	0.65511	373.35	-3.349
17	313	573.035	7.3675	0.55554	321.35	-8.352
18	556	581.523	7.5916	0.95026	550.68	5.315
19	831	587.811	7.3308	1.42385	840.30	-9.301
20	960	592.820	6.8664	1.64000	979.10	-19.101
21	1152	597.777	6.4846	1.94709	1170.63	-18.631
22	759	601.501	5.9325	1.28072	776.74	-17.742
23	607	605.216	5.4890	1.01488	618.29	-11.287
24	371	610.664	5.4807	0.60767	371.13	-0.126
25	298	617.205	5.6927	0.48019	295.46	2.542
26	378	632.989	7.7111	0.56853	349.67	28.326
27	373	642.391	8.0493	0.57580	368.14	4.859
28	443	655.597	9.0806	0.65923	426.11	16.891
29	374	666.385	9.4222	0.55668	369.26	4.743
30	660	679.556	10.1717	0.95445	642.19	17.807
31	1004	692.808	10.7879	1.42891	982.07	21.934
32	1153	703.487	10.7660	1.63980	1153.90	-0.898
33	1388	713.974	10.7103	1.94648	1390.71	-2.712
34	904	720.918	9.9571	1.27537	928.12	-24.118
35	715	725.603	8.9026	1.00898	741.75	-26.753
36	441	732.750	8.5514	0.60650	446.34	-5.336

(b) Point and 95 percent prediction interval forecasts

Period	Forecast	Lower	Upper
37	355.96	240.98	470.95
38	426.31	308.93	543.69
39	436.69	316.73	556.65
40	505.60	382.88	628.32
41	431.71	306.08	557.34
42	748.35	619.65	877.04
43	1132.57	1000.67	1264.47
44	1313.74	1178.51	1448.98
45	1576.09	1437.40	1714.78
46	1043.59	901.33	1185.84
47	834.24	688.32	980.17
48	506.65	356.96	656.35

FIGURE E.5 The MINITAB Graphical Forecasts When $\alpha = .2$, $\gamma = .2$, and $\delta = .2$

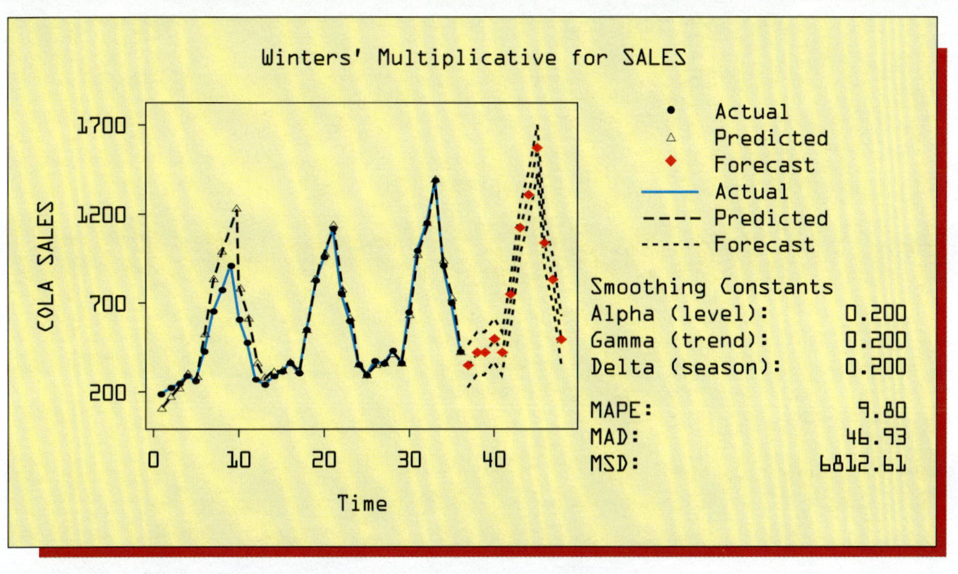

The reason that the 95 percent prediction intervals are so wide is that they can be shown to be functions of the historical forecast errors, which are very large in periods 1 through 12. The mean absolute forecast error in periods 13 through 36 can be calculated to be 12.98 and is more representative of Winters' method's accuracy than is the mean absolute forecast error in all 36 periods, which is 46.93 (see Figure E.5). Therefore, to obtain more reasonable prediction intervals, we might multiply the lengths of the prediction intervals by $12.98/46.93 \approx .28$. For example, Figure E.4(b) tells us that the 95 percent prediction interval for y_{37} is [240.98, 470.95], which has length $470.95 - 240.98 = 229.97$. Multiplying this length by .28, we obtain $(229.97)(.28) = 64.39$. Surrounding the point forecast 355.96 by a new half-length of $64.39/2 = 32.2$, we obtain a new 95 percent prediction interval of $[355.96 \pm 32.2] = [323.76,\ 388.16]$. The other 95 percent prediction intervals can be modified similarly.

The wide prediction intervals in Figure E.4(b) result from a combination of a short historical series (36 sales values) and MINITAB obtaining inaccurate initial estimates of the level, slope, and seasonal factors. When the historical series is long (for example, see Exercise 13.27, page 659), MINITAB usually obtains reasonable prediction intervals. Finally, note that MINITAB will not choose its own values of α, γ, and δ. However, the user can simply experiment with different combinations of values of these smoothing constants until a combination is found that produces the "best" results.

Exercises for Appendix E

CONCEPTS

E.1 When do we use double exponential smoothing?

E.2 When do we use Winters' method?

METHODS AND APPLICATIONS

E.3 Consider Figure E.1(a). Show how ℓ_2 and b_2 have been calculated from ℓ_1, b_1, and y_2. Also, show how $\hat{y}_{27}(24)$ in Figure E.1(b) has been calculated from ℓ_{24} and b_{24}.

E.4 Consider Figure E.4(a). Show how ℓ_{35}, b_{35}, and sn_{35} have been calculated from ℓ_{34}, b_{34}, y_{35}, and sn_{23}. Also, show how $\hat{y}_{38}(36)$ in Figure E.4(b) has been calculated from ℓ_{36}, b_{36}, and sn_{26}.

Answers to Most Odd-Numbered Exercises

Chapter 1

1.3 a. Quantitative
b. Quantitative
c. Qualitative
d. Quantitative
e. Qualitative

1.7 PepsiCo; ConAgra Foods; Archer Daniels; Campbell Soup; General Mills

1.9 a. 33276 58586
03427 09998
08178 14346
51259 24200
60268 07351
b. Between 36 and 48
40/65 = .615

1.11 a. People who oppose TV sex and violence
b. Doubtful
c. Highly doubtful

1.15 In control

1.17 Percentages out of control. Most business travel early in week; more help needed then.

1.19 Probably in control.

1.23 Nominative
Ordinal
Ordinal
Ordinal
Nominative
Nominative

1.33 Not in control; opinions may vary

1.35 b. 15, 7, 57, 42 and 59 minutes past the hour.

Chapter 2

2.3 a. Skewed to the right
b. Symmetrical and quite variable

2.5 b. Slightly skewed with a tail to the left

2.7 b. Symmetrical

2.9 An outlier that was an exceptional individual achievement.

2.15 a. 9.6, 10, 10
b. 103.33, 100, 90

2.17 a. Yes, $\bar{x} > 42$
b. Mean slightly < Median
A slight skewness to the left

2.19 a. Yes, $\bar{x} > 50$
b. Median = 50.65
Mean and median are very similar very little skewness

2.21 Somewhat skewed left; U.S. lowest

2.23 Skewed right; U.S. highest

2.25 Skewed right; U.S. above mean

2.27 a. Skewed right
b. About 33%; About 50%

2.33 10, 11.6, 3.4059

2.35 a. Revenue: 16.10; 26.6365; 5.1611
Profits: 4269; 1,180,247.09; 1086.3918
b. American $z = -.906$
US Airways: $z = 1.57$

2.37 a. Appropriate
b. [48.9312, 52.2188]; [47.2875, 53.8626]; [45.6436, 55.5064]
c. Yes
d. 67.5%, 95%, 100%
Yes

2.39 a. Somewhat reasonable
b. [40.3076, 45.5924]; [37.6652, 48.2348]; [35.0228, 50.8772]
c. Yes
d. 63%, 98.46%, 100%; Yes

2.41 a. [−72.99, 94.85], [−5.72, 31.72], [−47.87, 116.77]
c. 383.9, 72, 119.4
RS Internet Age is most risky; Franklin Income A is least risky

2.45 Trash bags:
a. 52.8, b. 50.65, c. 49.45,
d. 51.6, e. 48.4, f. 2.15

2.47 30 year rates higher; variability similar; Average of differences is .444

2.49 a. All categories
b. Most: strategic quality planning; quality and operational results. Least: Info. and analysis; human resource development and management.
c. Increase: leadership, human resource development, customer focus and satisfaction. Decrease: strategic quality planning, management of process quality. Others stayed about the same.
d. Leadership; strategic quality planning; human resource development; quality and operational results.

2.53 Ford, Chrysler and other imports gained in market share, while GM and Japanese decreased.

2.55 $\hat{p} = .541 > .5$, some evidence

2.59 Data scattered around a straight line with positive slope

2.67 a. No, or very slight
b. Yes, strong trend
c. Line graph
d. Probably not

2.71 a. Weighted = 13.559%
b. Unweighted = 10.72%

2.73 a. 4.6
b. 3.8289

2.75 51.5; 81.61; 9.0338

2.79 .4142

2.81 a. .39434
b. 2,139

2.87 a. [415, 661]
b. Yes

Chapter 3

3.3 b1. *AA*
b2. *AA, BB, CC*
b3. *AB, AC, BA, BC, CA, CB*
b4. *AA, AB, AC, BA, CA*
b5. *AA, AB, BA, BB*
c. 1/9, 1/3, 2/3, 5/9, 4/9

3.5 b1. *PPPN, PPNP, PNPP, NPPP*
b2. Outcomes with ≤2 *P*'s (11)
b3. Outcomes with ≥1 *P* (15)
b4. *PPPP, NNNN*
c. 1/4, 11/16, 15/16, 1/8

3.7 .15

3.11 a1. .25
a2. .40
a3. .10
c1. .55
c2. .45
c3. .45

3.13 a. 5/8
b. 21/40
c. 19/40
d. 3/8
e. 31/40

3.15 a. .205
b. .698
c. .606
d. .303

3.19 a. .6
b. .4
c. Dependent

3.21 .55

3.23 .1692

3.25 .31

3.27 b. .40
c. Yes, $P(FRAUD|FIRE) = P(FRAUD)$

3.29 a. .874
b. .996
c. .004

3.31 a. .10
b. .059, .068, .049, .037
c. .0256
d. .0151, .0174, .0125, .0095
e. .0801

3.33 a. .0295
b. .9705
c. Probably not

3.35 1/9, 1/9, 4/9

3.37 .04, .56, .26, .32

3.39 .902867

3.41 .943647

3.43 .721

3.45 .362

3.47 .502

3.49 Slight dependence

3.51 a. .2075
b. .25
c. .105
d. .42
e. Yes

3.53 a. 1, .96, .75, .75
b. .2169, .3123, .2530, .0723, .0361
c. .09, .1084, .83

3.55 a. 0
b. $P(A) \cdot P(B) > 0$
c. No: $P(A \mid B) = 0$ but $P(A) > 0$

3.57 a. Not independent
b. Not independent

Chapter 4

4.3 a. Discrete
b. Discrete
c. Continuous
d. Discrete
e. Discrete
f. Continuous
g. Continuous

4.5 $p(x) \geq 0$, each x

$$\sum_{\text{all } x} p(x) = 1$$

4.9 a. .8, .4
b. 1.15, .90967
c. 1.6, 2.1071

4.11 a. .667, .444, .667, [−.667, 2.001], [−1.334, 2.668]
b. 1.5, .75, .866, [−.232, 3.232], [−1.098, 4.098]
c. 2, 1, 1, [0, 4], [−1, 5]

4.13 b. $500

4.15 a.

x	$p(x)$
$400	.995
−$49,600	.005

b. $150
c. $1,250

4.17 −$5.60

4.19 a. $p(x) = .1099, .0879, .3077, .2967, .1978$
b. 3.38

4.23 a. $p(x) = \dfrac{5!}{x!\,(5-x)!}(.3)^x(.7)^{5-x}$
$x = 0, 1, 2, 3, 4, 5$
c. .1323
d. .9692
e. .8369
f. .0308
g. .1631
h. $\mu_x = 1.5, \sigma_x^2 = 1.05, \sigma_x = 1.024695$
i. [−.54939, 3.54939], .9692

4.25 a. $p(x) = \dfrac{15!}{x!\,(15-x)!}(.9)^x(.1)^{15-x}$
b1. .4509
b2. .9873
b3. .5491
b4. .1837
b5. .0022
c. No, $P(x \leq 9)$ is very small

4.27 a1. .0625
a2. .3125
b1. .4119
b2. .2517
b3. .0059
c. No, $P(x < 5)$ is very small

4.29 a. .9996, .0004
b. .4845, .5155
c. $p = 1/35$
d. .000040019

4.33 a. $\mu_x = 2, \sigma_x^2 = 2, \sigma_x = 1.414$
b. [−.828, 4.828], .9473
[−2.242, 6.242], .9955

4.35 a. .7851
b. .2149
c. .1912
d. .0088

4.37 a. Approximately zero
b. Rate of comas unusually high.

4.39 a.

x	$p(x)$
0	4/9
1	4/9
2	1/9

b. $p(x) = .16, .48, .36$
c. $p(x) = .12, .56, .32$

4.41 a. 2/3, 2/3
b. 1.2, .693
c. 1.2, .632
d. *b* and *c*
e. *b*

4.43 a. $12,000
b. At least $6,000

4.45 a. Binomial
$n = 8, p = .8$
b. .0104
c. No, probability is very small

4.47 a. .0498
b. .9962
c. .0038
d. .9574
e. .1157

4.49 .9995

4.51 .3232
Not much evidence against it

4.53 .0293
Claim probably not true

Chapter 5

5.7 $h = 1/125$

5.9 a. 3, 3, 1.73205
b. [1.268, 4.732], .57733

5.11 a. $f(x) = 1/20$ for $120 \leq x \leq 140$
c. .5
d. .25

5.13 $c = 1/6$

5.15 a. 4.5
b. 1.0, .57733

5.23 a. −1, one σ below μ
b. −3, three σ below μ
c. 0, equals μ
d. 2, two σ above μ
e. 4, four σ above μ

5.25 a. 2.33 d. −2.33
b. 1.645 e. −1.645
c. 2.05 f. −1.28

5.27 a. 696 f. 335.5
b. 664.5 g. 696
c. 304 h. 700
d. 283 i. 300
e. 717

5.29 a1. .9830
a2. .0033
a3. .0456
b. 947

5.31 a. .0013
b. Claim probably not true

5.33 .0424

5.35 a. 10%, 90%, −13.968
b. −1.402, 26.202

5.37 a. $[\mu \pm 2.33\sigma]$
b. [46.745, 54.405]

5.39 a. *A*: .3085
B: .4013
B is investigated more often
b. *A*: .8413
B: .6915
A is investigated more often
c. *B*
d. Investigate if cost variance exceeds $5,000
.5987

5.41 $\mu = 700, \sigma = 100$

5.43 Both np and $n(1-p) \geq 5$

5.45 a. $np = 80$ and
$n(1-p) = 120$
both ≥ 5
b1. .0558
b2. .9875
b3. .0125
b4. .0025
b5. .0015

5.47 a1. $np = 200$ and $n(1 - p) = 800$ both ≥ 5
a2. 200, 12.6491
a3. Less than .001
b. No

5.49 a. Less than .001
b. No

5.55 a. $3e^{-3x}$ for $x \geq 0$
c. .9502
d. .4226
e. .0025
f. 1/3, 1/9, 1/3
g. .9502

5.57 a. $(2/3)e^{-(2/3)x}$ for $x \geq 0$
c1. .8647
c2. .2498
c3. .0695
c4. .2835

5.59 a1. .1353
a2. .2325
a3. .2212
b. Probably not, probability is .2212

5.61 a. .0124
b. .3085
c. .0013

5.63 a. $f(x) = 1$ for $-.5 \leq x \leq .5$
c. .4
d. .8
e. 0, .2887
f. .5774

5.65 a. 10%, 90%, 3.464
b. 4.196, 5.804

5.67 15.053″

5.69 a. .2019
b. .3297

5.71 .0107

5.73 a. .2231, b. .1353

5.75 a. .0256 b. Yes

Chapter 6

6.7 a. 10, .16, .4
b. 500, .0025, .05
c. 3, .0025, .05
d. 100, .000625, .025

6.9 a. Normally distributed
No, sample size is large (≥ 30)
b. $\mu_{\bar{x}} = 20$, $\sigma_{\bar{x}} = .5$
c. .0228
d. .1093

6.11 a. Normal distribution because $n \geq 30$
b. .247
c. .0143
d. 1.43%, conclude $\mu < 6$

6.13 a. .2206
b. .0027
c. Yes

6.19 a. .5, .001, .0316
b. .1, .0009, .03
c. .8, .0004, .02
d. .98, .0000196, .004427

6.21 a. Approximately normal
b .9, .03
c. .0228, .8664, .6915

6.23 a. .0823
b. Perhaps, evidence not very strong

6.25 a1. .7372
a2. .9756

6.27 a. Less than .001
b. Yes

6.29 a. .3085
b. .0013
c. More difficult for average.
Yes.

6.31 a. .0014
b. Yes

6.33 a. .9544
b. .0062

6.35 a. Less than .001
b. Yes, conclude that $p < .5$

6.37 a. [49.151, 52.049]
b. [50.088, 51.112]
c. $n = 40$

6.39 a. Less than .001
b. Yes

6.41 a. Less than .001
b. Yes

Chapter 7

7.3 a. Longer
b. Shorter
c. Shorter
d. Longer

7.5 a. [49.608, 50.392]
b. [49.485, 50.515]
c. [49.566, 50.434]
d. [49.744, 50.256]
e. [49.4, 50.6]

7.7 a. [4.976, 5.944], [4.824, 6.096]
b. Yes, 95% interval is below 6
c. No, 99% interval extends above 6

7.9 a. [3.653, 7.707]
b. 3.653

7.11 a. [76.132, 89.068]
b. [85.748, 100.252]
c. Mean audit delay for public owner-controlled companies appears to be shorter

7.15 1.363, 2.201, 4.025
1.440, 2.447, 5.208

7.17 a. [3.442, 8.558]
b. Can be 95% confident, cannot be 99% confident

7.19 a. [13.065, 14.535]
b. Yes, 95% interval is below 17.

7.21 a. [786.609, 835.391]
b. Yes, 95% interval is above 750

7.23 [4.969, 5.951]; Yes

7.29 a. $n = 266$
b. $n = 465$

7.31 a. $n = 47$
b. $n = 328$

7.33 $n = 44$

7.35 a. $p = .5$
b. $p = .3$
c. $p = .8$

7.37 Part a. [.304, .496], [.286, .514], [.274, .526]
Part b. [.066, .134], [.060, .140], [.055, .145]
Part c. [.841, .959], [.830, .970], [.823, .977]
Part d. [.464, .736], [.439, .761], [.422, .778]

7.39 a. [.473, .610]
b. No, the interval extends below .5.

7.41 a. [.3804, .4596], no
b. [.5701, .6299], yes
c. 95% margin of error is .03

7.43 a. [.611, .729]
b. Yes, interval above .6

7.45 [.264, .344]
Yes, 95% interval exceeds .20.

7.47 a. $\hat{p} = .02$, [.0077, .0323]
b. $\hat{p} = .054$, [.034, .074]
c. Yes

7.49 Using $p = .73754$ and $z_{.005} = 2.576$, $n = 1429.13$ (or $n = 1430$)

7.53 a. [\$514.399, \$549.601]
b. \$5,559,932
[\$5,375,983.95, \$5,743, 880.05]
c. Claim is very doubtful

7.55 a. 2,954, [2,723, 3,185]
Yes, interval above 2,500
b. No, interval extends below 3,000

7.57 a. $n = 204$
b. $n = 371$

7.61 68.26%: [48.9312, 52.2188]
95.44%: [47.2874, 53.8626]
99.73%: [45.6436, 55.5064]
95% CI: [50.0492, 51.1008]

7.63 68.26%: [40.3076, 45.5924]
95.44%: [37.6652, 48.2348]
99.73%: [35.0228, 50.8772]
95% CI: [42.2952, 43.6048]

7.65 a. $\hat{p} = .3054$, [.2635, .3473]
b. Yes; yes
c. $n = 968$

7.67 2,301.28; [737.60, 3,864.96]

7.69 a. \$19,316,814; [\$16,541,476, \$22,092,152]
b. \$22,092,152

7.71 a. [25.1562, 27.2838]
b. Yes, not much more than 25

7.73 fa: [7.685%, 7.975%]; differs from 8.31%
dlcs: [9.108%, 17.732%]; does not differ from 11.71%
dms: [9.788%, 20.272%]; does not differ from 13.64%
dscs: [16.327%, 28.693%]; differs from 14.93%

7.75 [.61025, .66975]

7.77 a. [.796, .856]
b. Yes, interval is above .75

Chapter 8

8.1 H_0 status quo
H_a hoped for or suspected condition exists

8.5 Type I

8.7 The probability of Type II error becomes too large

8.9 a. H_0: $\mu \geq 6$ versus H_a: $\mu < 6$
b. Type I: decide $\mu < 6$ when $\mu \geq 6$
Type II: decide $\mu \geq 6$ when $\mu < 6$

8.11 a. H_0: $\mu = 16$ versus H_a: $\mu \neq 16$
b. Type I: readjust filler when not necessary
Type II: do not readjust when needed

8.13 There is a .05 probability that the network will advertise that the ZX-900 achieves a shorter mean stopping distance when it really does not.

8.17 1.28; reject H_0

8.19 2.33; reject H_0

8.21 p-value = .0062; Reject at all α except .001

8.23 $z = -2$

8.25 -1.645; reject H_0

8.27 -3.09; do not reject H_0

8.29 Strong

8.31 a. $z = -2.19$; Reject at $\alpha = .10, .05$
b. p-value = .0143; reject at an α of .10 or .05
c. Strong

8.33 $z = 4.8396$; $z_{.05} = 1.645$; reject H_0; p-value < .001; Yes

8.35 $z = -3.29$; run commercial; [56.489, 59.111]; μ is not substantially less than 60, but might be enough less than 60 to prevent more accidents

8.37 Use the point estimate and the confidence interval

8.39 $|z| = 3 > 1.645$; reject H_0

8.41 $|z| = 3 > 2.575$; reject H_0

8.43 p-value = .0026; reject H_0 with α = .10, .05 and .01, not with α = .001

8.45 a. $z = 2.37$; p-value = .0178; assign team
b. [2.958, 3.054]; some diameters outside limits

8.47 [16.0173, 16.0827]; reject H_0 because 16 is not within the confidence interval

8.51 $t = 2.33$; reject at .10 and .05, not at .01 and .001

8.53 a. $H_0: \mu \leq 3.5\%$ versus $H_a: \mu >$ 3.5%
b. $t = 3.62$; reject H_0 at $\alpha = .10$ and at $\alpha = .05$ and at $\alpha = .01$; very strong evidence

8.55 a. $H_0: \mu \leq 50$ versus $H_a: \mu > 50$
b. $t = 2.5$; reject H_0 at $\alpha = .10$ and at $\alpha = .05$ and at $\alpha = .01$; very strong evidence

8.57 p-value = .002261; reject at .10, .05, .01 but not at α = .001; very strong evidence

8.59 Most likely has practical importance

8.61 $t = -2.18$; reject H_0 at $\alpha = .05$; p-value = .0158; reject at .10 or .05

8.67 a. Yes e. Yes
b. No f. No
c. Yes g. Yes
d. Yes h. Yes

8.69 a. $z = -2.18$; do not reject H_0
b. .0292
c. Reject at .10, .05; do not reject at .01, .001

8.71 a. $H_0: p \leq .50$ versus $H_a: p > .50$
b. $z = 1.19$; do not reject at any α; little evidence
c. $z = 2.53$; very strong
d. $\hat{p} = .54$ based on much larger sample, stronger evidence p greater than .50

8.73 a. $H_0: p \leq .18$ versus $H_a: p > .18$
b. .0329; reject H_0 at .10, .05; do not at .01 or .001; strong evidence
c. Perhaps, subjective

8.75 a. $H_0: p = .95$ versus $H_a: p < .95$
b. $z = -14.68$; reject H_0 at each value of α; extremely strong evidence
c. Probably; $\hat{p} = .79$ far below claimed .95

8.79 a. .9279, .8315, .6772, .4840, .2946, .1492, .0618, .0207, .0055, .0012
b. No; $\beta = .2946$ when $\mu = 60.5$; increase the sample size
c. Power increases

8.81 $n = 246$

8.87 $\chi^2 = 6.72$; Reject H_0

8.89 [.0000738, .0003399]

8.91 a. $H_0: p \geq .05$ versus $H_a: p < .05$
b. $z = -2.43$; reject H_0 at .10, .05, and .01, not at .001; very strong evidence
c. p-value = .0075
d. Probably

8.93 a. p-value = .0043; Reject when α = .10, .05, .01 do not reject when α = .001
b. Very strong

8.95 a. $H_0: \mu \leq 1{,}200$ versus $H_a: \mu >$ 1,200
b. $t = 2.20$; reject H_0 at .10 and at .05; do not reject H_0 at .01 or at .001
c. $t = 3.72$; reject H_0 at each value of α; sample of $n = 100$ provides stronger evidence
d. Maybe
e. $t = 18.68$; reject H_0 at each value of α
e1. Yes
e2. Most likely

8.97 a. [.0157, .0419]
b. [22.641, 24.685]
c. [1203.14, 1279.26], [1219.217, 1263.183], [1489.291, 1559.909]

8.99 b. $t = -6.66$; reject H_0 (fa)
$t = .80$; do not reject (dlcs)
$t = .53$; do not reject (dms)
$t = 2.46$; reject H_0 (dscs)

8.101 Some evidence, reject H_0: $\mu = 30$ with $\alpha = .10$

8.103 a. $t = 4.9168$; reject H_0 with α = .001; extremely strong evidence
b. Opinions will vary. Estimated increase in expense on $100,000 investment is $440.

Chapter 9

9.1 a. $\mu_1 < \mu_2$ d. $\mu_1 > \mu_2$
b. $\mu_1 = \mu_2$ e. $\mu_1 > \mu_2$
c. $\mu_1 < \mu_2$ f. $\mu_1 \neq \mu_2$

9.5 a. [4.02, 5.98]; yes
b. $z = 10$; reject H_0; conclude $\mu_1 > \mu_2$
c. p-value = .0228; reject $H_0: \mu_1 - \mu_2 = 4$ at .10 and .05; do not reject at .01 or .001

9.7 a. [−20.12, −0.68]; yes, between .68 and 20.12 less
c. $z = -2.10$; reject H_0; conclude $\mu_1 < \mu_2$
d. p-value = .0179; reject H_0 at $\alpha = .10$, at $\alpha = .05$, and at $\alpha = .025$, but not at $\alpha = .01$ or at $\alpha = .001$; strong evidence $\mu_1 < \mu_2$

9.9 a. [−.05, .31]
b. No
c. $H_0: \mu_1 - \mu_2 \leq 0$ versus $H_a: \mu_1 - \mu_2 > 0$
d. $z = 1.41$; do not reject H_0; cannot conclude $\mu_1 > \mu_2$; cannot show to be harmful

9.11 a. $H_0: \mu_1 - \mu_2 = 0$ versus $H_a: \mu_1 - \mu_2 \neq 0$
b. $z = 5.06$; reject H_0 with $\alpha = .05$; μ_1 and μ_2 differ
c. p-value is less than .001; reject H_0 at each of the given values of α; extremely strong evidence
d. [.442, 1.358]

9.17 $t = 3.39$; reject H_0 with α = .10, .05, and .01; very strong evidence

9.19 For 9.16 assuming unequal variances: [23.503, 36.497]; yes, interval is above 20
For 9.17 assuming unequal variances: $t = 3.39$ with $df = 11$; p-value = .0030; Reject H_0 with α = .10, .05, and .01; very strong evidence.
For 9.18 assuming unequal variances: $t = 3.39$ with $df = 11$; p-value = .0061; Reject H_0 with α = .10, .05, and .01; very strong evidence.

9.21 a. $H_0: \mu_A - \mu_B \leq 0$ versus $H_a: \mu_A - \mu_B > 0$
b. $t = 1.97$; reject H_0 at $\alpha = .10$ and at $\alpha = .05$, but not at $\alpha = .01$ or $\alpha = .001$; strong evidence
c. [−12.01, 412.01]

9.23 a. $H_0: \mu_O - \mu_I = 0$ versus $H_a: \mu_O - \mu_I \neq 0$
b. $t = 2.31$ with 9 df; reject H_0 at .10 and .05, but not at .01 or .001; strong evidence
c. [$1.10, $100.90]

9.29 a. [100.141, 106.859]; yes [98.723, 108.277]; no
b. $t = 2.32$; strong evidence
c. $t = -4.31$; very strong evidence

9.31 a. $H_0: \mu_d = 0$; $H_a: \mu_d \neq 0$
b. $t = 9.22$; reject H_0 at each value of α
c. p-value = .000; reject H_0 at each value of α
d. [.1679, .2795]

9.33 a. $t = 6.18$; reject $H_0: \mu_d = 0$
b. Min 2.01; max 4.49; endpoints of 95% interval

9.35 a. $H_0: \mu_d = 0$ versus $H_a: \mu_d \neq 0$
b. $t = 3.89$; reject H_0 at all α except .001; yes
c. p-value = .006; reject H_0 at all α except .001; very strong evidence

9.39 $z = -10.14$; reject H_0 at each value of α; extremely strong evidence

9.41 a. $H_0: p_1 - p_2 = 0$ versus $H_a: p_1 - p_2 \neq 0$
b. $z = 3.63$; reject H_0 at each value of α
c. $H_0: p_1 - p_2 \leq .05$ versus $H_a: p_1 - p_2 > .05$
$z = 1.99$ and p-value = .0233; strong evidence
d. [.0509, .1711]; yes

9.43 p-value = .004; very strong evidence [−.057, −.011]; −.057

9.45 a. $z = 3.72$; reject $H_0: p_1 - p_2 = 0$ at $\alpha = .001$; [.029, .091]; largest: .091; smallest: .029

b. $z = -4.435$; reject H_0: $p_1 - p_2 = 0$ at $\alpha = .001$; [−.079, −.201]; largest: .079; smallest: .201

9.49 a. 2.96
b. 4.68
c. 3.16
d. 8.81

9.51 a. $F = 3.24$; do not reject
b. $F = 3.24$; do not reject

9.53 a. $F = 2.06$; do not reject H_0
b. p-value = .5052; do not reject H_0
c. Yes
d. $F = 2.06$

9.55 a. H_0: $\mu_T - \mu_B = 0$ versus H_a: $\mu_T - \mu_B \neq 0$
$t = 1.54$; cannot reject H_0 at any values of α; little or no evidence
b. [−.09, .73]

9.57 a. H_0: $\mu_d = 0$ versus H_a: $\mu_d > 0$
b. $t = 10.00$; reject H_0 at all levels of α
c. p-value = .000; reject H_0 at all levels of α; extremely strong evidence

9.59 a. $t = 8.251$; reject H_0: $\mu_O - \mu_{JVC} = 0$ at $\alpha = .001$
b. [$32.69, $55.31]; probably
c. $t = 2.627$; reject H_0: $\mu_O - \mu_{JVC} \leq 30$ at $\alpha = .05$

Chapter 10 (Answers to several Even-Numbered Exercises also given)

10.1 Factor = independent variables in a designed experiment
treatments = values of a factor (or combination of factors)
experimental units = entities to which treatments are assigned
response variable = the dependent variable (or variable of interest)

10.3 Response: time to stabilize emergency condition
Factor: display panel
Treatments: panels A, B, C
Experimental units: air traffic controllers

10.5 Constant variance, normality, independence

10.7 To determine which treatment means differ and to estimate how large the differences are.

10.9 a. $F = 184.57$; p-value = .000; reject H_0; shelf heights differ
b. bottom − middle: −21.4; [−25.12, −17.68]
bottom − top: 4.3; [.58, 8.02]
middle − top: 25.7; [21.98, 29.42]
Middle shelf maximizes mean sales
c. bottom − middle: [−24.45, −18.35]
bottom − top: [1.25, 7.35]
middle − top: [22.65, 28.75]
d. bottom: [53.65, 57.96]
middle: [75.04, 79.36]
top: [49.34, 53.66]

10.11 a. $F = 43.36$, p-value = .000; reject H_0; bottle designs differ
b. B − A: [11.56, 20.84]
C − A: [3.56, 12.84]
C − B: [−12.64, −3.36]
c. B − A: [12.41, 19.99]
C − A: [4.41, 11.99]
C − B: [−11.79, −4.21]
d. μ_A: [13.92, 19.28]
μ_B: [30.12, 35.48]
μ_C: [22.12, 27.48]

10.12 $F = 16.42$; p-value < .001; reject H_0; brands differ

10.13 Divot − Alpha: [38.41, 127.59]
Divot − Century: [50.21, 139.39]
Divot − Best: [−14.39, 74.79]
Century − Alpha: [−56.39, 32.79]
Century − Best: [−109.19, −20.01]
Best − Alpha: [8.21, 97.39]
Best and Divot appear to be most durable
Divot: [313.26, 359.94]
Best: [283.06, 329.74]
Alpha: [230.26, 276.94]
Century: [218.46, 265.14]

10.15 When differences between experimental units may be concealing any true differences between the treatments.

10.17 a. $F = 36.23$; p-value = .000; reject H_0; sales methods differ
b. $F = 12.87$; p-value = .007; reject H_0; salesman effects differ
c. Method 1 − Method 2: [−2.30, 2.96]
Method 1 − Method 3: [2.37, 7.63]
Method 1 − Method 4: [3.70, 8.96]
Method 2 − Method 3: [2.04, 7.30]
Method 2 − Method 4: [3.37, 8.63]
Method 3 − Method 4: [−1.30, 3.96]
Methods 1 and 2

10.19 a. $F = 441.75$ and p-value =.000; reject H_0; keyboard brand effects differ.
b. $F = 107.69$ and p-value =.000; reject H_0; specialist effects differ.
c. A − B: [8.55, 11.45]
A − C: [12.05, 14.95]
B − C: [2.05, 4.95]
Keyboard A

10.21 a. $F = 5.78$ and p-value =.0115; reject H_0; soft drink sales effects differ.
b. Coke Classic − New Coke: [7.99, 68.01]
Coke Classic − Pepsi: [−.71, 59.31]
New Coke − Pepsi: [−38.71, 21.31]
c. Yes, mean sales of Coke Classic were significantly higher than those for New Coke.

10.22 A combination of a level of factor 1 and a level of factor 2.

10.23 See Figure 10.11 on page 428 in the text.

10.25 a. Plot suggests little interaction. $F = .66$ and p-value = .681; do not reject H_0. Conclude no interaction.
b. $F = 26.49$ and p-value = .000; reject H_0; display panel effects differ.
c. $F = 100.80$ and p-value = .000; reject H_0; emergency condition effects differ.
d. A − B: [.49, 5.91]
A − C: [−6.81, −1.39]
B − C: [−10.01, −4.59]
e. 1 − 2: [−10.43, −4.17]
1 − 3: [−18.13, −11.87]
1 − 4: [.77, 7.03]
2 − 3: [−10.83, −4.57]
2 − 4: [8.07, 14.33]
3 − 4: [15.77, 22.03]
f. Panel *B*. No, there is no interaction.
g. [6.37, 12.63]

10.27 a. Plot suggests interaction exists. $F = 24.73$ and p-value = .001; reject H_0; conclude interaction exists. Cannot test separately.
b. House design *C* and foreman 1; [17.72, 19.88]

10.29 $F = 40.79$ and p-value < .0001; reject H_0; drug effects differ. All pairwise differences significant with $\alpha = .05$
Y − X: [9.18, 21.82]
Z − X: [−17.52, −4.88]
Z − Y: [−33.02, −20.38]
μ_Y: [34.73, 43.67]
All intervals are 95%.

10.31 Loan officer effects differ (p-value < .0001)
Evaluation method effects differ (p-value < .0001)
D − B: [−4.25, −3.25]
F − B: [−3.25, −2.25]
D − F: [−1.50, −.50]
4 − 1: [−4.58, −3.42]
3 − 1: [−3.58, −2.42]
2 − 1: [−1.91, −.75]
4 − 2: [−3.25, −2.09]
3 − 2: [−2.25, −1.09]
4 − 3: [−1.58, −.42]

10.33 F(int) = .09; do not reject H_0; conclude no interaction.
$F(1) = 3.31$; reject H_0, degree of attendance effects significant.
$F(2) = .23$; do not reject H_0; prior information effects not significant.

10.35 F(int) = 0.19 and p-value = .9019; do not reject H_0; conclude no interaction
$F(1) = 48.63$ and p-value = .000; reject H_0. Fertilizer type effects differ.
$F(2) = 78.90$ and p-value = .000; reject H_0. Wheat type effects differ.
Using Tukey comparisons: Fertilizer types *A* and *B* differ with $\alpha = .01$
Wheat types *M* and *N*, *M* and *O*, *M* and *P*, *O* and *P* each differ with $\alpha = .01$.

Chapter 11 (Answers to several Even-Numbered Exercises also given)

11.1 When the plot suggests a linear relationship between y and x.

11.3 β_1 = change in the mean value of y associated with a one unit increase in x
β_0 = mean value of y when $x = 0$

11.5 Plot has a straight line appearance (with a positive slope).

11.6 a. mean starting salary for marketing graduates with a 4.0 gpa
b. mean starting salary for marketing graduates with a 2.50 gpa
c. change in mean starting salary associated with a one point increase in gpa
d. mean starting salary for marketing graduates with a 0.00 gpa; can't graduate with a 0.00 gpa
e. all factors other than gpa; type of minor, job experience

11.7 Plot has a straight line appearance (with a positive slope).

11.8 a. mean service time when 4 copiers are serviced
b. mean service time when 6 copiers are serviced
c. change in mean service time associated with an additional copier serviced
d. mean service time when no copiers are serviced; no
e. all factors other than number of copiers serviced; work environment, number of distractions

11.9 plot looks reasonably linear

11.10 a. mean demand when price difference is .10.
b. mean demand when price difference is −.05.
c. change in mean demand per dollar increase in the price difference
d. mean demand when price difference equals 0; yes
e. all factors other than price difference; advertising budget, type of ads

11.11 b. the plot of y versus x appears linear (with a positive slope)

11.12 a. mean labor cost when batch size is 60
b. mean labor cost when batch size is 30
c. change in mean labor cost per unit increase in batch size
d. mean labor cost when batch size is zero; questionable
e. all factors other than batch size; wages, overtime

11.13 b. plot looks reasonably linear with a positive slope

11.14 a. mean sales price for 2000 ($x = 20$) sq. ft. homes
b. mean sales price for 1800 ($x = 18$) sq. ft. homes
c. change in mean sales price per one unit (100 square ft.) increase in home size
d. mean sales price when home size = 0; no
e. all factors other than home size; upkeep, location

11.15 The quality or goodness of the fit of the least squares line to the observed data.

11.17 Evaluate $\hat{y} = b_0 + b_1x$ for the given value of x.

11.19 a. $b_0 = 14.82$; $b_1 = 5.707$; no
b. $33,367.75

11.21 a. $b_0 = 7.814$; $b_1 = 2.665$; yes
b. 8.0805 (808,050 bottles)
c. .257 (about 26 cents)

11.23 a. $b_0 = 48.02$, $b_1 = 5.700$
c. $\hat{y} = 48.02 + 5.700\,x$
d. 162.02 ($162,020)

11.25 σ^2; σ That is, constant variance and standard deviation of the error term populations.

11.27 21.3002; 4.61521

11.29 74.67624; 8.64154

11.31 27.853025; 5.2776

11.35 a. $b_0 = 11.4641$; $b_1 = 24.6022$
b. $SSE = 191.7017$; $s^2 = 21.3002$; $s = 4.615$
c. $s_{b_1} = .8045$; $t = 30.580$
d. $t > 2.262$; reject H_0: $\beta_1 = 0$; strong evidence that regression relationship is significant.
e. $t > 3.250$; reject H_0: $\beta_1 = 0$; very strong evidence that regression relationship is significant.
f. p-value = .000; reject H_0: $\beta_1 = 0$ at all values of α. Extremely strong evidence regression relationship is significant.
g. [22.782, 26.422]
h. [21.987, 27.217]
i. $s_{b_0} = 3.4390$; $t = 3.334$
j. p-value = .0087; reject H_0: $\beta_0 = 0$ at all values of α except .001. Very strong evidence that the intercept is significant.
k. $SS_{xx} = 32.909$, $s_{b_0} = 3.439$, $s_{b_1} = .8045$

11.37 a. $b_0 = 18.4875$; $b_1 = 10.1463$
b. $SSE = 746.7624$; $s^2 = 74.6762$; $s = 8.6415$
c. $s_{b_1} = .0866$; $t = 117.1344$
d. Reject H_0: $\beta_1 = 0$ with $\alpha = .05$. Regression relationship is significant (strong evidence).
e. Reject H_0: $\beta_1 = 0$ with $\alpha = .01$. Regression relationship is significant (very strong evidence).
f. p-value = .000; reject H_0: $\beta_1 = 0$ at all values of α. Regression relationship is significant (extremely strong evidence).
g. [9.9533, 10.3393]
h. [9.872, 10.421]
i. $s_{b_0} = 4.6766$; $t = 3.9532$
j. p-value = .0027; reject H_0: $\beta_0 = 0$ at all values of α except $\alpha = .001$. Intercept is significant (very strong evidence).
k. $SS_{xx} = 9952.667$, $s_{b_0} = 4.6766$, $s_{b_1} = .0866$

11.39 [3.091, 5.770]

11.41 The distance between x_0 and $\bar{x}$

11.43 The smaller the distance value, the shorter the intervals

11.45 a. 109.873; [106.721, 113.025]
b. 109.873; [98.967, 120.779]
d. 113 minutes

11.47 a. 627.263; [621.054, 633.472]
b. 627.263; [607.032, 647.494]
c. [618.42, 636.10]; [598.48, 656.04]

11.49 2.3429; [1.7369, 2.9489]

11.51 a. 114.945; [110.604, 119.287]
b. 114.945; [102.024, 127.867]

11.55 19918.8428; $r^2 = .990$, $r = .995$

11.57 1,024,592.904; $r^2 = .999$, $r = .9995$

11.59 Exp. Var. = 5.1817
UnExp. Var. = 0.1343
Total Var. = 5.3160; $r^2 = .975$

11.63 Reject H_0: $\rho = 0$ at all four values of α

11.65 t-test for significance of β_1

11.67 a. $F = 935.149$
b. Reject H_0 with $\alpha = .05$; significant
c. Reject H_0 with $\alpha = .01$; significant
d. p-value less than .001; reject H_0 at all values of α; significant

11.69 a. $F = 13,720.4877$
b. Reject H_0 with $\alpha = .05$; significant
c. Reject H_0 with $\alpha = .01$; significant
d. p-value = .000; reject H_0 at all values of α; significant

11.71 a. $F = 154.2792$
b. Reject H_0 with $\alpha = .05$; significant
c. Reject H_0 with $\alpha = .01$; significant
d. p-value = .0002; reject H_0 at all values of α; significant

11.75 Approximate horizontal band appearance. No violations indicated.

11.77 No violations indicated.

11.79 Cyclical plot; $d = .473 < 1.27$; conclude positive autocorrelation exists; $4 - .473 = 3.527 > 1.45$; conclude no negative autocorrelation exists

11.81 Constant variance assumption violated

11.83 a. yes, plot appears linear
b. $b_0 = 306.619$; $b_1 = -27.714$
c. $\hat{y} = 306.619 - 27.714x$
d. p-value = .000; significant
e. for $2.10: 248.420; [244.511, 252.327]
for $2.75: 230.405; [226.697, 234.112]
for $3.10: 220.705; [216.415, 224.994]

11.85 a. We cannot
b. Possibly not; don't take up smoking

11.87 a. 10.0045; [8.494, 11.514]
b. 10.0045; [−.310, 20.318]

11.89 a. $F = 21.1299$ with p-value = .0002; significant relationship
b. $b_1 = 35.2877$; [19.2202, 51.3553]

11.91 $\hat{y} = 2.0572 + 6.3545(1/5) = 3.3281$

Chapter 12 (Answers to several Even-Numbered Exercises also given)

12.1 y: dependent variable $x_1, \ldots, x_k$: independent (predictor) variables

12.2 Mean value of y when the values of the independent variables are $x_1, x_2, \ldots, x_k$

12.3 Unknown regression parameters relating mean value of y to $x_1, \ldots, x_k$

12.4 Describes the effects on y of all factors other than $x_1, x_2, \ldots, x_k$

12.5 β_0 is the mean value of y when all predictor variables equal zero
β_1 is the change in mean y associated with a one unit increase in x_1 when all other predictor variables stay the same

12.7 a. Plots not very curved (see Table 12.4).
b. mean demand for Fresh when $x_1 = \$3.70$, $x_2 = \$3.90$, $x_3 = \$650{,}000$
c. β_0 = y-intercept has no practical meaning
β_1 = change in mean demand when x_1 increases by \$1 and x_2 and x_3 unchanged
β_2, β_3 similar to β_1
ε = effects on y of all factors other than x_1, x_2, x_3

12.9 SSE

12.11 a. $b_0 = 29.347$, $b_1 = 5.6128$, $b_2 = 3.8344$
b. $\hat{y} = 29.347 + 5.6128(20) + 3.8344(8) = 172.28$

12.13 a. $b_0 = 1946.8020$, $b_1 = .0386$, $b_2 = 1.0394$, $b_3 = -413.7578$
b. $\hat{y} = 1946.8020 + .0386(56194) + 1.0394(14077.88) - 413.7578(6.89) = 15896.25$
c. $17207.31 - 15896.25 = 1311.06$ greater than $\hat{y}$

12.14 σ^2, σ

12.15 a. proportion of total variation explained by the model
b. $\bar{R}^2$ avoids overestimating the importance of the independent variables

12.16 Tests to see if at least one independent variable is significant.

12.17 1. $SSE = 73.6$; $s^2 = 10.5$; $s = 3.24164$
2. total variation = 7447.5
unexplained variation = 73.6
explained variation = 7374
3. $R^2 = .99$; $\bar{R}^2 = .987$
4. F(model) = 350.87
5. F(model) $= 350.87 > F_{.05} = 4.74$; reject H_0: $\beta_1 = \beta_2 = 0$ with $\alpha = .05$. Model significant.
6. F(model) $= 350.87 > F_{.01} = 9.55$. Model significant with $\alpha = .01$.
7. p-value = .000; model significant at each value of α.

12.19 1. $SSE = 1{,}798{,}712.2$; $s^2 = 149{,}892.7$, $s = 387.1598$
2. total variation = 464,126,601.6
unexplained variation = 1,798,712.2
explained variation = 462,327,889.4
3. $R^2 = .9961$; $\bar{R}^2 = .9952$
4. F(model) = 1028.1309
5. F(model) $= 1028.1309 > F_{.05} = 3.49$; reject H_0: $\beta_1 = \beta_2 = \beta_3 = 0$ with $\alpha = .05$. Model significant.
6. F(model) $= 1028.1309 > F_{.01} = 5.95$. Model significant with $\alpha = .01$.
7. p-value < .001; model significant at each value of α.

12.22 1. $b_0 = 29.347$; $s_{b_0} = 4.891$; $t = 6.00$
$b_1 = 5.6128$; $s_{b_1} = .2285$; $t = 24.56$
$b_2 = 3.8344$; $s_{b_2} = .4332$; $t = 8.85$
2. β_0: $t = 6.00 > t_{.025} = 2.365$; reject H_0: $\beta_0 = 0$ with $\alpha = .05$
β_1: $t = 24.56 > 2.365$; reject H_0: $\beta_1 = 0$ with $\alpha = .05$
β_2: $t = 8.85 > 2.365$; reject H_0: $\beta_2 = 0$ with $\alpha = .05$
β_0, x_1, x_2 all significant with $\alpha = .05$
3. β_0: $t = 6.00 > t_{.005} = 3.499$; reject H_0: $\beta_0 = 0$ with $\alpha = .01$
β_1: $t = 24.56 > 3.499$; reject H_0: $\beta_1 = 0$ with $\alpha = .01$
β_2: $t = 8.85 > 3.499$; reject H_0: $\beta_2 = 0$ with $\alpha = .01$
β_0, x_1, x_2 all significant with $\alpha = .01$
4. For H_0: $\beta_0 = 0$, p-value $= 0.001 < \alpha = .01$; reject H_0 at $\alpha = .10, .05, .01$; β_0 significant at $\alpha = .10, .05, .01$, not at $\alpha = .001$.
For H_0: $\beta_1 = 0$, p-value = 0.000 < each value of α
Reject H_0: $\beta_1 = 0$, at each value of α
x_1 significant at each value of α
For H_0: $\beta_2 = 0$, p-value = 0.000 < each value of α
Reject H_0: $\beta_2 = 0$, at each value of α
x_2 significant at each value of α
5. β_0: [17.780, 40.914]
β_1: [5.072, 6.153]
β_2: [2.810, 4.860]
6. β_0: [12.233, 46.461]
β_1: [4.813, 6.412]
β_2: [2.319, 5.350]

12.23 1. $b_0 = 7.5891$, $s_{b_0} = 2.4450$, $t = 3.104$;
$b_1 = -2.3577$, $s_{b_1} = .6379$, $t = -3.696$;
$b_2 = 1.6122$, $s_{b_2} = .2954$, $t = 5.459$;
$b_3 = .5012$, $s_{b_3} = .1259$, $t = 3.981$;
2. β_0: $t = 3.104 > t_{.025} = 2.056$; reject H_0: $\beta_0 = 0$ with $\alpha = .05$;
β_1: $|t| = 3.696 > 2.056$; reject H_0: $\beta_1 = 0$ with $\alpha = .05$;
β_2: $t = 5.459 > 2.056$; reject H_0: $\beta_2 = 0$ with $\alpha = .05$;
β_3: $t = 3.981 > 2.056$; reject H_0: $\beta_3 = 0$ with $\alpha = .05$;
β_0, x_1, x_2, x_3 all significant with $\alpha = .05$
3. In each case, $|t| > t_{.005} = 2.779$; reject appropriate H_0 with $\alpha = .01$; β_0, x_1, x_2, x_3 all significant with $\alpha = .01$
4. For H_0: $\beta_0 = 0$, p-value $= .0046 < \alpha = .01$; reject H_0 at each α except $\alpha = .001$;
For H_0: $\beta_1 = 0$, p-value $= .0010 < \alpha = .01$; reject H_0 at each α except $\alpha = .001$;
For H_0: $\beta_2 = 0$, p-value $< .0001 < \alpha = .001$; reject H_0 at each value of α;
For H_0: $\beta_3 = 0$, p-value $= .0005 < \alpha = .001$; reject H_0 at each value of α;
β_0 and x_1 significant at $\alpha = .01$;
x_2 and x_3 significant at $\alpha = .001$;
5. 95% intervals: $[b_j \pm 2.056\, s_{b_j}]$;
β_0: [2.5633, 12.6149];
β_1: [−3.6690, −1.0464];
β_2: [1.0051, 2.2193];
β_3: [0.2424, 0.7599];
6. 99% intervals: $[b_j \pm 2.779\, s_{b_j}]$;
For example,
β_1: [−4.1304, −0.5850]

12.25 Distance of $x_1, x_2, \ldots, x_k$ from $\bar{x}_1, \bar{x}_2, \ldots, \bar{x}_k$

12.27 a. 172.28, [168.56, 175.99]
b. 172.28, [163.76, 180.80]
c. [166.79, 177.77], [159.68, 184.88]

12.29 [14906.24, 16886.26]
$y = 17{,}207.31$ is unusually high (above interval)

12.31 See page 557 in the text.

12.33 First interval shorter; model that uses x_4

12.35 Multiply x_1 by x_2 to form x_1x_2

12.37 a. 2.0122, 1.6633, 1.3144, .9655, .6166
b. 3.8342, 3.4853, 3.1364, 2.7875, 2.4386
c. Because the point estimates for part B are larger

12.39 a. For $x_1 = 13$: 108.93328
For $x_1 = 22$: 156.73012
b. For $x_1 = 13$: 129.75562
For $x_1 = 22$: 183.74788
c. As x_1 increases mean y increases at a faster rate when x_2 is higher

12.43 a. Linear plots with different y-intercepts for mutual and stock companies
b. β_2 = difference between mean times for mutual and stock companies
c. p-value < .001; reject H_0: $\beta_2 = 0$ with $\alpha = .05$ and $\alpha = .01$. Company type is significant. [4.9770, 11.1339]
d. No interaction

12.45 b. $F = 184.57$, p-value $< .001$; reject H_0. Display heights have different effects on mean sales
c. 21.4, −4.3, 25.7 [18.35, 24.45]; Reject H_0: $\beta_M = 0$; effect of middle height differs from bottom height [−7.35, −1.25]; Reject H_0: $\beta_T = 0$; effect of top height differs from bottom height
d. 77.2, [75.04, 79.36]; [71.486, 82.914]
e. [22.65, 28.75]; p-value $< .001$; Reject H_0: $\beta_M = 0$; effect of middle height differs from top height

12.47 a. Little or no interaction; interaction terms not needed
b. 8.61178 (861,178 bottles); [8.27089, 8.95266]; slightly longer

12.49 $(k - g)$ = number of parameters set equal to zero in H_0
$n - (k + 1)$ = denominator degrees of freedom

12.51 $F = 9.228 > F_{.01} = 4.31$. Reject H_0 at $\alpha = .05$ and .01

12.55 a. .9999; .9353; .9328; 9334.5; 8684.2; 23.0
b. BedDays, Load, Pop
c. $b_1 = -9.30$, $b_4 = -3.223$
d. Yes
e. Model 1; Model 2; Model 1; Model 2; Probably Model 2

12.59 a. Straight line appearance; normality assumption ok
b. Interpretations will vary

12.61 a. Yes
b. $\hat{y} = 1{,}239.70$ [1,167.32, 1,312.08] [878.68, 1,600.72]

12.65 Hospital 17: Model I Cook's D = 5.033, Model II Cook's D = 0.738
Hospital 15: Model I Cook's D = 0.541, Model II Cook's D = 1.442
Hospital 14: Stud. Del. Residual decreases from 4.558 (Model I) to 1.406 (Model II). Since $1.406 < t_{.025} = 2.179$, Hospital 14 no longer an outlier.

12.67 Odds = prob. of success ÷ prob. of failure; Odds ratio for x_j is proportional change in the odds for a one unit increase in x_j

12.69 a. $P(\text{Hire}|\text{Male}) = .628$
$P(\text{Hire}|\text{Female}) = .0062$
b. 271.429; yes, strong evidence $\beta_3 > 0$

12.71 At a specified square footage: adding rooms increases selling price, while adding bedrooms reduces selling price.

12.73 Run promotions during day games on weekdays.

12.75 a. β_5: $b_5 = 0.2137$ with p-value = .0022; effect of B versus A significant at $\alpha = .01$, but not at $\alpha = .001$; [.0851, .3423]
β_6: $b_6 = .3818$ with p-value less than .001; effect of C versus A significant at $\alpha = .001$; [.2551, .5085]
b. β_6: $b_6 = 0.1681$ with p-value = .0147; effect of C versus B significant at $\alpha = .05$; but not at $\alpha = .01$; [.0363, .2999]
d. Prediction interval for the third model is slightly shorter.

12.77 $|-4.96226| > 2$. Removing observation 17 will substantially change the point prediction of y_{17}.

Chapter 13

13.3 See page 636 in the text.

13.5 a. Straight line growth.
b. $\hat{y} = 290.089474 + 8.667669(21) = 472.1$

13.7 Square root ($y_t^{.5}$), Quartic root ($y_t^{.25}$), logarithmic ($\ln y_t$)

13.9 439.703, [389.915, 495.848]

13.11 See page 647 in the text.

13.13 See page 648 in the text.

13.15 $tr_t = 220.54 + 19.95\,t$

13.17 666.6, 881.6, 482.1, 299.9

13.19 a. 15.01, 40.54, 56.82, 22.02
b. [12.21, 17.81], [37.69, 43.39], [53.90, 59.74], [19.04, 25.00]

13.25 35,592.7; [31,325.5, 39,860]

13.27 810.04; [774.95, 845.13]

13.31 Method B; method A

13.37 b. 483, [401, 582]
c. 1.29289

Chapter 14

14.9 a. $\bar{x} = 5, 7, 6, 3, 7$; $R = 2, 4, 4, 2, 5$;
b. $\bar{\bar{x}} = 5.6$, $\bar{R} = 3.4$;
d. $\text{UCL}_{\bar{x}} = 9.0782$, $\text{LCL}_{\bar{x}} = 2.1218$; $\text{UCL}_R = 8.7516$, no LCL_R

14.11 b. Center $\text{line}_{\bar{x}} = 10.032$, $\text{UCL}_{\bar{x}} = 10.5167$, $\text{LCL}_{\bar{x}} = 9.5473$, Center $\text{line}_R = .84$, $\text{UCL}_R = 1.7758$, no LCL_R
d. Yes, R chart in control
e. $\bar{x}$ chart out of control; pressing machine not being properly adjusted
f. Center $\text{line}_{\bar{x}} = 10.2225$, $\bar{R} = .825$
g. $\text{UCL}_{\bar{x}} = 10.6985$, $\text{LCL}_{\bar{x}} = 9.7465$, Center $\text{line}_R = .825$, $\text{UCL}_R = 1.7440$, no LCL_R
h. Yes, both charts now in control

14.13 b. $\text{CL}_{\bar{x}} = 15.8$, $\text{UCL}_{\bar{x}} = 19.3389$, $\text{LCL}_{\bar{x}} = 12.2611$, $\text{CL}_R = 6.1333$, $\text{UCL}_R = 12.9658$, No LCL_R; yes
d. No, $\bar{x}$ chart out of control
e. No, both charts remain in control after die change
f. Yes, $\bar{x}$ chart badly out of control after die repair

14.15 a. $\text{CL}_{\bar{x}} = 841.45$, $\text{UCL}_{\bar{x}} = 845.2116$, $\text{LCL}_{\bar{x}} = 837.6884$, $\text{CL}_R = 5.16$, $\text{UCL}_R = 11.78$, no LCL_R; yes, both charts out of control
c. $\text{CL}_{\bar{x}} = 841.40$, $\text{UCL}_{\bar{x}} = 844.96$, $\text{LCL}_{\bar{x}} = 837.84$, $\text{CL}_R = 4.88$, $\text{UCL}_R = 11.14$, no LCL_R
d. R chart in control; yes, can use $\bar{x}$ chart
e. No, $\bar{x}$ chart out of control; process mean is changing
f. $\text{CL}_{\bar{x}} = 840.46$, $\text{UCL}_{\bar{x}} = 844.29$, $\text{LCL}_{\bar{x}} = 836.63$, $\text{CL}_R = 5.25$, $\text{UCL}_R = 11.98$, no LCL_R
g. Yes, all within control limits

14.17 a. $\text{CL}_{\bar{x}} = 15.99835$, $\text{UCL}_{\bar{x}} = 16.116685$, $\text{LCL}_{\bar{x}} = 15.880015$, $\text{CL}_R = .245$, $\text{UCL}_R = .4910$, no LCL_R
b. Both very near center line $\bar{R}$
c. Both very near center line $\bar{\bar{x}}$
d. Fills increase between 20 minutes after and 30 minutes after
e. Subgroup measurements 3 at a time—one subgroup each half hour.
f. $\text{UCL}_{\bar{x}} = 16.0418$, $\text{LCL}_{\bar{x}} = 15.95485$, $\text{UCL}_R = .1094$, no LCL_R
g. New R chart in control, new $\bar{x}$ chart out of control, process mean changing

14.21 a. Run 8 points below CL; Run 12 points above CL
b. Two points above UCL
c. No evidence
d. 2 of 3 points in zone A or beyond

14.23 Up A–B: 843.96
Up B–C: 842.70
Low B–C: 840.20
Low A–B: 838.94
Up A–B: 9.57
Up B–C: 7.37
Low B–C: 2.95
Low A–B: .75

14.29 a. [12.4644, 19.4188]
b. Max 19.4188 min; min 12.4644 min
c. Yes, max time less than 20 minutes
d. 20 min: 3.50 sigma; 30 min: 12.13 sigma

14.31 a. [.6518, 1.0416]
b. 1.0416 lb.

c. No; weights might be as low as .6518 lb.
d. .0681 or 6.81%

14.33 a. [50.9189, 54.2561]
b. Can be reduced by .4189 lb.; .4189(1,000,000)($2) = $837,800

14.35 .8736

14.39 UCL = .19, LCL = .01

14.41 a. UCL = .6217, LCL = .4323
b. In control, no assignable causes

14.43 a. UCL = .0853, LCL = .0187
b. UCL = .057, LCL = .005; yes

14.51 a. $UCL_{\bar{x}} = 5.35$, $LCL_{\bar{x}} = 3.51$
b. $UCL_R = 3.38$
c. In control

14.53 a. $UCL_{\bar{x}} = 5.08$, $LCL_{\bar{x}} = 3.92$, $UCL_R = 2.135$
b. Yes, in control
c. [3.20, 5.80]
d. Yes, capable
e. 3.45, .45

Chapter 15

15.3 a. $S = 4$; p-value = .375; do not reject H_0
b. $S = 5$; p-value = .031; reject H_0

15.5 a. p-value = .0059; reject H_0

15.7 a. $S_1 = 4$, $S_2 = 5$, $S = 5$
b. p-value = 1.0; do not reject H_0 at any α; conclude no difference

15.11 $T_1 = 120.5$; do not reject H_0; no difference

15.13 Differences exist

15.17 $T^- = 3$; reject H_0 at $\alpha = .02$

15.19 $T = 0$; reject H_0; conclude scores differ

15.23 Reject H_0; panels differ

15.25 $H = 14.36$; reject H_0; display heights differ

15.29 a. $r_s = -.721$
.648; yes
b. No

15.31 $r_s = 1.0$; reject H_0

15.33 $H = 14.36$
p-value = .001
Drugs differ

15.35 $T^+ = 1.0$
p-value = .004; decreased

15.37 $T_1 = 75$
p-value = .0066
Loan rates differ

Chapter 16

16.7 a. Each $E_i \geq 5$
b. $\chi^2 = 300.605$; reject H_0

16.9 a. $\chi^2 = 137.14$; reject H_0
b. Differences between brand preferences

16.11 a1. $(-\infty, 10.185)$
a2. (10.185, 14.147)
a3. (14.147, 18.108)
a4. (18.108, 22.069)
a5. (22.069, 26.030)
a6. $(26.030, \infty)$
b. 1.5, 9, 22, 22, 9, 1.5
c. Can use χ^2 test
e. 1, 9, 30, 15, 8, 2
$\chi^2 = 5.581$
f. Fail to reject; normal

16.13 Fail to reject H_0; normal

16.17 a.

		40%
		60%
20%	80%	

b.

16%	24%
40%	60%
80%	30%
4%	56%
6.67%	93.33%
20%	70%

c. $\chi^2 = 16.667$; reject H_0
d. Yes

16.19 a.

		24.24%
		22.73%
		53.03%
51.515%	48.485%	

b. For Heavy/Yes cell: cell: 18.18%; row: 75%; column: 35.29%
c. $\chi^2 = 6.86$; fail to reject H_0
d. Possibly; can reject H_0 at $\alpha = .05$

16.21 a. $\chi^2 = 16.384$; reject H_0
b. [−.216, −.072]

16.23 $\chi^2 = 65.91$; reject H_0; [.270, .376]

16.25 b. $\chi^2 = 20.941$; reject H_0
c. Dependent

16.27 $\chi^2 = 71.48$; reject H_0

Chapter 17

17.3 .571, .429

17.5 .502

17.7 a. .927
b. Yes

17.9 .174

17.15 Small facility

17.17 a. $10 million, $10.5 million, $3 million
b. Medium facility

17.19 a. $12.2 million
b. $1.7 million

17.21 a. *A*: 6.2, *B*: 5.2 *C*: 4.8
b. Location *A*
c. $1.8 million

17.23 a. Subcontract: $1.23
Expand: $1.57
Build: $1.35
b. Expand

17.29 a. .485, .8247, .0928, .0825
b. .300, .1667, .700, .1333
c. .215, .2325, .2093, .5581

17.31 a. 822
b. 580
c. 242
d. 242

17.35 a. .73, .9863, .0137
b. .27, .6667, .3333

17.37 a. Do not send, $14,958.90
b. Send, $14,500

17.45 Build large; $62 million

17.47 .5455

17.49 a. .186
c. 0.63
e. .833

17.51 b. Renew lease; $2,775,000
c. Sign; EVPI = $1,575,000

References

Abraham, B., and J. Ledolter. *Statistical Methods for Forecasting.* New York, NY: John Wiley & Sons, 1983.

Akaah, Ishmael P., and Edward A. Riordan. "Judgments of Marketing Professionals about Ethical Issues in Marketing Research: A Replication and Extension." *Journal of Marketing Research,* February 1989, pp. 112–20.

Ashton, Robert H., John J. Willingham, and Robert K. Elliott. "An Empirical Analysis of Audit Delay." *Journal of Accounting Research* 25, no. 2 (Autumn 1987), pp. 275–92.

Axcel, Amir. *Complete Business Statistics.* 3rd ed. Burr Ridge, IL: Irwin/McGraw-Hill, 1996.

Bayus, Barry L. "The Consumer and Durable Replacement Buyer." *Journal of Marketing* 55 (January 1991), pp. 42–51.

Beattie, Vivien, and Michael John Jones. "The Use and Abuse of Graphs in Annual Reports: Theoretical Framework and Empirical Study." *Accounting and Business Research* 22, no. 88 (Autumn 1992), pp. 291–303.

Blauw, Jan Nico, and Willem E. During. "Total Quality Control in Dutch Industry." *Quality Progress* (February 1990), pp. 50–51.

Blodgett, Jeffrey G., Donald H. Granbois, and Rockney G. Walters. "The Effects of Perceived Justice on Complainants' Negative Word-of-Mouth Behavior and Repatronage Intentions." *Journal of Retailing* 69, no. 4 (Winter 1993), pp. 399–428.

Bowerman, Bruce L., and Richard T. O'Connell. *Forecasting and Time Series: An Applied Approach.* 3rd ed. Belmont, CA: Duxbury Press, 1993.

Bowerman, Bruce L., and Richard T. O'Connell. *Linear Statistical Models: An Applied Approach.* 2nd ed. Boston, MA: PWS-KENT Publishing Company, 1990, pp. 457, 460–64, 729–974.

Box, G. E. P., and G. M. Jenkins. *Time Series Analysis: Forecasting and Control.* 2nd ed. San Francisco, CA: Holden-Day, 1976.

Boyd, Thomas C., and Timothy C. Krehbiel. "The Effect of Promotion Timing on Major League Baseball Attendance." *Sport Marketing Quarterly,* 1999, 8(4), pp. 23–34.

Brown, R. G. *Smoothing, Forecasting and Prediction of Discrete Time Series.* Englewood Cliffs, NJ: Prentice Hall, 1962.

Carey, John; Robert Neff; and Lois Therrien. "The Prize and the Passion." *Business Week* (Special 1991 bonus issue: The Quality Imperative), January 15, 1991, pp. 58–59.

Carslaw, Charles A. P. N., and Steven E. Kaplan. "An Examination of Audit Delay: Further Evidence from New Zealand." *Accounting and Business Research* 22, no. 85 (1991), pp. 21–32.

Cateora, Philip R. *International Marketing.* 9th ed. Homewood, IL: Irwin/McGraw-Hill, 1993, p. 262.

Clemen, Robert T. *Making Hard Decisions: An Introduction to Decision Analysis.* 2nd ed. Belmont, CA: Duxbury Press, 1996, p. 443.

Conlon, Edward J., and Thomas H. Stone. "Absence Schema and Managerial Judgment." *Journal of Management* 18, no. 3 (1992), pp. 435–54.

Cooper, Donald R., and C. William Emory. *Business Research Methods.* 5th ed. Homewood, IL: Richard D. Irwin, 1995, pp. 434–38, 450–51, 458–68.

Cuprisin, Tim. "Inside TV & Radio." *The Milwaukee Journal Sentinel,* April 26, 1995.

Dawson, Scott. "Consumer Responses to Electronic Article Surveillance Alarms." *Journal of Retailing* 69, no. 3 (Fall 1993), pp. 353–62.

Deming, W. Edwards. *Out of the Crisis.* Cambridge, MA: Massachusetts Institute of Technology Center for Advanced Engineering Study, 1986, pp. 18–96, 312–14.

Dielman, Terry. *Applied Regression Analysis for Business and Economics.* Belmont, CA: Duxbury Press, 1996.

Dillon, William R., Thomas J. Madden, and Neil H. Firtle. *Essentials of Marketing Research.* Homewood, IL: Richard D. Irwin Inc., 1993, pp. 382–84, 416–17, 419–20, 432–33, 445, 462–64, 524–27.

Dondero, Cort. "SPC Hits the Road." *Quality Progress,* January 1991, pp. 43–44.

Draper, N., and H. Smith. *Applied Regression Analysis.* 2nd ed. New York, NY: John Wiley & Sons, 1981.

Farnum, Nicholas R. *Modern Statistical Quality Control and Improvement.* Belmont, CA: Duxbury Press, 1994, p. 55.

Fitzgerald, Neil. "Relations Overcast by Cloudy Conditions." *CA Magazine,* April 1993, pp. 28–35.

Garvin, David A. *Managing Quality.* New York, NY: Free Press/Macmillan, 1988.

Gibbons, J. D. *Nonparametric Statistical Inference.* 2nd ed. New York: McGraw-Hill, 1985.

Gitlow, Howard; Shelly Gitlow; Alan Oppenheim; and Rosa Oppenheim. *Tools and Methods for the Improvement of Quality.* Homewood, IL: Richard D. Irwin, 1989, pp. 14–25, 533–53.

Guthrie, James P., Curtis M. Grimm, and Ken G. Smith. "Environmental Change and Management Staffing: A Reply." *Journal of Management* 19, no. 4 (1993), pp. 889–96.

Kuhn, Susan E. "A Closer Look at Mutual Funds: Which Ones Really Deliver?" *Fortune,* October 7, 1991, pp. 29–30.

Kumar, V., Roger A. Kerin, and Arun Pereira. "An Empirical Assessment of Merger and Acquisition Activity in Retailing." *Journal of Retailing* 67, no. 3 (Fall 1991), pp. 321–38.

Magee, Robert P. *Advanced Managerial Accounting.* New York, NY: Harper & Row, 1986, p. 223.

Mahmood, Mo Adam, and Gary J. Mann. "Measuring the Organizational Impact of Information Technology Investment: An Exploratory Study." *Journal of Management Information Systems* 10, no. 1 (Summer 1993), pp. 97–122.

Martocchio, Joseph J. "The Financial Cost of Absence Decisions." *Journal of Management* 18, no. 1 (1992), pp. 133–52.

Mendenhall, W., and J. Reinmuth. *Statistics for Management Economics.* 4th ed. Boston, MA: PWS-KENT Publishing Company, 1982.

The Miami University Report. Miami University, Oxford, OH, vol. 8, no. 26, 1989.

Moore, David S. *The Basic Practice of Statistics.* 2nd ed. New York: W. H. Freeman and Company, 2000.

Moore, David S., and George P. McCabe. *Introduction to the Practice of Statistics.* 2nd ed. New York: W. H. Freeman, 1993.

Morris, Michael H., Ramon A. Avila, and Jeffrey Allen. "Individualism and the Modern Corporation: Implications for Innovation and Entrepreneurship." *Journal of Management* 19, no. 3 (1993), pp. 595–612.

Neter, J., M. Kutner, C. Nachtsheim, and W. Wasserman. *Applied Linear Statistical Models.* 4th ed. Homewood, IL: Irwin/McGraw-Hill, 1996.

Neter, J., W. Wasserman, and M. H. Kutner. *Applied Linear Statistical Models.* 2nd ed. Homewood, IL: Richard D. Irwin, 1985.

Nunnally, Bennie H., Jr., and D. Anthony Plath. *Cases in Finance.* Burr Ridge, IL: Richard D. Irwin, 1995, pp. 12–1–12–7.

Olmsted, Dan, and Gigi Anders. "Turned Off." *USA Weekend,* June 2–4, 1995.

Ott, Lyman. *An Introduction to Statistical Methods and Data Analysis.* 2nd ed. Boston, MA: PWS-Kent, 1987.

SAS User's Guide. 1982 Edition. Cary, NC: SAS Institute, 1982.

Schaeffer, R. L., William Mendenhall, and Lyman Ott. *Elementary Survey Sampling.* 3rd ed. Boston, MA: Duxbury Press, 1986.

Scherkenbach, William. *The Deming Route to Quality and Productivity: Road Maps and Roadblocks.* Washington, D.C.: Ceepress Books, 1986.

Seigel, James C. "Managing with Statistical Models." SAE Technical Paper 820520. Warrendale, PA: Society for Automotive Engineers, Inc., 1982.

Sichelman, Lew. "Random Checks Find Loan Application Fibs." *The Journal-News* (Hamilton, Ohio), Sept. 26, 1992 (originally published in *The Washington Post*).

Siegel, Andrew F. *Practical Business Statistics.* 2nd ed. Homewood, IL: Richard D. Irwin, 1990, p. 588.

Silk, Alvin J., and Ernst R. Berndt. "Scale and Scope Effects on Advertising Agency Costs." *Marketing Science* 12, no. 1 (Winter 1993), pp. 53–72.

Stevenson, William J. *Production/Operations Management.* 6th ed. Homewood, IL : Irwin/McGraw-Hill, 1999, p. 228.

Thomas, Anisya S., and Kannan Ramaswamy. "Environmental Change and Management Staffing: A Comment." *Journal of Management* 19, no. 4 (1993), pp. 877–87.

Von Neumann, J., and O. Morgenstern. *Theory of Games and Economic Behavior.* 2nd ed. Princeton, N.J.: Princeton University Press, 1947.

Walton, Mary. *The Deming Management Method.* New York, NY: Dodd, Mead & Company, 1986.

Weinberger, Marc G., and Harlan E. Spotts. "Humor in U.S. versus U.K. TV Commercials: A Comparison." *Journal of Advertising* 18, no. 2 (1989), pp. 39–44.

Wright, Thomas A., and Douglas G. Bonett. "Role of Employee Coping and Performance in Voluntary Employee Withdrawal: A Research Refinement and Elaboration." *Journal of Management* 19, no. 1 (1993) pp. 147–61.

Photo Credits

Chapter 1
Page 2: Royalty Free/Corbis
Page 7: Bonnie Kamin/PhotoEdit, Inc.
Page 12: Steve Cole/Getty Images
Page 15: AP/Wide World Photos

Chapter 2
Page 42: Comstock Images/Getty Images
Page 60: Stockbyte-Platinum/Getty Images
Page 72: Getty Images
Page 89: AP/Wide World Photos
Page 97: Doug Menuez/Getty Images

Chapter 3
Page 126: Spencer Grant/PhotoEdit, Inc.
Page 134: Howard Grey/Getty Images
Page 145: Royalty Free/Corbis

Chapter 4
Page 158: Rick Friedman/Corbis
Page 165: Stone/Getty Images
Page 172: Claro Cortes IV/Reuters/Corbis
Page 183: Deborah Davis/Getty Images

Chapter 5
Page 194: Steve Mason/Getty Images
Page 210: Royalty Free/Corbis
Page 220: Stockbyte/PictureQuest

Chapter 6
Page 236: Pictor International/Pictor International, Ltd./PictureQuest
Page 241: Taxi/Getty Images
Page 246: Royalty Free/Corbis

Chapter 7
Page 260: No Credit Needed
Page 267: Susan Van Etten/PhotoEdit, Inc.
Page 283: Corbis
Page 291: Reportage/Getty Images

Chapter 8
Page 304: Tony Freeman/Photo Edit, Inc.
Page 306: Image Bank/Getty Images
Page 316: © NBC, Inc. Used with permission
Page 333: Ryan McVay/Getty Images

Chapter 9
Page 356: Comstock Images/Getty Images
Page 357: Keith Brofsky/Getty Images
Page 371: Corbis

Chapter 10
Page 402: Borland/Photolink/Getty Images
Page 405: Lena/Lena/Corbis
Page 426: Robert Llewellyn/Image State

Chapter 11
Page 448: Fisher/Thatcher/Getty Images
Page 450: Columbia Gas System 1995 Annual Report
Page 454: Royalty Free/Corbis

Chapter 12
Page 528: Royalty Free/Corbis
Page 560: Susan Van Etten/PhotoEdit, Inc.
Page 575: Ryan McVay/Getty Images
Page 604: Romilly Lockyer/Brand X Pictures/PictureQuest

Chapter 13
Page 632: Corbis
Page 635: Russell Illig/Getty Images
Page 637: Kelley-Mooney Photography/Corbis

Chapter 14
Page 674: Adam Crowley/Getty Images
Page 677: No Credit found

Chapter 15
Page 734: John A. Rizzo/Getty Images

Chapter 16
Page 764: Photo by Business Wire via Getty Images

Chapter 17
Page 792: Royalty Free/Corbis

Index

H

I

J

K

L

M

N

O

P

Q

R

S

T

U

V

W

X

Y

Z

Case Index

MegaStat® – Statistical Software for Excel

MegaStat is a full featured statistical add-in that is included on the CD-ROM with **Bowerman/O'Connell, *Business Statistics in Practice, Fourth Edition.***

MegaStat is always available from Excel's main menu.
Selecting a menu item pops up an easy to use dialog box. Regression analysis is shown below.

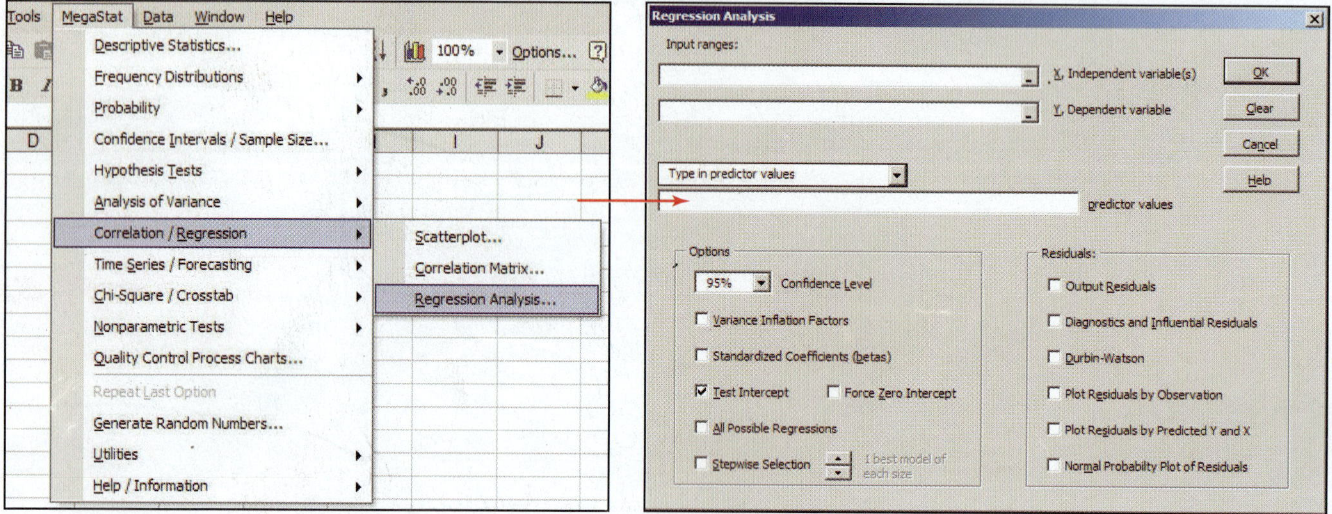

MegaStat includes the following features:

- Creates output sheets with carefully formatted output.
- AutoExpand feature allows quick data selection.
- Automatic detection of data labels.
- Completely separate from Excel's Data Analysis Tools. (The Data Analysis add-in does not have to be installed.)
- MegaStat corrects several computational problems with Excel and Data Analysis Tools.
- Computations involving factorials can handle factorials in excess of 1,000,000!
- The Stepwise Selection procedure provides a powerful new alternative to traditional stepwise regression.

MegaStat Contents:

Descriptive Statistics – standard output plus box plot, runs plot, stem & leaf, empirical rule, normal plot, normal curve, goodness of fit, etc.

Frequency Distributions – qualitative and quantitative (auto selection of interval width)

Probability – counting rules, discrete distributions (binomial, hypergeometric, Poisson), continuous distributions (normal, t, chi-square, and F)

Confidence Intervals & Sample Size – Intervals for means & proportions. Sample size determination for confidence intervals and hypothesis testing.

Hypothesis Tests – one and two group tests and confidence intervals for mean and proportion; tests for variances

ANOVA – One Factor, Randomized Blocks, Two-Factor (Includes graphical display and Tukey post-hoc analysis)

Regression – Scatterplot, Correlation Matrix, and Regression. Options for prediction intervals, VIFs and residual diagnostics. All Possible Regressions and Stepwise Selection. Non-contiguous independent variables can be selected without rearranging data.

Time Series / Forecasting – Curve Fit, Deseasonalization, Moving Average, and Exponential Smoothing

Chi-Square – Contingency Table, Crosstabulation, Goodness of Fit Test

Nonparametric Tests – includes nine of the most commonly used procedures

Quality Control Process Charts – charts for variables, proportion defective, and number of defects

Generate Random Numbers – fixed values or live functions for Uniform, Normal or Exponential distributions